A GUIDE BOOK OF
UNITED STATES COINS
MEGA RED™
2017

George Washington was president of the United States when the
first U.S. Mint was established in Philadelphia, Pennsylvania, in 1792.

THE OFFICIAL RED BOOK®

A GUIDE BOOK OF
UNITED STATES COINS
MEGA RED™
2017
2ND EDITION

R.S. YEOMAN

SENIOR EDITOR, KENNETH BRESSETT
WITH Q. DAVID BOWERS AND JEFF GARRETT

A Fully Illustrated Catalog of Useful Information on Colonial and Federal Coinage, 1616 to Date, With Detailed Photographs to Identify Your Coins and Retail Valuation Charts Indicating How Much They're Worth. Plus Illustrated Grading Instructions With Enlarged Images to Determine Your Coins' Conditions. Insider Tips on Treasures Waiting to be Discovered in Your Pocket Change; Advice on Smart Collecting; and More. Based on the Expertise of More Than 100 Professional Coin Dealers and Researchers. Also Featuring Entertaining Stories, Amazing Essays, and Astounding Facts and Figures About All Manner of Rare and Historical Coins of the United States of America.

A Guide Book of United States Coins™, Deluxe Edition
THE OFFICIAL RED BOOK OF UNITED STATES COINS™

THE OFFICIAL RED BOOK, MEGA RED, and
THE OFFICIAL RED BOOK OF UNITED STATES COINS
are trademarks of Whitman Publishing, LLC.

www.whitman.com

ISBN: 0794843921
Printed in the United States of America.

© 2016 Whitman Publishing, LLC
3101 Clairmont Road, Suite G, Atlanta GA 30329

Correspondence concerning this book may be directed to Whitman Publishing, Attn: Red Book Deluxe Edition, at the address above.

Whitman Publishing, LLC, does not deal in coins; the values shown herein are not offers to buy or sell but are included only as general information. Descriptions of coins are based on the most accurate data available, but could change with further research or discoveries.

Collect all the books in the Bowers Series. *A Guide Book of Morgan Silver Dollars* • *A Guide Book of Double Eagle Gold Coins* • *A Guide Book of United States Type Coins* • *A Guide Book of Modern United States Proof Coin Sets* • *A Guide Book of Shield and Liberty Head Nickels* • *A Guide Book of Flying Eagle and Indian Head Cents* • *A Guide Book of Washington and State Quarters* • *A Guide Book of Buffalo and Jefferson Nickels* • *A Guide Book of Lincoln Cents* • *A Guide Book of United States Commemorative Coins* • *A Guide Book of United States Tokens and Medals* • *A Guide Book of Gold Dollars* • *A Guide Book of Peace Dollars* • *A Guide Book of the Official Red Book of United States Coins* • *A Guide Book of Franklin and Kennedy Half Dollars* • *A Guide Book of Civil War Tokens* • *A Guide Book of Hard Times Tokens* • *A Guide Book of Mercury Dimes, Standing Liberty Quarters, and Liberty Walking Half Dollars* • *A Guide Book of Half Cents and Large Cents* • *A Guide Book of Barber Silver Coins* • *A Guide Book of Liberty Seated Silver Coins* • *A Guide Book of Modern U.S. Dollar Coins*

For a complete listing of numismatic reference books, supplies, and storage products,
visit Whitman Publishing online at www.whitman.com.

CONTENTS

CONTENTS

CONTENTS

CREDITS AND ACKNOWLEDGMENTS

CONTRIBUTORS TO THE SECOND
DELUXE EDITION RED BOOK

Senior Editor: Kenneth Bressett. Research Editor: Q. David Bowers. Valuations Editor: Jeff Garrett. Special Consultants: Philip Bressett, Robert Rhue, Troy Thoreson, and Ben Todd.

The following coin dealers and collectors have contributed pricing information to this edition:

Gary Adkins	Sheridan Downey	Donald H. Kagin	Robert M. Paul
Mark Albarian	Steve Ellsworth	Bradley S. Karoleff	Joel Rettew Jr.
Dominic Albert	Gerry Fortin	Jim Koenings	Joel Rettew Sr.
Buddy Alleva	John Frost	Richard A. Lecce	Greg Rohan
Richard S. Appel	Mike Fuljenz	Julian M. Leidman	Maurice Rosen
Mitchell A. Battino	John Gervasoni	Stuart Levine	Mark Salzberg
Richard M. August	Dennis M. Gillio	Kevin Lipton	Gerald R. Scherer Jr.
Lee J. Bellisario	Ronald J. Gillio	Denis W. Loring	Jeff Shevlin
Mark Borckardt	Rusty Goe	Dwight N. Manley	Roger Siboni
Larry Briggs	Ira M. Goldberg	David McCarthy	James Simek
Bill Bugert	Lawrence Goldberg	Robert T. McIntire	Rick Snow
H. Robert Campbell	Kenneth M. Goldman	Harry Miller	Scott Sparks
Elizabeth Coggan	J.R. Grellman	Lee S. Minshull	David M. Sundman
Alan Cohen	Tom Hallenbeck	Scott P. Mitchell	Anthony Terranova
Gary Cohen	Ash Harrison	Michael C. Moline	Rich Uhrich
James H. Cohen	Brian Hendelson	Charles Morgan	Frank Van Valen
Stephen M. Cohen	Brian Hodge	Casey Noxon	Fred Weinberg
Steve Contursi	Jesse Iskowitz	Paul Nugget	David Wnuck
Adam Crum	Steve Ivy	Mike Orlando	Mark S. Yaffe
Raymond Czahor	Amandeep Jassal	John M. Pack	
John Dannreuther	Joseph Jones	Joseph Parrella	

Special credit is due to the following for contributions to the *Guide Book of United States Coins, Deluxe Edition*: Gary Adkins, David W. Akers, John Albanese, David Allison, Jeff Ambio, the American Numismatic Society, Mitchell Battino, Jack Beymer, Doug Bird, Jon Alan Boka, Mark Borckardt, Q. David Bowers, Kenneth Bressett, Nicholas P. Brown, Roger W. Burdette, David J. Camire, Fonda Chase, Elizabeth Coggan, Greg Cohen, Ray Czahor, John W. Dannreuther, Beth Deisher, Dan Demeo, Cynthia Roden Doty, Richard Doty, Bill Eckberg, Michael Fahey, Bill Fivaz, Pierre Fricke, Jeff Garrett, Ira Goldberg, Lawrence Goldberg, Ken Goldman, J.R. Grellman Jr., Ron Guth, James Halperin, Greg Hannigan, Daniel W. Holmes Jr., Gwyn Huston, Walter Husak, Tom Hyland, Wayne Imbrogno, Steve Ivy, R.W. Julian, Brad Karoleff, David W. Lange, Julian Leidman, Jon Lerner, Littleton Coin Company, Denis W. Loring, John Lusk, Ron Manley, J.P. Martin, Jim Matthews, Chris Victor-McCawley, Jim McGuigan, Jack McNamara, Harry Miller, Paul Minshull, Scott Mitchell, Charles Moore, Dan Moore, Jim Neiswinter, Eric P. Newman, Numismatic Guaranty Corporation of America (NGC), Joel J. Orosz, John Pack, Michael Printz, Jim Reardon, Tom Reynolds, Marilyn Reback, Harry Salyards, Thomas Serfass, Neil Shafer, Jeff Shevlin, Craig Sholley, the Smithsonian Institution, Rick Snow, Max Spiegel, Lawrence R. Stack, Stack's Bowers Galleries, David M. Sundman, Jeff Swindling, James Taylor, Saul

Teichman, R. Tettenhorst, Scott Travers, Rich Uhrich, the U.S. Mint (Tom Jurkowsky, director of corporate communications; Michael White; Maria Goodwin, historian; Abby Gilbert, assistant historian), Frank Van Valen, Alan V. Weinberg, Fred Weinberg, Ken and Stephanie Westover, James Wiles, Ray Williams, Doug Winter, and David Wnuck.

Special credit is due to the following for service and data in the 2017 regular edition of the *Guide Book of United States Coins*: Stewart Blay, Roger W. Burdette, Frank J. Colletti, Columbus–America Discovery Group, Charles Davis, Tom DeLorey, David Fanning, Bill Fivaz, Kevin Flynn, Chuck Furjanic, James C. Gray, Charles Hoskins, R.W. Julian, Richard Kelly, George F. Kolbe, David W. Lange, G.J. Lawson, Andy Lustig, J.P. Martin, Syd Martin, Eric P. Newman, Ken Potter, P. Scott Rubin, Paul Rynearson, Mary Sauvain, Richard J. Schwary, Neil Shafer, Robert W. Shippee, Craig Smith, Jerry Treglia, Mark R. Vitunic, Holland Wallace, Weimar White, John Whitney, Raymond Williams, and John Wright.

Special credit is due to the following for service in past editions: David Akers, John Albanese, Lyman Allen, Jeff Ambio, Michael Aron, Philip E. Benedetti, Richard A. Bagg, Jack Beymer, George Blenker, Walter Breen, John Burns, Jason Carter, Marc Crane, Silvano DiGenova, Ken Duncan, Bob Entlich, John Feigenbaum, George Fitzgerald, Dennis Forgue, Harry Forman, George Fuld, Henry Garrett, William Gay, Harry Gittelson, J.R. Grellman, Ron Guth, John Hamrick, Stephen Hayden, Gene L. Henry, John W. Highfill, Karl D. Hirtzinger, Michael Hodder, John L. Howes, Robert Jacobs, James J. Jelinski, Larry Johnson, A.M. Kagin, Stanley Kesselman, Jerry Kimmel, Mike Kliman, Paul Koppenhaver, Robert B. Lecce, Ed Leventhal, Arnold Margolis, Chris McCawley, Glenn Miller, Paul Montgomery, Richard Nachbar, William P. Paul, Thomas Payne, Beth Piper, Doug Plasencia, Andrew Pollock III, John Porter, Mike Ringo, Cherie Schoeps, J.S. Schreiber, Hugh Sconyers, Robert Shaw, Arlie Slabaugh, Thomas Smith, William Spencer, Paul Spiegel, Lawrence R. Stack, Maurice Storck Sr., Charles Surasky, Anthony J. Swiatek, Steve Tanenbaum, Mark Van Winkle, Russell Vaughn, and Douglas Winter.

Special photo credits are due to the following: Al Adams, the American Numismatic Association, Angel Dee's Coins and Collectibles, the Architect of the Capitol (Washington, D.C.), Douglas F. Bird, J.H. Cline, Steve Contursi, Bill Fivaz, Ira & Larry Goldberg Coins & Collectibles, the estate of Bernard Heller, Heritage Auctions (www.ha.com), Littleton Coin Co., Tom Mulvaney, Numismatic Guaranty Corporation of America (NGC), PCGS, Doug Plasencia, Brent Pogue, Jim Pruitt, Sarasota Rare Coin Gallery, the Smithsonian Institution, Spectrum, Stack's Bowers Galleries, Superior Galleries, and the U.S. Mint.

HOW TO USE THIS BOOK

Numismatics, in its purest sense, is the study of items used as money. Today in the United States, as around the world, the term embraces the activities of a diverse community of hobbyists, historians, researchers, museum curators, and others who collect and study coins, tokens, paper money, and similar objects.

Since 1946 the *Guide Book of United States Coins* has served this community as the preeminent annual reference for coin specifications, mintages, values, photographs, and other information important to collectors and students. With more than 23 million copies in print since the first edition, the *Guide Book* (commonly known as the "Red Book") is well established as the most popular reference in numismatics—not to mention one of the best-selling nonfiction books in the history of American publishing. (In 1964 the 18th edition of the Red Book ranked number 5 on the national sales lists, at 1.2 million copies—higher than Dale Carnegie's *How to Win Friends and Influence People* at number 6, and John F. Kennedy's *Profiles in Courage* at number 9.)

Building on this strong foundation, the Deluxe Edition of the *Guide Book of United States Coins* is an expanded and enlarged volume intended to serve not only beginning collectors, but also intermediate to advanced coin collectors, professional coin dealers and auctioneers, researchers, and investors. It features more photographs, detailed higher-grade valuations, additional listings of die varieties and rare early Proof coins, certified-coin population data, auction records, and other resources that provide a wealth of information on every coin type ever made by the U.S. Mint. The Deluxe Edition also expands on the regular edition's coverage of collectible die varieties, with close-up photographs, valuations, and chart notes. It is a handy single-source guide that educates its users in auction and certification trends, retail valuations, and similar aspects of the marketplace.

Like the regular-edition Red Book, the Deluxe Edition includes information on colonial and early American coins and tokens as well as all federal series (copper half cents through gold double eagles). It also covers private and territorial gold pieces; Hard Times tokens; Civil War tokens; Confederate coins; Hawaiian, Puerto Rican, and Philippine coins; Alaskan tokens; misstrikes and errors; numismatic books; Proof and Mint sets; commemorative coins from 1892 to date; silver, gold, and platinum bullion coins; and other topics.

Readers of the *Guide Book of United States Coins, Deluxe Edition*, benefit from the following useful information.

The "Red Book" has become a popular collectible itself, with fans striving to acquire one of each edition dating back to number 1, published in November 1946 with a 1947 cover date. Rare early volumes can be worth $1,000 or more.

R.S. Yeoman, author of the original *Guide Book of United States Coins*, examining press proofs in 1969.

DENOMINATION INTRODUCTIONS

Each coinage denomination is discussed first in an overview of its history, major design types and sub-types, and general collectability by type. (The dollar denomination is divided into silver dollars, trade dollars, and modern dollars.) A second essay gives collectors a more in-depth analysis of specializing in that denomination. *These sections encapsulate decades of numismatic research and market observation, and they should be read in conjunction with the charts, photographs, and other information that follow.*

TYPE-BY-TYPE STUDIES

Within each denomination, each major coin type is laid out in chronological order. As in the regular-edition Red Book, the type's designer and its specifications (weight, composition, diameter, edge treatment, and production facilities) are given. Coinage designs are pictured at actual size except commemorative designs, which are standardized (one Mint State example and one Proof example, when available). Each type section includes summary text on the type's history; aspects of its striking, sharpness, and related characteristics; and its market availability. In-depth grading instructions, with enlarged illustrations, show how to grade each coin type, covering circulation strikes as well as Proofs.

CHARTS

The data charts include these elements:

	Mintage	Cert	Avg	%MS	G-4	VG-8	F-12	VF-20	EF-40	AU-50	MS-60 / PF-60	MS-63 / PF-63	MS-65 / PF-65
1840, Medium Letters (b)	(c)	47	40.0	15%	$140	$190	$275	$450	$800	$1,600	$3,750	$7,750	$23,500
Auctions: $2,233, MS-62, February 2015; $1,028, AU-58, January 2015; $259, EF-45, May 2015; $188, VF-30, September 2015													
1840, Small Letters, Proof	4–8	7	64.0										$100,000
Auctions: $30,550, PF-63, November 2013													
1840-O	855,100	130	49.0	27%	$42	$55	$70	$115	$190	$400	$900	$3,500	
Auctions: $2,350, MS-62, January 2015; $1,410, MS-60, June 2015; $212, EF-45, June 2015; $141, VF-30, June 2015													
1841	310,000	75	54.8	32%	$42	$60	$95	$150	$275	$450	$1,400	$2,800	$9,000
Auctions: $11,750, MS-65, May 2015; $4,230, MS-64, January 2015; $857, AU-58, June 2015; $364, EF-45, August 2015													
1841, Proof	4–8	6	64.5								$20,000	$45,000	$85,000
Auctions: $30,550, PF-64, September 2013													

b. The 1840, Medium Letters, half dollars were struck at the New Orleans Mint from a reverse die of the previous style, without mintmark. **c.** Included in circulation-strike 1840, Small Letters, mintage figure. **d.** Included in 1842, Medium Date, mintage figure.

Mintages. Mintage data is compiled from official Mint records whenever possible, and in other cases from more than 70 years of active numismatic research. In instances where the Mint's early records are in question or have been proven faulty, the official numbers are provided and further information is given in chart notes. For some early Proof coins for which no official mintage records exist, an estimated mintage, or the number of coins known in collections, is given. For modern issues (usually those minted within the past five years), the Mint has released production and/or sales numbers that are not yet officially finalized; these are given in italics.

Note that Mint reports are not always reliable for estimating the rarities of coins. In the early years of the Mint, coinage dies of previous years often were used until they became worn or broken. Certain reported quantities, particularly for gold and silver coins, cover the number of pieces struck and make no indication of the quantity that actually reached circulation. Many issues were deposited in the Treasury as backing for paper currency and later were melted without ever being released to the public.

Gold coins struck before August 1, 1834, are rare today because from 1821 onward (and at times before 1821) the gold in the coins was worth more than their face values, so they were struck as bullion and traded at a premium. Many were exported and melted for their precious-metal value.

Mintage figures shown for 1964 through 1966 are for coins bearing those dates. Some of these coins were struck in more than one year and at various mints, both with and without mintmarks. In recent years, mintage figures reported by the Mint have been revised several times and precise amounts remain uncertain.

Mintage figures shown in italics are estimates based on the most accurate information available. Numismatic research is constantly ongoing, and listed figures are sometimes revised, when new information becomes available.

Certified Populations. For each coin of a particular date and mint, a summary is provided of (1) the number of coins certified, (2) the average grade, on the standard 1–70 scale, of those coins graded, and (3) for circulation-strike coins, the percentage certified in Mint State.

These summaries provide the collector and investor with working data useful in comparing coins offered for sale or bid.

Certified population data is provided courtesy of Numismatic Guaranty Corporation of America (NGC), one of the nation's leading professional third-party grading firms.

It should be noted that for most coins, especially rare dates and varieties, the number certified actually represents the quantity of *submissions*, rather than the number of individual coins submitted. For example, a particular 1801 silver dollar that is submitted for certification five times would be counted the same as five individual coins. Such resubmissions can sometimes result in numbers close to or higher than a coin's entire surviving mintage.

Note, too, that the grade number assigned to a "slabbed" (graded and encapsulated) coin does not tell anything about the strength of that particular coin's strike, the quality of its planchet, whether it has been cleaned or dipped, or its overall eye appeal. Such factors are important to a coin's value. Two rare coins of the same date and variety, each with the same amount of surface wear and graded, for example, MS-63, will find different values in the marketplace if one is eye-pleasing and well struck, and the other is dull and poorly struck.

Valuations. Coin values shown in the Deluxe Edition are retail prices compiled from data and market observations provided by active coin dealers, auctioneers, and other qualified observers, under the direction and analysis of Valuations Editor Jeff Garrett and Senior Editor Kenneth Bressett and their consultants. In this guide book, values from under $1 up to several hundred dollars are for "raw" coins—that is, coins that have *not* been graded and encapsulated by a professional third-party grading service. Values near or above $500 reflect typical auction and retail prices seen for professionally certified coins. The valuations of professionally certified coins often are higher than what collectors normally pay for non-certified ("raw") coins. Values of certified coins may vary widely, depending on the grading service.

The coin market is so active in some categories that values can readily change after publication. Values are shown as a guide and are not intended to serve as a price list for any dealer's stock. A dash appearing in a valuations column indicates that coins in that grade exist even though there are no current retail or auction records for them. The dash does not necessarily mean that such coins are exceedingly rare. Italicized numbers indicate unsettled or speculative (estimated) values. A number of listings of rare coins lack valuations or dashes in certain grades, indicating that they are not available, or not believed to exist, in those grades. Proof coins are usually not shown with values in circulated grades.

For wholesale pricing, the *Handbook of United States Coins* (popularly called the Blue Book, and published since 1942), by R.S. Yeoman, contains average prices dealers nationwide will pay for U.S. coins. It is obtainable through most coin dealers, hobby shops, bookstores, and the Internet.

Auction Records. Multiple recent auction records are provided for nearly every coin (some exceptions being coins that are too common to sell individually at auction). Each record indicates:

the price paid for the coin (including any fees)

the grade of the coin

the date (month and year) of the auction

This combination of auction data gives valuable market information for each coin. It also serves as a springboard for further research. Many auction firms have online archives of coins sold, or else their auction catalogs can be studied using the information provided.

Chart notes. Additional information is provided for certain coins in chart notes. Historical background, die-variety diagnostics, notable market conditions, and other specific details are intended to further guide the collector and investor.

Abbreviations. These are some of the abbreviations you'll find in the charts.

%MS—Percentage of coins certified in Mint State

Avg—Average grade (on a 1–70 scale)

BN—Brown; descriptive of the coloration or toning on certain copper coins

Cam—Cameo

Cert—Certified population

DblDie—Doubled die

DCam—Deep Cameo

DMPL—Deep Mirror Prooflike

D/S—D Over S; a slash between words or letters represents an overdate or overmintmark

Dt—Date

Ex.—Extremely

FB—Full Bands

FBL—Full Bell Lines

FH—Full Head

FS—Full Steps

Horiz—Horizontal

Inv—Inverted

Knbd—Knobbed-Top

Lg—Large

Ltrd—Lettered

Ltrs—Letters

Med—Medium

Mintmk—Mintmark

Obv—Obverse

QuintDie—Quintupled Die

RB—Red and brown; descriptive of the mixture of mint red and brown coloration or toning on a copper coin

RD—Red; descriptive of the mint red color on an untoned copper coin

Rev—Reverse

RPD—Repunched Date

RPM—Repunched Mintmark

Sm—Small

SMS—Special Mint Set

Sq—Square

TransRev—Transitional Reverse

TripDie—Tripled Die

UCam—Ultra Cameo

Var—Variety

COLLECTING U.S. COINS
INVESTING IN RARE COINS

As with the regular edition of the *Guide Book of United States Coins*, those who edit, contribute to, and publish the Deluxe Edition advocate the collecting of coins for pleasure and educational benefits. A secondary consideration is that of investment, the profits of which are usually realized over the long term based on careful purchases. When it comes to investing in rare coins, knowledge is power.

USE COMMON SENSE

The rare-coin market combines some aspects of commodity trading with peculiarities seen more often among markets such as those for fine art, real estate, cut gemstones, and similar investments and collectibles. Armed with knowledge, an investor can have a very rewarding experience buying and selling rare coins. An uneducated investor can just as easily see substantial losses.

The regular edition of the *Guide Book of United States Coins* includes this bit of guidance, which bears repeating here: "The best advice given to anyone considering investing in rare coins is to use common sense." Any collector with common sense would think twice about buying a silver dollar at a flea market for less than its silver value. A common-sense collector who is offered a $1,000 coin from an "unsearched estate," or from a non-specialist who claims to know nothing of its provenance, would refuse it at $500— at least until a diligent examination was possible, and only with an iron-clad return policy and guarantee of authenticity. Profitable investment requires careful selection of qualified dealers (e.g., those professionally credentialed by groups such as the Professional Numismatists Guild [www.pngdealers.com] and the International Association of Professional Numismatists [www.iapn-coins.org]), and educated evaluation of the coins offered for sale.

LEARN ABOUT GRADING

In the past, coin grading was very subjective, and grade descriptions were far from universal. One dealer's "Choice Extremely Fine" might have been another's "About Uncirculated," and adjectives such as *gem* and *brilliant* varied in meaning from collector to collector. Today grading is still a subjective art striving to be an exact science, but progress has been made. The hobby's guidelines have been clearly standardized in systems such as the *Official American Numismatic Association Grading Standards for United States Coins,* and explored further in illustrated books such as *Grading Coins by Photographs: An Action Guide for the Collector and Investor.*

Today there are professional certification services such as NGC, PCGS, ICG, and ANACS that, for a fee, grade and authenticate coins, encapsulating them in sealed "slabs" with their grades noted. These are third-party firms, so called because they are neither buyer nor seller of the coins graded (which guarantees a professional level of impartiality to the process). Professional grading strives to be completely objective, but coins are graded by humans and not computers. This introduces the subjective element of *art* as opposed to *science.* A coin's grade, even if certified by a leading third-party grader (TPG), can be questioned by any collector or dealer—or even by the TPG that graded it, if the coin is resubmitted for a second look. Furthermore, within a given grade a keen observer will find coins that are low-quality, average, and high-quality for that grade. Such factors as luster, color, strength of strike, and overall eye appeal can make, for example, one MS-65 1914 Barber half dollar more visually attractive than another with the same grade. This gives the smart collector the opportunity to "cherrypick," or examine multiple slabbed coins and

The official coin-grading standards of the American Numismatic Association have been codified in book form. This gives every coin collector and dealer a universal "language"—although grading does remain an art as well as a science.

select the highest-quality example for the desired grade. This process builds a better collection than simply accepting a TPG's assigned grades, and is summed up in the guidance of "Buy the coin, not the slab." (Also, note that a coin certified as, for example, MS-64 might have greater eye appeal—and therefore be more desirable to a greater number of collectors—than a less attractive coin graded MS-65.)

Over the years, collectors have observed a trend nicknamed "gradeflation": the reinterpretation, in practice, of the standards applied to a given grade over time. For example, a coin evaluated by a leading TPG in 1994 as MS-63 might be graded today as MS-65 or even MS-66.

"Slabbed" coins are those that have been professionally graded and encapsulated by a third-party service such as ANACS, NGC, or PCGS.

Learn About What You're Buying

In addition to carefully vetting professional dealers, examining potential purchases for authenticity (see below for more on this topic), and studying the art and science of grading, an investor can profit by *learning* about coins. Each coin type has a cultural history that provides useful collecting/investing knowledge. For example, the Treasury Department often stored Morgan dollars by the thousands (and millions), so a bag of 1,000 Mint State dollars is not unheard of. On the other hand, the purchaser of a seemingly original bank-wrapped roll of 20 Mint State trade dollars would likely be left holding a pound of counterfeit coins.

Similarly, each coin type has a typical strike, surface quality, and related characteristics; knowledge of these features can help reveal fakes and lower-than-average-quality specimens. The investor who knows that a certain coin type is rarely encountered in a certain high grade is more alert to potential opportunities. Conversely, if a type is common in high grades, the savvy investor will pass on an average or below-average coin and wait for a sharper, more attractive example, knowing that time and the marketplace are on his side.

For these reasons, even if you consider yourself more *investor* than *collector*, it is recommended that you read every section of this Deluxe Edition that covers the coin series in which you are interested. The price and data charts provide one level of information, the denomination introductions another, the type summaries and grading guides yet others; combined, they offer a well-rounded education that prices alone cannot provide.

Understand the General Market

Coin values rise when (1) the economic trend is inflationary and speculators turn to tangible assets as a hedge, or when the number of collectors increases, while coin supplies remain stationary or decrease through attrition or melting; (2) dealers replace their stocks of coins only from collectors or other dealers, who expect a profit over what they originally paid; (3) speculators attempt to influence the market through selective buying; or (4) bullion (gold and silver) prices rise.

Coin values decline when (1) changes in collecting habits or economic conditions alter demand for certain coins; (2) speculators sell in large quantities; (3) hoards or large holdings are suddenly released and cannot be quickly absorbed by the normal market; or (4) bullion (gold and silver) prices decline.

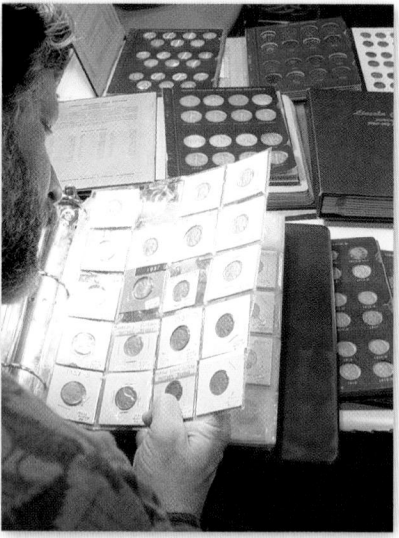

Attending a coin show gives you many opportunities to shop around, examine coins firsthand, talk to experienced collectors and dealers, and learn about the hobby.

Learn From the Experts

A rich numismatic world is available to the investor and collector who seek to learn. News weeklies such as *Coin World* and *Numismatic News* cover the hobby and its markets from many angles, as do a variety of monthly magazines (like *COINage* and *Coins*) and online blogs. Auction sale results, new U.S. Mint products, convention activities, market reports, and other information await the interested reader.

Web sites such as www.Whitman.com/RedBook, www.NumisMaster.com, and www.CoinFacts.com gather and present information from authoritative sources.

Organizations such as the American Numismatic Association (the ANA, online at www.money.org) and the American Numismatic Society (the ANS, at www.numismatics.org), as well as dozens of specialized groups focused on particular coins or series, offer resources and connections to collectors worldwide.

Every major American city and many smaller cities have coin shops where experienced dealers can be consulted for advice and opinions.

Coin shows are another venue for learning from seasoned collectors and investors. The ANA mounts popular shows annually, in different cities. Whitman Coin and Collectibles Expo (WhitmanExpo.com) hosts several shows yearly in Baltimore. Florida United Numismatists (FUN) organizes two shows in the winter and summer each year. All of these shows, and dozens of other local and regional conventions, offer opportunities to talk to other collectors and investors, meet market experts, listen to presentations, and examine hundreds of coins, tokens, and medals.

Books are another means of learning from the hobby's experts. Every collector and investor should have at least a basic numismatic library of standard references. (See the bibliography in the back of this volume.) In addition, nearly every specialty in American coins has one or more books devoted to greater in-depth exploration. Numismatic publishing has experienced a renaissance in recent years, making valuable knowledge more affordable and readily available than ever before. One book essential to the investor's understanding of the rare-coin market is a 672-page volume written by the "dean of American numismatics," Q. David Bowers. The *Expert's Guide to Collecting and Investing in Rare Coins* covers topics such as determining coin prices and values; focusing on rarity; quality and value for the smart buyer; coin-market fads, trends, and cycles; making of the modern market for rare coins; predicting the rare-coin market; techniques of smart buying and bidding; protecting your investment; and more. Robert W. Shippee's *Pleasure and Profit: 100 Lessons for Building and Selling a Collection of Rare Coins* offers first-hand insight from an experienced collector. Beth Deisher's *Cash In Your Coins: Selling the Rare Coins You've Inherited* advises on the selling side of the equation. These are just a few examples of the books awaiting today's collector.

In the long run, coin collectors—even those who seek mainly to profit financially from the hobby— are simply custodians of the relics they collect. Again, the regular edition of the *Guide Book of United States Coins* gives sound advice: "Those who treat rare coins with the consideration and respect they deserve will profit in many ways, not the least of which can be in the form of a sound financial return on one's investments of time and money."

SOME ASPECTS OF COLLECTING

The following topics—mints and mintmarks, checking your coins for authenticity, and coins from treasures and hoards as a key to understanding rarity and value—have proven very popular among collectors.

MINTS AND MINTMARKS

Mintmarks are small letters designating where coins were made. Coins struck at Philadelphia before 1979 (except five-cent pieces of 1942 to 1945) do not have mintmarks. Starting in 1979, a letter P was used on the dollar, and thereafter on all other denominations except the cent. The mintmark position is on the reverse of nearly all coins prior to 1965 (the cent is an exception), and on the obverse after 1967.

C—Charlotte, North Carolina (gold coins only; 1838–1861)

CC—Carson City, Nevada (gold and silver coins only; 1870–1893)

D—Dahlonega, Georgia (gold coins only; 1838–1861)

D—Denver, Colorado (1906 to date)

M—Manila (Philippines; 1920–1941; M not used in early years)

O—New Orleans, Louisiana (gold and silver coins only; 1838–1861; 1879–1909)

P—Philadelphia, Pennsylvania (1793 to date; P not used in early years)

S—San Francisco, California (1854 to date)

W—West Point, New York (1984 to date)

| Charlotte, North Carolina | Carson City, Nevada | Dahlonega, Georgia | Denver, Colorado | Manila, Philippines |

| New Orleans, Louisiana | Philadelphia, Pennsylvania | San Francisco, California | West Point, New York |

Prior to 1996 all dies for U.S. coins were made at the Philadelphia Mint. Some dies are now made at the Denver Mint. Dies for use at other mints are made with the appropriate mintmarks before they are shipped to those mints. Because this was a hand operation prior to 1985, the exact positioning and size of the mintmarks may vary slightly, depending on where and how deeply the punches were impressed. (For an example in this book, see the 1975-D Jefferson nickel.) This also accounts for double-punched and superimposed mintmarks such as the 1938-D, D Over D, and 1938-D, D Over S, Buffalo nickels. Polishing of dies may also alter the apparent size of fine details. Occasionally the mintmark is inadvertently left off a die sent to a branch mint, as was the case with some recent Proof cents, nickels, and dimes. Similarly, some 1982 dimes without mintmarks were made as circulation strikes. The mintmark M was used on coins made in Manila for the Philippines from 1925 through 1941.

Prior to 1900, punches for mintmarks varied greatly in size. This is particularly noticeable in the 1850 to 1880 period, in which the letters range from very small to very large. An attempt to standardize sizes started in 1892 with the Barber series, but exceptions are seen in the 1892-O half dollar and 1905-O dime, both of which have normal and "microscopic" mintmarks. A more or less standard-size, small mintmark was used on all minor coins starting in 1909, and on all dimes, quarters, and halves after the Barber series was replaced in 1916. Slight variations in mintmark size occur through 1945, with notable differences in 1928, when small and large S mintmarks were used.

In recent years a single D or S punch has been used to mark all branch-mint dies. The change to the larger D for Denver coins occurred in 1933. Nickels, dimes, quarter dollars, half dollars, and dollars of 1934 exist with either the old, smaller-size mintmark or the new, larger-size D. All other denominations of 1934 and after are standard. The San Francisco mintmark was changed to a larger size during 1941 and, with the exception of the half dollar, all 1941-S coins are known with either small or large mintmarks. Halves were not changed until 1942, and the 1942-S and 1943-S pieces exist both ways. The

1945-S dime with "microscopic" S is an unexplained use of a punch originally intended for Philippine coins of 1907 through 1920. In 1979, the punches were replaced. Varieties of some 1979 coins appear with either the old- or new-shaped S or D. The S punch was again replaced in 1981 with a punch that yielded a more distinct letter.

The mintmark application technique for Proof coins was changed in 1985, and for circulation-strike production in 1990 and 1991, when the letter was applied directly to the master die rather than being hand punched on each working die. At the same time, all the mintmark letters were made much larger and clearer than those of previous years.

CHECKING YOUR COINS FOR AUTHENTICITY

Coin collectors occasionally encounter counterfeit coins, or coins that have been altered so that they appear to be something other than what they really are. Any coin that does not seem to fit the description of similar pieces listed in this guide book should be looked upon with suspicion. Experienced coin dealers can usually tell quickly whether a coin is genuine, and would never knowingly sell spurious coins to a collector. Rare coins found in circulation or bought from a nonprofessional source should be examined carefully.

The risk of purchasing a spurious coin can be minimized through the use of common sense and an elementary knowledge of the techniques used by counterfeiters. It is well to keep in mind that the more popular a coin is among collectors and the public, the more likely it is that counterfeits and replicas will abound. Until recently, collector coins valued at under $100 were rarely replicated because of the high cost of making such items. The same was true of counterfeits made to deceive the public. Few counterfeit coins were made because it was more

These "coins" might appear authentic at first glance, but they're actually modern fakes, made to deceive unwary collectors.

profitable for the fakers to print paper money. Today, however, counterfeiters in Asia and elsewhere create fakes of a surprising variety of coins, most notably silver dollar types, but also smaller denominations.

The best way to detect counterfeit coins is to compare suspected pieces with others of the same issue. Carefully check size, color, luster, weight, edge devices, and design details. Replicas generally have less detail than their genuine counterparts when studied under magnification. Modern struck counterfeits made to deceive collectors are an exception to this rule. Any questionable gold coin should be referred to an expert for verification.

Cast forgeries are usually poorly made and of incorrect weight. Base metal is often used in place of gold or silver, and the coins are lightweight and often incorrect in color and luster. Deceptive cast pieces have been made using real metal content and modern dental techniques, but these too usually vary in quality and color.

Detection of alterations sometimes involves comparative examination of the suspected areas of a coin (usually mintmarks and date digits) at magnification ranging from 10x to 40x.

Coins of exceptional rarity or value should never be purchased without a written guarantee of authenticity. Professional authentication of rare coins for a fee is available with the services offered by commercial grading services, and by some coin dealers.

Three types of spurious coins you might encounter are replicas, counterfeits, and alterations.

Replicas. Reproductions of famous and historical coins have been distributed for decades by marketing firms and souvenir vendors. These pieces are often tucked away as curios by the original recipients, perhaps in a desk drawer or jewelry box, and later are found by others who believe they have discovered objects of great value. Genuine specimens of extremely rare and/or valuable coins are almost never found in unlikely places.

Most replicas are poorly made, often by the casting method (as opposed to being struck by dies), and are virtually worthless other than as novelties. They can sometimes be identified by a seam that runs around the edge of the piece where the two halves of the casting mold were joined together.

Counterfeits. For many centuries, counterfeiters have produced base-metal forgeries of gold and silver coins to deceive the public in the normal course of trade. These pieces are usually crudely made and easily detected on close examination. Crudely cast counterfeit copies of older coins are the most prevalent. These can usually be detected by the casting bubbles or pimples that can be seen with low-power magnification. Pieces struck from handmade dies are more deceptive, but the engravings do not match those of genuine mint products.

More recently, as coin collecting has gained popularity and rare-coin prices have risen, "numismatic" counterfeits (made not to pass in commerce, but for sale to unsuspecting collectors) have become more common. The majority of these are die-struck counterfeits of gold coins, mass produced overseas since 1950. Forgeries exist of most U.S. gold coins dated between 1870 and 1933, as well as all issues of the gold dollar and three-dollar gold piece. Most of these are very well made, as they were intended to pass the close scrutiny of collectors. Few gold coins of earlier dates have been counterfeited, but false 1799 ten-dollar gold pieces and 1811 five-dollar coins have been made. Gold coins in less than Extremely Fine condition are seldom counterfeited. For more information, including extensive illustrations, consult the *United States Gold Counterfeit Detection Guide*, by Bill Fivaz.

Silver dollars dated 1804, Lafayette commemorative dollars of 1900, several of the low-mintage commemorative half dollars, and 1795 half dimes have been forged in quantity. Minor-coin forgeries made in recent years are the 1909-S V.D.B. Lincoln cent; the 1914-D Lincoln cent; the 1955, Doubled Die Obverse, Lincoln cent; 1877 Indian Head cents; 1856 Flying Eagle cents; and, on a much smaller scale, a variety of dates of half cents and large cents. Nineteenth-century copies of colonial coins are also sometimes encountered (see the *Whitman Encyclopedia of Colonial and Early American Coins*).

Commonly seen modern-day counterfeits produced in China include Bust dollars; Liberty Seated dimes, quarters, halves, and dollars; Morgan dollars; and even American Silver Eagles, all of various dates and mintmarks—some fantastical (for example, Morgan dollars dated in the 1700s).

Alterations. Deceivers occasionally alter coins by the addition, removal, or change of a design feature (such as a mintmark or date digit) or by the polishing, sandblasting, acid etching, toning, or plating of the surface of a genuine piece. Among U.S. gold coins, only the 1927-D double eagle is commonly found with a deceptively added mintmark. On $2.50 and $5 gold coins, 1839 through 1856, New Orleans O mintmarks have been altered to C (for Charlotte, North Carolina) in a few instances.

More than a century ago, fraudsters imitated five-dollar gold pieces by gold-plating 1883 Liberty Head five-cent coins of the type without the word CENTS on the reverse. Other coins commonly created fraudulently through alteration include the 1799 large cent and the 1909-S, 1909-S V.D.B., 1914-D, 1922 "plain," and 1943 "copper" cents. The 1913 Liberty Head nickel has been extensively replicated by the alteration of 1903 and 1912 nickels. Scarce, high-grade Denver and San Francisco Buffalo nickels of the 1920s; 1916-D and 1942, 42 Over 41, dimes; 1918-S, 8 Over 7, quarters; 1932-D and -S quarters; and 1804 silver dollars have all been crafted by the alteration of genuine coins of other dates or mints.

COINS FROM TREASURES AND HOARDS:
A KEY TO UNDERSTANDING RARITY AND VALUE

The following discussion of coin treasures and hoards is derived from the writing of Q. David Bowers.

ELEMENTS OF RARITY

In many instances, the mintage of a coin can be a factor in its present-day rarity and value. However, across American numismatics there are many important exceptions, some very dramatic. As an introduction and example, in this book you will find many listings of Morgan silver dollars of 1878 through 1921 for which the mintage figure does not seem to correlate with the coin's price. For example, among such coins the 1901, of which 6,962,000 were made for circulation, is valued at $475,000 in MS-65. In the same series the 1884-CC, of which only 1,136,000 were struck, is listed at $500, or only a tiny fraction of the value of a 1901.

Why the difference? The explanation is that nearly all of the 6,962,000 dollars of 1901 were either placed into circulation at the time and became worn, or were melted generations ago. Very few were saved by collectors, and today MS-65 coins are extreme rarities. On the other hand, of the 1,166,000 1884-CC silver dollars minted, relatively few went into circulation. Vast quantities were sealed in 1,000-coin cloth bags and put into government storage. Generations later, as coin collecting became popular, thousands were paid out by the Treasury Department. Years after that, in the early 1960s, when silver metal rose in value, there was a "run" on long-stored silver dollars, and it was learned in March 1964 that 962,638 1884-CC dollars—84.7% of the original mintage—were still in the hands of the Treasury Department!

With this information, the price disparities become understandable. Even though the 1901 had a high mintage, few were saved, and although worn coins are common, gem MS-65 coins are rarities. In contrast, nearly all of the low-mintage 1884-CC dollars were stored by the government, and today most of them still exist, including some in MS-65 grade.

There are many other situations in which mintages are not particularly relevant to the availability and prices of coins today. Often a special circumstance will lead to certain coins' being saved in especially large quantities, later dramatically affecting the availability and value of such pieces. The following are some of those circumstances.

Excitement of a New Design. In the panorama of American coinage, some new designs have captured the fancy of the public, who saved them in large quantities when they were released. In many other instances new designs were ignored, and coins slipped into circulation unnoticed.

In 1909 great publicity was given to the new Abraham Lincoln portrait to be used on the one-cent piece, replacing the familiar Indian Head motif. On the reverse in tiny letters were the initials, V.D.B., of the coin's designer, Victor David Brenner. The occasion was the 100th anniversary of Lincoln's birth. Coinage commenced at the Philadelphia and San Francisco mints. In total, 27,995,000 1909 V.D.B., cents were struck and 484,000 of the 1909-S, V.D.B.

On August 2, 1909, the new cents were released to the public. A mad scramble ensued, and soon banks had to ration the number paid out to any single individual, this being particularly true in the East. (Interest in the West was less intense, and fewer coins were saved there.) A controversy arose as to the V.D.B. initials, and some newspaper notices complained that as Brenner had been paid for his work, there was no point in giving his initials a prominent place on the coins. Never mind that artists' initials had been used on other coins for a long time. As examples, the M initial of George T. Morgan appeared on both the obverse and reverse of silver dollars from 1878 onward; Chief Engraver Charles E. Barber was memorialized by a B on the neck of Miss Liberty on dimes, quarters, and half dollars from 1892 onward; and the recent (1907 onward) double eagles bore the monogram of Augustus Saint-Gaudens prominently on the obverse. In spite of these precedents, the offending V.D.B. initials were removed, and later 1909 and 1909-S cents were made without them.

Word spread that the cents with V.D.B. would be rare, and people saved even more of them. Today, the 1909 V.D.B. cents are readily available in Mint State. The 1909-S V.D.B., of lower mintage and of which far fewer were saved, lists for $1,500 in MS-63.

Other Popular First-Year Coins. Among other United States coins struck since 1792, these first-year-of-issue varieties (a partial list) were saved in large numbers and are especially plentiful today:

- **1837 Liberty Seated, No Stars, half dime.** Several thousand or more were saved, a large number for a half dime of the era. Apparently, their cameo-like appearance made them attractive curiosities at the time, the same being true of the dimes of the same year.

- **1837 Liberty Seated, No Stars, dime.** Somewhat more than a thousand were saved, a large number for a dime of the era.

- **1883 Liberty Head, Without CENTS, nickel.** The U.S. Mint expressed the value of this new design simply as "V," without mention of cents—not particularly unusual, as three-cent pieces of the era were simply denominated as "III." Certain people gold-plated the new nickels and passed them off as five-dollar gold coins of similar diameter. Soon, the Mint added the word CENTS. News accounts were printed that the "mistake" coins without CENTS would be recalled and would become very rare. Americans saved so many that today this variety is the most plentiful in Mint State of any Liberty Head nickel in the entire series from 1883 to 1913.

- **1892 and 1893 World's Columbian Exposition commemorative half dollars.** These, the first U.S. commemorative half dollars, were widely publicized, and hundreds of thousands were saved. Today they are very common in used condition, because quantities were eventually released into circulation as if they were regular half dollars.

- **MCMVII (1907) High-Relief gold twenty-dollar coin.** Although only about 12,000 were minted, at least 6,000 survive today, mostly in Mint State. Released in December 1907, the coin, by famous sculptor Augustus Saint-Gaudens, created a sensation, and soon examples were selling for $30 each. Today, Mint State coins are plentiful, but as the demand for them is extremely strong, choice specimens sell for strong prices. An MS-63 coin lists for $24,000.

- **1913 Buffalo nickel.** These were saved in large quantities, and today there are more Mint State coins of this year in existence than for any other issue of the next 15 years.

Many coins have been saved as special souvenirs. People often notice a new coinage design and will set examples aside from the first year of issue, making high-grade pieces available for later generations of collectors. Pictured: an 1883 No CENTS Liberty Head nickel, a steel 1943 cent, and a 1999 State quarter.

- **1916 Mercury dime.** In 1916, the Mercury dime's first year of issue, Americans saved many of the new coins from the Philadelphia and San Francisco mints. However, for some reason the low-mintage 1916-D was generally overlooked and today is very rare in Mint State.

- **1932 Washington quarter.** At the Philadelphia Mint, 5,504,000 were minted, and it is likely that several hundred thousand were saved, making them plentiful today. The 1932-D quarter was struck to the extent of 436,800, but for some reason was overlooked by the public, with the result that Mint State coins are rare today. On the other hand, of the 408,000 1932-S quarters struck, thousands were saved. Today, Mint State 1932-S quarters are at least 10 to 20 times more readily available than are equivalent examples of the higher-mintage 1932-D.

- **1943 zinc-coated steel cent.** The novel appearance of this coin resulted in many being saved as curiosities.

- **1964 Kennedy half dollar.** The popularity of the assassinated president was such that many of the hundreds of millions of 1964 half dollars were saved as souvenirs both at home and abroad. This was also the last year the 90% silver half dollar was made for circulation (later versions were 40% silver or copper-nickel), which further increased its popularity.

- **1999–2008 State quarters.** From 1999 to 2008, five different quarter dollar designs were produced each year, with motifs honoring the states in the order that they joined the Union. These coins were highly publicized, and hobby companies produced folders, albums, maps, and other holders to store and display them. A Treasury Department study estimated that 98 million Americans saved one or more sets of the coins, starting with the first one issued (Delaware) and continuing to the last (Hawaii).

- **2000 Sacagawea "golden dollar."** These coins, intended to be a popular substitute for paper dollars and to last much longer in circulation, were launched with great fanfare in 2000, and more than just a few were saved by the public. However, the coin did not catch on for general use in commerce. Later issues have been made for sale to collectors, but no quantities have been released for circulation.

COINS FEW PEOPLE NOTICED

In contrast to the examples above, most coins of new designs attracted no particular notice when they were first issued, and were not saved in unusual quantities. In sharp contrast to the highly popular Kennedy half dollar of 1964, its predecessor, the Franklin half dollar (launched in 1948), generated very little interest, and even numismatists generally ignored its debut—perhaps preferring the old Liberty Walking design, which had been a favorite.

Although a long list could be made, here is just a sampling of first-year-of-issue coins that were not noticed in their own time. Few were set aside in like-new condition. Consequently, today they range from scarce to rare in Mint State:

- **1793 half cent and cent.** As popular as these may be today, there is no known instance in which a numismatist or museum in 1793 deliberately saved pieces as souvenirs.

- **1794–1795 Flowing Hair half dimes, half dollars, and silver dollars.** The Flowing Hair coins, highly desired today, seem to have attracted little notice in their time, and again there is no record of any having been deliberately saved.

- **1807 and related Capped Bust coinages.** The Capped Bust and related coins of John Reich, assistant engraver at the Mint, were first used in 1807 on the silver half dollar and gold five-dollar piece, and later on certain other denominations. Today these are extremely popular with collectors, but in their time they were not noticed, and few were saved in Mint State.

- **1840 Liberty Seated dollar.** Examples are very scarce in Mint State today and are virtually unknown in gem preservation.

- **1892 Barber dime, quarter dollar, and half dollar.** In 1892 the new Liberty Head design by Charles E. Barber replaced the long-lived Liberty Seated motif. The new coins received bad press notices. Another factor detracting from public interest was the wide attention focused on the forthcoming commemorative half dollars of the World's Columbian Exposition. Not many of the new Barber coins were saved.

- **1938 Jefferson nickel.** Although the numismatic hobby was dynamic at the time, the new nickel design attracted little notice, and no unusual quantities were saved. The market was still reeling from the burst bubble of the 1935 through 1936 commemorative craze, and there was little incentive to save coins for investment.

THE 1962–1964 TREASURY RELEASE

The Bland-Allison Act of February 28, 1878, was a political boondoggle passed to accommodate silver-mining interests in the West. It mandated that the Treasury Department buy millions of ounces of silver each year and convert it to silver dollars. At the time, the world price of silver bullion was dropping, and there were economic difficulties in the Western mining states. From 1878 to 1904 and again in 1921, silver dollars of the Morgan design were minted under Bland-Allison and subsequent acts, to the extent of 656,989,387 pieces. From 1921 to 1928, and in 1934 and 1935, silver dollars of the Peace design were produced in the amount of 190,577,279 pieces.

Although silver dollars were used in commerce in certain areas of the West, paper currency by and large served the needs of trade and exchange. As these hundreds of millions of newly minted dollars were not needed, most were put up in 1,000-coin canvas bags and stored in Treasury vaults. In 1918, under terms of the Pittman Act, 270,232,722 Morgan dollars were melted. At the time, with World War I in its fifth year, the market for silver was temporarily strong, and there was a call for bullion to ship to India to shore up confidence in Britain's wartime government. No accounting was kept of the dates and mints involved in the destruction. Only the quantities were recorded (this procedure being typical when the Treasury melted old coins). However, hundreds of millions remained. Now and again there was a call for silver dollars for circulation, especially in the West; and in the East and Midwest there was a modest demand for pieces for use as holiday and other gifts; in such instances many were paid out. The example of the high-mintage 1901

Typical silver mining scene, late 1880s.

THE CARSON CITY SILVER DOLLARS THE LAST OF A LEGACY

The cover to a GSA flyer advertising the Treasury's hoard of Carson City silver dollars for sale.

dollar being rare in Mint State, as most were circulated, is reflective of this. Other coins were stored, such as the low-mintage 1884-CC, of which 84.7% were still in the hands of the Treasury as late as 1964! At this time the Treasury decided to hold back bags that were marked as having Carson City dollars, although in records of storage no account was made of them earlier.

Beginning in a significant way in the 1950s, silver dollars became very popular with numismatists. The rarest of all Morgan silver dollars by 1962 was considered to be the 1903-O. In that year's *Guide Book of United States Coins*, an Uncirculated coin listed for $1,500, the highest price for any variety. Experts estimated that fewer than a dozen Mint State coins existed in all of numismatics. It was presumed that most had been melted in 1918 under the Pittman Act.

A Carson City Morgan dollar from the Treasury release.

Then, in November 1962, during the normal payout of silver dollars as gifts for the holiday season, some long-sealed bags of coins were taken from a Philadelphia Mint vault that had remained under seal since 1929. It was soon found that brilliant 1903-O dollars were among these! A treasure hunt ensued, and hundreds of thousands of these former rarities were found. The rush was on!

From then until March 1964, hundreds of millions of Morgan and Peace dollars were emptied from government and bank storage. At one time a long line of people, some with wheelbarrows, formed outside of the Treasury Building in Washington, D.C., to obtain bags of dollars. Finally only about three million coins remained, mostly the aforementioned Carson City issues, which the Treasury decided to hold back. These were later sold at strong premiums in a series of auctions held by the General Services Administration (GSA). In the meantime, Morgan and Peace dollars became very large and important sections of the coin hobby, as they remain today. However, as can be seen, the combined elements of some coins' having been melted in 1918, others having been placed into circulation generations ago, and still others existing in Mint State from long-stored hoards, results in silver dollar prices that often bear little relation to mintage figures.

OTHER FAMOUS HOARDS

While the great Treasury release of 1962 through 1964 is the most famous of all hoards, quite a few others have attracted interest and attention over the years.

- **The Castine Hoard of Early Silver Coins (discovered in the 1840s).** From November 1840 through April 1841, Captain Stephen Grindle and his son Samuel unearthed many silver coins on their farm on the Bagaduce River about six miles from the harbor of Castine, Maine. The number of pieces found was not recorded, but is believed to have been between 500 and 2,000, buried in 1690 (the latest date observed) or soon afterward. Most pieces were foreign silver coins, but dozens of Massachusetts Pine Tree shillings and related silver coins were found. This hoard stands today as one of the most famous in American history.

- **The Bank of New York Hoard (1856).** Around 1856 a keg containing several thousand 1787 Fugio copper cents was found at the Bank of New York at 44 Wall Street. Each was in Mint State, most with brown toning. For many years these were given out as souvenirs and keepsakes to clients. By 1948, when numismatist Damon G. Douglas examined them, there were 1,641 remaining. Today, many remain at the bank and are appreciated for their history and value.

- **The Nichols Find of Copper Cents (by 1859).** In the annals of American numismatics, one of the most famous hoards is the so-called Nichols Find, consisting of 1796 and 1797 copper cents, Mint State, perhaps about 1,000 in total. These were distributed in the late 1850s by David Nichols. All were absorbed into the hobby community as of 1863, by which time they were worth $3 to $4 each, or less than a thousandth of their present-day value.

- **The Randall Hoard of Copper Cents (1860s).** Sometime soon after the Civil War, a wooden keg filled with as-new copper cents was located, said to have been beneath an old railroad platform in Georgia. Revealed were thousands of coins dated 1816 to 1820, with the 1818 and 1820 being the most numerous. Today, the Randall hoard accounts for most known Mint State examples of these particular dates.

- **The Colonel Cohen Hoard of 1773 Virginia Halfpennies (by the 1870s).** Sometime in the 1870s or earlier, Colonel Mendes I. Cohen, a Baltimore numismatist, obtained a cache of at least 2,200 Uncirculated 1773 Virginia halfpennies. These passed through several hands, and many individual pieces were dispersed along the way. As a result, today they are the only colonial (pre-1776) American coins that can be easily obtained in Mint State.

- **The Exeter Hoard of Massachusetts Silver (1876).** During the excavation of a cellar near the railroad station in Exeter, New Hampshire, a group of 30 to 40 Massachusetts silver shillings was found in the sand, amid the remains of what seemed to be a wooden box. All bore the date 1652 and were of the Pine Tree and Oak Tree types, plus, possibly, a rare Willow Tree shilling.

- **The Economite Treasure (1878).** In 1878 a remarkable hoard of silver coins was found in a subterranean storage area at Economy, Pennsylvania, in a building erected years earlier by the Harmony Society, a utopian work-share community. The March 1881 issue of the *Coin Collector's Journal* gave this inventory: Quarter dollars: 1818 through 1828, 400 pieces. Half dollars: 1794, 150; 1795, 650; 1796, 2; 1797, 1; 1801, 300; 1802, 200; 1803, 300; 1805 Over 04, 25; 1805, 600; 1806, 1,500; 1807, 2,000; 1815, 100. Common half dollars: 1808 through 1836, 111,356. Silver dollars: 1794, 1; 1795, 800; 1796, 125; 1797, 80; 1798 Small Eagle reverse, 30; 1798 Large Eagle reverse, 560; 1799 5 stars facing, 12; 1799, 1,250; 1800, 250; 1801, 1802, and 1803, 600. Foreign silver (French, Spanish, and Spanish-American), total face value: $12,600. Total face value of the hoard: $75,000. Other information indicates that most of the coins had been taken from circulation and showed different degrees of wear.

- **The Hoard of Miser Aaron White (before 1888).** Aaron White, a Connecticut attorney, distrusted paper money and even went so far as to issue his own token with the legend NEVER KEEP A PAPER DOLLAR IN YOUR POCKET TILL TOMORROW. He had a passion for saving coins and accumulated more than 100,000 pieces. After his death the coins were removed to a warehouse. Later, they were placed in the hands of dealer Édouard Frossard, who sold most of them privately and others by auction on July 20, 1888, billing them as "18,000 American and foreign copper coins and tokens selected from the Aaron White hoard." An overall estimate of the White hoard, as it existed before it was given to Frossard, was made by Benjamin P. Wright, and included these: "250 colonial and state copper coins, 60,000 copper large cents (which were mainly 'rusted' and spotted; 5,000 of the nicest ones were picked out and sold for 2¢ each), 60,000 copper-nickel Flying Eagle and Indian cents (apparently most dated 1862 and 1863), 5,000 bronze two-cent pieces, 200 half dollars, 100 silver dollars, 350 gold dollars, and 20,000 to 30,000 foreign copper coins."

- **The Collins Find of 1828 Half Cents (1894).** Circa 1894, Benjamin H. Collins, a Washington, D.C., numismatist, acquired a bag of half cents dated 1828, of the 13-stars variety. Historians believe that about 1,000 coins were involved, all bright Uncirculated. By the early 1950s all but a few hundred had been distributed in the marketplace, and by now it is likely that all have individual owners.

- **The Chapman Hoard of 1806 Half Cents (1906).** About 1906, Philadelphia dealer Henry Chapman acquired a hoard of 1806 half cents. Although no figure was given at the time, it is estimated that a couple hundred or so coins were involved. Most or all had much of their original mint red color, toning to brown, and with light striking at the upper part of the wreath.

- **The Baltimore Find (1934).** One of the most storied hoards in American numismatics is the Baltimore Find, a cache of at least 3,558 gold coins, all dated before 1857. On August 31, 1934, two young boys were playing in the cellar of a rented house at 132 South Eden Street, Baltimore, and found these coins hidden in a wall. Later, more were found in the same location. On May 2, 1935, many of the coins were sold at auction, by which time others had been sold quietly, some unofficially. This hoard included many choice and gem coins dated in the 1850s. Leonard Augsburger's award-winning *Treasure in the Cellar* tells the complete tale.

- **The New Orleans Bank Find (1982).** A few minutes past noon, on October 29, 1982, a bulldozer unearthed a cache of long-hidden silver coins, believed to have been stored in three wooden boxes in the early 1840s. They were mostly Spanish-American issues, but hundreds of United States coins, including 1840-O and 1841-O Liberty Seated quarters, were also found. Men in business suits, ladies in dresses, and others scrambled in the dirt and mud to find treasure. The latest-dated coin found was from 1842. This must have been a secret reserve of some long-forgotten merchant or bank.

- **Wells Fargo Hoard of 1908 $20 (1990s).** In the 1990s, dealer Ron Gillio purchased a hoard of 19,900 examples of the 1908, No Motto, double eagle. For a time these were stored in a Wells Fargo Bank branch, giving the name to the cache. All were Mint State, and many were of choice and gem quality. Offered in the market, these were dispersed over a period of several years.

- **Gold coins from abroad (turn of the 21st century).** In the late 20th and early 21st centuries, some exciting finds of Mint State double eagles were located in foreign banks. Involved were high-grade examples of some Carson City issues in the Liberty Head series and hundreds of scarce-mintmark varieties dated after 1923. As is often the case when hoards are discovered, pieces were filtered into the market without any publicity or an accounting of varieties found.

SUNKEN TREASURE

Throughout American history, tens of thousands of ships have been lost at sea and on inland waters. Only a handful of these vessels were reported as having had significant quantities of coins aboard. In recent decades, numismatists have been front-row center as wrecks from several sidewheel steamers lost in the 1850s and 1860s have yielded rare coins.

The SS *New York* was launched in 1837, carrying passengers between New York City and Charleston, South Carolina. The steamer was carrying $30,000 or more in money when she encountered an unexpected hurricane in the Gulf of Mexico on September 5, 1846. Captain John D. Phillips ordered the anchor dropped, hoping to ride out the storm. The wind and waves increased, however, and for two days those aboard watched as the rigging and other parts of the ship were torn apart. On September 7 the storm prevailed and the *New York* was overwhelmed, sinking into water 60 feet deep. An estimated 17 people—about one third of the passengers and crew—lost their lives. Decades later, in 2006 and 2007, treasure seekers recovered more than 2,000 silver coins and several hundred gold coins from the shipwreck. Most of the silver was heavily etched from exposure to the salt water, but certain of the gold coins were in high grades, including some of the finest known examples of their date and mint.

Eight years after the loss of the *New York*, the SS *Yankee Blade* was off the coast of Santa Barbara, California, steaming at full speed in a heavy fog. Captain Henry T. Randall believed the ship was in deep water far out to sea, and he was trying to establish a speed record—certain to be beneficial in advertising. In fact the steamer was amid the rockbound Channel Islands, and in the fog she smashed onto a rock and got hung up. The date was October 1, 1854. On board was some $152,000 in coins consigned by a banking house, plus other gold, and about 900 passengers and crew. Most of them escaped, but in the ensuing confusion before the *Yankee Blade* sank, between 17 and 50 lost their lives. Over the years most of the coins appear to have been recovered, under circumstances largely unknown. In 1948 the hull was found again and divers visited the wreck. Around 1977 more recoveries were yielded, including 200 to 250 1854-S double eagles. All showed microscopic granularity, possibly from the action of sea-bottom sand, and all had die cracks on the reverse. Little in the way of hard facts has ever reached print.

The wreck and recovery of the SS *Central America* was much better documented. The steamer was lost on September 12, 1857, carrying about $2.6 million in gold treasure, heading from Havana, Cuba, to New York City. A monster hurricane engulfed the ship on the 10th and 11th; Captain William Lewis Herndon enlisted the aid of male passengers to form a bucket brigade to bail water, but their efforts proved futile. The ship was swamped, and the captain ordered the American flag be flown upside-down, a signal of distress. The nearby brig *Marine* approached and nearly all of the *Central America*'s women and children were transferred over, along with some crew members, before the *Central America* was overwhelmed by the waves and went down, with Captain Herndon standing on the paddle box. The steamer ultimately settled 7,200 feet deep, and some 435 lives were lost. The wreck was found in 1987 and over time more than $100 million worth of treasure was brought to the surface. This included more than 5,400 mint-fresh 1857-S double eagles, hundreds of gold ingots (including one weighing 80 pounds), and other coins.

In the 1990s another sidewheel steamer was found: the SS *Brother Jonathan*, lost with few survivors as she attempted to return to safe harbor in Crescent City, California, after hitting stormy weather on her way north to Oregon (January 30, 1865). More than 1,000 gold coins were recovered from the wreck, including many Mint State 1865-S double eagles. Detailed files and photographs recorded every step of the recovery.

In 2003 another 1865 shipwreck was located: that of the SS *Republic*, lost off the coast of Georgia while en route from New York City to New Orleans on October 25, just months after the Civil War ended. The steamer sank in a hurricane along with a reported $400,000 in silver and gold. Recovery efforts brought up 51,000 coins and 14,000 other artifacts (bottles, ceramics, personal items, etc.). The coins included 1,400 double eagles dating from 1838 to 1858, and thousands from the 1850s and 1860s; plus more than 180 different examples of Liberty Seated half dollars, including five 1861-O die combinations attributed to Confederate control of the New Orleans mint. The most valuable single coin was a Mint State 1854-O double eagle, then valued at more than $500,000.

Shipwrecks continue to be found even today, and the hobby community eagerly awaits news of coins and treasure found amidst their watery resting places.

THE STORY OF AMERICAN MONEY

This introduction to U.S. coins is based on the work of the late Dr. Richard G. Doty,
senior curator of numismatics at the Smithsonian Institution.

Much of the early story of American coins focuses on the importation, adaptation, manufacture, and spread of a variety of monetary forms by the European colonizers of America and their descendants. To set the stage, though, we must first render an accounting of earlier peoples—Native Americans—and the monies they created.

Native Americans were more practical than Europeans—their monies were rooted in their immediate experience, in their proximate environment. While Europeans remained wedded to one particular monetary form, coinage, native peoples used what was there and did quite well.

But before we examine any examples in particular, we should realize that, regardless of time or place, any exchange medium must satisfy a number of requirements. If it does so, it will stand as viable money, likely to remain in fashion; if it does not, it will soon be replaced by something else. To be money, objects with *durability* have distinct advantages over their competitors. The aspiring monetary form should be *practical*, either directly or indirectly. It must be *easily quantifiable*. It must be of *moderate scarcity*, rare enough to possess an aura of desirability, plentiful enough so that everyone can see it and have at least a minimal chance of obtaining it. Finally, *beauty*, either for display or for other purposes, gives some potential trading objects an advantage over others (without being an absolute requirement for any of them). With these conditions met, nearly anything, either natural or manufactured, can become money.

Just what media the Native Americans used depended on their location, at least to a degree. Peoples occupying an area rich in fur-bearing animals would probably incorporate pelts into their monetary-exchange practices. But so might adjacent peoples who occupied areas where game was scarce. And while shells might form trading objects for coastal tribes, they might be known and used in the interior as well—at least in areas connected with the seacoast by reasonably easy communication.

THE EARLY AMERICAN "MONEY"

Hides and shells became the foundation of native monetary systems in the lands that would become the United States and Canada. In time, particular types of pelts and particular varieties of shells came to hold a special regard and became units or standards of value. The beaver's skin gained such a role, perhaps because the animal was regarded as sacred by many peoples. Skins of other animals were traded as multiples and fractions of one beaver, and when European commodities came to the tribes, the new goods too were tariffed in terms of so many to one "made" beaver (that is, a properly skinned and tanned pelt).

Elsewhere, shells, clams, and conchs were extremely important, for they were the raw materials behind the most important single type of native currency in all of North America. This was wanpanpiage, wampumpeage, or wampum.

Wampum is an old Algonquian word meaning "a string of white beads." Another term, *suckauhock*, was used for strings fashioned from purple beads, but the earliest European settlers tended to use the shortened term *wampum* indiscriminately, and their practice survives. Wampum consisted of short beads, cut from the shells of clams and conchs, drilled by hand, and strung. This means of trade appears to have originally seen employment when woven into patterned belts, for telling stories and conveying messages. It only gradually came into use as a display of wealth and, finally, as a unit of wealth. We know that it had achieved this final, crucial stage and was an accepted form of money before European settlement, for the explorer Jacques Cartier found it so employed in the mid-1530s. We believe we understand why it achieved popularity as a monetary form: under pre-industrial conditions, wampum was difficult to manufacture. It served as a unit of value because of the work and skill required to make it.

Wampum was popular on the Atlantic seaboard of North America, among both Native Americans and European newcomers. There was a parallel monetary form on the Pacific seaboard, based on the shell of a different sea creature, the dentalium (or tooth shell), but it never captured the attention of the European newcomers in the way that wampum did, and it played little role in post-contact economies.

To the south, other trading objects held sway. In Mexico, copper axe-shaped objects called *siccapili* (in modern Spanish *tajaderas*, "chopping knives") found popularity among Aztecs and their contemporaries—so much so that the earth is still yielding large numbers of them to the plows of modern farmers. Cacao beans were mainstays of the Aztec monetary system, and they illustrate one of the earliest instances of the debasement of a non-coin monetary form: the delicious contents of the cacao bean were sometimes scooped out and substituted with earth, the skin carefully replaced, and the extraction cleverly hidden.

Corn was also used as a trade commodity, and so was gold, either cast into bars or traded in transparent quills so that its purity could be seen by all. Hernán Cortés found tin circulating as money in several of the provinces through which he and his tiny band marched on their way to glory, but his compatriot Francisco Pizarro found much less to the south. The economy of the Inca Empire was paternalistic, socialistic—so planned, in fact, that commercial transactions (and thus the employment of money) were largely unnecessary. But it has been suggested that leaves of the coca plant—the source of a modern, international commodity called cocaine—may have enjoyed a limited monetary function prior to the Spanish conquest.

Elsewhere in the Americas, tribes in what became Venezuela appear to have used strings of shells, a form of money similar to wampum although probably not inspired by it. Some of the Brazilian peoples used arrows; others used stringed beads of snail shells. The latter practice persisted in Mato Grosso, Brazil, well into the 20th century.

The longevity of this particular form of money should alert us to an important fact about "primitive" monetary forms: they did not all obligingly disappear when the first Europeans arrived on American shores. While few of them displayed the persistence seen with the shell money of Mato Grosso (in part because few places in the Americas were as impenetrable as this jungle area in western Brazil), many of them were found as useful by new settlers as old, and they formed essential links between old economies and new.

Indeed, it is difficult to see how the numismatic history of the United States could have been written in the absence of the skins of fur-bearing animals and the shells of creatures of the sea. Along with commodities known to and developed by Native Americans (but not generally used by them for trade) and scant supplies of coinage and other trading objects brought from Europe, furs and shells would form most of the basis of our early money—but not all. A final ingredient was being created to the south, one whose influence would be so persistent and ultimately so potent that it would shape the very way we reckoned and fashioned our symbols of wealth.

Aztec *siccapili* or *tajadera*, an axe-shaped object used as money in Mexico; one was worth 8,000 cacao beans (like those pictured).

THE SPANISH CENTURIES

This final ingredient was the Spanish conquest of most of the Western Hemisphere. It began with Columbus's first voyage in 1492, and in some ways it is still going on, as the spread of Spanish language and culture across today's United States suggests. But it was far more active, and far less peaceful, five centuries ago.

At that time, nothing less than the wholesale exportation of one way of life (and a snuffing-out or radical transmutation of many others) was occurring. We have no idea how many millions died in the process—from new diseases, from new and merciless labor systems—but the event certainly stands as the greatest of all holocausts, the most massive population revolution in all of human history.

While it was running its course, a hybrid society was being created, and in it the Spanish worldview would predominate, first by force, later by tradition. Of course, one of the key elements in the Spanish world was the *coin*—and attached to it was the belief that this small metallic object and wealth were essentially interchangeable, simultaneous concepts. The idea did not originate in Spain, but when Spaniards carried it to the Americas, a number of interesting events took place. All of them stemmed from a central fact: the new lands contained vast quantities of silver and gold.

These metals were, of course, one of the primary reasons Spanish colonization began and was maintained. At first the newcomers were happy merely to appropriate what had been collected by someone else. These metals were sent back to the homeland and were quickly turned into coinage there.

Then, just as they were running through the last of the precious metals they had appropriated, Spain's people soon began finding new, raw sources of American gold and silver. At first this metal was simply refined on the spot and sent in ingot form to Sevilla, where it was turned into coinage and would soon benefit commerce in Spain and eventually all of Europe.

But metal in ingot form would be of no particular use to those who had actually found it. These people, in the Caribbean islands, Mexico, Peru, and Bolivia, were developing expanding consumer economies by the middle years of the 16th century—economies that needed coinage if they were to continue to expand.

And so an obvious though era-defining solution was devised: let the locals make their own coinage, following Spanish forms, denominations, and designs. It was obvious in part because of the primitive minting technology then in force: virtually anybody could make a creditable coin, provided the metal was at hand. But it defined the era because this was the first time anyone had ever done so in the Western Hemisphere. For the first time in human history, the concept and the making of coins spread beyond Europe and Asia, the lands of their birth.

THE EMERGENCE OF A STAPLE

By 1625 no fewer than eight mints had been established in Spanish America. Of them, several didn't last long (those at Santo Domingo, La Plata, Panama, and Cartagena), and two were sporadic (Bogotá and Lima). Two other mints were unqualified successes from the beginning: those of Mexico City, which struck its first coins in 1536, and Potosí, which entered production about four decades later. No final reckoning of the production of these facilities can ever be made, but the combined output of Mexico City and Potosí alone was several billion pieces.

Coins from these mints made their way into the pockets of local burghers, paused there only momentarily, then made their journey to Spain and flowed out of that country almost as soon as they entered it. They paid for wars; they furnished luxuries and even necessities that a local population—enamored of the instant wealth and good life promised by the coins—either could not or would not create at home. Those coins traveled in odd directions and found strange resting places: hordes of them have been discovered along the coast of China, suggesting that the commerce of the 17th century was far more complex than we had previously imagined.

We call these crude coins "cobs," the name perhaps derived from *cabo de barra*, "end of a bar." The name provides a clue to their manufacture. A rough ingot was cast, then crudely sliced into coin-size planchets or blanks. The blanks could be adjusted down to their desired weight by means of a file, after which they were struck by hand. Cobs were struck in both gold and silver, but silver predominated at most mints. Within the coinage of that metal, one denomination in particular came to overshadow all the others. This was the piece of eight, and it would finally become the most successful, longest-lived trade coin in all of human history.

Between its introduction (probably in the 1530s, though possibly somewhat earlier) and its demise, some 400 years would elapse. The piece of eight would be struck at half a dozen mints in Spain, and in more than two dozen mints in Spanish America and the independent successor states. The final examples would appear in 1949, when the failing Nationalist government of Chiang Kai-shek asked the Mexico City mint to strike several million pieces on its behalf as an alternative to its own inflated currency.

The piece of eight's brothers were the Joachimsthaler and its descendants: the Danish daler, the French écu, the British crown, and others, all of which came into being because of a greater abundance of silver during late-medieval and early-modern times. But the piece of eight overshadowed them all because it was able to draw on a larger source of metal than any of its competitors. Its persistence, and that of the other members of the series, surprises us when we least expect it. Consider, for example, that the New York Stock Exchange quoted securities in terms of an eighth of a point until 1997 because the *real*—the eighth of a piece of eight—was the lowest increment allowed on the Wall Street bourse!

Typical "cob" coins of the early 1600s.

INTERLOPERS!

The Spanish conquest did not occur in a vacuum. In Europe, honest amazement over Columbus's success turned quickly to envy, denial, and determined attempts to match it. When the interlopers were done, the map of the Spanish Empire would be greatly altered, and the seeds of a new country would be planted. In time, those seeds would grow into the United States of America.

An unusual Mexican cob, pre-1700. Despite its bizarre shape, the coin was of good Mexican silver, and that was what mattered to those who spent it.

The people who planted those particular seeds were Britons, but they were not the first to dispute Spanish exclusivity in the Americas. The first non-Spaniards to do something about the new transatlantic possibility were Spain's neighbors on the Iberian Peninsula, the Portuguese. Lisbon had been sending explorers down and around the African coast since the mid-1480s; in 1500, one of its captains, Pedro Álvares Cabral, just happened to get blown so far off course that he arrived at a new land altogether, on the far side of the Atlantic. This was named after a rosy-red dyewood found there—Brazil. By the 1530s the Portuguese were making a determined attempt to settle the vast new land that their captain had discovered.

Other Europeans soon entered the fray, first biting off bits of Spanish and Portuguese wealth; they would soon be biting off bits of Spanish and Portuguese *land*, as well. The wealth was appropriated first probably because it involved less of an outlay on the part of national governments. The original Iberian conquests had largely been affairs of private enterprise for public gain; so were many of the early efforts to redistribute the loot.

The first targets of attack were those Spanish vessels carrying home the rich American cargos of silver, gold, and other commodities. By the 1520s these vessels were being attacked and captured, their contents triumphantly carried into French harbors. The Spanish retaliated as best they could, arming their merchantmen and soon creating a convoy system featuring two main arrangements. In the first, vessels brought Spanish (and, increasingly, other European) goods one way, and carried gold, silver, and other American materials the other. In the second, convoys crossed the Pacific, voyaging all the way from Acapulco to the Philippines, carrying pieces of eight to Manila where they were traded for Chinese products, especially spices and silks.

This *flota* system made transport much safer, and it also made matters easier for royal bookkeepers back home because all legal trade was conducted and controlled through a single channel. However, raids on outlying vessels were common, especially when the scourge of hurricanes scattered members of the convoy. Indeed, the weather sent more vessels to the bottom than did Spain's enemies.

There were other ways of capitalizing on Spanish good fortune. A series of increasingly audacious captains, ranging from Hawkins to Drake to Morgan to Anson, conducted raids on Spanish-American cities. These were coastal sites, where rich cargos were gathered prior to shipment to Spain. One could move in quickly, pick up anything of value, and then decamp before the Spanish navy arrived on the scene. To this day, we are impressed by the massive walls of Campeche in Mexico and Cartagena in Colombia—those walls had to be thick if they were to keep out the likes of Sir Francis Drake and company!

Eventually they began doing more than simply raiding: they began wintering over, and what had been targets for looting became places for permanent settlement. As peoples from Scandinavia had with the rich towns on the coasts and rivers of England, Ireland, and France centuries earlier, Britons, French, Danes, Dutchmen, and Swedes began nibbling away at lands that their controllers were unable or unwilling to defend.

The enemies of Spain and Portugal turned up in the strangest places. We most certainly would not expect to see the enterprising Dutch in Brazil. But they were there, nevertheless, occupying the area around Recife for nearly a quarter of a century—and for the record, they were striking the first true Brazilian coins there in 1645, precisely half a century before the Portuguese got around to setting up their first mint at Rio. The French had been in Brazil nearly a hundred years before, but had minted no coins to mark the occasion.

So the islands and bits of the mainland were eaten away. In time, the useful theory of "no peace beyond the line" was proclaimed by Spain and its enemies. It was a way of ensuring that, regardless of peace treaties in Europe, warfare might continue in the Indies as Spain's competitors attempted to take—and Spain attempted to defend and retake—lands and property as the opportunity appeared.

Of course, we are especially interested in the fortunes of one particular group of interlopers, the English. To understand the coins of the United States, we must explore what the English and those who followed managed to do with their particular share of New World treasure.

THE THIRTEEN COLONIES AND THEIR MONIES

British colonization of the future United States began in earnest shortly after 1600. It was carried forward in a number of ways, by diverse peoples, and from a variety of motives. In Virginia, whose first settlement was loyally named *Jamestown* after the reigning British monarch, economic profit was the primary motive. In Massachusetts, a religious motive—the desire to commune with the Deity in a particular, though officially frowned-upon, fashion—led to the Pilgrim settlement at inhospitable Plymouth. A few miles to the north, a second settlement was established some 10 years later, in 1630. Unlike Plymouth, Boston was a going concern from the very beginning, perhaps because its founders were both people of conscience and people of business. Merchants of the town would soon be trading in a number of places where they had no business operating—with interesting effects upon America's money.

The economic and religious motives behind the founding of these colonies and others often were intertwined so completely that neither original colonizers nor subsequent historians could separate them. But this simple fact should not blind us to the complex nature of the fabric of America's early culture. The identity, color, and weave of that fabric would shift over time, as they still do today.

For example, dissenting Protestants were hardly the only sects represented in the new settlements. Maryland, which was first colonized at St. Mary's City in 1634, was meant as a haven for English Catholics. Other non-Anglican peoples came over too: Jews were represented by the 1640s at the latest, while Lutherans would be found here as early as the 1630s.

What's more, the fabric did in fact contain bold colors other than British red, as there was more than one colonizing country along the Eastern seaboard. Swedes penetrated the future Delaware, building Fort Christina (the future Wilmington—loyally named after their current monarch) in 1638, holding power there and along the adjacent rivers until 1655. The Dutch ejected them from that region and nearby settlements in New Jersey in 1655, leaving behind an architectural legacy in the form of the New World's first log cabins.

The Dutch remained the main players in the Middle Colonies, as well as Manhattan Island, until 1664, when Britons swept the Hollanders. Still, those areas long retained a determinedly non-English flavor, including a splendid, distinctly unusual tolerance for non-Christians. The Dutch also left another legacy to those who would follow: they had become accustomed to trading in the Native American monetary medium called wampum, to which they were introducing their English neighbors by the end of the 1620s.

By the mid-1600s, the British and their competitors were moving into new places ranging from Maine to Virginia. Settlers looking for economic opportunity and political liberty were advancing along the Connecticut River by the early and middle 1630s. Other pioneers in search of religious toleration were settling that smallest and quirkiest of British colonies, Rhode Island, just a few years later.

South of Virginia, colonization generally came later. South Carolina was set up as a proprietary colony, an arrangement tending to result in closer ties with the mother country than was usually the case elsewhere. North Carolina, home of the first and failed English colonial experiment at Roanoke in the 1580s, was one of the last places to be settled. The combination of coastal swamps and hostile Native Americans would long act to deter full European colonization of this area, and the European population of North Carolina would long remain modest.

English Catholics, under the protection of King Charles, colonized the region that would become Maryland. Here, they bargain with Native Americans.

That left Pennsylvania and Georgia. Both were "planned" settlements; unlike many other places, these two areas of British colonization were deliberately organized and selected, and they were brought into existence from a mixture of public and private goals. Pennsylvania was intended in part as a home for adherents of another non-Anglican religious sect facing difficulties at home, the Society of Friends (or Quakers). Though the Swedes and Dutch were there first, the pious Quakers had the better of the argument: in 1681, William Penn (to whose father King Charles II of England owed a good deal of money) accepted a royal grant to a vast new domain. This area was named after him—Pennsylvania, or "Penn's Woods."

The motives for founding Georgia were no less laudable. Led by James Oglethorpe, a number of British philanthropists were interested in establishing a haven where debtors might go to get a second chance in life. They shared their aspirations with the British government, which was interested in setting up a buffer zone between its established colonies to the north and Spanish Florida to the south. The goals of both groups coalesced in the founding of Savannah in 1733.

CHALLENGES—AND INNOVATIONS—FOR NEW ENGLAND

By the early years of the 18th century, British colonization had been underway for five generations. What had resulted was not one single, uninterrupted stretch of British red from Maine to Georgia, but a number of nuclei of varying sizes and fortunes, rather like beads on a string—with large spaces between one bead and another.

Despite extensive searching, these colonizers found no gold, no silver, and precious little copper. Indeed, nothing much would be found for more than 200 years. No metal meant no local coins. Combined with two other factors, this metallic dearth would ensure that the monetary development of the future United States could not and would not proceed on a "normal" and preferred path.

The European contribution to the monetary problem was a politico-economic theory of national wealth and power called *mercantilism*. Simply stated, mercantilism viewed a colony and its mother country in a fixed, monopolistic trading relationship, in which almost everything of value found in the ground or grown on the land was sent home. Furthermore, anything needed by the colonists that they could not produce themselves had to be sent from the mother country and paid for in the currency of the mother country. In other words, any coins that the colonies managed to accumulate should be remitted to the metropolis in payment for goods received under the closed economic arrangement.

If we apply the theory of mercantilism to the metal-poor British colonies along the Atlantic coast, logic tells us that the British government would hardly make an effort to export coinage to these shores when it was seeking to extract wealth from them. Furthermore, because trading was legally circumscribed, logic also suggests that the British colonies would remain coin-poor if the British metropolis remained true to the mercantilist idea. And this, of course, it did: hadn't mercantilism enriched the Spanish and the Portuguese?

The American contribution to the monetary crisis was a failure to satisfy the two conditions absolutely necessary for the functioning of a cashless economy: limited trading and a stable population. Had these two conditions been in force, all might have been well—but they weren't.

Almost from the beginning, these British colonies were economic and demographic successes, so that the monetary supply never had a chance of catching up with, much less surpassing, the monetary demand. Far from easily sending coinage back to Britain, people here could have used every spare piece of change that Britain could send. Along with the shortage of native precious metals, this inability of supply to ever meet demand would shape the story of American numismatics for a quarter of a millennium. It was even more important than the influence of mercantilism, as it continued to mold America's money long after the British and their theory had departed its shores.

Faced with perpetual lack and growing need, confronted with the very results of their success, the men and women of New England and the other colonies would replicate, create, try, reject, and redesign every monetary form ever invented anywhere else throughout the entire story of numismatics.

AMERICAN SOLUTIONS TO AMERICAN PROBLEMS

Their first investigations involved barter: if you don't have something, trade something else to get it. While theory tells us that anything can be swapped for anything else, logic tells us that some commodities have a better chance than others of becoming trading goods. The criteria mentioned earlier (durability, utility, scarcity, etc.) held true for the first colonists as they did for the Native Americans who witnessed their arrival.

The Europeans' list of preferred items included shot and powder, which were obviously useful in their new circumstances. It also contained nails, which may seem odd until we stop to think about it. Nails were obviously easily quantifiable, they were durable, they had utility, and they were very scarce in the beginning days of European settlement because they had to be imported from the old country. As such, nails were traded against British currency—a hundred of one size equal to six pence, a hundred of a larger size equal to ten pence, and so forth.

Other trade goods had a more direct connection with the land. In 1612 John Rolfe (who is perhaps better known as the husband of Pocahontas) saved the starving Virginia colony by putting in his first crop of tobacco, which could be traded for necessary supplies. The plant had come to Europe by the beginning of the 1560s, and by the late 1500s and early 1600s it was set to become Europe's latest craze. Consequently, Virginia's first legislature granted tobacco a monetary status in 1619, fixing its value at three shillings per pound for the best grade, half that for the lower grade.

Over the years, though, that high value descended precipitously. Bear in mind two of the primary conditions for the suitability of a commodity as money: it must be kept in short supply, and it must be durable. Tobacco proved to have neither property, as many residents of the Virginia colony soon began growing their own and thereby flooded the market. Also, the product itself was very susceptible to drying out or rotting. That, in turn, led to the development of "tobacco notes"—paper certificates issued against the value of the crop—which hinted at the direction American money would finally take.

Like the cultivation of tobacco, the trapping of wild animals for their pelts was adopted from Native Americans, and this would give colonists another form of commodity money—or rather several forms. While beaver was always the most popular pelt, and was the yardstick against which other pelts (and other goods, ranging from yards of cloth to thread, hats, shirts, and axes) were measured, otter skins were also popular, as were those of foxes and other animals. Furs were more popular in frontier areas than elsewhere, but their usage finally extended from the Atlantic to the Pacific, matching and anticipating the march of European settlement itself.

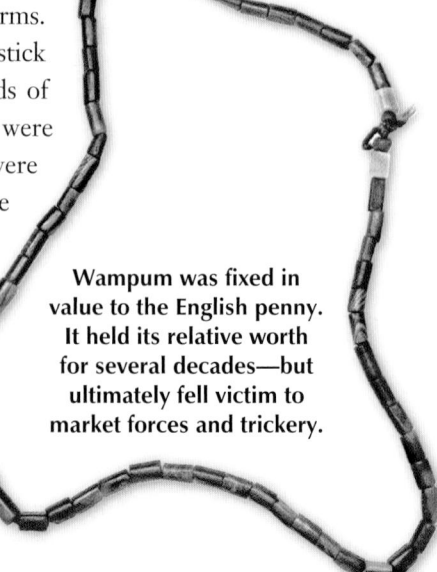

Wampum was fixed in value to the English penny. It held its relative worth for several decades—but ultimately fell victim to market forces and trickery.

One more commodity traded in the British colonies was the aforementioned wampum. Among the new arrivals to what would become the United States, the Dutch appear to have taken it up first: they would have obtained it from tribes on Long Island, a major center of wampum production for many years. In 1627 they carried it to Plymouth Colony, from whence it spread across New England and eventually to the South, where it was known as "roanoke."

As the incoming colonists happily embraced the medium as another partial solution to their chronic lack of cash, the established tribes began viewing it with increased favor as well, in part because their new neighbors seemed to take it so seriously. The growing popularity of this exchange medium led to two results that we might have anticipated: Wampum was overproduced, and it was adulterated.

When first introduced among European Americans, wampum was tariffed at so many beads to one English penny, in much the same manner as tobacco or nails. These fixed valuations began fraying in the late 1650s, however, as Native Americans—and enterprising Europeans as well—expanded production. Inevitably, wampum's value descended, and the last official use of the medium among Europeans appears to have taken place in the early 1690s. By then other monetary expedients were being pressed into service.

The counterfeiting of wampum, meanwhile, was achieved in Europe by the middle years of the 17th century and was sent to the New World along with other trading goods. A family of immigrants named Campbell began producing ceramic wampum later in the colonial period, and their operation continued until the closing years of the 19th century—which must represent a record of sorts for counterfeit money! Finally, other settlers discovered that the lower-valued white beads could be dyed to look like the more valuable purple variety; native tribes rarely fell for the adulteration, but it did gull the newcomers often enough.

EARLY AMERICAN COINAGE: MASSACHUSETTS

That grown men were playing childish tricks on each other suggests the monetary desperation in which they found themselves. Pelts, nails, tobacco, and wampum of varying plausibility—all would have been gladly cast aside at the sight of a coin. But no metal for such a coin existed. Even if it had, it would have to have been remitted to England, not retained in America. But one spot in the new lands was about to find a way around both limitations. That place was the town of Boston, and what Boston did must not only rank as a benchmark in the story of numismatics, but in that of the human spirit as well.

In 1652 the colonists of Massachusetts Bay began producing crude coins bearing a fancy NE (for "New England") on the obverse and the Roman numerals III, VI, or XII (for three, six, or twelve pence) on the reverse. They received the silver from illegal trade with the sugar islands of the Caribbean. The good people of Boston sent down rum, timber, and grain, and the good people of the Antilles sent back sugar and coins, mostly pieces of eight. These coins should have been sent on to England, but many of them were retained in Massachusetts, especially if they were lightweight or of poor silver quality (and, in fact, the mint at Potosí was then in the midst of a major scandal, corruptible minters having adulterated the silver coinage there).

In order to make the new coins unattractive to Britons and thereby keep them in circulation in the New World, local coiners deliberately made their new coins lightweight (compared to their British counterparts), while still expressing their denominations in British currency. This way, no London merchant would touch the coins (for he would have to go to the trouble of melting them down and selling them as bullion), but a Boston merchant would embrace them, for they would form part of a closed monetary system based on the familiar coins of the mother country.

Boston silversmith John Hull and his partner Robert Saunderson minted these coins between June and October 1652. Minting was stopped when it was realized that the tiny devices were easy targets for the clipper and the forger. The NE coins were soon followed by pieces of a more elaborate design, named after the type of tree occupying the central space on their obverses.

We call the earliest of these tree series "Willow Tree" pieces. They were made in tiny numbers between 1654 and 1660, double- and triple-struck, very rarely showing all of the designs on either side. They were followed by Oak Tree shillings and subdivisions (including a tiny twopence), and the Pine

Tree coins. The Pine Tree shilling is perhaps the most readily available of our early colonial issues; it is also among the most famous of all American coins and will repay a closer look.

On the obverse stands a pine tree. This tree may be an oblique reference to one of New England's few truly valuable exports at the time: timber for masts for the Royal Navy. Around the tree is the name of the colony, rendered as MASATHVSETS, a spelling that supposedly mimicked the sound of the original Native American name for the region. On the reverse, the remainder of the mint name is spelled out, along with the denomination XII, for twelve pence or one shilling, and the date.

It is this date that adds the final element of ingenuity to the Massachusetts silver coinage. With one exception, it is always rendered as 1652 (the exception is the Oak Tree twopence, dated 1662). This was the case for one of two reasons. First, the mint was founded in 1652. However, the second possibility is far more likely: the coins were deliberately and consistently dated 1652 to evade English law.

Under that law, the king enjoyed sole right of coinage. But in 1652, there was no king: Royal Charles's head had been separated from his body some three years earlier, and Cromwell's Commonwealth of England ruled in royalty's place. Surely regicides would scarcely look askance at a Massachusetts coinage.

In 1660 the English monarchy was restored, and there was an even greater reason to retain the old date on the coinage, as an issue dated 1652 could pass for an old coin struck when there was no king. As it turns out, King Charles had more important matters on his mind anyway, and he left the upstart coinage alone for the first two decades of his reign. During those years, the Oak Tree pieces were struck (down to 1667), as well as two issues of Pine Tree coins (between 1667 and 1674, and 1675 and 1682).

From top: Massachusetts Willow Tree shilling, Oak Tree shilling, and Pine Tree shilling.

Hull and Saunderson's contract with the Massachusetts General Court expired in 1682, and there seems to have been no talk about a renewal of the agreement. The tiny mint appears to have been working full bore for the last two years of its existence, as colonial authorities began receiving indications that the Crown was finally about to resume its prerogatives; they accordingly hurried their local coiners along. London did reassert its monopoly over the coinage, and soon enough Sir Edmund Andros was appointed as the new governor of a centralized, dictatorial administration embracing all of New England. Andros had instructions to bring the region to heel; they may have included a forced resumption of barter.

OTHER EARLY AMERICAN COINAGE

While Massachusetts was producing its own coinage, others were coping as best they could. Maryland had coinage produced *for* it; the Catholic noblemen who founded the colony wished to provide convenient money for their co-religionists, and Cecil Calvert, second Lord Baltimore, had been granted the right to coin.

Although none of it is dated, we know that this issue was minted during the winter of 1658–1659, but we have no idea by whom it was struck. It is commonly suggested that these coins were made at the Tower of London, but the members of the series—silver shillings, sixpence, fourpence or "groats," threepence, and a "denarium" or copper penny, of which fewer than ten are known—are well struck and far superior to most British coinage of the period.

The possible connection to the Tower Mint is even less plausible, as Calvert was not convicted of a crime when arrested and questioned in a London court about his coinage. For these reasons and others, Richard Doty, senior curator of numismatics for the Smithsonian Institution, suggested Ireland as a possible site for the Calvert mint: "The fabric of these pieces does not suggest the Tower Mint to me, and a Catholic island would have been a logical and sympathetic place to coin for a Catholic nobleman."

Interestingly, Ireland is linked to a second series circulating in the early colonies, although that link is anything but direct. A Quaker named Mark Newbie (or Newby) led a number of the faithful to settle in the vicinity of the modern city of Camden, New Jersey, and brought with him a cask containing £30 worth of coppers to distribute. These pieces—farthings and halfpennies—are named after him ("Newbie coppers"); they are alternately known as St. Patrick coppers, for that saint adorns their reverses. And that brings us back to Ireland.

The coppers weren't struck there—they had an English origin—but they *were* coined for Irish consumption. They were originally intended to pay Charles I's Catholic troops, who were engaged in fighting Cromwell's people in the Ulster Rebellion. The pieces are believed to have been made in Dublin circa 1663 to 1672, and were finally demonetized by the end of the 1670s. That was when Newbie came across these pieces and gave them a new lease on life.

The St. Patrick coinage's attractive appearance is augmented by a bit of yellow metal (brass, meant to resemble gold), splashed onto the copper during the minting process and positioned so that the king would appear to be receiving a golden crown. This care suggests a limited mintage, a suggestion belied by the known number of die combinations—more than 120 for the farthings alone. They may have been created by Nicholas Briot, using the roller method, but we know far less about these pieces than we would like.

The designs of the so-called St. Patrick coppers were similar for both the farthing- and halfpenny-sized coins. On the halfpenny, the saint is shown blessing the faithful, with the legend ECCE GREX—"Behold the Flock."

The same may be said for a curious issue featuring an elephant on its obverse, intended for British settlement in the Carolinas. We know that much because the reverse of this copper halfpenny token says GOD: PRESERVE: CAROLINA: AND THE: LORDS: PROPRIETORS. It is clearly related to another, much rarer issue with a reference to the northern colonies, whose reverse inscription reads GOD: PRESERVE: NEW: ENGLAND. Both pieces are dated 1694, and both pieces are connected to a third—which is where our mystery begins.

This third token has the arms of London, along with the legend GOD: PRESERVE: LONDON, but no date. Many believe this coin was struck prior to the others, the reverse legend perhaps referring to the plague and Great Fire besetting the English capital in 1665–1666. Others believe that the London token was struck at the same time as the two others, in the mid-1690s, although they are unable to explain the legend.

As for the elephant, it has been suggested the beast was put on the obverse by order of the Royal African Company, which had gotten the copper for the issue from West Africa. Consider, also, that golden guineas from the reign of Charles II and his immediate successors bore a tiny elephant to suggest the origins of the metal they contained.

We know a bit more about one last piece, a fleeting reminder of the attempt by James II to achieve control over the inhabitants of British North America. The issue would be made from tin—a most unstable coining material if used alone, but a sop to the miners of tin-rich Cornwall—and bear an equestrian portrait of the king. They were shipped across the Atlantic, but in the inhospitable climate of the New World, they deteriorated rapidly. Today an unblemished piece is a major rarity. We know why these pieces were made, under whose franchise (Richard Holt's, granted by the king), who designed them (the artist John Croker), and where they were struck (at the Royal Mint, in the Tower of London), but we are somewhat confused as to their denomination. The pieces bear the legend VAL. 24. PART. REAL. (value 1/24-real), suggesting they were to be tied to a Spanish or Spanish-American monetary system rather than a British or British-American one. But this denomination cannot be equated with anything in common use in Spain, Great Britain, or their colonies. Pieces of a similar size were struck at the Tower by James II and circulated as halfpence, and generations of collectors have assumed that these American coins had the same value, regardless of denomination. But it *would* be satisfying to know what James and his coiners had intended.

PAPER MONEY ON THE AMERICAN SCENE

With James's successors, the story of America's money would take an essential new path, one it would follow for the next two centuries. The new monarchs, King William III and Queen Mary, promptly became involved in a war with the French in Canada. This struggle for control of North America would persist through most of the ensuing three-quarters of a century, and it would eventually leave the English victorious, even as the seeds were being planted for their most resounding defeat.

For us, the essential fact is this: English colonists were expected to do their bit for a war effort that was being waged at least partly for their benefit. The first time they were asked to contribute was in 1690, when Massachusetts was asked to pay expenses for a military action by the British against the French in Canada. The request put the colony in a quandary, for there was a scarcity of cash with which to meet it.

Someone in the colonial government hit upon an interesting idea: why not issue official paper certificates to hire the troops and purchase the supplies? This scheme would work because the colony and its citizens knew that they would be reimbursed by the Crown at the end of the war. But because that was the case, the scheme was carried forward another crucial step: because reimbursement had been promised and everyone knew it, and because the paper would therefore circulate as readily as coinage, why not leave it in circulation rather than redeem it at the end of the war, in the process augmenting cash in a cash-strapped economy?

It was done. In 1690 and 1691, two issues with an aggregate face value of £40,000 were printed and circulated. The notes were receivable by the colonial treasurer in payment of taxes at a 5 percent premium, which was another way of ensuring their popularity and use. The paper-money practice soon spread elsewhere, and a new chapter in the global story of numismatics was under way.

The next half-century would see numerous notable developments in paper money, from the public note-issuing bank to engraving, typesetting, and Benjamin Franklin's nature prints.

A SNAPSHOT AT MID-CENTURY: 1750

The year 1750 is a good time to pause for a moment, to review the nature of America's money during the best years of the colonial period. Paper had come to lie at its heart. By that year, 12 of the 13 colonies either had issued paper or were currently doing so, and the 13th, Virginia, would join the parade in 1755. An amazing amount of bartering still occurred as well, and not all of it in the backcountry. However, as this volume is concerned primarily with coins, that is where we will focus.

SUPPLIES FROM THE MOTHERLAND

Great Britain occasionally sent over coins as payment for American participation in its ongoing saga with the French. A large number of halfpennies and farthings arrived on these shores in that very manner in 1749, part of a remittance to Massachusetts for the colony's expedition to capture Cape Breton from the French. Much of the rest of the remittance was made up of silver coin, which likely flowed back to England in short order; but the coppers did stay in America.

The colonists also used coins struck in England but without official British designs. For example, William Wood was contracted by King George I to produce two issues—one for use in Ireland and one for use in the colonies, both of which eventually came to circulate in the latter. The Irish coins featured a seated figure of Hibernia, the American coins a splendid open rose; their common obverse was a right-facing portrait of the king. They were well struck in a handsome alloy invented by Wood, one he called "Bath metal," consisting of three-quarters copper, slightly less than one-quarter zinc, and a tiny amount of silver—though not nearly enough to make the coins struck from it circulate at their stipulated value.

William Wood's Rosa Americana design declared the American Rose to be UTILE DULCI—"Useful and Pleasant." Despite the sweet words, his shortweight coins were a flop.

After the Irish pieces were violently rejected by their intended users out of a combination of outraged nationalism and anger over their short weight, some of the "Hibernia" pieces were later foisted on the colonies, where they met with a somewhat better reception than did Wood's coins specifically struck for American consumption.

Those pieces—issued in twopenny, penny, and halfpenny denominations and known as the "Rosa Americana" coinage—were less than half the weight they theoretically should have been. But more to the point, the Crown had not bothered to consult local assemblies before shipping the coins to New England and New York. Colonials refused to accept them, and the Massachusetts legislature issued emergency parchment money for one penny, twopence, and threepence even *before* Wood's coinage arrived. As a result, the Rosa Americana coinage was never effectively put into circulation in the North (although it did enter commerce in the South somewhat later), and its poor reception persuaded Wood to suspend production early in 1724.

OTHER EXTRANATIONAL ALTERNATIVES

British mints were not the only source of coins used in the British colonies. Regardless of theory and legality, reality found Americans trading all over the world, bringing back foreign coinage as they did so. Provided the coinage was of good gold or silver, it circulated in the colonies by weight, and elaborate tables were prepared and published that enabled businessmen to calculate what a certain coin should weigh and how much it was worth against another.

Thus, pieces from silver French écus to Turkish golden zeri mahbubs were traded. That being said, Americans did come to prefer one issue in particular over others (including anything British): this was the piece of eight. By now, they knew it as the "Mexican dollar" (because most of those coming their way originated at the busy mint at Mexico City) or the "Spanish milled dollar" (because Spain had introduced coining machinery to the Americas by this time, using it to strike the piece of eight). The coins that were struck, and which Americans used, were now indistinguishable from other 18th-century issues, save for one thing: their marvelous, evocative designs.

The obverse of the new piece of eight featured a splendid baroque crowned shield, along with the name and titles of the king of Spain, but it is the reverse that claims our attention. There, the Pillars of Hercules—which had been appearing on Spanish-American coins since the 1530s, a proclamation of the New World origins of the silver they contained—are wrapped by ribbons. It has been suggested that the dollar sign ($) was inspired by the right-hand ribbon.

Here and there, people were beginning to reckon their money in terms of Mexican dollars instead of English sterling. We should not be surprised; the American colonists had been using the piece of eight since the very beginning, and they were now more familiar with it than with several members of the British system, including that nation's closest equivalent, the crown. We know of the change from one system to another by the fact that various colonies begin printing paper

Did the American dollar sign ($) come from the reverse of the Spanish-American piece of eight? Notice the column at the right on this 1732 coin of King Philip V, struck in Mexico City.

money denominated in dollars rather than pounds. Massachusetts led the way in 1750, its notes backed by a deposit of pieces of eight it had recently received. Other colonies would eventually follow, in part because the denomination would soon have a new appeal—that of nationalism.

DOMESTIC EFFORTS

In addition to foreign coins, paper money, and "country pay" or barter, there were several issues of domestic coins: one in Virginia, another in Connecticut, and a third in Pennsylvania. The Virginia issue is known from precisely two examples, brass shilling tokens from the town of Gloucester, dated 1714. We know nothing about the reasons for the issue, beyond the fact that it seems to have been the idea of two local landowners, Christopher Righault and Samuel Dawson.

We know a bit more about the second issue, from Granby, Connecticut. In 1737 an enterprising owner of a copper mine in the region named Samuel Higley issued tokens denominated THE VALUE OF THREE PENCE. When his neighbors complained that his tokens were overvalued, he changed his obverse legend to VALUE ME AS YOU PLEASE, but still retained the III for three pence!

Samuel's brother John took over the mint upon the death of the former, striking undated pieces and a few more dated 1739. We have no idea of the original extent of the Higley issues, but eight obverse dies and five reverses are known. Because most show no signs of breakage, the mint's output could have been fairly extensive. Yet its tokens remain excessively rare today, for Higley's copper was so pure that it was frequently recycled into other uses.

The Pennsylvania issue came about in 1766, a product of the furor over the Stamp Act. James Smithers, a British gunsmith who had just immigrated to Philadelphia, poured all of the frustration felt by the colonials into his "halfpennies" and "farthings," pieces that may have begun as commemorative medalets but which ended up as part of the monetary supply. The portrait on the obverse is of William Pitt the Elder, one of the voices of reason on the British side during the Stamp

This William Pitt halfpenny token refers to the British politician's efforts to have the hated Stamp Act repealed: NO STAMPS.

Act crisis. His more famous son would eventually become prime minister in the 1780s, just in time to deal with an infant United States, created in part by those very policies of coercion that his father had deplored.

Added to these American tokens was an import, one that began with one message and ended with another. In 1760 an Irish buttonmaker named Roche struck halfpenny- and farthing-size copper tokens with the words VOCE POPULI surrounding the head on the obverse, and the word HIBERNIA surrounding a representation of Ireland on the reverse. He probably intended the obverse to remind Dubliners of the deposed Catholic Stuart regime or the virtues of home rule, for the portrait has been identified with the two Jacobite pretenders, while the legend surrounding it is Latin for "By the Voice of the People." But Roche's tokens were eventually shipped to America in large numbers, and colonists there embraced them because their obverse sentiment now seemed an appropriate commemoration of their own struggles against Mad King George.

Regardless of such odds and ends, the primary circulating medium in America was now paper money. Americans had used it to pay for wars on behalf of England; they were about to use it to fight a war *against* England. And when they did so, that previously trustworthy medium would betray their confidence.

THE WAR OF INDEPENDENCE AND ITS AFTERMATH

Of all of the world's wars for national sovereignty, that which created the United States of America is among the most confusing and complex. It has been said that a third of the American people were ardent patriots, another third remained loyal to the mother country, and the final third had no opinion but scrambled to get out of the way of the other two. This observation oversimplifies matters, but there is a grain of truth to it.

The war was generally more popular in New England than it was in the South—but the new nation's greatest general was a Virginian. And the war was fought to free a people. But which one? Certainly not Native Americans. Certainly not African-Americans. And certainly not women—although they might partake of the banquet as guests of their husbands and do the washing-up. Indeed, this was a most confusing war.

We do not even know when the complaining—the perennial practice and right of any colonial people—reached a point that might finally yield a bid for independence. We think it began to accelerate after the final victory against the French in 1763, when Britons and Americans fell to quarreling over the spoils of the war. In this way of thinking, the opening salvo was the Proclamation Act of 1763, wherein King George III drew a line from one end of the Appalachian chain to the other and forbade settlers to cross it. Americans were angered, but the crisis over the Sugar Act in 1764 and the much greater furor over the Stamp Act in 1765—both of which were seen by Britons as revenue-raising measures, and by Americans as intolerable affronts—kept the pot at a boil.

Still, all this doesn't tell us when, or why, the mutual estrangement began. It is obvious this falling-out had deep roots indeed, going back to when the first colonists left one world for another. The earliest settlers found that English habits and customs did not always work in an American setting; they discovered that makeshift, local expedients might actually serve better than orthodox, imported ones, and were branded hayseeds and hicks by their English cousins for doing so.

Through our numismatic examinations, we have already seen the slow process by which transplanted Englishmen were becoming Americans. We have seen it with the Pine Tree shilling, and we have especially seen it with paper money. Give the people who devised such clever monetary schemes a century and a half to evolve in new directions, and there was virtually no chance that they would *not* strike out on their own at one point or another.

But they would still do so with mixed feelings when that time finally came. The estrangement reached its flashpoint in the spring of 1775, when royalist governor Thomas Gage of Massachusetts sent British regulars to Concord to seize military supplies stored there by Americans. Alerted by Paul Revere and William Dawes, Americans assembled on the morning of April 19 on Lexington Green and fired the "shot heard round the world." Not all of their fellow colonists agreed with their stance, nor did all Britons agree with the response of the Redcoats who opposed them. On both sides of the Atlantic, war fever would take some time to build up, clarify, and capture the popular imagination. And it would never monopolize thinking in either place.

FINANCING THE WAR OF INDEPENDENCE

While military aid might in time be forthcoming from Britain's enemies, France and Spain—and golden onzas and silvery écus might come to America along with the soldiers and arms—the insurgents would first have to prove that their unaided cause was a going concern and that they had a chance of defeating England (or were at least capable of holding on until that country gave way). This caution on the part of Britain's former and potential enemies meant that American money would have to pay for an American war, and the form that money would take must be paper, for there was really no other possibility. After all, hadn't that same approach worked during the conflict between the English and the French in Canada?

What Americans failed to realize was that paper money had worked during earlier campaigns because Great Britain had directly or indirectly stood behind the currency being issued. The mother country was scarcely likely to do so in this case unless Americans succeeded in invading, defeating, and occupying it, and extracting such payment by force. Not even the most ardent patriot could have expected this scenario to take place.

Another reason why paper money had worked was that earlier American participation in wars had been limited and short lived. But this conflict would be different: it would go on year after year, and would involve enemy occupation of many of the most productive portions of the upstart nation, including several of its largest cities.

That being said, the revolutionaries did well enough for the first year or two. They had caught the British by surprise and had soon taken most of New England. But they failed in a bid to bring the blessings of liberty to the remainder of British North America, and despite the urgings of Benjamin Franklin and other leaders, Canada would remain in British hands.

Elsewhere, the tide began to move against them. They lost New York City in 1776, General George Washington being defeated at the Battle of Long Island that August. Sir William Howe took the national capital of Philadelphia a year later. A striking American victory at Saratoga in October 1777 would eventually mean a favorable turning for the war, because it would embolden France and Spain to enter the conflict on America's behalf. But it produced little of concrete benefit just yet, and Washington had his hands full simply keeping his army alive through the winter of 1777–1778 at Valley Forge.

America's money reflected all this. In the spring of 1775, the colonies (or "states," as they soon began calling themselves) began the issue of paper currency to pay for their portions of the fighting. So did a new, ad hoc national government, whose modest, temporary powers would eventually be made law under the Articles of Confederation. This central government issued what it called Continental Currency: Benjamin Franklin's old firm (he had taken on a partner named Hall before selling out entirely, and Hall had engaged a partner of his own named Sellers) printed the notes, which were denominated in terms of Spanish milled dollars.

The Continental Congress also had hopes of issuing a coinage, a symbol of its sovereignty, as a bolster to local morale, and as a backing for Continental Currency. When it came time to print the fifth issue of national paper, the dollar note was deliberately omitted, and was replaced with a Continental

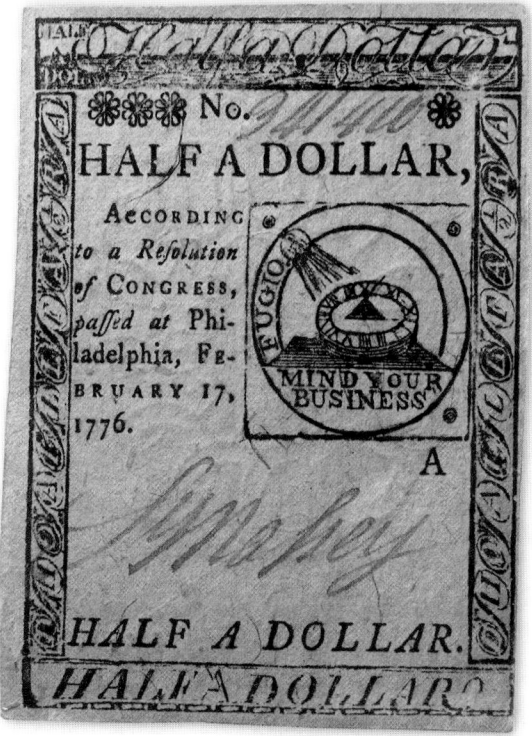

The notes issued by the Continental Congress were denominated in Spanish dollars.

dollar coin, struck from silver provided by the French. Elisha Gallaudet prepared dies for the new issue. He used the motifs—the sundial and the linked rings—from his earlier fractional paper currency.

The national government had no mint at this time, so Gallaudet set up his own facility, either in his hometown of Freehold, New Jersey, or in nearby Philadelphia. He made a few patterns in silver, a few more in brass, and more still in pewter. The latter alloy looked enough like silver to give a good idea of the appearance of the future coinage, but was at the same time soft enough not to damage his dies. Then the project ground to a halt. No French silver was forthcoming, and it soon became impractical to issue a dollar coin in any metal.

Some final observations about Continental Currency may be made. This money was issued from a number of places, reflecting the shifting fortunes of the patriot cause. While the first and last series were from Philadelphia—the original site of the national government—one in 1777 was circulated from Baltimore, while another in 1778 came from York, Pennsylvania—places to which the government had been forced to flee ahead of British troops. The York issue is particularly interesting, because it leads us to a major problem with Continental Currency: it was extensively counterfeited. It was forged by Americans, and there was nothing particularly new about that. But it was also forged by Britons; that *was* new, and contributed to the currency's problems.

THE DECLINE OF AMERICA'S NEW CURRENCY

If we assume that, at the time of the first issue of federal and state paper in the spring of 1775, $1.00 in national or, for example, Maryland-issued paper could purchase one Mexican piece of eight, we see matters as they were for the first 20 months of the war. By the beginning of 1777, Continental Currency was still standing firm, but that of several states was slipping: it then took $1.50 in Maryland notes to purchase that same Mexican dollar.

The autumn of that same year was the crucial point: in October, issues of the states ranged from a ratio of 1.09:1 to 3:1, and the value of Continental Currency had descended as well, down to 1.10:1. This was worrisome, but hardly fatal if it stopped there.

But it did not stop there. By March 1779, even though French and Spanish aid was coming in, state and federal currency alike had slipped to around 10:1 against the piece of eight. By then, the Continental Congress was printing the new, safer, bicolor notes, but it was increasingly unable to persuade anyone to accept them, other than the soldiers who received them as pay. The states had no better luck with their issues, and paper continued to slide. By April 1780, the ratio of Continental Currency to the Spanish dollar was 40:1, and the national government had decided not to issue any more. This was just as well, because by that time, it had circulated nearly a quarter-billion dollars' worth of paper. The states that continued to print money (and most did; what other choice had they?) saw its real value fall to a hundredth, and finally a thousandth, of its stated specie value. By then, they had printed as much money as the federal government, meaning that there was enough paper in circulation to purchase every house, factory, and farm in the new republic several times over—if there were anyone foolish enough to take this currency seriously.

So great was this problem that Congress and the states finally decided to do something about it. By a resolution passed on March 18, 1780, a new issue of paper was authorized, but it was one with a difference. This issue would consist of bills circulated by the states, exchangeable for Continental Currency at 40 to 1, the same value ratio that Continental notes now had against the Mexican dollar. The states of Maryland, Massachusetts, New Hampshire, New Jersey, New York, Pennsylvania, Rhode Island, and Virginia participated in the plan; the other states were either unwilling or unable to do so, or they were still occupied by British troops. In this way, more than $111,000,000 in Continental Currency was removed from circulation; a goodly amount of state paper was also lured in by the same law and destroyed.

In time, much of the remaining federal and state paper of the Revolutionary era was presented and redeemed for federal bonds under the funding plans of Alexander Hamilton and other Federalists. Some of the state issues stayed in circulation for some years, rendering continued (if suspect) service on the local economic scene. Other notes made their way into cupboards and jars, awaiting a redemption that never took place. And a new phrase entered into American English usage: "not worth a Continental," meaning worthless and useless. Americans had been badly mauled by their previously trustworthy exchange medium, and on the national level at least they would not soon forget the experience.

The Americans' war would eventually end, despite the collapse of the medium they had chosen to pay for it. Hoping to reverse the trend symbolized by the surrender of Philadelphia and the loss of the West, Great Britain had struck south, capturing the capitals of Georgia and South Carolina. Troops under Lord Cornwallis then swung north, hoping to roll up the American war effort before France and Spain could make a difference. Eventually, a siege resulted at Yorktown, and when Cornwallis surrendered his forces on October 19, 1781, the war was effectively over—although it would take two years of the canniest American diplomatic efforts to negotiate the peace, with the Treaty of Paris of 1783.

NEW COINS DURING A CRITICAL TRANSITION

After Yorktown, Americans were granted an opportunity they had never had before and would never have again. They had defeated an enemy and were therefore free to reject its monetary system as well. Additionally, because their own, makeshift monetary system had buckled, they were enabled and forced to reject it, too. What would they seek to erect in the places of these failed and rejected precursors? Would it work any better?

Americans kept some kinds of paper money, but not all. The states could and did issue such paper (normally expressed in dollar denominations, though not always) because they were sovereign entities. The large amounts of Spanish pieces of eight and French écus that had come in during the final stages of the war enabled states to back some of their notes with promises of specie payment—although this hard money soon left their treasuries and the states continued to print.

Several of the states also espoused a coinage of sorts. The only one to set up its own mint was Massachusetts. It had made a previous attempt to coin back in 1776, as had its neighbor New Hampshire, but the urgent demands of war and a shortage of copper had stopped both projects in the very beginning of the pattern stage. Now Massachusetts made a second, more successful attempt, and its coppers (which contained a generous amount of that metal) made numismatic history: they were the first American coins to bear the denominations CENT and HALF CENT.

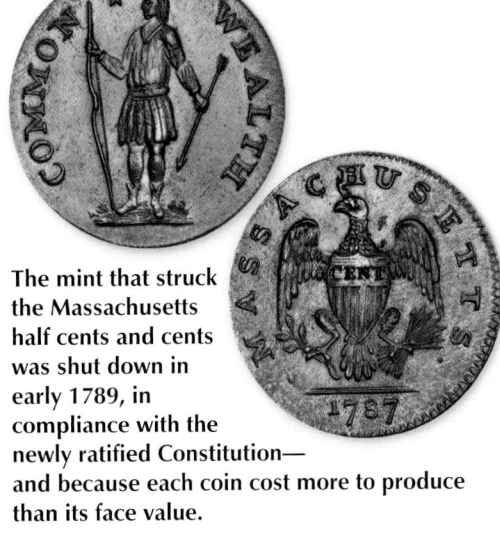

The mint that struck the Massachusetts half cents and cents was shut down in early 1789, in compliance with the newly ratified Constitution—and because each coin cost more to produce than its face value.

Other states allowed private mints to produce their coinage, resulting in generally lighter pieces and less artistic imagery. Between late 1785 and early 1789, several firms in Connecticut struck more than 340 varieties of halfpenny-size coppers. New York never got around to formally authorizing coinage, but a number of private mints would create money for it anyway. Their designs sometimes resembled English halfpennies, and sometimes incorporated elements from the state's coat of arms. New Jersey also contracted for its money, and the result was a copious coinage, struck at Rahway Mills, Elizabethtown, Morristown, New York City, and possibly on Staten Island. These coins—dated 1786, 1787, and 1788, but likely struck into 1789 and deliberately back-dated—are also of historical significance, as they were the first circulating American coins to bear the national shield (seen on many later federal issues) and the motto E PLURIBUS UNUM (seen on virtually all later federal issues).

None of the other states circulated its own coinage, although one of them, Virginia, saw the circulation of copper halfpence it had ordered in the final days of the colonial period. Virginia's royal charter of 1609 had given it the right to mint its own coins—the only one of the 13 colonies to enjoy this privilege. It had never set up its own mint due to lack of metal, but its Assembly authorized the Tower Mint to strike a copper coinage for it in May 1773. Some five tons' worth of coins were accordingly prepared and sent across the Atlantic.

By the time they arrived in Virginia, the first acts of the American Revolution were taking place. Thus, most of those Virginia halfpennies that had gotten into trade were soon pulled out, and hoarded for the duration of the war. After Yorktown, however, many did go into trade, where they passed from hand to hand in company with counterfeit and genuine British and Irish halfpence and the sponsored and unsponsored issues of several states—and of an adjacent, independent country: Vermont.

THE UNION GROWS

One of the last areas to be colonized, the Vermont Republic had sided with the Revolution, but it had also become involved in an acrimonious land dispute with its giant neighbor, New York. Until that dispute was settled, it would remain resolutely out of the Union. During that time, the country produced both notes and coins.

Reuben Harmon Jr. was chosen by the Vermont legislature to strike its copper coinage. His diemaker, William Coley of New York, incorporated the idea of the 14th entity into the reverse design of his coppers: here was an all-seeing eye (adapted from a contemporaneous British import, the Nova Constellatio copper), surrounded by 13 stars. The 14th star would be Vermont, and the region's aspirations of becoming a part of the new United States—as soon as those annoying New Yorkers saw matters its way—formed the basis of the reverse legend: STELLA. QUARTA. DECIMA., "The Fourteenth Star."

This reverse was close enough to those on the well-known Nova Constellatio coppers to encourage acceptance, but the landscape obverse Coley chose (or had chosen for him by the lawmakers) met with local resistance. As such, the design was changed, and Harmon and other coiners struck coppers until mid-1789 with a male head on the obverse and a seated female on the reverse.

Thus far, we have been talking mostly about copper coins, and with good reason: the great majority of coinages proposed and circulated during those years *were* copper—in part because of a scarcity of silver and gold. But there was one silver issue that managed to get into circulation, as well as one gold coin.

The circulating issue came from Annapolis, Maryland, and was the product of John Chalmers and Thomas Sparrow, who also engraved Maryland's paper money designs. The most common member of the series was the shilling, whose obverse bears clasped hands, an age-old symbol of amity. Meanwhile the reverse depicts the danger that can follow when friends have a falling-out. Here are two birds squabbling over a worm, oblivious to a serpent ready to attack them at any time. The message is clear enough in the light of current politics: if the states continue to squabble with each other—as they were indeed doing during the period of the Confederation—a greater enemy might destroy them.

Finally, we come to one of the most famous coins in American history, the gold Brasher doubloon. The coin's namesake, Ephraim Brasher of New York, may have struck coppers on a speculative basis. It has been suggested that the Brasher doubloons were patterns for a new copper coinage, struck in gold by way of a *douceur* or bribe to state legislators to secure the contract. If so, the ploy failed, but precisely seven doubloons with one design and an eighth and ninth with another design have survived.

Ephraim Brasher was a New York goldsmith and jeweler. He was also a neighbor and friend of George Washington's. In the late 1780s Brasher struck gold coins about equal in weight to the Spanish doubloon, equivalent to $16. The coins are punched with his initials, EB.

THE RISE OF A NEW CONSTELLATION

In 1783 Robert Morris, superintendent of finance under the Confederation, proposed an ambitious federal coinage. Had it been implemented, it would have meant a completely new direction for American numismatics: it would be fully decimal, with pieces ranging from 5 to 1,000 "units," the latter a silver coin weighing about two-thirds as much as the Mexican dollar. A handful of patterns were struck in Philadelphia, their simple designs featuring an all-seeing eye for the obverse, surrounded by 13 rays and stars, with the legend NOVA CONSTELLATIO, a "New Constellation" in the firmament of nations.

These coins never got beyond the pattern stage because their coiners never secured enough silver for more than a few trial pieces. But they did inspire Morris's assistant, Gouverneur Morris (no relation), to secure another coinage from another source. Gouverneur Morris went to England and partnered with coiner George Wyon to strike undenominated coppers very similar to the ill-fated Philadelphia patterns.

These pieces—dated 1783 and 1785 but apparently struck in 1785 and 1786—found a ready circulation in the United States, for their metal was good and their designs patriotic.

The Nova Constellatio coppers were hardly the only halfpenny-size imports at this time. Thomas Jefferson conceived of a new decimal coinage system based on an old coin, the Spanish or Mexican dollar, to be divided into hundredths. Someone in Congress suggested the name "decad" for the large copper piece that would sit on the bottom rung of the new monetary arrangement.

The name of this coin would eventually be changed to cent, but Thomas Wyon was asked to produce patterns in line with Congress's current idea. What resulted was perhaps the most iconographically loaded coin in early American history—and, ironically, it was struck by an Englishman. On the obverse, the goddess Diana leans against an altar while trampling on a crown. On the altar is a helmet, closely and deliberately resembling a liberty cap. Around her, we see the legend, INIMICA TYRANNIS AMERICANA—"America, Enemy of Tyrants."

There is one more message-bearing copper coin of the period worth mentioning: the "Georgius Triumpho" copper of 1783. The obverse head was probably intended to represent General Washington. The reverse introduces us to the subtleties of the 18th-century mind: a female, presumably representing liberty and independence, is enclosed in a framework with 13 vertical bars, and there are 4 fleurs-de-lis at the corners of the frame. The complete image probably means that American freedom is protected and secured through joint action of the states (the 13 bars), supported on all sides by aid from the French monarchy (the fleurs-de-lis).

Thus, by 1787 the nation's small change was composed of a confusing mixture of state coppers, British and Irish halfpennies, Morris's Nova Constellatio and other British speculative pieces—as well as large numbers of counterfeits manufactured on both sides of the Atlantic. Congress became convinced that a national standard must be issued under its aegis, a full-weight coin of good copper, against which everyone else's issues might be judged.

FLEDGLING ATTEMPTS

Not possessing a mint of its own, Congress had to contract for its money along with everyone else. It picked a Connecticut coiner named James Jarvis to do the work, and it picked the designs—Franklin's old sundial / linked rings concept, seen earlier on fractional notes and the Continental dollar in 1776.

Jarvis had been recommended by his friend Colonel William Duer, to whom he had paid a bribe of $10,000 for the contract. The obliging colonel helped him on his way, giving Jarvis more than 70,000 pounds of federally owned copper with which to begin work. This was a small fraction of what his contract called for, however, and he sailed for Europe in search of more metal.

He failed in his attempt, his somewhat shady reputation making industrialists wary of dealing with him. He finally returned home without his copper.

Meanwhile Jarvis's coining cronies had gotten the federal metal, and they were busily using it to coin lighter-weight Connecticut coppers! To minimize federal suspicion, they did strike some "Fugio" coppers on the federal pattern (their name comes from the obverse legend, the Latin for "I Fly," referring to time on the sundial; they are also known as "Franklin cents"), but fewer than 400,000 pieces were shipped to the treasurer of the United States on May 21, 1788, and Jarvis and his partners fled the country.

Fugio coppers are sometimes called "Franklin cents" because of their legends, attributed to Benjamin Franklin.

Fugio coppers proved unpopular with both the federal government (they were slightly under their legal weight and therefore useless if the federal government were serious about its reform) and with the people (who by this time were unfamiliar with the design). Very few went into circulation, and the government eventually sold what was left of the Fugio coins to a contractor with the unlikely name of Royal Flint.

As it would turn out, Flint was a friend of Colonel Duer's, and so we have come full circle. Flint went bankrupt before he could pay the government and was hauled off to jail. Duer joined him there a few years later; the Fugio story has no heroes.

But it did serve to symbolize what a growing number of people were saying: the government that had sponsored the coins must be strengthened, either reformed or scrapped altogether in favor of a more plausible, dignified, centralized government that would be taken seriously at home and abroad. The current central government could not tax, and it could not keep the peace. It was also incapable of being taken seriously by Europeans, as Britons moved against its newly won territories in the northwest, and Spaniards and others snubbed its diplomats in Europe.

A gathering had been held at Annapolis in September 1786 in the hopes of strengthening the Articles of Confederation. Few states bothered to send delegations, and the meeting broke up without concrete result—except for a promise to hold a second convention in Philadelphia the following spring. Then farmer and Revolutionary War veteran Daniel Shays and his disaffected peers (sinking in debt because they were not paid for their war service) swung into action, terrorizing parts of Massachusetts until dispersed by state militiamen in early 1787.

Shays' Rebellion turned the tide. It sent a shiver of horror through every merchant and creditor in the Republic, for if debtors could revolt in western Massachusetts, they could make trouble anywhere. That spring meeting at Philadelphia would be well attended indeed: out of its deliberations would come a new government, and a new chapter in the story of American numismatics. Most importantly, it would establish for the ages who could make money—and who could not.

"HARD MONEY" AND THE YOUNG REPUBLIC, 1789–1830

The 56 delegates who came to Philadelphia in May 1787 were entrusted with debating and enacting improvements to the Articles of Confederation—most notably, granting the national government the power of direct taxation. The hand of this group of "Federalist" debaters, led by Alexander Hamilton, was first seen in the decision to scrap the old edifice instead of tinkering with it. They wished the new nation to be taken seriously by the other members of the constellation of independent states, and they felt there were no means by which this might be accomplished if the current balance between state and national authority in America were to remain where it was. What's more, the Articles of Confederation, with their weak central control and strong local power (a balance that seemed to be increasingly favoring debtor farmers), were simply bad for business.

Joined to this was a certain snobbery on the part of Alexander Hamilton and many of his fellow delegates. It seemed undeniable that a government of the better sorts of people (or one made up of the rich, the well-born, and the able, in one Federalist's revealing words) was desirable and would be easier to achieve under a new political compact than under the current one. The members of this convention were in basic agreement on what they wanted, and they therefore managed to achieve it in the form of a written document, the Constitution of 1787.

The hands of the propertied delegates were visible throughout the document. States were expressly forbidden to interfere with contracts. The debt of the federal government was expressly recognized, its payment guaranteed. The central government was authorized to put down domestic uprisings. Federal judges were appointed for life, senators would be elected by state legislatures rather than by the people, and the president would receive a relatively long term—four years—and be chosen not by the people, but by an electoral college.

This national conservative trend would continue into the monetary arena. The uncontrolled emission of state and federal paper had threatened ruin to the mercantile classes along the Atlantic seaboard, so when it came time to discuss what sorts of money would be allowed and be created, and by whom, a permanent change was made. The Constitution's framers made their points most explicitly in two clauses of the first section of the new document.

Henceforth, states could not "coin Money; emit Bills of Credit [paper money]; [or] make any Thing but gold and silver Coin a Tender in Payment of Debts" (Article I, Section 10, paragraph 1). From then on, only the national government would have the authority to "coin Money, regulate the Value thereof, and of foreign Coin, and fix the Standard of Weights and Measures" (Article I, Section 8, paragraph 5). The Constitution did not state that the new central government could circulate paper money, and that vagueness was deliberate: Hamilton and his fellow framers were dedicated to the dream of making the United States a "hard money" country (based on specie—gold and silver coins) if this were humanly possible, but they also wanted the escape hatch of federal paper in case of extreme circumstances.

The new basic accord had to be ratified before its shortcomings could become manifest. The delegates to the Constitutional Convention finished their labors on September 8, 1787, sparking more than a year's worth of sincere debate. The tiny state of Delaware was first to swing into position behind the new compact (December 7, 1787) and within a month or so was joined by Pennsylvania, New Jersey, Georgia, and Connecticut. The ninth and crucial state, New Hampshire, ratified the Constitution on June 21, 1788.

Proving that governments can function without unanimity, George Washington was elected the first president by acclamation and got down to business with his new administration in New York City in April 1789, before both North Carolina, in November 1789, and Rhode Island, in May 1790, officially embraced the new system.

The Constitution laid the foundation for the new nation's money.

URGENT MATTERS FOR THE NEW NATION

Among the earliest concerns were finance and money. Alexander Hamilton had persuasively argued that the new government must be a model of fiscal honesty from the outset, and Article VI of the Constitution was sheer genius on the part of the young financier and his adherents. It recognized and assumed the debts of the states and former national government under the Articles of Confederation. This article did *not* specify payment in full—and the amount actually received, in the guise of long-term bonds, was not unduly generous—but the agreement to pay *anything* on notes already widely seen as worthless was a brilliant stroke and shifted loyalty on the part of the business community—which held most of the depreciated paper—away from the local and toward the new national government.

Because Hamilton and his colleagues distrusted paper, and because they were sincerely interested in underscoring the majesty and sovereignty of their new country and creation, they would have to do something about the coinage, and in fairly short order. State issues came to a halt in the spring of 1789, and a copper panic the following July drove both good coins and bad from circulation. A number of public and private groups and merchants took up the slack on the local level, and issues of small-change notes began appearing in commerce that summer. The bills were almost always denominated in pence, although those of the Bank of North America also proclaimed that they were worth one-ninetieth or three-ninetieths of a dollar, an attempt to express their value according to an old system, even as their issuers were moving toward a new.

As for the larger denominations, foreign gold and silver coinage would still be used when available. But the other earlier commercial mainstay was out: the states were no longer able to issue paper money, and the federal power was disinclined to do so. By 1790 there seemed a very real prospect that American business transactions would have to once again be carried on by barter and with Spanish-American currency.

At least the preliminary question of the identity of the American currency unit, and the relation of subordinate and multiple denominations to that unit and to each other, had effectively been answered by the end of the 1780s. In 1792 the law passed: the new American unit would be an old coin, the Spanish-American piece of eight, called by an old name, the dollar, but divided in a new fashion, decimally into dimes and cents.

Americans like to believe that they were the first to devise the concept of a stable, orderly arrangement of monetary denominations based on the number ten, but they were not. The ancient Greeks of Syracuse and other areas had dekadrachms, huge silver pieces equal to ten drachms. And that workhorse of the later Roman Republic and early Roman Empire, the silver denarius, was originally equal to ten copper asses. Neither ancient precursor left an indelible mark on the world's later money, and it would be another millennium and a half before the decimal monetary concept came to stay—this time in Russia, introduced in 1700 by Peter the Great.

That being said, Americans did not base their coinage arrangements on the Russian precedent, nor that of anyone else. On the contrary, the inhabitants of the fledgling United States would see their decimal coinage arrangement adopted around the world—first by Revolutionary France, then by Latin Europe and Latin America, and finally by the erstwhile enemy herself, when British coinage became decimal in 1971.

THE MINT ACT OF 1792

The United States enacted its decimal idea into law with the Mint Act of 1792. Passed on April 2, the law first proclaimed the establishment of a United States mint in the current national capital, Philadelphia, and determined the types of employees for the new facility and their salaries. Second, it established a decimal relationship between the members of the new coinage system and set down what those members would be, what quality and quantity of metal they would contain, and what images they might display.

Finally, the Mint Act guaranteed that the new coining facility would strike gold and silver for the public free of charge—an absolute necessity were the new operation to get the raw materials needed for coinage. What would the new coins be? As we might expect, they would center on the dollar, but the following chart shows all members of the proposed new system.

Metal	Name	Value ($)	Weight	Fineness
Gold	Eagle	10.00	270 grains (17.496 grams)	0.917
Gold	Half eagle	5.00	135 grains (8.748 grams)	0.917
Gold	Quarter eagle	2.50	67.5 grains (4.374 grams)	0.917
Silver	Dollar	1.00	416 grains (26.956 grams)	0.892
Silver	Half dollar	0.50	208 grains (13.478 grams)	0.892
Silver	Quarter dollar	0.25	104 grains (6.739 grams)	0.892
Silver	Disme	0.10	41.6 grains (2.696 grams)	0.892
Silver	Half disme	0.05	20.8 grains (1.348 grams)	0.892
Copper	Cent	0.01	264 grains (17.107 grams)	1.000
Copper	Half cent	0.005	132 grains (8.533 grams)	1.000

A few observations are in order. The word *disme* was shortened rather quickly to *dime*, which was how the word would be pronounced in any case. The copper cents and half cents had their weights reduced before coining began in earnest, as the price of copper had meanwhile risen. And the inclusion of a half cent brings a reminder that this was a hybrid system that treated an old coin in a new way.

That old coin, of course, was the piece of eight, which had always been divided into eight reales. It would continue to circulate beside its new American cousin—indeed it would *need* to continue to do so: it would be decades before there were enough American dollars in circulation to render Spanish-American coins unnecessary. Any American needing change for a real would also need a half cent, since the Spanish-American coin was worth 12-1/2 cents in the new reckoning.

Eight reales, four reales, two reales, and one real, all of the late 1700s.

Similarly, the quarter dollar would find a place in the new system, even though common sense tells us that one-fourth is not really part of a decimal arrangement. But the quarter would equal a coin with which all Americans had long been familiar, the two-real piece. And the quarter eagle ($2.50 gold piece), one suspects, was introduced because it expressed a decimal concept of sorts, equaling ten quarter dollars. In sum, this system was not completely decimal; rather, it contained comfortingly familiar elements in addition to those that were new, which is probably why it became so successful.

The Mint Act of 1792 set down designs for the new coinage in a fairly detailed fashion. Although there was a groundswell of sentiment in favor of depicting the president on the obverses of the new coins, Washington objected, saying it reminded him too much of monarchical practice. And so the Mint Act stipulated that one side of each coin be devoted to "an impression emblematic of liberty," with an inscription to that effect. Gold and silver coins were to incorporate an eagle, the national bird, onto their reverse designs, while reverses for cents and half cents were simply required to express the denomination.

The Mint Act and American coinage were not guaranteed or inevitable. In the years between 1789 and 1792, there was a good deal of talk about outsourcing the coinage to any of several private moneyers in Great Britain, Matthew Boulton's Soho Mint being the leading contender. Congress mulled over the idea of a foreign coiner, but while Boulton sent no samples, another British firm did. This was William and Alexander Walker, who commissioned John G. Hancock Sr. to prepare a handsome series of copper pattern cents as well as rarer pieces without denomination. The national legislature was impressed, but it was finally swayed by the arguments of Thomas Paine and Thomas Jefferson, who believed it simply made no sense to hold American coinage hostage to a European source in dangerous times.

LAYING THE MINT'S FOUNDATION

One of the prime movers in favor of a new coinage was Robert Morris, who had been behind the ill-fated trials of 1783. He found a temporary mint site in the cellar of a coach house belonging to a saw-maker named John Harper, who hired a self-taught diesinker, goldsmith, and silversmith named Peter Getz to cut the dies. Getz made strikings in copper and silver, presumably intended to represent cents and half dollars. Though Congress was not particularly taken with his artistry, Getz's efforts may have nudged Congress in the direction of passing the Mint Act.

Going forward, the government continued to use the coach house for minting purposes. Using dies engraved by Robert Birch, Harper's press struck the first American coin legally authorized by the new government, a half disme with a chubby portrait of Liberty on the obverse, and a scrawny eagle on the reverse. Some 1,500 of these pieces were struck on July 13, 1792.

At this point, the Mint Act was law, but the coining facility it had called into being had not yet opened. It would shortly do so, however: a site at Seventh Street and Sugar Alley was purchased for a trifle more than $4,000; the Republic received the deed on July 18 and the cornerstone was laid July 31. Now the mint proper could be erected.

As the walls were going up, designers and coiners began their work. Between September and December 1792 they experimented with three denominations. Someone contributed an obverse die for a disme companion to Birch's earlier half disme; it was married to a reverse by Birch, and the new chief coiner, Henry Voigt, struck a half dozen or so of the new coins in copper and in silver. Voigt's colleague, Joseph Wright, created a quarter dollar pattern with a charming young head of Liberty obverse and a standing eagle reverse. Two examples

About 1,500 half dismes were struck.

have survived in copper as well as an equal number in "white metal," a soft coining alloy composed mostly of tin.

Chief Coiner Voigt contributed a pattern himself, the "silver center" cent. This represented an attempt to create a coin worth a cent in a size more convenient than one made of pure copper. We do not know precisely how Voigt positioned the plug in the center of the planchet, and the difficulty he encountered appears to have tempted him to strike other patterns from the same dies wherein the silver was either mixed with the copper or was absent altogether. Fewer than 20 pieces of all types are known.

Finally, the man who had designed the half disme struck at one mint designed a cent struck at another. Robert Birch recycled his head from the silver half disme, turned it the other way, and struck a few cent trials in copper and one in white metal. The latter is particularly interesting because of a brief reverse legend, G*W Pt—for "George Washington President," the final gasp of the movement to honor the nation's chief executive on its coins.

These early pieces are among the most revered members of American numismatics, but with the exception of the Birch half disme, none would have been seen by the average citizen of the day. Still, that citizen was beginning to see the first "real" U.S. coins within a few months. In March 1793, the first issues—copper cents designed by Henry Voigt—began trickling from the new mint. For the obverse, Voigt employed a wild-haired, right-facing head of Liberty design that drew some criticism in the print media of the day. But the real adverse comment was reserved for his reverse, where Voigt reintroduced a design idea that had been in existence since 1776—linked rings, which began as a symbol of national unity but now appeared uncomfortably similar to a chain of slavery.

Mint director David Rittenhouse thus suggested a new design, and cents of this second type were struck through the summer of 1793. They were followed that September by a third attempt, the final contribution of the gifted Joseph Wright. Wright's Liberty borrowed heavily from Augustin Dupré's Libertas Americana medal of 1783, down to the Phrygian cap, an ancient symbol of the newly freed slave, behind her head. That motif, which also appeared on Wright's copper half cents struck between July and September 1793, would be incorporated into the designs of Wright's successors for a century after the engraver's untimely death in late 1793.

All told, the new mint struck 111,512 cents and 35,334 half cents that first year—not bad for a first effort, but scarcely guaranteed to alleviate American monetary difficulties on the lower end of the coinage scale. The new national coiners expanded their copper output the following year, and the year after that, but their fellow citizens still had recourse to more traditional sources for most of their small change. They kept those small-denomination, local notes in commerce, and they printed even more (sometimes denominated in cents, sometimes in pence). They also imported cent-sized tokens from Great Britain.

TOKEN COINAGE FOR CHANGING TIMES

By the beginning of the 1790s, Britons were experiencing a scarcity of official small change, making that which was suffered by Americans pale in comparison. The last time England had had legal copper money placed into circulation was two decades earlier, but as the country entered the beginning stages of the Industrial Revolution, vast amounts of low-value coinage would be needed to pay the new, salaried workers.

The Royal Mint was reluctant to provide public copper coins, and so private copper would fill in. Their issue began in North Wales in 1787, and by the middle of the next decade hundreds of merchants and firms across England, Scotland, Wales, and Ireland were busily providing the coppers that the Royal Mint would not. By that time, members of the upper and middle classes were beginning to treasure them for their collector interest as well as for their economic utility.

The collector coppers celebrated popular places, called attention to noteworthy historical events, and paid homage to the famous people of the day. It was probably inevitable that American personas and motifs would make their appearance, and while British collectors snapped up the more artistic creations featuring George Washington, the less popular appear to have been sent over to the United States to circulate there beside the new national cents.

The 1790s also saw British presses strike two types of copper tokens specifically intended for circulation among Americans—not simply sent there when rejected at home. The first of these was the Talbot, Allum & Lee cents of 1794–1795, ordered by a merchant house in New York City. These tokens found instant favor as cents—even though they were slightly lighter than the official issue—and the fledgling U.S. Mint found these coppers appealing as well. Needing rolled copper for half-cent planchets in the spring of 1795, Director Rittenhouse bought some 1,076 pounds of the tokens (around 52,000 of them) from William Talbot and recycled them into the national coining process.

The second made-for-America piece was created by Matthew Boulton for Philip Parry Price Myddelton in 1796. Myddelton had come into possession of a huge tract of land in Kentucky, and as part of his efforts to persuade impoverished British farmers and laborers to immigrate to the land, he enlisted Boulton to employ the talented Conrad Heinrich Küchler to design copper tokens for the project. However, these never got beyond the pattern stage, as in 1796 Myddelton was thrown into prison for his ambitious plan—to encourage the departure of British artisans was illegal.

SUCCESSES, CHALLENGES, AND INNOVATIONS

By the time of the Myddelton fiasco, the federal mint had managed to expand its production into metals other than copper. In October 1794, the first silver half dollars were coined, and on the 15th of that month the first representatives of the new American dollar also left the coining press. Of the latter, some 1,758 suitable for circulation were struck on that single day; no more were made until the following year.

Those dollars have much to say about the fledgling Mint and its first products. They were designed by Robert Scot, who would be responsible for most of America's coin designs over the next decade and a half. His dollar's Liberty head and eagle were criticized for their delicacy of execution, but that was hardly his fault: the new mint had no press strong enough to give its dollars a sharp impression, nor would it have until the following year—after which Scot's designs were seen to have improved.

The new dollars would serve as the flagship for American silver coins: any design changes adopted there were usually extended to lower denominations a year or two later. For example, when Scot abandoned his simple eagle for a heraldic one on the dollar, smaller silver coins replicated this substitution as well—as would gold coinage, which was first struck by the Mint in 1795 as eagles and their halves, designed once more by Robert Scot.

By the time the last of the legally mandated denominations—the quarter eagle, which appeared in mid-1796—was being coined, it was becoming apparent that at least a portion of the Mint's production could not be achieved in the ordinary

The first U.S. silver dollar was of the
Flowing Hair type, designed by Robert Scot.

way. The difficulty stemmed from two considerations: the low value of cents and half cents, and the time and trouble it took to make them.

Consider for a moment. If you were a Mint director in the late 1790s, and you had a set amount of money to produce during a given term, would you not prefer to meet it by striking eagles rather than cents? Those cents took as much labor to make as did the $10 pieces—more, in fact, because copper was harder to roll and strike than gold. And yet when you were finished, you had a cent instead of an eagle, and you still had virtually all of your coining left to do.

Rolling sheets was not the only problem; as far as anyone knew, the United States was still short of native coining metals. The simple winning of independence had done nothing to alleviate the shortage. Americans had little domestic gold or silver—or copper—which meant that their coiners had to scrounge for it. A 1798 cent exists overstruck on a halfpenny token from Anglesey, North Wales. One wonders whether this was accidental.

SEEKING ASSISTANCE

Of course, there *was* an area blessed with much copper and the technological wherewithal to turn it into blanks: Great Britain. By early 1796 the new U.S. Mint director, Elias Boudinot, was preparing to hold his nose and ask the old enemy for help.

Britain responded. Between 1796 and 1837, Cornish and Welsh copper was made into planchets of two sizes, then sent across the Atlantic to be elaborated into half cents and cents at Philadelphia. While two other firms participated, the favored agency was Boulton, Watt & Company—one more instance of the enterprising Matthew Boulton capitalizing on his ties with America. Boulton's planchets were made from the best copper, of the correct weight, and carefully finished, but they were not always available when needed.

On two occasions, their tardy delivery helped change the course of American numismatic history. The first was in the late 1790s, when Boulton delayed so long in sending copper that the U.S. Mint virtually ceased production in that metal, striking only a few thousand cents in 1799 and no half cents whatsoever between 1797 and 1800. The second occasion took place about 15 years later, but it was scarcely Soho's fault: the United States declared war on Great Britain in the spring of 1812, and the two countries remained hostile for nearly three years. During those years, the Mint struck no half cents and a dwindling number of cents, until it halted production altogether with the last of the 1814-dated coins. Cent coinage resumed in 1816 with the end of the war, and it steadily expanded through the 1820s.

By then, Americans were essentially doing business with only three of the ten denominations stipulated in the Mint Act: cents, half dollars, and half eagles. The cent was becoming essential on the lower end of the monetary scale, especially as the supply of genuine and counterfeit British and Irish halfpennies dwindled through attrition. The half dollar represented a handy amount of money in the United States, and the half eagle was popular because its gold value was conveniently close to other gold coins that Americans were using: the British guinea, the French louis d'or, and the Spanish-American double escudo.

But what about the other seven stars in the American monetary constellation? Several were unpopular and rarely produced because there existed better-known foreign coins that were preferred in trade. Thus, the half dime and dime yielded place to the half real and real, while the quarter dollar was rarely struck because people found it essentially duplicated the Latin American double real.

Other members could not be kept in circulation, most notably the silver dollar. This coin had been overvalued in relation to the piece of eight—it was slightly lighter and composed of slightly less-pure silver—and was thus swapped for pieces of eight in the West Indies, where it passed for par. The gold eagle suffered from similar problems; in 1803, France adopted a new silver-to-gold ratio of 15-1/2 to 1, and it became profitable to ship American gold coins to France for melting.

Seeking to end these evils, in 1804 an irate Boudinot suspended coinage of both eagles and dollars, a suspension that would hold for nearly four decades. The Mint director might have been relieved, for the policy meant that he had two fewer denominations to produce.

And this was a material consideration: the early U.S. Mint was a very inefficient coiner. Its equipment was ancient, made up of the castoffs and hand-me-downs of other countries and other coiners, as well as creaking machinery originally intended for other purposes. Its coiners were not masters of the craft, nor were its designers. The political climate was hostile, to say the least; the Mint regularly came up for review and could have been voted out of existence whenever such examination was made. It indeed came close to being abolished in 1800 and again in 1802; only an 11th-hour decision kept the facility open in the latter instance.

Not until May 19, 1828, would the U.S. Mint be authorized to remain "in force and operation, unless otherwise provided by law." But even by that period, its production had come nowhere close to meeting the demands of the people it attempted to serve.

FOREIGN COINS IN THE UNITED STATES

The same two conditions we saw at the beginning of America's story still held true. The country was metal-poor, and even with materials the Mint had no chance whatsoever of matching the needs of a population which was doubling every two decades. Thus, Americans would do as they had done since the beginning: they would turn to other people's coiners for help.

That being said, the Constitution granted the government the ability to ensure that their new federal creation played a key role in circulation regardless—Article I, Section 8, gave Congress the power to "regulate the Value . . . of foreign Coin." They exercised this power on February 9, 1793, when "an act regulating foreign coins, and for other purposes" was passed. The new law, which went into effect on the following first of

Various successors to the Spanish American piece of eight, such as this Peruvian 8 reales, were widely accepted in U.S. commerce.

July, demonetized all foreign coinage *except* the gold coins of Great Britain, Portugal, France, Spain, and Spanish America, and the silver coins of France and Spain. It also established values at which those coins were to circulate: for example, the Spanish dollar would be worth 100 cents, and its French equivalent 110.

The new law was intended as a stopgap. It stipulated that three years from the beginning of American silver and gold coinage, everything foreign except the Spanish and Spanish-American piece of eight would be demonetized. The reality was that the U.S. Mint simply could not make enough domestic coins to replace foreign ones, so Congress climbed down from its lofty but unattainable position of self-sufficiency, renewing the act in 1798, 1802, and 1806. The act was then allowed to expire, but foreign coins were allowed to circulate anyway. By 1816 an act renewing the circulation of foreign gold and silver coins was back on the books, and the provision was renewed periodically until the Act of 1857.

Which foreign coins circulated here? The Spanish and Spanish-American piece of eight led the way in silver, although coins like the Brazilian 960 reis (often a recycled Spanish-American peso, restruck at Bahia or Rio de Janeiro) gave it much competition in the 1810s and 1820s, as did the French five-franc piece, or piastre, in the 1830s.

In gold, British, French, Spanish-American, and Brazilian pieces held sway. The British guinea was important, but the last representatives of this denomination were struck in 1813. Four years later, its successor, the sovereign, emerged as a dominant player in international and intra-American commerce. In terms of sheer popularity, the sovereign would have frequently yielded place to the Spanish and Spanish-American onza or doubloon, particularly in border areas of the Old Southwest.

Aided by recurrent infusions of fresh foreign coinage, the American monetary system limped along. Had Americans had enough coinage of any kind for commercial use, they would have been satisfied; but even with the piece of eight, the sovereign, the gold of Brazil, and the silver of France, they were not receiving all the hard money they needed to keep up with their present and prospective rates of economic development.

What had been true before still held true now: America was a demographic and commercial success, but with an economy that constantly outpaced the orthodox money supply, they replied with an unorthodox one. Just as the Constitution was taking force, just as it was seeking to channel America's money in a particular direction, the prospective users of that money were cutting a path of their own with the paper note from the private bank. Between the years 1790 and 1865, private paper currency would reign.

GOLD!

The era of "rag" money—called "broken-bank notes" by the disrespectful and "obsolete notes" by the serious—lasted from approximately 1782 to 1866, coinciding rather nicely with the antebellum "first American republic." During this period, printers such as Jacob Perkins; Murray, Draper, Fairman & Company; and, later, the American Bank Note Company and National Bank Note Company would combat counterfeiting with ingenious new technologies and create numismatic works of art with their private bank currency. The miracle of 19th-century American growth simply could not have occurred without those paper notes, but the "rag" times would eventually end.

A combination of factors would soon ensure that the paper-money system that had taken three-quarters of a century to construct would only take a few years to demolish. One of these factors was the Civil War (see the following section). But earlier, the inevitability of the private note was challenged by a second, even more surprising event. For the first time in their history, Americans were getting enough precious metal, and enough expertise in coining it, to reduce their age-old dependence on paper.

The big discovery occurred approximately one week after the signing of the Treaty of Guadalupe Hidalgo, which ended the Mexican-American War and granted the United States title to Texas, New Mexico, Arizona, Nevada, Utah, part of Colorado, and California. A Mormon recent arrival to the West named James Marshall observed a glint of bright yellow—gold!—in the tailrace at a sawmill on the American River, near Sacramento. Nothing happened for several weeks because John Augustus Sutter (who owned the mill where the gold was found) did all he could to keep the discovery hidden.

But another Mormon named Sam Brannan wandered by, found out what had happened, and promptly rode back to San Francisco yelling, "Gold! Gold! Gold on the American River!" at the top of his lungs. And, as the saying goes, there went the neighborhood.

Within the next 18 months, some 75,000 gold seekers arrived from the East Coast, Europe, and even Australia. The effects of the California gold rush are almost too enormous to calculate. The discovery upset the old financial ratio between gold and silver, helping to precipitate a monetary instability that would last until both metals were removed from coinage more than 100 years later. It also inflamed tensions between North and South, as it became clear that California was bound to join the Union as a "free" state, therefore aligned with the North in foreign and domestic policy.

Thus, the California gold rush was one of the events leading to the American Civil War—and it would also help to ensure that the North would have the means with which to pursue it. For those interested in the story of America's money, the era has a double significance. First, it brought about a fascinating series of locally made coins, among the most interesting and historic issues in all of American numismatics. Second, the gold rush and related strikes elsewhere would mean that, combined with better coining technology, Americans would for the first time have enough domestic coinage for their monetary needs.

THE SMALLER SOUTHERN STRIKE

These were the great days of private gold coinage. Between 1848 and 1861, makeshift mints were established in California, Utah, Oregon, and Colorado to take advantage of the newly available precious metal, making it useful for local commerce and sending it back East for reworking there. In this, the private Western mints were similar to Spanish-American producers of pieces of eight. In both instances, the idea was to create a useful, feasible coinage *now*; those with artistic sensibilities could improve upon it later. Consequently we should not look for great artwork on these private issues.

Nor should we look for the first of them in California. We should look instead to an isolated area where North Carolina, South Carolina, and Georgia come together. Gold was found in that part of the world shortly before 1800, and, while it sparked nothing quite comparable with the California Gold Rush, there was enough precious metal in those layers and folds of the land to inspire a sizable mining scramble in the late 1820s, the eviction of Native Americans and their replacement by white settlers, and the appearance of private coiners by the early 1830s.

Templeton Reid—a sometime jeweler, gunsmith, watchmaker, and general handyman—was the first, setting up a mint in Milledgeville, Georgia, in 1830 and turning about $1,500 worth of metal into $2.50, $5, and $10 gold pieces. He soon packed up for Gainesville, where he struck a few hundred more coins between August and October 1830, but afterwards he seems to have abandoned coinage for nearly 20 years, relocating to Columbus, Georgia, where he engaged in creating and marketing new and better types of cotton gins.

Reid's coins were simple affairs, featuring his name and the denomination on one side, the origins of the precious metal and (usually) the date on the other. While he was criticized for creating lightweight coins, he made his money from pure gold, and so his coins were worth slightly more than their face value as bullion. This goes far toward explaining their extreme rarity today: most of them were melted down and recoined in Philadelphia.

You may be wondering how Templeton Reid managed to keep from being arrested: after all, if states could not coin money, how could an individual? The answer is that the framers of the Constitution apparently never anticipated that a private citizen would *want* to coin money, assuming instead that federal facilities would provide plentiful coinage for everyone. As we have seen, this did not occur. Private bank notes were one result. Private gold coinage was another.

Reid eventually struck one more coinage, this time shortly after the beginning of the rush to California. Numismatists long assumed that the coiner had followed the lure of metal west, as the coin is a $10 piece designated CALIFORNIA GOLD. But it

When the federal government failed to meet local coinage needs, enterprising Americans struck their own private money. Templeton Reid was one such entrepreneur—a jeweler, gunsmith, and inventor who turned his creativity to coins, including this $10 "Georgia Gold" piece.

now appears more likely that this coin (and a companion $25 piece that was stolen from the U.S. Mint Collection in 1858 and never recovered) was struck in Columbus. The elderly coiner was in no condition to travel and in fact died within a few months of his final foray into private moneying.

Not long after Reid's first issues, a family of German extraction named Bechtler set up shop near Rutherfordton, North Carolina—a few miles southeast of Asheville, a few miles northwest of the South Carolina and Georgia lines, and a local center for the gold trade. The family patriarch, Alt Christoph, soon made himself indispensable as the town's only jeweler and watchmaker. Meanwhile the locals petitioned Congress for a mint to turn their gold nuggets and dust into federal coinage. When they were ignored, they turned to the Bechtlers for help. Thus, the head of the clan was striking quarter and half eagles by July 1831, and by the end of the year, he had created an altogether new American coin: the gold dollar.

In time, the gold region got its mint—or rather two mints, one in Charlotte, North Carolina, and the other in Dahlonega, Georgia. Neither was an unqualified success, but they were enjoying enough trade by the end of the 1830s to persuade Alt Christoph to get out of the private minting business. In 1840 he transferred it to his son August, who moved the mint into the center of town and began striking gold dollars sometime in 1842, minting them in large numbers until his death in July 1846.

This brought a nephew into the trade: Christoph Jr. He continued to coin dollars and $5 pieces until the end of 1849 or the beginning of 1850. By then, the family's gold dollars were facing competition from official coins of the same denomination (first struck in Philadelphia in 1849), and this younger Christoph Bechtler seems to have given up the coining trade to concentrate on the family's earlier profession as a jeweler. Bechtler dollars and other coins continued to circulate alongside ordinary, federal products for many years; most of the surviving examples show evidence of a lengthy life in circulation.

California Gold: A Drama in Three Acts

Numismatist Walter Breen divided California private gold coinage into three main stages. The first began in the winter of 1848–1849 and continued through April 1850. A number of individuals and firms struck $5 and $10 coins at that time, and they created a number of circulating ingots as well. This first stage came to an end after the public learned that several of these issues were debased or contained less than their stated value in gold.

Local authorities then enacted legislation clamping down on private issues, but the laws were not enforceable, and another spate of private issues soon entered commerce. This second stage lasted until March 1851, and it was brought to a close by rumors that the new wave of private issues was also short-weight. No further private coins appeared during the remainder of 1851.

The third and final stage of California private coinage began in January 1852 and continued through 1856. While some new moneyers entered the field and placed their names on issues ranging up to $50, the most interesting event during this stage occurred on the lower end of the scale, as "fractional" gold coins—tariffed at 25¢ and 50¢, plus a related issue of dollars—entered commerce.

In the earliest stage, one of the first firms to strike coins was the Cincinnati Mining & Trading Company, which in 1849 struck a few different coins bearing a distinctive Liberty head with a feather headdress on the obverse and a unique left-facing eagle with a shield on the reverse. Both $5 and $10 coins were made, but their gold content was rumored to be low, and consequently almost all of the firm's products were soon pulled out of circulation and melted down. So were the issues of the Pacific Company, which were also struck in 1849, likely by hand with a sledgehammer.

One of the few firms to make a lasting contribution in this early period was Moffat & Company, which began issuing rectangular ingots in July 1849, graduating to normal coinage later that year. The concern's $5 and $10 gold pieces bore a deliberate similarity to ordinary U.S. gold coins.

The second stage of the California coinage saw the production of excessively rare rectangular ingots at a state assay office, but these soon yielded to orthodox coins: $5, $10, and, for the first time in California, $20 pieces. Two firms stood out here. Baldwin & Company was one, and their $10 gold piece depicting a *vaquero*, or Mexican cowboy, is among the most famous of all private gold issues. Schultz & Company, which set up shop behind the Baldwin mint and struck $5 pieces in 1851, was the other.

The third and final stage lasted for four years, and it saw a new player enter the field: the national government. In the autumn of 1850, a federal assay office of gold was created in San Francisco. It was granted the right to make ingots of refined gold, worth $50 each. A New York watchmaker named Augustus Humbert was appointed to assay the metal, and he, in turn, subcontracted the actual coining of it to Moffat & Company.

Whether or not anyone had so intended, Humbert's octagonal ingots (also called "slugs," or "Californians") entered circulation as ordinary coins—indeed, they were the principal accepted currency in California between 1851 and 1853. By 1852 Humbert was producing $10 as well as $50 ingots, and he added the double-eagle denomination in 1853. Humbert's ingots, with their distinctive eagle-and-shield obverses and engine-turned reverses, were better than anyone else's coins. They led naturally to an even more official coinage, as the assay office closed its doors in late 1853, and four months later a new branch of the U.S. Mint opened in its place.

But even after the establishment of the San Francisco Mint, private coining did not disappear; it persisted for some years. Kellogg & Company alone produced more $20 gold pieces in 1854 than the new federal facility, and those coins filled cashiers' tills in the mid-1850s, as did gigantic round $50 coins struck by two Hungarian veterans of the failed European revolutions of 1848, Count Samuel C. Wass and Agoston P. Molitor. Wass, Molitor & Company produced smaller coins as well, but they achieved immortality with those huge slugs, each of which contained more than a quarter of a troy pound of pure gold.

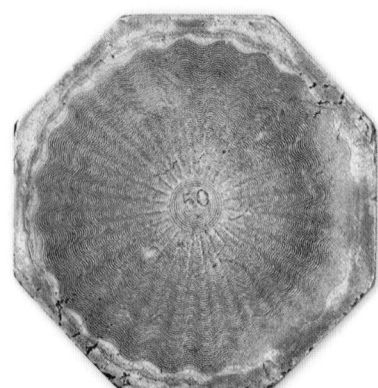

This 1851 $50 gold piece was struck by Moffat & Co. for Augustus Humbert, United States assayer of gold. These heavy coins were called "slugs" because they could knock a man out in a fight— or so the Wild West legend goes.

At the other end of the spectrum stood a motley assemblage of jewelers and dentists, people skilled at working with gold in small quantities. They now proceeded to create California "fractional" coins—tiny octagonal and round half dollars and quarters, as well as dollars. Most of the makers are anonymous, and their designs were simple. One thing is certain: coiners of fractional pieces had nothing whatsoever to do with makers of larger-denomination coins; the two groups were entirely separate.

OTHER REGIONS TAKE THE STAGE

The California gold rush had a ripple effect on the rest of the country. It influenced the tensions between North and South, but it was also responsible for smaller events of numismatic importance in Utah, Oregon, and Colorado. Neither of the first two areas had abundant gold of their own, but both had personal connections with California; many Oregon farmers had abandoned their plows and headed south at the first rumors of the gold strike, and recent migrants from Joseph Smith's peaceable Mormon kingdom near the Great Salt Lake (including the aforementioned Marshall and Brannan) accounted for many of the first prospectors to arrive in the Sacramento Valley.

UTAH: THE LAND OF THE HONEYBEE

Utah was settled in 1847 by followers of Joseph Smith, the martyred prophet of the Latter Day Saints. Led by Brigham Young, the faithful had trekked across the "Great American Desert" in search of a land so remote and so unpromising that other Americans would leave it (and them) alone. Their leader chose a site by the Great Salt Lake, and here the Mormons settled in July 1847.

They had only a limited and brief success in keeping other Americans out of Utah, however. Soon, victory in the Mexican War would grant the United States title to the American West—including the very area where Smith's disciples were building their theocratic state—and the California gold rush would result in thousands of "forty-niners" passing through the region. But the Mormons would stay where they were, and they would soon find that interlopers offered opportunities as well as threats.

Those heading west needed goods of all sorts and were prepared to pay high prices, and Mormon miners and others returning east bore gold, much of which was left behind in Utah. Thus, money could be made, and within a few months of the California strike, authorities in Utah were preparing to make it quite literally; Young enlisted the services of a British convert named John Mobourn Kay to make a distinctive local coinage, and a makeshift mint was in operation by the end of 1848.

The first coins struck were $10 pieces, some 46 of them, produced during the last month of 1848 but dated 1849. Production problems delayed an extension of the coinage until the following September, but from then through 1851, half eagles and quarter eagles were struck in some quantity, and a new denomination also entered American numismatic history: the double eagle, or $20 gold piece.

All of these coins used the same distinctive design, incorporating a three-pointed Phrygian crown—the emblem of the Mormon priesthood—and an abbreviated legend, G.S.L.C.P.G. ("Great Salt Lake City Pure Gold"). However, the gold in the Mormons' coins was *not* pure, and each denomination was only worth about 85 percent of its face value. In consequence, several thousand of the pieces were melted down in San Francisco, victims of the same backlash that was making instant rarities of the Pacific Company's coinage and other suspect issues.

At the end of the 1850s, the Mormon mint tried again, issuing half eagles notable for their incorporation of phonetic alphabet characters and the Mormon name for Utah, *Deseret*. By that time, it had a new source of gold—the region known as Colorado, where the yellow metal had been discovered in 1858. Alfred Cummings, governor of Utah Territory, finally quashed this coinage, but Colorado and its gold would soon write its own chapter in the story of private gold coinage.

This $5 gold piece shows a lion (hearkening to one of Brigham Young's nicknames, "Lion of the Lord"), an eagle, and a beehive. Deseret, Young's proposed named for the state of Utah, was the word for "honeybee" in the Book of Mormon.

OREGON: THE LAND OF "BEAVER MONEY"

The land of Oregon, occupied jointly by Americans and British for approximately three decades in the early 1800s, became sole property of the United States in 1846 and was formally organized as the Oregon Territory in 1848. Within a year, its citizens would be striking coinage from California gold.

The implements used to create this coinage still exist, housed at the Oregon Historical Society in Portland. Inspecting them makes one thing immediately apparent: the Oregon pioneers struck their eagles and half eagles *by hand*, using a sledgehammer instead of an orthodox coining press. Such a primitive way to coin money worked well enough in this instance for two reasons: Oregonian coiners were only making a few thousand pieces, and they were making them from a soft metal—pure gold from California.

The Oregon coinage was privately struck, but it had nearly begun as an official issue of the territory. Disputes over the value and measuring of gold dust led to a push for a territorial mint, but incoming governor Joseph Lane blocked the bill, arguing that such issues by a territory were illegal under the U.S. Constitution. Lane was on shaky ground; the Constitution indeed forbade coinage by states, but it said nothing about territories. He was the governor, though, and his word prevailed; if there was to be Oregon coinage, it would not be official, but private.

Soon, eight prominent businessmen founded the Oregon Exchange Company to strike those private coins. Their first issue, a $5 gold piece, bears on its obverse a beaver, whose valuable fur had inspired some of the earliest exploration and settlement of the region, and the initials T.O. (for "Territory of Oregon"). The reverse bears the denomination, the amount of gold, and the name of the issuer. Not long after, $10 pieces appeared, following the general designs of the $5 coins.

There was no attempt at assaying or standardization with this "beaver money," but to be on the safe side, the Oregonians made their coins' weights well *above* federal standards: when assayed at Philadelphia, the fives were found to be worth $5.50 and the tens $11. California bankers nevertheless valued them much lower, and they quickly melted down the great majority of the Oregon pieces to make a profit—perhaps 50 coins survive today. Actual coining came to a stop around September 1, 1849. By 1850 gold coins from California were arriving in Oregon in fair numbers, thus ending the monetary emergency that had led to the beaver money.

COLORADO: POLITICS, PIKES PEAK, AND PARSONS

Settlement of Colorado—acquired piecemeal between 1803, with the Louisiana Purchase, and 1848, with Mexico's official cession—began in earnest only after the discovery of gold on the South Platte River in July 1858. That summer brought a scramble comparable to the one in California a decade earlier. In this instance, conditions were even harsher: food was scarce, housing minimal, theft and violence rampant, and law enforcement nonexistent. The nearest secure source of many essential supplies was either Omaha, Nebraska, or St. Joseph, Missouri, and the neighboring Kansas Territory was in the midst of a bloody internal conflict.

Given their conditions, in 1859 Coloradans took the only logical step: they organized their own government, calling the region the "Territory of Jefferson," telling the federal government about it after the fact. By that time, gold dust and nuggets had become the universal media of exchange, and the inconveniences of such a system led to agitation for a local coinage. In 1860 it would be met by a firm calling itself Clark, Gruber & Company.

This concern was already doing business as a bank and assay office, but late in 1859, one of the principals made an arduous trip back East to purchase dies, presses, and the other necessities for a mint. In mid-January 1860, three lots were acquired in Denver City to house the new enterprise, and by early July the mint was ready to strike its first coinage. This was an up-to-date facility, and its output was impressive; between July and October 1860, some $120,000 of quarter eagles, half eagles, eagles, and double eagles was produced. The two lower denominations copied ordinary federal designs (Liberty's head for the obverse, and an eagle with a shield for the reverse), while the $10 and $20 pieces proudly displayed a romantic, if inaccurate, depiction of Pikes Peak on the obverse.

The "Pikes Peak" gold coins of Clark, Gruber & Company show a fanciful view of the famous landmark. The company also made coins with a traditional Liberty-head design.

After a temporary break during a harsh winter, Clark, Gruber & Company replaced Pikes Peak with Liberty on all denominations and struck approximately $240,000 in the next year, followed by $223,000 in 1862. Sadly, only a tiny percentage of these coins have survived, and this mint's days were soon numbered. The federal government never recognized the Jefferson Territory and instead organized the region as the Territory of Colorado in February 1861. Under national control, local enterprises such as private mints would face an uncertain future.

Indeed, the national government forced the sale of the mint in April 1863 on the pretext that the facility would be wanted for a federal facility in Denver. A national branch mint would indeed come into production on the site—but not until 1906. During its first 43 years, the facility would function only as an assay office.

Clark, Gruber & Company was by far the most prolific of the Colorado coiners, but there were two others, located elsewhere in the region. One of these was John J. Conway & Company, which set up shop in August 1861 at Georgia Gulch and made undated quarter eagles, half eagles, and eagles for a brief time. The other coiner was Dr. John D. Parsons, who set up a coining operation at Tarryall Mines, and in 1861 struck a few quarter eagles and half eagles with a most distinctive obverse design—it showed a quartz-reduction mill, used for separating gold from its rocky matrix. The operation came to an abrupt halt when Dr. Parsons ran out of gold, and today no more than half a dozen of his quarter eagles and three of his half eagles are known.

PRIVATE GOLD COINAGE DRAWS TO A CLOSE

The Colorado issues round out the period of private precious-metal coinage in the United States. There would be other strikes of gold and silver, but none of them produced a distinctive coinage. Why did they not? For one, private precious-metal coinage ceased because Congress declared it illegal in 1864. More importantly, though, times had changed.

The American Civil War was approaching its crescendo. The war would bring to a close the supremacy of local power and authority over national. The ending of that old tradition would inevitably have an effect on money; in the new climate, the private, local coin was an anachronism.

At the same time, the underpinnings that could bind the nation's disparate parts were expanding and improving. By 1864 the North was building a transcontinental railroad. Telegraphic communications were expanding as well, fostered by the war effort. What was emerging was the potential for a new, national economy, stretching from one coast to the other. The system would experience growing pains for the remainder of the century, but it would eventually mean that Americans would spend *national* coins when they used metallic money for trade.

And finally, the public coiner—the U.S. Mint—was getting better at the production of money, and was finally able to drive its competitors—the private coiners—from the field. Improvements at the main Philadelphia facility were underway by 1816; a fire at the beginning of the year had destroyed its old wooden millhouse, and Mint director Robert Maskell Patterson used the fire as an opportunity to incorporate a steam engine into the coining process. This engine powered the rolling operation—which at last gave this crucial step the power and precision it required—as well as the planchet-cutter, resulting in an increase in the Mint's productivity.

Mint personnel got better at their craft as well. They were asking Great Britain's Boulton, Watt & Company for technical advice in the mid-1820s, centering on the production of specimen strikes, or Proofs. By 1828 the minters were cautiously experimenting with restraining collars, which kept coins more consistent in shape and quality, and therefore more difficult to counterfeit.

By the end of the 1820s, congressional agitation to close the U.S. Mint had abated, and the institution faced an altogether different problem: space. Thus, the cornerstone for a new mint was laid by 1829, and the facility opened in January 1833. Next on the docket was to upgrade the old machinery; the key player here would be Franklin Peale, employed as all-purpose fact finder by Mint director Samuel Moore.

In this capacity Peale visited the more modern mints in Europe between 1833 and 1835. He investigated the facilities of the British Royal Mint, which used a type of coining press that Boulton had patented in 1790—essentially the traditional screw press, strengthened for connection to a new motive force, the steam engine. Peale also explored the mint in Karlsruhe, in the German grand duchy of Baden. Both there and in Paris he saw a different apparatus, one patented by Diedrich Uhlhorn in 1817 and lately improved upon by M. Thonnelier, which featured a toggle action and was more efficient with the steam power it received. What's more, since it did not coin by means of a screw—the most vulnerable and difficult-to-replace part of the Boulton apparatus—this machine was far more durable.

Peale was sold on the new press, and although he did not purchase one (not being empowered to in any case), he did manage to draw and memorize its essentials. He replicated them once he returned home in mid-1835, and by March 1836, a new press powered by the Mint's steam engine had been built and was striking its first coins. The improvement was clear from the outset: the new machinery could make twice or thrice as many coins as the old methods, and the resulting coins were also much more consistent in strike and finish.

Old ways and new: a half dollar struck in the traditional method (top), and another struck in a new way, by the power of steam (bottom); both were made in 1836.

THE MINT RISES TO PROMINENCE

Meanwhile more coinage metal was discovered. By 1837 a domestic source of copper had been found, breaking the Mint's 40-year dependence on planchets from Boulton, Watt & Company. Soon the Mint would find native suppliers of gold—in North Carolina and Georgia, mentioned earlier—and finally silver.

Just as significantly, Congress passed an Act in 1835 authorizing the establishment of branches of the U.S. Mint at Charlotte, North Carolina; Dahlonega, Georgia; and New Orleans, Louisiana. The first two towns were in convenient proximity to the mines that supplied Reid and the Bechtlers with bullion; and New Orleans was a convenient locale for a supply of precious metal too, in the form of coins from Mexico and elsewhere in Latin America. The Crescent City's economy was booming by the mid-1830s; why not help it along (and bolster local and national pride) by setting up a branch mint there as well?

Thus, by the spring of 1838, the United States had not one official coiner but four, all equipped with steam power and modern coining machinery. While the facilities at Dahlonega and Charlotte never reached expectations and were closed for good at the beginning of the Civil War, the mint in New Orleans was a success from the beginning, coining gold and silver on a regular basis until the outbreak of the conflict, and reopening in 1879 to remain in business for another 30 years.

As we have seen, a Western branch mint was opened in San Francisco in 1854. All the new mints (and the greater productivity of their parent at Philadelphia) led to a momentous decision some three years later, when Congress passed the Coinage Act of 1857, repealing "all former acts authorizing the currency of foreign gold and silver coins, and declaring the same a legal tender in payment for debts." For the first time in their history, the inhabitants of the United States felt confident enough about their own money to prohibit the use of other people's coins. And so all those pieces of eight, sovereigns, louis d'ors, thalers, and onzas assumed their present roles as parts of the nation's numismatic legacy—remembered with thanks, but no longer an active part of an ongoing story.

Ironically, the U.S. Mint would find itself unable to keep its own coins in circulation just four years later, when the quarreling between North and South deepened into a shooting war. In both places, uncertainty drove coinage into hiding and turned the American people back to their traditional expedient, the paper note, just as the potential seemed to have been achieved for banishing it once and for all.

FROM A CIVIL WAR TO A GILDED AGE

The Civil War meant and still means many things to Americans. It has produced feelings that have clarified, deepened, and changed over the past century and a half since the guns fell silent. But for all the complexity, the greatest lesson of the conflict is obvious: Americans would have to pay for the fine words enshrined in the Declaration of Independence with lives lived in a new way. They would have to actually take seriously the stirring phrase about the equality of *all* men.

The tremendously eventful 50 years that followed—called the "Gilded Age" after Mark Twain and Charles Dudley Warner's on-point satirical novel of the era—would see the nation struggle with that idea, all the while undergoing massive expansion and political change. The moniker could not be more apt; was not a *golden* age a period when humankind was at its best, transcending limitations of class, race, sex, and worldview? In reality, this was an age that posed as something solid and worthy, but whose gold plating was thin and easily worn away to reveal the bigotry and brass beneath.

Consider all that occurred between 1865 and 1914. The nation assumed its present borders when Alaska was added in 1867 and Hawaii in 1898, and it gained temporary and sometimes permanent control over other areas, too: the Philippines, Puerto Rico, Guam, the Canal Zone, and Guantánamo Bay. Meanwhile the continental states filled up thanks to increased immigration, improving transportation and communication, and advancing industry. The frontier finally disappeared.

These changes were for the better, or at least neutral, but they inevitably influenced some groups more than others, and caused immense friction and unrest virtually everywhere. Farmers lost their position at the head of the table, and Native Americans got shoved away altogether, locked up on reservations. African Americans saw most of what little they had won taken back in the South with the ending of Reconstruction; those who voyaged north found a scarcely more hospitable reception there. The organized labor movement experienced several sputtering beginnings, and though its days of success lay far distant in the next century, it was becoming increasingly apparent that those who owned the factories and firms owned a good deal more—including major portions of the state and federal governments.

The issue of tariffs and regional grudges caused tension between Democrats and Republicans, but the lasting truth was that the major parties both had an agenda that suited them and the economic elite while generally ignoring the real and worsening problems of the average citizen. As a result, the middle and late portions of the Gilded Age would see two movements for reform, speaking to the needs of the "forgotten man": the Populist and Progressive fronts, the latter of which would make more headway and help eradicate some of the worst social and industrial evils by the end of the period.

At bottom, all of this activity was tending in one direction: the country and its people were becoming ever more interconnected.

CURRENCY DURING THE CIVIL WAR

The Civil War was the defining experience of U.S. history—a true "watershed," to use a word ordinarily reserved by historians for far lesser events. The war split the country's story neatly down the middle;

in four short years the United States became a completely different country. And all this we have been saying about the country's history might be equally applied to its money.

In the four years of the Civil War, America's money would begin in familiar forms, then be constantly altered under pressure, and finally emerge with fundamentally new identities which remain today with minor modifications. Put most simply, the national government would be forced to acquire the same monopolistic powers over bills and notes that it had claimed over coins with the Coinage Act of 1857, as it became clear within six months of its start that the war must be fought and paid for by both sides with the time-honored expedient of paper money.

This money would take different forms, from the familiar private bank note to state notes and federal bills both Union and Confederate. All would be printed in mass quantities, whether by means of engraving, typesetting, or lithography. New media would emerge, including postage currency and bronze Civil War tokens.

Coinage, meanwhile, would be scarce, as gold and silver began disappearing from circulation in both the North and South shortly after the beginning of hostilities (thanks to the hoarding public). The mints at Charlotte, Dahlonega, and New Orleans all closed down in the spring of 1861. But coins would not disappear altogether. With the small number of coins it did produce during the period, the U.S. Mint concentrated on the lower end of the scale: cents bearing the new Indian Head design; a new two-cent piece introduced in 1864 (the first American coin to bear the motto "In God We Trust"); and a second three-cent piece to augment unwanted supplies of the first.

The two-cent coin was one of the shortest-lived series in U.S. coinage, being struck in a ten-year period that ended in 1873.

The three-cent piece takes a bit of explaining. The original version was introduced in 1851, when the postal rate for a first-class letter was lowered to 3¢, and was struck in quantity between then and 1853, first in silver, whose fineness was deliberately low, and later in the fineness current for all other American silver coins, 90 percent. The coiners at the U.S. Mint found their new, tiny coin so unpopular that production was drastically decreased and then ceased altogether in 1873; but early in 1865, they decided to try again—this time with a slightly larger coin struck in copper-nickel. They made a good many of the new pieces that first year, and the coins did in fact perform a modest service on the lower end of the monetary scale, but this version eventually proved as unpopular as the silver examples, and production stopped in 1889.

For what limited success federal coiners enjoyed on the base-metal end of the monetary column, they found even less when they turned to precious metals. Silver coins of the period—which bore Christian Gobrecht's Liberty Seated design, introduced in the late 1830s—were struck in very small number in the early 1860s, and most of them came from the branch mint at San Francisco rather than the parent facility at Philadelphia. In fact, the main U.S. mint virtually closed down at the end of 1861, and only half dollars were produced in a quantity comparable to that of pre-war years.

A similar pattern held for gold coins, most of which bore a rather pedestrian Liberty head with coronet, again designed by Gobrecht. The major exception was the slightly more attractive double eagle, designed by the man responsible for the current cent, the two-cent piece, and both three-cent pieces: James Barton Longacre. Whereas other gold denominations were struck in minuscule quantities after 1861, production of double eagles actually *ascended* through the war.

Virtually all of it, however, was accounted for by the San Francisco Mint, where the large gold coins were quickly struck and shipped east to bolster banking and the war effort. It would take the end of the armed conflict for America's metallic money to truly reemerge; meanwhile Reconstruction and new political ideas were shaping a distinctly new nation.

Money in the Gilded Age

The shift from the local to the national, from the particular to the universal, was implicit in the Northern victory of 1865; for the next half century, Americans would have civic calm at home, and thus they had the time and concentration necessary to determine where their new interconnections might lead. Part of the evidence that they were doing so comes from the money they were producing during the Gilded Age.

What do we see when we take a closer look? First, there is a return to coinage with the end of the Civil War. The uncertainty was over: once put in circulation, specie would remain there. Therefore, production of most denominations expanded, at least until the harsh economic times of the middle and later 1870s. The exceptions to this rule were those coins on the lower end of the scale, as issues of cents, two-cent pieces, and three-cent pieces were decreasing by the late 1860s.

On the upper end, the production of gold double eagles continued to rise through the 1870s. The production of these massive capstones increased because there seemed to be an endless supply of gold in the West, and the double eagle was the most efficient way to turn that resource into something useful. The great majority were struck at the San Francisco branch mint, assisted after 1870 by a new federal facility at Carson City, Nevada. This facility was erected primarily in response to the massive Comstock silver strike, but it was also a source of gold coinage until its closing in 1893.

While many of the new double eagles were sent back East, many more stayed near their point of origin—so many, in fact, that Congress had to alleviate the resultant banking nightmare with a new type of paper money, the National Gold Bank Note. Thus, while the national banking system and its notes proliferated throughout the country and homogenized currency, the federal government of the day might indeed respond to local monetary differences and act on behalf of influential interests on the state or regional level. Another example is the story of Western silver and the Morgan dollar.

A Question of Metals

The United States had long had a "bimetallic" monetary system, one based on two precious metals that were interchangeable with each other at a fixed ratio. This ratio had been established in 1834 at 16:1 (meaning that weight for weight, gold was worth 16 times as much as silver), and the system functioned adequately until the California Gold Rush upset the silver-to-gold ratio in favor of silver coinage. Congress responded to the subsequent melting and exportation of silver by reducing the precious-metal content of the half dollar, quarter, dime, and half dime, a measure that helped get silver coinage back into commerce until the emergency of the Civil War.

Not long before that crisis began, silver had been found near Virginia City, in the Nevada Territory (recently separated from the Utah Territory), and so much of it was shortly being taken from the ground there that the Union soon made Nevada into its own state. The nation's monetary system meanwhile acquired a headache of monumental size and duration, as the 16:1 ratio was again being upset—but this time in favor of gold. Matters worsened still in 1871, when the new German Empire adopted a strict gold standard, exporting nearly two-thirds of its silver stock, and adding more than $200 million of the metal to a market already glutted.

Mine owners and their congressional representatives were vocal in their distress, and the official reply was the Mint Act of February 12, 1873. The act gave with one hand and took away with the other: it put a slightly greater amount of silver in the half dollar, quarter, and dime, and it also created the silver trade dollar, which was intended to compete with the piece of eight in Far Eastern trade; but it halted production of the half dime, three-cent piece, and two-cent piece, and it closed out coinage of the normal silver dollar.

This was the famous "Crime of '73," which would soon become a rallying point for Western silver and Midwestern agrarian interests against the "goldbugs" of the East. Never mind that virtually no silver dollars had been struck during the 1860s and that no one wanted the three million or so that had been struck since 1870; for Western miners, the Mint Act of 1873 was outrage pure and simple, and they spent the next five years fighting to get it repealed. They would see success in 1878 with the passage of the Bland-Allison Act.

The act restored unlimited legal-tender status to silver dollars on the traditional standard, and it committed the U.S. Treasury to purchasing between two and four million dollars' worth of silver bullion each month for production of the new coins. The pieces were to have new designs by George T. Morgan, and his left-facing-portrait head of Liberty and more naturalistic reverse eagle represented a cautious attempt to bring more artistry to American coinage, a movement which gathered force as other denominations were redesigned after 1891. But for now, the dollar's new look was the last thing on most people's minds.

The reception and significance of the Morgan dollar varied wildly from place to place. The West was partially assuaged, because the region's silver production now had an outlet, and the new dollars were a circulating mainstay there for many years to come. They were also popular in the South, and millions were struck in New Orleans after the reopening of the federal branch mint there in 1879.

The Morgan silver dollar was struck by the millions starting in 1878.

THE ISSUE COMES TO A HEAD—AND THEN FADES

As the years went on, other groups grew progressively fonder of the Morgan dollar: medium and small farmers of the Midwest, West, and South, robbed of purchasing power in the 1880s and 1890s by a persistent agricultural depression, began to see the new silver dollars as a possible salvation. If the U.S. Mint coined them in unlimited numbers, then so much money would flood into the economy that the price of farm products would rise, and farmers could thus pay off their debts more easily than before.

But fortunately for the moneyed interests—who had a dislike and distrust of silver and rallied around gold—the Bland-Allison Act had stopped short of giving silver full bimetallic parity with gold at the old 16:1 ratio; it had also offered something less than completely "free" (unlimited) silver coinage. Both of these points would soon become rallying cries for miners and farmers. The Act did, however, allow for a massive coinage of cheap silver at inflated prices, a value-to-denomination ratio that became increasingly unrealistic as yet more silver poured from the mines and mints.

Along with the Morgan dollars, the Bland-Allison Act created a new type of paper currency, the Silver Certificate. This specialized note, originally intended to redeem the new dollars and later extended to the redemption of Legal Tender Notes issued during the Civil War, could not be exchanged for Gold Certificates. Nor would it remotely resemble any other type of federal paper money (the words "silver" and "silver dollars" dominating the designs), so anyone handed a Silver Certificate could immediately spot it and refuse it, demanding payment in a gold-based medium instead. But despite these measures and East Coast opposition, the new currency type gradually assumed a larger role in the national economy, as it was considerably easier to handle than the cumbrous coins it represented.

Today the debate over a gold standard versus a gold-and-silver standard may strike us as academic, but it had real and immediate connotations for those alive during the closing years of the 19th century. When miners and small farmers clamored for "the free and unlimited coinage of silver at the rate of sixteen to one," they were demanding recognition and respect for old ways of life that were now at risk. The fact that they could view endless coinage of a whitish metal with few nonmonetary applications as a panacea suggests that they were not being particularly realistic; but then, the same might be said for the opposition, who viewed the gold standard as sacred and any attempt to add silver as profane.

The issue came to a head in the presidential campaign of 1896, fought out against the backdrop of a miserable, three-year-long depression that had left factory workers unemployed and farmers and miners even worse off than before. Democratic candidate William Jennings Bryan hammered away at the Free Silver idea while Republican William McKinley's adherents spoke for gold coinage and a higher tariff. The latter—called "Big Bill McKinley, Advance Agent of Prosperity"—was elected, and sure enough, prosperity followed.

From this point, the issue of bimetallism faded in importance. When the Republic officially went on a gold standard in March 1900, Bryan and the Democrats railed and ran against it that fall—but no one cared and McKinley was reelected. He had more than prosperity on his side by that time; since he had taken office in March 1897, the United States had acquired an overseas empire. In the broader view of history, the new domains (and the fact that McKinley was reelected in part because of them) represented a historic shift in emphasis on the part of America's people; they were ready to look outward, and what they saw and how they reacted would amend the nature of their numismatic history in some very surprising ways.

New Empire, New Money

Change was in the air by the early 1870s. That the United States was looking abroad for economic gain was suggested by the new trade dollar; why mint such a coin for the Far Eastern trade if you were not interested in that trade yourself? And while the coin may not have lived up to expectations, Chinese merchants accepted it readily enough, until a fall in silver prices in 1876 resulted in millions of the coins recrossing the Pacific.

Another change: Prior to 1857, foreign coins were legal and common in circulation in the United States. By 1876 the Mint was actually beginning to coin for other countries—first for Venezuela, and later for other small nations in the Western Hemisphere, including the Dominican Republic in 1897, El Salvador in 1904, and Costa Rica in 1905. By 1906 it was supplying Mexico (in an interesting case of historical reciprocity), and the Mint would continue to extend its coinage production across Latin America during the first half of the 20th century.

In the 1880s, the U.S. Mint extended its attentions in another overseas direction—to Hawaii. The islands formed an independent kingdom in those days, but American missionaries had been preaching there since 1820, shortly followed by Yankee traders and businessmen. In 1847 an issue of copper keneta (cents) had been prepared for King Kamehameha III by a private mint in Attleboro, Massachusetts, but the issue was poorly received as the monarch's portrait was almost unrecognizable and the reverse denomination was misspelled.

American penetration of the islands increased its pace after 1849. In the early 1880s, King Kalākaua I desired another issue of Hawaiian coinage. His representative, sugar baron Claus Spreckels, approached the U.S. Mint with preliminary designs and a proposal for coining a million dollars' worth of silver into coinage for the island chain. The issue would consist of dala (dollars, on an exact par with the U.S. coin), hapalua (half dollars), hapaha (quarters), and umi keneta (ten-cent pieces)—making it possible to strike the entire issue on planchets left over from regular American coining—all of which were dated 1883.

Of course, Hawaii would eventually be annexed by the United States (1898) and later admitted to the Union, but this Pacific interest was an exception for the period as most of the U.S. Mint's foreign coining adventures were pursued in Spanish America. Two of the nations there for which the United States shortly would coin were Cuba and Panama, and there was a very good reason: the United States had helped create both countries in their modern forms.

In the case of Cuba, it was the Spanish-American War—that is, the U.S. military intervention in the Cuban War of Independence—that sparked the connection. From the time the war was won until 1902, the United States would occupy the island, and from then until 1915 American money would continue to circulate in the newly independent nation. After that, the Philadelphia Mint struck a new, distinctly Cuban coinage until the rise of Fidel Castro.

In the case of Panama, American desire for an interoceanic canal would prompt President Theodore Roosevelt to not only support a Panamanian revolt against controlling Colombia but also to act as midwife to the resultant new country. In this role the United States would strike no fewer than 6 new coins—based on a new coinage unit named for Vasco Núñez de Balboa—ranging from 1/2 to 50 centesimos. Interestingly, however, the mintages of those first issues of 1904 and most succeeding coinages were minuscule, as for the majority of business the country has preferred to use American coinage and American paper currency.

Charles Barber of the U.S. Mint designed this Hawaiian issue featuring King Kalākaua.

Finally, relevant to the topic of American imperialism and its numismatic importance, there was an outcome of the Spanish-American War that was just as important as Cuban independence: the American acquisition of Puerto Rico, Guam, and the Philippine Islands. The first two remain under U.S. control and still use U.S. coinage, and while the third is now independent and uses its own monetary system, the United States did strike coins for the Philippines for some time.

During the Philippines' days as a colony (1899–1935) and a commonwealth (1935–1946), Filipino coins were struck at every current American mint except New Orleans, and starting in 1920 at a new, special facility set up in Manila. The anomalous nature of the islands' status was demonstrated by the designs seen on their coinage: for obverses, a seated Filipino or a standing Filipina, for reverses, an American eagle surmounting an American shield. The coins were created by a local artist named Melecio Figueroa, and they were denominated in centavos and pesos.

A Renaissance in American Money

Theodore Roosevelt may be said to be the father of Panamanian numismatics, but numismatists know him far better in an American capacity: more than any other person, he was responsible for an artistic awakening in early 20th-century U.S. coinage. Once reelected in 1904, the energetic leader swung into action.

Roosevelt became involved in numismatics because he was deeply disgusted with the appearance of the American coins then in circulation. The old Gobrecht silver designs had been abandoned in 1891 in favor of new images for the dime, quarter, and half dollar, but these did not represent much of an improvement. Designer Charles E. Barber's Liberty head was acceptable, but his eagle was completely heraldic and appeared outdated even at the time it was introduced.

When it came to minor coinage, James B. Longacre's Indian Princess still graced the cent, more than 40 years after she had first appeared there. A copper-nickel five-cent piece, or "nickel," had been introduced in 1866, but its designs similarly failed to inspire. These included a fancy obverse shield and a reverse numeral by Longacre (used until 1883), and a trite obverse Liberty head and a large reverse "V" by Barber (used thereafter).

The designs of the gold coins annoyed President Roosevelt most of all. Ideas introduced by Gobrecht in 1838 and by Longacre in 1850 were still present on coins ranging from the quarter eagle to the double eagle. Surely, reasoned the president, the nation could do better than *that!*

He knew a gifted sculptor and medalist named Augustus Saint-Gaudens, who had been responsible for an attractive medal in a modern style portraying Christopher Columbus, created in conjunction with the 400th anniversary of the discovery of America. The politician and the artist had maintained contact over the years, and the latter responded magnificently to the former's call for help.

Saint-Gaudens's $10 gold piece featured a simple, left-facing Liberty with a feathered warbonnet (headgear added at the insistence of the president) and a naturalistic eagle inspired by an ancient Egyptian silver coin. His double eagle was still more ambitious, and it is arguably the most beautiful American coin. We see a figure of Liberty on the obverse, striding toward us in the dawn, holding the torch of freedom and the olive branch of peace. On the reverse, we see another eagle, this time soaring above the sun.

Saint-Gaudens would unfortunately die in the summer of 1907, and he never saw the completion of his project. Luckily, though, Barber would succeed in reducing the high relief of his prototypes, making them more practical for striking. This may have robbed the actual coins of a portion of their artistry, but even amended for the worse they were splendid coins.

Augustus Saint-Gaudens's gold double eagle is considered by many to be the most beautiful U.S. coin ever designed.

Roosevelt left office at the beginning of March 1909, also having secured the redesign of the quarter eagle and half eagle before he departed. These coins featured designs somewhat reminiscent of those on Saint-Gaudens's $10 piece, but struck *into* rather than *onto* the planchets, so that the fields of the new coins became their highest points. The innovative treatment engendered criticism (largely because it was assumed it would trap dirt and spread disease), but like the designs by Saint-Gaudens, these by Bela Lyon Pratt would serve on America's gold coinage until the final years of the medium itself.

Roosevelt's successor, William Howard Taft, continued the drive for greater numismatic artistry. A redesigned cent appeared during his first year in office, when Lithuanian immigrant Victor David Brenner created a new design to help the country mark the centenary of the birth of Abraham Lincoln. Slightly amended, Brenner's obverse portrait of "Honest Abe" is still in use; the reverse has changed from the original Wheat Ears, to the Lincoln Memorial (1959), to a set of four different reverses (2009 only, for the 200-year anniversary of Lincoln's birth), to the current Union Shield.

But back to the beginning of the 20th century: numismatic redesign continued after the Democratic Party regained national office in the election of 1912, and the five-cent piece was modified the following year. America's most artistic minor coin resulted: the Indian Head, or Buffalo, nickel showed what a gifted designer (in this case James Earle Fraser) could do with a humble coin in a base metal.

COMMEMORATIVES AND TOKENS

Another event in American numismatics during the Gilded Age was the creation of a coin for celebration rather than for commerce: the commemorative. Its origins in the United States date to 1892. The concept has much deeper roots elsewhere—coinage celebratory of a particular event or personage was known to the ancient Greeks, and was revived here and there in the Renaissance—but commemoratives truly gained popularity in Europe during the 19th century and their attraction eventually extended to the Americas as well.

While some earlier issues (such as the 1848 CAL. quarter eagle) could be considered commemorative coins, collectors begin the American series with a half dollar and quarter issued in conjunction with the World's Columbian Exposition in 1893. Half dollars with a head of Columbus on the obverse and a representation of the *Santa Maria* on the reverse—a collaborative effort between Charles Barber and George Morgan—were produced for sale in 1892 and 1893, while a quarter with Queen Isabella on the obverse and a female figure with a distaff and spindle on the reverse—the work of Barber alone—appeared in 1893. Some 5,000,000 of the half dollars were minted in Philadelphia, along with about 24,000 of the quarters.

From these modest beginnings, a numismatic industry would grow. Barber was responsible for a silver dollar celebrating George Washington and the Marquis de Lafayette dated 1900. The busy designer also tried his hand at a series of tiny commemorative gold dollars made for the Louisiana Purchase Exposition, dated 1903, and the Lewis and Clark Exposition, dated 1904 and 1905.

Meanwhile the career of another American monetary form, the token, was in decline. Like the celebratory coin, the private substitute for the regular coin had roots in the classical world, and we have seen this monetary form during the colonial period and the Civil War. During the Gilded Age, the locus of the token shifted West, as that region was chronically short of small change.

There were silver dollars and gold coins aplenty, but the mints at San Francisco, Carson City, and Denver (which began striking money in 1906) made far fewer small coins than large; they struck no cents until 1908 and no five-cent pieces until 1912. Furthermore, what smaller members of the silver series were struck tended to stay in large Western cities, to the detriment of merchants in small Western towns.

The latter responded as Americans had always addressed a monetary shortage: they obtained and circulated alternative money. Across the region, thousands of types of tokens, struck in brass, copper, zinc, aluminum, and even hard rubber, were called into service to expand the money supply. Because of the federal law of 1864 (which made private coinage illegal), these merchants' tokens generally promised payment in a specific article (a five-cent cigar, for instance) or "in trade," meaning that the customer might use the token as he pleased for the amount indicated on the piece.

These pieces formed a vital part of numismatic Americana during the Gilded Age, but their localism was more apparent than real. A handful of firms in New York and Chicago struck the majority of them. Here as elsewhere, diversity was yielding place to uniformity in the matter of America's money, a trend accelerated in the 20th century.

Tokens struck by merchants were one way to alleviate
the shortage of small-change coins in circulation.

ISOLATION, DEPRESSION, AND INTERVENTION: AMERICA, 1914–1945

Prior to 1940, a combination of distance, nationalism, and problems and prospects at home kept American attention firmly fixed on domestic affairs rather than foreign ones. This national tendency was never more evident than in the summer of 1914; when citizens of the New World heard that a conflagration had once more erupted in the Old, they heartily congratulated themselves on staying clear of it. They had problems enough at home.

Trusts were everywhere—those faceless octopi that restricted trade, held down wages, and squeezed the "little guy" to death. And along with the oil trust, sugar trust, steel trust, and the like, there was, it appeared, a "money trust." By the time President Woodrow Wilson was inaugurated on March 4, 1913, public opinion was demanding a dismantling of that beast, or at least its containment by the federal government. One way to keep it within bounds might be by exerting a greater federal control over the sinews of the banking system and the paper money employed in its operations. Thus the Federal Reserve Act of 1913 was born, and, in the following year, a new type of currency: the Federal Reserve Note.

The Federal Reserve Act divided the nation into 12 districts, each with a Federal Reserve Bank at its heart. The 12 districts, their cities, and the symbols that each must employ on the notes they issue are as follows:

District	City of Issue	Identification Symbol
1	Boston	1 or A
2	New York City	2 or B
3	Philadelphia	3 or C
4	Cleveland	4 or D
5	Richmond	5 or E
6	Atlanta	6 or F
7	Chicago	7 or G
8	St. Louis	8 or H
9	Minneapolis	9 or I
10	Kansas City, MO	10 or J
11	Dallas	11 or K
12	San Francisco	12 or L

Working in tandem with the Federal Reserve Board in Washington, each of the member banks had the theoretical power and obligation to advise on and act as a watchdog over banking activity within its district.

The Federal Reserve Notes of 1914 and later may have appeared to be local (or at least regional), but they were undeniably products of the national government. All were printed in Washington at the Bureau of Engraving and Printing. Among all the types of federal, state, and local currency issued in America over the past three centuries, this is the only one that has survived to the present.

FROM WORLD WAR I TO THE CRASH

American participation in the Great War (renamed the "First World War" when it became apparent that it would not be the last of its kind) was limited; the Yanks were not there for the first, and worst, of the fighting, and their vision of the conflict was therefore tinged with an aura of romance. This idealism was extremely significant for what happened next: there would be a paradigm shift, from concentration on domestic problems to a crusade to save Europe from itself, "to make the world safe for democracy," in the words of the American leader.

But when U.S. optimism collided with European reality (the Allies' desire to turn their victory in 1918 into a settling of old scores), the outcome was the worst of several possible combinations. Disillusioned, Americans would reject any substantive role in the new, postwar world order. Their disillusionment would extend to matters domestic as well, and the zeal for public reform would be replaced by one for private gain. Thus the Roaring Twenties, a supposedly golden age of unparalleled industrial growth, personal liberation, and new social, economic, and cultural icons: the automobile, the radio, and the flapper.

It was quite an era, but the golden dust of this new age was not scattered equally across the Republic, enriching all of its people. Accustomed to high commodity prices during the war, Midwestern and Southern farmers saw their incomes shrink and their debts rise after the beginning of the 1920s. Factory workers did poorly too, their wages held down by a new, anti-labor stance on the part of public officials. A determined managerial attempt to sell the concepts of the company union and the open shop kept wages depressed as well.

African Americans did still worse. Those who had migrated to the North before and during the war found that they were no more welcome there than they had been in the South. Women did slightly better; at least they now had the vote, and they could exert some influence on the national scene. But all in all, as the 1920s roared on, a disturbing fact became slowly apparent to those who wished to see it: much of the economic boom was based on hot air. All those new buildings, automobiles, radios, and other accessories of the New Era might someday disappear, when everyone's credit, and hence their ability to purchase them, ran out. If that ever happened, matters would become very interesting indeed.

And it happened, of course. In 1928 Herbert Hoover—a former secretary of commerce and one of the architects of the prosperous 1920s—was elected president of the United States. He was inaugurated in March 1929, and some seven months later, the house of cards tumbled down.

A DECLINE IN COINAGE AND PAPER MONEY

The hard times of the Great Depression had a variety of effects on American numismatics. For coinage, the years between 1929 and 1933 saw a decline in production, for those out of work would hardly need an abundance of new coins for their diminishing purchases. In the year of the stock-market crash, no fewer than eight coinage denominations were in current production at the U.S. Mint; the only American denominations not struck that year were dollars and eagles. In 1930 the total was six, and in 1931, four, where it remained in 1932 and 1933. Additionally, two of those four denominations were gold, which was of no earthly value to the average citizen, whose weekly wages were probably less than the value of the smaller denomination (the eagle), if they were being received at all. Only in 1934 did the quantity of denominations struck and coins minted begin rising.

Paper money was still being printed, but currency was now made in a new, smaller model. The types of notes in circulation remained what they had been prior to the crash—Federal Reserve bills, Silver Certificates, Legal Tender Notes, and the rest—but a standardization of design, if not of type, now set in. Of course, the nation's people were far more concerned about the soundness of their currency than the sameness of its designs; worry centered on locally issued National Bank Notes, as banks began failing immediately after the Wall Street crash in the autumn of 1929.

Despite President Hoover's optimism, the number of failures grew. Soon average citizens were taking their savings (if they had any) out of the bank and stuffing them under the mattress, where they could at least keep an eye on them. By late 1932, a crisis was reached; that November, Hoover lost his bid for reelection to Franklin Delano Roosevelt, but the nation would have to wait until the following March (when the new president was inaugurated) for any significant federal intervention.

Meanwhile governors began doing their bit on the state level to stop the hemorrhaging of the banking system by proclaiming "banking holidays," periods during which every bank within their jurisdiction would be forced to close its doors. The first state to take this action was Nevada. The closure was only supposed to last for 12 days, but it was extended indefinitely. By February 1933, other states were following in Nevada's wake, and by the time Hoover finally left the White House and Roosevelt moved in, virtually every bank in the country had shut down or was operating under extreme difficulties.

Once again faced with a shortage of "normal" money, Americans were forced to make money of their own beginning in 1931. In places, these efforts extended until 1939, but the core period coincided with the banking crisis of late 1932 and early 1933. During those few months, Americans gave their money a vitality and variety it had rarely enjoyed before and has never enjoyed since.

They constructed their makeshift money from a variety of materials, including paper, wood (there really were "wooden nickels" during these days), base metal, leather, fish skin, vulcanite, and—in a marvelous instance of history repeating itself—clamshells. A bewildering number of authorities stood behind those issues—large cities, small towns, companies and firms within those cities and towns, and mutual aid associations. This "Depression scrip" appeared in all 48 of the current states, as well as the Alaskan Territory. In short, there was a period of localism in currency fully comparable with that of the 19th century, if of shorter duration.

A citizen of Pismo Beach, California, could reimburse this clamshell for $1 at the Harter Drug Company.

ROOSEVELT AND A NEW DEAL

The incoming Roosevelt administration would take very determined steps to end the banking crisis that had inspired the locally issued scrip. The president proclaimed a national bank holiday on March 6, 1933, that would allow for careful examination of each bank's finances. Solvent banks gradually reopened their doors between the 13th and 15th of March, and those found unsound would stay closed.

This bold stroke, as well as Roosevelt's programs for other aspects of the economy and his self-assured attitude, brought a return of confidence to the nation and a return of normal money to the channels of commerce. It was originally thought that even *more* money in circulation would be necessary, and thus the Federal Reserve *Bank* Note (as opposed to the Federal Reserve Note) was formed as an interim national currency—but normal currency came back into circulation more quickly than anticipated, and the new notes were curtailed later in 1933.

Other types of money were being curtailed as well. Between 1933 and 1935, competing types of national paper currency were eclipsed by the Federal Reserve Note, and the Roosevelt administration concluded that National Banks' right to issue currency should be revoked. Other forms of currency fared scarcely better. The president also demonetized gold coinage (and Gold Certificates, the currency redeemable in gold coin), a policy he and a Democratic Congress would accomplish with successive laws passed in 1933 and 1934.

Under the new philosophy, the printing of the venerable National Bank Note came to a close in 1935; production of Silver Certificates was restricted to lower denominations; and most U.S. currency was made "redeemable in lawful money" rather than spelling out precisely what sort of coin might be received for each note. What Roosevelt and his advisors sought was a plausible currency that was also manageable, manipulable, and capable of expansion in times of depression and of contraction in times of inflation.

They found their solution in the Federal Reserve System with the Federal Reserve Note. Henceforth, this type of currency would reign supreme, and America's paper money would lose most of its individuality and localism. The state-chartered banks of the 1700s and 1800s, and the National Banks that succeeded them and continued the custom of locally issued currency, were history.

An Explosion of Commemoratives

Even as economic and social pressures and prospects (as well as Roosevelt's policies) were increasing "sameness" in American money, the federal government showed itself partial to celebrating the diversity and richness of American history. Beside the state guides produced by the Federal Writers' Workshops in the 1930s and 1940s, it found one of its most lasting expressions on the commemorative coin.

Commemorative coinage came to the United States with the Columbian Exposition celebrations of 1892–1893, and it took root in America by the first years of the new century. Commemoratives were issued from time to time during the 1910s and 1920s. Some of the most notable issues of the period would be the huge round and octagonal $50 pieces produced for the Panama-Pacific Exposition in 1915, as well as the new Peace silver dollar introduced at the end of 1921.

Commemorative coinage continued through the administrations of Harding and Coolidge, ordinarily restricted to a single denomination, the half dollar. Issues of that period tended to focus on events rather than places—battles of the American Revolution, the sesquicentennial of Independence, the centenary of the Monroe Doctrine—but the most successful of them celebrated a place as well as an epoch: the Oregon Trail.

The Oregon Trail half dollar is considered by many to have one of the most artful of U.S. commemorative designs.

The collapse of 1929 brought celebratory coinage to an abrupt end for four years. True, a commemorative was introduced for the bicentennial of George Washington's birth in 1932, but it soon transmogrified into that most pedestrian of 20th-century American circulating coins: the Washington quarter, which is still in production today. The real resumption of commemorative coinage began in 1934, accelerated in 1935, crested in 1936, and continued to enliven America's money through 1939, after which concern with overproduction and possible warfare put a damper on such numismatic enthusiasm.

But while it lasted, what a time it was! A fundamental shift had taken place, and while events would still receive their commemorative due, the real emphasis was now on the places where the events had occurred. Such celebration of local themes was underscored by the employment of local artists to create the designs for the new issues, and while some of the artistic attempts were more successful than others, the overall effect of the multiplicity of commemorative coins was a positive one. American collectors now look back to those days as a golden age of numismatics, even though their parents and grandparents may have thought that the spate of commemoratives was getting out of hand.

FRESH NEW CIRCULATING COINS

The period of the American commemorative coincided with one of the high points of American numismatic artistry on circulating coinage. True, the daring and beautiful designs of Pratt and Saint-Gaudens passed from the scene when gold coinage stopped in 1933, but these were great days indeed for silver and base-metal coinage.

John Flanagan's portrait of George Washington on the quarter dollar may have been a step down, artistically, compared to its dramatic predecessor by Hermon MacNeil. For other circulating denominations during the 1930s, the artistic flowering that Theodore Roosevelt had begun still held sway. Brenner's cent and Fraser's five-cent piece were in everyday use. The dime and half dollar were both redesigned in 1916, and Charles Barber's trite renditions were replaced by magnificent, authentically "patriotic" images by Adolph Alexander Weinman.

As with MacNeil's quarter, Weinman's dime and half dollar were designed just prior to American entry into the First World War, and the themes they incorporated suggested as much. For the dime, a realistic, left-facing head of Liberty imparted a new freshness to American numismatic design, although the wings on the goddess's cap, placed there to symbolize liberty of thought, were mistaken for the attributes of a god and the coin became known as the "Mercury" dime. Weinman's reverse brought an altogether new concept to American coinage: the fasces, emblem of unity, something obviously desired in the face of international danger.

Attractive as was his dime, this artist's half dollar was his greater contribution to U.S. numismatics, and it stands as the most beautiful circulating design ever created for that denomination. On the obverse, we see Liberty wearing an American flag and striding toward the dawn with a bundle of oak and laurel branches in the crook of her left arm; on the reverse is the American eagle, a splendidly naturalistic depiction of the bird.

By the time Weinman's dime and half dollar were replaced in the 1940s, James Earle Fraser's Buffalo nickel had passed from the scene as well, supplanted by Felix Schlag's design honoring Thomas Jefferson. The new coin marked a deepening of the trend away from symbolic representations and toward real people, a move already seen with the Lincoln cent of 1909 and the Washington quarter of 1932. This nickel is still in production today, although it has seen modifications in design over the years, some of them dramatic.

Weinman's Liberty Walking half dollar, like his dime, debuted in 1916 and was part of the U.S. Mint's lineup into the 1940s.

NEW STRUGGLES BRING NEW MONEY

After an uneasy armed truce lasting 21 years, the old adversaries of 1914 squared off once again; war broke out in September 1939, as expansionist Germany attempted one final bluff and found at last that there was a point beyond which the other side (Great Britain and France) would not retreat.

In the beginning, most Americans were quite happy to stay out of the conflict, as they had been in 1914. For the first two-thirds of a year, the war seemed to involve little more than politics, as Hitler absorbed Poland without opposition from his theoretical adversaries. But then came *Blitzkrieg*, as Germany overran Norway, Denmark, the Low Countries, and finally France itself, making the war look very real indeed.

Thus, as the 1940s began, the United States was uncertain. It did not want Germany and its allies to win the war, but getting deeply involved might be the only way to avoid that outcome. Then, as all eyes were on Europe, the event that would tip the scales occurred at a venue Americans regarded as a side-show, if they thought about it at all: on December 7, 1941, Japan attacked the United States at that splendid base the Navy had acquired from the Hawaiian monarchy back in 1887, Pearl Harbor.

Americans would henceforth be as deeply involved in the world conflict as anyone else, declaring war on the Japanese as well as their allies, Hitler's Germany and Mussolini's Italy. U.S. participation in the Second World War lasted some 45 months and left 292,131 dead and 671,801 wounded of the 16,353,659 men and women who served in its armed forces. It would also permanently change America's conduct abroad, as the nation embraced its larger role on the international scene.

But American participation in the Second World War changed even more at home than it did abroad. It planted seeds for future movements, including the empowerment of women and African Americans, groups that played key roles in the war efforts. The conflict was also a hotbed for technological development, resulting in new innovations both good (such as plastics, synthetic fibers centering on nylon, artificial lubricants, and new food products) and controversial (the Bomb).

Of course, the nationwide change also extended to coins and currency. In the case of the former, copper was removed from the cent at the end of 1942. Its alloy was changed to zinc-plated steel in 1943, and melted-down gun-shell casings in 1944, 1945, and 1946. Nickel was deemed a critical war material, too, and so a concoction of copper (56 percent), silver (35 percent), and manganese (9 percent) was introduced in October 1942 and used in the five-cent coin through 1945. More than half a billion coins were made from the threefold alloy, distinguished by their slightly different color and a large mintmark (including a new "P" for Philadelphia) over the dome of Monticello rather than a small one at its right side.

Changes in paper currency occurred more in peripheral areas. The new Hawaiian issues were simply ordinary Silver Certificates upon which a brown seal was substituted for the blue one appropriate to that type of currency. Additionally, the word HAWAII was overprinted twice in small letters on the face and once in gigantic letters on the back. The idea was that the distinctive notes, printed for circulation in Hawaii, could be declared irredeemable if the Japanese occupied the islands and seized the local banks. Notes were also issued for use of American troops in Europe and North Africa; some of this "Allied Military Currency" was denominated in dollars and some was denominated in the currencies of those countries in which U.S. soldiers served, but none was truly American currency.

Meanwhile the U.S. Mint's early activities in providing Latin American countries with coins were expanded dramatically during the war. The Mint continued to supply a number of old customers, and it also created "liberation" issues of several types. For the Philippines (which had had its own mint in Manila since 1920, but which had fallen to Japan early in the war), massive coin issues of the prewar types were prepared in Denver and San Francisco in 1944 and 1945, and placed in Philippine commerce as the islands were liberated by U.S. and local troops.

The U.S. Mint also served as temporary coiner for the Netherlands, supplying its possessions with money of the prewar type when the mother country was unable to do so. Finally, coins were prepared for liberated France and Belgium. Their extreme simplicity of design illustrates the urgency of the times. A two-franc coin was struck in brass for France, while the Mint found a handy way of recycling the unwanted steel-cent planchets of 1943, turning them into the Belgian double francs of 1944.

Thus the coinage and currency of an America at war. For all of the diversity of metals and types, and for all of the interesting experiments, the numismatic expedients of the Second World War left no permanent imprint on the story of the nation's money. When the fighting had ended, reality snapped back into its earlier, prewar mold: normal alloys returned and commemorative issues soon resumed. But an unintended and doleful new coin entered the monetary spectrum as well, and it might serve to symbolize the war and the events that had led up to it.

The coin was a dime, approved late in 1945, introduced early in 1946. The nation's new dime bore the head of the man who had dominated the American war effort and who had died in its pursuit: Franklin Delano Roosevelt. The coin is still in circulation today, linking Americans, many several generations removed from the war, with the man and the events.

COLD WAR AND BEYOND: 1946 TO THE PRESENT

The years since the end of the Second World War have been among the most eventful in American, and indeed human, history. The conflict convinced us that we must look outside our walls, and take larger responsibility for international affairs. Our new relationship meant hot wars in Korea and Vietnam, Kuwait, Afghanistan, and Iraq; a cold war with Russia; and an inability to enjoy the promised fruits of our earlier victory in 1945.

Meanwhile, on a domestic level we have seen several recessions; the longest economic boom in American history; the rise of the suburb and the decline of the central city; multiple cultural and technological revolutions; and a doubling of our population. Changes indeed, changes everywhere, except one place: until very recently, America's money scarcely changed at all.

Throughout history there was a dynamism at work in the coinage and currency of the United States, a dynamism spurred by and reflective of the larger events of the period. Yet here, against a background of some of the greatest alterations ever seen in ways of life, we still use American coinage and paper currency that would be recognizable to the average man and woman of 1946.

What happened? Why did the money become fixed in a single, virtually changeless pattern? And what does this say about larger issues?

The postwar decades of national stress played a major role in the unusual continuity of America's money. When people are constantly bombarded with threats and turmoil, they tend to take what comfort they can in prosaic objects that have "always" been with them in the same reliable form. Coins and paper money can fall into this category.

Between 1989 and 1991, the United States' major perceived foreign threat—the Soviet Union—removed itself from contention, and, for the first time since 1945, a real debate arose and still goes on about the designs on American coinage and paper currency, not only on the part of collectors but on the part of the wider public. Put most simply, America had more important matters on its mind until fairly recently; changes are taking place now that the nation has the leisure to look at its coins and notes with a more critical eye.

Of course, other forces have been at work, too. For example, when it comes to coinage, contemporary minters are mainly concerned with technological considerations; designs are adopted or rejected not primarily because of their looks, but because they will or will not translate well to an easy-to-mass-produce piece of metal. The arrangements that grace American circulating coinage are relatively successful from that standpoint. They are well balanced, obverse to reverse, so that designs on each side come up reasonably well in a single, quick blow of the press. And to the cry of the artist for reform of design comes the response of the minter: if it works, leave it alone. This is one reason for continuity on American coinage.

A new dime in 1946 would honor the fallen president who had rallied the United States throughout the war.

Another is the amount of verbiage that must, either by force of law or by force of tradition, be placed on the coinage. The elements that each coin must bear include the name of the country, a national motto ("E Pluribus Unum"), a second national motto ("In God We Trust"), a *third* national motto ("Liberty"), the denomination, the date, and the place of mintage, symbolized by a mintmark. Once you get all that onto a coin, you have precious little room for anything else, and if a design manages to cram everything in and still proves easy to coin, you will hold onto it very tightly.

AMERICAN MONEY IN STAGNATION

In 1959 the cent was changed in commemoration of Lincoln's 150th birthday and the half-century mark of the Lincoln cent itself. The martyred president continued to form the obverse design. But on the reverse, the "wheat ears" gave way to an attempt to depict the entire Lincoln Memorial—an attempt which found some success from a technological perspective, perhaps less from an artistic one.

Its comrades, the Washington quarter and the Jefferson nickel, seemingly have been in circulation forever. The quarter's basic designs date from 1932, and those of the nickel date from 1938. Both the dime and the half dollar were redesigned shortly after the end of the Second World War. Franklin Delano Roosevelt was placed on the obverse of the dime in 1946. The new dime's design was neat and compact.

In 1947 the last coins using the Weinman designs were struck, replaced by John R. Sinnock's less artistic designs featuring Benjamin Franklin on the obverse and the Liberty Bell on the reverse. In order to comply with the Mint Act of 1792, Sinnock added a tiny eagle to the right of the bell. This odd placement neatly summarizes the somewhat ungainly concept of the entire design, which came to an abrupt end in 1963. The next year saw another new design, this one by Gilroy Roberts and Frank Gasparro, paying homage to the martyred president, John Fitzgerald Kennedy. These designs still appear on half dollars, although the coins themselves are no longer released to banks for general distribution, and rarely appear in circulation.

Another coin that has seen its usage progressively restricted is the metallic dollar. Production for circulation was halted in 1935, and did not resume until 1971, when Frank Gasparro's new dollar appeared featuring a rendition of the *Apollo 11* insignia on the reverse and a left-facing head of President Dwight David Eisenhower on the obverse. The coin was struck only intermittently through 1978.

By that time, the dollar was not circulating except in certain areas of the West, such as the casinos of Las Vegas. In an attempt to increase the coin's convenience and appeal, and to create a more durable dollar than the paper one, the U.S. Mint reduced the coin's size, bringing out a smaller version in the spring of 1979 that replaced Eisenhower with groundbreaking feminist Susan B. Anthony. The Mint made more than 750 million dollars of this version in 1979, but the public was lukewarm about the new entry, and output shrank to less than 100 million in 1980 and less than 14 million in 1981.

The Susan B. Anthony dollar (1979–1999) continued with the reverse design of the earlier Eisenhower dollar.

The Mint then gave up and the coins were put in storage, where most of them still remain. A second release took place in 1999, but it proved no more successful than the first. Of course, no American coin actually contained silver by that point, and virtually none had since the mid-1960s; the United States removed silver from most of its coinage by the Act of July 23, 1965. The value of the precious metal had risen to the point where it eventually was worth the effort to melt down American coins for their silver. Since 1970, when the last of the half dollar's silver was removed, nearly every circulating American coin above five cents has consisted of the same metallic composition, with outer layers of 75 percent copper and 25 percent nickel bonded to cores of pure copper.

But the dime, quarter, and half dollar owed some of their continuing acceptance to their continuity of size and design—plus the fact that they were the *only* dimes, quarters, and halves provided by the government for public use. At the time of the introduction of the Anthony coin, the public already had a paper dollar, as well as a coin of a "real" dollar size: the Eisenhower dollar, which was reassuringly heavy, if not silver.

All of these changes—the elimination of precious metal, the melting of earlier issues, reductions in size (in the case of the dollar), and the freezing of designs—contributed to a curious fact in American numismatics. Fewer and fewer young people became interested in the hobby, for there was less and less to attract them to the coinage of their own country.

Collecting might be said to hinge upon the availability of objects with discernible differences, combined with the attractions of rarity and age. When the oldest coin one is likely to see in circulation is dated 1965; when it looks like every other coin in one's pocket and elsewhere; and when its numbers are counted in the billions, there is little reason to look at pocket change, little reason to collect it, little reason to venture into numismatics.

An Injection of Creative Change

The commemorative coin served as a partial solution to the dilemma. Three such issues were struck shortly after 1945, celebrating the centenary of the state of Iowa (issues of 1946); paying homage to the educator Booker T. Washington (issues of 1946 through 1951); and granting recognition to Booker T. Washington again, in conjunction with the scientist George Washington Carver (issues of 1951 through 1954). These two individuals were African Americans, and the commemoratives bearing their portraits suggested that members of this race were at least beginning to receive a measure of their due on American coins, anticipating their progress in wider matters.

But there was rather more to the Washington/Carver coin than appeared at first glance. It was promoted by one S.J. Phillips to provide funds "to oppose the spread of communism among Negroes in the interest of National Defense"; the coin appeared at the height of the Cold War, and the government was concerned about subversion in all aspects of society at the time. Phillips was deeply in debt from promoting the earlier half dollar for Booker T. Washington and needed money to pay off creditors and avoid lawsuits. In time, the real purpose of the Washington/Carver coin became common knowledge in Congress, and it cast a pall over the American commemorative lasting for a quarter of a century. Commemorative coinage came to a halt.

In 1975 and 1976, the reverses of the quarter dollar, half dollar, and dollar were redesigned to celebrate the bicentennial of the declaration of American independence. Of the three designs chosen (a Revolutionary War drummer for the quarter, Independence Hall for the half, and the Liberty Bell superimposed on the moon for the dollar), only the quarter design represented a real success; its artist, Jack L. Ahr, took the pains necessary to fit his concept into the circular constraints of a coin. Significantly, all three coins were released into commerce as normal issues, even though special presentation pieces could be purchased if desired.

The commemorative coin had been fully rehabilitated by the early 1980s. In 1982 the 250th anniversary of George Washington's birth was recorded on a new silver half dollar, struck only for collectors and not for circulation. That forecast the future. Since then, a large number of commemoratives have been struck in silver, and there has been a resumption of gold commemorative coinage as well.

It is worth noting that while most of the issues of the 1930s paid homage to places as well as people and events, therefore injecting a note of localism into a national coinage, the issues of the 1980s and later have swung away from localism and toward events, places, and persons of national significance. Their subject matter proclaims as much: the Olympic Games, American immigration, the Korean War, the bicentennial of Congress, the National Baseball Hall of Fame, to name just a few recent topics.

A NEW RENAISSANCE OF AMERICAN MONEY

In recent years, nothing less than a renaissance has taken place in America's coinage and currency. Hobbyists have made a determined effort to bring experimentation and localism back to these media and have found congressmen, senators, and numismatic writers sympathetic to the cause. It was slow going at the outset, but the rebirth is well under way.

The State quarters program is a case in point. Writers and hobby representatives such as Kenneth Bressett, Art Kagin, David Ganz, and Harvey Stack were hard at work promoting the idea as early as the beginning of the 1990s, but the first State quarters only came from the presses in 1999. A tremendous amount of pushing, shoving, and dedication had filled the intervening years, but all the effort was worth it; the State quarters did more to increase the ranks of casual and dedicated coin collectors than has any other program, or any other type of coinage, in all American history.

The idea for the program was to gain new collectors and retain old ones by putting coins with obvious differences into circulation. Contests were held in each state to select a unique reverse design, and the coins were issued at a rate of five per year in the same order that the states came into the Union. By doing all this, a sense of *history, place,* and *time* was distilled into a small, attractive object that everyone saw and all could afford.

While the quality of the designs varies, each of the coins does what it was intended to do: educate the public; show something of the variety of America; and function as solid, dependable money. The success of the program spawned a similar series of five-cent pieces, coins whose reverses allude to various aspects of the Lewis and Clark expedition while their obverses present us with various portraits of Thomas Jefferson, the president under whose aegis the historic trek took place. The idea was extended to include quarters for the District of Columbia and the five U.S. territories in 2009, followed by a series of National Park quarters starting in 2010. Even the lowly cent was refurbished, in 2009: celebrating Abraham Lincoln's 200th birthday, four new reverse designs were released, each emblematic of a major period in the martyred leader's life. Starting in 2010, the cent has featured a shield design, representing Lincoln's preservation of the Union.

In every case, the goal has been to produce money that everyone can afford to collect from circulation. For those so inclined, the Mint also strikes and sells Proof versions of these coins, along with a sizable run of other commemoratives and bullion coins in precious metals. One of the most successful of these ventures featured James Earle Fraser's designs for the nickel, successfully transferred to silver (in 2001) and gold (in 2006); here, the desire to commemorate merged with the desire to make something that would compete with other countries' bullion coins.

Finally, the past few years have witnessed other attempts at producing a small-sized circulating dollar coin. The first attempt featured Sacagawea on the obverse and a bald eagle in flight on the reverse, the latter standing as perhaps the most beautiful rendition of our national symbol to ever grace a base-metal coin. Struck in an alloy of copper, zinc, manganese, and nickel, the "golden" dollar was introduced in 2000 was struck until 2008.

And even while acceptance of the first golden dollar coin was in question, the popularity of the State quarters program emboldened the collecting fraternity to request a *second* dollar coin—or rather, a series. These coins (the same size as the first at 26.5 mm, a trifle larger than the quarter) celebrate the administration of every deceased American president from George Washington onward. These coins, which are currently being introduced at the rate of four per year, represent innovation: many of the presidential portraits face the viewer rather than appearing in profile; some mandatory wording (IN GOD WE TRUST and E PLURIBUS UNUM, as well as the actual year of issue) was for a time moved to the

Two new lines of "golden dollars" (the Sacagawea and the Presidential series) are among the U.S. Mint's innovations in recent years.

edge; and a depiction of the Statue of Liberty on the reverse stands in place of the word LIBERTY. Taking the place of the Sacagawea dollar, and running alongside the Presidential dollars, is the series of Native American dollars (2009 to date). These feature an annually changing design that honors the important contributions made by Indian tribes and individual Native Americans to the development and history of the United States.

LOOKING FORWARD

Will any of these new dollars be able to oust that traditional workhorse, the dollar bill? This seems unlikely unless special steps are taken. People are conservative when it comes to what they deem "normal" money, and they are likely to stick with what they know.

What about the survival of the one-cent piece? The 2009 Lincoln commemoratives are about the only pieces of good news for this most humble member of our monetary system. The price of copper rose in the early 1980s, so zinc was substituted for it, but recently the price of zinc has risen too. About the only remaining cheap metallic candidate is aluminum, but public opposition would be expected: we have come to regard aluminum as nearly worthless.

And there's still a larger problem: people simply don't use the cent as they once did. The coin's purchasing power has essentially disappeared. So the previously unmentionable is now being discussed: if we were to do away with the cent, would the Republic survive? Groups have sprung up to defend this hallowed member of the monetary system. Some are composed of traditionalists, who feel the cent must be saved, if only for its symbolic value; others represent the zinc industry, for which the billions of cents struck each year represent a significant profit.

And there is the question of what to do with all those unwanted cents. If we want to save the denomination, how do we get these billions of coins out of dresser drawers and piggy banks and back into trade? The simplest, most elegant solution might involve a permanent halt in production but continuing legality for those coins already struck. Since new cents would not be added to commerce, old ones would come out of hiding, perform at least a part of the role for which they had been created, become worn out, and quietly disappear.

The trials of the dollar and the eclipse of the cent should not cause alarm. At bottom, the American monetary system is always a work in progress. Change is inevitable, and if one world seems to be ending, another is beginning. Here and abroad, money is the product of *people*. And where there are people, there is always movement.

These developments are exciting for the hobbyist, but they are perhaps more important for the historian and student of numismatics: among other things, they proclaim that the exceptional, the unusual, and the local have by no means disappeared from America's media of exchange, and that what appeared at first glance to be a closing door is also an open one, welcoming, beckoning. Who knows where it may lead our people—and our money?

Colonial Issues

FOREIGN COINS IN THE COLONIES

Money had a rich history in America prior to the advent of the United States' national coinage in 1793. When coins tumbled off the presses from the first Philadelphia Mint the country was much more accustomed to coins from other lands. Prior to 1652 there was no local coinage and the only money in circulation was whatever came here from Europe through trade or travel. People were content to use currency, both old and new, whose value was based more on the metal content than on the issuer's reliability. Foreign money in America during the colonial period had become so embedded that it continued to be accepted as legal tender until discontinued by the Coinage Act of February 21, 1857. Coins of this era are so fundamental to American numismatics that every collection should include at least a sampling.

From the very beginning of commerce in America "hard money" was needed for trade with overseas nations. The largest quantity of coinage consisted of English crowns, shillings, and pence, and Spanish and Spanish-American silver pieces of eight, all of which circulated throughout colonial settlements until being sent back to England for critically needed supplies. Additional quantities of coins came from trading furs, lumber, and other exports that provided a limited but much needed supply of hard currency. Of equal importance to commerce were similar coins of other European countries. The large silver Dutch *leeuwendaalder* (Lyon or Lion dollar) and French *écu* saw extensive circulation, as did the Brazilian gold *peças*. Some New York bills of 1709 were even denominated in Lyon dollars. Distinguishing between the relative values of the multitude of different foreign currencies was not a simple task. To facilitate conversions, books and tables showed comparison prices for each currency.

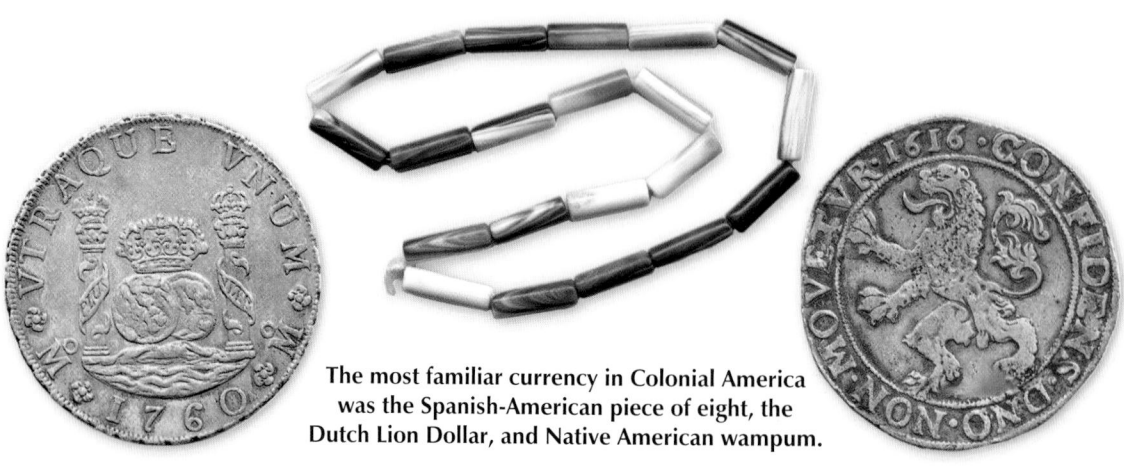

The most familiar currency in Colonial America was the Spanish-American piece of eight, the Dutch Lion Dollar, and Native American wampum.

The popular Spanish-American silver eight reales, Pillar dollar, or piece of eight, which was a radical departure from denominations in terms of English pounds, shillings, and pence, became a model for the American silver dollar, and its fractional parts morphed into the half-dollar and quarter-dollar coins that are now considered decimal fractions of the dollar. The American quarter dollar, which was similar in size and value to the Spanish two-real coin, took on the nickname "two bits"—a moniker that remains today. Similarly, the American one-cent coin has never totally lost its association with the English penny, and is still called that by anyone indifferent to numismatic accuracy.

Coins, tokens, paper money, and promissory notes were not the only media of exchange used during the early formation of the country. Many day-to-day transactions were carried on by barter and credit. Mixed into this financial morass were local trade items such as native wampum, hides, household goods, and tools. Records were kept in the traditional English pounds, shillings, and pence, but debts and taxes were paid in corn, beaver pelts, or money—money being whatever foreign coins were available. The terms "country pay" or "corn" referred to a number of different kinds of grain or even peas. Standard exchange rates were established and country pay was lawfully received at the colonial treasury for taxes.

Beyond these pre-federal considerations are the many kinds of private and state issues of coins and tokens that permeate the colonial period from 1616 to 1776. These are items that catch the attention and imagination of everyone interested in the history and development of early America. Yet, despite their enormous historical importance, forming a basic collection of such items is not nearly as daunting as one might expect.

The coins and tokens described in the next three sections of this book are fundamentally a major-type listing of the metallic money used throughout the pre-federal period. Many collectors use this as a guide to forming a basic set of these pieces. It is not encyclopedic in its scope. Beyond the basic types are numerous sub-varieties of some of the issues, and a wider range of European coins. Some collectors aim for the finest possible condition, while others find great enjoyment in pieces that saw actual circulation and use during the formative days of the country. There are no rules about how or what to collect other than to enjoy owning a genuine piece of early American history.

SPANISH-AMERICAN COINAGE IN THE NEW WORLD

Values shown for these silver coins are for the most common dates and mintmarked pieces of each issue. Similar pieces were struck at Spanish-American mints in Bolivia, Chile, Colombia, Guatemala, Mexico, Panama, Peru, and Santo Domingo.

COB COINAGE – KING PHILIP II (1556–1598) TO KING CHARLES III (1760–1772)

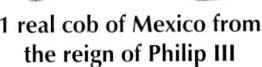

1 real cob of Mexico from the reign of Philip III	1668 2 reales cob struck in Potosi, from the reign of Charles II

	VG	F	VF	EF
Cob Type 1/2 Real (1556–1773)	$40	$90	$150	$400
Cob Type 1 Real (1556–1773)	$40	$100	$175	$425
Cob Type 2 Reales (1556–1773)	$90	$175	$250	$650
Cob Type 4 Reales (1556–1773)	$110	$250	$300	$800
Cob Type 8 Reales (1556–1773)	$150	$300	$500	$900

Values are for coins with partial or missing dates. Fully dated coins are valued much higher. Some cobs were also issued beyond these dates and until as late as 1773 in Bolivia.

PILLAR TYPE – KING PHILIP V (1732–1747), KING FERDINAND VI (1747–1760), AND KING CHARLES III (1760–1772)

1734 8 reales Pillar dollar from the reign of Philip V.   Spain 1722 2 reales "pistareen."

	VG	F	VF	EF
Pillar Type, 1/2 Real (1732–1772)	$15	$30	$75	$125
Pillar Type, 1 Real (1732–1772)	$30	$50	$80	$175
Pillar Type, 2 Reales (1732–1772)	$40	$65	$120	$300
Pillar Type, 4 Reales (1732–1772)	$150	$425	$750	$900
Pillar Type, 8 Reales (1732–1772)	$120	$200	$450	$675
Spanish 2 Reales "pistareen" (1716–1771)	$20	$30	$40	$65

BUST TYPE – KING CHARLES III (1772–1789), KING CHARLES IV (1789–1808), AND KING FERDINAND VII (1808–1825)

1807 8 reales Bust dollar from the reign of Charles IV.

	VG	F	VF	EF
Bust Type, 1/2 Real (1772–1825)	$10	$15	$35	$100
Bust Type, 1 Real (1772–1825)	$20	$35	$50	$120
Bust Type, 2 Reales (1772–1825)	$30	$50	$75	$180
Bust Type, 4 Reales (1772–1825)	$100	$300	$500	$800
Bust Type, 8 Reales (1772–1825)	$50	$75	$100	$250

Parallel issues of Spanish-American gold coins were made during this period. They saw extensive use for international trade and somewhat lesser use in domestic transactions in America. The Spanish silver pistareen was also a popular and convenient coin in circulation.

TYPICAL WORLD COINAGE USED IN COLONIAL AMERICA
NETHERLANDS SILVER COINAGE, 1601–1693

1640 1/2 Leeuwendaalder.

	VG	F	VF	EF
Netherlands, 1/2 Leeuwendaalder (1601–1653)	$50	$110	$225	$450
Netherlands, Leeuwendaalder "Lion Dollar" (1601–1693)	$50	$130	$275	$550

FRENCH SILVER COINAGE OF KING LOUIS XV (1715–1774) AND KING LOUIS XVI (1774–1792)

1791 écu from the reign of Louis XVI.

	VG	F	VF	EF
France, 1/2 Écu (1715–1792)	$20	$80	$150	$325
France, Écu (1715–1792)	$40	$100	$225	$375

See additional listings of French coins authorized for use in North America on pages 111–114.

BRITISH SILVER COINAGE OF KING CHARLES I (1625–1649) TO KING GEORGE III (1760–1820)

1639 6 pence from the reign of Charles I.   1787 shilling from the reign of George III.

	VG	F	VF	EF
England, Threepence (1625–1786)	$10	$25	$60	$90
England, Sixpence (1625–1787)	$20	$35	$80	$100
England, Shilling (1625–1787)	$30	$50	$100	$200
England, Half Crown (1625–1750)	$80	$150	$350	$600
England, Crown (1625–1730)	$200	$450	$800	$1,200

English copper coins and their imitations circulated extensively in early America and are described on pages 127–129.

Other items frequently used as money in early America included cut fractions of various silver coins. These were cut by private individuals. The quarter 8-reales coin was "two bits." Worn and cut portions of coins usually passed for change according to their weight.

BRITISH NEW WORLD ISSUES

SOMMER ISLANDS (BERMUDA)

This coinage, the first struck for the English colonies in the New World, was issued circa 1616. The coins were known as *Hogge Money* or *Hoggies*, from the wild hogs depicted on their obverses.

The Sommer Islands, as Bermuda was known at the time, were under the jurisdiction of the Virginia Company, a joint-stock mercantile venture formed under a British royal patent and headquartered in London. (This venture was actually undertaken by two companies: the Virginia Company of Plymouth, for what is now New England; and the Virginia Company of London, for the American South.)

English government of the islands had started a few years before the coins were issued—by accident! In 1609 Admiral Sir George Somers led a fleet bound from England to the New World, laden with relief supplies for the Virginia settlement of Jamestown. Somers and his ship were separated from the rest of the fleet in a strong storm, and they ran onto the reefs of the Bermuda Islands, some 700 miles from Virginia. (The islands were named for Juan de Bermúdez, who is believed to have stopped there some hundred years earlier.) For ten months Somers and his party were able to live on wild hogs and birds, local plants, and fish, building houses and a church. During this time they also constructed two small ships, in which, in May 1610, most of the shipwrecked colonists continued their interrupted journey to Virginia.

Bermuda became a separate entity of the Virginia Company of London, from November 1612 until June 29, 1615, when "the Governour and Company of the City of London for the Plantacon of the Somer Islands" (often called the Bermuda Company by historians) was officially incorporated under royal charter. This incorporation granted the right of coinage. The coins did not arrive in the islands until May 16, 1616, at the earliest, a year after Bermuda was under its new charter.

The pieces were struck on thin planchets of brass or copper, lightly silvered, in four denominations: shilling, sixpence, threepence, and twopence, each indicated by Roman numerals. A wild hog is the main device and appears on the obverse side of each coin. SOMMER ISLANDS is inscribed (misspelling both the English admiral's name and the corporation's) within beaded circles on the larger denominations. The reverse shows a full-rigged galleon, or carrack, with the flag of St. George on each of four masts.

"In an era when British silver shillings and fractions traded in commerce based on their intrinsic value," writes Q. David Bowers, "the Bermuda pieces were tokens of little value, a fiat currency that circulated in the manner that paper money would later be used worldwide—good as long as both parties had confidence in the value. As might be expected, these coins had little or no trade value other than within the islands, where they were mostly used at the company storehouse, exchanged for supplies" (*Whitman Encyclopedia of Colonial and Early American Coins*).

These coins of Bermuda did not circulate in North America, but they have traditionally been considered part of early "American" coinage. Sylvester S. Crosby, writing in his 1875 masterwork *Early Coins of America*, insisted that the Bermuda coins laid claim to being "the first ever struck for the English colonies in America," this despite the fact that the islands were not a part of the Virginia colony proper. The regular edition of the *Guide Book of United States Coins* has included them in its pre-federal coverage since the first edition, published in 1946.

Twopence · Threepence

Sixpence Obverse · Large Portholes Reverse · Small Portholes Reverse

Shilling Obverse · Small Sail Reverse · Large Sail Reverse

	AG	G	VG	F	VF	EF
Twopence, Large Star Between Legs	$4,250	$6,500	$9,000	$18,000	$50,000	$75,000
Twopence, Small Star Between Legs	$4,250	$6,500	$9,000	$18,000	$50,000	$75,000
Threepence	—	—	$75,000	$125,000	$175,000	—
Sixpence, Small Portholes	$3,500	$4,500	$7,500	$17,500	$50,000	$70,000
Sixpence, Large Portholes	$3,750	$4,750	$8,000	$20,000	$60,000	$90,000
Shilling, Small Sail	$4,750	$6,500	$11,000	$35,000	$65,000	$95,000
Shilling, Large Sail	$6,000	$10,000	$35,000	$65,000	$90,000	—

MASSACHUSETTS
"NEW ENGLAND" COINAGE (1652)

The earliest authorized medium of exchange in the New England settlements was wampum. The General Court of Massachusetts in 1637 ordered "that wampamege should passe at 6 a penny for any sume under 12 d." Wampum consisted of shells of various colors, ground to the size of kernels of corn. A hole was drilled through each piece so it could be strung on a leather thong for convenience and adornment.

Corn, pelts, and bullets were frequently used in lieu of coins, which were rarely available. Silver and gold coins brought over from England, Holland, and other countries tended to flow back across the Atlantic to purchase needed supplies. The colonists, thus left to their own resources, traded with the friendly Native Americans in kind. In 1661 the law making wampum legal tender was repealed.

Agitation for a standard coinage reached its height in 1651. England, recovering from a civil war between the Puritans and Royalists, ignored the colonists, who took matters into their own hands in 1652.

The Massachusetts General Court in 1652 ordered the first metallic currency—the New England silver threepence, sixpence, and shilling—to be struck in the English Americas (the Spaniards had established a mint in Mexico City in 1535). Silver bullion was procured principally in the form of mixed coinage from the West Indies. The mint was located in Boston, and John Hull was appointed mintmaster; his assistant was Robert Sanderson (or Saunderson). At first, Hull received as compensation one shilling threepence for every 20 shillings coined. This fee was adjusted several times during his term as mintmaster.

The planchets of the New England coins were struck with prepared punches twice (once for the obverse, and once for the reverse). First the letters NE were stamped, and then on the other side the numerical denomination of III, VI, or XII was added.

These are called "NE coins" today.

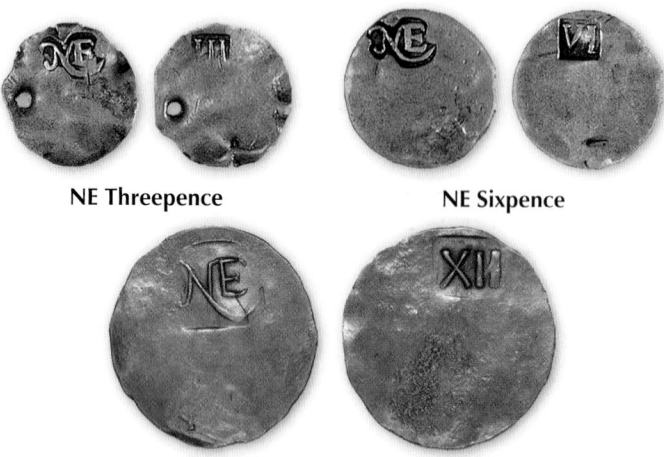

NE Threepence

NE Sixpence

NE Shilling

Early American coins in conditions better than those listed are rare and are consequently valued much higher.

	G	VG	F	VF	EF	AU
NE Threepence (a)				—		
NE Sixpence (b)	$55,000	$90,000	$175,000	$285,000	$400,000	$650,000
NE Shilling	$50,000	$80,000	$125,000	$175,000	$225,000	$310,000

a. Unique. b. 8 examples are known.

WILLOW TREE COINAGE (1653–1660)

The simplicity of the designs on the NE coins invited counterfeiting, and clipping or shaving of the edges by charlatans who sought to snip a little bit of metal from a lot of coins and thereby accumulate a pile of silver. Therefore, they were soon replaced by the Willow Tree series.

All of the Willow Tree coins bore the date 1652, when Oliver Cromwell was in power in Britain, after the English civil war and during the Interregnum government. In fact they were minted from 1653 to 1660. The date 1652 may have been used simply because this was the year the coinage was authorized. Output increased over the years, and the coins were plentiful in circulation.

These pieces, like all early American coins, were produced from handmade dies that are often individually distinctive. The tree in the design is known as a "willow" not from any official legislative records, and certainly not from lifelike resemblance to an actual willow tree, but from terminology dating from 1867 in an auction catalog of the Joseph Mickley Collection. To make the coins, a worker likely placed a silver planchet into a rocker press, which forced a curved upper die against a curved or flat bottom die. This would explain the slight elongation and gentle bend of many Willow Tree coins.

NEW ENGLAND is spelled out, instead of being abbreviated, as on the earlier NE coinage.

Among the four classes of Massachusetts silver coins—NE, Willow Tree, Oak Tree, and Pine Tree— the Willow Tree pieces are far and away the rarest today. The die varieties that can be found and identified are of interest to collectors who value each according to individual rarity. Values shown for type coins are for the most frequently seen die variety.

Threepence   Sixpence

Shilling

	G	VG	F	VF	EF
1652 Willow Tree Threepence (a)	—	—	—		
	Auctions: $587,500, VF, March 2015				
1652 Willow Tree Sixpence (b)	$20,000	$35,000	$70,000	$160,000	$250,000
	Auctions: $253,000, Unc., November 2005				
1652 Willow Tree Shilling	$20,000	$35,000	$60,000	$140,000	$225,000
	Auctions: $276,000, EF, November 2005				

a. 3 examples are known. **b.** 14 examples are known.

OAK TREE COINAGE (1660–1667)

The Oak Tree coins of Massachusetts were struck from 1660 to 1667, following the Willow Tree coinage. The 1662-dated twopence of this type was the only coin of the Willow Tree, Oak Tree, and Pine Tree series that did not bear the date 1652. Numismatists are divided on whether the twopence date of 1662 is an error, or a deliberate use of the year that the new denomination was authorized.

The obverse of these coins features a tree traditionally described by numismatists as an oak tree. Although it is deciduous, it does not closely resemble a specific species. On the reverse, NEW ENGLAND is spelled out, surrounding the date and denomination.

In 1660 the Commonwealth of England was dissolved and the British monarchy was restored under King Charles II. At the time, following longstanding tradition and law, the right to produce coins was considered to be a royal sovereign prerogative. Sylvester Crosby in *Early Coins of America* suggested that during the Massachusetts silver coinage period, numerous tributes—including ship masts, 3,000 codfish, and other material items—were sent to the king to placate him and postpone any action on the Massachusetts coinage question. As with many situations involving early American coinage, facts are scarce.

As with other types of Massachusetts silver, a number of die varieties of Oak Tree coinage can be collected and studied. In the marketplace they are seen far more often than are the two earlier types. They are valued according to their individual rarity. Values shown here are for the most frequently seen die varieties.

Twopence

Threepence

Sixpence

Shilling

	G	VG	F	VF	EF	AU	Unc.
1662 Oak Tree Twopence, Small 2	$600	$1,000	$1,800	$3,500	$6,000	$8,500	$13,000
1662 Oak Tree Twopence, Large 2	$600	$1,000	$1,800	$3,500	$6,000	$8,500	$13,000
1652 Oak Tree Threepence, No IN on Obverse	$725	$1,250	$3,000	$6,500	$11,000	$17,000	—
1652 Oak Tree Threepence, IN on Obverse	$725	$1,350	$3,250	$7,000	$13,000	$21,000	$50,000
1652 Oak Tree Sixpence, IN on Reverse	$800	$1,300	$3,200	$7,500	$16,000	$21,000	$40,000
1652 Oak Tree Sixpence, IN on Obverse	$800	$1,300	$3,200	$7,500	$14,000	$19,000	$35,000
1652 Oak Tree Shilling, IN at Left	$750	$1,250	$3,000	$7,000	$10,500	$16,000	$28,000
1652 Oak Tree Shilling, IN at Bottom	$750	$1,250	$3,000	$6,500	$10,000	$14,500	$26,000
1652 Oak Tree Shilling, ANDO	$900	$1,900	$4,000	$8,500	$15,000	$20,000	$34,000
1652 Oak Tree Shilling, Spiny Tree	$750	$1,250	$3,250	$7,000	$12,000	$17,000	$31,000

PINE TREE COINAGE (1667–1682)

The first Pine Tree coins were minted on the same-size planchets as the Oak Tree pieces, in denominations of threepence, sixpence, and shilling. Subsequent issues of the shilling were narrower in diameter and thicker. Large Planchet shillings ranged from 27 to 31 mm in diameter; Small Planchet shillings ranged from 22 to 26 mm in diameter.

The design of the Pine Tree coins borrowed from the flag of the Massachusetts Bay Colony, which featured a pine tree. On the reverse, NEW ENGLAND is spelled out, surrounding the date and a Roman numeral indicating the denomination (III, VI, or XII).

Large quantities of Pine Tree coins were minted. The coinage was abandoned in 1682. A proposal to renew coinage in 1686 was rejected by the General Court of Massachusetts.

As with other types of Massachusetts silver, a number of die varieties of Pine Tree coins are available for collecting and study. In the marketplace, they are valued according to their individual rarity. Values shown here are for the most often seen die varieties.

Threepence

Sixpence

Shilling, Large Planchet (1667–1674)

Shilling, Small Planchet (1675–1682)

	G	VG	F	VF	EF	AU	Unc.
1652 Threepence, Pellets at Trunk	$550	$800	$1,600	$3,200	$6,000	$9,000	$19,000
1652 Threepence, Without Pellets	$550	$800	$1,600	$3,250	$6,000	$9,000	$19,000
1652 Sixpence, Pellets at Trunk	$600	$925	$1,800	$3,600	$6,250	$10,000	$20,000
1652 Sixpence, Without Pellets	$600	$950	$1,900	$3,800	$6,750	$11,000	$21,000
1652 Shilling, Large Planchet (27–31 mm)							
Pellets at Trunk	$700	$1,100	$2,400	$5,000	$8,750	$14,000	$26,000
Without Pellets at Trunk	$700	$1,000	$2,300	$4,750	$8,500	$13,000	$25,000
No H in MASATUSETS	$800	$1,400	$3,000	$7,500	$13,500	$20,000	—
Ligatured NE in Legend	$700	$1,100	$2,400	$5,000	$8,750	$14,000	$26,000
1652 Shilling, Small Planchet (22–26 mm)	$600	$925	$2,200	$4,000	$6,800	$11,000	$25,000

MARYLAND
LORD BALTIMORE COINAGE

Cecil Calvert, the second Lord Baltimore, inherited from his father nearly absolute control over Maryland. Calvert believed he had the right to coin money for the colony, and in 1659 he ordered shillings, sixpences, and groats (four-penny pieces) from the Royal Mint in London and shipped samples to Maryland, to his brother Philip, who was then his secretary for the colony. Calvert's right to strike coins was upheld by Oliver Cromwell's government. The whole issue was small, and while his coins did circulate in Maryland at first, by 1700 they had largely disappeared from commerce.

Calvert's coins bear his portrait on the obverse, with a Latin legend calling him "Lord of Mary's Land." The reverses of the larger denominations bear his family coat of arms and the denomination in Roman numerals. There are several die varieties of each. Some of these coins are found holed and repaired. The copper penny, or denarium, is the rarest denomination, with only nine reported specimens, including some found in recent times by detectorists using electronic devices.

The silver groats (fourpence), sixpence, and shillings were used extensively in commerce, and today most examples show considerable wear. Typical grades include VG, Fine, and VF, often with surface marks or damage. Those graded AU or higher are major rarities. The silver pieces have an engrailed edge.

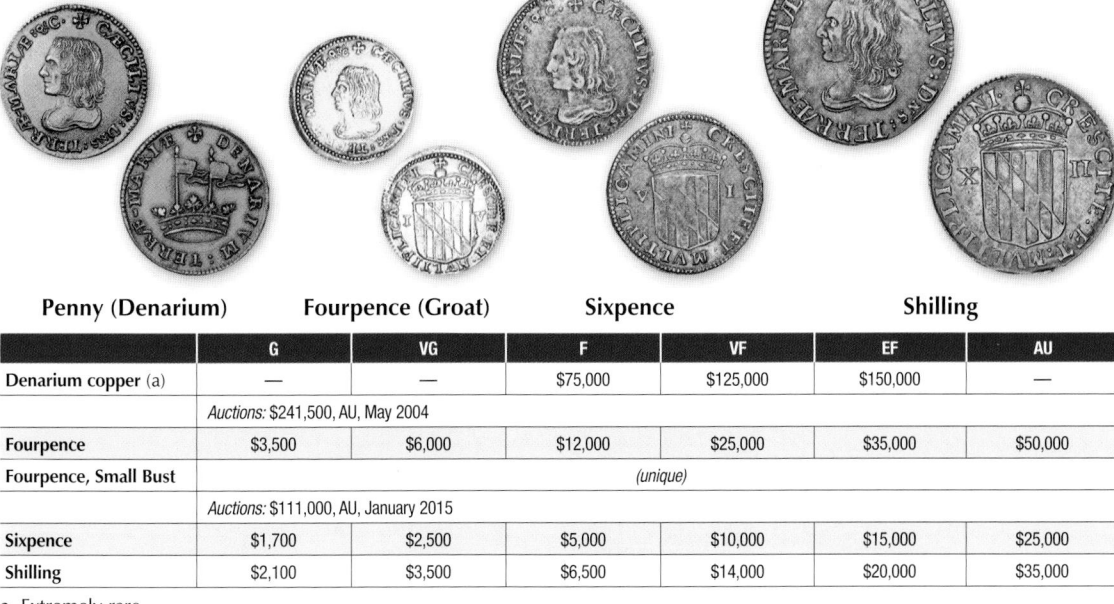

Penny (Denarium)   Fourpence (Groat)   Sixpence   Shilling

	G	VG	F	VF	EF	AU
Denarium copper (a)	—	—	$75,000	$125,000	$150,000	—
	Auctions: $241,500, AU, May 2004					
Fourpence	$3,500	$6,000	$12,000	$25,000	$35,000	$50,000
Fourpence, Small Bust	(unique)					
	Auctions: $111,000, AU, January 2015					
Sixpence	$1,700	$2,500	$5,000	$10,000	$15,000	$25,000
Shilling	$2,100	$3,500	$6,500	$14,000	$20,000	$35,000

a. Extremely rare.

NEW JERSEY
ST. PATRICK OR MARK NEWBY COINAGE

Mark Newby was a shopkeeper in Dublin, Ireland, in the 1670s and came to America in November 1681, settling in West Jersey (today's New Jersey). He brought with him a quantity of copper pieces, of two sizes, believed by numismatists to have been struck in Dublin circa 1663 to 1672. These are known as *St. Patrick coppers.* (Alternatively, they may have been struck for circulation in Ireland by Pierre Blondeau to fill an order made by the duke of Ormonde, but this has not been confirmed.) The larger-sized piece, called by collectors a *halfpenny*, bears the arms of the City of Dublin on the shield on the reverse. The smaller-sized piece, called a *farthing*, does not. Although neither bears a denomination, these are designations traditionally assigned by numismatists. Both sizes have reeded edges.

Newby became a member of the legislature of West Jersey, and under his influence the St. Patrick coinage was made legal tender by the General Assembly of New Jersey in May 1682. The legislature did not specify which size piece could circulate, only that the coin was to be worth a halfpenny in trade and that no one would be obliged to accept more than five shillings' worth (120 coins) in one payment. Some numismatists believe the larger-size coin was intended. However, many more farthing-size pieces are known than halfpennies, and numerous coins of the farthing size have been excavated by detectorists in New Jersey, while none of the larger coins have been found this way. Most numismatists believe that the smaller-sized piece was the one authorized as legal tender. Copper coins often circulated in the colonies at twice what they would have been worth in England.

The obverses show King David crowned, kneeling and playing a harp. The legend FLOREAT REX ("May the King Prosper") is separated by a crown. The reverse side of the halfpence shows St. Patrick with a crozier in his left hand and a trefoil in his right, and surrounded by people. At his left side is a shield. The legend is ECCE GREX ("Behold the Flock"). The farthing reverse shows St. Patrick driving away serpents and a dragon as he holds a metropolitan cross in his left hand. The legend reads QUIESCAT PLEBS ("May the People Be at Ease").

The decorative brass insert found on the coinage, usually over the crown on the obverse, was put there to make counterfeiting more difficult. On some pieces this decoration has been removed or does not show. Numerous die variations exist (more than 140 of the smaller coins, and 9 of the larger). The silver strikings, and a unique gold piece, were not authorized as legal tender, although many of the silver coins are heavily worn, suggesting that they were passed many times from hand to hand in commerce, perhaps at the value of a shilling.

St. Patrick "Farthing"

St. Patrick "Halfpenny"

	G	VG	F	VF	EF	AU
St. Patrick "Farthing"	$125	$300	$750	$2,500	$6,000	$14,000
Similar, Halo Around Saint's Head	$750	$1,500	$6,000	$15,000	$40,000	—
Similar, No C in QUIESCAT	$1,000	$4,000	$8,000	$17,000	—	—
St. Patrick "Farthing," Silver	$1,800	$3,200	$10,000	$18,000	$25,000	$35,000
St. Patrick "Farthing," Gold (a)						—
	Auctions: $184,000, AU, January 2005					
St. Patrick "Halfpenny"	$350	$800	$1,000	$2,500	$10,000	$18,000

a. Unique.

COINAGE AUTHORIZED BY BRITISH ROYAL PATENT

AMERICAN PLANTATIONS COINS (1688)

These tokens, struck in nearly pure tin, were the first royally authorized coinage for the British colonies in America. They were made under a franchise granted in August 1688 to Richard Holt, an agent for the owners of several tin mines. Holt proposed that the new issues be made with a Spanish monetary designation to increase their acceptance in the channels of American commerce, where Spanish-American coins were often seen. Thus the tokens are denominated as 1/24 part of a Spanish real.

The obverse shows an equestrian portrait of King James II in armor and flowing garments. The reverse features four heraldic shields (English, Scottish, French, and Irish) connected by chains. The edge is decorated with dots.

Numismatist Eric P. Newman has identified seven different obverse dies and an equal number of reverse dies. Most American Plantation tokens show black oxidation of the tin. Bright, unblemished original specimens are more valuable. (Around 1828 a London coin dealer acquired the original dies and arranged for restrikes to be made for sale. In high grades these pieces are seen more frequently in the marketplace than are originals. They are valuable but worth less than original strikes.)

	G	VG	F	VF	EF	AU	Unc.
(1688) James II Plantation 1/24 Real coinage							
1/24 Part Real	$225	$300	$500	$1,000	$1,750	$4,000	$7,000
1/24 Part Real, ET. HB. REX	$275	$400	$900	$2,000	$3,000	$8,000	$10,000
1/24 Part Real, Sidewise 4 in 24	$425	$1,000	$1,900	$4,500	$6,750	$11,000	$18,000
1/24 Part Real, Arms Transposed	$675	$1,750	$2,900	$6,750	$13,000	$19,000	—
1/24 Part Real, Restrike	$100	$150	$250	$450	$600	$850	$1,750

COINAGE OF WILLIAM WOOD (1722–1733)

William Wood, an English metallurgist, experimented with the production of several pattern coins (of halfpenny, penny, and twopence size) in 1717. In 1722 he was granted royal patents to mint coins for America and Ireland. At the time his productions were largely unpopular as money, but later generations of coin collectors have sought his Rosa Americana coins for their connections to colonial America. The Hibernia coins are similar in some respects; they have no connection with America but are sought as companion pieces.

ROSA AMERICANA COINS (1722–1723, 1733)

On July 12, 1722, William Wood obtained a patent from King George I to make coins for the American colonies. At the time the colonies were facing a serious shortage of circulating coins.

The first pieces Wood struck were undated. Later issues bear the dates 1722, 1723, 1724, and 1733. The Rosa Americana pieces were issued in three denominations—half penny, penny, and twopence—and were intended for America. This type had a fully bloomed rose on the reverse with the words ROSA AMERICANA UTILE DULCI ("American Rose—Useful and Sweet").

The obverse, common to both Rosa Americana and Hibernia pieces, shows the head of George I and the legend GEORGIUS D:G MAG: BRI: FRA: ET. HIB: REX ("George, by the Grace of God, King of Great Britain, France, and Ireland") or abbreviations thereof.

Despite Wood's best efforts, these Rosa Americana coins circulated in the colonies only to a limited extent. They eventually did see use as money, but it was back in England, and likely at values lower than their assigned denominations. (Each was about half the weight of its English counterpart coin.)

The 1733 twopence is a pattern that bears the bust of King George II facing to the left. It was issued by the successors to the original coinage patent, as William Wood had died in 1730.

The coins are made of a brass composition of copper and zinc (sometimes mistakenly referred to as *Bath metal*, an alloy proposed by Wood that would have also included a minute portion of silver). Planchet quality is often rough and porous because the blanks were heated prior to striking. Edges often show file marks.

	VG	F	VF	EF	AU	Unc.
(No date) Twopence, Motto in Ribbon *(illustrated)*	$200	$400	$700	$1,300	$3,200	$6,000
(No date) Twopence, Motto Without Ribbon (a)	—	—	—			

a. 3 examples are known.

	VG	F	VF	EF	AU	Unc.
1722 Halfpenny, VTILE DVLCI	$925	$2,250	$3,800	$6,750	$9,750	
1722 Halfpenny, D.G.REX ROSA AMERI. UTILE DULCI	$150	$200	$400	$925	$1,400	$3,500
1722 Halfpenny, DEI GRATIA REX UTILE DULCI	$150	$200	$400	$925	$1,400	$3,200

	VG	F	VF	EF	AU	Unc.
1722 Penny, GEORGIVS			$12,000	$17,500	$25,000	$30,000
1722 Penny, VTILE DVLCI	$170	$300	$700	$1,300	$2,750	$6,000
1722 Penny, UTILE DULCI	$150	$200	$400	$700	$1,300	$3,200

	VG	F	VF	EF	AU	Unc.
1722 Twopence, Period After REX	$150	$275	$600	$1,200	$2,400	$4,500
1722 Twopence, No Period After REX	$150	$275	$600	$1,200	$2,400	$4,500

	VG	F	VF	EF	AU	Unc.
1723 Halfpenny, Uncrowned Rose	$900	$1,750	$3,500	$5,000	$8,500	$11,000
1723 Halfpenny, Crowned Rose	$110	$170	$350	$750	$1,600	$3,900

	VG	F	VF	EF	AU	Unc.
1723 Penny *(illustrated)*	$100	$150	$350	$600	$1,000	$2,500
1723 Twopence	$150	$275	$400	$800	$1,300	$2,700

	EF	AU	Unc.
1724, 4 Over 3 Penny (pattern), DEI GRATIA	$7,500	$15,000	$22,000
1724, 4 Over 3 Penny (pattern), D GRATIA	$8,750	$20,000	$34,000
(Undated) (1724) Penny, ROSA: SINE: SPINA. (a)	$35,000	$45,000	—

a. 5 examples are known.

1724 Twopence (pattern)
Auctions: $25,300, Choice AU, May 2005

1733 Twopence (pattern), Proof

	Auctions: $63,250, Gem PF, May 2005

WOOD'S HIBERNIA COINAGE (1722–1724)

Around the same time that his royal patent was granted to strike the Rosa Americana coins for the American colonies, William Wood received a franchise to produce copper coins for circulation in Ireland. This was ratified on July 22, 1722. The resulting coins, likely struck in Bristol, England, featured a portrait of King George and, on the reverse, a seated figure with a harp and the word HIBERNIA. Their edges are plain. Denominations struck were farthing and halfpenny, with dates of 1722, 1723, and 1724. These Hibernia coins were unpopular in Ireland and faced vocal public criticism, including from satirist Jonathan Swift. "It was asserted that the issues for Ireland were produced without Irish advice or consent, that the arrangements were made in secret and for the private profit of Wood, and that the pieces were seriously underweight" (*Whitman Encyclopedia of Colonial and Early American Coins*). As a result, King George reduced the number of coins allowed by Wood's patent, and the franchise was retired completely in 1725 in exchange for Wood receiving a £24,000 pension over eight years. Some of the unpopular Hibernia coins, meanwhile, may have been sent to the American colonies to circulate as small change. Their popularity with American numismatists stems from the similarity of their obverses to those in the Rosa Americana series.

Numerous varieties exist.

| 1722, Hibernia Farthing | 1722, Hibernia Halfpenny, First Type | 1722, Hibernia Halfpenny, Ssecond Type | 1723, 3 Over 2 |

| 1724, Hibernia Farthing | 1724, Hibernia Halfpenny |

	G	VG	F	VF	EF	AU	Unc.
1722 Farthing, D: G: REX	$150	$500	$750	$2,200	$3,500	$7,500	$14,000
1722 Halfpenny, D: G: REX, Rocks at Right (pattern)	—	—	—	$8,000	$12,000	$20,000	$40,000
1722 Halfpenny, First Type, Harp at Left	$50	$100	$150	$300	$600	$900	$1,600
1722 Halfpenny, Second Type, Harp at Right	$45	$70	$100	$200	$550	$1,100	$2,000
1722 Halfpenny, Second Type, DEII (blunder)	$80	$150	$350	$800	$1,500	$2,000	$3,200
1723 Farthing, D.G.REX	$50	$100	$125	$250	$400	$550	$1,000
1723 Farthing, DEI. GRATIA. REX	$25	$50	$80	$125	$225	$400	$600
1723 Farthing (silver pattern)	$500	$1,500	$2,200	$3,500	$4,500	$6,500	$11,000
1723 Halfpenny, 3 Over 2 (a)	$45	$75	$150	$450	$850	$1,300	$2,400
1723 Halfpenny	$25	$45	$75	$125	$275	$400	$775
1723 Halfpenny (silver pattern)			—	—	—	—	—
1724 Farthing	$50	$125	$225	$750	$1,600	$2,250	$4,000
1724 Halfpenny	$45	$100	$150	$350	$700	$1,100	$2,200
1724 Halfpenny, DEI Above Head					—	—	

a. Varieties exist.

Virginia Halfpennies (1773–1774)

In 1773 the British Crown authorized coinage of copper halfpennies for the colony of Virginia, not to exceed 25 tons' weight. "This was the first and only colonial coinage authorized and produced in Britain for use in an American colony, thereby giving the Virginia pieces the unique claim of being the only true American colonial coinage" (*Whitman Encyclopedia of Colonial and Early American Coins*). The designs included a laurelled portrait of King George III and the royal coat of arms of the House of Hanover. The coins were struck at the Tower Mint in London. Their edges are plain.

Most Mint State pieces available to collectors today are from a hoard of some 5,000 or more of the halfpennies held by Colonel Mendes I. Cohen of Baltimore, Maryland, in the 1800s. Cohen came from a prominent banking family. His cache was dispersed slowly and carefully from 1875 until 1929, as the coins passed from his estate to his nieces and nephews. Eventually the remaining coins, numbering approximately 2,200, the property of Bertha Cohen, were dispersed in one lot in Baltimore. These pieces gradually filtered out, in groups and individually, into the wider numismatic marketplace.

The Proof patterns that were struck on a large planchet with a wide milled border are often referred to as pennies. The silver pieces dated 1774 are referred to as shillings, but they may have been patterns or trials for a halfpenny or a guinea.

Red Uncirculated pieces without spots are worth considerably more.

	G	VG	F	VF	EF	AU	Unc.
1773 Halfpenny, Period After GEORGIVS	$25	$50	$100	$150	$350	$500	$900
1773 Halfpenny, No Period After GEORGIVS	$35	$75	$140	$200	$400	$600	$1,200

1773, "Penny"   1774, "Shilling"

	PF
1773 "Penny"	$25,000
1774 "Shilling" (a)	$130,000

a. 6 examples are known.

EARLY AMERICAN AND RELATED TOKENS

ELEPHANT TOKENS (CA. 1672–1694)

LONDON ELEPHANT TOKENS

The London Elephant tokens were struck in London circa 1672 to 1694. Although they were undated, two examples are known to have been struck over 1672 British halfpennies. Most were struck in copper, but one was made of brass. Their legend, GOD PRESERVE LONDON, may have been a general plea for divine aid and not a specific reference to the outbreak of plague in 1665 or the great fire of 1666.

These pieces were not struck for the colonies, and they probably did not circulate widely in America, although a few may have been carried there by colonists. They are associated, through a shared obverse die, with the 1694 Carolina and New England Elephant tokens. They have a plain edge but often show the cutting marks from planchet preparation.

	VG	F	VF	EF	AU	Unc.
(1694) Halfpenny, GOD PRESERVE LONDON, Thick Planchet	$300	$550	$900	$1,750	$2,600	$4,200
(1694) Halfpenny, GOD PRESERVE LONDON, Thin Planchet	$500	$1,000	$3,000	$4,500	$6,750	$12,000
Similar, Brass (a)						
(1694) Halfpenny, GOD PRESERVE LONDON, Diagonals in Center of Shield	$700	$2,000	$6,000	$8,000	$15,000	$38,000
(1694) Halfpenny, Similar, Sword in Second Quarter of Shield	—	—	$20,000	—	—	—
(1694) Halfpenny, LON DON	$1,100	$2,250	$4,500	$8,500	$15,000	$24,000

a. Unique.

CAROLINA ELEPHANT TOKENS

Although no law is known authorizing coinage for Carolina, two very interesting pieces known as Elephant tokens were made with the date 1694. These copper tokens are of halfpenny denomination. The reverse reads GOD PRESERVE CAROLINA AND THE LORDS PROPRIETERS 1694.

The second and more readily available variety has the last word spelled PROPRIETORS. The correction was made on the original die, for the E shows plainly beneath the O. On the second variety the elephant's tusks nearly touch the milling.

The Carolina pieces were probably struck in England and perhaps intended as advertising to heighten interest in the Carolina Plantation. Another theory suggests they may have been related to or made for the Carolina coffee house in London.

	VG	F	VF	EF	AU	Unc.
1694 PROPRIETERS	$10,000	$30,000	$50,000	$60,000	$70,000	$125,000
1694 PROPRIETERS, O Over E	$5,000	$10,000	$20,000	$40,000	$60,000	$100,000

NEW ENGLAND ELEPHANT TOKENS

Like the Carolina tokens, the New England Elephant tokens are believed to have been struck in England, possibly as promotional pieces to increase interest in the American colonies, or perhaps related to the New England coffee house in London

	VG	F	VF	EF	AU
1694 NEW ENGLAND	$100,000	$120,000	$150,000	$185,000	—

NEW YORKE IN AMERICA TOKENS (1660S OR 1670S)

The New Yorke in America tokens are farthing or halfpenny tokens intended for New York, issued by Francis Lovelace, who was governor from 1668 until 1673. The tokens use the older spelling with a final "e" (YORKE), which predominated before 1710. The obverse shows Cupid pursuing the loveless butterfly-winged Psyche—a rebus on the name Lovelace. The reverse shows a heraldic eagle, identical to the one displayed in fesse, raguly (i.e., on a crenellated bar) on the Lovelace coat of arms. In weight, fabric, and die axis the tokens are similar to certain 1670 farthing tokens of Bristol, England, where they may have been struck. There is no evidence that any of these pieces ever circulated in America. Fewer than two dozen are believed to now exist.

	VG	F	VF	EF
(Undated) Brass or Copper	$10,000	$18,000	$30,000	$60,000
(Undated) Pewter	$10,000	$23,000	$33,000	$72,500

GLOUCESTER TOKENS (1714)

Sylvester S. Crosby, in his book *The Early Coins of America*, stated that these tokens appear to have been intended as a pattern for a shilling—a private coinage by Richard Dawson of Gloucester (county), Virginia. The only specimens known are struck in brass, although the denomination XII indicates that a silver coinage (one shilling) may have been planned. The building depicted on the obverse may represent some public building, possibly the courthouse.

Although neither of the two known examples shows the full legends, combining the pieces shows GLOVCESTER COVRTHOVSE VIRGINIA / RIGHAVLT DAWSON. ANNO.DOM. 1714. This recent discovery has provided a new interpretation of the legends, as a Righault family once owned land near the Gloucester courthouse. A similar, but somewhat smaller, piece possibly dated 1715 exists. The condition of this unique piece is too poor for positive attribution.

	F
1714 Shilling, brass (a)	$120,000

a. 2 examples are known.

HIGLEY OR GRANBY COPPERS (1737–1739)

Dr. Samuel Higley owned a private copper mine near Granby, Connecticut, in an area known for many such operations. Higley was a medical doctor, with a degree from Yale College, who also practiced blacksmithing and experimented in metallurgy. He worked his mine as a private individual, extracting particularly rich copper, smelting it, and shipping much of it to England. He also made his own dies for plain-edged pure-copper "coins" that he issued.

Legend has it that a drink in the local tavern cost three pence, and that Higley paid his bar tabs with his own privately minted coins, denominated as they were with the legend THE VALUE OF THREEPENCE. When his supply of such coppers exceeded the local demand, neighbors complained that they were not worth the denomination stated, and Higley changed the legends to read VALUE ME AS YOU PLEASE and I AM GOOD COPPER (but kept the Roman numeral III on the obverse).

After Samuel Higley's death in May 1737 his older brother John continued his coinage.

The Higley coppers were never officially authorized. There were seven obverse and four reverse dies. All are rare. Electrotypes and cast copies exist.

	AG	G	VG	F	VF
1737 THE VALVE OF THREE PENCE, CONNECTICVT, 3 Hammers	$10,000	$17,500	$40,000	$70,000	$120,000
1737 THE VALVE OF THREE PENCE, I AM GOOD COPPER, 3 Hammers (a)	$6,000	$20,000	$50,000	$80,000	$175,000
1737 VALUE ME AS YOU PLEASE, I AM GOOD COPPER, 3 Hammers	$10,000	$17,500	$40,000	$70,000	$125,000
1737 VALVE • ME • AS • YOU • PLEASE, I • AM • GOOD • COPPER, 3 Hammers (a)			$75,000		
(1737) VALUE • ME • AS • YOU • PLEASE, J • CUT • MY • WAY • THROUGH, Broad Axe	$10,000	$17,500	$40,000	$70,000	$120,000
(1737) THE • WHEELE • GOES • ROUND, Reverse as Above (b)					$376,000
1739 VALUE • ME • AS • YOU • PLEASE, J • CUT • MY • WAY • THROUGH, Broad Axe	$15,000	$25,000	$40,000	$60,000	$135,000

a. This issue has the CONNECTICVT reverse. 3 examples are known. **b.** Unique.

Hibernia–Voce Populi Coins

These coins, struck in the year 1760, were prepared by Roche, of King Street, Dublin, who was at that time engaged in the manufacture of buttons for the army. Like other Irish tokens, some could have found their way to colonial America and possibly circulated in the colonies with numerous other counterfeit halfpence and "bungtown tokens." There is no evidence to prove that Voce Populi pieces, which bear the legend HIBERNIA (Ireland) on the reverse, ever circulated in North America. Sylvester S. Crosby did not include them in *The Early Coins of America*, 1875. Nor were they covered in Wayte Raymond's *Standard Catalogue of United States Coins* (until Walter Breen revised the section on colonial coins in 1954, after which they were "adopted" by mainstream collectors). Various theories exist regarding the identity of the bust portrait on the obverse, ranging from kings and pretenders to the British throne, to the provost of Dublin College.

There are two distinct issues. Coins from the first, with a "short bust" on the obverse, range in weight from 87 to 120 grains. Those from the second, with a "long bust" on the obverse, range in weight from 129 to 154 grains. Most of the "long bust" varieties have the letter P on the obverse. None of the "short bust" varieties bear the letter P, and, judging from their weight, they may have been contemporary counterfeits.

Large-Letter Variety Farthing

Halfpenny

Halfpenny, "P" Before Face

VOOE POPULI

	G	VG	F	VF	EF	AU	Unc.
1760 Farthing, Large Letters	$200	$350	$600	$1,250	$2,000	$3,500	$7,000
1760 Farthing, Small Letters			$6,000	$22,000	$60,000	—	—
1760 Halfpenny	$65	$100	$170	$300	$525	$800	$1,000
1760 Halfpenny, VOOE POPULI	$90	$150	$225	$500	$650	$1,100	$3,250
1760 Halfpenny, P Below Bust	$110	$200	$300	$700	$1,000	$2,200	$5,500
1760 Halfpenny, P in Front of Face	$90	$175	$250	$600	$900	$1,700	$5,000

PITT TOKENS (CA. 1769)

William Pitt the Elder, the British statesman who endeared himself to America, is the subject of these brass or copper pieces, probably intended as commemorative medalets. The so-called halfpenny (the larger of the type's two sizes) served as currency during a shortage of regular coinage. The farthing-size tokens are rare.

The reverse legend (THANKS TO THE FRIENDS OF LIBERTY AND TRADE) refers to Pitt's criticism of the Crown's taxation of the American colonies, and his efforts to have the Stamp Act of March 22, 1765, repealed in 1766. The obverse bears a portrait and the legends THE RESTORER OF COMMERCE and NO STAMPS.

"Little is known concerning the circumstances of issue. Robert Vlack suggests that the pieces may have been designed by Paul Revere. Striking may have been accomplished around 1769 by James Smither (or Smithers) of Philadelphia" (*Whitman Encyclopedia of Colonial and Early American Coins*).

| Farthing | | | | Halfpenny | | | |

	G	VG	F	VF	EF	AU	Unc.
1766 Farthing	$3,500	$6,000	$12,000	$30,000	$42,000	—	
1766 Halfpenny		$500	$600	$1,200	$2,100	$3,250	$8,500
1766 Halfpenny, silvered				$1,800	$4,000	$5,500	$12,000

RHODE ISLAND SHIP MEDALS (CA. 1779)

The circumstances of the issue of these medals (or tokens) are mysterious. They were largely unknown to American coin collectors until 1864, when a specimen was offered in W. Elliot Woodward's sale of the Seavey Collection. It sold for $40—a remarkable price at the time.

The obverse shows the flagship of British admiral Lord Richard Howe at anchor, while the reverse depicts the retreat of American forces from Rhode Island in 1778. The inscriptions show that the coin was meant for a Dutch-speaking audience. The word *vlugtende* ("fleeing") appears on the earlier issues below Howe's flagship—an engraving error. After a limited number of pieces were struck with this word, it was removed on most coins. A wreath was added, eliminating the word *vlugtende*, after which the final coinage took place. It is believed the medal was struck in England circa 1779 or 1780 for the Dutch market, as propaganda to influence Dutch opinion against the American cause. Specimens are known in pinchbeck, copper, and pewter.

Rhode Island Ship Medal (1778–1779) Legend "vlugtende" Below Ship Wreath Below Ship

	VF	EF	AU	Unc.
With "vlugtende" (fleeing) Below Ship, Brass or copper		—		
Wreath Below Ship, Brass or copper	$1,000	$1,750	$3,250	$5,500
Without Wreath Below Ship, Brass or copper	$900	$1,700	$2,500	$5,000
Similar, Pewter	$3,500	$5,500	$8,500	$15,000

JOHN CHALMERS ISSUES (1783)

John Chalmers, a Maryland goldsmith and silversmith, struck a series of silver tokens of his own design in Annapolis in 1783. The dies were by Thomas Sparrow, another silversmith in the town. The shortage of change in circulation and the refusal of the American people to use underweight cut Spanish coins prompted the issuance of these pieces. (Fraudsters would attempt to cut five "quarters" or nine or ten "eighths" out of one Spanish silver dollar, thereby realizing a proportional profit when they were all spent.)

On the Chalmers threepence and shilling obverses, two clasped hands are shown, perhaps symbolizing unity of the several states; the reverse of the threepence has a branch encircled by a wreath. A star within a wreath is on the obverse of the sixpence, with hands clasped upon a cross utilized as the reverse type. On this denomination, the designer's initials TS (for Thomas Sparrow) can be found in the crescents that terminate the horizontal arms of the cross. The reverse of the more common shilling varieties displays two doves competing for a worm underneath a hedge and a snake. The symbolic message is thought to have been against the danger of squabbling with brethren over low-value stakes while a dangerous mutual enemy lurked nearby. The edges of these tokens are crudely reeded. There are only a few known examples of the shilling type with 13 interlinked rings, from which a liberty cap on a pole arises.

Threepence   Sixpence, Small Date   Sixpence, Large Date

Shilling, Birds, Long Worm   Shilling, Rings

	VG	F	VF	EF	AU
1783 Threepence	$2,000	$4,000	$8,000	$19,000	$37,500
1783 Sixpence, Small Date	$3,500	$7,500	$19,000	$32,000	$65,000
1783 Sixpence, Large Date	$2,600	$6,000	$15,000	$30,000	$60,000
1783 Shilling, Birds, Long Worm *(illustrated)*	$1,250	$2,500	$7,500	$14,000	$25,000
1783 Shilling, Birds, Short Worm	$1,200	$2,200	$6,500	$12,000	$22,500
1783 Shilling, Rings (a)	*$50,000*	*$100,000*	*$200,000*	—	—

a. 5 examples are known.

FRENCH NEW WORLD ISSUES

None of the coins of the French regime relate specifically to territories that later became part of the United States. They were all general issues for the French colonies of the New World. The coinage of 1670 was authorized by an edict of King Louis XIV dated February 19, 1670, for use in New France,

Acadia, the French settlements in Newfoundland, and the French West Indies. The copper coinage of 1717 to 1722 was authorized by edicts of 1716 and 1721 for use in New France, Louisiana, and the French West Indies.

COINAGE OF 1670

The coinage of 1670 consisted of silver 5 and 15 sols and copper 2 deniers (or "doubles"). A total of 200,000 of the 5 sols and 40,000 of the 15 sols was struck at Paris. Nantes was to have coined the copper, but did not; the reasons for this may never be known, since the archives of the Nantes Mint before 1700 were destroyed. The only known specimen is a pattern struck at Paris. The silver coins were raised in value by a third in 1672 to keep them circulating, but in vain. They rapidly disappeared, and by 1680 none were to be seen. Later they were restored to their original values. This rare issue should not be confused with the common 1670-A 1/12 ecu with reverse legend SIT. NOMEN. DOMINI. BENEDICTUM.

The 1670-A double de l'Amerique Françoise was struck at the Paris Mint along with the 5- and 15-sols denominations of the same date. All three were intended to circulate in France's North American colonies. Probably due to an engraving error, very few 1670-A doubles were actually struck. Today, only one is known to survive.

Copper Double

Silver 5 Sols

	VG	F	VF	EF	Unc.
1670-A Copper Double (a)			$225,000		
1670-A 5 Sols	$1,000	$2,000	$5,000	$7,000	$18,000
1670-A 15 Sols	$13,000	$32,000	$75,000	$125,000	—

a. Unique.

COINAGE OF 1717–1720

The copper 6 and 12 deniers of 1717 were authorized by an edict of King Louis XV (by order of the six-year-old king's regent, the duke of Orléans) dated December 1716, to be struck at Perpignan (mint-mark Q). The order could not be carried out, for the supply of copper was too brassy, and only a few pieces were coined. The issues of 1720 are popularly collected for their association with the John Law "Mississippi Bubble" venture.

1720 20 Sols

1717-Q 12 Deniers

1720 6 Deniers

	F	VF	EF
1717-Q 6 Deniers, No Crowned Arms on Reverse (a)			—
1717-Q 12 Deniers, No Crowned Arms on Reverse			$45,000
1720 Liard, Crowned Arms on Reverse, Copper	$350	$500	$900
1720 6 Deniers, Crowned Arms on Reverse, Copper	$550	$900	$1,750
1720 12 Deniers, Crowned Arms on Reverse, Copper	$400	$750	$1,500
1720 20 Sols, Silver	$375	$700	$1,500

a. Extremely rare.

BILLON COINAGE OF 1709–1760

The French colonial coins of 30 deniers were called *mousquetaires* because of the outlined cross on their reverse, evocative of the design on the short coats worn by French musketeers. These coins were produced at Metz and Lyon. The 15 deniers was coined only at Metz. The sou marque and the half sou were coined at almost every French mint, those of Paris being most common. The half sou of 1740 is the only commonly available date. Specimens of the sou marque dated after 1760 were not used in North America. A unique specimen of the 1712-AA 30 deniers is known in the size and weight of the 15-denier coins.

30 Deniers "Mousquetaire"   **Sou Marque (24 Deniers)**

	VG	F	VF	EF	AU	Unc.
1711–1713-AA 15 Deniers	$150	$300	$500	$1,000	$1,750	$4,000
1709–1713-AA 30 Deniers	$75	$100	$250	$400	$675	$1,500
1709–1713-D 30 Deniers	$75	$100	$250	$400	$675	$1,500
1738–1748 Half Sou Marque, various mints	$60	$100	$200	$350	$575	$1,200
1738–1760 Sou Marque, various mints	$50	$80	$125	$175	$300	$500

COINAGE OF 1721–1722

The copper coinage of 1721 and 1722 was authorized by an edict of King Louis XV dated June 1721. The coins were struck on copper blanks imported from Sweden. Rouen and La Rochelle struck pieces of nine deniers (one sou) in 1721 and 1722. New France received 534,000 pieces, mostly from the mint of La Rochelle, but only 8,180 were put into circulation, as the colonists disliked copper. In 1726 the rest of the issue was sent back to France.

In American coin catalogs of the 1800s, these coins were often called "Louisiana coppers."

	VG	F	VF	EF
1721-B (Rouen)	$500	$1,000	$3,500	$10,000
1721-H (La Rochelle)	$100	$175	$1,000	$2,500
1722-H	$100	$175	$1,000	$2,500
1722-H, 2 Over 1	$175	$275	$1,200	$4,000

FRENCH COLONIES IN GENERAL (1767)

These copper coins were produced for use in the French colonies and only unofficially circulated in Louisiana along with other foreign coins and tokens. Most were counterstamped RF (République Française) for use in the West Indies. The mintmark A signifies the Paris Mint. The edge is decorated with a double row of dots.

	VG	VF	EF	AU
1767 French Colonies, Sou	$120	$250	$700	$1,500
1767 French Colonies, Sou, counterstamped RF	$100	$200	$300	$600

Post-Colonial Issues

The coins explored in this section are classified as "post-colonial" because they came after the colonial period (some during the early months of rebellion; most after the official declaration of independence) but before the first federal Mint was established in Philadelphia in 1792.

Early American coins were produced from hand-engraved dies, which are often individually distinctive. For many types, the great number of die varieties that can be found and identified are of interest to collectors who value each according to its individual rarity. Values shown for type coins in this section are for the most common die variety of each.

SPECULATIVE ISSUES, TOKENS, AND PATTERNS

NOVA CONSTELLATIO COPPERS (1783–1786)

The Nova Constellatio coppers, dated 1783 and 1785 and without denomination, were struck in fairly large quantities in Birmingham, England, and were shipped to New York where they entered circulation. Apparently they resulted from a private coinage venture undertaken by Constable, Rucker & Co., a trading business formed by William Constable, John Rucker, Robert Morris, and Gouverneur Morris as equal partners. The designs and legends were copied from the denominated patterns dated 1783 made in Philadelphia (see page 151). A few additional coppers dated 1786 were made by an inferior diesinker.

"The Nova Constellatio coppers were well received and saw extensive use in commerce, as evidenced by the wear seen on typically specimens today," writes Q. David Bowers in the *Whitman Encyclopedia of Colonial and Early American Coins*. "Later, they were devalued, and many were used as undertypes (planchets) for Connecticut and, to a lesser extent, New Jersey and Vermont coppers."

1783, Pointed Rays,
Small U.S., CONSTELLATIO

1783, Pointed Rays,
Large U.S., CONSTELLATIO

	VG	F	VF	EF	AU	Unc.
1783, CONSTELLATIO, Pointed Rays, Small U.S.	$100	$200	$350	$700	$1,250	$2,750
1783, CONSTELLATIO, Pointed Rays, Large U.S.	$100	$225	$650	$1,100	$2,500	$6,750

1783, Blunt Rays, CONSTELATIO

1785, Blunt Rays, CONSTELATIO   1785, Pointed Rays, CONSTELATIO

	VG	F	VF	EF	AU	Unc.
1783, CONSTELATIO, Blunt Rays	$100	$225	$550	$1,050	$1,800	$5,750
1785, CONSTELATIO, Blunt Rays	$100	$225	$550	$1,200	$3,000	$7,200
1785, CONSTELLATIO, Pointed Rays	$100	$200	$375	$750	$1,200	$2,750
1785, Similar, Small, Close Date	$300	$600	$2,500	$4,500	$6,500	$15,000
1786, Similar, Small Date	$4,750	$8,000	$20,000	$30,000		

IMMUNE COLUMBIA PIECES (1785)

These pieces are considered private or unofficial coins. No laws describing them are known. There are several types bearing the seated figure of Justice. These pieces are stylistically related to the Nova Constellatio coppers, with the Immune Columbia motif with liberty cap and scale replacing the LIBERTAS and JUSTITIA design.

1785, Silver, 13 Stars   1785, Pointed Rays, CONSTELLATIO

	F	VF	EF
1785, Copper, 13 Stars	$15,000	$27,000	$45,000
1785, Silver, 13 Stars	$25,000	$50,000	$75,000
1785, Pointed Rays, CONSTELLATIO, Extra Star in Reverse Legend, Copper	$15,000	$27,000	$45,000
1785, Pointed Rays, CONSTELLATIO, Gold (a)			—
1785, Blunt Rays, CONSTELLATIO, Copper (b)		$50,000	—

Note: The gold specimen in the National Numismatic Collection (now maintained by the Smithsonian) was acquired in 1843 from collector Matthew A. Stickney in exchange for an 1804 dollar. **a.** Unique. **b.** 2 examples are known.

1785, George III Obverse

	G	VG	F	VF
1785, George III Obverse	$5,500	$8,500	$11,000	$16,000
1785, VERMON AUCTORI Obverse, IMMUNE COLUMBIA	$6,250	$10,000	$15,000	$40,000

1787, IMMUNIS COLUMBIA, Eagle Reverse

	VG	F	VF	EF	AU	Unc.
1787, IMMUNIS COLUMBIA, Eagle Reverse	$600	$1,000	$3,000	$4,500	$6,500	$11,000

Note: Believed to be a prototype for federal coinage; some were coined after 1787.

CONFEDERATIO AND OTHER SPECULATIVE PATTERNS

The Confederatio and associated coins are believed by some numismatists to be private proposals for patterns for America's early federal coinage. The 1785, Inimica Tyrannis America, variety may owe its design to a sketch by Thomas Jefferson. In all, 12 dies were presumed to have been used to strike coins in 13 combinations. No one knows for certain who made these coins, but some speculate the dies were produced by a combination of Walter Mould, John Bailey, and James Atlee in this country in connection with securing a federal-coinage contract. No documentation has been found. The pattern shield reverse ultimately found its way to the New Jersey state coinage.

America   Americana   Washington

Immunis   Eagle   Libertas et Justitia

Large Circle   Small Circle   Pattern Shield

The 1786, Immunis Columbia, with scrawny-eagle reverse is a related piece probably made by a different engraver or mint.

	VG	F	VF	EF	AU
1785 Inimica Tyrannis America, Large Circle (a,b)	$40,000	$70,000	$100,000	$175,000	$275,000
1785 Inimica Tyrannis Americana, Small Circle (c,d)	$30,000	$40,000	$50,000	$150,000	$250,000
1785 Inimica Tyrannis Americana, Large Circle, Silver (b,e)		$45,000 (f)			
1785 Gen. Washington, Large Circle (g,h)	$50,000	$75,000	$125,000	$250,000	
1786 Gen. Washington, Eagle (i,j)		$40,000			
(No Date) Gen. Washington, Pattern Shield (k,l)		$75,000	$100,000 (f)		$350,000
1786 Immunis, Pattern Shield (m,n)		$25,000	$50,000	$100,000	$125,000
1786 Immunis, 1785 Large Circle (o,j)					$100,000
1786 Eagle, Pattern Shield (p,e)					$200,000
1786 Eagle, 1785 Large Circle (q,j)		$50,000	$85,000		
1785 Libertas et Justitia, 1785 Large Circle (r,e)	$25,000				
1785 Small Circle, 1787 Excelsior Eagle (s,j)		$35,000			
1786 Immunis Columbia, Scrawny Eagle (l)			$50,000	$90,000	

a. America obverse, Large Circle reverse. b. 7 examples are known. c. Americana obverse, Small Circle reverse. d. 9 examples are known. e. 1 example is known. f. Damaged. g. Washington obverse, Large Circle reverse. h. 6 examples are known. i. Washington obverse, Eagle reverse. j. 2 examples are known. k. Washington obverse, Pattern Shield reverse. l. 3 examples are known. m. Immunis obverse, Pattern Shield reverse. n. 17 examples are known. o. Immunis obverse, Large Circle reverse. p. Eagle obverse, Pattern Shield reverse. q. Eagle obverse, Large Circle reverse. r. Libertas et Justitia obverse, Large Circle reverse. s. Small Circle obverse, 1787 Excelsior Eagle reverse. Image of the 1787 Excelsior eagle (facing right) is on page 126.

COINAGE OF THE STATES

NEW HAMPSHIRE (1776)

New Hampshire was the first of the states to consider the subject of coinage following the Declaration of Independence. On March 13, 1776, by which time the colonies were in rebellion but had not yet formally declared their independence, the New Hampshire House of Representatives established a committee to consider the minting of copper coins. The committee recommended such coinage as a way to facilitate small commercial transactions.

William Moulton was empowered to make a limited quantity of coins of pure copper authorized by the State House of Representatives in 1776. Although cast patterns were prepared, it is believed that they were not approved. Little of the proposed coinage was ever actually circulated.

Other purported patterns are of doubtful origin. These include a unique engraved piece and a rare struck piece with large initials WM on the reverse.

	G
1776 New Hampshire Copper	$100,000
Auctions: $172,500, VG-10, March 2012	

MASSACHUSETTS
MASSACHUSETTS UNOFFICIAL COPPERS (1776)

Presumably, in 1776, the year the colonies proclaimed their independence from Britain, three types of Massachusetts coppers were created. Very little is known about their origins or the circumstances of their production. Numismatic historians deduced them to be patterns until recent scholarship cast doubt on their authenticity as coppers of the Revolutionary War era.

The obverse of one of these coppers has a crude pine tree with "1d LM" at its base and the legend MASSACHUSETTS STATE. The reverse has a figure probably intended to represent the Goddess of Liberty, seated on a globe and holding a liberty cap and staff. A dog sits at her feet. The legend LIBERTY AND VIRTUE surrounds the figure, and the date 1776 is situated beneath.

Sylvester S. Crosby, writing in 1875 in *The Early Coins of America*, traced the provenance of this unique copper back to a grocer who sold it to a schoolboy around 1852. The grocer was from "the northerly part" of Boston, and he had "found it many years before while excavating on his premises, in the vicinity of Hull or Charter Street."

	VF
1776 Pine Tree Copper (a)	—

a. Unique, in the Massachusetts Historical Society collection.

A similar piece, probably from the same source as the Pine Tree copper, features a Native American standing with a bow on the obverse, with a worn legend that may read PROVINCE OF MASSA or similar. On the reverse is a seated figure and globe, visible partially visible legend (LIBERTATIS), and the date 1776 at bottom. The only known example was overstruck on a 1747 English halfpenny, and is holed.

	VG
1776 Indian Copper (a)	—

a. Unique.

A third Massachusetts piece is sometimes called the *Janus copper*. On the obverse are three heads, facing left, front, and right, with the legend STATE OF MASSA. 1/2 D. The reverse shows the Goddess of Liberty facing right, resting against a globe. The legend is GODDESS LIBERTY 1776.

	F
1776 Halfpenny, 3 Heads on Obverse (a)	—
Auctions: $44,650, Fine, January 2015; $40,000, Fine, November 1979	

a. Unique.

MASSACHUSETTS AUTHORIZED ISSUES (1787–1788)

An "Act for establishing a mint for the coinage of gold, silver and copper" was passed by the Massachusetts General Court on October 17, 1786. The next year, the council directed that the design of the copper coins should incorporate ". . . the figure of an indian with a bow & arrow & a star on one side, with the word 'Commonwealth,' the reverse a spread eagle with the words—'of Massachusetts A. D. 1787'—" (this wording would be slightly different in the final product).

The coinage of Massachusetts copper cents and half cents in 1787 and 1788 was under the direction of Captain Joshua Witherle of Boston. These were the first coins bearing the denomination *cent* as would be later established by Congress. They were produced in large quantities and are fairly plentiful today. The wear seen on many of the Massachusetts cents and half cents indicates that they enjoyed long circulation in commerce. Many varieties exist, the most valuable being that with arrows in the eagle's right talon.

Most of the dies for these coppers were made by Joseph Callender. Jacob Perkins of Newburyport also engraved some of the 1788 dies.

The mint was abandoned early in 1789, in compliance with the newly ratified U.S. Constitution, and because its production was unprofitable.

1787 Half Cent

1787 Cent, Obverse   Arrows in Right Talon   Arrows in Left Talon

	G	VG	F	VF	EF	AU	Unc.
1787 Half Cent	$100	$125	$225	$500	$750	$1,200	$2,800
1787 Cent, Arrows in Right Talon	$10,000	$16,000	$25,000	$50,000	$75,000	$100,000	$180,000
1787 Cent, Arrows in Left Talon	$100	$110	$200	$600	$1,250	$2,500	$6,000
1787 Cent, "Horned Eagle" (die break)	$110	$120	$225	$650	$1,300	$2,800	$7,000

1788 Half Cent

1788 Cent, Period After
MASSACHUSETTS

	G	VG	F	VF	EF	AU	Unc.
1788 Half Cent	$100	$125	$215	$550	$1,000	$1,500	$3,200
1788 Cent, Period After MASSACHUSETTS	$100	$110	$200	$500	$800	$1,750	$4,750
1788 Cent, No Period After MASSACHUSETTS	$115	$120	$250	$675	$1,500	$2,800	$6,000

CONNECTICUT (1785–1788)

Authority for establishing a mint near New Haven was granted by the state of Connecticut to Samuel Bishop, Joseph Hopkins, James Hillhouse, and John Goodrich in October 1785. They had petitioned the state's General Assembly for this right, noting the public need—small coins were scarce in circulation and many of those seen were counterfeits. Under the Assembly's grant, the four minters would pay the state's treasury an amount equal to 5 percent of the copper coins they produced. To make a profit, the minters would deduct this royalty, plus their other expenses (including materials, labor, and distribution), from the face value of the coins they struck.

Available records indicate that most of the Connecticut coppers were coined under a subcontract, by Samuel Broome and Jeremiah Platt, former New York merchants. Abel Buell was probably the principal diesinker. Many others were struck by Machin's Mills in Newburgh, New York, and were not authorized by Connecticut. These are as highly prized by collectors as are regular issues.

The Connecticut coppers were often struck crudely and on imperfect planchets. Numerous die varieties exist; over the years, collectors have given many of them distinctive nicknames.

1785 Copper, Bust Facing Left

1785 Copper, Bust Facing Right

1785 Copper, African Head

	G	VG	F	VF	EF	AU
1785 Copper, Bust Facing Left	$150	$250	$500	$1,500	$3,600	$8,000
1785 Copper, Bust Facing Right	$35	$60	$125	$475	$1,300	$3,500
1785 Copper, African Head	$70	$120	$400	$1,250	$3,500	$8,000

1786 Copper, ETLIB INDE

1786 Copper, Large Head Facing Right

1786 Copper, Mailed Bust Facing Left

1786 Copper, Draped Bust

1786 Copper, Mailed Bust Facing Left, Hercules Head

	G	VG	F	VF	EF	AU
1786 Copper, ETLIB INDE	$70	$140	$325	$850	$2,500	$7,000
1786 Copper, Large Head Facing Right	$250	$500	$1,500	$4,600	$10,000	
1786 Copper, Mailed Bust Facing Left	$40	$75	$140	$450	$1,100	$2,800
1786 Copper, Draped Bust	$75	$150	$400	$1,100	$2,750	$6,700
1786 Copper, Mailed Bust Facing Left, Hercules Head	$110	$200	$500	$2,000	$4,750	

1787 Copper, Small Head Facing Right, ETLIB INDE

1787 Copper, Muttonhead Variety

	G	VG	F	VF	EF	AU
1787 Copper, Small Head Facing Right, ETLIB INDE	$90	$150	$300	$1,600	$4,200	$8,500
1787 Copper, Liberty Seated Facing Right (a)		—				
1787, Mailed Bust Facing Right, INDE ET LIB	$100	$180	$400	$2,200	$5,000	
1787 Copper, Muttonhead	$100	$180	$400	$2,200	$5,000	$9,000

a. 2 examples are known.

1787 Copper, Mailed Bust Facing Left

1787 Copper, Laughing Head

1787 Copper, Reverse

	G	VG	F	VF	EF	AU
1787 Copper, Mailed Bust Facing Left	$40	$65	$120	$400	$1,000	$2,500
1787 Copper, Mailed Bust Facing Left, Laughing Head	$50	$100	$200	$500	$1,100	$2,300

**1787 Copper,
Horned Bust**

	G	VG	F	VF	EF	AU
1787 Copper, Mailed Bust Facing Left, Horned Bust	$40	$65	$120	$375	$750	$1,800
1787 Copper, Mailed Bust Facing Left, Hercules Head *(see 1786 for illustration)*	$400	$800	$2,000	$4,250	$8,000	—
1787 Copper, Mailed Bust Facing Left, Dated 1787 Over 1877	$80	$180	$600	$1,600	$4,750	—
1787 Copper, Mailed Bust Facing Left, 1787 Over 88	$175	$235	$700	$1,800	$5,000	—
1787 Copper, Mailed Bust Facing Left, CONNECT, INDE	$50	$125	$200	$600	$1,500	$3,000
1787 Copper, Mailed Bust Facing Left, CONNECT, INDL	$375	$700	$1,500	$3,200	$7,000	

1787 Copper, Draped Bust Facing Left

	G	VG	F	VF	EF	AU
1787 Copper, Draped Bust Facing Left	$30	$50	$80	$200	$500	$1,000
1787 Copper, Draped Bust Facing Left, AUCIORI	$40	$65	$100	$350	$900	$1,500
1787 Copper, Draped Bust Facing Left, AUCTOPI	$45	$75	$140	$500	$1,200	$2,200
1787 Copper, Draped Bust Facing Left, AUCTOBI	$45	$75	$140	$500	$1,200	$2,000
1787 Copper, Draped Bust Facing Left, CONNFC	$40	$60	$100	$400	$900	$1,500
1787 Copper, Draped Bust Facing Left, CONNLC	$75	$150	$250	$800	$3,000	—
1787 Copper, Draped Bust Facing Left, FNDE	$40	$65	$150	$400	$1,300	$2,400
1787 Copper, Draped Bust Facing Left, ETLIR	$40	$60	$125	$350	$1,000	$1,700
1787 Copper, Draped Bust Facing Left, ETIIB	$40	$60	$125	$350	$1,000	$1,800
1787 Copper, GEORGIVS III Obverse, INDE•ET Reverse	$1,500	$3,250	$3,500	—	—	—

1788 Copper, Mailed Bust Facing Right

	G	VG	F	VF	EF	AU
1788 Copper, Mailed Bust Facing Right	$40	$80	$150	$500	$1,300	$2,500
1788 Copper, GEORGIVS III Obverse *(Reverse as Above)*	$100	$210	$550	$1,550	$3,250	—
1788 Copper, Small Head *(see 1787 for illustration)*	$1,750	$4,000	$5,000	$12,000	$22,000	—

1788 Copper, Mailed Bust Facing Left   **1788 Copper, Draped Bust Facing Left**

	G	VG	F	VF	EF	AU
1788 Copper, Mailed Bust Facing Left	$45	$70	$175	$400	$1,100	$2,200
1788 Copper, Mailed Bust Facing Left, CONNLC	$55	$130	$250	$600	$1,800	$3,200
1788 Copper, Draped Bust Facing Left	$45	$70	$175	$400	$1,100	$2,200
1788 Copper, Draped Bust Facing Left, CONNLC	$85	$200	$450	$1,100	$2,500	$4,000
1788 Copper, Draped Bust Facing Left, INDL ET LIB	$80	$140	$300	$800	$2,000	$3,800

NEW YORK AND RELATED ISSUES (1780S)

No official state coinage for New York is known to have been authorized. However, a number of issues in copper and gold were made relating to the state, by a variety of different issuers.

BRASHER DOUBLOONS (1786–1787)

Among the most famous early American pieces coined before establishment of the U.S. Mint at Philadelphia were those produced by the well-known New York City silversmith, goldsmith, and jeweler Ephraim Brasher, who was a neighbor and friend of George Washington's when that city was the seat of the federal government.

The gold pieces Brasher made weighed about 408 grains and were valued at $15 in New York currency. They were approximately equal to the Spanish doubloon, which was equal to 16 Spanish dollars.

Pieces known as *Lima Style doubloons* were dated 1742, but it is almost certain that they were produced in 1786, and were the first efforts of Brasher to make a circulating coin for regional use. Neither of the two known specimens shows the full legends; but weight, gold content, and hallmark are all identical to those for the 1787-dated Brasher coins. An analogous cast imitation Lima style doubloon dated 1735 bears a hallmark attributed to Standish Barry of Baltimore, Maryland, circa 1787.

The design used on the 1787 Brasher doubloon features an eagle on one side and the arms of New York on the other. In addition to his impressed hallmark, Brasher's name appears in small letters on each of his coins. The unique 1787 gold half doubloon is struck from doubloon dies on an undersized planchet that weighs half as much as the larger coins. It is in the National Numismatic Collection in the Smithsonian Institution.

It is uncertain why Brasher produced these pieces. He may have produced them for his own account, charging a nominal fee to convert metal into coin. He was later commissioned by the government to test and verify other gold coins then in circulation. His hallmark EB was punched on each coin as evidence of its testing and its value. In some cases the foreign coins were weight-adjusted by clipping.

		EF
"1742" (1786) Lima Style gold doubloon (a)		$700,000
	Auctions: $690,000, EF-40, January 2005	

a. 2 examples are known.

		EF
1787 New York gold doubloon, EB on Breast		*$5,000,000*
	Auctions: $2,990,000, EF-45, January 2005	
1787 New York gold doubloon, EB on Wing		*$4,500,000*
	Auctions: $4,582,500, MS-63, January 2014	
1787 New York gold half doubloon (a)		—
Various foreign gold coins with Brasher's EB hallmark		*$5,000–$16,000*

a. Unique, in the Smithsonian Collection.

NEW YORK COPPER COINAGE

Several individuals petitioned the New York Legislature in early 1787 for the right to coin copper for the state, but a coinage was never authorized. Instead, a law was passed to regulate the copper coins already in use. Nevertheless, various unauthorized copper pieces were made privately and issued within the state.

One private mint known as Machin's Mills was organized by Captain Thomas Machin, a distinguished veteran of the Revolutionary War, and situated at the outlet of Orange Pond near Newburgh, New York. Shortly after this mint was formed, on April 18, 1787, it was merged with the Rupert, Vermont, mint operated by Reuben Harmon Jr., who held a coinage grant from the Republic of Vermont. The combined partnership agreed to conduct their business in New York, Vermont, Connecticut, or elsewhere if they could benefit by it (though their only known operation was the one at Newburgh).

The operations at Machin's Mills were conducted in secret and were looked upon with suspicion by the local residents. They minted several varieties of imitation George III halfpence, as well as counterfeit coppers of Connecticut and New Jersey. Only their Vermont coppers had official status.

Mints located in or near New York City were operated by John Bailey and Ephraim Brasher. They had petitioned the legislature on February 12, 1787, for a franchise to coin copper. The extent of their partnership, if any, and details of their operation are unknown. Studies of the state coinage show that they produced primarily the EXCELSIOR and NOVA EBORAC pieces of New York, and possibly the "running fox" New Jersey coppers.

Believed to be the bust of George Washington.

	G	VG	F	VF	EF	AU
1786, NON VI VIRTUTE VICI	$6,000	$10,000	$20,000	$40,000	$60,000	$90,000

1787 EXCELSIOR Copper, Large Eagle on Obverse

1787 EXCELSIOR Copper, Eagle on Globe Facing Left

	G	VG	F	VF	EF
1787 EXCELSIOR Copper, Eagle on Globe Facing Right	$2,750	$4,000	$8,500	$25,000	$60,000
1787 EXCELSIOR Copper, Eagle on Globe Facing Left	$2,750	$3,500	$8,000	$18,000	$40,000
1787 EXCELSIOR Copper, Large Eagle on Obverse, Arrows and Branch Transposed	$4,000	$6,500	$16,000	$33,000	$55,000

1787, George Clinton

1787, Indian and New York Arms

1787, Indian and Eagle on Globe

1787, Indian and George III Reverse

	G	VG	F	VF	EF
1787, George Clinton	$10,000	$20,000	$50,000	$100,000	$250,000
1787, Indian and New York Arms	$10,000	$18,000	$35,000	$50,000	$75,000
1787, Indian and Eagle on Globe	$10,000	$18,000	$30,000	$40,000	$50,000
1787, Indian and George III Reverse (a)		—			

a. 4 examples are known.

BRITISH COPPER COINS AND THEIR IMITATIONS
(INCLUDING MACHIN'S MILLS AND OTHER UNDERWEIGHT COINAGE OF *1786–1789*)

The most common copper coin used for small transactions in early America was the British halfpenny. Wide acceptance and the non–legal-tender status of these copper coins made them a prime choice for unauthorized reproduction by private individuals.

Many such counterfeits were created in America by striking from locally made dies, or by casting or other crude methods. Some were made in England and imported into this country. Pieces dated 1781 and 1785 seem to have been made specifically for this purpose, while others were circulated in both countries.

Genuine regal British halfpence and farthings minted in London and dated 1749 are of special interest to collectors because they were specifically sent to the North American colonies as reimbursement for participation in the expedition against Cape Breton, and circulated extensively throughout New England.

| *Genuine British halfpenny coppers of both George II (dated 1729–1754) and George III (dated 1770–1775) show finely detailed features within a border of close denticles; the 1 in the date looks like a J. They are boldly struck on good-quality planchets. Their weight is approximately 9.5 grams; their diameter, 29 mm.* | *British-made lightweight imitation halfpence are generally smaller in diameter and thickness, and weigh less than genuine pieces. Details are crudely engraved or sometimes incomplete. Inscriptions may be misspelled. Planchet quality may be poor.* |

	G	F	VF	EF	AU
1749, George II British farthing	$15	$35	$75	$175	$250
1749, George II British halfpenny	$20	$50	$100	$200	$300
1770–1775, George III British halfpenny (a)	$10	$20	$50	$100	$250
1770–1775, British imitation halfpenny (a)	$10	$15	$20	$100	$250

a. Values shown are for the most common variety. Rare pieces are sometimes worth significantly more.

During the era of American state coinage, New York diemaker James F. Atlee and/or other coiners minted unauthorized, lightweight, imitation British halfpence. These American-made false coins have the same or similar devices, legends, and, in some cases, dates as genuine regal halfpence, but they contain less copper. Their details are often poorly rendered or missing. Identification of American-made imitations has been confirmed by identifying certain punch marks (such as letters and numerals) and matching them to the distinct punch marks of known engravers.

There are four distinct groups of these halfpence, all linked to the regular state coinage. The first group was probably struck in New York City prior to 1786. The second group was minted in New York City in association with John Bailey and Ephraim Brasher during the first half of 1787. The third group was struck at Machin's Mills during the second half of 1787 and into 1788 or later. A fourth group, made by the Machin's Mills coiners, consists of pieces made from dies that were muled with false dies of the state coinages of Connecticut, Vermont, and New York. Pieces with very crude designs and other dates are believed to have been struck elsewhere in New England.

GEORGIVS/BRITANNIA
"MACHIN'S MILLS" COPPER HALFPENNIES MADE IN AMERICA

Dates used on these pieces were often "evasive," as numismatists describe them today. They include dates not used on genuine pieces and, sometimes, variations in spelling. They are as follows: 1771, 1772, 1774, 1775, and 1776 for the first group; 1747 and 1787 for the second group; and 1776, 1778, 1787, and 1788 for the third group. Pieces generally attributed to James Atlee can be identified by a single outline in the crosses (British Union) of Britannia's shield and large triangular denticles along the coin circumference. The more-valuable American-made pieces are not to be confused with the similar English-made George III counterfeits (some of which have identical dates), or with genuine British half-pence dated 1770 to 1775.

Group I coins dated 1771, 1772, 1774, 1775, and 1776 have distinctive bold designs but lack the fine details of the original coins. Planchets are generally of high quality.

Group II coins dated 1747 and 1787 are generally poorly made. The 1 in the date is not J-shaped, and the denticles are of various sizes. There are no outlines to the stripes in the shield.

Group III coins dated 1776, 1778, 1787, and 1788, struck at Machin's Mills in Newburgh, New York, are similar to coins of Group II, with their triangular-shaped denticles. Most have large dates and berries in the obverse wreath.

	AG	G	VG	F	VF	EF	AU
1747, GEORGIVS II. Group II	$125	$250	$400	$800	$3,500	$8,000	$20,000
1771, GEORGIVS III. Group I	$70	$100	$220	$325	$1,250	$3,000	$6,000
1772, GEORGIVS III. Group I	$80	$150	$250	$500	$1,600	$3,250	$8,000
1772, GEORGIUS III. Group I	$85	$200	$300	$750	$2,300	$4,500	—
1774, GEORGIVS III. Group I	$40	$80	$100	$225	$800	$2,500	$5,000
1774, GEORGIUS III. Group I	$80	$150	$225	$400	$1,750	$3,750	—
1775, GEORGIVS III. Group I	$35	$70	$100	$225	$700	$1,800	$4,750
1776, GEORGIVS III. Group III	$170	$325	$500	$950	$2,750	$6,750	—
1776, GEORCIVS III, Small Date	$1,000	$2,000	$4,500	$9,000	$18,000	$25,000	$35,000
1778, GEORGIVS III. Group III	$40	$70	$125	$275	$750	$2,500	$3,800
1784, GEORGIVS III	$200	$400	$800	$1,500	$3,200	$4,500	$7,500
1787, GEORGIVS III. Group II	$30	$75	$125	$225	$700	$1,400	$3,000
1787, GEORGIVS III. Group III	$30	$75	$125	$225	$700	$1,400	$3,000
1788, GEORGIVS III. Group III	$35	$80	$150	$275	$750	$1,500	$3,500

Note: Values shown are for the most common varieties in each category. Rare pieces can be worth significantly more. Also see related George III combinations under Connecticut, Vermont, and New York.

The muled coins of Group IV are listed separately with the Immune Columbia pieces and with the coins of Connecticut, Vermont, and New York. Other imitation coppers made by unidentified American makers are generally very crude and exceedingly rare. Cast copies of British coins probably circulated along with the imitations without being questioned. Counterfeits of silver Spanish-American coins and Massachusetts tree coins may have also been coined by American minters.

Nova Eborac Coinage for New York

An extensive issue of 1787-dated copper coins appeared, each with a bust on the obverse surrounded by NOVA EBORAC ("New York"). The reverse showed a seated goddess with a sprig in one hand and a liberty cap on a pole in the other hand, with the legend VIRT. ET. LIB. ("Virtue and Liberty") surrounding, and the date 1787 below. The letter punches used on this issue are identical to those used on the Brasher doubloon die. It is likely that John Bailey and Ephraim Brasher operated a minting shop in New York City and produced these and possibly other issues.

**1787, NOVA EBORAC, Reverse:
Seated Figure Facing Right**

**1787, NOVA EBORAC, Reverse:
Seated Figure Facing Left**

1787, NOVA EBORAC, Small Head

1787, NOVA EBORAC, Large Head

	AG	G	F	VF	EF	AU
1787, NOVA EBORAC, Seated Figure Facing Right	$50	$110	$225	$800	$1,500	$3,250
1787, NOVA EBORAC, Seated Figure Facing Left	$50	$90	$200	$600	$1,000	$2,000
1787, NOVA EBORAC, Small Head	$1,700	$4,000	$13,000	$25,000		
1787, NOVA EBORAC, Large Head	$500	$900	$2,000	$5,000		

NEW JERSEY (1786–1788)

On June 1, 1786, the New Jersey General Assembly granted to businessman and investor Thomas Goadsby, silversmith and assayer Albion Cox, and minter Walter Mould authority to coin three million coppers weighing six pennyweight and six grains (150 grains total, or 9.72 grams) apiece, to be completed by June 1788, on condition that they deliver to the state treasurer "one Tenth Part of the full Sum they shall strike." These coppers were to pass current at 15 to the shilling. Revolutionary War hero and New Jersey state legislator Matthias Ogden also played a significant financial and political role in the operation.

In an undertaking of this kind, the contractors purchased the metal and assumed all expenses of coining. The difference between these expenses and the total face value of the coins issued represented their profit.

Later, Goadsby and Cox asked authority to coin two-thirds of the total independently of Mould. Their petition was granted November 22, 1786. Mould was known to have produced his coins at Morristown, while Cox and Goadsby operated in Rahway. Coins with a diameter of 30 mm or more are generally considered Morristown products. Coins were also minted in Elizabethtown by Ogden and, without authority, by Machin's Mills.

The obverse shows design elements of the state seal, a horse's head with plow, and the legend NOVA CÆSAREA (New Jersey). The reverse has a United States shield and, for the first time on a coin, the legend E PLURIBUS UNUM (One Composed of Many). More than 140 varieties exist. The majority have the horse's head facing to the right; however, three of the 1788 date show the head facing left. Other variations have a sprig beneath the head, branches below the shield, stars, cinquefoils, a running fox, and other ornaments.

1786, Date Under
Plow Beam

1786 and 1787,
Pattern Shield

1786, Date Under
Plow, No Coulter

	AG	G	F	VF	EF
1786, Date Under Plow Beam			$85,000	$125,000	$200,000
1786, Date Under Plow, No Coulter	$500	$900	$3,000	$7,000	$10,000
1787, Pattern Shield (a)	$400	$700	$1,750	$3,000	$5,000

a. The so-called Pattern Shield reverse was also used on several speculative patterns. See page 117.

1786, Straight
Plow Beam,
Protruding Tongue

1786, Wide Shield

1786, Curved Plow
Beam, Bridle Variety

	AG	G	F	VF	EF	AU
1786, Straight Plow Beam (common varieties)	$25	$55	$175	$500	$850	$1,250
1786, Curved Plow Beam (common varieties)	$25	$55	$175	$500	$875	$1,500
1786, Protruding Tongue	$30	$70	$235	$600	$1,850	$4,500
1786, Wide Shield	$30	$75	$240	$650	$2,000	$5,000
1786, Bridle variety	$30	$75	$240	$650	$2,000	$5,000

1787, PLURIBS Error

1787, U Over S in PLURIBUS

1787, PLURIRUS Error

	AG	G	F	VF	EF	AU
1786, PLUKIBUS error	$30	$75	$250	$450	$1,700	$4,500
1787, PLURIBS error	$40	$125	$500	$1,600	$3,500	$7,500
1787, Second U Over S in PLURIBUS	$40	$160	$470	$1,100	$3,200	$5,000
1787, PLURIRUS error	$40	$160	$470	$1,100	$3,200	$5,500

1787, Sprig
Above Plow

1787, WM
Above Plow

1787, Hidden WM

	AG	G	F	VF	EF	AU
1787, Sprig Above Plow (common varieties)	$25	$65	$220	$650	$1,200	$2,500
1787, No Sprig Above Plow (common varieties)	$25	$65	$220	$550	$900	$1,600
1787, WM Above Plow (a)				—		
1787, Hidden WM in Sprig	$35	$75	$225	$675	$1,800	$3,500

a. Unique.

1787 Over 1887

1787, Camel Head

1787, Serpent Head

	AG	G	F	VF	EF	AU
1787, Date Over 1887	$200	$600	$3,000	$6,000	$15,000	—
1787, Camel Head (snout in high relief)	$30	$60	$200	$650	$900	$1,500
1787, Serpent Head	$35	$85	$400	$1,500	$3,750	$6,000
1787, Goiter Variety	$40	$75	$250	$700	$2,200	$4,500

**1788, Fox
Before Legend**

**1788, Indistinct
Coulter**

**1788, Fox
After Legend**

1788, Braided Mane

**1788, Head
Facing Left**

	AG	G	F	VF	EF	AU
1788, Horse's Head Facing Right, several varieties	$25	$60	$175	$550	$900	$1,600
1788, Horse's Head Facing Right, Running Fox Before Legend	$75	$150	$550	$2,000	$4,500	$9,000
1788, Similar, Indistinct Coulter	$150	$650	$2,500	$6,500	$15,000	—
1788, Horse's Head Facing Right, Running Fox After Legend	$9,000	$25,000	$75,000	$100,000	—	
1788, Braided Mane	$50	$300	$1,200	$3,500	$6,000	$12,000
1788, Horse's Head Facing Left	$175	$450	$1,750	$4,750	$12,000	—

REPUBLIC OF VERMONT (1785–1788)

The Republic of Vermont was not formally part of the Union in the 1780s. However, it considered itself American and allied with the original 13 colonies, having declared independence from Britain in January 1777 and having fought in the Revolutionary War. After the war Vermont sought political connection with the United States. Territorial disagreements with New York delayed its entry into the Union, but this was finally accomplished in 1791, when it was admitted as the 14th state. In the meantime, Vermont had already embarked on its own experiments in local coinage.

Reuben Harmon Jr., a storekeeper and entrepreneur of Rupert, Vermont, was granted permission by the Vermont House of Representatives to coin copper pieces for a period of two years beginning July 1, 1785. The well-known Vermont "Landscape" coppers were first produced in that year. The franchise was extended for eight years in 1786.

Harmon's mint was located in the northeast corner of Rupert near a stream known as Millbrook. Colonel William Coley, a New York goldsmith, made the first dies. Some of the late issues were made near Newburgh, New York, by the Machin's Mills coiners.

Most coppers made in Vermont were struck on poor and defective planchets. These included the landscape and Draped Bust Left varieties. Well-struck coins on smooth, full planchets command higher prices. Later pieces made at Machin's Mills are on high-quality planchets but usually have areas of weak striking.

1785, IMMUNE COLUMBIA

1785, VERMONTS   1785, Reverse   1785, VERMONTIS

1786, VERMONTENSIUM   1786, Baby Head

1786, Bust Left   1786, Reverse   1787, Reverse

	AG	G	VG	F	VF	EF	AU
1785, IMMUNE COLUMBIA	$4,250	$6,250	$10,000	$15,000	$40,000	—	—
1785, VERMONTS	$150	$275	$500	$750	$2,500	$4,250	$9,000
1785, VERMONTIS	$175	$325	$650	$1,400	$4,250	$10,000	$19,500
1786, VERMONTENSIUM	$110	$200	$350	$550	$1,350	$3,000	$5,500
1786, Baby Head	$200	$275	$400	$1,250	$3,000	$9,500	—
1786, Bust Left	$80	$125	$250	$650	$2,400	$4,000	—
1787, Bust Left	$3,000	$4,500	$10,500	$27,000	$42,000	—	—

1787, BRITANNIA

	AG	G	VG	F	VF	EF	AU
1787, BRITANNIA (a)	$45	$90	$120	$200	$450	$1,000	$2,200

a. The reverse of this coin is always weak.

1787, 1788, Bust Right (Several Varieties)

	AG	G	VG	F	VF	EF	AU
1787, Bust Right, several varieties	$60	$110	$150	$250	$900	$2,250	$4,000
1788, Bust Right, several varieties	$50	$90	$120	$225	$600	$1,400	$3,250
1788, Backward C in AUCTORI	$3,000	$4,500	$7,500	$17,500	$37,500	$75,000	
1788, *ET LIB* *INDE	$175	$300	$550	$1,250	$4,000	$10,000	—

1788, GEORGIVS III REX/ET•LIB+INDE+

	AG	G	VG	F	VF	EF	AU
1788, GEORGIVS III REX (a)	$300	$500	$900	$2,200	$4,500	$11,000	

a. This piece should not be confused with the common English halfpence with similar design and reverse legend BRITANNIA.

PRIVATE TOKENS AFTER CONFEDERATION

The formal ratification of the Articles of Confederation—the document signed amongst the original 13 colonies, which established the United States of America as a confederation of sovereign states and served as its first constitution—was accomplished in early 1781. A number of private coinages sprang up after confederation, intended to facilitate local commerce. These were not the products of the federal government, but were tokens issued by businesses and other private concerns.

NORTH AMERICAN TOKENS (DATED 1781)

These tokens were struck in Dublin, Ireland. The obverse shows the seated figure of Hibernia, the personification of Ireland, facing left. The date of issue is believed to have been much later than that shown on the token (1781). Like many Irish tokens, this issue found its way to America in limited quantities and was accepted in commerce near the Canadian border.

	VG	F	VF	EF	AU
1781, Copper or Brass	$60	$100	$200	$650	$1,300

BAR COPPERS (CA. 1785)

The Bar coppers are undated and of uncertain origin. They have 13 parallel and unconnected bars on one side. On the other side is the large roman-letter USA monogram. The design is virtually identical to that used on a Continental Army uniform button.

The significance of the design is clearly defined by its extreme simplicity. The separate 13 states (bars) unite into a single entity as symbolized by the interlocking letters (USA).

These pieces are believed to have first circulated in New York during November 1785, as mentioned in a report in the *New Jersey Gazette* of November 12, 1785. They may have been made in England. Although they are scarce, examples enter the marketplace with regularity, and nearly all are in higher grades.

John Adams Bolen (1826–1907), a numismatist and a master diesinker in Springfield, Massachusetts, struck copies of the Bar copper around 1862. On these copies, the letter A passes under, instead of over, the S. Bolen's intent was not to deceive, and he advertised his copies plainly as reproductions. But his skills were such that W. Elliot Woodward, a leading auctioneer of tokens and medals in the 1860s, vacillated between selling Bolen's copies and describing them as "dangerous counterfeits." Bolen copies of the Bar copper are highly collectible in their own right, but they are less valuable than the originals.

	G	VG	F	VF	EF	AU	Unc.
(Undated) (Circa 1785) Bar Copper	$500	$1,800	$3,000	$6,250	$9,000	$12,500	$21,000

AUCTORI PLEBIS TOKENS (1787)

These tokens are sometimes included with the coins of Connecticut, as they greatly resemble issues of that state. (The obverse features a draped male bust, possibly King George II, wearing laurels and facing left.) They were struck in England by an unknown maker, possibly for use in America.

	G	VG	F	VF	EF	AU	Unc.
1787, AUCTORI PLEBIS	$90	$110	$225	$450	$900	$1,600	$7,500

MOTT STORE CARDS (DATED 1789)

These 19th-century store cards have long been included in Early American coin collections because of the date they bear (1789). Most scholars believe these were produced no earlier than 1807 (and possibly in the Hard Times era of the late 1830s) as commemoratives of the founding of the Mott Company, and served as business cards. The firm, operated by Jordan Mott, was located at 240 Water Street, a fashionable section of New York at that time.

The obverse of the token features an eagle with wings spread and an American shield as a breastplate. The eagle holds an olive branch and arrows in his talons. Above is the date 1789, and around the rim is the legend CLOCKS, WATCHES, JEWELRY, SILVERWARE, CHRONOMETERS. The reverse of the token features a regulator clock with the legend MOTT'S N.Y. IMPORTERS, DEALERS, MANUFACTURERS OF GOLD & SILVER WARES.

	VG	F	VF	EF	AU	Unc.
"1789," Mott Token, Thick Planchet	$80	$175	$300	$450	$600	$1,200
"1789," Mott Token, Thin Planchet	$80	$200	$350	$800	$1,400	$2,500
"1789," Mott Token, Entire Edge Engrailed	$80	$300	$450	$1,000	$1,800	$3,200

STANDISH BARRY THREEPENCE (1790)

Standish Barry, of Baltimore, was a watch- and clockmaker, an engraver, and, later, a silversmith. In 1790 he circulated a silver threepence of his own fabrication. The tokens are believed to have been an advertising venture at a time when small change was scarce. The precise date on this piece may indicate that Barry intended to commemorate Independence Day, but there are no records to prove this. The head on the obverse is probably that of James Calhoun, who was active in Baltimore politics in the 1790s. The legend BALTIMORE TOWN JULY 4, 90, appears in the border. An enigmatic gold doubloon is also attributed to Barry (see page 121).

Nearly all examples of the silver threepence show significant wear, suggesting that they circulated for a long time.

	VG	F	VF	EF	AU
1790 Threepence	$10,000	$22,500	$50,000	$80,000	$110,000

ALBANY CHURCH PENNIES (1790)

The First Presbyterian Church of Albany, New York, authorized an issue of 1,000 copper uniface tokens in 1790. These passed at 12 to a shilling. They were used to encourage parishioner donations (at that time, there was a scarcity of small change in circulation). They were also intended to stop contributions of worn and counterfeit coppers (in the words of the church elders' resolution, "in order to add respect to the weekly collections"). Two varieties were made, one with the addition of a large D (the abbreviation for *denarium*, or penny, in the British monetary system) above the word CHURCH. All are rare, with fewer than a dozen of each variety known.

	VG	F	VF	EF
(Undated) (1790) Without D	$10,000	$15,000	$30,000	$50,000
(Undated) (1790) With D Added	$10,000	$15,000	$30,000	$50,000

KENTUCKY TOKENS (CA. 1792–1794)

These tokens were struck in England circa 1792 to 1794. Their obverse legend reads UNANIMITY IS THE STRENGTH OF SOCIETY; the central motif is a hand holding a scroll with the inscription OUR CAUSE IS JUST. The reverse shows a pyramid of 15 starbursts surrounded by rays. Each star in the triangle represents a state, identified by its initial letter. These pieces are usually called *Kentucky cents* or *Kentucky tokens* because the letter K (for Kentucky) happens to be at the top. Some of the edges are plain; others are milled with a diagonal reeding; and some have edge lettering that reads PAYABLE IN LANCASTER LONDON OR BRISTOL, PAYABLE AT BEDWORTH NUNEATON OR HINKLEY, or PAYABLE AT I. FIELDING, etc.

These are not known to have circulated in America. Rather, they were made as produced as collectibles, popular among English numismatists and others at the time. Likely more than 1,000 Kentucky tokens are in the hands of numismatists today.

	VF	EF	AU	Unc.
(1792–1794) Copper, Plain Edge	$185	$275	$450	$850
(1792–1794) Copper, Engrailed Edge	$500	$900	$1,350	$2,800
(1792–1794) Copper, Lettered Edge, PAYABLE AT BEDWORTH, etc.	—	—	—	—
(1792–1794) Copper, Lettered Edge, PAYABLE IN LANCASTER, etc.	$200	$300	$475	$950
(1792–1794) Copper, Lettered Edge, PAYABLE AT I. FIELDING, etc.	—	—	—	—

FRANKLIN PRESS TOKENS (1794)

These were English tradesman's tokens of the kind collected by English numismatists in the late 1700s and early 1800s. (As a group, they were popularly called Conder tokens, after James Conder, the man who first cataloged them for collectors.) The Franklin Press tokens did not circulate as money in America, but, being associated with a London shop where Benjamin Franklin once worked, they have long been included in American coin collections.

The obverse features a wood-frame printing press of the style that Benjamin Franklin would have operated by hand as a printer in England in 1725. He had left Philadelphia at the age of 18 to buy printing supplies in London and look for work. Around the central design is the legend SIC ORITOR DOCTRINA SURGETQUE LIBERTAS ("Thus Learning Advances and Liberty Grows"), and below is the date, 1794. The reverse legend reads PAYABLE AT THE FRANKLIN PRESS LONDON.

Most are plain-edged, but rare lettered-edge varieties exist, as well as a unique piece with a diagonally reeded edge.

	VG	VF	EF	AU	Unc.
1794 Franklin Press Token	$100	$250	$350	$550	$900
Similar, Edge Reads AN ASYLUM FOR THE OPPRESS'D OF ALL NATIONS			(unique)		
Similar, Edge Diagonally Reeded			(unique)		

TALBOT, ALLUM & LEE CENTS (1794–1795)

Talbot, Allum & Lee was a firm of importers engaged in the India trade and located at 241 Pearl Street, New York. It placed a large quantity of English-made coppers in circulation during 1794 and 1795.

ONE CENT appears on the 1794 issue, and the legend PAYABLE AT THE STORE OF on the edge. The denomination is not found on the 1795 reverse but the edge legend was changed to read WE PROMISE TO PAY THE BEARER ONE CENT. Rare plain-edged specimens of both dates exist. Exceptional pieces have edges ornamented or with lettering CAMBRIDGE BEDFORD AND HUNTINGDON.X.X.

It is estimated that more than 200,000 of these tokens were minted, though no original records have been located. Varieties and mulings are known; the values shown here are for the most common types.

Many undistributed tokens were sold to the Philadelphia Mint in a time of copper shortage. These were cut down and used by the Mint as planchets for coining 1795 and 1797 half cents.

1794 Cent, With NEW YORK   **1795 Cent**

	VG	F	VF	EF	AU	Unc.
1794 Cent, With NEW YORK	$65	$80	$225	$350	$550	$1,350
1794 Cent, Without NEW YORK	$500	$850	$2,750	$5,000	$7,500	$16,000
1795 Cent	$60	$80	$200	$300	$400	$800

MYDDELTON TOKENS (1796)

Philip Parry Price Myddelton was an Englishman who bought land in America after the Revolutionary War. He hoped to begin a vibrant farming community along the Ohio River and entice English crafts-men and workers to move there. To this end he contracted the design of a promotional token and had examples made in copper and silver. These tokens were struck at the Soho Mint of Boulton and Watt near Birmingham, England. Although their obverse legend reads BRITISH SETTLEMENT KENTUCKY, and Myddelton planned to order large quantities of the copper version for shipment to the United States, they were never actually issued for circulation in Kentucky. The entrepreneur was arrested in August 1796 and convicted in London for the crime of convincing hundreds of workers to leave England for America. He was jailed in Newgate prison for three and a half years, which ended his Kentucky plans.

The obverse of Myddelton's token shows Hope presenting two "little genii" (his description) to the goddess Liberty. She welcomes them with an open hand. At her feet is a flourishing sapling and a cornucopia representing America's bounty, and she holds a pole with a liberty cap. On the reverse, seated Britannia leans wearily on a downward-pointing spear, looking at the broken scale and fasces—symbols of unity, justice, and liberty—scattered at her feet.

Sylvester S. Crosby, in *The Early Coins of America*, remarked that "In beauty of design and execution, the tokens are unsurpassed by any piece issued for American circulation."

	PF
1796, Proof, Copper	$25,000
1796, Proof, Silver	$32,000

COPPER COMPANY OF UPPER CANADA TOKENS (EARLY 1800s)

These pieces were struck some time in the early 1800s. The obverse is the same as that of the Myddelton token. The new reverse refers to a Canadian firm, the Copper Company of Upper Canada, with the denomination ONE HALF PENNY. These tokens may have been made for numismatic purposes (for sale to collectors), or as part of the coiner's samples. Their maker is unknown. Restrikes were made in England in the 1890s.

	PF
1796, Proof, Copper	$10,000

CASTORLAND MEDALS (1796)

These medals, or "jetons," are dated 1796 and allude to a proposed French settlement known as Castorland. This was to be located on the Black River, in northern New York, not far from the Canadian border. Peter Chassanis of Paris had acquired land that he and others intended to parcel into large farms, with Chassanis heading the settlement's government, two commissaries residing at its seat, Castorville, and four commissaries headquartered in Paris. The medals were to be given as payment ("in recognition of the care which they may bestow upon the common concerns") to the Parisian directors of the colonizing company for their attendance at board meetings.

Some 20 French families, many of them aristocratic refugees from the French Revolution, moved to the settlement between 1796 and 1800. Challenges including sickness, harsh northern New York winters, loss of livestock, and theft of finances proved too much for the company, and Castorland was dissolved in 1814. Many of the surviving settlers moved to more prosperous American communities or returned to Europe.

The obverse of the Castorland medal features a profile portrait of the ancient goddess Sybele, associated with mountains, town and city walls, fertile nature, and wild animals. She wears a *corona muralis* ("walled crown"), laurels, and a draped head covering. The legend reads FRANCO-AMERICANA COLONIA, with CASTORLAND 1796 below. On the reverse the goddess Ceres, patroness of agriculture, stands at a maple with a sap drill while the tree's bounty flows into a waiting bucket. Ceres holds a cornucopia; at her feet are a sickle and a sheaf of wheat. A beaver at the bottom of the reverse further symbolizes Castorland and its resources (*castor* is French for "beaver," an animal crucial to the very profitable North American fur trade in the early 1800s). The legend, in Latin, is SALVE MAGNA PARENS FRUGUM—"Hail, Great Mother of Crops" (from Virgil).

Copy dies of the Castorland medal are still available and have been used at the Paris Mint for restriking throughout the years. Restrikes have a more modern look than originals; their metallic content (in French) is impressed on the edge: ARGENT (silver), CUIVRE (copper), or OR (gold).

	EF	AU	Unc.
1796, Original, Silver (reeded edge, unbroken dies)	$3,000	$4,500	$7,200
1796, Original, Silver (reverse rusted and broken)	$300	$600	$1,500
1796, Original, Bronze (reverse rusted and broken)	$200	$300	$700
(1796) Undated, Restrike, Silver (Paris Mint edge marks)		$30	$70
(1796) Undated, Restrike, Bronze (Paris Mint edge marks)		$20	$40

THEATRE AT NEW YORK TOKENS (CA. 1798)

These penny tokens were issued by Skidmore of London and illustrate the New Theatre (later known as the Park Theatre) in Manhattan, as it appeared circa 1797. The theater was New York City's attempt at a prestigious new level of entertainment, as the famous John Street Theatre (the "Birthplace of American Theater") was suffering from poor management and physical decay in the 1790s. The building's cornerstone was laid on May 5, 1795, and the theater opened on January 29, 1798, with a presentation of entertainments including Shakespeare's *As You Like It.*

The obverse of this copper token features a view of the playhouse building with the legend THE THEATRE AT NEW YORK AMERICA. The reverse shows an allegorical scene of a cornucopia on a dock, with bales, an anchor, and sailing ships. The legend reads MAY COMMERCE FLOURISH. The edge is marked I PROMISE TO PAY ON DEMAND THE BEARER ONE PENNY.

All known examples are struck in copper and have a Proof finish. They were made for collectors, not for use as advertising. Today examples are scarce, with about 20 known.

	EF
	PF
Penny, THE THEATRE AT NEW YORK AMERICA	—
Penny, THE THEATRE AT NEW YORK AMERICA, Proof	$26,000

NEW SPAIN (TEXAS) JOLA TOKENS (1817–1818)

In 1817 the Spanish governor of Texas, Colonel Manuel Pardo, authorized Manuel Barrera to produce 8,000 copper coins known as jolas. These crudely made pieces show the denomination ½ (real), the maker's initials and the date on the obverse, and a five-pointed star on the reverse.

The 1817 coins were withdrawn from circulation the following year and replaced by a similar issue of 8,000 pieces. These bear the date 1818 and the initials, JAG, of the maker, José Antonio de la Garza. Several varieties of each issue are known. All are rare.

	F	VF	EF
1817 1/2 Real	$15,000	$25,000	$50,000
1818 1/2 Real, Large or Small Size	$10,000	$25,000	$50,000

NORTH WEST COMPANY TOKENS (1820)

These tokens were probably valued at one beaver skin and struck in Birmingham, England, in 1820 by John Walker & Co. All but two known specimens are holed. Most have been found in Oregon in the region of the Columbia and Umpqua river valleys. They feature a portrait of King George IV on the obverse, with the legend TOKEN and the date 1820. The reverse shows a beaver in the wild, with the legend NORTH WEST COMPANY.

James A. Haxby, in the *Guide Book of Canadian Coins and Tokens*, writes, "The pieces actually issued for circulation were pierced at the top for suspension or stringing. Unholed copper strikes are known with plain or engrailed edge and are very rare. A number of pieces have been found buried in western Canada and as far south as central Oregon."

Holed Brass Token   **Unholed Copper Token**

	AG	G	VG	F	VF
1820, Copper or Brass (with hole)	$375	$800	$2,250	$4,250	$8,500
1820, Copper, unholed, plain or engrailed edge	—	—	—	—	—

WASHINGTON PIECES

Medals, tokens, and coinage proposals in this interesting series dated from 1783 to 1795 bear the portrait of George Washington. The likenesses in most instances were faithfully reproduced and were designed to honor the first president. Many of these pieces were of English origin and, although dated 1783, probably were made in the 1820s or later.

The legends generally signify a strong unity among the states and the marked display of patriotism that pervaded the new nation during that period. We find among some of these tokens an employment of what were soon to become the nation's official coin devices, namely, the American eagle, the United States shield, and stars. The denomination ONE CENT is used in several instances, while on some of the English pieces HALFPENNY will be found. Several of these pieces were private patterns for proposed coinage contracts.

GEORGIVS TRIUMPHO TOKENS

Although the head shown on these tokens bears a strong resemblance to that on some coins of King George III, many collectors consider the Georgivs Triumpho ("Triumphant George") tokens a commemorative of America's victory in the Revolutionary War.

The reverse side shows the Goddess of Liberty behind a framework of 13 bars and fleurs-de-lis. Holding an olive branch in her right hand and staff of liberty in her left, she is partially encircled by the words VOCE POPOLI ("By the Voice of the People") 1783.

	VG	F	VF	EF	AU	Unc.
1783, GEORGIVS TRIUMPHO	$110	$225	$500	$700	$1,200	$6,000

WASHINGTON PORTRAIT PIECES (1780s TO EARLY 1800s)

Military Bust. "The 1783-dated Washington Military Bust coppers bear a portrait, adapted (with a different perspective on the coin and a wreath added to the head) from a painting by Edward Savage," writes Q. David Bowers in the *Whitman Encyclopedia of Colonial and Early American Coins*. "These seem to have circulated in England as well as America. . . . Many varieties exist, but they are not well known outside of a circle of specialists. Accordingly, the opportunity exists to acquire rare die combinations for little premium over a regular issue."

The reverse features a seated female figure holding an olive branch and a pole topped by a liberty cap. Values shown are for the most common varieties.

1783, Large Military Bust, Point of Bust Close to W

1783, Small Military Bust

	F	VF	EF	AU	Unc.
1783, Large Military Bust	$75	$160	$350	$500	$1,750
1783, Small Military Bust, Plain Edge	$80	$175	$400	$750	$2,500
1783, Small Military Bust, Engrailed Edge	$100	$200	$550	$1,100	$3,000

Draped Bust. Draped Bust coppers dated 1783 depict Washington with the top of a toga draped over his shoulder. One variety includes a button at the folds in front of the toga. Another variety has no button, and has the initial "I" (for Ingram) in the toga, above the right side of the numeral 3 in the date. Both varieties feature a similar reverse design with a female figure seated on a rock, holding an olive branch and a pole surmounted by a liberty cap.

1783, Draped Bust, No Button   **With Button**

	F	VF	EF	AU	Unc.
1783, Draped Bust, No Button *(illustrated)*	$80	$160	$300	$500	$1,600
1783, Draped Bust, With Button (on Drapery at Neck)	$125	$225	$350	$700	$3,200
1783, Draped Bust, Copper Restrike, Plain Edge, Proof					$900
1783, Draped Bust, Copper Restrike, Engrailed Edge, Proof					$750
1783, Draped Bust, Silver Restrike, Engrailed Edge, Proof					$1,800

Unity States. The 1783-dated coppers with the legend UNITY STATES OF AMERICA were likely coined in the early 1800s at the Soho Mint in Birmingham, England. The obverse features a portrait of Washington in a toga and wearing laurels. The reverse is a copy of the wreath design on the copper cent produced by the Philadelphia Mint from 1796 to 1807, with UNITED spelled UNITY, perhaps as a way to evade charges of counterfeiting.

Despite the American denomination of this piece, they likely circulated in England (at the value of a halfpenny), as reflected by examples being found there in quantity in later years. They were imported into the United States as well, for use as a cent, and are mentioned in several counterfeit-detector publications in the 1850s.

1783, Unity States

	VG	VF	EF	AU	Unc.
1783, UNITY STATES	$100	$200	$325	$550	$1,400

Double Head. Although the Washington Double Head cents are undated, some numismatists assign them a date of 1783, given their resemblance to the Military Bust coppers that bear that date (even though those were probably struck years later). They were likely struck in Birmingham, England, by Edward Thomason sometime in the 1820s or later. They were made in England, as evidenced by many having been found there, but long after the Conder token era. They are denominated ONE CENT and, when exported to the United States, circulated along with Hard Times tokens of the 1830s.

Undated Double-Head Cent

	F	VF	EF	AU	Unc.
(Undated) Double-Head Cent	$100	$250	$425	$725	$2,400

Ugly Head. The so-called Ugly Head token is a medalet struck in copper and white-metal varieties, possibly satirical, and presumably of American origin. The token's legend reads WASHINGTON THE GREAT D.G. The abbreviation "D.G." on English coins stands for Dei Gratia ("By the Grace of God"), and the portrait appears to be wigless and possibly toothless, leading some numismatists to opine that the token is a satire on George Washington. Bowers notes that the token's date, 1784, has no particular significance in Washington's life. By that year the American Revolution was over and the general had retired his commission as commander-in-chief of the Continental Army. He would not assume the presidency until 1789. The reverse of the token features a design of linked rings with abbreviations for the British colonies, reminiscent of the 1776 Continental dollar.

1784, Ugly Head

	G
1784, Ugly Head, Copper	$100,000
Auctions: $20,000, Crude Good, December 1983	
1784, Ugly Head, Pewter	*(unique)*

Large and Small Eagle. Large Eagle and Small Eagle one-cent tokens dated 1791 were made in Birmingham, England, sponsored by merchants W. and Alex Walker of that city as proposals for official American coinage. Bowers writes in the *Whitman Encyclopedia of Colonial and Early American Coins* that the Walker firm "shipped a cask filled with these cents, estimated to be about 2,500 Large Eagle and 1,500 Small Eagle coins, to Thomas Ketland & Sons, a Philadelphia contact, to be distributed to legislators. The depiction of Washington was contrary to the president's own desires, who felt that having his image on coins would appear to have the 'stamp of royalty.'"

1791 Cent, Small Eagle Reverse,
Edge Lettered UNITED STATES OF AMERICA

1791 Cent, Large Eagle Reverse

	VG	F	VF	EF	AU	Unc.
1791 Cent, Small Eagle (Date on Reverse)		$475	$650	$800	$1,200	$2,750
1791 Cent, Large Eagle (Date on Obverse)	$150	$350	$550	$750	$1,100	$2,400

Liverpool. The Liverpool Halfpenny tokens were most likely made around 1793. They were intended for circulation as small change in England, although numismatists of the time also sought them for their collections. The obverse shows a uniformed bust of George Washington, as used on the Large Eagle one-cent tokens of 1791. The reverse features a sailing ship and the legend LIVERPOOL HALF-PENNY, a design used on various English Conder tokens.

1791 Liverpool Halfpenny

	VG	F	VF	EF	AU	Unc.
1791 Liverpool Halfpenny, Lettered Edge	$750	$1,100	$1,800	$3,000	$5,500	—

1792. An extensive series of 1792-dated Washington pieces was produced in many varieties, bearing no denomination. These apparently were made in England, and were collected by numismatists in addition to circulating as coinage substitutes in America.

1792 Cent, Small Eagle Reverse,
Edge Lettered UNITED STATES OF AMERICA

	VG	F	VF	EF
1792, WASHINGTON PRESIDENT, Eagle With 13 Stars Reverse				
PRESIDENT at Side of Bust, Copper				—
PRESIDENT, Silver			$125,000	—
PRESIDENT, Gold (a)			—	
PRESIDENT Extends Below Bust, Copper (a)				$117,000

a. Unique.

1792, WASHINGTON   **Legend Reverse**
PRESIDENT

	VG	F	VF	EF
1792, WASHINGTON PRESIDENT, Legend on Reverse				
Plain Edge, Copper	$2,750	$7,500	$18,000	$50,000
Lettered Edge, Copper	—	—	—	—

**(1792) Undated,
WASHINGTON
BORN VIRGINIA**

	VG	F	VF	EF
(1792) Undated, WASHINGTON BORN VIRGINIA, Eagle With 13 Stars Reverse *(reverse illustrated on previous page)*, Copper (a)		—		
(1792) Undated, WASHINGTON BORN VIRGINIA, Legend on Reverse				
Copper	$1,000	$1,800	$3,800	$7,000
Silver	—	—	—	—

a. 3 examples are known.

Peter Getz. Dies engraved by silversmith, mechanic, and inventor Peter Getz of Lancaster, Pennsylvania, are believed to have been made to produce a half dollar and a cent as a proposal to Congress for a private contract coinage before the Philadelphia Mint became a reality. These feature George Washington, in a military bust portrait, and a heraldic eagle.

1792, Small Eagle		**Large Eagle Reverse**		

	VG	F	VF	EF	AU	Unc.
1792, Small Eagle, Silver	—	—	—	$300,000		
	Auctions: $241,500, AU, May 2004					
1792, Small Eagle, Copper	$6,000	$12,000	$30,000	$50,000	$75,000	$150,000
	Auctions: $299,000, MS-64 BN, November 2006					
1792, Small Eagle, Ornamented Edge (Circles and Squares), Copper	—	—	—	$175,000		
	Auctions: $207,000, AU, November 2006					
1792, Small Eagle, Ornamented Edge, Silver (a)	—	—	$125,000	$200,000		
	Auctions: $391,000, Gem BU PL, May 2004					
1792, Large Eagle, Silver			—	—		
	Auctions: $34,500, EF, May 2004					

a. 4 examples are known.

Roman Head. The 1792-dated Roman Head cents show Washington in the style of an ancient Roman dignitary. These copper pieces were struck in England for collectors, as opposed to being intended for circulation. Their edge is lettered UNITED STATES OF AMERICA.

1792 Cent, Roman Head

	PF
1792 Cent, Roman Head, Lettered Edge UNITED STATES OF AMERICA, Proof	$90,000

Ship Halfpenny. The 1793 Ship Halfpenny tokens were struck from an overdated (3 Over 2) reverse die. These copper pieces were intended for collectors, but nearly all of them ended up in circulation in England. The more common lettered-edge variety reads PAYABLE IN ANGLESEY LONDON OR LIVERPOOL.

1793 Ship Halfpenny

	VG	F	VF	EF	AU	Unc.
1793 Ship Halfpenny, Lettered Edge	$100	$200	$400	$600	$850	$3,250
1793 Ship Halfpenny, Plain Edge (a)			—	—		

a. Rare.

1795 Copper. Copper tokens dated 1795 were made in large quantities as promotional pieces for the London firm of Clark & Harris, dealers in stoves and fireplace grates. The die work is attributed to Thomas Wyon, and numismatists believe the pieces were struck in Birmingham, England, for circulation in the British Isles (although collectors saved them as well).

The obverse features a right-facing portrait of George Washington in military uniform. Two varieties exist, Small Buttons and Large Buttons (describing the coats on his frock). The legend reads G. WASHINGTON: THE FIRM FRIEND TO PEACE & HUMANITY.

The reverse shows a fireplace with a coal grate, with legends PAYABLE BY CLARK & HARRIS 13. WORMWOOD St. BISHOPSGATE and LONDON 1795.

Most have a diagonally reeded edge, although some are edge-lettered as PAYABLE AT LONDON LIVERPOOL OR BRISTOL.

1795, Small Buttons   **1795, Large Buttons**

	F	VF	EF	AU	Unc.
1795, Large Buttons, Lettered Edge	$180	$350	$700	$1,500	$2,200
1795, Large Buttons, Reeded Edge	$80	$175	$300	$400	$700
1795, Small Buttons, Reeded Edge	$80	$200	$400	$725	$1,750

Liberty and Security. The Liberty and Security halfpenny and penny tokens were made in England in 1795 as collectibles, although the halfpence also circulated widely there as small change. Their designs consist of a portrait of George Washington, identified by name, and a heraldic eagle surmounting a stylized American shield, holding a sprig of olive and several arrows. Some of their edges are plain, and some are lettered with various phrases such as AN ASYLUM FOR THE OPPRESS'D OF ALL NATIONS and BIRMINGHAM REDRUTH & SWANSEA.

Varieties exist in copper and white metal, and with mulings of different reverses.

The common name of this series derives from the reverse legend, LIBERTY AND SECURITY.

1795, Liberty and Security Halfpenny

	F	VF	EF	AU	Unc.
1795 Halfpenny, Plain Edge	$110	$200	$500	$950	$2,650
1795 Halfpenny, LONDON Edge	$100	$210	$525	$750	$2,500
1795 Halfpenny, BIRMINGHAM Edge	$125	$250	$550	$1,100	$2,800
1795 Halfpenny, ASYLUM Edge	$200	$400	$1,100	$2,000	$5,500
1795 Penny, ASYLUM Edge	$2,500	$8,500	$12,500	$18,000	$32,500

(1795) Undated, Liberty and Security Penny, ASYLUM Edge

	F	VF	EF	AU	Unc.
(1795) Undated, Liberty and Security Penny	$275	$450	$650	$1,150	$2,250
Same, Corded Outer Rims	$600	$1,000	$1,800	$2,800	$5,000

North Wales. "The undated North Wales halfpenny issues, believed to have been struck in England in the early 1790s (usually listed as 1795, although this may be two or three years after they were coined), are part of the 'evasion halfpence' series. Accordingly, unlike Conder tokens, they were not created for collectors. None are known to have survived with sharp features and in high grades, as is characteristic of cabinet pieces" (*Whitman Encyclopedia of Colonial and Early American Coins*).

(1795) Undated, NORTH WALES Halfpenny

	G	F	VF	EF	AU
(1795) Undated, NORTH WALES Halfpenny	$90	$200	$500	$1,400	$2,800
(1795) Undated, Lettered Edge	$450	$1,450	$5,000	$8,000	—
(1795) Undated, Two Stars at Each Side of Harp	$2,200	$7,500	$13,500		

Success Tokens. Small and large types exist of these mysterious pieces of unknown date and purpose. Today known as Success tokens, they may have been souvenirs, perhaps struck to commemorate George Washington's second inauguration (March 1793), or 19th-century gaming tokens. They were struck in copper or brass and most likely were made in the mid-1800s. Specimens with original silvering are rare and are valued 20% to 50% higher than others. Varieties exist.

(Undated) Large Success Token   (Undated) Small Success Token

	F	VF	EF	AU	Unc.
(Undated) SUCCESS Token, Large, Plain or Reeded Edge	$250	$450	$750	$1,400	$2,750
(Undated) SUCCESS Token, Small, Plain or Reeded Edge	$300	$500	$800	$1,600	$3,000

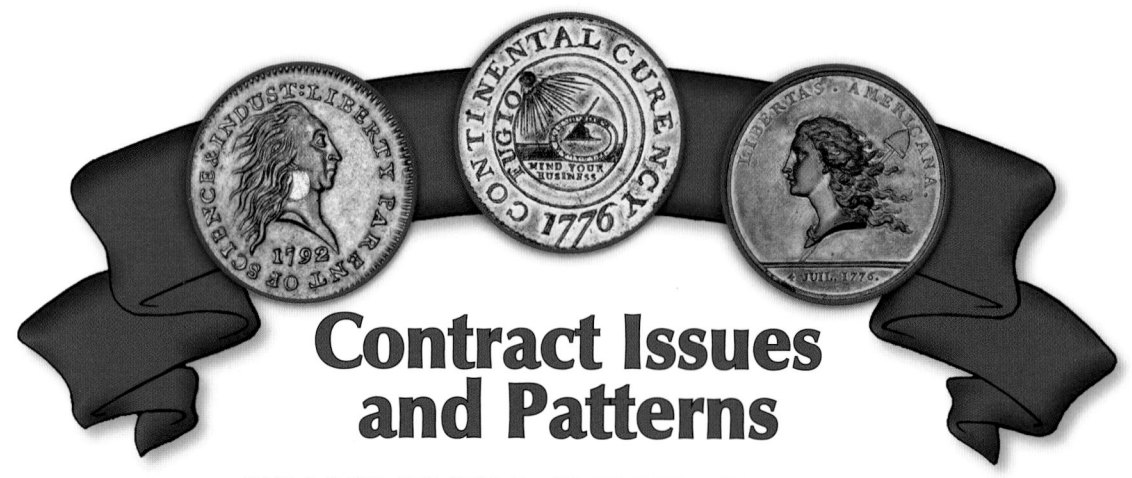

Contract Issues and Patterns

CONTINENTAL CURRENCY (1776)

The Continental Currency dollars (as they are known to numismatists) were made to serve in lieu of a paper dollar, but the exact nature of their monetary role is still unclear. They were the first dollar-sized coins ever attributed to the United States. One obverse die was engraved by someone whose initials were E.G. (thought to be Elisha Gallaudet) and is marked EG FECIT ("EG Made It"). Studies of the coinage show that there may have been two separate emissions made at different mints, one in New York City. The link design on the reverse was suggested by Benjamin Franklin and represents the former colonies.

Varieties result from differences in the spelling of the word CURRENCY and the addition of EG FECIT on the obverse. These coins were struck in pewter, brass, and silver. Pewter pieces served as a dollar, taking the place of a Continental Currency paper note. Brass and silver pieces may have been experimental or patterns. The typical grade encountered for a pewter coin is VF to AU. Examples in original bright Uncirculated condition are worth a strong premium.

Numerous copies and replicas of these coins have been made over the years. Authentication is recommended for all pieces.

| | CURRENCY | | CURENCY | |

	G	F	VF	EF	AU	Unc.
1776 CURENCY, Pewter (a)	$7,750	$12,000	$24,000	$36,000	$50,000	$75,000
1776 CURENCY, Brass (a)	$25,000	$40,000	$75,000	$135,000	$220,000	—
Auctions: $299,000, MS-63, July 2009						
1776 CURENCY, Silver (b)			$1,527,000			
Auctions: $1,410,000, MS-63, May 2014; $1,527,500, MS-62, January 2015; $1,527,500, EF-40, January 2015						
1776 CURRENCY, Pewter	$8,000	$13,000	$25,000	$37,500	$52,500	$80,000
1776 CURRENCY, EG FECIT, Pewter	$8,500	$15,000	$27,000	$40,000	$55,000	$85,000
Auctions: $546,250, MS-67, January 2012						

a. 2 varieties. b. 2 examples are known.

	G	F	VF	EF	AU	Unc.
1776 CURRENCY, EG FECIT, Silver (b)	—	—	—	—	$1,500,000
Auctions: $1,410,000, MS-63, May 2014						
1776 CURRENCEY, Pewter	—	—	$65,000		$175,000	—
1776 CURRENCY, Pewter, Ornamented Date (c)				$276,000	$329,000	
Auctions: $276,000, EF-45, July 2009						

b. 2 examples are known. **c.** 3 examples are known.

NOVA CONSTELLATIO PATTERNS (1783)

These Nova Constellatio pieces represent the first official patterns for a coinage of the United States. They were designed by Benjamin Dudley for Gouverneur Morris to carry out his ideas for a decimal coinage system. The 1,000-unit coin is a mark, the 500 a quint. These denominations, together with the small 100-unit piece, were designed to fit in with the many different values for foreign coins that constituted money in America at the time. These pattern pieces represent the first attempt at a decimal ratio, and were the forerunners of our present system of money values. Neither the proposed denominations nor the coins advanced beyond the pattern stage. These unique pieces are all dated 1783. There are two types of the quint. The copper "five" was first brought to the attention of collectors in 1980. Electrotype and cast copies exist.

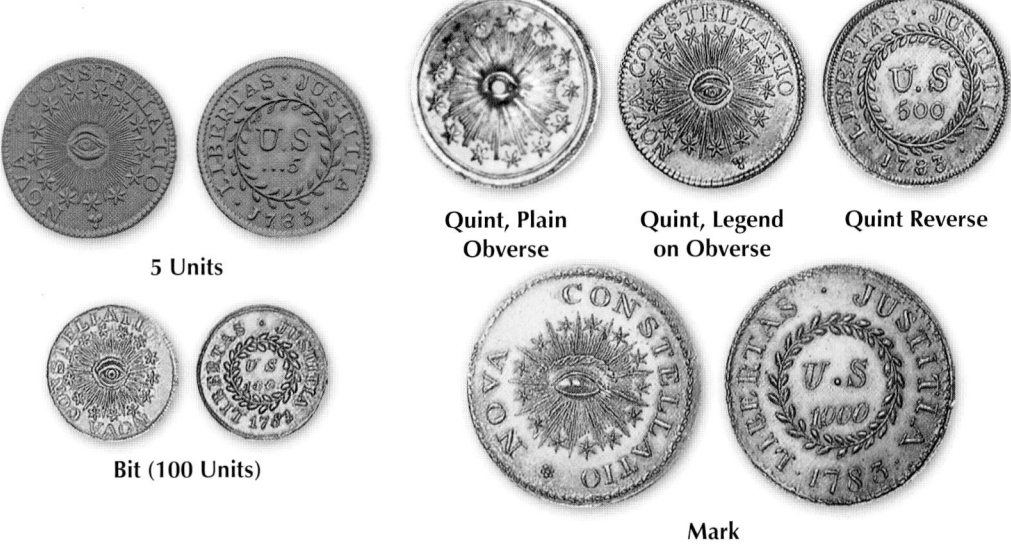

5 Units

Quint, Plain Obverse

Quint, Legend on Obverse

Quint Reverse

Bit (100 Units)

Mark

1783 (Five) "5," Copper	*(unique)*
1783 (Bit) "100," Silver, Decorated Edge	*(2 known)*
Auctions: $97,500, Unc., November 1979	
1783 (Bit) "100," Silver, Plain Edge	*(unique)*
Auctions: $705,000, AU-55, May 2014	
1783 (Quint) "500," Silver, Plain Obverse	*(unique)*
Auctions: $1,175,000, AU-53, April 2013	
1783 (Quint) "500," Silver, Legend on Obverse	*(unique)*
Auctions: $165,000, Unc., November 1979	
1783 (Mark) "1000," Silver	*(unique)*
Auctions: $190,000, Unc., November 1979	

FUGIO COPPERS (1787)

The first coins issued by authority of the United States for which contract information is known today were the "Fugio" pieces. Entries in the *Journal of Congress* supply interesting information about proceedings relating to this coinage. For example, the entry of Saturday, April 21, 1787, reads as follows: "That the board of treasury be authorized to contract for three hundred tons of copper coin of the federal standard, agreeable to the proposition of Mr. James Jarvis. . . . That it be coined at the expense of the contractor, etc."

On Friday, July 6, 1787, it was "[r]esolved, that the board of treasury direct the contractor for the copper coinage to stamp on one side of each piece the following device, viz: thirteen circles linked together, a small circle in the middle, with the words 'United States,' around it; and in the centre, the words 'We are one'; on the other side of the same piece the following device, viz: a dial with the hours expressed on the face of it; a meridian sun above on one side of which is the word 'Fugio,' [the intended meaning is *time flies*] and on the other the year in figures '1787,' below the dial, the words 'Mind Your Business.'"

The legends have been credited to Benjamin Franklin and are similar in some respects to the 1776 Continental Currency pewter and other coins.

These pieces were coined in New Haven, Connecticut. Most of the copper used in their coinage came from military stores or salvaged metal. The dies were made by Abel Buell of New Haven.

1787, WITH POINTED RAYS

The 1787, With Pointed Rays, was later replaced by the With Club Rays variety.

American Congress Pattern

Cross After Date

Label With Raised Rims

	G	VG	F	VF	EF	AU	Unc.
Obverse Cross After Date, No Cinquefoils							
Reverse Rays and AMERICAN CONGRESS				—	$300,000	$400,000	
Reverse Label with Raised Rims (a)					$35,000		
Reverse STATES UNITED	$300	$650	$1,000	$2,750	$5,500	$12,500	—
Reverse UNITED STATES	$275	$600	$900	$2,500	$5,200	$12,000	—

a. Extremely rare.

Cinquefoil After Date
These types, with pointed rays, have regular obverses punctuated with four cinquefoils (five-leafed ornaments).

	G	VG	F	VF	EF	AU	Unc.
STATES UNITED at Sides of Circle, Cinquefoils on Label	$150	$300	$600	$1,000	$1,500	$2,100	$4,000
STATES UNITED, 1 Over Horizontal 1	$225	$450	$1,000	$4,000	$8,500		
UNITED STATES, 1 Over Horizontal 1	$200	$400	$900	$3,500	$7,500		
UNITED STATES at Sides of Circle	$150	$300	$600	$1,000	$1,750	$2,200	$4,500
STATES UNITED, Label With Raised Rims, Large Letters in WE ARE ONE	$200	$450	$700	$2,200	$5,000	$10,000	$20,000
STATES UNITED, 8-Pointed Star on Label	$200	$400	$600	$1,000	$2,250	$4,750	$10,000
UNITED Above, STATES Below	$850	$1,750	$3,750	$9,000	$12,500	$19,500	—

1787, With Club Rays

The 1787, With Club Rays, is differentiated between concave and convex ends.

Rounded Ends   **Concave Ends**

	G	VG	F	VF	EF	AU
Club Rays, Rounded Ends	$200	$400	$800	$1,500	$2,750	$6,500
Club Rays, Concave Ends to Rays, FUCIO (C instead of G) (a)	$1,750	$3,750	$8,000	$24,000	$35,000	
Club Rays, Concave Ends, FUGIO, UNITED STATES	$2,000	$4,200	$10,000	$30,000	$40,000	$90,000
Club Rays, Similar, STATES UNITED Reverse		—	—		—	—

a. Extremely rare.

The so-called New Haven "restrikes" were made for Horatio N. Rust from dies recreated in 1859. These are distinguished by narrow rings on the reverse. At the time the fanciful story was given that teenaged C. Wyllys Betts discovered original dies in 1858 on the site of the Broome & Platt store in New Haven, where the original coins had been made.

New Haven Restrike.
Note narrow rings.

	EF	AU	Unc.
Gold (a)		—	—
Silver	$3,000	$4,250	$6,500
Copper or Brass	$400	$500	$800

a. 2 examples are known.

1792 PROPOSED COINAGE

Some members of the House of Representatives favored a depiction of the president's head on the obverse of each federal coin; others considered the idea an inappropriately monarchical practice. George Washington himself is believed to have expressed disapproval of the use of his portrait on American coins. The majority considered a figure emblematic of Liberty more appropriate, and the Senate finally concurred in this opinion. Robert Birch was an engraver employed to design proposed devices for American coins. He, perhaps together with others, engraved the dies for the disme and half disme. He also cut the dies for the large copper patterns known today as *Birch cents*. Most 1792 half dismes circulated and were considered to be official coinage, rather than patterns; they are summarized here and discussed in more detail under "Half Dismes."

1792 SILVER CENTER CENT

The dies for the 1792 cent with a silver center may have been cut by Henry Voigt. The coins are copper with a silver plug in the center. The idea was to create a coin with an intrinsic or melt-down value of a cent, but of smaller diameter than if it were made entirely of copper. On the obverse is a right-facing portrait of Miss Liberty, the legend LIBERTY PARENT OF SCIENCE & INDUSTRY, and the date 1792.

	F	VF	EF	AU
Cent, Silver Center (a)	$250,000	$450,000	$550,000	$650,000
Auctions: $1,997,500, MS-64, August 2014; $1,410,000, MS-63BN+, May 2014; $705,000, MS-61+, September 2014				
Cent, Without Silver Center (b)	$275,000	$400,000	$600,000	—
Auctions: $603,750, VF-30, January 2008				

a. 14 examples are known, including one unique specimen without plug. **b.** 9 examples are known.

1792 BIRCH CENT

On the large-diameter copper Birch cent, the portrait of Miss Liberty is "bright-eyed and almost smiling," as described in *United States Pattern Coins*. The legend LIBERTY PARENT OF SCIENCE & INDUSTRY surrounds the portrait. BIRCH is lettered on the truncation of her neck, for the engraver. On the reverse is a ribbon-tied wreath with the legend UNITED STATES OF AMERICA and the denomination in fractional terms of a dollar: 1/100. The edge of some examples is lettered TO BE ESTEEMED BE USEFUL (with punctuating stars).

G★W.Pt.

	F	VF	EF
Copper, Lettered Edge, TO BE ESTEEMED * BE USEFUL* (a)	$250,000	$650,000	$750,000
Auctions: $564,000, MS-61, January 2015			
Copper, Plain Edge (b)		$700,000	
Copper, Lettered Edge, TO BE ESTEEMED BE USEFUL * (b)		—	
Auctions: $2,585,000, MS-65H, January 2015			
White Metal, G*W.Pt. (George Washington President) Below Wreath (c)		—	

a. 8 examples are known. **b.** 2 examples are known. **c.** Unique.

1792 Half Disme

About 1,500 silver half dismes were struck in mid-August 1792 in the shop of John Harper, using equipment ordered for the Philadelphia Mint (the foundation stones of which would be laid on July 31). Nearly all were placed into circulation. In his annual address that autumn, President George Washington noted that these had been so distributed. Their obverse design is a portrait of Miss Liberty similar to the Birch cent's, but facing left. Its legend is abbreviated as LIB. PAR. OF SCIENCE & INDUSTRY. The reverse shows an eagle in flight, with UNI. STATES OF AMERICA around the top, and HALF DISME below.

	Mintage	AG	G	VG	F	VF	EF	AU	Unc.
Silver	1,500	$8,500	$20,000	$27,500	$40,000	$80,000	$100,000	$150,000	$300,000
	Auctions: $1,292,500, SP-67, August 2014								

1792 Disme

The 1792 pattern disme occurs in one silver variety and two copper varieties (plain-edged and the more readily available reeded-edge). The obverse legend is abbreviated as LIBERTY PARENT OF SCIENCE & INDUST., with the date 1792 below Miss Liberty's neck. The reverse features an eagle in flight, different in design from that of the half disme, with UNITED STATES OF AMERICA around the top of the coin and the denomination, DISME, below.

	F	EF	AU	Unc.
Silver (a)	$300,000	$500,000	$1,000,000	
	Auctions: $998,750, AU-50, January 2015			
Copper *(illustrated)* (b)	$135,000	$225,000	$450,000	$1,000,000
	Auctions: $1,057,500, MS-64, January 2015			

a. 3 examples are known. b. Approximately 15 examples are known.

1792 Quarter Dollar

Joseph Wright, an accomplished artist in the private sector, designed this pattern, thought to have been intended for a quarter dollar. Wright was George Washington's choice for the position of first chief engraver of the Mint, and he later designed the 1793, Liberty Cap, cent in that capacity, but died of yellow fever before being confirmed by Congress. Unique uniface trials of the obverse and reverse also exist.

	EF
1792, Copper *(illustrated)* (a)	$750,000
Auctions: $2,232,500, MS-63, January 2015	
1792, White Metal (b)	$325,000

a. 2 examples are known. **b.** 4 examples are known.

THE LIBERTAS AMERICANA MEDAL (1782)

The Liberty Cap coinage of the fledgling United States was inspired by the famous Libertas Americana medal, whose dies were engraved by Augustin Dupré in Paris in 1782 from a concept and mottoes proposed by Benjamin Franklin. To Franklin (then U.S. minister to France), the infant Hercules symbolized America, strangling two serpents representing the British armies at Saratoga and Yorktown. Minerva, with shield and spear, symbolized France as America's ally, keeping the British Lion at bay. Franklin presented gold examples of the medal to the French king and queen and silver strikings to their ministers, "as a monumental acknowledgment, which may go down to future ages, of the obligations we are under to this nation."

Between 100 and 125 original copper medals exist, and two dozen or more silver; the location of the two gold medals is unknown. Over the years the Paris Mint has issued additional medals that are appreciated and collected at a fraction of the cost for originals.

	PF-50	PF-60	PF-63	PF-65
Libertas Americana medal, Proof, Copper (a)	$8,000	$11,500	$16,500	$45,000
Libertas Americana medal, Proof, Silver (b)	$40,000	$80,000	$120,000	$180,000

a. 100 to 125 examples are known. **b.** At least 24 examples are known.

Half Cents
1793–1857

AN OVERVIEW OF HALF CENTS

Building a type set of the six different major designs in the half cent series can be a challenging and rewarding pursuit. The first design, with Liberty Head facing left with pole and cap, minted only in 1793, is scarce in all grades and will be the most difficult to locate. However, hundreds exist of this American classic, and many are fairly attractive.

The second type, with a *large* Liberty Head facing right with pole and cap, made only in 1794, is scarce with good eye appeal. Most are dark and rough. The next type, the *small* Liberty Head facing right, with pole and cap, is scarce, but enough are on the market that a collector can find a specimen without difficulty.

The Draped Bust half cents, struck from 1800 to 1808, are easily available as a type, including in higher grades. The Classic Head (1809–1836) and Braided Hair (1840–1857) are plentiful as types.

For the earlier half cent types there is ample opportunity for connoisseurship, for quality often varies widely, and every coin is apt to have a different appearance and "personality," even within the same grade.

FOR THE COLLECTOR AND INVESTOR: HALF CENTS AS A SPECIALTY

Collecting half cents by dates and major varieties has been a popular niche specialty for a long time. Some key issues in the series are the 1793; 1796, With Pole to Cap; 1796, Without Pole to Cap, (the most famous of all the rarities); 1802, 2 Over 0, With Reverse of 1800, (a single leaf at each side of the wreath apex, rare but somewhat obscure); 1831; and the Proof-only issues of 1836, 1840 through 1848, Small Date, and 1852.

As there are so many Proof varieties, and each of these is rare as well as expensive, many collectors opt to acquire only the circulation strikes. However, the Proofs are not nearly as expensive as one might think, probably because with so many different dates and varieties needed to complete a Proof collection, the prospect is daunting to many buyers. Proofs of most dates are available in both original and restrike forms. Although this rule is not without exceptions, the original strikings of the 1840–1848 and 1849, Small Date, half cents are usually described as having the Large Berries reverse, while restrikes are of the Small Berries reverse (within the Small Berries issues there are two dies—one with diagonal die striae below RICA, and the other with doubling at the ribbon wreath). Assembling Proofs by reverse varieties is a somewhat esoteric pursuit.

For an exhaustive study of die varieties of circulation strikes and Proofs, *Walter Breen's Encyclopedia of United States Half Cents, 1793–1857*, is definitive. Roger S. Cohen Jr.'s study, *American Half Cents, The "Little Half Sisters,"* gives detailed information on circulation strikes, but omits Proofs.

Die varieties are especially abundant among half cents of the first several types, 1793 to 1808. The year 1804 offers a panorama of dies, some of which have been studied as to die states, referring to the progression of use of a die as it develops wear, cracks, etc. Varieties of 1795 exist with and without the pole to the liberty cap, the Without Pole half cents being the result of a die being relapped (reground to dress the surface), during which process the pole was removed. On the other hand, the 1796, Without Pole, half cent was the result of a die-engraving error—the diecutter forgot to add it. Some half cents of 1795 and 1797 were struck on planchets cut from copper tokens issued by the New York City firm of Talbot, Allum & Lee. Upon close inspection, some of the design details of the tokens can still be seen.

One curious and readily available variety of the 1828 half cent has 12 stars instead of the standard 13. However, in choice Mint State the 12-stars issue becomes a rarity, for, unlike the 13-stars issue, none were ever found in hoards.

The Early American Coppers Club is a special-interest group emphasizing copper half cents and large cents. Its journal, *Penny-Wise*, provides much research, social, and collecting news and information.

LIBERTY CAP, HEAD FACING LEFT (1793)

Designer: *Henry Voigt.* **Weight:** *104 grains (6.74 grams).* **Composition:** *Copper.* **Diameter:* 21.2 to 24.6 mm.* **Edge:** *Lettered TWO HUNDRED FOR A DOLLAR.* **Mint:** *Philadelphia.*

Bowers-Whitman–4,
Cohen-4, Breen-4.

History. Among U.S. coinage, the Liberty Cap, Head Facing Left, design belongs to the small class of one-year-only types. Its design was inspired by Augustin Dupré's Libertas Americana medal. The Liberty Cap dies are often credited to Joseph Wright, who also cut the dies for the related cent, but they were more likely done by Henry Voigt.

Striking and Sharpness. Good-quality copper was used in these half cents, so they are often found light brown and on fairly smooth planchets. Unlike in later types, the borders on both sides are raised beads; certain of these beads can be weak, though this is not the norm. Some varieties are lightly defined at HALF CENT on the reverse, due to a combination of striking and shallow depth of letters in the die. This feature cannot be used in assigning a grade, as in lower grades (up to and including VG-8) these words may be completely missing.

Availability. Most half cents of 1793 are AG-3 to F-12. EF and AU examples are rare, and MS very rare (most being MS–60 to 63). Market grading is often liberal. Early American Coppers Club (EAC) "raw" grades often are lower than those of the certification services.

GRADING STANDARDS

MS-60 to 65 (Mint State). *Obverse:* In the lower ranges, MS–60 and 61, some light abrasions can be seen on the higher areas of the portrait. Luster in the field is incomplete, particularly in the center of the open areas. At the MS-63 level, luster should be complete, with no abrasions evident. In higher levels, the luster is deeper, and some original mint color may be seen. *Reverse:* In the lower ranges some abrasions are seen on the higher

1793; Bowers-Whitman–3, Cohen-3,
Breen-3. Graded MS-60BN.

areas of the leaves. Generally, luster is complete in all ranges, as the open areas are protected by the lettering and wreath. Otherwise, the same comments apply as for the obverse.

Illustrated coin: Well struck and nicely centered on the planchet, this example shows no sign of wear. Its color is a rich orange-brown overall, with a bit of darker gray-brown on the lower-right edge and field of the obverse. The faint roughness on the obverse is a flaw of the original planchet, and is not related to wear.

AU-50, 53, 55, 58 (About Uncirculated). *Obverse:* Friction is seen on the higher parts, particularly on the rounded cheek and on the higher strands of the hair. Friction and scattered marks are in the field, ranging from extensive at AU-50 to minimal at AU-58. Luster may be seen in protected areas, minimal at AU-50, but sometimes extensive on an AU-58 coin. Border beads, if well struck, are separate and boldly defined. *Reverse:* Friction

1793; BW-3, C-3, B-3. Graded AU-58.

is seen on the higher wreath leaves and (not as easy to discern) on the letters. The fields, protected by the designs, show friction, but not as noticeably as on the obverse. At AU–55 and 58 little if any friction is seen. The reverse may have original luster, toned brown, minimal on lower About Uncirculated grades, sometimes extensive at AU-58. Border beads, if well struck, are separate and boldly defined. Grading at the About Uncirculated level is mainly done by viewing the obverse.

Illustrated coin: Two tiny rim bruises can be seen, and some nicks can be seen as well under low magnification, none of which immediately draw the eye. This coin is about as good as can be found in this grade, as many examples of the date are porous.

EF-40, 45 (Extremely Fine). *Obverse:* Wear is seen on the portrait overall, with reduction or elimination of some separation of hair strands on the highest part. The cheek is ever so slightly flat on the highest part. Some leaves will retain some detail, especially where they join the stems. Luster is minimal or non-existent at EF-40 and may survive in traces in protected areas at EF-45. *Reverse:* Wear is seen on the highest wreath and rib-

1793; BW-3, C-3, B-3. Graded EF-45.

bon areas and the letters. Luster is minimal, but likely more noticeable than on the obverse, as the fields are protected by the designs and lettering.

Illustrated coin: The devices are crisp for the grade. Note the glossy golden-tan surfaces and the lack of meaningful contact marks.

VF-20, 30 (Very Fine). *Obverse:* Wear on the portrait has reduced the hair detail to indistinct or flat at the center on a VF-20 coin, with slightly more detail at VF-30. The thin, horizontal (more or less) ribbon near the top of the hair is distinct. The border beads are blended together, with many blurred or missing. No luster is seen. *Reverse:* The leaf details are nearly completely worn away at VF-20, and with slight detail at

1793; BW-3, C-3, B-3. Graded VF-30.

VF-30. The border beads are blended together, with many indistinct. Some berries in the sprays may be worn away, depending on the strike (on strong strikes they can be seen down into Very Good and Good grades). No luster is seen. HALF CENT may be weak, but is fully readable, on certain coins (such as BW-1, C-1, B-1) in which this feature was shallowly cut into the dies.

Illustrated coin: A small planchet crack at 8 o'clock on the obverse rim appears as struck. This planchet crack explains the softness of detail at the borders both in that area at 10 o'clock on the reverse.

F-12, 15 (Fine). *Obverse:* The hair details are mostly worn away, with about one-third visible, mainly at the edges. Border beads are weak or worn away in areas. F-15 shows slightly more detail. *Reverse:* The wreath leaves are worn flat, but their edges are distinct. HALF CENT may be missing on 1793 (Bowers-Whitman–1)—also true of lower grades given below. Border beads are weak or worn away in areas. F-15 shows slightly more detail.

1793; BW-3, C-3, B-3. Graded F-15.

Illustrated coin: Under magnification the surfaces are seen to be lightly porous.

VG-8, 10 (Very Good). *Obverse:* The portrait is well worn, although the eye can be seen, and the hair tips at the right show separation. Border beads are worn away, and the border blends into the field in most if not all of the periphery. LIBERTY and 1793 are bold. VG-10, not an official ANA grading designation, is sometimes applied to especially nice Very Good coins. *Reverse:* The wreath, bow, and lettering are seen in outline

1793; BW-4, C-4, B-4. Graded VG-8.

form, and some leaves and letters may be indistinct in parts. Border beads are worn away, and the border blends into the field in most if not all of the periphery.

Illustrated coin: The scratch from the E of LIBERTY to the base of the cap behind Liberty's head is less evident at the coin's unmagnified size.

G-4, 6 (Good). *Obverse:* The portrait is worn smooth and is seen only in outline form, although the eye position can be discerned. LIBERTY and 1793 are complete, although the date may be weak. *Reverse:* Extensive wear is seen overall. From half to two-thirds of the letters in UNITED STATES OF AMERICA and the fraction numerals are worn away. The reverse shows more evidence of wear than does the obverse,

1793; BW-2, C-2, B-2. Graded G-6.

and is key in assigning this grade. G-6 is often assigned to finer examples in this category.

AG-3 (About Good). *Obverse:* Wear is more extensive than on the preceding. The portrait is visible only in outline. LIBERTY is weak but usually fully discernible. 1793 is weak, and the bottoms of the digits may be worn away. *Reverse:* Parts of the wreath are visible in outline form, and all but a few letters are gone. Grading of AG-3 is usually done by the reverse.

1793; BW-3, C-3, B-3. Graded AG-3.

Fair-2 (Fair). *Obverse:* Worn nearly smooth. Date is partly visible, not necessarily clearly. Head of Miss Liberty is in outline form. Some letters of LIBERTY are discernible. *Reverse:* Worn nearly smooth. Peripheral letters are nearly all gone, with only vestiges remaining. Wreath is in outline form. HALF CENT ranges from readable to missing (the latter on certain die varieties as struck).

1793; BW-2, C-2, B-2. Graded Fair-2.

	Mintage	Cert	Avg	%MS	AG-3	G-4	VG-8	F-12	VF-20	EF-40	AU-50	MS-60BN	MS-63BN
1793	35,334	166	32.5	8%	$1,850	$3,750	$5,750	$9,500	$14,000	$24,000	$30,000	$60,000	$95,000

Auctions: $30,550, AU-53, March 2015; $18,800, AU-50, August 2015; $21,150, EF-45, January 2015; $16,450, EF-40, March 2015

LIBERTY CAP, HEAD FACING RIGHT (1794–1797)

Designer: *1794—Robert Scot; 1795–1797—Possibly Scot, John Smith Gardner, or other.*
Weight: *1794, thick planchet—6.74 grams; 1795–1797—5.44 grams.* **Composition:** *Copper.*
Diameter: *23.5 mm.* **Edge:** *1794, some of 1795, some of 1797—Lettered TWO HUNDRED FOR A DOLLAR; 1795, 1796, most of 1797—Plain; some of 1797—Gripped.* **Mint:** *Philadelphia.*

1794, High Relief Head; BW-9, C-9, B-9.

History. The design of the half cent changed in 1794 to a depiction, by Robert Scot, of Miss Liberty facing right. A smaller-headed portrait was used from 1795 on.

Striking and Sharpness. Half cents of 1794 usually are dark, with rough surfaces, and of low aesthetic quality. Most 1795's are on high-quality planchets, smooth and attractive, this being truer of the later plain-edge type than the early thick-planchet issue. Striking can be weak in areas. Often the denticles are incomplete on one or both sides. Many Small Head coins, particularly of 1795 to 1797, have very little detail on the hair, even in higher grades. Half cents of 1796 vary in quality; higher-grade pieces are usually attractive. Half cents of 1797 are usually seen in low grades and on poor planchets; striking varies widely, but is usually weak in areas. Denticles can be weak or can be prominent in various circulated grades, down to the lowest; on certain varieties of 1795 they are prominent even on well-worn coins. Grades must be assigned carefully, and expertise is recommended—combining knowledge of a given die variety and its relief or sharpness in the die, with observations of actual circulation wear. Grades of certified coins can vary widely in their interpretations.

Availability. As a general type, this issue is scarce, but available. Most are in lower grades, but VF and EF coins appear in the market with regularity.

GRADING STANDARDS

MS-60 to 70 (Mint State). *Obverse:* On MS–60 and 61 coins there are some traces of abrasion on the higher areas of the portrait. Luster in the field is incomplete, particularly in the center of the open areas. At MS-63, luster should be complete, and no abrasion is evident. At higher levels, the luster is deeper, and some original mint color may be seen. At MS-65 there are some scattered contact marks and possibly some traces of finger-

1794; BW-9, C-9, B-9. Graded MS-65.

prints or discoloration, but these should be minimal and not at all distracting. Above MS-65, a coin should approach perfection. *Reverse:* In the lower ranges some abrasions are seen on the higher areas of the leaves. Generally, luster is complete in all ranges, as the open areas are protected by the lettering and wreath. Otherwise, the same comments apply as for the obverse.

Illustrated coin: A spectacular coin of a year seldom seen in Mint State. Both sides have rich, brown surfaces. On the obverse the luster is light, while on the reverse it is not as noticeable. Note that the obverse die is in very high relief and of the Large Head style, while the reverse is in shallower relief.

AU-50, 53, 55, 58 (About Uncirculated). *Obverse:* Friction is seen on the higher parts, particularly the center of the portrait. Friction and scattered marks are in the field, ranging from extensive at AU-50 to minimal at AU-58. To reiterate: knowledge of the die variety is important. For certain shallow-relief dies (such as those of 1797) an About Uncirculated coin may appear to be in a lower grade. Luster may be seen in protected

1794; BW-1a, C-1a, B-1a. Graded AU-50.

areas, minimal at AU-50, but sometimes extensive on an AU-58 coin. *Reverse:* Friction is seen on the higher wreath leaves and (not as easy to discern) on the letters. The fields, protected by the designs, show friction, but not as noticeably as on the obverse. At AU–55 and 58 little if any friction is seen. The reverse may have original luster, toned brown, minimal on lower About Uncirculated grades, sometimes extensive on higher. Grading at the About Uncirculated level is mainly done by viewing the obverse.

Illustrated coin: Note faint ruddy highlights in the protected areas. The devices are boldly impressed. On this variety the 179 in the date was punched low into the die, partly effaced, then repunched in a higher position. On the reverse, a natural planchet fissure, small and as struck, runs from the rim through the M of AMERICA, and a smaller fissure runs from the rim to the E of AMERICA.

EF-40, 45 (Extremely Fine). *Obverse:* Wear is seen on the portrait overall, with some reduction or elimination of the separation of hair strands on the highest part. This varies by die variety, as some are better delineated than others. The cheek shows light wear. Luster is minimal or nonexistent at EF-40, and may survive in traces in protected areas (such as between the letters) at EF-45. *Reverse:* Wear is seen on the highest wreath and ribbon areas and the letters. Luster is minimal, but likely more noticeable than on the obverse, as the fields

1795, Pole to Cap, Lettered Edge;
BW-1, C-1, B-1. Graded EF-45.

are protected by the designs and lettering. Sharpness will vary depending on the die variety. Expect certain issues of 1794 and 1797 to be lighter.

Illustrated coin: This coin has bold details and excellent centering.

VF-20, 30 (Very Fine). *Obverse:* Wear on the portrait has reduced the hair detail to indistinct or flat at the center. The border denticles are blended together, with many indistinct. No luster is seen. Again, knowing details of the die variety is important. A VF–20 or 30 1797 is very different in appearance from a 1794, Large Head, in the same grade. *Reverse:* The leaf details are nearly completely worn away at VF-20, with slight

1797; BW-2, C-2. Graded VF-30.

detail at VF-30. The border denticles are blended together, with many indistinct. No luster is seen. The sharpness of details depends on the die variety. Half cents of 1797 require special care in their study.

Illustrated coin: Minor roughness is apparent at the center of both sides, undoubtedly a trace of microporosity from the blank planchet, although the devices are overall bold from a well executed strike.

F-12, 15 (Fine). *Obverse:* The hair details are mostly worn away, with about one-third visible, mainly at the edges. Border denticles are weak or worn away in areas. F-15 shows slightly more detail. *Reverse:* The wreath leaves are worn flat, but their edges are distinct. Border denticles are weak or worn away in areas. F-15 shows slightly more detail.

1794, High-Relief Head; BW-7, C-7, B-7. Graded F-15.

Illustrated coin: This late-die-state variety has a noticeable die crack in the E of UNITED.

VG-8, 10 (Very Good). *Obverse:* The portrait is well worn, although the eye can be seen, and the hair tips at the left show separation. Border denticles are worn away on some issues (not as much for 1795 coins), and the border blends into the field in most if not all of the periphery. LIBERTY and the date are bold. VG-10, not an official ANA grading designation, is sometimes applied to especially nice Very Good coins. *Reverse:* The

1794, High Relief Head; BW-9, C-9, B-9. Graded VG-8.

wreath, bow, and lettering are seen in outline form, and some leaves and letters may be indistinct in parts. Border denticles are worn away, and the border blends into the field in most if not all of the periphery. In certain die varieties and die states, especially of 1797, some letters may be very weak or missing.

Illustrated coin: This coin exhibits roughness in the fields, but the same does not apply to the devices.

G-4, 6 (Good). *Obverse:* The portrait is worn smooth and is seen only in outline form, although the eye position can be discerned. LIBERTY and the date are complete, although the date may be weak. Denticles are gone on some, but not all, die varieties. *Reverse:* Extensive wear is seen overall. From half to two-thirds of the letters in UNITED STATES OF AMERICA, and the fraction numerals, are worn away. Certain shallow-relief dies

1794; BW-2a, C-2a, B-2a. Graded G-4.

may have letters missing. G-6 is often assigned to finer examples in this category.

Illustrated coin: On this coin the surfaces are heavily worn, yet with considerable boldness of detail remaining on the obverse.

AG-3 (About Good). *Obverse:* Wear is more extensive than on the preceding. The portrait is visible only in outline. LIBERTY is weak but usually fully discernible. The date is weak, and the bottoms of the digits may be worn away. *Reverse:* Parts of the wreath are visible in outline form, and all but a few letters are gone. Grading of AG-3 is usually done by the reverse, as the obverse typically appears to be in a slightly higher grade. If split grading were used, more than just a few half cents of this type could be designated as G-4 / AG-3 or even G-6 / AG-3.

1795, Plain Edge, Punctuated Date; BW-5, C-4, B-4. Graded AG-3.

| 1794, Normal Head | 1794, High-Relief Head | 1795, With Pole | 1795, No Pole |

1795, Punctuated Date

	Mintage	Cert	Avg	%MS	AG-3	G-4	VG-8	F-12	VF-20	EF-40	AU-50	MS-60BN	MS-63BN
1794, All kinds	81,600												
1794, Normal Head		190	34.3	10%	$300	$575	$825	$1,500	$2,500	$5,000	$12,000	$22,500	$55,000
Auctions: $88,125, MS-63BN, April 2014													
1794, High-Relief Head		15	35.7	7%	$325	$600	$825	$1,600	$3,000	$6,200	$14,500	$25,000	$55,000
Auctions: $1,586, VF-20, October 2013													
1795, All kinds	139,690												
1795, Lettered Edge, With Pole		57	32.5	12%	$295	$570	$800	$1,500	$2,750	$6,000	$12,000	$17,000	$24,000
Auctions: $3,525, EF-40, September 2013; $2,820, VF-30, March 2015													
1795, Lettered Edge, Punctuated Date		5	19.2	0%	$295	$570	$800	$1,500	$3,000	$6,500	$12,000	$25,000	$45,000
Auctions: $12,925, AU-55, August 2013													
1795, Plain Edge, Punctuated Date		7	29.7	14%	$220	$475	$625	$1,200	$2,000	$4,800	$8,500	$14,000	$25,000
Auctions: $1,501, VF-20, August 2011													

| 1796, "Dr. Edwards" Copy | 1797, 1 Above 1 | 1797, Low Head |

	Mintage	Cert	Avg	%MS	AG-3	G-4	VG-8	F-12	VF-20	EF-40	AU-50	MS-60BN	MS-63BN
1795, Plain Edge, No Pole (a)		34	29.4	3%	$220	$475	$625	$1,200	$2,000	$4,800	$8,500	$14,000	$25,000
Auctions: $7,638, AU-55, June 2014													
1796, With Pole (b)	1,390	22	38.6	45%	$10,000	$18,000	$27,500	$37,500	$55,000	$75,000	$95,000	$150,000	
Auctions: $718,750, MS-65RB+, January 2014; $76,375, EF-40, August 2013													
1796, No Pole	(c)	1	62.0	100%	$17,500	$35,000	$65,000	$125,000	$180,000	$250,000	$300,000	$450,000	
Auctions: $891,250, MS-65BN, January 2014; $382, VG-8, September 2013													
1797, All kinds	127,840												
1797, 1 Above 1, Plain Edge		64	25.2	3%	$225	$425	$650	$1,100	$1,800	$4,000	$6,500	$15,000	
Auctions: $7,931, AU, March 2014													
1797, Plain Edge, Low Head		6	11.7	0%	$350	$575	$975	$2,250	$4,500	$15,000	—	—	—
Auctions: $1,495, VG-10, February 2012													
1797, Plain Edge		63	24.7	6%	$260	$475	$700	$1,250	$3,000	$6,000	$8,100	$16,000	
Auctions: $3,055, AU-50, April 2013; $823, F-12, August 2015; $400, VG-8, September 2015; $505, G-6, January 2015													
1797, Lettered Edge		4	14.3	0%	$700	$1,500	$3,000	$7,500	$17,500	$50,000	$75,000		
Auctions: $7,638, VG-10, November 2013													
1797, Gripped Edge		0	n/a		$20,000	$45,000	$75,000	$150,000	—	—	—		
Auctions: $195,500, G-6, September 2011													

a. Many of this date/variety were struck on cut-down cents (coins that had been rejected for circulation by Mint workers), or on planchets cut from English-made Talbot, Allum & Lee tokens (see the *Whitman Encyclopedia of Colonial and Early American Coins*).
b. The deceptive "Dr. Edwards" struck copy of this coin has a different head and larger letters, as pictured. c. Included in 1796, With Pole, mintage figure.

DRAPED BUST (1800–1808)

Designer: *Robert Scot.* Weight: *5.44 grams.* Composition: *Copper.*
Diameter: *23.5 mm.* Edge: *Plain.* Mint: *Philadelphia.*

1804, Crosslet 4, Stemless Wreath;
BW-10, C-12, B-11.

History. By the turn of the century the Draped Bust design was already familiar to Americans from its use on cents and silver coins. The motif was introduced to the half cent in 1800, and was used through 1808.

Striking and Sharpness. Striking varies. Weakness is often seen at the center of the obverse and on the wreath leaves on the reverse. Planchet quality is often porous and dark for 1802, 1803, 1807, and 1808 due to the copper stock used.

Availability. As a type, Draped Bust half cents are available in any grade desired, up to and including Mint State, the latter usually dated 1806 (occasionally 1800 and, less often, 1804). The year 1804 includes many different die varieties and die states. Apart from aspects of strike, cherrypicking for planchet quality is essential for 1802, 1803, 1807, and 1808.

GRADING STANDARDS

MS-60 to 70 (Mint State). *Obverse:* In the lower grades, MS–60 and 61, some slight abrasions can be seen on the higher areas of the portrait. Luster in the field is incomplete, particularly in the center of the open areas, which on this type are very extensive. At the MS-63 level, luster should be nearly complete, and no abrasions evident. In higher levels, the luster is complete and deeper and some original mint color may be seen. MS-64

1800; BW-1, C-1, B-1. Graded MS-62.

coins may have some slight discoloration or scattered contact marks. A well-graded MS-65 or higher coin has full, rich luster; no marks visible except under magnification; and a blend of brown toning or nicely mixed (not stained or blotchy) mint color and natural brown toning. *Reverse:* In the lower Mint State ranges some abrasions are seen on the higher areas of the leaves. Generally, luster is complete in all ranges, as the open areas are protected by the lettering and wreath. Sharpness of the leaves can vary by die variety, so check this aspect. Otherwise, the same comments apply as for the obverse.

AU-50, 53, 55, 58 (About Uncirculated). *Obverse:* Friction is seen on the higher parts, particularly the hair of Miss Liberty. Friction and scattered marks are in the field, ranging from extensive at AU-50 to minimal at AU-58. Luster may be seen in protected areas, minimal at AU-50, with more at AU-58. At AU-58 the field may retain some luster, as well. In all instances, the luster is lesser in area and in "depth" than on the reverse of this type.

1800; BW-1, C-1, B-1. Graded AU-58.

Reverse: Friction is evident on the higher wreath leaves and (not as easy to discern) on the letters. Again, the die variety should be checked. The fields, protected by the designs, show friction, but not as noticeably as on the obverse. At AU–55 and 58, little if any friction is seen. The reverse may have original luster, toned brown, minimal on lower About Uncirculated grades, often extensive at AU-58.

Illustrated coin: The motifs are very boldly rendered, except for partial weakness on the lower obverse and OF on the upper reverse, which is virtually missing due to the late die state.

EF-40, 45 (Extremely Fine). *Obverse:* Wear is seen on the portrait overall, with reduction or elimination of some separation of hair strands on the highest part. The cheek shows light wear. Luster is minimal or non-existent at EF-40, and may survive among the letters of LIBERTY at EF-45. *Reverse:* Wear is seen on the highest wreath and ribbon areas, and the letters. Luster is minimal, but likely more noticeable than on the obverse, as the fields are protected by the designs and lettering.

1800; BW-1, C-1, B-1. Graded EF-40.

VF-20, 30 (Very Fine). *Obverse:* Wear on the portrait has reduced the hair detail to indistinct or flat at the center. The border denticles are blended together, with many indistinct. No luster is seen. *Reverse:* The leaf details are nearly completely worn away at VF-20, and with slight detail at VF-30. The border denticles are blended together, with many indistinct. No luster is seen.

Illustrated coin: Struck from a later die state, the reverse shows a bisecting die crack.

1803; BW-1, C-1, B-1. Graded VF-20.

F-12, 15 (Fine). *Obverse:* The hair details are mostly worn away, with about one-third visible, mainly at the edges. Border denticles are weak or worn away in areas. F-15 shows slightly more detail. *Reverse:* The wreath leaves are worn flat, but their edges are distinct. HALF CENT may be missing on weakly struck varieties (also true of lower grades given below). Border denticles are weak or worn away in areas. F-15 shows slightly more detail.

Illustrated coin: This is the "Spiked Chin" variety, so called because of a thorn-like projection from the chin. The variety does not affect the grade.

1804, "Spiked Chin"; BW-5, C-8, B-7. Graded F-15.

VG-8, 10 (Very Good). *Obverse:* The portrait is well worn, although the eye can be seen, as can hints of hair detail (some at the left shows separation). Curls now appear as mostly solid blobs. Border denticles are worn away on most varieties, and the rim, although usually present, begins to blend into the field. LIBERTY and the date are bold. VG-10, not an official ANA grading designation, is sometimes applied to especially nice Very Good coins. *Reverse:* The wreath, bow, and lettering are seen in outline form, and some leaves and letters may be indistinct in parts. The border may blend into the field on some of the periphery.

1804, Plain 4, Stems to Wreath;
BW-12, C-11, B-12. Graded VG-10.

Illustrated coin: This coin is has many scratches, which detract from overall eye appeal.

G-4, 6 (Good). *Obverse:* The portrait is worn smooth and is seen only in outline form, although the eye position can be discerned. LIBERTY and the date are complete, although the date may be weak. The border blends into the field more extensively than on the preceding, but significant areas are still seen. *Reverse:* Extensive wear is seen overall. From one-half to two-thirds of the letters in UNITED STATES OF AMERICA and the fraction numerals are worn away. G-6 is often assigned to finer examples in this category.

1808, 8 Over 7; BW-2, C-2, B-2. Graded G-4.

Illustrated coin: A slightly off-center strike has allowed areas of heavier wear to creep in near the borders. There are many noticeable scratches on the obverse.

AG-3 (About Good). *Obverse:* Wear is more extensive than on the preceding. The portrait is visible only in outline. LIBERTY is weak but usually discernible. The date is weak, and the bottoms of the digits may be worn away, but must be identifiable. *Reverse:* Parts of the wreath are visible in outline form, and all but a few letters are gone.

1802, 2 Over 0; BW-2, C-2, B-2. Graded AG-3.

1st Reverse
(Style of 1800)

2nd Reverse
(Style of 1803)

1803, Normally Spaced 3

1803, Widely Spaced 3

1804, Plain 4

1804, Crosslet 4

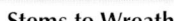

Stems to Wreath

Stemless Wreath

1804, "Spiked Chin"

	Mintage	Cert	Avg	%MS	AG-3	G-4	VG-8	F-12	VF-20	EF-40	AU-50	MS-60BN	MS-63BN
1800	202,908	202	45.1	30%	$40	$70	$90	$150	$300	$700	$1,000	$2,250	$4,000
	Auctions: $282, VF-35, May 2015; $329, VF-25, January 2015; $4,113, VF-20, June 2013												
1802, 2 Over 0, Reverse of 1800	(a)	2	2.0	0%	$10,000	$20,000	$35,000	$55,000	$80,000	$100,000	—		
	Auctions: $35,938, VG-8, April 2009												
1802, 2 Over 0, Second Reverse	20,266	46	9.3	0%	$350	$750	$1,700	$4,000	$12,500	$25,000	—		
	Auctions: $4,406, F-12, February 2013; $940, G-6, June 2015												
1803	(b)	193	32.1	10%	$35	$75	$100	$160	$325	$950	$1,500	$3,200	$7,000
	Auctions: $646, VF-35, August 2015; $376, VF-25, June 2015; $235, VF-30, February 2015; $153, VG-8, February 2015												
1803, Widely Spaced 3	92,000	22	31.0	9%	$35	$75	$100	$160	$325	$950	$1,500	$3,500	$7,500
	Auctions: $1,840, AU-55, April 2012												
1804, All kinds	1,055,312												
1804, Plain 4, Stems to Wreath		11	32.5	0%	$40	$75	$120	$200	$475	$1,300	$2,200	$4,000	
	Auctions: $4,994, AU-58, October 2013												
1804, Plain 4, Stemless Wreath		206	43.7	17%	$35	$70	$90	$120	$200	$365	$675	$1,300	$2,800
	Auctions: $940, AU-58, June 2015; $646, AU-55, October 2015; $588, AU-55, August 2015; $259, AU-50, May 2015												
1804, Crosslet 4, Stemless		57	54.8	46%	$35	$70	$90	$120	$200	$365	$675	$1,300	$2,800
	Auctions: $5,141, MS-64BN, September 2013; $376, EF-40, January 2015												
1804, Crosslet 4, Stems		117	45.4	17%	$35	$70	$90	$120	$200	$375	$675	$1,300	$2,800
	Auctions: $705, AU-55, March 2015; $470, EF-45, October 2015; $364, EF-40, April 2015; $282, VF-35, August 2015												
1804, "Spiked Chin"		390	43.5	13%	$35	$85	$100	$140	$250	$425	$850	$1,800	$3,600
	Auctions: $764, AU-53BN, September 2015; $646, AU-50, February 2015; $423, EF-45, June 2015; $247, EF-40, July 2015												

a. Included in 1800 mintage figure. b. Included in 1802, 2 Over 0, Second Reverse, mintage figure.

| 1805, Medium 5 | 1805, Small 5 | 1805, Large 5 |

| 1806, Small 6 | 1806, Large 6 | 1808, 8 Over 7 | 1808, Normal Date |

	Mintage	Cert	Avg	%MS	AG-3	G-4	VG-8	F-12	VF-20	EF-40	AU-50	MS-60BN	MS-63BN
1805, All kinds	814,464												
1805, Medium 5, Stemless		47	38.3	11%	$35	$70	$90	$120	$200	$400	$750	$1,350	$3,000
Auctions: $4,113, MS-64BN, April 2014; $517, EF-45, January 2015; $447, EF-40, January 2015													
1805, Small 5, Stems		7	13.9	0%	$500	$1,000	$1,650	$4,000	$8,000	$17,500	$55,000		
Auctions: $135, VF-20, April 2014													
1805, Large 5, Stems		29	34.1	0%	$35	$70	$90	$120	$225	$415	$850	$1,700	$3,750
Auctions: $1,293, AU-55, July 2015; $353, VF-35, June 2015; $223, VF-30, July 2015													
1806, All kinds	356,000												
1806, Small 6, Stems		20	29.7	0%	$90	$235	$425	$750	$1,650	$3,500	$9,000	$12,500	
Auctions: $5,464, AU, March 2014													
1806, Small 6, Stemless		127	45.6	18%	$35	$70	$90	$120	$175	$325	$675	$1,200	$2,900
Auctions: $823, AU-58, January 2015; $564, AU-50, September 2015; $517, AU-50, August 2015; $329, EF-45, February 2015													
1806, Large 6, Stems		90	50.8	43%	$35	$70	$90	$120	$175	$325	$675	$1,200	$2,900
Auctions: $5,581, MS-63RB, June 2014													
1807	476,000	274	37.0	7%	$35	$75	$100	$125	$200	$500	$1,000	$2,000	$3,750
Auctions: $1,175, AU-58, February 2013; $212, VF-20, May 2015													
1808, All kinds	400,000												
1808, Normal Date		134	30.2	1%	$35	$75	$100	$125	$220	$525	$1,300	$2,500	$5,000
Auctions: $823, AU-50, June 2014; $447, EF-45, January 2015; $200, VF-25, June 2015													
1808, 8 Over 7		46	20.0	0%	$80	$150	$350	$750	$2,000	$4,000	$10,000		
Auctions: $2,585, EF-40, April 2013													

CLASSIC HEAD (1809–1836)

Designer: *John Reich.* **Weight:** *5.44 grams.* **Composition:** *Copper.*
Diameter: *23.5 mm.* **Edge:** *Plain.* **Mint:** *Philadelphia.*

Circulation Strike
1835; BW-1, C-1, B-1.

Proof
1836; BW-1.

History. The Classic Head design (by Mint engraver John Reich) made its first appearance on the half cent in 1809, a year after it was adopted for the one-cent coin. A very similar motif of Miss Liberty was used on the quarter eagles and half eagles of the 1830s.

Striking and Sharpness. Coins of 1809 to 1811 usually have areas of light or incomplete striking. Grading coins of the early years requires special care and expertise. Sometimes coins as high as MS appear "blurry" in areas, due to the dies and striking. Those of later years are often found well struck and are easier to grade. Areas to check include the denticles and rims on both sides, the star centers and hair detail on the obverse, and the leaf detail on the reverse.

Availability. As a type this issue is found easily enough, although 1811 is scarce and 1831 and 1836 are notable rarities. MS coins from old hoards exist for certain of the later dates, particularly 1828, 1833, and 1835, but often have spotting, and many seen in the marketplace are cleaned or recolored. Care is advised. Although 1809–1811 half cents are often seen with extensive wear, those of the 1820s and 1830s are not often seen less than VF, as they did not circulate extensively.

GRADING STANDARDS

MS-60 to 70 (Mint State). *Obverse:* In the lower grades, MS–60 and 61, some slight abrasions can be seen on the portrait, most evident on the cheek, as the hair details are complex on this type. Luster in the field is complete or nearly complete. At MS-63, luster should be complete, and no abrasions are evident. In higher levels, the luster is complete and deeper, and some original mint color may be seen. MS-64 coins may have

1810; BW-1, C-1, B-1. Graded MS-64BN.

some slight discoloration or scattered contact marks. A well-graded MS-65 or higher coin has full, rich luster, with no marks visible except under magnification, and has a nice blend of brown toning or nicely mixed (not stained or blotchy) mint color and natural brown toning. Coins dated 1809 to 1811 may exhibit significant weakness of details due to striking (and/or, in the case of most 1811's, porous planchet stock). *Reverse:* In the lower Mint State grades, some abrasions are seen on the higher areas of the leaves. Mint luster is complete in all Mint State grades, as the open areas are protected by the lettering and wreath. Sharpness of the leaves can vary by die variety, so check this aspect. Otherwise, the same comments apply as for the obverse. Coins dated 1809 to 1811 may exhibit significant weakness of details due to striking (and/or, in the case of most 1811's, porous planchet stock).

Illustrated coin: Some surface marks on the coin holder obscure the reverse, but no such marks mar the surface of this sharply struck coin.

AU-50, 53, 55, 58 (About Uncirculated). *Obverse:* Friction is seen on the higher parts, particularly the cheek and hair (under magnification) of Miss Liberty. Friction and scattered marks are in the field, ranging from extensive at AU-50 to minimal at AU-58. Luster may be seen in protected areas, minimal at the AU-50 level, with more showing at AU-58. At AU-58 the field may retain some luster as well. *Reverse:* Friction is seen on the

1828, 12 Stars; BW-3, C-2, B-3. Graded AU-58.

higher wreath leaves and (not as easy to discern) on the letters. Again, half cents of 1809 to 1811 require special attention. The fields, protected by the designs, show friction, but not as noticeably as on the obverse. At AU–55 and 58, little if any friction is seen. The reverse may have original luster, toned brown, minimal on lower About Uncirculated grades, often extensive at AU-58.

EF-40, 45 (Extremely Fine). *Obverse:* Wear is seen on the portrait overall, with reduction or elimination of some separation of hair strands. The cheek shows light wear. Luster is minimal or nonexistent at EF-40 but may survive among the letters of LIB-ERTY at EF-45. *Reverse:* Wear is seen on the highest wreath and ribbon areas and the letters. Luster is minimal, but likely more noticeable than on the obverse, as the fields are protected by the designs and lettering.

1831, Original; BW-1, C-1, B-1. Graded EF-45.

VF-20, 30 (Very Fine). *Obverse:* Wear on the portrait has reduced the hair detail, but much can still be seen (in this respect the present type differs dramatically from earlier types). *Reverse:* The wreath details, except for the edges of the leaves, are worn away at VF-20, and have slightly more detail at VF-30.

Illustrated coin: This coin is lightly struck at the left-reverse border, despite overall bold striking elsewhere.

1811, Close Date; BW-3, C-3, B-2. Graded VF-30.

F-12, 15 (Fine). *Obverse:* The hair details are fewer than at the preceding level, but many are still present. Stars have flat centers. F-15 shows slightly more detail. *Reverse:* The wreath leaves are worn flat, but their edges are distinct. F-15 shows slightly more detail.

1809, Normal Date. Graded F-15.

VG-8, 10 (Very Good). *Obverse:* The portrait is well worn, although the eye and ear can be seen, as can some hair detail. The border is well defined in most areas. *Reverse:* The wreath, bow, and lettering are seen in outline form, and some leaves and letters may be indistinct in parts. The border is well defined in most areas.

1809, 9 Over Inverted 9; BW-6, C-5, B-5. Graded VG-10.

G-4, 6 (Good). *Obverse:* The portrait is worn smooth and is seen only in outline form. Much of LIBERTY on the headband is readable, but the letters are weak. The stars are bold in outline. Much of the rim can be discerned. *Reverse:* Extensive wear is seen overall. Lettering in UNITED STATES OF AMERICA ranges from weak but complete (although the ANA grading guidelines allow for only half to be readable; the ANA text

1811; BW-1, C-1, B-1. Graded G-6.

illustrates the words in full) to having perhaps a third of the letters missing. HALF CENT is usually bold.

Illustrated coin: While ultimately well-preserved for the grade, this coin is a bit rough in texture, with light pitting and traces of old, inactive surface build up.

AG-3 (About Good). *Obverse:* Wear is more extensive than on the preceding. The portrait is visible only in outline. A few letters of LIBERTY are discernible in the headband. The stars are weak or worn away on their outer edges. The date is light. *Reverse:* The wreath is visible in outline form. Most or even all of UNITED STATES OF AMER-ICA is worn away. HALF CENT is usually readable.

1811; BW-1, C-1, B-1. Graded AG-3.

PF-60 to 70 (Proof). Proofs were struck of various years in the 1820s and 1830s, with 1831 and 1836 being great rarities (these dates were also restruck at the Mint circa 1859 and later). Some prooflike circulation strikes (especially of the 1833 date) have been certified as Proofs. Except for the years 1831 and 1836, for which Proofs are unequivocal, careful study is advised when contemplating the purchase of a coin described as Proof.

1831, First Restrike; BW-1a, C-PR-2, B-2. Graded PF-66BN.

Blotchy and recolored Proofs are often seen, but hardly ever described as such. Probably fewer than 25 of the Proofs of this type are truly pristine—without one problem or another. *Obverse and Reverse:* Proofs that are extensively hairlined or have dull surfaces, this being characteristic of many issues (1831 and 1836 usually excepted), are graded PF–60 to 62 or 63. This includes artificially toned and recolored coins, a secret that isn't really secret among knowledgeable collectors and dealers, but is rarely described in print. To qualify as PF-65 or higher, hairlines should be microscopic, and there should be no trace of friction. Surfaces should be prooflike or, better, fully mirrored, without dullness.

Illustrated coin: Note the traces of mint red throughout and the blue iridescence of the reverse. The reverse die is severely cracked from the F in OF to the T of UNITED.

1809, Small 0 Inside 0   1809, 9 Over Inverted 9   1809, Normal Date

1811, Wide Date   1811, Close Date   1828, 13 Stars   1828, 12 Stars

	Mintage	Cert	Avg	%MS	G-4	VG-8	F-12	VF-20	EF-40	AU-50	MS-60BN	MS-63BN	MS-63RB
1809, All kinds	1,154,572												
1809, Normal Date		403	45.0	24%	$55	$65	$80	$100	$150	$300	$850	$1,500	$2,000
Auctions: $588, MS-61BN, June 2015; $823, AU-58, January 2015; $388, AU-55, March 2015; $176, AU-50, January 2015													
1809, Small o Inside 0		16	36.8	0%	$55	$80	$110	$160	$450	$900	$1,400	$5,000	
Auctions: $55, G-4, January 2013													
1809, 9 Over Inverted 9 (a)		228	49.9	19%	$55	$75	$100	$150	$375	$750	$1,300	$2,200	$3,000
Auctions: $1,116, AU-58, June 2015; $423, AU-50, January 2015; $306, EF-45, September 2015; $200, VF-30, May 2015													
1810	215,000	97	41.4	19%	$55	$75	$125	$270	$575	$1,000	$2,000	$3,200	$6,750
Auctions: $2,800, MS-63BN, April 2014; $376, VF-30, May 2015													
1811, All kinds	63,140												
1811, Wide Date		4	27.5	0%	$400	$800	$1,650	$2,750	$6,500	$10,000	$25,000	$50,000	
Auctions: $617, VF-20, January 2015; $564, VF-20, February 2015; $376, VF-20, August 2015													
1811, Close Date		6	23.7	0%	$375	$700	$1,600	$2,500	$6,500	$10,000	$25,000	$50,000	
Auctions: $26,450, AU-50, September 2011													
1811, Reverse of 1802, Unofficial Restrike (b)		5	63.8	100%					—	—	$16,000	$22,000	$27,500
Auctions: $23,000, MS-64BN, September 2008													
1825	63,000	282	48.9	25%	$55	$65	$80	$100	$200	$325	$900	$1,800	$3,000
Auctions: $529, MS-61BN, June 2015; $564, AU-55, May 2015; $282, AU-55, January 2015; $259, EF-45, June 2015													
1826	234,000	357	49.7	31%	$55	$65	$80	$90	$150	$300	$600	$1,000	$1,300
Auctions: $999, MS-63BN, August 2015; $764, MS-62BN, September 2015; $306, MS-61BN, May 2015; $165, EF-45, August 2015													
1828, All kinds	606,000												
1828, 13 Stars		136	49.3	38%	$50	$60	$70	$100	$120	$225	$350	$600	$1,000
Auctions: $1,028, MS-64RB, January 2015; $999, MS-64BN, January 2015; $590, MS-63BN, February 2015; $309, MS-62BN, September 2015													
1828, 12 Stars		218	50.6	25%	$50	$60	$75	$120	$250	$425	$1,300	$1,850	$3,500
Auctions: $2,468, MS-63BN, February 2014													
1829	487,000	348	51.4	45%	$50	$60	$70	$100	$140	$220	$400	$700	$1,100
Auctions: $482, MS-63BN, February 2015; $764, MS-61BN, June 2015; $517, AU-58, September 2015; $235, AU-53, September 2015													

a. Traditionally called 9 Over Inverted 9, but recent research shows it not to have an inverted digit. b. This coin is extremely rare.

| 1831, Proof, Restrike | Reverse, 1831–1836 | Reverse, 1840–1857 |

	Mintage	Cert	Avg	%MS	VG-8	F-12	VF-20	EF-40	AU-50	MS-60BN	MS-63BN	MS-63RB	MS-65RB
											PF-60BN	PF-63BN	PF-65BN
1831, Original (a)		6	52.0	50%					$50,000		—		
	Auctions: No auction records available.												
1831, Original, Proof (b)	2,200	6	54.7								$65,000	—	
	Auctions: $57,281, PF-60BN, January 2014												
1831, Restrike, Large Berries, Proof (Reverse of 1836)	*25–35*	9	65.7								$10,000	$15,000	$25,000
	Auctions: $47,000, PF-65RB, February 2014												
1831, Restrike, Small Berries, Proof (Reverse of 1840–1857)	*10–15*	0	n/a								$14,000	$21,500	$40,000
	Auctions: $63,250, PF-66BN, July 2009												
1832 (c)	51,000	430	52.9	38%	$50	$70	$85	$125	$200	$325	$475	$875	$4,000
	Auctions: $999, MS-64BN, June 2015; $306, MS-62BN, January 2015; $282, MS-61BN, May 2015; $259, AU-58, August 2015												
1832, Proof	*10–15*	1	64.0								$7,000	$10,000	$17,500
	Auctions: $44,063, PF-64BN, January 2014												
1833 (c)	103,000	619	58.2	66%	$50	$70	$85	$125	$200	$325	$450	$750	$3,500
	Auctions: $940, MS-64BN, February 2015; $823, MS-64BN, June 2015; $410, MS-63BN, May 2015; $212, AU-58, January 2015												
1833, Proof	*25–35*	15	64.1								$5,000	$6,000	$10,500
	Auctions: $11,163, PF-65BN, March 2013												
1834 (c)	141,000	638	55.8	50%	$50	$70	$85	$125	$200	$300	$450	$750	$3,500
	Auctions: $541, MS-64BN, January 2015; $423, MS-63BN, September 2015; $353, MS-62BN, March 2015; $259, AU-58, January 2015												
1834, Proof	*25–35*	13	64.8								$5,000	$6,000	$11,000
	Auctions: $18,800, PF-64RB, August 2013												
1835 (c)	398,000	1,206	55.6	55%	$50	$70	$85	$125	$200	$325	$450	$750	$3,500
	Auctions: $823, MS-64BN, August 2015; $646, MS-64, March 2015; $353, MS-63BN, May 2015; $329, MS-62BN, April 2015												
1835, Proof	*15–20*	2	64.0								$5,000	$6,000	$10,500
	Auctions: $11,163, PF-64RB, January 2014												
1836, Original, Proof	*140–240*	13	63.8								$6,000	$8,000	$12,500
	Auctions: $12,925, PF-64BN, April 2013												
1836, Restrike, Proof (Reverse of 1840–1857)	*8–15*	2	64.5								$9,000	$17,000	$30,000
	Auctions: No auction records available.												

a. Circulation strike. **b.** Beware of altered date. **c.** The figures given here are thought to be correct, although Mint records report these quantities for 1833 through 1836 rather than 1832 through 1835.

1837 "HALF CENT" TOKEN

The last circulation-strike half cents of the Classic Head design were minted in 1835, and Proofs of the series were made in 1836 (see next section). No half cents of any format were minted in 1837, 1838, or 1839—it would be 1840 before the denomination started up again, with the Braided Hair type.

To help fill that gap for date-by-date collectors, in the 1930s Wayte Raymond included in his "National" brand of coin albums a slot for a half cent–sized Hard Times token dated 1837. The token had been privately struck in the thousands as a supply of small change in the midst of the country's financial stagnation of the 1830s and early 1840s. It joined several hundred types of larger, cent-sized copper tokens, all privately manufactured and put into circulation by enterprising businesspeople, as substitutes for the federal government's half cents and large cents that were no longer circulating in any quantity.

Raymond's dignifying of the 1837 token brought about a new numismatic tradition. Half-cent collectors began to include the token—despite its not being official federal coinage—in their collections, and today the "Half Cent Worth of Pure Copper" is often found among their treasured coins.

	G-4	VG-8	F-12	VF-20	EF-40	AU-50	MS-60
1837 Token (*not a coin*)	$75	$85	$100	$140	$250	$350	$800

BRAIDED HAIR (1840–1857)

Designer: *Christian Gobrecht.* **Weight:** *5.44 grams.* **Composition:** *Copper.*
Diameter: *23 mm.* **Edge:** *Plain.* **Mint:** *Philadelphia.*

Circulation Strike	**Proof**
1853; BW-1, C-1, B-1.	*1843; BW-1, C-PO-4, B-1.*

History. The Braided Hair half cent debuted in 1840, a year after the same design was introduced on copper cents. There was scant commercial demand for this denomination, so only Proofs were struck from 1840 to 1848 and in 1852. (In 1849–1851 and 1853–1857 both Proofs and circulation strikes were made.) Ultimately the half cent was discontinued by the Act of February 21, 1857. After that point the coins were rapidly withdrawn from circulation, and by 1860 virtually all had disappeared from commerce.

Striking and Sharpness. Many if not most Braided Hair half cents are well struck, and nearly all are on good planchet stock. Check these points for sharpness: the denticles on both sides; the star centers and hair detail on the obverse; and the leaf detail on the reverse.

Availability. Because Braided Hair half cents were not struck for circulation until 1849 and they did not circulate after the 1850s, they never acquired extensive wear. Most coins grade EF-40 and finer. Lower grades are sometimes seen, but are not in demand.

GRADING STANDARDS

MS-60 to 70 (Mint State). *Obverse:* In the lower Mint State grades, MS–60 and 61, some slight abrasion can be seen on the portrait, most evidently on the cheek. Check the tip of the coronet as well. Luster in the field is complete, or nearly so. At MS-63, luster should be complete, and no abrasions evident. At higher levels, the luster is complete and deeper, and some original mint color may be seen. Mint frost on this type is usually

1849, Large Date; BW-3, C-1, B-4. Graded MS-63BN.

deep, sometimes satiny, but hardly ever prooflike. MS-64 coins may have some slight discoloration or scattered contact marks. A well-graded MS-65 or higher coin has full, rich luster; no contact marks visible except under magnification; and a nice blend of brown toning or nicely mixed (not stained or blotchy) mint color and natural brown toning. The late Walter Breen stated that he had never seen an 1853 (common date) half cent with extensive original mint color, but these are plentiful with brown-toned surfaces. *Reverse:* In the lower Mint State grades some abrasions are seen on the higher areas of the leaves. Mint luster is complete in all Mint State grades, as the open areas are protected by the lettering and wreath.

AU-50, 53, 55, 58 (About Uncirculated). *Obverse:* Wear is evident on the cheek, the hair above the forehead, and the tip of the coronet. Friction is evident in the field. At AU-58, luster may be present except in the center of the fields. As the grades go down to AU-50, wear is more evident on the portrait. Wear is seen on the stars, but is not as easy to discern as it is elsewhere. At AU-50 there is either no luster or only traces of luster close

1849, Large Date; BW-3, C-1, B-4. Graded AU-50.

to the letters and devices. *Reverse:* Wear is most evident on the highest areas of the leaves and the ribbon bow. Luster is present in the fields. As the grades go downward from AU-58 to 50, wear increases and luster decreases. At the AU-50 level there is either no luster or traces of luster close to the letters and devices.

Illustrated coin: This coin shows Full Details on both sides, and has eye-pleasing, light-brown surfaces.

EF-40, 45 (Extremely Fine). *Obverse:* Wear is more extensive on the portrait, including the cheek, hair, and coronet. The star centers are worn down slightly. Traces of luster are minimal, if at all existent. *Reverse:* The centers of the leaves are well worn, with detail visible only near the edges of the leaves and nearby, with the higher parts worn flat. Letters show significant wear. Luster, if present, is minimal.

1853; BW-1, C-1, B-1. Graded EF-40.

VF-20, 30 (Very Fine). *Obverse:* Wear is more extensive than at the preceding levels. Some of the strands of hair are fused together. The center radials of the stars are worn nearly completely away. *Reverse:* The leaves show more extensive wear, with details visible at the edges, and only minimally and not on all leaves. The lettering shows smooth, even wear.

The Braided Hair half cent is seldom collected in grades lower than VF-20.

1849, Large Date; BW-3, C-1, B-4. Graded VF-30.

PF-60 to 70 (Proof). For the issues of 1840 to 1848, the 1849, Small Date, and the issues of 1852, only Proofs were made, without related examples for circulation. All were restruck at the Mint. Generally, the quality of these Proofs is very good, with excellent striking of details and nice planchet quality. *Obverse and Reverse:* Superb gems at PF–65 and 66 show hairlines only under high magnification, and at PF–67 none are seen. The

1843, First Restrike; BW-2, C-SR-5, B-2. PF-64RB.

fields are deeply mirrorlike. There is no evidence of friction. At lower levels, hairlines increase, with a profusion at PF–60 to 62 (and also a general dullness of the fields). Typical color for an undipped coin ranges from light or iridescent brown to brown with some traces of mint color. Except for issues in the 1850s, Proofs are nearly always BN or, less often, RB. The rare Proofs of the 1840s are sometimes seen with light wear and can be classified according to the About Uncirculated and Extremely Fine comments above, except in place of "luster" read "Proof surface."

Illustrated coin: Overall this coin's surfaces are smooth, and the dominant sandy-olive patina belies semi reflective tendencies in the fields and gold, apricot and lilac undertones when viewed under direct light.

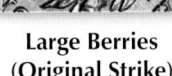

Large Berries	**Small Berries**
(Original Strike)	**(Restrike)**

	Mintage	Cert	Avg	%MS	VG-8	F-12	VF-20	EF-40	AU-50	MS-60BN	MS-63BN	MS-63RB	MS-65RB
										PF-60BN	PF-63BN	PF-65BN	
1840, Original, Proof	*125–150*	11	63.8							$5,350	$6,500	$9,250	
	Auctions: $7,475, PF-62BN, August 2006												
1840, Restrike, Proof	*21–25*	8	64.5							$5,350	$6,500	$9,250	
	Auctions: $25,850, PF-65RB, June 2014												
1841, Original, Proof	*150–250*	19	64.2							$4,350	$5,500	$8,750	
	Auctions: $21,150, PF-65BN, September 2013; $4,700, PF-58, September 2015												
1841, Restrike, Proof	*15–19*	8	64.6							$4,350	$5,500	$8,750	
	Auctions: $8,625, PF-66BN, June 2008												

1849, Small Date
(Proof Only)

1849, Large Date

	Mintage	Cert	Avg	%MS	VG-8	F-12	VF-20	EF-40	AU-50	MS-60BN	MS-63BN	MS-63RB	MS-65RB
											PF-60BN	PF-63BN	PF-65BN
1842, Original, Proof	120–180	5	63.4								$5,500	$7,000	$10,000
Auctions: $15,275, PF-64BN, February 2014													
1842, Restrike, Proof	35–45	10	64.7								$4,350	$5,500	$8,750
Auctions: $20,700, PF-65RB, April 2010													
1843, Original, Proof	125–200	6	62.7								$4,350	$5,500	$8,750
Auctions: $73,438, PF-65RD, April 2014													
1843, Restrike, Proof	37–44	7	64.7								$4,600	$5,700	$8,750
Auctions: $9,988, PF-64BN, February 2014													
1844, Original, Proof	120–180	9	62.9								$5,000	$6,000	$9,000
Auctions: $4,888, PF-50, May 2008													
1844, Restrike, Proof	21–26	2	65.5								$4,750	$5,750	$8,750
Auctions: $1,777, PF, February 2014													
1845, Original, Proof	110–170	3	65.0								$4,850	$6,000	$9,250
Auctions: $23,500, PF-64BN, April 2013													
1845, Restrike, Proof	20–24	9	64.4								$4,300	$5,400	$9,000
Auctions: $9,200, PF-65BN, October 2011													
1846, Original, Proof	125–200	9	63.8								$5,000	$6,000	$9,000
Auctions: $21,150, PF-64BN, January 2014													
1846, Restrike, Proof	19–24	7	65.1								$4,600	$5,750	$8,750
Auctions: $23,630, PF-66BN, June 2014; $15,275, PF-66BN, October 2015													
1847, Original, Proof	200–300	10	64.4								$5,000	$6,000	$9,250
Auctions: $5,288, PF-63BN, January 2014													
1847, Restrike, Proof	33–44	15	64.7								$4,500	$5,500	$8,500
Auctions: $15,275, PF-66BN, January 2014													
1848, Original, Proof	150–225	4	64.0								$5,350	$6,250	$9,250
Auctions: $10,350, PF-64RB, September 2003													
1848, Restrike, Proof	40–47	12	64.5								$4,500	$5,600	$8,500
Auctions: $6,169, PF-64BN, February 2014													
1849, Large Date	39,864	285	58.0	62%	$55	$70	$90	$150	$240	$500	$700	$900	$2,700
Auctions: $1,058, MS-63BN, February 2015; $541, MS-63, March 2015; $353, MS-62BN, October 2015; $329, AU-58, June 2015													
1849, Original, Small Date, Proof	70–90	4	59.0								$4,500	$5,500	$10,000
Auctions: $8,813, PF-64RB, April 2014													
1849, Restrike, Small Date, Proof	30–36	4	64.3								$4,850	$5,750	$9,750
Auctions: $7,344, PF-64BN, January 2014													
1850	39,812	237	57.8	58%	$55	$70	$90	$150	$240	$500	$700	$1,100	$3,000
Auctions: $1,880, MS-64BN, September 2013; $588, MS-62BN, March 2015													
1850, Proof	10–20	8	62.8								$5,000	$7,000	$13,000
Auctions: $5,875, PF-63BN, January 2014													
1851	147,672	786	58.4	63%	$50	$65	$80	$100	$175	$275	$550	$650	$2,000
Auctions: $1,175, MS-64RB, October 2015; $705, MS-64BN, August 2015; $441, MS-64, March 2015; $447, MS-63BN, January 2015													
1851, Proof	10–20	0	n/a								$7,000	$8,000	$20,000
Auctions: No auction records available.													

	Mintage	Cert	Avg	%MS	VG-8	F-12	VF-20	EF-40	AU-50	MS-60BN	MS-63BN PF-60BN	MS-63RB PF-63BN	MS-65RB PF-65BN
1852, Original, Proof	*225–325*	0	n/a									—	
Auctions: No auction records available.													
1852, Restrike, Proof	*110–140*	34	64.3								$4,000	$6,000	$9,000
Auctions: $6,463, PF, August 2013													
1853	129,694	996	60.9	79%	$50	$65	$80	$100	$175	$275	$550	$650	$1,700
Auctions: $940, MS-65BN, September 2015; $646, MS-64BN, August 2015; $329, MS-63BN, May 2015; $223, MS-61BN, May 2015													
1854	55,358	724	61.5	83%	$50	$65	$80	$100	$165	$275	$550	$650	$1,700
Auctions: $1,410, MS-65BN, August 2015; $541, MS-63RB, June 2015; $230, MS-62BN, September 2015; $161, MS-60, May 2015													
1854, Proof	*10–20*	4	64.3								$3,500	$4,500	$8,000
Auctions: $7,931, PF-65RB, February 2014; $7,344, PF-65RB, January 2015													
1855	56,500	1,038	61.9	86%	$50	$65	$80	$100	$165	$275	$550	$650	$1,600
Auctions: $940, MS-65BN, January 2015; $494, MS-64BN, September 2015; $376, MS-63BN, September 2015													
1855, Proof	*40–60*	18	64.2								$3,500	$4,500	$8,000
Auctions: $5,750, PF-64BN, August 2011													
1856	40,430	384	60.1	73%	$50	$65	$80	$125	$185	$275	$575	$675	$2,000
Auctions: $400, MS-63BN, August 2015; $306, MS-63BN, May 2015; $294, MS-63BN, June 2015; $153, AU-55, May 2015													
1856, Proof	*50–75*	21	64.2								$3,500	$4,500	$8,000
Auctions: $7,050, PF-65BN, January 2015; $8,519, PF, February 2014													
1857	35,180	585	60.9	80%	$75	$95	$125	$180	$260	$400	$650	$750	$2,500
Auctions: $823, MS-64BN, October 2015; $541, MS-63BN, July 2015; $376, MS-62BN, May 2015; $141, AU-50, January 2015													
1857, Proof	*75–100*	39	63.9								$3,500	$4,500	$8,000
Auctions: $14,100, PF-66RB, June 2014; $4,465, PF-64BN, January 2015													

Large Cents
1793–1857

AN OVERVIEW OF LARGE CENTS

Collecting one each of the major types of 1793–1857 copper cents can be a fascinating challenge. Early varieties were struck from hand-engraved dies, often on copper planchets of uncertain quality. It was not until 1836 that steam power was used to run coining presses at the Mint. All earlier issues were made by hand, by two men tugging on the weighted lever arm of a small screw-type press. As might be expected, this resulted in many variations in striking quality.

The first cents of 1793, the Chain varieties, are found with two major differences: AMERI. on the reverse, and the later version with AMERICA spelled out in full. These early issues have been highly desired from the beginning days of the numismatic hobby in America, and remain in the limelight today.

Wreath cents of 1793 occur with the edge displaying a vine and bars motif and also with lettering ONE HUNDRED FOR A DOLLAR. Liberty Cap cents of the 1793–1796 years have lettered edges (ONE HUNDRED FOR A DOLLAR) used in 1793, 1794, and part of 1795, and plain edges for most 1795 coins and all of 1796.

The Draped Bust type commenced partway through 1796 and was continued through 1807. This span includes the notably rare 1799, 9 Over 8, overdate and the 1799 as well as the somewhat rare 1804. Many interesting die varieties occur in this type, particularly with regard to errors on the reverse. The Classic Head cent, designed by John Reich, was introduced in 1808, and was continued through 1814. In 1815 no cents of this date were produced. Then in 1816 the Matron Head commenced, a new motif with a new reverse as well. With modifications this was continued through 1839, in which year the Braided Hair design by Christian Gobrecht made its appearance. Large cents were made continually through January 1857 and then discontinued.

FOR THE COLLECTOR AND INVESTOR: LARGE CENTS AS A SPECIALTY

For the enjoyment of copper cents 1793–1857 it is possible to go far beyond a type set. Today, varieties of the 1793–1814 cents are generally collected by Sheldon numbers (S-1, S-2, etc.), given first in *Early American Cents* and, later, in its revision, *Penny Whimsy*. Building upon this foundation, *Walter Breen's Encyclopedia of Early United States Large Cents, 1793–1814*, gives more information on this date range than available in any other single source.

Among dates and major varieties in the early range of the series, the 1793 issues Chain AMERI., Chain AMERICA, Wreath, and Liberty Cap, the 1799 (far and away the rarest date in the series), and the 1804 are key issues, each a part of an extensive series of more than 300 die varieties through and including 1814.

The most popular way to collect large cents is by basic varieties, mainly dates, overdates, and major varieties. Sometimes, a particular date is selected as a specialty for collecting die varieties by Sheldon numbers.

Generally, grades from Good to VF are popular objectives for the early series from 1793 to 1814, and for some varieties no better coins exist. EF, AU, and Mint State coins are available and are more likely to be sought by collectors of basic dates and major varieties, rather than by specialists seeing long runs of Sheldon numbers. Type-set collectors are also important in the market for high-grade pieces, where sights can be set high as there are fewer varieties to obtain. Accordingly, as a type-set collector one may aspire to own an AU or Mint State cent of the 1796–1807 Draped Bust type. However, for a specialist in die varieties, who wants to acquire more than 100 different specimens from this date range, such high grades might not be feasible to acquire.

Collecting cents of the later dates by basic varieties is an interesting pursuit, and one that is quite attainable in such grades as EF, AU, or even MS-60, most dates after the 1820s being readily available for relatively inexpensive prices. Key issues among 1816–1857 cents include 1823, 3 Over 2; 1823; 1824, 4 Over 2; 1839, 9 Over 6; and a few others. Collecting Braided Hair cents toward the end of the series, 1839 to 1857, is least expensive of all, and most major varieties can be obtained in such grades as MS–60 to 63, with lustrous brown surfaces, for reasonable figures.

FLOWING HAIR, CHAIN REVERSE (1793)

Designer: *Henry Voigt.* **Weight:** *13.48 grams.* **Composition:** *Copper.*
Diameter: *Average 26 to 27 mm.* **Edge:** *Vine and bars design.* **Mint:** *Philadelphia.*

Chain AMERI. Reverse
1793; Bowers-Whitman–1, Sheldon-1, Breen-1.

Chain AMERICA Reverse

Vine-and-Bars Edge

History. The first U.S. cents intended for circulation were struck at the Mint in Philadelphia from February 27 through March 12, 1793. These were of the Flowing Hair design, with a Chain reverse. Several varieties were struck, today these can be attributed by Bowers-Whitman numbers or Sheldon numbers. The first, or Bowers-Whitman–1, Sheldon-1, had AMERICA abbreviated as AMERI. A contemporary account noted that Miss Liberty appeared to be "in a fright," and that the chain motif on the reverse, 15 links intended to symbolize unity of the states in the Union, was an "ill omen" for a land of liberty; accordingly, the design was used for only a short time. The rims on both sides are raised, without denticles or beads.

Striking and Sharpness. The details of Miss Liberty's hair are often indistinct or missing, including on many higher-grade specimens. For all grades and varieties, the reverse is significantly sharper than the obverse. The portrait of Miss Liberty is shallow and is often weak, especially on the BW-1, S-1, variety (which is often missing the date). Note that early copper coins of all kinds may exhibit "tooling" (engraving done outside the Mint in order to simulate details that were worn away or weakly struck to begin with). Also, these old coppers have sometimes been burnished to smooth out areas of porosity. These alterations are considered to be damage, and they significantly decrease a coin's value.

Availability. Demand is higher than supply for all varieties, with fewer than 1,000 or so examples surviving today. Most are in lower grades, from Fair-2 to VG-8. Even heavily worn coins (still identifiable by the chain device) are highly collectible. VF and EF coins are few and far between, and AU and MS are very rare.

GRADING STANDARDS

MS-60 to 70 (Mint State). *Obverse:* In the lower Mint State grades, MS–60 and 61, some slight abrasions can be seen on the higher areas of the portrait. The large open field shows light contact marks and perhaps a few nicks. At MS-63 the luster should be complete, although some very light abrasions or contact marks may be seen on the portrait. At MS-64 or higher—a nearly impossible level for a Chain cent—there is no sign of abrasion anywhere. Mint color is not extensive on any known Mint State coin,

1793; Bowers-Whitman–4, Sheldon-3, Breen-4. Graded MS-66BN.

but traces of red-orange are sometimes seen around the rim and devices on both sides. *Reverse:* In the lower Mint State grades some abrasions are seen on the chain links. There is some abrasion in the field. At MS-63, luster should be unbroken. Some abrasion and minor contact marks may be evident. In still higher grades, luster is deep and there is no sign of abrasion.

Illustrated coin: This coin is sharply struck with full hair detail. It is the Cleneay-Jackman-Ryder specimen mentioned in Sheldon's *Penny Whimsy* as the unrivalled, finest-known example of this variety.

AU-50, 53, 55, 58 (About Uncirculated). *Obverse:* Light wear is seen on the highest areas of the portrait. Some luster is seen in the large open fields at the AU-58 level, less at AU-55, and little if any for AU–53 and 50. Scattered marks are normal and are most evident in the field. At higher levels, some vestiges of luster may be seen among the letters, numerals, and between the hair tips. *Reverse:* Light wear is most evident on the chain, as

1793; BW-4, S-3, B-4. Graded AU-53.

this is the most prominent feature. The letters show wear, but not as extensive. Luster may be seen at the 58 and 55 levels, usually slightly more on the reverse than on the obverse. Generally, the reverse grades higher than the obverse, usually by a step, such as an AU-50 obverse and an AU-53 reverse (such a coin would be listed as the lower of the two, or AU-50).

EF-40, 45 (Extremely Fine). *Obverse:* The center of the portrait is well worn, with the hair visible only in thick strands, although extensive detail remains in the hair tips at the left. No luster is seen. Contact marks are normal in the large expanse of open field, but should be mentioned if they are distracting. *Reverse:* The chain is bold and shows light wear. Other features show wear, as well—more extensive in appearance, as the relief is lower. The fields show some friction, but not as much as on the obverse.

1793; BW-4, S-3, B-4. Graded EF-45.

VF-20, 30 (Very Fine). *Obverse:* More wear is seen on the portrait, with perhaps half or slightly more of the hair detail showing, mostly near the left edge of the hair. The ear usually is visible (but might not be, depending on the sharpness of strike). The letters in LIBERTY show wear. The rim remains bold (more so than on the reverse). *Reverse:* The chain shows more wear than on the preceding, but is still bold. Other features show more wear and may be weak in areas. The rim may be weak in areas.

1793; BW-5, S-4, B-5. Graded VF-30.

F-12, 15 (Fine). *Obverse:* The hair details are mostly worn away, with about one-third visible, that being on the left. The rim is distinct on most examples. The bottoms of the date digits are weak or possibly worn away. *Reverse:* The chain is bold, as is the lettering within the chain. Lettering around the border shows extensive wear, but is complete. The rim may be flat in areas.

1793; BW-5, S-4, B-5. Graded F-15.

    Illustrated coin: The surface is generally smooth and even under close scrutiny reveals only minor roughness. Note the shallow reverse rim bruise outside the letters AM in AMERICA and some mild encrustation around the letter C in CENT and the nearby chain links.

VG-8, 10 (Very Good). *Obverse:* The portrait is well worn, although Miss Liberty's eye remains bold. Hair detail is gone at the center, but is evident at the left edge of the portrait. LIBERTY is always readable, but may be faded or partly missing on shallow strikes. The date is well worn, with the bottom of the numerals missing (published standards vary on this point, and it used to be the case that a full date was mandatory). *Reverse:* The chain

1793; BW-4, S-3, B-4. Graded VG-10.

remains bold, and the center letters are all readable. Border letters may be weak or incomplete. The rim is smooth in most areas.

    Illustrated coin: The coin is smooth in appearance with the worn areas showing lighter copper, while the fields have trace roughness and the classic black olive texture. Note the planchet flaw right of ONE, which appears as a void in the metal.

G-4, 6 (Good). *Obverse:* The portrait is worn smooth and is seen only in outline form, although the eye position can be discerned. LIBERTY may be weak. The date is weak, but the tops of the numerals can be discerned. *Reverse:* The chain is fully visible in outline form. Central lettering is mostly or completely readable, but light. Peripheral lettering is mostly worn away.

1793; BW-1, S-1, B-1. Graded G-4.

    Illustrated coin: Natural obverse planchet flaws, as struck, can be seen both at 12 o'clock on the rim and above and to the left of the date, with other faint fissuring seen on the reverse under low magnification.

AG-3 (About Good). *Obverse:* The portrait is visible as an outline. LIBERTY and the date are mostly or even completely worn away. Contact marks may be extensive. *Reverse:* The chain is fully visible in outline form. Traces of the central letters—or, on better strikes, nearly all of the letters—can be seen. Around the border all letters are worn away.

1793; BW-5, S-4, B-5. Graded AG-3.

	Mintage	Cert	Avg	%MS	AG-3	G-4	VG-8	F-12	VF-20	EF-40	AU-50	MS-60
1793, Chain, All kinds	36,103											
1793, AMERI. in Legend		36	24.0	8%	$5,500	$11,000	$17,500	$28,000	$45,000	$80,000	$175,000	$300,000
	Auctions: $440,625, MS-63BN, June 2014											
1793, AMERICA, Periods		15	23.8	0%	$4,500	$8,000	$15,000	$19,000	$37,500	$60,000	$120,000	$225,000
	Auctions: $22,325, AU-50, September 2013											
1793, AMERICA, No Periods		123	23.1	6%	$4,500	$7,500	$14,000	$18,000	$30,000	$55,000	$95,000	$180,000
	Auctions: $998,750, MS-65BN, January 2013											

FLOWING HAIR, WREATH REVERSE (1793)

Designer: *Henry Voigt.* **Weight:** *13.48 grams.* **Composition:** *Copper.* **Diameter:** *26 to 28 mm.* **Edge:** *Vine and bars design, or lettered ONE HUNDRED FOR A DOLLAR followed by either a single or a double leaf.* **Mint:** *Philadelphia.*

Vine-and-Bars Edge

1793, Sprung Die, Wreath Type,
Vine and Bars Edge; BW-12, S-6, B-7.

Lettered Edge
(ONE HUNDRED FOR A DOLLAR)

History. Between April 9 and July 17, 1793, the U.S. Mint struck and delivered 63,353 large copper cents. Most of these, and perhaps all, were of the Wreath type, although records do not specify when the design types were changed that year. The Wreath cent was named for the new reverse style. Both sides have raised beads at the border, similar to the style used on 1793 half cents.

Striking and Sharpness. These cents usually are fairly well struck, although high-grade pieces often exhibit some weakness on the highest hair tresses and on the leaf details. (On lower-grade pieces these areas are worn, so the point is moot.) Planchet quality varies widely, from smooth, glossy brown to dark and porous. The lettered-edge cents are often seen on defective planchets. Consult Sheldon's *Penny Whimsy (1793–1814)* and photographs to learn the characteristics of certain varieties. The borders have raised beads; on high-grade pieces these are usually very distinct, but they blend together on lower-grade coins and can sometimes be indistinct. The beads are not as prominent as those later used on the 1793 Liberty Cap cents.

Availability. At least several thousand examples exist of the different varieties of the type. Most are in lower grades, from AG-3 to VG-8, although Fine and VF pieces are encountered with regularity. Choice EF, AU, and finer coins see high demand. Some in MS have been billed as "specimen" or "presentation" coins, although this is supposition, as no records exist.

GRADING STANDARDS

MS-60 to 70 (Mint State). *Obverse:* On MS-60 and 61 coins there are some traces of abrasion on the higher areas of the portrait, most particularly the hair. As this area can be lightly struck, careful inspection is needed for evaluation, not as much in Mint State (as other features come into play), but in higher circulated grades. Luster in the field is incomplete at lower Mint State levels, but should be in generous quantity. At MS-63, luster should

1793; BW-12, S-6, B-7. Graded MS-66.

be complete, and no abrasion evident. At higher levels, the luster is deeper, and some original mint color may be seen. At MS-65 there might be some scattered contact marks and possibly bare traces of fingerprints or discoloration. Above MS-65, a coin should approach perfection. A Mint State 1793 Wreath cent is an object of rare beauty. *Reverse:* In the lower Mint State grades some abrasion is seen on the higher areas of the leaves. Generally, luster is complete in all grades, as the open areas are protected by the lettering and wreath. In many ways, the grading guidelines for this type follow those of the 1793 half cent—also with sprays of berries (not seen elsewhere in the series).

Illustrated coin: Remarkably, this coin displays some original Mint orange.

AU-50, 53, 55, 58 (About Uncirculated). *Obverse:* Friction is seen on the highest areas of the hair (which may also be lightly struck) and the cheek. Some scattered marks are normal in the field, ranging from more extensive at AU-50 to minimal at AU-58. *Reverse:* Friction is seen on the higher wreath leaves and (not as easy to discern) on the letters. The fields, protected by the designs (including sprays of berries at the center), show fric-

1793; BW-23, S-11c, B-16c. Graded AU-50.

tion, but not as noticeably as on the obverse. At AU–55 and 58, little if any friction is seen. Border beads, if well struck, are separate and boldly defined.

Illustrated coin: Note the clash marks on the obverse indicative of a late die state. Significant portions of the reverse wreath are clashed in the field from Liberty's nose to the base of the throat, below the bust around the leaf cluster, and between some of the strands of hair at the back of Liberty's head. Additionally, the letters MERICA in the word AMERICA are clashed in the right-obverse field, the letters becoming bolder toward the end of that word.

EF-40, 45 (Extremely Fine). *Obverse:* More extensive wear is seen on the high parts of the hair, creating mostly a solid mass (without detail of strands) of varying width in the area immediately to the left of the face. The cheek shows light wear. Luster is minimal or nonexistent at EF-40, and may survive in traces in protected areas (such as between the letters) at EF-45. *Reverse:* Wear is seen on the highest wreath and ribbon areas, and

1793; BW-17, S-9, B-12. Graded EF-40.

the letters. Luster is minimal, but likely more noticeable than on the obverse, as the fields are protected by the designs and lettering. Some of the beads blend together.

VF-20, 30 (Very Fine). *Obverse:* Wear on the hair is more extensive, and varies depending on the die variety and sharpness of strike. The ANA grading standards suggest that two-thirds of the hair is visible, which in practice can be said to be "more or less." More beads are blended together, but the extent of this blending depends on the striking and variety. Certain parts of the rim are smooth, with beads scarcely visible at all. No

1793; BW-12, S-6, B-7. Graded VF-25.

luster is seen. The date, LIBERTY, and hair ends are bold. *Reverse:* The leaf details are nearly completely worn away at VF-20, with slight detail at VF-30. The border beads are blended together, with many indistinct. Some berries in the sprays are light, but nearly all remain distinct. No luster is seen.

Illustrated coin: The surfaces are a bit rough overall with a few areas also revealing slight verdigris.

F-12, 15 (Fine). *Obverse:* The hair details are mostly worn away, with about one-third visible, mainly at the edges. The ANA grading standards suggest that half of the details are visible, seemingly applying to the total area of the hair. However, the visible part, at the left, also includes intermittent areas of the field. Beads are weak or worn away in areas. F-15 shows slightly more detail. By this grade, scattered light scratches, noticeable contact marks,

1793; BW-17, S-9, B-12. Graded F-12.

and the like are the rule, not the exception. These are not mentioned at all on holders and are often overlooked elsewhere, except in some auction catalogs and price lists. Such marks are implicit for coins in lower grades, and light porosity or granularity is common as well. *Reverse:* The wreath leaves are worn flat, but their edges are distinct. Border beads are weak or worn away in areas. F-15 shows slightly more detail.

Illustrated coin: Despite slight pock-marking on the obverse and scattered rim bruises, this coin features strong definition for an F-12 piece.

VG-8, 10 (Very Good). *Obverse:* The hair is well worn toward the face. Details at the left are mostly blended together in thick strands. The eye, nose, and lips often remain well defined. Border beads are completely gone, or just seen in traces, and part of the rim blends into the field. LIBERTY may be slightly weak. The 1793 date is fully visible, although there may be some lightness. Scattered marks are more common than on

1793; BW-23, S-11c, B-16c. Graded VG-8.

higher grades. *Reverse:* The wreath, bow, and lettering are seen in outline form, and some leaves and letters may be indistinct in parts. Most of the berries remain visible, but weak. Border beads are worn away, and the border blends into the field in most if not all of the periphery.

G-4, 6 (Good). *Obverse:* The hair is worn smooth except for the thick tresses at the left. The eye, nose, and lips show some detail. LIBERTY is weak, with some letters missing. The date is discernible, although partially worn away. The sprig above the date is usually prominent. The border completely blends into the field. *Reverse:* Extensive overall wear. The wreath is seen in outline form, with some areas weak. Usually ONE CENT remains

1793; BW-12, S-6, B-7. Graded G-4.

readable at the center. The border letters and fraction show extensive wear, with some letters very weak or even missing, although most should be discernible. Dark or porous coins may have more details on both sides in an effort to compensate for the roughness. Marks, edge bumps, and so on are normal.

Illustrated coin: Note minor surface roughness. Definition in the major devices is strong for this grade.

AG-3 (About Good). *Obverse:* Wear is more extensive than on the preceding. The eye, nose, and lips may still be discernible, and the sprig above the date can usually be seen. LIBERTY may be very weak or even missing. The date is gone, or just a trace will remain. *Reverse:* Parts of the wreath are visible in outline form. ONE CENT might be readable, but this is not a requirement. Most border letters are gone. If a coin is dark or porous

1793; BW-18, S-8, B-13. Graded AG-3.

it may be graded AG-3 and may be sharper than just described, with the porosity accounting for the lower grade.

Regular Sprig   **Strawberry Leaf**

	Mintage	Cert	Avg	%MS	AG-3	G-4	VG-8	F-12	VF-20	EF-40	AU-50	MS-60BN	MS-63BN
1793, Wreath, All kinds	63,353												
1793, Vine/Bars Edge		198	32.9	13%	$1,250	$3,000	$4,700	$7,000	$12,000	$20,000	$32,500	$55,000	$100,000
	Auctions: $176,250, MS-65BN, June 2015; $44,650, AU-55, August 2015; $14,688, VF-35, June 2015; $8,225, VF-20, September 2015												
1793, Lettered Edge		40	24.5	5%	$1,250	$3,000	$4,750	$7,500	$15,000	$27,500	$38,000	$80,000	$125,000
	Auctions: $18,800, F-15, January 2014												
1793, Strawberry Leaf †	(a)	1	12.0	0%	—	—	$450,000	$800,000					
	Auctions: $381,875, G-4, January 2014												

† Ranked in the *100 Greatest U.S. Coins* (fourth edition). **a.** 4 examples are known.

LIBERTY CAP (1793–1796)

Designer: *1793–1795, thick planchet—Probably Joseph Wright; 1795–1796, thin planchet—John Smith Gardner.* **Weight:** *1793–1795, thick planchet—13.48 grams; 1795–1796, thin planchet—10.89 grams.* **Composition:** *Copper.* **Diameter:** *Average 29 mm.* **Edge:** *1793–1795, thick planchet—Lettered ONE HUNDRED FOR A DOLLAR; 1795–1796, thin planchet—Plain.* **Mint:** *Philadelphia.*

Lettered Edge (1793–1795)

Reeded Edge (1795)

1794, Buckled Obverse; BW-17, S-27, B-9.

History. The Liberty Cap design was created in the summer of 1793 by artist and engraver Joseph Wright, who is also believed by some to have designed the 1793 half cent. On the cent, Miss Liberty faces to the right, rather than to the left (as on the half cent). Liberty Cap cents of 1793 have raised beaded borders. Other issues have denticles. Cents of 1794 and some of 1795 are on thick planchets with the edge lettered ONE HUNDRED FOR A DOLLAR, while those made later in 1795, and in 1796, are on thinner planchets and have a plain edge.

Striking and Sharpness. The depth of relief and striking characteristics vary widely, depending on the variety. Points to check are the details of the hair on Miss Liberty, the leaf details on the wreath, and the denticles on both sides. Generally, the earlier, thick-planchet issues are better strikes than are the thin-planchet coins. Plain-edge 1795 cents often have low or shallow rims. To determine the difference between lightness caused by shallow dies and lightness caused by wear, study the characteristics of the die variety involved (see in particular the reverses of 1793, BW-27, S-13, and 1793, BW-28 / BW-29, S-15 / S-12).

Availability. Cents of this type are readily available, although those of 1793 are rare and in great demand, and certain die varieties of the other dates are rare and can command high prices. Typical grades range from AG upward to Fine, VF, and, less often, EF. Attractive AU and MS coins are elusive, and when found are usually dated 1795, the thin planchet variety.

GRADING STANDARDS

MS-60 to 70 (Mint State). *Obverse:* On MS–60 and 61 coins there are some traces of abrasion on the higher areas of the portrait. Luster is incomplete, particularly in the field. At MS-63, luster should be complete, and no abrasion evident. At higher levels, the luster is deeper, and some original mint color may be seen on some examples. At the MS-65 level there may be some scattered contact marks and

1794; BW-12, S-22, B-6. Graded MS-62BN.

possibly some traces of fingerprints or discoloration, but these should be very minimal and not at all distracting. Generally, Liberty Cap cents of 1793 (in particular) and 1794 are harder to find with strong eye appeal than are those of 1795 and 1796. Mint State coins of 1795 often have satiny luster. Above MS-65, a coin should approach perfection, especially if dated 1795 or 1796. Certified Mint State cents can vary in their strictness of interpretation. *Reverse:* In the lower Mint State grades some abrasion is seen on the higher areas of the leaves. Generally, luster is complete in all grades, as the open areas are protected by the lettering and wreath. Often on this type the reverse is shallower than the obverse and has a lower rim.

Illustrated coin: Boldly struck on both the obverse and reverse, with strong hair separation evident on Liberty and some evidence of a central vein on each leaf. Note the small toning speck under the L of LIBERTY.

AU-50, 53, 55, 58 (About Uncirculated). *Obverse:* Very light wear is evident on the highest parts of the hair above and to the left of the ear. Friction is seen on the cheek and the liberty cap. Coins at this level are usually on smooth planchets and have nice eye appeal. Color is very important. Dark and porous coins are relegated to lower grades, even if AU-level sharpness is present. *Reverse:*

1794; BW-98, S-71, B-63. Graded AU-50.

Very light wear is evident on the higher parts of the leaves and the ribbon, and, to a lesser extent, on the lettering. The reverse may have original luster, toned brown, varying from minimal (at lower About Uncirculated grades) to extensive. Grading at the About Uncirculated level is mainly done by viewing the obverse, as many reverses are inherently shallow due to lower-relief dies.

Illustrated coin: Note the rough patch on and below Liberty's cap.

EF-40, 45 (Extremely Fine). *Obverse:* The center of the coin shows wear or a small, flat area, for most dies. Other hair details are strong. Luster is minimal or nonexistent at EF-40, and may survive in traces in protected areas (such as between the letters) at EF-45. *Reverse:* Wear is seen on the highest wreath and ribbon areas and the letters. Luster is minimal, but likely more noticeable than on the

1794; BW-18, S-28, B-10. Graded EF-40.

obverse, as the fields are protected by the designs and lettering. Sharpness varies depending on the die variety but is generally shallower than on the obverse, this being particularly true for many 1795 cents.

VF-20, 30 (Very Fine). *Obverse:* Wear on the portrait has reduced the hair detail to indistinct or flat at the center, and on most varieties the individual strands at the left edge are blended together. One rule does not fit all. The ANA grading standards suggest that 75% of the hair shows, while PCGS suggests 30% to 70% on varieties struck from higher-relief dies, and less than 50% for others. Examples such as this reflect the artistic, rather than sci-

1794, Head of 1794; BW-74, S-57, B-55. Graded VF-30.

entific, nature of grading. *Reverse:* The leaf details are nearly completely worn away at VF-20, and with slight detail at VF-30. Some border letters may be weak, and ditto for the central letters (on later variet-ies of this type). The border denticles are blended together with many indistinct. No luster is seen. The sharpness of details depends on the die variety.

F-12, 15 (Fine). *Obverse:* The hair details are mostly worn away, with about one-third visible, mainly at the lower edges. Border denticles are weak or worn away in areas, depending on the height of the rim when the coin was struck. F-15 shows slightly more detail. *Reverse:* The wreath leaves are worn flat, but their edges are distinct. Border den-ticles are weak or worn away in areas. F-15 shows slightly more detail. At this level and

1794, Head of 1794; BW-98, S-71, B-63. Graded F-15.

lower, planchet darkness and light porosity are common, as are scattered marks.

VG-8, 10 (Very Good). *Obverse:* The hair is more worn than on the preceding, with detail present only in the lower areas. Detail can differ, and widely, depending on the dies. Border denticles are worn away on some issues (not as much for 1793 and 1794 coins), and the border will blend into the field in areas in which the rim was low to begin with, or in areas struck slightly off center. LIBERTY and the date are bold. VG-10 is sometimes applied to especially nice Very Good coins. *Reverse:* The wreath, bow, and lettering are seen in outline form, and

1796; BW-1, S-91, B-1. Graded VG-8.

some leaves and letters may be indistinct in parts. Border denticles are worn away, and the border blends into the field in most if not all of the periphery. In certain die varieties and die states, especially of 1797, some letters may be very weak, or missing.

G-4, 6 (Good). *Obverse:* The portrait is worn smooth and is seen only in outline form, although the eye and nose can be discerned. LIBERTY and the date are complete, although the date may be weak. Denticles are gone on varieties struck with low or shallow rims. *Reverse:* Extensive wear is seen overall. From half to two-thirds of the letters in UNITED STATES OF AMERICA and the fraction numerals are worn away. Certain

1794, Starred Reverse; BW-59, S-48, B-38. Graded G-4.

shallow-relief dies may have letters missing. G-6 is often assigned to finer examples in this category. Darkness, porosity, and marks characterize many coins.

Illustrated coin: This coin is an example of the highly sought 1794, Starred Reverse, variety.

AG-3 (About Good). *Obverse:* Wear is more extensive than on the preceding. The portrait is visible only in outline. LIBERTY will typically have some letters worn away. The date is weak, but discernible. *Reverse:* Parts of the wreath are visible in outline form, and all but a few letters are gone. Grading of AG-3 is usually done by the reverse, as the obverse typically appears to be in a slightly higher grade.

1794, Starred Reverse; BW-59, S-48, B-38. Graded AG-3.

Illustrated coin: This coin is closer to G-4 on the obverse, but weak on the reverse, prompting a more conservative grade. While the reverse is worn nearly smooth, almost a third of the stars at the denticles, which mark this cent as a 1794, Starred Reverse, are visible.

Head of 1793 (1793–1794)
Head in high, rounded relief.

Head of 1794 (1794)
Well-defined hair;
hook on lowest curl.

Beaded Border (1793)

Denticle Border
(1794–1796)

	Mintage	Cert	Avg	%MS	AG-3	G-4	VG-8	F-12	VF-20	EF-40	AU-50	MS-60BN	MS-63BN
1793, Liberty Cap	11,056	26	15.3	0%	$3,200	$6,000	$12,000	$17,500	$45,000	$100,000	$200,000		
	Auctions: $21,150, F-12, July 2015; $3,760, VG-8, January 2015; $2,585, G-4, January 2015												

1794, Normal Reverse

1794, Starred Reverse

Head of 1795 (1794–1796)
*Head in low relief;
no hook on lowest curl.*

1795, "Jefferson Head"

	Mintage	Cert	Avg	%MS	AG-3	G-4	VG-8	F-12	VF-20	EF-40	AU-50	MS-60BN	MS-63BN
1794, All kinds	918,521												
1794, Head of 1793		19	16.2	11%	$575	$1,500	$3,000	$4,500	$10,000	$25,000	$45,000	$100,000	$175,000
	Auctions: $881,250, MS-64BN, January 2013												
1794, Head of 1794		303	33.2	5%	$150	$370	$550	$800	$1,800	$4,000	$6,000	$13,000	$25,000
	Auctions: $12,925, AU-55, June 2015; $9,988, AU-55, June 2015; $8,813, EF-45, June 2015; $2,468, VF-35, August 2015												
1794, Head in Low Relief		0	n/a		$150	$370	$550	$800	$1,800	$4,000	$6,000	$13,000	$25,000
	Auctions: No auction records available.												
1794, Exact Head of 1795 (a)		56	32.9	9%	$175	$400	$550	$850	$2,000	$5,000	$8,000	$25,000	$50,000
	Auctions: $329, VF-20, July 2015; $447, F-15, July 2015; $376, F-12, November 2015												
1794, Starred Reverse †		7	14.0	0%	$14,500	$16,500	$20,000	$45,000	$85,000	$225,000	$750,000		
	Auctions: $15,275, AG-3, October 2013												
1794, No Fraction Bar		5	33.0	20%	$200	$550	$650	$1,200	$2,700	$6,500	$15,000	$40,000	$75,000
	Auctions: $381,875, MS-64BN, January 2014												
1795, Lettered Edge	37,000	53	31.2	13%	$150	$350	$550	$1,000	$2,100	$5,250	$7,500	$11,000	$24,000
	Auctions: $79,313, MS-65BN, April 2013												
1795, Plain Edge	501,500	235	27.2	11%	$150	$325	$425	$650	$1,350	$3,000	$6,000	$8,500	$20,000
	Auctions: $21,150, MS-63BN, April 2013; $548, G-6, July 2015												
1795, Reeded Edge	(b)	0	n/a		$125,000	$275,000	$600,000						
	Auctions: $646,250, VG-10, January 2014												
1795, "Jefferson Head" (c)		1	10.0	0%	$10,000	$20,000	$34,000	$55,000	$125,000				
	Auctions: $184,000, VF-25, March 2012												
1795, "Jefferson Head," Lettered Edge (c)	(d)	0	n/a			—	$50,000	$85,000	$200,000				
	Auctions: No auction records available.												
1796, Liberty Cap	109,825	163	23.6	9%	$250	$400	$600	$1,200	$2,400	$5,500	$12,000	$25,000	$65,000
	Auctions: $141,000, MS-64RB, January 2014; $400, AG-3, February 2015; $376, AG-3, May 2015												

† Ranked in the *100 Greatest U.S. Coins* (fourth edition). **a.** The 1794 coin with Head of 1795 has a hooked curl but is in low relief. **b.** 9 examples are known. **c.** The "Jefferson Head" is not a regular Mint issue, but a design struck privately in an attempt to win a federal coinage contract. **d.** 3 examples are known.

DRAPED BUST (1796–1807)

Designer: *Robert Scot.* **Weight:** *10.89 grams.* **Composition:** *Copper.*
Diameter: *Average 29 mm.* **Edge:** *Plain.* **Mint:** *Philadelphia.*

1796, Reverse of 1797, Large Fraction;
BW-65, S-119, B-40.

History. The Draped Bust cent made its debut in 1796, following a coinage of Liberty Cap cents the same year. The motif, from a drawing by Gilbert Stuart, was first employed on certain silver dollars of 1795. (Its use on half cents did not take place until later, in 1800.) In 1798 Miss Liberty's head was slightly modified in design.

Striking and Sharpness. Most Draped Bust cents were struck on high-quality planchets. (This high planchet quality is less predictable for varieties of 1796, and almost never present for those of 1799 and 1800.) Detail sharpness differs by die variety. Weakness, when present, is usually on the hair behind the forehead, on the leaves in the upper part of the wreath, and among the denticles. However, a weak strike can show up in other areas as well. Many if not most Draped Bust cents are imperfectly centered, with the result that denticles can be bold on one side of a coin and light or even missing on the opposite side; this can occur on obverse as well as reverse. Typically this does not affect value. Certain Draped Bust cents of 1796 have semi-prooflike surfaces. Those of 1799 often have rough or porous surfaces and are found in lower grades.

Availability. As a type, Draped Bust cents are readily available, although the 1799, 9 Over 8, and 1799 are the keys to the series, and the 1804 is elusive. A different scenario evolves when considering engraving errors, repunched dates, and recut letters and numerals; many of these varieties are very difficult to locate. The eye appeal of these rarities usually is below par. Other years are generally available in high grades, VF and finer, well struck (except for some reverse leaves, in instances), on high-quality planchets, and with excellent eye appeal. Dark and porous coins are plentiful among coins graded below VF. True MS coins tend to be MS–60 to 63, when found.

GRADING STANDARDS

MS-60 to 70 (Mint State). *Obverse:* In the lower Mint State grades, MS–60 and 61, some slight abrasion can be seen on the higher areas of the portrait, especially the cheek, and the hair behind the forehead. Luster in the field is incomplete, particularly in the center of the open areas, which on this type are very open, especially at the right. At MS-63, luster should be nearly complete, and no abrasions evident. In higher levels, the lus-

1803, Small Date, Large Fraction;
BW-12, S-258, B-17. Graded MS-63BN.

ter is complete and deeper, and some original mint color should be seen. MS-64 coins may have some slight discoloration or scattered contact marks. A well-graded MS-65 or higher coin will have full, rich luster; no marks visible except under magnification; and a nice blend of brown toning or nicely mixed (not stained or blotchy) mint color and natural brown toning. *Reverse:* In the lower Mint State ranges some abrasions are seen on the higher areas of the leaves. Generally, luster is complete in all Mint State ranges, as the open areas are protected by the lettering and wreath. Sharpness of the leaves can vary by die variety, so check this aspect. Otherwise, the same comments apply as for the obverse.

Illustrated coin: This example is quite attractive despite the scratch on Liberty's bust and another through the D of UNITED. However, the left side of the reverse has toned differently from the rest of the coin's surfaces.

AU-50, 53, 55, 58 (About Uncirculated). *Obverse:* Friction is seen on the higher parts, particularly the hair of Miss Liberty and the cheek. Friction and scattered marks are in the field, ranging from more extensive at AU-50 to minimal at AU-58. Luster may be seen in protected areas, minimal at AU-50, more visible at AU-58. At AU-58 the field may retain some luster, as well. In many instances, the luster is smaller in area and lesser in "depth"

1803, Small Date, Large Fraction; BW-12, S-258, B-17. Graded AU-58.

than on the reverse of this type. Cents of this type can be very beautiful in About Uncirculated. *Reverse:* Friction is seen on the higher wreath leaves and (not as easy to discern) on the letters. Again, the die variety should be checked. The fields, though protected by the designs, show friction, but not as noticeably as on the obverse. At AU-55 and 58, little if any friction is seen. The reverse may have original luster, toned brown, minimal on lower About Uncirculated grades, often extensive at the AU-58 level. General rules for cents follow the half cents of the same type.

Illustrated coin: Note the die crack arcing through the lower-left obverse. This crack was also on the preceding coin, but is more noticeable here.

EF-40, 45 (Extremely Fine). *Obverse:* Wear is seen on the portrait overall, with reduction or elimination of some separation of hair strands on the highest part. By the standards of the Early American Coppers society, if the "spit curl" in front of Liberty's ear is missing, the coin is not EF. The cheek shows more wear than on higher grades, and the drapery covering the bosom is lightly worn on the higher areas. Often weakness in the separa-

1804, Original; BW-1, S-266, B-1. Graded EF-40.

tion of the drapery lines can be attributed to weakness in striking. Luster is minimal or nonexistent at EF-40, and may survive in amongst the letters of LIBERTY at EF-45. *Reverse:* Wear is seen on the highest wreath and ribbon areas, and on the letters. Luster is minimal, but likely more noticeable than on the obverse, as the fields are protected by the designs and lettering. The ANA grading standards state that at EF-45 nearly all of the "ribbing" (veins) in the leaves is visible, and that at EF-40 about 75% is sharp. In practice, striking plays a part as well, and some leaves may be weak even in higher grades.

Illustrated coin: This coin features a few small patches of porosity.

VF-20, 30 (Very Fine). *Obverse:* Wear on the portrait has reduced the hair detail further, especially to the left of the forehead. The rolling curls are solid or flat on their highest areas, as well as by the ribbon behind the hair. The border denticles are blended together, with many indistinct. No luster is seen. *Reverse:* The leaf details are nearly completely worn away at VF-20, and with slight detail at VF-30. The ANA grading

1805; BW-1, S-267, B-1. Graded VF-35.

standards are a bit stricter: 30% remaining at VF-20 and 50% at VF-30. In the marketplace, fewer details can be seen on most certified coins at these levels. The border denticles are blended together with many indistinct. No luster is seen.

F-12, 15 (Fine). *Obverse:* Many hair details are worn away, with perhaps one-half to one-third visible, mainly at the edges and behind the shoulder. Border denticles are weak or worn away in areas. F-15 shows slightly more detail. Porosity and scattered marks become increasingly common at this level and lower. *Reverse:* The wreath leaves are worn flat, but their edges are distinct. Little if anything remains of leaf vein details. Border denticles

1807, 7 Over 6; BW-2, S-273, B-3. Graded F-12.

are weak or worn away in areas. F-15 shows slightly more detail.

Illustrated coin: There are several distracting contact marks on the obverse of this coin. Note the 6 visible under the 7 in the date.

VG-8, 10 (Very Good). *Obverse:* The portrait is well worn, although the eye can be seen, as can hints of hair detail. Some hair at the left shows separation. Curls now appear as mostly solid blobs. Border denticles are worn away on most varieties, and the rim, although usually present, begins to blend into the field. LIBERTY and the date are bold in most areas, with some lightness toward the rim. VG-10 is sometimes applied to espe-

1807, Large Fraction. Graded VG-8.

cially nice Very Good coins. *Reverse:* The wreath, bow, and lettering are seen in outline form, and some leaves and letters may be indistinct in parts. The border may blend into the field on some of the periphery. The strength of the letters is dependent to an extent on the specific die variety.

G-4, 6 (Good). *Obverse:* The portrait is worn smooth and is seen only in outline form, although the eye position can be discerned and some curls can be made out. LIBERTY is readable, but the tops of the letters may fade away. The date is clearly readable, but the lower part of the numerals may be very weak or worn away. The border will blend into the field more extensively than on the preceding, but significant areas will still be seen. *Reverse:*

1799, 9 Over 8; BW-2, S-188, B-2. Graded G-6.

Extensive wear is seen overall. From one-half to two-thirds of the letters in UNITED STATES OF AMERICA and the fraction numerals are worn away. On most varieties, ONE CENT is fairly strong. G-6 is often assigned to finer examples in this category.

    Illustrated coin: This coin shows evidence of a past cleaning, but it has retoned.

AG-3 (About Good). *Obverse:* Wear is more extensive than on the preceding. The portrait is visible only in outline. LIBERTY is weak, partially worn away, but usually discernible. The date is weak, and the bottoms of the digits may be worn away, but must be identifiable. *Reverse:* Parts of the wreath are visible in outline form, and all but a few letters are gone. ONE CENT is usually mostly or completely discernible, depending on the variety.

1796, Reverse of 1797; BW-53, S-100, B-24. Graded AG-3.

    Illustrated coin: Early American Coppers has graded this same coin at Good.

Reverse of 1794 (1794–1796)
Note double leaf at top right;
14–16 leaves on left,
16–18 leaves on right.

Reverse of 1795 (1795–1798)
Note single leaf at top right;
17–21 leaves on left,
16–20 leaves on right.

Reverse of 1797 (1796–1807)
Note double leaf at top right; 16
leaves on left, 19 leaves on right.

1796, LIHERTY Error

1797, Wreath With Stems

1797, Stemless Wreath

Style 1 Hair
Found on all coins of 1796 and 1797, many 1798 varieties, and 1800, 1800 Over 1798.

Style 2 Hair
Found on coins of 1798–1807. Note the extra curl near shoulders.

1798, 8 Over 7

	Mintage	Cert	Avg	%MS	AG-3	G-4	VG-8	F-12	VF-20	EF-40	AU-50	MS-60BN	MS-63BN
1796, Draped Bust, All kinds	363,375												
1796, Reverse of 1794		34	14.4	0%	$120	$250	$600	$900	$2,750	$6,250	$12,500	$18,000	$26,500
Auctions: $11,750, AU-53, January 2014													
1796, Reverse of 1795		21	21.8	5%	$110	$175	$300	$650	$2,750	$6,500	$13,000	$19,500	$30,000
Auctions: $20,563, AU-58, January 2014; $764, G-6, October 2015; $646, G-6, October 2015													
1796, Reverse of 1797		24	19.2	13%	$110	$175	$300	$650	$2,000	$4,000	$6,500	$8,500	$14,000
Auctions: $28,200, MS-64BN, April 2013													
1796, LIHERTY Error		13	26.7	8%	$175	$350	$800	$1,400	$4,800	$12,000	$30,000	$60,000	$85,000
Auctions: $2,350, VF-20, August 2013													
1796, Stemless Reverse	(a)	0	n/a			$20,000							
Auctions: No auction records available.													
1797, All kinds	897,510												
1797, Gripped Edge, 1795-Style Reverse		16	22.3	0%	$60	$140	$250	$425	$1,000	$3,500	$7,750	$26,000	
Auctions: $1,351, VG-8, March 2013													
1797, Plain Edge, 1795-Style Reverse		12	12.7	0%	$60	$145	$265	$435	$1,200	$4,000	$8,250	$26,500	
Auctions: $940, EF-40, June 2014													
1797, 1797 Reverse, With Stems		190	33.2	19%	$55	$110	$190	$300	$975	$2,100	$3,600	$5,750	$14,000
Auctions: $41,125, MS-65RB, January 2013; $2,350, EF-45, March 2015; $999, F-15, June 2015; $129, F-12, March 2015													
1797, 1797 Reverse, Stemless		25	23.9	4%	$60	$135	$265	$550	$2,250	$6,750	$26,000	$60,000	
Auctions: $1,645, VF-25, January 2014													
1798, All kinds	1,841,745												
1798, 8 Over 7		20	25.7	5%	$60	$135	$275	$550	$3,000	$7,500	$14,000		
Auctions: $14,688, AU-58, February 2013													
1798, Reverse of 1796		10	16.3	0%	$50	$125	$250	$500	$2,000	$6,750	$9,500	$20,000	$35,000
Auctions: $3,290, VF-20, September 2013													
1798, Style 1 Hair		84	24.2	1%	$40	$100	$145	$250	$600	$2,200	$5,000	$10,000	$17,750
Auctions: $494, EF-40, June 2015; $494, VF-20, May 2015; $494, F-12, January 2015; $329, F-12, July 2015													
1798, Style 2 Hair		215	30.2	3%	$40	$100	$145	$250	$575	$1,950	$3,500	$8,350	$16,500
Auctions: $823, VF-30, August 2015; $940, VF-25, June 2015; $541, VF-20, January 2015; $376, F-12, January 2015													

a. 3 examples are known.

1799, 9 Over 8

1799, Normal Date

1800, 1800 Over 1798

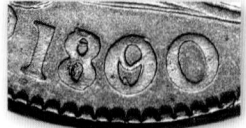

1800, 80 Over 79

1800, Normal Date

1801, Normal Reverse

1801, 3 Errors: 1/000, One Stem, and IINITED

1801, Fraction 1/000

1801, 1/100 Over 1/000

	Mintage	Cert	Avg	%MS	AG-3	G-4	VG-8	F-12	VF-20	EF-40	AU-50	MS-60BN	MS-63BN
1799, 9 Over 8	(b)	7	8.7	0%	$1,500	$3,500	$6,000	$15,000	$35,000	$100,000	$250,000	$600,000	
Auctions: $70,500, VF-25, January 2014													
1799, Normal Date	(b)	46	11.7	2%	$1,250	$2,750	$5,500	$10,500	$27,000	$85,000	$225,000	$500,000	
Auctions: $99,875, EF-35, January 2013; $32,900, VF-30, March 2015													
1800, All kinds	2,822,175												
1800, 1800 Over 1798, Style 1 Hair		26	25.1	4%	$35	$75	$135	$265	$1,500	$3,850	$7,000	$10,000	$14,000
Auctions: $2,585, G-6, January 2014													
1800, 80 Over 79, Style 2 Hair		61	23.3	7%	$35	$75	$120	$225	$600	$2,200	$4,000	$8,000	$25,000
Auctions: $19,388, MS-62BN, June 2014													
1800, Normal Date		144	24.9	10%	$35	$75	$120	$225	$550	$1,900	$3,000	$6,250	$14,000
Auctions: $70,500, MS-65BN, January 2013; $1,058, VF-25, June 2015; $705, VF-20, October 2015													
1801, All kinds	1,362,837												
1801, Normal Reverse		141	23.6	6%	$40	$75	$100	$225	$450	$1,250	$3,000	$7,500	$14,500
Auctions: $1,645, EF-40, February 2015; $112, VF-20, July 2015; $494, F-12, August 2015; $282, VG-10, July 2015													
1801, 3 Errors: 1/000, One Stem, and IINITED		22	19.5	9%	$75	$200	$350	$800	$2,700	$7,750	$13,500	$35,000	$115,000
Auctions: $3,525, EF-40, August 2013													
1801, Fraction 1/000		44	22.1	5%	$40	$75	$100	$250	$650	$2,200	$4,500	$12,500	$28,000
Auctions: $4,406, EF-40, January 2014													
1801, 1/100 Over 1/000		8	24.6	13%	$40	$80	$135	$275	$1,000	$2,500	$6,250	$15,000	$27,500
Auctions: $1,528, EF-45, January 2014													

b. Included in 1798, All kinds, mintage figure.

1802, Normal Reverse

1802, Fraction 1/000

1802, Stemless Wreath

1803, Small Date   1803, Large Date

*Note that Small Date varieties have a
blunt 1 in the date, and Large Date varieties
have a pointed 1 and noticeably larger 3.*

1803, Small Fraction

1803, Large Fraction

1803, 1/100 Over 1/000

1803, Stemless Wreath

	Mintage	Cert	Avg	%MS	AG-3	G-4	VG-8	F-12	VF-20	EF-40	AU-50	MS-60BN	MS-63BN
1802, All kinds	3,435,100												
1802, Normal Reverse		439	29.4	3%	$40	$65	$100	$200	$400	$1,000	$2,000	$4,500	$9,500
Auctions: $1,058, AU-50, January 2015; $881, EF-40, January 2015; $705, VF-35, January 2015; $617, VF-30, June 2015													
1802, Fraction 1/000		23	36.6	17%	$40	$75	$110	$220	$600	$1,700	$3,000	$7,200	$15,500
Auctions: $11,163, AU-55, January 2014													
1802, Stemless Wreath		47	30.7	4%	$40	$65	$100	$200	$500	$1,400	$2,750	$6,300	$13,500
Auctions: $2,938, AU-55, October 2013; $646, VF-25, January 2015; $470, VF-25, September 2015; $447, VF-25, August 2015													
1803, All kinds	3,131,691												
1803, Small Date, Small Fraction		165	30.5	6%	$40	$65	$100	$175	$350	$1,000	$1,450	$3,000	$8,500
Auctions: $423, EF-40, November 2015; $646, VF-30, July 2015; $541, VF-30, September 2015; $259, F-12, September 2015													
1803, Small Date, Large Fraction		103	31.3	9%	$40	$65	$100	$175	$350	$1,000	$1,450	$3,000	$8,500
Auctions: $18,800, MS-64BN, January 2014													
1803, Large Date, Small Fraction		3	12.0	0%	$2,400	$4,500	$8,500	$17,500	$35,000	$80,000			
Auctions: $15,275, VF-20, January 2014													
1803, Large Date, Large Fraction		6	45.0	17%	$50	$100	$175	$350	$1,500	$4,250	$8,500		
Auctions: $353, VF-20, August 2013													
1803, 1/100 Over 1/000		17	26.5	6%	$40	$85	$120	$240	$750	$2,200	$3,500	$6,750	$18,000
Auctions: $2,820, EF-45, September 2013													
1803, Stemless Wreath		15	29.7	13%	$40	$85	$120	$240	$750	$2,000	$2,750	$6,000	$17,000
Auctions: $8,225, AU-58, January 2014													

1804, Broken Dies
Bowers-Whitman–1c, Sheldon-266c.

Unofficial 1804 "Restrike"
Bowers-Whitman–3, Breen-1761, Pollock-6050.

Small 1807, 7 Over 6, Blunt 1

Large 1807, 7 Over 6, Pointed 1

1807, Small Fraction

1807, Large Fraction

1807, "Comet" Variety
Note the die break behind Miss Liberty's head.

	Mintage	Cert	Avg	%MS	AG-3	G-4	VG-8	F-12	VF-20	EF-40	AU-50	MS-60BN	MS-63BN
1804 (c)	96,500	93	16.6	1%	$750	$1,200	$2,500	$4,500	$8,500	$20,000	$50,000	$150,000	$650,000
	Auctions: $223,250, AU-55, January 2013												
1804, Unofficial Restrike of 1860 (d)		87	61.1	86%						$1,000	$1,100	$1,200	$1,450
	Auctions: $489, AU-55, August 2011												
1805	941,116	156	36.3	12%	$35	$60	$85	$175	$475	$1,200	$2,500	$5,250	$16,000
	Auctions: $940, VF-35, January 2015; $447, VF-20, February 2015; $376, VF-20, May 2015; $129, VG-10, May 2015												
1806	348,000	87	30.2	9%	$35	$70	$115	$225	$600	$2,000	$3,000	$8,500	$28,000
	Auctions: $3,819, AU-50, February 2013												

c. All genuine 1804 cents have a crosslet 4 in the date and a large fraction. The 0 in the date is in line with the O in OF on the reverse. **d.** Discarded Mint dies were used, circa 1860, to create "restrikes" (actually novodels or fantasies) of the scarce 1804 cent for collectors. These combine two unrelated dies: an altered 1803 die was used for the obverse, and a die of the 1820 cent for the reverse. The resulting coins cannot be confused with genuine 1804 cents.

	Mintage	Cert	Avg	%MS	AG-3	G-4	VG-8	F-12	VF-20	EF-40	AU-50	MS-60BN	MS-63BN
1807, All kinds	829,221												
1807, Small 1807, 7 Over 6, Blunt 1		7	13.7	0%	$1,200	$2,500	$4,500	$9,000	$20,000	$45,000	$150,000		
Auctions: $2,585, F-15, January 2014													
1807, Large 1807, 7 Over 6, Pointed 1		83	25.3	8%	$35	$60	$80	$185	$500	$1,200	$2,300	$5,850	$23,500
Auctions: $70,500, MS-65BN, April 2014; $764, VF-25, January 2015													
1807, Small Fraction		7	11.4	0%	$35	$60	$80	$200	$550	$1,750	$3,000	$6,000	$19,500
Auctions: $1,763, AU-50, August 2013													
1807, Large Fraction		28	18.5	0%	$35	$60	$80	$185	$450	$1,100	$2,300	$4,600	$16,500
Auctions: $5,750, AU-58, August 2011; $541, VF-25, October 2015; $364, VF-20, January 2015; $306, F-12, June 2015													
1807, "Comet" Variety		27	31.4	19%	$35	$75	$100	$225	$850	$2,650	$4,200	$10,500	$25,500
Auctions: $27,600, MS-61BN, February 2012													

CLASSIC HEAD (1808–1814)

Designer: *John Reich.* **Weight:** *10.89 grams.*
Composition: *Copper.* **Diameter:** *Average 29 mm.* **Edge:** *Plain.*

1810, 10 Over 09; BW-1, S-281, B-1.

History. The Classic Head design, by U.S. Mint assistant engraver John Reich, debuted in 1808. This cent type was minted through 1814. The quality of the coins' copper was poor during the War of 1812; the hostilities had ended the importation of high-quality planchets from England.

Striking and Sharpness. Striking sharpness varies, but often is poor. The cents of 1809 are notorious for having obverses much weaker than their reverses. Points to look for include sharpness of the denticles (which are often mushy, and in *most* instances inconsistent), star centers (a key area), hair details, and leaf details. Classic Head cents often are dark and porous due to the copper stock used.

Availability. Examples are readily available in grades from well worn to VF and EF, although overall quality often leaves much to be desired. AU and MS coins are elusive. Grading numbers do not mean much, as a connoisseur might prefer a high-quality EF-45 to a poorly struck MS-63. Overall eye appeal of obverse and reverse is often sub-par, a characteristic of this type.

GRADING STANDARDS

MS-60 to 70 (Mint State). *Obverse:* In the lower Mint State grades, MS–60 and 61, some slight abrasions can be seen on the portrait, most evidently on the cheek, as the hair details are complex on this type. Luster in the field is complete or nearly complete; the field is not as open on this type as on the Draped Bust issues. At MS-63, luster should be complete, and no abrasion evident. In higher levels, the luster is complete and deeper, and some orig-

1812, Large Date; BW-1, S-288, B-3. Graded MS-64BN.

inal mint color may be seen. MS-64 coins may have some slight discoloration or scattered contact marks. A well-graded MS-65 or higher coin will have full, rich luster; no marks visible except under magnification; and a nice blend of brown toning or nicely mixed (not stained or blotchy) mint color and natural brown toning. Incomplete striking of some details, especially the obverse stars, is the rule. *Reverse:* In the lower Mint State grades, some abrasion is seen on the higher areas of the leaves. Mint luster is complete in all Mint State grades, as the open areas are protected by the lettering and wreath. Sharpness of the leaves can vary by die variety, so check this aspect. Otherwise, the same comments apply as for the obverse.

Illustrated coin: The central devices are sharply struck and well preserved though obverse stars 1 through 5 are somewhat flat, as is virtually always seen on this type, and the reverse denticles from 8 o'clock to 11 o'clock are soft, which is also typical. This is one of the highest-graded Classic Head cents in existence.

AU-50, 53, 55, 58 (About Uncirculated). *Obverse:* Friction is seen on the higher parts, particularly the cheek. The hair will have friction and light wear, but will not be as obvious. Friction and scattered marks are in the field, ranging from more extensive at AU-50 to minimal at AU-58. Luster may be seen in protected areas, minimal at AU-50, but more visible at AU-58. At AU-58 the open field may retain some luster, as well.

1812, Large Date; BW-2, S-289, B-4. Graded AU-58.

Reverse: Friction is seen on the higher wreath leaves and on the letters. Fields, protected by the designs, show less friction. At the AU–55 and 58 levels little if any friction is seen. The reverse may have original luster, toned brown, minimal on lower About Uncirculated grades, often extensive at AU-58.

EF-40, 45 (Extremely Fine). *Obverse:* Wear is seen on the portrait overall, but most hair detail will still be present. The cheek shows light wear. Luster is minimal or nonexistent at EF-40, and may survive in among the letters of LIBERTY at EF-45. *Reverse:* Wear is seen on the highest wreath and ribbon areas and the letters. Leaf veins are visible except in the highest areas. Luster is minimal, but likely more noticeable than on the obverse, as the fields are protected by the designs and lettering.

1809; BW-1, S-280, B-1. Graded EF-40.

VF-20, 30 (Very Fine). *Obverse:* Wear on the portrait has reduced the hair detail, especially on the area to the right of the cheek and neck, but much can still be seen. *Reverse:* The wreath details, except for the edges of the leaves and certain of the tips (on leaves in lower relief), are worn away at VF-20, and with slightly more detail at VF-30.

1812, Large Date; BW-2, S-289, B-4. Graded VF-25.

F-12, 15 (Fine). *Obverse:* The hair details are fewer than on the preceding, but many are still present. The central hair curl is visible. Stars have flat centers. F-15 shows slightly more detail. The portrait on this type held up well to wear. *Reverse:* The higher areas of wreath leaves are worn flat, but their edges are distinct. F-15 shows slightly more detail.

Illustrated coin: This is a dark and somewhat porous example of what is considered to be the key issue of the Classic Head type.

1809; BW-1, S-280, B-1. Graded F-15.

VG-8, 10 (Very Good). *Obverse:* The portrait is well worn, although the eye and ear can be seen clearly. The hair is mostly blended, but some slight separation can be seen in areas. The border is raised in most or all areas. *Reverse:* The wreath is more worn than on the preceding grade, but there will still be some detail on the leaves. On most coins, ONE CENT is bold. Border letters are light or weak but are fully readable. The border is well defined in most areas.

1808. Graded VG-8.

G-4, 6 (Good). *Obverse:* The portrait is worn smooth and is seen only in outline form. Much or even all of LIBERTY on the headband is readable, but the letters are weak. The stars are weak, only in outline form, and several may be scarcely discernible. *Reverse:* Extensive wear is seen overall. Lettering in UNITED STATES OF AMERICA is weak, but completely discernible. The wreath is in outline, but still fairly bold, and ONE CENT is usually strong.

1808; BW-1, S-277, B-1. Graded G-6.

AG-3 (About Good). *Obverse:* Wear is more extensive than on the preceding. The portrait is visible only in outline. Most letters of LIBERTY are discernible, as this feature is in low relief. The stars are weak or worn away on their outer edges, and the date is light. *Reverse:* The wreath is visible in outline form but remains fairly strong. Most or even all of UNITED STATES OF AMERICA is worn away. ONE CENT is usually easily readable.

1808; BW-2, S-278, B-2. Graded AG-3.

1810, 10 Over 09

1810, Normal Date

1811, Last 1 Over 0

1811, Normal Date

1812, Small Date

1812, Large Date

1814, Plain 4

1814, Crosslet 4

	Mintage	Cert	Avg	%MS	AG-3	G-4	VG-8	F-12	VF-20	EF-40	AU-50	MS-60BN	MS-63BN
1808	1,007,000	102	34.1	17%	$30	$80	$150	$325	$750	$2,000	$3,500	$10,000	$17,500
Auctions: $25,850, MS-64BN, January 2013; $400, F-12, May 2015; $69, F-12, April 2015													
1809	222,867	64	30.1	8%	$50	$120	$250	$500	$1,500	$4,000	$5,000	$11,500	$25,000
Auctions: $28,200, MS-63BN, January 2013; $754, F-12, January 2015; $376, G-4, May 2015													
1810, All kinds	1,458,500												
1810, 10 Over 09		48	30.0	10%	$30	$80	$130	$325	$800	$1,700	$2,750	$8,000	$15,000
Auctions: $10,575, AU-55, April 2013													
1810, Normal Date		132	31.9	13%	$30	$80	$130	$325	$750	$1,600	$2,700	$8,000	$15,000
Auctions: $32,900, MS-64BN, January 2014; $376, EF-40, January 2015; $1,234, VF-35, January 2015; $940, VF-20, July 2015													
1811, All kinds	218,025												
1811, Last 1 Over 0		25	27.2	12%	$40	$85	$135	$500	$1,750	$5,250	$10,000	$25,000	$55,000
Auctions: $364, VF-20, August 2013; $2,585, VF-25, March 2015; $764, VG-10, August 2015; $176, AG-3, January 2015													
1811, Normal Date		74	30.8	15%	$45	$100	$150	$400	$1,000	$2,200	$5,500	$10,000	$20,000
Auctions: $23,500, MS-64BN, January 2013													
1812, All kinds	1,075,500												
1812, Small Date		34	30.9	6%	$25	$80	$130	$325	$750	$1,600	$2,500	$5,500	$12,000
Auctions: $44,063, MS-65RB, June 2014; $881, VF-30, August 2015; $94, F-12, March 2015; $153, VG-8, June 2015													
1812, Large Date		29	33.7	10%	$25	$50	$100	$250	$750	$1,600	$2,500	$5,500	$12,000
Auctions: $3,819, AU-55, January 2014													
1813	418,000	161	37.8	11%	$30	$60	$120	$325	$850	$1,750	$2,800	$6,000	$12,500
Auctions: $211,500, MS-65BN, January 2013; $940, AU-50, January 2015; $1,880, EF-40, March 2015; $1,116, VF-20, August 2015													
1814, All kinds	357,830												
1814, Plain 4		108	27.1	11%	$25	$80	$130	$325	$750	$1,600	$2,400	$5,000	$12,500
Auctions: $47,000, MS-65BN, April 2014; $223, VG-10, May 2015; $129, G-6, April 2015; $74, G-4, April 2015													
1814, Crosslet 4		84	30.1	13%	$25	$80	$130	$325	$750	$1,600	$2,400	$5,000	$12,500
Auctions: $1,028, VF-30, February 2015; $376, VF-20, November 2015; $188, VF-20, May 2015; $259, VG-10, May 2015													

MATRON HEAD (1816–1839)

Designer: *1816–1835, Matron Head—Possibly Robert Scot or John Birch; 1835–1839, Matron Head Modified—Christian Gobrecht.* **Weight:** *10.89 grams.* **Composition:** *Copper.* **Diameter:** *1816–1835, Matron Head—28 to 29 mm; 1835–1839, Matron Head Modified—27.5 mm.* **Edge:** *Plain.* **Mint:** *Philadelphia.*

Matron Head (1816–1835), Circulation Strike
1832; Newcomb-1.

Matron Head, Proof
1831; Newcomb-1.

Matron Head Modified (1835–1839), Circulation Strike
1838; Newcomb-5.

Matron Head Modified, Proof
1836; Newcomb-1.

History. The term *Matron Head* describes cents of 1816 to 1835 (none were struck in 1815). Engraver Christian Gobrecht experimented with various "Matron Head Modified" portraits in the later 1830s.

Striking and Sharpness. Planchet quality is generally very good for Liberty Head cents. Color tends to be lighter on coins of the 1830s than on earlier dates. Striking can vary. Points to check include the obverse stars (in particular), the highest hair details, and the leaves on the reverse. Denticles can range from sharp to weak, and centering is often irregular. The reverse design is essentially the same as that used on the Classic Head of 1808 to 1814, and can be graded the same way. This motif stood up to circulation particularly well.

Availability. As a type, Liberty Head cents are easily available. The scarcest date by far is 1823 (and the related 1823, 3 Over 2, overdate). Cents of 1816 to 1820 (particularly 1818 and 1820) are readily available in MS. Other MS coins are generally scarce, although those of the 1830s are more readily available than those of the teens and 1820s. Circulated examples exist in approximate relationship to their mintages. Planchet quality and striking sharpness vary in all grades.

GRADING STANDARDS

MS-60 to 70 (Mint State). *Obverse:* In the lower Mint State grades, MS–60 and 61, some slight abrasions can be seen on the portrait, most evidently on the cheek, which on this type is very prominent. Higher areas of the hair can be checked, particularly the top and back of Liberty's head, but do not confuse with lightness of strike. Luster in the

1817; N-2. Graded MS-63BN.

field is complete or nearly complete. At MS-63, luster should be complete, and no abrasion is evident.

In higher levels, the luster is complete and deeper, and some original mint color may be seen. MS-64 coins may have some minimal discoloration or scattered contact marks. A well-graded MS-65 or higher coin will have full, rich luster; no marks visible except under magnification; and a nice blend of brown toning or nicely mixed mint color and natural brown toning. Randall Hoard coins of the 1816 to 1820 years usually have much mint red and some black spotting. *Reverse:* In the lower Mint State grades some abrasion is seen on the higher areas of the leaves. Mint luster is complete in all Mint State grades, as the open areas are protected by the lettering and wreath. Sharpness of the leaves can vary by die variety, so check this aspect. Otherwise, the same comments apply as for the obverse.

Illustrated coin: Note the reverse die break running from NI of UNITED to OF A in OF AMERICA.

AU-50, 53, 55, 58 (About Uncirculated).

Obverse: Friction is seen on the higher parts, particularly the cheek. The hair has friction and light wear, usually most notable in the general area above BER of LIBERTY. Friction and scattered marks are in the field, ranging from extensive at AU-50 to minimal at AU-58. Luster may be seen in protected areas, minimal at the AU-50 level, more visible at AU-58. At AU-58 the field may retain some luster as well.

1820, 20 Over 19; N-10. Graded AU-58.

Reverse: Friction is seen on the higher wreath leaves and on the letters. Fields, protected by the designs, show friction. At the AU–55 and 58 levels little if any friction is seen. The reverse may have original luster, toned brown, minimal on lower About Uncirculated grades, often extensive at AU-58.

Illustrated coin: Flecks of darker patination spot both sides, but are particularly evident on the obverse.

EF-40, 45 (Extremely Fine). *Obverse:* Wear is seen on the portrait overall, but most hair detail is still present, except in higher areas. The cheek shows light wear. Luster is minimal or nonexistent at EF-40, and may survive in among the letters of LIBERTY at EF-45. *Reverse:* Wear is seen on the highest wreath and ribbon areas, and on the letters. Leaf veins are visible except in the highest areas. Luster is minimal, but likely more noticeable than on the obverse, as the fields are protected by the designs and lettering.

1816. Graded EF-45.

VF-20, 30 (Very Fine). *Obverse:* Wear on the portrait has reduced the hair detail, especially on the area to the right of the cheek and neck, but much can still be seen. *Reverse:* The wreath details, except for the edges of the leaves and certain of the tips (on leaves in lower relief), are worn away at VF-20, and with slightly more detail at VF-30.

1823; N2. Graded VF-20.

F-12, 15 (Fine). *Obverse:* The hair details are fewer than on the preceding, but still many are present. Wear is extensive above and below the LIBERTY coronet, with the area from the forehead to the coronet worn flat. Stars have flat centers. F-15 shows slightly more detail. *Reverse:* The higher areas of wreath leaves are worn flat, but their edges are distinct. F-15 shows slightly more detail.

1816. Graded F-15.

VG-8, 10 (Very Good). *Obverse:* The portrait is well worn, although the eye and ear can be seen clearly. The hair is mostly blended, but some slight separation can be seen in lower areas. The border is raised in most or all areas. *Reverse:* The wreath is more worn than on the preceding, but still there is some detail on the leaves. On most coins, ONE CENT is bold. Border letters are light or weak but are fully readable. The border is well defined in most areas.

1831, Large Letters; N-9. Graded VG-8.

Illustrated coin: A die break caused the internal cud which connects stars 3 through 5, and that broken die would have been retired shortly after striking this piece.

G-4, 6 (Good). *Obverse:* The portrait is worn smooth and is seen only in outline form. Much or even all of LIBERTY on the headband is readable, but the letters are weak, and L may be missing. The stars are weak. The rim is usually discernible all around. *Reverse:* Extensive wear is seen overall. Lettering in UNITED STATES OF AMERICA is weak, but completely discernible. The wreath is in outline, but still fairly bold, and ONE CENT

1830; N-9. Graded G-4.

is usually strong. The rim is usually faded into the field in many areas (depending on the die variety).

Illustrated coin: Note the lovely golden brown and rose surfaces.

AG-3 (About Good). *Obverse:* Wear is more extensive than on the preceding. The portrait is visible only in outline. Most letters of LIBERTY remain discernible in the headband, as this feature is in low relief. The stars are weak or worn away on their outer edges, and the date is light. *Reverse:* The wreath is visible in outline form, but remains fairly strong. Most of UNITED STATES OF AMERICA is worn away. ONE CENT is usually readable, but light.

1818; N-6. Graded AG-3.

1831, Large Letters; N-9. Graded PF-63BN.

PF-60 to 70 (Proof). Proofs were made for cents from 1817 onward. Often, what are called "Proofs" are only partially mirrorlike, and sometimes the striking is casual, e.g., with weakness on certain of the stars. Complicating the situation is the fact that all but one of the same die pairs were also used to make circulation strikes. Many misattributions were made generations ago, some of which have been perpetuated. Except among large-cent specialists, debate is effectively ended when a certification service seals a coin as a Proof (logic aside). True Proofs with deeply mirrored surfaces are in the small minority. *Obverse and Reverse:* Proofs that are extensively hairlined or have dull surfaces, this being characteristic of many issues (exceptions, when found, are usually dated in the 1830s) are graded PF–60 to 62 or 63. Artificially toned and recolored coins may be graded lower. To qualify as PF-65 or higher, hairlines should be microscopic, and there should be no trace of friction. Surfaces should be prooflike or, better, fully mirrored and without dullness.

Illustrated coin: This coin shows high quality for the grade. The surfaces are a light, reddish brown with areas of deep tan and hints of blue, green, gold and violet as well as considerable faded mint red on the reverse. This is one of two known Proof examples for the year.

1817, 13 Stars   **1817, 15 Stars**

	Mintage	Cert	Avg	%MS	G-4	VG-8	F-12	VF-20	EF-40	AU-50	MS-60BN / PF-63BN	MS-63BN / PF-64BN	MS-65BN / PF-65BN
1816	2,820,982	322	53.4	56%	$20	$30	$45	$100	$190	$300	$500	$700	$1,800
Auctions: $823, MS-63BN, October 2015; $259, AU-50, August 2015; $306, EF-45, April 2015; $69, EF-40, October 2015													
1817, All kinds	3,948,400												
1817, 13 Stars		452	52.9	54%	$20	$25	$40	$75	$140	$225	$450	$600	$1,550
Auctions: $1,293, MS-63BN, January 2015; $1,116, MS-63BN, January 2015; $1,175, MS-62BN, June 2015; $282, MS-60, June 2015													
1817, 15 Stars		46	50.1	24%	$30	$40	$50	$150	$600	$900	$2,800	$3,750	$35,000
Auctions: $9,400, VF-20, January 2014													
1817, Proof	2–3	1	63.0								$75,000	$100,000	$150,000
Auctions: $48,300, PF-66, July 2005													
1818	3,167,000	765	58.2	76%	$20	$25	$40	$75	$135	$225	$450	$600	$1,600
Auctions: $823, MS-64BN, September 2015; $764, MS-63RB, June 2015; $541, MS-62BN, October 2015; $494, MS-62BN, June 2015													

1819, Large Date   **1819, Small Date**   **1819, 9 Over 8**

1820, 20 Over 19   **1820, Large Date**   **1820, Small Date**
Note the 1 under the 2.   *Note the plain-topped 2.*   *Note the curl-topped 2.*

	Mintage	Cert	Avg	%MS	G-4	VG-8	F-12	VF-20	EF-40	AU-50	MS-60BN / PF-63BN	MS-63BN / PF-64BN	MS-65BN / PF-65BN
1819, All kinds	2,671,000												
1819, 9 Over 8		119	50.3	39%	$22	$30	$40	$85	$275	$375	$750	$1,300	$4,000
Auctions: $705, AU-58, October 2015; $259, EF-45, September 2015													
1819, Large Date		257	52.5	54%	$20	$25	$35	$70	$150	$300	$475	$700	$2,000
Auctions: $940, MS-63BN, August 2015; $259, AU-55, May 2015; $202, EF-40, September 2015													
1819, Small Date		102	54.9	61%	$20	$25	$35	$70	$150	$300	$475	$700	$2,000
Auctions: $1,293, MS-63BN, June 2015; $646, AU-58, October 2015; $282, AU-50, August 2015; $212, EF-40, May 2015													
1819, 9 Over 8, Proof	2–3	1	64.0								$30,000	$35,000	$50,000
Auctions: $32,200, PF-64BN, June 2005													
1820, All kinds	4,407,550												
1820, 20 Over 19		41	41.7	29%	$25	$30	$45	$110	$335	$550	$1,000	$1,600	$4,500
Auctions: $764, AU-55, August 2015													
1820, Large Date		107	57.5	72%	$20	$25	$35	$75	$175	$250	$400	$600	$1,250
Auctions: $1,293, MS-63BN, August 2015; $705, MS-63BN, January 2015; $588, MS-63BN, January 2015; $494, MS-60, September 2015													
1820, Small Date		37	51.9	54%	$20	$25	$35	$75	$250	$450	$900	$1,200	$2,800
Auctions: $4,994, MS-64BN, January 2014													
1820, Proof	8–15	3	63.7								$40,000	$50,000	$60,000
Auctions: $46,000, PF-64, November 2008													
1821 (a)	389,000	129	31.6	9%	$35	$55	$135	$375	$1,300	$2,300	$7,750	$11,000	
Auctions: $564, AU-50, January 2015; $494, VF-25, August 2015; $400, VF-20, January 2015; $129, VF-20, May 2015													
1821, Proof	4–6	3	63.0								$35,000	$50,000	$60,000
Auctions: $35,250, PF-62BN, August 2013													
1822	2,072,339	223	44.3	25%	$25	$30	$45	$120	$425	$700	$1,200	$1,800	$4,900
Auctions: $1,058, AU-58, June 2015; $793, AU-58, February 2015; $494, AU-55, January 2015; $517, AU-50, June 2015													
1822, Proof	4–6	3	63.3								$55,000	$65,000	
Auctions: $25,300, PF-63, March 2004													

a. Wide and closely spaced AMER varieties are valued the same.

1823, 3 Over 2

1824, 4 Over 2

Unofficial 1823 "Restrike"
Newcomb-3, Breen-1823, Pollock-6220.

1826, 6 Over 5

**Date Size, Through 1828
(Large, Narrow Date)**

**Date Size, 1828 and
Later (Small, Wide Date)**

	Mintage	Cert	Avg	%MS	G-4	VG-8	F-12	VF-20	EF-40	AU-50	MS-60BN / PF-63BN	MS-63BN / PF-64BN	MS-65BN / PF-65BN
1823, 3 Over 2	(b)	85	23.2	1%	$85	$150	$325	$750	$2,200	$4,500	$15,000	—	
Auctions: $1,645, VF-30, January 2015; $564, F-15, February 2015; $423, F-15, June 2015; $259, VG-10, May 2015													
1823, Normal Date	(b)	46	23.5	4%	$85	$150	$500	$1,250	$3,750	$7,500	$20,000	$30,000	$115,000
Auctions: $3,584, EF-35, January 2014													
1823, Unofficial Restrike (c)		61	63.3	97%			$450	$550	$925		$1,250	$1,500	$1,750
Auctions: $2,350, MS-64BN, December 2013													
1823, Proof	2–3	1	65.0								$65,000	$95,000	
Auctions: No auction records available.													
1823, 3 Over 2, Proof	5–8	3	64.3								$50,000	$60,000	
Auctions: $47,000, PF-64BN, June 2014													
1824, All kinds	1,262,000												
1824, 4 Over 2		42	37.1	12%	$25	$40	$85	$275	$1,500	$2,500	$7,500	$25,000	
Auctions: $423, VF-25BN, September 2015; $129, VG-10, May 2015; $94, VG-10, June 2015													
1824, Normal Date		129	42.4	17%	$20	$30	$45	$165	$500	$850	$2,400	$4,000	$8,000
Auctions: $564, EF-45, June 2015; $235, EF-40, January 2015; $259, VF-30, September 2015; $235, VF-30, May 2015													
1825	1,461,100	167	44.1	26%	$20	$30	$40	$100	$325	$650	$1,850	$2,750	$7,500
Auctions: $6,463, MS-64BN, January 2014													
1826, All kinds	1,517,425												
1826, 6 Over 5		19	52.1	47%	$25	$45	$100	$275	$975	$1,500	$2,800	$5,500	$20,000
Auctions: $10,575, MS-62BN, January 2014													
1826, Normal Date		261	48.5	35%	$20	$25	$40	$100	$250	$450	$900	$1,500	$3,100
Auctions: $3,290, MS-64, March 2015; $1,234, AU-58, August 2015; $376, AU-53, September 2015; $329, EF-40, June 2015													
1827	2,357,732	221	45.8	30%	$20	$25	$40	$100	$225	$425	$775	$1,400	$3,250
Auctions: $881, AU-58BN, October 2015; $576, AU-55, March 2015; $376, AU-53, May 2015; $259, EF-45, May 2015													
1827, Proof	5–8	2	64.0								$20,000	$25,000	$40,000
Auctions: $20,125, PF-64, March 2004													
1828, All kinds	2,260,624												
1828, Large Narrow Date		76	50.8	30%	$20	$25	$35	$75	$210	$400	$1,250	$1,750	$4,250
Auctions: $3,672, MS-64, March 2015; $881, AU-58, October 2015; $141, VF-30, January 2015													
1828, Small Wide Date		19	49.3	42%	$25	$30	$50	$120	$275	$650	$1,950	$3,500	$20,000
Auctions: $7,638, MS-64BN, February 2013													
1828, Proof	2–3	1	65.0										
Auctions: No auction records available.													

b. Included in 1824, All kinds, mintage figure. **c.** The unofficial 1823 "restrikes" (actually novodels or fantasies) were made at the same time (around 1860) and by the same people as those of 1804. The coins were made from a discarded obverse die of 1823 and an 1813 reverse die—both heavily rusted, producing surface lumps. Most examples have both dies cracked.

Large Letters (1808–1834)
*Note the size and proximity
of individual letters.*

Medium Letters (1829–1837)
*Note the isolation of the
letters, especially of STATES.*

	Mintage	Cert	Avg	%MS	G-4	VG-8	F-12	VF-20	EF-40	AU-50	MS-60BN / PF-63BN	MS-63BN / PF-64BN	MS-65BN / PF-65BN
1829, All kinds	1,414,500												
1829, Large Letters		42	48.0	36%	$20	$25	$35	$85	$200	$385	$650	$1,500	$5,200
Auctions: $646, AU-55, February 2015; $129, VF-25, February 2015													
1829, Medium Letters		16	42.8	19%	$20	$30	$110	$350	$800	$2,500	$6,500	$10,500	$17,000
Auctions: $7,050, AU-58, January 2014													
1829, Proof	2–3	1	64.0								$20,000	$25,000	$40,000
Auctions: $47,000, PF-64RB, January 2014													
1829, Bronzed, Proof	10–15	6	64.5								$18,000	$26,000	$40,000
Auctions: $41,125, PF-65BN, August 2013													
1830, All kinds	1,711,500												
1830, Large Letters		91	47.9	35%	$20	$25	$35	$70	$190	$300	$550	$1,000	$2,700
Auctions: $562, AU-55, August 2015; $646, AU-53, October 2015; $235, EF-40, May 2015; $153, VF-25, May 2015													
1830, Medium Letters		9	30.6	11%	$25	$40	$160	$500	$2,000	$4,100	$14,000	$25,000	$32,000
Auctions: $3,055, EF-40, June 2013													
1830, Proof	2–3	1	64.0								$25,000	$35,000	$150,000
Auctions: $16,500, PF-64, November 1988													
1831, All kinds	3,359,260												
1831, Large Letters		86	53.2	53%	$20	$25	$30	$65	$150	$250	$400	$700	$1,800
Auctions: $212, AU-53, July 2015; $224, AU-50, March 2015													
1831, Medium Letters		42	51.7	43%	$20	$25	$30	$65	$200	$350	$750	$1,600	$2,300
Auctions: $3,290, MS-62BN, January 2014													
1831, Proof	10–20	8	64.1								$14,500	$24,500	$50,000
Auctions: $30,550, PF-65BN, January 2014													
1832, All kinds	2,362,000												
1832, Large Letters		32	54.8	56%	$20	$25	$30	$65	$150	$250	$375	$650	$2,300
Auctions: $3,525, MS-65BN, January 2014; $306, AU-58, June 2015													
1832, Medium Letters		32	58.0	59%	$20	$25	$30	$85	$200	$550	$900	$1,200	$2,900
Auctions: $940, MS-62BN, July 2014													
1832, Proof	2–4	1	64.0										
Auctions: No auction records available.													
1833	2,739,000	269	52.2	45%	$20	$25	$30	$65	$150	$250	$375	$750	$2,600
Auctions: $423, AU-58, May 2015; $294, AU-53, May 2015; $223, EF-40, August 2015; $206, EF-40, June 2015													
1833, 3 Over 2, Proof	**(d)**	0	n/a										
Auctions: No auction records available.													

d. The mintage figure is unknown.

1834, Large 8, Large Stars, Large Reverse Letters
Newcomb-6.

1834, Large 8, Large Stars, Medium Reverse Letters
Newcomb-5.

1834, Large 8, Small Stars, Medium Reverse Letters
Newcomb-3.

1834, Small 8, Large Stars, Medium Reverse Letters
Newcomb-1.

	Mintage	Cert	Avg	%MS	G-4	VG-8	F-12	VF-20	EF-40	AU-50	MS-60BN / PF-63BN	MS-63BN / PF-64BN	MS-65BN / PF-65BN
1834, All kinds	1,855,100												
1834, Large 8, Stars, and Reverse Letters		14	44.4	7%	$20	$30	$75	$200	$550	$1,200	$2,250	$4,000	$8,500
Auctions: $2,820, AU-58, January 2014													
1834, Large 8 and Stars, Medium Letters		6	52.2	33%	$160	$325	$400	$1,000	$3,400	$6,500	$9,500	$12,000	$22,000
Auctions: $58,750, MS-65BN, January 2014; $253, AU-50, June 2015; $165, EF-40, January 2015													
1834, Large 8, Small Stars, Medium Letters		36	47.9	31%	$20	$25	$35	$65	$140	$240	$350	$625	$1,500
Auctions: $1,528, MS-63BN, January 2014													
1834, Small 8, Large Stars, Medium Letters		78	54.2	49%	$20	$25	$35	$65	$140	$240	$350	$625	$1,500
Auctions: $4,994, MS-66BN, January 2014; $823, AU-58, September 2015													
1834, Proof	6–8	4	65.0								$15,000	$21,000	$40,000
Auctions: $52,875, PF-60BN, January 2014													

1835, Large 8,
Large Stars,
Matron Head

1835, Small 8,
Small Stars,
Matron Head

Medium Letters
(1829–1837)

Small Letters
(1837–1839)

1835,
Matron
Head

1835, Head of 1836

1837
*Note the plain
hair cords.*

1837, Head of 1838
*Note the slim bust
and the beaded hair cords.*

1839, 1839 Over 1836
*Note the closed 9 and
the plain hair cords.*

1839, Silly Head
*Note the prominent lock
of hair at the forehead.*

1839, Booby Head

Note the shoulder tip. Also note the absence of a line under CENT.

	Mintage	Cert	Avg	%MS	G-4	VG-8	F-12	VF-20	EF-40	AU-50	MS-60BN / PF-63BN	MS-63BN / PF-64BN	MS-65BN / PF-65BN
1835, All kinds	3,878,400												
1835, Large 8 and Stars		13	53.7	46%	$20	$25	$35	$75	$225	$400	$750	$1,400	$2,100
Auctions: $16,450, MS-64BN, January 2013													
1835, Small 8 and Stars		47	46.9	30%	$20	$25	$35	$65	$175	$375	$475	$675	$1,750
Auctions: $3,819, MS-63BN, January 2014													
1835, Head of 1836		95	53.5	40%	$20	$25	$35	$55	$125	$250	$350	$550	$1,300
Auctions: $712, MS-62BN, August 2015; $646, AU-58, September 2015; $176, AU-50, October 2015; $106, AU-50, April 2015													
1836	2,111,000	231	52.3	47%	$20	$25	$35	$55	$125	$250	$350	$550	$1,300
Auctions: $881, MS-64BN, January 2015; $447, AU-58, September 2015; $259, AU-55, September 2015; $153, EF-45, August 2015													
1836, Proof	*6–8*	4	64.0								$15,000	$21,000	$40,000
Auctions: $47,000, PF-63RB, June 2014													
1837, All kinds	5,558,300												
1837, Plain Cord, Medium Letters		153	58.7	66%	$20	$25	$35	$55	$125	$250	$350	$550	$1,200
Auctions: $94, VF-35, February 2015													
1837, Plain Cord, Small Letters		26	55.0	50%	$20	$25	$35	$55	$125	$250	$375	$600	$1,500
Auctions: $411, AU-58, February 2014													
1837, Head of 1838		78	58.2	60%	$20	$25	$35	$45	$110	$200	$325	$500	$1,200
Auctions: $1,116, MS-64BN, January 2015; $646, MS-63BN, August 2015; $306, AU-58, August 2015; $235, AU-53, June 2015													
1837, Proof	*8–12*	7	64.0								$30,000		
Auctions: $27,025, PF-63BN, January 2014													
1838	6,370,200	870	55.6	58%	$20	$25	$35	$45	$120	$225	$335	$575	$1,325
Auctions: $1,028, MS-64BN, January 2015; $470, MS-63BN, January 2015; $223, AU-58, August 2015; $223, AU-55, May 2015													
1838, Proof	*10–20*	6	64.3								$14,000	$20,000	$38,000
Auctions: $64,625, PF-64RD, January 2014													
1839, All kinds	3,128,661												
1839, 1839 Over 1836, Plain Cords		55	13.8	0%	$225	$450	$1,250	$2,600	$9,000	$20,000	$65,000	$100,000	$250,000
Auctions: $5,581, EF-35, January 2014; $529, VG-8, January 2015													
1839, Head of 1838, Beaded Cords		97	55.0	44%	$20	$25	$32	$50	$115	$225	$325	$550	$1,450
Auctions: $1,645, MS-64BN, September 2013; $176, EF-45, February 2015; $141, EF-45, July 2015; $143, VF-35, September 2015													
1839, Silly Head		128	51.7	48%	$22	$26	$35	$75	$200	$400	$850	$1,200	$2,700
Auctions: $12,925, MS-67BN, January 2014; $160, EF-40, July 2015													
1839, Booby Head		214	53.3	50%	$20	$26	$35	$60	$150	$300	$675	$1,100	$2,350
Auctions: $470, AU-53, August 2015; $329, EF-40, May 2015; $141, VF-35, June 2015; $123, VF-25, September 2015													

BRAIDED HAIR (1839–1857)

Designer: *Christian Gobrecht.* **Weight:** *168 grains (10.89 grams).*
Composition: *Copper.* **Diameter:** *27.5 mm.* **Edge:** *Plain.* **Mint:** *Philadelphia.*

Circulation Strike
1856; N-8.

Proof

History. Christian Gobrecht's Braided Hair design was introduced in 1839. It loosely followed the design he had created for the 1838 gold eagle. On issues of 1839 through part of 1843, Miss Liberty's portrait is tilted forward, with the left tip of her neck truncation over the 8 of the date. For most issues of 1843 and all later dates her head is larger and aligned in a more vertical position, and the tip of her neck is over the first digit of the date. The reverse lettering was made larger beginning in 1844. The net result is that cents after 1843 are less delicate in appearance than are those of earlier dates. These coins were made in large quantities, except for their final year. They remained in circulation in the United States until the late 1850s, not long enough to be worn down to very low grades. (Some circulated in the eastern part of Canada through the 1860s, accounting for many of the more worn examples seen today.)

Striking and Sharpness. Sharpness can vary. On the obverse, the star centers can be weak, especially for dates in the 1850s, and, less often, there can be lightness on the front of the coronet and the hair. On the reverse the leaves can be light, but most are well struck. The denticles can be mushy and indistinct on either side, this being particularly true of dates in the early and mid-1850s. Flaky or laminated planchets can be a problem, again among coins of the 1850s, in which tiny pieces of metal fall away from the surface, leaving areas in the field that interrupt the luster on MS coins.

Availability. All dates of Braided Hair cents are readily available, with the 1857 somewhat less so (it was minted in January 1857 in low quantity; seemingly not all were released). The delicate-featured issues of 1839 to 1843 are becoming more difficult to find in EF or finer grades without surface problems. Cents dated in the 1850s are usually seen in VF or higher grades. Certain die varieties attributed by Newcomb numbers can be scarce or rare. For issues in the 1850s the differences can be microscopic, thus limiting their numismatic appeal and making them unattributable unless in high grades. Hoards were found of some dates, particularly 1850 to 1856, making MS coins of these years more readily available than would otherwise be the case. MS-64RD or higher coins with *original* color range from scarce to very rare for dates prior to 1850, but those of the 1850s are seen regularly (except for 1857). Coins below VF-20 are not widely collected and, for many issues, are too worn to attribute by die variety.

GRADING STANDARDS

MS-60 to 70 (Mint State). *Obverse:* In the lower Mint State grades, MS–60 and 61, some slight abrasions can be seen on the portrait, most evidently on the cheek. Check the tip of the coronet and the hair above the ear, as well. Luster in the field is complete or nearly so. At MS-63, luster should be complete, and no abrasion evident. If there is weakness on the hair it is due to light striking, not to wear; this also applies for the stars. In

1840, Large Date; N-7. Graded MS-64BN.

higher levels, the luster is complete and deeper, and some original mint color may be seen. Mint frost on this type is usually deep, sometimes satiny, but hardly ever prooflike. MS-64 coins may have some slight discoloration or scattered contact marks. A well-graded MS-65 or higher coin will have full, rich luster; no marks visible except under magnification; and a nice blend of brown toning or nicely mixed (not stained or blotchy) mint color and natural brown toning. MS-64RD or higher coins with original color range from scarce to very rare for dates prior to 1850, but those of the 1850s are seen regularly (except for 1857). *Reverse:* In the lower Mint State grades some abrasion is seen on the higher areas of the leaves. Mint luster is complete in all Mint State ranges, as the open areas are protected by the lettering and wreath. The quality of the luster is the best way to grade both sides of this type.

Illustrated coin: This coin is a light, golden olive with faint tints of pale green in places, with scattered red spotting on both the obverse and reverse. About half of the stars show their centers, but all of the stars are soft.

AU-50, 53, 55, 58 (About Uncirculated). *Obverse:* Wear is evident on the cheek, the hair above the ear, and the tip of the coronet. Friction is evident in the field. At AU-58, luster may be present except in the center of the fields. As the grade goes down to AU-50, wear becomes more evident on the cheek. Wear is seen on the stars, but is not as easy to discern as it is elsewhere and, in any event, many stars are weakly struck. At AU-50 there will be either no luster or only traces of luster close to the letters and devices. *Reverse:* Wear is most

1840, Large Date; N-8. Graded AU-58.

evident on the highest areas of the leaves and the ribbon bow. Luster is present in the fields. As grade goes down from AU-58 to 50, wear increases and luster decreases. At AU-50 there will be either no luster or just traces close to the letters and devices.

EF-40, 45 (Extremely Fine). *Obverse:* Wear is more extensive on the portrait, including the cheek, the hair above the ear, and the coronet. The star centers are worn down slightly (if they were sharply struck to begin with). Traces of luster are minimal, if at all existent. *Reverse:* The centers of the leaves are well worn, with detail visible only near the edges of the leaves and nearby, with the higher parts worn flat. Letters show significant wear. Luster, if present, is minimal.

1842, Large Date; N-6. Graded EF-45.

VF-20, 30 (Very Fine). *Obverse:* Wear is more extensive than on the preceding. Some of the strands of hair are fused together at the top of the head, above the ear, and on the shoulder. The center radials of the stars are nearly completely worn away. *Reverse:* The leaves show more extensive wear. Details are visible at the leaves' edges only minimally and not on all the leaves. The lettering shows smooth, even wear.

1842, Large Date; N-6. Graded VF-30.

F-12, 15 (Fine). *Obverse:* About two-thirds of the hair detail is visible. Extensive wear is seen below the coronet. On the coronet the beginning of the word LIBERTY shows wear, with L sometimes only partially visible. The hair behind the neck is flat. The stars are flat. *Reverse:* The leaves show more wear and are flat except for the lower areas. The ribbon has very little detail.

The Braided Hair large cent is seldom collected in grades lower than F-12.

1839, 9 Over 6; N-1. Graded F-12.

PF-60 to 70 (Proof). Except for the Proof 1841 cent, Proof Braided Hair cents before 1855 range from rare to very rare. Those from 1855 to 1857 are seen with some frequency. Most later Proofs are well struck and of nice quality, but there are exceptions. Most pieces from this era that have been attributed as Proofs really are such, but beware of deeply toned "Proofs" that are actually prooflike, or circulation strikes with polished fields, and

1841, Small Date; N-1. Graded PF-64RB.

recolored. *Obverse and Reverse:* Superb gems PF–65 and 66 show hairlines only under high magnification, and at PF-67 none are seen. The fields usually are deeply mirrorlike on issues after 1843, sometimes less so on earlier dates of this type. Striking should be sharp, including the stars (unlike the situation for many Proofs of the Matron Head type). There is no evidence of friction. In lower grades, hairlines are more numerous, with a profusion of them at the PF–60 to 62 levels, and there is also a general dullness of the fields. Typical color for an undipped coin ranges from light or iridescent brown to brown with some traces of mint color. Except for issues after 1854, Proofs are nearly always BN or, less often, RB. Prooflike pieces are sometimes offered as Proofs. Beware deeply toned "Proofs" and those that do not have full mirrorlike fields.

Illustrated coin: Early Proofs from this period are scarce to extremely rare. This example retains some mint orange in protected areas, as well as exhibiting hints of lilac and electric blue on the obverse.

Small Letters (1839–1843)

Large Letters (1843–1857)

1840, Large Date

1840, Small Date

1840, Small Date
Over Large 18

1842, Small Date

1842, Large Date

	Mintage	Cert	Avg	%MS	G-4	VG-8	F-12	VF-20	EF-40	AU-50	MS-60BN PF-63BN	MS-63BN PF-64BN	MS-65BN PF-65BN
1839	(a)	75	53.1	51%	$20	$25	$30	$50	$110	$265	$400	$650	$2,250 (b)
Auctions: $17,625, MS-65RB, January 2014; $1,293, MS-63BN, January 2015; $176, EF-40, May 2015													
1840, All kinds	2,462,700												
1840, Large Date		93	56.1	53%	$20	$25	$30	$35	$85	$200	$300	$500	$1,200
Auctions: $14,100, MS-64RD, January 2013													
1840, Small Date		49	55.9	51%	$20	$25	$30	$35	$85	$200	$300	$500	$1,200
Auctions: $541, MS-61BN, August 2015; $259, MS-60, October 2015; $400, AU-58, February 2015													
1840, Small Date Over Large 18		9	43.8	33%	$20	$25	$30	$50	$200	$400	$900	$1,600	$2,350
Auctions: $16,100, MS-65RB, September 2011													
1840, Proof	15–20	7	64.3								$7,000	$10,500	$20,000
Auctions: $14,100, PF-63RB, January 2014													
1841, Small Date	1,597,367	147	53.7	49%	$20	$25	$35	$50	$125	$250	$450	$950	$1,650 (c)
Auctions: $4,113, MS-66BN, June 2014													
1841, Proof	30–50	20	64.3								$6,000	$9,500	$16,000
Auctions: $21,150, PF-65RB, August 2013													
1842, All kinds	2,383,390												
1842, Small Date		48	53.6	48%	$20	$25	$30	$35	$90	$220	$375	$650	$2,200 (d)
Auctions: $23,500, MS-64RD, January 2014													
1842, Large Date		132	52.9	48%	$20	$25	$30	$35	$85	$150	$300	$500	$1,800 (c)
Auctions: $1,175, MS-63BN, August 2015; $881, MS-63BN, June 2015; $259, AU-55, April 2015; $188, AU-55, June 2015													
1842, Proof	10–20	6	64.3								$7,000	$11,000	$20,000
Auctions: $14,100, PF-64BN, January 2014													

a. Included in 1839, All kinds, mintage figure on page 216. **b.** Value in MS-65RB is $4,500. **c.** Value in MS-65RB is $3,000. **d.** Value in MS-65RB is $4,000.

1844, 44 Over 81

Head of 1840
("Petite Head," 1839–1843)

Head of 1844
("Mature Head," 1843–1857)

1847, 7 Over "Small 7"

1846, Small Date
*Note the squat date
and the closed 6.*

1846, Medium Date
*Note the medium date
height and the ball-top 6.*

1846, Tall Date
*Note the vertically
stretched date and
the open-mouthed 6.*

1851, 51 Over 81
*These are not true
overdates, but are three
of the more spectacular
of several date-punch
blunders of the 1844–
1854 period. The so-called
overdates of 1844 and
1851 each have the date
punched upside down,
then corrected normally.*

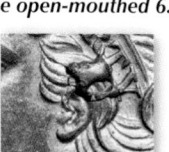

1855, Upright 5's

1855, Slanting 5's

1855, Knob on Ear

	Mintage	Cert	Avg	%MS	G-4	VG-8	F-12	VF-20	EF-40	AU-50	MS-60BN	MS-63BN	MS-65BN
											PF-63BN	PF-64BN	PF-65BN
1843, All kinds	2,425,342												
1843, Petite Head, Small Letters		163	55.8	62%	$20	$25	$30	$35	$85	$160	$300	$450	$1,750
Auctions: $1,293, MS-63BN, January 2015; $588, MS-63BN, August 2015; $494, AU-58, August 2015; $376, AU-58, August 2015													
1843, Petite Head, Large Letters		56	53.3	48%	$20	$30	$45	$80	$210	$320	$825	$1,500	$2,300
Auctions: $4,406, MS-64BN, January 2014													
1843, Mature Head, Large Letters		51	48.6	41%	$20	$25	$30	$45	$150	$275	$550	$900	$2,100
Auctions: $9,988, MS-64RB, January 2014													
1843, Proof	10–20	9	64.4								$7,000	$11,000	$20,000
Auctions: $25,850, PF-66RB, June 2014													
1844, Normal Date	2,398,752	196	53.4	47%	$20	$25	$30	$40	$85	$160	$300	$500	$1,500
Auctions: $8,225, MS-65BN, January 2014; $940, MS-62BN, June 2015; $141, AU-53, January 2015													
1844, 44 Over 81	(e)	38	44.3	26%	$35	$40	$60	$120	$250	$550	$1,200	$2,750	$5,500
Auctions: $1,175, MS-60BN, January 2014; $212, VF-25, August 2015													
1844, Proof	10–20	6	64.5								$13,000	$20,000	$30,000
Auctions: $55,813, PF-65RD, January 2014													
1845	3,894,804	332	55.1	58%	$20	$25	$30	$35	$75	$135	$225	$375	$1,200
Auctions: $881, MS-64BN, January 2015; $423, MS-63BN, March 2015; $353, MS-62BN, May 2015; $176, AU-53, January 2015													
1845, Proof	8–12	5	63.8								$8,000	$15,000	$23,000
Auctions: $16,450, PF-64BN, April 2013													

e. Included in 1844, Normal Date, mintage figure.

| | Mintage | Cert | Avg | %MS | G-4 | VG-8 | F-12 | VF-20 | EF-40 | AU-50 | MS-60BN | MS-63BN | MS-65BN |
											PF-63BN	PF-64BN	PF-65BN
1846, All kinds	4,120,800												
1846, Small Date		280	54.5	60%	$20	$25	$30	$35	$75	$135	$225	$350	$1,200
Auctions: $494, MS-64BN, February 2015; $329, MS-62BN, February 2015; $129, AU-53, February 2015; $119, AU-50, April 2015													
1846, Medium Date		34	57.6	68%	$20	$25	$30	$35	$85	$150	$250	$400	$1,350
Auctions: $705, MS-61BN, March 2013													
1846, Tall Date		58	48.1	41%	$25	$30	$35	$50	$150	$225	$500	$950	$1,800
Auctions: $56, VF-30, September 2011													
1846, Proof	*8–12*	2	66.0								$8,000	$15,000	$23,000
Auctions: $30,550, PF-65BN, June 2014													
1847	6,183,669	735	56.6	62%	$20	$25	$30	$40	$75	$135	$225	$350	$950
Auctions: $646, MS-64BN, August 2015; $881, MS-63BN, August 2015; $188, MS-62BN, June 2015; $223, MS-61BN, September 2015													
1847, 7 Over "Small 7"	**(f)**	34	52.0	47%	$25	$35	$45	$75	$175	$420	$1,000	$1,350	$2,750
Auctions: $9,694, MS-65BN, January 2014													
1847, Proof	*8–12*	1	64.0								$8,000	$15,000	$23,000
Auctions: $31,050, PF-65RB, February 2011													
1848	6,415,799	770	55.7	57%	$20	$25	$30	$35	$75	$130	$225	$350	$925
Auctions: $1,175, MS-65BN, January 2015; $223, MS-62BN, January 2015; $259, AU-58, January 2015; $129, AU-55, October 2015													
1848, Proof	*15–20*	10	64.6								$10,000	$15,000	$23,000
Auctions: $14,100, MS-64BN, August 2013													
1849	4,178,500	437	55.3	54%	$20	$25	$30	$35	$85	$150	$250	$450	$1,200
Auctions: $317, MS-62, March 2015; $259, AU-58, October 2015; $353, AU-50, July 2015; $84, EF-40, May 2015													
1849, Proof	*6–10*	4	64.3								$8,500	$16,000	$25,000
Auctions: $23,500, PF-65RB, August 2013													
1850	4,426,844	966	60.1	78%	$20	$25	$30	$35	$60	$125	$180	$230	$650 **(g)**
Auctions: $1,058, MS-65BN, January 2015; $376, MS-64BN, January 2015; $286, MS-63BN, February 2015; $259, AU-58, June 2015													
1850, Proof	*6–10*	3	65.0								$10,000	$17,000	$28,000
Auctions: $19,550, PF-64RB, February 2011													
1851, Normal Date	9,889,707	1,397	58.5	69%	$20	$25	$30	$35	$60	$125	$180	$230	$650 **(g)**
Auctions: $1,058, MS-65BN, August 2015; $411, MS-64BN, May 2015; $306, MS-64BN, October 2015; $100, AU-50, April 2015													
1851, 51 Over 81	**(h)**	94	57.4	66%	$25	$35	$45	$65	$200	$250	$500	$1,000	$2,400
Auctions: $1,763, MS-65BN, June 2014; $329, AU-55, May 2015													
1852	5,063,094	1,319	60.0	74%	$20	$25	$30	$35	$60	$125	$180	$230	$635 **(i)**
Auctions: $881, MS-65BN, October 2015; $764, MS-65BN, January 2015; $353, MS-64BN, January 2015; $129, AU-55, February 2015													
1852, Proof	*4–6*	1	65.0								$10,000	$35,000	$65,000
Auctions: $47,150, PF-64BN, February 2011													
1853	6,641,131	2,084	59.9	74%	$20	$25	$30	$35	$60	$125	$180	$230	$635 **(i)**
Auctions: $2,115, MS-65RD, January 2015; $588, MS-64RB, January 2015; $235, MS-63BN, January 2015; $212, MS-62BN, June 2015													
1854	4,236,156	1,127	58.4	65%	$20	$25	$30	$35	$60	$125	$180	$230	$650 **(g)**
Auctions: $360, MS-64BN, October 2015; $282, MS-63BN, May 2015; $212, MS-62BN, January 2015; $141, AU-58, January 2015													
1854, Proof	*4–6*	5	64.6								$8,500	$10,000	$14,000
Auctions: $28,200, PF-65RB, June 2014													
1855, All kinds	1,574,829												
1855, Upright 5's		387	58.3	64%	$20	$25	$30	$35	$60	$125	$180	$230	$635 **(i)**
Auctions: $1,116, MS-65RB, January 2015; $400, MS-64BN, June 2015; $282, MS-63BN, July 2015; $200, MS-62BN, January 2015													
1855, Slanting 5's		100	58.4	62%	$20	$25	$30	$35	$65	$130	$200	$275	$1,250 **(j)**
Auctions: $353, MS-62BN, November 2015; $200, MS-61BN, June 2015; $141, MS-60, January 2015; $153, AU-53, June 2015													
1855, Slanting 5's, Knob on Ear		138	56.7	50%	$20	$30	$45	$55	$110	$225	$400	$525	$2,150
Auctions: $259, AU-50, July 2015; $153, EF-45, September 2015; $100, EF-40, August 2015													
1855, Proof	*15–20*	10	64.5								$5,500	$7,000	$10,000
Auctions: $8,050, PF-64RB August 2011													

f. Included in 1847 mintage figure. **g.** Value in MS-65RB is $1,200. **h.** Included in 1851, Normal Date, mintage figure. **i.** Value in MS-65RB is $1,150. **j.** Value in MS-65RB is $2,000.

1856, Upright 5	**1856, Slanting 5**	**1857, Large Date**	**1857, Small Date**

	Mintage	Cert	Avg	%MS	G-4	VG-8	F-12	VF-20	EF-40	AU-50	MS-60BN / PF-63BN	MS-63BN / PF-64BN	MS-65BN / PF-65BN
1856, All kinds	2,690,463												
1856, Upright 5		239	58.8	63%	$20	$25	$30	$35	$65	$130	$225	$270	$675 (g)
	Auctions: $725, MS-65BN, January 2015; $705, MS-64RB, January 2015; $482, MS-64BN, January 2015; $165, AU-58, September 2015												
1856, Slanting 5		369	57.5	60%	$20	$25	$30	$35	$65	$130	$225	$270	$675 (g)
	Auctions: $999, MS-66BN, June 2015; $764, MS-65BN, February 2015; $259, MS-63BN, February 2015; $223, MS-62BN, February 2015												
1856, Proof	40–60	21	64.7								$5,000	$7,000	$10,000
	Auctions: $25,850, PF-66RB, November 2013												
1857, All kinds	333,546												
1857, Large Date		592	58.1	61%	$60	$80	$100	$125	$200	$300	$400	$750	$1,200
	Auctions: $823, MS-64BN, January 2015; $558, MS-62, March 2015; $141, AU-50, July 2015; $223, EF-45, October 2015												
1857, Small Date		232	55.8	46%	$65	$85	$110	$135	$200	$310	$430	$800	$1,500
	Auctions: $940, MS-64BN, January 2015; $646, MS-63BN, August 2015; $494, MS-62BN, January 2015; $353, AU-55, September 2015												
1857, Large Date, Proof	100–150	33	64.5								$5,000	$7,000	$12,500
	Auctions: No auction records available.												
1857, Small Date, Proof	15–20	8	65.1								$6,000	$8,000	$13,000
	Auctions: $52,875, PF-65RD, April 2014												

Note: Numismatic anachronisms dated 1868 were struck in nickel and in copper, featuring the large cent design last used in 1857. These likely were quietly and unofficially sold by Mint employees to collectors. They are classified as Judd-610 and 611 in *United States Pattern Coins*. **g.** Value in MS-65RB is $1,200.

THE PASSING OF THE LARGE CENT AND HALF CENT

By 1857 the U.S. Mint's costs for manufacturing and distributing its half cents and large cents had risen so high that Mint Director James Ross Snowden reported that the copper coins "barely paid expenses." Both denominations had become unpopular, and they rarely circulated outside the nation's larger cities. With this pressure, change was on the horizon. The Treasury Department had recent precedent to tinker with coinage sizes and compositions. For several years in the early 1850s the Mint had issued silver coins of reduced weight, as a way to discourage their melting and export (the coins' silver content had been greater than their face values). On the heels of this coinage reform, new legislation in 1857 replaced the large copper cent with a smaller copper-nickel coin of the same value, and terminated the half cent outright.

The coinage legislation of 1857 brought important benefits to the United States. Under its terms, Spanish coins were redeemed for melting at the Mint and exchanged for the new, small cents. The old-fashioned reckoning of business transactions in Spanish *reales* and *medios*, British shillings, and other currencies was (officially, at least) abandoned, and the American decimal system was popularized. Citizens found the new small cent to be convenient, and it quickly became a favored and useful means of retail trade. Tens of millions would be minted before the decade closed.

The hobby of coin collecting experienced a boom when the large cent and half cent passed away. Casual observers set aside the obsolete coins as mementoes of a time gone by, while more experienced collectors sought to assemble collections composed of one of each date. Over the ensuing decades the study and collecting of these old coppers has become more and more specialized while still attracting hobby newcomers. Their devoted enthusiasts appreciate the coins' historical connections and cultural significance.

Small Cents
1856 to Date

This study of U.S. small cents is based on the work of Q. David Bowers,
a numismatic professional, and author in the field, for more than 60 years.

THE BIRTH OF THE SMALL CENT

LARGE COPPER CENTS OF 1793 TO 1857

Authorized by the Mint Act of April 2, 1792, the first copper large cents were struck at the Philadelphia Mint in February 1793. Each large cent type featured the head of Miss Liberty on the obverse. Early types were made from hand-engraved dies with many interesting variations. As time went on, engraving techniques improved, and various mechanical processes were introduced into the production of large cents. The wide variations seen in the hand-cut dies of 1793 cents were replaced by much subtler differences by the early 1800s. In 1832 the production of coins was shifted to the second United States Mint, a Greek Revival building designed by architect William Strickland. This facility remained in use until 1901.

Throughout the early 1800s the copper cent was the most popular, the most ubiquitous, of American coins. A handful of pennies could buy a dinner, an overnight stay in a hotel, or passage on a coach drawn by a span of horses. As the passport to many delights, the large cent endeared itself to everyone, resulting in collecting mania when it began fading from circulation in 1857.

TRANSITION OF THE COPPER CENT

By the late 1840s the cost of producing the large, heavy copper cents had risen sharply, reducing the profit their coinage made for the Mint. At the time, copper cents (and also half cents, made in much smaller numbers) were produced as a source of revenue for the Mint. Raw copper would be bought, or blank planchets ready for coining would be acquired from a supplier. Finished cents would be placed into circulation for face value, with the Mint account recording the profit made after metal and production

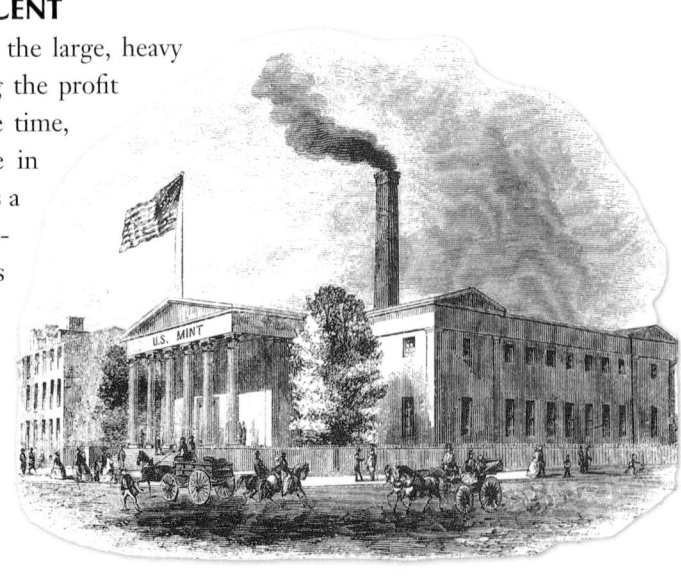

The second Philadelphia Mint began production of coins in 1832 and continued in use until 1901.

costs were deducted. In contrast, silver and gold coins were made only at the request of depositors of these precious metals, who would pay a very small fee for refining and coinage, yielding little profit to the Mint. These depositors requested specific denominations, such as dollars or half eagles, to be coined from their precious metals. Because of their profitability, copper cents were produced continuously (except for 1815), while mintages of gold and silver coins were very erratic.

Starting in 1849, the Mint began making an effort to find a replacement for the 168-grain copper large cent, which was considered cumbersome to handle and too expensive to produce. The Mint experimented with reduced-diameter and lower-weight cents as early as 1850 with several annular (ring-shaped) designs in various metals. The difference between metal cost and face value was a source of profit that was carefully studied and guarded by the Mint.

In 1851 and early 1852 the price of copper subsided somewhat, and the sense of urgency for a new cent diminished within the Treasury Department. In late 1852 and in 1853 the price rose again—at one point to 42¢ per

A steam-powered coining press, introduced in the 1830s, at work in the 1850s.

pound. The Mint estimated that when the price was more than 40¢ per pound (which was enough metal to make 42-2/3 one-cent pieces), a loss was sustained due to the costs of manufacturing. In 1853 some patterns were struck in a nickel-copper composition, utilizing an 1853 quarter eagle obverse die with a pattern reverse die; these pieces appeared silvery in the manner of Feuchtwanger cents, which were produced as cent substitutes in 1837.

Momentum for a new-style cent of lighter weight and smaller diameter increased sharply in 1854 and 1855 when really serious investigation began. Some of the pattern cents of these two years used an adaptation of Christian Gobrecht's flying eagle design created in 1838 for use on half dollars. Other 1854 and 1855 pattern cents displayed Liberty Heads. One notable variant was made by mechanically copying the obverse of an 1854, Liberty Seated, dollar (the crossbar and diagonal element did not copy well, and the date appeared as 1851).

In spring 1856, James Booth, the Mint's melter and refiner, concluded that a mixture of 88 parts copper and 12 parts nickel would be ideal for a new cent. This alloy became known as copper-nickel. Booth suggested that a weight of 72 grains would be convenient, as this was equivalent to 80 pieces to the Troy pound (although the avoirdupois pound, rather than the Troy measure, was usually employed for base metals). The resultant coins were to be of small diameter, and they were made fairly thick to eliminate any confusion with silver coins at a glance. The result was the 1856, Flying Eagle, cent—the first small cent.

In 1837 Dr. Lewis Feuchtwanger proposed that his special alloy be used for federal cents. Congress did not accept the idea. Feuchtwanger commissioned large quantities to be made for his own account. These small-diameter cents were widely accepted in commerce during the Panic of 1837 when all coins were scarce in circulation. (shown at 200%)

An 1854, Liberty Seated, silver dollar was placed into a portrait lathe and mechanically copied and reduced—a curious procedure—to create the obverse die for a pattern cent variety known as Judd-157.

Judd-173 is one of several varieties of large-diameter Flying Eagle pattern cents made in 1854 and 1855.

DESIGNS OF SMALL CENTS

Small cents have been produced in a variety of designs.

Types include:

> Flying Eagle (1856–1858)
> Indian Head (1859–1909)
>> Copper-Nickel, Indian Head, Laurel Wreath Reverse (1859)
>> Copper-Nickel, Indian Head, Oak Wreath With Shield Reverse (1860–1864)
>> Bronze, Indian Head, Oak Wreath With Shield Reverse (1864–1909)
> Lincoln, Wheat Ears Reverse (1909–1958)
>> Bronze, Lincoln, Wheat Ears Reverse (1909–1942)
>> Zinc-Coated Steel, Lincoln, Wheat Ears Reverse (1943)
>> Bronze, Lincoln, Wheat Ears Reverse (1944–1958)
> Lincoln, Memorial Reverse (1959–2008)
>> Copper Alloy, Lincoln, Memorial Reverse (1959–1982)
>> Copper-Plated Zinc, Lincoln, Memorial Reverse (1982–2008)
> Lincoln, Bicentennial Reverses (2009)
> Lincoln, Shield Reverse (2010 to Date)

COLLECTING SMALL CENTS

WAYS TO COLLECT

Flying Eagle cents of 1856 to 1858 are usually collected in combination with Indian Head cents of 1859 to 1909. These two series are very popular today and have been for a long time. For those with an advanced interest, the Flying Eagle and Indian Head Collectors' Society, nicknamed the Fly-In Club, can be contacted on the Internet (www.fly-inclub.org). The club publishes *Longacre's Ledger*, named for James B. Longacre, the designer of both the Flying Eagle and the Indian Head cent.

Flying Eagle cents can be collected by the basic varieties listed in the regular edition of the *Guide Book of United States Coins*, or by using the present text many other varieties can be contemplated. The key to the series is the famous 1856 Flying Eagle cent, but there are other elusive issues as well. Among these are the three 1857 varieties struck from clashed dies. Rick Snow's *The Flying Eagle & Indian Cent Attribution Guide*, vols. 1 and 2, are a source for extremely detailed information for advanced collectors.

Most Indian Head cents were made in large quantities, but some are considered scarce or rare in relation to the demand for them, this being especially true for examples in higher–Mint State grades. These rarities include the 1864, With L, cent (with the initial L engraved on the ribbon for Longacre, the designer); the somewhat scarce 1871 and 1872 cents; the especially elusive 1877 cent; and the low-mintage 1909-S cent. Among Proof Indian Head cents the 1864, With L, is one of the great classics of the second half of the 19th century.

Without a doubt, Lincoln cents are the single most popular series in numismatics. First coined in 1909 and still being made, they have seen several changes in reverse designs and metal compositions. Most Lincoln cents in general circulation date from 1959 onward. Cents of 1909 to 1958 with the Wheat Ears reverse—nicknamed "wheaties"—are few and far between. Even among varieties this side of 1959 there are some that have strong value, often considerably stronger in very high grades.

If you aspire to collect one Lincoln cent of each date and major variety the key issue in circulated grades is the 1909-S V.D.B., certainly one of the best-known key 20th-century coins. The next rarest, when circulated coins are considered, is the 1914-D cent. In upper echelons of Mint State there are a number of *condition rarities.* A gem 1911-S cent, to pick one of many examples, is rarer than a gem 1909-S V.D.B. cent, but in worn grades the 1911-S cent is very common.

There are a number of unusual varieties beyond standard dates and mintmarks that are highly desired by Lincoln cent collectors. The 1922-D, No D, cent is a 1922-D cent struck from a die in which the D was filled in. As no Philadelphia cents were made this year, the 1922-D, No D, is sometimes collected as a filler in place of a Philadelphia coin. The 1955, Doubled Die Obverse, cent is scarce in all grades and, in relation to the demand, is rare in Mint State. Several other doubled dies are hard to find, with the 1969-S, Doubled Die Obverse, being a major rarity. The 1990 Proof cent that should have an S mintmark but doesn't is another elusive issue.

How to Be a Smart Buyer

Now to buying coins for your collection and enjoyment. Although one set of information does not necessarily fit all, the characteristics of small cents are quite similar for the Flying Eagle, Indian Head, and Lincoln series. The main exception is that copper-nickel alloy was used on Flying Eagle cents and on Indian Head cents through spring 1864 and is not subject to the toning and coloration that affects later bronze coins which are classified as brown (BN), red-brown (RB), and red (RD).

In the marketplace today the vast majority of small cents are simply given a grading abbreviation such as EF-40, MS-63, and so on. For bronze cents the suffixes BN, RB, and RD are given to coins in the Mint State range. In relatively recent times the two leading certification services, the Professional Coin Grading Service (PCGS) and the Numismatic Guaranty Corporation of America (NGC), have added suffixes to their grades such as plus signs, stars, terms like *Cameo*, etc. These suffixes are elusive of precise definition, and in any event countless millions of coins were certified in the years before such additional designations were used. The Certified Acceptance Corporation (CAC), an independent authentication service, will, for a fee, add a sticker to a certified coin's holder if its experts consider a coin to be a nice example within its assigned certified grade. Rick Snow's Eagle Eye Photo Seal, first used in 1996, is applied to Flying Eagle and Indian Head cents that he views as being of nice quality.

Even with the aid of these certifications, there is no way other than carefully examining a coin or a high-resolution image of it that you can tell if it is sharply struck in all areas, is on a flawless planchet, and has great aesthetic or eye appeal. For my money an 1857, Flying Eagle, cent in MS-63 grade, sharply struck, deeply lustrous, and very attractive is a better buy than an MS-65 cent with lightly struck areas and dull surfaces. Another catch is the color system. Some BN bronze coins have significant areas of mint red, more so than those certified as RB. A tremendous number of RD bronze coins have tiny flecks or streaks, or are not fully red. Many of these have been dipped to gain their brightness. The following catalog points out instances where this is very common, such as among Proof RD Indian Head cents before 1890 and all Matte Proof cents from 1909 through 1916. Adding a further complication is that some coins tone or change color while in certified holders, causing the color designation in the certified grade to be erroneous.[1] A coin listed as RD may appear blotchy. This often happens to dipped BN and RB cents that become RD, but do not have stable surfaces.

The preceding is *good news* for you!

By carefully cherrypicking (a term popularized by Bill Fivaz and J.T. Stanton) for quality, you can often buy a superb coin for no more than others pay for dull, unattractive pieces. While this makes common sense, or so it would seem, reality is that more than 90% of buyers do no more than read the grading label on a holder. A holder will *never* say, "MS-63 with carbon spots," or "AU-50 with light scratch on the reverse." Most buyers are not aware that there can be huge differences in quality within a single grade.

Here are several hypothetical coins and their grade descriptions:

1863 MS-64.
1863 MS-65.

1907 MS-65 RD.
1907 MS-66 RD.

1911 Matte Proof BN.
1911 Matte Proof RD.

Here are the same coins with comments in parentheses as to how a smart buyer might see them:

1863 MS-64. (Sharply struck, bright, and with superb eye appeal.)
1863 MS-65. (Rather dull surfaces. The tips of the feathers in the headdress are weakly struck.)

1907 MS-65 RD. (Nicely struck, brilliant surfaces, no flecks or streaks.)
1907 MS-66 RD. (Nicely struck, but sprinkled with tiny flecks on the obverse.)

1911 Matte Proof BN. (Richly lustrous surfaces with a hint of blue.)
1911 Matte Proof RD. (Likely dipped, with unstable surfaces, as *original* RD Matte Proofs are as scarce as hen's teeth.)

Be warned that such connoisseurship will limit what you will want to buy at auction or in other offerings. You will need to spend much more time in your searches.

A SMALL CENT, EXAMINED

This 1926-S cent demonstrates what cherry-picking and connoisseurship are all about. This very weakly struck cent was certified as MS-63RD by a leading service. Both dies are extremely worn, with the reverse showing a "ghost" outline of the obverse. In addition, the dies were probably spaced too widely apart. Probably, any connoisseur would rather have a sharply struck AU-58 coin for a *tiny fraction* of the price! In this instance the holder labeled and certified as "1926-S MS-63RD" has no real meaning for a smart buyer.

A 1926-S, Lincoln, Wheat Ears Reverse, cent. Graded MS-63RD.

ASPECTS OF SHARPNESS

Except for Proofs, small cents were made to be used in commerce. The various mints are coin factories challenged to turn out as many coins as possible, as quickly as possible, with as little expense as possible. Assuming that all of the obverse dies made for a given date of a cent were used, here are some fiscal-year figures for the average number of coins struck per obverse die:

1862 cent (copper-nickel): 143,240

1865 cent (bronze, a softer metal than copper-nickel): 331,115

1898 cent: 252,900

1903 cent: 478,049

1912 cent (average for each of three mints): 315,787

Modern cent on Schuler press: 500,000+

Although most dies held up well, in nearly all instances coins made later in a die's life show some indistinct areas.

A major cause of weakness was in the striking process for many cents. In a coining press the farther the dies are spaced apart, the longer they will last. Spacing them too closely increases breakage. In some areas of American numismatics such wide die spacing led to weak higher areas such as the reverse bands on Mercury dimes (1916 through 1945), Liberty's head and shield on Standing Liberty quarters (1916 through 1930), and the head and left hand on Liberty Walking half dollars (1916 through 1947). As a standout example, there seems to be no such thing as a sharply struck 1923-S in the last series.

For Flying Eagle cents of 1856 through 1858 the key places to check for light strike are the eagle's head and tail on the obverse and the highest leaves on the reverse. Beyond that, check the denticles (which can be mushy). Each of the basic varieties does exist sharply struck.

A detail of a Flying Eagle cent with strong detail in the tail feathers.

A detail of a Flying Eagle cent with weakness in the tail feathers.

For Indian Head cents the key area on the obverse is the headdress. On many, sometimes most for certain issues, the feather tips are flat and indistinct. Cents of 1863 are particularly notable in this respect.

A detail of a certified MS-66 1864 copper-nickel cent that sold for thousands of dollars based on its grade, as no one cared that some of the feathers were weak.

A detail of another 1864 cent in a lower grade that sold for far less money, but is sharply struck and with nice eye appeal.

For Lincoln cents with the Wheat Ears Reverse (1909 through 1958), the area to check first is Lincoln's shoulder. This element is raised, and on many coins the metal did not fill the die recess completely. The result is that even on Mint State coins there can be many tiny nicks and marks on the shoulder—characteristics from the original surface of the planchet. Also check the O of ONE on the reverse, which is opposite the high-relief shoulder. After learning about and studying these weaknesses, most sophisticated buyers find such coins intolerable. The catch is that finding a sharp one, which is possible, may take a long time.

A detail of a certified MS-66RD 1925-D, Lincoln, Wheat Ears Reverse, cent with countless abrasions on Lincoln's shoulder as a result of the coin not being struck fully.

A weakly struck 1943-S zinc-coated steel cent. The 4 in the date is mostly gone, and the top of WE TRUST is weak.

For Lincoln cents with the Memorial Reverse (1959–2008) the striking varies. Until the relief of Lincoln's shoulder was considerably reduced in 1984, the letters E PL of E PLURIBUS were typically quite shallow.[2] After the portrait adjustment, the sharpness on a typical coin increased. As a general rule, check all points for sharpness. Die wear usually manifests itself with graininess in the Lincoln, Memorial Reverse, type and the later reverses of 1909 onward were made in large quantities, so finding a sharp Lincoln cent should be no problem. This is especially true for Lincoln, Bicentennial Reverse, cents (2009) and Lincoln, Shield Reverse, cents (2010 to the present).

ASPECTS OF PLANCHET QUALITY AND METALLIC COMPOSITION

The planchets or blank disks used to strike coins were typically of high quality, fairly consistent weight, and of well mixed alloy. Problems stemming from the planchets are few and far between. When they do occur they are usually in the form of laminations or thin flakes of metal separating.

Sometimes, the alloy elements did not mix completely. For certain bronze Indian Head cents a "woodgrain" effect can be seen on high-grade coins with brown (BN) toning. This was caused by the tin and zinc, which made up 5% of the alloy, not being completely mixed. When a copper ingot of this alloy was rolled out and distended during the making of planchet strips (from which planchets are cut), these unmixed particles were distended as well. Woodgrain effect can be very attractive and sometimes adds to the appeal of an RB coin.

The planchets for the 1909-S, Indian Head; 1909-S, V.D.B.; 1909-S; and some 1910-S cents exhibit a light gold-brown woodgrain effect in many instances. A wider commentary was given by David W. Lange in an article in *The Numismatist*, "San Francisco Mint Cents 1908–24," August 2002, that included this:

A 1910-S cent with a distinctive yellowish tinge and a light woodgrain effect (delicate toning streaks with a diagonal orientation).

One thing I've noticed while examining Uncirculated bronze coins produced by the San Francisco Mint from the onset of coinage there in 1908 through roughly 1924 is that they have some very distinctive features. These often enable one to identify them as "S" Mint products before seeing the mintmark. Though the alloy used for United States cents was prescribed by law, there are peculiarities seemingly unique to cents made at San Francisco.

When entirely untoned, "S" Mint bronze coins have a very pale, brassy color unlike that of the more reddish or coppery cents from the Philadelphia and Denver Mints. For the period described, however, "S" Mint cents are seldom seen untoned. The only issues commonly encountered in that condition are the widely hoarded 1909-S cents, both with and without the designer's initials "V.D.B." Subsequent dates through the mid-1920s are typically toned to various degrees, though many have survived with partial mint color.

In later years the planchets for Lincoln cents were of more uniform consistency at the various mints, resulting in coins of an orange-red color. There are some exceptions, and certain cents are a warmer red. Cents of 1943 are of distinctive zinc-coated steel. Those of 1944 to 1946 are sometimes called brass, as the composition is 95% copper and 5% zinc, without the tin that defines bronze. The color difference is not often noticeable.

The copper-coated zinc planchets introduced in 1982 caused all sorts of problems. Many coins became discolored, or bubbles or blisters erupted on the surface, or the coins became blotchy. This problem extended through 1983, but was corrected after that—although on occasion some unattractive coins were still minted. Flaking of the copper coating, or sections of a cent with the copper missing, are not unusual. These are in the category of mint errors.

"Light colored" cents were reported in the Collectors' Clearinghouse column of *Coin World* on May 23, 1983. Not long afterward, nearly 20 were sent in by readers:

Mint officials say that the brass-colored plating is composed of 10% zinc and 90% copper rather than 100% copper. "That's why they are light in color," they explained. They believed that as time went on, those cents would turn a "mustard" color.

David W. Lange suggests that such coating, or an alloy close to it, has been used since 1983. "It adheres better and reduces blistering."[3] The color of finished cents can vary slightly, however. Zinc proportions can vary among modern cents. This is so because zinc planchets can become trapped in the copper plating tank and dissolve into the plating solution. Authentic cents with this feature have been reported by Ken Potter to include 1985-D (most often encountered), 1997, 1997-D, and 1998 cents.[4] Doubtless, others will be found. As these can be simulated artificially, authentication is recommended if a coin costs a substantial amount. Otherwise, buy from a respected seller.

ASPECTS OF ORIGINAL COLOR AND TONING

When a bronze Indian Head cent of, say, 1865 or a Lincoln cent of 1915 left the coining press it had a bright, shiny, orange-red color on both sides and on the edge (as viewed edge-on). As the minting process creates heat, the newly made coin was warm, even hot to the touch. Immediately, it was subjected to the atmosphere, which in any mint consisted of the normal nitrogen-oxygen composition, plus traces of human breath, heating or industrial fumes, various suspended particles, and more. Copper is a chemically active metal, and the cent began to acquire normal light toning—at first hardly perceptible.

At the mint the coin was run through a mechanical counting machine, then put into a canvas bag for shipping. No care was taken to keep the bag from moisture, and in storage, handling, and shipping some dampness was probably acquired. Prior to the establishment of the Federal Reserve System in 1913, the mints as well as the Sub-Treasury offices (until about 1920 or 1921) shipped cents directly to banks and other customers.[5] Subsequently, they have been distributed through the Federal Reserve. In the 20th century and later, many cents were put up in 50-coin paper rolls. Many were put into bags of $50 face value, filled with either loose coins or rolls.

After distribution, the typical coin was paid into circulation, or perhaps in the 19th century it was saved in a cast-iron bank or, later, in a piggy bank or other type, or maybe it was acquired by a numismatist. As the years went by, the cent acquired more toning. If carefully kept in a dry environment away from heat and light, the toning would be minimized. Otherwise the coin would acquire a tinge or whisper of light brown with a pleasing softening of the orange-red color overall. If kept in a coin cabinet tray or in a paper envelope, it would typically acquire a deeper brown toning. Cents kept in seaside areas often gained tiny black flecks from microscopic particles of sea salt in the air. Those kept in homes in which sulfur fumes, even in small quantity, were emitted from furnaces tended to tone as did those subjected to smog or fumes in a city. Original mint red (RD) faded to red and brown (RB) then to brown (BN). The vast majority of bronze cents from 1864 into the 20th century acquired toning in this way.

In contrast, coins acquired by numismatists in the 19th and early 20th centuries that were stored in paper envelopes tended to remain brilliant, sometimes with just a trace of toning. Beginning in a large way in the 1930s, cents kept in quantity in bank-wrapped rolls remained brilliant.

BN, RB, and RD: Color and Price

In many instances, in today's price hierarchy coins with full brilliance certified as RD (red) command prices far in excess of those with the same grade number that are called BN (brown) or RB (red-brown). And yet, from the standpoint of eye appeal and general desirability, a BN coin can often be nicer than an RD coin. Nowhere is this more evident than in Matte Proofs from 1909 to 1916, which were hardly ever seen with RD surfaces until the second half of the 20th century. By that time the "brilliant is best" philosophy had characterized the vast majority of the coin market, and toned copper and silver coins were often dipped in a silver-dip solution to make them bright. Others were cleaned with silver polish. Over a period of time these coins retoned, after which they were usually cleaned again. Similarly, it became popular to brighten copper coins by dipping, not by the use of polish. Such coins became brilliant. To give them a whisper of toning, such as might be acquired by aging, they were subjected to being warmed for a short period of time.

Beginning in a significant way with the auction of the Garrett Collection from 1979 to 1981, coins with very attractive original toning brought high prices at auction. Many of these had been collected by T. Harrison Garrett in the 1870s and 1880s and carefully preserved over time. Dipping and redipping of silver coins slowed down, and an industry was born to add artificial iridescent or other toning to bright silver coins. Today, if you examine offerings of Proof silver coins of the 19th century you will find very few

An 1883 cent, graded PF-65RB, showing original color. Unfortunately, such coins are often dipped to make them RD.

certified above PF-66, and many are certified from PF–60 to 64. If it was not for such cleaning, almost every Proof 19th century coin would be PF-67 or higher today. In practice, few are. This is the testimony to widespread cleaning. Today, the certification services do not call Proofs that are not gems "cleaned," despite the fact that they may be so. However, any Capped Bust or later 19th-century silver coin, excepting silver dollars from the Treasury hoard, if brilliant is routinely certified as cleaned.

Today, it is the opinion of Q. David Bowers that the vast majority of RD Proof Indian Head cents dated before 1890 have been dipped and ditto for nearly all Matte Proof Lincoln cents from 1909 to 1916. Most of these are routinely certified as RD. Lacking chemical improvement, nearly all would grade BN or RB.

Long-time collector and dealer Sam Lukes told of an acquaintance who has specialized in turning BN (brown) and RB (red and brown) Mint State Lincoln cents into ones that could be certified as RD (red). This was achieved by dipping the coin into a solution, then freezing the coin for a day, and then wrapping it in a special bag and freezing it again, after which he would leave it on a counter for several hours to return to room temperature.

Many of these were sent to grading services and certified as RD. Some were even crossed over to other services for even higher Mint State RD grades. Unfortunately, some of these "gems" later became spotted within their holders.[6] Many services, perhaps all, make no guarantees against coins becoming blotchy or spotted after certification. In Bowers's experience, this does *not* happen to coins with *original* mint red-orange color. However, if a copper coin gives a hint of being dipped at the time of certification, such as having splotches, it is often rejected as "damaged."

An MS-65RD Indian Head or Lincoln cent of a rare variety, original or new color, if certified often commands much more than one certified as BN or RB. You are usually home safe with RD Lincoln cents this side of 1930, but for earlier ones be careful. In any event, avoid coins with flecks, splotches, or stains no matter the color.

ASPECTS OF EYE APPEAL

Beauty is in the eye of the beholder. To many, a sparkling, brilliant copper-nickel Flying Eagle cent or a richly lustrous brown Proof or Mint State Indian Head cent is of rare beauty. The same goes for early Lincoln cents in various shades of brown and red and brown. In any scenario, whether a coin is called BN, RB, or RD, the presence of flecks or spots is a minus. No question about it. According to Q. David Bowers, blotchy and mottled coloration is a negative as well, but someone else might think that such a coin is a rare and beautiful find.

As you examine cents in your exploration of the series and search for nice pieces, you will come to like the coloration and appearance of some, and not like others. If you are contemplating a coin and cannot determine if it is beautiful, or if you find it borderline, simply wait for another opportunity. Flying Eagle, Indian Head, and Lincoln cents are plentiful in nearly all grades (although original color may be much scarcer depending on the issue), and an opportunity passed today will likely recur next month or next year.

At coin club meetings, at viewing sessions for auctions, at displays of copper coins at conventions, likely there will be an opportunity to find several collectors who are experienced in the field. These series each have essentially the same aspects of quality and connoisseurship. Discuss color, eye appeal, and anything else. You will find that most experienced collectors are very willing, even enthusiastic, to help anyone seeking to learn. The Internet is a wonderful resource as well.

As to dealers in stores and at shows, some are as friendly as can be, while others have little or no time for idle chat that does not result in an immediate sale. Simply find a dealer who appreciates your growing interest. When you do, take caution if he or she is busy with another customer, to ask when it might be convenient to return when the pace is more leisurely. It is also good etiquette to buy *something* if you take up a lot of time—perhaps a numismatic book or magnifying glass or the like.

While beauty is in the eye of the beholder, I am sure that with experience, a group of cents you pick out as having good eye appeal will be found to be attractive to others as well.

ASPECTS OF RARITY

How rare is it? After "How much is it worth?" this is usually the most-asked question, especially by collectors who have not studied a series.

Rarity is relative. In the context of Lincoln cents from 1909 to date, the most famous rarity is the 1909-S with the initials V.D.B. on the reverse. A glance at *A Guide Book of United States Coins* reveals that only 484,000 were struck—this number being fewer than any other regular date and mintmark in the entire series. Today, probably more than 100,000 exist in various worn grades from Good-4 to VF-35 and thousands from EF-40 to AU-58.

The key is that coins are *rare* only in the context of other coins—with relation to a given series or specialty. Beyond that, *rare* is the usual term describing the field of collectible coins, whether they exist in large numbers or if only a few are around.

Collectors and dealers all consider the 1909-S V.D.B. cent to be rare. This is *in the context of the demand for it.* There are fewer of these around than any other Lincoln cent date or mintmark when the entire population is considered. However, a Mint State 1909-S V.D.B. cent is very common in comparison to a 1939 Arkansas commemorative half dollar, of which only 2,104 were struck. The 2017 *Guide Book of United States Coins* values a gem MS-65 Arkansas half dollar at $1,905, or a fraction of the cost of a gem 1909-S V.D.B. Lincoln cent. The explanation is that hundreds of thousands of people have albums and boards and collect Lincoln cents, but relatively few collect early commemorative half dollars (curiously enough!).

A variety that is rare only in high grade, but which is plentiful in low grades, is a *condition rarity.* An example is provided by the 1926-S cent of which 4,550,000 were coined, or nine times more than of the 1909-S V.D.B. cent, but of which no more than a couple dozen MS-65 coins with original red color survive today. The reason is that the 1909-S V.D.B. cent was widely saved at the time of issue (see page 375), while in 1926, before the era of albums and folders, few people collected Lincoln cents by mintmarks. The novelty of 1909-dated cents had passed.

STRATEGIES FOR BUYING SMALL CENTS

A SIMPLE SYSTEM

You can be among the best buyers that the field of Lincoln cents has ever known!

By now in the present text you have read about grade, striking sharpness, cleaning, eye appeal, and many other things—certainly a lot to absorb. Add the element of time and a few field trips—visits to coin stores and conventions—and you will turn theory into practice. The fact that you have progressed this far shows you have the interest. Don't rush. Lincoln cents are one of the most *complex* series in American numismatics, in respect to locating truly choice coins.

Most buyers of Lincoln cents—at least more than 90%, perhaps more than 95%—buy Lincoln cents only by considering the grade and price. A simple 1-1/2" or 2"–square coin holder with a cellophane center, displaying a cent, may be marked "MS-65RD." Or a certification-service plastic "slab" may be so marked. The coin itself can be any Lincoln cent in any grade—a common 1910 cent in Good-4, or a 1960, Small Date, cent in MS-67RD, or anything else. With this information, a price guide is consulted, or multiple guides—price information is everywhere.

Under the preceding scenario, Mr. Average Buyer will see that he has an MS-65RD cent offered at, say, $400, and prices listed in *Coin World, Numismatic News,* the *Guide Book of United States Coins,* and other places range from $500 to $600. Obviously, the $400 price is a great bargain!

Or, *Coin World, Numismatic News,* the *Guide Book of United States Coins,* and other places will indicate a range of $250 to $325. Obviously, the $400 coin is vastly overpriced!

Mr. Average Buyer is driven by price. The actual appearance of the coin is of little concern. The label MS-65RD in a grading-service holder is all that he wants. No research needed. The coin *must be* great, or it wouldn't have been certified in such a high grade!

With this guide in hand *you* are equipped to think more clearly. Let us suppose that instead of simply being marked MS-65RD, the coin is further described by the seller as "weakly struck on the head and rims, as usual." It probably won't be; *you* as a smart buyer will have to add this description on your own, after looking at it. With this new information, it would seem that if the coin were listed in guides at $500 to $600, this coin would not be worth buying for $400. No longer is it a bargain.

Now, let us suppose that a coin is marked as MS-65RD and further described as, "needle-sharp strike on both sides, a rarity as such—in fact, the only coin of this sharpness I have seen in the past 10 years." With this new information, it would seem that if price guides listed it at the range of $250 to $325, it would be a bargain at $400!

If you agree with this, you are on your way to being a smart buyer!

In short, if you want to be a connoisseur and form a truly outstanding collection of Lincoln cents, there is much more than just the grading numbers to consider. Numbers, while important, are not necessarily any more significant than other aspects such as quality and eye appeal. Many smart buyers would rather have an MS-65RB cent with Full Details and attractive original toning than an MS-67RD with planchet abrasions and weak features. The first coin, if rare in that form, could be worth much more than the catalog value, while the second coin would not be worth purchasing at half catalog price.

If you are considering forming a set of small cents and want superb coins, learn what and what not to expect in the marketplace, using the tips specific to small cents that follow. As small cents, and Lincoln cents in particular, are a very complex, sophisticated series, these denomination-specific tips are invaluable:

NUMERICAL GRADE ASSIGNED TO THE COIN

With a listing of the coins and grades you need, when you visit a dealer's shop, attend a convention, or surf the Internet you can focus on the items you need and ignore the vast majority of other offerings. If Flying Eagle, Indian Head, or Lincoln cents represent a new area for you, do some window shopping on the Internet for a few days before making purchases. For Lincoln cents from the 1930s onward it is best to buy these at a coin show or in a dealer's shop, as sharpness of strike and eye appeal vary widely, but it is not financially feasible for most dealers to illustrate them on the Internet or describe them in detail. Another plan is to align yourself with a mail-order seller of these and state that you want only needle-sharp coins, without graininess on Lincoln's shoulder, that are bright with no flecks or streaks. In less time than you realize, you will learn the fundamentals of grading.

Most mail-order dealers have not sorted their later-dates by sharpness, so you might offer to pay slightly more for their effort to do so for best results. In a coin shop, if you spend time browsing and asking questions but do not see coins you want to buy, it is nice to make a courtesy purchase of a coin or a book or two. Forming warm relationships with several friendly dealers will be an asset throughout your collecting career.

EYE APPEAL AT FIRST GLANCE

Go slowly and buy later dates first, these in the Indian Head series being from 1879 to 1909 and in the Lincoln series from the 1930s to the present. In that way any mistakes you make will be inexpensive. There is absolutely no need to compromise on the aspect of eye appeal. Q. David Bowers states that he is not aware of even a single date or mintmark that does not exist, and in multiples, with excellent eye appeal. In contrast, if you were a collector of Vermont copper coins of 1785 to 1788 by die varieties, there are some for which the finest known specimens might be Fine or Very Fine, and there are other varieties that are not known to exist sharply struck.

EVALUATING SHARPNESS AND RELATED FEATURES

The next step is to examine the cent for sharpness, using the extensive information given earlier (see page 229) and also checking the individual date and mintmark listings in the following catalog. Aspire to acquire a coin that has full details on both sides—including the portrait, lettering, and rim, and struck from fresh dies. *This is the single most difficult problem for pre-1934 cents.*

Also check for surface quality. Is the luster satiny or frosty, with full sheen—or is the coin struck from overused dies showing metal flow and granularity? Again, assigned numerical grades reveal nothing about this. Is the planchet of good quality, or is it rough? For Proof cents across the board the surface quality is nearly always excellent. For circulation strikes this can vary dramatically.

ESTABLISHING A FAIR MARKET PRICE

As an example, an MS-66 1943 zinc-coated steel cent is easy to find sharply struck and with superb eye appeal. As such coins are common, you should pay in the range of current market price.

On the other hand, if at this point you have a sharply struck, beautiful 1863 copper-nickel Indian Head cent or a Lincoln cent from the Denver or San Francisco mint from the 1920s that usually is found weakly struck, don't become obsessed with the market price. If you have to pay a 50% premium to get it, do so. However, more often than not you will be able to buy a sharply struck coin with strong eye appeal at current market or just slightly above, for the seller will not be concerned with sharpness, and may not care about original color either.

COLLECTING BEYOND THE BASICS

SPECIALIZED VARIETIES AND TEXTS

Beyond dates, mintmarks, and basic varieties (such as are listed in the regular edition of *A Guide Book of United States Coins*) there is a wonderland of other varieties—some major, others trivial—to consider. Most of these are unknown to the general numismatic community and with some patience can be cherry-picked by paying no more than for a regular date or mintmark. The bibliography lists various references that are useful in this regard. The following, however, are essential and are highly recommended:

The *Cherrypickers' Guide to Rare Die Varieties of United States Coins*, by Bill Fivaz and J.T. Stanton, has been the standard reference for many years for varieties in all series from half cents to double eagles. Over time it has expanded and is now in multiple volumes. The sixth edition, volume 1, includes small cents. Varieties are illustrated and have been given FS numbers that include the denomination of the coin, in this instance 01 for small cents, followed by the date and mintmark (if there is a mintmark), followed by the sequential "identifier" number. Identifiers have these number ranges:

101–200: Obverse doubled die variety.
301–399: Obverse date variety.
401–499: Obverse variety, miscellaneous.
501–699: Mintmark variety.
701–799: Miscellaneous variety.
801–899: Reverse doubled die.
901–999: Reverse variety, miscellaneous.

FS varieties are evaluated using the Universal Rarity Scale, which has consistent divisions and has been popular in many specialized texts:

Universal Rarity Scale

URS-1 = 1 known, unique	URS-14 = 4,001–8,000
URS-2 = 2 known	URS-15 = 8,001–16,000
URS-3 = 3 or 4	URS-16 = 16,001–32,000
URS-4 = 5–8	URS-17 = 32,001–64,000
URS-5 = 9–16	URS-18 = 64,001–125,000
URS-6 = 17–32	URS-19 = 125,001–250,000
URS-7 = 33–64	URS-20 = 250,001–500,000
URS-8 = 65–125	URS-21 = 500,001–1,000,000
URS-9 = 124–250	URS-22 = 1,000,001–2,000,000
URS-10 = 251–500	URS-23 = 2,000,001–4,000,000
URS-11 = 501–1,000	URS-24 = 4,000,001–8,000,000
URS-12 = 1,001–2,000	URS-25 = 8,000,001–16,000,000
URS-13 = 2,001–4,000	URS-26> = same progression

For Flying Eagle and Indian Head cents the essential reference is the aptly named *The Flying Eagle & Indian Cents Attribution Guide*, third edition, vols. 1 and 2, by Rick Snow. Published in 2014, these books tell you all you will ever want to know about varieties from trivial to essential, with much interesting history, rarity information, and other useful content. Snow numbers are used to identify the varieties.

CONECA, the acronym for Combined Organizations of Numismatic Error Collectors of America, maintains www.conecaonline.org, which lists many of the die varieties described in the Lincoln cents section of the following catalog. These varieties are listed with key identifying letters such as:

DDO: Doubled-Die Obverse.
DDR: Doubled-Die Reverse.
OMM: Overmintmark (sometimes spelled as *over mintmark*, this refers to one mintmark stamped over a *different* mintmark in the die).
RPM: Repunched Mintmark.

The *Authoritative Reference on Lincoln Cents*, second edition, by John Wexler and Kevin Flynn, contains many marvelous photographs, including varieties not in the Fivaz-Stanton or CONECA studies. The *Complete Guide to Lincoln Cents*, by David W. Lange, is a "walk" through the series with authoritative comments on each of the dates, mintmarks, and major varieties.

Among Flying Eagle, Indian Head, and Lincoln cents new and interesting varieties are continually discovered. Probably 50% or more of those listed in the above books were not described in any book 25 years ago.

FLYING EAGLE (1856–1858)

Designer: *James B. Longacre.* **Weight:** *4.67 grams.* **Composition:** *.880 copper, .120 nickel.*
Diameter: *19 mm.* **Edge:** *Plain.* **Mint:** *Philadelphia.*

Circulation Strike   **Proof**

THE 1856 FLYING EAGLE CENT PATTERNS

Americans of the mid-1850s had grown up with the old copper large cents that had been in circulation ever since they were introduced in 1793. Mint officials figured that the public would require some education to understand the change to a lightweight, small-diameter, lightly hued, copper-nickel cent.

Accordingly, beginning in late November 1856, approximately 1,000 or more 1856-dated pattern Flying Eagle cents were struck for distribution to newspaper editors, congressmen, and other individuals of influence, with some coins held in reserve for distribution to numismatists. Included in the disseminated 1856 Flying Eagle cents were one to each senator and representative; four to President Franklin Pierce; about 200 to the Committee on Coinage, Weights, and Measures; and other pieces to Treasury Department officials. However, it seems that any congressman who wanted a few extra pieces had no trouble getting them. Exactly how many promotional pieces of the 1856 Flying Eagle cent were struck in 1856 and early 1857 is not known, and it could have been far in excess of 1,000 coins.

These initial specimens of the 1856 Flying Eagle cent were "Uncirculated" as they were made in the circulation-strike format, not struck in the style of Proofs, and were intended to be similar in finish to what the average citizen would see when mass production of the new cents began. The "advertising campaign" was a success, and the Coinage Act of February 21, 1857, was signed into law, making the copper-nickel Flying Eagle cent a reality.

BROTHER JONATHAN'S NEW BABY.

A cartoon in *Harper's Weekly,* February 21, 1857.
"Brother Jonathan" was a popular nickname for
the United States of America at the same time.

NOT A RED CENT.

We give you, out of the abundance of the liberal resources of our establishment, a "counterfeit presentment" of the new cent.

You see for yourselves the patriotic design—the wreath entwined with the vine and Indian corn on the one side, and that everlasting American eagle, "spreading its wings and soaring aloft," on the other. The bird, by-the-by, has rather an anserine than an aquiline look, and is said to be the same as once was set loose upon golden wings in a previous issue of half-eagles, but having been again caged, in consequence of its barn-yard fowl appearance, is now to be turned adrift for a humbler flight.

The cut gives an exact representation of the size, with the exception of the thickness, which is about equal to that of two half-eagles put together. The composition is of copper and nickel. As the former metal has become dearer, from the fact of its supply not having kept up with the manufacturing demand for it, the Government gains by the alloy, as, although the nickel is comparatively dear, the quantity used of the mixed metal is smaller. The intrinsic value at one time of the single copper cent was only 1-50th part of the dollar; now, with the heightened value of copper, it has risen to nearly 1-86th. The new cent only costs 1-65th part of the dollar.

Provided the act of Congress, which establishes the new cent, becomes a law, which it has not as yet, we think the public will be a gainer by the new coin. Its smaller size makes it much more convenient for handling, and less burdensome for transportation, while the neater look and the freedom from the *brassy* odor, renders it much more acceptable to fastidious delicacy. Ladies may now venture to touch with their ungloved fingers small change without being, like Lady Macbeth, unable to wash out with Cologne, or any other toilet detersive, the "damned spot" of a base contamination.

There is a great deal that is interesting in the history of the old American cent, which we would like to have eliminated. Will our "Notes and Queries" tell us something about the old Washington Penny, for which eager collectors are willing, it is said, to pay for in weight of gold? Let us know something, also, about the whereabouts of these rarities. Franklin, as well as Washington, we believe, has honored the penny with his name. What was his design? Is it a fact, that at one time, our cents—eagle, stars, and all—were manufactured in Great Britain, at the celebrated Soho Works of Birmingham, belonging to Bolton and the great Watt, and imported in the gross by our hardware merchants, and sold at large profits to small dealers for their own purposes?

We will lose an American proverb, now widely circulated, by the issue of the new coin. "He's not worth a *red* cent" will be of such general application that it will not have any specific meaning, and will be of course dropped, for the new cent is not red, being of a gray, silvery aspect.

Harper's Weekly informed readers of
the new cent on February 7, 1857.

EARLY REVIEWS OF THE NEW CENT

The *Buffalo Commercial Advertiser*, January 8, 1857, printed this after a pattern cent had been inspected:

The New Cent: The editor of the Providence, R.I. *Journal* has been permitted to see one of the new cents just struck off at the Mint. He describes it as a little larger than a dime, and nearly twice as thick. On one side is a flying eagle, with the inscription 'United States of America, 1856,' around the circle: On the other is 'One Cent' within a wreath. It is altogether the *handsomest* coin of so low a denomination that we have ever seen.

In its issue of February 7, 1857, *Harper's Weekly* inserted an illustration of an 1856, Flying Eagle, cent and furnished this commentary:

You see for yourselves the patriotic design—the wreath entwined with the vine and Indian corn on the one side, and that everlasting American eagle, 'spreading its wings and soaring aloft,' on the other. The bird, by-the-by, has rather an anserine than an aquiline look, and is said to be the same as once was set loose upon golden wings in a previous issue of half eagles, but having been again caged, in consequence of its barn-yard fowl appearance, is now to be turned adrift for a humbler flight. . . .

The account went on to suggest that the old phrase, "Not worth a red cent," would be of no use now that copper cents were to be replaced, "for the new cent is not red, being of a gray, silvery aspect."

The *Baltimore Sun* gave this overview on February 27, 1857, less than a week after the new cent had been authorized:

The New Cent

The director of the United States Mint, in a letter to the secretary of the Treasury, thus describes the new cent which is about to be issued:

The obverse is a flying eagle with the legend "United States of America," and the date of the piece. The reverse is simply a wreath, composed of the staple productions of our country, encircling the denomination. The propriety simplicity and symmetry of this arrangement, I think, is apparent by an inspection of the coin. The wreath is similar in design to the three dollar gold coin, but the greater thickness of the cent enables it to be brought out in higher and more perfect relief, and it fills more completely the face of the coin.

The devices and general appearance of this cent—its thickness and the smooth edge—render it so dissimilar as to prevent its being mistaken for any of the other denominations. The last named characteristic will enable persons of defective vision, or where there is an absence of light, to ascertain the denomination. . . .

The *Philadelphia Ledger* says:

"The intrinsic value of the new cent is about seventy-five percent of its nominal value, and the government, therefore, can afford to coin the new cents and redeem all of the Spanish coins at par without suffering any loss or subjecting the people to any. In a few days the Mint will be ready to distribute the new coinage, and the distribution will be made at the expense of the Mint; that is, the coin will be sent to the various cities whence the distribution takes place, and there, through the government agents, it will be paid out for Spanish coin, or for any other, at the convenience of the purchaser. Due notice will be given by circulars and in the newspapers when, where, how, and in what quantities the distribution will be made."

On March 14, 1857, the cent was reviewed by *Frank Leslie's Illustrated Newspaper*:

The New Cent

We are soon to witness the advent of the new cent, which we trust will eventually take the place of the present miserable "copper device," which is so large and coarse withal that a few [dimes' worth] will load you down past convenient locomotion and make your pockets and hands offensive with a strange metallic taint.

We have seen "the new specimen" and must congratulate the public that we shall have a currency that shows some little progress in the art of coining. We have made no progress at the Mint for fifty years, so far as the stamping of gold and silver is concerned, but the new cent promises a better era, and we may soon have coins not only intrinsically valuable, but also attractive from their tasteful device. . . .

COINAGE OF THE NEW CENT

The Coinage Act of 1857 abolished the old, large cents and provided for the production of the new-format cents made of 88% copper and 12% nickel, weighing 72 grains (with the tolerance in weight to be no greater than 4 grains per coin). Although not specified by law, the diameter was ultimately set at 3/4 of an inch (thus laying four coins end to end is a handy way to measure 3 inches, a convenience if a ruler is not at hand).[7]

The design of the new cent was not specified, but was to be whatever the director of the Mint wanted, so long as approval was secured from the secretary of the Treasury.

While the Act was in its draft stages there was a provision that the new cents be legal tender up to a total of 10¢ per transaction, this proviso did not appear in the final version. This was hardly novel, as the old-style cents were not legal tender either (the Mint Act of April 2, 1792, regulating the coinage, gave legal-tender status to silver and gold coins only). As cents were not legal tender, anyone including government officials could refuse to accept them!

The Coinage Act of 1857 also made the use of foreign currency illegal and provided for the redemption of large cents and certain foreign coins along with the issuance of the new copper-nickel cents. Flying Eagle cents were struck in quantity beginning in April 1857, and they were stockpiled for several weeks awaiting their initial release.

MOTIFS ON THE FLYING EAGLE CENT

James Longacre's new obverse design for the cent depicted an eagle flying to the left, with UNITED STATES OF AMERICA around the obverse border, and the date below. Longacre adopted the eagle motif created 20 years earlier by Christian Gobrecht (after designs by Titian Peale) and used on the 1836 silver dollar. This design was said to have been modeled from a real eagle, Peter, once a mascot at the Philadelphia Mint, although contemporary information about the legendary Peter is elusive today.

The reverse was a copy of the "agricultural" wreath containing, as usually stated, "wheat, corn, cotton, and tobacco," devised by Longacre earlier for use on the 1854 gold $1 coins and $3 coins.[8] In modern literature the cotton leaves are often referred to as *maple* leaves, as they more closely resemble the latter in a botanical sense; besides, few numismatists are aware of what a cotton leaf looks like.[9] However, cotton leaf is correct. The wreath composition, beginning at the ribbon, seems to be: tobacco, wheat, corn, cotton, and a corn ear, the last figure hardly true to nature.[10]

The agricultural wreath
on the reverse of the
1854 $3 gold coin.

The agricultural wreath on
the reverse of the new
Flying Eagle cent.

While the reincarnation of Peter the eagle on the Flying Eagle cent and the re-use of an old wreath created a design admired by numismatists and others, it remains a puzzle why original motifs were not used on such a momentous change in the most ubiquitous of all American coin denominations. However, at the time the cent received very little attention in either the Engraving Department or the director's office at the Mint. This denomination was more or less taken for granted. When experiments in new and artistic motifs were undertaken, likely as not they were in precious-metal denominations.[11]

Moreover, Chief Engraver Longacre was known for the slow pace at which he performed his work. Perhaps Mint Director James Ross Snowden thought it would simplify matters if new motifs did not have to be created. It was far from the last time Longacre updated a denomination with a motif used elsewhere in U.S. coinage.

Apparently, much of the new artistic work on various coins, patterns, and medals was eventually (after October 1857) given to *Assistant* Engraver Anthony C. Paquet, whose contribution to the small-cent field is just now beginning to be recognized for its true importance.

New Cents for Old Coins

A fascinating account of what happened when the new Flying Eagle cent made its debut was printed in the *Philadelphia Bulletin*, May 25, 1857:

The New Cents

Every man and boy in the crowd had his package of coin with them. Some had their rouleaux of Spanish coin done up in bits of newspaper wrapped in handkerchiefs, while others had carpet bags, baskets and other carrying contrivances, filled with coppers—"very cheap and filling," like boarding-house fare.

The officiating priest in the temple of mammon had anticipated this grand rush and crush, and every possible preparation was made in anticipation of it. Conspicuous among these arrangements was the erection of a neat wooden building in the yard [interior courtyard] of the mint, a special accommodation of the great crowd of money-changers. This temporary structure was furnished with two open windows which faced the south. Over one of these windows were inscribed the words CENTS FOR CENTS, and over the other CENTS FOR SILVER. Inside the little office were scales and other apparatus for weighing and testing coin, a goodly pile of bags containing the newly-struck compound of nickel and copper, and a detachment of weighers, clerks, etc. . . .

These lines soon grew to be of unconscionable length, and to economize space they were wound around and around like the convulsions of a snake of a whimsical turn of mind. The clerks and the weighers exerted themselves to the utmost to meet the demands of all comers, and to deal out the little canvas bags to all who were entitled to receive them; the crowd grew apace, and we estimated that at one time there could not have been less than 1,000 persons in the zigzag lines, weighed down with small change, and waiting patiently for their turn.

Those who were served rushed into the street with their moneybags, and many of them were immediately surrounded by an outside crowd, who were willing to buy out in small lots and in advance on first cost. We saw quite a number of persons on the steps of the mint dealing out the new favorites in advance of from 30% to 100%, and some of the outside purchasers even huckstered out the coin again in smaller lots at a still heavier advance. The great majority of those who came out "made tracks" with their bags of money, and not an omnibus [horse-drawn enclosed carriage] went eastward past the mint for several hours that did not, like the California steamers, carry "specie [used fancifully, as this term denotes gold and silver coins] in the hands of the passengers."

Those who made their way homeward a-foot attracted the attention of passersby by their display of specie bags, and we doubt much whether, in the history of the mint, there was ever so great a rush inside the building, or so animated a scene outside of it. It was, in effect, at once a funeral of the old coppers and of the ancient Spanish coins, and the giving of a practical working existence to the new cents.

On May 25, 1857, the day that the 1857 Flying Eagle cent made its debut, Mint Director James Ross Snowden wrote to the secretary of the Treasury, James Guthrie:

> The demand for them is enormous. . . . We had on hand this morning $30,000 worth, that is, 3,000,000 pieces. Nearly all of this amount will be paid out today. The coinage will go forward, however, at the rate of 100,000 or more pieces per day and the demand will be met as well as we can.

SUBSEQUENT REVIEWS OF THE NEW CENT

There was much to say about the new cents in the popular press when the coins reached circulation.

The *Albany Evening Journal* printed this on June 3, 1857:

James Ross Snowden, director of the Mint from 1853 to 1861.

The New Cent

The new cent coin wins opinions anything but golden. Its color—like copper counterfeiting pinchbeck, and blushing at being caught in the cheat—is the ground of objection for some. Others revile the ambiguous figure which the Mint officers interpret to mean a flying eagle, but which to the uninstructed resembles a table napkin or a pen wiper got up for sale at a fancy fair.

The latest objection we have noticed is that children swallow it with great consequent irritation of the stomach and bowels, from the corrosive nature of the metals of which it is composed. There is just one good thing in the new cent. It weighs precisely the hundredth part of a pound. People inclined to decimals may turn it to some purpose as a convenient mode of determining fractional weights: six pence worth is an ounce; three of them can be sent by mail for three cents more.

Those of our readers who desire to see what the new cent ought to have been in color and material can step into the State Library and admire the beautiful collection of bronze medals of the French kings, presented by Napoleon the Little. They are nearly black. A cent of this hue could not be mistaken for a half eagle or a dime, while the present abortion is a compromise hint between the two. Our Mint is the more inexcusable, because the French have, within the past three years, replaced their old and cumbrous copper coinage by one of bronze, in which the defect of weight was compensated not so much by superior value in the material as by artistic taste and elegance of the devices and execution. Their example was before us for instruction and imitation.

Who cares whether a penny is worth the hundredth part of a dollar, or only one hundred and fiftieth? Not a soul. It is a mere counter's change, not designed for keeping. But our Mint is scrupulous on this point. Honesty, which has deserted pretty nearly every other civil department of the federal government, still keeps a lingering foothold there. And this it comes that an administration which sticks at no outrage upon liberty—whose effigy is banished from the cent—insists on mixing preposterous German silver with its copper, to the end that the purchaser of a penny may get his dirty pennysworth. So did the Pharisees pay tithes of mint, anise, and cumin while neglecting the weightier matters of law.

The San Francisco *Daily Globe*, July 2, 1857, included this:

The New Cent

We have received from Berford & Company of the Atlantic and Pacific Express, the new cent coin. It is a neat and appropriate institution, less in circumference than the five dollar piece, much thicker. It is smooth on the edge and has a shade between silver and copper. On one side it is partly encircled with the words

'United States of America' and the date 1857. In the center is a representation of an eagle flying. Reverse, a wreath with a bow knot encircling the words 'One Cent.'

We do not agree with the New York *Times*, when it says, "the eagerness to get hold of the new coin we do not quite understand, for a less attractive specimen of the numismatic art than the new cent we do not remember to have seen. Its great and only recommendation is that there is not much of it. The color is far from pleasing, and it will not improve with age. The design of an eagle on the wing is simply an estate, and the execution of the die so poor and feeble that it can hardly be made out. The new cent is so vaguely and feebly executed that it requires a very lively imagination to discover a likeness to anything in the wreath enclosing the words which determine its value."

We think it is a very convenient coin and creditable to the Mint. We understand that the reason for representing the eagle on the wing is, because he is supposed to be on a *new scent*, [a pun on the words *cent* and *ascent*, as well as the phrase *on a new scent*] as witness Cuba, Mexico, Central America, &c.

LATER RESPONSES TO THE FLYING EAGLE DESIGN

In 1904 President Theodore Roosevelt visited the Smithsonian Institution and viewed the ancient Greek coins on display. Dissatisfied with the current American coin motifs, particularly the silver and gold denominations, he proposed changing all of the designs from the cent to the $20 double eagle. He enlisted Augustus Saint-Gaudens, America's most famous sculptor, to undertake this commission. Working from his studio in Cornish, New Hampshire (today a popular National Historic Site), the artist spent most time with the $20 coin. In a letter to the president on June 28, 1906, he stated for the reverse of the double eagle he was going to use:

> . . . a flying eagle, a modification of the device which was used on the cent of 1857. I had not seen that coin for many years, and was so impressed by it that I thought if carried out with some modification, nothing better could be done. It is by all odds the best design on any American coin.

Correspondence continued, models were made (including a Flying Eagle cent), and in time his version of a flying eagle was adopted for the reverse of the double eagle. Saint-Gaudens died of cancer on August 3, 1907, after which his work for $10 and $20 coins was carried on by his assistant, Henry Hering. (Also see introductory material on page 355 relating to the sculptor's idea for cents.) The new double eagle was released into circulation in December 1907. With some changes the design was continued through early 1933, after which production of gold coins for circulation ceased forever.

In his book *Numismatic Art in America*, Cornelius Vermeule, of the Boston Museum of Fine Arts, praised Gobrecht's design as seen on early silver dollars and later adapted for the copper-nickel cent:

> The famous flying eagle . . . is one of the greatest symphonies of die design and cutting to be performed on any flan at any period in the history of Western civilization. This is cold observation, not mere national pride.
>
> Only the most sensitive, most penetrating photograph can bring out the bold yet subtle relief and foreshortening of the bird as he flies across our vision from right front to left rear. Feathers, wing tips, beak, and curled talon are presented with a naturalistic power and precision as advanced in American numismatic art as was Benedetto Pistrucci's 1818 portrait of aged George III [on British coinage]. . . .
>
> This vision of the national bird on the wing was as magnificent a presentation in depth, detail, and silhouette as the human mind could conceive and the human hand translate into the mechanics of coining processes. . . .

In view of the admiration of Saint-Gaudens, Vermeule, and others for Longacre's "recycled" design borrowed from Gobrecht's adaptation of Titian Peale's artwork—and the enthusiasm collectors have for Flying Eagle cents today—perhaps it is all for the best that some new motif was not created in the 1850s at the Mint when experiments to eliminate the cumbersome large copper cent were conducted.

FLYING EAGLE CENTS FOR CIRCULATION, 1857 THROUGH 1858

By most accounts, the new small-diameter Flying Eagle cents were a great success. More than 17 million were made for circulation in 1857, followed by more than 24 million in 1858. The old-style large copper cents became an anachronism within the following decade.[12]

However, the Mint was not satisfied with the Flying Eagle design. Parts of the relatively large Flying Eagle motif on the obverse were opposite the heavy agricultural wreath on the reverse in the coining press. Because of this, at the moment of striking the demand was made for metal to flow into opposing deep orifices which could not be completely filled under normal die spacing and production conditions. The result was that a number of coins showed weaknesses, particularly at the eagle's head and tail.

"HIGH LEAF" AND "LOW LEAF" ISSUES OF 1856 THROUGH 1858

On "High Leaf" reverses the leaves closest to CENT extend into the field next to CENT on one or both sides, while on "Low Leaf" reverses, both leaves end below the baseline of the word CENT.

1856 cents: All originals (Mint State as well as worn pieces) have High Leaf as do nearly all Proofs. Only two coins (1856, Snow-4), both Proofs, were seen with Low Leaf, these also having the 1856 date on the obverse shallowly punched in the die; presumably, these are clear candidates for having been struck no earlier than 1858, as many "1856" Proofs were struck after 1856; these are unique among 1856 cents in that cotton leaves 1 and 2 on the wreath are incised rather than in relief.

One "High Leaf" variety has the words ONE CENT rotated slightly in a clockwise direction, thus lifting the C in CENT above its normal orientation; in this instance the leaf is long as in the High Leaf style, but it does not extend above the baseline; this is described in Walter Breen's *Encyclopedia of United States and Colonial Proof Coins, 1722–1977* (from Breen dies 1-A) and in Rick Snow's text (1856, Snow-1).

1857 cents: All have High Leaf.

1858, 8 Over 7, cents: All have High Leaf.

1858, Large Letters, cents: Proofs have High Leaf; sometimes the High Leaf is thin or imperfect. Circulation strikes come with both High Leaf and Low Leaf, the Large Letters, Low Leaf, coins being scarcer. The Low Leaf reverse occurs with sub-varieties: the E in ONE is either open (the style usually seen) or closed (quite scarce).

1858, Small Letters, cents: Proofs exist of both types, with the Low Leaf the most often seen. Fewer than 10 are known of the High Leaf.[13] Among circulation strikes, the overwhelming majority are of the Low Leaf variety. The Low Leaf reverse occurs with sub-varieties: the E in ONE is either open (the style usually seen) or closed (quite scarce). The switch to Small Letters extended the life of the dies.

GRADING STANDARDS

Caveat: These grading standards do not take sharpness of strike into account.

MS-60 to 70 (Mint State). *Obverse:* Contact marks, most obvious in the field, are evident at MS-60, diminishing at MS–61, 62, and higher. The eagle, the feathers of which usually hide marks, shows some evidence of contact as well. At Gem MS-65 or finer there is no trace of friction or rubbing. A few tiny nicks or marks may be seen, but none are obvious. At MS-67 and higher levels the coin will approach perfection. A theoretically perfect MS-70 will

1858; Snow-11. Graded MS-64.

have no marks at all evident, even under a strong magnifier. Although in practice this is not always consistent, at MS-66 and higher there should be no staining or other problems, and the coin should have good eye appeal overall. *Reverse:* Check the higher parts of the wreath for slight abrasions at MS–60 to 62. Otherwise, the above guidelines apply.

Illustrated coin: The surfaces display a healthy satin luster, as well as an iridescent rose and golden-tan patina. The coin is sharply and evenly struck and offers razor-sharp definition.

AU-50, 53, 55, 58 (About Uncirculated). *Obverse:* At AU-50, light wear is seen on the breast of the eagle, the top edge of the closest wing, and, less so, on the head. As both the head and tail tip can be lightly struck, these are not reliable indicators of grade. Luster is present in traces among the letters. At higher About Uncirculated levels the evidence of wear diminishes. An AU-58 coin will have nearly full luster, but friction is seen in the fields, as

1858. Graded AU-53.

are some marks. *Reverse:* At AU-50, light wear is seen on the ribbon bow and the highest areas of the leaves. Some luster is seen (more than on the obverse). Friction is evident, as are some marks, but these will not be as distracting as those on the obverse, as the heavy wreath and lettering are more protective of the reverse field. In higher grades, wear is less, and at AU-58 nearly full luster—or even completely full luster—is seen.

Illustrated coin: The reverse features a large rim cud.

EF-40, 45 (Extremely Fine). *Obverse:* Wear is more extensive, especially on the eagle's breast and the top of the closest wing. Wear will also show on the other wing in the area below OF. Marks may be more extensive in the field. The wear is slightly greater at EF-40 than at EF-45, although in the marketplace these two grades are not clearly differentiated. *Reverse:* More wear shows on the higher areas of the wreath, but most detail

1858, Small Letters. Graded EF-40.

will still be present. There may be tinges of luster in protected areas, more likely at EF-45 than at EF-40.

VF-20, 30 (Very Fine). *Obverse:* Wear is appreciable, with the breast feathers gone over a larger area and with more wear on the wings. The tail shows significant wear, negating the question as to whether it was well struck originally. Marks are more extensive, although across all grades the durable copper-nickel metal resisted heavy marks and cuts; any such should be separately described. Staining and spotting, not related to grade, is

1858, Small Letters. Graded VF-20.

common. Cherrypicking (examining multiple coins, all slabbed at the same grade level, and selecting the finest of them) at this and lower grades will yield nice coins in any given category. *Reverse:* The wreath is worn flat in the higher and medium–relief areas, although some detail is seen in the lower areas close to the field. ONE / CENT may be slightly weak, depending on the quality of the original strike. Marks are fewer than on the obverse.

F-12, 15 (Fine). *Obverse:* The eagle shows extensive wear, with about half of the feathers gone. Some detail is still seen, especially on the underside of the closest wing, above the breast. *Reverse:* Wear is even more extensive, with the wreath nearing flatness, but still with some detail in the lower areas.

1857. Graded F-12.

VG-8, 10 (Very Good). *Obverse:* On the obverse the eagle is clear in outline form, but only a small number of feathers can be discerned, mostly above the breast. Letters and the date show extensive wear but are complete and clear. *Reverse:* The wreath is now mostly an outline, although some lower-relief features can be differentiated. ONE / CENT may be weak (depending on the strike).

1858, Small Letters. Graded VG-10.

G-4, 6 (Good). *Obverse:* The eagle is nearly completely flat, with just a few feathers, if any, discernible. The rim is worn down, making the outer parts of the letters and the lower part of the date slightly weak, but all are readable. *Reverse:* The wreath is basically in outline form, with hardly any detail. ONE / CENT is weak, usually with CENT weakest. The rim is worn down.

1857. Graded G-4.

AG-3 (About Good). *Obverse:* Wear is extensive, but most of the eagle is visible in outline form. The letters are mostly worn away, with vestiges remaining here and there. The date is partially worn away at the bottom, but is distinct and readable. *Reverse:* The wreath is so worn that it cannot be distinguished from the field in areas, usually toward the top. ONE / CENT is mostly gone, but much of CENT can be discerned (unless the coin was a weak strike to begin with).

1857. Graded AG-3.

PF-60 to 70 (Proof). *Obverse and Reverse:* Gem PF-65 coins have very few hairlines, and these are visible only under a strong magnifying glass. At the PF-67 level or higher there should be no evidence of hairlines or friction at all. PF-60 coins can be dull from repeated dipping and cleaning (remember, hairlines on any Proof were caused by cleaning with an abrasive agent; they had no hairlines when struck). At PF-63 the mirrorlike fields should

1858, Large Letters. Graded PF-65.

be attractive, and hairlines should be minimal, best seen when the coin is held at an angle to the light. No rubbing is seen. PF-64 coins are even nicer.

Illustrated coin: The fields of this coin are highly reflective for a nickel-alloy Proof cent.

Flying Eagle Cents of 1856

KEYS TO COLLECTING: In recent times there has been an increased interest in minute die varieties of Flying Eagle cents. Rick Snow has taken the lead with these and Indian Head cents by publishing detailed studies on these two series.

HOARDS OF 1856 FLYING EAGLE CENTS: The quoted material in the following commentary concerning three famous hoards of 1856 Flying Eagle cents is the research of John F. Jones and was published in 1944:[14]

Leeds Hoard: "The first whom we shall mention was R.B. Leeds. He was, at the time of his death, the oldest resident of Atlantic City, N.J. (about 55 miles from Philadelphia). Henry Chapman sold Mr. Leeds' collection on November 27–28, 1906. In the catalogue he stated:

" 'For many years he was an ardent collector, turning his attention to accumulating all the examples he could of certain dates, his especial hobby being 1856 Eagle cents of which he had 109 specimens, the greatest collection ever offered of this very rare cent. Mr. Leeds was a firm believer in the rarity and value of this coin, and bought all that he could for many years past. The advance of the past 10 years has proved his judgment to have been correct.' "

Rice Hoard: "George W. Rice, a wealthy building contractor of Detroit, Michigan, who began collecting coins in 1864, accumulated the largest hoard of the little 1856 Flying Eagle cents ever gathered together, numbering 756 pieces. . . . In 1911 he sold this hoard of 756 Eagle cents through Henry Chapman."

Beck Hoard: John Andrew Beck was born in Chestnut Ridge, Pennsylvania, on January 5, 1859, Beck spent part of his youth with his parents in Texas, but the family was forced to return to the Keystone State because of Indian depredations in the West. In Pennsylvania, Beck's father engaged in drilling for brine (a source of salt) near Pittsburgh. After his father's death, John and his brothers maintained the business. John subsequently acquired 100% interest in the enterprise, and for a number of years traveled around western Pennsylvania selling salt, groceries, and other goods. Later, he went into the oil business.

At the age of 10 Beck collected his first coins. The passion grew, and as an adult he developed a special interest and hoarding instinct for gold, especially territorial issues, many of which he bought through the Chapman brothers of Philadelphia. At some unrecorded point he became interested in 1856 Flying Eagle cents and decided to hoard them as well.

"No doubt Beck bought many of the Leeds and Rice 1856 cents, as the greater portion of those cents were enclosed in Henry Chapman's envelopes (marked with their cost), proving they came principally from Philadelphia. However, one country coin dealer wrote that 'he sold Mr. Beck at least 50 or 60 of his Eagle cents.' For years he had a standing offer with all coin dealers of $10 for each 1856 Flying Eagle cent obtained, regardless of condition."

Beck passed away on January 27, 1924. His estate was handled by the Pittsburgh National Bank & Trust Company. Beck had been a director of several banks which were merged into this institution. An inventory of Beck's numismatic estate revealed 531 specimens of the 1856 Flying Eagle cent. In the early 1970s the Beck estate coins were consigned to the Quality Sales Corporation, which was operated by Abner Kreisberg and Jerry Cohen. A few were auctioned to set price levels, and the majority were then sold privately. Q. David Bowers had an early opportunity, perhaps the very first, to inspect and select from the coins. All were covered with "vault grime," which was easily removed with the application of the inert chemical acetone (which is highly flammable and must be used with great care).

1856 IN NUMISMATICS: In 1856 extensive repairs were done to the Philadelphia Mint, in order to render the facilities, it was said, "entirely fireproof." The arrangements of certain rooms and the flow of coins and bullion were changed, and vaults were made more secure—this last improvement being made in the aftermath of earlier defalcations and investigations involving the theft of coin and bullion deposits.

1856 • **Circulation-strike mintage:** 2,000 estimated; certainly, more than 1,000 were struck.

Availability in Mint State: *MS–60 to 64:* In these grades this issue is very rare, especially examples that are original, choice, frosty, and without any prooflike surfaces. In any event, the distinction between circulation strikes and Proofs is rarely clear for this issue—except for two extremes: lustrous and frosty Uncirculated coins (which are very rare) and deep mirror Proofs (which are somewhat elusive). Most specimens in high grades are prooflike and were struck as Proofs. *MS-65 and higher:* Several hundred examples are known in MS-65 or higher. Among these, uncleaned, brilliant, lustrous, and frosty coins are in the minority. Most graded as Mint State by commercial services are prooflike (and thus arguably Mint State) or Proofs and were probably restrikes made after 1857. (See 1856, Proof, commentary on page 249.)

Availability in circulated grades: This issue is rare. Probably about 500 to 800 exist, including originals and quite a few Proofs that entered circulation after being erroneously spent, the latter category being comprised primarily of restrikes. Typically circulated coins are evenly worn and have a yellowish-brown color. Most are in grades from Fine to EF. Very few remained undetected in circulation long enough to wear down to such levels as Good or Very Good.

Characteristics of striking: This issue is usually well struck. On a very few pieces there is weak striking on the eagle's head and tail.

Notes: *Circulation-strike production:* Multiple circulation-strike obverse dies were made with the 1856 date in late 1856 and early 1857, before the Act of February 21, 1857. At least seven were left undated and were used in 1857 for coins bearing that date.[15] These dies each have the "Style of 1856" lettering. R.W. Julian has located Mint records showing that only two pairs of dies were actually made in 1856, presumably two obverses and two reverses. Thus it seems that the additional obverses were made early in 1857.[16]

Die-finish commentary: It is likely that "originals" were struck with prooflike fields at first, then with a satiny finish as the dies wore. However, complicating the matter is the situation that some original dies with the satiny finish seem to have been later resurfaced and given prooflike or Proof finish.

	Cert	Avg	%MS	G-4	VG-8	F-12	VF-20	EF-40	AU-50	MS-60BN	MS-63BN	MS-65
1856 †	0	n/a		$6,500	$7,500	$9,000	$11,000	$12,500	$13,500	$16,000	$20,000	$55,000

† Ranked in the *100 Greatest U.S. Coins* (fourth edition).

1856, Proof • Proof mintage: 1,500 to 2,500.

Proof commentary: These were restrikes struck in 1858 or later from several die pairs with the Style of 1856 obverse letters. Most Proofs are toned yellow-brown, often with surfaces that fall far short of mirrorlike (the typical 1856 Proof cent compares in no way with the gem mirror quality of selected 1857 Proof and 1858 Proof Flying Eagle cents). This is due in large part to the way they were made; apparently, the dies on 1856 Proof Flying Eagle cents were not as polished as their later Proof cousins in the series.[17] Flying Eagle cents of 1856 are of very slightly smaller diameter than are those of 1857 and 1858, and they are on slightly thicker planchets.[18]

More than 1,000 Proof 1856 cents, some seeming more prooflike than like mirrored Proofs, exist today, and they are far more plentiful than those of 1857 and 1858 combined. Most are of the 1856, Snow-9 variety (with a center dot on the reverse under the top-left serif of the N in CENT) and are properly described as restrikes. Certified holders and most catalog descriptions make note of no such distinction. Quite possibly, underscoring the status of individual 1856 Proof cents as restrikes is moot if all prooflike and Proof coins are restrikes anyway.

	Cert	Avg	%MS	PF-60	PF-63BN	PF-65BN
1856, Proof	415	58.3	78%	$16,000	$20,000	$27,500

Flying Eagle Cents of 1857

KEYS TO COLLECTING: Most collectors seek a single 1857 Flying Eagle cent to illustrate the date. Beyond that, acquiring one each of the clashed die varieties is a sporting challenge. These are very worthwhile additions to a set. Obtaining one each of the two letter styles is worthwhile, with the Style of 1856 being rare (although because it is not often attributed by sellers, there is the strong possibility of finding one and not having to pay an additional premium).

In the early 20th century Commodore W.C. Eaton of the U.S. Navy took a fancy to minute die varieties of 1857 and 1858 cents and was joined in the pursuit by his friend F.R. Alvord (today best remembered for his fantastic collection of half cents sold at auction by S. Hudson Chapman in June 1924). They examined thousands of cents of these two dates. These cents were obtained simply enough by writing to dealers and asking them to forward their stocks. Alvord did most, if not all, of the research on the 1857 cents, and Eaton compiled the results. The result of their work, "The Eagle Cents of 1857," was published in *The Numismatist* in May 1921. Some of the varieties they identified were not from different dies, but were from doubling due to die chatter in the coining press.

The reference books by Rick Snow are recommended as a guide for specialists.

TWO LETTER STYLES: There are two styles of obverse letters on 1857 Flying Eagle cents, distinguished as follows:

Type of 1856 (old style): The bases of the A and M in AMERICA are barely touching, and the base of the M is aligned slightly high where it meets the base of the A. The center serifs of the E's in UNITED, STATES, and AMERICA are solidly connected to the upper arms of the E's. In UNITED the outer edge of the diagonal in N is notched toward the bottom. In the O in OF the opening is somewhat "boxy" or "squared" at the corners (in auction catalog photographs and other illustrations this feature is often the best for quick identification). Only one in about every two or three–dozen 1857 cents is of this style.

A detail of the Type of 1856 lettering at OF AMERICA.

Type of 1857 (new style): The bases of the A and M in AMERICA are solidly touching, and the base of the M is aligned properly where it meets the base of the A. The center serifs of the E's in UNITED, STATES, and AMERICA are not connected to the upper arms of the E's. In UNITED the outer edge of the diagonal in N is perfect. In the O in OF the opening is somewhat rounded on its ends. This is the style usually seen.

A detail of the Type of 1857 lettering at OF AMERICA.

1857 CENTS FROM CLASHED DIES: Among 1857 Flying Eagle cents there is a subset of three different varieties struck from dies that clashed with those of other denominations. These were errors made during the set-up process when a cent die was placed in a coining press and a die of another denomination had not been removed and was opposite to it.

1857 IN NUMISMATICS: A wave of nostalgia swept across the country as the old copper cents began disappearing from circulation. The familiar "pennies" of childhood would soon be gone. Many people tried to collect as many different dates as they could find. Numismatics was on its way to becoming a dynamic hobby!

1857 • Circulation-strike mintage: 17,450,000.

Availability in Mint State: *MS–60 to 64:* This issue is readily available in these grades. *MS-65 and higher:* Examples are quite rare in relation to the demand for them. Possibly fewer than 500 exist. Coins with good strike and eye appeal are in the minority among these coins.

Availability in circulated grades: This issue is very common in circulated grades.

	Cert	Avg	%MS	G-4	VG-8	F-12	VF-20	EF-40	AU-50	MS-60BN	MS-63BN	MS-65
1857	3,623	53.1	60%	$30	$40	$50	$60	$150	$215	$380	$900	$3,500

Varieties: The 1857, Type of 1856, variety probably accounts for less than a tenth of the 1857 circulation-strike population. See page 251 for illustration.

1857, Type of 1856, Repunched Date (FS-01-1857-401a): This variety is also identified as 1857, Snow-1. Its rarity is URS-12. In addition to having the old style of lettering, this variety has a date showing signs of earlier punching to the left of the 8, 5, and 7.

1857, Type of 1856 (FS-01-1857-401b): This variety is also identified as 1857, Snow-2. Its rarity is URS-12. See page 250 for detail.

A detail of the 1857, Type of 1856, Repunched Date (FS-01-1857-401a), overdate.

	EF-40	AU-50	MS-60	MS-63	MS-65
FS-01-1857-401a	$400	$900	$1,500	$4,000	$15,000
FS-01-1857-401b	$250	$500	$900	$1,500	$4,500

1857, Reverse 25¢ Clash •

Circulation-strike mintage: Included in 1857 circulation-strike mintage.

Availability in Mint State: *MS–60 to 64:* 8 to 12 examples are known in these grades. Mint State coins are highly prized. *MS-65 and higher:* 3 or 4 examples are known in these grades.

Availability in circulated grades: 70 to 90 examples exist in circulated grades. This variety is very scarce.

On the left, a composite figure showing how the cent die clashed with the quarter die; on the right, the clashed cent face.

Notes: This variety is identified by Fivaz and Stanton as FS-01-1857-901 and can also be identified as 1857, Snow-8. Its rarity is URS-9.

This variety of 1857 Flying Eagle cent shows on its reverse the outline, in mirror image, of the center of an 1857 Liberty Seated quarter dollar reverse die. You can see the eagle's head, neck, and shoulders (the top of its wings).

The impression from the quarter dollar die is slightly deeper at the top part of the reverse (showing the eagle's head and shoulders) than at the bottom part. All clash marks are within the cent's wreath. On the left, opposite the O in ONE, a clash mark emerges from the wreath, goes through a corn ear leaf, continues upward through tips of wreath elements, passes below the wreath "bud" or tip at the top left of the wreath (which was called a wheat tip by Breen, but is it the end of an ear of corn?), and enters the bud at top right, just below its tip. This represents the shoulder, top of the neck, and top of the head of the eagle on the reverse of the Liberty Seated quarter. Another part of the clash mark emerges from the wreath on the upper inside right, curves irregularly to the left and downward through the left serif tip of the top right of the N, through the upright of the right side of the N, curving right to the E, continuing through E in the top area where the middle serif of E joins the upright of the E, extending upward through the top arm of the E, and curving gracefully upward and to the right, then downward to the tip of a corn ear leaf. This represents the bottom of the eagle's head, neck, and shoulder. These clashes are very distinct. Less distinct are vestiges of shield stripes among the letters C and E of CENT and extending to the right of the N and parts of the eagle's lower wing outline and leg below the right of the N of CENT and extending to the lower left of the T. The clash mark design is oriented in the same direction as the cent reverse design.

	Cert	Avg	%MS	EF-40	AU-50	MS-60BN	MS-63BN
1857, Reverse 25¢ Clash	37	44.2	35%	$230	$450	$850	$2,750

1857, Obverse 50¢ Clash •

Circulation-strike mintage: Included in 1857 circulation-strike mintage.

Availability in Mint State: *MS–60 to 64:* 50 to 100 examples are known in these grades. *MS-65 and higher:* An estimated 8 to 12 examples exist in these grades.

Availability in circulated grades: 200 to 400 examples exist in these grades.[19]

On the left, a composite figure showing how the cent die clashed with the half dollar die; on the right, the clashed cent face.

Notes: This variety is identified by Fivaz and Stanton as FS-01-1857-402 and can also be identified as 1857, Snow-9. Its rarity is URS-11.

This variety of 1857, Flying Eagle, cent shows on its obverse the outline, in mirror image, of the center of an 1857, Liberty Seated, half dollar obverse die. You can see parts of Miss Liberty's arm, the liberty cap pole, the drapery of her gown, and other features. The 1857 Flying Eagle cent obverse die clashed with the obverse die of a half dollar when both were in the press at the same time (the illustration superimposes this cent variety on the reversed image of a half dollar).

This clash is very prominent on the obverse of the Flying Eagle cent. The dies seem to have had absolutely parallel faces when clashing, thus yielding bold impressions. A clash mark extends from the left rim of the cent, upward and diagonally to the right, through the top curve of the eagle's beak, across the field, and to the underside of the wing. A clash mark emerges from the top of the same wing, slightly left of the intersection with the right-side wing, and curves to the left in the direction toward the ST of STATES, but it fades before reaching those letters. The preceding features are part of Miss Liberty's leg and the far side of her upraised arm on the half dollar. In the field below the TA of STATES there is an elongated U-shaped clash, combining with another U-shaped clash to its right, the latter extending upward through the second T of STATES and the upper left of the E. This represents part of Miss Liberty's arm, her neck, and the liberty cap pole. On the right side of the cent is an especially prominent clash line beginning at the rim above the M of AMERICA, continuing downward through the top right of the E and progressing deeper into the letters RICA, touching the top tip of the eagle's tail, and then turning sharply right for a short distance to exit to the rim—this clash line representing an impression of Miss Liberty's lowered arm. Additional clash marks, lighter in definition, abound in the field above and below the eagle's tail, and these are Miss Liberty's skirt lines. The clash-mark design is oriented in the same direction as the cent obverse design.

	Cert	Avg	%MS	EF-40	AU-50	MS-60BN	MS-63BN
1857, Obverse 50¢ Clash	121	34.6	26%	$230	$450	$800	$1,250

1857, Obverse $20 Clash •

Circulation-strike mintage: Included in 1857 circulation-strike mintage.

Availability in Mint State: No Mint State examples are known.

Availability in circulated grades: 50 to 75 examples exist in circulated grades.

On the left, a composite figure showing how the cent die clashed with the double eagle die; on the right, the clashed cent face.

Notes: This variety is identified by Fivaz and Stanton as FS-01-1857-403 and can also be identified as 1857, Snow-7. Its rarity is URS-7.

The third variety of 1857 Flying Eagle cent shows on its obverse the outline, in mirror image, of the center of an 1857 Liberty Head double eagle obverse die. You can see nearly all of the left, right, and bottom outlines of Miss Liberty's portrait. The 1857 Flying Eagle cent obverse die clashed with the obverse die of a double eagle when both were in the press at the same time (the illustration superimposes this cent variety on the reversed image of a double eagle). This variety is nearly always seen in worn grades. A Mint State example is a great rarity.

The obverse Flying Eagle cent die came into forced contact with a die used to coin the obverse of a Liberty Head double eagle. This double eagle die impressed a positive, coin-like image on the cent die, which created a mirror image (backward) outline on Flying Eagle cents struck from this die.

On the left obverse of the Flying Eagle cent an irregular clash mark begins at the lower-left rim and continues upward to the underside of the eagle's head where the lower beak meets the neck feathers; a clash mark exits the top of the beak in front of the nostril and continues through the lower right of U of UNITED and the upper left of the N to the border. This represents the outline of the back of Miss Liberty's hair and hair bun on the double eagle die. On the right side of the Flying Eagle cent an irregular clash mark begins at the rim above F and continues irregularly through the AME of America, below the RI, grazing the lower part of CA, to the top of the tail. This represents the lower part of the forehead, the nose, the lips, and the chin of Miss Liberty on the double eagle die. From the eagle's claw a clash mark curves slightly right and downward to the rim—this representing an outline of Miss Liberty's neck from the double eagle die. The facial features of Miss Liberty are dramatic and unequivocal, once you spend a few moments adjusting the alignment of the coin. Parts of the outline of Miss Liberty's neck truncation including a faint J.B.L. (for Longacre's initials) from the double eagle die are seen at the bottoms of the numerals 185 of the date. The clash mark design is oriented in the same direction as the cent obverse design.

	Cert	Avg	%MS	EF-40	AU-50	MS-60BN
1857, Obverse $20 Clash	19	19.1	0%	$2,400	$6,000	$15,000

1857, Proof • **Proof mintage:** 50 to 100.

Proof commentary: Years ago most 1857 Flying Eagle cents offered under the designation "Proof" were not in fact Proofs. In recent decades the problem has been diminished sharply, but not completely eliminated, by the certification services. Accordingly, listings of Proofs in many 19th and 20th–century auction catalogs are not correct. Careful attribution of Proofs did not begin in a widespread way until the late 1980s.

True Proofs are very rare, more so than generally realized. Walter Breen states that most Proofs were made in May 1857 from a die with file marks over the NI of UNITED, one file mark joining the left upright of I to the rim,[20] but whether his proposed date is accurate is uncertain. On these Proofs the reverse has the leaf on the left at the C of CENT high. All known 1857 Proofs are of the Style of 1857 lettering. These were probably released to collectors on or after May 25, 1857 (the day that circulation strikes were first distributed to an eager public). Only a few dozen *true* Proofs are known of this date.

	Cert	Avg	%MS	PF-60	PF-63BN	PF-65BN
1857, Proof	35	63.9		$5,000	$8,500	$25,000

Flying Eagle Cents Overdated 1858

KEYS TO COLLECTING: This overdate, not obvious except under magnification, was discovered by Walter Breen circa 1957. The variety was slow in being publicized, and when it was, there was little demand for it. That changed as more collectors paid attention to the *Guide Book of United States Coins* listing, and auction catalogers showcased higher-grade pieces. Today the overdate is very popular and is highly desired. It is listed as no. 3 among the top 20 most popular of all unusual varieties by Larry R. Steve and Kevin Flynn in *A Comprehensive Guide to Selected Rare Flying Eagle and Indian Cent Die Varieties.*

Nearly all coins in existence show wear. In lower grades, up to F-12 or so, the overdate feature is often indistinct. Such low-grade examples should be avoided. Under magnification EF and AU coins show the overdate clearly. Choice and gem Mint State coins are very rare.

1858, 8 Over 7 • Circulation-strike mintage: Included in 1858, Large Letters, circulation-strike mintage.

Availability in Mint State: *MS–60 to 64:* 45 to 65 examples exist in these grades. *MS-65 and higher:* 12 to 16 examples exist in these grades.

Availability in circulated grades: 300 to 400 examples exist in circulated grades.

Notes: This variety is identified by Fivaz and Stanton as FS-01-1858-301. It can also be identified as 1858, Snow-1. Its rarity is URS-10. Late-die-state examples are worth considerably less, as the visibility of the tip of the 7 decreased over use of the die.

A detail of the 1858, 8 Over 7
(FS-01-1858-301), overdate.

The 1858, 8 Over 7, overdate is not easily distinguished on lower grades; demand for overdates without the tip of the 7 visible is low. Two obverse dies are known for 1858, 8 Over 7. The overdate varieties are both Large Letters style. This entry discusses the first, and most sought after, overdate, while the second is mentioned in the varieties following the main entry.

This is one of the most subtle of American overdates, and it is identifiable by a prominent vestige of the upper right of the 7 in the field beyond the upper right of the second 8. In addition there is a triangular "island," perhaps unrelated to a date punch, in the field high above and slightly right of the first 8. There are early and late die states, with the early state showing the tip of the under-digit 7 more clearly. On the early die state the right-side tip of the eagle's wing is connected; on later die states (not illustrated here) the tip appears as a separate "island."

The obverse die has a small, triangular (raised) die mark in the field between the date and the eagle's breast; this may have been caused by the inadvertent contact of the upper-left corner of the base of the digit 1 in the four-digit date logotype with the working die (a conclusion reached by Chris Pilliod). This overdate appears to be lightly struck on the obverse (actually, the dies were shallowly defined, causing weakness in areas). The tip of the wing near the border is barely connected, and on late die states it is disconnected, but this is not definitive as other non-overdate cents of this date sometimes occur with a broken wingtip.[21] On the reverse the two cotton leaves at the upper left are weak on all specimens seen.

	Cert	Avg	%MS	G-4	VG-8	F-12	VF-20	EF-40	AU-50	MS-60BN	MS-63BN	MS-65
1858, 8 Over 7	179	53.0	53%	$75	$100	$200	$400	$850	$1,500	$3,650	$10,000	$50,000

	F-12	VF-20	EF-40	AU-50	MS-60	MS-63	MS-65
1858, 8 Over 7, Late Die State	$100	$150	$250	$400	$700	$1,000	$5,500

Varieties: *FS-01-1858-302:* This variety can also be identified as 1858, Snow-7. Its rarity is URS-5. This, the second overdate, just shows tiny traces of the upper left of the 1 and less of the 7; UNITED is doubled. The second 1858, 8 Over 7, obverse die lacks the triangular mark in the field of the first. The overdate is not very clear. Some opt not to include this in a variety collection.

A detail of the 1858, 8 Over 7 (FS-01-1858-302), overdate.

	F-12	VF-20	EF-40	AU-50	MS-60	MS-63	MS-65
FS-01-1858-302	$300	$500	$1,000	$2,000	$4,500	$7,500	$25,000

Flying Eagle Cents of 1858

KEYS TO COLLECTING: As a date, 1858 is much scarcer than 1857, but enough examples are around that it will not be a stumbling block. The market price is less than might be expected considering it is at least five times harder to find an 1858 than an 1857. Circulated coins are very common. In gem grades of MS-64 or finer the 1858, Large Letters, is more available than the 1858, Small Letters, though most of the 1858 cents struck were Small Letters cents.

Specialists often see all four varieties of 1858 cents: Large Letters, High Leaf; Large Letters, Low Leaf; Small Letters, Medium Leaf; and Small Letters, Low Leaf.

1858 IN NUMISMATICS: As of June 30, 1858, Mint Director James Ross Snowden reported that $16,602 value *by weight* of old large cents had been exchanged for the new Flying Eagle cents in 1857, and that $31,404 value by weight had been exchanged thus far in 1858. Presumably, this equaled about 5 million large cents.[22]

The following is from *The Bankers' Magazine*, December 1858, and was reprinted from the *Philadelphia Bulletin*. The effect that the new cents had on numismatics is reflected:

> Since the circulation of the new 'nickels,' coin collectors have been eagerly searching for rare coppers of the old kind, for they will soon be very scarce. We know of one collector who boasts of every copper known to be struck in America, except three or four. Numismatics has become as much a 'rage' as opera-going, chess-playing, sailing on the Delaware, rowing on the Schuylkill, exercising in the gymnasium; and the votaries of the fancy pursue it with a zeal and ardor worthy of the immortal old buck.
>
> One collector was indefatigable enough to pick out from nearly 100,000 coins a cabinet of 400 or 500, which he considered at least worth $500; but just after he had made his selection his premises were broken open, and the rare and precious coins were carried off by some rascally burglar, who valued them at about the price of old copper.

1858, Large Letters • Circulation-strike

mintage: The lesser portion of 24,600,000.

Availability in Mint State: *MS–60 to 64:* 2,500 to 4,000 examples exist in these grades. *MS-65 and higher:* 500 to 600 examples exist in these grades.

Availability in circulated grades: This issue is very common in any grade desired.

Characteristics of striking: Some coins are lightly struck, but enough sharp coins survive to satisfy the demand for them.

Notes: The bottoms of A and M in AMERICA are connected. The letters are thinner and taller than on the Small Letters variety. The eagle's beak exhibits a blunt top and thick bottom.

	Cert	Avg	%MS	G-4	VG-8	F-12	VF-20	EF-40	AU-50	MS-60BN	MS-63BN	MS-65
1858, Large Letters	1,614	48.2	47%	$30	$40	$50	$60	$150	$215	$400	$950	$3,750

1858, Large Letters, Proof • Proof

mintage: 100 estimated.

Proof commentary: Until 1992 PCGS listed *all* Proof 1858 cents as Large Letters cents in its *Population Report*, but no more than 90 to 130 Large Letters Proofs were struck. At least two obverse dies were used; one displaying delicate repunching of letters and with tiny die defects below the first 8 and the 5 of the date; the other displaying light repunching of the first A in AMERICA.[23] Proofs have the High Leaf style reverse (see commentary on 1858 reverse varieties on page 255). An estimated 50 to 80 are known today in PF–60 to 64, and 18 to 22 are known in PF–65 or finer grades.

	Cert	Avg	%MS	PF-60	PF-63BN	PF-65BN
1858, Large Letters, Proof	35	64.7		$5,000	$8,500	$25,000

1858, Small Letters • Circulation-strike mintage: The greater portion of 24,600,000.

Availability in Mint State: *MS–60 to 64:* 1,750 to 2,500 examples are known in these grades. *MS-65 and higher:* 120 to 175 examples are known in these grades. This issue is very hard to find at this level, and even more so with good eye appeal.

Availability in circulated grades: Worn coins are very common.

Characteristics of striking: Most examples are well struck.

Notes: The bottoms of A and M in AMERICA do not touch. The letters are shorter and thicker than on the Large Letters variety; there is less open field in the enclosed spaces. The eagle's beak exhibits a sharply pointed tip and a thin and pointed bottom. Also, feathers on the eagle's neck appear more "ruffed" than on the Large Letters variety or on earlier (1856 and 1857) Flying Eagle cents.[24] Q. David Bowers has seen no Mint documentation on the 1858, Small Letters, cents, a letter style which may have been employed to minimize the metal flow in both directions in the dies, thus permitting the head and tail of the eagle on the obverse to be struck more sharply than it is on the Large Letters style. It is probable that one of Paquet's punch fonts intended for another denomination—possibly the dime—was used to create the 1858, Small Letters, cent.[25]

	Cert	Avg	%MS	G-4	VG-8	F-12	VF-20	EF-40	AU-50	MS-60BN	MS-63BN	MS-65
1858, Small Letters	1,823	46.6	42%	$30	$40	$50	$60	$150	$215	$400	$950	$3,750

1858, Small Letters, Proof • Proof

mintage: 200 estimated.

Proof commentary: Today these are rare at any Proof level, and probably fewer than 25 are known in grades from PF–60 to 64, with perhaps 7 to 9 in PF–65 or finer grades. Perhaps all were struck for inclusion in the original 12-coin sets of copper-nickel pattern coins for this year. Most true Proofs were probably sold singly. Most Proofs seen of 1858 are of the Large Letters variety. Some Proofs are not deeply mirrored and display myriad parallel die-finish lines—and while these no doubt were struck as Proofs, they are more apt to be called prooflike Mint State by numismatists today and classified as such by the certification services. These have a mixture of mint luster and mirror surfaces. They are not figured in the survival estimates given here. The Eliasberg Collection 1858, Small Letters, cent (lot 609) was described as "MS-65, prooflike." It was from a 12-piece set of (mostly) pattern cents sold in the Richard B. Winsor Collection sale by the Chapman brothers, 1895, and undoubtedly, it was intended as a Proof. Similarly, Rick Snow commented:

> I handled a prooflike 1858 Small Letters cent from the same dies as the Proof and pattern pieces. It was not struck strongly and thus was not an impaired Proof. I think it was struck for inclusion in one of the pattern sets, but under careless conditions as can be seen on many different varieties of 1858 pattern cents.[26]

	Cert	Avg	%MS	PF-60	PF-63BN	PF-65BN
1858, Small Letters, Proof	25	64.2		$5,000	$8,500	$25,000

INDIAN HEAD (1859–1909)

Variety 1 (Copper-Nickel, Laurel Wreath Reverse, 1859):
Designer: *James B. Longacre.* Weight: *4.67 grams.* Composition: *.880 copper, .120 nickel.*
Diameter: *19 mm.* Edge: *Plain.* Mint: *Philadelphia.*

**Copper-Nickel,
Laurel Wreath Reverse,
Without Shield (1859)**

**Copper-Nickel,
Laurel Wreath Reverse,
Without Shield, Proof**

Variety 2 (Copper-Nickel, Oak Wreath With Shield, 1860–1864):
Designer: *James B. Longacre.* Weight: *4.67 grams.* Composition: *.880 copper, .120 nickel.*
Diameter: *19 mm.* Edge: *Plain.* Mint: *Philadelphia.*

**Copper-Nickel,
Oak Wreath Reverse,
With Shield (1860–1864)**

**Copper-Nickel,
Oak Wreath Reverse,
With Shield, Proof**

Variety 3 (Bronze, 1864–1909): Designer: *James B. Longacre.*
Weight: *3.11 grams.* Composition: *.950 copper, .050 tin and zinc.*
Diameter: *19 mm.* Edge: *Plain.* Mints: *Philadelphia and San Francisco.*

**Bronze, Oak Wreath Reverse,
With Shield (1864–1909)**

**Bronze, Oak Wreath Reverse,
With Shield, Proof**

THE INDIAN HEAD CENT CREATED AND COINED

In early 1858 Chief Engraver James B. Longacre and Assistant Engraver Anthony C. Paquet worked to prepare new designs for the obverse of the copper-nickel cent. The Flying Eagle cent, made first as a pattern in 1856 and then for circulation in 1857 and 1858, was difficult to strike up properly. Often the parts of the eagle nearest the border on the obverse would be lightly defined. The use of the Small Letters style on the obverse of the 1858 cent did not help reduce striking difficulties as may have been hoped. One proposed solution to this was a modified small or "skinny" flying eagle cent obverse, the eagle reduced in size and located mostly at the center of the coin. On this coin, the lower-relief eagle was probably the work of an unidentified artist (it does not resemble Longacre's work), and the lettering seems to have been by Paquet.[27]

Several different new reverse designs were made by Anthony C. Paquet and James B. Longacre. These consisted of one style with an oak wreath, another with an oak wreath and broad ornamented shield, and a third with an open laurel wreath. The two oak wreath styles each had a few laurel leaves on the bottom of the wreath immediately to the left of the bow.[28] A pencil sketch in the National Portrait Gallery shows a laurel wreath similar to that used on the 1859 cent and is attributed to Longacre; however, as it is not signed, perhaps the attribution is tentative, and the sketch could have been assigned to his credit as chief engraver.[29] Two varieties of the laurel wreath were made: one, with five groups of leaves on each side, and the other, scarcer variety, with six.[30] Paquet is the other potential designer for this reverse motif.

Among 11 pattern designs and die combinations created by Longacre and Paquet in 1858 was one featuring Longacre's fanciful portrait of an Indian on the obverse and Paquet's open laurel wreath on the reverse. The obverse depicted *Miss* Liberty, hardly a Native American, wearing an Indian chief's war bonnet. The facial features bear many similarities to the face used on Longacre's 1854 $3 gold coin and, to a lesser extent, his 1849 gold $1 and $20 gold pieces—enough to suggest that these were used as sources—but there are differences in the face as well.

Mint Director Snowden described the motif as "an Indian head with a falling crown of feathers."[31]

Quite probably, patterns of this format were available by spring 1858, for on April 12 a Mr. Howard wrote to Director Snowden:

In 1858 sets of 11 pattern cents plus one prooflike 1858, Small Letters, cent were made available to collectors. Judd-193 combines a regular 1858 Flying Eagle die with a pattern reverse of oak and other leaves surmounted by an ornate shield. (shown at 200%)

The obverse of Judd-203 has a small or "skinny" eagle while the reverse has an open wreath of oak and other leaves. (shown at 200%)

This Indian Head galvano, a larger model of the portrait that would be miniaturized and engraved onto the coin hub by means of a lathe, probably preceded certain of the pattern issues. The headband is blank and bordered by rows of tiny dashes. The bust end is pointed, but not identical to that used on 1858 pattern and 1859 regular-issue cents. There are also some slight differences among the feathers. (shown at 200%)

I have learned that a new pattern piece for the cent has been struck off at the Mint, having upon the obverse a head resembling that of the three dollar piece, and on the reverse a shield at the top of the olive and oak wreath.

I beg leave to inquire of you if you will use your efforts to procure me one specimen only. For which I will give you any price you choose to ask if it is not over five dollars.[32]

This pattern, Judd-209, with the Indian Head obverse and laurel wreath reverse, is a transitional pattern with similar motifs to those adopted for circulation in 1859.

Knowledge about the new cent design was certainly widespread by early that summer, for R. Coulton Davis (a Philadelphia druggist who was an avid collector of pattern coins) wrote to Director Snowden on June 24, 1858, indicating that a Boston newspaper had just carried a favorable story about the proposed new Indian design.[33] On June 26, 1858, Augustus B. Sage, writing on behalf of the newly formed American Numismatic and Archaeological Society, contacted Snowden regarding a specimen of the new Indian Head cent for the Society and another for his own collection.[34]

THE INDIAN HEAD MOTIF

In a letter dated August 21, 1858, to the director of the Mint, James Ross Snowden, Longacre observed:[35]

I allude more especially to the design on the obverse . . . Why should we in seeking a type for the illustration or symbol of a nation that need not hold itself lower than the Roman virtue or the science of Greece, prefer the barbaric period of a remote and distant people, from which to draw an emblem of nationality, to the aboriginal period of our own land? . . . Why not be American from the spring-head within our own domain?

From the copper shores of Lake Superior to the silver mountains of Potosi, from the Ojibwa to the Araucanian, the feathered tiara is as characteristic of the primitiveness of our hemisphere, as the turban is of the Asiatic. Nor is there anything in its decorative character, repulsive to the association of Liberty, with the intelligent American.

On November 4, 1858, Director Snowden discussed Longacre's motif in a letter to the secretary of the Treasury, Howell Cobb, noting in part:

The obverse . . . presents an ideal head of America—the drooping plumes of the North American Indian give it the character of North America . . . and that so far from being modeled on any human features in the Longacre family, or any Indians, these were based squarely on the classical profiles on ancient sculpture. . . . In any event, the feathered headdress was certainly intended in at least two instances to be that of the Indian, the artists at the Mint evidently not realizing the absurd incongruity of placing this most masculine attribute of the warrior brave on the head of a woman . . .

Earlier, in 1854, Longacre had used a "feathered tiara" on the new designs for the gold dollar and $3 gold piece. However, it was differently styled than the new headdress, which is typically likened to a war bonnet, used on the 1858 and later Indian Head cents.

An apocryphal legend that Longacre's young daughter Sarah posed as the model after borrowing the headdress of an Indian chief has long endured, but in actuality the image is probably a composite of an ideal classical head and a war bonnet observed elsewhere. Longacre himself stated the facial profile was copied from a statue, *Venus Accroupie* (Venus Crouching), apparently studied by him either in a Philadelphia museum or at the Vatican in Italy.[36] The above-quoted letter from Snowden to Cobb seemingly addresses the "Sarah question" via the sentence denying the representation of "any human features in the Longacre family."

A photograph of Sarah Longacre (born on February 20, 1828, and thus hardly a little girl, as the apocryphal story about the Indian chief proposed, when either the 1854 $3 gold piece or the 1858 pattern Indian Head cents were made) taken on her wedding day in 1847 is inconclusive, but it does show her face to be an equal or better candidate for the visage on the coin than the somewhat unlikely profile of the aforementioned Venus (both images are presented in juxtaposition in *Longacre's Ledger*, July 1992, p. 19). The attribution of the portrait will probably never be decided to everyone's satisfaction, especially absent any surviving information from Longacre stating that his daughter Sarah was or was not the model.

With regard to the "absurd incongruity of placing this most masculine attribute of the warrior brave on the head of a woman," history repeated itself in 1907 when Augustus Saint-Gaudens decked Miss Liberty in a feathered headdress on the new $10 gold coin. However, ethnologically correct male Indians in headdresses were used elsewhere in the American monetary system, most notably on the $5 Silver Certificate paper currency in the Series of 1899, Bela Lyon Pratt's designs for the new $2.50 gold coins and $5 gold coins of 1908, and James Earle Fraser's Indian Head, or Buffalo, nickel of 1913.

In 1859 Longacre's Indian Head design became standard on the copper-nickel cent, and 36,400,000 examples were coined for circulation. As it turned out, the laurel wreath reverse was only used this year on the cent. It was not forgotten completely, however, and in 1865 it was adapted for use on the new nickel three-cent denomination.

Indian Head cents were struck each year. Some mintages were reduced, notably the 1877 as that was an economic recession year. In 1908 and 1909 coins were struck at the San Francisco Mint, the first branch-mint coinage of any minor (copper or nickel) denomination.

The San Francisco Mint.

RECEPTION OF THE INDIAN HEAD CENT

Examples of the new Indian Head cent were distributed to newspapers in December 1858.

An early commentary appeared in Virginia's *Alexandria Gazette*, January 1, 1859:

> The new cent is out. Instead of the suspicious looking eagle on one side of its illustrious predecessor it has the design of a beautiful Indian girl with a circlet of feathers radiating from a bandeau around her head, inscribed with the word "Liberty." On the other side is the denominational term "one cent" encircled by a wreath.

On January 5, 1859, the *New York Tribune* printed this, displaying some confusion and dissatisfaction as to the portrait of the woman wearing the headdress:

> The year 1859 is chiefly marked by the introduction of a new penny. Hercules, or rather the statue of that mythical personage, was told by his foot. So the majestic art of this country may be told by this penny.
>
> The Goddess of Liberty is represented by an Indian squaw—that is to say, there is a lady with the Greek outline, except that the lips are cantankerously thin, and without the pulp of emotional loveliness; a lady with this expression, wearing a head-dress of aquiline feathers in the true Indian style.
>
> The customary absence of relief to the configuration which distinguishes modern coins from ancient, coupled with the necessary want of color, makes the face as mean and tame as possible, not to say unnatural and of the pancake order of high art. "O Liberty, what crimes are committed in thy name."
>
> True, Madame Roland; and not the least are such abominations as this penny of 1859. A Grecian American squaw—a latitudinally flat-headed one into the bargain, as a representative of Liberty! Delicious idealism!

On the same day the Washington *Daily Union* included this more matter-of-fact description:

> The new cent ordered by the secretary of the Treasury is now in the process of coinage at Philadelphia and will be distributed in January or February.
>
> The obverse presents an ideal head of America; the drooping plumes of the North American Indian give it the character of North America. The head is intended as an illustration of "Liberty." The reverse is a plain laurel wreath enclosing the words ONE CENT; weight 72 grains, or three-twentieths of a troy ounce—eighty-eight percent copper and twelve percent nickel.

The Cleveland *Plain Dealer* printed this favorable review of the new design on January 13, 1859:

> *Another New Cent:* It is of the same size and composed of the same metal as the old cent, but it is much prettier in its device. The reverse, like the old cent, has a wreath surrounding the legend "one cent," but the obverse has, fortunately, discarded the hideous and screeching bird of prey with which the old cent was disfigured, and in its place has the head of an Indian woman with a coronal of feathers, and in the band the noble word of "Liberty." Around the sides are the words, "The United States of America," and the date 1859. They begin to circulate here.

COUNTERSTAMPED AND OVERSTRUCK COINS

Many Indian Head cents were privately marked with punches and placed into circulation to broadcast a message. Possibly the most curious of these is the variety issued by W. Bell, an Erie, Pennsylvania, dry-goods retailer who obtained a quantity of 1859 cents, ground off the reverse of each, and counterstamped them with an advertisement for his business.

Dr. G.G. Wilkins of Pittsfield, New Hampshire, stamped many copper-nickel Indian Head cents and a few early bronze issues with his name. In their time such pieces must have served as advertisement for his dental practice, or perhaps for one or another of his activities (operating an eating house, selling patent medicines, etc.). Somewhat rarer are early-date Indian Head cents stamped OIL OF ICE, one of many patent medicines made by George H. Goodwin of Exeter, New Hampshire. In Blendon, Michigan, in the 1870s, Perry E. Ballou, a phrenologist (a person who examines head bumps and contours with the object of offering conclusions about the personality of the subject), stamped Indian Head cents and other coins with P.E. BALLOU / PHRENOLOGIST. These pieces are also quite rare, and Q. David Bowers has seen only one or two over the course of his career.

A selection of Indian Head cents counterstamped with various advertising motifs. These were "little billboards" that passed hand to hand to promote products and services. (shown at 200%)

Numerous privately produced Civil War store cards and patriotic tokens of the 1863 era exist overstruck on copper-nickel cents, and these range in availability from merely scarce to very rare. Among patriotic-type Civil War tokens, about 65 to 70 different varieties are known.[37] Additional varieties of store cards (advertising tokens) are overstruck and are also scarce to rare.

Parts of the original Indian Head cent designs and inscriptions are still visible on the tokens if one looks closely, and if you are lucky, the date will be readable as well. The reason for striking tokens on these cents is not known, for it seems that little commercial advantage would have been gained by taking current cents at face value, running them through a coining press, and delivering them to a merchant. It can be said that there may have been some advertising advantage, but if so, it would have been easier to have made the same token designs on thin bronze planchets which could have been purchased for less than 1¢ each. Quite possibly, such

A patriotic Civil War token, made using Fuld dies 26 and 418, overstruck on an 1863 Indian Head cent with much of the cent design still visible. (shown at 200%)

overstruck pieces—which exist today to the extent of several hundred pieces, and usually in Mint State—were made to the order of J.N.T. Levick, Edward Groh (curator of the collection of the American Numismatic and Archaeological Society), and other token aficionados active in the 1860s. It seems likely that these pieces were mainly produced to create token varieties in copper-nickel metal, rather than to specifically make overstrikes, as no special effort seems to have been made to preserve the original Indian Head cent designs.

In 1859 (presumably) a dry-goods retailer obtained a supply of new Indian Head cents, ground off their reverses on a lathe, and stamped on each this inscription: FOR / BARGAINS / IN / DRY GOODS / GO TO / W. BELL'S / 5 EXCHANGE / ERIE Pa. This store card is listed by Dr. George Fuld in his catalog as number PA-360-A-1do. Perhaps 40 to 80 of these pieces are known today.

In 1862 John B. Schiller, proprietor of the Sazerac Coffee House and an importer of spirits in New Orleans, counterstamped 1860 Indian Head cents with J.B. Shiller on the obverse and X (meaning 10 cents) on the reverse. These served as small change when the city was occupied by Confederate forces (Fuld variety LA-670-A-1d).

A woman strikes coins at the Philadelphia Mint as visitors watch. Souvenir coins could be purchased from the cashier for face value, and many visitors took cents home with them.

While Indian Head cents counterstamped with advertisements or overstruck with token dies can have significant numismatic value, running in some instances into the hundreds of dollars, much more common are cents that were stamped with stray marks. Such pieces bear initials, numbers, or other punches not attributable today to any source, and these pieces are usually considered damaged coins. For example, a VF-20 1860 cent if counterstamped with OIL OF ICE would be worth more than $100—equal to many multiples of the VF-20 price for an unstamped coin—but if marked with a stray punch such as the letter "A" it would be considered damaged and worth only a dollar or two.

An 1859 Indian Head cent with the reverse planed off and stamped with the advertisement of W. Bell, an Erie, Pennsylvania merchant. (PA-360-A-1do) (shown at 200%)

Counterstamps of J.B Schiller on the obverse and reverse of an 1860 cent to create a coin worth 10 cents in commerce. (Fuld LA-670-A-1d) (shown at 200%)

PROOF MINTAGES

Government records of the total quantities struck of minor Proof coins (those made of copper-nickel, bronze, and nickel alloy) before 1878 do not exist. Although the *Guide Book of United State Coins* lists estimated mintage figures for Proof Indian Head cents of the 1859–1877 years, these seem to be based upon the figures for *silver* coins of the same years. While those who bought silver sets usually also bought Proof Indian Head cents, many extra Proof cents were sold singly and in groups. The mintages of Proof cents and silver Proof coins were often different, sometimes dramatically so.

In the following catalog estimated figures based on the research of Q. David Bowers are used for Proof distribution in the years before 1878. After that time official Mint figures are used.

Among Proof copper-nickel cents of 1860 through 1864, the scarcest dates are 1860 and 1861, and the most plentiful is 1862.

In the 1880s the Mint went wild with the striking of Proof cents, and so many unsold pieces piled up that they were wholesaled to Eastern dealers, and supplies remained on the market for generations afterward, at least until the 1950s.

COLLECTING PROOF INDIAN HEAD CENTS

Selecting Indian Head cents for quality is probably even more important for Proofs than for circulation strikes. While an MS-60 circulation strike can be very attractive, as can an MS-61, in general Proof coins in lower grades such as PF-60 and PF-61 tend to be spotted, stained, mottled, or just plain ugly.

Unless you come upon some very special low-grade Proofs, I suggest using PF-63 as a starting search point, at least for the bronze issues. The copper-nickel Proofs of 1859 to 1864 are sometimes decent in grades such as PF-60 or PF-61, but bronze Proofs rarely are. In general, Proof copper-nickel Indian Head cents survived in nicer condition than did Proof bronze cents, as bronze is a more chemically active alloy.

For bronze cents, even at the PF-63 level and continuing up to whatever higher Proof grades you want to buy, it is essential to cherrypick. While some microscopic "flyspecks" are normal on most Proofs, avoid big spots, oxidation and corrosion patches, and other detractions.

There is a strange situation among Proof Indian Head cents of the bronze series from 1864 to 1909: sometimes a carefully selected brown or red-brown Proof coin can be more attractive than a red one with spots—and a heck of a lot cheaper, too! Likely, a very carefully chosen collection of PF-63BN and PF-64BN Proofs would be a finer assemblage that a quickly purchased run of PF-65RD coins, especially if the red coins had problems (as they often do).

In the 1880s the Mint produced a record number of Proof cents. Many of these were not distributed to the public, but at year's end, or early the following year, they were sold in bulk to dealers. Large numbers, still in thin tissue-paper wrappings, remained in hoards through the mid-point of the 20th century. Today these can often be recognized by having virtually flawless gem surfaces, toned a rich medium brown (from the sulfur in the tissue paper), and with nuances of blue or purple iridescence of incredible beauty.

The amazing situation today is that such a gem might cost much less on the market than a spotted or defective PF-65RD coin!

In general, the quality of Proofs made at the Mint declined from the 1880s through the 1890s, and some of the latter decade are very sloppily made.

Michael G. Fahey, senior numismatist at ANACS, commented concerning the fact that relatively few Proofs of the late 1880s have been certified in comparison to their large mintages:[38]

> One possible explanation for such a low percentage is the poor quality of Proof minor coins from this era. There may be hundreds of Proof coins that are trading as circulation strikes due to their appearance. Also, poorly made Proofs are typically downgraded, due to their substandard eye appeal.

Choose slowly and carefully. A hurry-up set of miscellaneous-quality Proofs could probably be built in a few months, except, perhaps, for the 1864, With L, rarity. A superb-quality set might well take several years to assemble even if your checking account has no limits.

Proofs from about 1902 through 1909, and especially of the year 1903, have the portrait semi-polished rather than frosty. This is normal.

GRADING STANDARDS

Caveat: These grading standards do not take sharpness of strike into account.

MS-60 to 70 (Mint State). *Obverse:* Contact marks, most obvious in the field, are evident at MS-60, diminishing at MS–61, 62, and higher. This abrasion is most noticeable on copper-nickel cents, for it blends in with the background on bronze issues. The cheek of the Indian and the field show some evidence as well. Typical color is BN, occasionally RB at MS–63 and 64, unless dipped to be RD. At gem MS-65 or finer there is no trace of abra-

1860, Pointed Bust. Graded MS-63.

sion. A few tiny nicks or marks may be seen, but none are obvious. At MS-67 and finer the coin will approach perfection. Check "RD" coins for originality. A theoretically perfect MS-70 will have no marks at all, even under a strong magnifier. Although in practice this is not always consistent, at MS-66 and higher there should be no staining or other problems, and the coin should have good eye appeal overall. *Reverse:* Check the high parts of the wreath for abrasion. Otherwise the above comments apply.

Illustrated coin: The surfaces display satin luster and a lovely pinkish-tan patina.

AU-50, 53, 55, 58 (About Uncirculated). *Obverse:* At AU-50, wear is most noticeable on the hair above the ear, on the central portion of the ribbon, on the curl to the right of the ribbon, and near the feather tips, although the last is not a reliable indicator due to striking. Luster is present, but mostly in protected areas. At AU–53 and 55, wear is less. At AU-58 friction is evident, rather than actual wear. Luster, toned brown, is nearly complete at

1861. Graded AU-55.

AU-58, but may be incomplete in the field. *Reverse:* At AU-50, light wear is seen on the ribbon and the higher-relief areas of the leaves, while the lower areas retain their detail. Some luster may be present in protected areas. At AU–53 and 55, wear is less and luster is more extensive. An AU-58 coin will have nearly full luster and show only light friction.

EF-40, 45 (Extremely Fine). *Obverse:* Wear is more extensive, but all of LIBERTY is very clear. Wear is seen on the hair above and below the ear, on the central portion of the ribbon, and on the feather tips. Overall the coin is bold. Scattered marks are normal for this and lower grades, most often seen on the cheek and in the field. *Reverse:* The higher-relief parts of the leaves and ribbon bow show light wear, but details are sharp in lower

1861. Graded EF-45.

areas. Some tiny lines in the vertical stripes in the shield may be blended. Scattered marks may be present, but on all grades they are usually fewer on the reverse than on the obverse.

VF-20, 30 (Very Fine). *Obverse:* Wear is more extensive. LIBERTY shows significant wear on BE, but it is sharp overall. Most hair detail is gone. The feather tips show greater wear (the extent of which will depend on the original strike). The ribbon and hair no longer show separation. *Reverse:* Wear is more extensive than at the preceding level, and many tiny vertical lines are fused together. Detail is still good on lower levels of the leaves.

1870, Shallow N. Graded VF-30.

F-12, 15 (Fine). *Obverse:* Traditionally, the word LIBERTY should be fully readable, but weak on the higher letters of LIB. PCGS suggests this is true, but not if a coin was lightly struck. Full or incomplete, well-struck or lightly struck, no matter what the coin, most buyers still want the word to be discernible. Other areas have correspondingly more wear than on the next-higher grade. *Reverse:* The higher areas of the leaves and the bow show

1870. Graded F-15.

wear. The shield shows greater wear than at the preceding level. Overall, the reverse appears to be less worn than the obverse, this being generally true of all circulated grades.

VG-8, 10 (Very Good). *Obverse:* A total of at least three letters in LIBERTY must be visible. This can be a combination of several partial letters. PCGS does not adhere to this rule and suggests that wear on the feathers is a better indicator. The rim may blend into the field in areas, depending on striking. *Reverse:* Wear is even more extensive. Leaves on the left have hardly any detail, while those on the right may have limited detail. The rim is complete.

1870, Bold N. Graded VG-10.

G-4, 6 (Good). *Obverse:* The coin is worn flat, with the portrait visible mostly in outline form, with only slight indication of feathers. Lettering and date are complete. Part of the rim is usually gone. At G-6, the rim is clearer. *Reverse:* The wreath is nearly flat, although some hints of detail may be seen on the right side. All letters are readable, although the inscription is light at the center (on issues from the 1870s onward). The rim is discernible all around, but is light in areas. At G-6 the rim is clearly delineated.

1877. Graded G-6.

 Illustrated coin: The date is actually quite sharp for this grade.

AG-3 (About Good). *Obverse:* Most letters are worn away, as is the rim. The portrait is in outline form. The date is clearly readable, but may be weak or missing at the bottom. *Reverse:* Extensive wear prevails, although the rim will usually be more discernible than on the obverse. Most lettering, or sometimes all, is readable.

1877. Graded AG-3.

PF-60 to 70 (Proof). *Obverse and Reverse:* Gem PF-65 coins will have very few hairlines, and these are visible only under a strong magnifying glass. At any level and color, a Proof with hairlines likely (though not necessarily) has been cleaned. At PF-67 or higher there should be no evidence of hairlines or friction at all. Such a coin is fully original. PF-60 coins can be dull from repeated dipping and cleaning and are often toned iridescent colors. At

1868. Graded PF-64RB.

PF-63 the mirrorlike fields should be attractive, and hairlines should be minimal. These are easiest to see when the coin is held at an angle to the light. No rubbing is seen. PF-64 coins are even nicer.

Indian Head Cents of 1859

KEYS TO COLLECTING: Enough were minted that today there is no problem finding one in just about any desired grade. Brilliant gems are particularly beautiful, even more so if sharply struck.

NUMISMATIC CURIOSITY: The Stuart C. Levine, M.D., Collection, lot 2209, sold in April 1986 by Bowers and Merena, was an 1859 Indian Head cent obverse die impression deeply struck on an 1857 silver half dime. The obverse of the half dime was flattened by the cent die. The reverse of the half dime was more or less intact, but wavy; perhaps the half dime had been placed face-up on a piece of leather during the striking process. Described as AU-55, the piece was pedigreed to the George F. Seavey and Lorin G. Parmelee collections in the 19th century and to the Charles L. Ruby Collection sale held in 1974 by Superior Galleries.

1859 • **Circulation-strike mintage:** 36,400,000.

Availability in Mint State: *MS–60 to 64:* Mint State coins are plentiful, with most being MS–60 to 64. The population is perhaps 2,000 to 3,000. *MS-65 and higher:* MS-65 and higher coins are elusive in relation to the demand for them. An estimated 400 or more exist.

Availability in circulated grades: This issue is very plentiful, mostly in lower circulated grades.

Characteristics of striking: Many are lightly struck.

Notes: This date stands alone among regular-issue Indian Head cents as the only variety with a laurel wreath on the reverse.

	Cert	Avg	%MS	G-4	VG-8	F-12	VF-20	EF-40	AU-50	MS-60BN	MS-63BN	MS-65
1859	2,123	57.1	63%	$15	$20	$25	$55	$110	$200	$285	$625	$2,800

Varieties: *1859, Repunched Date (FS-01-1859-301):* This variety can also be identified as 1859, Snow-1. Its rarity is URS-7. Strong traces of an earlier date are seen southwest of the final date. There are other 1859, Repunched Date, cents, but this variety is rarest and worth the greatest premium.

A detail of the repunched date. Note the flag of the earlier 1 protruding to the left of the final 1.

	EF-40	AU-50	MS-60	MS-63	MS-65
FS-01-1859-301	$800	$1,250	$2,000	$4,000	$10,000

1859, Proof • **Proof mintage:** 800 to 1,000.

Proof commentary: Proofs have laurel leaves in clusters of 6; should one be found with leaves in clusters of 5 it may represent a very early striking, or even a pattern. Proof mintage records do not exist for Indian Head cents prior to 1878; figures given here are estimates of those actually distributed based on the research of Q. David Bowers. There is no way of knowing if larger quantities were made and later melted (such data exist for certain silver coins but for few minor issues).

In 1859 the cost for an individual Proof cent was face value plus postage. As of 1860 the cost was twice face value, or 2¢, at the Mint.[39] Prior to 1860 there was no premium attached.

Probably more than 700 exist today. PF-65 and finer coins with good eye appeal are scarce. 1859 Proof Indian Head cents, the only year of Indian Head cents with the laurel wreath reverse, have traditionally commanded premium prices over, say, Proof Indian Head cents of 1860 and 1861, which exist in markedly lower numbers. As the 1859 has been more expensive, more in demand, and more the focus of attention, a proportionately higher percentage of extant pieces have been sent to the certification services.

	Cert	Avg	%MS	PF-63BN	PF-64BN	PF-65BN
1859, Proof	188	64.4		$1,500	$2,500	$4,500

1859, Oak Wreath With Shield
Reverse • Circulation-strike mintage: 1,000+.

Availability in Mint State: *MS–60 to 64:* Probably about 500 to 750 exist today. Nearly all are in Mint State, mostly in grades MS–63 to 64. *MS-65 and higher:* This issue is rare in this grade. Probably fewer than 100 examples are known.

Availability in circulated grades: Probably no more than a handful exist.

Characteristics of striking: Sometimes examples are seen with slight weakness on the shield.

Notes: This is the famous 1859 transitional Indian Head cent, with the obverse being from the regular die and the reverse being the oak wreath and shield style, which became regularly used in 1860. Traditionally it is listed as a pattern, Judd-228, but it is more likely that it is a regular issue made in limited numbers at the end of 1859. Nearly all were made with lustrous finish, in the manner of circulating coins.

The origin of the new modified design is related by a letter from Director Snowden to the Treasury Department, on December 13, 1859, stating that a change of the reverse design would be desirable, and enclosing specimens to illustrate the new concept. On December 14, 1859, Secretary of the Treasury Howell Cobb approved the new design. As no further action was necessary to approve the change (no act of Congress, for example), the design became official at that point. Soon afterward perhaps a thousand or so circulation-strike pieces (not Proof patterns) were made by combining an 1859 obverse with the reverse of 1860 to augment the few samples made earlier.

Over the years some authors and editors have incorporated these into the regular series, most notably in the listing in the final edition of the *Standard Catalogue of United States Coins*, published in 1957. This insertion was at the behest of editor John J. Ford Jr., who was the successor to Wayte Raymond's involvement in the *Standard Catalogue of United States Coins*. Q. David Bowers recalls finding several specimens of the Obverse of 1859, Reverse of 1860, transitional cent in dealers' stocks as regular issues. Nearly all specimens are very sharply struck, brilliant, and lustrous. He has never seen a well-worn one, although Walter Breen in his 1988 *Complete Encyclopedia of U.S. and Colonial Coins* stated that "many survivors are in Fine to EF grades." This assertion is patently wrong in the opinion of modern researchers; Breen often made things up if he did not know or was not sure of an answer. Rick Snow suggests (in a letter to Q. David Bowers, April 10, 1996) that many of these pieces may have been stored at the Mint and distributed to collectors in the late 1870s, about the same time that leftover Proof 1862 cents were released.

	Cert	Avg	%MS	MS-63BN
1859, Oak Wreath With Shield, experimental reverse	0	n/a		$2,000

1859, Oak Wreath With Shield
Reverse, Proof • Proof mintage: Unknown.

Proof commentary: Only a few examples have been attributed as Proofs, nearly always with prooflike rather than deep mirror Proof surfaces. These are sharply struck on the shield. Very few mirror Proofs exist, if any.

Indian Head Cents of 1860

KEYS TO COLLECTING: Circulated coins are common. Lower-level Mint State coins are plentiful in relation to the demand for them. MS-65 coins with excellent eye appeal are in the minority. Pointed Bust coins are rare and in high levels of Mint State they are extremely rare.

This is the first year for which all cents featured the Oak Wreath With Shield reverse.

TWO BUST STYLES: There are two styles of the obverse portrait for this year. On one the truncation of the bust is pointed, and on the other it is round.

THE MINTING PROCESS: The following account of the minting process in 1860 is excerpted from *A Description of Ancient and Modern Coins, in the Cabinet Collection at the Mint of the United States*, by Mint Director James Ross Snowden, 1860:

> The ingots [of coinage alloy metal] are first brought to a red heat in order to anneal and render them sufficiently ductile to be rolled with facility; they are then passed between hardened steel rollers, driven by a steam engine, which are so arranged that they can be adjusted with the greatest nicety in order to reduce the bar very nearly to the exact thickness required for the coin. In this form they are taken to the *drawing bench*, driven by the same engine, in which the strip is drawn slowly through the *drawing dies*, or plates of the hardest steel accurately adjusted to reduce the strips to their proper thickness. The strip, thus prepared, is next passed through the *cutting press*, also moved by steam, and pieces or *planchets* of the proper size are cut from it. The punch moves with such rapidity that 160 pieces on an average are cut out in one minute. At the completion of this part of the process, which leaves the strip full of holes, it is folded up and returned to the melting pot.
>
> The planchets are now carried to the coining room, where, in order to raise the edge of the planchet to protect the surface of the coin, they are passed through the *milling machine*. The planchets are fed to this machine through an upright tube, and as they descend from the lower aperture, they are caught upon the edge of a revolving wheel and carried about a quarter of a revolution, during which the edge is compressed and forced up—the space between the wheel and the rim being a little less than the diameter of the planchet. This apparatus moves so nimbly, that 560 half dimes can be milled in a minute; but for large pieces the average is about 120.
>
> The planchets [at least for gold and silver coins] are next to be cleaned, annealed, and whitened. . . .
>
> The planchets are now ready to receive the last impression which is to render them a perfect coin. This most important office is performed by the *coining press*, which we have before mentioned. This machine receives the planchets in a tube from the hand of a workman; as the coin reaches the bottom of the tube it is seized between a pair of fingers and carried forward and deposited within a steel collar between the dies; and while the fingers are expanding and returning for another planchet, the dies close upon the one within the collar, and by a rotary motion are made to impress it silently but powerfully. The fingers, as they again close upon a planchet at the mouth of the tube, also seize the coin, and while conveying a second planchet on to the die, carry the coin off, dropping it into a box provided for the purpose—and this operation is repeated *ad infinitum*. These coining-presses are of various sizes to suit the different denominations of coins. The usual speed of striking is 60 pieces per minute for the half dollar; 75 for the quarter dollar; and 90 for the dime and half dime [and Indian Head cent].
>
> The coining dies, it will be necessary to state, are prepared by engravers specially maintained at the Mint for the purpose. The process of engraving a die consists in cutting the devices and legends in soft steel, those parts being depressed which in the coin appear in relief. This having been finished and hardened, constitutes an "original die"; which being the result of a tedious and difficult task is deemed

too precious to be directly employed in striking coins, but is used for *multiplying dies*. It is first used to impress another piece of soft steel, which then presents the appearance of a coin, and is called a *hub*. This hub being hardened, is used to impress other pieces of steel in like manner, which being exactly like the original die, are hardened and used for striking the coins. A pair of these will, on an average,[40] perform two weeks' work.

LARGE COPPER CENTS RETIRED: The *Annual Report of the Director of the Mint* for the fiscal year ending June 30, 1860, informed readers about the retirement of large cents and the unprecedented spread of the small cent:

The new [copper-nickel] cents have heretofore been issued in exchange for the fractions of the Spanish and Mexican dollar, and for the old copper cents. As the Spanish and Mexican pieces were received at their nominal value, large amounts of these coins have been brought to the melting-pot, and thus the community has been relieved from an irregular and depreciated currency. But it has required the issue of a large amount of cents, and induced a temporary redundancy of that coin in some of the eastern cities. They are gradually, however, being distributed to all parts of our country, including a portion of the southern states, where the copper cent was scarcely known as a circulating medium. Since the passage of the Act of 25th of June, 1860, the issues have been limited to exchanges for the copper cents, except the supplying of the government offices with the new issue, and distant parts of the country in limited amounts. In order to accelerate the process of relieving the community from the cumbrous and inconvenient copper cents, the Mint now pays the expenses of transportation on them, and will make returns in the new issues. This arrangement will tend to relieve the country from a burdensome currency, without increasing the amount of circulation of that denomination of coins.

AMPLE SUPPLIES OF NEW CENTS: The *Bankers' Magazine* included this in its October 1860 issue:

The Flood of Cents. There is much feeling manifested in this city at the persistence of the Philadelphia Mint coinage of cents, the market is so flooded with them. The answer of the Mint is, that there is a constant demand, to meet which they must continue to coin. This demand comes from those who care nothing for the inconvenience of the community, or who do not experience any of the evils of the great surplus of cents, and are therefore inconsiderate enough to order new pieces from the Mint to meet their payments. Banks, and a variety of other institutions and establishments which have to provide change, prefer an elegant new cent to a dirty old one, and will order from the Mint a constant supply as fast as their stock is exhausted. Of course, as they are not obliged to receive them back, they care little how many are afloat. Thus the evil goes on increasing every day.

There are 10 million cents at this moment in New York over and above the want of the community, and they serve no purpose except to rob the poor of the daily commission on their hard earnings. There is no way to get rid of them; they are sold every day at a depreciation, and immediately put into circulation to be paid out and sold over again. There is but one way to remedy the evil. Let the secretary of the Treasury order the Mint at once to stop the coinage. If there is any demand for them, orders can be filled here at this moment, at a discount of one year's interest. Congress should then give the people the privilege of exchanging them at the Mint for silver; this would at once meet the 'demand' at the Mint, and the director would take care that there were not too many coined, if the surplus were allowed to go back to its source.

1860 IN NUMISMATICS: Snowden was directed to cut back coinage operations. Copper-nickel cents were in oversupply and no new gold dollars were needed.

An article by W.C. Prime, "Coin in America," in *Harper's New Monthly Magazine*, March 1860, gave an overview of American coinage, including a rarity scale for copper and silver coins and a commentary, "Collections of Coins."

1860, Rounded Bust • Circulation-strike mintage: About 90% of 20,566,000.

Availability in Mint State: *MS–60 to 64:* An estimated 1,500 to 2,250 exist, most in grades MS–60 to 63. *MS-65 and higher:* MS-65 coins with excellent eye appeal are scarce. Several hundred exist.

Availability in circulated grades: This issue is very common in circulated grades.

Characteristics of striking: Most pieces are fairly well struck, but specimens are sometimes seen with pebbly or grainy surfaces due to protracted die use.

A detail of the truncation of the bust, which is round.

Notes: This is the style of 1860 with the rounded neck tip.

	Cert	Avg	%MS	G-4	VG-8	F-12	VF-20	EF-40	AU-50	MS-60BN	MS-63BN	MS-65
1860, Rounded Bust	1,243	59.5	74%	$10	$15	$20	$35	$70	$110	$185	$250	$1,200

1860, Pointed Bust • Circulation-strike mintage: About 10% of 20,566,000.

Availability in Mint State: *MS–60 to 64:* This issue is very rare in these grades, but as most collectors are content with a single example of an 1860 cent, whether Pointed Bust or Round Bust, the prices for these coins in these grades are not as high as their objective rarity would suggest. *MS-65 and higher:* This issue is an unappreciated rarity in these grades.

Availability in circulated grades: The Pointed Bust, the bust style used in 1859, is considerably the rarer of the two bust styles, and in grades up to MS-63 it is worth a sharp premium over the Rounded Bust.

A detail of the truncation of the bust, which is pointed.

Characteristics of striking: Striking varies for this issue, but it is usually sharp.

Notes: The variety differences are not widely publicized and most certified holders do not mention the bust style. The 1860, Pointed Bust, is thus a prime coin for cherrypicking. This variety's Fivaz-Stanton identification is FS-01-1860-401. This Fivaz-Stanton designation encompasses several Snow varieties. Its rarity is URS-13.

	Cert	Avg	%MS	G-4	VG-8	F-12	VF-20	EF-40	AU-50	MS-60BN	MS-63BN	MS-65
1860, Pointed Bust	151	58.8	73%	$20	$25	$30	$50	$100	$165	$300	$575	$3,250

1860, Rounded Bust, Proof • Proof

mintage: 1,000+.

Proof commentary: Proofs are fairly scarce. Probably 500 to 700 exist, mostly in grades below PF-65. All Proofs for this year are of the Broad Bust style. One specimen of the Narrow Bust cent has been certified as a Proof, but according to Rick Snow, "it is blatantly not a Proof."[41] The first recorded delivery by the coiner of U.S. Proof cents took place on March 8, 1860, when 1,000 or more pieces were delivered along with 1,000 silver Proof sets.[42] Many of these Proof sets never found buyers. The Mint was optimistic in its production quantities of silver Proof coins (no records exist for copper-nickel cents) from 1859 through 1861, after which mintages were scaled back to more closely conform to actual sales. It is believed that each silver Proof set sold during the era was accompanied by a copper-nickel cent, and that, in addition, extra Proof cents were minted. The cost of individual Proof cents at the Mint was 2¢ plus postage.

	Cert	Avg	%MS	PF-63BN	PF-64BN	PF-65BN
1860, Rounded Bust, Proof	56	64.7		$1,000	$2,200	$3,500

Indian Head Cents of 1861

KEYS TO COLLECTING: This date has the lowest mintage for any copper-nickel Indian Head cent. However, enough 1861 cents survive today that examples are obtainable in all grades.

1861 IN NUMISMATICS: The American Civil War broke out. The Charlotte, Dahlonega, and New Orleans mints fell into Confederate hands. Redeemed half cents and old-style large cents (under the Act of February 21, 1857) provided the sole source for the 88% copper part of the copper-nickel alloy this year.[43] The slowing of such redemptions to a trickle may have been responsible in part for the low mintage figure. Further, all newly-minted cents of this date were paid out in exchange for redeemed coins.

1861 • Circulation-strike mintage:

10,100,000.

Availability in Mint State: *MS–60 to 64:* Today 1,500 or so exist in these grades. Among Mint State coins brilliant, frosty pieces are scarce. *MS-65 and higher:* An estimated 400 to 500 or so exist in these grades. MS-65 and higher coins with good eye appeal are seldom seen.

Availability in circulated grades: These coins are plentiful in circulated grades, but they remain the scarcest of the copper-nickel Indian Head cents.

Characteristics of striking: Usually examples are seen fairly well struck, but there are exceptions.

	Cert	Avg	%MS	G-4	VG-8	F-12	VF-20	EF-40	AU-50	MS-60BN	MS-63BN	MS-65
1861	1,181	56.4	66%	$25	$35	$45	$60	$110	$175	$225	$325	$1,100

1861, Proof • Proof mintage: 800 to 1,000.

Proof commentary: Mintage estimates vary widely, and Q. David Bowers has seen numbers as low as 100 and as high as 1,000. Examples are scarce. The Proof reverse die was not well made, and coins struck from it lack the deep mirror surface which is characteristic of Proofs of the following year, 1862. On the obverse, the date is boldly impressed into die. Sometimes the rims of Proofs are rounded, rather than sharp or "square."[44] Deeply mirrored PF-65 or finer coins are rare.

In 1977 in his *Encyclopedia of United States and Colonial Proof Coins 1722–1977*, Walter Breen stated, "Many marketed as Proofs are in fact early circulation strikes," and that "possibly only a little over 100" true Proofs survive. The Breen estimates are often on the low side, based mainly upon what he had personally seen; of course, there were many he had not seen or had reliably reported to him. Still, the Proof 1861 cent seems to be rarer than generally realized, but not as rare as the Proof 1860. Most coins certified as Proofs by the leading services are Proofs, but they are not always mirrorlike for the reasons noted above.

	Cert	Avg	%MS	PF-63BN	PF-64BN	PF-65BN
1861, Proof	80	64.2		$1,500	$3,400	$6,750

Indian Head Cents of 1862

KEYS TO COLLECTING: Cents of this year are very common. Circulation strikes are available in any grade desired through MS-65 or so. Many are softly struck.

COINLESS AMERICA: Although there had been engagements between the South and the North since the Battle of Bull Run in July 1861, neither side could claim victories that might lead to the end of the war. The treasuries of both countries (and by now the Confederate States of America was considered by the world, if not by the Union, to be independent) were depleted. To raise funds Congress, under the Legal Tender Act of February 25, 1862, authorized the issuance of $150,000,000 in Legal Tender Notes, less the amount of Demand Notes still in circulation. Unlike the Demand Notes the new bills were not redeemable in gold or silver coin, but were simply the government's promise to pay in the future.

At the time silver coins were still aplenty in Northern commerce. Gold coins were available from banks and exchange brokers, but only at a premium. In the meantime, federal silver and gold coins had been absent from commerce in the South since the summer of 1861. This was reflected by a May 1862 account of the Army's purchase of goods from Virginia citizens: "Silver Money. Some of the Virginians are delighted with the silver money which they get from our army in exchange for the things they sell, not having seen any for a year."[45]

When Legal Tender Notes were placed into circulation, public distrust of money increased. Silver coins from three-cent pieces to dollars were sought after by citizens who wanted to hold "hard money," and by early summer all were gone. Federal coins in circulation consisted only of Flying Eagle and Indian Head cents and the occasional stray old copper cent. Inflation was rampant, and with the depreciation of paper money in terms of gold and silver, prices of goods rose steadily.

In the second week of July even one-cent pieces disappeared into the hands of hoarders. For the first time before or since, the United States was coinless! In the absence of coins to pay for newspapers, haircuts, beer, lunches, and other goods, a wide variety of monetary substitutes reached circulation in flood proportion. The Act of July 17, 1862, sought to remedy the situation, at least in part, and made *postage and other stamps* legal tender in amounts up to $5 for certain debts (the government still had to pay interest on federal bonds in gold coins). This caused a great deal of excitement as the public took the view that stamps could buy anything. Various merchants and others had small paper envelopes printed to their order, with their name and a number such as 25 or 50 printed to indicate the face value of the stamps within. John Gault, who had recently come to New York City from Boston, patented the encased postage stamp. These consisted of a brass frame with advertising on the back and, on the face, a pane of clear mica behind which was a postage stamp; they were made by the Scovill Manufacturing Company in Waterbury, Connecticut.[46] Merchants, towns, railroads, banks, and others circulated millions of small paper scrip notes, typically with values of 3¢, 5¢, 10¢, 25¢, and 50¢. The Act of July 17, 1862, also prohibited the use of tokens as money, but their use as a money substitute flourished as well.[47]

In the meantime, the Mint was trying its best to produce copper cents, but generous production of cents did little to help the situation. The *North American* reported that in July, 3,682,236 cents were struck, and:

> At an early hour, there were not less than 150 boys and men, and 31 young ladies and girls, awaiting a supply of pennies. The boys and men carried shot bags, cigar boxes, baskets, and all sorts of contrivances in which to carry off the much-needed coin. The girls principally carried neat baskets. When the distribution came to be made, the girls were first served, to the intense chagrin of the men, who had been standing on a single foot, alternately, upon the sidewalk for two or three hours. The men and boys were not attended to until the last girl had departed.[48]

MINT INVENTORIES OF CENTS AND NOTES ABOUT THEM:[49] The quantity of undistributed Indian Head cents on hand at the Mint at various times during this era dramatically reflects the scarcity in the summer of 1862:

1861, August 31: 420,505 cents on hand. A comfortable supply.
1861, October 31: 92,290. Supplies were becoming low, and this foretold a larger mintage for 1862.
1862, January 31: 737,935. A comfortable supply.
1862, April 30: 940,379. A comfortable supply.
1862, August 31: 368.
1862, December 1: 254.

Supplies remained adequate at the Mint through at least July 3, 1862, as evidenced by correspondence from the Mint to a bank, noting that an order for one-cent pieces would be shipped in "a day or two."

In contrast, an order received by the Mint on July 20, 1862, for 5,000 cents was not shipped until September 12! From this time until well into the year 1864, the Mint was not able to ship cents on a timely basis, and delays up to four months were experienced.

On December 1, 1862, Mint Director James Pollock wrote to the secretary of the Treasury, Salmon P. Chase, to inform him that the Mint had the capacity to coin 240,000 or more cents per day, but sometimes only 90,000 were struck, with a good average day's production being about 160,000. Chief among the problems affecting steady coinage was the lack of a reliable supply of nickel, although copper stocks (primarily on hand from melted-down "large" cents) remained adequate. Nickel from the Lancaster Gap mine in Pennsylvania became unavailable in early autumn 1862 due to difficulties with the smelting process resulting in a temporary cessation of operation, and for several weeks there was no other significant domestic supply.[50] By December 1, the metal was again provided to the Mint. Seeking to diversify the sources, Director Pollock increased the amount of nickel obtained overseas through the agencies of Irving Van Wart & Co., C. Robbins, and Fleitmann & Weirss.[51]

In November 1862 it cost about 48¢ to make 100 copper-nickel cents. Nickel cost about $1.65 to $1.75 per pound when imported from Europe and was not easy to obtain even at that price, as the Civil War in America affected imports and exports. Copper ranged in price from 25¢ to 34¢ per pound and did not pose an acquisition problem. By early 1863, nearly all nickel was being obtained from Europe, although some small quantities may have come from Lancaster County, Pennsylvania.

HOARD OF MINT STATE 1862 CENTS SOLD IN 1918: On January 25 and 26, 1918, Thomas L. Elder conducted an auction featuring the Robert Hewitt and B.C. Bartlett collections. Lot 318 was described as "1862 C. Nickel. Bright. Unc. 125 pcs." This was followed by lots 319 to 323, each described as "Bright Unc." and each containing 100 coins. Then came lot 324, also of 100 coins, "Unc. Red." Apparently, these were toned. Lot 325 featured 50 specimens, "Unc. Bright." To this point 775 pieces of Mint State 1862 cents had been offered. Then followed three lots of 100 coins each, described as containing mixed cents dated from 1857 to 1862, each including "many" 1862 cents, but without the precise number given. Accordingly, it is probable that the Elder hoard consisted of about 1,000 specimens of this date.[52]

1862 IN NUMISMATICS: The Union took over New Orleans, including the Mint. It was not until years later in 1879 that coinage was again conducted there, after which silver and gold issues were produced, but no cents.

In the absence of federal coins, all of which had disappeared from circulation in the East and Midwest by July (see page 275), the Postage Currency bills, encased postage stamps, and cent-size tokens attracted the attention of numismatists. Within a year they would be widely collected.

1862 • **Circulation-strike mintage:** 28,075,000.

Availability in Mint State: *MS–60 to 64:* Several thousand or more examples are known in this grade. High-level Mint State coins, sharply struck and with good eye appeal, are scarce. *MS-65 and higher:* 500 or more exist in this grade. This figure is surprisingly low given what the mintage might suggest.

Availability in circulated grades: This issue is very common in circulated grades.

Characteristics of striking: Among higher-grade coins, cherrypicking for quality is advisable, as most of these cents are lightly struck, especially in the feather details. Some have grainy or pebbly surfaces from being struck from well-used dies.

Notes: Mintage climbed this year due to unprecedented war-driven demand. Hoarding of circulating coinage, which had begun in December 1861, went out of control in the second week of July, 1862, at which time all coins including one-cent pieces disappeared from circulation. The Civil War continued to rage.

	Cert	Avg	%MS	G-4	VG-8	F-12	VF-20	EF-40	AU-50	MS-60BN	MS-63BN	MS-65
1862	1,851	61.1	82%	$10	$15	$20	$30	$50	$75	$110	$200	$1,000

1862, Proof • **Proof mintage:** 1,500 to 2,000.

Proof commentary: Proofs of this year are readily available up to and past PF-65 grades.

One can suppose that there was a rush for 1862 Proofs because of the circumstances going on in the economy at the time; the rush for Mint State 1862 cents probably created a crossover demand for extra Proofs. Moreover, apparently a group of undistributed Proofs was found at the Mint in the late 1870s and sold to numismatists at that time.[53]

	Cert	Avg	%MS	PF-63BN	PF-64BN	PF-65BN
1862, Proof	310	64.7		$900	$1,300	$2,500

Indian Head Cents of 1863

KEYS TO COLLECTING: With a record mintage of 49,840,000 cents, the 1863 is the most plentiful of the copper-nickel issues. They are easy to find today in all grades, although coins with needle-sharp detail are scarcer and worth a special premium. Many are dull and unattractive. Among Mint State coins a numerical grade may be one thing, but quality may be another thing entirely. Experts have seen multiple sharp MS-63 coins for this year that have better appearance and aesthetic value than poorly struck MS-65 coins.

CENTS REMAIN SCARCE: In the year 1863 copper-nickel Indian Head cents remained scarce despite the widespread availability of other media of exchange, including encased postage stamps, privately minted Civil War tokens, and paper Fractional Currency notes.

On June 30, 1925, the Treasury Department stated that a grand total of 200,772,000 copper-nickel cents had been coined in the Flying Eagle and Indian Head series through 1864, and as of 1925 some 120,043,446 remained outstanding.[54]

In early 1863 nearly all nickel used to make cents was imported from Europe (also see page 277 under 1862).[55] By March 1863, Mint Director Pollock informed Treasury Secretary Chase that the cost to produce 100 copper-nickel cents was about 60¢ per hundred, not including an estimated 20¢ per hundred for labor. By March 1863, due to uncertainties concerning the outcome of the Civil War, the continued public hoarding of silver coins pushed the price of older silver coins to a 40% premium in terms of federal paper money. In other words, it cost more than $140 in federal "greenback" notes to buy $100 face value of silver coins at a bullion exchange or broker.

During the first half of 1863, cent coinage was at a record monthly average pace of about 4.5 million coins. Despite this, the Mint fell far behind in filling orders. One order for cents received on March 16, 1863, was not filled until mid-September! In late 1863, production of cents slowed somewhat, due to erratic supplies of nickel metal. Meanwhile, privately issued copper and bronze tokens were popular in commerce, foreshadowing the end of the copper-nickel cent.

From the 1863 *Mint Report:*

> The coinage and issue of the nickel cent during the year has been very large—almost unprecedented. The demand still continues, and every effort has been made to supply it. This coin has been distributed to every part of the country, and orders for large amounts are daily received. The profits pay all expenses and distribution of the cent.
>
> A great benefit to the country was effected by the Act of 1857, reducing the size of the cent. It is to be regretted that the idea still prevailed that it was necessary to put into the coin, if not an equivalent, at least a large proportion of real value. To this end, and for other reasons, an alloying metal was sought which should command a comparatively high price in the market, without being properly a *precious* metal. Nickel, possessing the requisite value and suitable qualities, was selected. It was then worth about $2 per pound; though it has since been much lower in price. . . .
>
> The change was well intended, but the experience of other countries, and indeed of our own, has taught us that it was an unnecessary liberality; and that all the nickel we have thus used has been so much money wasted. In France, they had formerly a copper *sous*, or five centimes, about the same as our cent in legal value—weighing 154 grains troy; but the five centimes of the present day weighs only half as much. This latter is a mixture called *bronze*, and is composed of 95% copper, the remainder being tin and zinc, which adds nothing to the cost, but gives character and prestige to the coin. The mixture is less oxidizable and more cleanly [*sic*] than copper.

This account went on to note that even if a cent be made in a new alloy and be intrinsically worth just 1/10 of its face value, it should be made anyway. It would be a cent, by law, to everyone using it. Further:

> If any further proof of this fact should be demanded, we have only to refer to our own recent experience when illegal cents [today called Civil War tokens], or false tokens the size of the legal cent, were made and freely passed—although they contained no nickel, weighed on the average about 51 grains, and worth not more than one-fifth of a cent. Not less than three hundred varieties of those false and illegal tokens, or cents, have been made and issued; and until suppressed, were freely used as coin by the public. They were in direct violation of the laws of the United States, and the prosecution of certain parties issuing them have deterred others, and will soon drive them altogether from circulation.

Next followed a plea requesting that nickel should be eliminated from the cent, and, contrary to the paean to nickel coinage given in 1856:

> Nickel derives its name from a certain unpleasant allusion,[56] indicating its character, and which, in a metallurgic sense, it honestly deserves. It is very obstinate in the melting pot, requiring the fiercest fire even when in alloy with copper. It commonly makes a hard mixture, destructive to dies, and all the contiguous parts of the coining machinery.

Further, nickel found little use in the arts, the director commented.

Thus was laid the foundation for the elimination of nickel in the cent and the implementation of bronze (which would take place the next year, 1864).

The same account went on to say that while current copper-nickel cents were in strong demand, "they are little used in the Western and Southern states." Of course, the Civil War was going on, and it would have been an unlikely scenario for freshly-minted copper-nickel cents to have been shipped there.

By June 20, 1863, old-style large cents in the value of $287,536 had been exchanged for copper-nickel cents. Presumably this value was on a one-to-one exchange; if so, the number of pieces involved was 28,753,600.[57] Copper-nickel cents continued to sell at a premium in terms of paper money and were traded by speculators and brokers.

PATTERN CENTS IN BRONZE: The following letter (here lightly edited and quoted in part) was sent from Mint Director James Pollock to Secretary of the Treasury Salmon P. Chase regarding the problems with copper-nickel:

> Bronze, composed of 95% copper, 3% tin, and 2% zinc, makes a beautiful and ductile alloy. This change of material of the cent is not only desirable in itself as an improvement in the quality and appearance of the coin, but becomes an absolute necessity from the advanced, and still advancing, price of nickel (for a supply of which we are at present entirely dependent upon the foreign market, paying for it in gold or its equivalent), the great uncertainty of procuring an adequate supply for the future from any source at a price within the legal limit . . . the difficulty of melting, the destruction of dies and machinery, etc., thus increasing the cost of production. . . .
>
> It is not proposed to change the size and devices of the cent, only the weight. The weight of the new coin would be 48 grains or 1/10th of an ounce troy. Enclosed I send you specimens of the bronze cent, which is very superior in every respect to the *slumpy* nickel.

While the precise definition of *slumpy* is unknown, from its context you can be sure it was intended as a pejorative word. The bronze cents referred to were patterns (today known as Judd-299 and Pollock-359), and Proofs were struck with medal-type alignment with the obverse and reverse dies aligned in the same direction (rather than coin alignment, or 180° apart); some non-Proofs—exceedingly rare today—were struck with normal coin alignment.[58] The Proof patterns with medal-type alignment were struck on bronze planchets that were darkened before striking; thus, specimens in cabinets today have a glossy brown surface if they have not been cleaned. Those patterns with coin alignment may have been struck with a brilliant finish.

The new bronze cents weighed 48 grains, a figure devised by Director Pollock as being a convenient measure: 1/10 of a *troy* ounce, even though the avoirdupois ounce (1/10 of which equals 43.75 grains) was regularly used as the measure for base metals at the Mint. A survey of privately issued copper tokens in circulation revealed that they weighed on average 51 grains.[59]

1863 • Circulation-strike mintage: 49,840,000.

Availability in Mint State: *MS–60 to 64:* This issue is plentiful in these grades. Mint State coins are often dull or stained, or are struck from worn dies, giving a "greasy" rather than lustrous aspect to the surfaces, especially in the obverse fields. Cherrypick for quality. ***MS–65 and higher:*** 700 to 950 examples exist.

Availability in circulated grades: This issue is very common in circulated grades.

Characteristics of striking: Many are lightly struck, particularly on the feather tips. This issue and the 1864 copper-nickel are notorious in this regard.

	Cert	Avg	%MS	G-4	VG-8	F-12	VF-20	EF-40	AU-50	MS-60BN	MS-63BN	MS-65
1863	2,491	61.0	81%	$10	$15	$20	$30	$50	$75	$110	$200	$1,000

1863, Doubled-Die Reverse • Circulation-strike

mintage: Included in 1863 circulation-strike mintage figure.

Commentary: This variety's Fivaz-Stanton identification is FS-01-1863-801. It can also be identified as 1863, Snow-10. Three or four examples are believed to exist in all grades. Strong doubling is evident on the right leaves of the wreath as well as the upper left leaves, to a lesser extent.

A detail of the doubling on the reverse at the wreath.

	Cert	Avg	%MS	EF-40	AU-50	MS-60BN	MS-63BN	MS-65
1863, Doubled-Die Reverse	2	62.5	100%	$200	$375	$450	$950	$3,000

1863, Proof • Proof mintage: 800 to 1,000.

Proof commentary: Proofs are readily available proportional to the demand for them.

	Cert	Avg	%MS	PF-63BN	PF-64BN	PF-65BN
1863, Proof	144	64.3		$900	$1,300	$2,500

Copper-Nickel Indian Head Cents of 1864

KEYS TO COLLECTING: This is the most difficult copper-nickel cent to find with really nice aesthetic appeal. Nowhere else in the copper-nickel Indian Head cent series is there such a variation in quality among specimens in a given grade (although serious competition for the cellar position is mounted by the 1863).

1864, Copper-Nickel • Circulation-strike mintage: 13,740,000.

Availability in Mint State: *MS–60 to 64:* This issue is relatively easy to find in these grades, but well-struck pieces are scarce. More than 1,000 are known. *MS-65 and higher:* Several hundred at least exist in these grades.

Availability in circulated grades: This issue is scarcer than the 1862 and 1863 in circulated grades, but it is still plentiful.

Characteristics of striking: This date is usually seen weakly struck especially at the tips of the Indian's headdress feathers, and cherrypicking is advised. In Mint State average or weak strikes for this year generally sell below market value. Copper-nickel cents dated 1864 were struck early in the year, with the last coinage occurring in early May.

Notes: R.W. Julian has presented evidence that the combined figures for copper-nickel and bronze cents of 1864 are about 1.2 million coins too high.[60]

	Cert	Avg	%MS	G-4	VG-8	F-12	VF-20	EF-40	AU-50	MS-60BN	MS-63BN	MS-65
1864, Copper-Nickel	1,558	58.6	74%	$20	$30	$40	$55	$100	$150	$200	$325	$1,350

1864, Copper-Nickel, Proof • Proof mintage: 800 to 1,000.

Proof commentary: Estimates of the rarity of this issue vary widely, and some have called it a major rarity. These Proof cents were struck in the early months of the year and were distributed with Proof sets through at least the end of May 1864 and perhaps later as well (to deplete any inventory). Really choice Proofs are quite scarce. In 1977 in his *Encyclopedia of United States and Colonial Proof Coins* Walter Breen stated that possibly 370 or more were struck, but that it is rarer than that figure would suggest. The research of Q. David Bowers, however, shows this issue is likely to be the most available Oak Wreath With Shield Reverse Proof copper-nickel cent aside from the 1862 Proof cent. The order of rarity is probably as follows: 1860, Proof (the rarest); 1861, Proof; 1863, Proof; 1864, Proof; and 1862, Proof (the most available). The Proof obverse die used to strike these coins was also employed to strike bronze Proofs.

	Cert	Avg	%MS	PF-63BN	PF-64BN	PF-65BN
1864, Copper-Nickel, Proof	151	64.3		$900	$1,300	$2,500

Bronze Indian Head Cents of 1864

KEYS TO COLLECTING: Examples of 1864 bronze cents are readily available in nearly any grade desired. Nearly all are sharply struck.

ADVENT OF THE NEW BRONZE CENT: On March 17, 1864, Mint Director James Pollock sent a copper-nickel cent on a thin planchet, weighing 48 grains, to the Treasury Department as a suggestion that this alloy could be retained for the cent, and bronze could be used for the new two-cent piece (due to political considerations discussed on page 278), but the change to bronze prevailed for the cent.[61] At the Mint the officers had been impressed by the fact that thin bronze Civil War tokens were circulating by the millions. Bronze seemed to be a good alternative for the heavier and harder copper-nickel cent, which had been more difficult to strike sharply.

The new bronze cent was coined under authority of the Act of April 22, 1864, which set the alloy and made the coins legal tender up to a maximum of 10¢. (Also see note under 1865.) However, hoarding of cents by the public and speculators continued through at least early summer 1864, as noted on page 284.

From the 1864 *Mint Report:*

> The substitution of the bronze alloy for the nickel mixture, as authorized by Congress, has been highly successful. The demand for the one- and two-cent pieces has been unprecedented, and every effort has been made to meet it. The demand still continues, although the number daily issued largely exceeds that of any former period. Large quantities are hoarded, and thus kept from circulation. They have also been bought and sold by small brokers at a premium; this has induced individuals to collect them for the purpose of sale, thus producing a scarcity and inconvenience to the public that ought not to exist. . . .

Following the passage of the aforementioned legislation, coinage of copper-nickel cents continued through early May, in order to use up supplies of nickel and the alloy on hand.[62] The first bronze ingots for the 48-grain bronze coinage were prepared on May 13, 1864, after which assays were made. The quantity of tin ranged from 3% to 3.2% and zinc formed about 2.2% of the composition, with the balance being copper. On May 20, 1864, a shipment of 50,000 of the new cents went to the Treasury Department in Washington.

In June 1864 a contract was made with Holmes, Booth & Hayden of Waterbury, Connecticut, for the firm to supply pre-made bronze planchets for cents and two-cent pieces, these to be used in addition to those made at the Mint. The Connecticut firm supplied its first planchets on July 5 (this being the date of their arrival at the Mint), and by the end of October more than 50 tons of cent and two-cent planchets had been delivered.[63]

BRONZE ALLOY DIFFERENCES: The copper used to coin bronze 1864 (and 1864, With L) cents seems to have been of a special quality, for specimens that are toned brown have an especially rich appearance. Such differences in metal quality exist elsewhere in the series and are subtle. Doubtless, if extremely refined non-destructive elemental analysis were ever made, the typical bronze cent of 1864, 1907, and 1908-S would all be found to have slightly different metallic compositions.

NEW REVERSE HUB: The 1864 bronze cent marked the introduction of the new reverse hub with the bottom of the N in ONE and, to a lesser extent, the tops of the EN in CENT shallow in the die; this would continue in use until a new hub was made in 1870.

WHARTON PROTESTS THE BRONZE CENT: Joseph Wharton, owner of America's only significant nickel mine, did not take kindly to the impending adoption of the new bronze format, and in a letter dated February 15, 1864, he began a counterattack on the new cent, giving four reasons why the copper-nickel format should be retained (critical commentary is shown in brackets):

1. The copper-nickel cent yielded a good coinage profit to the Treasury [but not as great as a bronze cent would yield].
2. He was ready to begin supplying good quantities of nickel to the Mint [but added that he could not completely satisfy the Mint's requirements; meanwhile, foreign supplies were becoming increasingly erratic].
3. The difficulty of coining the hard nickel metal alloy provided a better defense against counterfeiting than would bronze [but in practice, cents never were a popular denomination with counterfeiters; too much trouble for the yield obtained].
4. "Unnecessary changes" in the coinage of a great nation such as the United States should be avoided whenever possible.

He distributed a pamphlet dated April 15, 1864, in which he went even further and suggested that as part of a revised coinage system, one-cent pieces should have 25% nickel and 75% copper—or more than twice as much nickel as was currently in the copper-nickel cent!

Pollock discussed the Wharton letter and other aspects of the Wharton campaign with other Mint officials, and it was agreed that Wharton's political connections to the Treasury Department and to the Mint were so strong, that, indeed, nickel should be continued in cent coinage, but that the copper-nickel cents could be reduced in weight from 72 grains to the same 48 grains that had been proposed for the bronze issue; meanwhile, bronze could be used for a new denomination, the two-cent piece. Although Treasury Secretary Chase must have been confused by Pollock's turnabout, Chase ignored the new advice and proposed that the original bill (providing for the new bronze cent) be passed, and it was—as the Act of April 22, 1864. However, while Wharton may have lost his anti–bronze cent campaign, he won his war with the Mint in that the subsequent advent of the nickel three-cent piece in 1865 and the Shield nickel five-cent piece in 1866 assured that his coffers would remain overflowing.[64]

REWRITING HISTORY: With the advent of the bronze cent the old copper-nickel alloy was a thing of the past. Or, was it? One interesting thing about reading old *Mint Reports* and National Archives data is the finding of numerous inconsistencies, including the re-invention of old ideas and denial of earlier facts. In this vein someone at the Mint, probably not the director (but, who knows?), attempted to rewrite history a few decades later, for the *Annual Report of the Director of the Mint for the Fiscal Year Ending June 30, 1911*, which contains this amazing commentary on page 9:

> The composition of the [Lincoln] 1-cent piece, 95 per cent copper and 5 per cent tin and zinc, is unsatisfactory. The coins soon become dull and dirty in appearance and, when exposed to the salt air of the seacoast, are rendered unfit for circulation. This is particularly noticeable of coins which lie for a time in slot machines. They are offered for redemption in bad condition and must be remelted. When handled in the Treasury offices and mints an objectionable dust arises from them.
>
> The act adopting the present composition was passed in 1864, prior to which date the 1-cent piece was issued under the Act of February 21, 1857, which provided for a composition of 88% copper and 12% nickel. The Mint officials have always regarded the change as a backward step, and in the opinion of the bureau the percentage of nickel should have been increased instead of reduced.

This sort of thing makes numismatic research a lot of fun!

1864, No L • Circulation-strike mintage: Most of 39,233,714.

Availability in Mint State: *MS–60 to 64:* This issue is the most plentiful of the early-date bronze cents in these grades. Mint State coins often show a mixture of orange and brown nicely blended, sometimes with a woodgrain effect. Fully brilliant coins turn up with frequency, more so than any other bronze cents of this era. As with all bronze Indian Head cents it is important to differentiate between *original* brilliance and *dipped* brilliance. *MS-65 and higher:* Examples are readily available in BN and RB, and these are often very attractive. RD coins without any flecks or problems are rare.

Availability in circulated grades: This issue is common in circulated grades, but it is scarcer than the very common issues of 1879 through 1909.

Characteristics of striking: Most examples are well struck, except for some struck from late states of dies used to coin copper-nickel cents.[65]

Notes: The mintage for 1864-dated bronze cents is given as 39,233,714 in the *Guide Book of United States Coins.* This figure includes an estimated 5,000,000 to 7,500,000 with L on the ribbon (see entry below). However, as noted under the 1864 copper-nickel cent (see page 281), R.W. Julian has presented evidence that the combined figures for copper-nickel and bronze cents of 1864 are about 1.2 million coins too high.[66]

	Cert	Avg	%MS	G-4	VG-8	F-12	VF-20	EF-40	AU-50	MS-60BN	MS-63BN	MS-65RB	MS-65RD
1864, No L	1,322	60.1	84%	$15	$20	$25	$45	$70	$90	$115	$150	$400	$1,000

1864, With L • Circulation-strike

mintage: 5,000,000 to 7,500,000 of 39,233,714.

Availability in Mint State: *MS–60 to 64:* This issue is fairly scarce in these grades. Mint State coins can be very attractive if they appear glossy brown or with a smoothly blended mixture of red and brown, often with a wood-grain effect. Original (undipped, uncleaned) full-red specimens are rare. *MS-65 and higher:* Several hundred at least exist in these grades, mostly BN and RB examples. Often these have nice eye appeal.

Availability in circulated grades: This issue is slightly scarce in these grades. Many years ago, when looking through a large hoard of 1864 bronze cents, Q. David Bowers found that about 1/3 had the L on the ribbon. Very worn 1864 bronze cents with pointed a truncation can be identified as 1864, With L, cents even if the L is worn away, but such coins do not bring any more than a regular bronze coin price.

Characteristics of striking: This issue is usually well struck. Sometimes examples are from clashed dies with traces of the reverse wreath outline visible in the obverse field. The bottom of the N in ONE and, to a lesser extent, the tops of the EN in CENT are always shallow, as on the die; this would continue until a new hub was made in 1870.

Notes: Examples exist in all circulation-strike grades from well-worn to Mint State and are not major rarities, although the fame of the variety has given it a special aura and the status of a key issue. The number of 1864, With L, cents struck was not separately recorded, but it is part of the more than 39,000,000 bronze cents struck this year. 1864, With L, cents were made from 18 or more obverse dies.

Adding the L onto the ribbon: Late in 1864 the tiny initial L was added to the ribbon at the bottom of the Indian's headdress for the engraver James B. Longacre. The tip of the neck truncation is pointed on the 1864, With L, cent (rather than rounded as on the earlier 1864 bronze cents and copper-nickel cents dating back to 1860).

British Connection Disputed: Walter Breen reported that many 1864, With L, cents were shipped to England, probably during and after the Civil War, and that thousands were repatriated during the 1950s through the 1970s.[67] However, Q. David Bowers spent much time in England during the 1960s, bought many American coins, gained an excellent knowledge of which issues were common there and which were not, and is not aware of any such preponderance of 1864, With L, cents, although occasional pieces were seen.[68]

Further, most if not all 1864, With L, cents were placed into circulation in 1864 in the Union (Northern) states. There was no particular reason that quantities of these cents should have been shipped to

England. On the contrary, bronze cents were never international trade coins and, further, as England carried out considerable trade with the Confederacy during the war, due to the cotton from the South needed for British mills, the export of Union-made 1864, With L, cents seems even more unlikely.

	Cert	Avg	%MS	G-4	VG-8	F-12	VF-20	EF-40	AU-50	MS-60BN	MS-63BN	MS-65RB	MS-65RD
1864, With L	1,457	51.9	50%	$55	$80	$150	$200	$275	$375	$425	$600	$1,800	$5,000

Varieties: *1864, Bronze, Circular Lathe Lines (FS-01-1864-1401):* This variety can also be identified as 1864, Snow-11. This variety has a rarity of URS-8. Concentric lathe lines are seen on the obverse in the area of the ear.

A detail of the circular lathe lines on the portrait.

1864, With L, Repunched Date (FS-01-1864-2304): Different varieties of the 1864, With L, cent with repunched date numerals are seen with some frequency and may comprise about 1/3 of known pieces. Several different varieties have the date triple punched. This particularly curious variety (also identified as 1864, Snow-5; 1864, FND-005) not only has a triple date, but at one time was believed

A detail of the repunched date.

to be from a working die punched with two working hubs—first with an 1864, No L, hub with rounded neck tip and, second, with an 1864, With L, hub with pointed neck tip; the jury is still out on whether this description is accurate. This variety has a rarity of URS-10.

Perhaps a newcomer in the Engraving Department was doing much of the date punching at the Mint in 1864, for the high frequency of repunching has no counterpart in quantity among the earlier copper-nickel Indian Head cents. Witness as examples the vastly larger mintages of the 1864 copper-nickel and the 1864, No L, cents that exist with relatively few repunchings.

It seems likely that these endemic repunchings on the 1864, With L, cent can be ascribed to William H. Key, who signed on at the Mint as an assistant engraver in October 1864, which would have been just about the time of production for the 1864, With L, cent. However, Key was not an amateur, as he had worked with his family's diecutting and token-making business prior to his employment at the Mint. Thomas K. DeLorey suggests that perhaps an inexperienced person had been hired, his ineptness discovered, and subsequently Key was hired to *replace* him.[69]

1864, With L, cents in copper-nickel: A few 1864 cents with the L were struck on thick copper-nickel planchets, at least some of them from Die Pair 1 described under Proofs on page 288. Several Proofs are known and three VF specimens from non-Proof dies exist.[70] These admit of a small possibility that circulation-strike 1864, With L, cents were struck in the copper-nickel format (listed today as patterns; Judd-358, Pollock-249). If so, this means that the 1864, With L, hub was in use before the 1864, No L, bronze circulation-strike coinage. If this was the case, then it would suggest that many 1864, No L, dies had been made early in the year and used for copper-nickel as well as the later bronze coinage, but that one or more 1864, With L, dies were on hand in spring 1864 when copper-nickel coinage was still in progress.

	VF-20	EF-40	AU-50	MS-60	MS-63	MS-65
FS-01-1864-1401	$50	$100	$175	$250	$300	$500
FS-01-1864-2304	$300	$400	$500	$600	$750	$2,200

1864, No L, Proof • Proof mintage: 150+.

Proof commentary: Most extant specimens show brown toning. It has been conjectured that bronzed (with dark brown surfaces) Proofs may have been issued; certainly this was true of the related bronze Proof patterns dated 1863 (Judd-299, Pollock-359, both on thin planchets with medal alignment).[71] Many if not most "red" PF-63, PF-64, and PF-65 coins on the market have been dipped. Rick Snow concurs that Proof 1864, No L, bronze cents were probably issued with bronzed surfaces.[72] Thus, prices given for "red" Proofs below—taken from market listings—should be taken with a large grain of salt; the situation needs more research to determine if there are any red coins that are not direct results of dipping. In contrast, Proof 1864 cents with L on the ribbon were struck with bright or "red" surfaces (see next listing).

Proofs were struck from at least three different obverse dies, one of which was used earlier to make copper-nickel Proofs.[73] The *Guide Book of United States Coins* suggests that just 150+ Proofs were made, an enticingly low number that is often quoted, but Q. David Bowers suspects this estimate may be on the low side. The + probably represents several hundred coins. In 1977 in his *Encyclopedia of United States and Colonial Proof Coins, 1722–1977*, Walter Breen stated that only 100 or so were struck. Bowers estimates 400 to 500 were struck.

	Cert	Avg	%MS	PF-63BN	PF-64RB	PF-65RD
1864, No L, Proof	151	64.3		$500	$1,750	$9,000

1864, With L, Proof • Proof mintage: 20+.

Proof commentary: The number of Proofs minted is not known. The *Guide Book of United States Coins* suggests 20 coins, a figure that may well be close to true number, as this issue is a prime rarity in Proof format. Q. David Bowers notes that one badly stained Mint State coin is in a certified Proof holder and is likely to remain there. Some examples of Proof 1864, With L, cents and other Proof cents after 1864 were called "copper" die trials by Adams and Woodin in their 1913 text. Bowers had occasion to purchase and closely examine many such "copper pattern" pieces from the Woodin estate via Sol Kaplan in the 1950s. He is skeptical of all such "copper" attributions and suspects that elemental analysis will reveal that any such pieces are, in fact, bronze.

Proof cents of both die pairs seem to be of about the same rarity. Rick Snow compiled a listing of 13 known specimens in a 1994 article that reveals that all but two (Marks Collection and Anderson-Dupont collection specimens) have spots, fingerprints, or other defects.

Over the years Q. David Bowers has handled perhaps five or six Proof coins of this issue. Probably fewer than 15 can be traced with certainty, two gems of which are currently held in a certain Eastern estate and were not mentioned in previous studies of Indian Head cents.

Pricing for these Proofs in particular tend to vary at auction depending upon the quality of the coin and market conditions at the time.

Unlike the 1864, No L, bronze Proof cents, perhaps all of which may have been issued with a dark or bronzed surface, the Proof 1864, With L, cents were definitely issued with a brilliant finish.

Notes: *Two die pairs:* Proofs for the 1864, With L, were struck from two different die pairs:[74]

Die Pair 1 (originals): The date is farther to the left on this die pair than on the other, with the 1 in the date directly below the neck tip. There is no spine from the curl below Liberty's ear (see Die Pair 2 for comparison). Rick Snow says: "The obverse die is polished somewhat unevenly, with more space between the denticles at 3:00 and 9:00 than at 12:00 and 6:00. The reverse die was used earlier to strike some 1864 (No L) bronze Proof cents."[75] This is the original die pair.[76]

Die Pair 2 (restrikes): The date is significantly to the right of the tip of the neck, with the left side of the 1 in the date being an obvious point for inspection. A tiny spine (about 1.5 mm) extends downward to the left from the curl below Liberty's ear into Liberty's neck. The reverse seems to be from the same die used to strike the 1863, With L, pattern cents, but in a later state.[77] Rick Snow[78] and Q. David Bowers believe these were made for collectors in 1871; i.e., they are restrike issues. (See the Norweb Collection, Part I, 1987, lot 156, for an example of Die Pair 2.) John Dannreuther reports that Proof 1864, Small Motto, two-cent pieces also exist in restrike form and suggests that they may have been struck around 1871.[79]

Issuing scenario for Proofs: The scenario for the issuance of Proof 1864, With L, cents may well have been as follows:

Late in 1864 the new hub with L on the ribbon was introduced into the cent series. Proofs produced at that time were made of the new style and routinely sold to collectors who ordered them. Such orders would have straggled in, for traditionally most Proof minor coins were sold early in any given year. At the time, *there was no numismatic interest in or knowledge of the hub change,* and no coin collectors noticed that certain late-1864 bronze Proofs had the L on ribbon. For that reason, the mintage was small and simply limited to those needed to fill regular orders as they came in.

By 1871 collectors were aware of the tiny L on the ribbon and sought to buy 1864, With L, Proof, bronze cents, but specimens were few and far between. The solution was a simple one: A new obverse Proof die dated 1864, with the L on the ribbon was created, and additional Proofs were made. The evidence for this is provided by this die sequence in the words of Rick Snow, here lightly paraphrased and expanded:[80]

Among 1864, With L, Proof cents, the reverse of Die Pair 1 has been matched to the reverse of a regular 1864, No L, bronze cent. Thus, Die Pair 1 can definitely be assigned "original Proof" status. A copper-nickel 1864, With L, cent [a pattern: Judd-358, Pollock-429] I have in stock is also a Die Pair 1 coin and was probably struck in 1864.

The aluminum strikings of the 1864, With L, cent (J-361, P-432) and the 1863, With L, cents in various metals (J-301, P-363 in bronze; J-302, P-365 in copper-nickel; J-403, P-367 in aluminum) are all paired with the same reverse used to create 1864, With L, Proof bronze cents from Die Pair 2, but these various patterns are from an earlier die state. This indicates that the 1863, With L, cents were struck before the Die Pair 2 1864, With L, bronze Proofs.

However—and here is the telling part—this same reverse die can be found on 1869 aluminum strikings (J-671, P-747) and regular-issue Proof 1870 and 1871 bronze cents. The striking order of this reverse die—as observed from coins together at the same time for side-by-side comparison—is as follows:

1863, With L, pattern in bronze (Pointed Bust)
1863, With L, pattern in copper-nickel (Pointed Bust)
1869 pattern in aluminum
1870 regular bronze Proof
1871 regular bronze Proof (variety with 71 apart)
1864, With L, regular bronze Proof
1871 regular bronze Proof (variety with 71 numerals close)

This clearly shows that the Die Pair 2 Proof 1864, With L, cents were struck no earlier than 1871 and were made as restrikes for the collector market. It also shows that in 1871 the Mint was making up restrikes for numismatists.

This restriking activity from the 1871 era is not a revelation, as, for example, the so-called Proof restrike 1801, 1802, and 1803 dollars are believed to have been made around this time, and a glance at the Judd or Pollock books will reveal many unusual mulings and off-metal strikes created around this time as well. Of course, restrikes are avidly collected in their own right, and in some instances (such as Proof half cents of the 1830s and 1840s) rare varieties of restrikes sometimes bring higher prices than originals.

	Cert	Avg	%MS	PF-63BN	PF-64RB
1864, With L, Proof	5	64.4		$15,000	$45,000

Indian Head Cents of 1865

KEYS TO COLLECTING: The 1865 is readily available in just about any grade desired. There are two styles of 5 in the date, but not much attention has been paid to them.

1865 IN NUMISMATICS: The Act of March 3, 1864, lowered the legal tender of the bronze cent from a maximum of 10¢ per transaction to just 4¢. The intent of the legislation was to prevent large debts to be paid in bulk bronze cents rather than government paper money (such as Fractional Currency notes). At the time silver and gold coins did not circulate except on the West Coast.

In June 1865 the *New York Journal of Commerce* commented:[81]

> But why can we not have the head of Washington on our coinage now? The cent is the coin in most common use, and on that it ought to be placed. We respectfully urge it on the attention of the director of the Mint. Let us have a few patterns with the head of Washington submitted to the Treasury Department, and do a good thing by thus adopting the memory of Washington as a special object of veneration.

Chief Engraver Longacre did not respond with any cent patterns, but this suggestion may have influenced the production in 1865 and 1866 of several pattern nickel five-cent pieces (in anticipation of the launching of this new denomination in 1866) with the portrait of Washington.

1865 • **Circulation-strike mintage:** 35,429,286.

Availability in Mint State: *MS–60 to 64:* This and the 1864, No L, are the two most plentiful early bronze cents in Mint State. Fully brilliant or nearly brilliant specimens are especially attractive and are in the distinct minority among Mint State coins. Some have a wood-grain type of toning as also seen on 1864 bronze cents (also see commentary under 1909-S on page 351). Original bright-red specimens are somewhat on the rare side, but as 1865 is a common date overall (when all grades are considered), bright-red coins have never brought especially high prices. *MS-65 and higher:* This issue is easy to find in these grades. Most examples are BN or RB.

Availability in circulated grades: This issue is common in circulated grades within the context of its era. As recently as the 1950s, when quantities of unsorted worn Indian Head cents were common in public hands and were often brought to coin dealers for valuation, it was usual to find 1864 and 1865 bronze cents in multiples.

Characteristics of striking: This issue is usually fairly well struck. The bottom of the N in ONE and, to a lesser extent, the tops of the EN in CENT are always shallow as on the die; this would continue until a new hub was made in 1870.

	Cert	Avg	%MS	G-4	VG-8	F-12	VF-20	EF-40	AU-50	MS-60BN	MS-63BN	MS-65RB	MS-65RD
1865	967	60.9	83%	$15	$20	$25	$30	$45	$65	$90	$150	$600	$1,750

Varieties: *"Plain" and "Fancy" 5:* Two different date logotype punches were used for 1865 cents, usually called the "Plain 5" and "Fancy 5" varieties.[82]

Plain 5: These issues display shorter serifs on the base of the 1, a small projection from the lower right of the upper curve of the 8, a truncated ball at the top of the 6, a somewhat "bent" left side to the upright attached to the top of the 5, and the flag of the 5 with a gently curved top.

A detail showing the
Plain 5 in the date.

Fancy 5: These issues have longer serifs at the base of the 1, no projection on the 8, a normal knob or ball on the 6, a straight left side to the upright attached to the top of the 5, and the flag of the 5 with the top flat for about 40% of its surface to the left, then dipping in an arc for the remaining 60%.

A detail showing the
Fancy 5 in the date.

Rick Snow's book, *Flying Eagle & Indian Cent Attribution Guide*, third edition, describes these in detail as does *A Comprehensive Guide to Selected Rare Flying Eagle and Indian Cent Die Varieties* by Larry R. Steve and Kevin Flynn. The marketplace has taken virtually no notice of these differences, price-wise. Rick Snow reports that the Plain 5 varieties are slightly scarcer than the Fancy 5 issues. Inasmuch as Proofs are of the Plain 5 variety and were made beginning earlier in the year, it is assumed that among circulation strikes the Plain 5 variety preceded the Fancy 5.

The variety called "1865/4" by Walter Breen[83] and others has been considered by certain authorities to be Plain 5 Over Fancy 5, but at present it is viewed, per Fivaz and Stanton, who list it as FS-1865-1302, as simply a repunched Plain 5 date over a defective 5; not an overdate.

1865, Die Gouge in Headdress • Circulation-strike

mintage: Included in 1865 circulation-strike mintage figure.

Commentary: This variety's Fivaz-Stanton identification is FS-01-1865-1401. It can also be identified as 1865, Snow-14. Its rarity is URS-5. A heavy arc, part of an incomplete circle, is seen through the headdress. This marking is a lathe line.

A detail of the die gouge
through the headdress.

	Cert	Avg	%MS	AU-50	MS-60BN	MS-63BN
1865, Die Gouge in Headdress	0	n/a		$500	$750	$1,200

1865, Doubled-Die Reverse •

Circulation-strike mintage: Included in 1865 circulation-strike mintage figure.

Commentary: This variety's Fivaz-Stanton identification is FS-01-1865-1801. It can also be identified as 1865, Snow-2. Its rarity is URS-7. This variety displays the Fancy 5 (see page 290). The reverse displays strong doubling, primarily on the left side, which is especially evident at ONE CENT. This variety is one of the most popular varieties in the Indian Head cent series.

A detail of the doubling on ONE CENT.

	Cert	Avg	%MS	EF-40	AU-50	MS-60BN	MS-63BN
1865, Doubled-Die Reverse	10	41.6	40%	$800	$1,100	$2,200	$5,500

1865, Proof • **Proof mintage:** 750 to 1,000.

Proof commentary: All examples have Plain 5 in the date. Most are toned brown or brown with only traces of red. Original bright-red, unspotted gems are very hard to find.

	Cert	Avg	%MS	PF-63BN	PF-64RB	PF-65RD
1865, Proof	142	64.3		$375	$800	$7,500

Indian Head Cent, 1866

KEYS TO COLLECTING: This is fairly scarce as a date, the beginning of the tough-to-find era of Indian Head cents that would extend through the early 1870s. In the 1950s, when it was not uncommon to find cigar boxes filled with cents, Q. David Bowers relates that he always picked out the dates from 1866 to 1878 inclusive and set them aside as scarce.

1866 IN NUMISMATICS: From the 1866 *Mint Report:* "The demand from the small coin, both bronze [1¢, 2¢] and nickel [3¢, 5¢], was very great during the year, and the coinage was regulated to meet the demand. They were distributed to all parts of the United States, but principally to the Western and Southern states."[84]

Part of this was probably due to peace following the Civil War, and the lack of circulating coins in the South (whose merchants and other interests during the Civil War had issued very few private tokens). However, it is doubtful if many were circulated in the *far* West.

1866 • Circulation-strike mintage: 9,826,500.

Availability in Mint State: *MS–60 to 64:* This issue is elusive in these grades. Most examples are BN or RB. Original (undipped) red specimens are several orders rarer than RB pieces. *MS-65 and higher:* Beginning with this year and continuing through 1877 true gems exist by a couple hundred or more for each date, but superb quality is elusive. Most examples are BN and RB.

Availability in circulated grades: This issue is slightly scarce in circulated grades.

Characteristics of striking: Striking is often satisfactory, although one rule hardly fits all examples of this issue. The bottom of the N in ONE and, to a lesser extent, the tops of the EN in CENT are always shallow, as on the die; this would continue until a new hub was made in 1870. Three different obverse dies of this year show severe sinking at their centers, causing the obverse of each coin struck from these dies to bulge and to wear rapidly at that point.[85]

	Cert	Avg	%MS	G-4	VG-8	F-12	VF-20	EF-40	AU-50	MS-60BN	MS-63BN	MS-65RB	MS-65RD
1866	1,012	54.8	60%	$50	$65	$80	$100	$190	$250	$290	$380	$1,500	$5,250

Varieties: Repunched date varieties exist for this date and are described by Snow, as well as in the Steve-Flynn text.

    1866, Doubled-Die Obverse (FS-01-1866-101): One variety of this year (1866, Snow-1; 1866, FND-001) has sharp doubling at ERTY in the headband, but this variety is not widely known; the striking is actually *tripled*, but according to Larry Steve the tripling can only be seen on well-struck specimens of very early die states.[86]

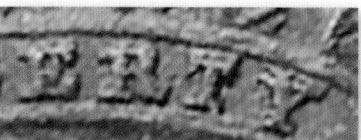

A detail of the doubling at ERTY.

	VF-20	EF-40	AU-50	MS-60	MS-63	MS-65
FS-01-1866-101	$200	$350	$600	$750	$1,200	$3,500

1866, Proof • Proof mintage: 725 to 1,100.

Proof commentary: Most are in grades below PF-65 and are BN or RB. RD gems are rare. Proofs have an irregular surface to Miss Liberty's cheek and certain other head and neck features, probably the result of die rust. The obverse die field is more basined than normal. Bright-red Proofs are very hard to find. Most "red" Proofs have been dipped (ditto for other red Proofs in the series).

	Cert	Avg	%MS	PF-63BN	PF-64RB	PF-65RD
1866, Proof	126	64.5		$400	$600	$5,000

Indian Head Cents of 1867

KEYS TO COLLECTING: The 1867 cent is a scarce date in all grades.

1867 IN NUMISMATICS: By 1867 minor coins were still circulating in large numbers in the aftermath of the Civil War; these included the Indian Head cent, two-cent piece, nickel three-cent piece, and the new nickel five-cents. Silver coins were absent from the channels of commerce in the Eastern and Midwest United States (but they circulated on the West Coast).

1867 • **Circulation-strike mintage:** 9,821,000.

Availability in Mint State: *MS–60 to 64:* This issue is quite elusive in this grade. Most are BN or RB. Original bright-red specimens were rare even years ago and are more elusive today; most "Brilliant Uncirculated" pieces on the market have been dipped. *MS-65 and higher:* More examples are available for this issue in these grades than for the 1866 cent, but they are still scarce in relation to the demand for them.

Availability in circulated grades: This issue is scarce in circulated grades.

Characteristics of striking: Striking varies for this issue, but it is usually on the sharp side. The bottom of the N in ONE and, to a lesser extent, the tops of the EN in CENT are always shallow, as on the die; this would continue until a new hub was made in 1870.

	Cert	Avg	%MS	G-4	VG-8	F-12	VF-20	EF-40	AU-50	MS-60BN	MS-63BN	MS-65RB	MS-65RD
1867	990	53.5	60%	$50	$70	$90	$135	$230	$275	$300	$400	$1,600	$6,000

Varieties: *1867, Repunched Date (FS-01-1867-301):* This variety can also be identified as 1867, Snow-1. Its rarity is URS-10. Protruding above the last two digits of the date are prominent remnants of an earlier date. Called 1867, 1867 Over 67, this variety was first publicized in the February-March 1959 issue of *Empire Topics* (the predecessor of the *Rare Coin Review*), which suggested the undertype was from a smaller font. Modern scholarship holds that just one date logotype was used, but the digits 67 of the undertype do appear smaller.

A detail of the repunched date.

	VF-20	EF-40	AU-50	MS-60	MS-63	MS-65
FS-01-1867-301	$500	$600	$800	$1,000	$1,500	$5,000

1867, Proof • **Proof mintage:** 850 to 1,100.

Proof commentary: Most examples are RB. Some may have "thin letters" on the obverse (see Walter Breen, *Encyclopedia of United States and Colonial Proof Coins, 1722–1877*, p. 132), but this may be from a lapped or repolished die; certainly it is not a distinct variety. The certification services routinely call coins RD even if they have corrosion spots.[87] In all instances, PF-65RD coins are scarcer and more desirable if they are spotless.

	Cert	Avg	%MS	PF-63BN	PF-64RB	PF-65RD
1867, Proof	189	64.4		$400	$600	$5,000

Indian Head Cents of 1868

KEYS TO COLLECTING: The 1868 along with the 1866, 1869, and 1870 is considered to be semi-scarce in all circulation-strike grades.

1868 IN NUMISMATICS: From the 1868 *Mint Report:*

> The purchase of the nickel-copper [*sic;* this was common terminology at the Mint at the time; the writer was simply listing the more valuable metal in the alloy first] cents, composed of 88% copper and 12% nickel, still continues, payment being made in the three- and five-cent nickel coins. The amount purchased to the close of the fiscal year [June 30] was $260,482.04. This operation results in a small profit to the United States and serves to reduce the redundancy of cent coins.

1868 • Circulation-strike mintage: 10,266,500.

Availability in Mint State: *MS–60 to 64:* This issue is rare in these grades. Most examples are fully or at least partly brown. Bright-red cents of this date are seen more often than are those of the somewhat comparable (mintage-wise) 1867, but in absolute terms they are extremely rare. As is the case for all "Brilliant Uncirculated" Indian Head cents, the majority offered as such on the market have been dipped. *MS-65 and higher:* Several hundred or more exist in these grades, mostly BN and RB.

Availability in circulated grades: This issue is scarce in circulated grades.

Characteristics of striking: Striking varies for this issue, but it is often weak or of average sharpness, usually not as sharp as, for example, a typical cent of 1867. The bottom of the N in ONE and, to a lesser extent, the tops of the EN in CENT are always shallow, as on the die; this would continue until a new hub was made in 1870.

	Cert	Avg	%MS	G-4	VG-8	F-12	VF-20	EF-40	AU-50	MS-60BN	MS-63BN	MS-65RB	MS-65RD
1868	949	54.1	61%	$40	$50	$70	$125	$170	$220	$250	$360	$925	$4,000

Varieties: *Die clashed with nickel three-cent piece:* An interesting and rare 1868 nickel three-cent piece was discovered by Chris Pilliod and described in *Coin World*, March 4, 1996:

> I discovered . . . in late 1994 at a public auction in Michigan an 1868 copper-nickel three cent coin with a clover-leaf pattern smack in the middle of Liberty's neck . . . The obverse die of this three-cent coin was clashed with the reverse of an Indian Head cent, and what appears as a three-leaf clover is in fact an oak leaf from the wreath of the cent. Several smaller leaves and a portion of the ribbon may be seen in back of Liberty's forehead. Apparently the clashing also occurred at an oblique angle [rather than during the die set-up process in which both dies would have been firmly mounted in the press]. . . . Additional searching has uncovered several additional examples beyond the discovery piece . . . I speculate they occurred when the operator was changing over a minting press from one denomination to a different one. Doubtless the Mint used presses interchangeably for coins of similar diameters. The operator may have inadvertently fired the press before completing the turnover of dies . . .[88]

Separately, Chris Pilliod noted that as of early April 1996, he knew of several EF specimens and one AU piece. His estimate of scarcity is more than 30 known.[89] The Indian Head cent reverse die was in the anvil or fixed part of the set-up in the coining press, while the obverse for the nickel three-cent piece was in the hammer die position. As Chris Pilliod suggests, this clashing was probably inadvertent and was caused by mismatched dies in the press during the press set-up process (much in the manner that 1857 clashed die Flying Eagle cents were created; see page 250). Question: Is there an 1868 Indian Head cent showing on its reverse evidence of clash marks from the obverse of a nickel three-cent piece?[90]

1868, Proof • **Proof mintage:** 750 to 1,000.

Proof commentary: On April 27, 1868, 100 Proof Indian Head cents were delivered along with an equivalent number of silver Proof sets, indicating that it was the practice to include cent Proofs with silver sets at the time. In addition, for 15¢ payable in silver or gold (the government would not accepts its own paper money at par!), a minor Proof set could be purchased, this containing the Indian Head cent, two-cent piece, nickel three-cent piece, and Shield nickel—yielding a total face value 11¢.[91]

Most are RB. Some Proofs—apparently somewhat less than half of the known pieces—have the obverse and reverse dies aligned in the same direction, rather than the usual 180° apart; this variation has not been widely noted and bears no significant premium.

	Cert	Avg	%MS	PF-63BN	PF-64RB	PF-65RD
1868, Proof	133	64.4		$375	$550	$5,000

Indian Head Cents of 1869

KEYS TO COLLECTING: The 1869 is considered to be semi-scarce in all circulation-strike grades.

1869 IN NUMISMATICS: James B. Longacre, who created the Flying Eagle and Indian Head designs and had been Mint engraver since 1844, died on January 1, 1869. William Barber, who had worked as an assistant since 1865, became chief engraver in the same month. Without doubt he had punched his share of four-digit date logotypes into Indian Head cent dies between 1865 and 1869, and possibly later as well. Coins from Longacre's estate were auctioned a year later, on January 21, 1870, by M. Thomas & Sons.

1869 • **Circulation-strike mintage:** 6,420,000.

Availability in Mint State: *MS–60 to 64:* This issue is scarce in these grades. Usually examples are fully or partly brown. Original red examples are rare. *MS-65 and higher:* Several hundred or more exist in these grades, most of which are BN or RB. Full *original* red coins are rare for this and other dates of the era.

Availability in circulated grades: This issue is scarce in circulated grades.

Characteristics of striking: Striking varies, but this issue is usually sharp. The bottom of the N in ONE and, to a lesser extent, the tops of the EN in CENT are always shallow, as on the die; this would continue until a new hub was made in 1870.

	Cert	Avg	%MS	G-4	VG-8	F-12	VF-20	EF-40	AU-50	MS-60BN	MS-63BN	MS-65RB	MS-65RD
1869	1,023	47.0	49%	$85	$120	$235	$335	$445	$550	$600	$700	$1,800	$4,750

1869, 9 Over 9 • Circulation-strike

mintage: Included in the 1869 circulation-strike mintage.

Commentary: A number of repunched dates exist. This variety, whose Fivaz-Stanton identification is FS-01-1869-301, slightly resembles an overdate, 1869, 9 Over 8, and for many years it was listed as such, including in the *Guide Book of United States Coins.* Today it is known to be a repunched date, showing secondary digits under the 6 and 9. The rarity for this variety is URS-12.

A detail of the repunched date.

	Cert	Avg	%MS	G-4	VG-8	F-12	VF-20	EF-40	AU-50	MS-60BN	MS-63BN	MS-65RB
1869, 9 Over 9	369	42.0	37%	$125	$225	$450	$575	$725	$825	$975	$1,200	$2,400

1869, Proof • Proof distribution (esti-

mate): 850 to 1,100.

Proof commentary: 600 or more exist today. Most are RB. Some were sloppily made. As is true of all Proofs of this era, bright-red gems without spots are quite rare. Proofs were struck from at least two different obverse dies, one with very slight repunching of the last date digit. Rick Snow suggests that about one in 20 coins from this latter die have medallic alignment.[92]

	Cert	Avg	%MS	PF-63BN	PF-64RB	PF-65RD
1869, Proof	175	64.4		$380	$650	$3,000

Indian Head Cents of 1870

KEYS TO COLLECTING: The 1870 cents are scarce in all grades, particularly so in Mint State.

1870 CENT CLASHED DIE WITH 1870 NICKEL FIVE-CENT PIECE:
An interesting and rare 1870 Shield nickel five-cent piece was discovered by Ken Hill in 1994. Its obverse shows clash-mark impressions of the obverse of an Indian Head cent. The face and headdress of Miss Liberty appear clearly and in an inverted position in the background areas between the shield stripes on the nickel. The Indian Head cent obverse die was in the hammer (or top, movable part) of the set-up in the coining press, while the obverse for the Shield nickel was in the anvil or stake position at the bottom. This clashing was probably inadvertent and was caused by mismatched dies in the press during the press set-up process (much in the manner that 1857 clashed die Flying Eagle cents were created; see page

A detail of a Shield nickel, the die for which had clashed with an Indian Head cent die.

250). These are rare. No Indian Head cent variety has been found showing related traces of the Shield nickel design.

MISPLACED DATES: At least two varieties are known which show parts of the date logotype in the denticles below the correctly placed 1870, apparently the result of the four-digit punch coming into hard contact with the working die while not being even near the correct position. They are varieties of 1870, Bold N, and 1870, Doubled-Die Reverse, cents.

REVERSE HUB DIFFERENCES SHOWING BOLD AND SHALLOW N: Several minor reverse die differences occur and are given descriptions below. Market interest varies when it comes to differentiating the Bold N and Shallow N varieties:

Reverse hub C (introduced in 1864 with the bronze coinage; in use through 1869 and intermittently until 1877): This reverse style is called "Shallow N" by the *Guide Book of United States Coins*. The E's appear with T-shaped serifs at their centers. The bottom of the N in ONE and tops of the EN in CENT are in low relief. This style was used from 1864 through 1870 and intermittently later (as on 1877 circulation strikes, for example).

A detail of the Shallow N in ONE.

Reverse hub D (introduced in 1870 and used on some cents through 1877, and all after that date): This reverse style is called "Bold N" by the *Guide Book of United States Coins*. The E's appear with flared or trumpet-shaped serifs at their centers. The N in ONE is in normal relief. This style was used on most cents through 1909.

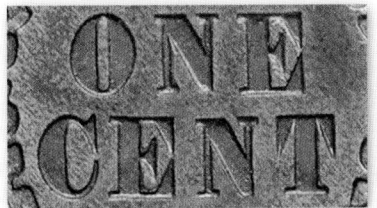

A detail of the Bold N in ONE.

Reverse hub D Over C: Hub D struck over hub C shows doubling, especially at the top left of the E in CENT. The E in ONE has a T-shaped serif at its center, while the E in CENT has a flared serif. This reverse style is seen on some 1870 cents.

1870, Shallow N • Circulation-strike

mintage: The greater portion of 5,275,000.

Availability in Mint State: *MS–60 to 64:* Most examples in these grades are BN or RB. Choice coins are elusive. Original bright-red coins are rare and sometimes have a yellowish cast to them, due no doubt to the alloy. *MS-65 and higher:* This issue is very scarce in these grades. Only a few hundred exist.

Availability in circulated grades: This issue is quite scarce in circulated grades.

Characteristics of striking: Striking varies on this issue, but examples can be found well defined. Die characteristics vary.

See page 297 for details comparing the Shallow N and Bold N.

	Cert	Avg	%MS	G-4	VG-8	F-12	VF-20	EF-40	AU-50	MS-60BN	MS-63BN	MS-65RB
1870, Shallow N	4	41.5	25%	$80	$100	$220	$320	$400	$500	$550	$900	$1,600

1870, Bold N • Circulation-strike

mintage: The lesser portion of 5,275,000.

Availability in Mint State: *MS–60 to 64:* Most examples in these grades are BN or RB. Choice coins are elusive. Original bright-red coins are rare and sometimes have a yellowish cast to them, due no doubt to the alloy. *MS-65 and higher:* This issue is very scarce in these grades. Only a few hundred exist.

Availability in circulated grades: Bold N coins are slightly scarcer than Shallow N coins for the year 1870.

Characteristics of striking: Striking varies on this issue, but examples can be found well defined. Die characteristics vary.

See page 297 for details comparing the Shallow N and Bold N.

	Cert	Avg	%MS	G-4	VG-8	F-12	VF-20	EF-40	AU-50	MS-60BN	MS-63BN	MS-65RB	MS-65RD
1870, Bold N	921	48.2	49%	$55	$75	$200	$280	$375	$450	$500	$850	$1,300	$4,000

Varieties: *1870, Doubled-Die Obverse, Repunched Date, Misplaced Date (FS-01-1870-102):* The most startling 1870 misplaced date, in the view of Q. David Bowers, is this variety, also known as 1870, Snow-5, and 1870, FND-001. It shows the upper part of a 0 protruding from the denticles below the 7 of the date. A secondary 8 can also be seen in the bottom loop of the 8. There is also strong doubling at LIBERTY.

A detail of the date showing misplaced digits.

	VF-20	EF-40	AU-50	MS-60	MS-63
FS-01-1870-102	$1,500	$2,000	$2,500	$4,000	$7,500

1870, Doubled-Die Reverse •

Circulation-strike mintage: Included in 1870, Shallow N, circulation-strike mintage.

Commentary: The Fivaz-Stanton identification for this variety is FS-01-1870-801. Its rarity is URS-9. This is a very popular doubled die. The doubling can be seen on ONE CENT, both sides of the wreath, and the top of the shield. A later die state has a small die crack from 11:30 to the wreath at two o'clock. 1870, Snow-2, displays this reverse, but it is also listed as FS-1870-101 (a doubled-die obverse with a repunched date). This is the strongest doubled-die reverse of several for this date. Most Mint State pieces are RB. Fully red examples command higher prices.

A detail showing the doubling on the reverse.

	Cert	Avg	%MS	EF-40	AU-50	MS-60BN	MS-63BN	MS-65RB	MS-65RD
1870, Doubled-Die Reverse	9	62.6	89%	$575	$750	$850	$1,000	$2,500	$4,000

Varieties: *1870, Misplaced Date, Doubled-Die Reverse (FS-01-1870-302):* This misplaced date (also known as 1870, FND-004) is best seen under strong magnification. It shows a garbled mess of digit segments (at least eight according to Larry R. Steve and Kevin Flynn, though Fivaz and Stanton speculate that as many as twelve are present) within the denticles.

A detail showing the misplaced date.

	VF-20	EF-40	AU-50	MS-60	MS-63
FS-01-1870-302	$500	$700	$1,000	$1,250	$2,000

1870, Shallow N, Proof • Proof

mintage: The greater portion of 1,000+.

Proof commentary: Most are RB. Quite a few cleaned specimens are around, seemingly more than for any other date of this immediate era. This date also seems to be susceptible to spotting. Original bright-red Proofs are rare.

At least two obverse dies were used, one of which shows repunching on the 8 of the date.

See page 297 for details comparing the Shallow N and Bold N.

	Cert	Avg	%MS	PF-63BN	PF-64RB	PF-65RD
1870, Shallow N, Proof	0	n/a		$325	$525	$1,900

1870, Bold N, Proof • **Proof mintage:** The lesser portion of 1,000+.

Proof commentary: The comments for this issue are similar to those for the Shallow N Proof, listed previously. This is less common than the Shallow N Proof, but Q. David Bowers has never seen a want list that differentiated between these two varieties of Proofs.

Note: See page 297 for details comparing the Shallow N and Bold N.

	Cert	Avg	%MS	PF-63BN	PF-64RB	PF-65RD
1870, Bold N, Proof	(a)			$425	$725	$2,500

a. Included in certified population for 1870, Shallow N, Proof.

Indian Head Cents of 1871

KEYS TO COLLECTING: The 1871 cent is one of the classic scarcities in the series, in a class with the 1872 and slightly scarcer than it. It is sought after in all grades. It is very scarce in Mint State.

TWO DATE LOGOTYPES ON PROOFS: Two different logotypes were used on Proofs this year. The usually seen style is the Wide Date; this is found on the vast majority of circulation strikes and most Proofs. Quite rare is the Close Date. A search of photographic files indicates that Close Date Proofs form just a tiny minority, probably fewer than 1 in 5 or 1 in 10 Proofs examined. These same two four-digit logotype punches were also used on dies for bronze two-cent pieces; there the rarity is just the opposite: most 1871 two-cent pieces are of the Close Date style.[93]

1871 IN NUMISMATICS: Up to this year the primary Mint source for copper to refine for coinage into cents was from obsolete copper half cents and large cents redeemed by the Treasury. The copper in 100 lightly worn large cents was sufficient to make more than 350 bronze Indian Head cents.[94]

In 1871 copper-nickel Flying Eagle and Indian Head cents began to be redeemed in very large quantities, although they were only lightly worn in most instances. In this year 8,569,848 were redeemed by the Treasury.

The Act of March 3, 1871, provided that copper and other token coins (minor coins with no important intrinsic value) could be exchanged for federal greenback notes when presented in quantities of $20 or more. At the time there was a glut of minor coin, and the cent's legal-tender limit of 4¢ per transaction (due to the Act of March 3, 1864) made it impossible to use the coins in large transactions. The redundancy of bronze cents at the time no doubt contributed to the reduced mintage figures for new cents in 1871.

Silver and gold coins remained absent from commerce except on the West Coast. Active markets continued as usual in such coins, as bankers and exchange houses bought and sold them at a premium. On one occasion a single steamship left New York City with 65 tons of silver coins aboard.[95] Gold coins were flying away as well, depleting domestic supplies.

1871, Shallow N • Circulation-strike

mintage: The lesser portion of 3,929,500.

Availability in Mint State: *MS–60 to 64:* This issue is rare at this level. Examples are generally brown or brown with traces of red. ***MS-65 and higher:*** Examples are very rare if they appear with a generous amount of original red color. This coin is a key to the series at this level.

See page 297 for details comparing the Shallow N and Bold N.

Availability in circulated grades: This issue is even rarer than the 1871, Bold N, cent. This is the rarest small cent date of the 1870s. See the following entry for more information.

Characteristics of striking: The striking on this issue is usually fairly strong.

	Cert	Avg	%MS	G-4	VG-8	F-12	VF-20	EF-40	AU-50	MS-60BN	MS-63BN	MS-65RB
1871, Shallow N	2	54.0	0%	$130	$180	$325	$450	$575	$650	$775	$1,000	$2,600

1871, Bold N • Circulation-strike

mintage: The greater portion of 3,929,500.

Availability in Mint State: *MS–60 to 64:* This issue is rare in these grades. It is one of the top several key issues in the series. Original bright-red specimens are exceedingly hard to find, but their market price is dampened by the offering of dipped coins. In general, the 1871 Indian Head cent can hold its own with the 1872 in any rarity contest, but

See page 297 for details comparing the Shallow N and Bold N.

the latter date is much more publicized. ***MS-65 and higher:*** This issue is one of the most difficult dates to find in the series in these grades.

Availability in circulated grades: This issue is rare in the context of the series. It is one of the key issues in circulated grades. In fact, in grades from Good through Fine, this is believed to be the rarest date in the 1870–1879 span, excluding the 1877.[96] This empirical observation is backed by the relative mintage figures for the decade.

Characteristics of striking: The striking on this issue is usually fairly strong.

	Cert	Avg	%MS	G-4	VG-8	F-12	VF-20	EF-40	AU-50	MS-60BN	MS-63BN	MS-65RB	MS-65RD
1871, Bold N	2	54.0	0%	$70	$85	$250	$350	$475	$525	$550	$800	$2,350	$7,000

1871, Shallow N, Proof • Proof

mintage: The lesser portion of 960+.

Proof commentary: The Shallow N Proof is less common than the Bold N Proof. See the following entry for more information. Two date logotypes were used on Proofs of this year: for more information see page 300.

See page 297 for details comparing the Shallow N and Bold N.

	Cert	Avg	%MS	PF-63BN	PF-64RB	PF-65RD
1871, Shallow N, Proof	1,042	46.5		$500	$875	$2,350

1871, Bold N, Proof • Proof mintage: The greater portion of 960+.

Proof commentary: 1871 Proofs are in especially strong demand due to the overall rarity (of both circulation strikes and Proofs) of the date; however, this means that certification figures are skewed, as a higher percentage of the known pieces of this date have been submitted than is usually the case for a given population. Choice Proofs are elusive. Many have been cleaned. In addition, many Proofs were carelessly made. In this year the Mint restruck specimens of the 1864, With L, Proof bronze cent and certain other delicacies. Two date logotypes were used on Proofs of this year: for more information see page 300.

Note: See page 297 for details comparing the Shallow N and Bold N.

	Cert	Avg	%MS	PF-63BN	PF-64RB	PF-65RD
1871, Bold N, Proof	(a)			$325	$600	$2,150

a. Included in certified population for 1871, Shallow N, Proof.

Indian Head Cents of 1872

KEYS TO COLLECTING: At the time there were many bronze coins in circulation. In response the Mint reduced its production of new Indian Head cents.

DATE NUMERALS: Date numerals are compact and in a straight line for this issue; this alignment would continue through and including 1880. The 1872 and 1873 dates are given in especially small numerals. (The 1872 nickel three-cent piece also has a small, compact date, but it is slightly curved.)

DIE VARIETIES: Most circulation-strike 1872 cents have the date positioned very low, with the space between the bottom of the 1 in the date and the denticles being about 1/3 to 1/4 of that from the top of the 1 to the neck. However, a few circulation strikes have the date slightly higher, though not centered, and a few have the date centered (as on Proofs). The date positions of a Low Date circulation strike and a Centered Date Proof are dramatically different when the two are compared side by side. A doubled-die obverse discovered by Larry R. Steve was reported on the first page of the April 12, 1993, edition of *Coin World*.

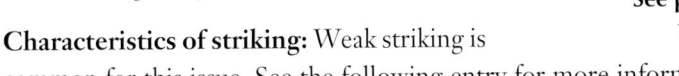

BROKEN-TOP "D" HUB: Certain Indian Head cents of 1872 through 1875 have the top of the D in UNITED missing. This was caused by a defect in the working hub.[97]

1872 IN NUMISMATICS: In 1872 5,751,073 copper-nickel cents of 1857 to 1864 were redeemed by the Treasury.

1872, Shallow N • Circulation-strike

mintage: The lesser portion of 4,042,000.

Availability in Mint State: This issue is slightly rarer in all Mint State grades than the following entry.

Availability in circulated grades: This issue is slightly rarer in all circulated grades than the following entry.

Characteristics of striking: Weak striking is common for this issue. See the following entry for more information.

See page 297 for details comparing the Shallow N and Bold N.

	Cert	Avg	%MS	G-4	VG-8	F-12	VF-20	EF-40	AU-50	MS-60BN	MS-63BN	MS-65RB
1872, Shallow N	5	33.8	0%	$100	$170	$370	$425	$575	$700	$950	$1,250	$4,500

1872, Bold N • Circulation-strike

mintage: The greater portion of 4,042,000.

Availability in Mint State: *MS–60 to 64:* This is a key issue in these grades. It is more publicized than the 1871, but ever so slightly less rare. Attractive specimens are hard to find. Some Mint State coins of this era have yellowish-orange fields with streaky brown flecks sprinkled over the surfaces, such flecks often being oriented in a particular direction;

See page 297 for details comparing the Shallow N and Bold N.

this is due to imperfectly mixed alloy distending during the strip-rolling process. *MS-65 and higher:* This issue is very scarce in these grades, but RD examples, while rare, are seen more often than they are for 1871.

Availability in circulated grades: This issue is rare; a key date. Within the 1870s only the 1877 and 1871 are harder to find in circulated grades.

Characteristics of striking: Shallow N (scarcer) and Bold N varieties exist, but in the marketplace these differences are rarely described. Most examples of this issue are somewhat indifferently struck; they are hardly needle sharp. Specialist Carl Herkowitz observed that about 10 coins out of 35 are notably weak.[98]

	Cert	Avg	%MS	G-4	VG-8	F-12	VF-20	EF-40	AU-50	MS-60BN	MS-63BN	MS-65RB	MS-65RD
1872, Bold N	1,218	43.8	38%	$90	$140	$300	$375	$500	$650	$785	$1,150	$4,000	$17,000

1872, Bold N, Proof • Proof mintage: 850 to 1,100.

Proof commentary: 1872 Proofs are in especially strong demand due to the overall rarity (of both circulation strikes and Proofs) of the date; however, this means that certification figures are skewed, as a higher percentage of the known pieces of this date have been submitted than is usually the case for a given population. Choice Proofs are elusive. Many have been cleaned. In addition, many Proofs were carelessly made.

See page 297 for details comparing the Shallow N and Bold N.

Beginning with this year, a reverse die with a "blob" or bulge at the top-right, downward arm of the T in CENT was used to strike Proofs; this die was used for other Proof dates along with other (normal) reverse dies through 1878. This is a die flaw or accident and does not represent an intended change.

On all Proofs seen the date is centered, with the space between the top of the 1 and the neck being about the same as the space between the bottom of the 1 and the denticles.

Q. David Bowers suggests that bright-red Proofs are a bit easier to find (but are still rare) for this date than for 1870 or 1871, but opinions differ. Most 1872 Proofs he has seen are a nice blend of red and brown. In anyone's book, a gem Proof of this scarce date is a winner.

	Cert	Avg	%MS	PF-63BN	PF-64RB	PF-65RD
1872, Bold N, Proof	226	64.3		$400	$700	$4,300

Indian Head Cents of 1873

KEYS TO COLLECTING: The 1873, Close 3, cent is much the scarcer of the two date varieties of this year, quite possibly three or four times scarcer than the Open 3 issue. However, many numismatists desire just one specimen of the date and do not collect by varieties; thus, the price differential between the two varieties is not as great as it might otherwise be. Notwithstanding this, the awareness of the Close and Open 3 varieties in the collecting community has grown by leaps and bounds in recent years, thus widening the price differential. Much of this new demand is due to the dissemination of information in the Snow and Steve-Flynn books, as well as through *Longacre's Ledger.*

TWO DATE VARIETIES: Indian Head cents of 1873 were made with Close 3 in the date (all Proofs plus some circulation strikes) and Open 3 in the date (no Proofs, some circulation strikes). At a quick glance the 1873, Close 3, date, made early in the year, resembled "1878," as the knobs on the 3 were close together. The Open 3 was created by filing away most of the bottom knob on the 3 of the date logotype and trimming the knob to a smaller size; dies punched with this modified date logotype are called Open 3.

A detail showing the Close 3 in 1873.

BACKGROUND: On January 18, 1873, A. Loudon Snowden, chief coiner at the Philadelphia Mint, wrote to James Pollock, director of the Mint, to state in part:[99]

A detail showing the Open 3 in 1873.

I desire in a formal manner to direct your attention to the "figures" used in dating the dies for the present year.

They are so heavy, and the space between each so very small that upon the smaller gold and silver, and upon the base coins it is almost impossible to distinguish with the naked eye, whether the last figure is an eight or a three . . .

Snowden recommended that new "sets of figures" be made at an early date. Presumably, there were many dies already on hand with what later became known as the "Close 3," and these were not destroyed, but were used later in the due course of business, to be replaced at a still later date with the new "Open 3" dies.

On both varieties of the 1873 cent the date numerals are compact and in a straight line; this alignment would continue through and including 1880. The years 1872 and 1873 are in especially small numerals.

1873 IN NUMISMATICS: In 1873 2,641,157 copper-nickel cents of 1857 to 1864 were redeemed by the Treasury. The Coinage Act of February 12, 1873, abolished the bronze two-cent piece, silver three-cent piece, and half dime, stopped coinage of the Liberty Seated silver dollar, and provided for the production of a new denomination, the trade dollar.

1873, Close 3 • Circulation-strike

mintage: 2,000,000 estimated out of a total of 11,676,500 total cents minted this year.

Availability in Mint State: *MS–60 to 64:* This issue is rare in these grades. The elusive nature of Mint State 1873, Close 3, cents continues to grow as the variety becomes increasingly popular and well known. *MS–65 and higher:* This issue is seldom seen in these grades. Original, brilliant-red specimens are very rare.

See page 304 for images showing the Close 3 and Open 3.

Availability in circulated grades: This issue is scarce in circulated grades.

Characteristics of striking: Usually striking is fairly strong on this issue.

Notes: *Alignment of date numerals:* On both varieties of 1873 cents the date numerals are compact and in a straight line; this alignment would continue through and including 1880.

	Cert	Avg	%MS	G-4	VG-8	F-12	VF-20	EF-40	AU-50	MS-60BN	MS-63BN	MS-65RB	MS-65RD
1873, Close 3	287	54.6	59%	$25	$35	$65	$125	$185	$235	$410	$550	$2,500	$10,000

1873, Close 3, Doubled LIBERTY •

Circulation-strike mintage: Included in 1873, Close 3, circulation-strike mintage.

Commentary: This variety was first published in the October 1958 issue of *Empire Topics* (published by Q. David Bowers and James F. Ruddy trading as Empire Coin Co.) in the article, "Blundered Dies of U.S. and Colonial Coinage," by Walter Breen. Later a different but similar variety was discovered.

See page 304 for images showing the Close 3 and Open 3.

	Cert	Avg	%MS	G-4	VG-8	F-12	VF-20	EF-40	AU-50	MS-60BN	MS-63BN	MS-65RB
1873, Close 3, Doubled LIBERTY	96	43.1	28%	$200	$350	$825	$1,750	$2,500	$5,250	$7,500	$13,500	$57,500

Varieties: *Type I (FS-01-1873-101):* This variety can also be identified as 1873, Snow-1. Its rarity is URS-9. This format is sharp, with all the letters of LIBERTY doubled; this is the most desirable variety. Probably fewer than 75 examples exist in MS-60 or finer. An MS-64 or MS-65BN coin, if properly graded, is a rarity.

A detail showing the doubling
on LIBERTY for FS-01-1873-101.

	VF-20	EF-40	AU-50	MS-60	MS-63	MS-65
FS-01-1873-101	$2,000	$3,000	$4,000	$7,500	$14,000	$70,000

Type II (FS-01-1873-102): This variety can also be identified as 1873, Snow-2. Its rarity is URS-8. This variety has only the first several letters of LIBERTY slightly doubled. It is scarcer than the preceding variety, but it is in lesser demand, as the doubling is not as noticeable. Fivaz and Stanton call this variety "somewhat of a step-sister to FS-01-1873-101 which exhibits stronger doubling."

A detail showing the doubling
on LIBERTY for FS-01-1873-102.

	VF-20	EF-40	AU-50	MS-60	MS-63	MS-65
FS-01-1873-102	$250	$350	$500	$750	$2,000	$5,000

1873, Open 3 • Circulation-strike

mintage: 9,676,500 estimated[100] out of a total of 11,676,500 minted this year.

Availability in Mint State: *MS–60 to 64:* This issue is scarce in these grades. Bright-red specimens are especially scarce. Beginning with this year, brilliant specimens are seen with more frequency than for any other date since 1865. ***MS-65 and higher:*** This issue is rare in these grades, and surprisingly so. Probably fewer than 150 examples exist in these grades.

See page 304 for images showing the Close 3 and Open 3.

Availability in circulated grades: This variety is scarce in circulated grades, but not nearly as scarce as the Close 3 variety.

Characteristics of striking: Striking varies; strong pieces can be found for this issue.

Notes: *Alignment of date numerals:* On both varieties of 1873 cents the date numerals are compact and in a straight line; this alignment would continue through and including 1880.

	Cert	Avg	%MS	G-4	VG-8	F-12	VF-20	EF-40	AU-50	MS-60BN	MS-63BN	MS-65RB	MS-65RD
1873, Open 3	542	53.8	54%	$20	$30	$50	$85	$160	$190	$250	$325	$1,275	$7,500

1873, Close 3, Proof • Proof

mintage: 1,500 to 2,000.

Proof commentary: All Proofs minted were of the Close 3 style. Dies for Proofs were made early in the year when the Close 3 was the norm; no later dies were produced. Proofs are seen with some frequency today but are still fairly elusive. Bright-red gems are especially hard to find.

See page 304 for images showing the Close 3 and Open 3.

Only one (rather than two, as has been sometimes stated) Proof obverse die was used, this having the word LIBERTY very faintly doubled—not at all to the degree of the aforementioned 1873, Close 3, Doubled LIBERTY, circulation strikes, but still discernible.[101]

All Proofs have a high-relief "blob" as the right arm of the T in CENT; this die had been in use since 1872 (see note under 1872, Bold N, Proof, on page 304).

	Cert	Avg	%MS	PF-63BN	PF-64RB	PF-65RD
1873, Close 3, Proof	231	64.2		$265	$550	$2,050

Indian Head Cents of 1874

KEYS TO COLLECTING: This date is somewhat scarce, as are other dates in the mid-1870s (1873 through 1876 in particular), but it is not in the same league with the especially scarce 1871, 1872, or 1877.

DATE NUMERAL SIZE: Date numerals are larger than in 1872 and 1873, and they appear in a straight line; this alignment would continue through and including 1880.

1874 IN NUMISMATICS: In 1874 3,015,870 copper-nickel cents of 1857 to 1864 were redeemed by the Treasury. Popular series with collectors included cents from 1793 to 1874, silver coins before 1839, and gold coins dated from 1795 to 1834. Tokens and medals were widely popular and occupied much space in auction catalogs. Ancient coins and foreign crowns (dollar-sized silver coins) were eagerly sought as well. The leading numismatic centers of the day were New York, Philadelphia, and Boston.

1874 • Circulation-strike mintage: 14,187,500.

Availability in Mint State: *MS–60 to 64:* This issue is fairly scarce in these grades. It is quite elusive in bright-red state, especially in comparison to the cents of only a few years earlier. *MS-65 and higher:* This issue is scarce in these grades, but it is more available at this level than the earlier dates of this decade are. Nice RB coins are seen with some frequency.

Availability in circulated grades: This issue is scarce in circulated grades.

Characteristics of striking: This issue is usually struck sharp.

	Cert	Avg	%MS	G-4	VG-8	F-12	VF-20	EF-40	AU-50	MS-60BN	MS-63BN	MS-65RB	MS-65RD
1874	920	57.5	68%	$20	$25	$45	$65	$100	$150	$225	$250	$725	$3,500

1874, Proof • Proof mintage: 1,000 to 1,200.

Proof commentary: Proofs were coined from an obverse die having the 4 in the date first punched slightly too low and then corrected. No "perfect date" Proof 1874 has come to light.[102] Bright-red gems are quite scarce, especially so in the experience of Q. David Bowers. He has seen very few over the years.

The repunched date 1874, Proof, obverse die is also believed to have been used to make some circulation strikes.[103]

Some Proofs have a high-relief "blob" as the right arm of the T in CENT; this die had been in use since 1872 (see note under 1872, Bold N, Proof, on page 304).

	Cert	Avg	%MS	PF-63BN	PF-64RB	PF-65RD
1874, Proof	164	64.4		$250	$400	$2,100

Indian Head Cents of 1875

KEYS TO COLLECTING: This cent is popular as a date in the 1870s, but it is not in the same rarity category as the 1871, 1872, 1877, or even the 1876.

DATE NUMERALS: The date numerals are larger than in 1872 and 1873, and they are in straight line; this alignment would continue through and including 1880.

1875 IN NUMISMATICS: In 1875 2,204,701 copper-nickel cents of 1857 to 1864 were redeemed by the Treasury.

1875 • Circulation-strike mintage: 13,528,000.

Availability in Mint State: *MS–60 to 64:* This issue is slightly scarcer in all combined Mint State grades than the preceding issue is, but, in the experience of Q. David Bowers, brilliant pieces are slightly easier to find than for the 1874 (opinions differ on this). **MS-65 and higher:** Many hundreds of examples exist in these grades, and nice RD coins are seen with some frequency.

Availability in circulated grades: This issue is somewhat scarce in circulated grades.

Characteristics of striking: Striking is usually sharp for this issue, but it varies.

	Cert	Avg	%MS	G-4	VG-8	F-12	VF-20	EF-40	AU-50	MS-60BN	MS-63BN	MS-65RB	MS-65RD
1875	858	56.8	70%	$20	$35	$60	$75	$120	$160	$235	$260	$900	$3,750

1875, Dot Reverse • Circulation-strike mintage: Included in 1875 circulation-strike mintage figure.

Commentary: The Fivaz-Stanton identification for this variety is FS-01-1875-801. It can also be identified as 1875, Snow-16. Its rarity is URS-5. A few 1875 cents have a raised dot near the left top of the N of ONE. In August 1875 Mint employee George Mitchell was suspected of stealing cents. A reverse die was marked with a dot, and Mitchell operated the coining press using this die. Upon later examination Mitchell was found to have marked coins on his person. It is thought that cents with this dot were the telltale coins involved in this incident.[104]

A detail of the dot on the N of ONE.

	Cert	Avg	%MS	MS-63BN
1875, Dot Reverse	0	n/a		—

1875, Proof • **Proof mintage:** 1,000 to 1,250.

Proof commentary: Proofs were coined from at least three, possibly four, obverse dies, one (1875, Snow-2) having traces of a previous 5 slightly above the 5 in the date, another (1875, Snow-1) with minor evidence of doubling on the 1 and 8 of the date. See the Snow text for more information on these and other die varieties. In bright-red gem preservation this is a very scarce date.

The Proof die for 1875, Snow-1, described above, was also used to make some circulation strikes.[105]

Some Proofs have a high-relief "blob" as the right arm of the T in CENT; this die had been in use since 1872 (see note under 1872, Bold N, Proof, on page 304).

Proofs of this year were poorly made; the Mint was derelict in its duties to numismatists. Today, *choice* full-red Proofs are very hard to find.[106]

	Cert	Avg	%MS	PF-63BN	PF-64RB	PF-65RD
1875, Proof	180	64.2		$250	$500	$4,000

Indian Head Cents of 1876

KEYS TO COLLECTING: This date is fairly scarce in all grades.

DATE NUMERALS: The date numerals are in a straight line; this alignment would continue through and including 1880. The date is usually boldly punched into the die on these issues.

1876 IN NUMISMATICS: In 1876 3,106,895 copper-nickel cents of 1857 to 1864 were redeemed by the Treasury and melted.[107]

1876 • **Circulation-strike mintage:** 7,944,000.

Availability in Mint State: *MS–60 to 64:* This issue is scarce in these grades, especially if it is fully brilliant and red (original, undipped). In the late 1970s a roll of 50 gem Mint State coins owned by Allen Harriman was dispersed in the market.[108] It is not known what the grade distribution would be today. *MS-65 and higher:* This issue is quite scarce, even surprisingly so, in these grades. It is a rarity if it is original RD.

Availability in circulated grades: This is the scarcest date since 1872 in circulated grades.

Characteristics of striking: Sometimes this issue is lightly struck at the lower part of the portrait.

	Cert	Avg	%MS	G-4	VG-8	F-12	VF-20	EF-40	AU-50	MS-60BN	MS-63BN	MS-65RB	MS-65RD
1876	847	54.1	61%	$35	$40	$70	$135	$225	$240	$300	$390	$1,000	$3,000

1876, Proof • Proof mintage: 1,500 to 2,000.

Proof commentary: More Proofs than usual seem to have been minted this year. Perhaps the holding of the Centennial Exhibition in Philadelphia that year increased demand with visitors to the Mint. Bright-red Proofs are occasionally seen, much more often than for 1874 and 1875.

Walter Breen noted that one variety with a large knob to the top of the 6 in the date had been reported to him; this variety resulting from the use of a dime date logotype.[109]

Some Proofs have a high-relief "blob" as the right arm of the T in CENT; this die had been in use since 1872 (see note under 1872, Bold N, Proof, on page 304).

	Cert	Avg	%MS	PF-63BN	PF-64RB	PF-65RD
1876, Proof	211	64.5		$250	$450	$1,900

Indian Head Cents of 1877

KEYS TO COLLECTING: The 1877 Indian Head cent is front row, center as the most publicized, most desired single date in the Indian Head cent series and has been for generations. When they were placed into circulation in 1877 hardly any attention was paid to them. Interested collectors bought Proofs. Later, when numismatists began collecting Indian Head cents from general circulation the elusive nature of the 1877 was recognized.

DATE NUMERALS: The date numerals of the 1877 cent are in a straight line; this alignment would continue through and including 1880. The numerals are in shallow relief.

AN EARLY SEARCH FOR 1877 CENTS: The following appeared as "He 'Kept Books' on the 1877 Cents," *The Numismatist*, September 1915, p. 319:

> A correspondent of the *New York Sun* gives the result of his mathematical computations on the bronze cent of 1877, in a recent issue of that paper, as follows:
>
> "Herewith find observations on the humble bronze cent bearing date 1877:
>
> "Noticing that this date formed a very small proportion of the dates to be found in a handful of pennies, it occurred to me to start a memorandum record. So in 1881 I began with 1,250 [mixed cents] procured from the bank and found six dated 1877, showing that in the general circulation it then constituted 0.0048% of the output. In 1883, when the number examined had reached 2,950, eleven of that date had appeared, equivalent to 0.0037%. In May 1884, 7,500 had yielded 24, or 0.0032%. An intermission then took place, and on February 10, 1896, 10,100 had returned only 24—not one having been found in the additional lot—or 0.0023%. The final entry, November 27, 1897, brought the total to 28,450 with 35 of the 1877, or 0.0012% [of the coins examined].
>
> "The foregoing shows in a striking manner how the 1877 cent in 16 years had moved toward the vanishing point. What it is today I do not know. I believe, however, that it would take a very long day's work to secure even one out of a batch of 10,000. . . ."

1877 IN NUMISMATICS: In 1877 2,870,433 copper-nickel cents of 1857 to 1864 were redeemed by the Treasury. Some were reissued.[110] The national economy remained slow, and 1877 saw a slight setback, noticeable enough that some called it the Panic of 1877. The effects were not long lasting, however.

Still, commerce was sluggish and there was little call for minor coins to make small change. The Indian Head cent mintage dipped to just 852,500 pieces—a record low in that series for any year of production, before or after.

1877 • **Circulation-strike mintage:** 852,500.

Availability in Mint State: *MS–60 to 64:* In Mint State, this is the rarest of all Indian Head cent dates. When seen, examples are usually fully or partially brown. Original full–mint red, uncleaned, and undipped coins are great rarities. Certification does not always help matters, as some dipped coins have been certified RD; cherrypicking is a must. *MS-65 and higher:* A couple hundred or so examples of this issue exist in these grades.

Availability in circulated grades: This is the rarest of the Philadelphia Mint Indian Head cents. This is the key to a set of the series. Certified populations are heavily skewed in favor of the 1877 due to the value of examples in any grade—since even low-grade examples are worth quite a lot, this coin is sent for certification even in low grades, making the total number certified higher than for coins which are only certified in Mint State. More 1877 cents have been certified than just about any other Indian Head cent—a good point for newcomers to the hobby to consider. Among cents of all dates, expensive coins have a far larger percentage of their overall population certified than do inexpensive issues.

Caveat: Cast and struck counterfeits exist, as do altered dates; buy this issue only if it is accompanied by a guarantee.

Characteristics of striking: Most examples are somewhat lightly struck. Markers for genuine coins include:[111] the second 7 in the date is *slightly* larger than the first, this being most noticeable at the bottoms of the 7's; the lower portion of the N in ONE and, to a lesser extent, the tops of EN in CENT on the reverse are weak (sometimes described as "shallow"). Some coins with evidence of circulation are "spent" Proofs and have strong central letter details.[112]

In 1996 Q. David Bowers saw a high-grade circulation-strike 1877 with OF AMERICA flatly struck, while the other features of the coin were quite sharp. An impaired piece such as this is worth considerably less than an average or above-average strike.

	Cert	Avg	%MS	G-4	VG-8	F-12	VF-20	EF-40	AU-50	MS-60BN	MS-63BN	MS-65RB	MS-65RD
1877	3,037	23.5	11%	$900	$1,100	$1,550	$2,000	$2,500	$3,000	$3,800	$4,500	$15,000	$25,000

1877, Proof • **Proof mintage:** 1,250 to 1,500.

Proof mintage commentary: The mintage of this and other Proofs prior to 1878 is not certainly known. The *Guide Book of United States Coins* suggests "900+." Most probably the 1877 Proof Indian Head cents, three-cent pieces and Shield nickels were sold in minor sets, and the Proof mintages of all three are the same. However, fewer of the Proof 1877 cents seem to have survived.

Proof die commentary: Proofs are usually seen BN or RB, sometimes with a very attractive woodgrain effect.

Proofs were struck from at least three different obverse and three different reverse dies, one of which has a blob at the right arm of the T—this is the die first used in 1872.[113] Unlike the situation with circulation strikes, the N in ONE and the EN in CENT on the reverse are bold on Proofs.[114]

Rick Snow expands on the above:[115]

> 3 obverse, 3 reverse dies. All are from the bold N reverse die (one is the defective T with blob). One die pair seems to have struck a quantity that are singly struck, exhibiting weak denticles, rounded rims and slight weakness in the headdress. Some of these have made it into circulation and in no way resemble Proofs once worn down to EF, although they were intended as such. Counterfeits from transfer dies usually have the bold N reverse (from a later, cheaper date) but using the bold N is not a conclusive way to identify these counterfeits.

Some Proofs (Snow's PR-1) have a high-relief "blob" as the right arm of the T in CENT; this die had been in use since 1872 (see note under 1872, Bold N, Proof, on page 304).

	Cert	Avg	%MS	PF-63BN	PF-64RB	PF-65RD
1877, Proof	262	63.7		$2,600	$4,500	$12,000

Indian Head Cents of 1878

KEYS TO COLLECTING: This date is scarce in all grades, the last Philadelphia Mint Indian Head cent to be in this category, although the 1885 and 1894 come close. In general, 1878 marks the end of the old order of Indian Head cents, after which circulation-strike quantities increased dramatically.

DATE NUMERALS: The date numerals are in a straight line; this alignment would continue through and including 1880.

1878 IN NUMISMATICS: In 1878 1,993,125 copper-nickel cents of 1857 to 1864 were redeemed by the Treasury.

1878 • Circulation-strike mintage: 5,797,500.

Availability in Mint State: *MS–60 to 64:* Many Mint State coins show considerable red. Bright, original red pieces are much more available than are those of the late 1860s and early 1870s. In the late 1970s a roll of 50 gem Mint State coins owned by Allen Harriman was dispersed in the market.[116] It is not known what the grading distribution would be today. *MS-65 and higher:* Hundreds exist in these grades, including many nice RB coins.

Availability in circulated grades: This issue is scarce in circulated grades.

Characteristics of striking: This issue is usually well struck.

	Cert	Avg	%MS	G-4	VG-8	F-12	VF-20	EF-40	AU-50	MS-60BN	MS-63BN	MS-65RB	MS-65RD
1878	790	55.4	67%	$35	$45	$60	$110	$200	$275	$325	$380	$950	$2,500

1878, Proof • Proof mintage: 2,350.

Proof commentary: This is not a low-mintage Proof date, but 1878 Proof cents are in demand due to the scarcity of related circulation strikes. Bright-red gems are scarce, but this is the most available of any Proof Indian Head cent date up to this point in time at that level of quality.

Proofs were made from at least two obverse dies, one with repunching at the base of the 1 in the date. Some Proofs have "square" or wire rims, while others are rounded, the latter more in the style of a circulation strike although these are definitely Proofs. Some Proofs have a high-relief "blob" as the right arm of the T in CENT; this die had been in use since 1872 (see note under 1872, Bold N, Proof, on page 304).

This is the first year for which precise coinage figures are known for Proof bronze Indian Head cents. The first Proof mintage figures were a part of the chief coiner's report of January 31, 1878. Earlier mintage figures found in numismatic references (the *Guide Book of United States Coins*, for example) are primarily guesses based upon the number of silver Proofs struck each year, the silver Proof mintages having been recorded from 1859 onward.

	Cert	Avg	%MS	PF-63BN	PF-64RB	PF-65RD
1878, Proof	330	64.3		$235	$450	$1,500

Indian Head Cents of 1879

KEYS TO COLLECTING: This year inaugurates a run of mostly common Philadelphia Mint cents that continues through 1909. Some are slightly scarcer than others, as subsequently noted.

NUMERAL ALIGNMENT: This is the next-to-last year with the date numerals in a straight line.

1879 IN NUMISMATICS: In 1879 870,342 copper-nickel cents of 1857 to 1864 were redeemed by the Treasury.

In February 1879 Horatio C. Burchard became director of the Mint, and he would remain in the position until 1885.

From the 1879 *Mint Report:*

> Owing to the general increased business activity in the country an unusually heavy demand has been created for the minor coins, and the mint at Philadelphia has been called upon to furnish one-cent pieces in excess of its capacity for striking this denomination of coin, and at the same time execute the quota of standard silver dollars [Morgan dollars mandated by the Bland-Allison Act of 1878] required by law.

1879 • Circulation-strike mintage: 16,228,000.

Availability in Mint State: *MS–60 to 64:* This issue is readily available in these grades, although it is not as plentiful as some issues of the following decade. Most examples are BN or RB. *MS-65 and higher:* Examples in these grades are easily found.

Availability in circulated grades: This issue is common in circulated grades.

Characteristics of striking: Striking varies for this issue. It is difficult in many instances to make a blanket statement about striking quality for issues in which dozens of die pairs were used and for which striking continued over a longer period of time than usual during the year.

	Cert	Avg	%MS	G-4	VG-8	F-12	VF-20	EF-40	AU-50	MS-60BN	MS-63BN	MS-65RB	MS-65RD
1879	849	61.1	84%	$8	$12	$20	$40	$70	$80	$90	$140	$425	$1,400

1879, Proof • Proof mintage: 3,200.

Proof commentary: Proofs were coined from at least two obverse dies. One has the date slightly to the left, with the serif of 1 nearly in line with the bust point. The second has the base of the 1 in the date slightly repunched and has traces of slight repunching on the 8 and 9 as well (as noted by Breen in his *Encyclopedia of United States and Colonial Proof Coins, 1722–1977*).

High-quality pieces with rich, brown-toned surfaces, often with a nuance of iridescent blue (especially when viewed at a certain angle to the light), are from long-term hoards that passed into dealers' hands. The same comment applies for issues of the 1880s and some of the 1890s, until the Mint began reducing the mintage quantities. Also see commentary in 1883, Proof, on page 319.

	Cert	Avg	%MS	PF-63BN	PF-64RB	PF-65RD
1879, Proof	381	64.5		$150	$325	$1,200

Indian Head Cents of 1880

KEYS TO COLLECTING: At the time of issue many collectors acquired an example, but there was no particular excitement for this date.

DATE PECULIARITIES: The date logotype on some circulation strikes and on Proofs is defective and shows some irregularities in the relief of the numerals.

The date is in a straight line; later years have the date slightly curved to complement the border curve, but in a different arc (1881 is a hybrid of the two styles; see page 316). The large, widely spaced numerals of 1880 are much easier to read than the compact, smaller letters of 1872, the first issue of the straight-line date sequence.

1880 IN NUMISMATICS: In 1880 577,130 copper-nickel cents of 1857 to 1864 were redeemed by the Treasury.

From the 1880 *Mint Report:*

> Notwithstanding the large number of cents struck, the demand for this denomination of coin has been so great that the Mint at Philadelphia—the only mint at which minor coins are struck—has been unable to manufacture a sufficient supply to promptly fill the orders received, although the bronze alloy has been purchased in the form of manufactured blanks or planchets ready for striking, and thus greatly lessened the amount of labor required.

1880 • **Circulation-strike mintage:** 38,961,000.

Availability in Mint State: *MS–60 to 64:* This issue is readily available in these grades within the context of the 1880s. In general, Mint State cents of the 1880s are often brighter (more brilliant) and less spotted than those of the 1890s, although there are certainly many spotted and stained coins with dates from 1880 to 1889. *MS-65 and higher:* Examples are easily found in these grades, including original RD coins. This comment is applicable to most Philadelphia Mint dates from here to the end of the series.

Availability in circulated grades: This issue is common in circulated grades.

Characteristics of striking: Striking varies for his issue.

	Cert	Avg	%MS	G-4	VG-8	F-12	VF-20	EF-40	AU-50	MS-60BN	MS-63BN	MS-65RB	MS-65RD
1880	726	62.6	92%	$5	$7	$9	$12	$30	$60	$80	$130	$400	$1,300

1880, Doubled-Die Obverse, Reverse Clash • Circulation-strike mintage: Included in 1880 circulation-strike mintage figure.

Commentary: The Fivaz-Stanton identification for this variety is FS-01-1880-101. This variety can also be identified as 1880, Snow-1. Its rarity is URS-8. LIBERTY is slightly doubled in the headband. However, the main attraction of this variety is a very prominent clash area on the reverse, to the right of the shield and through the NE of ONE. The clash displays denticles and was caused by an obverse die clashing with a blank die that was subsequently hubbed into an Indian Head cent reverse die.[117]

A detail of the reverse clash.

	Cert	Avg	%MS	AU-50	MS-60BN	MS-63BN	MS-65RB	MS-65RD
1880, Doubled-Die Obverse, Reverse Clash	7	62.0	86%	$390	$750	$1,500	$2,000	$2,900

1880, Proof • Proof mintage: 3,955.

Proof commentary: In the 1880s the Mint produced a record number of Proof cents. Many of these were not distributed to the public, but at year's end, or early the following year, were sold in bulk to dealers. Large numbers, still in thin tissue-paper wrappings, remained in hoards through the mid-point of the 20th century. Today these can often be recognized by having virtually flawless gem surfaces, toned a rich medium brown (from the sulfur in the tissue paper), and with nuances of blue or purple iridescence of incredible beauty.

Proofs were struck from at least two obverse dies, one with slight traces of repunching at the upper part of the second 8 in the date.

Pieces with rich, brown-toned surfaces are from long-term hoards that passed into dealers' hands; see commentary in 1879, Proof, on page 314.

	Cert	Avg	%MS	PF-63BN	PF-64RB	PF-65RD
1880, Proof	399	64.4		$150	$325	$1,200

Indian Head Cents of 1881

KEYS TO COLLECTING: At the time of issue many collectors acquired an example, but there was no particular excitement for this date.

1881 IN NUMISMATICS: In 1881 81,393 copper-nickel cents of 1857 to 1864 were redeemed by the Treasury. By the end of this year the redemption of these old-style cents totaled 31,681,967. Redemption would continue for many decades thereafter, and figures would be listed in the *Annual Mint Report* issues. The quantities of cents redeemed each year diminished sharply over the following years. By mid-1909 more than 80 million copper-nickel small cents had been redeemed, or close to 40% of the total issued. According to Treasury reports, tens of millions of copper-nickel cents are still unredeemed. Such reports, while interesting, are known to be inaccurate in some areas. For example, during the 19th century the Treasury had no record of even a single copper half cent ever being redeemed, while it is known that some must have been.

1881 • Circulation-strike mintage: 39,208,000.

Availability in Mint State: *MS–60 to 64:* This issue is common in these grades, although many such examples are spotted; this is especially true of brilliant red specimens. *MS-65 and higher:* This issue is common in these grades in the context of the series.

Availability in circulated grades: This issue is common in circulated grades.

Characteristics of striking: Striking varies for this issue, but sharp examples can be found. On the other hand, a noticeable number were struck from worn dies and show wavy, granular fields.

	Cert	Avg	%MS	G-4	VG-8	F-12	VF-20	EF-40	AU-50	MS-60BN	MS-63BN	MS-65RB	MS-65RD
1881	750	62.5	93%	$5	$6	$8	$10	$25	$35	$60	$90	$315	$1,350

1881, Proof • Proof mintage: 3,575.

Proof commentary: Pieces with rich, brown-toned surfaces are from long-term hoards; see commentary in 1879, Proof, on page 314.

Notes: *Date peculiarities:* The 1881 date is irregular, with the central 88 misaligned, the first 18 digits appearing as if straight, and the final 81 appearing as if curved; this is sort of a hybrid between a straight date (as used for the last time in 1880) and a curved date as used in later years. Curious!

	Cert	Avg	%MS	PF-63BN	PF-64RB	PF-65RD
1881, Proof	393	64.6		$150	$325	$1,200

Indian Head Cents of 1882

KEYS TO COLLECTING: At the time of issue many collectors acquired an example, but there was no excitement for this particular date.

1882 IN NUMISMATICS: This statement comes from the 1882 *Mint Report*: "The demand for small coins, as has been noticed in other countries, increases with business activity, and is a favorable indication of the frequency of actual exchanges and of a prosperous condition of the country."

1882 • Circulation-strike mintage: 38,578,000.

Availability in Mint State: *MS–60 to 64:* This issue is common in these grades among cents of this era. ***MS-65 and higher:*** Gem original red pieces at this level are scarce if unspotted.

Availability in circulated grades: This issue is common in circulated grades.

Characteristics of striking: Striking varies for this issue.

	Cert	Avg	%MS	G-4	VG-8	F-12	VF-20	EF-40	AU-50	MS-60BN	MS-63BN	MS-65RB	MS-65RD
1882	771	62.9	93%	$5	$6	$8	$10	$25	$35	$60	$90	$315	$1,350

1882, Misplaced Date • Circulation-strike mintage: Included in 1882 circulation-strike mintage figure.

Commentary: The Fivaz-Stanton identification for this variety is FS-01-1882-302. It can also be identified as 1882, Snow-6. Its rarity is URS-6. This variety shows *two* separate traces of a stray numeral 1 on Miss Liberty's neck at the fourth and fifth beads (counting from the left), as well as the bases of two more 1's, between the first and second beads and in the hair curl behind the ribbon.

A detail of the stray 1's in
Miss Liberty's necklace.

	Cert	Avg	%MS	AU-50	MS-60BN	MS-63BN	MS-65RB
1882, Misplaced Date	4	64.5	100%	$450	$875	$1,700	$6,000

1882, Proof • Proof mintage: 3,100.

Proof commentary: Proofs were struck from two or more different obverse dies.

Pieces with rich, brown-toned surfaces are from long-term hoards; see commentary in 1879, Proof, on page 314. In this era the Mint made far more Proofs than it could sell during the year. Bright-red gems are on the rare side, especially so if they are without spots.

	Cert	Avg	%MS	PF-63BN	PF-64RB	PF-65RD
1882, Proof	397	64.7		$150	$325	$1,000

Indian Head Cents of 1883

KEYS TO COLLECTING: Indian Head cents of this date are easily available in nearly any grade desired.

DATE NUMERALS: The date numerals are quite widely spaced; this characteristic is also seen on 1883 Shield nickels.

1883 • Circulation-strike mintage: 45,591,500.

Availability in Mint State: *MS–60 to 64:* This issue is common in these grades. As is true of all dates of this era, bright, original-red pieces are seen much less frequently than toned examples. *MS-65 and higher:* Examples are available easily enough in these grades. Usually they are brown or red and brown. Many red coins are recolored.

Availability in circulated grades: This issue is common in these grades.

Characteristics of striking: Striking varies for this issue.

	Cert	Avg	%MS	G-4	VG-8	F-12	VF-20	EF-40	AU-50	MS-60BN	MS-63BN	MS-65RB	MS-65RD
1883	760	62.7	92%	$5	$6	$8	$10	$25	$35	$60	$90	$315	$1,350

1883, Proof • Proof mintage: 6,609.

Proof commentary: Proofs were struck from at least two obverse dies, the scarcer die showing the 3 of 1883 repunched.

This is the high-water mark for Proof Indian Head cent mintage. In this year there was a speculative rush at the Mint for Proof nickel five-cent pieces, which were produced in three design types (Shield; Liberty Head, Without CENTS; and Liberty Head, With CENTS) to the extent of more than 17,000 Proofs. Many of these 1883 Proof cents and nickels went to the general public, rather than to numismatists, and today the Proofs are not as commonly available as mintage figures would seem to indicate. It is easy to envision that an excited new collector, eager to get a Proof specimen of the "rare" 1883 Liberty Head, With CENTS, nickel, but forced to acquire a "minor Proof set" also containing an Indian Head cent and a nickel three-cent piece, simply spent the two unwanted denominations.

Many Proofs of this and other high-mintage dates of the era remained unsold and later went in bulk to David U. Proskey and other dealers; old-time dealers Wayte Raymond and William Pukall still had these available in thin paper mint wrappers as late as the 1950s (Q. David Bowers recalls buying many from these sources). Nearly all of these were toned a beautiful medium-brown color, often with blue iridescent highlights. Also see commentary in 1879, Proof, on page 314. Bright-red Proofs are scarce.

	Cert	Avg	%MS	PF-63BN	PF-64RB	PF-65RD
1883, Proof	577	64.6		$150	$325	$1,200

Indian Head Cents of 1884

KEYS TO COLLECTING: The 1884 cent and the 1886 have both been considered as slightly rarer dates in the decade, but neither is as scarce as the 1885.

1884 • Circulation-strike mintage: 23,257,800.

Availability in Mint State: *MS–60 to 64:* This is one of the scarcer issues of the 1880s in these grades, but there are many in existence. *MS-65 and higher:* Bright-red gems are quite a bit more elusive than generally realized at this level. Q. David Bowers notes that he has seen relatively few bright-red gems for this issue over the years. Examples are otherwise easy to find in these grades, but they are scarcer than for the earlier dates in the decade.

Availability in circulated grades: This issue is common in circulated grades.

Characteristics of striking: Striking varies, but is usually good, for this issue.

	Cert	Avg	%MS	G-4	VG-8	F-12	VF-20	EF-40	AU-50	MS-60BN	MS-63BN	MS-65RB	MS-65RD
1884	703	62.7	92%	$5	$7	$10	$14	$27	$40	$75	$120	$450	$1,650

1884, Proof • **Proof mintage:** 3,942.

Proof commentary: Unsold quantities remained at the Mint and were wholesaled. Typically examples are seen with much brown on the surface. See commentary in 1879, Proof, on page 314.

	Cert	Avg	%MS	PF-63BN	PF-64RB	PF-65RD
1884, Proof	496	64.8		$150	$325	$1,200

Indian Head Cents of 1885

KEYS TO COLLECTING: The 1885 is generally considered to be the scarcest Philadelphia Mint Indian Head cent after 1878.

1885 IN NUMISMATICS: From the 1885 *Mint Report* (covering the fiscal year that ended June 30, 1885—note that mintage figures for the dates mentioned will not be congruent with the figures given below, as they are for the total number of cents struck *during the fiscal year* and not the total number of cents struck *bearing a given date*):

> 40,571,962 cents [were] struck in [fiscal year] 1884 at an estimated cost of $20,000, and 17,571,670 struck in [fiscal year] 1885 at a cost of some $15,000 (which is about the estimate of the Superintendent of the Mint at Philadelphia) for the reason that the planchets for this coinage are purchased. The cost of coinage therefore is principally the cost of striking.

1885 • **Circulation-strike mintage:** 11,761,594.

Availability in Mint State: *MS–60 to 64:* This issue is the scarcest circulation strike of the 1880s. In the era when these were made, most collectors bought Proofs and ignored circulation strikes. The survival of Mint State coins is a matter of chance. Gems are elusive, especially if with significant mint red. By far the majority of Mint State coins are of medium-brown coloration. This issue is always in strong demand in these grades due to its appeal as an elusive date. *MS-65 and higher:* This is the scarcest date of the decade in these grades, but 1886, when both types are combined, gives the 1885 a run for the money and may be scarcer if in full original RD.

Availability in circulated grades: This issue is slightly scarce in circulated grades. It is the key issue of the 1880s. However, enough exist that finding one will be no problem.

Characteristics of striking: This issue is usually seen well struck.

	Cert	Avg	%MS	G-4	VG-8	F-12	VF-20	EF-40	AU-50	MS-60BN	MS-63BN	MS-65RB	MS-65RD
1885	671	62.1	87%	$8	$9	$15	$30	$65	$80	$110	$200	$650	$2,100

1885, Proof • Proof mintage: 3,790.

Proof commentary: Proofs were struck from at least four different obverse dies, two of which can be readily differentiated by the position of the 1 in the date in relation to the neck tip, one with the 1 directly under the tip and the other with the 1 positioned farther to the right.[118]

Rick Snow commented:

> Many of the Proofs of these high-mintage years were struck only once, leaving rounded rims, weak denticles and weakness on the portrait. Some dies have also been used for regular production after they were retired for Proof production, making attributing some Proofs extremely difficult.[119]

Proofs are usually seen with BN or RB; they are rarely full red (unless dipped). Pieces with rich, brown-toned surfaces are from long-term hoards; see commentary in 1879, Proof, on page 314. Many 1885 and 1886 (both types) Proof cents have nice purple iridescence over brown surfaces.[120] However, 1885 remained in old-time hoards in smaller quantities than some of the other dates as it was considered to have greater demand (pressure was put on Proofs because of the relative scarcity of circulation strikes), and examples were sold into the market at a more rapid rate.

John Dannreuther commented that for Proof cents of 1885 and both types of 1886, purple is the main color for most of the deeply toned coins examined by PCGS.[121] Vast numbers of Proofs have been made brilliant by dipping.

Writing in the October 1943 issue of *The Numismatist*, Marvin Winsett was enthusiastic about Indian Head cents. As part of an extended commentary he noted:[122] "Both the Uncirculated and Proof bronze Indian cents are usually toned in a wide variety of color shades. My own 1885 Proof is a brilliant purple color. Perfect brilliant red coins are scarce and usually command a higher price."

	Cert	Avg	%MS	PF-63BN	PF-64RB	PF-65RD
1885, Proof	462	64.9		$150	$325	$1,200

Indian Head Cents of 1886

KEYS TO COLLECTING: As a date the 1886 has always been considered to be second scarcest of the 1880s (1885 is scarcest).

TWO VARIETIES OF 1886 CENTS: Variety 1 and Variety 2 of 1886, Indian Head, cents were not widely known until the 1950s and not widely collected until later in the 20th century when Walter Breen, Rick Snow, the *Guide Book of United States Coins*, and other entities publicized them. The first knowledge of these varieties was attributed to James Reynolds of Flint, Michigan, June 1949, in "Cent Design Changed in 1886," *The Numismatic Scrapbook Magazine*.

A detail of the last headdress feather on Variety 1 cents, pointing between the I and C of AMERICA.

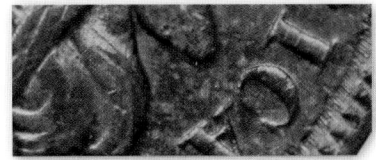

A detail of the last headdress feather on Variety 2 cents, pointing between the C and A of AMERICA.

1886 IN NUMISMATICS: During the 1886 Christmas season at Macy's store in New York City there was a shortage of one-cent pieces. According to one account, Jerome B. Wheeler, a partner in the firm, journeyed to Washington to personally see the secretary of the Treasury and persuade him to secure an order with the director of the Philadelphia Mint for "$10,000 in brand new copper cents."[123]

1886, Variety 1 • Circulation-strike

mintage: 13,000,000+ estimated of 17,650,000 total cents produced for the year.

Availability in Mint State: *MS–60 to 64:* This variety is scarce in these grades, but it is more often seen than Variety 2. *MS-65 and higher:* Bright-red gems are rare at this level for this issue, especially if they are problem free (certification is no help in this regard).

Availability in circulated grades: This variety is slightly scarce within the context of the 1880s.

Characteristics of striking: This variety is usually found fairly sharp.

   On the Variety 1 the last feather of the headdress points between the I and the C of AMERICA. See page 321 for a detail shot.

	Cert	Avg	%MS	G-4	VG-8	F-12	VF-20	EF-40	AU-50	MS-60BN	MS-63BN	MS-65RB	MS-65RD
1886, Variety 1	406	56.8	60%	$6	$8	$20	$50	$140	$175	$200	$250	$975	$4,000

1886, Variety 2 • Circulation-strike

mintage: 4,000,000+ estimated of 17,650,000 total cents produced for the year.

Availability in Mint State: *MS–60 to 64:* This variety is quite scarce in these grades, especially with good aesthetic characteristics as the grades increase. However, many exist in low–Mint State levels without brilliance.[124]

MS-65 and higher: This variety is worth a strong premium if a gem example is found. Bright-red gems are especially elusive. The price differential for this variety and Variety 1 is a phenomenon of recent years; earlier, the difference in availability was largely unknown.

Availability in circulated grades: This variety is slightly scarce within the context of the 1880s, but it is common enough in well-worn grades.

Characteristics of striking: Striking is usually sharp for this issue.

   On the Variety 2 the last feather of the headdress points between the C and the A of AMERICA. See page 321 for a detail shot.

	Cert	Avg	%MS	G-4	VG-8	F-12	VF-20	EF-40	AU-50	MS-60BN	MS-63BN	MS-65RB	MS-65RD
1886, Variety 2	475	57.8	68%	$7	$12	$25	$75	$175	$220	$325	$500	$2,900	$14,000

1886, Variety 1, Proof • Proof

mintage: 2,490 estimated of 4,290 total Proof cents produced for the year.

Proof commentary: The Variety 1 pieces are slightly more plentiful in Proof format, based upon a new study by Rick Snow who estimates a revised Proof mintage of for Variety 1 and 1,800 for Variety 2.[125] Pieces with rich, brown-toned surfaces are from long-term hoards; see commentary in 1879, Proof, on page 314. The typical coin has a rich brown surface with some nuances of blue and purple, with the latter color being quite plentiful on Proofs of 1886 (both types) and also 1885.[126] Q. David Bowers recalls removing quite a few Proofs from this era from their original Mint wrappers, remnants of a hoard bought from an old-time dealer.

	Cert	Avg	%MS	PF-63BN	PF-64RB	PF-65RD
1886, Variety 1, Proof	123	64.6		$150	$325	$1,800

1886, Variety 2, Proof • Proof

mintage: 1,800 estimated of 4,290 total Proof cents produced for the year.

Proof commentary: The Variety 1 pieces are slightly more plentiful in Proof format, based upon a new study by Rick Snow who estimates a revised Proof mintage of 2,490 for Variety 1 and 1,800 for Variety 2. See note given in 1886, Variety 1, Proof, entry on page 322.

Pieces with rich, brown-toned surfaces are from long-term hoards; see commentary under 1879, Proof, and under 1886, Variety 1, Proof, on pages 314 and 322, respectively. Many 1885 and 1886 (both types) Proof cents have nice purple iridescence over brown surfaces.[127] Brian Wagner noted:

> In seven years of observing certified Indian cents I have never seen a red specimen of the 1886, Variety 2, in Proof. I consider this date to be the scarcest of the bronze Indian cents in red Proof except for the 1864, With L, Proof. This coin is also infrequently encountered in red and brown or even in brown Proof.[128]

John Dannreuther commented that for Proof cents of 1885 and both types of 1886, purple is the main color for most of the deeply toned coins examined by PCGS.[129] "Red" Proofs usually are dipped coins. One Proof obverse die has a repunched date; this die was also used to make some circulation strikes.[130]

	Cert	Avg	%MS	PF-63BN	PF-64RB	PF-65RD
1886, Variety 2, Proof	74	64.4		$350	$750	$10,000

Indian Head Cents of 1887

KEYS TO COLLECTING: This is another readily available date from an era in which cents of most years exist in quantity.

A POSSIBILITY TO LOOK FOR: In 1887 a number of unused 1886 dies were overdated, including at least three different dies for nickel three-cent pieces (two Proof dies and one circulation strike) and multiple dies for Morgan dollars. It would not be surprising if an 1887, 7 Over 6, cent turns up someday, but so far Q. David Bowers has never heard even a rumor of one.

1887 IN NUMISMATICS: In 1886 and 1887 there was a distribution problem with one-cent pieces and other minor coins. They were piling up in Sub-Treasury offices, which redeemed them when presented "in sums not less than $20." Meanwhile, remote areas as well as urban centers were suffering from a shortage of the same coins. Adams Express Co. had the contract for shipping minor coins.

The 1887 *Mint Report* noted (in "bureaucratese"):

> Part of the demand for minor coin, which has arisen to an unprecedented extent during the latter part of the last 12 months [since January 1887], during the first part of which period the coinage of minor coin had not been resumed since February 16, 1885, is at least unreasonable, it having appeared that, in the exercise of a preference for fresh coin, applications to the mint at Philadelphia for large sums of minor coin have been from the very cities where an accumulation was reported in the Sub-Treasuries.

Stated simply, the Mint director felt that it was unreasonable that parties in certain cities should request newly minted Indian Head cents and Liberty Head nickels from the Mint while stocks of these same denominations existed in Treasury facilities in the same cities.

The account further stated that certain merchants who received large quantities of current coins and turned them into the Sub-Treasuries were the same people who asked for "fresh" coins of the same type from the Mint. Mint Director James P. Kimball suggested, among other ideas, that the Treasury be given the power "to discriminate against unreasonable demands for new coin when current old coin is available."

The *American Journal of Numismatics*, July 1887, reported that up to this year, "in San Francisco the smallest coin has been the dime, whilst in St. Louis and New Orleans, nothing circulates less than the 5¢ nickel." It was related that recently merchants had introduced small denominations, "so that large quantities of 5¢ and 1¢ pieces are now forwarded by the Mint to California and Oregon, where they are delivered free of expense, by the government."

1887 • **Circulation-strike mintage:** 45,223,523.

Availability in Mint State: *MS–60 to 64:* This issue is plentiful in Mint State for the era. Often examples display much red, but spotting is a problem (ditto for other dates of this generation). *MS-65 and higher:* This issue is common in these grades in the context of the series.

Availability in circulated grades: This issue is common in circulated grades.

Characteristics of striking: Striking varies for this issue. It is sometimes seen softly struck from worn dies, giving a granular appearance to the fields, particularly on the obverse.

	Cert	Avg	%MS	G-4	VG-8	F-12	VF-20	EF-40	AU-50	MS-60BN	MS-63BN	MS-65RB	MS-65RD
1887	605	62.1	92%	$3	$4	$5	$8	$18	$28	$55	$80	$575	$1,700

1887, Doubled-Die Obverse •

Circulation-strike mintage: Included in 1887 circulation-strike mintage figure.

Commentary: This variety, known as FS-01-1887-101 or 1887, Snow-1, shows slight doubling at the TY of LIBERTY and more noticeable doubling at OF AMERICA. It is quite rare, with a rarity of URS-9.

A detail of the doubling on OF AMERICA on the obverse.

	Cert	Avg	%MS	EF-40	AU-50	MS-60BN	MS-63BN	MS-65RB
1887, Doubled-Die Obverse	26	42.4	19%	$250	$490	$1,000	$2,500	$8,000

1887, Proof • **Proof mintage:** 2,960.

Proof commentary: Most Proofs show toning; red Proofs are very rare. Pieces with rich, brown-toned surfaces are from long-term hoards; see commentary in 1879, Proof, on page 314. Some Proofs were carelessly made (for further information, consult Breen, *Encyclopedia of United States and Colonial Proof Coins, 1722–1977*). Clerks at the Mint were very casual with their handling of Proofs during this era.

	Cert	Avg	%MS	PF-63BN	PF-64RB	PF-65RD
1887, Proof	324	64.4		$150	$300	$3,500

Indian Head Cents Overdated 1888

KEYS TO COLLECTING: The record production this year took its toll in accuracy, and a number of dies of this year show repunching or other errors (which, of course, is good news for numismatists). From the 1888 *Mint Report:* "During the fiscal year [which ended June 30] the minor coinage was the largest in the history of the Mint at Philadelphia. . . ." It was noted that during the year 275,557.55 pounds of cent planchets had been delivered to the Mint, and the cost for these was $74,026.69.

1888, Last 8 Over 7 • **Circulation-strike mintage:** Unknown. Probably very small and on the order of just a few thousand pieces of the total 1888 circulation-strike mintage (see page 326).

Availability in Mint State: *MS–60 to 64:* Only a few dozen or so are known in these grades, mostly BN with some RB. *MS-65 and higher:* Estimates of examples existing in these grades range from *no* conservatively graded coins known to just more than a dozen liberally graded ones.

Availability in circulated grades: This variety is very rare in circulated grades. The population is smaller than 50.

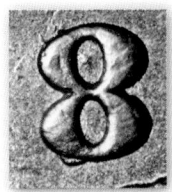

A detail showing the 8 over 7 in the date.

Characteristics of striking: This variety is found primarily with average sharpness.

Notes: *The "Ruddy Variety":* This variety is known as FS-01-1888-301 (1888, Snow-1; 1888, FND-001). Two specimens of this overdate, both in Mint State, were discovered by James F. Ruddy in 1970 in a small cache of Indian Head cents found in the attic of a mansion in Virginia.[131] Both had a distinctive "cud" die break on the left rim at the 9:00 position. One was sold to Robert Marks and the other to Julian Leidman. These remain the finest-known examples and are tentatively represented by MS-63RB prices, although they certainly could grade higher, even *much* higher. Q. David Bowers assessed them personally, but he has not seen them in years and does not remember them well enough to equate them to today's numbers.

This is often called the "Ruddy Variety"[132] Since Jim Ruddy's discovery, the variety has become widely publicized, but even so, only two more Mint State pieces have come to light, plus perhaps up to two-dozen worn examples. The market prices are highly volatile for this variety, as specimens are few and far between, especially in higher grades.

Rick Snow commented that only 13 specimens are confirmed.

	Cert	Avg	%MS	G-4	VG-8	F-12	VF-20	EF-40	AU-50	MS-60BN	MS-63BN
1888, Last 8 Over 7	12	38.3	17%	$1,200	$1,500	$2,000	$3,500	$7,500	$17,500	$23,000	$35,000

Indian Head Cents of 1888

KEYS TO COLLECTING: Cents of this year are easily found in nearly any grade desired.

1888 IN NUMISMATICS: The 1888 *Mint Report* gives an interesting insight into which areas of the country used minor coins. No new Indian Head cents were sent to Arizona, Idaho, Montana, New Mexico, or Utah. Relatively low amounts were sent to other Western states. The state of West Virginia received more cents than all three West Coast states combined. Here is the report of Indian Head cents distributed:

Alabama: 120,000
Arizona: None
Arkansas: 100,000
California: 62,000
Colorado: 87,000
Connecticut: 685,000
Dakota: 87,500
Delaware: 160,000
District of Columbia: 20,000
Florida: 45,500
Georgia: 352,000
Idaho: None

Illinois: 4,900,500
Indiana: 926,000
Iowa: 996,000
Kansas: 441,500
Kentucky: 270,000
Louisiana: 60,000
Maine: 199,000
Maryland: 987,000
Massachusetts: 2,446,000
Michigan: 1,599,000
Minnesota: 790,500
Mississippi: 4,000

Missouri: 332,000
Montana: None
Nebraska: 462,000
New Hampshire: 316,000
New Jersey: 1,183,000
New Mexico: None
New York: 11,016,800
North Carolina: 253,000
Ohio: 2,747,500
Oregon: 12,000
Pennsylvania: 4,006,500

Rhode Island: 515,000
South Carolina: 124,500
Tennessee: 253,000
Texas: 6,000
Utah: None
Vermont: 148,000
Virginia: 337,500
Washington: 12,000
West Virginia: 96,000
Wisconsin; 852,000
Wyoming: None

Statistics such as the above indicate why cents were not struck at Western mints during the 19th century: there was only a trivial demand for them.

1888 • Circulation-strike mintage: 37,489,832 (including 1888, 8 Over 7).

Availability in Mint State: *MS–60 to 64:* This issue is available in all Mint State levels, but sharply struck gems are elusive. *MS-65 and higher:* Bright-red gems, if unspotted and never dipped, are in the rarity class. As always, cherrypicking is advised, as coins can be certified as "MS-65RD" and still have spots. Spotty coins, even if graded MS-65RD, will sell for far less than hand-picked gems.

Availability in circulated grades: This issue is common in circulated grades.

	Cert	Avg	%MS	G-4	VG-8	F-12	VF-20	EF-40	AU-50	MS-60BN	MS-63BN	MS-65RB	MS-65RD
1888	746	60.0	86%	$3	$4	$5	$8	$22	$27	$65	$130	$725	$2,250

1888, Proof • Proof mintage: 4,582.

Proof commentary: Most Proofs show toning; red Proofs are very rare. Pieces with rich, brown-toned surfaces are from long-term hoards; see commentary in 1879, Proof, on page 314. Proofs of this year were made and handled carelessly at the Mint.

At least two different obverses were used to coin Proofs this year, one of which displays misplaced digits in the denticles.

	Cert	Avg	%MS	PF-63BN	PF-64RB	PF-65RD
1888, Proof	276	64.2		$150	$315	$3,500

Indian Head Cents of 1889

KEYS TO COLLECTING: At the time of issue many collectors acquired an example, but there was no particular excitement for this date.

1889 IN NUMISMATICS: In order to avoid unnecessary coinage of minor coins, the superintendent of the Philadelphia Mint was instructed to refuse requests from merchants for newly minted coins if the same people were located in a city with a federal Sub-Treasury that had a supply of older but still current designs on hand.[133]

1889 • Circulation-strike mintage: 48,866,025.

Availability in Mint State: *MS–60 to 64:* This issue is available in all Mint State grades; high-grade, fully brilliant, undipped, uncleaned coins are scarcer. *MS-65 and higher:* This issue is common in these grades in the context of the series. Bright-red, undipped, and unspotted gems are particularly elusive and have a straw-like golden color.[134]

Availability in circulated grades: This issue is common in circulated grades.

Characteristics of striking: Striking quality varies. Some examples have pebbly surfaces from worn dies.

	Cert	Avg	%MS	G-4	VG-8	F-12	VF-20	EF-40	AU-50	MS-60BN	MS-63BN	MS-65RB	MS-65RD
1889	766	62.3	93%	$3	$4	$5	$7	$18	$27	$60	$80	$400	$2,000

1889, Proof • Proof mintage: 3,336.

Proof commentary: Proofs are often seen spotted. Pieces with rich, brown-toned surfaces are from long-term hoards; see commentary in 1879, Proof, on page 314.

Most Proofs are from a clashed obverse die with part of the C in CENT visible in front of Miss Liberty. On the reverse in the corresponding area, the outline of Miss Liberty's forehead is seen.

	Cert	Avg	%MS	PF-63BN	PF-64RB	PF-65RD
1889, Proof	276	64.3		$150	$315	$1,750

Indian Head Cents of 1890

KEYS TO COLLECTING: At the time of issue many collectors acquired an example, but there was no particular excitement for this date.

"BLOB" 9: The 9 in the date has the bottom ball touching the top curve of the 9; on worn pieces the connection appears continuous. This blob-type 9 appears on various Indian Head cents of the 1890s and 1900s until 1909, in which year the 9 was redesigned to an open configuration. The appearance of the 9 on cents from 1890 to 1908 is most blob-like when the date logotype was punched deeply into the working die. On dies with the logotype punched lightly, there is a small separation between the bottom ball and the top curve.

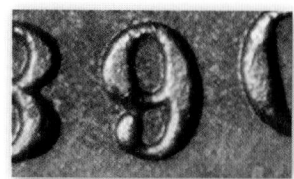

A detail of the blob at the bottom of the 9 in the date.

SOURCES OF PLANCHETS: In February 1890 the Mint entered into a contract with the Scovill Manufacturing Co., of Waterbury, Connecticut, for the supply of 500,000 pounds of one-cent blanks at $0.1994 per pound.[135]

The *American Journal of Numismatics*, April 1890, p. 95, related this:

> The copper used in the manufacture of pennies is of the very best quality. The metal is shipped in bulk from the mines to the factories of Merchant & Co., in Connecticut. There it is rolled and stamped out in circles of the requisite size. These circles are perfectly plain, with the exception of the raised or milled edge. At this stage the pieces intended for pennies are as bright as gold pieces. . . . In this condition they are delivered to the Mint. 100 pennies weigh exactly one pound. When these pieces reach the Mint they are subjected to the finishing process, which consists in stamping them with the denomination, lettering, and characters seen on the coins when they reach the public. . . . The copper pennies require a pressure of 10 tons avoirdupois. . . ."

1890 • Circulation-strike mintage: 57,180,114.

Availability in Mint State: *MS–60 to 64:* This issue is available in all Mint State grades; high-grade, fully brilliant, undipped, and uncleaned coins are scarcer. *MS-65 and higher:* This issue is common in these grades in the context of the series. Sharply struck RD gems are rare, especially if they are unspotted.

Availability in circulated grades: This issue is common in circulated grades.

Characteristics of striking: Most examples are indifferently struck.

	Cert	Avg	%MS	G-4	VG-8	F-12	VF-20	EF-40	AU-50	MS-60BN	MS-63BN	MS-65RB	MS-65RD
1890	701	62.8	94%	$3	$4	$5	$7	$16	$27	$60	$80	$410	$1,150

1890, Proof • **Proof mintage:** 2,740.

Proof commentary: Proofs are often seen spotted. Pieces with rich, brown-toned surfaces are from long-term hoards; see commentary in 1879, Proof, on page 314.

	Cert	Avg	%MS	PF-63BN	PF-64RB	PF-65RD
1890, Proof	265	64.1		$150	$315	$1,650

Indian Head Cents of 1891

KEYS TO COLLECTING: This is another date that is readily available in any desired grade.

"BLOB" 9: The 9 in the date has the bottom ball touching the top curve of the 9; on worn pieces the connection appears continuous. The 1891 is similar to the 1890 in this regard. This situation occurs on some later dates as well, especially on circulation strikes with the date logotype punched deeply into the working die. See page 328 for a detail showing the Blob 9.

1891 IN NUMISMATICS: On April 4, 1891, the Treasury Department sent a circular letter to artists inviting new designs for silver coins (designs of which had been called "inelegant"), but the bronze cent was not mentioned.[136]

1891 • **Circulation-strike mintage:** 47,070,000.

Availability in Mint State: *MS–60 to 64:* This issue is available in all Mint State grades. *MS-65 and higher:* This issue is common in these grades in the context of the series. Gem, fully RD, undipped, and uncleaned coins are scarcer.

Availability in circulated grades: This issue is common in circulated grades.

Characteristics of striking: Striking varies for this issue. In general, cents of the 1890s are not deeply and sharply struck.

	Cert	Avg	%MS	G-4	VG-8	F-12	VF-20	EF-40	AU-50	MS-60BN	MS-63BN	MS-65RB	MS-65RD
1891	819	62.7	94%	$3	$4	$5	$7	$15	$27	$60	$80	$400	$1,100

1891, Doubled-Die Obverse •

Circulation-strike mintage: Included in 1891 circulation-strike mintage.

Commentary: The Fivaz-Stanton identification for this variety is FS-01-1891-101. It can also be identified as 1891, Snow-1. Its rarity is URS-7. The doubling on this variety is evident on LIBERTY and STATES OF AMERICA, which shows a decreasing spread of doubling from left to right.

A detail showing doubling on the obverse.

	Cert	Avg	%MS	EF-40	AU-50	MS-60BN	MS-63BN
1891, Doubled-Die Obverse	12	45.9	25%	$250	$450	$775	$1,150

1891, Proof • Proof mintage: 2,350.

Proof commentary: Proofs are fairly scarce at the gem level. Pieces with rich, brown-toned surfaces are from long-term hoards; see commentary in 1879, Proof, on page 314. For 1891, Proof mintage is reduced in quantity from the average of the 1880s, and the downward trend would continue.

	Cert	Avg	%MS	PF-63BN	PF-64RB	PF-65RD
1891, Proof	283	64.2		$150	$315	$1,375

Indian Head Cents of 1892

KEYS TO COLLECTING: Building a "short set" of Indian Head cents of 1879 to 1909 is a pleasant pursuit. Nearly all years, including this one, are readily available in any grade desired.

MELTDOWN: During fiscal year 1892 (which began July 1, 1891, and ended June 30, 1892) Indian Head cents in the amount of 1,429,087 were made from melted-down minor coins that were no longer current, primarily bronze two-cent pieces.[137]

The following scenario, discussed in depth in vol. 1, issue 4, of *Longacre's Ledger*, details how unscrupulous planchet suppliers drove the Mint to melt down more old cents for recoining:[138] in July 1892 the Mint solicited bids for bronze cent planchets and nickel-alloy five-cent planchets from three sources including Benedict & Burnham Manufacturing Co. (of Waterbury, Connecticut, a firm also numismatically remembered for having issued Hard Times tokens circa 1837), Scovill Manufacturing Co. (also of Waterbury, and also a former issuer of Hard Times tokens), and Merchant & Co. (of Philadelphia).

When the bids arrived they were found to be "nearly equal" and each a sharp advance over the latest contract price, leading Mint Director E.O. Leech, in a letter dated August 25, 1892, to call the bids a "put up job." As a result, Leech ordered the Sub-Treasury in New York City to ship to the Mint $50,000 face value of older bronze cents (five million coins) for melting and recoinage. It seems logical that these cents would have been of earlier dates, perhaps mainly of the 1860s and 1870s, as there would have been no point in returning lightly worn pieces of the 1880s and very early 1890s.

1892 • Circulation-strike mintage: 37,647,087.

Availability in Mint State: *MS–60 to 64:* This issue is available in all Mint State grades. *MS-65 and higher:* This issue is common in these grades in the context of the series. Gem, fully RD, undipped, and uncleaned coins are scarcer. This can be said of any Indian Head cent of the era, but is more appropriate to the 1880s and 1890s than to the 1900s.

Availability in circulated grades: This issue is common in circulated grades.

Characteristics of striking: Striking varies for this issue.

	Cert	Avg	%MS	G-4	VG-8	F-12	VF-20	EF-40	AU-50	MS-60BN	MS-63BN	MS-65RB	MS-65RD
1892	733	63.0	95%	$3	$4	$5	$8	$20	$27	$60	$80	$375	$1,100

1892, Proof • Proof mintage: 2,745.

Proof commentary: Proofs are fairly scarce in grades PF-65 or finer if they have good eye appeal.

	Cert	Avg	%MS	PF-63BN	PF-64RB	PF-65RD
1892, Proof	303	64.4		$150	$315	$1,200

Indian Head Cents of 1893

KEYS TO COLLECTING: This is another popular and readily available date across the range of grades.

1893 • Circulation-strike mintage: 46,640,000.

Availability in Mint State: *MS–60 to 64:* This issue is available in all Mint State grades. *MS-65 and higher:* This issue is common in these grades in the context of the series. Gem, fully brilliant, undipped, uncleaned coins are scarcer—although they are more available for this date than they are for coins from the preceding several years.

Availability in circulated grades: This issue is common in circulated grades.

	Cert	Avg	%MS	G-4	VG-8	F-12	VF-20	EF-40	AU-50	MS-60BN	MS-63BN	MS-65RB	MS-65RD
1893	868	63.1	95%	$3	$4	$5	$8	$20	$27	$60	$80	$320	$900

1893, Proof • **Proof mintage:** 2,195.

Proof commentary: This was a recession year in the American economy. Presumably, Proof coins were among luxury goods bought in smaller quantities.

	Cert	Avg	%MS	PF-63BN	PF-64RB	PF-65RD
1893, Proof	265	64.2		$150	$315	$1,300

Indian Head Cents of 1894

KEYS TO COLLECTING: The 1894 is popular as the lowest-mintage Indian Head cent of the 1890s. The Doubled Date variety is eagerly sought. Hundreds are known in Mint State due to the large mintage. Most MS-65 coins are RB with a nice quotient of RD.

1894 IN NUMISMATICS: There was a glut of one-cent pieces and nickels, and in April 1894 coinage of these two denominations was suspended. A few months later, cent coinage resumed.[139]

1894 • **Circulation-strike mintage:** 16,749,500.

Availability in Mint State: *MS–60 to 64:* This issue is readily available in these grades, but it brings a premium due to its low mintage within the decade. *MS-65 and higher:* This issue is common in these grades in the context of the series, but it is not as common as its contemporaries due to the lower mintage this year. Blazing gems are scarce. Most gems are somewhat orange in color.

Availability in circulated grades: This issue is common overall in circulated grades, but it is the least-seen date of the 1890s.

Characteristics of striking: This issue is generally of average sharpness.

	Cert	Avg	%MS	G-4	VG-8	F-12	VF-20	EF-40	AU-50	MS-60BN	MS-63BN	MS-65RB	MS-65RD
1894	801	61.6	88%	$5	$6	$15	$20	$50	$70	$85	$115	$385	$1,100

1894, Doubled Date • Circulation-strike mintage: Included in 1894 circulation-strike mintage figure.

Commentary: The Fivaz-Stanton identification for this variety is FS-01-1894-301. This variety can also be identified as 1894, Snow-1. Its rarity is URS-9. Prominent traces of an earlier date are seen to the right of the final date. The repunching is spectacular, and this certainly is the "king" of repunched dates among Indian Head cents. It is listed as No. 4 among the top 20 most popular of all unusual Indian Head cent varieties, by Larry R. Steve and Kevin Flynn in *A Comprehensive Guide to Selected Rare Flying Eagle and Indian Cent Die Varieties.* As the average production for an obverse die this year was 304,536 coins, this may give a ballpark figure for the mintage of this variety.

A detail of the doubled date.

	Cert	Avg	%MS	G-4	VG-8	F-12	VF-20	EF-40	AU-50	MS-60BN	MS-63BN	MS-65RB	MS-65RD
1894, Doubled Date	94	49.0	56%	$30	$40	$65	$130	$225	$385	$675	$1,200	$4,000	$10,000

1894, Proof • Proof mintage: 2,632.

Proof commentary: This Proof date is popular due to the low mintage of related circulation strikes. Bright-red gems are especially elusive.

	Cert	Avg	%MS	PF-63BN	PF-64RB	PF-65RD
1894, Proof	296	64.1		$150	$315	$1,200

Indian Head Cents of 1895

KEYS TO COLLECTING: The 1895 cent blends in with others of its era as having no particularly notable features, although elsewhere in numismatics the silver dollars of this date became scarce to rare.

STRONG DEMAND: Herman Kratz, superintendent of the Philadelphia Mint, wrote to R.E. Preston, the Mint director, on December 17, 1895:[140]

> The demand for one-cent bronzes is on the increase daily and if it continues at this rate, we will be unable to supply the wants as promptly as should be done from institutions of this character. I have decided if it meets you[r] approval to run the presses until 8 p.m. each day until such time as the orders for one-cent bronzes are filled, to allow each employee who works, over-time at the rate they are paid. . . .

Much if not most of this demand was caused by the rapidly expanding popularity of coin-operated vending and amusement devices that used cents.

1895 • **Circulation-strike mintage:** 38,341,574.

Availability in Mint State: *MS–60 to 64:* This issue is available in all Mint State grades. *MS-65 and higher:* This issue is common in these grades in the context of the series. Brilliant, undipped, and uncleaned coins are scarcer, but there are enough around that finding one will not be a problem.

Availability in circulated grades: This issue is common in circulated grades.

Characteristics of striking: This issue is usually lightly struck.

	Cert	Avg	%MS	G-4	VG-8	F-12	VF-20	EF-40	AU-50	MS-60BN	MS-63BN	MS-65RB	MS-65RD
1895	879	62.8	95%	$3	$4	$5	$8	$15	$25	$45	$65	$200	$800

1895, Proof • **Proof mintage:** 2,062.

Proof commentary: Proofs are fairly scarce. Multiple dies were used, including one with a repunched 9 in the date and another with a repunched 895. The 1895 Proof set has always been especially popular due to the Barber dime and the rare Morgan silver dollar, these being in demand due to the rarity of circulation strikes for the dime and the apparent non-existence of circulation-strike dollars of this date.

	Cert	Avg	%MS	PF-63BN	PF-64RB	PF-65RD
1895, Proof	274	64.5		$160	$315	$1,200

Indian Head Cents of 1896

KEYS TO COLLECTING: The 1896 is yet another easily available date.

DIES: In fiscal-year 1896 (July 1, 1895, to June 30, 1896) 286 dies for Indian Head cents were made.[141] It is presumed these were used to strike cents dated both 1895 and 1896. Using some ballpark assumptions (reality probably varied somewhat) this equals 143 pairs of dies. Assuming an average annual coinage during the period of about 39 million cents, and assuming all dies were used, this equates to around 272,000 Indian Head cents per die pair, a figure that squares nicely with separate figures published by the government. Thus, a particular die variety of the era (e.g., an 1894, Doubled Date) may have been made to the extent of about this many coins.

1896 • **Circulation-strike mintage:** 39,055,431.

Availability in Mint State: *MS–60 to 64:* This issue is available in all Mint State grades. *MS-65 and higher:* High-grade, fully brilliant, undipped, and uncleaned coins are scarcer than generally realized. Most of these are a deep, reddish color.

Availability in circulated grades: This issue is common in circulated grades.

Characteristics of striking: Striking varies for this issue; however, it is often lightly defined.

	Cert	Avg	%MS	G-4	VG-8	F-12	VF-20	EF-40	AU-50	MS-60BN	MS-63BN	MS-65RB	MS-65RD
1896	666	62.6	94%	$3	$4	$5	$8	$15	$25	$45	$65	$220	$925

1896, Proof • Proof mintage: 1,862.

Proof commentary: This was the first year since 1877 that the mintage dipped below 2,000 Proofs. All grades are scarce today, with bright-red gems being especially so.

	Cert	Avg	%MS	PF-63BN	PF-64RB	PF-65RD
1896, Proof	226	64.3		$150	$300	$1,350

Indian Head Cents of 1897

KEYS TO COLLECTING: As is true of other Indian Head cents of the era, the 1897 is common across the board.

1897 • Circulation-strike mintage: 50,464,392.

Availability in Mint State: *MS–60 to 64:* This issue is available in all Mint State grades. *MS-65 and higher:* High-grade, fully brilliant, undipped, and uncleaned coins are scarcer. Sharply struck coins are scarce.

Availability in circulated grades: This issue is common in circulated grades.

Characteristics of striking: This issue is usually lightly struck.

	Cert	Avg	%MS	G-4	VG-8	F-12	VF-20	EF-40	AU-50	MS-60BN	MS-63BN	MS-65RB	MS-65RD
1897	834	62.9	94%	$3	$4	$5	$8	$15	$25	$45	$65	$200	$925

Varieties: *"Blob" 9:* On some circulation strikes the date logotype was impressed too deeply into the working die, and the bottom part of the 9 in the date appears as a blob, with no open area to the right of the ball. See page 328 for a detail showing the Blob 9.

 Variety with "spur" from neck (1897, Misplaced Date, FS-01-1897-401): One curious variety (also known as 1897, Snow-1; Breen-2030; and 1897, FND-001) has the bottom-left serif of the 1 in the date protruding from the neck into the field just above the necklace. A date logotype was probably tapped against the working die as a test to see if the die had been hardened.[142]

A detail showing the spur of the misplaced 1 at the neck.

	VF-20	EF-40	AU-50	MS-60	MS-63
FS-01-1897-401	$200	$350	$750	$1,000	$2,500

1897, Proof • Proof mintage: 1,938.

Proof commentary: Proofs are scarce. This is generally true for Proofs of the 1890s and even more so for those of the early 20th century.

	Cert	Avg	%MS	PF-63BN	PF-64RB	PF-65RD
1897, Proof	255	64.5		$150	$300	$1,200

Indian Head Cents of 1898

KEYS TO COLLECTING: This is another readily available issue.

OUR AMERICAN PENNIES: From the Trenton, New Jersey, *Evening Times*, February 3, 1898:

They Are the Most Agile Coins Issued by Uncle Sam: The little penny is the most agile coin that bears the face of the goddess of liberty. If all the pennies that are now in circulation in the United States were piled one upon another, when the pile was finished it would be 100 times as big as the giant Goddess of Liberty that enlightens a small part of the world in New York harbor. If those same pennies were laid edge to edge they would extend from San Francisco to St. Petersburg. It is also true that the tall pile of them referred to would be 4,000 times the height of the Eiffel tower, the tallest in the world.[143]

All the pennies in the United States are stamped at the Philadelphia Mint, but they are not, as most people suppose, made there. The government buys the blank coppers on which the design is stamped from a western firm, each 1,000 cents costing $1.25. So 100 cents with a face value of one dollar cost the government less than one-fifth of the sum. As a result of all this, Uncle Sam makes a profit on his pennies that would drive a pawnbroker to suicide with envy. This would not be true if all of the pennies that are coined were presented for redemption. They never are, however, for fully one-fifth of them seemingly go out of existence in mysterious ways. All the ways in which the pennies are lost are as multifarious as the sins of the usurer. If the lost pennies were weighed, it is estimated that they would tip the scale at 2,500 pounds.

When the blanks from which the cents are made reach the Mint they are first cut into long strips. These strips are run through a stamping machine which cuts them out, imprints the design and drops them into boxes. Then they are run through a sorting machine, which throws out any that are imperfectly made, and the rest pass on to a broad table, where they are counted, not by hand, but by means of a grooved case into which they fall 500 at a time. Then they are tied up in canvas bags ready to be shipped away as they are called for.

One would think that the penny would be the last coin to be counterfeited, but as a matter of fact there are more spurious cents than there are [spurious] dollars or dimes. A pound of copper, enough to make 100 cents, can be bought for 11 cents, so that the counterfeiters can make a good profit if they are skillful enough. So many bad pennies come to the United States Treasury that some of the Secret Service men are at work all the time, looking for the men who make them.

"The hardest working member of the whole coin family is the penny," said Superintendent Milman, of the New York Sub-Treasury, the other day, as he watched the unloading of an express wagon piled high with canvas bags of the copper coins. "It is the errand boy of the money world and a remarkably spry youngster, too, who covers a lot of ground in the course of a year. It is also preeminently the children's coin, though I dare say there are a lot of interesting things about it that those whose sticky fingers help to keep it under motion do not know. For instance, cents often come to us at a rate of a million a day. The Sub-Treasury is the clearing house of these coins for the metropolitan district and we handle an immense number of them in the course of the year. That lot just coming in contains $5,000 worth and represents a day's collection from a single big slot-machine company.

"Perhaps before the day is over a delivery truck from one of the great department stores will be down here after $10,000 worth—1,000,000 pieces. That often happens, and it shows the way they come and go. Here" leading the way to the room occupied by what is known as the minor coin division, "you see the way we handle them."

The part of the room which held the money was protected by a railing of heavy iron bars and behind these bars clerks were busily at work. In one corner, piled as high as the men's heads, were the canvas bags, each with its thousand coins, just as they had been brought in. On the opposite side three clerks were busy counting off from a great heap of loose pennies.

"Perhaps there are 500,000,000 one-cent pieces here now," continued the superintendent, "possibly more. The stock is growing now, and has been since the beginning of the year. That is to say, there are more people who have pennies which they want to exchange for bills than there are who bring us large denominations and get cents for them. The cents are as good as calendars for us.

"For several weeks before Christmas we don't take in many; the children were saving them up to buy presents. All those that passed into the hands of the candy men, toy dealers, and other shop keepers about December 25 are coming back to us now. But they will go out again by and by. Every fall, when school opens, the pennies begin to come in fast. The children are spending more for candy and such things. During the summer months they accumulate on our hands, for then the youngsters are not spending so many. Whenever there is a storm, a spell of bad weather, or anything that keeps the penny-spending population at home we can see the difference in the numbers that come to us.

"So there are many ways in which we can trace the connection between the children and the cents, and it may interest the youngsters to know that they have a great deal to do with the circulation of this particular coin. Perhaps the two things which have the most to do with the great increase in the circulation of pennies in recent years are the slot machines and the bargain stores.

"The craze for 49-cent and 99-cent bargains requires a great many pennies in the way of change, and, as I have said, it is no unusual thing for the big department stores to take $10,000 worth at a time. Most of them come back to us by the way of the slot machines, which have come to be wonderful in number and variety.

"There are Kinetoscope views, phonographs, automatic music boxes, candy and chewing-gum sellers, weighing machines, lifting machines, and a hundred and one others standing at every hand and coaxing the pennies from their owners' pockets. The result of all this has been that the government has hard work some of the time in maintaining the supply, and can hardly make pennies fast enough to keep up with the growth in the demand for them."[144]

1898 IN NUMISMATICS: In England "the outbreak of slot machines was noted as long ago as 1898 as the cause of heavy coinage of pence."[145] Meanwhile, in America a proliferation of coin-in-the-slot devices prompted record coinages of cents and nickels.

1898 • **Circulation-strike mintage:** 49,821,284.

Availability in Mint State: *MS–60 to 64:* This issue is available in all Mint State grades. *MS-65 and higher:* High-grade, fully brilliant, undipped, and uncleaned coins are scarce. Less-choice MS-65 coins are common, as is true of other dates of the era.

Availability in circulated grades: This issue is common in circulated grades.

Characteristics of striking: Mostly, examples are lightly struck.

	Cert	Avg	%MS	G-4	VG-8	F-12	VF-20	EF-40	AU-50	MS-60BN	MS-63BN	MS-65RB	MS-65RD
1898	899	62.8	93%	$3	$4	$5	$8	$15	$25	$45	$65	$195	$575

1898, Proof • **Proof mintage:** 1,795.

Proof commentary: Proofs of this date are scarce, as are most of the Proofs of this era.

	Cert	Avg	%MS	PF-63BN	PF-64RB	PF-65RD
1898, Proof	261	64.8		$150	$300	$1,200

Indian Head Cents of 1899

KEYS TO COLLECTING: Although circulation-strike cents of this era are common, assembling a nicely matched set in Mint State is not as simple a task as it may seem at first, in particular if attention is paid to aesthetic quality.

1899 • **Circulation-strike mintage:** 53,598,000.

Availability in Mint State: *MS–60 to 64:* This is the most plentiful issue of the 1890s at all Mint State levels, including gem bright-red examples.[146] *MS-65 and higher:* This issue is common in these grades in the context of the series.

Availability in circulated grades: This issue is common in circulated grades.

Characteristics of striking: Striking varies for this issue, but most examples are lightly struck.

	Cert	Avg	%MS	G-4	VG-8	F-12	VF-20	EF-40	AU-50	MS-60BN	MS-63BN	MS-65RB	MS-65RD
1899	1,456	63.4	95%	$3	$4	$5	$8	$15	$25	$45	$65	$195	$460

1899, Proof • **Proof mintage:** 2,031.

Proof commentary: Proofs of this date are scarce, as are most of the Proofs of this era.

	Cert	Avg	%MS	PF-63BN	PF-64RB	PF-65RD
1899, Proof	255	64.7		$150	$300	$1,200

Indian Head Cents of 1900

KEYS TO COLLECTING: This is another readily available issue.

CENTS IN GOLD: At least three circulation-strike 1900 cents struck on gold quarter eagle planchets exist and were probably made as curiosities (rather than occurring as legitimate mint errors).[147] The same is likely true for one (verified) or more pieces struck in silver. These pieces are from a slightly rusted reverse die. One gold striking, weighing 65.8 grains, appeared in the Quality Sales Corporation offering of the John A. Beck Collection, Part I, January 1975, as lot 609. There, it was pedigreed to B.G. Johnson and the Col. E.H.R. Green Collection (this must have been an outside consignment to the sale, not originating from the Beck estate, as Beck died in 1924, at which time Green was just *beginning* his collection; B.G. Johnson assisted with the sale of the Green coins after 1936). This same coin later appeared in the Superior Galleries section of Auction '89, July 1989, as lot 856; then, again in Bowers and Merena, Inc.'s the American Numismatic Association 1891–1991 Centennial Auction, August 1991, as lot 4103, where it was tentatively credited to George T. Morgan, assistant engraver at the Mint at the time. Gold strikings are also known for cents of 1905 and 1906; see page 345.

1900 IN NUMISMATICS: In 1900 and 1901 George E. Roberts, director of the Mint, recommended that cents and nickels be manufactured at the New Orleans and San Francisco mints, for thus "the demand for the Southwestern and Pacific Coast states and territories could be supplied much more economically than at present."[148] By this time the previously small demand from those sections had increased markedly, but it was still not comparable to demand in the East and Midwest.

1900 • **Circulation-strike mintage:** 66,831,502.

Availability in Mint State: *MS–60 to 64:* This issue is readily available in these grades. A few rolls came on the market in the 1950s and 1960s. However, bright, original-red pieces are a bit harder to find than conventional wisdom suggests.[149] *MS-65 and higher:* This issue is very common in these grades in the context of the series.

Availability in circulated grades: This issue is common in circulated grades.

Characteristics of striking: Striking on this issue varies.

	Cert	Avg	%MS	G-4	VG-8	F-12	VF-20	EF-40	AU-50	MS-60BN	MS-63BN	MS-65RB	MS-65RD
1900	961	62.8	94%	$2	$3	$5	$6	$10	$20	$40	$60	$170	$460

1900, Proof • Proof mintage: 2,062.

Proof commentary: Proofs are scarce. It is a curious situation that as circulation-strike mintages became larger, Proof mintages trended smaller. Per Walter Breen, *Encyclopedia of United States and Colonial Proof Coins, 1722–1977*, the mintage figure of 2,262 published elsewhere is a typographical error.

	Cert	Avg	%MS	PF-63BN	PF-64RB	PF-65RD
1900, Proof	252	64.7		$150	$300	$1,200

Indian Head Cents of 1901

KEYS TO COLLECTING: There was no particular excitement at the time over this date or other dates of the era, but newly minted cents were collected as part of the Indian Head series.

1901 IN NUMISMATICS: Among souvenirs sold at the Pan-American Exposition in Buffalo, New York, were Indian Head cents in round aluminum "frames" bearing inscriptions relating to the event. Coins later removed from these frames are somewhat "shrunken" in diameter and sometimes also show part of the lettering from the frame impressed on the rim of the cent; those unaware of the Exposition cents sometimes mistake these for "mint errors."

1901 • Circulation-strike mintage: 79,609,158.

Availability in Mint State: *MS–60 to 64:* This issue is readily available in these grades. A few rolls came on the market in the 1950s, at which time they were plentiful in the marketplace. Today such coins are usually seen one at a time. *MS-65 and higher:* This issue is very common in these grades in the context of the series.

Availability in circulated grades: This issue is common in circulated grades.

Characteristics of striking: Striking varies for this issue, as might be expected from most coins struck from so many pairs of dies.

	Cert	Avg	%MS	G-4	VG-8	F-12	VF-20	EF-40	AU-50	MS-60BN	MS-63BN	MS-65RB	MS-65RD
1901	1,689	63.2	96%	$2	$3	$5	$6	$10	$20	$40	$60	$170	$440

1901, Proof • Proof mintage: 1,985.

Proof commentary: This Proof has one of the lower mintages. As is true of other Proofs of this era, the demand for the 1901 is diminished due to the common nature of related circulation strikes.

Rick Snow commented on "wipe lines" on Proofs of 1901 to 1907:[150]

Early-die-state Proofs of this era generally show an 'orange peel' effect if the planchets are annealed at a too-high temperature. On cents from 1901 to 1907 (except 1906), there are what I call *wipe lines* on these early-die-state coins. When the coin is viewed at one angle, a deep mirror surface is evident. When viewed at another angle there are a profusion of parallel striations, which look like hairlines. These are not problems with the coin. These are lines caused by a wiping of the die with a heavy cloth (probably) while the die was soft. The lines then transfer to the coin. After the die has been in use awhile, these lines fade. After the die is repolished they disappear completely."

Q. David Bowers usually refers to these as "die finish lines." Alternatively to Snow's "wiping" theory, they may have been caused by polishing the die on a buffing wheel. John Dannreuther noted that similar lines are found on Proof Liberty Head nickels of this decade.[151]

	Cert	Avg	%MS	PF-63BN	PF-64RB	PF-65RD
1901, Proof	284	64.8		$150	$300	$1,200

Indian Head Cents of 1902

KEYS TO COLLECTING: Cents of 1902 are common in all grades, but fully struck pieces with needle-sharp feather details are scarce.

1902 IN NUMISMATICS: There is said to have been a plague of counterfeit cents during this period, and during fiscal year 1902 some 96,995 pieces were detected by the Treasury Department. The runner-up in "popularity" with counterfeiters was the quarter dollar, which returned 5,125 counterfeit pieces to the Treasury Department. Surprisingly, only 11 spurious gold coins were found.[152] Even more surprising is that today very few collectors are aware of such pieces; certainly the numismatic community would like to know how they differed from authentic pieces.

The *Annual Report of the Director of the Mint*, 1902, told that the amount of pressure required for stamping a silver dollar was 160 tons, while a pressure of 35 tons was needed for a quarter eagle, 155 tons for a double eagle, 98 tons for a half dollar, 35 tons for a dime, and 40 tons for a cent. A large coining press at the Mint was driven by a 7.5-horsepower electric motor running at 950 rpm and could strike 90 coins per minute.

A small coining press—such as one used to strike Indian Head cents—was run by a 3-horsepower motor at 1,050 rpm and could strike 100 pieces per minute. This was equivalent to 6,000 coins per hour, not allowing for down time.

1902 • Circulation-strike mintage: 87,374,704.

Availability in Mint State: *MS–60 to 64:* This issue is common in these grades. Most are lightly struck (no wonder, considering the record number of coins produced per die during this year). Bright-red specimens are scarcer for this date than are those of the preceding several years. *MS-65 and higher:* This issue is very common in these grades in the context of the series.

Availability in circulated grades: This issue is common in circulated grades.

Characteristics of striking: Most specimens are lightly struck.

	Cert	Avg	%MS	G-4	VG-8	F-12	VF-20	EF-40	AU-50	MS-60BN	MS-63BN	MS-65RB	MS-65RD
1902	1,635	62.7	94%	$2	$3	$5	$6	$10	$20	$40	$60	$170	$485

1902, Proof • Proof mintage: 2,018.

Proof commentary: Proofs are scarce due to the low mintage, but among surviving pieces there are more bright-red coins than for other dates of this era.[153] Some early Proof strikings are seen with "wipe lines," a.k.a. die finish lines (see comment under 1901, Proof, on page 340).

	Cert	Avg	%MS	PF-63BN	PF-64RB	PF-65RD
1902, Proof	285	64.6		$150	$300	$1,200

Indian Head Cents of 1903

KEYS TO COLLECTING: There was no particular excitement with this or other dates of the era, but they were collected as part of the later 1879–1909 series.

A VISIT TO THE NEW MINT: A visitors' guide, *The United States Mint at Philadelphia*, by James Rankin Young, was published in 1903 and contained many views and descriptions of the new Mint facilities (first occupied in 1901). Excerpts relating to one-cent pieces follow:

The twenty-five coining presses now used are supposed to be the best designed machines in the Mint, and represent the gradual development of a press installed in 1874. . . . Ten new presses were installed when the mint was moved into its new quarters. These presses . . . were built at the shops of the T.C. Dill Machine Co. in Philadelphia.

The dies are adjusted in the coining press by a skilled operator, the adjustment requiring the services of a man of long experience. The blanks are then fed into a tube at the front of the machine. In doing this the women who feed the machines shake the blanks in the palm of their hand, getting them in a column ready to go into the tube, and incidentally detecting any false or nicked blank that may have escaped the vigilance of the workers at the selecting tables. A pair of [mechanical] fingers takes the disc from the bottom of the feed tube and carries it in between the upper and lower die, where it is held in position by a collar. . . . The stamp then descends. The obverse of the coin is struck on the top of the blank and the reverse on the lower side. . . . When the pressure is released the lower die forces the coin out of the collar and the fingers force it back into its channel, at the same time carrying a new blank into the collar. Despite the fact that many tons pressure are put on each coin stamped, this whole operation is done in a moment, and from 80 to 100 coins are thrown into the can at the bottom of the machine every minute. . . .

Since 1899 experiments have been regularly conducted aiming at improvements in the various minting processes. The results of this spirit of enterprise are visible today in every department. . . .

Practically all the nickel comes from the mines at the Gap, in Lancaster County, Pennsylvania, and the copper from the Lake Superior mints. The nickel and copper is received already refined, stamped, and milled [with raised rims], ready to have the design stamped on it by the coining presses, making it coin. . . . Large box-loads of blanks for pennies are received here daily. The blanks are scooped out and placed in big metal pans [one side of a balance-arm scale], when they are weighed and emptied into trucks [iron-wheeled carts], four or five feet high, in which they are transferred to the coiner. An average of twenty-two tons of bronze and nickel per month are weighed on these scales. . . .

The five cent (nickel) and the one cent (bronze) pieces are all issued from the Philadelphia Mint. The blanks are purchased under contract, and the millions of little pieces sent out yearly are all stamped in the building. The presses are constantly running on these coins, as the demand from the country is a never-ceasing one. The Cashier ships daily to banks and business firms throughout the United States thousands upon thousands of the nickel and bronze pieces, the demand being particularly heavy during the weeks preceding the Christmas holidays. For the work thus done the Cashier has two office assistants, a shipping clerk, and five to six packers. . . .

Visitors to the Mint invariably find their way to the Cashier's office before leaving the building. The visit is not complete unless some newly-minted coins are carried away as "souvenirs," the bright cent generally catching the fancy of the stranger. . . .

The actual shipping of coin from the Mint building is done in a room on the north side of the area in the basement. Here the bags of coin are packed into small heavy kegs, about twenty of which constitute a wagon load. From here they are transferred to the various express companies, who are under contract and bond to do all the transportation for the government. . . .

In a single room in the southern end of the second floor of the building is the Medal Room, a department under the Coiner though almost an independent mint in itself. All the Proof coins . . . and medals are made in this room. . . . Against the wall are two electrically driven hydraulic presses, capable respectively of a pressure of 400 and 300 tons to the square inch, and next to them the two hydraulic pumps. Off in an out-of-the-way corner is the old-fashioned hand screw press, with its long arms and heavy weights. The foreman, growing reminiscent, tells how, as a helper, he used to get these arms going round at such a gait that they would move the whole machine.

The Proof sets of coins are made under the government supervision to be preserved for record, or sold to collectors. The face of the dies used in stamping these sets have been given an extra fine finish, and glisten as though they had been nickel-plated. The blanks for coins are annealed and stamped by the hydraulic press. . . .

The "business office" of the Medal Department is in a room on the right side of the corridor as you enter the Cabinet [Mint Collection room]. Proof sets of the half dozen silver and minor coins [Indian Head cent, Liberty nickel, Barber dime, Barber quarter, Barber half dollar, Morgan dollar] are sold for $2.50, while Proof sets of the four gold coins [$2.50, $5, $10, $20] cost $38.50. Any one of the gold coins can be bought at a premium of twenty-five cents, and a Proof nickel and cent may be had for eight cents, but the Proof sets of silver coins will not be separated.

1903 • Circulation-strike mintage:
85,092,703.

Availability in Mint State: *MS–60 to 64:* This issue is common at all Mint State levels. *MS-65 and higher:* This issue is very common in these grades in the context of the series.

Availability in circulated grades: This issue is common in circulating grades.

Characteristics of striking: Most examples are not sharply struck on the feather ends.

	Cert	Avg	%MS	G-4	VG-8	F-12	VF-20	EF-40	AU-50	MS-60BN	MS-63BN	MS-65RB	MS-65RD
1903	1,506	62.7	94%	$2	$3	$5	$6	$10	$20	$40	$60	$170	$440

1903, Proof • **Proof mintage:** 1,790.

Proof commentary: This Proof has one of the lower mintages. The portrait is lightly polished in the dies, not frosty. The feather tips are usually weak.

Some early Proof strikings are seen with "wipe lines," a.k.a. die finish lines (see comment under 1901, Proof, on page 340).

	Cert	Avg	%MS	PF-63BN	PF-64RB	PF-65RD
1903, Proof	251	64.6		$150	$300	$1,200

Indian Head Cents of 1904

KEYS TO COLLECTING: The 1904 is very common. As is true of all of these later-date cents, seek a sharply struck coin. Quality can vary widely.

DATE NUMERALS: The 4 in 1904 is tilted to the right (on both circulation strikes and Proofs), so that the base of the 4 is not parallel to the curve of the denticles, but tilts downward to the right (the left base of the 4, if extended, would intersect the 0 at its lower-right outside curve). By contrast, the base of the 4 in the dates 1864, 1884, and 1894 is oriented parallel to the denticles (the 1874 cent has a straight date, so comparisons are not relevant).

A detail showing the tilted 4 in the date.

1904 • **Circulation-strike mintage:** 61,326,198.

Availability in Mint State: *MS–60 to 64:* This issue is common in these grades. A few rolls of this date have come on the market in recent decades. Often Mint State cents of this date are bright orange-red. *MS-65 and higher:* This issue is very common in these grades in the context of the series.

Availability in circulated grades: This issue is common in circulated grades.

Characteristics of striking: Striking varies for this issue, but sharp pieces can be found.

	Cert	Avg	%MS	G-4	VG-8	F-12	VF-20	EF-40	AU-50	MS-60BN	MS-63BN	MS-65RB	MS-65RD
1904	1,292	62.8	94%	$2	$3	$5	$6	$10	$20	$40	$60	$170	$460

1904, Proof • **Proof mintage:** 1,817.

Proof commentary: Traces of a misplaced 9 are seen in the denticles below the correctly positioned 9.[154] This date is one of the lower mintages and is especially hard to find preserved in gem RD. Some early Proof strikings are seen with "wipe lines," a.k.a. die finish lines (see comment under 1901, Proof, on page 340).

	Cert	Avg	%MS	PF-63BN	PF-64RB	PF-65RD
1904, Proof	238	64.2		$150	$300	$1,200

Indian Head Cents of 1905

KEYS TO COLLECTING: At the time of issue many collectors acquired an example, but there was no particular excitement for this date.

In 1996 John Dannreuther reported that a large group of nominally "Uncirculated" 1905 cents came on the market, but that these were in fact circulated pieces that had been treated, possibly with cyanide or another etching agent, and then given a brilliant color—the color will wipe off these coins![155] Such coins would have little value to the serious numismatist.

GOLD STRIKING: One specimen of this date is known struck in gold, undoubtedly a delicacy made for numismatic sale (see related entries under 1900, page 339, and 1906, below) rather than a true mint error.[156]

1905 • **Circulation-strike mintage:** 80,717,011

Availability in Mint State: *MS–60 to 64:* This issue is common at all Mint State levels. *MS-65 and higher:* This issue is very common in these grades in the context of the series.

Availability in circulated grades: This issue is common in circulated grades.

Characteristics of striking: Most examples are lightly struck on the feather ends.

	Cert	Avg	%MS	G-4	VG-8	F-12	VF-20	EF-40	AU-50	MS-60BN	MS-63BN	MS-65RB	MS-65RD
1905	1,530	62.9	94%	$2	$3	$5	$6	$10	$20	$40	$60	$170	$490

1905, Proof • **Proof mintage:** 2,152.

Proof commentary: Proofs are scarce. Some early Proof strikings are seen with "wipe lines," a.k.a. die finish lines (see comment under 1901, Proof, on page 340).

	Cert	Avg	%MS	PF-63BN	PF-64RB	PF-65RD
1905, Proof	253	64.5		$150	$300	$1,200

Indian Head Cents of 1906

KEYS TO COLLECTING: Again we have the situation—prevalent for the 1890s and 1900s—that an issue is plentiful in circulation-strike form but truly scarce in Proof format.

PLANCHETS: In 1906, for the first time in many years, planchets for one-cent pieces were made within the Philadelphia Mint. However, 216,000 pounds avoirdupois of ready-made planchets were also purchased from the outside for $59,540.[157]

GOLD STRIKING: One specimen is known struck in gold, undoubtedly a delicacy made for numismatic sale (see related entries under 1900, page 339 and 1905, above) rather than a true mint error.[158]

OVERVIEW OF CENTS: *The Numismatist*, May 1906, carried an article, "New Design for Copper Cent," which contained some information and misinformation. Excerpts:

A change in the design of the small bronze cent, which has made its appearance each year since its adoption, in 1864, is being considered by a Congressional committee, and experiments are also underway looking to the use of a new metal, either pure nickel or aluminum, to take the place of that now used, which is 95% copper and 5% zinc.

The contemplated change is the outcome of the agitation in favor of new designs for United States coins of all denominations, not a single one of the present series seeming to meet with general favor. Expert numismatists go so far as to say that never in the history of this country has it been represented by a less artistic set of coins. . . .

In 1808 the old style of Liberty Head, with flowing hair and face to the right, was superseded by a new and handsome head, with hair bound, facing to the left. . . . There was not a really handsome head borne by any cent issued after 1809 [sic; actually, the design of 1808, called the Classic Head today, was continued through 1814], each succeeding year the design apparently becoming more indifferent that its predecessor, while in 1839 there appeared varieties now known to collectors by the titles of "Booby Head" and "Silly Head" cents. . . .

Of recent years very few pattern cent dies have been made, though quite a number of cents have been struck at the Mint from the regular dies in various metals other than those ordinarily used. It would thus appear that the designers are now content with the present style of cent, but many of those interested in coins are not so well pleased, and will gladly welcome a change.

As it turned out, a number of shield-design cents had been made in 1896. While some were sold to collectors, many dozens were retained at the Mint and exchanged with William H. Woodin circa 1910. In the early 1950s these turned up in or near Woodin's home in Berwick, Pennsylvania, and were acquired by Robert K. Botsford, of Nescopeck, Pennsylvania, and sold to Q. David Bowers.

1906 IN NUMISMATICS: At 10:59 a.m., Thursday, February 1, 1906, Superintendent F.M. Downer gave a signal, and as part of a public ceremony the first official Denver Mint coins were struck.

The Philadelphia Mint charged 8¢ for a set of minor Proof coins with the Indian Head cent and Liberty Head nickel, $1.50 for a set with the dime, quarter, and half dollar, plus the minor coins, and $38.50 for a set of gold Proofs with the $2.50, $5, $10, and $20 gold pieces (representing $37.50 in face value for the set). Gold coins could also be ordered singly for 25¢ above face value. Current federal coins did not attract much interest at the time. The market was led by early coinage as well as colonials, tokens, medals, patterns, and other specialties.

1906 • Circulation-strike mintage:
96,020,530.

Availability in Mint State: *MS–60 to 64:* This issue is common at all Mint State levels. Philadelphia Mint coins of this decade are usually priced by coin type rather than by date. Although some levels are scarcer than others, there are still enough around to fill the demand. *MS-65 and higher:* This issue is very common in these grades in the context of the series.

Availability in circulated grades: This issue is common in circulated grades.

Characteristics of striking: Striking varies for this issue.

	Cert	Avg	%MS	G-4	VG-8	F-12	VF-20	EF-40	AU-50	MS-60BN	MS-63BN	MS-65RB	MS-65RD
1906	1,742	62.4	92%	$2	$3	$5	$6	$10	$20	$40	$60	$170	$440

1906, Proof • Proof mintage: 1,725.

Proof commentary: This Proof has one of the lower mintages. Dies were typically fully mirrored; no "wipe lines" are seen on early states of these Proofs.[159]

	Cert	Avg	%MS	PF-63BN	PF-64RB	PF-65RD
1906, Proof	224	64.4		$150	$300	$1,200

Indian Head Cents of 1907

KEYS TO COLLECTING: The 1907 is the most common Indian Head cent in terms of circulation strikes. It is available in all grades.

Proofs are quite scarce as, indeed, are most Proof issues of the 1890s and 1900s. However, the price structure is such that more plentiful Proofs of the 1880s often sell for higher prices than these scarcer issues.

PLANCHETS: The manufacture of bronze cent planchets continued within the Mint, but in fiscal-year 1907 190,000 pounds avoirdupois of finished blanks were purchased on contract for $65,550.[160]

CENT STRUCK IN GOLD: At the 1952 convention of the American Numismatic Association, California dealer Abe Kosoff sold Eastern dealer Bill Mertes a 1907 Indian Head cent struck in gold. The price was $40, which was about 15 times the amount a bronze Proof of the same date might have sold for at the time. The *New York Times* carried a story on August 19 stating that "a 1907 Indian cent" had sold for $40, neglecting to mention that the cent in question was struck in gold. Other newspapers picked up the news. For the next several days coin dealers were deluged with telephone calls and visits from members of the public who had ordinary bronze 1907 cents—the commonest date of the series, a coin worth about 5¢ if well worn—hoping to get $40 for it.

The *Numismatic Scrapbook Magazine*, September 1952, told of the incident and went on to give a theory concerning the origin of the gold issue:

> There are several Indian cents of various dates known that are struck in gold. During the time that the Indian head type was being struck the Mint was also coining gold coins. The gold cents happened the same way that a nickel on a cent blank turns up occasionally today; a stray blank planchet in the wrong press.

(Also see commentary under the 1900 cent listing on page 339.)

1907 IN NUMISMATICS: Working in his studio in Cornish, New Hampshire, America's best-known living sculptor, Augustus Saint-Gaudens, was busy redesigning the nation's coinage. By the time of his death on August 3, 1907, he had completed most work for his Indian Head $10 gold piece and MCMVII $20 gold piece designs and had sketched new motifs for a one-cent piece. While the $10 and $20 gold pieces were made in coinage form by the end of the year, his designs for the new cent were not developed sufficiently to be put into use.

In September Frank A. Leach became director of the Mint (though he was confirmed by the Senate later, on February 12, 1908). Liberty Head $2.50 and $20 gold coins were minted for the last time. Liberty Head $5 gold coins would be discontinued in 1908.

1907 • **Circulation-strike mintage:** 108,137,143.

Availability in Mint State: *MS–60 to 64:* This issue is common at all of these levels. A few rolls in these grades came on the market in the 1950s and 1960s. *MS-65 and higher:* This issue has the highest mintage of all Indian Head cents and is perhaps the most common in these grades.

Availability in circulated grades: This issue is common in circulated grades.

Characteristics of striking: Striking varies for this issue.

	Cert	Avg	%MS	G-4	VG-8	F-12	VF-20	EF-40	AU-50	MS-60BN	MS-63BN	MS-65RB	MS-65RD
1907	1,875	62.3	93%	$2	$3	$5	$6	$10	$20	$40	$60	$170	$440

1907, Proof • **Proof mintage:** 1,475.

Proof commentary: Paradoxically, while 1907 has the highest mintage of any circulation-strike Indian Head cent, it has the lowest Proof mintage of its era. There was a financial panic that year, and many buyers of Proof coins sat on the sidelines. Several years ago a client of coin dealer and numismatic scholar Q. David Bowers, John Jay Pittman, spent several years trying to find a nice Proof of this date. Bright-red Proofs are especially elusive.

Many Proof strikings are seen with "wipe lines," a.k.a. die finish lines. The 1907 is particularly well known for this feature. (See comment under 1901, Proof, on page 340).

	Cert	Avg	%MS	PF-63BN	PF-64RB	PF-65RD
1907, Proof	214	64.4		$150	$300	$1,250

Indian Head Cents of 1908

KEYS TO COLLECTING: The 1908 is readily available, but it is always considered to be a slightly scarcer date in Mint State.

1908 IN NUMISMATICS: 1908 is the first year cents were struck by more than just one mint. The San Francisco Mint produced the 1908-S cent.

1908 • **Circulation-strike mintage:** 32,326,317.

Availability in Mint State: *MS–60 to 64:* This issue is readily available in Mint State, although dealer and numismatic scholar Q. David Bowers does not recall ever having had a full roll of original Mint State coins. This issue is scarcer than any date of the decade up to this point. *MS-65 and higher:* This issue is slightly scarce in these grades in the context of the series. Most undipped coins are BN or RB. Full original RD coins are scarce.

Availability in circulated grades: This issue is common in circulating grades.

Characteristics of striking: Striking varies for this issue, but it is mostly average, neither sharp nor weak.

	Cert	Avg	%MS	G-4	VG-8	F-12	VF-20	EF-40	AU-50	MS-60BN	MS-63BN	MS-65RB	MS-65RD
1908	1,605	63.1	95%	$2	$3	$5	$6	$10	$20	$40	$60	$170	$440

1908, Proof • Proof mintage: 1,620.

Proof commentary: This Proof has a very low mintage for the era. Sometimes examples are seen red with brown blotches. Assembling a beautiful set of Proof Indian Head cents dated in the 1900s is far more difficult than putting one together from the 1880s.

	Cert	Avg	%MS	PF-63BN	PF-64RB	PF-65RD
1908, Proof	286	64.7		$150	$300	$1,200

1908-S • Circulation-strike mintage: 1,115,000.

Availability in Mint State: *MS–60 to 64:* In Mint State, 1908-S cents are fairly scarce, but they are more available than the low mintage implies, as collectors saved them at the time of issue. In more than 60 years of being a rare-coin dealer Q. David Bowers has seen only one original, bank-wrapped roll of 50 pieces, and this roll was owned by James F. Ruddy in the mid-1950s. "However," he says, "I have always thought that the 1908-S is harder to find than the 1909-S Indian Head cent, and in terms of rarity in Mint State it far eclipses the celebrated 1909-S V.D.B. Lincoln cent." The 1908-S cents and 1909-S Indian Head cents (and also 1909-S V.D.B. Lincoln cents) were struck on bronze planchets of a more straw-colored alloy, different to the experienced eye from the deeper red used for Philadelphia Mint cents (this difference can only be seen on cents that have not been cleaned, dipped, or retoned). Sometimes this issue exhibits a wood-grain type of toning, but it is not as prominent as on 1909-S Indian Head cents. *MS-65 and higher:* This issue is scarce in these grades for such a late issue. Full original RD coins are especially scarce.

Availability in circulated grades: This issue is rare in circulated grades in the context of the Indian Head series. It is a key issue. Circulated specimens are most often seen in grades from Fine to VF or EF. Well-worn pieces (AG and G) are rarer, but not more desirable.

Characteristics of striking: The striking for this issue is of average quality. The reverse is usually sharper than the obverse. The feather tips are nearly always weak, but there are scattered exceptions. Rick Snow reports seeing an original roll of 50 Mint State coins with all pieces having the final A in AMERICA very weak.[161]

Notes: *Keys to collecting:* This is the first branch-mint coin of this denomination, and it is always in demand. The 1908-S is scarcer in Mint State than is generally believed, due no doubt to most pieces being put into circulation before widespread public interest arose in "rare" cents.

No minor coins at other mints: In the American West most transactions were completed in silver and gold coins, and on the West Coast one-cent pieces were rarely seen, nor was there any call for them. Because of this, no minor coins were struck at Western mints until the 1908-S cent.

From the fiscal-year 1909 *Mint Report:*

> The manufacture of United States minor coin was instituted at this mint during the year [1908], and on November 27, 1908, the first 1-cent pieces ever made at the San Francisco Mint were delivered by the coiner to the superintendent. The 1-cent bronze pieces struck during the [1909 fiscal year extending from July 1, 1908 to June 30, 1909] amounted to $14,240. . . . The bronze coins manufactured at this mint during the year were made on the silver presses. Two new presses for bronze coining are now being installed to handle this class of work.

A specimen of the 1908-S cent was subsequently added to the Mint Collection in Philadelphia. This cabinet did not normally include branch-mint coins (of earlier issues in the silver and gold series), nor did the 1908-S inclusion signal a major policy change. By 1914 no 1909-S Indian Head cent had been added.[162]

	Cert	Avg	%MS	G-4	VG-8	F-12	VF-20	EF-40	AU-50	MS-60BN	MS-63BN	MS-65RB	MS-65RD
1908-S	3,002	45.0	35%	$90	$100	$125	$145	$175	$250	$290	$400	$850	$2,300

Varieties: The May 1912 issue of *The Numismatist* contained this comment from Commodore W.C. Eaton, whose earlier scholarship included several commentaries on varieties of Lincoln small cents:

> I find that in my various listings of the sub-varieties of the San Francisco cents I have missed one. Mr. Henry Mitchell of Philadelphia has kindly written me concerning his discovery that there are two varieties in the position of the mint mark in the S.F. Indian Head of 1908. In one the 'S' is midway between the ribbon end on the left and the stem on the right; in the other the 'S' is nearer the ribbon end. I do not know how I overlooked this variety as I find I have both, my duplicates all being of the latter type.
>
> If all collectors were as obliging as Mr. Mitchell in reporting their discoveries we would be pretty certain to make this list complete.[163]

Today all of these dies can be found in *Flying Eagle & Indian Cents,* third edition, by Richard E. Snow.

Indian Head Cents of 1909

KEYS TO COLLECTING: 1909 is the last year of Indian Head cents production and cents of this year are in slightly greater demand as such. However, the 1909 cent is not particularly scarce in higher grades. The 1909-S is rarer in those grades in relation to demand.

MASTER DIE CHANGE: Beginning this year the date was included in the master die and impressed at the same time as the other design features into the working die. Thus, from 1909 onward—including in the Lincoln series—there are no more repunched date numerals (later doubled-die obverses are from the entire die being double punched, not just the date).

In 1909 the initial L (for Longacre) on the headdress ribbon was enlarged slightly.

The 9 in the date, which often displayed blob-like characteristics on coins dated from 1890 through 1908, was reconfigured to a more open appearance, with greater separation between the bottom ball and the top curve. See expanded commentary and detail shot under 1890 on page 328.

PLANCHETS: For the first time in many years *all* planchets were made within Mint facilities.[164]

1909 • Circulation-strike mintage: 14,368,470.

Availability in Mint State: *MS–60 to 64:* Undipped, uncleaned, brilliant Mint State coins are reddish-orange and are colored differently from the 1909-S. *MS-65 and higher:* This issue is available easily enough in these grades, but it is scarce in the context of Philadelphia Mint cents of the two preceding decades. Most examples are BN or RB.

Availability in circulated grades: This is a slightly scarcer date in worn grades due to its lower mintage.

Characteristics of striking: Striking for this issue varies, but it is usually better than average.

	Cert	Avg	%MS	G-4	VG-8	F-12	VF-20	EF-40	AU-50	MS-60BN	MS-63BN	MS-65RB	MS-65RD
1909	2,174	62.4	94%	$12	$15	$17	$20	$25	$30	$45	$65	$175	$440

1909, Proof • Proof mintage: 2,175.

Proof commentary: This Proof is fairly scarce. Usually it displays a rich, red-orange color if it is brilliant. This date has often sold for a premium, due not so much to its scarcity as to its status as the last year in the series.

	Cert	Avg	%MS	PF-63BN	PF-64RB	PF-65RD
1909, Proof	256	64.6		$150	$300	$1,300

1909-S • Circulation-strike mintage: 309,000.

Availability in Mint State: *MS–60 to 64:* This issue is fairly scarce in these grades, although it is more available by far than Mint State coins of higher mintages of such dates as 1866 through 1872 and 1877. This is because in 1909 there was an awareness in numismatics of low mintages that was not present in the hobby earlier. Planchets usually display light straw-colored or yellow streaks, sometimes subtle, sometimes giving a wood-grain toning effect similar to that seen on bronze cents of the mid-1860s (although the cents of the 1860s are reddish, not yellowish, in cast). This characteristic is probably true of all undipped original 1909-S Indian Head cents (the same planchet characteristics are seen on the later 1909-S V.D.B. Lincoln cents). *MS-65 and higher:* This issue is rare in proportion to demand, but at least several thousand or so exist. Most are RB.

Availability in circulated grades: This issue is rare in circulated grades. Usually circulated examples are seen Fine or better. Both struck and cast counterfeits exist of this cent, as do pieces with phony mintmarks added later; buy this cent with a written guarantee of authenticity, without exception.

Characteristics of striking: Striking is usually lightly defined and this cent is always lacking feather tip details, not due to striking, but to lack of definition in the working die. On the reverse the shield is usually well struck, however.[165] There were only two reverse dies used; these are illustrated in *Flying Eagle & Indian Cents*, third edition, by Richard E. Snow.

Notes: *Keys to collecting:* This issue has the lowest mintage of any regular issue in the series; just 309,000. Numismatists were aware of the desirability of the variety, and quite a few coins were saved (in contrast, circulation-strike 1877 cents were ignored in the year of their issue and became very rare). However, the old-style 1909-S Indian Head cents were vastly eclipsed by the new Lincoln cents released on August 2, 1909, and they soon were forgotten by all but a few.

A reminiscence by Q. David Bowers:

In the early 1950s I received a price list from B. Max Mehl (1884–1957), a famous Fort Worth, Texas, dealer who was then in the twilight years of his illustrious career. He offered for sale an Uncirculated 1909-S cent for $10. Mehl at that time issued such price lists only occasionally and did not necessarily keep up with the rapidly advancing rare-coin market. Recognizing the 1909-S offered at this price as a bargain, I telephoned him in Fort Worth to order one. He responded with a cheery commentary that went something like this:

"I know the 1909-S Indians are worth a lot more than ten dollars now, but I have had these for a long time. I like to read your ads in the *Numismatic Scrapbook*, and I wish you luck in your career. How many 1909-S cents do you want?"

	Cert	Avg	%MS	G-4	VG-8	F-12	VF-20	EF-40	AU-50	MS-60BN	MS-63BN	MS-65RB	MS-65RD
1909-S	3,185	39.8	29%	$450	$500	$600	$700	$750	$900	$1,050	$1,200	$2,500	$5,250

LINCOLN, WHEAT EARS REVERSE (1909–1958)

Variety 1 (Bronze, 1909–1942): **Designer:** *Victor D. Brenner.* **Weight:** *3.11 grams.*
Composition: *.950 copper, .050 tin and zinc.* **Diameter:** *19 mm.*
Edge: *Plain.* **Mints:** *Philadelphia, Denver, and San Francisco.*

Variety 1, Bronze
(1909–1942)

Variety 1, Bronze,
Matte Proof

Mintmark location, all varieties 1909 to
date, is on the obverse below the date.

Variety 2 (Steel, 1943): **Weight:** *2.70 grams.* **Composition:** *Steel, coated with zinc.*
Diameter: *19 mm.* **Edge:** *Plain.* **Mints:** *Philadelphia, Denver, and San Francisco.*

Variety 2, Steel (1943)

Variety 1 Resumed (1944–1958): **Weight:** *3.11 grams.*
Composition: *1944–1946—.950 copper and .050 zinc; 1947–1958—.950 copper and .050 tin and zinc.*
Diameter: *19 mm.* **Edge:** *Plain.* **Mints:** *Philadelphia, Denver, and San Francisco.*

Variety 1 Resumed, Bronze
(1944–1958)

Variety 1 Resumed, Bronze,
Mirror Proof

THE BIRTH OF A POPULAR DESIGN

On August 2, 1909, the new Lincoln cent made its debut, and the long-lived Indian Head cent design became part of history. With slight modifications, the Lincoln obverse has continued in use through today, making the various Lincoln cent types the most familiar of U.S. coins. Despite calls that the "penny" is obsolete in commerce, more have been made in recent generations than in the earlier decades of the design.

Over the years Lincoln, Wheat Ears Reverse, cents were minted in response to the demand for them in banking and commercial circles. When small change was scarce, such as during both world wars, cent mintages rose to high levels. When the country was in a recession or depression, as in 1921 and 1922, or 1930 through 1933, there were adequate stocks of cents on hand, and new mintages were small.

COLLECTING LINCOLN, WHEAT EARS REVERSE, CENTS

When Lincoln, Wheat Ears Reverse, cents were first released in August 1909 they attracted wide attention. The new coins and the background of their design were featured in articles in *The Numismatist* and elsewhere, including in popular magazines and newspapers. The first issues had V.D.B., the initials of sculptor-designer Victor D. Brenner, on the reverse. Complaints were voiced that such placement was a free advertisement for a man who had been paid for his work—never mind that at the same time the initials of other artists were prominent on certain other coins, such as the ASG monogram for Augustus Saint-Gaudens on the obverse of the $20 gold piece. The Treasury stopped distributing the cents featuring the initials, and the public thought the coins would have great value. Large numbers of this variety were hoarded.

Numismatic interest in Lincoln, Wheat Ears Reverse, cents was strong at the beginning, but it soon faded. From 1910 through the early 1930s, many different dates and mintmarks were produced. Few collectors saved them, with the result that the low-mintage 1914-D eventually became recognized as scarce in any grade and rare in Mint State. Other varieties also proved to be elusive to a later generation of enthusiasts.

Collectors habits changed in 1931 when the low-mintage 1931-S cent was publicized, and collectors and dealers hoarded quantities of the issue. Overnight it became popular to save bank-wrapped rolls of 50 coins. In the depth of the Depression these rolls were not costly, and the allure of increasing value was an incentive for investors.

In the early 1930s Wayte Raymond promoted his series of "National" coin albums. These consisted of cardboard pages with openings for various dates and mintmarks of Lincoln, Wheat Ears

A National coin album marketed by Wayte Raymond through Scott Stamp & Coin Co.

Reverse, cents and other coins. The mintage for each issue was given below the appropriate opening. Clear, cellulose-acetate slides covered the front and back, permitting an instant view of a collection as it expanded. J.K. Post of Neenah, Wisconsin, marketed his "Lincoln Penny Collector," a cardboard sheet with openings into which coins could be pressed. His coin-board business was acquired by Whitman Publishing, and the company later launched coin folders with expanded storage capacity and protection as well as coin albums.

All of a sudden, collecting Lincoln cents by date and mintmark became popular. It was learned that certain earlier issues were hard to find, especially in Mint State. Values doubled and tripled, and doubled and tripled again.

From the 1940s onward Whitman Publishing's coin folders for Lincoln cents sold by the millions. Hundreds of thousands of people became numismatists after filling in their folders from pocket change, striving to complete their collections by finding rare issues. Whitman's *Guide Book of United States Coins*, launched in 1946 with a 1947 cover date, became the standard source for prices, and has been published annually since then.

Today, Lincoln cents remain as popular as ever. Most in circulation date from 1959 onward, with the Lincoln Memorial reverse. Older coins called "wheaties" are seldom seen.

Designing and Distributing the Lincoln Cent
Roosevelt and Brenner

In the autumn of 1908, a well-known sculptor, Victor David Brenner, was selected by President Theodore Roosevelt to model his portrait for use on the obverse of a medal to honor workers on the Panama Canal, a project still in progress at the time (opening ceremonies would held in 1914). During Roosevelt's sitting for Brenner in the summer of 1908, it seems that the two discussed American coinage designs and the work left unfinished by the death of Saint-Gaudens. The latter sculptor had passed away on August 3, 1907, leaving most of his 1905 commission to redesign all coins, from the cent to the double eagle, unfinished.

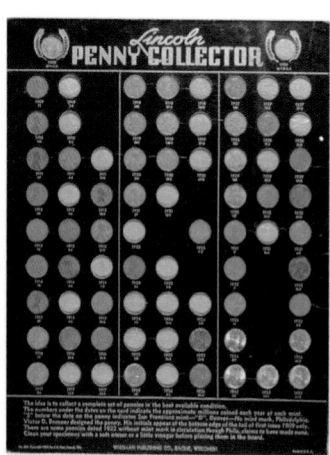

A Whitman Lincoln Penny Collector board of 1935, after Whitman Publishing acquired the rights from J.K. Post. Such inexpensive storage devices sold widely and prompted hundreds of thousands of hobbyists to collect cents.

A Whitman Lincoln cent folder from the 1960s.

First page of the Lincoln cent section in the first edition (1947) of *A Guide Book of United States Coins.*

Victor D. Brenner in his studio with a statue of Lincoln.

The official presidential portrait of President Theodore Roosevelt, painted in 1903 by John Singer Sargent.

Augustus Saint-Gaudens in 1905.

Although Saint-Gaudens had made some sketches and even models for a new cent of the Flying Eagle design, nothing further had been done. (Also see page 243.) The president admired Brenner's portrait of Lincoln, created in 1907 on a rectangular copper plaque.

Later in the year, when the idea of a Lincoln coin came to the forefront of Roosevelt's mind, Brenner was contacted by Mint Director Frank Leach at the behest of the president. The artist accepted the commission, with a stipend of $1,000. Already into the project by January 4, 1909, he commented, "I was thinking of embodying the portrait of Mr. Lincoln on the cent piece, and find that it will compose very well." Brenner simply took his plaque portrait and adapted it for use on a coin.

The idea of this artist creating the new cent design met with Roosevelt's approval. By that time the Indian Head cent had been in circulation since 1859, and it was ripe for a change. Within two weeks Brenner had prepared preliminary models of the new cent.

Victor David Brenner

By 1909 Brenner, born Viktoras Barnauskas (though variant spellings occur) in Shavli (a city then in Russia, later known as Siauliai, Lithuania) on June 12, 1871, was the most *numismatically aware* of American sculptors. He had studied under his father, a sculptor and engraver. The young Brenner's talents were very impressive. He emigrated to America aboard the

Sketches and models by Augustus Saint-Gaudens for a proposed Flying Eagle cent design, the model using the eagle that was finalized on the $20 gold coin.

Brenner's 1907 copper plaque of Lincoln.

steamship *Gellert*, and arrived on May 17, 1890. In the United States he was known as Victor David Brenner. In New York City he gained employment as an engraver of jewelry and repairer of watches. Beginning in 1891 he studied at the Academy of Design and the Cooper Union, Art Students' League.

Brenner at a bench finessing details on a model for a medal.

Sculpture and medals were his primary interest. From 1898 to 1901 Brenner studied art in Paris, under Louis Oscar Roty (in particular), Alexander Charpentier, and others, during which time he exhibited his work at the Paris Salon and the Exposition Universelle in 1900, earning bronze medals from each. He was a member of the American Numismatic and Archaeological Society, for which he served as an instructor at the Society's School for Die-Cutting. Brenner also joined the American Numismatic Association.

In the course of his work Brenner operated a Janvier portrait reduction lathe to create hubs to make dies to strike art medals for the Deitsch brothers, makers of jewelry, buckles, and ornaments. Much of his work was displayed in New York City and featured in the *Catalogue of Medals and Plaques by Victor D. Brenner, Exhibited at the Grolier Club, March 7 to March 23, 1907*, for which Brenner wrote the introduction. His plaque of Lincoln, made and sold this year, was widely admired.

By that time he was well known in American art circles. In 1909 a medal from Brenner's models was produced by the Gorham Manufacturing Company for the Lincoln centennial, featuring the same portrait used on his 1907 plaque. His 1910 booklet, *The Art of the Medal*, was published by the American Numismatic Society (which had dropped "and Archaeological" from its name in 1908).

After receiving his commission from the Treasury Department Brenner hoped to design coins besides the cent, but his offers were never accepted by the Mint. In addition to his single fling with circulating coinage, Brenner was very successful with his medallic art and enjoyed recognition and prosperity. He completed only one large-scale sculpture, *Song to Nature (Zeus and Persephone)*, a fountain in Schenley Park in Pittsburgh, Pennsylvania.

On April 4, 1924, the designer of the Lincoln cent died in New York City, survived by his wife of 11 years, Anna. Over a long period of years, Brenner's work has formed the focus of displays at the American Numismatic Society and elsewhere and articles by numismatists in various journals. The definitive reference for his work as a medalist is *Who's Who Among American Medalists*, by D. Wayne Johnson, 2015.

PROGRESS OF THE LINCOLN CENT DESIGN

Victor D. Brenner's design for the Lincoln cent evolved from a series of different designs, not only for the cent, but for other denominations the artist hoped to modify. Brenner envisioned himself as the heir to the unfinished work of Saint-Gaudens. However, when no commissions for other coins were given to the artist, Brenner settled down to working on the cent alone.

Leach wrote to Brenner with some advice on the coin's reverse, February 9, 1909:

> The subject of the design for the reverse of the penny has been discussed by the President and the Secretary and myself, and it was decided that owing to the law permitting of only one figure emblematic of Liberty to be on the coin, and the desire that the coin should be plain and simple, your suggestion of the female figure, left with me yesterday, is rejected; and you are requested to submit another design which shall be in compliance with the memorandum furnished you yesterday.

Brenner replied to Leach, February 10, 1909:

> I beg also to acknowledge receipt of your letter dated Feb. 9th, fixing the designs for the cent piece for the obverse to have the portrait of Mr. Lincoln with the word Liberty and the date of the coinage, for the reverse to have United States of America, One Cent and E Pluribus Unum. I shall submit my arrangement of the design to you shortly.

Chief Engraver Charles E. Barber wrote to Brenner the same month, furnishing him advice on sculpting for coinage:

> Your letter of the 10th inst, received and the contents have been discussed with the Director who I understand has given you certain instructions regarding the design. Mr. Leach tells me that he has explained to you that he desired the field of the coin to be finished with a fixed radius or curve, therefore the model must be made with a fixed radius.
>
> I find in your Lincoln medal that the field in front of the face is one plane while the field at the back of the head is an entirely different plane. This you will see will never do as we have to finish the field of the dies mechanically in order to comply with the wish of the Director, namely to have the field finished smooth and one radius. In making your design you must avoid as much as possible one bold part of your design coming opposite another on the other side of the coin, as that would be fatal to the coining of the piece.
>
> In regard to what relief you had better adopt, I am sorry to say that I cannot give you any fixed instructions as so much depends upon the design of both sides and the particular metal the design is for, also the area of the coin.
>
> You can look at the [Indian Head] cent, judge from that, and that is the extent of the relief that can be successfully used for the one cent coin, and you will also see that for the point of utility, that the design is good, as it is so arranged that no one point comes in opposition to another, and as these coins are struck by tons every year, not thousands, but millions and if the usual average per pair of dies was not produced, the Coiner would condemn the dies at once.
>
> In designing for a coin you must give due weight to the mechanical requirements of coinage and remember that great quantities of coin are demanded against time, and therefore, everything that can be done to simplify both the making of the dies and the production of the coin, must be considered.
>
> You also know that the coins drop from the press at the rate of 120 per minute and that unlike a medal there is no bronzing or finishing of any description, no chance to bring out the design by coloring. It comes from the press one color and that is the color of the metal whatever that may be.

Brenner's sketches and a model proposing a standing figure emblematic of Liberty. The model is signed V.D. BRENNER at the bottom of the obverse.

Brenner wrote again to Leach when he submitted his final design, February 26, 1909:

> I have the honor to inform you that I have today expressed to you the completed models of the Lincoln penny also the molds of the same. I trust you will find them satisfactory. I will appreciate the permission of examining the hubs before they are hardened, and should any retouching be necessary, to do so under the supervision of Mr. Barber.

Leach passed along Brenner's submission to Superintendent John Landis of the Philadelphia Mint, February 27, 1909:

These galvanos were made circa March 1909. The obverse portrait is slightly smaller, lacks the motto, certain portrait details are different, and LIBERTY is in taller letters and placed lower in regard to Lincoln's jacket, than on the adopted 1909 die. The reverse is signed *Brenner* at the bottom.

I send you by express today the models adopted by the President of the design for the proposed new issue of the one cent piece. I notice that Mr. Brenner insists upon putting his name in full on the obverse side. I am sorry to have to disappoint him in this matter, but after consultation with the Secretary of the Treasury upon the subject it was decided that only his initials could be permitted, and that in an unobtrusive way.

Mr. Brenner writes me that he desires to see the hub in time to have touched up any imperfections that he might notice. I wish you would advise me whether or not his request is practicable. As soon as the dies are ready and proof [pattern or sample] pieces struck I shall be pleased to be advised of the fact.

A brass galvano with compass scribe lines around the border. These marks were made as part of the study to see how much of the shoulder should be shown and how close the top of the portrait should be to the border.

Brenner was cooperative regarding his name and moved his surname in full to the bottom of the reverse in italic type, stating to Leach on March 4:

I fully agree with you that my name on the obverse looks obtrusive, and thanks for calling my attention to it. I shall take it out, and put it in small letters on the reverse near the rim.

Further correspondence dealt with slight revisions and retouchings requested by the artist. Chief Engraver Barber conceded that he would not resist these, as he had been humiliated by accusations leveled against him by numismatists (Henry Chapman in particular) and others that he had interfered with the art of Augustus Saint-Gaudens and Bela Lyon Pratt, and he wished to be spared this indignity in the future.

Significantly, the motto "In God We Trust" was not being considered as the new cent was being developed, possibly because President Roosevelt felt that the name of the Deity on coinage was a sacrilege. In any event, the inscription did not appear on the Indian Head cent currently in use. The inscription would be added after incoming president William H. Taft was inaugurated in March. The idea came from Director Leach and Chief Engraver Barber, as related in this letter Leach wrote to Brenner on May 22:

I have to inform you that I was not satisfied with the first proof of the Lincoln cent. I found that you had not dropped the Lincoln portrait down so that the head would come nearer the center of the coin, a matter I called your attention to when we were discussing the model. This is necessary to get the best result in bringing out the details of the features in striking the coin. Therefore, I had Mr. Barber make me a proof of this change, and as this left so much blank space over the top we concluded that it would be better to put on the motto "In God We Trust."

This change has made a marked improvement in the appearance of the coin. I cannot send a sample, but if you feel enough interest in the matter it would be better for you to go down to Philadelphia where Mr. Barber can explain and show you what has been done. . . .

The Numismatist carried this piece in June describing the cent's final iteration before production:

Information from Washington indicates that the now long anticipated Lincoln cent will not be issued before August. When examples from the supposed completed dies were submitted to President Taft, it is said that he asked for the motto IN GOD WE TRUST to be placed on the coin. We are pleased to be able to give what we believe is the first description of the coin design as now decided upon.

The obverse will have the head of Lincoln (facing right) as modeled by sculptor Brenner, with IN GOD WE TRUST above, in the field, at left, will be the word LIBERTY, at right below center, 1909. The center of the reverse in five regular lines will bear the inscription E.P.U. [E PLURIBUS UNUM, which was spelled out on the finished coin] / ONE / CENT / UNITED STATES / OF AMERICA, with two unjoined branches surrounding.

THE DIES AND COINAGE

In New York City, Henri Weil, using the Janvier portrait-reduction lathe imported from France by the Deitsch brothers, created the final hub from a brass casting of the model. The Mint eventually used this hub to make *obverse* dies. Brenner had asked the Mint for permission to use the Deitsches' lathe. Brenner was at the shop supervising as Weil did the work. Henri and Felix Weil, by that time, were in business as the Medallic Art Company. At the time, the Mint had a Janvier lathe, but no one was comfortable using it. The fee to Weil was $100. In the meantime, the Mint used its Hill portrait-reduction lathe for most of its work, including some of Brenner's proposals in model form as well as the hub for the reverse die.

The work in New York was done prior to adding the motto IN GOD WE TRUST, which was done at the Mint after the change was directed by President Taft. Brenner suggested that it be placed near the top rim on the obverse. In May, Chief Engraver Barber supervised the making of 13 pattern strikings, all of which were certified as having been destroyed after they were inspected. Director Leach commanded that no samples be sent out, not even to Brenner.

Beginning on June 10 the Philadelphia Mint struck more than 25 million cents in anticipation of their release. A news item of the time stated that the cents would be struck in an alloy of 95% copper, 3% tin, and 2% zinc, a more precise definition than that usually given, 95% copper and 5% tin and zinc. On July 1 the Mint closed for summer vacation, with a supply of the new coins on hand.

Minting in San Francisco began in July. Only since the year before, and not in large quantities, had this denomination been minted in San Francisco. Cents had been used on the West Coast for a long time, though in limited numbers compared to gold and silver coins, but the establishing acts for the branch mints did not provide for coinage other than in silver or gold.[166]

After coinage had commenced in Philadelphia, after the fact on July 14, Secretary of the Treasury Franklin MacVeagh officially approved the Lincoln cent design. Standards remained the same as for the Indian Head cent: the diameter was 0.75 inches (with a tolerance of plus or minus 0.0025 inches); weight was 48 grains (with a tolerance of plus or minus 2 grains); and the composition was a bronze alloy of 95% copper, and a slight alloy change to 3% tin and 2% zinc. The administratively approved thickness of a finished coin was 0.062 inches.[167] In practice this figure varied due to the height of the rim.

RELEASE OF THE LINCOLN CENTS

The new cents were scheduled to be released on August 2. Stocks had been supplied to banks that had ordered them, as well as to the Treasury and its Sub-Treasury branches (including Boston, Chicago, New York City, Chicago, and St. Louis), and all was set to go. Both mints had produced what they considered would be adequate quantities.

Interest had been high in the public press, with newspaper accounts about the new design, and collectors as well as ordinary citizens looked forward to getting the coins. On the morning of August 2, long lines of eager buyers formed at the Treasury Building in Washington and in many other places. Although early applicants often obtained cents by the hundreds, soon the quantities were rationed.

Early birds, mostly newsboys and messengers, line up at the New York Sub-Treasury on August 4, 1909, awaiting their turn to buy Lincoln cents.

The Philadelphia Mint limited the payout to just two coins per person, while buyers at the Sub-Treasury in New York City could get 100 coins at a time while they lasted. In the meantime, orders that had been placed by mail were on hand at both mints, and these perhaps totaled several thousand coins.

In San Francisco the coins available to the public on August 2 were quickly gone. Among the lucky recipients was young Gobel Ziemer, who acquired a handful, then upon leaving the Mint saw dozens of people milling around, talking about the coins, and youngsters with a supply selling them for 3¢ each or two for 5¢.[168]

Outside the Philadelphia Mint, sales at a quarter each were reported before the price settled down to a few cents. Newsboys, always on the lookout to make a dollar here and there, were early birds in many lines at banks across the country, getting cents by the hundreds before the demand was realized. They soon sold their prize coins at a profit, especially when the tellers ran out of coins—many before closing time on the first day. Banks telegraphed requests for additional coins to the two mints, but were told that supplies were exhausted for the time being.

Numismatists making inquiries were ignored in some instances and in others told that none of the new cents were available. This included Matte Proofs that were supposed to have been made for collectors. No record has been found of anyone in the hobby contacting the Philadelphia Mint in early August and consummating a satisfactory transaction for multiple coins. Confusion reigned.

IN THE POPULAR PRESS

The *New York Times* reported on August 6, 1909, that the new cent was particularly popular with New York's black population as a result of Lincoln's connection to the emancipation of slaves. While this clipping has been received uncritically by some numismatists since that time, the 100-word article does call its own objectiveness into question by focusing on the *superstitiousness* of black cent enthusiasts—a common racial stereotype levied against American black communities at the time. The article closes, "Jewelers were kept busy making charms of the coins, which many colored people believe will bring good luck," but it is worth noting that Americans were purchasing such mementos across racial lines.

From the *Boston Daily Globe*, August 13, 1909:

Dollar for a Cent
South Egremont Farmer Gets 28 Lincoln Coins
Mr. Baldwin Liked Their Looks and Urged Boys to Collect Them

Great Barrington, Aug 12—In the little hamlet of South Egremont, the new cent brought record breaking prices for Berkshire County. Ephraim Baldwin, a well-to-do farmer, was just delighted with the Lincoln cents for they looked so much like gold and he told the youngsters that he would pay them one dollar for each one they could get for him.

The little village was searched, and every farmer who had been to town for some time was ordered to look through his collection of change to see if he had one of the new coins. There were 28 in all gathered and Mr. Baldwin paid the price of $28 for them.

The other extreme was reached in Pittsfield where a business house sold two Lincoln pennies for a cent as an advertising scheme.

THE V.D.B. CONTROVERSY
AUGUST 4, 1909

This article from the *New York Times*, August 5, suggests that Secretary of the Treasury Franklin MacVeagh had not seen the cent prior to its release, and was surprised that the initials V.D.B. appeared at the bottom of the reverse. His decision to remove them caused further demand for the coins on August 4, when news of the change circulated in the streets. The story, printed the next day, also tells of the great excitement in the city when the cents were released, similar to the above account of the activity in Washington.

From the *New York Times*:

New Dies Ordered for Lincoln Cents

WASHINGTON, Aug. 5. Secretary of the Treasury MacVeagh has decided to stop the minting of the new Lincoln cents. New dies will be prepared as soon as possible, substituting for the initials of the designer the single initial "B" in an obscure part of the design. None of the cents issued so far will be called in, but the minting will be stopped because a sufficient supply is on hand. The initials V.D.B. are those of the designer, V.D. Brenner of New York, and the single initial will be, it is considered, a sufficient recognition of his work.

This decision created much surprise, as the Treasury Department announced yesterday that the new coins would be in circulation for the present at least, and that the use of the initials on them was in line with a custom that had prevailed for years. This prominence, however, awakened widespread criticism, and today's action followed further consideration of the matter.

Mr. MacVeagh said today that he did not know that the initials would appear in embossed form on the pennies, and that he was surprised when he saw them. It has been customary to allow designers to cut initials into the design somewhere, but they have usually been so small as to require a magnifying glass to discover them.

Sub-Treasury is Besieged
Reserves Called to Handle Crowds

With the Lincoln cent craze two days old, the Sub-Treasury yesterday was cleaned out of its supply and had to send hurried calls to Washington for reinforcements. All day long, from the time the office opened, a constant string of men and boys filed into the building where the shiny little "V.D.B." coins were being doled out in exchange for other currency.

So great did the crush become to Pine Street, from Nassau to William Street, that the police reserves had to be called out. They were obliged eventually to establish lines at either end of the street.

They Will Drop Two Initials and Show Only "B."
Designer Brenner Displeased.

While this "run on the Treasury" was going on, the news of Secretary MacVeagh's decision to stop the minting of any more coins with the initials of the artist, Victor D. Brenner, was received. Mr. Brenner was greatly cast down when he heard of it. At his studio, at 114 Twenty-Eighth Street, he declared that a serious injustice would be done him if the Secretary's order was carried out.

"If I find that this order has gone forth," said Mr. Brenner, "I shall write to Mr. MacVeagh about it. He should consult me before doing anything of the sort. It is a courtesy that is due me. . . .

"When my design was accepted by the Treasury, my full name was upon the coin. Secretary Cortelyou, with whom I had my dealings, assured me that my name should remain upon it. Mr. Leach of the Mint at Philadelphia understood this, too. When I received the first die of the coin, my name was there; just as I had engraved it. They sent me another die later, and on this my initials appeared instead of the whole name. I thought that was an exceedingly peculiar thing for them to do, but I decided to say nothing.

"Now that they are going to cut down the initials to one, I feel that I have a right to object. Why should they deny this courtesy to me? On all the coins with the exception of the cent with the Indian head the sculptor's initials have been allowed. You will find the initials of Saint-Gaudens upon the $20 and $10 gold pieces, and those of Bela Lyon Pratt upon the $5 and $2.50 pieces. Upon the silver dollars there is the initial 'M,' and on all other silver coins the initial 'B.'

"I am delighted," Mr. Brenner added, "that so much attention has been directed to the new cents. That pleases me, but the taking of my initials off takes half the satisfaction away."

Cents Sell Three for a Nickel, But They Are Not Worth It

Not in the history of the Sub-Treasury has there been a more feverish scramble to exchange money than has been witnessed since the Mint turned out these new cents. Wall Street, as it looked on yesterday, recalled the excitement about some of the institutions which suspended payment during the panic of two years ago.

While those who sought the brilliant little coins were impelled by the expectation that the cents, if mintage was stopped, would someday be worth infinitely more than their face value, numismatic experts coldly figured that the collectors were only fooling themselves. B.L. Belden, Director of the American Numismatic Society, calculated that, possibly in 25 years each of the coins might be worth 5 cents. The danger of a shortage in supply, however, has been minimized, he said, by the fact that 2,000,000 of them have been minted, and professional collectors have gathered up all they want of them.

The Sub-Treasury officials early in the day found themselves overwhelmed by the crowds. They soon found it necessary to close up two of the windows facing the corridor and place on them placards reading: "Positively no Lincoln pennies here."

Only at one window were the coins dished out, and most of those who received them stationed themselves at street corners to sell them. Three for 5 cents was the market price. "Here you are, three Lincoln cents for a nickel" was the call heard all over town.

Banks felt the demand upon them for the "V.D.B." issue, and the drain became so great by noon that the bank supply by the Sub-Treasury was limited to $10 lots. Even then just before closing hour the last cent had been passed over the counter. Exact figures were not obtainable, but it was stated that the Sub-Treasury on Wednesday received 300,000 cents and another allotment came in early yesterday morning.

A clerk in a Pine Street banking house was arrested by one of the police reserves while standing on the steps of his office. When he was told to move on he replied he had a right [to be] there. The lieutenant at the John Street Station, which heard the complaint, promptly ordered his release and lectured the policeman for having arrested him.

A cigar firm, which has a number of branches in the city, sent batches of the new cents to its stores yesterday morning, telling the clerks to give them to customers who asked for them in change. It was not long before the news got out, and the clerks were kept hard at it issuing "V.D.B." coins until the supply was exhausted. It did not take long.

Coinage was halted after August 4, and no more cents were struck until about August 12.

In fact, Treasury Secretary Franklin MacVeagh *had* seen and approved of the V.D.B. initials earlier, as revealed by the memorandum sent by Assistant Secretary of the Treasury C.D. Norton to MacVeagh, from a meeting held with Barber in Washington on the afternoon of August 6, 1909:

> Mr. Barber . . . of the Philadelphia Mint is here, and I should be glad to have you meet him before he returns to Philadelphia, if possible.
>
> The first issue of the Lincoln coin was exactly similar to the present issue except that the Lincoln head was placed near the top of the coin, and more of the bust was showing, and there was no motto "In God We Trust." In the second and final edition, the only change was that the head was brought nearer to the center of the coin, part of the shoulders were cut off, and the motto "In God We Trust" was set above.
>
> On the reverse side there has been no change. V.D.B.'s initials were in the samples which were showed to you and the president [Taft], Mr. Barber states. . . .[169]

BEHIND THE SCENES

The *Times* story of "widespread criticism" about the use the V.D.B. initials may have been something related in a communication from the Treasury Department, or there may have been another source. None of the dozens of newspaper accounts read by numismatic researcher Q. David Bowers, published before August 5, reveal any such dissatisfaction. Later, much folklore was invented surrounding the incident, stating that the artist's initials constituted advertising for a private individual, or even that when the Treasury Department "discovered" Brenner was Jewish, this caused the change in their attitude toward the sculptor. None of this is reflected in any contemporary Treasury records or printed accounts seen by Bowers.

It seems that if Secretary of the Treasury Franklin MacVeagh had seen a coin prior to its release, he did not look at it carefully. Apparently clueless that the ASG monogram of Augustus Saint-Gaudens was currently appearing even more prominently on the obverse of $20 gold coins, he sought to find out why Brenner's initials had been allowed.

A letter from Philadelphia Mint Superintendent John H. Landis to Assistant Secretary of the Treasury C.D. Norton, August 4, 1909, stated:

> As requested in your communication over the telephone this morning I have investigated the matter of the designer's initials on the Lincoln cent and find they were authorized by the Director of the Mint in his letter of February 27, 1909, a copy of which I enclose. The design, as completed, was approved by the Honorable Secretary of the Treasury and the Director of the Mint July 15, 1909, a copy of which is also enclosed.

A cartoon in *The Numismatist,* combined issue of September and October 1909, mocks the inconsistency of attitudes toward Brenner's initials as opposed to Saint-Gaudens's.

I would say that it was proposed that the initial of Mr. Brenner's last name only be used, but as this was the same as that on the present subsidiary silver coins designed by Mr. Barber, it was not distinctive enough and the three initials had to be used.

All the United States coins, with the exception of the eagle and the five-cent nickel piece, have the initials or monogram of the designer upon them.

The information that all current coins except two designs had the engraver identified seems to have made no difference to MacVeagh. He still had a problem with V.D.B. On the August 5 Assistant Secretary of the Treasury Norton wrote to his boss:

The letter B could be engraved in the mother die easily, but The V.D.B. cannot be erased from the mother die because it is intaglio. To make a new mother die with an inconspicuous B and without the V.D.B. would take at least fourteen days.

This delay can be avoided by simply erasing the V.D.B. from the hub and having no B whatever on the coin. From the amended hub the coinage dies can be rapidly and promptly struck off within three days and the mint can continue the coinage of the pennies for which there is a great demand (and in which there is a great profit to the government).

Mr. Barber favors cutting off the initials and leaving them off entirely. This is not unusual as there are no initials on the five-cent piece and formerly there were no initials on the eagle, half eagle or quarter eagle. On the other hand it is not unusual to have an initial show on a coin. St. Gaudens' initials appear on the gold pieces, Pratt's in the half eagle and quarter eagle, etc. I have before me a French five-franc piece coined in 1870 on which Barre's full name appears. On another piece coined in 1831, the name E.A. Oudine appears. An Italian 20 centime piece bears the full name of both the engraver and designer.

There are two reasons why Mr. Barber favors erasing the initials from the new penny; first, because it involves a delay of only three days in coining operations instead of a delay of about fourteen days. Second, because if the B is placed in an inconspicuous place, he fears that it may be confused with the B which now appears on the half-dollar which was engraved by himself. He is not willing to be held personally responsible for the Lincoln penny which he has always opposed and does not regard as a successful coin.

During the first two weeks of August, 1909, newspapers across the country told of the distribution of the new Lincoln cent. Selected accounts reflect the excitement, some mentioning the artist's V.D.B. initials. This lengthy and especially detailed account is from the *Washington Post*, August 5, 1909:

New Cents Will Stay

Not to Be Called in Because of Designer's Initials

Precedent in Other Coins: All Except the Old Penny and the Nickel Give Credit to the Artist. Treasury Besieged by Mob Clamoring for Lincoln Penny, But It is Said There Will Be Enough for All.

The demand for the new Lincoln cent almost has reached the stages of a frenzy throughout the country. In Washington it has assumed mob-like proportions, because of a false report that the issue was to be recalled. Persons of all races, sexes, and ages have become seized with a wild speculative mania. The United States Treasury sustained a three-hour "run" yesterday, unprecedented for tumult, and in all 80,000 of the ornate coins were given out—$800 worth.

From all the sub-treasuries of the country requests poured in on the Philadelphia Mint for new supplies of the coinage. The San Francisco Mint is making a small quantity, about $5,000 so far, for the Pacific slope, but the rest of the country is being supplied from Philadelphia. Two hundred and sixty thousand dollars of the pennies have been coined there, and the minting will continue. There is no prospect that there will be a shortage of supply.

According to the Treasury officials, the country gets excited over a new coin nowadays in a manner that must be described as nothing short of frenzy. In anticipation of the issue of the new pennies, orders have been flooding the Mint and Treasury offices.

Banks have joined in the clamorous appeal, for to them it is becoming an important business advantage to be able to supply customers with shining new money.

About 3,000 persons, boys and old men predominating, were awarded allotments yesterday. They began coming in large numbers shortly before 11:00 and kept surging and clamoring until the gates were promptly closed at 2:00.

Doorkeeper Kept Busy

"In all my years on this post I never have seen the like," complained the veteran doorkeeper when 2:00 finally came and he could "shoo" the newsboys away. "I have had to stand here for hours fighting people off. I wonder what's the matter with the people, anyway? They're getting crazy. I haven't had a chance to get a bite to eat, and I am completely worn out."

The mob about the corridor and steps was at times 600 strong, desperately struggling to get to the window where the coins were issued. At first all was tumult, for it had never been dreamed that police regulation would be necessary. It was soon seen, however, that system must be established, and a line of the penny applications was formed from the window, stretching, serpent-like, up and down the long corridor and out to the steps in front of the main entrance.

Boys at once set up a thriving business. The gatekeeper and Treasury officials had to accord them the same rights as any other citizen of the land, and as they could burrow through the crowd they got to the window first. Then they went out into the mob and began selling the coins to those who saw that it was impossible for them to reach the disbursing window in reasonable time. The rates fluctuated, from 3 cents to 5 cents each, the latter being the prevailing price. About 400 persons who were turned away when the doors were closed at 2:00 afforded a harvest for the youthful speculators.

Eager for Speculation

Aged men also were numerous in the throng. One of them came rushing up, perspiring and breathless, demanding to be shown where he might get the new coins. When the inquiry was made of him why he was so frantically eager for the pennies, he replied, "Don't you know, they are going to sell for a big premium? I want to get $25 worth." He was very much crestfallen when informed that not more than 25 pennies could be had, by one applicant.

From an office with a large working force came a young man. His fellow-employees had entrusted to him to get a supply of the new pennies. His role of purchasing agent did not work, however. He got 25 pennies for himself, but the rest of the office force must go to the Treasury in person.

It was explained yesterday that the Treasury has an abundant supply of the coins, or can easily provide itself from the Philadelphia Mint. The chief difficulty it has to contend with is the unpacking of the pennies from the kegs in which they come, and the sealing up in the little envelopes, the working force not being adequate for a penny-mad populace.

There is a strong demand for coins fresh from the mint, but the erroneous report that the new pennies would be withdrawn from circulation because the initials of the designer, Victor D. Brenner, appear on them, added greatly to the excitement in Washington. Such action would at once have sent them up to a high premium among coin collectors, and it was at once made apparent that a large part of Washington's population is keenly alert to pick up easy money. Unfortunately, the highly built hopes must be dashed to the ground, for the government is going to continue minting the pennies in abundant supply.

Designers Receive Credit

Almost all the coins in circulation bear the initials of the designers, the nickel and old penny being the only exceptions. Look at the handsome throat of the goddess, where it begins to taper off on the dime, and you will use the letter B. That is the initial of Barber, the designer. The 25-cent and 50-cent pieces bear the same stamp, showing the same authorship. On the dollar the letter M is to be found—Morgan being its designer. The $5 and $2.50 pieces carry the initials of Bigelow [*sic*; should be Bela Lyon] Pratt down to posterity, and the $10 and $20 coins are initialed by Saint-Gaudens.

The practice of giving designers credit for their work, just as painters affix their names, began in 1849, when the letter L first appeared on a double eagle, a man named Longacre then being the chief designer for the mint. . . .

The Mint authorities do not undertake to account for the remarkable interest that is taken throughout the country for new coins. In part, it is explained by the demand of fashionable women in the large cities to be supplied with clean, undefiled coin at the banks. Many bankers, therefore, are sending to the mints for new issues, even though forced to pay the expense of expressage. The sub-treasuries in the respective cities could furnish plenty of coin without this extra cost, but when milady imperiously throws back a money piece that has gathered a trifle of filth from circulation and makes the demand, "Oh, give me some new money," her desires must be gratified, just as it is always good policy to cater to the wishes of business customers.

Procured Clean Money

A New York bank ran out of clean, untainted money recently, and it found that it could obtain a supply of the shining, spick and span variety only at the New Orleans Mint. Though the cost of this long-distance expressage was considerable, the bank unhesitatingly sent on for the money, in order to satisfy the requirements of patrons.

Connecticut is said to be the only state from which no demand for freshly made coin has come, the explanation ventured being that up there the people are eager for any kind of coin, so long as it is coin of the realm.

The Treasury has a postal card prepared for answering inquiries in numismatics, and it is set forth that "no coins of the United States have been called in." The nearest thing to this was the suspension of the Saint-Gaudens double eagles, which was found necessary because they could not be stacked.

New Yorkers Seek Coins

New York, Aug. 4. Wall Street found diversion today in the sight of a line of applicants for the new Lincoln pennies, which stretched from the door of the United States Sub-Treasury. A report that the coins might be withdrawn from circulation because of the questioned legality of the issue with the initials of the designer upon the face [*sic*] of the coin, drew the coin collectors to the financial district in swarms.

Not more than a dollar's worth was given each applicant, and a premium was demanded by the possessors of the bright, new 1-cent pieces, in the belief that official action might result in making the coins comparatively rare.

Assistant Treasurer Terry said today that his attention had been directed to the matter, but that he had received no instructions from Washington to discontinue the distribution of the pennies.[170]

Coinage was halted after August 4, and no more cents were struck until about August 12.

BRENNER'S REACTION

Brenner reacted unfavorably, as the August 5 *New York Times* article mentioned, but he revealed that an alteration had been made to the cent that was even more important to him. This reflects that he had not seen an example of the new cent prior to its official release. Also on August 5, he wrote this to Abram Piatt Andrew, Mint director designate, the successor to Landis:

Much has been said for and against my initials on the Lincoln cent, and as the designer of same, it was natural for me to express indignation to their being taken off. In reality there is a feature in the new cent which was brought in without my knowledge, and which concerns me most. Lincoln's bust in my design was to touch the edge of the coin. In the minted cents, the bust is separated from the border. This feature makes my coin lose much of its artistic beauty.

I beg you Sir, before more cents are minted, and before new dies are made, to kindly consider, and advise.

On August 7, MacVeagh directed that the V.D.B. initials be removed from the design, without mentioning anything in relation to Brenner's other concerns.

AUGUST *12, 1909*

Mint correspondence reveals that Chief Engraver Charles E. Barber had barely tolerated the "intrusion" of outside artist Brenner into the Mint domain of designing coins, following in the footsteps of the much-detested, by Barber, Augustus Saint-Gaudens. As noted earlier, Barber acquiesced to letting Brenner complete the work to avoid more criticism for interfering with other artists. Barber was viewed as incompetent or worse by much of the community of medal sculptors and by most numismatists. Hence this poignant comment about Barber given in the August 5 letter to MacVeagh on page 364: "He is not willing to be held personally responsible for the Lincoln penny which he has always opposed and does not regard as a successful coin."

This reveals that Barber's unfavorable view of the Lincoln cent must have been well known within the Treasury Department in Washington, not just inside the Mint in Philadelphia. It must have been an especially bitter pill when, soon, numismatic catalogs and *The Numismatist* praised Brenner's new cent to the skies.

In August 1909, at their annual convention, members of the American Numismatic Association passed a resolution protesting the removal of the V.D.B. initials. Over the next several months, articles pointed out the inconsistency of MacVeagh's decision to do so.

Brenner sent this letter on August 12 to Farran Zerbe, president of the American Numismatic Association:

It is mighty hard for me to express my sentiments with reference to the initials on the cent. The name of the artist on a coin is essential for the student of history as it enables him to trace environments and conditions of the time said coin was produced. Much fume has been made about my initials as a means of advertisement; such is not the case. The very talk the initials has brought out has done more good for numismatics than it could do me personally. The cent not alone represents in part my art, but it represents *the type of art of our period*.

The conventionalizing of the sheaves of wheat was done by me with much thought and I feel that with the prescribed wording no better design could be obtained. The cent will wear out two of the last ones in time, due entirely to the hollow surface.

The original design had *Brenner* on it, and that was changed to the initials. Of course the issue rests with the numismatic bodies, and Europe will watch the outcome with interest.[171]

On the same day, August 12, Superintendent Landis sent 100 of the new V.D.B.-less cents to Director Leach, indicating that production of the revised version was underway by that time.

In Europe the October issue of *The Numismatic Circular*, published by Spink & Son, carried a request from Horatio R. Storer, M.D., of Newport, Rhode Island, that the matter be brought up for vote at the next meeting of the British Numismatic Society. Comments from Storer were quoted:

Probably through professional jealousy, the propriety of Mr. V.D. Brenner's initials appearing upon it was challenged . . . My own opinion is that for an artist to attach his initials or signature on coins or medals has the same advantage as for a painter to place his name upon the canvas. In both instances, the historical interest is increased, the pecuniary worth enhanced, and the standards of the ideal conception and mechanical execution materially advanced.

CHANGES AND EVOLUTION OF THE DESIGN

In August 1909 the controversial V.D.B. initials were dropped.

The next design change took place in 1918 when the tiny incuse or intaglio V.D.B. letters were added to the bottom edge of the Lincoln portrait on the obverse, a modification that hardly anyone noticed and which drew no complaints. These letters were sharpened in 1921.

In 1943 copper was a strategic metal needed for munitions and other ordnance in World War II. In this year the composition of the Lincoln cent was changed to zinc-coated steel. This proved to be unsatisfactory, as the cents became dull and stained and, beyond that, some users mistook them for dimes.

Thought was given in 1952 to redesigning the obverse of the Lincoln cent, and models and galvanos were made adapting a model made in 1911 by James Earle Fraser, but no serious consideration was given to the idea.

The new third Philadelphia Mint which was occupied beginning in 1901.

Finally, in 1959, the 50th anniversary of the Lincoln cent, a new reverse by assistant engraver Frank Gasparro was adopted. Featured was a front view of the Lincoln Memorial with the artist's initials in tiny letters at the lower right.

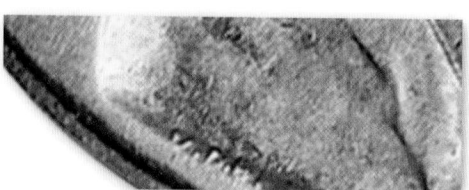

The V.D.B. initials on the shoulder of a Lincoln cent of 1918.

A 1952 proposal for redesigning the obverse of the Lincoln cent, adopting a model by James Earle Fraser made in 1911. This design bears the same inscriptions, arranged differently, and Lincoln facing to the left.

The coining room at the Philadelphia Mint. Lincoln cents were struck on knuckle-action presses.

One of various galvanos made in 1958 to test the radius, curvature (basining), and other aspects of the new reverse introduced in 1959. This is #1 per the inscriptions on the border of the galvano (shown in detail view).

REVIEW OF THE DESIGN

In his book *Numismatic Art in America*, Cornelius Vermeule, the foremost numismatic art critic of the 20th century, gave this review of the Lincoln, Wheat Ears Reverse, cent:

> Brenner, a pupil of Louis-Oscar Roty (1846–1911) in Paris, had instructed at the coin- and medal-designing and die-cutting class in 1901–1902 that opened at the National Academy under the direction of the Academy of Design and the American Numismatic and Archaeological Society. Morey wrote that there was a 'rare combination of qualities of good relief in miniature in Brenner's work, namely, clear contours that nevertheless coax the light and shade, and an economy of forms with sufficient area left to the unworked field.'[172]
>
> These characteristics are visible in the tiny tondo of the cent, a durable coin because Brenner cleverly made the surfaces slightly convex with a raised rim. He succeeded in conveying the feeling that a photograph of Lincoln has been turned into a three-dimensional experience in metal. An aura of impressionism hovers about the hair and beard, and presentation of the subject in everyday dress seems natural enough. Photographic realism is itself a major numismatic advance, but when it is taken in connection with a famous person in everyday clothing a giant stride has been made away from the Greco-Roman or neo-Pheidian French Libertys of the earlier coinage.
>
> Brenner's reverse, simple lettering flanked by ears of grain, took much thought on the part of the artist, as his correspondence reveals, and this modest design served well until the 150th anniversary of Lincoln's birth when it was replaced by Frank Gasparro's reverse showing the mausoleum-like Lincoln Memorial in full frontal view.

PROOF LINCOLN CENTS

Proof Lincoln cents for collectors have been made intermittently since the advent of the design in 1909. These were sold at a premium as part of a minor Proof set that also included a nickel five-cent piece. From the outset Proofs were made with a matte or satin finish inspired by medals made at the Paris Mint in the 19th century. Matte Proof finishes in slight variations were made first on Assay Commission medals at the Philadelphia Mint. Beginning in 1908 a Sand Blast Proof finish was given to gold coins, after which, in 1909 and 1910, a Satin Proof finish was employed, followed by a reversion to Sand Blast Proof for gold coins of 1911 to 1915. These gold-coin finishes were never used on lower denominations.

Beginning early in 1909 continuing through midsummer, cent Proofs with a mirror finish were made of the Indian Head design. Matte Proof 1909 V.D.B., cents were available to collectors beginning in August. Their distribution was erratic at best, especially after the design was altered to eliminate the initials. Requests from collectors and dealers were mostly ignored. Likely, many if not most 1909 V.D.B. Matte Proofs were destroyed or, as some have suggested, put into circulation. Whatever the scenario, such Proofs are rare today. Matte Proof cents continued in production through and including 1916, in which year only 600 were struck. This Proof style was very unpopular with collectors and dealers, and many complaints were raised regarding the finish, but to no avail.

When issued, Matte Proofs were wrapped in thin, rather stiff tissue paper. This caused them to tone to brown or brown with hints of blue. Most Matte Proofs in existence today retain this color—dipped coins and very few originals excepted.

A Matte Proof 1916 cent, from the last year this Proof format was used.

In 1936, after a lapse of 20 years, Proof cents were again struck. These were of the mirror-field style and were available singly or as part of five-coin sets, the latter selling for $1.81. Certain early strikes of the year 1937 have a somewhat satiny appearance. Production of Proofs was halted after 1942 due to the war effort.

A Mirror Proof 1936 cent with all devices, including the portrait, polished in the dies.

In 1950 Proofs became available again, only as part of five-coin sets for $2.10. These continued the mirror style. Certain early 1950 coins are somewhat satiny. Production continued through the end of the Lincoln, Wheat Ears Reverse, design.

Some scattered Lincoln, Wheat Ears Reverse, Proofs since 1950 can be found with Cameo or frosted contrast on the higher points, and can command sharp premiums.

GRADING STANDARDS

Caveat: These grading standards do not take sharpness of strike into account.

MS-60 to 70 (Mint State). *Obverse and Reverse:* At MS-65 and higher, the luster is rich on all areas, except perhaps the shoulder (which may be grainy and show original planchet surface). There is no rubbing, and no contact marks are visible except under magnification. Coins with full or nearly full mint orange-red color can be designated RD; those with full or nearly full brown-toned surfaces can be designated BN; and those with a sub-

1909-S, V.D.B. Graded MS-64RB.

stantial percentage of red-orange and of brown can be called RB. Ideally, MS-65 or finer coins should have good eye appeal, which in the RB category means nicely blended colors, not stained or blotched. Below MS-65, full RD coins become scarce, and at MS-60 to 62 they are virtually non-existent, unless they have been dipped. Copper is a very active metal, and influences that define the grade—such as slight abrasions, contact marks, and so on—also affect the color. The ANA grading standards allow for "dull" and/or "spotted" coins at MS-60 and 61, as well as incomplete luster. In the marketplace, interpretations often vary widely. BN and RB coins at MS-60 and 61 are apt to be more attractive than (dipped) RD coins.

Illustrated coin: The rose-orange color of this cent is better than is usually expected for a coin graded Red Brown. Note some toning streaks on the obverse, lighter than the surrounding surfaces, across Lincoln's forehead and nose.

AU-50, 53, 55, 58 (About Uncirculated). *Obverse:* Slight wear shows on Lincoln's cheekbone to the left of his nose, and also on his beard. At AU-55 or 58 there may be some hints of mint red-orange. Most coins in About Uncirculated are BN, but they are seldom designated by color. *Reverse:* Slight wear is evident on the stalks of wheat to the left and right. Otherwise, the same standards apply as for the obverse.

1920-S. Graded AU-58.

EF-40, 45 (Extremely Fine). *Obverse:* Light wear is seen on Lincoln's portrait, and hair detail is gone on the higher areas, especially above the ear. *Reverse:* Light wear is seen overall, but the parallel lines in the wheat stalks are clearly separated.

1914-D. Graded EF-45.

VF-20, 30 (Very Fine). *Obverse:* Lincoln's portrait is worn all over, with most hair detail gone at the center. Hair separation is seen at the back and the top of the head, but hairs are blended together. The jaw outline is clear. The center of the ear is defined and the bowtie is clear. The date and lettering is sharp. *Reverse:* More wear is seen, but still the lines in the wheat stalks are separated. Lettering shows wear but is very clear.

   Illustrated coin: This coin features even wear and few marks.

1922-D, No D. Graded VF-20.

F-12, 15 (Fine). *Obverse:* More wear is seen overall. Hair definition is less. The center of the ear is partially visible. The jaw outline and bowtie are clear. *Reverse:* Most lines in the wheat stalks are either weak or blended with others, but more than half of the separating lines are clear.

   Illustrated coin: Other than one deep contact mark in the cheek, the surfaces are smooth.

1922-D, No D. Graded F-15.

VG-8, 10 (Very Good). *Obverse:* The portrait is more worn, with only slight hair strands visible (thick strands blended). The ear opening is visible. The bowtie and jacket show fewer details. *Reverse:* The lines in the wheat stalks are blended together in flat areas. Perhaps 40% to 50% of the separating lines can be seen. The rim may be weak in areas.

1909-S. Graded VG-10.

G-4, 6 (Good). *Obverse:* The portrait is well worn. Some slight details are seen at the top of the head and the bottom of the coat. LIBERTY is weak. The rim may touch or blend with the tops of the letters forming IN GOD WE TRUST. The date and mintmark (if any) are very clear. *Reverse:* The wheat stalks are flat, with just a few scattered details visible.

1914-D. Graded G-6.

AG-3 (About Good). *Obverse:* Wear is extensive. The portrait is mostly in outline form, with only scattered details visible. LIBERTY is weak and perhaps with some letters missing. IN GOD WE TRUST blends in with the rim, and several letters are very weak or missing. *Reverse:* The rim is worn down to blend with the outside of the wheat stalks in some areas, although some hints of the edge of the stalks can be seen. Lettering is weak, with up to several letters missing.

1913-D. Graded AG-3.

PF-60 to 70 (Matte Proof). *Obverse and Reverse:* At the Matte PF-65 level or higher there are no traces of abrasion or contact marks. Color will range from brown (BN)—the most common—to brown with significant tinges of mint red-orange (RB), or with much mint color (RD). Most RD coins have been dipped. Some tiny flecks are normal on coins certified as PF-65 but should be microscopic or absent above that. Coins in the PF-60 to 63 range are BN or sometimes RB—almost impossible to be RD unless dipped. Lower-grade Proofs usually have poor eye appeal.

1909, V.D.B. Matte Proof. Graded PF-68RD.

Illustrated coin: Most of the red tint is medium orange, but there is a faint pink tint to the upper-left obverse.

PF-60 to 70 (Mirror Proof). *Obverse and Reverse:* PF-65 and higher coins are usually RB (colors should be nicely blended) or RD, the latter with bright red-orange fading slightly to hints of brown. Some tiny flecks are normal on coins certified as PF-65 but should be microscopic or absent above that. PF-60 and 61 coins can be dull, stained, or spotted but still have some original mint color. Coins with fingerprints must be given a low numerical grade. Lower-grade Proofs usually have poor eye appeal.

1936. Mirror Proof. Graded PF-66RD.

Illustrated coin: The mirrored surfaces are free of blemish.

Lincoln, Wheat Ears Reverse, Cents of 1909

KEYS TO COLLECTING: Cents of the inaugural year in the Lincoln series have always been popular. The focus is on the 1909-S V.D.B. cent the most famous "popular rarity" among 20th-century coins. Enough examples are around to satisfy demand, which is such that these are expensive in all grades. The Philadelphia version is common and is affordable in high grades—a popular coin for inclusion in type sets. Generally, cents of this year are well struck and have excellent eye appeal.

1909, V.D.B. • **Circulation-strike mintage:** 27,995,000.

Availability in Mint State: *MS–60 to 64:* Hundreds of thousands of examples exist in these grades. *MS-65 and higher:* Countless thousands of examples exist in these grades. Mostly these are BN and RB coins, but thousands of RD coins have been certified, and hundreds have been certified at the MS-67RD level. Above that grade, RD coins are rarities.

Availability in circulated grades: This issue is very common in circulated grades, including in VF to AU. Some of these high-grade circulated coins were saved at the time of issue and then spent years later.

Characteristics of striking: Most examples are well struck with Full Details, with excellent definition of Lincoln's hair, the lettering, and other features. Some have the V.D.B. initials weakly defined, usually at the top of the letters. Coins displaying this weakness should be avoided. David W. Lange reports, "1909 V.D.B. and 1909-S V.D.B. cents have higher, broader rims than do the initial-less cents that replaced them, a fact that becomes very evident on worn pieces, as these do not conform to standard grading descriptions."[173]

	Cert	Avg	%MS	G-4	VG-8	F-12	VF-20	EF-40	AU-50	MS-60BN	MS-63BN	MS-65RD
1909, V.D.B.	11,231	63.4	96%	$15	$16	$17	$18	$19	$20	$25	$30	$165

1909, V.D.B., Proof • Proof mintage:

1,194; however, as few as 420 may have left the Mint, while the remainder were destroyed and the copper recoined without the V.D.B. initials. See the following Proof commentary for more discussion.

Proof commentary: Proofs of this year are of the grainy or Matte Proof style, struck from dies the faces of which were lightly etched—completely unlike the mirror Proofs in the predecessor Indian Head cent series. The rims on both the obverse and reverse are perfectly flat (not rounded) and do not have the matte finish. Viewed edge-on, the edges are *mirrorlike*, unlike circulation strikes. Today, since most examples are encapsulated, you need to take the word of a grading service that a Matte Proof is indeed such. At the same time Q. David Bowers recommends that you only buy a coin certified by one of the top several services, and then have it checked by another expert.

As to the frequency of misattributed "Matte Proofs," this comment was given regarding lot 375 in New Netherlands' 51st sale, in June 1958: "Nine out of every ten offered will not stand up to critical examination." To the casual glance, many Matte Proofs do not look distinctive, and for this reason they were unpopular at the time of issue.

The mintage of the 1909 V.D.B. Matte Proof has been stated as 420 for many years. As researcher Roger W. Burdette and others have reported, figures for Proof mintage of this era, particularly for the cent, nickel, and gold coins, are subject to question. The mintage of 1,194 Matte Proofs has been suggested by Kevin Flynn. Although Mint data supports this suggestion, surviving examples, including the number seen by certification services, suggest that far fewer ever reached numismatic channels. Q. David Bowers suggests the most accurate estimate is much closer to the 420 figure earlier reported. Not long after these Proofs were struck Lyman H. Low wrote: "Minor Proof sets of the first issue of Lincoln cents cannot be had at the Mint. The supply of Proof cents of that issue is long since exhausted. There were only 420 of them made, and they are therefore rather rare."[174] To this can be added a modern comment by David W. Lange, a consummate student of Lincoln cents, "The gross mintage may have been 1,194 coins, but I suspect that the removal of the initials prompted the Mint to destroy more than half of the Proof Lincolns on hand, leaving the net distribution at or near the traditional figure of 420 pieces."[175]

Correspondence of the era reveals that collectors and dealers found it almost impossible to order Matte Proofs in early August 1909. It could be that distribution was suppressed and those on hand were destroyed or put into circulation.

A pristine (undipped) Matte Proof usually will have light-brown toning overall, but some have mint red-orange at the centers. Years ago coins with full *original* mint color were almost unheard of. Today, many have been certified. Any Matte Proof that is bright overall is virtually always a cleaned or dipped coin. Q. David Bowers has never seen an *original* bright, red-orange coin.

Laura Sperber and Q. David Bowers recently discussed certified coins that in some instances were selling for double list prices and in other instances for half, as holders give no indication concerning quality. Here, Sperber comments on a certain "low end" 1909 V.D.B. cent:

> Having been in the coin business for over 40 years and working to assemble one of the very finest collections ever, I can tell you, even in today's hard-charging, third party–grading dominated marketplace, quality really does matter. Even in the "slabs" today there is still high end and low end. There was just a 1909, VDB, Proof-66RB cent in an auction. It brought only $23,000 as it was a totally inferior coin. Had it been what the grade implied to intending bidders, it would have sold for an easy $50,000+. I can

tell you, in down or slower markets, all you ever see are the low-end coins. They become like rocks and are harder to trade. It does not matter if [the coin in question] is a common date or a classic rarity. My motto of 40 years, "There is no substitution for quality," has yet to be proven wrong.[176]

Notes: *Keys to collecting:* The 1909 V.D.B. cent is readily available in any and all grades from well-worn to gem Mint State, the latter usually appears with original orange color, either full or partial. Luster varies from frosty to matte, the latter often mistaken for Matte Proof finish. MS-65RD and higher certified coins abound, giving you a wide choice if you prefer to buy coins in certified holders. It is fortunate for collectors that this very short-lived type, certainly one of the greatest "story coins" in American numismatics, is the most affordable of all early Lincoln cents. There should be room for one in *every collection:* this is at the same time a landmark coin and inexpensive.

	Cert	Avg	%MS	PF-63RB	PF-64RB
1909, V.D.B., Proof	56	65.0		$5,500	$12,000

1909-S, V.D.B. • Circulation-strike
mintage: 484,000.

Availability in Mint State: *MS–60 to 64:* Many thousands of examples exist of this issue in these grades, but the unrelenting demand for this, the most famous Lincoln cent, has caused the market value to go onward and upward over a long period of years. Most Mint State coins have original color, which is a yellowish-orange (different in color from the Philadelphia version; David W. Lange calls the San Francisco coin "brassy") due to a slightly different alloy mix. The same distinctive color is seen on pristine (undipped) 1908-S cents and 1909-S Indian Head cents. On the other hand, a "RD" 1909-S V.D.B. that is orange, without the yellow tint, is most certainly likely to have been dipped and processed. There are quite a few of these dipped "beauties" around, including in certified holders. In all levels of Mint State the 1909-S V.D.B. is the most plentiful mintmark issue of its era, a record it does not yield until the late 1920s. It is much easier to find than the regular 1909-S, made later, although the regular 1909-S has a much higher mintage (see page 351). *MS-65 and higher:* Many thousands of examples exist in these grades. They are mostly BN and RB, although more than a thousand MS-65RD coins have been certified. At the MS-66RD level about 200 or so have been certified, and only a few have been certified in grades beyond that.

Availability in circulated grades: Probably 100,000 or more exist in grades from AG through VF, many of these having been plucked out of circulation after "penny boards" and albums became popular in the 1930s. Fewer are available in higher circulated grades such as EF and AU. This is the key issue among basic dates and mintmarks in the Lincoln cent series.

Characteristics of striking: The typical 1909-S V.D.B. cent is very well struck with Full Details, but some have the V.D.B. initials slightly weak, usually at the top. Avoid such weak coins. Sam Lukes relates an instance in which someone paid $92,000 for a slabbed MS-67RD example, although "the most important part of the coin, the designer's initials, were weakly struck and mushy."[177] This serves to illustrate that some people will buy just about anything if the label on a holder is appealing, never mind the coin itself! Likely, the typical reader of this book would get more enjoyment from paying $5,000 or so for an MS-65RD example with Full Details. Matters such as this provide lively points for discussion at coin club meetings and anywhere else that collectors gather.

The S mintmark punch on early San Francisco Lincoln cents has a tiny raised-dot flaw within the upper loop, noted David W. Lange. This S punch was used into 1917, when a slightly larger letter replaced it.

Notes: *Keys to collecting:* This is the be-all and end-all object of desire in the Lincoln cent series, the Holy Grail (as David W. Lange suggests). It is by no means the rarest Lincoln cent. Certain of the die varieties (although not basic dates and mintmarks) are more elusive.

Examples are available in just about any grade desired, although attractive well-worn coins in grades such as VF and EF are rarer than are AU and Mint State coins.

Caveat: There are thousands of fakes on the market. Some of these have been made by adding an S to a Philadelphia coin, but some are die struck. Insist on buying an example certified by one of several leading certification services. Avoid buying *any* "raw" 1909-S V.D.B. such as might be found on the Internet, or "from an old-time collection," etc.—and be suspicious of bargains!

Early numismatic sales: George J. Fuld told of a story from John Zug, the Bowie, Maryland, mail-order dealer, who stated that he obtained 25,000 examples at face value from the San Francisco Mint at the time of issue, then sold them around 1918 for 1-3/4¢ each. Although it is certain that John Zug, Henry Chapman, and some other dealers had working stocks of such pieces, Q. David Bowers is not aware of any single hoard running into the tens of thousands of pieces. If such an arrangement by Zug took place, it should be verifiable by Mint correspondence, none of which has come to light thus far to support his claim. Likely, Zug was simply telling a "big story," as old-time dealers liked to do.

In *The Numismatist*, July 1910, these and other cents of the era were offered in quantity:

> For Sale . . . Pennies in lots of 500 each kind. Lincoln V.D.B.-S, cir. and unc., 6¢; all unc., 8¢. Lincoln 1909-S, no initials, unc., 3¢; 1910 do., 2¢. Indian 1908-S, cir. and unc., 6¢; all unc., 8¢. Indian 1909-S, cir. and unc., 7¢; all unc., 10¢. In lots of 100 each kind 1¢ each additional. California Loan Office, Oakland, Cal.

Arthur M. Kagin related this anecdote to Q. David Bowers:

> In early 1952 I received an inquiry from a California collector asking for an offer on an Uncirculated roll of 1909-S, V.D.B., cents, I offered him $500 per roll. Each roll had 50 coins in it. About 10 days later five rolls arrived. About two weeks after sending him the check another five rolls arrived. In sending him the check I stated that I would buy all he had at the same price as I didn't want him to break the market by offering a large quantity at one time. About four or five months later a number of ads appeared in the *Numismatic Scrapbook Magazine* offering Uncirculated 1909-S V.D.B. cents at $12 to $15 each. Apparently, he had sold more rolls to other people.

	Cert	Avg	%MS	G-4	VG-8	F-12	VF-20	EF-40	AU-50	MS-60BN	MS-63BN	MS-65RD
1909-S, V.D.B. †	8,413	44.6	41%	$700	$800	$850	$900	$1,100	$1,200	$1,350	$1,500	$4,500

† Ranked in the *100 Greatest U.S. Coins* (fourth edition).

Varieties: *Mehl's Numismatic Monthly*, January 1916, included this from a correspondent:

> The variations of the late issues of one and five cent pieces was brought to my attention through the catalog of a dealer who priced two 1909 Lincoln V.D.B. cents of the S. mint, one of which had the S. mint mark under the 0 of the date and the other had the S between the first 9 and the 0. As a collector of the cent series and being in the part of the country where the S mint mark is most frequently seen, I began a search for the above two varieties with remarkable results. The number of different varieties that I found before I finally got the ones I originally started out to find have made a very large collection for me, not only in the Lincoln head but the Indian head cents as well.

1909 • Circulation-strike mintage: 72,702,618.

Availability in Mint State: *MS–60 to 64:* Most examples are brown in these grades, though some appear with original mint red. *MS-65 and higher:* This issue is very common in these grades, but many fewer examples exist than for the lower-mintage V.D.B. variety. Most examples are BN or RB. More than 1,000 MS-65RD examples and more than 500 MS-66RD examples have been certified. The top grade for this issue seems to be MS-67RD.

Availability in circulated grades: This issue is common in these grades. Most are in grades from G to VF.

Characteristics of striking: Striking is nearly always sharp for this issue.

	Cert	Avg	%MS	G-4	VG-8	F-12	VF-20	EF-40	AU-50	MS-60BN	MS-63BN	MS-65RD
1909	1,660	63.4	97%	$4	$5	$6	$7	$8	$12	$17	$20	$160

1909, Proof • Proof mintage: 2,618.

Proof commentary: Three obverse dies were used to coin Matte Proof cents of this variety, one of which had been used for the V.D.B. Two reverse dies were employed. Most examples are well struck and have Full Details *except for* minute planchet marks on the shoulder. These Proofs are scarce today. Most pristine (undipped) coins are a rich, light-brown color. Some have original red-orange color on one or both sides, but they are *never* fully brilliant in the experience of Q. David Bowers—never mind that many dozens have been certified as such. On December 16 Virgil M. Brand wrote to the secretary of the Treasury stating that he needed 100 each of the three Proof cent varieties of the year (Indian Head, the Lincoln cent with V.D.B., and the Lincoln cent without the initials) and had been ordering such sets in quantity for 20 years, with no problems. Always, Proofs of the types of a given year were available throughout the year, as in 1883 when there were three types of nickel five-cent pieces. Seemingly, however, Brand's request was ignored.[178]

	Cert	Avg	%MS	PF-63RB	PF-64RB	PF-65RD
1909, Proof	243	64.6		$675	$1,150	$2,700

1909-S • Circulation-strike mintage: 1,825,000.

Availability in Mint State: *MS–60 to 64:* This issue is scarce in any and all grades from well-worn to Mint State, in the context of the Lincoln series. Q. David Bowers has only seen one bank-wrapped roll offered for sale, and that was owned by David Nethaway in the 1950s. *MS-65 and higher:* MS-65RD and slightly higher-grade coins are easy enough to find and are usually quite attractive. The population tops out at MS-67RD. BN and RB coins are more plentiful in all grades than RD coins. Undipped coins will have a slightly yellowish tint, similar to the 1909-S V.D.B (see page 375).

Availability in circulated grades: This is one of the scarcer early varieties in circulated grades. Most examples are in grades from G to VF. Beginning in the 1930s, the low mintage of the regular 1909-S attracted many, who plucked them from circulation—initially in grades of Fine to VF and though such finds were worn down to G-4 if they were found in the early 1950s.

Characteristics of striking: This issue is usually very well struck with Full Details.

Notes: *Keys to collecting:* One of the obverse dies used on the 1909-S V.D.B. cents was also used for the 1909-S (without V.D.B.). Five obverse dies were used for the 1909-S. Some reverses show minute traces of the V.D.B. having been filed off.

	Cert	Avg	%MS	G-4	VG-8	F-12	VF-20	EF-40	AU-50	MS-60BN	MS-63BN	MS-65RD
1909-S	3,316	40.2	38%	$100	$110	$125	$150	$225	$250	$300	$350	$1,050

Varieties: *1909-S, Repunched Mintmark, S Over Seemingly Slightly Smaller S (FS-01-1909S-1501):* This variety can also be identified as CONECA 1909-S, RPM-001. Its rarity is URS-10. A clear, well-formed slightly earlier S was over-punched with a second S; the first S must have been from the same punch as the final S, because only one S punch was used this year.[179] The first S, not being deep in the die, appears to be smaller. The double-punched mintmark is very clearly defined under low magnification.

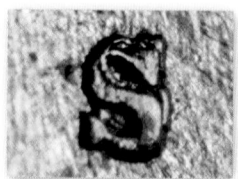

A detail of the repunched mintmark.

	VF-20	EF-40	AU-50	MS-60	MS-63	MS-65
FS-01-1909S-1501	$200	$300	$350	$400	$600	$850

1909-S, S Over Horizontal S •

Circulation-strike mintage: Included in 1909-S circulation-strike mintage.

Commentary: This variety's Fivaz-Stanton identification is FS-01-1909S-1502. It can also be identified as CONECA 1909-S, RPM-002. Its rarity is URS-12. Several hundred examples of this variety have been certified as MS-65RD, and dozens as MS-66RD. Although there are several varieties of 1909-S cents with repunched mintmarks, this one is particularly desirable, as the first S was punched in horizontally and then corrected. The variety was not publicized until the 1970s and is still not widely known today, although it is listed in the

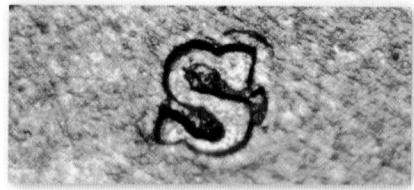

A detail of the repunched mintmark.

regular edition of the *Guide Book of United States Coins.* As the die continued in use, the undertype erroneous S became less visible. Find a decent strike, as most are, but don't hold out for perfection.

	Cert	Avg	%MS	G-4	VG-8	F-12	VF-20	EF-40	AU-50	MS-60BN	MS-63BN	MS-65RD
1909-S, S Over Horizontal S	549	50.4	64%	$110	$115	$135	$160	$235	$285	$340	$370	$1,250

Lincoln, Wheat Ears Reverse, Cents of 1910

KEYS TO COLLECTING: Cents of this date are common in worn grades. Mint State coins are plentiful as well. Evaluating populations of this or most any other Philadelphia Mint cent, remember that they are usually severely underreported, since these coins are not as valuable as the branch-mint issues.

Minting took place at Philadelphia and San Francisco. Large quantities of the 1909 cents with V.D.B. were spent, as the public tired of the novelty of holding onto examples of the design, and by now there were ample coins of the new design in circulation. Cent production in 1910 year reached a record of 152,846,218, the most of any year since copper cents were first struck in 1793. The record would be broken in 1916 and again multiple times after that.

VICE OF THE PENNY ARCADES: From *Leslie's Weekly New York Observer and Chronicle,* August 11, 1910:

> Wherever there is a 'penny arcade' in New York to-day there may be seen the vicious, insinuating placards, and, not infrequently, photographs that justify in a measure the curious expectations of the child who drops its penny in the slot. Statistics prove, furthermore, that this holds true in the majority of cities and towns in the United States where "penny arcades" obtain, and in Chicago, San Francisco and a hundred other cities of lesser size the penny-picture machines have been supplemented slyly, in an off corner, with five-cent machines, the exhibitions to be seen in which may not be described on clean white paper. . . .

EVA TANGUAY: From the Cleveland *Plain Dealer,* October 23, 1910:

> **Noisy Eva Throws Good Money Away:** The 'I don't care' idea has gone so far with Eva Tanguay that she is indulging in the uncommon habit of throwing away money. She has made special arrangements with the Philadelphia Mint authorities whereby she receives newly coined pennies each day which she throws to her audiences at the matinee and evening performances. She will continue the practice at B.F. Keith's Hippodrome next week.

Tanguay was the most prominent actress in vaudeville at the time. She described herself and her act as wild, a mixture of the risqué with the farcical. When singing *Oh, You Money* (a punning title), she would wear a jacket made of copper one-cent pieces, and from an additional supply throw hundreds of them into the audience. Her usual sign-off song, *I Don't Care What Happens to Me,* earned her the famous nickname, "the I Don't Care Girl." This and other suggestive titles such as *It's All Been Done Before But Not the Way I Do It* and *I Want Someone to Go Wild With Me* appealed to what the trade papers called "TBM" audiences, a term referring to the "tired business man" who after work slipped into a vaudeville or burlesque show for a change of pace before going home to his wife and kids.

1910, V.D.B.: A 1910 cent with barely discernible vestiges of the first 1909 V.D.B. die was described in *Coin World,* June 7, 2004.

1910 IN NUMISMATICS: The hobby of coin collecting was in an expansion phase, and a number of collectors and dealers emphasized that numismatics was at once relaxing, interesting, challenging, and a good store of value. High on the popularity list were colonial coins, early copper cents, patterns, tokens, and medals. Current issues of mintmarked coins attracted hardly any attention.

Coin collections and inventories were usually kept in paper envelopes measuring 2x2 inches square, in pill envelopes available from drugstores, in cabinets, or in drawer-lined safes. There were no albums or folders and would not be until the late 1920s, gaining wide popularity in the 1930s.

1910 • Circulation-strike mintage: 146,801,218.

Availability in Mint State: MS–60 to 64: This issue is common in these grades. **MS-65 and higher:** Coins that are MS-65RD or higher are scarce, numbering a little under 1,000 known. Most of these have original color.

Availability in circulated grades: This issue is very common in circulated grades in the context of early Lincoln cents.

Characteristics of striking: Nearly all examples are well struck on both the obverse and reverse. Coins with close to Full Details can be found for this and most early dates, *except* for graininess on Lincoln's shoulder. To find one with truly Full Details, some patience and the use of a medium-strength magnifying glass are all you need.

	Cert	Avg	%MS	G-4	VG-8	F-12	VF-20	EF-40	AU-50	MS-60BN	MS-63BN	MS-65RD
1910	1,217	63.4	95%	$0.35	$0.50	$1	$1.50	$4	$10	$18	$25	$230

1910, Proof • Proof mintage: 4,083.

Proof commentary: These are Matte Proofs. Most pristine (undipped) coins are a rich, light-brown color. Some have original red-orange color on one or both sides, but these are never fully brilliant—never mind that dozens of "RD gems" have been certified in recent decades. In the context of Matte Proofs, this is one of the more plentiful issues in the marketplace. The first delivery of Matte Proofs was on January 7, 1910, and consisted of 483 acceptable coins from 498 struck. The Mint is said to have kept quantities of these on hand after 1910, eventually selling them to dealers including William L. Pukall. *All* of these remainder coins were toned a rich brown with hints of blue, without exception.[180]

A unique-at-the-time Matte Proof 1910 cent with traces of V.D.B. on the reverse, discovered in 1991 by Bill Fivaz, sold for $2,400 in the Society of Lincoln Cent Collectors' 121st mail-bid sale in the mid-1990s. The reverse does not match that of other Matte Proof 1910 cents. It has abrasion lines near the lower rim (where the initials V.D.B. were on certain 1909 cents) and a spot congruent to the position where the reverse die used for Matte Proof 1909 V.D.B. cents had a die chip. It was graded PF-65BN by ANACS.

	Cert	Avg	%MS	PF-63RB	PF-64RB	PF-65RD
1910, Proof	244	64.2		$550	$1,100	$2,550

1910-S • Circulation-strike mintage: 6,045,000.

Availability in Mint State: *MS–60 to 64:* Mint State coins are seen with some frequency and usually have light toning. Carbon spots and flecks are usually not a problem, except on coins that were dipped decades ago and are now slightly retoned. A blazing gem with original color is scarce if it is also sharply struck, with good eye appeal. On such coins, the rims and edges will have light toning. Mint State coins with *original* color have distinctive hues. **MS-65 and higher:** Gems with good color and nice eye appeal are not rarities, but they require some effort to track down, in view of the great demand for them. Examples that are RD and with original color number in the hundreds—which is not many in relation to the demand for them. BN and RB coins are common. Bowers and Merena Galleries distributed a small hoard of 50 of these from a bank-wrapped roll in 1994.

Availability in circulated grades: This issue is slightly scarce in circulated grades in the context of the era.

Characteristics of striking: This issue is typically well struck, with the usual exception that some graininess can appear on Lincoln's shoulder.

Notes: *Keys to collecting:* Obverse mintmark positions vary slightly, as they do on all branch-mint coins Some 1910-S cents are said to have traces of a V.D.B. having been removed (*Walter Breen's Complete Encyclopedia of U.S. and Colonial Coins*, 1978); whether such pieces, if they exist, would stand up to modern scrutiny by experts can only be conjectured.

	Cert	Avg	%MS	G-4	VG-8	F-12	VF-20	EF-40	AU-50	MS-60BN	MS-63BN	MS-65RD
1910-S	1,277	57.1	77%	$17	$20	$22	$25	$45	$80	$100	$120	$635

Varieties: *1910-S, Repunched Mintmark (FS-01-1910S-501):* This variety can also be identified as CONECA 1910-S, RPM-001. Its rarity is URS-7. This 1910-S, Repunched Mintmark, variety is dramatically repunched, the earlier mintmark being partially visible in a slightly lower vertical position with enough traces remaining that the horizontal elements of the undertype are very distinct. Most are in circulated grades.

A detail of the repunched mintmark.

1910-S, Repunched Mintmark (FS-01-1910S-502): This variety can also be identified as CONECA 1910-S, RPM-002. Its rarity is URS-8. This is a companion to the preceding variety. This 1910-S, Repunched Mintmark, variety is dramatically repunched, the earlier mintmark being partially visible in a slightly higher vertical position with enough traces remaining that the horizontal elements of the undertype are very distinct. Most examples of this variety are in circulated grades.

A detail of the repunched mintmark.

	VF-20	EF-40	AU-50	MS-60	MS-63	MS-65
FS-01-1910S-501	$50	$75	$125	$150	$200	$500
FS-01-1910S-502	$40	$50	$95	$125	$175	$450

Lincoln, Wheat Ears Reverse, Cents of 1911

KEYS TO COLLECTING: Lincoln cents of this year are usually attractive, although exceptions occur in some grades and mintmarks, as noted in the following entries. Sharp striking is the rule.

DENVER COINAGE: In 1911 the Denver Mint, a facility that had opened in 1906, struck Lincoln cents for the first time, inaugurating a policy (which would continue for decades with some exceptions) of striking cents at three mints each year. Coinage continued in San Francisco.

DIE LIFE IN SAN FRANCISCO: The superintendent of the San Francisco Mint reported, "The life of a die for one-cent pieces is about 150,000 coins." Uncirculated coins were available directly from the Mint to interested collectors for face value plus a nominal postage and handling charge.

The Denver Mint.

1911 • **Circulation-strike mintage:** 101,177,787.

Availability in Mint State: *MS–60 to 64:* This is one of the more plentiful issues of this series in these grades. Most examples are BN or RB. *MS-65 and higher:* This issue is available easily enough in these grades, with hundreds known. RD coins without stains or flecks are elusive.

Availability in circulated grades: This issue is common in circulated grades. Most examples are G to VF.

Characteristics of striking: Striking varies for this issue from quite sharp, including the shoulder of Lincoln—these being Full Details coins—to fairly sharp, with some original graininess on Lincoln's shoulder (but other features well defined), to light in areas. A sharp one can be found without great difficulty.

	Cert	Avg	%MS	G-4	VG-8	F-12	VF-20	EF-40	AU-50	MS-60BN	MS-63BN	MS-65RD
1911	671	63.4	96%	$0.45	$0.65	$1.50	$2.50	$6	$11	$21	$50	$400

1911, Proof • **Proof mintage:** 1,725.

Proof commentary: At least two qualities of surface exist on Matte Proof cents of this year: some are more satiny, and later examples are less so. Most pristine (undipped) coins are a rich, light-brown color. Some have original red-orange color on one or both sides, but these are never fully brilliant, although about three dozen have been certified as PF-65RD or higher—some of which might be duplicate listings of the same particular coin. An example from the Bowers and Merena, Inc., sale of the Walter H. Childs Collection, August 30, 1999, lot 78, was purchased directly from the Mint by the Childs family in 1909 and held in the same family since that time, but it has different die characteristics from those described in the

Lange and Wexler-Flynn texts. It was cataloged by Q. David Bowers: he describes it as an unquestioned Matte Proof.

	Cert	Avg	%MS	PF-63RB	PF-64RB	PF-65RD
1911, Proof	206	64.3		$550	$1,050	$3,400

1911-D • Circulation-strike mintage: 12,672,000.

Availability in Mint State: *MS–60 to 64:* This issue is common in worn grades, as the mintage suggests, but at any Mint State level this is a scarce issue—although this scarcity is not generally recognized. Mint State coins that are sharply struck with Full Details and without defects are especially scarce, and ones with full original red are very rare. This is a poster example of a coin to be cherrypicked. Most collectors are not aware of how elusive they are. ***MS-65 and higher:*** This issue is rare in these grades when it is RD, problem-free, and without flecks or spots. Probably fewer than 250 such coins exist. Add RD coins that have been recolored and BN and RB coins, and there are several thousand examples in these grades.

Availability in circulated grades: This issue is common in circulated grades.

Characteristics of striking: Most have light striking in one area or another, such as the higher parts of the Lincoln portrait, and the rim may be weak in areas. David W. Lange observed:

> Although most examples are rather softly struck, a few very sharp specimens may be found. When found in Mint State, these sharper coins are almost always brown or with minimal red. It seems that most of the fully red pieces fall into the softly struck category. This is true of many early Lincoln cents and can be quite frustrating to collectors. It appears that the smoother surfaces of softly struck cents actually imparted some preservative quality to them which is lacking in the more textured coins with fuller strikes. Cleaned and retoned coins are also very common for this date. Although nearly all of these are rejected by the major grading services, a few of the most professional jobs may slip past.

	Cert	Avg	%MS	G-4	VG-8	F-12	VF-20	EF-40	AU-50	MS-60BN	MS-63BN	MS-65RD
1911-D	805	58.6	77%	$6	$7	$10	$20	$50	$75	$95	$125	$1,400

1911-S • Circulation-strike mintage: 4,026,000.

Availability in Mint State: *MS–60 to 64:* The ideal 1911-S at this level is a lustrous brown example. Some patience is need to find one that is just right. Many with traces of red tend to have spots. ***MS-65 and higher:*** Mint State coins at the MS-65RD level and higher come on the market with some frequency, but some have flecks or spots. Finding a truly great coin combining quality surfaces and sharp detail will take some time. Mint State coins with *original* color have distinctive hues. Over a long period of years Q. David Bowers has seen fewer than 100 examples meeting these standards.

Availability in circulated grades: This issue is readily available in circulated grades. It is very popular, as these and other early San Francisco cents are scarce in relation to dates of a couple decades later. Many branch-mint coins from this decade were plucked out of circulation as duplicates when filling albums became widely popular in the 1930s.

Characteristics of striking: Striking is usually somewhat light on the higher points of this issue, but Full Details pieces do exist. Since most collectors are not aware of the difference, once again you, as a knowledgeable collector, have an advantage when buying.

	Cert	Avg	%MS	G-4	VG-8	F-12	VF-20	EF-40	AU-50	MS-60BN	MS-63BN	MS-65RD
1911-S	968	48.7	50%	$50	$55	$60	$65	$85	$110	$185	$235	$2,750

Varieties: *1911-S, Repunched Mintmark (FS-01-1911S-501):* This variety can also be identified as CONECA 1911-S, RPM-001. Its rarity is URS-4. There is also a very similar repunched mintmark identified as CONECA 1911-S, RPM-002. The repunched mintmark varieties are often sought by specialists. These show slight repunching left of the final S.

A detail of the repunched mintmark.

	VF-20	EF-40	AU-50	MS-60	MS-63	MS-65
FS-01-1911S-501	$75	$100	$125	$200	$325	$1,000

Lincoln, Wheat Ears Reverse, Cents of 1912

KEYS TO COLLECTING: Most cents of this year are fairly well struck, except at the borders. Quality can vary, especially among higher grades, as noted in the following entries.

DIE USE: The average number of cents struck per die during this fiscal year, according to the Wexler-Flynn text, are: Philadelphia, 345,136 per obverse die, 355,880 per reverse die; Denver, 381,075 per obverse die, 323,337 per reverse die; San Francisco, 221,152 per obverse die, 192,305 per reverse die.

MINTMARKS ON CENTS: W.C. Eaton contributed this to *The Numismatist*, March 1912:

> I have to now report that the Denver Mint is already using, or has used, three different dies for the cents of 1912, at least the 'D' has been cut in three slightly differing places. In the first two a prolongation of the '1' downward would cut the right edge of the 'D' but in one case the 'D' is perceptibly nearer the '9' than in the other. In the third variety the '1' prolonged would miss the 'D' altogether and the 'D' is smaller than in either of the first two varieties. These three varieties were all mixed in one lot of 25 I have just received from the Mint.

The shipment Eaton received reflects the courtesy of the various mints at the time. On most occasions they furnished collectors with quantities of desired coins, charging only postage.

EVA TANGUAY: Eva Tanguay continued to evolve and publicize the use of Lincoln, Wheat Ears Reverse, cents in her performances. From the *Boston Journal*, March 23, 1912:

> *Keith's Theatre:* Eva Tanguay to shower audiences with pennies: Eva Tanguay, "the Madcap Genius of Mirth and Song," and the highest-salaried artiste on the American stage today, comes to B.F. Keith's Theatre next week for a limited engagement of one week only. As an entertainer Eva Tanguay stands in a class by herself. This season Miss Tanguay has been unusually fortunate in the selection of her songs. . . . Among the best is *Oh, You Money.* . . . Her new costumes . . . include a gown covered entirely with bright new Lincoln pennies. This is worn by Miss Tanguay in her famous *Money* song, and during the chorus she throws handfuls of real money into the audience to be taken home as souvenirs.

1912 • Circulation-strike mintage: 68,153,060.

Availability in Mint State: *MS–60 to 64:* This issue is scarce in these grades. Most examples are BN or RB. Many have stains or problems. ***MS-65 and higher:*** Gems with full *original* color and without carbon spots or flecks are *extremely rare*. In 1981 Stephen G. Manley, in *The Lincoln Cent,* stated without qualification: "The 1912 is the biggest sleeper of the Lincoln cent series in the upper grades." Today, hundreds have been certified as MS-65RD or higher, but it is uncertain how Manley would evaluate them. Modern viewing reveals that quality coins without spots and with original color remain elusive.

Availability in circulated grades: This issue is common in circulated grades.

Characteristics of striking: Most examples are fairly well struck, although there are exceptions.

	Cert	Avg	%MS	G-4	VG-8	F-12	VF-20	EF-40	AU-50	MS-60BN	MS-63BN
1912	646	63.1	95%	$1.25	$1.65	$2.25	$5.50	$13	$25	$35	$50

1912, Proof • Proof mintage: 2,172.

Proof commentary: These are Matte Proofs. Most pristine (undipped) coins are a rich, light-brown color and have a finely granular surface. Some have original red-orange color on one or both sides, but in Q. David Bowers's experience these are never fully brilliant. This Proof date is quite *rare,* more so than the low mintage suggests.

	Cert	Avg	%MS	PF-63RB	PF-64RB	PF-65RD
1912, Proof	218	64.3		$550	$1,050	$6,250

1912-D • Circulation-strike mintage: 10,411,000.

Availability in Mint State: *MS–60 to 64:* Lower-range Mint State coins are easily enough found. Cherrypicking for quality is essential. ***MS-65 and higher:*** Gems with full *original* color, with sharply struck surfaces in all areas including the borders, are rare. Probably fewer than 200 exist. As MS-65BN and RB coins can often be very beautiful and cost but a fraction of RD coins, these are well worth exploring.

Availability in circulated grades: This issue is slightly scarce in circulated grades.

Characteristics of striking: This issue is often well struck at the center, but weak or slightly "fuzzy" at the periphery, due to use of worn dies. David W. Lange adds:

> While most 1912-D cents are well struck in their centers they tend to have an 'expanded' look to them. . . . The lettering and numerals, including both date and mintmark, appear larger than normal. This is a form of die wear that seems to be peculiar to the Denver Mint issues.

	Cert	Avg	%MS	G-4	VG-8	F-12	VF-20	EF-40	AU-50	MS-60BN	MS-63BN	MS-65RD
1912-D	607	57.2	71%	$7	$8	$10	$25	$65	$100	$170	$240	$1,850

1912-S • Circulation-strike mintage: 4,431,000.

Availability in Mint State: *MS–60 to 64:* This issue is scarce in these grades. Many examples in this range have been dipped and retoned. *MS-65 and higher:* Gems with full *original* color and free of flecks are rare. David W. Lange acutely observes: "The fact that most of the surviving high-grade examples have been dipped at some point is not clearly reflected in the certified population data, as some leeway seems to have been given for this very scarce date." This comment is something of a reality check for many, perhaps the majority of collectors, who read the labels on holders, but are clueless about such aspects as originality of color or, for that matter, quality of strike. The idea that *leeway* is given in certifying some dipped coins should not come as a surprise to you at this point in this text, but it should serve as a caution when buying rare issues. Mint State coins with *original* color have distinctive hues.

Availability in circulated grades: This issue is readily available in these grades, many being left over from supplies of duplicates plucked out of circulation in the 1930s and 1940s.

Characteristics of striking: This issue is usually seen fairly well struck. A sharp coin is a reasonable expectation.

	Cert	Avg	%MS	G-4	VG-8	F-12	VF-20	EF-40	AU-50	MS-60BN	MS-63BN	MS-65RD
1912-S	823	50.0	57%	$24	$26	$29	$40	$75	$110	$180	$255	$3,500

Lincoln, Wheat Ears Reverse, Cents of 1913

KEYS TO COLLECTING: There are no rarities for this year, but high-level branch-mint coins are scarce in comparison to those later in the decade.

DIE USE: The average number of cents struck per die during this fiscal year, according to the Wexler-Flynn text, are: Philadelphia, 337,752 per obverse die, 323,621 per reverse die; Denver, 501,364 per obverse die, 391,309 per reverse die; San Francisco, 218,275 per obverse die, 160,835 per reverse die.

1913 • Circulation-strike mintage: 76,532,352.

Availability in Mint State: *MS–60 to 64:* This issue is common in these grades in the context of the series. *MS-65 and higher:* Examples are fairly plentiful in these grades, although full RD coins with *original* color and with excellent eye appeal are scarce or even rare. BN and RB coins exist by the thousands.

Availability in circulated grades: Well-worn examples picked out of circulation from the 1930s onward are plentiful. As is true of most Lincoln cents after 1909, up to the early 1920s, EF and AU coins—which might have been picked out of circulation in the teens and 1920s if only there had been more widespread interest—are scarce.

Characteristics of striking: Most examples are well struck, although there are exceptions.

	Cert	Avg	%MS	G-4	VG-8	F-12	VF-20	EF-40	AU-50	MS-60BN	MS-63BN	MS-65RD
1913	673	62.5	94%	$0.85	$1	$2	$4	$18	$27	$35	$55	$420

1913, Proof • Proof mintage: 2,983.

Proof commentary: These are Matte Proofs. Most pristine (undipped) coins are a rich, light-brown color. Some have original red-orange color on one or both sides, but these are never fully brilliant, although dozens have been certified PF-65RD or higher. This is the most plentiful date of the Matte Proof Lincoln, Wheat Ears Reverse, cents.

	Cert	Avg	%MS	PF-63RB	PF-64RB	PF-65RD
1913, Proof	319	64.5		$500	$1,050	$2,450

1913-D • Circulation-strike mintage: 15,804,000.

Availability in Mint State: *MS–60 to 64:* Many examples exist in these grades, most being BN or RB. *MS-65 and higher:* Many examples have been certified in these grades, but problem-free gems are in the minority. A gem-RD coin with sharp strike is a rarity—a quest for the cherrypicker.

Availability in circulated grades: This issue is relatively plentiful in circulated grades.

Characteristics of striking: Most examples have areas of weakness. Full Details examples are hard to find.

	Cert	Avg	%MS	G-4	VG-8	F-12	VF-20	EF-40	AU-50	MS-60BN	MS-63BN	MS-65RD
1913-D	599	58.1	76%	$3	$3.50	$4.50	$10	$50	$70	$110	$175	$2,200

1913-S • Circulation-strike mintage: 6,101,000.

Availability in Mint State: *MS–60 to 64:* Mint State coins are elusive, and gems with original color and sharp strike are rare. The advantage of being a smart buyer and cherrypicking is implied by David W. Lange's comment that many coins certified as RD "just barely make the cut." Words to heed! Mint State coins with *original* color have distinctive hues. *MS-65 and higher:* RD gems at this level with *original* color and no problems are rare, and probably fewer than 100 exist. To build a set of basic Lincoln cent dates and mintmarks in MS-65RD, with original color, would probably take a year or so. Disregard the requirement for original color and just read inscriptions on holders and probably less than a month will be required. The cost for the coins under either discipline is the same.

Availability in circulated grades: This is a scarce issue in all grades, in the context of the Lincoln, Wheat Ears Reverse, series. Most in existence were picked out of circulation from the 1930s onward and tend to grade from Good to Fine or so.

Characteristics of striking: Most examples show some lightness, but not as egregiously as on the 1913-D.

	Cert	Avg	%MS	G-4	VG-8	F-12	VF-20	EF-40	AU-50	MS-60BN	MS-63BN	MS-65RD
1913-S	739	49.4	56%	$14	$17	$20	$31	$60	$100	$175	$225	$5,000

Lincoln, Wheat Ears Reverse, Cents 1914

KEYS TO COLLECTING: Philadelphia cents are plentiful in low grades but are elusive in Mint State combined with good eye appeal. Most are sharply struck. The 1914-D is front-row, center for attention and has been an object of desire ever since thousands of collectors started filling albums in the 1930s. The 1914-S is scarce in a combination of high grade and good eye appeal.

1914 IN NUMISMATICS: The government announced a 1¢ tax on all telegraph and telephone messages costing more than 15 cents. The Philadelphia Mint anticipated a need for more cents to make change and, in the autumn, shipped extra supplies to banks.[181]

1914 • Circulation-strike mintage: 75,238,432.

Availability in Mint State: *MS–60 to 64:* This issue is readily available in these grades, though it is often lacking eye appeal. *MS-65 and higher:* MS-65BN and RB coins are easy to find. RD coins with original color probably exist only to the extent of a couple hundred pieces.

Availability in circulated grades: This issue is common in circulated grades.

Characteristics of striking: Most examples are very well struck—a pleasant surprise. Full Details coins, while not plentiful, will not be hard to find.

	Cert	Avg	%MS	G-4	VG-8	F-12	VF-20	EF-40	AU-50	MS-60BN	MS-63BN	MS-65RD
1914	705	60.7	87%	$0.75	$1	$2	$6	$20	$40	$55	$70	$450

1914, Proof • Proof mintage: 1,365.

Proof commentary: Collector dislike of Matte Proofs continued, and the mintage of such declined to half of what it was in the preceding year. Most pristine (undipped) coins are a rich, light-brown color. Some have original red-orange color on one or both sides, but these are never fully brilliant in Q. David Bowers's experience with pristine coins, despite dozens of pieces having been certified as such.

Notes: *"Mirror Proofs":* Several decades ago a group of mirror-style "Proofs" for this year appeared on the market, but these were quickly proven fake. Occasionally, examples from this hoax still come on the market.

	Cert	Avg	%MS	PF-63RB	PF-64RB	PF-65RD
1914, Proof	157	64.7		$550	$1,100	$2,450

1914-D • Circulation-strike mintage: 1,193,000.

Availability in Mint State: *MS–60 to 64:* Lower-range Mint State coins are rare. Walter Breen wrote of this issue that a "hoard of at least 700 Uncirculated specimens existed until the early 1950s." In the 1970s two rolls of Uncirculated coins, 100 pieces total, turned up in Hawaii (although another account says they appeared in the Philippine Islands). Q. David Bowers examined several pieces said to have been from that source, and they were all spotted red and brown. Also in the 1970s, Q. David Bowers bought a half-roll of Uncirculated coins from a New Zealand source. There is a lot of value to be found in glossy brown coins, sometimes with a hint of red, that do not have stains, flecks, or other problems. A hand-picked MS-64BN coin is a better option than an MS-65RD with flecks, and at a tiny fraction of the price. *MS-65 and higher:* Gems with *original* color, and with no flecks or spots, are very rare. Nearly all have carbon spots of varying sizes, unless they have been dipped or cyanided. A gem with good eye appeal and sharp strike will be a prize when found. This date and mintmark, one of the most challenging in the series, offers many treasure-hunting opportunities!

Availability in circulated grades: The 1914-D is a rarity in all grades. Notice of this low-mintage issue was not widespread until albums and folders became popular in the 1930s, by which time many coins had been worn down to levels of VG or so after just 20 to 25 years of circulation.[182] From that time the search was on, and many examples were retrieved from circulation, but far fewer were found in circulation than for any other issues in the series except the 1909-S V.D.B. Most circulated examples range from G to VF in grade.

Characteristics of striking: Most examples are fairly well struck, but many have some lightness on Lincoln's hair details and shoulder, and at the tops of the letters. Others are flat at the rims. Six obverse dies were used, and perhaps as many as seven reverses.

Notes: *Keys to collecting:* While the 1909-S, V.D.B., cent is more famous, the 1914-D in Mint State is dozens of times rarer, as in 1914 there was minimal interest in collecting current coins by mintmarks. The era of albums and folders was two decades in the future.

As to the relative number of 1914-D cents in circulation in 1938 and their quality, *The Numismatic Scrapbook Magazine* printed this in that year:

> Goldblatt Bros. department stores started in business in 1914. They recently offered a "soda" to anyone presenting a 1914 cent at their fountains.
>
> Kenneth D. McQuigg inquired as to how many were presented and received a letter stating that 2,463 were turned in. Of these, 29 were D mint and 40 S mint. McQuigg states that most of the coins were worn and over 95 percent were below Good.

Caveat: Fakes of the 1914-D cent abound. Until sophisticated die-struck forgeries came on the market in quantities, from the 1960s to date, most were crude. Many were made by altering the first 4 of a 1944-D cent (which, unlike a real 1914-D cent, has tiny initials V.D.B. on the shoulder).

Frank Trask supplied this comment:

> As most experienced collectors and dealers know the 1914-D cent is far rarer in coin circles than the 1909-S, V.D.B., which has a low mintage of 484,000 or less than half of the 1914-D. The 1909-S, V.D.B., is easily found on dealer's tables, often in EF and higher grades. In contrast, at the many Western coin shows in which I have a table each year it is rare to find very many dealers at any coin show that have 1914-D cents for sale. And when they do it is far more likely that they will be in VG to EF condition, rather than Mint State or even close.[183]

	Cert	Avg	%MS	G-4	VG-8	F-12	VF-20	EF-40	AU-50	MS-60BN	MS-63BN	MS-65RD
1914-D	4,711	25.0	9%	$200	$250	$300	$425	$875	$1,500	$2,000	$3,000	$17,000

1914-S • Circulation-strike mintage: 4,137,000.

Availability in Mint State: *MS–60 to 64:* Mint State coins are few and far between for this issue. Nearly all are toned BN, or are RB. The bronze planchets used at San Francisco this year and the next seem to have been prone to toning quickly. David W. Lange notes:

> Mint State coins which have not been cleaned at some point (and these are few in number) will be fairly dark, precluding the designation RD in all but a few instances. . . . A deterrent to finding a desirable coin is the conflict between strike and color. It seems that sharply struck coins are invariably dark, while the few bright examples tend to be mushy.

MS-65 and higher: MS-65RD coins with *original* color are very difficult to locate, especially if they are well struck. Probably fewer than 100 examples exist with these qualities. Add BN and RB examples to that number and the population is still probably below 1,000.

Availability in circulated grades: The 1914-S is scarce in lower circulated grades and is rare at the EF and AU levels.

Characteristics of striking: Most examples of this issue are fairly sharp, but some are weak.

Notes: *Keys to collecting:* In the early 1930s the 1914-S was recognized as one of the two key issues in Mint State, ranking in price with the 1914-D (though initially ranking higher than the 1914-D) and valued higher than the 1909-S, V.D.B. Later, this distinction faded, and while the 1914-S is still regarded as scarce, it is no longer a subject of publicity in this regard. Beware gem RD cents that have been dipped.

	Cert	Avg	%MS	G-4	VG-8	F-12	VF-20	EF-40	AU-50	MS-60BN	MS-63BN	MS-65RD
1914-S	738	44.8	37%	$24	$28	$30	$40	$85	$175	$325	$460	$8,150

Lincoln, Wheat Ears Reverse, Cents of 1915

KEYS TO COLLECTING: This is the last year in which most cents were fairly sharply struck. The branch-mint coins are elusive in Mint State.

1915 IN NUMISMATICS: In 1915 there were no basic books on collecting U.S. coins, no references with mintage figures and prices, and no grading standards. There was very little interest in collecting Lincoln cents by date and mint, and no notice was taken of the recent 1914-D being scarce or desirable. This is *key* to understanding the rarity of such coins today.

1915 • Circulation-strike mintage: 29,092,120.

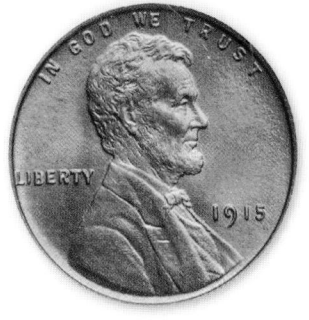

Availability in Mint State: *MS–60 to 64:* Although the mintage of the 1915 is low for a Philadelphia Mint cent, it is nonetheless common in all grades up to and including gem Mint State. *MS-65 and higher:* RD coins without problems are rare.

Availability in circulated grades: This issue is common in circulated grades. Most circulated examples are Good to Fine. These and other early Philadelphia Mint issues were easily found in circulation until the 1960s, when they started becoming scarce.

Characteristics of striking: This issue is usually sharp. David W. Lange noted:

> The obverse master die for the cents of 1915 from all three mints appears to have been manually enhanced. The cents of this date are similar to those of earlier years yet, when coined from fresh working dies, they possess superior detail in Lincoln's hair and beard. This reworking proved so successful that for the cents of 1916 a new master hub was prepared incorporating these changes, but to an even finer state of detail.

	Cert	Avg	%MS	G-4	VG-8	F-12	VF-20	EF-40	AU-50	MS-60BN	MS-63BN	MS-65RD
1915	590	60.3	85%	$1.75	$2.50	$5	$18	$60	$70	$90	$105	$875

1915, Proof • Proof mintage: 1,150.

Proof commentary: These are Matte Proofs. They are rare today. Most pristine (undipped) coins are a rich, light-brown color. Some have original red-orange color on one or both sides, but these are never fully brilliant.

	Cert	Avg	%MS	PF-63RB	PF-64RB	PF-65RD
1915, Proof	127	64.7		$600	$1,200	$3,500

1915-D • Circulation-strike mintage: 22,050,000.

Availability in Mint State: *MS–60 to 64:* Mint State coins are seen with frequency in the marketplace, but coins with *original* color, without spots, and sharply struck are rare. *MS-65 and higher:* This issue is rare in these grades if problem-free. Population reports offer no clue to the eye appeal or overall quality. Most examples are BN or RB.

Availability in circulated grades: This issue is common in circulated grades in the context of branch-mint Lincoln, Wheat Ears Reverse, cents. This issue was plentiful in circulation into the 1950s.

Characteristics of striking: Many are lightly defined on the higher areas due to tired dies or the dies being spaced too far apart in the press.

	Cert	Avg	%MS	G-4	VG-8	F-12	VF-20	EF-40	AU-50	MS-60BN	MS-63BN	MS-65RD
1915-D	906	57.8	79%	$2	$3	$4	$7	$22	$45	$85	$120	$1,100

1915-S • **Circulation-strike mintage:** 4,833,000.

Availability in Mint State: *MS–60 to 64:* Mint State coins are seen with frequency, but these are usually toned and sometimes blotchy. The bronze used this year, and in 1914 at San Francisco, seemed to turn dark quickly. Many if not most "brilliant" coins on the market in recent generations have been dipped or processed. Coins with *original* mint red-orange, and without flecks or spots, are rare. Mint State coins with *original* color have distinctive hues. *MS-65 and higher:* Examples are very rare in these grades if they are RD and completely free of problems. This is the earliest condition rarity among regular Lincoln, Wheat Ears Reverse, varieties. Cherrypick for quality. Many RB coins are nicer overall than those certified as RD.

Availability in circulated grades: The 1915-S is scarce in all grades, especially at higher levels, these including from EF-40 upward.

Characteristics of striking: Most examples are fairly well struck, but there are many exceptions. Sharp coins can be found with some persistence.

	Cert	Avg	%MS	G-4	VG-8	F-12	VF-20	EF-40	AU-50	MS-60BN	MS-63BN	MS-65RD
1915-S	640	47.5	49%	$20	$25	$30	$35	$70	$135	$200	$235	$5,000

Lincoln, Wheat Ears Reverse, Cents of 1916

KEYS TO COLLECTING: Sharp strikes may require some searching for this year, though they exist in large numbers. The increased output of cents, fueled by a rising economy tied to manufacturing for European allies, resulted in the mints paying less attention to quality.

DIE USE: The average number of cents struck per die during this fiscal year, according to the Wexler-Flynn text, were: Philadelphia, 378,786 per obverse die, 371,400 per reverse die; Denver, 180,690 per obverse die, 103,669 per reverse die; San Francisco, 484,658 per obverse die, 484,685 per reverse die.

DIE ENHANCEMENT: The master hub for the obverse of the cent was sharpened this year, giving more detail to Lincoln's hair as was done now and again over the years.[184]

"BIG SHORTAGE OF PENNIES": The *Philadelphia Inquirer*, October 21, 1916:

> New York, Oct. 20. A serious shortage of pennies is confronting the country, according to information obtained at the Sub-Treasury in Wall Street today. An unprecedented increase in the use of 1-cent pieces with the warring countries controlling the copper market by long-term contracts has affected this condition.
>
> In the South and West many department and chain stores have been opened recently, and these have caused a tremendous demand for pennies in a territory where the 5-cent piece had been the smallest coin in use.

One suggestion to relieve the condition is that the millions of pennies in the slot machines throughout the country be compelled to disgorge their gleanings daily instead of weekly or monthly as is now the custom. Many millions of pennies remain out of circulation in these vending and weighing machines for months at a time.[185]

1916 • Circulation-strike mintage: 131,833,677.

Availability in Mint State: *MS–60 to 64:* This issue is plentiful in all grades including Mint State. Sharply struck coins with original mint red-orange and no flecks or spots are scarce, however. *MS-65 and higher:* Problem-free BN and RB coins are common in these grades, and RD coins are relatively easy to find as well.

Availability in circulated grades: This issue is common in circulated grades. Most circulated examples are G to VF.

Characteristics of striking: Many examples are found with exquisite sharpness from the strengthened hub this year. Full Details coins await your discovery. There are also, however, many from dies that were spaced too widely apart or overly worn.

	Cert	Avg	%MS	G-4	VG-8	F-12	VF-20	EF-40	AU-50	MS-60BN	MS-63BN	MS-65RD
1916	841	63.0	96%	$0.30	$0.50	$0.75	$2	$8	$13	$18	$35	$300

1916, Proof • Proof mintage: 1,050.

Proof commentary: Authentic Matte Proofs are rare. Often, circulation strikes fool even the experts, unless die characteristics are examined under a microscope. True Proofs should have a *flat rim.* Most pristine (undipped) coins are a rich, light-brown color. Some have original red-orange color on one or both sides, but these are never fully brilliant. In 1916 a United States Proof set consisted of just two coins: the Buffalo nickel and Lincoln cent, both in matte finish. Collectors had been critical of Matte, Sand Blast, and Satin Proofs from the beginning, and orders were so small that they were no longer worthwhile for the Mint to strike.

	Cert	Avg	%MS	PF-63RB	PF-64RB	PF-65RD
1916, Proof	97	64.7		$1,250	$2,500	$12,000

1916-D • Circulation-strike mintage: 35,956,000.

Availability in Mint State: *MS–60 to 64:* This issue is easy to find in these grades. Usually examples are BN, sometimes with traces of RD. *MS-65 and higher:* Examples are rare in these grades if RD and problem free; this cent is a condition rarity. BN and RB coins are slightly scarce.

Availability in circulated grades: This issue is common in circulated grades.

Characteristics of striking: Sharpness for this issue varies due to the use of worn dies and the presence of too much space between dies in the press. Improperly annealed planchets may have been a factor as well. Many sharp examples exist, however, the desirability of which is enhanced by the modified hub this year.

	Cert	Avg	%MS	G-4	VG-8	F-12	VF-20	EF-40	AU-50	MS-60BN	MS-63BN	MS-65RD
1916-D	765	60.7	85%	$1	$1.75	$3	$6	$15	$35	$75	$150	$2,850

1916-S • **Circulation-strike mintage:** 22,510,000.

Availability in Mint State: *MS–60 to 64:* Pristine Mint State coins will nearly always show some light fading and, often, a wood-grain effect. *MS-65 and higher:* Likely, a coin that is 100% brilliant, including the edges, has been dipped. Mint State coins with *original* color have distinctive hues and are first-class rarities in relation to the demand for them. In a marketplace in which the 1909-S V.D.B. cent is famous it is often overlooked that in MS-65RD some later branch-mint coins such as this one are dozens of times rarer!

Availability in circulated grades: This issue is common in circulated grades. Most circulated examples are G to VG. In the 1950s Lincoln, Wheat Ears Reverse, cents of 1909 and the following decade could be found in circulation easily enough, the 1909-S V.D.B., 1909-S, and 1914-D cents excepted. The others were available in proportion to their mintages.

Characteristics of striking: This issue is often seen well struck, but there are many exceptions.

	Cert	Avg	%MS	G-4	VG-8	F-12	VF-20	EF-40	AU-50	MS-60BN	MS-63BN	MS-65RD
1916-S	753	58.6	75%	$1.75	$2.25	$3.50	$8	$25	$50	$105	$175	$7,500

Lincoln, Wheat Ears Reverse, Cents of 1917

KEYS TO COLLECTING: Cents of this year are very common, though sharply struck coins in high grades with excellent eye appeal are more rare.

DIE-HUB WEAR: The obverse master hub die used for all dies and mints began to show signs of wear, which would continue for decades through 1968.

STAMPS USED WHEN CENTS WERE SCARCE: Buoyed by the wartime economy, mintages of coins were generous across the board. However, this did not help the nationwide shortage of "pennies" that was constantly and widely reported in the press during the year. Odd prices due to new taxes were a main cause of the shortage. Beyond that, inflation caused the prices of many items formerly retailing for a nickel to be increased by a cent or two. The Treasury Department and others appealed to citizens, including children, to empty their savings banks and put cents back into circulation. Reminiscent of the shortage of 1862, in many places *postage stamps* were being used to make change!

CAVEAT CONCERNING THE SO-CALLED 1917 "MATTE PROOF" CENTS: Walter Breen in his 1988 *Complete Encyclopedia of U.S. and Colonial Coins* states that an unknown number of Proofs were "clandestinely made." These started coming on the market in the 1960s along with "Matte Proof" commemorative coins and other previously unknown productions, some signed by letters of "authentication" by Breen. These pieces are not authentic. Today, many of Breen's authentication letters are dismissed by numismatic scholars.

1917 • **Circulation-strike mintage:** 196,429,785.

Availability in Mint State: *MS–60 to 64:* This issue is common in these grades. It could even be considered a "no-problem" date, although usual care should be exercised to avoid spotted and dipped coins. *MS-65 and higher:* Examples are easy to find in these grades, including coins with nice eye appeal.

Availability in circulated grades: This issue is common in circulated grades.

Characteristics of striking: Many sharp coins exist, rivaling certain 1916 cents. There are many unsatisfactory strikes, however, and it will pay to ignore these.

	Cert	Avg	%MS	G-4	VG-8	F-12	VF-20	EF-40	AU-50	MS-60BN	MS-63BN	MS-65RD
1917	748	60.7	91%	$0.30	$0.40	$0.50	$2	$4	$10	$16	$32	$425

1917, Doubled-Die Obverse •

Circulation-strike mintage: Included in 1917 circulation-strike mintage.

This variety's Fivaz-Stanton identification is FS-01-1917-101. It can also be identified as CONECA 1917, DDO-001. Its rarity is URS-8. Although this variety was little known years ago, it has been publicized in modern times and has leapt to the forefront of in-demand varieties. In 1998 Sam Lukes bought a small group of these, the finest of which was subsequently graded as MS-65RD by PCGS, and sold for $18,750.

A detail of the doubling at the date.

A detail of the doubling at TRUST.

	Cert	Avg	%MS	G-4	VG-8	F-12	VF-20	EF-40	AU-50	MS-60BN	MS-63BN	MS-65RD
1917, Doubled-Die Obverse	70	35.3	17%	$85	$145	$225	$450	$1,000	$1,600	$2,750	$5,750	$19,500

1917-D • **Circulation-strike mintage:** 55,120,000.

Availability in Mint State: *MS–60 to 64:* Mint State coins are plentiful, but most are weakly struck, and many have spots from earlier cleaning. *MS-65 and higher:* A sharply struck original-color gem is a rare bird indeed, a sleeper if you can find one! Again, certification service numbers do not reflect either sharpness or eye appeal, leaving many opportunities for alert buyers.

Availability in circulated grades: This issue is common in grades of G and VG, but progressively less common as the grade level rises.

Characteristics of striking: Most examples range from below average to wretched in terms of sharpness. Exceptions exist but are very rare, especially in higher grades.

	Cert	Avg	%MS	G-4	VG-8	F-12	VF-20	EF-40	AU-50	MS-60BN	MS-63BN	MS-65RD
1917-D	627	60.0	82%	$0.80	$1	$1.75	$4.50	$35	$50	$80	$125	$2,750

1917-S • Circulation-strike mintage: 32,620,000.

Availability in Mint State: *MS–60 to 64:* This issue is easy to find in these grades, although quality varies widely. *MS-65 and higher:* A sharply struck MS-65RD or higher coin, without spots and with excellent eye appeal, is a *rarity*, although few non-specialists know this. Mint State coins with *original* color have distinctive hues.

Availability in circulated grades: This issue is common in circulated grades. Most examples are well worn. As is true of other early Philadelphia Mint Lincoln cents, while many were picked out of circulation to place in boards and albums in the 1930s, duplicates of common dates were not saved. In the 1950s and 1960s *any* early Lincoln cent was apt to be saved. By that time most were in grades such as G and VG.

Characteristics of striking: Substandard is the rule for sharpness this year in San Francisco, similar to the situation at Denver. There are exceptions.

Notes: *Mintmark punches:* Cent dies made early this year had the S mintmark added by the same punch used since 1909. Later this year, a new punch with a slightly larger S was placed into use.

	Cert	Avg	%MS	G-4	VG-8	F-12	VF-20	EF-40	AU-50	MS-60BN	MS-63BN	MS-65RD
1917-S	454	59.5	81%	$0.50	$0.65	$1	$2.50	$10	$25	$75	$160	$13,000

Lincoln, Wheat Ears Reverse, Cents of 1918

KEYS TO COLLECTING: Repeating a familiar scenario, cents of this year are very common in lower grades and with light or average strike. Branch-mint coins that are well struck and have superb eye appeal are few and far between. In all instances cherrypicking for quality is advised.

V.D.B. ADDED: In this year the initials V.D.B. were restored to the cent, now in tiny letters on the edge of Lincoln's shoulder.

1918 • Circulation-strike mintage: 288,104,634.

Availability in Mint State: *MS–60 to 64:* This issue is common in these grades. Most examples are BN, some are RB. RD coins nearly always have problems. *MS-65 and higher:* This is one of the more available issues of the decade in these grades.

Availability in circulated grades: This issue is common in circulated grades.

Characteristics of striking: Striking is usually well defined for this issue, but there are exceptions.

	Cert	Avg	%MS	G-4	VG-8	F-12	VF-20	EF-40	AU-50	MS-60BN	MS-63BN	MS-65RD
1918	593	63.2	96%	$0.20	$0.30	$0.50	$1.50	$3	$8	$16	$27	$330

1918-D • Circulation-strike mintage: 47,830,000.

Availability in Mint State: *MS–60 to 64:* This issue is fairly scarce in these grades. *MS-65 and higher:* This issue is available readily enough with a typical strike (see "Characteristics of striking"). Sharply struck RD examples without problems are major condition rarities.

Availability in circulated grades: This issue is common in circulated grades.

Characteristics of striking: Lack of detail is the rule. While worn dies are part of the cause, it seems likely that the Denver Mint in particular, and the San Francisco Mint to a lesser extent, spaced the dies slightly too widely apart. This same situation exists for many branch-mint coins of other denominations from the World War I era through the 1920s.

	Cert	Avg	%MS	G-4	VG-8	F-12	VF-20	EF-40	AU-50	MS-60BN	MS-63BN	MS-65RD
1918-D	480	59.0	76%	$0.75	$1.25	$2.50	$4	$12	$35	$80	$140	$3,500

1918-S • Circulation-strike mintage: 34,680,000.

Availability in Mint State: *MS–60 to 64:* Mint State coins are not rare in lower levels, or with brown or red and brown toning. *MS-65 and higher:* MS-65RD coins are rare, as certification data shows. If you are a connoisseur, and want one that is sharply struck and with no flecks, be prepared for a challenging search that might take a year or more!

Availability in circulated grades: This issue is common in circulated grades.

Characteristics of striking: Examples are usually poorly struck. Exceptions are few and far between.

	Cert	Avg	%MS	G-4	VG-8	F-12	VF-20	EF-40	AU-50	MS-60BN	MS-63BN	MS-65RD
1918-S	542	59.9	77%	$0.50	$1	$2	$3	$11	$32	$80	$185	$9,500

Lincoln, Wheat Ears Reverse, Cents of 1919

KEYS TO COLLECTING: Quality can be elusive for the Denver and San Francisco issues. Study and observation are needed to determine quality, for nearly all public offerings do not address sharpness or strike or eye appeal. The rule in the marketplace seems to be "say nothing that is even slightly negative or a coin will not sell." Certified holders do not address the several factors needed to create a special coin. Also beneficial to sellers is that most buyers look only at grading labels. As a reader of this detailed text, you will be much more informed.

1919 IN NUMISMATICS: The coin market was quiet and did not participate in the inflation that characterized many aspects of the American scene. In May, Henry Chapman advertised: "1919 regular coinage, 1c, 5c, 10c, 25c, 50c Unc. Set $1.10."

1919 • Circulation-strike mintage: 392,021,000.

Availability in Mint State: *MS–60 to 64:* These are common enough, but it is advised to cherrypick for sharpness of strike and eye appeal. *MS-65 and higher:* This issue is common in these grades. Spots are not much of a problem. A nice gem will be an easy find, for a change. Hooray!

Availability in circulated grades: This issue is very common in circulated grades. Most circulated examples are G or VG.

Characteristics of striking: Most examples are well struck this year, due to careful adjustment of the coining presses and properly annealed planchets.

	Cert	Avg	%MS	G-4	VG-8	F-12	VF-20	EF-40	AU-50	MS-60BN	MS-63BN	MS-65RD
1919	785	63.3	95%	$0.20	$0.30	$0.40	$1	$3.25	$5	$14	$28	$230

1919-D • Circulation-strike mintage: 57,154,000.

Availability in Mint State: *MS–60 to 64:* This issue is common in these grades, but examples many have problems. *MS-65 and higher:* At a casual glance, the 1919-D is a common issue among gem cents from the Denver Mint— unless, that is, you desire a choice or gem specimen that is well struck, with original color. Such a coin is very scarce. Many pieces with original mint color are mottled or irregular.

Availability in circulated grades: This issue is common in circulated grades. Most are well worn.

Characteristics of striking: Most examples show lightness of striking in some areas, particularly at the center of the obverse and the periphery of the reverse. Wavy surfaces from overused dies are often seen, particularly on the reverse.

	Cert	Avg	%MS	G-4	VG-8	F-12	VF-20	EF-40	AU-50	MS-60BN	MS-63BN	MS-65RD
1919-D	581	61.6	89%	$0.50	$0.75	$1	$4	$10	$32	$65	$110	$2,400

1919-S • Circulation-strike mintage: 139,760,000.

Availability in Mint State: *MS–60 to 64:* This issue is common in these grades, although most examples are lightly struck. *MS-65 and higher:* Sharply struck pieces with original color are in the minority in these grades, and finding one will be a challenge. Mint State coins with *original* RD color have distinctive hues.

Availability in circulated grades: This issue is common in circulated grades. G and VG are typical grades.

Characteristics of striking: Nearly all examples are lightly struck in one area or another.

	Cert	Avg	%MS	G-4	VG-8	F-12	VF-20	EF-40	AU-50	MS-60BN	MS-63BN	MS-65RD
1919-S	643	60.5	82%	$0.20	$0.40	$1	$2	$6	$18	$50	$115	$6,000

Lincoln, Wheat Ears Reverse, Cents of 1920

KEYS TO COLLECTING: Coins from all three mints are common enough, although Denver and San Francisco coins are elusive in high Mint State grades, sharply struck.

1920 IN NUMISMATICS: The *Annual Report of the Director of the Mint* for the fiscal year (ending June 30, 1920) noted:

> At the Philadelphia mint 357,000,000 cents were coined during this year; the average per pair of dies is more than 450,000 pieces. This result stands alone in our records, and such an average can only be obtained by the most painstaking care in the selection of the steel in every succeeding operation until the dies are set in the coining presses.

1920 • Circulation-strike mintage: 310,165,000.

Availability in Mint State: *MS–60 to 64:* This issue is easy to find in these grades. *MS-65 and higher:* This is a common date in these grades in the context of the era, and choice and gem examples are plentiful in the marketplace. Many examples have been dipped.

Availability in circulated grades: This issue is common in circulated grades. Most circulated examples are in low grades.

Characteristics of striking: The strike is usually decent on examples of this issue for the era, but the dies were not made with the sharp detail seen a decade earlier in the series. Overused dies show graininess.

	Cert	Avg	%MS	G-4	VG-8	F-12	VF-20	EF-40	AU-50	MS-60BN	MS-63BN	MS-65RD
1920	696	63.2	96%	$0.20	$0.30	$0.35	$0.50	$2.25	$4	$15	$28	$220

1920-D • Circulation-strike mintage: 49,280,000.

Availability in Mint State: *MS–60 to 64:* These are elusive if sharply struck. As always, seeking quality will pay dividends. Probably not one in five MS-63 coins, for example, combines sharp strike and eye appeal. *MS-65 and higher:* Finding a *sharply struck* gem with *original color* is almost, but not quite, an impossibility. The 1920-D is another great challenge for the connoisseur. David W. Lange notes that most gems certified as "RD aren't really [and have] a subdued red bordering on red/brown or a peculiar pink color," concluding, "for those who place more emphasis on the certified grade than on the coin itself, this may not matter, but experienced collectors will recognize the difference."

Availability in circulated grades: This issue is common in circulated grades.

Characteristics of striking: The typical 1920-D is a miserable strike, with a lack of detail on Lincoln's hair, the usual microscopic planchet marks on the shoulder, and an uneven field and indistinct edges of letters on the reverse. Probably poor annealing of planchets and poor press adjustment combined to cause these problems.

	Cert	Avg	%MS	G-4	VG-8	F-12	VF-20	EF-40	AU-50	MS-60BN	MS-63BN	MS-65RD
1920-D	497	60.5	84%	$1	$2	$3	$6.50	$19	$40	$80	$110	$2,050

1920-S • Circulation-strike mintage: 46,220,000.

Availability in Mint State: *MS–60 to 64:* This issue is easy to find in these grades. Most RD coins are recolored. *MS-65 and higher:* While average examples are easily enough found MS-65BN or RB or higher, finding a choice RD coin sharply struck with original color is nearly impossible. As a general rule, an MS-65BN or RB coin is much nicer that a numerically lower but brilliant MS-64RD.

Availability in circulated grades: This issue is common in circulated grades.

Characteristics of striking: Most 1920-S cents are poorly struck, with indistinct details on the higher areas on the obverse, and with the reverse often blurry. Tired, overused dies seem to have been the rule at San Francisco this year. Seeking a truly Full Details coin may be like tilting at a windmill, and this is one issue for which you may have to compromise. It is rather curious that only Lincoln-cent specialists are aware of this. Most dealers would be surprised to learn of the rarity of a choice coin of this date and mint.

	Cert	Avg	%MS	G-4	VG-8	F-12	VF-20	EF-40	AU-50	MS-60BN	MS-63BN	MS-65RD
1920-S	518	59.4	75%	$0.50	$0.65	$1.50	$2.25	$10	$35	$110	$185	$10,000

Lincoln, Wheat Ears Reverse, Cents of 1921

KEYS TO COLLECTING: Because of reduced demand no cents were struck at the Denver Mint. Philadelphia cents are readily available. San Francisco cents are slightly scarce, but not enough to be ranked as key issues.

SHARPENING OF THE V.D.B. INITIALS: The master obverse die, beginning in 1921, had the initials V.D.B. sharpened. This appears to have been done by hand engraving into the hub.

1921 IN NUMISMATICS: Demand for new coins fell, and mintages were generally low, creating varieties that would be recognized as key issues by a later generation of numismatists. In recent years coinage had reached record levels, and now it receded.

1921 • Circulation-strike mintage: 39,157,000.

Availability in Mint State: *MS–60 to 64:* Although sharply struck coins are rare on a relative basis, enough Mint State coins exist that finding one *can* be done, with patience. In the 1950s this was the one date, among Philadelphia cents of the early 1920s, that occasionally was seen in roll quantities—one or two at a time—with the pieces typically being a bright yellow-orange hue. *MS-65 and higher:* This issue is relatively easy to find in these grades, including with original RD color.

Availability in circulated grades: This issue is common in circulated grades.

Characteristics of striking: Most examples are weakly struck or struck from tired, overused dies. This is one of the most poorly struck Philadelphia Mint cents of the era.

	Cert	Avg	%MS	G-4	VG-8	F-12	VF-20	EF-40	AU-50	MS-60BN	MS-63BN	MS-65RD
1921	554	62.8	94%	$0.50	$0.60	$1.30	$2.10	$9	$22	$50	$80	$345

1921-S • Circulation-strike mintage: 15,274,000.

Availability in Mint State: *MS–60 to 64:* Sharply struck coins with good eye appeal are elusive. Coins that are 63 and 64 "RD" usually have spotting or other problems. A far less expensive lustrous BN coin is a better buy. ***MS-65 and higher:*** Gem Mint State coins with BN or RB color are very elusive, and for *original* RD examples are almost impossible to find.

Availability in circulated grades: Circulated examples are scarce in the context of the series, due to the low mintage.

Characteristics of striking: Most coins are struck with light definition of details on higher points or from worn dies. The S mintmark can be weak. Sharp examples are rare.

Notes: The low mintage is explained by David W. Lange:

> All 1921-S cents were coined early in the year, before a nationwide recession slowed business activity. Due to a lack of demand from banks, the San Francisco Mint still had in its vaults on June 30, 1922 some 15,493,230 cents of earlier years awaiting distribution. Thus, no more were coined [in San Francisco] until the latter part of 1923.

	Cert	Avg	%MS	G-4	VG-8	F-12	VF-20	EF-40	AU-50	MS-60BN	MS-63BN	MS-65RD
1921-S	675	57.6	65%	$1.50	$2.25	$3.50	$7	$35	$75	$135	$190	$11,500

Lincoln, Wheat Ears Reverse, Cents of 1922

KEYS TO COLLECTING: All cents this year were struck at the Denver Mint. Quality can vary widely, as discussed in the following entries. Illogically, the weaker the strike, the more valuable a 1922-D cent is!

WEAKLY STRUCK CENTS: Curiously, poorly struck coins and those from worn dies are desirable for this year (see pages 402 and 403). These have a weak D mintmark or no D mintmark at all, furnishing a substitute for a mintmarkless 1922 in a year when no coins were struck at the Philadelphia Mint. Advanced specialists may want to acquire a regular 1922-D and also one with a weak or, better yet, completely missing D. Twenty obverse dies were prepared for coinage, but it is not known if all were used. Twenty-seven reverses were on hand, but, again, it is possible not all were used.

A detail of the 1922-D mintmark.

A detail of the 1922-D, No D, mintmark.

A detail of the 1922-D, Weak D, mintmark.

1922 IN NUMISMATICS: Demand for copper, nickel, and silver American coinage hit a low point for the era, except for Peace silver dollars, which were made in record numbers due to special legislation. With a nationwide slump in the economy, there was little need for new cents. Mintage of cents was accomplished only at Denver, as noted.

1922-D • Circulation-strike mintage: 7,160,000.

Availability in Mint State: *MS–60 to 64:* Original Mint State coins are found here and there in the marketplace. Q. David Bowers remarks that he has never seen a roll of 50. ***MS-65 and higher:*** Gem, high-grade, Mint State coins with original color are very scarce, and some effort will be needed to find one in

See page 401 for mintmark detail.

a combination of high quality, sharp strike, and good eye appeal.

Availability in circulated grades: The 1922-D has been a numismatic favorite for a long time, a date and mintmark widely saved in the 1930s when it became popular to look for key issues in circulation. Circulated examples are common in relation to the demand for them.

Characteristics of striking: Striking for this issue ranges from sharp to very weak,though many pieces with weak striking fall into the category of the next variety listed.

	Cert	Avg	%MS	G-4	VG-8	F-12	VF-20	EF-40	AU-50	MS-60BN	MS-63BN	MS-65RD
1922-D	1,573	41.7	44%	$20	$21	$25	$27	$40	$75	$110	$165	$2,000

1922-D, No D • Circulation-strike mintage: Included in 1922-D circulation-strike mintage.

Availability in Mint State: *MS–60 to 64:* This issue is rare in these grades in relation to the demand for it. Most examples are BN. ***MS-65 and higher:*** This issue is extremely rare in these grades. Most examples are BN, some with hints of red.

See page 401 for mintmark detail.

Availability in circulated grades: This issue is rare in relation to the demand for it.

Characteristics of striking: Some 1922-D cents were struck from obverse dies that were so weak that the D was not visible, or only barely visible. The desired issue is from die pair No. 2 (described under "Die history" below), with the D mintmark deliberately effaced (in the process of removing some die damage that occurred in the coining press). Buy only coins from die pair No. 2; all others are simply "Weak D" coins.

Notes: This variety's Fivaz-Stanton identification is FS-01-1922-402.

Die history: When dies were first put into use they produced regular 1922-D cents. Then they weakened as the die became worn from extensive use. It is thought that the D was completely ground off of one die—that die being from pair No. 2—when it was relapped, or resurfaced, to reduce surface roughness and extend its life. Cents of 1922-D struck without a mintmark *always* have a very weakly detailed obverse in other areas as well. The reverse can range from weak to fairly sharp, depending upon the die.

In his column in *Hobbies* magazine, July 1939, Thomas L. Elder marveled at the interest shown in a "D-less D Cent at Auction," which was bright red. Bids ranged from $1 to $5.25, with 25 bidders competing.

The ANACS staff, writing in *The Numismatist*, July 1982, consolidated comments and research by others, and described the specific characteristics of die pairs used to strike 1922 cents with a weak or missing D. Die pair No. 2, with no D visible, was described as starting with a fresh pair of dies. The two dies clashed (met in the coining press without a planchet between them), causing clash marks on both sides. According to the ANACS scenario, the obverse die was lightly dressed or filed, to remove the clash marks, and in the process the D was removed completely. The reverse die was discarded and replaced by a new one. Thus 1922 cents with no D whatever were produced at the Denver Mint.

Not admired by all: Many veteran collectors pooh-poohed the 1922, No D, cent as nothing more than a defective coin. *The Numismatist* printed this in May 1945:

> In 1922 the U.S. Government coined 7,160,000 Lincoln head cents at the Denver Mint. None was coined at Philadelphia or San Francisco. Some of these cents are poorly struck and show only a faint outline or no sign of the D mintmark. That's all there is to the story. Collectors who feel they "must" own a 1922 cent with an obliterated mintmark should use a tack-hammer on the mintmark of a well struck specimen. With a little practice they will become as expert as the next fellow.

This disdainful philosophy was often heard into the 1950s. Since then the publicity given to auction offerings and the listing of the variety in standard guides has muted such criticism.

In *Looking Through Lincoln Cents*, 2005 edition, Charles D. Daughtrey commented: "It is my opinion that all 1922 'no D' cents are common, grease filled or worn out dies, and that none of them should have ever gained the attention or value they currently demand."

Caveat: Beware normal 1922-D cents from which unscrupulous people have removed the D mintmark. Buying a 1922, No D, cent from a leading certification service, and only from die pair No. 2, is strongly suggested.

	Cert	Avg	%MS	G-4	VG-8	F-12	VF-20	EF-40	AU-50	MS-60BN	MS-63BN
1922, No D	3,133	21.4	2%	$600	$750	$1,000	$1,250	$2,500	$4,500	$10,000	$20,000

1922-D, Weak D • Circulation-strike

mintage: Included in 1922-D circulation-strike mintage.

Availability in Mint State: *MS–60 to 64:* This issue is scarce in these grades. *MS-65 and higher:* This issue is rare in these grades. Most examples are BN or BN with hints of RD.

Availability in circulated grades: This issue is scarce in circulated grades.

See page 401 for mintmark detail.

Characteristics of striking: This variety is known from at least two pairs of dies, both of which became worn to a point where the D is barely visible. The rest of the obverse is weakly detailed as well. The reverse quality can range from weak to sharp: reverse dies were replaced as needed, and not necessarily at the same time as obverse dies.

Caveat: Some of these, with a little raised area or a hint of a D, have been offered as "No D" or "Plain." This is simply profiteering. The same coins were called "Weak D" or similar years ago. A coin that shows a hint of a D is *not* a 1922 "No D" and is not particularly rare.

Notes: This variety's Fivaz-Stanton identification is FS-01-1922-401.

	Cert	Avg	%MS	G-4	VG-8	F-12	VF-20	EF-40	AU-50	MS-60BN	MS-63BN
1922, Weak D	515	16.6	3%	$25	$35	$50	$70	$160	$200	$350	$1,000

Lincoln, Wheat Ears Reverse, Cents of 1923

KEYS TO COLLECTING: Philadelphia coins are common, San Francisco cents exist in much smaller numbers across the grading spectrum. No Denver Mint cents were made.

1923 IN NUMISMATICS: Cents were struck only at Philadelphia and San Francisco. Many but not all of the planchets were provided through a contract with the Scovill Manufacturing Co. of Waterbury, Connecticut.

1923 • Circulation-strike mintage: 74,723,000.

Availability in Mint State: *MS–60 to 64:* This issue is common in these grades. *MS-65 and higher:* This issue is common across the board, but sharply struck coins are in the minority; however, there are enough of them to satisfy the demand.

Availability in circulated grades: This issue is common in circulated grades.

Characteristics of striking: Striking varies for this issue from Full Details to poor. Keep in mind that as the hubs and master dies were used during this decade, details in Lincoln's hair became less distinct. A 1923 cent struck from carefully spaced new dies will not be as detailed as a 1916 cent (the year the details were sharpened). The shoulder of Lincoln continued to be lightly struck on most cents of this decade. This is detected today by examining the area under high magnification to see if there are any minute nicks and marks from the original planchet.

	Cert	Avg	%MS	G-4	VG-8	F-12	VF-20	EF-40	AU-50	MS-60BN	MS-63BN	MS-65RD
1923	571	63.2	97%	$0.35	$0.45	$0.65	$1	$5	$9.50	$15	$30	$360

1923-S • Circulation-strike mintage: 8,700,000.

Availability in Mint State: *MS–60 to 64:* This issue is plentiful in these grades with BN or RB color. Many if not most RD coins are either recolored or have other problems. Probably not one in 10 is a "keeper" for the connoisseur. *MS-65 and higher:* This issue is rare in these grades if RD, and very rare if sharp. The majority of "brilliant" Lincoln, Wheat Ears Reverse, cents have been dipped. Reflecting sophisticated thinking, David W. Lange stated that he would rather have a sharp AU example than a weakly struck Mint State coin. Mint State coins with *original* color have distinctive hues.

Availability in circulated grades: This issue is somewhat scarce in all circulated grades, although it is not generally considered a key date. This was one of the mintmark varieties that collectors saved in quantity during the 1930s, when looking through pocket change first became popular.

Characteristics of striking: Striking for this issue is usually weak, sometimes *very* weak. Most connoisseurs who land a sharp coin buy one toned brown or red and brown.

	Cert	Avg	%MS	G-4	VG-8	F-12	VF-20	EF-40	AU-50	MS-60BN	MS-63BN	MS-65RD
1923-S	418	56.7	62%	$4	$6	$7	$10	$40	$90	$220	$390	$17,000

Lincoln, Wheat Ears Reverse, Cents of 1924

KEYS TO COLLECTING: Philadelphia cents are common. The 1924-D is a semi-key issue, the nature of which was realized in the 1930s when many people began looking through pocket change for scarce issues. The San Francisco cents are elusive in higher grades. Sharpness of strike can be elusive across the board for cents this year.

1924 IN NUMISMATICS: It was back to business as usual, and for the first time since 1920, cents were struck at all three mints. Obituaries of the year included Lincoln cent designer Victor D. Brenner.

1924 • **Circulation-strike mintage:** 75,178,000.

Availability in Mint State: *MS–60 to 64:* This issue is common in these grades in the context of the early and mid-1920s. *MS-65 and higher:* Sharply struck gems with original color are not difficult to locate, but careful inspection is advised.

Availability in circulated grades: This issue is common in circulated grades.

Characteristics of striking: Many examples are weak, but many others are sharp. Quality is mixed, but there are enough around that this is not a problem.

	Cert	Avg	%MS	G-4	VG-8	F-12	VF-20	EF-40	AU-50	MS-60BN	MS-63BN	MS-65RD
1924	398	63.1	95%	$0.20	$0.30	$0.40	$0.85	$5	$10	$24	$50	$375

1924-D • **Circulation-strike mintage:** 2,520,000.

Availability in Mint State: *MS–60 to 64:* Mint State coins are scarce, and higher-level examples with original color, sharp details, and no spots are rare today. *MS-65 and higher:* Even BN and RB coins are on the scarce side in relation to the demand for them in these grades. More RD coins exist than for certain higher-mintage coins of earlier times, but not many are problem free.

Availability in circulated grades: Registering the lowest mintage since 1914-D, the 1924-D has always been considered a semi-key issue. Many were saved from pocket change in the 1930s and later.

Characteristics of striking: Usually examples appear with weakness, which is often attributed to worn dies, but perhaps most likely comes from the dies being spaced too far apart in the press. Sometimes the left and right borders are light, and on some strikes the D mintmark is not bold.

	Cert	Avg	%MS	G-4	VG-8	F-12	VF-20	EF-40	AU-50	MS-60BN	MS-63BN	MS-65RD
1924-D	1,167	43.4	37%	$40	$45	$50	$60	$125	$175	$300	$350	$12,500

1924-S • **Circulation-strike mintage:** 11,696,000.

Availability in Mint State: *MS–60 to 64:* This issue is scarce in these grades. Most are BN or tinged RB. *MS-65 and higher:* Although the mintage of the 1924-S is multiples of its Denver cousin, in gem Mint State, with original color, the 1924-S eclipses it in rarity—as well as nearly all other cents of this decade!—though the reason for this is unknown today.

Availability in circulated grades: Circulated coins can be found in just about any grade, but most are G or VG.

Characteristics of striking: Usually stiking for this issue is weakly defined in areas. Exceptions are few and far between.

Notes: *Delayed distribution:* It is likely that 1924-S cents were not released into circulation until 1925.

	Cert	Avg	%MS	G-4	VG-8	F-12	VF-20	EF-40	AU-50	MS-60BN	MS-63BN
1924-S	484	55.7	64%	$1.30	$1.50	$2.75	$5.50	$20	$75	$125	$225

Lincoln, Wheat Ears Reverse, Cents of 1925

KEYS TO COLLECTING: The following information on the characteristics of strike for the 1925-D and the 1925-S cents is what connoisseurship is all about. The secret is that if you find a sharp coin it likely will cost no more as 95% or more of buyers are clueless as to sharpness.

1925 • **Circulation-strike mintage:** 139,949,000.

Availability in Mint State: *MS–60 to 64:* This issue is common in these grades. *MS-65 and higher:* This issue is common in gem Mint State, sharply struck and with original color.

Availability in circulated grades: This issue is common in circulated grades.

Characteristics of striking: Most examples are well struck, but there are the inevitable exceptions.

	Cert	Avg	%MS	G-4	VG-8	F-12	VF-20	EF-40	AU-50	MS-60BN	MS-63BN	MS-65RD
1925	812	64.2	98%	$0.20	$0.25	$0.35	$0.60	$3	$6.50	$10	$20	$135

1925-D • **Circulation-strike mintage:** 22,580,000.

Availability in Mint State: *MS–60 to 64:* This issue is common in these grades. *MS-65 and higher:* A gem that is sharply struck and has original mint color is a *rarity*. If you are a typical buyer, you'll find a gem to satisfy you quickly. If you are a connoisseur, perhaps a decade hence you will still be looking for the perfect coin. Ease of collecting always leads to fading of enthusiasm. Seeking sharply struck, mintmarked Lincoln cents of the 1920s will keep you on your toes.

Availability in circulated grades: This issue is common in circulated grades.

Characteristics of striking: This issue is usually weakly struck, which one might think would be embarrassing to the Treasury Department—but no one cared. (During this decade, branch-mint Buffalo nickels, Standing Liberty quarters, and Liberty Walking halves were also miserably struck in most instances.) David W. Lange notes:

> 1925-D vies with 1925-S for the title of most poorly made issue in the entire Lincoln series. It's difficult to believe that the dies for the 1925-D cents were ever new, as sharply rendered specimens are essentially unknown. Gross distortion of the design elements (particularly toward the peripheries) is the norm for these coins. It's quite possible that the [dies were not properly hardened]. This would have led to premature erosion.

	Cert	Avg	%MS	G-4	VG-8	F-12	VF-20	EF-40	AU-50	MS-60BN	MS-63BN	MS-65RD
1925-D	627	61.1	87%	$0.85	$1.30	$2.45	$4	$13	$30	$75	$90	$3,750

1925-S • Circulation-strike mintage: 26,380,000.

Availability in Mint State: *MS–60 to 64:* This issue is scarce in Mint State, and usually dipped when seen. *MS–65 and higher:* This issue is truly rare when certified as MS-65RD. As to a *sharply struck* specimen certified MS-65RD, such a coin would be the find of the year. Good luck!

Availability in circulated grades: This issue is common in circulated grades. Most circulated examples are Good to Fine.

Characteristics of striking: This issue exhibits poor striking, keeping the Denver cents company in this regard.

	Cert	Avg	%MS	G-4	VG-8	F-12	VF-20	EF-40	AU-50	MS-60BN	MS-63BN	MS-65RD
1925-S	488	59.7	79%	$0.75	$1	$1.85	$2.75	$12	$30	$90	$200	$18,000

Lincoln, Wheat Ears Reverse, Cents of 1926

KEYS TO COLLECTING: The 1926-S is a semi-key date. The Philadelphia cents are very common. The 1926-D is common as well, except in a combination of high grade and sharp strike.

1926 • Circulation-strike mintage: 157,088,000.

Availability in Mint State: *MS–60 to 64:* This issue is common in these grades. *MS–65 and higher:* This issue is plentiful in MS-65RD and higher, including well-struck examples.

Availability in circulated grades: This issue is common in circulated grades. Most circulated examples are Good to Fine, a comment appropriate to other cents of the era.

Characteristics of striking: Usually well struck.

	Cert	Avg	%MS	G-4	VG-8	F-12	VF-20	EF-40	AU-50	MS-60BN	MS-63BN	MS-65RD
1926	1,017	64.5	99%	$0.20	$0.25	$0.30	$0.50	$2	$4	$8	$18	$110

1926-D • Circulation-strike mintage: 28,020,000.

Availability in Mint State: *MS–60 to 64:* This issue is easy to find in these grades. Most examples are BN or RB. *MS-65 and higher:* This issue is easy to find in these grades if BN or RB, but super rare if an original RD piece, sharply struck, is sought.

Availability in circulated grades: This issue is very common in circulated grades.

Characteristics of striking: The striking for this issue is poor, as a rule. David W. Lange attributes this to a combination of "dies displaying advanced wear," poor die steel, and low-quality planchets, but Q. David Bowers suggests that improper die spacing was also a significant factor. Find a Full Details coin and you've hit a numismatic World Series home run with the bases loaded.

Notes: *Keys to collecting:* This issue is common in circulated grades and readily available in Mint State as well, except that most brilliant coins have been cleaned. However, Sol Taylor and David W. Lange write that the 1926-D is usually unattractive, dull, and, per Lange, "Those coins graded MS-65RD by the grading services will not be equal in their aesthetic qualities to a 1926 in the same certified grade." (Again, an alert for naïve buyers who believe all certified coins in a given grade are the same!) Gems with original color, sharply struck, are exceedingly rare.

	Cert	Avg	%MS	G-4	VG-8	F-12	VF-20	EF-40	AU-50	MS-60BN	MS-63BN	MS-65RD
1926-D	482	59.9	82%	$1.35	$1.75	$3.50	$5.25	$14	$32	$85	$125	$3,550

1926-S • Circulation-strike mintage: 4,550,000.

Availability in Mint State: *MS–60 to 64:* This issue is rare in these grades, especially if a problem-free example is sought. *MS-65 and higher:* As to certified MS-65RD coins, when David W. Lange wrote his book in 1995, there was just one—count it—just one example certified in this grade. By 2015 PCGS had certified 2. This is *the* rarity among pristine (undipped) Mint State Lincoln cents. A few years ago Sam Lukes, a Lincoln cent specialist for many years, stated that *he* has never seen a 1926-S that he would call MS-65RD. Another well-known specialist in Lincoln cents, who prefers to be referenced as "S.B.," a connoisseur and careful buyer, mentioned to Q. David Bowers some years ago that he had never seen an MS-65 cent with full *original* red, but he had had many RB ones offered to him, and took detailed notes on each. Lo and behold! Some of those former red and brown coins somehow became "RD" and were offered to him again, though he noticed the deception. Presumably, most of these were caught by the certification services if submitted.

Availability in circulated grades: Examples remain scarce in circulated grades in comparison to higher-mintage issues.

Characteristics of striking: Usually example appear with indistinct areas: striking for this issue is generally sub-par. Exceptions are rare. It seems likely that Full Details coins were struck on especially soft planchets and toned very quickly. Weak strikes that have much of the original color were probably struck on harder planchets, which tended to tone more slowly.

Notes: *Keys to collecting:* The low mintage has hallmarked this as a key issue ever since collectors began plucking coins from circulation in the 1930s.

A small cache of 14 RB Uncirculated pieces was sold, against a then-current Raymond *Standard Catalogue* valuation of $25 for Uncirculated, in several lots by New Netherlands in their 50th Sale, December 1957. They realized about $15 to $25 each. Some were described as weakly struck, but probably all were weakly struck to some degree.

	Cert	Avg	%MS	G-4	VG-8	F-12	VF-20	EF-40	AU-50	MS-60BN	MS-63BN	MS-65RD
1926-S	861	54.7	53%	$9	$10	$13	$17	$35	$75	$155	$325	$90,000

Lincoln, Wheat Ears Reverse, Cents of 1927

KEYS TO COLLECTING: In worn grades all issues of this year are common. In high grades with sharp details the two branch-mint varieties are slightly scarce.

HUB WEAR: The detail in new dies continued to decline due to wear on the hubs. Still, in this context, many fairly sharp coins were made, especially at the Philadelphia Mint.

1927 • **Circulation-strike mintage:** 144,440,000.

Availability in Mint State: *MS–60 to 64:* This issue is common in these grades. *MS-65 and higher:* This issue is common in these grades, including sharply struck coins.

Availability in circulated grades: This issue is common in circulated grades.

Characteristics of striking: This issue is usually well struck.

	Cert	Avg	%MS	G-4	VG-8	F-12	VF-20	EF-40	AU-50	MS-60BN	MS-63BN	MS-65RD
1927	747	63.8	97%	$0.20	$0.25	$0.30	$0.60	$2	$3.50	$10	$20	$135

1927-D • **Circulation-strike mintage:** 27,170,000.

Availability in Mint State: *MS–60 to 64:* This issue is common in these grades. *MS-65 and higher:* Full *original* RD coins with sharp details are elusive.

Availability in circulated grades: This issue is common in circulated grades.

Characteristics of striking: Most examples have weakness in areas, but enough were struck well enough that sharp examples are encountered with frequency in the marketplace.

	Cert	Avg	%MS	G-4	VG-8	F-12	VF-20	EF-40	AU-50	MS-60BN	MS-63BN	MS-65RD
1927-D	567	61.2	86%	$1.25	$1.75	$2.75	$3.75	$7.50	$25	$62	$85	$2,100

1927-S • **Circulation-strike mintage:** 14,276,000.

Availability in Mint State: *MS–60 to 64:* This issue is common in these grades. However, Mint State examples are usually weakly struck. *MS-65 and higher:* Examples are plentiful in these grades if they are typically struck. They are extremely rare if they are sharp, with a generous quotient of original mint color. This situation is really amazing in that the absolute *rarity* of original mint-red Lincoln cents with sharp details is almost completely unknown to the general collecting public!

Availability in circulated grades: This issue is common in circulated grades.

Characteristics of striking: The striking of this issue is usually miserable. Sharp examples are rare. David W. Lange wrote that, for his collection, he sold a nearly full RD Mint State coin and kept "an attractive and original red/brown example which grades only AU-58, yet it possesses an absolutely needle-sharp strike." This situation will seem to be very strange to the typical collector!

	Cert	Avg	%MS	G-4	VG-8	F-12	VF-20	EF-40	AU-50	MS-60BN	MS-63BN	MS-65RD
1927-S	431	60.0	79%	$1.50	$2	$3	$5	$15	$40	$85	$140	$7,750

Lincoln, Wheat Ears Reverse, Cents of 1928

KEYS TO COLLECTING: In worn grades all issues of this year are common. In high grades with sharp details the two branch-mint varieties are slightly scarce.

1928 IN NUMISMATICS: The economy was robust, and this called for extensive coinage of new cents at the three mints.

M.L. Beistle, a manufacturer of cardboard and paper products in Shippensburg, Pennsylvania, launched his "Unique Coin Holders" album pages. Later, these were marketed aggressively by Wayte Raymond and helped contribute to the coin boom of the mid-1930s. In the meantime, sales seem to have been slow.

1928 • **Circulation-strike mintage:** 134,116,000.

Availability in Mint State: *MS–60 to 64:* This issue is common in these grades. *MS-65 and higher:* This issue is common in all grades, including well-struck gems with full original color just beginning to naturally fade.

Availability in circulated grades: This issue is common in circulated grades.

Characteristics of striking: Most examples are well struck.

	Cert	Avg	%MS	G-4	VG-8	F-12	VF-20	EF-40	AU-50	MS-60BN	MS-63BN	MS-65RD
1928	836	63.9	98%	$0.20	$0.25	$0.30	$0.60	$2	$3	$9	$13	$120

1928-D • Circulation-strike mintage: 31,170,000.

Availability in Mint State: *MS–60 to 64:* This issue is common in Mint State up to about MS-64. *MS-65 and higher:* MS-65RD coins with original color are somewhat scarce. BN and RB coins in these grades are plentiful.

Availability in circulated grades: This issue is common in circulated grades.

Characteristics of striking: Many examples are lightly defined, though others are sharp. Enough sharp coins are around that finding one will not be a problem.

	Cert	Avg	%MS	G-4	VG-8	F-12	VF-20	EF-40	AU-50	MS-60BN	MS-63BN	MS-65RD
1928-D	513	61.8	87%	$0.75	$1	$1.75	$3	$5.50	$17	$37	$80	$1,200

1928-S • Circulation-strike mintage: 17,266,000.

Availability in Mint State: *MS–60 to 64:* This issue is common in all grades up to about MS-64BN and RB. *MS-65 and higher:* MS-65RD coins with sharp strike are rarities. With normal strike they are quite scarce.

Availability in circulated grades: This issue is common in circulated grades.

Characteristics of striking: Striking is usually weak for this issue. David W. Lange calls them "mushy."

	Cert	Avg	%MS	G-4	VG-8	F-12	VF-20	EF-40	AU-50	MS-60BN	MS-63BN	MS-65RD
1928-S	341	60.8	84%	$1	$1.60	$2.75	$3.75	$9.50	$30	$75	$100	$4,000

Varieties: *1928-S, Large S and Small S Mintmarks:* The difference between the small S and the large S is dramatic. The large S is the rarer of the two and accounts for perhaps no more than 5% to 10% of those known. These command a premium to variety specialists.[186]

A detail showing the small mintmark.

The 1928-S, Large S Mintmark, can be identified as FS-01-1928S-501, or as CONECA 1928-S, MMS-003. It has a rarity of URS-14.

The large mintmark has a very "fat" or heavy diagonal at the center and flat edges at the upper right and lower left to the serifs. The small mintmark is, of course, smaller and has blobs at the serifs. A similar difference is found among 1941-S cents (see page 430), these being better known than the 1928-S. Collector interest in the 1928-S mintmarks is minimal, and you should be able to buy either without paying a premium. The 1928-S, Small S, is priced in the 1928-S chart, above.

A detail showing the large mintmark.

	VF-20	EF-40	AU-50	MS-60	MS-63	MS-65
FS-01-1928S-501	$15	$25	$50	$95	$150	$950

Lincoln, Wheat Ears Reverse, Cents of 1929

KEYS TO COLLECTING: In worn grades all are common. The Denver and San Francisco coins are slightly scarce in higher grades, but enough exist that finding nice examples will be no problem. In this and other commentaries it is *implicit* that cherrypicking for sharp strike is desirable. Such coins cost no more, but take time to find.

ODD CENTS: Newspaper accounts stated that certain 1929 cents, on which the head of Lincoln was "too small," turned up in Evanston, Illinois. These must have been counterfeits despite this report:

> Federal authorities were called in. They telegraphed the government mints and found that the pennies, instead of being counterfeit, were of imperfect coinage, and that they should never have been put into circulation. Mint officials asked that the imperfect coins be withdrawn from circulation at once. But Evanston coin collectors, learning of the situation, began bidding $1 each for the pennies. . . . The pennies bear the date 1929. The Lincoln head is considerably smaller than on other pennies, and the edges are rough.

1929 IN NUMISMATICS: New 1929 coins began piling up in bank vaults, adding to limited supplies of 1927 and 1928 issues. Somehow, the demand for cents in commerce had slowed. When coin collecting became very popular in 1934, some of these older rolls were found and saved.

1929 • **Circulation-strike mintage:** 185,262,000.

Availability in Mint State: *MS–60 to 64:* This issue is plentiful in all of these grades. *MS-65 and higher:* This issue is common in these grades. Cents of this year and the next several years have a deeper red-orange color than coins of later or earlier dates.

Availability in circulated grades: This issue is common in circulated grades.

Characteristics of striking: Examples are usually sharply struck, but there are exceptions.

	Cert	Avg	%MS	G-4	VG-8	F-12	VF-20	EF-40	AU-50	MS-60BN	MS-63BN	MS-65RD
1929	969	64.4	98%	$0.20	$0.25	$0.30	$0.75	$2	$4	$8	$14	$105

1929-D • **Circulation-strike mintage:** 41,730,000.

Availability in Mint State: *MS–60 to 64:* This issue is easy to find overall in these grades, but sharply struck coins are slightly scarce. *MS-65 and higher:* This issue is common in these grades in the context of branch-mint cents of the 1920s. MS-65RD and higher are rare, if sharply struck, but otherwise readily available.

Availability in circulated grades: This issue is common in circulated grades.

Characteristics of striking: Examples usually appear with weakness in areas. Some are sharp, however. Full Details coins can be found.

Notes: *Keys to collecting:* This issue is common in all grades through Mint State, though sharp strikes become more difficult to obtain at higher grade levels.

	Cert	Avg	%MS	G-4	VG-8	F-12	VF-20	EF-40	AU-50	MS-60BN	MS-63BN	MS-65RD
1929-D	426	63.0	94%	$0.40	$0.85	$1.25	$2.25	$5.50	$13	$25	$37	$550

1929-S • Circulation-strike mintage: 50,148,000.

Availability in Mint State: *MS–60 to 64:* This issue is common in these grades. The quality of striking varies. *MS-65 and higher:* The same comment as for the 1929-D applies.

Availability in circulated grades: This issue is common in circulated grades.

Characteristics of striking: Striking for this issue is a mixed bag, with most examples having weakness to one degree or another. Full Details coins exist, however.

Notes: *Keys to collecting:* This issue is common in all grades through gem–Mint State RD. Sharpness adds a challenge, and well-struck coins are in the minority.

	Cert	Avg	%MS	G-4	VG-8	F-12	VF-20	EF-40	AU-50	MS-60BN	MS-63BN	MS-65RD
1929-S	679	63.4	96%	$0.50	$0.90	$1.65	$2.35	$5.80	$14	$21	$29	$475

Lincoln, Wheat Ears Reverse, Cents of 1930

KEYS TO COLLECTING: Many bank-wrapped rolls were saved in this era, but far fewer than would be the case in 1934 and later.

1930 IN NUMISMATICS: In 1930 a Mint State 1909-S V.D.B. cent would have cost you 25¢: a price not much different from five years earlier or, for that matter, two or three years later.

The Scott Stamp & Coin Company, operated by Wayte Raymond, began to market its "National" albums made by Beistle—presaging a new world of collecting. Raymond commented that the company had discontinued selling coins some years earlier because: "At that time the collection of coins required bulky cabinets; such things as were available were not only expensive but were ugly in appearance. They had no place in the home, excepting perhaps some out of the way corner in the cellar." The annual American Numismatic Association convention was held at the Statler Hotel in Buffalo in August. Membership was 1,196. The year 1930 closed on a favorable note. In complete contravention to the national economy, the hobby of coin collecting was strong and growing stronger. The Scott albums had a lot to do with this.

1930 • Circulation-strike mintage: 157,415,000.

Availability in Mint State: This issue is common. From this year forward MS-65 coins are very plentiful, and quite a few are in even higher grades (and are mainly sought by those in the PCGS registry set competition). For grade-by-grade data for each issue both PCGS and NGC offer reports on the populations they have certified online. Over time the number of coins certified in various grades.

Availability in circulated grades: This issue is common in circulated grades.

Characteristics of striking: Striking quality varies for this issue. Most examples are fairly well struck, considering that the hub dies had been losing detail since 1916.

Notes: *Keys to collecting:* This issue is common in any desired grade, including MS-65RD and beyond, sharply struck.

	Cert	Avg	%MS	G-4	VG-8	F-12	VF-20	EF-40	AU-50	MS-60BN	MS-63BN	MS-65RD
1930	3,546	65.3	100%	$0.15	$0.20	$0.25	$0.50	$1.25	$2	$6	$10	$43

1930-D • Circulation-strike mintage: 40,100,000.

Availability in Mint State: This issue is common in all grades through gem Mint State, sharply struck, but this is the scarcest of the three issues of this year.

Availability in circulated grades: This issue is common in circulated grades.

Characteristics of striking: Quality of striking is mixed for this issue; sharp strikes are available, but they are in the minority.

	Cert	Avg	%MS	G-4	VG-8	F-12	VF-20	EF-40	AU-50	MS-60BN	MS-63BN	MS-65RD
1930-D	671	64.2	98%	$0.20	$0.25	$0.30	$0.55	$2.50	$4	$12	$28	$115

Varieties: Most examples seem to have a large D mintmark, but in the December 1953 issue of the *Numismatic Scrapbook Magazine*, Arlie Slabaugh reported a small D mintmark. In actuality, for the "large" D, the same D punch (normally employed from 1917 to 1932) was used, but punched more deeply into a working die. One rare variety has the 0 in the date filled in, due to the center breaking away from the working die.

1930-S • Circulation-strike mintage: 24,286,000.

Availability in Mint State: This issue is common in all grades, including gems with sharp details and original mint red-orange color.

Availability in circulated grades: This issue is common in circulated grades.

Characteristics of striking: Examples are usually fairly well struck, making this issue a standout in comparison to the typical San Francisco cent of the 1920s.

	Cert	Avg	%MS	G-4	VG-8	F-12	VF-20	EF-40	AU-50	MS-60BN	MS-63BN	MS-65RD
1930-S	1,535	64.8	99%	$0.20	$0.25	$0.30	$0.60	$1.75	$6	$10	$12	$90

Lincoln, Wheat Ears Reverse, Cents of 1931

KEYS TO COLLECTING: The 1931-S is a key to the series, at least with regard to finding them in circulation after the early 1940s. Today, examples are readily available in all grades. The higher-mintage 1931-D is much scarcer in Mint State as few people paid attention to it. Philadelphia cents are common.

1931 • Circulation-strike mintage: 19,396,000.

Availability in Mint State: This issue is common in all grades, including sharply struck gems with original color. It is important to remember that "common" in this context is *rare* in comparison to *any* date and mintmark struck in 1934 or later. Cents of 1931 never were readily available in quantities of bank-wrapped rolls, and Q. David Bowers does not recall ever handling one (and his activity as a dealer began in 1953).

Availability in circulated grades: This issue is common in circulated grades.

Characteristics of striking: Examples are usually well struck.

	Cert	Avg	%MS	G-4	VG-8	F-12	VF-20	EF-40	AU-50	MS-60BN	MS-63BN	MS-65RD
1931	658	64.0	97%	$0.50	$0.75	$1	$1.50	$4	$9	$20	$35	$125

1931-D • Circulation-strike mintage: 4,480,000.

Availability in Mint State: This issue is readily available, but far scarcer than its lower-mintage cousin, the 1931-S, in gem Mint State with sharp details. Rolls and other quantities of the 1931-D were generally overlooked by dealers and collectors in this era, and few were saved.

Availability in circulated grades: This issue is common in any and all grades, but it is a semi-key issue among cents of this decade.

Characteristics of striking: Examples are usually well struck.

	Cert	Avg	%MS	G-4	VG-8	F-12	VF-20	EF-40	AU-50	MS-60BN	MS-63BN	MS-65RD
1931-D	769	59.6	70%	$5	$6	$7	$8.50	$13.50	$37	$60	$70	$875

1931-S • Circulation-strike mintage: 866,000.

Availability in Mint State: Examples are very common in Mint State, as at least several hundred thousand exist. These cents were often traded as bank-wrapped rolls of 50 coins in the early 1950s. Until the coin market boom that began in 1960, rolls of 1931-S cents turned up more often than any other Lincoln cent before 1934. Later, the rolls were broken apart, and today Mint State 1931-S coins are usually seen one at a time.

Availability in circulated grades: This issue is very scarce in circulated grades in the context of the series. In the 1950s when Lincoln cents dating back to 1909 could be found in circulation, examples of the 1931-S were the third-rarest cents in terms of those found in circulation, trailing by a significant distance the 1909-S V.D.B. and 1914-D cents.

Characteristics of striking: Striking varies for this issue, but it is usually above average. Sharp coins can be found, but they are in the minority.

Notes: *Keys to collecting:* A key to the series, the 1931-S is a famous issue due to its low mintage. Plentiful in Mint State or close and rare in worn grades, it has attracted attention for a long time. This issue was not widely released in 1931, but held by the Treasury. Later, specimens were made available for face value to collectors and investors, probably resulting in at least half of them being saved in Mint State. Today these remain readily available in gem quality with good strike, but spotting can be a problem. Many have been dipped.

Walter Breen reported that the Maurice Scharlack hoard contained "over 200,000 red Uncirculated specimens, many weak." Q. David Bowers reports that he has found no confirmation of this quantity, which seems to be overly large for one dealer, and David W. Lange is skeptical of the figure as well. Scharlack was known for his hoarding of 1922-D cents. Breen often added a generous measure of guesswork to his research.[187] In the mid-1950s Bowers bought a cigar box full of rolls (more than a thousand coins) from Dayton dealer James Kelly.

David W. Lange supplied this letter written in 1985 by veteran dealer Norman Shultz, of Salt Lake City, Utah:

> The 1931-S cents were sent to the Federal Reserve Bank here in 1935—500,000 of them. One of the fellows working here called me and told me they had these, and how many did I want? In 1935 money was scarce with any coin dealer, and I took a $20 sack. I sold it to a lawyer for the Southern Pacific in Los Angeles for 40¢ each. A year later he sold them back to me for 30¢ each. This will give you some idea how tight money was. The bank would not lend me money to buy coins even when I offered to put up face value in rare coins.[188]

	Cert	Avg	%MS	G-4	VG-8	F-12	VF-20	EF-40	AU-50	MS-60BN	MS-63BN	MS-65RD
1931-S	4,613	55.0	60%	$60	$75	$85	$100	$125	$150	$175	$195	$550

Lincoln, Wheat Ears Reverse, Cents of 1932

KEYS TO COLLECTING: Cents of this year, made only at Philadelphia and Denver, are common in all grades.

1932 IN NUMISMATICS: The Treasury Department accommodated collectors by offering recent as well as older issues of Uncirculated coins from its stocks. The cost was just face value plus postage. Included were these Lincoln cents: 1929, 1929-S, 1930, 1930-D, 1930-S, 1931, 1931-D, 1931-S, 1932, and 1932-D. Alert collectors and dealers descended upon the opportunity, particularly focusing on the low-mintage 1931-S cents, of which at least several hundred thousand were purchased and squirreled away for investment and stock. At the Philadelphia, Denver, and San Francisco mints, coinage production was at low levels, and some denominations, continuing the trend from 1931, were not produced at all.

1932 • Circulation-strike mintage: 9,062,000.

Availability in Mint State: The production this year hit an all-time low for the Philadelphia Mint Lincoln cent. Despite this, today there are enough examples around, having been picked from circulation or saved in rolls, to fill numismatic demand. Singles in MS-65RD with sharp details are easily enough found.

Availability in circulated grades: This issue is common in circulated grades.

Characteristics of striking: Striking varies for this issue, but enough sharp examples exist that finding one will not be a problem.

	Cert	Avg	%MS	G-4	VG-8	F-12	VF-20	EF-40	AU-50	MS-60BN	MS-63BN	MS-65RD
1932	717	64.4	97%	$1.50	$1.75	$2	$2.50	$4.50	$12	$20	$28	$115

1932-D • Circulation-strike mintage: 10,500,000.

Availability in Mint State: Examples are readily available in any desired grade, up to MS-65RD and beyond, sharply struck. They are scarce, however, in the context of any and all issues 1934 and later. Q. David Bowers does not recall ever having had an original 50-coin roll of these, though, in contrast, he has had hundreds of rolls of 1931-S cents.

Availability in circulated grades: This issue is common in circulate grades.

Characteristics of striking: Striking varies for this issue, but finding a sharp example will not be difficult.

	Cert	Avg	%MS	G-4	VG-8	F-12	VF-20	EF-40	AU-50	MS-60BN	MS-63BN	MS-65RD
1932-D	444	63.7	93%	$1.50	$1.75	$2.50	$2.75	$4.50	$11	$19	$28	$155

Lincoln, Wheat Ears Reverse, Cents of 1933

KEYS TO COLLECTING: Cents of this year, made only at Philadelphia and Denver, are common in all grades.

1933 IN NUMISMATICS: Although by this time the 1931-S cent had attracted attention for its low mintage, scarcely any attention was paid to the new issues of 1933, the last year for which this would be true. President Roosevelt stopped the production of gold coins and called for the surrender of those held by the public and banks, except a personal quantity of up to $100 face value and rare coins kept for numismatic purposes. At the several mints the production of new copper, nickel, and silver coins was low, as it had been in recent years.

1933 • Circulation-strike mintage: 14,360,000.

Availability in Mint State: This issue is scarce in terms of mintage, but enough were saved, including in gem Mint State, that finding an ideal coin will be easy.

Availability in circulated grades: This issue is common in circulated grades.

Characteristics of striking: Striking is often sharp for this issue, but there are exceptions.

	Cert	Avg	%MS	G-4	VG-8	F-12	VF-20	EF-40	AU-50	MS-60BN	MS-63BN	MS-65RD
1933	697	64.7	98%	$1.50	$1.75	$2.50	$3	$6.25	$13	$20	$30	$115

1933-D • **Circulation-strike mintage:** 6,200,000.

Availability in Mint State: Examples are readily available on the numismatic market, including well-struck gems with original color. They are scarce or even rare, however, in comparison to issues of 1934 and later.

Availability in circulated grades: This issue is common in circulated grades.

Characteristics of striking: Examples are usually well struck. Sharp coins are easy to find. In this year, a new, larger D mintmark was used; it would remain the standard for decades.

	Cert	Avg	%MS	G-4	VG-8	F-12	VF-20	EF-40	AU-50	MS-60BN	MS-63BN	MS-65RD
1933-D	1,029	64.3	97%	$3.50	$3.75	$5.50	$7.25	$12	$19	$26	$30	$135

Lincoln, Wheat Ears Reverse, Cents of 1934

KEYS TO COLLECTING: This was the first year that bank-wrapped rolls of Uncirculated Lincoln cents were saved in large quantities. As demand for cents for circulation increased, banks and the Treasury tapped into the stocks in their vaults, including some cents dating back to the late 1920s.

In the 1950s it was common to buy and sell $50 face-value bags of cents from 1934 to date. Robert Friedberg, for one, bought these in quantity for sale in the leased coin boutiques he operated in various department stores. The key to such a group was the 1939-D cent, this being a scarcer bag than the others. After the late 1950s such quantities no longer traded, but the buying and selling of 50-coin rolls was a dynamic activity.

From 1934 onward, all standard circulation-strike dates and mintmarks are common in relation to the demand for them. On an absolute basis, the later the year, the more common the coins. Accordingly, from this year onward we give a general commentary relating to Mint State coins. Striking varied over the years, but with many millions made each year, finding sharp examples is not difficult.

1934 IN NUMISMATICS: In 1934 the first large edition of Wayte Raymond's *Standard Catalogue of United States Coins* was issued, to be followed by 18 editions through the late 1950s.

1934 • **Circulation-strike mintage:** 219,080,000.

Commentary: This is a common date in any and all grades. Millions were saved at the time of issue, initiating the interest in saving rolls as an investment in the hobby. This is the starting gate for all later dates and mintmarks being available in multiple-roll quantities until the rolls started to be broken up in the 1960s and 1970s. From here forward, among regular dates and mintmarks, MS-65RD coins are plentiful in relation to the demand for them, although some are more elusive than others. For most of these through the 1980s MS-65RD is the target grade of choice for many collectors. MS-66RD and 67RD coins are usually readily available but more expensive, as they are often in certified holders that necessitated incurring a certification fee. The certified population records of NGC and PCGS indicate availability in even higher grades exists. Most dates and mintmarks have relatively few certified MS-68 or higher until recent decades.

Notes: ***Date numeral:*** The 3 in the date has a *long, pointed tail* at the bottom, unlike all other 3 digits in the series to date, and unlike the 3 used later in this decade; this pointed-tail style was again used in 1943 and was not employed again after that.

A detail of the 3 in the date, showing a long, pointed tail.

	Cert	Avg	%MS	G-4	VG-8	F-12	VF-20	EF-40	AU-50	MS-60BN	MS-63BN	MS-65RD
1934	2,048	65.7	100%	$0.15	$0.18	$0.20	$0.30	$1	$4	$10	$12	$37

1934, Double-Die Obverse •

Circulation-strike mintage: Included in 1934 circulation-strike mintage figure.

Commentary: The Fivaz-Stanton identification for this variety is FS-01-1934-101. It can also be identified as CONECA 1934, DDO-004. Its rarity is URS-4. The remains of a secondary 9 and 3 can be seen southeast of the date.

A detail of the date showing the secondary 9 and 3 below.

	Cert	Avg	%MS	PF-63RB
1934, Doubled-Die Obverse	3	58.0	67%	$300

1934-D • Circulation-strike mintage: 28,446,000.

Commentary: This issue is common in all Mint State grades, although this is the scarcest issue of 1934 and later. It is sufficiently scarce that some offerings of roll sets in the 1950s (when such were stock-in-trade on the market) started with the three mint varieties of 1935 rather than 1934, as rolls of 1934-D were seldom seen.

	Cert	Avg	%MS	G-4	VG-8	F-12	VF-20	EF-40	AU-50	MS-60BN	MS-63BN	MS-65RD
1934-D	910	64.8	99%	$0.20	$0.25	$0.50	$0.75	$2.25	$7.50	$22	$25	$62

Lincoln, Wheat Ears Reverse, Cents of 1935

KEYS TO COLLECTING: From 1934 onward, all standard circulation-strike dates and mintmarks are common in relation to the demand for them, and with many millions made each year, finding sharp examples is not difficult. Accordingly, from 1934 on we give a general commentary relating to Mint State coins.

1935 IN NUMISMATICS: Collecting coins by dates and mintmarks became popular due to the wide sales of boards and albums for storage and display. In Uncirculated grades, key issues among Lincoln cents were the 1913-D, 1913-S, 1914, 1914-D, 1914-S (especially hard to find and valued at about $2 a piece), 1915, 1924-D, and 1924-S. The 1909-S V.D.B. was still around in roll quantities and was apt to sell for 25¢ or so each. Whitman Publishing sold "penny boards," which had been invented by J.K. Post of Neenah, Wisconsin. These sold like hotcakes. Commemorative coins were as hot as a firecracker. By year's end, 1935 stood as the most dynamic 12-month period the numismatic hobby had ever known.

1935 • Circulation-strike mintage: 245,388,000.

Commentary: This issue is common in all grades including sharply struck MS-65RD and higher.

	Cert	Avg	%MS	G-4	VG-8	F-12	VF-20	EF-40	AU-50	MS-60BN	MS-63BN	MS-65RD
1935	1,911	65.7	99%	$0.15	$0.18	$0.20	$0.25	$0.50	$1	$3	$5	$33

1935-D • Circulation-strike mintage: 47,000,000.

Commentary: This issue is common in all grades through gem MS-65RD and higher, although it is necessarily seen less often than its higher-mintage Philadelphia counterpart. Striking can vary, and more than just a few are weakly struck. Sharp examples survive but constitute a tiny minority of coins in the marketplace. Finding one can be a challenge in comparison to most other cents of this decade.

	Cert	Avg	%MS	G-4	VG-8	F-12	VF-20	EF-40	AU-50	MS-60BN	MS-63BN	MS-65RD
1935-D	1,336	65.7	100%	$0.15	$0.18	$0.20	$0.25	$0.50	$2	$5	$6	$39

1935-S • Circulation-strike mintage: 38,702,000.

Commentary: Quality varies widely for the 1935-S, with some examples being weakly struck and others having irregular toning. Finding a choice gem is doable, but cherry-picking is advised—perhaps more so than for any other Lincoln cent in this *decade*. Get set for an enjoyable treasure hunt for a sharp coin.

	Cert	Avg	%MS	G-4	VG-8	F-12	VF-20	EF-40	AU-50	MS-60BN	MS-63BN	MS-65RD
1935-S	840	64.8	99%	$0.15	$0.18	$0.25	$0.50	$2	$5	$12	$17	$60

Lincoln, Wheat Ears Reverse, Cents of 1936

KEYS TO COLLECTING: From 1934 onward, all standard circulation-strike dates and mintmarks are common in relation to the demand for them, and with many millions made each year, finding sharp examples is not difficult. Accordingly, from 1934 on we give a general commentary relating to Mint State coins.

1936 IN NUMISMATICS: Proof coins were offered to collectors for the first time since 1916. Proofs were available as a set from the cent to the half dollar for $1.91. In addition desired coins could be ordered singly. Meanwhile, with all of the commemorative excitement, few collectors were interested in ordering the new Proof coins.

1936 • Circulation-strike mintage: 309,632,000.

Commentary: This issue is very common in any grade desired. Striking varies, but it is mostly sharp.

	Cert	Avg	%MS	G-4	VG-8	F-12	VF-20	EF-40	AU-50	MS-60BN	MS-63BN	MS-65RD
1936	2,677	65.5	98%	$0.15	$0.18	$0.25	$0.50	$1.50	$2.60	$5	$7	$30

1936, Doubled-Die Obverse •

Circulation-strike mintage: Included in 1936 circulation-strike mintage.

Commentary: The Fivaz-Stanton identification for this variety is FS-01-1936-101. It can also be identified as CONECA 1936, DDO-001. Its rarity is URS-10. This variety was not widely known until recent times (a listing in the regular edition of *A Guide Book of United States Coins* has helped to publicize it). The variety shows distinctive doubling when viewed under low-power magnification. Several varieties exist and are described in detail by John Wexler and Kevin Flynn in *The Authoritative Reference on Lincoln Cents*. Bill Fivaz and J.T. Stanton's *Cherrypickers' Guide to Rare Die Varieties of United States Coins* lists three of them. Most are well struck. These are very elusive, and gems, if found, are apt to be very expensive.

A detail of the doubling at 1936.

A detail of the doubling at LIBERTY.

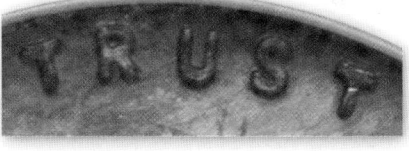

A detail of the doubling at TRUST.

	Cert	Avg	%MS	F-12	VF-20	EF-40	AU-50	MS-60BN	MS-63BN
1936, Doubled-Die Obverse	57	42.9	23%	$75	$125	$200	$350	$500	$1,500

1936, Proof • Proof mintage: 5,569.

Proof commentary: The earliest Proofs of this year had only partially mirrored surfaces and were satiny. Today, these are called Type I issues. Soon the fully mirrored format, with the polished area on the dies including the portrait and other features, was used. The mirror-finish coins are seen more often.

	Cert	Avg	%MS	PF-63RB	PF-64RB	PF-65RD
1936, Proof	719	64.0		$200	$485	$2,750

1936-D • Circulation-strike mintage: 40,620,000.

Commentary: This issue is common in all grades through gem MS-65 and higher.

	Cert	Avg	%MS	G-4	VG-8	F-12	VF-20	EF-40	AU-50	MS-60BN	MS-63BN	MS-65RD
1936-D	1,685	65.9	100%	$0.15	$0.20	$0.30	$0.50	$1	$2	$4	$7	$21

1936-S • Circulation-strike mintage: 29,130,000.

Commentary: Saved in large quantities at the time of issue, the 1936-S is common today in any desired grade. Later mintages in the *billions* would make the 1936-S and other cents of the 1930s seem rare by comparison. In 1936 and today, the number of available gems exceeded the number of numismatists seeking them.

	Cert	Avg	%MS	G-4	VG-8	F-12	VF-20	EF-40	AU-50	MS-60BN	MS-63BN	MS-65RD
1936-S	1,233	65.5	100%	$0.15	$0.25	$0.40	$0.55	$1	$3	$5	$6	$25

Lincoln, Wheat Ears Reverse, Cents of 1937

KEYS TO COLLECTING: From 1934 onward, all standard circulation-strike dates and mintmarks are common in relation to the demand for them, and with many millions made each year, finding sharp examples is not difficult. Accordingly, from 1934 on we give a general commentary relating to Mint State coins.

SAN FRANCISCO MINT: The new San Francisco Mint began striking coins this year. Cents were struck at the old San Francisco Mint early in the year, then in the autumn, in the new facility.

REEDED EDGE CAPER: In 1941 at the American Numismatic Association convention held that year in Philadelphia, Ira Z. Reed, a well-known Philadelphia dealer, offered pairs of 1937 Lincoln cents and Buffalo nickels with *reeded edges* for sale. These were sold as novelties, as they were not Mint products. Somehow, the intent of these novelties was forgotten, and in time both were later listed as rarities in *A Guide Book of United States Coins*. By now they have been discredited and delisted for a long time.

1937 IN NUMISMATICS: In *The Numismatist* in June, editor Frank Duffield noted: "Anyone, without the expenditure of even a dollar, may start a collection of small cents. This makes that series of coins attractive to both sexes of all ages. Its attractiveness has been stimulated by the cardboard holders for the series placed on the market by novelty dealers." A brilliant Uncirculated 1909-S V.D.B. cent cost about $2 in the

The new San Francisco Mint first occupied in 1937, replacing the facility in use since 1874.

marketplace, or nearly 10 times its market price of a decade earlier and up from just 50¢ a few years before. Other Lincoln, Wheat Ears Reverse, cents in this grade were priced as follows:

1909-S: $1	1911-S: $1.75	1912-S: 90¢	1913-S: $2.75	1914-S: $2.75
1910-S: 50¢	1911-D: $1.25	1912-D: $1.75	1913-D: $2.25	1914-D: $8

Whitman Publishing continued to offer penny boards for 25¢—"developing . . . the numismatists of tomorrow," an advertisement noted.

In the meantime many scarce and rare coins had been rescued by bank and Treasury employees who had substituted common coins for them. Large quantities of formerly scarce varieties were sold to New York dealers especially.

1937 • Circulation-strike mintage: 309,170,000.

Commentary: This issue is common in any and all grades desired. Most examples are sharply struck.

	Cert	Avg	%MS	G-4	VG-8	F-12	VF-20	EF-40	AU-50	MS-60BN	MS-63BN	MS-65RD
1937	3,958	66.0	100%	$0.15	$0.20	$0.30	$0.50	$1	$2	$3	$5	$15

1937, Proof • Proof mintage: 9,320.

Proof commentary: These are readily available in proportion to the number minted. Many have been dipped, then later acquired spots, and then were redipped. Pristine coins will always have gentle toning. There are no exceptions to this rule.

	Cert	Avg	%MS	PF-63RB	PF-64RB	PF-65RD
1937, Proof	849	64.4		$65	$90	$350

1937-D • Circulation-strike mintage: 50,430,000.

Commentary: Overall, this is a high-quality issue. It is common in all grades, including sharply struck in MS-65RD and higher.

	Cert	Avg	%MS	G-4	VG-8	F-12	VF-20	EF-40	AU-50	MS-60BN	MS-63BN	MS-65RD
1937-D	2,525	66.2	100%	$0.15	$0.20	$0.25	$0.40	$1	$3	$5	$6	$17

1937-S • **Circulation-strike mintage:** 34,500,000.

Commentary: Examples are common today, including those in gem preservation. Sharpness can vary.

	Cert	Avg	%MS	G-4	VG-8	F-12	VF-20	EF-40	AU-50	MS-60BN	MS-63BN	MS-65RD
1937-S	1,565	65.9	100%	$0.15	$0.20	$0.30	$0.40	$1	$3	$5	$8	$22

Lincoln, Wheat Ears Reverse, Cents of 1938

KEYS TO COLLECTING: From 1934 onward, all standard circulation-strike dates and mintmarks are common in relation to the demand for them, and with many millions made each year, finding sharp examples is not difficult. Accordingly, from 1934 on we give a general commentary relating to Mint State coins.

1938 IN NUMISMATICS: The coin market continued to be robust for just about all coins except commemoratives, the investment market for these having collapsed in late 1936.

1938 • **Circulation-strike mintage:** 156,682,000.

Commentary: This issue is usually well struck. It is common in Mint State, including grades MS-65 and finer.

	Cert	Avg	%MS	G-4	VG-8	F-12	VF-20	EF-40	AU-50	MS-60BN	MS-63BN	MS-65RD
1938	2,084	66.1	100%	$0.15	$0.20	$0.30	$0.40	$1	$2	$4	$7	$16

1938, Proof • **Proof mintage:** 14,734.

Proof commentary: Examples are plentiful, in keeping with the mintage. Due to dipping and spotting (from glue in the cellophane envelopes in which they were issued as well as from cleaning), pristine gems are scarce. These always have delicate toning.

	Cert	Avg	%MS	PF-63RB	PF-64RB	PF-65RD
1938, Proof	992	64.5		$60	$80	$200

1938-D • **Circulation-strike mintage:** 20,010,000.

Commentary: This issue is common in Mint State, including grades MS-65 and finer.

	Cert	Avg	%MS	G-4	VG-8	F-12	VF-20	EF-40	AU-50	MS-60BN	MS-63BN	MS-65RD
1938-D	2,051	66.1	100%	$0.20	$0.30	$0.50	$0.80	$1.25	$3	$4	$7	$17

1938-S • **Circulation-strike mintage:** 15,180,000.

Commentary: Despite the relatively small mintage, quantities were saved by collectors, dealers, and investors. Gems are readily available today.

	Cert	Avg	%MS	G-4	VG-8	F-12	VF-20	EF-40	AU-50	MS-60BN	MS-63BN	MS-65RD
1938-S	2,536	66.1	100%	$0.40	$0.50	$0.60	$0.75	$1.10	$3	$4	$6	$21

Varieties: *1938-S, Large S Over Seemingly Small S (FS-01-1938S-501):* This variety can also be identified as CONECA 1938-S, RPM-001. Its rarity is URS-10. An S was first punched into the die lightly, making it appear smaller, and then overpunched deeply with a stronger and larger impression of the same punch.[189]

A detail of the repunched mintmarks.

1938-S, Triple-Punched Mintmark (FS-1938S-502): This variety can also be identified as CONECA 1938-S, RPM-002. Its rarity is URS-11. This is one of the most interesting mintmark repunchings in the Lincoln series. All three S mintmarks are clearly visible.

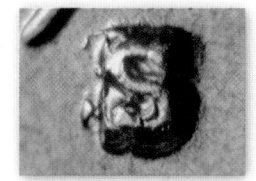

A detail of the repunched mintmarks.

	VF-20	EF-40	AU-50	MS-60	MS-63	MS-65
FS-01-1938S-501	$5	$7.50	$10	$15	$25	$35
FS-01-1938S-502	$5	$7.50	$10	$15	$25	$35

Lincoln, Wheat Ears Reverse, Cents of 1939

KEYS TO COLLECTING: From 1934 onward, all standard circulation-strike dates and mintmarks are common in relation to the demand for them, and with many millions made each year, finding sharp examples is not difficult. Accordingly, from 1934 on we give a general commentary relating to Mint State coins.

1939 IN NUMISMATICS: Wayte Raymond offered a complete collection of Uncirculated Lincoln cents from 1909 to 1938 for $80 in this year.

1939 • Circulation-strike mintage: 316,466,000.

Commentary: This issue is common in Mint State, including grades MS-65 and finer.

	Cert	Avg	%MS	G-4	VG-8	F-12	VF-20	EF-40	AU-50	MS-60BN	MS-63BN	MS-65RD
1939	3,008	66.1	100%	$0.15	$0.18	$0.20	$0.25	$0.50	$1	$2	$4	$14

1939, Proof • Proof mintage: 13,520.

Proof commentary: Examples are readily available, but pristine, undipped gems are in the minority. In one variety, the second 9 in the date appears smaller, due to overpolishing of the die.

	Cert	Avg	%MS	PF-63RB	PF-64RB	PF-65RD
1939, Proof	987	64.7		$55	$70	$180

1939-D • Circulation-strike mintage: 15,160,000.

Commentary: This issue is common in absolute terms, but scarce in the context of Lincoln, Wheat Ears Reverse, cents of the era. Among rolls of cents from 1934 onward, this is the key issue. The low mintage was widely recognized at the time of issue, and

large quantities of rolls were saved by collectors. Gems are available easily enough. In 1946 this cent was well known as a key issue. In that year, dealer R. Green of Chicago offered rolls of 50 Uncirculated coins "for investment" at $3.60—certainly a fortunate purchase for anyone at the time.

	Cert	Avg	%MS	G-4	VG-8	F-12	VF-20	EF-40	AU-50	MS-60BN	MS-63BN	MS-65RD
1939-D	1,667	66.1	100%	$0.50	$0.60	$0.65	$0.85	$1.25	$3	$4	$5	$18

1939-S • Circulation-strike mintage: 52,070,000.

Commentary: Although enough examples were saved that they are common today, most have unsatisfactory luster and are not from sharp dies. Cherrypicking for quality is advised and costs no more than the alternative.

	Cert	Avg	%MS	G-4	VG-8	F-12	VF-20	EF-40	AU-50	MS-60BN	MS-63BN	MS-65RD
1939-S	3,276	66.0	100%	$0.15	$0.20	$0.30	$0.75	$1	$2.50	$3	$4	$16

Lincoln, Wheat Ears Reverse, Cents of 1940

KEYS TO COLLECTING: From 1934 onward, all standard circulation-strike dates and mintmarks are common in relation to the demand for them, and with many millions made each year, finding sharp examples is not difficult. Accordingly, from 1934 on we give a general commentary relating to Mint State coins.

1940 IN NUMISMATICS: The coin hobby remained strong in 1940, with continuing emphasis on starting out by collecting Lincoln cents from circulation. Gold coins were very popular. Dealers had smiles on their faces.

1940 • Circulation-strike mintage: 586,810,000.

Commentary: Examples are very common, including well-struck gems. Grades above MS-65 exist and are often sought by builders of PCGS and NGC registry sets.

	Cert	Avg	%MS	G-4	VG-8	F-12	VF-20	EF-40	AU-50	MS-60BN	MS-63BN	MS-65RD
1940	2,533	66.1	100%	$0.15	$0.18	$0.20	$0.40	$0.60	$1	$2	$3	$14

1940, Proof • Proof mintage: 15,872.

Proof commentary: This issue is plentiful in proportion to its mintage. Pristine, undipped coins are in the minority.

	Cert	Avg	%MS	PF-63RB	PF-64RB	PF-65RD
1940, Proof	978	64.5		$45	$60	$170

1940-D • **Circulation-strike mintage:** 81,390,000.

Commentary: This issue is readily available in almost any grade desired, including at the gem level, MS-65 or finer.

	Cert	Avg	%MS	G-4	VG-8	F-12	VF-20	EF-40	AU-50	MS-60BN	MS-63BN	MS-65RD
1940-D	1,470	66.2	100%	$0.15	$0.18	$0.25	$0.60	$0.75	$2	$3	$4	$15

1940-S • **Circulation-strike mintage:** 112,940,000.

Commentary: Minted in large quantities, the 1940-S is easily obtainable today in just about any grade desired. A few were made with the obverse and reverse aligned instead of the standard 180° difference.

	Cert	Avg	%MS	G-4	VG-8	F-12	VF-20	EF-40	AU-50	MS-60BN	MS-63BN	MS-65RD
1940-S	2,580	66.1	100%	$0.15	$0.18	$0.20	$0.50	$1	$1.75	$3	$5	$15

Lincoln, Wheat Ears Reverse, Cents of 1941

KEYS TO COLLECTING: From 1934 onward, all standard circulation-strike dates and mintmarks are common in relation to the demand for them, and with many millions made each year, finding sharp examples is not difficult. Accordingly, from 1934 on we give a general commentary relating to Mint State coins.

1941 IN NUMISMATICS: The *Handbook of United States Coins*, by R.S. Yeoman, a listing of standard prices paid by dealers, was issued by Whitman Publishing. Whitman introduced its three-panel, folding, blue-cardboard coin albums, successors to the "penny board" sheets and related products.

In *The Numismatist* in January, "A Study of Lincoln Cents," an article by Louis I. Kane, discussed the variations in mintmark positions observed on such issues as the 1928-S, 1929-D, and 1930-S issues:

> The position of mintmarks seems to rove all along the year. In some years the mintmark starts from the extreme left and continues horizontally to the end of the date, then it may start from the extreme left and drop diagonally, or it will begin at some point under the second numeral of the date and zigzag about. Very interesting, no?

1941 • **Circulation-strike mintage:** 887,018,000.

Commentary: This issue is common through the MS-65RD and slightly higher levels.

	Cert	Avg	%MS	G-4	VG-8	F-12	VF-20	EF-40	AU-50	MS-60BN	MS-63BN	MS-65RD
1941	2,844	65.9	99%	$0.15	$0.18	$0.20	$0.30	$0.60	$1.50	$2	$3	$14

Varieties: *1941, Thick Planchet:* Some cents were made from planchet stock that was too thick. These are properly considered mint errors, but since many were made it is worthwhile to make note of them. These turned up in Chicago later in the year. In the November issue of *Numismatic Scrapbook Magazine*, the superintendent of the Mint, Edwin H. Dressel, commented in part to Lee F. Hewitt, editor:

> In view of the extremely heavy demands for coinage, and the fact that we have a greatly augmented working force, mistakes, such as you mention, could be due to the inexperience of the new employee during his period of training.

1941, Doubled-Die Obverse: Three varieties with doubled obverses exist. These varieties exhibit slight doubling, best observed on the letters, such as the boldly doubled B in LIBERTY on FS-01-1941-101; IN GOD WE TRUST on FS-01-1941-102; and the TY of LIBERTY on FS-01-1941-103. FS-01-1941-103 also exhibits noticeable doubling on Lincoln's earlobe.

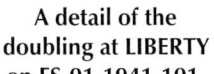

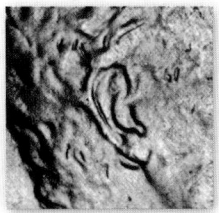

| A detail of the doubling at LIBERTY on FS-01-1941-101. | Details of the doubling at IN GOD WE TRUST on FS-01-1941-102. | A detail of the doubling at LIBERTY on FS-01-1941-103. | A detail of Lincoln's doubled earlobe on FS-01-1941-103. |

	VF-20	EF-40	AU-50	MS-60	MS-63	MS-65
FS-01-1941-101	$25	$50	$75	$100	$200	$300
FS-01-1941-102	$25	$50	$75	$100	$200	$300
FS-01-1941-103	$25	$50	$75	$100	$200	$300

1941, Proof • Proof mintage: 21,100.

Proof commentary: This issue is readily available in proportion to the Proof mintage. Pristine gems are in the minority, but these are more available than for issues in the 1930s.

	Cert	Avg	%MS	PF-63RB	PF-64RB	PF-65RD
1941, Proof	1,062	64.4		$40	$55	$165

1941-D • Circulation-strike mintage: 128,700,000.

Commentary: This issue is common through the MS-65RD and slightly higher levels. Some examples are lightly struck.

	Cert	Avg	%MS	G-4	VG-8	F-12	VF-20	EF-40	AU-50	MS-60BN	MS-63BN	MS-65RD
1941-D	1,773	66.4	100%	$0.15	$0.18	$0.20	$0.50	$1	$3	$4	$5	$15

1941-S • Circulation-strike mintage: 92,360,000.

Commentary: Gems are common, but cherry-picking is advised. Some are either weak in areas or lack eye appeal, or both.

	Cert	Avg	%MS	G-4	VG-8	F-12	VF-20	EF-40	AU-50	MS-60BN	MS-63BN	MS-65RD
1941-S	2,495	66.1	100%	$0.15	$0.18	$0.30	$0.50	$1	$3	$4	$5	$15

Varieties: *1941-S, Large and Small S Mintmarks:* The difference is dramatic. The large S is the rarer of the two and accounts for about 5% to 10% of the population. Enough exist in relation to the demand that these can usually be found for no extra cost.[190] (A similar difference is found among 1928-S cents; see page 411.) The large mintmark on the 1941-S is heavy at the upper left curve, thin at the center, and slightly

A detail of the Large S mintmark.

heavier at the lower right. The edge of the top-right serif is vertical, while the lower-left serif is more of a blob. The small mintmark is, of course, smaller, and it is similar in general appearance to that of the 1928-S with the small S mintmark. Although these varieties have been discussed in print many times, collector interest is not strong. There should be room for one of each in your collection.

Lincoln, Wheat Ears Reverse, Cents of 1942

KEYS TO COLLECTING: From 1934 onward, all standard circulation-strike dates and mintmarks are common in relation to the demand for them, and with many millions made each year, finding sharp examples is not difficult. Accordingly, from 1934 on we give a general commentary relating to Mint State coins.

1942 IN NUMISMATICS: Because copper was needed for military use, production of cents was curtailed dramatically in July. Experiments were made with other materials for coinage including fiber and plastic. After continuous production since 1936, Proof coins were suspended following the 1942 coinage because Mint facilities had a more important use in the war effort. Proof coinage would be resumed in 1950.

While national focus was on the war, collectors were reminded that numismatics offered an escape from everyday reality—a chance to relax and enjoy, if only for brief periods. The hobby of numismatics grew by leaps and bounds, not necessarily as a method of relaxing, but as a place to put money when consumer goods were scarce. The investment record of coins had been phenomenal since the mid-1930s, and this created even more attention and demand.

1942 • Circulation-strike mintage: 657,796,000.

Commentary: This issue is common in all grades, although sharpness can vary.

	Cert	Avg	%MS	G-4	VG-8	F-12	VF-20	EF-40	AU-50	MS-60BN	MS-63BN	MS-65RD
1942	2,588	65.9	100%	$0.15	$0.18	$0.20	$0.25	$0.50	$0.75	$1	$2	$14

1942, Proof • Proof mintage: 32,600.

Proof commentary: Examples are available easily enough, but pristine, undipped gems are scarce. Such coins will have light toning but can still be called RD by the services. This is the last year of Proofs until 1950.

	Cert	Avg	%MS	PF-63RB	PF-64RB	PF-65RD
1942, Proof	1,601	64.1		$41	$58	$175

1942-D • Circulation-strike mintage: 206,698,000.

Commentary: This issue is common through the MS-65RD and slightly higher levels.

	Cert	Avg	%MS	G-4	VG-8	F-12	VF-20	EF-40	AU-50	MS-60BN	MS-63BN	MS-65RD
1942-D	3,174	66.1	100%	$0.15	$0.18	$0.20	$0.25	$0.50	$0.85	$1	$2	$14

1942-S • Circulation-strike mintage: 85,590,000.

Commentary: Again, this is an issue which can be found in nearly any grade desired. Die spacing and die wear resulted in many coins with traces of lightness, but some basic searching should enable you to find a Full Details example.

	Cert	Avg	%MS	G-4	VG-8	F-12	VF-20	EF-40	AU-50	MS-60BN	MS-63BN	MS-65RD
1942-S	2,033	66.0	99%	$0.15	$0.18	$0.20	$0.25	$0.50	$0.85	$1	$2	$14

Lincoln, Wheat Ears Reverse, Cents of 1943

KEYS TO COLLECTING: From 1934 onward, all standard circulation-strike dates and mintmarks are common in relation to the demand for them, and with many millions made each year, finding sharp examples is not difficult. Accordingly, from 1934 on we give a general commentary relating to Mint State coins.

1943 IN NUMISMATICS: As copper was viewed as a strategic metal, its use was discontinued in cents and as an alloy in nickel. Cents struck in 1943 were made of zinc-coated steel. Bright coins were sometimes confused with dimes. The steel cents quickly spotted and became dull. In 1944 copper alloy was resumed.

In 1943 there was cash aplenty in citizens' pockets, rare coins became an increasing focus of investment interest, making the market, even for commemoratives (which touched bottom in 1941), trend upward. Abe Kosoff's sale of the Michael F. Higgy Collection in September saw many 20th-century coins sell for multiples of the latest catalog values. The market caught fire and would remain hot for the next several years.

1943 • Circulation-strike mintage: 684,628,670.

Commentary: This issue was struck in zinc-coated steel. These are very common in grades from VF to spotted Mint State. Opt for a pristine Gem Mint State example, and be "picky." There is not much money at stake. Such coins with no spotting are in the distinct minority, but when these are found they are very beautiful. Coating pieces with clear fingernail polish to prevent oxidation was a common and effective practice; such residue can be removed harmlessly by acetone. Sharp coins exist aplenty. Some show lightness in the higher areas. Some have a weak 4 in the date. Some have letters missing, and these are not rare.

	Cert	Avg	%MS	F-12	VF-20	EF-40	AU-50	MS-63BN	MS-65	MS-66	MS-67	MS-68
1943	9,085	66.1	100%	$0.30	$0.35	$0.40	$0.50	$2.50	$8	$35	$90	$1,200

1943, Bronze • Circulation-strike mintage: Included in 1943 circulation-strike mintage figure.

Commentary: This is numismatically classified as an off-metal error, not a regular circulation issue. For years there had been rumors that a few 1943 cents had been made in bronze instead of the zinc-coated steel standard. In November 1952, Lee F. Hewitt, in *The Numismatic Scrapbook Magazine*, wrote: "While numismatists have kept their collective eagle-eyes open for that possibility of a stray bronze blank getting mixed in with the steel ones—to date no genuine 1943 cents in bronze have been reported." In February 1958 the *Scrapbook* printed this from an Illinois numismatist: "As all 1943 cents are made of steel they can be case hardened and pressed into a piece of soft polished steel. This die can then be hardened and pressed into another cent." Since that time more than two dozen have been reported coming in from many different directions, some of which are open to question, but at least a dozen of which are believed to be genuine.[191]

	Cert	Avg	%MS	AU-50
1943, Bronze †	8	56.6	25%	$200,000

† Ranked in the *100 Greatest U.S. Coins* (fourth edition).

1943, Silver • Circulation-strike mintage: Included in 1943 circulation-strike mintage figure.

Commentary: A few Lincoln cents were struck in error on silver planchets intended for Mercury dimes. These are highly prized today, and only a handful are known. This is numismatically classified as an off-metal error, not a regular circulation issue.

	Cert	Avg	%MS	EF-40	AU-50
1943, Silver	0	n/a		$3,000	$4,500

1943-D • Circulation-strike mintage: 217,660,000.

Commentary: This issue was struck in zinc-coated steel. These are readily available in gem Mint State. Attractiveness varies, but finding a beautiful example will be no problem. Usually they are fairly well struck, although there are exceptions. Examples are common in gem Mint State.

	Cert	Avg	%MS	F-12	VF-20	EF-40	AU-50	MS-63BN	MS-65	MS-66	MS-67	MS-68
1943-D	6,285	66.3	100%	$0.35	$0.40	$0.45	$0.75	$3	$10	$35	$90	$1,300

Varieties: *1943-D, Bronze:* This variety is a mint error—an off-metal strike. One reported example is graded MS-64.[192]

1943-D, Boldly Doubled Mint-mark • Circulation-strike mintage: Included in 1943-D circulation-strike mintage.

Commentary: This variety's Fivaz-Stanton identification is FS-01-1943D-501. It can also be identified as CONECA 1943-D, RPM-001. Its rarity is URS-9. Exhibiting prominent repunching, this variety is in strong demand. Its composition of zinc-coated steel adds interest.

A detail of the doubled mintmark.

	Cert	Avg	%MS	F-12	VF-20	EF-40	AU-50	MS-63BN	MS-65	MS-66	MS-67
1943-D, Boldly Doubled Mintmark	28	64.0	100%	$40	$50	$60	$60	$100	$1,400	$2,500	$10,000

1943-S • Circulation-strike mintage: 191,550,000.

Commentary: This issue was struck in zinc-coated steel. It is similar in many ways to the 1943 and 1943-D cents. Gems are common, but they are in the minority of extant specimens. It is usually fairly well struck, although there are exceptions.

	Cert	Avg	%MS	F-12	VF-20	EF-40	AU-50	MS-63BN	MS-65	MS-66	MS-67	MS-68
1943-S	6,901	66.0	100%	$0.40	$0.65	$0.75	$1	$6	$20	$50	$135	$2,000

Varieties: *1943-S, Bronze:* This variety is a mint error—an off-metal strike. Perhaps a half dozen or so examples exist.[193]

Lincoln, Wheat Ears Reverse, Cents of 1944

KEYS TO COLLECTING: From 1934 onward, all standard circulation-strike dates and mintmarks are common in relation to the demand for them, and with many millions made each year, finding sharp examples is not difficult. Accordingly, from 1934 on we give a general commentary relating to Mint State coins.

OFF-METAL STRIKINGS: Apparently, quite a few 1944 cents were made on 1943 zinc-coated steel planchets, since dozens have been certified as genuine by ANACS. Some details are weak on these pieces. Perhaps the first report of these was in the February 1959 issue of the *Numismatic Scrapbook Magazine*. Such pieces are classified as off-metal errors. One, reported to have come from a lady friend of Chief Engraver John R. Sinnock, was auctioned in 1981 for $3,500.

1944 IN NUMISMATICS: Steel cents were discontinued and bronze was used in an alloy of 95% copper and 5% zinc, without tin. As tin is not present, this alloy is sometimes called brass. The color is more like bronze that the normal yellow associated with brass. This alloy was used through 1946.

1944 • Circulation-strike mintage: 1,435,400,000.

Commentary: This issue is common as can be, as might be expected from its billion-plus coinage. Striking varies for this issue, but sharp examples can be found with ease.

	Cert	Avg	%MS	VF-20	EF-40	AU-50	MS-63RB	MS-65RB	MS-65RD	MS-67RD
1944	3,553	65.9	100%	$0.10	$0.20	$0.35	$1	$5	$12	$65

1944-D • Circulation-strike mintage: 430,578,000.

Commentary: Gems abound, and lower-grade pieces are common as well. This issue is usually well struck.

	Cert	Avg	%MS	VF-20	EF-40	AU-50	MS-63RB	MS-65RB	MS-65RD	MS-67RD
1944-D	3,675	65.7	98%	$0.10	$0.20	$0.35	$0.85	$4	$14	$85

1944-D, D Over S • Circulation-strike mintage: 500,000 estimated of the 1944-D circulation-strike mintage.

Commentary: The D mintmark has been punched over an erroneous S. Only a tiny fraction of 1944-D cents have this feature, but it is still likely that thousands exist. More than 200 have been certified as MS-64RD

See page 435 for details of the overmintmarks.

or higher, with far fewer BN and RB examples, simply because they are less valuable, although more plentiful.

	Cert	Avg	%MS	VF-20	EF-40	AU-50	MS-63RB	MS-65RB	MS-65RD
1944-D, D Over S	97	53.5	51%	$125	$175	$235	$450	$700	$2,500

Varieties: There are two varieties of the overmintmark. Probably a couple hundred thousand to half a million of Variety 1 were coined (judging from a typical die life), although the number could have been much smaller if the error was noticed and the die was retired from service. Variety 2 was made in larger numbers. Both were relatively unknown a generation ago. As is true of virtually all die varieties within the series, the opportunity for cherrypicking is excellent.

Caveat: Some coins were certified simply as 1944, D Over S, before Variety 1 and Variety 2 were separately used on labels. Accordingly, population reports are not accurate with regard to these varieties.

1944-D, D Over S (FS-01-1944D-511): This variety can also be identified as CONECA 1944-D, OMM-001. Its rarity is URS-12. The more desirable and significantly rarer Variety 1 has the earlier S protruding above the D. For the specialist this is one of the most desirable die varieties in the Lincoln cent series.

A detail of the FS-01-1944D-511 overmintmark.

1944-D, D Over S (FS-01-1944D-512): This variety can also be identified as CONECA 1944-D, OMM-002. Its rarity is URS-12. The usually seen Variety 2 has the S protruding below the D. While it is a cousin to the preceding variety, this overmintmark is not as distinctive.

A detail of the FS-01-1944D-512 overmintmark.

	EF-40	AU-50	MS-60	MS-63	MS-65
FS-01-1944D-511	$150	$165	$275	$375	$900
FS-01-1944D-512	$75	$95	$150	$300	$600

1944-S • Circulation-strike mintage: 282,760,000.

Commentary: This issue is common in all grades. Examples are often lightly defined in areas, so some looking will need to be done to find a sharp one.

Notes: *Keys to collecting:* Two styles of S mintmarks were used. The earlier style has serifs and the later (and scarcer) style has rounded ends and is more compact. This later style continued in use the next year.

	Cert	Avg	%MS	VF-20	EF-40	AU-50	MS-63RB	MS-65RB	MS-65RD	MS-67RD
1944-S	5,292	66.1	100%	$0.15	$0.20	$0.35	$0.85	$4	$13	$110

Lincoln, Wheat Ears Reverse, Cents of 1945

KEYS TO COLLECTING: From 1934 onward, all standard circulation-strike dates and mintmarks are common in relation to the demand for them, and with many millions made each year, finding sharp examples is not difficult. Accordingly, from 1934 on we give a general commentary relating to Mint State coins.

1945 IN NUMISMATICS: Mintage of cents continued at a high level due to the war in progress and the demand for more coins in circulation. The brass alloy was continued this year.

Prices of just about every numismatic piece went up, and up some more.

1945 • Circulation-strike mintage: 1,040,515,000.

Commentary: Due to the quantity of surviving Mint State coins, a satisfactory gem can be found with ease, but many are blotchy. One variety displays a heavy die crack connecting the two wheat stalks on the reverse.

	Cert	Avg	%MS	VF-20	EF-40	AU-50	MS-63RB	MS-65RB	MS-65RD
1945	2,645	65.7	100%	$0.10	$0.20	$0.35	$0.85	$2	$8

1945-D • Circulation-strike mintage: 266,268,000.

Commentary: This issue is common in gem grade, but some looking may be required to attain an example with strong eye appeal because many are unattractive. Striking varies, but many sharp strikes exist.

	Cert	Avg	%MS	VF-20	EF-40	AU-50	MS-63RB	MS-65RB	MS-65RD	MS-67RD
1945-D	4,020	66.0	100%	$0.10	$0.20	$0.35	$0.85	$2	$9	$140

1945-S • Circulation-strike mintage: 181,770,000.

Commentary: Gems abound, but they are scarcer than for the higher mintage issues of the era. Eye appeal can vary. Striking varies for this issue, with some examples weakly defined.

	Cert	Avg	%MS	VF-20	EF-40	AU-50	MS-63RB	MS-65RB	MS-65RD	MS-67RD
1945-S	3,935	66.3	100%	$0.15	$0.20	$0.35	$0.85	$2	$9	$95

Lincoln, Wheat Ears Reverse, Cents of 1946

KEYS TO COLLECTING: From 1934 onward, all standard circulation-strike dates and mintmarks are common in relation to the demand for them, and with many millions made each year, finding sharp examples is not difficult. Accordingly, from 1934 on we give a general commentary relating to Mint State coins.

1946 IN NUMISMATICS: The *Guide Book of United States Coins*, written by R.S. Yeoman with the technical assistance of Stuart Mosher, was published with a 1947 cover date.

1946 • Circulation-strike mintage: 991,655,000.

Commentary: Repeating a familiar scenario, gems are common. Color varies from reddish to red-orange, with no difference in value. Striking varies, but sharp examples are common. The numeral 4 in the date is of unusual shape on all cents.

	Cert	Avg	%MS	VF-20	EF-40	AU-50	MS-63RB	MS-65RB	MS-65RD
1946	1,621	65.4	99%	$0.10	$0.20	$0.35	$0.60	$2	$14

1946-D • Circulation-strike mintage: 315,690,000.

Commentary: This issue is common in all grades, including gems with original color. Many are weakly struck due to wide die spacing, but sharp examples can be found.

	Cert	Avg	%MS	VF-20	EF-40	AU-50	MS-63RB	MS-65RB	MS-65RD	MS-67RD
1946-D	2,296	66.0	100%	$0.10	$0.20	$0.35	$0.60	$2	$10	$300

1946-S • Circulation-strike mintage: 198,100,000.

Commentary: Gems are common, including those with original color, but sharpness can be a problem—easily enough overcome by cherrypicking. Poor die spacing plus overused dies combined to create many inadequate pieces.

	Cert	Avg	%MS	VF-20	EF-40	AU-50	MS-63RB	MS-65RB	MS-65RD	MS-67RD
1946-S	4,162	65.9	100%	$0.15	$0.20	$0.35	$0.60	$2	$10	$135

1946-S, S Over D • Circulation-strike

mintage: Unknown, but likely several hundred thousand, included in the 1946-S circulation-strike mintage.

Commentary: The Fivaz-Stanton identification for this variety is FS-01-1946S-511. It can also be identified as CONECA 1946-S, OMM-001. Its rarity is URS-9. Some imagination may be required to see the D under the S. Accordingly, this variety is not widely collected. Most examples found so far have been in lower grades. Probably many remain in numismatic hands as regular 1946-S cents that have not been examined. John Wexler and Kevin Flynn commented in 1996: "This

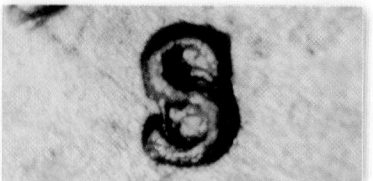

A detail of the overmintmark.

is an extremely difficult variety to find in any grade; very rare in Mint State." The listing of the variety in the *Guide Book of United States Coins* has focused attention on it. Today, more than 50 MS-65RD coins have been certified. No doubt there are many others to be discovered, and still others that will not be submitted unless lower grades of this variety come to have higher market values. As to the total number known, perhaps an estimate between 500 and 1,000 would be realistic.

	Cert	Avg	%MS	VF-20	EF-40	AU-50	MS-63RB	MS-65RD
1946-S, S Over D	18	61.7	83%	$35	$75	$125	$240	$575

Lincoln, Wheat Ears Reverse, Cents of 1947

KEYS TO COLLECTING: From 1934 onward, all standard circulation-strike dates and mintmarks are common in relation to the demand for them, and with many millions made each year, finding sharp examples is not difficult. Accordingly, from 1934 on we give a general commentary relating to Mint State coins.

ALLOY CHANGE: In 1947 the alloy for cents was modified slightly to add 1% tin to 95% copper and 4% zinc. This combination was used through 1962, after which zinc was not used until the entirely different cent stock of 1982.

1947 IN NUMISMATICS: All seemed to be well in the marketplace, at least on the surface. Privately, some dealers worried whether recent record auction prices would hold.[194]

1947 • Circulation-strike mintage:

190,555,000.

Commentary: Gems with original color are in the distinct minority, but enough exist to fill the demand. Striking varies for this issue, but most examples are sharp.

	Cert	Avg	%MS	VF-20	EF-40	AU-50	MS-63RB	MS-65RB	MS-65RD
1947	1,323	65.5	100%	$0.10	$0.20	$0.40	$1	$3	$12

1947-D • Circulation-strike mintage: 194,750,000.

Commentary: This issue is common in all grades. Gems, of course, are a tiny minority, but in absolute terms enough exist to make them readily available. The strike is usually quite good.

	Cert	Avg	%MS	VF-20	EF-40	AU-50	MS-63RB	MS-65RB	MS-65RD	MS-67RD
1947-D	1,914	65.8	100%	$0.10	$0.20	$0.40	$0.60	$2	$10	$650

1947-S • Circulation-strike mintage: 99,000,000.

Commentary: Examples are common in all grades, including gem, but cherrypicking is advised for strike as many have areas of weakness.

	Cert	Avg	%MS	VF-20	EF-40	AU-50	MS-63RB	MS-65RB	MS-65RD	MS-67RD
1947-S	2,720	66.0	100%	$0.20	$0.25	$0.50	$0.85	$2	$12	$175

Lincoln, Wheat Ears Reverse, Cents of 1948

KEYS TO COLLECTING: From 1934 onward, all standard circulation-strike dates and mintmarks are common in relation to the demand for them, and with many millions made each year, finding sharp examples is not difficult. Accordingly, from 1934 on we give a general commentary relating to Mint State coins.

1948 IN NUMISMATICS: Beginning this year and continuing through about 1951, fewer Uncirculated rolls were saved by investors because the coin market was in a slump. After having had a run-up in prices for several years, followed by a hint of chill in 1947, in 1948 the rare-coin market caught a cold. Prices declined in many series, especially for expensive issues.

1948 • Circulation-strike mintage: 317,570,000.

Commentary: This issue is common in all grades up to and including MS-65RD, or higher. Mintages of this era were reduced from the immediately preceding years, but the quantities were still large. Most examples are sharply struck.

	Cert	Avg	%MS	VF-20	EF-40	AU-50	MS-63RB	MS-65RB	MS-65RD
1948	1,293	65.6	100%	$0.10	$0.20	$0.35	$0.85	$2	$15

1948-D • Circulation-strike mintage: 172,637,500.

Commentary: This issue is common in all grades, including original gems. Striking varies, but finding a sharp coin will be easy to do.

	Cert	Avg	%MS	VF-20	EF-40	AU-50	MS-63RB	MS-65RB	MS-65RD	MS-67RD
1948-D	1,707	65.7	100%	$0.10	$0.20	$0.35	$0.60	$2	$11	$900

1948-S • Circulation-strike mintage: 81,735,000.

Commentary: This issue is common in all grades, but not nearly as common as higher-mintage issues of the era. Many have weaknesses, but sharp examples can be found.

	Cert	Avg	%MS	VF-20	EF-40	AU-50	MS-63RB	MS-65RB	MS-65RD	MS-67RD
1948-S	2,707	66.0	100%	$0.20	$0.30	$0.35	$1	$3	$9	$150

Lincoln, Wheat Ears Reverse, Cents of 1949

KEYS TO COLLECTING: From 1934 onward, all standard circulation-strike dates and mintmarks are common in relation to the demand for them, and with many millions made each year, finding sharp examples is not difficult. Accordingly, from 1934 on we give a general commentary relating to Mint State coins.

1949 IN NUMISMATICS: Gilroy Roberts, chief engraver at the Mint, stated that since at least 1947 the typical die for the cent had been used for 800,000 to 1,000,000 impressions or more.

Early American Cents, by Dr. William H. Sheldon, was published. This introduced the Sheldon grading system ranging from 1 to 70, which was initially intended to be the basis of a market formula to calculate prices of coins.

1949 • Circulation-strike mintage: 217,775,000.

Commentary: This issue is common in all grades. David W. Lange notes:

Common are pieces having a pattern of shallow stains which has been described as 'cob webbing.' An unappealing feature which often affects every coin in a roll, it's common for many Philadelphia Mint cents dated 1949–1952. It was almost certainly caused by some chemical treatment of the planchets prior to coining, but why it appears particularly for these years is not known.

Such comments are a good reason for you to acquire Lange's *Complete Guide to Lincoln Cents.*

	Cert	Avg	%MS	VF-20	EF-40	AU-50	MS-63RB	MS-65RB	MS-65RD
1949	1,034	65.7	100%	$0.10	$0.20	$0.35	$1	$3	$15

1949-D • Circulation-strike mintage: 153,132,500.

Commentary: Common in all grades. Higher-grade examples are not rare and are usually sought by those building PCGS and NGC registry sets, a comment applicable to all cents of this era and later.

	Cert	Avg	%MS	VF-20	EF-40	AU-50	MS-63RB	MS-65RB	MS-65RD
1949-D	1,599	65.6	100%	$0.10	$0.20	$0.35	$1	$3	$14

1949-S • Circulation-strike mintage: 64,290,000.

Commentary: This issue is common in all grades, but fewer rolls were saved of it than was the case for issues earlier in the decade. This was a recession time in the coin-investment market. On examples, details vary from weak to sharp.

	Cert	Avg	%MS	VF-20	EF-40	AU-50	MS-63RB	MS-65RB	MS-65RD	MS-67RD
1949-S	3,136	66.1	100%	$0.25	$0.30	$0.35	$2	$4	$16	$200

Lincoln, Wheat Ears Reverse, Cents of 1950

KEYS TO COLLECTING: From 1934 onward, all standard circulation-strike dates and mintmarks are common in relation to the demand for them, and with many millions made each year, finding sharp examples is not difficult. Accordingly, from 1934 on we give a general commentary relating to Mint State coins.

1950 IN NUMISMATICS: The numeral 5 introduced on cents of this date had a long tail at the bottom, quite unlike the compact 5 used in earlier years. In 1950 the Philadelphia Mint produced 51,386 Proof sets, the first produced since 1942. The cost of a set was $2.10. These went on sale on July 17, with a limit of five sets per person. Interest was good, but there was little excitement.

1950 • Circulation-strike mintage: 272,635,000.

Commentary: This issue is common in all grades, but it is scarcer in Mint State than those issued shortly before 1948 or after 1951. Saving bank-wrapped rolls lessened in popularity during this quiet break in the market: only contrarians did it. Gems with original bright color are slightly scarce.

	Cert	Avg	%MS	VF-20	EF-40	AU-50	MS-63RB	MS-65RB	MS-65RD	MS-67RD
1950	1,141	65.6	100%	$0.10	$0.20	$0.35	$0.85	$2	$18	$1,000

1950, Proof • Proof mintage: 51,386.

Proof commentary: The earlier Proofs of the year have a hybrid finish that is mirror-like, but with some satiny graininess. Later strikes, these being the majority, are from highly polished dies. Some of the deeply mirrored pieces have slightly satiny or "frosted" portraits. These are especially desirable to the specialists who seek them. The terms "Cameo" and "Ultra Cameo" are used by grading services, but in any event the cameo effect on these pieces is much less distinctive than that found on modern Proof Lincoln cents (which are now deliberately made with cameo contrast).

	Cert	Avg	%MS	PF-65RD	PF-66RD	PF-67RD
1950, Proof	1,410	65.3		$70	$90	$750

1950-D • Circulation-strike mintage: 334,950,000.

Commentary: This issue is common in all grades, with the highest production of any mint this year. Striking varies for this issue, but many sharp coins are in the offing. Again, relatively few bank-wrapped rolls were saved. On a relative basis, gem coins with full original color are scarce today, but on an absolute basis, there are enough around to satisfy the needs of those who seek them.

	Cert	Avg	%MS	VF-20	EF-40	AU-50	MS-63RB	MS-65RB	MS-65RD
1950-D	1,822	65.7	100%	$0.10	$0.20	$0.35	$0.60	$2	$17

1950-S • Circulation-strike mintage: 118,505,000.

Commentary: This issue is common in all grades, but scarce in comparison to Philadelphia and Denver cents of the era. Relatively few rolls were saved. David W. Lange notes that many 1950-S and 1951-S cents have dark streaking, probably from some chemical used in one of the processes not having been thoroughly rinsed away. Enough gems survive, however, to fill numismatic needs. Increasingly, higher-grade pieces are being picked through for submission to the certification services.

	Cert	Avg	%MS	VF-20	EF-40	AU-50	MS-63RB	MS-65RB	MS-65RD
1950-S	1,946	65.9	100%	$0.15	$0.25	$0.35	$0.85	$2	$13

Lincoln, Wheat Ears Reverse, Cents of 1951

KEYS TO COLLECTING: From 1934 onward, all standard circulation-strike dates and mintmarks are common in relation to the demand for them, and with many millions made each year, finding sharp examples is not difficult. Accordingly, from 1934 on we give a general commentary relating to Mint State coins.

1951 IN NUMISMATICS: The marketplace remained quiet across the board, the last year for which this can be said. A set of Mint State Lincoln, Wheat Ears Reverse, cent dates and mintmarks from 1934 to 1950 cost about $2.50.

1951 • Circulation-strike mintage: 284,576,000.

Commentary: This issue is common in all grades, including gems with original color. Sharp striking is the rule for examples of this issue.

	Cert	Avg	%MS	VF-20	EF-40	AU-50	MS-63RB	MS-65RB	MS-65RD
1951	921	65.7	100%	$0.10	$0.25	$0.35	$0.70	$2	$18

1951, Proof • Proof mintage: 57,500.

Proof commentary: Most examples survive in choice to gem grades, although many have been dipped. Cameo contrast on the 1951 Proof cent is harder to find than on any other cent from 1950 to 1970—notes Rick Tomaska in *Cameo and Brilliant Proof Coinage of the 1950 to 1970 Era.*

	Cert	Avg	%MS	PF-65RD	PF-66RD	PF-67RD
1951, Proof	1,320	65.6		$65	$85	$225

1951-D • Circulation-strike mintage: 625,355,000.

Commentary: This issue is common in all grades. Most examples are well struck.

	Cert	Avg	%MS	VF-20	EF-40	AU-50	MS-63RB	MS-65RB	MS-65RD	MS-67RD
1951-D	2,361	65.7	100%	$0.10	$0.12	$0.35	$0.60	$2	$9	$750

1951-D, D Over S • Circulation-strike

mintage: Probably several hundred thousand of each variety, included in the 1951-D circulation-strike mintage.

Commentary: There are two varieties of 1951-D, D Over S. The Wexler-Flynn text suggests that overmintmarks are simply repunched D mintmarks, but this view is not commonly accepted.

See below for details of the overmintmarks.

	Cert	Avg	%MS	MS-63RB
1951-D, D Over S	17	64.2	100%	$100

Varieties: *1951-D, D Over S, Centered S (FS-01-1951D-511):* This variety can also be identified as CONECA 1951-D, OMM-001. Its rarity is URS-9. Traces of an earlier S, particularly the curved upper left, are seen centered under the final S.

A detail of the
Centered S in the D
Over S overmintmark.

1951-D, D Over S, Low S (FS-01-1951D-512): This variety can also be identified as CONECA 1951-D, OMM-2. Its rarity is URS-9. Traces of an earlier S are seen, particularly the curved bottom that extends below the D.

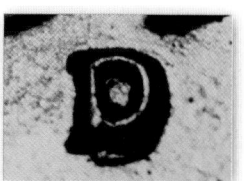

A detail of the Low S
in the D Over S
overmintmark.

	EF-40	AU-50	MS-60	MS-63	MS-65
FS-01-1951D-511	$25	$40	$60	$100	$150
FS-01-1951D-512	$25	$40	$60	$100	$150

1951-S • Circulation-strike mintage:

136,010,000.

Commentary: Examples are common in all grades, including gems with original color. Many are weak, but sharp coins can be found.

	Cert	Avg	%MS	VF-20	EF-40	AU-50	MS-63RB	MS-65RB	MS-65RD	MS-67RD
1951-S	1,474	65.9	100%	$0.25	$0.30	$0.50	$1	$3	$11	$550

Lincoln, Wheat Ears Reverse, Cents of 1952

KEYS TO COLLECTING: From 1934 onward, all standard circulation-strike dates and mintmarks are common in relation to the demand for them, and with many millions made each year, finding sharp examples is not difficult. Accordingly, from 1934 on we give a general commentary relating to Mint State coins.

1952 IN NUMISMATICS: At the Mint, thought was given to changing the Lincoln cent to a design by James Earle Fraser, and pattern pieces were struck. The election of Dwight D. Eisenhower (a Republican, as Lincoln had been) and a strong demand for circulating coins of various denominations put an end to the idea.

The slump in the coin market ended, activity became intense, and excitement prevailed.

1952 • Circulation-strike mintage: 186,775,000.

Commentary: This issue is common in all grades. Examples are usually well struck.

	Cert	Avg	%MS	VF-20	EF-40	AU-50	MS-63RB	MS-65RB	MS-65RD	MS-67RD
1952	1,163	65.7	100%	$0.10	$0.15	$0.35	$1	$3	$16	$3,500

1952, Proof • Proof mintage: 81,980.

Proof commentary: Proofs are plentiful in proportion to their mintage. Cameo contrast Proofs are not "deep."

	Cert	Avg	%MS	PF-65RD	PF-66RD	PF-67RD
1952, Proof	1,377	65.9		$50	$75	$130

1952-D • Circulation-strike mintage: 746,130,000.

Commentary: This issue is common in all grades. Examples are usually well struck.

	Cert	Avg	%MS	VF-20	EF-40	AU-50	MS-63RB	MS-65RB	MS-65RD
1952-D	2,372	65.7	100%	$0.10	$0.15	$0.25	$0.75	$2	$9

1952-D, D Over S • Circulation-

strike mintage: Several hundred thousand or more, included in 1952-D circulation-strike mintage figure.

Commentary: This variety's Fivaz-Stanton identification is FS-01-1952D-511. It can also be identified as CONECA 1952-D, OMM-001. Its rarity is URS-9. Traces of an earlier S are seen, particularly the curved bottom that extends below the D. It is similar in this respect to the 1951-D, D Over S, Low S (see page 444).

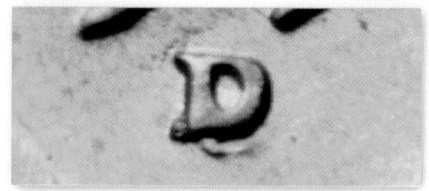

A detail of the D mintmark over an earlier S.

	EF-40	AU-50	MS-60	MS-63	MS-65
1952-D, D Over S (FS-01-1952D-511)	$25	$40	$60	$100	$150

1952-S • Circulation-strike mintage:

137,800,004.

Commentary: This issue is common in all grades, although it is scarcer in circulated grades than are circulated-grade coins from the other two mints. The commonness of Mint State coins from San Francisco this year was caused by a change in investment-collecting patterns. Beginning in a strong way this year, rolls of S-marked coins became especially popular with investors, resulting in proportionately more being saved than of the Philadelphia and Denver coins. In absolute terms, however, there are more than enough to go around today. Many are weakly defined, but there are enough sharp coins that finding one will not be a problem.

	Cert	Avg	%MS	VF-20	EF-40	AU-50	MS-63RB	MS-65RB	MS-65RD	MS-67RD
1952-S	1,809	66.0	100%	$0.15	$0.20	$0.35	$2	$4	$13	$450

Lincoln, Wheat Ears Reverse, Cents of 1953

KEYS TO COLLECTING: From 1934 onward, all standard circulation-strike dates and mintmarks are common in relation to the demand for them, and with many millions made each year, finding sharp examples is not difficult. Accordingly, from 1934 on we give a general commentary relating to Mint State coins.

1953 IN NUMISMATICS: The hobby of coin collecting continued to grow with enthusiasm everywhere. Prices rose, and many dealers offered to pay more than *Guide Book of United States Coins* list prices.

1953 • Circulation-strike mintage: 256,755,000.

Commentary: This issue is common in all grades. Most examples are well struck.

	Cert	Avg	%MS	VF-20	EF-40	AU-50	MS-63RB	MS-65RB	MS-65RD
1953	1,180	65.5	99%	$0.10	$0.15	$0.20	$0.50	$1	$18

1953, Proof • Proof mintage: 128,800.

Proof commentary: This issue is easily available due to the high mintage. Examples with deep-cameo contrast are rare.

	Cert	Avg	%MS	PF-65RD	PF-66RD	PF-67RD
1953, Proof	1,957	66.3		$30	$40	$100

1953-D • Circulation-strike mintage: 700,515,000.

Commentary: This issue is common in all grades, as might be expected from such a high-mintage issue. Most examples are sharply struck.

	Cert	Avg	%MS	VF-20	EF-40	AU-50	MS-63RB	MS-65RB	MS-65RD
1953-D	2,279	65.7	100%	$0.10	$0.15	$0.20	$0.50	$1	$11

1953-S • Circulation-strike mintage: 181,835,000.

Commentary: This issue is common in all grades, but slightly scarcer than cents of the other two mints, particularly Denver. Some coins are discolored. Bank-wrapped rolls were saved with a passion because S-marked coins were a great favorite with investors. Striking varies, but it is usually good.

	Cert	Avg	%MS	VF-20	EF-40	AU-50	MS-63RB	MS-65RB	MS-65RD	MS-67RD
1953-S	2,972	66.0	100%	$0.10	$0.15	$0.20	$0.60	$2	$12	$300

Lincoln, Wheat Ears Reverse, Cents of 1954

KEYS TO COLLECTING: From 1934 onward, all standard circulation-strike dates and mintmarks are common in relation to the demand for them, and with many millions made each year, finding sharp examples is not difficult. Accordingly, from 1934 on we give a general commentary relating to Mint State coins.

1954 IN NUMISMATICS: The market was strong, as it had been since 1952, and was getting better each month. Proof sets and rolls were in strong demand, but all series did well.

1954 • Circulation-strike mintage: 71,640,050.

Commentary: This issue is common in all grades, although on a comparative basis, well-struck coins with original red surfaces and superb eye appeal are few and far between. Most examples are somewhat dark, as made. The relatively low mintage for a Philadelphia Mint cent of this era encouraged the saving of rolls by investors. Striking is often poor, which is rather curious, considering the technology available at the time and the general reputation of the Philadelphia Mint for turning out well-struck coins.

	Cert	Avg	%MS	VF-20	EF-40	AU-50	MS-63RB	MS-65RB	MS-65RD
1954	1,286	65.4	100%	$0.25	$0.35	$0.45	$0.60	$2	$27

1954, Proof • Proof mintage: 233,300.

Proof commentary: Examples are readily available in proportion to the mintage. Gems are easy to find, as are those with cameo contrast.

	Cert	Avg	%MS	PF-65RD	PF-66RD	PF-67RD
1954, Proof	2,160	66.5		$20	$30	$60

1954-D • Circulation-strike mintage: 251,552,500.

Commentary: This issue is common in all grades, including superb gem Mint State. Many if not most examples were well struck.

	Cert	Avg	%MS	VF-20	EF-40	AU-50	MS-63RB	MS-65RB	MS-65RD
1954-D	3,042	65.9	100%	$0.10	$0.12	$0.20	$0.50	$1	$10

1954-S • Circulation-strike mintage: 96,190,000.

Commentary: This issue is common in all grades. Gem Mint State coins with original color and needle-sharp strike require some pursuit. Rolls were saved with a vengeance by investors—thousands and thousands of them. Striking varies, with many being poorly struck. Some have a die crack or defect linking the BE of LIBERTY, giving rise to the term "LIBIERTY," a variety that attracted modest attention at one time, but now is mostly forgotten. Shane Anderson's *Complete Lincoln Cent Encyclopedia* makes special note of these.

	Cert	Avg	%MS	VF-20	EF-40	AU-50	MS-63RB	MS-65RB	MS-65RD
1954-S	6,648	66.0	100%	$0.10	$0.12	$0.20	$0.50	$1	$8

Lincoln, Wheat Ears Reverse, Cents of 1955

KEYS TO COLLECTING: From 1934 onward, all standard circulation-strike dates and mintmarks are common in relation to the demand for them, and with many millions made each year, finding sharp examples is not difficult. Accordingly, from 1934 on we give a general commentary relating to Mint State coins.

1955 IN NUMISMATICS: The announced closing of the San Francisco Mint caused a mad scramble for rolls of cents and dimes, the only denominations struck there. To observers, it seemed this move would close forever this chapter in history. Presses were removed from the mint, other government offices were installed. Eventually on July 11, 1962, the title "Mint" changed to "Assay Office."

1955 • Circulation-strike mintage: 330,958,200.

Commentary: This issue is common overall, although sharply struck gem MS-65 examples with full original color are scarce in the context of the series. Many cents of this date and mint have die cracks at the center of the obverse, probably from improperly tempered steel dies. Such coins are sometimes called the "cracked skull" variety. The striking is usually below par.

	Cert	Avg	%MS	VF-20	EF-40	AU-50	MS-63RB	MS-65RB	MS-65RD
1955	1,860	65.0	97%	$0.10	$0.12	$0.15	$0.35	$1	$19

1955, Doubled-Die Obverse •
Circulation-strike mintage: Included in 1955 circulation-strike mintage.

Commentary: The Fivaz-Stanton identification for this variety is FS-01-1955-101. It can also be identified as CONECA 1955, DDO-001. Its rarity is URS-15. By almost any evaluation, the 1955, Doubled Die Obverse, cent is the most famous die variety in the Lincoln cent series. The date and all obverse

For details of the doubling, see page 450.

lettering are dramatically doubled. As to how the coins were made, Q. David Bowers inquired at the Philadelphia Mint and learned that, on a particular day in 1955, several presses were coining cents, dumping the coins into a box where they were then collected and mixed with the cents from other coining presses. According to an account he received from a Mint official not long afterward, late in the afternoon, a Mint inspector noticed the

A detail of the doubling at the date.

bizarre doubled cents and removed the offending die. By that time, somewhat more than 40,000 cents had been produced, about 24,000 of which had been mixed with normal cents from other presses. The decision was made to destroy the cents still in the box, and to release into circulation the 24,000 or so pieces which were mixed with other cents.

Sydney C. Engel, chief coiner at the time, reminisced with his version of the story in *Coin World*, August 19, 1970, noting that when he arrived at the Mint one morning in 1955, his assistant approached him with a magnifying glass and a few newly struck 1955, Doubled Die Obverse, cents in hand. As a line of trucks waited to pick up newly struck coins for transport to the Federal Reserve, Engel had to decide whether to destroy about 10 million cents (the previous night's production from all dies, which had been mixed together) including the 20,000 to 24,000 doubled die cents, or to release all of them, including the error cents, into circulation. Weighing this decision, Engel decided to order the coins shipped, doubled dies and all, "as the lesser of two evils."

The Mint had no reason to believe that these would attract attention or have value with collectors. They were simply viewed as defective coins. It is likely that about 3,000 to 4,000 1955, Doubled Die Obverse, cents exist today. *All genuine pieces have the reverse die misaligned about 5% from the normal 180° rotation.* Many counterfeits exist, so it is recommended that you buy only coins that have been certified by one of the leading services. A few other obverse dies exist with very minor doubling. The *doubled die* term was applied by Kenneth Bressett when the coin was first listed in the *Guide Book of United States Coins* a few years later. Earlier they had been known as "shift" cents and by other designations.

The first dealer to take notice of and buy the unusual coins from the public was James F. Ruddy, of the Triple Cities Coin Exchange, Johnson City, New York. This was before anything had appeared about the variety in the numismatic press. Many if not most of these were found by buyers of 23-cent packs of cigarettes, which were vended in machines for 25¢ each with two "refund" cents under the cellophane on one side of the pack. The local newspaper caught the story, and Jim offered to pay 25 cents each for all coins offered to him. Before long he had too many, with no apparent resale market in sight, and he stopped buying.[195]

It is to be remembered that at the time there was virtually no numismatic interest in what many called "freak" coins, a fact that is hard to believe today. Wide interest in off-center coins began in the late 1950s when Michael Kolman Jr., of the Federal Coin Exchange in Cleveland, began buying and selling them. Die-struck varieties and the like were launched in 1963 when Frank G. Spadone, a Newark, New Jersey, publisher, wrote and issued the *Major Variety and Oddity Guide of United States Coins.*[196] In 1990 enthusiasm for such coins went into high gear when the first edition of the *Cherrypickers' Guide to Rare Die Varieties,* by Bill Fivaz and J.T. Stanton, was published.

	Cert	Avg	%MS	VF-20	EF-40	AU-50	MS-63RB	MS-65RB	MS-65RD
1955, Doubled-Die Obverse †	3,347	58.8	48%	$1,600	$1,750	$2,000	$3,500	$10,000	$30,000

† Ranked in the *100 Greatest U.S. Coins* (fourth edition).

1955, Proof • Proof mintage: 378,200.

Proof commentary: This issue is common in the context of the series. Proof sets were a popular investment at the time. Cameo-contrast coins are not hard to find.

	Cert	Avg	%MS	PF-65RD	PF-66RD	PF-67RD
1955, Proof	3,842	67.1		$18	$30	$50

1955-D • Circulation-strike mintage: 563,257,500.

Commentary: This issue is common in all grades, including gems with original color. The strike is often poor, and you may have to view multiple coins to find one that is sharp.

	Cert	Avg	%MS	VF-20	EF-40	AU-50	MS-63RB	MS-65RB	MS-65RD
1955-D	3,505	65.6	99%	$0.10	$0.12	$0.15	$0.35	$1	$9

1955-S • Circulation-strike mintage: 44,610,000.

Commentary: This issue is very scarce in circulated grades. It is extremely common in Mint State, since millions of coins were snapped up by dealers and collectors. The strike is usually sub-par; few are needle-sharp. Cents for the year were last coined by March

24. In August 1958 the Oakland Coin Shop (operated by Leo A. Young and his son Gary) had many bags of rolls of this issue stacked along one wall. Walter Breen (in his *Complete Encyclopedia of U.S. amd Colonial Coins*, 1988) states that Robert Friedberg, who operated several dozen coin boutiques as leased facilities in department stores, had seven million examples.

	Cert	Avg	%MS	VF-20	EF-40	AU-50	MS-63RB	MS-65RB	MS-65RD	MS-67RD
1955-S	11,738	66.1	100%	$0.20	$0.30	$0.40	$0.85	$3	$8	$145

Lincoln, Wheat Ears Reverse, Cents of 1956

KEYS TO COLLECTING: From 1934 onward, all standard circulation-strike dates and mintmarks are common in relation to the demand for them, and with many millions made each year, finding sharp examples is not difficult. Accordingly, from 1934 on we give a general commentary relating to Mint State coins.

1956 IN NUMISMATICS: The coin market was very strong, with rolls and Proof sets leading the way. Lincoln cents remained the single most popular series to collect, most often inserted into blue Whitman coin folders. Albums, including National, Popular, and Meghrig albums, were often used for storing higher-grade collections. Plastic holders were becoming increasingly popular, but mostly for use in series with fewer coins than Lincoln cents.

1956 • Circulation-strike mintage: 420,745,000.

Commentary: This issue is common in all grades, although needle-sharp gems with original color are scarcer than one might expect, due to poor workmanship at the mint.

	Cert	Avg	%MS	VF-20	EF-40	AU-50	MS-63RB	MS-65RB	MS-65RD
1956	2,147	65.7	100%	$0.10	$0.12	$0.15	$0.35	$1	$13

1956, Proof • Proof mintage: 669,384.

Proof commentary: Proofs are very common, and they are usually very attractive. Cameo-contrast coins are in the minority, but they are readily available.

	Cert	Avg	%MS	PF-65RD	PF-66RD	PF-67RD
1956, Proof	3,612	67.2		$10	$25	$30

1956-D • Circulation-strike mintage: 1,098,201,100.

Commentary: This issue is common in all grades. Most examples are sharply struck.

	Cert	Avg	%MS	VF-20	EF-40	AU-50	MS-63RB	MS-65RB	MS-65RD	MS-67RD
1956-D	3,812	65.6	99%	$0.10	$0.12	$0.15	$0.30	$1	$9	$2,750

1956-D, D Above Shadow D •

Circulation-strike mintage: Included in 1956-D circulation-strike mintage.

Commentary: This variety's Fivaz-Stanton identification is FS-1956D-508. It can also be identified as CONECA 1956-D, RPM-008. Its rarity is URS-11. This 1956-D variety with the mintmark sharply doubled—first punched too low, and now visible as a distinct but somewhat ghostlike image—was reported by several readers in the *Numismatic Scrapbook Magazine*, in May 1962. Today the variety is scarce, but it is not widely known except among readers of specialized variety texts, although many gems have been certified. In my opinion, this is one of the most interesting repunched mintmarks in the entire series.

Detail of the
repunched
mintmark.

	Cert	Avg	%MS	VF-20	EF-40	AU-50	MS-63RB	MS-65RD
1956-D, D Above Shadow D	99	63.3	90%	$10	$25	$30	$35	$170

Lincoln, Wheat Ears Reverse, Cents of 1957

KEYS TO COLLECTING: From 1934 onward, all standard circulation-strike dates and mintmarks are common in relation to the demand for them, and with many millions made each year, finding sharp examples is not difficult. Accordingly, from 1934 on we give a general commentary relating to Mint State coins.

1957 IN NUMISMATICS: The market for modern Proof sets crashed. It had been rising steadily in the 1950s. Many sets from 1936 onward dropped 40% to 50% in value. In most other categories the market was hot and prices rose.

1957 • **Circulation-strike mintage:** 282,540,000.

Commentary: This issue is common in all grades. It is usually well struck.

	Cert	Avg	%MS	VF-20	EF-40	AU-50	MS-63RB	MS-65RB	MS-65RD	MS-67RD
1957	2,307	65.7	100%	$0.10	$0.12	$0.15	$0.30	$1	$15	$1,350

1957, Proof • Proof mintage: 1,247,952.

Proof commentary: Examples of this issue are common, and usually attractive. Cameo-contrast Proofs are scarcer, often with the contrast on only one side. During this era, cameo Proofs were not deliberately made, but the Proof finish on some specimens resulted from early strikes being made from incompletely polished dies—before they self-polished from extended use.

	Cert	Avg	%MS	PF-65RD	PF-66RD	PF-67RD
1957, Proof	3,913	67.2		$10	$25	$30

1957-D • Circulation-strike mintage: 1,051,342,000.

Commentary: This issue is common in all grades, as might be expected from a mintage that crossed the billion line. Most are well struck.

	Cert	Avg	%MS	VF-20	EF-40	AU-50	MS-63RB	MS-65RB	MS-65RD
1957-D	4,456	65.7	99%	$0.10	$0.12	$0.15	$0.30	$1	$9

Lincoln, Wheat Ears Reverse, Cents of 1958

KEYS TO COLLECTING: From 1934 onward, all standard circulation-strike dates and mintmarks are common in relation to the demand for them, and with many millions made each year, finding sharp examples is not difficult. Accordingly, from 1934 on we give a general commentary relating to Mint State coins.

1958 IN NUMISMATICS: In *The Numismatist* in September 1958, Daniel D. Wiseman of Austin, Minnesota, related that he and his wife had just finished an endeavor that occupied a full year: looking through a million cents. While they found no 1909-S V.D.B. coins, they picked out seven 1909-S cents, five 1914-D cents, "nearly a roll of 1924-D," and three 1931-S cents. Other finds included more than 35 Indian Head cents.

1958 • Circulation-strike mintage: 252,525,000.

Commentary: This issue is common in all grades. Most examples are well struck.

	Cert	Avg	%MS	VF-20	EF-40	AU-50	MS-63RB	MS-65RB	MS-65RD	MS-67RD
1958	3,244	65.7	100%	$0.10	$0.12	$0.15	$0.30	$1	$9	$450

1958, Doubled-Die Obverse •

Circulation-strike mintage: Included in 1958 circulation-strike mintage.

Commentary: This variety's Fivaz-Stanton identification is FS-01-1958-101. It can also be identified as CONECA 1958, DDO-001. Its rarity is URS-2. The doubling on the date of this variety is very slight, but on the lettering it is dramatic. The Collector's Clearinghouse feature in *Coin World* observed that it was more dramatic than on the 1972, Doubled Die Obverse, but not comparable to that on the 1955, Doubled Die Obverse. This variety was discovered around 1960 by Charles Ludovico, a collector who had been looking through a $50 face-value bag of 1958

**Details of the doubling at
IN GOD WE TRUST and LIBERTY.**

cents. Walter Breen, in his 1988 *Complete Encyclopedia of U.S. amd Colonial Coins*, noted that the doubling is plainest on LIBERTY and the motto. The *Cherrypickers' Guide To Rare Die Varieties of United States Coins* notes: "The authors feel this variety never reached the general population. To the best of our knowledge the only known specimens came either directly or indirectly from an employee of the U.S. Mint in Philadelphia. . . ." In *Coin World*, October 17, 2005, editor Beth Deisher wrote:

> The finer of two known specimens of the 1958 Lincoln, Doubled-Die Obverse, cent has been purchased by New York collector Stewart Blay in a private transaction for 'in excess of $100,000,' setting a record for a doubled-die cent. Professional Coin Grading Service graded the coin Mint State-65 red in late September during the Long Beach Coin and Stamp Expo.

The account noted that the other piece had been graded by ANACS around the time it sold privately on July 12, 1996, for $25,025, as MS-64RD. In 2000 it was given the same grade by PCGS and it sold for $57,500. There is an essay on this on pages 371 through 373 of the Wexler-Flynn book, *The Authoritative Reference on Lincoln Cents*.

	Cert	Avg	%MS	MS-63RB
1958, Doubled-Die Obverse	0	n/a		—

1958, Proof • **Proof mintage:** 875,652.

Proof commentary: The mintage fell sharply from the year before due to the 1957 crash in the market for modern Proof sets. This issue is common and usually attractive. Cameo-contrast pieces are less often seen, and those with deep contrast are rare.

	Cert	Avg	%MS	PF-65RD	PF-66RD	PF-67RD
1958, Proof	3,814	67.2		$8	$20	$30

1958-D • Circulation-strike mintage: 800,953,300.

Commentary: This issue is common in all grades. Most examples are well struck.

	Cert	Avg	%MS	VF-20	EF-40	AU-50	MS-63RB	MS-65RB	MS-65RD	MS-67RD
1958-D	5,628	65.8	100%	$0.10	$0.12	$0.15	$0.30	$1	$8	$425

LINCOLN, MEMORIAL REVERSE (1959–2008)

Copper Alloy (1959–1982): **Designer:** *Victor D. Brenner (obverse), Frank Gasparro (reverse).*
Weight: *3.11 grams.* **Composition:** *1959–1962—.950 copper, .050 tin and zinc; 1962–1982—*
.950 copper, .050 zinc. **Diameter:** *19 mm.* **Edge:** *Plain.* **Mints:** *Philadelphia, Denver, and San Francisco.*

Copper Alloy (1959–1982)   **Copper Alloy, Proof**

Copper-Plated Zinc (1982 to date): **Designer:** *Victor D. Brenner (obverse),*
Frank Gasparro (reverse). **Weight:** *2.5 grams.* **Composition:** *copper-plated zinc*
(core: .992 zinc, .008 copper, with a plating of pure copper; total content .975 zinc, .025 copper).
Diameter: *19 mm.* **Edge:** *Plain.* **Mints:** *Philadelphia, Denver, and San Francisco.*

Copper-Plated Zinc (1982–2008)   **Copper-Plated Zinc, Proof**

A NEW REVERSE

In 1959 the Lincoln Memorial reverse design by Frank Gasparro was introduced. Through several changes in metal composition the Lincoln cent obverse and Lincoln Memorial reverse remained in use through 2008.

Through the pages of the monthly journals—*Numismatic News, Numismatic Scrapbook Magazine,* and *The Numismatist*—collectors were generally kept aware when Lincoln cents caused national attention or, at other times, excitement within the hobby. However, this time it was different. Apparently, no one in the Treasury Department thought to give advance notice of an announcement from James Hagerty, press secretary to President Dwight D. Eisenhower:

For Sunday Morning Release, December 21, 1958

President Eisenhower approved today the recommendation of the Secretary of the Treasury Robert B. Anderson for the minting of a new reverse side of the one cent Lincoln coin as a feature of the Lincoln Sesquicentennial observance. Production of the changed coin will begin January second.

In recommending the change on the Lincoln cent, the secretary of the Treasury and Department officials have been working with the Lincoln Sesquicentennial Commission, of which Senator John

Sherman Cooper of Kentucky is chairman. The portrait of Lincoln by Victor D. Brenner on the face of the cent will remain unchanged. The new reverse will portray the Lincoln Memorial, as viewed from the front of the entrance. Above the Memorial is the motto, "E Pluribus Unum," and above this, following the curve of the border, the words, "United States of America," below the Memorial, also following the curve, will appear the denomination "One Cent." These inscriptions are required by law to appear in United States coins. The new permanent design was done by Frank Gasparro of the Philadelphia Mint, and selected by Secretary Anderson and the Director of the Mint William H. Brett. Both Philadelphia and Denver Mints, which will begin production of the changed coin early in January, will have a supply for distribution on Lincoln's birthday, February 12.

More than 25 billion Lincoln cents of the present design have been minted since its adoption in 1909.

Apparently, discussions of designs, preparation of models, and other internal Mint activities relating to the design change had been taking place over a period of at least several months, while Mint and other governmental officials left the numismatic community in the dark.

It was subsequently learned that four engravers at the Mint had been invited to submit designs appropriate to the 150th anniversary of Lincoln's birth. Suggestions were bandied about, including the favorite of the Lincoln Sesquicentennial Commission, a depiction of the president's birthplace cabin in Kentucky. Perhaps the recent (1946 to 1951) use of another cabin on the reverse of the unloved commemorative half dollars depicting Booker T. Washington turned the Mint staff away from that idea. In any event, Frank Gasparro's entry was chosen from the 23 received. The selection was made by the secretary of the Treasury, Robert B. Anderson, and the director of the Mint, William H. Brett. Models were made in preparation for coining, as were hubs and other equipment. President Eisenhower gave his approval on December 20, and the announcement was made the next day.

At the time Gasparro was one of several assistants to Chief Engraver Gilroy Roberts, who had held the senior post since July 22, 1948. Gasparro selected the Lincoln Memorial in Washington, D.C., as his subject, although he had never personally viewed it.[197]

The motif was familiar of course, and, among other places, had appeared on the back of $5 notes since 1929. The engraver thought the combination of Lincoln's portrait with a colonnaded building on the reverse was a nice classical touch (similar in arrangement to certain ancient coins). This time there was no dispute about identifying the engraver. Gasparro's initials, FG, were placed in the field to the right of the building.

The Lincoln Memorial in real life.

The Lincoln Memorial on the back of a $5 note.

The Lincoln Memorial on the reverse of a Lincoln cent.

A galvano of the Memorial reverse showing a level of detail, such as on Lincoln's statue, seldom seen on finished coins.

An article by Maxwell Talleyrand, "Artists and the Lincoln Cent," in the *Numismatic Scrapbook Magazine*, quoted these comments from the artist:

My first inspiration for the Lincoln Memorial reverse of the one-cent goes back to a number of Greek coins I observed, an ideal head on the obverse and a temple portal on the reverse with a deity in the portal. In fact, the Lincoln Memorial is Greek Classical in design, lending itself very well to a coin in linear design and detail.

The conception of this design for the Lincoln reverse was an accumulation of thumbnail sketches and ideas of a Lincoln coin going back ten years while I have been associated with the Mint. I have always been a great admirer of Lincoln, having made various sculptures of him in the past.

I remembered seeing several elevation plans for the Lincoln Memorial during its construction, at the Philadelphia Public Library, and I referred to these actual frontal elevation plans for correct proportions. In these plans the figure of Lincoln is an integral part of the Memorial; on the coin you can see this seated figure in the center of the portal as it is in the building at Washington, D.C. With the aid of a strong glass full details of the figure can be seen.

I feel that the design of the Lincoln Memorial on the reverse of the one-cent is a fitting token of esteem to this great president as it shows a national shrine.

Unfortunately, during actual production of the new cent, the intricate details of the Lincoln statue either were not transferred to the working dies or did not strike up properly, for even some *Proofs* do not show the features sharply. From 1909 until it was lowered in 1984, the relief of Lincoln's shoulder was high. For Memorial reverse cents beginning in 1959 this had the effect of making the E PL of E PLURIBUS weak on the reverse. Accordingly, finding sharply struck coins from 1959 to 1984 requires cherrypicking.[198]

With a nod to John R. Sinnock's design of the 1948 Franklin half dollar, on the Lincoln Memorial reverse the name of the country was given as UNITED STATES oF AMERICA, with a curious small "o," the result of thoughtful artistic license in both cases.

Coinage proceeded apace at the Philadelphia and Denver mints on January 2, 1959, and on February 12, the 150th anniversary of Lincoln's birth, the cents were officially released through banks. Inevitably, as also happens with postage stamps before the authorized date, some escaped early into the hands of delighted collectors.

In some areas of the country there was a rush to get the new cents, *The Numismatist* reported in March. In many other districts, however, there was less interest. The wild times of early August 1909 were not repeated. Within a short time there were more than enough coins to supply demand in most areas. Many of the new coins were deliberately held back, which caused a shortage in some areas during the summer. On August 10, 1959, the Federal Reserve Bank of San Francisco sent a notice to bankers in its district, noting in part:

Immediately prior to February 12, 1959, a supply of the new coin was issued in observance of the Lincoln Sesquicentennial celebration. However, only a nominal supply of the new cent was issued at that time inasmuch as there was a sizeable backlog of 1958 mintage cents available for distribution. Subsequently, when the supply of 1958 cents was exhausted, the 1959 cent was issued in large quantities.

During the first half of this calendar year, the Philadelphia and Denver Mints produced over 560,000,000 pieces of the 1959 mintage as compared with 489,000,000 pieces of the 1958 mintage during the first half of the year 1958. These have been distributed in the usual manner through the Federal Reserve banks and branches to the commercial banks.

Contrary to some rumors there are no errors in the design [such as the small "o" in oF] or construction of the new 1959 Lincoln cent, and the change is a permanent one which by law must remain in effect for the next twenty-five years. No coins of the old design were manufactured after December 31, 1958.

One rumor, which was erroneous, has been prevailing to the effect that the new coin is being withdrawn from circulation, and another rumor that a limited mintage is expected is unfounded, as indicated by the high mintage in the first half of 1959.

Recently there has developed an unprecedented demand for cents which may be due in part to these distorted and erroneous statements. This large demand has overtaxed the wrapping facilities at some of our offices on occasion, making it necessary for such offices to ration the supply of wrapped cents available to the member banks. Additional supplies of cents are being received from the Denver Mint at frequent intervals, but even so, the demand for cents has reduced the available supply of that coin at some offices to the point where we feel we should request our member banks to cooperate first, by not holding excessive stocks of cents in their vaults and, second, by not ordering from us in amounts beyond normal needs:

As has been the case in the past, shortages of any single denomination coin are quickly overcome, and it is expected that with the quieting of the rumors which have existed about the new cents, more than adequate stocks will be available at all our offices.

Reviews by numismatists were mixed. Don Taxay, in *The U.S. Mint and Coinage*, 1966, suggested that the building looked like a "trolley car." One wag, picking up on a review of a building James Thurber once submitted to Harold Ross, editor of the *New Yorker*, offered the comment that the Memorial "was pretty ugly and a little big for its surroundings."

The latter part of this view was, as noted, shared by Gasparro, who had hoped the Memorial would have been smaller. Others liked it—as a fresh look on a design that had become timeworn.

Harry J. Forman, a prominent Philadelphia dealer in bags and rolls of modern coins, told Q. David Bowers that several customers had used the occasion to start "bag sets" of Lincoln cents, hoping to maintain them by date and mint as the years went on.

By 1968 the hubs had become worn, and on the obverse some detail was lost. In 1969 a revision was made with adjustments that included moving IN GOD WE TRUST farther from the rim, slightly modifying the tail of the R of LIBERTY, and strengthening the hair details. Cornelius Vermeule describes the changes in *Numismatic Art in America*:

Ten years later Brenner's obverse underwent certain modifications designed to bring Lincoln's bust back to the sharpness of the original issues and their immediate successors. By 1968 the master die was producing a blurry image with lettering intruding into the rim. On the new master die [of 1969] the highest wave of Lincoln's hair was centered under the W of WE, the details of the beard were restored, and the bow tie took on something of its pristine vigor. The word LIBERTY was made shorter, with narrower, taller letters, and a greater swing to the tail of the R. The results are eminently successful, a reminder that the clarity and precision of a restyled older masterpiece can easily surpass timid new designs in modern coinage.

Obverses of the 1968-S (old hub)
and the 1969-S (new hub) cents.

Although minor adjustments had been made to the obverse hubs now and again, from 1909 onward Lincoln's shoulder was in fairly high relief. This caused the *majority* of circulation strikes to have weakness in that area. As there were no design details there, the weakness can be detected by looking for tiny nicks and other marks from the surface of the original planchet; these were not obliterated during the coining process. In 1984 an adjustment to the hub was made, and thenceforth this area was fairly sharp on most strikes.

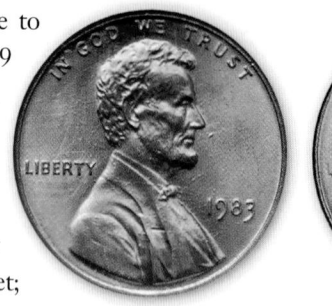

A 1983 cent made from the old hub, with Lincoln's shoulder in high relief—a focus point for many nicks and marks—and a 1984-D cent made from the new hub, showing the shoulder in low relief and with slightly different details.

Due to the rising cost of copper, partway through 1982 the composition of the cent was changed to copper-coated zinc. In 2009, the 100th anniversary of the Lincoln cent, four different reverse designs were used, each depicting a period in Lincoln's life.

CONTINUING POPULARITY OF THE LINCOLN CENT

Although in early 1964 the half dollar was selected to memorialize the martyred President John F. Kennedy, as it was the largest circulating coin of the realm, consideration was given to having a one-cent piece. Models were prepared and galvanos made. On the obverse was the portrait of Kennedy by Chief Engraver Gilroy Roberts, as used on the half dollar. On the reverse was a sturdy oak tree, the symbol of strength. This was resurrected from a proposed design by James Earle Fraser, never adopted, for a 1915 Panama-Pacific International Exposition commemorative quarter dollar. Beyond this activity nothing further was done with the Kennedy one-cent pieces.

In the 1960s for his weekly column in *Coin World*, Q. David Bowers set about to see what a cent could buy on its own. He was able to find just three things: you could buy a one-cent postage stamp; a gumball in a vending machine could be yours; or, in Disneyland, a hand-cranked Mutoscope "peep show" machine delivered about two minutes of flickering images upon receipt of a single coin.

Despite calls that the "penny" is obsolete in commerce, more have been made in recent generations than in the earlier decades of the design. The huge production of Lincoln cents since that time has had nothing to do with the cent's buying power, but is the result of being needed for change in transactions that involve sales tax, a feature of all but a few states. Odd prices such as 99¢, $1.99, and the like also require cents in change. It has been sug-

Galvanos for a proposed 1964 John F. Kennedy cent. The reverse design hailed from a proposal made in 1915.

gested that the manufacture of cents should be dropped, and nickel five-cent pieces become the lowest denomination. However, this idea has not been popular with the public. As an unexpected consequence of the need for small cents, many stores have a "Take a penny, leave a penny" dish inviting customers to have a few for free!

MUTOSCOPES

"THE BACKBONE OF THE ARCADE BUSINESS"

The marvelous growth of the Penny Vaudeville business is well known. Dozens of Arcades were opened last year, in which the Mutoscope proved itself the greatest money-earner of all coin-operated machines. The privilege of free exchange of pictures keeps it fresh and up-to-date. Our new Type E Mutoscope embodies improvements, suggested by years of experience, that make it the acme of perfection. Price $50. We have a few Type D Machines at $40. Special prices when ordered in quantities.

American Mutoscope and Biograph Co.

TYPE E.   116 N. BROADWAY, LOS ANGELES.   11 E. 14th Street, NEW YORK.

A Mutoscope cent-operated peep show from the turn of the 20th century. Costing $50, these hand-cranked machines were popular in arcades, amusement parks, and other places of entertainment, often paying for themselves within a year of purchase by cents fed into the coin slot. The Mutoscope at Disneyland was a holdover from this bygone era.

LINCOLN, MEMORIAL REVERSE, PROOFS

Proofs were made from the first year of the Lincoln, Memorial Reverse, cent through and including 1964. In 1965 there was a nationwide hoarding of coins, including cents. As related later on page 474, Mint Director Eva Adams found numismatists to be squarely to blame and punished them by discontinuing the making of Proofs and by eliminating mintmarks on coins. In reality, collectors had little to do with the shortage. The general public took up the hoarding craze.

In 1965, 1966, and 1967 Special Mint Sets, as they were called, were made available to collectors. The coins had high-quality satin finish with some hints of mirror finish.

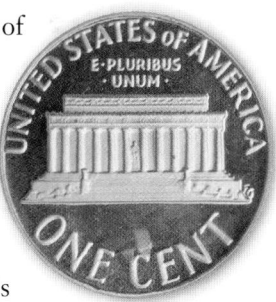

In 1968 Proof sets became available once again. Five-piece sets were struck and packaged at the San Francisco Mint and, for the first time, bore S mintmarks. These continue to the present day. Minting technology improved along the way, with the result that modern Proof cents have what grading services call Cameo, Deep Cameo, or Ultra Deep Cameo grades for Proofs, although the interpretation of these terms has varied. In the early 1990s a new rotary polishing system for planchets was introduced, giving them a better finish for Proof production.[199]

A Proof 1979-S cent with frosted surfaces.

Today's Proofs all have frosted high areas and can be graded PF–69 or 70.

GRADING STANDARDS

Caveat: These grading standards do not take sharpness of strike into account.

MS-60 to 70 (Mint State). *Obverse and Reverse:* At MS-65 and higher, the luster is rich on all areas, except perhaps the shoulder (which may be grainy and show original planchet surface). There is no rubbing, and no contact marks are visible except under magnification. Coins with full or nearly full mint orange-red color can be designated RD; those with full or nearly full brown-toned surfaces can be designated BN; and those with a sub-

1998-D. Graded MS-68.

stantial percentage of red-orange and of brown can be called RB. Ideally, MS-65 or finer coins should have good eye appeal, which in the RB category means nicely blended colors, not stained or blotched. Below MS-65, full RD coins become scarce, and at MS–60 to 62 they are virtually non-existent, unless they have been dipped. Copper is a very active metal, and influences such as slight abrasions, contact marks, and so on that define the grade also affect the color. The ANA grading standards allow for "dull" and/or "spotted" coins at MS–60 and 61, as well as incomplete luster. In the marketplace, interpretations often vary widely. BN and RB coins at MS–60 and 61 are apt to be more attractive than (dipped) RD coins.

AU-50, 53, 55, 58 (About Uncirculated).
Obverse: Same guidelines as for the preceding type except that tinges of original mint-red are sometimes seen on coins that have not been cleaned. *Reverse:* Slight wear is seen on the Lincoln Memorial, particularly on the steps, the columns, and the horizontal architectural elements above.

Illustrated coin: The doubling of the obverse die of this popular variety is easily visible to the naked eye.

1969-S, Double Die Obverse. Graded AU-58.

EF-40, 45 (Extremely Fine). *Obverse:* Light wear is seen on Lincoln's portrait, and hair detail is gone on the higher areas, especially above the ear. *Reverse:* Most detail is gone from the steps of the Lincoln Memorial, and the columns and other higher-relief architectural elements show wear.

The Lincoln cent with Memorial reverse is seldom collected in grades lower than EF-40.

1962-D. Graded EF-40.

PF-60 to 70 (Proof). *Obverse and Reverse:* PF-65 and higher coins are usually RB (colors should be nicely blended) or RD, the latter with bright red-orange fading slightly to hints of brown. Some tiny flecks are normal on coins certified as PF-65 but should be microscopic or absent above that. PF–60 and 61 coins can be dull, stained, or spotted and still have some original mint color. Coins with fingerprints must be given a low numerical grade. Lower-grade Proofs usually have poor eye appeal. Generally, Proofs below PF-64 are not desired by most collectors.

1959. Graded PF-69RD Cameo.

Lincoln, Memorial Reverse, Cents of 1959

1959 IN NUMISMATICS: As noted on page 457, the Lincoln cent was modified by Chief Engraver Frank Gasparro—the Lincoln Memorial reverse replaced the "wheat ears" motif that had been in use since 1909. From this point on, when weakness is evident on cents, it will be evident on the portrait as before, but now also on the tiny figure of Lincoln within the Memorial and the shrubbery. Of course, it is important to check the rim and all other features as well. 1958 and 1959 were good years for the collector, investor, and dealer alike. Anyone who purchased Proof sets at the reduced prices of those years would have no trouble in doubling or tripling his or her investment capital within the next five years, in the boom market of the early 1960s.

1959 • Circulation-strike mintage: 609,715,000.

Commentary: This issue is common through the MS-65RD level and even higher. The E PL of E PLURIBUS on the reverse can be weak—a comment which is applicable to all circulation-strike issues through 1983.

	Cert	Avg	%MS	MS-63RB	MS-65RD	MS-66RD	MS-67RD
1959	1,464	65.7	100%	$0.20	$0.30	$37	$550

1959, Proof • Proof mintage: 1,149,291.

Proof commentary: This issue is common, and usually the examples seen are choice. Cameo contrast (better yet, deep cameo) coins are very popular and are often purchased in appropriately marked certified holders.

	Cert	Avg	%MS	PF-65RD	PF-67RD	PF-67Cam	PF-68DCam
1959, Proof	3,729	67.3		$3	$22	$55	$865

1959-D • Circulation-strike mintage: 1,279,760,000.

Commentary: This issue is common in gem Mint State. Sharpness of strike varies, so cherrypick for sharpness.

	Cert	Avg	%MS	MS-63RB	MS-65RD	MS-66RD	MS-67RD
1959-D	1,221	65.8	100%	$0.50	$0.55	$25	$475

Varieties: *A curiosity:* Beginning in the 1980s, a purported 1959-D cent with the old-style "wheat ears" reverse made the news. A Secret Service agent who had taken a counterfeit detection course with the American Numismatic Association suggested it was genuine, but his teacher, J.P. Martin, stated that while he had no specific evidence it was a counterfeit, his "gut instinct" was that it was not a Mint product. PCGS founder David Hall stated he thought it was a fake. Others suggested it was genuine. Current thought is that no such genuine pieces exist.

1959-D, Triple-Punched Mintmark (FS-01-1959D-501): This variety can also be identified as CONECA 1959-D, RPM-001. Its rarity is URS-12. This mintmark is dramatically repunched. Examples are easy to find.

A detail showing the triple-punched mintmark.

	EF-40	AU-50	MS-60	MS-63	MS-65
FS-01-1959D-501	$3	$5	$8	$10	$20

Lincoln, Memorial Reverse, Cents of 1960

LARGE DATE AND SMALL DATE CENTS: At the Philadelphia and San Francisco mints cents were made with two date sizes. The Large Date has the top of the 1 in the date significantly lower than the top of the adjacent 9. On the Small Date the tops of 1 and 9 are at the same level.

A detail showing the Large Date.

The Small Date cents were made first. It was found at the Philadelphia Mint that the 0 in the date was too small, and that the interior might break away on the die, causing the numeral to fill in (as it actually did on certain 1930-D, Lincoln, Wheat Ears Reverse, cents and 1960 nickels of the Jefferson design). The date was made larger, but this alteration was not announced. Soon Large Date cents replaced the Small Dates, and they were made in much larger quantities. At the Denver Mint the Small

A detail showing the Small Date.

Date dies were used much longer before being replaced. The difference was not publicized until May, after which time Mint Director William H. Brett, apparently acting on general policy and without specific knowledge, stated that all were from the same master hub, and that there was no difference. Later, the Mint admitted that a change had indeed been made.

1960 IN NUMISMATICS: At a New Netherlands Coin Co. sale on April 22, a gem Uncirculated 1909-S, V.D.B., cent fetched $100, and a 1914-D, brilliant Uncirculated, cent "with traces of tarnish," commanded $245. In May dealers Abner Kreisberg and Jerry Cohen offered a roll set (50 coins per roll) of Lincoln cents from 1934 to 1959, for $1,300.

Also in May, newspapers and television programs across America carried accounts of the fabulous, valuable, and rare 1960, Small Date, cents. It was estimated that about two million of these were made in Philadelphia, and a much larger quantity in Denver. This electrified the numismatic community. Accounts were published of $50 face-value bags (5,000 coins) selling for $12,000 or more. In August Mint Director William H. Brett pooh-poohed the idea that 1960 Small Date cents would have any lasting value, noting that by August 23, some 235,915,000 cents (this figure including both the Small Date and the Large Date cents) had been produced at the Philadelphia Mint.

The inauguration of *Coin World* on April 21, the vast publicity and hoopla that developed for the 1960, Small Date, cent, and an expanded interest in coins in general served to ignite the market. Prices rose across the board, starting a boom that would last until 1964. Numismatics was a hot topic nationwide, and newcomers rushed to get in on anticipated large profits in the offing.

1960, Large Date • Circulation-

strike mintage: The vast majority of 586,405,000.

Commentary: This issue is common in gem Mint State. Sharpness of strike varies, so cherrypick for sharpness.

See page 464 for details comparing the Large Date and the Small Date.

	Cert	Avg	%MS	MS-63RB	MS-65RD	MS-66RD
1960, Large Date	1,694	65.5	100%	$0.20	$0.30	$30

1960, Small Date • Circulation-

strike mintage: Estimated 2,075,000 by David W. Lange—a tiny percentage of the total mintage for Philadelphia cents (586,405,000) of this date.

Commentary: This is by far the more elusive of the two Philadelphia Mint varieties. Many Small Date cents were saved by numismatists, with the result that examples, including well-struck choice and gem coins with original color, are readily available today. Circulated coins are very scarce. Most are well struck.

See page 464 for details comparing the Large Date and the Small Date.

David W. Lange estimated the specific mintage of the Small Date:

> Some 2,075,000 cents were coined at the Philadelphia Mint in January before production was halted. None were struck in February, and then cents alone were coined in March and April as the mint attempted to make up for lost production. It's a reasonable assumption that the two million cents of January represent the total production of small-date 1960-P cents for circulation. The fact that the large date coins were found so early in the year tends to reinforce this theory. The balance of the 1960-P cent seems to have been of the large date variety.

	Cert	Avg	%MS	MS-63RB	MS-65RD	MS-66RD
1960, Small Date	1,165	65.5	100%	$3	$7	$38

1960, Large Date, Proof • Proof

mintage: Around 90% of 1,691,602.

Proof commentary: These constitute the vast majority of 1960 cent Proofs, probably more than 1,600,000 coins. Most survive as gems today.

See page 464 for details comparing the Large Date and the Small Date.

	Cert	Avg	%MS	PF-65RD	PF-67RD	PF-67Cam	PF-68DCam
1960, Large Date, Proof	3,338	67.3		$2	$26	$45	$375

Varieties: *1960, Large Date Over Small Date Proofs (FS-01-1960-101 and FS-01-1960-103):* These reflect squeezing of more than one Small Date die with a Large Date hub. Very slight doubling is seen at one side of the date numerals. Multiple dies have been identified. These seem to be quite scarce, perhaps with a mintage of up to 5,000 coins per error die. FS-01-1960-103 is actually a tripled die, with a Large Date hub having been impressed twice over a Small Date hub.

| A detail showing doubling caused by overpunching on FS-01-1960-101. | Details showing doubling caused by overpunching on FS-01-1960-102. | Details showing doubling caused by overpunching on FS-01-1960-103. |

	PF-63	PF-65	PF-66	PF-67
FS-01-1960-101	$250	$450	$600	$750
FS-01-1960-103	$250	$450	$600	$750

1960, Small Date, Proof • Proof

mintage: Around 10% of 1,691,602.

Proof commentary: Most examples survive as choice or gem specimens. With a mintage of perhaps 170,000 pieces, the Small Date is scarce in comparison to the Large Date. That figure is sufficiently large, however, that in the early 21st century there are enough in existence to give one to every unduplicated name in the ANA membership list and the subscriber lists to *Coin World* and *Numismatic News.* Population reports reveal that more Small Date than Large Date coins have been certified; this is because the Small Dates are worth more and thus more practical to have certified.

See page 464 for details comparing the Large Date and the Small Date.

	Cert	Avg	%MS	PF-65RD	PF-67RD	PF-67Cam	PF-68DCam
1960, Small Date, Proof	2,520	67.2		$22	$37	$75	$2,300

1960-D, Large Date • Circulation-

strike mintage: Around 70% of 1,580,884,000.

Commentary: This issue is common in gem Mint State.

See page 464 for details comparing the Large Date and the Small Date.

	Cert	Avg	%MS	MS-63RB	MS-65RD	MS-66RD	MS-67RD
1960-D, Large Date	1,059	65.4	98%	$0.20	$0.30	$30	

Varieties: A variety once called 1960-D, Large Date, D Over Horizontal D, has been disproved as such, and it is now considered a triple-punched D.

1960-D, Small Date • Circulation-strike mintage: Around 30% of 1,580,884,000.

Commentary: This issue is common in gem Mint State. It is common in all grades, including sharply struck gems. While these were made in lesser numbers than the Large Date, hundreds of millions were certainly created. When the Small Dates were discovered, some thought that the Denver coins

See page 464 for details comparing the Large Date and the Small Date.

were nearly as scarce as the Philadelphia issues, but this did not prove to be the case. It might be conjectured that Small Date dies sent to Denver were kept in use until they were retired. There was no awareness, until May, of the date-size differences, so coinage may have continued up to that time, or even longer. Sharpness of strike varies, so cherrypick for sharpness.

	Cert	Avg	%MS	MS-63RB	MS-65RD	MS-66RD	MS-67RD
1960-D, Small Date	1,418	65.6	100%	$0.20	$0.30	$30	$1,850

1960-D, D Over D, Small Date Over Large Date • Circulation-strike mintage: Included in 1960-D, Small Date, circulation-strike mintage.

Commentary: The Fivaz-Stanton identification for this variety is FS-01-1960D-101/501. It can also be identified as CONECA 1960-D, DDO-001/RPM-100. Its rarity is URS-9. On this variety the final D mintmark is tilted slightly to the left, with an earlier D mintmark, appearing ghostlike, mostly protruding above it. It also exhibits the Small Date punched over the Large Date. This is one of the most interesting varieties in the series—a "twofer" that shows both the date and mintmark with distinguishing features. These constitute only a tiny fraction of the 1960-D, Large Date, mintage.

See page 464 for details comparing the Large Date and the Small Date.

A detail showing the repunched mintmark and date.

Enough exist, however, including certified coins, that finding an example will be no problem.

	Cert	Avg	%MS	MS-63RB	MS-65RD	MS-66RD
1960-D, D Over D, Small Date Over Large Date	265	64.2	98%	$200	$400	$2,000

Lincoln, Memorial Reverse, Cents of 1961

1961 IN NUMISMATICS: In a January message, American Numismatic Association president Admiral Oscar H. Dodson stated that 1960, Small Date, cents were the "bottom rung of an adventurous and inspiring ladder." The excitement of the 1960, Small Date, cent had faded, but its effects remained, since there were now tens of thousands of newcomers in the hobby, all eager to explore other series. The investment market for rare coins was in high gear, led by series readily available in "investment grades" such as Uncirculated rolls, commemoratives, and Proof sets. News reporter Margo Russell was named as editor of *Coin World* after editor D. Wayne Johnson, who had been with the publication since its inception, resigned in a wage dispute. Russell would serve with distinction until her retirement in 1985 and would win nearly every important numismatic award.

1961 • Circulation-strike mintage: 753,345,000.

Commentary: This issue is common in gem Mint State. For any of this year's issues, cherry-pick for quality, as sharpness varies—a comment applicable through 1983.

	Cert	Avg	%MS	MS-63RB	MS-65RD	MS-66RD
1961	780	65.1	99%	$0.15	$0.30	$50

1961, Proof • Proof mintage: 3,028,244.

Proof commentary: This issue is common. Usually examples are found at the gem level, and very attractive. Deep-cameo Proofs are seen much less often than those with polished portraits.

	Cert	Avg	%MS	PF-65RD	PF-67RD	PF-67Cam	PF-68DCam
1961, Proof	3,842	67.2		$1.50	$23	$40	$375

1961-D • Circulation-strike mintage: 1,753,266,700.

Commentary: This issue is common in gem Mint State. Sharpness of strike varies, with some weakly struck or with poor luster. This does not represent a problem if you are willing to search for an attractive specimen. There are many Full Details coins available because the mintage was so large.

	Cert	Avg	%MS	MS-63RB	MS-65RD	MS-66RD	MS-67RD
1961-D	959	65.4	99%	$0.15	$0.30	$70	$100

Varieties: 1961-D, D Over Horizontal D (FS-01-1961D-501): This variety can also be identified as CONECA 1961-D, RPM-001. Its rarity is URS-14. The first D was entered into the die far on its side, rotated to the left, not quite to the extent of being horizontal, but dramatic in appearance. The second D was punched in the correct orientation. This variety is scarce in comparison to regular coins, but likely hundreds of thousands were struck.

A detail showing the correctly oriented D over the earlier misaligned D.

	AU-50	MS-60	MS-63	MS-65
FS-01-1961D-501	$2	$5	$10	$35

Lincoln, Memorial Reverse, Cents of 1962

ALLOY CHANGE: The alloy for the cent was changed this year from 95% copper, 5% tin and zinc (as it had been since 1947), to 95% copper, 5% zinc. The latter alloy can be referred to as *brass*, because *bronze* is defined as copper with tin and, sometimes, other metals added, while brass is copper and zinc. The *Guide Book of United States Coins* calls the new composition "copper alloy" as it does not have a brassy yellow color.

1962 IN NUMISMATICS: On July 1, 1962, the government changed the designation of the San Francisco Mint to the San Francisco Assay Office. The San Francisco Mint name was not restored until March 1, 1988. The S mintmark was used while the San Francisco facility operated under both names. In the present text "San Francisco Mint" is used in many instances in relation to activities which were accomplished under the Assay Office name.

Contrary to the national economy, the coin market was on fire as the boom, ignited in 1960, continued to expand. Prices rose for almost all American series, from half cents to double eagles. Many coin shops opened, to the extent that within the next two years, Chet Krause, publisher of *Numismatic News*, estimated that there were 6,000 or so nationwide. Just about every medium-size town had two or more, and large cities were apt to have more than a dozen.

1962 • **Circulation-strike mintage:** 606,045,000.

Commentary: This issue is common in gem Mint State. Various die doublings and variations are found this year and for others of the era and are delineated in the Wexler-Flynn text. Most of these varieties can be purchased without paying a premium. Sharply struck coins are readily available.

	Cert	Avg	%MS	MS-63RB	MS-65RD	MS-66RD
1962	1,038	65.6	100%	$0.15	$0.30	$50

1962, Proof • Proof mintage: 3,218,019.

Proof commentary: Examples are very common, including superb gems. Deep-cameo Proofs are scarce.

	Cert	Avg	%MS	PF-65RD	PF-67RD	PF-67Cam	PF-68DCam
1962, Proof	3,996	67.3		$1.50	$10	$15	$100

1962-D • Circulation-strike mintage: 1,793,148,140.

Commentary: This issue is common in gem Mint State.

	Cert	Avg	%MS	MS-63RB	MS-65RD	MS-66RD	MS-67RD
1962-D	855	65.5	99%	$0.15	$0.30	$75	$250

Lincoln, Memorial Reverse, Cents of 1963

1963 IN NUMISMATICS: Teletype systems linked several hundred dealers by 1962 and 1963, and at one time the Professional Numismatists Guild even had its own network. These noisy machines were fitted in a hinged, green metal case with a clear glass panel on the front. The *Coin Dealer Newsletter* was launched and using Teletype data as a basis, listed bid and ask prices for rolls, Proof sets, and other items.

1963 • Circulation-strike mintage: 754,110,000.

Commentary: This issue is common in gem Mint State.

	Cert	Avg	%MS	MS-63RB	MS-65RD	MS-66RD
1963	1,451	65.3	100%	$0.15	$0.30	$60

1963, Proof • **Proof mintage:** 3,075,645.

Proof commentary: Examples are plentiful. Cameo-contrast coins are easily obtained as well. In January 2004 a coin that had been certified as "Proof-70 Deep Cameo" by PCGS had developed carbon spots on the obverse. David Hall, president of PCGS, announced that the coin had sold for $40,250 in the Heritage sale in January. PCGS "ate" the coin and refunded the cost. Hall said coins can "turn" even after being sealed in an inert case by the grading service. "It's part of the market for top-graded copper coins. It just happens. It's part of what you have to deal with when you buy, sell, or grade top-quality copper."[200] PCGS no longer guarantees the stability of color on the copper coins it certifies. Though unrelated to this incident, it seems that dipped RD coins are especially prone to "turning."[201]

	Cert	Avg	%MS	PF-65RD	PF-67RD	PF-67Cam	PF-68DCam
1963, Proof	4,509	67.5		$1.50	$10	$14	$55

1963-D • **Circulation-strike mintage:** 1,774,020,400.

Commentary: This issue is common in gem Mint State, although PCGS has certified none higher than MS-66, the only date or mintmark of this general era for which that can be said. Sharpness of strike varies. It is to be remembered that the obverse hub dies, slowly but surely over the decades, lost detail, with the result that a cent of 1963 (or any other year in this era) will not hold a candle in detail to a cent of 1916 (when details were sharpened). A "good" strike in the modern era is one that, taking the hub into consideration, is good within the context of the era.

	Cert	Avg	%MS	MS-63RB	MS-65RD	MS-66RD	MS-67RD
1963-D	612	65.4	100%	$0.15	$0.30	$100	$475

Lincoln, Memorial Reverse, Cents of 1964

IRREGULAR DATING PROCEDURE: On September 28 the San Francisco Assay Office began to make planchets for cents and five-cent pieces. On September 1, *1965*, the first time since 1955, the former San Francisco Mint began striking Lincoln cents. The dies were backdated to 1964 and did not have an S mintmark. Of the total mintage of 2,648,575,000 of mintmarkless 1964 cents, made in the style of the Philadelphia Mint, about 92% were struck in Philadelphia and 8% in San Francisco. The Denver Mint's 1964-D cents were all struck in Denver in calendar-year 1964.

1964 IN NUMISMATICS: This was one of the most pivotal years in numismatics. The government laid plans that would dramatically affect coinage, including Lincoln cents. The great investment boom was still red hot early in 1964, but cooling winds of change soon arose. Counterfeits of key U.S. coins plagued the marketplace. The American Numismatic Association published plans for a headquarters building. (The location of Colorado Springs was decided upon and announced early in the next year.) In other ANA business, the Hall of Fame was instituted (and would become a very popular feature at the headquarters), and records were changed from paper files to IBM magnetic tape.

In the meantime, the world price of silver metal was rising, despite the U.S. Treasury trying to maintain a uniform market value of $1.28 per ounce. The Treasury cache of older-date silver dollars, which had been draining since November 1962, became further depleted, until in March it was announced that only about three million were left, and no more would be paid out. In the same month the new Kennedy silver half dollar made its debut, and millions of coins were snapped up by the public—leaving none for general circulation. Citizens rushed to hoard ordinary silver dimes, quarters, and half dollars that had been in circulation, and bank supplies became short. Soon the problem spread to common Lincoln cents, which virtually disappeared from pocket change, precipitating the worst coin shortage since the Civil War. The Treasury Department announced that the silver content of the dime, quarter, and half dollar would be reduced or eliminated entirely, in view of rising world prices of this precious metal. It became difficult for stores to make change, and some merchants paid premiums for rolls of common Lincoln cents to use in their cash registers.

Eva Adams, director of the Mint, blamed this nationwide shortage on *coin collectors*, not the public, causing great consternation in numismatic circles. As punishment, mintmarks on coins were to be eliminated and the production of Proof sets was to be discontinued. The market for rare coins remained very strong, although behind the scenes there were many worries about the price stability of rolls and Proof sets, these being investors' favorites.

1964 • Circulation-strike mintage: 2,648,575,000.

Commentary: This issue is common in gem Mint State. Cents of the 1964 "Philadelphia" issue include some made in *1965 in San Francisco*, but without mintmarks (see page 469). Sharpness of strike varies, but so many were made that a relatively sharp example can be found easily.

	Cert	Avg	%MS	MS-63RB	MS-65RD	MS-66RD
1964	731	65.2	100%	$0.15	$0.30	$65

1964, Proof • Proof mintage: 3,950,762.

Proof commentary: Usually examples are seen in gem preservation, sometimes from dies that were too vigorously polished, removing design detail. Cameo Proofs, while in the minority, are plentiful. These are the last of the Philadelphia Mint Proofs. No more Proofs were made until 1968, when the San Francisco Assay Office (the San Francisco Mint) was employed in striking them.

	Cert	Avg	%MS	PF-65RD	PF-67RD	PF-67Cam	PF-68DCam
1964, Proof	8,295	67.8		$1.50	$10	$11	$23

1964-D • **Circulation-strike mintage:** 3,799,071,500.

Commentary: This issue is common in gem Mint State. Coins were struck from 1964-D dies in calendar year 1965 as well. Sharpness varies, and surfaces are often poor. Decent examples exist, however.

	Cert	Avg	%MS	MS-63RB	MS-65RD	MS-66RD
1964-D	463	65.4	99%	$0.15	$0.30	$42

Lincoln, Memorial Reverse, Cents of 1965

NO MINTMARKS: After the passage of the Coinage Act of 1965, the Treasury moved 10 coin presses from the Denver Mint to the San Francisco Assay Office (earlier known as the San Francisco Mint), after which production of Lincoln cents commenced on September 1. The S mintmark was eliminated from these coins, and they were backdated 1964, to discourage hoarding. Production of cents with the 1965 date did not begin until December 29, 1965. Most of the cents of this date were struck in calendar-year 1966 at the Denver Mint, and a lesser number at the San Francisco Assay Office, but without mintmarks. This production continued until July 1966. Only 1,085,000 1965-dated cents were actually struck in that year. Unfortunately, there is no die difference to distinguish these.

1965 IN NUMISMATICS: In January 1965 the coin market, to anyone reading *Coin World* or *Numismatic News*, seemed to be robust. Behind the scenes, however, seasoned collectors and dealers worried that the investment bubble, which began in 1960, would burst—the rate of price increases had been slowing. The bellwether roll of 40 1950-D nickels, now at $1,200, seemed to be vulnerable, as did many other rolls and Proof sets, these being investors' favorites. Special deals were being made to move such investment-type items.

Buyers became scarce. All of a sudden, it was sell time. By the summer, the 1950-D nickel roll was advertised for just $750 and headed further south. Meanwhile, the prices of scarce and rare coins remained strong, as reflected in price lists and auction results.

On July 23 President Lyndon B. Johnson signed the Coinage Act of 1965, which changed the metallic content of higher-denomination coins to clad compositions and had other provisions, including making *any* coins previously struck at a federal mint legal tender. This inadvertently restored monetary status to the 19th-century trade dollar, which had been demonetized. Also, pattern coins, 1933 double eagles, and other coins that some suggested might not be legal tender were officially made so.

Mint Director Eva Adams implemented her plan to mete out punishment to coin collectors for supposedly causing the nationwide shortage of circulated Lincoln cents and other coins. She eliminated mintmarks on coins struck at the Denver and San Francisco mints and stopped the production of Proof sets. Moreover, she extended the date 1964 to December 29, 1965, for Lincoln cents and Jefferson nickels. These restrikes (for that is what they were) bore no special markings. However, collectors were not completely overlooked—in the absence of Proof sets, the Mint made Special Mint Sets (SMSs) with coins from specially polished dies (which were not of full mirror Proof quality). The San Francisco Assay Office (San Francisco Mint), which had not been involved in coinage until the production of mintmarkless coins this year, resumed punching planchets for cents and nickels.

1965 • Circulation-strike mintage: 1,497,224,900.

Commentary: This issue is common in gem Mint State. It was struck at all three mints, mostly in calendar-year 1966 (see page 469). Gems with good visual appeal are in the minority. Sharpness of strike varies, as does planchet quality.

	Cert	Avg	%MS	MS-63RB	MS-65RD	MS-66RD
1965	399	65.9	100%	$0.20	$0.50	$27

1965, Special Mint Set • Special Mint Set (SMS) mintage: 2,360,000.

Special Mint Set commentary: About 62,000 went unsold. Special Mint Sets (SMSs) were made at the San Francisco Assay Office (the erstwhile San Francisco Mint) and sold at a premium to collectors, from this year through 1967 as a consolation for Proofs not being issued. These are well struck, from partially polished dies, and usually very appealing. Some are quite mirrorlike. The success of these led to the San Francisco Assay Office being selected to make Proof sets beginning in 1968.[202] Normal planchets, instead of those carefully prepared and selected, were used. Most are not particularly distinctive, except for some that are prooflike. Some have handling marks, reflective of indifferent care taken at the Mint. Production from 1965-dated dies took place in early 1966. These cents are desirable and widely collected by specialists. Cherrypick for quality, and seek those that are somewhat prooflike.

	Cert	Avg	%MS	PF-65RD	PF-67RD	MS-66RD	MS-67RD
1965, Special Mint Set	1,653	66.3	100%	$11	$55		

Lincoln, Memorial Reverse, Cents of 1966

1966 IN NUMISMATICS: Production of Special Mint Sets continued in lieu of Proofs. Striking of cents bearing this date took place at all three mints beginning in July 1966, as it had when the mints were restriking 1965-dated coins. Mint Director Eva Adams was viewed as Public Enemy No. 1 by many numismatists. Mainly due to a campaign promoted by *Numismatic News*, Felix O. Schlag, the designer of the Jefferson nickel in 1938, whose initials had not appeared on the coins, finally gained recognition when FS was placed on the obverse, creating a "new type" for numismatists.

There were few happy numismatic campers. Long faces were everywhere. There was a nationwide scramble to pluck all pre-1965 silver coins from circulation, and not enough clad dimes and quarters (those with no silver content) had been struck to make up the shortage. Coin conventions and coin shops were noisy with the clatter of mechanical counters that processed quantities of silver-content coins brought by the public.

1966 • **Circulation-strike mintage:** 2,188,147,783.

Commentary: This issue, struck at all three mints, is common in gem Mint State.

	Cert	Avg	%MS	MS-63RB	MS-65RD	MS-66RD
1966	285	65.5	99%	$0.20	$0.50	$60

1966, Special Mint Set • **Special Mint Set (SMS) mintage:** 2,261,583.

Special Mint Set commentary: About 114,000 went unsold. SMS coins of this date were struck from polished planchets and slightly polished dies, giving an improvement over the 1965 issues. Some show handling marks, which are usually minor. Nearly all are very attractive and closely resemble Proofs, yielding coins that are well worth owning, a significant improvement over the SMS of the previous year.

	Cert	Avg	%MS	PF-65RD	PF-67RD
1966, Special Mint Set	2,150	66.7	100%	$10	$25

Lincoln, Memorial Reverse, Cents of 1967

1967 IN NUMISMATICS: This was the last year of Special Mint Sets, and also of placing no mintmark on coins struck at the Denver and San Francisco branch mints (although in the 1970s, the practice would resume, when San Francisco struck circulation cents without mintmarks). All Lincoln cents dated 1967 were actually struck in calendar year 1967, and no earlier-dated cents were made.

Mint Director Eva Adams supported Senate bill S.1008, to repeal the prohibition of mintmarks on U.S. coins. Perhaps she was beginning to "get religion" and see the collectors' side of things? Some light was seen at the end of a dark numismatic tunnel. For the year, however, Lincoln cents and other coins remained mintmarkless.

1967 • **Circulation-strike mintage:** 3,048,667,100.

Commentary: This issue, struck at all three mints, is common in gem Mint State. The striking is usually quite good in the context of the era.

	Cert	Avg	%MS	MS-63RB	MS-65RD	MS-66RD
1967	196	65.5	99%	$0.20	$0.50	$90

1967, Special Mint Set • Special Mint Set (SMS) mintage: 1,863,344.

Special Mint Set commentary: About 27,000 went unsold. Quality reached a high level, and most coins resemble full Proofs. Some have cameo contrast and are especially desirable.

	Cert	Avg	%MS	MS-65RD	MS-67RD
1967, Special Mint Set	2,325	66.8	100%	$11	$42

Lincoln, Memorial Reverse, Cents of 1968

1968 IN NUMISMATICS: The mintage of Lincoln cents returned to normal in Philadelphia, Denver, and San Francisco, producing cents with a D mintmark, not seen since 1964, and S-marked coins, not seen since 1955. Proof cents, now with an S mintmark, were made for the first time since 1964. The San Francisco Assay Office (San Francisco Mint) cents, struck for circulation, were eagerly sought and traded actively, usually in roll or bag quantities, by individuals who were keenly aware of the S-mintmarked coins' absence since 1955.

Proof set production was resumed, now at the San Francisco Assay Office (which would retain this name officially until 1988, though mintage had resumed and the name *San Francisco Mint* appears in most popular usage), with each Proof being given an S mintmark.

1968 • Circulation-strike mintage: 1,707,880,970.

Commentary: This issue is common in gem Mint State. Eye appeal can vary from example to example. Sharpness of strike varies, so cherrypick to find one with better-than-average sharpness—although by this year the portrait had many indistinct areas.

	Cert	Avg	%MS	MS-63RB	MS-65RD	MS-66RD
1968	325	65.5	100%	$0.25	$0.60	$33

1968-D • Circulation-strike mintage: 2,886,269,600.

Commentary: This issue is common in all grades. Usually this issue was well struck in relation to the dies themselves, considering that by this time, the details on the master hub were often light.

	Cert	Avg	%MS	MS-63RB	MS-65RD	MS-66RD
1968-D	665	65.3	99%	$0.15	$0.40	$27

1968-S • **Circulation-strike mintage:** 258,270,001.

Commentary: This issue is common in all grades, although in circulation this and subsequent S-marked coins are seen infrequently in comparison to Philadelphia and Denver issues. Very popular with investors, bags of 1968-S cents found a ready market. Sharpness of strike varies; it is often weak because the portrait was "mushy" by this time.

	Cert	Avg	%MS	MS-63RB	MS-65RD	MS-66RD
1968-S	810	65.4	99%	$0.15	$0.40	$29

1968-S, Proof • **Proof mintage:** 3,041,506.

Proof commentary: Usually examples are attractive and seen at the gem level. Over-polishing of the dies removed lower-relief details on some. Cameo and deep-cameo coins are especially desired. Certification figures for this issue are of little meaning, although those building registry sets can take note of what has been certified at PF-68RD and higher—this comment holding true for later Proofs as well. Of the 3,041,506 Proof cents struck this year, only a tiny fraction have been submitted for certification. *Be careful of any Proofs of this era that are billed as "rare" only because of low population-report figures.*

	Cert	Avg	%MS	PF-65RD	PF-67RD	PF-67Cam	PF-68DCam
1968-S, Proof	1,126	67.2		$1	$12	$16	$50

Lincoln, Memorial Reverse, Cents of 1969

MODIFIED PORTRAIT: In 1969 the obverse was modified, with small differences in several areas, and sharpening of features throughout. The relief of the obverse was lowered, permitting more consistent striking of details. A quick way to identify the modification is to check the highest wave of Lincoln's hair. On issues of 1969 and later it is directly under the W of WE. Earlier, it was to the left, between GOD and WE. The modifications ended a generation of coins that lacked needle-sharp details due to wear on hub dies. A quick way to discern the differences in sharpness is by comparing a Proof 1968-S with one of 1969-S.

1969 • **Circulation-strike mintage:** 1,136,910,000.

Commentary: This issue is common in gem Mint State. Sharpness of strike varies.

	Cert	Avg	%MS	MS-63RB	MS-65RD	MS-66RD
1969	406	65.7	100%	$0.35	$0.70	$55

1969-D • Circulation-strike mintage: 4,002,832,200.

Commentary: This issue is common in gem Mint State. Sharpness varies, but most examples are well struck.

	Cert	Avg	%MS	MS-63RB	MS-65RD	MS-66RD
1969-D	642	65.3	99%	$0.15	$0.30	$28

1969-S • Circulation-strike mintage: 544,375,000.

Commentary: This issue is common on an absolute basis. It was popular with investors, and large quantities were saved in gem Mint State. It is scarce in circulation in comparison to Philadelphia and Denver coins. Sharpness of strike varies.

	Cert	Avg	%MS	MS-63RB	MS-65RD	MS-66RD
1969-S	829	64.4	95%	$0.15	$0.50	$65

1969-S, Doubled-Die Obverse •

Circulation-strike mintage: Included in 1969-S circulation-strike figure.

Commentary: This variety's Fivaz-Stanton identification is FS-01-1969S-101. It can also be identified as CONECA 1969-S, DDO-001. Its rarity is URS-6. The date and lettering are well doubled on the obverse, not as dramatically as for the 1955, Doubled Die Obverse, but appearing especially clear under low magnification. Gems exist, as the population data indicates, but they are rare. Discovery of this variety made front-page news in *Coin World,* July 8, 1970. The Secret Service went on a witch hunt for these, believing they were counterfeit. By the time these were acknowledged as legitimate, five genuine coins had been destroyed (see the Wexler-Flynn text for details and identification of the cast of characters in this sorry situation).

Caveat: Some 1969-S circulation strikes, from regular dies but with "machine doubling" or die chatter during the coining process, have

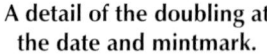

A detail of the doubling at the date and mintmark. | A detail of the doubling at LIBERTY.

Details of the doubling at IN GOD WE TRUST.

been offered or even certified (but not by one of the top three or four services) as the 1969-S, Doubled Die Obverse. Machine-doubled coins will have the S mintmark doubled, whereas the true 1969-S, Doubled Die Obverse, does not.

	Cert	Avg	%MS	MS-63RB
1969-S, Doubled-Die Obverse ‡	15	58.6	47%	$75,000

‡ Ranked in the *100 Greatest U.S. Modern Coins.*

1969-S, Proof • Proof mintage: 2,943,631.

Proof commentary: Usually examples are of high quality. Cameo Proofs, especially, are in demand. David W. Lange reported that some were struck from a broken die, and these are rare.

	Cert	Avg	%MS	PF-65RD	PF-67RD	PF-67Cam	PF-68DCam
1969-S, Proof	1,258	67.2		$1	$11	$13	$33

Lincoln, Memorial Reverse, Cents of 1970

TWO DATE VARIETIES: Two hub varieties were made this year, with different size dates. The Large Date hub was used on Philadelphia and Denver cents, and both Large and Small Date hubs were used on San Francisco cents. From the Wexler-Flynn text, *The Authoritative Reference on Lincoln Cents:*

A detail of the Small Date.

> **1970 Philadelphia, Denver, and San Francisco Large Date:** Thinner space between digits. Inside of 0 larger. Top of 7 below 9 and 0. Top of 0 comes to a point. Bottom of 7 comes to a point. LIBERTY has clear, distinct letters.

> **1970-S Small Date:** More space between digits. Inside of 0 smaller. Top of 7 even with top of 9 and 0. Top of 0 well rounded; bottom of 7 is squared. LIBERTY usually has mushy letters with the TY much weaker.

A detail of the Large Date.

1970 IN NUMISMATICS: James F. Ruddy launched *Photograde,* a photographic guide to grading coins, which became a runaway bestseller and inspired confidence in those who used it. Ruddy also announced the discovery of the 1888, 8 Over 7, Indian Head cent after finding two in a Virginia estate.

1970 • Circulation-strike mintage: 1,898,315,000.

Commentary: This issue was struck using the Large Date hub only. It is common in gem Mint State. Sharpness varies from example to example.

	Cert	Avg	%MS	MS-63RB	MS-65RD	MS-66RD	MS-67RD
1970	376	65.6	100%	$0.30	$0.65	$25	$250

1970-D • Circulation-strike mintage: 2,891,438,900.

Commentary: This issue was struck using the Large Date hub only. It is common in gem Mint State. Sharpness varies from example to example.

	Cert	Avg	%MS	MS-63RB	MS-65RD	MS-66RD	MS-67RD
1970-D	531	65.0	100%	$0.15	$0.30	$70	$900

1970-S, Small Date (High 7) •
Circulation-strike mintage: The lesser portion of 690,560,004.

Commentary: This issue is very scarce. It is a key issue among modern Lincoln cents.

For details comparing the Small Date and Large Date see page 479.

	Cert	Avg	%MS	MS-63RB	MS-65RD	MS-66RD
1970-S, Small Date (High 7)	789	64.5	100%	$25	$55	$240

1970-S, Large Date (Low 7) •
Circulation-strike mintage: The greater portion of 690,560,004.

Commentary: S-marked cents of this era are few and far between in general circulation. Bags and rolls of the 1970-S, Large Date, were widely hoarded, thus gems are easy to find in quantity. Examples are usually well struck. This issue is scarce in circulation due to the hoarding of Mint State coins.

For details comparing the Small Date and Large Date see page 479.

	Cert	Avg	%MS	MS-63RB	MS-65RD	MS-66RD	MS-67RD
1970-S, Large Date (Low 7)	1,339	64.8	98%	$0.20	$0.50	$30	$950

1970-S, Doubled-Die Obverse •

Circulation-strike mintage: Included in 1970-S, Large Date, circulation-strike mintage.

Commentary: The Fivaz-Stanton identification for this variety is FS-01-1970S-101. It can calso be identified as CONECA 1970-S, DDO-001. Its rarity is URS-5. This variety, made with the Large Date hub, has received very little publicity over the years, but it is now listed in *A Guide Book of United States Coins*, with the result that additional pieces may come to light. At present the variety is rare, and, who knows, it may remain so.

For details comparing the Small Date and Large Date see page 479.

A detail of the doubling at the date and mintmark.

A detail of the doubling at LIBERTY.

A detail of the doubling at IN GOD.

	Cert	Avg	%MS	MS-65RD
1970-S, Doubled-Die Obverse	12	63.1	83%	—

1970-S, Small Date (High 7), Proof •

Proof mintage: A small portion of 2,632,810.

Proof commentary: This issue is very scarce. Deep cameo Proofs are especially rare. The valuable Small Dates are certified in larger numbers than the more common Large Dates because of their increased worth over the common variety.

For details comparing the Small Date and Large Date see page 479.

	Cert	Avg	%MS	PF-65RD	PF-67RD	PF-67Cam
1970-S, Small Date (High 7), Proof	513	66.6		$40	$65	$150

1970-S, Large Date (Low 7), Proof • Proof mintage: Most of 2,632,810.

Proof commentary: This Proof is common.

For details comparing the Small Date and Large Date see page 479.

	Cert	Avg	%MS	PF-65RD	PF-67RD	PF-67Cam	PF-68DCam
1970-S, Large Date (Low 7), Proof	1,121	66.9		$1	$15	$25	$65

Lincoln, Memorial Reverse, Cents of 1971

1971 IN NUMISMATICS: Although the market crash of 1965 was history, little buying energy was evident in Lincoln cents and other 20th-century series.

1971 • Circulation-strike mintage: 1,919,490,000.

Commentary: This issue is common in gem Mint State. Sharpness of strike varies. In this era many $50 face-value bags were bought by investors.

	Cert	Avg	%MS	MS-63RB	MS-65RD	MS-66RD
1971	630	65.4	99%	$0.25	$0.60	$25

1971, Doubled Die Obverse •

Circulation-strike mintage: Included in 1971 circulation-strike mintage figure.

Commentary: The Fivaz-Stanton identification for this variety is FS-01-1971-101. It can also be identified as CONECA 1971, DDO-001. Its rarity is URS-9. Strong doubling is apparent on LIBERTY and IN GOD WE TRUST, with less noticeable doubling also on the date. This is a very recognizable variety.

A detail showing the doubling at LIBERTY.

A detail showing the doubling at IN GOD.

	Cert	Avg	%MS	MS-65RD
1971, Doubled-Die Obverse	27	63.3	93%	$50

1971-D • Circulation-strike mintage: 2,911,045,600.

Commentary: This issue is common in gem Mint State. Sharpness of strike varies.

	Cert	Avg	%MS	MS-63RB	MS-65RD	MS-66RD	MS-67RD
1971-D	239	65.4	100%	$0.20	$0.50	$24	$500

1971-S • Circulation-strike mintage: 525,133,459.

Commentary: This issue is very common, because at the time San Francisco coins in rolls were especially appealing to investors. Examples are usually well struck.

	Cert	Avg	%MS	MS-63RB	MS-65RD	MS-66RD
1971-S	414	65.4	98%	$0.20	$0.50	$50

1971-S, Proof • Proof mintage: 3,220,733.

Proof commentary: Usually examples are of superb quality, including many with cameo contrast. *Deep*-cameo coins are scarce. The following two listings are popular varieties of this Proof cent.

	Cert	Avg	%MS	PF-65RD	PF-67RD	PF-67Cam	PF-68DCam
1971-S, Proof	1,244	67.2		$1	$18	$30	$120

1971-S, Doubled Die Obverse, Proof • Proof mintage: Included in 1971-S, Proof, mintage.

Commentary: There are multiple varieties of 1971-S, Doubled Die Obverse, Proofs.

Varieties: One variety—FS-01-1971S-103— has very light doubling and is worth substantially less than the other two varieties.

	Cert	Avg	%MS	PF-65RD	PF-67RD	PF-67Cam
1971-S, Doubled-Die Obverse, Proof	94	66.5		$40	$150	$200

1971-S, Doubled Die Obverse, Proof (FS-01-1971S-101): This variety can also be identified as CONECA 1971-S, DDO-001. Its rarity is URS-8. Strong doubling of the obverse can be seen under magnification on IN GOD, TRUST, and LIBERTY. There is slight doubling on the date. In American numismatics not many Proof dies show noticeable doubling.

A detail showing the doubling at LIBERTY on FS-01-1971S-101.

1971-S, Doubled Die Obverse, Proof (FS-01-1971S-102): This variety can also be identified as CONECA 1971-S, DDO-002. Its rarity is URS-6. Strong doubling can be seen under magnification on IN GOD WE TRUST and LIBERTY. There is no doubling on the date. This is much rarer than the preceding doubled-die obverse.

A detail showing the doubling at LIBERTY on FS-01-1971S-102.

	PF-63	PF-65	PF-66	PF-67
FS-01-1971S-101	$250	$450	$600	$750
FS-01-1971S-102	$500	$750	$1,100	$1,500

Lincoln, Memorial Reverse, Cents of 1972

1972 IN NUMISMATICS: Plastic holders were in vogue for storing and displaying individual coins as well as sets. Paper envelopes continued to be standard for dealers' inventories. "Whizzing," the use of a wire brush to change the surface of circulated coins by adding fake luster, was a large problem for coin buyers who did not have enough knowledge to discern such altered coins.

1972 • Circulation-strike mintage: 2,933,255,000.

Commentary: This issue is common in gem Mint State. Usually examples are well struck, but care is still needed to acquire a well-struck example.

	Cert	Avg	%MS	MS-63RB	MS-65RD	MS-66RD
1972	592	65.1	96%	$0.15	$0.30	$32

1972, Doubled Die Obverse •

Circulation-strike mintage: Included in 1972 circulation-strike mintage figure.

Commentary: There are several varieties featuring this doubling.

	Cert	Avg	%MS	MS-63RB	MS-65RD	MS-66RD	MS-67RD
1972, Doubled-Die Obverse	2,288	64.3	99%	$400	$650	$1,050	$5,500

Varieties: *1972, Doubled Die Obverse (FS-01-1972-101):* This variety can also be identified as CONECA 1972, DDO-001. Its rarity is URS-14. This variety is from a strong, dramatic doubled die. John Wexler suggested that 75,000 were released, many more than the 20,000 estimated by Sol Taylor. No information has been seen by numismatic researcher Q. David Bowers as to why this and the next die were removed from use. Today, this is one of the most popular varieties in the Lincoln series.

A detail showing the doubling at LIBERTY on FS-01-1972-101.

1972, Doubled Die Obverse (FS-01-1972-102): This variety can also be identified as CONECA 1972, DDO-002. Its rarity is URS-16. This variety shows slight doubling. Other genuine obverse dies with lesser doubling exist for this issue. Counterfeits are also common. Q. David Bowers advises to buy coins certified by the leading services.

A detail showing the light doubling at the date on FS-01-1972-102.

	AU-50	MS-60	MS-63	MS-65
FS-01-1972-101	$240	$300	$400	$600
FS-01-1972-102	$20	$50	$70	$100

1972-D • Circulation-strike mintage: 2,665,071,400.

Commentary: This issue is common in gem Mint State.

	Cert	Avg	%MS	MS-63RB	MS-65RD	MS-66RD
1972-D	228	65.2	97%	$0.15	$0.30	$28

1972-S • Circulation-strike mintage: 376,939,108.

Commentary: This issue is common in all grades, although diluted in circulation by greater numbers of Philadelphia and Denver cents. Sharp coins are easily found.

	Cert	Avg	%MS	MS-63RB	MS-65RD	MS-66RD	MS-67RD
1972-S	299	65.0	98%	$0.25	$0.75	$78	$1,000

1972-S, Proof • Proof mintage: 3,260,996.

Proof commentary: Examples are common, including with cameo contrast.

	Cert	Avg	%MS	PF-65RD	PF-67RD	PF-67Cam	PF-68DCam
1972-S, Proof	794	67.3		$1	$15	$20	$35

Lincoln, Memorial Reverse, Cents of 1973

REVERSE HUB MODIFICATION: The reverse hub was modified slightly: the initials FG, for Frank Gasparro, were considerably enlarged and some design details were sharpened. In the next year the size of FG was reduced slightly.

1973 • Circulation-strike mintage: 3,728,245,000.

Commentary: This issue is common in gem Mint State. On any of the cents of this era, check the high points of Lincoln on the obverse, and on the reverse check the tiny statue at the center of the Memorial, and the shrubbery.

	Cert	Avg	%MS	MS-63RB	MS-65RD	MS-66RD	MS-67RD
1973	417	65.7	100%	$0.15	$0.30	$37	$600

1973-D • Circulation-strike mintage: 3,549,576,588.

Commentary: This issue is common in gem Mint State.

	Cert	Avg	%MS	MS-63RB	MS-65RD	MS-66RD
1973-D	429	65.6	100%	$0.15	$0.30	$37

1973-S • Circulation-strike mintage: 317,177,295.

Commentary: This issue is common in gem Mint State. In circulation, however, they are few and far between in comparison to the issues of Philadelphia and Denver. When these first came out they were the object of wild and frantic speculation, with $50 face-value bags

selling for $700 or more, because the Mint was slow in releasing them, and it seemed to some that a rarity was in the offing. With good judgment, Mint Director Mary Brooks directed that remaining stocks be mixed with Denver and Philadelphia coins and placed into circulation. This was mostly done in 1974 and effectively removed the possibility of anyone getting more $50 bags (while at the same time making the coins available to collectors looking through pocket change). Usually all are well struck.

	Cert	Avg	%MS	MS-63RB	MS-65RD	MS-66RD
1973-S	335	65.3	99%	$0.25	$0.85	$200

1973-S, Proof • Proof mintage: 2,760,339.

Proof commentary: This issue is common. Most Proofs of this era and later have deep-cameo contrast, although labeling varies on certified holders.

	Cert	Avg	%MS	PF-65RD	PF-67RD	PF-67Cam	PF-68DCam
1973-S, Proof	252	67.5		$1	$13	$16	$30

Lincoln, Memorial Reverse, Cents of 1974

WEST POINT BULLION DEPOSITORY: In the summer, the West Point Bullion Depository, with a staff of about 50 people, was marshaled into service as a mint to strike cents. Millions of coins were produced there, but since they bore no mintmark, they were not collectible as such.

HUB CHANGES: The designer's initials were slightly reduced, but remained larger than on the 1972-style cent (see a discussion of the initial changes under 1973, page 482). Two obverse hub changes were made: one with very sharp details was used only in 1974; the other, with less detail, was used through 1982. David W. Lange calls the first the Large Date and the second the Small Date, although he notes that the only *significant* distinction is that on the Small Date the date is farther from the border. These varieties have not attracted wide notice in the collecting community and are not listed in the *Guide Book of United States Coins*. David W. Lange discussed the changes of this year:

> Of particular interest to collectors, at least those with sharp eyes, are the subtle changes that occurred during 1974. The obverse master hub created in 1969 and used thereafter through 1973 was replaced with a dramatically sharpened portrait for the 1974 cent coinage. In addition to more distinct lettering, numeral 7 of the date received a shorter horizontal segment and a long, curving arc to its diagonal segment. Finally, the Lincoln bust was given a more robust character, his wavy hair being bolder and more sharply delineated from his ear.
>
> Dies generated from this new and very attractive obverse hub were used by all four mints active at that time. This included West Point which, like Philadelphia, coined cents without a mintmark. Strangely, however, this obverse hub was replaced with another one midway through 1974, resulting in two subtypes for the Lincoln cents dated 1974. This hub, too, was used to sink dies for all the mints, resulting in a total of six collectable cent varieties for 1974. All of the 1974-S proofs appear to be from the first hub, as the proofs were made early in that year.
>
> The second obverse of 1974 differed from the first in being of faintly lower relief and having duller details in Lincoln's hair. A noticeable blending of Lincoln's ear with the surrounding hair further aggravated this loss of boldness. Finally, the new master hub had been mechanically reduced to a slightly

smaller diameter than the first. This provided greater separation of peripheral elements from the coin's border, but it also made the entire design slightly smaller overall. This is perhaps most noticeable in the greater distance between the date and adjacent border on the revised hub.[203]

1974 ALUMINUM CENTS: In late 1973, the rising price of copper prompted the Mint to investigate making cents in aluminum. Seven different alloys, combining various metals with 96% aluminum, were tested using 1974-dated dies. Mint Director Mary Brooks passed out samples, making no statement that they had to be returned. They went to nine congressmen and four senators, and some went to Mint staff. Others went to Treasury officials. Apparently, no account of the distribution was made, because no one thought these pieces would become numismatically interesting, rare, or valuable. News of this excited collectors, and it was hoped that some would reach the market, where they certainly would become expensive rarities. Brooks sought to have the recipients bring their coins back, but 14 remained missing. The FBI and others got into the act and interviewed the congressmen, whose recollections were fuzzy at best—complete with denials that such coins had ever been received—and no more were returned. Mint records reveal that 1,571,167 such aluminum cents were struck in anticipation of their use. Speculation arose in numismatic circles as to the legality of these aluminum cents if an example should come to light. The matter was moot—none had been seen in the marketplace. Then in 2001, one surfaced and was featured in *Numismatic News*, in a February 20 article by Alan Herbert. The coin is said to have been found after a congressman had dropped it on the floor of the Rayburn Office Building, by Albert Toven, a U.S. Capitol police officer. Seeking to return it, Toven was told by the congressman to keep it. In 2005 it was certified as AU-58 by the Independent Coin Grading Company (ICG). Less than two months later, it had "graduated" from the AU level to MS-62 in a PCGS holder. A discussion printed in *Coin World* ("Aluminum 1¢ Changes Grade," by Paul Gilkes, October 17, 2005) quoted ICG founder Keith Love as saying, "The ICG graders were unanimous in calling the coin AU-58." David Hall, principal at PCGS, stated that graders there all pronounced it to be Uncirculated. Another example is in the National Numismatic Collection in the Smithsonian Institution.

EXPERIMENTAL CENTS: Some experimental coins, in bronze-clad steel, were also made, as were strikings of approximately cent-sized coins from dies with "nonsense" inscriptions, to test various compositions.

1974 IN NUMISMATICS: The collecting of mint error coins, which had been dismissed a generation earlier as "freaks," was by now a very popular pursuit.

Whizzed coins continued to be a problem, and much ink was used to describe them in print. Almost single-handedly, ANACS and its supporters attenuated the flood of counterfeits and other deceptive pieces coming into the market, closed down numerous whizzing and processing operations, and made numerous recommendations which resulted in the suspension or expulsion of American Numismatic Association members engaged in such practices.

The year 1974 closed on an optimistic note. Limited-edition Franklin Mint medals continued to be in the limelight, sharing attention with modern world Proof sets, limited-edition crowns, and other pieces of recent manufacture. In the United States series, gold coins and silver dollars continued their popularity, and other series were also doing well. Emphasis was on scarcities and rarities, and year by year prices escalated. In 1974 prices were far higher than even five years earlier in 1969. While some of this increase can be explained by an influx of new people into the hobby, this was only part of the story, for the membership rolls of the American Numismatic Association had increased only moderately, and the subscriber rolls of *Coin World* had actually decreased from a high point in the 1960s. Most dealers and hobby insiders attributed the increase to a vast expansion of investment interest. A typical buyer had investment in mind, and was apt to write much larger checks than the numismatist or hobbyist buying pieces for a collection. This investment interest was to continue and by a decade later it almost completely dominated certain portions of the rare-coin field.

1974 • Circulation-strike mintage: 4,232,140,523.

Commentary: This issue is common in gem Mint State. Some pieces were struck at West Point, but were made without mintmarks. Mintmarkless coins struck at West Point cannot be differentiated from Philadelphia issues. Usually examples are well struck.

	Cert	Avg	%MS	MS-63RB	MS-65RD	MS-66RD	MS-67RD
1974	363	65.9	100%	$0.15	$0.30	$27	$175

1974-D • Circulation-strike mintage: 4,235,098,000.

Commentary: This issue is common in gem Mint State. Sharpness of strike varies.

	Cert	Avg	%MS	MS-63RB	MS-65RD	MS-66RD	MS-67RD
1974-D	335	65.6	100%	$0.15	$0.30	$23	$100

1974-S • Circulation-strike mintage: 409,426,660.

Commentary: This issue is common in gem Mint State. In circulation, these and other San Francisco cents of the era are scarce in proportion to those from Philadelphia and Denver. Many were released mixed with Denver and Philadelphia cents, as had been done with the 1973-S. Sharpness of strike varies. This was the last year that circulation-strike cents made at San Francisco bore an S mintmark.

	Cert	Avg	%MS	MS-63RB	MS-65RD	MS-66RD	MS-67RD
1974-S	173	65.2	100%	$0.25	$0.75	$100	$750

1974-S, Proof • Proof mintage: 2,612,568.

Proof commentary: Cameo contrast is the rule for these Proofs, with deep cameos being in the minority but still plentiful. Proofs are from the new hub, used only this year, with the portrait details slightly sharper.

	Cert	Avg	%MS	PF-65RD	PF-67RD	PF-67Cam	PF-68DCam
1974-S, Proof	276	67.2		$1	$13	$16	$30

Lincoln, Memorial Reverse, Cents of 1975

1975 • **Circulation-strike mintage:** 5,451,476,142.

Commentary: This issue is common in gem Mint State. Mintmarkless coins struck at West Point and San Francisco cannot be differentiated from Philadelphia issues. Usually examples are well struck. Nearly 10 *billion* cents were struck this year at four minting facilities. Circulation-strike cents, produced at the San Francisco Assay Office (San Francisco Mint) by the many millions, were made without S mintmarks, giving them the appearance of Philadelphia coins. Mint Director Mary Brooks thought that this would minimize the hoarding of such cents, which, no doubt, it did.

	Cert	Avg	%MS	MS-63RB	MS-65RD	MS-66RD	MS-67RD
1975	341	65.8	100%	$0.15	$0.30	$29	$150

1975-D • **Circulation-strike mintage:** 4,505,275,300.

Commentary: This issue is common in gem Mint State. Sharpness of strike varies.

	Cert	Avg	%MS	MS-63RB	MS-65RD	MS-66RD	MS-67RD
1975-D	196	65.7	100%	$0.15	$0.30	$28	$350

1975-S, Proof • **Proof mintage:** 2,845,450.

Commentary: These Proofs were mostly made with cameo contrast, and made much less often with deep-cameo contrast. This issue is popular as a "Proof only" date because, while the San Francisco Assay Office (San Francisco Mint) struck cents for circulation, these did not have a mintmark and appeared the same as Philadelphia issues. From this year onward, S-marked Proofs have this special cachet, and are thus essential for the completion of a date-and-mintmark collection.

	Cert	Avg	%MS	PF-65RD	PF-67RD	PF-67Cam	PF-68DCam
1975-S, Proof	488	67.2		$3.50	$13	$16	$30

Lincoln, Memorial Reverse, Cents of 1976

1976 • Circulation-strike mintage: 4,674,292,426.

Commentary: This issue is common in gem Mint State. Sharp strikes can be easily found among the large quantities coined. Some were struck at West Point. Mintmarkless coins struck at West Point cannot be differentiated from Philadelphia issues.

	Cert	Avg	%MS	MS-63RB	MS-65RD	MS-66RD	MS-67RD
1976	174	65.9	99%	$0.15	$0.30	$27	$55

1976-D • Circulation-strike mintage: 4,221,592,455.

Commentary: This issue is common in gem Mint State. Sharpness varies, but nice examples can be found.

	Cert	Avg	%MS	MS-63RB	MS-65RD	MS-66RD	MS-67RD
1976-D	116	65.3	100%	$0.15	$0.30	$35	$750

1976-S, Proof • Proof mintage: 4,149,730.

Proof commentary: This Proof is common with typical cameo contrast. Deep-cameo cents are in the minority. Proof-set production reached a new high this year, due to demand for American Bicentennial coins. By year's end, however, some sets remained unsold.

	Cert	Avg	%MS	PF-65RD	PF-67RD	PF-67Cam	PF-68DCam
1976-S, Proof	755	67.1		$3.20	$13	$16	$30

Lincoln, Memorial Reverse, Cents of 1977

1977 IN NUMISMATICS: "Overdate" 1977, 7 Over 6, cents caused some notice this year, but these were found to be counterfeits.

1977 • Circulation-strike mintage:
4,469,930,000.

Commentary: This issue is common in gem Mint State. Some were struck at West Point. Mintmarkless coins struck at West Point cannot be differentiated from Philadelphia issues. Full Details coins are common.

	Cert	Avg	%MS	MS-63RB	MS-65RD	MS-66RD	MS-67RD
1977	262	66.1	100%	$0.15	$0.30	$55	$130

1977-D • Circulation-strike mintage:
4,194,062,300.

Commentary: This issue is common in gem Mint State. Sharpness of strike varies.

	Cert	Avg	%MS	MS-63RB	MS-65RD	MS-66RD	MS-67RD
1977-D	409	65.2	100%	$0.15	$0.30	$90	$650

1977-S, Proof • Proof mintage:
3,251,152.

Proof commentary: This issue is common. Usually examples are found with cameo contrast; less often, with deep-cameo contrast.

	Cert	Avg	%MS	PF-65RD	PF-67RD	PF-67Cam	PF-68DCam
1977-S, Proof	416	68.2		$2.50	$13	$16	$30

Lincoln, Memorial Reverse, Cents of 1978

1978 • **Circulation-strike mintage:** 5,558,605,000.

Commentary: This issue is common in gem Mint State. Some were struck at West Point and San Francisco. Mintmarkless coins struck at San Francisco and West Point cannot be differentiated from Philadelphia issues. Full Details coins are common.

	Cert	Avg	%MS	MS-63RB	MS-65RD	MS-66RD	MS-67RD
1978	170	65.6	99%	$0.15	$0.30	$80	$625

1978-D • **Circulation-strike mintage:** 4,280,233,400.

Commentary: This issue is common in gem Mint State. Sharpness of strike varies.

	Cert	Avg	%MS	MS-63RB	MS-65RD	MS-66RD	MS-67RD
1978-D	175	65.5	100%	$0.15	$0.30	$75	$425

1978-S, Proof • **Proof mintage:** 3,127,781.

Proof commentary: This issue is common. Deep-cameo contrast was the norm, not the exception, continuing from this year onward.

	Cert	Avg	%MS	PF-65RD	PF-67RD	PF-67Cam	PF-68DCam
1978-S, Proof	440	67.5		$2.50	$13	$16	$30

Lincoln, Memorial Reverse, Cents of 1979

1979 • **Circulation-strike mintage:** 6,018,515,000.

Commentary: This issue is common in gem Mint State. Sharpness varies, with sharply defined coins common. Some were struck at San Francisco and West Point. Mintmarkless coins struck at San Francisco and West Point cannot be differentiated from Philadelphia issues.

	Cert	Avg	%MS	MS-63RB	MS-65RD	MS-66RD	MS-67RD
1979	614	66.5	100%	$0.15	$0.30	$20	$70

1979-D • Circulation-strike mintage: 4,139,357,254.

Commentary: This issue is common in gem Mint State. Sharp strikes can be easily found. Examples exist without the FG initials on the reverse, resulting from either weak striking or, more likely, dressing the face of the die too harshly. In many other instances in this era, the FG initials can be weak in areas. Both the weak and missing FG pieces are of little commercial importance.

	Cert	Avg	%MS	MS-63RB	MS-65RD	MS-66RD
1979-D	281	65.5	100%	$0.15	$0.30	$60

1979-S, Type 1, Proof • Proof mintage: The greater portion of 3,677,175.

Commentary: This variety was made with an old-style S punch, filled in at the center, making it appear as a blob. Deep-cameo contrast is the norm for this variety.

A detail of the old style with a filled S.

	Cert	Avg	%MS	PF-65RD	PF-67RD	PF-67Cam	PF-68DCam
1979-S, Type 1, Proof	561	68.3		$5	$11	$13	$17

1979-S, Type 2, Proof • Proof mintage: The lesser portion of 3,677,175.

Commentary: This variety was made with a new punch, well defined at the center. It is the scarcer of the two varieties, but not dramatically so. Deep-cameo contrast is also the norm for this variety. These S-mintmark variations are known across the other Proof denominations, and are considered scarce only for the Kennedy half dollar and the Susan B. Anthony dollar. This same punch was used in 1980.

A detail of the new style with an open S.

	Cert	Avg	%MS	PF-65RD	PF-67RD	PF-67Cam	PF-68DCam
1979-S, Type 2, Proof	740	68.1		$6	$17	$20	$30

Lincoln, Memorial Reverse, Cents of 1980

1980 IN NUMISMATICS: By 1979 coin investment was one of the hottest things going, and by early 1980 prices were riding a crest. Numerous editors of newsletters, "hard money" advocates, and others proclaimed that anyone holding paper dollars was a fool, an idiot, or worse. Gold (and to a lesser extent, silver) was the only way to go. In January, gold hit a new high of $873 per ounce, and silver hit $49.50 per ounce. From that point it was down, down, and down some more. On January 18, Allen Harriman, editor of the *Coin Dealer Newsletter*, remarked: "With both silver and gold bullion soaring into new uncharted ranges, trading in many areas of the coin market becomes more uncertain each day—if not each hour!" By this time, most *serious numismatists* were sitting on the sidelines and not buying any of the hot coins that investors were lapping up. In March dealers and investors zipped up their wallets, buyers of "investment grade" coins were nowhere to be seen, and the market for such coins plunged, this being the talk of the Central States show in Lincoln, Nebraska. Lincoln cents, ignored by nearly all investors, were not affected by the market crash, nor were colonial coins, tokens and medals, early copper coins, early silver, and other series with a solid base of collectors.

Soft clear polyvinyl chloride (PVC) envelopes had become a very popular way to store coins, and many collectors, dealers, and auction houses used them. Alarms were sounded as collectors began to notice damage to coins stored in such a manner, including this warning by Edward Cohen in *The Numismatist*:

> I am greatly concerned about long term storage of coins in vinyl flips. I, as well as a close friend, have noticed green corrosion developing on copper, copper-nickel, brass, and other base metal coins stored in these flips. We both use quality flips. Corrosion starts to appear after two years and is most evident after two years as a green circle on flip. After 10 years, corrosion is well into central surface of coin. Base metal coins within a few years lose their brilliance.
>
> For coins stored in Mylar, cardboard holders I have never had a problem. I get no sympathy from dealers in this matter. I believe collectors should know about the problem. Subsequently warnings about vinyl flips were issued in the hobby, but, curiously, the manufacturers and distributors of same remained silent on the subject. Countless coins, particularly those containing copper or nickel, were damaged.
>
> Many of these were rescued, at least partially, by dipping to remove the PVC, in solvents such as ammonia and acetone, then dipping, to restore brilliance, in another solution.

The American Numismatic Association board of governors expanded the official grading standards, in the Uncirculated range, to include intermediate grades MS-63 and MS-67. The Numismatic Bibliomania Society, a club for devotees of numismatic literature, was formed. (Visit www.coinbooks.org for more information.)

In July 1979 Mint Director Stella B. Hackel revealed a new plan for mintmarks, noting that a P mintmark would appear on all coins from the cent to the dollar made at Philadelphia in 1980—except this:

> In 1980, one-cent coins produced for circulation in Philadelphia, Denver, San Francisco, and the West Point Bullion Depository will bear no mintmarks. At present there is considerable withdrawal from circulation by collectors of 'D' marked one-cent coins. Elimination of any distinction among coins struck at the four Mint locations should increase the circulating one-cent pool. With the exception of the one-cent coins, the 'D' mintmark will continue to appear on all other denominations struck at Denver. All Proof coins, including the Proof one-cent coin, and the Susan B. Anthony dollar coins produced for circulation by the San Francisco Assay Office will bear the 'S' mintmark.

The plan did not come to pass, and Denver Mint cents continued to bear a D mintmark.

The West Point Bullion Depository (later renamed West Point Mint) began striking ounce and half-ounce American Arts Gold Medallions. Collectors largely ignored them; the program ended in 1984. (For more information, see *American Gold and Silver: U.S. Mint Collector and Investor Coins and Medals, Bicentennial to Date.*)

1980 • Circulation-strike mintage: 7,414,705,000.

Commentary: This issue is common in gem Mint State. Sharp strikes can be easily found. Some were struck at San Francisco and West Point. Mintmarkless coins struck at San Francisco and West Point cannot be differentiated from Philadelphia issues.

	Cert	Avg	%MS	MS-63RB	MS-65RD	MS-66RD	MS-67RD
1980	177	65.3	100%	$0.15	$0.30	$27	$125

1980, Doubled-Die Obverse •

Circulation-strike mintage: Included in 1980 circulation-strike mintage.

Commentary: This variety's Fivaz-Stanton identification is FS-01-1980-101. It can also be identified as CONECA 1980, DDO-001. Its rarity is URS-11. There is strong doubling on the date and LIBERTY, but virtually none on IN GOD WE TRUST.

A detail showing the doubling on the date.

A detail showing the doubling at LIBERTY.

	Cert	Avg	%MS	MS-63RB	MS-65RD
1980, Doubled-Die Obverse	231	61.7	79%	$225	$350

1980-D • Circulation-strike mintage: 5,140,098,660.

Commentary: This issue is common in gem Mint State. A larger D mintmark was implemented this year. Sharp strikes can be easily found.

	Cert	Avg	%MS	MS-63RB	MS-65RD	MS-66RD	MS-67RD
1980-D	265	65.3	99%	$0.15	$0.30	$40	$400

1980-S, Proof • **Proof mintage:** 3,554,806.

Proof commentary: These Proofs are common. They were made with deep cameo contrast.

	Cert	Avg	%MS	PF-65RD	PF-67RD	PF-67Cam	PF-68DCam
1980-S, Proof	871	68.4		$2.50	$10	$11	$15

Lincoln, Memorial Reverse, Cents of 1981

1981 IN NUMISMATICS: Lincoln cents were more widely used than ever in circulation. Although there were virtually no goods or services that could be bought for one cent alone, the coin was necessary in making change, since all but a handful of states had sales taxes. Although mintages had reached record highs in recent times, in 1981, the Treasury stocks were alarmingly low. An inventory at the end of the year showed "only" 140 million held by the Mint and about 470 million held by the Federal Reserve Bank system. In the most recent fiscal year (ending June 30, 1981), according to a report by Mint Director Donna Pope, the Mint was able to strike only about 13.32 billion, short of the 15.3 billion the Federal Reserve requested.

1981 • **Circulation-strike mintage:** 7,491,750,000.

Commentary: This issue is common in gem Mint State. Sharpness of strike varies. Some were struck in San Francisco and West Point. Mintmarkless coins struck at San Francisco and West Point cannot be differentiated from Philadelphia issues. David W. Lange noted that cents sold by the Bureau of the Mint as part of Mint sets for this year are often discolored, probably due to some rinse used at the Mint.

	Cert	Avg	%MS	MS-63RB	MS-65RD	MS-66RD	MS-67RD
1981	156	65.3	99%	$0.15	$0.30	$35	$125

1981-D • **Circulation-strike mintage:** 5,373,235,677.

Commentary: This issue is common in gem Mint State. Sharpness of strike varies.

	Cert	Avg	%MS	MS-63RB	MS-65RD	MS-66RD	MS-67RD
1981-D	191	65.5	99%	$0.15	$0.30	$40	$225

1981-S, Type 1, Proof • Proof mintage: The greater part of 4,063,083.

Commentary: This variety was punched with an S that was filled in at the center, making it appear as a blob. Deep-cameo contrast is the norm for this Proof. The 1981-S, Type 1, Proof was made by the 1979-S, Type 2, Proof punch, now eroded, and the filled S on this issue is different in appearance from the filled S on the 1979-S, Type 1, Proof.

A detail of the old style with a filled S.

	Cert	Avg	%MS	PF-65RD	PF-67RD	PF-67Cam	PF-68DCam
1981-S, Type 1, Proof	1,036	68.3		$3	$10	$11	$15

1981-S, Type 2, Proof • Proof mintage: The lesser part of 4,063,083.

Commentary: This mintmark was made from a new S punch, which was well defined at the center. It is in the distinct minority among Proofs of 1981-S (the Bureau of the Mint estimated 599,000 coins), and thus of considerable value. Deep-cameo contrast is the rule for this variety. Mintmark size differences in 1981 are also known for the other denominations.

A detail of the new style with an open S.

	Cert	Avg	%MS	PF-65RD	PF-67RD	PF-67Cam	PF-68DCam
1981-S, Type 2, Proof	637	67.9		$15	$28	$38	$55

Lincoln, Memorial Reverse, Cents of 1982

SMALL DATES AND LARGE DATES: A new obverse hub, known as the Small Date, was introduced this year, having slightly lower relief and the sharpened lettering. What is now known as the Large Date variety is, as David W. Lange points out, the same as the *Small Date* of 1974. Confused? An easy way to differentiate them is that, on the Large Date, the tops of 98 are above the tops of 1 and 2; while on the Small Date, the tops of the numerals are even. The first Small Date cents were struck on September 3, 1982.

A detail showing the Large Date.

Further, this differential comes from the Wexler-Flynn text, *The Authoritative Reference on Lincoln Cents:*

1982, Large Date: Larger digits, mushy letters. LIBERTY distinct, well defined letters. Larger bust, close to rim. IN GOD closer to rim, mushy. WE TRUST closer to rim, mushy.

A detail showing the Small Date.

1982, Small Date: Date has smaller, sharper digits. Smaller bust. IN GOD farther from rim, much sharper letters. WE TRUST farther from rim, much sharper letters.

COPPER-COATED ZINC CENTS: The Bureau of the Mint converted cent production from copper alloy (95% copper, 5% zinc) to copper-coated zinc, a move that made the production of cents more profitable, in the face of the high market price of copper. Released early in the year, the new coins contained 99.2% zinc and 0.8% copper as a coating. The new coins weighed about 25% less than the brass versions. All Proofs were struck in brass this year. The copper-coated zinc cents were soon found to be prone to discoloration and, less often, flaking or bubbling. Due to technology most problems with the new composition were solved over time.

This is the first of several galvanos made by Mint engraver Sherl Joseph Winter in 1982 to test the curvature of the field of the cent, as well as other aspects.

1982 IN NUMISMATICS: Never a part of the investment segment of the market, Lincoln cents continued to be very popular, although problems of erratic grading and the dipping and cleaning of coins continued for collectors seeking bargains in retail advertisements. Bullion prices continued to be depressed, with negative effects on the market for common silver and gold coins traded in quantity. Grading in the marketplace was often wild and undisciplined with such offerings as MS-65+++ and the like, showing no consistency. Overgraded coins were sold without regulation and were eagerly purchased by bargain seekers who, somehow, thought that the leading numismatic periodicals were policing their advertisers.

1982, Large Date, Copper Alloy •

Circulation-strike mintage: Part of 10,712,525,000 (includes both metals).

Commentary: This issue is common in gem Mint State. It is slightly more common than the Small Date. Sharp strikes can be easily found. Some were struck in San Francisco and West Point. Mintmarkless cents struck at the two other mints cannot be differentiated from Philadelphia strikes.

See page 498 and above for details comparing the Large Date and the Small Date.

	Cert	Avg	%MS	MS-63RB	MS-65RD	MS-66RD	MS-67RD
1982, Large Date, Copper Alloy	121	65.0	100%	$0.20	$0.35	$25	$55

1982, Small Date, Copper Alloy •

Circulation-strike mintage: Part of 10,712,525,000 (includes both metals).

Commentary: This issue is common in gem Mint State. It is slightly less common than the Large Date, but still exceedingly plentiful. Sharp coins abound, although many of this era are weak on the reverse at the E PL of E PLURIBUS, which is true of cents from 1959 to 1983. Some were struck in San Francisco and West Point. Mintmarkless cents struck at the two other mints cannot be differentiated from Philadelphia strikes.

See pages 498 and 499 for details comparing the Large Date and the Small Date.

	Cert	Avg	%MS	MS-63RB	MS-65RD	MS-66RD	MS-67RD
1982, Small Date, Copper Alloy	139	65.3	100%	$0.30	$0.50	$45	$125

1982-D, Copper Alloy •

Circulation-strike mintage: Part of 6,012,979,368 (includes both metals).

Commentary: This issue has a widely-spaced AM in AMERICA as usually seen. This issue is common in gem Mint State. All copper alloy 1982-D cents are Large Dates. These were coined until October 21. Sharp strikes can be easily found.

See pages 498 and 499 for details comparing the Large Date and the Small Date.

	Cert	Avg	%MS	MS-63RB	MS-65RD	MS-66RD	MS-67RD
1982-D	137	65.3	99%	$0.15	$0.30	$20	$35

1982-S, Copper Alloy, Proof •

Proof mintage: 3,857,479.

Proof commentary: These Proofs were made with deep-cameo contrast. Examples are common. All Proof cents this year are in copper alloy and of the Large Date style. It has been said (by Breen in 1988, and Lange in 1995) that some Small Date Proofs were made, but destroyed.

See pages 498 and 499 for details comparing the Large Date and the Small Date.

	Cert	Avg	%MS	PF-65RD	PF-67RD	PF-67Cam	PF-68DCam
1982-S, Copper Alloy, Proof	464	68.1		$2.50	$10	$11	$15

1982, Large Date, Copper-Plated Zinc • Circulation-strike mintage: Part of 10,712,525,000 (includes both metals).

Commentary: This issue is common in gem Mint State. Discolored coins of this and other copper-plated zinc issues can be bypassed—there are enough nice ones to be found. Sharp coins are the rule. Some were struck in San Francisco and West Point. Mintmarkless cents struck at the two other mints cannot be differentiated from Philadelphia strikes.

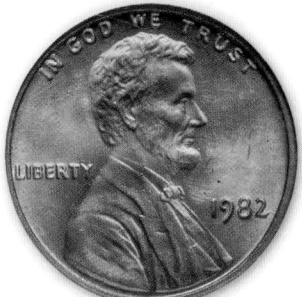 

See pages 498 and 499 for details comparing the Large Date and the Small Date.

	Cert	Avg	%MS	MS-63RB	MS-65RD	MS-66RD	MS-67RD
1982, Large Date, Copper-Plated Zinc	370	66.3	100%	$0.35	$0.50	$35	$60

1982, Small Date, Copper-Plated Zinc • Circulation-strike mintage: Part of 10,712,525,000 (includes both metals).

Commentary: This issue is common in gem Mint State. Sharp strikes can be easily found. Some were struck in San Francisco and West Point. Mintmarkless cents struck at the two other mints cannot be differentiated from Philadelphia strikes.

See pages 498 and 499 for details comparing the Large Date and the Small Date.

	Cert	Avg	%MS	MS-63RB	MS-65RD	MS-66RD	MS-67RD
1982, Small Date, Copper-Plated Zinc	385	66.5	100%	$0.50	$0.85	$35	

1982-D, Large Date, Copper-Plated Zinc • Circulation-strike mintage: Part of 6,012,979,368 (includes both metals).

Commentary: This issue is common in gem Mint State. Sharp strikes are common.

See pages 498 and 499 for details comparing the Large Date and the Small Date.

	Cert	Avg	%MS	MS-63RB	MS-65RD	MS-66RD	MS-67RD
1982-D, Large Date, Copper-Plated Zinc	245	66.4	100%	$0.20	$0.40	$25	$45

1982-D, Small Date, Copper-Plated Zinc • Circulation-strike

mintage: Part of 6,012,979,368 (includes both metals).

Commentary: This issue is common in gem Mint State. Sharp strikes can be easily found.

See pages 498 and 499 for details comparing the Large Date and the Small Date.

	Cert	Avg	%MS	MS-63RB	MS-65RD	MS-66RD	MS-67RD
1982-D, Small Date, Copper-Plated Zinc	239	66.2	100%	$0.15	$0.30	$15	$275

Lincoln, Memorial Reverse, Cents of 1983

1983 IN NUMISMATICS: Lincoln cents continued to be popular with collectors, but relatively few made them a long-term specialty. Copper-coated zinc continued as the standard composition; discolored and irregular surfaces (e.g., tiny blisters or bubbles caused by the metals not bonding properly) were annoying to numismatists.

1983 • Circulation-strike mintage:

Most of 7,752,355,000.

Commentary: This issue is common in gem Mint State. Avoid discolored coins and those with surface bubbling or problems. Sharp strikes can be easily found. Some, from dies finished too vigorously, have the FG initials weak or missing, and others lack the bottom of the E in CENT (making it look like an F). These are more curious than valuable. Some were struck in San Francisco and West Point. Mintmarkless coins struck at San Francisco and West Point cannot be differentiated from Philadelphia issues. Several examples struck in solid brass (pre-1982 composition) have been reported.

	Cert	Avg	%MS	MS-63RB	MS-65RD	MS-66RD	MS-67RD
1983	238	65.5	97%	$0.15	$0.30	$15	$45

1983, Doubled Die Reverse •

Circulation-strike mintage: Lesser portion of 7,752,355,000.

Commentary: This variety's Fivaz-Stanton identification is FS-01-1983-801. It can also be identified as CONECA 1983, DDR-001. Its rarity is URS-14. Doubling is strong on all the peripheral letters on this variety. First reported in the summer of 1983, these doubled-die coins were later found, according to Walter Breen, in limited numbers in the Lewistown, Pennsylvania, area (with others in northern Florida, per Sol Taylor). All examples are seen with extensive die-finishing lines (i.e., microscopic raised lines) on the obverse, and this should not affect the certified grade.

A detail showing the doubling at UNITED.   A detail showing the doubling at ONE CENT.

	Cert	Avg	%MS	MS-63RB	MS-65RD	MS-66RD	MS-67RD
1983, Doubled-Die Reverse	970	64.9	98%	$250	$385	$550	$1,200

1983-D • Circulation-strike mintage: 6,467,199,428.

Commentary: This issue is common in gem Mint State. Avoid discolored coins and those with surface bubbling or problems. Sharp strikes are aplenty.

	Cert	Avg	%MS	MS-63RB	MS-65RD	MS-66RD	MS-67RD
1983-D	220	66.6	100%	$0.15	$0.30	$15	$31

1983-S, Proof • Proof mintage: 3,279,126.

Proof commentary: These Proofs were made with deep-cameo contrast. They are "Quite subject to discoloration," observes David W. Lange, who comments that a fiberboard insert in the Proof set packaging, used beginning this year, may make the problem worse. "Only time will tell whether these coins can survive." Removing these and any other Proofs from such holders should solve the potential problem.

	Cert	Avg	%MS	PF-65RD	PF-67RD	PF-67Cam	PF-68DCam
1983-S, Proof	563	68.4		$3	$10	$11	$15

Lincoln, Memorial Reverse, Cents of 1984

DIE RELIEF CHANGED: The relief of Lincoln's shoulder was lowered this year, thus reducing the problem of weakness in this area, which had characterized the series since its inception in 1909. For Memorial Reverse cents 1959 to this point, the E PL of E PLURIBUS was often weak. After this time, the minute planchet marks on Lincoln's shoulder, which had long been a source of annoyance to connoisseurs, were minimized, and the reverse letters were sharper.[204]

1984 • Circulation-strike mintage: 8,151,079,000.

Commentary: This issue is common in gem Mint State. Avoid discolored coins and those with surface bubbling or problems. Sharp strikes can be easily found. Some were struck in San Francisco and West Point. Mintmark-less coins struck at San Francisco cannot be differentiated from Philadelphia issues.

	Cert	Avg	%MS	MS-63RB	MS-65RD	MS-66RD	MS-67RD
1984	190	65.7	99%	$0.15	$0.30	$15	$35

1984, Doubled Ear • Circulation-strike mintage: Included in 1984 circulation-strike mintage.

Commentary: This variety's Fivaz-Stanton identification is FS-01-1984-101. It can also be identified as CONECA 1984, DDO-001. Its rarity is URS-15. This variety can be discerned under low magnification and shows part of an extra earlobe below and slightly to the left of Lincoln's ear, the result of doubling when the working die was made. More than 1,000 have been certified as MS-65RD or higher, suggesting perhaps that the total mintage was only in the low tens of thousands. This variety is listed in the regular edition of the *Guide Book of United States Coins,* sharply increasing the demand for and awareness of it.

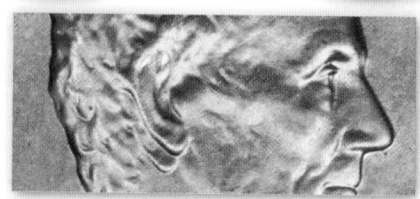

A detail of the doubled ear.

	Cert	Avg	%MS	MS-63RB	MS-65RD	MS-66RD	MS-67RD
1984, Doubled Ear	550	65.5	99%	$175	$230	$350	$425

1984-D • Circulation-strike mintage: 5,569,238,906.

Commentary: This issue is common in gem Mint State. Avoid discolored coins and those with surface bubbling or problems. Sharp strikes are common.

	Cert	Avg	%MS	MS-63RB	MS-65RD	MS-66RD	MS-67RD
1984-D	200	66.1	99%	$0.15	$0.30	$15	$35

1984-S, Proof • Proof mintage: 3,065,110.

Proof commentary: These were made with deep-cameo contrast. Examples are common.

	Cert	Avg	%MS	PF-65RD	PF-67RD	PF-67Cam	PF-68DCam
1984-S, Proof	487	68.9		$4	$10	$11	$15

Lincoln, Memorial Reverse, Cents of 1985

1985 • Circulation-strike mintage: 5,648,489,887.

Commentary: This issue is common in gem Mint State. Most examples are very attractive. Sharp strikes are plentiful. Some were struck in San Francisco and West Point. Mintmarkless coins struck at West Point cannot be differentiated from Philadelphia issues.

	Cert	Avg	%MS	MS-63RB	MS-65RD	MS-66RD	MS-67RD
1985	520	66.4	100%	$0.15	$0.30	$15	$35

1985-D • Circulation-strike mintage: 5,287,339,926.

Commentary: This issue is common in gem Mint State. Most examples are very pleasing in appearance. A larger D mintmark was used this year. Sharp strikes are common.

Varieties: *1985-D, Brass-Plated Cent:* These are "light colored" cents, inadvertently made with about 90% copper and 10% zinc coating (due to zinc contamination of the copper plating bath for planchets) instead of 100% copper. The 1985-D is the most-often encountered date and mintmark displaying this anomalous variety.

	Cert	Avg	%MS	MS-63RB	MS-65RD	MS-66RD	MS-67RD
1985-D	358	66.8	99%	$0.15	$0.30	$15	$29

1985-S, Proof • Proof mintage: 3,362,821.

Proof commentary: These Proofs are made with deep-cameo contrast. Examples are common.

Notes: *Mintmark added to master die:* Beginning this year, the S mintmark was added to the master die to make Proofs. This eliminated positional differences in mintmarks. (This policy was extended to circulation-strike master dies in 1990.) A larger S mintmark was introduced this year.

	Cert	Avg	%MS	PF-65RD	PF-67RD	PF-67Cam	PF-68DCam
1985-S, Proof	546	68.9		$5	$11	$12	$15

Lincoln, Memorial Reverse, Cents of 1986

MINOR HUB MODIFICATION: A new obverse hub was introduced this year, known as the Small Date, in slightly lower relief and with the lettering sharpened. What is known as the Large Date variety is, as David W. Lange points out, the same as the Small Date of 1974. Confused? An easy way to tell the Large Date and Small Date of 1986 apart: On the Large Date the tops of the 98 are above the tops of the 1 and 2; on the Small Date, the tops of the numerals are even.

1986 • Circulation-strike mintage: 4,491,395,493.

Commentary: This issue is common in all grades including gem Mint State.

	Cert	Avg	%MS	MS-63RB	MS-65RD	MS-66RD	MS-67RD
1986	255	66.6	100%	$0.15	$0.30	$15	$35

1986-D • Circulation-strike mintage: 4,442,866,698.

Commentary: This issue is common in gem Mint State. Excellent eye appeal is the rule for this issue. Coins with Full Details are plentiful.

	Cert	Avg	%MS	MS-63RB	MS-65RD	MS-66RD	MS-67RD
1986-D	287	66.8	100%	$0.15	$0.30	$15	$35

1986-S, Proof • Proof mintage: 3,010,497.

Proof commentary: These Proofs were made with deep-cameo contrast. This issue is common.

	Cert	Avg	%MS	PF-65RD	PF-67RD	PF-67Cam	PF-68DCam
1986-S, Proof	497	68.9		$7	$11	$12	$15

Lincoln, Memorial Reverse, Cents of 1987

1987 • Circulation-strike mintage: 4,682,466,931.

Commentary: This issue is common in gem Mint State. Most coins are very attractive. Sharply struck coins are common.

	Cert	Avg	%MS	MS-63RB	MS-65RD	MS-66RD	MS-67RD
1987	349	66.8	100%	$0.15	$0.30	$15	$29

1987-D • Circulation-strike mintage: 4,879,389,514.

Commentary: This issue is common in gem Mint State. Nearly all are very attractive— this comment being true for nearly all cents of the era. Many examples of this issue are sharp.

	Cert	Avg	%MS	MS-63RB	MS-65RD	MS-66RD	MS-67RD
1987-D	477	66.6	100%	$0.15	$0.30	$15	$32

1987-S, Proof • Proof mintage: 4,227,728.

Proof commentary: These Proofs were made with deep-cameo contrast. This issue is common.

	Cert	Avg	%MS	PF-65RD	PF-67RD	PF-67Cam	PF-68DCam
1987-S, Proof	738	68.9		$5	$10	$11	$13

Lincoln, Memorial Reverse, Cents of 1988

1988 IN NUMISMATICS: In 1988 the U.S. Mint's Uncirculated coin sets, made for collectors, began including coins that were struck from new or fresh dies. In the past the sets had included a random mix that included all manner of die states. These coins, often highly reflective, were included in the sets from 1988 until they were replaced in 2005 with the so-called satin-finish coins.[205]

On March 1, 1988, the name San Francisco *Mint* was restored. Since July 1, 1962, the official designation had been the San Francisco *Assay Office*, although most numismatists began calling it the San Francisco Mint again when coinage was resumed there in 1965 following a 10-year hiatus.

1988 • Circulation-strike mintage: 6,092,810,000.

Commentary: This issue is common in gem Mint State. Most examples are very attractive. Full Details coins are common.

	Cert	Avg	%MS	MS-63RB	MS-65RD	MS-66RD	MS-67RD
1988	214	66.3	99%	$0.15	$0.30	$20	$40

Varieties: *1988, Reverse Design Change (FS-01-1988-901):* This variety can also be identified as CONECA 1988, RDV-006. Its rarity is URS-11. This variety has been mistakenly called the Wide AM. There may be some difference in the placement of these letters, but it is almost impossible to discern. The primary difference on this variety is that the G in the initials FG has a flared stem, rather than the stick-straight stem of the standard issue. Most likely what happened is that the reverse dies that were to become standard in 1989, with a flared G, were used in late 1988 for circulation strikes in Philadelphia and Denver.[206]

A detail showing the new designer's initials on FS-01-1988-901.

A detail showing the doubled ear on FS-01-1988-101.

1988, Doubled-Ear Die (FS-01-1988-101): This variety can also be identified as CONECA 1988, DDO-003. Its rarity is URS-2. This die shows Lincoln's earlobe doubled (see detail above). Only two of this variety have been found so far.[207]

	AU-50	MS-60	MS-63	MS-65
FS-01-1988-901	$10	$20	$30	$50
FS-01-1988-101	$75	$100	$200	$300

1988-D • Circulation-strike mintage: 5,253,740,443.

Commentary: This issue is common in gem Mint State. Most are very attractive. Full Details coins are common.

	Cert	Avg	%MS	MS-63RB	MS-65RD	MS-66RD	MS-67RD
1988-D	269	66.6	100%	$0.15	$0.30	$15	$25

Varieties: *1988-D, Reverse Design Change (FS-01-1988D-901):* This variety can also be identified as CONECA 1988-D, RDV-006. Its rarity is URS-11. This variety has been mistakenly called the Wide AM. There may be some difference in the placement of these letters, but it is almost impossible to discern. The primary difference on this variety is that the G in the initials FG has a flared stem, rather than the stick-straight stem of the standard issue. Most likely what happened is that the reverse dies that were to become standard in 1989, with a flared G, were used in late 1988 for circulation strikes in Philadelphia and Denver. See page 508 for a detail showing the new style of designer's initials.

	AU-50	MS-60	MS-63	MS-65
FS-01-1988D-901	$20	$40	$60	$90

1988-S, Proof • Proof mintage: 3,262,948.

Commentary: These were made with deep-cameo contrast. This issue is common.

	Cert	Avg	%MS	PF-65RD	PF-67RD	PF-67Cam	PF-68DCam
1988-S, Proof	453	68.9		$9	$11	$12	$13

Lincoln, Memorial Reverse, Cents of 1989

1989 IN NUMISMATICS: Lincoln cents were excluded from the investment excitement. A leading investment writer said, "Sell all copper." Not much attention was paid to the 1909-S, V.D.B.; 1914-D; 1955, Doubled Die Obverse, or any other Lincoln cents.

1989 • Circulation-strike mintage: 7,261,535,000.

Commentary: This issue is common in gem Mint State. Nice eye appeal is the rule, not the exception for examples of this issue. Full Details coins are easily acquired.

	Cert	Avg	%MS	MS-63RB	MS-65RD	MS-66RD	MS-67RD
1989	333	66.5	100%	$0.15	$0.30	$15	$25

1989-D • Circulation-strike mintage: 5,345,467,111.

Commentary: This issue is common in gem Mint State. Most examples are very attractive. Full Details coins are abundant.

	Cert	Avg	%MS	MS-63RB	MS-65RD	MS-66RD	MS-67RD
1989-D	332	66.4	100%	$0.15	$0.30	$15	$31

1989-S, Proof • **Proof mintage:** 3,220,194.

Proof commentary: These Proofs are made with deep-cameo contrast. This issue is common.

	Cert	Avg	%MS	PF-65RD	PF-67RD	PF-67Cam	PF-68DCam
1989-S, Proof	580	68.9		$9	$11	$12	$13

Lincoln, Memorial Reverse, Cents of 1990

HUB CHANGES: Changes, lessening the relief slightly, were made to the obverse and reverse hubs. The V.D.B. initials on Lincoln's shoulder were made slightly larger and much more noticeable. Reverse details, including the Lincoln statue and foliage, were made sharper. Minor adjustments were made in letter spacing, and the stem of the G in the initials FG was given a flare reminiscent of a serif.

MINTMARKS: Beginning this year, mintmarks were placed on the master dies for circulation-strike coins, and not punched separately into working dies. (This had been done with Proofs beginning in 1985.) Hence, mintmark-position variations came to an end. Beginning this year, any doubled obverse dies would have the mintmark doubled as well.

1990 IN NUMISMATICS: By 1989 and early 1990, *collectors* were no longer significant buyers of "investment grade" coins. They sat on the sidelines on these, since they had been priced far beyond what seasoned numismatists would pay. Instead, they concentrated on early copper coins, colonials, obsolete bank notes, Washington medals, and other traditional numismatic series. Finally, in early 1990, the investment market ran out of steam. Few new buyers appeared. Offered coins found no investment buyers and, at 1989 levels, few collectors were even slightly interested. The market collapsed, and many commemoratives, Peace dollars, and other favorites eventually descended to *small fractions* of their 1989 prices.

Several years later, collectors resumed buying.

1990 • **Circulation-strike mintage:** 6,851,765,000.

Commentary: This issue is common in gem Mint State. Most examples are very attractive. Sharp strikes, having more detail than previously due to the modified hubs (see above), can be easily found.

	Cert	Avg	%MS	MS-63RB	MS-65RD	MS-66RD	MS-67RD
1990	210	66.6	100%	$0.15	$0.30	$19	$36

1990-D • Circulation-strike mintage: 4,922,894,533.

Commentary: This issue is common in gem Mint State. Most examples are very attractive. Full Details coins are common.

	Cert	Avg	%MS	MS-63RB	MS-65RD	MS-66RD	MS-67RD
1990-D	298	66.8	100%	$0.15	$0.30	$15	$25

1990-S, Proof • Proof mintage (with S mintmark): 3,299,559.

Proof commentary: These Proofs are made with deep-cameo contrast. This issue is common.

	Cert	Avg	%MS	PF-65RD	PF-67RD	PF-67Cam	PF-68DCam
1990-S, Proof	829	69.0		$5	$10	$11	$13

1990, No S, Proof • Proof mintage (without S mintmark): 100 to 250 have been estimated struck, these included in the 1990-S, Proof, mintage figure.

Commentary: This variety's Fivaz-Stanton identification is FS-01-1990-101. It can also be identified as CONECA 1990, MMO-001. Its rarity is URS-5. This is a dramatic error, the omission of the S mintmark having escaped the notice of at least 14 people during the die preparation and the coining processes, as Shane Anderson notes in *The Complete Lincoln Cent Encyclopedia*. Apparently, a mintmarkless circulation-strike die had been given a mirror finish. At one time, the Mint provided information that an estimated 3,700 were coined without the S, and all but 145 were shipped, those 145 having been destroyed when the error was discovered. Later, a Mint official stated that there were no facts on hand regarding the number struck, the figure 3,700 was an unsupported guess, and it was not known how many had been shipped. In 1995 David W. Lange commented: "A figure in the range of 100–150 is probable, though many purchasers of 1990-S Proof sets who are not in tune with hobby news may have such coins and not yet know it." In 1996 John Wexler and Kevin Flynn stated, "Currently there are about 250 known."

	Cert	Avg	%MS	PF-65RD	PF-67RD
1990, No S, Proof	67	67.8		$4,000	$5,500

Lincoln, Memorial Reverse, Cents of 1991

1991 • Circulation-strike mintage: 5,165,940,000.

Commentary: This issue is common in gem Mint State. Most examples are very attractive. Because these and other similar coins are so *cheap*, you may have to visit a coin shop to buy them—their value is not sufficient to merit their listing in catalogs and advertisements. Full Details coins are abundant.

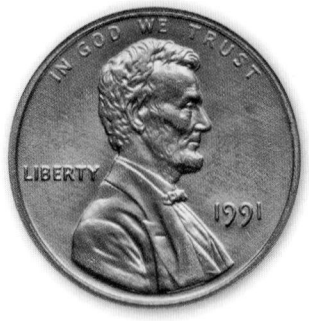 

	Cert	Avg	%MS	MS-63RB	MS-65RD	MS-66RD	MS-67RD
1991	201	66.7	100%	$0.15	$0.30	$14	$25

1991-D • Circulation-strike mintage: 4,158,446,076.

Commentary: This issue is common in gem Mint State. Most examples are very pleasing to the eye. Full Details coins are common.

	Cert	Avg	%MS	MS-63RB	MS-65RD	MS-66RD	MS-67RD
1991-D	343	66.8	100%	$0.15	$0.30	$14	$25

1991-S, Proof • Proof mintage: 2,867,787.

Commentary: These Proofs were made with deep-cameo contrast. This issue is common.

	Cert	Avg	%MS	PF-65RD	PF-67RD	PF-67Cam	PF-68DCam
1991-S, Proof	830	69.1		$12	$13	$14	$16

Lincoln, Memorial Reverse, Cents of 1992

HUB CHANGES: The obverse hubs were changed slightly this year, part of a continuing process to increase the sharpness of the coins made on high-speed presses. The reverse die with the new design for 1993 was inadvertently used on a few 1992 cents.[208] On the 1993 die the AM of AMERICA is very closely spaced, the foot of the A is microscopically higher than the foot of the M, and the G of FG has a straight vertical line. This design was also accidentally used on some Proof cents of 1998 and 1999.

1992 • **Circulation-strike mintage:** 4,648,905,000.

Commentary: Most bear the Wide AM; for the Close AM, see the next entry. This issue is common in gem Mint State. See above for narrative.

	Cert	Avg	%MS	MS-63RB	MS-65RD	MS-66RD	MS-67RD
1992	521	67.0	100%	$0.15	$0.30	$14	$25

1992, Close AM • **Circulation-strike mintage:** Included in 1992 circulation-strike mintage figure.

Commentary: The Fivaz-Stanton identification for this variety is FS-01-1992-901. It can also be identified as CONECA 1992, RDV-007. Its rarity is URS-5. The letters AM of AMERICA almost touch; FG is close to the building (this is the style regularly used in 1993). This variety is extremely rare in relation to the demand for it. See above for narrative.

A detail showing the Close AM.

	Cert	Avg	%MS	MS-63RB	MS-65RD
1992, Close AM ‡	6	60.5	67%	—	—

‡ Ranked in the *100 Greatest U.S. Modern Coins*.

1992-D • **Circulation-strike mintage:** 4,448,673,300.

Commentary: Most bear the Wide AM; for the Close AM, see the next entry. This issue is easily found in gem Mint State. Most examples are very pretty. Full Details coins are easily found.

	Cert	Avg	%MS	MS-63RB	MS-65RD	MS-66RD	MS-67RD
1992-D	295	66.7	99%	$0.15	$0.30	$14	$25

1992-D, Close AM • Circulation-strike mintage: Included in 1992-D circulation-strike mintage figure.

Commentary: The Fivaz-Stanton identification for this variety is FS-01-1992D-901. It can also be identified as CONECA 1992-D, RDV-007. Its rarity is URS-9. The letters AM of AMERICA almost touch; FG is close to the building (this is the style regularly used in 1993). These must have been struck very late in the year, and are very rare, although as with any of these "AM" varieties, doubtless more await identification—for at present they are not widely known, despite listings in the *Guide Book of United States Coins.* Still, by now it is reasonable to suppose that only a few of the existing examples have been found.

A detail showing the Close AM.

	Cert	Avg	%MS	MS-63RB	MS-65RD
1992-D, Close AM ‡	17	60.6	71%	—	—

‡ Ranked in the *100 Greatest U.S. Modern Coins.*

1992-S, Proof • Proof mintage: 4,176,560.

Proof commentary: All of these Proofs were made with the Wide AM and deep-cameo contrast. This issue is common.

	Cert	Avg	%MS	PF-65RD	PF-67RD	PF-67Cam	PF-68DCam
1992-S, Proof	1,745	69.0		$5	$10	$11	$12

Lincoln, Memorial Reverse, Cents of 1993

1993 • Circulation-strike mintage: 5,684,705,000.

Commentary: This issue is common in gem Mint State. Sharp coins are readily available.

	Cert	Avg	%MS	MS-63RB	MS-65RD	MS-66RD	MS-67RD
1993	262	66.9	100%	$0.15	$0.30	$14	$25

1993-D • Circulation-strike mintage: 6,426,650,571.

Commentary: This issue is common in gem Mint State. Most examples are very attractive. Full Details coins are plentiful.

	Cert	Avg	%MS	MS-63RB	MS-65RD	MS-66RD	MS-67RD
1993-D	410	66.9	100%	$0.15	$0.30	$14	$25

1993-S, Proof • Proof mintage: 3,394,792.

Proof commentary: These Proofs were made with deep-cameo contrast. This issue is common.

	Cert	Avg	%MS	PF-65RD	PF-67RD	PF-67Cam	PF-68DCam
1993-S, Proof	1,685	68.8		$9	$10	$11	$12

Lincoln, Memorial Reverse, Cents of 1994

HUB ALTERATION: The obverse hub was altered to sharply lower the relief of Lincoln's shoulder, giving it an unnatural appearance when carefully examined.

1994 • Circulation-strike mintage: 6,500,850,000.

Commentary: This issue is common in gem Mint State. Most examples are very attractive. Full Details examples are easily found.

	Cert	Avg	%MS	MS-63RB	MS-65RD	MS-66RD	MS-67RD
1994	190	66.7	99%	$0.15	$0.30	$14	$25

1994-D • Circulation-strike mintage: 7,131,765,000.

Commentary: This issue is common in gem Mint State. Most examples are very attractive. Full Details coins are plentiful.

	Cert	Avg	%MS	MS-63RB	MS-65RD	MS-66RD	MS-67RD
1994-D	271	66.8	99%	$0.15	$0.30	$15	$27

1994-S, Proof • Proof mintage: 3,269,923.

Proof commentary: These Proofs were made with deep-cameo contrast. This issue is common.

	Cert	Avg	%MS	PF-65RD	PF-67RD	PF-67Cam	PF-68DCam
1994-S, Proof	1,440	68.9		$9	$11	$12	$13

Lincoln, Memorial Reverse, Cents of 1995

1995 • Circulation-strike mintage: 6,411,440,000.

Commentary: This issue is common in gem Mint State. Most have great eye appeal. Sharp coins are everywhere.

	Cert	Avg	%MS	MS-63RB	MS-65RD	MS-66RD	MS-67RD
1995	318	66.6	100%	$0.15	$0.30	$15	$30

1995, Doubled Die Obverse •

Circulation-strike mintage: Included in 1995 circulation-strike mintage figure.

Commentary: The Fivaz-Stanton identification for this variety is FS-01-1995-101. It can also be identified as CONECA 1995, DDO-001. Its rarity is URS-21. There was a free-for-all in the coin hobby when it was discovered, early in the year, that some Lincoln cents were slightly doubled on the obverse—not significantly at the date, but noticeably at LIBERTY and at certain letters of IN GOD WE TRUST.

A detail of the doubling at IN GOD.

A detail of the doubling at LIBERTY.

	Cert	Avg	%MS	MS-63RB	MS-65RD	MS-66RD	MS-67RD
1995, Doubled-Die Obverse ‡	18,090	67.2	100%	$35	$50	$90	$220

‡ Ranked in the *100 Greatest U.S. Modern Coins.*

1995-D • Circulation-strike mintage: 7,128,560,000.

Commentary: This issue is common in gem Mint State. Full Details coins are plentiful.

	Cert	Avg	%MS	MS-63RB	MS-65RD	MS-66RD	MS-67RD
1995-D	283	66.9	99%	$0.15	$0.30	$15	$35

Varieties: *1995-D, Doubled Die Obverse (FS-01-1995D-103):* This variety can also be identified as CONECA 1995-D, DDO-003. Its rarity is URS-5. On this variety doubling is most prominent on IN GOD WE TRUST.

A detail of the doubling at the date and mintmark.

Details of the doubling at GOD WE TRUST.

	AU-50	MS-60	MS-63	MS-65
FS-01-1995D-103	$175	$250	$350	$500

1995-S, Proof • Proof mintage: 2,797,481.

Proof commentary: These Proofs were made with deep-cameo contrast. This issue is common.

	Cert	Avg	%MS	PF-65RD	PF-67RD	PF-67Cam	PF-68DCam
1995-S, Proof	1,441	69.0		$9	$11	$12	$13

Lincoln, Memorial Reverse, Cents of 1996

1996 IN NUMISMATICS: More people became seriously interested in collecting Lincoln cents as books by David W. Lange and the team of John Wexler and Kevin Flynn gained distribution. Sol Taylor's Society of Lincoln Cent Collectors continued to draw members.

1996 • Circulation-strike mintage: 6,612,465,000.

Commentary: This variety has the Close AM. The Wide AM variety of this year has been delisted following the discovery that the discovery piece was a fantasy constructed from two separate coins. Nearly all examples of this issue are very attractive. Full Details coins are common.

	Cert	Avg	%MS	MS-63RB	MS-65RD	MS-66RD	MS-67RD
1996	234	66.8	100%	$0.15	$0.30	$12	$18

1996-D • Circulation-strike mintage: 6,510,795,000.

Commentary: This issue is common in all grades including gem Mint State. Most examples are very attractive. Full Details coins are plentiful.

	Cert	Avg	%MS	MS-63RB	MS-65RD	MS-66RD	MS-67RD
1996-D	418	66.9	100%	$0.15	$0.30	$12	$18

1996-S, Proof • Proof mintage: 2,525,265.

Proof commentary: These Proofs are made with deep-cameo contrast. This issue is common.

	Cert	Avg	%MS	PF-65RD	PF-67RD	PF-67Cam	PF-68DCam
1996-S, Proof	1,307	69.0		$4.50	$9	$10	$12

Lincoln, Memorial Reverse, Cents of 1997

HUB CHANGES: "Lincoln to Get a Face Lift for 1997," by Paul Gilkes, *Coin World*, November 11, 1996, included this:

> Refinements are in store for 1997 to three of the coin denominations used for circulation and in numismatic collector sets. Lincoln's getting a facelift and spruced-up wardrobe. . . . George E. Hunter, the Mint's assistant director for process and quality control, said major strengthening of details has been

done on the plaster models for the 1997 obverses of both the Lincoln cent and Kennedy half dollar to improve the overall looks and the reverse of the Washington quarter for striking improvements. . . . Lincoln's facial details and his coat will be strengthened, "Which will be a noticeable improvement," Hunter said. "The modifications are being made to the plaster models—one of the early stages of die manufacturing—to improve the aesthetic looks of the nation's longest-enduring and most-produced coin design. Not everybody will notice the differences," Hunter said. "Some people wouldn't know if we changed the designs [completely]. The savvy collector will see a little more sharpened and strengthened details." . . . The cent can average 600,000 or more strikes per die. While design enhancements were undertaken, die production capabilities at all stages are also being revamped.

1997 • Circulation-strike mintage: 4,622,800,000.

Commentary: This issue is common in gem Mint State. Most examples are very attractive. Sharp coins are easy to find.

	Cert	Avg	%MS	MS-63RB	MS-65RD	MS-66RD	MS-67RD
1997	169	66.4	100%	$0.15	$0.30	$15	$42

Varieties: *1997, Brass-Plated:* These "light colored" cents were inadvertently made with about 90% copper and 10% zinc coating (instead of 100% copper) due to zinc contamination of the copper-plating bath for planchets.

1997, Doubled Ear • Circulation-strike mintage: Included in 1997 circulation-strike mintage figure.

Commentary: The Fivaz-Stanton identification for this variety is FS-01-1997-101. It can also be identified as CONECA 1997, DDO-001. Its rarity is URS-9. Doubling on the ear makes it appear as if Lincoln has a second earlobe.

A detail of the doubled ear.

	Cert	Avg	%MS	MS-63RB	MS-65RD	MS-66RD	MS-67RD
1997, Doubled Ear	43	65.3	100%	$275	$500		

1997-D • Circulation-strike mintage: 4,576,555,000.

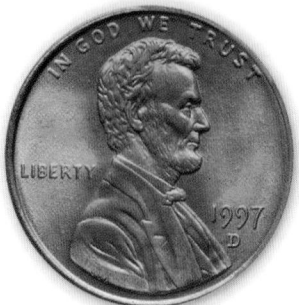

Commentary: This issue is common in gem Mint State. Most examples are very attractive. Full Details coins are plentiful.

	Cert	Avg	%MS	MS-63RB	MS-65RD	MS-66RD	MS-67RD
1997-D	227	66.7	100%	$0.15	$0.30	$14	$30

Varieties: *1997-D, Brass-Plated:* These "light colored" cents were inadvertently made with about 90% copper and 10% zinc coating (instead of 100% copper) due to zinc contamination of the copper-plating bath for planchets.

1997-S, Proof • Proof mintage: 2,796,678.

Proof commentary: These Proofs are made with deep-cameo contrast. This issue is common.

	Cert	Avg	%MS	PF-65RD	PF-67RD	PF-67Cam	PF-68DCam
1997-S, Proof	1,241	69.0		$10	$12	$13	$14

Lincoln, Memorial Reverse, Cents of 1998

1998 • Circulation-strike mintage: 5,032,155,000.

Commentary: Most examples of this issue are Close AM. For Wide AM, see the next entry. This issue is easy to find in all grades including gem Mint State, with nice eye appeal. Full Details coins are plentiful.

	Cert	Avg	%MS	MS-63RB	MS-65RD	MS-66RD	MS-67RD
1998	167	66.3	98%	$0.15	$0.30	$12	$18

Varieties: *1998, Brass-Plated:* These "light colored" cents were inadvertently made with about 90% copper and 10% zinc coating (instead of 100% copper) due to zinc contamination of the copper-plating bath for planchets.

1998, Wide AM • Circulation-strike

mintage: Included in 1998 circulation-strike mintage figure.

Commentary: This variety's Fivaz-Stanton identification is FS-01-1998-901. It can also be identified as CONECA 1998, RDV-006. Its rarity is URS-11. The letters AM of AMER-ICA have significant space between them on this variety; FG is distant from the building. This variety is scarce.

A detail showing the AM on a regular 1998 cent.　　A detail of the Wide AM.

	Cert	Avg	%MS	MS-63RB	MS-65RD	MS-66RD	MS-67RD
1998, Wide AM ‡	297	65.0	97%	$12	$25	$40	$600

‡ Ranked in the *100 Greatest U.S. Modern Coins.*

1998-D • Circulation-strike mintage: 5,225,353,500.

Commentary: This issue is common in gem Mint State. Most examples are very attractive. Full Details coins are common.

	Cert	Avg	%MS	MS-63RB	MS-65RD	MS-66RD	MS-67RD
1998-D	203	66.8	100%	$0.15	$0.30	$17	$57

1998-S, Proof • Proof mintage: 2,086,507.

Proof commentary: This issue usually displays the Wide AM. For Close AM, see the next entry. These Proofs were made with deep-cameo contrast. Examples are common.

	Cert	Avg	%MS	PF-65RD	PF-67RD	PF-67Cam	PF-68DCam
1998-S, Proof	1,489	68.9		$9	$10	$11	$12

1998-S, Close AM, Proof • Proof

mintage: Included in 1998-S, Proof, mintage.

Proof commentary: This variety's Fivaz-Stanton identification is FS-01-1998S-901. It can also be identified as CONECA 1998-S, RDV-007. Its rarity is URS-7. This circulation-strike design (see 1992, Close AM, on page 513 for a related variety and further explanation) was inadvertently used to make some Proof dies of 1998-S and 1999-S. This variety was first publicized by Ken Potter in *Numismatic News*, May 3, 2005.

A detail showing the AM on a regular 1998-S, Proof, cent.

A detail of the Close AM.

	Cert	Avg	%MS	PF-65RD	PF-67RD	PF-67Cam	PF-68DCam
1998-S, Close AM, Proof	106	68.9	100%	$475	$525	$575	$700

Lincoln, Memorial Reverse, Cents of 1999

HUB MODIFICATION: The hair on Lincoln was sharpened slightly this year.

1999 • Circulation-strike mintage: 5,237,600,000.

Commentary: This issue usually displays the Close AM. For Wide AM, see the next entry. This issue is common in gem Mint State. Most examples are very attractive. Sharp coins are readily available.

	Cert	Avg	%MS	MS-63RB	MS-65RD	MS-66RD	MS-67RD
1999	246	65.6	100%	$0.15	$0.30	$13	$30

1999, Wide AM • Circulation-strike

mintage: Included in 1999 circulation-strike mintage figure.

Commentary: This variety's Fivaz-Stanton identification is FS-01-1999-901. It can also be identified as CONECA 1999, RDV-006. Its rarity is URS-11. The letters AM of AMERICA have significant space between them; FG is distant from the building. Examples are rare.

See page 521 for details comparing the regular AM with the Wide AM.

	Cert	Avg	%MS	MS-65RD	MS-67RD
1999, Wide AM ‡	174	64.4	95%	$500	$1,500

‡ Ranked in the *100 Greatest U.S. Modern Coins*.

1999-D • Circulation-strike mintage: 6,360,065,000.

Commentary: This issue is common in gem Mint State. Full Details coins are plentiful.

	Cert	Avg	%MS	MS-63RB	MS-65RD	MS-66RD	MS-67RD
1999-D	253	66.9	100%	$0.15	$0.30	$12	$25

1999-S, Proof • Proof mintage: 3,347,966.

Proof commentary: This issue usually displays the Wide AM. For Close AM, see the next entry. The regular Proof die with Wide AM in AMERICA was made with deep-cameo contrast, and examples are common.

	Cert	Avg	%MS	PF-65RD	PF-67RD	PF-67Cam	PF-68DCam
1999-S, Proof	5,829	69.1		$6	$9	$10	$12

1999-S, Close AM, Proof • Proof mintage: Included in 1999-S, Proof, mintage.

Proof commentary: This variety's Fivaz-Stanton identification is FS-01-1999S-901. It can also be identified as CONECA 1999-S, RDV-007. Its rarity is URS-9. The letters AM of AMERICA almost touch; FG is close to the building (the style regularly used on circulation strikes this year). This variety was first publicized by Ken Potter in *Numismatic News*, on April 12, 2005.

See page 521 for details comparing the regular AM with the Wide AM.

	Cert	Avg	%MS	PF-65RD	PF-67RD	PF-67Cam	PF-68DCam
1999-S, Close AM, Proof	308	68.3		$80	$100	$125	$190

Lincoln, Memorial Reverse, Cents of 2000

2000 • Circulation-strike mintage: 5,503,200,000.

Commentary: This issue usually displays the Close AM. For Wide AM, see the next entry. This issue is common in gem Mint State. Most examples are very beautiful.

	Cert	Avg	%MS	MS-63RB	MS-65RD	MS-66RD	MS-67RD
2000	863	65.8	100%	$0.15	$0.30	$12	$25

2000, Wide AM • Circulation-strike mintage: Included in 2000 circulation-strike mintage figure.

Commentary: The Fivaz-Stanton identification for this variety is FS-01-2000-901. It can also be identified as CONECA 2000, RDV-006. Its rarity is URS-14. This variety was inadvertently made with the Proof reverse design with wide AM in AMERICA.

See page 521 for details comparing the regular AM with the Wide AM.

	Cert	Avg	%MS	MS-63RB	MS-65RD	MS-66RD	MS-67RD
2000, Wide AM	885	65.6	100%	$10	$20	$35	$55

2000-D • Circulation-strike mintage: 8,774,220,000.

Commentary: This issue is easy to find in all grades including gem Mint State, and it is usually attractive. Full Details coins are common.

	Cert	Avg	%MS	MS-63RB	MS-65RD	MS-66RD	MS-67RD
2000-D	194	66.7	100%	$0.15	$0.30	$12	$25

2000-S, Proof • Proof mintage: 4,047,993.

Proof commentary: These Proofs were made with deep-cameo contrast. Examples are common.

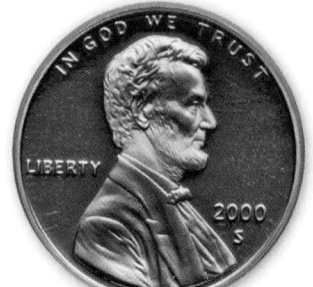 

	Cert	Avg	%MS	PF-65RD	PF-67RD	PF-67Cam	PF-68DCam
2000-S, Proof	5,607	69.1		$4	$7	$8	$11

Lincoln, Memorial Reverse, Cents of 2001

2001 IN NUMISMATICS: The trading activity in Lincoln cents had begun to incorporate Internet images, which gave buyers a view of the actual color of each coin, although without the possibility of ascertaining whether the color was original.

2001 • Circulation-strike mintage: 4,959,600,000.

Commentary: This issue is common in gem Mint State. Most examples are very attractive. Full Details coins are common.

	Cert	Avg	%MS	MS-63RB	MS-65RD	MS-66RD	MS-67RD
2001	97	66.8	100%	$0.15	$0.30	$11	$18

2001-D • Circulation-strike mintage: 5,374,990,000.

Commentary: This issue is common in gem Mint State. Most examples are very attractive. Full Details coins are everywhere.

	Cert	Avg	%MS	MS-63RB	MS-65RD	MS-66RD	MS-67RD
2001-D	181	66.9	100%	$0.15	$0.30	$11	$18

2001-S, Proof • Proof mintage: 3,184,606.

Proof commentary: These Proofs were made with deep-cameo contrast. This issue is common.

	Cert	Avg	%MS	PF-65RD	PF-67RD	PF-67Cam	PF-68DCam
2001-S, Proof	4,429	69.1		$4	$7	$8	$11

Lincoln, Memorial Reverse, Cents of 2002

2002 • **Circulation-strike mintage:** 3,260,800,000.

Commentary: This issue is common in all grades including gem Mint State. Most examples are very attractive. Full Details coins are plentiful.

	Cert	Avg	%MS	MS-63RB	MS-65RD	MS-66RD	MS-67RD
2002	111	67.3	100%	$0.15	$0.30	$11	$16

2002-D • **Circulation-strike mintage:** 4,028,055,000.

Commentary: This issue is common in gem Mint State.

	Cert	Avg	%MS	MS-63RB	MS-65RD	MS-66RD	MS-67RD
2002-D	135	67.2	100%	$0.15	$0.30	$12	$19

2002-S, Proof • **Proof mintage:** 3,211,995.

Proof commentary: These Proofs were made with deep-cameo contrast. This issue is common.

	Cert	Avg	%MS	PF-65RD	PF-67RD	PF-67Cam	PF-68DCam
2002-S, Proof	4,773	69.1		$4	$7	$8	$11

Lincoln, Memorial Reverse, Cents of 2003

2003 • **Circulation-strike mintage:** 3,300,000,000.

Commentary: This issue is common in gem Mint State. Most examples are very attractive.

Notes: *One example is the Holy Grail of Lincoln cents:* An MS-70 RD (PCGS) cent—the first circulation-strike Lincoln cent ever to receive this certification—sold for $15,120

on September 28, 2006, in a Teletrade auction. "This coin is the Holy Grail of Lincoln cents and something for which we have been searching for two decades," Jaime Hernandez, PCGS price-guide editor, said.[209] Proof and SMS Lincoln cents had received this grade in the past, but no circulation-strike Lincoln cent had been graded so high.

	Cert	Avg	%MS	MS-63RB	MS-65RD	MS-66RD	MS-67RD
2003	260	67.0	100%	$0.15	$0.30	$11	$16

2003-D • Circulation-strike mintage:
3,548,000,000.

Commentary: This issue is common in gem Mint State. Most examples are very attractive. Full Details coins are common.

	Cert	Avg	%MS	MS-63RB	MS-65RD	MS-66RD	MS-67RD
2003-D	150	66.3	100%	$0.15	$0.30	$10	$15

2003-S, Proof • Proof mintage:
3,298,439.

Proof commentary: These Proofs are made with deep-cameo contrast. This issue is common.

	Cert	Avg	%MS	PF-65RD	PF-67RD	PF-67Cam	PF-68DCam
2003-S, Proof	7,816	69.1		$4	$7	$8	$11

Lincoln, Memorial Reverse, Cents of 2004
2004 • Circulation-strike mintage:
3,379,600,000.

Commentary: This issue is common in gem Mint State. Full Details coins are plentiful.

	Cert	Avg	%MS	MS-63RB	MS-65RD	MS-66RD	MS-67RD
2004	151	66.8	100%	$0.15	$0.30	$10	$20

2004-D • Circulation-strike mintage: 3,456,400,000.

Commentary: This issue is common in gem Mint State. Most examples are very attractive. Full Details coins abound.

	Cert	Avg	%MS	MS-63RB	MS-65RD	MS-66RD	MS-67RD
2004-D	127	66.4	100%	$0.15	$0.30	$10	$18

2004-S, Proof • Proof mintage: 2,965,422.

Proof commentary: These Proofs are made with deep-cameo contrast. This issue is common.

	Cert	Avg	%MS	PF-65RD	PF-67RD	PF-67Cam	PF-68DCam*
2004-S, Proof	5,300	69.1		$4	$7	$8	$11

Lincoln, Memorial Reverse, Cents of 2005

2005 IN NUMISMATICS: In 2005 the Uncirculated coins sold in sets to collectors by the U.S. Mint adopted a satin finish, replacing the somewhat prooflike finish that had been the standard since 1988.[210] As in Aesop's fables, the tortoise Lincoln cent specialty continued on its merry way, while the hare "trophy coins" in other series captured headlines. High-grade modern cents with low population numbers continued to bring strong prices.

2005 • Circulation-strike mintage: 3,935,600,000.

Commentary: This issue is common in gem Mint State. Most examples are very attractive.

	Cert	Avg	%MS	MS-63RB	MS-65RD	MS-66RD	MS-67RD
2005	2,569	67.3	100%	$0.15	$0.30	$10	$25

2005, Satin Finish •

Mintage: 1,160,000.

Commentary: From 2005 to 2010 the U.S. Mint issued Uncirculated sets with a special satin finish. These sets, made using burnished blanks and sandblasted dies, have in many cases been broken out of their original packaging to give collectors access to individual Satin Finish coins. The grading services sometimes grade such coins with the designation "SP" instead of "MS."

	Cert	Avg	%MS	MS-63RB	MS-65RD	MS-66RD	MS-67RD
2005, Satin Finish	2,383	67.2	100%	$5	$10	$15	$20

2005-D • Circulation-strike mintage: 3,764,450,500.

Commentary: This issue is common in gem Mint State. Sharp strikes can be found easily.

	Cert	Avg	%MS	MS-63RB	MS-65RD	MS-66RD	MS-67RD
2005-D	10,780	69.1	100%	$0.15	$0.30	$20	$40

2005-D, Satin Finish •

Mintage: 1,160,000.

Commentary: From 2005 to 2010 the U.S. Mint issued Uncirculated sets with a special satin finish. These sets, made using burnished blanks and sandblasted dies, have in many cases been broken out of their original packaging to give collectors access to individual Satin Finish coins. The grading services sometimes grade such coins with the designation "SP" instead of "MS."

	Cert	Avg	%MS	MS-63RB	MS-65RD	MS-66RD	MS-67RD
2005-D, Satin Finish	2,259	66.9	100%	$5	$10	$15	$20

2005-S, Proof • Proof mintage: 3,344,679.

Proof commentary: These Proofs were made with deep-cameo contrast. This issue is common.

	Cert	Avg	%MS	PF-65RD	PF-67RD	PF-67Cam	PF-68DCam
2005-S, Proof	2,482	66.9		$4	$7	$8	$11

Lincoln, Memorial Reverse, Cents of 2006

2006 • **Circulation-strike mintage:** 4,290,000,000.

Commentary: This issue is common in gem Mint State. Sharp strikes can be found easily.

	Cert	Avg	%MS	MS-63RB	MS-65RD	MS-66RD	MS-67RD
2006	1,428	67.0	100%	$0.15	$0.30	$10	$18

2006, Satin Finish • Mintage: 847,361.

Commentary: From 2005 to 2010 the U.S. Mint issued Uncirculated sets with a special satin finish. These sets, made using burnished blanks and sandblasted dies, have in many cases been broken out of their original packaging to give collectors access to individual Satin Finish coins. The grading services sometimes grade such coins with the designation "SP" instead of "MS."

	Cert	Avg	%MS	MS-63RB	MS-65RD	MS-66RD	MS-67RD
2006, Satin Finish	1,358	67.1	100%	$5	$10	$15	$20

2006-D • Circulation-strike mintage: 3,944,000,000.

Commentary: This issue is common in gem Mint State. Sharp strikes can be found easily.

	Cert	Avg	%MS	MS-63RB	MS-65RD	MS-66RD	MS-67RD
2006-D	1,198	66.7	100%	$0.15	$0.30	$13	$25

2006-D, Satin Finish • Mintage: 847,361.

Commentary: From 2005 to 2010 the U.S. Mint issued Uncirculated sets with a special satin finish. These sets, made using burnished blanks and sandblasted dies, have in many cases been broken out of their original packaging to give collectors access to individual Satin Finish coins. The grading services sometimes grade such coins with the designation "SP" instead of "MS."

	Cert	Avg	%MS	MS-63RB	MS-65RD	MS-66RD	MS-67RD
2006-D, Satin Finish	1,070	66.8	100%	$5	$10	$15	$20

2006-S, Proof • Proof mintage: 3,054,436.

Proof commentary: These Proofs were made with deep-cameo contrast. This issue is common.

	Cert	Avg	%MS	PF-65RD	PF-67RD	PF-67Cam	PF-68DCam
2006-S, Proof	5,178	69.2		$4	$7	$8	$11

Lincoln, Memorial Reverse, Cents of 2007

2007 IN AMERICA: Despite talk that the cents should be discontinued because they cost more than face value to produce, they remained a mainstay in everyday commerce and retailing.

2007 IN NUMISMATICS: "Melt a cent, go to prison" was the title of an article by Paul Gilkes in the January 1, 2007, issue of *Coin World* that stated:

> U.S. Mint officials implemented interim regulations Dec. 15, delegated through the Treasury Department, that restrict the melting, exportation and treatment of 1-cent and 5-cent coins and that include prison terms and fines for violations. The regulations are in reaction to rising production costs for the Lincoln cent, which are 73 percent higher than face value, and for the Jefferson 5-cent coin, which are nearly 69 percent over face value.

2007 • Circulation-strike mintage: 3,762,400,000.

Commentary: This issue is common in gem Mint State.

	Cert	Avg	%MS	MS-63RB	MS-65RD	MS-66RD	MS-67RD
2007	532	67.0	100%	$0.15	$0.30	$16	$30

2007, Satin Finish • Mintage: 895,628.

Commentary: From 2005 to 2010 the U.S. Mint issued Uncirculated sets with a special satin finish. These sets, made using burnished blanks and sandblasted dies, have in many cases been broken out of their original packaging to give collectors access to individual Satin Finish coins. The grading services sometimes grade such coins with the designation "SP" instead of "MS."

	Cert	Avg	%MS	MS-63RB	MS-65RD	MS-66RD	MS-67RD
2007, Satin Finish	271	66.9	100%	$5	$10	$15	$20

2007-D • Circulation-strike mintage: 3,638,800,000.

Commentary: This issue is common in gem Mint State.

	Cert	Avg	%MS	MS-63RB	MS-65RD	MS-66RD	MS-67RD
2007-D	323	66.1	100%	$0.15	$0.30	$16	$33

2007-D, Satin Finish • Mintage: 895,628.

Commentary: From 2005 to 2010 the U.S. Mint issued Uncirculated sets with a special satin finish. These sets, made using burnished blanks and sandblasted dies, have in many cases been broken out of their original packaging to give collectors access to individual Satin Finish coins. The grading services sometimes grade such coins with the designation "SP" instead of "MS."

	Cert	Avg	%MS	MS-63RB	MS-65RD	MS-66RD	MS-67RD
2007-D, Satin Finish	212	66.3	100%	$5	$10	$15	$20

2007-S, Proof • Proof mintage: 2,577,166.

Proof commentary: These Proofs were made with deep-cameo contrast. This issue is common.

	Cert	Avg	%MS	PF-65RD	PF-67RD	PF-67Cam	PF-68DCam
2007-S, Proof	4,623	69.1		$4	$7	$8	$11

Lincoln, Memorial Reverse, Cents of 2008

2008 IN NUMISMATICS: The doctoring of coins was a popular subject for debate. Countless Morgan dollars in particular now had rainbow and other colorful toning, far more than had ever been seen in the market before. "Gradeflation" was endemic, and across the board the leading certification services often bumped MS-63 to MS-64, MS-64 to MS-65, and so on. This was a win-win situation for the owners of the coins, who came to believe their coins were worth more, and for the grading services that collected more fees.

In March the American Numismatic Association appointed well-known Ohio dealer Larry Shepherd to be the new executive director. "His short term priority is to stabilize the organization," wrote David Harper, editor of *Numismatic News*.[211] The passion for otherwise very common coins bringing high prices was the subject of this comment by *Coin World* market analyst Mark Ferguson:

Coins graded as perfect Mint State and Proof 70 lack dealer buyback support, and the supply grows as more are graded as such, which could lead to a correction in market values for particular coins that have advanced to levels beyond ridiculousness, according to many seasoned collectors and dealers.[212]

2008 • Circulation-strike mintage: 2,558,800,000.

Commentary: This issue is common in gem Mint State.

	Cert	Avg	%MS	MS-63RB	MS-65RD	MS-66RD	MS-67RD
2008	215	67.3	100%	$0.15	$0.30	$12	$18

2008, Satin Finish • Mintage: 745,464.

Commentary: From 2005 to 2010 the U.S. Mint issued Uncirculated sets with a special satin finish. These sets, made using burnished blanks and sandblasted dies, have in many cases been broken out of their original packaging to give collectors access to individual Satin Finish coins. The grading services sometimes grade such coins with the designation "SP" instead of "MS."

	Cert	Avg	%MS	MS-63RB	MS-65RD	MS-66RD	MS-67RD
2008, Satin Finish	141	67.8	100%	$5	$10	$15	$20

2008-D • Circulation-strike mintage: 2,849,600,000.

Commentary: This issue is common in gem Mint State.

	Cert	Avg	%MS	MS-63RB	MS-65RD	MS-66RD	MS-67RD
2008-D	193	66.7	100%	$0.15	$0.30	$15	$31

2008-D, Satin Finish • Mintage: 745,464.

Commentary: From 2005 to 2010 the U.S. Mint issued Uncirculated sets with a special satin finish. These sets, made using burnished blanks and sandblasted dies, have in many cases been broken out of their original packaging to give collectors access to individual Satin Finish coins. The grading services sometimes grade such coins with the designation "SP" instead of "MS."

	Cert	Avg	%MS	MS-63RB	MS-65RD	MS-66RD	MS-67RD
2008-D, Satin Finish	106	67.4	100%	$5	$10	$15	$20

2008-S, Proof • **Proof mintage:** 2,169,561.

Proof commentary: These Proofs were made with deep-cameo contrast. This issue is common.

	Cert	Avg	%MS	PF-65RD	PF-67RD	PF-67Cam	PF-68DCam
2008-S, Proof	3,663	69.1		$4	$7	$8	$11

LINCOLN, BICENTENNIAL REVERSES (2009)

Designer: *Victor D. Brenner (obverse); see image captions for reverse designers.*
Weight: *Regular-issue coins—2.5 grams; special coins included in collector sets—3.1 grams.*
Composition: *Regular-issue coins—copper-plated zinc (core: .992 zinc, .008 copper, with a plating of pure copper; total content .975 zinc, .025 copper); special coins included in collector sets—.950 copper, .005 tin and zinc.* **Diameter:** *19 mm.* **Edge:** *Plain.* **Mints:** *Philadelphia, Denver, and San Francisco.*

Circulation Strike

Birth and Early Childhood
Reverse designer: Richard Masters.

Formative Years
Reverse designer: Charles Vickers.

Professional Life
Reverse designer: Joel Iskowitz.

Presidency
Reverse designer: Susan Gamble.

Proof

Birth and Early Childhood, Proof

Formative Years, Proof

Professional Life, Proof

Presidency, Proof

A NEW TRIBUTE TO LINCOLN ON THE CENT

Congress established the Lincoln Bicentennial Commission to plan events to honor the president on the 200th anniversary of his birth in 2009. These included a ceremony to rededicate the Lincoln Memorial in Washington, re-enactments of the Lincoln-Douglas debates, various programs, and even a ceremony to dedicate the obscure Lincoln Memorial Garden in Lincoln City, Indiana. Very few of these events attracted significant attention from the news media.

Title III of the Presidential $1 Coin Act of 2005 included this about the Lincoln cent:

SEC. 301. FINDINGS.

The Congress finds as follows:

(1) Abraham Lincoln, the 16th president, was one of the Nation's greatest leaders, demonstrating true courage during the Civil War, one of the greatest crises in the nation's history.

(2) Born of humble roots in Hardin County (present-day LaRue County), Kentucky, on February 12, 1809, Abraham Lincoln rose to the Presidency through a combination of honesty, integrity, intelligence, and commitment to the United States.

(3) With the belief that all men are created equal, Abraham Lincoln led the effort to free all slaves in the United States.

(4) Abraham Lincoln had a generous heart, with malice toward none and with charity for all.

(5) Abraham Lincoln gave the ultimate sacrifice for the country he loved, dying from an assassin's bullet on April 15, 1865.

(6) All Americans could benefit from studying the life of Abraham Lincoln, for Lincoln's life is a model for accomplishing the "American dream" through honesty, integrity, loyalty, and a lifetime of education.

(7) The year 2009 will be the bicentennial anniversary of the birth of Abraham Lincoln.

(8) Abraham Lincoln was born in Kentucky, grew to adulthood in Indiana, achieved fame in Illinois, and led the nation in Washington, D.C.

(9) The so-called "Lincoln cent" was introduced in 1909 on the 100th anniversary of Lincoln's birth, making the obverse design the most enduring on the nation's coinage.

(10) President Theodore Roosevelt was so impressed by the talent of Victor David Brenner that the sculptor was chosen to design the likeness of President Lincoln for the coin, adapting a design from a plaque Brenner had prepared earlier.

(11) In the nearly 100 years of production of the "Lincoln cent", there have been only 2 designs on the reverse: the original, featuring 2 wheat-heads in memorial style enclosing mottoes, and the current representation of the Lincoln Memorial in Washington, D.C.

(12) On the occasion of the bicentennial of President Lincoln's birth and the 100th anniversary of the production of the Lincoln cent, it is entirely fitting to issue a series of 1-cent coins with designs on the reverse that are emblematic of the 4 major periods of President Lincoln's life.

SEC. 302. REDESIGN OF THE LINCOLN CENT FOR 2009.

(a) IN GENERAL—During the year 2009, the Secretary of the Treasury shall issue 1-cent coins in accordance with the following design specifications:

(1) OBVERSE.—The obverse of the 1-cent coin shall continue to bear the Victor David Brenner likeness of President Abraham Lincoln.

(2) REVERSE.—The reverse of the coins shall bear 4 different designs each representing a different aspect of the life of Abraham Lincoln, such as—

(A) his birth and early childhood in Kentucky;

(B) his formative years in Indiana;

(C) his professional life in Illinois; and

(D) his presidency, in Washington, D.C.

(b) ISSUANCE OF REDESIGNED LINCOLN CENTS IN 2009.—

(1) ORDER.—The 1-cent coins to which this section applies shall be issued with 1 of the 4 designs referred to in subsection (a)(2) beginning at the start of each calendar quarter of 2009.

(2) NUMBER.—The Secretary shall presc ribe, on the basis of such factors as the Secretary determines to be appropriate, the number of 1-cent coins that shall be issued with each of the designs selected for each calendar quarter of 2009.

(c) DESIGN SELECTION.—The designs for the coins specified in this section shall be chosen by the Secretary—

(1) after consultation with the Abraham Lincoln Bicentennial Commission and the Commission of Fine Arts; and

(2) after review by the Citizens Coinage Advisory Committee.

SEC. 303. REDESIGN OF REVERSE OF 1-CENT COINS AFTER 2009.

The design on the reverse of the 1-cent coins issued after December 31, 2009, shall bear an image emblematic of President Lincoln's preservation of the United States of America as a single and united country.

SEC. 304. NUMISMATIC PENNIES WITH THE SAME METALLIC CONTENT AS THE 1909 PENNY.

The Secretary of the Treasury shall issue 1-cent coins in 2009 with the exact metallic content as the 1-cent coin contained in 1909 in such number as the Secretary determines to be appropriate for numismatic purposes.

SEC. 305. SENSE OF THE CONGRESS.

It is the sense of the Congress that the original Victor David Brenner design for the 1-cent coin was a dramatic departure from previous American coinage that should be reproduced, using the original form and relief of the likeness of Abraham Lincoln, on the 1-cent coins issued in 2009.

Members of the Mint's Artistic Infusion Program and staff sculptor-engravers were invited to submit designs, and 38 were received. Upon reviewing the results, several prominent numismatists expressed dissatisfaction, mainly suggesting that the somewhat complex scenes would have been better suited to coins of larger diameter. These ideas were adopted:

Birth and Early Childhood: The motif showed the log cabin in Kentucky in which Lincoln was born in 1809. It was designed by Richard Masters, a member of the Mint's Artistic Infusion Program, and modeled by Mint medallic sculptor Jim Licaretz.

Formative Years: Designed and modeled by Mint sculptor-engraver Charles Vickers, this showed Lincoln, famous as a rail-splitter, setting his mallet aside to sit on a log and read a book.

Professional Life: This design shows lawyer and political debater Lincoln standing near the Illinois State Capitol in Springfield. It was designed by Joel Iskowitz of the Artistic Infusion Program and modeled by Mint sculptor-engraver Don Everhart.

Presidency: The motif is a view of the United States Capitol with the dome still under construction as it appeared during the Civil War. It was designed by Artistic Infusion Program member Susan Gamble and modeled by Mint medallic sculptor Joseph Menna.

Painted by George P.A. Healy, Abraham Lincoln's official presidential portrait captures the president in thoughtful repose.

In the American economy 2009 was a time of recession. Recently, great problems had arisen in many sectors, including banking, real estate, and investment securities. The need for new cents for circulation was much less than it had been earlier. Distribution of the 2009 coins was done by the Federal Reserve System, which placed the coins with banks specifically calling for them. Each of the four designs was launched in sequence, not at the same time. There was no nationwide program to promote collector interest, distribution was widely scattered, and anyone looking to build a set from circulating change was likely to be disappointed. In terms of coin programs it was a non-event.

Circulation strikes were made in copper-plated zinc, the composition in use since 1982. The overall quality of sharpness and strike was excellent, with most coins grading well above MS-65. For the numismatic trade a bronze alloy of 95% copper and 5% tin and zinc was used—this being the alloy first used for cents with the Indian Head design in 1864 and continued through many of the early Lincoln cents. These had a special satin finish and were sold in sets.

GRADING STANDARDS

Caveat: These grading standards do not take sharpness of strike into account.

MS-60 to 70 (Mint State). *Obverse and Reverse:* At MS-65 and higher, luster is rich on all areas; there is no rubbing, and no contact marks are visible except under magnification. Coins with full or nearly full mint orange-red color can be designated RD; those with a substantial percentage of red-orange and of brown can be called RB; and those with full (or nearly full) brown-toned surfaces can be designated BN. Some 2009 cents, even from original rolls and bags, have surface marks that look like water spots.

2009-D, Formative Years. Graded MS-67RD.

The Lincoln Bicentennial cent is seldom collected in grades lower than MS-60.

PF-60 to 70 (Proof). *Obverse and Reverse:* PF-65 and higher coins are RB (with colors nicely blended) or RD, the latter with bright red-orange color sometimes fading to hints of brown. Some tiny flecks are normal on coins certified as PF-65 but should be microscopic or absent above that level. PF-60 and 61 coins can be dull, stained, or spotted and still have some original mint luster. Proof coins with fingerprints are impaired and must be given a lower numerical grade. Lower-

2009-S, Birthplace and Early Childhood.
Graded PF-70RD Deep Cameo.

grade Proofs usually have poor eye appeal. Generally, Proofs of these types below PF-65 are not desired by most collectors.

Lincoln, Bicentennial Reverses, Cents of 2009

2009, Birth and Early Childhood, Copper-Coated Zinc • Circulation-strike mintage: 284,400,000.

Commentary: This issue is common in gem Mint State. Most examples are brilliant, well struck, and of very high quality, grading far above MS-65. Some of the various 2009 types in this composition have water spot–like stains and should be avoided.

Notes: *Distribution problems and the launch ceremony:* The American economy was in a recession. What might have been a nationally dynamic release of the new Lincoln cents was delayed because banks were sufficiently stocked with old cents and did not need any new ones. About this time, banks around the country slowed down and in many instances stopped ordering Presidential dollars, Sacagawea dollars, and other coins for their customers. On February 23, Paul Gilkes reported in *Coin World*:

> The Feb. 12 nationwide release of the first of four Lincoln cents to be issued in 2009 may be delayed because Federal Reserve Banks and coin terminals are saturated with cents. Orders for new coins are not being placed because of the state of the U.S. economy, according to published reports, but unconfirmed by U.S. Mint officials. . . . As of Feb. 6, U.S. Mint officials were reported to be considering offering Denver and Philadelphia Mint circulation strikes in rolls at the Mint's Web site, but there was no indication whether customers would be offered an option similar to its Direct Ship program . . . in order to get the coins in circulation. Larue High School in Hodgenville, Ky., may be the only place Feb. 12 that collectors can definitely and immediately obtain the first Lincoln cent, which shows a log cabin representative of Abraham Lincoln's birthplace. . . .

Low mintage: Due to the slow economy and reduced needs for cents, the mintage for 2009 was projected to reach record lows for recent years. "If production of the remaining three Lincoln cents for 2009 stays at the level of the first coin, the total of 2.5 billion or so cents would be less than half the number of cents produced in 2008 and the lowest combined circulation-cent total in some 40 years," Paul Gilkes proposed in an article in *Coin World*, April 27, 2009.

	Cert	Avg	%MS	MS-63RB	MS-65RD	MS-66RD	MS-67RD
2009, Birth and Early Childhood, Copper-Coated Zinc	13,948	65.8	100%	$0.15	$0.30	$12	$20

2009, Birth and Early Childhood, Copper, Satin Finish • Mintage: 784,614.

Commentary: Cents in this composition were sold to the numismatic trade. Nearly all examples are brilliant, sharply struck, and grade MS–69 or 70.

Notes: *Bronze planchets:* Paul Gilkes reported on the Mint's preparations to strike coins in the copper alloy originally used for Lincoln cents in *Coin World*, March 9, 2009:

The U.S. Mint has placed orders for coin strip to make planchets to strike 2009 Lincoln cents for coin sets in the same alloy used in the first Lincoln bronze cents, introduced into circulation in 1909. The composition of the original planchets from 1909, each weighing 3.1 grams, is 95% copper, 5% tin and zinc. U.S. Mint spokesman Michael White said Feb. 20 that cents from 1909 were sampled and the tin level set at 2% for the new planchets. . . . White said Feb. 18 that the coinage strip for the cents to be made for inclusion in the numismatic cents was ordered from Olin Brass, located in East Alton, Ill., one of two Mint vendors that supplies the U.S. Mint with coinage strip for copper-nickel 5-cent coins; copper-nickel clad dimes, quarter dollars, and half dollars; and manganese-brass clad Presidential dollars and Native American dollar coins. The cent strip will be shipped to Jarden Zinc Products in Greeneville, Tenn., where blanks will first be punched from the coinage strip and then processed into 'ready-to-strike' planchets with upset, or raised rims. Mint officials have not disclosed whether production has commenced on either the Proof or Uncirculated Mint set versions of the cent in the 1909 composition. . . .

	Cert	Avg	%MS	MS-68RD	MS-69RD
2009, Birth and Early Childhood, Copper, Satin Finish	1,587	67.7	100%	$15	$45

2009-D, Birth and Early Childhood, Copper-Coated Zinc •

Circulation-strike mintage: 350,400,000.

Commentary: This issue is common in gem Mint State. Some of the various 2009 types in this composition have water spot–like stains and should be avoided.

	Cert	Avg	%MS	MS-63RB	MS-65RD	MS-66RD	MS-67RD
2009-D, Birth and Early Childhood, Copper-Coated Zinc	4,953	65.9	100%	$0.15	$0.30	$12	$20

2009-D, Birth and Early Childhood, Copper, Satin Finish • Mintage: 784,614.

Commentary: All of these cents were sold at a premium to collectors. Nearly all examples are brilliant, sharply struck, and grade MS–69 or 70.

	Cert	Avg	%MS	MS-68RD	MS-69RD
2009-D, Birth and Early Childhood, Copper, Satin Finish	1,671	67.7	100%	$17	$95

2009-S, Birth and Early Childhood, Copper, Proof • Proof mintage: 2,995,615.

Proof commentary: These Proofs were made with deep-cameo contrast. Most examples are brilliant and grade PF–69 or 70.

	Cert	Avg	%MS	PF-65RD	PF-67RD	PF-67Cam	PF-68DCam
2009-S, Birth and Early Childhood, Copper, Proof	14,376	69.1		$4	$7	$8	$11

2009, Formative Years, Copper-Coated Zinc • Circulation-strike

mintage: 376,000,000.

Commentary: This issue is common in gem Mint State. Some of the various 2009 types in this composition have water spot–like stains and should be avoided.

Notes: *Launch Ceremony:* Paul Gilkes reported on the launch of this design in *Coin World*, June 1, 2009:

> Threatening weather failed to dampen the enthusiasm of the thousands of collectors and other members of the public who traveled to Lincoln State Park in Lincoln City, Ind., for a May 14 event launching the second 2009 Lincoln cent. Participants were afforded opportunities to acquire rolls of the second of four circulating commemorative Lincoln cents to be issued in 2009 marking Lincoln's 200th birthday. The second design reflects his formative years as a youth and young man in Indiana. . . . After a nearly hour-long ceremony May 14 staged by the U.S. Mint at the park's 1,500-seat Lincoln Amphitheatre, representatives from Freedom National Bank in nearby Dale, Ind., began exchanging 50-coin rolls containing cents struck at the Philadelphia Mint for cash, for a minimum of two rolls, up to a maximum of six rolls (temporarily reduced to four, at the request of U.S. Mint officials, but then the six-roll maximum was reinstated just before the exchange began), during their first pass through the line.

	Cert	Avg	%MS	MS-63RB	MS-65RD	MS-66RD	MS-67RD
2009, Formative Years, Copper-Coated Zinc	27,039	65.9	100%	$0.15	$0.30	$12	$20

Varieties: *Doubled-die reverses:* The *Cherrypickers' Guide to Rare Die Varieties of United States Coins* notes: "Numerous doubled-die reverses appear on Lincoln cents of the Formative Years design. These are localized on the left hand, most often in what appears to be an extra index finger or thumb. The circulation-strike doubled die reverses listed here all exhibit either a strong or very strong spread." (Also see 2009-S, Formative Years, Copper, Proof on page 542).

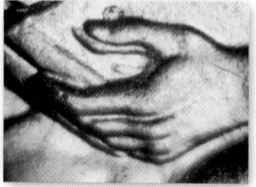

Detail of the "extra" fingers on FS-01-2009-FS801.

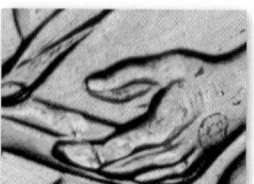

Detail of the "extra" fingers on FS-01-2009-FS802.

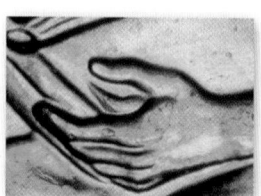

Detail of the "extra" fingers on FS-01-2009-FS803.

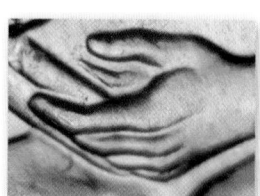

Detail of the "extra" fingers on FS-01-2009-FS804.

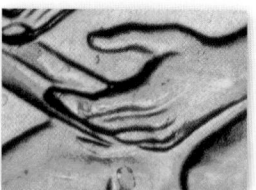

Detail of the "extra" fingers on FS-01-2009-FS805.

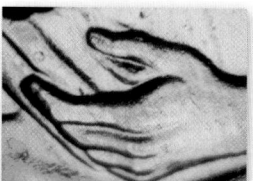

Detail of the "extra" fingers on FS-01-2009-FS806.

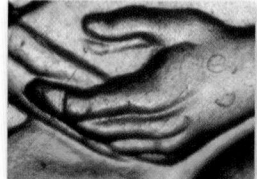

Detail of the "extra" fingers on FS-01-2009-FS807.

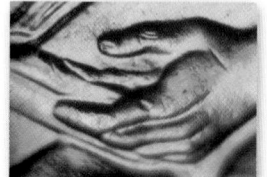

Detail of the "extra" fingers on FS-01-2009-FS808.

	AU-50	MS-60	MS-63	MS-65
FS-01-2009-801, 802, 803, 804, 805, 806, 807, and 808	$5	$10	$20	$40

2009, Formative Years, Copper, Satin Finish • Mintage: 784,614.

Commentary: All of these cents were sold at a premium to collectors. Nearly all examples are brilliant, sharply struck, and grade MS–69 or 70.

	Cert	Avg	%MS	MS-68RD	MS-69RD
2009, Formative Years, Copper, Satin Finish	1,486	67.6	100%	$15	$45

2009-D, Formative Years, Copper-Coated Zinc • Circulation-strike mintage: 363,600,000.

Commentary: This issue is common in gem Mint State. Some of the various 2009 types in this composition have water spot–like stains and should be avoided.

	Cert	Avg	%MS	MS-63RB	MS-65RD	MS-66RD	MS-67RD
2009-D, Formative Years, Copper-Coated Zinc	2,644	65.9	100%	$0.15	$0.30	$12	$20

2009-D, Formative Years, Copper, Satin Finish • Mintage: 784,614.

Commentary: All of these cents were sold at a premium to collectors. Nearly all examples are brilliant, sharply struck, and grade MS–69 or 70.

	Cert	Avg	%MS	MS-68RD	MS-69RD
2009-D, Formative Years, Copper, Satin Finish	1,521	67.5	100%	$15	$200

2009-S, Formative Years, Copper, Proof • Proof mintage: 2,995,615.

Proof commentary: These Proofs were made with deep-cameo contrast. This issue is common. Most examples are brilliant and grade PF–69 or 70.

	Cert	Avg	%MS	PF-65RD	PF-67RD	PF-67Cam	PF-68DCam
2009-S, Formative Years, Copper, Proof	14,267	69.1		$4	$7	$8	$11

Varieties: *2009-S, Doubled-Die Reverse (FS-01-2009S-801):* This is the most popular doubled-die reverse for the Formative Years Proof. See 2009, Formative Years, Copper-Coated Zinc, on page 540 for more doubled dies of this design.

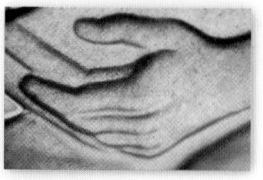

Detail of the "extra" fingers.

	PF-64	PF-65	PF-66	PF-67
FS-01-2009S-801	$75	$150	$250	$350

2009, Professional Life, Copper-Coated Zinc • Circulation-strike

mintage: 316,000,000.

Commentary: This issue is common in gem Mint State. Some of the various 2009 types in this composition have water spot–like stains and should be avoided.

Notes: *Launch Ceremony:* Paul Gilkes reported on the launch of this design in *Coin World*, August 31, 2009:

> Die-hard collectors, dealers and others converged on the Old State Capitol in Springfield, Ill., for the opportunity to exchange cash Aug. 13 for rolls of the 2009, Lincoln, Professional Life, cent. The cent depicts on its reverse a standing portrait of Lincoln as though delivering a speech, with the Old State Capitol in the background over his left shoulder. . . .

	Cert	Avg	%MS	MS-63RB	MS-65RD	MS-66RD	MS-67RD
2009, Professional Life, Copper-Coated Zinc	17,466	66.0	100%	$0.15	$0.30	$12	$20

2009, Professional Life, Copper, Satin Finish • Mintage: 784,614.

Commentary: All of these cents were sold at a premium to collectors. Nearly all examples are brilliant, sharply struck, and grade MS–69 or 70.

	Cert	Avg	%MS	MS-68RD	MS-69RD
2009, Professional Life, Copper, Satin Finish	1,835	67.8	100%	$15	$45

2009-D, Professional Life, Copper-Coated Zinc • Circulation-strike

mintage: 336,000,000.

Commentary: This issue is common in gem Mint State. Some of the various 2009 types in this composition have water spot–like stains and should be avoided.

	Cert	Avg	%MS	MS-63RB	MS-65RD	MS-66RD	MS-67RD
2009-D, Professional Life, Copper-Coated Zinc	1,947	66.0	100%	$0.15	$0.30	$12	$20

2009-D, Professional Life, Copper, Satin Finish • Mintage: 784,614.

Commentary: All of these cents were sold at a premium to collectors. Nearly all examples are brilliant, sharply struck, and grade MS–69 or 70.

	Cert	Avg	%MS	MS-68RD	MS-69RD
2009-D, Professional Life, Copper, Satin Finish	1,482	67.6	100%	$15	$200

2009-S, Professional Life, Copper, Proof • Proof mintage: 2,995,615.

Proof commentary: These Proofs were made with deep-cameo contrast. This issue is common. Most are brilliant and grade PF–69 or 70.

	Cert	Avg	%MS	PF-65RD	PF-67RD	PF-67Cam	PF-68DCam
2009-S, Professional Life, Copper, Proof	14,322	69.1		$4	$7	$8	$11

2009, Presidency, Copper-Coated Zinc • Circulation-strike mintage: 129,600,000.

Commentary: This issue is common in gem Mint State. Some of the various 2009 types in this composition have water spot–like stains and should be avoided.

Notes: *Launch ceremony: Numismatic News* reported on December 1, 2009:

> The weather did not cooperate with the Nov. 12 launch of the fourth and final Lincoln cent design ceremony on the lawn of the U.S. Capitol Building at the Ulysses S. Grant Memorial in Washington, D.C., but some 250 people eagerly awaited the opportunity to trade folding money for Uncirculated rolls of the new coins. Heading up the list of dignitaries that braved the rain from the remnants of Hurricane Ida was Mint Director Ed. Moy. He was joined by Donald R. Kennon, chief historian of the U.S. Capitol Historical Society and Eileen R. Mackevich, executive director of the Abraham Lincoln Bicentennial Commission. . . .

	Cert	Avg	%MS	MS-63RB	MS-65RD	MS-66RD	MS-67RD
2009, Presidency, Copper-Coated Zinc	4,457	65.9	100%	$0.15	$0.30	$12	$20

2009, Presidency, Copper, Satin Finish • Mintage: 784,614.

Commentary: All of these cents were sold at a premium to collectors. Nearly all examples are brilliant, sharply struck, and grade MS–69 or 70.

	Cert	Avg	%MS	MS-68RD	MS-69RD
2009, Presidency, Copper, Satin Finish	1,488	67.6	100%	$15	$45

2009-D, Presidency, Copper-Coated Zinc • Circulation-strike mintage: 198,000,000.

Commentary: This issue is common in gem Mint State. Some of the various 2009 types in this composition have water spot–like stains and should be avoided.

	Cert	Avg	%MS	MS-63RB	MS-65RD	MS-66RD	MS-67RD
2009-D, Presidency, Copper-Coated Zinc	1,369	65.9	100%	$0.15	$0.30	$12	$20

2009-D, Presidency, Copper, Satin Finish • Mintage: 784,614.

Commentary: All of these cents were sold at a premium to collectors. Nearly all examples are brilliant, sharply struck, and grade MS–69 or 70.

	Cert	Avg	%MS	MS-68RD	MS-69RD
2009-D, Presidency, Copper, Satin Finish	1,592	67.6	100%	$15	$200

2009-S, Presidency, Copper, Proof • Proof mintage: 2,995,615.

Proof commentary: These Proofs were made with deep-cameo contrast. This issue is common. Most are brilliant and grade PF–69 or 70.

	Cert	Avg	%MS	PF-65RD	PF-67RD	PF-67Cam	PF-68DCam
2009-S, Presidency, Copper, Proof	14,535	69.1		$4	$7	$8	$11

LINCOLN, SHIELD REVERSE (2010 TO DATE)

Designer: *Victor D. Brenner (obverse) and Lyndall Bass (reverse).*
Weight: *2.5 grams.* **Composition:** *Copper-plated zinc (core: .992 zinc, .008 copper, with a plating of pure copper; total content .975 zinc, .025 copper).*
Diameter: *19 mm.* **Edge:** *Plain.* **Mints:** *Philadelphia, Denver, and San Francisco.*

Circulation Strike

Proof

ANOTHER REVERSE

It was thought by many that the Lincoln Memorial reverse would be used again beginning in 2010. The Treasury Department decided differently and solicited new design ideas. A shield motif designed by Lyndall Bass, a member of the Artistic Infusion Program, was selected as the new design. Modeling was done by Mint medallic sculptor Joseph Menna. It was revealed November 12, 2009, during the launch ceremony for the 2009 Presidency reverse cent in a ceremony held at the United States Capitol.

Paul Gilkes reported on the launch of this design in *Coin World*, March 1, 2010:

> More than 1,000 collectors and members of the general public braved sub-freezing temperatures Feb. 11 in Springfield, Ill., for the opportunity to obtain rolls of 2010 Lincoln, Union Shield cents during official release ceremonies of the coin at the Abraham Lincoln Presidential Museum. It took less than three hours following the festivities for employees of U.S. Bank's Adam Street branch to distribute 1 million of the new coins wrapped in 50-coin rolls to attendees, who began waiting in line outside as much as five hours before the 9:30 a.m. program began inside the museum. U.S. Mint Director Edmund C. Moy was joined by Jan Grimes, acting executive director of the Abraham Lincoln Presidential Library and Museum, and ALPLM's curator, James Cornelius, in the coin launch ceremonies. . . .

The design, which was quite similar to various reverses used on privately issued Civil War tokens in the early 1860s, elicited many complaints. However, after due consideration, most numismatists came to like it as an improvement on the Lincoln Memorial style.

The features of the Lincoln portrait on the obverse were modified slightly to conform with the details in the original Brenner design of 1909.

MODERN TECHNOLOGY

By this time and for some years the mints had been using ultra–high speed Schuler presses for coining circulation strikes of various denominations. Arranged in banks of machines, the presses struck coins at a speed of more than a dozen a second, faster than the eye can see.

The output of each was carried on a conveyor to a line containing many trays to receive the output of multiple presses, after which they were conveyed to storage in huge Kevlar bags for shipment to the Federal Reserve System. The following images were taken at the Denver Mint in 2015.[213]

A side view of one of a row of
Schuler presses minting Lincoln cents.

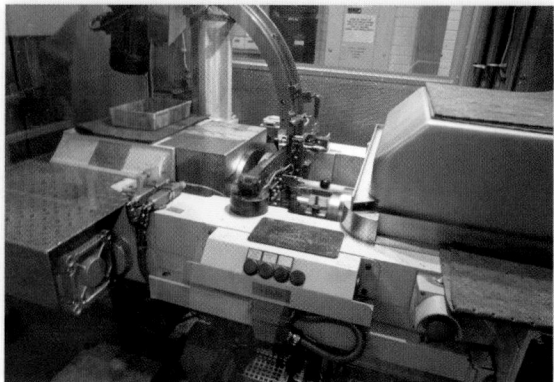

The interior of the SP-61
(Schuler Press no. 61) coining press.

Cents on a small conveyor emerging
from the coining press.

The back end of the Schuler press,
where struck coins emerge. The small
red container at the right is marked
"Condemn," where misstruck and other
unsatisfactory (except to numismatists)
coins are tossed, to be destroyed.

2015-D cents
hot (literally)
off the press.

Lincoln cents collecting in a small bin that
was later emptied onto another conveyor.

A conveyor system with
bins containing thousands
of 2015-D cents, the output
from multiple presses.

Grading Standards

Caveat: These grading standards do not take sharpness of strike into account.

MS-60 to 70 (Mint State). *Obverse and Reverse:* At MS-65 and higher, luster is rich on all areas; there is no rubbing, and no contact marks are visible except under magnification. Coins with full or nearly full mint orange-red color can be designated RD; those with a substantial percentage of red-orange and of brown can be called RB; and those with full (or nearly full) brown-toned surfaces can be designated BN. Some 2009

2011-D. Graded MS-67RD.

cents, even from original rolls and bags, have surface marks that look like water spots.

The Lincoln, Shield Reverse, cent is seldom collected in grades lower than MS-60.

PF-60 to 70 (Proof). *Obverse and Reverse:* PF-65 and higher coins are RB (with colors nicely blended) or RD, the latter with bright red-orange color sometimes fading to hints of brown. Some tiny flecks are normal on coins certified as PF-65 but should be microscopic or absent above that level. PF–60 and 61 coins can be dull, stained, or spotted and still have some original mint luster. Proof coins with fingerprints are impaired and must

2012-S. Graded PF-70RD Deep Cameo.

be given a lower numerical grade. Lower-grade Proofs usually have poor eye appeal. Generally, Proofs of this type below PF-65 are not desired by most collectors.

Lincoln, Shield Reverse, Cents of 2010

2010 IN NUMISMATICS: Bright-red copper coins that change color after being certified were the subject of new restrictions: "Since environmental factors can create changes in the color of copper beyond our control, we will not be guaranteeing the color of copper coins graded or sold after Jan. 1, 2010," PCGS announced.

2010 • **Circulation-strike mintage:** 1,963,630,000.

Commentary: This issue is common in gem Mint State.

	Cert	Avg	%MS	MS-63RB	MS-65RD	MS-66RD	MS-67RD
2010	6,843	65.5	100%	$0.15	$0.30	$10	$18

2010, Satin Finish • Mintage: 583,897.

Commentary: From 2005 to 2010 the U.S. Mint issued Uncirculated sets with a special satin finish. These sets, made using burnished blanks and sandblasted dies, have in many cases been broken out of their original packaging to give collectors access to individual Satin Finish coins. The grading services sometimes grade such coins with the designation "SP" instead of "MS."

	Cert	Avg	%MS	MS-63RB	MS-65RD	MS-66RD	MS-67RD
2010, Satin Finish	270	67.1	100%	$5	$10	$15	$20

2010-D • Circulation-strike mintage: 2,047,200,000.

Commentary: Despite sometimes being labeled "Satin Finish," this is a regular issue. It is common in gem Mint State.

	Cert	Avg	%MS	MS-63RB	MS-65RD	MS-66RD	MS-67RD
2010-D	2,314	65.9	100%	$0.15	$0.30	$10	$18

2010-D, Satin Finish • Mintage: 583,897.

Commentary: From 2005 to 2010 the U.S. Mint issued Uncirculated sets with a special satin finish. These sets, made using burnished blanks and sandblasted dies, have in many cases been broken out of their original packaging to give collectors access to individual Satin Finish coins. The grading services sometimes grade such coins with the designation "SP" instead of "MS."

	Cert	Avg	%MS	MS-63RB	MS-65RD	MS-66RD	MS-67RD
2010-D, Satin Finish	357	67.6	100%	$5	$10	$15	$20

2010-S, Proof • Proof mintage: 1,689,364.

Proof commentary: These Proofs were made with deep-cameo contrast. Nearly all examples are well struck, brilliant, and in grades of PF–69 and 70.

	Cert	Avg	%MS	PF-65RD	PF-67RD	PF-67Cam	PF-68DCam
2010-S, Proof	5,601	69.1		$7	$7.50	$8	$11

Lincoln, Shield Reverse, Cents of 2011

2011 IN NUMISMATICS: The rising price of copper and nickel, a concern for many years, prompted the Mint to experiment with other metals during this era.

2011 • **Circulation-strike mintage:** 2,402,400,000.

Commentary: This issue is common in gem Mint State.

	Cert	Avg	%MS	MS-63RB	MS-65RD	MS-66RD	MS-67RD
2011	472	66.3	100%	$0.15	$0.30	$10	$18

2011-D • **Circulation-strike mintage:** 2,536,140,000.

Commentary: This issue is common in gem Mint State.

	Cert	Avg	%MS	MS-63RB	MS-65RD	MS-66RD	MS-67RD
2011-D	267	66.8	100%	$0.15	$0.30	$10	$18

2011-S, Proof • **Proof mintage:** 1,673,010.

Proof commentary: These Proofs were made with deep-cameo contrast. Nearly all examples are well struck, brilliant, and in grades of PF–69 and 70. For any and all of these later-era Proofs most survived in the condition as issued.

	Cert	Avg	%MS	PF-65RD	PF-67RD	PF-67Cam	PF-68DCam
2011-S, Proof	6,230	69.1		$7	$7.50	$8	$11

Lincoln, Shield Reverse, Cents of 2012

2012 • Circulation-strike mintage: 3,132,000,000.

Commentary: This issue is common in gem Mint State.

	Cert	Avg	%MS	MS-63RB	MS-65RD	MS-66RD	MS-67RD
2012	275	67.0	100%	$0.15	$0.30	$10	$18

2012-D • Circulation-strike mintage: 2,883,200,000.

Commentary: This issue is common in gem Mint State.

	Cert	Avg	%MS	MS-63RB	MS-65RD	MS-66RD	MS-67RD
2012-D	169	66.9	100%	$0.15	$0.30	$10	$18

2012-S, Proof • Proof mintage: 1,237,415.

Proof commentary: These Proofs were made with deep-cameo contrast. Nearly all examples are well struck, brilliant, and in grades of PF–69 and 70.

	Cert	Avg	%MS	PF-65RD	PF-67RD	PF-67Cam	PF-68DCam
2012-S, Proof	552	66.2		$7	$7.50	$8	$11

Lincoln, Shield Reverse, Cents of 2013

2013 • Circulation-strike mintage: 3,750,400,000.

Commentary: This issue is common in gem Mint State.

	Cert	Avg	%MS	MS-63RB	MS-65RD	MS-66RD	MS-67RD
2013	356	66.8	100%	$0.15	$0.30	$10	$18

2013-D • Circulation-strike mintage: 3,319,600,000.

Commentary: This issue is common in gem Mint State.

	Cert	Avg	%MS	MS-63RB	MS-65RD	MS-66RD	MS-67RD
2013-D	2,034	69.1	100%	$0.15	$0.30	$10	$18

2013-S, Proof • Proof mintage: 1,237,976.

Proof commentary: These Proofs were made with deep cameo contrast. Nearly all examples are well struck, brilliant, and in grades of PF–69 and 70.

	Cert	Avg	%MS	PF-65RD	PF-67RD	PF-67Cam	PF-68DCam
2013-S, Proof	2,423	69.2		$7	$7.50	$8	$11

Lincoln, Shield Reverse, Cents of 2014

2014 • Circulation-strike mintage:
3,990,800,000.

Commentary: This issue is common in gem Mint State.

	Cert	Avg	%MS	MS-63RB	MS-65RD	MS-66RD	MS-67RD
2014	588	66.8	100%	$0.15	$0.30	$10	$15

2014-D • Circulation-strike mintage:
4,155,600,000.

Commentary: This issue is common in gem Mint State.

	Cert	Avg	%MS	MS-63RB	MS-65RD	MS-66RD	MS-67RD
2014-D	594	66.7	100%	$0.15	$0.30	$10	$15

2014-S, Proof • Proof mintage:
670,425.

Proof commentary: These Proofs were made with deep-cameo contrast. Nearly all examples are well struck, brilliant, and in grades of PF–69 and 70.

	Cert	Avg	%MS	PF-65RD	PF-67RD	PF-67Cam	PF-68DCam
2014-S, Proof	3,944	69.3		$7	$7.50	$8	$11

Lincoln, Shield Reverse, Cents of 2015

2015 • Circulation-strike mintage:
4,464,100,000.

Commentary: This issue is common in gem Mint State.

	Cert	Avg	%MS	MS-63RB	MS-65RD	MS-66RD	MS-67RD
2015	29	66.9	100%	$0.15	$0.30	$10	$15

2015-D • Circulation-strike mintage: 4,424,800,000.

Commentary: This issue is common in gem Mint State.

	Cert	Avg	%MS	MS-63RB	MS-65RD	MS-66RD	MS-67RD
2015-D	35	66.5	100%	$0.15	$0.30	$10	$15

2015-S, Proof • Proof mintage: 1,022,410.

Proof commentary: These Proofs were made with deep-cameo contrast. Nearly all examples are well struck, brilliant, and in grades of PF–69 and 70.

	Cert	Avg	%MS	PF-65RD	PF-67RD	PF-67Cam	PF-68DCam
2015-S, Proof	810	69.3		$7	$7.50	$8	$11

Lincoln, Shield Reverse, Cents of 2016

2016 • Circulation-strike mintage: Not known at press time.

Commentary: This issue is common in gem Mint State.

	Cert	Avg	%MS	MS-63RB	MS-65RD	MS-66RD	MS-67RD
2016	0	n/a		$0.15	$0.30	$10	$15

2016-D • Circulation-strike mintage: Not known at press time.

Commentary: This issue is common in gem Mint State.

	Cert	Avg	%MS	MS-63RB	MS-65RD	MS-66RD	MS-67RD
2016-D	0	n/a		$0.15	$0.30	$10	$15

2016-S, Proof • Proof mintage: Not known at press time.

Proof commentary: These Proofs were made with deep-cameo contrast. Nearly all examples are well struck, brilliant, and in grades of PF–69 and 70.

	Cert	Avg	%MS	PF-65RD	PF-67RD	PF-67Cam	PF-68DCam
2016-S, Proof	0	n/a		$7	$7.50	$8	$11

Two-Cent Pieces
1864–1873

AN OVERVIEW OF TWO-CENT PIECES

The two-cent piece was introduced in 1864. Made of bronze, it was designed by U.S. Mint chief engraver James B. Longacre, and was the first circulating U.S. coin to bear the motto IN GOD WE TRUST. At the time, coins were scarce in circulation because of the ongoing Civil War and the public's tendency to hoard hard currency, and silver and gold issues were entirely absent. Treasury officials felt that the two-cent piece would prove to be very popular as a companion to the Indian Head cent. However, the introduction of the nickel three-cent piece in 1865 negated much of this advantage, the production of two-cent pieces declined, and by 1873, when the denomination was discontinued, its only coinage consisted of Proofs for collectors.

A full "type set" of the two-cent piece consists of but a single coin. Most available in Mint State are the issues of 1864 and 1865, often seen with original mint orange color fading to natural brown. Proofs are available for all years.

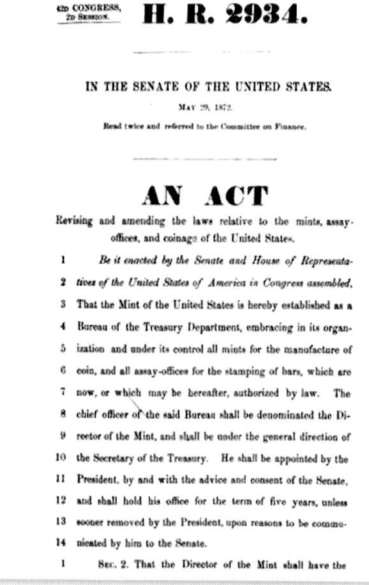

The Coinage Act of 1873 eliminated not only the two-cent piece but also the three-cent silver and half dime.

FOR THE COLLECTOR AND INVESTOR: TWO-CENT PIECES AS A SPECIALTY

Two-cent pieces can be collected by date and variety. A basic display consists of an 1864, Large Motto; 1864, Small Motto (rare); 1873, Close 3; and 1873, Open 3, the latter two being available only in Proof format. Some specialists opt to include just one of the 1873 varieties.

Collectors should select both circulation strikes and Proofs with care, for the number of truly choice *original* (unprocessed, undipped, not retoned) coins is but a small percentage of the whole. As a type, though, the two-cent piece is readily available for collecting.

Several specialized studies of two-cent pieces have been published over a long span of years, the first of significance being "Two-Cent Pieces of the United States," by S.W. Freeman, published in the *Numismatist*, June 1954.

TWO-CENT PIECES (1864–1873)

Designer: *James B. Longacre.* **Weight:** *6.22 grams.*
Composition: *.950 copper, .050 tin and zinc.* **Diameter:** *23 mm.*
Edge: *Plain.* **Mint:** *Philadelphia.*

Circulation Strike   **Proof**

History. The two-cent piece, struck in bronze like the new Indian Head cents, made its debut under the Mint Act of April 22, 1864. Coins of all kinds were scarce in circulation at the time, due to hoarding. The outcome of the Civil War was uncertain, and Americans desired "hard money." Many millions of two-cent pieces were struck in 1864, after which the mintage declined, due to once-hoarded Indian Head cents becoming available again and to the new nickel three-cent coins being introduced in 1865. Continually decreasing quantities were made through 1872, and only Proofs were struck in the coin's final year, 1873.

Striking and Sharpness. Points to check for sharpness on the obverse include WE in the motto, the leaves, and the horizontal shield lines. On the reverse check the wreath details and the border letters. Check the denticles on both sides. Most coins are quite well struck.

Availability. Most MS coins are dated 1864 or 1865, after which the availability declines sharply, especially for the issue of 1872. Among 1864 coins most seen are of the Large Motto variety. Small Motto coins are elusive. Coins with much or nearly all *original* mint red-orange color are rare for the later years, with most in the marketplace being recolored. The 1864, Small Motto, Proof, is a great rarity, with fewer than two dozen estimated to exist. Coins of 1873 were made only in Proof format, of the Close 3 and Open 3 styles. Proofs of most dates are easily enough acquired. Very few have original color. Do not overlook the many nice brown and red-and-brown pieces on the market (some investors acquire only "red" copper coins, leaving many great values among others). Refer to the comments under Proof Indian Head cents.

GRADING STANDARDS

MS-60 to 70 (Mint State). *Obverse and Reverse:* At MS-65 and higher, the luster is rich on all areas. There is no rubbing, and no contact marks are visible except under magnification. Coins with full or nearly full mint orange-red color can be designated RD (the color on this is often more orange than red), those with full or nearly full brown-toned surfaces can be designated BN, and those with a substantial percentage of red-orange

1864, Large Motto, RPD; Leone-9. Graded MS-66RD.

and of brown can be called RB. Ideally, MS-65 or finer coins should have good eye appeal, which in the RB category means nicely blended colors, not stained or blotched, the latter problem mostly with dipped and irregularly retoned coins. Below MS-65, full RD coins become scarce, although MS-64RD coins can be attractive. These usually have more flecks and tiny spots, while the color remains bright. At MS–60 to 62, RD coins are virtually nonexistent, unless they have been dipped. The ANA standards allow for "dull" and/or "spotted" coins at MS–60 and 61 as well as incomplete luster. As a rule, MS–60 to 63BN coins can be fairly attractive if not spotted or blotched, but those with hints of color usually lack eye appeal.

AU-50, 53, 55, 58 (About Uncirculated).
Obverse: WE shows light wear, this being the prime place to check. The arrowheads and leaves also show light wear. At AU-50, level wear is more noticeable. At AU–53 and 55, wear is less. At AU-58, friction is evident, rather than actual wear. Luster, toned brown, is nearly complete at AU-58, but may be incomplete in the field. *Reverse:* At AU-50, light wear is seen on the ribbon and the higher-relief areas of the leaves and grains, while the lower areas retain their detail. Some luster may be present in protected areas. At AU–53 and 55, wear is lesser and luster is more extensive. An AU-58 coin will have nearly full luster and show only light friction.

1871. Graded AU-58.

EF-40, 45 (Extremely Fine). *Obverse:* Wear is more extensive. WE shows wear extensively, but still is clear. The leaves lack detail on their highest points. Some scattered marks are normal at this and lower grades. *Reverse:* The higher-relief parts of the leaves and ribbon bow show further wear, as do other areas.

1864, Small Motto. Graded EF-45.

VF-20, 30 (Very Fine). *Obverse:* WE is clear, but not strong. Leaves show more wear, as do all other areas. *Reverse:* Still more wear is seen, but the leaves still are separately defined. The wheat grains are very clear.

1864, Small Motto. Graded VF-20.

F-12, 15 (Fine). *Obverse:* WE is the defining factor and is very weak, but readable, if only barely. Other areas show more wear. The edges of some leaves are gone, blending them into adjacent leaves. *Reverse:* Wear is more extensive. Near the apex of the wreath the edges of some leaves are gone, blending them into adjacent leaves. The grains of wheat are clear, but some are slightly weak.

Illustrated coin: WE is very weak.

1872. Graded F-15.

VG-8, 10 (Very Good). *Obverse:* WE is gone, although the ANA grading standards and *Photograde* suggest "very weak." IN GOD and TRUST are readable, but some areas may be weak. The inner edges of most leaves are gone. *Reverse:* The wear appears to be less extensive than on the obverse. All lettering is bold. A few grains of wheat may be well worn or even missing.

1872. Graded VG-8.

G-4, 6 (Good). *Obverse:* Wear is more extensive, and the leaf bunches are in flat clumps. IN GOD and TRUST are very worn, with a letter or two not visible. *Reverse:* All letters are clear. The wreath is mostly in outline on G-4. On G-6, perhaps half the grains are visible.

1864, Small Motto. Graded G-4.

AG-3 (About Good). *Obverse:* The motto shows only a few letters. The leaves are flat. Only a few horizontal shield stripes can be seen. *Reverse:* The wreath is in outline form. The letters are weak, with 20% to 40% worn away entirely.

1872. Graded AG-3.

PF-60 to 70 (Proof). *Obverse and Reverse:* Gem PF-65 two-cent pieces will have very few hairlines, and these visible only under a strong magnifying glass. At any level and color, a Proof with hairlines has likely been cleaned, a fact usually overlooked. At PF-67 or higher there should be no evidence of hairlines or friction at all. Such a coin is fully original. PF-60 coins can be dull from repeated dipping and cleaning and are often toned iridescent colors or have mottled surfaces. At PF-63, the mirrorlike fields should be attractive, and hairlines should be minimal, most easily seen when the coin is held at an angle to the light. No rubbing is seen. PF-64 coins are even nicer. As a general rule, Proofs of 1873 are of very high quality but, unless dipped or cleaned, are nearly always toned light brown.

1872. Graded PF-64RD.

1864, Small Motto

1864, Large Motto

1865, Plain 5

1865, Fancy 5

	Mintage	Cert	Avg	%MS	G-4	F-12	VF-20	EF-40	AU-50	MS-60BN	MS-63BN	MS-64BN	MS-65RD
											PF-63BN	PF-64BN	PF-65RB
1864, Small Motto (a)	**(b)**	599	52.4	65%	$225	$400	$600	$850	$1,000	$1,500	$1,750	$2,000	$12,500
Auctions: $2,232, MS-65BN, January 2015; $1,410, MS-61BN, January 2015; $763, EF-45, October 2015; $646, EF-45, August 2015													
1864, Large Motto (c)	19,822,500	3,783	61.1	86%	$15	$25	$30	$50	$80	$110	$175	$200	$1,250
Auctions: $1,116, MS-66BN, June 2015; $305, MS-65BN, May 2015; $129, MS-63BN, January 2015; $111, AU-58, October 2015													
1864, Small Motto, Proof † (d)	**(e)**	8	64.8								$18,500	$20,000	$55,000
Auctions: $105,750, PF-66RD, June 2014													
1864, Large Motto, Proof	100+	132	64.6								$550	$775	$2,500
Auctions: $3,760, PF-66BN, October 2015; $3,642, PF-66BN, January 2015; $3,535, PF-65RB, August 2015; $646, PF-62BN, February 2015													
1865 (f)	13,640,000	2,464	60.8	84%	$15	$25	$30	$50	$80	$110	$175	$200	$1,250
Auctions: $540, MS-65RB, May 2015; $399, MS-65BN, February 2015; $646, MS-64RD, August 2015; $199, MS-64BN, January 2015													
1865, Proof	500+	156	64.7								$450	$525	$1,200
Auctions: $2,820, PF-66RB, October 2015; $3,290, PF-65RB, June 2015; $1,997, PF-65RB, January 2015; $1,178, PF-65BN, January 2015													
1866	3,177,000	520	59.1	76%	$20	$30	$35	$50	$80	$120	$175	$220	$2,000
Auctions: $1,692, MS-65RD, July 2015; $587, MS-64RD, January 2015; $517, MS-64RB, October 2015; $212, MS-64BN, April 2015													
1866, Proof	725+	169	64.7								$450	$525	$1,200
Auctions: $4,700, PF-66RB, July 2015; $1,527, PF-65RB, January 2015; $1,175, PF-65RB, September 2015; $470, PF-64BN, January 2015													

† Ranked in the *100 Greatest U.S. Coins* (fourth edition). **a.** The circulated Small Motto is distinguished by a wider D in GOD, and the first T in TRUST nearly touching the ribbon crease at left. **b.** Included in circulation-strike 1864, Large Motto, mintage figure. **c.** The circulated Large Motto is distinguished by a narrow D in GOD, and a 1 mm gap between the first T in TRUST and the ribbon crease. **d.** 20 to 30 examples are known. **e.** Included in 1864, Large Motto, Proof, mintage figure. **f.** Circulated varieties show the tip of the 5 either plain or fancy (curved).

1867, Doubled-Die Obverse
FS-02-1867-101.

1869, Doubled-Die Obverse
FS-02-1869-101.

	Mintage	Cert	Avg	%MS	G-4	F-12	VF-20	EF-40	AU-50	MS-60BN	MS-63BN / PF-63BN	MS-64BN / PF-64BN	MS-65RD / PF-65RB
1867	2,938,750	570	59.8	81%	$20	$30	$35	$50	$80	$130	$190	$235	$3,250
Auctions: $646, MS-64RB, August 2015; $423, MS-64RB, October 2015; $282, MS-64BN, February 2015; $141, MS-61BN, May 2015													
1867, Doubled-Die Obverse (g)	(h)	59	43.5	36%	$100	$200	$300	$600	$850	$1,400	$2,750	$3,200	
Auctions: $22,325, MS-65RD, January 2014													
1867, Proof	625+	202	64.7								$450	$525	$1,200
Auctions: $940, PF-65RB, August 2015; $763, PF-65BN, September 2015; $646, PF-64BN, January 2015													
1868	2,803,750	570	59.6	79%	$20	$36	$50	$75	$110	$150	$225	$375	$4,000
Auctions: $1,292, MS-65RB, January 2015; $1,057, MS-65RB, October 2015; $834, MS-64RB, June 2015; $211, MS-63BN, February 2015													
1868, Proof	600+	187	64.8								$450	$525	$1,200
Auctions: $470, PF-64BN, January 2015													
1869	1,546,500	500	59.3	77%	$25	$40	$55	$80	$125	$160	$225	$375	$3,500
Auctions: $2,820, MS-65RD, September 2015; $1,540, MS-65RB, January 2015; $763, MS-65BN, July 2015; $329, MS-64BN, June 2015													
1869, Doubled-Die Obverse	(i)	0	n/a							$600	$900	$1,250	
Auctions: No auction records available.													
1869, Proof	600+	233	64.6								$450	$525	$1,250
Auctions: $2,820, PF-66RB, July 2015; $1,527, PF-66RB, October 2015; $1,881, PF-65RD, September 2015; $822, PF-65BN, January 2015													
1870	861,250	385	57.6	74%	$35	$55	$85	$135	$200	$275	$300	$575	$4,500
Auctions: $1,762, MS-65RB, August 2015; $329, MS-63RB, October 2015; $258, MS-62BN, May 2015; $62, EF-40, January 2015													
1870, Proof	1,000+	274	64.5								$450	$575	$1,275
Auctions: $3,290, PF-67BN, July 2015; $1,821, PF-65RD, February 2015; $1,116, PF-65RB, January 2015; $705, PF-65BN, September 2015													
1871	721,250	545	57.6	71%	$40	$85	$110	$150	$225	$300	$375	$800	$5,500
Auctions: $1,292, MS-64RD, January 2015; $1,008, MS-64RB, August 2015; $411, MS-64BN, June 2015; $282, MS-61BN, July 2015													
1871, Proof	960+	273	64.6								$450	$575	$1,275
Auctions: $8,233, PF-66RD, July 2015; $2,115, PF-65RB, August 2015; $1,057, PF-64RB, February 2015; $881, PF-64RB, January 2015													
1872	65,000	320	35.4	28%	$400	$600	$800	$1,050	$1,650	$2,800	$3,600	$3,900	$22,500
Auctions: $5,405, MS-65BN, September 2015; $2,350, MS-62BN, January 2015; $1,997, MS-61BN, October 2015; $493, VG-10, February 2015													
1872, Proof	950+	341	64.5								$900	$950	$1,300
Auctions: $1,762, PF-66RB, June 2015; $1,410, PF-65BN, August 2015; $1,292, PF-65BN, February 2015; $2,820, PF-64BN, June 2015													
1873, Close 3, Proof	400	275	64.0								$3,200	$3,500	$4,300
Auctions: $4,700, PF-66BN, June 2015; $3,535, PF-65RB, October 2015; $3,290, PF-64RB, August 2015; $2,381, PF-64BN, January 2015													
1873, Open 3, Proof (Alleged Restrike)	200	125	63.6								$3,100	$3,250	$4,000
Auctions: $11,162, PF-66RB, October 2015; $5,640, PF-66BN, January 2015; $2,820, PF-63BN, September 2015; $2,232, PF-62BN, January 2015													

g. This variety is somewhat common in low-end circulated grades, but is considered rare in EF and AU, and very rare in MS.
h. Included in circulation-strike 1867 mintage figure. **i.** Included in circulation-strike 1869 mintage figure.

Three-Cent Pieces
1851–1889

AN OVERVIEW OF THREE-CENT PIECES

SILVER THREE-CENT PIECES

The silver three-cent piece or *trime* is one of the more curious coins in American numismatics. The rising price of silver in 1850 created a situation in which silver coins cost more to produce than their face value. Mintages dropped sharply and older pieces disappeared from circulation. In 1851 a solution was provided by the three-cent piece. Instead of being made with 90% silver content, the fineness was set at 75%. Accordingly, the coins were worth less intrinsically, and there was no advantage in melting them. Large quantities were made through 1853. In that year, the standards for regular silver coins were changed, and other denominations reappeared on the marketplace, making the trime unnecessary. Mintages dropped beginning in 1854, until 1873, when production amounted to just 600 Proofs for collectors.

Of the three varieties of trimes, Variety 2 (1854–1858) is at once the scarcest and, by far, the most difficult to find with a sharp strike. In fact, not one in fifty Variety 2 coins is needle sharp. Curiously, when such pieces are found they are likely to be dated 1855, the lowest-mintage issue of the type. Trimes of the Variety 1 design (1851–1853) vary widely in striking, but can be found sharp. Variety 3 coins (1859–1873) often are sharp.

Mint State coins are readily found for Variety 1 and are usually in grades from MS–60 to 63 or so, although quite a few gems are around with attractive luster. Sharply struck gems are another matter and require some searching to find. Mint State Variety 2 trimes are all rare, and when seen are apt to be miserably struck and in lower grades. Variety 3 coins are readily found in Mint State, including in MS–65 and higher grades.

The term *trime* was first used by the director of the United States Mint, James Ross Snowden, at the time of the coins' production.

Proofs were made of all years, but not in quantity until 1858, when an estimated 210 were struck. For all dates after 1862, high-grade Proofs are much more readily available today than are Mint State coins. Circulated examples are available of all three varieties. While extensively worn coins of Variety 1 are available, most Variety 2 coins are Fine or better and most Variety 3 pieces are VF or better.

FOR THE COLLECTOR AND INVESTOR:
SILVER THREE-CENT PIECES AS A SPECIALTY

Trimes cover a fairly long span of years and embrace several design types, but comprise no "impossible" rarities. Accordingly, it is realistic to collect one of each Philadelphia Mint coin from 1851 to 1873 plus the 1851-O. There are two overdates in the series, 1862, 2 Over 1 (which is distinct and occurs only in circulation-strike format), and 1863, 3 Over 2 (only Proofs, and not boldly defined), which some specialists collect and others ignore. A curious variety of 1852 has the first digit of the date over an inverted 2.

Typically, a high-grade set includes Mint State examples of all issues 1851 through 1857 and Proofs after that date. As noted, Variety 2 trimes usually are very poorly struck, save the occasionally encountered sharp 1855. As an example, a specialist in the series who found an 1856 with needle-sharp details, at three times the regular market price, might be well advised to buy it. After 1862, Mint State coins are rare for most dates. The formation of a choice Mint State set 1851 through 1872 plus a Proof 1873 would be a formidable challenge.

A set of circulated coins can be gathered through and including 1862, after which such pieces become very rare. Most later dates will have to be acquired on a catch-as-catch-can basis, perhaps by acquiring impaired Proofs for certain of the years.

NICKEL THREE-CENT PIECES

Nickel three-cent pieces were introduced in 1865 to help fill the need for coins in circulation. At the time, silver and gold issues were hoarded, and were available only at a premium. The nickel three-cent piece joined the Indian Head cent and the new (as of 1864) two-cent piece. The coin proved to be very popular in its time, and millions were struck. In 1866 the nickel five-cent piece was introduced, after which time the demand for the nickel three-cent piece diminished somewhat. However, pieces were made in quantity until 1876. In that year silver coins again returned to circulation, and mintages for the nickel three-cent piece dropped sharply. Only Proofs were made in 1877 and 1878. In later years, mintages ranged from small to modest, except for 1881.

Mint State coins are readily available for the early years, although many if not most have weak striking in areas or are from clashed dies. Pristine, sharp Mint State coins on the market are mostly of later years, in the 1880s, where such pieces are the rule, not the exception.

FOR THE COLLECTOR AND INVESTOR:
NICKEL THREE-CENT PIECES AS A SPECIALTY

Nickel three-cent coins are interesting to collect by date sequence from 1865 to 1889. Varieties are provided by the 1873, Close 3, and 1873, Open 3, and the 1887, 7 Over 6, overdate. A set of Mint State coins is considerably more difficult to form than a run of Proofs. A hand-selected set of well-struck coins MS-65 or finer could take several years to complete.

Among Proofs, the rarest year is 1865, probably followed by the "perfect date" (not overdate) 1887. Proofs of the 1860s and early 1870s are scarce in PF-65 with excellent strike and eye appeal. Proofs of the latter decade of coinage are much more readily available and usually are choice.

SILVER THREE-CENT PIECES (TRIMES) (1851–1873)

Variety 1 (1851–1853): **Designer:** *James B. Longacre.* **Weight:** *0.80 gram.*
Composition: *.750 silver, .250 copper.* **Diameter:** *14 mm.*
Edge: *Plain.* **Mints:** *Philadelphia and New Orleans.*

Variety 1 (1851–1853)   Variety 1, Proof

Variety 2 (1854–1858): **Designer:** *James B. Longacre.* **Weight:** *0.75 gram.*
Composition: *.900 silver, .100 copper.* **Diameter:** *14 mm.* **Edge:** *Plain.* **Mint:** *Philadelphia.*

Variety 2 (1854–1858)   Variety 2, Proof

Variety 3 (1859–1873): **Designer:** *James B. Longacre.* **Weight:** *0.75 gram.*
Composition: *.900 silver, .100 copper.* **Diameter:** *14 mm.* **Edge:** *Plain.* **Mint:** *Philadelphia.*

Variety 3 (1859–1873)   Variety 3, Proof

History. In 1850 Americans began hoarding their silver coins, as the flood of gold from California made silver disproportionately valuable. To provide a small coin for commerce, the Mint introduced the silver three-cent piece, or *trime*. These were .750 fine (as opposed to the standard .900 fineness), and contained less than 3¢ of metal, so there was no incentive to hoard or melt them. Three different designs were made, Variety 1 of which was struck from 1851 to 1853. These coins were popular in their time and circulated widely. These are distinguished from the other two designs by having no outline or frame around the obverse star. The Act of February 21, 1853, reduced the amount of silver in other denominations (from the half dime to the half dollar, but not the dollar), which discouraged people from hoarding them. The tiny trime lost the public's favor, and mintages decreased.

In 1854 the design was changed considerably, creating Variety 2, which was made through 1858. The alloy was modified to the standard for other issues and the weight was lightened. A raised border was added to the obverse star plus two line frames around it. On the reverse an olive branch was placed above the III and a bundle of arrows below it. This new motif proved to be very difficult to strike up properly.

In 1859 the design was modified again, creating Variety 3. Demand for the denomination continued to be small, and after 1862 very few were made for circulation, as silver coins were hoarded by the war-weary public and began to trade at a premium. Under the Coinage Act of 1873 the trime was discontinued, and that year only Proofs were struck. Also in that year, nearly the entire production of non-Proof coins of 1863 to 1872 was melted.

Striking and Sharpness. On the Variety 1 obverse the tiny shield at the center of the star often lacks certain details. On the reverse check the details and strength of the III. On both sides check the rims. Needle-sharp coins are in the minority. Sharpness of strike has been nearly completely overlooked in the marketplace.

Trimes of Variety 2 are usually poorly struck, with some or all of these characteristics: obverse lettering weak in places; frames around the star of inconsistent strength or missing in certain areas; shield weak in places; reverse stars irregular and poorly formed; olive branch and arrows weak in areas; weak or irregular rims. Now and then a sharp 1855 is found.

Most Variety 3 trimes are sharply struck. Points to look for include full outlines around the star, full shield on the star, and full leaf details and sharp stars.

Most Proofs are needle sharp and have mirrored surfaces, although some of the late 1860s and early 1870s can have slightly grainy or satiny lustrous surfaces. Striking quality varies. Lint marks and surface problems are not unusual. Careful examination is recommended.

Availability. Circulated examples of the Variety 1 trimes are plentiful. MS coins are often seen, although the 1851-O is scarce in MS and high circulated grades. Most MS coins are lustrous and attractive, especially at 63 and above. Circulated Variety 2 coins are scarce in all grades, particularly so at MS-64 and higher. With a needle-sharp strike, MS-65 and higher are *rarities*. Among Variety 3 trimes, circulated coins of the years 1859 to 1862 are easy to find. All later dates range from scarce to rare in circulation-strike format. MS-63 and better coins 1865 and later are very rare. A few Proofs were made in the early 1850s and are great rarities today. After 1857, production increased to an estimated 210 or so in 1858, through 500 to 700 or so as a yearly average in the 1860s to 1873.

GRADING STANDARDS

MS-60 to 70 (Mint State). *Obverse and Reverse:* At MS-60, some abrasion and very minor contact marks are evident, most noticeably on the obverse star and the C ornament on the reverse. At MS-63, abrasion is hard to detect except under magnification. An MS-65 coin will have no abrasion. Luster should be full and rich (not grainy). Grades above MS-65 are defined by having fewer marks as perfection is approached. Most high-grade Mint State coins are of the Variety 3 design.

1853, Variety 1. Graded MS-66.

AU-50, 53, 55, 58 (About Uncirculated). *Obverse:* Light wear is most obvious on the star arms and shield on Variety 1, and on the points of the frames on Variety 2 and Variety 3. At AU-50, luster is evident, but only on part of the field. At AU-58 luster is nearly complete. *Reverse:* Light wear is seen on the C ornament and III. On Variety 2 and 3, light wear is seen on the leaves and arrows.

Illustrated coin: This is sharply struck, as are most Variety 3 trimes.

1863, Variety 3. Graded AU-50.

EF-40, 45 (Extremely Fine). *Obverse:* More wear is seen, most noticeable on the ridges of the star arms, this in addition to more wear on the frames (Variety 2 and Variety 3). Luster is absent, or seen only in traces. *Reverse:* More wear is seen on the C ornament and III. On Variety 2 and Variety 3 more wear is seen on the leaves and arrows.

1869, Variety 3. Graded EF-45.

VF-20, 30 (Very Fine). *Obverse:* Further wear reduced the relief of the star. On Variety 2 and Variety 3 the frames show further wear and begin to blend together. The center shield shows wear, and its border is indistinct in areas, but its horizontal and vertical stripes are fully delineated (unless the coin was weakly struck). *Reverse:* Still more wear is seen on the C ornament and III. On Variety 2 and Variety 3 the high-relief areas of the

1862, Variety 3. Graded VF-30.

leaves and the feathers of the arrow are partially worn away. Stars are flat at their centers (on sharply struck coins in addition to, as expected, on weak strikes).

F-12, 15 (Fine). *Obverse:* The star is worn so as to have lost most of its relief. On Variety 2 and Variety 3 the frames are mostly blended together. The center shield shows wear, and its border is flat (or else showing only slight separation of its two outlines), but its horizontal and vertical stripes still are delineated (unless the coin was weakly struck). *Reverse:* Still more wear is seen on the C ornament and III. On Variety 2 and Variety 3 the

1851, Variety 1. Graded F-12.

high-relief areas of the leaves, and the feathers of the arrow, have slight if any detail. Stars are flat. The designs within the C ornament are missing much detail.

VG-8, 10 (Very Good). *Obverse:* The border is incomplete in places, but all lettering is bold. The horizontal and vertical stripes within the shield begin to blend together, but most remain well delineated. *Reverse:* Still more wear is seen on all areas. The designs within the C ornament have more detail gone.

   Illustrated coin: The obverse of this coin shows VG wear, but if the dent in the star was considered it would grade lower.

1852, Variety 1. Graded VG-10.

G-4, 6 (Good). *Obverse:* The border is worn into the tops of the letters and the bottom of the date. The shield is blended into the star, and only traces of the shield outline remain. In this grade most coins seen are Variety 1. *Reverse:* The border is worn into the outer parts of the stars. Additional wear is seen in all other areas.

1851, Variety 1. Graded G-6.

AG-3 (About Good). *Obverse:* The star is flat. Strong elements of the shield are seen, but the tiny lines are mostly or completely blended together. Lettering and date are weak and partially missing, but the date must be identifiable. In this grade most coins seen are Variety 1. *Reverse:* The border is worn into the stars, with outer elements of the stars now gone. Additional wear is seen in all other areas. The designs within the C ornament are only in outline form.

1853, Variety 1. Graded AG-3.

PF-60 to 70 (Proof). *Obverse and Reverse:* Proofs that are extensively cleaned and have many hairlines, or that are dull and grainy, are lower level, such as PF–60 to 62. These are difficult to verify as Proofs. For a trime with medium hairlines and good reflectivity, an assigned grade of PF-64 is indicated, and with relatively few hairlines, gem PF-65. PF-66 should have hairlines so delicate that magnification is needed to see them. Above that, a Proof should be free of such lines.

1857, Variety 2. Graded PF-66.

Illustrated coin: Note the remarkable sharpness of strike, particularly evident on the obverse.

	Mintage	Cert	Avg	%MS	G-4	VG-8	F-12	VF-20	EF-40	AU-50	MS-60 PF-63	MS-63 PF-64	MS-65 PF-65
1851	5,447,400	1,259	61.1	88%	$25	$45	$50	$70	$80	$150	$180	$275	$800
	Auctions: $3,055, MS-67, July 2015; $2,115, MS-66, June 2015; $1,292, MS-66, September 2015; $446, MS-64, January 2015												
1851, Proof (a)		0	n/a								—		
	Auctions: No auction records available.												
1851-O	720,000	474	58.7	74%	$40	$60	$75	$100	$175	$250	$450	$700	$3,000
	Auctions: $11,163, MS-67, July 2014; $12,925, MS-66, December 2013; $793, MS-62, October 2014; $317, AU-55, October 2014												

a. 1 or 2 examples are known.

1852, 1 Over Inverted 2
FS-3S-1852-301.

1853, Repunched Date
FS-3S-1853-301.

1854, Repunched Date
FS-3S-1854-301.

	Mintage	Cert	Avg	%MS	G-4	VG-8	F-12	VF-20	EF-40	AU-50	MS-60	MS-63	MS-65
											PF-63	PF-64	PF-65
1852, 1 Over Inverted 2 (b)	(c)	1	61.0	100%					$775	$950	$1,150	$1,425	$1,950
Auctions: No auction records available.													
1852	18,663,500	1,607	58.3	80%	$25	$45	$50	$70	$80	$150	$180	$275	$800
Auctions: $2,643, MS-67, June 2015; $1,057, MS-66, July 2015; $1,028, MS-66, August 2015; $705, MS-65, January 2015													
1852, Proof (d)		0	n/a								—		
Auctions: No auction records available.													
1853	11,400,000	864	54.7	68%	$25	$45	$50	$60	$80	$150	$180	$275	$800
Auctions: $1,233, MS-66, June 2015; $587, MS-65, October 2015; $423, MS-64, January 2015; $152, AU-58, September 2015													
1853, Repunched Date (e)	(f)	0	n/a						$100	$200	$260	$300	$1,000
Auctions: No auction records available.													
1854	671,000	379	59.6	75%	$40	$55	$60	$70	$120	$225	$350	$700	$2,500
Auctions: $3,290, MS-66, June 2015; $2,820, MS-65, January 2015; $646, MS-62, September 2015; $199, AU-53, April 2015													
1854, Repunched Date (g)	(h)	0	n/a						$185	$325	$500	$800	$3,500
Auctions: No auction records available.													
1854, Proof	25–35	8	64.1								$12,000	$15,000	$35,000
Auctions: $41,125, PF-65, June 2014; $14,688, PF-64, October 2014													
1855	139,000	148	54.4	56%	$40	$65	$75	$125	$200	$350	$600	$1,100	$7,500
Auctions: $9,400, MS-66, August 2015; $1,645, MS-64, January 2015; $399, AU-55, April 2015; $305, EF-45, July 2015													
1855, Proof	30–40	24	64.8								$5,000	$8,500	$14,000
Auctions: $21,150, PF-66Cam, October 2014; $8,225, PF-64, October 2014													
1856	1,458,000	347	58.3	71%	$40	$45	$50	$70	$120	$235	$360	$700	$3,000
Auctions: $1,292, MS-64, July 2015; $1,086, MS-64, October 2015; $329, MS-62, May 2015; $352, AU-58, April 2015													
1856, Proof	40–50	31	64.5								$4,300	$6,500	$17,000
Auctions: $21,738, PF-66, January 2014													
1857	1,042,000	355	58.5	77%	$40	$45	$50	$70	$120	$235	$360	$700	$2,500
Auctions: $5,405, MS-66, January 2015; $2,820, MS-65, September 2015; $940, MS-64, October 2015; $646, AU-58, April 2015													
1857, Proof	60–80	37	64.6								$3,750	$5,000	$12,000
Auctions: $15,863, PF-66, June 2014													
1858	1,603,700	635	57.8	69%	$40	$45	$50	$70	$120	$235	$360	$700	$2,500
Auctions: $5,875, MS-67, July 2015; $1,821, MS-65, February 2015; $1,116, MS-64, September 2015; $353, AU-58, April 2015													
1858, Proof	210	107	64.6								$2,750	$4,500	$7,500
Auctions: $12,925, PF-67, August 2015; $6,462, PF-65, October 2015													
1859	364,200	335	60.8	79%	$40	$45	$50	$60	$90	$175	$215	$300	$1,000
Auctions: $1,762, MS-66, January 2015; $1,645, MS-66, September 2015; $881, MS-65, October 2015; $763, MS-65, August 2015													
1859, Proof	800	116	64.1								$750	$1,100	$2,000
Auctions: $4,700, PF-66Cam, August 2015; $2,643, PF-66, June 2015; $1,880, PF-65, January 2015; $1,586, PF-64Cam, February 2015													
1860	286,000	333	58.4	65%	$40	$45	$50	$60	$90	$175	$215	$300	$1,000
Auctions: $434, MS-64, October 2015; $317, MS-63, April 2015; $211, MS-61, May 2015; $166, AU-55, January 2015													
1860, Proof	1,000	78	63.8								$750	$1,200	$4,500
Auctions: $4,935, PF-65, August 2015													

b. An inverted 2 is visible beneath the primary 1. "A secondary date punch was obviously punched into the die in an inverted orientation and then corrected after some effacing of the die" (*Cherrypickers' Guide to Rare Die Varieties,* sixth edition, volume I). c. Included in circulation-strike 1852 mintage figure. d. 1 example is known. e. Secondary digits are visible to the north of the primary 1 and 8. This repunched date can be detected on lower-grade coins. f. Included in 1853 mintage figure. g. Secondary digits are visible to the west of the primary digits on the 8 and 5. h. Included in circulation-strike 1854 mintage figure.

1862, 2 Over 1
FS-3S-1862-301.

	Mintage	Cert	Avg	%MS	G-4	VG-8	F-12	VF-20	EF-40	AU-50	MS-60	MS-63	MS-65
											PF-63	PF-64	PF-65
1861	497,000	842	60.9	78%	$40	$45	$50	$60	$90	$175	$215	$300	$1,000
Auctions: $2,938, MS-67, June 2015; $1,410, MS-66, January 2015; $519, MS-64, August 2015; $164, AU-53, May 2015
1861, Proof	1,000	91	64.1								$750	$1,000	$2,000
Auctions: $3,055, PF-66, June 2015; $2,351, PF-66, September 2015; $1,175, PF-65, January 2015
1862, 2 Over 1 (i)	(j)	334	63.6	91%	$40	$45	$50	$60	$95	$190	$240	$350	$1,050
Auctions: $1,762, MS-66, June 2015; $881, MS-65, August 2015; $540, MS-64, February 2015; $329, AU-58, April 2015
1862	343,000	1,131	62.7	89%	$40	$45	$50	$60	$90	$175	$215	$285	$950
Auctions: $2,585, MS-67, September 2015; $1,116, MS-66, June 2015; $734, MS-65, January 2015; $223, AU-58, April 2015
1862, Proof	550	139	64.1								$750	$1,000	$2,000
Auctions: $2,127, PF-66, October 2015; $2,115, PF-65, January 2015; $1,527, PF-65, August 2015; $646, PF-63, June 2015
1863	21,000	86	64.2	97%	$300	$325	$350	$375	$435	$550	$800	$1,100	$2,250
Auctions: $7,050, MS-67, January 2015; $5,875, MS-67, October 2015
1863, So-Called 3 Over 2, Proof	(k)	0	n/a								$1,800	$3,600	$6,250
Auctions: $8,812, PF-67, January 2015; $5,875, PF-65, August 2015; $5,405, PF-64, October 2015
1863, Proof	460	140	64.3								$750	$1,000	$1,400
Auctions: $3,995, PF-66Cam, January 2015; $1,703, PF-65Cam, January 2015
1864	12,000	91	63.4	92%	$300	$325	$350	$375	$435	$550	$650	$1,000	$2,250
Auctions: $3,760, MS-66, October 2015; $1,116, MS-63, June 2015; $1,880, AU-58, January 2015
1864, Proof	470	175	64.6								$750	$1,000	$1,400
Auctions: $2,585, PF-66, August 2015; $3,055, PF-65Cam, January 2015; $1,116, PF-65, July 2015; $1,088, PF-64Cam, August 2015
1865	8,000	108	62.6	87%	$325	$350	$425	$450	$475	$575	$675	$1,100	$2,500
Auctions: $5,170, MS-67, August 2015; $4,230, MS-66, October 2015; $1,527, MS-64, January 2015; $2,232, MS-63, January 2015
1865, Proof	500	155	64.4								$750	$1,000	$1,400
Auctions: $3,642, PF-67, October 2015; $3,995, PF-66, June 2015; $1,645, PF-65, August 2015; $3,290, PF-64, January 2015
1866	22,000	84	62.9	88%	$300	$325	$350	$400	$425	$500	$600	$1,000	$2,500
Auctions: $11,750, MS-67, October 2015; $8,812, MS-66, October 2015; $998, EF-40, January 2015; $940, EF-40, July 2015
1866, Proof	725	208	64.2								$750	$1,000	$1,400
Auctions: $6,462, PF-67, January 2015; $1,762, PF-66, August 2015; $1,292, PF-64, September 2015; $705, PF-63, July 2015
1867	4,000	43	62.3	86%	$325	$350	$425	$450	$475	$525	$675	$1,300	$7,500
Auctions: $14,100, MS-65, October 2015; $4,465, MS-64, August 2015; $3,643, MS-64, September 2015; $1,292, AU-50, July 2015
1867, Proof	625	264	64.4								$750	$1,000	$1,400
Auctions: $1,762, PF-66, September 2015; $1,527, PF-65, August 2015; $998, PF-64, January 2015; $822, PF-64, July 2015

i. A secondary 1 is evident beneath the 2 of the date. "This overdate is believed to be due more to economy (the Mint having used a good die another year) than to error. Circulated examples are about as common as the regular-dated coin" (*Cherrypickers' Guide to Rare Die Varieties*, sixth edition, volume I). **j.** Included in circulation-strike 1862 mintage figure. **k.** Included in 1863, Proof, mintage figure.

	Mintage	Cert	Avg	%MS	F-12	VF-20	EF-40	AU-50	MS-60	MS-63	MS-64	MS-65	MS-66
											PF-63	PF-64	PF-65
1868	3,500	35	60.7	86%	$425	$450	$475	$550	$690	$1,400	$2,300	$6,250	$15,000
Auctions: $21,150, MS-66, October 2015; $10,575, MS-64, January 2015; $5,405, AU-58, July 2015													
1868, Proof	600	274	64.1								$750	$1,000	$1,400
Auctions: $3,525, PF-66, October 2015; $1,410, PF-66, January 2015; $1,997, PF-65, August 2015; $940, PF-63, September 2015													
1869	4,500	49	62.4	86%	$425	$475	$525	$600	$700	$1,400	$2,100	$3,200	$5,750
Auctions: $9,987, MS-65, October 2015; $4,230, MS-64, October 2015; $1,645, MS-62, August 2015; $940, EF-40, July 2015													
1869, Proof	600	181	64.4								$750	$1,000	$1,400
Auctions: $7,050, PF-67, August 2015; $1,880, PF-66, January 2015; $1,645, PF-65, October 2015; $423, PF-62, June 2015													
1869, So-Called 9 Over 8, Proof (a)	(b)	0	n/a								$2,000	$3,000	$5,750
Auctions: $9,987, PF-66, August 2015													
1870	3,000	91	61.7	80%	$425	$450	$475	$550	$675	$1,300	$1,850	$4,800	$6,250
Auctions: $7,116, MS-66, October 2015; $470, EF-40, May 2015													
1870, Proof	1,000	243	64.1								$750	$1,000	$1,400
Auctions: $1,880, PF-66, January 2015; $1,762, PF-65, September 2015; $1,762, PF-64, October 2015; $3,055, PF-63, October 2015													
1871	3,400	158	63.7	92%	$425	$450	$475	$500	$650	$1,000	$1,400	$1,950	$3,000
Auctions: $3,290, MS-67, June 2015; $1,880, MS-66, February 2015; $1,645, MS-64, January 2015; $1,086, MS-63, November 2015													
1871, Proof	960	231	64.1								$750	$1,000	$1,400
Auctions: $2,291, PF-66, January 2015; $1,527, PF-65, September 2015; $881, PF-63, July 2015; $646, PF-61, June 2015													
1872	1,000	48	61.5	85%	$450	$475	$500	$600	$1,000	$1,800	$2,500	$5,200	$9,000
Auctions: $54,050, MS-67, February 2015; $14,100, MS-67, August 2015; $4,935, MS-65, October 2015; $2,540, AU-50, January 2015													
1872, Proof	950	233	64.2								$750	$1,000	$1,400
Auctions: $11,750, PF-67Cam, January 2015; $2,585, PF-66, August 2015; $3,290, PF-65, October 2015; $1,645, PF-65, August 2015													
1873, Close 3, Proof (a)	600	380	64.1								$2,000	$2,500	$2,800
Auctions: $3,055, PF-66Cam, June 2015													

a. Proof only. **b.** Included in 1869, Proof, mintage figure.

NICKEL THREE-CENT PIECES (1865–1889)

Designer: *James B. Longacre.* **Weight:** *1.94 grams.* **Composition:** *.750 copper, .250 nickel.*
Diameter: *17.9 mm.* **Edge:** *Plain.* **Mint:** *Philadelphia.*

Circulation Strike

Proof

History. The copper-nickel three-cent coin debuted in the final year of the Civil War, 1865. The American public was still hoarding silver coins (a situation that would continue until 1876), including the silver three-cent piece. The highest-denomination coin remaining in circulation at the time was the recently introduced two-cent piece. After 1875, when silver coins circulated once again, the three-cent denomination became redundant and mintages dropped. The last pieces were coined in 1889.

Striking and Sharpness. On the obverse check the hair and other portrait details. On the reverse the tiny vertical lines in the Roman numeral III can be weak. Check the denticles on both sides of the coin. Among circulation strikes, clashed dies are common, particularly for the earlier high-mintage years. Generally, coins of the 1860s and 1870s have weakness in one area or another. Many if not most of the 1880s are well struck. Proofs from 1878 onward often have satiny or frosty fields, rather than mirrored surfaces, and resemble circulation strikes.

Availability. Circulated examples of dates from 1865 to the mid-1870s are readily available. MS coins, particularly from the 1860s, are easily found, but often have areas of weakness or lack aesthetic appeal. MS coins of the 1880s are readily found for most dates (except for 1883, 1884, 1885, and 1887), some of them probably sold as Proofs. Many Proofs of the era had slight to extensive mint luster. Proofs were struck of all dates and can be found easily enough in the marketplace. The rarest is the first year of issue, 1865, of which only an estimated 500 or so were made. The vast majority of 1865s have a repunched date. Second rarest (not counting PF-only date of 1877) is the 1887 (perfect date, not the overdate) with a production of about 1,000 coins. Proofs of the years 1865 to 1876 can be difficult to find as true gems, while later Proofs are nearly all gems.

GRADING STANDARDS

MS-60 to 70 (Mint State). *Obverse and Reverse:* Mint luster is complete in the obverse and reverse fields. Lower grades such as MS–60, 61, and 62 can show some evidence of abrasion. This is usually on the area of the hair to the right of the face (on the obverse), and on the highest parts of the wreath (on the reverse). Abrasion can appear as scattered contact marks elsewhere. At MS-63, these marks are few, and on MS-65

1865. Graded MS-61.

they are fewer yet. In grades above MS-65, marks can only be seen under magnification.

AU-50, 53, 55, 58 (About Uncirculated). *Obverse:* Light wear is seen on the portrait, most notably on the upper cheek and on the hair to the right of the face. Mint luster is present in the fields, ranging from partial at AU-50 to nearly complete at AU-58. All details are sharp, unless lightly struck. *Reverse:* Light wear is seen on the top and bottom horizontal edges of the III and the wreath. Luster is partial at AU-50, increasing

1881. Graded AU-55.

to nearly full at AU-58. All details are sharp, unless lightly struck.

EF-40, 45 (Extremely Fine). *Obverse:* More wear is seen on the cheek and the hair to the right of the face and neck. The hair to the right of the coronet beads shows light wear. *Reverse:* The wreath still shows most detail on the leaves. Some wear is seen on the vertical lines within III (but striking can also cause weakness). Overall the reverse appears to be very bold.

1889. Graded EF-40.

VF-20, 30 (Very Fine). *Obverse:* Most hair detail is gone, with a continuous flat area to the right of the face and neck, where the higher hair strands have blended together. The hair to the right of the coronet beads shows about half of the strands. *Reverse:* Higher details of the leaves are worn away; the central ridges are seen on some. Wear on the vertical lines in III has caused some to merge, but most are separate.

1880. Graded VF-25.

F-12, 15 (Fine). *Obverse:* Wear is more extensive. The forehead blends into the hair above it. About 10% to 29% of the hair detail to the right of the coronet remains, and much detail is seen lower, at the right edge opposite the ear and neck. Denticles are distinct. *Reverse:* The top (highest-relief) part of most leaves is flat. Many vertical lines in III are fused. Denticles are distinct.

1882. Graded F-15.

VG-8, 10 (Very Good). *Obverse:* Less hair detail shows. Denticles all are clear. *Reverse:* The leaves show more wear. The inner edges of some leaves are worn away, causing leaves to merge. Only about half, or slightly fewer, of the lines in III are discernible.

1865. Graded VG-10.

G-4, 6 (Good). *Obverse:* Most hair details are gone, but some remain at the lower right. The rim is worn smooth in areas, and many denticles are missing. The lettering is weak, but readable. *Reverse:* The leaves mostly are worn flat. Very few lines remain in III. The rim is worn smooth in areas, and many denticles are missing.

1867. Graded G-4.

AG-3 (About Good). *Obverse:* The rim is worn away and into the tops of most of the letters. The date remains bold. *Reverse:* The rim is worn away and into some of the leaves.

1867. Graded AG-3.

PF-60 to 70 (Proof). *Obverse and Reverse:* PF–60, 61, and 62 coins show varying amounts of hairlines in the field, decreasing as the grade increases. Fields may be dull or cloudy on lower-level pieces. At PF-65, hairlines are visible only under magnification and are very light; the cheek of Miss Liberty does not show any friction or "album slide marks." Above PF-65, hairlines become fewer, and in ultra-high grades are nonexistent, this mean-

1878. Graded PF-65.

ing that the coins have never been subject to wiping or abrasive cleaning. At PF-65 or better, expect excellent aesthetic appeal. Blotched, deeply toned, or recolored coins are sometimes seen at Proof levels from PF–60 through 65 or even 66 and should be avoided, but these are less often seen than on contemporary Proof nickel five-cent pieces.

1866, Doubled-Die Obverse
FS-3N-1866-101.

	Mintage	Cert	Avg	%MS	G-4	VG-8	VF-20	EF-40	AU-50	MS-60	MS-63 / PF-63	MS-65 / PF-65	MS-66 / PF-66
1865	11,382,000	1,996	59.8	78%	$15	$20	$30	$40	$65	$100	$160	$550	$1,200
	Auctions: $1,880, MS-66, January 2015; $399, MS-64, May 2015; $199, MS-61, November 2015; $111, AU-58, June 2015												
1865, Proof	500+	198	64.7								$1,500	$5,000	$8,000
	Auctions: $3,995, PF-66, September 2015; $3,760, PF-65, February 2015; $3,760, PF-65, September 2015; $2,820, PF-65, September 2015												
1866	4,801,000	788	60.1	81%	$18	$20	$28	$40	$65	$100	$160	$550	$1,500
	Auctions: $7,637, MS-67, August 2015; $1,527, MS-66, June 2015; $111, MS-63, February 2015; $89, MS-62, April 2015												
1866, Doubled-Die Obverse (a)	(b)	5	48.4	20%				$150	$250	$350	$450	$1,000	
	Auctions: No auction records available.												
1866, Proof	725+	298	64.5								$350	$1,100	$2,000
	Auctions: $2,820, PF-66, January 2015; $1,880, PF-66, September 2015; $1,527, PF-65, August 2015; $1,292, PF-65, June 2015												

a. Moderate doubling is visible on AMERICA and on portions of the hair. "The dies clashed midway through the obverse's life. Mid– and late–die-state coins exhibit the clash marks and die cracks as progression occurs. This variety has proven extremely scarce" (*Cherrypickers' Guide to Rare Die Varieties*, sixth edition, volume I). b. Included in circulation-strike 1866 mintage figure.

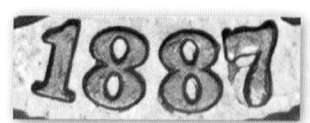

1887, 7 Over 6, Proof
FS-3N-1887-302.

	Mintage	Cert	Avg	%MS	G-4	VG-8	VF-20	EF-40	AU-50	MS-60	MS-63	MS-65	MS-66
											PF-63	PF-65	PF-66
1867	3,915,000	608	59.3	75%	$15	$20	$30	$40	$65	$100	$160	$700	$1,800
	Auctions: $238, MS-64, January 2015; $141, MS-63, February 2015; $111, MS-62, May 2015; $79, AU-58, August 2015												
1867, Proof	625+	314	64.7								$350	$850	$1,500
	Auctions: $9,400, PF-68, July 2015; $1,880, PF-66, January 2015; $1,527, PF-66, September 2015; $763, PF-65, August 2015												
1868	3,252,000	573	60.2	79%	$15	$20	$30	$40	$65	$100	$160	$600	$1,200
	Auctions: $881, MS-66, August 2015; $822, MS-65, January 2015; $111, MS-63, February 2015; $117, MS-62, April 2015												
1868, Proof	600+	294	64.8								$350	$1,100	$1,600
	Auctions: $1,065, PF-66, January 2015; $1,116, PF-65, September 2015; $705, PF-65, August 2015; $446, PF-64, January 2015												
1869	1,604,000	391	60.8	82%	$15	$20	$30	$40	$65	$125	$185	$750	$1,500
	Auctions: $1,292, MS-66, August 2015; $141, MS-63, February 2015; $105, MS-62, February 2015; $129, MS-61, November 2015												
1869, Proof	600+	380	64.7								$350	$750	$1,250
	Auctions: $5,170, PF-67, July 2015; $881, PF-66, January 2015; $1,028, PF-65, October 2015; $705, PF-65, January 2015												
1870	1,335,000	411	60.9	82%	$20	$25	$30	$40	$65	$140	$195	$725	$1,450
	Auctions: $223, MS-64, March 2015; $164, MS-63, November 2015; $129, MS-62, May 2015; $84, AU-58, April 2015												
1870, Proof	1,000+	350	64.5								$350	$850	$1,250
	Auctions: $1,175, PF-66, January 2015; $763, PF-65, September 2015; $329, PF-64, April 2015; $235, MS-61, November 2015												
1871	604,000	239	60.7	84%	$20	$25	$30	$40	$65	$140	$195	$750	$1,500
	Auctions: $3,525, MS-67, January 2015; $2,723, MS-66, September 2015; $2,350, MS-66, February 2015; $282, MS-64, May 2015												
1871, Proof	960+	381	64.5								$350	$800	$1,250
	Auctions: $5,875, PF-67Cam, October 2015; $940, PF-66, February 2015; $763, PF-65, January 2015; $258, PF-63, November 2015												
1872	862,000	189	60.0	78%	$20	$25	$30	$40	$65	$150	$210	$1,200	$2,200
	Auctions: $881, MS-66, January 2015; $940, MS-65, October 2015; $211, MS-63, May 2015; $117, MS-62, July 2015												
1872, Proof	950+	434	64.5								$350	$750	$1,150
	Auctions: $4,700, PF-66, February 2015; $1,600, PF-66, July 2015; $505, PF-65, June 2015; $293, PF-63, November 2015												
1873, Close 3	390,000	105	56.9	69%	$20	$25	$30	$40	$65	$150	$210	$1,400	$2,750
	Auctions: $2,232, MS-66, August 2015; $423, MS-64, June 2015; $399, MS-64, October 2015; $237, MS-63, February 2015												
1873, Open 3	783,000	89	56.0	73%	$20	$25	$30	$40	$70	$160	$350	$2,750	$7,500
	Auctions: $3,055, MS-65, January 2015; $587, MS-64, June 2015; $223, MS-63, October 2015; $199, MS-63, May 2015												
1873, Close 3, Proof	1,100+	445	64.4								$350	$750	$1,250
	Auctions: $969, PF-66, August 2015; $734, PF-65, June 2015; $540, PF-65, January 2015; $290, PF-64, November 2015												
1874	790,000	187	58.5	73%	$20	$25	$30	$40	$65	$150	$210	$1,200	$2,000
	Auctions: $2,115, MS-66, October 2015; $188, MS-63, August 2015; $176, MS-62, January 2015; $79, AU-58, February 2015												
1874, Proof	700+	344	64.7								$350	$750	$1,100
	Auctions: $601, PF-66, January 2015; $564, PF-66, October 2015; $587, PF-65, June 2015; $329, PF-64, April 2015												
1875	228,000	232	62.2	90%	$20	$25	$35	$45	$80	$175	$225	$800	$1,500
	Auctions: $646, MS-65, August 2015; $329, MS-64, November 2015; $446, AU-58, April 2015; $129, AU-55, May 2015												
1875, Proof	700+	268	64.4								$350	$1,100	$1,650
	Auctions: $998, PF-65, January 2015; $646, PF-65, June 2015; $470, PF-64, January 2015; $305, PF-64, October 2015												
1876	162,000	123	58.4	73%	$20	$25	$35	$50	$110	$200	$260	$1,600	$2,250
	Auctions: $1,880, MS-66, June 2015; $1,292, MS-65, February 2015; $940, MS-64, July 2015; $616, AU-58, May 2015												
1876, Proof	1,150+	414	64.6								$350	$750	$1,100
	Auctions: $1,057, PF-66, September 2015; $881, PF-66, July 2015; $517, PF-65, January 2015; $540, PF-64, May 2015												
1877, Proof (c)	900	467	64.9								$2,000	$3,750	$5,000
	Auctions: $9,987, PF-67Cam, August 2015; $3,525, PF-66Cam, January 2015; $2,820, PF-66, October 2015; $3,760, PF-65Cam, June 2015												
1878, Proof (c)	2,350	692	64.8								$1,000	$1,100	$1,350
	Auctions: $1,527, PF-67, August 2015; $822, PF-66, October 2015; $646, PF-63, January 2015; $374, PF-60, May 2015												

c. Proof only.

	Mintage	Cert	Avg	%MS	G-4	VG-8	VF-20	EF-40	AU-50	MS-60	MS-63 / PF-63	MS-65 / PF-65	MS-66 / PF-66
1879	38,000	176	57.7	72%	$60	$70	$90	$125	$175	$300	$400	$850	$1,200
Auctions: $998, MS-66, July 2015; $1,057, MS-65, August 2015; $575, MS-65, January 2015; $258, AU-53, May 2015
1879, Proof	3,200	944	65.1								$400	$650	$800
Auctions: $2,820, PF-68, January 2015; $998, PF-67, July 2015; $675, PF-66Cam, August 2015; $411, PF-65, May 2015
1880	21,000	198	59.0	78%	$90	$110	$150	$200	$220	$350	$410	$850	$1,250
Auctions: $705, MS-65, August 2015; $564, MS-64, January 2015; $296, MS-63, October 2015; $211, MS-60, May 2015
1880, Proof	3,955	977	65.0								$400	$600	$800
Auctions: $540, PF-66, June 2015; $470, PF-66, January 2015; $376, PF-65, November 2015; $298, PF-64, April 2015
1881	1,077,000	603	59.3	73%	$20	$25	$30	$40	$65	$125	$185	$650	$1,000
Auctions: $493, MS-65, July 2015; $152, MS-63, July 2015; $94, MS-62, August 2015; $89, AU-58, October 2015
1881, Proof	3,575	1,005	65.2								$375	$600	$800
Auctions: $3,760, PF-68, February 2015; $1,057, PF-67, February 2015; $587, PF-66, January 2015; $282, PF-63, April 2015
1882	22,200	118	50.0	42%	$110	$125	$180	$225	$275	$400	$500	$1,200	$2,500
Auctions: $587, MS-64, January 2015; $199, VF-30, February 2015; $164, VF-25, October 2015; $164, F-15, July 2015
1882, Proof	3,100	1,029	65.1								$400	$600	$800
Auctions: $4,230, PF-68, January 2015; $446, PF-65, March 2015; $258, PF-62, August 2015; $199, PF-60, May 2015
1883	4,000	49	53.2	49%	$175	$225	$350	$500	$700	$1,200	$2,500	$5,000	$15,000
Auctions: $15,275, MS-66, September 2015; $2,820, MS-62, July 2015; $822, AU-55, August 2015; $1,057, AU-53, January 2015
1883, Proof	6,609	1,523	64.8								$400	$600	$800
Auctions: $5,287, PF-68, January 2015; $705, PF-66, February 2015; $376, PF-65, November 2015; $235, PF-64, January 2015
1884	1,700	32	51.5	41%	$450	$500	$650	$850	$1,250	$2,500	$5,500	$12,500	$20,000
Auctions: $3,055, MS-61, January 2015; $2,585, MS-61, June 2015; $1,997, EF-45, February 2015; $1,292, EF-40, January 2015
1884, Proof	3,942	1,179	64.8								$400	$600	$800
Auctions: $998, PF-67, October 2015; $734, PF-66, August 2015; $376, PF-65, January 2015; $305, PF-64, February 2015
1885	1,000	36	57.2	67%	$500	$650	$1,200	$2,000	$3,000	$4,500	$6,000	$12,500	$17,500
Auctions: $16,450, MS-66, June 2015; $5,170, MS-62, January 2015; $3,055, EF-45, July 2015
1885, Proof	3,790	996	64.7								$400	$600	$800
Auctions: $646, PF-66, June 2015; $340, PF-64, February 2015; $329, PF-64, January 2015; $258, PF-60, August 2015
1886, Proof (c)	4,290	1,053	64.7								$400	$650	$825
Auctions: $900, PF-67, January 2015; $505, PF-66, January 2015; $517, PF-65, August 2015; $329, PF-64, February 2015
1887	5,001	114	55.9	61%	$275	$325	$350	$400	$500	$550	$675	$1,500	$2,250
Auctions: $1,703, MS-66, August 2015; $763, MS-63, July 2015; $705, EF-45, January 2015
1887, Proof	2,960	357	64.3								$400	$850	$1,000
Auctions: $1,880, PF-67, June 2015; $540, PF-65, July 2015; $517, PF-65, January 2015; $423, PF-64, May 2015
1887, 7 Over 6, Proof (d)	(e)	492	64.9								$425	$750	$950
Auctions: $2,585, PF-66, August 2015; $998, PF-66, October 2015; $517, PF-64Cam, January 2015; $376, PF-62, August 2015
1888	36,501	303	59.4	69%	$50	$65	$75	$90	$150	$300	$400	$850	$1,350
Auctions: $1,527, MS-67, January 2015; $564, MS-65, September 2015; $305, MS-63, May 2015; $446, AU-58, February 2015
1888, Proof	4,582	1,074	64.8								$400	$600	$800
Auctions: $3,055, PF-68, October 2015; $1,762, PF-67, February 2015; $600, PF-66, January 2015; $446, PF-65, February 2015
1889	18,125	246	59.8	68%	$80	$100	$135	$220	$250	$350	$450	$850	$1,350
Auctions: $1,645, MS-66, January 2015; $795, MS-66, June 2015; $188, AU-55, May 2015; $176, AU-50, July 2015
1889, Proof	3,436	1,064	65.0								$400	$600	$800
Auctions: $734, PF-67, January 2015; $646, PF-66, August 2015; $399, PF-65, September 2015; $282, PF-64, January 2015

c. Proof only. d. Strong remnants of the underlying 6 are evident on either side of the lower portion of the 7, with the 1 and both 8's clearly repunched. This Proof overdate is relatively common; note that the regular date can be valued higher than the variety. e. Included in 1887, Proof, mintage figure.

Nickel
Five-Cent Pieces
1866 to Date

AN OVERVIEW OF NICKEL FIVE-CENT PIECES

Five-cent pieces made of nickel were introduced in 1866, in an era in which the silver half dime as well as other silver denominations were not seen in circulation. More than a dozen designs and their variations have graced the "nickel" in the past 140-plus years.

While Shield nickels of both varieties are slightly scarce in upper Mint State levels, they are within the financial reach of most collectors. Proofs are available of each variety, but the 1866–1867, With Rays, and the 1913 Buffalo, Variety 1, issues are rare.

The quality of strike presents a challenge across the various types of nickel five-cent pieces, most particularly with the 1866–1867, With Rays, for there are fewer possibilities from which to choose. Although 1913–1938 Buffalo, Variety 2, nickels are often poorly struck, there are enough sharp ones that finding a choice example should present no great challenge for the collector.

FOR THE COLLECTOR AND INVESTOR: FIVE-CENT PIECES AS A SPECIALTY

Shield nickels of the 1866–1883 era are often collected by date sequence. A full set includes 1866 and 1867, With Rays, plus 1867 to 1883, Without Rays. In addition, there is the 1879, 9 Over 8, overdate, which is found only in Proof format but is readily available (constituting perhaps a third or so of the Proof mintage of 3,200 for the 1879 year) and the 1883, 3 Over 2 (scarce, and available only as a circulation strike).

Circulation strikes are available of all Shield nickel dates, 1866 to 1883, except 1877 and 1878, which were made only in Proof format. A set of Proofs can be completed except for the 1867, With Rays, which is exceedingly rare in Proof, with an estimated population of fewer than two dozen coins. Most 1878 Proofs are frosty and appear not much different from Mint State, but only Proofs were made this year.

In circulated grades, Shield nickels are available in proportion to their mintage figures. The dates 1879 to 1881 had high Proof mintages (in the context of Proof figures), but low circulation-strike mintages, and thus they are key dates in the latter format. In other words, a gem MS-65 1880 Shield nickel (16,000 coined, but few were saved, as collectors acquired Proofs instead) is exceedingly rare today. In the same year 3,955 Proofs were struck, all were preserved by collectors and dealers, and today the Proof 1880 is one of the most plentiful dates.

Liberty Head nickels of the 1883, Without CENTS (or "No CENTS"), variety are plentiful in Mint State and also in Proof. Later dates With CENTS, through 1912, are generally available in proportion to their mintages. The 1885 and 1886 are considered to be key dates. Proofs are readily collectible, although pristine high-quality examples can be hard to find. The 1912-D and 1912-S are scarce. In 1913 an estimated five Liberty Head nickels were privately made, and today stand as famous rarities.

Among Buffalo nickels, 1913 to 1938, the different dates and mints can be collected easily enough in circulated grades, although certain issues such as 1913-S, Variety 2; 1921-S; and 1926-S are on the scarce side. An overdate, 1918-D, 8 Over 7, is a rarity at all grade levels. Curious varieties are provided by the very rare 1916, Doubled Date; the scarce 1937-D, 3-Legged (the die was heavily polished, resulting in some loss of detail); and the fascinating and readily available 1938-D, D Over S, overmintmark.

In choice or gem Mint State most branch-mint Buffalo nickels, 1914–1927, are fairly scarce, and some are

Popularized in the 1890s and throughout the beginning of the 1900s, coin-operated machines took cents and other denominations, but the coin of choice was the nickel. Pictured is a postcard for Horn & Hardart restaurants, 1930s, where patrons would serve themselves with such coin-operated devices.

quite rare. Most branch-mint coins of the 1920s are lightly struck in one area or another, with the 1926-D being particularly infamous in this regard. Sharply struck examples of such varieties are worth much more than lightly struck ones, although the grading services take no particular note of such differences. Matte Proofs of dates 1913 to 1916 were struck, and mirror-finish Proofs were made in 1936 and 1937. These exist today in proportion to their mintages.

Jefferson nickels from 1938 to date are readily collectible in Mint State and Proof format. Many otherwise common varieties can be very rare if sharply struck.

SHIELD (1866–1883)

Designer: *James B. Longacre.* **Weight:** *5 grams.* **Composition:** *.750 copper, .250 nickel.*
Diameter: *20.5 mm.* **Edge:** *Plain.* **Mint:** *Philadelphia.*

Variety 1, Rays Between Stars
(1866–1867)

Variety 1, Rays Between Stars,
Proof

Variety 2, Without Rays
(1867–1883)

Variety 2, Without Rays, Proof

History. The nickel five-cent piece was introduced in 1866. At the time, silver coins (except the trime) did not circulate in the East or Midwest. The new denomination proved popular, and "nickels" of the Shield variety were made continuously from 1866 to 1883. All 1866 nickels have rays between the stars on the reverse, as do a minority of 1867 issues, after which this feature was dropped. In 1877 and 1878 only Proofs were made, with no circulation strikes. The design, by Chief Engraver James B. Longacre, is somewhat similar to the obverse of the two-cent piece. Some Shield nickels were still seen in circulation in the 1930s, by which time most had been worn nearly smooth.

Striking and Sharpness. Sharpness can be a problem for Shield nickels in the 1860s through 1876, much less so for later years. On the obverse the horizontal shield stripes, vertical stripes, and leaves should be checked. The horizontal stripes in particular can be blended together. On the reverse the star centers can be weak. Check all other areas as well. Die cracks are seen on *most* circulation-strike Shield nickels, and do not affect value. Proof Shield nickels were struck of all dates 1866 to 1883, including two varieties of 1867 (With Rays, a great rarity, and the usually seen Without Rays). Fields range from deeply mirrorlike to somewhat grainy in character to mirror-surface, depending on a given year. Many of 1878, a date struck only in Proof format, have *lustrous* surfaces or prooflike surfaces combined with some luster, resembling a circulation strike. While most Proofs are sharp, some have weakness on the shield on the obverse and/or the star centers on the reverse. Lint marks or tiny recessed marks from scattered debris on the die faces are sometimes encountered, especially on issues of the 1870s, but not factored into the grade in commercial certification unless excessive.

Availability. Circulated coins generally are available in proportion to their mintage quantities (exceptions being the 1873, Open 3, and 1873, Close 3, varieties, which tend to be elusive in all grades despite their relatively high mintage). MS coins are similarly available, except that 1880 is a rarity. Those dated 1882 and 1883 are plentiful.

Grading Standards

MS-60 to 70 (Mint State). *Obverse and Reverse:* At MS-60 some abrasion and very minor contact marks are evident, most noticeably on high points of the shield on the obverse and the field on the reverse. Sometimes light striking on the shield and stars can be mistaken for light wear, and marks on the numeral 5 on the reverse can be from the original planchet surface not struck up fully. At MS-63 abrasions are hard to detect except

1873, Open 3. Graded MS-66.

under magnification. An MS-65 coin will have no abrasion. Luster should be full and rich (not grainy). Grades above MS-65 are defined by having no marks that can be seen by the naked eye. Higher-grade coins display deeper luster or virtually perfect prooflike surfaces, depending on the dies used.

  Illustrated coin: Note the faint golden toning along the obverse border.

AU-50, 53, 55, 58 (About Uncirculated). *Obverse:* Light wear is on the outside edges of the leaves, the frame of the shield, and the horizontal stripes (although the stripes can also be weakly struck). Mint luster is present in the fields, ranging from partial at AU-50 to nearly complete at AU-58. All details are sharp, unless lightly struck. *Reverse:* Light wear is seen on the numeral 5, and friction is seen in the field, identifiable as a change of color (loss of luster).

1867, Rays. Graded AU-58.

Luster is partial at AU-50, increasing to nearly full at AU-58. All details are sharp, unless lightly struck.

EF-40, 45 (Extremely Fine). *Obverse:* Nearly all shield border and leaf detail is visible. Light wear is seen on the shield stripes (but the horizontal stripes can be weakly struck). *Reverse:* More wear is seen on the numeral 5. The radial lines in the stars (if sharply struck to begin with) show slight wear. The field shows more wear.

1867, Rays. Graded EF-40.

VF-20, 30 (Very Fine). *Obverse:* The frame details and leaves show more wear, with much leaf detail gone. The shield stripes show more wear, and some of the vertical lines will begin to blend together. *Reverse:* More wear is seen overall, but some radial detail can still be seen on the stars.

1868. Graded VF-20.

F-12, 15 (Fine). *Obverse:* Most leaves are flat and have little detail, but will remain outlined. The shield frame is mostly flat. Most horizontal lines are blended together, regardless of original strike. Many vertical lines in the stripes are blended together. IN GOD WE TRUST is slightly weak. *Reverse:* All areas are in outline form except for slight traces of the star radials. Lettering is bold.

1867, Without Rays. Graded F-12.

VG-8, 10 (Very Good). *Obverse:* Many leaves are flat and blended with adjacent leaves. The frame is blended and has no details. Only a few horizontal lines may show. Vertical lines in the stripes are mostly blended. IN GOD WE TRUST is weak. *Reverse:* All elements are visible only in outline form. The rim is complete.

1879. Graded VG-10.

G-4, 6 (Good). *Obverse:* The shield and elements are seen in outline form except the vertical stripe separations. IN GOD WE TRUST is weak, and a few letters may be missing. *Reverse:* The rim is mostly if not completely worn away and into the tops of the letters.

 Illustrated coin: Overall this coin is slightly better than G-4, but the 5 in the date is weak, making G-4 an appropriate attribution.

1881. Graded G-4.

AG-3 (About Good). *Obverse:* The rim is worn down and blended with the wreath. Only traces of IN GOD WE TRUST can be seen. The date is fully readable. *Reverse:* The rim is worn down and blended with the letters, some of which may be missing.

1880. Graded AG-3.

PF-60 to 70 (Proof). *Obverse and Reverse:* PF–60, 61, and 62 coins show varying amounts of hairlines in the reverse field in particular, decreasing as the grade increases. Fields may be dull or cloudy on lower-level pieces. At PF-65, hairlines are visible only under magnification and are very light and usually only on the reverse. Above PF-65, hairlines become fewer, and in ultra-high grades are nonexistent, this meaning that the coins have never

1882. Graded PF-66.

been subject to wiping or abrasive cleaning. At PF-65 or better, expect excellent aesthetic appeal.

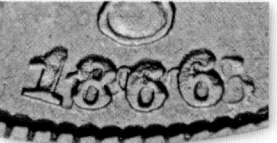

1866, Repunched Date
Several varieties exist.

	Mintage	Cert	Avg	%MS	G-4	VG-8	F-12	VF-20	EF-40	AU-50	MS-60 PF-63	MS-63 PF-65	MS-65 PF-66
1866, Rays	14,742,500	1,676	59.9	77%	$30	$45	$50	$100	$160	$240	$275	$425	$2,000
	Auctions: $2,056, MS-65, January 2015; $616, MS-64, February 2015; $176, MS-60, August 2015; $211, AU-58, May 2015												
1866, Repunched Date (a)	(b)	25	49.7	40%	$60	$100	$175	$250	$450	$1,000	$1,500	$3,500	
	Auctions: $12,925, MS-64, August 2014; $8,813, MS-64, October 2014; $1,293, AU-50, March 2013; $1,175, AU-50, August 2014												
1866, Rays, Proof	600+	273	64.7								$1,850	$3,250	$4,500
	Auctions: $2,585, PF-66, September 2015; $3,055, PF-65, January 2015; $1,997, PF-64, January 2015; $1,057, PF-61, October 2015												

a. There are at least five similar, very strong repunched dates for 1866; the values shown are typical for each. **b.** Included in circulation-strike 1866, Rays, mintage figure.

1873, Close 3	1873, Open 3	1873, Close 3, Doubled-Die Obverse

Several varieties exist. Pictured are
FS-05-1873-101 (left) and FS-05-1873-102 (right).

	Mintage	Cert	Avg	%MS	G-4	VG-8	F-12	VF-20	EF-40	AU-50	MS-60 / PF-63	MS-63 / PF-65	MS-65 / PF-66
1867, Rays	2,019,000	581	58.8	70%	$35	$50	$65	$130	$190	$285	$375	$500	$3,000
Auctions: $998, MS-64, January 2015; $705, MS-64, October 2015; $517, MS-63, June 2015; $117, EF-40, January 2015													
1867, Rays, Proof †	25+	31	64.5								$3,250	$45,000	$65,000
Auctions: $64,625, PF-66, January 2015; $25,850, PF-65, August 2015; $34,075, PF-64, August 2015													
1867, No Rays	28,890,500	896	60.2	76%	$25	$30	$35	$50	$65	$110	$140	$225	$800
Auctions: $1,116, MS-66, October 2015; $705, MS-65, January 2015; $305, MS-64, May 2015; $111, MS-60, February 2015													
1867, No Rays, Proof	600+	259	64.3								$475	$2,000	$3,500
Auctions: $3,760, PF-66, September 2015; $2,115, PF-66, October 2015; $1,410, PF-65, February 2015; $376, PF-63, January 2015													
1867, No Rays, Pattern Reverse, Proof (c)	(d)	2	65.5	100%							$6,500	$14,000	
Auctions: $3,760, PF-66, June 2015													
1868	28,817,000	876	60.2	77%	$25	$30	$35	$50	$65	$110	$140	$225	$700
Auctions: $1,762, MS-66, October 2015; $164, MS-63, January 2015; $69, MS-60, May 2015; $111, AU-55, February 2015													
1868, Proof	600+	216	64.7								$385	$1,250	$1,750
Auctions: $1,762, PF-66, September 2015; $1,116, PF-65, June 2015; $822, PF-65, January 2015; $270, PF-63, April 2015													
1869	16,395,000	520	60.2	82%	$25	$30	$35	$50	$65	$110	$140	$225	$750
Auctions: $587, MS-65, September 2015; $246, MS-64, May 2015; $176, AU-58, January 2015; $56, AU-50, February 2015													
1869, Proof	600+	348	64.6								$385	$750	$1,250
Auctions: $3,055, PF-67, June 2015; $1,116, PF-66, July 2015; $881, PF-65, January 2015; $646, PF-65, August 2015													
1870	4,806,000	232	58.7	78%	$30	$35	$60	$80	$90	$140	$210	$300	$1,500
Auctions: $4,465, MS-66, February 2015; $1,292, MS-64, January 2015; $423, MS-64, August 2015; $340, MS-64, March 2015													
1870, Proof	1,000+	317	64.3								$385	$750	$1,250
Auctions: $1,292, PF-66, October 2015; $763, PF-65, January 2015; $646, PF-65, October 2015; $258, PF-63, June 2015													
1871	561,000	102	55.5	68%	$80	$100	$150	$215	$280	$350	$450	$625	$1,500
Auctions: $3,055, MS-65, January 2015; $1,292, MS-65, January 2015; $211, AU-50, January 2015; $123, F-12, June 2015													
1871, Proof	960+	330	64.5								$425	$800	$1,250
Auctions: $1,527, PF-66, September 2015; $1,410, PF-66, August 2015; $881, PF-65, October 2015; $646, PF-65, January 2015													
1872	6,036,000	272	58.8	72%	$35	$45	$75	$100	$125	$175	$235	$300	$1,250
Auctions: $1,997, MS-66, January 2015; $1,410, MS-65, June 2015; $423, MS-64, October 2015; $258, AU-58, April 2015													
1872, Proof	950+	358	64.8								$385	$700	$1,000
Auctions: $3,055, PF-67, July 2015; $2,585, PF-67, September 2015; $998, PF-66, January 2015; $493, PF-65, January 2015													
1873, Close 3	436,050	63	59.8	75%	$30	$40	$60	$100	$140	$200	$325	$585	$2,250
Auctions: $1,997, MS-65, August 2015; $822, MS-64, January 2015													
1873, Close 3, Doubled-Die Obverse (e)	(f)	15	56.9	60%				$600	$1,000	$2,000	$3,500	$7,000	$10,000
Auctions: $1,880, MS-64, February 2015													
1873, Open 3	4,113,950	89	59.6	80%	$30	$35	$60	$80	$100	$140	$210	$300	$2,000
Auctions: $2,115, MS-66, July 2015; $1,880, MS-66, August 2015; $763, MS-64, October 2015; $600, MS-64, May 2015													
1873, Close 3, Proof	1,100+	365	64.5								$385	$700	$1,000
Auctions: $2,820, PF-67, January 2015; $1,292, PF-66, October 2015; $376, PF-64, February 2015; $258, PF-63, May 2015													

† Ranked in the *100 Greatest U.S. Coins* (fourth edition). **c.** These were made from a pattern (Judd-573) reverse die that is slightly different than the regular Without Rays design. **d.** 21 to 30 examples are known. **e.** There are several varieties of 1873, Close 3, Doubled-Die Obverse. The values shown are representative of the more avidly sought varieties; others command smaller premiums. **f.** Included in circulation-strike 1873, Close 3, mintage figure.

1883, 3 Over 2
Several varieties exist, as well as pieces with a recut 3. Pictured are FS-05-1883-301 (left) and FS-05-1883-305 (right).

	Mintage	Cert	Avg	%MS	G-4	VG-8	F-12	VF-20	EF-40	AU-50	MS-60 PF-63	MS-63 PF-65	MS-65 PF-66
1874	3,538,000	167	60.7	79%	$30	$40	$65	$80	$120	$170	$250	$325	$1,500
	Auctions: $5,170, MS-66, October 2015; $881, MS-65, January 2015; $282, MS-63, August 2015; $188, AU-58, January 2015												
1874, Proof	700+	304	64.6								$385	$800	$1,100
	Auctions: $3,290, PF-67, September 2015; $2,115, PF-66, January 2015; $340, PF-64, May 2015; $258, PF-63, January 2015												
1875	2,097,000	161	59.2	79%	$45	$60	$100	$130	$160	$220	$275	$360	$1,500
	Auctions: $5,640, MS-66, January 2015; $3,290, MS-66, October 2015; $229, AU-55, May 2015; $188, AU-50, January 2015												
1875, Proof	700+	293	64.4								$425	$1,250	$1,850
	Auctions: $3,290, PF-67, August 2015; $1,527, PF-66, January 2015; $881, PF-65, July 2015; $517, PF-64, March 2015												
1876	2,530,000	259	61.3	86%	$40	$55	$80	$115	$145	$190	$260	$325	$1,000
	Auctions: $940, MS-65, June 2015; $376, MS-64, August 2015; $105, AU-55, January 2015; $164, AU-50, January 2015												
1876, Proof	1,150+	403	64.6								$385	$750	$1,000
	Auctions: $2,350, PF-67, February 2015; $998, PF-66, July 2015; $763, PF-65, August 2015; $376, PF-64, January 2015												
1877, Proof (g)	900	423	64.5								$3,400	$4,500	$5,000
	Auctions: $9,987, PF-67, September 2015; $6,462, PF-66, July 2015; $4,230, PF-65, June 2015; $3,525, PF-64, January 2015												
1878, Proof (g)	2,350	616	64.4								$1,250	$1,750	$2,000
	Auctions: $1,880, PF-67, January 2015; $2,232, PF-66, July 2015; $1,233, PF-65, January 2015; $1,265, PF-64, June 2015												
1879	25,900	86	56.5	71%	$375	$475	$600	$660	$725	$750	$1,000	$1,250	$2,500
	Auctions: $10,575, MS-67, July 2015; $1,880, MS-63, September 2015; $1,762, MS-62, February 2015; $1,410, AU-55, January 2015												
1879, Proof	3,200	572	64.8								$500	$650	$800
	Auctions: $6,462, PF-68, January 2015; $564, PF-65, August 2015; $352, PF-64, May 2015; $282, PF-62, October 2015												
1879, 9 Over 8, Proof (h)	(i)	0	n/a								$725	$850	$1,100
	Auctions: $2,361, PF-67, June 2015; $646, PF-65, August 2015; $470, PF-64, January 2015; $305, AU-58, November 2015												
1880	16,000	38	46.3	24%	$475	$560	$675	$980	$1,300	$4,000	$6,500	$10,000	$50,000
	Auctions: $117,500, MS-66, January 2015; $3,995, AU-53, October 2015												
1880, Proof	3,955	901	64.0								$500	$700	$850
	Auctions: $6,462, PF-68, January 2015; $3,995, PF-67, October 2015; $505, PF-65, January 2015; $423, PF-64, May 2015												
1881	68,800	160	47.4	49%	$250	$300	$425	$510	$600	$775	$850	$1,000	$1,950
	Auctions: $2,585, MS-66, January 2015; $2,350, MS-66, October 2015; $822, AU-58, January 2015; $940, AU-50, June 2015												
1881, Proof	3,575	827	64.9								$500	$700	$850
	Auctions: $1,292, PF-67, July 2015; $616, PF-66, October 2015; $493, PF-65, January 2015; $250, PF-62, April 2015												
1882	11,472,900	1,065	59.1	81%	$25	$30	$35	$50	$65	$110	$150	$225	$650
	Auctions: $734, MS-66, February 2015; $493, MS-65, January 2015; $235, MS-64, October 2015; $129, MS-62, May 2015												
1882, Proof	3,100	936	65.1								$385	$600	$850
	Auctions: $15,275, PF-67, August 2015; $1,116, PF-66, August 2015; $705, PF-66, January 2015; $352, PF-64, May 2015												
1883	1,451,500	1,758	61.9	83%	$25	$30	$35	$50	$65	$110	$150	$225	$650
	Auctions: $1,057, MS-66, January 2015; $223, MS-64, April 2015; $164, MS-63, September 2015; $84, AU-55, August 2015												
1883, 3 Over 2 (j)	(k)	40	58.3	65%	$250	$325	$650	$950	$1,250	$1,750	$2,100	$2,500	$5,500
	Auctions: $7,050, MS-65, January 2015; $1,527, MS-63, January 2015; $1,292, MS-60, June 2015; $1,175, AU-58, January 2015												
1883, Proof	5,419	1,139	64.8								$385	$600	$850
	Auctions: $6,462, PF-68, January 2015; $470, PF-65, March 2015; $329, PF-64, August 2015; $282, PF-63, October 2015												

g. Proof only. **h.** This variety is confirmed only with Proof finish, although Breen mentions two circulation strikes and further mentions that there are "at least two varieties" (*Walter Breen's Complete Encyclopedia of U.S. and Colonial Coins*). In the *Guide Book of Shield and Liberty Head Nickels*, Bowers discusses research and theories from Breen, DeLorey, Spindel, and Julian, noting that the variety's overdate status is "not determined." **i.** Included in 1879, Proof, mintage figure. **j.** Several varieties exist. For more information, see the *Cherrypickers' Guide to Rare Die Varieties*, sixth edition, volume I. "Beware of 1882 Shield nickels with a filled-in, blobby 2, as these are very frequently offered as 1883, 3 Over 2. This is possibly the single most misunderstood coin in all U.S. coinage." (Howard Spindel, communication to Q. David Bowers, quoted in *A Guide Book of Shield and Liberty Head Nickels*.) **k.** Included in circulation-strike 1883 mintage figure.

LIBERTY HEAD (1883–1912)

Designer: *Charles E. Barber.* **Weight:** *5 grams.* **Composition:** *.750 copper, .250 nickel.*
Diameter: *21.2 mm.* **Edge:** *Plain.* **Mints:** *Philadelphia, Denver, and San Francisco.*

Variety 1, Without CENTS
(1883)

Variety 1, Without CENTS, Proof

Variety 2, With CENTS
(1883–1912)

Mintmark locations is on the reverse, to the left of CENTS.

Variety 2, With CENTS, Proof

History. Liberty Head nickels were popular in their time, minted in large quantities most years, and remained in circulation through the 1940s, by which time most were worn down to grades such as AG-3 and G-4. Stray coins could still be found in the early 1950s. Serious numismatic interest in circulated examples began in the 1930s with the popularity of Whitman and other coin boards, folders, and albums. Many of the scarcer dates were picked from circulation at that time. The five known 1913 Liberty Head nickels were not an authorized Mint issue, and were never placed into circulation.

Striking and Sharpness. Many Liberty Head nickels have areas of light striking. On the obverse, this is often seen at the star centers, particularly near the top border. The hair above the forehead can be light as well, and always is thus on 1912-S (the obverse die on this San Francisco issue is slightly bulged). On the reverse, E PLURIBUS UNUM can vary in sharpness of strike. Weakness is often seen at the wreath bow and on the ear of corn to the left (the kernels in the ear can range from indistinct to bold). Even Proofs can be weakly struck in areas. Mint luster can range from minutely pebbly or grainy (but still attractive) to a deep, rich frost. Some later Philadelphia coins show stress marks in the field, particularly the obverse, from the use of "tired" dies. This can be determined only by observation, as "slabbed" grades for MS coins do not indicate the quality of the luster or surfaces. Proof Liberty Head nickels were struck of all dates 1883 to 1912, plus both varieties of 1883 (with and without CENTS). The fields range from deeply mirrorlike to somewhat grainy character to mirror-surface, depending on a given year. While most Proofs are sharp, some have weakness at the star centers and/or the kernels on the ear of corn to the left of the ribbon bow. These weaknesses are overlooked by the certification services. Generally, later issues are more deeply mirrored than are earlier ones. Some years in the 1880s and 1890s can show graininess, a combination of mint luster and mirror quality. Lint marks or tiny recessed marks from scattered debris on the die faces are sometimes encountered, but not factored into third-party–certified grades unless excessive.

Availability. All issues from 1883 to 1912 are readily collectible, although the 1885 (in particular), 1886, and 1912-S are considered to be key dates. Most readily available are well-worn coins in AG-3 and G-4. As a class, VF, EF, and AU pieces are very scarce in relation to demand. MS coins are generally scarce in the 1880s, except for the 1883, Without CENTS, which is plentiful in all grades. MS pieces are less scarce in the 1890s and are easily found for most 20th-century years, save for 1909, 1912-D, and 1912-S, all of which are elusive.

GRADING STANDARDS

MS-60 to 70 (Mint State). *Obverse and Reverse:* Mint luster is complete in the obverse and reverse fields. Lower grades such as MS–60, 61, and 62 can show some evidence of abrasion, usually on the portrait on the obverse and highest parts of the wreath on the reverse, and scattered contact marks elsewhere. At MS-63 these marks are few, and at MS-65 they are fewer yet. In grades above MS-65, marks can only be seen under magnification.

1894. Graded MS-65.

AU-50, 53, 55, 58 (About Uncirculated). *Obverse:* Light wear is seen on the portrait and on the hair under LIB. Mint luster is present in the fields, ranging from partial at AU-50 to nearly complete at AU-58. All details are sharp, unless lightly struck. *Reverse:* Light wear is seen on the V, the other letters, and the wreath. Luster is partial at AU-50, increasing to nearly full at AU-58. All details are sharp, unless lightly struck.

1885. Graded AU-58.

EF-40, 45 (Extremely Fine). *Obverse:* Nearly all hair detail is visible, save for some lightness above the forehead. Stars show radial lines (except for those that may have been lightly struck). Overall bold appearance. *Reverse:* The wreath still shows most detail on the leaves. Denticles are bold inside the rim.

1885. Graded EF-40.

VF-20, 30 (Very Fine). *Obverse:* Letters in LIBERTY are all well defined. Hair detail is seen on the back of the head and some between the ear and the coronet. Denticles are bold. Some stars show radial lines. *Reverse:* Detail is seen in the wreath leaves. Lettering and denticles are bold, although E PLURIBUS UNUM may range from medium-light to bold (depending on the strike).

1888. Graded VF-20.

F-12, 15 (Fine). *Obverse:* All of the letters in LIBERTY are readable, although the I may be quite weak. The detail beginning at the front of hair is visible. Denticles are well defined. *Reverse:* Detail of the leaves begins to fade in the wreath. Denticles are well defined all around the border. E PLURIBUS UNUM has medium definition, and is complete.

1885. Graded F-15.

VG-8, 10 (Very Good). *Obverse:* Three or more letters in LIBERTY can be discerned. This can be a combination of two full letters and two or more partial letters. Some hair detail shows at the back of the head. The rim is well outlined and shows traces of most or even all denticles. *Reverse:* The wreath and lettering are bold, but in outline form. E PLURIBUS UNUM is readable, but may be weak. The rim is complete all around, with traces of most denticles present.

1885. Graded VG-8.

G-4, 6 (Good). *Obverse:* The rim is complete all around. Some denticles show on the inside of the rim. The date, Liberty head, and stars are in outline form. No letters of LIBERTY are visible in the coronet. *Reverse:* V and the wreath are visible in outline form. Most letters are complete, but may be faint. E PLURIBUS UNUM is very weak (this feature can vary, and on some G-4 coins it is better defined). The rim is complete in most areas, but may blend with the field in some parts.

1885. Graded G-6.

AG-3 (About Good). *Obverse:* The head is outlined, with only the ear hole as a detail. The date is well worn; the bottom of the digits can be weak or incomplete. The stars are solid, without detail; some may be incomplete. The rim is indistinct or incomplete in some areas. *Reverse:* Details are nearly all worn away, showing greater effects of wear than does the obverse. V is in outline form. The wreath is in outline form, and may be

1885. Graded AG-3.

indistinct in areas. Lettering ranges from faint to missing, but with some letters readable. The rim is usually worn down into the letters.

PF-60 to 70 (Proof). *Obverse and Reverse:* PF–60, 61, and 62 coins show varying amounts of hairlines in the field, decreasing as the grade increases. Fields may be dull or cloudy on lower-level pieces. At PF-65, hairlines are visible only under magnification and are very light; the cheek of Miss Liberty does not show any abrasion or "album slide marks." Above PF-65, hairlines become fewer, and in ultra-high grades are nonexistent, this meaning that

1883, With CENTS. Graded PF-66 Deep Cameo.

the coins have never been subject to wiping or abrasive cleaning. At PF-65 or better, expect excellent aesthetic appeal. Blotched, deeply toned, or recolored coins can be found at most Proof levels from PF–60 through 65 or even 66, and should be avoided. Watch for artificially toned lower-grade Proofs colored to mask the true nature of the fields.

Illustrated coin: This Proof shows spotting in the fields.

	Mintage	Cert	Avg	%MS	G-4	VG-8	F-12	VF-20	EF-40	AU-50	MS-60	MS-63	MS-65
											PF-63	PF-64	PF-65
1883, Without CENTS	5,474,300	7,195	63.3	93%	$7	$8	$9	$11	$15	$18	$35	$50	$225
Auctions: $3,525, MS-67, January 2015; $282, MS-66, June 2015; $164, MS-65, April 2015; $329, MS-64, October 2015													
1883, Without CENTS, Proof	5,219	1,009	64.6								$300	$450	$800
Auctions: $4,935, PF-67, August 2015; $3,055, PF-67, January 2015; $1,057, PF-66, January 2015; $379, PF-64, August 2015													
1883, With CENTS	16,026,200	1,038	61.3	84%	$20	$30	$35	$55	$85	$120	$150	$200	$600
Auctions: $5,875, MS-66, October 2015; $2,115, MS-66, January 2015; $1,292, MS-66, June 2015; $258, MS-64, February 2015													
1883, With CENTS, Proof	6,783	719	64.6								$275	$400	$700
Auctions: $881, PF-64, January 2015; $851, PF-66, September 2015; $822, PF-65, July 2015; $188, PF-63, May 2015													
1884	11,270,000	466	59.2	79%	$20	$30	$35	$55	$85	$130	$190	$300	$1,600
Auctions: $5,405, MS-66, January 2015; $1,997, MS-66, February 2015; $1,351, MS-65, September 2015; $353, MS-64, June 2015													
1884, Proof	3,942	785	64.5								$250	$375	$650
Auctions: $3,055, PF-67, June 2015; $763, PF-66, January 2015; $399, PF-65, April 2015; $376, PF-64, May 2015													
1885	1,472,700	839	26.9	26%	$550	$600	$850	$1,000	$1,350	$1,700	$2,000	$3,250	$8,500
Auctions: $12,925, MS-66, February 2015; $7,637, MS-65, July 2015; $2,115, MS-60, January 2015; $3,055, AU-58, September 2015													
1885, Proof	3,790	812	64.7								$1,300	$1,400	$1,500
Auctions: $2,232, PF-67, January 2015; $1,762, PF-66, June 2015; $1,292, PF-65, October 2015; $1,086, PF-64Cam, August 2015													
1886	3,326,000	767	29.1	28%	$275	$320	$425	$500	$700	$825	$1,000	$2,500	$6,500
Auctions: $16,450, MS-66, January 2015; $4,465, MS-65, August 2015; $1,763, MS-63, June 2015; $763, AU-55, August 2015													
1886, Proof	4,290	801	64.6								$650	$675	$950
Auctions: $2,115, PF-67, January 2015; $969, PF-65, February 2015; $793, PF-65, October 2015; $558, PF-64, May 2015													
1887	15,260,692	474	62.0	88%	$15	$20	$35	$50	$75	$110	$140	$195	$800
Auctions: $5,405, MS-66, January 2015; $616, MS-65, August 2015; $258, MS-64, March 2015; $176, MS-63, May 2015													
1887, Proof	2,960	574	64.3								$250	$375	$650
Auctions: $2,500, PF-67, January 2015; $705, PF-66, June 2015; $211, PF-63, October 2015; $141, PF-62, March 2015													
1888	10,167,901	399	58.2	81%	$30	$40	$60	$120	$175	$220	$275	$340	$1,000
Auctions: $5,170, MS-66, January 2015; $763, MS-65, August 2015; $235, MS-62, February 2015; $199, AU-58, May 2015													
1888, Proof	4,582	786	64.5								$250	$375	$650
Auctions: $3,642, PF-67, February 2015; $525, PF-66, January 2015; $423, PF-65, October 2015; $247, PF-64, May 2015													
1889	15,878,025	573	63.2	95%	$15	$20	$30	$50	$75	$120	$140	$175	$750
Auctions: $1,600, MS-66, January 2015; $705, MS-65, July 2015; $350, MS-64, October 2015; $141, MS-62, April 2015													
1889, Proof	3,336	629	64.6								$250	$375	$650
Auctions: $446, PF-66, January 2015; $493, PF-65, January 2015; $399, PF-65, October 2015; $182, PF-63, July 2015													

**1899, Repunched Date,
Early Die State**

**1899, Repunched Date,
Late Die State**

FS-05-1899-301.

	Mintage	Cert	Avg	%MS	G-4	VG-8	F-12	VF-20	EF-40	AU-50	MS-60 / PF-63	MS-63 / PF-64	MS-65 / PF-65
1890	16,256,532	337	62.0	90%	$10	$20	$25	$40	$65	$110	$160	$200	$950
	Auctions: $16,450, MS-67, October 2015; $4,935, MS-66, January 2015; $705, MS-65, July 2015; $188, MS-62, February 2015												
1890, Proof	2,740	474	64.1								$250	$375	$650
	Auctions: $2,467, PF-67, February 2015; $376, PF-65, January 2015; $376, PF-65, October 2015; $282, PF-64, May 2015												
1891	16,832,000	430	62.7	92%	$7	$12	$25	$45	$70	$125	$160	$200	$800
	Auctions: $10,575, MS-67, January 2015; $3,290, MS-65, August 2015; $211, MS-64, October 2015; $141, MS-61, May 2015												
1891, Proof	2,350	475	64.4								$250	$375	$650
	Auctions: $2,820, PF-67, February 2015; $705, PF-66, January 2015; $282, PF-64, November 2015; $141, PF-62, May 2015												
1892	11,696,897	461	62.4	92%	$6	$10	$20	$40	$65	$110	$140	$160	$1,000
	Auctions: $1,762, MS-66, January 2015; $822, MS-65, February 2015; $258, MS-64, October 2015; $141, MS-63, May 2015												
1892, Proof	2,745	514	64.4								$250	$375	$650
	Auctions: $625, PF-66, January 2015; $517, PF-65, October 2015; $282, PF-64, August 2015; $184, PF-63, May 2015												
1893	13,368,000	468	62.9	94%	$6	$10	$20	$40	$65	$110	$140	$160	$800
	Auctions: $1,880, MS-66, January 2015; $1,527, MS-65, February 2015; $176, MS-62, May 2015; $123, MS-61, October 2015												
1893, Proof	2,195	465	64.5								$250	$375	$650
	Auctions: $1,292, PF-66, July 2015; $517, PF-65, September 2015; $458, PF-65, January 2015; $434, PF-65, October 2015												
1894	5,410,500	350	58.8	79%	$20	$35	$100	$165	$240	$300	$350	$425	$1,200
	Auctions: $4,935, MS-66, January 2015; $1,527, MS-65, August 2015; $493, MS-64, October 2015; $352, MS-63, May 2015												
1894, Proof	2,632	456	64.3								$250	$375	$650
	Auctions: $1,292, PF-67, October 2015; $564, PF-66, January 2015; $540, PF-65, July 2015; $117, PF-60, May 2015												
1895	9,977,822	356	62.2	92%	$6	$8	$22	$45	$70	$115	$140	$200	$1,500
	Auctions: $21,150, MS-67, July 2015; $2,232, MS-66, September 2015; $2,585, MS-65, January 2015; $1,292, MS-65, June 2015												
1895, Proof	2,062	432	64.2								$250	$375	$650
	Auctions: $3,995, PF-67, January 2015; $646, PF-66, August 2015; $399, PF-65, May 2015; $258, PF-64, February 2015												
1896	8,841,058	326	61.6	89%	$9	$18	$35	$65	$90	$150	$190	$265	$1,800
	Auctions: $4,582, MS-66, June 2015; $1,997, MS-65, January 2015; $319, MS-64, September 2015; $211, AU-58, May 2015												
1896, Proof	1,862	420	64.4								$250	$375	$650
	Auctions: $646, PF-66, October 2015; $587, PF-65, January 2015; $282, PF-64, February 2015; $139, PF-62, May 2015												
1897	20,426,797	465	62.5	93%	$4	$5	$12	$27	$45	$70	$100	$160	$850
	Auctions: $4,700, MS-66, January 2015; $1,057, MS-65, July 2015; $616, MS-64, August 2015; $129, MS-63, February 2015												
1897, Proof	1,938	463	64.7								$250	$375	$650
	Auctions: $4,022, PF-68, January 2015; $352, PF-65, November 2015; $176, PF-63, May 2015; $111, PF-60, February 2015												
1898	12,530,292	421	62.7	94%	$4	$5	$12	$27	$45	$75	$150	$185	$800
	Auctions: $881, MS-66, January 2015; $763, MS-65, January 2015; $646, MS-65, August 2015; $293, AU-58, May 2015												
1898, Proof	1,795	431	64.5								$250	$375	$650
	Auctions: $505, PF-66, January 2015; $364, PF-65, October 2015; $258, PF-64, September 2015; $164, PF-63, May 2015												
1899	26,027,000	749	62.8	94%	$2	$3	$8	$20	$30	$60	$90	$140	$550
	Auctions: $4,230, MS-66, January 2015; $470, MS-65, April 2015; $188, MS-64, May 2015; $119, MS-63, September 2015												
1899, Repunched Date (a)	**(b)**	0	n/a						$85	$150	$190	$240	$800
	Auctions: No auction records available.												
1899, Proof	2,031	460	64.7								$250	$375	$650
	Auctions: $1,410, PF-67, July 2015; $423, PF-65, January 2015; $258, PF-64, September 2015; $176, PF-63, May 2015												

a. "The loop of a 9, or possibly (but unlikely) an 8, is evident within the lower loop of the second 9. Some specialists believe this to be an 1899/8 overdate. However, we feel it is simply a repunched date, with the secondary 9 far to the south of the primary 9 at the last digit" (*Cherrypickers' Guide to Rare Die Varieties*, sixth edition, volume I). **b.** Included in circulation-strike 1899 mintage figure.

1900, Doubled-Die Reverse
FS-05-1900-801.

	Mintage	Cert	Avg	%MS	G-4	VG-8	F-12	VF-20	EF-40	AU-50	MS-60 PF-63	MS-63 PF-64	MS-65 PF-65
1900	27,253,733	846	63.1	95%	$2	$3	$8	$15	$30	$65	$90	$140	$500
	Auctions: $7,050, MS-67, January 2015; $646, MS-66, July 2015; $117, MS-63, November 2015; $111, MS-62, February 2015												
1900, Doubled-Die Reverse (c)	**(d)**	4	61.5	75%					$110	$160	$235	$310	$875
	Auctions: No auction records available.												
1900, Proof	2,262	478	64.8								$250	$375	$650
	Auctions: $5,640, PF-68, January 2015; $675, PF-66, August 2015; $387, PF-65, May 2015; $340, PF-64, March 2015												
1901	26,478,228	767	62.9	96%	$2	$3	$5	$13	$30	$60	$85	$135	$475
	Auctions: $8,812, MS-67, January 2015; $1,399, MS-66, October 2015; $317, MS-65, May 2015; $141, MS-64, July 2015												
1901, Proof	1,985	518	64.9								$250	$375	$650
	Auctions: $940, PF-67, January 2015; $587, PF-66, September 2015; $446, PF-65, October 2015; $305, PF-64, January 2015												
1902	31,487,561	765	62.5	93%	$2	$3	$4	$13	$30	$60	$85	$135	$475
	Auctions: $5,405, MS-67, January 2015; $399, MS-65, July 2015; $282, MS-64, February 2015; $152, MS-64, November 2015												
1902, Proof	2,018	473	64.7								$250	$375	$650
	Auctions: $1,028, PF-67, January 2015; $646, PF-66, June 2015; $399, PF-65, March 2015; $317, PF-64, October 2015												
1903	28,004,935	850	62.9	95%	$2	$3	$4	$13	$30	$60	$85	$135	$475
	Auctions: $5,287, MS-67, September 2015; $1,645, MS-66, January 2015; $423, MS-65, August 2015; $176, MS-64, April 2015												
1903, Proof	1,790	543	64.9								$250	$375	$650
	Auctions: $540, PF-66, October 2015; $376, PF-65, September 2015; $293, PF-64, January 2015; $129, PF-61, May 2015												
1904	21,403,167	716	63.1	95%	$2	$3	$4	$13	$30	$60	$85	$135	$475
	Auctions: $1,292, MS-66, January 2015; $352, MS-65, August 2015; $176, MS-64, February 2015; $144, MS-63, April 2015												
1904, Proof	1,817	485	64.3								$250	$375	$650
	Auctions: $998, PF-66, January 2015; $365, PF-65, October 2015; $258, PF-64, April 2015; $179, PF-63, May 2015												
1905	29,825,124	867	62.6	93%	$2	$3	$4	$13	$30	$60	$85	$135	$475
	Auctions: $2,585, MS-66, January 2015; $352, MS-65, October 2015; $159, MS-64, May 2015; $105, MS-63, February 2015												
1905, Proof	2,152	461	64.6								$250	$375	$650
	Auctions: $3,525, PF-67, June 2015; $2,585, PF-66, February 2015; $1,410, PF-66, October 2015; $285, PF-64, January 2015												
1906	38,612,000	632	61.6	88%	$2	$3	$4	$13	$30	$60	$85	$135	$650
	Auctions: $5,875, MS-66, January 2015; $423, MS-65, August 2015; $152, MS-64, May 2015; $211, MS-63, February 2015												
1906, Proof	1,725	453	64.6								$250	$375	$650
	Auctions: $3,290, PF-68, August 2015; $1,527, PF-67, October 2015; $1,292, PF-67, January 2015; $587, PF-66, June 2015												
1907	39,213,325	619	61.7	89%	$2	$3	$4	$13	$30	$60	$85	$135	$750
	Auctions: $1,645, MS-66, July 2015; $470, MS-65, August 2015; $188, MS-64, May 2015; $84, MS-61, March 2015												
1907, Proof	1,475	370	64.7								$250	$375	$650
	Auctions: $2,350, PF-67, February 2015; $616, PF-66, June 2015; $540, PF-66, January 2015; $253, PF-64, September 2015												
1908	22,684,557	568	61.4	90%	$2	$3	$4	$13	$30	$60	$85	$135	$700
	Auctions: $2,115, MS-66, January 2015; $705, MS-65, August 2015; $176, MS-64, October 2015; $111, MS-63, May 2015												
1908, Proof	1,620	447	64.6								$250	$375	$650
	Auctions: $8,225, PF-68, October 2015; $2,115, PF-67, January 2015; $763, PF-66, February 2015; $517, PF-65, June 2015												

c. Doubling on this very popular variety is evident on all reverse design elements, including the V, with a stronger spread on the lower quadrant of the reverse. **d.** Included in circulation-strike 1900 mintage figure.

1913, Liberty Head

	Mintage	Cert	Avg	%MS	G-4	VG-8	F-12	VF-20	EF-40	AU-50	MS-60 / PF-63	MS-63 / PF-64	MS-65 / PF-65
1909	11,585,763	417	60.6	85%	$3	$4	$5	$15	$32	$75	$100	$140	$750
Auctions: $1,645, MS-66, October 2015; $793, MS-65, August 2015; $705, MS-65, February 2015; $99, MS-62, May 2015													
1909, Proof	4,763	1,342	65.0								$250	$375	$650
Auctions: $1,086, PF-67, October 2015; $493, PF-66, January 2015; $258, PF-64, February 2015; $117, PF-60, April 2015													
1910	30,166,948	657	61.4	87%	$2	$3	$4	$13	$30	$60	$85	$135	$500
Auctions: $2,585, MS-66, January 2015; $211, MS-64, September 2015; $130, MS-63, May 2015; $60, AU-58, June 2015													
1910, Proof	2,405	702	64.9								$250	$375	$650
Auctions: $6,462, PF-68, January 2015; $587, PF-66, June 2015; $399, PF-65, November 2015; $282, PF-64, April 2015													
1911	39,557,639	1,262	62.3	92%	$2	$3	$4	$13	$30	$60	$85	$135	$475
Auctions: $1,762, MS-66, January 2015; $376, MS-65, February 2015; $141, MS-64, October 2015; $99, MS-63, May 2015													
1911, Proof	1,733	585	64.7								$250	$375	$650
Auctions: $600, PF-66, January 2015; $365, PF-65, October 2015; $258, PF-64, June 2015; $170, PF-63, February 2015													
1912	26,234,569	1,107	61.8	91%	$2	$3	$4	$13	$30	$60	$85	$135	$475
Auctions: $446, MS-65, January 2015; $141, MS-64, April 2015; $94, MS-63, September 2015; $74, AU-58, June 2015													
1912, Proof	2,145	583	64.5								$250	$375	$650
Auctions: $2,232, PF-67, January 2015; $910, PF-66, July 2015; $489, PF-65, April 2015; $199, PF-63, October 2015													
1912-D	8,474,000	792	60.1	87%	$3	$4	$10	$38	$85	$175	$300	$400	$1,850
Auctions: $4,230, MS-66, January 2015; $1,703, MS-65, July 2015; $646, MS-64, September 2015; $305, MS-63, May 2015													
1912-S	238,000	1,394	33.6	42%	$175	$240	$285	$500	$850	$1,400	$1,750	$2,000	$5,500
Auctions: $5,170, MS-66, July 2015; $3,525, MS-65, January 2015; $2,585, MS-65, October 2015; $1,997, MS-64, February 2015													
1913 † (e)		0	n/a									$3,500,000	
Auctions: No auction records available.													
1913, Proof † (e)		2	47.5								$3,500,000	$3,750,000	
Auctions: $3,290,000, PF-64, January 2014; $3,172,500, PF-63, April 2013													

† Ranked in the *100 Greatest U.S. Coins* (fourth edition). **e.** An estimated five 1913 Liberty Head nickels (four circulation-strike and one Proof) were struck under irregular circumstances at the Mint. Some researchers consider them all to be Proofs. They were dispersed and are now held in various public and private collections.

INDIAN HEAD OR BUFFALO (1913–1938)

Designer: *James Earle Fraser.* **Weight:** *5 grams.* **Composition:** *.750 copper, .250 nickel.*
Diameter: *21.2 mm.* **Edge:** *Plain.* **Mints:** *Philadelphia, Denver, and San Francisco.*

**Variety 1, FIVE CENTS
on Raised Ground (1913)**

*Mintmark location for all
varieties is on the reverse,
below FIVE CENTS.*

**Variety 1, FIVE CENTS
on Raised Ground, Proof**

**Variety 2, FIVE CENTS
in Recess (1913–1938)**

**Variety 2, FIVE CENTS in Recess,
Matte Proof (1913–1916)**

**Variety 2, FIVE CENTS in
Recess, Satin Proof (1936)**

**Variety 2, FIVE CENTS in Recess,
Mirror Proof (1936–1937)**

History. The Indian Head nickel five-cent piece today is almost universally known as the "Buffalo" nickel, after the American bison on the reverse. The design made its debut in 1913. James Earle Fraser, a sculptor well known in the private sector, was its creator. The obverse features an authentic portrait of a Native American, modeled as a composite from life, with three subjects posing. Unlike any preceding coin made for circulation, the Buffalo nickel had little in the way of open, smooth field surfaces. Instead, most areas on the obverse and reverse were filled with design elements or, especially on the reverse, an irregular background, as on a bas-relief plaque. Soon after the first coins were released, it was thought that the inscription FIVE CENTS, on a high area of the motif, would wear too quickly. The Mint modified the design to lower the ground under the bison, which had been arranged in the form of a mound (on what became known as Variety 1). The flat-ground design is called Variety 2.

Striking and Sharpness. Most circulation-strike Buffalo nickels are poorly struck in one or more areas, and for many Denver and San Francisco issues of the 1920s the striking is very poor. However, enough sharp strikes exist among common dates of the 1930s that one can be found with some patience. Certification services do not reflect the quality of strike on their labels, so examine carefully. The matter of striking sharpness on Buffalo nickels is an exceedingly important aspect for the connoisseur (who might prefer, for example, a sharply struck coin in AU-58 over a fully lustrous MS example with much shallower detail). Points to check on the obverse include the center of the coin, especially the area immediately above the tie on the braid. On the reverse check the fur on the head of the bison, and the fur "line" above the bison's shoulder on its back. On both sides, examine the overall striking of letters and other details.

Availability. Among circulated varieties of standard dates and mintmarks, availability is in proportion to their mintages. Among early issues the 1913-S, Variety 2, is the scarcest. The date wore away more quickly on the Variety 1 coins than on the modified design used from later 1913 through the end of the series. In the 1920s the 1926-S is the hardest to find. Collectors sought Buffalo nickels from circulation until the 1960s, after which most were gone. By that time the dates in the teens were apt to have their dates completely worn away, or be AG-3 or G-4. Among MS nickels, the issues of 1913 were saved in quantity as novelties, although 1913-S, Variety 2, is slightly scarce. Philadelphia Mint issues are readily available through the 1920s, while MS-63 and finer mintmarked issues from 1914 to 1927 can range from scarce to rare. From 1931 to 1938, all dates and mintmarks were saved in roll quantities, and all are plentiful today. Many Buffalo nickels in MS are very rare if with Full Details, this being especially true for mintmarked issues after 1913, into the early 1930s. Sharpness of strike is not noted on certification holders, but a connoisseur would probably rather own a Full Details coin in MS-65 than an MS-66 or higher with a flat strike.

Proofs. Proof Buffalo nickels are of two main styles. Matte Proofs were made from 1913 to 1916 and are rare. These have minutely granular or matte surfaces, are sharply struck with Full Details of the design on both sides, and have edges (as viewed edge-on) that are mirrored, a distinctive figure. These are easily confused with circulation strikes except for the features noted. Certified holders usually list these simply as "Proof," not "Matte Proof." Some early Proofs of 1936 have satiny rather than mirror-like fields. Later Proofs of 1936 and all of 1937 have a mirror surface in the fields. The motifs of the 1936 and 1937 mirror Proofs are lightly polished in the die (not frosty or matte).

GRADING STANDARDS

MS-60 to 70 (Mint State). *Obverse and Reverse:* Mint luster is complete in the obverse and reverse fields, except in areas not fully struck up, in which graininess or marks from the *original planchet surface* can be seen. Lower grades such as MS–60, 61, and 62 can show some evidence of abrasion, usually on the center of the obverse above the braid, and on the reverse at the highest parts of the bison. These two checkpoints are often areas of light

1937-D. Graded MS-67.

striking, so abrasion must be differentiated from original planchet marks. At MS-63 evidences of abrasion are few, and at MS-65 they are fewer yet. In grades above MS-65, a Buffalo nickel should be mark-free.

AU-50, 53, 55, 58 (About Uncirculated). *Obverse:* Light wear is seen on the highest area of the cheek, to the left of the nose, this being the most obvious checkpoint. Light wear is also seen on the highest-relief areas of the hair. Luster is less extensive, and wear more extensive, at AU-50 than at higher grades. An AU-58 coin will have only slight wear and will retain the majority of luster. *Reverse:* Light wear is seen on the shoulder

1925-S. Graded AU-53.

and hip, these being the key checkpoints. Light wear is also seen on the flank of the bison and on the horn and top of the head. Luster is less extensive, and wear more extensive, at AU-50 than at higher grades. An AU-58 coin will have only slight wear and will retain the majority of luster.

EF-40, 45 (Extremely Fine). *Obverse:* More wear is seen on the cheek (in particular) and the rest of the face. The center of the coin above the braid is mostly smooth. Other details are sharp. *Reverse:* More wear is evident. The tip of the horn is well defined on better strikes. The shoulder, flank, and hip show more wear. The tip of the tail may be discernible, but is mostly worn away.

1937-D. Graded EF-40.

VF-20, 30 (Very Fine). *Obverse:* The hair above the braid is mostly flat, but with some details visible. The braid is discernible. The feathers lack most details. On Variety 1 coins the date is light. *Reverse:* Wear is more extensive, with most fur detail on the high area of the shoulder gone, the tip of the tail gone, and the horn flat. Ideally the tip of the horn should show, but in the marketplace many certified coins do not show this. On some coins this is due to a shallow strike.

1937-D, 3-Legged. Graded VF-20.

Illustrated coin: On this highly desirable variety one of the buffalo's forelegs has been polished off of the die, probably as the result of an attempt to remove clash marks.

F-12, 15 (Fine). *Obverse:* Only slight detail remains in the hair above the braid. Some of the braid twists are blended together. LIBERTY is weak, and on some coins the upper part of the letters is faint. The rim still is separate. On all coins, the date shows extensive wear. On Variety 1 coins it is weak. *Reverse:* The horn is half to two-thirds visible. Fur details are gone except on the neck at the highest part of the back.

1918-D. Graded F-12.

VG-8, 10 (Very Good). *Obverse:* Hair details above the braid are further worn, as is the hair at the top of the head. Most braid twists are blended together. The rim is worn down to the tops of the letters in LIBERTY. The date is light on all coins and very weak on those of Variety 1. *Reverse:* The base of the horn is slightly visible. Fur details are worn more, but details can still be seen on the neck and top of the back. The hip and flank beneath are worn flat.

1913-D. Graded VG-8.

G-4, 6 (Good). *Obverse:* Scarcely any hair details are seen at the center, and the braid is flat. The rim and tops of the letters in LIBERTY are blended. The date is weak but readable, with at least the last two numerals showing on earlier issues. *Reverse:* The rim is worn to blend into the tops of some or all letters in UNITED STATES OF AMERICA (except for Variety 1). E PLURIBUS UNUM and FIVE CENTS are full, and the mintmark, if any, is clear. The front part of the bison's head blends into the rim.

1918-D, 8 Over 7. Graded G-4.

AG-3 (About Good). *Obverse:* The head is mostly flat, but the facial features remain clear. LIBERTY is weak and partly missing. The date may be incomplete but must be identifiable. *Reverse:* Further wear is seen. On Variety 1 coins, UNITED STATES OF AMERICA is full and readable. On the Variety 2 the rim is worn further into the letters. The reverse of the Variety 1 nickels is bolder as the overall grade is defined by the date, which wore away more quickly than on the Variety 2.

1913-D, Variety 2. Graded AG-3.

PF-60 to 70 (Matte Proof). *Obverse and Reverse:* Most Matte Proofs are in higher grades. Those with abrasion or contact marks can be graded PF–60 to 62; these are not widely desired. PF-64 can have some abrasion. Tiny flecks are not common, but are sometimes seen. At the Matte PF-65 level or higher there will no traces of abrasion or flecks. Differences between higher-grade Proofs are highly subjective, and one certified at PF-65 can be similar to another at PF-67, and vice-versa.

1915. Graded Matte PF-67.

PF-60 to 70 (Mirror Proof). *Obverse and Reverse:* Most mirror Proofs are in higher grades. PF–60 to 62 coins can have abrasion or minor handling marks, but are usually assigned such grades because of staining or blotches resulting from poor cleaning. PF–63 and 64 can have minor abrasion and staining. Tiny flecks are not common, but are sometimes seen, as are dark stripe lines from the glued seams in the cellophane envelopes used by the Mint. PF-65

1937. Graded Mirror PF-66.

and higher coins should be free of stains, flecks, and abrasion of any kind. Differences between higher-grade Proofs are highly subjective, and one certified PF-65 can be similar to another at PF-67, and vice-versa.

1913, Variety 1,
3-1/2 Legged
FS-05-1913-901.

1914, 4 Over 3
FS-05-1914-101.

	Mintage	Cert	Avg	%MS	G-4	VG-8	F-12	VF-20	EF-40	AU-50	MS-60	MS-63	MS-65
											PF-63	PF-64	PF-65
1913, Variety 1	30,992,000	7,987	64.1	96%	$12	$15	$16	$20	$25	$35	$45	$60	$170
Auctions: $822, MS-67, February 2015; $211, MS-66, March 2015; $129, MS-65, January 2015; $84, MS-64, August 2015													
1913, Variety 1, 3-1/2 Legged (a)	**(b)**	0	n/a						$400	$500	$750	$1,500	$10,000
Auctions: $10,350, MS-64, April 2009													
1913, Variety 1, Proof	1,520	310	65.4								$1,200	$1,800	$3,250
Auctions: $7,637, PF-67, July 2015; $4,230, PF-66, June 2015; $3,760, PF-66, January 2015; $2,115, PF-64, January 2015													
1913-D, Variety 1	5,337,000	2,213	62.6	89%	$15	$20	$24	$34	$42	$60	$75	$80	$300
Auctions: $1,997, MS-67, June 2015; $329, MS-66, February 2015; $199, MS-65, August 2015; $84, MS-64, January 2015													
1913-S, Variety 1	2,105,000	1,540	60.2	81%	$45	$50	$60	$70	$90	$110	$130	$180	$650
Auctions: $2,585, MS-66, January 2015; $998, MS-64, August 2015; $164, MS-63, October 2015; $152, MS-62, February 2015													
1913, Variety 2	29,857,186	1,980	62.8	91%	$10	$12	$14	$17	$22	$30	$40	$80	$300
Auctions: $2,820, MS-67, January 2015; $564, MS-66, October 2015; $493, MS-66, July 2015; $223, MS-65, March 2015													
1913, Variety 2, Proof	1,514	242	65.3								$1,000	$1,600	$2,250
Auctions: $3,525, PF-67, January 2015; $3,231, PF-66, October 2015; $1,762, PF-66, February 2015; $1,645, PF-65, January 2015													
1913-D, Variety 2	4,156,000	1,262	52.0	55%	$120	$150	$175	$200	$235	$260	$300	$400	$900
Auctions: $1,997, MS-66, January 2015; $310, MS-63, June 2015; $211, AU-58, May 2015; $170, EF-45, February 2015													
1913-S, Variety 2	1,209,000	1,718	47.2	45%	$340	$400	$450	$500	$600	$750	$900	$1,100	$3,250
Auctions: $3,055, MS-65, January 2015; $1,645, MS-62, February 2015; $727, MS-60, August 2015; $446, AU-58, May 2015													
1914	20,664,463	1,541	58.2	78%	$20	$22	$25	$30	$35	$45	$60	$85	$400
Auctions: $8,225, MS-67, January 2015; $1,116, MS-66, October 2015; $246, MS-64, February 2015; $79, MS-63, May 2015													
1914, 4 Over 3 (c)	**(d)**	0	n/a		$200	$250	$325	$525	$1,000	$1,500	$2,800	$6,250	$25,000
Auctions: $8,338, MS-64, April 2012													
1914, Proof	1,275	419	65.4								$1,000	$1,500	$2,200
Auctions: $6,462, PF-67, February 2015; $2,820, PF-66, August 2015; $1,762, PF-66, January 2015; $1,527, PF-65, August 2015													
1914-D	3,912,000	1,234	51.1	54%	$90	$125	$160	$220	$325	$400	$450	$550	$1,300
Auctions: $587, MS-64, January 2015; $376, MS-63, May 2015; $340, AU-58, February 2015; $211, EF-45, October 2015													
1914-S	3,470,000	1,493	57.2	69%	$26	$38	$45	$65	$90	$160	$200	$425	$1,700
Auctions: $1,468, MS-65, July 2015; $305, MS-63, March 2015; $235, MS-62, November 2015; $123, AU-58, January 2015													
1915	20,986,220	1,452	62.3	89%	$6	$8	$9	$15	$25	$45	$60	$90	$300
Auctions: $4,700, MS-67, January 2015; $540, MS-66, February 2015; $940, MS-65, August 2015; $111, MS-64, October 2015													
1915, Proof	1,050	346	65.2								$1,000	$1,600	$2,250
Auctions: $8,812, PF-67, August 2015; $4,817, PF-67, June 2015; $3,760, PF-67, October 2015; $1,645, PF-66, January 2015													
1915-D	7,569,000	985	57.7	62%	$20	$35	$40	$70	$130	$160	$270	$350	$1,700
Auctions: $376, MS-64, September 2015; $258, MS-63, January 2015; $236, MS-62, May 2015; $124, AU-58, February 2015													
1915-S	1,505,000	804	48.0	51%	$50	$75	$115	$200	$400	$500	$650	$1,000	$3,000
Auctions: $3,525, MS-66, October 2015; $3,704, MS-65, August 2015; $1,527, MS-64, June 2015; $1,057, MS-63, January 2015													

a. The reverse die was heavily polished, possibly to remove clash marks, resulting in a die with most of the bison's front leg missing. **b.** Included in circulation-strike 1913, Variety 1, mintage figure. **c.** The straight top bar of the underlying 3 is visible at the top of the 4. The start of the 3's diagonal is seen on the upper right, outside of the 4. On some coins, a hint of the curve of the lower portion of the 3 shows just above the crossbar of the 4. **d.** Included in circulation-strike 1914 mintage figure.

1916, Doubled-Die Obverse
FS-05-1916-101.

1916, Missing Designer's Initial
FS-05-1916-401.

1918, Doubled-Die Reverse
FS-05-1918-801.

1918-D, 8 Over 7
FS-05-1918D-101.

	Mintage	Cert	Avg	%MS	G-4	VG-8	F-12	VF-20	EF-40	AU-50	MS-60 / PF-63	MS-63 / PF-64	MS-65 / PF-65
1916	63,497,466	2,046	61.8	88%	$6	$7	$8	$10	$14	$25	$50	$85	$300
Auctions: $564, MS-66, January 2015; $235, MS-65, February 2015; $94, MS-64, November 2015; $62, MS-63, July 2015												
1916, Doubled-Die Obverse (e)	(f)	102	39.2	12%	$2,200	$4,000	$7,750	$11,000	$18,500	$32,000	$60,000	$150,000	
Auctions: $30,550, AU-55, January 2014; $28,200, AU-55, August 2014												
1916, Missing Initial (g)	(f)	0	n/a					$135	$200	$280	$375	$600	
Auctions: $341, AU-55, February 2014												
1916, Proof	600	173	65.4								$1,200	$2,000	$3,500
Auctions: $4,230, PF-66, January 2015; $4,113, PF-66, October 2015; $2,820, PF-64, August 2015; $2,232, PF-64, January 2015												
1916-D	13,333,000	1,216	59.4	73%	$16	$28	$30	$45	$90	$120	$175	$260	$1,500
Auctions: $1,086, MS-65, January 2015; $493, MS-64, February 2015; $235, MS-63, April 2015; $158, MS-62, November 2015												
1916-S	11,860,000	940	58.9	71%	$10	$15	$20	$40	$90	$125	$190	$275	$1,600
Auctions: $3,290, MS-66, January 2015; $2,592, MS-65, February 2015; $1,880, MS-65, October 2015; $188, MS-62, July 2015												
1917	51,424,019	972	61.7	88%	$8	$9	$10	$12	$16	$35	$60	$150	$475
Auctions: $705, MS-66, January 2015; $376, MS-65, August 2015; $176, MS-64, April 2015; $94, MS-62, October 2015												
1917-D	9,910,000	906	54.1	59%	$18	$30	$50	$85	$150	$275	$350	$750	$2,400
Auctions: $1,880, MS-65, October 2015; $1,233, MS-64, October 2015; $793, MS-63, January 2015; $329, AU-58, February 2015												
1917-S	4,193,000	749	48.9	48%	$22	$40	$75	$115	$200	$375	$450	$1,200	$3,750
Auctions: $4,230, MS-66, January 2015; $1,527, MS-64, June 2015; $1,028, MS-63, August 2015; $616, MS-62, October 2015												
1918	32,086,314	620	60.5	83%	$6	$7	$8	$16	$32	$50	$125	$325	$1,100
Auctions: $1,292, MS-65, January 2015; $399, MS-64, July 2015; $305, MS-63, April 2015; $211, MS-63, August 2015												
1918, Doubled-Die Reverse (h)	(i)	4	43.0	25%	$190	$260	$375	$525	$1,450	$2,300	$3,500	$7,000	
Auctions: $170, VF-20, August 2013												
1918-D, 8 Over 7 † (j)	(k)	792	19.8	6%	$1,000	$1,500	$2,700	$5,500	$8,500	$12,000	$34,000	$57,500	$265,000
Auctions: $1,292, VG-10, March 2015; $940, G-6, January 2015; $822, G-6, July 2015; $763, G-4, January 2015												
1918-D	8,362,000	720	46.8	45%	$22	$40	$65	$135	$225	$350	$450	$1,050	$3,250
Auctions: $5,875, MS-66, January 2015; $2,937, MS-65, July 2015; $575, AU-58, February 2015; $423, AU-58, October 2015												
1918-S	4,882,000	653	53.4	62%	$14	$27	$55	$110	$200	$325	$585	$2,750	$18,000
Auctions: $2,820, MS-63, February 2015; $998, MS-62, January 2015; $399, AU-55, June 2015; $235, EF-45, August 2015												
1919	60,868,000	1,146	62.2	89%	$2.25	$3	$3.50	$8	$15	$32	$55	$125	$485
Auctions: $5,875, MS-67, January 2015; $1,645, MS-66, August 2015; $1,410, MS-65, June 2015; $188, MS-64, October 2015												
1919-D	8,006,000	712	47.5	41%	$15	$30	$75	$135	$260	$350	$600	$1,500	$6,500
Auctions: $1,762, MS-64, January 2015; $1,410, MS-63, June 2015; $519, AU-58, October 2015; $305, AU-53, November 2015												
1919-S	7,521,000	778	49.7	44%	$9	$20	$50	$125	$260	$375	$625	$1,800	$12,500
Auctions: $2,585, MS-64, August 2015; $1,292, MS-63, February 2015; $493, AU-58, October 2015; $282, AU-55, January 2015												

† Ranked in the *100 Greatest U.S. Coins* (fourth edition). **e.** The date, chin, throat, feathers, and the tie on the braid are all doubled. "Beware of 1916 nickels with strike doubling on the date offered as this variety. . . . The true doubled die must look like the coin shown here" (*Cherrypickers' Guide to Rare Die Varieties*, sixth edition, volume I). **f.** Included in circulation-strike 1916 mintage figure. **g.** The initial F, for Fraser—normally below the date—is clearly absent. Some dies exist with a partially missing or weak initial; these do not command the premium of the variety with a completely missing initial. **h.** Doubling is most obvious to the north on E PLURIBUS UNUM. Some coins show a die crack from the rim to the bison's rump, just below the tail. **i.** Included in 1918 mintage figure. **j.** "Look for the small die crack immediately above the tie on the braid, leading slightly downward to the Indian's jaw. The beginning of this die break can usually be seen even on lower-grade coins" (*Cherrypickers' Guide to Rare Die Varieties*, sixth edition, volume I). **k.** Included in 1918-D mintage figure.

	Mintage	Cert	Avg	%MS	G-4	VG-8	F-12	VF-20	EF-40	AU-50	MS-60 / PF-63	MS-63 / PF-64	MS-65 / PF-65
1920	63,093,000	883	62.2	90%	$1.50	$2.50	$3	$7	$14	$30	$65	$145	$625
	Auctions: $1,116, MS-66, September 2015; $705, MS-65, February 2015; $176, MS-64, January 2015; $117, MS-63, April 2015												
1920-D	9,418,000	729	51.9	57%	$8	$15	$32	$115	$275	$325	$585	$1,400	$4,750
	Auctions: $3,525, MS-65, January 2015; $1,645, MS-64, June 2015; $881, MS-63, October 2015; $705, MS-62, February 2015												
1920-S	9,689,000	747	53.1	56%	$4.50	$12	$28	$100	$200	$300	$575	$1,850	$17,500
	Auctions: $8,812, MS-65, September 2015; $2,585, MS-64, January 2015; $1,410, MS-63, August 2015; $881, AU-58, February 2015												
1921	10,663,000	763	60.2	81%	$4	$6	$8	$24	$50	$75	$150	$320	$700
	Auctions: $1,527, MS-66, January 2015; $1,116, MS-65, August 2015; $376, MS-64, April 2015; $258, MS-63, October 2015												
1921-S	1,557,000	1,142	32.0	21%	$75	$125	$200	$550	$950	$1,200	$1,600	$2,100	$7,250
	Auctions: $2,585, MS-64, October 2015; $646, AU-50, January 2015; $399, VF-30, August 2015; $199, VF-20, February 2015												
1923	35,715,000	954	62.5	89%	$2	$3	$4	$6	$13	$35	$65	$160	$575
	Auctions: $9,400, MS-67, August 2015; $1,880, MS-66, January 2015; $470, MS-65, April 2015; $176, MS-64, May 2015												
1923-S	6,142,000	1,197	51.1	58%	$8	$10	$30	$135	$300	$400	$600	$900	$7,000
	Auctions: $4,347, MS-65, January 2015; $1,086, MS-64, August 2015; $387, AU-58, May 2015; $282, AU-53, November 2015												
1924	21,620,000	659	62.2	89%	$1.50	$2	$5	$10	$24	$42	$75	$160	$750
	Auctions: $2,115, MS-66, January 2015; $724, MS-65, September 2015; $352, MS-64, March 2015; $188, MS-63, July 2015												
1924-D	5,258,000	814	47.8	52%	$8.50	$12	$30	$85	$235	$325	$390	$765	$3,500
	Auctions: $4,465, MS-65, January 2015; $1,880, MS-64, September 2015; $763, AU-58, April 2015; $223, EF-45, July 2015												
1924-S	1,437,000	1,068	28.8	16%	$15	$32	$110	$475	$1,150	$1,700	$2,300	$3,700	$11,000
	Auctions: $5,287, MS-64, July 2015; $1,292, AU-50, June 2015; $470, EF-40, January 2015; $105, F-15, September 2015												
1925	35,565,100	1,004	63.6	95%	$3	$3.50	$4	$8	$15	$32	$42	$100	$350
	Auctions: $4,230, MS-67, June 2015; $446, MS-66, January 2015; $352, MS-65, March 2015; $152, MS-64, August 2015												
1925-D	4,450,000	789	53.0	65%	$10	$20	$40	$95	$185	$265	$400	$750	$4,000
	Auctions: $940, MS-64, February 2015; $472, MS-62, January 2015; $470, MS-61, July 2015; $352, AU-58, July 2015												
1925-S	6,256,000	878	48.9	48%	$5	$9	$18	$90	$180	$250	$475	$1,850	$20,000
	Auctions: $1,762, MS-64, January 2015; $1,292, MS-63, July 2015; $188, AU-50, May 2015; $135, EF-40, February 2015												
1926	44,693,000	1,455	63.6	96%	$1.25	$1.75	$2.50	$5	$10	$20	$32	$75	$190
	Auctions: $3,760, MS-67, June 2015; $587, MS-66, January 2015; $376, MS-66, November 2015; $152, MS-65, September 2015												
1926-D	5,638,000	869	53.7	67%	$10	$18	$28	$110	$185	$300	$350	$500	$3,000
	Auctions: $3,995, MS-65, July 2015; $1,410, MS-64, January 2015; $376, MS-63, April 2015; $258, MS-62, November 2015												
1926-S	970,000	1,791	29.4	11%	$25	$45	$100	$375	$900	$2,650	$4,500	$8,500	$95,000
	Auctions: $11,750, MS-64, January 2015; $2,350, AU-58, February 2015; $1,997, AU-53, June 2015; $705, EF-45, September 2015												
1927	37,981,000	1,069	63.5	95%	$1.25	$1.75	$2.50	$4	$12	$21	$35	$80	$245
	Auctions: $446, MS-66, November 2015; $423, MS-66, January 2015; $164, MS-65, September 2015; $223, MS-64, August 2015												
1927, Presentation Strike, Proof (l)	(m)	5	65.0									$30,000	$48,000
	Auctions: $43,125, SP-65, January 2012												
1927-D	5,730,000	778	59.7	83%	$2.50	$6	$7	$32	$80	$135	$180	$310	$6,500
	Auctions: $4,935, MS-65, January 2015; $646, MS-64, October 2015; $376, MS-63, May 2015; $188, AU-58, September 2015												
1927-S	3,430,000	653	54.9	55%	$1.50	$2	$3	$5	$34	$95	$185	$550	$2,000	$14,500
	Auctions: $3,525, MS-64, January 2015; $1,116, MS-62, October 2015; $329, AU-58, August 2015; $282, AU-55, February 2015												
1928	23,411,000	903	63.3	92%	$1.25	$1.75	$2.50	$5	$13	$23	$32	$80	$280
	Auctions: $5,875, MS-67, June 2015; $793, MS-66, September 2015; $258, MS-65, October 2015; $258, MS-65, November 2015												
1928-D	6,436,000	1,551	63.1	97%	$1.50	$2.50	$5	$15	$45	$50	$60	$110	$600
	Auctions: $517, MS-65, September 2015; $481, MS-65, August 2015; $129, MS-64, January 2015; $99, MS-63, February 2015												
1928-S	6,936,000	726	60.3	79%	$1.75	$2	$2.50	$11	$26	$110	$260	$550	$3,250
	Auctions: $7,343, MS-65, October 2015; $2,115, MS-65, January 2015; $822, MS-64, August 2015; $458, MS-63, February 2015												

l. Some experts believe that certain 1927 nickels were carefully made circulation strikes; such pieces are sometimes certified as "Examples" or "Presentation Strikes." Professional numismatic opinions vary. See Bowers, *A Guide Book of Buffalo and Jefferson Nickels*. m. The mintage figure is unknown.

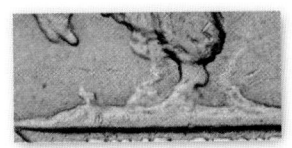

1935, Doubled-Die Reverse
FS-05-1935-801.

1936-D, 3-1/2 Legged
FS-05-1936D-901.

	Mintage	Cert	Avg	%MS	G-4	VG-8	F-12	VF-20	EF-40	AU-50	MS-60 / PF-63	MS-63 / PF-64	MS-65 / PF-65
1929	36,446,000	1,221	63.0	94%	$1.25	$1.50	$2.50	$4	$12	$20	$40	$75	$300
	Auctions: $5,402, MS-66, January 2015; $305, MS-65, March 2015; $258, MS-64, August 2015; $152, MS-64, October 2015												
1929-D	8,370,000	749	62.5	93%	$1.25	$2	$2.50	$7	$32	$45	$60	$130	$1,100
	Auctions: $763, MS-65, October 2015; $376, MS-64, February 2015; $282, MS-64, January 2015; $129, MS-63, May 2015												
1929-S	7,754,000	911	62.8	91%	$1.25	$1.50	$2	$4	$12	$25	$55	$80	$375
	Auctions: $340, MS-65, January 2015; $329, MS-65, October 2015; $129, MS-64, April 2015; $79, MS-63, May 2015												
1930	22,849,000	1,464	63.2	93%	$1.25	$1.50	$2.50	$4	$11	$20	$35	$75	$220
	Auctions: $517, MS-66, January 2015; $329, MS-66, August 2015; $199, MS-65, February 2015; $176, MS-64, June 2015												
1930-S	5,435,000	755	62.5	91%	$1.25	$1.50	$2.50	$4	$14	$35	$65	$120	$385
	Auctions: $1,880, MS-66, January 2015; $364, MS-65, February 2015; $188, MS-64, August 2015; $111, MS-63, May 2015												
1931-S	1,200,000	2,079	61.8	89%	$15	$16	$20	$25	$35	$55	$65	$100	$300
	Auctions: $616, MS-66, August 2015; $1,057, MS-65, January 2015; $517, MS-65, October 2015; $111, MS-64, May 2015												
1934	20,213,003	1,139	63.4	91%	$1.25	$1.50	$2.50	$4	$10	$18	$50	$65	$300
	Auctions: $1,938, MS-67, January 2015; $481, MS-66, February 2015; $258, MS-65, October 2015; $199, MS-65, June 2015												
1934-D	7,480,000	1,207	63.0	95%	$1.50	$2.50	$4	$9	$20	$45	$80	$125	$550
	Auctions: $1,880, MS-66, October 2015; $188, MS-64, August 2015; $152, MS-64, January 2015; $117, MS-63, April 2015												
1935	58,264,000	1,622	63.4	92%	$1	$1.50	$1.75	$2	$3	$10	$22	$45	$120
	Auctions: $851, MS-67, January 2015; $229, MS-66, March 2015; $164, MS-66, September 2015; $117, MS-65, May 2015												
1935, Doubled-Die Reverse (n)	(o)	176	30.9	6%	$45	$55	$100	$160	$500	$1,300	$4,000	$6,000	$25,000
	Auctions: $329, EF-40, January 2015; $282, VF-35, January 2015; $95, VF-20, July 2015												
1935-D	12,092,000	1,297	63.4	96%	$1	$1.50	$2.50	$6	$18	$42	$75	$85	$400
	Auctions: $2,232, MS-67, January 2015; $1,410, MS-66, September 2015; $352, MS-65, March 2015; $89, MS-64, May 2015												
1935-S	10,300,000	1,387	63.6	96%	$1	$1.50	$2	$2.50	$4	$18	$55	$70	$210
	Auctions: $2,585, MS-67, January 2015; $305, MS-66, October 2015; $164, MS-65, March 2015; $74, MS-64, May 2015												
1936	118,997,000	3,275	64.1	92%	$1	$1.50	$1.75	$2	$3	$9	$22	$40	$80
	Auctions: $352, MS-67, May 2015; $105, MS-66, March 2015; $339, MS-64, August 2015; $305, AU-58, October 2015												
1936, Proof, Both kinds	4,420												
1936, Satin Finish, Proof		632	65.8								$1,150	$1,400	$1,675
	Auctions: $6,462, PF-68, July 2015; $2,585, PF-67, June 2015; $1,527, PF-67, October 2015; $1,527, PF-66, January 2015												
1936, Brilliant Finish, Proof		561	65.5								$1,275	$1,650	$2,500
	Auctions: $5,875, PF-68, August 2015; $3,290, PF-67, July 2015; $1,762, PF-66, February 2015; $1,762, PF-65, January 2015												
1936-D	24,814,000	2,316	64.0	97%	$1	$1.50	$1.75	$2	$4	$12	$38	$45	$100
	Auctions: $1,527, MS-67, January 2015; $123, MS-66, November 2015; $117, MS-66, February 2015; $69, MS-65, April 2015												
1936-D, 3-1/2 Legged (p)	(q)	0	n/a		$600	$1,000	$1,500	$3,500	$4,500	$12,500			
	Auctions: $3,290, AU-50, January 2014												
1936-S	14,930,000	1,636	64.4	97%	$1	$1.50	$1.75	$2	$4	$12	$38	$45	$95
	Auctions: $822, MS-67, January 2015; $270, MS-66, February 2015; $188, MS-66, November 2015; $94, MS-65, May 2015												

n. Strong doubling is evident on FIVE CENTS, E PLURIBUS UNUM, and the eye, horn, and mane of the bison. This variety (FS-05-1935-801) is extremely rare above VF, and fewer than a dozen are known in MS. Do not mistake it for the more moderately doubled FS-05-1935-803, which commands much lower premiums. **o.** Included in 1935 mintage figure. **p.** The right front leg has been partially polished off the die—similar to the 1937-D, 3-Legged, variety, but not as severe. (This variety is not from the same die as the 1937-D.) Fewer than 40 are known in all grades. Incorrectly listed by Breen as 1936-P. **q.** Included in 1936-D mintage figure.

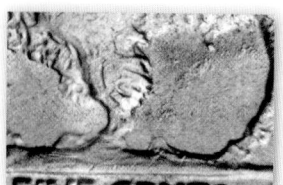

1937-D, 3-Legged
FS-05-1937D-901.

1938-D, D Over S
FS-05-1938D-511.

	Mintage	Cert	Avg	%MS	G-4	VG-8	F-12	VF-20	EF-40	AU-50	MS-60	MS-63	MS-65
											PF-63	PF-64	PF-65
1937	79,480,000	7,790	65.2	98%	$1	$1.50	$1.75	$2	$3	$9	$22	$40	$60
Auctions: $3,995, MS-68, January 2015; $1,059, MS-67, October 2015; $340, MS-67, February 2015; $94, MS-66, August 2015													
1937, Proof	5,769	1,601	65.6								$1,250	$1,500	$1,750
Auctions: $3,525, PF-68, August 2015; $3,055, PF-67, January 2015; $1,351, PF-66, July 2015; $1,292, PF-65, June 2015													
1937-D	17,826,000	4,256	64.9	97%	$1	$1.50	$1.75	$3	$4	$10	$32	$42	$60
Auctions: $540, MS-67, January 2015; $423, MS-67, February 2015; $69, MS-66, June 2015; $48, MS-65, March 2015													
1937-D, 3-Legged (r)	(s)	6,415	49.8	27%	$550	$600	$650	$750	$1,200	$1,450	$2,500	$5,000	$35,000
Auctions: $822, AU-55, February 2015; $822, AU-53, August 2015; $646, EF-45, July 2015; $493, F-12, January 2015													
1937-S	5,635,000	3,600	65.0	99%	$1	$1.50	$1.75	$3	$6	$9	$32	$42	$65
Auctions: $881, MS-67, October 2015; $446, MS-67, January 2015; $62, MS-66, March 2015; $52, MS-64, June 2015													
1938-D	7,020,000	32,054	65.7	100%	$3.50	$4	$4.50	$4.75	$5	$8	$22	$36	$60
Auctions: $188, MS-67, October 2015; $129, MS-67, January 2015; $50, MS-66, February 2015; $28, MS-65, August 2015													
1938-D, D Over D	(t)	2,620	65.6	100%	$4.50	$6.50	$9	$11	$20	$25	$45	$50	$75
Auctions: $822, MS-67, October 2015; $564, MS-67, January 2015; $129, MS-66, February 2015; $60, MS-65, June 2015													
1938-D, D Over S (u)	(t)	2,120	65.2	99%	$5.50	$8	$10	$14	$20	$32	$55	$80	$160
Auctions: $646, MS-67, August 2015; $517, MS-66, November 2015; $188, MS-66, March 2015; $94, MS-65, January 2015													

r. The reverse die was polished heavily, perhaps to remove clash marks, resulting in the shaft of the bison's right front leg missing. Beware altered examples fraudulently passed as genuine. "Look for a line of raised dots from the middle of the bison's belly to the ground as one of the diagnostics on the genuine specimen" (*Cherrypickers' Guide to Rare Die Varieties*, sixth edition, volume I). **s.** Included in 1937-D mintage figure. **t.** Included in 1938-D mintage figure. **u.** There are five different D Over S dies for this date. Varieties other than the one listed here (FS-05-1938D-511) command smaller premiums.

JEFFERSON (1938–2003)

Designer: *Felix Schlag.* **Weight:** *5 grams.* **Composition:** *1938–1942, 1946–2003—.750 copper, .250 nickel; 1942–1945—.560 copper, .350 silver, .090 manganese, with net weight .05626 oz. pure silver.* **Diameter:** *21.2 mm.* **Edge:** *Plain.* **Mints:** *Philadelphia, Denver, and San Francisco.*

Circulation Strike

Mintmark location, 1938–1941 and 1946–1964, is on the reverse, to the right of Monticello.

Mintmark location, 1942–1945, is on the reverse, above Monticello.

Proof

Wartime Silver Alloy (1942–1945)

Mintmark location, 1968–2004, is on the obverse, near the date.

Wartime Silver Alloy, Proof

History. The Jefferson nickel, designed by Felix Schlag in a public competition, made its debut in 1938, and has been a numismatic favorite since. The obverse features a portrait of Thomas Jefferson after the famous bust by Jean Antoine Houdon, and the reverse a front view of Jefferson's home, Monticello.

From partway through 1942 to the end of 1945 a copper-silver-manganese alloy replaced the traditional 75% copper and 25% nickel composition. This was to help save nickel for the war effort. These silver-content coins bear a distinctive P, D, or S mintmark above the dome of Monticello. Starting in 1966, Felix Schlag's initials, FS, were added below the presidential bust. The coinage dies were remodeled to strengthen the design in 1971, 1972, 1977, and 1982. The mintmark position, originally on the reverse to the right of Monticello, was moved to the obverse starting in 1968.

Striking and Sharpness. On the obverse, check for weakness on the portrait, especially in the lower jaw area. On the reverse, most circulation strikes have weak details on the six steps of Monticello, especially under the third pillar from the left, as this section on the reverse was opposite in the dies (in the press) from the high parts of the Jefferson portrait, and metal could not effectively flow in both directions at once. Planchet weight allowance was another cause, the dies being spaced slightly too far apart. Jefferson nickels can be classified as "Full Steps" (FS) if either five or six of Monticello's porch steps (with the top step counting as one) are clear. Notations of 5FS or 6FS can indicate the number of visible steps. It is easier to count the incuse lines than the raised steps. If there are four complete, unbroken lines, the coin qualifies as Full Steps (with five steps); five complete, unbroken lines indicate six full steps. There must be no nicks, cuts, or scratches interrupting the incuse lines. It is difficult to determine a full five-step count on the 1938 and some 1939 issues, as the steps are wavy and ill-defined; a great deal of subjectivity is common for these dates. Even if the steps are mostly or fully defined, check other areas to determine if a coin has Full Details overall. Interestingly, nickels of the 1950s and 1960s are among the most weakly struck. The silver-content coins of the 1940s usually are well struck. Some nickels of the 1950s to 1970s discolored easily, perhaps due to some impurities in the alloy. Proofs were struck from 1938 to 1942, 1950 to 1964, and 1968 to 2003. All have mirror fields. Striking is usually with Full Details, although there are scattered exceptions. Most survivors are in high grade, PF-64 and upward. Most since the 1970s have frosted or cameo contrast on the higher features. Special Mint Set (SMS) coins were struck in lieu of Proofs from 1965 to 1967; these in some instances closely resemble Proofs.

Availability. All basic dates and mintmarks were saved in roll quantities. Scarce issues in MS include 1939-D and 1942-D. The low-mintage 1950-D was a popular speculation in its time, and most of the mintage went into numismatic hands, making MS coins common today. Many different dates and mints are rare if with 5FS or 6FS; consult *A Guide Book of Buffalo and Jefferson Nickels* for details.

GRADING STANDARDS

MS-60 to 70 (Mint State). *Obverse and Reverse:* Mint luster is complete in the obverse and reverse fields, except in areas not fully struck up, in which graininess or marks from the *original planchet surface* can be seen. This may include the jaw, the back of Jefferson's head, and the higher-relief central features of Monticello. The highest parts of the design may have evidence of abrasion and/or contact marks in lower MS grades. Lower grades such

1939. Graded MS-66.

as MS–60, 61, and 62 can show some evidence of abrasion, usually on the same areas that display weak striking. At MS-63, evidences of abrasion are few, and at MS-65 they are fewer yet. In grades above MS-65, a Jefferson nickel should be mark-free.

AU-50, 53, 55, 58 (About Uncirculated). *Obverse:* The cheekbone and the higher points of the hair show light wear, more at AU-50 than at AU-58. Some mint luster will remain on some AU-55 and most AU-58 coins. *Reverse:* The central part of Monticello shows light wear, but is difficult to evaluate as this area often shows weakness of strike. Some mint luster will remain on some AU-55 and most AU-58 coins.

1943-P, 3 Over 2. Graded AU-58.

EF-40, 45 (Extremely Fine). *Obverse:* More wear is evident on the cheekbone. The higher parts of the hair are without detail. *Reverse:* Monticello shows wear overall. The bottom edge of the triangular area above the columns at the center are worn away.

1942-D, D Over Horizontal D. Graded EF-40.

VF-20, 30 (Very Fine). *Obverse:* Most hair detail is lost, except for the back of the head and lower area. The cheekbone is flat and mostly blended into the hair at the right. *Reverse:* Many shallow-relief architectural features are worn away. The windows remain clear and the four columns are distinct.

The Jefferson nickel is seldom collected in grades lower than VF-20.

1945-P, Doubled-Die Reverse. Graded VF-20.

PF-60 to 70 (Proof). *Obverse and Reverse:* Most Proof Jefferson nickels are in higher grades. Those with abrasion or contact marks can be graded PF–60 to 62 or even 63; these are not widely desired by collectors. PF-64 can have some abrasion. Tiny flecks are sometimes seen on coins of 1938 to 1942, as are discolorations (even to the extent of black streaks); these flaws are from cellophane holders. You should avoid such coins. Undipped Proofs of

1975-S. Graded PF-70 Deep Cameo.

the early era often have a slight bluish or yellowish tint. At PF-65 or higher there are no traces of abrasion or flecks. Evaluation of differences between higher-grade Jefferson Proofs is highly subjective; one certified at PF-65 might be similar to another at PF-67, and vice-versa. Striking is typically with full details, although there are scattered exceptions. At PF–69 and 70 there are no traces of abrasion, contact marks, or other flaws.

Five Steps

Six Steps

1939, Doubled-Die Reverse
FS-05-1939-801.

	Mintage	Cert	Avg	%MS	VF-20	EF-40	AU-50	MS-60	MS-63	MS-65 / PF-65	MS-65FS / PF-66	MS-67 / PF-67
1938	19,496,000	919	65.5	98%	$0.50	$1	$1.50	$3	$4	$16	$150	$200
Auctions: $188, MS-66, August 2015; $164, MS-66, May 2015; $141, MS-66, September 2015; $141, MS-66, October 2015												
1938, Proof	19,365	1,254	65.5							$125	$175	$400
Auctions: $1,997, PF-68, October 2015; $1,057, PF-68, January 2015; $399, PF-67, July 2015; $94, PF-66, August 2015												
1938-D	5,376,000	2,348	66.2	100%	$1.50	$2	$3	$7	$9	$14	$125	$150
Auctions: $881, MS-67, August 2015; $423, MS-67, January 2015; $141, MS-66, February 2015; $111, MS-66, September 2015												
1938-S	4,105,000	1,160	65.8	99%	$2.50	$3	$3.50	$4.50	$8	$16	$270	$600
Auctions: $282, MS-67, January 2015; $305, MS-66, February 2015; $258, MS-66, October 2015; $129, MS-65, May 2015												
1939	120,615,000	1,270	65.0	93%	$0.25	$0.50	$1	$2	$2.50	$12	$47	$225
Auctions: $1,116, MS-67FS, January 2015; $223, MS-66FS, February 2015; $36, MS-66, April 2015; $223, MS-65FS, February 2015												
1939, Doubled-Die Reverse (a)	(b)	266	55.0	55%	$80	$110	$150	$200	$375	$1,000	$2,400	$4,500
Auctions: $89, EF-40, November 2014; $86, EF-40, November 2014; $70, EF-40, November 2014; $7,050, EF-40, August 2013												
1939, Proof	12,535	898	65.4							$125	$175	$400
Auctions: $2,115, PF-67, January 2015; $447, PF-67, February 2015; $129, PF-66, August 2015; $84, PF-65, October 2015												
1939-D	3,514,000	1,321	65.4	97%	$10	$13	$30	$60	$90	$120	$500	$450
Auctions: $282, MS-67, January 2015; $129, MS-67, May 2015; $188, MS-66, November 2015; $135, MS-66, January 2015												
1939-S	6,630,000	714	65.0	96%	$2	$5	$10	$18	$35	$70	$400	$450
Auctions: $1,528, MS-67, November 2013; $764, MS-66FS, June 2015; $247, MS-65FS, November 2014; $229, MS-65FS, September 2014												
1940	176,485,000	669	65.8	98%	$0.25	$0.40	$0.75	$1	$1.50	$15	$45	$250
Auctions: $1,320, MS-67FS, July 2015; $1,028, MS-67FS, February 2015; $153, MS-67, July 2015; $79, MS-65FS, November 2015												
1940, Proof	14,158	902	65.4							$125	$160	$600
Auctions: $6,463, PF-68, October 2015; $259, PF-67, January 2015; $94, PF-66, May 2015; $79, PF-65, June 2015												
1940-D	43,540,000	1,391	65.9	99%	$0.35	$0.50	$1	$2	$2.50	$15	$45	$150
Auctions: $229, MS-67FS, November 2013												
1940-S	39,690,000	425	65.5	99%	$0.35	$0.50	$1	$2.25	$3	$12	$70	$350
Auctions: $5,170, MS-67FS, June 2015; $282, MS-67FS, May 2015; $125, MS-66FS, February 2015; $69, MS-66FS, January 2015												
1941	203,265,000	656	65.8	99%	$0.20	$0.30	$0.50	$0.75	$1.50	$12	$65	$250
Auctions: $1,528, MS-68, September 2013; $940, VF-20, October 2014												
1941, Proof	18,720	1,073	65.4							$90	$150	$600
Auctions: $200, PF-67, April 2015; $112, PF-66, May 2015; $106, PF-66, May 2015; $60, PF-65, August 2015												
1941-D	53,432,000	1,375	66.1	99%	$0.25	$0.40	$1.50	$2.50	$3.50	$12	$45	$80
Auctions: $1,058, MS-67FS, June 2015; $166, MS-67FS, February 2015; $69, MS-67, February 2015; $54, MS-67, February 2015												
1941-S (c)	43,445,000	296	65.5	98%	$0.30	$0.50	$1.50	$3	$4	$12	$80	$625
Auctions: $2,585, MS-66FS, April 2014; $282, MS-66FS, November 2014; $259, MS-66FS, January 2015; $106, MS-66FS, August 2015												

a. Very strong doubling is evident to the east of the primary letters, most noticeably on MONTICELLO and FIVE CENTS. Lesser doubling is also visible on UNITED STATES OF AMERICA and the right side of the building. **b.** Included in circulation-strike 1939 mintage figure. **c.** Large and small mintmark varieties exist.

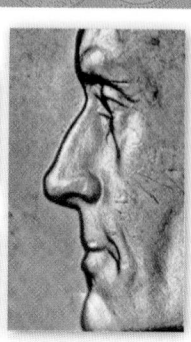

1942-D, D Over Horizontal D
FS-05-1942D-501.

1943-P, 3 Over 2
FS-05-1943P-101.

1943-P, Doubled-Die Obverse
The *"Doubled Eye"* variety. FS-05-1943P-106.

	Mintage	Cert	Avg	%MS	VF-20	EF-40	AU-50	MS-60	MS-63	MS-65	MS-65FS	MS-67
										PF-65	PF-66	PF-67
1942	49,789,000	682	65.2	99%	$0.30	$0.45	$1.25	$4	$6	$15	$85	$250
Auctions: $4,700, MS-66FS, July 2015; $1,763, MS-66FS, July 2015; $188, MS-66FS, August 2015												
1942, Proof	29,600	1,817	65.7							$90	$130	$200
Auctions: $1,410, PF-68, January 2015; $423, PF-67, June 2015; $118, PF-66, May 2015; $79, PF-66, January 2015												
1942-D	13,938,000	1,240	65.7	99%	$1	$2	$5	$28	$38	$60	$80	$380
Auctions: $541, MS-67FS, January 2015; $494, MS-67FS, July 2015; $100, MS-66FS, January 2015; $89, MS-66FS, February 2015												
1942-D, D Over Horizontal D (d)	(e)	82	48.8	30%	$75	$200	$500	$1,500	$3,000	*$10,000*		
Auctions: $15,275, MS-66, April 2013; $764, AU-58, October 2014; $329, AU-50, August 2014; $44, F-12, September 2014												
1942-P, Silver	57,873,000	4,488	66.3	100%	$2	$2.50	$3.25	$7	$12	$20	$75	$50
Auctions: $764, MS-67FS, September 2015; $153, MS-67, September 2015; $129, MS-66FS, January 2015												
1942-P, Proof, Silver	27,600	2,783	65.5							$180	$250	$275
Auctions: $230, PF-67, January 2015; $223, PF-67, January 2015; $100, PF-66, January 2015; $74, PF-64, March 2015												
1942-S	32,900,000	4,267	66.2	100%	$2	$2.50	$3.25	$7	$12	$25	$200	$100
Auctions: $2,820, MS-67FS, August 2015; $176, MS-66FS, January 2015; $153, MS-66FS, January 2015; $54, MS-65FS, September 2015												
1943-P, 3 Over 2 (f)	(g)	312	55.2	65%	$50	$100	$165	$225	$260	$700	$1,100	$2,850
Auctions: $588, MS-66, October 2015; $539, MS-65, January 2015; $376, MS-64, January 2015; $333, MS-63, June 2015												
1943-P	271,165,000	5,222	65.8	98%	$2	$2.50	$3	$5	$8	$20	$40	$65
Auctions: $881, MS-67FS, June 2015; $646, MS-67FS, January 2015; $118, MS-67, August 2015; $62, MS-66FS, June 2015												
1943-P, Doubled-Die Obverse (h)	(g)	129	62.3	82%	$25	$40	$60	$90	$160	$650	$1,000	$2,200
Auctions: $1,293, MS-66FS, September 2015; $940, MS-66FS, July 2015; $823, MS-66, June 2015; $411, MS-65, October 2015												
1943-D	15,294,000	8,430	66.2	100%	$2	$3.50	$4	$6	$12	$20	$45	$55
Auctions: $3,760, MS-67FS, August 2015; $1,645, MS-67FS, July 2015; $62, MS-66FS, September 2015; $30, MS-66, September 2015												
1943-S	104,060,000	5,273	66.2	100%	$2	$2.50	$3	$5	$8	$20	$50	$70
Auctions: $1,645, MS-67FS, February 2015; $517, MS-67FS, January 2015; $94, MS-66FS, January 2015; $69, MS-66FS, June 2015												
1944-P (i)	119,150,000	3,425	66.0	100%	$2	$2.50	$3.25	$7	$12	$30	$80	$125
Auctions: $259, MS-67, February 2015; $223, MS-67, February 2015; $212, MS-67, February 2015; $106, MS-67, May 2015												
1944-D	32,309,000	5,742	66.3	100%	$2	$2.50	$3	$6	$12	$25	$35	$70
Auctions: $1,528, MS-67FS, July 2015; $1,410, MS-67FS, January 2015; $100, MS-66FS, January 2015; $79, MS-66FS, April 2015												
1944-S	21,640,000	5,253	66.2	100%	$2	$2.50	$3	$5	$10	$22	$160	$80
Auctions: $5,170, MS-67FS, July 2015; $2,350, MS-67FS, January 2015; $329, MS-66FS, January 2015; $188, MS-65FS, January 2015												

Note: Genuine examples of some wartime dates were struck in nickel, in error. **d.** The initial D mintmark was punched into the die horizontally, then corrected. "This is the rarest of the major Jefferson nickel varieties in Mint State" (*Cherrypickers' Guide to Rare Die Varieties*, sixth edition, volume I). **e.** Included in 1942-D mintage figure. **f.** "This popular variety was created when the die was first hubbed with a 1942-dated hub, then subsequently hubbed with a 1943-dated hub. The diagonal of the 2 is visible within the lower opening of the 3. Doubling is also visible on LIBERTY and IN GOD WE TRUST. . . . There is at least one 1943-P five-cent piece that has a faint, short die gouge extending upward from the lower ball of the 3; this is often mistaken for the overdate" (*Cherrypickers' Guide to Rare Die Varieties*, sixth edition, volume I). **g.** Included in 1943-P mintage figure. **h.** This variety is nicknamed the "Doubled Eye." Doubling is visible on the date, LIBERTY, the motto, and, most noticeably, Jefferson's eye. **i.** 1944 nickels without mintmarks are counterfeit.

1945-P, Doubled-Die Reverse
FS-05-1945P-803.

	Mintage	Cert	Avg	%MS	VF-20	EF-40	AU-50	MS-60	MS-63	MS-65 / PF-65	MS-65FS / PF-66	MS-67 / PF-67
1945-P	119,408,100	3,565	65.8	100%	$2	$2.50	$3	$5	$8	$20	$125	$750
	Auctions: $9,988, MS-67FS, July 2015; $329, MS-67, October 2015; $223, MS-66FS, January 2015; $58, MS-66, January 2015											
1945-P, DblDie Reverse (j)	(k)	212	64.2	95%	$20	$30	$50	$75	$130	$800	$7,000	
	Auctions: $400, MS-65, January 2015; $353, MS-65, February 2015; $212, MS-65, January 2015; $176, MS-64, January 2015											
1945-D	37,158,000	5,922	66.3	100%	$2	$2.50	$3	$5	$8	$20	$40	$125
	Auctions: $705, MS-67FS, January 2015; $54, MS-66FS, May 2015; $50, MS-66FS, January 2015; $48, MS-66FS, May 2015											
1945-S	58,939,000	6,087	66.2	100%	$2	$2.50	$3	$5	$8	$20	$200	$150
	Auctions: $3,055, MS-67FS, August 2015; $1,116, MS-67FS, January 2015; $1,058, MS-66FS, January 2015											
1946	161,116,000	287	65.0	98%	$0.25	$0.30	$0.35	$0.75	$2.50	$15	$200	
	Auctions: $1,763, MS-67, December 2013; $259, MS-65FS, May 2015; $259, MS-65FS, December 2014; $153, MS-65FS, January 2015											
1946-D	45,292,200	878	65.5	99%	$0.35	$0.40	$0.45	$1	$2.50	$12	$35	$500
	Auctions: $2,350, MS-67FS, September 2015; $1,528, MS-67FS, January 2015; $1,175, MS-67FS, October 2015;											
1946-S	13,560,000	761	65.6	99%	$0.40	$0.45	$0.50	$1	$2	$11	$125	$125
	Auctions: $353, MS-66FS, December 2014; $306, MS-66FS, July 2015; $223, MS-66FS, October 2014; $529, MS-66FS, April 2014											
1947	95,000,000	414	65.4	99%	$0.25	$0.30	$0.35	$0.75	$1.75	$12	$65	$135
	Auctions: $3,760, MS-67FS, January 2015; $564, MS-66FS, July 2015; $153, MS-66FS, February 2015; $150, MS-66FS, January 2015											
1947-D	37,822,000	720	65.7	100%	$0.30	$0.35	$0.40	$0.90	$1.75	$11	$30	$150
	Auctions: $940, MS-67FS, October 2015; $79, MS-66FS, January 2015; $74, MS-66FS, May 2015; $69, MS-66FS, November 2015											
1947-S	24,720,000	371	65.2	99%	$0.40	$0.45	$0.50	$1	$1.75	$12	$50	$750
	Auctions: $2,056, MS-66FS, June 2014											

Note: Genuine examples of some wartime dates were struck in nickel, in error. **j.** There are several collectible doubled-die reverses for this date. Values are for the variety pictured (FS-05-1945P-801), with a strongly doubled reverse. The doubling spread increases from left to right. **k.** Included in 1945-P mintage figure.

1949-D, D Over S
FS-05-1949D-501.

	Mintage	Cert	Avg	%MS	MS-60	MS-63	MS-65	MS-65FS	MS-66	MS-66FS / PF-65	MS-67 / PF-66	MS-67FS / PF-67
1948	89,348,000	226	65.2	99%	$1	$1.50	$10	$200	$75	$1,750		
	Auctions: $112, MS-65FS, January 2015; $106, MS-65FS, July 2015											
1948-D	44,734,000	602	65.7	100%	$1.60	$4	$10	$30	$45	$90	$150	
	Auctions: $588, MS-67FS, January 2015; $112, MS-66FS, November 2015											
1948-S	11,300,000	740	66.0	100%	$1.50	$2.50	$9	$45	$40	$280	$175	
	Auctions: $7,050, MS-67FS, January 2015; $4,935, MS-67FS, July 2015; $517, MS-67, January 2015											
1949-P	60,652,000	273	65.2	99%	$2.50	$9	$12	$1,750	$35			
	Auctions: $1,553, MS-65FS, February 2010											
1949-D	36,498,000	689	65.4	99%	$1.50	$6	$10	$50	$25	$185	$225	
	Auctions: $734, MS-67, January 2015; $411, MS-67, July 2014; $84, MS-67, December 2014											
1949-D, D Over S (a)	(b)	66	63.0	95%	$150	$200	$500	$1,800	$1,200			
	Auctions: $564, MS-66, January 2015; $541, MS-66, January 2015; $541, MS-66, July 2015; $494, MS-66, October 2015											
1949-S	9,716,000	334	65.4	99%	$1.75	$5	$10	$275	$50	$1,500		
	Auctions: $15,275, MS-67FS, January 2014; $235, MS-65FS, November 2014; $188, MS-65FS, November 2014											

a. The top serif of the S is visible to the north of the D, with the upper left loop of the S visible to the west of the D. "This variety is quite rare in Mint State and highly sought after. Some may still be found in circulated grades. Some examples have been located in original Mint sets" (*Cherrypickers' Guide to Rare Die Varieties,* sixth edition, volume I). **b.** Included in 1949-D mintage figure.

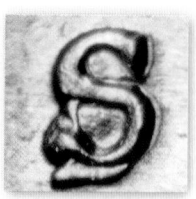

1954-S, S Over D
FS-05-1954S-501.

	Mintage	Cert	Avg	%MS	MS-60	MS-63	MS-65	MS-65FS	MS-66	MS-66FS	MS-67	MS-67FS
										PF-65	PF-66	PF-67
1950	9,796,000	486	65.7	100%	$2	$3.25	$8	$175	$60	$500		
Auctions: $106, MS-65FS, January 2015; $94, MS-65FS, July 2015												
1950, Proof	51,386	1,429	66.1							$75	$85	$125
Auctions: $329, PF-68, October 2015; $188, PF-68, August 2015; $141, PF-66Cam, November 2015; $50, PF-65, July 2015												
1950-D	2,630,030	4,033	65.5	100%	$14	$16	$25	$60	$70	$150	$275	$2,750
Auctions: $1,293, MS-67FS, August 2015; $250, MS-67, January 2015; $306, MS-66FS, February 2015; $118, MS-66FS, February 2015												
1951	28,552,000	291	65.4	100%	$3	$6.50	$15	$425	$80	$2,000		
Auctions: $1,880, MS-66FS, February 2015; $282, MS-66FS, August 2015; $259, MS-65FS, January 2015; $235, MS-65, August 2015												
1951, Proof	57,500	1,733	66.7							$65	$75	$120
Auctions: $823, PF-68Cam, January 2015; $705, PF-68Cam, October 2015; $129, PF-67Cam, June 2015; $58, PF-67, February 2015												
1951-D	20,460,000	620	65.7	100%	$4	$7	$11	$80	$30	$300	$575	
Auctions: $2,820, MS-66FS, June 2013												
1951-S	7,776,000	475	65.7	100%	$1.50	$2	$12	$200	$55	$1,000		
Auctions: $646, MS-67, August 2015; $194, MS-67, September 2015; $1,293, MS-66FS, January 2015; $881, MS-66FS, January 2015												
1952	63,988,000	257	65.5	100%	$1	$4	$9	$950	$175	$2,000	$400	
Auctions: $259, MS-66FS, July 2014; $259, MS-64FS, November 2014; $476, AU-55, April 2014												
1952, Proof	81,980	1,768	66.9							$45	$60	$75
Auctions: $176, PF-67Cam, January 2015; $153, PF-67Cam, December 2015; $64, PF-66Cam, December 2015; $26, PF-66, March 2015												
1952-D	30,638,000	413	65.7	100%	$3.50	$6.25	$15	$200	$35	$600	$500	
Auctions: $16,450, MS-67FS, July 2015; $12,338, MS-67FS, January 2015; $329, MS-66FS, August 2015; $112, MS-65FS, January 2015												
1952-S	20,572,000	696	65.6	100%	$1	$1.50	$12	$300	$35	$2,500		
Auctions: $235, MS-65FS, August 2015; $212, MS-65FS, January 2015												
1953	46,644,000	268	65.4	100%	$0.25	$0.75	$8	$3,000	$80	$4,000		
Auctions: $129, PF-67Cam, December 2015; $26, PF-66Cam, August 2015; $54, PF-66, June 2015												
1953, Proof	128,800	2,406	67.1							$45	$50	$65
Auctions: $15,275, PF-68DCam, April 2013; $65, PF-68, September 2014; $135, PF-67Cam, November 2014; $35, PF-67, July 2014												
1953-D	59,878,600	608	65.6	100%	$0.25	$0.75	$9	$225	$40	$900	$650	
Auctions: $129, MS-67, January 2015; $1,880, MS-66FS, July 2015; $135, MS-65FS, August 2015; $141, MS-65, October 2015												
1953-S	19,210,900	488	65.2	100%	$0.75	$1	$10	$5,000	$100			
Auctions: $1,293, MS-64FS, June 2013												
1954	47,684,050	320	65.0	100%	$1	$1.50	$15	$375	$25	$2,000	$250	
Auctions: $999, MS-66FS, November 2014; $259, MS-65FS, January 2015; $207, MS-65FS, February 2010												
1954, Proof	233,300	2,678	67.3							$22	$40	$55
Auctions: $5,875, PF-68DCam, March 2013												
1954-D	117,183,060	272	64.2	98%	$0.60	$1	$30	$700	$100		$250	
Auctions: $646, MS-65FS, January 2015; $282, MS-65FS, August 2015; $200, MS-65FS, August 2015; $176, MS-65FS, August 2015												
1954-S	29,384,000	703	64.7	99%	$1.75	$2	$15	$4,000	$165			
Auctions: $1,410, MS-64FS, January 2015; $764, MS-64FS, October 2015												
1954-S, S Over D (c)	(d)	177	63.3	95%	$26	$40	$160	$500	$1,000			
Auctions: $329, MS-66, January 2015; $159, MS-65, April 2015; $147, MS-65, February 2015; $84, MS-64, April 2015												

c. The overall strength of the strike is the important factor in this overmintmark's value. **d.** Included in 1954-S mintage figure.

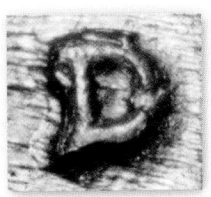

1955-D, D Over S
FS-05-1955D-501.

	Mintage	Cert	Avg	%MS	MS-60	MS-63	MS-65	MS-65FS	MS-66	MS-66FS PF-65	MS-67 PF-66	MS-67FS PF-67
1955	7,888,000	416	65.0	100%	$0.75	$1	$15	$900	$100			
Auctions: $382, MS-65FS, April 2014												
1955, Proof	378,200	4,346	67.6							$18	$30	$45
Auctions: $1,175, PF-68DCam, October 2015; $646, PF-68DCam, August 2015; $69, PF-66, July 2015; $54, PF-63, May 2015												
1955-D	74,464,100	414	64.5	98%	$0.50	$0.75	$20	$4,500	$150			
Auctions: $165, MS-66, August 2014; $69, MS-66, November 2015; $999, MS-64FS, February 2013												
1955-D, D Over S (e)	(f)	149	63.9	95%	$36	$57.50	$175	$500	$1,000			
Auctions: $823, MS-66, August 2015; $165, MS-65, January 2015; $50, MS-63, November 2015												
1956	35,216,000	688	65.4	100%	$0.50	$0.75	$20	$80	$45	$275		$4,000
Auctions: $588, MS-66FS, June 2014												
1956, Proof	669,384	3,748	67.5							$5	$25	$40
Auctions: $47, PF-69, October 2014; $5,581, PF-68DCam, June 2013												
1956-D	67,222,940	456	65.5	100%	$0.50	$0.75	$20	$675	$35	$3,000	$500	
Auctions: $911, MS-65FS, February 2013												
1957	38,408,000	419	65.0	100%	$0.50	$0.75	$15	$125	$80	$2,600		
Auctions: $441, MS-66FS, April 2014												
1957, Proof	1,247,952	3,615	67.4							$4	$12	$20
Auctions: $881, PF-68Cam, June 2013												
1957-D	136,828,900	609	65.4	100%	$0.50	$0.70	$15	$150	$35	$2,750		
Auctions: $1,087, MS-66FS, August 2015; $376, MS-66FS, August 2015; $259, MS-66FS, August 2015; $188, MS-66FS, January 2015												
1958	17,088,000	275	64.3	100%	$0.60	$0.80	$12	$700				
Auctions: $1,116, MS-66FS, November 2014; $764, MS-65, January 2014; $42, MS-64FS, June 2015												
1958, Proof	875,652	3,402	67.4							$8	$12	$20
Auctions: $7,050, PF-68DCam, April 2013												
1958-D	168,249,120	711	65.4	99%	$0.40	$0.50	$12	$50	$50	$100		$3,250
Auctions: $1,763, MS-67FS, December 2013												
1959	27,248,000	552	65.3	99%	$0.25	$0.50	$10	$80	$125	$1,000		
Auctions: $165, MS-66FS, August 2015; $165, MS-66FS, August 2015; $153, MS-66FS, January 2015; $30, MS-65FS, May 2015												
1959, Proof	1,149,291	3,403	67.4							$3	$10	$20
Auctions: $7,050, PF-69DCam, April 2013; $1,293, PF-68DCam, September 2014; $494, PF-67DCam, August 2015												
1959-D	160,738,240	460	65.4	99%	$0.25	$0.50	$8	$250	$50	$2,250		
Auctions: $306, MS-66FS, July 2015; $223, MS-66FS, January 2015; $118, MS-65FS, January 2015; $107, MS-65FS, September 2015												
1960	55,416,000	372	65.2	99%	$0.25	$0.50	$8	$1,750	$70			
Auctions: $1,495, MS-65FS, February 2010												
1960, Proof	1,691,602	3,787	67.4							$3	$10	$18
Auctions: $6,463, PF-69DCam, March 2013; $229, PF-69Cam, September 2014												
1960-D	192,582,180	371	65.4	99%	$0.25	$0.50	$10		$100		$500	
Auctions: $223, MS-66, February 2013												

e. There are 10 or more different D Over S varieties for 1955. Values shown are for the strongest (FS-05-1955D-501); others command smaller premiums. **f.** Included in 1955-D mintage figure.

	Mintage	Cert	Avg	%MS	MS-60	MS-63	MS-65	MS-65FS	MS-66	MS-66FS PF-65	MS-67 PF-66	MS-67FS PF-67
1961	73,640,100	365	65.5	100%	$0.25	$0.50	$20	$2,500	$60	$3,500		
	Auctions: $2,530, MS-65FS, February 2010											
1961, Proof	3,028,144	3,944	67.3							$3	$10	$18
	Auctions: $1,763, PF-69DCam, April 2013											
1961-D	229,342,760	309	65.0	100%	$0.25	$0.50	$20	$6,000	$200		$2,000	
	Auctions: $11,163, MS-64FS, February 2013											
1962	97,384,000	364	65.2	99%	$0.25	$0.50	$10	$50	$30	$600	$425	
	Auctions: $21,150, MS-67FS, August 2013											
1962, Proof	3,218,019	4,289	67.3							$3	$10	$18
	Auctions: $823, PF-69DCam, September 2013											
1962-D	280,195,720	202	64.5	98%	$0.25	$0.50	$30					
	Auctions: $89, MS-63FS, November 2014; $118, MS-63FS, June 2013											
1963	175,776,000	619	65.4	100%	$0.25	$0.50	$10	$150	$40	$1,200		
	Auctions: $541, MS-66FS, July 2015; $79, MS-65FS, January 2015											
1963, Proof	3,075,645	4,853	67.4							$3	$10	$18
	Auctions: $329, PF-69UCam, July 2015; $317, PF-69DCam, December 2014; $823, PF-69DCam, September 2013											
1963-D	276,829,460	185	64.0	97%	$0.25	$0.50	$30	$7,500				
	Auctions: $7,475, MS-65FS, February 2010											
1964	1,024,672,000	333	65.2	99%	$0.25	$0.50	$8	$325	$60	$2,000		
	Auctions: $881, MS-66FS, July 2015; $147, MS-65, January 2015; $129, MS-64, August 2015; $62, MS-64, August 2015											
1964, Proof	3,950,762	8,499	68.1							$3	$10	$18
	Auctions: $176, PF-69DCam, January 2015; $112, PF-69DCam, January 2015; $94, PF-69UCam, July 2015											
1964-D	1,787,297,160	411	65.1	99%	$0.25	$0.50	$5	$750	$55	$4,000		
	Auctions: $2,350, MS-66FS, January 2015; $969, MS-66FS, January 2015; $282, MS-65FS, January 2015											
1965	136,131,380	335	65.8	99%	$0.25	$0.50	$5	$50	$25	$250	$200	
	Auctions: $165, MS-67, December 2014; $646, MS-66, August 2013											
1965, Special Mint Set ‡	2,360,000	2,439	66.6	100%						$5 (g)	$20	$45
	Auctions: $5,288, PF-67DCam, July 2014; $123, PF-67Cam, September 2014; $79, PF-67Cam, January 2015											
1966	156,208,283	110	65.1	97%		$0.25	$5	$50	$25	$250	$200	
	Auctions: $56, MS-66, July 2014; $322, MS-65DCam, February 2010											
1966, Special Mint Set ‡	2,261,583	2,242	66.8	100%						$5 (h)	$20	$35
	Auctions: $329, PF-67Cam, July 2015; $94, PF-67Cam, January 2015											
1967	107,325,800	289	65.5	99%		$0.25	$5	$50	$25	$250	$200	
	Auctions: $132, MS-66, February 2013											
1967, Special Mint Set ‡	1,863,344	2,651	66.8	100%						$5 (i)	$20	$30
	Auctions: $188, PF-68Cam, August 2015; $823, PF-67DCam, July 2015; $40, PF-67Cam, February 2015											

‡ Ranked in the *100 Greatest U.S. Modern Coins.* **g.** Value in PF-64FS is $10; in PF-65FS, $55. **h.** Value in PF-64FS is $10; in PF-65FS, $65. **i.** Value in PF-64FS is $10; in PF-65FS, $60.

	Mintage	Cert	Avg	%MS	MS-63	MS-64FS	MS-65	MS-65FS	MS-66	MS-66FS PF-66	MS-67 PF-67Cam	MS-67FS PF-69DC
1968-D	91,227,880	629	65.5	100%	$0.25		$4		$35			
	Auctions: No auction records available.											
1968-S	100,396,004	307	65.6	100%	$0.25	$475	$5	$1,350	$35	$4,000	$275	
	Auctions: No auction records available.											
1968-S, Proof	3,041,506	1,413	67.8							$4	$16	$115
	Auctions: $4,406, PF-65, August 2013											
1969-D	202,807,500	442	65.5	100%	$0.25	$10	$4		$115			
	Auctions: $94, MS-66, February 2013											
1969-S	120,165,000	201	65.0	100%	$0.25		$2		$350			
	Auctions: $188, PF-69DCam, January 2015											
1969-S, Proof	2,934,631	1,346	67.8							$4	$10	$400
	Auctions: $282, PF-69DCam, November 2014; $1,116, PF-69DCam, June 2013											

	Mintage	Cert	Avg	%MS	MS-63	MS-64FS	MS-65	MS-65FS	MS-66	MS-66FS	MS-67 / PF-66	MS-67FS / PF-67Cam	MS-67FS / PF-69DC
1970-D	515,485,380	505	64.9	100%	$0.25		$10		$180				
Auctions: $200, MS-63, August 2013; $200, MS-62, July 2014; $176, MS-62, August 2015													
1970-S	238,832,004	225	64.9	100%	$0.25	$225	$8	$400	$225	$650			
Auctions: $999, MS-66FS, December 2013; $89, MS-64FS, November 2014													
1970-S, Proof	2,632,810	1,317	67.7								$4	$15	$300
Auctions: $499, PF-69DCam, September 2013; $411, PF-69DCam, September 2014; $376, PF-69DCam, January 2015													

	Mintage	Cert	Avg	%MS	MS-63	MS-64FS	MS-65	MS-65FS	MS-66	MS-66FS	MS-67 / PF-66	MS-67FS / PF-67Cam	MS-69FS / PF-69DC
1971	106,884,000	271	64.8	99%	$0.75	$10	$3	$30	$50	$130			
Auctions: $127, MS-66FS, February 2010													
1971-D	316,144,800	674	66.0	100%	$0.30	$10	$3	$20	$30	$60		$750	
Auctions: $646, MS-67FS, August 2013													
1971, No S, Proof ‡ (a)	1,655	101	67.6								$1,250	$1,500	$8,000
Auctions: $1,704, PF-69Cam, August 2015; $881, PF-68Cam, October 2015; $1,175, PF-67Cam, January 2015; $940, PF-67, January 2015													
1971-S, Proof	3,220,733	1,300	67.7								$8	$20	$600
Auctions: $1,528, PF-69DCam, June 2013													
1972	202,036,000	123	65.2	99%	$0.25	$10	$3	$40	$60	$300			
Auctions: $141, MS-66FS, November 2014; $276, MS-66FS, March 2012													
1972-D	351,694,600	165	64.9	99%	$0.25	$10	$3	$40	$75	$350			
Auctions: $212, MS-63, November 2014; $823, MS-63, August 2013													
1972-S, Proof	3,260,996	1,006	67.6								$8	$20	$120
Auctions: $58, PF-69DCam, November 2015; $52, PF-69DCam, November 2015; $42, PF-69DCam, October 2015													
1973	384,396,000	221	65.1	100%	$0.25	$10	$3	$30	$45	$150	$110		
Auctions: $103, MS-66FS, February 2013													
1973-D	261,405,000	252	65.4	100%	$0.25	$10	$3	$25	$30	$60	$90		
Auctions: $353, MS-65, February 2014													
1973-S, Proof	2,760,339	301	67.8								$7	$15	$30
Auctions: $44, PF-69DCam, September 2009													
1974	601,752,000	230	64.9	100%	$0.25	$40	$3	$175	$35	$900			
Auctions: $110, MS-65FS, March 2014; $54, MS-65FS, January 2015; $46, MS-65FS, November 2014													
1974-D	277,373,000	155	65.2	99%	$0.25	$15	$3	$40	$45	$150		$1,550	
Auctions: $34, MS-66FS, November 2014; $200, MS-62, April 2013													
1974-S, Proof	2,612,568	382	67.1								$8	$12	$20
Auctions: $25, PF-69DCam, March 2008													
1975	181,772,000	221	65.5	100%	$0.50	$20	$3	$50	$50	$300			
Auctions: $2,820, MS-67FS, January 2015; $129, MS-66FS, August 2015													
1975-D	401,875,300	152	65.3	100%	$0.25	$15	$3	$60	$55	$300			
Auctions: $176, MS-66FS, August 2015; $153, MS-64FS, August 2015													
1975-S, Proof	2,845,450	533	67.9								$8	$12	$20
Auctions: $42, PF-68Cam, August 2013													
1976	367,124,000	89	64.7	100%	$0.45	$30	$3	$175	$37	$675		$3,250	
Auctions: $1,265, MS-66FS, February 2012													
1976-D	563,964,147	215	65.0	100%	$0.45	$10	$3	$30	$40	$300			
Auctions: $235, MS-65, February 2014; $94, MS-64, July 2014													
1976-S, Proof	4,149,730	808	67.8								$8	$12	$20
Auctions: $36, PF-70DCam, January 2010													

‡ Ranked in the *100 Greatest U.S. Modern Coins*. **a.** 1971, Proof, nickels without the S mintmark were made in error after an assistant engraver forgot to punch a mintmark into a die. The U.S. Mint estimates that 1,655 such error coins were struck.

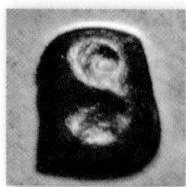

**1979-S, Filled S
(Type 1), Proof**

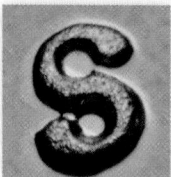

**1979-S, Clear S
(Type 2), Proof**

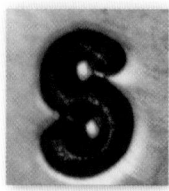

**1981-S, Rounded S
(Type 1), Proof**

**1981-S, Flat S
(Type 2), Proof**

	Mintage	Cert	Avg	%MS	MS-63	MS-64FS	MS-65	MS-65FS	MS-66	MS-66FS	MS-67	MS-67FS	MS-69FS
											PF-66	PF-67Cam	PF-69DC
1977	585,376,000	146	65.3	100%	$0.25	$70	$3	$150	$48	$1,000			
Auctions: $306, MS-65, September 2015; $881, MS-64, October 2014; $329, MS-63, September 2013													
1977-D	297,313,422	220	64.8	100%	$0.50	$10	$3	$35	$40	$275			
Auctions: $940, MS-68, August 2013													
1977-S, Proof	3,251,152	730	68.3								$7	$12	$20
Auctions: $1,116, PF-70DCam, April 2013													
1978	391,308,000	149	65.2	100%	$0.25	$35	$3	$175	$55	$900			
Auctions: $43, MS-64, July 2014; $259, MS-64, September 2013; $282, MS-63, October 2014													
1978-D	313,092,780	227	64.8	100%	$0.25	$15	$3	$40	$55	$100			
Auctions: $104, MS-66FS, February 2010													
1978-S, Proof	3,127,781	723	68.6								$7	$12	$20
Auctions: $165, PF-70DCam, February 2015; $153, PF-70DCam, February 2015; $129, PF-70DCam, July 2015													
1979	463,188,000	119	65.1	99%	$0.25	$40	$3	$300	$50	$1,000			
Auctions: $200, MS-63, January 2015; $129, MS-60, September 2015													
1979-D	325,867,672	286	64.8	99%	$0.25	$10	$4	$30	$37	$150			
Auctions: $182, MS-66FS, February 2013													
1979-S, Proof, Both kinds	3,677,175												
1979-S, Type 1, Proof		788	68.6								$7	$12	$22
Auctions: $1,763, PF-70DCam, June 2013													
1979-S, Type 2, Proof		860	68.8								$8	$13	$30
Auctions: $646, PF-70DCam, June 2013													
1980-P	593,004,000	171	65.5	100%	$0.25	$10	$4	$45	$30	$250			
Auctions: $329, MS-64, January 2015; $259, MS-65, January 2015; $240, MS-64, January 2015; $188, MS-60, January 2015													
1980-D	502,323,448	150	65.0	99%	$0.25	$10	$3	$20	$60	$250			
Auctions: $217, MS-66FS, February 2013													
1980-S, Proof	3,554,806	1,009	68.7								$7	$12	$20
Auctions: No auction records available.													
1981-P	657,504,000	195	65.6	99%	$0.25	$100	$3	$500	$50	$3,500			
Auctions: $282, MS-66, January 2015; $223, MS-62, January 2015													
1981-D	364,801,843	177	65.0	100%	$0.25	$10	$3	$30	$35	$180			
Auctions: $206, MS-66FS, June 2014													
1981-S, Proof, Both kinds	4,063,083												
1981-S, Type 1, Proof		1,173	68.6								$7	$12	$20
Auctions: $1,528, PF-70DCam, June 2013													
1981-S, Type 2, Proof		1,015	68.9								$10	$13	$30
Auctions: $3,525, PF-70DCam, April 2013													
1982-P	292,355,000	37	64.6	95%	$5	$12	$10	$50	$35	$325			
Auctions: $881, MS-67, February 2014; $2,350, MS-62, September 2014; $306, MS-62, February 2015													
1982-D	373,726,544	71	65.0	97%	$2	$25	$6	$55	$30	$400			
Auctions: $374, MS-66FS, February 2010													
1982-S, Proof	3,857,479	854	68.8								$8	$12	$20
Auctions: No auction records available.													

	Mintage	Cert	Avg	%MS	MS-63	MS-64FS	MS-65	MS-65FS	MS-66	MS-66FS	MS-67 / PF-66	MS-67FS / PF-67Cam	MS-69FS / PF-69DC
1983-P	561,615,000	41	64.1	93%	$2	$60	$9	$400	$60	$1,500			
Auctions: $141, MS-64, January 2015; $64, MS-64, January 2015; $36, MS-64, August 2015													
1983-D	536,726,276	44	64.5	95%	$1.50	$15	$4	$175	$35	$875			
Auctions: $863, MS-66FS, June 2010; $112, MS-65FS, November 2014													
1983-S, Proof	3,279,126	793	68.8								$8	$12	$20
Auctions: $1,528, PF-70DCam, June 2013													
1984-P	746,769,000	144	65.4	100%	$1	$10	$3	$25	$40	$100			
Auctions: $66, MS-66FS, February 2013													
1984-D	517,675,146	136	65.1	99%	$0.25	$10	$3	$30	$65	$275			
Auctions: $36, MS-65FS, February 2013													
1984-S, Proof	3,065,110	602	68.6								$10	$12	$20
Auctions: $705, PF-70DCam, June 2013													
1985-P	647,114,962	129	65.5	100%	$0.50	$25	$3	$50	$60	$325			
Auctions: $89, MS-66FS, November 2014; $70, MS-66FS, November 2014; $259, MS-62, November 2013													
1985-D	459,747,446	114	65.3	100%	$0.50	$10	$3	$40	$40	$225		$1,850	
Auctions: $196, MS-66FS, June 2010													
1985-S, Proof	3,362,821	635	68.9								$8	$12	$20
Auctions: $1,528, PF-70DCam, June 2013													
1986-P	536,883,483	139	65.7	100%	$0.50	$10	$3	$50	$35	$200			
Auctions: $705, MS-66FS, August 2015; $99, MS-66FS, February 2013; $47, MS-66FS, November 2014													
1986-D	361,819,140	114	65.4	100%	$1	$10	$3	$35	$50	$275			
Auctions: $253, MS-66FS, February 2010													
1986-S, Proof	3,010,497	490	68.9								$9	$13	$20
Auctions: $3,525, PF-70DCam, April 2013													
1987-P	371,499,481	382	66.0	100%	$0.25	$10	$2.75	$15	$60	$65		$225	
Auctions: $329, MS-67FS, June 2014													
1987-D	410,590,604	345	65.6	100%	$0.25	$10	$3.50	$20	$30	$150			
Auctions: $173, MS-67FS, April 2008													
1987-S, Proof	4,227,728	633	68.9								$8	$12	$20
Auctions: $558, PF-70DCam, June 2013													
1988-P	771,360,000	124	65.8	100%	$0.25	$12	$3	$30	$35	$140			
Auctions: $329, MS-67, August 2013; $79, MS-64, August 2015; $69, MS-64, July 2014													
1988-D	663,771,652	192	65.3	99%	$0.25	$10	$3	$35	$32	$125			
Auctions: $165, MS-67, June 2014													
1988-S, Proof	3,262,948	572	68.7								$9	$13	$25
Auctions: $823, PF-70DCam, June 2013													
1989-P	898,812,000	217	65.9	100%	$0.25	$10	$2.75	$20	$25	$35		$650	
Auctions: $18, AU-50, August 2013													
1989-D	570,842,474	142	65.1	100%	$0.25	$12	$2.75	$40	$35	$180			
Auctions: $188, MS-66FS, February 2013													
1989-S, Proof	3,220,194	607	69.0								$8	$12	$20
Auctions: $82, PF-70DCam, May 2013													
1990-P	661,636,000	157	66.0	99%	$0.25	$10	$2.75	$20	$25	$40			
Auctions: $24, MS-66FS, October 2009													
1990-D	663,938,503	127	65.0	99%	$0.25	$9	$2.75	$30	$45	$200			
Auctions: $129, MS-67FS, June 2014													
1990-S, Proof	3,299,559	864	69.1								$8	$12	$20
Auctions: $441, PF-69DCam, June 2014													

	Mintage	Cert	Avg	%MS	MS-63	MS-64FS	MS-65	MS-65FS	MS-66	MS-66FS	MS-67	MS-67FS	MS-69FS
											PF-66	PF-67Cam	PF-69DC
1991-P	614,104,000	96	65.6	100%	$0.30	$10	$2.75	$45	$35	$190			
Auctions: $90, MS-66FS, February 2013													
1991-D	436,496,678	103	65.3	100%	$0.30	$10	$2.75	$25	$35	$160			
Auctions: $76, MS-66FS, February 2013													
1991-S, Proof	2,867,787	773	69.1								$10	$12	$20
Auctions: $64, PF-70DCam, August 2013													
1992-P	399,552,000	144	65.9	100%	$1.50	$10	$3	$20	$28	$50		$1,650	
Auctions: $88, MS-67FS, August 2013													
1992-D	450,565,113	121	65.2	100%	$0.25	$10	$2.75	$30	$30	$160			
Auctions: $72, MS-66FS, February 2013													
1992-S, Proof	4,176,560	1,508	69.1								$8	$12	$20
Auctions: $45, PF-70DCam, May 2013													
1993-P	412,076,000	130	65.8	100%	$0.25	$10	$1	$30	$35	$75			
Auctions: $68, MS-66FS, February 2013													
1993-D	406,084,135	174	65.4	100%	$0.25	$10	$1	$20	$20	$40	$100	$375	
Auctions: $374, MS-67FS, February 2010													
1993-S, Proof	3,394,792	1,549	69.0								$8	$12	$20
Auctions: $47, PF-70DCam, October 2009													
1994-P	722,160,000	162	66.0	100%	$0.25	$10	$2.50	$25	$25	$100	$35		
Auctions: $235, MS-70, January 2015; $881, MS-63, April 2013													
1994-P, Special Uncirculated ‡ (b)	167,703	1,669	68.9	100%	$50	$75	$75	$125	$125	$150	$250	$450	
Auctions: $123, MS-70, November 2014; $66, MS-69FS, March 2013; $40, MS-69, September 2014; $38, MS-69, November 2014													
1994-D	715,762,110	102	64.8	99%	$0.25	$10	$1	$30	$35	$100	$50		
Auctions: $92, MS-66FS, February 2013													
1994-S, Proof	3,269,923	1,394	69.1								$8	$12	$20
Auctions: $33, PF-70DCam, April 2013													
1995-P	774,156,000	187	66.2	100%	$0.25	$20	$1	$40	$20	$90	$25	$250	
Auctions: $499, MS-65, August 2013; $141, MS-63, July 2014													
1995-D	888,112,000	59	65.0	98%	$0.50	$10	$1	$25	$25	$200	$35	$1,000	
Auctions: $940, MS-67FS, April 2014													
1995-S, Proof	2,797,481	1,355	69.1								$10	$13	$20
Auctions: $79, PF-70DCam, February 2010													
1996-P	829,332,000	195	65.7	100%	$0.25	$18	$1	$20	$25	$30	$35	$350	
Auctions: $129, MS-64, January 2015; $69, MS-64, January 2015													
1996-D	817,736,000	224	65.3	100%	$0.25	$20	$1	$22	$25	$35	$35	$200	
Auctions: $161, MS-67FS, February 2010													
1996-S, Proof	2,525,265	1,391	69.1								$8	$12	$25
Auctions: $56, PF-70DCam, February 2010													
1997-P	470,972,000	79	65.9	100%	$0.50	$10	$2	$45	$25	$175	$50	$350	
Auctions: $306, MS-70FS, July 2015; $118, MS-69FS, February 2015													
1997-P, Special Uncirculated ‡ (b)	25,000	936	69.3	100%	$200	$100	$225	$300	$300	$375	$450	$800	
Auctions: $200, MS-70FS, October 2014; $499, MS-70FS, June 2014; $223, MS-69FS, November 2014; $118, MS-69FS, November 2014													
1997-D	466,640,000	95	65.2	99%	$1	$15	$2	$50	$20	$100	$25	$500	
Auctions: $33, MS-66FS, June 2014													
1997-S, Proof	2,796,678	1,365	69.3								$8	$12	$25
Auctions: $36, PF-70DCam, December 2009													

‡ Ranked in the *100 Greatest U.S. Modern Coins*. **b.** Special "frosted" Uncirculated nickels were included in the 1993, Thomas Jefferson, commemorative dollar packaging (sold in 1994) and in the 1997, Botanic Garden, sets. They resemble Matte Proof coins.

	Mintage	Cert	Avg	%MS	MS-63	MS-64FS	MS-65	MS-65FS	MS-66	MS-66FS	MS-67 / PF-66	MS-67FS / PF-67Cam	MS-69FS / PF-69DC
1998-P	688,272,000	90	65.1	100%	$0.35	$8	$1	$35	$45	$125	$110	$400	
Auctions: $176, MS-65, July 2014; $940, MS-64, August 2014; $42, MS-62, November 2014													
1998-D	635,360,000	96	64.1	97%	$0.35	$10	$1	$100	$60	$450	$150		
Auctions: $66, MS-65FS, November 2014; $90, MS-65FS, June 2014													
1998-S, Proof	2,086,507	1,561	69.3								$8	$12	$25
Auctions: $47, PF-70DCam, November 2009													
1999-P	1,212,000,000	197	65.4	97%	$0.25	$10	$1	$10	$25	$75	$35	$250	
Auctions: $56, MS-65FS, August 2015; $46, MS-64FS, August 2015; $40, MS-65FS, August 2015; $23, MS-63, August 2015													
1999-D	1,066,720,000	172	65.5	99%	$0.25	$8	$1	$15	$30	$300	$50		
Auctions: $106, MS-64, September 2015; $89, MS-64, August 2015													
1999-S, Proof	3,347,966	6,107	69.1								$9	$12	$25
Auctions: $42, PF-70DCam, September 2009													
2000-P	846,240,000	114	65.6	100%	$0.25	$10	$1	$12	$18	$35	$25	$500	
Auctions: $470, MS-67FS, August 2013													
2000-D	1,509,520,000	171	65.9	99%	$0.25	$10	$1	$12	$18	$50	$25	$500	
Auctions: $613, MS-67FS, July 2015; $36, MS-65, August 2015; $56, MS-64FS, August 2015; $56, MS-63, August 2015													
2000-S, Proof	4,047,993	6,463	69.1								$7	$12	$25
Auctions: $17, PF-69DCam, March 2014													
2001-P	675,704,000	87	65.8	99%	$0.25	$8	$1	$10	$12	$20	$25	$40	
Auctions: $50, MS-67FS, June 2013													
2001-D	627,680,000	66	65.6	98%	$0.25	$8	$1	$10	$12	$20	$25	$130	
Auctions: $138, MS-67FS, February 2010													
2001-S, Proof	3,184,606	4,969	69.2								$7	$12	$25
Auctions: $17, PF-69DCam, March 2014													
2002-P	539,280,000	72	65.5	100%	$0.25	$8	$1	$10	$12	$20	$30	$75	
Auctions: $72, MS-67FS, June 2014													
2002-D	691,200,000	57	65.3	95%	$0.25	$8	$1	$10	$12	$90			
Auctions: $74, MS-66FS, February 2013													
2002-S, Proof	3,211,995	5,397	69.1								$7	$12	$25
Auctions: $15, PF-69DCam, February 2013													
2003-P	441,840,000	181	65.7	99%	$0.25	$8	$1	$10	$12	$20	$22	$50	
Auctions: $1,058, MS-68FS, November 2013													
2003-D	383,040,000	129	65.1	100%	$0.25	$8	$1	$15	$12	$80			
Auctions: $86, MS-66FS, February 2013													
2003-S, Proof	3,298,439	9,139	69.2								$7	$12	$25
Auctions: $15, PF-69DCam, March 2014													

WESTWARD JOURNEY (2004–2005)

Designers: *See image captions for designers.* **Weight:** *5 grams.* **Composition:** *.750 copper, .250 nickel.* **Diameter:** *21.2 mm.* **Edge:** *Plain.* **Mints:** *Philadelphia, Denver, and San Francisco.*

| Westward Journey, Obverse (2004) Designer: Felix Schlag. | Peace Medal Reverse (2004) Designer: Norman E. Nemeth. | Keelboat Reverse (2004) Designer: Al Maletsky. | Westward Journey, Obverse (2005) Designer: Joe Fitzgerald. | American Bison Reverse (2005) Designer: Jamie Franki. | Ocean in View Reverse (2005) Designer: Joe Fitzgerald. |

| Westward Journey, Obverse, Proof | Peace Medal Reverse, Proof | Keelboat Reverse, Proof | Westward Journey, Obverse, Proof | American Bison Reverse, Proof | Ocean in View Reverse, Proof |

Mintmark location, 2005, is on the obverse, near the date (2004 location is the same as previous years).

History. In 2004 special designs commemorating the Westward Journey (Lewis and Clark expedition) were introduced. They utilized the previous obverse design paired with two different reverse designs, one representing the Peace Medals given out by Lewis and Clark, the other showing the keelboat that provided much of their transportation. Two new reverse designs were introduced for 2005, showing the American Bison and a representation of Clark's journal entry upon spotting what he thought was the Pacific Ocean (in actuality, they were still approximately 20 miles from the coast). They were paired with a new obverse, a tightly cropped profile of Jefferson facing right.

Striking and Sharpness. On the obverse, check for weakness on the portrait. Proofs were struck for each design. All have mirror fields. Most have frosted or cameo contrast on the higher features.

Availability. All basic dates and mintmarks were saved in roll quantities.

GRADING STANDARDS

MS-60 to 70 (Mint State). *Obverse and Reverse:* Mint luster is complete in the obverse and reverse fields. Check the higher parts of the obverse and reverse for abrasion and contact marks.

The Westward Journey nickels are seldom collected in grades lower than MS-60.

2004-D, Peace Medal. Graded MS-66.

PF-60 to 70 (Proof). *Obverse and Reverse:* Evaluation of differences between higher-grade Jefferson Proofs is highly subjective; one certified at PF-65 might be similar to another at PF-67, and vice-versa. All Proof Westward Journey nickels have mirror fields. Striking is typically with full details, although there are scattered exceptions. Nearly all Westward Journey nickel Proofs are as issued, in PF–69 or 70.

2005-S, Ocean in View. Graded PF-70 Ultra Cameo.

	Mintage	Cert	Avg	%MS	MS-63	MS-65 / PF-65	MS-66 / PF-67	MS-67 / PF-69DC
2004-P, Peace Medal	361,440,000	2,112	63.7	97%	$0.25	$0.75	$8	$50
Auctions: $200, MS-67, February 2013								
2004-D, Peace Medal	372,000,000	513	65.6	100%	$0.25	$0.75	$5	$30
Auctions: $374, MS-68, February 2010								
2004-S, Peace Medal, Proof	2,992,069	11,895	69.2			$8	$12	$25
Auctions: $15, PF-69DCam, March 2014								
2004-P, Keelboat	366,720,000	269	65.6	100%	$0.25	$0.75	$5	$20
Auctions: $299, MS-68, February 2010								
2004-D, Keelboat	344,880,000	324	65.9	100%	$0.25	$0.75	$5	$20
Auctions: No auction records available.								
2004-S, Keelboat, Proof	2,965,422	11,908	69.2			$8	$12	$25
Auctions: $31, PF-70DCam, November 2013								
2005-P, American Bison	448,320,000	4,275	66.7	100%	$0.35	$1.25	$8	$30
Auctions: $28, MS-69, January 2010								
2005-P, American Bison, Satin Finish	1,160,000	3,709	67.0	100%	$0.50	$1	$3	$10
Auctions: No auction records available.								
2005-D, American Bison	487,680,000	4,584	66.1	100%	$0.35	$1.25	$8	$25
Auctions: $388, MS-66, June 2014; $170, MS-64, November 2014; $26, MS-64, November 2014; $84, MS-64, November 2014								
2005-D, American Bison, Satin Finish	1,160,000	3,219	66.6	100%	$0.50	$1	$3	$10
Auctions: No auction records available.								
2005-S, American Bison, Proof	3,344,679	19,259	69.2			$10	$14	$30
Auctions: $34, PF-70DCam, July 2013								
2005-P, Ocean in View	394,080,000	3,286	66.5	100%	$0.25	$0.75	$6	$25
Auctions: $19, MS-66, February 2010								
2005-P, Ocean in View, Satin Finish	1,160,000	3,040	66.7	100%	$0.50	$1	$3	$10
Auctions: No auction records available.								
2005-D, Ocean in View	411,120,000	3,481	66.5	100%	$0.25	$0.75	$5	$22
Auctions: $15, MS-65, August 2009								
2005-D, Ocean in View, Satin Finish	1,160,000	3,248	66.6	100%	$0.50	$1	$3	$10
Auctions: No auction records available.								
2005-S, Ocean in View, Proof	3,344,679	18,964	69.2			$8	$12	$25
Auctions: $21, PF-70DCam, November 2013								

JEFFERSON MODIFIED (2006 TO DATE)

Designers: *Jamie Franki (obverse)* and *Felix Schlag (reverse)*. **Weight:** *5 grams.* **Composition:** *.750 copper, .250 nickel.* **Diameter:** *21.2 mm.* **Edge:** *Plain.* **Mints:** *Philadelphia, Denver, and San Francisco.*

Circulation Strike

Mintmark location, 2006 to date, is on the obverse, below the date.

Proof

History. 2006 saw the return of Felix Schlag's reverse design showing a front view of Jefferson's home, Monticello. It also featured the debut of another new Jefferson portrait on the obverse, this time in three-quarters profile.

Striking and Sharpness. On the obverse, check for weakness on the portrait. Jefferson nickels can be classified as "Full Steps" (FS) if either five or six of Monticello's porch steps (with the top step counting as one) are clear. Notations of 5FS or 6FS can indicate the number of visible steps. It is easier to count the incuse lines than the raised steps. If there are four complete, unbroken lines, the coin qualifies as Full Steps (with five steps); five complete, unbroken lines indicate six full steps. There must be no nicks, cuts, or scratches interrupting the incuse lines. Even if the steps are mostly or fully defined, check other areas to determine if a coin has Full Details overall. Proofs were struck; all have mirror fields. Striking is usually with Full Details, although there are scattered exceptions. Most survivors are in high grade, PF-64 and upward. Most have frosted or cameo contrast on the higher features.

Availability. All basic dates and mintmarks were saved in roll quantities.

GRADING STANDARDS

MS-60 to 70 (Mint State). *Obverse and Reverse:* Mint luster is complete in the obverse and reverse fields. Check the higher parts of the obverse and reverse for abrasion and contact marks.

The Jefferson Modified nickel is seldom collected in grades lower than MS-60.

2011-P. Graded MS-67FS.

PF-60 to 70 (Proof). *Obverse and Reverse:* Evaluation of differences between higher-grade Jefferson Proofs is highly subjective; one certified at PF-65 might be similar to another at PF-67, and vice-versa. All Proof Jefferson Modified nickels have mirror fields. Striking is typically with full details, although there are scattered exceptions. Nearly all Jefferson Modified nickel Proofs are as issued, in PF-69 or 70.

2006-S. Graded PF-70 Deep Cameo.

	Mintage	Cert	Avg	%MS	MS-63	MS-65	MS-65FS	MS-66	MS-66FS	MS-67	MS-67FS / PF-65	MS-68FS / PF-67	MS-69FS / PF-69DC
2006-P, Monticello	693,120,000	281	65.3	100%	$0.25	$0.75	$4	$3	$5	$8	$10	$20	$30
Auctions: $705, MS-67FS, July 2014; $19, MS-64FS, January 2013													
2006-P, Monticello, Satin Finish	847,361	1,233	66.8	100%	$0.50	$1	$2	$3	$5	$10			
Auctions: No auction records available.													
2006-D, Monticello	809,280,000	319	65.7	100%	$0.25	$0.75	$5	$4	$6	$9	$22	$30	$50
Auctions: $11, MS-67, July 2008													
2006-D, Monticello, Satin Finish	847,361	1,341	66.9	100%	$0.50	$1	$2	$3	$5	$10			
Auctions: No auction records available.													
2006-S, Monticello, Proof	3,054,436	7,347	69.3								$5	$12	$25
Auctions: $32, PF-70DCam, April 2013													
2007-P	571,680,000	46	65.1	100%	$0.25	$0.50	$4	$3	$5	$8	$10	$20	$30
Auctions: $11, MS-68FS, July 2008													
2007-P, Satin Finish	895,628	252	66.3	100%	$0.50	$1	$2	$3	$5	$10			
Auctions: No auction records available.													
2007-D	626,160,000	28	64.8	100%	$0.25	$0.50	$5	$4	$6	$9	$22	$30	$50
Auctions: $14, MS-68FS, July 2008													
2007-D, Satin Finish	895,628	217	66.2	100%	$0.50	$1	$2	$3	$5	$10			
Auctions: No auction records available.													
2007-S, Proof	2,577,166	5,528	69.3								$4	$12	$30
Auctions: $15, PF-69DCam, May 2013													
2008-P	279,840,000	94	65.5	100%	$0.25	$0.50	$4	$3	$5	$8	$10	$20	$30
Auctions: No auction records available.													
2008-P, Satin Finish	745,464	84	66.9	100%	$0.50	$1	$2	$3	$5	$10			
Auctions: No auction records available.													
2008-D	345,600,000	60	64.9	100%	$0.25	$0.50	$5	$4	$6	$9	$22	$30	$50
Auctions: No auction records available.													
2008-D, Satin Finish	745,464	104	67.0	100%	$0.50	$1	$2	$3	$5	$10			
Auctions: No auction records available.													
2008-S, Proof	2,169,561	4,113	69.5								$4	$12	$30
Auctions: $56, PF-70DCam, June 2009													
2009-P	39,840,000	209	65.3	100%	$0.30	$0.70	$4	$3	$5	$8	$10	$20	$30
Auctions: No auction records available.													
2009-P, Satin Finish	784,614	191	67.0	100%	$0.50	$1	$2	$3	$5	$10			
Auctions: No auction records available.													
2009-D	46,800,000	161	65.1	100%	$0.30	$0.70	$5	$4	$6	$9	$22	$30	$50
Auctions: No auction records available.													
2009-D, Satin Finish	784,614	196	67.0	100%	$0.50	$1	$2	$3	$5	$10			
Auctions: No auction records available.													
2009-S, Proof	2,179,867	6,201	69.3								$4	$12	$30
Auctions: $79, PF-70UCam, November 2009													
2010-P	260,640,000	73	65.8	100%	$0.25	$0.50	$4	$3	$5	$8	$10	$20	$30
Auctions: $15, MS-67FS, June 2013													
2010-P, Satin Finish	583,897	82	66.9	100%	$0.50	$1	$2	$3	$5	$10			
Auctions: No auction records available.													
2010-D	229,920,000	109	65.9	100%	$0.25	$0.50	$5	$4	$6	$9	$22	$30	$50
Auctions: No auction records available.													
2010-D, Satin Finish	583,897	96	67.4	100%	$0.50	$1	$2	$3	$5	$10			
Auctions: No auction records available.													

	Mintage	Cert	Avg	%MS	MS-63	MS-65	MS-65FS	MS-66	MS-66FS	MS-67	MS-67FS / PF-65	MS-68FS / PF-67	MS-69FS / PF-69DC
2010-S, Proof	1,689,216	4,229	69.3								$4	$12	$30
Auctions: $62, PF-70DCam, June 2013													
2011-P	450,000,000	180	66.5	100%	$0.25	$0.50	$4	$3	$5	$8	$10	$20	$30
Auctions: No auction records available.													
2011-D	540,240,000	233	66.6	100%	$0.25	$0.50	$5	$4	$6	$9	$22	$30	$50
Auctions: No auction records available.													
2011-S, Proof	1,453,276	5,735	69.3								$4	$12	$30
Auctions: $35, PF-70DCam, June 2013													
2012-P	464,640,000	113	66.7	100%	$0.25	$0.50	$4	$3	$5	$8	$10	$20	$30
Auctions: No auction records available.													
2012-D	558,960,000	114	66.7	100%	$0.25	$0.50	$5	$4	$6	$9	$20	$27	$40
Auctions: No auction records available.													
2012-S, Proof	1,237,415	2,205	69.5								$4	$12	$30
Auctions: No auction records available.													
2013-P	607,440,000	98	66.4	100%	$0.25	$0.50	$4	$3	$5	$8	$10	$20	$30
Auctions: No auction records available.													
2013-D	615,600,000	92	66.6	100%	$0.25	$0.50	$5	$4	$6	$9	$20	$27	$40
Auctions: No auction records available.													
2013-S, Proof	802,460	2,287	69.4								$4	$12	$30
Auctions: No auction records available.													
2014-P	635,520,000	137	67.0	100%	$0.25	$0.50	$4	$3	$5	$8	$10	$20	$30
Auctions: No auction records available.													
2014-D	570,720,000	148	67.1	100%	$0.25	$0.50	$5	$4	$6	$9	$20	$27	$40
Auctions: No auction records available.													
2014-S, Proof	665,100	2,760	69.3								$4	$12	$30
Auctions: No auction records available.													
2015-P	752,880,000	0	n/a		$0.25	$0.50	$4	$3	$5	$8	$10	$20	$30
Auctions: No auction records available.													
2015-D	846,720,000	0	n/a		$0.25	$0.50	$5	$4	$6	$9	$20	$27	$40
Auctions: No auction records available.													
2015-S, Proof	1,022,410	0	n/a								$4	$12	$30
Auctions: No auction records available.													
2016-P		0	n/a		$0.25	$0.50	$5	$4	$6	$9	$20	$27	$40
Auctions: No auction records available.													
2016-D		0	n/a		$0.25	$0.50	$5	$4	$6	$9	$20	$27	$40
Auctions: No auction records available.													
2016-S, Proof		0	n/a								$4	$12	$30
Auctions: No auction records available.													

Half Dismes
1792

AN OVERVIEW OF HALF DISMES

Half dimes or five-cent silver coins were provided for in the Mint Act of April 2, 1792. The spelling was stated as *half disme*. The latter word (likely pronounced "dime," as in modern usage, but perhaps in some places as "deem," in the French mode) was used intermittently in government correspondence for years afterward, but on coins dated 1794 and beyond it appeared only as *dime*.

President George Washington, in his fourth annual message to the House of Representatives, November 6, 1792, referred to the half disme:

> In execution of the authority given by the Legislature, measures have been taken for engaging some artists from abroad to aid in the establishment of our Mint; others have been employed at home. Provision has been made of the requisite buildings, and these are now putting into proper condition for the purposes of the establishment.
>
> There has also been a small beginning in the coinage of half-dismes; the want of small coins in circulation calling the first attention to them. The regulation of foreign coins, in correspondence with the principles of our national Coinage, as being essential to their due operation, and to order in our money-concerns, will, I doubt not, be resumed and completed.

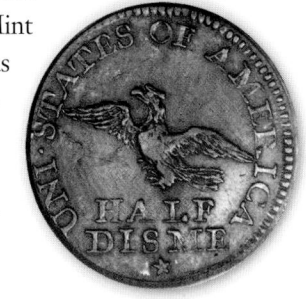

The 1792 half dismes are studied in *United States Pattern Coins* (the hobby's standard reference on pattern coins and experimental and trial pieces), and some numismatists have traditionally referred to them as patterns. It is true that they were struck at a private shop in Philadelphia while the official Mint buildings were still in planning. However, several factors point to their status as regular circulating coins. The half disme was authorized as a federal issue by congressional legislation. Its mintage was considerable—some 1,500 or so pieces—and, as noted by President Washington, the coins were meant to alleviate the national need for small change. Furthermore, nearly all surviving examples show signs of extensive wear.

The 1792 half dismes are not commonly collected, simply because they are not common coins; only 200 to 300 are estimated to still exist. However, their rarity, the romance of their connection to the nation's founding, and the mysteries and legends surrounding their creation make them a perennial favorite among numismatists.

The 1792 half disme has often been considered to be a pattern by some numismatists. Nevertheless, the coins entered circulation as currency over the next decade.

HALF DISME (1792)

Designer: *Unknown (possibly Robert Birch).* **Weight:** *1.35 grams.*
Composition: *.8924 silver, .1076 copper.* **Diameter:** *16.5 mm.*
Edge: *Reeded.* **Mint:** *John Harper's shop, Philadelphia.*

*Judd-7, Pollock-7,
Logan-McCloskey–1.*

History. Rumors and legends are par for the course with the 1792 half disme. Martha Washington is sometimes said to have posed for the portrait of Miss Liberty, despite the profile's dissimilarity to life images of the first lady. Longstanding numismatic tradition says that President George Washington had his own silver tableware taken to the mint factory to be melted down, with these little coins being the result. Whether these Washingtonian connections are true or not, other facts are certain: while the Philadelphia Mint was in the planning stage (its cornerstone would be laid on July 31, 1792), dies were being cut for the first federal coinage of that year. The designer may have been Robert Birch, a Mint engraver who created (or helped create) the dies for the half disme, the disme, and other coins. The half dismes were struck in a private facility owned by saw-maker John Harper, in mid-July. It is believed, from Thomas Jefferson's records, that 1,500 were made. Most were placed into circulation. The coin's designs, with a unique head of Miss Liberty and an outstretched eagle, would not be revived when normal production of the half dime denomination started at the Mint's official facilities in 1795.

Striking and Sharpness. These coins usually are fairly well struck, but with some lightness on Miss Liberty's hair above her ear, and on the eagle's breast. Some examples have adjustment marks from the planchet being filed to adjust the weight prior to striking.

Availability. Most of the estimated 200 to 300 surviving coins show extensive wear. Some AU and MS coins exist, several in choice and gem state, perhaps from among the four examples that Mint Director David Rittenhouse is said to have reserved for himself.

GRADING STANDARDS

MS-60 to 70 (Mint State). *Obverse:* No wear is visible. Luster ranges from nearly full at MS-60 to frosty at MS-65 or higher. Toning often masks the surface, so careful inspection is required. *Reverse:* No wear is visible. The field around the eagle is lustrous, ranging from not completely full at MS-60 to deep and frosty at MS-65 and higher.

1792. Graded MS-64.

AU-50, 53, 55, 58 (About Uncirculated).
Obverse: Light wear is seen on the cheek and on the hair (not as easily observable, as certain areas of the hair may be lightly struck). Luster ranges from light and mostly in protected areas at AU-50, to extensive at AU-58. Friction is evident in the field, less so in the higher ranges. *Reverse:* Light wear is seen on the eagle, but is less noticeable on the letters. Luster ranges from light and mostly in protected areas at AU-50, to extensive at AU-58. Friction is evident in the field, less in the higher ranges.

1792. Graded AU-55.

EF-40, 45 (Extremely Fine). *Obverse:* The hair shows medium wear to the right of the face and on the bust end. The fields have no luster. Some luster may be seen among the hair strands and letters. *Reverse:* The eagle shows medium wear on its breast and the right wing, less so on the left wing. HALF DISME shows wear. The fields have no luster. Some luster may be seen among the design elements and letters.

1792. Graded EF-40.

VF-20, 30 (Very Fine). *Obverse:* More wear is seen on the hair, including to the right of the forehead and face, where only a few strands may be seen. The hair tips at the right are well detailed. The bust end is flat on its high area. Letters all show light wear. *Reverse:* The eagle displays significant wear, with its central part flat and most of the detail missing from the right wing. Letters all show light wear.

1792. Graded VF-30.

F-12, 15 (Fine). *Obverse:* The portrait, above the neck, is essentially flat, but details of the eye, the nose, and, to a lesser extent, the lips can be seen. The bust end and neck truncation are flat. Some hair detail can be seen to the right of the neck and behind the head, with individual strands blended into heavy groups. Both obverse and reverse at this grade and lower are apt to show marks, minor digs, and other evidence of handling.

1792. Graded F-12.

Reverse: Wear is more advanced than on a Very Fine coin, with significant reduction of the height of the lettering, and with some letters weak in areas, especially if the rim nearby is flat.

VG-8, 10 (Very Good). *Obverse:* The head has less detail than a Fine coin and is essentially flat except at the neck. Some hair, in thick strands, can be seen. The letters show extensive wear, but are readable. *Reverse:* The eagle is mostly flat, and the letters are well worn, some of them incomplete at the borders. Detail overall is weaker than on the obverse.

1792. Graded VG-10.

G-4, 6 (Good). *Obverse:* There is hardly any detail on the portrait, except that the eye can be seen, as well as some thick hair tips. The date is clear. Around the border the edges of the letters are worn away, and some are weak overall. *Reverse:* The eagle is only in outline form. The letters are very worn, with some missing.

1792. Graded G-6.

AG-3 (About Good). *Obverse:* Extreme wear has reduced the portrait to an even shallower state. Around the border some letters are worn away completely, some partially. The 1792 date can be seen but is weak and may be partly missing. *Reverse:* Traces of the eagle will remain and there are scattered letters and fragments of letters. Most of the coin is worn flat.

Illustrated coin: The scratches on the obverse should be noted.

1792. Graded AG-3.

	Mintage	Cert	Avg	%MS	AG-3	G-4	VG-8	F-12	VF-20	EF-40	AU-50	MS-60	MS-62
1792 †	1,500	43	49.1	42%	$8,500	$20,000	$27,500	$40,000	$75,000	$110,000	$175,000	$325,000	$400,000
	Auctions: $212,750, AU-58, March 2012												

† Ranked in the *100 Greatest U.S. Coins* (fourth edition).

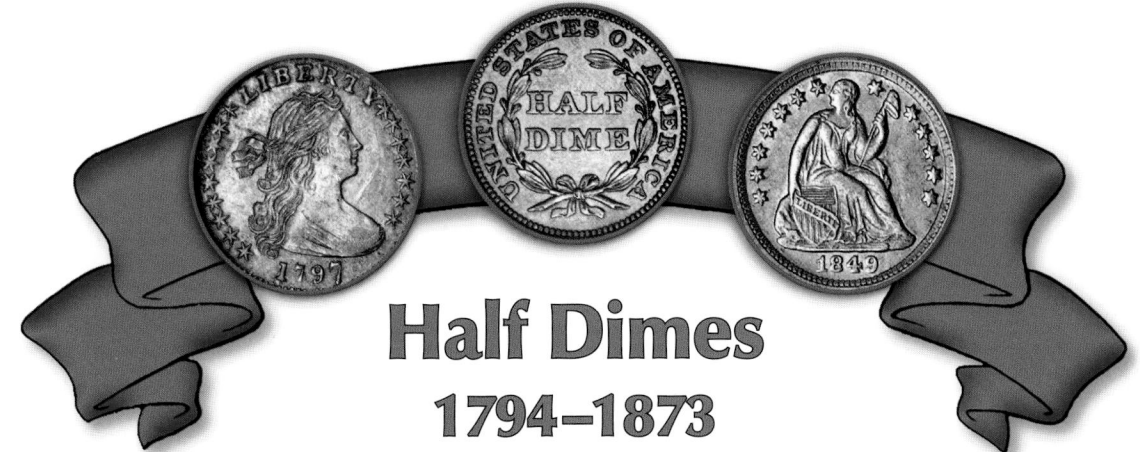

Half Dimes
1794–1873

AN OVERVIEW OF HALF DIMES

The first half dimes, dated 1794 and of the Flowing Hair type, were not actually struck until 1795. In that year additional half dimes with the 1795 date were made. In 1796 and 1797 the short-lived Draped Bust obverse combined with the Small Eagle reverse was used, after which no half dimes were struck until 1801. From that year through 1805, excepting 1804, the Draped Bust obverse was used in combination with the Heraldic Eagle reverse. Then followed a long span of years without any coinage of the denomination. In 1829 the laying of the cornerstone for the second Philadelphia Mint precipitated a new issue, the Capped Bust design, some examples of which were made for the ceremony. Production was resumed for circulation, and half dimes of this motif were made through 1837. In that year the Liberty Seated motif, by Christian Gobrecht, was introduced, to be continued without interruption through 1873, although there were a number of design modifications and changes during that span.

Assembling a set of the different half-dime types is a challenge for the collector. The 1794 and 1795, Flowing Hair, half dimes are fairly scarce at all levels and are quite rare in choice Mint State. Then come the Draped Bust obverse, Small Eagle reverse half dimes of 1796 and 1797. In the late 1960s, researcher Jim Ruddy found that of the various silver types (including the more famous 1796–1797 half dollars), half dimes of this type were the hardest to complete a photographic set of, from the lowest grades to the highest.

Draped Bust obverse, Heraldic Eagle reverse half dimes of the 1800–1805 years are scarce in all grades, more so than generally realized. In Mint State they are very rare, although on occasion some dated 1800 turn up (not often for the others). Finding a *sharply struck* example is next to impossible, and a collector may have to give up on this aspect and settle for one that has some weakness in areas.

Capped Bust half dimes and the several variations of Liberty Seated half dimes will pose no problem at all, and with some small amount of patience a collector will be able to find a sharply struck example in nearly any grade desired.

FOR THE COLLECTOR AND INVESTOR: HALF DIMES AS A SPECIALTY

Collecting half dimes by early die varieties of 1794–1837, and/or by dates and mintmarks (beginning with the 1838-O), has captured the fancy of many numismatists over the years. As these coins are so small it is necessary to have a magnifying glass when studying the series—something the collector of silver dollars and double eagles does not need.

One of the earlier enthusiasts in the field was Philadelphia attorney and numismatist Harold P. Newlin, who in 1883 issued *A Classification of the Early Half Dimes of the United States.* Newlin's two

favorite varieties were the 1792 half disme and the rare 1802, and after reading his enticing prose about the desirability of each, no doubt some collectors in 1883 put both coins on their "must have" lists.

Among early half dimes the rarest and most expensive is the 1802. In 1883 Newlin listed just 16 examples known to him. Although no one has compiled an up-to-date registry, it is likely that fewer than 30 exist. Most are well worn. Other early half dimes range from rare to very rare.

Capped Bust half dimes of the 1829–1837 years are all easily available as dates, but some of the die varieties are very rare. Today, most half dimes on the market are not attributed by varieties, making the search for such things rewarding when a rarity is found for the price of a regular coin.

In 1978 the numismatic world was startled to learn that Chicago dealer Edward Milas had located an 1870-S half dime, a variety not earlier known to exist and not listed in the annual Mint reports. Other than this coin, still unique today, the dates and mints in the Liberty Seated series 1837 to 1873-S are readily collectible by date and mint, with no great rarities. There are several very curious varieties within that span, the most interesting of which may be the 1858, Over Inverted Date. The date was first punched into the die upside down, the error was noted, and then it was corrected.

The new design upon the resumption of the denomination in 1829 was created by Chief Engraver William Kneass. It is thought to have been based upon an earlier design by John Reich.

FLOWING HAIR (1794–1795)

Designer: *Unknown.* **Engraver:** *Robert Scot.*
Weight: *1.35 grams.* **Composition:** *.8924 silver, .1076 copper.*
Diameter: *Approximately 16.5 mm.* **Edge:** *Reeded.* **Mint:** *Philadelphia.*

Logan-McCloskey–3.

History. Half dimes dated 1794 and 1795, of the Flowing Hair type, were all struck in the calendar year 1795, although dies were ready by the end of 1794. The Flowing Hair motif was also used on half dollars and silver dollars of the same years, but not on other denominations.

Striking and Sharpness. Many Flowing Hair half dimes have problems of one sort or another, including adjustment marks (from the planchet being filed down to proper weight) and/or light striking in some areas. On the obverse, check the hair and stars, and on the reverse the breast of the eagle. It may not be possible to find a *needle-sharp* example, but with some extensive searching a fairly decent strike can be obtained. Sharp striking and excellent eye appeal add dramatically to the value.

Availability. Examples appear on the market with frequency, typically in lower circulated grades. Probably 250 to 500 could be classified as MS, most of these dated 1795. Some searching is needed to locate choice examples in any grade. As a rule, half dimes are more readily available than are half dollars and dollars of the same design, and when found are usually more attractive and have fewer problems.

GRADING STANDARDS

MS-60 to 70 (Mint State). *Obverse:* At MS-60 some abrasion and contact marks are evident, most noticeably on the cheek and in the fields. Luster is present, but may be dull or lifeless, and interrupted in patches. At MS-63, contact marks are very few, and abrasion is hard to detect except under magnification. An MS-65 coin has no abrasion, and contact marks are so minute as to require magnification. Luster should be full and rich. Coins

1795; LM-10. Graded MS-63.

graded above MS-65 are more theoretical than actual for this type—but they do exist, and are defined by having fewer marks as perfection is approached. *Reverse:* Comments apply as for the obverse, except that abrasion and contact marks are most noticeable on the eagle at the center. The field area is small and is protected by lettering and the wreath, and in any given grade shows fewer marks than on the obverse.

Illustrated coin: This coin reveals increased olive and blue iridescence under bright light. The central weakness is typical for the striking of this die marriage.

AU-50, 53, 55, 58 (About Uncirculated). *Obverse:* Light wear is seen on the hair area immediately to the left of the face and neck, on the cheek, and on the top of the neck truncation, more so at AU-50 than at AU-53 or 55. An AU-58 coin will have minimal traces of wear. An AU-50 will have luster in protected areas among the stars and letters, with little in the open fields or on the portrait. At AU-58, most luster is present in the fields, but is worn

1794; LM-3. Graded AU-55.

away on the highest parts of the motifs. *Reverse:* Light wear is seen on the eagle's body and right wing. At AU-50, detail is lost in most feathers in this area. However, striking can play a part, and some coins are weak to begin with. Light wear is seen on the wreath and lettering. Luster is the best key to actual wear. This will range from perhaps 20% remaining in protected areas at AU-50 to nearly full mint bloom at AU-58.

Illustrated coin: Liberty's hair displays impressive detail for this grade.

EF-40, 45 (Extremely Fine). *Obverse:* More wear is evident on the portrait, especially on the hair to the left of the face and neck; the cheek; and the tip of the neck truncation. Excellent detail remains in low-relief areas of the hair. The stars show wear, as do the date and letters. Luster, if present at all, is minimal and in protected areas. *Reverse:* The eagle, this being the focal point to check, shows more wear. Observe in combination with a knowl-

1794; LM-2. Graded EF-40.

edge of the die variety, to determine the sharpness of the coin when it was first struck. Some were flat at the center at the time they were made. Additional wear is on the wreath and letters, but many details are present. Some luster may be seen in protected areas, and if present is slightly more abundant than on the obverse.

VF-20, 30 (Very Fine). *Obverse:* The hair is well worn at the VF-20 level, less so at VF-30. The strands are blended so as to be heavy. The cheek shows only slight relief, and the tip of the neck truncation is flat. The stars have more wear, making them appear larger (an optical illusion). *Reverse:* The body of the eagle shows few if any feathers, while the wings have about half of the feathers visible, depending on the strike. The leaves lack

1795; LM-8. Graded VF-30.

detail and are in outline form. Scattered, non-disfiguring marks are normal for this and lower grades. Any major defects should be noted separately.

F-12, 15 (Fine). *Obverse:* Wear is more extensive than on a Very Fine coin, reducing the definition of the thick strands of hair. The cheek has less detail, and the stars appear larger. The rim is distinct and many denticles remain visible. *Reverse:* Wear is more extensive. Now, feather details are reduced, mostly remaining on the right wing. The wreath and lettering are more worn, and the rim is usually weak in areas, although some denticles can be seen.

1794; LM-1. Graded F-12.

Illustrated coin: Two light adjustment marks on the lower left of the portrait date from the time of striking.

VG-8, 10 (Very Good). *Obverse:* The portrait is mostly seen in outline form, with most hair strands gone, although the tips at the lower left are clear. The ear is discernible, as is the eye. The stars appear larger still, again an illusion. The rim is weak in areas. LIBERTY and the date are readable and usually full, although some letters may be weak at their tops. *Reverse:* The eagle is mostly an outline, although some traces of feathers may be seen

1795; LM-9. Graded VG-8.

in the tail and the lower part of the inside of the right wing. The rim is worn, as are the letters, with some weak, but the motto is readable.

G-4, 6 (Good). *Obverse:* Wear is more extensive, and some stars may be missing or only partially visible. The head is an outline, although a few elements of thick hair strands may be seen. The eye is visible only in outline form. The rim is well worn or even missing. LIBERTY is worn, and parts of some letters may be missing, but elements of all are readable. The date is readable, but worn. *Reverse:* The eagle is flat and discernible in outline

1795; LM-8. Graded G-6.

form. The wreath is well worn. Some of the letters may be partly missing. At this level some "averaging" can be done. If the letters are stronger than usual in one area, but some are missing in another area, the coin can still qualify as G-4.

Illustrated coin: There are several adjustment marks on the obverse, but this coin lacks the bisecting obverse die crack typical of later issues struck from this die pair. The reverse die on this coin was rotated 20 degrees out of the normal alignment.

AG-3 (About Good). *Obverse:* Wear is so extensive that the coin is barely identifiable. The head is in outline form, LIBERTY is mostly gone, and the date, while readable, may be partially missing. *Reverse:* The reverse is well worn with parts of the wreath and lettering missing.

1794; LM-4. Graded AG-3.

	Mintage	Cert	Avg	%MS	AG-3	G-4	VG-8	F-12	VF-20	EF-40	AU-50	MS-60	MS-63
1794	(a)	141	51.0	42%	$850	$1,500	$1,800	$2,400	$3,750	$7,500	$10,000	$17,500	$30,000
Auctions: $129,250, MS-65, August 2014; $5,875, EF-45, March 2015; $6,463, EF-40, August 2014; $4,313, VF-30, April 2012													
1795	86,416	392	49.5	34%	$550	$1,350	$1,600	$1,850	$3,250	$6,000	$8,000	$12,500	$21,000
Auctions: $94,000, MS-67, April 2013; $73,438, MS-66, September 2015; $58,750, MS-65, March 2015; $734, F-12, September 2015													

a. Included in 1795 mintage figure.

DRAPED BUST, SMALL EAGLE REVERSE (1796–1797)

Designer: *Probably Gilbert Stuart.* **Engraver:** *Robert Scot.*
Weight: *1.35 grams.* **Composition:** *.8924 silver, .1076 copper.*
Diameter: *Approximately 16.5 mm.* **Edge:** *Reeded.* **Mint:** *Philadelphia.*

LM-2.

History. Although the Draped Bust obverse design was used on various copper and silver coins circa 1795 to 1808, it was employed in combination with the *Small Eagle* reverse only on silver coins of 1795 to 1798—for the half dime series, only in 1796 and 1797.

Striking and Sharpness. Most 1796–1797 half dimes are weak in at least one area. Points to check for sharpness include the hair of Miss Liberty, the centers of the stars, the bust line, and, on the reverse, the center of the eagle. Check for planchet adjustment marks (these are infrequent). Denticles around the border are usually decent, but may vary in strength from one part of the border to another. Sharp striking and excellent eye appeal add to the value dramatically.

Availability. This type is fairly scarce in *any* grade; in MS-63 and finer, no more than a few dozen examples have been traced. As is advisable for other early silver types, beware of deeply toned or vividly iridescent-toned pieces whose flawed surface characters are obscured by the toning, but which are offered as MS; in truth some of these are barely better than EF.

GRADING STANDARDS

MS-60 to 70 (Mint State). *Obverse:* At MS-60 some abrasion and contact marks are evident, most noticeably on the cheek, on the drapery, and in the right field. Luster is present, but may be dull or lifeless, and interrupted in patches. At MS-63, contact marks are very few, and abrasion is hard to detect except under magnification, although this type is sometimes graded liberally due to its rarity. An MS-65 coin has no abrasion, and contact

1797, 16 Stars; LM-2, Valentine-4. Graded MS-62.

marks are so minute as to require magnification. Luster should be full and rich. Coins graded above MS-65 are more theoretical than actual for this type—but they do exist, and are defined by having fewer marks as perfection is approached. *Reverse:* Comments apply as for the obverse, except that abrasion and marks are most noticeable on the eagle at the center, a situation complicated by the fact that this area was often flatly struck. Grading is best done by the obverse, then verified by the reverse. The field area is small and is protected by lettering and the wreath, and in any given grade shows fewer marks than on the obverse.

Illustrated coin: Note the clash marks in the right obverse field, which are typical for this die variety.

AU-50, 53, 55, 58 (About Uncirculated). *Obverse:* Light wear is seen on the hair area above the ear and extending to left of the forehead, on the ribbon, and on the bosom—more so at AU-50 than at AU-53 or 55. An AU-58 coin has minimal traces of wear. An AU-50 coin has luster in protected areas among the stars and letters, with little in the open fields or on the portrait. At AU-58, most luster is present in the fields, but is worn away on the high-

1796, LIKERTY; LM-1. Graded AU-50.

est parts of the motifs. *Reverse:* Light wear is seen on the eagle's body (keep in mind this area might be lightly struck) and edges of the wings. Light wear is seen on the wreath and lettering. Luster is the best key to actual wear. This ranges from perhaps 20% remaining in protected areas at AU-50 to nearly full mint bloom at AU-58.

Illustrated coin: This is the LIKERTY variety, its fanciful name derived from the top and bottom lines of the B being defective.

EF-40, 45 (Extremely Fine). *Obverse:* More wear is evident on the upper hair area and the ribbon and on the drapery and bosom. Excellent detail will remain in low relief areas of the hair. The stars show wear as will the date and letters. Luster, if present at all, is minimal and in protected areas. *Reverse:* The eagle shows more wear, this being the focal point to check. On most examples, many feathers remain on the interior areas of the wings.

1796, LIKERTY; LM-1. Graded EF-40.

Check the eagle in combination with a knowledge of the die variety to determine the sharpness of the coin when it was first struck. Additional wear is evident on the wreath and letters, but many details are present. Some luster may be seen in protected areas and, if present, is slightly more abundant than on the obverse.

VF-20, 30 (Very Fine). *Obverse:* The higher-relief areas of hair are well worn at VF-20, less so at VF-30. The drapery and bosom show extensive wear. The stars have more wear, making them appear larger (an optical illusion seen on most worn silver coins of this era). *Reverse:* The body of the eagle shows few if any feathers, while the wings have about half of the feathers visible, depending on the strike. The leaves lack most detail

1796, LIKERTY; LM-1. Graded VF-30.

and are in outline form. Scattered, non-disfiguring marks are normal for this and lower grades; any major distractions should be noted separately.

F-12, 15 (Fine). *Obverse:* Wear is more extensive than on a Very Fine coin. Wear is particularly noticeable on the hair, face, and bosom, and the stars appear larger. About half the hair detail remains, most noticeably behind the neck and shoulder. The rim may be partially worn away and may blend into the field. *Reverse:* Wear is more extensive. Feather details are diminished, with fewer than half remaining on the wings. The wreath

1797, 13 Stars; LM-4. Graded F-15.

and lettering are worn further, and the rim is usually weak in areas, although some denticles can be seen.

VG-8, 10 (Very Good). *Obverse:* The portrait is mostly seen in outline form, with most hair strands gone, although there is some definition at the back of the hair and behind the shoulder. The ear is discernible, as is the eye. The stars appear larger still, again an illusion. The rim is weak in areas. LIBERTY and the date are readable and usually full, although some letters may be weak at their tops. *Reverse:* The eagle is mostly an outline,

1796, LIKERTY; LM-1. Graded VG-8.

with parts blending into the field (on lighter strikes). The rim is worn, as are the letters, with some weak, but the motto is readable.

G-4, 6 (Good). *Obverse:* Wear is more extensive, and some stars may be partly missing. The head is an outline. The eye is visible only in outline form. The rim is well worn or even missing in areas. LIBERTY is worn, and parts of some letters may be missing, but elements of all should be readable. The date is readable, but worn. *Reverse:* The eagle is flat and discernible in outline form, and may be blending into the field. The wreath is well

1797, 16 Stars. Graded G-4.

worn. Some of the letters may be partly missing. At this level some "averaging" can be done. If the letters are stronger than usual in one area, but some are missing in another area, the coin can still qualify as G-4.

AG-3 (About Good). *Obverse:* Wear is so extensive that the coin is barely identifiable. The head is in outline form. LIBERTY is mostly gone, as are some of the stars. The date, while readable, may be partially worn away. *Reverse:* The reverse is well worn, with parts of the wreath and lettering missing.

1796, LIKERTY; LM-1. Graded AG-3.

1796, 6 Over 5		1796, LIKERTY

1797, 15 Stars	1797, 16 Stars	1797, 13 Stars

	Mintage	Cert	Avg	%MS	AG-3	G-4	VG-8	F-12	VF-20	EF-40	AU-50	MS-60	MS-63
1796, 6 Over 5	10,230	15	52.2	67%	$700	$1,500	$1,800	$3,500	$5,000	$9,500	$15,000	$25,000	$45,000
	Auctions: $31,725, MS-63, August 2013												
1796	(a)	18	50.7	33%	$1,000	$1,800	$2,200	$3,500	$5,000	$8,750	$13,500	$17,500	$35,000
	Auctions: No auction records available.												
1796, LIKERTY (b)	(a)	54	48.7	30%	$700	$1,500	$1,800	$3,450	$4,750	$8,750	$12,500	$16,000	$35,000
	Auctions: $17,625, MS-61, September 2013; $1,586, Fair-2, October 2014; $676, Fair-2, October 2014												
1797, 15 Stars	44,527	34	47.2	21%	$700	$1,500	$1,800	$3,450	$4,750	$8,750	$12,500	$16,000	$25,000
	Auctions: $70,500, MS-64, June 2014; $7,638, AU-55, October 2014; $7,638, AU-53, March 2015; $494, G-4, September 2015												
1797, 16 Stars	(c)	24	45.9	38%	$700	$1,500	$1,800	$3,450	$4,750	$8,750	$12,500	$16,000	$25,000
	Auctions: $54,344, MS-65, June 2014; $734, Fair-2, October 2014; $1,763, Fair-2, August 2014												
1797, 13 Stars	(c)	6	46.8	0%	$750	$2,000	$3,500	$4,500	$6,500	$13,500	$25,000	$40,000	$65,000
	Auctions: $25,850, AU-55, February 2013												

a. Included in 1796, 6 Over 5, mintage figure. **b.** A die imperfection makes the B in LIBERTY somewhat resemble a K. **c.** Included in 1797, 15 Stars, mintage figure.

DRAPED BUST,
HERALDIC EAGLE REVERSE (1800–1805)

Designer: *Robert Scot.* **Weight:** *1.35 grams.* **Composition:** *.8924 silver, .1076 copper.*
Diameter: *Approximately 16.5 mm.* **Edge:** *Reeded.* **Mint:** *Philadelphia.*

LM-1.

History. The combination of Draped Bust obverse / Heraldic Eagle reverse was used in the silver half dime series from 1800 to 1805. The obverse style, standardized with 13 stars, is the same as used in 1796 and 1797. During this span the rare 1802 was produced, and none were minted with the date 1804.

Striking and Sharpness. Most 1800–1805 half dimes are lightly struck in one area or another. The obverse stars usually show some weakness. On many coins the central details of Miss Liberty are not sharp. On the reverse the upper right of the shield and the adjacent part of the eagle's wing are often soft, and several or even most stars may be lightly defined (sharp stars show sharply peaked centers); high parts of the clouds are often weak. The area on the reverse opposite the bosom of Miss Liberty may be flat or weak, due to the metal having to flow in both directions when the coins were struck. (The area curving obliquely up and to the right of the eagle's head—exactly mirroring the curvature of the bust on the obverse—is especially prone to weakness of strike.) Denticles are likely to be weak or missing in areas. Many have Mint-caused adjustment marks, from overweight planchets being filed down to proper specifications. In summary, *a sharply struck coin is a goal, not necessarily a reality.* In this series, sharp striking and excellent eye appeal will add to a coin's value dramatically, this being particularly true for all issues from 1801 to 1805.

Availability. This is a challenging type to find with nice eye appeal. Many toned pieces have been recolored to hide flaws or to improve eye appeal. Some are porous or have other problems. The majority of pieces surviving today are dated 1800, and nearly all of the AU or finer coins are of this date.

GRADING STANDARDS

MS-60 to 70 (Mint State). *Obverse:* At MS-60 some abrasion and contact marks are evident, most noticeably on the cheek, on the drapery, and in the right field. Luster is present, but may be dull or lifeless, and interrupted in patches. At MS-63, contact marks are very few, and abrasion is hard to detect except under magnification, although this type is sometimes graded liberally due to its rarity. An MS-65 coin will have no abrasion,

1800; LM-1, V-1. Graded MS-63.

and contact marks are so minute as to require magnification. Luster should be full and rich. Coins graded above MS-65 are more theoretical than actual for this type—but they do exist, and are defined by having fewer marks as perfection is approached. *Reverse:* Comments apply as for the obverse, except that abrasion and contact marks are most noticeable on the eagle's neck, the tips of the wing, and the tail. The field area is complex—with stars above the eagle, the arrows and olive branch, and other features, there is not much open space. Accordingly, marks will not be as noticeable as on the obverse.

AU-50, 53, 55, 58 (About Uncirculated). *Obverse:* Light wear is seen on the hair area above the ear and extending to left of the forehead, on the ribbon, and on the bosom, more so at AU-50 than at AU–53 or 55. An AU-58 coin will have minimal traces of wear. An AU-50 coin will have luster in protected areas among the stars and letters, with little in the open fields or on the portrait. At AU-58, most luster is present in the fields,

1803, Large 8; LM-2. Graded AU-58.

but is worn away on the highest parts of the motifs. *Reverse:* Comments as for Mint State coins, except that the eagle's neck, the tips and top of the wings, the clouds, and the tail show noticeable wear, as do other features. Luster ranges from perhaps 20% remaining in protected areas at AU-50 to nearly full mint bloom at AU-58. Often the reverse of this type retains much more luster than the obverse.

Illustrated coin: Note the areas of rich, blue toning.

EF-40, 45 (Extremely Fine). *Obverse:* More wear is evident on the upper hair area and the ribbon, and on the drapery and bosom. Excellent detail remains in low-relief areas of the hair. The stars show wear, as do the date and letters. Luster, if present at all, is minimal and only in protected areas. *Reverse:* Wear is greater than on an About Uncirculated coin, overall. The neck lacks feather detail on its highest points. Feathers lose some detail near

1800; LM-1. Graded EF-45.

the edges of the wings, and some areas of the horizontal lines in the shield may be blended together. Some traces of luster may be seen, more so at EF-45 than at EF-40.

Illustrated coin: The obverse cud break is as struck.

VF-20, 30 (Very Fine). *Obverse:* The higher-relief areas of hair are well worn at VF-20, less so at VF-30. The drapery and bosom show extensive wear. The stars have more wear, making them appear larger (an optical illusion seen on most worn silver coins of this era). *Reverse:* Wear is greater, including on the shield and wing feathers. Star centers are flat. Other areas have lost detail as well.

1800; LM-1. Graded VF-20.

F-12, 15 (Fine). *Obverse:* Wear is more extensive than on a Very Fine coin, particularly noticeable on the hair, face, and bosom, and the stars appear larger. About half the hair detail remains, most noticeably behind the neck and shoulder. The rim may be partially worn away and may blend into the field. *Reverse:* Wear is even more extensive, with the shield and wing feathers being points to observe. The incuse E PLURIBUS UNUM

1801; LM-2. Graded F-15.

may have a few letters worn away. The clouds all seem to be connected. The stars are weak. Parts of the border and lettering may be weak.

VG-8, 10 (Very Good). *Obverse:* The portrait is mostly seen in outline form, with most hair strands gone, although there is some definition at the back of the hair and behind the shoulder. The ear is discernible, as is the eye. The stars appear larger still, again an illusion. The rim is weak in areas. LIBERTY and the date are readable and usually full, although some letters may be weak at their tops. *Reverse:* Half or so of the letters in the

1800; LM-1. Graded VG-8.

motto are worn away. Most feather details are worn away, although separation of some of the lower feathers may be seen. Some stars are faint. The border blends into the field in areas, and some letters are weak.

G-4, 6 (Good). *Obverse:* Some stars may be partly missing. The head is an outline. The eye is visible only in outline form. The rim is well worn or even missing in areas. LIBERTY is worn, and parts of some letters may be missing, but elements of all should be readable. The date is readable, but worn. *Reverse:* The upper part of the eagle is flat, and feathers are noticeable only at the lower edge of the wings and do not have detail. The upper part of the

1801; LM-2. Graded G-6.

shield is flat. Only a few letters of the motto can be seen. The rim is worn extensively, and a few letters may be missing.

AG-3 (About Good). *Obverse:* Wear is so extensive that the coin is barely identifiable. The head is in outline form. LIBERTY is mostly gone; same for the stars. The date, while readable, may be partially worn away. *Reverse:* Extensive wear is seen overall, with the rim worn away and some areas worn smooth. The eagle can be discerned in outline form, but not necessarily completely. A few stray motto letters may remain.

1800. Graded AG-3.

1800, LIBEKTY

	Mintage	Cert	Avg	%MS	AG-3	G-4	VG-8	F-12	VF-20	EF-40	AU-50	MS-60	MS-63
1800	24,000	161	45.8	24%	$450	$1,000	$1,500	$2,000	$3,000	$6,000	$8,500	$12,500	$21,500
	Auctions: $25,850, MS-64, August 2014; $4,994, AU-50, October 2014; $2,350, EF-40, November 2014; $676, EF-40, October 2015												
1800, LIBEKTY (a)	16,000	44	45.3	30%	$450	$1,200	$1,750	$2,500	$3,250	$6,200	$8,500	$13,000	$22,000
	Auctions: $31,725, MS-64, April 2014; $3,086, VF-25, October 2014; $617, Fair-2, October 2014												

a. A defective die punch gives the R in LIBERTY the appearance of a K.

| 1803, Large 8 | 1803, Small 8 |

	Mintage	Cert	Avg	%MS	AG-3	G-4	VG-8	F-12	VF-20	EF-40	AU-50	MS-60	MS-63
1801	27,760	27	36.8	19%	$450	$1,500	$2,000	$3,000	$4,000	$6,500	$10,000	$16,000	$27,500
Auctions: $5,581, EF-40, February 2014													
1802 †	3,060	2	50.0	0%	$20,000	$33,000	$44,000	$60,000	$125,000	$250,000	$325,000		
Auctions: $352,500, AU-50, June 2014													
1803, Large 8	37,850	8	39.9	25%	$450	$1,000	$1,300	$2,000	$3,000	$6,500	$9,000	$14,000	$25,000
Auctions: $7,050, AU-50, February 2014													
1803, Small 8	(b)	2	58.0	50%	$450	$1,000	$1,400	$2,500	$3,250	$7,000	$10,000	$20,000	$35,000
Auctions: $5,922, EF-35, April 2013; $999, Fair-2, October 2014													
1805	15,600	27	31.3	4%	$450	$1,000	$1,300	$2,750	$3,500	$9,000	$20,000	$55,000	
Auctions: $9,400, EF-45, August 2013; $729, AG-3, August 2014; $793, Fair-2, October 2014													

† Ranked in the *100 Greatest U.S. Coins* (fourth edition). **b.** Included in 1803, Large 8, mintage figure.

CAPPED BUST (1829–1837)

Engraver: *William Kneass, after a design by John Reich.* **Weight:** *1.35 grams (changed to 1.34 grams in 1837).* **Composition:** *.8924 silver, .1076 copper (changed to .900 silver, .100 copper in 1837).* **Diameter:** *Approximately 15.5 mm.* **Edge:** *Reeded.* **Mint:** *Philadelphia.*

Circulation Strike
LM-7.

Proof
LM-4.

History. Half dimes of the Capped Bust design were first struck the morning of July 4, 1829, to be included in the cornerstone time capsule of the new (second) Philadelphia Mint building and, presumably, to have some inexpensive coins on hand for distribution as souvenirs. Engraver John Reich's design was not new; it had been used on half dollars as early as 1807. It was logical to employ it on the new half dime, a coin that had not been made since 1805. The new half dimes proved popular and remained in circulation for many years.

Striking and Sharpness. Striking varies among Capped Bust half dimes, and most show lightness in one area or another. On the obverse, check the hair details to the left of the eye, as well as the star centers. On the reverse, check the eagle's feathers and neck. The motto, which can be a problem on certain other coins of this design (notably half dollars), is usually bold on the half dimes. Denticles range from well defined to somewhat indistinct, and, in general, are sharper on the obverse than on the reverse.

Proofs. Proofs were struck in small quantities, generally as part of silver Proof sets, although perhaps some were made to mark the Mint cornerstone event mentioned above; facts are scarce. True Proofs have fully mirrored fields. Scrutinize deeply toned pieces (deep toning often masks the true nature of a coin, e.g., if it is not a true Proof, or if it has been cleaned or repaired). Some pieces attributed as "Proofs" are not Proofs. This advice applies across the entire Capped Bust silver series.

Availability. Finding an example in any desired grade should not be a challenge. Finding one with Full Details will take more time. Connoisseurship is required at the MS level, given the high value of these coins.

GRADING STANDARDS

MS-60 to 70 (Mint State). *Obverse:* At MS-60 some abrasion and contact marks are evident, most noticeably on the cheek, on the hair below the left part of LIBERTY, and on the area near the drapery clasp. Luster is present, but may be dull or lifeless, and interrupted in patches. At MS-63, contact marks are very few, and abrasion is hard to detect except under magnification. An MS-65 coin has no abrasion, and has contact marks so minute as to require magnification.

1830; LM-3. Graded MS-65.

Luster should be full and rich, usually more so on half dimes than larger coins of the Capped Bust type. Grades above MS-65 are seen now and again, and are defined by having fewer marks as perfection is approached. *Reverse:* Comments apply as for the obverse, except that abrasion and contact marks are most noticeable on the eagle's neck, the top of the wings, the claws, and the flat band that surrounds the incuse motto. The field is mainly protected by design elements and does not show abrasion as much as does the obverse.

AU-50, 53, 55, 58 (About Uncirculated). *Obverse:* Light wear is seen on the cap, the hair below LIBERTY, the hair near the clasp, and the drapery at the bosom. At AU-58, the luster is extensive except in the open area of the field, especially to the right. At AU–50 and 53, luster remains only in protected areas. *Reverse:* Wear is visible on the eagle's neck, the top of the wings, the claws, and the flat band above the eagle. An AU-58 coin will have

1829; LM-4. Graded AU-58.

nearly full luster. At AU–50 and 53, there will still be significant luster, more than on the obverse.

Illustrated coin: Note the rings of toning on the obverse, displaying russet, cobalt, and rosy iridescence.

EF-40, 45 (Extremely Fine). *Obverse:* Wear is most noticeable on the higher areas of the hair. The cap shows more wear, as does the cheek. Stars, usually protected by the rim, still show their centers (unless lightly struck). Luster, if present, is in protected areas among the star points and close to the portrait. *Reverse:* The wings show wear on the higher areas of the feathers, and some details are lost. Feathers in the neck are light. The eagle's claws and the

1837, Small 5 C.; LM-4. Graded EF-40.

leaves show wear. Luster may be present in protected areas, even if there is little or none on the obverse.

VF-20, 30 (Very Fine). *Obverse:* Wear has caused most of the hair to be combined into thick tresses without delicate features. The curl on the neck is flat. Most stars, unless they were weakly struck, retain their interior lines. *Reverse:* Wear is most evident on the eagle's neck, to the left of the shield, and on the leaves and claws. Most feathers in the wing remain distinct.

1834; LM-2. Graded VF-30.

F-12, 15 (Fine). *Obverse:* Wear is more extensive, with much of the hair blended together. The drapery is indistinct at its upper edge. Stars have lost some detail at the centers, but still have relief (are not flat). *Reverse:* Wear is more extensive, now with only about half of the feathers remaining on the wings. Some of the horizontal lines in the shield may be worn away.

1830; LM-6. Graded F-12.

VG-8, 10 (Very Good). *Obverse:* The hair is less distinct, with the area surrounding the face blended into the facial features. LIBERTY is complete, but weak in areas. The stars are nearly flat, although some interior detail can be seen on certain strikings. *Reverse:* Feathers are fewer and mostly appear on the right wing. Other details are weaker. All lettering remains easily visible.

1829. Graded VG-8.

G-4, 6 (Good). *Obverse:* The portrait is mostly in outline, with few interior details discernible. LIBERTY may still be readable or may be partially worn away, depending on the variety. Stars are flat at their centers. *Reverse:* The eagle mostly is in outline form, although some feathers can be seen in the right wing. All letters around the border are clear. E PLURIBUS UNUM may be weak, sometimes with a few letters worn away.

1829; LM-8. Graded G-6.

AG-3 (About Good). *Obverse:* The portrait is an outline, although traces of LIBERTY can still be seen. The rim is worn down, and some stars are weak. The date remains clear. *Reverse:* The reverse shows more wear overall than the obverse, with the rim indistinct in areas and many letters worn away.

1835, Small Date, Large 5 C. Graded AG-3.

PF-60 to 70 (Proof). *Obverse and Reverse:* Proofs that are extensively cleaned and have many hairlines, or that are dull and grainy, are lower level, such as PF–60 to 62. These are not of great interest to specialists unless they are of rare die varieties (such as 1829, LM–1 to 3, described in the image caption). With medium hairlines, an assigned grade of PF-64 may be in order, and with relatively few hairlines, gem PF-65. PF-66 should have

1829; LM-2, V-3. Graded PF-67+.

hairlines so delicate that magnification is needed to see them. Above that, a Proof should be free of such lines. Grading is highly subjective with early Proofs, and eye appeal also is a factor.

Illustrated coin: Stunning in sharpness of strike and attractiveness of toning, this coin is the finest-known Proof of this type.

	Mintage	Cert	Avg	%MS	G-4	VG-8	F-12	VF-20	EF-40	AU-50	MS-60	MS-63	MS-65
											PF-60	PF-63	PF-65
1829	1,230,000	735	58.0	65%	$75	$90	$135	$190	$250	$300	$400	$925	$3,000
	Auctions: $881, MS-63, October 2015; $705, MS-63, January 2015; $353, MS-60, June 2015; $329, AU-58, September 2015												
1829, Proof	20–30	8	64.4								$4,500	$10,000	$35,000
	Auctions: $36,719, PF-65Cam, January 2014												
1830	1,240,000	624	57.9	67%	$55	$75	$80	$125	$185	$250	$375	$850	$2,500
	Auctions: $852, MS-63, October 2015; $646, MS-62, February 2015; $400, MS-60, May 2015; $353, AU-58, August 2015												
1830, Proof	10–15	3	64.7								$4,500	$12,500	$37,000
	Auctions: $49,938, PF-66, September 2013; $30,550, PF-64, August 2014												
1831	1,242,700	785	60.0	71%	$55	$75	$80	$125	$185	$250	$375	$850	$2,500
	Auctions: $564, MS-62, June 2015; $376, MS-61, October 2015; $259, MS-60, March 2015; $212, AU-58, January 2015												
1831, Proof	20–30	1	67.0								$4,500	$12,500	$38,000
	Auctions: $73,438, PF-67, January 2014												
1832	965,000	964	59.1	69%	$55	$75	$80	$125	$185	$250	$375	$850	$2,500
	Auctions: $823, MS-63, June 2015; $541, MS-62, January 2015; $376, MS-61, March 2015; $247, AU-55, March 2015												
1832, Proof	5–10	2	64.0								$5,000	$13,000	$40,000
	Auctions: $19,550, PF-64, March 2004												
1833	1,370,000	635	58.7	67%	$55	$75	$80	$125	$185	$250	$375	$850	$2,500
	Auctions: $8,813, MS-67, January 2015; $764, MS-63, January 2015; $470, MS-62, January 2015; $282, MS-60, August 2015												

1834, 3 Over Inverted 3
FS-H10-1834-301.

1835, Small Date

1835, Large Date

Small 5 C.

Large 5 C.

	Mintage	Cert	Avg	%MS	G-4	VG-8	F-12	VF-20	EF-40	AU-50	MS-60	MS-63	MS-65
											PF-60	PF-63	PF-65
1834	1,480,000	611	58.9	67%	$55	$75	$80	$125	$185	$250	$375	$850	$2,500
	Auctions: $6,463, MS-67, September 2015; $646, MS-63, October 2015; $517, MS-62, August 2015; $282, AU-55, June 2015												
1834, 3 Over Inverted 3	(a)	22	54.8	50%	$55	$80	$100	$150	$250	$500	$600	$1,200	$4,000
	Auctions: $376, AU-55, October 2015												
1834, Proof	25–35	14	65.0								$4,500	$10,000	$30,000
	Auctions: $32,900, PF-66, November 2013; $12,925, PF-64, October 2014; $14,100, PF-64, August 2014												
1835, All kinds	2,760,000												
1835, Large Date and 5 C.		53	56.2	60%	$55	$75	$80	$125	$185	$250	$375	$850	$2,500
	Auctions: $376, AU-58, March 2015; $188, AU-50, February 2015; $129, AU-50, July 2015; $89, EF-45, May 2015												
1835, Large Date, Small 5 C.		22	57.9	50%	$55	$75	$80	$125	$185	$250	$375	$850	$2,500
	Auctions: $376, MS-62, September 2015												
1835, Small Date, Large 5 C.		30	55.4	60%	$55	$75	$80	$125	$185	$250	$375	$850	$2,500
	Auctions: $165, MS-60, May 2015												
1835, Small Date and 5 C.		42	56.6	62%	$55	$75	$80	$125	$185	$250	$375	$850	$2,500
	Auctions: $494, MS-62, June 2015; $400, MS-62, June 2015; $400, MS-61, July 2015												
1835, Proof		0	n/a								$5,000	$13,000	
	Auctions: No auction records available.												
1836, Small 5 C.	1,900,000	42	54.3	50%	$55	$75	$80	$125	$185	$250	$375	$850	$2,500
	Auctions: $153, EF-45, May 2015												
1836, Large 5 C.	(b)	28	56.7	68%	$55	$75	$80	$125	$185	$250	$375	$850	$2,500
	Auctions: $423, AU-58, October 2015; $201, AU-55, February 2015; $74, AU-50, February 2015; $129, EF-45, January 2015												
1836, 3 Over Inverted 3	(b)	33	55.2	55%	$65	$85	$100	$150	$250	$475	$675	$1,200	$3,750
	Auctions: $329, AU-58, January 2015												
1836, Proof	5–10	2	65.5								$4,500	$10,000	$35,000
	Auctions: $47,000, PF-66, February 2014												
1837, Small 5 C.	871,000	33	58.6	67%	$65	$85	$100	$185	$300	$500	$975	$2,100	$10,000
	Auctions: $1,880, MS-63, June 2013												
1837, Large 5 C.	(c)	29	51.7	48%	$55	$75	$80	$125	$185	$250	$400	$850	$3,500
	Auctions: $5,288, MS-65, March 2015; $159, AU-50, March 2015; $118, AU-50, June 2015; $129, VF-35, February 2015												
1837, Proof (d)	5–10	0	n/a								$6,500	$14,000	$37,500
	Auctions: No auction records available.												

a. Included in circulation-strike 1834 mintage figure. **b.** Included in 1836, Small 5 C., mintage figure. **c.** Included in 1837, Small 5 C., mintage figure. **d.** The 1837, Proof, coin is untraced.

LIBERTY SEATED (1837–1873)

Variety 1, No Stars on Obverse (1837–1838): **Designer:** *Christian Gobrecht.*
Weight: *1.34 grams.* **Composition:** *.900 silver, .100 copper.*
Diameter: *15.5 mm.* **Edge:** *Reeded.* **Mints:** *Philadelphia and New Orleans.*

**Variety 1, No Stars
on Obverse (1837–1838)**
    **Variety 1, No Stars
on Obverse, Proof**

Variety 2, Stars on Obverse (1838–1853): **Designer:** *Christian Gobrecht.*
Weight: *1.34 grams.* **Composition:** *.900 silver, .100 copper.* **Diameter:** *15.5 mm.*
Edge: *Reeded.* **Mints:** *Philadelphia and New Orleans.*

**Variety 2, Stars on
Obverse (1838–1853)**
    **Variety 2, Stars
on Obverse, Proof**

Variety 3, Arrows at Date, Reduced Weight (1853–1855):
Designer: *Christian Gobrecht.* **Weight:** *1.24 grams.* **Composition:** *.900 silver, .100 copper.*
Diameter: *15.5 mm.* **Edge:** *Reeded.* **Mints:** *Philadelphia and New Orleans.*

**Variety 3, Arrows at Date,
Reduced Weight (1853–1855)**
    **Variety 3, Arrows at Date,
Reduced Weight, Proof**

Variety 2 Resumed, With Weight Standard of Variety 3 (1856–1859):
Designer: *Christian Gobrecht.* **Weight:** *1.24 grams.* **Composition:** *.900 silver, .100 copper.*
Diameter: *15.5 mm.* **Edge:** *Reeded.* **Mints:** *Philadelphia and New Orleans.*

**Variety 2 Resumed, Weight
Standard of Variety 3 (1856–1859)**
    **Variety 2 Resumed, Weight
Standard of Variety 3, Proof**

Variety 4, Legend on Obverse (1860–1873): **Designer:** *Christian Gobrecht.*
Weight: *1.24 grams.* **Composition:** *.900 silver, .100 copper.* **Diameter:** *15.5 mm.*
Edge: *Reeded.* **Mints:** *Philadelphia, New Orleans, and San Francisco.*

**Variety 4, Legend on
Obverse (1860–1873)**
    *Mintmark location,
1860–1869 and
1872–1873, is on the
reverse, below the bow.*
    *Mintmark location,
1870–1872, is on the
reverse, above the bow.*
    **Variety 4, Legend
on Obverse, Proof**

History. The Liberty Seated design without obverse stars, known as Variety 1, was used in the half dime and dime series only at the Philadelphia Mint in 1837 and the New Orleans Mint in 1838 (1838-O). The motif, by Christian Gobrecht, follows the obverse inaugurated on the 1836 silver dollar. Miss Liberty has no drapery at her elbow. In 1838 13 obverse stars were added, and in 1840 a restyling (drapery added to the elbow) by Robert Ball Hughes appeared. Arrows were added to the sides of the date starting in 1853, through 1855; these denoted the reduction of weight under the terms of the Act of February 21, 1853. The earlier design resumed in 1856. The reverse design stayed the same during these changes. In 1860 on the half dime the legend UNITED STATES OF AMERICA was moved to the obverse, in place of the stars. The reverse displayed a "cereal wreath" (as it was called in Mint records) enclosing the words HALF DIME.

Striking and Sharpness. For half dimes dated 1837 to 1838, check the highest parts of the Liberty Seated figure (especially the head and horizontal shield stripes) and, on the reverse, the leaves. Check the denticles on both sides. These coins are very attractive, and the starless obverse gives them a cameo-like appearance. For half dimes dated 1838 to 1859, strike quality varies widely. Most from 1838 to 1852 are sharper than later ones, but there are exceptions. (Coins with "mushy" details are especially common among the high-mintage dates of the mid- to late 1850s.) On the obverse, check the star centers, the head and center of Miss Liberty, and the denticles. On the reverse, check the wreath leaves and denticles. Excellent strike and deeply mirrored fields characterized nearly all Proofs. Points to check on coins dated 1860 to 1873 include the head of Miss Liberty on the obverse, the wreath details on the reverse (particularly at the inside upper left, above the H of HALF) and the denticles on both sides. Generally, MS coins have excellent luster, although some struck from relapped dies tend to be prooflike and with many striae. The word LIBERTY is not an infallible guide to grading at lower levels, as on some dies the shield was in lower relief, and the letters wore away less quickly. This guideline should be used in combination with other features. Generally, Proofs are well made, with deeply mirrored fields, although some of the late 1860s and early 1870s can have weak areas. Average quality in the marketplace is higher than for larger Liberty Seated denominations.

Availability. Liberty Seated half dimes are easily available as a type, but with many scarce varieties. The Philadelphia coins are easily available in all grades. The 1838-O is a rarity in true Mint State, often is over-graded, and typically has low eye appeal. Such issues as 1849-O and 1846 are extreme rarities at the true MS level. San Francisco coins, first made in 1863, are rare in MS for the first several years. Grades above MS-65 are seen with regularity, more often than the related No Stars dimes. Quality varies widely, and many MS coins are artificially toned.

Proofs. It is likely that at least several dozen Proofs were made of the 1837 half dime, although perhaps more were made of the related dime. Today, attractive examples exist and are rare. Nearly all designated as Proofs are, indeed, Proofs. If you aspire to acquire one, select an example with deep mirror surfaces. 1858 was the first year Proofs were widely sold to collectors, and an estimated 210 silver sets were distributed. (Proofs were made of earlier dates, but in much smaller numbers.) It is believed that 800 Proofs were struck of 1859, of which slightly more than 400 found buyers. From 1860 to 1873, Proof coins were made in fair quantities each year and are readily available today. The quality of Proofs on the market varies widely, mainly due to cleaning and dipping. Patience and care are needed to find a choice example.

GRADING STANDARDS

MS-60 to 70 (Mint State). *Obverse:* At MS-60 some abrasion and contact marks are evident, most noticeably on the bosom, thighs, and knees. Luster is present, but may be dull or lifeless, and interrupted in patches in the large open field. At MS-63, contact marks are very few, and abrasion is hard to detect except under magnification. An MS-65 coin has no abrasion, and contact marks are so minute as to require magnification. Luster

1844-O, Small O; V-2. Graded MS-64.

should be full and rich, except for Philadelphia (but not San Francisco) half dimes of the early and mid-1860s. Most Mint State coins of 1861 to 1865, Philadelphia issues, will have extensive die striae (from the dies being incompletely finished). Some low-mintage Philadelphia issues may be prooflike (and some may even be mislabeled as Proofs). Clashmarks are common in this era. Half dimes of this type can be very beautiful at this level. *Reverse:* Comments apply as for the obverse except that in lower Mint State grades abrasion and contact marks are most noticeable on the highest parts of the leaves and the ribbon, less so on HALF DIME. The field is mainly protected by design elements and does not show abrasion as much as does the open-field obverse on a given coin.

Illustrated coin: This coin was struck in medallic alignment, as is seen with multiple examples of 1844-O, V-2.

AU-50, 53, 55, 58 (About Uncirculated). *Obverse:* Light wear is seen on the thighs and knees, bosom, and head. At AU-58, the luster is extensive, but incomplete. Friction is seen in the large open field. At AU–50 and 53, luster is less. *Reverse:* Wear is noticeable on the leaves and ribbon. An AU-58 coin has nearly full luster—more so than on the obverse, as the design elements protect the small field areas. At AU–50 and 53, there still is significant luster, more than on the obverse.

1853, Arrows. Graded AU-50.

EF-40, 45 (Extremely Fine). *Obverse:* Further wear is seen on all areas, especially the thighs and knees, bosom, and head. Little or no luster is seen. *Reverse:* Further wear is seen on all areas, most noticeably at the leaves to each side of the wreath apex, and on the ribbon bow knot. Leaves retain details except on the higher areas.

1852-O. Graded EF-40.

VF-20, 30 (Very Fine). *Obverse:* Further wear is seen. Most details of the gown are worn away, except in the lower-relief areas above and to the right of the shield. Hair detail is gone on the higher points. *Reverse:* Wear is more extensive. The highest leaves are flat, particularly the larger leaves at the top of the wreath.

1846. Graded VF-35.

F-12, 15 (Fine). *Obverse:* The seated figure is well worn, but with some detail above and to the right of the shield. LIBERTY on the shield is fully readable, but weak in areas. *Reverse:* Most detail of the leaves is gone. The rim is worn but remains bold, and most if not all denticles are visible.

1844-O; V-6. Graded F-15.

VG-8, 10 (Very Good). *Obverse:* The seated figure is more worn, but some detail can be seen above and to the right of the shield. The shield is discernible. In LIBERTY at least three letters are readable but very weak at VG-8; a few more appear at VG-10. *Reverse:* Further wear has combined the details of most leaves. The rim is complete, but weak in areas. On most coins the reverse appears to be in a slightly higher grade than the obverse.

1846. Graded VG-10.

G-4, 6 (Good). *Obverse:* The seated figure is worn smooth. At G-4 there are no letters in LIBERTY remaining. At G-6, traces of one or two can be seen. *Reverse:* Wear is more extensive. The leaves are all combined and in outline form. The rim is clear but well worn and missing in some areas, causing the outer parts of the peripheral letters to be worn away in some instances. On most coins the reverse appears to be in a slightly higher grade than the obverse.

Illustrated coin: This is a No Stars variety.

1837, Small Date. Graded G-4.

AG-3 (About Good). *Obverse:* The seated figure is mostly visible in outline form, with no detail. The rim is worn away. The date remains clear. *Reverse:* Many if not most letters are worn away, as are parts of the wreath, though this and the interior letters are discernible. The rim can usually be seen, but is weak.

Illustrated coin: This is a No Stars variety.

1837, Small Date. Graded AG-3.

PF-60 to 70 (Proof). *Obverse and Reverse:* Proofs that are extensively cleaned and have many hairlines, or that are dull and grainy, are lower level, such as PF–60 to 62. These are not widely desired, save for the rare (in any grade) date of 1846. Both the half dime and dime Proofs of 1837 were often cleaned, resulting in coins which have lost much of their mirror surface. With medium hairlines and good reflectivity, a grade of PF-64 is

1873. Graded PF-66 Ultra Cameo.

assigned, and with relatively few hairlines, gem PF-65. In various grades hairlines are most easily seen in the obverse field. PF-66 should have hairlines so delicate that magnification is needed to see them. Above that, a Proof should be free of such lines.

1837, Small Date *Note the flat-topped 1.*	**1837, Large Date** *Note the pointed-top 1.*	**No Drapery From Elbow** (1837–1840)	**Drapery From Elbow** (Starting 1840)

	Mintage	Cert	Avg	%MS	G-4	VG-8	F-12	VF-20	EF-40	AU-50	MS-60	MS-63	MS-65
											PF-60	PF-63	PF-65
1837, Small Date	1,405,000	47	58.4	68%	$40	$55	$80	$145	$235	$500	$725	$1,100	$3,400
Auctions: $7,050, MS-67, January 2015; $1,175, MS-64, July 2015; $705, MS-63, January 2015; $793, MS-62, June 2015													
1837, Large Date	(a)	30	61.7	83%	$40	$55	$80	$145	$235	$500	$700	$1,000	$3,000
Auctions: $8,225, MS-67, January 2015; $3,290, MS-66, September 2015; $2,115, MS-65, September 2015; $541, MS-62, January 2015													
1837, Proof	15–20	10	64.3								$6,500	$14,000	$37,500
Auctions: $105,750, PF-67, June 2014													
1838-O, No Stars	70,000	41	46.9	32%	$90	$150	$235	$550	$850	$1,250	$2,400	$8,500	$32,000
Auctions: $21,150, MS-65, October 2015; $17,625, MS-64, October 2015; $7,050, MS-62, October 2015; $4,700, MS-62, July 2015													

a. Included in 1837, Small Date, mintage figure.

1838, Normal Stars

1838, Small Stars

1840-O, No Drapery, Normal Reverse
Note four-leaf cluster next to DIME.

1840-O, No Drapery, Transitional Reverse
Note three-leaf cluster next to DIME.

	Mintage	Cert	Avg	%MS	G-4	VG-8	F-12	VF-20	EF-40	AU-50	MS-60 / PF-60	MS-63 / PF-63	MS-65 / PF-65
1838, No Drapery, Large Stars	2,225,000	715	60.7	77%	$18	$21	$28	$35	$75	$175	$250	$420	$1,700
Auctions: $5,523, MS-67, October 2015; $2,585, MS-66, January 2015; $999, MS-65, January 2015; $705, MS-64, January 2015													
1838, No Drapery, Small Stars	(a)	52	57.6	62%	$22	$30	$55	$100	$185	$360	$560	$1,100	$3,750
Auctions: $3,290, MS-66, October 2015; $2,820, MS-65, October 2015; $423, AU-58, October 2015; $306, AU-55, February 2015													
1838, Proof	4–5	2	64.5								$10,000	$12,500	$50,000
Auctions: $129,250, PF-67, October 2014; $182,125, PF-66, January 2014													
1839, No Drapery	1,069,150	308	60.5	74%	$20	$25	$30	$40	$75	$160	$260	$420	$1,800
Auctions: $5,405, MS-66, October 2015; $1,175, MS-65, February 2015; $400, MS-63, January 2015; $329, MS-60, October 2015													
1839, Proof	5–10	3	64.7								$10,000	$12,500	$37,500
Auctions: $27,600, PF-65Cam, April 2008													
1839-O, No Drapery	1,291,600	76	52.0	43%	$20	$25	$30	$40	$80	$170	$525	$1,850	$6,250
Auctions: $16,450, MS-67, May 2015; $7,050, MS-65, October 2015; $1,998, MS-63, January 2015; $1,175, MS-62, August 2015													
1840, No Drapery	1,034,000	296	60.2	75%	$20	$25	$30	$35	$75	$175	$260	$420	$2,000
Auctions: $6,000, MS-67, August 2015; $2,585, MS-66, October 2015; $1,293, MS-65, October 2015; $470, MS-64, January 2015													
1840, No Drapery, Proof	5–10	3	65.7								$10,000	$12,500	$40,000
Auctions: $30,550, PF-64, April 2014													
1840-O, No Drapery	695,000	54	51.7	26%	$20	$23	$30	$40	$85	$285	$725	$2,250	$15,000
Auctions: $18,213, MS-66, June 2014; $11,163, MS-65, October 2015; $141, EF-45, July 2014; $80, VF-25, September 2014													
1840-O, No Drapery, Transitional Reverse (b)	100	0	n/a						$800	$1,250	$1,600		
Auctions: $431, F-15, November 2011													
1840, Drapery	310,085	64	59.4	77%	$25	$40	$55	$120	$210	$360	$460	$825	$2,700
Auctions: $3,995, MS-65, October 2015; $1,763, MS-65, August 2015; $329, AU-55, April 2015													
1840, Drapery, Proof	(c)	0	n/a										
Auctions: No auction records available.													
1840-O, Drapery	240,000	41	46.6	12%	$30	$55	$110	$160	$425	$1,250	$3,100	$8,200	
Auctions: $9,988, AU-58, October 2015; $282, VF-30, September 2015													
1841	1,150,000	180	61.0	81%	$16	$20	$30	$35	$75	$160	$210	$325	$1,300
Auctions: $1,528, MS-66, January 2015; $1,175, MS-65, October 2015; $940, MS-65, October 2015; $141, AU-55, January 2015													
1841, Proof	10–20	4	64.3								$10,000	$15,000	$32,500
Auctions: $28,200, PF-65, October 2014; $46,000, PF-65, January 2008													
1841-O	815,000	53	51.4	26%	$20	$24	$35	$50	$110	$300	$665	$1,525	$6,000
Auctions: $8,225, MS-66, October 2015; $3,173, MS-64, October 2015; $470, AU-55, April 2015													

a. Included in 1838, No Drapery, Large Stars, mintage figure. **b.** "This rare transitional variety exhibits large letters and open or split buds on the reverse die, along with a small O mintmark. The key diagnostic of the variety is three-leaf clusters on either side of the word DIME, while the common reverse has four-leaf clusters" (*Cherrypickers' Guide to Rare Die Varieties*, sixth edition, volume II). **c.** The mintage figure is unknown.

1848, Medium Date	1848, Large Date	1849, So-Called 9 Over 6 FS-H10-1849-302.	1849, 9 Over 8 FS-H10-1849-301.

	Mintage	Cert	Avg	%MS	G-4	VG-8	F-12	VF-20	EF-40	AU-50	MS-60 PF-60	MS-63 PF-63	MS-65 PF-65
1842	815,000	183	59.9	70%	$16	$20	$27	$35	$75	$160	$210	$325	$1,250
	Auctions: $3,055, MS-66, May 2015; $1,058, MS-66, October 2015; $652, MS-64, August 2015; $400, MS-63, July 2015												
1842, Proof	*10–20*	4	64.8								$8,000	$12,000	$22,500
	Auctions: $12,075, PF-64, January 2010												
1842-O	350,000	37	46.4	24%	$30	$40	$65	$185	$525	$825	$1,275	$2,250	$12,500
	Auctions: $18,800, MS-66, May 2015; $13,513, MS-66, October 2015; $1,998, MS-63, October 2015; $1,763, MS-63, October 2015												
1843	815,000	235	59.5	69%	$16	$20	$27	$35	$75	$160	$210	$325	$1,400
	Auctions: $1,645, MS-66, October 2015; $676, MS-63, October 2015; $259, MS-62, August 2015; $165, AU-58, April 2015												
1843, 1843 Over 1843, Proof	*10–20*	1	67.0								$8,000	$12,000	$22,500
	Auctions: $55,813, PF-67, January 2014												
1844	430,000	166	61.8	86%	$16	$20	$27	$35	$75	$160	$210	$325	$1,400
	Auctions: $1,058, MS-66, January 2015; $1,293, MS-65, October 2015; $823, MS-64, October 2015; $423, MS-63, October 2015												
1844, Proof	*15–25*	6	64.5								$8,000	$12,000	$25,000
	Auctions: $35,250, PF-67, February 2014; $12,925, PF-64, October 2014												
1844-O	220,000	34	39.3	12%	$80	$115	$200	$550	$1,100	$3,200	$5,600	$11,000	$25,000
	Auctions: $7,050, MS-64, October 2015; $1,293, EF-45, January 2015; $317, EF-40, January 2015; $494, VF-30, September 2015												
1845	1,564,000	218	59.1	69%	$16	$20	$27	$35	$75	$160	$210	$325	$1,100
	Auctions: $3,995, MS-67, May 2015; $1,175, MS-66, June 2015; $793, MS-64, October 2015; $306, MS-63, March 2015												
1845, Proof	*10–15*	6	65.3								$9,000	$14,000	$30,000
	Auctions: $64,625, PF-68, January 2014												
1846	27,000	55	30.7	2%	$350	$525	$900	$1,250	$2,750	$4,600	$11,000	$25,000	
	Auctions: $2,115, VF-25, January 2015; $1,998, VF-20, July 2015; $1,293, G-8, June 2015; $1,116, G-8, January 2015												
1846, Proof	*10–20*	8	65.4								$8,000	$12,000	$26,000
	Auctions: $35,250, PF-66, June 2014												
1847	1,274,000	216	58.7	69%	$16	$20	$27	$35	$75	$160	$225	$500	$1,250
	Auctions: $1,763, MS-66, January 2015; $940, MS-65, January 2015; $447, MS-64, April 2015; $259, MS-63, January 2015												
1847, Proof	*8–12*	3	64.7								$8,000	$12,000	$24,000
	Auctions: $38,188, PF-67, October 2014; $36,719, PF-66Cam, April 2014												
1848, Medium Date	668,000	97	57.7	57%	$16	$20	$27	$35	$75	$160	$250	$500	$2,750
	Auctions: $3,525, MS-65, May 2015; $1,293, MS-64, June 2015; $447, MS-63, February 2015; $329, AU-58, April 2015												
1848, Large Date	(d)	33	57.4	55%	$22	$32	$45	$65	$130	$285	$575	$1,600	$3,500
	Auctions: $14,100, MS-66, May 2015; $1,645, MS-62, September 2015; $470, AU-58, February 2015; $306, AU-53, February 2015												
1848, Proof	*6–8*	2	65.0								$9,000	$14,000	$25,000
	Auctions: $63,250, PF-66, July 2008												
1848-O	600,000	77	62.1	84%	$22	$25	$35	$60	$120	$250	$410	$720	$2,200
	Auctions: $12,338, MS-67, January 2014												
1849, All kinds	1,309,000												
1849, 9 Over 6 (e)		38	56.5	66%	$25	$35	$40	$60	$125	$225	$500	$1,200	$2,250
	Auctions: $2,585, MS-65, June 2014; $200, MS-60, September 2014												
1849, 9 Over Widely Placed 6 (f)		21	54.5	48%	$30	$40	$60	$100	$175	$260	$620	$1,400	$2,750
	Auctions: $5,405, MS-67, October 2015; $541, MS-62, March 2015; $306, MS-62, April 2015; $270, AU-58, April 2015												

d. Included in 1848, Medium Date, mintage figure. **e.** Fivaz and Stanton contend that this is actually a 9 Over 8 overdate (*Cherrypickers' Guide to Rare Die Varieties*, sixth edition, volume II). **f.** The 4 of the date is at least triple punched, with one secondary 4 south and one east of the primary 4. There is also a secondary numeral east of the lower portion of the 9.

	Mintage	Cert	Avg	%MS	G-4	VG-8	F-12	VF-20	EF-40	AU-50	MS-60	MS-63	MS-65
											PF-60	PF-63	PF-65
1849, Normal Date		146	58.2	59%	$20	$25	$30	$40	$75	$160	$235	$520	$1,600
Auctions: $4,406, MS-67, June 2014; $270, MS-61, November 2014; $188, AU-58, November 2014													
1849, Proof	8–12	5	65.0								$8,000	$12,000	$25,000
Auctions: $22,325, PF-65, June 2014													
1849-O	140,000	54	49.5	35%	$30	$40	$85	$220	$475	$1,200	$2,500	$4,200	$10,000
Auctions: $4,465, MS-64, October 2015; $1,528, MS-61, September 2015; $1,293, AU-53, January 2015; $223, VF-30, February 2015													
1850	955,000	230	61.4	83%	$18	$22	$28	$40	$75	$160	$220	$350	$1,200
Auctions: $7,050, MS-67, October 2015; $1,116, MS-66, March 2015; $705, MS-65, July 2015; $494, MS-64, June 2015													
1850, Proof	8–12	4	64.0								$12,000	$20,000	$45,000
Auctions: $57,500, PF-65, January 2008													
1850-O	690,000	67	55.1	52%	$25	$30	$40	$65	$120	$310	$750	$1,650	$4,000
Auctions: $11,456, MS-67, January 2015; $7,638, MS-66, October 2015; $1,293, MS-63, October 2015; $212, AU-50, September 2015													
1851	781,000	159	59.0	74%	$18	$22	$28	$40	$75	$160	$210	$325	$1,200
Auctions: $8,813, MS-67, May 2015; $4,171, MS-67, January 2015; $646, MS-64, October 2015; $235, MS-62, April 2015													
1851-O	860,000	117	56.9	57%	$25	$30	$35	$50	$110	$235	$525	$850	$3,850
Auctions: $5,170, MS-66, May 2015; $4,465, MS-65, October 2015; $588, MS-62, March 2015; $376, MS-61, February 2015													
1852	1,000,500	183	61.9	84%	$18	$22	$28	$40	$75	$160	$210	$325	$1,200
Auctions: $1,410, MS-66, October 2015; $705, MS-65, January 2015; $317, MS-63, March 2015; $141, AU-58, September 2015													
1852, Proof	10–15	9	64.2								$8,000	$12,000	$25,000
Auctions: $30,550, PF-65, January 2014; $19,975, PF-65, June 2015; $14,100, PF-64, October 2014													
1852-O	260,000	53	51.9	40%	$30	$40	$75	$135	$260	$525	$865	$2,000	$8,250
Auctions: $646, AU-58, August 2015; $353, AU-50, January 2015; $206, AU-50, June 2015; $84, VF-20, June 2015													
1853, No Arrows	135,000	136	59.9	79%	$35	$45	$75	$135	$260	$500	$750	$1,200	$2,500
Auctions: $2,510, MS-66, July 2015; $1,880, MS-65, September 2015; $1,175, MS-64, January 2015; $940, MS-63, January 2015													
1853-O, No Arrows	160,000	31	34.9	6%	$200	$300	$425	$750	$2,250	$3,500	$6,200	$12,500	$35,000
Auctions: $32,900, MS-65, October 2014; $25,850, MS-65, October 2014; $3,819, AU-55, April 2013; $1,175, VF-25, January 2015													
1853, With Arrows	13,210,020	1,258	57.5	61%	$20	$25	$30	$35	$70	$140	$200	$310	$1,450
Auctions: $7,638, MS-67, August 2015; $1,880, MS-66, August 2015; $470, MS-64, January 2015; $259, MS-63, January 2015													
1853, With Arrows, Proof (g)	3–5	1	64.0								$20,000	$25,000	
Auctions: No auction records available.													
1853-O, With Arrows	2,200,000	95	53.6	48%	$20	$25	$35	$50	$75	$160	$275	$925	$3,400
Auctions: $15,275, MS-67, October 2015; $5,405, MS-66, October 2015; $376, MS-61, October 2015; $259, AU-58, September 2015													
1854	5,740,000	630	58.5	70%	$20	$25	$30	$35	$65	$140	$230	$325	$1,500
Auctions: $7,050, MS-67, October 2015; $1,645, MS-66, June 2015; $1,116, MS-65, January 2015; $494, MS-64, February 2015													
1854, Proof	15–25	11	64.5								$4,750	$8,500	$14,000
Auctions: $9,694, PF-65, August 2013													
1854-O	1,560,000	101	58.6	65%	$20	$24	$35	$45	$75	$155	$285	$775	$3,600
Auctions: $15,275, MS-67, October 2015; $4,465, MS-66, October 2015; $1,058, MS-64, October 2015; $999, MS-63, October 2015													
1855	1,750,000	250	60.3	75%	$20	$25	$30	$35	$65	$130	$210	$350	$2,200
Auctions: $8,813, MS-67, February 2015; $2,585, MS-66, July 2015; $1,293, MS-65, July 2015; $353, MS-63, August 2015													
1855, Proof	15–25	20	65.1								$4,750	$8,500	$14,000
Auctions: $21,150, PF-66, June 2014; $11,750, PF-65, October 2014; $8,519, PF-65, June 2015													
1855-O	600,000	81	58.7	67%	$20	$25	$35	$55	$175	$200	$575	$1,100	$4,200
Auctions: $4,230, MS-65, October 2015; $84, VF-35, April 2015													
1856	4,880,000	472	59.9	74%	$18	$22	$25	$35	$65	$130	$185	$320	$1,200
Auctions: $1,410, MS-66, October 2015; $846, MS-65, January 2015; $447, MS-63, May 2015; $212, MS-63, January 2015													
1856, Proof	40–60	25	64.8								$2,500	$4,500	$8,500
Auctions: $8,813, PF-65, October 2015; $4,230, PF-64, October 2015; $4,113, PF-64, July 2015													
1856-O	1,100,000	96	55.7	35%	$18	$22	$25	$55	$110	$265	$575	$1,000	$2,350
Auctions: $3,408, MS-66, October 2015; $1,645, MS-65, October 2015; $470, AU-58, April 2015; $235, AU-55, January 2015													

g. This coin is extremely rare.

1858, Repunched High Date
FS-H10-1858-301.

1858, Over Inverted Date
FS-H10-1858-302.

1860, Obverse of 1859, Reverse of 1860
Transitional pattern, with stars (Judd-247).

	Mintage	Cert	Avg	%MS	G-4	VG-8	F-12	VF-20	EF-40	AU-50	MS-60 PF-60	MS-63 PF-63	MS-65 PF-65
1857	7,280,000	845	59.9	76%	$18	$22	$25	$35	$65	$130	$185	$320	$1,100
Auctions: $6,463, MS-68, September 2015; $2,585, MS-67, September 2015; $1,058, MS-66, June 2015; $646, MS-65, January 2015													
1857, Proof	*40–60*	29	65.0								$2,200	$3,000	$5,500
Auctions: $21,738, PF-67Cam, January 2014; $7,050, PF-66, August 2014; $4,935, PF-66, May 2015													
1857-O	1,380,000	231	57.8	63%	$18	$22	$25	$45	$70	$200	$375	$500	$1,600
Auctions: $3,525, MS-67, June 2015; $1,293, MS-66, October 2015; $1,058, MS-65, October 2015; $329, MS-62, October 2015													
1858	3,500,000	734	60.9	81%	$18	$22	$25	$35	$65	$130	$185	$320	$1,100
Auctions: $2,800, MS-67, January 2015; $999, MS-66, September 2015; $881, MS-65, January 2015; $388, MS-64, March 2015													
1858, Repunched High Date (h)	(i)	6	43.2	17%	$40	$60	$100	$150	$235	$350	$650	$1,200	$3,000
Auctions: $135, AU-50, November 2014; $65, VF-30, July 2011													
1858, Over Inverted Date (j)	(i)	28	55.9	50%	$40	$60	$100	$150	$220	$325	$625	$1,100	$2,750
Auctions: $7,638, MS-65, February 2014													
1858, Proof	*300*	84	64.1								$850	$1,400	$4,500
Auctions: $3,055, PF-65Cam, October 2015; $823, PF-62, September 2015													
1858-O	1,660,000	232	60.1	77%	$18	$22	$30	$50	$80	$155	$265	$450	$1,450
Auctions: $517, MS-64, August 2015; $470, MS-64, October 2015; $435, MS-63, May 2015; $212, MS-61, April 2015													
1859	340,000	250	62.0	84%	$18	$22	$30	$45	$80	$130	$220	$425	$1,250
Auctions: $5,640, MS-68, January 2015; $3,290, MS-67, October 2015; $2,585, MS-67, August 2015; $329, MS-63, October 2015													
1859, Proof	*800*	233	64.0								$550	$1,250	$3,500
Auctions: $5,640, PF-66Cam, September 2015; $3,525, PF-66, October 2015; $2,585, PF-65, October 2015; $1,293, PF-64, March 2015													
1859, Obverse of 1859 (With Stars), Reverse of 1860, Proof (k)	*20*	6	63.5								$19,000	$35,000	$55,000
Auctions: $34,500, PF-63, August 2010													
1859-O	560,000	121	60.9	76%	$20	$25	$35	$50	$130	$210	$285	$375	$1,950
Auctions: $4,935, MS-66, October 2015; $881, MS-64, October 2015; $423, MS-63, August 2015; $282, MS-62, October 2015													
1860, Obverse of 1859 (With Stars), Reverse of 1860 (l)	*100*	57	64.4	100%							$2,500 $3,000	$3,750	$5,600
Auctions: $5,750, MS-66, February 2012													
1860, Legend on Obverse	798,000	529	62.3	86%	$16	$20	$25	$30	$50	$85	$160	$260	$800
Auctions: $2,115, MS-67, January 2015; $881, MS-66, January 2015; $705, MS-65, January 2015; $447, MS-64, January 2015													
1860, Proof	1,000	115	64.4								$350	$550	$1,500
Auctions: $2,115, PF-66Cam, July 2014; $$3,290, PF-66Cam, April 2014; 1,528, PF-65Cam, July 2014													
1860-O	1,060,000	241	59.9	74%	$16	$20	$25	$30	$50	$100	$200	$320	$950
Auctions: $7,050, MS-67, August 2015; $1,116, MS-65, October 2015; $447, MS-64, June 2015; $259, MS-63, October 2015													

h. The date was first punched into the die very high, then corrected and punched into its normal location. The original high-date punch is clearly visible within the upper portions of the primary date. **i.** Included in circulation-strike 1858 mintage figure. **j.** The date was first punched into the die in an inverted orientation, and then corrected. The bases of the secondary digits are evident above the primary digits. **k.** This transitional issue, made surreptitiously at the Mint for a private collector, has the new Liberty Seated die made in the old style of 1859, but with the date of 1860. The reverse is the regular die of 1860, with a cereal wreath. Classified as Judd-267 (*United States Pattern Coins*, tenth edition). **l.** Classified as Judd-232 (*United States Pattern Coins*, tenth edition), this features the obverse design of 1859 and the reverse of 1860.

1861, So-Called 1 Over 0
FS-H10-1861-301.

	Mintage	Cert	Avg	%MS	G-4	VG-8	F-12	VF-20	EF-40	AU-50	MS-60 PF-60	MS-63 PF-63	MS-65 PF-65
1861	3,360,000	647	59.5	71%	$16	$20	$25	$30	$50	$85	$160	$260	$750
Auctions: $2,820, MS-67, October 2015; $1,763, MS-66, August 2015; $617, MS-65, August 2015; $329, MS-64, January 2015													
1861, So-Called 1 Over 0	(m)	0	n/a		$35	$45	$50	$90	$250	$375	$600	$900	$2,000
Auctions: $3,290, MS-66, October 2015; $1,645, MS-65, June 2015; $1,293, MS-64, January 2015; $588, MS-62, February 2015													
1861, Proof	1,000	96	64.4								$350	$550	$1,500
Auctions: $6,169, PF-67, June 2014													
1862	1,492,000	684	62.3	86%	$25	$30	$45	$55	$65	$110	$180	$260	$750
Auctions: $2,115, MS-67, January 2015; $494, MS-65, January 2015; $329, MS-64, January 2015; $259, MS-63, August 2015													
1862, Proof	550	188	64.4								$350	$550	$1,500
Auctions: $3,760, PF-67Cam, June 2015; $1,293, PF-66Cam, October 2015; $960, PF-65, August 2015; $541, PF-63, September 2015													
1863	18,000	119	61.9	88%	$160	$185	$235	$300	$475	$625	$725	$950	$1,600
Auctions: $9,988, MS-68, October 2015; $3,995, MS-67, January 2015; $1,645, MS-66, October 2015; $1,410, MS-66, July 2015													
1863, Proof	460	181	64.1								$350	$550	$1,500
Auctions: $3,760, PF-67, October 2015; $4,700, PF-66Cam, October 2015; $1,293, PF-66, March 2015; $1,175, PF-65, January 2015													
1863-S	100,000	94	60.1	76%	$30	$40	$45	$55	$160	$320	$750	$1,000	$3,000
Auctions: $4,935, MS-66, October 2015; $4,230, MS-65, October 2015; $1,645, MS-64, October 2015; $764, MS-60, June 2015													
1864	48,000	49	58.7	80%	$325	$440	$500	$725	$925	$1,100	$1,200	$1,350	$2,450
Auctions: $2,585, MS-65, January 2015; $1,410, MS-64, July 2015; $646, MS-64, January 2015; $541, MS-63, June 2015													
1864, Proof	470	148	64.2								$350	$550	$1,500
Auctions: $4,700, PF-67, August 2014; $4,259, PF-67, June 2014; $1,175, PF-66, September 2015													
1864-S	90,000	60	54.8	53%	$45	$55	$100	$135	$285	$440	$725	$1,400	$3,750
Auctions: $4,935, MS-66, October 2015; $2,115, MS-64, October 2015; $224, VF-35, August 2015													
1865	13,000	54	57.5	74%	$275	$340	$425	$550	$675	$750	$850	$1,250	$2,000
Auctions: $7,638, MS-67, October 2015; $376, G-6, February 2015													
1865, Proof	500	165	64.1								$350	$550	$1,500
Auctions: $1,763, PF-66Cam, July 2015; $1,116, PF-65Cam, August 2015; $764, PF-64Cam, September 2015; $435, PF-63, March 2015													
1865-S	120,000	56	53.4	43%	$30	$40	$50	$75	$175	$550	$950	$2,100	$5,000
Auctions: $881, AU-55, January 2015; $212, EF-40, June 2015													
1866	10,000	62	59.1	81%	$325	$375	$425	$550	$650	$700	$825	$1,200	$2,500
Auctions: $5,640, MS-67, January 2015; $3,055, MS-66, October 2015; $940, MS-61, October 2015; $999, EF-45, January 2015													
1866, Proof	725	169	64.0								$350	$550	$1,500
Auctions: $19,975, PF-67DCam, January 2015; $2,820, PF-65DCam, January 2015; $580, PF-64, June 2015; $541, PF-63, July 2015													
1866-S	120,000	77	58.5	61%	$30	$40	$50	$65	$160	$375	$475	$950	$3,500
Auctions: $7,638, MS-66, May 2015; $3,760, MS-65, October 2015; $564, MS-61, April 2015; $482, AU-58, April 2015													
1867	8,000	86	60.3	85%	$450	$525	$625	$750	$850	$925	$1,100	$1,400	$2,000
Auctions: $2,585, MS-66, October 2015; $8,813, MS-65, October 2015; $1,410, MS-63, September 2015													
1867, Proof	625	223	64.5								$350	$550	$1,500
Auctions: $1,528, PF-66Cam, August 2015; $999, PF-65, January 2015; $823, PF-64Cam, July 2015; $705, PF-64, October 2015													
1867-S	120,000	62	57.8	58%	$25	$35	$50	$65	$160	$325	$575	$1,200	$3,200
Auctions: $3,055, MS-66, February 2015; $2,585, MS-65, August 2015; $881, MS-63, January 2015; $458, AU-58, April 2015													

m. Included in circulation-strike 1861 mintage figure.

1872, Doubled-Die Obverse
FS-H10-1872-101.

	Mintage	Cert	Avg	%MS	G-4	VG-8	F-12	VF-20	EF-40	AU-50	MS-60	MS-63	MS-65
											PF-60	PF-63	PF-65
1868	88,600	76	60.5	84%	$55	$65	$120	$185	$325	$475	$675	$900	$1,700
	Auctions: $4,230, MS-67, October 2015; $517, AU-58, April 2015												
1868, Proof	600	177	64.1								$350	$550	$1,500
	Auctions: $2,585, PF-66Cam, February 2015; $1,058, PF-65Cam, October 2015; $588, PF-64, September 2015; $376, PF-62, May 2015												
1868-S	280,000	146	61.2	71%	$16	$20	$30	$35	$45	$130	$320	$600	$2,200
	Auctions: $5,170, MS-66, October 2015; $1,410, MS-65, October 2015; $282, MS-62, April 2015; $212, MS-60, January 2015												
1869	208,000	105	62.9	87%	$16	$20	$30	$35	$45	$160	$260	$400	$1,100
	Auctions: $3,760, MS-67, May 2015; $1,880, MS-66, October 2015; $1,058, MS-65, July 2015; $999, MS-65, October 2015												
1869, Proof	600	220	64.3								$350	$550	$1,500
	Auctions: $2,585, PF-67Cam, June 2015; $2,115, PF-67, January 2015; $1,410, PF-66, January 2015; $588, PF-64, January 2015												
1869-S	230,000	80	60.9	80%	$16	$20	$30	$35	$45	$130	$320	$800	$3,750
	Auctions: $4,465, MS-67, May 2015; $3,290, MS-65, October 2015; $306, AU-58, April 2015; $282, AU-55, April 2015												
1870	535,000	291	60.7	79%	$16	$20	$25	$30	$45	$80	$150	$275	$900
	Auctions: $2,820, MS-67, September 2015; $949, MS-66, October 2015; $235, MS-62, February 2015; $129, MS-62, May 2015												
1870, Proof	1,000	179	64.2								$350	$550	$1,500
	Auctions: $1,293, PF-66Cam, October 2015; $764, PF-64Cam, July 2015; $541, PF-63, September 2015; $259, PF-62, May 2015												
1870-S † (n)		1	63.0	100%							$1,500,000		
	Auctions: $661,250, MS-63, July 2004												
1871	1,873,000	491	60.6	76%	$16	$20	$25	$30	$45	$80	$150	$275	$800
	Auctions: $1,410, MS-66, August 2015; $400, MS-64, May 2015; $361, MS-64, July 2015; $62, AU-55, January 2015												
1871, Proof	960	206	64.2								$350	$550	$1,500
	Auctions: $2,468, PF-67Cam, August 2015; $1,175, PF-65Cam, August 2015; $1,293, PF-66, January 2015; $823, PF-64, January 2015												
1871-S	161,000	120	60.8	69%	$18	$22	$32	$65	$80	$180	$310	$500	$2,200
	Auctions: $423, MS-64, January 2015; $235, MS-62, May 2015; $259, MS-61, April 2015; $208, AU-58, April 2015												
1872	2,947,000	412	59.8	74%	$16	$20	$25	$30	$45	$80	$150	$275	$800
	Auctions: $3,760, MS-67, May 2015; $1,469, MS-66, August 2015; $376, MS-64, May 2015; $106, AU-58, April 2015												
1872, DblDie Obv (o)	(p)	8	48.6	0%					$200	$300	$550	$800	
	Auctions: $89, EF-45, August 2011												
1872, Proof	950	179	64.2								$350	$550	$1,500
	Auctions: $3,525, PF-67Cam, March 2015; $1,058, PF-65Cam, October 2015; $999, PF-64Cam, October 2015												
1872-S, All kinds	837,000												
1872-S, Mintmark above bow		167	61.7	80%	$20	$25	$30	$45	$50	$80	$150	$275	$750
	Auctions: $2,468, MS-67, May 2015; $764, MS-66, July 2015; $529, MS-65, January 2015; $282, MS-63, April 2015												
1872-S, Mintmark below bow		156	61.9	79%	$20	$25	$30	$45	$50	$80	$150	$275	$750
	Auctions: $2,585, MS-67, January 2015; $1,058, MS-66, September 2015; $353, MS-64, January 2015; $282, MS-63, March 2015												
1873, Close 3 (q)	712,000	145	59.7	74%	$16	$20	$25	$30	$45	$80	$150	$275	$850
	Auctions: $2,820, MS-67, October 2015; $1,528, MS-66, January 2015; $165, MS-62, January 2015; $100, MS-60, May 2015												
1873, Proof	600	244	64.3								$350	$550	$1,500
	Auctions: $1,528, PF-66, March 2015; $1,469, PF-66, June 2015; $1,293, PF-65, January 2015; $580, PF-64, June 2015												
1873-S Close 3 (q)	324,000	259	62.3	85%	$16	$20	$25	$30	$45	$80	$150	$275	$750
	Auctions: $1,175, MS-66, October 2015; $646, MS-65, June 2015; $423, MS-64, August 2015; $376, MS-64, November 2015												

† Ranked in the *100 Greatest U.S. Coins* (fourth edition). **n.** The 1870-S coin is unique. **o.** "Doubling is evident on UNITED STATES OF AMERICA and on most elements of Miss Liberty. AMERICA is the strongest point" (*Cherrypickers' Guide to Rare Die Varieties*, sixth edition, volume II). **p.** Included in circulation-strike 1872 mintage figure. **q.** Close 3 only.

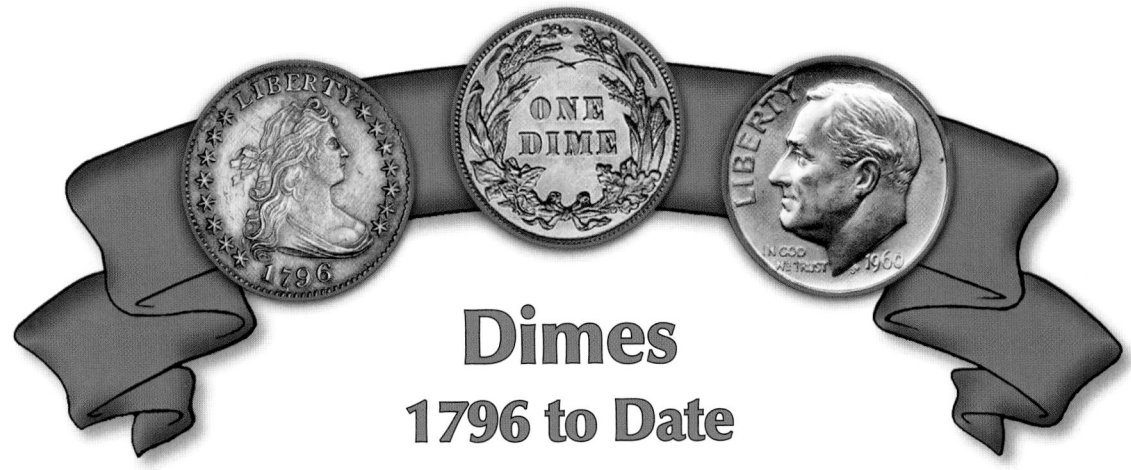

Dimes
1796 to Date
AN OVERVIEW OF DIMES

A collection of dimes ranging from 1796 to date includes many interesting issues. As a type, none are super-rare, but earlier types, combining low mintages with commonly weak striking, can be a challenge for the collector.

The 1796–1797 dime with Draped Bust obverse, Small Eagle reverse, is the rarest of the dime types by far, with fewer than 50,000 pieces minted. These hail from an era in which there was no numismatic interest in saving such coins. Finding a choice example in whatever grade desired will require time and effort.

Then comes the Draped Bust obverse, Heraldic Eagle reverse type, made from 1798 through 1807 (except for 1799). Today these are available easily enough in circulated grades, but are elusive in Mint State. Nearly all are lightly struck—another challenge. Capped Bust dimes of the 1809–1828 years also require connoisseurship to locate a sharply struck specimen. For all of these early types some compromise with perfection is required.

Later Capped Bust dimes of 1828 to 1837 can be found well struck, as can be the later variations within the Liberty Seated type. Barber, Mercury, and Roosevelt dimes are easy to find in just about any grade desired.

Proofs are most readily available from the Liberty Seated era to the present and are sometimes included in type sets, usually answering the call for sharply struck pieces, as most (but not all) were made with care.

FOR THE COLLECTOR AND INVESTOR: DIMES AS A SPECIALTY

Dimes have been a very popular denomination to collect on a systematic basis. Generally, interest is separated into different eras. Those of the early years, the Draped Bust and Capped Bust issues, 1796 to 1837, are enthusiastically sought not only for dates and major varieties (as, for example, those listed in the charts to follow), but also by more rarefied die varieties. Aficionados use the book *Early United States Dimes, 1796–1837*, whose listings are by JR numbers, for John Reich, the designer of the Capped Bust silver issues. The

Controversy over Chief Engraver John R. Sinnock's design arose after claims that Sinnock had borrowed his design from Selma Burke's bas relief, as seen at the Recorder of Deeds building in Washington, D.C.

John Reich Collectors Society (www.jrcs.org), publisher of the *John Reich Journal*, serves as a forum for the exchange of ideas and new information.

Among early varieties, the 1796; 1797, 16 Stars; and 1797, 13 Stars, are each rare in all grades. Dimes with the Heraldic Eagle reverse, 1798–1807, are generally scarce, but not prohibitively rare, although Mint State coins are elusive. Among the reverse dies some were shared with contemporary quarter eagles of like design and diameter—feasible as there is no indication of denomination on them. Indeed, there was no mark of value on any dime until 1809.

Among Classic Head dimes of the 1809–1828 years, the 1822 is the key date and is especially rare in high grades. Among the modified Classic Head dimes of 1829–1837, all varieties listed in this book are available without difficulty. An example of how a newly discovered variety can be considered unique or exceedingly rare, and later be recognized as plentiful, is provided by the 1830, 30 Over 29, overdate, first publicized by Don Taxay in 1970 in *Scott's Comprehensive Catalogue of United States Coinage* (cover-dated 1971). The overdate was then considered one of a kind, but since then dozens more have been identified.

Liberty Seated dimes of the various varieties have been a popular specialty over a long period of time. There are no impossible rarities except for the unique 1873-CC, Without Arrows, but certain other varieties are very hard to find, including the Carson City issues of the early 1870s.

Barber dimes can be collected by date and mint from 1892 to 1916, except for the 1894-S, of which only 24 are believed to have been struck, with only about 10 accounted for today. The other Barber varieties range from common to scarce. Mercury dimes, 1916–1945, have an enthusiastic following. The key issues are 1916-D (in particular); 1921; 1921-D; 1942, 2 Over 1; and 1942-D, 2 Over 1. Roosevelt dimes from 1946 to date can easily be collected by date and mint and are very popular.

DRAPED BUST, SMALL EAGLE REVERSE (1796–1797)

Designer: *Probably Gilbert Stuart.* **Engraver:** *Robert Scot.*
Weight: *2.70 grams.* **Composition:** *.8924 silver, .1076 copper.*
Diameter: *Approximately 19 mm.* **Edge:** *Reeded.* **Mint:** *Philadelphia.*

John Reich-2.

History. Dimes were first minted for circulation in 1796. There are no records of publicity surrounding their debut. The coins featured the Draped Bust obverse, as used on cents and other silver coins, combined with the Small Eagle reverse. Some 1796 dimes exhibit prooflike surfaces, suggesting that they may have been "presentation pieces," but no records exist to confirm this possibility.

Striking and Sharpness. Most dimes of this type have weakness or problems in one area or another, usually more so on those dated 1797. Points to check for sharpness include the hair of Miss Liberty, the drapery lines on the bust, the centers of the stars, and, on the reverse, the breast and wing feathers of the eagle. Also check for adjustment marks. A sharply struck coin is a goal, not necessarily a reality. Sharp striking and excellent eye appeal add dramatically to the value.

Availability. This is the rarest and most expensive type in the dime series. Within any desired grade, examples should be selected with great care, as many have problems of one sort or another. MS coins are especially rare; when seen they are usually dated 1796. Dimes of 1797 are much rarer in all grades, and nearly impossible to find in MS-63 or finer.

GRADING STANDARDS

MS-60 to 70 (Mint State). *Obverse:* At MS-60, some abrasion and contact marks are evident, most noticeably on the cheek, the drapery, and the right field. Luster is present, but may be dull or lifeless, and interrupted in patches. At MS-63, contact marks are very few, and abrasion is hard to detect except under magnification, although this type is sometimes graded liberally due to its rarity. An MS-65 coin has no abrasion, and contact

1796; JR-3. Graded MS-63.

marks are so minute as to require magnification. Luster should be full and rich. Coins graded above MS-65 are more theoretical than actual for this type—but they do exist, and are defined by having fewer marks as perfection is approached. *Reverse:* Comments apply as for the obverse, except that abrasion and marks are most noticeable on the eagle at the center, a situation complicated by the fact that this area was sometimes lightly struck. The field area is small and is protected by lettering and the wreath, and in any given grade shows fewer marks than on the obverse.

Illustrated coin: This coin is one of only two known with this triangular rim break on the reverse. The dies were likely discarded shortly after the break occurred. Also note the die break from the rim break to the eagle's left wing.

AU-50, 53, 55, 58 (About Uncirculated). *Obverse:* Light wear is seen on the hair area above the ear and extending to left of the forehead, on the ribbon, and on the bosom, more so at AU-50 than at AU-53 or 55. An AU-58 coin has minimal traces of wear. An AU-50 coin has luster in protected areas among the stars and letters, with little in the open fields or on the portrait. At AU-58, most luster is present in the fields, but is worn

1796; JR-3. Graded AU-50.

away on the highest parts of the motifs. Generally, grading guidelines for this dime type follow those of the related half dimes. *Reverse:* Light wear is seen on the eagle's body (keep in mind that the higher parts of this area might be lightly struck) and the edges of the wings. Light wear is seen on the wreath and lettering. Luster is the best key to actual wear. This ranges from perhaps 20% remaining in protected areas (at AU-50) to nearly full mint bloom (at AU-58).

EF-40, 45 (Extremely Fine). *Obverse:* More wear is evident on the upper hair area and the ribbon, and on the drapery and bosom. Excellent detail remains in low-relief areas of the hair. The stars show wear as do the date and letters. Luster, if present at all, is minimal and in protected areas. *Reverse:* The eagle shows more wear, this being the focal point to check. Many feathers remain on the interior areas of the wings. Additional wear is

1796; JR-5. Graded EF-45.

on the wreath and letters, but many details are present. Some luster may be seen in protected areas, and if present is slightly more abundant than on the obverse.

Illustrated coin: Note the single adjustment mark running across the eagle's chest. Most examples of this die variety bear similar adjustment marks at varying angles.

VF-20, 30 (Very Fine). *Obverse:* The higher-relief areas of hair are well worn at VF-20, less so at VF-30. The drapery and bosom show extensive wear. The stars have more wear, making them appear larger (an optical illusion seen on most worn silver coins of this era). *Reverse:* The body of the eagle shows few if any feathers, while the wings have about half of the feathers visible, depending on the strike. At VF-30 more than half of the

1796; JR-6. Graded VF-30.

feathers may show. The leaves lack most detail and are in outline form. Scattered, non-disfiguring marks are normal for this and lower grades. Any major defects should be noted separately.

F-12, 15 (Fine). *Obverse:* Wear is more extensive than on a Very Fine coin, particularly noticeable on the hair, face, and bosom, and the stars appear larger. About half the hair detail remains, most noticeably behind the neck and shoulder. The rim may be partially worn away and blend into the field. *Reverse:* Wear is more extensive. Now, feather details are diminished, with fewer than half remaining on the wings. The wreath and lettering

1796; JR-4. Graded F-12.

are worn further, and the rim is usually weak in areas, although some denticles can be seen.

Illustrated coin: This coin falls at the low end of the Fine range.

VG-8, 10 (Very Good). *Obverse:* The portrait is mostly seen in outline form, with most hair strands gone, although there is some definition at the back of the hair and behind the shoulder. The ear is discernible, as is the eye. The stars appear larger still, again an illusion. The rim is weak in areas. LIBERTY and the date are readable and usually full, although some letters may be weak at their tops. *Reverse:* The eagle is mostly an outline

1796; JR-4. Graded VG-8.

with parts blending into the field (on lighter strikes). The rim is worn, as are the letters, with some weak, but the motto is readable.

G-4, 6 (Good). *Obverse:* Wear is more extensive, and some stars may be partly missing. The head is an outline. The eye is visible only in outline form. The rim is well worn or even missing in areas. LIBERTY is worn, and parts of some letters may be missing, but elements of all should be readable. The date is readable, but worn. *Reverse:* The eagle is flat and discernible in outline form, and may be blending into the field. The wreath is well worn. Some of the letters may be partly missing. At this level some "averaging" can be done. If the letters are stronger than usual in one area, but some are missing in another area, the coin can still qualify as G-4.

1796; JR-6. Graded G-4.

AG-3 (About Good). *Obverse:* Wear is so extensive that the coin is barely identifiable. The head is in outline form. LIBERTY is mostly gone, same for the stars. The date, while readable, may be partially worn away. *Reverse:* The reverse is well worn with parts of the wreath and lettering missing.

1796; JR-2. Graded AG-3.

1797, 16 Stars

1797, 13 Stars

	Mintage	Cert	Avg	%MS	AG-3	G-4	VG-8	F-12	VF-20	EF-40	AU-50	MS-60	MS-63
1796	22,135	254	49.0	40%	$1,000	$2,200	$3,500	$5,000	$7,000	$11,500	$14,000	$23,000	$35,000 (a)
	Auctions: $793,125, MS-68, August 2014; $881,250, MS-67, June 2014; $32,900, MS-63, March 2015; $17,625, MS-62, September 2015												
1797, All kinds	25,261												
1797, 16 Stars		20	45.6	35%	$1,100	$2,500	$3,750	$5,500	$7,500	$12,000	$18,000	$35,000	$55,000
	Auctions: $35,250, MS-62, April 2014												
1797, 13 Stars		23	27.1	4%	$1,200	$2,800	$4,000	$5,500	$8,000	$13,500	$20,000	$50,000	$100,000
	Auctions: $38,188, AU-58, April 2014												

a. Value in MS-65 is $85,000.

DRAPED BUST, HERALDIC EAGLE REVERSE (1798–1807)

Designer: *Robert Scot.* **Weight:** *2.70 grams.* **Composition:** *.8924 silver, .1076 copper.*
Diameter: *Approximately 19 mm.* **Edge:** *Reeded.* **Mint:** *Philadelphia.*

JR-3.

History. Dimes of this style were minted each year from 1798 to 1807 (with the exception of 1799 and 1805). The designs follow those of other silver coins of the era.

Striking and Sharpness. Nearly all have one area or another of light striking. On the obverse, check the hair details and drapery lines, and the star centers. On the reverse, the upper right of the shield and the adjacent part of the eagle's wing often are soft, and several or even most stars may be lightly defined (sharp stars show sharply peaked centers); high parts of the clouds are often weak. Denticles are likely to be weak or missing in areas on either side. Expect to compromise on the strike; a sharply struck coin is a goal, not necessarily a reality. Certain reverse dies of this type were also used to coin quarter eagles. Sharp striking and excellent eye appeal dramatically add to a Draped Bust dime's value, this being particularly true for the dates most often seen in MS: 1805 and 1807 (which are usually weakly struck, especially 1807).

Availability. Although certain die varieties are rare, the basic years are available, with 1805 and 1807 being the most often seen. As a class, MS coins are rare. Again, when seen they are usually dated 1805 or 1807, and have areas of striking weakness. Coins of 1801 through 1804 are scarce in VF and higher grades, very scarce in AU and better.

GRADING STANDARDS

MS-60 to 70 (Mint State). *Obverse:* At MS-60 some abrasion and contact marks are evident, most noticeably on the cheek, the drapery at the shoulder, and the right field. Luster is present, but may be dull or lifeless, and interrupted in patches. At MS-63, contact marks are very few, and abrasion is hard to detect except under magnification. An MS-65 coin has no abrasion, and contact marks are so minute as to require magnifica-

1802; JR-4. Graded MS-62.

tion. Luster should be full and rich. Coins graded above MS-65 are more theoretical than actual for this type—but they do exist, and are defined by having fewer marks as perfection is approached. *Reverse:* Comments apply as for the obverse, except that abrasion and marks are most noticeable on the eagle's neck, the tips of the wing, and the tail. The field area is complex, without much open space, given the stars above the eagle, the arrows and olive branch, and other features. Accordingly, marks are not as noticeable as on the obverse.

Illustrated coin: Attractive luster and toning increase the eye appeal and desirability of this coin, despite softer-than-average striking. More than one important 20th-century collector has called this the finest dime of its kind.

AU-50, 53, 55, 58 (About Uncirculated).
Obverse: Light wear is seen on the hair area above the ear and extending to left of the forehead, on the ribbon, and on the drapery at the shoulder, more so at AU-50 than at AU-53 or 55. An AU-58 coin has minimal traces of wear. An AU-50 coin has luster in protected areas among the stars and letters, with little in the open fields or on the portrait. At AU-58, most luster is present in the fields, but is worn

1800; JR-2. Graded AU-50.

away on the highest parts of the motifs. *Reverse:* Comments as preceding, except that the eagle's neck, the tips and top of the wings, the clouds, and the tail now show noticeable wear, as do other features. As always, a familiarity with a given die variety will help differentiate striking weakness from actual wear. Luster ranges from perhaps 20% remaining in protected areas (at AU-50) to nearly full mint bloom (at AU-58). Often the reverse of this type will retain much more luster than the obverse.

EF-40, 45 (Extremely Fine). *Obverse:* More wear is evident on the upper hair area and the ribbon and on the drapery and bosom. Excellent detail remains in low-relief areas of the hair. The stars show wear, as do the date and letters. Luster, if present at all, is minimal and in protected areas. *Reverse:* The neck lacks feather detail on its highest points. Feathers have lost some detail near the edges of the wings, and some areas of the horizontal lines

1802; JR-2. Graded EF-45.

in the shield may be blended together, particularly at the right (an area that is also susceptible to weak striking). Some traces of luster may be seen, more so at EF-45 than at EF-40.

   Illustrated coin: Note the die crack on the reverse from above OF to below the eagle's left foot. There is also some die clashing evident in the field behind the eagle. This reverse was used to coin dimes long after it was damaged.

VF-20, 30 (Very Fine). *Obverse:* The higher-relief areas of hair are well worn at VF-20, less so at VF-30. The drapery and bosom show extensive wear. The stars have more wear, making them appear larger (an optical illusion seen on most worn silver coins of this era). *Reverse:* Wear is greater, including on the shield and wing feathers. Star centers are flat. Other areas have lost detail, as well. E PLURIBUS UNUM is complete (this incuse feature tended to wear away slowly).

1801; JR-1. Graded VF-20.

   Illustrated coin: Here is a problem-free example with normal wear for this grade.

F-12, 15 (Fine). *Obverse:* Wear is more extensive than on a Very Fine coin, particularly noticeable on the hair, face, and bosom, and the stars appear larger. About half the hair detail remains, most noticeably behind the neck and shoulder. The rim may be partially worn away and blend into the field. *Reverse:* Wear is even more extensive, with the shield and wing feathers being points to observe. About half of the feathers are visible

1805; JR-2. Graded F-15.

(depending on striking). E PLURIBUS UNUM may have a few letters worn away. The clouds all seem to be connected. The stars are weak. Parts of the border and lettering may be weak.

 Illustrated coin: There are some digs in the fields of both the obverse and reverse.

VG-8, 10 (Very Good). *Obverse:* The portrait is mostly seen in outline form, with most hair strands gone, although there is some definition at the back of the hair and behind the shoulder. The ear may be discernible. The eye is evident. The stars appear larger still, again an illusion. The rim is weak in areas. LIBERTY and the date are readable and usually full, although some letters may be weak at their tops. *Reverse:* Half or so of the

1798, 8 Over 7; JR-2. Graded VG-8.

letters in the motto are worn away. Most feathers are worn away, although separation of some may be seen. Some stars are faint. The border blends into the field in areas, and some letters are weak. Sharpness can vary widely depending on the die variety. At this level, grading by the obverse first, then checking the reverse, is recommended.

G-4, 6 (Good). *Obverse:* Some stars may be partly missing. The head is an outline. The eye is visible only in outline form. The rim is well worn or even missing in areas. LIBERTY is worn, and parts of some letters may be missing, but elements of all should be readable. The date is readable, but worn. *Reverse:* The upper part of the eagle is flat, and feathers are noticeable at the lower edge of the wing. Some scattered feather detail may or may not be seen. The

1807; JR-1. Graded G-4.

upper part of the shield is flat or nearly so, depending on the variety. Only a few letters of the motto can be seen, although this depends on the variety. The rim is worn extensively, and a few letters may be missing.

AG-3 (About Good). *Obverse:* Wear is very extensive, and some stars and letters are extremely weak or missing entirely. The date is readable. *Reverse:* Extensive wear is seen overall, with the rim worn away and some areas worn smooth. The eagle can be discerned in outline form, but not necessarily completely. A few stray motto letters may remain. Sometimes the obverse can be exceedingly worn (but the date must be readable) and the reverse with more detail, or vice-versa.

1803; JR-3. Graded AG-3.

1798, 8 Over 7

**1798, 8 Over 7,
16 Stars on Reverse**

**1798, 8 Over 7,
13 Stars on Reverse**

1798, Large 8

1798, Small 8

	Mintage	Cert	Avg	%MS	AG-3	G-4	VG-8	F-12	VF-20	EF-40	AU-50	MS-60	MS-63
1798, All kinds	27,550												
1798, 8 Over 7, 16 Stars on Reverse		54	51.3	57%	$350	$800	$1,200	$1,500	$2,500	$3,500	$5,000	$8,000	$18,000
	Auctions: $88,125, MS-65, November 2013												
1798, 8 Over 7, 13 Stars on Reverse		6	41.5	17%	$350	$1,000	$2,200	$4,250	$7,000	$10,000	$20,000	$55,000	
	Auctions: $58,750, MS-62, January 2014												
1798, Large 8		23	47.8	30%	$325	$750	$1,000	$1,500	$2,500	$3,750	$4,500	$8,500	$20,000 (a)
	Auctions: $70,500, MS-63, June 2014; $499, AG-3, August 2014												
1798, Small 8		4	33.3	25%	$350	$800	$1,100	$1,750	$3,500	$5,500	$12,500	$25,000	$40,000
	Auctions: $103,500, MS-64, January 2012												
1800	21,760	56	42.1	13%	$325	$750	$1,000	$1,500	$3,000	$4,000	$8,000	$22,500	$45,000
	Auctions: $352,500, MS-66, June 2014; $259, Fair-2, October 2014												
1801	34,640	35	32.7	17%	$325	$750	$1,100	$2,000	$3,750	$6,000	$11,000	$30,000	$48,500
	Auctions: $4,406, VF-25, February 2014; $411, Fair-2, August 2014												
1802	10,975	40	32.3	15%	$500	$1,500	$2,000	$3,000	$5,000	$10,000	$17,500	$35,000	
	Auctions: $67,563, MS-62, September 2013												
1803	33,040	35	30.5	11%	$350	$800	$1,250	$1,800	$3,200	$6,000	$10,000	$45,000	
	Auctions: $35,250, AU-53, August 2013; $823, Fair-2, November 2014												

a. Value in MS-65 is $50,000.

| 1804, 13 Stars on Reverse | 1804, 14 Stars on Reverse | 1805, 4 Berries | 1805, 5 Berries |

	Mintage	Cert	Avg	%MS	AG-3	G-4	VG-8	F-12	VF-20	EF-40	AU-50	MS-60	MS-63
1804, All kinds	8,265												
1804, 13 Stars on Reverse		2	55.0	0%	$750	$2,000	$4,000	$8,500	$15,000	$30,000	$75,000		
Auctions: $48,175, EF-45, April 2013													
1804, 14 Stars on Reverse		8	32.1	13%	$800	$2,250	$4,250	$9,000	$20,000	$40,000	$85,000		
Auctions: $367,188, MS-63, April 2013													
1805, All kinds	120,780												
1805, 4 Berries		275	41.9	39%	$250	$600	$900	$1,400	$2,000	$3,000	$4,000	$7,500	$14,000 **(b)**
Auctions: $49,938, MS-66, April 2014													
1805, 5 Berries		39	34.4	23%	$250	$600	$900	$1,400	$2,200	$3,400	$4,500	$9,000	$20,000
Auctions: $1,998, VF-20, June 2013													
1807	165,000	276	44.4	37%	$250	$550	$850	$1,300	$2,000	$2,750	$3,750	$6,500	$11,500 **(c)**
Auctions: $55,813, MS-65, June 2014; $2,587, AU-53, August 2014; $317, G-4, October 2014													

b. Value in MS-65 is $40,000. c. Value in MS-65 is $38,500.

CAPPED BUST (1809–1837)

Variety 1, Wide Border (1809–1828): **Designer:** *John Reich.*
Weight: *2.70 grams.* **Composition:** *.8924 silver, .1076 copper.*
Diameter: *Approximately 18.8 mm.* **Edge:** *Reeded.* **Mint:** *Philadelphia.*

**Variety 1, Wide Border
(1809–1828)
JR-3.**

**Variety 1, Wide Border, Proof
JR-12.**

Variety 2, Modified Design (1828–1837): **Designer:** *John Reich.*
Weight: *2.70 grams (changed to 2.67 grams, .900 fine in 1837).*
Composition: *.8924 silver, .1076 copper.*
Diameter: *Approximately 18.5 mm.* **Edge:** *Reeded.* **Mint:** *Philadelphia.*

**Variety 2, Modified Design
(1828–1837)**

**Variety 2, Modified Design,
Proof
JR-4.**

History. The wide-border dimes were struck intermittently from 1809 to 1828. The design, by John Reich, closely follows that inaugurated with the Capped Bust half dollars of 1807. New equipment at the U.S. Mint was used to make the 1828, Small Date, dimes, and those subsequent. The slightly modified design includes smaller denticles or beads in the border and other minor differences, and they are of uniform diameter. The 2 in the 1828, Small Date, dime has a square (not curled) base.

Striking and Sharpness. Many if not most Wide Border dimes have areas of light striking. On the obverse, check the star centers, the hair details, and the drapery at the bosom. On the reverse, check the eagle, especially the area in and around the upper right of the shield. Denticles are sometimes weak, but are usually better defined on the reverse than on the obverse. The height of the rims on both sides can vary, and coins with a low rim or rims tend to show wear more quickly. Most dimes of the modified design (Variety 2) are fairly well struck, with fewer irregularities of strike than those of 1809 to 1828. On the obverse, check the hair and the brooch. The stars usually are sharp, but don't overlook them. On the reverse, check the details of the eagle. The denticles usually are sharp.

Availability. There are no extremely rare dates in this series, so all are available to collectors, but certain die varieties range from rare to extremely rare. In MS, most are scarce and some rare. The dates of the early 1830s to 1835 are the most readily available. Those exhibiting a strong strike, with Full Details, command a premium, especially the earlier dates. Most have nice eye appeal.

Proofs. Proof Capped Bust dimes of 1809 to 1828 were struck in small numbers, likely mostly as part of presentation sets. As is the case with any and all early Proofs, you should insist on a coin with deeply and fully (not partially) mirrored surfaces, well struck, and with good contrast. Carefully examine deeply toned pieces (deep toning can mask the true nature of a coin, e.g., if it is not a true Proof, or if it has been cleaned or repaired). More than just a few pieces attributed as "Proofs" are not Proofs at all. Proofs were made of each year from 1828 to 1837 and are rare. Beware of "Proofs" that have deeply toned surfaces or fields that show patches of mint frost. Buy slowly and carefully.

GRADING STANDARDS

MS-60 to 70 (Mint State). *Obverse:* The rims are more uniform for the 1828–1837 variety than for the 1809–1828 variety, striking is usually very sharp, and any abrasion occurs evenly on both sides. At MS-60 some abrasion and contact marks are evident, most noticeably on the cheek and on the area near the drapery clasp. Luster is present, but may be dull or lifeless, and interrupted in patches. At MS-63, contact marks are very few, and

1831; JR-5. Graded MS-64.

abrasion is hard to detect except under magnification. An MS-65 coin has no abrasion, and contact marks are so minute as to require magnification. Luster should be full and rich. Grades above MS-65 are seen now and again, and are defined by having fewer marks as perfection is approached. *Reverse:* Comments apply as for the obverse, except that abrasion and contact marks are most noticeable on the eagle's neck, the top of the wings, the claws, and the flat band that surrounds the incuse motto. The field is mainly protected by design elements and does not show abrasion as much as does the obverse.

AU-50, 53, 55, 58 (About Uncirculated).
Obverse: The rims are more uniform for the 1828–1837 variety than for the 1809–1828 variety, striking is usually very sharp, and any abrasion occurs evenly on both sides. Light wear is seen on the cap, the hair below LIBERTY, the hair near the clasp, and the drapery at the bosom. At AU-58, the luster is extensive except in the open area of the field, especially to the right. At AU–50 and 53, lus-

1814; JR-5. Graded AU-55.

ter remains only in protected areas. As is true of all high grades, sharpness of strike can affect the perception of wear. *Reverse:* Wear is evident on the eagle's neck, the top of the wings, and the claws. An AU-58 has nearly full luster. At AU-50 and 53, there still is significant luster, more than on the obverse.

Illustrated coin: The stars on this coin are weakly struck.

EF-40, 45 (Extremely Fine). *Obverse:* The rims are more uniform for the 1828–1837 variety than for the 1809–1828 variety, striking is usually very sharp, and the wear occurs evenly on both sides. Wear is more extensive, most noticeable on the higher areas of the hair. The cap shows more wear, as does the cheek. Stars still show their centers (unless lightly struck, and *many* are). Luster, if present, is in protected areas among the star points and close to the portrait. *Reverse:* The wings show wear on the higher areas of the feathers (par-

1834, Large 4; JR-1. Graded EF-40.

ticularly on the right wing), and some details are lost. Feathers in the neck are light. The eagle's claws show wear. Luster may be present in protected areas, even if there is little or none on the obverse.

VF-20, 30 (Very Fine). *Obverse:* The rims are more uniform for the 1828–1837 variety than for the 1809–1828 variety, striking is usually very sharp, and wear occurs evenly on both sides. Wear is more extensive, and most of the hair is combined into thick tresses without delicate features. The curl on the neck is flat. Unless they were weakly struck to begin with, most stars retain their interior lines. *Reverse:* Wear is most evident on the eagle's

1825. Graded VF-30.

neck, to the left of the shield, and on the leaves and claws. Most feathers in the wing remain distinct.

F-12, 15 (Fine). *Obverse:* The rims are more uniform for the 1828–1837 variety than for the 1809–1828 variety, striking is usually very sharp, and wear occurs evenly on both sides. (For both varieties the striking is not as important at this and lower grades.) Wear is more extensive, with much of the hair blended together. The drapery is indistinct along part of its upper edge. Stars have lost detail at the center and some may be flat. The height of

1821; JR-7. Graded F-15.

obverse rim is important in the amount of wear the coin has received. *Reverse:* Wear is more extensive, now with only about a third to half of the feathers remaining on the wings, more on the wing to the left. Some of the horizontal lines in the shield may be worn away.

VG-8, 10 (Very Good). *Obverse:* The hair is less distinct, with the area surrounding the face blended into the facial features. LIBERTY is complete, but weak in areas. Stars are nearly flat. *Reverse:* Feathers are fewer and mostly visible on the eagle's left wing. Other details are weaker. All lettering remains easily readable, although some letters may be faint.

1822; JR-1. Graded VG-8.

G-4, 6 (Good). *Obverse:* The portrait is mostly in outline, with few interior details discernible. LIBERTY may still be readable or may be partially worn away, depending on the variety (this varies due to the strike characteristics of some die marriages). Stars are flat at their centers. *Reverse:* The eagle is mostly in outline form, although some feathers can be seen in the right wing. All letters around the border are clear on a sharp strike;

1820, Large 0. Graded G-4.

some letters are light or missing on a coin with low rims. E PLURIBUS UNUM may be weak, often with some letters worn away.

    Illustrated coin: This is an attractive, problem-free coin at this grade.

AG-3 (About Good). *Obverse:* The portrait is an outline, although traces of LIBERTY can still be seen. The rim is worn down, and some stars are weak. The date remains clear although weak toward the rim. *Reverse:* The reverse shows more wear overall than the obverse, with the rim indistinct in areas and many if not most letters worn away.

1811, 11 Over 09; JR-1. Graded AG-3.

PF-60 to 70 (Proof). *Obverse and Reverse:* Generally, Proof dimes of the 1828–1837 variety are of better quality than the 1809–1828 variety and have Full Details in almost all areas. Proofs of this type can have areas of light striking, such as at the star centers. Proofs that are extensively cleaned and have many hairlines, or that are dull and grainy, are lower level, such as PF-60 to 62. These are not of great interest to specialists unless they

1835; JR-4. Graded PF-65 Cameo.

are of rare die varieties. A PF-64 has fewer hairlines, but they are obvious, perhaps slightly distracting. A Gem PF-65 should have fewer still and full mirrored surfaces (no trace of cloudiness or dullness). PF-66 should have hairlines so delicate that magnification is needed to see them. Above that, a Proof should be free of such lines. Grading is highly subjective with early Proofs, and eye appeal also is a major factor.

Illustrated coin: Note the awkward mix of numerals in the date. Punches of different sizes were used, and the 3 in particular looks clumsy and large in comparison to the 8 and the 5.

| 1811, 11 Over 09 | 1814, Small Date | 1814, Large Date | 1814, STATESOFAMERICA |

	Mintage	Cert	Avg	%MS	G-4	VG-8	F-12	VF-20	EF-40	AU-50	MS-60	MS-63	MS-65
											PF-60	PF-63	PF-65
1809	51,065	47	37.9	38%	$200	$300	$550	$900	$1,800	$2,500	$4,500	$7,500	$25,000
	Auctions: $31,725, MS-64, June 2014												
1811, 11 Over 09	65,180	61	42.3	30%	$120	$200	$300	$625	$1,700	$2,200	$4,000	$6,500	$27,500
	Auctions: $8,225, MS-64, February 2014												
1814, All kinds	421,500												
1814, Small Date		33	56.3	61%	$55	$85	$125	$275	$725	$1,200	$2,500	$5,000	$16,000
	Auctions: $5,875, MS-64, January 2014; $259, EF-40, October 2014												
1814, Large Date		30	50.8	53%	$40	$50	$75	$185	$600	$1,000	$2,000	$4,000	$12,500
	Auctions: $999, AU-50, June 2015; $588, EF-40, August 2015												
1814, STATESOFAMERICA		14	45.5	43%	$60	$90	$120	$300	$900	$1,500	$3,000	$5,000	$15,000
	Auctions: $374, VG-10, February 2012												

1820, Large 0

1820, STATESOFAMERICA

1820, Small 0

1821, Large Date

1821, Small Date

1823, 3 Over 2

1823, 3 Over 2, Small E's

1823, 3 Over 2, Large E's

1824, 4 Over 2

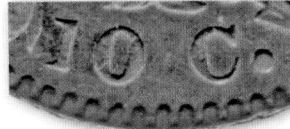
1824 and 1827,
Flat Top 1

1824 and 1827,
Pointed Top 1

	Mintage	Cert	Avg	%MS	G-4	VG-8	F-12	VF-20	EF-40	AU-50	MS-60	MS-63	MS-65
											PF-60	PF-63	PF-65
1820, All kinds	942,587												
1820, Large 0		9	41.7	33%	$40	$45	$60	$125	$500	$675	$1,400	$2,750	$12,500
	Auctions: $1,939, AU-58, January 2015; $911, AU-53, July 2015; $764, AU-53, August 2015; $223, AU-50, May 2015												
1820, Small 0		45	40.1	22%	$40	$45	$60	$150	$600	$700	$1,500	$3,500	$15,000
	Auctions: $1,293, MS-60, February 2014												
1820, STATESOFAMERICA		13	47.5	46%	$50	$75	$150	$250	$750	$1,250	$3,000	$5,000	$15,000
	Auctions: $67,563, MS-66, June 2014; $1,176, EF-40, January 2015; $441, F-12, August 2014												
1820, Proof	2–5	1	66.0								$12,000	$20,000	$65,000
	Auctions: $80,500, PF-66, February 2008												
1821, All kinds	1,186,512												
1821, Small Date		67	46.7	46%	$35	$50	$75	$150	$525	$850	$1,750	$3,500	$14,000
	Auctions: $5,581, MS-64, March 2013; $1,175, MS-60, August 2014; $764, EF-45, June 2015												
1821, Large Date		108	38.0	19%	$35	$50	$60	$135	$520	$800	$1,700	$3,250	$13,500
	Auctions: $1,058, AU-55, July 2015; $823, AU-53, February 2015; $564, EF-45, January 2015; $153, EF-40, May 2015												
1821, Proof	5–8	4	64.5								$8,000	$18,000	$40,000
	Auctions: $55,200, PF-65, April 2005												
1822	100,000	44	32.7	32%	$1,200	$2,100	$3,200	$4,800	$8,000	$11,000	$15,000	$25,000	
	Auctions: $70,500, MS-66, February 2013												
1822, Proof (a)	2–5	0	n/a								$15,000	$25,000	$70,000
	Auctions: $440,625, PF-66Cam, June 2014												
1823, 3 Over 2, All kinds	440,000												
1823, 3 Over 2, Small E's		8	38.1	25%	$35	$50	$60	$120	$450	$800	$1,500	$3,000	$14,000
	Auctions: $8,813, MS-65, June 2014												
1823, 3 Over 2, Large E's		16	38.5	44%	$35	$50	$60	$120	$450	$800	$1,500	$3,000	$15,000
	Auctions: $7,050, MS-65, April 2013												

a. This coin is extremely rare.

1828, Large Date,
Curl Base 2 (Variety 1)

1828, Small Date,
Square Base 2 (Variety 2)

1829, Curl Base 2

1829, Small 10 C.

1829, Medium 10 C.

1829, Large 10 C.

	Mintage	Cert	Avg	%MS	G-4	VG-8	F-12	VF-20	EF-40	AU-50	MS-60 PF-60	MS-63 PF-63	MS-65 PF-65
1824, 4 Over 2, Flat Top 1 in 10 C.	510,000	10	25.8	0%	$40	$65	$110	$375	$800	$1,500	$2,250	$4,000	$17,500
Auctions: No auction records available.													
1824, 4 Over 2, Pointed Top 1 in 10 C.	(b)	2	14.5	0%	$300	$700	$1,200	$2,500	$4,250				
Auctions: No auction records available.													
1824, 4 Over 2, Proof	4–6	4	66.0								$8,000	$18,000	$40,000
Auctions: $42,550, PF-65, July 2005													
1825	(b)	119	48.9	45%	$35	$50	$75	$150	$500	$900	$2,000	$3,500	$12,000
Auctions: $823, AU-53, July 2015; $564, AU-50, June 2015; $341, VF-30, August 2015; $282, VF-20, February 2015													
1825, Proof	4–6	3	65.0								$8,000	$18,000	$40,000
Auctions: $18,400, PF-63, June 2011													
1827, Flat Top 1 in 10 C.	1,215,000	2	10.0	0%	$225	$375	$900	$1,250	$1,800	$3,000			
Auctions: No auction records available.													
1827, Pointed Top 1 in 10 C.	(c)	0	n/a		$35	$50	$65	$125	$450	$700	$1,500	$3,000	$13,500
Auctions: $517, AU-53, June 2015; $881, AU-50, October 2015; $541, AU-50, June 2015; $400, EF-45, October 2015													
1827, Proof	10–15	7	65.4								$8,000	$18,000	$40,000
Auctions: $120,750, PF-67, February 2008													
1828, Variety 1, Large Date, Curl Base 2	(d)	29	44.8	24%	$50	$80	$130	$300	$625	$1,200	$2,250	$5,500	
Auctions: $4,113, AU-58, November 2013													
1828, Variety 2, Small Date, Square Base 2	(e)	54	47.8	41%	$40	$50	$75	$150	$400	$750	$1,300	$2,500	$12,000
Auctions: $2,820, MS-63, April 2013													
1828, Proof	4–6	2	64.0								$8,500	$18,000	$32,500
Auctions: $29,900, PF-65, February 2008													
1829, All kinds	770,000												
1829, Curl Base 2 (f)		8	6.0	0%	$7,000	$10,000	$15,000	$25,000					
Auctions: $7,638, VG-8, June 2014													
1829, Small 10 C.		57	41.1	33%	$32	$40	$45	$100	$375	$475	$1,200	$2,000	$8,000
Auctions: $764, AU-58, June 2015; $588, AU-53, July 2015; $329, AU-53, May 2015; $282, EF-45, April 2015													
1829, Medium 10 C.		8	37.5	38%	$35	$40	$45	$100	$400	$600	$1,700	$3,200	$8,500
Auctions: $717, AU-55, August 2013													
1829, Large 10 C.		16	42.3	25%	$35	$45	$60	$125	$425	$750	$2,000	$4,000	$12,000
Auctions: $259, F-12, November 2013													
1829, Proof	6–10	4	63.5								$7,500	$15,000	$30,000
Auctions: $37,375, PF-66, June 2002													

b. Included in 1824, 4 Over 2, Flat Top 1 in 10 C., mintage figure. **c.** Included in 1827, Flat Top 1 in 10 C., mintage figure. **d.** 1828, Variety 1 and Variety 2, have a combined mintage of 125,000. **e.** 1828, Variety 1 and Variety 2, have a combined mintage of 125,000. **f.** Only one working die for the 1829 dime coinage featured a curled 2, rather than the normal square-based 2. Nearly all known examples are in low grades.

1830, 30 Over 29

1830, Large 10 C.

1830, Small 10 C.

1833, Last 3 Normal

1833, Last 3 High

1834, Small 4

1834, Large 4

	Mintage	Cert	Avg	%MS	G-4	VG-8	F-12	VF-20	EF-40	AU-50	MS-60 / PF-60	MS-63 / PF-63	MS-65 / PF-65
1830, All kinds	510,000												
1830, 30 Over 29 (g)		41	53.1	44%	$40	$60	$110	$200	$450	$650	$1,300	$4,000	$12,000
Auctions: $23,500, MS-66, June 2014; $270, VF-35, December 2014; $212, VF-35, July 2015													
1830, Large 10 C.		0	n/a		$35	$40	$45	$80	$325	$500	$1,200	$2,500	$9,000
Auctions: $823, MS-61, June 2015; $200, AU-50, February 2015; $306, EF-45, July 2015; $123, EF-40, January 2015													
1830, Small 10 C.		5	35.6	40%	$35	$40	$45	$80	$375	$650	$1,200	$2,500	$9,000
Auctions: $1,221, MS-63, January 2012													
1830, Proof (h)	5–8	3	64.0								$7,500	$15,000	$30,000
Auctions: $18,800, PF-63, April 2014													
1831	771,350	363	52.6	50%	$35	$40	$45	$80	$300	$450	$1,000	$2,000	$7,500
Auctions: $999, MS-62, January 2015; $1,880, AU-58, January 2015; $646, AU-55, October 2015; $541, AU-55, June 2015													
1831, Proof	15–25	12	65.2								$7,500	$15,000	$30,000
Auctions: $58,750, PF-66Cam, January 2014													
1832	522,500	346	51.5	49%	$35	$40	$45	$80	$300	$450	$1,000	$2,000	$7,500
Auctions: $646, AU-55, October 2015; $575, AU-55, October 2015; $223, EF-40, January 2015; $141, VF-30, May 2015													
1832, Proof (i)	2–5	0	n/a								—		
Auctions: No auction records available.													
1833, All kinds	485,000												
1833		389	49.2	45%	$35	$40	$45	$80	$300	$450	$1,000	$2,000	$7,500
Auctions: $1,543, AU-58, August 2015; $646, AU-55, February 2015; $353, AU-55, May 2015; $400, AU-53, February 2015													
1833, Last 3 High		32	47.3	38%	$35	$40	$45	$80	$300	$450	$1,000	$2,000	$7,500
Auctions: $17,625, MS-66, April 2013													
1833, Proof	5–10	5	65.6								$8,000	$15,000	$40,000
Auctions: $13,800, PF-64, January 2009													
1834, All kinds	635,000												
1834, Small 4		14	34.1	21%	$35	$40	$45	$80	$300	$450	$1,500	$2,250	$9,000
Auctions: $1,116, MS-62, June 2015; $940, AU-58, October 2015; $676, AU-55, July 2015; $447, AU-53, August 2015													
1834, Large 4		64	42.1	30%	$35	$40	$45	$80	$300	$450	$1,000	$2,000	$7,500
Auctions: $270, MS-60, February 2015; $447, AU-55, August 2015; $423, AU-53, May 2015													
1834, Proof	5–10	3	65.7								$7,500	$15,000	$30,000
Auctions: $35,250, PF-65, October 2014													

g. The tail of the 2 is evident to the right of the lower curve of the 3. The very top of the 9 is evident below the 0. Surface doubling from the initial 1829 punch is also evident on the 8. There are three of four known dies of this overdate; all are similar and command similar values. Today the variety is known to be more common than thought in the early 1970s, when it was first publicized. **h.** Values are for JR-6. A very few Proof versions of the 1830, 30 Over 29, dime are known. A PF-60, JR-4, sold at auction in January 2012 for $5,750. **i.** This coin is extremely rare.

	Mintage	Cert	Avg	%MS	G-4	VG-8	F-12	VF-20	EF-40	AU-50	MS-60	MS-63	MS-65
											PF-60	PF-63	PF-65
1835	1,410,000	615	48.8	43%	$35	$40	$45	$80	$300	$450	$1,000	$2,000	$7,500
Auctions: $1,058, AU-58, February 2015; $764, AU-58, January 2015; $282, EF-45, January 2015; $188, EF-40, May 2015													
1835, Proof	5–10	7	64.6								$7,500	$15,000	$30,000
Auctions: $41,125, PF-65Cam, April 2014													
1836	1,190,000	280	49.5	41%	$35	$40	$45	$80	$300	$450	$1,000	$2,000	$7,500
Auctions: $646, AU-58, July 2015; $376, EF-45, September 2015; $240, EF-45, August 2015; $200, EF-40, May 2015													
1836, Proof	2–5	3	63.7								$8,500	$15,000	$37,500
Auctions: $6,900, PF-66, September 1998													
1837	359,500	183	50.8	52%	$35	$40	$45	$80	$300	$450	$1,000	$2,000	$7,500
Auctions: $400, AU-50, May 2015; $125, VF-35, February 2015; $129, VF-25, January 2015; $123, VF-25, February 2015													
1837, Proof	2–5	1	64.0								$8,500	$15,000	$40,000
Auctions: $23,000, MS-64 Specimen, April 2010													

LIBERTY SEATED (1837–1891)

Variety 1, No Stars on Obverse (1837–1838): **Designer:** *Christian Gobrecht.*
Weight: *2.67 grams.* **Composition:** *.900 silver, .100 copper.* **Diameter:** *17.9 mm.*
Edge: *Reeded.* **Mints:** *Philadelphia and New Orleans.*

**Variety 1, No Stars on Obverse
(1837–1838)**

**Variety 1, No Stars on Obverse,
Proof**

Variety 2, Stars on Obverse (1838–1853): **Designer:** *Christian Gobrecht.*
Weight: *2.67 grams.* **Composition:** *.900 silver, .100 copper.* **Diameter:** *17.9 mm.*
Edge: *Reeded.* **Mints:** *Philadelphia, New Orleans, and San Francisco.*

**Variety 2, Stars on Obverse
(1838–1853)**

Mintmark location,
1837–1860 (Variety 2),
is on the reverse,
above the bow.

**Variety 2, Stars on Obverse,
Proof**

Variety 3, Stars on Obverse, Arrows at Date, Reduced Weight (1853–1855):
Designer: *Christian Gobrecht.* **Weight:** *2.49 grams.* **Composition:** *.900 silver, .100 copper.*
Diameter: *17.9 mm.* **Edge:** *Reeded.* **Mints:** *Philadelphia, New Orleans, and San Francisco.*

**Variety 3, Stars on Obverse,
Arrows at Date, Reduced
Weight (1853–1855)**

**Variety 3, Stars on Obverse,
Arrows at Date, Reduced
Weight, Proof**

Variety 2 Resumed, With Weight Standard of Variety 3 (1856–1860):
Designer: *Christian Gobrecht.* **Weight:** *2.49 grams.* **Composition:** *.900 silver, .100 copper.*
Diameter: *17.9 mm.* **Edge:** *Reeded.* **Mints:** *Philadelphia, New Orleans, and San Francisco.*

Variety 2 Resumed,
Weight Standard of Variety 3
(1856–1860)

Variety 2 Resumed, Weight
Standard of Variety 3, Proof

Variety 4, Legend on Obverse (1860–1873): **Designer:** *Christian Gobrecht.*
Weight: *2.49 grams.* **Composition:** *.900 silver, .100 copper.* **Diameter:** *17.9 mm.*
Edge: *Reeded.* **Mints:** *Philadelphia, New Orleans, San Francisco, and Carson City.*

Variety 4, Legend on Obverse
(1860–1873)

Mintmark location,
1860 (Variety 4)–1891,
is on the reverse,
below the bow.

Variety 4, Legend
on Obverse, Proof

Variety 5, Legend on Obverse, Arrows at Date, Increased Weight (1873–1874):
Designer: *Christian Gobrecht.* **Weight:** *2.50 grams.* **Composition:** *.900 silver, .100 copper.*
Diameter: *17.9 mm.* **Edge:** *Reeded.* **Mints:** *Philadelphia, New Orleans, San Francisco, and Carson City.*

Variety 5, Legend on Obverse,
Arrows at Date, Increased
Weight (1873–1874)

Variety 5, Legend on Obverse,
Increased Weight, Proof

Variety 4 Resumed, With Weight Standard Variety of 5 (1875–1891):
Designer: *Christian Gobrecht.* **Weight:** *2.50 grams.* **Composition:** *.900 silver, .100 copper.*
Diameter: *17.9 mm.* **Edge:** *Reeded.* **Mints:** *Philadelphia, New Orleans, San Francisco, and Carson City.*

Variety 4 Resumed,
Weight Standard Variety of 5
(1875–1891)

Variety 4 Resumed, Weight
Standard Variety of 5, Proof

History. The first of the Liberty Seated designs, with no stars on the obverse, was inspired by Christian Gobrecht's silver dollar of 1836. The reverse features a different motif, with a wreath and inscription. This variety was made only at the Philadelphia Mint in 1837 and at the New Orleans Mint in 1838. Liberty Seated dimes of the Stars on Obverse varieties were first made without drapery at Miss Liberty's elbow. These early issues have the shield tilted sharply to the left. Drapery was added in 1840, and the shield reoriented, this being the style of the 1840s onward. Variety 3 coins (minted in part of 1853, and all of

1854 and 1855) have arrows at the date, signifying the reduction in weight brought on by the Coinage Act of February 21, 1853. The earlier design resumed in 1856 at the new weight standard. Liberty Seated dimes were made in large quantities, and circulated widely. In 1860 the Liberty Seated design continued with UNITED STATES OF AMERICA replacing the stars on the obverse. A new reverse featured what the Mint called a "cereal wreath," encircling ONE DIME in two lines. In 1873 the dime was increased in weight to 2.50 grams (from 2.49); arrows at the date in 1873 and 1874 indicate this change, making Variety 5. Variety 4 (without the arrows) resumed from 1875 and continued to the end of the series in 1891.

Striking and Sharpness. Coins of these varieties usually are fairly well struck for the earlier years, somewhat erratic in the 1870s, and better from the 1880s to 1891. Many Civil War dimes of Philadelphia, 1861 to 1865, have parallel die striae from the dies not being finished (this being so for virtually all silver and gold issues of that period). Some dimes, especially dates from 1879 to 1881, are found prooflike. Check the highest parts of the Liberty Seated figure (especially the head and horizontal shield stripes), the star centers, and, on the reverse, the leaves. Check the denticles on both sides. Avoid coins struck from "tired" or overused dies, as evidenced by grainy rather than lustrous fields (on higher-grade coins). Issues of the Carson City Mint in the early 1870s, particularly 1873-CC, With Arrows, are often seen with porous surfaces (a post-striking effect).

Note that the word LIBERTY on the shield is not an infallible key to attributing lower grades. On some dies such as those of the early 1870s the shield was in low relief on the coins and wore away slowly, with the result that part or all of the word can be readable in grades below F-12.

Availability. The 1837 is readily available in all grades, including MS-65 and higher. The 1838-O is usually seen with wear and is a rarity if truly MS-63 or above. Beware coins with deep or vivid iridescent toning, which often masks friction or evidence of wear. Coins with uniformly grainy etching on both sides have been processed and should be avoided. The 1838 to 1860 dimes are plentiful as a rule, although certain dates and varieties are rare. Most MS coins on the market are dated in the 1850s and are often found MS–63 to 65. While certain issues of the 1860s through 1881 range from scarce to very rare, those from 1882 to 1891 are for the most part very common, even in MS-63 and finer.

Proofs. Examples of Proofs have deep-mirror surfaces and are mostly quite attractive. Proofs of 1837 (but not 1838-O) were struck in an unknown small quantity, but seemingly more than the related 1837 half dime. Proofs were made of most years and are mostly available from 1854 onward, with 1858 and especially 1859 being those often seen. Some Proofs of the 1860s and early 1870s can be carelessly struck, with areas of lightness and sometimes with lint marks. Those of the mid-1870s onward are usually sharply struck and without problems. Proof Liberty Seated dimes of this variety were made continuously from 1860 to 1891. They exist today in proportion to their mintages. Carefully examine deeply toned pieces to ensure the toning does not hide flaws.

GRADING STANDARDS

MS-60 to 70 (Mint State). *Obverse:* At MS-60, some abrasion and contact marks are evident, most noticeably on the bosom and thighs and knees. Luster is present, but may be dull or lifeless, and interrupted in patches in the large open field. At MS-63, contact marks are very few, and abrasion is hard to detect except under magnification. An MS-65 coin has no abrasion, and contact marks are so minute as to require magnification. Luster

1876-CC, Variety 1. Graded MS-64.

should be full and rich, except for Philadelphia (but not San Francisco) dimes of the early and mid-1860s. Most Mint State coins of the 1861 to 1865 years, Philadelphia issues, have extensive die striae (from not completely finishing the die). Some low-mintage Philadelphia issues may be prooflike. Clashmarks are common in this era. This is true of contemporary half dimes as well. Half dimes of this type can be very beautiful at this level. Grades above MS-65 are seen with regularity, more so than for the related No Stars dimes. *Reverse:* Comments apply as for the obverse, except that in lower Mint State grades abrasion and contact marks are most noticeable on the highest parts of the leaves and the ribbon, less so on ONE DIME. At MS-65 or higher there are no marks visible to the unaided eye. The field is mainly protected by design elements and does not show abrasion as much as does the open-field obverse on a given coin.

Illustrated coin: Note the blend of pink, lilac, and gold tones.

AU-50, 53, 55, 58 (About Uncirculated).
Obverse: Light wear is seen on the thighs and knees, bosom, and head. At AU-58, the luster is extensive, but incomplete. Friction is seen in the large open field. At AU–50 and 53, luster is less. *Reverse:* Wear is evident on the leaves (especially at the top of the wreath) and ribbon. An AU-58 coin has nearly full luster, more so than on the obverse, as the design elements protect the small field areas. At AU–50 and 53, there still is significant luster, more than on the obverse.

1838-O, No Stars; F-101. Graded AU-58.

EF-40, 45 (Extremely Fine). *Obverse:* Further wear is seen on all areas, especially the thighs and knees, bosom, and head. Little or no luster is seen. *Reverse:* Further wear is seen on all areas, most noticeably at the leaves to each side of the wreath apex and on the ribbon bow knot. Leaves retain details except on the higher areas.

1838-O, No Stars; F-102. Graded EF-45.

VF-20, 30 (Very Fine). *Obverse:* Further wear is seen. Most details of the gown are worn away, except in the lower-relief areas above and to the right of the shield. Hair detail is mostly or completely gone. *Reverse:* Wear is more extensive. The highest leaves are flat.

1872-CC; F-101. Graded VF-30.

F-12, 15 (Fine). *Obverse:* The seated figure is well worn, with little detail remaining. LIBERTY on the shield is fully readable but weak in areas. On the 1838–1840 subtype Without Drapery, LIBERTY is in higher relief and will wear more quickly; ER may be missing, but other details are at the Fine level. *Reverse:* Most detail of the leaves is gone. The rim is worn but bold, and most if not all denticles are visible.

1874-CC. Graded F-15.

VG-8, 10 (Very Good). *Obverse:* The seated figure is more worn, but some detail can be seen above and to the right of the shield. The shield is discernible. In LIBERTY at least three letters are readable but very weak at VG-8; a few more visible at VG-10. On the 1838–1840 subtype Without Drapery, LIBERTY is in higher relief, and at Very Good only one or two letters may be readable. However, LIBERTY is not an infallible

1843-O; F-101. Graded VG-8.

way to grade this type, as some varieties have the word in low relief on the die, so it wore away slowly. *Reverse:* Further wear has combined the details of most leaves. The rim is complete, but weak in areas. The reverse appears to be in a slightly higher grade than the obverse.

G-4, 6 (Good). *Obverse:* The seated figure is worn smooth. At G-4 there are no letters in LIBERTY remaining on most (but not all) coins. At G-6, traces of one or two can be seen (except on the early No Drapery coins). *Reverse:* Wear is more extensive. The leaves are all combined and in outline form. The rim is well worn and missing in some areas, causing the outer parts of the peripheral letters to be worn away in some instances. On

1873-CC. Graded G-4.

most coins the reverse appears to be in a slightly higher grade than the obverse.

    Illustrated coin: The scratch on the obverse lessens the desirability of this coin.

AG-3 (About Good). *Obverse:* The seated figure is mostly visible in outline form, with no detail. The rim is worn away. The date remains clear. *Reverse:* Many if not most letters are worn away, at least in part. The wreath and interior letters are discernible. The rim is weak.

1874-CC. Graded AG-3.

PF-60 to 70 (Proof). *Obverse and Reverse:* Proofs that are extensively cleaned and have many hairlines, or that are dull and grainy, are lower level, such as PF–60 to 62. These command less attention than more visually appealing pieces, save for the scarce (in any grade) dates of 1844 and 1846, and 1863 through 1867. Both the half dime and dime Proofs of 1837 were often cleaned, resulting in coins that have lost much of their mirror surface. With

1886. Graded PF-67.

medium hairlines and good reflectivity, an assigned grade of PF-64 is indicated, and with relatively few hairlines, Gem PF-65. In various grades hairlines are most easily seen in the obverse field. PF-66 should have hairlines so delicate that magnification is needed to see them. Above that, a Proof should be free of such lines.

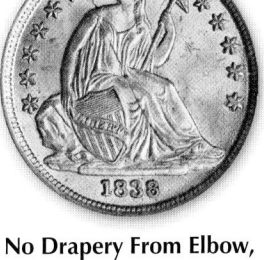 

1837, Large Date	**1837, Small Date**	**No Drapery From Elbow, Tilted Shield (1838–1840)** **Drapery From Elbow, Upright Shield (1840–1891)**

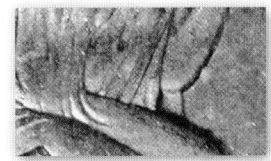

1838, Small Stars	**1838, Large Stars**	**1838, So-Called Partial Drapery**

	Mintage	Cert	Avg	%MS	G-4	F-12	VF-20	EF-40	AU-50	MS-60	MS-63	MS-64	MS-65
										PF-60	PF-63	PF-65	
1837, All kinds	682,500												
1837, Large Date		35	51.8	46%	$45	$100	$300	$500	$700	$1,100	$1,800	$4,000	$7,750
Auctions: $4,700, MS-65, January 2015; $3,290, MS-64, January 2015; $1,293, AU-58, January 2015; $470, AU-50, January 2015													
1837, Small Date		34	54.3	47%	$50	$120	$325	$525	$725	$1,200	$2,000	$4,500	$8,500
Auctions: $3,055, MS-64, February 2015; $2,358, MS-64, February 2015; $1,058, AU-58, July 2015; $282, AU-50, January 2015													
1837, Proof	25–35	26	63.9							$8,500	$15,000	$40,000	
Auctions: $30,550, PF-65, January 2015													
1838-O, Variety 1	489,034	165	42.2	19%	$60	$140	$400	$750	$1,200	$3,000	$6,500	$10,000	$20,000
Auctions: $6,463, MS-64, January 2015; $999, AU-55, January 2015; $646, VF-35, January 2015; $376, VF-25, February 2015													
1838, Variety 2, All kinds	1,992,500												
1838, Small Stars		74	57.7	68%	$30	$55	$80	$175	$400	$700	$1,350	$2,000	$4,000
Auctions: $10,575, MS-67, October 2015; $2,820, MS-65, June 2015; $188, EF-45, May 2015													
1838, Large Stars		374	59.6	69%	$25	$30	$40	$135	$250	$375	$850	$1,100	$3,000
Auctions: $5,640, MS-67, July 2015; $2,350, MS-65, January 2015; $999, MS-64, January 2015; $881, MS-64, January 2015													
1838, Partial Drapery (a)		22	62.0	77%	$30	$60	$100	$200	$500	$850	$2,000		
Auctions: $1,293, MS-62, January 2015; $89, VF-20, February 2015													
1838, Proof (b)	2–3	0	n/a										
Auctions: $161,000, PF-67Cam, January 2008													

a. The so-called "partial drapery" is not a design variation; rather, it is evidence of die clashing from the E in DIME on the reverse.
b. The 1838, Proof, dime may be unique.

**1839-O,
Repunched
Mintmark**

**1841-O, Transitional
Reverse, Small O**

**1841-O, Transitional
Reverse, Large O**

**Regular Reverse
Style of 1841-O**

	Mintage	Cert	Avg	%MS	G-4	F-12	VF-20	EF-40	AU-50	MS-60	MS-63	MS-64	MS-65
											PF-60	PF-63	PF-65
1839	1,053,115	234	60.7	71%	$20	$30	$40	$135	$250	$400	$850	$1,100	$3,000
Auctions: $9,988, MS-67, May 2015; $1,410, MS-64, September 2015; $764, MS-63, February 2015; $388, AU-55, June 2015													
1839, Proof	4–5	3	64.3								$7,000	$10,000	$45,000
Auctions: $36,719, PF-66, April 2013													
1839-O	1,291,600	87	54.2	47%	$25	$40	$45	$135	$275	$450	$1,500	$3,000	$7,000
Auctions: $15,863, MS-67, May 2015; $823, AU-55, October 2015; $764, AU-50, June 2015; $470, AU-50, June 2015													
1839-O, Repunched Mintmark	(c)	1	30.0	0%				$150	$325	$750	$1,500		
Auctions: $13,800, MS-66+, February 2012													
1839-O, Proof	2–3	1	65.0									$25,000	$75,000
Auctions: $74,750, PF-65, October 2008													
1840, No Drapery	981,500	136	56.5	59%	$20	$25	$40	$135	$250	$400	$850	$1,500	$4,000
Auctions: $1,998, MS-65, June 2015; $188, MS-60, June 2015; $165, AU-55, January 2015; $212, AU-50, February 2015													
1840, No Drapery, Proof	4–5	5	64.8								$10,000	$15,000	$30,000
Auctions: $27,600, PF-65Cam, August 2007													
1840-O, No Drapery	1,175,000	30	43.9	20%	$25	$40	$55	$230	$800	$2,500	$6,000	$15,000	
Auctions: $376, AU-50, June 2015; $206, AU-50, June 2015; $423, EF-45, September 2015; $188, VF-30, November 2015													
1840, Drapery	377,500	23	47.8	30%	$35	$90	$175	$300	$450	$1,200	$5,500	$10,000	$25,000
Auctions: $27,025, MS-64, May 2015; $2,585, MS-62, January 2015; $84, VF-20, January 2015													
1841 (d)	1,622,500	81	59.0	68%	$20	$30	$35	$60	$140	$350	$650	$1,200	$3,000
Auctions: $223, AU-55, March 2015; $212, AU-55, January 2015; $141, AU-53, August 2015; $79, AU-53, January 2015													
1841, Proof (d)	2–3	1	63.0									$65,000	
Auctions: $41,125, PF-63Cam, October 2014													
1841, No Drapery, Proof	2–3	2	60.0									$75,000	
Auctions: $305,500, PF-67, November 2013													
1841-O	2,007,500	83	48.8	25%	$25	$35	$50	$85	$225	$900	$1,800	$3,500	$6,500
Auctions: $353, AU-55, June 2015; $329, AU-53, January 2015; $259, AU-53, July 2015; $106, EF-45, June 2015													
1841-O, Transitional Reverse, Small O (e)	(f)	4	9.3	0%									
Auctions: $940, G-6, June 2013													
1841-O, Transitional Reverse, Large O (e)	(f)	3	8.3	0%									
Auctions: $2,611, F-12, January 2014													
1842	1,887,500	182	50.8	47%	$20	$30	$35	$50	$125	$400	$650	$1,000	$3,000
Auctions: $4,700, MS-66, May 2015; $3,760, MS-66, January 2015; $3,290, MS-65, June 2015; $881, MS-64, August 2015													
1842, Proof	6–10	4	63.8								$10,000	$15,000	$40,000
Auctions: $37,375, PF-65Cam, April 2008													
1842-O	2,020,000	37	46.4	24%	$25	$35	$70	$265	$1,300	$2,500	$5,000	$7,500	$20,000
Auctions: $14,100, MS-65, May 2015; $306, AU-50, August 2015; $447, EF-45, February 2015; $141, VF-35, January 2015													

c. Included in circulation-strike 1839-O mintage figure. **d.** Two examples are known of 1841, No Drapery, Small Stars, Upright Shield. One is a Proof and the other is a circulation strike in VF. **e.** The 1841-O, Transitional Reverse, varieties were struck with a reverse die that was supposed to have been discontinued in 1840, but saw limited use into 1841. Note the closed buds (not open, as in the regular reverse die of 1841); also note that the second leaf from the left (in the group of four leaves to the left of the bow knot) reaches only halfway across the bottom of the U in UNITED. **f.** Included in 1841-O mintage figure.

	Mintage	Cert	Avg	%MS	G-4	F-12	VF-20	EF-40	AU-50	MS-60	MS-63	MS-64	MS-65
											PF-60	PF-63	PF-65
1843	1,370,000	74	57.6	55%	$20	$30	$35	$50	$125	$400	$800	$1,250	$3,500
	Auctions: $8,225, MS-66, June 2014												
1843, Proof	*10–15*	10	64.3								$5,000	$10,000	$25,000
	Auctions: $25,850, PF-66, June 2014												
1843-O	150,000	48	23.3	0%	$85	$350	$850	$3,500	$10,000	$35,000			
	Auctions: $423, F-12, February 2015; $206, VG-10, January 2015; $84, G-3, June 2015												
1844	72,500	98	24.1	9%	$200	$450	$700	$1,200	$1,800	$4,000	$12,000	$20,000	$35,000
	Auctions: $705, VF-30, July 2015; $447, VF-30, February 2015; $439, VF-20, May 2015; $212, F-12, February 2015												
1844, Proof	*4–8*	2	64.0								$18,000	$32,500	$65,000
	Auctions: $44,063, PF-65, October 2014; $31,725, PF-64, May 2015												
1845	1,755,000	153	59.1	69%	$20	$30	$35	$50	$125	$400	$800	$1,250	$3,500
	Auctions: $4,935, MS-66, May 2015; $3,290, MS-65, January 2015; $423, MS-62, January 2015; $364, AU-58, April 2015												
1845, Proof	*6–10*	5	64.8								$7,500	$12,500	$35,000
	Auctions: $19,975, PF-65, April 2013												
1845-O	230,000	44	32.0	5%	$25	$75	$250	$850	$2,500	$7,500			
	Auctions: $123,376, MS-69, May 2015; $541, AU-50, June 2015; $865, EF-40, January 2015; $364, VF-25, January 2015												
1846	31,300	56	25.0	2%	$200	$475	$950	$2,500	$8,500	$15,000	$45,000		
	Auctions: $11,456, AU-58, January 2015; $764, VF-20, February 2015; $646, F-12, January 2015; $401, VG-10, February 2015												
1846, Proof	*8–12*	7	63.9								$10,000	$15,000	$40,000
	Auctions: $31,725, PF-65, March 2013												
1847	245,000	37	51.8	35%	$20	$40	$70	$125	$350	$950	$4,000	$6,500	$10,000
	Auctions: $5,581, MS-63, February 2014; $4,700, MS-63, October 2014; $229, EF-45, November 2014												
1847, Proof	*3–5*	1	66.0								$8,000	$13,000	$40,000
	Auctions: $35,250, PF-66Cam, March 2013; $44,063, PF-66, October 2014												
1848	451,500	68	56.1	59%	$20	$32	$50	$85	$150	$550	$900	$1,500	$6,500
	Auctions: $6,463, MS-65, May 2015; $400, AU-58, April 2015; $100, AU-55, January 2015												
1848, Proof	*10–15*	9	64.6								$5,000	$10,000	$25,000
	Auctions: $27,025, PF-66, February 2013												
1849	839,000	75	56.1	60%	$20	$30	$40	$60	$125	$300	$900	$1,500	$3,500
	Auctions: $74, EF-45, January 2015; $46, VF-30, April 2015												
1849, Proof	*4–6*	3	65.3								$10,000	$15,000	$40,000
	Auctions: $35,250, PF-65, August 2013												
1849-O	300,000	82	46.2	24%	$25	$50	$125	$300	$750	$2,500	$5,500	$11,000	
	Auctions: $5,288, MS-64, January 2015; $3,525, MS-63, June 2015; $617, AU-55, January 2015; $165, AU-50, July 2015												
1850	1,931,500	147	55.8	62%	$20	$30	$40	$60	$125	$300	$700	$1,500	$4,500
	Auctions: $1,645, MS-65, October 2015; $940, MS-64, June 2015; $646, MS-63, January 2015; $123, AU-58, January 2015												
1850, Proof	*4–6*	4	64.5								$10,000	$15,000	$40,000
	Auctions: $44,650, PF-67, May 2015; $19,975, PF-64, May 2015												
1850-O	510,000	25	41.4	24%	$25	$40	$90	$175	$375	$1,200	$2,600	$4,500	$6,500
	Auctions: $823, AU-58, January 2015; $1,058, AU-55, July 2015; $74, VF-20, August 2015												
1851	1,026,500	74	56.3	59%	$20	$30	$40	$60	$125	$350	$850	$1,400	$5,000
	Auctions: $20,563, MS-67, June 2013; $8,225, MS-67, May 2015; $170, AU-53, October 2014												
1851-O	400,000	37	49.2	16%	$25	$40	$80	$175	$450	$2,000	$3,750	$6,500	$15,000
	Auctions: $15,275, MS-65, May 2015; $165, EF-40, January 2015; $106, EF-40, June 2015												
1852	1,535,500	96	57.2	64%	$20	$30	$40	$60	$125	$300	$700	$1,200	$3,000
	Auctions: $5,640, MS-67, February 2015; $2,468, MS-65, June 2015; $376, MS-62, May 2015												
1852, Proof	*5–10*	8	64.4								$5,000	$10,000	$25,000
	Auctions: $8,225, PF-62, January 2014												
1852-O	430,000	52	55.4	54%	$30	$50	$140	$250	$350	$1,600	$2,750	$4,000	$12,500
	Auctions: $259, EF-40, January 2015; $129, VF-20, January 2015												

	Mintage	Cert	Avg	%MS	G-4	F-12	VF-20	EF-40	AU-50	MS-60	MS-63	MS-64	MS-65
											PF-60	PF-63	PF-65
1853, No Arrows	95,000	109	55.0	72%	$100	$275	$475	$625	$725	$900	$1,350	$1,850	$2,500
Auctions: $200, EF-45, January 2015; $306, VF-20, February 2015; $118, F-15, May 2015; $176, VG-10, February 2015													
1853, With Arrows	12,173,000	888	58.8	68%	$20	$25	$30	$50	$175	$300	$675	$950	$1,750
Auctions: $3,995, MS-67, January 2015; $2,820, MS-66, June 2015; $1,704, MS-65, January 2015; $881, MS-64, January 2015													
1853, Proof	5–10	5	64.6								$15,000	$30,000	$75,000
Auctions: $52,875, PF-66, June 2014; $34,075, PF-65, October 2014; $14,100, PF-62, October 2014													
1853-O	1,100,000	47	45.2	15%	$25	$50	$100	$275	$500	$1,750	$3,500	$5,500	$10,000
Auctions: $1,880, AU-55, June 2015; $200, EF-40, July 2015; $89, VF-25, August 2015; $54, VF-25, January 2015													
1854	4,470,000	252	58.2	62%	$20	$25	$30	$50	$175	$300	$675	$950	$1,850
Auctions: $4,465, MS-67, June 2015; $6,463, MS-66, May 2015; $1,234, MS-65, February 2015; $881, MS-64, February 2015													
1854, Proof	8–12	9	65.0								$8,000	$15,000	$40,000
Auctions: $25,850, PF-65Cam, April 2013; $19,975, PF-65, October 2014; $17,625, PF-65, January 2015													
1854-O	1,770,000	89	57.7	73%	$20	$25	$45	$85	$200	$400	$1,000	$1,500	$3,250
Auctions: $8,225, MS-66, May 2015; $646, MS-62, August 2015													
1855	2,075,000	100	60.4	74%	$20	$25	$30	$60	$185	$325	$850	$1,300	$2,850
Auctions: $1,116, MS-64, January 2015; $1,058, MS-64, February 2015; $646, MS-63, June 2015; $153, AU-55, January 2015													
1855, Proof	8–12	15	64.9								$8,000	$15,000	$40,000
Auctions: $38,188, PF-67Cam, March 2013													
1856, All kinds	5,780,000												
1856, Large Date		26	46.9	19%	$18	$22	$36	$60	$160	$400	$1,000	$2,000	$15,000
Auctions: $6,463, MS-64, October 2015; $2,233, MS-63, October 2015													
1856, Small Date		92	52.2	48%	$16	$20	$30	$50	$130	$300	$600	$950	$2,250
Auctions: $1,763, MS-65, January 2015; $494, MS-63, October 2015; $188, AU-58, July 2015; $129, AU-58, January 2015													
1856, Proof	40–50	26	64.4								$2,500	$4,500	$15,000
Auctions: $25,850, PF-67, June 2014													
1856-O	1,180,000	58	53.5	48%	$18	$25	$35	$65	$250	$800	$1,350	$2,250	$5,000
Auctions: $3,672, MS-65, October 2014; $1,469, MS-63, November 2013; $74, AU-50, February 2015; $147, EF-45, November 2014													
1856-S	70,000	23	42.8	9%	$120	$375	$600	$1,250	$1,700	$3,800	$15,000	$20,000	$45,000
Auctions: $1,410, VF-30, January 2015; $341, G-6, January 2015													
1857	5,580,000	514	59.5	71%	$16	$20	$30	$50	$130	$300	$650	$900	$1,950
Auctions: $2,233, MS-66, January 2015; $1,763, MS-66, June 2015; $376, MS-63, May 2015; $235, MS-62, August 2015													
1857, Proof	45–60	36	64.6								$2,000	$3,750	$6,500
Auctions: $7,638, PF-66, October 2015; $2,820, PF-64, June 2015													
1857-O	1,540,000	231	57.8	63%	$18	$25	$35	$70	$200	$425	$750	$1,000	$2,350
Auctions: $2,468, MS-66, May 2015; $1,998, MS-66, June 2015; $423, MS-62, February 2015; $212, AU-55, August 2015													
1858	1,540,000	140	59.7	72%	$16	$20	$30	$50	$130	$300	$650	$850	$2,000
Auctions: $4,935, MS-67, June 2015; $2,585, MS-66, June 2015													
1858, Proof	(g)	81	64.5								$1,000	$2,000	$4,500
Auctions: $10,575, PF-67, May 2015; $5,170, PF-66, January 2015; $1,645, PF-64, January 2015; $1,410, PF-63, March 2015													
1858-O	290,000	48	55.5	40%	$25	$40	$85	$135	$300	$600	$1,000	$2,500	$5,500
Auctions: $517, AU-58, January 2015; $188, EF-45, April 2015													
1858-S	60,000	29	37.6	10%	$100	$225	$450	$900	$1,600	$3,800	$15,000	$22,500	
Auctions: $1,116, EF-40, January 2015; $999, VF-35, March 2015; $646, VF-20, January 2015; $306, F-12, February 2015													
1859	429,200	153	62.3	86%	$20	$22	$32	$60	$140	$300	$650	$850	$2,000
Auctions: $376, MS-63, September 2015; $341, MS-62, March 2015; $40, AU-53, January 2015; $112, AU-50, September 2015													
1859, Proof	(g)	213	64.5								$950	$1,500	$4,000
Auctions: $6,463, PF-67Cam, October 2015; $4,230, PF-66Cam, June 2015; $4,230, PF-66, January 2015; $2,350, PF-65, January 2015													

g. The mintage figure is unknown.

**1859 Pattern Dime: Obverse of 1859,
Reverse of 1860, Proof**
Judd-233

**1861, Six Vertical
Shield Lines**

	Mintage	Cert	Avg	%MS	G-4	F-12	VF-20	EF-40	AU-50	MS-60	MS-63	MS-64	MS-65
											PF-60	PF-63	PF-65
1859, Obverse of 1859, Reverse of 1860, Proof (h)	(i)	12	64.7								$10,000	$18,500	$25,000
Auctions: $5,875, PF-67Cam, October 2014; $4,113, PF-66Cam, July 2014; $3,672, PF-66Cam, October 2014; $2,585, PF-65, July 2014
1859-O	480,000	119	58.6	68%	$20	$25	$60	$95	$275	$400	$850	$1,150	$2,250
Auctions: $5,405, MS-67, June 2015; $494, MS-63, February 2015; $329, MS-61, January 2015; $106, AU-50, February 2015
1859-S	60,000	21	29.2	10%	$100	$300	$650	$1,500	$4,000	$11,000	$27,500	$40,000	$85,000
Auctions: $376, EF-40, February 2015; $200, F-12, January 2015; $447, G-6, February 2015
1860-S, Variety 2	140,000	42	45.1	17%	$35	$60	$150	$400	$950	$2,500	$5,000	$8,500	$25,000
Auctions: $37,600, MS-65, May 2015; $1,998, MS-62, May 2015; $999, AU-58, March 2015; $823, AU-50, January 2015
1860, Variety 4	606,000	122	62.6	88%	$16	$20	$32	$40	$100	$200	$325	$450	$1,150
Auctions: $11,163, MS-67, May 2015; $1,410, MS-66, June 2015; $1,880, MS-65, January 2015; $423, MS-64, June 2015
1860, Variety 4, Proof	1,000	158	64.5								$350	$750	$1,750
Auctions: $5,405, PF-68, August 2015; $6,463, PF-67, October 2014; $1,646, PF-65+, September 2014; $734, PF-64, July 2014
1860-O, Variety 4	40,000	45	29.6	7%	$325	$850	$1,800	$4,000	$8,000	$15,000		$65,000	
Auctions: $64,625, MS-64, May 2015; $2,350, VF-35, February 2015; $999, VF-20, September 2015
1861 (j)	1,883,000	142	58.9	75%	$16	$22	$30	$40	$100	$200	$325	$450	$1,150
Auctions: $3,290, MS-66, January 2015; $764, MS-65, January 2015; $376, MS-64, January 2015; $259, MS-63, January 2015
1861, Proof	1,000	103	63.9								$350	$750	$2,000
Auctions: $6,463, PF-67Cam, May 2015; $676, PF-64, March 2015; $764, PF-63, August 2015
1861-S	172,500	25	44.6	32%	$40	$110	$200	$450	$1,000	$3,500	$8,500		
Auctions: $51,700, MS-66, January 2015; $823, EF-40, February 2015; $764, VF-25, February 2015; $235, VF-20, January 2015
1862	847,000	181	62.2	89%	$16	$25	$30	$40	$100	$185	$350	$500	$1,150
Auctions: $1,763, MS-66, July 2015; $881, MS-65, January 2015; $400, MS-64, January 2015; $306, MS-62, February 2015
1862, Proof	550	104	63.7								$350	$750	$2,000
Auctions: $1,998, AU-50, August 2015; $2,115, EF-45, June 2015; $505, VF-25, August 2015; $259, VF-20, November 2015
1862-S	180,750	18	39.1	28%	$45	$90	$200	$675	$1,000	$2,500	$5,000	$8,000	
Auctions: $35,250, MS-65, October 2014; $646, AU-50, October 2014; $646, VF-30, April 2014; $388, VF-25, July 2014
1863	14,000	41	57.3	83%	$310	$600	$750	$900	$1,100	$1,300	$1,800	$2,500	$4,000
Auctions: $5,170, MS-66, May 2015; $2,820, MS-63, January 2015; $881, G-6, August 2015
1863, Proof	460	159	64.5								$325	$700	$1,750
Auctions: $16,450, PF-67DCam, January 2015; $4,230, PF-66Cam, October 2015; $1,880, PF-65Cam, February 2015; $529, PF-63, October 2015
1863-S	157,500	30	52.2	33%	$40	$60	$120	$350	$700	$1,500	$6,500	$12,500	$30,000
Auctions: $30,550, MS-66, May 2015; $881, EF-45, January 2015; $153, F-15, January 2015

h. In 1859 the Mint made a dime pattern, of which some 13 to 20 examples are known. These "coins without a country" do not bear the nation's identity (UNITED STATES OF AMERICA). They are transitional pieces, not made for circulation, but struck at the time that the dime's legend was being transferred from the reverse to the obverse (see Variety 4). For more information, consult *United States Pattern Coins*, 10th edition (Judd). **i.** The mintage figure is unknown. **j.** The dime's dies were modified slightly in 1861. The first (scarcer) variety has only five vertical lines in the top part of the shield.

	Mintage	Cert	Avg	%MS	G-4	F-12	VF-20	EF-40	AU-50	MS-60	MS-63	MS-64	MS-65
											PF-60	PF-63	PF-65
1864	11,000	43	57.0	74%	$225	$425	$575	$875	$1,100	$1,200	$1,750	$2,500	$5,500
	Auctions: $940, AU-50, January 2015; $999, VF-25, January 2015												
1864, Proof	470	155	64.3								$325	$700	$1,750
	Auctions: $1,645, PF-66, October 2015; $3,525, PF-65, March 2015; $823, PF-64, June 2015; $764, PF-64, January 2015												
1864-S	230,000	38	48.0	42%	$55	$120	$210	$375	$600	$1,500	$1,900	$4,000	$6,500
	Auctions: $1,528, MS-62, January 2015; $1,293, MS-61, March 2015; $1,058, AU-55, February 2015; $153, VF-30, January 2015												
1865	10,000	53	55.6	72%	$250	$550	$700	$800	$950	$1,200	$2,000	$2,500	$3,500
	Auctions: $14,688, MS-67, October 2014; $9,988, MS-67, November 2013; $3,916, MS-66, June 2015; $1,528, EF-40, October 2014												
1865, Proof	500	116	64.1								$350	$750	$2,000
	Auctions: $2,703, PF-66Cam, October 2015; $1,087, PF-63Cam, October 2015; $1,058, PF-63, October 2015; $1,058, PF-63, October 2015												
1865-S	175,000	26	39.7	15%	$65	$275	$475	$750	$2,200	$6,750	$12,000	$25,000	$40,000
	Auctions: $5,875, MS-62, January 2015; $517, AU-50, January 2015; $823, VF-35, January 2015; $212, VF-30, January 2015												
1866	8,000	43	55.8	77%	$450	$1,100	$1,400	$1,600	$1,750	$2,000	$2,500	$2,750	$3,250
	Auctions: $4,465, MS-66, May 2015; $3,760, MS-66, June 2015; $3,055, MS-66, January 2015; $1,880, MS-62, June 2015												
1866, Proof	725	165	64.4								$325	$700	$1,750
	Auctions: $1,058, PF-65, June 2015; $823, PF-64, July 2015												
1866-S	135,000	32	40.1	34%	$40	$75	$135	$350	$600	$1,250	$5,500	$8,500	$17,500
	Auctions: $14,100, MS-66, May 2015; $588, EF-40, August 2015; $541, EF-40, January 2015; $165, VF-20, June 2015												
1867	6,000	46	60.8	85%	$400	$750	$900	$1,000	$1,250	$1,500	$2,000	$2,500	$4,000
	Auctions: $11,163, MS-68, June 2014; $2,468, MS-64, July 2014; $1,763, MS-63, February 2015												
1867, Proof	625	133	64.2								$325	$700	$1,750
	Auctions: $5,170, PF-67Cam, May 2015; $2,233, PF-66Cam, June 2015; $1,293, PF-64Cam, July 2015; $940, PF-64Cam, July 2015												
1867-S	140,000	30	49.2	47%	$32	$100	$170	$425	$700	$1,250	$3,000	$5,000	$8,000
	Auctions: $2,585, MS-62, January 2015; $2,233, MS-62, June 2015; $447, AU-50, April 2015; $376, VF-30, January 2015												
1868	464,000	41	56.8	76%	$18	$30	$40	$65	$150	$300	$850	$1,500	$4,000
	Auctions: $118, EF-45, April 2015; $62, EF-40, January 2015												
1868, Proof	600	156	63.9								$325	$700	$1,750
	Auctions: $1,058, PF-64Cam, October 2015; $577, PF-63Cam, January 2015												
1868-S	260,000	22	51.2	59%	$20	$35	$70	$125	$225	$400	$1,000	$2,500	$5,000
	Auctions: $541, AU-53, March 2015; $89, EF-40, March 2015												
1869	256,000	27	53.0	56%	$18	$30	$65	$100	$200	$400	$900	$1,750	$3,250
	Auctions: $7,638, MS-67, May 2015; $79, AU-50, January 2015; $125, VF-25, September 2015												
1869, Proof	600	178	64.1								$325	$700	$1,750
	Auctions: $1,175, PF-65Cam, March 2015; $1,100, PF-65, January 2015; $823, PF-64, June 2015; $475, PF-63Cam, July 2015												
1869-S	450,000	56	60.8	80%	$18	$25	$50	$150	$250	$400	$800	$1,300	$3,000
	Auctions: $3,995, MS-66, May 2015; $2,585, MS-65, January 2015; $764, MS-62, March 2015; $306, AU-53, March 2015												
1870	470,500	71	60.5	80%	$16	$25	$30	$50	$100	$200	$450	$800	$1,650
	Auctions: $588, MS-64, January 2015; $129, MS-60, January 2015												
1870, Proof	1,000	158	64.1								$325	$700	$1,750
	Auctions: $7,050, PF-67, January 2014												
1870-S	50,000	34	40.7	35%	$250	$400	$475	$600	$850	$1,800	$2,750	$3,500	$6,000
	Auctions: $1,116, AU-53, March 2015; $646, VF-30, July 2015; $223, VF-20, January 2015; $306, VG-8, February 2015												
1871	906,750	71	59.7	68%	$16	$25	$30	$50	$150	$250	$425	$850	$1,600
	Auctions: $259, MS-62, July 2015; $235, AU-58, January 2015; $56, AU-50, January 2015												
1871, Proof	960	146	64.0								$325	$700	$1,750
	Auctions: $1,645, PF-66, January 2015; $1,116, PF-64, January 2015; $200, PF-60, September 2015												
1871-CC	20,100	21	36.0	24%	$2,500	$5,200	$8,000	$12,500	$22,500	$50,000	$100,000	$150,000	$275,000
	Auctions: $270,250, MS-65, October 2014; $27,025, AU-55, May 2013; $6,463, AU-50, July 2014; $3,525, EF-40, January 2015												
1871-S	320,000	28	55.6	46%	$25	$80	$140	$225	$300	$850	$2,500	$4,000	$10,000
	Auctions: $4,230, MS-64, October 2015; $364, EF-45, March 2015; $69, VF-20, January 2015; $40, VF-20, February 2015												

1872, Doubled-Die Reverse
FS-10-1872-801.

1873, With Arrows,
Doubled-Die Obverse
FS-10-1873-101.

1873, Close 3   **1873, Open 3**

	Mintage	Cert	Avg	%MS	G-4	F-12	VF-20	EF-40	AU-50	MS-60	MS-63	MS-64	MS-65
											PF-60	PF-63	PF-65
1872	2,395,500	81	58.7	73%	$18	$25	$30	$40	$90	$175	$300	$650	$1,100
	Auctions: $17,625, MS-68, May 2015; $494, MS-64, January 2015; $176, MS-62, May 2015; $69, MS-60, January 2015												
1872, Doubled-Die Reverse (k,l)	(m)	2	37.5	0%	$50	$75	$150	$250	$350	$750			
	Auctions: $425, VF-20, May 2008												
1872, Proof	950	146	63.8								$325	$700	$1,750
	Auctions: $999, PF-65, January 2015; $881, PF-65, January 2015												
1872-CC	35,480	40	26.4	0%	$500	$2,000	$4,000	$7,500	$17,500	$50,000	$200,000		
	Auctions: $182,125, MS-63, May 2015; $2,233, EF-40, January 2015; $1,410, EF-40, February 2015; $1,293, VF-20, June 2015												
1872-S	190,000	23	54.2	48%	$25	$85	$140	$225	$400	$1,200	$3,500	$7,500	$25,000
	Auctions: $28,200, MS-65, May 2015; $1,647, MS-60, March 2015; $376, EF-40, January 2015; $69, VF-30, January 2015												
1873, No Arrows, Close 3	1,506,800	42	57.9	62%	$16	$22	$25	$40	$90	$150	$250	$650	$1,500
	Auctions: $6,463, MS-67, June 2014; $259, AU-58, October 2014												
1873, No Arrows, Open 3	60,000	35	51.0	40%	$20	$50	$75	$130	$200	$600	$1,500	$4,500	$15,000
	Auctions: $9,400, MS-64, August 2013; $353, AU-55, October 2014; $259, AU-55, October 2014; $259, AU-55, February 2015												
1873, No Arrows, Close 3, Proof	600	176	64.3								$325	$700	$1,750
	Auctions: $14,100, PF-68Cam, May 2015; $8,813, PF-67Cam, January 2015; $1,116, PF-65Cam, June 2015												
1873-CC, No Arrows † (n,o)	12,400	0	n/a								—		—
	Auctions: $891,250, MS-65, July 2004; $1,840,000, MS-65, August 2012												
1873, With Arrows	2,377,700	185	57.2	63%	$18	$26	$55	$150	$300	$550	$900	$1,650	$4,000
	Auctions: $11,750, MS-66, June 2015; $2,233, MS-65, January 2015; $400, MS-62, May 2015; $329, MS-61, March 2015												
1873, With Arrows, Doubled-Die Obverse (p)	(q)	4	27.8	25%	$150	$250	$500	$1,500	$5,000	$20,000			
	Auctions: $3,220, VF-25, October 2011												
1873, With Arrows, Proof	500	107	64.2								$750	$1,500	$5,000
	Auctions: $9,988, PF-67Cam, September 2014; $9,988, PF-66Cam, September 2014; $16,450, PF-67, November 2013												
1873-CC, With Arrows	18,791	39	16.8	3%	$2,700	$5,000	$8,500	$17,000	$40,000	$50,000	$100,000		$225,000
	Auctions: $3,290, AU-50, January 2015; $3,290, EF-40, January 2015; $2,820, EF-40, February 2015; $7,638, VF-35, January 2015												
1873-S	455,000	59	63.0	92%	$22	$35	$60	$175	$450	$1,000	$2,000	$3,500	$7,500
	Auctions: $3,890, MS-64, January 2015; $2,233, MS-64, January 2015; $1,058, MS-62, March 2015; $46, AU-50, January 2015												

† Ranked in the *100 Greatest U.S. Coins* (fourth edition). **k.** The first die hubbing was almost completely obliterated by the second, which was rotated about 170 degrees from the first. The key indicators of this variety are inside the opening of the D, and near the center arm of the E in ONE. **l.** This coin is considered rare. **m.** Included in circulation-strike 1872 mintage figure. **n.** Most of the mintage of 1873-CC (Without Arrows) was melted after the law of 1873, affecting the statuses and physical properties of U.S. coinage, was passed. **o.** This coin is considered unique. **p.** Doubling is evident on the shield and on the banner across the shield. Although well known for decades, very few examples of this variety have been reported. **q.** Included in circulation-strike 1873, With Arrows, mintage figure.

1875-CC, Mintmark Above Bow — **1875-CC, Mintmark Below Bow** — **1876-CC, Variety 1 Reverse** — **1876-CC, Variety 2 Reverse** *FS-10-1876CC-901.*

	Mintage	Cert	Avg	%MS	G-4	F-12	VF-20	EF-40	AU-50	MS-60	MS-63 / PF-60	MS-64 / PF-63	MS-65 / PF-65
1874	2,940,000	268	57.8	66%	$18	$25	$55	$150	$310	$600	$1,000	$1,400	$4,500
Auctions: $15,275, MS-67, June 2015; $3,525, MS-66, August 2015; $4,230, MS-65, August 2015; $447, MS-62, February 2015													
1874, Proof	700	185	63.8								$750	$1,500	$5,000
Auctions: $3,772, PF-65Cam, October 2015; $2,820, PF-65, October 2015; $1,175, PF-64, March 2015; $764, PF-63Cam, July 2015													
1874-CC	10,817	12	34.9	8%	$4,500	$12,500	$18,000	$25,000	$45,000	$90,000	$165,000		
Auctions: $6,463, EF-40, January 2015; $2,585, G-3, February 2015; $4,230, Fair-2, January 2015													
1874-S	240,000	47	58.1	70%	$25	$65	$110	$225	$500	$900	$2,000	$3,250	$6,500
Auctions: $505, AU-58, March 2015; $306, AU-50, February 2015													
1875	10,350,000	416	61.4	87%	$15	$20	$25	$35	$80	$150	$250	$400	$750
Auctions: $5,170, MS-67, May 2015; $1,116, MS-66, August 2015; $541, MS-65, January 2015; $353, MS-64, February 2015													
1875, Proof	700	160	64.4								$300	$650	$1,500
Auctions: $5,405, PF-67Cam, October 2015; $1,200, PF-66Cam, October 2015; $999, PF-65, June 2015; $458, PF-62Cam, September 2015													
1875-CC, All kinds	4,645,000												
1875-CC, Above Bow		142	53.4	58%	$28	$35	$50	$70	$150	$325	$500	$1,250	$2,500
Auctions: $5,170, MS-67, September 2015; $3,760, MS-66, January 2015; $3,525, MS-65, October 2015; $823, MS-64, January 2015													
1875-CC, Below Bow		67	55.6	67%	$28	$35	$50	$70	$125	$350	$550	$1,400	$2,750
Auctions: $4,230, MS-65, May 2015; $1,880, MS-65, August 2015													
1875-S, All kinds	9,070,000												
1875-S, Below Bow		69	57.1	71%	$15	$20	$25	$35	$85	$160	$250	$400	$1,000
Auctions: $2,233, MS-66, May 2015; $999, MS-66, October 2015; $940, MS-65, August 2015; $600, MS-65, October 2015													
1875-S, Above Bow		32	62.7	81%	$15	$20	$25	$35	$85	$160	$275	$500	$1,400
Auctions: $3,055, MS-66, May 2015; $1,880, MS-66, July 2015; $705, MS-63, August 2015; $400, MS-63, March 2015													
1876	11,460,000	340	61.5	87%	$15	$20	$25	$35	$80	$150	$250	$400	$800
Auctions: $1,880, MS-67, January 2015; $969, MS-66, August 2015; $900, MS-66, August 2015; $705, MS-65, June 2015													
1876, Proof	1,250	158	63.7								$300	$650	$1,500
Auctions: $3,525, PF-67, May 2015; $494, PF-63, March 2015; $282, PF-61, March 2015													
1876-CC	8,270,000	374	55.1	66%	$27	$32	$45	$65	$100	$230	$450	$550	$1,350
Auctions: $9,988, MS-67, January 2015; $2,056, MS-66, September 2015; $1,146, MS-65, January 2015; $353, MS-60, October 2015													
1876-CC, Variety 2 Reverse (r)	(s)	3	56.3	33%				$250	$350	$600	$1,250		
Auctions: $3,738, MS-64, February 2012													
1876-CC, Proof	3–4	5	65.2								$40,000		$75,000
Auctions: $38,188, PF-65, October 2014													
1876-S	10,420,000	99	59.2	76%	$15	$20	$25	$35	$80	$150	$250	$450	$1,750
Auctions: $2,401, MS-66, June 2015; $2,056, MS-66, August 2015; $388, MS-64, March 2015; $100, MS-60, January 2015													
1877	7,310,000	160	61.9	87%	$15	$20	$25	$35	$80	$150	$250	$450	$850
Auctions: $1,645, MS-66, October 2015; $764, MS-65, June 2015; $247, MS-63, January 2015; $188, MS-62, January 2015													
1877, Proof	510	121	63.9								$300	$650	$1,500
Auctions: $1,880, PF-65, October 2015; $940, PF-64, January 2015; $329, PF-62, October 2015; $176, PF-60, May 2015													
1877-CC	7,700,000	443	58.1	76%	$27	$32	$45	$65	$100	$230	$500	$850	$2,000
Auctions: $4,935, MS-67, January 2015; $2,115, MS-66, July 2015; $1,116, MS-65, January 2015; $881, MS-64, August 2015													
1877-S	2,340,000	90	61.8	87%	$15	$20	$25	$35	$80	$150	$300	$650	$1,500
Auctions: $494, MS-64, May 2015; $353, MS-64, March 2015; $129, AU-58, January 2015													

r. The scarce Variety 2 reverse exhibits a single point to the end of the left ribbon; the common Variety 1 reverse has a split at the ribbon's end. **s.** Included in circulation-strike 1876-CC mintage figure.

	Mintage	Cert	Avg	%MS	G-4	F-12	VF-20	EF-40	AU-50	MS-60	MS-63	MS-64	MS-65
											PF-60	PF-63	PF-65
1878	1,677,200	89	61.7	88%	$15	$20	$25	$35	$80	$150	$250	$425	$900
	Auctions: $5,170, MS-67, May 2015; $1,645, MS-66, October 2015; $376, MS-63, May 2015; $188, MS-62, October 2015												
1878, Proof	800	167	64.0								$300	$650	$1,500
	Auctions: $2,233, PF-66Cam, August 2015; $1,058, PF-65Cam, August 2015; $881, PF-64, January 2015; $676, PF-64, March 2015												
1878-CC	200,000	74	50.9	64%	$150	$250	$350	$420	$625	$1,250	$2,000	$2,750	$4,000
	Auctions: $7,638, MS-67, May 2015; $541, EF-45, January 2015; $235, EF-40, January 2015; $353, VF-25, February 2015												
1879	14,000	214	63.3	93%	$200	$325	$400	$500	$550	$575	$650	$800	$1,100
	Auctions: $2,174, MS-67, January 2015; $3,525, MS-66, June 2015; $494, MS-63, January 2015												
1879, Proof	1,100	304	64.2								$300	$650	$1,500
	Auctions: $4,935, PF-68, May 2015; $2,115, PF-67Cam, January 2015; $1,116, PF-65Cam, July 2015; $999, PF-65, October 2015												
1880	36,000	151	61.3	86%	$150	$250	$350	$400	$500	$650	$700	$800	$1,250
	Auctions: $1,763, MS-67, January 2015; $646, MS-63, June 2015; $376, EF-45, June 2015; $223, F-12, January 2015												
1880, Proof	1,355	312	64.5								$300	$650	$1,500
	Auctions: $1,058, PF-65Cam, January 2015; $664, PF-64, March 2015; $646, PF-64, February 2015; $376, PF-60, May 2015												
1881	24,000	87	55.6	71%	$160	$260	$375	$425	$525	$675	$775	$875	$1,300
	Auctions: $8,225, MS-67, May 2015; $2,820, MS-67, August 2015; $823, MS-64, January 2015; $646, MS-62, July 2015												
1881, Proof	975	251	64.6								$300	$650	$1,500
	Auctions: $4,583, PF-67Cam, January 2015; $1,116, PF-66Cam, July 2015; $1,234, PF-66, February 2015; $1,012, PF-65, January 2015												
1882	3,910,000	375	63.0	92%	$15	$20	$25	$35	$80	$150	$250	$400	$750
	Auctions: $1,645, MS-67, January 2015; $600, MS-65, June 2015; $400, MS-64, November 2015; $176, MS-63, March 2015												
1882, Proof	1,100	345	64.6								$300	$650	$1,500
	Auctions: $2,586, PF-67, August 2015; $1,763, PF-66Cam, January 2015; $1,175, PF-66, January 2015; $705, PF-64, January 2015												
1883	7,674,673	472	61.6	88%	$15	$20	$25	$35	$80	$150	$250	$400	$750
	Auctions: $1,586, MS-67, September 2015; $1,234, MS-66, September 2015; $712, MS-65, August 2015; $329, MS-64, January 2015												
1883, Proof	1,039	307	64.4								$300	$650	$1,500
	Auctions: $2,350, PF-67, January 2015; $1,188, PF-66, August 2015; $3,760, PF-65, August 2015; $705, PF-64Cam, January 2015												
1884	3,365,505	386	63.2	91%	$15	$20	$25	$35	$80	$150	$250	$400	$750
	Auctions: $2,585, MS-67, May 2015; $1,528, MS-66, January 2015; $329, MS-64, June 2015; $212, MS-63, January 2015												
1884, Proof	875	310	64.9								$300	$650	$1,500
	Auctions: $3,290, PF-67Cam, August 2015; $1,763, PF-66Cam, September 2015; $1,116, PF-65Cam, October 2015; $1,002, PF-65, March 2015												
1884-S	564,969	58	59.8	72%	$20	$32	$60	$100	$300	$750	$1,100	$1,500	$5,000
	Auctions: $14,100, MS-66, October 2015; $1,175, MS-64, July 2015; $999, MS-63, March 2015; $705, MS-61, June 2015												
1885	2,532,497	349	63.0	92%	$15	$20	$25	$35	$80	$150	$250	$400	$750
	Auctions: $8,813, MS-67, August 2015; $764, MS-66, January 2015; $194, MS-63, January 2015; $129, MS-61, November 2015												
1885, Proof	930	286	64.8								$300	$650	$1,500
	Auctions: $5,640, PF-68Cam, August 2015; $4,465, PF-67Cam, May 2015; $1,351, PF-66Cam, October 2015; $1,293, PF-65Cam, August 2015												
1885-S	43,690	57	34.4	25%	$400	$800	$1,400	$2,200	$4,000	$5,500	$8,500	$15,000	$27,500
	Auctions: $1,645, VF-35, January 2015; $1,175, VF-25, January 2015; $505, F-12, October 2015; $499, VG-8, October 2015												
1886	6,376,684	593	62.3	89%	$15	$20	$25	$35	$80	$150	$250	$400	$750
	Auctions: $1,293, MS-67, July 2015; $1,116, MS-66, June 2015; $1,293, MS-65, January 2015; $353, MS-64, November 2015												
1886, Proof	886	288	64.6								$300	$650	$1,500
	Auctions: $1,998, PF-67, July 2015; $1,528, PF-66, June 2015; $999, PF-65, January 2015; $999, PF-65, January 2015												
1886-S	206,524	57	59.7	79%	$30	$50	$75	$135	$200	$600	$1,000	$2,000	$3,500
	Auctions: $8,813, MS-67, October 2014; $4,700, MS-66, September 2014; $6,463, MS-66, June 2013; $2,585, MS-65, October 2014												
1887	11,283,229	565	61.1	85%	$15	$20	$25	$35	$80	$150	$250	$400	$750
	Auctions: $2,820, MS-67, May 2015; $1,528, MS-66, January 2015; $588, MS-65, January 2015; $423, MS-64, February 2015												
1887, Proof	710	207	64.5								$300	$650	$1,500
	Auctions: $3,173, PF-67Cam, September 2015; $3,525, PF-66, October 2015; $1,058, PF-65Cam, May 2015; $999, PF-65, June 2015												
1887-S	4,454,450	259	60.3	81%	$15	$20	$25	$35	$80	$150	$300	$450	$1,000
	Auctions: $6,463, MS-67, June 2015; $1,586, MS-66, May 2015; $999, MS-65, October 2015; $423, MS-64, August 2015												

**1891-O, O Over
Horizontal O**
FS-10-1891o-501.

**1891-S, Repunched
Mintmark**
FS-10-1891S-501.

	Mintage	Cert	Avg	%MS	G-4	F-12	VF-20	EF-40	AU-50	MS-60	MS-63	MS-64	MS-65
											PF-60	PF-63	PF-65
1888	5,495,655	310	61.4	86%	$15	$20	$25	$35	$80	$150	$250	$400	$750
Auctions: $1,293, MS-66, August 2015; $423, MS-64, October 2015; $217, MS-63, October 2015; $89, AU-58, January 2015													
1888, Proof	832	210	64.5								$300	$650	$1,500
Auctions: $3,995, PF-67Cam, May 2015; $1,410, PF-66Cam, July 2015; $1,351, PF-65Cam, August 2015; $1,200, PF-65Cam, September 2015													
1888-S	1,720,000	70	57.6	64%	$15	$20	$25	$35	$100	$250	$850	$1,150	$3,000
Auctions: $501, MS-63, March 2015; $390, MS-62, October 2015; $56, AU-50, October 2015													
1889	7,380,000	341	61.7	86%	$15	$20	$25	$35	$80	$150	$250	$400	$750
Auctions: $3,819, MS-67, January 2015; $2,350, MS-66, January 2015; $517, MS-64, October 2015; $176, MS-63, July 2015													
1889, Proof	711	177	64.6								$300	$650	$1,500
Auctions: $4,700, PF-68, October 2015; $1,939, PF-67, July 2015; $1,175, PF-66, January 2015; $1,058, PF-65, October 2015													
1889-S	972,678	81	60.3	65%	$20	$30	$50	$80	$150	$450	$1,000	$1,250	$3,250
Auctions: $2,115, MS-65, January 2015; $329, MS-62, March 2015; $74, AU-55, January 2015; $129, AU-50, September 2015													
1890	9,910,951	565	61.6	86%	$15	$20	$25	$35	$80	$150	$250	$400	$750
Auctions: $4,700, MS-67, September 2015; $1,058, MS-66, October 2015; $588, MS-65, June 2015; $282, MS-64, February 2015													
1890, Proof	590	210	64.5								$300	$650	$1,500
Auctions: $1,939, PF-66Cam, August 2015; $1,410, PF-66, February 2015; $1,116, PF-66, July 2015													
1890-S, Large S	1,423,076	106	60.3	78%	$18	$25	$55	$85	$150	$350	$700	$1,000	$1,500
Auctions: $6,169, MS-66, May 2015; $676, MS-64, March 2015; $1,293, MS-63, September 2015; $270, MS-62, January 2015													
1890-S, Small S (t)	(u)	(v)						—	—	—			
Auctions: $1,208, MS-65, February 2006													
1891	15,310,000	979	61.9	86%	$15	$20	$25	$35	$80	$150	$250	$450	$750
Auctions: $1,645, MS-67, July 2015; $1,116, MS-66, March 2015; $588, MS-65, January 2015; $282, MS-64, October 2015													
1891, Proof	600	224	64.8								$300	$650	$1,500
Auctions: $6,463, PF-67Cam, November 2013													
1891-O	4,540,000	208	59.9	83%	$15	$20	$30	$50	$100	$175	$350	$550	$1,500
Auctions: $2,000, MS-66, September 2015; $1,528, MS-65, January 2015; $306, MS-63, August 2015; $60, AU-50, June 2015													
1891-O, O Over Horizontal O (w)	(x)	2	51.5	0%	$60	$120	$150	$225	$1,000	$3,000			
Auctions: $253, AU-58, May 2010													
1891-O, Proof (y)	2–3	2	66.0										
Auctions: No auction records available.													
1891-S	3,196,116	172	62.2	88%	$15	$20	$25	$35	$80	$175	$300	$450	$850
Auctions: $881, MS-66, August 2015; $764, MS-65, January 2015; $235, MS-63, March 2015; $141, MS-61, January 2015													
1891-S, Repunched Mintmark (z)	(aa)	0	n/a						$200	$225	$500		
Auctions: $5,750, MS-66, September 2010													

t. This coin is considered rare. **u.** Included in 1890-S, Large S, mintage figure. **v.** Included in certified population for 1890-S, Large S. **w.** The primary O mintmark was punched over a previously punched horizontal O. **x.** Included in circulation-strike 1891-O mintage figure. **y.** This coin is considered extremely rare. **z.** The larger primary S mintmark (known as the medium S) was punched squarely over the smaller S, which is evident within both loops. **aa.** Included in 1891-S mintage figure.

BARBER OR LIBERTY HEAD (1892–1916)

Designer: *Charles E. Barber.* **Weight:** *2.50 grams.* **Composition:** *.900 silver, .100 copper* *(net weight: .07234 oz. pure silver).* **Diameter:** *17.9 mm.* **Edge:** *Reeded.*
Mints: *Philadelphia, Denver, New Orleans, and San Francisco.*

Circulation Strike

Mintmark location is on the reverse, below the bow.

Proof

History. This dime belongs to a suite of silver coins (including the quarter and half dollar) designed by U.S. Mint chief engraver Charles E. Barber. It features a large Liberty Head styled similarly to contemporary French coinage. The reverse of the dime continues the "cereal wreath" motif of the late Liberty Seated era.

Striking and Sharpness. Check the details of the hair on the obverse. The reverse usually is sharp. If weakness is seen, it is typically in the wreath details. The denticles usually are sharp on the obverse and reverse. The Proofs of 1892 to 1901 usually have cameo contrast between the designs and the mirror fields. Later Proofs vary in contrast.

Availability. With the exception of the rare 1894-S, of which fewer than a dozen are known, all dates and mintmarks are collectible. Probably 90% or more of the survivors are in lower grades such as AG-3 and G-4. The word LIBERTY in the headband, a key to grading, tended to wear away quickly. Relatively few are in grades from Fine upward. MS coins are somewhat scarce, this being especially true of the branch-mint issues. MS-63 and finer Barber dimes usually are from the Philadelphia Mint or, if from a branch mint, are dated after 1905. Proof Barber dimes survive in proportion to their mintages. Choice and Gem examples are more easily found among dimes than among quarters and half dollars of this type. All were originally sold in silver-coin sets.

GRADING STANDARDS

MS-60 to 70 (Mint State). *Obverse:* At MS-60, some abrasion and contact marks are evident, most noticeably on the cheek and the obverse field to the right. Luster is present, but may be dull or lifeless. Many Barber coins have been cleaned, especially of the earlier dates. At MS-63, contact marks are very few; abrasion still is evident, but less than at lower levels. An MS-65 coin may have minor abrasion on the cheek, but contact marks are so minute as to require magnification. Luster should be full and rich. *Reverse:* Comments apply as for the

1910. Graded MS-65.

obverse, except that in lower Mint State grades abrasion and contact marks are most noticeable on the highest parts of the leaves and the ribbon, less so on ONE DIME. At MS-65 or higher, there are no marks visible to the unaided eye. The field is mainly protected by design elements and does not show abrasion as much as does the obverse on a given coin.

Illustrated coin: The striking on this example is razor sharp.

AU-50, 53, 55, 58 (About Uncirculated). *Obverse:* Light wear is seen on the head, especially on the forward hair under LIBERTY. At AU-58, the luster is extensive, but incomplete, especially on the higher parts and in the right field. At AU–50 and 53, luster is less. *Reverse:* Wear is seen on the leaves and ribbon. An AU-58 coin will have nearly full luster, more so than on the obverse, as the design elements protect the small field areas. At AU–50 and 53, there still is significant luster.

1910. Graded AU-53.

EF-40, 45 (Extremely Fine). *Obverse:* Further wear is seen on the head. The hair above the forehead lacks most detail. LIBERTY shows wear but still is strong. *Reverse:* Further wear is seen on all areas, most noticeably at the wreath and ribbon. Leaves retain excellent details except on the higher areas.

1895-O. Graded EF-40.

VF-20, 30 (Very Fine). *Obverse:* The head shows more wear, now with nearly all detail gone in the hair above the forehead. LIBERTY shows wear, but is complete. The leaves on the head all show wear, as does the upper part of the cap. *Reverse:* Wear is more extensive. The details in the highest leaves are weak or missing, but in lower levels the leaf details remain strong.

1914-S. Graded VF-30.

F-12, 15 (Fine). *Obverse:* The head shows extensive wear. LIBERTY, the key place to check, is weak, especially at ER, but is fully readable. The ANA grading standards and *Photograde* adhere to this. PCGS suggests that lightly struck coins "may have letters partially missing." Traditionally, collectors insist on full LIBERTY. *Reverse:* Much detail of the leaves in the higher areas is gone. The rim remains bold.

1901-S. Graded F-12.

    Illustrated coin: LIBERTY is readable, but letters ER are light.

VG-8, 10 (Very Good). *Obverse:* A net of three letters in LIBERTY must be readable. Traditionally LI is clear, and after that there is a partial letter or two. *Reverse:* Further wear has made the wreath flat; now only in outline form with only a few traces of details. The rim is complete.

1903-S. Graded VG-10.

G-4, 6 (Good). *Obverse:* The head is in outline form, with the center flat. Most of the rim is there. All letters and the date are full. *Reverse:* The leaves are all combined and in outline form. The rim is weak in areas.

1895-O. Graded G-6.

AG-3 (About Good). *Obverse:* The lettering is readable, but the parts near the border may be worn away. The date is clear. *Reverse:* The wreath and interior letters are partially worn away. The rim is weak.

1895-O. Graded AG-3.

PF-60 to 70 (Proof). *Obverse and Reverse:* Proofs that are extensively cleaned and have many hairlines, or that are dull and grainy, are lower level, such as PF–60 to 62. These are not widely desired, save for the rare (in any grade) year of 1895, and even so most collectors would rather have a lustrous MS-60 than a dull PF-60. With medium hairlines and good reflectivity, an assigned grade of PF-64 is indicated. Tiny horizontal lines on Miss Liberty's cheek, known

1911. Graded PF-67 Deep Cameo.

as *slide marks*, from National and other album slides scuffing the relief of the cheek, are endemic among Barber silver coins. With noticeable marks of this type, the highest grade assignable is PF-64. With relatively few hairlines, a rating of PF-65 can be given. PF-66 should have hairlines so delicate that magnification is needed to see them. Above that, a Proof should be free of any hairlines or other problems.

   Illustrated coin: Proof dimes of 1911 are rare (only 543 minted), but one with a Deep Cameo finish, as displayed by this coin, is *extremely* rare. The coin is fully struck on both sides, and has neither a blemish nor a trace of toning.

1893, 3 Over 2

1897, Repunched Date
FS-10-1897-301.

	Mintage	Cert	Avg	%MS	G-4	VG-8	F-12	VF-20	EF-40	AU-50	MS-60	MS-63	MS-65
											PF-60	PF-63	PF-65
1892	12,120,000	1,325	61.6	85%	$7	$7.50	$18	$25	$30	$80	$135	$225	$600
	Auctions: $4,700, MS-67, January 2015; $823, MS-66, June 2015; $494, MS-65, July 2015; $306, MS-64, January 2015												
1892, Proof	1,245	293	64.6								$300	$600	$1,500
	Auctions: $2,233, PF-66Cam, February 2015; $1,058, PF-65Cam, January 2015; $1,058, PF-65, January 2015; $646, PF-64, January 2015												
1892-O	3,841,700	235	58.3	73%	$12	$15	$35	$50	$75	$95	$175	$350	$1,250
	Auctions: $4,994, MS-66, February 2013												
1892-S	990,710	147	49.8	57%	$65	$120	$190	$240	$280	$330	$425	$775	$4,000
	Auctions: $6,463, MS-66, January 2015; $1,175, MS-64, January 2015; $764, MS-63, February 2015; $517, MS-62, September 2015												
1893, 3 Over 2 (a)	(b)	0	n/a		$140	$150	$160	$175	$200	$300	$700	$1,800	$5,250
	Auctions: $3,055, MS-64, January 2015; $2,233, MS-63, January 2015; $1,763, MS-63, June 2015; $1,528, MS-62, February 2015												
1893	3,339,940	297	59.4	81%	$8	$12	$20	$30	$45	$80	$150	$250	$800
	Auctions: $8,225, MS-67, January 2015; $564, MS-65, January 2015; $341, MS-64, August 2015; $165, MS-63, May 2015												
1893, Proof	792	269	65.0								$300	$600	$1,500
	Auctions: $21,150, PF-69, August 2015; $5,953, PF-68, January 2015; $999, PF-65, March 2015; $646, PF-64, October 2015												
1893-O	1,760,000	173	52.0	64%	$30	$45	$120	$150	$190	$230	$325	$600	$2,000
	Auctions: $4,935, MS-67, October 2015; $1,763, MS-65, February 2015; $999, MS-64, August 2015; $376, AU-58, May 2015												
1893-S (c)	2,491,401	138	53.3	64%	$15	$25	$37	$60	$90	$150	$290	$700	$3,000
	Auctions: $118, AU-50, May 2015; $64, EF-45, January 2015; $50, EF-40, February 2015												
1894	1,330,000	217	50.8	61%	$30	$45	$120	$160	$180	$220	$325	$500	$1,000
	Auctions: $3,525, MS-67, May 2015; $1,175, MS-65, October 2015; $517, MS-64, January 2015; $180, AU-58, January 2015												
1894, Proof	972	319	64.9								$300	$600	$1,500
	Auctions: $1,204, PF-66, March 2015; $823, PF-64, June 2015; $646, PF-64, January 2015; $646, PF-64, January 2015												
1894-O	720,000	132	28.3	17%	$70	$95	$200	$275	$425	$600	$1,450	$2,500	$12,500
	Auctions: $37,600, MS-67, May 2015; $8,813, MS-64, October 2015; $5,875, MS-64, September 2015; $1,351, MS-60, January 2015												
1894-S, Proof † (d)	24	6	64.5									$1,500,000	$2,000,000
	Auctions: $1,552,500, PF-64, October 2007; $1,997,500, PF-66, January 2016												
1895	690,000	172	43.9	49%	$80	$160	$325	$475	$550	$625	$725	$1,200	$2,500
	Auctions: $5,640, MS-66, October 2015; $1,116, MS-64, June 2015; $764, MS-63, October 2015; $423, AU-50, September 2015												
1895, Proof	880	322	65.0								$300	$600	$1,500
	Auctions: $4,465, PF-68Cam, September 2015; $1,058, PF-66Cam, September 2015; $1,175, PF-66, October 2015; $764, PF-63, October 2015												
1895-O	440,000	285	19.2	9%	$375	$550	$850	$1,250	$2,400	$3,400	$6,000	$10,000	$22,500
	Auctions: $1,293, EF-40, January 2015; $793, EF-40, July 2015; $588, VF-20, October 2015; $617, VG-10, February 2015												
1895-S	1,120,000	212	47.3	55%	$42	$60	$135	$190	$240	$310	$500	$1,000	$4,500
	Auctions: $3,760, MS-65, June 2015; $2,468, MS-65, October 2015; $1,175, MS-64, January 2015; $881, MS-62, February 2015												
1896	2,000,000	136	56.1	74%	$10	$22	$50	$75	$100	$120	$175	$500	$1,150
	Auctions: $1,293, MS-66, October 2015; $1,528, MS-65, June 2015; $400, MS-64, January 2015; $353, MS-63, August 2015												
1896, Proof	762	250	64.9								$300	$600	$1,500
	Auctions: $15,275, PF-68Cam, June 2014; $1,763, PF-67, March 2015; $676, PF-64, July 2014; $588, PF-64, July 2014												
1896-O	610,000	120	29.9	23%	$80	$160	$290	$350	$450	$650	$1,000	$2,400	$7,000
	Auctions: $11,750, MS-65, October 2015; $4,935, MS-65, June 2015; $3,290, AU-58, July 2015; $676, EF-45, June 2015												
1896-S	575,056	151	40.8	49%	$80	$150	$280	$335	$400	$550	$850	$1,500	$3,750
	Auctions: $5,875, MS-66, August 2015; $3,055, MS-65, October 2015; $2,820, MS-65, January 2015; $447, AU-53, April 2015												

† Ranked in the *100 Greatest U.S. Coins* (fourth edition). **a.** Overlaid photographs indicate this is not a true overdate. **b.** Included in circulation-strike 1893 mintage figure. **c.** Boldly doubled mintmark. **d.** The reason for the low mintage of the Proof 1894-S dime is unknown. Popular theories, among others, include a rounding out of the Mint's record books, or a special presentation to bankers visiting the San Francisco Mint. Fewer than a dozen examples are known to exist. Five of these coins were reserved for assay.

	Mintage	Cert	Avg	%MS	G-4	VG-8	F-12	VF-20	EF-40	AU-50	MS-60	MS-63	MS-65
											PF-60	PF-63	PF-65
1897	10,868,533	445	61.1	84%	$4	$5	$8	$15	$32	$75	$135	$225	$575
Auctions: $2,585, MS-67, January 2015; $2,200, MS-67, August 2015; $541, MS-65, January 2015; $270, MS-64, January 2015													
1897, Repunched Date (e)	(f)	1	63.0	100%						$80	$120	$200	
Auctions: No auction records available.													
1897, Proof	731	248	64.8								$300	$600	$1,500
Auctions: $5,889, PF-68Cam, January 2015; $3,819, PF-68, March 2015; $2,938, PF-67, January 2015; $999, PF-66, January 2015													
1897-O	666,000	129	36.6	39%	$65	$115	$280	$375	$475	$600	$900	$1,500	$4,000
Auctions: $5,640, MS-66, May 2015; $4,230, MS-66, June 2015; $1,998, MS-64, July 2015; $353, EF-40, August 2015													
1897-S	1,342,844	105	49.7	51%	$18	$35	$90	$120	$175	$260	$450	$1,000	$3,500
Auctions: $5,170, MS-66, May 2015; $2,585, MS-65, October 2015; $1,410, MS-64, August 2015; $259, MS-60, March 2015													
1898	16,320,000	493	60.2	81%	$4	$5	$8	$12	$26	$75	$130	$225	$575
Auctions: $1,028, MS-66, September 2015; $646, MS-65, January 2015; $306, MS-64, January 2015; $153, MS-63, February 2015													
1898, Proof	735	293	65.2								$300	$600	$1,500
Auctions: $1,998, PF-67, June 2015; $1,087, PF-66, July 2015; $1,058, PF-65, March 2015; $646, PF-64, January 2015													
1898-O	2,130,000	90	51.6	59%	$12	$26	$85	$140	$190	$280	$450	$1,100	$3,000
Auctions: $3,760, MS-65, January 2015; $2,115, MS-65, January 2015; $153, AU-50, July 2015; $107, VF-25, January 2015													
1898-S	1,702,507	66	53.1	58%	$8	$15	$32	$45	$80	$150	$375	$1,200	$3,250
Auctions: $2,115, MS-64, September 2015; $141, AU-53, July 2015; $89, AU-50, February 2015; $84, AU-50, January 2015													
1899	19,580,000	350	59.4	79%	$4	$5	$8	$12	$25	$75	$130	$225	$575
Auctions: $6,169, MS-68, September 2015; $1,645, MS-66, August 2015; $1,058, MS-66, October 2015; $230, MS-64, April 2015													
1899, Proof	846	245	64.8								$300	$600	$1,500
Auctions: $1,410, PF-66, October 2015; $999, PF-66, January 2015; $999, PF-65, January 2015; $646, PF-64, July 2015													
1899-O	2,650,000	121	49.0	54%	$10	$18	$65	$95	$140	$225	$400	$1,100	$3,500
Auctions: $1,998, MS-64, September 2015; $940, MS-63, June 2015; $764, MS-63, June 2015; $84, EF-40, January 2015													
1899-S	1,867,493	104	58.1	71%	$8.50	$16	$32	$35	$45	$110	$300	$750	$2,250
Auctions: $6,463, MS-67, January 2015; $100, AU-53, April 2015													
1900	17,600,000	256	60.1	79%	$4	$5	$8	$12	$25	$75	$125	$225	$650
Auctions: $5,405, MS-67, September 2015; $2,585, MS-66, June 2015; $482, MS-65, April 2015; $306, MS-64, October 2015													
1900, Proof	912	236	64.7								$300	$600	$1,500
Auctions: $2,350, PF-67Cam, January 2015; $1,146, PF-66Cam, July 2015; $999, PF-65, January 2015; $646, PF-64, January 2015													
1900-O	2,010,000	107	44.7	42%	$18	$38	$110	$160	$220	$360	$650	$1,000	$4,500
Auctions: $3,995, MS-66, May 2015; $2,115, MS-64, February 2015; $764, MS-61, February 2015; $141, AU-50, May 2015													
1900-S	5,168,270	161	57.0	55%	$5	$6	$12	$20	$30	$75	$175	$425	$1,500
Auctions: $4,230, MS-66, May 2015; $3,525, MS-66, June 2015; $764, MS-64, January 2015; $42, AU-50, January 2015													
1901	18,859,665	310	60.5	80%	$4	$5	$7	$10	$26	$75	$125	$225	$575
Auctions: $999, MS-66, February 2015; $423, MS-65, January 2015; $259, MS-64, January 2015; $176, MS-63, July 2015													
1901, Proof	813	248	64.7								$300	$600	$1,500
Auctions: $14,100, PF-68, May 2015; $1,645, PF-67, January 2015; $999, PF-66, January 2015; $940, PF-65, July 2015													
1901-O	5,620,000	113	52.5	50%	$4	$5.50	$16	$28	$75	$180	$450	$850	$3,000
Auctions: $1,763, MS-64, September 2015; $1,175, MS-64, October 2015; $423, MS-62, April 2015; $135, AU-55, January 2015													
1901-S	593,022	136	34.5	25%	$80	$150	$350	$450	$550	$675	$1,050	$1,750	$5,000
Auctions: $2,350, MS-64, September 2015; $377, AU-50, May 2015; $376, EF-40, November 2015; $259, VF-30, January 2015													
1902	21,380,000	235	56.7	68%	$4	$5	$6	$8	$25	$75	$125	$225	$600
Auctions: $259, MS-64, January 2015; $212, MS-64, August 2015; $200, MS-64, September 2015; $100, AU-58, March 2015													
1902, Proof	777	206	64.2								$300	$600	$1,500
Auctions: $1,116, PF-66, October 2015; $999, PF-65, January 2015; $646, PF-64, January 2015; $423, PF-63, November 2015													
1902-O	4,500,000	124	54.8	57%	$4	$6	$15	$32	$65	$150	$400	$1,000	$3,750
Auctions: $1,410, MS-64, September 2015; $1,399, MS-64, September 2015; $356, AU-58, January 2015; $123, AU-53, April 2015													
1902-S	2,070,000	91	50.4	54%	$9	$20	$55	$80	$140	$200	$400	$1,000	$3,000
Auctions: $235, AU-58, August 2015; $153, AU-55, January 2015; $106, AU-50, May 2015; $94, VF-35, February 2015													

e. More than one repunched date exists for 1897. This listing is for FS-10-1897-301 (see the *Cherrypickers' Guide to Rare Die Varieties*, sixth edition, volume II), one of the most dramatic RPDs of the series. The secondary digits of the date are evident west of the primary digits. f. Included in circulation-strike 1897 mintage figure.

1905-O, Normal O   **1905-O, Micro O**

	Mintage	Cert	Avg	%MS	G-4	VG-8	F-12	VF-20	EF-40	AU-50	MS-60	MS-63	MS-65
											PF-60	PF-63	PF-65
1903	19,500,000	169	57.7	71%	$4	$5	$6	$8	$25	$75	$125	$250	$1,000
Auctions: $1,998, MS-66, May 2015; $1,528, MS-66, October 2015; $259, MS-64, January 2015; $165, MS-63, January 2015													
1903, Proof	755	215	64.4								$300	$600	$1,500
Auctions: $2,233, PF-67, October 2015; $1,058, PF-66, January 2015; $1,058, PF-66, July 2015; $329, PF-62, January 2015													
1903-O	8,180,000	181	55.2	44%	$5	$6	$14	$25	$55	$110	$275	$550	$3,500
Auctions: $8,813, MS-67, May 2015; $2,350, MS-65, July 2015; $881, MS-64, February 2015; $306, AU-58, July 2015													
1903-S	613,300	123	33.7	24%	$85	$130	$350	$475	$725	$875	$1,100	$1,500	$2,750
Auctions: $3,055, MS-66, May 2015; $2,820, MS-66, June 2015; $1,058, AU-58, January 2015; $282, AU-50, October 2015													
1904	14,600,357	197	59.4	79%	$4	$5	$6	$9	$25	$75	$125	$250	$1,250
Auctions: $2,585, MS-66, May 2015; $1,763, MS-66, January 2015; $306, MS-64, January 2015; $50, AU-58, January 2015													
1904, Proof	670	224	64.3								$300	$600	$1,500
Auctions: $2,233, PF-67Cam, March 2015; $1,821, PF-67, January 2015; $1,080, PF-66, October 2015; $1,146, PF-65Cam, January 2015													
1904-S	800,000	131	41.0	38%	$45	$75	$160	$235	$325	$475	$800	$1,500	$4,000
Auctions: $10,117, MS-66, January 2015; $400, AU-55, August 2015; $376, AU-55, May 2015; $153, EF-40, January 2015													
1905	14,551,623	200	58.1	72%	$4	$5	$6	$10	$25	$75	$125	$240	$650
Auctions: $1,528, MS-66, January 2015; $1,293, MS-66, September 2015; $517, MS-65, September 2015; $235, MS-64, September 2015													
1905, Proof	727	212	64.7								$300	$600	$1,500
Auctions: $4,465, PF-68, January 2015; $2,800, PF-67, July 2015; $1,000, PF-65Cam, June 2015; $940, PF-65, July 2015													
1905-O	3,400,000	165	55.6	72%	$5	$10	$35	$60	$100	$150	$300	$500	$1,250
Auctions: $1,998, MS-66, October 2015; $1,645, MS-65, October 2015; $564, MS-64, January 2015; $153, AU-58, August 2015													
1905-O, Micro O	(g)	37	32.6	14%	$25	$50	$110	$160	$175	$275	$600	$3,500	
Auctions: $4,113, MS-62, June 2014; $282, VF-25, August 2014; $223, VF-25, October 2014													
1905-S	6,855,199	188	56.6	61%	$4	$6	$9	$20	$40	$95	$250	$325	$1,000
Auctions: $1,528, MS-66, October 2015; $141, MS-61, January 2015; $69, MS-60, October 2015													
1906	19,957,731	380	59.0	76%	$4	$5	$6	$10	$25	$75	$125	$225	$550
Auctions: $3,525, MS-67, July 2015; $259, MS-64, May 2015; $212, MS-64, July 2015; $165, MS-63, April 2015													
1906, Proof	675	190	64.6								$300	$600	$1,500
Auctions: $1,645, PF-67, January 2015; $1,050, PF-65, January 2015; $646, PF-64, January 2015; $447, PF-63, October 2015													
1906-D	4,060,000	115	55.8	72%	$4	$5	$8	$15	$35	$80	$175	$400	$1,400
Auctions: $3,055, MS-66, May 2015; $646, MS-64, July 2015; $182, MS-62, August 2015; $118, AU-58, October 2015													
1906-O	2,610,000	145	58.5	81%	$6	$14	$45	$75	$110	$130	$200	$300	$1,050
Auctions: $4,935, MS-67, August 2015; $1,116, MS-66, January 2015; $764, MS-65, June 2015; $153, MS-60, February 2015													
1906-S	3,136,640	124	57.9	74%	$4	$6	$13	$25	$45	$110	$275	$550	$1,200
Auctions: $4,465, MS-66, May 2015; $1,763, MS-66, August 2015; $999, MS-64, August 2015; $212, AU-58, August 2015													
1907	22,220,000	466	58.0	77%	$4	$5	$6	$10	$25	$75	$125	$225	$550
Auctions: $705, MS-66, August 2015; $329, MS-65, May 2015; $259, MS-64, January 2015; $165, MS-63, May 2015													
1907, Proof	575	185	64.7								$300	$600	$1,500
Auctions: $6,463, PF-68, May 2015; $2,115, PF-67, January 2015; $1,351, PF-66, January 2015; $600, PF-64, January 2015													
1907-D	4,080,000	87	57.3	71%	$4	$5	$10	$20	$45	$110	$300	$900	$2,000
Auctions: $1,293, MS-65, June 2015; $1,175, MS-64, July 2015; $1,058, MS-64, July 2015; $494, MS-63, June 2015													
1907-O	5,058,000	164	58.0	76%	$4	$7	$30	$45	$70	$110	$200	$375	$1,100
Auctions: $1,645, MS-66, January 2015; $400, MS-64, February 2015; $153, MS-63, May 2015; $212, MS-62, June 2015													
1907-S	3,178,470	104	54.9	52%	$4	$6	$15	$27	$75	$150	$400	$750	$2,250
Auctions: $1,070, MS-64, July 2015; $482, MS-62, February 2015; $79, AU-55, January 2015; $106, AU-50, July 2015													

g. Included in 1905-O mintage figure.

	Mintage	Cert	Avg	%MS	G-4	VG-8	F-12	VF-20	EF-40	AU-50	MS-60 / PF-60	MS-63 / PF-63	MS-65 / PF-65
1908	10,600,000	332	59.9	83%	$4	$5	$6	$10	$25	$75	$125	$225	$550
Auctions: $1,293, MS-66, June 2015; $499, MS-65, January 2015; $259, MS-64, February 2015; $240, MS-64, July 2015													
1908, Proof	545	191	64.7								$300	$600	$1,500
Auctions: $1,528, PF-67, September 2015; $1,410, PF-66, June 2015; $940, PF-65, January 2015; $622, PF-64, June 2015													
1908-D	7,490,000	203	55.0	62%	$4	$5	$6	$10	$30	$75	$130	$300	$850
Auctions: $646, MS-65, July 2015; $588, MS-65, February 2015; $200, MS-63, July 2015; $60, AU-53, February 2015													
1908-O	1,789,000	117	55.8	69%	$6	$12	$45	$65	$95	$150	$300	$600	$1,250
Auctions: $1,528, MS-66, August 2015; $764, MS-64, June 2015; $447, MS-63, June 2015; $182, AU-58, April 2015													
1908-S	3,220,000	98	56.2	58%	$4	$6	$15	$25	$45	$170	$350	$800	$1,500
Auctions: $4,700, MS-67, August 2015; $153, AU-53, July 2015; $42, EF-45, January 2015													
1909	10,240,000	309	59.1	81%	$4	$5	$6	$10	$25	$75	$125	$225	$550
Auctions: $881, MS-66, May 2015; $212, MS-64, April 2015; $170, MS-63, July 2015; $118, MS-62, July 2015													
1909, Proof	650	259	64.6								$300	$600	$1,500
Auctions: $1,528, PF-67, October 2015; $1,058, PF-65Cam, February 2015; $881, PF-65, January 2015; $646, PF-64, January 2015													
1909-D	954,000	105	54.1	66%	$8	$20	$60	$90	$140	$225	$500	$1,000	$2,000
Auctions: $3,055, MS-66, May 2015; $212, AU-53, May 2015; $100, EF-40, July 2015													
1909-O	2,287,000	117	55.7	68%	$5	$8	$13	$25	$70	$150	$250	$575	$1,500
Auctions: $4,935, MS-66, May 2015; $2,820, MS-66, July 2015; $999, MS-64, February 2015; $235, AU-53, April 2015													
1909-S	1,000,000	95	51.5	63%	$9	$20	$80	$130	$180	$310	$550	$1,400	$2,500
Auctions: $9,400, MS-67, September 2015; $9,988, MS-66, May 2015; $517, MS-62, July 2015; $235, MS-60, October 2015													
1910	11,520,000	484	60.1	84%	$4	$5	$6	$10	$24	$75	$125	$2,225	$5,500
Auctions: $1,410, MS-66, October 2015; $646, MS-65, February 2015; $259, MS-64, February 2015; $188, MS-63, February 2015													
1910, Proof	551	217	64.7								$300	$600	$1,500
Auctions: $8,813, PF-68, May 2015; $1,880, PF-67, August 2015; $1,058, PF-66, October 2015; $646, PF-64, January 2015													
1910-D	3,490,000	93	57.1	72%	$4	$5	$10	$20	$48	$95	$220	$450	$1,300
Auctions: $3,643, MS-66, January 2015; $1,293, MS-64, June 2015; $588, MS-63, August 2015; $353, AU-58, October 2015													
1910-S	1,240,000	74	53.6	58%	$6	$9	$50	$70	$110	$180	$425	$700	$2,000
Auctions: $7,344, MS-67, June 2014; $2,820, MS-66, July 2014; $411, MS-62, July 2014													
1911	18,870,000	965	60.0	84%	$4	$5	$6	$10	$24	$75	$125	$225	$550
Auctions: $1,116, MS-66, September 2015; $401, MS-65, August 2015; $243, MS-64, February 2015; $165, MS-63, May 2015													
1911, Proof	543	227	64.9								$300	$600	$1,500
Auctions: $3,760, PF-67Cam, January 2015; $1,528, PF-66Cam, July 2015; $860, PF-65, September 2015; $646, PF-64, January 2015													
1911-D	11,209,000	267	57.7	73%	$4	$5	$6	$10	$24	$75	$125	$225	$500
Auctions: $3,525, MS-67, June 2015; $370, MS-65, September 2015; $306, MS-64, September 2015; $118, MS-62, May 2015													
1911-S	3,520,000	200	61.2	84%	$4	$5	$10	$20	$40	$100	$200	$375	$850
Auctions: $4,818, MS-67, September 2015; $1,410, MS-66, August 2015; $734, MS-65, July 2015; $529, MS-64, February 2015													
1912	19,349,300	1,003	59.7	82%	$4	$5	$6	$10	$24	$75	$125	$225	$550
Auctions: $2,056, MS-67, May 2015; $911, MS-66, January 2015; $400, MS-65, August 2015; $240, MS-64, January 2015													
1912, Proof	700	183	64.5								$300	$600	$1,500
Auctions: $2,350, PF-67, August 2015; $1,020, PF-65, September 2015; $999, PF-65, January 2015; $588, PF-64, January 2015													
1912-D	11,760,000	363	54.2	65%	$4	$5	$6	$10	$24	$75	$125	$225	$650
Auctions: $6,169, MS-67, August 2015; $6,169, MS-66, May 2015; $517, MS-65, September 2015; $306, MS-64, November 2015													
1912-S	3,420,000	175	60.0	74%	$4	$5	$6	$12	$32	$90	$170	$300	$700
Auctions: $1,293, MS-66, June 2013; $999, MS-65, May 2015; $206, MS-62, July 2014; $206, MS-62, August 2014													

	Mintage	Cert	Avg	%MS	G-4	VG-8	F-12	VF-20	EF-40	AU-50	MS-60 PF-60	MS-63 PF-63	MS-65 PF-65
1913	19,760,000	852	57.8	77%	$4	$5	$6	$10	$24	$75	$125	$225	$500
	Auctions: $564, MS-66, October 2015; $999, MS-65, October 2015; $200, MS-64, April 2015; $118, MS-62, April 2015												
1913, Proof	622	200	64.1								$300	$600	$1,500
	Auctions: $4,935, PF-67Cam, May 2015; $3,290, PF-66Cam, July 2015; $2,056, PF-66, October 2015; $1,036, PF-65, September 2015												
1913-S	510,000	219	36.7	39%	$35	$55	$125	$190	$250	$320	$500	$800	$1,500
	Auctions: $2,967, MS-66, October 2015; $1,058, MS-63, June 2015; $881, MS-63, October 2015; $617, MS-61, June 2015												
1914	17,360,230	874	59.0	82%	$4	$5	$6	$10	$24	$75	$125	$240	$575
	Auctions: $2,703, MS-67, January 2015; $1,763, MS-66, June 2015; $564, MS-65, January 2015; $259, MS-64, October 2015												
1914, Proof	425	168	64.5								$300	$600	$1,500
	Auctions: $3,055, PF-67, January 2015; $650, PF-64, January 2015; $470, PF-63, October 2015												
1914-D	11,908,000	552	55.6	69%	$4	$5	$6	$10	$24	$75	$125	$240	$575
	Auctions: $823, MS-66, October 2015; $470, MS-65, January 2015; $165, MS-63, February 2015; $118, AU-58, May 2015												
1914-S	2,100,000	172	58.5	78%	$4	$5	$10	$18	$40	$80	$175	$325	$1,250
	Auctions: $1,645, MS-66, October 2015; $881, MS-65, August 2015; $646, MS-64, March 2015; $400, MS-64, February 2015												
1915	5,620,000	381	58.9	81%	$4	$5	$6	$10	$24	$75	$125	$240	$500
	Auctions: $1,880, MS-67, June 2015; $1,175, MS-66, May 2015; $235, MS-64, February 2015; $141, MS-62, January 2015												
1915, Proof	450	145	64.3								$300	$600	$1,500
	Auctions: $1,763, PF-67, January 2015; $999, PF-65, August 2015; $940, PF-64, October 2015; $153, PF-60, August 2015												
1915-S	960,000	146	57.0	66%	$7	$12	$35	$50	$70	$140	$275	$475	$1,250
	Auctions: $1,998, MS-66, January 2015; $1,200, MS-65, June 2015; $823, MS-64, August 2015; $517, MS-64, October 2015												
1916	18,490,000	1,304	59.1	80%	$4	$5	$6	$10	$24	$75	$125	$240	$500
	Auctions: $646, MS-66, January 2015; $588, MS-65, January 2015; $242, MS-64, January 2015; $120, MS-62, January 2015												
1916-S	5,820,000	342	59.9	77%	$4	$5	$6	$10	$24	$75	$125	$240	$650
	Auctions: $2,233, MS-66, January 2015; $1,058, MS-66, June 2015; $282, MS-64, May 2015; $188, MS-63, October 2015												

WINGED LIBERTY HEAD OR "MERCURY" (1916–1945)

Designer: *Adolph A. Weinman.* **Weight:** *2.50 grams.* **Composition:** *.900 silver, .100 copper (net weight .07234 oz. pure silver).* **Diameter:** *17.9 mm.* **Edge:** *Reeded.* **Mints:** *Philadelphia, Denver, and San Francisco.*

  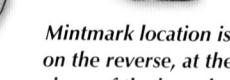  

Circulation Strike

Mintmark location is on the reverse, at the base of the branch.

Proof

History. In 1916 a new dime, designed by sculptor Adolph A. Weinman (who also created the half dollar that debuted that year), replaced Charles Barber's Liberty Head type. Officially Weinman's design was known as the Winged Liberty Head, but numismatists commonly call the coin the *Mercury* dime, from Miss Liberty's wing-capped resemblance to the Roman god. The reverse depicts a fasces (symbolic of strength in unity) and an olive branch (symbolic of peaceful intentions). Production was continuous from 1916 to 1945, except for 1922, 1932, and 1933.

Striking and Sharpness. Many Mercury dimes exhibit areas of light striking, most notably in the center horizontal band across the fasces, less so in the lower horizontal band. The bands are composed of two parallel lines with a separation or "split" between. The term Full Bands, abbreviated FB, describes coins with both parallel lines in the center band distinctly separated. *In addition*, some dimes may display weak striking in other areas (not noted by certification services or others), including at areas of Liberty's hair, the rim, and the date. Dimes of 1921 in particular can have FB but poorly struck dates. Proof dies were completely polished, including the portrait.

Availability. Certain coins, such as 1916-D; 1921-P; 1921-D; 1942, 2 Over 1; and 1942-D, 2 Over 1, are elusive in any grade. Others are generally available in lower circulated grades, although some are scarce. In MS many of the issues before 1931 range from scarce to rare. If with FB and also sharply struck in other areas, some are rare. MS coins usually are very lustrous. In the marketplace certain scarce early issues such as 1916-D, 1921, and 1921-D are often graded slightly more liberally than are later varieties. Proofs were minted from 1936 to 1942 and are available in proportion to their mintages.

GRADING STANDARDS

MS-60 to 70 (Mint State). *Obverse:* At MS-60, some abrasion and contact marks are evident on the highest part of the portrait, including the hair immediately to the right of the face and the upper left part of the wing. At MS-63, abrasion is slight at best, less so for MS-64. Album slide marks on the cheek, if present, should not be at any grade above MS-64. An MS-65 coin should display no abrasion or contact marks except under mag-

1928. Graded MS-66FB.

nification, and MS-66 and higher coins should have none at all. Luster should be full and rich. *Reverse:* Comments apply as for the obverse, except that the highest parts of the fasces, these being the horizontal bands, are the places to check. The field is mainly protected by design elements and does not show contact marks readily.

AU-50, 53, 55, 58 (About Uncirculated). *Obverse:* Light wear is seen on the cheek, the hair immediately to the right of the face, the left edge of the wing, and the upper right of the wing. At AU-58, the luster is extensive, but incomplete, especially on the higher parts and in the field. At AU–50 and 53, luster is less. *Reverse:* Light wear is seen on the higher parts of the fasces. An AU-58 coin has nearly full luster, more so than on the obverse, as the

1942, 2 Over 1. Graded AU-50.

design elements protect the field areas. At AU–50 and 53, there still is significant luster. Generally, the reverse appears to be in a slightly higher grade than the obverse.

EF-40, 45 (Extremely Fine). *Obverse:* Further wear is seen on the head. Many of the hair details are blended together, as are some feather details at the left side of the wing. *Reverse:* The horizontal bands on the fasces may be fused together. The diagonal bands remain in slight relief against the vertical lines (sticks).

1942-D, 2 Over 1; FS-101. Graded EF-45.

VF-20, 30 (Very Fine). *Obverse:* The head shows more wear, now with the forehead and cheek mostly blending into the hair. More feather details are gone. *Reverse:* Wear is more extensive, but the diagonal and horizontal bands on the fasces still are separated from the thin vertical sticks.

1942-D, 2 Over 1; FS-101. Graded VF-20.

F-12, 15 (Fine). *Obverse:* The head shows more wear, the hair has only slight detail, and most of the feathers are gone. In the marketplace a coin in F-12 grade usually has slightly less detail than stated by the ANA grading standards or *Photograde*, from modern interpretations. *Reverse:* Many of the tiny vertical sticks in the fasces are blended together. The bands can be barely discerned and may be worn away at the highest-relief parts.

1916-D. Graded F-12.

VG-8, 10 (Very Good). *Obverse:* Wear is more extensive on the portrait, and only a few feathers are seen on the wing. The outlines between the hair and cap and of the wing are distinct. Lettering is clear, but light in areas. *Reverse:* The rim is complete, or it may be slightly worn away in areas. Only a few traces of the vertical sticks remain in the fasces. Current interpretations in the marketplace are given here and are less strict than those

1921. Graded VG-8.

listed by the ANA grading standards and *Photograde*. Often, earlier issues are graded more liberally than are later dates.

G-4, 6 (Good). *Obverse:* Wear is more extensive, with not all of the outline between the hair and the wing visible. The rim is worn into the edges of the letters and often into the bottom of the last numeral in the date. *Reverse:* The rim is worn away, as are the outer parts of the letters. The fasces is flat or may show a hint of a vertical stick or two. The leaves are thick from wear. The mintmark, if any, is easily seen.

1916-D. Graded G-4.

AG-3 (About Good). *Obverse:* The rim is worn further into the letters. The head is mostly outline all over, except for a few indicates of edges. Folds remain at the top of the cap. The date is clearly visible. *Reverse:* The rim is worn further into the letters. The mintmark, if any, is clear but may be worn away slightly at the bottom. The apparent wear is slightly greater on the reverse than on the obverse.

1916-D. Graded AG-3.

PF-60 to 70 (Proof). *Obverse and Reverse:* Proofs that are extensively cleaned and have many hairlines, or that are dull and grainy, are lower level, such as PF–60 to 62. These are not widely desired, and represent coins that have been mistreated. With medium hairlines and good reflectivity, assigned grades of PF–63 or 64 are appropriate. Tiny horizontal lines on Miss Liberty's cheek, known as *slide marks*, from National and other album slides

1942. Graded PF-67.

scuffing the relief of the cheek, are common; coins with such marks should not be graded higher than PF-64, but sometimes are. With relatively few hairlines and no noticeable slide marks, a rating of PF-65 can be given. PF-66 should have hairlines so delicate that magnification is needed to see them. Above that, a Proof should be free of any hairlines or other problems.

Full Bands

	Mintage	Cert	Avg	%MS	G-4	VG-8	F-12	VF-20	EF-40	AU-50	MS-60	MS-63	MS-65
1916	22,180,080	2,737	62.6	94%	$4	$5	$7	$8	$15	$25	$35	$48	$150
	Auctions: $1,175, MS-67FB, January 2015; $112, MS-65FB, May 2015; $84, MS-64FB, January 2015; $39, MS-63, August 2015												
1916-D † (a)	264,000	4,089	10.6	5%	$1,000	$1,500	$2,600	$4,200	$6,000	$9,000	$13,500	$16,000	$25,000
	Auctions: $13,513, MS-63FB, January 2015; $10,006, MS-62, June 2015; $8,343, MS-60, September 2015; $9,988, AU-58FB, January 2015												
1916-S	10,450,000	987	58.7	86%	$4	$6	$9	$12	$20	$25	$42	$65	$215
	Auctions: $823, MS-67, January 2015; $282, MS-66, January 2015; $212, MS-65, February 2015; $79, MS-64, May 2015												
1917	55,230,000	824	62.3	89%	$3	$3.25	$3.50	$6	$8	$12	$30	$60	$170
	Auctions: $881, MS-66FB, January 2015; $282, MS-65FB, January 2015; $106, MS-64FB, February 2015; $69, MS-63FB, January 2015												
1917-D	9,402,000	575	60.9	80%	$4.50	$6	$11	$22	$45	$95	$145	$350	$1,050
	Auctions: $4,230, MS-67FB, August 2015; $4,700, MS-65FB, January 2015; $823, MS-64FB, January 2015; $282, MS-62FB, February 2015												
1917-S	27,330,000	592	61.5	83%	$3	$3.25	$4	$7	$12	$30	$60	$180	$500
	Auctions: $940, MS-66, October 2015; $1,028, MS-65FB, January 2015; $329, MS-64, May 2015; $94, MS-62, August 2015												

† Ranked in the *100 Greatest U.S. Coins* (fourth edition). **a.** Beware of altered or otherwise spurious mintmarks.

	Mintage	Cert	Avg	%MS	G-4	VG-8	F-12	VF-20	EF-40	AU-50	MS-60	MS-63	MS-65
1918	26,680,000	443	62.0	86%	$3	$4	$6	$12	$25	$40	$70	$125	$425
	Auctions: $1,058, MS-66FB, October 2015; $1,116, MS-65FB, January 2015; $188, MS-63FB, May 2015; $176, MS-63FB, May 2015												
1918-D	22,674,800	523	60.9	84%	$3	$4	$6	$12	$24	$50	$125	$250	$600
	Auctions: $1,880, MS-66, September 2015; $1,204, MS-65, January 2015; $282, MS-64, August 2015; $141, MS-63, August 2015												
1918-S	19,300,000	407	61.5	86%	$3	$3.25	$5	$10	$18	$40	$120	$275	$725
	Auctions: $3,055, MS-66, January 2015; $764, MS-65, October 2015; $376, MS-64, January 2015; $200, MS-62, May 2015												
1919	35,740,000	501	62.0	87%	$3	$3.25	$4	$6	$10	$30	$45	$150	$375
	Auctions: $1,058, MS-66FB, January 2015; $881, MS-65FB, January 2015; $188, MS-64FB, January 2015; $141, MS-62FB, February 2015												
1919-D	9,939,000	397	60.7	84%	$4	$7	$12	$24	$35	$75	$200	$450	$1,600
	Auctions: $32,900, MS-65FB, August 2015; $3,290, MS-64FB, January 2015; $388, MS-63, December 2015; $447, MS-62, May 2015												
1919-S	8,850,000	283	59.1	66%	$3.50	$4	$8	$16	$35	$75	$200	$450	$1,200
	Auctions: $1,645, MS-65FB, August 2015; $823, MS-65, January 2015; $705, MS-64, January 2015; $447, MS-63, January 2015												
1920	59,030,000	796	63.3	95%	$3	$3.25	$3.50	$5	$8	$15	$35	$75	$260
	Auctions: $646, MS-66FB, February 2015; $470, MS-65FB, January 2015; $130, MS-64FB, February 2015; $106, MS-64FB, February 2015												
1920-D	19,171,000	424	61.2	83%	$3	$3.50	$4.50	$8	$20	$45	$145	$350	$775
	Auctions: $1,351, MS-66, October 2015; $306, MS-64, February 2015; $182, MS-60, May 2015; $165, AU-58, May 2015												
1920-S	13,820,000	293	61.4	81%	$3.25	$4	$5	$8	$18	$45	$145	$325	$1,450
	Auctions: $5,170, MS-65FB, July 2015; $4,465, MS-65FB, June 2015; $1,880, MS-64FB, February 2015; $1,763, MS-64FB, February 2015												
1921	1,230,000	1,271	25.2	18%	$65	$80	$130	$320	$600	$925	$1,200	$2,200	$3,500
	Auctions: $5,170, MS-65FB, August 2015; $2,821, MS-64FB, January 2015; $2,350, MS-62FB, September 2015; $2,350, MS-61FB, June 2015												
1921-D	1,080,000	1,362	24.6	18%	$80	$130	$210	$420	$775	$1,250	$1,500	$2,600	$3,500
	Auctions: $7,050, MS-65FB, January 2015; $3,231, MS-64FB, October 2015; $823, MS-60, June 2015; $564, AU-50, June 2015												
1923 (b)	50,130,000	904	63.1	93%	$3	$3.25	$3.50	$5	$7	$16	$30	$45	$130
	Auctions: $940, MS-67FB, June 2015; $423, MS-66FB, January 2015; $282, MS-65FB, April 2015; $79, MS-64FB, August 2015												
1923-S	6,440,000	321	59.6	75%	$3	$4	$8	$18	$65	$105	$160	$400	$1,250
	Auctions: $1,700, MS-66, January 2015; $1,293, MS-65, August 2015; $764, MS-64, May 2015; $470, MS-63, January 2015												
1924	24,010,000	524	63.8	96%	$3	$3.25	$4	$6	$15	$30	$45	$100	$210
	Auctions: $2,115, MS-67FB, October 2015; $823, MS-66FB, October 2015; $329, MS-65FB, May 2015; $188, MS-64FB, June 2015												
1924-D	6,810,000	440	60.9	84%	$3.50	$4.50	$8	$24	$70	$110	$175	$500	$950
	Auctions: $1,763, MS-66FB, August 2015; $1,175, MS-65FB, January 2015; $705, MS-64FB, May 2015; $447, MS-63FB, January 2015												
1924-S	7,120,000	344	60.1	77%	$3.50	$4	$6	$10	$60	$110	$200	$525	$1,250
	Auctions: $3,525, MS-64FB, October 2015; $588, MS-64, January 2015; $1,058, MS-63FB, February 2015; $823, MS-62, June 2015												
1925	25,610,000	342	62.7	89%	$3	$3.25	$4	$5	$10	$20	$30	$85	$225
	Auctions: $2,585, MS-67FB, October 2015; $881, MS-65FB, January 2015; $306, MS-65, January 2015; $188, MS-64, April 2015												
1925-D	5,117,000	298	59.1	69%	$4	$5	$12	$45	$120	$200	$375	$800	$1,700
	Auctions: $11,750, MS-67FB, October 2015; $2,115, MS-66FB, October 2015; $2,938, MS-65FB, January 2015; $881, MS-63FB, February 2015												
1925-S	5,850,000	259	60.4	77%	$3.25	$4	$8	$18	$70	$110	$180	$500	$1,400
	Auctions: $3,995, MS-65FB, January 2015; $1,998, MS-64FB, September 2015; $423, MS-62, January 2015; $188, MS-60, May 2015												
1926	32,160,000	702	63.3	93%	$3	$3.25	$3.50	$5	$7	$16	$25	$65	$250
	Auctions: $3,055, MS-67FB, October 2015; $999, MS-66FB, February 2015; $259, MS-65FB, January 2015; $141, MS-64FB, October 2015												
1926-D	6,828,000	449	61.5	86%	$3.25	$4.50	$6	$10	$28	$50	$125	$275	$600
	Auctions: $1,528, MS-65FB, October 2015; $969, MS-64FB, February 2015; $376, MS-63FB, August 2015; $282, MS-63, May 2015												
1926-S	1,520,000	382	46.3	34%	$13	$15	$26	$60	$250	$450	$825	$1,500	$2,850
	Auctions: $4,113, MS-64FB, October 2015; $1,880, MS-64, January 2015; $1,528, MS-62, June 2015; $705, AU-58, October 2015												
1927	28,080,000	533	62.5	92%	$3	$3.25	$3.50	$5	$7	$15	$30	$60	$150
	Auctions: $2,115, MS-67FB, October 2015; $541, MS-66FB, January 2015; $212, MS-65FB, January 2015; $199, MS-64FB, January 2015												
1927-D	4,812,000	271	59.1	69%	$3.50	$5.50	$8	$25	$80	$100	$200	$400	$1,200
	Auctions: $2,585, MS-66FB, October 2015; $2,820, MS-66, January 2015; $646, MS-64, January 2015; $541, MS-63, May 2015												
1927-S	4,770,000	224	60.2	78%	$3.25	$4	$6	$12	$28	$50	$275	$550	$1,400
	Auctions: $3,303, MS-66, July 2015; $999, MS-65, January 2015; $1,116, MS-64, January 2015; $353, MS-60, January 2015												

b. Dimes dated 1923-D or 1930-D are counterfeit.

1928-S, Small S

1928-S, Large S
FS-10-1928S-501.

1929-S, Doubled-Die Obverse
FS-10-1929S-101.

	Mintage	Cert	Avg	%MS	G-4	VG-8	F-12	VF-20	EF-40	AU-50	MS-60	MS-63	MS-65
1928	19,480,000	446	63.7	95%	$3	$3.25	$3.50	$5	$7	$18	$30	$55	$130
	Auctions: $1,293, MS-67FB, January 2015; $558, MS-66FB, January 2015; $306, MS-65FB, June 2015; $141, MS-64FB, December 2015												
1928-D	4,161,000	271	59.9	80%	$4	$5	$8	$20	$50	$95	$175	$360	$850
	Auctions: $4,113, MS-66FB, June 2015; $2,115, MS-65FB, January 2015; $1,175, MS-64FB, January 2015; $646, MS-63FB, July 2015												
1928-S (c)	7,400,000	5	59.0	60%	$3	$3.25	$4	$6	$16	$45	$150	$320	$400
	Auctions: $3,525, MS-66FB, June 2015; $764, MS-66, January 2015; $1,116, MS-65FB, January 2015; $200, MS-62FB, January 2015												
1929	25,970,000	862	64.2	96%	$3	$3.25	$3.50	$5	$6	$12	$22	$35	$75
	Auctions: $1,058, MS-67FB, October 2015; $823, MS-66FB, January 2015; $129, MS-66, February 2015; $35, MS-63, October 2015												
1929-D	5,034,000	1,197	64.3	98%	$3	$3.50	$5	$8	$15	$24	$30	$36	$75
	Auctions: $1,410, MS-67FB, June 2015; $564, MS-66FB, October 2015; $282, MS-65FB, May 2015; $89, MS-64FB, August 2015												
1929-S	4,730,000	396	63.2	91%	$3	$3.25	$3.75	$5	$10	$20	$35	$45	$125
	Auctions: $3,055, MS-67FB, January 2015; $212, MS-66, February 2015; $353, MS-65FB, January 2015; $46, AU-58, April 2015												
1929-S, Doubled-Die Obverse (d)	(e)	4	58.5	50%								$150	$200
	Auctions: $170, AU-58, December 2009												
1930 (b)	6,770,000	427	63.4	92%	$3	$3.25	$3.50	$5	$8	$16	$30	$50	$125
	Auctions: $7,050, MS-67FB, June 2015; $2,115, MS-66FB, February 2015; $471, MS-65FB, January 2015; $212, MS-64FB, January 2015												
1930-S	1,843,000	295	62.9	91%	$3	$4	$5	$7	$15	$45	$80	$150	$210
	Auctions: $11,163, MS-67FB, January 2015; $3,173, MS-66FB, August 2015; $881, MS-65FB, June 2015; $470, MS-65, May 2015												
1931	3,150,000	457	63.3	92%	$3	$3.10	$4	$6	$10	$22	$35	$70	$150
	Auctions: $3,055, MS-67, March 2015; $1,116, MS-66FB, October 2015; $764, MS-65FB, July 2015; $112, MS-65, February 2015												
1931-D	1,260,000	552	62.3	91%	$8	$9	$12	$20	$35	$60	$90	$140	$280
	Auctions: $1,763, MS-67FB, January 2015; $646, MS-66FB, January 2015; $306, MS-65FB, January 2015; $176, MS-64FB, January 2015												
1931-S	1,800,000	407	60.3	84%	$4	$5	$6	$10	$16	$45	$90	$150	$300
	Auctions: $764, MS-67, January 2015; $259, MS-65, May 2015; $212, MS-64, May 2015; $129, MS-63, February 2015												

b. Dimes dated 1923-D or 1930-D are counterfeit. **c.** Two mintmark styles exist: Large S (scarce) and Small S (common). About 80% of 1928-S dimes are of the Small S style. The scarcer Large S is worth about two to three times the values listed (which are for the Small S). **d.** Moderate doubling is evident on the date and IN GOD WE TRUST. **e.** Included in 1929-S mintage figure.

	Mintage	Cert	Avg	%MS	F-12	VF-20	EF-40	AU-50	MS-60	MS-63	MS-65	MS-65FB	MS-66
											PF-65	PF-66	PF-67
1934	24,080,000	934	64.5	97%	$2.75	$3	$3.25	$16	$25	$35	$50	$140	$65
	Auctions: $1,293, MS-67FB, January 2015; $235, MS-66FB, February 2015; $200, MS-65FB, May 2015; $32, MS-62FB, November 2015												
1934-D	6,772,000	677	64.3	96%	$2.75	$3	$8	$33	$50	$60	$85	$325	$230
	Auctions: $881, MS-67FB, October 2015; $705, MS-66FB, September 2015; $447, MS-66FB, January 2015												
1935	58,830,000	1,439	65.1	97%	$2.75	$3	$3.25	$7	$10	$15	$35	$75	$60
	Auctions: $329, MS-67FB, May 2015; $94, MS-66FB, January 2015; $165, MS-65FB, April 2015; $38, MS-64FB, August 2015												
1935-D	10,477,000	497	63.9	94%	$2.75	$3	$8	$26	$35	$50	$90	$525	$325
	Auctions: $2,350, MS-67FB, September 2015; $1,116, MS-66FB, January 2015; $881, MS-66FB, October 2015; $517, MS-65FB, February 2015												
1935-S	15,840,000	609	65.0	98%	$2.75	$3	$5	$16	$22	$30	$40	$350	$80
	Auctions: $2,820, MS-67FB, January 2015; $435, MS-66FB, January 2015; $255, MS-65FB, February 2015; $94, MS-63FB, April 2015												

1936-S, Possible Overdate
FS-10-1936S-110.

	Mintage	Cert	Avg	%MS	F-12	VF-20	EF-40	AU-50	MS-60	MS-63	MS-65 PF-65	MS-65FB PF-66	MS-66 PF-67
1936	87,500,000	1,964	65.1	97%	$2.75	$3	$3.25	$7	$10	$18	$30	$90	$48
	Auctions: $3,643, MS-68FB, October 2015; $881, MS-67FB, January 2015; $94, MS-66FB, October 2015; $74, MS-66FB, June 2015												
1936, Proof	4,130	1,086	65.0								$1,250	$1,650	$4,500
	Auctions: $1,998, PF-67, January 2015; $1,293, PF-66, January 2015; $1,410, PF-65, January 2015; $646, PF-64, January 2015												
1936-D	16,132,000	585	64.2	94%	$2.75	$3	$6	$16	$25	$40	$55	$275	$80
	Auctions: $1,351, MS-67FB, August 2015; $259, MS-66FB, January 2015; $235, MS-65FB, October 2015												
1936-S	9,210,000	1,038	65.4	99%	$2.75	$3	$3.25	$13	$23	$30	$38	$95	$55
	Auctions: $881, MS-67FB, February 2015; $646, MS-67FB, June 2015; $176, MS-66FB, May 2015; $56, MS-66, August 2015												
1936-S, Possible Overdate (a)	**(b)**	0	n/a								$600		
	Auctions: $1,500, MS-65FB, November 2011												
1937	56,860,000	4,022	65.7	99%	$2.75	$3	$3.25	$7	$10	$15	$30	$60	$40
	Auctions: $764, MS-68FB, January 2015; $388, MS-67FB, September 2015; $188, MS-67FB, August 2015												
1937, Proof	5,756	1,240	65.4								$650	$750	$750
	Auctions: $9,988, PF-68, January 2015; $4,935, PF-67, January 2015; $376, PF-66, May 2015; $411, PF-65, March 2015												
1937-D	14,146,000	982	65.3	98%	$2.75	$3	$4	$12	$21	$30	$45	$100	$85
	Auctions: $541, MS-67FB, January 2015; $282, MS-67FB, September 2015; $94, MS-66FB, January 2015; $89, MS-65FB, April 2015												
1937-S	9,740,000	987	65.5	98%	$2.75	$3	$3.25	$12	$20	$30	$40	$185	$80
	Auctions: $4,465, MS-68FB, June 2015; $2,233, MS-67, August 2015; $212, MS-66FB, May 2015; $188, MS-65FB, October 2015												
1938	22,190,000	1,588	65.5	99%	$2.75	$3	$3.25	$7	$10	$15	$30	$85	$55
	Auctions: $400, MS-67FB, January 2015; $329, MS-67FB, May 2015; $74, MS-66FB, January 2015; $64, MS-66FB, February 2015												
1938, Proof	8,728	1,785	65.4								$300	$500	$800
	Auctions: $18,800, PF-69, August 2015; $1,880, PF-68, September 2015; $764, PF-67, January 2015; $282, PF-66, June 2015												
1938-D	5,537,000	1,715	65.5	99%	$2.75	$3	$4	$11	$18	$25	$35	$65	$75
	Auctions: $212, MS-67FB, February 2015; $79, MS-66FB, February 2015; $44, MS-65FB, September 2015												
1938-S	8,090,000	965	65.2	97%	$2.75	$3	$3.50	$12	$20	$28	$42	$160	$80
	Auctions: $588, MS-67FB, October 2015; $541, MS-67FB, October 2015; $141, MS-66FB, May 2015; $112, MS-65FB, August 2015												
1939	67,740,000	3,246	65.8	98%	$2.75	$3	$3.25	$6	$8	$12	$26	$180	$40
	Auctions: $188, MS-68, May 2015; $1,116, MS-67FB, January 2015; $69, MS-67, May 2015; $188, MS-66FB, January 2015												
1939, Proof	9,321	1,974	65.9								$250	$300	$425
	Auctions: $2,820, PF-68, January 2015; $331, PF-67, June 2015; $200, PF-66, May 2015; $165, PF-65, January 2015												
1939-D	24,394,000	3,405	65.7	99%	$2.75	$3	$3.25	$6	$8	$12	$32	$55	$60
	Auctions: $9,694, MS-69FB, June 2015; $1,410, MS-68FB, January 2015; $129, MS-67FB, April 2015; $44, MS-66FB, June 2015												
1939-S	10,540,000	785	65.1	98%	$2.75	$3	$4	$13	$23	$30	$42	$725	$110
	Auctions: $2,585, MS-67FB, September 2015; $1,293, MS-66FB, August 2015; $940, MS-66FB, January 2015												
1940	65,350,000	3,294	65.7	98%	$2.75	$3	$3.25	$5	$7	$12	$30	$50	$45
	Auctions: $400, MS-67FB, September 2015; $200, MS-67FB, August 2015; $165, MS-67FB, May 2015; $112, MS-67FB, February 2015												
1940, Proof	11,827	2,167	65.6								$225	$285	$400
	Auctions: $2,056, PF-68, January 2015; $329, PF-67, June 2015; $153, PF-66, December 2015; $141, PF-64, January 2015												
1940-D	21,198,000	2,380	65.5	99%	$2.75	$3	$3.25	$5	$7	$14	$35	$50	$50
	Auctions: $999, MS-68FB, October 2015; $329, MS-67FB, June 2015; $44, MS-66FB, January 2015; $38, MS-65FB, August 2015												
1940-S	21,560,000	2,468	65.6	99%	$2.75	$3	$3.25	$6	$8	$15	$35	$100	$40
	Auctions: $617, MS-67FB, January 2015; $376, MS-67FB, October 2015; $94, MS-66FB, February 2015; $56, MS-65FB, January 2015												

a. "The secondary image of a 2 is evident beneath the 3 of the date. Most evident is the flat portion of the base of the underlying 2. Remains of what is likely a secondary 9 are evident to the left of the primary 9. Many die polish marks are also evident throughout the surface of the obverse. No doubling is evident on other elements. . . . The length of time between the striking of the last 1929-dated coins and this 1936 coin would seem to eliminate the possibility of a 2 underlying the 3. However, examination has matched the shapes on the image under the 3 to that of the 2 on 1929-dated dimes. Stranger things have happened. Keep in mind that 1936 was during the Great Depression, when Mint personnel wanted to save money whenever possible." (*Cherrypickers' Guide to Rare Die Varieties*, sixth edition, volume II) **b.** Included in 1936-S mintage figure.

1941-S, Small S

1941-S, Large S
FS-10-1941S-511.

1942, 42 Over 41
FS-10-1942-101.

1942-D, 42 Over 41, Repunched Mintmark
FS-10-1942D-101.

1943-S, Trumpet Tail Mintmark
FS-10-1943S-511.

	Mintage	Cert	Avg	%MS	F-12	VF-20	EF-40	AU-50	MS-60	MS-63	MS-65 / PF-65	MS-65FB / PF-66	MS-66 / PF-67
1941	175,090,000	4,376	65.3	97%	$2.75	$3	$3.25	$5	$7	$12	$30	$50	$45
Auctions: $940, MS-68FB, January 2015; $646, MS-67FB, August 2015; $235, MS-67FB, January 2015; $40, MS-67, September 2015													
1941, Proof	16,557	2,767	65.5								$200	$250	$375
Auctions: $3,055, PF-68, January 2015; $423, PF-67, January 2015; $141, PF-66, January 2015; $140, PF-65, February 2015													
1941-D	45,634,000	3,279	65.3	98%	$2.75	$3	$3.25	$6	$8	$14	$25	$50	$32
Auctions: $1,234, MS-68FB, January 2015; $588, MS-67FB, January 2015; $153, MS-67FB, September 2015; $46, MS-66FB, April 2015													
1941-S	43,090,000	4,507	65.6	99%	$2.75	$3	$3.25	$5	$7	$12	$30	$50	$38
Auctions: $259, MS-67FB, September 2015; $235, MS-67FB, April 2015; $165, MS-67FB, May 2015; $153, MS-67FB, January 2015													
1941-S, Large S (c)	**(d)**	30	54.8	63%							$325		
Auctions: $120, MS-63, June 2010													
1942, 42 Over 41 (e)	**(f)**	1,683	40.4	7%	$625	$800	$1,000	$1,750	$2,500	$4,500 (g)	$15,000	$45,000	$20,000
Auctions: $1,116, AU-58, January 2015; $646, AU-53, January 2015; $470, EF-40, January 2015; $400, VF-30, February 2015													
1942	205,410,000	5,137	65.1	97%	$2.75	$3	$3.25	$4.50	$6	$12	$30	$50	$45
Auctions: $911, MS-67FB, January 2015; $135, MS-67, September 2015; $46, MS-67, September 2015; $44, MS-66FB, April 2015													
1942, Proof	22,329	4,093	65.7								$200	$250	$375
Auctions: $1,821, PF-68, January 2015; $212, PF-67, January 2015; $165, PF-66, January 2015; $165, PF-65, December 2015													
1942-D, 42 Over 41 (h)	**(i)**	960	37.2	10%	$675	$850	$1,100	$1,850	$2,600	$4,750 (j)	$10,000	$32,000	$12,000
Auctions: $940, AU-55, February 2015; $853, AU-50, January 2015; $588, EF-40, June 2015; $400, VF-25, February 2015													
1942-D	60,740,000	4,295	64.7	95%	$2.75	$3	$3.25	$4.50	$6	$12	$28	$48	$45
Auctions: $881, MS-68FB, October 2015; $153, MS-67FB, March 2015; $125, MS-67FB, February 2015; $46, MS-66FB, January 2015													
1942-S	49,300,000	1,772	65.1	97%	$2.75	$3	$3.25	$6	$8	$20	$30	$150	$50
Auctions: $400, MS-67FB, January 2015; $153, MS-66FB, January 2015; $89, MS-65FB, September 2015; $200, MS-63FB, November 2015													
1943	191,710,000	5,179	65.4	98%	$2.75	$3	$3.25	$4.50	$6	$12	$27	$55	$35
Auctions: $2,233, MS-67FB, June 2015; $1,880, MS-67FB, June 2015; $881, MS-67FB, July 2015; $118, MS-67, May 2015													
1943-D	71,949,000	5,603	65.5	99%	$2.75	$3	$3.25	$4.50	$6	$15	$30	$50	$45
Auctions: $1,880, MS-68FB, October 2015; $306, MS-67FB, February 2015; $123, MS-67FB, January 2015; $120, MS-67FB, February 2015													
1943-S	60,400,000	3,315	65.8	99%	$2.75	$3	$3.25	$5	$7	$16	$30	$70	$40
Auctions: $3,525, MS-68FB, October 2015; $1,410, MS-67FB, October 2015; $353, MS-67FB, January 2015; $58, MS-67, September 2015													
1943-S, Trumpet Tail Mintmark (k)	**(l)**	7	62.6	71%							$450	$750	$500
Auctions: $130, MS-62, December 2011													

c. This is the "Trumpet Tail" S mintmark, which is rare for this date. The upper serif points downward and the lower serif is rounded, like the bell of a trumpet. There are several dies known for the Large S dime, including one that is repunched. For more information, see the *Cherrypickers' Guide*. **d.** Included in 1941-S mintage figure. **e.** Doubling is evident in the 42 over 41 overdate, and slightly evident on IN GOD WE TRUST. Values for this variety fluctuate. **f.** Included in circulation-strike 1942 mintage figure. **g.** Value in MS-64 is $7,200. **h.** Doubling is evident in the 42 over 41 overdate, slightly evident on IN GOD WE TRUST, and as a D over D repunched mintmark (slanted west). Values for this variety fluctuate. **i.** Included in 1942-D mintage figure. **j.** Value in MS-64 is $7,200. **k.** This variety is considerably rarer than the 1941-S, Large S, which also features a Trumpet S mintmark. It is extremely rare in MS, and examples with FB command a significant premium. The top serif of the S points downward, with the lower serif rounded, much like the bell of a trumpet. **l.** Included in 1943-S mintage figure.

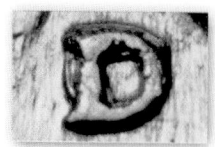
1945-D, D Over Horizontal D
FS-10-1945D-506.

1945-S, S Over Horizontal S
FS-10-1945S-503.

1945-S, Normal S

1945-S, Micro S
FS-10-1945S-512.

	Mintage	Cert	Avg	%MS	F-12	VF-20	EF-40	AU-50	MS-60	MS-63	MS-65	MS-65FB	MS-66
											PF-65	PF-66	PF-67
1944	231,410,000	6,230	65.4	98%	$2.75	$3	$3.25	$4.50	$6	$12	$25	$80	$45
	Auctions: $12,925, MS-68FB, August 2015; $1,586, MS-67FB, October 2015; $1,116, MS-67FB, January 2015; $129, MS-65, November 2015												
1944-D	62,224,000	7,323	65.8	99%	$2.75	$3	$3.25	$5	$7	$15	$30	$50	$48
	Auctions: $1,175, MS-68FB, July 2015; $764, MS-68FB, October 2015; $188, MS-67FB, February 2015; $112, MS-67FB, February 2015												
1944-S	49,490,000	5,376	65.8	99%	$2.75	$3	$3.25	$5	$7	$15	$30	$55	$50
	Auctions: $294, MS-68, February 2015; $200, MS-67FB, September 2015; $129, MS-67, February 2015; $176, MS-66FB, September 2015												
1945	159,130,000	6,597	65.5	99%	$2.75	$3	$3.25	$4.50	$6	$12	$28	$10,000	$45
	Auctions: $58, MS-67, January 2015; $56, MS-67, April 2015; $38, MS-66, September 2015; $212, MS-60, September 2015												
1945-D	40,245,000	7,093	65.7	100%	$2.75	$3	$3.25	$4.50	$6	$12	$26	$45	$50
	Auctions: $200, MS-67FB, September 2015; $165, MS-67FB, January 2015; $141, MS-67FB, May 2015; $112, MS-67FB, November 2015												
1945-D, D Over Horizontal D (m)	(n)	5	50.2	0%							$950		
	Auctions: No auction records available.												
1945-S	41,920,000	6,103	65.9	99%	$2.75	$3	$3.25	$4.50	$6	$12	$30	$125	$40
	Auctions: $1,058, MS-68, January 2015; $186, MS-67, June 2015; $129, MS-66FB, September 2015; $100, MS-66FB, September 2015												
1945-S, S Over Horizontal S (o)	(p)	0	n/a								$950		
	Auctions: No auction records available.												
1945-S, Micro S (q)	(p)	1,115	65.2	98%	$3.25	$3.50	$6	$18	$30	$40	$100	$650	$120
	Auctions: $823, MS-67, September 2015; $129, MS-66, June 2015; $100, MS-65, September 2015; $48, MS-64, August 2015												

m. The first D mintmark was punched into the die horizontally and then corrected. **n.** Included in 1945-D mintage figure. **o.** The first S mintmark was punched into the die horizontally and then corrected. **p.** Included in 1945-S mintage figure. **q.** The S mintmark is significantly smaller than that of the normal S punch. This variety has the only mintmark punch of this type and size known to have been used during the 1940s. It was originally used for Philippine coins of 1907 through 1920.

ROOSEVELT (1946 TO DATE)

Silver (1946–1964, and some modern Proofs): **Designer:** *John R. Sinnock.*
Weight: *2.50 grams.* **Composition:** *.900 silver, .100 copper (net weight: .07234 oz. pure silver).*
Diameter: *17.9 mm.* **Edge:** *Reeded.* **Mints:** *Philadelphia, Denver, San Francisco, and West Point.*

Silver, Circulation Strike

Mintmark location is on the reverse, to the left of the fasces.

Silver, Proof

Clad (1965 to date): **Designer:** *John R. Sinnock.* **Weight:** *2.27 grams.*
Composition: *Outer layers of copper-nickel (.750 copper, .250 nickel) bonded to inner core of pure copper.*
Diameter: *17.9 mm.* **Edge:** *Reeded.* **Mints:** *Philadelphia, Denver, and San Francisco.*

Clad, Circulation Strike

Mintmark location is on the obverse, above the date.

Clad, Proof

History. After President Franklin D. Roosevelt died in 1945, the Treasury rushed to create a coin in his honor. The ten-cent denomination was particularly appropriate, given the president's active support of the March of Dimes' fundraising efforts to cure polio. The obverse of the coin bears Roosevelt's profile portrait, while the reverse features a torch flanked by branches of olive and oak.

Striking and Sharpness. Compared to earlier coinage series, collectors and dealers have paid relatively little attention to the sharpness of Roosevelt dimes. The obverse portrait is such that lightness of strike on the higher points is difficult to detect. On the reverse, check the leaves and the details of the torch. Some with complete separation on the lower two bands have been called Full Torch (FT) or Full Bands (FB), but interest in this distinction seems to be minimal in today's marketplace.

Availability. All are common, although some are more common than others. MS coins in higher grades are usually very lustrous.

Note: Values of common-date silver coins have been based on a silver current bullion price of $15.50 per ounce, and may vary with the prevailing spot price.

GRADING STANDARDS

MS-60 to 70 (Mint State). *Obverse:* At MS-60, some abrasion and contact marks are evident on the cheek, the hair above the ear, and the neck. At MS-63, abrasion is slight at best, less so for MS-64. An MS-65 coin should display no abrasion or contact marks except under magnification, and MS-66 and higher coins should have none at all. Luster should be full and rich. *Reverse:* Comments apply as for

1955-D. Graded MS-68FB.

the obverse, except that the highest parts of the torch, flame, and leaves are the places to check. On both sides the fields are protected by design elements and do not show contact marks readily.

AU-50, 53, 55, 58 (About Uncirculated). *Obverse:* Light wear is seen on the cheek and higher-relief part of the hair. At AU-58, the luster is extensive, but incomplete, especially on the higher parts and in the field. At AU–50 and 53, luster is less. *Reverse:* Light wear is seen on the higher parts of the torch and leaves. An AU-58 coin has nearly full luster. At AU–50 and 53, there still is significant luster.

1962-D. Graded AU-58.

EF-40, 45 (Extremely Fine). *Obverse:* Further wear is seen on the head. Some details are gone in the hair to the right of the forehead. *Reverse:* Further wear is seen on the torch, but the vertical lines are visible, some just barely. The higher-relief details in the leaves, never strong to begin with, are worn away.

The Roosevelt dime is seldom collected in grades lower than EF-40.

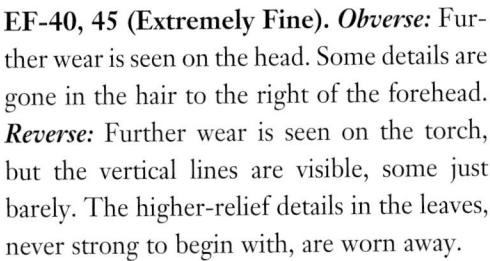

1950-S. Graded EF-40.

PF-60 to 70 (Proof). *Obverse and Reverse:* Proofs that are extensively cleaned and have many hairlines, or that are dull and grainy, are lower level, such as PF–60 to 62. These are not widely desired, and represent coins that have been mistreated. Fortunately, only a few Proof Roosevelt dimes are in this category. With medium hairlines and good reflectivity, assigned grades of PF–63 or 64 are appropriate. PF–65 may have hairlines so delicate that magnification is needed to see them. Above that, a Proof should be free of any hairlines or other problems.

1983-S, No S. Graded PF-69 Deep Cameo.

Illustrated coin: The S mintmark is missing from this popular variety.

	Mintage	Cert	Avg	%MS	EF-40	MS-63	MS-65	MS-66	MS-67	MS-67FB
								PF-65	PF-66	PF-67
1946	255,250,000	1,667	66.0	100%	$2	$4.25	$12	$28	$110	$400
	Auctions: $764, MS-67FB, June 2015; $235, MS-67FB, January 2015; $165, MS-67FB, February 2015; $58, MS-67, March 2015									
1946-D	61,043,500	2,141	66.1	100%	$2	$4.25	$14	$30	$100	$200
	Auctions: $999, MS-68FB, June 2015; $646, MS-67FB, July 2015; $153, MS-67FB, February 2015; $106, MS-67FB, August 2015									
1946-S	27,900,000	2,582	66.3	100%	$2	$4.50	$20	$32	$90	$175
	Auctions: $1,234, MS-68FB, October 2015; $282, MS-67FB, September 2015; $153, MS-67FB, September 2015; $141, MS-66FB, July 2015									
1947	121,520,000	1,343	65.6	97%	$2	$6	$12	$24	$55	$500
	Auctions: $1,645, MS-68FB, June 2015; $223, MS-67FB, January 2015; $646, MS-67, August 2015									
1947-D	46,835,000	1,170	66.2	100%	$2	$6.50	$12	$24	$30	$400
	Auctions: $270, MS-67FB, August 2014; $1,763, MS-67FB, November 2013; $259, MS-67FB, January 2015									
1947-S	34,840,000	2,057	66.3	100%	$2	$6	$12	$30	$110	$250
	Auctions: $764, MS-68, August 2015; $588, MS-67FB, August 2015; $165, MS-67FB, February 2015; $64, MS-65, August 2015									
1948	74,950,000	1,085	66.0	100%	$2	$4.25	$12	$30	$85	$350
	Auctions: $259, MS-67FB, January 2015; $200, MS-67FB, February 2015; $176, MS-67FB, August 2015; $147, MS-67FB, September 2015									
1948-D	52,841,000	1,255	66.2	100%	$2	$6	$12	$30	$85	$150
	Auctions: $2,820, MS-68FB, June 2015; $2,233, MS-68FB, July 2015; $94, MS-67FB, September 2015; $89, MS-67FB, February 2015									
1948-S	35,520,000	1,551	66.3	100%	$2	$5.50	$12	$32	$100	$150
	Auctions: $118, MS-67FB, February 2015; $112, MS-67FB, January 2015; $89, MS-67FB, July 2015; $74, MS-67FB, February 2015									
1949	30,940,000	1,176	65.9	99%	$3	$27	$38	$65	$125	$825
	Auctions: $541, MS-67FB, February 2015; $100, MS-66FB, February 2015									
1949-D	26,034,000	1,749	66.1	100%	$3	$12	$20	$35	$105	$300
	Auctions: $106, MS-67FB, March 2015; $100, MS-67FB, January 2015; $30, MS-66FB, January 2015; $30, MS-66FB, February 2015									
1949-S	13,510,000	2,335	66.2	99%	$5	$45	$55	$75	$190	$1,250
	Auctions: $1,175, MS-67FB, October 2015; $200, MS-66FB, May 2015; $188, MS-66FB, February 2015									
1950	50,130,114	1,363	65.9	99%	$3	$13	$16	$35	$135	$300
	Auctions: $999, MS-67FB, June 2015; $646, MS-67FB, August 2015; $212, MS-67FB, November 2015; $188, MS-67FB, January 2015									
1950, Proof	51,386	1,397	66.3					$50	$65	$120
	Auctions: $353, PF-67Cam, December 2015; $52, PF-67, August 2015; $129, PF-66Cam, January 2015; $42, PF-66, September 2015									
1950-D	46,803,000	1,649	66.3	100%	$2	$6	$12	$28	$90	$150
	Auctions: $1,410, MS-68FB, June 2014; $86, MS-67, July 2014; $165, MS-67+, November 2014; $123, MS-67, November 2014									

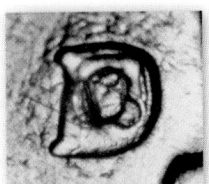

1950-D, D Over S
FS-10-1950D-501.

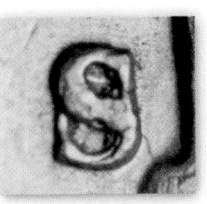

1950-S, S Over D
FS-10-1950S-501.

	Mintage	Cert	Avg	%MS	EF-40	MS-63	MS-65	MS-66	MS-67	MS-67FB
								PF-65	PF-66	PF-67
1950-D, D Over S (a)	**(b)**	0	n/a			$400	$650	$825	$1,100	
Auctions: No auction records available.										
1950-S	20,440,000	1,476	66.2	99%	$5	$38	$55	$75	$135	$425
Auctions: $259, MS-67FB, January 2015; $200, MS-67FB, August 2015; $153, MS-67, January 2015; $84, MS-66FB, February 2015										
1950-S, S Over D (c)	**(d)**	0	n/a			$250	$400	$750	$1,000	$1,675
Auctions: $159, MS-66, August 2014; $84, MS-65, June 2014; $57, MS-64, November 2014										
1951	103,880,102	1,510	66.1	100%	$2	$4.25	$10	$30	$110	$325
Auctions: $3,290, MS-68FB, July 2015; $2,350, MS-67FB, January 2015; $1,410, MS-67FB, October 2015; $69, PF-67, August 2015										
1951, Proof	57,500	1,746	66.7					$50	$65	$100
Auctions: $23,500, PF-68DCam, January 2014; $123, PF-67Cam, September 2014; $125, PF-67Cam, November 2014; $411, PF-69, July 2014										
1951-D	56,529,000	940	66.1	100%	$2	$4	$10	$28	$130	$300
Auctions: $3,290, MS-68FB, January 2015; $153, MS-67FB, January 2015; $89, MS-67FB, January 2015										
1951-S	31,630,000	1,571	66.4	100%	$3	$14	$25	$45	$110	$250
Auctions: $1,763, MS-68FB, October 2015; $705, MS-68, October 2015; $141, MS-67FB, January 2015; $120, MS-67FB, October 2015										
1952	99,040,093	1,031	65.9	100%	$2	$4.25	$10	$30	$85	$500
Auctions: $282, MS-67FB, January 2015; $282, MS-67FB, August 2015; $259, MS-67FB, June 2015; $129, MS-67FB, August 2015										
1952, Proof	81,980	1,427	66.7					$35	$50	$85
Auctions: $881, PF-68Cam, November 2014; $1,116, PF-68Cam, April 2013; $188, PF-67Cam, June 2015; $165, PF-66Cam, November 2014										
1952-D	122,100,000	1,153	66.1	100%	$2	$4.25	$9	$25	$30	$325
Auctions: $1,234, MS-67FB, June 2015; $823, MS-67FB, August 2015; $188, MS-67FB, August 2015; $118, MS-67FB, January 2015										
1952-S	44,419,500	1,667	66.3	100%	$3	$8	$12	$35	$75	$500
Auctions: $588, MS-68, September 2015; $881, MS-67FB, September 2015; $259, MS-67FB, January 2015; $141, MS-67FB, February 2015										
1953	53,490,120	832	65.9	100%	$2	$4	$8	$15	$90	$750
Auctions: $823, MS-67FB, January 2015; $376, MS-67, January 2015; $129, MS-66FB, October 2015; $112, MS-66FB, October 2015										
1953, Proof	128,800	2,081	66.8					$38	$55	$80
Auctions: $106, PF-67Cam, June 2015; $84, PF-67Cam, August 2015; $74, PF-67Cam, August 2015										
1953-D	136,433,000	1,126	66.1	100%	$2	$4	$9	$20	$45	$350
Auctions: $1,410, MS-68FB, July 2015; $176, MS-67FB, January 2015										
1953-S	39,180,000	2,698	66.3	100%	$3	$4	$9	$25	$65	$575
Auctions: $999, MS-67FB, January 2015; $353, MS-67FB, August 2015; $94, MS-67, February 2015										
1954	114,010,203	1,336	65.9	100%	$2	$4	$8	$20	$32	$650
Auctions: $165, MS-67FB, September 2014; $129, MS-67FB, November 2014; $83, MS-66FB, August 2014; $56, MS-66FB, January 2015										
1954, Proof	233,300	2,584	67.1	100%				$18	$25	$30
Auctions: $141, PF-68Cam, July 2015; $94, PF-67Cam, August 2015; $69, PF-67Cam, October 2015										
1954-D	106,397,000	985	66.0		$2	$4	$9	$14	$30	$350
Auctions: $129, MS-67FB, January 2015; $129, MS-67FB, July 2015; $58, MS-67FB, August 2015; $36, MS-67, January 2015										
1954-S	22,860,000	2,099	66.2	100%	$2	$4	$9	$16	$40	$400
Auctions: $212, MS-67FB, December 2014; $1,116, MS-67FB, August 2013; $79, MS-67, August 2014										

a. The diagonal stroke of the initially punched S mintmark is visible within the opening of the primary D mintmark. The lower curve of the S is evident on the lower right curve of the D. **b.** Included in 1950-D mintage figure. **c.** The S mintmark is punched squarely over a previously punched D. CONECA lists this coin as an S Over Inverted S, indicating that the line enclosing the lower loop is that of the long upper serif on an inverted S. However, Fivaz and Stanton, in the *Cherrypickers' Guide to Rare Die Varieties*, sixth edition, volume II, "believe this to be an [overmintmark] (actually S/S/D) because the long upper serif of an S would not enclose the lower opening. In addition, the curve of the face of a D is clearly evident in the upper opening." **d.** Included in 1950-S mintage figure.

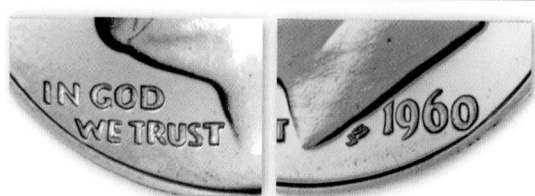

1960, Doubled-Die Obverse, Proof
FS-10-1960-102. Various die states exist.

	Mintage	Cert	Avg	%MS	EF-40	MS-63	MS-65	MS-66 / PF-65	MS-67 / PF-66	MS-67FB / PF-67
1955	12,450,181	2,310	66.0	100%	$2	$4	$8	$16	$25	$1,250
	Auctions: $26, MS-68FB, August 2015; $50, MS-67, February 2015									
1955, Proof	378,200	3,972	67.4					$15	$20	$25
	Auctions: $881, PF-68DCam, April 2013; $28, PF-67, November 2014									
1955-D	13,959,000	1,483	65.6	100%	$2	$4	$8	$15	$24	$250
	Auctions: $247, MS-67FB, August 2015; $212, MS-67FB, January 2015									
1955-S	18,510,000	3,322	66.0	100%	$2	$4	$8	$15	$60	$3,050
	Auctions: $2,585, MS-67FB, September 2015; $1,645, MS-67FB, August 2015; $235, MS-67FB, August 2015; $69, MS-66FB, January 2015									
1956	108,640,000	2,201	66.2	100%	$2	$3	$6	$14	$45	$1,000
	Auctions: $705, MS-67FB, July 2015; $646, MS-67FB, June 2015; $110, MS-66FB, January 2015; $79, MS-66FB, February 2015									
1956, Proof	669,384	3,700	67.5					$8	$10	$18
	Auctions: $56, PF-68Cam, August 2015									
1956-D	108,015,100	1,003	66.1	100%	$2	$3	$6	$15	$35	$500
	Auctions: $306, MS-67FB, January 2015; $235, MS-67FB, May 2015; $141, MS-67FB, May 2015									
1957	160,160,000	2,224	66.2	100%	$2	$3	$6	$14	$65	$2,000
	Auctions: $1,998, MS-67FB, April 2014; $21, MS-67, November 2014									
1957, Proof	1,247,952	4,142	67.5					$5	$8	$25
	Auctions: $4,113, PF-69DCam, January 2014									
1957-D	113,354,330	1,517	66.1	100%	$2	$3	$6	$14	$20	$500
	Auctions: $1,293, MS-68FB, January 2015; $259, MS-67FB, January 2015; $212, MS-67FB, March 2015									
1958	31,910,000	2,233	66.3	100%	$2	$3	$7	$15	$55	$2,500
	Auctions: $106, MS-66FB, February 2015; $79, MS-66FB, January 2015; $54, MS-66FB, February 2015									
1958, Proof	875,652	3,198	67.4					$5	$8	$10
	Auctions: $2,585, PF-69DCam, April 2013									
1958-D	136,564,600	1,682	66.2	100%	$2	$3	$7	$14	$45	$150
	Auctions: $881, MS-68FB, August 2015; $188, MS-67FB, May 2015; $84, MS-67FB, October 2015; $74, MS-67FB, January 2015									
1959	85,780,000	1,481	65.9	100%	$2	$3	$6	$15	$35	$500
	Auctions: $1,528, MS-67FB, June 2014									
1959, Proof	1,149,291	3,659	67.6					$5	$8	$10
	Auctions: $235, PF-69Cam, August 2015									
1959-D	164,919,790	1,070	66.1	100%	$2	$3	$6	$14	$25	$150
	Auctions: $1,763, MS-67FB, June 2015; $94, MS-67FB, January 2015; $40, MS-67FB, January 2015									
1960	70,390,000	1,203	65.9	100%	$2	$3	$6	$14	$25	$800
	Auctions: $2,938, MS-67FB, June 2014; $1,645, MS-67FB, February 2015; $470, MS-67FB, August 2014; $80, MS-66FB, October 2014									
1960, Proof	1,691,602	4,579	67.5					$5	$10	$18
	Auctions: $165, PF-69UCam, July 2015; $135, PF-66Cam, September 2015									
1960, Doubled-Die Obverse, Proof	(e)	68	66.5					$150	$250	
	Auctions: $106, PF-67, November 2014; $129, PF-67, June 2013; $127, PF-67, March 2012									
1960-D	200,160,400	918	66.0	100%		$3	$5	$15	$70	$700
	Auctions: $1,087, MS-67FB, January 2015; $705, MS-67FB, August 2015; $423, MS-67FB, February 2015									

e. Included in 1960, Proof, mintage figure.

1963, Doubled-Die Reverse
FS-10-1963-805.

1963-D, Doubled-Die Reverse
FS-10-1963D-801.

1963, Doubled-Die Reverse, Proof
FS-10-1963-802. Other varieties exist

	Mintage	Cert	Avg	%MS	EF-40	MS-63	MS-65	MS-66	MS-67	MS-67FB
								PF-65	PF-66	PF-67
1961	93,730,000	1,175	65.9	100%	$2	$3	$5	$12	$35	$1,000
Auctions: $823, MS-67FB, January 2015										
1961, Proof	3,028,244	4,614	67.4					$5	$8	$12
Auctions: $141, PF-69UCam, July 2015; $129, PF-69UCam, October 2015										
1961-D	209,146,550	868	65.9	100%	$2	$3	$5	$12	$25	$700
Auctions: $411, MS-67FB, November 2014; $259, MS-67FB, December 2014; $306, MS-67FB, October 2013; $259, MS-67FB, August 2015										
1962	72,450,000	1,363	65.9	100%	$2	$3	$5	$12	$40	$400
Auctions: $564, MS-67FB, January 2015; $259, MS-67FB, January 2015										
1962, Proof	3,218,019	4,276	67.3					$5	$8	$10
Auctions: $176, PF-69UCam, July 2015; $140, PF-69UCam, September 2015										
1962-D	334,948,380	1,002	66.0	99%	$2	$3	$5	$12	$30	$300
Auctions: $999, MS-67FB, June 2015; $165, MS-67FB, January 2015										
1963	123,650,000	1,129	65.9	99%	$2	$3	$5	$12	$30	$3,000
Auctions: $5,581, MS-67FB, February 2014										
1963, Doubled-Die Reverse (f)	(g)	11	63.3	91%		$25	$38	$90		
Auctions: No auction records available.										
1963, Proof	3,075,645	5,812	67.5					$5	$8	$10
Auctions: $141, PF-69DCam, February 2015; $129, PF-69UCam, July 2015; $46, PF-68UCam, May 2015; $36, PF-68UCam, May 2015										
1963, Doubled-Die Reverse, Proof (h)	(i)	522	66.9					$150	$250	
Auctions: $129, PF-67DCam, December 2014; $100, PF-68, December 2014										
1963-D	421,476,530	1,072	65.8	99%	$2	$3	$5	$12	$30	$1,500
Auctions: $382, MS-67FB, December 2014; $2,115, MS-67FB, September 2013; $115, MS-66FB, November 2014; $42, MS-66FB, January 2015										
1963-D, Doubled-Die Reverse (j)	(k)	14	63.6	93%		$125	$225	$300		
Auctions: $94, MS-66, September 2014										

f. Doubling is evident on UNITED, E PLURIBUS, the olive branch, and the stem. Lesser doubling is also visible on ONE DIME.
g. Included in circulation-strike 1963 mintage figure. **h.** Several less-valuable 1963, Proof, DDRs exist. Values shown are for
FS-10-1963-802. **i.** Included in 1963, Proof, mintage figure. **j.** Doubling is evident on all reverse lettering, with the most obvious
doubling on AMERICA and on the top of the flame. Most MS examples are MS-63 and lower. **k.** Included in 1963-D mintage figure.

1964-D, Doubled-Die Reverse
FS-10-1964D-801. Other varieties exist.

1967, Doubled-Die Obverse
FS-10-1967-101.

1968-S, Doubled-Die Obverse, Proof
FS-10-1968S-102.

1968-S, No Mintmark, Proof
FS-10-1968S-501.

	Mintage	Cert	Avg	%MS	EF-40	MS-63	MS-65	MS-66 / PF-65	MS-67 / PF-66	MS-67FB / PF-67
1964 (l)	929,360,000	1,414	65.7	99%	$2	$3	$5	$12	$30	$500
Auctions: $141, MS-67FB, August 2015; $112, MS-67, October 2015; $79, MS-67, January 2015; $306, MS-65, August 2015										
1964, Proof	3,950,762	11,992	67.8	100%				$5	$8	$10
Auctions: $188, PF-70, October 2015; $100, PF-69DCam, January 2015; $69, PF-69DCam, January 2015										
1964-D (l)	1,357,517,180	1,684	65.7	98%	$2	$3	$5	$12	$50	$400
Auctions: $270, MS-67FB, September 2014; $235, MS-67FB, September 2014; $940, MS-67+, July 2014										
1964-D, Doubled-Die Reverse (m)	(n)	18	57.2	22%	$35	$100	$160	$235	$450	$750
Auctions: $165, MS-64, November 2014; $62, EF-45, November 2014										
1965	1,652,140,570	104	65.8	98%			$2.50	$6	$25	$1,000
Auctions: $1,293, MS-67FB, June 2015; $106, MS-63, May 2015										
1965, Special Mint Set ‡	2,360,000	2,414	67.1					$11	$13	$17
Auctions: $176, PF-67Cam, November 2014										
1966	1,382,734,540	181	66.2	97%			$2.25	$6	$30	$1,000
Auctions: $2,820, MS-68FB, November 2013; $153, MS-68, July 2014; $141, MS-68, July 2014										
1966, Special Mint Set ‡	2,261,583	2,140	67.2					$11	$13	$20
Auctions: $176, PF-68Cam, October 2014										
1967	2,244,007,320	168	64.5	84%			$2	$5	$25	$750
Auctions: No auction records available.										
1967, Doubled-Die Obverse (o)	(p)	0	n/a				$400	$600	$850	
Auctions: No auction records available.										
1967, Special Mint Set ‡	1,863,344	2,571	67.1					$12	$14	$18
Auctions: $2,300, MS-69Cam, March 2010										
1968	424,470,400	189	65.8	99%			$2	$5	$25	$900
Auctions: $382, MS-67FB, September 2014; $236, MS-67FB, December 2014; $1,116, MS-67FB, December 2013										
1968-D	480,748,280	655	66.2	100%			$2	$5	$20	$125
Auctions: $141, AU-58, November 2013										
1968-S, Proof	3,041,506	1,178	67.9					$2	$4	$6
Auctions: $13, PF-70Cam, March 2009										
1968-S, Doubled-Die Obverse, Proof (q)	(r)	12	67.0					$350	$500	$750
Auctions: $74, PF-67, March 2012										
1968-S, No Mintmark, Proof ‡ (s)	(r)	9	67.9					$12,000	$14,500	$16,000
Auctions: $22,325, PF-68, November 2014; $21,150, PF-68, July 2015										

‡ Ranked in the *100 Greatest U.S. Modern Coins.* **l.** The 9 in the date has either a pointed tail or a straight tail. **m.** There are several varieties of 1964-D with a doubled-die reverse. The variety pictured and valued here is FS-10-1964D-801. For more information, see the *Cherrypickers' Guide to Rare Die Varieties,* sixth edition, volume II. **n.** Included in 1964-D mintage figure. **o.** This is a very rare doubled die. Its doubling is evident on IN GOD WE TRUST, the date, and the designer's initials. **p.** Included in circulation-strike 1967 mintage figure. **q.** There are several 1968-S, Proof, doubled-die obverse varieties. The one listed here is FS-10-1968S-102 (see the *Cherrypickers' Guide to Rare Die Varieties,* sixth edition, volume II). **r.** Included in 1968-S, Proof, mintage figure. **s.** The S mintmark was inadvertently left off the coinage die; this defect was probably discovered before the end of the die's life.

1970, Doubled-Die Reverse
FS-10-1970-801.

	Mintage	Cert	Avg	%MS	EF-40	MS-63	MS-65	MS-66 / PF-65	MS-67 / PF-66	MS-67FB / PF-67
1969	145,790,000	90	65.1	99%			$3	$6	$30	
Auctions: $176, MS-66FB, December 2014; $470, MS-67, April 2014										
1969-D	563,323,870	760	66.0	100%			$2	$6	$25	$1,000
Auctions: $17, MS-64, August 2013										
1969-S, Proof	2,394,631	995	68.1					$2	$4	$6
Auctions: $206, PF-69DCam, October 2009										
1970	345,570,000	152	64.4	96%			$2	$6	$35	
Auctions: $52, MS-67, October 2014; $55, MS-66, June 2014										
1970, Doubled-Die Reverse (t)	(u)	4	62.3	75%			$300	$650	$1,000	
Auctions: $56, MS-65, June 2009										
1970-D	754,942,100	502	65.1	99%			$2	$5	$35	
Auctions: $16, MS-65FB, November 2014; $200, MS-61, January 2014										
1970-S, Proof	2,632,810	1,068	67.7	100%				$2	$4	$6
Auctions: $17, PF-70DCam, August 2009										
1970-S, No Mintmark, Proof ‡ (s)	(v)	168	67.6					$800	$900	$1,000
Auctions: $1,293, PF-68Cam, September 2015; $646, PF-68Cam, September 2015; $541, PF-67, January 2015; $517, PF-67, July 2015										
1971	162,690,000	68	64.9	100%			$2.50	$6	$40	
Auctions: $276, MS-66FB, January 2012										
1971-D	377,914,240	140	65.7	100%			$2.25	$6	$40	$700
Auctions: $109, MS-67FB, April 2012										
1971-S, Proof	3,220,733	1,263	68.1					$2	$4	$6
Auctions: $15, PF-68DCam, August 2009										
1972	431,540,000	90	65.0	99%			$2	$6	$60	
Auctions: $79, MS-67, November 2014										
1972-D	330,290,000	173	65.7	100%			$2	$6	$40	$800
Auctions: $141, MS-67FB, December 2014										
1972-S, Proof	3,260,996	1,139	68.0					$2	$4	$6
Auctions: $127, PF-70DCam, October 2009										
1973	315,670,000	85	65.2	100%			$2	$5	$70	$1,200
Auctions: $59, MS-67, November 2014										
1973-D	455,032,426	140	65.4	100%			$2	$6	$50	$500
Auctions: $84, MS-67FB, December 2014										
1973-S, Proof	2,760,339	416	67.7					$2	$4	$6
Auctions: $489, PF-70DCam, October 2009										
1974	470,248,000	52	65.0	100%			$2	$5	$25	
Auctions: $52, MS-67, March 2004										
1974-D	571,083,000	105	65.4	100%			$2	$5	$25	$1,000
Auctions: $51, MS-67, October 2007										
1974-S, Proof	2,612,568	350	67.9					$2	$4	$6
Auctions: $69, PF-70DCam, October 2009										

‡ Ranked in the *100 Greatest U.S. Modern Coins*. **s.** The S mintmark was inadvertently left off the coinage die; this defect was probably discovered before the end of the die's life. **t.** Doubling on this extremely rare variety is evident on all reverse lettering, especially on UNITED STATES OF AMERICA, with slightly weaker doubling on ONE DIME. **u.** Included in circulation-strike 1970 mintage figure. **v.** Included in 1970-S, Proof, mintage figure.

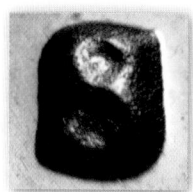

**1979-S, Filled S
(Type 1), Proof**

**1979-S, Clear S
(Type 2), Proof**

	Mintage	Cert	Avg	%MS	EF-40	MS-63	MS-65	MS-66 / PF-65	MS-67 / PF-66	MS-67FB / PF-67
1975	585,673,900	116	65.3	99%			$2	$5	$25	$1,000
Auctions: $112, MS-66FB, November 2014										
1975-D	313,705,300	186	66.2	99%			$2	$5	$30	$600
Auctions: $270, MS-68, July 2014; $84, MS-67FB, December 2014; $423, MS-67FB, August 2015										
1975-S, Proof	2,845,450	508	68.0					$2.50	$4	$6
Auctions: $1,610, PF-70DCam, January 2010										
1975-S, No Mintmark, Proof (s)	(w)	0	n/a					$38,000	$40,000	$45,000
Auctions: $349,600, PF-68, August 2011										
1976	568,760,000	127	66.1	100%			$2	$5	$25	$1,200
Auctions: $1,035, MS-68, January 2012										
1976-D	695,222,774	128	65.7	97%			$2	$5	$45	$1,200
Auctions: $100, MS-67FB, December 2014										
1976-S, Proof	4,149,730	837	68.1					$2.75	$4	$6
Auctions: $30, PF-70Dcam, December 2009										
1977	796,930,000	177	65.9	100%			$2	$5	$25	$1,200
Auctions: $64, MS-66FB, October 2008										
1977-D	376,607,228	105	65.6	100%			$2	$5	$25	$1,200
Auctions: $64, MS-65FB, December 2007										
1977-S, Proof	3,251,152	785	68.5					$2.50	$4	$6
Auctions: $69, PF-70DCam, January 2010										
1978	663,980,000	79	65.7	99%			$2	$5	$30	$1,200
Auctions: $17, MS-65, August 2008										
1978-D	282,847,540	73	65.8	100%			$2	$5	$25	
Auctions: $100, MS-66FB, December 2014										
1978-S, Proof	3,127,781	707	68.9					$2.50	$4	$6
Auctions: $104, PF-70DCam, February 2010										
1979	315,440,000	136	65.8	100%			$2	$5	$30	
Auctions: $21, MS-66, December 2007										
1979-D	390,921,184	113	65.7	100%			$2	$5	$30	
Auctions: $28, MS-67, December 2004										
1979-S, Type 1, Proof	3,677,175	854	69.0					$2.50	$4	$6
Auctions: $74, PF-70DCam, January 2010										
1979-S, Type 2, Proof	(x)	1,020	69.2					$5	$6	$8
Auctions: $58, PF-70DCam, August 2014; $50, PF-70DCam, February 2015										
1980-P	735,170,000	128	65.8	99%			$2	$5	$25	
Auctions: $26, MS-67, March 2004										
1980-D	719,354,321	84	65.8	100%			$2	$5	$30	
Auctions: $13, MS-66, February 2008										
1980-S, Proof	3,554,806	1,071	68.5					$2.50	$4	$6
Auctions: $40, PF-70DCam, October 2009										

s. The S mintmark was inadvertently left off the coinage die; this defect was probably discovered before the end of the die's life.
w. Included in 1975-S, Proof, mintage figure. **x.** Included in 1979-S, Type 1, Proof, mintage figure.

1981-S, Rounded S (Type 1), Proof

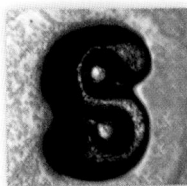

1981-S, Flat S (Type 2), Proof

1982, No Mintmark, Strong Strike
FS-10-1982-501.

1982, No Mintmark, Weak Strike
FS-10-1982-502.

	Mintage	Cert	Avg	%MS	EF-40	MS-63	MS-65	MS-66	MS-67	MS-67FB
								PF-65	PF-66	PF-67
1981-P	676,650,000	192	66.0	99%			$2	$5	$40	$70
Auctions: $329, MS-68FB, December 2014; $129, MS-65, January 2013										
1981-D	712,284,143	305	66.5	100%			$2	$5	$20	$80
Auctions: $123, MS-68FB, December 2014										
1981-S, Type 1, Proof	4,063,083	1,225	68.8					$2.50	$4	$6
Auctions: $56, PF-70DCam, December 2009										
1981-S, Type 2, Proof	(y)	620	69.0					$5.50	$6	$8
Auctions: $159, PF-70DCam, August 2014										
1982, No Mintmark, Strong Strike ‡ (z)	(aa)	55	65.3	100%			$150	$300	$650	$1,800
Auctions: $282, MS-66, February 2015; $259, MS-66, July 2015; $188, MS-65, October 2015; $123, MS-64, May 2015										
1982, No Mintmark, Weak Strike ‡ (z)	(aa)	406	64.2	92%			$85	$130	$300	
Auctions: No auction records available.										
1982-P	519,475,000	187	66.2	98%			$7.50	$18	$50	$1,000
Auctions: $153, MS-67FB, December 2014; $56, MS-67, November 2014										
1982-D	542,713,584	122	65.9	98%			$2.50	$6	$25	$700
Auctions: $1,410, MS-67FB, April 2014; $118, MS-67FB, December 2014										
1982-S, Proof	3,857,479	748	69.0					$2.50	$4	$6
Auctions: $74, PF-70DCam, December 2009										
1983-P	647,025,000	114	65.8	96%			$6.50	$15	$30	$250
Auctions: $489, MS-68, April 2012										
1983-D	730,129,224	50	65.8	96%			$3.25	$8.50	$25	$200
Auctions: $223, MS-68, November 2014; $188, MS-68, December 2013										
1983-S, Proof	3,279,126	829	69.2					$3	$4	$6
Auctions: $150, PF-70DCam, December 2009										
1983-S, No Mintmark, Proof (s) ‡	(bb)	145	68.8					$750	$850	$1,000
Auctions: $764, PF-69DCam, September 2015; $676, PF-69UCam, October 2015; $646, PF-68DCam, September 2015										
1984-P	856,669,000	144	66.5	100%			$2	$5	$20	$100
Auctions: $212, MS-68FB, December 2014										
1984-D	704,803,976	104	65.4	100%			$2.25	$5	$20	$150
Auctions: $94, MS-67FB, May 2012										
1984-S, Proof	3,065,110	556	69.1					$2.50	$4	$6
Auctions: $106, PF-70DCam, March 2013										
1985-P	705,200,962	114	66.5	100%			$2.25	$5	$25	$150
Auctions: $66, MS-67FB, November 2014; $64, MS-67FB, August 2015										
1985-D	587,979,970	177	66.8	100%			$2.25	$5	$30	$100
Auctions: $129, MS-68FB, December 2014										
1985-S, Proof	3,362,821	622	69.1					$3	$4	$6
Auctions: $16, PF-69DCam, August 2009										

‡ Ranked in the *100 Greatest U.S. Modern Coins*. **s.** The S mintmark was inadvertently left off the coinage die; this defect was probably discovered before the end of the die's life. **y.** Included in 1981-S, Type 1, Proof, mintage figure. **z.** The P mintmark was omitted from this working die. There are two versions of this variety: one with a strong strike, and one with a weak strike. The strong strike is far more valuable and in demand than the weak. **aa.** Included in 1982-P mintage figure. **bb.** Included in 1983-S, Proof, mintage figure.

	Mintage	Cert	Avg	%MS	EF-40	MS-63	MS-65	MS-66 PF-65	MS-67 PF-66	MS-67FB PF-67
1986-P	682,649,693	160	65.9	99%			$2.50	$5	$20	$800
Auctions: $89, MS-67FB, December 2014										
1986-D	473,326,970	170	66.3	99%			$2.50	$5	$20	$700
Auctions: $999, MS-67FB, August 2015; $123, MS-67FB, December 2014										
1986-S, Proof	3,010,497	465	69.1					$4	$5	$7
Auctions: $48, PF-70DCam, April 2013										
1987-P	762,709,481	122	66.3	99%			$2	$5	$25	$800
Auctions: $259, MS-67FB, December 2014										
1987-D	653,203,402	148	66.1	99%			$2	$5	$20	$200
Auctions: $382, MS-67FB, December 2014										
1987-S, Proof	4,227,728	624	69.1					$3	$4	$6
Auctions: $15, PF-69DCam, August 2009										
1988-P	1,030,550,000	128	65.8	96%			$2	$5	$35	$225
Auctions: $103, MS-64, July 2014										
1988-D	962,385,489	144	66.3	99%			$2	$5	$40	$100
Auctions: $165, MS-68FB, December 2014										
1988-S, Proof	3,262,948	432	69.1					$4	$5	$7
Auctions: $60, PF-70DCam, May 2013										
1989-P	1,298,400,000	130	66.1	99%			$2	$5	$20	$100
Auctions: $106, MS-68FB, December 2014; $45, MS-65, July 2014; $129, MS-63, January 2015										
1989-D	896,535,597	181	66.4	99%			$2	$6	$20	$75
Auctions: $242, MS-68FB, April 2012										
1989-S, Proof	3,220,194	451	69.1					$4	$5	$6
Auctions: $15, PF-69DCam, August 2009										
1990-P	1,034,340,000	72	66.0	97%			$2	$6	$20	$1,000
Auctions: $27, MS-67, March 2004										
1990-D	839,995,824	95	66.2	98%			$2	$4	$25	$1,100
Auctions: $12, MS-67, March 2004										
1990-S, Proof	3,299,559	646	69.3					$2.50	$4	$6
Auctions: $56, PF-70DCam, December 2009										
1991-P	927,220,000	58	66.3	98%			$2	$4	$20	$100
Auctions: $27, MS-67, March 2004										
1991-D	601,241,114	68	65.8	100%			$2	$4	$20	$200
Auctions: $127, MS-67, May 2012										
1991-S, Proof	2,867,787	656	69.4					$4	$5	$7
Auctions: $31, PF-70DCam, June 2014										
1992-P	593,500,000	75	67.0	100%			$2	$5	$35	$150
Auctions: $322, MS-67FB, May 2010										
1992-D	616,273,932	66	66.2	100%			$2	$4	$30	$200
Auctions: $99, MS-67FB, April 2012										
1992-S, Proof	2,858,981	485	69.5					$3	$4	$6
Auctions: $53, PF-70DCam, December 2009										
1992-S, Proof, Silver	1,317,579	1,285	69.2					$6	$7	$8
Auctions: $36, PF-70DCam, October 2014										
1993-P	766,180,000	113	66.4	97%			$2	$4	$30	$250
Auctions: $53, MS-67FB, April 2012										
1993-D	750,110,166	79	65.9	100%			$2	$4	$25	$500
Auctions: $15, MS-66FB, October 2008										
1993-S, Proof	2,633,439	510	69.4					$5	$6	$7
Auctions: $62, PF-70DCam, December 2009										
1993-S, Proof, Silver	761,353	1,043	69.2					$7	$8	$9
Auctions: $94, PF-70DCam, February 2010										

	Mintage	Cert	Avg	%MS	EF-40	MS-63	MS-65	MS-66	MS-67	MS-67FB
								PF-65	PF-66	PF-67
1994-P	1,189,000,000	106	66.5	97%			$2	$4	$25	$200
	Auctions: $76, MS-67FB, June 2014									
1994-D	1,303,268,110	58	65.5	98%			$2	$4	$25	$300
	Auctions: $130, MS-64, July 2014; $79, MS-64, August 2015									
1994-S, Proof	2,484,594	443	69.5					$5	$6	$8
	Auctions: $59, PF-70DCam, October 2009									
1994-S, Proof, Silver	785,329	971	69.2					$8	$9	$10
	Auctions: $96, PF-70DCam, May 2013									
1995-P	1,125,500,000	66	66.9	100%			$2	$4	$30	$500
	Auctions: $21, MS-66FB, August 2009									
1995-D	1,274,890,000	84	66.1	98%			$2	$5	$35	$425
	Auctions: $259, MS-67FB, December 2014; $18, MS-65FB, November 2014									
1995-S, Proof	2,117,496	413	69.5					$10	$16	$20
	Auctions: $84, PF-70DCam, December 2009									
1995-S, Proof, Silver	679,985	1,070	69.1					$14	$23	$30
	Auctions: $100, PF-70DCam, May 2013									
1996-P	1,421,163,000	152	66.7	98%			$2	$4	$25	$30
	Auctions: $66, MS-65, July 2015; $50, MS-65, August 2015									
1996-D	1,400,300,000	186	66.2	99%			$2	$4	$20	$75
	Auctions: $11, MS-67FB, October 2008									
1996W ‡ (cc)	1,457,000	5,094	66.5	100%		$20	$30	$50	$100
	Auctions: $282, MS-68FB, April 2014; $62, MS-68, September 2015; $42, MS-67, October 2014									
1996-S, Proof	1,750,244	438	69.4					$3	$6	$8
	Auctions: $42, PF-70DCam, February 2010									
1996-S, Proof, Silver	775,021	994	69.1					$8	$10	$15
	Auctions: $88, PF-70DCam, May 2013									
1997-P	991,640,000	66	66.6	98%			$2	$6	$60	$100
	Auctions: $26, MS-67FB, November 2014									
1997-D	979,810,000	72	66.1	99%			$2	$6	$65	$100
	Auctions: $11, MS-65FB, October 2008									
1997-S, Proof	2,055,000	345	69.6					$8	$10	$15
	Auctions: $69, PF-70DCam, December 2009									
1997-S, Proof, Silver	741,678	1,084	69.2					$12	$22	$24
	Auctions: $46, PF-70DCam, May 2013									
1998-P	1,163,000,000	78	66.8	99%			$2	$3	$18	$100
	Auctions: $11, MS-66FB, September 2008									
1998-D	1,172,250,000	71	66.0	99%			$2	$3	$15	$100
	Auctions: $118, MS-67FB, December 2014									
1998-S, Proof	2,086,507	324	69.5					$4	$6	$8
	Auctions: $17, PF-69DCam, August 2009									
1998-S, Proof, Silver	878,792	1,182	69.3					$6	$8	$10
	Auctions: $79, PF-70DCam, February 2010									
1999-P	2,164,000,000	121	66.8	98%			$2	$3	$15	$30
	Auctions: $3,055, MS-64, January 2014; $36, MS-64, July 2014; $30, MS-64, August 2015; $38, MS-63, November 2014									
1999-D	1,397,750,000	110	66.4	99%			$2	$3	$15	$40
	Auctions: $1,610, MS-69FB, April 2010									
1999-S, Proof	2,543,401	2,371	69.2					$4	$6	$8
	Auctions: $67, PF-70DCam, January 2010									
1999-S, Proof, Silver	804,565	3,688	69.2					$7	$8	$12
	Auctions: $76, PF-70DCam, May 2013									

‡ Ranked in the *100 Greatest U.S. Modern Coins.* **cc.** Issued in Mint sets only, to mark the 50th anniversary of the design.

	Mintage	Cert	Avg	%MS	EF-40	MS-63	MS-65	MS-66 / PF-65	MS-67 / PF-66	MS-67FB / PF-67
2000-P	1,842,500,000	58	65.3	88%			$2	$3	$15	$30
Auctions: $66, MS-65, July 2014; $26, MS-64, July 2014; $823, MS-64, June 2013; $45, MS-63, July 2014										
2000-D	1,818,700,000	76	66.3	96%			$2	$3	$15	$30
Auctions: $11, MS-68FB, September 2008										
2000-S, Proof	3,082,572	1,398	69.2					$2.50	$4	$7
Auctions: $59, PF-70DCam, December 2009										
2000-S, Proof, Silver	965,421	4,300	69.3					$5	$6	$8
Auctions: $28, PF-70DCam, April 2013										
2001-P	1,369,590,000	56	66.5	100%			$2	$3	$12	$30
Auctions: $79, MS-64, November 2014										
2001-D	1,412,800,000	69	66.2	94%			$2	$3	$12	$30
Auctions: No auction records available.										
2001-S, Proof	2,294,909	1,132	69.4					$2.50	$4	$7
Auctions: $50, PF-70DCam, December 2009										
2001-S, Proof, Silver	889,697	3,747	69.4					$5	$6	$8
Auctions: $36, PF-70UCam, February 2010										
2002-P	1,187,500,000	33	66.6	97%			$2	$3	$12	$30
Auctions: $11, MS-68FB, September 2008										
2002-D	1,379,500,000	39	66.4	97%			$2	$3	$12	$30
Auctions: $14, MS-68FB, October 2008										
2002-S, Proof	2,319,766	1,575	69.3					$2.50	$4	$7
Auctions: $44, PF-70DCam, December 2009										
2002-S, Proof, Silver	892,229	3,548	69.4					$5	$6	$8
Auctions: $42, PF-70UCam, March 2010										
2003-P	1,085,500,000	140	66.0	100%			$2	$3	$10	$30
Auctions: $11, MS-68FB, October 2008										
2003-D	986,500,000	99	65.7	100%			$2	$3	$10	$30
Auctions: $11, MS-68FB, September 2008										
2003-S, Proof	2,172,684	3,515	69.3					$2.50	$4	$7
Auctions: $52, PF-70DCam, March 2010										
2003-S, Proof, Silver	1,125,755	4,524	69.3					$4.50	$5	$8
Auctions: $38, PF-70UCam, March 2010										
2004-P	1,328,000,000	112	66.6	100%			$2	$3	$8	$30
Auctions: $94, MS-68FB, December 2014										
2004-D	1,159,500,000	72	66.8	100%			$2	$3	$8	$35
Auctions: $21, MS-68FB, October 2008										
2004-S, Proof	1,789,488	1,424	69.3					$3	$5	$7
Auctions: $69, PF-70DCam, October 2009										
2004-S, Proof, Silver	1,175,934	4,445	69.5					$5	$6	$8
Auctions: $40, PF-70DCam, November 2013										
2005-P	1,412,000,000	42	67.0	100%			$2	$3	$8	$65
Auctions: $129, MS-67FB, December 2014; $74, MS-67FB, November 2014										
2005-P, Satin Finish	1,160,000	101	68.3	100%	$1	$2	$3			
Auctions: No auction records available.										
2005-D	1,423,500,000	95	66.1	99%			$2	$3	$8	$80
Auctions: $47, MS-67FB, November 2014; $106, MS-67FB, December 2014										
2005-D, Satin Finish	1,160,000	2,292	66.9	100%	$1	$2	$3			
Auctions: No auction records available.										
2005-S, Proof	2,275,000	6,088	69.3					$2.50	$4	$7
Auctions: $40, PF-70DCam, December 2009										

	Mintage	Cert	Avg	%MS	EF-40	MS-63	MS-65	MS-66	MS-67	MS-67FB
								PF-65	PF-66	PF-67
2005-S, Proof, Silver	1,069,679	5,465	69.5					$5	$6	$8
Auctions: $40, PF-70DCam, November 2013										
2006-P	1,381,000,000	110	65.8	99%			$2	$3	$6	$22
Auctions: $94, MS-67FB, December 2014										
2006-P, Satin Finish	847,361	1,180	66.9	100%	$1	$2	$3			
Auctions: No auction records available.										
2006-D	1,447,000,000	96	66.1	100%			$2	$3	$6	$22
Auctions: No auction records available.										
2006-D, Satin Finish	847,361	1,135	66.8	100%	$1	$2	$3			
Auctions: $16, MS-69FB Satin, September 2008										
2006-S, Proof	2,000,428	1,980	69.4					$2.50	$4	$7
Auctions: $69, PF-70DCam, October 2009										
2006-S, Proof, Silver	1,054,008	2,977	69.5					$5	$6	$8
Auctions: $56, PF-70UCam, February 2010										
2007-P	1,047,500,000	20	66.3	100%			$2	$3	$6	$22
Auctions: $59, MS-67FB, December 2014; $223, MS-64, June 2013										
2007-P, Satin Finish	895,628	199	66.4	100%	$1	$2	$3			
Auctions: No auction records available.										
2007-D	1,042,000,000	178	66.2	100%			$2	$3	$6	$22
Auctions: $53, MS-67FB, December 2014										
2007-D, Satin Finish	895,628	226	66.6	100%	$1	$2	$3			
Auctions: No auction records available.										
2007-S, Proof	1,702,116	1,669	69.6					$2.50	$4	$7
Auctions: $40, PF-70DCam, December 2009										
2007-S, Proof, Silver	875,050	3,476	69.6					$5	$6	$8
Auctions: $26, PF-69DCam, February 2013										
2008-P	391,000,000	20	66.0	100%			$2	$3	$5	$22
Auctions: $188, MS-67FB, December 2014; $100, MS-66FB, November 2014										
2008-P, Satin Finish	745,464	66	67.8	100%	$1	$2	$3			
Auctions: No auction records available.										
2008-D	624,500,000	95	66.2	100%			$2	$3	$5	$22
Auctions: No auction records available.										
2008-D, Satin Finish	745,464	84	68.2	100%	$1	$2	$3			
Auctions: No auction records available.										
2008-S, Proof	1,405,674	1,303	69.7					$2.50	$4	$7
Auctions: $56, PF-70DCam, October 2009										
2008-S, Proof, Silver	763,887	3,758	69.8					$5	$6	$8
Auctions: $36, PF-70UCam, March 2010										
2009-P	96,500,000	254	65.7	100%			$2	$3	$5	$22
Auctions: No auction records available.										
2009-P, Satin Finish	784,614	111	67.7	100%	$1	$2	$3			
Auctions: No auction records available.										
2009-D	49,500,000	156	66.0	100%			$2	$3	$5	$22
Auctions: No auction records available.										
2009-D, Satin Finish	784,614	171	68.4	100%	$1	$2	$3			
Auctions: No auction records available.										
2009-S, Proof	1,482,502	3,350	69.6					$2.50	$4	$7
Auctions: $23, PF-69DCam, February 2013										
2009-S, Proof, Silver	697,365	3,888	69.7					$5	$6	$8
Auctions: $40, PF-70UCam, March 2010										

	Mintage	Cert	Avg	%MS	EF-40	MS-63	MS-65	MS-66 PF-65	MS-67 PF-66	MS-67FB PF-67
2010-P	557,000,000	128	66.6	100%			$2	$3	$4	$20
Auctions: $259, MS-68FB, August 2015; $65, MS-68FB, December 2014;										
2010-P, Satin Finish	583,897	99	68.2	100%	$1	$2	$3			
Auctions: No auction records available.										
2010-D	562,000,000	107	66.2	100%			$2	$3	$4	$20
Auctions: $44, MS-67FB, December 2014										
2010-D, Satin Finish	583,897	96	68.4	100%	$1	$2	$3			
Auctions: No auction records available.										
2010-S, Proof	1,103,815	1,357	69.5					$2.50	$4	$7
Auctions: No auction records available.										
2010-S, Proof, Silver	585,401	3,777	69.7					$5	$6	$8
Auctions: No auction records available.										
2011-P	748,000,000	197	67.3	100%			$2	$3	$4	$20
Auctions: $84, MS-69FB, December 2014										
2011-D	754,000,000	197	67.1	100%			$2	$3	$4	$20
Auctions: No auction records available.										
2011-S, Proof	1,098,835	2,327	69.5					$2.50	$4	$7
Auctions: No auction records available.										
2011-S, Proof, Silver	574,175	4,723	69.7					$5	$6	$8
Auctions: No auction records available.										
2012-P	808,000,000	93	67.0	100%			$2	$3	$4	$20
Auctions: $499, MS-69FB, December 2014; $564, MS-60, July 2015										
2012-D	868,000,000	99	66.8	100%			$2	$3	$4	$20
Auctions: No auction records available.										
2012-S, Proof	841,972	1,375	69.5					$2.50	$4	$7
Auctions: No auction records available.										
2012-S, Proof, Silver	395,443	1,556	69.8					$5	$6	$8
Auctions: No auction records available.										
2013-P	1,086,500,000	85	66.8	100%			$2	$3	$4	$20
Auctions: No auction records available.										
2013-D	1,025,500,000	112	67.1	100%			$2	$3	$4	$20
Auctions: No auction records available.										
2013-S, Proof	802,460	1,737	69.6					$2.50	$4	$7
Auctions: No auction records available.										
2013-S, Proof, Silver	419,719	0	n/a					$5	$6	$8
Auctions: No auction records available.										
2014-P	1,125,500,000	132	67.3	100%			$2	$3	$4	$20
Auctions: No auction records available.										
2014-D	1,177,000,000	0	n/a				$2	$3	$4	$20
Auctions: No auction records available.										
2014-S, Proof	665,100	1,367	69.5					$2.50	$4	$7
Auctions: No auction records available.										
2014-S, Proof, Silver	393,037	2,829	69.8					$5	$6	$8
Auctions: No auction records available.										
2015-P	1,497,510,000						$2	$3	$4	$20
Auctions: No auction records available.										
2015-D	1,543,500,000						$2	$3	$4	$20
Auctions: No auction records available.										
2015-S, Proof	669,960							$2.50	$4	$7
Auctions: No auction records available.										

	Mintage	Cert	Avg	%MS	EF-40	MS-63	MS-65	MS-66	MS-67	MS-67FB
								PF-65	PF-66	PF-67
2015-S, Proof, Silver	352,450							$5	$6	$8
Auctions: No auction records available.										
2015-W, Proof, Silver	74,430	5,993	69.5					$15	$25	$40
Auctions: No auction records available.										
2015-P, Reverse Proof, Silver	74,430	6,269	69.5					$20	$30	$50
Auctions: No auction records available.										
2016-P							$2	$3	$4	$20
Auctions: No auction records available.										
2016-D							$2	$3	$4	$20
Auctions: No auction records available.										
2016-S, Proof								$2.50	$4	$7
Auctions: No auction records available.										
2016-S, Proof, Silver								$5	$6	$8
Auctions: No auction records available.										

Twenty-Cent Pieces
1875–1878

AN OVERVIEW OF TWENTY-CENT PIECES

The twenty-cent piece, made in silver, proved to be the shortest-lived denomination in American coinage history. The coins were struck in quantity in their first year of issue, 1875, after which it was learned that the public confused them with quarter dollars. Mintages dropped sharply, and in 1877 and 1878 coinage was limited to just Proofs for collectors.

Both sides of the twenty-cent piece were designed by U.S. Mint chief engraver William Barber. The obverse is simply an adaptation of the Liberty Seated motif earlier used on other denominations. The reverse is new and depicts a perched eagle (of the same general appearance as introduced by Barber on the 1873 silver trade dollar).

Only one twenty-cent piece is needed for inclusion in a type set. By far the most readily available in Mint State is the 1875-S, followed by the 1875-CC. These are often somewhat lightly struck on the reverse, particularly near the top of the eagle's wings. The 1875 and 1876 Philadelphia coins are occasionally encountered in Mint State and are usually well struck.

Proofs are readily available for all years, 1875 through 1878.

Senator John P. Jones was involved with the minting of the twenty-cent piece silver coin.

FOR THE COLLECTOR AND INVESTOR: TWENTY-CENT PIECES AS A SPECIALTY

A full date-and-mintmark set of twenty-cent pieces consists of the 1875, 1875-CC, 1875-S, 1876, 1876-CC, 1877, and 1878, the latter two years being available only in Proof format. The great challenge in forming a set is the 1876-CC, of which 10,000 were minted, but, seemingly, all but about two dozen were melted. Those that do survive are typically encountered in Mint State and are widely heralded when they are offered at auction.

LIBERTY SEATED (1875–1878)

Designer: *William Barber.* **Weight:** *5 grams.* **Composition:** *.900 silver, .100 copper.*
Diameter: *22 mm.* **Edge:** *Plain.* **Mints:** *Philadelphia, Carson City, and San Francisco.*

Circulation Strike

*Mintmark location
is on the reverse,
below the eagle.*

Proof

History. The twenty-cent coin debuted in 1875 as a convenient denomination to make change in the West (at the time silver coins did not circulate in the East or Midwest). The coins sometimes were confused with quarter dollars, given their similar Liberty Seated design on the obverse, and their similar size. The quantity minted dropped considerably in 1876, and in 1877 and 1878 only Proofs were struck. Despite the brief time of their production, these coins were still seen in circulation through the early 1900s, by which time they were often casually used as quarters. Proof coins were made of all years 1875 to 1878.

Striking and Sharpness. Areas of weakness are common. On the obverse, check the head of Miss Liberty and the stars. The word LIBERTY is *raised* on this coin, a curious departure from other Liberty Seated coins of the era, on which it is recessed or incuse (the Gobrecht silver dollars of 1836 and 1839 being exceptions). On the reverse, check the eagle's feathers, especially the top of the wing on the left, but other areas can be weak as well. Some 1875-S coins are highly prooflike. The 1877 and 1878 are Proof-only issues with no related circulation strikes. Most have been cleaned or even lightly polished. Many Proofs in the marketplace have been convincingly retoned to mask problems. Proofs are usually well struck, but more than just a few are somewhat flat on the hair details of Miss Liberty.

Availability. Most often seen is the high-mintage 1875-S, although the 1875 and 1875-CC are encountered with frequency. The 1876 is quite scarce and when seen is usually in high grades and well struck. The 1876-CC is a rarity, and only about two dozen are known, nearly all of which are MS. The eye appeal of MS coins can vary widely. The number of letters in LIBERTY on certain coins graded from VG through VF can vary widely in the marketplace. Proofs most often seen are those of 1875 and 1876. For some unexplained reason, high-quality Proofs of the series' final two years are very hard to find.

GRADING STANDARDS

MS-60 to 70 (Mint State). *Obverse:* At MS-60, some abrasion and contact marks are evident, most noticeably on the bosom and thighs and knees. Luster is present, but may be dull or lifeless. At MS-63, contact marks are very few, and abrasion is hard to detect except under magnification. An MS-65 coin has no abrasion, and contact marks are sufficiently minute as to require magnification. Check the knees of Liberty and the right field.

1875; BF-1. Graded MS-64.

Luster should be full and rich. *Reverse:* Comments apply as for the obverse, except that in lower–Mint State grades abrasion and contact marks are most noticeable on the eagle's breast and the top of the wing to the left. At MS-65 or higher, there are no marks visible to the unaided eye. The field is mainly protected by design elements and does not show abrasion as much as does the obverse on a given coin.

Illustrated coin: Semi-Proof surfaces contrast nicely against the frosted devices of this well-struck piece.

AU-50, 53, 55, 58 (About Uncirculated). *Obverse:* Light wear is seen on the thighs and knees, bosom, and head. At AU-58, the luster is extensive but incomplete, especially in the right field. At AU–50 and 53, luster is less. *Reverse:* Very light wear is evident on the eagle's breast (the prime focal point) and at the top of the wings. An AU-58 coin will have nearly full luster, more so than on the obverse, as the design elements protect the small field areas. At AU–50 and 53, there still are traces of luster.

1875-CC. Graded AU-55.

EF-40, 45 (Extremely Fine). *Obverse:* Further wear is seen on all areas, especially the thighs and knees, bosom, and head. Little or no luster is seen on most coins. From this grade downward, sharpness of strike of the stars and the head does not matter to connoisseurs. *Reverse:* More wear is evident on the eagle's breast and the top of the wings. Some feathers may be blended together, but most details are defined.

1875-S. Graded EF-45.

VF-20, 30 (Very Fine). *Obverse:* Further wear is seen. Most details of the gown are worn away, except in the lower-relief areas above and to the right of the shield. Hair detail is mostly or completely gone. As to whether LIBERTY should be completely readable, this seems to be a matter of debate. On many coins in the marketplace the word is weak or missing one to several letters. ANA grading standards and PCGS require full

1875-S. Graded VF-30.

LIBERTY. *Reverse:* Wear is more extensive, but at least three-quarters of the feathers in the breast and wings are distinct. At VF-30 the head is flat with distinct details; head details are less distinct at VF-20.

F-12, 15 (Fine). *Obverse:* The seated figure is well worn, but with some detail above and to the right of the shield. LIBERTY has at least three letters visible (per ANA grading standards). In the marketplace, some have more letters missing. *Reverse:* Wear is extensive, with about half of the feathers flat or blended with others and head details are indistinct except for the eye.

1875-CC. Graded F-15.

VG-8, 10 (Very Good). *Obverse:* The seated figure is more worn, but some detail can be seen above and to the right of the shield. The shield is discernible. In LIBERTY a letter or two may be visible per ANA grading standards. In the marketplace, many have no letters. *Reverse:* Further wear has flattened about half of the feathers. Those remaining are on the inside of the wings. The rim is full and shows many if not most denticles.

1875-S. Graded VG-10.

G-4, 6 (Good). *Obverse:* The seated figure is worn nearly smooth, but with some slight detail above and to the right of the shield. At G-4, there are no letters in LIBERTY remaining. On some at the G-6 level, there may be a trace of letters. *Reverse:* Most feathers in the eagle are gone. The border lettering is weak. The rim is visible partially or completely (depending on the strike).

1875-CC. Graded G-6.

AG-3 (About Good). *Obverse:* The seated figure is mostly visible in outline form, with only a hint of detail. Much of the rim is worn away. The date remains clear. *Reverse:* The border letters are partially worn away. The eagle is mostly in outline form, but with a few details discernible. The rim is weak or missing.

1875-CC. Graded AG-3.

PF-60 to 70 (Proof). *Obverse and Reverse:* Proofs that are extensively cleaned and have many hairlines, or that are dull and grainy, are lower level, such as PF–60 to 62. These are not widely desired. With medium hairlines and good reflectivity, an assigned grade of PF-64 is indicated, and with relatively few hairlines, Gem PF-65. In various grades hairlines are most easily seen in the obverse field. PF-66 should have hairlines so delicate that

1877. Graded PF-61.

magnification is needed to see them. Above that, a Proof should be free of such lines.

Illustrated coin: Lovely frosted devices are complemented by indigo toning in the peripheries of the fields.

	Mintage	Cert	Avg	%MS	G-4	VG-8	F-12	VF-20	EF-40	AU-50	MS-60	MS-63	MS-65
											PF-60	PF-63	PF-65
1875	38,500	484	53.6	50%	$235	$270	$350	$420	$550	$700	$900	$1,600	$5,500
	Auctions: $1,292, MS-64, August 2015; $940, MS-62, July 2015; $881, MS-61, January 2015; $352, AU-50, February 2015												
1875, Proof	1,200	255	63.5								$1,500	$3,000	$8,500
	Auctions: $7,050, PF-65, August 2015; $4,465, PF-64Cam, July 2015; $3,995, PF-64, January 2015; $2,585, PF-63Cam, October 2015												
1875-CC	133,290	968	39.1	32%	$400	$450	$550	$750	$1,100	$1,800	$2,250	$3,500	$10,500
	Auctions: $7,050, MS-65, August 2015; $2,820, MS-62, January 2015; $2,056, MS-62, September 2015; $1,116, AU-55, June 2015												
1875-S (a)	1,155,000	3,162	49.5	47%	$110	$120	$150	$175	$250	$400	$650	$1,250	$3,250
	Auctions: $6,462, MS-66, June 2015; $2,467, MS-65, March 2015; $540, MS-61, January 2015; $352, AU-53, April 2015												
1875-S, Proof	10–20	2	63.0								$15,000	$25,000	
	Auctions: No auction records available.												
1876	14,750	438	58.2	65%	$210	$275	$350	$420	$500	$650	$950	$1,500	$6,000
	Auctions: $15,275, MS-66, June 2015; $4,700, MS-65, July 2015; $4,465, MS-65, January 2015; $940, AU-58, October 2015												
1876, Proof	1,150	305	63.6								$1,500	$3,000	$8,500
	Auctions: $25,850, PF-68, August 2015; $4,230, PF-64, February 2015; $3,995, PF-64, January 2015; $3,760, PF-63Cam, October 2015												
1876-CC †	10,000	7	64.6	100%						$175,000	$250,000	$375,000	$575,000
	Auctions: $564,000, MS-65, January 2013												
1877, Proof	510	261	63.6								$4,500	$6,000	$11,000
	Auctions: $7,637, PF-65, July 2015; $7,050, PF-64Cam, August 2015; $6,494, PF-64, January 2015; $3,995, PF-62, June 2015												
1878, Proof	600	316	63.6								$4,250	$5,250	$10,500
	Auctions: $11,162, PF-65Cam, August 2015; $5,405, PF-64, January 2015; $4,935, PF-63Cam, August 2015; $3,290, PF-63, August 2014												

† Ranked in the *100 Greatest U.S. Coins* (fourth edition). **a.** There are at least two misplaced-date die varieties of the 1875-S twenty-cent piece. These do not command a premium in the marketplace. A repunched mintmark is likewise common.

Quarter Dollars
1796 to Date

AN OVERVIEW OF QUARTER DOLLARS

In 1796 the first silver quarters were struck at the Philadelphia Mint. The Draped Bust obverse in combination with the Small Eagle reverse was produced only in this year, after which no pieces of this denomination were produced until 1804. At that time the Draped Bust obverse was continued, but now with the Heraldic Eagle reverse. The coinage proved to be brief and lasted only through 1807, after which no quarters were struck until 1815. The new quarters dated 1815 were of the Capped Bust style, by John Reich. These were produced intermittently through 1838. The Liberty Seated motif, by Christian Gobrecht, made its debut in 1838 and was produced continuously through 1891, with several modifications in design and metallic content over the years. The Liberty Head quarter, today called the Barber quarter after its designer, was introduced in 1892 and minted continuously through 1916. The obverse features the head of Miss Liberty, and the reverse a heraldic eagle. In late 1916 the Standing Liberty by Hermon A. MacNeil became the new design. This was produced through 1930, except for 1922. Some changes to both the obverse and reverse were made partway through 1917.

The Washington quarter dollar was struck in 1932 to observe the 200th anniversary of the birth of our first president. Washington quarters have been struck continuously since then, except for 1933, and with none dated 1975. In 1976 a special Bicentennial motif was introduced. Beginning in 1999 the State quarters were launched, issued at the rate of five per year, covering all 50 states, each coin having its own distinctive design. After this successful and popular program came quarter dollars with motifs celebrating the District of Columbia and U.S. territories. A similar program commemorating national parks started in 2010 and is slated to run through 2021.

While there are no super-rarities among the different *types* of quarter dollars, the first one, the 1796 with Draped Bust obverse and Small Eagle reverse, is hard to find and expensive in all grades. The values are, of course, justified by the great demand for this single-year type.

**Quarter-dollar designers
Hermon A. MacNeil and John Flanagan.**

The collector's greatest challenge in finding a decent strike is in the short-lived 1804–1807 type with the Heraldic Eagle reverse. Sufficient quantities were made that examples from these years are not rarities, but nearly all are weakly struck. Quarters of the 1815–1828 Capped Bust, large planchet, type are available easily enough in worn grades but are scarce to rare in Mint State. Some cherrypicking (close examination for high quality within a given grade) is needed to find a sharp strike.

Respite from the sharp-strike difficulty is at last found with the 1831–1838 type, Capped Bust, small diameter, and without E PLURIBUS UNUM. Most are quite nicely struck. Also, for the first time Mint State coins are generally available with frequency in the marketplace, although those with good eye appeal are in the distinct minority.

The Liberty Seated quarters of the several types made from 1838 to 1891 are generally available in proportion to their mintages, with an allowance for the earlier dates being scarcer than the later ones—as they had a longer time to become worn or lost. Many quarters of earlier dates were melted circa 1850 to 1853, when the price of silver rose on international markets, making such coins worth slightly more than 25 cents in melt-down value.

Barber quarters, 1892–1916, present no difficulty for the collector, except that there is a challenge to find an example with sharp striking overall, including in the telltale area on the reverse at and near the eagle's leg to the right. MS-65 and better Barber quarters are scarcer than generally known (the same can be said for Barber half dollars). Proofs were sold to collectors and saved, and thus they are available in proportion to their mintages, with probably 70% to 80% surviving today.

The Variety 1 Standing Liberty quarter is a rarity if dated 1916, for only 52,000 were struck, and not many were saved. The feasible alternative is the 1917, Variety 1, which is often seen in Mint State, sharply struck, and very beautiful. Standing Liberty quarters of the Variety 2 design, minted from partway through 1917 to 1930, often are weakly struck on the head of Miss Liberty and on the shield rivets, and sometimes other places as well. Diligent searching is needed to locate a nice example.

Washington quarters also present no difficulty for collectors. The State, D.C./Territorial, and America the Beautiful (National Park) reverses are appealing in their diversity and make a fascinating study in themselves.

FOR THE COLLECTOR AND INVESTOR: QUARTER DOLLARS AS A SPECIALTY

The formation of a specialized collection of quarter dollars from 1796 to date, by dates, mints, and major varieties, is a considerable challenge. As a class, quarters are considerably more difficult to acquire than are either dimes or half dollars. Relatively few numismatists have ever concentrated on the entire series.

The 1796 is rare and popular both as a date and a type. The 1804, although elusive in worn grades, is of commanding importance if in AU or Mint State. The 1823, 3 Over 2, is a classic rarity and is nearly always encountered well worn. From the same decade the 1827 is famous. Although Mint records indicate that 4,000 circulation strikes were produced in calendar-year 1827, they were probably struck from 1825-dated or earlier dies, as no unequivocal circulation strike has ever been located. There are, however, a dozen or so Proofs. Originals are distinguished by the 2 (in the 25 C. denomination) having a curved base, while restrikes, also very rare, have a square-base 2.

One of the unsolved mysteries in numismatics involves certain quarter dollars dated 1815 (the die variety known as Browning-1) and 1825, 5 Over 3 (Browning-2), which are often seen counterstamped, above the cap, with either an E or an L. Hundreds exist. As other quarter-dollar die varieties were made during this period, but only these two bear counterstamps, it may be that this was done either at the Mint or elsewhere before they were generally distributed.

Ard W. Browning's 1925 text, *The Early Quarter Dollars of the United States, 1796–1838*, remains the standard reference on the series, together with new information added here and there, including in issues of the *John Reich Journal*, the magazine of the John Reich Collectors Society, and in more recently published books.

The panorama of Liberty Seated quarters from 1838 to 1891 is highlighted by several rarities, notably the 1842, Small Date (known only in Proof format), and the 1873-CC, Without Arrows (of which only five are known, at least three being Mint State). The others are generally available, but some can be almost impossible to find in Mint State, the 1849-O, certain early San Francisco issues, and Carson City coins of the early 1870s being well known in this regard. From the mid-1870s onward Mint State coins are generally available, including choice and gem pieces. Proofs from 1858 onward can be found in proportion to their mintages, with later dates often being seen with higher numerical designations than are earlier ones.

Barber quarters are collectible by date and mint, although the "big three" rarities, the 1896-S, 1901-S, and 1913-S, are expensive and hard to find.

Standing Liberty quarters, 1916–1930, represent a short-lived series, one easy enough to collect in grades up to MS-63, except for the rare 1918-S, 8 Over 7, overdate. Finding higher-grade coins that are sharply struck is another matter entirely, and over the years few sets of this nature have been assembled.

Washington quarters are all collectible, with no great rarities. However, in relation to the demand for them, certain early issues are elusive, the 1932-D being a well-known example. Modern issues, including the Bicentennial, State, D.C./Territorial, and National Park coins, are at once plentiful, inexpensive, and interesting.

The Early Quarter Dollars OF THE United States 1796-1838

By A.W. Browning
Completely Updated by Walter Breen
New Foreword by Q. David Bowers

A copy of Ard W. Browning's 1925 text, *The Early Quarter Dollars of the United States, 1796–1838*.

DRAPED BUST, SMALL EAGLE REVERSE (1796)

Designer: *Probably Gilbert Stuart.* **Engraver:** *Robert Scot.*
Weight: *6.74 grams.* **Composition:** *.8924 silver, .1076 copper.*
Diameter: *Approximately 27.5 mm.* **Edge:** *Reeded.* **Mint:** *Philadelphia.*

Browning-2.

History. The Philadelphia Mint coined its first quarter dollar in 1796. Its design followed that of other silver U.S. coins. Only 6,146 were made, followed by a production hiatus until 1804, by which time a new reverse was used. Thus the 1796 was isolated as a single-year type.

Striking and Sharpness. On the obverse, check the hair details and the star centers. Most are well struck. On the reverse, most are well struck except for the head of the eagle, which can be shallow or flat, especially on the Browning-2 variety (there are two known die varieties for this year, Browning-1 being the rarer). Rarely is a Full Details coin encountered. The denticles are unusually bold and serve to frame the motifs. Check for planchet adjustment marks (from overweight planchets being filed down at the Mint to achieve proper weight). A few pieces have carbon streaks, which lower their value. Sharp striking (as on Browning-2) will add to the value. Most MS examples have excellent eye appeal.

Availability. Examples are available in all grades from well worn to superb MS. Nearly all of the latter are highly prooflike, but there are some exceptions. Although hundreds of circulated examples exist, demand for this famous coin exceeds supply in the marketplace, making public offerings a scene of excitement and strong bidding. Hundreds of higher-grade examples also survive, many of them prooflike and attractive. They attract great attention when offered for sale.

GRADING STANDARDS

MS-60 to 70 (Mint State). *Obverse:* At MS-60, some abrasion and contact marks are evident, most noticeably on the cheek, the drapery, and the right field. Luster is present, but may be dull or lifeless, and interrupted in patches. On prooflike coins the contact marks are more prominent. At MS-63, contact marks are very few, and abrasion is hard to detect except under magnification, although this type is sometimes graded liberally due to its

1796; Browning-2. Graded MS-62.

rarity. An MS-65 coin has no abrasion, and contact marks are so minute as to require magnification. Luster should be full and rich. Grades above MS-65 are defined by having fewer marks as perfection is approached. *Reverse:* Comments apply as for the obverse, except that abrasion and contact marks are most noticeable on the eagle at the center, a situation complicated by the fact that this area is typically flatly struck (except on the Browning-2 variety). Grading is best done by the obverse, then verified by the reverse. The field area is small and is protected by lettering and the wreath and in any given grade shows fewer marks than on the obverse.

Illustrated coin: This coin is well struck on the obverse, and the weak striking on the eagle's breast and head is typical of this issue.

AU-50, 53, 55, 58 (About Uncirculated). *Obverse:* Light wear is seen on the hair area above the ear and extending to left of the forehead, on the ribbon, on the drapery at the shoulder, and on the high points of the bust line, more so at AU-50 than at AU–53 or 55. An AU-58 coin has minimal traces of wear. An AU-50 coin has luster in protected areas among the stars and letters, with little in the open fields or on the portrait. At AU-58, most

1796; Browning-2. Graded AU-58.

luster remains in the fields, but is worn away on the highest parts of the motifs. *Reverse:* Light wear is seen on the eagle's body (keep in mind this area is nearly always lightly struck) and the edges of the wings. Light wear is seen on the wreath and lettering. Luster is the best key to actual wear. This ranges from perhaps 20% remaining in protected areas (at AU-50) to nearly full mint bloom (at AU-58).

EF-40, 45 (Extremely Fine). *Obverse:* More wear is evident on the upper hair area and the ribbon, and on the drapery and bosom. Excellent detail remains in low-relief areas of the hair. The stars show wear as do the date and letters. Luster, if present at all, is minimal and in protected areas. *Reverse:* The eagle shows more wear, this being the focal point to check. Most feathers remain on the interior areas of the wings. Additional wear is on

1796; Browning-1. Graded EF-40.

the wreath and letters, but many details are present. Some luster may be seen in protected areas and if present is slightly more abundant than on the obverse.

VF-20, 30 (Very Fine). *Obverse:* The higher-relief areas of hair are well worn at VF-20, less so at VF-30, although much detail remains on the areas below the ear. The drapery and bosom show extensive wear. The stars have more wear, making them appear larger (an optical illusion seen on most worn silver coins of this era). *Reverse:* The body of the eagle shows few if any feathers, while the wings have about half of the feath-

1796; Browning-2. Graded VF-30.

ers visible, mostly on the right wing, depending on the strike. The leaves lack most detail and are in outline form. Scattered, non-disfiguring marks are normal for this and lower grades. Any major defects should be noted separately.

F-12, 15 (Fine). *Obverse:* Wear is more extensive than on a Very Fine coin, particularly noticeable on the hair, face, and bosom. The stars appear larger. About half the hair detail remains, most noticeably behind the neck and shoulder. The denticles remain strong (while on most other silver denominations of this design they become weak at this grade level). *Reverse:* Wear is more extensive. Now feather details are diminished, with

1796; Browning-2. Graded F-12.

fewer than half remaining on the wings. The wreath and lettering are worn further, and the rim is slightly weak in areas, although most denticles can be seen.

VG-8, 10 (Very Good). *Obverse:* The portrait is mostly seen in outline form, with most hair strands gone, although there is some definition at the back of the hair and behind the shoulder. The ear is discernible, as is the eye. The stars appear larger still, again an illusion. The rim is weak in areas. Most denticles are seen, some of them even bold. LIBERTY and the date are readable and usually full, although some letters may be weak

1796; Browning-2. Graded VG-10.

at their tops (the high rim and denticles protect the design more on the quarter dollar than on other silver coins of this type). *Reverse:* The eagle is mostly an outline, with parts blending into the field (on lighter strikes), although some slight feather detail can be seen on the right wing. The rim is worn, as are the letters, with some weak, but the motto is readable. Most denticles remain clear.

G-4, 6 (Good). *Obverse:* Wear is more extensive. The head is an outline. The rim still is present, as are most of the denticles, most well defined. LIBERTY is worn, but complete. The date is bold. *Reverse:* The eagle is flat and discernible in outline form, blending into the field in areas. The wreath is well worn. Some of the letters may be partly missing. Some rim areas and denticles are discernible. At this level some "averaging" can

1796; Browning-1. Graded G-4.

be done. If the letters are stronger than usual in one area, but some are missing in another area, the coin can still qualify as G-4.

AG-3 (About Good). *Obverse:* Wear is so extensive that the coin is barely identifiable. The head is in outline form, LIBERTY is mostly gone, same for the stars, and the date, while readable, may be partially worn away. *Reverse:* The reverse is well worn, with parts of the wreath and lettering missing.

1796; Browning-2. Graded AG-3.

	Mintage	Cert	Avg	%MS	AG-3	G-4	VG-8	F-12	VF-20	EF-40	AU-50	MS-60	MS-63
1796 †	6,146	181	34.5	20%	$7,000	$12,000	$17,000	$25,000	$35,000	$47,500	$52,500	$70,000	$160,000
	Auctions: $881,250, SP-66, August 2014; $52,875, AU-58, August 2014; $64,625, AU-55, August 2014; $8,225, G-4, January 2015												

† Ranked in the *100 Greatest U.S. Coins* (fourth edition).

DRAPED BUST, HERALDIC EAGLE REVERSE (1804–1807)

Designer: *Robert Scot.* **Weight:** *6.74 grams.* **Composition:** *.8924 silver, .1076 copper.*
Diameter: *Approximately 27.5 mm.* **Edge:** *Reeded.* **Mint:** *Philadelphia.*

Browning-4.

History. Early on, the U.S. Mint's production of silver coins in any given year depended on requests made by depositors of silver; they were not made for the Mint's own account. After 1796 no quarters were struck until 1804. When production started up again, the Draped Bust obverse was used, but with the new Heraldic Eagle reverse—similar to that on other silver (and gold) denominations of the time. The Heraldic Eagle design was patterned after the Great Seal of the United States.

Striking and Sharpness. Virtually all examples are lightly struck in one area or another. On the obverse, check the hair details and the star centers. On the reverse, check the shield, stars, feathers, and other design elements. The denticles and rims on both sides often have problems. Quarters of 1807 are usually the lightest struck. Also check for planchet adjustment marks (where an overweight planchet was filed down by a Mint worker to reach acceptable standards). Sharp striking and excellent eye appeal add to a coin's value. This series often is misgraded due to lack of understanding of its strike anomalies.

Availability. All dates are collectible, with 1804 being scarcer than the others and a rarity in MS. Those of 1805, 1806, and 1807 are readily available in the marketplace, usually in circulated grades although MS examples are sometimes seen. Some die varieties are rare. High-grade coins with Full Details are very rare.

GRADING STANDARDS

MS-60 to 70 (Mint State). *Obverse:* At MS-60, some abrasion and contact marks are evident, most noticeably on the cheek, the drapery, and the right field. Luster is present, but may be dull or lifeless, and interrupted in patches. At MS-63, contact marks are very few, and abrasion is hard to detect except under magnification. An MS-65 coin will have no abrasion, and contact marks are so minute as to require magnification. Luster should be

1806; Browning-9. Graded MS-66.

full and rich. Coins graded above MS-65 are more theoretical than actual for this type—but they do exist, and are defined by having fewer marks as perfection is approached. As noted in the introduction, expect weakness in some areas. *Reverse:* Comments apply as for the obverse, except that abrasion and contact marks are most noticeable on the eagle's neck, the tips of the wing, and the tail. The field area is complex, without much open space, given the stars above the eagle, the arrows and olive branch, and other features. Accordingly, marks are not as noticeable as on the obverse.

   Illustrated coin: This coin is lightly struck on the right obverse stars and at the center of the reverse. Some planchet adjustment marks are mostly hidden. Some tiny carbon streaks are on the obverse (seemingly typical for Browning-9).

AU-50, 53, 55, 58 (About Uncirculated). *Obverse:* Light wear is seen on the hair area above the ear and extending to left of the forehead, on the ribbon, and on the drapery at the shoulder, more so at AU-50 than at AU–53 or 55. An AU-58 coin has minimal traces of wear. An AU-50 coin has luster in protected areas among the stars and letters, with little in the open fields or on the portrait. At AU-58, most luster is present in the fields, but is worn away on the highest parts of the motifs.

1804; Browning-1. Graded AU-58.

Reverse: Comments as preceding, except that the eagle's neck, the tips and top of the wings, the clouds, and the tail now show noticeable wear, as do other features. Luster ranges from perhaps 20% remaining in protected areas (at AU-50) to nearly full mint bloom (at AU-58). Often the reverse retains much more luster than the obverse, more so on quarter dollars than on other denominations of this design.

Illustrated coin: Lightly struck on the obverse stars. The reverse has some light areas but is sharp overall. A few planchet adjustment marks are visible. Abundant luster and good eye appeal rank this as an exceptional example of this date, the most difficult of the type to find in high grades.

EF-40, 45 (Extremely Fine). *Obverse:* More wear is evident on the upper hair area and the ribbon, and on the drapery at the shoulder and the bosom. Excellent detail remains in low-relief areas of the hair. The stars show wear, as do the date and letters (note: on most coins of this type the stars are softly struck). Luster, if present at all, is minimal and in protected areas. *Reverse:* Wear is greater than on an About Uncirculated coin, overall. The

1804; Browning-1. Graded EF-45.

neck lacks feather detail on its highest points. Feathers have lost some detail near the edges of the wings, and some areas of the horizontal lines in the shield may be blended together. Some traces of luster may be seen, more so at EF-45 than at EF-40.

VF-20, 30 (Very Fine). *Obverse:* The higher-relief areas of hair are well worn at VF-20, less so at VF-30. The drapery and bosom show extensive wear. The stars have more wear, making them appear larger (an optical illusion seen on most worn silver coins of this era). *Reverse:* Wear is greater, including on the shield and wing feathers, although more than half of the feathers are defined. Star centers are flat. Other areas have lost

1804; Browning-1. Graded VF-30.

detail as well. Some letters in the motto may be missing, depending on the strike.

F-12, 15 (Fine). *Obverse:* Wear is more extensive than on a Very Fine coin, particularly noticeable on the hair, face, and bosom. The stars appear larger. About half the hair detail remains with the tresses fused so as to appear thick, most noticeably behind the neck and shoulder. The rim may be partially worn away and blend into the field. *Reverse:* Wear is even more extensive, with the shield and wing feathers being points to observe.

1804; Browning-1. Graded F-12.

About half of the feathers can be seen. The incuse E PLURIBUS UNUM may have a few letters worn away. The clouds all seem to be connected. The stars are weak. Parts of the border and lettering may be weak. As with most quarters of this type, peculiarities of striking can account for some weakness.

VG-8, 10 (Very Good). *Obverse:* The portrait is mostly seen in outline form, with most hair strands gone, although there is slight definition at the back of the hair and behind the shoulder. The ear is discernible, as is the eye. The stars appear larger still, again an illusion. The rim is weak in areas. LIBERTY and the date are readable and usually full, although some letters may be weak at their tops. *Reverse:* Wear is more extensive. Half

1804; Browning-1. Graded VG-8.

or so of the letters in the motto are worn away. Most feathers are worn away, although separation of some of the lower feathers may be seen. Some stars are faint. The border blends into the field in areas (depending on striking), and some letters are weak.

G-4, 6 (Good). *Obverse:* Wear is more extensive, and some stars may be partly missing. The head is an outline. The eye is visible only in outline form. The rim is well worn or even missing in areas. LIBERTY is worn, and parts of some letters may be missing, but elements of all should be readable. The date is readable, but worn. *Reverse:* Wear is more extensive. The upper part of the eagle is flat, and feathers are noticeable only at some (but

1804; Browning-1. Graded G-4.

not necessarily all) of the lower edge of the wings, and do not have detail. The shield lacks most of its detail. Only a few letters of the motto can be seen (depending on striking). The rim is worn extensively, and a few letters may be missing.

AG-3 (About Good). *Obverse:* Wear is so extensive that the coin is barely identifiable. The head is in outline form, LIBERTY is mostly gone. Same for the stars. The date, while readable, may be partially worn away. *Reverse:* Extensive wear is seen overall, with the rim worn away and some areas worn smooth. The eagle can be discerned in outline form, but not necessarily completely. A few stray motto letters may remain. Sometimes the obverse appears to be more worn than the reverse, or vice-versa.

1804; Browning-1. Graded AG-3.

1806, 6 Over 5

	Mintage	Cert	Avg	%MS	AG-3	G-4	VG-8	F-12	VF-20	EF-40	AU-50	MS-60	MS-63
1804	6,738	126	17.4	4%	$2,200	$4,250	$6,000	$8,500	$13,000	$25,000	$45,000	$85,000	$165,000
	Auctions: $82,250, AU-55, November 2013; $7,638, F-12, March 2015; $1,351, Fair-2, January 2015												
1805	121,394	338	24.6	7%	$200	$475	$600	$1,000	$1,800	$3,750	$5,250	$10,000	$20,000
	Auctions: $946, F-15, January 2015; $709, VG-10, June 2015; $564, VG-8, January 2015; $552, VG-8, March 2015												
1806, All kinds	206,124												
1806, 6 Over 5		133	27.4	9%	$250	$600	$750	$1,100	$1,725	$4,000	$6,000	$11,500	$22,500
	Auctions: $152,750, MS-66, November 2013; $1,116, VG-10, October 2014; $646, VG-10, March 2015												
1806		501	24.5	9%	$225	$500	$650	$950	$1,600	$3,600	$5,250	$10,000	$16,500
	Auctions: $1,528, VF-20, March 2015; $764, VF-20, August 2015; $529, VF-20, January 2015; $470, F-12, February 2015												
1807	220,643	258	24.2	13%	$225	$500	$650	$950	$1,600	$3,600	$5,250	$10,000	$16,500
	Auctions: $764, VG-10, June 2015; $676, VG-10, March 2015; $494, VG-8, July 2015; $424, G-6, June 2015												

CAPPED BUST (1815–1838)

Variety 1, Large Diameter (1815–1828): **Designer:** *John Reich.*
Weight: *6.74 grams.* **Composition:** *.8924 silver, .1076 copper.*
Diameter: *Approximately 27 mm.* **Edge:** *Reeded.* **Mint:** *Philadelphia.*

Variety 1, Large Diameter (1815–1828)
Browning-1.

Variety 1, Large Diameter, Proof
Browning-4.

Variety 2, Reduced Diameter, Motto Removed (1831–1838):
Designer: *William Kneass.* **Weight:** *6.74 grams (changed to 6.68 grams, .900 fine, in 1837).*
Composition: *.8924 silver, .1076 copper.* **Diameter:** *24.3 mm.* **Edge:** *Reeded.* **Mint:** *Philadelphia.*

Variety 2, Reduced Diameter,
Motto Removed (1831–1838)
Browning-1.

Variety 2, Reduced Diameter,
Motto Removed, Proof

History. The Capped Bust design, by John Reich, was introduced on the half dollar of 1807 but was not used on the quarter until 1815. The difference between the Large Diameter and the Reduced Diameter types resulted from the introduction of the close collar in 1828. Capped Bust, Reduced Diameter, quarter dollars are similar in overall appearance to the preceding type, but with important differences. The diameter is smaller, E PLURIBUS UNUM no longer appears on the reverse, and the denticles are smaller and restyled using a close collar.

Striking and Sharpness. Striking sharpness of Capped Bust, Large Diameter, quarters varies. On the obverse, check the hair of Miss Liberty, the broach clasp (a particular point of observation), and the star centers. On this type the stars are often well defined (in contrast with half dollars of the same design). On the reverse, check the neck of the eagle and its wings, and the letters. The details of the eagle often are superbly defined. Check the scroll or ribbon above the eagle's head for weak or light areas. Examine the denticles on both sides. When weakness occurs it is usually in the center. Proofs were struck for inclusion in sets and for numismatists. Some deeply toned coins, and coins with patches of mint luster, have been described as Proofs but are mostly impostors, some of which have been certified or have "papers" signed by Walter Breen. Be careful! Nearly all coins of the Capped Bust, Reduced Diameter, Motto Removed, variety are very well struck. Check all areas for sharpness. Some quarters of 1833 and 1834 are struck from rusted or otherwise imperfect dies and can be less attractive than coins from undamaged dies. Avoid any Proofs that show patches of mint frost or that are darkly toned.

Availability. Most quarters of the Large Diameter variety range from slightly scarce to rare, with the 1823, 3 Over 2, and the 1827 being famous rarities. Typical coins range from well worn to Fine and VF. AU and MS coins are elusive (and are usually dated before the 1820s), and gems are particularly rare. All authentic Proofs are rarities. Examples of the Reduced Diameter, Motto Removed, variety are readily available of all dates, including many of the first year of issue. Mint frost ranges from satiny (usual) to deeply frosty. Proofs were struck of all dates for inclusion in sets and for sale or trade to numismatists; avoid deeply toned pieces, and seek those with deep and full (not partial) mirror surfaces and good contrast.

GRADING STANDARDS

MS-60 to 70 (Mint State). *Obverse:* At MS-60, some abrasion and contact marks are evident, most noticeably on the cheek, the hair below LIBERTY, and the area near the drapery clasp. Luster is present, but may be dull or lifeless, and interrupted in patches. At MS-63, contact marks are very few, and abrasion is hard to detect except under magnification. An

1831, Large Letters; Browning-5. Graded MS-62.

MS-65 coin has no abrasion, and contact marks are so minute as to require magnification. Luster should be full and rich. Grades above MS-65 are seen now and again and are defined by having fewer marks as perfection is approached. Grading for Reduced Diameter, Motto Removed, examples is similar, except the rims are more uniform, striking is usually very sharp, and the wear occurs evenly on both sides. *Reverse:* Comments apply as for the obverse, except that abrasion and contact marks are most noticeable on the eagle's neck, the top of the wings, the claws, and the flat band that surrounds the incuse motto. The field is mainly protected by design elements and does not show abrasion as much as does the obverse on a given coin.

AU-50, 53, 55, 58 (About Uncirculated).

Obverse: Light wear is seen on the cap, the hair below LIBERTY, the curl on the neck, the hair near the clasp, and the drapery. At AU-58, the luster is extensive except in the open area of the field, especially to the right. At AU–50 and 53, luster remains only in protected areas. Grading for Reduced Diameter, Motto Removed, examples is similar, except the rims are more uniform, striking is usually

1834; Browning-2. Graded AU-55.

very sharp, and the wear occurs evenly on both sides. *Reverse:* Wear is evident on the eagle's neck, the top of the wings, the claws, and the flat band above the eagle. An AU-58 coin has nearly full luster. At AU–50 and 53, there still is significant luster, more than on the obverse. Generally, light wear is most obvious on the obverse.

EF-40, 45 (Extremely Fine).

Obverse: Wear is more extensive, most noticeably on the higher areas of the hair. The cap shows more wear, as does the cheek. Most or all stars have some radial lines visible (unless lightly struck, as many are). Luster, if present, is in protected areas among the star points and close to the portrait. Grading for Reduced Diameter, Motto Removed, examples is similar, except the rims are more uniform, striking is

1831, Small Letters; Browning-4. Graded EF-40.

usually very sharp, and the wear occurs evenly on both sides. *Reverse:* The wings show wear on the higher areas of the feathers, and some details are lost. Feathers in the neck are light on some (but not on especially sharp strikes). The eagle's claws and the leaves show wear. Luster may be present in protected areas, even if there is little or none on the obverse.

VF-20, 30 (Very Fine). *Obverse:* Wear is more extensive, and most of the hair is combined into thick tresses without delicate features. The curl on the neck is flat. Details of the drapery are well defined at the lower edge. Unless they were weakly struck, the stars are mostly flat although a few may retain radial lines. Grading for Reduced Diameter, Motto Removed, examples is similar, except the rims are more uniform, striking is usually very sharp, and the wear occurs evenly on both sides. *Reverse:* Wear is most evident on the eagle's neck, to the left of the shield, and on the leaves and claws. Most feathers in the wing remain distinct, but some show light wear. Overall, the reverse on most quarters at this level shows less wear than the obverse.

1828. Graded VF-20.

F-12, 15 (Fine). *Obverse:* Wear is more extensive, with much of the hair blended together. The drapery is indistinct at its upper edge. The stars are flat. Grading for Reduced Diameter, Motto Removed, examples is similar, except the rims are more uniform, striking is usually very sharp, and the wear occurs evenly on both sides. *Reverse:* Wear is more extensive, now with only about half of the feathers remaining on the wings. The claws on the right are fused at their upper parts.

1815. Graded F-15.

VG-8, 10 (Very Good). *Obverse:* The hair is less distinct, with the area above the face blended into the facial features. LIBERTY is complete, but can be weak in areas. At the left the drapery and bosom are blended together in a flat area. The rim is worn away in areas, and blends into the field. *Reverse:* Feathers are fewer and mostly on the eagle's wing to the left. Other details are weaker. E PLURIBUS UNUM is weak, perhaps with some letters missing. All border lettering remains easily readable.

1828, 25 Over 50 C.; Browning-3. Graded VG-10.

Illustrated coin: Gunmetal toning in the fields contrasts nicely with the lighter devices. The overpunched denomination shows signs of the 50 punched first into the die to the left of both 2 and 5.

G-4, 6 (Good). *Obverse:* The portrait is mostly in outline, with few interior details discernible. LIBERTY may still be readable or may be partially worn away, depending on the variety. Most or all of the border is worn away, and the outer parts of the stars are weak. *Reverse:* The eagle mostly is in outline form, although some feathers can be seen in the wing to the left. All letters around the border are clear. E PLURIBUS UNUM is mostly or completely worn away.

1815; Browning-1. Graded G-4.

AG-3 (About Good). *Obverse:* The portrait is an outline. Most of LIBERTY can still be seen. Stars are weak or missing toward what used to be the rim. The date remains clear, but may be weak at the bottom. *Reverse:* The reverse shows more wear than at G-4, but parts of the rim may remain clear.

1825, 5 Over 4; Browning-3. Graded AG-3.

PF-60 to 70 (Proof). *Obverse and Reverse:* Proofs that are extensively cleaned and have many hairlines, or that are dull and grainy, are lower level, such as PF–60 to 62. While any early Proof coin will attract attention, lower-level examples are not of great interest to specialists unless they are of rare die varieties. With medium hairlines, an assigned grade of PF-64 may be in order and with relatively few, Gem PF-65. PF-66 should have

1833; Browning-1. Graded PF-64 Cameo.

hairlines so delicate that magnification is needed to see them. Above that, a Proof should be free of such lines. Grading is highly subjective with early Proofs, and eye appeal also is a factor.

Illustrated coin: This coin features frosted devices and reflective fields, though the fields are marred by some light scratches.

1818, 8 Over 5   **1818, Normal Date**

	Mintage	Cert	Avg	%MS	AG-3	G-4	VG-8	F-12	VF-20	EF-40	AU-50	MS-60	MS-63
											PF-60	PF-63	PF-65
1815	89,235	167	43.4	36%	$75	$135	$200	$300	$550	$1,600	$2,200	$3,500	$7,000
	Auctions: $999, VF-30, October 2014; $635, F-15, September 2014; $499, VG-8, September 2014; $353, VG-8, June 2015												
1818, 8 Over 5	361,174	108	52.6	58%	$40	$100	$175	$225	$450	$1,500	$2,200	$3,500	$6,500
	Auctions: $176,250, MS-67, November 2013; $270, F-15, July 2014; $259, F-12, October 2014; $88, G-6, July 2014												
1818, Normal Date	(a)	506	40.3	29%	$40	$100	$150	$200	$425	$1,450	$2,200	$3,500	$6,500
	Auctions: $823, VF-35, February 2015; $764, VF-35, January 2015; $674, VF-35, October 2015; $517, VF-35, October 2015												

a. Included in 1818, 8 Over 5, mintage figure.

| **1819, Small 9** | **1819, Large 9** | **1820, Small 0** | **1820, Large 0** |

| **1822, 25 Over 50 C.** | **1823, 3 Over 2** | **1824, 4 Over 2** |

| **1825, 5 Over 2** | **1825, 5 Over 4** |

| | Mintage | Cert | Avg | %MS | AG-3 | G-4 | VG-8 | F-12 | VF-20 | EF-40 | AU-50 | MS-60 | MS-63 |
											PF-60	PF-63	PF-65
1819, Small 9	144,000	42	21.3	10%	$40	$100	$150	$200	$425	$1,450	$2,200	$3,500	$7,500
Auctions: $646, EF-45, September 2014; $646, EF-40, June 2015; $353, VF-20, September 2014; $243, VF-20, May 2015
1819, Large 9	**(b)**	25	36.4	12%	$40	$100	$150	$200	$425	$1,450	$2,200	$3,500	$14,000
Auctions: $23,501, MS-64, November 2013; $764, VF-25, July 2014; $282, VG-10, October 2014
1820, Small 0	127,444	19	37.2	21%	$40	$100	$150	$200	$425	$1,450	$2,200	$3,500	$6,750
Auctions: $3,055, AU-55, February 2014; $441, VF-20, September 2014; $176, G-6, July 2014; $94, G-6, July 2014
1820, Large 0	**(c)**	27	38.6	19%	$40	$100	$170	$225	$500	$1,550	$2,500	$3,500	$10,000
Auctions: $41,125, MS-66, November 2013
1820, Proof	*6–10*	2	65.5									$45,000	$130,000
Auctions: $97,750, PF-64, May 2008
1821	216,851	256	39.3	24%	$40	$100	$150	$200	$425	$1,450	$2,200	$3,500	$7,500
Auctions: $646, VF-30, January 2015; $1,293, VF-25, June 2015; $764, VF-25, July 2015; $112, G-6, November 2014
1821, Proof	*6–10*	4	65.3									$40,000	$100,000
Auctions: $94,000, PF-65, October 2014; $82,250, PF-65, August 2015; $51,750, PF-64, April 2009
1822	64,080	126	37.1	17%	$55	$110	$190	$265	$500	$1,550	$2,600	$4,000	$12,000
Auctions: $25,850, MS-64, November 2013
1822, 25 Over 50 C.	**(d)**	14	35.3	21%	$825	$2,100	$4,750	$6,000	$8,500	$15,000	$24,000	$42,500	$75,000
Auctions: No auction records available.
1822, Proof	*6–10*	2	65.5									$50,000	$175,000
Auctions: $229,125, PF-65, January 2014
1823, 3 Over 2	17,800	7	42.7	14%	$20,000	$32,000	$38,000	$50,000	$65,000	$80,000	$100,000	$225,000	
Auctions: $17,625, G-4, February 2014
1823, 3 Over 2, Proof	*2–4*	0	n/a									$175,000	
Auctions: $396,563, PF-64, June 2014
1824, 4 Over 2	168,000	81	25.5	4%	$300	$650	$1,000	$1,700	$3,000	$5,000	$15,000	$25,000	$65,000
Auctions: $35,250, MS-62, June 2014; $1,293, VG-10, January 2015; $999, VG-8, August 2014
1824, 4 Over 2, Proof	*2–4*	1	63.0									$50,000	
Auctions: No auction records available.
1825, 5 Over 2	**(e)**	17	34.9	0%	$85	$175	$200	$300	$750	$2,500	$8,000	$16,000	$27,500
Auctions: $3,290, VF-30, February 2014; $159, G-6, July 2014; $94, G-4, July 2014
1825, 5 Over 4	**(e)**	153	43.1	22%	$50	$100	$150	$200	$450	$1,500	$2,200	$3,500	$6,500
Auctions: $1,495, EF-45, April 2012
1825, 5 Over 4 Over 3, Proof	*6–10*	0	n/a									$40,000	
Auctions: $4,313, PF-63, January 2010

b. Included in 1819, Small 9, mintage figure. **c.** Included in circulation-strike 1820, Small 0, mintage figure. **d.** Included in circulation-strike 1822 mintage figure. **e.** Included in circulation-strike 1824, 4 Over 2, mintage figure.

1827, Original, Proof
Curl-Base 2 in 25 C.

1827, Restrike, Proof
Square-Base 2 in 25 C.

1828, 25 Over 50 C.

	Mintage	Cert	Avg	%MS	AG-3	G-4	VG-8	F-12	VF-20	EF-40	AU-50	MS-60	MS-63
											PF-60	PF-63	PF-65
1827, 7 Over 3, Original, Proof †	*20–30*	4	52.5								$100,000	$175,000	$550,000
Auctions: $411,250, PF-64, June 2014													
1827, 7 Over 3, Restrike, Proof	*20–30*	10	64.2									$50,000	$115,000
Auctions: $69,000, PF-66, July 2009													
1828	102,000	181	42.0	27%	$40	$100	$150	$200	$425	$1,450	$2,200	$3,500	$8,000
Auctions: $764, VF-35, January 2015; $400, VF-25, June 2015; $176, VG-10, May 2015; $106, G-6, August 2015													
1828, 25 Over 50 C.	(f)	18	39.4	17%	$100	$200	$350	$700	$1,600	$3,000	$4,000	$15,000	$75,000
Auctions: $352,500, MS-67, November 2013; $117,500, MS-63, August 2014													
1828, Proof	*8–12*	6	64.2								$15,000	$40,000	$100,000
Auctions: $82,250, PF-65, June 2014													

† Ranked in the *100 Greatest U.S. Coins* (fourth edition). *Note:* Although 4,000 1827 quarters were reported to have been made for circulation, their rarity today (only one worn piece is known, and it could be a circulated Proof) suggests that this quantity was for coins struck in calendar-year 1827 but bearing an earlier date, probably 1825. **f.** Included in circulation-strike 1828 mintage figure.

1831, Small Letters
Browning-2.

1831, Large Letters
Browning-6.

	Mintage	Cert	Avg	%MS	G-4	VG-8	F-12	VF-20	EF-40	AU-50	MS-60	MS-63	MS-65
											PF-60	PF-63	PF-65
1831, Small Letters	398,000	65	49.5	22%	$70	$100	$125	$150	$400	$750	$1,300	$4,500	$27,500
Auctions: $853, AU-50, July 2015; $341, AU-50, July 2015; $382, EF-45, April 2015; $376, EF-45, June 2015													
1831, Large Letters	(a)	44	49.8	30%	$70	$100	$125	$150	$400	$750	$1,300	$4,500	$30,000
Auctions: $6,463, MS-64, October 2015; $3,525, MS-63, January 2015; $1,175, MS-60, February 2015; $423, EF-45, September 2015													
1831, Large Letters, Proof	*20–25*	1	65								$15,000	$22,500	$75,000
Auctions: $141,000, PF-66, January 2014; $28,200, PF-63, October 2015													
1832	320,000	178	46.1	28%	$70	$100	$125	$150	$425	$750	$1,300	$5,000	$32,500
Auctions: $400, EF-45, May 2015; $212, EF-40, May 2015; $259, VF-35, July 2015; $176, VF-30, October 2015													

a. Included in 1831, Small Letters, mintage figure.

1834, O Over F in OF
FS-25-1834-901.

	Mintage	Cert	Avg	%MS	G-4	VG-8	F-12	VF-20	EF-40	AU-50	MS-60 / PF-60	MS-63 / PF-63	MS-65 / PF-65
1833	156,000	190	47.4	28%	$80	$110	$135	$200	$475	$850	$1,600	$5,500	$35,000
	Auctions: $764, AU-50, June 2015; $646, AU-50, March 2015; $353, EF-45, August 2015; $306, VF-35, May 2015												
1833, O Over F in OF (b)	(c)	11	40.2	9%	$85	$120	$165	$235	$500	$900	$1,700	$6,000	$35,000
	Auctions: No auction records available.												
1833, Proof	10–15	5	64.8								$15,000	$25,000	$90,000
	Auctions: $46,000, PF-65Cam, April 2009												
1834	286,000	580	46.4	28%	$70	$100	$125	$150	$400	$750	$1,300	$4,500	$25,000
	Auctions: $28,200, MS-66, January 2015; $8,519, MS-64, January 2015; $6,463, MS-64, August 2015; $4,230, MS-63, October 2015												
1834, O Over F in OF (b)	(d)	55	46.0	15%	$80	$110	$150	$200	$450	$850	$1,600	$5,700	$33,500
	Auctions: $1,116, AU-58, November 2014; $588, AU-50, October 2014												
1834, Proof	20–25	8	64.9								$15,000	$22,500	$75,000
	Auctions: $235,000, PF-66, November 2013												
1835	1,952,000	596	43.2	16%	$70	$100	$125	$150	$400	$750	$1,300	$4,500	$27,500
	Auctions: $611, MS-60, January 2015; $823, AU-55, August 2015; $223, AU-55, July 2015; $764, AU-53, October 2015												
1835, Proof	10–15	5	64.2								$15,000	$35,000	$100,000
	Auctions: $25,850, PF-63, August 2013												
1836	472,000	219	39.3	17%	$70	$100	$125	$150	$400	$750	$1,300	$4,700	$40,000
	Auctions: $940, AU-53, January 2015; $823, AU-53, February 2015; $558, EF-45, November 2014; $329, EF-40, May 2015												
1836, Proof	8–12	2	65.5								$15,000	$25,000	$100,000
	Auctions: $97,750, PF-67, January 2006												
1837	252,400	286	48.5	33%	$70	$100	$125	$150	$400	$750	$1,300	$4,500	$25,000
	Auctions: $646, AU-55, November 2014; $823, AU-50, January 2015; $306, EF-40, November 2014; $200, VF-30, January 2015												
1837, Proof	8–12	2	66								$15,000	$25,000	$90,000
	Auctions: $132,250, PF-67, August 2006												
1838	366,000	266	46.0	27%	$70	$100	$125	$150	$400	$750	$1,300	$4,500	$25,000
	Auctions: $82,250, MS-67, September 2015; $646, EF-45, August 2015; $576, EF-45, March 2015; $423, EF-40, August 2015												
1838, Proof	8–12	2	66.0								$25,000	$35,000	$100,000
	Auctions: $48,875, PF-64, July 2011												

b. The OF is re-engraved with the letters connected at the top, and the first A in AMERICA is also re-engraved. Other identifying characteristics: there is no period after the C in the denomination, and the 5 and C are further apart than normal. **c.** Included in circulation-strike 1833 mintage figure. **d.** Included in circulation-strike 1834 mintage figure.

LIBERTY SEATED (1838–1891)

Variety 1, No Motto Above Eagle (1838–1853): **Designer:** *Christian Gobrecht.*
Weight: *6.68 grams.* **Composition:** *.900 silver, .100 copper.* **Diameter:** *24.3 mm.*
Edge: *Reeded.* **Mints:** *Philadelphia and New Orleans.*

Variety 1 (1838–1853)

Mintmark location is on the reverse, below the eagle, for all varieties.

Variety 1, Proof

Variety 2, Arrows at Date, Rays Around Eagle (1853): **Designer:** *Christian Gobrecht.*
Weight: *6.22 grams.* **Composition:** *.900 silver, .100 copper.* **Diameter:** *24.3 mm.*
Edge: *Reeded.* **Mints:** *Philadelphia and New Orleans.*

Variety 2 (1853)   Variety 2, Proof

Variety 3, Arrows at Date, No Rays (1854–1855): **Designer:** *Christian Gobrecht.*
Weight: *6.22 grams.* **Composition:** *.900 silver, .100 copper.* **Diameter:** *24.3 mm.*
Edge: *Reeded.* **Mints:** *Philadelphia, New Orleans, and San Francisco.*

Variety 3 (1854–1855)   Variety 3, Proof

Variety 1 Resumed, With Weight Standard of Variety 2 (1856–1865):
Designer: *Christian Gobrecht.* **Weight:** *6.22 grams.* **Composition:** *.900 silver, .100 copper.*
Diameter: *24.3 mm.* **Edge:** *Reeded.* **Mints:** *Philadelphia, New Orleans, and San Francisco.*

Variety 1 Resumed, Weight   Variety 1 Resumed, Weight
Standard of Variety 2 (1856–1865)   Standard of Variety 2, Proof

Variety 4, Motto Above Eagle (1866–1873): **Designer:** *Christian Gobrecht.*
Weight: *6.22 grams.* **Composition:** *.900 silver, .100 copper.* **Diameter:** *24.3 mm.*
Edge: *Reeded.* **Mints:** *Philadelphia, San Francisco, and Carson City.*

Variety 4 (1866–1873)   Variety 4, Proof

Variety 5, Arrows at Date (1873–1874): **Designer:** *Christian Gobrecht.*
Weight: *6.25 grams.* **Composition:** *.900 silver, .100 copper.* **Diameter:** *24.3 mm.*
Edge: *Reeded.* **Mints:** *Philadelphia, San Francisco, and Carson City.*

Variety 5 (1873–1874)   Variety 5, Proof

Variety 4 Resumed, With Weight Standard of Variety 5 (1875–1891):
Designer: *Christian Gobrecht.* **Weight:** *6.25 grams.* **Composition:** *.900 silver, .100 copper.*
Diameter: *24.3 mm.* **Edge:** *Reeded.* **Mints:** *Philadelphia, New Orleans, and San Francisco.*

Variety 4 Resumed, Weight
Standard of Variety 5 (1875–1891)

Variety 4 Resumed, Weight
Standard of Variety 5, Proof

History. The long-running Liberty Seated design was introduced on the quarter dollar in 1838. Early issues lack drapery at Miss Liberty's elbow and have small lettering on the reverse. Drapery was added in 1840 and continued afterward. In 1853 a reduction in the coin's weight was indicated with the addition of arrows at the date and rays on the reverse (in the field around the eagle). The rays were omitted after 1853, but the arrows were retained through 1855. The motto IN GOD WE TRUST was added to the reverse in 1866. Arrows were placed at the date in the years 1873 and 1874 to denote the change of weight from 6.22 to 6.25 grams. The new weight, without the arrows, continued through 1891.

Striking and Sharpness. On the obverse, check the head of Miss Liberty and the star centers. If these are sharp, then check the central part of the seated figure. On the reverse, check the eagle, particularly the area to the lower left of the shield. Check the denticles on both sides. Generally, the earliest issues are well struck, as are those of the 1880s onward. The word LIBERTY is not an infallible guide to grading at lower levels, as on some dies the shield was in lower relief, and the letters wore away less quickly. This guideline should be used in combination with examining other features. Some Proofs (1858 is an example) have lint marks, and others can have light striking (particularly in the 1870s and 1880s). Avoid "problem" coins and those with deep or artificial (and often colorful) toning.

Availability. Coins of this type are available in proportion to their mintages. MS coins can range from rare to exceedingly rare, as they were mostly ignored by numismatists until the series ended. Quality can vary widely, especially among branch-mint coins. Proofs of the earlier years are very rare. Beginning with 1856, they were made in larger numbers, and from 1859 onward the yearly production was in the multiple hundreds. Proofs of the later era are readily available today; truly choice and gem pieces with no distracting hairlines are in the minority and will require diligent searching.

GRADING STANDARDS

MS-60 to 70 (Mint State). *Obverse:* At MS-60, some abrasion and contact marks are evident, most noticeably on the bosom and thighs and knees. Luster is present, but may be dull or lifeless. At MS-63, contact marks are very few, and abrasion is hard to detect except under magnification. An MS-65 coin has no abrasion, and contact marks are sufficiently minute as to require magnification. Check the knees of Liberty and the right

1853, Repunched Date, No Arrows or Rays; FS-301. Graded MS-67.

field. Luster should be full and rich. Most Mint State coins of the 1861 to 1865 years, Philadelphia issues, have extensive die striae (from not completely finishing the die). *Reverse:* Comments apply as for the obverse, except that in lower Mint State grades abrasion and contact marks are most noticeable on the eagle's neck, the claws, and the top of the wings (harder to see there, however). At MS-65 or higher there are no marks visible to the unaided eye. The field is mainly protected by design elements and does not show abrasion as much as does the obverse on a given coin.

Illustrated coin: Note the delicate toning in the fields. In addition to hints of green, rose, and teal there is a good deal of luster as well.

AU-50, 53, 55, 58 (About Uncirculated). *Obverse:* Light wear is seen on the thighs and knees, bosom, and head. At AU-58, the luster is extensive, but incomplete, especially in the right field. At AU–50 and 53, luster is less. *Reverse:* Wear is evident on the eagle's neck, claws, and top of the wings. An AU-58 coin has nearly full luster, more so than on the obverse, as the design elements protect the small field areas. At AU–50 and 53, there still are traces of luster.

1891. Graded AU-53.

EF-40, 45 (Extremely Fine). *Obverse:* Further wear is seen on all areas, especially the thighs and knees, bosom, and head. Little or no luster is seen on most coins. From this grade downward, sharpness of strike of the stars and the head does not matter to connoisseurs. *Reverse:* Further wear is evident on the eagle's neck, claws, and wings. Some feathers in the right wing may be blended together.

1843. Graded EF-40.

VF-20, 30 (Very Fine). *Obverse:* Further wear is seen. Most details of the gown are worn away, except in the lower-relief areas above and to the right of the shield. Hair detail is mostly or completely gone. *Reverse:* Wear is more extensive, with more feathers blended together, especially in the right wing. The area below the shield shows more wear.

Illustrated coin: The surfaces of this coin are unusually smooth and problem free for the issue.

1860-S. Graded VF-20.

F-12, 15 (Fine). *Obverse:* The seated figure is well worn, but with some detail above and to the right of the shield. LIBERTY is readable but weak in areas. *Reverse:* Wear is extensive, with about half of the feathers flat or blended with others.

1854-O. Graded F-12.

VG-8, 10 (Very Good). *Obverse:* The seated figure is more worn, but some detail can be seen above and to the right of the shield. The shield is discernible. In LIBERTY at least the equivalent of two or three letters (can be a combination of partial letters) must be readable but can be very weak at VG-8, with a few more visible at VG-10. However, LIBERTY is not an infallible guide to grade this type, as some varieties had the word in low relief on

1872-CC. Graded VG-10.

the die, so it wore away slowly. *Reverse:* Further wear has flattened all but a few feathers, and the horizontal lines of the shield are indistinct. The leaves are only in outline form. The rim is visible all around, as are the ends of most denticles.

Illustrated coin: Note the faint red toning evident in areas of this otherwise pleasingly gray coin.

G-4, 6 (Good). *Obverse:* The seated figure is worn smooth. At G-4 there are no letters in LIBERTY remaining on most (but not all) coins; some coins, especially of the early 1870s, are exceptions. At G-6, traces of one or two can barely be seen. *Reverse:* The designs are only in outline form, although some vertical shield stripes can be seen on some. The rim is worn down, and tops of the border letters are weak or worn away, although the inscription can still be read.

1872-CC. Graded G-6.

AG-3 (About Good). *Obverse:* The seated figure is mostly visible in outline form, with only a hint of detail. Much of the rim is worn away. The date remains clear. *Reverse:* The border letters are partially worn away. The eagle is mostly in outline form, but with a few details discernible. The rim is weak or missing.

1862-S. Graded AG-3.

PF-60 to 70 (Proof). *Obverse and Reverse:* Proofs that are extensively cleaned and have many hairlines, or that are dull and grainy, are lower level, such as PF–60 to 62. These are not widely desired by connoisseurs. With medium hairlines and good reflectivity, an assigned grade of PF-64 is appropriate and with relatively few hairlines, Gem PF-65. In various grades hairlines are most easily seen in the obverse field. PF-66 should have hairlines so delicate that magnification is needed to see them. Above that, a Proof should be free of such lines.

1860. Graded PF-65.

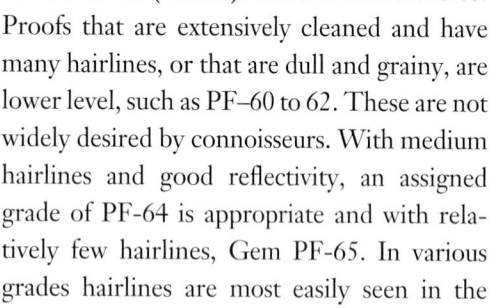

| 1839, No Drapery | 1840-O, Drapery | 1840-O, Drapery, Normal O | 1840-O, Drapery, Large O |

Coins designated Deep Cameo or Ultra Cameo bring a premium of 50% to 100% above listed values.

	Mintage	Cert	Avg	%MS	G-4	VG-8	F-12	VF-20	EF-40	AU-50	MS-60	MS-63	MS-65
											PF-60	PF-63	PF-65
1838, No Drapery	466,000	183	53.9	44%	$35	$40	$60	$100	$375	$750	$2,000	$6,750	$35,000
	Auctions: $3,055, MS-63, January 2015; $591, AU-53, January 2015; $794, AU-50, January 2015; $364, EF-45, March 2015												
1838, Proof	2–3	0	n/a						(extremely rare)				
	Auctions: No auction records available.												
1839, No Drapery	491,146	149	51.7	30%	$35	$40	$60	$100	$375	$750	$1,850	$5,000	$45,000
	Auctions: $940, AU-58, June 2015; $1,116, AU-55, September 2015; $823, AU-53, January 2015; $764, AU-53, June 2015												
1839, Proof (a)	2–3	1	65.0										$500,000
	Auctions: $270,250, PF-65, October 2014; $411,250, PF-65, April 2013												
1840-O, No Drapery	382,200	138	47.3	24%	$40	$45	$70	$120	$400	$800	$2,000	$8,000	$40,000
	Auctions: $199,750, MS-67, May 2015; $19,975, MS-65, May 2015; $3,533, MS-63, June 2015; $1,410, MS-62, September 2015												
1840, Drapery	188,127	43	51.1	30%	$25	$30	$55	$100	$180	$300	$950	$4,500	$25,000
	Auctions: $17,625, MS-66, May 2015; $16,450, MS-64, October 2015; $423, AU-53, June 2015; $306, AU-53, May 2015												
1840, Drapery, Proof	5–8	2	64.5										$75,000
	Auctions: $99,889, PF-65, August 2013												
1840-O, Drapery	43,000	73	50.6	34%	$30	$50	$70	$110	$210	$500	$1,300	$4,000	$20,000
	Auctions: $16,450, MS-65, May 2015; $2,585, MS-63, March 2015; $1,410, MS-62, October 2015; $1,293, AU-58, October 2015												
1840-O, Drapery, Large O (b)	(c)	0	n/a							$4,750	$9,000		
	Auctions: $3,220, MS-63, December 2010												

a. This piece is unique. **b.** The O mintmark punch is about 25% larger than normal. There are two known reverse dies for this variety, with one showing doubled denticles. **c.** Included in 1840-O, Drapery, mintage figure.

1842, Small Date	1842, Large Date	1842-O, Small Date	1842-O, Large Date
Philadelphia Small Date is Proof only.			

	Mintage	Cert	Avg	%MS	G-4	VG-8	F-12	VF-20	EF-40	AU-50	MS-60 / PF-60	MS-63 / PF-63	MS-65 / PF-65
1841	120,000	67	56.8	61%	$45	$70	$100	$150	$250	$325	$900	$2,500	$12,000
Auctions: $28,200, MS-66, May 2015; $8,225, MS-65, October 2015; $6,463, MS-65, October 2015; $1,528, AU-58, August 2015													
1841, Proof	3–5	1	66.0								$65,000	$100,000	$200,000
Auctions: $235,000, PF-66, April 2013													
1841-O	452,000	67	54.9	52%	$30	$45	$60	$80	$175	$320	$800	$1,900	$15,000
Auctions: $1,763, MS-63, August 2015; $646, AU-58, February 2015; $353, AU-53, June 2015; $306, AU-50, June 2015													
1842, Large Date (d)	88,000	43	51.9	33%	$75	$100	$160	$250	$350	$650	$1,750	$4,500	$12,500
Auctions: $1,175, AU-58, August 2015; $423, EF-45, July 2015; $423, EF-40, May 2015; $318, VF-30, January 2015													
1842, Small Date, Proof † (e)	3–5	2	65.0									$60,000	$125,000
Auctions: $164,500, PF-66, January 2015; $282,000, PF-65, October 2014; $258,500, PF-65, August 2013													
1842-O, All kinds	769,000												
1842-O, Small Date		17	25.4	6%	$350	$550	$1,000	$1,900	$3,750	$7,500	$20,000	$75,000	
Auctions: $12,925, AU-55, October 2015; $1,763, F-12, August 2015; $1,028, VG-10, August 2015; $940, VG-8, June 2015													
1842-O, Large Date		54	38.0	28%	$30	$50	$70	$110	$220	$600	$1,750	$4,500	
Auctions: $3,290, MS-63, November 2014; $423, MS-60, July 2015; $306, AU-53, November 2014; $141, AU-50, May 2015													
1843	645,600	95	58.1	56%	$25	$30	$35	$45	$85	$175	$450	$1,250	$6,500
Auctions: $4,935, MS-65, May 2015; $483, MS-61, May 2015; $188, AU-55, March 2015; $141, EF-45, May 2015													
1843, Proof	10–15	4	61.0								$12,500	$20,000	$45,000
Auctions: $64,625, PF-66, April 2013													
1843-O	968,000	54	44.1	15%	$30	$45	$60	$125	$250	$800	$2,250	$8,500	$25,000
Auctions: $19,975, MS-64, May 2015; $7,050, MS-64, May 2015; $3,290, EF-45, October 2015; $1,880, EF-40, February 2015													
1844	421,200	89	55.8	47%	$25	$30	$35	$45	$85	$175	$525	$1,500	$8,000
Auctions: $4,935, MS-64, June 2015; $940, MS-61, June 2015; $306, AU-53, May 2015; $100, AU-50, November 2014													
1844, Proof (f)	3–5	1	66.0										
Auctions: $276,000, PF-66, July 2009													
1844-O	740,000	49	50.3	31%	$30	$45	$60	$85	$200	$360	$1,500	$3,000	$10,000
Auctions: $1,880, MS-63, July 2015; $259, AU-50, July 2015; $141, VF-25, January 2015; $69, VF-20, November 2014													
1845	922,000	129	56.1	49%	$25	$30	$35	$45	$80	$160	$450	$1,250	$6,000
Auctions: $705, MS-62, September 2015; $517, MS-62, February 2015; $494, AU-58, August 2015; $423, AU-58, August 2015													
1845, Proof	6–8	7	64.6									$30,000	$55,000
Auctions: $31,725, PF-65, October 2015; $26,438, PF-64, September 2015; $25,850, PF-64, August 2015													
1846	510,000	79	55.3	43%	$25	$30	$35	$50	$85	$180	$600	$1,500	$16,000
Auctions: $22,325, MS-66, January 2014													
1846, Proof	15–20	11	64.5								$5,000	$10,000	$30,000
Auctions: $25,850, PF-65, April 2013													
1847	734,000	67	54.8	48%	$25	$30	$35	$45	$80	$160	$575	$1,500	$10,000
Auctions: $10,575, MS-65, May 2015; $1,410, MS-63, July 2015; $940, AU-58, May 2015; $705, AU-58, October 2015													
1847, Proof	6–8	4	65.3								$5,000	$10,000	$35,000
Auctions: $17,625, PF-66, October 2015; $28,200, PF-65, November 2013; $14,688, PF-64, July 2014													
1847-O	368,000	37	43.9	16%	$35	$50	$75	$150	$800	$1,800	$4,500	$12,500	
Auctions: $8,225, MS-62, October 2015; $4,230, AU-58, August 2015; $1,293, EF-45, June 2015; $376, VF-20, August 2015													

† Ranked in the *100 Greatest U.S. Coins* (fourth edition). **d.** The Large Date was used on the Philadelphia Mint's 1842 coins struck for circulation. **e.** For the Philadelphia Mint's quarters of 1842, the Small Date was used on Proofs only. **f.** 2 examples are known.

1853, Repunched Date, No Arrows or Rays
FS-25-1853-301.

1853, 3 Over 4 (Arrows at Date, Rays Around Eagle)
FS-25-1853-1301.

	Mintage	Cert	Avg	%MS	G-4	VG-8	F-12	VF-20	EF-40	AU-50	MS-60 PF-60	MS-63 PF-63	MS-65 PF-65
1848	146,000	38	49.0	34%	$25	$35	$60	$100	$175	$300	$1,150	$4,000	$15,000
	Auctions: $5,170, MS-64, January 2015; $4,230, MS-63, October 2015; $1,116, AU-55, January 2015; $494, EF-45, June 2015												
1848, Proof	5–8	2	65.0								$5,000	$10,000	$30,000
	Auctions: $64,625, PF-66, October 2014; $55,813, PF-66, August 2013; $22,325, PF-65, January 2015												
1849	340,000	93	53.7	33%	$25	$30	$45	$75	$160	$250	$800	$2,000	$12,000
	Auctions: $11,163, MS-65, August 2015; $8,813, MS-65, May 2015; $8,225, MS-65, August 2015; $1,116, MS-63, January 2015												
1849, Proof	5–8	3	64.3								$5,000	$10,000	$27,500
	Auctions: $32,900, PF-65, January 2014												
1849-O	(g)	42	34.2	14%	$450	$600	$1,100	$2,400	$6,000	$7,750	$15,000	$20,000	
	Auctions: $24,675, MS-64, May 2015; $17,625, MS-63, January 2015; $7,050, AU-55, August 2015; $7,050, AU-53, January 2015												
1850	190,800	34	57.7	56%	$30	$45	$65	$95	$175	$240	$1,000	$3,500	$11,000
	Auctions: $13,513, MS-65, October 2015; $3,055, MS-64, November 2014; $1,293, MS-60, November 2014; $306, AU-50, June 2015												
1850, Proof	5–8	2	63.5										
	Auctions: $258,500, PF-68, August 2013												
1850-O	412,000	65	52.8	42%	$30	$45	$65	$95	$175	$475	$1,600	$3,500	$15,000
	Auctions: $9,400, MS-64, October 2015; $3,525, MS-63, August 2015; $447, EF-40, February 2015; $212, VF-35, May 2015												
1851	160,000	40	50.7	33%	$35	$50	$75	$125	$200	$300	$1,000	$2,000	$9,500
	Auctions: $4,935, MS-65, October 2015; $646, EF-45, August 2015; $764, EF-40, January 2015; $517, VF-35, August 2015												
1851-O	88,000	37	27.7	8%	$150	$275	$500	$1,000	$1,500	$3,000	$8,000	$32,500	
	Auctions: $881, VF-20, June 2015; $823, F-12, August 2015; $764, VG-10, August 2015; $376, G-4, January 2015												
1852	177,060	53	56.0	58%	$45	$55	$95	$135	$225	$300	$675	$1,500	$7,000
	Auctions: $99,875, MS-68, May 2015; $18,800, MS-66, October 2015; $3,760, MS-65, July 2015; $646, EF-45, August 2015												
1852, Proof	5–8	1	65.0										$75,000
	Auctions: $105,750, PF-65, April 2013												
1852-O	96,000	26	31.1	8%	$175	$250	$400	$1,000	$2,250	$4,500	$9,000	$40,000	
	Auctions: $21,150, MS-62, May 2015; $18,800, MS-62, October 2015; $999, F-15, January 2015; $764, VG-10, August 2015												
1853, Repunched Date, No Arrows or Rays (h)	44,200	42	48.5	48%	$300	$400	$625	$800	$1,500	$2,500	$3,500	$5,500	$12,000
	Auctions: $32,900, MS-67, June 2015; $19,975, MS-66, October 2015; $9,400, MS-65, October 2015; $3,760, EF-40, June 2015												
1853, Variety 2	15,210,020	1,246	50.0	34%	$25	$30	$35	$50	$175	$300	$1,000	$2,500	$12,500
	Auctions: $17,625, MS-65, August 2015; $11,163, MS-65, August 2015; $9,988, MS-65, February 2015; $7,638, MS-65, October 2015												
1853, Variety 2, 3 Over 4 (i)	(j)	51	42.5	22%	$35	$70	$110	$225	$350	$675	$2,000	$5,500	$40,000
	Auctions: $9,988, MS-64, October 2014; $617, EF-45, August 2015; $423, VF-35, September 2015; $282, VF-25, February 2015												
1853, Variety 2, Proof	10–15	5	65.2								$30,000	$50,000	$140,000
	Auctions: $141,000, PF-66Cam, August 2013; $64,625, PF-64, October 2014; $41,125, PF-64, May 2015												
1853-O, Variety 2	1,332,000	94	45.7	17%	$25	$45	$60	$75	$250	$1,100	$3,250	$10,000	$30,000
	Auctions: $17,625, MS-64, October 2015; $1,293, AU-53, August 2015; $1,058, EF-45, February 2015; $306, EF-45, May 2015												

g. Included in 1850-O mintage figure. **h.** The secondary 5 and 3 are evident south of the primary digits. In the past, this variety was erroneously attributed as a 53 Over 2 overdate. This is the only die known for 1853 that lacks the arrows and rays. **i.** In addition to the 3 punched over a 4, there is also evidence of the repunched 8 and 5 (weaker images slightly north and west of the primary digits). The right arrow shaft is also doubled, north of the primary. "On well-worn or late-die-state specimens, the doubling of the arrow shaft may be the only evidence of the overdate. This is the only quarter dollar date known to be punched over the *following* year!" (*Cherrypickers' Guide to Rare Die Varieties*, sixth edition, volume II). **j.** Included in 1853, Variety 2, mintage figure.

1854-O, Normal O

1854-O, Huge O

**1856-S,
S Over Small S**
FS-25-1856S-501.

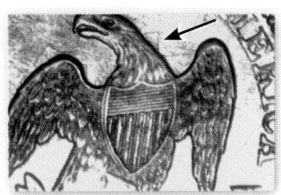
**1857, Clashed
Reverse Die**
FS-25-1857-901.

	Mintage	Cert	Avg	%MS	G-4	VG-8	F-12	VF-20	EF-40	AU-50	MS-60	MS-63	MS-65
											PF-60	PF-63	PF-65
1854	12,380,000	672	52.2	36%	$25	$30	$35	$45	$75	$225	$500	$1,100	$6,500
	Auctions: $8,225, MS-65, October 2015; $4,230, MS-65, February 2015; $4,230, MS-65, June 2015; $1,998, MS-64, September 2015												
1854, Proof	20–30	10	64.3								$10,000	$20,000	$50,000
	Auctions: $30,550, PF-66, April 2013												
1854-O, Normal O	1,484,000	100	45.5	34%	$30	$35	$45	$55	$100	$275	$1,200	$2,500	$15,000
	Auctions: $23,500, MS-66, October 2015; $15,275, MS-65, January 2015; $14,100, MS-65, October 2015; $247, AU-50, October 2015												
1854-O, Huge O (k)	(l)	61	19.2	0%	$900	$1,250	$2,000	$2,500	$6,000	$12,000			
	Auctions: $4,994, EF-45, February 2013; $705, G-6, August 2014; $558, AG-3, July 2014												
1855	2,857,000	179	53.9	40%	$25	$30	$35	$45	$85	$225	$575	$1,450	$12,000
	Auctions: $27,025, MS-67, May 2015; $17,625, MS-66, October 2015; $23,406, MS-65, July 2015; $1,116, MS-63, March 2015												
1855, Proof	20–30	10	64.6								$8,500	$17,500	$45,000
	Auctions: $28,200, PF-66, October 2014; $21,150, PF-65Cam, April 2013; $8,225, PF-62, October 2015												
1855-O	176,000	33	44.4	33%	$40	$65	$110	$275	$400	$2,000	$4,750	$12,000	
	Auctions: $82,250, MS-67, May 2015; $12,925, MS-63, October 2015; $823, VF-20, August 2015; $235, VF-20, September 2014												
1855-S	396,400	31	41.1	16%	$40	$60	$85	$175	$350	$1,200	$3,000	$8,500	$30,000
	Auctions: $19,975, MS-65, January 2015; $15,275, MS-64, May 2015; $7,050, MS-63, October 2015; $423, EF-40, May 2015												
1855-S, Proof	1–2	1	64.0					*(unique)*					
	Auctions: $176,250, PF-64, August 2013												
1856	7,264,000	264	53.5	45%	$25	$30	$35	$45	$75	$175	$350	$600	$4,000
	Auctions: $3,525, MS-66, January 2015; $3,290, MS-66, July 2015; $5,288, MS-66, October 2015; $3,231, MS-66, June 2015												
1856, Proof	40–50	28	64.0								$3,500	$6,000	$15,000
	Auctions: $12,959, PF-66, August 2014; $11,750, PF-66, May 2015; $12,925, PF-65, January 2015; $9,400, PF-65, October 2015												
1856-O	968,000	76	47.8	21%	$25	$45	$55	$65	$80	$250	$1,100	$2,500	$12,000
	Auctions: $11,163, MS-65, March 2015; $4,230, MS-64, October 2015; $940, AU-58, January 2015; $259, AU-50, September 2015												
1856-S, All kinds	286,000												
1856-S		24	41.7	25%	$40	$60	$100	$200	$1,500	$2,250	$6,500	$15,000	$40,000
	Auctions: $441, EF-40, July 2015; $259, EF-40, June 2015; $646, VF-20, August 2015; $423, VF-20, May 2015												
1856-S, S Over Small S (m)		5	19	0%	$200	$325	$750	$2,500	$7,500	$15,000	—		
	Auctions: $28,200, AU-58, June 2014												
1857	9,644,000	552	55.1	55%	$25	$30	$35	$45	$75	$175	$350	$600	$3,000
	Auctions: $14,100, MS-67, June 2015; $12,925, MS-67, September 2015; $10,575, MS-67, August 2015; $10,575, MS-67, October 2015												
1857, Clashed Rev Die (n)	(o)	5	50.2	40%					$500	$750			
	Auctions: No auction records available.												
1857, Proof	40–50	34	63.9								$3,250	$4,750	$13,500
	Auctions: $7,050, PF-66, January 2015; $6,463, PF-66, June 2015; $2,820, PF-63, January 2015; $2,233, PF-62, June 2015												
1857-O	1,180,000	80	50	23%	$30	$40	$50	$60	$150	$400	$1,200	$3,000	
	Auctions: $7,050, MS-64, October 2015; $2,820, MS-63, October 2015; $2,585, MS-63, October 2015; $1,880, MS-63, August 2015												
1857-S	82,000	41	49.4	22%	$60	$110	$200	$375	$600	$1,200	$3,000	$8,750	
	Auctions: $11,163, MS-64, October 2015; $8,813, MS-64, October 2015; $940, EF-40, August 2015; $588, VF-30, July 2015												

k. The Huge O mintmark is very large, extremely thick on the left side, and irregular, suggesting that it was punched into the die by hand. **l.** Included in 1854-O mintage figure. **m.** A larger S mintmark was punched over a much smaller S mintmark, the latter probably intended for half-dime production. **n.** The reverse clashed with the reverse die of an 1857 Flying Eagle cent. Images of the cent reverse die are easily visible on either side of the eagle's neck, within the shield, and below the eagle's left wing. **o.** Included in circulation-strike 1857 mintage figure.

	Mintage	Cert	Avg	%MS	G-4	VG-8	F-12	VF-20	EF-40	AU-50	MS-60 / PF-60	MS-63 / PF-63	MS-65 / PF-65
1858	7,368,000	418	54.7	52%	$25	$30	$35	$45	$75	$175	$350	$600	$3,500
Auctions: $17,625, MS-67, May 2015; $3,760, MS-66, October 2015; $3,290, MS-66, October 2015; $2,703, MS-65, October 2015													
1858, Proof	*300*	71	63.5								$1,500	$2,500	$6,500
Auctions: $28,200, PF-67, September 2015; $9,400, PF-66, October 2014; $7,638, PF-66, October 2015; $4,935, PF-65, February 2015													
1858-O	520,000	44	49.3	16%	$30	$40	$45	$65	$125	$350	$1,800	$7,500	$30,000
Auctions: $14,100, MS-65, October 2015; $21,150, MS-64, May 2015; $7,638, MS-62, October 2015; $94, EF-45, September 2014													
1858-S	121,000	38	38.0	3%	$50	$75	$250	$650	$2,250	$5,000	$15,000	—	
Auctions: $35,250, MS-62, May 2015; $28,200, MS-62, October 2015; $8,813, AU-58, October 2015; $1,645, VF-35, August 2015													
1859	1,343,200	144	55.1	49%	$25	$30	$35	$45	$80	$175	$400	$1,100	$5,000
Auctions: $3,878, MS-65, January 2015; $3,819, MS-65, January 2015; $3,055, MS-65, September 2015; $1,645, MS-64, August 2015													
1859, Proof	800	156	64.1								$1,050	$2,250	$5,750
Auctions: $17,625, PF-67, May 2015; $7,638, PF-66, October 2015; $4,583, PF-65Cam, September 2015; $1,998, PF-64Cam, January 2015													
1859-O	260,000	44	51.5	25%	$25	$40	$50	$65	$135	$400	$1,250	$4,000	$12,500
Auctions: $793, AU-55, January 2015; $423, AU-53, August 2015; $329, AU-50, February 2015; $329, AU-50, March 2015													
1859-S	80,000	22	29.3	0%	$100	$200	$350	$650	$4,500	$15,000	—		
Auctions: $9,988, AU-50, October 2015; $6,756, EF-45, January 2015; $940, VF-25, July 2015; $1,028, VG-10, August 2015													
1860	804,400	123	55.5	41%	$25	$30	$35	$45	$80	$175	$400	$1,000	$5,500
Auctions: $200, MS-60, May 2015; $130, AU-50, May 2015; $118, EF-40, November 2015; $94, EF-40, August 2015													
1860, Proof	1,000	108	64.0								$750	$1,200	$5,500
Auctions: $21,150, PF-68, May 2015; $7,050, PF-66, February 2015; $5,875, PF-66, October 2015; $3,525, PF-65, August 2015													
1860-O	388,000	78	55.1	40%	$30	$45	$55	$65	$95	$375	$1,000	$2,250	$12,500
Auctions: $3,055, MS-64, July 2015; $1,350, MS-63, September 2015; $1,028, MS-62, June 2015; $176, AU-50, October 2015													
1860-S	56,000	21	27.3	0%	$600	$1,000	$2,000	$5,000	$9,500	$20,000	$50,000		
Auctions: $15,275, AU-50, January 2015; $8,813, EF-45, January 2015; $8,225, EF-45, September 2015; $8,049, EF-40, August 2015													
1861	4,853,600	620	57.4	56%	$25	$30	$33	$45	$80	$175	$350	$750	$3,500
Auctions: $12,925, MS-67, August 2015; $11,750, MS-67, September 2015; $3,760, MS-66, September 2015; $2,350, MS-65, September 2015													
1861, Proof	1,000	103	63.6								$750	$1,200	$5,500
Auctions: $10,575, PF-67, October 2015; $6,169, PF-66, January 2015; $5,405, PF-66, October 2015; $1,410, PF-64, January 2015													
1861-S	96,000	29	30.4	0%	$250	$450	$900	$2,000	$3,500	$10,000			
Auctions: $21,150, AU-58, May 2015; $1,293, VF-20, February 2015; $1,469, F-15, August 2015; $940, F-12, August 2015													
1862	932,000	165	57.4	62%	$25	$30	$33	$50	$85	$175	$350	$750	$4,000
Auctions: $7,638, MS-67, June 2015; $3,995, MS-66, October 2015; $1,293, MS-64, October 2015; $999, MS-64, October 2015													
1862, Proof	550	133	63.7								$750	$1,200	$5,500
Auctions: $9,988, PF-67Cam, October 2015; $6,463, PF-66, May 2015; $6,169, PF-66, October 2015; $1,998, PF-64, August 2015													
1862-S	67,000	45	44.9	24%	$55	$85	$150	$325	$800	$1,800	$3,800	$10,000	
Auctions: $6,463, MS-62, October 2015; $3,525, MS-62, January 2015; $2,115, AU-53, July 2015; $447, VF-25, August 2015													
1863	191,600	64	56.9	66%	$40	$50	$75	$130	$240	$375	$650	$1,100	$4,500
Auctions: $4,935, MS-65, October 2015; $1,586, MS-64, January 2015; $881, MS-62, June 2015; $823, MS-61, June 2015													
1863, Proof	460	156	63.6								$750	$1,200	$5,000
Auctions: $8,519, PF-67, January 2015; $5,875, PF-66, October 2015; $2,585, PF-64, August 2015; $1,998, PF-64, June 2015													
1864	93,600	59	53.7	59%	$75	$100	$160	$225	$325	$475	$800	$2,100	$5,500
Auctions: $35,250, MS-67, May 2015; $14,100, MS-66, October 2015; $494, AU-50, September 2015; $646, EF-45, August 2015													
1864, Proof	470	187	63.9								$750	$1,200	$5,500
Auctions: $3,760, PF-65Cam, October 2015; $2,585, PF-64Cam, January 2015; $1,528, PF-64, January 2015; $1,410, PF-63Cam, July 2015													
1864-S	20,000	42	30.4	14%	$600	$900	$1,200	$2,700	$3,800	$5,500	$12,000	$25,000	
Auctions: $28,200, MS-64, October 2015; $3,525, EF-40, August 2015; $2,585, VF-30, January 2015; $1,293, F-15, January 2015													
1865	58,800	48	48.1	33%	$100	$125	$175	$250	$425	$575	$1,000	$1,850	$8,000
Auctions: $32,900, MS-67, January 2015; $1,645, MS-62, August 2015; $400, VF-35, April 2015; $153, VF-20, October 2015													
1865, Proof	500	180	64.0								$750	$1,200	$5,500
Auctions: $23,500, PF-68, May 2015; $12,925, PF-67Cam, October 2015; $5,405, PF-66Cam, October 2015; $8,225, PF-66, September 2015													
1865-S	41,000	41	50.4	44%	$150	$250	$350	$500	$1,000	$1,750	$3,000	$6,000	$15,000
Auctions: $64,625, MS-66, February 2014; $999, EF-40, October 2014; $764, VF-35, February 2015; $200, G-4, September 2014													

	Mintage	Cert	Avg	%MS	G-4	VG-8	F-12	VF-20	EF-40	AU-50	MS-60 PF-60	MS-63 PF-63	MS-65 PF-65
1866	16,800	43	53.0	65%	$600	$750	$900	$1,100	$1,600	$1,850	$2,200	$2,750	$6,500
Auctions: $1,410, VF-25, August 2015; $1,175, VF-25, November 2015; $1,058, VF-25, August 2015; $999, VF-20, June 2015													
1866, No Motto, Proof † (p)	1	0	n/a					*(unique)*					
Auctions: No auction records available.													
1866, Proof	725	158	64.0								$500	$1,000	$2,500
Auctions: $19,975, PF-68, November 2013													
1866-S	28,000	25	30.5	20%	$400	$800	$1,200	$1,800	$3,250	$5,000	$7,000	$14,000	$34,500
Auctions: $25,263, MS-65, October 2014; $1,293, VF-30, September 2014; $1,175, VF-20, October 2014; $764, F-12, June 2015													
1867	20,000	32	44.4	38%	$400	$600	$700	$800	$1,350	$1,650	$2,250		$8,500
Auctions: $9,400, MS-64, October 2015; $6,463, MS-63, October 2015; $3,760, MS-63, October 2015; $1,528, AU-55, October 2015													
1867, Proof	625	176	64.0								$500	$1,000	$2,500
Auctions: $3,525, PF-66, October 2015; $2,703, PF-64Cam, October 2015; $1,116, PF-64, October 2015; $764, PF-63, September 2015													
1867-S	48,000	18	26.0	11%	$400	$600	$850	$1,250	$2,250	$7,500	$11,500	$20,000	
Auctions: $88,125, MS-67, May 2015; $17,625, MS-64, June 2015; $3,525, EF-45, June 2015; $1,410, VF-25, June 2015													
1868	29,400	32	52.3	56%	$150	$225	$300	$375	$550	$650	$1,200	$2,200	$9,000
Auctions: $8,225, MS-65, October 2015; $7,050, MS-65, August 2015; $400, EF-40, May 2015; $354, EF-40, August 2015													
1868, Proof	600	157	63.5								$500	$1,000	$2,500
Auctions: $4,465, PF-66, January 2015; $3,055, PF-66, October 2015; $2,820, PF-65, January 2015; $2,233, PF-65, September 2015													
1868-S	96,000	41	40.6	27%	$100	$150	$275	$600	$900	$1,500	$3,500	$7,750	$25,000
Auctions: $82,250, MS-67, August 2015; $18,800, MS-66, August 2015; $14,100, MS-64, October 2015; $999, EF-40, July 2015													
1869	16,000	24	43.5	46%	$400	$550	$750	$1,000	$1,400	$1,800	$2,250	$3,000	$12,000
Auctions: $1,028, VF-25, August 2015; $646, VF-20, July 2015; $764, F-12, August 2015; $541, G-6, April 2015													
1869, Proof	600	174	63.5								$500	$1,000	$2,500
Auctions: $18,800, PF-67Cam, November 2013; $4,818, PF-67, October 2015; $3,290, PF-66, October 2015; $445, PF-53, September 2014													
1869-S	76,000	30	39.2	17%	$100	$200	$400	$550	$750	$1,000	$2,750	$6,500	$15,000
Auctions: $9,988, MS-64, October 2015; $564, VF-25, July 2015; $400, F-15, August 2015; $447, F-12, February 2015													
1870	86,400	33	50.8	36%	$50	$100	$150	$200	$275	$550	$800	$2,200	$8,750
Auctions: $8,813, MS-66, May 2015; $382, EF-45, November 2014; $306, EF-45, April 2015; $212, EF-40, May 2015													
1870, Proof	1,000	162	63.5								$500	$975	$2,600
Auctions: $6,169, PF-67, October 2014; $3,290, PF-66, January 2015; $1,087, PF-64, January 2015; $1,763, PF-63, January 2015													
1870-CC	8,340	27	26.6	4%	$10,000	$14,000	$18,500	$25,000	$35,000	$80,000	$200,000		
Auctions: $188,000, AU-55, May 2015; $70,500, AU-53, January 2014; $10,281, VG-8, August 2015													
1871	118,200	44	54.3	59%	$50	$100	$150	$200	$275	$450	$600	$1,500	$7,000
Auctions: $32,900, MS-67, June 2014; $6,484, MS-65, October 2015; $1,175, MS-63, June 2015; $259, AU-50, May 2015													
1871, Proof	960	142	63.6								$500	$975	$2,600
Auctions: $15,275, PF-68, May 2015; $4,706, PF-67, October 2015; $3,055, PF-66, August 2015; $2,820, PF-66, January 2015													
1871-CC	10,890	13	25.0	8%	$8,000	$12,000	$18,000	$25,000	$50,000	$75,000	$100,000		$350,000
Auctions: $352,500, MS-65, June 2014; $79,313, AU-55, October 2015; $11,163, VG-8, August 2015; $8,225, G-6, July 2015													
1871-S	30,900	26	51.7	54%	$900	$1,200	$1,750	$2,250	$3,500	$4,500	$6,750	$10,000	$17,500
Auctions: $17,625, MS-65, October 2015; $4,406, AU-58, March 2015; $2,115, VF-25, August 2015; $2,527, F-12, September 2015													
1872	182,000	60	52.5	45%	$30	$40	$60	$115	$250	$450	$650	$2,000	$7,500
Auctions: $6,025, MS-65, August 2015; $2,820, MS-64, February 2015; $2,115, MS-63, August 2015; $541, AU-58, August 2015													
1872, Proof	950	179	64.0								$500	$950	$2,200
Auctions: $6,756, PF-67Cam, October 2015; $2,820, PF-66, June 2015; $2,585, PF-65Cam, March 2015; $1,528, PF-65, January 2015													
1872-CC	22,850	28	21.0	4%	$1,650	$2,250	$3,600	$5,250	$9,000	$17,000	$40,000		
Auctions: $3,567, F-15, August 2015; $1,410, F-12, July 2015; $1,645, G-6, August 2015; $1,087, Fair-2, June 2015													
1872-S	83,000	20	43.1	45%	$1,600	$2,700	$3,600	$6,500	$8,000	$10,000	$15,000	$25,000	$55,000
Auctions: $10,575, MS-63, October 2015; $8,225, AU-55, June 2015; $4,700, F-15, August 2015; $3,995, F-15, August 2015													

† Ranked in the *100 Greatest U.S. Coins* (fourth edition). **p.** The unique 1866, Proof, quarter dollar without motto (as well as the half dollar and dollar of the same design) is not mentioned in the Mint director's report. "Not a pattern, but a muling created at a later date as a numismatic rarity" (*United States Pattern Coins*, tenth edition). Saul Teichman dates its creation to the 1870s. It is classified as Judd-536.

1873, Close 3   **1873, Open 3**

	Mintage	Cert	Avg	%MS	G-4	VG-8	F-12	VF-20	EF-40	AU-50	MS-60 / PF-60	MS-63 / PF-63	MS-65 / PF-65
1873, Variety 4, Close 3	40,000	13	32.5	23%	$375	$600	$900	$1,300	$2,350	$4,500	$18,000	$40,000	
Auctions: $9,988, AU-58, April 2014													
1873, Variety 4, Open 3	172,000	35	57.1	63%	$30	$45	$65	$125	$200	$300	$500	$1,100	$5,500
Auctions: $7,638, MS-66, May 2015; $3,290, MS-64, February 2015; $1,939, MS-64, June 2015; $1,763, MS-63, June 2015													
1873, Variety 4, Proof	600	173	63.6								$500	$950	$2,200
Auctions: $11,750, PF-67Cam, August 2015; $5,170, PF-67Cam, July 2015; $4,700, PF-66Cam, October 2015; $1,880, PF-65, June 2015													
1873-CC, Variety 4 † (q)	4,000	3	56.7	67%				—	$85,000	$115,000	$150,000	$400,000	
Auctions: $431,250, MS-63, January 2009													
1873, Variety 5	1,271,200	259	55.4	49%	$25	$30	$40	$60	$225	$425	$850	$1,650	$4,000
Auctions: $1,188, MS-63, September 2013													
1873, Variety 5, Proof	540	151	63.7								$900	$1,450	$7,000
Auctions: $14,100, PF-67, October 2015; $5,405, PF-66, September 2015; $2,820, PF-64Cam, January 2015; $2,585, PF-64, June 2015													
1873-CC, Variety 5	12,462	21	22.0	5%	$5,000	$8,000	$11,500	$17,000	$20,000	$35,000	$75,000	$125,000	
Auctions: $176,250, MS-64, May 2015; $76,375, AU-55, October 2015; $4,465, G-6, July 2015; $4,818, G-4, August 2015													
1873-S, Variety 5	156,000	64	50.5	36%	$50	$75	$125	$175	$350	$500	$1,500	$6,000	$20,000
Auctions: $18,800, MS-65, May 2015; $13,513, MS-65, October 2015; $11,163, MS-65, October 2015; $5,640, MS-64, October 2015													
1874	471,200	98	56.2	53%	$25	$30	$40	$65	$200	$450	$900	$1,550	$4,700
Auctions: $5,875, MS-66, November 2014; $1,528, MS-63, August 2014; $564, AU-58, May 2015; $89, EF-40, September 2015													
1874, Proof	700	260	64.0								$900	$1,450	$7,000
Auctions: $17,625, PF-67, May 2015; $7,050, PF-66, October 2015; $2,233, PF-64, February 2015; $1,998, PF-64, March 2015													
1874-S	392,000	155	60.5	78%	$25	$35	$65	$115	$265	$485	$950	$1,450	$3,750
Auctions: $18,800, MS-67, June 2015; $9,988, MS-67, October 2015; $4,465, MS-66, October 2015; $3,525, MS-65, June 2015													
1875	4,292,800	327	58.6	68%	$25	$30	$35	$45	$65	$160	$275	$550	$1,800
Auctions: $2,233, MS-66, October 2015; $1,528, MS-65, January 2015; $494, MS-63, September 2015; $376, MS-62, August 2015													
1875, Proof	700	165	63.8								$500	$900	$2,200
Auctions: $9,988, PF-68Cam, January 2015; $8,225, PF-67Cam, October 2015; $1,800, PF-65Cam, January 2015; $1,116, PF-64Cam, July 2015													
1875-CC	140,000	51	47.8	31%	$200	$350	$450	$600	$1,000	$2,100	$3,000	$6,750	$32,000
Auctions: $49,350, MS-66, February 2015; $30,550, MS-65, August 2015; $589, VF-25, August 2015; $564, VF-25, June 2015													
1875-S	680,000	100	56.2	60%	$35	$45	$70	$115	$200	$300	$600	$1,400	$3,750
Auctions: $6,580, MS-66, January 2015; $3,055, MS-65, October 2014; $68, EF-40, November 2014; $165, VF-35, May 2015													
1876	17,816,000	579	57.1	64%	$25	$30	$35	$45	$65	$160	$275	$550	$1,850
Auctions: $10,575, MS-67, May 2015; $8,225, MS-67, September 2015; $3,290, MS-66, October 2015; $999, MS-65, October 2015													
1876, Proof	1,150	222	63.8								$500	$900	$2,200
Auctions: $32,900, PF-68, May 2015; $10,281, PF-68, October 2015; $2,585, PF-66, January 2015; $1,645, PF-65Cam, July 2015													
1876-CC	4,944,000	374	48.5	44%	$45	$65	$75	$125	$200	$300	$600	$1,300	$4,500
Auctions: $9,400, MS-66, May 2015; $3,672, MS-65, August 2015; $646, MS-63, August 2015; $517, MS-62, September 2015													
1876-S	8,596,000	307	59.5	71%	$25	$30	$35	$45	$65	$160	$275	$550	$2,250
Auctions: $5,640, MS-66, May 2015; $4,230, MS-66, August 2015; $1,645, MS-65, August 2015; $541, MS-62, March 2015													

† Ranked in the *100 Greatest U.S. Coins* (fourth edition). **q.** 6 examples are known.

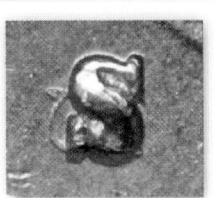

**1877-S, S Over
Horizontal S**
FS-25-1877S-501.

	Mintage	Cert	Avg	%MS	G-4	VG-8	F-12	VF-20	EF-40	AU-50	MS-60 / PF-60	MS-63 / PF-63	MS-65 / PF-65
1877	10,911,200	419	60.0	76%	$25	$30	$35	$45	$65	$160	$275	$550	$1,800
Auctions: $3,055, MS-67, July 2015; $2,938, MS-67, September 2015; $2,056, MS-66, September 2015; $940, MS-64, February 2015													
1877, Proof	510	147	63.9								$500	$900	$2,200
Auctions: $22,325, PF-68Cam, May 2015; $4,700, PF-67, October 2015; $3,055, PF-66Cam, January 2015; $1,528, PF-65, January 2015													
1877-CC (r)	4,192,000	506	55.9	66%	$45	$65	$75	$85	$120	$220	$475	$900	$2,500
Auctions: $15,289, MS-67, July 2015; $5,640, MS-66, October 2015; $3,525, MS-66, July 2015; $1,410, MS-64, July 2015													
1877-S	8,996,000	374	59.0	73%	$25	$30	$35	$45	$65	$160	$275	$550	$1,650
Auctions: $3,055, MS-67, October 2015; $1,528, MS-66, October 2015; $1,293, MS-65, October 2015; $705, MS-64, October 2015													
1877-S, S Over Horizontal S (s)	(t)	46	58.8	59%	$30	$45	$85	$150	$250	$400	$800	$2,200	$5,000
Auctions: $23,500, MS-66, June 2014; $1,645, MS-63, July 2014; $217, EF-45, November 2014													
1878	2,260,000	118	58.0	69%	$25	$30	$35	$45	$65	$160	$260	$550	$2,900
Auctions: $3,055, MS-66, October 2015; $2,585, MS-66, August 2015; $2,233, MS-65, June 2015; $1,763, MS-65, October 2015													
1878, Proof	800	200	63.6								$500	$900	$2,200
Auctions: $21,150, PF-68, May 2015; $3,525, PF-67, October 2015; $3,525, PF-66Cam, August 2015; $3,760, PF-66, January 2015													
1878-CC	996,000	266	55.3	62%	$55	$70	$85	$120	$200	$300	$700	$1,500	$4,000
Auctions: $823, MS-62, September 2015; $306, AU-50, August 2015; $235, AU-50, October 2015; $282, EF-40, April 2015													
1878-S	140,000	31	53.9	61%	$125	$230	$360	$525	$700	$1,300	$2,250	$4,000	$17,500
Auctions: $14,100, MS-65, January 2015; $1,528, AU-50, June 2015; $882, EF-40, August 2015; $823, VF-30, July 2015													
1879	13,600	213	63.3	92%	$175	$250	$325	$450	$525	$650	$725	$850	$2,250
Auctions: $23,500, MS-68, May 2015; $4,700, MS-67, May 2015; $1,998, MS-66, September 2015; $1,410, MS-65, January 2015													
1879, Proof	1,100	304	63.9								$500	$900	$2,200
Auctions: $3,995, PF-67, August 2015; $3,525, PF-67, May 2015; $1,821, PF-66, January 2015; $1,294, PF-65, January 2015													
1880	13,600	134	62.9	89%	$150	$225	$300	$400	$500	$600	$700	$850	$2,250
Auctions: $4,935, MS-67, October 2015; $3,525, MS-67, October 2015; $2,115, MS-66, July 2015; $1,293, MS-64, March 2015													
1880, Proof	1,355	378	64.3								$500	$900	$2,200
Auctions: $21,150, PF-68, May 2015; $7,638, PF-68, January 2015; $3,055, PF-67, October 2015; $2,585, PF-66Cam, January 2015													
1881	12,000	103	59.5	82%	$250	$300	$350	$400	$450	$500	$625	$850	$2,500
Auctions: $4,465, MS-67, October 2015; $2,350, MS-66, October 2015; $494, MS-60, May 2015; $447, VF-20, August 2015													
1881, Proof	975	294	64.3								$500	$900	$2,200
Auctions: $7,638, PF-68Cam, January 2015; $8,225, PF-68, October 2015; $2,350, PF-66Cam, January 2015; $1,880, PF-66, June 2015													
1882	15,200	76	59.9	82%	$300	$350	$400	$450	$500	$650	$625	$900	$2,250
Auctions: $19,975, MS-68, September 2015; $14,100, MS-68, May 2015; $646, AU-50, August 2015; $517, EF-45, August 2015													
1882, Proof	1,100	308	64.3								$500	$900	$2,200
Auctions: $18,800, PF-68Cam, May 2015; $9,400, PF-67DCam, February 2015; $4,465, PF-67, October 2015; $6,463, PF-66DCam, August 2015													
1883	14,400	83	60.1	87%	$300	$350	$400	$450	$550	$600	$625	$900	$2,500
Auctions: $4,700, MS-66, October 2015; $2,820, MS-66, June 2015; $2,350, MS-65, July 2015; $1,236, MS-64, July 2015													
1883, Proof	1,039	348	64.3								$500	$900	$2,200
Auctions: $8,225, PF-68, October 2015; $7,638, PF-67, May 2015; $2,350, PF-66Cam, September 2015; $1,645, PF-65, January 2015													

r. The 1877-CC quarter with fine edge-reeding is scarcer than that with normally spaced reeding; in the marketplace, there is no price differential. **s.** This variety, known since the 1950s, was caused by an initial S mintmark being punched into the die horizontally, and then corrected with an upright S mintmark. **t.** Included in 1877-S mintage figure.

	Mintage	Cert	Avg	%MS	G-4	VG-8	F-12	VF-20	EF-40	AU-50	MS-60	MS-63	MS-65
											PF-60	PF-63	PF-65
1884	8,000	99	57.3	78%	$325	$375	$425	$475	$550	$600	$700	$900	$2,000
Auctions: $8,519, MS-67, June 2015; $3,290, MS-66, October 2015; $881, AU-53, August 2015; $564, VF-35, August 2015
1884, Proof	875	282	64.5								$500	$900	$2,200
Auctions: $3,643, PF-67, October 2015; $2,115, PF-66, July 2015; $1,800, PF-66, June 2015; $2,115, PF-65, March 2015
1885	13,600	87	60.3	78%	$175	$235	$300	$375	$450	$550	$675	$1,100	$2,750
Auctions: $6,756, MS-67, May 2015; $3,055, MS-66, August 2015; $3,290, MS-65, October 2015; $705, MS-62, October 2015
1885, Proof	930	264	64.3								$500	$900	$2,200
Auctions: $5,881, PF-67Cam, June 2015; $4,700, PF-67, October 2015; $2,820, PF-67, January 2015; $1,998, PF-66Cam, January 2015
1886	5,000	42	58.3	79%	$700	$750	$800	$900	$1,000	$1,100	$1,200	$1,500	$3,200
Auctions: $6,169, MS-66, August 2015; $2,115, MS-65, October 2015; $1,410, MS-64, June 2015; $1,116, VF-30, August 2015
1886, Proof	886	296	64.4								$500	$900	$2,200
Auctions: $11,750, PF-68, May 2015; $12,925, PF-67Cam, October 2015; $21,150, PF-67, August 2015; $4,230, PF-66Cam, March 2015
1887	10,000	107	61.9	86%	$400	$500	$600	$700	$800	$900	$1,000	$1,300	$2,050
Auctions: $4,935, MS-67, October 2015; $2,585, MS-66, October 2015; $2,295, MS-66, January 2015; $999, MS-62, August 2015
1887, Proof	710	231	64.4								$500	$900	$2,200
Auctions: $7,638, PF-68, January 2015; $3,760, PF-67, October 2015; $2,350, PF-66Cam, January 2015; $1,880, PF-66, August 2015
1888	10,001	133	63.2	94%	$200	$245	$325	$425	$500	$650	$700	$1,000	$2,050
Auctions: $5,640, MS-67, May 2015; $3,760, MS-67, October 2015; $2,350, MS-66, January 2015; $1,351, MS-65, January 2015
1888, Proof	832	223	64.2								$500	$900	$2,200
Auctions: $3,525, PF-67, January 2015; $3,055, PF-66Cam, August 2015; $1,528, PF-65, January 2015; $282, PF-60, August 2015
1888-S	1,216,000	148	56.5	67%	$25	$30	$35	$45	$70	$160	$300	$850	$3,000
Auctions: $7,638, MS-66, May 2015; $6,463, MS-66, October 2015; $3,525, MS-65, September 2015; $1,528, MS-64, June 2015
1889	12,000	176	63.0	90%	$250	$300	$350	$400	$500	$600	$700	$850	$1,800
Auctions: $4,700, MS-67, January 2015; $3,525, MS-66, October 2015; $1,880, MS-65, January 2015; $1,116, MS-64, June 2015
1889, Proof	711	193	64.6								$500	$900	$2,200
Auctions: $15,275, PF-68, May 2015; $8,519, PF-68, October 2015; $1,880, PF-66, January 2015; $1,645, PF-65Cam, January 2015
1890	80,000	186	62.5	87%	$60	$75	$100	$125	$175	$300	$525	$775	$1,850
Auctions: $10,589, MS-68, June 2015; $3,995, MS-67, January 2015; $2,233, MS-66, October 2015; $2,350, MS-65, October 2015
1890, Proof	590	231	64.8								$500	$900	$2,200
Auctions: $4,700, PF-67Cam, September 2015; $3,643, PF-66Cam, January 2015; $1,500, PF-65, June 2015; $1,410, PF-64, August 2015
1891	3,920,000	662	60.7	77%	$25	$30	$35	$45	$65	$160	$260	$550	$1,800
Auctions: $4,230, MS-67, May 2015; $1,998, MS-65, June 2015; $1,763, MS-66, September 2015; $1,645, MS-66, January 2015
1891, Proof	600	242	64.6								$500	$900	$2,200
Auctions: $15,275, PF-67, October 2015; $3,760, PF-67, October 2015; $2,820, PF-66, January 2015; $1,528, PF-64Cam, October 2015
1891-O	68,000	40	41.1	40%	$250	$450	$750	$1,300	$2,250	$3,200	$4,400	$8,500	$30,000
Auctions: $28,200, MS-65, May 2015; $22,325, MS-65, January 2015; $14,100, MS-63, August 2015; $1,293, F-15, August 2015
1891-S	2,216,000	195	59.1	72%	$25	$30	$35	$45	$70	$160	$260	$550	$2,000
Auctions: $3,055, MS-66, May 2015; $1,645, MS-65, October 2015; $823, MS-64, October 2015; $564, MS-63, June 2015

BARBER OR LIBERTY HEAD (1892–1916)

Designer: *Charles E. Barber.* **Weight:** *6.25 grams.*
Composition: *.900 silver, .100 copper (net weight .18084 oz. pure silver).*
Diameter: *24.3 mm.* **Edge:** *Reeded.* **Mints:** *Philadelphia, Denver, New Orleans, and San Francisco.*

| Circulation Strike | Mintmark location is on the reverse, below the eagle. | Proof |

History. The Liberty Head design was by Charles E. Barber, chief engraver of the U.S. Mint. Barber quarters feature the same obverse motif used on dimes and half dollars of the era, with the designer's initial, B, found at the truncation of the neck of Miss Liberty. The reverse depicts a heraldic eagle holding an olive branch in one talon and arrows in the other, along with a ribbon reading E PLURIBUS UNUM.

Striking and Sharpness. On the obverse, check the hair details and other features. On the reverse, the eagle's leg at the lower right and the arrows can be weak. Also check the upper–right portion of the shield and the nearby wing. Once these coins entered circulation and acquired wear, the word LIBERTY on the headband tended to disappear quickly. Most Proofs are sharply struck, although more than just a few are weak on the eagle's leg at the lower right and on certain parts of the arrows. The Proofs of 1892 to 1901 usually have cameo contrast between the designs and the mirror fields. Later Proofs vary in their contrast.

Availability. Barber quarters in Fine or better grade are scarce. Today, among circulation strikes, 90% or more in existence are G-4 or below. MS coins are available of all dates and mints, but some are very elusive. The 1896-S, 1901-S, and 1913-S are the key dates in all grades. Proofs exist in proportion to their mintages. Choicer examples tend to be of later dates.

GRADING STANDARDS

MS-60 to 70 (Mint State). *Obverse:* At MS-60, some abrasion and contact marks are evident, most noticeably on the cheek and the obverse field to the right. Luster is present, but may be dull or lifeless. Many Barber coins have been cleaned, especially of the earlier dates. At MS-63, contact marks are very few. Abrasion still is evident, but less than at lower levels. Indeed, the cheek of Miss Liberty virtually showcases abrasion. An MS-65 coin

1896-S. Graded MS-65.

may have minor abrasion, but contact marks are so minute as to require magnification. Luster should be full and rich. *Reverse:* Comments apply as for the obverse, except that in lower Mint State grades abrasion and contact marks are most noticeable on the head and tail of the eagle and on the tips of the wings. At MS-65 or higher, there are no marks visible to the unaided eye. The field is mainly protected by design elements, and often appears to grade a point or two higher than the obverse.

Illustrated coin: This brilliant coin shows full satin luster.

AU-50, 53, 55, 58 (About Uncirculated). *Obverse:* Light wear is seen on the head, especially on the forward hair under LIBERTY. At AU-58, the luster is extensive but incomplete, especially on the higher parts and in the right field. At AU–50 and 53, luster is less. *Reverse:* Wear is evident on the head and tail of the eagle and on the tips of the wings. At AU–50 and 53, there still is significant luster. An AU-58 coin (as determined by the obverse) can have the reverse appear to be full Mint State.

1911-D. Graded AU-50.

EF-40, 45 (Extremely Fine). *Obverse:* Further wear is seen on the head. The hair above the forehead lacks most detail. LIBERTY shows wear, but still is strong. *Reverse:* Further wear is seen on the head and tail of the eagle and on the tips of the wings, most evident at the left and right extremes of the wings. At this level and below, sharpness of strike on the reverse is not important.

Illustrated coin: Note the subtle lilac and gold toning.

1913-S. Graded EF-40.

VF-20, 30 (Very Fine). *Obverse:* The head shows more wear, now with nearly all detail gone in the hair above the forehead. LIBERTY shows wear, but is complete. The leaves on the head all show wear, as does the upper part of the cap. *Reverse:* Wear is more extensive, particularly noticeable on the outer parts of the wings, the head, the shield, and the tail.

Illustrated coin: The dig and discoloration in Liberty's cheek decrease the appeal of this example.

1896-S. Graded VF-20.

F-12, 15 (Fine). *Obverse:* The head shows extensive wear. LIBERTY, the key place to check, is weak, especially at ER, but is fully readable. The ANA grading standards and *Photograde* adhere to this. PCGS suggests that lightly struck coins "may have letters partially missing." Traditionally, collectors insist on full LIBERTY. *Reverse:* More wear is seen on the reverse in the places as above. E PLURIBUS UNUM is light, with one to several letters worn away.

1913-S. Graded F-15.

VG-8, 10 (Very Good). *Obverse:* A net of three letters in LIBERTY must be readable. Traditionally, LI is clear, and after that there is a partial letter or two. *Reverse:* Further wear has smoothed more than half of the feathers in the wing. The shield is indistinct except for a few traces of interior lines. The motto is partially worn away. The rim is full, and many if not most denticles can be seen.

1914-S. Graded VG-10.

G-4, 6 (Good). *Obverse:* The head is in outline form, with the center flat. Most of the rim is there. All letters and the date are full. *Reverse:* The eagle shows only a few feathers, and only a few scattered letters remain in the motto. The rim may be worn flat in some or all of the area, but the peripheral lettering is clear.

1913-S. Graded G-4.

AG-3 (About Good). *Obverse:* The stars and motto are worn, and the border may be indistinct. Distinctness varies at this level. The date is clear. Grading is usually determined by the reverse. *Reverse:* The rim is gone and the letters are partially worn away. The eagle is mostly flat, perhaps with a few hints of feathers.

1901-S. Graded AG-3.

PF-60 to 70 (Proof). *Obverse and Reverse:* Proofs that are extensively cleaned and have many hairlines, or that are dull and grainy, are lower level, such as PF–60 to 62. These are not widely desired by collectors. With medium hairlines and good reflectivity, an assigned grade of PF-64 is appropriate. Tiny horizontal lines on Miss Liberty's cheek, known as slide marks, from National and other album slides scuffing the relief of the

1913. Graded PF-68 Cameo.

cheek, are endemic on all Barber silver coins. With noticeable marks of this type, the highest grade assignable is PF-64. With relatively few hairlines, a rating of PF-65 can be given. PF-66 should have hairlines so delicate that magnification is needed to see them. Above that, a Proof should be free of any hairlines or other problems.

Illustrated coin: Exceptional fields offset the bright devices to high advantage.

1892, Variety 1 Reverse   **1892, Variety 2 Reverse**
Note position of wing tip relative to E in UNITED.

Coins designated Deep Cameo or Ultra Cameo bring a premium of 50% to 100% above listed values.

	Mintage	Cert	Avg	%MS	G-4	VG-8	F-12	VF-20	EF-40	AU-50	MS-60	MS-63	MS-65
											PF-60	PF-63	PF-65
1892 (a)	8,236,000	1,701	60.4	73%	$9	$10	$26	$45	$75	$130	$235	$440	$1,000
	Auctions: $9,988, MS-68, January 2015; $2,820, MS-67, July 2015; $1,528, MS-66, August 2015; $1,058, MS-65, August 2015												
1892, Proof	1,245	401	64.7								$450	$800	$1,750
	Auctions: $2,820, PF-65DCam, April 2015; $940, PF-64Cam, January 2015; $2,468, PF-64, August 2015; $560, PF-63, September 2015												
1892-O	2,460,000	432	59.6	69%	$15	$20	$45	$60	$95	$160	$300	$475	$1,550
	Auctions: $14,100, MS-68, October 2015; $9,106, MS-67, October 2015; $3,055, MS-66, August 2015; $1,645, MS-65, August 2015												
1892-S	964,079	129	49.0	51%	$30	$50	$80	$130	$200	$300	$475	$1,050	$4,250
	Auctions: $14,100, MS-66, January 2015; $3,055, MS-65, July 2015; $447, AU-55, October 2015; $646, EF-45, May 2015												
1893	5,444,023	322	57.8	69%	$9	$10	$26	$45	$75	$130	$235	$440	$1,250
	Auctions: $1,058, MS-65, January 2015; $470, MS-64, October 2015; $259, MS-61, May 2015; $165, MS-60, May 2015												
1893, Proof	792	302	65.0								$450	$800	$1,750
	Auctions: $8,813, PF-68, September 2015; $5,170, PF-67Cam, January 2015; $2,115, PF-66Cam, January 2015; $1,528, PF-65Cam, February 2015												
1893-O	3,396,000	218	56.9	64%	$10	$14	$30	$60	$110	$170	$275	$500	$1,750
	Auctions: $8,225, MS-67, October 2015; $2,938, MS-66, February 2015; $1,412, MS-65, January 2015; $517, MS-64, September 2015												
1893-S	1,454,535	109	50.4	60%	$20	$35	$60	$110	$175	$300	$425	$1,000	$6,000
	Auctions: $20,563, MS-67, October 2015; $4,700, MS-66, August 2015; $7,638, MS-65, September 2015; $223, EF-45, May 2015												
1894	3,432,000	183	57.5	72%	$9	$10	$35	$50	$95	$150	$240	$450	$1,250
	Auctions: $3,760, MS-66, May 2015; $1,116, MS-65, June 2015; $60, EF-40, May 2015												
1894, Proof	972	341	64.8								$450	$800	$1,750
	Auctions: $8,225, PF-68, May 2015; $3,055, PF-67, January 2015; $2,585, PF-66Cam, October 2015; $1,450, PF-65, January 2015												
1894-O	2,852,000	154	55.2	65%	$10	$20	$45	$70	$130	$230	$325	$725	$2,000
	Auctions: $11,163, MS-67, May 2015; $9,988, MS-66, October 2015; $1,763, MS-65, January 2015; $259, AU-55, May 2015												
1894-S	2,648,821	209	58.4	73%	$10	$15	$40	$60	$120	$210	$325	$725	$2,000
	Auctions: $17,625, MS-67, May 2015; $1,410, MS-65, January 2015; $2,820, MS-64, October 2015; $588, MS-62, August 2015												
1895	4,440,000	235	55.8	69%	$10	$14	$30	$45	$80	$140	$250	$500	$1,350
	Auctions: $2,820, MS-66, October 2015; $1,175, MS-65, January 2015; $1,651, MS-64, March 2015; $411, MS-63, May 2015												
1895, Proof	880	278	65.0								$450	$800	$1,750
	Auctions: $9,988, PF-68Cam, January 2015; $4,935, PF-67Cam, October 2015; $3,761, PF-66, March 2015; $588, PF-63, July 2015												
1895-O	2,816,000	121	52.8	57%	$12	$20	$50	$70	$140	$230	$400	$900	$2,450
	Auctions: $1,528, MS-65, January 2015; $423, AU-58, May 2015; $470, AU-55, February 2015; $69, EF-40, May 2015												
1895-S	1,764,681	121	47.8	48%	$20	$32	$70	$120	$170	$275	$420	$1,050	$3,500
	Auctions: $8,225, MS-68, January 2015; $2,585, MS-64, August 2015; $823, MS-63, August 2015; $705, MS-62, January 2015												
1896	3,874,000	203	56.7	76%	$10	$14	$30	$45	$80	$135	$250	$425	$1,000
	Auctions: $3,760, MS-66, February 2015; $764, MS-65, June 2015; $541, MS-64, October 2015; $165, AU-55, May 2015												
1896, Proof	762	328	65.4								$450	$800	$1,750
	Auctions: $8,225, PF-68Cam, February 2015; $4,465, PF-67Cam, January 2015; $1,645, PF-66, January 2015; $1,061, PF-64Cam, January 2015												
1896-O	1,484,000	166	35.8	32%	$55	$85	$200	$320	$550	$800	$1,000	$2,000	$6,500
	Auctions: $9,988, MS-66, January 2015; $1,410, MS-63, September 2015; $999, MS-62, August 2015; $1,116, AU-58, January 2015												
1896-S	188,039	461	12.3	8%	$900	$1,500	$2,400	$3,800	$5,000	$7,000	$10,000	$17,500	$47,500
	Auctions: $1,998, F-12, February 2015; $1,175, VG-10, September 2015; $900, G-6, October 2015; $588, G-4, January 2015												

a. There are two varieties of the 1892 reverse. Variety 1: the eagle's wing covers only half of the E in UNITED; Variety 2: the eagle's wing covers most of the E. Coins of Variety 1 are somewhat scarcer.

	Mintage	Cert	Avg	%MS	G-4	VG-8	F-12	VF-20	EF-40	AU-50	MS-60 / PF-60	MS-63 / PF-63	MS-65 / PF-65
1897	8,140,000	300	56.1	69%	$9	$14	$26	$40	$70	$120	$240	$450	$1,250
	Auctions: $5,640, MS-67, May 2015; $2,350, MS-66, September 2015; $329, MS-62, January 2015; $79, EF-45, June 2015												
1897, Proof	731	270	64.8								$450	$800	$1,750
	Auctions: $9,988, PF-68Cam, August 2015; $9,988, PF-68, May 2015; $1,410, PF-65Cam, February 2015; $881, PF-64, February 2015												
1897-O	1,414,800	125	37.6	34%	$40	$65	$180	$340	$385	$600	$850	$1,800	$3,300
	Auctions: $14,100, MS-67, May 2015; $20,563, MS-66, October 2015; $3,055, MS-65, August 2015; $2,115, MS-64, March 2015												
1897-S	542,229	186	27.3	24%	$120	$150	$300	$550	$825	$1,000	$1,600	$1,900	$6,500
	Auctions: $36,425, MS-67, May 2015; $7,050, MS-66, July 2015; $1,998, AU-58, January 2015; $1,528, AU-50, January 2015												
1898	11,100,000	377	52.6	61%	$9	$10	$26	$45	$70	$125	$225	$425	$1,000
	Auctions: $4,700, MS-67, October 2015; $1,763, MS-66, October 2015; $764, MS-65, January 2015; $705, MS-64, August 2015												
1898, Proof	735	323	65.6								$450	$800	$1,750
	Auctions: $23,500, PF-69Cam, October 2015; $4,700, PF-67DCam, January 2015; $2,233, PF-66, October 2015; $1,469, PF-65, March 2015												
1898-O	1,868,000	88	47.1	49%	$15	$28	$70	$140	$300	$390	$625	$1,500	$8,750
	Auctions: $11,750, MS-66, January 2015; $764, AU-58, January 2015; $329, AU-50, January 2015; $212, EF-45, July 2015												
1898-S	1,020,592	77	51.2	49%	$11	$25	$40	$55	$100	$200	$400	$1,400	$7,500
	Auctions: $7,050, MS-65, June 2015; $4,935, MS-64, August 2015; $881, AU-58, January 2015; $541, AU-55, July 2015												
1899	12,624,000	397	50.5	58%	$9	$10	$26	$45	$75	$125	$240	$425	$1,100
	Auctions: $1,293, MS-66, January 2015; $823, MS-65, January 2015; $188, AU-58, September 2015; $165, AU-55, February 2015												
1899, Proof	846	198	64.9								$450	$800	$1,750
	Auctions: $5,876, PF-67Cam, July 2015; $1,998, PF-66Cam, August 2015; $494, PF-62, August 2015												
1899-O	2,644,000	107	55.6	60%	$11	$18	$35	$70	$120	$260	$400	$800	$2,500
	Auctions: $12,925, MS-67, August 2015; $4,818, MS-66, October 2015; $2,820, MS-65, January 2015; $1,058, MS-64, June 2015												
1899-S	708,000	58	53.7	48%	$27	$40	$95	$110	$140	$270	$425	$1,400	$3,750
	Auctions: $9,988, MS-67, June 2015; $940, AU-58, January 2015; $329, AU-55, January 2015; $376, AU-53, May 2015												
1900	10,016,000	303	57.2	73%	$9	$10	$26	$45	$75	$125	$240	$425	$1,100
	Auctions: $10,575, MS-67, May 2015; $1,184, MS-65, January 2015; $588, MS-64, July 2015; $317, MS-63, October 2015												
1900, Proof	912	271	64.8								$450	$800	$1,750
	Auctions: $7,344, PF-68, May 2015; $3,290, PF-67Cam, October 2015; $2,585, PF-66Cam, January 2015; $1,293, PF-65, January 2015												
1900-O	3,416,000	118	51.8	58%	$12	$26	$65	$110	$150	$310	$525	$850	$3,250
	Auctions: $17,626, MS-68, May 2015; $12,925, MS-67, October 2015; $7,050, MS-66, August 2015; $2,350, MS-65, June 2015												
1900-S	1,858,585	127	52.4	31%	$10	$15	$35	$55	$80	$130	$350	$1,000	$4,500
	Auctions: $10,575, MS-67, May 2015; $6,169, MS-66, August 2015; $341, MS-61, May 2015; $259, AU-58, January 2015												
1901	8,892,000	324	47.4	57%	$9	$10	$26	$45	$80	$135	$240	$425	$1,100
	Auctions: $2,115, MS-66, October 2015; $940, MS-65, January 2015; $423, MS-64, May 2015; $329, MS-63, May 2015												
1901, Proof	813	255	64.8								$450	$800	$1,750
	Auctions: $5,875, PF-68, July 2015; $3,995, PF-67, October 2015; $1,528, PF-66, March 2015; $1,293, PF-65, January 2015												
1901-O	1,612,000	84	32.3	21%	$40	$60	$140	$275	$550	$750	$950	$1,850	$5,000
	Auctions: $2,585, MS-63, January 2015; $940, AU-50, July 2015; $705, EF-40, June 2015; $212, F-15, February 2015												
1901-S	72,664	330	8.4	4%	$5,250	$10,000	$16,500	$23,000	$30,000	$36,000	$40,000	$50,000	$85,000
	Auctions: $18,800, VF-25, January 2015; $14,100, F-12, September 2015; $7,638, VG-8, January 2015; $5,405, G-6, October 2015												
1902	12,196,967	322	53.7	58%	$9	$10	$26	$45	$65	$120	$240	$425	$1,100
	Auctions: $7,638, MS-67, May 2015; $2,233, MS-66, October 2015; $999, MS-65, January 2015; $656, MS-64, June 2015												
1902, Proof	777	229	64.3								$450	$800	$1,750
	Auctions: $2,820, PF-67, October 2015; $3,055, PF-66, October 2015; $1,410, PF-66, January 2015; $646, PF-63, January 2015												
1902-O	4,748,000	106	50.2	44%	$10	$16	$50	$85	$140	$225	$475	$1,300	$3,750
	Auctions: $28,200, MS-68, May 2015; $7,050, MS-66, October 2015; $1,763, MS-64, August 2015; $823, MS-63, July 2015												
1902-S	1,524,612	112	54.5	57%	$14	$22	$55	$90	$160	$240	$500	$950	$3,000
	Auctions: $3,995, MS-66, August 2015; $2,233, MS-65, January 2015; $1,410, MS-64, August 2015; $705, MS-63, September 2015												

	Mintage	Cert	Avg	%MS	G-4	VG-8	F-12	VF-20	EF-40	AU-50	MS-60	MS-63	MS-65
											PF-60	PF-63	PF-65
1903	9,759,309	139	54.0	56%	$9	$10	$26	$45	$65	$120	$240	$450	$2,000
	Auctions: $9,400, MS-66, October 2015; $423, MS-64, May 2015; $353, MS-64, November 2015; $94, AU-53, April 2015												
1903, Proof	755	288	65.1								$450	$800	$1,750
	Auctions: $5,875, PF-68, May 2015; $3,290, PF-66, August 2015; $823, PF-64, February 2015; $589, PF-62, February 2015												
1903-O	3,500,000	98	49.5	40%	$10	$12	$40	$60	$120	$275	$425	$1,200	$4,250
	Auctions: $32,900, MS-67, May 2015; $3,055, MS-65, October 2015; $176, AU-50, July 2015; $101, EF-45, November 2014												
1903-S	1,036,000	86	56.7	71%	$15	$25	$45	$85	$150	$275	$425	$850	$1,800
	Auctions: $19,975, MS-67, May 2015; $4,230, MS-66, October 2015; $1,821, MS-65, September 2015; $1,000, MS-62, May 2015												
1904	9,588,143	173	54.3	57%	$9	$10	$26	$45	$70	$120	$240	$425	$1,100
	Auctions: $5,170, MS-66, October 2015; $141, AU-55, August 2015; $125, AU-55, May 2015; $64, EF-40, March 2015												
1904, Proof	670	264	64.7								$450	$800	$1,750
	Auctions: $5,405, PF-68, June 2015; $4,230, PF-67, January 2015; $1,528, PF-66, July 2015; $823, PF-64, October 2015												
1904-O	2,456,000	137	46.7	41%	$30	$40	$85	$150	$240	$450	$800	$1,300	$2,400
	Auctions: $41,125, MS-67, June 2014												
1905	4,967,523	221	46.8	53%	$30	$35	$50	$65	$70	$120	$240	$440	$1,100
	Auctions: $2,233, MS-66, October 2015; $1,293, MS-66, October 2015; $999, MS-65, July 2015; $353, MS-63, November 2015												
1905, Proof	727	248	64.6								$450	$800	$1,750
	Auctions: $3,878, PF-67, January 2015; $3,173, PF-66, September 2015; $1,293, PF-65, February 2015; $881, PF-64, August 2015												
1905-O	1,230,000	93	43.4	46%	$40	$60	$120	$220	$260	$350	$475	$1,250	$6,000
	Auctions: $11,750, MS-67, October 2015; $5,170, MS-65, September 2015; $2,585, MS-64, August 2015; $833, MS-62, January 2015												
1905-S	1,884,000	117	45.5	43%	$30	$40	$75	$100	$105	$225	$350	$1,000	$3,500
	Auctions: $3,055, MS-65, August 2015; $1,175, MS-64, September 2015; $646, MS-62, June 2015; $84, VF-30, July 2015												
1906	3,655,760	202	58.8	79%	$9	$10	$26	$45	$70	$120	$240	$425	$1,100
	Auctions: $2,820, MS-66, June 2014												
1906, Proof	675	206	64.9								$450	$800	$1,750
	Auctions: $16,450, PF-68, May 2015; $2,233, PF-66, August 2015; $1,410, PF-65, January 2015; $1,351, PF-65, September 2015												
1906-D	3,280,000	127	59.2	77%	$9	$10	$30	$50	$70	$145	$250	$450	$1,850
	Auctions: $9,400, MS-67, May 2015; $823, MS-64, January 2015; $235, AU-58, October 2015; $58, EF-40, April 2015												
1906-O	2,056,000	140	60.1	78%	$9	$10	$40	$60	$100	$200	$300	$550	$1,350
	Auctions: $11,750, MS-67, October 2015; $5,640, MS-67, May 2015; $2,233, MS-66, October 2015; $1,666, MS-65, September 2015												
1907	7,132,000	384	56.7	66%	$9	$10	$26	$40	$65	$120	$240	$425	$1,100
	Auctions: $6,463, MS-67, October 2015; $1,998, MS-66, October 2015; $705, MS-65, January 2015; $376, MS-64, May 2015												
1907, Proof	575	293	65.0								$450	$800	$1,750
	Auctions: $5,170, PF-67Cam, August 2015; $2,115, PF-66, July 2015; $1,293, PF-65Cam, September 2015; $940, PF-64Cam, October 2015												
1907-D	2,484,000	109	54.7	69%	$9	$10	$26	$48	$70	$175	$250	$650	$2,400
	Auctions: $1,058, MS-64, July 2015; $999, MS-64, July 2015; $150, AU-53, July 2015; $141, AU-50, May 2015												
1907-O	4,560,000	194	55.4	68%	$9	$10	$26	$45	$70	$135	$275	$500	$1,750
	Auctions: $9,988, MS-68, January 2015; $10,575, MS-67, October 2015; $1,293, MS-65, August 2015; $552, MS-64, July 2015												
1907-S	1,360,000	74	55.1	73%	$10	$18	$45	$70	$140	$280	$475	$1,200	$4,500
	Auctions: $6,463, MS-66, September 2015; $5,405, MS-66, October 2015; $3,564, MS-65, August 2015; $223, EF-45, July 2015												
1908	4,232,000	241	58.5	73%	$9	$10	$26	$45	$70	$120	$240	$425	$1,100
	Auctions: $1,116, MS-66, January 2015; $940, MS-65, June 2015; $447, MS-64, January 2015; $329, MS-63, January 2015												
1908, Proof	545	190	64.8								$450	$800	$1,750
	Auctions: $5,170, PF-67, October 2015; $1,528, PF-66, February 2015; $1,175, PF-65, June 2015; $823, PF-64, July 2015												
1908-D	5,788,000	262	52.0	57%	$9	$10	$26	$45	$70	$120	$240	$425	$1,200
	Auctions: $2,585, MS-66, October 2015; $1,058, MS-65, August 2015; $306, MS-62, February 2015; $94, AU-50, May 2015												
1908-O	6,244,000	249	53.7	69%	$9	$10	$26	$45	$65	$120	$240	$425	$1,100
	Auctions: $764, MS-65, October 2015; $235, MS-62, January 2015; $176, AU-58, April 2015; $112, AU-53, August 2015												
1908-S	784,000	128	47.5	57%	$18	$38	$85	$165	$325	$465	$750	$1,200	$4,250
	Auctions: $7,050, MS-67, October 2015; $2,963, MS-65, January 2015; $1,763, MS-64, January 2015; $1,293, MS-63, September 2015												

	Mintage	Cert	Avg	%MS	G-4	VG-8	F-12	VF-20	EF-40	AU-50	MS-60 PF-60	MS-63 PF-63	MS-65 PF-65
1909	9,268,000	520	55.8	67%	$9	$10	$26	$45	$65	$120	$240	$425	$1,100
	Auctions: $3,055, MS-66, May 2015; $999, MS-65, January 2015; $494, MS-64, September 2015; $247, MS-62, May 2015												
1909, Proof	650	275	64.8								$450	$800	$1,750
	Auctions: $13,513, PF-68, May 2015; $1,704, PF-66, February 2015; $1,058, PF-64, January 2015; $719, PF-63Cam, June 2015												
1909-D	5,114,000	304	50.1	53%	$9	$10	$26	$45	$85	$150	$240	$425	$1,200
	Auctions: $9,400, MS-67, May 2015; $1,293, MS-66, October 2015; $2,350, MS-65, October 2015; $705, MS-64, January 2015												
1909-O	712,000	85	38.0	46%	$42	$100	$400	$650	$1,000	$1,800	$3,000	$3,750	$7,500
	Auctions: $21,150, MS-67, May 2015; $1,175, VF-35, February 2015; $1,116, VF-25, October 2015; $180, VG-10, February 2015												
1909-S	1,348,000	111	50.1	63%	$9	$10	$35	$55	$90	$185	$285	$750	$1,750
	Auctions: $12,925, MS-67, May 2015; $2,585, MS-66, January 2015; $1,763, MS-65, January 2015; $182, AU-55, September 2015												
1910	2,244,000	202	55.2	74%	$9	$10	$26	$45	$80	$140	$240	$425	$1,100
	Auctions: $1,528, MS-66, January 2015; $711, MS-65, January 2015; $676, MS-64, August 2015; $176, AU-58, June 2015												
1910, Proof	551	272	65.1								$450	$800	$1,750
	Auctions: $2,703, PF-67Cam, September 2015; $1,998, PF-65Cam, January 2015; $911, PF-64Cam, October 2015; $881, PF-64Cam, October 2015												
1910-D	1,500,000	130	53.7	62%	$10	$11	$45	$70	$125	$240	$350	$900	$1,500
	Auctions: $4,818, MS-67, October 2015; $447, MS-62, February 2015; $376, MS-61, April 2015; $212, AU-55, August 2015												
1911	3,720,000	290	58.6	73%	$9	$10	$26	$45	$70	$125	$240	$425	$1,100
	Auctions: $3,055, MS-66, August 2015; $764, MS-65, February 2015; $470, MS-64, January 2015; $329, MS-63, October 2015												
1911, Proof	543	233	65.2								$450	$800	$1,750
	Auctions: $7,050, PF-68Cam, February 2015; $3,290, PF-67Cam, October 2015; $2,585, PF-66Cam, October 2015; $1,704, PF-65Cam, October 2015												
1911-D	933,600	115	42.6	43%	$30	$40	$150	$300	$400	$600	$850	$1,300	$5,000
	Auctions: $4,113, MS-65, June 2015; $764, MS-62, January 2015; $705, AU-58, January 2015; $353, EF-45, April 2015												
1911-S	988,000	171	59.3	78%	$9	$10	$55	$85	$165	$280	$375	$750	$1,400
	Auctions: $2,585, MS-66, January 2015; $1,998, MS-66, October 2015; $1,880, MS-65, September 2015; $617, AU-58, January 2015												
1912	4,400,000	446	57.8	76%	$9	$10	$26	$45	$70	$120	$240	$425	$1,100
	Auctions: $8,225, MS-67, May 2015; $1,410, MS-66, September 2015; $823, MS-65, January 2015; $235, MS-62, February 2015												
1912, Proof	700	217	64.6								$450	$800	$1,750
	Auctions: $19,975, PF-68Cam, May 2015; $3,055, PF-67, February 2015; $2,820, PF-67, March 2015; $1,175, PF-64Cam, September 2015												
1912-S	708,000	108	52.1	64%	$20	$30	$65	$90	$125	$220	$400	$925	$1,750
	Auctions: $11,163, MS-68, May 2015; $5,875, MS-67, June 2015; $1,763, MS-65, January 2015; $1,880, MS-64, August 2015												
1913	484,000	139	48.0	50%	$22	$35	$100	$180	$400	$525	$900	$1,200	$3,750
	Auctions: $3,055, MS-65, October 2015; $2,585, MS-65, February 2015; $1,998, MS-65, October 2015; $588, AU-58, August 2015												
1913, Proof	613	245	64.5								$450	$850	$1,800
	Auctions: $4,230, PF-67Cam, July 2015; $1,483, PF-66, January 2015; $2,585, PF-65, August 2015; $1,175, PF-64Cam, January 2015												
1913-D	1,450,800	182	54.2	63%	$12	$15	$35	$60	$85	$175	$275	$450	$1,100
	Auctions: $6,756, MS-67, July 2015; $1,704, MS-66, October 2015; $705, MS-64, August 2015; $376, MS-63, May 2015												
1913-S	40,000	478	11.0	9%	$1,650	$2,200	$5,000	$7,500	$10,000	$12,750	$15,000	$20,000	$30,000
	Auctions: $35,250, MS-66, June 2015; $3,995, F-12, July 2015; $1,998, VG-10, August 2015; $1,763, VG-8, June 2015												
1914	6,244,230	662	55.6	68%	$9	$10	$22	$40	$65	$120	$240	$425	$1,100
	Auctions: $1,763, MS-66, October 2015; $823, MS-65, January 2015; $447, MS-64, June 2015; $329, MS-63, May 2015												
1914, Proof	380	205	64.8								$450	$950	$1,900
	Auctions: $7,050, PF-68, October 2014; $3,525, PF-67, October 2015; $2,938, PF-67, November 2014; $1,763, PF-66, June 2015												
1914-D	3,046,000	347	55.7	69%	$9	$10	$22	$40	$65	$120	$240	$425	$1,100
	Auctions: $4,700, MS-67, October 2015; $2,938, MS-66, June 2015; $676, MS-65, August 2015; $364, MS-63, August 2015												
1914-S	264,000	385	16.5	13%	$125	$180	$375	$550	$825	$975	$1,400	$1,650	$3,000
	Auctions: $3,290, MS-64, January 2015; $2,468, MS-63, July 2015; $999, AU-50, January 2015; $646, VF-35, January 2015												

	Mintage	Cert	Avg	%MS	G-4	VG-8	F-12	VF-20	EF-40	AU-50	MS-60	MS-63	MS-65
											PF-60	PF-63	PF-65
1915	3,480,000	492	56.1	72%	$9	$10	$22	$40	$65	$120	$240	$425	$1,100
Auctions: $2,350, MS-66, May 2015; $881, MS-65, January 2015; $401, MS-64, August 2015; $376, MS-63, May 2015													
1915, Proof	450	177	64.3								$450	$1,000	$2,000
Auctions: $15,275, PF-68, May 2015; $3,055, PF-67, January 2015; $1,234, PF-65, January 2015; $830, PF-64, June 2015													
1915-D	3,694,000	642	58.0	74%	$9	$10	$22	$40	$70	$120	$240	$425	$1,100
Auctions: $4,935, MS-67, May 2015; $1,410, MS-66, August 2015; $999, MS-65, January 2015; $388, MS-64, October 2015													
1915-S	704,000	210	51.2	59%	$25	$40	$60	$85	$115	$200	$285	$475	$1,300
Auctions: $8,225, MS-67, May 2015; $2,820, MS-66, January 2015; $2,468, MS-65, September 2015; $259, MS-62, August 2015													
1916	1,788,000	439	57.1	71%	$9	$10	$22	$40	$70	$120	$240	$425	$1,000
Auctions: $3,055, MS-67, October 2015; $1,293, MS-66, August 2015; $940, MS-65, August 2015; $400, MS-64, March 2015													
1916-D	6,540,800	1,500	59.0	76%	$9	$10	$22	$40	$70	$120	$240	$425	$1,000
Auctions: $3,525, MS-67, March 2015; $1,528, MS-66, January 2015; $1,058, MS-65, January 2015; $541, MS-64, January 2015													

STANDING LIBERTY (1916–1930)

Variety 1, No Stars Below Eagle (1916–1917): **Designer:** *Hermon A. MacNeil.*
Weight: *6.25 grams.* **Composition:** *.900 silver, .100 copper (net weight .18084 oz. pure silver).*
Diameter: *24.3 mm.* **Edge:** *Reeded.* **Mints:** *Philadelphia, Denver, and San Francisco.*

**Variety 1, No Stars Below Eagle
(1916–1917)**

*Mintmark location is on the
obverse, at the top left of
the date, for both varieties.*

Variety 2, Stars Below Eagle (1917–1930): **Designer:** *Hermon A. MacNeil.*
Weight: *6.25 grams.* **Composition:** *.900 silver, .100 copper (net weight .18084 oz. pure silver).*
Diameter: *24.3 mm.* **Edge:** *Reeded.* **Mints:** *Philadelphia, Denver, and San Francisco.*

**Variety 2, Stars Below Eagle
(1917–1930)**

History. The Standing Liberty quarter dollar, designed by sculptor Hermon A. MacNeil (whose initial, M, is located above and to the right of the date), was greeted with wide acclaimed from its first appearance. All of 1916 and many of 1917 are of the Variety 1 design, with the right breast of Miss Liberty exposed on the obverse and with no stars below the eagle on the reverse. Variety 2 of the Standing Liberty design was introduced in 1917 and continued to the end of the series. Miss Liberty is clothed in a jacket of chainmail armor, and the reverse is slightly redesigned, with stars below the eagle. These changes came at the suggestion of the designer, Hermon A. MacNeil.

Striking and Sharpness. Many if not most 1916 quarters are somewhat lightly struck on the head and body of Miss Liberty. The 1917, Variety 1, quarters usually are quite well struck. When light striking is found, it is usually on the higher-relief parts of the head, the right knee (not as obvious), and the rivets on the left side of the shield. The 1917 Philadelphia Mint coins are usually sharper than the other varieties of this type. Most coins of the Variety 2 design have areas of light striking. On the obverse these are most notable on the head of Miss Liberty and on the shield, the latter often with the two lower-left rivets weak or missing and with the center emblem on the shield weak. The center of the standing figure can be weak as well, as can the upper-left area at and near the date. After 1924 the date was slightly recessed, eliminating that problem. On the reverse, check the eagle's breast. A misleading term, Full Head (FH), is widely used to describe quarters that have only *partial* head details; such coins often actually have the two lower-left shield rivets poorly struck or not visible at all. Most third-party grading services define these criteria for "Full Head" designation (in order of importance): a full, unbroken hairline from Liberty's brow down to the jawline; all three leaves on the head showing; and a visible ear hole.

Availability. The 1916 quarter is the key to the series. Examples tend to be liberally graded in the real-life marketplace, especially in EF and AU, this in contrast to more careful grading for the less valuable 1917 issues. Circulated coins of 1916 and 1917 often have the date worn partly away, due to the high position of this feature in the design. Among Variety 2 coins, the 1918-S, 8 Over 7, is recognized as the key issue, and the 1919-D, 1921, 1923-S, and 1927-S as quite scarce. MS coins are readily available for most issues, but Full Details coins can be *extreme* rarities. Circulated coins dated from 1917 through 1924 often have the date worn partly away, due to the high position of this feature in the design. On MS coins the luster usually is rich and attractive. No Proof coins of this type were officially issued, but specimen strikings dated 1917 are known to exist.

GRADING STANDARDS

MS-60 to 70 (Mint State). *Obverse:* At MS-60 some abrasion and contact marks are evident on the higher areas, which are also the areas most likely to be weakly struck. This includes the rivets on the shield to the left and the central escutcheon on the shield, the head, and the right leg of Miss Liberty. The luster may not be complete in those areas on weakly struck coins, even those certified above MS-65—the *original planchet surface*

1919. Graded MS-65FH.

may be revealed as it was not smoothed out by striking. Accordingly, grading is best done by evaluating abrasion and mint luster as it is observed. Luster may be dull or lifeless at MS–60 to 62 but should have deep frost at MS-63 or better, particularly in the lower-relief areas. At MS-65 or better, it should be full and rich. *Reverse:* Striking is usually quite good, permitting observation of luster in all areas. Check the eagle's breast and the surface of the right wing. Luster may be dull or lifeless at MS–60 to 62 but should have deep frost at MS-63 or better, particularly in the lower-relief areas. At MS-65 or better, it should be full and rich.

    Illustrated coin: See the subtle notes of gold, blue, and pink on this lustrous example.

AU-50, 53, 55, 58 (About Uncirculated). *Obverse:* Light wear is seen on the figure of Miss Liberty, especially noticeable around her midriff and right knee. The shield shows wear, as does the highest part of the sash where it crosses Miss Liberty's waist. At AU-58 the luster is extensive, but incomplete on the higher areas, although it should be nearly full in the panels of the parapet to the left and right, and in the upper field. At AU–50 and 53, luster is less. *Reverse:* Wear is most evident on the eagle's breast, the edges of both wings, and the interior area of the right wing. Luster is nearly complete at AU-58, but at AU-50, half or more is gone.

1917-S, Variety 1. Graded AU-53.

EF-40, 45 (Extremely Fine). *Obverse:* Wear is more extensive, with the higher parts of Miss Liberty now without detail and the front of the right leg flat. The shield is worn. On coins dated from 1917 to 1924 the date shows wear at the top (on those of 1925 to 1930, with the date recessed, the numbers are bold). Little or no luster is seen, except perhaps among the letters. *Reverse:* The eagle shows more wear, with the surface of the right wing being mostly flat. Little or no luster is evident.

1927-S. Graded EF-45.

VF-20, 30 (Very Fine). *Obverse:* Wear is more extensive. The higher-relief areas of Miss Liberty are flat, and the sash crossing her waist is mostly blended into it (some sharply struck pieces being exceptions). The left side of the shield is mostly flat, although its outline can be seen. On quarters dated 1917 to 1924 the top of the date shows more wear. *Reverse:* The eagle shows further wear, with the body blending into the wing above

1919-S. Graded VF-20.

it. Much feather detail is gone from the wing to the left (on quarters dated 1925 to 1930; less so for those dated 1917 to 1924). Most detail is gone from the right wing.

F-12, 15 (Fine). *Obverse:* Miss Liberty is worn nearly flat. Most detail in her gown is gone, except to the left of her leg and below her knee to the right. The stars on the parapet are well worn, with some indistinct. The top of the date is weak. Quarters of the rare 1916 date are slightly weaker than those of 1917 in this and lower grades. On quarters of 1917 to 1924 the top of the date is weak. On those dated 1925 to 1930 the date remains strong.

1917-D. Graded F-12.

Reverse: The eagle shows further wear, this being greater on 1925 to 1930 issues than on the earlier dates.

VG-8, 10 (Very Good). *Obverse:* The obverse is worn further, with fewer details in the skirt, and part of the shield border to the left blended into the standing figure. The date is partially worn away at the top, and quarters from 1917 to 1924 have less detail. Those from 1925 to 1930 retain more detail, and the date is full. *Reverse:* The eagle is worn further, with only about a third of the feathers now discernible, these mostly on the wing to the left.

1921. Graded VG-10.

G-4, 6 (Good). *Obverse:* The wear is more extensive. Most coins have the stars missing, the standing figure flat, and much of the date worn away, although still clearly identifiable. Quarters of 1925 to 1930 show more detail and the date is clear. *Reverse:* The eagle is mostly in outline form, with only a few feather details visible. The rim is worn into the letters, and on quarters of 1916 to 1924, E PLURIBUS UNUM is very faint; it is clear on quarters of later dates.

1927-S. Graded G-6.

AG-3 (About Good). *Obverse:* The obverse is worn nearly smooth, and the date is mostly gone. On some coins just one or two digits are seen. Fortunately, those digits are usually on the right, such as a trace of just a 6, which will identify the coin as a 1916. On quarters of 1925 to 1930 the wear is more extensive than for G-4, but most features are discernible and the date is clear. *Reverse:* The eagle is flat, and the border is worn down further.

1921. Graded AG-3.

On quarters of 1916 to 1924, E PLURIBUS UNUM is extremely faint or even missing in areas; it remains readable on quarters of later dates.

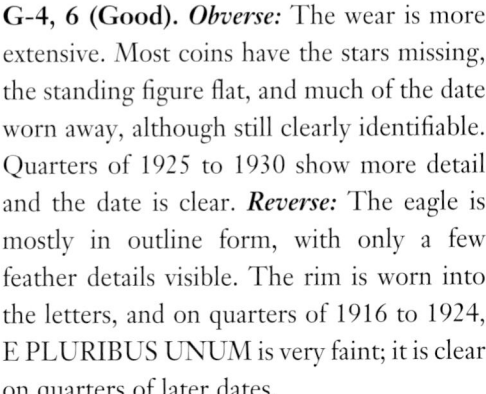

Full Head Details, Variety 1
Note the excellently defined cheek, facial features, and wreath.

Full Head Details, Variety 2
Note the full unbroken hairline from brow to neck, all three leaves clearly visible in Liberty's cap, and a visible ear hole.

Pedestal Date
(1917–1924)

Recessed Date
(1925–1930)

1918-S, 8 Over 7
FS-25-1918S-101.

	Mintage	Cert	Avg	%MS	G-4	VG-8	F-12	VF-20	EF-40	AU-50	MS-60	MS-63	MS-65FH
1916 †	52,000	864	44.8	48%	$2,600	$5,500	$6,750	$7,500	$10,000	$11,500	$15,000	$16,500	$35,000
	Auctions: $146,875, MS-67FH, January 2015; $52,875, MS-66FH, January 2015; $18,800, MS-64FH, October 2015; $19,975, MS-63, June 2015												
1917, Variety 1	8,740,000	6,559	59.8	79%	$25	$45	$65	$90	$110	$200	$250	$350	$1,100
	Auctions: $4,465, MS-67FH, August 2015; $8,225, MS-66FH, October 2015; $1,821, MS-65FH, January 2015; $646, MS-64FH, February 2015												
1917-D, Variety 1	1,509,200	1,885	59.5	75%	$30	$55	$80	$120	$200	$250	$325	$425	$1,850
	Auctions: $2,585, MS-67, July 2015; $2,585, MS-66FH, August 2015; $3,055, MS-65FH, February 2015; $1,058, MS-64FH, January 2015												
1917-S, Variety 1	1,952,000	1,156	55.5	67%	$40	$70	$110	$150	$210	$285	$350	$475	$3,000
	Auctions: $5,405, MS-66FH, February 2015; $2,703, MS-65FH, June 2015; $705, MS-64FH, June 2015; $364, MS-63, January 2015												
1917, Variety 2	13,880,000	1,538	60.4	78%	$25	$40	$55	$70	$100	$150	$210	$275	$900
	Auctions: $2,585, MS-67, January 2015; $3,525, MS-66FH, February 2015; $1,998, MS-65FH, August 2015; $353, MS-64, October 2015												
1917-D, Variety 2	6,224,400	824	58.6	68%	$45	$55	$85	$110	$150	$210	$260	$350	$3,000
	Auctions: $5,875, MS-66FH, October 2015; $3,995, MS-65FH, August 2015; $1,880, MS-64FH, August 2015; $646, MS-63, August 2015												
1917-S, Variety 2	5,552,000	791	59.2	71%	$45	$60	$90	$120	$160	$225	$260	$350	$3,250
	Auctions: $4,935, MS-66FH, February 2015; $3,525, MS-65FH, August 2015; $1,410, MS-66, October 2015; $400, MS-64, October 2015												
1918	14,240,000	875	60.7	75%	$20	$25	$30	$35	$55	$90	$150	$225	$1,750
	Auctions: $3,525, MS-67, June 2015; $7,638, MS-66FH, August 2015; $1,543, MS-65FH, August 2015; $282, MS-63, November 2015												
1918-D	7,380,000	723	58.2	63%	$25	$40	$75	$90	$145	$200	$275	$400	$4,000
	Auctions: $5,405, MS-66FH, June 2015; $8,813, MS-65FH, February 2015; $646, MS-64, August 2015; $282, MS-62, January 2015												
1918-S	11,072,000	954	56.2	63%	$20	$25	$35	$45	$60	$120	$200	$300	$12,000
	Auctions: $27,025, MS-67FH, August 2015; $22,325, MS-66FH, October 2015; $21,150, MS-65FH, May 2015; $2,350, MS-64FH, February 2015												
1918-S, 8 Over 7 † (a)	(b)	334	40.5	19%	$1,600	$2,200	$3,500	$5,000	$8,000	$13,000	$19,000	$30,000	$250,000
	Auctions: $188,000, MS-64FH, June 2014; $24,675, AU-58FH, July 2014; $3,819, VF-20, October 2014												
1919	11,324,000	1,092	60.6	77%	$35	$45	$60	$80	$100	$135	$185	$250	$1,500
	Auctions: $8,520, MS-67FH, August 2015; $1,058, MS-66, August 2015; $1,939, MS-65FH, August 2015; $1,293, MS-64FH, August 2015												
1919-D	1,944,000	459	47.0	37%	$85	$120	$200	$400	$600	$800	$950	$1,600	$23,500
	Auctions: $6,463, MS-66, August 2015; $49,350, MS-65FH, August 2015; $18,800, MS-64FH, August 2015; $2,585, MS-63, June 2015												
1919-S	1,836,000	479	47.5	34%	$80	$110	$175	$350	$550	$750	$900	$1,500	$27,500
	Auctions: $6,463, MS-66, August 2015; $24,675, MS-64FH, June 2015; $1,880, MS-63, January 2015; $881, AU-58, October 2015												

† Ranked in the *100 Greatest U.S. Coins* (fourth edition). **a.** This clear overdate was caused by the use of two differently dated hubs when the die was made. "Because of the boldness of the 7, this variety can be confirmed easily in low grades. . . . This variety is extremely rare in high grades. We recommend authentication because alterations do exist. Genuine specimens have a small die chip above the pedestal, just to the left of the lowest star on the right" (*Cherrypickers' Guide to Rare Die Varieties*, sixth edition, volume II). **b.** Included in 1918-S mintage figure.

	Mintage	Cert	Avg	%MS	G-4	VG-8	F-12	VF-20	EF-40	AU-50	MS-60	MS-63	MS-65FH
1920	27,860,000	1,735	61.0	78%	$15	$20	$30	$35	$55	$100	$160	$230	$1,500
Auctions: $9,400, MS-67, January 2015; $1,528, MS-66, February 2015; $3,290, MS-65FH, August 2015; $470, MS-64FH, October 2015													
1920-D	3,586,400	395	53.4	54%	$50	$60	$80	$120	$165	$225	$350	$800	$6,500
Auctions: $10,575, MS-67, June 2015; $16,450, MS-66FH, October 2015; $4,465, MS-64FH, February 2015; $999, MS-64, March 2015													
1920-S	6,380,000	578	57.6	63%	$20	$25	$35	$50	$65	$140	$270	$750	$22,500
Auctions: $8,813, MS-66, February 2015; $1,880, MS-65, August 2015; $4,818, MS-64FH, January 2015; $646, MS-63, October 2015													
1921	1,916,000	1,065	44.2	43%	$175	$225	$500	$700	$800	$1,150	$1,600	$2,200	$5,000
Auctions: $18,800, MS-66FH, May 2015; $6,463, MS-66, February 2015; $2,820, MS-65, October 2015; $3,055, MS-64FH, January 2015													
1923	9,716,000	1,550	61.5	83%	$15	$20	$30	$38	$55	$100	$170	$240	$4,000
Auctions: $2,350, MS-67, February 2015; $4,465, MS-65FH, August 2015; $329, MS-64, June 2015; $306, MS-62FH, February 2015													
1923-S	1,360,000	791	48.2	43%	$280	$425	$750	$1,100	$1,500	$2,000	$2,600	$3,250	$6,500
Auctions: $4,935, MS-66, August 2015; $4,935, MS-65, June 2015; $3,290, MS-64, January 2015; $3,067, MS-63, January 2015													
1924	10,920,000	1,122	60.7	80%	$15	$20	$25	$35	$55	$110	$185	$275	$1,400
Auctions: $20,563, MS-68, January 2015; $14,100, MS-67FH, October 2015; $2,820, MS-66FH, June 2015; $470, MS-65, March 2015													
1924-D	3,112,000	1,540	62.4	89%	$55	$70	$100	$140	$195	$230	$325	$375	$4,500
Auctions: $999, MS-67, September 2015; $18,800, MS-66FH, March 2015; $4,700, MS-65FH, August 2015; $364, MS-64, November 2015													
1924-S	2,860,000	594	58.4	69%	$26	$33	$45	$65	$130	$250	$350	$900	$5,500
Auctions: $3,760, MS-66, July 2015; $5,875, MS-65FH, March 2015; $1,116, MS-64, September 2015; $1,058, MS-63FH, August 2015													
1925	12,280,000	1,195	61.1	82%	$7.50	$8	$10	$20	$45	$100	$160	$250	$1,000
Auctions: $3,055, MS-67, August 2015; $5,405, MS-66FH, May 2015; $1,116, MS-65FH, August 2015; $235, MS-64, July 2015													
1926	11,316,000	1,254	61.5	81%	$7.50	$8	$9	$20	$45	$100	$150	$250	$2,000
Auctions: $3,760, MS-67, September 2015; $2,585, MS-66FH, October 2015; $353, MS-65, March 2015; $646, MS-64FH, October 2015													
1926-D	1,716,000	2,222	63.1	97%	$7.50	$10	$22	$40	$80	$140	$180	$250	$24,000
Auctions: $564, MS-66, January 2015; $400, MS-65, December 2015; $447, MS-64, November 2015; $270, MS-63, August 2015													
1926-S	2,700,000	429	54.8	58%	$7.50	$10	$15	$28	$110	$225	$375	$775	$25,000
Auctions: $4,935, MS-66, February 2015; $17,625, MS-65FH, January 2015; $4,465, MS-62FH, January 2015; $552, AU-58, March 2015													
1927	11,912,000	1,457	60.4	76%	$7.50	$8	$9	$17	$35	$80	$140	$225	$1,100
Auctions: $2,820, MS-67, August 2015; $7,050, MS-66FH, August 2015; $447, MS-65, August 2015; $764, MS-64FH, March 2015													
1927-D	976,000	972	59.9	86%	$15	$20	$30	$75	$150	$220	$270	$310	$3,000
Auctions: $6,463, MS-66FH, June 2015; $793, MS-66, August 2015; $2,585, MS-65FH, August 2015; $353, MS-64, May 2015													
1927-S	396,000	1,167	27.0	12%	$40	$50	$130	$350	$1,250	$3,000	$5,000	$7,000	$175,000
Auctions: $1,293, AU-55, January 2015; $2,233, AU-53, September 2015; $1,645, AU-50, January 2015; $1,175, EF-45, September 2015													
1928	6,336,000	966	61.1	80%	$7.50	$8	$9	$17	$40	$80	$140	$225	$1,750
Auctions: $1,058, MS-67, January 2015; $3,525, MS-66FH, September 2015; $1,410, MS-65FH, August 2015; $306, MS-64, June 2015													
1928-D	1,627,600	1,446	63.1	92%	$7.50	$8	$9	$17	$35	$80	$150	$235	$5,000
Auctions: $517, MS-66, January 2015; $423, MS-65, March 2015; $353, MS-64, July 2015; $223, MS-63, February 2015													
1928-S (c)	2,644,000	1,426	62.8	90%	$7.50	$8	$9	$22	$40	$90	$140	$235	$900
Auctions: $4,700, MS-67FH, January 2015; $1,410, MS-66, February 2015; $1,293, MS-65FH, October 2015; $400, MS-64, November 2015													
1929	11,140,000	1,852	61.5	81%	$7.50	$8	$9	$17	$35	$80	$140	$225	$900
Auctions: $1,528, MS-66FH, February 2015; $646, MS-65FH, August 2015; $423, MS-64FH, October 2015; $235, MS-64, April 2015													
1929-D	1,358,000	978	60.7	76%	$7.50	$8	$9	$17	$40	$80	$140	$230	$5,000
Auctions: $5,405, MS-67, July 2015; $1,116, MS-66, February 2015; $423, MS-65, November 2015; $329, MS-64, October 2015													
1929-S	1,764,000	1,386	61.6	83%	$7.50	$8	$9	$17	$35	$80	$140	$225	$850
Auctions: $4,935, MS-67FH, February 2015; $1,381, MS-66FH, July 2015; $353, MS-65, October 2015; $235, MS-64, May 2015													
1930	5,632,000	3,510	61.9	80%	$7.50	$8	$9	$17	$35	$80	$140	$225	$850
Auctions: $2,820, MS-67, February 2015; $1,175, MS-66FH, January 2015; $734, MS-65FH, August 2015; $423, MS-64FH, May 2015													
1930-S	1,556,000	1,066	61.8	84%	$7.50	$8	$9	$17	$35	$80	$140	$225	$850
Auctions: $2,820, MS-67FH, January 2015; $793, MS-66, January 2015; $494, MS-65, March 2015; $365, MS-64FH, August 2015													

c. Large and small mintmarks exist; their values are the same.

WASHINGTON, EAGLE REVERSE (1932–1998)

Designer: *John Flanagan.* **Weight:** *Silver issue—6.25 grams; clad issue—5.67 grams; silver Proofs—6.25 grams.* **Composition:** *Silver issue—.900 silver, .100 copper (net weight .18084 oz. pure silver); clad issue—outer layers of copper nickel (.750 copper, .250 nickel) bonded to inner core of pure copper; silver Proofs—.900 silver, .100 copper (net weight .18084 oz. pure silver).* **Diameter:** *24.3 mm.* **Edge:** *Reeded.* **Mints:** *Philadelphia, Denver, and San Francisco.*

Circulation Strike

Proof

 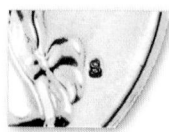

Mintmark location, 1932–1964, is on the reverse, below the eagle.

Mintmark location, 1965 to date, is on the obverse, to right of the hair ribbon.

Bicentennial variety: **Designers:** *John Flanagan and Jack L. Ahr.* **Weight:** *Silver issue—5.75 grams; copper-nickel issue—5.67 grams.* **Composition:** *Silver issue—outer layers of .800 silver, .200 copper bonded to inner core of .209 silver, .791 copper (net weight .0739 oz. pure silver); copper-nickel issue—outer layers of .750 copper, .250 nickel bonded to inner core of pure copper.* **Diameter:** *24.3 mm.* **Edge:** *Reeded.* **Mints:** *Philadelphia, Denver, and San Francisco.*

Bicentennial variety

Bicentennial variety, Proof

History. The Washington quarter, designed by New York sculptor John Flanagan, originally was intended to be a commemorative coin, but it ultimately was produced as a regular circulation issue. The obverse is inspired by a famous bust by Jean Antoine Houdon. Flanagan's initials, JF, are at the base of Washington's neck. The reverse features a modernistic eagle perched on a quiver of arrows, with wings unfolding. In October 1973, the Treasury Department announced an open contest for the selection of suitable designs for the Bicentennial reverses of the quarter, half dollar, and dollar, with $5,000 to be awarded to each winner. Twelve semifinalists were chosen, and from these the symbolic entry of Jack L. Ahr was selected for the quarter reverse. It features a military drummer facing left, with a victory torch encircled by 13 stars at the upper left. Except for the dual dating, "1776–1976," the obverse remained unchanged. Pieces with this dual dating were coined during 1975 and 1976. They were struck for general circulation and included in all the U.S. Mint's offerings of Proof and Uncirculated coin sets. (The grading instructions below are for the regular Eagle Reverse variety.)

Striking and Sharpness. The relief of both sides of the Washington quarter issues from 1932 to 1998 is shallow. Accordingly, any lightness of strike is not easily seen. Nearly all are well struck. On all quarters of 1932 and some of 1934, the motto IN GOD WE TRUST is light, as per the design. It was strengthened in 1934.

Availability. The 1932-D and -S are key issues but not rarities. All others are readily available in high grades, but some are scarcer than others. Proof dates available are 1936 to 1942 and 1950 to 1964 (from the Philadelphia Mint) and 1968 to 1998 (from San Francisco). Certain later Proofs are available in clad metal as well as silver strikings. Special Mint Set (SMS) coins were struck in lieu of Proofs from 1965 to 1967; these in some instances closely resemble Proofs. The majority of Proofs made in recent decades are in high levels, PF–66 to 68 or higher.

Note: Values of common-date silver coins have been based on the current bullion price of silver, $15.50 per ounce, and may vary with the prevailing spot price.

GRADING STANDARDS

MS-60 to 70 (Mint State). *Obverse:* At MS-60, some abrasion and contact marks are evident on the hair above the ear and at the top of the head below the E of LIBERTY. At MS-63, abrasion is slight at best, less so for MS-64. An MS-65 coin should display no abrasion or contact marks except under magnification, and MS-66 and higher coins should have none at all. Luster should be full and rich. *Reverse:* Comments apply as for the

1939-D. Graded MS-64.

obverse, except that the eagle's breast and legs are the places to check. On both sides the fields are protected by design elements and do not show contact marks readily.

AU-50, 53, 55, 58 (About Uncirculated). *Obverse:* Light wear is seen on the cheek, the high areas of the hair, and the neck. At AU-58, the luster is extensive but incomplete, especially on the higher parts and in the field. At AU–50 and 53, luster is less. *Reverse:* Light wear is seen on the breast, legs, and upper edges of the wings of the eagle. An AU-58 coin has nearly full luster. At AU–50 and 53, there still is significant luster.

1932-S. Graded AU-55.

EF-40, 45 (Extremely Fine). *Obverse:* Further wear is seen on the head. Higher-relief details are gone in the hair. The higher-relief parts of the neck show wear, most noticeably just above the date. *Reverse:* Further wear is seen on the eagle. Most breast feathers, not strong to begin with, are worn away.

1932-D. Graded EF-40.

VF-20, 30 (Very Fine). *Obverse:* Most hair detail is worn away, except above the curls. The delineation between the temple and the edge of the hair is faint. The curl by the ear is worn flat. Tips of the letters in LIBERTY and the date digits touch the rim in some instances. *Reverse:* More details of the eagle are worn away, and the outlines of the feathers in the wing, while nearly all present, are faint. Tips of the letters touch the rim in some instances on this and lower grades, but this can vary from coin to coin depending on the strength of the rim.

1942-D, Doubled-Die Obverse; FS-101. Graded VF-30.

F-12, 15 (Fine). *Obverse:* Most of the hair is worn flat, with no distinction between the face and the beginning of the hair. There is some detail remaining just above and below the curls. *Reverse:* More feathers are worn away. The end of the branch at the left is worn so as to blend into the wing. The edge of the rim is barely visible and in some areas is worn away. (In this and the Very Good grade, opinions concerning the rim vary in the ANA grading standards and in *Photograde*; PCGS is silent on the matter.)

1932-D. Graded F-12.

VG-8, 10 (Very Good). *Obverse:* Further wear is seen on the head, with most of the upper part of the curls now blending into the hair above. *Reverse:* The rim is worn into the tops of the letters. There is no detail on the leaves. About half of the feathers are outlined, but only faintly.

1932-S. Graded VG-10.

G-4, 6 (Good). *Obverse:* Further wear is seen in all areas. On 1932 and some 1934 coins the IN GOD WE TRUST motto is so worn that some letters are missing. *Reverse:* The rim is worn further into the letters. Fewer details are seen on the eagle's wing. On both sides the coin appears to be "worn flat," with little in relief.

1932-D. Graded G-4.

AG-3 (About Good). *Obverse:* Wear is more extensive, with about half of the letters gone. *Reverse:* Wear is more extensive, with about half of the letters gone. Slight detail remains in the eagle's wings. The mintmark, if any, is very clear.

1942. Graded AG-3.

PF-60 to 70 (Proof). *Obverse and Reverse:* Proofs that are extensively cleaned and have many hairlines, or that are dull and grainy, are lower level, such as PF–60 to 62. These are not widely desired, and represent coins that have been mistreated. Most low-level Proofs are of the 1936 to 1942 dates. With medium hairlines and good reflectivity, assigned grades of PF–63 or 64 are appropriate. PF–66 should have hairlines so delicate that magnification is needed to see them. Above that, a Proof should be free of any hairlines or other problems.

1974-S. Graded PF-70 Deep Cameo.

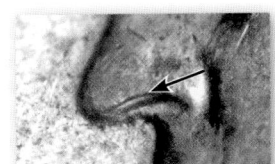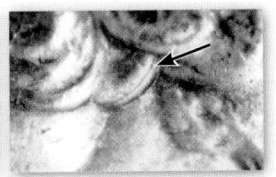

1932, Doubled-Die Obverse
FS-25-1932-101.

	Mintage	Cert	Avg	%MS	VG-8	F-12	VF-20	EF-40	AU-50	MS-60	MS-62	MS-63	MS-65
1932	5,404,000	1,958	62.5	87%	$8	$9	$10	$11	$15	$25	$40	$60	$410
Auctions: $8,813, MS-67, June 2015; $1,763, MS-66, January 2015; $505, MS-65, January 2015; $64, MS-64, February 2015													
1932, DblDie Obv (a)	(b)	23	56.9	30%						$350	$400	$500	$800
Auctions: $235, MS-62, December 2013													
1932-D	436,800	3,859	40.2	28%	$175	$190	$250	$300	$400	$1,050	$1,200	$1,500	$12,000
Auctions: $9,988, MS-65, January 2015; $1,351, MS-63, February 2015; $1,058, MS-61, January 2015; $541, AU-58, January 2015													
1932-S	408,000	4,734	46.6	40%	$175	$190	$225	$275	$300	$450	$750	$850	$4,500
Auctions: $2,299, MS-65, January 2015; $1,586, MS-64, January 2015; $617, MS-63, January 2015; $356, AU-58, January 2015													

a. The doubling is evident on the earlobe, the nostril, and the braid of hair. **b.** Included in 1932 mintage figure.

1934, Doubled-Die Obverse
FS-25-1934-101.

1934, Light Motto
FS-25-1934-401.

1934, Heavy Motto
FS-25-1934-403.

	Mintage	Cert	Avg	%MS	VG-8	F-12	VF-20	EF-40	AU-50	MS-60	MS-62	MS-63	MS-65
1934, All kinds	31,912,052												
1934, Doubled-Die Obverse (c)		192	41.1	30%	$75	$85	$200	$300	$600	$1,000	$1,500	$1,900	$4,250
	Auctions: $306, AU-55, May 2015; $329, AU-50, May 2015; $129, F-12, February 2015												
1934, Light Motto (d)		303	63.4	89%	$7.50	$7.75	$8	$10	$24	$60	$80	$135	$385
	Auctions: $447, MS-66, August 2015; $259, MS-66, July 2015; $235, MS-65, January 2015; $176, MS-64, January 2015												
1934, Heavy Motto (e)		63	62.8	81%	$7.50	$7.75	$8	$10	$15	$30	$40	$50	$135
	Auctions: $470, MS-66, September 2014; $100, MS-65, May 2015; $88, MS-65, August 2014; $118, MS-64, July 2014												
1934-D	3,527,200	1,298	61.3	78%	$7.50	$8	$12	$25	$85	$250	$280	$340	$850
	Auctions: $1,058, MS-66, January 2015; $646, MS-65, June 2015; $447, MS-64, July 2015; $165, AU-55, October 2015												
1935	32,484,000	1,949	64.5	94%	$7.50	$7.75	$8	$9	$10	$22	$30	$35	$135
	Auctions: $2,820, MS-67, January 2015; $2,115, MS-67, September 2015; $147, MS-66, August 2015; $69, MS-65, June 2015												
1935-D	5,780,000	1,240	61.8	81%	$7.50	$8	$10	$20	$125	$240	$265	$275	$625
	Auctions: $517, MS-66, January 2015; $306, MS-64, August 2015; $213, MS-62, August 2015; $141, AU-58, October 2015												
1935-S	5,660,000	1,374	62.7	84%	$7.50	$8	$9	$15	$38	$100	$120	$135	$300
	Auctions: $999, MS-67, January 2015; $282, MS-65, May 2015; $141, MS-64, September 2015; $79, MS-62, March 2015												

c. Very strong doubling is visible on the motto, LIBERTY, and the date. **d.** "Notice the considerable weakness in the letters of the motto. In addition, the center point of the W is pointed" (*Cherrypickers' Guide to Rare Die Varieties*, sixth edition, volume II). **e.** The motto has very thick letters, and the central apex of the W is pointed, rising slightly above the other letters.

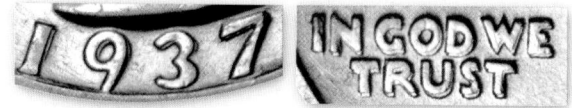

1937, Doubled-Die Obverse
FS-25-1937-101.

	Mintage	Cert	Avg	%MS	EF-40	AU-50	MS-60	MS-63	MS-65	MS-66	MS-67
									PF-64	PF-65	PF-67
1936	41,300,000	1,712	64.7	96%	$8	$10	$25	$35	$120	$200	$550
	Auctions: $306, MS-67, May 2015; $247, MS-67, October 2015; $89, MS-66, July 2015; $79, MS-65, April 2015										
1936, Proof	3,837	964	64.4						$1,400	$1,800	$7,500
	Auctions: $6,463, PF-67, June 2015; $1,528, PF-66, February 2015; $1,058, PF-65, October 2015; $541, PF-64, January 2015										
1936-D	5,374,000	1,161	60.5	75%	$55	$250	$525	$800	$1,100	$1,750	$8,000
	Auctions: $1,528, MS-66, June 2015; $705, MS-64, January 2015; $646, MS-62, February 2015; $429, AU-58, May 2015										
1936-S	3,828,000	1,419	63.8	95%	$15	$50	$120	$140	$325	$650	$2,000
	Auctions: $1,528, MS-67, September 2015; $517, MS-66, October 2015; $188, MS-65, February 2015; $106, MS-64, April 2015										
1937	19,696,000	1,119	64.4	96%	$8	$12	$25	$35	$90	$200	$600
	Auctions: $6,463, MS-68, June 2015; $881, MS-67, January 2015; $148, MS-66, September 2015; $74, MS-65, August 2015										
1937, Doubled-Die Obverse (a)	(b)	45	26.2	11%	$700	$1,500	$2,450	$3,800	$12,000	$18,000	
	Auctions: $1,778, MS-63, April 2013; $494, VF-35, July 2015; $188, F-12, November 2014										
1937, Proof	5,542	960	65.1						$450	$600	$1,100
	Auctions: $1,410, PF-67, January 2015; $412, PF-66, November 2015; $306, PF-65, October 2015; $141, PF-62, August 2015										
1937-D	7,189,600	1,184	64.0	95%	$15	$30	$70	$90	$150	$375	$1,400
	Auctions: $1,116, MS-67, August 2015; $235, MS-66, July 2015; $106, MS-65, January 2015; $79, MS-64, July 2015										
1937-S	1,652,000	1,143	63.4	93%	$35	$95	$150	$250	$400	$750	$2,000
	Auctions: $705, MS-66, June 2015; $295, MS-65, September 2015; $212, MS-64, May 2015; $200, MS-63, March 2015										

a. Very strong doubling is evident on the motto, LIBERTY, the date, and the end of the braid ribbons. "This variety is considered one of the most important in the series" (*Cherrypickers' Guide to Rare Die Varieties*, sixth edition, volume II). **b.** Included in circulation-strike 1937 mintage figure.

1942-D, Doubled-Die Obverse
FS-25-1942D-101.

1942-D, Doubled-Die Reverse
FS-25-1942D-801.

| | Mintage | Cert | Avg | %MS | EF-40 | AU-50 | MS-60 | MS-63 | MS-65 | MS-66 | MS-67 |
									PF-64	PF-65	PF-67
1938	9,472,000	1,092	63.6	90%	$15	$45	$95	$110	$210	$350	$850
	Auctions: $734, MS-67, October 2015; $494, MS-67, June 2015; $212, MS-66, July 2015; $141, MS-65, January 2015										
1938, Proof	8,045	1,233	65.0						$275	$350	$850
	Auctions: $1,058, PF-67, June 2015; $235, PF-66, October 2015; $153, PF-65, May 2015; $94, PF-63, February 2015										
1938-S	2,832,000	1,388	64.2	96%	$20	$55	$105	$140	$230	$350	$800
	Auctions: $705, MS-67, August 2015; $188, MS-66, January 2015; $155, MS-65, March 2015; $129, MS-64, September 2015										
1939	33,540,000	1,898	65.2	97%	$8	$12	$15	$25	$60	$100	$200
	Auctions: $1,293, MS-68, September 2015; $764, MS-67, June 2015; $64, MS-66, July 2015; $56, MS-65, August 2015										
1939, Proof	8,795	1,229	65.4						$235	$275	$600
	Auctions: $3,055, PF-68, September 2015; $517, PF-67, January 2015; $165, PF-66, July 2015; $112, PF-64, February 2015										
1939-D	7,092,000	1,387	64.7	97%	$11	$20	$40	$50	$115	$175	$750
	Auctions: $494, MS-67, May 2015; $129, MS-66, August 2015; $74, MS-65, January 2015; $36, MS-63, September 2015										
1939-S	2,628,000	1,150	63.8	93%	$20	$60	$95	$135	$300	$475	$1,400
	Auctions: $764, MS-67, January 2015; $282, MS-66, September 2015; $223, MS-65, February 2015; $100, MS-62, March 2015										
1940	35,704,000	1,370	65.1	97%	$8	$9	$17	$35	$60	$115	$400
	Auctions: $15,275, MS-68, January 2015; $705, MS-67, June 2015; $46, MS-66, May 2015; $28, MS-64, November 2015										
1940, Proof	11,246	1,497	65.4						$175	$225	$425
	Auctions: $1,821, PF-68, June 2015; $541, PF-67, September 2015; $106, PF-66, January 2015; $100, PF-65, February 2015										
1940-D	2,797,600	1,226	64.2	95%	$24	$65	$120	$165	$300	$425	$1,250
	Auctions: $564, MS-67, June 2015; $353, MS-66, January 2015; $147, MS-64, August 2015; $153, MS-63, February 2015										
1940-S	8,244,000	1,204	65.1	97%	$9	$16	$21	$32	$65	$120	$500
	Auctions: $423, MS-67, January 2015; $69, MS-66, April 2015; $50, MS-65, August 2015; $28, MS-64, November 2015										
1941	79,032,000	1,718	65.3	98%	$7.50	$8	$10	$14	$45	$80	$300
	Auctions: $259, MS-67, September 2015; $200, MS-67, January 2015; $38, MS-66, April 2015; $36, MS-65, May 2015										
1941, Proof	15,287	1,806	65.4						$140	$175	$425
	Auctions: $329, PF-67, March 2015; $100, PF-66, November 2015; $79, PF-65, January 2015; $72, PF-64, September 2015										
1941-D	16,714,800	1,015	64.9	97%	$8	$13	$32	$55	$70	$200	$1,250
	Auctions: $470, MS-67, June 2015; $112, MS-66, January 2015; $94, MS-66, November 2015; $69, MS-63, September 2015										
1941-S	16,080,000	1,191	64.7	96%	$8	$11	$28	$55	$70	$185	$1,000
	Auctions: $705, MS-67, January 2015; $376, MS-67, October 2015; $106, MS-66, February 2015; $69, MS-65, March 2015										
1942	102,096,000	1,226	64.8	96%	$7.50	$8	$9	$10	$35	$200	$800
	Auctions: $823, MS-67, October 2015; $282, MS-67, January 2015; $141, MS-66, September 2015; $79, MS-66, October 2015										
1942, Proof	21,123	2,239	65.2						$135	$150	$385
	Auctions: $10,575, PF-68, June 2015; $235, PF-67, January 2015; $79, PF-65, May 2015; $56, PF-64, December 2015										
1942-D	17,487,200	1,256	65.2	99%	$8	$10	$17	$20	$40	$200	$400
	Auctions: $223, MS-67, July 2015; $207, MS-67, January 2015; $69, MS-66, January 2015; $58, MS-66, November 2015										
1942-D, DblDie Obv (c)	(d)	56	33.4	9%	$350	$750	$1,800	$4,000	$6,000	$10,500	
	Auctions: $823, MS-64, June 2014; $1,207, AU-55, April 2013; $188, AU-50, August 2014										
1942-D, DblDie Rev (e)	(d)	20	45.6	40%		$385	$750	$1,250	$2,250	$5,000	
	Auctions: $5,875, MS-66, August 2013										
1942-S	19,384,000	1,301	64.0	93%	$10	$20	$70	$115	$175	$375	$850
	Auctions: $400, MS-67, January 2015; $235, MS-66, April 2015; $118, MS-65, June 2015; $84, MS-64, September 2015										

c. Doubling is evident, with a very strong spread, on LIBERTY, the date, and the motto. **d.** Included in 1942-D mintage figure.
e. Doubling on this popular variety is most prominent on the eagle's beak, the arrows, and the branch above the mintmark.

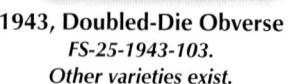

1943, Doubled-Die Obverse
FS-25-1943-103.
Other varieties exist.

1943-S, Doubled-Die Obverse
FS-25-1943S-101.

	Mintage	Cert	Avg	%MS	EF-40	AU-50	MS-60	MS-63	MS-65	MS-66	MS-67
									PF-64	PF-65	PF-67
1943	99,700,000	2,065	65.1	97%	$7.50	$8	$9	$10	$40	$100	$350
Auctions: $223, MS-67, September 2015; $165, MS-67, January 2015; $36, MS-66, January 2015											
1943, DblDie Obverse (f)	**(g)**	14	54.6	50%	$300	$500	$1,600	$3,500	$5,500	$8,000	
Auctions: $30, VF-20, March 2012											
1943-D	16,095,600	1,104	65.2	98%	$8	$15	$28	$39	$60	$120	$800
Auctions: $282, MS-67, August 2015; $217, MS-67, January 2015; $52, MS-66, January 2015; $32, MS-65, February 2015											
1943-S	21,700,000	1,283	65.1	98%	$9	$13	$26	$42	$60	$120	$900
Auctions: $6,463, MS-68, July 2015; $734, MS-67, January 2015; $89, MS-66, May 2015; $62, MS-66, November 2015											
1943-S, DblDie Obv (h)	**(i)**	122	45.7	48%	$200	$350	$500	$1,000	$2,600	$6,250	$8,250
Auctions: $1,528, MS-64, June 2015; $1,293, MS-64, August 2015; $705, MS-64, January 2015; $79, EF-40, August 2015											
1944	104,956,000	2,225	65.4	98%	$7.50	$8	$9	$10	$32	$60	$500
Auctions: $282, MS-67, October 2015; $165, MS-67, July 2015; $36, MS-66, August 2015											
1944-D	14,600,800	1,947	65.7	99%	$8	$10	$17	$20	$40	$70	$400
Auctions: $10,575, MS-68, August 2015; $235, MS-67, September 2015; $165, MS-67, January 2015; $50, MS-66, April 2015											
1944-S	12,560,000	1,864	65.7	99%	$8	$10	$14	$20	$35	$60	$350
Auctions: $317, MS-67, February 2015; $176, MS-67, September 2015; $48, MS-66, August 2015; $129, MS-65, April 2015											
1945	74,372,000	1,554	65.1	99%	$7.50	$8	$9	$10	$38	$150	$650
Auctions: $16,450, MS-68, January 2015; $2,350, MS-68, October 2015; $329, MS-67, August 2015; $58, MS-66, January 2015											
1945-D	12,341,600	1,207	65.4	99%	$8	$12	$18	$25	$40	$70	$1,000
Auctions: $364, MS-67, September 2015; $329, MS-67, May 2015; $42, MS-64, April 2015											
1945-S	17,004,001	1,612	65.4	99%	$7.50	$8	$9	$13	$35	$60	$750
Auctions: $353, MS-67, October 2015; $236, MS-67, May 2015; $69, MS-66, July 2015; $54, MS-66, May 2015											
1946	53,436,000	1,004	65.2	98%	$7	$8	$9	$10	$40	$100	$1,500
Auctions: $353, MS-67, September 2015; $306, MS-67, July 2015; $74, MS-66, January 2015; $20, MS-64, September 2015											
1946-D	9,072,800	2,562	65.6	100%	$7.50	$8	$9	$10	$45	$80	$650
Auctions: $306, MS-67, November 2015; $165, MS-67, January 2015; $34, MS-65, September 2015											
1946-S	4,204,000	5,795	65.5	100%	$7	$8	$9	$10	$40	$60	$350
Auctions: $235, MS-67, March 2015; $223, MS-67, November 2015; $58, MS-66, October 2015; $46, MS-66, August 2015											
1947	22,556,000	1,597	65.5	99%	$7.50	$8	$11	$19	$42	$80	$350
Auctions: $176, MS-67, August 2015; $153, MS-67, October 2015; $56, MS-66, September 2015											
1947-D	15,338,400	2,628	65.7	100%	$7.50	$8	$11	$17	$40	$60	$250
Auctions: $147, MS-67, December 2015; $84, MS-67, May 2015; $52, MS-66, July 2015; $38, MS-65, April 2015											
1947-S	5,532,000	4,717	65.7	100%	$7	$8	$9	$15	$32	$55	$250
Auctions: $646, MS-68, September 2015; $165, MS-67, December 2015; $40, MS-66, May 2015; $21, MS-65, July 2015											
1948	35,196,000	2,230	65.5	99%	$7	$8	$9	$10	$35	$60	$300
Auctions: $135, MS-67, November 2015; $112, MS-67, January 2015; $69, MS-66, May 2015; $52, MS-66, October 2015											
1948-D	16,766,800	1,542	65.3	99%	$7.50	$8	$13	$18	$55	$100	$750
Auctions: $2,585, MS-67, January 2015; $74, MS-66, February 2015; $52, MS-66, September 2015; $46, MS-65, May 2015											
1948-S	15,960,000	2,595	65.5	99%	$7	$8	$9	$13	$45	$70	$250
Auctions: $153, MS-67, November 2015; $118, MS-67, January 2015; $129, MS-66, February 2015; $74, MS-66, October 2015											

f. Doubling is very strong on the motto, LIBERTY, and the date. **g.** Included in 1943 mintage figure. **h.** Very strong doubling is visible on the motto, LIBERTY, the designer's initials, and the date. "Values for this variety are generally firm, but do change with market conditions and demand fluctuations" (*Cherrypickers' Guide to Rare Die Varieties*, sixth edition, volume II). **i.** Included in 1943-S mintage figure.

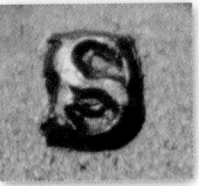
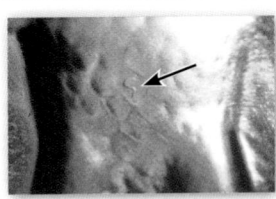

1950-D, D Over S
FS-25-1950D-601.
Other varieties exist.

1950-S, S Over D
FS-25-1950S-601.

1952, Die Damage, Proof
"Superbird" variety.
FS-25-1952-901.

	Mintage	Cert	Avg	%MS	EF-40	AU-50	MS-60	MS-63	MS-65 PF-64	MS-66 PF-65	MS-67 PF-67
1949	9,312,000	1,379	65.2	98%	$10	$14	$35	$47	$70	$115	$300
Auctions: $329, MS-67, August 2015; $282, MS-67, January 2015; $84, MS-66, April 2015; $74, MS-66, October 2015											
1949-D	10,068,400	1,476	65.2	99%	$8	$12	$16	$38	$50	$110	$600
Auctions: $4,700, MS-68, September 2015; $223, MS-67, July 2015; $74, MS-66, January 2015; $74, MS-65, August 2015											
1950	24,920,126	1,350	65.5	99%	$7	$8	$9	$10	$35	$70	$450
Auctions: $529, MS-67, September 2014; $282, MS-67, September 2015; $223, MS-67, January 2015; $52, MS-66, February 2015											
1950, Proof	51,386	1,819	65.9						$70	$100	$150
Auctions: $881, PF-67Cam, January 2015; $106, PF-67, August 2015; $317, PF-66Cam, May 2015; $42, PF-66, August 2015											
1950-D	21,075,600	1,469	64.8	97%	$7	$8	$9	$10	$35	$70	$800
Auctions: $206, MS-67, November 2015; $170, MS-67, May 2015; $56, MS-66, October 2015											
1950-D, D Over S (j)	(k)	124	48.3	30%	$150	$225	$325	$550	$3,000	$12,000	—
Auctions: $1,880, MS-64, June 2015; $1,469, MS-64, September 2015; $176, AU-58, June 2015; $100, EF-45, August 2015											
1950-S	10,284,004	1,440	64.6	95%	$7.50	$8	$12	$16	$45	$60	$400
Auctions: $259, MS-67, September 2015; $235, MS-67, January 2015; $106, MS-66, September 2015; $74, MS-66, April 2015											
1950-S, S Over D (l)	(m)	100	53.8	57%	$150	$250	$350	$500	$1,500	$2,800	$5,000
Auctions: $1,880, MS-66, September 2015; $705, MS-65, June 2015; $588, MS-64, February 2015; $306, AU-58, May 2015											
1951	43,448,102	1,538	65.5	99%	$7	$8	$9	$10	$25	$50	$300
Auctions: $450, MS-67, September 2014; $282, MS-67, September 2014; $206, MS-67, November 2015; $176, MS-67, January 2015											
1951, Proof	57,500	1,792	66.0						$65	$90	$125
Auctions: $1,645, PF-68Cam, June 2015; $1,293, PF-68Cam, June 2015; $1,234, PF-68Cam, November 2014; $176, PF-66Cam, February 2015											
1951-D	35,354,800	1,573	65.4	99%	$7	$8	$9	$10	$35	$60	$575
Auctions: $284, MS-67, March 2015; $235, MS-67, July 2015; $76, MS-66, March 2015; $66, MS-66, October 2015											
1951-S	9,048,000	1,543	65.8	100%	$7.50	$8	$10	$15	$40	$80	$350
Auctions: $2,115, MS-68, September 2015; $229, MS-67, February 2015; $176, MS-67, September 2015; $79, MS-66, February 2015											
1952	38,780,093	1,198	65.5	99%	$7.50	$8	$9	$10	$25	$60	$250
Auctions: $494, MS-68, January 2015; $165, MS-67, January 2015; $141, MS-67, December 2015; $42, MS-66, December 2015											
1952, Proof	81,980	1,726	66.3						$45	$75	$100
Auctions: $69, PF-67, August 2015; $46, PF-66, March 2015; $42, PF-66, August 2015; $212, PF-65Cam, May 2015											
1952, Die Damage, Proof (n)	(o)	(p)							$250	$500	
Auctions: $3,525, PF-66DCam, April 2014											
1952-D	49,795,200	985	65.2	99%	$7	$8	$9	$10	$40	$100	$2,500
Auctions: $3,878, MS-67, September 2015; $3,055, MS-67, January 2015; $84, MS-66, February 2015; $69, MS-66, October 2015											
1952-S	13,707,800	1,855	65.7	100%	$7.50	$8	$12	$20	$42	$80	$150
Auctions: $4,935, MS-68, October 2015; $153, MS-67, January 2015; $141, MS-67, September 2015; $94, MS-66, October 2015											

j. The upper left curve of the underlying S is visible west and north of the D mintmark. Most Mint State specimens have brilliant surfaces. **k.** Included in 1950-D mintage figure. **l.** Most Mint State specimens have a frosty luster, rather than the brilliant surface seen on most of this year's Mint State D Over S coins. **m.** Included in 1950-S mintage figure. **n.** "There is an unusual S-shaped mark on the breast of the eagle. The cause of this mark is unknown. The nickname for this well-known variety is, suitably, 'Superbird'!" (*Cherrypickers' Guide to Rare Die Varieties*, sixth edition, volume II). **o.** Included in 1952, Proof, mintage figure. **p.** Included in certified population for 1952, Proof.

	Mintage	Cert	Avg	%MS	EF-40	AU-50	MS-60	MS-63	MS-65	MS-66	MS-67
									PF-64	PF-65	PF-67
1953	18,536,120	967	65.3	99%	$7.50	$8	$9	$10	$40	$80	$450
	Auctions: $447, MS-67, February 2015; $423, MS-67, January 2015; $52, MS-66, April 2015; $42, MS-66, June 2015										
1953, Proof	128,800	3,197	66.7						$45	$60	$80
	Auctions: $1,293, PF-69Cam, October 2015; $7,638, PF-68DCam, October 2015; $52, PF-67, September 2015; $40, PF-66, August 2015										
1953-D	56,112,400	1,039	65.0	99%	$7	$8	$9	$10	$35	$100	$1,500
	Auctions: $1,528, MS-67, January 2015; $1,058, MS-67, October 2015; $177, MS-66, October 2015; $54, MS-66, April 2015										
1953-S	14,016,000	2,439	65.6	100%	$7	$8	$9	$10	$34	$60	$300
	Auctions: $235, MS-67, January 2015; $129, MS-67, September 2015; $341, MS-66, February 2015; $62, MS-66, July 2015										
1954	54,412,203	2,123	65.4	99%	$7	$8	$9	$10	$34	$60	$300
	Auctions: $2,820, MS-67+, September 2014; $223, MS-67, October 2014; $200, MS-67, September 2015; $129, MS-67, January 2015										
1954, Proof	233,300	3,837	67.0						$25	$35	$60
	Auctions: $376, PF-69Cam, March 2015; $42, PF-68, August 2015; $411, PF-67DCam, January 2015; $42, PF-66, September 2015										
1954-D	42,305,500	1,186	65.2	100%	$7	$8	$9	$10	$35	$60	$2,250
	Auctions: $2,115, MS-67, January 2015; $705, MS-67, August 2015; $79, MS-66, November 2015; $54, MS-66, April 2015										
1954-S	11,834,722	4,496	65.6	100%	$7	$8	$9	$10	$36	$60	$400
	Auctions: $368, MS-67, November 2014; $200, MS-67, January 2015; $182, MS-67, November 2014; $182, MS-67, March 2015										
1955	18,180,181	2,533	65.4	99%	$7	$8	$9	$10	$27	$60	$700
	Auctions: $353, MS-67, September 2014; $282, MS-67, October 2014; $259, MS-67, June 2015; $212, MS-67, September 2015										
1955, Proof	378,200	5,248	67.3						$25	$35	$50
	Auctions: $1,175, PF-69UCam, January 2015; $764, PF-68UCam, August 2015; $200, PF-67DCam, April 2015										
1955-D	3,182,400	2,853	64.5	100%	$7.50	$8	$9	$10	$60	$400	$1,500
	Auctions: $2,350, MS-66, April 2012										
1956	44,144,000	3,304	65.7	100%	$7	$8	$9	$10	$21	$50	$150
	Auctions: $306, MS-67, May 2015; $129, MS-67, September 2015; $36, MS-65, September 2015; $588, MS-64, October 2014										
1956, Proof	669,384	6,152	67.5						$15	$25	$50
	Auctions: $1,293, PF-69DCam, September 2015; $329, PF-69Cam, August 2015; $89, PF-68UCam, May 2015; $32, PF-68, July 2015										
1956-D	32,334,500	1,026	65.4	100%	$7	$8	$9	$10	$27	$60	$2,000
	Auctions: $447, MS-67, September 2015; $423, MS-67, January 2015; $48, MS-66, September 2015; $26, MS-66, September 2015										
1957	46,532,000	2,203	65.7	99%	$7	$8	$9	$10	$27	$50	$125
	Auctions: $1,528, MS-68, July 2015; $79, MS-67, January 2015; $69, MS-67, September 2015; $22, MS-66, September 2015										
1957, Proof	1,247,952	5,066	67.3						$15	$25	$45
	Auctions: $188, PF-69Cam, January 2015; $588, PF-68UCam, July 2015; $353, PF-68, May 2015; $200, PF-67DCam, July 2015										
1957-D	77,924,160	1,760	65.6	99%	$7	$8	$9	$10	$25	$60	$275
	Auctions: $1,293, MS-68, September 2015; $259, MS-67, January 2015; $176, MS-67, November 2015; $36, MS-65, February 2015										
1958	6,360,000	3,989	65.8	100%	$7.50	$8	$9	$10	$20	$50	$100
	Auctions: $79, MS-67, February 2015; $69, MS-67, November 2015; $62, MS-67, August 2014; $69, MS-67, November 2014										
1958, Proof	875,652	3,968	67.1						$15	$30	$40
	Auctions: $1,528, PF-68DCam, September 2014; $764, PF-68DCam, November 2014; $235, PF-67DCam, October 2015										
1958-D	78,124,900	2,271	65.6	99%	$7	$8	$9	$10	$25	$50	$250
	Auctions: $353, MS-68, September 2015; $235, MS-67, June 2015; $118, MS-66, November 2015; $30, MS-65, September 2015										
1959	24,384,000	1,698	65.5	100%	$7	$8	$9	$10	$25	$50	$850
	Auctions: $2,585, MS-67, January 2015; $1,763, MS-67, September 2015; $282, MS-66, April 2015; $60, MS-65, August 2015										
1959, Proof	1,149,291	4,454	67.3						$12	$25	$35
	Auctions: $9,400, PF-69DCam, November 2014; $881, PF-68DCam, September 2014; $705, PF-68UCam, November 2015										
1959, Doubled-Die Obverse, Proof (q)	(r)	80	66.4						$185	$300	
	Auctions: $150, PF-65, February 2012										
1959-D	62,054,232	1,403	65.1	99%	$7	$8	$9	$10	$25	$60	$1,350
	Auctions: $646, MS-67, August 2015; $470, MS-67, June 2015; $68, MS-66, November 2015; $16, MS-65, November 2014										

q. Dramatic doubling is evident on all obverse lettering, especially IN GOD WE TRUST. There are at least five different doubled-die obverses for this date; the one featured here is FS-25-1959-101. r. Included in 1959, Proof, mintage figure.

	Mintage	Cert	Avg	%MS	EF-40	AU-50	MS-60	MS-63	MS-65	MS-66	MS-67
									PF-64	PF-65	PF-67
1960	29,164,000	1,187	65.4	100%	$7	$8	$9	$10	$20	$80	$950
Auctions: $1,058, MS-67, June 2015; $764, MS-67, September 2015; $100, MS-66, November 2015; $50, MS-66, August 2015											
1960, Proof	1,691,602	4,732	67.0						$11	$20	$30
Auctions: $2,115, PF-69DCam, September 2014; $999, PF-69DCam, July 2015; $764, PF-69DCam, November 2014; $217, PF-68DCam, November 2014											
1960-D	63,000,324	905	65.1	99%	$7	$8	$9	$10	$20	$50	$1,900
Auctions: $2,233, MS-67, January 2015; $2,115, MS-67, April 2014; $92, MS-66, September 2014											
1961	37,036,000	1,112	65.2	99%	$7	$8	$9	$10	$15	$60	$1,500
Auctions: $3,995, MS-67, June 2015; $946, MS-67, June 2015; $940, MS-67, September 2015; $764, MS-67, January 2015											
1961, Proof	3,028,244	6,081	67.2						$11	$20	$30
Auctions: $1,058, PF-69DCam, June 2015; $881, PF-69DCam, September 2015; $282, PF-69UCam, July 2015; $88, PF-68DCam, November 2014											
1961-D	83,656,928	767	64.9	99%	$7	$8	$9	$10	$15	$150	$3,000
Auctions: $7,638, MS-67, July 2014; $7,638, MS-67, August 2014; $129, MS-66, November 2015; $112, MS-66, June 2015											
1962	36,156,000	1,405	65.4	99%	$7	$8	$9	$10	$15	$60	$1,000
Auctions: $881, MS-67, February 2015; $353, MS-67, August 2015; $100, MS-66, August 2015; $52, MS-66, November 2015											
1962, Proof	3,218,019	5,662	67.1						$11	$20	$30
Auctions: $823, PF-69DCam, June 2015; $447, PF-69UCam, July 2015; $94, PF-68DCam, September 2015											
1962-D	127,554,756	758	64.8	98%	$7	$8	$9	$10	$15	$120	$2,000
Auctions: $4,759, MS-67, January 2015; $1,293, MS-67, June 2015; $212, MS-66, January 2015; $165, MS-66, June 2015											
1963	74,316,000	1,931	65.4	99%	$7	$8	$9	$10	$15	$60	$1,000
Auctions: $1,410, MS-67, February 2015; $940, MS-67, July 2015; $18, MS-66, April 2015; $2,115, MS-62, September 2014											
1963, Proof	3,075,645	6,926	67.4						$11	$20	$30
Auctions: $223, PF-69DCam, November 2014; $212, PF-69DCam, May 2015; $200, PF-69UCam, July 2015; $22, PF-67DCam, April 2015											
1963-D	135,288,184	785	65.0	98%	$7	$8	$9	$10	$15	$60	$1,000
Auctions: $969, MS-67, October 2015; $435, MS-67, June 2015; $74, MS-66, June 2015; $69, MS-66, November 2015											
1964	560,390,585	1,854	64.9	98%	$7	$8	$9	$10	$15	$50	$1,000
Auctions: $447, MS-67, January 2015; $353, MS-67, September 2015; $153, MS-66, October 2015											
1964, Proof	3,950,762	9,586	67.8						$11	$20	$30
Auctions: $329, PF-69DCam, January 2015; $282, PF-69UCam, January 2015; $259, PF-69UCam, July 2015											
1964-D	704,135,528	2,027	64.8	96%	$7	$8	$9	$10	$15	$50	$650
Auctions: $517, MS-67, June 2015; $447, MS-67, January 2015; $56, MS-66, February 2015											

1966, Doubled-Die Reverse
FS-25-1966-801.

	Mintage	Cert	Avg	%MS	MS-63	MS-65	MS-66	MS-67
						PF-65	PF-67Cam	PF-68DC
1965	1,819,717,540	253	64.8	95%	$1	$9	$30	$175
Auctions: $317, MS-67Cam, August 2015; $141, MS-67Cam, January 2015; $223, MS-67, March 2015; $188, MS-67, January 2015								
1965, Special Mint Set ‡	2,360,000	2,731	66.8			$12	$375	—
Auctions: $505, MS-67Cam, January 2014; $588, MS-67Cam, September 2014; $441, MS-67Cam, October 2014								
1966	821,101,500	90	64.8	94%	$1	$7	$30	$120
Auctions: $376, MS-67, January 2015; $259, MS-67, September 2014; $353, MS-63, January 2015; $212, MS-63, July 2015								
1966, Doubled-Die Reverse (a)	(b)	2	58.0	50%	$900	$1,400	$2,250	
Auctions: $920, EF-45, April 2012								
1966, Special Mint Set ‡	2,261,583	2,653	66.9			$12	$135	—
Auctions: $1,293, MS-68Cam, June 2014; $4,113, MS-68Cam, September 2014; $84, MS-67Cam, November 2014								

‡ Ranked in the *100 Greatest U.S. Modern Coins*. **a.** Very strong doubling is visible on all reverse lettering. Note that this is not the 1966 Special Mint Set issue. **b.** Included in circulation-strike 1966 mintage figure.

**1968-S, Doubled-Die
Reverse, Proof**
FS-25-1968S-801.

1970-D, Doubled-Die Obverse
FS-25-1970D-101.

	Mintage	Cert	Avg	%MS	MS-63 / PF-65	MS-65 / PF-67Cam	MS-66 / PF-67Cam	MS-67 / PF-68DC
1967	1,524,031,848	124	65.7	97%	$1	$6	$35	$180
	Auctions: $118, MS-68, January 2015; $188, MS-67, January 2015; $141, MS-67, November 2015; $95, MS-67, January 2015							
1967, Special Mint Set ‡	1,863,344	3,187	67.0			$12	$50	—
	Auctions: $212, MS-68Cam, September 2014; $188, MS-68Cam, August 2013							
1968	220,731,500	216	65.8	98%	$1.25	$8	$25	$100
	Auctions: $159, MS-67, July 2014; $141, MS-67, January 2015; $123, MS-67, September 2014; $84, MS-67, July 2015							
1968-D	101,534,000	688	66.0	100%	$1.10	$6	$15	$55
	Auctions: $123, MS-67, March 2013							
1968-S, Proof	3,041,506	1,085	67.4			$5	$15	$150
	Auctions: $194, PF-64, May 2013							
1968-S, Doubled-Die Reverse, Proof (c)	**(d)**	23	66.1			$165		
	Auctions: $196, PF-66, March 2012							
1969	176,212,000	98	64.8	96%	$3	$10	$35	$300
	Auctions: $3,290, MS-67, January 2015; $141, MS-66, January 2015; $135, MS-66, June 2014; $123, MS-66, September 2014							
1969-D	114,372,000	582	65.8	99%	$2.50	$10	$25	$75
	Auctions: $1,998, MS-68, July 2014; $72, MS-67, July 2014; $69, MS-67, April 2015; $200, MS-63, July 2015							
1969-S, Proof	2,934,631	1,447	67.9			$5	$15	$100
	Auctions: $617, PF-69DCam, December 2013							
1970	136,420,000	280	65.3	100%	$1	$10	$40	$100
	Auctions: $153, MS-67, August 2014; $441, MS-67, September 2014; $2,115, MS-67, November 2013; $30, MS-66, July 2014							
1970-D	417,341,364	1,138	65.8	99%	$1	$6	$10	$35
	Auctions: $2,926, MS-68, January 2014; $40, MS-67, December 2015; $182, AU-55, July 2014; $69, EF-45, September 2015							
1970-D, Doubled-Die Obverse (e)	**(f)**	2	59.5	50%	$300	$375	$500	
	Auctions: $2,875, MS-65, January 2012							
1970-S, Proof	2,632,810	1,177	67.9			$5	$15	$125
	Auctions: $705, PF-69DCam, June 2013; $1,175, PF-67Cam, October 2014							
1971	109,284,000	131	64.7	99%	$1	$6	$50	$150
	Auctions: $306, MS-66, August 2015; $212, MS-66, August 2015; $123, MS-66, September 2014; $89, MS-66, August 2015							
1971-D	258,634,428	264	65.9	100%	$1	$6	$20	$100
	Auctions: $4,113, MS-68, September 2013; $86, MS-67, July 2014; $182, MS-67, September 2014; $235, MS-62, October 2015							
1971-S, Proof	3,220,733	1,236	67.8			$5	$15	$300
	Auctions: $1,058, PF-69DCam, December 2013							
1972	215,048,000	226	65.7	100%	$1	$6	$25	$175
	Auctions: $588, MS-67, November 2013							
1972-D	311,067,732	607	66.2	100%	$1	$6	$18	$30
	Auctions: $3,055, MS-68, January 2014; $259, MS-65, October 2014							
1972-S, Proof	3,260,996	966	68.0			$5	$10	$30
	Auctions: $411, PF-65Cam, August 2013							

‡ Ranked in the *100 Greatest U.S. Modern Coins*. **c.** Doubling is evident on all reverse lettering around the rim and the left tips. **d.** Included in 1968-S, Proof, mintage figure. **e.** This extremely rare variety (fewer than a half dozen known) shows very strong doubling on the date, IN GOD WE TRUST, and the ERTY of LIBERTY. **f.** Included in 1970-D mintage figure.

1979-S, Filled S
(Type 1), Proof

 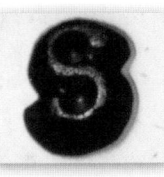

1979-S, Clear S
(Type 2), Proof

	Mintage	Cert	Avg	%MS	MS-63	MS-65	MS-66	MS-67
					PF-65	PF-67Cam	PF-68DC
1973	346,924,000	140	65.3	99%	$1	$6	$25	$175
Auctions: $1,116, MS-67, September 2013								
1973-D	232,977,400	156	65.1	99%	$1	$6	$25	$175
Auctions: $1,410, MS-65, February 2014								
1973-S, Proof	2,760,339	416	68.1	100%		$5	$10	$20
Auctions: $96, PF-67, March 2013								
1974	801,456,000	116	65.1	98%	$1	$6	$25	$175
Auctions: $382, MS-67, November 2013								
1974-D	353,160,300	162	65.4	99%	$1	$7	$25	$75
Auctions: $1,763, MS-64, September 2013								
1974-S, Proof	2,612,568	427	68.1			$5	$10	$20
Auctions: $7,015, PF-70DCam, April 2012								
1776–1976, Copper-Nickel Clad ‡	809,784,016	454	65.5	99%	$1.25	$6	$15	$50
Auctions: $306, MS-62, February 2014								
1776–1976-D, Copper-Nickel Clad	860,118,839	762	65.5	98%	$1.25	$6	$15	$60
Auctions: $66, MS-67, March 2013								
1776–1976-S, Silver Clad	11,000,000	1,120	66.1	100%	$4	$7	$15	$40
Auctions: $129, MS-68, October 2014; $100, MS-68, January 2015; $78, MS-68, August 2014								
1776–1976-S, Proof, Copper-Nickel Clad	7,059,099	1,712	68.0			$5	$10	$20
Auctions: $253, PF-70DCam, January 2015; $212, PF-70DCam, July 2015; $141, PF-70DCam, November 2015								
1776–1976-S, Proof, Silver Clad	4,000,000	3,307	68.1			$8	$12	$25
Auctions: $376, PF-70DCam, January 2015; $282, PF-70DCam, July 2015; $235, PF-70DCam, October 2015								
1977	468,556,000	125	65.5	98%	$1	$6	$20	$100
Auctions: $123, MS-67, September 2014; $52, MS-66, August 2015; $100, MS-60, September 2015								
1977-D	256,524,978	101	65.0	98%	$1	$6	$25	$125
Auctions: $229, MS-67, September 2014								
1977-S, Proof	3,251,152	811	68.7			$5	$10	$20
Auctions: $70, PF-70DCam, August 2014; $103, PF-70DCam, November 2014; $90, PF-70DCam, May 2013								
1978	521,452,000	160	65.4	99%	$1	$6	$20	$100
Auctions: $165, MS-67, January 2015; $470, MS-65, February 2015; $247, MS-65, August 2015; $259, MS-60, July 2015								
1978-D	287,373,152	140	65.4	99%	$1	$6	$25	$175
Auctions: $26, MS-66, August 2014								
1978-S, Proof	3,127,781	714	68.8			$5	$10	$16
Auctions: $61, PF-70DCam, August 2014; $80, PF-70DCam, May 2013; $12, PF-70DCam, March 2015								
1979	515,708,000	171	65.8	99%	$1	$6	$25	$125
Auctions: $411, MS-66, June 2014; $200, MS-64, February 2015; $176, MS-64, November 2014								
1979-D	489,789,780	139	65.5	99%	$1	$6	$25	$125
Auctions: $441, MS-67, September 2013								
1979-S, Proof, All kinds (g)	3,677,175							
1979-S, Type 1 ("Filled" S), Proof		930	68.8			$5	$10	$16
Auctions: $68, PF-70DCam, August 2014								
1979-S, Type 2 ("Clear" S), Proof		981	69.0			$6	$12	$25
Auctions: $529, PF-70DCam, September 2014; $76, PF-70DCam, August 2014; $72, PF-70DCam, September 2014								

‡ Ranked in the *100 Greatest U.S. Modern Coins*. **g.** The mintmark style was changed during 1979 Proof production, creating two distinctly different types. "The Type 2 is the rare variety, and is easily distinguished from the common Type 1. The Type 1 has a very indistinct blob, whereas the Type 2 shows a well-defined S" (*Cherrypickers' Guide to Rare Die Varieties*, sixth edition, volume II).

1981-S, Rounded S
(Type 1), Proof

1981-S, Flat S
(Type 2), Proof

	Mintage	Cert	Avg	%MS	MS-63	MS-65	MS-66	MS-67
						PF-65	PF-67Cam	PF-68DC
1980-P	635,832,000	367	65.9	99%	$1	$6	$18	$85
Auctions: $74, MS-65, November 2015; $56, MS-62, August 2015; $141, AU-58, January 2015								
1980-D	518,327,487	153	65.5	99%	$1	$6	$20	$175
Auctions: $1,380, MS-67, February 2007								
1980-S, Proof	3,554,806	1,121	68.7			$5	$10	$16
Auctions: $79, PF-70DCam, May 2013								
1981-P	601,716,000	269	66.0	100%	$1	$6	$15	$100
Auctions: $176, MS-65, August 2013								
1981-D	575,722,833	304	65.6	99%	$1	$6	$15	$150
Auctions: $259, MS-67, September 2013								
1981-S, Proof, All kinds (h)	4,063,083							
1981-S, Type 1 ("Rounded" S), Proof		1,310	68.8			$4	$8	$16
Auctions: $70, PF-70DCam, May 2013								
1981-S, Type 2 ("Flat" S), Proof		862	69.0			$6	$12	$25
Auctions: $705, PF-70DCam, April 2013								
1982-P	500,931,000	150	65.5	99%	$7	$30	$60	$240
Auctions: $646, MS-67, January 2015; $282, MS-63, September 2015; $353, AU-50, January 2015								
1982-D	480,042,788	219	65.5	99%	$5	$18	$60	$200
Auctions: $30, MS-66, March 2013								
1982-S, Proof	3,857,479	912	69.0			$4	$8	$16
Auctions: $103, PF-70DCam, May 2014; $56, PF-70DCam, September 2014; $47, PF-70DCam, November 2014								
1983-P ‡	673,535,000	752	65.0	99%	$30	$65	$200	$400
Auctions: $74, MS-66, July 2014; $74, MS-66, September 2014; $423, AU-58, January 2015								
1983-D	617,806,446	101	65.2	100%	$10	$45	$150	$500
Auctions: $1,058, MS-67, June 2014; $108, MS-66, August 2014; $92, MS-66, September 2014; $84, MS-66, January 2015								
1983-S, Proof	3,279,126	860	68.8			$4	$8	$16
Auctions: $72, PF-70DCam, September 2014; $90, PF-70DCam, August 2013								
1984-P	676,545,000	152	65.3	97%	$2	$10	$20	$125
Auctions: $1,058, MS-67, September 2013								
1984-D	546,483,064	86	64.6	98%	$2	$12	$65	$300
Auctions: $764, MS-67, September 2013								
1984-S, Proof	3,065,110	619	69.0			$4	$8	$16
Auctions: $80, PF-70DCam, May 2013; $55, PF-70DCam, August 2014; $50, PF-70DCam, August 2015								
1985-P	775,818,962	177	65.5	98%	$2	$15	$25	$100
Auctions: $764, MS-65, June 2014								
1985-D	519,962,888	186	65.7	99%	$1	$9	$25	$100
Auctions: $66, MS-66, March 2013								
1985-S, Proof	3,362,821	680	69.0			$4	$8	$16
Auctions: $86, PF-70DCam, May 2013								

‡ Ranked in the *100 Greatest U.S. Modern Coins*. **h.** The mintmark style was changed during the 1981 Proof production, creating two distinct types. "The Type 2 is the rare variety, and is not easily distinguished from the common Type 1. For most collectors, the easiest difference to discern on the Type 2 is the flatness on the top curve of the S, which is rounded on the Type 1. Additionally, the surface of the Type 2 mintmark is frosted, and the openings in the loops slightly larger" (*Cherrypickers' Guide to Rare Die Varieties*, sixth edition, volume II).

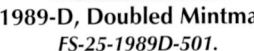

1989-D, Doubled Mintmark
FS-25-1989D-501.

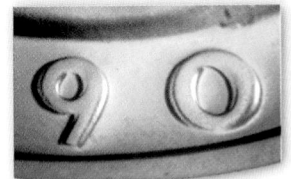

1990-S, Doubled-Die Obverse, Proof
FS-25-1990S-101.

	Mintage	Cert	Avg	%MS	MS-63	MS-65	MS-66	MS-67
						PF-65	PF-67Cam	PF-68DC
1986-P	551,199,333	172	65.0	98%	$2.50	$12	$30	$125
Auctions: $129, MS-64, October 2014; $103, MS-66, September 2014; $100, MS-66, August 2015; $30, MS-66, November 2014								
1986-D	504,298,660	201	65.6	99%	$6	$18	$25	$100
Auctions: $104, MS-66, November 2007								
1986-S, Proof	3,010,497	588	69.1			$4	$8	$16
Auctions: $39, PF-70DCam, August 2013								
1987-P	582,499,481	119	65.2	99%	$1	$9	$40	$200
Auctions: $59, MS-66, December 2007								
1987-D	655,594,696	143	65.6	99%	$1	$6	$20	$150
Auctions: $676, MS-67, January 2015; $66, MS-66, September 2014								
1987-S, Proof	4,227,728	816	69.0			$4	$8	$16
Auctions: No auction records available.								
1988-P	562,052,000	157	65.2	99%	$1.25	$15	$30	$175
Auctions: $66, MS-66, March 2013								
1988-D	596,810,688	139	65.5	100%	$1	$10	$20	$125
Auctions: $66, MS-66, November 2007								
1988-S, Proof	3,262,948	534	69.1			$4	$8	$16
Auctions: $55, PF-70DCam, August 2013								
1989-P	512,868,000	128	65.1	98%	$1	$12	$30	$150
Auctions: $216, MS-66, August 2009								
1989-D	896,535,597	118	65.3	97%	$1	$7	$25	$125
Auctions: $70, MS-66, March 2013								
1989-D, Repunched Mintmark (i)	(j)	0	n/a		$20	$25	$50	
Auctions: No auction records available.								
1989-S, Proof	3,220,194	610	68.9			$4	$8	$16
Auctions: $79, PF-70DCam, January 2010								
1990-P	613,792,000	149	65.9	99%	$1	$10	$20	$100
Auctions: $282, MS-64, June 2014								
1990-D	927,638,181	163	65.9	100%	$1	$10	$20	$125
Auctions: $646, MS-68, April 2014; $52, MS-67, August 2014								
1990-S, Proof	3,299,559	803	69.2			$4	$8	$16
Auctions: $53, PF-68DCam, April 2013								
1990-S, Doubled-Die Obverse, Proof ‡ (k)	(l)	5	68.2			$225	$700	
Auctions: $4,888, PF-70DCam, April 2012								
1991-P	570,968,000	126	66.0	99%	$1	$12	$30	$100
Auctions: $90, MS-66, November 2007								
1991-D	630,966,693	85	65.4	100%	$1	$12	$30	$225
Auctions: $66, MS-66, March 2013								
1991-S, Proof	2,867,787	773	69.3			$4	$8	$16
Auctions: $69, PF-70DCam, January 2010								

‡ Ranked in the *100 Greatest U.S. Modern Coins.* **i.** The secondary D mintmark is visible west of the primary D. **j.** Included in 1989-D mintage figure. **k.** Very strong doubling is visible on the date and the mintmark, with slightly less dramatic doubling on IN GOD WE TRUST. **l.** Included in 1990-S, Proof, mintage figure.

	Mintage	Cert	Avg	%MS	MS-63	MS-65	MS-66	MS-67
						PF-65	PF-67Cam	PF-68DC
1992-P	384,764,000	129	65.9	100%	$1.50	$16	$35	$225
	Auctions: $242, MS-66, February 2008							
1992-D	389,777,107	114	65.4	99%	$1	$16	$35	$225
	Auctions: $1,763, MS-67, November 2013; $47, MS-66, July 2014							
1992-S, Proof	2,858,981	579	69.2			$4	$8	$16
	Auctions: $50, PF-70DCam, January 2010							
1992-S, Proof, Silver	1,317,579	1,344	69.1			$9	$12	$22
	Auctions: $109, PF-70DCam, January 2010							
1993-P	639,276,000	173	66.1	98%	$1	$7	$20	$85
	Auctions: $86, MS-67, August 2014; $306, MS-64, June 2014; $282, MS-64, February 2015							
1993-D	645,476,128	147	65.9	99%	$1	$7	$25	$100
	Auctions: $1,298, MS-67, January 2015; $59, MS-67, August 2014; $101, MS-66, September 2014; $36, AU-58, July 2014							
1993-S, Proof	2,633,439	579	69.3			$4	$8	$16
	Auctions: $58, PF-70DCam, May 2013							
1993-S, Proof, Silver	761,353	1,070	69.0			$9	$12	$22
	Auctions: $70, PF-70DCam, August 2013							
1994-P	825,600,000	124	66.0	100%	$1	$10	$25	$100
	Auctions: $70, MS-66, March 2013							
1994-D	880,034,110	108	65.1	96%	$1	$10	$30	$150
	Auctions: $123, MS-66, September 2014; $212, MS-64, July 2014							
1994-S, Proof	2,484,594	545	69.3			$4	$8	$16
	Auctions: $69, PF-70DCam, January 2010							
1994-S, Proof, Silver	785,329	994	69.0			$9	$14	$25
	Auctions: $76, PF-70DCam, September 2014; $96, PF-70DCam, May 2013							
1995-P	1,004,336,000	128	66.6	100%	$1.25	$14	$20	$65
	Auctions: $129, MS-67, March 2013							
1995-D	1,103,216,000	133	66.1	100%	$1	$13	$20	$75
	Auctions: $165, MS-67, September 2014; $38, MS-64, July 2015							
1995-S, Proof	2,117,496	433	69.4			$8	$10	$20
	Auctions: $69, PF-70DCam, January 2010							
1995-S, Proof, Silver	679,985	1,083	69.0			$9	$14	$25
	Auctions: $68, PF-70DCam, September 2014; $69, PF-70DCam, November 2014; $135, PF-70DCam, May 2013							
1996-P	925,040,000	201	66.5	100%	$1	$10	$18	$30
	Auctions: $441, MS-68, March 2013							
1996-D	906,868,000	212	66.3	100%	$1	$10	$18	$30
	Auctions: $447, MS-68, March 2013; $165, MS-64, November 2014; $79, MS-63, January 2015							
1996-S, Proof	1,750,244	517	69.3			$5	$8	$18
	Auctions: $84, PF-70DCam, January 2010							
1996-S, Proof, Silver	775,021	1,059	69.0			$9	$14	$25
	Auctions: $76, PF-70DCam, May 2013							
1997-P	595,740,000	107	66.3	100%	$1	$11	$18	$40
	Auctions: $15, MS-60, January 2013							
1997-D	599,680,000	115	66.1	99%	$1	$12	$18	$40
	Auctions: $66, MS-67, March 2013							
1997-S, Proof	2,055,000	438	69.5			$5	$8	$18
	Auctions: $69, PF-70DCam, January 2010							
1997-S, Proof, Silver	741,678	1,113	69.2			$9	$14	$25
	Auctions: $89, PF-70DCam, January 2010							

	Mintage	Cert	Avg	%MS	MS-63	MS-65	MS-66	MS-67
					PF-65	PF-67Cam	PF-68DC
1998-P	896,268,000	151	66.6	99%	$1	$7	$18	$40
	Auctions: $364, MS-68, September 2014; $329, MS-68, June 2014; $306, MS-66, January 2015; $159, MS-64, November 2014							
1998-D	821,000,000	134	65.4	97%	$1	$7	$20	$75
	Auctions: $1,528, MS-67+, January 2015;$364, MS-67, September 2014; $32, MS-66, June 2014; $69, MS-63, August 2015							
1998-S, Proof	2,086,507	484	69.5		$6	$8	$18	
	Auctions: $9,988, PF-65, August 2014							
1998-S, Proof, Silver	878,792	1,276	69.2		$9	$12	$22	
	Auctions: $70, PF-70DCam, May 2013							

WASHINGTON, STATE, D.C., AND TERRITORIAL (1999–2009)

Designers: *John Flanagan (obverse); see image captions for reverse designers.* **Weight:** *Clad issue—5.67 grams; silver Proofs—6.25 grams.* **Composition:** *Clad issue—Outer layers of copper-nickel (.750 copper, .250 nickel) bonded to inner core of pure copper; silver Proofs—.900 silver, .100 copper (net weight .18084 oz. pure silver).* **Diameter:** *24.3 mm.* **Edge:** *Reeded.* **Mints:** *Clad issue—Philadelphia, Denver, and San Francisco; silver Proofs—San Francisco.*

Circulation Strike

Proof

History. In 1999 the U.S. Mint introduced a new program of State quarters (officially called the United States Mint 50 State Quarters® Program). These were released at the rate of five new reverse designs each year, in combination with a restyled obverse, through 2008. Each design honored the state the coin was issued for, and they were released in public celebrations in the order in which the states joined the Union. The coins became very popular, adding millions of Americans to the ranks of everyday coin collectors, and are still widely collected with enthusiasm. In 2009 the Mint released a similar program of quarter dollars for Washington, D.C., and the five U.S. territories. Circulation strikes were made at the Philadelphia and Denver mints, and special silver-content and Proof issues at San Francisco. Each coin combines a modified obverse depicting George Washington, without a date. The reverses are distinctive and bear the date of issue, the date of statehood (for the State quarters), and other design elements. Each state or district/territory selected its own design.

Some State quarters were accidentally made with "disoriented" dies and are valued higher than ordinary pieces. Normal U.S. coins have dies oriented in coin alignment, such that the reverse appears upside down when the coin is flipped from right to left. Values for the rotated-die quarters vary according to the amount of shifting. The most valuable are those that are shifted 180 degrees, so that both sides appear upright when the coin is turned over (called *medal alignment*).

Striking and Sharpness. State quarters can have light striking on the highest area of the obverse. On the reverse there can be weak areas, depending on the design, seemingly more often seen on Denver Mint coins. Some in the State quarter series were struck through grease, obliterating portions of both the obverse (usually) and reverse designs.

Availability. All modern quarters are readily available in high grades. Typical MS coins are MS–63 and 64 with light abrasion. MS-65 and higher coins are in the minority, but enough exist that finding them is no problem. Around MS-68 many issues are scarce, and higher grades are scarcer yet.

Proofs. State and D.C./Territorial quarter dollar Proofs are made in San Francisco. For certain later issues of Washington quarters as well as State, D.C., and Territorial issues, Proofs are available in copper-nickel–clad metal as well as silver strikings. On some Proofs over-polishing of dies eliminated some details, as on part of the WC (for William Cousins) initials on certain 1999 Delaware pieces.

GRADING STANDARDS

MS-60 to 70 (Mint State). *Obverse:* At MS-60, some abrasion and contact marks are evident on the highest-relief parts of the hair and the cheek. At MS-63, abrasion is slight at best, less so at MS-64. An MS-65 coin should display no abrasion or contact marks except under magnification, and MS-66 and higher coins should have none at all. Luster should be full. *Reverse:* Check the highest-relief areas of the design (these differ from coin to coin). Otherwise, comments are as for the obverse.

2004-D, Wisconsin, Extra Leaf Low. Graded MS-66.

AU-50, 53, 55, 58 (About Uncirculated). *Obverse:* Light wear is seen on the cheek, the high areas of the hair, and the neck. At AU-58, the luster is extensive, but incomplete, especially on the higher parts and in the field. At AU–50 and 53, luster is less. About Uncirculated coins usually lack eye appeal. *Reverse:* Light wear is seen on the higher-relief areas. Otherwise, comments are as for the obverse.

2004-D, Wisconsin, Extra Leaf High. Graded AU-58.

State, D.C., and Territorial quarter dollars are seldom collected in grades lower than AU-50.

PF-60 to 70 (Proof). *Obverse and Reverse:* These coins are so recent, and as only a few have been cleaned, most approach perfection and can be designated PF–68 to 70, the latter only if no contact marks or other problems can be seen under magnification. A cleaned coin with extensive hairlines would not be collectible for most numismatists and would be classified at a lower level such as PF–60 to 63. Those with lighter hairlines qualify for PF–64 or 65.

2008-S, Alaska. Graded PF-70 Ultra Cameo.

1999, Delaware
Reverse designer:
William Cousins.

1999, Pennsylvania
Reverse designer:
John Mercanti.

1999, New Jersey
Reverse designer:
Alfred Maletsky.

1999, Georgia
Reverse designer:
T. James Ferrell.

1999, Connecticut
Reverse designer:
T. James Ferrell.

	Mintage	Cert	Avg	%MS	AU-50	MS-63	MS-65	MS-66	MS-67
							PF-65	PF-66DC	PF-69DC
1999-P, Delaware	373,400,000	1,214	66.0	100%	$0.50	$1.25	$3	$25	$55
1999-D, Delaware	401,424,000	1,347	66.0	100%	$0.50	$1.25	$3	$25	$55
1999-S, Delaware, Proof	3,713,359	6,715	69.2				$7	$8	$20
1999-S, Delaware, Proof, Silver	804,565	12,596	69.0				$30	$35	$50
1999-P, Pennsylvania	349,000,000	1,102	66.1	100%	$0.50	$1.25	$3	$25	$55
1999-D, Pennsylvania	358,332,000	978	65.9	100%	$0.50	$1.25	$3	$25	$55
1999-S, Pennsylvania, Proof	3,713,359	6,483	69.2				$7	$8	$20
1999-S, Pennsylvania, Proof, Silver	804,565	12,037	69.1				$30	$35	$50
1999-P, New Jersey	363,200,000	1,055	66.2	100%	$0.50	$1.25	$3	$25	$55
1999-D, New Jersey	299,028,000	1,179	66.0	100%	$0.50	$1.25	$3	$25	$55
1999-S, New Jersey, Proof	3,713,359	6,480	69.2				$7	$8	$20
1999-S, New Jersey, Proof, Silver	804,565	12,132	69.1				$30	$35	$50
1999-P, Georgia	451,188,000	1,153	65.7	99%	$0.50	$1.25	$3	$25	$55
1999-D, Georgia	488,744,000	1,155	65.8	99%	$0.50	$1.25	$3	$25	$55
1999-S, Georgia, Proof	3,713,359	6,517	69.2				$7	$8	$20
1999-S, Georgia, Proof, Silver	804,565	12,226	69.1				$30	$35	$50
1999-P, Connecticut	688,744,000	1,236	65.6	99%	$0.50	$1.25	$3	$25	$55
1999-D, Connecticut	657,880,000	2,271	65.4	100%	$0.50	$1.25	$3	$25	$55
1999-S, Connecticut, Proof	3,713,359	6,553	69.3				$7	$8	$20
1999-S, Connecticut, Proof, Silver	804,565	12,045	69.1				$30	$35	$50

2000, Massachusetts
Reverse designer:
Thomas D. Rogers Sr.

2000, Maryland
Reverse designer:
Thomas D. Rogers Sr.

2000, South Carolina
Reverse designer:
Thomas D. Rogers Sr.

2000, New Hampshire
Reverse designer:
William Cousins.

2000, Virginia
Reverse designer:
Edgar Z. Steever.

	Mintage	Cert	Avg	%MS	AU-50	MS-63	MS-65	MS-66	MS-67
							PF-65	PF-66DC	PF-69DC
2000-P, Massachusetts	628,600,000	810	66.2	100%	$0.35	$1	$2	$15	$40
2000-D, Massachusetts	535,184,000	652	66.1	100%	$0.35	$1	$2	$15	$40
2000-S, Massachusetts, Proof	4,020,172	4,621	69.2				$3	$4	$15
2000-S, Massachusetts, Proof, Silver	965,421	9,669	69.2				$8	$10	$20
2000-P, Maryland	678,200,000	622	65.9	99%	$0.35	$1	$2	$15	$40
2000-D, Maryland	556,532,000	636	66.0	100%	$0.35	$1	$2	$15	$40
2000-S, Maryland, Proof	4,020,172	4,524	69.2				$3	$4	$15
2000-S, Maryland, Proof, Silver	965,421	9,799	69.2				$8	$10	$20

| | Mintage | Cert | Avg | %MS | AU-50 | MS-63 | MS-65 | MS-66 | MS-67 |
							PF-65	PF-66DC	PF-69DC
2000-P, South Carolina	742,576,000	601	66.1	100%	$0.35	$1	$2	$15	$40
2000-D, South Carolina	566,208,000	739	66.3	100%	$0.35	$1	$2	$15	$40
2000-S, South Carolina, Proof	4,020,172	4,576	69.2				$3	$4	$15
2000-S, South Carolina, Proof, Silver	965,421	9,461	69.2				$8	$10	$20
2000-P, New Hampshire	673,040,000	554	65.6	99%	$0.35	$1	$2	$15	$40
2000-D, New Hampshire	495,976,000	570	66.0	100%	$0.35	$1	$2	$15	$40
2000-S, New Hampshire, Proof	4,020,172	4,582	69.2				$3	$4	$15
2000-S, New Hampshire, Proof, Silver	965,421	9,453	69.1				$8	$10	$20
2000-P, Virginia	943,000,000	665	66.1	100%	$0.35	$1	$2	$15	$40
2000-D, Virginia	651,616,000	588	66.1	99%	$0.35	$1	$2	$15	$40
2000-S, Virginia, Proof	4,020,172	4,566	69.2				$3	$4	$15
2000-S, Virginia, Proof, Silver	965,421	9,594	69.2				$8	$10	$20

2001, New York
Reverse designer:
Alfred Maletsky.

2001, North Carolina
Reverse designer:
John Mercanti.

2001, Rhode Island
Reverse designer:
Thomas D. Rogers Sr.

2001, Vermont
Reverse designer:
T. James Ferrell.

2001, Kentucky
Reverse designer:
T. James Ferrell.

| | Mintage | Cert | Avg | %MS | AU-50 | MS-63 | MS-65 | MS-66 | MS-67 |
							PF-65	PF-66DC	PF-69DC
2001-P, New York	655,400,000	388	66.1	100%	$0.35	$1	$2	$15	$40
2001-D, New York	619,640,000	461	66.2	100%	$0.35	$1	$2	$15	$40
2001-S, New York, Proof	3,094,140	3,668	69.2				$3	$8	$15
2001-S, New York, Proof, Silver	889,697	7,731	69.2				$10	$15	$20
2001-P, North Carolina	627,600,000	377	66.3	100%	$0.35	$1	$2	$15	$40
2001-D, North Carolina	427,876,000	406	66.3	100%	$0.35	$1	$2	$15	$40
2001-S, North Carolina, Proof	3,094,140	3,758	69.2				$3	$8	$15
2001-S, North Carolina, Proof, Silver	889,697	7,665	69.2				$10	$15	$20
2001-P, Rhode Island	423,000,000	311	66.0	100%	$0.35	$1	$2	$15	$40
2001-D, Rhode Island	447,100,000	360	66.0	100%	$0.35	$1	$1.25	$15	$40
2001-S, Rhode Island, Proof	3,094,140	3,358	69.2				$3	$8	$15
2001-S, Rhode Island, Proof, Silver	889,697	7,737	69.2				$10	$15	$20
2001-P, Vermont	423,400,000	1,872	65.7	100%	$0.35	$1	$2	$15	$40
2001-D, Vermont	459,404,000	374	66.3	100%	$0.35	$1	$2	$15	$40
2001-S, Vermont, Proof	3,094,140	3,531	69.3				$3	$8	$15
2001-S, Vermont, Proof, Silver	889,697	7,795	69.3				$10	$15	$20
2001-P, Kentucky	353,000,000	388	66.3	100%	$0.35	$1.25	$1.50	$16	$40
2001-D, Kentucky	370,564,000	296	66.2	100%	$0.35	$1.25	$1.50	$16	$40
2001-S, Kentucky, Proof	3,094,140	3,394	69.3				$3	$8	$15
2001-S, Kentucky, Proof, Silver	889,697	7,689	69.2				$10	$15	$20

2002, Tennessee
Reverse designer:
Donna Weaver.

2002, Ohio
Reverse designer:
Donna Weaver.

2002, Louisiana
Reverse designer:
John Mercanti.

2002, Indiana
Reverse designer:
Donna Weaver.

2002, Mississippi
Reverse designer:
Donna Weaver.

	Mintage	Cert	Avg	%MS	AU-50	MS-63	MS-65	MS-66	MS-67
							PF-65	PF-66DC	PF-69DC
2002-P, Tennessee	361,600,000	303	66.5	100%	$0.75	$1.75	$3	$18	$40
2002-D, Tennessee	286,468,000	304	66.4	100%	$0.75	$1.75	$3	$18	$40
2002-S, Tennessee, Proof	3,084,245	2,945	69.2				$3	$5	$15
2002-S, Tennessee, Proof, Silver	892,229	7,553	69.2				$8	$10	$20
2002-P, Ohio	217,200,000	344	66.7	100%	$0.35	$1	$1.25	$10	$30
2002-D, Ohio	414,832,000	281	66.2	100%	$0.35	$1	$1.25	$10	$30
2002-S, Ohio, Proof	3,084,245	2,932	69.3				$3	$5	$15
2002-S, Ohio, Proof, Silver	892,229	7,648	69.2				$8	$10	$20
2002-P, Louisiana	362,000,000	261	66.7	100%	$0.35	$1	$1.25	$10	$30
2002-D, Louisiana	402,204,000	213	66.3	100%	$0.35	$1	$1.25	$10	$30
2002-S, Louisiana, Proof	3,084,245	2,940	69.2				$3	$5	$15
2002-S, Louisiana, Proof, Silver	892,229	7,365	69.2				$8	$10	$20
2002-P, Indiana	362,600,000	306	66.5	99%	$0.35	$1	$1.25	$10	$30
2002-D, Indiana	327,200,000	239	66.4	100%	$0.35	$1	$1.25	$10	$30
2002-S, Indiana, Proof	3,084,245	2,964	69.2				$3	$5	$15
2002-S, Indiana, Proof, Silver	892,229	7,484	69.2				$8	$10	$20
2002-P, Mississippi	290,000,000	277	66.2	100%	$0.35	$1	$1.25	$10	$30
2002-D, Mississippi	289,600,000	223	66.4	100%	$0.35	$1	$1.25	$10	$30
2002-S, Mississippi, Proof	3,084,245	3,000	69.3				$3	$5	$15
2002-S, Mississippi, Proof, Silver	892,229	7,747	69.2				$8	$10	$20

2003, Illinois
Reverse designer:
Donna Weaver.

2003, Alabama
Reverse designer:
Norman E. Nemeth.

2003, Maine
Reverse designer:
Donna Weaver.

2003, Missouri
Reverse designer:
Alfred Maletsky.

2003, Arkansas
Reverse designer:
John Mercanti.

	Mintage	Cert	Avg	%MS	AU-50	MS-63	MS-65	MS-66	MS-67
							PF-65	PF-66DC	PF-69DC
2003-P, Illinois	225,800,000	254	66.0	100%	$0.50	$1.50	$2	$12	$32
2003-D, Illinois	237,400,000	2,063	65.2	100%	$0.50	$1.50	$2	$12	$32
2003-S, Illinois, Proof	3,408,516	5,611	69.3				$3	$5	$15
2003-S, Illinois, Proof, Silver	1,125,755	8,369	69.2				$8	$9	$20
2003-P, Alabama	225,000,000	271	65.7	100%	$0.35	$1	$1.25	$10	$30
2003-D, Alabama	232,400,000	2,060	65.1	100%	$0.35	$1	$1.25	$10	$30
2003-S, Alabama, Proof	3,408,516	5,697	69.3				$3	$5	$15
2003-S, Alabama, Proof, Silver	1,125,755	8,362	69.2				$8	$9	$20

	Mintage	Cert	Avg	%MS	AU-50	MS-63	MS-65	MS-66	MS-67
							PF-65	PF-66DC	PF-69DC
2003-P, Maine	217,400,000	243	65.8	100%	$0.35	$1	$1.25	$10	$30
2003-D, Maine	231,400,000	2,062	65.2	100%	$0.35	$1	$1.25	$10	$30
2003-S, Maine, Proof	3,408,516	5,564	69.2				$3	$5	$15
2003-S, Maine, Proof, Silver	1,125,755	8,253	69.2				$8	$9	$20
2003-P, Missouri	225,000,000	258	65.9	99%	$0.35	$1	$1.25	$10	$30
2003-D, Missouri	228,200,000	2,073	65.2	100%	$0.35	$1	$1.25	$10	$30
2003-S, Missouri, Proof	3,408,516	5,755	69.3				$3	$5	$15
2003-S, Missouri, Proof, Silver	1,125,755	8,355	69.2				$8	$9	$20
2003-P, Arkansas	228,000,000	232	65.8	100%	$0.35	$1	$1.25	$10	$30
2003-D, Arkansas	229,800,000	2,108	65.2	100%	$0.40	$1	$1.25	$10	$30
2003-S, Arkansas, Proof	3,408,516	5,703	69.3				$3	$5	$15
2003-S, Arkansas, Proof, Silver	1,125,755	8,391	69.2				$8	$9	$20

2004, Michigan
*Reverse designer:
Donna Weaver.*

2004, Florida
*Reverse designer:
T. James Ferrell.*

2004, Texas
*Reverse designer:
Norman E. Nemeth.*

2004, Iowa
*Reverse designer:
John Mercanti.*

2004, Wisconsin
*Reverse designer:
Alfred Maletsky.*

**2004-D, Wisconsin,
Normal Reverse**

**2004-D, Wisconsin,
Extra Leaf High**
FS-25-2004D-WI-5901.

**2004-D, Wisconsin,
Extra Leaf Low**
FS-25-2004D-WI-5902.

	Mintage	Cert	Avg	%MS	AU-50	MS-63	MS-65	MS-66	MS-67
							PF-65	PF-66DC	PF-69DC
2004-P, Michigan	233,800,000	2,351	65.2	100%	$0.35	$0.75	$1	$10	$30
2004-D, Michigan	225,800,000	397	67.3	100%	$0.35	$0.75	$1	$10	$30
2004-S, Michigan, Proof	2,740,684	3,859	69.3				$3	$5	$15
2004-S, Michigan, Proof, Silver	1,769,786	9,781	69.3				$8	$10	$20
2004-P, Florida	240,200,000	2,339	65.2	100%	$0.35	$0.75	$1	$10	$30
2004-D, Florida	241,600,000	301	66.9	100%	$0.35	$0.75	$1	$10	$30
2004-S, Florida, Proof	2,740,684	3,785	69.3				$3	$5	$15
2004-S, Florida, Proof, Silver	1,769,786	9,602	69.2				$8	$10	$20
2004-P, Texas	278,800,000	2,378	65.2	100%	$0.35	$0.75	$1	$10	$30
2004-D, Texas	263,000,000	314	66.9	100%	$0.35	$0.75	$1	$10	$30
2004-S, Texas, Proof	2,740,684	3,901	69.3				$3	$5	$15
2004-S, Texas, Proof, Silver	1,769,786	10,006	69.3				$8	$10	$20
2004-P, Iowa	213,800,000	2,304	65.1	100%	$0.35	$0.75	$1	$10	$30
2004-D, Iowa	251,400,000	280	66.9	100%	$0.35	$0.75	$1	$10	$30
2004-S, Iowa, Proof	2,740,684	3,940	69.4				$3	$5	$15
2004-S, Iowa, Proof, Silver	1,769,786	9,884	69.3				$8	$10	$20

| | Mintage | Cert | Avg | %MS | AU-50 | MS-63 | MS-65 | MS-66 | MS-67 |
							PF-65	PF-66DC	PF-69DC
2004-P, Wisconsin	226,400,000	2,541	65.2	100%	$0.35	$0.75	$1	$10	$30
2004-D, Wisconsin	226,800,000	2,787	65.7	100%	$0.35	$0.75	$1	$10	$30
2004-D, Wisconsin, Extra Leaf High ‡ (a)	(b)	4,731	64.8	96%	$75	$150	$200	$300	$500
2004-D, Wisconsin, Extra Leaf Low ‡ (a)	(b)	6,372	64.9	97%	$50	$130	$165	$275	$450
2004-S, Wisconsin, Proof	2,740,684	3,931	69.3				$3	$5	$15
2004-S, Wisconsin, Proof, Silver	1,769,786	10,018	69.3				$8	$10	$20

‡ Ranked in the *100 Greatest U.S. Modern Coins*. **a.** Some 2004-D, Wisconsin, quarters show one of two different die flaws on the reverse, in the shape of an extra leaf on the corn. **b.** Included in 2004-D, Wisconsin, mintage figure.

2005, California
Reverse designer: Don Everhart.

2005, Minnesota
Reverse designer: Charles Vickers.

2005, Oregon
Reverse designer: Donna Weaver.

2005, Kansas
Reverse designer: Norman E. Nemeth.

2005, West Virginia
Reverse designer: John Mercanti.

| | Mintage | Cert | Avg | %MS | AU-50 | MS-63 | MS-65 | MS-66 | MS-67 |
							PF-65	PF-66DC	PF-69DC
2005-P, California	257,200,000	456	65.9	100%	$0.30	$0.75	$1.10	$10	$30
2005-P, California, Satin Finish	1,160,000	2,835	67.0	100%	$1	$2	$3	$5	$12
2005-D, California	263,200,000	282	66.2	99%	$0.30	$0.75	$1.10	$10	$30
2005-D, California, Satin Finish	1,160,000	2,515	66.9	100%	$1	$2	$3	$5	$12
2005-S, California, Proof	3,262,960	8,592	69.3				$3	$4.50	$15
2005-S, California, Proof, Silver	1,678,649	10,846	69.4				$8	$10	$20
2005-P, Minnesota	239,600,000	360	65.1	98%	$0.30	$0.75	$1	$10	$30
2005-P, Minnesota, Satin Finish	1,160,000	2,955	67.2	100%	$1	$2	$3	$5	$12
2005-D, Minnesota	248,400,000	174	66.1	99%	$0.30	$0.75	$1	$10	$30
2005-D, Minnesota, Satin Finish	1,160,000	2,733	67.1	100%	$1	$2	$3	$5	$12
2005-S, Minnesota, Proof	3,262,960	8,555	69.3				$3	$4.50	$15
2005-S, Minnesota, Proof, Silver	1,678,649	10,597	69.4				$8	$10	$20
2005-P, Oregon	316,200,000	253	65.1	100%	$0.30	$0.75	$1	$10	$30
2005-P, Oregon, Satin Finish	1,160,000	3,001	67.2	100%	$1	$2	$3	$5	$12
2005-D, Oregon	404,000,000	137	66.2	100%	$0.30	$0.75	$1	$10	$30
2005-D, Oregon, Satin Finish	1,160,000	2,732	67.1	100%	$1	$2	$3	$5	$12
2005-S, Oregon, Proof	3,262,960	8,518	69.3				$3	$4.50	$15
2005-S, Oregon, Proof, Silver	1,678,649	10,588	69.4				$8	$10	$20
2005-P, Kansas	263,400,000	330	65.1	98%	$0.30	$0.75	$1	$10	$30
2005-P, Kansas, Satin Finish	1,160,000	2,553	66.8	100%	$1	$2	$3	$5	$12
2005-D, Kansas	300,000,000	227	66.2	100%	$0.30	$0.75	$1	$10	$30
2005-D, Kansas, Satin Finish	1,160,000	2,641	67.0	100%	$1	$2	$3	$5	$12
2005-S, Kansas, Proof	3,262,960	8,573	69.3				$3	$4.50	$15
2005-S, Kansas, Proof, Silver	1,678,649	10,713	69.3				$8	$10	$20
2005-P, West Virginia	365,400,000	299	65.3	100%	$0.30	$0.75	$1	$10	$30
2005-P, West Virginia, Satin Finish	1,160,000	2,827	67.0	100%	$1	$2	$3	$5	$12
2005-D, West Virginia	356,200,000	180	66.2	99%	$0.30	$0.75	$1	$10	$30
2005-D, West Virginia, Satin Finish	1,160,000	2,427	66.9	100%	$1	$2	$3	$5	$12
2005-S, West Virginia, Proof	3,262,960	8,584	69.3				$3	$4.50	$15
2005-S, West Virginia, Proof, Silver	1,678,649	10,716	69.4				$8	$10	$20

2006, Nevada
Reverse designer:
Don Everhart.

2006, Nebraska
Reverse designer:
Charles Vickers.

2006, Colorado
Reverse designer:
Norman E. Nemeth.

2006, North Dakota
Reverse designer:
Donna Weaver.

2006, South Dakota
Reverse designer:
John Mercanti.

	Mintage	Cert	Avg	%MS	AU-50	MS-63	MS-65	MS-66	MS-67
							PF-65	PF-66DC	PF-69DC
2006-P, Nevada	277,000,000	273	66.1	100%	$0.30	$0.75	$1	$10	$30
2006-P, Nevada, Satin Finish	847,361	1,047	66.6	100%	$1	$2	$3	$5	$12
2006-D, Nevada	312,800,000	356	66.5	100%	$0.30	$0.75	$1	$10	$30
2006-D, Nevada, Satin Finish	847,361	1,276	66.9	100%	$1	$2	$3	$5	$12
2006-S, Nevada, Proof	2,882,428	5,951	69.4				$3	$4.50	$15
2006-S, Nevada, Proof, Silver	1,585,008	9,544	69.5				$8	$9	$20
2006-P, Nebraska	318,000,000	141	66.0	100%	$0.30	$0.75	$1	$10	$30
2006-P, Nebraska, Satin Finish	847,361	1,334	67.0	100%	$1	$2	$3	$5	$12
2006-D, Nebraska	273,000,000	263	66.5	100%	$0.30	$0.75	$1	$10	$30
2006-D, Nebraska, Satin Finish	847,361	1,590	67.2	100%	$1	$2	$3	$5	$12
2006-S, Nebraska, Proof	2,882,428	5,953	69.4				$3	$4.50	$15
2006-S, Nebraska, Proof, Silver	1,585,008	9,434	69.5				$8	$9	$20
2006-P, Colorado	274,800,000	251	66.2	100%	$0.30	$0.75	$1	$10	$30
2006-P, Colorado, Satin Finish	847,361	1,182	66.8	100%	$1	$2	$3	$5	$12
2006-D, Colorado	294,200,000	422	66.4	100%	$0.30	$0.75	$1	$10	$30
2006-D, Colorado, Satin Finish	847,361	1,505	67.2	100%	$1	$2	$3	$5	$12
2006-S, Colorado, Proof	2,882,428	5,940	69.4				$3	$4.50	$15
2006-S, Colorado, Proof, Silver	1,585,008	9,528	69.5				$8	$9	$20
2006-P, North Dakota	305,800,000	182	65.8	99%	$0.30	$0.75	$1	$10	$30
2006-P, North Dakota, Satin Finish	847,361	1,136	66.8	100%	$1	$2	$3	$5	$12
2006-D, North Dakota	359,000,000	261	66.2	100%	$0.30	$0.75	$1	$10	$30
2006-D, North Dakota, Satin Finish	847,361	1,539	67.1	100%	$1	$2	$3	$5	$12
2006-S, North Dakota, Proof	2,882,428	5,951	69.4				$3	$4.50	$15
2006-S, North Dakota, Proof, Silver	1,585,008	9,529	69.5				$8	$9	$20
2006-P, South Dakota	245,000,000	162	66.0	100%	$0.30	$0.75	$1	$10	$30
2006-P, South Dakota, Satin Finish	847,361	1,312	66.9	100%	$1	$2	$3	$5	$12
2006-D, South Dakota	265,800,000	187	66.3	99%	$0.30	$0.75	$1	$10	$30
2006-D, South Dakota, Satin Finish	847,361	1,546	67.1	100%	$1	$2	$3	$5	$12
2006-S, South Dakota, Proof	2,882,428	5,959	69.5				$3	$4.50	$15
2006-S, South Dakota, Proof, Silver	1,585,008	9,524	69.5				$8	$9	$20

2007, Montana
Reverse designer:
Don Everhart.

2007, Washington
Reverse designer:
Charles Vickers.

2007, Idaho
Reverse designer:
Don Everhart.

2007, Wyoming
Reverse designer:
Norman E. Nemeth.

2007, Utah
Reverse designer:
Joseph Menna.

	Mintage	Cert	Avg	%MS	AU-50	MS-63	MS-65	MS-66	MS-67
							PF-65	PF-66DC	PF-69DC
2007-P, Montana	257,000,000	111	66.1	100%	$0.30	$0.75	$1	$10	$30

	Mintage	Cert	Avg	%MS	AU-50	MS-63	MS-65 / PF-65	MS-66 / PF-66DC	MS-67 / PF-69DC
2007-P, Montana, Satin Finish	895,628	319	66.5	100%	$1	$2	$3	$5	$12
2007-D, Montana	256,240,000	153	65.9	99%	$0.30	$0.75	$1	$10	$30
2007-D, Montana, Satin Finish	895,628	317	66.5	100%	$1	$2	$3	$5	$12
2007-S, Montana, Proof	2,374,778	3,424	69.5				$3	$4.50	$15
2007-S, Montana, Proof, Silver	1,313,481	7,937	69.4				$8	$9	$20
2007-P, Washington	265,200,000	136	66.1	100%	$0.30	$0.75	$1	$10	$30
2007-P, Washington, Satin Finish	895,628	303	66.4	100%	$1	$2	$3	$5	$12
2007-D, Washington	280,000,000	147	66.0	99%	$0.30	$0.75	$1	$10	$30
2007-D, Washington, Satin Finish	895,628	336	66.7	100%	$1	$2	$3	$5	$12
2007-S, Washington, Proof	2,374,778	3,213	69.5				$3	$4.50	$15
2007-S, Washington, Proof, Silver	1,313,481	7,893	69.4				$8	$9	$20
2007-P, Idaho	294,600,000	73	65.8	100%	$0.30	$0.75	$1	$10	$30
2007-P, Idaho, Satin Finish	895,628	342	66.6	100%	$1	$2	$3	$5	$12
2007-D, Idaho	286,800,000	116	66.2	100%	$0.30	$0.75	$1	$10	$30
2007-D, Idaho, Satin Finish	895,628	324	66.5	100%	$1	$2	$3	$5	$12
2007-S, Idaho, Proof	2,374,778	3,230	69.5				$3	$4.50	$15
2007-S, Idaho, Proof, Silver	1,313,481	7,945	69.4				$8	$9	$20
2007-P, Wyoming	243,600,000	63	65.0	100%	$0.30	$0.75	$1	$10	$30
2007-P, Wyoming, Satin Finish	895,628	282	66.1	100%	$1	$2	$3	$5	$12
2007-D, Wyoming	320,800,000	127	65.9	99%	$0.30	$0.75	$1	$10	$30
2007-D, Wyoming, Satin Finish	895,628	326	66.4	100%	$1	$2	$3	$5	$12
2007-S, Wyoming, Proof	2,374,778	3,154	69.4				$3	$4.50	$15
2007-S, Wyoming, Proof, Silver	1,313,481	7,806	69.3				$8	$9	$20
2007-P, Utah	255,000,000	127	65.6	100%	$0.30	$0.75	$1	$10	$30
2007-P, Utah, Satin Finish	895,628	299	66.3	100%	$1	$2	$3	$5	$12
2007-D, Utah	253,200,000	190	66.2	100%	$0.30	$0.75	$1	$10	$30
2007-D, Utah, Satin Finish	895,628	325	66.6	100%	$1	$2	$3	$5	$12
2007-S, Utah, Proof	2,374,778	3,174	69.5				$3	$4.50	$15
2007-S, Utah, Proof, Silver	1,313,481	7,950	69.4				$8	$9	$20

2008, Oklahoma
Reverse designer: Phebe Hemphill.

2008, New Mexico
Reverse designer: Don Everhart.

2008, Arizona
Reverse designer: Joseph Menna.

2008, Alaska
Reverse designer: Charles Vickers.

2008, Hawaii
Reverse designer: Don Everhart.

	Mintage	Cert	Avg	%MS	AU-50	MS-63	MS-65 / PF-65	MS-66 / PF-66DC	MS-67 / PF-69DC
2008-P, Oklahoma	222,000,000	68	65.7	99%	$0.30	$0.75	$1	$10	$30
2008-P, Oklahoma, Satin Finish	745,464	102	67.3	100%	$1	$2	$3	$5	$12
2008-D, Oklahoma	194,600,000	99	66.2	100%	$0.30	$0.75	$1	$10	$30
2008-D, Oklahoma, Satin Finish	745,464	81	67.1	100%	$1	$2	$3	$5	$12
2008-S, Oklahoma, Proof	2,078,112	3,509	69.5				$3	$5	$18
2008-S, Oklahoma, Proof, Silver	1,192,908	8,364	69.5				$8	$10	$22
2008-P, New Mexico	244,200,000	83	65.4	100%	$0.30	$0.75	$1	$10	$30
2008-P, New Mexico, Satin Finish	745,464	84	67.1	100%	$1	$2	$3	$5	$12
2008-D, New Mexico	244,400,000	113	66.3	100%	$0.30	$0.75	$1	$10	$30
2008-D, New Mexico, Satin Finish	745,464	64	67.0	100%	$1	$2	$3	$5	$12

	Mintage	Cert	Avg	%MS	AU-50	MS-63	MS-65 / PF-65	MS-66 / PF-66DC	MS-67 / PF-69DC
2008-S, New Mexico, Proof	2,078,112	3,571	69.4				$3	$5	$18
2008-S, New Mexico, Proof, Silver	1,192,908	8,225	69.5				$8	$10	$22
2008-P, Arizona	244,600,000	119	65.7	100%	$0.30	$0.75	$1	$10	$30
2008-P, Arizona, Satin Finish	745,464	94	67.3	100%	$1	$2	$3	$5	$12
2008-D, Arizona	265,000,000	48	65.9	98%	$0.30	$0.75	$1	$10	$30
2008-D, Arizona, Satin Finish	745,464	70	67.2	100%	$1	$2	$3	$5	$12
2008-S, Arizona, Proof	2,078,112	3,657	69.6				$3	$5	$18
2008-S, Arizona, Proof, Silver	1,192,908	8,595	69.5				$8	$10	$22
2008-P, Alaska	251,800,000	48	65.3	100%	$0.30	$0.75	$1	$10	$30
2008-P, Alaska, Satin Finish	745,464	97	67.3	100%	$1	$2	$3	$5	$12
2008-D, Alaska	254,000,000	59	65.7	100%	$0.30	$0.75	$1	$10	$30
2008-D, Alaska, Satin Finish	745,464	70	66.8	100%	$1	$2	$3	$5	$12
2008-S, Alaska, Proof	2,078,112	3,491	69.5				$3	$5	$18
2008-S, Alaska, Proof, Silver	1,192,908	8,523	69.5				$8	$10	$22
2008-P, Hawaii	254,000,000	124	65.3	100%	$0.30	$0.75	$1	$10	$30
2008-P, Hawaii, Satin Finish	745,464	92	67.1	100%	$1	$2	$3	$5	$12
2008-D, Hawaii	263,600,000	58	65.7	100%	$0.30	$0.75	$1	$10	$30
2008-D, Hawaii, Satin Finish	745,464	78	67.0	100%	$1	$2	$3	$5	$12
2008-S, Hawaii, Proof	2,078,112	3,514	69.4				$3	$10	$25
2008-S, Hawaii, Proof, Silver	1,192,908	8,534	69.4				$8	$10	$22

2009, District of Columbia
Reverse designer: Don Everhart.

2009, Puerto Rico
Reverse designer: Joseph Menna.

2009, Guam
Reverse designer: Jim Licaretz.

2009, American Samoa
Reverse designer: Charles Vickers.

2009, U.S. Virgin Islands
Reverse designer: Joseph Menna.

2009, Northern Mariana Islands
Reverse designer: Phebe Hemphill.

	Mintage	Cert	Avg	%MS	AU-50	MS-63	MS-65 / PF-65	MS-66 / PF-66DC	MS-67 / PF-69DC
2009-P, District of Columbia	83,600,000	86	66.1	100%	$0.50	$1	$1.50	$10	$30
2009-P, District of Columbia, Satin Finish	784,614	229	67.6	100%	$1	$2	$3	$5	$12
2009-D, District of Columbia	88,800,000	119	66.4	100%	$0.50	$1	$1.50	$10	$30
2009-D, District of Columbia, Satin Finish	784,614	233	67.9	100%	$1	$2	$3	$5	$12
2009-S, District of Columbia, Proof	2,113,478	4,149	69.6				$3	$4.50	$15
2009-S, District of Columbia, Proof, Silver	996,548	6,461	69.7				$8	$9	$20
2009-P, Puerto Rico	53,200,000	90	65.9	100%	$0.50	$1	$1.50	$10	$30
2009-P, Puerto Rico, Satin Finish	784,614	166	67.5	100%	$1	$2	$3	$5	$12
2009-D, Puerto Rico	86,000,000	82	66.6	100%	$0.50	$1	$1.50	$10	$30
2009-D, Puerto Rico, Satin Finish	784,614	211	67.8	100%	$1	$2	$3	$5	$12
2009-S, Puerto Rico, Proof	2,113,478	4,132	69.6				$3	$4.50	$15
2009-S, Puerto Rico, Proof, Silver	996,548	6,639	69.7				$8	$9	$20

| | Mintage | Cert | Avg | %MS | AU-50 | MS-63 | MS-65 | MS-66 | MS-67 |
							PF-65	PF-66DC	PF-69DC
2009-P, Guam	45,000,000	41	66.1	100%	$0.50	$1	$1.50	$10	$30
2009-P, Guam, Satin Finish	784,614	214	67.4	100%	$1	$2	$3	$5	$12
2009-D, Guam	42,600,000	64	66.6	100%	$0.50	$1	$1.50	$10	$30
2009-D, Guam, Satin Finish	784,614	187	67.6	100%	$1	$2	$3	$5	$12
2009-S, Guam, Proof	2,113,478	4,035	69.6				$3	$4.50	$15
2009-S, Guam, Proof, Silver	996,548	6,403	69.7				$8	$9	$20
2009-P, American Samoa	42,600,000	104	66.5	100%	$0.50	$1	$1.50	$10	$30
2009-P, American Samoa, Satin Finish	784,614	273	67.8	100%	$1	$2	$3	$5	$12
2009-D, American Samoa	39,600,000	134	67.0	100%	$0.50	$1	$1.50	$10	$30
2009-D, American Samoa, Satin Finish	784,614	307	68.3	100%	$1	$2	$3	$5	$12
2009-S, American Samoa, Proof	2,113,478	4,199	69.6				$3	$4.50	$15
2009-S, American Samoa, Proof, Silver	996,548	6,542	69.7				$8	$9	$20
2009-P, U.S. Virgin Islands	41,000,000	65	66.8	100%	$0.75	$1	$1.50	$12	$32
2009-P, U.S. Virgin Islands, Satin Finish	784,614	266	67.2	100%	$1	$2	$3	$5	$12
2009-D, U.S. Virgin Islands	41,000,000	68	66.8	100%	$0.75	$1	$1.50	$12	$32
2009-D, U.S. Virgin Islands, Satin Finish	784,614	300	67.8	100%	$1	$2	$3	$5	$12
2009-S, U.S. Virgin Islands, Proof	2,113,478	4,174	69.6				$3	$4.50	$15
2009-S, U.S. Virgin Islands, Proof, Silver	996,548	6,513	69.7				$8	$9	$20
2009-P, Northern Mariana Islands	35,200,000	105	66.7	100%	$0.50	$1	$1.50	$10	$30
2009-P, Northern Mariana Islands, Satin Finish	784,614	277	67.9	100%	$1	$2	$3	$5	$12
2009-D, Northern Mariana Islands	37,600,000	104	66.7	100%	$0.50	$1	$1.50	$10	$30
2009-D, Northern Mariana Islands, Satin Finish	784,614	263	67.7	100%	$1	$2	$3	$5	$12
2009-S, Northern Mariana Islands, Proof	2,113,478	4,176	69.6				$3	$4.50	$15
2009-S, Northern Mariana Islands, Proof, Silver	996,548	6,499	69.7				$8	$9	$20

WASHINGTON, AMERICA THE BEAUTIFUL™ (2010 TO DATE)

Designers: *John Flanagan (obverse); see image captions for reverse designers.* **Weight:** *Clad issue—5.67 grams; silver Proofs—6.25 grams.* **Composition:** *Clad issue—Outer layers of copper-nickel (.750 copper, .250 nickel) bonded to inner core of pure copper; silver Proofs—.900 silver, .100 copper (net weight .18084 oz. pure silver).* **Diameter:** *24.3 mm.* **Edge:** *Reeded.* **Mints:** *Clad issue—Philadelphia, Denver, and San Francisco; silver Proofs—San Francisco.*

Circulation Strike

Proof

History. In 2010 the U.S. Mint introduced a new program of quarters honoring national parks and historic sites in each state, the District of Columbia, and the five U.S. territories. It will run through 2021. These are released at the rate of five new reverse designs each year, in combination with the obverse found on the State and D.C./Territorial quarters of previous years. Circulation strikes are made at the Philadelphia and Denver mints, and special silver-content and Proof issues at San Francisco. Each coin combines a modified obverse depicting George Washington, without a date. The reverses are distinctive and bear the date of issue and a special design showcasing a national park in the state, district, or territory. The official title of the series is the America the Beautiful™ Quarters Program; popularly, they are known as National Park quarters.

In 2012, the U.S. Mint introduced a new innovation in the National Park quarters program. For the first time since the 1950s, the San Francisco Mint is being used to produce quarters in a non-Proof format. These Uncirculated coins are made in limited quantities for collectors. They can be purchased directly from the Mint for a premium above their face value, as opposed to being released into circulation like normal quarters. Unlike the Uncirculated S-mintmark Bicentennial quarters dated 1976, which were 40% silver and sold only in sets, the S-mintmark National Park quarters are of normal copper-nickel–clad composition and are sold in bags of 100 and rolls of 40 coins. Thus the 2012-S coins are considered the first circulation-strike quarters made at San Francisco since 1954. The S-mintmark coins have been made of each National Park design from 2012 to date.

Striking and Sharpness. These quarters can have light striking on the highest area of the obverse. On the reverse there can be weak areas, depending on the design, seemingly more often seen on Denver Mint coins.

Availability. All modern quarters are readily available in high grades. Typical MS coins are MS–63 and 64 with light abrasion. MS-65 and higher coins are in the minority, but enough exist that finding them is no problem. Around MS-68 many issues are scarce, and higher grades are scarcer yet. The S-mintmark coins are proportionally scarce compared to Philadelphia and Denver issues, and are not seen in circulation. They are available for direct purchase from the U.S. Mint in their year of issue, and from the secondary market after that.

Proofs. National Park quarter dollar Proofs are made in San Francisco. For certain later issues, Proofs are available in clad metal as well as silver strikings. On some Proofs over-polishing of dies has eliminated some details.

GRADING STANDARDS

MS-60 to 70 (Mint State). *Obverse:* At MS-60, some abrasion and contact marks are evident on the highest-relief parts of the hair and the cheek. At MS-63, abrasion is slight at best, less so at MS-64. An MS-65 coin should display no abrasion or contact marks except under magnification, and MS-66 and higher coins should have none at all. Luster should be full. *Reverse:* Check the highest-relief areas of the design (these differ from coin to coin). Otherwise, comments are as for the obverse.

2010-D, Hot Springs (AR). Graded MS-68.

PF-60 to 70 (Proof). *Obverse and Reverse:* These coins are so recent, and as only a few have been cleaned, most approach perfection and can be designated PF–68 to 70, the latter only if no contact marks or other problems can be seen under magnification. A cleaned coin with extensive hairlines would not be collectible for most numismatists and would be classified at a lower level such as PF–60 to 63. Those with lighter hairlines qualify for PF–64 or 65.

2010-S, Grand Canyon (AZ).
Graded PF-69 Ultra Cameo.

2010, Hot Springs National Park (AR)
Reverse designer: Don Everhart.

2010, Yellowstone National Park (WY)
Reverse designer: Don Everhart.

2010, Yosemite National Park (CA)
Reverse designer: Joseph Menna.

2010, Grand Canyon National Park (AZ)
Reverse designer: Phebe Hemphill.

2010, Mt. Hood National Forest (OR)
Reverse designer: Phebe Hemphill.

| | Mintage | Cert | Avg | %MS | AU-50 | MS-63 | MS-65 | MS-66 | MS-67 |
							PF-65	PF-66DC	PF-69DC
2010-P, Hot Springs National Park (AR)	35,600,000	696	66.1	100%	$0.50	$0.75	$1	$10	$30
2010-P, Hot Springs National Park (AR), Satin Finish	583,897	347	67.5	100%	$1	$2	$3	$5	$12
2010-D, Hot Springs National Park (AR)	34,000,000	1,541	65.6	100%	$0.50	$0.75	$1	$10	$30
2010-D, Hot Springs National Park (AR), Satin Finish	583,897	374	67.6	100%	$1	$2	$3	$5	$12
2010-S, Hot Springs National Park (AR), Proof	1,402,889	4,041	69.5				$3	$4.50	$15
2010-S, Hot Springs, National Park (AR), Proof, Silver	859,417	11,220	69.6				$8	$9	$20
2010-P, Yellowstone National Park (WY)	33,600,000	441	66.1	100%	$0.50	$0.75	$1	$10	$30
2010-P, Yellowstone National Park (WY), Satin Finish	583,897	317	67.4	100%	$1	$2	$3	$5	$12
2010-D, Yellowstone National Park (WY)	34,800,000	758	65.8	100%	$0.50	$0.75	$1	$10	$30
2010-D, Yellowstone National Park (WY), Satin Finish	583,897	336	67.4	100%	$1	$2	$3	$5	$12
2010-S, Yellowstone National Park (WY), Proof	1,404,259	4,081	69.5				$3	$4.50	$15
2010-S, Yellowstone National Park (WY), Proof, Silver	859,417	11,228	69.7				$8	$9	$20
2010-P, Yosemite National Park (CA)	35,200,000	286	66.1	100%	$0.50	$0.75	$1.25	$12	$30
2010-P, Yosemite National Park (CA), Satin Finish	583,897	359	67.3	100%	$1	$2	$3	$5	$12
2010-D, Yosemite National Park (CA)	34,800,000	615	66.0	100%	$0.50	$0.75	$1.25	$12	$30
2010-D, Yosemite National Park (CA), Satin Finish	583,897	378	67.4	100%	$1	$2	$3	$5	$12
2010-S, Yosemite National Park (CA), Proof	1,401,522	4,006	69.5				$3	$4.50	$15
2010-S, Yosemite National Park (CA), Proof, Silver	859,417	11,130	69.6				$8	$9	$20
2010-P, Grand Canyon National Park (AZ)	34,800,000	372	66.3	100%	$0.50	$0.75	$1	$10	$30
2010-P, Grand Canyon National Park (AZ), Satin Finish	583,897	361	67.5	100%	$1	$2	$3	$5	$12
2010-D, Grand Canyon National Park (AZ)	35,400,000	626	66.1	100%	$0.50	$0.75	$1	$10	$30
2010-D, Grand Canyon National Park (AZ), Satin Finish	583,897	400	67.7	100%	$1	$2	$3	$5	$12
2010-S, Grand Canyon National Park (AZ), Proof	1,401,462	3,993	69.5				$3	$4.50	$15
2010-S, Grand Canyon National Park (AZ), Proof, Silver	859,417	11,146	69.6				$8	$9	$20
2010-P, Mt. Hood National Forest (OR)	34,400,000	205	66.1	100%	$0.50	$0.75	$1	$10	$30
2010-P, Mt. Hood National Forest (OR), Satin Finish	583,897	318	67.4	100%	$1	$2	$3	$5	$12
2010-D, Mt. Hood National Forest (OR)	34,400,000	408	65.6	100%	$0.50	$0.75	$1	$10	$30
2010-D, Mt. Hood National Forest (OR), Satin Finish	583,897	414	67.5	100%	$1	$2	$3	$5	$12
2010-S, Mt. Hood National Forest (OR), Proof	1,398,106	4,008	69.4				$3	$4.50	$15
2010-S, Mt. Hood National Forest (OR), Proof, Silver	859,417	11,325	69.6				$8	$9	$20

2011, Gettysburg National Military Park (PA)
Reverse designer: Joel Iskowitz.

2011, Glacier National Park (MT)
Reverse designer: Barbara Fox.

2011, Olympic National Park (WA)
Reverse designer: Susan Gamble.

2011, Vicksburg National Military Park (MS)
Reverse designer: Thomas Cleveland.

2011, Chickasaw National Recreation Area (OK)
Reverse designer: Donna Weaver.

	Mintage	Cert	Avg	%MS	AU-50	MS-63	MS-65	MS-66	MS-67
							PF-65	PF-66DC	PF-69DC
2011-P, Gettysburg National Military Park (PA)	30,800,000	742	66.3	100%	$0.50	$0.75	$1.25	$12	$30
2011-D, Gettysburg National Military Park (PA)	30,400,000	291	66.5	100%	$0.50	$0.75	$1.25	$12	$30
2011-S, Gettysburg National Military Park (PA), Proof	1,273,068	2,752	69.5				$3	$4.50	$15
2011-S, Gettysburg National Military Park (PA), Proof, Silver	722,076	5,980	69.7				$8	$9	$20
2011-P, Glacier National Park (MT)	30,400,000	269	67.2	100%	$0.50	$0.75	$1	$10	$30
2011-D, Glacier National Park (MT)	31,200,000	439	65.8	100%	$0.50	$0.75	$1	$10	$30
2011-S, Glacier National Park (MT), Proof	1,269,422	2,750	69.6				$3	$4.50	$15
2011-S, Glacier National Park (MT), Proof, Silver	722,076	6,136	69.7				$8	$9	$20
2011-P, Olympic National Park (WA)	30,400,000	294	67.1	100%	$0.50	$0.75	$1	$10	$30
2011-D, Olympic National Park (WA)	30,600,000	544	66.2	100%	$0.50	$0.75	$1	$10	$30
2011-S, Olympic National Park (WA), Proof	1,268,231	2,763	69.6				$3	$4.50	$15
2011-S, Olympic National Park (WA), Proof, Silver	722,076	5,960	69.7				$8	$9	$20
2011-P, Vicksburg National Military Park (MS)	30,800,000	270	66.8	100%	$0.50	$0.75	$1	$10	$30
2011-D, Vicksburg National Military Park (MS)	33,400,000	449	66.3	100%	$0.50	$0.75	$1	$10	$30
2011-S, Vicksburg National Military Park (MS), Proof	1,268,623	2,757	69.5				$3	$4.50	$15
2011-S, Vicksburg National Military Park (MS), Proof, Silver	722,076	6,003	69.7				$8	$9	$20
2011-P, Chickasaw National Recreation Area (OK)	73,800,000	307	67.2	100%	$0.45	$0.50	$1	$10	$30
2011-D, Chickasaw National Recreation Area (OK)	69,400,000	420	66.2	100%	$0.45	$0.50	$1	$10	$30
2011-S, Chickasaw National Recreation Area (OK), Proof	1,266,825	2,745	69.5				$3	$4.50	$15
2011-S, Chickasaw National Recreation Area (OK), Proof, Silver	722,076	5,917	69.6				$8	$9	$20

2012, El Yunque National Forest (PR)
Reverse designer: Gary Whitley.

2012, Chaco Culture National Historical Park (NM)
Reverse designer: Donna Weaver.

2012, Acadia National Park (ME)
Reverse designer: Barbara Fox.

2012, Hawai'i Volcanoes National Park (HI)
Reverse designer: Charles L. Vickers.

2012, Denali National Park and Preserve (AK)
Reverse designer: Susan Gamble.

	Mintage	Cert	Avg	%MS	AU-50	MS-63	MS-65	MS-66	MS-67
							PF-65	PF-66DC	PF-69DC
2012-P, El Yunque National Forest (PR)	25,800,000	557	66.1	100%	$0.50	$0.75	$1	$10	$30
2012-D, El Yunque National Forest (PR)	25,000,000	234	66.8	100%	$0.50	$0.75	$1	$10	$30
2012-S, El Yunque National Forest (PR) (a)	1,680,140	609	66.4	100%		$1	$2	$12	$35
2012-S, El Yunque National Forest (PR), Proof	1,012,094	2,020	69.3				$3	$4.50	$15
2012-S, El Yunque National Forest (PR), Proof, Silver	608,060	4,818	69.7				$8	$9	$20
2012-P, Chaco Culture National Historical Park (NM)	22,000,000	139	67.2	100%	$0.50	$0.75	$1	$10	$30
2012-D, Chaco Culture National Historical Park (NM)	22,000,000	341	66.2	100%	$0.50	$0.75	$1	$10	$30
2012-S, Chaco Culture National Historical Park (NM) (a)	1,389,020	374	66.5	100%		$1	$2	$12	$35
2012-S, Chaco Culture National Historical Park (NM), Proof	961,464	2,010	69.3				$3	$4.50	$15
2012-S, Chaco Culture National Historical Park (NM), Proof, Silver	608,060	4,568	69.7				$8	$9	$20
2012-P, Acadia National Park (ME)	24,800,000	339	65.6	100%	$0.50	$0.75	$1	$10	$30
2012-D, Acadia National Park (ME)	21,606,000	106	66.7	100%	$0.50	$0.75	$1	$10	$30
2012-S, Acadia National Park (ME) (a)	1,409,120	447	66.3	100%		$1	$2	$12	$35
2012-S, Acadia National Park (ME), Proof	962,038	2,012	69.3				$3	$4.50	$15
2012-S, Acadia National Park (ME), Proof, Silver	608,060	4,737	69.7				$8	$9	$20

a. Not issued for circulation. From 2012 to date, the San Francisco Mint has made Uncirculated S-mintmark quarters of each design in the National Park series. These can be purchased by collectors directly from the U.S. Mint, in bags of 100 or rolls of 40 coins, for a premium above face value.

	Mintage	Cert	Avg	%MS	AU-50	MS-63	MS-65 / PF-65	MS-66 / PF-66DC	MS-67 / PF-69DC
2012-P, Hawai'i Volcanoes National Park (HI)	46,200,000	129	67.1	100%	$0.50	$0.75	$1	$10	$30
2012-D, Hawai'i Volcanoes National Park (HI)	78,600,000	393	66.1	100%	$0.45	$0.50	$1	$10	$30
2012-S, Hawai'i Volcanoes National Park (HI) (a)	1,409,120	402	66.4	100%	$0.45	$0.50	$1	$12	$35
2012-S, Hawai'i Volcanoes National Park (HI), Proof	962,447	2,015	69.3				$3	$4.50	$15
2012-S, Hawai'i Volcanoes National Park (HI), Proof, Silver	608,060	4,875	69.7				$8	$9	$20
2012-P, Denali National Park and Preserve (AK)	135,400,000	144	67.0	100%	$0.40	$0.50	$1	$10	$30
2012-D, Denali National Park and Preserve (AK)	166,600,000	434	66.2	100%	$0.40	$0.50	$1	$10	$30
2012-S, Denali National Park and Preserve (AK) (a)	1,409,220	520	66.2	100%		$1	$2	$12	$35
2012-S, Denali National Park and Preserve (AK), Proof	959,602	2,016	69.3				$3	$4.50	$15
2012-S, Denali National Park and Preserve (AK), Proof, Silver	608,060	4,764	69.7				$8	$9	$20

a. Not issued for circulation. From 2012 to date, the San Francisco Mint has made Uncirculated S-mintmark quarters of each design in the National Park series. These can be purchased by collectors directly from the U.S. Mint, in bags of 100 or rolls of 40 coins, for a premium above face value.

2013, White Mountain National Forest (NH) *Reverse designer: Phebe Hemphill.*	**2013, Perry's Victory and International Peace Memorial (OH)** *Reverse designer: Don Everhart.*	**2013, Great Basin National Park (NV)** *Reverse designer: Ronald D. Sanders.*	**2013, Fort McHenry National Monument and Historic Shrine (MD)** *Reverse designer: Joseph Menna.*	**2013, Mount Rushmore National Memorial (SD)** *Reverse designer: Joseph Menna.*

	Mintage	Cert	Avg	%MS	AU-50	MS-63	MS-65 / PF-65	MS-66 / PF-66DC	MS-67 / PF-69DC
2013-P, White Mountain National Forest (NH)	68,800,000	536	66.5	100%	$0.50	$0.75	$1	$10	$30
2013-D, White Mountain National Forest (NH)	107,600,000	292	67.1	100%	$0.50	$0.75	$1	$10	$30
2013-S, White Mountain National Forest (NH) (a)	1,606,900	341	66.4	100%		$1	$2	$12	$35
2013-S, White Mountain National Forest (NH), Proof	989,803	1,865	69.5				$3	$4.50	$15
2013-S, White Mountain National Forest (NH), Proof, Silver	467,691	4,913	69.7				$8	$9	$20
2013-P, Perry's Victory and Int'l Peace Memorial (OH)	107,800,000	461	66.5	100%	$0.50	$0.75	$1	$10	$30
2013-D, Perry's Victory and Int'l Peace Memorial (OH)	131,600,000	261	67.2	100%	$0.50	$0.75	$1	$10	$30
2013-S, Perry's Victory and Int'l Peace Memorial (OH) (a)	1,425,860	255	66.4	100%		$1	$2	$12	$35
2013-S, Perry's Victory and Int'l Peace Memorial (OH), Proof	947,815	1,839	69.5				$3	$4.50	$15
2013-S, Perry's Victory and Int'l Peace Memorial (OH), Proof, Silver	467,691	4,797	69.7				$8	$9	$20
2013-P, Great Basin National Park (NV)	122,400,000	212	66.9	100%	$0.50	$0.75	$1	$10	$30
2013-D, Great Basin National Park (NV)	141,400,000	439	66.5	100%	$0.50	$0.75	$1	$10	$30
2013-S, Great Basin National Park (NV) (a)	1,316,500	291	66.9	100%		$1	$2	$12	$35
2013-S, Great Basin National Park (NV), Proof	945,777	1,838	69.5				$3	$4.50	$15
2013-S, Great Basin National Park (NV), Proof, Silver	467,691	4,969	69.7				$8	$9	$20
2013-P, Ft. McHenry Nat'l Monument / Historic Shrine (MD)	120,000,000	482	66.5	100%	$0.50	$0.75	$1	$10	$30
2013-D, Ft. McHenry Nat'l Monument / Historic Shrine (MD)	151,400,000	295	67.2	100%	$0.50	$0.75	$1	$10	$30
2013-S, Ft. McHenry Nat'l Monument / Historic Shrine (MD) (a)	1,313,680	480	67.1	100%		$1	$2	$12	$35
2013-S, Ft. McHenry Nat'l Monument / Historic Shrine (MD), Proof	946,380	1,835	69.5				$3	$4.50	$15
2013-S, Ft. McHenry National Monument / Historic Shrine (MD), Proof, Silver	467,691	4,927	69.7				$8	$9	$20

a. Not issued for circulation. From 2012 to date, the San Francisco Mint has made Uncirculated S-mintmark quarters of each design in the National Park series. These can be purchased by collectors directly from the U.S. Mint, in bags of 100 or rolls of 40 coins, for a premium above face value.

	Mintage	Cert	Avg	%MS	AU-50	MS-63	MS-65	MS-66	MS-67
							PF-65	PF-66DC	PF-69DC
2013-P, Mount Rushmore National Memorial (SD)	231,800,000	188	66.9	100%	$0.50	$0.75	$1	$10	$30
2013-D, Mount Rushmore National Memorial (SD)	272,400,000	434	66.3	100%	$0.50	$0.75	$1	$10	$30
2013-S, Mount Rushmore National Memorial (SD) (a)	1,373,260	437	66.9	100%		$1	$2	$12	$35
2013-S, Mount Rushmore National Memorial (SD), Proof	958,853	1,837	69.5				$3	$4.50	$15
2013-S, Mount Rushmore National Memorial (SD), Proof, Silver	467,691	4,935	69.7				$8	$9	$20

a. Not issued for circulation. From 2012 to date, the San Francisco Mint has made Uncirculated S-mintmark quarters of each design in the National Park series. These can be purchased by collectors directly from the U.S. Mint, in bags of 100 or rolls of 40 coins, for a premium above face value.

2014, Great Smoky Mountains National Park (TN)
Reverse designer: Chris Costello.

2014, Shenandoah National Park (VA)
Reverse designer: Phebe Hemphill.

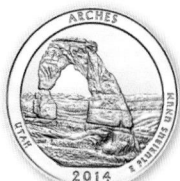

2014, Arches National Park (UT)
Reverse designer: Donna Weaver.

2014, Great Sand Dunes National Park (CO)
Reverse designer: Don Everhart.

2014, Everglades National Park (FL)
Reverse designer: Joel Iskowitz.

	Mintage	Cert	Avg	%MS	AU-50	MS-63	MS-65	MS-66	MS-67
							PF-65	PF-66DC	PF-69DC
2014-P, Great Smoky Mountains National Park (TN)	73,200,000	402	66.6	100%	$0.50	$0.75	$1	$10	$30
2014-D, Great Smoky Mountains National Park (TN)	99,400,000	250	67.5	100%	$0.50	$0.75	$1	$10	$30
2014-S, Great Smoky Mountains National Park (TN) (a)	1,360,780	473	66.7	100%		$1	$2	$12	$35
2014-S, Great Smoky Mountains National Park (TN), Proof	881,896	1,981	69.5				$3	$4.50	$15
2014-S, Great Smoky Mountains National Park (TN), Proof, Silver	472,107	4,143	69.7				$8	$9	$20
2014-P, Shenandoah National Park (VA)	112,800,000	401	66.4	100%	$0.50	$0.75	$1	$10	$30
2014-D, Shenandoah National Park (VA)	197,800,000	228	67.5	100%	$0.50	$0.75	$1	$10	$30
2014-S, Shenandoah National Park (VA) (a)	1,260,700	682	66.9	100%		$1	$2	$12	$35
2014-S, Shenandoah National Park (VA), Proof	846,441	1,975	69.5				$3	$4.50	$15
2014-S, Shenandoah National Park (VA), Proof, Silver	472,107	4,145	69.7				$8	$9	$20
2014-P, Arches National Park (UT)	214,200,000	240	67.3	100%	$0.50	$0.75	$1	$10	$30
2014-D, Arches National Park (UT)	251,400,000	284	67.4	100%	$0.50	$0.75	$1	$10	$30
2014-S, Arches National Park (UT) (a)	1,226,220	563	66.8	100%		$1	$2	$12	$35
2014-S, Arches National Park (UT), Proof	844,775	1,978	69.5				$3	$4.50	$15
2014-S, Arches National Park (UT), Proof, Silver	472,107	4,273	69.7				$8	$9	$20
2014-P, Great Sand Dunes National Park (CO)	159,600,000	179	67.4	100%	$0.50	$0.75	$1	$10	$30
2014-D, Great Sand Dunes National Park (CO)	171,800,000	218	67.7	100%	$0.50	$0.75	$1	$10	$30
2014-S, Great Sand Dunes National Park (CO) (a)	1,170,500	822	67.1	100%		$1	$2	$12	$35
2014-S, Great Sand Dunes National Park (CO), Proof	843,238	1,974	69.5				$3	$4.50	$15
2014-S, Great Sand Dunes National Park (CO), Proof, Silver	472,107	4,139	69.7				$8	$9	$20
2014-P, Everglades National Park (FL)	157,601,200	194	67.3	100%	$0.50	$0.75	$1	$10	$30
2014-D, Everglades National Park (FL)	142,400,000	272	67.6	100%	$0.50	$0.75	$1	$10	$30
2014-S, Everglades National Park (FL) (a)	1,173,720	0	n/a			$1	$2	$12	$35
2014-S, Everglades National Park (FL), Proof	856,139	1,976	69.5				$3	$4.50	$15
2014-S, Everglades National Park (FL), Proof, Silver	472,107	4,141	69.7				$8	$9	$20

a. Not issued for circulation. From 2012 to date, the San Francisco Mint has made Uncirculated S-mintmark quarters of each design in the National Park series. These can be purchased by collectors directly from the U.S. Mint, in bags of 100 or rolls of 40 coins, for a premium above face value.

| 2015, Homestead National Monument of America (NE) *Reverse designer: Ronald D. Sanders.* | 2015, Kisatchie National Forest (LA) *Reverse designer: Susan Gamble.* | 2015, Blue Ridge Parkway (NC) *Reverse designer: Frank Morris.* | 2015, Bombay Hook National Wildlife Refuge (DE) *Reverse designer: Joel Iskowitz.* | 2015, Saratoga National Historical Park (NY) *Reverse designer: Barbara Fox.* |

	Mintage	Cert	Avg	%MS	AU-50	MS-63	MS-65 PF-65	MS-66 PF-66DC	MS-67 PF-69DC
2015-P, Homestead National Monument of America (NE)	214,400,000	40	67.0	100%	$0.50	$0.75	$1	$10	$30
2015-D, Homestead National Monument of America (NE)	248,600,000	2	66.0	100%	$0.50	$0.75	$1	$10	$30
2015-S, Homestead National Monument of America (NE) (a)	1,135,460	404	66.9	100%		$2	$3	$12	$35
2015-S, Homestead National Monument of America (NE), Proof	764,611	394	69.5	100%			$3	$4.50	$15
2015-S, Homestead National Monument of America (NE), Proof, Silver	447,489	788	69.4	100%			$8	$9	$20
2015-P, Kisatchie National Forest (LA)	397,200,000	45	67.2	100%	$0.50	$0.75	$1	$10	$30
2015-D, Kisatchie National Forest (LA)	379,600,000	34	66.9	100%	$0.50	$0.75	$1	$10	$30
2015-S, Kisatchie National Forest (LA) (a)	1,081,560	241	67.0	100%		$2	$3	$12	$35
2015-S, Kisatchie National Forest (LA), Proof	730,469	328	69.4	100%			$3	$4.50	$15
2015-S, Kisatchie National Forest (LA), Proof, Silver	447,489	787	69.4	100%			$8	$9	$20
2015-P, Blue Ridge Parkway (NC)	325,616,000	22	66.5	100%	$0.50	$0.75	$1	$10	$30
2015-D, Blue Ridge Parkway (NC)	505,200,000	9	66.9	100%	$0.50	$0.75	$1	$10	$30
2015-S, Blue Ridge Parkway (NC) (a)	1,049,500	0	n/a			$2	$3	$12	$35
2015-S, Blue Ridge Parkway (NC), Proof	731,823	328	69.4	100%			$3	$4.50	$15
2015-S, Blue Ridge Parkway (NC), Proof, Silver	447,489	787	69.4	100%			$8	$9	$20
2015-P, Bombay Hook National Wildlife Refuge (DE)	275,000,000	40	67.1	100%	$0.50	$0.75	$1	$10	$30
2015-D, Bombay Hook National Wildlife Refuge (DE)	206,400,000	34	66.9	100%	$0.50	$0.75	$1	$10	$30
2015-S, Bombay Hook National Wildlife Refuge (DE) (a)	923,960	0	n/a			$2	$3	$12	$35
2015-S, Bombay Hook National Wildlife Refuge (DE), Proof	728,412	328	69.4	100%			$3	$4.50	$15
2015-S, Bombay Hook National Wildlife Refuge (DE), Proof, Silver	447,489	786	69.4	100%			$8	$9	$20
2015-P, Saratoga National Historical Park (NY)	223,000,000	19	66.9	100%	$0.50	$0.75	$1	$10	$30
2015-D, Saratoga National Historical Park (NY)	215,800,000	24	67.0	100%	$0.50	$0.75	$1	$10	$30
2015-S, Saratoga National Historical Park (NY) (a)	888,380	0	n/a			$2	$3	$12	$35
2015-S, Saratoga National Historical Park (NY), Proof	743,133	328	69.4	100%			$3	$4.50	$15
2015-S, Saratoga National Historical Park (NY), Proof, Silver	447,489	788	69.3	100%			$8	$9	$20

a. Not issued for circulation. From 2012 to date, the San Francisco Mint has made Uncirculated S-mintmark quarters of each design in the National Park series. These can be purchased by collectors directly from the U.S. Mint, in bags of 100 or rolls of 40 coins, for a premium above face value.

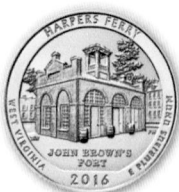

2016, Shawnee National Forest (IL)
Reverse designer: Justin Kunz.

2016, Cumberland Gap National Historic Park (KY)
Reverse designer: Barbara Fox.

2016, Harpers Ferry National Historical Park (WV)
Reverse designer: Thomas Hipschen.

2016, Theodore Roosevelt National Park (ND)
Reverse designer: Joel Iskowitz.

2016, Fort Moultrie at Fort Sumter National Monument (SC)
Reverse designer: Richard Scott.

| | Mintage | Cert | Avg | %MS | AU-50 | MS-63 | MS-65 | MS-66 | MS-67 |
							PF-65	PF-66DC	PF-69DC
2016-P, Shawnee National Forest (IL)		0	n/a		$0.50	$0.75	$1	$10	$30
2016-D, Shawnee National Forest (IL)		0	n/a		$0.50	$0.75	$1	$10	$30
2016-S, Shawnee National Forest (IL) (a)		0	n/a			$2	$3	$12	$35
2016-S, Shawnee National Forest (IL), Proof		0	n/a				$3	$4.50	$15
2016-S, Shawnee National Forest (IL), Proof, Silver		0	n/a				$8	$9	$20
2016-P, Cumberland Gap National Historical Park (KY)		0	n/a		$0.50	$0.75	$1	$10	$30
2016-D, Cumberland Gap National Historical Park (KY)		0	n/a		$0.50	$0.75	$1	$10	$30
2016-S, Cumberland Gap National Historical Park (KY) (a)		0	n/a			$2	$3	$12	$35
2016-S, Cumberland Gap National Historical Park (KY), Proof		0	n/a				$3	$4.50	$15
2016-S, Cumberland Gap National Historical Park (KY), Proof, Silver		0	n/a				$8	$9	$20
2016-P, Harpers Ferry National Historical Park (WV)		0	n/a		$0.50	$0.75	$1	$10	$30
2016-D, Harpers Ferry National Historical Park (WV)		0	n/a		$0.50	$0.75	$1	$10	$30
2016-S, Harpers Ferry National Historical Park (WV) (a)		0	n/a			$2	$3	$12	$35
2016-S, Harpers Ferry National Historical Park (WV), Proof		0	n/a				$3	$4.50	$15
2016-S, Harpers Ferry National Historical Park (WV), Proof, Silver		0	n/a				$8	$9	$20
2016-P, Theodore Roosevelt National Park (ND)		0	n/a		$0.50	$0.75	$1	$10	$30
2016-D, Theodore Roosevelt National Park (ND)		0	n/a		$0.50	$0.75	$1	$10	$30
2016-S, Theodore Roosevelt National Park (ND) (a)		0	n/a			$2	$3	$12	$35
2016-S, Theodore Roosevelt National Park (ND), Proof		0	n/a				$3	$4.50	$15
2016-S, Theodore Roosevelt National Park (ND), Proof, Silver		0	n/a				$8	$9	$20
2016-P, Fort Moultrie (Fort Sumter National Monument) (SC)		0	n/a		$0.50	$0.75	$1	$10	$30
2016-D, Fort Moultrie (Fort Sumter National Monument) (SC)		0	n/a		$0.50	$0.75	$1	$10	$30
2016-S, Fort Moultrie (Fort Sumter National Monument) (SC) (a)		0	n/a			$2	$3	$12	$35
2016-S, Fort Moultrie (Fort Sumter National Monument) (SC), Proof		0	n/a				$3	$4.50	$15
2016-S, Fort Moultrie (Fort Sumter National Monument) (SC), Proof, Silver		0	n/a				$8	$9	$20

a. Not issued for circulation. From 2012 to date, the San Francisco Mint has made Uncirculated S-mintmark quarters of each design in the National Park series. These can be purchased by collectors directly from the U.S. Mint, in bags of 100 or rolls of 40 coins, for a premium above face value.

Half Dollars
1794 to Date

AN OVERVIEW OF HALF DOLLARS

Many hobbyists consider a collection of half dollars to be one of the most satisfying in the American series. The panorama of designs is extensive, ranging from the early Flowing Hair issues of 1794 and 1795 down to classic 20th-century motifs and the presidential portrait of the present day. The large size of half dollar coins makes them convenient to view and easy to enjoy.

Among the types, the 1794–1795 Flowing Hair half dollar is readily available in circulated grades and rare in Mint State, but at any level is hard to find well struck and without adjustment marks (evidence of where a Mint worker filed an overweight planchet down to proper weight). Most on the market are dated 1795. Careful selection for quality is advised.

The next type, dated 1796–1797 with a Draped Bust obverse and Small Eagle reverse, is the scarcest in the American silver series excepting the 1839 Gobrecht dollar. (However, the latter is available in Proof restrike form, yielding choice and gem examples, so it can be considered in a different category from the circulation-strike 1796–1797 half dollar type.) It might not be possible to be particular, but, finances permitting, a collector should take some time and endeavor to find an example that is sharply struck on both sides. Needle-sharp striking is more of a theory than a practicality, and some compromise in this regard may be necessary.

Half dollars of the 1801–1807 type, with the obverse as preceding but now with the Heraldic Eagle reverse, are plentiful enough in worn grades but somewhat scarce in Mint State. Striking is seldom needle-sharp and ranges from average to very poor. However, there are enough coins in the marketplace that collectors can afford to take their time and seek a sharp strike.

Capped Bust half dollars with a lettered edge, 1807–1836, abound in just about any grade desired. Again, striking is a consideration, and some searching is needed for a high-quality strike. Generally, those in the late 1820s and the 1830s are better struck than are those of earlier dates, the earlier coins being scarcer and more expensive in any event.

The short-lived type of 1836–1837, Capped Bust with a reeded edge and with the denomination spelled as 50 CENTS, is available easily enough through the high-mintage 1837, but most have problems with the quality of striking. Then comes the 1838–1839 type of the same obverse style, its reverse modified with a slightly different eagle and with the denomination as HALF DOL. Generally these are fairly well struck.

Liberty Seated half dollars of the several styles within the series, 1839–1891, admit of no great rarities for the type collector, save for the 1839, No Drapery, in levels of MS-63 and finer. However, among the earlier types in particular, sharply struck pieces are in the minority. Curiously, the most readily available Mint State Liberty Seated half dollars also are the lowest-mintage issues, the dates 1879 and later, as these were recognized as desirable at the time of issue and were widely saved.

Barber half dollars were not popular in their time, and while Proofs exist in proportion to their production figures, few circulation-strike coins were saved by collectors and Mint State examples are quite scarce today. In fact, as a type, a Barber half dollar dated 1900 or later in Mint State is the scarcest of all silver issues of that century. Well-struck MS-63 and better Barber half dollars, with the upper-right corner of the shield and the leg at lower right showing full details, are significantly scarcer than generally realized.

Liberty Walking half dollars, minted from 1916 to 1947, are plentiful in all grades. Again, some attention should be made to striking sharpness, which makes the search become more intense. Fortunately there are countless thousands of MS-63 and finer coins of the 1940s on the market, giving collectors a wide choice. Then come Franklin half dollars, made only from 1948 to 1963, with representative coins easy enough to acquire in about any grade desired. Kennedy half dollars exist in several varieties, all of which are available without any problem. Among these and other modern coins care needs to be taken for value received versus price paid. Modern issues in, for example, MS–65 and 66, selected for quality, are for many collectors preferable to MS–69 or 70 coins offered at a much higher price.

The release of the Franklin half dollar was announced to the coin-collecting world on the front page of the *Numismatist*, June 1948.

For the Collector and Investor: Half Dollars as a Specialty

Many collectors over the years have pursued half dollars by date, mint, and variety. Except for the series of copper cents, half dollars are the most generally available coins over a nearly continuous span, making them possible to collect for reasonable cost. Also, enough die varieties exist that this can form another focus of interest and importance.

In general, the half dollars of the early era form a concentration in themselves. Die varieties can be attributed by Overton numbers, as listed by Al C. Overton in his immensely popular *Early Half Dollar Die Varieties 1794–1836*. Glenn R. Peterson's book, *The Ultimate Guide to Attributing Bust Half Dollars*, is also useful in this regard. The John Reich Collectors Society (www.jrcs.org) publishes the *John Reich Journal* and serves as a forum for the exchange of information, updates, news about die varieties, and the like.

Among rarities in the early years, the 1796 and 1797 half dollars with the Draped Bust obverse and Small Eagle reverse are perhaps the most famous, needed for variety collections as well as one example for a type set. Variety enthusiasts aspire to get two of 1796—one with 15 stars on the obverse and the other with 16 stars—plus the 1797.

Draped Bust half dollars from 1801 through 1807 have a number of rare die varieties (as listed by Overton), but the basic varieties are easy enough to find. The 1805, 5 Over 4, overdate is particularly popular, as there was no "perfect date" 1804, and this is the closest collectors can come to it.

A vast and interesting field in early American numismatics is that of the Capped Bust half dollar, 1807–1836, with a lettered edge. Several hundred different die combinations exist, and many collectors are active in their pursuit, using the Overton book as a road map. All the major varieties are readily collectible except the 1817, 7 Over 4, overdate, of which only about a half dozen exist. The 1815, 5 Over 2, is considered the key issue among the specific dates (rather than varieties of dates). The majority of these survive in VF grade, not often lower and not often higher either—an interesting situation. During the 1820s vast quantities of these were transferred among banks, not wearing down from as much hand-to-hand circulation as they might have otherwise. While many if not most of the varieties listed herein can be obtained in Mint State, most collectors opt for VF or EF, these grades showing the necessary details but also permitting a budget to be stretched to include more varieties, rather than just a few high-grade pieces. Choice and gem examples can be found here and there, and are most plentiful among the later dates.

Among the Capped Bust half dollars of reduced size, 1836–1837, the 1836 is a key date, with fewer than 5,000 believed to have been minted. The next type, 1838 and 1839, Capped Bust, reeded edge, with a modified eagle on the reverse, includes the famous 1838-O rarity, of which only 20 are said to have been struck (per a note published in 1894 in the catalog of the Friesner Collection). These have a prooflike surface. Interestingly, they were not struck until 1839. In the same year, 1839-O half dollars were also struck, to the extensive quantity of 178,976 pieces; they are unusual as the mintmark is on the obverse, an odd placement for the era.

Within the series of Liberty Seated half dollars, collectors generally seek the varieties listed herein, although certain dedicated specialists will consult the *Complete Guide to Liberty Seated Half Dollars*, by Randy Wiley and Bill Bugert—a volume that delineates many interesting features, including the number of different reeds on the edges of certain coins.

Among Liberty Seated half dollars there is just one "impossible" rarity, that being the 1853-O coin without arrows at the date. Only three exist, and each shows extensive wear. At the San Francisco Mint, half dollars were first struck in 1855, and at the Carson City Mint in 1870. Generally, large quantities were minted of most dates and mintmark varieties of Liberty Seated half dollars, making them readily obtainable today. Except for the later dates, 1879 to 1891, Mint State pieces are generally scarce, gems especially so. Many specialists in half dollars belong to the Liberty Seated Collectors Club (LSCC, at www.lsccweb.org) and receive its magazine, *The Gobrecht Journal*.

Proof Liberty Seated halves can be collected by date sequence from 1858 onward. Survivors exist in proportion to their mintage quantities. Generally those before the mid-1870s often are found cleaned or hairlined, and more care is needed in selecting choice examples than is necessary for the later dates.

Barber half dollars were made continuously from 1892 through 1915, in such quantities that today there are no great rarities in the series. However, a number of issues are quite scarce, even in well-worn grades, and in MS-63 and better many are difficult to find. These coins had little honor in the era in which they were issued, and few numismatists saved them. Proofs were made each year from 1892 to 1915 and today can be obtained in proportion to their mintages. However, those of 1914 and 1915 are hard to find with choice, original surfaces—decades ago a collector hoarded these two dates and polished the ones in his possession.

Liberty Walking half dollars are popular to collect by date and mint. Scarce varieties include the 1917-S with obverse mintmark, the three issues of 1921, and the low mintage 1938-D, although the latter is not inordinately expensive. Mint State pieces are most readily available for 1916 and 1917, and then especially so in the 1930s and 1940s. Striking quality can be a problem, particularly for issues of the mid-1920s and also the later dates. For example, with a needle-sharp strike the 1923-S is an extreme rarity. Among later coins the 1940-S and 1941-S often are weakly struck.

Franklin half dollars minted from 1948 through 1963 have been very popular in recent decades. The complete series of dates and mintmarks is short and contains no scarce or rare pieces in higher grades such as MS–63 and 64. However, if you consider the element of sharp striking, usually defined as Full Bell Lines (FBL) on the reverse, certain otherwise common dates become elusive. Proofs of most years can also be readily collected.

Kennedy half dollars are easily enough collected, and so many have been made by this time that nearly 200 date-and-mintmark combinations extend from 1964 to present, including a gold version that marks the design's 50th anniversary. The wise collector will select coins that have a meeting point between a high grade such as MS–65 or 66 (or equivalent Proofs) and a reasonable price.

FLOWING HAIR (1794–1795)

Designer: *Robert Scot.* **Weight:** *13.48 grams.*
Composition: *.8924 silver, .1076 copper.* **Diameter:** *Approximately 32.5 mm.*
Edge: *FIFTY CENTS OR HALF A DOLLAR with decorations between the words.* **Mint:** *Philadelphia.*

Overton-105.

History. The Flowing Hair design inaugurated the half-dollar denomination. They were immediately popular, as was evident in 1795, when many depositors of silver at the Philadelphia Mint asked for half dollars in return. The same motif was used on half dimes and silver dollars of the same years. Early half dollars have been extensively collected by die varieties, of which many exist for most dates. Valuations given below are in each case for the most readily available variety; scarcer ones, as listed by Overton, generally command higher prices.

Striking and Sharpness. Many have problems of one sort or another, including adjustment marks from the planchet being filed down to proper weight and mushy denticles. On the obverse, check the hair details and the stars. On the reverse, check the breast of the eagle in particular. As with other silver coins of this design, it may not be possible to find a *needle-sharp* example, but with some extensive searching a fairly decent strike can be obtained. Sharp striking and excellent eye appeal add to the value dramatically. However, very few 1794 and 1795 halves are uniformly sharp on both sides.

Availability. Probably 3,500 to 6,000 circulated Flowing Hair half dollars exist. Most are dated 1795, the 1794 being considered a rare date (though not among the great U.S. coin rarities). Typical grades are Good to Fine. EF and AU grades are elusive in regard to the total population. Probably 100 or so could be graded MS (nearly all of them 1795). Unlike half dollars of the 1796–1797 type, none of these are known to have been made with prooflike surfaces.

GRADING STANDARDS

MS-60 to 70 (Mint State). *Obverse:* At MS-60, some abrasion and contact marks are evident, most noticeably on the cheek and in the fields. This denomination, heavier than the half dime of the same design, was more susceptible to contact and other outside influences. A typical half dollar certified at MS–60 or 61 today might well have been designated as About Uncirculated a generation ago. Luster is present, but may be dull or lifeless, and

1795; Overton-110a. Graded MS-63.

interrupted in patches, perhaps as much from old cleaning as from contact the coin may have received. At MS-63, contact marks are very few, and abrasion is present, but not as noticeable. An MS-65 coin has no abrasion, and contact marks are very few. Luster should be full and rich. Higher grades are seldom seen in this type, but are defined in theory by having fewer marks as perfection is approached. *Reverse:* Comments apply as for the obverse, except that abrasion and contact marks are most noticeable on the eagle at the center. This area is often lightly struck, so in all grades do not mistake weak striking for actual wear. Knowledge of specific die varieties is helpful in this regard. The field area is small and is protected by lettering and the wreath, and in any given grade shows fewer marks than on the obverse.

Illustrated coin: This is a well-struck example with superb eye appeal.

AU-50, 53, 55, 58 (About Uncirculated).

1795; O-116. Graded AU-55.

Obverse: Light wear is seen on the hair area immediately to the left of the face and above the forehead, on the cheek, and, to a lesser extent, on the top of the neck truncation, more so at AU-50 than at AU–53 or 55. An AU-58 coin has minimal traces of wear. An AU-50 coin has luster in protected areas among the stars and letters, with little in the open fields or on the portrait. At AU-58, much luster is present in the fields but is worn away on the highest parts of the motifs. *Reverse:* Light wear is seen on the eagle's body and the upper part of both wings. On well-struck pieces the details of the wing features are excellent. At AU-50, detail is lost in some feathers in this area. However, striking can play a part, as some coins were weakly struck to begin with. Light wear is seen on the wreath and lettering, but is harder to discern. Luster is the best key to actual wear. This will range from perhaps 20% remaining in protected areas (at AU-50) to nearly full mint bloom (at AU-58), although among certified coins the amounts of luster can vary widely.

Illustrated coin: Significant luster remains in protected areas on this attractive early half dollar.

EF-40, 45 (Extremely Fine).

1794; O-101. Graded EF-40.

Obverse: More wear is evident on the portrait, especially on the hair to the left of and above the forehead, and in the back below the LI of LIBERTY. The tip of the neck truncation shows flatness, and the cheek is worn. Excellent detail remains in low-relief areas of the hair. The stars show wear, as do the date and letters. Luster, if present at all, is minimal and in protected areas. *Reverse:* The eagle shows more wear on the body and on the tops of the wings. Interior wing detail is good on most coins (depending on the variety and the striking), and the tail feathers can be discerned. Additional wear is on the wreath and letters, but many details are present. Some luster may be seen in protected areas and if present is slightly more abundant than on the obverse.

Illustrated coin: Note some lightness of the stars at the right and at the reverse center, as struck. The scrape on the reverse below the ribbon knot was mentioned by the cataloger in an auction offering.

VF-20, 30 (Very Fine). *Obverse:* The hair is well worn at VF-20, less so at VF-30, and is most noticeable in the upper part of the head, the area above the level of the eye, and extending to the back. The strands are blended as to be heavy. The cheek shows only slight relief, and the tip of the neck truncation is flat. The stars have more wear, making them appear larger (an optical illusion). Scattered marks are common on half dollars at this level

1795; O-109. Graded VF-20.

and below, and should be mentioned if particularly serious. *Reverse:* The body of the eagle shows few if any feathers, while the wings have perhaps a quarter or a third of the feathers visible depending on the strike, with sharper strikes having up to half visible (as PCGS suggests). *Photograde* and the ANA grading standards suggest half of the feathers on all, which may be the case on coins that were well struck to begin with. The leaves lack detail and are in outline form. Scattered, non-disfiguring marks are normal for this and lower grades. Any major defects should be noted separately.

Illustrated coin: On this variety in this grade, the denticles are especially prominent on each side. Such aspects vary from coin to coin.

F-12, 15 (Fine). *Obverse:* Wear is more extensive than on the preceding, with less hair visible. The ear position can be seen, as can the eye. The cheek is nearly flat, and the stars appear larger. The rim is distinct and most denticles remain visible. *Reverse:* Wear is more extensive. Now, feather details are fewer, mostly remaining on the wing to the left. The wreath and lettering are more worn, and the rim is usually weak in areas, although most denticles can be seen.

1795; O-107. Graded F-12.

VG-8, 10 (Very Good). *Obverse:* The portrait is mostly seen in outline form, with most hair strands gone save for an area centered behind the neck. The hair tips at the lower left are clear. The eye location is barely discernible. The stars appear larger still and often quite bold, again an illusion. The rim is weak in areas. LIBERTY and the date are readable and usually full, although some letters may be weak at their tops. *Reverse:* The

1795; O-109. Graded VG-8.

eagle is mostly an outline, although traces of the separation between the body and the right wing can sometimes be seen. The rim is worn, as are the letters, with some weak, but the motto is readable. On many coins the rim remains fairly prominent.

Illustrated coin: Note a spot, a tiny edge bruise, and some adjustment marks. A cataloger mentioned that "the top of the obverse is slightly soft due to axial misalignment"—a technical note. On any half dollar of this era, knowledge of the varieties and peculiarities of striking is useful.

G-4, 6 (Good). *Obverse:* Wear is more extensive, and some stars may be missing or only partially visible. The head is an outline, although a few elements of thick hair strands may be seen. The rim is well worn or even missing. LIBERTY is worn, and parts of some letters may be missing, but elements of all should be readable. The date is readable, but worn. *Reverse:* The eagle is flat and discernible in outline form. The wreath is well

1794; O-106. Graded G-6.

worn. Some of the letters may be partly missing. At this level some "averaging" can be done. If the letters are stronger than usual in one area, but some are missing in another area, the coin can still qualify as G-4. Often on this type in lower grades the reverse is more detailed than the obverse.

AG-3 (About Good). *Obverse:* Wear is very extensive. The head is in outline form (perhaps partly blended into the field). LIBERTY is mostly gone. The date, while readable, may be partially worn away. Some stars are missing. *Reverse:* The reverse is well worn, with parts of the wreath and lettering very weak or even missing. The details that remain and those that do not is often dependent on the particular die variety.

1795; O-116. Graded AG-3.

1795, Normal Date

1795, Recut Date

1795, Two Leaves Under Each Wing

1795, Three Leaves Under Each Wing

	Mintage	Cert	Avg	%MS	AG-3	G-4	VG-8	F-12	VF-20	EF-40	AU-50	AU-55	MS-60
1794	23,464	338	21.8	2%	$2,750	$4,500	$7,750	$12,500	$23,000	$38,000	$75,000	$105,000	$150,000
Auctions: $152,750, MS-61, June 2014; $18,800, VF-30, August 2014; $12,925, VF-20, August 2014; $11,750, VG-10, August 2014													
1795, All kinds (a)	299,680												
1795, Normal Date		1,073	24.3	5%	$650	$1,000	$1,450	$2,750	$3,900	$11,000	$19,000	$21,000	$42,000
Auctions: $129,250, MS-62, November 2013; $1,998, F-12, March 2015; $881, G-6, September 2015; $705, AG-3, June 2015													
1795, Recut Date		25	22.9	0%	$650	$1,000	$1,450	$2,750	$3,900	$11,000	$20,500	$25,000	$45,000
Auctions: $1,651, F-12, March 2014; $1,645, VG-8, September 2014													
1795, 3 Leaves Under Each Wing		15	25.0	0%	$1,100	$2,200	$3,000	$4,600	$8,500	$20,000	$40,000	$42,000	$65,000
Auctions: $8,519, VF, March 2014													

a. Varieties of 1795 are known with the final S in STATES over a D; with the A in STATES over an E; and with the Y in LIBERTY over a star. All are scarce. Some 1794 and 1795 half dollars were weight-adjusted by insertion of a silver plug in the center of the blank planchet before the coin was struck.

DRAPED BUST, SMALL EAGLE REVERSE (1796–1797)

Designer: *Robert Scot.* **Weight:** *13.48 grams.*
Composition: *.8924 silver, .1076 copper.* **Diameter:** *Approximately 32.5 mm.*
Edge: *FIFTY CENTS OR HALF A DOLLAR with decorations between words.* **Mint:** *Philadelphia.*

O-101.

History. Robert Scot's Draped Bust design is similar to that used on the half dime, dime, quarter, and silver dollar of this era. In 1796 and 1797 there was little demand for half dollars and the combined mintage for the two years was therefore low. Among design types of U.S. silver coins made in circulation-strike format this is the Holy Grail—a classic rarity, with no common date in the series.

Striking and Sharpness. On the obverse, check the hair details and the stars. On the reverse, first check the breast of the eagle, but examine other areas as well. Also check the denticles on both sides. Look especially for coins that do not have significant adjustment marks (from an overweight planchet being filed down to correct specifications). Coins of this denomination are on average better struck than are half dimes, dimes, quarters (which have reverse problems), and dollars in the Draped Bust suite.

Availability. Examples are rare in any grade—survivors likely number only in the hundreds of coins. MS examples are particularly rare, and when seen are nearly always dated 1796. Some of these have partially prooflike surfaces. Any half dollar of this type has strong market demand.

GRADING STANDARDS

MS-60 to 70 (Mint State). *Obverse:* At MS-60, some abrasion and contact marks are evident, most noticeably on the cheek, the drapery at the shoulder, and the right field. Also check the hair to the left of the forehead. Luster is present, but may be dull or lifeless, and interrupted in patches. At MS-63, contact marks are few, and abrasion is hard to detect, although this type is sometimes graded liberally due to its rarity. An MS-65 coin has

1797; O-101a. Graded MS-66.

no abrasion, and contact marks are so minute as to require magnification. Luster should be full and rich. Coins graded above MS-65 are more theoretical than actual for this type, although some notable pieces have crossed the auction block. These are defined by having fewer marks as perfection is approached. *Reverse:* Comments apply as for the obverse, except that abrasion and contact marks are most noticeable on the eagle at the center, a situation that should be evaluated by considering the original striking (which can be quite sharp, but with many exceptions). The field area is small and is protected by lettering and the wreath, and in any given grade shows fewer marks than on the obverse.

Illustrated coin: This superb gem has prooflike surfaces.

AU-50, 53, 55, 58 (About Uncirculated). *Obverse:* Light wear is seen on the hair area above the ear and extending to the left of the forehead, on the ribbon, and on the drapery at the shoulder, more so at AU-50 than at AU–53 or 55. An AU-58 coin has minimal traces of wear. An AU-50 coin has luster in protected areas among the stars and letters, with little in the open fields or on the portrait. At AU-58, most luster is present in the fields, but is worn

1797; O-101a. Graded AU-50.

away on the highest parts of the motifs. *Reverse:* Light wear is seen on the eagle's body and the edges of the wings. Light wear is seen on the wreath and lettering. Luster is the best key to actual wear. This ranges from perhaps 20% remaining in protected areas (at AU-50) to nearly full mint bloom (at AU-58).

EF-40, 45 (Extremely Fine). *Obverse:* More wear is evident on the upper hair area, particularly to the left of the forehead and also below the LI of LIBERTY, in the ribbon, and on the drapery and bosom. Excellent detail remains in low-relief areas of the hair. The stars show wear as do the date and letters. Luster, if present at all, is minimal and in protected areas. *Reverse:* The eagle shows more wear, this being the focal point to

1796, 15 Stars; O-101. Graded EF-40.

check. Many feathers remain on the interior areas of the wings. Additional wear is on the wreath and letters, but many details are present. Some luster may be seen in protected areas and if present is slightly more abundant than on the obverse.

VF-20, 30 (Very Fine). *Obverse:* The higher-relief areas of hair are well worn at VF-20, less so at VF-30. The drapery and bosom show extensive wear. The stars have more wear. *Reverse:* The body of the eagle shows few if any feathers, while the wings have about half or more of the feathers visible, depending on the strike. The leaves lack most detail and are outlined. Scattered, non-disfiguring marks are normal for this and

1796, 16 Stars; O-103. Graded VF-20.

lower grades; major defects should be noted separately.

F-12, 15 (Fine). *Obverse:* Wear is more extensive than on a Very Fine coin, particularly noticeable on the hair, face, and bosom. The stars appear larger (an optical illusion). About half the hair detail remains, most noticeably behind the neck and shoulder. The rim may be partially worn away and blend into the field, but on many coins it remains intact. *Reverse:* Wear is more extensive. Now, feather details are diminished,

1797; O-101a. Graded F-15.

with fewer than half remaining on the wings. The wreath and lettering are worn further, and the rim is usually weak in areas, but most denticles can be seen.

VG-8, 10 (Very Good). *Obverse:* The portrait is mostly seen in outline form, with most hair strands gone, although there is some definition at the back of the hair and behind the shoulder. The ear is barely discernible and the eye is fairly distinct. The stars appear larger still, again an illusion. The rim is weak in areas, but shows most denticles. LIBERTY and the date are readable and usually full, although some letters may be weak at their

1796, 16 Stars; O-102. Graded VG-10.

tops. *Reverse:* The eagle is mostly an outline, with parts blending into the field (on lighter strikes). The rim is worn, as are the letters, with some weak, but the motto is readable.

G-4, 6 (Good). *Obverse:* Wear is more extensive, and some stars may be partly missing. The head is an outline. The eye is visible only in outline form. The rim is well worn or even missing in areas, but many denticles remain. LIBERTY is worn. The letters and date are weak but fully readable. *Reverse:* The eagle is flat and discernible in outline form, and may be blending into the field. The wreath is well worn. Some of the letters may

1797. Graded G-4.

be partly missing. At this level some "averaging" can be done. If the letters are stronger than usual in one area, but some are missing in another area, the coin can still qualify as G-4.

AG-3 (About Good). *Obverse:* Wear is so extensive that the coin is barely identifiable. The head is in outline form. LIBERTY is mostly gone; same for the stars. The date, while readable, may be partially worn away. *Reverse:* The reverse is well worn, with parts of the wreath and lettering missing. On most coins the reverse shows more wear than the obverse.

1797. Graded AG-3.

1796, 15 Stars

1796, 16 Stars

	Mintage	Cert	Avg	%MS	AG-3	G-4	VG-8	F-12	VF-20	EF-40	AU-50	AU-58	MS-60
1796, 15 Stars †	(a)	19	42.6	37%	$23,000	$34,000	$40,000	$52,000	$70,000	$110,000	$165,000	$220,000	$290,000
Auctions: No auction records available.													
1796, 16 Stars †	(a)	13	32.0	23%	$23,000	$36,500	$43,500	$56,000	$71,000	$110,000	$170,000	$250,000	$305,000
Auctions: $470,000, MS-63, November 2013													
1797, 15 Stars †	3,918	53	28.5	8%	$23,000	$34,000	$40,000	$52,000	$70,000	$110,000	$165,000	$220,000	$290,000
Auctions: $1,292,500, MS-65+, August 2014; $282,000, MS-63, June 2014													

† Ranked in the *100 Greatest U.S. Coins* (fourth edition). **a.** Included in 1797, 15 Stars, mintage figure.

DRAPED BUST, HERALDIC EAGLE REVERSE (1801–1807)

Designer: *Robert Scot.* **Weight:** *13.48 grams.*
Composition: *.8924 silver, .1076 copper.* **Diameter:** *Approximately 32.5 mm.*
Edge: *FIFTY CENTS OR HALF A DOLLAR with decorations between words.* **Mint:** *Philadelphia.*

O-101.

History. The half dollar's Draped Bust, Heraldic Eagle design is similar to that of other silver coins of the era. While dies were prepared for the 1804 half dollar, none were minted in that year, despite Mint reports that state otherwise.

Striking and Sharpness. Most have light striking in one area or another. On the obverse, check the hair details and, in particular, the star centers. On the reverse, check the stars above the eagle, the clouds, the details of the shield, and the eagle's wings. Check the denticles on both sides. Adjustment marks are sometimes seen, from overweight planchets being filed down to correct weight, but not as often as on earlier half dollar types. Typically, the earlier years are better struck; many of 1806 and nearly all of 1807 are poorly struck. Sharp striking and excellent eye appeal add to the value dramatically, this being particularly true for those of 1805 to 1807, which are often weak (particularly 1807).

Availability. Earlier years are scarce in the marketplace, beginning with the elusive 1801 and including the 1802, after which they are more readily available. Some die varieties are scarce. Most MS coins are dated 1806 and 1807, but all are scarce. Finding sharply struck high-grade coins is almost impossible, a goal more than a reality.

GRADING STANDARDS

MS-60 to 70 (Mint State). *Obverse:* At MS-60, some abrasion and contact marks are evident, most noticeably on the cheek, the drapery at the shoulder, and the right field. Luster is present, but may be dull or lifeless, and interrupted in patches. At MS-63, contact marks are very few, and abrasion is hard to detect except under magnification. An MS-65 coin has no abrasion, and contact marks are so minute as to require magnifica-

1803, Large 3; O-101. Graded MS-63.

tion. Luster should be full and rich. Coins grading above MS-65 are more theoretical than actual for this type—but they do exist, and are defined by having fewer marks as perfection is approached. Later years usually have areas of flat striking. *Reverse:* Comments apply as for the obverse, except that abrasion and contact marks are most noticeable on the eagle's neck, the tips of the wing, and the tail. The field area is complex, without much open space, given the stars above the eagle, the arrows and olive branch, and other features. Accordingly, marks are not as noticeable as on the obverse.

Illustrated coin: This is an extraordinary strike with superb eye appeal. A connoisseur might prefer this coin to an MS-65 example with flat striking.

AU-50, 53, 55, 58 (About Uncirculated). *Obverse:* Light wear is seen on the hair area above the ear and extending to left of the forehead, on the ribbon, and on the bosom, more so at AU-50 than at AU–53 or 55. An AU-58 coin has minimal traces of wear. An AU-50 coin has luster in protected areas among the stars and letters, with little in the open fields or on the portrait. At AU-58, most luster is present in the fields, but is worn

1806, Pointed 6, No Stem; O-109. Graded AU-50.

away on the highest parts of the motifs. *Reverse:* Comments as preceding, except that the eagle's neck, the tips and top of the wings, the clouds, and the tail now show noticeable wear, as do other features. Luster ranges from perhaps 20% remaining in protected areas (at AU-50) to nearly full mint bloom (at AU-58). Often the reverse of this type retains much more luster than the obverse.

Illustrated coin: This example has gray and lilac toning.

EF-40, 45 (Extremely Fine). *Obverse:* More wear is evident on the upper hair area and the ribbon, and on the drapery and bosom. Excellent detail remains in low-relief areas of the hair. The stars show wear, as do the date and letters. Luster, if present at all, is minimal and in protected areas. *Reverse:* Wear is greater than on an About Uncirculated coin, overall. The neck lacks feather detail on its highest points. Feathers have lost some detail

1807; O-105. Graded EF-40.

near the edges of the wings, and some areas of the horizontal lines in the shield may be blended together. Some traces of luster may be seen, more so at EF-45 than at EF-40.

Illustrated coin: Light striking at the obverse center is normal for this die variety.

VF-20, 30 (Very Fine). *Obverse:* The higher-relief areas of hair are well worn at VF-20, less so at VF-30. The drapery on the shoulder and the bosom show extensive wear. The stars have more wear, making them appear larger (an optical illusion seen on most worn silver coins of this era). *Reverse:* Wear is greater, including on the shield and wing feathers. Half to two-thirds of the feathers are visible. Star centers are flat. Other areas have lost detail as well.

1806, 6 Over Inverted 9; O-111a. Graded VF-30.

Illustrated coin: Note the cud break on the reverse rim over the E in UNITED.

F-12, 15 (Fine). *Obverse:* Wear is more extensive than on a Very Fine coin, particularly noticeable on the hair, face, and bosom. The stars appear larger. About half the hair detail remains, most noticeably behind the neck and shoulder, but the fine hair is now combined into thicker tresses. The rim may be partially worn away and blend into the field. *Reverse:* Wear is even more extensive, with the shield and wing feathers being

1805; O-109. Graded F-15.

points to observe. The incuse E PLURIBUS UNUM may have half or more of the letters worn away (depending on striking). The clouds all appear connected. The stars are weak. Parts of the border and lettering may be weak.

VG-8, 10 (Very Good). *Obverse:* The portrait is mostly seen in outline form, with most hair strands gone, although there is some definition at the back of the hair and behind the shoulder. The ear is discernible as is the eye. The stars appear larger still, again an illusion. The rim is weak in areas. LIBERTY and the date are readable and usually full, although some letters may be weak at their tops. *Reverse:* Wear is more extensive. Half

1805, 5 Over 4; O-103. Graded VG-8.

or more of the letters in the motto are worn away. Most feathers are worn away, although separation of some of the lower feathers may be seen. Some stars are faint (depending on the strike). The border blends into the field in areas and some letters are weak.

G-4, 6 (Good). *Obverse:* Wear is more extensive, and some stars may be partly missing. The head is mostly an outline, although some hair strand outlines may be visible on some strikings. The rim is well worn or even missing in areas. LIBERTY is worn, and parts of some letters may be missing, but elements should be readable. The date is readable, but worn. *Reverse:* Wear is more extensive. The upper part of the eagle is flat. Feathers are

1805; O-111. Graded G-4.

noticeable only at the lower edge of the wings, and do not have detail. The upper part of the shield is flat or mostly so (depending on the strike). Only a few letters of the motto can be seen. The rim is worn extensively, and a few letters may be missing.

AG-3 (About Good). *Obverse:* Wear is so extensive that the coin is barely identifiable. The head is in outline form. LIBERTY is mostly gone; same for the stars. The date, while readable, may be partially worn away. *Reverse:* Extensive wear is seen overall, with the rim worn away and some areas worn smooth. The eagle can be discerned in outline form, but not necessarily completely. A few stray motto letters may remain.

1801. Graded AG-3.

	Mintage	Cert	Avg	%MS	G-4	VG-8	F-12	VF-20	EF-40	AU-50	AU-55	MS-60	MS-63
1801	30,289	141	28.6	2%	$800	$1,200	$2,400	$3,500	$6,750	$16,000	$21,000	$45,000	$160,000
	Auctions: $329,000, MS-64, November 2013; $4,700, EF-40, March 2015; $576, G-4, October 2014; $517, AG-3, July 2015												
1802	29,890	99	31.8	1%	$750	$1,200	$2,500	$3,500	$7,750	$17,000	$25,000	$60,000	
	Auctions: $70,500, AU-58, August 2013; $3,173, VF-20, August 2014; $2,115, F-15, August 2014												

| 1803, Small 3 | 1803, Large 3 | 1805, 5 Over 4 | 1805, Normal Date |

   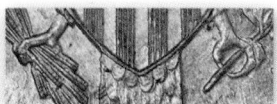

| 1806, 6 Over 5 | 1806, 6 Over Inverted 6 | 1806, Stem Not Through Claw | 1806, Stem Through Claw |

1806, Knobbed-Top 6, Large Stars
With traces of overdate.

1806, Knobbed-Top 6, Small Stars

	Mintage	Cert	Avg	%MS	G-4	VG-8	F-12	VF-20	EF-40	AU-50	AU-55	MS-60	MS-63
1803, All kinds	188,234												
1803, Small 3		40	38.8	3%	$350	$475	$550	$1,000	$2,600	$6,000	$10,000	$21,000	$65,000
	Auctions: $49,938, MS-62, June 2014												
1803, Large 3		118	32.3	4%	$325	$425	$500	$900	$2,050	$5,000	$7,000	$16,000	$40,000
	Auctions: $1,763, EF-40, March 2015; $881, VF-30, June 2015; $752, VF-25, March 2015; $552, VF-20, March 2015												
1805, All kinds	211,722												
1805, 5 Over 4		115	33.5	2%	$290	$440	$875	$1,600	$3,500	$7,500	$12,750	$30,000	$85,000
	Auctions: $152,750, MS-65, November 2013; $3,525, EF-45, August 2014; $3,290, EF-40, August 2014; $9,106, VG-8, March 2015												
1805, Normal Date		407	32.5	2%	$260	$325	$450	$850	$2,250	$5,000	$6,600	$16,000	$35,000
	Auctions: $4,406, AU-50, March 2015; $2,350, EF-45, May 2015; $1,528, VF-25, September 2015; $617, F-15, August 2015												
1806, All kinds	839,576												
1806, 6 Over 5		204	33.3	3%	$265	$350	$450	$900	$2,200	$5,000	$6,500	$12,000	$26,000
	Auctions: $21,150, MS-61, November 2013; $881, VF-30, September 2014; $794, VF-25, January 2015; $764, VF-20, July 2014												
1806, 6 Over Inverted 6		69	27.3	1%	$300	$450	$925	$1,450	$3,750	$7,000	$12,500	$27,500	$38,000
	Auctions: $28,200, MS-61, November 2013; $999, F-12, September 2014; $940, F-12, August 2014; $999, Fair-2, August 2014												
1806, Knobbed 6, Large Stars (Traces of Overdate)		37	29.5	0%	$250	$300	$400	$700	$2,000	$5,000	$7,000	$10,000	$21,500
	Auctions: $2,364, EF-40, August 2013												
1806, Knobbed 6, Small Stars		39	30.6	0%	$250	$300	$400	$700	$2,000	$5,000	$7,000	$11,000	$30,000
	Auctions: $2,350, EF-45, January 2014; $435, F-15, July 2014												
1806, Knobbed 6, Stem Not Through Claw		0	n/a		$35,000	$55,000	$85,000	$115,000	$200,000				
	Auctions: $126,500, EF-40, January 2009												
1806, Pointed 6, Stem Through Claw		277	33.0	6%	$250	$300	$400	$700	$1,750	$4,500	$5,250	$8,500	$20,000
	Auctions: $35,250, MS-64, November 2013; $7,638, AU-53, August 2014; $447, F-12, October 2015; $327, VG-10, February 2015												
1806, Pointed 6, Stem Through Claw, E Over A in STATES		8	21.3	0%	$400	$900	$1,600	$3,200	$7,500	$20,000			
	Auctions: No auction records available.												
1806, Pointed 6, Stem Not Through Claw		110	36.6	7%	$250	$300	$400	$700	$2,000	$5,500	$5,750	$9,500	$20,000
	Auctions: $12,925, MS-62, November 2013; $3,840, AU-55, August 2014; $1,293, EF-40, January 2015; $881, VF-30, July 2015												
1807	301,076	1,104	33.9	7%	$250	$300	$400	$700	$1,800	$5,000	$5,500	$9,000	$20,000
	Auctions: $1,528, EF-40, March 2015; $588, VF-20, February 2015; $400, F-12, August 2015; $306, VG-10, May 2015												

CAPPED BUST, LETTERED EDGE (1807–1836)

Designer: *John Reich.* **Weight:** *13.48 grams.*
Composition: *.8924 silver, .1076 copper.* **Diameter:** *Approximately 32.5 mm.*
Edge: *1807–1814—FIFTY CENTS OR HALF A DOLLAR;*
1814–1831—star added between DOLLAR and FIFTY;
1832–1836—vertical lines added between words. **Mint:** *Philadelphia.*

First Style (1807–1808)
O-104.

Remodeled Portrait and Eagle
(1809–1836)
O-109.

Remodeled Portrait and Eagle, Proof
O-103.

History. The Capped Bust design was created by Mint assistant engraver John Reich; the motif was widely used, in several variations, on much of the era's coinage. Reich was the first artist to consistently include the denomination in his designs for U.S. gold and silver coins. The half dollar, minted continuously from 1807 to 1836, except 1816, was the largest silver coin of the realm at the time (silver dollars had not been struck since 1804).

Striking and Sharpness. On the obverse, check the hair and broach details. The stars are often flatly struck on Capped Bust half dollars, much more so than on other denominations. On the reverse, check the motto band and the eagle's head, and the wing to the left, as well as other areas (the neck feathers, often lightly struck on other denominations of Capped Bust silver, are usually fairly sharp on half dollars). The E PLURIBUS UNUM band is often weak in the area left of its center; this does not normally occur on other Capped Bust silver coins. Inspect the denticles on both sides. Generally, later dates are better struck than are earlier ones. Many half dollars have semi-prooflike surfaces, or patches of mirror-like character interspersed with luster. Others can have nearly full prooflike surfaces, with patches of luster being in the minority (and often in the left obverse field); some of these have been mischaracterized as "Proofs." Some issues from the early 1830s have little digs or "bite marks" on the portrait, possibly from some sort of a gadget used to eject them from the press. Unlike the Capped Bust half dime, dime, and quarter dollar, the half dollar is particularly subject to very wide variations in striking quality.

True Proofs have deeply mirrored surfaces. Impostors are often seen, with deeply toned surfaces or with patches of mint luster. This situation is more prevalent with half dollars than with any other Capped Bust denomination. Proceed slowly, and be careful. There are some crushed-lettered-edge ("CLE")

Proofs of the 1833 to 1835 era that are especially beautiful and are more deeply mirrorlike than original issues. Some of these are restrikes (not necessarily an important consideration, but worth mentioning), believed to have been made at the Mint beginning in the spring of 1859.

Availability. Examples of most dates and overdates are easily found in just about any grade desired, from Fine and VF to MS. (As the largest silver coin struck between 1803 and 1836, these half dollars spent much of their time in bags, transferred from bank to bank, rather than wearing down in circulation.) The later years are the most readily available and are also seen in higher average grades. Many die varieties range from scarce to rare. Proofs were made in limited numbers for presentation purposes and for distribution to numismatists.

GRADING STANDARDS

MS-60 to 70 (Mint State). *Obverse:* At MS-60, some abrasion and contact marks are evident, most noticeably on the cheek, the hair below the left part of LIBERTY, the cap, and the front part of the bosom and drapery. These areas also coincide with the highest parts of the coin and are thus susceptible to lightness of strike. Complicating matters is that when an area is lightly struck, and the planchet is not forced into the deepest parts

1827, Square Base 2; O-104. Graded MS-60.

of the die, the *original planchet surface* (which may exhibit scuffing and nicks) is visible. A lightly struck coin can have virtually perfect luster in the fields, deep and rich, and yet appear to be "worn" on the higher parts, due to the lightness of strike. This is a very sophisticated concept and is hard to quantify. In practice, the original planchet surface will usually be considered as wear on the finished coin, which of course is not true. Such grades as high About Uncirculated and low Mint State levels are often assigned to pieces that, if well struck, would be MS–64 and 65. As a matter of practicality, but not of logic, you will need to do the same. If a coin has original planchet abrasions, but otherwise is a Gem, those abrasions must be taken into consideration. Apart from this, on well-struck coins in lower Mint State grades, luster is present, but may be dull or lifeless, and interrupted in patches. At MS-63, on a well-struck coin, contact marks are very few, and abrasion is hard to detect except under magnification. A well-struck MS-65 coin has no abrasion, and contact marks are so minute as to require magnification. Luster should be full and rich. Grades above MS-65 are seen now and again and are defined by having fewer marks as perfection is approached. *Reverse:* Comments apply as for the obverse, except that nearly all coins with weak striking on the obverse (so as to reveal original planchet surface) do not show such original surface on the reverse, except perhaps on the motto ribbon. Accordingly, market grading is usually by the obverse only, even if the reverse seems to be in much better preservation. On well-struck coins, abrasion and contact marks are most noticeable on the eagle's head, the top of the wings, the claws, and the flat band that surrounds the incuse motto. The field is mainly protected by design elements and does not show abrasion as much as does the obverse on a given coin.

Illustrated coin: This is an exceptional coin at the low Mint State level.

AU-50, 53, 55, 58 (About Uncirculated).
Obverse: Light wear is seen on the cheek, the hair below the left part of LIBERTY, the cap, and the front part of the bosom and drapery. Some of this apparent "wear" may be related to the original planchet surface (as noted under Mint State, above), but at the About Uncirculated level the distinction is less important. On a well-struck coin, at AU-58 the luster is exten-sive except in the open area of the field, espe-

1820, Curl Base 2, Small Date; O-103. Graded AU-55.

cially to the right. At AU–50 and 53, luster remains only in protected areas. *Reverse:* Wear is evident on the eagle's head, the top of the wings, the claws, and the flat band above the eagle. An AU-58 coin has nearly full luster. At AU–50 and 53, there still is significant luster, more than on the obverse.

  Illustrated coin: An attractive coin by any measure, this has light toning and ample areas of original luster.

EF-40, 45 (Extremely Fine). *Obverse:* Wear is more extensive, most noticeably on the higher areas of the hair. The cap shows more wear, as does the cheek. Luster, if present, is in protected areas among the star points and close to the portrait. *Reverse:* The wings show wear on the higher areas of the feathers, and some details are lost. The top of the head and the beak are flat. The eagle's claws and the leaves show wear. Luster may be present in protected areas, even if there is little or none on the obverse.

1810; O-110. Graded EF-45.

  Illustrated coin: This coin probably was lightly cleaned years ago so as to give a light silver color, which added some hairlines, but now it has halo toning around the borders that adds attractiveness.

VF-20, 30 (Very Fine). *Obverse:* Wear is more extensive, and most of the hair is com-bined into thick tresses without delicate fea-tures. The curl on the neck is flat. The cap shows significant wear at its top, and the left part of the drapery and bosom is nearly flat. Stars are flat at their centers (even if sharply struck to begin with). *Reverse:* Wear is most evident on the eagle's head, the tops of the wings, and the leaves and claws. Nearly all feathers in the wing remain distinct.

1815, 5 Over 2; O-101. Graded VF-30.

  Illustrated coin: The areas of wear appear exaggerated due to the light toning, a feature often observed on half dollars of this date but not as often among other years.

F-12, 15 (Fine). *Obverse:* Wear is more extensive, with much of the hair blended together. The drapery is indistinct on most of its upper edge. The stars are flat at their centers. LIBERTY remains bold. *Reverse:* Wear is more extensive, now with only about half of the feathers remaining on the wings, more on the right wing. The head shows the eye, nostril, and beak but no details. The claws show more wear. Other features are worn as well, but not as noticeable as the key points mentioned.

1827, Square Base 2; O-122. Graded F-12.

VG-8, 10 (Very Good). *Obverse:* The hair is less distinct, with the forehead blended into the hair above. LIBERTY is complete, but may be slightly weak in areas. The stars are flat. The rim is distinct, with most if not all denticles visible. *Reverse:* Feathers are fewer and mostly on the right wing, although sharp strikes can show detail in both wings. Other details are weaker. All lettering remains easily readable.

1831; O-120. Graded VG-8.

Illustrated coin: This coin was cleaned and partially retoned. It is sharply struck on the reverse.

G-4, 6 (Good). *Obverse:* The portrait is mostly in outline, with few interior details discernible. LIBERTY may still be readable or may be partially worn away, depending on the variety. The rim is weak, but distinct in most areas. *Reverse:* The eagle is mostly in outline form, although some feathers can be seen in the right wing. All letters around the border are clear. E PLURIBUS UNUM may be weak. Overall, a typical coin has the reverse in a slightly higher grade than the obverse.

1808. Graded G-4.

AG-3 (About Good). *Obverse:* The portrait is an outline, although some of LIBERTY can still be seen. The rim is worn down, and some stars are blended into it. The date remains clear, but is weak at the bottom (on most but not all). *Reverse:* At this level the reverse shows more wear overall than the obverse, with the rim indistinct in areas and many letters worn away. This is an interesting turnabout from the situation of most G-4 coins.

1824. Graded AG-3.

PF-60 to 70 (Proof). *Obverse and Reverse:* Proofs of this type have confused experts for a long time (as have large copper cents of the same era). Proofs that were extensively cleaned and therefore have many hairlines, or that are dull and grainy, are lower level, such as PF–60 to 62. While any early Proof half dollar will generate interest among collectors, lower levels are not of great interest to specialists unless they are of rare die varieties. With medium

1836; O-108. Graded PF-64 Cameo.

hairlines, an assigned grade of PF-64 may be in order and with relatively few, Gem PF-65. PF-66 should have hairlines so delicate that magnification is needed to see them. Above that, a Proof should be free of such lines. Grading is highly subjective with early Proofs, with eye appeal being a major factor.

1807, Small Stars

1807, Large Stars

1807, Large Stars, 50 Over 20

1807, "Bearded" Liberty

1808, 8 Over 7

	Mintage	Cert	Avg	%MS	G-4	F-12	VF-20	EF-40	AU-50	AU-55	MS-60 / PF-63	MS-63 / PF-64	MS-65 / PF-65
1807, All kinds	750,500												
1807, Small Stars		33	36.3	6%	$140	$450	$850	$2,400	$5,000	$6,000	$9,000	$16,000	$65,000
	Auctions: $28,200, MS-61, January 2014; $999, EF-40, August 2014; $823, VF-25, January 2015; $329, VG-10, January 2015												
1807, Large Stars		36	38.2	8%	$120	$350	$700	$1,700	$3,500	$5,000	$8,000	$15,000	$85,000
	Auctions: $152,750, MS-65, November 2013												
1807, Large Stars, 50 Over 20		140	40.1	6%	$110	$325	$650	$1,400	$2,700	$3,750	$5,750	$11,000	$33,500
	Auctions: $1,293, EF-45, January 2015; $940, VF-35, February 2015; $764, VF-35, January 2015; $282, VG-10, February 2015												
1807, "Bearded" Liberty (a)		34	29.6	0%	$500	$975	$2,100	$4,000	$9,500	$13,000	$27,500	—	
	Auctions: $8,225, VF-30, January 2014												
1808, All kinds	1,368,600												
1808, 8 Over 7		193	41.8	10%	$100	$150	$275	$650	$1,500	$2,000	$4,200	$10,000	
	Auctions: $21,150, MS-65, November 2013; $676, EF-45, January 2015; $705, EF-40, July 2014; $388, VF-35, October 2014												
1808		579	42.0	15%	$75	$110	$190	$375	$1,000	$1,200	$3,000	$6,000	$19,000
	Auctions: $1,175, AU-50, August 2015; $705, EF-45, March 2015; $259, VF-20, April 2015; $212, F-15, March 2015												

a. Also called the Bearded Goddess variety; a die crack gives the illusion of long whiskers growing from Miss Liberty's chin.

1809, xxxx Edge
Experimental edge has
"xxxx" between the words.

1809, ||||| Edge
Experimental edge has
"|||||" between the words.

1811, (18.11), 11 Over 10
The date is "punctuated" with a period.

1811, Small 8

1811, Large 8

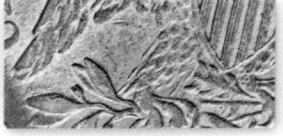

1812, 2 Over 1, Small 8

1812, 2 Over 1, Large 8

1812, Two Leaves Below Wing

1812, Single Leaf Below Wing

	Mintage	Cert	Avg	%MS	G-4	F-12	VF-20	EF-40	AU-50	AU-55	MS-60	MS-63	MS-65
											PF-63	PF-64	PF-65
1809, All kinds	1,405,810												
1809, Normal Edge		604	43.7	15%	$75	$110	$190	$375	$900	$1,500	$3,000	$5,500	$19,000
Auctions: $764, AU-55, February 2015; $494, EF-40, April 2015; $353, VF-35, August 2015; $165, F-15, January 2015													
1809, xxxx Edge		54	38.6	4%	$90	$135	$230	$475	$1,000	$2,750	$5,000	$7,000	
Auctions: $1,645, AU-50, April 2014; $411, VF-25, July 2014													
1809, IIIII Edge		129	39.9	9%	$90	$135	$230	$475	$1,200	$3,000	$4,000	$7,300	$22,000
Auctions: $38,188, MS-66, April 2014													
1810	1,276,276	680	43.5	14%	$75	$110	$170	$315	$800	$1,400	$3,500	$5,750	$18,000
Auctions: $646, AU-53, January 2015; $505, AU-50, June 2015; $447, EF-40, June 2015; $282, VF-35, October 2015													
1811, All kinds	1,203,644												
1811, (18.11), 11 Over 10		121	42.7	11%	$80	$135	$235	$650	$1,400	$2,500	$4,000	$10,000	
Auctions: $6,463, AU-58, January 2014; $423, VF-35, August 2015; $494, VF-30, June 2015$411, VF-25, October 2014													
1811, Small 8		217	45.3	18%	$75	$125	$170	$325	$700	$1,200	$2,500	$4,500	$17,000
Auctions: $999, AU-55, January 2015; $1,175, AU-53, February 2015; $494, VF-35, March 2015; $188, VF-20, June 2015													
1811, Large 8		60	47.0	3%	$75	$125	$170	$325	$800	$1,500	$3,000	$5,000	$17,250
Auctions: $1,880, AU-58, January 2015; $329, EF-45, June 2015; $494, EF-40, October 2015; $282, VF-35, March 2015													
1812, All kinds	1,628,059												
1812, 2 Over 1, Small 8		121	44.2	21%	$80	$150	$225	$400	$1,200	$2,000	$3,400	$6,000	$18,000
Auctions: $1,293, AU-55, July 2014; $306, VF-30, March 2015; $248, VF-25, October 2015; $182, F-15, October 2015													
1812, 2 Over 1, Large 8		18	37.6	6%	$3,500	$6,000	$10,000	$13,000	$24,000	$30,000	$40,000	—	
Auctions: $14,100, AU-58, August 2013; $8,225, VF-30, August 2014													
1812		973	47.5	26%	$75	$110	$160	$265	$700	$950	$2,200	$3,600	$14,000
Auctions: $44,063, MS-65, November 2013; $441, AU-50, October 2014; $470, EF-45, August 2014; $324, EF-40, October 2014													
1812, Single Leaf Below Wing		2	31.5	0%	$750	$1,300	$2,400	$3,750	$7,000	$12,000	$17,000	$30,000	
Auctions: No auction records available.													

1813, 50 C. Over UNI.

1814, 4 Over 3

1814, E Over A in STATES

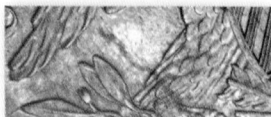

1814, Two Leaves Below Wing

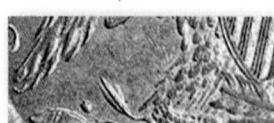

1814, Single Leaf Below Wing

1815, 5 Over 2

1817, 7 Over 3

1817, 7 Over 4

1817, Dated 181.7
The date is "punctuated" with a period between the second 1 and the 7.

1817, Two Leaves Below Wing

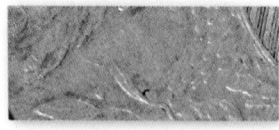

1817, Single Leaf Below Wing

	Mintage	Cert	Avg	%MS	G-4	F-12	VF-20	EF-40	AU-50	AU-55	MS-60 PF-63	MS-63 PF-64	MS-65 PF-65
1813, All kinds	1,241,903												
1813		643	45.8	19%	$70	$110	$160	$265	$700	$1,000	$2,250	$4,500	$16,000
		Auctions: $881, AU-53, September 2015; $423, EF-45, January 2015; $353, EF-40, May 2015; $212, VF-30, October 2015											
1813, 50 C. Over UNI		76	48.4	22%	$90	$160	$235	$450	$1,400	$2,600	$3,500	$6,000	
		Auctions: $24,675, MS-64, June 2014											
1814, All kinds	1,039,075												
1814, 4 Over 3		107	41.4	13%	$115	$200	$325	$750	$1,750	$2,500	$3,750	$6,500	$19,000
		Auctions: $1,175, EF-45, June 2015; $823, EF-40, September 2015; $353, VF-35, March 2015; $482, VF-25, February 2015											
1814, E Over A in STATES		29	40.9	7%	$95	$150	$250	$475	$1,500	$2,500	$4,000	$6,000	
		Auctions: $4,700, AU-55, January 2014; $505, VF-35, July 2014											
1814		585	48.1	24%	$70	$120	$175	$265	$800	$1,300	$2,500	$4,500	$14,000
		Auctions: $22,325, MS-65, November 2013; $3,290, MS-62, August 2014; $705, AU-50, October 2014; $382, EF-45, September 2014											
1814, Single Leaf Below Wing		22	34.2	0%	$80	$125	$225	$550	$1,750	$2,250	$3,200	$6,000	
		Auctions: $3,408, AU-50, August 2014; $705, EF-40, November 2013; $159, VF-20, October 2014											
1815, 5 Over 2	47,150	241	43.7	11%	$1,250	$2,200	$3,500	$5,150	$10,000	$13,000	$17,500	$32,000	
		Auctions: $117,500, MS-64, November 2013; $5,581, EF-40, March 2015; $4,700, VF-30, August 2014; $2,820, Fair-2, October 2014											
1817, All kinds	1,215,567												
1817, 7 Over 3		154	41.0	15%	$135	$275	$525	$975	$2,500	$3,500	$5,000	$12,500	$42,500
		Auctions: $28,200, MS-64, November 2013; $823, AU-50, January 2015; $541, F-15, October 2015; $499, F-15, July 2014											
1817, 7 Over 4 † (b)		1	35.0	0%	$60,000	$150,000	$200,000	$250,000	$350,000				
		Auctions: $184,000, VF-20, August 2010											
1817, Dated 181.7		29	44.4	10%	$75	$125	$180	$350	$1,750	$2,500	$3,500	$7,500	$22,000
		Auctions: $3,055, AU-58, August 2013; $529, VF-30, July 2014											
1817		551	44.2	17%	$70	$100	$150	$275	$700	$1,100	$2,000	$4,000	$15,500
		Auctions: $508, AU-53, January 2015; $541, AU-50, June 2015; $325, EF-45, May 2015; $153, F-12, August 2015											
1817, Single Leaf Below Wing		12	41.5	8%	$95	$135	$190	$475	$1,000	$1,650	$2,750	$4,500	
		Auctions: $3,055, AU-55, April 2013											

† Ranked in the *100 Greatest U.S. Coins* (fourth edition). **b.** 8 examples are known.

| 1818, First 8 Small, Second 8 Over 7 | 1818, First 8 Large, Second 8 Over 7 | 1819, Small 9 Over 8 | 1819, Large 9 Over 8 |

| 1820, 20 Over 19, Square Base 2 | 1820, 20 Over 19, Curl Base 2 | 1820, Curl Base, No Knob 2, Small Date | 1820, Square Base, Knob 2, Large Date |

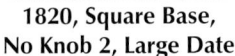

1820, Square Base, No Knob 2, Large Date

1820, Broken Serifs on E's
Compare with normal serifs on 1834, Large Letters, reverse.

	Mintage	Cert	Avg	%MS	G-4	F-12	VF-20	EF-40	AU-50	AU-55	MS-60 PF-63	MS-63 PF-64	MS-65 PF-65
1818, All kinds	1,960,322												
1818, 8 Over 7, Small 8		57	45.6	12%	$90	$130	$160	$375	$950	$1,900	$2,900	$6,500	$18,500
Auctions: $881, AU-53, August 2014; $499, EF-40, September 2014; $270, VF-35, March 2015; $165, F-15, October 2015													
1818, 8 Over 7, Large 8		71	43.5	10%	$90	$135	$200	$425	$925	$1,800	$2,900	$6,500	$19,500
Auctions: $1,645, AU-55, January 2015; $999, AU-50, September 2014; $764, EF-40, August 2014; $212, VF-25, October 2015													
1818		703	47.3	17%	$70	$100	$140	$235	$600	$975	$2,200	$4,000	$13,500
Auctions: $2,174, MS-62, May 2015; $1,528, AU-55, January 2015; $353, EF-45, January 2015; $235, EF-40, May 2015													
1818, Proof	3–5	4	65.5								$50,000	$75,000	$105,000
Auctions: $100,625, PF-65, April 2011													
1819, All kinds	2,208,000												
1819, Small 9 Over 8		60	40.3	5%	$75	$120	$160	$275	$750	$1,200	$1,750	$3,500	$16,000
Auctions: $588, AU-50, July 2015; $353, EF-45, May 2015; $235, VF-35, May 2015; $141, VF-20, May 2015													
1819, Large 9 Over 8		140	45.9	9%	$80	$140	$200	$300	$750	$1,400	$2,000	$3,600	$16,500
Auctions: $734, AU-53, October 2014; $1,763, AU-50, September 2015; $329, EF-40, January 2015; $206, Fair-2, October 2014													
1819		511	44.9	17%	$70	$100	$140	$220	$450	$700	$1,500	$3,000	$14,500
Auctions: $823, AU-55, February 2015; $646, AU-53, July 2015; $259, EF-40, May 2015; $400, VF-35, October 2015													
1820, All kinds	751,122												
1820, 20 Over 19, Square 2		43	41.9	14%	$100	$140	$230	$475	$1,150	$2,000	$2,650	$7,000	$22,000
Auctions: $15,863, MS-63, January 2014; $3,819, AU-58, August 2014; $382, VF-30, July 2014													
1820, 20 Over 19, Curl Base 2		61	42.9	3%	$90	$135	$200	$450	$1,100	$1,800	$2,350	$6,000	$18,500
Auctions: $8,225, MS-63, January 2014; $1,028, AU-50, January 2015; $940, AU-50, March 2015; $470, VF-35, May 2015													
1820, Curl Base 2, Small Dt		34	50.5	15%	$85	$130	$170	$340	$1,000	$1,750	$2,000	$5,000	$15,000
Auctions: $823, AU-50, January 2015; $705, AU-53, January 2015; $376, VF-35, March 2015; $165, F-12, August 2015													
1820, Sq Base Knob 2, Lg Dt		60	49.7	12%	$80	$125	$150	$300	$850	$1,600	$2,000	$5,000	$16,000
Auctions: $18,800, MS-64, January 2014; $517, MS-60, August 2015; $1,880, AU-55, October 2014; $411, EF-40, March 2015													
1820, Sq Base No Knob 2, Large Date		59	46.8	10%	$80	$125	$150	$300	$850	$1,600	$2,000	$5,000	$16,000
Auctions: $61,688, MS-65, June 2014; $1,293, AU-53, March 2015; $259, AU-50, August 2015; $1,058, EF-45, July 2014													
1820, Broken Serifs on E's		9	41.6	22%	$475	$800	$1,600	$3,000	$6,000	$6,250	$7,000	$12,000	$40,000
Auctions: $4,888, VF-35, December 2011													
1820, Proof	3–5	1	63.0								$50,000	$75,000	$105,000
Auctions: No auction records available.													

1822, So-called 2 Over 1

1823, Normal Date

1823, Broken 3

1823, Patched 3

1823, Ugly 3

1824, Normal Date

1824, 4 Over 1

1824, 4 Over
Various Dates
Probably 4 Over 2 Over 0.

1824, 4 Over 4
4 Over 4 varieties are easily mistaken for the scarcer 4 Over 1. Note the distance between the 2's and 4's in each.

	Mintage	Cert	Avg	%MS	G-4	F-12	VF-20	EF-40	AU-50	AU-55	MS-60	MS-63	MS-65
											PF-63	PF-64	PF-65
1821	1,305,797	658	47.2	17%	$70	$100	$130	$225	$650	$800	$1,400	$3,000	$13,000
Auctions: $447, AU-50, May 2015; $282, EF-45, March 2015; $306, EF-40, August 2015; $84, VG-10, February 2015													
1821, Proof	3–5	3	64.0								$50,000	$75,000	$105,000
Auctions: No auction records available.													
1822, All kinds	1,559,573												
1822		735	48.8	26%	$70	$100	$130	$225	$450	$800	$1,200	$2,850	$14,000
Auctions: $823, AU-55, February 2015; $282, EF-40, April 2015; $153, VF-35, May 2015; $94, F-15, February 2015													
1822, So-called 2 Over 1		104	49.3	23%	$100	$140	$250	$375	$800	$1,150	$1,600	$3,750	$16,000
Auctions: $1,410, MS-60, November 2013; $1,645, EF-45, September 2014; $306, VF-30, October 2014													
1822, Proof	3–5	1	64.0								$50,000	$75,000	$105,000
Auctions: $55,813, PF-64, June 2014													
1823, All kinds	1,694,200												
1823, Broken 3		50	41.6	16%	$80	$135	$225	$550	$1,500	$2,500	$3,750	$7,500	$25,000
Auctions: $23,500, MS-64, November 2013													
1823, Patched 3		49	49.4	33%	$75	$110	$185	$425	$1,200	$2,000	$4,000	$7,500	$20,000
Auctions: $4,113, MS-63, March 2015; $1,410, AU-50, January 2015; $353, EF-45, February 2015; $165, VF-25, May 2015													
1823, Ugly 3		23	46.2	17%	$75	$150	$250	$450	$1,000	$2,500	$4,500	$7,500	$18,000
Auctions: $4,113, AU-55, January 2014													
1823, Normal		880	48.3	23%	$70	$100	$130	$180	$500	$800	$1,250	$2,500	$13,500
Auctions: $94,000, MS-67, November 2013; $3,290, MS-64, August 2014; $2,115, MS-62, August 2014; $1,410, MS-62, August 2014													
1823, Proof	3–5	1	63.0								$50,000	$75,000	$105,000
Auctions: $80,500, PF-63, April 2011													
1824, All kinds	3,504,954												
1824, 4 Over Various Dates		63	44.0	10%	$70	$110	$140	$220	$750	$1,300	$1,700	$3,100	$12,000
Auctions: $11,163, MS-64, June 2014; $1,116, AU-53, August 2015; $306, VF-25, February 2015; $129, F-15, September 2015													
1824, 4 Over 1		91	49.5	35%	$75	$115	$150	$220	$750	$1,300	$1,700	$3,100	$15,000
Auctions: $799, AU-53, September 2014; $529, AU-53, September 2014; $517, AU-50, January 2015; $353, EF-40, October 2015													
1824, 4 Over 4 (c)		150	48.7	21%	$75	$110	$140	$210	$700	$1,200	$1,500	$2,950	$12,000
Auctions: $558, AU-50, August 2014; $558, AU-50, July 2014; $458, AU-50, January 2015; $235, VF-30, October 2015													
1824, Normal		1,105	47.7	23%	$75	$100	$130	$200	$600	$850	$1,150	$2,000	$14,000
Auctions: $10,575, MS-65, January 2015; $2,820, MS-63, March 2015; $223, EF-45, March 2015; $94, F-15, August 2015													

c. 2 varieties.

1827, 7 Over 6　　　　**1827, Square Base 2**　　　　**1827, Curl Base 2**

1828, Curl Base,　　**1828, Curl Base, Knob 2**　　**1828, Square Base 2,**　　**1828, Square Base 2,**
No Knob 2　　　　　　　　　　　　　　　　　　**Large 8's**　　　　　　**Small 8's**

1828, Large Letters　　　　　　**1828, Small Letters**

	Mintage	Cert	Avg	%MS	G-4	F-12	VF-20	EF-40	AU-50	AU-55	MS-60	MS-63	MS-65
											PF-63	PF-64	PF-65
1825	2,943,166	1,247	51.0	26%	$75	$100	$130	$200	$450	$700	$1,150	$2,000	$12,000
	Auctions: $541, AU-58, January 2015; $176, EF-45, March 2015; $188, EF-40, March 2015; $112, VF-30, July 2015												
1825, Proof	3–5	1	66.0								$50,000	$75,000	$105,000
	Auctions: $32,200, PF-62, May 2008												
1826	4,004,180	1,856	51.2	27%	$75	$100	$130	$200	$400	$525	$1,150	$2,000	$9,500
	Auctions: $1,058, MS-61, January 2015; $881, AU-55, September 2015; $182, EF-40, March 2015; $89, VF-30, January 2015												
1826, Proof	3–5	1	65.0								$50,000	$75,000	$105,000
	Auctions: $76,375, PF-65, September 2013												
1827, All kinds	5,493,400												
1827, 7 Over 6		173	51.2	24%	$80	$120	$160	$240	$600	$900	$1,500	$3,000	$13,000
	Auctions: $18,800, MS-65, November 2013; $764, AU-55, October 2014												
1827, Square Base 2		691	49.2	17%	$75	$100	$130	$200	$500	$700	$1,200	$2,100	$10,000
	Auctions: $764, MS-60, June 2015; $494, AU-55, January 2015; $329, AU-50, May 2015; $165, EF-40, July 2015												
1827, Curl Base 2		55	50.1	11%	$75	$100	$130	$200	$500	$800	$1,500	$2,500	$10,000
	Auctions: $8,813, MS-64, January 2014												
1827, Proof	5–8	3	64.7								$50,000	$75,000	$105,000
	Auctions: $21,150, PF-62, September 2013												
1828, All kinds	3,075,200												
1828, Curl Base No Knob 2		82	51.4	18%	$70	$95	$130	$200	$550	$850	$1,200	$2,000	$10,000
	Auctions: $5,875, MS-65, March 2015; $940, AU-58, June 2015; $764, AU-55, October 2015; $247, EF-45, April 2015												
1828, Curl Base Knob 2		36	52.3	22%	$70	$95	$130	$200	$700	$950	$1,300	$2,500	$12,000
	Auctions: $19,975, MS-65, April 2013; $382, AU-58, July 2014; $259, EF-45, May 2015												
1828, Square Base 2, Large 8's		49	49.3	10%	$70	$95	$130	$200	$550	$750	$1,150	$2,000	$9,000
	Auctions: $32,900, MS-66, November 2013; $306, AU-50, October 2014; $112, EF-45, October 2014												
1828, Square Base 2, Small 8's, Large Letters		307	49.9	19%	$65	$90	$120	$200	$525	$700	$1,150	$2,000	$9,000
	Auctions: $329, AU-50, October 2015; $223, EF-45, January 2015; $192, VF-35, May 2015; $188, VF-30, October 2015												
1828, Square Base 2, Small 8's and Letters		27	49.5	4%	$75	$105	$150	$250	$600	$750	$1,500	$3,000	$11,000
	Auctions: $30,550, MS-65, April 2014; $411, AU-50, July 2014												

1829, 9 Over 7   1830, Small 0   1830, Large 0

1830, Large Letters

Experimental Edge of 1830
Raised segment lines angled to the right.

Experimental Edge of 1830–1831
Raised segment lines angled to the left.

Edge Adopted for Coinage, 1830–1836
Straight vertical lines.

1832, Large Letters Reverse
Note the prominent die crack.

	Mintage	Cert	Avg	%MS	G-4	F-12	VF-20	EF-40	AU-50	AU-55	MS-60 / PF-63	MS-63 / PF-64	MS-65 / PF-65
1829, All kinds	3,712,156												
1829, 9 Over 7		223	51.6	25%	$70	$110	$145	$225	$600	$750	$1,500	$3,500	$18,000
Auctions: $2,115, MS-61, January 2015; $558, AU-53, September 2014; $353, EF-45, July 2014; $141, VF-25, October 2015													
1829		1048	48.9	23%	$60	$80	$110	$180	$400	$500	$1,000	$2,000	$10,000
Auctions: $16,450, MS-66, March 2015; $1,058, AU-55, January 2015; $306, AU-50, June 2015; $153, EF-45, March 2015													
1829, Large Letters		30	54.4	27%	$65	$90	$120	$200	$400	$550	$1,200	$2,500	$10,500
Auctions: $194, AU-50, September 2013													
1829, Proof	6–9	5	64.2								$40,000	$65,000	$95,000
Auctions: $102,813, PF-64, January 2014													
1830, All kinds	4,764,800												
1830, Small 0		528	47.9	13%	$65	$90	$120	$180	$375	$550	$1,000	$2,100	$10,000
Auctions: $1,410, MS-61, January 2015; $589, AU-58, August 2015; $217, EF-45, July 2015; $100, VF-25, September 2015													
1830, Large 0		132	51.0	17%	$65	$90	$120	$180	$375	$550	$1,000	$2,100	$10,000
Auctions: $41,125, MS-66, November 2013; $588, AU-58, July 2014; $482, AU-55, July 2014; $353, AU-53, July 2014													
1830, Large Letters		12	33.3	8%	$1,400	$2,950	$3,800	$4,800	$9,000	$14,000	$17,500	$22,000	
Auctions: $2,990, VF-35, October 2011													
1830, Proof	3–5	2	64.5								$40,000	$65,000	$95,000
Auctions: $41,400, PF-64, January 2005													
1831	5,873,660	1,888	51.9	26%	$65	$90	$120	$180	$375	$500	$1,000	$2,000	$10,000
Auctions: $922, MS-61, January 2015; $541, AU-58, August 2015; $306, AU-53, October 2015; $153, EF-40, February 2015													
1831, Proof	3–5	2	64.5								$40,000	$65,000	$95,000
Auctions: $79,313, PF-65, April 2013													
1832, All kinds	4,797,000												
1832		1,698	51.4	24%	$60	$80	$110	$180	$375	$500	$1,000	$2,000	$10,000
Auctions: $999, MS-62, January 2015; $764, AU-58, January 2015; $212, EF-45, March 2015; $112, VF-35, October 2015													
1832, Large Letters		76	50.3	13%	$60	$80	$110	$180	$375	$500	$1,000	$2,000	$10,000
Auctions: $4,406, MS-64, November 2013; $364, AU-55, July 2014; $382, AU-50, August 2014													
1832, Proof	6–9	4	65.3								$40,000	$65,000	$95,000
Auctions: $29,900, PF-63, January 2008													

1834, Large Date　　**1834, Small Date**　　**1834, Large Letters**　　**1834, Small Letters**

1836, Over 1336

	Mintage	Cert	Avg	%MS	G-4	F-12	VF-20	EF-40	AU-50	AU-55	MS-60 / PF-63	MS-63 / PF-64	MS-65 / PF-65
1833	5,206,000	1,660	51.2	23%	$60	$80	$110	$180	$375	$500	$1,000	$2,000	$10,000
Auctions: $353, AU-55, February 2015; $317, AU-53, August 2015; $270, AU-50, May 2015; $188, EF-45, April 2015												
1833, Proof	1–2	2	63.0										
Auctions: No auction records available.												
1833, Crushed Lettered Edge, Proof	3–5	2	64.5								$40,000	$65,000	$95,000
Auctions: No auction records available.												
1834, All kinds	6,412,004												
1834, Large Date and Letters		138	51.1	19%	$60	$80	$110	$180	$375	$500	$1,000	$2,000	$9,000
Auctions: $564, AU-58, January 2015; $135, EF-45, May 2015; $159, EF-40, July 2015; $153, VF-35, February 2015												
1834, Large Date, Small Letters		211	50.5	18%	$60	$80	$110	$180	$375	$500	$1,000	$2,000	$9,000
Auctions: $823, AU-58, January 2015; $447, AU-55, August 2015; $376, AU-53, June 2015; $200, EF-45, April 2015												
1834, Small Date, Stars, Letters		410	49.5	14%	$60	$80	$110	$180	$375	$500	$1,000	$2,000	$9,000
Auctions: $764, AU-58, February 2015; $350, AU-55, May 2015; $120, EF-40, January 2015; $94, VF-35, September 2015												
1834, Proof	8–12	7	64.6								$40,000	$65,000	$95,000
Auctions: $23,710, PF-63, November 2013												
1834, Crushed Lettered Edge, Proof	3–5	2	65.0								$40,000	$65,000	$95,000
Auctions: No auction records available.												
1835	5,352,006	1015	50.1	21%	$60	$80	$110	$180	$375	$500	$1,000	$2,000	$9,000
Auctions: $881, AU-58, August 2015; $350, AU-55, February 2015; $212, EF-45, August 2015; $141, VF-35, October 2015												
1835, Proof	5–8	2	63.0								$40,000	$65,000	$95,000
Auctions: $43,125, PF-64, August 2007												
1835, Crushed Lettered Edge, Proof	3–5	2	65.0								$40,000	$65,000	$95,000
Auctions: No auction records available.												
1836, All kinds	6,545,000												
1836		1,524	49.2	21%	$60	$80	$110	$180	$375	$500	$1,000	$2,000	$9,000
Auctions: $823, AU-58, August 2015; $282, AU-50, January 2015; $100, VF-30, August 2015; $94, VF-25, October 2015												
1836, 1836 Over 1336		59	48.8	14%	$80	$100	$130	$225	$475	$700	$1,200	$2,500	$10,000
Auctions: $2,703, MS-64, August 2014; $499, AU-53, July 2014; $270, AU-50, March 2015; $194, VF-35, December 2014												
1836, 50 Over 00		48	50.4	19%	$90	$130	$175	$335	$925	$1,500	$2,100	$3,900	
Auctions: $1,645, AU-55, February 2013												
1836, Beaded Border on Reverse (d)		42	44.5	17%	$85	$120	$140	$250	$525	$675	$1,300	$2,400	$9,500
Auctions: $494, AU-53, May 2015; $212, EF-45, February 2015; $153, VF-35, September 2015 $112, EF-40, November 2014												
1836, Lettered Edge, Proof	8–12	5	64.4								$40,000	$65,000	$95,000
Auctions: $96,938, PF-66, November 2013												
1836, 50 Over 00, Proof	3–5	2	64.5								$50,000	$80,000	$115,000
Auctions: $81,937, PF-65, October 2006												

d. The same beaded-border reverse die was used for Proofs of 1833, 1834, and 1835 with the crushed edge lettering; all are very rare.

CAPPED BUST, REEDED EDGE (1836–1839)

Designer: *Christian Gobrecht.* **Weight:** *13.36 grams.* **Composition:** *.900 silver, .100 copper.*
Diameter: *30 mm.* **Edge:** *Reeded.* **Mint:** *Philadelphia.*

Reverse 50 CENTS (1836–1837)

Reverse 50 CENTS, Proof

Reverse HALF DOL. (1838–1839)

Mintmark
location is
on the obverse,
above the date.

Reverse HALF DOL., Proof

History. This half dollar type features a slight restyling of John Reich's Capped Bust design, modified by Christian Gobrecht. It is of smaller diameter than the preceding type, and made with a reeded edge. The reverse is of two variations: the 1836–1837, with 50 CENTS; and the 1838–1839, with HALF DOL.

Striking and Sharpness. The key points for observation are the stars on the obverse. On the reverse, check the border letters and the details of the eagle. The 1839-O nearly always shows die cracks, often extensive (these have no effect on desirability or market value).

Availability. The 1836 is rare. The 1838-O is a famous rarity, and the 1839-O is scarce. The others are easily available in nearly any grade desired, with 1837 being the most common. Proofs are occasionally encountered of the year 1836 and are quite rare. Authentic Proofs of 1837 exist but for all practical purposes are unobtainable. Most 1838-O (a rarity) and a few 1839-O coins have been called branch-mint Proofs.

GRADING STANDARDS

MS-60 to 70 (Mint State). *Obverse and Reverse:* Grading guidelines are the same as for the 1807–1836 type, except on this type the rims are more uniform. On the 1836–1837 dates the reverse rim is generally lower than the obverse, causing the reverse to wear slightly more quickly. On the 1838–1839 type (with slightly different lettering) the wear occurs evenly on both sides, and light striking showing areas of the original planchet on the obverse does not occur here.

1837. Graded MS-62.

Illustrated coin: This example displays light gray toning with a sprinkling of gold over fully lustrous surfaces.

AU-50, 53, 55, 58 (About Uncirculated).
Obverse and Reverse: Grading guidelines are
the same as for the 1807–1836 type, except on
this type the rims are more uniform. On the
1836–1837 dates the reverse rim is generally
lower than the obverse, causing the reverse to
wear slightly more quickly. On the 1838–1839
type (with slightly different lettering) the wear
occurs evenly on both sides.

1836. Graded AU-53.

EF-40, 45 (Extremely Fine). *Obverse and
Reverse:* Grading guidelines are the same as
for the 1807–1836 type, except on this type
the rims are more uniform. On the 1836–1837
dates the reverse rim is generally lower than
the obverse, causing the reverse to wear
slightly more quickly. On the 1838–1839 type
(with slightly different lettering) the wear
occurs evenly on both sides.

1836. Graded EF-40.

VF-20, 30 (Very Fine). *Obverse and
Reverse:* Grading guidelines are the same as
for the 1807–1836 type, except on this type
the rims are more uniform. On the 1836–1837
dates the reverse rim is generally lower than
the obverse, causing the reverse to wear
slightly more quickly. On the 1838–1839 type
(with slightly different lettering) the wear
occurs evenly on both sides.

1836. Graded VF-20.

F-12, 15 (Fine). *Obverse and Reverse:* Grading guidelines are the same as for the 1807–
1836 type, except on this type the rims are
more uniform. On the 1836–1837 dates the
reverse rim is generally lower than the obverse,
causing the reverse to wear slightly more
quickly. On the 1838–1839 type (with slightly
different lettering) the wear occurs evenly on
both sides.

1839-O. Graded F-15.

VG-8, 10 (Very Good). *Obverse and Reverse:* Grading guidelines are the same as for the 1807–1836 type, except on this type the rims are more uniform. On the 1836–1837 dates the reverse rim is generally lower than the obverse, causing the reverse to wear slightly more quickly. On the 1838–1839 type (with slightly different lettering) the wear occurs evenly on both sides.

1836. Graded VG-10.

G-4, 6 (Good). *Obverse and Reverse:* Grading guidelines are the same as for the 1807–1836 type, except on this type the rims are more uniform. On the 1836–1837 dates the reverse rim is generally lower than the obverse, causing the reverse to wear slightly more quickly. On the 1838–1839 type (with slightly different lettering) the wear occurs evenly on both sides.

1838. Graded G-4.

AG-3 (About Good). *Obverse and Reverse:* Grading guidelines are the same as for the 1807–1836 type, except on this type the rims are more uniform. On the 1836–1837 dates the reverse rim is generally lower than the obverse, causing the reverse to wear slightly more quickly. On the 1838–1839 type (with slightly different lettering) the wear occurs evenly on both sides.

1836. Graded AG-3.

PF-60 to 70 (Proof). *Obverse and Reverse:* Proofs in grades of PF–60 to 62 show extensive hairlines and cloudiness. At PF–63, hairlines are obvious, but the mirrored fields are attractive. PF–64 and 65 coins have fewer hairlines, but they still are obvious when the coin is slowly turned while held at an angle to the light. PF-66 coins require a magnifier to discern hairlines, and higher grades should have no hairlines.

1836. Graded PF-64 Cameo.

1839, Regular Letters Reverse

1839, Small Letters Reverse

	Mintage	Cert	Avg	%MS	G-4	F-12	VF-20	EF-40	AU-50	AU-55	MS-60 / PF-60	MS-63 / PF-63	MS-65 / PF-65
1836	1,200+	208	48.9	18%	$1,000	$1,650	$2,000	$3,250	$5,000	$6,000	$9,000	$19,000	$63,500
Auctions: $38,188, MS-64, October 2014; $423, AU-58, September 2015; $4,113, AU-53, March 2015; $3,290, EF-45, March 2015													
1836, Reeded Edge, Proof	10–15	10	63.7								$30,000	$45,000	$90,000
Auctions: $32,900, PF-63, April 2013													
1837	3,629,820	1,464	54	36%	$70	$100	$135	$215	$475	$675	$1,200	$2,750	$16,500
Auctions: $11,456, MS-64, March 2015; $1,645, MS-62, January 2015; $425, AU-55, June 2015; $247, EF-45, August 2015													
1837, Proof	4–6	2	63.5								$30,000	$50,000	$100,000
Auctions: $32,200, PF-62, July 2008													
1838	3,546,000	1,105	53	28%	$70	$100	$135	$225	$475	$675	$1,200	$2,750	$18,000
Auctions: $17,625, MS-66, May 2015; $1,645, MS-62, January 2015; $588, AU-55, January 2015; $235, EF-45, June 2015													
1838, Proof	3–5	0	n/a								$30,000	$50,000	$100,000
Auctions: $129,250, PF-64, April 2014													
1838-O, Proof † (a)	20	3	63.7								$500,000	$750,000	
Auctions: $763,750, PF-64, January 2014													
1839	1,392,976	497	51.2	25%	$65	$100	$145	$225	$500	$750	$1,400	$3,100	$30,000
Auctions: $5,288, MS-64, March 2015; $470, AU-55, January 2015; $259, EF-45, June 2015; $235, EF-40, June 2015													
1839, Small Letters Reverse (b)		2	52.5	0%		$40,000	$55,000		$65,000				
Auctions: $50,025, AU-50, January 2010													
1839, Reeded Edge, Proof (c)	n/a	0	n/a								—		
Auctions: No auction records available.													
1839-O	116,000	270	47.2	19%	$220	$700	$1,000	$1,750	$2,100	$2,500	$3,500	$6,500	$42,500
Auctions: $129,250, MS-66, June 2014; $1,528, VF-25, June 2015; $881, VG-8, May 2015; $376, AG-3, October 2015													
1839-O, Proof	5–10	5	63.2								$100,000	$150,000	$250,000
Auctions: $92,000, PF-63, March 2012													

† Ranked in the *100 Greatest U.S. Coins* (fourth edition). **a.** The 1838-O, Proof, was the first branch-mint half dollar, though it was not mentioned in the Mint director's report. The New Orleans chief coiner stated that only 20 were struck. **b.** Extremely rare. **c.** Unverified.

LIBERTY SEATED (1839–1891)

Variety 1, No Motto Above Eagle (1839–1853): **Designer:** *Christian Gobrecht.*
Weight: *13.36 grams.* **Composition:** *.900 silver, .100 copper.* **Diameter:** *30.6 mm.*
Edge: *Reeded.* **Mints:** *Philadelphia and New Orleans.*

Mintmark location is on the reverse, below the eagle, for all varieties.

Variety 1 (1839–1853) Variety 1, Proof

Variety 2, Arrows at Date, Rays Around Eagle (1853): **Designer:** *Christian Gobrecht.*
Weight: *12.44 grams.* **Composition:** *.900 silver, .100 copper.* **Diameter:** *30.6 mm.*
Edge: *Reeded.* **Mints:** *Philadelphia and New Orleans.*

Variety 2 (1853) Variety 2, Proof

Variety 3, Arrows at Date, No Rays (1854–1855): **Designer:** *Christian Gobrecht.*
Weight: *12.44 grams.* **Composition:** *.900 silver, .100 copper.* **Diameter:** *30.6 mm.*
Edge: *Reeded.* **Mints:** *Philadelphia, New Orleans, and San Francisco.*

Variety 3 (1854–1855) Variety 3, Proof

Variety 1 Resumed, With Weight Standard of Variety 2 (1856–1866):
Designer: *Christian Gobrecht.* **Weight:** *12.44 grams.* **Composition:** *.900 silver, .100 copper.*
Diameter: *30.6 mm.* **Edge:** *Reeded.* **Mints:** *Philadelphia, New Orleans, and San Francisco.*

Variety 1 Resumed, Weight Standard
of Variety 2 (1856–1866)

Variety 1 Resumed, Weight Standard
of Variety 2, Proof

Variety 4, Motto Above Eagle (1866–1873): **Designer:** *Christian Gobrecht.*
Weight: *12.44 grams.* **Composition:** *.900 silver, .100 copper.* **Diameter:** *30.6 mm.*
Edge: *Reeded.* **Mints:** *Philadelphia, San Francisco, and Carson City.*

Variety 4 (1866–1873)   **Variety 4, Proof**

Variety 5, Arrows at Date (1873–1874): **Designer:** *Christian Gobrecht.*
Weight: *12.50 grams.* **Composition:** *.900 silver, .100 copper.* **Diameter:** *30.6 mm.*
Edge: *Reeded.* **Mints:** *Philadelphia, San Francisco, and Carson City.*

Variety 5 (1873–1874)   **Variety 5, Proof**

Variety 4 Resumed, With Weight Standard of Variety 5 (1875–1891): **Designer:** *Christian Gobrecht.*
Weight: *12.50 grams.* **Composition:** *.900 silver, .100 copper.* **Diameter:** *30.6 mm.*
Edge: *Reeded.* **Mints:** *Philadelphia, San Francisco, and Carson City.*

Variety 4 Resumed, Weight Standard   **Variety 4 Resumed, Weight Standard**
of Variety 5 (1875–1891)   **of Variety 5, Proof**

History. Half dollars of the Liberty Seated type were struck every year from 1839 to 1891. The designs varied slightly over the years, but with the basic obverse and reverse motifs remaining the same (e.g., from 1842 to 1853 the coins bore a modified reverse with large letters in the legend, and in 1846 the date size was enlarged). Large quantities were made until 1879, at which time there was a glut of silver coins in commerce. After that mintages were reduced.

The earliest Liberty Seated half dollars, dated 1839, lacked drapery at Miss Liberty's elbow. In that year Robert Ball Hughes modified Christian Gobrecht's design by adding drapery, a feature that continued for the rest of the series.

Striking and Sharpness. On the obverse, first check the head of Miss Liberty and the star centers. On coins of the Arrows at Date variety, especially 1855, the word LIBERTY tends to wear faster compared to earlier and later varieties. On the reverse, check the eagle at the lower left. Afterward, check all other features. Generally, the higher-mintage issues are the least well struck, and many New Orleans Mint coins can be lightly struck, particularly those of the 1850s. The luster on MS coins usually is very attractive. Resurfaced dies often are prooflike, some with the drapery polished away (as with 1877-S, in particular). Above and beyond issues of strike, the Small Letters coins of 1839 to 1842 have narrower, lower rims that afforded less protection to the central devices of the reverse. In contrast, the No Motto, Large Letters, coins have wider, higher rims that tend to better protect the central devices. Many pre–Civil War dates, particularly of the 1840s, show evidence of extensive die polishing in the fields (especially evident in the open expanses of the obverse). From grades of EF downward, sharpness of strike of the stars and the head does not matter to connoisseurs. Quality is often lacking, with lint marks seen on some issues of the late 1850s and early 1860s. Light striking is occasionally seen on the star centers and the head of Miss Liberty; connoisseurs avoid coins with this detraction, but most buyers will not be aware. Slide marks (usually seen on the right knee) from coin albums can be a problem, more so on Liberty Seated halves than on lower denominations of this design.

Availability. Collecting these coins is a popular pursuit with many enthusiasts. Examples of the higher-mintage dates are readily available, with earlier years being much scarcer than later ones. Most often seen among MS coins are issues from the mid-1870s onward. Circulated coins from well worn through AU can be found of most dates and mintmarks; these are avidly sought. Proofs were made in most years, with production beginning in a particularly significant way in 1858, when an estimated 210 silver sets were sold. Today, Proofs from 1858 through 1891 are readily available.

GRADING STANDARDS

MS-60 to 70 (Mint State). *Obverse:* At MS-60, some abrasion and contact marks are evident, most noticeably on the bosom and thighs and knees. Luster is present, but may be dull or lifeless. At MS-63, contact marks are very few, and abrasion is hard to detect except under magnification. An MS-65 coin has no abrasion, and contact marks are sufficiently minute as to require magnification. Check the knees of Liberty and the right field. Luster

1856-O. Graded MS-63.

should be full and rich. Most Mint State coins of the 1861 to 1865 years, Philadelphia issues, have extensive die striae (from dies not being completely finished); note that these are *raised* (whereas cleaning hairlines are incuse). *Reverse:* Comments as preceding, except that in lower Mint State grades abrasion and contact marks are most noticeable on the eagle's head, neck, and claws, and the top of the wings (harder to see there, however). At MS-65 or higher there are no marks visible to the unaided eye. The field is mainly protected by design elements and does not show abrasion as much as does the obverse on a given coin.

AU-50, 53, 55, 58 (About Uncirculated). *Obverse:* Light wear is seen on the thighs and knees, bosom, and head. At AU-58, the luster is extensive, but incomplete, especially in the right field. At AU–50 and 53, luster is less. *Reverse:* Wear is evident on the eagle's neck, the claws, and the top of the wings. An AU-58 coin has nearly full luster, more so than on the obverse, as the design elements protect the small field areas. At AU–50 and 53, there still are traces of luster.

1841-O. Graded AU-55.

Illustrated coin: Gray toning is evident on this coin. The reverse is lightly struck, a characteristic that should not be mistaken for wear.

EF-40, 45 (Extremely Fine). *Obverse:* Further wear is seen on all areas, especially the thighs and knees, bosom, and head. Little or no luster is seen on most coins. From this grade downward, sharpness of strike of stars and the head does not matter to connoisseurs. *Reverse:* Further wear is evident on the eagle's neck, claws, and wings.

1839, No Drapery From Elbow. Graded EF-40.

VF-20, 30 (Very Fine). *Obverse:* Further wear is seen. Most details of the gown are worn away, except in the lower-relief areas above and to the right of the shield. Hair detail is mostly or completely gone. *Reverse:* Wear is more extensive, with some of the feathers blended together.

1839, No Drapery From Elbow. Graded VF-20.

F-12, 15 (Fine). *Obverse:* The seated figure is well worn, but with some detail above and to the right of the shield. LIBERTY is readable but weak in areas, perhaps with a letter missing (a slightly looser interpretation than the demand for full LIBERTY a generation ago). *Reverse:* Wear is extensive, with about a third to half of the feathers flat or blended with others.

1842-O, Small Date. Graded F-12.

VG-8, 10 (Very Good). *Obverse:* The seated figure is more worn, but some detail can be seen above and to the right of the shield. The shield is discernible, but the upper-right section may be flat and blended into the seated figure. In LIBERTY at least the equivalent of two or three letters (can be a combination of partial letters) must be readable, possibly very weak at VG-8, with a few more visible at VG-10. In the marketplace and among certified coins, parts of

1873-CC, Arrows at Date. Graded VG-8.

two letters seem to be allowed. Per PCGS, "localized weakness may obscure some letters." LIBERTY is *not* an infallible guide: some varieties have the word in low relief on the die, so it wore away slowly. *Reverse:* Further wear has flattened all but a few feathers, and many if not most horizontal lines of the shield are indistinct. The leaves are only in outline form. The rim is visible all around, as are the ends of most denticles.

G-4, 6 (Good). *Obverse:* The seated figure is worn nearly smooth. At G-4 there are no letters in LIBERTY remaining on most (but not all) coins; some coins, especially of the early 1870s, are exceptions. At G-6, traces of one or two can barely be seen and more details can be seen in the figure. *Reverse:* The eagle shows only a few details of the shield and feathers. The rim is worn down, and the tops of the border letters are weak or worn away, although the inscription can still be read.

1873, No Arrows, Open 3. Graded G-6.

AG-3 (About Good). *Obverse:* The seated figure is visible in outline form. Much or all of the rim is worn away. The date remains clear. *Reverse:* The border letters are partially worn away. The eagle is mostly in outline form, but with a few details discernible. The rim is weak or missing.

1873, No Arrows, Open 3. Graded AG-3.

PF-60 to 70 (Proof). *Obverse and Reverse:* Proofs that are extensively cleaned and have many hairlines, or that are dull and grainy, are lower level, such as PF–60 to 62. These are not widely desired, save for the low mintage (in circulation-strike format) years from 1879 to 1891. With medium hairlines and good reflectivity, an assigned grade of PF-64 is appropriate, and with relatively few hairlines, Gem PF-65. In various grades hairlines are

1889. Graded PF-65.

most easily seen in the obverse field. PF-66 should have hairlines so delicate that magnification is needed to see them. Above that, a Proof should be free of such lines.

					G-4	VG-8	F-12	VF-20	EF-40	AU-50	MS-60	MS-63	MS-65
No Drapery From Elbow (1839) 		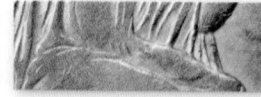 Drapery From Elbow (Starting 1839)											
	Mintage	Cert	Avg	%MS	G-4	VG-8	F-12	VF-20	EF-40	AU-50	MS-60	MS-63	MS-65
											PF-60	PF-63	PF-65
1839, No Drapery From Elbow	(a)	169	46.9	15%	$45	$120	$400	$600	$1,400	$2,800	$6,500	$30,000	$160,000
Auctions: $2,180, EF-40, January 2015; $881, VF-30, June 2015; $705, VF-25, August 2015; $595, VF-20, February 2015													
1839, No Drapery, Proof	4–6	6	63.2								$100,000	$135,000	$250,000
Auctions: $223,250, PF-64, November 2013													
1839, Drapery From Elbow	1,972,400	164	51.7	34%	$42	$55	$65	$100	$175	$350	$850	$2,300	$18,000
Auctions: $4,230, MS-64, January 2015; $541, AU-55, January 2015; $564, AU-53, January 2015; $541, AU-50, May 2015													
1839, Drapery, Proof	1–2	1	64.0									$115,000	$250,000
Auctions: $184,000, PF-64, April 2008													
1840, Small Letters	1,435,008	233	51.5	27%	$50	$60	$75	$125	$175	$300	$650	$1,300	$6,000
Auctions: $5,640, MS-65, October 2015; $329, AU-50, February 2015													

a. Included in circulation-strike 1839, Drapery From Elbow, mintage figure.

Small Letters in Legend (1839–1841)	1840 (Only), Medium Letters, Large Eagle	Large Letters in Legend (1842–1853)

1842, Small Date	1842, Medium Date

	Mintage	Cert	Avg	%MS	G-4	VG-8	F-12	VF-20	EF-40	AU-50	MS-60 / PF-60	MS-63 / PF-63	MS-65 / PF-65
1840, Medium Letters (b)	(c)	47	40.0	15%	$140	$190	$275	$450	$800	$1,600	$3,750	$7,750	$23,500
Auctions: $2,233, MS-62, February 2015; $1,028, AU-58, January 2015; $259, EF-45, May 2015; $188, VF-30, September 2015													
1840, Small Letters, Proof	4–8	7	64.0										$100,000
Auctions: $30,550, PF-63, November 2013													
1840-O	855,100	130	49.0	27%	$42	$55	$70	$115	$190	$400	$900	$3,500	
Auctions: $2,350, MS-62, January 2015; $1,410, MS-60, June 2015; $212, EF-45, June 2015; $141, VF-30, June 2015													
1841	310,000	75	54.8	32%	$42	$60	$95	$150	$275	$450	$1,400	$2,800	$9,000
Auctions: $11,750, MS-65, May 2015; $4,230, MS-64, January 2015; $857, AU-58, June 2015; $364, EF-45, August 2015													
1841, Proof	4–8	6	64.5								$20,000	$45,000	$85,000
Auctions: $30,550, PF-64, September 2013													
1841-O	401,000	115	51.0	28%	$42	$55	$65	$100	$215	$400	$950	$3,500	$19,000
Auctions: $27,025, MS-66, May 2015; $447, AU-53, July 2015; $259, EF-45, May 2015; $153, VF-30, July 2015													
1842, Sm Date, Sm Letters	(d)	0	n/a						$4,500	$7,500	$17,500		
Auctions: $99,875, MS-64, June 2014													
1842, Medium Date	2,012,764	140	50.6	21%	$42	$55	$65	$100	$150	$325	$875	$2,100	$7,000
Auctions: $2,585, MS-64, October 2015; $353, MS-60, August 2015; $360, AU-58, May 2015; $129, EF-40, September 2015													
1842, Sm Date, Lg Letters	(d)	58	52.0	28%	$42	$55	$65	$100	$150	$350	$1,175	$3,450	$23,000
Auctions: $21,150, MS-65, April 2014; $2,585, MS-63, January 2015; $306, EF-45, May 2015; $176, VF-25, August 2015													
1842, Sm Date, Lg Ltrs, Proof	4–8	5	64.2								$15,000	$27,500	$60,000
Auctions: $44,063, PF-66, June 2014													
1842-O, Sm Date, Sm Letters	203,000	34	37.2	6%	$575	$925	$1,400	$2,350	$4,500	$8,000	$18,500	$39,000	
Auctions: $35,250, MS-62, January 2014; ; $3,760, EF-40, January 2015; $764, VG-10, November 2014; $823, VG-8, September 2014													
1842-O, Med Date, Lg Letters	754,000	66	48.3	24%	$42	$55	$60	$100	$150	$350	$1,100	$4,250	$17,500
Auctions: $19,975, MS-65, January 2015; $517, AU-50, July 2015; $282, EF-45, July 2015; $212, VF-35, January 2015													
1843	3,844,000	225	50.9	28%	$42	$55	$65	$100	$150	$250	$500	$1,200	$7,750
Auctions: $4,935, MS-65, January 2015; $201, AU-50, January 2015; $212, EF-45, August 2015; $89, VF-25, March 2015													
1843, Proof	4–8	3	63.7								$15,000	$27,500	$60,000
Auctions: $70,500, PF-65Cam, August 2013; $44,063, PF-64, October 2014													
1843-O	2,268,000	106	51.5	41%	$60	$65	$70	$100	$150	$250	$700	$2,200	$15,000
Auctions: $3,290, MS-63, January 2015; $764, AU-58, August 2015; $646, AU-55, June 2015; $223, EF-40, January 2015													

b. The 1840, Medium Letters, half dollars were struck at the New Orleans Mint from a reverse die of the previous style, without mintmark. c. Included in circulation-strike 1840, Small Letters, mintage figure. d. Included in 1842, Medium Date, mintage figure.

1846, Medium Date

1844-O, Doubled Date
FS-50-1844o-301.

1846, Tall Date

1846-O, Medium Date

1846-O, Tall Date

1847, 7 Over 6
FS-50-1847-301.

	Mintage	Cert	Avg	%MS	G-4	VG-8	F-12	VF-20	EF-40	AU-50	MS-60 PF-60	MS-63 PF-63	MS-65 PF-65
1844	1,766,000	143	54.3	37%	$42	$55	$65	$100	$150	$250	$600	$1,650	$12,500
	Auctions: $12,338, MS-65, May 2015; $223, AU-50, August 2015; $129, EF-45, May 2015; $247, EF-40, February 2015												
1844, Proof	3–6	1	62.0										$125,000
	Auctions: $149,500, PF-66Cam, January 2008												
1844-O	2,005,000	109	47.0	32%	$42	$55	$70	$110	$175	$300	$900	$2,750	$13,500
	Auctions: $10,575, MS-64, May 2015; $764, AU-58, January 2015; $295, AU-50, October 2015; $376, EF-45, October 2015												
1844-O, Doubled Date (e)	(f)	19	42.6	5%	$600	$800	$1,250	$1,600	$2,750	$6,000	$12,000		
	Auctions: $6,463, AU-55, February 2013; $115, VG-8, July 2014; $235, Fair-2, October 2014												
1845	589,000	57	50.9	25%	$60	$70	$80	$120	$240	$400	$1,000	$3,350	$15,000
	Auctions: $3,055, MS-64, January 2015; $447, AU-55, June 2015; $536, AU-53, January 2015; $235, VF-30, January 2015												
1845, Proof	3–6	3	65.0								$15,000	$30,000	$67,500
	Auctions: $57,500, PF-64, May 2008												
1845-O	2,094,000	115	46.1	23%	$42	$55	$65	$100	$150	$300	$725	$2,250	$12,000
	Auctions: $329, AU-50, November 2015; $259, AU-50, November 2015; $353, EF-45, May 2015; $223, EF-40, August 2015												
1845-O, No Drapery (g)	(h)	18	51.4	22%	$50	$70	$80	$130	$275	$500	$1,400	$4,800	
	Auctions: $6,463, MS-64, June 2014												
1846, All kinds	2,210,000												
1846, Medium Date		73	51.6	29%	$42	$50	$55	$85	$150	$400	$800	$1,550	$12,000
	Auctions: $1,293, MS-63, January 2015; $705, AU-58, June 2015; $223, AU-50, May 2015; $165, EF-40, August 2015												
1846, Tall Date		105	53.3	30%	$42	$50	$60	$85	$140	$500	$900	$2,750	
	Auctions: $881, AU-58, September 2015; $588, AU-53, October 2015; $423, AU-53, May 2015; $317, EF-45, April 2015												
1846, 6 Over Horizontal 6 (i)		39	49.0	21%	$190	$260	$300	$500	$750	$1,500	$3,800	$11,000	$25,000
	Auctions: $7,050, MS-62, June 2014												
1846, Med Letters, Proof	15–20	11	63.5								$11,000	$21,000	$50,000
	Auctions: $28,200, PF-64, October 2014; $23,500, PF-63, January 2014; $14,100, PF-63, March 2015												
1846-O, Medium Date	2,304,000	94	43.7	20%	$42	$50	$55	$85	$140	$300	$1,050	$3,400	$12,000
	Auctions: $2,820, MS-62, January 2015; $588, AU-55, January 2015; $376, AU-53, July 2015; $153, VF-35, March 2015												
1846-O, Tall Date	(j)	29	37.6	7%	$175	$285	$375	$600	$1,350	$2,500	$7,500	$12,000	
	Auctions: $1,528, EF-45, January 2015; $881, VF-30, June 2015; $306, F-15, June 2015; $360, VG-10, January 2015												
1847, 7 Over 6 (k)	(l)	5	49.8	40%	$1,800	$2,500	$3,250	$4,500	$7,400	$16,000	$30,000		
	Auctions: $17,038, AU-55, May 2015; $5,875, AU-50, August 2014; $8,225, VF-35, August 2014; $5,640, VF-35, January 2015												
1847	1,156,000	113	52.5	25%	$42	$50	$65	$85	$185	$250	$500	$1,350	$7,000
	Auctions: $8,813, MS-65, May 2015; $1,410, MS-63, February 2015; $235, AU-53, May 2015; $165, EF-40, October 2015												
1847, Proof	15–20	10	63.5								$11,000	$21,000	$50,000
	Auctions: $12,338, PF-63, August 2013												
1847-O	2,584,000	93	50.6	32%	$50	$65	$70	$90	$195	$300	$800	$2,750	$18,500
	Auctions: $30,550, MS-66, May 2015; $1,880, MS-62, January 2015; $378, AU-53, February 2015; $176, EF-40, October 2015												

e. This rare variety shows all four numerals protruding from the rock above the primary date. **f.** Included in 1844-O mintage figure. **g.** The drapery is missing because of excessive polishing of the die. **h.** Included in 1845-O mintage figure. **i.** This variety can be detected in low grades. **j.** Included in 1846-O, Medium Date, mintage figure. **k.** Remains of an underlying 6 are visible below and between the primary 4 and 7. "The overdate might not be evident on later die states" (*Cherrypickers' Guide to Rare Die Varieties*, sixth edition, volume II). **l.** Included in circulation-strike 1847 mintage figure.

	Mintage	Cert	Avg	%MS	G-4	VG-8	F-12	VF-20	EF-40	AU-50	MS-60 / PF-60	MS-63 / PF-63	MS-65 / PF-65
1848	580,000	67	54.3	45%	$45	$60	$100	$180	$275	$500	$1,000	$1,750	$7,600
	Auctions: $7,638, MS-64, January 2015; $617, AU-55, March 2015; $341, EF-45, August 2015; $235, VF-35, May 2015												
1848, Proof	4–8	2	66.0								$13,000	$27,500	$60,000
	Auctions: $34,075, PF-64, June 2014												
1848-O	3,180,000	106	48.9	25%	$42	$50	$65	$85	$210	$285	$875	$2,200	$12,000
	Auctions: $940, AU-58, January 2015; $999, AU-55, June 2015; $306, EF-45, July 2015; $141, VF-35, August 2015												
1849	1,252,000	104	56.1	38%	$45	$65	$75	$90	$225	$400	$975	$2,450	$18,000
	Auctions: $10,575, MS-65, January 2015; $517, AU-58, June 2015; $400, AU-53, August 2015; $294, EF-45, March 2015												
1849, Proof	4–8	4	65.0								$13,000	$27,500	$60,000
	Auctions: $70,500, PF-66, January 2014; $38,188, PF-66, October 2014; $18,800, PF-63, October 2015												
1849-O	2,310,000	75	49.7	28%	$45	$65	$75	$90	$170	$300	$850	$2,500	$13,500
	Auctions: $793, AU-55, January 2015; $564, AU-53, January 2015; $153, VF-35, January 2015; $129, VF-30, August 2015												
1850	227,000	91	54.3	35%	$240	$325	$450	$600	$775	$1,000	$1,800	$4,000	$19,500
	Auctions: $117,500, MS-67, May 2015; $15,275, MS-65, November 2013; $764, EF-40, August 2015; $447, Fair-2, October 2014												
1850, Proof	4–8	4	63.8								$13,000	$27,500	$60,000
	Auctions: $20,125, PF-64, July 2009												
1850-O	2,456,000	90	54.5	44%	$42	$50	$60	$80	$175	$300	$650	$1,375	$9,000
	Auctions: $28,200, MS-66, May 2015; $329, AU-50, May 2015; $259, EF-40, November 2015; $165, VF-35, August 2015												
1851	200,750	52	58.6	65%	$750	$850	$1,000	$1,400	$1,750	$2,100	$2,500	$4,000	$13,500
	Auctions: $49,938, MS-66, June 2014; $2,820, AU-58, January 2015; $1,645, EF-45, September 2014; $881, Fair-2, October 2014												
1851-O	402,000	53	54.6	47%	$42	$50	$120	$140	$200	$350	$800	$2,000	$12,000
	Auctions: $999, AU-55, January 2015; $940, AU-53, September 2015; $588, EF-45, November 2015; $376, VF-35, August 2015												
1852	77,130	75	56.5	53%	$350	$475	$600	$850	$975	$1,400	$2,300	$3,100	$10,000
	Auctions: $12,338, MS-66, October 2014; $3,525, MS-62, January 2015; $2,115, AU-58, January 2015; $1,410, AU-53, July 2014												
1852, Proof	3–6	3	62.7									$35,000	$85,000
	Auctions: $74,750, PF-65, July 2008												
1852-O	144,000	43	44.7	12%	$70	$150	$275	$400	$775	$1,400	$3,500	$10,000	$29,500
	Auctions: $1,116, EF-40, June 2015; $940, VF-20, February 2015; $823, F-15, July 2015; $764, F-15, September 2015												
1852-O, Proof	2–3	1	62.0									$37,500	
	Auctions: $24,150, PF-62, May 2001												
1853-O, Variety 1 † (m)		1	40.0	0%	$200,000	$275,000	$350,000	$500,000					
	Auctions: $368,000, VF-35, October 2006; $199,750, VG-8, August 2015												
1853, Variety 2	3,532,708	1,094	50.7	26%	$42	$50	$65	$110	$265	$550	$1,450	$3,500	$22,000
	Auctions: $73,438, MS-66, January 2015; $28,200, MS-66, May 2015; $282, EF-45, October 2015; $165, VF-35, August 2015												
1853, Variety 2, Proof	5–10	4	65.0									$50,000	$150,000
	Auctions: $117,500, PF-65, October 2014; $184,000, PF-65, January 2012; $94,000, PF-64, October 2014												
1853-O, Variety 2	1,328,000	208	44.8	17%	$50	$60	$80	$160	$350	$750	$2,750	$6,500	$32,000
	Auctions: $12,338, MS-64, January 2015; $1,058, AU-55, August 2015; $259, EF-40, January 2015; $176, VF-25, June 2015												
1854	2,982,000	482	52.9	29%	$42	$50	$65	$80	$130	$325	$650	$1,700	$8,400
	Auctions: $1,645, MS-63, February 2015; $282, AU-55, June 2015; $153, EF-40, January 2015; $79, VF-30, January 2015												
1854, Proof	15–20	15	64.8								$8,500	$13,500	$30,000
	Auctions: $70,500, PF-67, November 2013												
1854-O	5,240,000	719	51.5	32%	$42	$50	$65	$80	$130	$325	$650	$1,700	$8,400
	Auctions: $5,405, MS-65, January 2015; $470, MS-61, September 2015; $494, AU-58, August 2015; $94, VF-35, January 2015												

† Ranked in the *100 Greatest U.S. Coins* (fourth edition). **m.** 4 examples are known.

1855, 1855 Over 854
FS-50-1855-301.

	Mintage	Cert	Avg	%MS	G-4	VG-8	F-12	VF-20	EF-40	AU-50	MS-60	MS-63	MS-65
											PF-60	PF-63	PF-65
1855, All kinds	759,500												
1855, 1855 Over 854		52	47.4	25%	$75	$90	$175	$300	$425	$675	$2,250	$4,500	$19,000
Auctions: $353, AU-50, November 2014; $588, EF-45, January 2015; $423, EF-45, July 2015; $411, VF-35, December 2014													
1855, Normal Date		148	54.8	39%	$42	$50	$65	$80	$135	$325	$750	$1,750	$11,000
Auctions: $881, AU-58, June 2015; $329, AU-53, January 2015; $176, EF-45, January 2015; $118, VF-35, August 2015													
1855, 55 Over 54, Proof	*1–2*	0	n/a								$10,000	$22,000	$60,000
Auctions: $30,550, PF-64, June 2014													
1855, Proof	*15–20*	9	64.6								$7,500	$12,500	$35,000
Auctions: $41,125, PF-66Cam, June 2014													
1855-O	3,688,000	513	53.0	30%	$42	$50	$65	$80	$135	$325	$750	$1,750	$9,500
Auctions: $705, MS-62, September 2015; $423, AU-58, May 2015; $172, EF-45, March 2015; $100, VF-35, May 2015													
1855-S	129,950	53	33.4	6%	$350	$550	$850	$1,750	$3,500	$7,600	$24,000	—	
Auctions: $41,125, MS-61, October 2014; $14,688, AU-55, January 2015; $8,225, AU-53, July 2014; $423, G-4, October 2015													
1855-S, Proof	*2–3*	1	65.0									$150,000	
Auctions: $276,000, PF-65, August 2011													
1856	938,000	118	53.3	35%	$42	$50	$65	$85	$130	$225	$500	$1,100	$5,750
Auctions: $16,450, MS-66, May 2015; $376, AU-58, November 2015; $188, AU-50, March 2015; $176, EF-45, March 2015													
1856, Proof	*20–30*	21	64.3								$4,000	$6,500	$23,000
Auctions: $17,625, PF-65, October 2014; $17,625, PF-65, November 2013													
1856-O	2,658,000	261	53.5	42%	$42	$50	$65	$100	$135	$225	$500	$1,100	$6,000
Auctions: $4,818, MS-65, January 2015; $470, MS-61, September 2015; $282, AU-53, May 2015; $141, EF-45, July 2015													
1856-S	211,000	35	42.5	11%	$42	$50	$175	$325	$625	$1,275	$4,250	$13,000	
Auctions: $12,925, MS-63, May 2015; $3,055, AU-58, January 2015; $881, VF-35, August 2015; $499, VF-35, October 2014													
1857	1,988,000	230	52.9	34%	$42	$50	$65	$85	$125	$250	$500	$1,100	$4,800
Auctions: $3,525, MS-65, January 2015; $764, MS-63, September 2015; $400, AU-58, July 2015; $282, AU-55, August 2015													
1857, Proof	*30–50*	38	63.8								$3,000	$4,500	$27,500
Auctions: $23,500, PF-66, June 2013													
1857-O	818,000	77	48.6	12%	$42	$50	$65	$90	$170	$300	$1,050	$3,500	$12,000
Auctions: $517, AU-58, June 2015; $259, AU-53, May 2015; $212, EF-45, August 2015; $182, EF-40, June 2015													
1857-S	158,000	37	47.1	22%	$60	$90	$175	$325	$775	$1,350	$4,850	$18,000	$35,000
Auctions: $61,688, MS-66, June 2014; $400, EF-40, August 2014; $176, VG-8, October 2014													
1858	4,225,700	580	52.9	31%	$42	$50	$65	$85	$125	$225	$450	$1,100	$5,100
Auctions: $1,058, MS-63, January 2015; $423, AU-58, August 2015; $259, AU-55, October 2015; $147, EF-45, February 2015													
1858, Proof	*300+*	64	63.8								$1,400	$2,250	$8,000
Auctions: $7,050, PF-65, February 2015; $6,756, PF-65, January 2015; $6,463, PF-64, October 2015; $1,821, PF-63, October 2015													
1858-O	7,294,000	462	48.4	20%	$42	$50	$65	$85	$130	$225	$475	$1,200	$10,000
Auctions: $411, MS-61, June 2015; $470, AU-58, January 2015; $141, EF-45, September 2015; $123, EF-40, March 2015													
1858-S	476,000	65	50.0	20%	$45	$55	$70	$120	$260	$450	$1,100	$4,000	$12,000
Auctions: $505, AU-53, March 2015; $423, AU-50, August 2015; $400, EF-45, November 2015; $235, VF-30, February 2015													

1861-O, Cracked Obverse Die
FS-50-1861o-401.

	Mintage	Cert	Avg	%MS	G-4	VG-8	F-12	VF-20	EF-40	AU-50	MS-60	MS-63	MS-65
											PF-60	PF-63	PF-65
1859	747,200	180	54.5	36%	$42	$50	$65	$85	$120	$250	$500	$1,100	$5,250
	Auctions: $18,213, MS-67, May 2015; $1,293, MS-61, January 2015; $329, AU-55, October 2015; $153, EF-40, August 2015												
1859, Proof	800	149	63.6								$1,150	$1,600	$7,250
	Auctions: $12,925, PF-67, October 2015; $7,050, PF-66, January 2015; $4,004, PF-65, September 2015; $4,700, PF-64, August 2015												
1859-O	2,834,000	231	48.7	22%	$42	$50	$65	$85	$120	$225	$450	$1,275	$7,500
	Auctions: $9,988, MS-66, May 2015; $541, MS-62, September 2015; $376, AU-55, February 2015; $141, EF-40, September 2015												
1859-S	566,000	70	56.2	53%	$45	$55	$70	$105	$225	$350	$1,050	$3,000	$14,500
	Auctions: $47,000, MS-68, May 2015; $646, AU-55, February 2015; $329, EF-40, May 2015; $306, EF-40, August 2015												
1860	302,700	77	56.0	42%	$42	$50	$65	$85	$135	$275	$600	$1,100	$5,400
	Auctions: $940, MS-62, January 2015; $423, AU-55, October 2015; $400, AU-55, May 2015; $247, EF-45, March 2015												
1860, Proof	1,000	132	63.9								$750	$1,600	$5,900
	Auctions: $29,375, PF-67, May 2015; $2,585, PF-64, January 2015; $1,998, PF-63, July 2015; $1,410, PF-63, June 2015												
1860-O	1,290,000	244	53.5	39%	$45	$55	$70	$100	$145	$250	$475	$1,300	$6,000
	Auctions: $940, MS-63, January 2015; $306, AU-55, May 2015; $235, AU-50, May 2015; $206, EF-45, August 2015												
1860-S	472,000	69	52.9	36%	$50	$70	$75	$100	$180	$300	$1,000	$3,500	$15,000
	Auctions: $1,116, AU-58, July 2015; $646, AU-55, October 2014; $165, AU-50, November 2014; $282, EF-40, April 2015												
1861	2,887,400	467	55.9	48%	$50	$60	$75	$90	$130	$235	$525	$1,100	$5,250
	Auctions: $10,575, MS-66, January 2015; $306, AU-53, May 2015; $165, EF-45, February 2015; $112, VF-35, October 2015												
1861, Proof	1,000	109	63.7								$750	$1,600	$5,900
	Auctions: $1,351, PF-63, September 2015; $823, PF-61, July 2014; $764, PF-60, January 2015												
1861-O (n)	2,532,633	293	51.3	40%	$55	$65	$80	$100	$140	$275	$500	$1,100	$5,500
	Auctions: $2,820, MS-64, January 2015; $1,528, AU-53, June 2015; $259, EF-45, March 2015; $212, F-15, October 2015												
1861-O, Cracked Obv (o)	(p)	28	37.1	4%	$200	$300	$500	$800	$1,500	$2,500	$4,500	—	
	Auctions: $16,450, MS-62, October 2014; $11,750, AU-58, September 2013; $4,700, EF-40, August 2014; $3,525, EF-40, August 2014												
1861-S	939,500	95	50.1	33%	$50	$65	$80	$95	$150	$300	$775	$2,350	$13,500
	Auctions: $3,760, MS-64, January 2015; $588, AU-55, June 2015; $259, EF-40, September 2015; $112, VF-20, August 2015												
1862	253,000	75	54.3	58%	$45	$65	$85	$110	$190	$400	$800	$1,300	$6,000
	Auctions: $18,800, MS-66, May 2015; $881, MS-62, July 2015; $282, EF-45, August 2015; $259, EF-40, February 2015												
1862, Proof	550	202	63.7								$750	$1,600	$5,900
	Auctions: $9,988, PF-65Cam, February 2015; $4,935, PF-65, February 2015; $4,230, PF-65, October 2015; $4,113, PF-65, March 2015												
1862-S	1,352,000	108	44.6	18%	$45	$60	$75	$85	$150	$275	$750	$2,400	$15,000
	Auctions: $42,300, MS-66, May 2015; $1,058, MS-61, February 2015; $793, AU-55, January 2015; $223, EF-40, August 2015												
1863	503,200	91	56.3	57%	$45	$60	$75	$90	$155	$350	$800	$1,175	$5,750
	Auctions: $24,675, MS-67, January 2015; $212, AU-50, February 2015; $329, EF-45, February 2015; $270, VF-30, December 2014												
1863, Proof	460	139	63.5								$750	$1,600	$5,900
	Auctions: $7,638, PF-66, October 2015; $4,700, PF-65, February 2015; $2,468, PF-64, March 2015; $2,233, PF-64, January 2015												
1863-S	916,000	118	54.2	39%	$45	$60	$75	$90	$145	$265	$700	$1,975	$14,000
	Auctions: $3,408, MS-64, January 2015; $588, AU-55, January 2015; $165, EF-40, September 2015; $84, VF-20, October 2015												

n. The 1861-O mintage includes 330,000 half dollars struck by the United States government; 1,240,000 struck for the State of Louisiana after it seceded from the Union; and 962,633 struck after Louisiana joined the Confederate States of America. All of these coins were made from federal dies, rendering it impossible to distinguish one from another with but one exception. **o.** In 1861, the New Orleans Mint used a federal obverse die and a Confederate reverse die to strike a handful of Confederate half dollars. That particular obverse die was also paired with a regular federal reverse die to strike some 1861-O half dollars, which today are popular among collectors, especially in higher grades. Their identifying feature is a die crack running from the denticles to the right of the sixth star down to Miss Liberty's nose (and to her shoulder below her jaw). **p.** Included in 1861-O mintage figure.

	Mintage	Cert	Avg	%MS	G-4	VG-8	F-12	VF-20	EF-40	AU-50	MS-60	MS-63	MS-65
											PF-60	PF-63	PF-65
1864	379,100	96	56.7	61%	$45	$60	$75	$100	$175	$550	$1,000	$1,600	$8,000
Auctions: $999, MS-62, July 2015; $646, AU-53, August 2015; $376, AU-50, September 2015; $306, EF-40, February 2015													
1864, Proof	470	156	63.7								$750	$1,600	$5,900
Auctions: $2,233, PF-64, September 2015; $1,175, PF-62, June 2015; $940, PF-62, September 2015; $676, PF-60, October 2015													
1864-S	658,000	68	41.8	21%	$45	$60	$75	$100	$210	$400	$900	$3,100	$15,000
Auctions: $4,700, MS-63, February 2015; $940, AU-55, January 2015; $247, VF-30, August 2015; $235, VF-25, May 2015													
1865	511,400	78	53.7	50%	$45	$60	$75	$100	$235	$500	$1,100	$2,000	$7,000
Auctions: $32,900, MS-67, May 2015; $3,290, MS-64, February 2015; $764, AU-53, June 2015; $282, EF-40, August 2015													
1865, Proof	500	201	63.9								$750	$1,600	$5,900
Auctions: $7,050, PF-66, July 2015; $4,465, PF-65Cam, June 2015; $4,700, PF-65, January 2015; $2,115, PF-64, October 2015													
1865-S	675,000	69	46.4	25%	$45	$60	$75	$100	$210	$500	$1,200	$2,900	$75,000
Auctions: $42,300, MS-65, May 2015; $705, AU-53, June 2015; $282, EF-40, May 2015; $247, VF-35, August 2015													
1866-S, Variety 1	60,000	66	28.6	12%	$450	$600	$875	$1,250	$2,300	$3,400	$6,000	$20,000	$65,000
Auctions: $164,500, MS-67, November 2013; $2,585, EF-45, August 2014; $1,410, VF-35, July 2014; $676, F-12, July 2014													
1866, Variety 4	744,900	111	51.7	50%	$50	$70	$80	$100	$145	$235	$500	$1,350	$5,850
Auctions: $5,170, MS-66, January 2015; $282, AU-53, May 2015; $200, EF-45, May 2015; $118, VF-25, August 2015													
1866, Variety 4, Proof	725	119	63.7								$700	$1,500	$3,900
Auctions: $3,643, PF-66, January 2015; $3,525, PF-66, July 2015; $2,115, PF-64Cam, November 2014; $1,116, PF-63, October 2015													
1866, No Motto, Proof † (q)	1	1	62.0								$750		$3,900
Auctions: No auction records available.													
1866-S, Variety 4	994,000	69	46.7	28%	$45	$55	$70	$85	$180	$275	$675	$2,250	$13,000
Auctions: $881, AU-55, January 2015; $259, EF-45, May 2015; $223, EF-40, August 2015; $176, VF-30, January 2015													
1867	449,300	62	51.1	40%	$42	$50	$80	$130	$210	$300	$700	$2,000	$8,000
Auctions: $999, AU-58, January 2015; $235, EF-45, May 2015; $329, EF-40, May 2015; $259, VF-35, July 2015													
1867, Proof	625	173	64.0								$700	$1,500	$3,600
Auctions: $8,225, PF-66Cam, October 2015; $3,995, PF-65Cam, February 2015; $3,290, PF-64Cam, January 2015; $793, PF-62, July 2015													
1867-S	1,196,000	94	51.1	28%	$42	$50	$65	$85	$145	$300	$775	$2,300	$12,500
Auctions: $1,116, AU-58, January 2015; $306, AU-53, January 2015; $176, EF-45, October 2015; $188, VF-30, June 2015													
1868	417,600	47	52.1	38%	$50	$60	$90	$175	$275	$400	$800	$1,500	$7,000
Auctions: $9,988, MS-65, May 2015; $1,175, MS-63, January 2015; $494, AU-55, July 2015; $259, VF-30, May 2015													
1868, Proof	600	163	63.7								$700	$1,500	$3,600
Auctions: $4,230, PF-66, February 2015; $2,585, PF-65, August 2015; $823, PF-62, July 2015; $564, PF-61, March 2015													
1868-S	1,160,000	75	49.0	16%	$45	$50	$65	$85	$145	$275	$800	$1,800	$9,500
Auctions: $17,625, MS-66, May 2015; $564, AU-55, January 2015; $353, AU-53, November 2015; $349, AU-53, March 2015													
1869	795,300	131	53.8	33%	$42	$50	$65	$85	$145	$250	$525	$1,300	$5,600
Auctions: $1,293, MS-62, June 2015; $376, AU-55, October 2015; $200, EF-45, May 2015; $200, EF-40, May 2015													
1869, Proof	600	152	63.6								$700	$1,500	$3,600
Auctions: $7,638, PF-67, May 2015; $6,169, PF-67, September 2015; $1,410, PF-64, January 2015; $1,293, PF-64, February 2015													
1869-S	656,000	56	48.4	38%	$42	$50	$65	$85	$165	$300	$825	$2,600	$7,500
Auctions: $259, AU-50, November 2015; $189, AU-50, August 2015; $141, EF-40, May 2015; $94, EF-40, February 2015													
1870	633,900	82	50.9	35%	$42	$50	$65	$85	$140	$225	$500	$1,250	$6,000
Auctions: $1,058, MS-62, January 2015; $376, AU-53, November 2015; $212, EF-40, August 2015; $165, VF-30, January 2015													
1870, Proof	1,000	129	63.2								$700	$1,350	$3,600
Auctions: $1,645, PF-64, March 2015; $1,528, PF-64, May 2015; $1,175, PF-63, September 2015; $1,058, PF-63, January 2015													
1870-CC	54,617	63	26.8	6%	$1,750	$2,750	$4,400	$8,200	$16,000	$32,000	$85,000	—	
Auctions: $17,625, EF-45, January 2015; $11,750, EF-45, January 2015; $7,050, VF-30, January 2015; $5,875, VF-25, March 2015													
1870-S	1,004,000	48	45.2	19%	$42	$50	$65	$90	$170	$450	$1,200	$3,750	$15,000
Auctions: $1,293, AU-55, January 2015; $376, EF-45, January 2015; $306, EF-40, May 2015; $176, VF-25, February 2015													

† Ranked in the *100 Greatest U.S. Coins* (fourth edition). **q.** Classified as Judd-538 (*United States Pattern Coins*, tenth edition). This fantasy piece was deliberately struck for pharmacist and coin collector Robert Coulton Davis, likely around 1869 or in the early 1870s, along with the No Motto Proof quarter and dollar of the same date.

1873, Close 3   **1873, Open 3**

	Mintage	Cert	Avg	%MS	G-4	VG-8	F-12	VF-20	EF-40	AU-50	MS-60 PF-60	MS-63 PF-63	MS-65 PF-65
1871	1,203,600	154	53.5	40%	$42	$50	$65	$85	$130	$250	$500	$1,150	$5,350
Auctions: $3,525, MS-64, May 2015; $223, AU-50, March 2015; $176, EF-45, October 2015; $91, VF-30, March 2015
1871, Proof	960	165	63.3								$700	$1,300	$3,600
Auctions: $4,230, PF-66, January 2015; $2,703, PF-65, January 2015; $1,410, PF-64, June 2015; $1,058, PF-63, January 2015
1871-CC	153,950	50	28.4	6%	$400	$700	$900	$1,500	$3,200	$5,000	$15,000	$55,000	
Auctions: $76,375, MS-64, May 2015; $3,055, EF-45, January 2015; $1,998, VF-30, January 2015; $259, AG-3, November 2015
1871-S	2,178,000	118	47.9	23%	$45	$50	$65	$85	$120	$250	$600	$1,500	$7,000
Auctions: $2,611, MS-64, May 2015; $294, AU-53, July 2015; $165, EF-45, November 2015; $112, EF-40, August 2015
1872	880,600	86	50.3	29%	$45	$50	$65	$85	$120	$285	$500	$1,400	$5,500
Auctions: $1,528, MS-62, February 2015; $329, AU-55, August 2015; $223, AU-50, May 2015; $153, AU-50, January 2015
1872, Proof	950	156	63.6								$700	$1,300	$3,600
Auctions: $5,523, PF-65Cam, June 2015; $4,935, PF-65Cam, January 2015; $4,465, PF-65Cam, February 2015
1872-CC	257,000	96	29.0	1%	$200	$300	$500	$1,050	$2,500	$4,250	$20,000	$70,000	
Auctions: $4,230, AU-53, January 2015; $447, F-12, October 2015; $282, VG-8, May 2015; $129, AG-3, October 2015
1872-S	580,000	49	47.4	27%	$45	$50	$65	$125	$240	$400	$1,300	$3,000	$13,000
Auctions: $2,820, MS-63, February 2015; $1,028, AU-55, June 2015; $353, EF-45, April 2015; $306, VF-30, May 2015
1873, Close 3, Variety 4	587,000	78	48.8	26%	$45	$55	$70	$110	$175	$300	$620	$1,200	$5,100
Auctions: $1,410, AU-58, July 2015; $212, AU-53, May 2015; $176, EF-45, July 2015; $94, EF-40, May 2015
1873, Open 3, Variety 4	214,200	16	34.2	0%	$3,100	$4,250	$5,500	$6,750	$8,000	$12,000	$21,000	$50,000	
Auctions: $55,813, MS-61, October 2014; $21,150, AU-58, January 2015; $4,230, VG-8, January 2015; $3,290, VG-8, August 2014
1873, Variety 4, Proof	600	178	63.8								$700	$1,300	$3,600
Auctions: $8,813, PF-66, June 2015; $3,290, PF-65, February 2015; $1,410, PF-64, September 2015; $618, PF-61, June 2015
1873-CC, Variety 4	122,500	48	33.2	15%	$250	$450	$750	$1,350	$2,000	$4,500	$11,000	$37,000	$65,000
Auctions: $5,053, AU-50, January 2015; $423, G-6, August 2015; $306, G-6, October 2015; $206, AG-3, November 2015
1873-S, Variety 4 (r)	5,000	0	n/a										
Auctions: No auction records available.
1873, Variety 5	1,815,200	279	51.3	36%	$45	$50	$65	$100	$230	$425	$950	$1,950	$17,500
Auctions: $1,293, AU-58, January 2015; $259, EF-45, November 2015; $159, VF-35, August 2015; $107, VF-25, February 2015
1873, Variety 5, Proof	800	141	63.7								$1,000	$2,650	$11,000
Auctions: $12,925, PF-66, September 2014; $6,463, PF-65, March 2015; $2,174, PF-63, June 2015; $1,763, PF-63, January 2015
1873-CC, Variety 5	214,560	105	37.6	14%	$225	$325	$475	$975	$2,000	$3,750	$7,500	$20,000	$52,000
Auctions: $2,497, EF-45, January 2015; $764, VF-20, June 2015; $376, VG-10, October 2015; $176, AG-3, November 2015
1873-S, Variety 5	228,000	45	46.8	20%	$55	$80	$130	$250	$450	$750	$2,500	$6,000	$35,000
Auctions: $705, AU-50, May 2015; $364, AU-50, November 2015; $208, EF-40, October 2015; $165, VF-20, May 2015
1874	2,359,600	359	53.6	42%	$45	$50	$65	$100	$230	$400	$950	$1,875	$17,000
Auctions: $25,850, MS-66, May 2015; $200, MS-60, October 2015; $364, AU-53, June 2015; $259, EF-45, August 2015
1874, Proof	700	207	63.4								$1,000	$2,650	$11,000
Auctions: $11,750, PF-66, January 2015; $6,169, PF-65, June 2015; $4,465, PF-64Cam, June 2015; $1,469, PF-62, August 2015
1874-CC	59,000	68	32.9	16%	$700	$1,300	$1,800	$2,400	$4,650	$8,250	$15,000	$28,000	$77,500
Auctions: $94,000, MS-65, May 2015; $44,650, MS-64, January 2015; $1,293, VG-10, October 2014; $1,410, VG-8, September 2014
1874-S	394,000	55	51.7	45%	$45	$50	$80	$190	$375	$700	$1,700	$3,500	$25,000
Auctions: $15,275, MS-65, January 2015; $4,406, MS-64, March 2015; $1,116, AU-55, June 2015; $282, VF-35, August 2015

r. The 1873-S, No Arrows, half dollar is unknown in any collection.

1877, 7 Over 6
FS-50-1877-301.

	Mintage	Cert	Avg	%MS	G-4	VG-8	F-12	VF-20	EF-40	AU-50	MS-60	MS-63	MS-65
											PF-60	PF-63	PF-65
1875	6,026,800	370	54.2	50%	$38	$45	$65	$80	$100	$200	$475	$800	$4,000
Auctions: $1,410, MS-64, January 2015; $1,116, MS-63, August 2015; $376, AU-58, April 2015; $129, EF-45, March 2015
1875, Proof	700	132	63.7								$700	$1,300	$3,200
Auctions: $12,925, PF-67, May 2015; $4,465, PF-66, February 2015; $3,055, PF-65Cam, January 2015; $810, PF-62, March 2015
1875-CC	1,008,000	152	46.7	39%	$55	$85	$120	$150	$250	$375	$900	$2,400	$8,500
Auctions: $881, AU-55, July 2015; $999, AU-53, January 2015; $881, AU-50, January 2015; $353, VF-30, May 2015
1875-S	3,200,000	273	58.5	70%	$38	$45	$65	$80	$100	$200	$475	$800	$4,000
Auctions: $2,820, MS-65, January 2015; $646, MS-63, August 2015; $329, AU-55, November 2015; $165, EF-45, August 2015
1876	8,418,000	406	53.8	48%	$38	$45	$65	$80	$100	$200	$475	$800	$4,000
Auctions: $3,055, MS-65, March 2015; $588, MS-62, February 2015; $176, AU-53, January 2015; $94, VF-35, January 2015
1876, Proof	1,150	214	63.5								$700	$1,300	$3,200
Auctions: $3,055, PF-65Cam, February 2015; $1,410, PF-64, November 2014; $1,116, PF-62Cam, August 2014; $646, PF-61, September 2014
1876-CC	1,956,000	206	48.9	43%	$50	$65	$90	$110	$180	$300	$725	$1,500	$5,100
Auctions: $1,528, AU-58, January 2015; $212, VF-35, August 2015; $212, VF-25, February 2015; $69, VG-10, March 2015
1876-S	4,528,000	210	53.8	50%	$38	$45	$65	$80	$100	$200	$475	$800	$4,000
Auctions: $3,173, MS-65, January 2015; $212, AU-55, July 2015; $176, AU-50, May 2015; $118, EF-45, June 2015
1877	8,304,000	358	53.8	53%	$38	$45	$65	$80	$100	$200	$475	$800	$4,000
Auctions: $6,463, MS-67, May 2015; $376, AU-58, July 2015; $200, EF-45, November 2015; $71, EF-40, March 2015
1877, 7 Over 6 (s)	(t)	0	n/a			$275	$450	$625	$900	$1,350	$3,000	$12,000	
Auctions: $3,335, MS-62, August 2009
1877, Proof	510	167	63.5								$700	$1,300	$3,200
Auctions: $11,750, PF-66Cam, February 2015; $3,290, PF-66, October 2015; $1,528, PF-64, January 2015; $881, PF-62, March 2015
1877-CC	1,420,000	236	52.9	62%	$55	$65	$80	$125	$200	$350	$800	$2,000	$5,000
Auctions: $7,931, MS-66, May 2015; $960, AU-58, January 2015; $212, VF-20, May 2015; $100, VG-10, June 2015
1877-S	5,356,000	506	56.5	57%	$38	$45	$65	$80	$100	$200	$475	$800	$4,000
Auctions: $19,975, MS-67, May 2015; $353, AU-58, March 2015; $206, AU-50, January 2015; $153, EF-45, August 2015
1878	1,377,600	104	54.1	51%	$38	$45	$65	$90	$120	$200	$485	$850	$4,250
Auctions: $705, MS-62, January 2015; $259, AU-50, November 2015; $119, VF-35, June 2015; $84, F-12, May 2015
1878, Proof	800	228	64.1								$700	$1,300	$3,200
Auctions: $35,250, PF-68, May 2015; $4,935, PF-66Cam, October 2015; $1,998, PF-64, January 2015; $969, PF-63, January 2015
1878-CC	62,000	47	28.0	17%	$700	$1,150	$2,200	$2,500	$3,500	$5,000	$9,000	$22,500	$50,000
Auctions: $64,625, MS-65, June 2014; $1,763, VG-10, September 2014; $881, G-4, November 2014
1878-S	12,000	12	39.8	50%	$30,000	$40,000	$50,000	$65,000	$67,500	$70,000	$80,000	$120,000	$195,000
Auctions: $199,750, MS-64, June 2014; $58,750, AU-50, August 2014
1879	4,800	253	60.9	83%	$275	$315	$365	$415	$525	$675	$850	$1,150	$4,000
Auctions: $2,938, MS-65, January 2015; $940, AU-55, June 2015; $881, AU-53, June 2015; $705, EF-40, January 2015
1879, Proof	1,100	315	63.7								$700	$1,300	$3,200
Auctions: $8,225, PF-67Cam, February 2015; $2,468, PF-65, March 2015; $1,410, PF-64, January 2015; $911, PF-62, March 2015
1880	8,400	104	59.7	79%	$265	$300	$340	$375	$525	$675	$850	$1,150	$4,000
Auctions: $8,225, MS-67, May 2015; $4,230, MS-66, January 2015; $1,293, AU-58, June 2015; $1,087, AU-55, June 2015
1880, Proof	1,355	376	63.8								$700	$1,300	$3,200
Auctions: $7,050, PF-66Cam, August 2015; $2,938, PF-66, January 2015; $1,645, PF-64, July 2015

s. The top portion of a 6 is visible on the upper surface of the last 7. **t.** Included in circulation-strike 1877 mintage figure.

	Mintage	Cert	Avg	%MS	G-4	VG-8	F-12	VF-20	EF-40	AU-50	MS-60 PF-60	MS-63 PF-63	MS-65 PF-65
1881	10,000	108	56.5	76%	$265	$300	$340	$375	$525	$675	$850	$1,150	$4,250
Auctions: $9,400, MS-67, June 2014													
1881, Proof	975	326	63.9								$700	$1,300	$3,200
Auctions: $9,400, PF-68, May 2015; $6,698, PF-67, July 2014; $2,820, PF-65Cam, July 2014; $2,938, PF-65, September 2014													
1882	4,400	77	58.6	75%	$280	$310	$350	$400	$535	$675	$850	$1,150	$4,250
Auctions: $4,700, MS-65, January 2015; $2,291, MS-64, January 2015; $646, VF-25, October 2015; $470, VG-8, October 2015													
1882, Proof	1,100	320	64.0								$700	$1,300	$3,200
Auctions: $15,275, PF-67Cam, November 2013; $6,463, PF-66DCam, August 2014; $6,169, PF-65DCam, August 2014													
1883	8,000	98	57.0	71%	$280	$310	$350	$400	$535	$675	$850	$1,225	$4,000
Auctions: $5,640, MS-66, May 2015; $1,116, MS-61, June 2015; $911, AU-58, June 2015; $306, AG-3, October 2015													
1883, Proof	1,039	330	64.0								$700	$1,300	$3,200
Auctions: $11,163, PF-67Cam, October 2014; $7,638, PF-67Cam, November 2014; $1,998, PF-64Cam, March 2015; $1,528, PF-63Cam, June 2015													
1884	4,400	97	60.6	87%	$325	$375	$425	$525	$625	$850	$1,100	$1,500	$4,000
Auctions: $21,150, MS-67, January 2015; $15,275, MS-67, June 2014; $1,234, EF-45, July 2015; $517, VG-10, October 2015													
1884, Proof	875	224	63.9								$700	$1,300	$3,200
Auctions: $7,931, PF-67, May 2015; $2,233, PF-65, September 2015; $1,528, PF-64, August 2015; $764, PF-61, January 2015													
1885	5,200	76	56.4	70%	$325	$375	$425	$525	$625	$850	$950	$1,500	$4,250
Auctions: $4,230, MS-66, January 2015; $1,998, MS-63, January 2015; $1,058, AU-55, February 2015; $1,410, EF-45, January 2015													
1885, Proof	930	303	64.1								$700	$1,300	$3,200
Auctions: $5,758, PF-67, September 2015; $2,585, PF-65Cam, September 2015; $1,351, PF-63Cam, March 2015; $823, PF-61, July 2015													
1886	5,000	88	57.4	78%	$400	$475	$575	$700	$800	$900	$1,100	$1,500	$4,250
Auctions: $25,850, MS-67, May 2015; $617, AU-50, June 2015; $646, VG-10, August 2015; $517, VG-8, October 2015													
1886, Proof	886	243	63.9								$700	$1,300	$3,200
Auctions: $11,163, PF-67Cam, August 2015; $3,290, PF-66, June 2015; $2,585, PF-65, January 2015; $1,116, PF-62, June 2015													
1887	5,000	115	57.3	73%	$450	$500	$600	$700	$800	$875	$1,000	$1,400	$4,250
Auctions: $24,675, MS-67, June 2014; $1,116, AU-50, August 2014; $734, EF-40, October 2014													
1887, Proof	710	184	64.2								$700	$1,300	$3,200
Auctions: $29,375, PF-68DCam, November 2013													
1888	12,001	127	57.2	71%	$250	$300	$350	$400	$475	$650	$800	$1,150	$4,000
Auctions: $8,813, MS-67, January 2015; $4,230, MS-66, January 2015; $852, AU-50, March 2015; $447, VG-10, October 2015													
1888, Proof	832	218	63.8								$700	$1,300	$3,200
Auctions: $8,225, PF-67, July 2015; $3,760, PF-66, February 2015; $2,820, PF-65, October 2015; $2,350, PF-64Cam, January 2015													
1889	12,000	112	55.9	69%	$250	$300	$350	$400	$475	$650	$800	$1,150	$4,000
Auctions: $8,225, MS-66, May 2015; $2,115, MS-64, January 2015; $823, AU-55, June 2015; $588, VF-25, October 2015													
1889, Proof	711	198	63.9								$700	$1,300	$3,200
Auctions: $2,820, PF-66, August 2015; $2,115, PF-65, March 2015; $2,233, PF-64, January 2015; $1,175, PF-63, June 2015													
1890	12,000	101	58.4	77%	$250	$300	$350	$400	$475	$650	$800	$1,150	$4,000
Auctions: $676, MS-60, February 2015; $705, AU-50, September 2015; $676, AU-50, June 2015; $411, VG-8, October 2015													
1890, Proof	590	209	64.4								$700	$1,300	$3,200
Auctions: $9,988, PF-67Cam, May 2015; $2,585, PF-65, January 2015; $1,645, PF-64Cam, February 2015; $823, PF-62Cam, January 2015													
1891	200,000	174	57.7	71%	$50	$65	$100	$125	$150	$225	$450	$1,150	$4,000
Auctions: $423, AU-55, November 2015; $541, AU-53, May 2015; $141, VF-35, August 2015; $125, VF-30, October 2015													
1891, Proof	600	191	64.2								$700	$1,300	$3,200
Auctions: $5,405, PF-67, January 2015; $4,230, PF-66, February 2015; $1,410, PF-64, January 2015; $1,175, PF-63, June 2015													

BARBER OR LIBERTY HEAD (1892–1915)

Designer: *Charles E. Barber.* **Weight:** *12.50 grams.* **Composition:** *.900 silver, .100 copper.*
Diameter: *30.6 mm.* **Edge:** *Reeded.* **Mints:** *Philadelphia, Denver, New Orleans, and San Francisco.*

Mintmark
location is
on the reverse,
below the eagle.

Circulation Strike   **Proof**

History. Charles E. Barber, chief engraver of the U.S. Mint, crafted the eponymous "Barber" or Liberty Head half dollars along with similarly designed dimes and quarters of the same era. His initial, B, is at the truncation of Miss Liberty's neck. Production of the coins was continuous from 1892 to 1915, stopping a year before the dime and quarter of the same design.

Striking and Sharpness. On the obverse, check Miss Liberty's hair details and other features. On the reverse, the eagle's leg at the lower right and the arrows often are weak, and there can be weakness at the upper right of the shield and the nearby wing area. At EF and below, sharpness of strike on the reverse is not important. Most Proofs are sharply struck, although many are weak on the eagle's leg at the lower right and on certain parts of the arrows and/or the upper-right area of the shield and the nearby wing. The Proofs of 1892 to 1901 usually have cameo contrast between the designs and the mirror fields. Those of 1914 and 1915 are often with extensive hairlines or other problems.

Availability. Most examples seen in the marketplace are well worn. There are no rarities in the Barber half dollar series, although some are scarcer than others. Coins that are Fine or better are much scarcer—in particular the San Francisco Mint issues of 1901, 1904, and 1907. MS coins are available of all dates and mints, but some are very elusive. Proofs exist in proportion to their mintages. Choicer examples tend to be of later dates, similar to other Barber coins.

GRADING STANDARDS

MS-60 to 70 (Mint State). *Obverse:* At MS-60, some abrasion and contact marks are evident, most noticeably on the cheek and the obverse field to the right. Luster is present, but may be dull or lifeless. Many Barber coins have been cleaned, especially of the earlier dates. At MS-63, contact marks are very few; abrasion still is evident but less than at lower levels. Indeed, the cheek of Miss Liberty vir-

1909. Graded MS-62.

tually showcases abrasion. This is even more evident on a half dollar than on lower denominations. An MS-65 coin may have minor abrasion, but contact marks are so minute as to require magnification. Luster should be full and rich. *Reverse:* Comments apply as for the obverse, except that in lower Mint State grades abrasion and contact marks are most noticeable on the head and tail of the eagle and on the tips of the wings. At MS-65 or higher there are no marks visible to the unaided eye. The field is mainly protected by design elements, so the reverse often appears to grade a point or two higher than the obverse.

Illustrated coin: On this example, mottled light-brown toning appears over lustrous surfaces.

AU-50, 53, 55, 58 (About Uncirculated). *Obverse:* Light wear is seen on the head, especially on the forward hair under LIBERTY. At AU-58, the luster is extensive but incomplete, especially on the higher parts and in the right field. At AU–50 and 53, luster is less. *Reverse:* Wear is seen on the head and tail of the eagle and on the tips of the wings. At AU–50 and 53, there still is significant luster. An AU-58 coin (as determined by the obverse) can have the reverse appear to be full Mint State.

1915-D. Graded AU-53.

    Illustrated coin: Areas of original Mint luster can be seen on this coin, more so on the reverse than on the obverse.

EF-40, 45 (Extremely Fine). *Obverse:* Further wear is seen on the head. The hair above the forehead lacks most detail. LIBERTY shows wear but still is strong. *Reverse:* Further wear is seen on the head and tail of the eagle and on the tips of the wings, most evident at the left and right extremes of the wings At this level and below, sharpness of strike on the reverse is not important.

1908. Graded EF-45.

VF-20, 30 (Very Fine). *Obverse:* The head shows more wear, now with nearly all detail gone in the hair above the forehead. LIBERTY shows wear, but is complete. The leaves on the head all show wear, as does the upper part of the cap. *Reverse:* Wear is more extensive, particularly noticeable on the outer parts of the wings, the head, the shield, and the tail.

1897-S. Graded VF-30.

    Illustrated coin: This coin is seemingly lightly cleaned.

F-12, 15 (Fine). *Obverse:* The head shows extensive wear. LIBERTY, the key place to check, is weak, especially at ER, but is fully readable. The ANA grading standards and *Photograde* adhere to this. PCGS suggests that lightly struck coins "may have letters partially missing." Traditionally, collectors insist on full LIBERTY. *Reverse:* More wear is seen on the reverse, in the places as above. E PLURIBUS UNUM is light, with one to several letters worn away.

1909-O. Graded F-12.

VG-8, 10 (Very Good). *Obverse:* A net of three letters in LIBERTY must be readable. Traditionally LI is clear, and after that there is a partial letter or two. *Reverse:* Further wear has smoothed more than half of the feathers in the wing. The shield is indistinct except for a few traces of interior lines. The motto is partially worn away. The rim is full, and many if not most denticles can be seen.

1915-S. Graded VG-8.

G-4, 6 (Good). *Obverse:* The head is in outline form, with the center flat. Most of the rim is there and all letters and the date are full. *Reverse:* The eagle shows only a few feathers, and only a few scattered letters remain in the motto. The rim may be worn flat in some or all of the area, but the peripheral lettering is clear.

Illustrated coin: On this coin the obverse is perhaps G-6 and the reverse AG-3. The grade might be averaged as G-4.

1892-O. Graded G-4.

AG-3 (About Good). *Obverse:* The stars and motto are worn, and the border may be indistinct. Distinctness varies at this level. The date is clear. Grading is usually determined by the reverse. *Reverse:* The rim is gone and the letters are partially worn away. The eagle is mostly flat, perhaps with a few hints of feathers. Usually, the obverse appears to be in a slightly higher grade than the reverse.

1896-S. Graded AG-3.

PF-60 to 70 (Proof). *Obverse and Reverse:* Proofs that are extensively cleaned and have many hairlines, or that are dull and grainy, are lower level, such as PF–60 to 62; these are not widely desired. With medium hairlines and good reflectivity, an assigned grade of PF-64 is appropriate. Tiny horizontal lines on Miss Liberty's cheek, known as slide marks, from National and other album slides scuffing the relief of the cheek, are endemic on all Barber

1914. Graded PF-61.

silver coins. With noticeable marks of this type, the highest grade assignable is PF-64. With relatively few hairlines, a rating of PF-65 can be given. PF-66 should have hairlines so delicate that magnification is needed to see them. Above that, a Proof should be free of any hairlines or other problems.

Illustrated coin: This is an attractive coin at the relatively low PF-61 grade.

1892-O, Normal O   **1892-O, Micro O**
FS-50-1892o-501.

	Mintage	Cert	Avg	%MS	G-4	VG-8	F-12	VF-20	EF-40	AU-50	MS-60 / PF-60	MS-63 / PF-63	MS-65 / PF-65
1892	934,000	972	59.2	74%	$27	$40	$70	$115	$210	$350	$525	$1,000	$2,600
Auctions: $39,950, MS-68, October 2015; $1,116, MS-64, January 2015; $353, AU-55, May 2015; $247, EF-45, September 2015													
1892, Proof	1,245	371	64.5								$600	$1,200	$3,100
Auctions: $7,639, PF-68, January 2015; $9,400, PF-67UCam, October 2015; $4,700, PF-66, January 2015; $2,585, PF-64DCam, August 2015													
1892-O	390,000	414	35.8	35%	$300	$380	$500	$600	$675	$750	$900	$1,600	$3,700
Auctions: $47,000, MS-68, August 2015; $588, AU-55, October 2015; $725, AU-53, January 2015; $200, G-4, February 2015													
1892-O, Micro O (a)	(b)	12	28.9	33%	$2,500	$4,250	$5,500	$7,500	$12,000	$18,500	$28,000	$40,000	$80,000
Auctions: $36,014, MS-63, June 2014													
1892-S	1,029,028	306	28.9	24%	$235	$340	$400	$500	$575	$700	$975	$2,250	$4,500
Auctions: $30,550, MS-67, October 2015; $646, EF-40, January 2015; $259, VG-8, June 2015; $188, G-6, November 2015													
1893	1,826,000	282	54.6	54%	$20	$30	$80	$160	$210	$325	$550	$1,200	$4,300
Auctions: $28,200, MS-67, August 2015; $1,058, MS-64, October 2015; $212, EF-40, September 2015; $306, VF-35, January 2015													
1893, Proof	792	277	64.5								$600	$1,200	$3,100
Auctions: $18,800, PF-68Cam, August 2015; $4,530, PF-67, February 2015; $1,265, PF-63Cam, June 2015; $564, PF-61, September 2015													
1893-O	1,389,000	212	51.5	61%	$35	$70	$130	$220	$350	$425	$700	$1,500	$8,500
Auctions: $18,800, MS-66, July 2015; $1,880, MS-64, March 2015; $505, MS-60, September 2015; $588, AU-53, July 2015													
1893-S	740,000	247	22.1	18%	$140	$210	$500	$650	$850	$1,200	$1,900	$4,500	$22,000
Auctions: $12,925, MS-65, February 2015; $1,763, AU-58, August 2015; $388, F-12, October 2015; $212, VG-10, February 2015													
1894	1,148,000	225	48.0	55%	$30	$50	$110	$200	$300	$375	$550	$1,100	$3,000
Auctions: $17,625, MS-67, October 2015; $306, AU-55, May 2015; $223, EF-40, May 2015; $188, VF-30, January 2015													
1894, Proof	972	311	64.3								$600	$1,200	$3,100
Auctions: $4,406, PF-67, June 2015; $4,113, PF-66, May 2015; $1,293, PF-64, July 2015; $3,055, PF-63, January 2015													
1894-O	2,138,000	191	49.5	57%	$25	$35	$90	$170	$300	$375	$550	$1,100	$5,400
Auctions: $14,100, MS-66, August 2015; $999, AU-58, June 2015; $194, VF-20, August 2015; $106, F-15, January 2015													
1894-S	4,048,690	227	46.3	48%	$22	$25	$70	$140	$215	$375	$600	$1,500	$8,500
Auctions: $8,813, MS-66, May 2015; $1,175, MS-63, June 2015; $329, AU-50, September 2015; $212, VF-25, June 2015													
1895	1,834,338	202	49.7	54%	$18	$25	$70	$140	$210	$400	$575	$950	$3,200
Auctions: $5,170, MS-66, October 2015; $1,058, MS-64, January 2015; $517, AU-55, October 2015; $306, AU-50, May 2015													
1895, Proof	880	357	64.6								$600	$1,200	$3,100
Auctions: $3,819, PF-67, March 2015; $3,290, PF-66, June 2015; $2,100, PF-65, November 2014; $1,755, PF-65, October 2015													
1895-O	1,766,000	152	40.4	39%	$40	$60	$130	$180	$260	$385	$625	$1,300	$6,000
Auctions: $25,850, MS-67, October 2015; $541, AU-50, July 2015; $176, EF-45, January 2015; $79, VG-10, February 2015													
1895-S	1,108,086	174	50.4	63%	$30	$55	$140	$250	$300	$385	$625	$1,400	$6,500
Auctions: $11,163, MS-66, August 2015; $794, AU-55, July 2015; $355, VF-30, January 2015; $94, F-12, May 2015													
1896	950,000	127	50.1	57%	$20	$25	$90	$160	$240	$365	$575	$950	$5,000
Auctions: $25,850, MS-67, October 2015; $1,293, MS-64, September 2015; $852, MS-63, January 2015; $176, VF-25, January 2015													
1896, Proof	762	269	64.4								$600	$1,200	$3,100
Auctions: $7,050, PF-67Cam, October 2015; $1,880, PF-64, August 2015; $940, PF-63, February 2015; $881, PF-62, June 2015													
1896-O	924,000	118	25.5	14%	$50	$70	$210	$340	$550	$825	$3,500	$8,500	$24,000
Auctions: $88,125, MS-67, August 2015; $3,525, AU-55, October 2015; $646, VF-30, January 2015; $435, VF-20, May 2015													
1896-S	1,140,948	179	25.4	23%	$115	$165	$240	$385	$575	$825	$1,550	$3,700	$9,500
Auctions: $23,500, MS-66, May 2015; $1,528, EF-45, September 2015; $881, VF-35, October 2015; $212, VG-8, February 2015													

a. This variety "was created when an O mintmark punch for quarters was used in place of the regular, larger mintmark intended for use on half dollar dies. . . . Many examples show strong strike doubling on reverse" (*Cherrypickers' Guide to Rare Die Varieties*, sixth edition, volume II). **b.** Included in 1892-O mintage figure.

	Mintage	Cert	Avg	%MS	G-4	VG-8	F-12	VF-20	EF-40	AU-50	MS-60 PF-60	MS-63 PF-63	MS-65 PF-65
1897	2,480,000	238	52.4	54%	$20	$22	$45	$95	$200	$375	$575	$950	$3,250
	Auctions: $19,388, MS-67, August 2015; $212, EF-45, January 2015; $141, VF-30, May 2015; $52, F-15, September 2015												
1897, Proof	731	325	64.8								$600	$1,200	$3,100
	Auctions: $61,688, PF-69UCam, August 2015; $18,800, PF-68DCam, January 2015; $5,875, PF-67Cam, October 2015; $4,465, PF-65Cam, January 2015												
1897-O	632,000	273	17.2	11%	$160	$230	$500	$750	$1,050	$1,300	$2,000	$4,000	$8,000
	Auctions: $25,850, MS-67, October 2015; $940, VF-25, January 2015; $259, VG-10, August 2015; $129, G-6, November 2015												
1897-S	933,900	249	21.9	18%	$150	$220	$350	$550	$800	$1,100	$1,900	$3,750	$6,750
	Auctions: $35,250, MS-67, May 2015; $4,230, AU-58, August 2015; $282, F-12, November 2015; $176, VG-8, May 2015												
1898	2,956,000	230	50.1	50%	$18	$20	$45	$95	$200	$375	$575	$950	$3,200
	Auctions: $37,600, MS-67, October 2015; $5,170, MS-66, January 2015; $482, AU-58, June 2015; $353, AU-53, January 2015												
1898, Proof	735	267	64.9								$600	$1,200	$3,100
	Auctions: $15,275, PF-68Cam, January 2015; $12,925, PF-67Cam, August 2015; $2,938, PF-66Cam, September 2015; $1,528, PF-64Cam, January 2015												
1898-O	874,000	128	33.8	29%	$38	$90	$240	$400	$540	$650	$1,200	$3,200	$8,000
	Auctions: $22,325, MS-67, October 2015; $2,233, AU-50, January 2015; $553, VF-30, July 2015; $212, F-12, August 2015												
1898-S	2,358,550	141	42.1	28%	$30	$48	$90	$185	$340	$450	$925	$3,600	$9,000
	Auctions: $4,700, MS-64, January 2015; $3,564, MS-64, September 2015; $823, AU-55, August 2015; $247, VF-30, January 2015												
1899	5,538,000	369	49.8	46%	$18	$20	$45	$95	$200	$375	$575	$1,000	$3,400
	Auctions: $19,975, MS-67, August 2015; $400, AU-58, April 2015; $376, AU-55, September 2015; $112, VF-30, February 2015												
1899, Proof	846	212	64.4								$600	$1,200	$3,100
	Auctions: $11,163, PF-68, August 2015; $3,290, PF-66Cam, October 2015; $1,234, PF-64Cam, March 2015; $646, PF-62, July 2015												
1899-O	1,724,000	134	41.4	42%	$25	$35	$80	$165	$275	$400	$685	$1,600	$7,500
	Auctions: $11,750, MS-66, May 2015; $3,760, MS-65, August 2015; $2,820, AU-58, January 2015; $141, VF-30, November 2015												
1899-S	1,686,411	128	46.9	37%	$25	$40	$90	$175	$300	$400	$685	$2,150	$5,900
	Auctions: $17,625, MS-67, August 2015; $764, AU-58, January 2015; $259, EF-45, June 2015; $141, VF-25, November 2015												
1900	4,762,000	362	52.4	55%	$17	$19	$45	$95	$200	$375	$575	$950	$3,300
	Auctions: $19,975, MS-67, October 2015; $4,700, MS-66, May 2015; $376, AU-58, August 2015; $147, VF-35, December 2015												
1900, Proof	912	286	64.6								$600	$1,200	$3,100
	Auctions: $10,869, PF-68Cam, October 2015; $7,638, PF-67Cam, August 2015; $2,115, PF-65, February 2015; $940, PF-63, January 2015												
1900-O	2,744,000	105	39.2	30%	$18	$25	$60	$170	$280	$435	$875	$3,400	$13,000
	Auctions: $37,600, MS-67, May 2015; $30,550, MS-66, August 2015; $5,170, MS-64, January 2015; $376, AU-50, May 2015												
1900-S	2,560,322	125	45.5	27%	$17	$19	$45	$100	$210	$375	$650	$2,400	$8,100
	Auctions: $22,325, MS-67, May 2015; $14,100, MS-66, October 2015; $470, AU-58, January 2015; $353, AU-53, February 2015												
1901	4,268,000	328	50.7	44%	$17	$18	$45	$95	$200	$375	$550	$950	$3,700
	Auctions: $17,625, MS-67, August 2015; $376, AU-58, January 2015; $165, VF-30, October 2015; $123, VF-25, April 2015												
1901, Proof	813	269	64.5								$600	$1,200	$3,100
	Auctions: $32,900, PF-69Cam, August 2015; $9,106, PF-68, September 2015; $1,175, PF-64, January 2015; $881, PF-63, March 2015												
1901-O	1,124,000	83	43.2	45%	$17	$26	$80	$230	$350	$475	$1,350	$4,850	$13,500
	Auctions: $6,169, MS-64, August 2015; $1,528, AU-55, September 2015; $470, VF-35, July 2015; $317, VF-20, August 2015												
1901-S	847,044	103	25.5	17%	$32	$55	$165	$350	$700	$1,250	$2,250	$10,000	$15,500
	Auctions: $11,750, MS-65, August 2015; $2,703, AU-55, September 2015; $1,410, EF-45, January 2015; $188, F-15, August 2015												
1902	4,922,000	290	49.9	44%	$17	$18	$45	$95	$200	$375	$550	$950	$3,750
	Auctions: $14,100, MS-67, October 2015; $517, MS-62, February 2015; $541, AU-58, February 2015; $84, VF-25, January 2015												
1902, Proof	777	241	64.1								$600	$1,200	$3,100
	Auctions: $4,113, PF-67, March 2015; $4,230, PF-66Cam, February 2015; $2,233, PF-65, January 2015; $1,293, PF-64, January 2015												
1902-O	2,526,000	139	44.8	39%	$17	$20	$55	$105	$220	$400	$800	$3,550	$9,200
	Auctions: $16,450, MS-67, August 2015; $1,763, MS-63, October 2015; $1,528, AU-58, June 2015; $129, VF-30, April 2015												
1902-S	1,460,670	82	43.4	44%	$19	$28	$65	$150	$250	$400	$800	$2,800	$7,750
	Auctions: $28,200, MS-67+, August 2015; $10,575, MS-66, October 2015; $5,170, MS-65, August 2015; $5,170, MS-64, October 2015												

	Mintage	Cert	Avg	%MS	G-4	VG-8	F-12	VF-20	EF-40	AU-50	MS-60	MS-63	MS-65
											PF-60	PF-63	PF-65
1903	2,278,000	120	48.8	47%	$17	$18	$45	$95	$200	$375	$550	$1,500	$7,200
	Auctions: $12,925, MS-66, May 2015; $4,230, MS-65, June 2015; $588, AU-58, June 2015; $165, VF-30, January 2015												
1903, Proof	755	260	64.5								$600	$1,200	$3,100
	Auctions: $12,925, PF-68, May 2015; $4,348, PF-66Cam, January 2015; $2,938, PF-66, June 2015; $1,382, PF-64, February 2015												
1903-O	2,100,000	178	50.9	53%	$17	$18	$55	$125	$210	$400	$675	$1,600	$8,200
	Auctions: $9,988, MS-66, May 2015; $4,230, MS-65, August 2015; $646, AU-55, January 2015; $353, EF-45, January 2015												
1903-S	1,920,772	118	45.4	52%	$17	$19	$60	$130	$230	$400	$675	$1,700	$4,900
	Auctions: $17,625, MS-67, May 2015; $1,763, AU-58, July 2015; $308, EF-40, January 2015; $153, VF-25, February 2015												
1904	2,992,000	199	49.5	45%	$17	$18	$35	$85	$200	$375	$550	$1,000	$4,100
	Auctions: $4,465, MS-66, August 2015; $250, AU-55, May 2015; $259, EF-45, May 2015; $89, VF-25, January 2015												
1904, Proof	670	257	64.3								$600	$1,200	$3,100
	Auctions: $12,925, PF-68, October 2015; $3,878, PF-67, October 2015; $2,820, PF-66, July 2015; $2,291, PF-65, January 2015												
1904-O	1,117,600	90	39.8	24%	$22	$35	$95	$235	$400	$600	$1,250	$3,750	$10,750
	Auctions: $12,925, MS-66, October 2015; $2,233, MS-60, June 2015; $705, AU-55, June 2015; $881, EF-45, January 2015												
1904-S	553,038	188	21.6	10%	$48	$115	$340	$775	$1,500	$2,300	$9,500	$19,500	$39,000
	Auctions: $91,063, MS-67, August 2015; $3,055, EF-45, July 2015; $2,820, VF-35, January 2015; $353, F-12, October 2015												
1905	662,000	125	46.9	49%	$25	$29	$85	$185	$265	$375	$600	$1,600	$5,500
	Auctions: $16,450, MS-67, October 2015; $4,583, MS-65, January 2015; $823, AU-58, July 2015; $223, EF-45, February 2015												
1905, Proof	727	214	64.1								$600	$1,200	$3,100
	Auctions: $9,106, PF-68, August 2015; $2,585, PF-66, October 2015; $2,350, PF-65, March 2015; $1,645, PF-64, January 2015												
1905-O	505,000	128	47.9	63%	$30	$45	$125	$225	$325	$450	$750	$1,750	$4,200
	Auctions: $56,400, MS-68, January 2015; $8,813, MS-67, October 2015; $2,233, AU-58, June 2015; $118, F-12, January 2015												
1905-S	2,494,000	126	40.9	37%	$16	$19	$53	$140	$240	$400	$650	$1,950	$8,500
	Auctions: $14,100, MS-67, August 2015; $1,410, AU-58, August 2015; $259, EF-45, April 2015; $179, VF-30, May 2015												
1906	2,638,000	362	51.7	55%	$16	$17	$45	$95	$200	$375	$550	$950	$3,000
	Auctions: $15,275, MS-67, August 2015; $2,703, MS-65, March 2015; $329, AU-53, January 2015; $188, EF-45, May 2015												
1906, Proof	675	258	64.5								$600	$1,200	$3,100
	Auctions: $10,869, PF-68, May 2015; $4,230, PF-67, October 2015; $2,938, PF-66, July 2015; $2,176, PF-65, January 2015												
1906-D	4,028,000	284	48.0	46%	$16	$17	$45	$95	$200	$375	$550	$950	$3,000
	Auctions: $47,000, MS-67, May 2015; $423, AU-58, June 2015; $223, EF-45, August 2015; $118, VF-30, February 2015												
1906-O	2,446,000	128	41.1	35%	$16	$19	$42	$95	$200	$400	$625	$1,400	$5,500
	Auctions: $18,800, MS-67, May 2015; $7,050, MS-66, October 2015; $282, EF-45, September 2015; $94, F-15, June 2015												
1906-S	1,740,154	130	49.2	50%	$16	$19	$53	$115	$210	$375	$625	$1,400	$4,750
	Auctions: $15,275, MS-67, May 2015; $940, MS-62, February 2015; $1,058, AU-55, January 2015; $212, VF-25, January 2015												
1907	2,598,000	318	54.3	63%	$16	$17	$45	$95	$200	$375	$550	$950	$2,800
	Auctions: $3,995, MS-66, January 2015; $881, MS-63, October 2015; $282, AU-53, May 2015; $165, VF-35, February 2015												
1907, Proof	575	187	64.3								$600	$1,200	$3,100
	Auctions: $18,800, PF-68, June 2014												
1907-D	3,856,000	338	48.6	48%	$16	$17	$45	$95	$200	$375	$550	$950	$2,800
	Auctions: $3,055, MS-66, October 2015; $1,116, MS-63, August 2015; $353, AU-53, April 2015; $112, VF-30, May 2015												
1907-O	3,946,600	294	49.4	55%	$16	$17	$45	$95	$200	$375	$550	$950	$2,800
	Auctions: $16,450, MS-67, August 2015; $306, AU-50, January 2015; $153, EF-40, August 2015; $212, VF-35, May 2015												
1907-S	1,250,000	97	36.7	32%	$18	$30	$85	$185	$375	$650	$1,275	$5,700	$11,000
	Auctions: $17,625, MS-67, October 2015; $2,585, AU-53, January 2015; $450, VF-35, May 2015; $165, F-15, May 2015												
1908	1,354,000	191	52.2	60%	$16	$17	$45	$95	$200	$375	$550	$950	$2,800
	Auctions: $12,925, MS-67, August 2015; $2,233, MS-65, June 2015; $1,058, MS-64, March 2015; $911, MS-63, January 2015												
1908, Proof	545	178	64.3								$600	$1,200	$3,100
	Auctions: $7,050, PF-68, October 2015; $2,115, PF-65, June 2015; $823, PF-63, September 2015; $764, PF-62, June 2015												
1908-D	3,280,000	364	46.5	45%	$16	$17	$45	$95	$200	$375	$550	$950	$2,600
	Auctions: $22,325, MS-68, October 2015; $2,350, MS-65, March 2015; $306, AU-55, January 2015; $176, EF-45, September 2015												
1908-O	5,360,000	293	46.6	48%	$16	$17	$45	$95	$200	$375	$550	$950	$2,600
	Auctions: $15,275, MS-67, August 2015; $793, MS-63, June 2015; $646, AU-58, January 2015; $646, AU-53, May 2015												
1908-S	1,644,828	101	38.0	41%	$16	$25	$75	$160	$275	$435	$875	$2,400	$5,100
	Auctions: $7,050, MS-66, August 2015; $3,819, MS-65, March 2015; $3,055, MS-64, January 2015; $2,585, AU-58, August 2015												

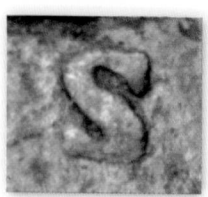

1909-S, Inverted Mintmark
FS-50-1909S-501.

1911-S, Repunched Mintmark
FS-50-1911S-501.

	Mintage	Cert	Avg	%MS	G-4	VG-8	F-12	VF-20	EF-40	AU-50	MS-60 / PF-60	MS-63 / PF-63	MS-65 / PF-65
1909	2,368,000	473	49.4	54%	$16	$17	$45	$95	$200	$375	$550	$950	$3,250
	Auctions: $3,760, MS-66, May 2015; $447, AU-55, February 2015; $306, AU-53, October 2015; $165, EF-40, January 2015												
1909, Proof	650	283	64.5								$600	$1,200	$3,100
	Auctions: $11,163, PF-68Cam, May 2015; $1,880, PF-64, January 2015; $940, PF-63, October 2015; $881, PF-62, June 2015												
1909-O	925,400	153	36.2	37%	$18	$22	$65	$175	$375	$650	$1,400	$1,650	$4,800
	Auctions: $$16,450, MS-66, May 2015; $2,820, MS-64, September 2015; $705, AU-50, July 2015; $106, F-15, August 2015												
1909-S	1,764,000	152	36.0	32%	$16	$17	$45	$95	$200	$375	$600	$1,300	$4,100
	Auctions: $17,625, MS-67, May 2015; $3,525, MS-65, January 2015; $329, EF-45, January 2015; $259, EF-40, February 2015												
1909-S, Inverted Mintmark (c)	(d)	0	n/a							$425	$675	$1,550	
	Auctions: $11,750, MS-67, October 2015; $4,406, MS-66, November 2014; $141, VF-35, June 2015; $206, VF-30, August 2014												
1910	418,000	168	47.1	51%	$20	$30	$95	$175	$320	$410	$600	$1,100	$3,400
	Auctions: $8,225, MS-66, August 2015; $646, MS-61, September 2015; $764, AU-58, October 2015; $188, VF-25, May 2015												
1910, Proof	551	255	64.6								$600	$1,200	$3,100
	Auctions: $15,275, PF-68, October 2015; $5,875, PF-67Cam, January 2015; $1,175, PF-64, August 2015												
1910-S	1,948,000	131	37.7	34%	$18	$20	$35	$95	$200	$375	$650	$2,000	$5,750
	Auctions: $15,275, MS-67, October 2015; $376, AU-50, January 2015; $147, VF-35, October 2015; $141, VF-30, May 2015												
1911	1,406,000	325	53.5	60%	$16	$17	$45	$95	$200	$375	$550	$950	$2,600
	Auctions: $4,702, MS-66, August 2015; $494, MS-62, January 2015; $306, AU-55, January 2015; $129, VF-30, January 2015												
1911, Proof	543	236	64.5								$600	$1,200	$3,100
	Auctions: $16,450, PF-67, October 2015; $1,175, PF-64, October 2015; $588, PF-62, September 2015; $541, PF-61, June 2015												
1911-D	695,080	151	51.3	58%	$16	$17	$45	$95	$200	$375	$550	$950	$3,500
	Auctions: $15,275, MS-67, October 2015; $2,115, MS-65, September 2015; $1,704, MS-64, June 2015; $1,177, MS-64, July 2015												
1911-S	1,272,000	112	37.0	32%	$18	$20	$40	$100	$210	$385	$650	$1,500	$5,200
	Auctions: $42,300, MS-67, August 2015; $3,532, MS-65, August 2015; $118, VF-30, April 2015; $106, VF-25, February 2015												
1911-S, Repunched Mintmark (e)	(f)	0	n/a							$475	$750	$1,600	$5,400
	Auctions: $4,888, MS-65, December 2009												
1912	1,550,000	391	51.7	57%	$16	$17	$45	$95	$200	$375	$550	$950	$2,600
	Auctions: $15,275, MS-66, May 2015; $2,233, MS-65, January 2015; $1,116, MS-64, January 2015												
1912, Proof	700	197	64.0								$600	$1,200	$3,100
	Auctions: $8,813, PF-68, May 2015; $4,465, PF-67, January 2015; $1,763, PF-65, October 2015; $881, PF-63, June 2015												
1912-D	2,300,800	573	50.5	54%	$16	$17	$45	$95	$200	$375	$550	$950	$2,600
	Auctions: $4,700, MS-66, October 2015; $353, AU-58, February 2015; $176, EF-40, May 2015; $94, VF-20, July 2015												
1912-S	1,370,000	224	41.7	46%	$16	$18	$45	$100	$200	$425	$600	$1,150	$4,100
	Auctions: $12,338, MS-67, August 2015; $376, AU-50, October 2015; $200, EF-40, January 2015; $129, VF-25, January 2015												
1913	188,000	420	18.9	13%	$75	$90	$210	$425	$650	$825	$1,350	$2,000	$4,500
	Auctions: $8,225, MS-66, October 2015; $494, VF-20, June 2015; $79, VG-8, February 2015; $59, G-6, August 2015												
1913, Proof	627	196	64.0								$700	$1,300	$3,200
	Auctions: $3,055, PF-66, October 2015; $1,293, PF-64, August 2015; $940, PF-63, June 2015; $541, PF-62, June 2015												
1913-D	534,000	267	53.3	54%	$16	$17	$45	$95	$200	$375	$550	$950	$4,350
	Auctions: $7,050, MS-66, August 2015; $282, AU-55, July 2015; $353, AU-53, April 2015; $306, EF-40, November 2015												
1913-S	604,000	152	43.9	51%	$16	$25	$55	$120	$275	$400	$635	$1,375	$3,900
	Auctions: $21,150, MS-67, October 2015; $12,925, MS-66, September 2015; $1,763, MS-64, January 2015												

c. The S mintmark was punched into the die upside-down (with the top slightly wider than the base). d. Included in 1909-S mintage figure. e. The lower serif of the underlying mintmark is visible protruding from the primary serif. f. Included in 1911-S mintage figure.

	Mintage	Cert	Avg	%MS	G-4	VG-8	F-12	VF-20	EF-40	AU-50	MS-60	MS-63	MS-65
											PF-60	PF-63	PF-65
1914	124,230	479	21.4	18%	$150	$170	$315	$550	$775	$900	$1,400	$2,100	$7,500
	Auctions: $9,988, MS-65, January 2015; $2,585, AU-58, September 2015; $294, F-15, May 2015; $129, VG-8, February 2015												
1914, Proof	380	173	64.5								$800	$1,450	$3,400
	Auctions: $5,875, PF-67, October 2015; $4,700, PF-66, June 2015; $2,056, PF-64, October 2015; $423, PF-58, June 2015												
1914-S	992,000	187	41.7	44%	$16	$20	$40	$100	$200	$400	$600	$1,150	$4,350
	Auctions: $22,325, MS-66, February 2015; $235, EF-40, January 2015; $118, VF-25, May 2015; $79, F-15, March 2015												
1915	138,000	513	16.3	7%	$110	$140	$285	$375	$575	$850	$1,350	$2,250	$5,750
	Auctions: $11,750, MS-66, August 2015; $881, AU-50, February 2015; $764, EF-40, January 2015; $223, F-15, October 2015												
1915, Proof	450	177	64.5								$800	$1,400	$3,400
	Auctions: $15,275, PF-68, May 2015; $2,703, PF-66, January 2015; $3,290, PF-65, October 2015; $1,528, PF-64, August 2015												
1915-D	1,170,400	651	53.1	59%	$16	$17	$45	$95	$200	$375	$550	$950	$2,600
	Auctions: $4,465, MS-66, July 2015; $188, AU-50, February 2015; $188, EF-45, October 2015; $165, EF-40, May 2015												
1915-S	1,604,000	498	49.5	56%	$16	$17	$45	$95	$200	$375	$550	$950	$2,600
	Auctions: $8,225, MS-67, August 2015; $588, AU-58, October 2015; $112, VF-25, May 2015; $52, F-12, February 2015												

LIBERTY WALKING (1916–1947)

Designer: *Adolph A. Weinman.* **Weight:** *12.50 grams.*
Composition: *.900 silver, .100 copper (net weight .36169 oz. pure silver).*
Diameter: *30.6 mm.* **Edge:** *Reeded.* **Mints:** *Philadelphia, Denver, and San Francisco.*

Circulation Strike   Proof

Mintmark location,
1916–1917, is on the
obverse, below the motto.

Mintmark location,
1917–1947, is on the
reverse, below the branch.

History. The Liberty Walking half dollar was designed by Adolph A. Weinman, the sculptor who also created the Mercury or Winged Liberty Head dime. His monogram appears under the tips of the eagle's wing feathers. Mintage was intermittent from 1916 to 1947, with none struck in 1922, 1924, 1925, 1926, 1930, 1931, and 1932. On the 1916 coins and some of the 1917 coins, the mintmark is located on the obverse, below IN GOD WE TRUST. Other coins of 1917, and those through 1947, have the mintmark on the reverse, under the pine branch.

Striking and Sharpness. Most circulation-strike Liberty Walking half dollars are lightly struck. In this respect they are similar to Standing Liberty quarters of the same era. On the obverse, the key points to check are Miss Liberty's left hand, the higher parts and lines in the skirt, and her head; after that, check all other areas. *Very few* coins are sharply struck in these areas, and for some issues sharp strikes might not exist at all. On the reverse, check the breast of the eagle.

Proofs were made beginning in 1936 and continuing through 1942. The entire die was polished (including the figure of Miss Liberty and the eagle), generating coins of low contrast. Proofs are usually fairly well struck. Most Proofs of 1941 are from over-polished dies, with the AW monogram of the designer no longer present. Striking sharpness can vary. Seek coins with full head and left-hand details.

Availability. All dates and mintmarks are readily collectible, although some, such as 1917-S (obverse mintmark), 1919-D, the three issues of 1921, and 1938-D, are scarce. Earlier years are often seen with extensive wear. MS coins are most often seen of the three issues of 1916, the 1917, and those of 1933 to 1947. Collectors saved the issues of the 1940s in large quantities, making the coins common today. As noted, coins with Full Details can range from scarce to extremely rare for certain dates. Half dollars dated 1928-D are counterfeit.

Note: Values of common-date silver coins have been based on the current bullion price of silver, $15.50 per ounce, and may vary with the prevailing spot price.

GRADING STANDARDS

MS-60 to 70 (Mint State). *Obverse:* At MS-60, some abrasion and contact marks are evident on the higher areas, which are also the areas most likely to be weakly struck. This includes Miss Liberty's left arm, her hand, and the areas of the skirt covering her left leg. The luster may not be complete in those areas on weakly struck coins (even those certified above MS-65)—the *original planchet surface* may be revealed, as it was not smoothed out by strik-

1917. Graded MS-65.

ing. Accordingly, grading is best done by evaluating abrasion as it is observed *in the right field*, plus evaluating the mint luster. Luster may be dull or lifeless at MS–60 to 62, but should have deep frost at MS-63 or better, particularly in the lower-relief areas. At MS-65 or better, it should be full and rich. Sometimes, to compensate for flat striking, certified coins with virtually flawless luster in the fields, evocative of an MS–65 or 66 grade, are called MS-63 or a lower grade. Such coins would seem to offer a lot of value for the money, if the variety is one that is not found with Full Details (1923-S is one of many examples). *Reverse:* Striking is usually better, permitting observation of luster in all areas except the eagle's body, which may be lightly struck. Luster may be dull or lifeless at MS–60 to 62, but should have deep frost at MS-63 or better, particularly in the lower-relief areas. At MS-65 or better, it should be full and rich.

Illustrated coin: This is a lustrous gem example.

AU-50, 53, 55, 58 (About Uncirculated). *Obverse:* Light wear is seen on the higher-relief areas of Miss Liberty, the vertical area from her head down to the date. At AU-58, the luster in the field is extensive, but is interrupted by friction and light wear. At AU–50 and 53, luster is less. *Reverse:* Wear is most evident on the eagle's breast immediately under the neck feathers, the left leg, and the top of the left wing. Luster is nearly complete at AU-58, but at AU-50 half or more is gone.

1921. Graded AU-50.

EF-40, 45 (Extremely Fine). *Obverse:* Wear is more extensive, with the higher parts of Miss Liberty now without detail, and with no skirt lines visible directly over her left leg. Little or no luster is seen. *Reverse:* The eagle shows more wear overall, with the highest parts of the body and left leg worn flat.

1919. Graded EF-40.

VF-20, 30 (Very Fine). *Obverse:* Wear is more extensive, and Miss Liberty is worn mostly flat in the line from her head to her left foot. Her skirt is worn, but most lines are seen, except over the leg and to the left and right. The lower part of her cape (to the left of her waist) is worn. *Reverse:* The eagle is worn smooth from the head to the left leg, and the right leg is flat at the top. Most feathers in the wings are delineated, but weak.

1921-S. Graded VF-20.

F-12, 15 (Fine). *Obverse:* Wear is more extensive, now with only a few light lines visible in the skirt. The rays of the sun are weak below the cape, and may be worn away at their tips. *Reverse:* Wear is more extensive, with most details now gone on the eagle's right leg. Delineation of the feathers is less, and most in the upper area and right edge of the left wing are blended together.

1918-S. Graded F-12.

VG-8, 10 (Very Good). *Obverse:* Wear is slightly more extensive, but the rim still is defined all around. The tops of the date numerals are worn and blend slightly into the ground above. *Reverse:* Wear is more extensive. On the left wing only a few feathers are delineated, and on the shoulder of the right wing most detail is gone. Detail in the pine branch is lost and it appears as a clump.

1921-D. Graded VG-8.

G-4, 6 (Good). *Obverse:* Miss Liberty is worn flat, with her head, neck, and arms all blended together. Folds can be seen at the bottom of the skirt, but the lines are worn away. The rim is worn done into the tops of some of the letters. *Reverse:* All areas show more wear. The rim is worn down into the tops of some of the letters, particularly at the top border.

1917-S, Obverse Mintmark. Graded G-4.

AG-3 (About Good). *Obverse:* Wear is more extensive. The sun's rays are nearly all gone, the motto is very light and sometimes incomplete, and the rim is worn down into more of the letters. *Reverse:* Wear is more extensive, with the eagle essentially worn flat. The rim is worn down into more of the letters.

1918. Graded AG-3.

PF-60 to 70 (Proof). *Obverse and Reverse:* Proofs that are extensively cleaned and have many hairlines, or that are dull and grainy, are lower level, such as PF–60 to 62. These are not widely desired, and represent coins that have been mistreated. With medium hairlines and good reflectivity, assigned grades of PF–63 or 64 are appropriate. Tiny horizontal lines on Miss Liberty's leg, known as slide marks, from National and other album slides scuffing the relief of the cheek, are common; coins with such marks should not be graded higher than PF-64, but sometimes are. With relatively few hairlines and no noticeable slide marks, a rating of PF-65 can be given. PF-66 should have hairlines so delicate that magnification is needed to see them. Above that, a Proof should be free of any hairlines or other problems.

1939. Graded PF-65.

Illustrated coin: This example is a brilliant gem Proof.

	Mintage	Cert	Avg	%MS	G-4	VG-8	F-12	VF-20	EF-40	AU-50	MS-60	MS-63	MS-65
											PF-64	PF-65	PF-67
1916	608,000	1,512	53.4	70%	$50	$55	$90	$160	$225	$265	$350	$650	$2,200
	Auctions: $35,250, MS-67, August 2015; $588, MS-61, August 2015; $329, AU-55, May 2015; $118, F-15, February 2015												
1916-D, Obverse Mintmark	1,014,400	1,724	52.3	65%	$50	$60	$85	$135	$215	$240	$360	$725	$2,600
	Auctions: $4,935, MS-66, August 2015; $400, AU-58, October 2015; $200, EF-45, February 2015; $141, VF-25, February 2015												
1916-S, Obverse Mintmark	508,000	1,025	35.2	40%	$120	$140	$275	$435	$650	$800	$1,200	$2,100	$6,000
	Auctions: $9,988, MS-65, June 2015; $1,821, AU-58, August 2015; $411, VF-25, January 2015; $160, VG-10, December 2015												

	Mintage	Cert	Avg	%MS	G-4	VG-8	F-12	VF-20	EF-40	AU-50	MS-60 / PF-64	MS-63 / PF-65	MS-65 / PF-67
1917	12,292,000	2,205	61.8	84%	$18	$19	$19.50	$21	$40	$70	$150	$210	$1,100
	Auctions: $2,233, MS-66, June 2015; $353, MS-64, August 2015; $118, MS-61, April 2015; $94, AU-58, February 2015												
1917-D, Obverse Mintmark	765,400	982	53.8	61%	$25	$35	$80	$150	$240	$325	$600	$1,150	$7,500
	Auctions: $32,900, MS-66, August 2015; $5,640, MS-65, September 2015; $705, AU-58, February 2015; $282, EF-45, April 2015												
1917-S, Obverse Mintmark	952,000	557	44.1	43%	$27	$50	$140	$375	$750	$1,300	$2,750	$5,500	$23,000
	Auctions: $152,750, MS-67, August 2015; $21,150, MS-65, August 2015; $376, VF-35, February 2015; $112, F-12, January 2015												
1917-D, Reverse Mintmark	1,940,000	597	54.2	50%	$18	$19	$45	$145	$280	$515	$950	$2,200	$16,000
	Auctions: $28,200, MS-66, August 2015; $1,410, AU-58, February 2015; $470, AU-53, November 2015; $141, VF-30, June 2015												
1917-S, Reverse Mintmark	5,554,000	887	58.3	69%	$18	$19	$20	$35	$70	$170	$425	$1,800	$12,000
	Auctions: $37,600, MS-66, August 2015; $10,869, MS-65, January 2015; $541, AU-58, October 2015; $212, EF-45, February 2015												
1918	6,634,000	783	58.5	68%	$18	$19	$20	$65	$155	$265	$625	$1,250	$4,500
	Auctions: $32,900, MS-66, August 2015; $4,230, MS-65, June 2015; $306, AU-55, May 2015; $84, VF-35, August 2015												
1918-D	3,853,040	755	54.6	60%	$18	$19	$38	$100	$250	$475	$1,300	$3,500	$30,000
	Auctions: $99,875, MS-66, August 2015; $35,250, MS-65, August 2015; $84, VF-30, January 2015; $40, F-15, September 2015												
1918-S	10,282,000	908	57.8	67%	$18	$19	$20	$35	$80	$200	$475	$1,750	$16,000
	Auctions: $18,800, MS-65, August 2015; $4,700, MS-64, March 2015; $376, AU-55, May 2015; $123, EF-45, January 2015												
1919	962,000	552	44.0	43%	$25	$32	$78	$265	$515	$825	$1,350	$3,500	$6,800
	Auctions: $54,050, MS-67, August 2015; $32,900, MS-66, May 2015; $4,113, MS-64, January 2015; $1,116, AU-53, October 2015												
1919-D	1,165,000	598	41.4	38%	$26	$40	$115	$345	$825	$1,900	$4,500	$13,000	$160,000
	Auctions: $30,550, MS-64, August 2015; $1,939, AU-50, July 2015; $1,058, EF-45, September 2015; $106, F-12, January 2015												
1919-S	1,552,000	482	40.4	29%	$20	$30	$85	$275	$815	$1,600	$3,250	$8,750	$25,000
	Auctions: $42,300, MS-66, August 2015; $11,750, MS-64, January 2015; $2,233, AU-50, June 2015; $764, EF-40, January 2015												
1920	6,372,000	849	59.9	76%	$18	$19	$20	$45	$80	$160	$325	$700	$4,200
	Auctions: $7,050, MS-66, January 2015; $564, MS-63, August 2015; $329, AU-58, April 2015; $123, EF-45, August 2015												
1920-D	1,551,000	363	44.9	46%	$18	$20	$75	$250	$450	$925	$2,500	$4,500	$15,000
	Auctions: $54,050, MS-66, August 2015; $2,585, AU-58, June 2015; $823, EF-45, June 2015; $235, VF-25, March 2015												
1920-S	4,624,000	509	52.6	53%	$18	$18.50	$23	$90	$230	$475	$875	$3,000	$14,000
	Auctions: $58,750, MS-66, August 2015; $999, AU-58, January 2015; $376, EF-45, August 2015; $141, VF-35, April 2015												
1921	246,000	1,258	19.6	15%	$175	$220	$350	$775	$1,700	$2,900	$5,750	$7,500	$20,000
	Auctions: $54,050, MS-66, August 2015; $10,575, MS-64, January 2015; $1,410, VF-35, August 2015; $176, VG-8, January 2015												
1921-D	208,000	1,471	17.3	12%	$250	$375	$525	$850	$2,500	$5,000	$8,000	$14,000	$35,000
	Auctions: $94,000, MS-66, August 2015; $3,290, EF-40, March 2015; $1,175, VF-20, January 2015; $259, VG-8, February 2015												
1921-S	548,000	1,163	20.1	9%	$48	$80	$250	$800	$4,500	$7,500	$20,000	$32,000	$110,000
	Auctions: $117,500, MS-65, August 2015; $8,813, AU-53, March 2015; $3,055, EF-40, January 2015; $229, F-15, May 2015												
1923-S	2,178,000	441	50.2	51%	$13	$15	$30	$110	$365	$1,050	$2,100	$4,500	$16,000
	Auctions: $25,850, MS-66, August 2015; $2,233, MS-62, September 2015; $1,645, AU-55, February 2015; $376, EF-40, September 2015												
1927-S	2,392,000	621	57.2	70%	$13	$15	$18	$50	$160	$450	$1,200	$2,050	$9,750
	Auctions: $44,650, MS-66, August 2015; $969, AU-55, August 2015; $707, AU-53, June 2015; $259, EF-45, October 2015												
1928-S (a,b)	1,940,000	496	55.4	64%	$13	$15	$19	$75	$180	$500	$1,250	$3,000	$10,000
	Auctions: $25,850, MS-66, August 2015; $8,813, MS-65, September 2015; $1,410, AU-58, June 2015; $940, AU-55, January 2015												
1929-D	1,001,200	871	58.1	61%	$12	$15	$18	$30	$100	$190	$400	$800	$2,700
	Auctions: $5,405, MS-66, May 2015; $646, MS-63, August 2015; $282, AU-55, January 2015; $118, EF-45, August 2015												
1929-S	1,902,000	788	58.0	69%	$12	$15	$18	$35	$115	$230	$425	$1,200	$3,000
	Auctions: $3,290, MS-66, January 2015; $1,293, MS-64, October 2015; $400, AU-58, September 2015; $106, EF-45, May 2015												
1933-S	1,786,000	965	57.6	58%	$12	$15	$18	$20	$60	$240	$635	$1,500	$3,200
	Auctions: $25,850, MS-67, June 2015; $1,410, MS-63, September 2015; $705, AU-58, January 2015; $282, AU-55, May 2015												
1934	6,964,000	2,469	63.5	91%	$9	$10	$11	$16	$19	$26	$75	$100	$400
	Auctions: $5,405, MS-67, August 2015; $118, MS-64, October 2015; $94, MS-63, August 2015; $79, MS-61, March 2015												
1934-D (a)	2,361,000	1,383	62.7	89%	$9	$10	$11	$16	$35	$85	$140	$250	$1,300
	Auctions: $3,819, MS-66, August 2015; $306, MS-64, June 2015; $223, MS-63, September 2015; $141, AU-50, October 2015												
1934-S	3,652,000	887	60.7	72%	$9	$10	$11	$16	$30	$90	$325	$750	$3,500
	Auctions: $30,550, MS-67, August 2015; $2,585, MS-65, July 2015; $1,001, MS-64, January 2015; $79, AU-53, January 2015												

a. Large and small mintmark varieties exist. **b.** Half dollars dated 1928-D are counterfeit.

1936, Doubled-Die Obverse
FS-50-1936-101.

	Mintage	Cert	Avg	%MS	G-4	VG-8	F-12	VF-20	EF-40	AU-50	MS-60	MS-63	MS-65
											PF-64	PF-65	PF-67
1935	9,162,000	2,484	63.6	93%	$9	$10	$11	$16	$19	$25	$40	$70	$275
Auctions: $11,750, MS-68, October 2015; $4,935, MS-67, August 2015; $200, MS-65, August 2015; $89, MS-64, February 2015													
1935-D	3,003,800	1,000	62.5	88%	$9	$10	$11	$16	$30	$65	$140	$300	$2,000
Auctions: $8,225, MS-66, May 2015; $1,821, MS-65, August 2015; $259, MS-62, January 2015; $100, MS-60, November 2015													
1935-S	3,854,000	863	62.0	84%	$9	$10	$11	$16	$26	$95	$250	$465	$2,800
Auctions: $5,640, MS-66, January 2015; $1,293, MS-64, October 2015; $564, MS-63, August 2015; $259, AU-58, March 2015													
1936	12,614,000	3,421	64.0	94%	$9	$10	$11	$16	$18	$25	$45	$75	$210
Auctions: $1,528, MS-67, June 2015; $306, MS-66, September 2015; $212, MS-65, January 2015; $89, MS-64, August 2015													
1936, DblDie Obv (c)	**(d)**	0	n/a		$500	$600							
Auctions: $940, MS-65, December 2013; $235, MS-65, January 2015													
1936, Proof	3,901	1,348	64.8								$2,600	$3,250	$10,000
Auctions: $14,689, PF-67, June 2015; $4,348, PF-66, July 2015; $2,820, PF-65, January 2015; $1,175, PF-62, October 2015													
1936-D	4,252,400	1,715	63.6	94%	$9	$10	$11	$16	$20	$50	$85	$120	$400
Auctions: $4,935, MS-67, August 2015; $2,585, MS-66, February 2015; $212, MS-64, September 2015; $79, MS-63, June 2015													
1936-S	3,884,000	1,293	63.5	94%	$9	$10	$11	$16	$22	$60	$130	$200	$750
Auctions: $19,975, MS-67, August 2015; $881, MS-65, January 2015; $329, MS-64, May 2015; $217, MS-63, September 2015													
1937	9,522,000	3,152	63.9	93%	$9	$10	$11	$16	$18	$25	$40	$70	$215
Auctions: $1,528, MS-67, June 2015; $270, MS-66, July 2015; $259, MS-65, January 2015; $84, MS-64, August 2015													
1937, Proof	5,728	1,547	65.2								$650	$950	$1,600
Auctions: $5,640, PF-68, January 2015; $2,115, PF-67, August 2015; $564, PF-64, January 2015; $470, PF-63, October 2015													
1937-D	1,676,000	1,168	63.0	89%	$9	$10	$11	$16	$32	$100	$215	$265	$650
Auctions: $5,170, MS-67, August 2015; $482, MS-65, October 2015; $235, MS-63, January 2015; $153, AU-58, January 2015													
1937-S	2,090,000	1,262	63.7	94%	$9	$10	$11	$16	$25	$60	$165	$210	$625
Auctions: $8,813, MS-67, August 2015; $353, MS-65, October 2015; $247, MS-64, February 2015; $129, MS-62, July 2015													
1938	4,110,000	2,235	63.4	92%	$9	$10	$11	$18	$20	$45	$70	$160	$300
Auctions: $2,585, MS-67, January 2015; $212, MS-65, September 2015; $123, MS-63, May 2015; $46, AU-55, May 2015													
1938, Proof	8,152	1,842	65.4								$500	$775	$1,350
Auctions: $14,100, PF-68, January 2015; $764, PF-66, August 2015; $734, PF-65, June 2015; $430, PF-64, October 2015													
1938-D	491,600	2,838	42.3	40%	$55	$65	$90	$100	$160	$225	$425	$550	$1,300
Auctions: $5,640, MS-67, June 2015; $1,410, MS-65, July 2015; $400, AU-58, February 2015; $176, EF-45, January 2015													
1939	6,812,000	3,634	64.3	94%	$9	$10	$11	$16	$18	$26	$40	$65	$155
Auctions: $8,225, MS-68, August 2015; $194, MS-66, September 2015; $118, MS-65, January 2015; $84, MS-64, September 2015													
1939, Proof	8,808	1,976	65.6								$450	$700	$1,000
Auctions: $4,935, PF-68, August 2015; $570, PF-66, March 2015; $646, PF-65, February 2015; $388, PF-64, July 2015													
1939-D	4,267,800	2,882	64.3	96%	$9	$10	$11	$16	$18	$25	$43	$75	$145
Auctions: $4,700, MS-67, January 2015; $270, MS-66, October 2015; $165, MS-65, August 2015; $94, MS-64, February 2015													
1939-S	2,552,000	1,959	64.4	96%	$9	$10	$11	$16	$26	$70	$150	$180	$240
Auctions: $12,925, MS-68, September 2015; $564, MS-66, October 2015; $153, MS-64, April 2015; $74, AU-58, June 2015													
1940	9,156,000	4,052	64.3	96%	$9	$10	$11	$16	$18	$22	$35	$55	$120
Auctions: $7,050, MS-68, August 2015; $294, MS-66, January 2015; $89, MS-65, September 2015; $94, MS-64, April 2015													
1940, Proof	11,279	2,314	65.5								$450	$575	$1,000
Auctions: $3,290, PF-68, January 2015; $517, PF-66, June 2015; $423, PF-65, October 2015; $376, PF-64, February 2015													
1940-S	4,550,000	3,024	63.9	97%	$9	$10	$11	$16	$18	$35	$45	$80	$280
Auctions: $27,025, MS-67, June 2015; $823, MS-66, October 2015; $235, MS-65, August 2015; $112, MS-64, February 2015													

c. No examples have yet been discovered grading better than Fine. "Extremely strong doubling is evident on the date. Less doubling is evident on IN GOD WE TRUST, the skirt, and some other elements" (*Cherrypickers' Guide to Rare Die Varieties*, sixth edition, volume II). Several varieties exist; this one is FS-50-1936-101. **d.** Included in circulation-strike 1936 mintage figure.

1945, Missing Designer's Initials
FS-50-1945-901.

	Mintage	Cert	Avg	%MS	G-4	VG-8	F-12	VF-20	EF-40	AU-50	MS-60 PF-64	MS-63 PF-65	MS-65 PF-67
1941	24,192,000	11,031	64.2	94%	$9	$10	$11	$16	$18	$22	$35	$55	$100
Auctions: $2,938, MS-68, January 2015; $588, MS-67, August 2015; $79, MS-65, February 2015; $46, MS-64, October 2015													
1941, Proof (e)	15,412	2,606	65.3								$450	$575	$900
Auctions: $7,050, PF-68, August 2015; $646, PF-67, October 2015; $400, PF-65, September 2015; $400, PF-64, February 2015													
1941-D	11,248,400	5,839	64.4	96%	$9	$10	$11	$16	$18	$22	$38	$65	$125
Auctions: $881, MS-67, January 2015; $176, MS-66, November 2015; $118, MS-65, July 2015; $67, MS-64, May 2015													
1941-S	8,098,000	5,775	63.2	92%	$9	$10	$11	$16	$18	$26	$75	$120	$600
Auctions: $35,250, MS-67, August 2015; $1,293, MS-66, January 2015; $141, MS-64, April 2015; $64, MS-61, June 2015													
1942	47,818,000	16,275	63.9	93%	$9	$10	$11	$16	$18	$22	$40	$60	$100
Auctions: $3,290, MS-67+, February 2015; $129, MS-66, July 2015; $84, MS-65, August 2015; $46, MS-64, October 2015													
1942, Proof	21,120	4,344	65.6								$450	$575	$900
Auctions: $4,465, PF-68, June 2015; $1,528, PF-67+, August 2015; $400, PF-65, October 2015; $470, PF-64, January 2015													
1942-D	10,973,800	4,246	64.3	96%	$9	$10	$11	$16	$18	$20	$40	$80	$200
Auctions: $834, MS-67, June 2015; $212, MS-66, January 2015; $165, MS-65, October 2015; $84, MS-64, February 2015													
1942-S (a)	12,708,000	4,510	63.7	96%	$9	$10	$11	$16	$18	$22	$40	$80	$330
Auctions: $1,116, MS-66, February 2015; $306, MS-65, January 2015; $94, MS-64, November 2015; $118, MS-63, February 2015													
1943	53,190,000	16,507	63.9	93%	$9	$10	$11	$16	$18	$20	$35	$50	$100
Auctions: $21,150, MS-68, August 2015; $1,293, MS-67+, January 2015; $74, MS-64+, April 2015; $40, MS-63, February 2015													
1943-D	11,346,000	5,092	64.7	97%	$9	$10	$11	$16	$18	$24	$48	$75	$190
Auctions: $4,935, MS-68, June 2015; $646, MS-67, February 2015; $94, MS-64, August 2015; $40, MS-62, October 2015													
1943-S	13,450,000	5,179	64.0	97%	$9	$10	$11	$16	$18	$25	$42	$60	$240
Auctions: $6,463, MS-67, August 2015; $4,465, MS-66+, February 2015; $200, MS-65, August 2015; $69, MS-64, May 2015													
1944	28,206,000	9,675	63.9	95%	$9	$10	$11	$16	$18	$20	$35	$50	$105
Auctions: $3,525, MS-67, August 2015; $76, MS-65, March 2015; $56, MS-64, October 2015; $32, MS-60, March 2015													
1944-D	9,769,000	6,109	64.6	98%	$9	$10	$11	$16	$18	$20	$40	$60	$105
Auctions: $1,528, MS-67+, September 2015; $183, MS-66, January 2015; $118, MS-65, March 2015; $89, MS-64, February 2015													
1944-S	8,904,000	6,100	64.0	98%	$9	$10	$11	$16	$18	$24	$40	$63	$325
Auctions: $3,290, MS-66+, June 2015; $376, MS-65, July 2015; $84, MS-64, February 2015; $44, MS-62, October 2015													
1945	31,502,000	13,365	64.0	96%	$9	$10	$11	$16	$18	$20	$35	$50	$100
Auctions: $1,645, MS-67, July 2015; $89, MS-65, October 2015; $94, MS-64, August 2015; $44, MS-63, February 2015													
1945, Missing Initials	(f)	18	57.4	67%							$100	$150	$250
Auctions: $705, MS-64, January 2014													
1945-D	9,966,800	8,837	64.8	98%	$9	$10	$11	$17.50	$18	$20	$35	$60	$120
Auctions: $14,100, MS-68, August 2015; $4,465, MS-67+, August 2015; $94, MS-65, May 2015; $64, MS-64, February 2015													
1945-S	10,156,000	7,467	64.3	99%	$9	$10	$11	$17.50	$18	$24	$38	$55	$120
Auctions: $6,463, MS-67, January 2015; $212, MS-66, August 2015; $106, MS-65, April 2015; $74, MS-64, February 2015													

a. Large and small mintmark varieties exist. **e.** The variety without the designer's initials was created by the over-polishing of dies.
f. Included in 1945 mintage figure.

1946, Doubled-Die Reverse
FS-50-1946-801.

	Mintage	Cert	Avg	%MS	G-4	VG-8	F-12	VF-20	EF-40	AU-50	MS-60	MS-63	MS-65
											PF-64	PF-65	PF-67
1946	12,118,000	6,848	64.0	96%	$9	$10	$11	$17.50	$18	$20	$37	$50	$120
	Auctions: $3,525, MS-67, August 2015; $176, MS-66, April 2015; $112, MS-65, April 2015; $94, MS-64, September 2015												
1946, DblDie Rev (g)	(h)	171	51.1	37%	$20	$24	$28	$40	$65	$125	$275	$550	$2,500
	Auctions: $2,233, MS-64, January 2015; $188, AU-58, April 2015; $84, EF-45, August 2015; $79, F-15, April 2015												
1946-D	2,151,000	13,075	64.8	100%	$9	$10	$11	$17.50	$22	$32	$47	$60	$105
	Auctions: $3,760, MS-67, August 2015; $141, MS-66, January 2015; $60, MS-64, October 2015; $42, MS-62, October 2015												
1946-S	3,724,000	8,555	64.7	99%	$9	$10	$11	$17.50	$18	$25	$43	$58	$100
	Auctions: $8,225, MS-67, October 2015; $217, MS-66, February 2015; $100, MS-65, July 2015; $89, MS-64, May 2015												
1947	4,094,000	7,439	64.3	98%	$9	$10	$11	$17.50	$18	$25	$48	$60	$110
	Auctions: $9,400, MS-67, February 2015; $188, MS-66, November 2015; $123, MS-65, July 2015; $64, MS-64, October 2015												
1947-D	3,900,600	8,310	64.6	99%	$9	$10	$11	$17.50	$18	$30	$45	$60	$105
	Auctions: $5,640, MS-67, August 2015; $182, MS-66, April 2015; $129, MS-65, September 2015; $69, MS-64, July 2015												

g. Very strong doubling is visible on E PLURIBUS UNUM, the eagle's wing feathers and left wing, and the branch. h. Included in 1946 mintage figure.

FRANKLIN (1948–1963)

Designer: *John R. Sinnock.* **Weight:** *12.50 grams.*
Composition: *.900 silver, .100 copper (net weight .36169 oz. pure silver).*
Diameter: *30.6 mm.* **Edge:** *Reeded.* **Mints:** *Philadelphia, Denver, and San Francisco.*

Circulation Strike

Mintmark location is on the reverse, above the beam.

Proof

History. U.S. Mint chief engraver John R. Sinnock developed a motif for a silver half dime in 1942; it was proposed but never adopted for regular coinage. In 1948, the year after Sinnock died, his Franklin half dollar was introduced, its design an adaptation of his earlier half dime motif. The Liberty Bell is similar to that used by Sinnock on the 1926 Sesquicentennial commemorative half dollar modeled from a sketch by John Frederick Lewis. The designs were finished by Sinnock's successor, chief engraver Gilroy Roberts. The coin-collecting community paid little attention to the Franklin half dollar at the time, but today the coins are widely collected.

Striking and Sharpness. Given the indistinct details of the obverse, sharpness of strike usually is ignored. On the reverse, if the bottom lines of the Liberty Bell are complete the coin may be designated as Full Bell Lines (FBL). Virtually all Proofs are well struck.

Availability. All dates and mintmarks are easily available in grades from VF upward. Lower-level MS coins can be unattractive due to contact marks and abrasion, particularly noticeable on the obverse.

High-quality gems are generally inexpensive, although varieties that are rare with FBL can be costly amid much competition in the marketplace. Most collectors seek MS coins. Grades below EF are not widely desired. Proofs were made from 1950 to 1963 and are available today in proportion to their mintages. Those with cameo-frosted devices are in the minority and often sell for strong premiums.

Note: Values of common-date silver coins have been based on the current bullion price of silver, $15.50 per ounce, and may vary with the prevailing spot price.

GRADING STANDARDS

MS-60 to 70 (Mint State). *Obverse:* At MS-60, some abrasion and contact marks are evident on the cheek, on the hair left of the ear, and the neck. At MS-63, abrasion is slight at best, less so for MS-64. An MS-65 coin should display no abrasion or contact marks except under magnification, and MS-66 and higher coins should have none at all. Luster should be full and rich. As details are shallow on this design, the amount and "depth" of luster is important to grading. *Reverse:* General comments apply as for the obverse. The points to check are the bell harness, the words PASS AND STOW on the upper area of the Liberty Bell, and the bottom of the bell.

1951-S. Graded MS-65.

   Illustrated coin: Satiny brilliance is seen on the obverse of this coin, light golden toning on the reverse.

AU-50, 53, 55, 58 (About Uncirculated). *Obverse:* At AU-50, medium wear is evident on the portrait, and most of the luster in the field is gone. At AU-53, wear is less and luster is more extensive. AU–55 and 58 coins show much luster. Wear is noticeable on the portrait and, to a lesser extent, in the field. *Reverse:* At AU-50, medium wear is evident on most of the Liberty Bell, and most of the luster in the field is gone. At AU-53, wear is slightly less. AU–55 and 58 coins show much luster. Light wear is seen on the higher areas of the bell.

1949-D. Graded AU-50.

EF-40, 45 (Extremely Fine). *Obverse:* Wear is more extensive, and some hair detail (never strong to begin with) is lost. There is no luster. *Reverse:* Wear is seen overall. The inscription on the bell is weak, and the highest parts of the bottom horizontal lines are worn away. There is no luster.

   The Franklin half dollar is seldom collected in grades lower than EF-40.

1955. Graded EF-40.

PF-60 to 70 (Proof). *Obverse and Reverse:* Proofs that are extensively cleaned and have many hairlines, or that are dull and grainy, are lower level, such as PF–60 to 62. These are not widely desired, and represent coins that have been mistreated. Fortunately, only a few Proof Franklin half dollars are in this category. With medium hairlines and good reflectivity, assigned grades of PF–63 or 64 are appropriate. PF–66 should have hairlines

1950. Graded PF-65 Cameo.

so delicate that magnification is needed to see them. Above that, a Proof should be free of any hairlines or other problems.

Full Bell Lines

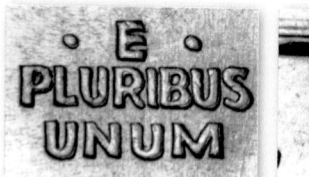

1948, Doubled-Die Reverse
FS-50-1948-801.

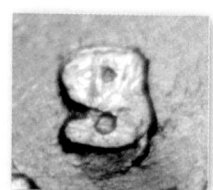

1949-S, Repunched Mintmark
FS-50-1949S-501.

	Mintage	Cert	Avg	%MS	VF-20	EF-40	MS-60	MS-63	MS-64	MS-65	MS-65FBL	MS-66	MS-66FBL
											PF-64	PF-65	PF-65DC
1948	3,006,814	4,069	64.1	97%	$9	$11	$20	$27	$35	$80	$140	$300	$350
	Auctions: $3,760, MS-67FBL, September 2015; $1,410, MS-66FBL+, June 2015; $84, MS-65FBL, August 2015; $46, MS-64FBL, August 2015												
1948, Doubled-Die Reverse (a)	(b)	32	63.8	100%				$75	$125	$200	$300	$550	
	Auctions: No auction records available.												
1948-D	4,028,600	3,855	64.0	98%	$9	$11	$20	$24	$30	$115	$185	$600	$800
	Auctions: $19,975, MS-67FBL, January 2015; $12,925, MS-67FBL, July 2015; $135, MS-65FBL, February 2015; $74, MS-64, January 2015												
1949	5,614,000	2,706	63.1	89%	$12	$18	$40	$70	$75	$120	$155	$350	$550
	Auctions: $1,469, MS-66FBL+, September 2015; $212, MS-65FBL, November 2015; $188, MS-65FBL, July 2015; $62, MS-64FBL, January 2015												
1949-D	4,120,600	2,804	63.3	95%	$12	$18	$45	$75	$90	$500	$750	$2,500	$10,000
	Auctions: $2,820, MS-66FBL, January 2015; $400, MS-65FBL, January 2015; $141, MS-64FBL, February 2015; $44, MS-63FBL, July 2015												
1949-S	3,744,000	3,200	63.9	95%	$12	$20	$65	$95	$115	$140	$500	$225	$750
	Auctions: $6,463, MS-67FBL, June 2015; $259, MS-66, September 2015; $200, MS-65FBL, May 2015; $74, MS-64, January 2015												
1949-S, Doubled Mintmark (c)	(d)	9	60.7	67%				$120	$170	$280	$350	$575	
	Auctions: $223, MS-65, January 2014												
1950	7,742,123	2,363	63.6	93%	$9	$11	$30	$35	$55	$110	$190	$385	$575
	Auctions: $18,213, MS-67FBL, August 2015; $1,528, MS-66FBL, January 2015; $259, MS-65, February 2015; $56, MS-64FBL, November 2015												
1950, Proof	51,386	3,274	64.8								$425	$475	$10,000
	Auctions: $4,230, PF-67, January 2015; $7,638, PF-66Cam, October 2015; $1,645, PF-65Cam, July 2015; $376, PF-64, June 2015												
1950-D	8,031,600	2,426	63.4	95%	$9	$11	$26	$40	$70	$250	$375	$900	$1,350
	Auctions: $2,585, MS-66FBL, January 2015; $1,058, MS-66FBL, June 2015; $235, MS-65FBL, May 2015; $46, MS-64FBL, August 2015												

a. Doubling is visible on E PLURIBUS UNUM, UNITED, HALF DOLLAR, the dots, and the Liberty Bell's clapper. "There are several similar, yet lesser, DDRs for this date" (*Cherrypickers' Guide to Rare Die Varieties*, sixth edition, volume II). The variety listed and pictured is FS-50-1948-801. **b.** Included in 1948 mintage figure. **c.** The secondary mintmark is visible south of the primary. CONECA lists two other repunched mintmarks for this date; the one illustrated and listed here is FS-50-1949S-501. **d.** Included in 1949-S mintage figure.

1951-S, Doubled-Die Reverse
FS-50-1951S-801.

1955, Clashed Obverse Die "Bugs Bunny" variety
FS-50-1955-401.

	Mintage	Cert	Avg	%MS	VF-20	EF-40	MS-60	MS-63	MS-64	MS-65	MS-65FBL / PF-64	MS-66 / PF-65	MS-66FBL / PF-65DC
1951	16,802,102	2,576	63.9	95%	$9	$11	$14	$24	$35	$70	$235	$225	$775
Auctions: $1,410, MS-66FBL, July 2015; $200, MS-66, July 2015; $235, MS-65FBL, September 2015; $44, MS-65, January 2015													
1951, Proof	57,500	3,341	64.9								$320	$375	$2,500
Auctions: $4,465, PF-68, June 2015; $3,290, PF-67Cam, February 2015; $494, PF-65Cam, July 2015; $259, PF-64, March 2015													
1951-D	9,475,200	2,022	63.6	96%	$9	$11	$30	$45	$70	$150	$250	$650	$1,000
Auctions: $764, MS-66FBL, January 2015; $141, MS-65FBL, July 2015; $84, MS-64FBL, April 2015; $28, MS-63FBL, July 2015													
1951-S	13,696,000	2,671	64.1	97%	$9	$11	$25	$35	$50	$70	$400	$275	$1,100
Auctions: $1,645, MS-67, October 2015; $588, MS-66FBL, July 2015; $176, MS-64FBL, January 2015; $46, MS-63, May 2015													
1951-S, DblDie Rev (e)	(f)	9	64.4	100%				$80	$110	$275	$725	$900	
Auctions: $188, MS-65, January 2014													
1952	21,192,093	2,665	64.0	96%	$9	$11	$14	$23	$32	$70	$125	$225	$430
Auctions: $4,935, MS-67FBL, July 2015; $200, MS-66FBL, February 2015; $94, MS-65FBL, February 2015; $48, MS-64FBL, November 2015													
1952, Proof	81,980	3,854	65.3								$180	$230	$4,500
Auctions: $3,821, PF-67Cam, August 2015; $8,813, PF-66DCam, June 2015; $260, PF-66, October 2015; $118, PF-64, January 2015													
1952-D	25,395,600	2,352	63.8	97%	$9	$11	$14	$23	$32	$125	$180	$600	$1,150
Auctions: $564, MS-66FBL, January 2015; $176, MS-65FBL, September 2015; $129, MS-65FBL, February 2015													
1952-S	5,526,000	2,507	64.5	99%	$12	$17	$50	$70	$80	$100	$750	$225	$2,850
Auctions: $21,150, MS-67FBL, February 2015; $1,645, MS-67, January 2015; $129, MS-66, July 2015; $423, MS-64FBL, January 2015													
1953	2,668,120	2,088	64.0	98%	$9	$10	$14	$27	$40	$100	$635	$450	$2,750
Auctions: $2,233, MS-66FBL, January 2015; $306, MS-66, March 2015; $646, MS-65FBL, October 2015; $129, MS-64FBL, May 2015													
1953, Proof	128,800	5,154	65.6								$125	$190	$1,400
Auctions: $4,230, PF-68Cam, August 2015; $2,585, PF-66DCam, January 2015; $165, PF-66, February 2015; $84, PF-64, May 2015													
1953-D	20,900,400	3,113	63.9	98%	$9	$10	$14	$23	$38	$110	$175	$550	$725
Auctions: $494, MS-66FBL, February 2015; $112, MS-65FBL, February 2015; $74, MS-65, May 2015; $56, MS-64FBL, October 2015													
1953-S	4,148,000	5,043	64.8	100%	$9	$10	$25	$35	$48	$70	$25,500	$350	
Auctions: $2,233, MS-67, January 2015; $447, MS-66, June 2015; $21,150, MS-65FBL, September 2015; $100, MS-65, September 2015													
1954	13,188,202	4,141	64.2	99%	$9	$10	$14	$20	$30	$70	$120	$300	$1,100
Auctions: $1,880, MS-66FBL, July 2015; $823, MS-66FBL, October 2015; $153, MS-65FBL, January 2015; $38, MS-64FBL, July 2015													
1954, Proof	233,300	6,891	66.2								$65	$85	$425
Auctions: $14,100, PF-68DCam, October 2015; $270, PF-67, May 2015; $129, PF-66Cam, May 2015; $34, PF-64, August 2015													
1954-D	25,445,580	5,065	64.1	99%	$9	$10	$14	$24	$28	$90	$140	$375	$800
Auctions: $588, MS-66FBL, June 2015; $353, MS-66, February 2015; $89, MS-65FBL, January 2015; $54, MS-65, May 2015													
1954-S	4,993,400	7,912	64.7	100%	$12	$14	$16	$24	$35	$50	$250	$240	$1,050
Auctions: $1,763, MS-67, July 2015; $194, MS-66, November 2015; $188, MS-65FBL, September 2015; $56, MS-64FBL, February 2015													
1955	2,498,181	7,260	64.1	99%	$18	$22	$25	$30	$40	$55	$115	$150	$425
Auctions: $1,763, MS-66FBL, January 2015; $52, MS-65, September 2015; $38, MS-64FBL, April 2015; $40, MS-63FBL, April 2015													
1955, Clashed Obverse Die (g)	(h)	534	62.6	100%				$48	$65	$130	$350	$265	$700
Auctions: $423, MS-66FBL, February 2013; $129, MS-64FBL, September 2014; $76, MS-64FBL, September 2014													
1955, Proof	378,200	11,489	66.9								$65	$75	$425
Auctions: $4,700, PF-68DCam, October 2015; $212, PF-68, January 2015; $165, PF-67Cam, March 2015; $141, PF-66, August 2015													

e. Doubling is evident on the eagle's tail feathers and left wing, as well as on E PLURIBUS UNUM. This variety is FS-50-1951S-801.
f. Included in 1951-S mintage figure. g. This variety, popularly known as the "Bugs Bunny," has evidence of clash marks that appear as two buckteeth on Benjamin Franklin. h. Included in circulation-strike 1955 mintage figure.

1957, Tripled-Die Reverse, Proof
FS-50-1957-801.

1959, Doubled-Die Reverse
FS-50-1959-801.

	Mintage	Cert	Avg	%MS	VF-20	EF-40	MS-60	MS-63	MS-64	MS-65	MS-65FBL	MS-66	MS-66FBL
											PF-64	PF-65	PF-65DC
1956	4,032,000	9,607	64.3	100%	$9	$10	$14	$25	$28	$42	$100	$80	$275
	Auctions: $353, MS-67, January 2015; $176, MS-66FBL, September 2015; $106, MS-66, July 2015; $60, MS-65FBL, December 2015												
1956, Proof	669,384	4,634	67.1								$35	$45	$100
	Auctions: $2,820, PF-69DCam, September 2015; $329, PF-69, February 2015; $118, PF-68, February 2015; $376, PF-67, July 2015												
1957	5,114,000	4,519	64.7	100%	$9	$10	$14	$19	$25	$40	$125	$85	$225
	Auctions: $$1,763, MS-67FBL, October 2015; $329, MS-67, January 2015; $94, MS-66FBL, October 2015; $48, MS-66, October 2015												
1957, Proof	1,247,952	15,966	67.0								$25	$28	$250
	Auctions: $2,585, PF-69Cam, September 2015; $112, PF-68, June 2015; $90, PF-67, July 2015; $84, PF-66Cam, February 2015												
1957, Tripled-Die Reverse, Proof (i)	(j)	4	65.8								$75	$90	$800
	Auctions: No auction records available.												
1957-D	19,966,850	4,933	64.4	99%	$9	$10	$14	$19	$23	$40	$75	$85	$375
	Auctions: $3,055, MS-67FBL, October 2015; $764, MS-67, October 2015; $212, MS-66FBL, February 2015; $123, MS-65, August 2015												
1958	4,042,000	6,274	64.7	99%	$9	$10	$14	$19	$24	$45	$125	$80	$350
	Auctions: $4,700, MS-67FBL, January 2015; $400, MS-67, February 2015; $353, MS-67, September 2015; $44, MS-66, April 2015												
1958, Proof	875,652	11,874	66.8								$32	$38	$675
	Auctions: $705, PF-69Cam, July 2015; $2,115, PF-67UCam, July 2015; $153, PF-67Cam, March 2015; $20, PF-63, September 2015												
1958-D	23,962,412	6,154	64.5	99%	$9	$10	$14	$18	$19	$45	$70	$75	$475
	Auctions: $$1,175, MS-67FBL, October 2015; $588, MS-67, January 2015; $153, MS-66FBL, February 2015; $20, MS-64, May 2015												
1959	6,200,000	4,518	64.3	99%	$9	$10	$14	$18	$20	$70	$225	$800	$1,750
	Auctions: $1,763, MS-66FBL, January 2015; $154, MS-65FBL, May 2015; $84, MS-65, November 2015; $46, MS-64, May 2015												
1959, Doubled-Die Reverse (k)	(l)	54	63.9	98%			$85	$90	$120	$450	$1,125		
	Auctions: $431, MS-65FBL, March 2011												
1959, Proof	1,149,291	13,091	66.8								$18	$22	$2,000
	Auctions: $1,529, PF-68Cam, January 2015; $423, PF-67Cam, February 2015; $341, PF-67Cam, March 2015; $235, PF-66Cam, October 2015												
1959-D	13,053,750	4,493	64.3	99%	$9	$10	$14	$18	$22	$90	$140	$775	$1,050
	Auctions: $1,528, MS-66FBL, August 2015; $470, MS-66, January 2015; $118, MS-65FBL, February 2015; $89, MS-65FBL, September 2015												
1960	6,024,000	4,182	64.2	99%	$9	$10	$14	$18	$19	$100	$225	$550	$2,000
	Auctions: $1,293, MS-66FBL, January 2015; $1,058, MS-66FBL, September 2015; $176, MS-65FBL, February 2015; $153, MS-65FBL, November 2014												
1960, Proof	1,691,602	15,497	66.8								$18	$22	$100
	Auctions: $646, PF-69, January 2015; $1,369, PF-68UCam, July 2015; $176, PF-68Cam, March 2015; $46, PF-66, August 2015												
1960, Doubled-Die Obverse, Proof (m)	(n)	72	66.2								$80	$95	$400
	Auctions: $160, PF-67, May 2012												
1960-D	18,215,812	3,643	64.0	99%	$9	$10	$14	$18	$28	$200	$450	$900	$4,250
	Auctions: $1,645, MS-66FBL, February 2015; $331, MS-65FBL, August 2015; $112, MS-65, July 2015; $28, MS-64FBL, January 2015												

i. A closely tripled image is evident on E PLURIBUS UNUM, portions of UNITED STATES OF AMERICA, and HALF DOLLAR. **j.** Included in 1957, Proof, mintage figure. **k.** Strong doubling is evident on the eagle; doubling is also visible on E PLURIBUS UNUM, UNITED, and portions of the Liberty Bell. **l.** Included in circulation-strike 1959 mintage figure. **m.** Doubling is visible on LIBERTY, TRUST, and the date. **n.** Included in 1960, Proof, mintage figure.

1961, Doubled-Die Reverse, Proof
FS-50-1961-801.

	Mintage	Cert	Avg	%MS	VF-20	EF-40	MS-60	MS-63	MS-64	MS-65	MS-65FBL PF-64	MS-66 PF-65	MS-66FBL PF-65DC
1961	8,290,000	4,366	64.2	99%	$9	$10	$14	$18	$25	$75	$900	$600	$5,000
	Auctions: $8,225, MS-66FBL, July 2015; $881, MS-66, September 2015; $40, MS-65, July 2015; $84, MS-64FBL, May 2015												
1961, Proof	3,028,244	20,119	66.8								$25	$30	$125
	Auctions: $1,880, PF-68DCam, January 2015; $306, PF-68Cam, January 2015; $129, PF-68, July 2015; $84, PF-67Cam, May 2015												
1961, Doubled-Die Reverse, Proof (o)	(p)	86	65.6								$2,200	$2,900	
	Auctions: $4,935, PF-67, August 2015; $2,350, PF-65, June 2014; $1,880, PF-64, July 2014												
1961-D	20,276,442	3,369	64.1	99%	$9	$10	$14	$18	$25	$110	$450	$1,000	$3,000
	Auctions: $3,302, MS-66FBL, February 2015; $1,175, MS-66, January 2015; $423, MS-65FBL, January 2015; $79, MS-65, October 2015												
1962	9,714,000	3,159	64.1	99%	$9	$10	$14	$18	$25	$90	$1,750	$750	$11,000
	Auctions: $7,638, MS-66FBL, October 2015; $1,645, MS-65FBL, January 2015; $200, MS-64FBL, February 2015; $36, MS-63FBL, July 2015												
1962, Proof	3,218,019	25,985	66.7								$22	$27	$60
	Auctions: $153, PF-68Cam, July 2015; $212, PF-67UCam, April 2015; $26, PF-67, September 2015; $56, PF-66Cam, April 2015												
1962, Doubled-Die Obverse, Proof (q)	(r)	0	n/a								$25	$30	$150
	Auctions: No auction records available.												
1962-D	35,473,281	4,093	64.0	99%	$9	$10	$14	$18	$25	$120	$450	$1,000	$3,500
	Auctions: $4,230, MS-66FBL, January 2015; $60, MS-65, March 2015; $22, MS-64, October 2015; $38, MS-63FBL, March 2015												
1963	22,164,000	11,358	64.3	99%	$9	$10	$14	$18	$19	$40	$1,150	$750	$2,500
	Auctions: $$17,625, MS-66FBL, October 2015; $1,880, MS-65FBL, January 2015; $1,116, MS-65FBL, October 2015; $330, MS-64FBL, January 2015												
1963, Proof	3,075,645	24,848	66.8								$22	$26	$52
	Auctions: $364, PF-69, February 2015; $1,998, PF-68DCam, September 2015; $118, PF-68Cam, January 2015; $129, PF-67Cam, June 2015												
1963-D	67,069,292	8,713	64.1	98%	$9	$10	$14	$18	$19	$45	$175	$350	$1,050
	Auctions: $1,175, MS-66FBL, July 2015; $282, MS-65FBL, September 2015; $153, MS-65FBL, March 2015; $36, MS-64FBL, April 2015												

o. Other reverse doubled dies exist for this date. The variety pictured and listed here (FS-50-1961-801) is by far the most dramatic. Very strong doubling is evident on the reverse lettering. **p.** Included in 1961, Proof, mintage figure. **q.** Doubling is visible on the 62 of the date and on WE TRUST. **r.** Included in 1962, Proof, mintage figure.

KENNEDY (1964 TO DATE)

Designers: *Gilroy Roberts and Frank Gasparro.* **Weight:** *1964, modern silver Proofs, and 2014 silver—12.50 grams; 1965–1970—11.50 grams; 1971 to date—11.34 grams.* **Composition:** *1964 and modern silver Proofs—.900 silver, .100 copper (net weight .36169 oz. pure silver); 1965–1970—outer layers of .800 silver and .200 copper bonded to inner core of .209 silver, .791 copper (net weight .1479 oz. pure silver); 1971 to date—outer layers of copper-nickel (.750 copper, .250 nickel) bonded to inner core of pure copper; 2014 gold—.9999 gold (net weight .75 oz. pure gold).* **Diameter:** *30.6 mm.* **Edge:** *Reeded.* **Mints:** *Philadelphia, Denver, and San Francisco.*

Circulation Strike

Proof

Mintmark location, 1964, is on the reverse, below the claw holding the branch.

Mintmark location, 1968 to date, is on the obverse, above the date.

Bicentennial variety: **Designers:** *Gilroy Roberts and Seth Huntington.* **Weight:** *Silver clad—11.50 grams; copper-nickel clad—11.34 grams.* **Composition:** *Silver clad—outer layers of .800 silver, .200 copper bonded to inner core of .209 silver, .791 copper (net weight .14792 oz. pure silver); copper-nickel clad—outer layers of copper-nickel (.750 copper, .250 nickel) bonded to inner core of pure copper.* **Diameter:** *30.6 mm.* **Edge:** *Reeded.* **Mints:** *Philadelphia, Denver, and San Francisco.*

Bicentennial variety

Bicentennial variety, Proof

50th Anniversary varieties: **Designers:** *Gilroy Roberts and Frank Gasparro.*
Weight: *Gold—23.33 grams; silver Proofs and Unc.—12.50 grams; copper-nickel clad—*
11.34 grams. **Composition:** *Gold—.9999 gold (net weight .75 oz. pure gold); silver—.900 silver,*
.100 copper (net weight .36169 oz. pure silver); copper-nickel clad—outer layers of copper-nickel
(.750 copper, .250 nickel) bonded to inner core of pure copper. **Diameter:** *30.6 mm.*
Edge: *Reeded.* **Mints:** *Philadelphia, Denver, San Francisco, and West Point.*

50th Anniversary variety, gold

50th Anniversary variety, Uncirculated

**50th Anniversary variety,
Enhanced Uncirculated**

50th Anniversary variety, Proof

50th Anniversary variety, Reverse Proof

History. Kennedy half dollars, minted from 1964 to date, were struck in 90% silver the first year, then with 40% silver content through 1970, and in later years in copper-nickel (except for special silver issues made for collectors and a gold issue in 2014). The obverse, by Chief Engraver Gilroy Roberts, features a portrait of President John F. Kennedy, while the reverse, by Frank Gasparro, displays a modern version of a heraldic eagle.

The 1976 Bicentennial coin shows Philadelphia's Independence Hall, a design by Seth G. Huntington. The obverse was unchanged except for the dual dating 1776–1976. The Bicentennial half dollars were struck during 1975 and 1976 and were used for general circulation as well as being included in Proof and Uncirculated sets for 1975 and 1976.

The year 2014 brought several special issues to mark the 50th year of the Kennedy half dollar: a .9999 fine gold version containing three-quarters of an ounce of pure gold; a Proof in silver; a Reverse Proof in silver; an Enhanced Uncirculated in silver; and an Uncirculated in silver. These coins are dual-dated 1964–2014 on the obverse. They were offered for sale by the U.S. Mint in a number of packages and options.

Striking and Sharpness. Nearly all are well struck. Check the highest points of the hair on the obverse and the highest details on the reverse.

Availability. All issues are common in high circulated grades as well as MS and Proof.

Proofs and Special Mint Set Coins. Proofs of 1964 were struck at the Philadelphia Mint. Those from 1968 to date have been made in San Francisco. All are easily obtained. Most from the 1970s to date have cameo contrast. Special Mint Set (SMS) coins were struck in lieu of Proofs from 1965 to 1967; in some instances, these closely resemble Proofs. Silver Proofs have been struck in recent years, for Silver Proof sets and for the 2014 50th Anniversary issue (which also includes a Reverse Proof). In 1998, a special Matte Proof silver Kennedy half dollar was struck for inclusion in the Robert F. Kennedy commemorative coin set.

Note: Values of common-date silver coins have been based on the current bullion price of silver, $15.50 per ounce, and may vary with the prevailing spot price.

GRADING STANDARDS

MS-60 to 70 (Mint State). *Obverse:* At MS-60, some abrasion and contact marks are evident on the cheek, and on the hair to the right of the forehead and temple. At MS-63, abrasion is slight at most, and less so for MS-64. An MS-65 coin should display no abrasion or contact marks except under magnification, and MS-66 and higher coins should have none at all. Luster should be full and rich. *Reverse:* Comments apply as for the obverse, except that the highest parts of the eagle at the center are the key places to check.

1964-D. Graded MS-66.

AU-50, 53, 55, 58 (About Uncirculated). *Obverse:* Light wear is seen on the cheek and higher-relief area of the hair below the part, high above the ear. At AU-58, the luster is extensive but incomplete, especially on the higher parts and in the field. At AU–50 and 53, luster is less. *Reverse:* Light wear is seen on the higher parts of the eagle. At AU–50 and 53 there still is significant luster.

1964. Graded AU-55.

EF-40, 45 (Extremely Fine). *Obverse:* Further wear is seen on the head. More details are gone on the higher parts of the hair. *Reverse:* Further wear is seen on the eagle in particular, but also on other areas in high relief (including the leaves, arrowheads, and clouds).

The Kennedy half dollar is seldom collected in grades lower than EF-40.

1964. Graded EF-45.

PF-60 to 70 (Proof). *Obverse and Reverse:* Proofs that are extensively cleaned and have many hairlines, or that are dull and grainy, are lower level, such as PF–60 to 62. There are not many of these in the marketplace. With medium hairlines and good reflectivity, assigned grades of PF–63 or 64 are appropriate. With relatively few hairlines a rating of PF-65 can be given. PF-66 should have hairlines so delicate that magnification is needed to see them. Above that, a Proof should be free of any hairlines or other problems.

1964. Graded PF-66.

1964, Doubled-Die Obverse
FS-50-1964-102.

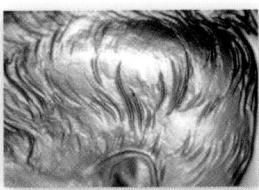

1964, Heavily Accented Hair, Proof
FS-50-1964-401.

1964-D, Doubled-Die Obverse
FS-50-1964D-101.

1964-D, Repunched Mintmark
FS-50-1964D-502.

| | Mintage | Cert | Avg | %MS | MS-60 | MS-63 | MS-65 | MS-66 | MS-67 |
							PF-65	PF-67Cam	PF-68DC
1964	273,304,004	7,729	64.4	98%	$11	$12	$20	$40	$625
	Auctions: $1,234, MS-67, October 2015; $118, MS-66, January 2015; $34, MS-65, April 2015; $37, MS-64, April 2015								
1964, Doubled-Die Obverse (a)	(b)	13	64.6	100%		$35	$65	$250	
	Auctions: $69, MS-65, June 2015; $52, MS-64, August 2015; $34, MS-64, August 2015								
1964, Proof	3,950,762	28,156	67.5				$20	$45	$200
	Auctions: $4,700, PF-70, August 2015; $4,230, PF-69DCam, August 2015; $364, PF-68DCam, January 2015								
1964, Heavily Accented Hair, Proof ‡ (c)	(d)	11,367	66.5				$45	$180	$4,900
	Auctions: $1,645, PF-69, June 2015; $212, PF-67, April 2015; $89, PF-65, September 2015; $40, PF-63, October 2015								
1964-D	156,205,446	4,377	64.3	99%	$11	$12	$20	$40	$800
	Auctions: $2,291, MS-67, February 2015; $1,880, MS-67, January 2015; $69, MS-65, January 2015; $60, MS-65, August 2015								
1964-D, Doubled-Die Obverse (e)	(f)	29	61.9	69%		$45	$70	$150	
	Auctions: $60, MS-66, November 2011; $89, MS-65, June 2015; $36, MS-64, August 2015								
1964-D, Repunched Mintmark (g)	(f)	24	63.3	92%		$45	$65	$125	
	Auctions: $130, AU-55, June 2010								

‡ Ranked in the *100 Greatest U.S. Modern Coins*. **a.** There are several doubled-die obverses for the 1964 Kennedy half dollar. The one pictured and listed is FS-50-1964-102. **b.** Included in circulation-strike 1964 mintage figure. **c.** This variety "is identifiable by the enhanced hairline in the central area of the hair, just below the part. However, the easiest way to identify the variety is the weak or broken lower left serif of the I (in LIBERTY)" (*Cherrypickers' Guide to Rare Die Varieties*, sixth edition, volume II). **d.** Included in 1964, Proof, mintage figure. **e.** Doubling on this variety is evident on the date, IN GOD WE TRUST, the designer's initials, and the LI and TY of LIBERTY. "This is a very popular variety. It is extremely rare above MS-65" (*Cherrypickers' Guide to Rare Die Varieties*, sixth edition, volume II). There are other doubled-die obverses for 1964-D. The one pictured and listed is FS-50-1964D-101. **f.** Included in 1964-D mintage figure. **g.** There are several repunched mintmarks for 1964-D. The one listed is FS-50-1964D-502.

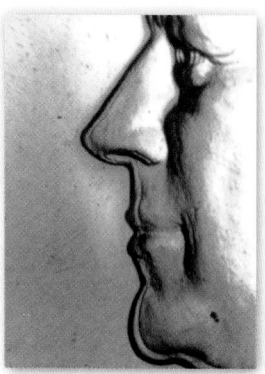
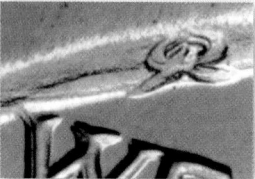

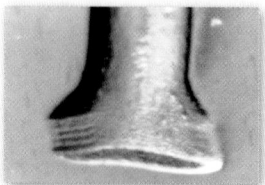

1966, Doubled-Die Obverse, Special Mint Set
FS-50-1966-103.

1967, Quintupled-Die Obverse, Special Mint Set
FS-50-1967-101.

	Mintage	Cert	Avg	%MS	MS-63	MS-65	MS-66	MS-67
					PF-65	PF-67Cam	PF-68DC	
1965	65,879,366	857	64.6	98%	$6	$17	$150	$650
Auctions: $470, MS-67, January 2015; $282, MS-67, October 2015; $259, MS-66, July 2015								
1965, Special Mint Set ‡	2,360,000	9,522	66.6			$11	$175	
Auctions: $118, PF-66Cam, November 2014; $1,998, PF-66DCam, January 2014								
1966	108,984,932	774	64.5	97%	$6	$25	$170	$400
Auctions: No auction records available.								
1966, Special Mint Set ‡	2,261,583	11,013	66.8			$11	$80	
Auctions: $376, MS-68, September 2015; $1,410, MS-67, October 2015; $94, MS-67, July 2015								
1966, Special Mint Set, Doubled-Die Obverse (a)	(b)	175	66.5	100%		$85	$325	
Auctions: $176, MS-67, October 2015; $153, MS-67, September 2015; $69, MS-66, October 2015								
1967	295,046,978	1,072	64.5	96%	$6	$22	$95	$750
Auctions: $17,625, MS-68, August 2015; $3,525, MS-67, October 2015; $100, MS-67, October 2015								
1967, Special Mint Set ‡	1,863,344	10,051	66.7			$15	$60	
Auctions: $200, PF-68, September 2014; $734, PF-67DCam, November 2014								
1967, Special Mint Set, Quintupled-Die Obverse (c)	(d)	28	66.5			$135	$500	
Auctions: $345, SP-66, February 2012								
1968-D	246,951,930	2,172	64.8	98%	$6	$20	$45	$235
Auctions: $1,763, MS-67, January 2015; $1,293, MS-67, October 2015; $46, MS-66, April 2015								
1968-S, Proof	3,041,506	6,822	67.7			$10	$22	$50
Auctions: $10,575, PF-70DCam, August 2015; $329, PF-69DCam, August 2015								
1969-D	129,881,800	1,492	64.6	99%	$6	$30	$225	$1,100
Auctions: $1,116, MS-67, September 2015; $235, MS-66, January 2015; $188, MS-66, October 2015								
1969-S, Proof	2,934,631	10,090	67.9			$10	$23	$45
Auctions: $224, PF-69DCam, January 2014								
1970-D ‡	2,150,000	4,090	64.3	100%	$20	$42	$215	$775
Auctions: $4,935, MS-67, October 2015; $329, MS-66, September 2015; $235, MS-66, September 2015								
1970-S, Proof	2,632,810	8,879	67.9			$15	$30	$50
Auctions: $306, PF-69DCam, January 2015; $282, PF-69DCam, January 2015								
1971	155,164,000	162	64.2	95%	$3	$15	$45	$200
Auctions: $170, MS-66, May 2014								
1971-D	302,097,424	776	65.1	95%	$3	$10	$22	$70
Auctions: $235, MS-67, January 2015; $112, MS-67, March 2015; $100, MS-66, July 2015								
1971-S, Proof	3,220,733	5,075	67.9			$4	$20	$100
Auctions: $1,821, PF-67, July 2013								

‡ Ranked in the *100 Greatest U.S. Modern Coins*. **a.** There are several doubled-die obverse varieties of the 1966, Special Mint Set, half dollar. The one listed is FS-50-1966-103, with strong doubling evident on the profile, IN GOD WE TRUST, the eye, the hair, and the designer's initials. **b.** Included in 1966, Special Mint Set, mintage figure. **c.** "A prominent quintupled (at least) spread is evident on RTY of LIBERTY, with strong multiple images on all obverse lettering and portions of the hair" (*Cherrypickers' Guide to Rare Die Varieties*, sixth edition, volume II). **d.** Included in 1967, Special Mint Set, mintage figure.

**1972, Doubled-Die
Obverse**
FS-50-1972-101.

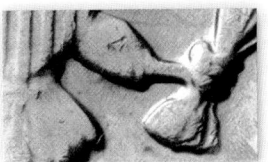

**1972-D, Missing
Designer's Initials**
FS-50-1972D-901.

	Mintage	Cert	Avg	%MS	MS-63 / PF-65	MS-65 / PF-67Cam	MS-66 / PF-68DC	MS-67 / PF-68DC
1972	153,180,000	238	64.8	96%	$3	$15	$50	$290
Auctions: $36, MS-66, July 2014								
1972, Doubled-Die Obverse (e)	(f)	2	58.0	0%	$140	$165	$225	$450
Auctions: $90, AU-50, March 2011								
1972-D	141,890,000	409	65.2	97%	$3	$10	$23	$100
Auctions: $153, MS-67, November 2015; $94, MS-67, October 2015; $17, MS-66, July 2015								
1972-D, Missing Initials	(g)	4	58.3	25%	$50	$75	$150	$250
Auctions: $380, EF-45, October 2009								
1972-S, Proof	3,260,996	3,838	68.0		$4	$16	$25	
Auctions: $92, PF-69DCam, June 2014								
1973	64,964,000	170	64.6	96%	$3	$15	$45	$155
Auctions: $282, MS-67, August 2014; $153, MS-67, October 2015; $38, MS-66, October 2015								
1973-D	83,171,400	341	65.1	98%	$3	$11	$20	$170
Auctions: $329, MS-67, July 2014; $206, MS-67, October 2015								
1973-S, Proof	2,760,339	750	68.2		$3	$16	$25	
Auctions: $2,350, PF-70DCam, December 2011								
1974	201,596,000	176	64.3	95%	$3	$20	$35	$145
Auctions: $3,290, MS-67, October 2015; $2,350, MS-67, August 2014; $37, MS-66, March 2008								
1974-D	79,066,300	273	64.6	94%	$3	$15	$35	$175
Auctions: $382, MS-67, August 2014; $259, MS-67, October 2015; $65, MS-65, June 2014								
1974-D, Doubled-Die Obverse ‡ (h)	(i)	429	63.8	95%	$40	$100	$200	$450
Auctions: $411, MS-66, July 2014; $135, MS-65, July 2014; $28, MS-63, October 2014								
1974-S, Proof	2,612,568	789	68.1		$4	$9	$18	
Auctions: $4,406, PF-70DCam, March 2014								
1776–1976, Copper-Nickel Clad ‡	234,308,000	394	64.2	95%	$3	$15	$50	$125
Auctions: $1,998, MS-67, August 2014; $2,350, MS-62, February 2014								
1776–1976-D, Copper-Nickel Clad	287,565,248	686	65.0	98%	$3	$15	$25	$375
Auctions: $1,116, MS-67, October 2015; $79, MS-65, August 2015; $999, AU-58, August 2015								
1776–1976-S, Silver Clad	11,000,000	1,277	66.0	100%	$8	$10	$15	$30
Auctions: $217, MS-68, July 2014; $188, MS-68, October 2015; $153, MS-68, September 2015; $141, MS-68, May 2015								
1776–1976-S, Proof, Copper-Nickel Clad	7,059,099	1,896	67.8		$4	$13	$18	
Auctions: $3,290, PF-70DCam, January 2015; $2,585, PF-70DCam, July 2015; $2,233, PF-70DCam, August 2015								
1776–1976-S, Proof, Silver Clad (j)	4,000,000	3,462	68.2		$12	$15	$25	
Auctions: $881, PF-70DCam, January 2015; $881, PF-70DCam, July 2015; $750, PF-70DCam, August 2015								
1977	43,598,000	301	65.4	99%	$3	$12	$28	$120
Auctions: $1,116, MS-67, November 2014; $764, MS-67, June 2014; $259, MS-67, August 2014								
1977-D	31,449,106	134	64.9	98%	$3	$15	$22	$85
Auctions: $176, MS-67, August 2014; $153, MS-67, October 2015; $21, MS-66, August 2007								
1977-S, Proof	3,251,152	1,207	68.7		$4	$9	$15	
Auctions: $141, PF-70DCam, February 2015; $129, PF-70DCam, March 2015; $106, PF-70DCam, August 2015								

‡ Ranked in the *100 Greatest U.S. Modern Coins*. **e.** Doubling is strongly evident on IN GOD WE TRUST and on the date. This variety is very rare above MS-65. **f.** Included in 1972 mintage figure. **g.** Included in 1972-D mintage figure. **h.** Strong doubling is visible on IN GOD WE TRUST, the date, and LIBERTY. **i.** Included in 1974-D mintage figure. **j.** Mintage figures for 1976-S silver coins are approximate. Many were melted in 1982.

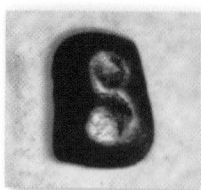

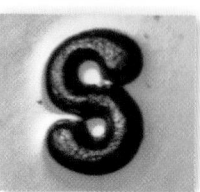

1979-S, Filled S (Type 1), Proof	1979-S, Clear S (Type 2), Proof	1981-S, Rounded S (Type 1), Proof	1981-S, Flat S (Type 2), Proof

	Mintage	Cert	Avg	%MS	MS-63 PF-65	MS-65 PF-67Cam	MS-66 PF-68DC	MS-67
1978	14,350,000	221	65.2	99%	$3	$12	$20	$150
	Auctions: $411, MS-67, August 2014; $212, MS-67, October 2015; $19, MS-66, July 2008							
1978-D	13,765,799	172	65.1	100%	$3	$10	$23	$150
	Auctions: $881, MS-67, August 2014; $18, MS-66, September 2008							
1978-S, Proof	3,127,781	1,408	68.8			$3	$12	$18
	Auctions: $106, PF-70DCam, February 2015; $89, PF-70DCam, June 2015; $84, PF-70DCam, October 2015; $74, PF-70DCam, May 2015							
1979	68,312,000	261	65.2	98%	$3	$10	$25	$150
	Auctions: $423, MS-67, July 2014; $306, MS-67, October 2015; $188, MS-64, September 2015; $764, AU-58, July 2015							
1979-D	15,815,422	230	65.2	100%	$3	$12	$25	$160
	Auctions: $823, MS-67, October 2015; $764, MS-67, August 2014; $11, MS-66, September 2008							
1979-S, Proof, All kinds (k)	3,677,175							
1979-S, Type 1, Proof		1,974	68.9			$3	$11	$14
	Auctions: $200, PF-70DCam, April 2012							
1979-S, Type 2, Proof		1,485	69.0			$25	$27	$30
	Auctions: $588, PF-70DCam, February 2013							
1980-P	44,134,000	218	65.5	99%	$3	$10	$17	$35
	Auctions: $129, MS-67, July 2014; $129, MS-67, October 2015; $42, MS-67, October 2015							
1980-D	33,456,449	142	64.8	98%	$3	$15	$55	$175
	Auctions: $4,935, MS-68, October 2015; $212, MS-67, October 2015; $138, MS-66, September 2008; $65, MS-66, October 2015							
1980-S, Proof	3,554,806	2,055	68.8			$3	$12	$15
	Auctions: $135, PF-70DCam, July 2015; $106, PF-70DCam, November 2015; $100, PF-70DCam, October 2015							
1981-P	29,544,000	305	65.4	99%	$3	$12	$25	$260
	Auctions: No auction records available.							
1981-D	27,839,533	120	64.3	98%	$3	$18	$40	$350
	Auctions: $1,880, MS-67, August 2014; $50, MS-66, June 2014							
1981-S, Proof, All kinds (l)	4,063,083							
1981-S, Type 1, Proof		2,295	68.8			$3	$12	$15
	Auctions: $259, PF-70DCam, June 2013							
1981-S, Type 2, Proof		956	68.9			$25	$29	$33
	Auctions: $2,585, PF-70DCam, November 2013							
1982-P	10,819,000	175	64.8	97%	$7	$23	$70	$425
	Auctions: $153, MS-66, October 2015; $74, MS-65, October 2015; $69, MS-65, August 2015; $42, MS-64, October 2015							
1982-D	13,140,102	236	65.4	99%	$7	$18	$40	$325
	Auctions: $3,290, MS-67, November 2013; $999, MS-67, August 2014; $823, MS-67, October 2015; $141, MS-66, October 2015							
1982-S, Proof	3,857,479	1,408	69.0			$4	$12	$15
	Auctions: $529, PF-70DCam, June 2013							

k. The mintmark style of 1979-S, Proof, coins was changed during production, resulting in two distinct types. The scarcer, well-defined Type 2 is easily distinguished from the more common blob-like Type 1. **l.** The mintmark style of the 1981-S, Proof, coins was changed during production, creating two different types. The scarcer Type 2 is not easily distinguished from the common Type 1. Type 2 is flat on the top curve of the S, compared to Type 1, which has a more rounded top. The surface of Type 2 is frosted, and the openings in the loops are slightly larger.

**1988-S, Doubled-Die
Obverse, Proof**
FS-50-1988S-101.

	Mintage	Cert	Avg	%MS	MS-63 / PF-65	MS-65 / PF-67Cam	MS-66 / PF-68DC	MS-67
1983-P	34,139,000	308	65.2	98%	$8	$22	$45	$200
Auctions: $147, MS-65, April 2014								
1983-D	32,472,244	93	64.9	96%	$7	$15	$30	$330
Auctions: $1,645, MS-67, August 2014; $646, MS-67, October 2015; $13, MS-66, October 2008								
1983-S, Proof	3,279,126	1,453	69.0			$4	$12	$15
Auctions: $115, PF-70DCam, August 2013								
1984-P	26,029,000	191	65.5	99%	$3	$12	$38	$250
Auctions: $1,116, MS-67, August 2014; $940, MS-67, October 2015; $98, MS-66, September 2008								
1984-D	26,262,158	173	65.1	99%	$3	$17	$40	$350
Auctions: $3,290, MS-67, October 2015; $2,820, MS-67, August 2014; $11, MS-66, September 2008								
1984-S, Proof	3,065,110	1,023	69.0			$4	$12	$15
Auctions: $382, PF-70DCam, June 2013								
1985-P	18,706,962	226	66.0	100%	$5	$15	$25	$90
Auctions: $123, MS-67, July 2014; $62, MS-67, October 2015								
1985-D	19,814,034	334	66.1	100%	$5	$12	$15	$45
Auctions: $159, MS-67, July 2014; $112, MS-67, October 2015								
1985-S, Proof	3,362,821	1,237	69.0			$4	$12	$15
Auctions: $135, PF-70DCam, November 2015; $106, PF-70DCam, August 2013								
1986-P	13,107,633	254	66.0	100%	$6	$13	$28	$70
Auctions: $282, MS-67, July 2014; $118, MS-67, October 2015; $112, MS-67, August 2015								
1986-D	15,336,145	347	66.1	100%	$5	$11	$20	$45
Auctions: $57, MS-67, July 2014								
1986-S, Proof	3,010,497	898	69.0			$4	$12	$15
Auctions: $106, PF-70DCam, October 2015; $94, PF-70DCam, March 2015; $94, PF-70DCam, July 2015								
1987-P ‡ (m)	2,890,758	387	65.6	100%	$5	$15	$30	$100
Auctions: $4,113, MS-68, October 2015; $3,290, MS-68, August 2014; $223, MS-67, October 2015								
1987-D ‡ (m)	2,890,758	521	66.0	100%	$5	$12	$23	$50
Auctions: $3,055, MS-68, October 2015; $2,585, MS-68, August 2014; $21, MS-67, October 2008								
1987-S, Proof	4,227,728	1,541	69.0			$4	$12	$15
Auctions: $96, PF-70DCam, August 2013								
1988-P	13,626,000	193	65.8	99%	$5	$15	$28	$90
Auctions: $282, MS-67, July 2014; $153, MS-67, October 2015								
1988-D	12,000,096	317	66.2	100%	$4	$12	$25	$40
Auctions: $57, MS-67, July 2014								
1988-S, Proof	3,262,948	1,086	69.1			$4	$12	$15
Auctions: $113, PF-70DCam, May 2013								
1988-S, Doubled-Die Obverse, Proof (n)	(o)	12	68.8	100%		$110	$160	
Auctions: $260, PF-68UCam, February 2011								

‡ Ranked in the *100 Greatest U.S. Modern Coins*. **m.** Not issued for circulation; included with Mint and Souvenir sets. **n.** Clear doubling is visible on IN GOD WE TRUST, the date, and the mintmark. Some doubling is also evident on LIBERTY and the mintmark. **o.** Included in 1988-S, Proof, mintage figure.

	Mintage	Cert	Avg	%MS	MS-63	MS-65	MS-66	MS-67
						PF-65	PF-67Cam	PF-68DC
1989-P	24,542,000	252	65.6	99%	$4	$15	$23	$90
	Auctions: $282, MS-67, October 2015; $259, MS-67, July 2014							
1989-D	23,000,216	302	66.0	100%	$3	$11	$18	$60
	Auctions: $129, MS-67, July 2014; $74, MS-67, October 2015							
1989-S, Proof	3,220,194	1,037	69.0			$5	$12	$20
	Auctions: $123, PF-70DCam, May 2013							
1990-P	22,278,000	174	65.8	100%	$3	$11	$22	$150
	Auctions: $259, MS-67, October 2015; $200, MS-66, November 2015; $153, MS-66, November 2015; $106, MS-65, November 2014							
1990-D	20,096,242	211	65.6	100%	$3	$16	$32	$200
	Auctions: $31, MS-66, October 2008							
1990-S, Proof	3,299,559	1,178	69.1			$5	$12	$18
	Auctions: $82, PF-70DCam, May 2013							
1991-P	14,874,000	212	66.1	100%	$4	$12	$25	$200
	Auctions: $217, MS-67, July 2014; $165, MS-67, October 2015							
1991-D	15,054,678	238	65.8	100%	$4	$15	$30	$300
	Auctions: $920, MS-67, September 2008; $329, MS-67, August 2014; $294, MS-67, October 2015							
1991-S, Proof	2,867,787	1,086	69.3			$10	$14	$20
	Auctions: $68, PF-70DCam, July 2013							
1992-P	17,628,000	191	66.0	100%	$2	$11	$22	$25
	Auctions: $2,350, MS-68, August 2014; $11, MS-67, October 2008							
1992-D	17,000,106	132	66.1	100%	$3	$10	$18	$30
	Auctions: $147, MS-67, August 2014; $30, MS-67, August 2014; $46, MS-67, July 2014							
1992-S, Proof	2,858,981	688	69.2			$5	$14	$20
	Auctions: $35, PF-70DCam, May 2013							
1992-S, Proof, Silver	1,317,579	2,029	69.1			$17	$20	$25
	Auctions: $92, PF-70DCam, July 2013							
1993-P	15,510,000	326	66.4	99%	$3	$11	$20	$40
	Auctions: $58, MS-67, July 2014							
1993-D	15,000,006	592	66.0	100%	$3	$10	$22	$60
	Auctions: $2,585, MS-68, August 2014; $11, MS-66, October 2008							
1993-S, Proof	2,633,439	749	69.3			$8	$17	$23
	Auctions: $31, PF-70DCam, May 2013							
1993-S, Proof, Silver	761,353	1,563	69.1			$27	$30	$37
	Auctions: $99, PF-70DCam, May 2014							
1994-P	23,718,000	407	65.8	100%	$3	$10	$20	$55
	Auctions: $2,115, MS-68, August 2014; $10, MS-66, October 2008							
1994-D	23,828,110	191	65.8	100%	$3	$10	$20	$75
	Auctions: $364, MS-67, July 2014; $141, MS-67, October 2015							
1994-S, Proof	2,484,594	709	69.3			$8	$17	$23
	Auctions: $45, PF-70DCam, May 2013							
1994-S, Proof, Silver	785,329	1,495	69.1			$26	$33	$35
	Auctions: $206, PF-70DCam, February 2013							
1995-P	26,496,000	225	66.2	100%	$3	$10	$17	$40
	Auctions: $55, MS-67, July 2014							
1995-D	26,288,000	287	66.2	100%	$3	$10	$20	$50
	Auctions: $2,585, MS-68, August 2014; $13, MS-67, October 2008							
1995-S, Proof	2,117,496	656	69.3			$16	$20	$25
	Auctions: $66, PF-70DCam, August 2013							
1995-S, Proof, Silver ‡	679,985	1,178	69.1			$38	$40	$45
	Auctions: $135, PF-70DCam, May 2014							

‡ Ranked in the *100 Greatest U.S. Modern Coins.*

	Mintage	Cert	Avg	%MS	MS-63	MS-65	MS-66	MS-67
						PF-65	PF-67Cam	PF-68DC
1996-P	24,442,000	321	66.2	99%	$3	$10	$17	$35
	Auctions: $247, MS-68, July 2014; $165, MS-68, October 2015							
1996-D	24,744,000	310	66.2	100%	$3	$10	$17	$35
	Auctions: $1,293, MS-68, August 2014; $999, MS-68, January 2015; $11, MS-67, October 2008							
1996-S, Proof	1,750,244	654	69.2			$10	$15	$22
	Auctions: $66, PF-70DCam, August 2013							
1996-S, Proof, Silver	775,021	1,426	69.0			$30	$35	$40
	Auctions: $135, PF-70DCam, August 2013							
1997-P	20,882,000	159	66.2	99%	$3	$12	$30	$80
	Auctions: $60, MS-67, July 2014							
1997-D	19,876,000	259	65.9	100%	$3	$13	$30	$90
	Auctions: $646, MS-68, June 2013; $123, MS-67, July 2014; $79, MS-67, October 2015							
1997-S, Proof	2,055,000	560	69.3			$12	$20	$25
	Auctions: $76, PF-70DCam, August 2013							
1997-S, Proof, Silver	741,678	1,567	69.2			$30	$40	$50
	Auctions: $96, PF-70DCam, August 2013							
1998-P	15,646,000	203	66.3	100%	$3	$15	$35	$70
	Auctions: $76, MS-67, July 2014							
1998-D	15,064,000	187	65.9	99%	$3	$11	$20	$70
	Auctions: $62, MS-67, July 2014							
1998-S, Proof	2,086,507	669	69.4			$10	$17	$23
	Auctions: $56, PF-70DCam, August 2013							
1998-S, Proof, Silver	878,792	1,801	69.3			$18	$25	$35
	Auctions: $88, PF-70DCam, August 2013							
1998-S, Matte Finish Proof, Silver ‡ (p)	*62,000*	2,159	69.2			$125		
	Auctions: $270, PF-70, November 2014; $441, PF-70, July 2014; $113, PF-69, November 2014							
1999-P	8,900,000	227	66.2	100%	$3	$10	$20	$30
	Auctions: $2,115, MS-69, June 2013; $823, MS-68, August 2014							
1999-D	10,682,000	227	66.2	100%	$3	$10	$16	$23
	Auctions: $1,998, MS-68, August 2014; $10, MS-66, October 2008							
1999-S, Proof	2,543,401	3,423	69.3			$13	$16	$20
	Auctions: $90, PF-70DCam, May 2013							
1999-S, Proof, Silver	804,565	5,453	69.1			$25	$30	$32
	Auctions: $147, PF-70DCam, August 2013							
2000-P	22,600,000	118	66.0	100%	$3	$10	$17	$35
	Auctions: $764, MS-68, August 2014; $48, MS-67, October 2008							
2000-D	19,466,000	217	66.1	100%	$3	$10	$20	$40
	Auctions: $123, MS-67, July 2014; $94, MS-67, October 2015							
2000-S, Proof	3,082,483	2,701	69.3			$5	$12	$16
	Auctions: $58, PF-70DCam, May 2013							
2000-S, Proof, Silver	965,421	6,518	69.2			$14	$18	$20
	Auctions: $78, PF-70DCam, May 2013							
2001-P	21,200,000	388	65.5	100%	$3	$8	$15	$28
	Auctions: $176, MS-68, September 2015; $60, MS-68, October 2015							
2001-D	19,504,000	437	65.8	100%	$3	$8	$13	$28
	Auctions: $247, MS-68, July 2014; $153, MS-68, October 2015							
2001-S, Proof	2,294,909	2,052	69.3			$6	$10	$13
	Auctions: $76, PF-70DCam, May 2013							
2001-S, Proof, Silver	889,697	4,802	69.2			$15	$21	$23
	Auctions: $90, PF-70DCam, May 2013							

‡ Ranked in the *100 Greatest U.S. Modern Coins*. **p.** Minted for inclusion in the Robert F. Kennedy commemorative set (along with an RFK commemorative dollar).

	Mintage	Cert	Avg	%MS	MS-63	MS-65	MS-66	MS-67
						PF-65	PF-67Cam	PF-68DC
2002-P (q)	3,100,000	211	65.6	100%	$3	$8	$15	$30
Auctions: $182, MS-68, June 2014; $135, MS-68, January 2015; $129, MS-68, October 2015; $118, MS-68, July 2014								
2002-D (q)	2,500,000	230	65.8	100%	$3	$9	$20	$40
Auctions: $2,115, MS-69, June 2013								
2002-S, Proof	2,319,766	2,098	69.2			$5	$13	$16
Auctions: $60, PF-70DCam, May 2013								
2002-S, Proof, Silver	892,229	5,050	69.3			$14	$18	$20
Auctions: $61, PF-70DCam, May 2013								
2003-P (q)	2,500,000	268	65.8	100%	$3	$9	$20	$30
Auctions: $59, MS-67, July 2014								
2003-D (q)	2,500,000	251	65.8	100%	$3	$8	$16	$25
Auctions: $51, MS-67, July 2014								
2003-S, Proof	2,172,684	4,119	69.2			$5	$12	$16
Auctions: $62, PF-70DCam, August 2015; $35, PF-70DCam, May 2013								
2003-S, Proof, Silver	1,125,755	5,983	69.2			$14	$18	$20
Auctions: $76, PF-70DCam, November 2014; $82, PF-70DCam, May 2014								
2004-P (q)	2,900,000	247	66.2	100%	$3	$8	$17	$30
Auctions: $100, MS-67, October 2015; $86, MS-67, July 2014								
2004-D (q)	2,900,000	392	66.3	100%	$3	$8	$16	$25
Auctions: $423, MS-68, July 2014; $235, MS-68, October 2015								
2004-S, Proof	1,789,488	1,874	69.2			$13	$17	$24
Auctions: $66, PF-70DCam, August 2013								
2004-S, Proof, Silver	1,175,934	5,841	69.2			$20	$22	$23
Auctions: $69, PF-70DCam, January 2013								
2005-P (q)	3,800,000	232	66.0	100%	$4	$18	$25	$75
Auctions: $470, MS-67, October 2015; $42, MS-66, July 2014								
2005-P, Satin Finish (q)	1,160,000	2,502	67.0	100%	$2	$5	$8	$15
Auctions: No auction records available.								
2005-D (q)	3,500,000	262	66.3	100%	$4	$15	$23	$40
Auctions: $1,116, MS-68, August 2014; $11, MS-66, October 2008								
2005-D, Satin Finish (q)	1,160,000	2,176	66.7	100%	$2	$5	$8	$15
Auctions: No auction records available.								
2005-S, Proof	2,275,000	7,119	69.2			$5	$12	$16
Auctions: $66, PF-70DCam, August 2013								
2005-S, Proof, Silver	1,069,679	7,246	69.3			$12	$18	$20
Auctions: $74, PF-70DCam, January 2013								
2006-P (q)	2,400,000	201	66.7	100%	$2	$9	$22	$26
Auctions: $42, MS-69, January 2009; $764, MS-68, August 2014; $376, MS-68, October 2015								
2006-P, Satin Finish (q)	847,361	1,356	66.8	100%	$2	$5	$8	$15
Auctions: No auction records available.								
2006-D (q)	2,000,000	191	66.3	100%	$2	$7	$15	$28
Auctions: $82, MS-67, July 2014; $60, MS-67, October 2015								
2006-D, Satin Finish (q)	847,361	1,351	66.8	100%	$2	$5	$8	$15
Auctions: No auction records available.								
2006-S, Proof	2,000,428	2,774	69.3			$5	$12	$16
Auctions: $46, PF-70DCam, August 2013								
2006-S, Proof, Silver	1,054,008	4,109	69.4			$12	$18	$20
Auctions: $76, PF-70DCam, August 2013								
2007-P (q)	2,400,000	172	66.5	100%	$2	$6	$11	$17
Auctions: $270, MS-68, July 2014; $100, MS-68, October 2015								

q. Not issued for circulation. Sold directly to the public in rolls and small bags.

	Mintage	Cert	Avg	%MS	MS-63	MS-65	MS-66	MS-67
						PF-65	PF-67Cam	PF-68DC
2007-P, Satin Finish (q)	895,628	351	66.8	100%	$2	$5	$8	$15
Auctions: No auction records available.								
2007-D (q)	2,400,000	135	66.1	100%	$2	$6	$15	$30
Auctions: $15, MS-69, January 2009								
2007-D, Satin Finish (q)	895,628	373	66.9	100%	$2	$5	$8	$15
Auctions: No auction records available.								
2007-S, Proof	1,702,116	2,841	69.3			$5	$12	$16
Auctions: $64, PF-70DCam, January 2013								
2007-S, Proof, Silver	875,050	3,685	69.4			$14	$19	$22
Auctions: $86, PF-70DCam, August 2013								
2008-P (q)	1,700,000	208	66.3	100%	$2	$8	$20	$40
Auctions: $1,410, MS-68, August 2014; $12, SP-67, April 2012								
2008-P, Satin Finish (q)	745,464	78	67.0	100%	$2	$5	$8	$15
Auctions: No auction records available.								
2008-D (q)	1,700,000	101	65.9	100%	$2	$8	$20	$45
Auctions: $24, MS-66, June 2011								
2008-D, Satin Finish (q)	745,464	55	66.8	100%	$2	$5	$8	$15
Auctions: No auction records available.								
2008-S, Proof	1,405,674	1,780	69.3			$5	$12	$16
Auctions: $71, PF-70DCam, November 2013								
2008-S, Proof, Silver	763,887	3,767	69.4			$14	$20	$23
Auctions: $66, PF-70DCam, August 2013								
2009-P (q)	1,900,000	179	66.2	100%	$2	$6	$12	$25
Auctions: $1,998, MS-68, August 2014; $6, MS-66, November 2011								
2009-P, Satin Finish (q)	784,614	207	67.1	100%	$2	$5	$8	$15
Auctions: No auction records available.								
2009-D (q)	1,900,000	133	66.2	100%	$2	$6	$12	$30
Auctions: $27, MS-66, February 2012								
2009-D, Satin Finish (q)	784,614	229	67.4	100%	$2	$5	$8	$15
Auctions: No auction records available.								
2009-S, Proof	1,482,502	3,613	69.3			$5	$12	$16
Auctions: $31, PF-70DCam, May 2013								
2009-S, Proof, Silver	697,365	4,586	69.3			$14	$18	$20
Auctions: $41, PF-70DCam, May 2013								
2010-P (q)	1,800,000	217	66.6	100%	$2	$6	$12	$25
Auctions: $23, MS-67, July 2014								
2010-P, Satin Finish (q)	583,897	201	67.1	100%	$2	$5	$8	$15
Auctions: No auction records available.								
2010-D (q)	1,700,000	150	66.2	100%	$2	$6	$12	$25
Auctions: $3,995, MS-68, August 2015; $101, MS-67, July 2014; $48, MS-67, October 2015								
2010-D, Satin Finish (q)	583,897	304	67.6	100%	$2	$5	$8	$15
Auctions: No auction records available.								
2010-S, Proof	1,103,815	1,288	69.3			$5	$12	$16
Auctions: $48, PF-70DCam, August 2013								
2010-S, Proof, Silver	585,401	4,186	69.6			$14	$18	$20
Auctions: $48, PF-70DCam, May 2013								
2011-P (q)	1,750,000	427	66.7	100%	$2	$6	$12	$25
Auctions: $229, MS-68, July 2014; $176, MS-68, October 2015								
2011-D (q)	1,700,000	352	66.5	100%	$2	$6	$12	$25
Auctions: $1,116, MS-68, August 2014; $1,058, MS-68, August 2014; $33, MS-67, January 2012								

q. Not issued for circulation. Sold directly to the public in rolls and small bags.

	Mintage	Cert	Avg	%MS	MS-63	MS-65	MS-66	MS-67
						PF-65	PF-67Cam	PF-68DC
2011-S, Proof	1,098,835	2,310	69.4			$5	$12	$16
Auctions: $21, PF-70UCam, March 2012								
2011-S, Proof, Silver	574,175	4,981	69.7			$14	$18	$20
Auctions: $39, PF-70DCam, August 2014; $36, PF-70DCam, April 2012								
2012-P (q)	1,800,000	232	66.8	100%	$2	$6	$12	$25
Auctions: No auction records available.								
2012-D (q)	1,700,000	251	66.7	100%	$2	$6	$12	$25
Auctions: No auction records available.								
2012-S, Proof	843,705	1,808	69.3			$5	$12	$16
Auctions: $51, PF-70DCam, May 2013								
2012-S, Proof, Silver	445,612	1,998	69.6			$14	$18	$20
Auctions: No auction records available.								
2013-P (q)	5,000,000	290	66.9	100%	$2	$6	$12	$25
Auctions: No auction records available.								
2013-D (q)	4,600,000	317	67.0	100%	$2	$6	$12	$25
Auctions: No auction records available.								
2013-S, Proof	*854,785*	1,897	69.4			$5	$12	$16
Auctions: No auction records available.								
2013-S, Proof, Silver	467,691	2,223	69.6			$14	$18	$20
Auctions: No auction records available.								
2014-P (q,r)	2,500,000	389	66.8	100%	$2	$6	$12	$25
Auctions: No auction records available.								
2014-P, Proof, Silver (s)	*219,173*	0	n/a				$30	$40
Auctions: No auction records available.								
2014-D (q,r)	2,100,000	620	67.3	100%	$2	$6	$12	$25
Auctions: No auction records available.								
2014-D, Proof, Silver (s)	*219,173*	0	n/a				$30	$40
Auctions: No auction records available.								
2014-S, Enhanced Uncirculated, Silver (s)	*219,173*	0	n/a				$30	$40
Auctions: No auction records available.								
2014-S, Proof	*767,977*	2,555	69.3			$5	$12	$16
Auctions: No auction records available.								
2014-S, Proof, Silver	472,107	5,089	69.5			$14	$18	$20
Auctions: No auction records available.								
2014-W, Reverse Proof, Silver (s)	*219,173*	0	n/a				$30	$40
Auctions: No auction records available.								
2014-W, 50th Anniversary, Proof, Gold (t)	73,772	0	n/a					
Auctions: No auction records available.								
2015-P (q)	2,300,000	87	66.8	100%	$2	$6	$12	$25
Auctions: No auction records available.								
2015-D (q)	2,300,000	88	66.8	100%	$2	$6	$12	$25
Auctions: No auction records available.								
2015-S, Proof	*669,960*	371	69.2	100%		$5	$12	$16
Auctions: No auction records available.								

q. Not issued for circulation. Sold directly to the public in rolls and small bags. **r.** To celebrate the 50th anniversary of the Kennedy half dollar, in 2014 the U.S. Mint issued an Uncirculated two-coin set featuring a Kennedy half dollar from Philadelphia and one from Denver. **s.** Featured in the 2014 half dollar silver-coin collection released by the U.S. Mint to commemorate the 50th anniversary of the Kennedy half dollar. **t.** First gold half dollar offered by the U.S. Mint. It commemorates the 50th anniversary of the first release of the Kennedy half dollar in 1964. Dual-dated 1964–2014.

	Mintage	Cert	Avg	%MS	MS-63	MS-65	MS-66	MS-67
						PF-65	PF-67Cam	PF-68DC
2015-S, Proof, Silver	*352,450*	399	69.5	100%		$14	$18	$20
Auctions: No auction records available.								
2016-P (q)					$2	$6	$12	$25
Auctions: No auction records available.								
2016-D (q)					$2	$6	$12	$25
Auctions: No auction records available.								
2016-S, Proof						$5	$12	$16
Auctions: No auction records available.								
2016-S, Proof, Silver						$14	$18	$20
Auctions: No auction records available.								

q. Not issued for circulation. Sold directly to the public in rolls and small bags.

Silver Dollars
1794–1935

AN OVERVIEW OF SILVER DOLLARS

The silver dollar was authorized by Congress on April 2, 1792, and first coined in 1794. This denomination includes some of the most popular series in American numismatics.

The first coin of the denomination, the Flowing Hair dollar, is easy enough to obtain (given the proper budget) in grades from VF through low Mint State. Striking usually ranges from poor to barely acceptable, and adjustment marks (from an overweight planchet being filed down to correct weight) are often seen. Accordingly, careful examination is needed to find a good example.

The silver dollar with the Draped Bust obverse in combination with the Small Eagle reverse was made from 1795 through 1798, with most examples being dated 1796 or 1797. Today both the 1796 and 1797 exist in about the same numbers. Although mintage figures refer to the quantities produced in the given calendar year, these do not necessarily refer to the dates on the coins themselves, as Mint workers would use coinage dies into the next calendar year. Silver dollars of this type are fairly scarce. Sharpness of strike presents a challenge to the collector, and usually there are weaknesses in details, particularly on the reverse eagle.

The 1798 to 1804 type features a Draped Bust obverse and Heraldic Eagle reverse. Many such coins exist, mostly in grades from VF through lower Mint State levels. Striking can be indifferent, but the population of surviving coins is such that collectors have more to choose from, and can select for quality.

The Gobrecht silver dollars of 1836 (starless obverse, stars on reverse, plain edge) and 1839 (stars on obverse, starless reverse, reeded edge) present a special challenge in the formation of a type set. For quite a few years these were considered by numismatists to be *patterns*, and thus anyone forming a type set of regular-issue U.S. coins did not have to notice them. However, in recent decades, research by R.W. Julian (in particular), Walter Breen, and others, has revealed that the vast majority of 1836 and 1839 silver dollars originally produced were put into circulation at face value. Accordingly, they were coins of the realm at the time, were spent as currency, and are deserving of a place among regular coinage types.

The 1836 Gobrecht dollar is easy enough to find in today's marketplace, although expensive. The original production amounted to 1,600 coins, to which an unknown number of restrikes can be added. The main problem arises with the 1839, made only to the extent of 300 pieces. Those that exist today nearly always have abundant signs of circulation. This is the rarest of all major U.S. coin design types, even outclassing the 1796–1797 half dollar and the 1808 quarter eagle.

In 1840 the regular Liberty Seated dollar made its appearance, with the reverse depicting a perched eagle holding an olive branch and arrows. This style was continued through 1873, with minor modifications over the years; for example, in 1866 the motto IN GOD WE TRUST was added to the reverse. Generally, Liberty Seated dollars can be easily enough found in circulated grades from VF up, as well as low Mint State levels. MS-63 and higher pieces are in the minority, particularly of the 1840–1865 type.

Morgan silver dollars, made by the hundreds of millions from 1878 through 1921, are easily found, with the 1881-S being at once the most common of all varieties existing today in gem condition and also usually seen with sharp strike and nice appearance.

Peace silver dollars of 1921 through 1935 exist in large quantities. Some collectors select the first year of issue, 1921, as a separate type, as the design is in high relief. The 1921 is plentiful in Mint State, but rarely is found sharply struck at the obverse and reverse center. Later Peace dollars with shallow relief abound in MS-63 and finer grades, although strike quality can be a problem.

The Peace dollar was the last of the United States' circulating .900 fine silver dollars. One final type of dollar coin was produced in the large 38.1 mm format—the Eisenhower dollar, often colloquially called a "silver dollar" even though its regular issues were made of copper and nickel. Since the Eisenhower dollar, U.S. coins of this denomination have been produced in smaller diameters and in base metals. These modern dollars are explored

Anthony de Francisci, designer of the Peace dollar, used his wife Teresa (ranked in the *100 Greatest Women on Coins*) as the model for his Miss Liberty.

in detail in the next chapter. The U.S. Mint has also produced various *commemorative* silver dollars from 1900 to date, and the one-ounce American Silver Eagle bullion coin has a denomination of one dollar. These coins are covered in the Commemoratives and Bullion sections, respectively.

FOR THE COLLECTOR AND INVESTOR: SILVER DOLLARS AS A SPECIALTY

Generally, silver dollars of the 1794–1803 years are collected by dates and major types.

Although the 1794, of which an estimated 135 or so exist today, is famous and expensive, other varieties are eminently affordable in such grades as VF and EF. Beyond the listings herein there is a rich panorama of die varieties, most extensively delineated in the 1993 two-volume study *Silver Dollars and Trade Dollars of the United States: A Complete Encyclopedia*. This built upon earlier works, including J.W. Haseltine's *Type Table of United States Dollars, Half Dollars and Quarter Dollars*, and, especially, the long-term standard work by M.H. Bolender, *The United States Early Silver Dollars from 1794 to 1803*. In many instances among early dollars the number of aficionados desiring a particularly rare die combination may be even smaller than the population of coins available—with the result that not much premium has to be paid.

The 1804 silver dollar is a study in itself. None were actually produced in the year 1804. Several were made in 1834 as presentation pieces for foreign dignitaries, and even later examples were made for private collectors. Only a handful exist of this classic rarity, the "King of American Coins."

After 1803 it is a long jump to 1836, when silver dollars (of the Gobrecht design) were again struck for circulation. In 1839 more Gobrecht dollars were struck, with the design modified. In addition to the listings in this book are a number of other die combinations, edge and metal varieties, etc., including pieces of the year 1838, most of which are pattern restrikes (studied in *United States Pattern Coins*). These are avidly desired and collected.

Forming a specialized collection of Liberty Seated dollars from 1840 through 1873 has been a pursuit of many collectors over the years. Generally, the Philadelphia Mint dates are available without difficulty, although the 1851 and 1852 are typically acquired as Proof restrikes—originals of both years being prohibitively rare. Most difficult to find in higher grades are coins of the branch mints, including the famous 1870-S, of which only 10 are known to exist and for which no mintage quantity figure was ever listed in official reports. Branch-mint pieces, starting with the 1846-O, were placed into circulation and used extensively. Beginning in 1870, dollars of this type were struck at Carson City; these also are seen with evidence of circulation. The only exceptions to this are certain dollars of 1859-O and 1860-O which turned up in very "baggy" Mint State preservation (showing contact marks from other coins) among Treasury hoards, to the extent of several thousand pieces of both dates combined.

Morgan silver dollars from 1878 through 1921 are one of the most active and popular series in American numismatics. Approximately 100 different major varieties can be collected, although certain unusual varieties (not basic dates and mintmarks) can be dropped from a collection or added as desired. The vast majority of Morgan dollars can be found in Mint State. When these coins were first minted there was little need for them in circulation, and hundreds of millions of coins piled up in Treasury and other vaults. Although many were melted in 1918, enough remained that untold millions exist today in the hands of the public.

Varieties such as the 1881-S are common and are normally seen in high grades with sharp strike, but others with high mintages, the 1886-O and 1896-O being examples, are quite rare in MS-63 and finer, and when seen usually have rather poor eye appeal. Accordingly, quite a bit of discernment is recommended for the savvy collector.

Peace silver dollars, minted from 1921 to 1935, include the High Relief style of 1921, and the shallow-relief motif of 1922 to 1935. A basic set of 24 different dates and mintmarks is easily enough obtained, including in Mint State. The most elusive is the 1934-S.

FLOWING HAIR (1794–1795)

Engraver: *Robert Scot.* **Weight:** *26.96 grams.* **Composition:** *.900 silver, .100 copper (net weight 0.78011 oz. pure silver).* **Diameter:** *Approximately 39–40 mm.* **Edge:** *HUNDRED CENTS ONE DOLLAR OR UNIT with decorations between words.* **Mint:** *Philadelphia.*

Bowers-Borckardt–27, Bolender-5.

History. The first U.S. silver dollars were of the Flowing Hair design. In 1794 only 1,758 were released for circulation (slightly fewer than were struck), and the next year nearly 100 times that amount. These coins were popular in their time and circulated for decades afterward. Many were used in international trade, particularly in the Caribbean.

Striking and Sharpness. On the obverse, check the hair details. It is essential to check the die variety, as certain varieties were struck with very little detail at the center. Accordingly, high-grade examples can appear to be well worn on the hair. Check the star centers, as well. On the reverse, check the breast and wings of the eagle. All 1794 dollars are lightly struck at the lower left of the obverse (often at portions of the date) and to a lesser extent the corresponding part of the reverse. Many coins of both dates have planchet adjustment marks (from overweight blanks being filed down to proper weight before striking), often heavy and sometimes even disfiguring; these are not noted by the certification services. Expect weakness in some areas on dollars of this type; a coin with Full Details on both sides is virtually unheard of. Sharp striking and excellent eye appeal add to the value dramatically. These coins are very difficult to find problem-free, even in MS.

Availability. The 1794 is rare in all grades, with an estimated 125 to 135 known, including a handful in MS. The 1795 is easily available, with an estimated 4,000 to 7,500 still existing, although some die varieties range from scarce to rare. Many if not most have been dipped at one time or another, and many have been retoned, often satisfactorily. The existence of *any* luster is an exception between EF-40 and AU-58. MS coins are quite scarce (perhaps 150 to 250 existing, most dated 1795), especially at MS-63 or above.

Varieties listed herein are those most significant to collectors, but numerous minor variations may be found because each of the early dies was made individually. (Values of varieties not listed in this guide depend on collector interest and demand.) Blanks were weighed before the dollars were struck and over-weight pieces were filed to remove excess silver. Coins with old adjustment marks from this filing process may be worth less than the values shown here. Some Flowing Hair dollars were weight-adjusted through insertion of a small (8 mm) silver plug in the center of the blank planchet before the coin was struck.

GRADING STANDARDS

MS-60 to 70 (Mint State). *Obverse:* At MS-60, some abrasion and contact marks are evident, most noticeably on the cheek and in the fields. Luster is present, but may be dull or lifeless, and interrupted in patches. At MS-63, contact marks are very few, and abrasion is light and not obvious. An MS-65 coin has little or, better yet, no abrasion, and contact marks are minute. Luster should be full

1794; BB-1, Bolender-1. Graded MS-64. Fully brilliant and highly lustrous.

and rich. Coins graded above MS-65 are more theoretical than actual for this type—but they do exist, and are defined by having fewer marks as perfection is approached. *Reverse:* Comments apply as for the obverse, except that abrasion and contact marks are most noticeable on the eagle at the center, although most dollars of this type are lightly struck in the higher points of that area. The field area is small and is protected by lettering and the wreath and in any given grade shows fewer marks than on the obverse.

Illustrated coin: Like all 1794 dollars, this coin is weak at the left obverse and the corresponding part of the reverse. Planchet flaws are seen at stars 3 and 5. The center obverse is very well struck.

AU-50, 53, 55, 58 (About Uncirculated). *Obverse:* Light wear is seen on the hair area immediately to the left of the face and neck (except for those flatly struck there), on the cheek, and on the top of the neck truncation, more so at AU-50 than at AU–53 or 55. An AU-58 coin has minimal traces of wear. An AU-50 coin has luster in protected areas among the stars and letters, with little luster in the open fields or the portrait. Some certified coins have

1795, Two Leaves; BB-21, Bolender-1. Graded AU-58.

virtually no luster, but are considered high quality in other aspects. At AU-58, most luster is partially present in the fields. On any high-grade dollar, luster is often a better key to grading than is the appearance of wear. *Reverse:* Light wear is seen on the eagle's body and the upper edges of the wings. At AU-50, detail is lost for some of the feathers in this area. However, some coins are weak to begin with. Light wear is seen on the wreath and lettering. Again, luster is the best key to actual wear. This ranges from perhaps 20% remaining in protected areas (at AU-50) to two-thirds or more (at AU-58). Generally, the reverse has more luster than the obverse.

Illustrated coin: This coin shows above-average striking sharpness on the obverse.

EF-40, 45 (Extremely Fine). *Obverse:* More wear is evident on the portrait, especially on the hair to the left of the face and neck (again, remember that some varieties were struck with flatness in this area), the cheek, and the tip of the neck truncation. Excellent detail remains in low-relief areas of the hair. The stars show wear, as do the date and letters. Luster, if present at all, is minimal and in protected areas. *Reverse:* The eagle shows more

1795, Three Leaves; BB-26, Bolender-12a. Graded EF-40.

wear, this being the focal point to check. Most or nearly all detail is well defined. These aspects should be reviewed in combination with knowledge of the die variety, to determine the sharpness of the coin when it was first struck. Most silver dollars of this type were flat at the highest area of the center at the time they were made, as this was opposite the highest point of the hair in the press when the coins were struck. Additional wear is on the wreath and letters, but many details are present. Some luster may be seen in protected areas, and if present is slightly more abundant than on the obverse.

Illustrated coin: On the obverse, a massive die crack extends upward through the 7 of the date.

VF-20, 30 (Very Fine). *Obverse:* The hair is well worn at VF-20, less so at VF-30. On well-struck varieties the weakness is in the area left of the temple and cheek. The strands are blended as to be heavy. The cheek shows only slight relief. The stars have more wear, making them appear larger (an optical illusion). *Reverse:* The body of the eagle shows few if any feathers, while the wings have a third to half of the feathers visible, depending on the strike. The leaves

1795, Two Leaves; BB-21, Bolender-1. Graded VF-20.

lack most detail, but veins can be seen on a few. Scattered, non-disfiguring marks are normal for this and lower grades. Any major defects should be noted separately.

Illustrated coin: Light rim bumps should be noted. This coin features attractive medium toning.

F-12, 15 (Fine). *Obverse:* Wear is more extensive than on the preceding, reducing the definition of the thick strands of hair. The cheek has less detail, but the eye is usually well defined. On most coins, the stars appear larger. The rim is distinct in most areas, and many denticles remain visible. *Reverse:* Wear is more extensive. Now, feather details are fewer, mostly remaining on the wing to the left and at the extreme tip of the wing on the

1795, Three Leaves; BB-27, Bolender-5. Graded F-12.

right. As always, the die variety in question can have an influence on this. The wreath and lettering are worn further. The rim is usually complete, with most denticles visible.

Illustrated coin: This variety is flatly struck on the head, and examples in higher grades show no detail at the center. Note the smooth, even wear with some marks.

VG-8, 10 (Very Good). *Obverse:* The portrait is mostly seen in outline form, with most hair strands gone, although some are visible left of the neck, and the tips at the lower left are clear. The eye is distinct. The stars appear larger still, again an illusion. LIBERTY and the date are readable and usually full, although some letters may be weak at their tops. The rim is usually complete, and many denticles can be seen. *Reverse:* The eagle is mostly an outline, although some traces of feathers may be seen in the tail and the lower part of the inside of the right wing. The rim is worn, as are the letters, with some weak, but the motto is readable.

1795, Two Leaves; BB-11, Bolender-3. Graded VG-10.

   Illustrated coin: This coin shows some microscopic granularity overall. It is an interesting variety with a silver plug inserted at the center of the planchet prior to minting, to slightly increase the weight; this feature can barely be seen in outline form.

G-4, 6 (Good). *Obverse:* Wear is more extensive. LIBERTY and the stars are all there, but weak. The head is an outline, although the eye can still be seen. The rim is well worn or even missing. LIBERTY is worn, and parts of some letters may be missing, but elements of all should be readable. The date is readable, but worn. *Reverse:* The eagle is flat and discernible in outline form. The wreath is well worn. Some of the letters may be partly miss-

1795, Two Leaves; BB-11, Bolender-1. Graded G-6.

ing. At this level some "averaging" can be done. If the letters are stronger than usual in one area, but some are missing in another area, the coin can still qualify as G-4.

   Illustrated coin: This is an attractive example with smooth, even wear and a few defects.

AG-3 (About Good). *Obverse:* Wear is extensive, but some stars and letters can usually be discerned. The head is in outline form. The date, while readable, may be partially worn away. *Reverse:* The reverse is well worn, with parts of the wreath and lettering missing.

1795, Three Leaves. Graded AG-3.

**1795, Two Leaves
Beneath Each Wing**

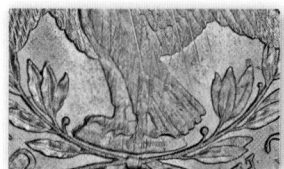

**1795, Three Leaves
Beneath Each Wing**

1795, Silver Plug
BB-15, Bolender-7.

	Mintage	Cert	Avg	%MS	AG-3	G-4	VG-8	F-12	VF-20	EF-40	AU-50	MS-60	MS-63
1794 †	1,758	35	38.0	17%	$37,500	$65,000	$95,000	$115,000	$150,000	$275,000	$350,000	$700,000	$1,600,000
Auctions: $305,500, EF-40, January 2014; $223,250, VF-35, August 2014													
1794, Silver Plug (a)	(b)	1	66.0	100%									
Auctions: $10,016,875, SP-66, January 2013													
1795, All kinds	160,295												
1795, Two Leaves		190	32.1	6%	$1,100	$1,750	$2,500	$4,350	$5,750	$13,500	$20,000	$70,000	$175,000
Auctions: $25,850, AU-55, August 2013; $4,994, VF-35, August 2014; $5,993, VF-30, August 2014; $3,819, VF-25, October 2014													
1795, Three Leaves		172	34.9	3%	$1,100	$1,750	$2,500	$4,100	$5,500	$12,000	$19,500	$65,000	$160,000
Auctions: $822,500, SP-64, August 2014; $12,925, AU-50, August 2014; $5,523, VF-20, May 2015; $3,819, F-15, March 2015													
1795, Silver Plug		35	33.3	6%	$1,500	$2,800	$4,750	$8,500	$16,000	$27,500	$45,000	$150,000	
Auctions: $99,875, AU-55, August 2013													

† Ranked in the *100 Greatest U.S. Coins* (fourth edition). **a.** This unique piece, graded SP-66, shows evidence of planchet adjustment marks, as well as traces of a silver plug that was added to bring the coin's weight up to specification. **b.** Included in 1794 mintage figure.

DRAPED BUST, SMALL EAGLE REVERSE (1795–1798)

Designer: *Robert Scot.* **Weight:** *26.96 grams.* **Composition:** *.8924 silver, .1076 copper (net weight .77352 oz. pure silver).* **Diameter:** *Approximately 39–40 mm.* **Edge:** *HUNDRED CENTS ONE DOLLAR OR UNIT with decorations between words.* **Mint:** *Philadelphia.*

BB-51, Bolender-14.

History. The Draped Bust silver dollar with the Small Eagle reverse, inaugurated in 1795, brought the first appearance of this popular obverse portrait—a depiction of Miss Liberty that later was used on other silver denominations as well as copper half cents and cents. The motif was continued into 1798. Production of the Draped Bust silver dollars started at the end of the year on a new mint press that was first used for striking Flowing Hair dollars that summer. Draped Bust dollars circulated widely, especially outside the United States, and in the Caribbean in particular.

Striking and Sharpness. On the obverse, check the highest areas of the hair, the bust line, and the centers of the stars. On the reverse, check the feathers on the eagle's breast and wings. Examine the denticles. Planchet adjustment marks (from the filing down of overweight blanks) are common and should be avoided. Studying die varieties can be helpful for accurate grading. For example, the Small Letters reverse, a long-lived die design used from 1795 to 1798, has shallow relief and is usually seen with a low rim, with the result that its grade is lower than that of the obverse. On some reverse dies the eagle has very little detail. Fairly sharp striking (not necessarily Full Details) and excellent eye appeal add to the value dramatically.

Availability. These silver dollars are readily available as a type, although certain varieties range from scarce to very rare. MS coins are elusive and when seen are usually of the 1795 date, sometimes with prooflike surfaces. Most coins have been dipped and/or retoned, some successfully. These coins acquired marks more readily than did smaller denominations, and such are to be expected (but should be noted along with the grade, if distracting). Careful buying is needed to obtain coins with good eye appeal. Many AU examples are deeply toned and recolored.

The Smithsonian's National Numismatic Collection includes a unique Specimen 1794 dollar, plugged, and a unique Specimen 1797 10 Stars Left, 6 Stars Right, dollar.

GRADING STANDARDS

MS-60 to 70 (Mint State). *Obverse:* At MS-60, some abrasion and contact marks are evident, most noticeably on the cheek, the drapery at the shoulder, and the right field. Luster is present, but may be dull or lifeless, and interrupted in patches. At MS-63, contact marks are few, and abrasion is harder to detect. Many coins listed as Mint State are deeply toned, making it impossible to evaluate abrasion and even light wear; these are best avoided completely. An MS-65 coin has

1796, Small Date, Large Letters; BB-61, Bolender-2. Graded MS-60.

no abrasion, and contact marks are so minute as to require magnification. Luster should be full and rich. Coins grading above MS-65 are more theoretical than actual for this type—but they do exist, and are defined by having fewer marks as perfection is approached. *Reverse:* Comments apply as for the obverse, except that abrasion and contact marks are most noticeable on the eagle at the center, a situation complicated by the fact that this area was often flatly struck, not only on the famous Small Letters dies used from 1795 to 1798, but on some others as well. Grading is best done by the obverse, then verified by the reverse. In the Mint State category the amount of luster is usually a good key to grading. The field area is small and is protected by lettering and the wreath, and in any given grade shows fewer marks than on the obverse.

Illustrated coin: Note the tiny dig near Miss Liberty's ear. This coin is fairly well struck overall, but with some lightness on the eagle's body and leg on the right. It has excellent eye appeal.

AU-50, 53, 55, 58 (About Uncirculated). *Obverse:* Light wear is seen on the hair area above the ear and extending to left of the forehead, on the ribbon, and on the drapery at the shoulder, more so at AU-50 than at AU–53 or 55. An AU-58 coin has minimal traces of wear. An AU-50 coin has luster in protected areas among the stars and letters, with little in the open fields or on the portrait. At AU-58, most luster is present in the fields, but is worn away on the highest parts of the motifs. At this level

1797, Stars 9x7, Large Letters; BB-73, Bolender-1. Graded AU-50.

there are many deeply toned and recolored coins, necessitating caution when buying. *Reverse:* Light wear is seen on the eagle's body (keep in mind this area might be lightly struck) and edges of the wings. Light wear is seen on the wreath and lettering. Luster is the best key to actual wear. This ranges from perhaps 20% remaining in protected areas (at AU-50) to nearly full mint bloom (at AU-58).

Illustrated coin: This coin has some lightness of strike, but is better than average. It has some dings and marks, but these are not immediately obvious; without them, the coin might grade higher. This illustrates the many variables on these large, heavy coins. No single rule fits all.

EF-40, 45 (Extremely Fine). *Obverse:* More wear is evident on the upper hair area and the ribbon, and on the drapery and bosom. Excellent detail remains in low-relief areas of the hair. The stars show wear, as do the date and letters. Luster, if present at all, is minimal and in protected areas. For any and all dollars of this type, knowledge of die variety characteristics is essential to grading. Once again, one rule does not fit all. *Reverse:* The eagle, this being the focal point to check, shows

1796, Small Date, Large Letters; BB-61, Bolender-4. Graded EF-40.

more wear. On most strikings, the majority of feathers remain on the interior areas of the wings. Additional wear is on the wreath and letters, but many details are present. Some luster may be seen in protected areas and if present is slightly more abundant than on the obverse.

Illustrated coin: Some marks are on the neck and a small pit is above the eagle's beak.

VF-20, 30 (Very Fine). *Obverse:* The higher-relief areas of hair are well worn at VF-20, less so at VF-30. The drapery and bosom show extensive wear, usually resulting in loss of most detail below the neck. The stars have more wear, making them appear larger. *Reverse:* The body of the eagle shows few if any feathers, while the wings have about half of the feathers visible, depending on the strike. The leaves lack most detail and are in outline form. Scattered, non-disfiguring

1797, Stars 9x7, Small Letters; BB-72, Bolender-2. Graded VF-20.

marks are normal for this and lower grades. Any major defects should be noted separately.

Illustrated coin: This is the particularly famous Small Letters die (one of three Small Letters dies used for this type) first used in 1795 and last used in 1798. Used on 1795 BB-51, later 1796 BB-62, BB-63, and BB-66 now relapped, 1797 BB-72, and 1798 BB-81. The rims are low, and the eagle is in low relief. For coins struck from this particular reverse die, grading must be done by the obverse only.

F-12, 15 (Fine). *Obverse:* Wear is more extensive than on a Very Fine coin, particularly noticeable on the hair, face, and bosom. The stars appear larger. About half the hair detail remains, most noticeably behind the neck and shoulder. The rim shows wear but is complete or nearly so, with most denticles visible. *Reverse:* Wear is more extensive. Now, feather details are diminished, with relatively few remaining on the wings. The wreath and lettering are worn further, and

1796, Large Date, Small Letters; BB-65, Bolender-5. Graded F-12.

the rim is usually weak in areas, although most denticles can be seen.

Illustrated coin: This is not the long-lived Small Letters die discussed above; this Small Letters die was used only in 1796. It is distinguished by a piece out of the die at the lower right of the reverse.

VG-8, 10 (Very Good). *Obverse:* The portrait is worn further, with much detail lost in the area above the level of the ear, although the curl over the forehead is delineated. There is some definition at the back of the hair and behind the shoulder, with the hair now combined to form thick strands. The ear is discernible, as is the eye. The stars appear larger still, again an illusion. The rim is weak in areas. LIBERTY and the date are readable and usually full. The rim is worn away in areas, although many denticles can still be discerned. *Reverse:* The eagle is mostly an outline, with parts blending into the field (on lighter strikes). The rim is worn, as are the letters, with some weak, but the motto is readable.

1796, Small Date, Large Letters;
BB-61, Bolender-4. Graded VG-10.

Illustrated coin: Note the vertical scratches on the cheek.

G-4, 6 (Good). *Obverse:* Wear is more extensive, and some stars may be partly missing. The head is an outline. The eye is visible only in outline form. The rim is well worn or even missing in areas. LIBERTY is worn, and parts of some letters may be missing, but elements of all should be readable. The date is readable, but worn. Usually the date is rather bold. *Reverse:* The eagle is flat and discernible in outline form, and may be blending into the field. The wreath is well worn. Some of the letters may be partly missing (for some shallow-relief dies with low rims). At this level some "averaging" can be done. If the letters are stronger than usual in one area, but some are missing in another area, the coin can still qualify as G-4. This general rule is applicable to most other series as well.

1797, Stars 9x7, Large Letters;
BB-73, Bolender-1. Graded G-4.

Illustrated coin: This is a well-circulated coin with several edge bumps.

AG-3 (About Good). *Obverse:* Wear is very extensive, but most letters and stars should be discernible. The head is in outline form. The date, while readable, may be partially worn away. *Reverse:* The reverse is well worn, with parts of the wreath and lettering missing. At this level, the reverse usually gives much less information than does the obverse.

1796, Large Date, Small Letters;
BB-65, Bolender-5a. Graded AG-3.

1795, Off-Center Bust

1795, Centered Bust

1796, Small Date

1796, Large Date

Small Letters

Large Letters

1797, 10 Stars Left, 6 Right

1797, 9 Stars Left, 7 Right

1798, 15 Stars on Obverse

1798, 13 Stars on Obverse

	Mintage	Cert	Avg	%MS	AG-3	G-4	VG-8	F-12	VF-20	EF-40	AU-50	MS-60	MS-63
1795, All kinds	42,738												
1795, Off-Center Bust		98	39.0	7%	$960	$1,450	$2,150	$3,500	$5,100	$10,750	$15,500	$60,000	$110,000
Auctions: $910,625, MS-66, November 2013; $30,550, AU-58, August 2014; $12,925, EF-45, August 2014; $1,528, G-4, July 2015													
1795, Centered Bust		37	39.1	16%	$960	$1,450	$2,150	$3,500	$5,100	$10,750	$16,500	$55,000	$150,000
Auctions: $17,625, AU-50, March 2013; $7,638, EF-45, August 2014; $7,050, EF-45, August 2014; $3,995, EF-40, June 2015													
1796, All kinds	79,920												
1796, Small Date, Small Letters (a)		25	41.2	4%	$825	$1,550	$2,100	$3,800	$5,500	$10,750	$15,000	$62,500	$150,000
Auctions: $1,175,000, MS-65, April 2013; $4,406, VF-30, August 2014; $3,290, F-12, October 2014													
1796, Small Date, Large Letters		48	36.9	2%	$825	$1,550	$2,100	$3,800	$5,500	$10,750	$15,000	$75,000	$200,000
Auctions: $352,500, MS-63, November 2013; $7,638, EF-45, August 2014; $5,111, VF-30, September 2014													
1796, Large Date, Small Letters		50	34.2	6%	$825	$1,550	$2,100	$3,400	$5,250	$10,500	$15,000	$62,500	$160,000
Auctions: $12,338, AU-50, August 2014; $13,513, AU-50, August 2013; $3,055, VF-20, August 2014													
1797, All kinds	7,776												
1797, 10 Stars Left, 6 Right		112	38.5	6%	$850	$1,550	$2,000	$3,000	$5,000	$10,000	$14,750	$62,000	$125,000
Auctions: $440,625, MS-64, November 2013; $4,406, VF-25, August 2014													
1797, 9 Stars Left, 7 Right, Large Letters		85	36.6	5%	$850	$1,550	$2,000	$3,100	$6,000	$10,750	$15,300	$63,000	$135,000
Auctions: $381,875, MS-64, November 2013; $5,288, VF-30, August 2014; $2,820, F-12, August 2014													
1797, 9 Stars Left, 7 Right, Small Letters		34	32.4	3%	$1,200	$1,800	$2,750	$3,900	$8,200	$16,250	$32,500	$110,000	
Auctions: $164,500, MS-62, November 2013; $7,638, VF-20, August 2014													
1798, All kinds (b)	327,536												
1798, 15 Stars on Obverse		32	37.4	6%	$1,100	$1,750	$2,650	$3,800	$8,000	$16,000	$24,500	$84,000	$155,000
Auctions: $258,500, MS-63, November 2013; $6,169, VF-35, August 2014; $9,988, VF-25, August 2014													
1798, 13 Stars on Obverse		31	38.5	6%	$1,000	$1,700	$2,100	$3,500	$7,750	$15,000	$20,000	$150,000	
Auctions: $129,250, AU-58, November 2013; $9,106, EF-40, August 2014													

a. 3 varieties. b. The Mint struck 327,536 silver dollars in 1798, but did not record how many of each type (Small Eagle reverse and Heraldic Eagle reverse).

DRAPED BUST, HERALDIC EAGLE REVERSE (1798–1804)

Designer: *Robert Scot.* **Weight:** *26.96 grams.* **Composition:** *.8924 silver, .1076 copper (net weight .77352 oz. pure silver).* **Diameter:** *Approximately 39–40 mm.* **Edge:** *HUNDRED CENTS ONE DOLLAR OR UNIT with decorations between words.* **Mint:** *Philadelphia.*

Circulation Strike
BB-241, Bolender-6.

Proof (Restrike)
BB-302.

History. The design of the silver dollar closely follows that of other silver coins of the era. The two earliest reverse dies of 1798 have five vertical lines in the stripes in the shield. All dollar dies thereafter have four vertical lines. Production of the Draped Bust dollar continued through early 1804, but in that year the coins were struck from earlier-dated dies.

1804 silver dollars were first struck in 1834 from 1804-dated dies prepared at that time. (As a class these can be called *novodels*, rather than *restrikes*, as no originals were ever made in 1804.) The 1804 dollars were produced in Proof format. Later, probably circa 1859, a new reverse die was made up and combined with the earlier 1804 obverse (made in 1834). Those coins made in 1834 and around that time are today known as Class I dollars, whereas those made with a different reverse, beginning in 1859 and continuing perhaps through the 1870s, are known as Class III. An intermediate variety, from the Class III die combination but with a plain instead of lettered edge, is in the Smithsonian Institution's National Numismatic Collection and is known as Class II. All varieties combined comprise 15 different specimens. The 1804 dollar has been called the "King of American Coins" for well over a century and has achieved great fame. Interested numismatists are directed to *The Fantastic 1804 Dollar, Tribute Edition* (2009).

Striking and Sharpness. Very few of these coins have Full Details. On the obverse, check the highest points of the hair, the details of the drapery, and the centers of the stars. On the reverse, check the shield, the eagle, the stars above the eagle, and the clouds. Examine the denticles on both sides. Planchet adjustment marks are often seen, from overweight blanks being filed down to proper specifications, but they usually are lighter than on the earlier silver dollar types. The relief of the dies and the height of the rims can vary, affecting sharpness. Sharp striking and excellent eye appeal add to the value dramatically. Top-grade MS coins, when found, usually are dated 1800.

Availability. This is the most readily available type among the early silver dollars. Most often seen are the dates 1798 and 1799. Many varieties are available in any grade desired, although MS–63 and 65 coins are elusive. Other die varieties are rare at any level. As with other early dollars, connoisseurship is needed to acquire high-quality coins. These silver dollars usually have problems. To evaluate one for the market it is necessary to grade it, determine its quality of striking, and examine the characteristics of its surface. Nearly all have been dipped or cleaned.

Proofs. There were no Proofs coined in the era this type was issued. Years later, in 1834, the U.S. Mint made up new dies with the 1804 date and struck an unknown number of Proofs, perhaps a dozen or so, for inclusion in presentation Proof sets for foreign dignitaries. Today these are called Class I 1804 dollars. Eight examples are known, one of which shows circulation. The finest by far is the Sultan of Muscat coin, which approaches perfection. Circa 1858 or 1859 the Mint prepared a new obverse die dated 1804 and struck an unknown number of examples for private sale to collectors and dealers—the Class III dollars. No records were kept. These were artificially worn to give them the appearance of original dollars struck in 1804.

Sometime between circa 1858 and the 1870s, the Mint prepared new obverse dies dated 1801, 1802, and 1803, and struck Proof dollars for secret sale to the numismatic market. Many if not most were distributed through J.W. Haseltine, a Philadelphia dealer who had close connections with Mint officials. Today these are known as "Proof restrikes." All are rare, the 1801 being particularly so.

Class I 1804 dollars typically show hairlines and light abrasion. Grading is usually very liberal, in view of the fame of this rarity (not that this is logical). Circulated examples of Class I and Class III 1804 dollars have been graded using prefixes such as EF and AU. Proof restrikes of 1801 to 1803 generally survive in much higher grades, PF-64 or finer.

GRADING STANDARDS

MS-60 to 70 (Mint State). *Obverse:* At MS-60, some abrasion and contact marks are evident, most noticeably on the cheek, the drapery, and the right field. Luster is present, but may be dull or lifeless, and interrupted in patches. At MS-63, contact marks are very few, and abrasion is hard to detect except under magnification. Knowledge of the die variety is desirable, but on balance the portraits on this type are usually quite well

1798, 10 Arrows; BB-108, Bolender-13. Graded MS-63.

struck. An MS-65 coin has no abrasion, and contact marks are so minute as to require magnification. Luster should be full and rich. Coins grading above MS-65 are more theoretical than actual for this type—but they do exist and are defined by having fewer marks as perfection is approached. *Reverse:* Comments apply as for the obverse, except that abrasion and contact marks are most noticeable on the eagle's neck, the tips of the wing, and the tail. The field area is complex, without much open space, given the stars above the eagle, the arrows and olive branch, and other features. Accordingly, marks will not be as noticeable as on the obverse.

Illustrated coin: This coin is well struck, essentially problem free, and with superb eye appeal.

AU-50, 53, 55, 58 (About Uncirculated). *Obverse:* Light wear is seen on the hair area above the ear and extending to left of the forehead, on the ribbon, and on the drapery and bosom, more so at AU-50 than AU-53 or 55. An AU-58 coin has minimal traces of wear. An AU-50 coin has luster in protected areas among the stars and letters, with little in the open fields or on the portrait. At AU-58, much luster is present in the fields, but is worn away on the highest parts of the

1799, Irregular Date, 13-Star Reverse; BB-152, Bolender-15. Graded AU-50.

motifs. *Reverse:* Comments as preceding, except that the eagle's neck, the tips and top of the wings, the clouds, and the tail now show noticeable wear, as do other features. Luster ranges from perhaps 20% remaining in protected areas (at AU-50) to nearly full mint bloom (at AU-58). Sometimes the reverse of this type retains much more luster than the obverse, this being dependent on the height of the rim and the depth of the strike (particularly at the center).

Illustrated coin: This is an attractive and problem-free coin.

EF-40, 45 (Extremely Fine). *Obverse:* More wear is evident on the upper hair area and the ribbon, and on the drapery and bosom. The shoulder is a key spot to check for wear. Excellent detail remains in low-relief areas of the hair. The stars show wear, as do the date and letters. Luster, if present at all, is minimal and in protected areas. *Reverse:* Wear is greater than on an AU coin, overall. The neck has lost its feather detail on the highest points. Feathers have lost some detail near the edges of the

1802, Narrow Normal Date; BB-241, Bolender-6. Graded EF-45.

wings. Some traces of luster may be seen, more so at EF-45 than at EF-40.

Illustrated coin: This is an attractive example retaining some mint luster. It has above-average striking sharpness.

VF-20, 30 (Very Fine). *Obverse:* The higher-relief areas of hair are well worn at VF-20, less so at VF-30. The drapery at the shoulder and the bosom show extensive wear. The stars have more wear, making them appear larger (an optical illusion seen on most worn silver coins of this era). *Reverse:* Wear is greater, including on the shield and the wing feathers. Most of the feathers on the wings are clear. The star centers are flat. Other areas have lost detail as well.

1799; BB-157, Bolender-5. Graded VF-20.

Illustrated coin: Some scratches appear on the portrait. This coin was cleaned long ago and now is retoned. It is a typical early dollar at this grade.

F-12, 15 (Fine). *Obverse:* Wear is more extensive than on a Very Fine coin, particularly on the hair, face, and bosom. The stars appear larger. About half the hair detail remains, most noticeably behind the neck and shoulder. The rim may be partially worn away and blend into the field. *Reverse:* Wear is even more extensive, with the shield and wing feathers being points to observe. Half or slightly more of the feathers will remain clear. The incuse E PLURIBUS UNUM

1798, Pointed 9, Close Date; BB-122, Bolender-14. Graded F-12.

may have a few letters worn away. The clouds all seem to be connected except on varieties in which they are spaced apart. The stars are weak. Parts of the border and lettering may be weak.

Illustrated coin: This coin was cleaned long ago. Cleaning and retoning is common on dollars of this era, but often is not noted by the grading services.

VG-8, 10 (Very Good). *Obverse:* The portrait is mostly seen in outline form, with most hair strands gone, although there is some definition at the back of the hair and behind the shoulder. The ear is discernible, as is the eye. The stars appear larger still, again an illusion. The rim is weak in areas. LIBERTY and the date are readable and usually full, although some letters may be weak at their tops. *Reverse:* Wear is more extensive. Half

1799. Graded VG-8.

or more of the letters in the motto are worn away. Most feathers are worn away, although separation of some of the lower feathers may be seen at the edges of the wings. Some stars are faint or missing. The border blends into the field in areas and some letters are weak. As always, a particular die variety can vary in areas of weakness.

G-4, 6 (Good). *Obverse:* Wear is more extensive, and some stars may be partly missing. The head is an outline. The eye is visible only in outline form. The rim is well worn or even missing in areas. LIBERTY is worn, and parts of some letters may be missing, but elements of all should be readable. The date is readable, but worn. *Reverse:* Wear is more extensive. The upper part of the eagle is flat. The feathers are noticeable only at the lower

1799; BB-169, Bolender-21. Graded G-4.

edge of the wings, sometimes incompletely, and do not have detail. The upper part of the shield is mostly flat. Only a few letters of the motto can be seen, if any at all. The rim is worn extensively, and the letters are well worn, but the inscription should be readable.

Illustrated coin: This coin has some marks, but is respectable for the grade.

AG-3 (About Good). *Obverse:* Wear is so extensive that the coin is barely identifiable. The head is in outline form. LIBERTY is mostly gone; same for the stars. The date, while readable, may be partially worn away. *Reverse:* Extensive wear is seen overall, with the rim worn away and some areas worn smooth. The eagle can be discerned in outline form, but not necessarily completely. A few stray motto letters may remain.

1799. Graded AG-3.

PF-60 to 70 (Proof). *Obverse and Reverse:* For lower Proof levels, extensive abrasion is seen in the fields, or even evidence of circulation (the Mickley example of the 1804 Class I, earlier graded as AU-50, was certified as PF-62 by a leading certification service in 2008). Numbers assigned by grading services have been erratic. No rules are known, and grading has not been consistent.

1804, Class I. Proof.

1798, Knob 9

1798, Pointed 9

1798, Pointed 9, Close Date

1798, Pointed 9, Wide Date

Five Vertical Lines in Shield's Stripes

Four Vertical Lines in Shield's Stripes

1798, Pointed 9, 10 Arrows

1798, Pointed 9, 4 Berries

1799, 99 Over 98, 15-Star Reverse

1799, 99 Over 98, 13-Star Reverse

1799, Irregular Date, 15-Star Reverse

1799, Irregular Date, 13-Star Reverse

1799, Irregular Date

1799, Normal Date

1800, Very Wide Date, Low 8

1800, "Dotted Date"

1799, 8 Stars Left, 5 Stars Right

1800, Only 12 Arrows   1800, AMERICAI

	Mintage	Cert	Avg	%MS	G-4	VG-8	F-12	VF-20	EF-40	AU-50	MS-60 / PF-63	MS-63 / PF-64	MS-65 / PF-65
1798, Knob 9, 5 Vertical Lines	(a)	3	35.0	0%	$900	$1,150	$1,650	$2,800	$4,700	$8,500	$22,000	$70,000	—
Auctions: $10,063, AU-50, September 2011													
1798, Knob 9, 4 Vertical Lines	(a)	8	50.9	25%	$900	$1,150	$1,650	$2,800	$4,700	$8,800	—		
Auctions: $9,775, AU-50, September 2011													
1798, Knob 9, 10 Arrows	(a)	7	37.9	0%	$900	$1,150	$1,650	$2,800	$4,700	$8,800	—		
Auctions: $7,175, AU-53, September 2013													
1798, Pointed 9, Close Date	(a)	146	37.8	3%	$900	$1,150	$1,650	$2,800	$4,700	$8,800	$22,000	$70,000	$165,000
Auctions: $5,302, AU-50, October 2014; $4,348, EF-45, July 2015; $3,290, EF-40, March 2015; $940, VG-10, January 2015													
1798, Pointed 9, Wide Date	(a)	160	36.2	6%	$900	$1,150	$1,650	$2,800	$4,700	$8,500	$22,000	$70,000	$165,000
Auctions: $3,290, EF-45, October 2015; $3,525, EF-40, August 2015; $2,115, VF-30, June 2015; $911, VF-20, September 2015													
1798, Pointed 9, 5 Vertical Lines	(a)	52	37.6	2%	$900	$1,150	$1,650	$2,800	$4,700	$8,800	$25,000	—	—
Auctions: $8,225, AU-53, September 2013													
1798, Pointed 9, 10 Arrows	(a)	56	32.2	4%	$950	$1,200	$1,750	$3,100	$4,900	$9,250	$23,500	$80,000	—
Auctions: $6,463, AU-53, August 2015; $3,760, EF-40, June 2015; $1,763, VF-20, March 2015; $1,410, F-15, March 2015													
1798, Pointed 9, 4 Berries	(a)	31	31.3	0%	$900	$1,150	$1,650	$2,800	$4,700	$8,500	$21,500	$67,500	$165,000
Auctions: $4,465, AU-53, September 2015; $3,290, EF-40, September 2015; $2,233, VF-30, January 2015													
1799, All kinds	423,515												
1799, 99 Over 98, 15-Star Reverse (b)		45	44.8	20%	$960	$1,350	$1,800	$2,850	$5,200	$8,700	$23,000	$57,000	—
Auctions: $29,375, MS-62, August 2014; $4,406, EF-45, September 2014; $1,528, F-12, October 2015; $852, F-12, September 2015													
1799, 99 Over 98, 13-Star Reverse		35	37.1	9%	$950	$1,250	$1,750	$2,700	$4,700	$8,400	$22,400	$56,500	—
Auctions: $852, F-12, November 2014; $646, AG-3, July 2015													
1799, Irregular Date, 15-Star Reverse		14	32.2	0%	$950	$1,150	$1,550	$2,550	$4,700	$8,500	$23,000	—	—
Auctions: $3,055, VF-35, September 2013													
1799, Irregular Date, 13-Star Reverse		27	37.7	7%	$950	$1,150	$1,550	$2,550	$4,700	$8,200	$22,000	$56,500	$190,000
Auctions: $99,875, MS-64, August 2013; $2,409, VF-30, October 2014													
1799, Normal Date		1,905	36.1	5%	$900	$1,150	$1,550	$2,550	$4,700	$8,200	$22,400	$56,500	$190,000
Auctions: $5,875, AU-53, March 2015; $1,998, VF-25, May 2015; $1,998, VF-20, November 2015; $1,645, F-15, August 2015													
1799, 8 Stars Left, 5 Right		34	39.5	6%	$1,000	$1,350	$1,900	$3,100	$5,750	$13,500	$32,500	$92,500	—
Auctions: $41,125, MS-61, November 2013; $646, VG-8, November 2014													
1800, All kinds	220,920												
1800, Very Wide Date, Low 8		19	39.1	0%	$900	$1,100	$1,600	$2,500	$4,600	$8,500	$24,500	$60,000	—
Auctions: $11,750, AU-53, January 2014; $8,813, AU-53, August 2014; $2,233, VF-30, March 2015; $1,763, F-15, August 2014													
1800, "Dotted Date" (c)		33	39.8	12%	$900	$1,150	$1,650	$2,600	$5,200	$8,500	$24,500	$59,000	$190,000
Auctions: $11,750, AU-55, August 2014; $9,988, AU-53, August 2013; $2,350, VF-30, October 2014; $999, VF-20, January 2015													
1800, Only 12 Arrows		31	40.5	13%	$900	$1,100	$1,600	$2,500	$4,600	$8,500	$24,500	$60,000	—
Auctions: $6,463, AU-50, September 2013; $2,938, EF-40, March 2015; $1,880, VF-25, August 2014													
1800, Normal Dies		822	37.1	2%	$900	$1,100	$1,600	$2,500	$4,600	$8,500	$24,000	$56,500	$190,000
Auctions: $17,625, AU-58, August 2014; $12,925, AU-55, August 2014; $2,233, VF-30, November 2015; $494, VG-8, July 2015													
1800, AMERICAI (d)		40	39.2	10%	$900	$1,100	$1,600	$2,500	$4,600	$8,100	$26,500	—	—
Auctions: $223,250, MS-65, November 2013													

Note: The two earliest reverse dies of 1798 have five vertical lines in the stripes in the shield. All dollar dies thereafter have four vertical lines. **a.** The Mint struck 327,536 silver dollars in 1798, but did not record how many of each type (Small Eagle reverse and Heraldic Eagle reverse). **b.** The engraver of the reverse die accidentally engraved 15 stars, instead of the 13 needed to represent the original Colonies. He attempted to cover the two extra stars under the leftmost and rightmost clouds, but their points stick out slightly. **c.** The "dotted" date is the result of die breaks. **d.** A reverse-die flaw resulted in what appears to be a sans-serif letter I after AMERICA. "Perhaps from a punch or from a stray piece of metal during the die making process" (Bowers, *Silver Dollars & Trade Dollars of the United States*).

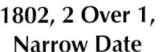

1802, 2 Over 1, Narrow Date

1802, 2 Over 1, Wide Date

1802, Narrow Normal Date

1802, Wide Normal Date

1803, Small 3

1803, Large 3

	Mintage	Cert	Avg	%MS	G-4	VG-8	F-12	VF-20	EF-40	AU-50	MS-60 PF-63	MS-63 PF-64	MS-65 PF-65
1801	54,454	302	37.7	5%	$900	$1,100	$1,600	$2,500	$4,900	$8,350	$29,500	$82,500	$250,000
	Auctions: $329,000, MS-65, November 2013; $3,525, EF-40, October 2014; $764, VG-8, January 2015												
1801, Restrike, Proof † (e)	*2 known*	1	66.0									$1,000,000	$1,500,000
	Auctions: No auction records available.												
1802, All kinds	41,650												
1802, 2 Over 1, Narrow Date		20	40.7	15%	$950	$1,200	$1,800	$2,600	$5,000	$9,100	$30,000	$68,500	—
	Auctions: $11,750, AU-58, February 2013; $2,115, VF-30, January 2015; $2,820, VF-20, October 2014												
1802, 2 Over 1, Wide Date		32	34.5	6%	$1,000	$1,250	$1,900	$2,700	$5,250	$11,100	$32,000	$71,000	—
	Auctions: $6,463, AU-53, January 2015; $4,465, EF-40, February 2015; $2,820, VF-25, January 2015; $2,585, VF-25, October 2015												
1802, Narrow Normal Date		55	41.4	15%	$950	$1,200	$1,700	$2,500	$4,900	$8,100	$23,500	$68,500	$240,000
	Auctions: $54,050, MS-63, January 2015; $25,850, MS-61, May 2015; $12,925, AU-55, June 2015; $2,350, VF-25, January 2015												
1802, Wide Normal Date		8	40.4	0%	$1,000	$1,250	$1,850	$2,800	$5,000	$10,100	$36,000	$76,000	$300,000
	Auctions: $10,869, AU-55, August 2013												
1802, Restrike, Proof † (e)	*4 known*	3	64.0								$400,000	$600,000	$1,000,000
	Auctions: $920,000, PF-65Cam, April 2008												
1803, All kinds	85,634												
1803, Small 3		65	38.1	8%	$1,000	$1,200	$1,800	$2,800	$5,000	$9,000	$27,000	$71,000	—
	Auctions: $117,500, MS-63, November 2013; $2,585, VF-35, October 2014; $2,350, VF-30, August 2014; $999, F-12, July 2014												
1803, Large 3		68	38.7	4%	$1,000	$1,200	$1,800	$2,800	$5,000	$9,000	$27,000	$71,000	—
	Auctions: $6,463, EF-45, August 2014; $2,174, VF-20, March 2015; $1,410, VF-20, August 2015; $646, VF-20, August 2015												
1803, Restrike, Proof † (e)	*3 known*	7	65.6								$400,000	$600,000	$1,000,000
	Auctions: $851,875, PF-66, January 2013												

† Ranked in the *100 Greatest U.S. Coins* (fourth edition). **e.** "The Proof silver dollars of 1801, 1802, and 1803 are all extremely rare, valuable, and desirable, although none of them were made anywhere near the dates on the coins, nor do they share any die characteristics with any real silver dollars made from 1801 to 1803" (*100 Greatest U.S. Coins*, fourth edition).

1804 Dollar, Proof   **1804, First Reverse, Proof**   **1804, Second Reverse, Proof**

Note the position of the words STATES OF in relation to the clouds.

	Mintage	Cert	Avg	%MS	G-4	VG-8	F-12	VF-20	EF-40	AU-50	MS-60 / PF-63	MS-63 / PF-64	MS-65 / PF-65
1804, First Reverse, Class I, Proof (f)	8 known	6	50.0								$4,000,000	$4,500,000	$6,000,000
Auctions: $3,877,500, PF-62, August 2013													
1804, Second Reverse, Restrike, Class III, Proof (f)	6 known	4	59.3										
Auctions: $2,300,000, PF-58, April 2009; $1,880,000, PF-55, August 2014													
1804, Second Reverse, Restrike, Plain Edge, Class II, Proof (f,g)	1	0	n/a										
Auctions: No auction records available.													
1804, Electrotype of Unique Plain-Edge Specimen (f,h)	4	0	n/a										
Auctions: No auction records available.													

f. The 1804 dollars as a group are ranked among the *100 Greatest U.S. Coins*. **g.** The plain-edge restrike is in the Smithsonian's National Numismatic Collection. **h.** These electrotypes were made by the U.S. Mint.

GOBRECHT (1836–1839)

No Stars on Obverse, Stars on Reverse (1836):
Designer: *Christian Gobrecht.* **Weight:** *26.96 grams.*
Composition: *.8924 silver, .1076 copper (net weight .77352 oz. pure silver).*
Diameter: *39–40 mm.* **Edge:** *Plain.*

No Stars on Obverse, Stars on Reverse

Stars on Obverse, No Stars on Reverse (1838–1839): **Designer:** *Christian Gobrecht.*
Weight: *26.73 grams.* **Composition:** *.900 silver, .100 copper*
(net weight .77345 oz. pure silver). **Diameter:** *39–40 mm.* **Edge:** *Reeded.*

Stars on Obverse, No Stars on Reverse

History. Suspension of silver dollar coinage was lifted in 1831, but it was not until 1835 that steps were taken to resume their production. Late that year, Mint Director R.M. Patterson had engraver Christian Gobrecht prepare a pair of dies based on motifs by Thomas Sully and Titian Peale. The first obverse die, dated 1836, bore the seated figure of Miss Liberty with the inscription C. GOBRECHT F. ("F." for the Latin word *Fecit*, or "made it") in the field above the date. On the reverse die was a large eagle flying left, surrounded by 26 stars and the legend UNITED STATES OF AMERICA • ONE DOLLAR •. It is unknown whether coins were struck from these dies at that time. A new obverse die with Gobrecht's name on the base of Liberty was prepared, and in December 1836, a thousand plain-edged pieces were struck for circulation. These coins weighed 416 grains, the standard enacted in 1792.

The feeder mechanism that was used, apparently designed for coins of half dollar size or smaller, damaged the reverse die's rim. Attempts were made to solve the problem by rotating the reverse die at various times during the striking run, but this only extended the damage to both sides of the rim. The original 1836 issue is thus known in multiple die alignments:

Die Alignment I—head of Liberty opposite DO in DOLLAR; eagle flying upward.

Die Alignment II—head of Liberty opposite ES in STATES; eagle flying upward.

Die Alignment IV—head of Liberty opposite F in OF; eagle flying level.

Original 1836 die orientation using either "coin" or "medal" turn.

Die alignment of original issues dated 1838 and 1839.

Restrikes were made from the late 1850s through the early 1870s. They were struck using the original obverse die and a different reverse die with cracks through NITED STATES O and OLLA, and in a different alignment:

Die Alignment III—head of Liberty opposite N of ONE; eagle flying level.

In January 1837, the standard weight for the dollar was lowered to 412-1/2 grains, and on January 8, 1837, Benjamin Franklin Peale wrote an internal memorandum to Mint Director Patterson noting, among other things, that the new dollar had received much criticism for looking too medallic, rather than like a coin. Peale felt this was due to the "smooth" edge and suggested striking with a segmented, lettered-edge collar like one he had seen in France. In March 1837, the dies of 1836 were used to strike 600 pieces (whether with plain or reeded edge is unknown). According to reports, the results were unsatisfactory and the coins were destroyed—although a single example, with a reeded edge, is known. It is unclear whether it was part of the March striking, from an earlier 1837 striking caused by the Peale memo, or struck at some later period.

Pattern pieces were struck in 1838 using modified dies with Gobrecht's name removed from the base, 13 stars added to the obverse, and the 26 stars removed from the reverse. These were struck in alignment IV using a reeded-edge collar. In 1839, 300 pieces were struck for circulation, also in alignment IV. Both of these were restruck in alignment III and possibly alignment IV in the late 1850s through early 1870s.

Striking and Sharpness. Striking is usually very good. Check the details on Miss Liberty's head and the higher parts of the eagle. Note that the word LIBERTY is raised.

Availability. 1836 Gobrecht dollars are available in grades from so-called Very Fine upward (the coins were struck as Proofs, and worn examples are properly designated as PF-30, PF-40, and so on; however, sometimes they are found graded as Fine, VF, and EF for levels below PF-50). Most in the marketplace range from PF–50 to 62. Most have contact marks. Truly pristine PF-65 and better examples are very elusive. The demand for these coins is intense. For the 1839, circulated grades typically are PF-50 or higher, often with damage. Pristine Proofs are available, but virtually all are restrikes.

GRADING STANDARDS

PF-60 to 70 (Proof). *Obverse and Reverse:* Many Proofs have been extensively cleaned and have many hairlines and dull fields. This is more applicable to 1836 than to 1839. Grades are PF–60 to 61 or 62. With medium hairlines and good reflectivity, an assigned grade of PF-64 is appropriate, and with relatively few hairlines, Gem PF-65. In various grades hairlines are most easily seen in the obverse field. PF-66 should have hairlines so

1839. Graded PF-65.

delicate that magnification is needed to see them. Above that, a Proof should be free of such lines.

Illustrated coin: This is a restrike made at the Mint in or after spring 1859.

PF-50, 53, 55, 58 (Proof). *Obverse:* Light wear is seen on the thighs and knees, bosom, and head. At PF-58, the Proof surface is extensive, but the open fields show abrasion. At PF–50 and 53, most if not all mirror surface is gone and there are scattered marks. *Reverse:* Wear is most evident on the eagle's breast and the top of the wings. Mirror surface ranges from perhaps 60% complete (at PF-58) to none (at PF-50).

1836. Graded PF-58.

Illustrated coin: This original 1836 Gobrecht dollar, of which 1,000 were coined in 1836, is nicely toned and has excellent eye appeal.

PF-40 to 45 (Proof). *Obverse:* Further wear is seen on all areas, especially the thighs and knees, bosom, and head. The center of LIBERTY, which is in relief, is weak. Most at this level and lower are the 1836 issues. *Reverse:* Further wear is evident on the eagle, including the back edge of the closest wing, the top of the farthest wing, and the tail.

1836. Graded PF-45.

PF-20, 25, 30, 35 (Proof). *Obverse:* Further wear is seen. Many details of the gown are worn away, but the lower-relief areas above and to the right of the shield remain well defined. Hair detail is mostly or completely gone. LIBERTY is weak at the center. *Reverse:* Even more wear is evident on the eagle, with only about 60% of the feathers visible.

1836. Graded PF-20.

	Cert	Avg	%MS	PF-20	PF-40	PF-50	PF-60	PF-62	PF-63	PF-64	PF-65
1836. C. GOBRECHT F. on base. Judd-60. Plain edge, no stars on obverse, stars in field on reverse. Die alignment I, ↑↓. Circulation issue. 1,000 struck (a)	214	55.6		$12,500	$15,000	$18,000	$25,000	$27,000	$40,000	$75,000	$150,000
	Auctions: $29,900, PF-62, April 2012										
1836. As above. Plain edge. Judd-60. Die alignment II and die alignment IV, ↑↑. Circulation issue struck in 1837. 600 struck (a)	**(b)**			$13,000	$16,000	$21,000	$25,000	$30,000	$45,000	$75,000	$150,000
	Auctions: $16,100, PF-58, March 2012										

a. Originals. Although these are listed in Judd as patterns, they are considered circulation strikes. b. Included in 1836, C. GOBRECHT F. on base, certified population.

	Cert	Avg	%MS	PF-20	PF-40	PF-50	PF-60	PF-62	PF-63	PF-64	PF-65
1838. Obverse stars added around border, reeded edge. Judd-84. Designer's name removed. Reverse eagle flying in plain field. Die alignment IV, ↑↑.	29	62.3					$70,000	$75,000	$85,000	$100,000	$150,000
Auctions: $83,375, PF-64, July 2008											
1839. As above. Reeded edge. Judd-104. Die alignment IV, ↑↑. Circulation issue. 300 struck	47	62.7		$15,000	$17,500	$22,500	$29,000	$38,500	$55,000	$80,000	$150,000
Auctions: $18,975, PF-45, November 2011											

Restrike

	Cert	Avg	%MS	PF-20	PF-40	PF-50	PF-60	PF-62	PF-63	PF-64	PF-65
1836. Name below base; eagle in starry field; plain edge. Judd-58. Die alignment III, ↑↓, and die alignment IV, ↑↑. (a)	12(b)	64.0		$17,500	$30,000	$70,000	$75,000	$75,500	$100,000	$125,000	$150,000
Auctions: $34,500, PF-63, April 2012											
1836. Name on base; plain edge. Judd 60. Die alignment III, ↑↓. (a,c)	(d)			$15,000	$20,000	$23,500	$26,000	$35,000	$55,000	$90,000	$150,000
Auctions: $18,975, PF-61, September 2010											
1836. C. GOBRECHT F. on base. Judd-61. Reeded edge. No stars on obverse, stars in field on reverse. Die alignment IV, ↑↑. (a)	0	n/a					*(extremely rare)*				
Auctions: $195,000, PF-63, May 2003											
1838. Designer's name removed; reeded edge. Judd-84. Die alignment III, ↑↓, and die alignment IV, ↑↑. (a)	(d)			$25,000	$30,000	$35,000	$47,500	$62,500	$85,000	$125,000	
Auctions: $83,375, PF-64, March 2012											
1839. Designer's name removed; eagle in plain field; reeded edge. Judd-104. Die alignment III, ↑↓, and die alignment IV, ↑↑. (a)	(d)			$20,000	$25,000	$37,500	$42,500	$50,000	$65,000	$100,000	
Auctions: $51,750, PF-64, April 2012											

Note: Restrikes were produced from the late 1850s to the 1870s, and are not official Mint issues. They were all oriented in either die alignment III (coin turn) or die alignment IV (medal turn), with the eagle flying level. Almost all were struck from a cracked reverse die. For detailed analysis of these pieces, consult *United States Pattern Coins*, tenth edition. **a.** Restrikes. Listed in Judd as patterns. **b.** Many originals were certified as restrikes in years past. This figure includes some of these originals. **c.** 30 to 40 are known. **d.** Included in figure for first listing with this Judd number, as the grading services do not consistently distinguish between originals and restrikes.

LIBERTY SEATED (1840–1873)

No Motto (1840–1865): **Designer:** *Christian Gobrecht.* **Weight:** *26.73 grams.*
Composition: *.900 silver, .100 copper (net weight .77344 oz. pure silver).*
Diameter: *38.1 mm.* **Edge:** *Reeded.* **Mints:** *Philadelphia, New Orleans, and San Francisco.*

Mintmark location is on the reverse, below the eagle, for all varieties.

No Motto
(1840–1865)

No Motto, Proof

With Motto IN GOD WE TRUST (1866–1873): **Designer:** *Christian Gobrecht.*
Weight: *26.73 grams.* **Composition:** *.900 silver, .100 copper (net weight .77344 oz. pure silver).*
Diameter: *38.1 mm.* **Edge:** *Reeded.* **Mints:** *Philadelphia, Carson City, and San Francisco.*

With Motto
IN GOD
WE TRUST
(1866–1873)a

With Motto
IN GOD
WE TRUST,
Proof

History. The Liberty Seated dollar was minted every year from 1840 to 1873, with an obverse design modified from that of the 1839 Gobrecht dollar. On the reverse, the flying eagle of the Gobrecht dollar was replaced with a perched eagle similar to that of contemporary quarter and half dollars. The dollars, minted in modest numbers, circulated in the United States through 1850. In that year the rising value of silver on the international markets brought the cost of minting each coin to more than $1. Production continued for the international, rather than domestic, market, through 1873, when the trade dollar took the Liberty Seated dollar's place.

Striking and Sharpness. On the obverse, check the head of Miss Liberty and the centers of the stars. On the reverse, check the feathers of the eagle. The denticles usually are sharp. Dollars of 1857 usually are weakly struck, but have semi-prooflike surfaces. The word LIBERTY is in a high-relief area on the coin, with the result that it wore away quickly. Therefore this feature cannot be used as the only guide to grading an obverse. From EF downward, strike sharpness in the stars and the head does not matter to connoisseurs. Proof coins were made for all dates. All of 1851 and 1853 are restrikes, as are most of 1852. In 1858 only Proofs were struck, to the extent of an estimated 210 pieces, with no related circulation strikes. Most early dates were restruck at the Mint, augmenting the supply of originals. Nearly all Proofs are very well struck.

Availability. All issues from 1840 to 1850 are available in proportion to their mintages. Those of 1851 to the late 1860s are either scarce or rare in circulated grades, and in MS they range from rare to extremely rare, despite generous mintages in some instances. The later-date coins were shipped to China and later melted. Coins of the 1870s are more readily available, although some are scarce to rare. Today, Proofs from 1858 to 1873 are readily available, but high-quality examples with superb eye appeal are in the minority. Most Proofs prior to 1860 survive only in grades below PF-65 if strict grading is applied.

GRADING STANDARDS

MS-60 to 70 (Mint State). *Obverse:* At MS-60, some abrasion and contact marks are evident, most noticeably on the bosom and thighs and knees. Luster is present, but may be dull or lifeless. At MS-63, contact marks are very few, and abrasion is minimal. An MS-65 coin has no abrasion in the fields (but may have a hint on the knees), and contact marks are trivial. Check the knees of Liberty and the right field. Luster should be full and

1864. Graded MS-65.

rich on later issues, not necessarily so for dates in the 1840s. Most Mint State coins of the 1861 to 1865 years, Philadelphia issues, have extensive die striae (from not completely finishing the die). *Reverse:* Comments apply as for the obverse, except that in lower Mint State grades, abrasion and marks are most noticeable on the eagle's head, the neck, the claws, and the top of the wings (harder to see there, however). At MS-65 or higher, there are no marks visible to the unaided eye. The field is mainly protected by design elements and does not show abrasion as much as does the obverse on a given coin.

Illustrated coin: The fields show striations from incomplete polishing of the dies, but this does not affect the grade.

AU-50, 53, 55, 58 (About Uncirculated). *Obverse:* Light wear is seen on the thighs and knees, bosom, and head. At AU-58, the luster is extensive but incomplete, especially in the right field. At AU–50 and 53, luster is less. *Reverse:* Wear is visible on the eagle's neck, the claws, and the top of the wings. An AU-58 coin has nearly full luster. At AU–50 and 53, there still are traces of luster.

Illustrated coin: This is an attractive example with much of the original luster.

1842. Graded AU-58.

EF-40, 45 (Extremely Fine). *Obverse:* Further wear is seen on all areas, especially the thighs and knees, bosom, and head. Little or no luster is seen on most coins. From this grade downward, strike sharpness in the stars and the head does not matter to connoisseurs. *Reverse:* Further wear is evident on the eagle's neck, claws, and the wings, although on well-struck coins nearly all details are sharp.

1846. Graded EF-40.

VF-20, 30 (Very Fine). *Obverse:* Further wear is seen. Many details of the gown are worn away, but the lower-relief areas above and to the right of the shield remain well defined. Hair detail is mostly or completely gone. The word LIBERTY is weak at BE (PCGS allows BER to be missing "on some coins"). *Reverse:* Wear is more extensive, with some feathers blended together, especially on the neck for a typical coin. Detail remains quite good overall.

1854. Graded VF-20.

F-12, 15 (Fine). *Obverse:* The seated figure is well worn, but with some detail above and to the right of the shield. BER in LIBERTY is visible only in part or missing entirely. *Reverse:* Wear is extensive, with about a third to half of the feathers flat or blended with others.

   Illustrated coin: The reverse is stronger than the obverse on this coin.

1872-CC. Graded F-12.

VG-8, 10 (Very Good). *Obverse:* The seated figure is more worn, but some detail can be seen above and to the right of the shield. The shield is discernible, but the upper-right section may be flat and blended into the seated figure. In LIBERTY two or three letters, or a combination totaling that, are readable. *Reverse.* Further wear has flattened half or slightly more of the feathers (depending on the strike). The rim is visible all around,

1871-CC. Graded VG-8.

as are the ends of the denticles. A Very Good Liberty Seated dollar usually has more detail overall than a lower-denomination coin of the same design.

G-4, 6 (Good). *Obverse:* The seated figure is worn nearly smooth. The stars and date are complete, but may be weak toward the periphery. *Reverse:* The eagle shows only a few details of the shield and feathers. The rim is worn down. The tops of the border letters are weak or worn away, although the inscription can still be read.

1850-O. Graded G-6.

AG-3 (About Good). *Obverse:* The seated figure is visible in outline form. Much or all of the rim is worn away. The stars are weak and some may be missing. The date remains clear. *Reverse:* The border letters are partially worn away. The eagle is mostly in outline form, but with a few details discernible. The rim is weak or missing.

1872. Graded AG-3.

PF-60 to 70 (Proof). *Obverse and Reverse:* Proofs that are extensively cleaned and have many hairlines, or that are dull and grainy, are lower level, such as PF–60 to 62. These are not widely desired, except for use as fillers for the dates (most circulation-strike dollars are rare after 1849 and before 1870). The rarities of 1851, 1852, and 1858 are in demand no matter what the grade. With medium hairlines and good reflectivity, an assigned grade of PF-64 is appropriate, and with relatively few hairlines, gem PF-65. In various grades hairlines are most easily seen in the obverse field. PF-66 should have hairlines so delicate that magnification is needed to see them. Above that, a Proof should be free of such lines.

1861. Graded PF-63.

Illustrated coin: The frosty cameo motifs on this example contrast with the deeply mirrored fields.

1851, Original,
High Date

1851, Restrike,
Proof
Date is centered.

1852, Original

1852, Restrike,
Proof

	Mintage	Cert	Avg	%MS	VG-8	F-12	VF-20	EF-40	AU-50	MS-60 / PF-60	MS-63 / PF-63	MS-65 / PF-65
1840	61,005	258	49.9	20%	$350	$375	$475	$750	$1,500	$4,000	$19,000	$110,000
Auctions: $12,925, MS-63, October 2015; $1,240, EF-45, January 2015; $705, VF-35, August 2015; $517, VF-25, January 2015												
1840, Proof	40–60	27	63.3							$25,000	$40,000	$85,000
Auctions: $85,188, PF-64Cam, April 2013												
1841	173,000	264	50.5	20%	$325	$350	$450	$700	$1,000	$2,750	$8,000	$90,000
Auctions: $2,820, MS-62, January 2015; $1,528, AU-58, January 2015; $541, EF-45, August 2015; $400, VF-35, February 2015												
1841, Proof	10–15	4	63.0							$70,000	$150,000	$250,000
Auctions: $94,000, PF-64, October 2014; $141,000, PF-64, April 2013												
1842	184,618	592	49.1	14%	$300	$325	$425	$600	$950	$2,400	$5,000	$90,000
Auctions: $11,163, MS-64, May 2015; $1,528, AU-58, June 2015; $646, EF-45, January 2015; $423, VF-35, June 2015												
1842, Proof	10–15	8	63.3							$35,000	$65,000	$110,000
Auctions: $57,281, PF-65, August 2013												
1843	165,100	494	48.3	12%	$300	$325	$425	$600	$950	$2,400	$7,000	$100,000
Auctions: $3,055, MS-62, June 2015; $940, AU-55, August 2015; $517, EF-45, January 2015; $411, F-15, June 2015												
1843, Proof	10–15	7	63.3							$30,000	$50,000	$110,000
Auctions: $52,875, PF-64, August 2013												
1844	20,000	158	51.6	15%	$300	$350	$425	$800	$1,250	$5,000	$14,000	$100,000
Auctions: $3,055, AU-58, January 2015; $940, AU-50, July 2015; $541, VF-30, January 2015; $541, VF-25, March 2015												
1844, Proof	10–15	8	63.9							$30,000	$50,000	$110,000
Auctions: $70,500, PF-65, April 2013; $44,063, PF-64, October 2014												
1845	24,500	177	50.4	11%	$325	$375	$450	$800	$1,500	$9,000	$25,000	$150,000
Auctions: $31,725, MS-63, May 2015; $5,170, MS-61, June 2015; $2,350, AU-58, January 2015; $676, VF-30, January 2015												
1845, Proof	10–15	11	63.8							$30,000	$45,000	$80,000
Auctions: $141,000, PF-67, August 2013												

	Mintage	Cert	Avg	%MS	VG-8	F-12	VF-20	EF-40	AU-50	MS-60 PF-60	MS-63 PF-63	MS-65 PF-65
1846	110,600	495	50.7	16%	$300	$325	$425	$650	$1,000	$2,500	$5,500	$90,000
	Auctions: $6,463, MS-64, October 2015; $2,585, MS-61, January 2015; $1,175, AU-55, June 2015; $570, EF-40, July 2015											
1846, Proof	10–15	14	62.9							$30,000	$45,000	$105,000
	Auctions: $94,000, PF-66, April 2013											
1846-O	59,000	177	47.0	11%	$300	$375	$450	$800	$1,400	$7,250	$17,000	$100,000
	Auctions: $70,501, MS-64, January 2015; $4,230, MS-60, January 2015; $881, EF-40, January 2015; $505, VF-20, March 2015											
1847	140,750	508	50.7	16%	$300	$325	$425	$600	$850	$2,700	$5,500	$90,000
	Auctions: $5,875, MS-64, October 2015; $4,700, MS-63, October 2015; $2,115, AU-58, August 2015; $793, EF-45, October 2015											
1847, Proof	10–15	16	63.9							$22,000	$30,000	$60,000
	Auctions: $35,250, PF-65, October 2014; $41,125, PF-65, April 2013											
1848	15,000	92	50.0	11%	$375	$500	$700	$1,100	$1,500	$4,750	$13,000	$90,000
	Auctions: $47,000, MS-64, May 2015; $5,993, MS-61, September 2014; $2,350, AU-55, January 2015; $646, EF-40, January 2015											
1848, Proof	10–15	10	64.2							$30,000	$40,000	$80,000
	Auctions: $117,500, PF-67, August 2013											
1849	62,600	292	53.6	26%	$300	$325	$425	$700	$1,000	$2,600	$6,750	$90,000
	Auctions: $2,585, MS-62, June 2015; $1,763, AU-58, January 2015; $588, EF-40, August 2015; $400, VF-35, March 2015											
1849, Proof	10–15	9	63.9							$34,000	$50,000	$80,000
	Auctions: $129,250, PF-67, April 2013											
1850	7,500	114	54.9	32%	$550	$750	$1,100	$1,800	$2,500	$6,500	$14,000	$90,000
	Auctions: $7,638, MS-61, July 2015; $3,995, MS-60, January 2015; $4,230, AU-58, February 2015; $2,996, AU-53, February 2015											
1850, Proof	20–30	16	63.9							$25,000	$30,000	$55,000
	Auctions: $51,406, PF-66, August 2013; $19,975, PF-64, October 2014											
1850-O	40,000	145	43.7	10%	$350	$500	$750	$1,450	$3,200	$11,500	$25,000	$120,000
	Auctions: $3,055, AU-50, July 2015; $2,350, EF-45, January 2015; $823, VF-30, January 2015; $646, F-15, October 2015											
1851, Original, High Date † (a)	1,300	26	61.1	73%	$7,500	$10,500	$15,000	$20,000	$27,500	$35,000	$65,000	$140,000
	Auctions: $70,500, MS-64, January 2015; $42,300, MS-63, May 2015; $28,200, AU-58, September 2015											
1851, Restrike, Proof (a)	35–50	18	62.9							$31,000	$38,500	$80,000
	Auctions: $99,875, PF-65Cam, April 2014											
1852, Original † (a)	1,100	19	59.8	68%	$6,000	$10,000	$13,500	$17,500	$27,500	$40,000	$60,000	$140,000
	Auctions: $70,500, MS-63, January 2015; $34,075, AU-58, June 2014; $23,500, AU-50, September 2014											
1852, Original, Proof (a)	20–30	3	64.3							$43,500	$50,000	$77,500
	Auctions: $57,500, PF-65Cam, January 2009											
1852, Restrike, Proof (a)	20–30	15	63.7							$30,000	$40,000	$70,000
	Auctions: $70,500, PF-65, June 2014											
1853	46,110	153	57.7	53%	$350	$450	$650	$1,100	$1,300	$3,200	$7,250	$85,000
	Auctions: $2,350, AU-58, February 2015; $1,410, AU-53, September 2015; $1,293, EF-45, January 2015											
1853, Restrike, Proof (b)	15–20	6	63.7							$37,000	$57,500	$110,000
	Auctions: $152,750, PF-66Cam, August 2013; $105,750, PF-66, October 2014; $16,318, PF-58, October 2015											
1854	33,140	46	55.6	43%	$1,500	$2,500	$3,000	$4,150	$5,500	$9,000	$13,000	$95,000
	Auctions: $21,738, MS-64, May 2015; $6,169, AU-58, January 2015; $5,053, EF-45, June 2015; $4,465, VF-35, August 2015											
1854, Proof	40–60	17	63.8							$16,500	$23,500	$57,500
	Auctions: $49,938, PF-66, April 2013; $21,150, PF-64, May 2015; $15,275, PF-62, August 2014											
1855	26,000	57	53.9	32%	$1,250	$1,500	$2,250	$4,000	$4,750	$7,500	$25,000	$90,000
	Auctions: $7,050, AU-58, October 2015; $4,700, AU-50, January 2015; $4,465, AU-50, August 2015; $5,640, EF-45, August 2015											
1855, Proof	40–60	21	64.0							$16,000	$25,000	$42,500
	Auctions: $45,531, PF-66, August 2013											

† Ranked in the *100 Greatest U.S. Coins* (fourth edition). **a.** Silver dollars of 1851 are found in two formats: originals struck for circulation and Proof restrikes made years later. Silver dollars of 1852 are found in these formats and also as original Proofs. "As part of [Mint Director] James Ross Snowden's restriking activities in 1859, Proof examples of certain rare silver dollars of earlier dates were made, including the 1851 and 1852. For the 1851 dollar, the original die (with four-date digit logotype slanting slightly upward and the date close to the base of Liberty) probably could not be located in 1859. In any event, a different die, not originally used in 1851, with the date horizontal and centered, was employed. Whether this die was created new in 1859 and given an 1851 date, or whether it was made in 1851 and not used at that time, is not known" (*United States Pattern Coins*, tenth edition). **b.** Made at the Mint from postdated dies circa 1862.

	Mintage	Cert	Avg	%MS	VG-8	F-12	VF-20	EF-40	AU-50	MS-60 PF-60	MS-63 PF-63	MS-65 PF-65
1856	63,500	54	52.5	30%	$425	$525	$750	$1,600	$3,500	$5,000	$15,000	$85,000
	Auctions: $4,230, AU-58, January 2015; $3,290, EF-45, January 2015; $1,763, VF-20, June 2015; $1,234, F-15, October 2015											
1856, Proof	*40–60*	37	63.6							$13,000	$18,000	$32,500
	Auctions: $30,550, PF-65, October 2014; $27,025, PF-65, April 2013; $23,500, PF-65, May 2015; $13,513, PF-64, January 2015											
1857	94,000	87	58.8	70%	$425	$525	$750	$1,550	$1,900	$3,250	$9,250	$85,000
	Auctions: $76,375, MS-66, May 2015; $10,575, MS-64, October 2015; $5,405, AU-58, January 2015; $2,233, EF-45, January 2015											
1857, Proof	*50–70*	28	64.0							$13,500	$18,500	$33,500
	Auctions: No auction records available.											
1858, Proof (c)	300	72	62.4							$14,000	$19,000	$38,000
	Auctions: $11,456, PF-63, October 2014; $11,163, PF-63, September 2015; $14,100, PF-62, August 2015; $9,400, PF-61, January 2015											
1859	255,700	78	55.4	44%	$325	$425	$525	$750	$1,225	$2,500	$6,000	$85,000
	Auctions: $8,813, MS-64, January 2015; $5,170, MS-63, July 2015; $3,290, MS-61, June 2015; $1,880, AU-55, February 2015											
1859, Proof	800	152	63.9							$4,750	$8,500	$20,000
	Auctions: $5,640, PF-64, January 2015; $5,405, PF-64, June 2015; $3,258, PF-62, January 2015; $2,088, PF-60, January 2015											
1859-O	360,000	624	53.3	49%	$300	$325	$425	$600	$850	$2,050	$5,150	$65,000
	Auctions: $2,820, MS-62, February 2015; $764, AU-53, September 2015; $329, VF-25, February 2015; $259, F-15, September 2015											
1859-S	20,000	139	47.1	17%	$415	$550	$850	$1,700	$3,350	$13,000	$29,000	$130,000
	Auctions: $17,625, MS-63, September 2015; $10,575, MS-62, October 2015; $1,763, EF-45, January 2015; $1,410, VF-20, August 2015											
1860	217,600	116	56.8	52%	$300	$400	$525	$650	$850	$2,100	$5,100	$75,000
	Auctions: $6,463, MS-64, August 2015; $1,175, AU-53, July 2015; $823, AU-50, January 2015; $564, EF-40, January 2015											
1860, Proof	1,330	154	63.7							$4,750	$6,500	$15,000
	Auctions: $64,625, PF-67, April 2013; $24,675, PF-66, May 2015; $22,325, PF-66, October 2015; $4,230, PF-63, July 2015											
1860-O	515,000	897	54.1	53%	$300	$325	$425	$600	$785	$1,900	$3,750	$60,000
	Auctions: $6,169, MS-64, January 2015; $853, AU-55, June 2015; $541, EF-45, January 2015; $494, EF-40, June 2015											
1861	77,500	74	55.6	59%	$775	$1,100	$1,400	$2,250	$3,000	$3,450	$5,850	$65,000
	Auctions: $50,525, MS-65, May 2015; $8,225, MS-64, November 2014; $2,585, MS-60, June 2015; $3,055, EF-45, January 2015											
1861, Proof	1,000	100	63.4							$4,750	$6,500	$15,000
	Auctions: $4,994, PF-63Cam+, September 2014; $76,375, PF-66, June 2014											
1862	11,540	89	55.6	63%	$700	$1,100	$1,400	$2,100	$3,200	$6,500	$9,000	$65,000
	Auctions: $31,725, MS-64, June 2014; $12,925, MS-64, November 2014; $5,405, AU-53, January 2015; $3,525, EF-40, November 2014											
1862, Proof	550	166	63.3							$4,750	$6,500	$15,000
	Auctions: $38,775, PF-67, January 2015; $35,250, PF-67, August 2015; $6,169, PF-64, January 2015; $2,820, PF-62, January 2015											
1863	27,200	82	55.0	60%	$800	$1,100	$1,200	$1,600	$2,000	$3,575	$7,000	$65,000
	Auctions: $9,988, MS-64, August 2015; $8,813, MS-64, January 2015; $3,055, AU-53, July 2015; $1,763, EF-40, January 2015											
1863, Proof	460	147	63.7							$4,750	$7,500	$18,000
	Auctions: $129,250, PF-69, April 2013; $18,800, PF-66, May 2015; $9,988, PF-65, August 2014; $3,760, PF-63, January 2015											
1864	30,700	85	49.2	28%	$425	$500	$700	$1,000	$1,600	$3,575	$7,500	$60,000
	Auctions: $47,000, MS-65, May 2015; $1,058, AU-50, January 2015; $1,998, EF-45, October 2015; $1,528, EF-45, March 2015											
1864, Proof	470	161	63.5							$4,750	$6,500	$15,000
	Auctions: $52,875, PF-68, April 2013											
1865 (d)	46,500	74	51.3	34%	$400	$450	$650	$1,600	$2,100	$3,000	$7,500	$80,000
	Auctions: $5,405, MS-61, October 2015; $3,408, AU-55, January 2015; $1,116, AU-50, January 2015; $1,763, EF-40, February 2015											
1865, Proof	500	191	63.9							$4,750	$6,500	$15,000
	Auctions: $19,975, PF-66, August 2015; $10,575, PF-65, June 2015; $4,600, PF-63Cam, August 2015; $3,995, PF-63, July 2015											

c. Proof only. d. There is a common doubled-die reverse variety for 1865, which does not command a premium in today's market. "Doubling is evident only on the U of UNITED. . . . This is probably the most common variety for this date" (*Cherrypickers' Guide to Rare Die Varieties*, sixth edition, volume II).

1869, Repunched Date
FS-S1-1869-302.
Other varieties exist.

	Mintage	Cert	Avg	%MS	VG-8	F-12	VF-20	EF-40	AU-50	MS-60 / PF-60	MS-63 / PF-63	MS-65 / PF-65
1866	48,900	108	51.7	34%	$300	$390	$550	$850	$1,100	$2,300	$5,500	$65,000
Auctions: $4,230, MS-63, January 2015; $2,291, MS-61, January 2015; $1,293, AU-50, August 2015; $823, EF-45, January 2015												
1866, Proof	725	239	63.6							$3,800	$5,750	$14,000
Auctions: $19,975, PF-66Cam, October 2015; $17,625, PF-66Cam, May 2015; $6,463, PF-64, October 2015												
1866, No Motto, Proof † (e)	*2 known*	2	64.0							—		
Auctions: No auction records available.												
1867	46,900	68	50.7	40%	$300	$365	$525	$850	$1,050	$2,200	$5,300	$70,000
Auctions: $$11,163, MS-64, June 2015; $8,813, MS-64, October 2015; $881, AU-50, February 2015; $881, EF-40, January 2015												
1867, Proof	625	218	63.4							$3,900	$5,750	$14,000
Auctions: $56,400, PF-65, May 2015; $47,588, PF-65, October 2015; $5,405, PF-64Cam, January 2015; $2,938, PF-63, June 2015												
1868	162,100	109	49.0	17%	$300	$350	$475	$800	$1,150	$2,400	$7,000	$65,000
Auctions: $705, AU-50, January 2015; $764, EF-45, September 2015; $764, EF-40, January 2015; $423, EF-40, September 2015												
1868, Proof	600	209	63.7							$3,800	$5,750	$14,000
Auctions: $3,290, PF-63, September 2015; $2,291, PF-62, August 2015; $2,115, PF-62, January 2015; $1,763, PF-61, October 2014												
1869	423,700	135	51.9	35%	$300	$340	$425	$750	$1,050	$2,300	$5,250	$65,000
Auctions: $3,995, MS-63, September 2015; $4,230, MS-62, January 2015; $494, VF-30, June 2015; $423, VF-25, May 2015												
1869, Repunched Date (f)	(g)	0	n/a							$3,800	$5,750	$14,000
Auctions: $4,406, MS-62, October 2014												
1869, Proof	600	206	63.5							$3,800	$5,750	$14,000
Auctions: $9,988, PF-64DCam, October 2014; $6,463, PF-64Cam, October 2014; $5,875, PF-64Cam, November 2014												
1870	415,000	227	49.2	27%	$300	$325	$425	$600	$950	$2,100	$4,750	$55,000
Auctions: $56,400, MS-65+, May 2015; $1,175, AU-55, March 2015; $470, VF-35, January 2015; $400, VF-25, August 2015												
1870, Proof	1,000	214	63.3							$3,800	$5,750	$14,000
Auctions: $17,625, PF-66Cam, September 2015; $9,106, PF-65, October 2015; $5,405, PF-64Cam, August 2015; $3,055, PF-63, July 2015												
1870-CC	11,758	217	41.0	8%	$800	$1,400	$2,250	$4,250	$8,000	$26,000	$40,000	—
Auctions: $19,975, AU-58+, August 2015; $6,463, AU-50, January 2015; $4,230, EF-40, October 2015; $1,998, F-12, September 2015												
1870-S †	(h)	4	47.0	0%	$200,000	$275,000	$450,000	$650,000	$1,000,000	$1,500,000	—	—
Auctions: $763,750, EF-40, January 2014												
1871	1,073,800	749	46.4	22%	$300	$325	$425	$600	$1,050	$2,100	$4,650	$50,000
Auctions: $50,525, MS-65, January 2015; $705, AU-50, March 2015; $470, EF-45, June 2015; $306, VF-20, December 2015												
1871, Proof	960	199	63.0							$3,800	$5,750	$14,000
Auctions: $21,150, PF-66, January 2015; $15,863, PF-66, October 2015; $4,700, PF-64, September 2015; $1,998, PF-61, October 2015												
1871-CC	1,376	47	41.6	9%	$3,500	$4,850	$7,250	$15,000	$22,000	$75,000	$175,000	—
Auctions: $5,640, AU-50, January 2015; $11,163, VF-35, January 2015; $4,935, VF-25, January 2015; $3,760, F-12, January 2015												

† Ranked in the *100 Greatest U.S. Coins* (fourth edition). **e.** The 1866, No Motto, dollar is classified as Judd-540 (*United States Pattern Coins*). Two examples of this fantasy piece are known; at least one was deliberately struck for pharmacist and coin collector Robert Coulton Davis, likely around 1869 or in the early 1870s, along with the No Motto Proof quarter and half dollar of the same date. The three-coin set is on display at the American Numismatic Association's Edward C. Rochette Money Museum in Colorado Springs. "A second 1866 'No Motto' silver dollar resurfaced in the 1970s before entering a private Midwestern collection in the early 1980s. After not meeting its auction reserve price in September 2003, the coin was sold privately for nearly a million dollars some time later" (*100 Greatest U.S. Coins*, fourth edition). **f.** There are several repunched dates known for 1869. The one listed is FS-S1-1869-302. The top flag of a secondary 1 is evident midway between the primary 1 and the 8. **g.** Included in circulation-strike 1869 mintage figure. **h.** The Mint shows no record of 1870-S dollars being struck, but about a dozen are known to exist. The 1870-S silver dollars may have been struck as mementos of the laying of the cornerstone of the San Francisco Mint (May 25, 1870).

	Mintage	Cert	Avg	%MS	VG-8	F-12	VF-20	EF-40	AU-50	MS-60 / PF-60	MS-63 / PF-63	MS-65 / PF-65
1872	1,105,500	552	44.5	18%	$300	$325	$425	$600	$950	$2,050	$4,700	$50,000
	Auctions: $14,100, MS-64, August 2015; $940, AU-53, January 2015; $329, F-15, August 2015; $176, G-4, February 2015											
1872, Proof	950	178	63.1							$3,800	$5,750	$14,000
	Auctions: $9,988, PF-65, August 2015; $8,813, PF-65, March 2015; $7,638, PF-64, May 2015; $1,410, PF-60, January 2015											
1872-CC	3,150	87	41.0	16%	$3,000	$4,500	$5,000	$8,500	$13,000	$28,000	$100,000	$300,000
	Auctions: $28,200, MS-62, October 2015; $11,750, AU-53, February 2015; $5,640, EF-45, August 2015; $2,468, VG-10, February 2015											
1872-S	9,000	111	43.4	12%	$500	$675	$950	$1,975	$3,500	$12,000	$37,500	
	Auctions: $7,050, MS-61, October 2015; $6,463, AU-58, January 2015; $1,528, EF-40, October 2015; $1,410, VF-35, January 2015											
1873	293,000	178	52.6	40%	$375	$400	$450	$600	$975	$2,100	$4,850	$60,000
	Auctions: $58,750, MS-65, May 2015; $11,750, MS-64+, January 2015; $881, EF-45, October 2015; $646, VF-35, February 2015											
1873, Proof	600	186	63.3							$3,800	$5,750	$14,000
	Auctions: $16,450, PF-65Cam+, August 2014; $9,988, PF-65, June 2015; $16,450, PF-64, August 2015; $940, PF-60, January 2015											
1873-CC	2,300	26	43.4	15%	$7,000	$11,000	$24,000	$32,000	$55,000	$115,000	$190,000	$500,000
	Auctions: $105,750, MS-61, May 2015; $56,400, AU-55, August 2015; $35,250, EF-45, November 2014; $11,163, EF-40, January 2015											
1873-S (i)	700	0	n/a									
	Auctions: No auction records available.											

i. The 1873-S is unknown in any collection, public or private, despite Mint records indicating that 700 were struck. None have ever been seen.

MORGAN (1878–1921)

Designer: *George T. Morgan.* **Weight:** *26.73 grams.* **Composition:** *.900 silver, .100 copper (net weight .77344 oz. pure silver).* **Diameter:** *38.1 mm.* **Edge:** *Reeded.* **Mints:** *Philadelphia, New Orleans, Carson City, Denver, and San Francisco.*

Mintmark location is on the reverse, below the bow.

Circulation Strike

Proof

History. The Morgan dollar, named for English-born designer George T. Morgan, was struck every year from 1878 to 1904, and again in 1921. The coin's production benefited Western silver interests by creating an artificial federal demand for the metal, whose market value had dropped sharply by 1878. Hundreds of millions of the coins, stored in cloth bags of 1,000 each, piled up in government vaults. In the 1900s some were melted, but immense quantities were bought by collectors and investors; today they are the most widely collected of all coins of their era.

Striking and Sharpness. On coins of 1878 to 1900, check the hair above Miss Liberty's ear and, on the reverse, the breast feathers of the eagle. These are weak on many issues, particularly those of the New Orleans Mint. From 1900 to 1904 a new reverse hub was used, and breast feathers, while discernible, are not as sharp. In 1921 new dies were made in lower relief, with certain areas indistinct. Many Morgan dollars have partially or fully prooflike surfaces. These are designated as Prooflike (PL), Deep Prooflike (DPL), or Deep Mirror Prooflike (DMPL). Certification practices can be erratic, and some DMPL-certified coins are not fully mirrored. All prooflike coins tend to emphasize contact marks, with the result that lower MS levels can be unattractive. *A Guide Book of Morgan Silver Dollars* (Bowers) and other references furnish information as to which dates and mintmarks are easily found with Full Details and which usually are weak, as well as the availability of the various levels of prooflike surface.

Proofs were struck from 1878 to 1904, with those of 1878 to 1901 generally having cameo contrast, and 1902 to 1904 having the portrait lightly polished in the die. Some are lightly struck; check the hair above Liberty's ear (in particular), and the eagle's breast feathers. In 1921 many so-called Zerbe Proofs (named thus after numismatic entrepreneur Farran Zerbe), with many microscopic die-finish lines, were made. A very few deeply mirrored 1921 coins were made, called Chapman Proofs (after coin dealer Henry Chapman, who started marketing them shortly after their production). Some Zerbe Proofs have been miscertified as Chapman Proofs.

Availability. All dates and mints of Morgan dollars are available in grades from well worn to MS. Some issues such as certain Carson City coins are rare if worn and common in MS. Other issues such as the 1901 Philadelphia coins are common if worn and are rarities at MS-65. The 1889-CC and 1893-S, and the Proof 1895, are considered to be the key issues. Varieties listed herein are some of those most significant to collectors. Numerous other variations exist, studied in the *Cherrypickers' Guide to Rare Die Varieties* and other specialized texts. Values shown herein are for the most common pieces. Values of varieties not listed in this guide depend on collector interest and demand.

Note: Values of common-date silver coins have been based on the current bullion price of silver, $15.50 per ounce, and may vary with the prevailing spot price.

GRADING STANDARDS

MS-60 to 70 (Mint State). *Obverse:* At MS-60, some abrasion and contact marks are evident, most noticeably on the cheek and on the hair above the ear. The left field also shows such marks. Luster is present, but may be dull or lifeless. At MS-63, contact marks are extensive but not distracting. Abrasion still is evident, but less than at lower levels. Indeed, the cheek of Miss Liberty showcases abrasion. An MS-65 coin may have minor abrasion, but

1895-O. Graded MS-61.

contact marks are so minute as to require magnification. Luster should be full and rich. Coins with prooflike surfaces such as PL, DPL, and DMPL display abrasion and contact marks much more noticeably than coins with frosty surfaces; in grades below MS-64 many are unattractive. With today's loose and sometimes contradictory interpretations, many at MS-64 appear to have extensive marks as well. *Reverse:* Comments apply as for the obverse, except that in lower Mint State grades abrasion and contact marks are most noticeable on the eagle's breast. At MS-65 or higher there are no marks visible to the unaided eye. The field is mainly protected by design elements, so the reverse often appears to grade a point or two higher than the obverse. A Morgan dollar can have an MS-63 obverse and an MS-65 reverse, as was indeed the nomenclature used prior to the single-number system. A careful cataloger may want to describe each side separately for a particularly valuable or rare Morgan dollar. An example with an MS-63 obverse and an MS-65 reverse should have an overall grade of MS-63, as the obverse is traditionally given prominence.

Illustrated coin: This is a lustrous and attractive example.

AU-50, 53, 55, 58 (About Uncirculated). *Obverse:* Light wear is seen on the cheek and, to a lesser extent, on the hair below the coronet. Generally, the hair details mask friction and wear and it is not as easy to notice as on the cheek and in the fields. At AU-58, the luster is extensive, but incomplete, especially on the higher parts and in the left field. At AU–50 and 53, luster is less, but still is present. PL, DPL, and DMPL coins are not widely desired at these levels, as the marks are too distracting. *Reverse:* Wear is evident on the head, breast, wing tips, and, to a lesser extent, in the field. An AU-58 coin (as determined by the obverse) can have a reverse that appears to be full Mint State. (Incidentally, this is also true of Barber quarter dollars and half dollars.)

1889-CC. Graded AU-58.

Illustrated coin: This is a lustrous example of the rarest Carson City Morgan dollar. As is typical of AU-58 dollars of this design, the reverse appears to be full Mint State, as the field is protected by the design elements.

EF-40, 45 (Extremely Fine). *Obverse:* Further wear is seen on the cheek in particular. The hair near the forehead and temple has flatness in areas, most noticeable above the ear. Some luster can be seen in protected areas on many coins, but is not needed to define the EF-40 and 45 grades. *Reverse:* Further wear is seen on the breast of the eagle (most noticeably), the wing tips, and the leaves.

1879-CC. Graded EF-40.

VF-20, 30 (Very Fine). *Obverse:* The head shows more wear, now with most of the detail gone in the areas adjacent to the forehead and temple. The lower area has most hair fused into large strands. *Reverse:* Wear is more extensive on the breast and on the feathers in the upper area of the wings, especially the right wing, and on the legs. The high area of the leaves has no detail.

1889-CC. Graded VF-20.

F-12, 15 (Fine). *Obverse:* The head shows more wear, with most hair detail gone, and with a large flat area above the ear. Less detail is seen in the lower curls. *Reverse:* More wear is seen on the reverse, with the eagle's breast and legs flat and about a third of the feather detail gone, mostly near the tops of the wings.

1893-S. Graded F-15.

VG-8, 10 (Very Good). *Obverse:* More hair details are gone, especially from the area from the top of the head down to the ear. The details of the lower part of the cap are gone. The rim is weak in areas, and some denticles are worn away. *Reverse:* Further wear has smoothed more than half of the feathers in the wing. The leaves are flat except for the lowest areas. The rim is weak in areas.

1892-CC. Graded VG-8.

G-4, 6 (Good). *Obverse:* The head is in outline form, with most details gone. LIBERTY still is readable. The eye position and lips are discernible. Most of the rim is worn away. *Reverse:* The eagle shows some feathers near the bottom of the wings, but nearly all others are gone. The leaves are seen in outline form. The rim is mostly worn away. Some letters have details toward the border worn away.

The Morgan dollar is seldom collected in grades lower than G-4.

Illustrated coin: Here is a well-worn example of this key issue.

1893-S. Graded G-4.

PF-60 to 70 (Proof). *Obverse and Reverse:* Dull, grainy Proofs, or extensively cleaned ones with many hairlines, are lower level (PF–60 to 62). Only the 1895 is desirable at such low grades. Those with medium hairlines and good reflectivity may grade at about PF-64, and with relatively few hairlines, Gem PF-65. Hairlines are most easily seen in the obverse field. Horizontal slide marks on Miss Liberty's cheek, caused by clear slides on some coin albums, are common. PF-66 may have hairlines so delicate that magnification is needed to see them. Above that, a Proof should be free of such lines, including slide marks.

1898. Graded PF-64.

First Reverse
Eight tail feathers.

Second Reverse
Parallel top arrow feather,
concave breast.

Third Reverse
Slanted top arrow feather,
convex breast.

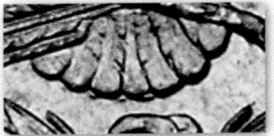

1878, Doubled
Tail Feathers
FS-S1-1878-032.

1878, 8 Feathers,
Obverse Die Gouge
The "Wild Eye" variety.
VAM-14.11. FS-S1-1878-014.11.

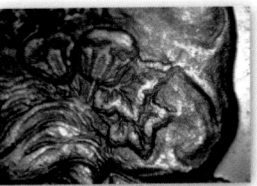
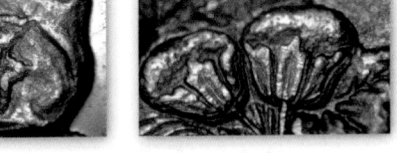

1878, 7 Over 8 Tail Feathers, Tripled Leaves
VAM-44. FS-S1-1878-044.

	Mintage	Cert	Avg	%MS	VF-20	EF-40	AU-50	MS-60	MS-63	MS-64	MS-64DMPL / PF-60	MS-65 / PF-63	MS-65DMPL / PF-65
1878, 8 Feathers	749,500	11,859	62.1	94%	$75	$90	$120	$180	$285	$475	$4,000	$1,600	$21,000
Auctions: $1,586, MS-65, January 2015; $212, MS-62, May 2015; $125, AU-55, February 2015; $89, EF-45, May 2015													
1878, 8 Feathers, Obverse Die Gouge (a)	(b)	6	60.0	67%				$8,000	$13,000	$24,000			
Auctions: $16,100, MS-62, August 2011													
1878, 7 Feathers, All kinds	9,759,300												
1878, 7 Over 8, Clear Doubled Feathers	(c)	2,368	61.6	91%	$50	$55	$75	$190	$275	$475	$5,200	$2,300	$16,000
Auctions: $1,410, MS-64, January 2015; $223, MS-63, August 2015; $188, MS-62, June 2015; $52, EF-45, February 2015													
1878, 7 Over 8, Tripled Leaves (d)	(c)	22	50.8	23%				$5,900	$12,000	$23,000			
Auctions: $820, MS-65, September 2015; $206, MS-64, January 2015; $106, MS-62, June 2015; $62, AU-58, February 2015													
1878, 7 Feathers, 2nd Reverse (e)	(c)	14,131	62.4	95%	$45	$48	$60	$90	$150	$250	$2,200	$1,050	$11,000
Auctions: $3,760, MS-66, January 2015; $176, MS-63, June 2015; $84, MS-61, February 2015; $62, AU-55, April 2015													
1878, 7 Feathers, 3rd Reverse (e)	(c)	5,195	61.6	91%	$45	$48	$50	$110	$250	$450	$5,500	$1,800	$23,000
Auctions: $3,055, MS-65+, January 2015; $2,703, MS-64+, August 2015; $223, MS-63, November 2015; $84, MS-61, January 2015													

a. Two spikes protrude from the front of Liberty's eye. "Fewer than a dozen specimens are known of this Top 100 variety and any sale is a landmark event" (*Cherrypickers' Guide to Rare Die Varieties*, sixth edition, volume II). **b.** Included in circulation-strike 1878, 8 Feathers, mintage figure. **c.** Included in circulation-strike 1878, 7 Feathers, mintage figure. **d.** Called the "King of VAMs" (Van Allen / Mallis varieties), this variety shows three to five weak tail feathers under the seven primary feathers. On the obverse, tripling is evident on the cotton bolls and the leaves, and doubling on LIBERTY. Values are fluid for this popular variety. **e.** The Second Reverse is sometimes known as "Concave Breast" or "Reverse of 1878." The Third Reverse is sometimes known as "Round Breast" or "Reverse of 1879."

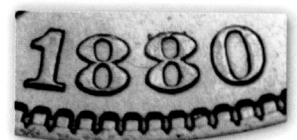

1880, 80 Over 79
VAM-6. FS-S1-1880-006.

	Mintage	Cert	Avg	%MS	VF-20	EF-40	AU-50	MS-60	MS-63	MS-64	MS-64DMPL	MS-65	MS-65DMPL
											PF-60	PF-63	PF-65
1878, 8 Feathers, Proof	500	135	64.2								$3,500	$4,500	$8,500
Auctions: $70,500, PF-67, January 2015; $11,163, PF-65Cam, January 2015; $14,100, PF-64Cam+, August 2015; $5,053, PF-64, August 2015													
1878, 7 Feathers, 2nd Reverse, Proof	250	101	63.6								$3,750	$5,600	$11,500
Auctions: $8,225, PF-63, March 2015; $6,463, PF-63, August 2015; $4,700, PF-63, October 2014; $6,463, PF-62, September 2014													
1878, 7 Feathers, 3rd Reverse, Proof (e)	(f)	5	62.4								$60,000	$115,000	$200,000
Auctions: $155,250, PF-64, November 2004													
1878-CC	2,212,000	24,440	60.9	90%	$120	$140	$180	$400	$475	$575	$2,800	$1,850	$10,000
Auctions: $6,463, MS-66, January 2015; $188, AU-55, February 2015; $141, EF-45, June 2015; $106, VF-20, May 2015													
1878-S	9,774,000	44,455	63.1	98%	$45	$47	$48	$65	$100	$120	$2,000	$310	$10,000
Auctions: $8,225, MS-67, January 2015; $306, MS-65, November 2015; $79, MS-63, May 2015; $2,703, EF-45, February 2015													
1879	14,806,000	11,373	62.7	95%	$35	$37	$40	$55	$95	$155	$2,100	$825	$15,000
Auctions: $2,468, MS-66, January 2015; $617, MS-65, November 2015; $141, MS-64, February 2015; $118, MS-60, August 2015													
1879, Proof	1,100	327	64.2								$3,200	$4,300	$6,000
Auctions: $14,100, PF-67Cam, August 2015; $4,583, PF-64Cam, January 2015; $2,585, PF-63, January 2015; $1,763, PF-62, August 2015													
1879-CC, CC Over CC	756,000	2,051	49.1	51%	$290	$770	$1,700	$4,200	$6,750	$10,000	$42,000	$40,000	$60,000
Auctions: $4,700, MS-62, March 2015; $1,058, EF-45, January 2015; $541, VF-35, September 2015; $176, VG-10, February 2015													
1879-CC, Clear CC	(g)	3,527	49.0	59%	$290	$750	$2,200	$4,500	$8,000	$11,000	$25,000	$28,000	$47,500
Auctions: $21,150, MS-65, September 2015; $9,694, MS-64, January 2015; $705, EF-40, July 2015; $481, VF-35, July 2015													
1879-O	2,887,000	8,543	61.4	84%	$40	$42	$47	$90	$250	$600	$4,250	$4,000	$22,000
Auctions: $17,625, MS-66, August 2015; $3,525, MS-65, January 2015; $112, MS-61, May 2015; $56, AU-55, March 2015													
1879-O, Proof (h)	4–8	5	64.4									$150,000	$200,000
Auctions: $176,250, PF-64, August 2013													
1879-S, 2nd Reverse	9,110,000	2,257	60.4	81%	$40	$45	$70	$190	$625	$1,500	$8,000	$5,500	$21,000
Auctions: $3,290, MS-65, January 2015; $1,704, MS-64, January 2015; $84, AU-55, August 2015; $200, AU-53, May 2015													
1879-S, 3rd Reverse	(i)	100,310	64.2	100%	$35	$37	$39	$55	$65	$80	$500	$170	$1,300
Auctions: $5,758, MS-68, June 2015; $1,351, MS-67, January 2015; $112, MS-64, September 2015; $282, MS-63, November 2015													
1880	12,600,000	13,430	62.8	96%	$35	$37	$39	$50	$80	$160	$1,150	$750	$6,900
Auctions: $4,230, MS-66, June 2015; $588, MS-65, October 2015; $141, MS-64, July 2015; $194, AU-53, February 2015													
1880, 80 Over 79 (j)	(k)	1	45.0	0%	$37	$39	$55	$100	$675	$850		$3,300	
Auctions: $764, AU-58, January 2015; $200, AU-55, February 2015; $176, AU-53, November 2014; $153, AU-50, January 2015													
1880, Proof	1,355	429	64.8								$3,200	$4,000	$6,000
Auctions: $10,575, PF-67Cam, August 2015; $9,988, PF-66Cam+, June 2015; $6,169, PF-65, August 2015; $2,585, PF-62, March 2015													

e. The Second Reverse is sometimes known as "Concave Breast" or "Reverse of 1878." The Third Reverse is sometimes known as "Round Breast" or "Reverse of 1879." **f.** Included in 1878, 7 Feathers, Proof, mintage figure. **g.** Included in 1879-CC, CC Over CC, mintage figure. **h.** Some numismatists classify these as Deep Mirror Prooflike circulation strikes, rather than as Proofs. **i.** Included in 1879-S, 2nd Reverse, mintage figure. **j.** Several die varieties exist; values shown are for the most common. **k.** Included in circulation-strike 1880 mintage figure.

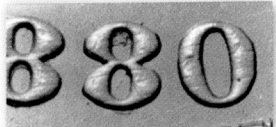
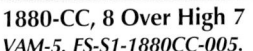

1880-CC, 8 Over High 7
VAM-5. FS-S1-1880CC-005.

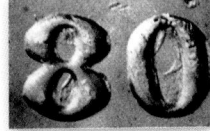

1880-CC, 80 Over 79
VAM-4. FS-S1-1880CC-004.

1880-CC, 8 Over Low 7
VAM-6. FS-S1-1880CC-006.

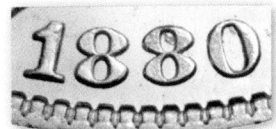

1880-O, 80 Over 79
VAM-4. FS-S1-1880o-004.

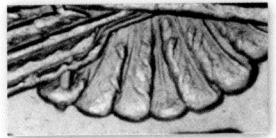

1880-O, Die Gouge
The "Hangnail" variety.
VAM-49. FS-S1-1880o-049.

	Mintage	Cert	Avg	%MS	VF-20	EF-40	AU-50	MS-60	MS-63	MS-64	MS-64DMPL PF-60	MS-65 PF-63	MS-65DMPL PF-65
1880-CC, All kinds	591,000												
1880-CC, 80 Over 79, 2nd Reverse (l)		1,175	62.9	99%	$220	$285	$350	$600	$700	$1,150	$5,000	$2,700	$20,000
Auctions: $8,225, MS-66, March 2015; $1,058, MS-64, January 2015; $734, MS-63, March 2015; $129, G-4, January 2015													
1880-CC, 8 Over 7, 2nd Reverse		328	63.4	100%	$210	$285	$325	$550	$650	$1,050	$5,000	$2,200	$20,000
Auctions: $1,998, MS-64, August 2015; $881, MS-64, July 2015; $588, MS-62, August 2015; $235, VG-10, August 2015													
1880-CC, 8 Over High 7, 3rd Reverse (m)		556	63.4	100%	$210	$275	$325	$500	$600	$700	$2,450	$1,200	$9,000
Auctions: $852, MS-64+, March 2015; $588, MS-64, January 2015; $541, MS-63, September 2015; $529, MS-63, December 2015													
1880-CC, 8 Over Low 7, 3rd Reverse (n)		457	63.5	100%	$270	$365	$475	$600	$640	$750	$2,700	$1,275	$9,000
Auctions: $1,763, MS-65, March 2015; $905, MS-64, September 2015; $764, MS-64, June 2015; $494, MS-63, August 2015													
1880-CC, 3rd Reverse	0	n/a			$210	$275	$325	$500	$600	$700	$2,450	$1,200	$9,000
Auctions: $18,800, MS-67, January 2015; $259, EF-45, February 2015; $200, VF-25, September 2015; $112, G-6, July 2015													
1880-O, All kinds	5,305,000												
1880-O, 80 Over 79 (o)		229	59.1	66%	$35	$37	$48	$150	$625	$2,500	$8,000		
Auctions: $353, MS-63, January 2015; $341, MS-63, September 2015; $353, AU-58, January 2015; $165, AU-58, March 2015													
1880-O		9,596	60.6	76%	$35	$37	$43	$90	$400	$1,650	$7,250	$25,000	$62,500
Auctions: $14,100, MS-65, January 2015; $329, MS-63, November 2015; $64, AU-58, August 2015; $48, AU-55, February 2015													
1880-O, Die Gouge (p)		190	55.8	37%	$200	$450	$900	$2,000	—				
Auctions: $15,275, MS-65, January 2015; $94, AU-58, March 2015; $74, AU-58, January 2015; $69, AU-58, February 2015													
1880-S, All kinds	8,900,000												
1880-S, 80 Over 79		202	63.8	98%	$35	$40	$46	$55	$80	$125	$450	$300	$1,500
Auctions: $435, MS-66, January 2015; $188, MS-65, October 2015; $112, MS-64, April 2015; $94, MS-64, February 2015													
1880-S, 0 Over 9		836	64.0	100%	$35	$40	$46	$63	$80	$125	$450	$300	$1,500
Auctions: $1,058, MS-66+, January 2015; $176, MS-65, April 2015; $129, MS-64, May 2015; $89, MS-63, September 2015													
1880-S		148,482	64.2	100%	$35	$37	$39	$50	$65	$80	$450	$170	$1,000
Auctions: $12,925, MS-68, February 2015; $3,525, MS-65, January 2015; $282, MS-64, November 2015; $182, MS-63, May 2015													

l. The top crossbar and diagonal stem of an underlying 79 are clearly seen within the 8. Extensive polishing marks are visible within the 0. **m.** An almost complete 7 is visible inside the last 8 of the date. The top edge of the 7 touches the top inside of the 8. **n.** A complete 7 is visible inside the last 8 of the date. The crossbar of the underlying 7 can be seen in the top loop and the diagonal of the 7 is visible in the lower loop. **o.** The crossbar of the underlying 7 is visible within the upper loop of the second 8. The 1 and the first 8 are slightly doubled to the right. **p.** On the reverse of the "Hangnail" variety, a die gouge runs from the bottom of the arrow feather, across the feathers, and out the eagle's rightmost tail feather. On the obverse, the top-left part of the second 8 has a spike.

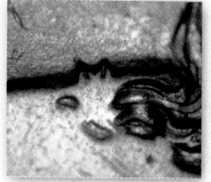

1881-O, Repunched Mintmark
VAM-5. FS-S1-1881o-005.

1882-O, O Over S
VAM-4. FS-S1-1882o-004.

	Mintage	Cert	Avg	%MS	VF-20	EF-40	AU-50	MS-60	MS-63	MS-64	MS-64DMPL / PF-60	MS-65 / PF-63	MS-65DMPL / PF-65
1881	9,163,000	10,626	63.2	98%	$35	$37	$42	$53	$80	$170	$1,375	$750	$19,500
Auctions: $2,350, MS-66, August 2015; $588, MS-65, June 2015; $118, MS-64, October 2015; $79, MS-63, January 2015													
1881, Proof	984	262	64.2								$3,200	$4,000	$6,000
Auctions: $5,581, PF-65Cam, July 2014; $8,813, PF-67, August 2014; $14,100, PF-67, October 2014; $2,468, PF-63, January 2015													
1881-CC	296,000	21,076	63.2	98%	$400	$425	$440	$500	$600	$650	$1,200	$950	$3,000
Auctions: $7,050, MS-67+, October 2015; $517, MS-64, January 2015; $470, MS-61, April 2015; $306, VF-20, March 2015													
1881-O	5,708,000	17,054	62.6	95%	$35	$37	$39	$50	$75	$190	$900	$1,400	$18,000
Auctions: $10,575, MS-66, June 2015; $3,290, MS-65+, August 2015; $129, MS-64, July 2015; $48, AU-58, June 2015													
1881-O, Repunched Mintmark (q)	(r)	10	62.0	100%			$80	$110	$250	—	$1,450	$1,600	
Auctions: $218, MS-64, March 2012													
1881-O, Doubled-Die Obverse (s)	(r)	26	56.7	27%		$175	$400	—	—				
Auctions: $150, AU-50, September 2011													
1881-S	12,760,000	242,970	64.1	100%	$35	$37	$39	$50	$65	$80	$475	$165	$1,000
Auctions: $5,405, MS-68+, January 2015; $129, MS-65, September 2015; $74, MS-64+, May 2015; $188, MS-63, November 2015													
1882	11,100,000	19,182	63.2	99%	$35	$37	$39	$50	$70	$120	$1,000	$550	$6,500
Auctions: $3,173, MS-66+, August 2015; $112, MS-64+, March 2015; $61, MS-63, June 2015; $294, AU-58, January 2015													
1882, Proof	1,100	356	64.4								$3,200	$4,000	$6,000
Auctions: $14,688, PF-67Cam, October 2015; $9,400, PF-66DCam, August 2015; $4,935, PF-65, January 2015; $4,465, PF-64, January 2015													
1882-CC	1,133,000	38,865	63.3	99%	$110	$120	$145	$210	$250	$275	$625	$550	$1,900
Auctions: $6,463, MS-67, January 2015; $129, AU-53, May 2015; $112, EF-40, June 2015; $84, VG-8, February 2015													
1882-O	6,090,000	17,239	62.9	96%	$35	$37	$42	$50	$85	$135	$1,300	$1,500	$5,200
Auctions: $4,583, MS-66, July 2015; $84, MS-64, February 2015; $56, MS-62, February 2015; $54, AU-55, July 2015													
1882-O, O Over S (t)	(u)	3,792	56.7	42%	$50	$70	$120	$235	$775	$2,000	$8,500	$50,000	$62,500
Auctions: $911, MS-63, March 2015; $376, MS-62, July 2015; $94, AU-58, January 2015; $42, VF-35, April 2015													
1882-S	9,250,000	77,714	64.2	100%	$35	$37	$39	$50	$70	$80	$950	$200	$3,800
Auctions: $4,465, MS-68, October 2015; $1,058, MS-67, July 2015; $176, MS-65, August 2015; $84, MS-64, January 2015													
1883	12,290,000	22,894	63.7	99%	$35	$37	$39	$50	$75	$110	$450	$220	$1,600
Auctions: $5,875, MS-67+, October 2015; $188, MS-65, May 2015; $89, MS-64, January 2015; $60, MS-63, August 2015													
1883, Proof	1,039	296	64.0								$3,200	$4,000	$6,000
Auctions: $16,450, PF-67, January 2015; $8,225, PF-66Cam, January 2015; $2,468, PF-63, June 2015; $1,410, PF-61, September 2015													
1883-CC	1,204,000	51,365	63.6	99%	$110	$120	$145	$210	$240	$265	$525	$500	$1,300
Auctions: $3,760, MS-67, January 2015; $4,230, MS-66+, January 2015; $423, MS-65, November 2015; $229, MS-61, July 2015													
1883-O	8,725,000	126,054	63.4	100%	$35	$37	$39	$50	$65	$80	$500	$165	$1,450
Auctions: $2,585, MS-67, January 2015; $129, MS-65, October 2015; $74, MS-64, August 2015; $79, MS-62, February 2015													
1883-O, Proof (v)	*4–8*	2	64.0									$125,000	$175,000
Auctions: $270,250, PF-67Cam, April 2013													
1883-S	6,250,000	5,435	55.5	34%	$35	$53	$140	$750	$2,500	$6,000	$75,000	$45,000	$125,000
Auctions: $17,625, MS-65, September 2015; $1,351, MS-61, June 2015; $341, AU-58, January 2015; $50, EF-45, May 2015													

q. A diagonal image, the remains of one or two additional O mintmark punches, is visible within the primary O. **r.** Included in 1881-O mintage figure. **s.** Clear doubling is evident on the back outside of Liberty's ear **t.** Several varieties exist. **u.** Included in 1882-O mintage figure. **v.** "A numismatic tradition exists, dating back well over a century, that 12 full Proofs were struck of the 1883-O Morgan dollar. And, they may have been, although the differentiation between a cameo DMPL and a 'branch mint Proof' would be difficult to explain" (*A Guide Book of Morgan Silver Dollars*, fourth edition).

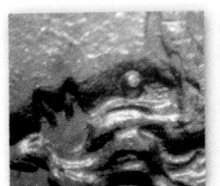 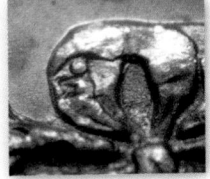

1884, Large Dot
VAM-3. FS-S1-1884-003.

 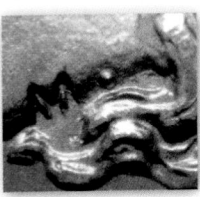

1884, Small Dot
VAM-4. FS-S1-1884-004.

1885, Die Chip
VAM-8. FS-S1-1885-008.

1886, Repunched Date
VAM-20. FS-S1-1886-020.

	Mintage	Cert	Avg	%MS	VF-20	EF-40	AU-50	MS-60	MS-63	MS-64	MS-64DMPL / PF-60	MS-65 / PF-63	MS-65DMPL / PF-65
1884, All kinds	14,070,000												
1884		17,503	63.4	98%	$35	$37	$39	$50	$75	$110	$850	$375	$5,000
Auctions: $25,850, MS-68, January 2015; $1,880, MS-66, October 2015; $94, MS-64, February 2015; $64, MS-63, July 2015													
1884, Large Dot (w)		91	54.8	42%			$55	$85	$250	—			
Auctions: $80, MS-62, May 2014; $74, AU-55, September 2014													
1884, Small Dot (w)		228	61.9	91%			$65	$90	$350	—			
Auctions: $182, MS-63, September 2014; $153, MS-63, February 2015; $141, MS-63, September 2014; $123, MS-63, July 2015													
1884, Proof	875	208	64.3								$3,200	$4,000	$6,000
Auctions: $8,813, PF-66Cam, July 2015; $4,259, PF-65, March 2015; $4,406, PF-64Cam, March 2015; $3,760, PF-63Cam, January 2015													
1884-CC	1,136,000	59,116	63.6	100%	$140	$150	$160	$210	$240	$265	$550	$500	$1,300
Auctions: $5,170, MS-67, June 2015; $423, MS-65, November 2015; $306, MS-64, February 2015; $223, MS-62, March 2015													
1884-O	9,730,000	203,691	63.5	100%	$35	$37	$39	$50	$65	$80	$450	$165	$1,000
Auctions: $2,585, MS-67, January 2015; $188, MS-65, June 2015; $74, MS-64, September 2015; $188, MS-63, February 2015													
1884-S	3,200,000	7,643	52.6	6%	$40	$60	$290	$7,200	$35,000	$115,000	$135,000	$235,000	$275,000
Auctions: $123,375, MS-64, January 2015; $22,325, MS-62, August 2015; $1,528, AU-58, September 2015; $118, EF-45, October 2015													
1885	17,787,000	75,834	63.7	100%	$35	$37	$39	$50	$65	$80	$450	$165	$1,000
Auctions: $2,174, MS-67, October 2015; $147, MS-65, August 2015; $764, MS-64, October 2015; $329, MS-63, November 2015													
1885, Die Chip (x)	(y)	6	61.7	83%			$70	$95	$550	—			
Auctions: No auction records available.													
1885, Proof	930	253	64.3								$3,200	$4,000	$6,000
Auctions: $9,400, PF-66Cam, June 2015; $7,050, PF-65, July 2015; $4,935, PF-64Cam, August 2015; $2,938, PF-63, July 2015													
1885-CC	228,000	20,815	63.5	99%	$550	$570	$590	$700	$825	$875	$1,300	$1,100	$2,400
Auctions: $14,100, MS-67, October 2015; $2,468, MS-66+, January 2015; $676, MS-62, July 2015; $423, F-12, February 2015													
1885-O	9,185,000	199,588	63.7	100%	$35	$37	$39	$50	$65	$80	$450	$165	$1,000
Auctions: $37,600, MS-68, January 2015; $329, MS-66, November 2015; $118, MS-64, November 2015; $74, MS-63, February 2015													
1885-S	1,497,000	6,316	61.0	83%	$50	$63	$110	$250	$315	$675	$5,000	$1,800	$45,000
Auctions: $4,700, MS-66, June 2015; $1,645, MS-65, May 2015; $212, MS-60, April 2015; $79, AU-50, January 2015													
1886	19,963,000	129,293	63.8	100%	$35	$37	$39	$50	$65	$80	$475	$165	$1,300
Auctions: $4,465, MS-68, June 2015; $1,293, MS-67, August 2015; $176, MS-65, November 2015; $62, MS-64, May 2015													
1886, RPD (z)	(aa)	10	60.1	70%			$2,250	$3,500	$5,750	—			
Auctions: $3,819, MS-64, September 2013													
1886, Proof	886	240	64.1								$3,200	$4,000	$6,000
Auctions: $8,813, PF-67, October 2014; $5,875, PF-66, October 2014; $5,405, PF-66, January 2015; $1,939, PF-62, July 2015													

w. A raised dot, either Large or Small, is visible after the designer's initial and on the reverse ribbon. "These dots varieties are thought to have been used as some sort of identifier" (*Cherrypickers' Guide to Rare Die Varieties*, sixth edition, volume II). **x.** A large, raised die chip is evident below the second 8. **y.** Included in circulation-strike 1885 mintage figure. **z.** Repunching is especially evident in the base of the 1, and the lower loop of the 6. **aa.** Included in circulation-strike 1886 mintage figure.

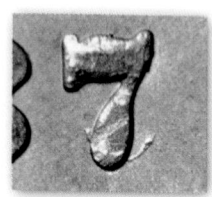

1887, 7 Over 6
VAM-2.
FS-S1-1887-002.

1887-O, 7 Over 6
VAM-3. FS-S1-1887o-003.

1888-O, Obverse Die Break
The "Scarface" variety.
VAM-1B. FS-S1-1888o-001b.

1888-O, Doubled-Die Obverse
The "Hot Lips" variety.
VAM-4. FS-S1-1888o-004.

	Mintage	Cert	Avg	%MS	VF-20	EF-40	AU-50	MS-60	MS-63	MS-64	MS-64DMPL	MS-65	MS-65DMPL
											PF-60	PF-63	PF-65
1886-O	10,710,000	5,797	55.8	30%	$39	$45	$75	$900	$3,500	$11,000	$70,000	$185,000	$300,000
Auctions: $12,338, MS-64, January 2015; $1,293, MS-61, June 2015; $317, AU-58, July 2015; $282, AU-50, April 2015													
1886-O, Clashed Die (bb)	(cc)	11	51.5	0%			$225	$950	$5,750	—			
Auctions: $282, AU-58, July 2015; $176, AU-55, August 2015; $89, AU-50, January 2015; $31, EF-45, March 2015													
1886-S	750,000	4,559	60.0	75%	$78	$105	$150	$350	$500	$850	$8,500	$3,250	$27,000
Auctions: $5,875, MS-66, August 2015; $423, MS-63, May 2015; $188, AU-58, March 2015; $90, EF-45, January 2015													
1887, 7 Over 6	(dd)	1,024	62.5	94%	$48	$70	$165	$400	$500	$750	$4,750	$1,800	$26,000
Auctions: $764, MS-64, August 2015; $400, MS-63, January 2015; $376, MS-62, December 2015; $353, MS-61, January 2015													
1887	20,290,000	186,672	63.7	100%	$35	$37	$39	$50	$65	$80	$450	$165	$1,000
Auctions: $1,087, MS-67, August 2015; $2,585, MS-66, January 2015; $69, MS-63, February 2015; $40, AU-58, September 2015													
1887, Proof	710	220	64.3								$3,200	$4,000	$6,000
Auctions: $17,038, PF-67, May 2015; $3,055, PF-64, October 2015; $3,408, PF-63, January 2015; $823, PF-60, January 2015													
1887-O, 7 Over 6	(ee)	566	60.7	84%	$48	$70	$165	$400	$500	$750	$4,750	$1,800	$26,000
Auctions: $5,581, MS-64, January 2014; $1,586, MS-63, January 2015; $705, MS-60, October 2014; $447, MS-60, January 2015													
1887-O	11,550,000	9,654	62.3	95%	$35	$42	$55	$70	$150	$400	$1,700	$2,750	$13,500
Auctions: $2,585, MS-65, January 2015; $306, MS-64, August 2015; $129, MS-63, October 2015; $94, MS-62, March 2015													
1887-S	1,771,000	6,732	61.3	81%	$40	$45	$50	$135	$300	$750	$7,000	$2,600	$27,500
Auctions: $4,465, MS-66, August 2015; $3,525, MS-65+, September 2015; $176, MS-62, September 2015; $79, AU-58, February 2015													
1888	19,183,000	46,695	63.6	99%	$35	$37	$39	$50	$65	$80	$450	$250	$2,400
Auctions: $4,935, MS-67, July 2015; $376, MS-66, October 2015; $166, MS-65, August 2015; $96, MS-64+, January 2015													
1888, Proof	833	196	63.9								$3,200	$4,000	$6,000
Auctions: $24,675, PF-66Cam, April 2013; $5,288, PF-65, October 2015													
1888-O	12,150,000	24,305	63.2	99%	$35	$37	$39	$50	$75	$115	$500	$625	$4,500
Auctions: $4,583, MS-66, January 2015; $94, MS-64, September 2015; $69, MS-63, November 2015; $517, AU-58, January 2015													
1888-O, Obverse Die Break (ff)	(gg)	47	61.7	98%			$2,250	$4,750	$8,650				
Auctions: $14,688, MS-64, December 2013													
1888-O, Doubled-Die Obverse (hh)	(gg)	821	32.2	1%	$145	$290	$900	$20,000	$30,000	—			
Auctions: $6,169, MS-66, January 2015; $764, MS-64, August 2015; $235, AU-58, December 2015; $141, EF-45, March 2015													
1888-S	657,000	5,104	58.8	71%	$175	$185	$205	$315	$500	$1,000	$2,850	$3,500	$15,500
Auctions: $6,169, MS-66, January 2015; $764, MS-64, August 2015; $235, AU-58, December 2015; $141, EF-45, March 2015													

bb. Clashing of the E of LIBERTY is evident between the eagle's tail feathers and the bow on the wreath **cc.** Included in 1886-O mintage figure. **dd.** Included in circulation-strike 1887 mintage figure. **ee.** Included in 1887-O mintage figure. **ff.** A major die break runs from the rim between E and P, through the field, and all the way across Liberty's face and neck. This variety is nicknamed "Scarface." **gg.** Included in 1888-O mintage figure. **hh.** Doubling is visible on the lips (especially), nose, eye, chin, entire profile, and part of the hair. This variety is nicknamed "Hot Lips."

1889, Die Break
The "Bar Wing" variety.
VAM-22. FS-S1-1889-022.

1889-O, Clashed Die
VAM-1A. FS-S1-1889o-001a.

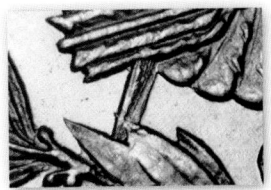

1890-CC, Die Gouge
The "Tailbar" variety.
VAM-4. FS-S1-1890CC-004.

1890-O, Die Gouges
The "Comet" variety.
VAM-10. FS-S1-1890o-010.

	Mintage	Cert	Avg	%MS	VF-20	EF-40	AU-50	MS-60	MS-63	MS-64	MS-64DMPL	MS-65	186,672
											PF-60	PF-63	PF-65
1889	21,726,000	45,509	63.2	98%	$35	$37	$39	$50	$70	$90	$700	$380	$3,600
Auctions: $5,004, MS-66+, January 2015; $235, MS-65, September 2015; $84, MS-64, February 2015; $64, MS-63, July 2015													
1889, Die Break (ii)	(jj)	109	59.2	67%			$80	$150	$285	$325		$2,500	
Auctions: $182, MS-63, September 2014; $106, MS-62, February 2015; $89, MS-62, September 2014; $84, MS-61, September 2014													
1889, Proof	811	191	64.2								$3,200	$4,000	$6,000
Auctions: $12,925, PF-66Cam, August 2015; $3,290, PF-64Cam, January 2015; $3,055, PF-64, January 2015; $3,290, PF-63, January 2015													
1889-CC	350,000	4,646	33.1	11%	$1,250	$3,000	$8,000	$26,000	$50,000	$85,000	$95,000	$325,000	$350,000
Auctions: $16,450, MS-61, January 2015; $7,344, AU-53, February 2015; $705, VG-10, June 2015; $376, AG-3, August 2015													
1889-O	11,875,000	4,597	60.3	84%	$35	$37	$55	$185	$400	$1,000	$6,500	$7,500	$17,500
Auctions: $8,813, MS-65+, January 2015; $646, MS-64, July 2015; $200, MS-61, October 2015; $64, AU-55, January 2015													
1889-O, Clashed Die (kk)	(ll)	42	37.9	2%			$975	$2,000	—	—			
Auctions: $4,465, MS-61, August 2015; $940, AU-58, August 2015; $740, AU-55, January 2015; $217, VF-35, March 2015													
1889-S	700,000	6,349	60.9	77%	$60	$75	$105	$275	$375	$675	$5,500	$2,200	$37,500
Auctions: $3,055, MS-66, August 2015; $223, MS-61, March 2015; $135, AU-58, January 2015; $94, AU-53, December 2015													
1890	16,802,000	17,205	62.8	97%	$35	$37	$43	$53	$95	$175	$2,500	$2,050	$20,000
Auctions: $2,820, MS-65+, June 2015; $194, MS-64+, March 2015; $141, MS-64, January 2015; $74, MS-63, August 2015													
1890, Proof	590	229	64.8								$3,200	$4,000	$6,000
Auctions: $88,125, PF-69DCam, April 2013; $12,925, PF-66Cam, July 2014; $4,259, PF-64Cam, November 2014													
1890-CC	2,309,041	7,940	55.9	75%	$110	$140	$190	$500	$900	$1,500	$2,800	$5,000	$13,750
Auctions: $28,200, MS-66, August 2015; $5,405, MS-65, February 2015; $282, AU-58, July 2015; $118, VF-35, December 2015													
1890-CC, Die Gouge (mm)	(nn)	432	46.9	48%			$650	$1,150	$2,950	—			
Auctions: $3,760, MS-63, January 2015; $911, AU-55, January 2015; $470, EF-45, January 2015; $223, F-12, November 2015													
1890-O	10,701,000	9,365	62.5	97%	$35	$37	$49	$75	$105	$325	$1,500	$2,500	$9,250
Auctions: $2,585, MS-65, June 2015; $376, MS-64+, July 2015; $94, MS-63, December 2015; $79, MS-62, January 2015													
1890-O, Die Gouges (oo)	(pp)	57	61.0	84%			$65	$90	$260	—		$2,100	
Auctions: $2,233, MS-65, February 2015; $1,410, MS-64+, July 2015; $306, MS-64, September 2015; $188, MS-63, January 2015													
1890-S	8,230,373	9,527	62.3	91%	$35	$37	$45	$70	$105	$325	$3,200	$1,400	$9,250
Auctions: $4,230, MS-66+, January 2015; $1,087, MS-65, September 2015; $329, MS-64+, August 2015; $84, MS-62, February 2015													

ii. A die break is visible on the top of the eagle's right wing. This variety is nicknamed the "Bar Wing." Different obverse die pairings exist. **jj.** Included in circulation-strike 1889 mintage figure. **kk.** The E of LIBERTY is visible in the field below the eagle's tail feathers and slightly left of the bow. This variety is extremely rare in Mint State, and unknown above MS-61. **ll.** Included in 1889-O mintage figure. **mm.** A heavy die gouge extends from between the eagle's first tail feather and the lowest arrow feather to the leaves in the wreath below. "This is an extremely popular and highly marketable variety, especially in Mint State" (*Cherrypickers' Guide to Rare Die Varieties*, sixth edition, volume II). This variety is nicknamed the "Tailbar." **nn.** Included in 1890-CC mintage figure. **oo.** Die gouges are evident to the right of the date. This variety is nicknamed the "Comet." **pp.** Included in 1890-O mintage figure.

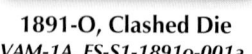

1891-O, Clashed Die
VAM-1A. FS-S1-1891o-001a.

1891-O, Pitted Reverse Die
VAM-1B. FS-S1-1891o-001b.

	Mintage	Cert	Avg	%MS	VF-20	EF-40	AU-50	MS-60	MS-63	MS-64	MS-64DMPL / PF-60	MS-65 / PF-63	MS-65DMPL / PF-65
1891	8,693,556	7,184	61.6	91%	$35	$40	$45	$75	$220	$750	$6,900	$8,000	$23,000
Auctions: $12,925, MS-65+, October 2015; $564, MS-64, July 2015; $89, MS-62, December 2015; $50, AU-58, January 2015													
1891, Proof	650	222	64.5								$3,200	$4,000	$6,000
Auctions: $4,583, PF-65, October 2015; $3,525, PF-64Cam, January 2015; $3,408, PF-64Cam, January 2015; $2,938, PF-63, August 2015													
1891-CC	1,618,000	10,984	59.7	85%	$110	$140	$190	$450	$775	$1,275	$4,500	$5,000	$32,000
Auctions: $4,935, MS-65, August 2015; $881, MS-63, January 2015; $282, AU-58, December 2015; $206, EF-45, March 2015													
1891-O	7,954,529	4,648	61.3	90%	$35	$40	$55	$200	$400	$825	$7,250	$7,500	$36,500
Auctions: $8,225, MS-65, June 2015; $517, MS-64, September 2015; $235, MS-62, January 2015; $79, AU-58, February 2015													
1891-O, Clashed Die (qq)	(rr)	139	36.8	1%			$235	$400	$1,500	—			
Auctions: $517, AU-53, January 2015; $153, AU-50, June 2015; $79, AU-50, November 2014; $48, F-12, November 2014													
1891-O, Pitted Reverse Die (ss)	(rr)	9	51.9	0%			$370		—	—			
Auctions: $4,700, MS-65, June 2014; $3,055, MS-65, October 2014; $3,290, MS-65, November 2014; $2,585, MS-64, October 2014													
1891-S	5,296,000	6,300	62.3	91%	$35	$40	$45	$70	$160	$350	$3,200	$1,750	$20,000
Auctions: $5,640, MS-66, June 2015; $1,234, MS-65, September 2015; $118, MS-63, December 2015; $46, AU-58, May 2015													
1892	1,036,000	4,645	60.1	73%	$43	$53	$90	$300	$525	$1,200	$3,200	$5,250	$18,000
Auctions: $4,230, MS-65+, January 2015; $1,704, MS-64, August 2015; $84, AU-53, December 2015; $46, VF-35, May 2015													
1892, Proof	1,245	365	64.4								$3,200	$4,000	$6,000
Auctions: $14,100, PF-67, January 2015; $6,169, PF-65Cam, October 2015; $3,878, PF-64, August 2015; $2,350, PF-63, September 2015													
1892-CC	1,352,000	5,973	55.3	72%	$285	$450	$690	$1,500	$2,400	$3,200	$9,000	$9,250	$36,000
Auctions: $22,913, MS-66, August 2015; $7,638, MS-65, September 2015; $588, AU-53, February 2015; $458, EF-45, December 2015													
1892-O	2,744,000	5,214	60.8	84%	$40	$48	$70	$290	$425	$1,050	$20,000	$7,500	$50,000
Auctions: $3,525, MS-65, January 2015; $1,763, MS-64+, August 2015; $306, MS-62, September 2015; $259, MS-61, March 2015													
1892-S	1,200,000	3,810	40.8	1%	$140	$300	$1,650	$40,000	$65,000	$115,000	$145,000	$190,000	$250,000
Auctions: $20,563, AU-58, August 2015; $329, EF-45, August 2015; $147, VF-35, January 2015; $94, F-15, September 2015													
1893	378,000	4,792	51.9	46%	$225	$275	$400	$725	$1,100	$2,300	$32,500	$8,500	$67,500
Auctions: $10,313, MS-65+, June 2015; $350, AU-55, December 2015; $235, EF-45, January 2015; $147, VG-10, February 2015													
1893, Proof	792	245	64.0								$3,200	$4,000	$6,000
Auctions: $35,250, PF-68, May 2015; $3,995, PF-64, October 2015; $1,763, PF-62, January 2015; $911, PF-58, February 2015													
1893-CC	677,000	4,090	40.9	43%	$625	$1,500	$2,400	$5,000	$8,500	$16,000	$46,000	$70,000	$85,000
Auctions: $25,850, MS-64+, July 2015; $5,170, MS-62, August 2015; $2,350, AU-50, January 2015; $705, VF-30, February 2015													
1893-CC, Proof (tt)	4–8	10	63.8									$125,000	$175,000
Auctions: $149,500, PF-65, August 2011													
1893-O	300,000	3,335	42.1	21%	$325	$475	$775	$2,850	$6,500	$17,000	$105,000	$200,000	$275,000
Auctions: $11,163, MS-64, March 2015; $5,170, MS-62, January 2015; $1,351, AU-55, February 2015; $235, VF-20, June 2015													
1893-S † (uu,vv)	100,000	2,899	21.0	1%	$5,200	$9,000	$20,000	$120,000	$225,000	$350,000	$400,000	$650,000	$750,000
Auctions: $282,000, MS-63, July 2015; $25,850, AU-55, January 2015; $6,200, VF-35, September 2015; $3,760, F-12, February 2015													

qq. The evidence of a clashed die is visible below the eagle's tail feathers and slightly left of the bow, where the E in LIBERTY has been transferred from the obverse die. **rr.** Included in 1891-O mintage figure. **ss.** Pitting on the reverse is visible around the ONE and on the bottom of the wreath above and between ONE and DOLLAR. This variety is rare in circulated grades, and unknown in Mint State. **tt.** Some numismatists classify these as Deep Mirror Prooflike circulation strikes, rather than as Proofs. **uu.** "All 1893-S Morgan dollars were struck from a single die pairing. Genuine 1893-S silver dollars display a diagonal die scratch in the top of the T in LIBERTY. This diagnostic can be seen even on very low-grade examples" (*100 Greatest U.S. Coins*, fourth edition). **vv.** Beware of altered or otherwise fraudulent mintmarks.

1899-O, Micro O
*VAM-4, 5, 6, 31, and
32. FS-S1-1899o-501.*

	Mintage	Cert	Avg	%MS	VF-20	EF-40	AU-50	MS-60	MS-63	MS-64	MS-64DMPL	MS-65	MS-65DMPL
											PF-60	PF-63	PF-65
1894 (vv)	110,000	3,575	46.7	27%	$1,250	$1,350	$1,700	$3,400	$4,900	$9,500	$60,000	$40,000	$90,000
Auctions: $28,200, MS-65, January 2015; $881, VF-35, July 2015; $823, F-15, February 2015; $541, G-6, October 2015													
1894, Proof	972	345	64.2								$3,500	$5,000	$7,000
Auctions: $44,063, PF-67Cam, April 2013; $14,100, PF-66Cam, October 2014													
1894-O	1,723,000	4,801	50.8	22%	$60	$115	$260	$950	$4,750	$11,500	$29,000	$65,000	$65,000
Auctions: $19,388, MS-64+, June 2015; $2,104, MS-62, July 2015; $212, AU-55, February 2015; $56, VF-30, May 2015													
1894-S	1,260,000	3,312	55.8	64%	$95	$150	$450	$825	$1,200	$2,400	$22,000	$7,000	$35,000
Auctions: $18,800, MS-66, March 2015; $8,225, MS-65, August 2015; $411, AU-55, February 2015; $212, EF-45, April 2015													
1895, Proof † (ww)	880	369	62.3								$50,000	$55,000	$70,000
Auctions: $58,750, PF-65Cam, January 2015; $58,750, PF-64Cam, November 2014; $42,300, PF-63Cam, January 2015													
1895-O	450,000	5,491	39.8	3%	$400	$600	$1,200	$14,500	$50,000	$80,000	$140,000	$165,000	$240,000
Auctions: $79,313, MS-64, January 2015; $24,675, MS-62, July 2015; $852, AU-50, February 2015; $353, EF-40, September 2015													
1895-O, Proof (tt)	2–3	5	64.0				*(extremely rare)*						
Auctions: $528,750, PF-66, June 2013													
1895-S	400,000	2,834	37.1	28%	$900	$1,200	$1,800	$3,900	$6,250	$11,000	$19,500	$26,000	$40,000
Auctions: $11,750, MS-64+, January 2015; $3,055, AU-58, August 2015; $1,087, EF-45, October 2015; $400, F-12, December 2015													
1896	9,976,000	52,284	63.5	99%	$35	$37	$39	$50	$65	$90	$450	$250	$1,200
Auctions: $3,055, MS-67, January 2015; $764, MS-66+, July 2015; $80, MS-64, March 2015; $94, MS-63, October 2015													
1896, Proof	762	277	64.9								$3,200	$4,000	$6,000
Auctions: $39,950, PF-68DCam, February 2015; $19,975, PF-68, October 2014; $3,672, PF-63DCam, November 2014; $1,528, PF-60, July 2014													
1896-O	4,900,000	6,273	54.7	22%	$39	$43	$160	$1,500	$8,000	$42,000	$60,000	$175,000	$200,000
Auctions: $17,038, MS-63, August 2015; $1,500, MS-61, June 2015; $176, AU-55, January 2015; $58, EF-45, October 2015													
1896-S	5,000,000	1,702	49.0	43%	$70	$220	$775	$2,100	$3,750	$5,750	$57,500	$17,500	$100,000
Auctions: $15,275, MS-65, July 2015; $9,106, MS-64, June 2015; $1,293, AU-55, January 2015; $200, EF-40, December 2015													
1897	2,822,000	16,982	63.4	98%	$35	$37	$39	$50	$75	$100	$500	$350	$3,700
Auctions: $6,463, MS-67, July 2015; $1,533, MS-66+, January 2015; $235, MS-65, October 2015; $79, MS-64, December 2015													
1897, Proof	731	213	64.4								$3,200	$4,000	$6,000
Auctions: $7,050, PF-66, June 2015; $4,935, PF-65, February 2015; $2,056, PF-62, September 2014; $881, PF-60, November 2014													
1897-O	4,004,000	6,342	55.5	24%	$35	$41	$100	$850	$4,750	$16,500	$37,500	$65,000	$75,000
Auctions: $9,988, MS-64, October 2015; $4,700, MS-63, August 2015; $1,182, MS-61, July 2015; $259, AU-58, December 2015													
1897-S	5,825,000	8,097	62.8	93%	$35	$37	$45	$85	$150	$200	$1,100	$650	$3,000
Auctions: $5,170, MS-67, August 2015; $1,293, MS-66, January 2015; $306, MS-64, October 2015; $46, AU-58, September 2015													
1898	5,884,000	21,664	63.5	98%	$35	$37	$39	$50	$65	$80	$450	$175	$1,025
Auctions: $5,170, MS-67, January 2015; $206, MS-65, November 2015; $84, MS-64, August 2015; $142, MS-63, May 2015													
1898, Proof	735	252	64.8								$2,900	$4,000	$6,000
Auctions: $25,850, PF-68Cam, January 2015; $21,150, PF-68, May 2015; $9,400, PF-65DCam, January 2015; $3,055, PF-63, August 2015													
1898-O	4,440,000	70,139	63.9	100%	$35	$37	$39	$50	$65	$80	$450	$175	$1,025
Auctions: $2,820, MS-67, June 2015; $470, MS-66+, August 2015; $129, MS-65, August 2015; $84, MS-64, January 2015													
1898-S	4,102,000	3,304	59.7	68%	$40	$50	$100	$275	$475	$650	$3,250	$2,400	$13,750
Auctions: $15,275, MS-66+, August 2015; $764, MS-64, January 2015; $282, MS-61, September 2015; $129, AU-58, March 2015													

† Ranked in the *100 Greatest U.S. Coins* (fourth edition). **tt.** Some numismatists classify these as Deep Mirror Prooflike circulation strikes, rather than as Proofs. **vv.** Beware of altered or otherwise fraudulent mintmarks. **ww.** Mint records indicate that 12,000 1895 Morgan dollars were struck for circulation; however, none have ever been seen. In order to complete their collections, date-by-date collectors are forced to acquire one of the 880 Proofs struck that year, causing much competition for this, "The King of the Morgan Dollars."

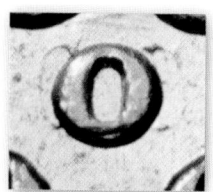
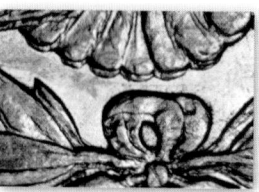
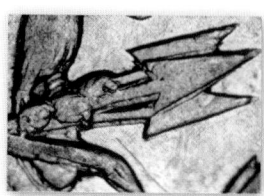

1900-O, Obverse Die Crack
VAM-29A. FS-S1-1900o-029a.

1900-O, O Over CC
Various VAMs.
FS-S1-1900o-501.

1901, Doubled-Die Reverse
The "Shifted Eagle" variety. VAM-3. FS-S1-1901-003.

	Mintage	Cert	Avg	%MS	VF-20	EF-40	AU-50	MS-60	MS-63	MS-64	MS-64DMPL	MS-65	MS-65DMPL
											PF-60	PF-63	PF-65
1899	330,000	9,996	61.4	88%	$180	$200	$225	$265	$300	$400	$1,200	$925	$2,300
Auctions: $4,465, MS-66, August 2015; $259, MS-63, October 2015; $141, AU-53, December 2015; $165, EF-45, March 2015
1899, Proof	846	226	64.2								$3,200	$4,000	$6,000
Auctions: $22,325, PF-68, June 2015; $9,988, PF-67, June 2015; $2,820, PF-63, January 2015; $1,410, PF-61, July 2015
1899-O	12,290,000	55,628	63.7	100%	$35	$37	$39	$50	$65	$90	$500	$210	$1,650
Auctions: $4,230, MS-67, August 2015; $940, MS-66+, January 2015; $282, MS-66, September 2015; $79, MS-64, November 2015
1899-O, Micro O (xx)	(yy)	596	37.1	3%			$140	$375	$1,000	—			
Auctions: $306, AU-55, September 2015; $200, AU-53, October 2015; $69, AU-50, January 2015; $84, EF-45, January 2015
1899-S	2,562,000	2,985	60.4	75%	$48	$65	$140	$380	$500	$825	$3,800	$2,150	$23,000
Auctions: $37,600, MS-67, August 2015; $3,995, MS-66, January 2015; $411, MS-61, August 2015; $121, AU-55, February 2015
1900	8,830,000	31,799	63.6	98%	$35	$37	$39	$50	$65	$80	$9,000	$170	$40,000
Auctions: $8,225, MS-67, February 2015; $3,290, MS-66+, February 2015; $223, MS-65, October 2015; $63, MS-63, June 2015
1900, Proof	912	273	64.3								$3,200	$4,000	$6,000
Auctions: $8,813, PF-67, January 2015; $7,050, PF-65Cam, August 2015; $5,170, PF-65, January 2015; $2,174, PF-62, March 2015
1900-O	12,590,000	42,871	63.7	99%	$35	$37	$39	$50	$65	$80	$1,100	$170	$5,750
Auctions: $2,585, MS-67, January 2015; $1,175, MS-66+, September 2015; $135, MS-65, June 2015; $94, MS-63, November 2015
1900-O, Obverse Die Break (zz)	(aaa)	69	28.8	6%		$700		—	—				
Auctions: $306, AU-58, January 2015; $153, EF-40, October 2014; $112, VF-30, February 2015; $94, VF-25, July 2015
1900-O, O Over CC (bbb)	(aaa)	3,158	59.7	82%	$65	$105	$170	$325	$725	$950	$8,500	$2,100	$19,000
Auctions: $1,293, MS-64, January 2015; $447, MS-62, December 2015; $235, AU-58, June 2015; $153, EF-40, February 2015
1900-S	3,540,000	3,993	60.8	76%	$40	$48	$90	$300	$400	$650	$19,000	$1,800	$35,000
Auctions: $2,233, MS-65+, January 2015; $306, MS-62, June 2015; $129, AU-58, March 2015; $50, EF-45, September 2015
1901 (ccc)	6,962,000	4,712	53.9	15%	$50	$115	$280	$3,500	$15,750	$50,000	$70,000	$475,000	
Auctions: $51,700, MS-64, August 2015; $19,975, MS-63, January 2015; $7,050, MS-62, June 2015; $353, AU-55, February 2015
1901, Doubled-Die Reverse (ddd)	(eee)	108	41.3	2%	$375	$1,100	$1,900	$4,500	—				
Auctions: $41,125, MS-62, August 2013
1901, Proof	813	276	63.8								$3,200	$4,100	$6,500
Auctions: $28,200, PF-68, May 2015; $12,925, PF-67, August 2015; $7,050, PF-65Cam, June 2015; $2,820, PF-62Cam, July 2015
1901-O	13,320,000	37,017	63.7	100%	$35	$37	$39	$50	$65	$80	$1,200	$175	$8,500
Auctions: $19,975, MS-67, March 2015; $4,465, MS-66+, January 2015; $223, MS-65, August 2015; $94, MS-64, June 2015
1901-S	2,284,000	2,595	58.9	71%	$45	$65	$200	$525	$850	$1,200	$21,000	$3,500	$30,000
Auctions: $42,300, MS-67, February 2015; $9,400, MS-66, August 2015; $282, AU-58, September 2015; $42, EF-40, January 2015

xx. The O mintmark is smaller than normal; its punch was probably intended for a Barber half dollar. Five different dies are known, all scarce. **yy.** Included in 1899-O mintage figure. **zz.** A die break is visible from the rim through the date to just below the lower point of the bust. This variety is very rare in Mint State. **aaa.** Included in 1900-O mintage figure. **bbb.** An O mintmark was punched into the die over a previously punched CC mintmark. There are at least seven different dies involved; the one pictured is VAM-9. **ccc.** Beware of a fraudulently removed mintmark intended to make a less valuable 1901-O or 1901-S appear to be a 1901 dollar. **ddd.** Doubling is visible on the eagle's tail feathers, and also on IN GOD WE TRUST, as well as on the arrows, wreath, and bow. This variety is nicknamed the "Shifted Eagle." It is very rare in Mint State. **eee.** Included in circulation-strike 1901 mintage figure.

1903-S,
Small S
Mintmark
VAM-2.
FS-S1-1903S-002.

	Mintage	Cert	Avg	%MS	VF-20	EF-40	AU-50	MS-60	MS-63	MS-64	MS-64DMPL / PF-60	MS-65 / PF-63	MS-65DMPL / PF-65
1902	7,994,000	5,881	63.2	96%	$35	$37	$45	$55	$135	$180	$13,000	$475	$20,000
	Auctions: $5,405, MS-67, June 2015; $1,645, MS-66, September 2015; $129, MS-64, August 2015; $106, MS-63, January 2015												
1902, Proof	777	234	64.3								$3,200	$4,000	$6,000
	Auctions: $9,400, PF-67, January 2015; $11,750, PF-66, August 2015; $5,053, PF-65, February 2015; $2,820, PF-63, January 2015												
1902-O	8,636,000	67,015	63.6	100%	$35	$37	$45	$55	$65	$80	$2,800	$175	$13,500
	Auctions: $15,275, MS-67, February 2015; $3,055, MS-66+, June 2015; $200, MS-65+, September 2015; $89, MS-64, May 2015												
1902-S	1,530,000	3,474	57.5	70%	$140	$190	$275	$380	$650	$875	$8,000	$2,800	$14,000
	Auctions: $6,463, MS-66, August 2015; $646, MS-63, June 2015; $259, AU-58, December 2015; $79, F-12, January 2015												
1903	4,652,000	12,358	63.4	96%	$50	$55	$65	$78	$90	$120	$7,500	$320	$22,500
	Auctions: $3,526, MS-67, August 2015; $1,293, MS-66+, October 2015; $223, MS-65, February 2015; $89, MS-64, December 2015												
1903, Proof	755	268	64.3								$3,200	$4,000	$6,000
	Auctions: $3,995, PF-64, January 2015; $3,819, PF-64, March 2015; $3,055, PF-63, August 2015; $1,998, PF-62, January 2015												
1903-O	4,450,000	7,804	63.0	98%	$340	$350	$365	$415	$450	$475	$1,800	$625	$6,400
	Auctions: $3,760, MS-67, January 2015; $2,585, MS-66+, June 2015; $823, MS-65, September 2015; $376, MS-64, December 2015												
1903-S	1,241,000	2,431	34.3	12%	$205	$350	$1,600	$4,500	$7,000	$8,000	$15,000	$11,000	$38,000
	Auctions: $7,638, MS-64, January 2015; $6,770, MS-63, January 2015; $2,115, AU-55, October 2015; $188, VF-35, November 2015												
1903-S, Small S (fff)	(ggg)	135	23.4	1%				$6,400	—	—			
	Auctions: $588, VF-30, January 2015; $329, VF-20, January 2015; $112, VG-10, May 2015; $94, G-4, February 2015												
1904	2,788,000	4,373	61.9	89%	$40	$47	$55	$100	$260	$575	$42,500	$2,850	$60,000
	Auctions: $9,988, MS-66, August 2015; $2,233, MS-65, September 2015; $376, MS-64, January 2015; $79, AU-58, October 2015												
1904, Proof	650	290	63.9								$3,200	$4,000	$6,000
	Auctions: $22,325, PF-68, May 2015; $7,638, PF-66, March 2015; $3,995, PF-64+, February 2015; $2,820, PF-64, January 2015												
1904-O	3,720,000	131,951	63.7	100%	$35	$37	$39	$50	$65	$80	$450	$165	$1,150
	Auctions: $4,465, MS-67, January 2015; $400, MS-66, September 2015; $153, MS-65, July 2015; $74, MS-64+, February 2015												
1904-S	2,304,000	2,114	46.7	32%	$80	$200	$500	$2,500	$4,500	$5,750	$13,000	$11,000	$22,000
	Auctions: $16,450, MS-66, June 2015; $4,935, MS-64, August 2015; $2,350, AU-58, January 2015; $200, EF-45, December 2015												
1921	44,690,000	107,003	63.4	99%	$32	$34	$35	$42	$50	$65	$7,750	$160	$11,500
	Auctions: $3,055, MS-66+, January 2015; $182, MS-65, May 2015; $100, MS-64, September 2015; $129, MS-62, August 2015												
1921, Zerbe Proof (hhh)	150–250	74	64.1								$5,250	$8,000	$11,000
	Auctions: $29,375, PF-66, August 2015; $11,163, PF-65, June 2015; $11,163, PF-64, January 2015; $9,401, SP-63, August 2015												
1921, Chapman Proof (iii)	25–40	1	66.0								$35,000	$40,000	$70,000
	Auctions: $61,688, PF-65, April 2013												
1921-D	20,345,000	16,216	63.0	94%	$32	$34	$35	$50	$70	$120	$7,500	$375	$12,000
	Auctions: $3,760, MS-66, August 2015; $259, MS-65, August 2015; $112, MS-64, December 2015; $100, AU-53, January 2015												
1921-S	21,695,000	12,921	62.8	95%	$32	$34	$35	$50	$80	$160	$12,000	$1,200	$30,000
	Auctions: $3,819, MS-66, January 2015; $852, MS-65, February 2015; $84, MS-64, May 2015; $69, MS-63, October 2015												
1921-S, Zerbe Proof (hhh)	1–2	0	n/a									$90,000	$140,000
	Auctions: $117,500, PF-65, August 2013												

fff. The S mintmark is smaller than normal, possibly intended to be punched into a Barber half dollar die. **ggg.** Included in 1903-S mintage figure. **hhh.** "Pieces called Zerbe Proofs are simply circulation strikes with a semi-prooflike character, not as nice as on the earlier-noted [mirrorlike] prooflike pieces, struck from dies that were slightly polished, but that retained countless minute striae and preparation lines. In the view of the writer [Bowers], Zerbe Proofs have no basis in numismatic fact or history, although opinions differ on the subject. It seems highly unlikely that these were produced as Proofs for collectors. If indeed they were furnished to Farran Zerbe, a leading numismatic entrepreneur of the era, it is likely that they were simply regular production pieces. Zerbe had a fine collection and certainly knew what a brilliant Proof should look like, and he never would have accepted such pieces as mirror Proofs" (*A Guide Book of Morgan Silver Dollars,* fourth edition). **iii.** Breen stated that 12 Chapman Proofs were minted (*Walter Breen's Encyclopedia of U.S. and Colonial Proof Coins, 1792–1977*); Bowers estimates fewer than 30 (*A Guide Book of Morgan Silver Dollars,* fourth edition). These are sometimes called *Chapman Proofs* because Philadelphia coin dealer Henry Chapman advertised them for sale within a few months of their production.

PEACE (1921–1935)

Designer: *Anthony de Francisci.* **Weight:** *26.73 grams.*
Composition: *.900 silver, .100 copper (net weight .77344 oz. pure silver).*
Diameter: *38.1 mm.* **Edge:** *Reeded.* **Mints:** *Philadelphia, Denver, and San Francisco.*

Mintmark location is on the reverse, to the left of the tail feathers.

Circulation Strike

Proof

History. In 1921, following the melting of more than 270 million silver dollars as legislated by the Pittman Act of 1918, the U.S. Treasury struck millions more silver dollars of the Morgan type while a new Peace dollar was in development. Sculptor and medalist Anthony de Francisci created the Peace design, originally intended as a commemorative of the end of the hostilities of the Great War. The obverse features a flowing-haired Miss Liberty wearing a spiked tiara, and the reverse an eagle perched before the rising sun. The designer's monogram is located in the field of the coin under the neck of Miss Liberty. Coins of 1921 were struck in high relief; this caused weakness at the centers, so the design was changed to low relief in 1922. The dollars were struck until 1928, then again in 1934 and 1935. Legislation dated August 3, 1964, authorized the coinage of 45 million silver dollars, and 316,076 dollars of the Peace design dated 1964 were struck at the Denver Mint in 1965. Plans for completing this coinage were subsequently abandoned and all of these coins were melted. None were preserved or released for circulation; details are found in *A Guide Book of Peace Dollars* (Burdette).

Striking and Sharpness. Peace dollars of 1921 are always lightly struck at the center of the obverse, with hair detail not showing in an area. The size of this flat spot can vary. For this and other Peace dollars, check the hair detail at the center and, on the reverse, the feathers on the eagle. Many coins are struck from overly used dies, giving a grainy appearance to the fields, particularly the obverse. On many Peace dollars tiny white "milk spots" are seen, left over from when they were struck; these are not as desirable in the marketplace as unspotted coins.

Availability. All dates and mintmarks are readily available. Although some are well worn, they are generally collected in EF and finer grades. MS coins are available for each, with the 1934-S considered to be the key date. San Francisco issues of the 1920s, except for 1926-S, are often heavily bagmarked from coming into contact with other coins during shipment, storage, and other handling. The appearance of luster varies from issue to issue and can be deeply frosty, or—in the instance of Philadelphia Mint coins of 1928, 1934, and 1935—satiny or "creamy."

Proofs. Some Sandblast Proofs were made in 1921 and a limited issue in 1922 in high relief. These are rare today. Seemingly, a few Satin Proofs were also made in 1921. Sandblast Proofs of 1922 have a peculiar whitish surface in most instances, sometimes interrupted by small dark flecks or spots. There are a number of impostors among certified "Proofs."

Note: Values of common-date silver coins have been based on the current bullion price of silver, $15.50 per ounce, and may vary with the prevailing spot price.

GRADING STANDARDS

MS-60 to 70 (Mint State). *Obverse:* At MS-60, some abrasion and contact marks are evident, most noticeably on the cheek and on the hair to the right of the face and forehead. Luster is present, but may be dull or lifeless. At MS-63, contact marks are extensive but not distracting. Abrasion still is evident, but less than at lower levels. MS-64 coins are slightly finer. Some Peace dollars have whitish "milk spots" in the field; while these are

1921. Graded MS-64.

not caused by handling, but seem to have been from liquid at the mint or in storage, coins with these spots are rarely graded higher than MS–63 or 64. An MS-65 coin may have minor abrasion, but contact marks are so minute as to require magnification. Luster should be full and rich on earlier issues, and either frosty or satiny on later issues, depending on the date and mint. *Reverse:* At MS-60 some abrasion and contact marks are evident, most noticeably on the eagle's shoulder and nearby. Otherwise, comments apply as for the obverse.

Illustrated coin: Note the scattered marks that are practically definitive of the grade. The high relief of this particular year results in light striking at the center; this is normal and not to be mistaken for wear.

AU-50, 53, 55, 58 (About Uncirculated). *Obverse:* Light wear is seen on the cheek and the highest-relief areas of the hair. The neck truncation edge also shows wear. At AU-58, the luster is extensive, but incomplete. At AU–50 and 53, luster is less but still present. *Reverse:* Wear is evident on the eagle's shoulder and back. Otherwise, comments apply as for the obverse.

1934-S. Graded AU-53.

Illustrated coin: This coin shows medium and somewhat mottled toning. Luster is still seen in protected areas.

EF-40, 45 (Extremely Fine). *Obverse:* Further wear is seen on the highest-relief areas of the hair, with many strands now blended together. Some luster can usually be seen in protected areas on many coins, but is not needed to define the EF–40 and 45 grades. *Reverse:* Further wear is seen on the eagle, and the upper 60% of the feathers have most detail gone, except for the delineation of the edges of rows of feathers. PEACE shows light wear.

1928. Graded EF-40.

VF-20, 30 (Very Fine). *Obverse:* More wear shows on the hair, with more tiny strands now blended into heavy strands. *Reverse:* Further wear has resulted in very little feather detail except on the neck and tail. The rock shows wear. PEACE is slightly weak.

1934-D. Graded VF-30.

F-12, 15 (Fine). *Obverse:* Most of the hair is worn flat, with thick strands blended together, interrupted by fewer divisions than on higher grades. The rim is full. *Reverse:* Fewer feather details show. Most of the eagle, except for the tail feathers and some traces of feathers at the neck, is in outline only. The rays between the left side of the eagle and PEACE are weak and some details are worn away.

The Peace dollar is seldom collected in grades lower than F-12.

1921. Graded F-12.

PF-60 to 70 (Proof). *Obverse and Reverse:* Proofs of both types usually display very few handling marks or defects. To qualify as Satin PF-65 or Sandblast PF-65 or finer, contact marks must be microscopic.

1921. Satin Finish Proof.

1921, Line Through L
VAM-3. FS-S1-1921-003.

	Mintage	Cert	Avg	%MS	VF-20	EF-40	AU-50	MS-60	MS-62	MS-63	MS-64	MS-65	MS-66
											PF-60	PF-63	PF-65
1921, High Relief	1,006,473	14,436	59.2	76%	$110	$140	$150	$275	$375	$450	$850	$2,100	$6,500
	Auctions: $70,500, MS-67, August 2015; $4,700, MS-66, January 2015; $282, MS-62, December 2015; $153, AU-50, February 2015												
1921, High Relief, Line Through L (a)	**(b)**	55	60.7	80%			$225	$315	$400	$500	$900	$2,500	
	Auctions: $940, MS-63, June 2013												
1921, Satin Finish Proof	10–20	17	63.6								$30,000	$50,000	$75,000
	Auctions: $32,200, PF-64, July 2009												
1921, Sandblast Finish Proof	5–8	3	64.0									$60,000	$85,000
	Auctions: $99,875, PF-66, January 2014; $129,250, PF-64, August 2014												

a. A ray runs through the first L in DOLLAR, instead of behind it. b. Included in 1921, High Relief, mintage figure.

1922, Die Break in Field
VAM-1F. FS-S1-1922-001f.

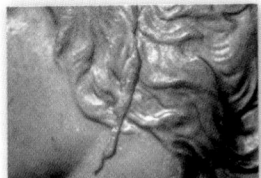

1922, Die Break at Ear
The "Ear Ring" variety.
VAM-2A. FS-S1-1922-002a.

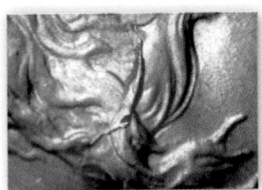

1922, Die Break in Hair
The 1922 "Extra Hair" variety.
VAM-2C. FS-S1-1922-002c.

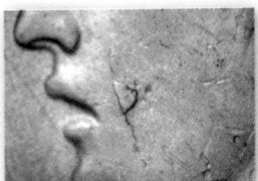

1922, Die Break on Cheek
The "Scar Cheek" variety.
VAM-5A. FS-S1-1922-005a.

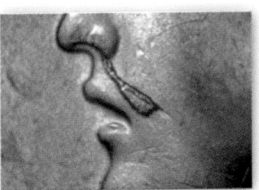

1922, Die Break at Nose
The "Moustache" variety.
VAM-12A. FS-S1-1922-012a.

	Mintage	Cert	Avg	%MS	VF-20	EF-40	AU-50	MS-60	MS-62	MS-63	MS-64	MS-65	MS-66
											PF-60	PF-63	PF-65
1922, High Relief (c)	35,401	0	n/a				—				—		
Auctions: No auction records available.													
1922, Normal Relief	51,737,000	187,004	63.5	99%	$25	$28	$30	$32	$35	$40	$60	$125	$600
Auctions: $11,163, MS-67, August 2015; $1,175, MS-66, March 2015; $176, MS-65, February 2015; $188, MS-64, October 2015													
1922, Die Break in Field (d)	(e)	29	58.4	41%				$400	$800	$1,750	$2,500		
Auctions: $1,528, MS-64, December 2013; $58, AU-55, September 2014													
1922, Die Break at Ear (f)	(e)	47	58.6	53%				$290	$650	$1,400	$2,300		
Auctions: $1,293, MS-63, December 2013													
1922, Die Break in Hair (g)	(e)	114	56.9	56%				$90	$180	$300	$385		
Auctions: $153, MS-64, February 2015; $76, MS-62, March 2015; $74, MS-62, October 2014; $69, MS-61, September 2014													
1922, Die Break on Cheek (h)	(e)	24	60.1	67%				$190	$400	$550			
Auctions: $259, MS-63, February 2015; $165, MS-63, February 2015; $165, MS-61, February 2015; $200, AU-58, September 2014													
1922, Die Break at Nose (i)	(e)	129	58.7	48%				$90	$200	$325	$500	$975	
Auctions: $223, MS-62, January 2015; $212, MS-62, March 2015; $129, AU-58, February 2015; $112, AU-58, September 2015													
1922, High Relief, Sandblast Finish Proof	10–15	12	64.6									$100,000	$140,000
Auctions: $329,000, PF-67, January 2014													
1922, Low Relief, Sandblast Finish Proof	3–6	3	65.3									$100,000	$150,000
Auctions: $35,200, PF-65, November 1988													
1922, Low Relief, Satin Finsih Proof	3–6	2	64.0									$100,000	$150,000
Auctions: $44,850, PF-60, November 2009													
1922-D	15,063,000	7,036	63.1	94%	$28	$30	$33	$50	$55	$85	$150	$625	$2,200
Auctions: $39,950, MS-67, August 2015; $7,050, MS-66+, February 2015; $734, MS-65+, October 2015; $153, MS-64, January 2015													
1922-S	17,475,000	5,765	62.3	92%	$28	$30	$33	$50	$60	$95	$300	$2,400	$20,000
Auctions: $8,813, MS-66, January 2015; $4,230, MS-65+, August 2015; $259, MS-64, February 2015; $36, AU-58, September 2015													

c. 1 example is known. **d.** A die break is visible in the field above DOLLAR. "This variety has turned out to be much rarer than previously thought, and is very scarce in grades above EF" (*Cherrypickers' Guide to Rare Die Varieties*, sixth edition, volume II). **e.** Included in 1922, Normal Relief, mintage figure. **f.** A major die break near Liberty's ear, dangling down to her neck, gives this variety its nickname, the "Ear Ring." Several die states are known. **g.** An irregular line of raised metal runs along the back of Liberty's hair. This is called the "Extra Hair" variety. Several die states are known. **h.** Liberty's cheek has a raised, almost triangular chunk of metal along a vertical die break. Also, the reverse is lightly tripled. This variety, called the "Scarface," is very scarce in Mint State. **i.** A die break is visible running from Liberty's nose along the top of her mouth. This is known as the "Moustache" variety.

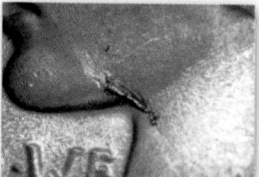

1923, Die Break at Jaw
The "Whisker Jaw" variety.
VAM-1A. FS-S1-1923-001a.

1923, Die Break in Hair
The 1923 "Extra Hair"
variety. VAM-1B.
FS-S1-1923-001b.

1923, Die Break on
O in DOLLAR
The "Tail on O" variety.
VAM-1C. FS-S1-1923-001c.

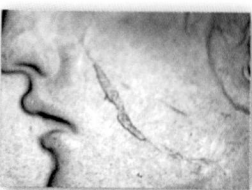

1923, Die Break on Cheek
The "Whisker Cheek" variety.
VAM-1D. FS-S1-1923-001d.

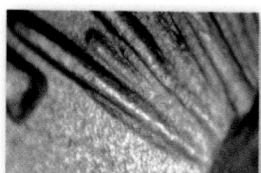

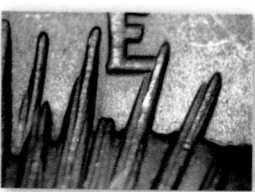

1923, Doubled-Die Obverse
The "Double Tiara" variety. VAM-2. FS-S1-1923-002.

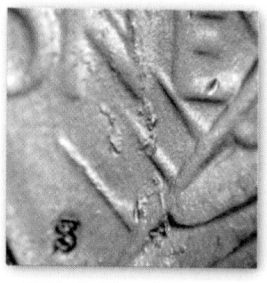

1923-S, Pitted Reverse
VAM-1C. FS-S1-1923S-001c.

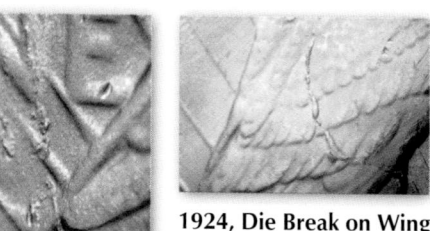

1924, Die Break on Wing
The "Broken Wing" variety.
VAM-5A. FS-S1-1924-005a.

	Mintage	Cert	Avg	%MS	VF-20	EF-40	AU-50	MS-60	MS-62	MS-63	MS-64	MS-65	MS-66
											PF-60	PF-63	PF-65
1923	30,800,000	285,969	63.7	100%	$25	$28	$30	$32	$35	$40	$60	$125	$550
Auctions: $4,465, MS-67, January 2015; $940, MS-66+, February 2015; $64, MS-64, May 2015; $40, MS-62, July 2015													
1923, Die Break at Jaw (j)	(k)	180	61.5	81%			$80	$125	$175	$265	$550		$1,250
Auctions: $282, MS-65, February 2015; $141, MS-64, March 2015; $129, MS-64, January 2015; $76, MS-62, March 2015													
1923, Die Break in Hair (l)	(k)	74	61.5	86%			$125	$200	$300	$400	$600		
Auctions: $400, MS-65, February 2015; $59, MS-64, September 2014; $115, MS-63, August 2014; $84, MS-63, September 2014													
1923, Die Break on O (m)	(k)	65	58.9	72%			$275	$650	$1,150	$1,800			
Auctions: $2,468, MS-65, April 2014													
1923, Die Break on Cheek (n)	(k)	91	60.4	68%			$165	$250	$350	$475	$875		
Auctions: $206, MS-64, March 2015; $235, MS-63, February 2015; $165, MS-62, August 2015; $200, AU-55, June 2015													
1923, DblDie Obverse (o)	(k)	65	61.9	83%			$58	$75	$100	$160	$375		
Auctions: $329, MS-65, February 2015; $129, MS-62, January 2015; $74, MS-62, July 2015; $129, AU-58, February 2015													
1923-D	6,811,000	3,486	62.2	89%	$28	$30	$40	$70	$90	$160	$375	$1,300	$4,750
Auctions: $17,625, MS-66+, August 2015; $282, MS-64, September 2015; $123, MS-63, October 2015; $46, AU-55, January 2015													
1923-S	19,020,000	6,280	62.1	91%	$28	$30	$36	$55	$70	$90	$450	$6,000	$30,000
Auctions: $4,230, MS-65, January 2015; $705, MS-64, February 2015; $112, MS-63, June 2015; $38, AU-58, November 2015													
1923-S, Pitted Reverse (p)	(q)	28	58.5	54%			$125	$250	—	$450	$975		
Auctions: $282, MS-63, December 2013													
1924	11,811,000	44,326	63.8	99%	$25	$28	$30	$32	$35	$40	$60	$125	$650
Auctions: $12,925, MS-67, August 2015; $1,293, MS-66+, January 2015; $217, MS-65, September 2015													
1924, Die Break on Wing (r)	(s)	48	61.2	77%			$130	$200	$375	$475			
Auctions: $2,233, MS-67, January 2015; $423, MS-64, January 2015; $282, MS-63, February 2015; $106, MS-62, August 2014													
1924-S	1,728,000	4,171	60.6	73%	$28	$40	$60	$220	$400	$500	$1,300	$8,500	$43,500
Auctions: $11,163, MS-65, June 2015; $4,230, MS-64+, January 2015; $353, MS-62, October 2015; $79, AU-58, April 2015													

j. A die break bridges Liberty's cheek and jaw. This is the "Whisker Jaw" variety. **k.** Included in 1923 mintage figure. **l.** A significant die break runs diagonally across the strands of Liberty's hair; die breaks may also be visible toward the back of her hair. This variety is nicknamed the 1923 "Extra Hair." **m.** A die break trails from the O of DOLLAR. This variety, called the "Tail on O," is very rare in any grade. **n.** A die break runs down Liberty's cheek toward the junction of the chin and neck. This is the "Whisker Cheek" variety. **o.** Doubling is most evident in the wide spread on the rays of Liberty's tiara, especially those under the BER of LIBERTY. This is the "Double Tiara" variety. **p.** "Pitting runs from the eagle's back tail-feathers, just to the right of the mintmark, upward to the N in ONE. . . . This is the most important Pitted Reverse variety in the Peace dollar series" (*Cherrypickers' Guide to Rare Die Varieties,* sixth edition, volume II). **q.** Included in 1923-S mintage figure. **r.** A dramatic die break runs down and across the entire width of the eagle's back. This is the "Broken Wing" variety. **s.** Included in 1924 mintage figure.

1925, Missing Ray
VAM-5. FS-S1-1925-005.

1926-S, Reverse Dot
The "Extra Berry" variety.
VAM-4. FS-S1-1926S-004.

1934-D, Doubled-Die Obverse, Small D
VAM-4. FS-S1-1934D-004.

	Mintage	Cert	Avg	%MS	VF-20	EF-40	AU-50	MS-60	MS-62	MS-63	MS-64	MS-65	MS-66
											PF-60	PF-63	PF-65
1925	10,198,000	49,714	63.9	99%	$25	$28	$30	$32	$35	$40	$60	$125	$600
Auctions: $5,405, MS-67, January 2015; $1,528, MS-66, June 2015; $123, MS-65+, March 2015; $74, MS-64, February 2015
1925, Missing Ray (t)	(u)	82	62.8	90%			$65	$85	$100	$145	$250	$400	
Auctions: $129, MS-64, December 2013; $200, MS-63, February 2015; $59, MS-62, September 2014; $47, MS-62, September 2014
1925-S	1,610,000	5,677	61.8	87%	$28	$32	$45	$100	$180	$280	$900	$27,500	—
Auctions: $24,675, MS-65, January 2015; $3,055, MS-64, January 2015; $112, MS-62, July 2015; $130, AU-58, November 2015
1926	1,939,000	9,055	63.2	97%	$28	$32	$37	$52	$100	$110	$140	$600	$2,100
Auctions: $3,760, MS-66, August 2015; $376, MS-65, September 2015; $106, MS-64, June 2015; $94, AU-58, January 2015
1926-D	2,348,700	3,595	62.3	87%	$28	$32	$44	$85	$140	$230	$410	$1,000	$2,500
Auctions: $47,000, MS-67, August 2015; $3,760, MS-66, August 2015; $1,528, MS-65, January 2015; $153, MS-63, May 2015
1926-S	6,980,000	5,892	62.4	90%	$28	$32	$38	$60	$75	$120	$300	$1,100	$4,850
Auctions: $6,463, MS-66, August 2015; $1,058, MS-65, September 2015; $206, MS-64, November 2015; $84, MS-63, January 2015
1926-S, Reverse Dot (v)	(w)	40	56.4	50%			$55	$90	$140	$200	$360		
Auctions: $165, MS-64, September 2014; $223, MS-63, February 2015; $129, MS-63, September 2015; $61, AU-58, November 2014
1927	848,000	5,774	62.0	89%	$39	$42	$50	$85	$120	$200	$625	$2,900	$23,000
Auctions: $23,500, MS-66, September 2015; $3,290, MS-65, January 2015; $79, MS-61, December 2015; $54, AU-58, March 2015
1927-D	1,268,900	3,417	60.9	78%	$39	$45	$75	$180	$250	$400	$1,050	$4,750	$25,000
Auctions: $9,988, MS-65+, January 2015; $793, MS-64, August 2015; $79, AU-55, March 2015; $74, AU-53, September 2015
1927-S	866,000	3,946	61.2	82%	$39	$45	$75	$200	$265	$600	$1,300	$9,750	$45,000
Auctions: $8,225, MS-65, January 2015; $1,763, MS-64, June 2015; $470, MS-63+, October 2015; $259, MS-62, August 2015
1928	360,649	7,694	58.8	66%	$300	$340	$375	$500	$600	$850	$1,250	$4,500	$25,000
Auctions: $39,950, MS-66, August 2015; $7,050, MS-65, January 2015; $400, AU-58, May 2015; $235, EF-40, February 2015
1928-S	1,632,000	5,327	60.6	76%	$39	$48	$65	$200	$300	$475	$1,100	$20,000	—
Auctions: $42,300, MS-65+, August 2015; $2,585, MS-64+, February 2015; $470, MS-63, November 2015; $94, AU-55, May 2015
1934	954,057	5,404	62.4	89%	$44	$45	$50	$115	$170	$225	$375	$750	$3,000
Auctions: $11,750, MS-66+, January 2015; $1,175, MS-65, September 2015; $494, MS-64, May 2015; $69, AU-58, December 2015
1934-D (x)	1,569,500	5,014	60.9	78%	$44	$45	$50	$150	$250	$375	$600	$2,100	$4,900
Auctions: $10,575, MS-66, August 2015; $1,880, MS-64+, June 2015; $306, MS-63, November 2015; $64, AU-58, February 2015
1934-D, DblDie Obv, Sm D (y)	(z)	61	55.6	48%	$115	$185	$375	$750	$900	$1,650			
Auctions: $999, MS-63, January 2015; $306, MS-62, September 2015; $364, AU-58, January 2015; $353, AU-55, February 2015
1934-S	1,011,000	3,755	50.4	34%	$80	$175	$500	$2,500	$3,200	$4,400	$7,000	$9,000	$27,500
Auctions: $32,900, MS-66, August 2015; $9,988, MS-65+, January 2015; $6,463, MS-64, February 2015
1935	1,576,000	6,997	62.7	91%	$44	$45	$50	$85	$90	$125	$275	$800	$2,500
Auctions: $9,988, MS-66+, June 2015; $517, MS-65, October 2015; $129, MS-63, February 2015; $94, MS-62, July 2015
1935-S (aa)	1,964,000	3,539	61.1	80%	$44	$50	$88	$275	$325	$500	$675	$1,500	$4,000
Auctions: $16,450, MS-66+, August 2015; $881, MS-64, February 2015; $400, MS-63, May 2015; $153, AU-58, September 2015
1964-D (bb)	316,076	0	n/a					*(none known to exist)*					
Auctions: No auction records available.

t. This variety is the result of a reverse die polished with too much gusto. The partially effaced remains of bold clash marks are evident, but the topmost internal ray is missing. **u.** Included in 1925 mintage figure. **v.** A raised circular dot of metal is visible to the left of the bottom olive leaf. This is nicknamed the "Extra Berry" variety. **w.** Included in 1926-S mintage figure. **x.** Varieties exist with small and large mintmarks. **y.** The obverse shows strong doubling on most letters of IN GOD WE TRUST, the rays on the right, and especially on Liberty's profile. The mintmark is a small D, shaped much like that of the 1920s-era D punches. **z.** Included in 1934-D mintage figure. **aa.** Varieties exist with either three or four rays below ONE. They are valued equally in the marketplace. **bb.** The entire mintage of 1964-D Peace dollars was melted by government order. Deceptive reproductions exist.

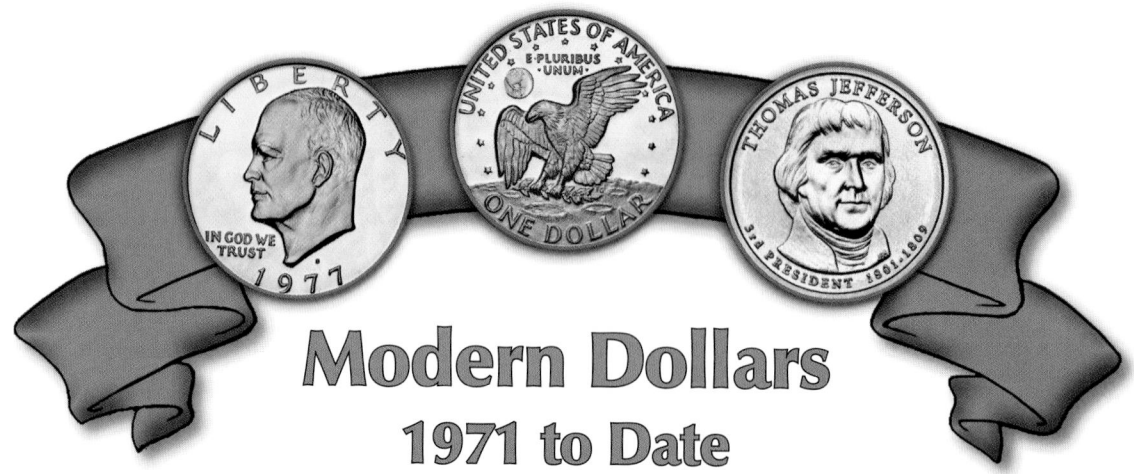

Modern Dollars
1971 to Date

AN OVERVIEW OF MODERN DOLLARS

After the last Peace dollars rolled off the presses at the San Francisco and Philadelphia mints in 1935, there was a long lapse in silver dollar coinage until 1965. In that year the Denver Mint struck Peace dollars dated 1964—the start of production of 45 million coins authorized by legislation of August 3, 1964. This coinage ultimately was stopped after 316,076 of the new Peace dollars were made; they were held back from being released into circulation and melted. It would be another six years before the United States had a new dollar coin, and it would not be silver.

Production of the next dollar started in 1971. The coin was the size of the 20th century's earlier silver dollars, but made in copper-nickel for circulation (and, in much smaller quantities, in .400 fine silver for collectors). Its motifs honor the late President Dwight D. Eisenhower, and the *Apollo 11* spaceflight that had landed the first men on the Moon in 1969.

Silver dollars had long since disappeared from circulation, but there was demand for dollar coins in Las Vegas, Reno, and other centers of legalized gambling. Casinos otherwise had to depend on gaming chips and tokens.

The Eisenhower dollar was minted from 1971 to 1978, with those made in 1975 and 1976 being dual-dated 1776–1976 for the national bicentennial. In 1979 the "Ike" dollar was replaced by a smaller-format coin, the Susan B. Anthony dollar, honoring the famous women's-rights leader. Its reverse design shows an eagle landing on the Moon, similar to that of its predecessor (this design had in turn been based on the official insignia of the *Apollo 11* mission). The Anthony dollar was struck in 1979, 1980, and 1981; then, in 1999 an additional final mintage of more than 40 million coins was produced to meet the needs of the vending-machine industry until distribution of the next year's new-design dollars could begin.

Presidential golden dollars cover the span from the 1st president of the United States, George Washington, to the 40th president, Ronald Reagan.

The year 2000 marked the debut of the first of several types of "golden" dollars, so called for the lustrous color of their manganese-brass surfaces. First came the Sacagawea dollar, minted from 2000 to 2008, with its conceptualized portrait of the young Shoshone Native American interpreter and guide who assisted the Lewis and Clark expedition of the early 1800s. A series of Native American dollars, each celebrating a different aspect of Native culture and historical importance, which began in 2009 and is ongoing today, is an offshoot of the Sacagawea dollar. And, since 2007, the golden-dollar format has been the canvas for a series of presidential portrait dollars honoring the nation's chief executives.

FOR THE COLLECTOR AND INVESTOR: MODERN DOLLARS AS A SPECIALTY

Eisenhower dollars, Susan B. Anthony dollars, and the golden dollars of various types are all easily found in today's marketplace. Dealers often have an abundance on hand of every date, mint, and most varieties. Banks sometimes have small quantities of Eisenhower or Anthony dollars. The current series are available directly from the U.S. Mint in collector formats and in rolls and bags of circulation strikes.

Eisenhower dollars are easily obtained in choice Mint State, although some of the coins made for circulation, especially of the earlier years, tend to be blemished with contact marks from jostling other coins during minting, transportation, and storage. Gems can be elusive. The Mint issued many options for collectors, including Proofs and .400 fine silver issues. Specialists look for die varieties including modified features, doubled dies, changes in depth of relief in the design, and other popular anomalies and variations that increase the challenge of building an extensive collection in what is otherwise a fairly short coinage series. Some Denver Mint dollars of 1974 and 1977 are also known to be struck in error, in silver clad composition rather than the intended copper-nickel.

Anthony dollars, too, are easy to assemble into a complete, high-grade collection of dates and mints. Specialists can focus on both varieties of 1979-P (Narrow Rim and Wide Rim), and varieties of S mint-mark styles among the Proofs. Even these are common enough to easily acquire. Those seeking a harder challenge can search for the elusive 1980-S, Repunched Mintmark, Proof.

The Sacagawea dollar series includes several uncommon varieties that make an otherwise easy-to-collect type more challenging. The 2000-P coins include popular die varieties as detailed herein. Later dates were struck in smaller quantities and not issued for circulation, but still are readily available in high grades in the numismatic marketplace.

Native American dollars of 2009 to date are readily available in high grades.

The Presidential dollar series includes some error varieties with plain edges, instead of the normal lettered edge. These can be added to a date-and-mintmark collection for reasonable premiums. Otherwise the entire series is readily collectible from the secondary market and, for the current year of issue, in quantity directly from the U.S. Mint.

EISENHOWER (1971–1978)

Designer: *Frank Gasparro.* **Weight:** *Silver issue—24.59 grams; copper-nickel issue—22.68 grams.*
Composition: *Silver issue—40% silver, 60% copper, consisting of outer layers of .800 silver, .200 copper bonded to inner core of .209 silver, .791 copper (net weight .3161 oz. pure silver); copper-nickel issue—outer layers of .750 copper, .250 nickel bonded to inner core of pure copper.*
Diameter: *38.1 mm.* **Edge:** *Reeded.* **Mints:** *Philadelphia, Denver, and San Francisco.*

Circulation
Strike

Proof

Mintmark location is
on the obverse, between
the bust and the date.

Bicentennial variety: Designers: *Frank Gasparro and Dennis R. Williams.*
Weight: *Silver issue—24.59 grams; copper-nickel issue—22.68 grams.*
Composition: *Silver issue—outer layers of .800 silver, .200 copper bonded
to inner core of .209 silver, .791 copper (net weight .3161 oz. pure silver);
copper-nickel issue—outer layers of .750 copper, .250 nickel bonded to inner core of pure copper.*
Diameter: *38.1 mm.* **Edge:** *Reeded.* **Mints:** *Philadelphia, Denver, and San Francisco.*

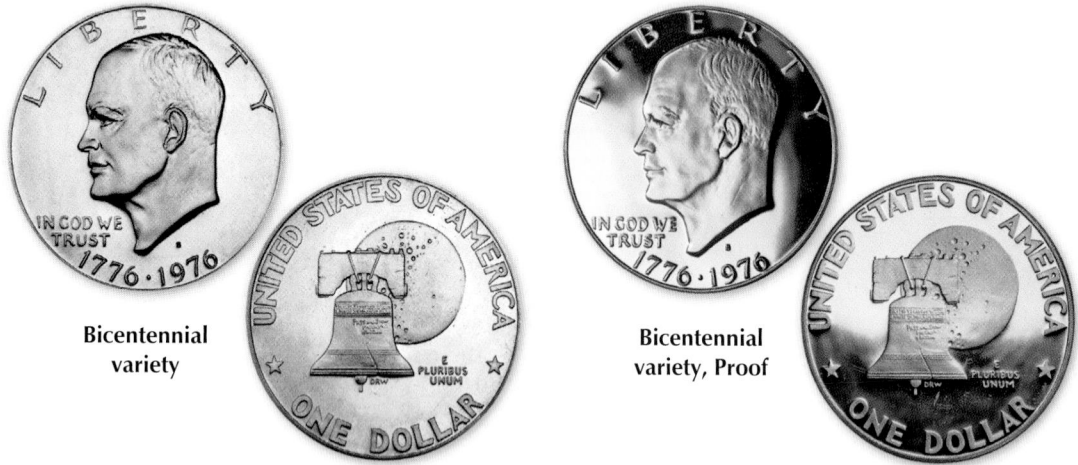

Bicentennial
variety

Bicentennial
variety, Proof

History. Honoring both President Dwight D. Eisenhower and the first landing of man on the Moon, this coin is the work of Chief Engraver Frank Gasparro, whose initials are on the truncation of the president's neck and below the eagle. The reverse is an adaptation of the official *Apollo 11* insignia. Collectors' coins were struck in 40% silver composition and sold by the Mint at a premium, and the circulation issue (for years a staple of the casino trade) was made in copper-nickel.

The dies for the Eisenhower dollar were modified several times by changing the relief, strengthening the design, and making Earth (above the eagle) more clearly defined.

Low-relief (Variety 1) dies, with a flattened Earth and three islands off the coast of Florida, were used for all copper-nickel issues of 1971, Uncirculated silver coins of 1971, and most copper-nickel coins of 1972.

High-relief (Variety 2) dies, with a round Earth and weak or indistinct islands, were used for all Proofs of 1971, all silver issues of 1972, and the reverse of some exceptional and scarce Philadelphia copper-nickel coins of 1972.

Improved high-relief reverse dies (Variety 3) were used for late-1972 Philadelphia copper-nickel coins and for all subsequent issues. Modified high-relief dies were also used on all issues beginning in 1973.

A few 1974-D and 1977-D dollars were made, in error, in silver clad composition.

A special reverse design was selected for the nation's Bicentennial. Nearly a thousand entries were submitted after the Treasury announced an open competition in October 1973. After the field was narrowed down to 12 semifinalists, the judges chose a rendition of the Liberty Bell superimposed on the Moon to appear on the dollar coins. The obverse remained unchanged except for the dual date 1776–1976, which appeared on all dollars made during 1975 and 1976. These dual-dated coins were included in the various offerings of Proof and Uncirculated coins made by the Mint. They were also struck for general circulation. The lettering was slightly modified early in 1975 to produce a more attractive design.

Striking and Sharpness. Striking generally is very good. For circulation strikes, on the obverse check the high parts of the portrait, and on the reverse, the details of the eagle. Nearly all Proofs are well struck and of high quality.

Availability. MS coins are common in the marketplace, although several early varieties are elusive at MS-65 or higher grades. Lower grades are not widely collected. Proofs were made of the various issues (both copper-nickel clad and silver clad from 1971 to 1976; copper-nickel only in 1977 and 1978). All are readily available in the marketplace today.

Note: Values of common-date silver coins have been based on the current bullion price of silver, $15.50 per ounce, and may vary with the prevailing spot price.

GRADING STANDARDS

MS-60 to 70 (Mint State). *Obverse:* At MS-60, some abrasion and contact marks are evident, most noticeably on the cheek, jaw, and temple. Luster is present, but may be dull or lifeless. At MS-63, contact marks are extensive but not distracting. Abrasion still is evident, but less than at lower levels. MS-64 coins are slightly finer. An MS-65 coin may have minor abrasion, but contact marks are so minute as to require magnification. Luster

1971-S. Graded MS-65.

should be full and rich. *Reverse:* At MS-60, some abrasion and contact marks are evident, most noticeably on the eagle's breast, head, and talons. Otherwise, the same comments apply as for the obverse.

AU-50, 53, 55, 58 (About Uncirculated). *Obverse:* Light wear is seen on the higher-relief areas of the portrait. At AU-58, the luster is extensive, but incomplete. At AU–50 and 53, luster is less but still present. *Reverse:* Further wear is evident on the eagle, particularly the head, breast, talons, and tops of the wings. Otherwise, the same comments apply as for the obverse.

The Eisenhower dollar is seldom collected in grades lower than AU-50.

1972. Graded AU-50.

PF-60 to 70 (Proof). *Obverse and Reverse:* Proofs that are extensively cleaned and have many hairlines, or that are dull and grainy, are lower level, such as PF–60 to 62. There are not many of these in the marketplace. With medium hairlines and good reflectivity, assigned grades of PF–63 or 64 are appropriate. With relatively few hairlines a rating of PF-65 can be given. PF-66 may have hairlines so delicate that magnification is needed

1776–1976-S, Bicentennial. Graded PF-68.

to see them. Above that, a Proof should be free of any hairlines or other problems.

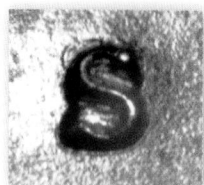

1971-S, Repunched Mintmark, Silver Clad

1971-S, Polished Die, Silver Clad
The "Peg Leg R" variety.

1971-S, Doubled-Die Obverse, Proof

1972-S, Silver Clad, Doubled-Die Obverse, Proof

1973-S, Silver Clad, Doubled-Die Obverse, Proof

	Mintage	Cert	Avg	%MS	EF-40	MS-63	MS-65	MS-66
						PF-65	PF-67Cam	PF-68DC
1971, Copper-Nickel Clad, Reverse A ‡ (a)	47,799,000	1,458	64.0	97%	$2.25	$6	$120	$1,000
1971-D, Copper-Nickel Clad, Variety 1, Reverse A	68,587,424	2,622	64.8	98%	$3.50	$5	$100	$250
1971-D, Copper-Nickel Clad, Variety 2, Reverse B	(b)	0	n/a		$2	$5	$50	$130
1971-S, Silver Clad, Reverse A	6,868,530	3,671	65.3	100%		$13	$20	$40
1971-S, Silver Clad, Repunched Mintmark (c,d)	(e)	6	64.7	100%			$225	$350
1971-S, Silver Clad, Polished Die (f)	(e)	0	n/a				$125	$250
1971-S, Silver Clad, Proof, Reverse A	4,265,234	5,200	68.1			$14	$15	$25
1971-S, Silver Clad, DblDie Obv, Proof (g,h)	(i)	21	68.0			$90	$150	
1972, Copper-Nickel Clad, All kinds	75,890,000							
1972, Copper-Nickel Clad, Variety 1, Reverse A (j)		1,247	64.0	98%	$2	$5	$140	$7,000
1972, Copper-Nickel Clad, Variety 2, Reverse D ‡ (k)		498	62.3	87%	$7	$80	$1,300	$8,500
1972, Copper-Nickel Clad, Variety 3, Reverse E (l)		971	64.2	98%	$2.50	$5	$125	$900
1972-D, Copper-Nickel Clad, Reverse A	92,548,511	1,505	64.6	97%	$2	$5	$30	$150
1972-S, Silver Clad	2,193,056	4,355	66.5	100%		$13	$15	$20
1972-S, Silver Clad, Proof	1,811,631	3,794	68.2			$14	$15	$25
1972-S, Silver Clad, Doubled-Die Obverse, Proof (g)	(n)	21	67.9					—
1973, Copper-Nickel Clad ‡ (o)	2,000,056	1,013	64.4	100%		$13	$65	$750
1973-D, Copper-Nickel Clad ‡ (p)	2,000,000	983	64.5	100%		$13	$50	$275
1973-S, Copper-Nickel Clad (q)	(r)	0	n/a					
1973-S, Silver Clad	1,883,140	2,917	66.3	100%		$14	$18	$35
1973-S, Copper-Nickel Clad, Proof	2,760,339	1,125	68.1			$14	$16	$30
1973-S, Silver Clad, Proof	1,013,646	3,229	68.1			$35	$37	$50
1973-S, Silver Clad, DblDie Obv, Proof (m)	(k)	1	67.0					—

‡ Ranked in the *100 Greatest U.S. Modern Coins*. Only issued in Mint sets. **a.** Auction: $823, MS-66, August 2015. **b.** Included in 1971-D, Copper-Nickel Clad, Variety 1, mintage figure. **c.** A secondary S is visible protruding northwest of the primary S. "This is one of fewer than a half dozen RPMs known for the entire series" (*Cherrypickers' Guide to Rare Die Varieties*, sixth edition, volume II). **d.** Auction: $253, MS-66, July 2011. **e.** Included in circulation-strike 1971-S, Silver Clad, mintage figure. **f.** The left leg of the R in LIBERTY was overpolished. This is popularly known as the "Peg Leg R" variety. **g.** Strong doubling is visible on IN GOD WE TRUST, the date, and LIBER of LIBERTY. There are at least two doubled-die obverses for this date (valued similarly); the one listed is FS-S1-1971S-103. "This obverse is also paired with a minor doubled-die reverse" (*Cherrypickers' Guide to Rare Die Varieties*, sixth edition, volume II). **h.** Auction: $2,585, PF-69Cam, January 2016. **i.** Included in 1971-S, Proof, Silver Clad, mintage figure. **j.** Auction: $1,528, MS-66, August 2015. **k.** Auction: $329, MS-64+, May 2015. **l.** Auction: $2,820, MS-66, January 2015. **m.** A medium spread of doubling is evident on IN GOD WE TRUST, LIBERTY, and slightly on the date. **n.** Included in 1972-S, Proof, Silver Clad, mintage figure. **o.** Auction: $940, MS-66, January 2015. **p.** Auction: $12,925, MS-67, June 2013. **q.** Two reported to exist. **r.** Included in 1973-D, Copper-Nickel Clad, mintage figure. **s.** Included in 1973-S, Proof, Silver Clad, mintage figure.

	Mintage	Cert	Avg	%MS	EF-40	MS-63	MS-65	MS-66
						PF-65	PF-67Cam	PF-68DC
1974, Copper-Nickel Clad	27,366,000	1,163	64.5	99%	$2	$6	$60	$550
1974-D, Copper-Nickel Clad	45,517,000	7,517	65.0	100%	$2	$6	$38	$130
1974-S, Silver Clad	1,900,156	3,733	66.5	100%		$13	$20	$25
1974-S, Copper-Nickel Clad, Proof	2,612,568	970	68.0			$10	$15	$30
1974-S, Silver Clad, Proof	1,306,579	3,682	68.2			$15	$16	$30
1776–1976, Copper-Nickel Clad, Variety 1 (t)	4,019,000	856	64.1	100%	$2	$8	$160	$1,250
1776–1976, Copper-Nickel Clad, Variety 2	113,318,000	3,025	64.9	99%	$2	$5	$30	$125
1776–1976-D, Copper-Nickel Clad, Variety 1	21,048,710	1,855	64.8	100%	$2	$5	$50	$185
1776–1976-D, Copper-Nickel Clad, Variety 2	82,179,564	5,426	65.0	100%	$2	$5	$28	$60
1776–1976-S, Copper-Nickel Clad, Variety 1, Proof ‡ (u)	2,845,450	1,214	67.8			$12	$15	$30
1776–1976-S, Copper-Nickel Clad, Variety 2, Proof	4,149,730	1,683	68.1			$8	$12	$30
1776–1976, Silver Clad, Variety 2		0	n/a					
1776–1976, Silver Clad, Variety 2, Proof		0	n/a			—		
1776–1976-S, Silver Clad, Variety 1	11,000,000	2,662	66.2	100%		$17	$20	$30
1776–1976-S, Silver Clad, Variety 1, Proof	4,000,000	4,166	68.1			$19	$20	$35
1977, Copper-Nickel Clad	12,596,000	2,433	65.0	100%	$2	$6	$35	$135
1977-D, Copper-Nickel Clad	32,983,006	15,370	65.1	100%	$2	$6	$35	$170
1977-S, Copper-Nickel Clad, Proof	3,251,152	1,722	68.4			$10	$15	$25
1978, Copper-Nickel Clad	25,702,000	962	64.8	99%	$2	$6	$45	$160
1978-D, Copper-Nickel Clad	33,012,890	4,885	65.0	100%	$2	$5.50	$40	$125
1978-S, Copper-Nickel Clad, Proof	3,127,781	1,811	68.5			$10	$15	$25

‡ Ranked in the *100 Greatest U.S. Modern Coins*. Only issued in Mint sets. **t.** Auction: $129, MS-65, January 2015. **u.** Auction: $2,820, PF-70DCam, October 2015.

SUSAN B. ANTHONY (1979–1999)

Designer: *Frank Gasparro.* **Weight:** *8.1 grams.*
Composition: *Outer layers of copper-nickel (.750 copper, .250 nickel) bonded to inner core of pure copper.* **Diameter:** *26.5 mm.*
Edge: *Reeded.* **Mints:** *Philadelphia, Denver, and San Francisco.*

Circulation Strike

Mintmark location is on the obverse, above the left tip of the bust.

Proof

History. The Susan B. Anthony dollar was designed by Frank Gasparro, chief engraver of the U.S. Mint, following a congressional mandate. It features a portrait of the famous suffragette, along with an eagle-and-Moon motif reduced from the coin's larger predecessor, the Eisenhower dollar. Legislators hoped that these so-called mini-dollars would be an efficient substitute for paper dollars, which wear much more quickly in circulation. A large mintage in 1979 was followed by smaller quantities in 1980 and 1981, and then a hiatus of almost 20 years. The coins were not popular in circulation, with some members of the public complaining that they were too easily confused with the similarly sized quarter dollar. A final coinage of Anthony dollars was struck in 1999—a stopgap measure to ensure the Treasury's supply of dollar coins before the Sacagawea dollar was launched in 2000.

Striking and Sharpness. Most are well struck, but check the highest areas of both sides.

Availability. Susan B. Anthony dollars are readily available in MS, although those of 1981 are less common than those of 1979 and 1980. Circulated coins are not widely sought by collectors. Proofs were made of all issues and are readily available today.

GRADING STANDARDS

MS-60 to 70 (Mint State). *Obverse:* At MS-60, some abrasion and contact marks are evident, most noticeably on the cheek and upper center of the hair. Luster is present, but may be dull or lifeless. At MS-63, contact marks are extensive but not distracting. Abrasion still is evident, but less than at lower levels. MS-64 coins are slightly finer. An MS-65 coin may have minor abrasion, but contact marks are so minute as to require magnification. Lus-

1980-D. Graded MS-65.

ter should be full and rich. *Reverse:* At MS-60, some abrasion and contact marks are evident, most noticeably on the eagle's breast, head, and talons. Otherwise, the same comments apply as for the obverse.

AU-50, 53, 55, 58 (About Uncirculated). *Obverse:* Light wear is seen on the higher-relief areas of the portrait. At AU-58, the luster is extensive but incomplete. At AU-50 and 53, luster is less but still present. *Reverse:* Further wear is evident on the eagle, particularly the head, breast, talons, and tops of the wings. Otherwise, the same comments apply as for the obverse.

The Susan B. Anthony dollar is seldom collected in grades lower than AU-50.

1979-D. Graded AU-50.

PF-60 to 70 (Proof). *Obverse and Reverse:* Proofs that are extensively cleaned and have many hairlines, or that are dull and grainy, are lower level, such as PF-60 to 62. This comment is more theoretical than practical, as nearly all Proofs have been well kept. With medium hairlines and good reflectivity, assigned grades of PF–63 or 64 are appropriate. With relatively few hairlines a rating of PF-65

1979-S, Type 2. Graded PF-70 Deep Cameo.

can be given. PF-66 may have hairlines so delicate that magnification is needed to see them. Above that, all the way to PF-70, a Proof should be free of any hairlines or other problems under strong magnification.

1979-P, Narrow Rim
The "Far Date" variety.

1979-P, Wide Rim
The "Near Date" variety.

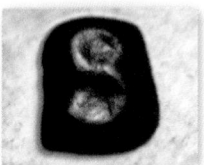
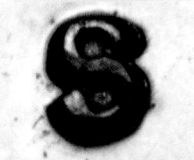

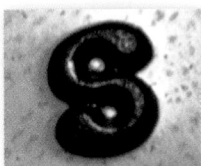
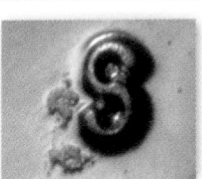

| 1979-S, Filled S (Type 1), Proof | 1979-S, Clear S (Type 2), Proof | 1981-S, Rounded S (Type 1), Proof | 1981-S, Flat S (Type 2), Proof | 1980-S, Repunched Mintmark, Proof *FS-C1-1980S-501* |

	Mintage	Cert	Avg	%MS	MS-63	MS-64	MS-65	MS-66
							PF-65	PF-68DC
1979-P, Narrow Rim (a)	360,222,000	647	64.9	97%	$6	$7	$10	$20
1979-P, Wide Rim ‡ (a,b)	(c)	1,331	64.6	96%	$38	$38	$55	$135
1979-D	288,015,744	805	65.4	98%	$7	$8	$12	$25
1979-S	109,576,000	614	65.4	99%	$6	$7	$10	$20
1979-S, Type 1, Proof (d)	3,677,175	3,997	68.9				$7	$10
1979-S, Type 2, Proof ‡ (d,e)	(f)	2,659	68.8				$70	$75
1980-P	27,610,000	1,132	65.8	100%	$5	$6	$10	$15
1980-D	41,628,708	1,000	65.7	100%	$5	$6	$10	$15
1980-S	20,422,000	864	65.3	100%	$10	$12	$15	$25
1980-S, Proof	3,554,806	3,861	68.9				$6	$10
1980-S, RPM, Proof (g)		0	n/a				—	—
1981-P (h)	3,000,000	828	65.6	100%	$12	$14	$20	$55
1981-D (h)	3,250,000	991	65.7	100%	$10	$12	$15	$25
1981-S ‡ (h)	3,492,000	629	64.6	100%	$20	$25	$35	$250
1981-S, Type 1, Proof	4,063,083	4,522	68.9				$6	$10
1981-S, Type 2, Proof ‡ (i)	(j)	2,593	68.7				$160	$170
1999-P (k)	29,592,000	668	66.2	100%	$3	$5	$10	$15
1999-D (k)	11,776,000	850	66.5	100%	$3	$5	$10	$15
1999-P, Proof (l)	750,000	5,220	69.3				$20	$27.50

‡ Ranked in the *100 Greatest U.S. Modern Coins*. **a.** The obverse design was modified in 1979 to widen the border rim. Late issues of 1979-P and subsequent issues have the wide rim. The 1979-P Wide Rim dollar is nicknamed the "Near Date" because the numerals are closer to the rim. **b.** Auction: $259, MS-67, January 2015. **c.** Included in 1979-P, Narrow Rim, mintage figure. **d.** The S mintmark punch was changed in 1979 to create a clearer mintmark. **e.** Auction: $188, PF-70DCam, June 2015. **f.** Included in 1979-S, Variety 1, Proof, mintage figure. **g.** "The remnants of a previously punched S appear left of the primary S. . . . Very few specimens of this variety have surfaced to date" (*Cherrypickers' Guide to Rare Die Varieties*, sixth edition, volume II). **h.** 1981-P, -D, and -S dollars were issued only in Mint Sets. **i.** Auction: $764, PF-70DCam, February 2015. **j.** Included in 1981-S, Variety 1, Proof, mintage figure. **k.** Dies for the 1999 dollars were further modified to strengthen details on the reverse. **l.** The mintage reflects the total for the Proof coins dated 1999, which were sold through 2003.

SACAGAWEA (2000–2008)

Designers: *Glenna Goodacre (obverse), Thomas D. Rogers Sr. (reverse).*
Weight: *8.1 grams.* **Composition:** *Pure copper core with outer layers of manganese brass (.770 copper, .120 zinc, .070 manganese, and .040 nickel).*
Diameter: *26.5 mm.* **Edge:** *Plain.* **Mints:** *Philadelphia, Denver, and San Francisco; 22-karat gold experimental specimens dated 2000-W were struck at West Point in 1999.*

Circulation Strike

Mintmark location is on the obverse, below the date.

Proof

History. The Sacagawea dollar was launched in 2000, with a distinctive golden color and a plain edge to distinguish it from other denominations or coins of similar size. (One complaint leveled against the Susan B. Anthony dollar was that it too closely resembled the quarter dollar; both were silvery, with reeded edges, and with only about two millimeters' difference in diameter.) The new coinage alloy and the change in appearance were mandated by the United States Dollar Coin Act of 1997. The core of the coin is pure copper, and the golden outer layer is of manganese brass. The obverse shows a modern artist's conception of Sacagawea, the Shoshone Indian who assisted the Lewis and Clark expedition, and her infant son, Jean Baptiste. (No known contemporary portraits of them exist.) The reverse shows an eagle in flight.

In 1999, about a dozen Sacagawea dollars were struck in 22-karat gold at the West Point Mint, as experimental or presentation pieces. These featured a prototype reverse design with boldly detailed tail feathers on the eagle. The following year, a small number of early circulation strikes from the Philadelphia Mint also featured that same prototype design. These are popularly called "Cheerio" dollars, as the coins were packaged as a promotion in boxes of Cheerios cereal (their unusual nature was not recognized at the time). Today collectors seek them as rare and desirable varieties.

In addition to the regular Uncirculated or Mint State coins produced in large quantities, smaller numbers of Satin Finish dollars were made of the 2005 to 2008 years, Philadelphia and Denver mints. Sold at an additional premium, most of these exist today in grades of MS-67 and upward and are designated SP (Specimen) or SMS (Special Mint Set) by the commercial grading services.

Several distinct finishes can be identified on the Sacagawea dollars as a result of the Mint's attempts to adjust the dies, blanks, strikes, or finishing to produce coins with minimal spotting and better surface color. One group of 5,000 pieces, dated 2000 and with a special finish, was presented to sculptor Glenna Goodacre in payment for the obverse design. These have since entered the numismatic market and command a significant premium.

Another peculiarity in the Sacagawea series is a numismatic mule (a coin made from mismatched dies)—the combination of an undated State quarter obverse and a Sacagawea dollar reverse. Examples of this error are extremely rare.

Striking and Sharpness. Most are very well struck. Weakness sometimes is evident on the higher design points. Special issues are uniformly sharply struck.

Availability. These coins are common in high grades, and are usually collected in MS and Proof.

GRADING STANDARDS

MS-60 to 70 (Mint State). *Obverse:* At MS-60, some abrasion and contact marks are evident, most noticeably on the cheekbone and the drapery near the baby's head. Luster is present, but may be dull or lifeless. At MS-63, contact marks are extensive but not distracting. Abrasion still is evident, but less than at lower levels. MS-64 coins are slightly finer. An MS-65 coin may have minor abrasion, but contact marks are so minute as to require magnification. Luster should be full and rich. *Reverse:* At MS-60, some abrasion and contact marks are evident, most noticeably on the eagle's breast. Otherwise, the same comments apply as for the obverse.

2006-D. Graded MS-65.

AU-50, 53, 55, 58 (About Uncirculated). *Obverse:* Light wear is seen on cheekbone, drapery, and elsewhere. At AU-58, the luster is extensive, but incomplete. At AU–50 and 53, luster is less but still present. *Reverse:* Further wear is evident on the eagle. Otherwise, the same comments apply as for the obverse.

The Sacagawea dollar is seldom collected in grades lower than AU-50.

2000-P. Graded AU-55.

PF-60 to 70 (Proof). *Obverse and Reverse:* Proofs that are extensively cleaned and have many hairlines, or that are dull and grainy, are lower level, such as PF–60 to 62. This comment is more theoretical than practical, as nearly all Proofs have been well kept. With medium hairlines and good reflectivity, assigned grades of PF–63 or 64 are appropriate. With relatively few hairlines a rating of PF-65 can be given. PF-66 may have hair-

2002-S. Graded PF-69.

lines so delicate that magnification is needed to see them. Above that, all the way to PF-70, a Proof should be free of any hairlines or other problems under strong magnification.

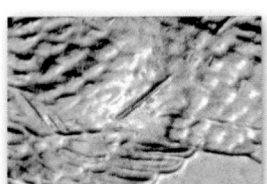
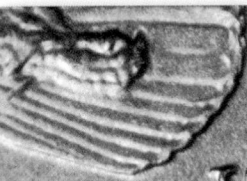

| 2000-P, Reverse Die Aberrations *The "Speared Eagle" variety.* | 2000-P, Normal Feathers | 2000-P, Boldly Detailed Tail Feathers |

	Mintage	Cert	Avg	%MS	MS-64	MS-65 PF-65	MS-66 PF-69DC
2000-P	767,140,000	5,746	66.7	100%	$2.50	$5	$12
2000-P, Reverse Die Aberrations (a,b)	(c)	73	67.4	100%		$775	$1,500
2000-P, Goodacre Presentation Finish ‡ (d,e)	5,000	85	66.1	100%	$450	$500	$600
2000-P, Boldly Detailed Tail Feathers ‡ (f,g)	5,500	2	64.0	100%		$4,000	$6,000
2000-D	518,916,000	7,411	66.4	100%	$4	$8	$15
2000-S, Proof	4,047,904	15,782	69.1			$12	$25
2001-P	62,468,000	674	67.1	100%	$2	$4	$6
2001-D	70,939,500	393	65.9	100%	$2	$4	$6
2001-S, Proof	3,183,740	11,099	69.2			$50	$70

‡ Ranked in the *100 Greatest U.S. Modern Coins*. **a.** Two spike-like die aberrations appear through the breast of the eagle. This variety is nicknamed the "Speared Eagle." **b.** Auction: $2,012, MS-67, January 2012. **c.** Included in 2000-P mintage figure. **d.** A group of 5,000 coins, dated 2000 and with a special finish, were presented to sculptor Glenna Goodacre in payment for the obverse design. **e.** Auction: $541, MS-68, June 2015. **f.** The feathers of the eagle are finely enhanced. This is nicknamed the "Cheerios" variety, as the coins were included as a promotion in boxes of Cheerios cereal. **g.** Auction: $8,195, MS-67, September 2008.

	Mintage	Cert	Avg	%MS	MS-64	MS-65 PF-65	MS-66 PF-69DC
2002-P (h)	3,865,610	387	67.1	100%	$2	$4	$10
2002-D (h)	3,732,000	354	66.3	100%	$2	$4	$8
2002-S, Proof	3,211,995	9,230	69.2			$18	$30
2003-P (h)	3,080,000	683	66.7	100%	$3	$5	$8
2003-D (h)	3,080,000	599	66.1	100%	$3	$5	$8
2003-S, Proof	3,298,439	12,539	69.2			$16	$30
2004-P (h)	2,660,000	557	66.8	100%	$2	$4	$8
2004-D (h)	2,660,000	683	66.6	100%	$2	$4	$8
2004-S, Proof	2,965,422	12,029	69.2			$16	$30
2005-P (h)	2,520,000	350	66.3	100%	$7	$10	$20
2005-P, Satin Finish (h)	1,160,000	4,000	67.0	100%	$3	$5	$12
2005-D (h)	2,520,000	593	66.2	100%	$7	$10	$20
2005-D, Satin Finish (h)	1,160,000	3,702	66.6	100%	$3	$5	$12
2005-S, Proof	3,344,679	17,472	69.2			$15	$20
2006-P (h)	4,900,000	377	66.1	100%	$2	$4	$8
2006-P, Satin Finish (h)	847,631	1,549	66.9	100%	$3	$5	$12
2006-D (h)	2,800,000	578	65.9	100%	$2	$4	$8
2006-D, Satin Finish (h)	847,631	1,496	66.9	100%	$3	$5	$12
2006-S, Proof	3,054,436	8,483	69.3			$15	$20
2007-P (h)	3,640,000	554	66.7	100%	$3	$5	$8
2007-P, Satin Finish (h)	895,628	557	67.0	100%	$3	$5	$12
2007-D (h)	3,920,000	869	66.5	100%	$3	$5	$8
2007-D, Satin Finish (h)	895,628	615	66.9	100%	$3	$5	$12
2007-S, Proof	2,577,166	8,708	69.2		$3	$5	$12
2008-P (h)	1,820,000	209	66.4	100%	$3	$5	$8
2008-P, Satin Finish (h)	745,464	261	67.1	100%	$3	$5	$12
2008-D (h)	1,820,000	634	66.7	100%	$3	$5	$8
2008-D, Satin Finish (h)	745,464	333	67.2	100%	$3	$5	$12
2008-S, Proof	2,169,561	6,285	69.2			$15	$20

h. Not issued for circulation.

NATIVE AMERICAN (2009 TO DATE)

Designers: *Glenna Goodacre (obverse); see image captions for reverse designers.*
Weight: *8.1 grams.* **Composition:** *Pure copper core with outer layers of manganese brass (.770 copper, .120 zinc, .070 manganese, and .040 nickel).*
Diameter: *26.5 mm.* **Edge:** *Lettered.* **Mints:** *Philadelphia, Denver, and San Francisco.*

Circulation Strike   **Mintmark location is on the rim.**   **Proof**

History. Since 2009, the reverse of the golden dollar has featured an annually changing design that memorializes Native Americans and, in the words of the authorizing legislation, "the important contributions made by Indian tribes and individual Native Americans to the development [and history] of the United States." The coins are marked (incuse) on their edges with the year of minting, the mintmark, and the legend E PLURIBUS UNUM. The Native American $1 Coin Act also specified that at least 20% of the total mintage of dollar coins in any given year (including Presidential dollars) will be Native American dollars. Production of all dollar coins minted after 2011 has been limited to numismatic sales (Proofs and other collector formats, and circulation strikes in rolls and bags available directly from the U.S. Mint); none are issued for circulation, as they have proven unpopular in commerce.

The obverse of the Native American dollar coin is a modified version of the Sacagawea dollar, featuring that coin's central portraits (of Sacagawea and Jean Baptiste), and the legends LIBERTY and IN GOD WE TRUST. The date and mintmark, as noted above, are on the coin's edge. Each new reverse design is chosen by the secretary of the Treasury following consultation with the Senate Committee on Indian Affairs, the Congressional Native American Caucus of the House of Representatives, the Commission of Fine Arts, and the National Congress of American Indians. Design proposals are also reviewed by the Citizens Coinage Advisory Committee.

In addition to the regular Uncirculated or Mint State coins produced in large quantities, smaller numbers of Satin Finish dollars were made of the 2009-P, 2009-D, 2010-P, and 2010-D issues. Sold at an additional premium, most of these exist today in grades of MS-67 and upward and are designated SP (Specimen) or SMS (Special Mint Set) by the commercial grading services. 50,000 2014-D coins were made with Enhanced Uncirculated finish and were sold at an extra premium. Most of these grade MS–68 to 70. In 2015 at the West Point Mint 90,000 2015-W dollars were struck with Enhanced Uncirculated finish. These are unique up to this time as the only collectible West Point dollars in any of the three "golden dollar" series (Sacagawea, Native American, and Presidential). Nearly all are in grades MS–68 to 70.

Some error coins have been discovered without edge lettering.

Striking and Sharpness. Most examples are very well struck. Check the higher points of the design. Special issues are uniformly sharply struck.

Availability. Native American dollars are common in high grades, and are usually collected in MS and Proof. Distribution for public circulation has been slow despite Mint efforts such as the $1 Coin Direct Ship program (intended "to make $1 coins readily available to the public, at no additional cost [including shipping], so they can be easily introduced into circulation—particularly by using them for retail transactions, vending, and mass transit"). Proofs have been made each year and are readily available.

GRADING STANDARDS

MS-60 to 70 (Mint State). *Obverse:* At MS-60, some abrasion and contact marks are evident, most noticeably on the cheekbone and the drapery near the baby's head. Luster is present, but may be dull or lifeless. At MS-63, contact marks are extensive but not distracting. Abrasion still is evident, but less than at lower levels. MS-64 coins are slightly finer. An MS-65 coin may have minor abrasion, but contact marks are so minute as to require magnification. Luster should be full and rich. *Reverse:* At MS-60, some abrasion and contact marks are evident, most noticeably on the eagle's breast. Otherwise, the same comments apply as for the obverse.

2009-P, Three Sisters. Graded MS-68.

Native American dollars are seldom collected in grades lower than MS-60.

PF-60 to 70 (Proof). *Obverse and Reverse:* Proofs that are extensively cleaned and have many hairlines, or that are dull and grainy, are lower level, such as PF-60 to 62. This comment is more theoretical than practical, as nearly all Proofs have been well kept. With medium hairlines and good reflectivity, assigned grades of PF–63 or 64 are appropriate. With relatively few hairlines a rating of PF-65 can be given. PF-66 may have hairlines so delicate that magnification is needed to see them. Above that, all the way to PF-70, a Proof should be free of any hairlines or other problems under strong magnification.

2009-S, Three Sisters. Graded PF-70 Deep Cameo.

Three Sisters (2009)
Reverse designer:
Norman E. Nemeth.

Great Law of Peace (2010)
Reverse designer:
Thomas Cleveland.

Wampanoag Treaty (2011)
Reverse designer:
Richard Masters.

Trade Routes in the 17th Century (2012)
Reverse designer:
Thomas Cleveland.

Treaty With the Delawares (2013)
Reverse designer:
Susan Gamble.

Native Hospitality (2014)
Reverse designer:
Chris Costello.

Mohawk Ironworkers (2015)
Reverse designer:
Ronald D. Sanders.

Code Talkers (2016)
Reverse designer:
Thomas D. Rogers Sr.

	Mintage	Cert	Avg	%MS	MS-64	MS-65 / PF-65	MS-66 / PF-69DC
2009-P, Three Sisters	39,200,000	340	66.1	100%	$3	$5	$8
2009-P, Three Sisters, Satin Finish	784,614	564	67.3	100%	$3	$5	$12
2009-D, Three Sisters	35,700,000	262	65.3	100%	$3	$5	$8
2009-D, Three Sisters, Satin Finish	784,614	428	67.2	100%	$3	$5	$12
2009-S, Three Sisters, Proof	2,179,867	9,798	69.3			$10	$17
2010-P, Great Law	32,060,000	462	66.0	100%	$3	$5	$8
2010-P, Great Law, Satin Finish	583,897	294	67.4	100%	$3	$5	$12
2010-D, Great Law	48,720,000	362	65.8	100%	$3	$5	$8
2010-D, Great Law, Satin Finish	583,897	373	67.5	100%	$3	$5	$12
2010-S, Great Law, Proof	1,689,216	6,193	69.2			$10	$17
2011-P, Wampanoag Treaty	29,400,000	365	66.7	100%	$3	$5	$8
2011-D, Wampanoag Treaty	48,160,000	407	67.0	100%	$3	$5	$8
2011-S, Wampanoag Treaty, Proof	1,453,276	7,758	69.2			$15	$18
2012-P, Trade Routes	2,800,000	222	67.2	100%	$3	$5	$8
2012-D, Trade Routes	3,080,000	1,329	67.4	100%	$3	$5	$8
2012-S, Trade Routes, Proof	1,189,445	4,315	69.3			$15	$18

	Mintage	Cert	Avg	%MS	MS-64	MS-65	MS-66
						PF-65	PF-69DC
2013-P, Treaty With the Delawares	1,820,000	324	67.0	100%	$3	$5	$8
2013-D, Treaty With the Delawares	1,820,000	1,264	67.1	100%	$3	$5	$8
2013-S, Treaty With the Delawares, Proof	1,222,180	4,189	69.5			$15	$18
2014-P, Native Hospitality	3,080,000	205	67.0	100%	$3	$6	$9
2014-D, Native Hospitality	2,800,000	530	67.3	100%	$3	$6	$9
2014-D, Native Hospitality, Enhanced Unc.	50,000	1,477	68.9	100%	$8	$10	$15
2014-S, Native Hospitality, Proof	1,144,154	6,341	69.3			$15	$18
2015-P, Mohawk Ironworkers	2,800,000	27	66.4	100%	$3	$5	$6
2015-D, Mohawk Ironworkers	2,240,000	21	66.8	100%	$3	$5	$6
2015-S, Mohawk Ironworkers, Proof	*974,883*	1,273	69.4			$10	$15
2015-W, Mohawk Ironworkers, Enhanced Unc.	*84,059*	114	69.5	100%	$15	$20	$25
2016-P, Code Talkers					$3	$5	$6
2016-D, Code Talkers					$3	$5	$6
2016-S, Code Talkers, Proof						$10	$15

PRESIDENTIAL (2007–2016)

Designers: *Various (obverse); Don Everhart (reverse).* **Weight:** *8.1 grams.*
Composition: *Pure copper core with outer layers of manganese brass (.770 copper, .120 zinc, .070 manganese, and .040 nickel).* **Diameter:** *26.5 mm.* **Edge:** *Lettered.* **Mints:** *Philadelphia, Denver, and San Francisco.*

Obverse Style,
2007–2008,
Circulation Strike
No motto on obverse.

Obverse Style,
2009–2016,
Circulation Strike
Motto beneath portrait.

Common Reverse,
Circulation Strike

Proof

Date, Mintmark, and
Mottos Incused on Edge
IN GOD WE TRUST
moved to obverse in 2009.

History. Presidential dollars debuted in 2007 and are scheduled for issue at the rate of four designs per year through 2015, with the program's two final coins issued in 2016. The series starts with George Washington and continues in order of office. Living presidents are ineligible, so the program is slated to end with Gerald Ford. Each coin has a common reverse showing the Statue of Liberty. The series began with the date, mintmark, and mottos IN GOD WE TRUST and E PLURIBUS UNUM incused on the edge of the coins; in 2009 IN GOD WE TRUST was moved from the edge to the obverse after some public criticism of the "Godless dollars."

In December 2011, Secretary of the Treasury Timothy Geithner directed that the U.S. Mint suspend minting and issuing circulating Presidential dollars. "Regular circulating demand for the coins will be met through the Federal Reserve Bank's existing inventory of circulating coins minted prior to 2012," the Mint announced. Collector formats, however, have continued to be issued.

In addition to the regular Uncirculated or Mint State coins produced in large quantities, smaller numbers of Satin Finish dollars were made of the 2007 to 2010 years, Philadelphia and Denver Mints. Sold at an additional premium, most of these exist today in grades of MS-67 and upward and are designated SP (Specimen) or SMS (Special Mint Set) by the commercial grading services. Catching collectors, dealers, and others by surprise, the Coin and Chronicles sets of Presidential dollars were introduced in 2015. A small number of additional (to the regular Uncirculated) coins were made with Reverse Proof finish and sold at a sharp premium as part of Coin and Chronicles sets, which also included a brochure and a medal. Most collectors desired only the dollar. The Eisenhower and Truman sets, the first offered, sold out quickly, leaving many Mint clients disappointed. Letters of protest filled the columns of Coin World and Numismatic News when the only option to secure them seemed to be paying double or triple issue price on eBay and other venues. These were carefully produced, and nearly all grade MS–68 to 70. "First strike" and other notations on holders add little or nothing to the resale value of these or other modern coins.

Some Presidential dollars were inadvertently struck with the edge lettering missing. A 2009-D, John Tyler, variety has the wrong date, 2010, on the edge.

Striking and Sharpness. These usually are well struck, but check the higher-relief parts of each side. Special issues are uniformly sharp.

Availability. Presidential dollars are very common in MS. Most have from a few too many bagmarks, with true MS-65 and better coins in the minority.

GRADING STANDARDS

MS-60 to 70 (Mint State). *Obverse:* At MS-60, some abrasion and contact marks are evident, most noticeably on the highest-relief areas of the portrait, the exact location varying with the president depicted. Luster is present, but may be dull or lifeless. At MS-63, contact marks are extensive but not distracting. Abrasion still is evident, but less than at lower levels.

2007-P, Washington. Graded MS-68.

MS-64 coins are slightly finer. An MS-65 coin may have minor abrasion, but contact marks are so minute as to require magnification. Luster should be full and rich. *Reverse:* At MS-60, some abrasion and contact marks are evident, most noticeably on the cheek and arm. Otherwise, the same comments apply as for the obverse.

AU-50, 53, 55, 58 (About Uncirculated). *Obverse:* Light wear is seen on the portrait, most prominently on the higher-relief areas. At AU-58, the luster is extensive, but incomplete. At AU–50 and 53, luster is less, but still is present. *Reverse:* Further wear is evident on statue. Otherwise, the same comments apply as for the obverse.

2007-P, Madison. Graded AU-53.

Presidential dollars are seldom collected in grades lower than AU-50.

PF-60 to 70 (Proof). *Obverse and Reverse:* Proofs that are extensively cleaned and have many hairlines, or that are dull and grainy, are lower level, such as PF–60 to 62. This comment is more theoretical than practical, as nearly all Proofs have been well kept. With medium hairlines and good reflectivity, assigned grades of PF–63 or 64 are appropriate. With relatively few hairlines a rating of PF-65

2007-S, Madison. Graded PF-65.

can be given. PF-66 may have hairlines so delicate that magnification is needed to see them. Above that, all the way to PF-70, a Proof should be free of any hairlines or other problems under strong magnification.

2007, Washington

2007, J. Adams

2007, Jefferson

2007, Madison

	Mintage	Cert	Avg	%MS	MS-64	MS-65	MS-66
						PF-65	PF-69DC
2007-P, Washington	176,680,000	17,781	65.0	100%	$1.50	$3	$6
2007-P, Washington, Satin Finish	895,628	755	66.3	100%	$3	$5	$12
2007-P, Washington, Plain Edge ‡ (a,b)	(c)	43,444	64.7	100%	$40	$50	$100
2007-D, Washington	163,680,000	14,553	65.1	100%	$1.50	$3	$5
2007-D, Washington, Satin Finish	895,628	923	66.9	100%	$3	$5	$12
2007-S, Washington, Proof	3,965,989	45,127	69.2			$10	$18
2007-P, J. Adams	112,420,000	20,133	64.6	100%	$1.50	$3	$6
2007-P, J. Adams, Satin Finish	895,628	821	66.4	100%	$3	$5	$12
2007-D, J. Adams	112,140,000	5,848	65.0	100%	$1.50	$3	$6
2007-D, J. Adams, Satin Finish	895,628	905	67.0	100%	$3	$5	$12
2007-S, J. Adams, Proof	3,965,989	44,883	69.2			$10	$18
2007-P, Jefferson	100,800,000	4,975	65.3	100%	$1.50	$3	$6
2007-P, Jefferson, Satin Finish	895,628	888	66.5	100%	$3	$5	$12
2007-D, Jefferson	102,810,000	5,648	65.3	100%	$1.50	$3	$6
2007-D, Jefferson, Satin Finish	895,628	914	66.9	100%	$3	$5	$12
2007-S, Jefferson, Proof	3,965,989	44,976	69.2			$10	$18
2007-P, Madison	84,560,000	2,670	65.4	100%	$1.50	$3	$6
2007-P, Madison, Satin Finish	895,628	862	66.6	100%	$3	$5	$12
2007-D, Madison	87,780,000	3,011	65.4	100%	$1.50	$3	$6
2007-D, Madison, Satin Finish	87,780,000	877	66.9	100%	$3	$5	$12
2007-S, Madison, Proof	3,965,989	45,239	69.2			$10	$18

‡ Ranked in the *100 Greatest U.S. Modern Coins*. **a.** Some circulation-strike Washington dollars are known without the normal edge lettering (date, mintmark, IN GOD WE TRUST, and E PLURIBUS UNUM). **b.** Auction: $235, MS-67, September 2015. **c.** Included in 2007-P, Washington, mintage figure.

2008, Monroe

2008, J.Q. Adams

2008, Jackson

2008, Van Buren

	Mintage	Cert	Avg	%MS	MS-64	MS-65	MS-66
						PF-65	PF-69DC
2008-P, Monroe	64,260,000	2,227	65.5	100%	$1.50	$3	$6
2008-P, Monroe, Satin Finish	745,464	379	66.9	100%	$3	$5	$12
2008-D, Monroe	60,230,000	1,792	65.3	100%	$1.50	$3	$6
2008-D, Monroe, Satin Finish	745,464	398	67.1	100%	$3	$5	$12
2008-S, Monroe, Proof	3,083,940	24,163	69.2			$10	$16
2008-P, J.Q. Adams	57,540,000	2,570	65.9	100%	$1.50	$3	$6
2008-P, J.Q. Adams, Satin Finish	745,464	392	66.9	100%	$3	$5	$12
2008-D, J.Q. Adams	57,720,000	2,053	65.7	100%	$1.50	$3	$6
2008-D, J.Q. Adams, Satin Finish	745,464	398	67.1	100%	$3	$5	$12
2008-S, J.Q. Adams, Proof	3,083,940	24,169	69.3			$10	$16

	Mintage	Cert	Avg	%MS	MS-64	MS-65	MS-66
						PF-65	PF-69DC
2008-P, Jackson	61,180,000	3,002	65.7	100%	$1.50	$3	$6
2008-P, Jackson, Satin Finish	745,464	370	67.1	100%	$3	$5	$12
2008-D, Jackson	61,070,000	1,931	65.2	100%	$1.50	$3	$6
2008-D, Jackson, Satin Finish	745,464	401	67.3	100%	$3	$5	$12
2008-S, Jackson, Proof	3,083,940	24,139	69.2			$10	$16
2008-P, Van Buren	51,520,000	1,394	65.8	100%	$1.50	$3	$6
2008-P, Van Buren, Satin Finish	745,464	372	66.7	100%	$3	$5	$12
2008-D, Van Buren	50,960,000	932	65.2	100%	$1.50	$3	$6
2008-D, Van Buren, Satin Finish	745,464	374	67.0	100%	$3	$5	$12
2008-S, Van Buren, Proof	3,083,940	24,203	69.3			$10	$16

| 2009, W.H. Harrison | 2009, Tyler | 2009, Polk | 2009, Taylor |

	Mintage	Cert	Avg	%MS	MS-64	MS-65	MS-66
						PF-65	PF-69DC
2009-P, W.H. Harrison	43,260,000	1,121	65.5	100%	$1.50	$3	$6
2009-P, W.H. Harrison, Satin Finish	784,614	483	67.3	100%	$3	$5	$12
2009-D, W.H. Harrison	55,160,000	1,153	65.2	100%	$1.50	$3	$6
2009-D, W.H. Harrison, Satin Finish	784,614	451	67.5	100%	$3	$5	$12
2009-S, W.H. Harrison, Proof	2,809,452	17,897	69.2			$8	$15
2009-P, Tyler	43,540,000	1,019	65.3	100%	$1.50	$3	$6
2009-P, Tyler, Satin Finish	784,614	324	67.1	100%	$3	$5	$12
2009-D, Tyler	43,540,000	999	65.2	100%	$1.50	$3	$6
2009-D, Tyler, Satin Finish	784,614	277	67.0	100%	$3	$5	$12
2009-D, Tyler, 2010 Edge	(d)	10	66.0	100%	—	—	—
2009-S, Tyler, Proof	2,809,452	17,866	69.2			$8	$15
2009-P, Polk	46,620,000	1,033	66.0	100%	$1.50	$3	$6
2009-P, Polk, Satin Finish	784,614	396	67.3	100%	$3	$5	$12
2009-D, Polk	41,720,000	769	65.4	100%	$1.50	$3	$6
2009-D, Polk, Satin Finish	784,614	369	67.3	100%	$3	$5	$12
2009-S, Polk, Proof	2,809,452	17,872	69.2			$8	$15
2009-P, Taylor	41,580,000	779	65.7	100%	$1.50	$3	$6
2009-P, Taylor, Satin Finish	784,614	467	67.6	100%	$3	$5	$12
2009-D, Taylor	36,680,000	782	65.6	100%	$1.50	$3	$6
2009-D, Taylor, Satin Finish	784,614	414	67.4	100%	$3	$5	$12
2009-S, Taylor, Proof	2,809,452	18,031	69.3			$8	$15

d. Included in 2009-D, Tyler, mintage figure.

| 2010, Fillmore | 2010, Pierce | 2010, Buchanan | 2010, Lincoln |

	Mintage	Cert	Avg	%MS	MS-64	MS-65 PF-65	MS-66 PF-69DC
2010-P, Fillmore	37,520,000	861	65.6	100%	$1.50	$3	$6
2010-P, Fillmore, Satin Finish	583,897	413	67.3	100%	$3	$5	$12
2010-D, Fillmore	36,960,000	601	65.2	100%	$1.50	$3	$6
2010-D, Fillmore, Satin Finish	583,897	563	67.5	100%	$3	$5	$12
2010-S, Fillmore, Proof	2,224,827	15,287	69.2			$10	$18
2010-P, Pierce	38,220,000	759	65.6	100%	$1.50	$3	$6
2010-P, Pierce, Satin Finish	583,897	428	67.4	100%	$3	$5	$12
2010-D, Pierce	38,360,000	689	65.5	100%	$1.50	$3	$6
2010-D, Pierce, Satin Finish	583,897	579	67.6	100%	$3	$5	$12
2010-S, Pierce, Proof	2,224,827	15,237	69.2			$8	$15
2010-P, Buchanan	36,820,000	354	65.6	100%	$1.50	$3	$6
2010-P, Buchanan, Satin Finish	583,897	424	67.2	100%	$3	$5	$12
2010-D, Buchanan	36,540,000	493	65.3	100%	$1.50	$3	$6
2010-D, Buchanan, Satin Finish	583,897	557	67.5	100%	$3	$5	$12
2010-S, Buchanan, Proof	2,224,827	15,310	69.2			$8	$15
2010-P, Lincoln	49,000,000	724	65.5	100%	$1.50	$3	$6
2010-P, Lincoln, Satin Finish	583,897	673	67.1	100%	$3	$5	$12
2010-D, Lincoln	48,020,000	375	65.2	100%	$1.50	$3	$6
2010-D, Lincoln, Satin Finish	583,897	917	67.4	100%	$3	$5	$12
2010-S, Lincoln, Proof	2,224,827	16,017	69.2			$8	$15

| 2011, A. Johnson | 2011, Grant | 2011, Hayes | 2011, Garfield |

	Mintage	Cert	Avg	%MS	MS-64	MS-65 PF-65	MS-66 PF-69DC
2011-P, A. Johnson	35,560,000	384	66.7	100%	$1.50	$3	$6
2011-D, A. Johnson	37,100,000	372	67.0	100%	$1.50	$3	$6
2011-S, A. Johnson, Proof	1,972,863	8,096	69.2			$8	$15
2011-P, Grant	38,080,000	424	66.8	100%	$1.50	$3	$6
2011-D, Grant	37,940,000	392	67.0	100%	$1.50	$3	$6
2011-S, Grant, Proof	1,972,863	8,158	69.2			$8	$15
2011-P, Hayes	37,660,000	385	66.5	100%	$1.50	$3	$6
2011-D, Hayes	36,820,000	392	67.1	100%	$1.50	$3	$5
2011-S, Hayes, Proof	1,972,863	8,236	69.3			$8	$15
2011-P, Garfield	37,100,000	337	66.4	100%	$1.50	$3	$6
2011-D, Garfield	37,100,000	346	67.0	100%	$2	$3	$6
2011-S, Garfield, Proof	1,972,863	8,230	69.2			$8	$15

2012, Arthur	2012, Cleveland, First Term	2012, B. Harrison	2012, Cleveland, Second Term

	Mintage	Cert	Avg	%MS	MS-64	MS-65	MS-66
						PF-65	PF-69DC
2012-P, Arthur (e)	6,020,000	707	66.8	100%	$2	$3	$6
2012-D, Arthur (e)	4,060,000	281	67.1	100%	$2	$3	$6
2012-S, Arthur, Proof	1,438,743	4,873	69.3			$9	$16
2012-P, Cleveland, First Term (e)	5,460,000	737	66.7	100%	$2	$3	$6
2012-D, Cleveland, First Term (e)	4,060,000	251	66.9	100%	$2	$3	$6
2012-S, Cleveland, First Term, Proof	1,438,743	4,899	69.3			$9	$16
2012-P, B. Harrison (e)	5,640,001	725	66.6	100%	$2	$3	$6
2012-D, B. Harrison (e)	4,200,000	251	67.1	100%	$2	$3	$6
2012-S, B. Harrison, Proof	1,438,743	4,853	69.3			$9	$16
2012-P, Cleveland, Second Term (e)	10,680,000	691	66.6	100%	$2	$3	$6
2012-D, Cleveland, Second Term (e)	3,920,000	258	67.1	100%	$2	$3	$6
2012-S, Cleveland, Second Term, Proof	1,438,743	4,847	69.3			$9	$16

e. Not issued for circulation.

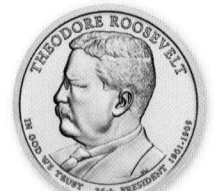

2013, McKinley	2013, T. Roosevelt	2013, Taft	2013, Wilson

	Mintage	Cert	Avg	%MS	MS-64	MS-65	MS-66
						PF-65	PF-69DC
2013-P, McKinley (e)	4,760,000	745	67.1	100%	$2	$3	$6
2013-D, McKinley (e)	3,365,100	153	67.0	100%	$2	$3	$6
2013-S, McKinley, Proof	1,488,798	4,922	69.5			$9	$16
2013-P, T. Roosevelt (e)	5,310,700	1,008	67.1	100%	$2	$3	$6
2013-D, T. Roosevelt (e)	3,920,000	291	66.6	100%	$2	$3	$6
2013-S, T. Roosevelt, Proof	1,503,943	4,955	69.5			$9	$16
2013-P, Taft (e)	4,760,000	876	67.1	100%	$2	$3	$6
2013-D, Taft (e)	3,360,000	210	67.0	100%	$2	$3	$6
2013-S, Taft, Proof	1,488,798	4,872	69.5			$9	$16
2013-P, Wilson (e)	4,620,000	949	67.4	100%	$2	$3	$6
2013-D, Wilson (e)	3,360,000	195	67.2	100%	$2	$3	$6
2013-S, Wilson, Proof	1,488,798	4,868	69.5			$9	$16

e. Not issued for circulation.

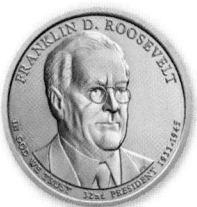

2014, Harding	2014, Coolidge	2014, Hoover	2014, F.D. Roosevelt

	Mintage	Cert	Avg	%MS	MS-64	MS-65	MS-66
						PF-65	PF-69DC
2014-P, Harding (e)	6,160,000	260	66.9	100%	$2	$3	$6
2014-D, Harding (e)	3,780,000	215	67.0	100%	$2	$3	$6
2014-S, Harding, Proof	1,373,569	3,848	69.5			$9	$16
2014-P, Coolidge (e)	4,480,000	304	67.2	100%	$2	$3	$6
2014-D, Coolidge (e)	3,780,000	186	67.3	100%	$2	$3	$6
2014-S, Coolidge, Proof	1,373,569	3,868	69.4			$9	$16
2014-P, Hoover (e)	4,480,000	246	67.0	100%	$2	$3	$6
2014-D, Hoover (e)	3,780,000	195	67.2	100%	$2	$3	$6
2014-S, Hoover, Proof	1,373,569	3,850	69.4			$9	$16
2014-P, F.D. Roosevelt (e)	4,760,000	291	67.1	100%	$2	$3	$6
2014-D, F.D. Roosevelt (e)	3,920,000	158	67.2	100%	$2	$3	$6
2014-S, F.D. Roosevelt, Proof	1,392,619	3,865	69.4			$9	$16

e. Not issued for circulation.

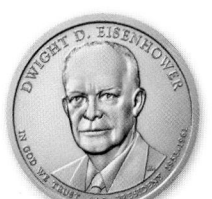

2015, Truman	2015, Eisenhower	2015, Kennedy	2015, L.B. Johnson

	Mintage	Cert	Avg	%MS	MS-64	MS-65	MS-66
						PF-65	PF-69DC
2015-P, Truman (e)	4,900,000	30	66.8	100%	$2	$3	$5
2015-D, Truman (e)	3,500,000	32	66.9	100%	$2	$3	$5
2015-S, Truman, Proof	1,191,876	1,477	69.4			$6	$15
2015-S, Truman, Reverse Proof	16,812	144	69.0			$175	$225
2015-P, Eisenhower (e)	4,900,000	15	66.2	100%	$2	$3	$5
2015-D, Eisenhower (e)	3,645,998	11	66.8	100%	$2	$3	$5
2015-S, Eisenhower, Proof	1,191,876	1,470	69.4			$6	$15
2015-S, Eisenhower, Reverse Proof	16,744	155	68.8			$150	$200
2015-P, Kennedy (e)	6,160,000	34	66.2	100%	$2	$3	$5
2015-D, Kennedy (e)	5,180,000	27	66.9	100%	$2	$3	$5
2015-S, Kennedy, Proof	1,191,876	1,485	69.4			$6	$15
2015-S, Kennedy, Reverse Proof	49,051	136	69.0			$80	$125
2015-P, L.B. Johnson (e)	7,840,000	17	66.8	100%	$2	$3	$5
2015-D, L.B. Johnson (e)	4,200,000	29	66.9	100%	$2	$3	$5
2015-S, L.B. Johnson, Proof	1,191,876	1,472	69.4			$6	$15
2015-S, L.B. Johnson, Reverse Proof	23,905	0	n/a				

e. Not issued for circulation.

2016, Nixon

2016, Ford

The design for the 2016 Ronald Reagan Presidential dollar was not finalized at the time of publication.

	Mintage	Cert	Avg	%MS	MS-64	MS-65	MS-66
						PF-65	PF-69DC
2016-P, Richard M. Nixon (e)					$2	$3	$5
2016-D, Richard M. Nixon (e)					$2	$3	$5
2016-S, Richard M. Nixon, Proof						$6	$15
2016-P, Gerald Ford (e)					$2	$3	$5
2016-D, Gerald Ford (e)					$2	$3	$5
2016-S, Gerald Ford, Proof						$6	$15
2016-P, Ronald Reagan (e)					$2	$3	$5
2016-D, Ronald Reagan (e)					$2	$3	$5
2016-S, Ronald Reagan, Proof						$6	$15
2016-S, Ronald Reagan, Reverse Proof					$60	$75	$90

e. Not issued for circulation.

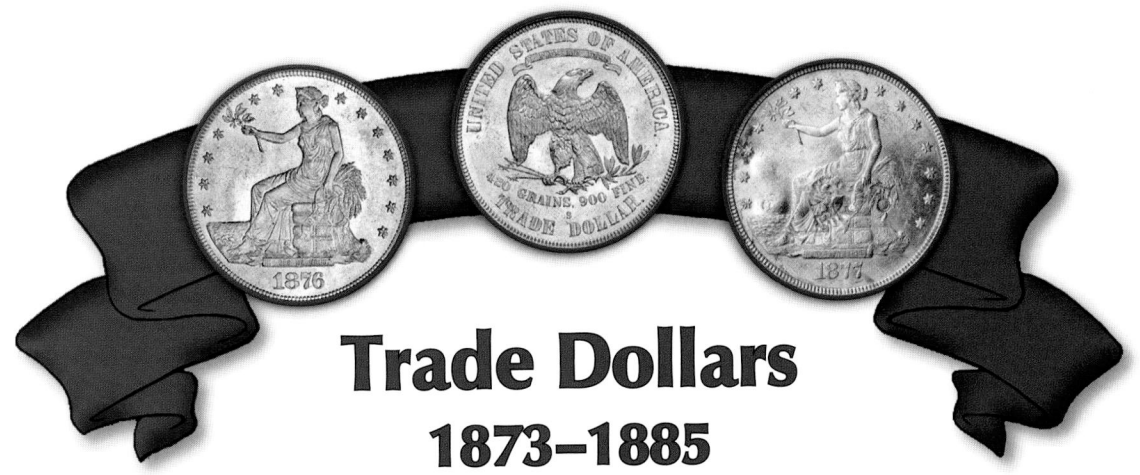

Trade Dollars
1873–1885

AN OVERVIEW OF TRADE DOLLARS

A new denomination, the silver trade dollar, was authorized by the Coinage Act of 1873. This provided that a coin weighing 420 grains, of .900 fine silver, be struck for use in the export trade. By comparison, contemporary Liberty Seated silver dollars weighed 412.5 grains. Produced in quantity from 1873 through 1878, the trade dollars were a great success, particularly in China, where merchants preferred silver to gold and would not accept paper money of any kind. Coinage would have continued except for passage of the Bland-Allison Act of February 28, 1878, which authorized the government to buy millions of ounces of silver each year and resume the production of standard silver dollars (which had not been minted since 1873). The trade dollar was discontinued forthwith; however, Proof impressions were made for numismatists through 1883, plus a small quantity of Proofs distributed privately in 1884 and 1885, coins of these last two issues being great rarities today.

Choosing a trade dollar for a type set is easy enough to do, the choices being a circulation strike, which requires some connoisseurship, or a Proof, most of which are sharply struck and attractive. Enough exist in both formats that collectors will easily find a nice example, except that MS-65 and better pieces are elusive.

FOR THE COLLECTOR AND INVESTOR: TRADE DOLLARS AS A SPECIALTY

There are two great rarities among trade dollars: the Proof-only 1884, of which just ten are known, and the Proof-only 1885, of which only five are known. Neither was produced openly, and examples were sold for the private profit of Mint officials, going to John W. Haseltine, a Philadelphia dealer who was a favored outlet for such things. The existence of these coins was not generally known to numismatists until 1907–1908, when examples began to appear on the market. As to the mintage figures, the numbers five and ten have no official origin, but are said to represent the number once held by Haseltine. Relatively few numismatists have been able to afford examples of these two dates.

William Barber's Amazonian design, featuring a seated Columbia with eagle and sword, was rejected by Mint authorities for being too militaristic.

Beyond the above, a complete collection of trade dollars of the 1873 to 1883 years can be formed with some effort. Proofs were made of each year during this span, and after 1878 *only* Proofs were made, at the Philadelphia Mint, with no branch-mint issues. Proofs had greater appeal than Mint State circulation strikes to collectors of an earlier era, and more were saved, with the result that Proofs of the otherwise common dates 1873 to 1877 are much harder to find today, especially in choice condition.

Circulation strikes were regularly minted from 1873 through 1878, with production greatest at the San Francisco and Carson City mints, these being closest to eastern Asia, where the coins were used in commerce. Some trade dollars (but not many) went into domestic circulation (they were legal tender until that status was repealed on July 22, 1876). Later, after 1876, they traded widely in the United States but were valued by their silver content, not their face value. In 1878 the 412.5-grain Morgan dollar was worth $1.00 in circulation, while the heavier 420-grain trade dollar was worth only its melt-down value of about $0.90.

Very few of the circulating issues were saved by numismatists, with the result today that assembling a collection in choice or gem Mint State can be a great challenge. The key issue is the 1878-CC, with the lowest mintage by far in the series—scarce in any and all grades. As trade dollars became numismatically popular in the United States, thousands were repatriated from China, often bearing Chinese characters called *chopmarks*, which were applied by bankers and merchants. More often than not the imported coins had been harshly cleaned in China, as the owners thought shiny coins were more desirable. However, many choice and undamaged pieces were imported as well. The pieces with chopmarks are collectible in their own right in view of their historical significance.

Collectors are warned that many modern counterfeit trade dollars lurk in the marketplace.

TRADE DOLLAR (1873–1885)

Designer: *William Barber.* **Weight:** *27.22 grams.*
Composition: *.900 silver, .100 copper (net weight .7874 oz. pure silver).*
Diameter: *38.1 mm.* **Edge:** *Reeded.* **Mints:** *Philadelphia, Carson City, and San Francisco.*

Mintmark location is on the reverse, below the fineness.

Circulation Strike

Proof

History. Trade dollars were minted under the Coinage Act of 1873. Containing 420 grains of .900 fine silver, they were heavier than the Liberty Seated dollar (of 412.5 grains). They were made for use in the China export trade and proved to be a great success. Some circulated at par in the United States, until they were demonetized by the Act of July 22, 1876, after which they circulated at their silver value, which was slightly lower than their face value. The Bland-Allison Act of 1878 provided for the new "Morgan" silver dollar, and trade dollars were discontinued, although Proofs continued to be made through 1885. Modifications to the trade dollar design are distinguished as follows.

Reverse 1: With a berry under the eagle's left talon; the lowest arrowhead ends over the 0 in 420. (Used on all coins from all mints in 1873 and 1874, and occasionally in 1875 and 1876.)

Reverse 2: Without an extra berry under the talon; the lowest arrowhead ends over the 2 in 420. (Used occasionally at all mints from 1875 through 1876, and on all coins from all mints 1877 through 1885.)

Obverse 1: The ends of the scroll point to the left; the extended hand has only three fingers. (Used on coins at all mints, 1873 through 1876.)

Obverse 2: The ends of the scroll point downward; the extended hand has four fingers. (Used in combination with Reverse 2 on one variety of 1876-S, and on all coins at all mints from 1877 through 1885.)

Striking and Sharpness. Weakness is often seen. On the obverse, check Miss Liberty's head and the star centers first. On the reverse, check the feathers on the eagle, particularly on the legs. Luster can range from dull to deeply frosty. In EF and lower grades, strike sharpness on the stars and the head does not matter to connoisseurs. Some Proofs are lightly struck on the head and the stars on the obverse and the leg feathers of the eagle on the reverse.

Availability. The 1878-CC is a rarity. Other dates and mintmarks are readily collected in grades from EF to MS. Lower grades are not often seen, for these coins did not circulate for a long time. Many used in China have counterstamps, called *chopmarks*, which are of interest to collectors. On an MS-63 or better coin a chopmark will decrease its value, but on EF and AU coins specialists eagerly seek them. MS coins are mostly in the lower ranges, often with unsatisfactory surfaces. True gems are very scarce. Proofs for collectors were made from 1873 to 1883 in quantity to supply the demand. In addition, a few were secretly made in 1884 and 1885. Most survivors are of high quality today, although gems of the 1873 to 1877 years are much harder to find than are those of 1878 to 1883.

Note: In recent years a flood of modern counterfeit trade dollars, many coming from China, has deluged the market.

GRADING STANDARDS

MS-60 to 70 (Mint State). *Obverse:* At MS-60, some abrasion and contact marks are evident, most noticeably on the left breast, left arm, and left knee. Luster is present, but may be dull or lifeless. Many of these coins are light in color or even brilliant, having been repatriated from China, and have been cleaned to remove sediment and discoloration. At MS-63, contact marks are very few, and abrasion is minimal. An MS-65 coin has

1875-S, Reverse 1. Graded MS-61.

no abrasion in the fields (but may have a hint on the higher parts of the seated figure), and contact marks are trivial. Luster should be full and rich. *Reverse:* Comments apply as for the obverse, except that in lower Mint State grades abrasion and contact marks are most noticeable on the eagle's head, the claws, and the top of the wings. At MS-65 or higher there are no marks visible to the unaided eye. The field is mainly protected by design elements and does not show abrasion as much as does the obverse on a given coin.

Illustrated coin: Some friction in the fields is seen, but much of the original luster remains.

AU-50, 53, 55, 58 (About Uncirculated).
Obverse: Light wear is seen on the knees, bosom, and head. At AU-58, the luster is extensive but incomplete. At AU–50 and 53, luster is less. *Reverse:* Wear is visible on the eagle's head, the claws, and the top of the wings. An AU-58 coin will have nearly full luster. At AU–50 and 53, there still are traces of luster.

1876, Reverse 2. Graded AU-53.

  Illustrated coin: This example shows light, even wear. Most of the luster is gone, except in protected areas, but it has excellent eye appeal for the grade.

EF-40, 45 (Extremely Fine). *Obverse:* Further wear is seen on all areas, especially the head, the left breast, the left arm, the left leg, and the bale on which Miss Liberty is seated. Little or no luster is seen on most coins. From this grade downward, strike sharpness on the stars and the head does not matter to connoisseurs. *Reverse:* Further wear is evident on the eagle's head, legs, claws, and wings, although on well-struck coins nearly all feather details on the wings are sharp.

1876-CC, Reverse 1. Graded EF-40.

VF-20, 30 (Very Fine). *Obverse:* Further wear is seen on the seated figure, although more than half the details of her dress are visible. Details of the wheat sheaf are mostly intact. IN GOD WE TRUST and LIBERTY are clear. *Reverse:* Wear is more extensive; some feathers are blended together, with two-thirds or more still visible.

1877-S. Graded VF-30.

F-12, 15 (Fine). *Obverse:* The seated figure is further worn, with fewer details of the dress visible. Most details in the wheat sheaf are clear. Both mottos are readable, but some letters may be weak. *Reverse:* Wear is extensive, with about half to nearly two-thirds of the feathers flat or blended with others. The eagle's left leg is mostly flat. Wear is seen on the raised E PLURIBUS UNUM, and one or two letters may be missing.

1873-CC. Graded F-12.

  The trade dollar is seldom collected in grades lower than F-12.

PF-60 to 70 (Proof). *Obverse and Reverse:* Proofs that are extensively cleaned and have many hairlines, or that are dull and grainy, are lower level, such as PF–60 to 62. These are not widely desired. With medium hairlines and good reflectivity, an assigned grade of PF-64 is appropriate, and with relatively few hairlines, gem PF-65. In various grades hairlines are most easily seen in the obverse field. PF-66 may have hairlines so delicate

1882. Graded PF-62.

that magnification is needed to see them. Above that, a Proof should be free of such lines.

Illustrated coin: This coin has medium-gray toning overall.

Chopmarked Trade Dollar

Examples of chopmarks.

	Mintage	Cert	Avg	%MS	VG-8	F-12	VF-20	EF-40	AU-50	MS-60	MS-63	MS-64	MS-65
										PF-60	PF-63	PF-65
1873	396,900	175	57.9	66%	$145	$175	$225	$325	$650	$1,050	$3,150	$5,500	$13,000
	Auctions: $3,760, MS-64, August 2015; $3,668, MS-64, January 2015; $646, AU-55, September 2015; $588, AU-50, March 2015												
1873, Proof	600	170	63.2								$1,750	$3,300	$8,500
	Auctions: $8,225, PF-65, March 2015; $3,055, PF-64, September 2015; $3,055, PF-63Cam, June 2015; $2,720, PF-62Cam, July 2015												
1873-CC	124,500	128	53.0	28%	$325	$500	$700	$1,250	$2,000	$9,000	$20,000	$49,000	$110,000
	Auctions: $3,290, AU-58, February 2015; $3,290, AU-55, February 2015; $2,233, EF-45, February 2015; $1,645, EF-45, September 2015												
1873-S	703,000	103	59.6	71%	$175	$200	$300	$450	$675	$1,750	$4,000	$5,500	$18,000
	Auctions: $3,995, MS-63, July 2015; $2,820, MS-63, June 2015; $646, AU-55, March 2015; $165, VF-30, September 2015												

Reverse 1
*Arrowheads end over 0;
berry under eagle's left talon.*

Reverse 2
*Arrowheads end over 2;
no berry under talon.*

Obverse 1
*Hand has three fingers;
scroll points left.*

Obverse 2
*Hand has four fingers;
scroll points downward.*

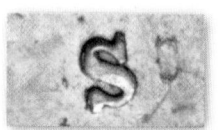

1875-S, S Over CC
FS-T1-1875S-501.

	Mintage	Cert	Avg	%MS	VG-8	F-12	VF-20	EF-40	AU-50	MS-60	MS-63	MS-64	MS-65
										PF-60	PF-63	PF-65
1874	987,100	146	58.0	64%	$145	$175	$225	$300	$425	$1,200	$2,500	$4,000	$14,000
	Auctions: $9,400, MS-65, August 2015; $2,350, MS-63, January 2015; $823, AU-58, September 2015; $400, EF-45, October 2015												
1874, Proof	700	209	63.2							$1,750	$3,100	$8,500
	Auctions: $8,813, PF-66, January 2015; $11,456, PF-65Cam, October 2015; $3,878, PF-64Cam, August 2015; $2,468, PF-62, October 2015												
1874-CC	1,373,200	240	58.1	62%	$300	$400	$475	$650	$1,000	$3,000	$7,000	$12,500	$35,000
	Auctions: $14,100, MS-64, October 2015; $7,050, MS-63, August 2015; $3,525, MS-61, September 2015; $2,233, AU-58, July 2015												
1874-S	2,549,000	324	59.6	68%	$140	$160	$185	$245	$325	$900	$2,000	$3,250	$13,000
	Auctions: $1,645, MS-63, July 2015; $1,129, MS-62, September 2015; $911, MS-61, July 2015; $376, AU-53, July 2015												
1875	218,200	104	57.9	70%	$240	$375	$525	$750	$1,250	$2,600	$5,000	$7,500	$20,000
	Auctions: $1,175, AU-53, September 2015; $541, AU-50, June 2015; $353, EF-40, April 2015; $1,763, VF-30, January 2015												
1875, Reverse 2	(a)	1	64.0	100%	$240	$375	$525	$750	$1,250	$2,600	$4,650	$9,000	$21,000
	Auctions: $4,888, MS-64, April 2012												
1875, Proof	700	229	63.3							$1,750	$3,300	$8,500
	Auctions: $28,200, PF-66, May 2015; $7,638, PF-65, August 2015; $3,290, PF-64Cam, June 2015; $2,233, PF-62, July 2015												
1875-CC, All kinds	1,573,700												
1875-CC		310	55.8	50%	$275	$375	$475	$575	$850	$2,500	$6,000	$11,500	$35,000
	Auctions: $823, MS-60, June 2015; $969, AU-53, December 2015; $646, EF-40, June 2015; $376, VF-25, February 2015												
1875-CC, Reverse 2		0	n/a		$280	$400	$525	$750	$1,075	$2,500	$5,750	$10,000	$35,000
	Auctions: $1,610, AU-58, January 2012												
1875-S, All kinds	4,487,000												
1875-S		947	60.3	77%	$140	$155	$165	$260	$350	$900	$1,700	$3,000	$11,000
	Auctions: $1,058, MS-62, August 2015; $881, MS-61, September 2015; $447, AU-58, April 2015; $282, EF-45, December 2015												
1875-S, Reverse 2		5	61.4	80%	$145	$165	$190	$300	$400	$1,175	$2,350	$3,400	$11,000
	Auctions: $69,000, MS-67, January 2012												
1875-S, S Over CC (b)		58	58.9	52%	$265	$400	$525	$1,000	$1,700	$5,000	$13,000	$22,500	$57,500
	Auctions: $24,675, MS-64, May 2015; $4,113, MS-61, January 2015; $2,585, AU-58, October 2015; $823, AU-50, June 2015												

a. Included in circulation-strike 1875 mintage figure. **b.** A weak C from the underlying CC mintmark is visible to the right of the S mintmark.

1876-CC, Doubled-Die Reverse
FS-T1-1876CC-801.

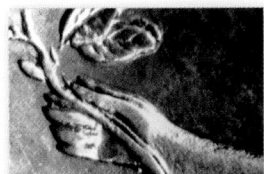 

1876-S, Doubled-Die Obverse
FS-T1-1876S-101.

| | Mintage | Cert | Avg | %MS | VG-8 | F-12 | VF-20 | EF-40 | AU-50 | MS-60 | MS-63 | MS-64 | MS-65 |
											PF-60	PF-63	PF-65
1876	455,000	452	59.6	77%	$140	$155	$190	$250	$335	$1,050	$2,400	$3,200	$12,000
Auctions: $400, MS-60, May 2015; $494, AU-55, August 2015; $212, AU-50, February 2015; $212, EF-45, June 2015
1876, Obverse 2, Reverse 2 (c)	**(d)**	0	n/a							—			
Auctions: No auction records available.
1876, Reverse 2	**(d)**	1	55.0	0%	$140	$155	$190	$250	$335	$900	$2,000	$3,200	$11,000
Auctions: $2,760, MS-64, April 2012
1876, Proof	1,150	285	62.8							$1,750	$3,100	$8,500
Auctions: $15,275, PF-66Cam, October 2015; $3,760, PF-64Cam, June 2015; $2,703, PF-63, January 2015; $1,410, PF-60, February 2015
1876-CC, All kinds	509,000												
1876-CC		139	55.6	42%	$350	$450	$575	$775	$2,000	$6,250	$27,000	$37,000	$100,000
Auctions: $2,585, AU-55, February 2015; $646, AU-50, September 2014; $499, EF-40, July 2014; $485, VF-30, November 2014
1876-CC, Reverse 1	1	53.0	0%	$245	$325	$600	$875	$2,350	$7,250	$29,500	$40,000	$115,000
Auctions: $3,220, MS-60, February 2006
1876-CC, Doubled-Die Reverse (e)		32	55.3	28%				$1,550	$2,100	$11,000	—		
Auctions: $2,350, MS-60, February 2014; $1,087, AU-50, June 2015; $382, AU-50, September 2014
1876-S, All kinds	5,227,000												
1876-S		844	57.4	58%	$140	$155	$165	$260	$350	$900	$1,700	$3,000	$11,000
Auctions: $1,175, MS-62, January 2015; $705, AU-58, May 2015; $400, AU-55, October 2015; $200, EF-40, October 2015
1876-S, Doubled-Die Obverse (f)		0	n/a					$1,400	$1,750	$2,200			
Auctions: No auction records available.
1876-S, Reverse 2		3	57.0	0%	$140	$155	$165	$260	$350	$900	$1,700	$3,000	$11,000
Auctions: $1,506, MS-63, September 2011
1876-S, Obverse 2, Reverse 2		1	58.0	0%	$165	$200	$300	$500	$850	$1,500	$2,650	$3,700	$13,500
Auctions: $1,495, MS-60 CAC, August 2011

c. Extremely rare. **d.** Included in circulation-strike 1876 mintage figure. **e.** Doubling is visible on the branches on the right, the eagle's talons, the right wing tip, and the eagle's beak; and is very strong on E PLURIBUS UNUM. Weaker doubling is seen on UNITED STATES OF AMERICA. "Considered by most to be the strongest reverse doubled die in the series, this variety is one of the highlights of the trade dollar varieties and is thought to be extremely rare in grades above AU" (*Cherrypickers' Guide to Rare Die Varieties*, sixth edition, volume II). **f.** Doubling is visible on Liberty's hand, chin, and left foot, and on the olive branch. "This DDO is easily the rarest doubled die in the series, and is considered extremely rare in grades above AU. Most known examples are cleaned. The variety is known as the king of the trade dollar varieties" (*Cherrypickers' Guide to Rare Die Varieties*, sixth edition, volume II).

1877, Doubled-Die Obverse
FS-T1-1877-101.

1877-S, Repunched Date
FS-T1-1877S-301.

1877-S, Doubled-Die Reverse
FS-T1-1877S-801.

1877-S, Doubled-Die Reverse
FS-T1-1877S-802.

1878-S, Doubled-Die Reverse
FS-T1-1878S-801.

	Mintage	Cert	Avg	%MS	VG-8	F-12	VF-20	EF-40	AU-50	MS-60	MS-63 PF-60	MS-64 PF-63	MS-65 PF-65
1877	3,039,200	618	52.4	46%	$160	$180	$200	$275	$350	$900	$2,000	$3,250	$12,500
Auctions: $16,450, MS-65, October 2015; $1,528, MS-63, January 2015; $588, AU-58, June 2015; $165, VF-35, August 2015													
1877, DblDie Obv (g)	(h)	2	60.0	50%				$300	$400	$1,250			
Auctions: No auction records available.													
1877, Proof	510	200	63.5								$1,750	$3,250	$8,750
Auctions: $3,055, PF-64, March 2015; $3,290, PF-63Cam, June 2015; $1,528, PF-60, January 2015; $1,293, PF-60, June 2015													
1877-CC	534,000	128	55.5	56%	$285	$425	$550	$675	$1,000	$3,500	$12,500	$28,500	$65,000
Auctions: $14,100, MS-64, March 2015; $7,638, MS-63, February 2015; $6,463, MS-62, November 2014; $564, AU-50, June 2015													
1877-S	9,519,000	1,476	55.1	52%	$140	$155	$165	$245	$325	$1,000	$2,050	$3,100	$11,000
Auctions: $6,463, MS-65, January 2015; $1,351, MS-63, October 2015; $212, EF-45, March 2015; $136, VF-30, June 2015													
1877-S, Repunched Date (i)	(j)	0	n/a						$550	$800	$1,600		
Auctions: $250, EF-45, May 2010													
1877-S, DblDie Rev (k)	(j)	2	55.5	0%					$300	$425	$1,300		
Auctions: No auction records available.													
1877-S, DblDie Rev (l)	(j)	6	52.7	50%					$300	$400	$1,200		
Auctions: $1,323, MS-62, April 2011													
1878	0	n/a							$1,500				
Auctions: No auction records available.													
1878, Proof	900	344	63.6								$1,750	$3,250	$8,750
Auctions: $12,338, PF-66, May 2015; $6,463, PF-65Cam, August 2015; $8,813, PF-64DCam, September 2015													
1878-CC (m)	97,000	86	49.0	31%	$700	$1,175	$1,675	$3,750	$5,000	$14,000	$35,000	$75,000	$110,000
Auctions: $18,800, MS-62, May 2015; $12,338, MS-61, February 2015; $10,575, AU-58, June 2015; $3,525, EF-40, January 2015													
1878-S	4,162,000	1051	52.3	41%	$140	$155	$165	$260	$350	$900	$1,700	$3,000	$10,000
Auctions: $28,200, MS-66, May 2015; $2,703, MS-64, August 2015; $329, AU-55, January 2015; $200, EF-40, October 2015													
1878-S, DblDie Rev (n)	(o)	13	53.5	38%					$450	$550	$1,300		
Auctions: $1,000, MS-62, August 2011													

g. Doubling on this rare variety is evident on the wheat stalks, LIBERTY, IN GOD WE TRUST, and stars 11, 12, and 13. **h.** Included in circulation-strike 1877 mintage figure. **i.** A secondary 7 protrudes prominently south from the last 7. **j.** Included in 1877-S mintage figure. **k.** Doubling is visible on E PLURIBUS UNUM, the ribbon, and UNITED STATES OF AMERICA. There are at least two different doubled-die reverses for 1877-S; this one is FS-T1-1877S-801. "Considered a highlight of the trade dollar varieties" (*Cherrypickers' Guide to Rare Die Varieties*, sixth edition, volume II). **l.** Minor doubling is visible on nearly all reverse lettering, especially on 420 GRAINS. This reverse doubled die is more common than the preceding; it is listed as FS-T1-1877S-802. **m.** On July 19, 1878, a quantity of 44,148 trade dollars was melted by the Mint. Many of these may have been 1878-CC. **n.** Strong doubling is visible on the entire lower left of the reverse, on the arrow points and shafts, and on 420 GRAINS; slight doubling is evident on the motto. Rare in AU and higher grades. There are at least two doubled-die reverses for this date; the one listed is FS-T1-1878S-801. **o.** Included in 1878-S mintage figure.

	Mintage	Cert	Avg	%MS	VG-8	F-12	VF-20	EF-40	AU-50	MS-60	MS-63	MS-64	MS-65
											PF-60	PF-63	PF-65
1879, Proof	1,541	554	63.8								$1,750	$3,200	$8,750
Auctions: $15,863, PF-67Cam, January 2015; $8,813, PF-66Cam, September 2015; $5,053, PF-65+, September 2015; $1,763, PF-62, January 2015													
1880, Proof	1,987	701	63.5								$1,750	$3,200	$8,750
Auctions: $15,275, PF-67, August 2015; $11,750, PF-66UCam, January 2015; $3,408, PF-64Cam, January 2015; $2,585, PF-63, January 2015													
1881, Proof	960	422	63.8								$1,750	$3,200	$8,750
Auctions: $$8,225, PF-66, May 2015; $4,818, PF-65, October 2015; $4,700, PF-64Cam+, September 2015; $1,763, PF-62, January 2015													
1882, Proof	1,097	529	63.9								$1,750	$3,200	$8,750
Auctions: $19,975, PF-66DCam, August 2015; $5,405, PF-65, August 2015; $3,760, PF-64Cam, October 2015; $3,055, PF-63Cam, August 2015													
1883, Proof	979	487	63.7								$1,750	$3,200	$8,750
Auctions: $14,100, PF-66Cam, August 2015; $7,638, PF-65, August 2015; $4,935, PF-64Cam, June 2015; $2,374, PF-63, January 2015													
1884, Proof † (p)	10	7	64.1									$550,000	$1,000,000
Auctions: $998,750, PF-65, January 2014													
1885, Proof † (p)	5	2	62.0									$2,000,000	$2,500,000
Auctions: $1,006,250, PF-62, November 2004													

† Ranked in the *100 Greatest U.S. Coins* (fourth edition). **p.** Trade dollars of 1884 and 1885 were unknown to the numismatic community until 1907 and 1908. None are listed in the Mint director's report, and numismatists believe that they are not a part of the regular Mint issue but were produced secretly for private sale to collectors.

Gold Dollars
1849–1889

AN OVERVIEW OF GOLD DOLLARS

Coinage of the gold dollar was authorized by the Act of March 3, 1849, after the start of the California Gold Rush.

Although a case could be made for designating the Small Head, Open Wreath, gold dollar as a separate type, it is not generally collected as such. Instead, pieces dated from 1849 through 1854 (whether Open Wreath or Close Wreath) are collectively designated as Type 1. Examples today are readily available in all grades, although truly choice and gem Mint State pieces are in the minority.

In contrast, the Type 2 design, produced at the Philadelphia Mint in part of 1854, and at the Philadelphia, Charlotte, Dahlonega, and New Orleans mints in 1855, and only at the San Francisco Mint in 1856, is a great challenge. Examples are scarcer in all grades than are those of types 1 and 3. Choice and gem coins are especially rare. Striking is a great problem, and while some sharp pieces exist, probably 80% or more have areas of weakness, typically at the 85 (center two digits) of the date, but also often on the headdress and elsewhere. Further, the borders are sometimes imperfect.

Type 3 gold dollars, made from 1856 through 1889, are easier to acquire in nearly any grade desired, including choice and gem Mint State. Most are well struck and in Mint State have excellent eye appeal. Among Type 3 gold dollars the dates from 1879 through 1889 inclusive are most often seen, as these were widely saved by coin dealers and collectors at the time and did not circulate to any appreciable extent. Gold dollar coins also were popular as Christmas gifts in the late 1800s. Some of these have very low mintage figures, making them very appealing to today's collectors.

FOR THE COLLECTOR AND INVESTOR: GOLD DOLLARS AS A SPECIALTY

North Carolina Representative James Iver McKay was among the proponents for the introduction of a gold dollar coin. He introduced a bill to authorize the denomination into the House of Representatives on February 20, 1849.

Forming a specialized collection of gold dollars is a fascinating pursuit, one that has drawn the attention of many numismatists over the years. A complete run of date-and-mintmark issues from 1849 through 1889 includes no impossible rarities, although the 1875, with just 20 Proofs and 400 circulation strikes made, is the key date and can challenge collectors. While the dollars of 1879 through 1889 often have remarkably low mintages, they were saved in quantity, and certain of these dates are easily obtainable (although not necessarily inexpensive).

The branch-mint gold dollars of the early years present a special challenge. Among the Charlotte Mint varieties the 1849 comes with an Open Wreath (of which just five are presently known, with a rumor of a sixth) and with a Close Wreath, the latter being scarce but available. Later Charlotte gold dollars, extending through 1859, range from scarce to rare. The 1857-C is notorious for its poor striking.

Gold dollars were struck at the Dahlonega Mint from 1849 through 1861. In the latter year the facility was under the control of the Confederate States of America, and thus the 1861-D gold dollars, rare in any event, are even more desirable as true Confederate coins. The New Orleans Mint also produced gold dollars, which in general are better struck than those of the Charlotte and Dahlonega mints. From 1854 intermittently to 1860, and then in 1870, gold dollars were struck in San Francisco. These Western issues are usually sharply defined and range from scarce to rare. In particular, choice and gem Mint State pieces are elusive.

LIBERTY HEAD (1849–1854)

Designer: *James B. Longacre.* **Weight:** *1.672 grams.*
Composition: *.900 gold, .100 copper (net weight .04837 oz. pure gold).*
Diameter: *13 mm.* **Edge:** *Reeded.* **Mints:** *Philadelphia,*
Charlotte, Dahlonega, New Orleans, and San Francisco.

| Open Wreath Reverse | Close Wreath Reverse | Proof | Mintmark location is on the reverse, below the wreath. |

History. U.S. Mint chief engraver James Barton Longacre designed the nation's gold dollars. This first type measured 13 mm in diameter, which proved to be inconvenient, and the two later types were enlarged to 15 mm.

Striking and Sharpness. As a rule, Type 1 gold dollars struck in Philadelphia are sharper than those of the Charlotte and Dahlonega mints. On the obverse, check the highest areas of the hair below the coronet. On the reverse, check the wreath and the central two figures in the date. On both sides check the denticles, which can be mushy or indistinct (particularly on Charlotte and Dahlonega coins, which often have planchet roughness as well).

Availability. All dates and mintmarks are readily collectible, save for the 1849-C, Open Wreath, variety. MS coins often are found for the Philadelphia issues but can be elusive for the branch mints. Charlotte and Dahlonega coins often have striking problems. The few gold dollars of this type that are less than VF in grade usually are damaged or have problems. Although a few Proofs were coined in the early years, they are for all practical purposes unobtainable. Only about a dozen are known.

GRADING STANDARDS

MS-60 to 70 (Mint State). *Obverse:* At MS–60 to 62, there is abrasion on the hair below the coronet (an area that can be weakly struck as well) and on the cheeks. Marks may be seen. At MS-63, there may be slight abrasion. Luster is irregular. At MS-64, abrasion is less. Luster is rich on most coins, less so on Charlotte and Dahlonega varieties. At MS-65 and above, luster is deep and frosty. At MS-66 and higher, no marks at all are visible

1854, Close Wreath. Graded MS-62.

without magnification. *Reverse:* On MS–60 to 62 coins, there is abrasion on the 1, the highest parts of the leaves, and the ribbon. Otherwise, the same comments apply as for the obverse.

Illustrated coin: Some friction is visible on the portrait and in the fields.

AU-50, 53, 55, 58 (About Uncirculated). *Obverse:* Light wear on the hair below the coronet and the cheek is very noticeable at AU-50, and progressively less at higher levels to AU-58. Luster is minimal at AU-50 and scattered and incomplete at AU-58. Some tiny nicks and contact marks are to be expected and should be mentioned if they are distracting. *Reverse:* Light wear on the 1, the wreath, and the ribbon characterize an AU-50 coin,

1853-D. Graded AU-58.

progressively less at higher levels to AU-58. Otherwise, the same comments apply as for the obverse.

Illustrated coin: Much of the luster remains, especially in protected areas.

EF-40, 45 (Extremely Fine). *Obverse:* Medium wear is seen on the hair below the coronet, extending to near the bun, and on the curls below. Detail is partially gone on the hair to the right of the coronet. Luster is gone on most coins. *Reverse:* Light wear is seen overall, and the highest parts of the leaves are flat. Luster is gone.

1849-C, Close Wreath. Graded EF-45.

VF-20, 30 (Very Fine). *Obverse:* Most hair detail is gone, except in the lower-relief areas and on the lower curls. Star centers are flat. *Reverse:* The wreath and other areas show more wear. Most detail is gone on the higher-relief leaves.

This gold dollar is seldom collected in grades lower than VF-20.

1851-D. Graded VF-25.

PF-60 to 70 (Proof). *Obverse and Reverse:* PF–60 to 62 coins have extensive hairlines and may have nicks and contact marks. At PF-63, hairlines are prominent, but the mirror surface is very reflective. PF-64 coins have fewer hairlines. At PF-65, hairlines should be minimal and mostly seen only under magnification. One cannot be "choosy" with Proofs of this type, as only a few exist.

1849, Open Wreath. Proof.

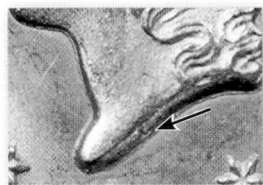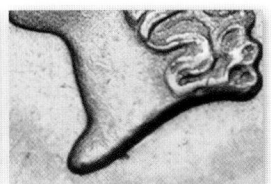

| | 1849, With L | 1849, No L |

	Mintage	Cert	Avg	%MS	VF-20	EF-40	AU-50	AU-55	AU-58	MS-60	MS-63	MS-64	MS-65
													PF-60
1849, Open Wreath, So-Called Small Head, With L (a)	688,567	963	60.9	74%	$215	$250	$285	$300	$350	$900	$1,550	$2,500	$5,000
	Auctions: $1,763, MS-64, June 2015; $705, MS-62, January 2015; $188, AU-58, January 2015; $235, AU-50, July 2015												
1849, Open Wreath, So-Called Small Head, No L (a)	(b)	390	62.2	86%	$250	$300	$375	$400	$475	$1,100	$2,000	$2,750	$5,750
	Auctions: $4,935, MS-65, July 2015; $1,293, MS-63, January 2015; $881, MS-61, February 2015; $823, MS-60, October 2015												
1849, Open Wreath, So-Called Large Head (a)	(b)	0	n/a		$215	$250	$275	$295	$325	$600	$1,250	$2,100	$5,000
	Auctions: $3,760, MS-65, January 2015; $1,495, MS-64, April 2012												
1849, Close Wreath	(b)	482	61.6	80%	$215	$250	$275	$295	$325	$600	$1,250	$2,100	$5,000
	Auctions: $25,850, MS-66, August 2015; $705, MS-62, August 2015; $376, AU-58, August 2015; $329, AU-50, March 2015												
1849, Open Wreath, So-Called Small Head, No L, Proof (c)	unknown	3	62.7						*(extremely rare)*				
	Auctions: No auction records available.												
1849-C, Open Wreath (d)	(b)	2	32.5	0%	$200,000	$225,000	$250,000	$300,000	$450,000	$550,000	$650,000		
	Auctions: $3,220, AU-58, April 2012												
1849-C, Close Wreath	11,634	101	55.9	33%	$1,300	$1,850	$2,800	$3,750	$5,250	$8,500	$16,500	$32,500	
	Auctions: $49,350, MS-64, August 2015; $10,281, MS-62, September 2013; $1,058, AU-50, January 2015; $2,820, EF-45, July 2014												
1849-D, Open Wreath	21,588	0	n/a		$1,350	$2,000	$2,850	$3,250	$3,750	$5,500	$12,500	$21,500	$55,000
	Auctions: $22,325, MS-64, April 2013; $4,465, MS-62, January 2015; $3,760, MS-61, January 2015; $2,585, AU-55, September 2014												
1849-O, Open Wreath	215,000	0	n/a		$245	$325	$425	$550	$600	$1,100	$3,750	$7,000	$12,500
	Auctions: $11,750, MS-65, March 2015; $999, MS-61, September 2015; $423, AU-58, June 2015; $259, EF-45, November 2015												

a. It is now well known that the so-called Small Head and Large Head coins are from the same punch. **b.** Included in 1849, Open Wreath, So-Called Small Head, With L, mintage figure. **c.** 2 to 3 examples are known. **d.** This coin is extremely rare.

	Mintage	Cert	Avg	%MS	VF-20	EF-40	AU-50	AU-55	AU-58	MS-60	MS-63	MS-64	MS-65
													PF-60
1850	481,953	542	59.9	67%	$215	$250	$265	$285	$300	$425	$1,100	$2,000	$5,500
	Auctions: $32,900, MS-67, August 2015; $2,585, MS-64, October 2015; $447, MS-61, June 2015; $235, AU-55, January 2015												
1850, Proof (e)	*unknown*	0	n/a										$100,000
	Auctions: No auction records available.												
1850-C	6,966	80	54.6	25%	$1,350	$1,750	$2,500	$4,250	$6,250	$8,500	$32,500		
	Auctions: $24,675, MS-63, February 2015; $19,975, MS-63, January 2014; $17,625, MS-63, November 2014; $1,939, EF-45, July 2014												
1850-D	8,382	97	54.6	25%	$1,500	$2,000	$3,000	$5,000	$7,250	$11,000	$26,000	$37,500	
	Auctions: $3,290, AU-55, January 2015; $3,204, AU-50, July 2014												
1850-O	14,000	197	58.2	43%	$300	$500	$950	$1,350	$2,000	$3,200	$7,000	$14,500	
	Auctions: $2,532, MS-61, April 2012												
1851	3,317,671	4,468	61.1	80%	$215	$250	$265	$285	$300	$425	$800	$1,000	$3,750
	Auctions: $3,995, MS-66, July 2015; $329, MS-61, January 2015; $229, AU-55, April 2015; $1,528, EF-45, September 2015												
1851-C	41,267	398	57.2	34%	$1,250	$1,550	$2,000	$2,250	$2,550	$3,200	$6,250	$12,500	$25,000
	Auctions: $5,376, MS-63, January 2015; $3,525, MS-62, June 2015; $2,468, AU-58, March 2015; $2,056, AU-55, January 2015												
1851-D	9,882	139	58.0	41%	$1,500	$1,800	$2,450	$2,750	$3,250	$5,000	$15,500	$22,500	$45,000
	Auctions: $14,688, MS-64, October 2014; $7,638, MS-62, February 2015; $4,113, AU-58, October 2014; $2,233, AU-50, March 2015												
1851-O	290,000	900	58.5	46%	$235	$285	$350	$425	$450	$850	$2,250	$5,500	$9,500
	Auctions: $12,925, MS-65, August 2015; $764, MS-61, January 2015; $270, AU-55, November 2015; $194, EF-45, January 2015												
1852	2,045,351	4,023	61.2	80%	$215	$250	$265	$285	$300	$425	$800	$1,000	$3,750
	Auctions: $4,700, MS-66, July 2015; $470, MS-63, August 2015; $259, AU-58, May 2015; $235, AU-55, August 2015												
1852-C	9,434	150	57.2	41%	$1,500	$1,850	$2,100	$2,750	$3,000	$4,250	$11,500	$16,500	$30,000
	Auctions: $15,863, MS-64, February 2013; $2,128, AU-55, October 2014; $2,585, AU-53, July 2014; $1,880, EF-40, July 2015												
1852-D	6,360	107	56.4	26%	$1,500	$2,000	$2,600	$3,600	$4,850	$8,750	$27,500		
	Auctions: $4,230, AU-58, February 2015; $4,994, AU-55, July 2014; $4,230, EF-45, January 2015												
1852-O	140,000	475	56.9	33%	$240	$285	$450	$700	$850	$1,400	$4,250	$10,500	$22,500
	Auctions: $37,600, MS-65, August 2015; $2,497, MS-63, January 2015; $541, AU-58, January 2015; $237, AU-53, June 2015												
1853	4,076,051	10,644	61.2	81%	$215	$250	$265	$285	$300	$425	$800	$1,000	$3,750
	Auctions: $20,575, MS-67, August 2015; $881, MS-64, February 2015; $353, MS-61, August 2015; $235, AU-55, November 2015												
1853-C	11,515	130	57.0	37%	$1,350	$1,600	$2,100	$2,600	$3,500	$4,750	$13,500	$26,000	$40,000
	Auctions: $14,100, MS-64, January 2014; $4,406, MS-62, August 2014; $9,988, MS-62, October 2014; $1,593, EF-40, July 2014												
1853-D	6,583	132	57.7	30%	$1,400	$1,850	$2,500	$4,250	$5,500	$8,750	$26,000	$35,000	$55,000
	Auctions: $17,038, MS-63, June 2015; $8,225, MS-62, June 2015; $6,933, MS-61, January 2015; $3,055, AU-55, October 2014												
1853-O	290,000	1,285	59.5	57%	$235	$255	$335	$425	$450	$825	$2,150	$5,000	$11,000
	Auctions: $23,500, MS-66, August 2015; $1,058, MS-62, January 2015; $259, AU-55, June 2015; $212, AU-50, February 2015												
1854	855,502	3,749	61.5	86%	$215	$250	$265	$285	$300	$425	$800	$1,000	$3,750
	Auctions: $19,975, MS-67, August 2015; $5,170, MS-66, August 2015; $376, MS-62, November 2015; $282, AU-55, October 2015												
1854, Proof	*unknown*	0	n/a		*(unique, in the Bass Foundation Collection)*								
	Auctions: No auction records available.												
1854-D	2,935	75	56.1	33%	$1,850	$2,450	$4,750	$6,500	$7,750	$11,500	$35,000	$65,000	
	Auctions: $7,638, MS-61, October 2015; $6,465, AU-58, July 2015; $5,640, AU-58, January 2015; $4,113, EF-45, July 2014												
1854-S	14,632	148	58.5	39%	$400	$550	$950	$1,150	$1,350	$2,500	$5,750	$13,500	$30,000
	Auctions: $56,400, MS-65, August 2015; $2,820, MS-62, January 2015; $1,528, AU-58, January 2015; $1,058, AU-53, February 2015												

e. 2 examples are known.

INDIAN PRINCESS HEAD, SMALL HEAD (1854–1856)

Designer: *James B. Longacre.* **Weight:** *1.672 grams.*
Composition: *.900 gold, .100 copper (net weight .04837 oz. pure gold).* **Diameter:** *15 mm.*
Edge: *Reeded.* **Mints:** *Philadelphia, Charlotte, Dahlonega, New Orleans, San Francisco.*

Circulation Strike

*Mintmark location
is on the reverse,
below the wreath.*

Proof

History. The Type 2 gold dollar, with the diameter increased from 13 mm to 15 mm, was first made in 1854. The headdress is decorated with *ostrich* plumes, which would not have been used in any genuine Native American headgear. The design proved difficult to strike, leading to its modification in 1856.

Striking and Sharpness. On the obverse, check the highest area of the hair below the coronet and the tips of the feathers. Check the letters. On the reverse, check the ribbon bow knot and in particular the two central digits of the dates. Examine the digits on both sides. Nearly all have problems. This type is often softly struck in the centers, with weak hair detail and the numerals 85 in the date sometimes faint— this should not be confused with wear. The 1855-C and 1855-D coins are often poorly struck and on rough planchets.

Availability. All Type 2 gold dollars are collectible, but the Charlotte and Dahlonega coins are rare. With patience, Full Details coins are available of 1854, 1855, and 1856-S, but virtually impossible to find for the branch-mint issues of 1855. The few gold dollars of this type that are less than VF in grade usually are damaged or have problems. Proofs exist of the 1854 and 1855 issues, but were made in very small quantities.

GRADING STANDARDS

MS-60 to 70 (Mint State). *Obverse:* At MS–60 to 62, there is abrasion on the hair below the band lettered LIBERTY (an area that can be weakly struck as well), on the tips of the feather plumes, and throughout the field. Contact marks may also be seen. At MS-63, there should be only slight abrasions. Luster is irregular. At MS-64, abrasions and marks are less. Luster is rich on most coins, less so on Charlotte and Dahlonega issues. At

1854. Graded MS-61.

MS-65 and above, luster is deep and frosty, with no marks at all visible without magnification at MS-66 and higher. *Reverse:* At MS–60 to 62, there may be abrasions on the 1, on the highest parts of the leaves, on the ribbon knot, and in the field. Otherwise, the same comments apply as for the obverse.

Illustrated coin: Some loss of luster is evident in the fields, but strong luster remains among the letters and in other protected areas. Good eye appeal is elusive for this type.

AU-50, 53, 55, 58 (About Uncirculated). *Obverse:* Light wear on the hair below the coronet, the cheek, and the tips of the feather plumes is very noticeable at AU-50, progressively less at higher levels to AU-58. Luster is minimal at AU-50 and scattered and incomplete at AU-58. Some tiny nicks and contact marks are to be expected and should be mentioned if they are distracting. *Reverse:* Light wear on the 1, the wreath, and the ribbon knot characterize an AU-50 coin, progressively less at higher levels to AU-58. Otherwise, the same comments apply as for the obverse.

1855. Graded AU-55.

Illustrated coin: This coin was lightly struck at the center. Clash marks appear on both sides, most prominent within the wreath on the reverse.

EF-40, 45 (Extremely Fine). *Obverse:* Medium wear is seen on the hair below the coronet and on the feather plume tips. Detail is partially gone on the hair, although the usual light striking may make this moot. Luster is gone on most coins. *Reverse:* Light wear is seen overall, and the highest parts of the leaves are flat. Luster is gone on most coins.

Illustrated coin: This coin was lightly struck at the centers, but overall has extraordinary quality.

1855-C. Graded EF-40.

VF-20, 30 (Very Fine). *Obverse:* Most hair detail is gone, except at the back of the lower curls. The feather plume ends are flat. *Reverse:* The wreath and other areas show more wear. Most detail is gone on the higher-relief leaves.

This gold dollar is seldom collected in grades lower than VF-20.

Illustrated coin: This coin is well worn, but has an exceptionally bold date, indicating that it must have been a very sharp strike.

1854. Graded VF-25.

PF-60 to 70 (Proof). *Obverse and Reverse:* PF–60 to 62 coins have extensive hairlines and may have nicks and contact marks. At PF-63, hairlines are prominent, but the mirror surface is very reflective. PF-64 coins have fewer hairlines. At PF-65, hairlines should be minimal and mostly seen only under magnification. There should be no nicks or marks. PF-66 and higher coins have no marks or hairlines visible to the unaided eye.

1854. Graded PF-66.

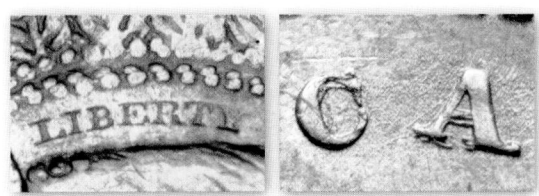

1854, Doubled-Die Obverse
FS-G1-1854-1101.

	Mintage	Cert	Avg	%MS	VF-20	EF-40	AU-50	AU-55	MS-60	MS-62	MS-63	MS-64	MS-65
											PF-63	PF-64	PF-65
1854	783,943	5,823	57.3	28%	$350	$500	$600	$725	$1,700	$3,000	$6,500	$12,000	$27,500
Auctions: $51,700, MS-66, August 2015; $1,880, MS-62, January 2015; $402, AU-53, October 2015; $329, EF-40, August 2015													
1854, Doubled-Die Obverse (a)	(b)	13	55.9	8%					$2,500	$5,500	$7,500	$12,500	
Auctions: $3,738, MS-62, December 2011													
1854, Proof	4 known	5	64.6								$200,000	$300,000	$425,000
Auctions: $218,500, PF-64DCam, March 2009													
1855	758,269	5,391	57.2	29%	$350	$500	$600	$725	$1,700	$3,000	$6,500	$12,000	$27,500
Auctions: $54,050, MS-66, August 2015; $4,230, MS-63, January 2015; $640, AU-58, February 2015; $529, EF-40, April 2015													
1855, Proof	unknown	6	64.8								$165,000	$225,000	$325,000
Auctions: $397,800, PF, September 2013													
1855-C	9,803	186	51.5	9%	$1,850	$4,000	$8,500	$12,500	$26,000	$40,000			
Auctions: $24,675, MS-61, January 2015; $7,638, AU-55, June 2015; $5,611, AU-50, June 2015; $4,230, EF-40, June 2015													
1855-D	1,811	41	53.3	12%	$8,500	$15,000	$25,000	$27,500	$50,000	$65,000	$100,000	$165,000	
Auctions: $164,500, MS-64, August 2015; $8,225, AU-50, July 2015; $52,875, EF-45, July 2014													
1855-O	55,000	507	54.8	14%	$575	$1,000	$1,700	$2,500	$8,000	$15,000	$32,500	$45,000	
Auctions: $3,525, AU-58, June 2015; $2,585, AU-55, January 2015; $1,998, AU-50, July 2015; $705, VF-25, January 2015													
1856-S	24,600	212	54.7	16%	$950	$1,450	$2,250	$3,250	$7,500	$15,000	$28,500	$47,500	
Auctions: $52,875, MS-64, February 2013; $5,640, AU-58, January 2015; $3,290, AU-58, January 2015; $282, VF-20, August 2015													

a. Check for strong doubling on UNITED STATES OF AMERICA, the beads in the headdress, the feathers, and portions of LIBERTY.
b. Included in circulation-strike 1854 mintage figure.

INDIAN PRINCESS HEAD, LARGE HEAD (1856–1889)

Designer: *James B. Longacre.* **Weight:** *1.672 grams.*
Composition: *.900 gold, .100 copper (net weight .04837 oz. pure gold).* **Diameter:** *15 mm.*
Edge: *Reeded.* **Mints:** *Philadelphia, Charlotte, Dahlonega, and San Francisco.*

Circulation Strike   **Proof**

History. The design of the Indian Princess Head was modified in 1856. The new Type 3 portrait is larger and in shallower relief. After this change, most (but not all) gold dollars were struck with strong detail. Gold dollars of this type did not circulate extensively after 1861, except in the West. As they did not see heavy use, today most pieces are EF or better. MS coins are readily available, particularly of the dates 1879 through 1889 (during those years the coins were popular among investors and speculators, and many were saved). These gold dollars were very popular with jewelers, who would purchase them at a price of $1.50 for use in a variety of ornaments.

Striking and Sharpness. These dollars usually are well struck, but many exceptions exist. Charlotte and Dahlonega coins are usually weak in areas and can have planchet problems. On all coins, check the hair details on the obverse. The word LIBERTY may be only partially present or missing completely, as the dies were made this way for some issues, particularly in the 1870s; this does not affect their desirability. On the reverse, check the ribbon knot and the two central date numerals. Check the denticles on both sides. Copper stains are sometimes seen on issues of the 1880s due to incomplete mixing of the alloy. Many coins of the 1860s onward have highly prooflike surfaces.

Availability. All Type 3 gold dollars are collectible, but many issues are scarce. Most MS-65 or finer coins are dated from 1879 to 1889. The few gold dollars of this type that are less than VF usually are damaged or have problems. Proofs were made of all years. Most range from rare to very rare, some dates in the 1880s being exceptions. Some later dates have high Proof mintages, but likely many of these coins were sold to the jewelry trade (as the Mint was reluctant to release circulation strikes to this market sector). Such coins were incorporated into jewelry and no longer exist as collectible coins.

GRADING STANDARDS

MS-60 to 70 (Mint State). *Obverse:* At MS–60 to 62, there is abrasion on the hair below the band lettered LIBERTY (an area that can be weakly struck as well), on the tips of the feather plumes, and throughout the field. Contact marks may also be seen. At MS-63, there should be only slight abrasions. Luster is irregular. At MS-64, abrasions and marks are less. Luster is rich on most coins, less so on Charlotte and Dahlonega issues. At

1878. Graded MS-67.

MS-65 and above, luster is deep and frosty, with no marks at all visible without magnification at MS-66 and higher. *Reverse:* At MS-60 to 62, there may be abrasions on the 1, on the highest parts of the leaves, on the ribbon knot, and in the field. Otherwise, the same comments apply as for the obverse.

Illustrated coin: This exceptionally high-grade coin has superb eye appeal.

AU-50, 53, 55, 58 (About Uncirculated). *Obverse:* Light wear on the hair below the coronet, the cheek, and the tips of the feather plumes is very noticeable at AU-50, progressively less at higher levels to AU-58. Luster is minimal at AU-50 and scattered and incomplete at AU-58. Some tiny nicks and contact marks are to be expected and should be mentioned if they are distracting. *Reverse:* Light wear on the 1, the wreath, and the ribbon

1857-C. Graded AU-58.

knot characterize an AU-50 coin, progressively less at higher levels to AU-58. Otherwise, the same comments apply as for the obverse.

Illustrated coin: The obverse field is slightly bulged. This coin is lightly struck at the center, unusual for most Type 3 gold dollars, but sometimes seen on Charlotte and Dahlonega varieties. Among 1857-C gold dollars this coin is exceptional. Most have poor striking and/or planchet problems.

EF-40, 45 (Extremely Fine). *Obverse:* Medium wear is seen on the hair below the coronet and on the feather plume tips. Detail is partially gone on the hair, although the usual light striking may make this moot. Luster is gone on most coins. *Reverse:* Light wear is seen overall, and the highest parts of the leaves are flat. Luster is gone on most coins.

1859-S. Graded EF-40.

VF-20, 30 (Very Fine). *Obverse:* Most hair detail is gone, except at the back of the lower curls. The feather plume ends are flat. *Reverse:* The wreath and other areas show more wear. Most detail is gone on the higher-relief leaves.

This gold dollar is seldom collected in grades lower than VF-20.

Illustrated coin: This coin is lightly struck at the center obverse, as well as at the U and IC in the border lettering. It is lightly struck at the center of the reverse.

1859-D. Graded VF-20.

PF-60 to 70 (Proof). *Obverse and Reverse:* PF-60 to 62 coins have extensive hairlines and may have nicks and contact marks. At PF-63, hairlines are prominent, but the mirror surface is very reflective. PF-64 coins have fewer hairlines. At PF-65, hairlines should be minimal and mostly seen only under magnification. There should be no nicks or marks. PF-66 and higher coins have no marks or hairlines visible to the unaided eye.

1884. Graded PF-68.

Illustrated coin: This splendid cameo Proof is one of the finest graded.

	Mintage	Cert	Avg	%MS	VF-20	EF-40	AU-50	AU-55	MS-60	MS-62	MS-63	MS-64	MS-65
											PF-63	PF-64	PF-65
1856, All kinds	1,762,936												
1856, Upright 5		326	59.0	49%	$275	$300	$375	$450	$650	$850	$1,500	$2,000	$7,500
	Auctions: $16,450, MS-66, July 2015; $1,998, MS-64, September 2015; $447, MS-61, September 2015; $259, AU-55, September 2015												
1856, Slant 5		1,416	59.3	55%	$245	$250	$265	$285	$575	$650	$900	$1,150	$2,850
	Auctions: $42,300, MS-68, August 2015; $400, MS-62, January 2015; $306, AU-58, June 2015; $212, AU-50, November 2015												
1856, Slant 5, Proof	*unknown*	5	66.0								$30,000	$35,000	$65,000
	Auctions: $30,550, PF, January 2013												
1856-D	1,460	34	55.5	15%	$3,750	$5,750	$8,000	$11,000	$27,500	$42,500	$80,000		
	Auctions: $11,750, AU-58, September 2013; $7,050, EF-45, July 2014												

1862, Doubled-Die Obverse
FS-G1-1862-101.

	Mintage	Cert	Avg	%MS	VF-20	EF-40	AU-50	AU-55	MS-60	MS-62	MS-63	MS-64	MS-65
											PF-63	PF-64	PF-65
1857	774,789	1,273	60.1	64%	$245	$250	$265	$285	$575	$650	$900	$1,200	$2,850
Auctions: $51,700, MS-68, August 2015; $823, MS-64, October 2015; $353, MS-61, September 2015; $329, AU-50, October 2015													
1857, Proof	unknown	6	64.8								$17,500	$20,000	$38,500
Auctions: $16,100, PF-63Cam, June 2008													
1857-C	13,280	153	53.8	7%	$1,350	$1,750	$3,000	$5,000	$11,000	$20,000	—		
Auctions: $8,813, MS-61, January 2015; $3,290, AU-55, March 2015; $3,102, AU-55, January 2015; $3,055, EF-45, January 2015													
1857-D	3,533	96	55.3	17%	$1,500	$2,400	$3,750	$4,850	$10,000	$15,000			
Auctions: $5,581, AU-58, April 2013; $3,525, AU-53, October 2014; $2,238, EF-45, July 2014													
1857-S	10,000	112	54.2	15%	$450	$750	$1,250	$2,000	$5,750	$8,500	$20,000	$35,000	
Auctions: $3,995, MS-61, January 2015; $3,775, MS-61, June 2015; $2,350, AU-55, July 2014; $999, AU-53, January 2015													
1858	117,995	243	60.1	62%	$245	$250	$265	$285	$575	$650	$950	$1,400	$5,000
Auctions: $51,700, MS-68, August 2015; $1,410, MS-63, September 2015; $282, AU-55, July 2015; $235, AU-53, January 2015													
1858, Proof	unknown	14	64.5								$13,500	$15,000	$30,000
Auctions: $32,900, PF-66Cam+, November 2014; $79,313, PF, March 2014													
1858-D	3,477	108	55.4	29%	$1,500	$2,250	$3,750	$4,750	$8,500	$12,500	$19,500	$37,500	$60,000
Auctions: $7,638, MS-61, December 2013; $4,230, AU-58, February 2015; $1,439, AU-50, September 2014; $1,998, EF-45, July 2014													
1858-S	10,000	101	54.2	12%	$385	$675	$1,300	$1,750	$5,500	$9,000	$15,000	$18,500	$30,000
Auctions: $25,850, MS-64, August 2015; $7,050, MS-62, June 2015; $4,348, MS-61, August 2015; $852, AU-50, January 2015													
1859	168,244	405	60.6	72%	$245	$250	$255	$285	$575	$675	$900	$1,100	$2,500
Auctions: $37,600, MS-68, August 2015; $1,998, MS-65, August 2015; $376, MS-61, August 2015; $282, AU-58, January 2015													
1859, Proof	80	13	64.8								$10,000	$12,000	$17,500
Auctions: $22,325, PF-64, August 2013													
1859-C	5,235	78	57.0	28%	$1,400	$2,000	$3,500	$6,000	$10,000	$15,000	$25,000		
Auctions: $15,275, MS-63, June 2015; $5,640, AU-58, June 2015; $4,465, AU-55, July 2015; $2,585, AU-50, August 2015													
1859-D	4,952	109	57.0	29%	$1,600	$2,250	$3,250	$4,750	$8,750	$12,000	$22,500	$32,500	$55,000
Auctions: $11,750, MS-62, June 2013; $3,290, AU-55, July 2014; $3,055, AU-53, February 2015; $911, AU-50, November 2014													
1859-S	15,000	150	52.2	10%	$300	$575	$1,250	$1,900	$5,000	$8,500	$15,000	$24,000	
Auctions: $6,169, MS-62, February 2013; $3,760, MS-61, January 2015; $1,469, AU-58, June 2015; $306, EF-40, September 2015													
1860	36,514	163	61.2	80%	$245	$250	$275	$300	$575	$675	$1,250	$2,250	$7,500
Auctions: $10,869, MS-65, August 2015; $881, MS-63, September 2015; $646, MS-61, August 2015; $329, AU-55, February 2015													
1860, Proof	154	19	64.8								$8,000	$10,000	$15,000
Auctions: $27,600, PF-66, January 2012													
1860-D	1,566	65	54.9	20%	$3,000	$4,250	$7,500	$9,750	$18,500	$27,500	$50,000	$70,000	
Auctions: $42,300, MS-64, February 2013; $11,750, AU-50, June 2015; $6,463, EF-40, July 2014													
1860-S	13,000	150	56.2	27%	$350	$500	$775	$1,100	$2,650	$4,000	$6,000	$12,500	$30,000
Auctions: $31,725, MS-65, August 2015; $1,998, MS-61, January 2015; $1,116, AU-55, January 2015; $317, AU-50, October 2015													
1861	527,150	1,439	61.3	84%	$245	$250	$265	$285	$575	$675	$750	$1,400	$2,500
Auctions: $32,900, MS-67, August 2015; $2,585, MS-65, September 2015; $494, MS-61, January 2015; $212, EF-45, January 2015													
1861, Proof	349	16	64.8								$8,000	$11,000	$15,000
Auctions: $17,625, PF-65Cam, October 2014													
1861-D	1,250	27	58.1	37%	$22,500	$30,000	$40,000	$57,500	$72,500	$85,000	$115,000	$135,000	$185,000
Auctions: $111,625, MS-63, June 2013; $70,500, MS-61, January 2015; $30,550, EF-45, July 2014													
1862	1,361,355	3,019	61.7	88%	$245	$250	$265	$285	$575	$650	$750	$1,100	$2,250
Auctions: $25,850, MS-67, August 2015; $4,230, MS-66, August 2015; $353, MS-61, April 2015; $223, AU-55, January 2015													
1862, DblDie Obv (a)	(b)	17	61.6	82%	$750	$1,500	$2,000	$2,500	$4,000	$4,750	$5,750		
Auctions: $675, MS-62, February 2011; $447, AU-50, April 2015													

a. Doubling, visible on the entire obverse, is most evident on the tops of the hair curls and the feathers. **b.** Included in circulation-strike 1862 mintage figure.

	Mintage	Cert	Avg	%MS	VF-20	EF-40	AU-50	AU-55	MS-60	MS-62	MS-63 PF-63	MS-64 PF-64	MS-65 PF-65
1862, Proof	35	19	64.9								$8,000	$11,000	$17,000
Auctions: $7,475, PF-63UCam, April 2008													
1863	6,200	36	61.5	75%	$1,350	$2,000	$3,250	$4,500	$6,000	$8,750	$10,500	$13,500	$22,500
Auctions: $193,875, MS-68, August 2015; $10,575, MS-64, October 2014; $8,813, MS-63, April 2013; $5,434, AU-55, July 2014													
1863, Proof	50	18	65.2								$9,000	$12,500	$20,000
Auctions: $58,750, PF, February 2013													
1864	5,900	70	61.3	79%	$500	$850	$1,350	$1,500	$2,000	$2,750	$4,500	$6,500	$10,000
Auctions: $70,500, MS-68, August 2015; $705, MS-60, October 2014; $1,293, AU-55, July 2014; $235, AU-50, March 2015													
1864, Proof	50	14	64.2								$9,000	$12,500	$20,000
Auctions: $32,200, PF-66UCam, October 2011													
1865	3,725	40	62.5	85%	$600	$900	$1,100	$1,350	$2,000	$2,750	$4,750	$5,500	$10,000
Auctions: $15,275, MS-66, August 2015; $12,925, MS-65, July 2015; $3,055, MS-61, October 2014; $1,116, EF-45, July 2014													
1865, Proof	25	13	65.2								$9,000	$12,500	$20,000
Auctions: $25,300, PF-65, August 2011													
1866	7,100	75	62.3	84%	$400	$500	$750	$900	$1,250	$1,550	$2,150	$3,000	$5,000
Auctions: $23,500, MS-67, August 2015; $4,700, MS-66, January 2015; $1,175, MS-62, January 2015; $646, AU-55, January 2015													
1866, Proof	30	19	65.4								$9,000	$12,500	$20,000
Auctions: $27,600, PF-67UCam, August 2007													
1867	5,200	76	61.5	71%	$450	$525	$700	$850	$1,200	$1,500	$2,000	$2,750	$5,000
Auctions: $9,400, MS-66, August 2015; $1,763, MS-63, January 2015; $1,058, MS-61, January 2015; $823, MS-60, February 2015													
1867, Proof	50	13	63.5								$7,500	$12,500	$20,000
Auctions: $19,975, PF-66Cam, August 2014													
1868	10,500	126	61.0	79%	$285	$425	$525	$625	$1,000	$1,500	$2,000	$2,750	$4,500
Auctions: $35,250, MS-68, August 2015; $5,940, MS-66, June 2015; $881, MS-61, October 2015; $329, MS-60, May 2015													
1868, Proof	25	9	64.4								$7,500	$14,000	$20,000
Auctions: $29,900, PF-66UCam+, August 2011													
1869	5,900	91	61.6	82%	$350	$475	$700	$800	$1,150	$1,600	$2,250	$2,750	$5,500
Auctions: $42,300, MS-68, August 2015; $2,115, MS-64, January 2015; $1,293, MS-62, September 2015; $940, AU-58, January 2015													
1869, Proof	25	10	64.0								$7,500	$12,500	$20,000
Auctions: $19,975, PF-65Cam, April 2014													
1870	6,300	112	61.6	77%	$325	$450	$675	$750	$1,000	$1,500	$2,000	$2,750	$5,500
Auctions: $18,800, MS-67, August 2015; $1,410, MS-63, January 2015; $676, MS-61, July 2015; $588, AU-58, September 2015													
1870, Proof	35	9	62.6								$7,500	$12,500	$20,000
Auctions: $17,625, PF-64, January 2014													
1870-S	3,000	56	60.0	61%	$500	$825	$1,250	$1,750	$2,750	$4,000	$8,000	$12,500	$27,500
Auctions: $35,250, MS-68, August 2015; $3,878, MS-62, January 2015; $3,525, AU-58, September 2015; $1,293, AU-50, January 2015													
1871	3,900	119	62.2	88%	$315	$450	$575	$675	$900	$1,100	$1,900	$2,250	$4,000
Auctions: $35,250, MS-68, August 2015; $823, MS-61, October 2014; $412, MS-60, September 2014; $852, AU-58, July 2014													
1871, Proof	30	4	66.3								$8,000	$12,500	$20,000
Auctions: $27,600, PF-65DCam, November 2011													
1872	3,500	72	60.6	72%	$315	$525	$575	$700	$1,000	$1,250	$2,250	$3,000	$5,000
Auctions: $14,100, MS-67, August 2015; $1,528, MS-63, October 2015; $764, AU-58, January 2015; $517, AU-55, June 2015													
1872, Proof	30	15	64.2								$8,000	$12,500	$20,000
Auctions: $4,888, PF-61, March 2011													
1873, Close 3	1,800	114	60.4	70%	$425	$750	$1,100	$1,150	$1,700	$2,500	$4,250	$7,500	$15,000
Auctions: $1,529, MS-62, August 2015; $1,293, MS-61, April 2015; $1,183, MS-61, September 2015; $832, AU-58, June 2015													
1873, Open 3	123,300	2,219	61.8	91%	$245	$250	$265	$285	$525	$675	$800	$950	$2,000
Auctions: $35,250, MS-68, August 2015; $1,410, MS-64, January 2015; $541, MS-63, August 2015; $353, MS-60, June 2015													
1873, Close 3, Proof	25	6	63.0								$15,000	$22,500	$35,000
Auctions: $30,550, PF-65, August 2014													
1874	198,800	3,846	62.2	94%	$245	$250	$265	$285	$525	$650	$700	$800	$1,350
Auctions: $10,575, MS-68, October 2015; $940, MS-65, January 2015; $341, MS-61, June 2015; $259, AU-53, June 2015													

	Mintage	Cert	Avg	%MS	VF-20	EF-40	AU-50	AU-55	MS-60	MS-62	MS-63	MS-64	MS-65
											PF-63	PF-64	PF-65
1874, Proof	20	7	64.4								$12,000	$15,000	$25,000
Auctions: $12,650, PF-64UC+, August 2010													
1875	400	32	61.3	81%	$2,750	$4,500	$5,500	$6,500	$8,500	$10,000	$17,500	$25,000	$40,000
Auctions: $76,375, MS-66, August 2015; $22,325, MS-64, April 2013; $2,820, MS-60, October 2014; $5,875, AU-53, July 2014													
1875, Proof	20	11	64.1								$18,500	$30,000	$40,000
Auctions: $55,813, PF-66DCam, November 2013													
1876	3,200	144	61.5	78%	$325	$375	$500	$600	$750	$1,000	$1,350	$1,500	$3,500
Auctions: $28,200, MS-67, October 2015; $940, MS-62, July 2014; $588, AU-55, September 2014; $646, AU-50, October 2014													
1876, Proof	45	17	64.7								$7,000	$11,000	$15,000
Auctions: $34,075, PF-66DCam, June 2013; $16,450, PF-65DCam, September 2014													
1877	3,900	180	62.1	84%	$300	$375	$525	$600	$800	$1,000	$1,400	$1,550	$3,500
Auctions: $12,338, MS-67, August 2015; $541, AU-58, June 2015; $423, AU-55, August 2015; $329, AU-55, January 2015													
1877, Proof	20	16	64.7								$8,000	$11,000	$15,000
Auctions: $7,638, PF, February 2014													
1878	3,000	150	61.8	87%	$300	$350	$525	$600	$775	$900	$1,200	$1,450	$3,250
Auctions: $32,900, MS-67, August 2015; $2,849, MS-65, August 2015; $1,175, MS-62, October 2014; $764, MS-61, July 2014													
1878, Proof	20	13	64.3								$7,500	$11,000	$15,000
Auctions: $19,550, PF-65DCam, January 2012													
1879	3,000	206	63.4	93%	$265	$300	$325	$375	$650	$800	$1,150	$1,300	$2,750
Auctions: $5,640, MS-67, July 2015; $4,113, MS-66, August 2015; $1,175, MS-64, January 2015; $270, AU-55, January 2015													
1879, Proof	30	9	64.3								$6,500	$10,500	$15,000
Auctions: $8,225, PF, August 2013													
1880	1,600	297	65.5	99%	$265	$300	$325	$375	$575	$700	$1,000	$1,150	$2,350
Auctions: $8,813, MS-68, January 2015; $7,050, MS-68, June 2015; $2,849, MS-67, August 2015; $2,585, MS-66, January 2015													
1880, Proof	36	30	64.5								$5,500	$10,500	$12,000
Auctions: $18,800, PF-65DCam, February 2013													
1881	7,620	385	64.8	97%	$250	$285	$325	$375	$575	$700	$1,000	$1,150	$2,350
Auctions: $12,925, MS-68, August 2015; $2,644, MS-67, October 2015; $1,645, MS-66, October 2015; $517, MS-63, March 2015													
1881, Proof	87	27	64.7								$5,000	$8,500	$12,500
Auctions: $2,820, PF-60, September 2014; $19,975, PF, March 2014													
1882	5,000	211	64.3	97%	$250	$285	$325	$375	$575	$700	$1,000	$1,150	$2,350
Auctions: $16,450, MS-68, August 2015; $1,998, MS-66, September 2015; $1,645, MS-66, August 2015; $646, MS-62, July 2014													
1882, Proof	125	35	65.3								$5,000	$8,500	$11,500
Auctions: $20,563, PF-67UCam, January 2015; $8,813, PF-64DCam, November 2014; $15,275, PF, August 2013													
1883	10,800	490	64.1	97%	$250	$285	$350	$400	$575	$700	$1,000	$1,150	$2,350
Auctions: $18,800, MS-68, August 2015; $4,230, MS-67, September 2015; $3,055, MS-64, January 2015; $564, MS-62, January 2015													
1883, Proof	207	49	65.0								$5,000	$8,000	$11,500
Auctions: $9,400, PF-65Cam, February 2013													
1884	5,230	227	63.4	97%	$250	$285	$325	$375	$575	$700	$1,000	$1,150	$2,350
Auctions: $8,225, MS-68, July 2015; $3,995, MS-67, June 2015; $705, MS-64, January 2015; $588, MS-62, June 2015													
1884, Proof	1,006	63	65.3								$5,000	$6,750	$10,500
Auctions: $29,250, PF, September 2013													
1885	11,156	453	63.6	95%	$250	$285	$325	$375	$575	$700	$1,000	$1,150	$2,350
Auctions: $7,638, MS-68, June 2015; $1,763, MS-66, June 2015; $1,175, MS-65, October 2015; $235, AU-55, January 2015													
1885, Proof	1,105	113	64.9								$5,000	$6,750	$10,500
Auctions: $16,450, PF-66, August 2015; $9,400, PF-65Cam, July 2014; $28,200, PF, August 2013													
1886	5,000	316	63.2	97%	$250	$285	$325	$375	$575	$700	$1,000	$1,150	$1,800
Auctions: $4,113, MS-67, January 2015; $1,645, MS-65, February 2015; $470, MS-61, July 2015; $282, AU-50, January 2015													
1886, Proof	1,016	72	64.4								$5,000	$6,750	$10,500
Auctions: $18,800, PF-67Cam, August 2014; $13,513, PF-67Cam, January 2015; $14,100, PF-66Cam, January 2015													

	Mintage	Cert	Avg	%MS	VF-20	EF-40	AU-50	AU-55	MS-60	MS-62	MS-63	MS-64	MS-65
											PF-63	PF-64	PF-65
1887	7,500	479	63.8	99%	$250	$285	$325	$375	$575	$675	$825	$1,000	$1,750
	Auctions: $35,250, MS-68, August 2015; $1,645, MS-66, October 2015; $494, MS-63, January 2015; $306, MS-60, November 2015												
1887, Proof	1,043	61	64.7								$5,000	$6,750	$10,500
	Auctions: $10,575, PF-65DCam, September 2013; $10,288, PF-65Cam+, October 2014; $4,700, PF-64Cam, January 2015												
1888	15,501	729	63.8	98%	$250	$285	$325	$375	$575	$650	$700	$800	$1,350
	Auctions: $15,275, MS-68, August 2015; $2,961, MS-67, July 2015; $1,645, MS-66, January 2015; $881, MS-64, February 2015												
1888, Proof	1,079	94	64.5								$5,000	$6,750	$10,500
	Auctions: $18,800, PF-66DCam, April 2013												
1889	28,950	1,974	64.2	98%	$250	$285	$325	$375	$575	$650	$700	$800	$1,350
	Auctions: $8,225, MS-68, August 2015; $3,055, MS-67, July 2015; $764, MS-64, January 2015; $400, MS-62, October 2015												
1889, Proof	1,779	35	64.2								$5,000	$6,750	$10,500
	Auctions: $12,925, PF-66Cam, April 2013												

Gold Quarter Eagles ($2.50) 1796–1929

AN OVERVIEW OF GOLD QUARTER EAGLES

The quarter eagle, denominated at one-fourth of an eagle, or $2.50, was authorized by the Act of April 2, 1792. Early types in the series range from rare to very rare. The first, the 1796 without stars on the obverse, Heraldic Eagle motif on the reverse, is a classic, one of the most desired of all pieces needed for a type set, and accordingly expensive. Most examples are in such grades as EF and AU.

Quarter eagles with stars on the obverse and with the Heraldic Eagle reverse were produced from 1796 intermittently through 1807. Today they exist in modest numbers, particularly in grades such as EF and AU, but on an absolute basis are fairly rare.

The standalone 1808 Draped Bust type, by John Reich, of which only 2,710 were minted, is the rarest single type coin in the entire American copper, nickel, silver, and gold series, possibly excepting the 1839 Gobrecht dollar (in a different category, as Proof restrikes were made). Examples of the 1808 can be found in various grades from VF through AU, and only rarely higher.

The next style of quarter eagle, from 1821 through 1827, is scarce, but when seen is usually in grades such as EF, AU, or even the low levels of Mint State. The same can be said for the modified quarter eagle of 1829 through early 1834.

Finally, with the advent of the Classic Head in late 1834, continuing through 1839, quarter eagles become more readily available. Examples can be found in nearly any grade from VF into the lower levels of Mint State. Then come the Liberty Head quarter eagles, minted continuously from 1840 through 1907, in sufficient numbers and for such a long time that it is not difficult to obtain an example to illustrate the type, with choice and gem Mint State coins being plentiful for the dates of the early 20th century.

The last quarter eagles are of the Indian Head type, minted from 1908 through 1929. These pieces are plentiful today, but grading can be difficult, as they were struck in sunken relief and the highest part on the coin is the field (this area was immediately subject to contact marks and wear). Although many opportunities exist in the marketplace, a collector should approach a purchase with care, seeking an example that has frosty, lustrous fields.

FOR THE COLLECTOR AND INVESTOR: GOLD QUARTER EAGLES AS A SPECIALTY

Collecting quarter eagles by dates, mintmarks, and major varieties is a very appealing pursuit. Although many are scarce and rare—this description applies to any variety from 1796 through early 1834—none are truly impossible to obtain. Among the Classic Head issues of 1834–1839, branch-mint coins are especially scarce in higher grades.

Liberty Head quarter eagles, produced continuously from 1840 through 1907, include a number of key issues, such as the famous 1854-S (usually seen in well-circulated grades), the Proof-only 1863 (of which only 30 were struck), and a number of elusive mintmarks. Of particular interest is the 1848 coin with CAL. counterstamped on the reverse, signifying that the coin was made from gold bullion brought to the Philadelphia Mint in a special shipment from California.

CAPPED BUST TO RIGHT (1796–1807)

Designer: *Robert Scot.* **Weight:** *4.37 grams.* **Composition:** *.9167 gold, .0833 silver and copper.*
Diameter: *Approximately 20 mm.* **Edge:** *Reeded.* **Mint:** *Philadelphia.*

No Stars on Obverse (1796)
Bass-Dannreuther–2.

Stars on Obverse (1796–1807)
Bass-Dannreuther–3.

History. The first quarter eagles were struck intermittently during the late 1790s and early 1800s, with consistently small mintages. The earliest issues of 1796 lack obverse stars. They likely circulated domestically, rather than being exported in international trade.

Striking and Sharpness. Most have light striking in one area or another. On the obverse, check the hair details and the stars. On the reverse, check the shield, stars, and clouds. Examine the denticles on both sides. Planchet adjustment marks (from a coin's overweight planchet being filed down to correct specifications) are seen on many coins and are not noted by the certification services. On high-grade coins the luster usually is very attractive. Certain reverse dies of this type were also used to make dimes of the era, which were almost exactly the same diameter.

Availability. Most Capped Bust to Right quarter eagles in the marketplace are EF or AU. MS coins are elusive; when seen, they usually are of later dates.

GRADING STANDARDS

MS-60 to 70 (Mint State). *Obverse:* At MS-60, some abrasion and contact marks are evident, most noticeably on the hair to the left of Miss Liberty's forehead and on the higher-relief areas of the cap. On the No Stars quarter eagles, there is some abrasion in the field—more so than the With Stars coins, on which the field is more protected. Luster is present, but may be dull or lifeless, and

1802, 2 Over 1. Graded MS-61.

interrupted in patches. At MS-63, contact marks are few, and abrasion is very light. An MS-65 coin will have hardly any abrasion, and contact marks are so minute as to require magnification. Luster should be full and rich. Coins grading above MS-65 exist more in theory than in reality for this type—but they do exist, and are defined by having fewer marks as perfection is approached. *Reverse:* Comments apply as for the obverse, except that abrasion and contact marks are most noticeable on the upper part of the eagle and the clouds. The field area is complex; there is not much open space, with stars above the eagle, the arrows and olive branch, and other features. Accordingly, marks are not as noticeable as on the obverse.

Illustrated coin: Some friction appears on the higher areas of this example, but the fields retain nearly full luster, and the coin overall has nice eye appeal.

AU-50, 53, 55, 58 (About Uncirculated).

Obverse: Light wear is seen on the cheek, the hair immediately to the left of the face, and the cap, more so at AU-50 than at AU–53 or 55. An AU-58 coin has minimal traces of wear. An AU-50 coin has luster in protected areas among the stars and letters, with little in the open fields or on the portrait. At AU-58 most luster is present in the fields, but is worn away on the highest parts of the motifs. The

1796, No Stars; BD-2. Graded AU-58.

1796 No Stars type has less luster in any given grade. *Reverse:* Comments as for Mint State, except that the eagle's neck, the tips and top of the wings, the clouds, and the tail now show noticeable wear, as do other features. Luster ranges from perhaps 40% remaining in protected areas at AU-50 to nearly full mint bloom at AU-58. Often the reverse of this type retains much more luster than does the obverse.

EF-40, 45 (Extremely Fine). *Obverse:* Wear

is evident all over the portrait, with some loss of detail in the hair to the left of Miss Liberty's face. Excellent detail remains in low-relief areas of the hair, such as the front curl and the back of the head. The stars show wear, as do the date and letters. Luster, if present at all, is minimal and in protected areas. *Reverse:* Wear is greater than at the About Uncirculated level. The neck lacks feather detail on its

1802; BD-1. Graded EF-45.

highest points. Feathers have lost some detail near the edges of the wings, and some areas of the horizontal lines in the shield may be blended together. Some traces of luster may be seen, more so at EF-45 than at EF-40. Overall, the reverse appears to be in a slightly higher grade than the obverse.

VF-20, 30 (Very Fine). *Obverse:* The

higher-relief areas of hair are well worn at VF-20, less so at VF-30. The stars are flat at their centers. *Reverse:* Wear is greater, including on the shield and wing feathers. The star centers are flat. Other areas have lost detail as well. E PLURIBUS UNUM is easy to read.

The Capped Bust to Right quarter eagle is seldom collected in grades lower than VF-20.

1796, With Stars; BD-3. Graded VF-30.

	Mintage	Cert	Avg	%MS	F-12	VF-20	EF-40	AU-50	AU-55	AU-58	MS-60	MS-63	MS-64
1796, No Stars on Obverse	963	34	57.3	35%	$42,500	$65,000	$95,000	$120,000	$150,000	$200,000	$250,000	$500,000	$750,000 (a)
Auctions: $64,625, EF-40, August 2014; $94,000, VF-30, December 2013													
1796, Stars on Obverse	432	25	58.3	48%	$35,000	$47,500	$70,000	$95,000	$130,000	$165,000	$185,000	$400,000	$600,000 (b)
Auctions: $102,813, AU-58, March 2014; $223,250, AU-58, November 2014													
1797	427	16	49.5	13%	$18,500	$27,500	$40,000	$72,500	$125,000	$150,000	$187,500	$235,000	$375,000
Auctions: $105,750, AU-53, April 2013													

a. Value in MS-65 is $1,600,000. **b.** Value in MS-65 is $1,600,000.

1798, Close Date	1798, Wide Date	1804, 13-Star Reverse	1804, 14-Star Reverse

	Mintage	Cert	Avg	%MS	F-12	VF-20	EF-40	AU-50	AU-55	AU-58	MS-60	MS-63	MS-64
1798, All kinds	1,094												
1798, Close Date		20	57.3	30%				$30,000	$43,500	$55,000	$67,500	$125,000	
Auctions: $18,800, AU-50, August 2014													
1798, Wide Date	(c)							$30,000	$43,500	$55,000	$67,500	$125,000	
Auctions: $70,500, AU-58, November 2014; $44,063, AU-50, June 2014													
1802	3,035	73	56.5	34%	$6,000	$8,500	$13,000	$17,500	$20,000	$23,500	$32,500	$75,000	$200,000
Auctions: $20,563, AU-58, August 2014; $21,150, AU-58, March 2013; $16,450, AU-50, August 2014; $15,275, EF-45, August 2014													
1804, 13-Star Reverse	(d)	3	50.0	0%	$75,000	$100,000	$125,000	$325,000	$500,000	$650,000			
Auctions: $322,000, AU-58, July 2009													
1804, 14-Star Reverse	3,327	61	53.0	18%	$5,250	$9,000	$14,000	$18,000	$21,000	$25,000	$35,000	$150,000	
Auctions: $44,063, MS-62, April 2014; $70,501, MS-62, November 2014; $21,738, AU-58, November 2014; $19,975, AU-55, August 2014													
1805	1,781	54	54.9	31%	$5,750	$9,500	$14,000	$18,000	$21,000	$23,500	$32,500	$125,000	
Auctions: $32,900, MS-60, March 2015; $20,563, AU-58, August 2014; $23,500, AU-55, November 2014; $14,100, AU-53, October 2014													
1806, 6 Over 4, 8 Stars Left, 5 Right	1,136	26	53.6	35%	$5,750	$9,500	$14,000	$18,000	$21,000	$23,500	$32,500	$150,000	
Auctions: $30,550, MS-61, June 2014; $22,325, AU-58, August 2014; $21,150, AU-58, August 2014; $20,563, AU-58, October 2014													
1806, 6 Over 5, 7 Stars Left, 6 Right	480	15	57.2	47%	$12,000	$15,000	$20,000	$40,000	$57,500	$67,500	$95,000	$275,000	
Auctions: $67,563, AU-About Uncirculated, February 2014													
1807	6,812	115	55.7	37%	$5,750	$8,500	$13,250	$17,000	$20,000	$23,500	$32,500	$75,000	$175,000 (e)
Auctions: $44,063, MS-62, March 2014; $24,675, AU-58, March 2015; $17,625, AU-55, August 2014; $11,750, AU-50, November 2014													

c. Included in certified population for 1798, Close Date. **d.** Included in 1804, 14-Star Reverse, mintage figure. **e.** Value in MS-65 is $300,000.

DRAPED BUST TO LEFT, LARGE SIZE (1808)

Designer: *John Reich.* **Weight:** *4.37 grams.* **Composition:** *.9167 gold, .0833 silver and copper.* **Diameter:** *Approximately 20 mm.* **Edge:** *Reeded.*

History. John Reich's Draped Bust was an adaptation of the design introduced in 1807 on the half dollar. On the quarter eagle it was used for a single year only, with fewer than 3,000 coins struck, making it the rarest of the major gold coin types (indeed, the rarest of any U.S. coin type).

Striking and Sharpness. All examples are lightly struck on one area or another, particularly the stars and rims. The rims are low and sometimes missing or nearly so (on the obverse), causing quarter eagles of this type to wear more quickly than otherwise might be the case. Sharpness of strike is overlooked by most buyers.

Availability. Examples are rare in any grade. Typical grades are EF and AU. Lower grades are seldom seen, as the coins did not circulate to any great extent. Gold coins of this era were not seen in circulation after 1821, so they did not get a chance to acquire significant wear.

GRADING STANDARDS

MS-60 to 70 (Mint State). *Obverse:* At MS-60, some abrasion and contact marks are seen on the cheek, on the hair below the LIBERTY inscription, and on the highest-relief folds of the cap. Luster is present, but may be dull or lifeless, and interrupted in patches. At MS-63, contact marks are few, and abrasion is very light. Abrasion is even less at MS-64. (Discussion of such high grades in these early coins starts to enter the realm of

1808; BD-1. Graded MS-63.

theory.) Quarter eagles of this type are almost, but not quite, non-existent in a combination of high grade and nice eye appeal. *Reverse:* Comments apply as for the obverse, except that abrasion is most noticeable on the eagle's neck and highest area of the wings.

Illustrated coin: Superbly struck, this coin is a "poster example" with few peers.

AU-50, 53, 55, 58 (About Uncirculated). *Obverse:* Light wear is seen on the cheek and higher-relief areas of the hair and cap. Friction and scattered marks are in the field, ranging from extensive at AU-50 to minimal at AU-58. The low rim affords little protection to the field of this coin, but the stars in relief help. Luster may be seen in protected areas, minimal at AU-50, but less so at AU-58. At AU-58 the field retains some lus-

1808. Graded AU-50.

ter as well. *Reverse:* Comments are as for a Mint State coin, except that the eagle's neck, the top of the wings, the leaves, and the arrowheads now show noticeable wear, as do other features. Luster ranges from perhaps 40% remaining in protected areas at AU-50 to nearly full mint bloom at AU-58. Often the reverse of this type retains much more luster than does the obverse, as on this type the motto, eagle, and lettering protect the surrounding flat areas.

Illustrated coin: Note some lightness of strike.

EF-40, 45 (Extremely Fine). *Obverse:* More wear is seen on the portrait, the hair, the cap, and the drapery near the clasp. Luster is likely to be absent on the obverse due to the low rim. *Reverse:* Wear is more extensive on the eagle, including the top of the wings, the head, the top of the shield, and the claws. Some traces of luster may be seen in protected areas, more so at EF-45 than at EF-40.

1808. Graded EF-40.

VF-20, 30 (Very Fine). *Obverse:* Wear on the portrait has reduced the hair detail, especially to the right of the face and the top of the head, but much can still be seen. *Reverse:* Wear on the eagle is greater, and details of feathers near the shield and near the top of the wings are weak or missing. All other features show wear, but most are fairly sharp. Generally, Draped Bust gold coins at this grade level lack eye appeal.

1808. Graded VF-20.

The Draped Bust to Left, Large Size, quarter eagle is seldom collected in grades lower than VF-20.

Illustrated coin: This is a nice, problem-free example of a lower but very desirable grade for this rare issue.

	Mintage	Cert	Avg	%MS	F-12	VF-20	EF-40	AU-50	AU-55	AU-58	MS-60	MS-62	MS-63	MS-64
1808	2,710	46	54.6	33%	$30,000	$45,000	$60,000	$90,000	$105,000	$120,000	$150,000	$275,000	$450,000	$750,000
	Auctions: $126,900, MS-60, January 2013; $80,781, AU-55, August 2014													

CAPPED HEAD TO LEFT (1821–1834)

Designer: *John Reich.* **Weight:** *4.37 grams.* **Composition:** *.9167 gold, .0833 silver and copper.* **Diameter:** *1821–1827—approximately 20 mm; 1829–1834—approximately 18.2 mm.* **Edge:** *Reeded.* **Mint:** *Philadelphia.*

Circulation Strike
BD-1.

Proof

History. Capped Head to Left quarter eagles dated 1821 through 1827 have a larger diameter and larger letters, dates, and stars than those of 1829 to 1834. The same grading standards apply to both. Gold coins of this type did not circulate in commerce, because their face value was lower than their bullion value. Many legislators, who had the option to draw their pay in specie (silver and gold coinage), took advantage of this fact to sell their salaries at a premium for paper money. Most wear was due to use as pocket pieces, or from minor handling.

Striking and Sharpness. Most Capped Head to Left quarter eagles are well struck. On the obverse, check the hair details (which on the Large Diameter style can be light in areas) and the stars. On the reverse, check the eagle. On both sides inspect the denticles. Fields are often semi-prooflike on higher grades.

Availability. All Capped Head to Left quarter eagles are rare. Grades typically range from EF to MS, with choice examples in the latter category being scarce, and gems being very rare. Proof coins were made on a limited basis for presentation and for sale to numismatists. All Proof examples are exceedingly rare today, and are usually encountered only when great collections are dispersed.

GRADING STANDARDS

MS-60 to 70 (Mint State). *Obverse:* At MS-60, some abrasion and contact marks are seen on the cheek, on the hair below the LIBERTY inscription, and on the highest-relief folds of the cap. Luster is present, but may be dull or lifeless, and interrupted in patches. At MS-63, contact marks are few, and abrasion is very light. Abrasion is even less at MS-64. (Discussion of such high grades in these early coins starts to enter the realm of theory.) Quarter eagles of this type are almost, but not quite, non-existent in a combination of high grade and nice eye appeal. *Reverse:* Comments apply as for the obverse, except that abrasion is most noticeable on the eagle's neck and highest area of the wings.

1827, BD-1. Graded MS-65.

Illustrated coin: This is a well-struck lustrous gem.

AU-50, 53, 55, 58 (About Uncirculated). *Obverse:* Light wear is seen on the cheek and higher-relief areas of the hair and cap. Friction and scattered marks are in the field, ranging from extensive at AU-50 to minimal at AU-58. The low rim affords little protection to the field of this coin, but the stars in relief help. Luster may be seen in protected areas, minimal at AU-50, but less so at AU-58. At AU-58 the field retains some luster as well.

1833; BD-1. Graded AU-53.

Reverse: Comments are as for a Mint State coin, except that the eagle's neck, the top of the wings, the leaves, and the arrowheads now show noticeable wear, as do other features. Luster ranges from perhaps 40% remaining in protected areas at AU-50 to nearly full mint bloom at AU-58. Often the reverse of this type retains much more luster than does the obverse, as on this type the motto, eagle, and lettering protect the surrounding flat areas.

EF-40, 45 (Extremely Fine). *Obverse:* More wear is seen on the portrait, the hair, the cap, and the drapery near the clasp. Luster is likely to be absent on the obverse due to the low rim. *Reverse:* Wear is more extensive on the eagle, including the top of the wings, the head, the top of the shield, and the claws. Some traces of luster may be seen in protected areas, more so at EF-45 than at EF-40.

1821; BD-1. Graded EF-40.

The Capped Head to Left quarter eagle is seldom collected in grades lower than EF-40.

PF-60 to 70 (Proof). *Obverse and Reverse:*

PF–60 to 62 coins have extensive hairlines and may have nicks and contact marks. At PF-63, hairlines are prominent, but the mirror surface is very reflective. PF-64 coins have fewer hairlines. At PF-65, hairlines should be minimal and mostly seen only under magnification. There should be no nicks or marks. PF-66 and higher coins should have no marks or hairlines visible to the unaided eye.

1824, 4 Over 1. Proof.

	Mintage	Cert	Avg	%MS	F-12	VF-20	EF-40	AU-50	AU-55	AU-58	MS-60	MS-63 / PF-63	MS-65 / PF-64
1821	6,448	20	57.4	40%	$6,750	$9,000	$13,500	$16,000	$17,500	$23,500	$35,000	$75,000	
Auctions: $44,063, MS-62, March 2014													
1821, Proof	3–5	3	64.7									$275,000	$450,000
Auctions: $241,500, PF-64Cam, January 2007													
1824, 4 Over 1	2,600	30	56.7	37%	$6,750	$9,500	$14,000	$16,500	$18,750	$25,000	$35,000	$80,000	
Auctions: $18,800, AU-58, August 2013													
1824, 4 Over 1, Proof	3–5	0	n/a		*(unique, in the Smithsonian's National Numismatic Collection)*								
Auctions: No auction records available.													
1825	4,434	49	58.8	55%	$6,750	$8,000	$13,000	$15,500	$17,500	$23,500	$32,500	$65,000	
Auctions: $141,000, MS-65, November 2014; $105,750, MS-64, March 2014; $38,188, MS-62, July 2014; $32,900, MS-61, August 2014													
1825, Proof (a)	unknown	0	n/a										
Auctions: No auction records available.													
1826, 6 Over 6	760	7	55.0	0%	$10,000	$12,500	$17,000	$25,000	$32,500	$40,000	$62,500		
Auctions: $44,063, AU-58, August 2014; $45,531, AU-55, September 2013; $27,025, AU-55, November 2014													
1826, 6 Over 5, Proof (b)	unknown	0	n/a										
Auctions: No auction records available.													
1827	2,800	23	58.6	65%	$6,500	$9,500	$13,100	$17,500	$19,500	$32,500	$35,000	$65,000	
Auctions: $58,750, MS-63, September 2014; $21,150, AU-58, August 2014; $28,200, AU-55, February 2013													
1827, Proof (c)	unknown	0	n/a										
Auctions: No auction records available.													
1829	3,403	44	60.0	64%	$6,000	$7,500	$9,500	$13,000	$17,000	$18,500	$24,000	$35,000	$100,000
Auctions: $41,125, MS-63, June 2013; $12,925, AU-55, August 2014													
1829, Proof	2–4	0	n/a		*(extremely rare; 2–3 known)*								
Auctions: No auction records available.													
1830	4,540	46	60.1	52%	$6,000	$7,500	$9,500	$13,000	$17,000	$18,500	$24,000	$35,000	$85,000
Auctions: $29,375, MS-63, November 2013; $24,675, MS-62, November 2014; $22,913, MS-62, November 2014													
1830, Proof (d)	unknown	0	n/a										
Auctions: No auction records available.													
1831	4,520	65	60.3	66%	$6,000	$7,500	$9,500	$13,000	$17,000	$18,500	$24,000	$35,000	$85,000
Auctions: $28,200, MS-63, September 2014; $18,800, AU-58, February 2013; $15,863, AU-58, August 2014													
1831, Proof	6–10	2	64.5									$100,000	$150,000
Auctions: $30,550, PF-60, September 2013													
1832	4,400	41	57.0	41%	$6,000	$7,500	$9,500	$13,000	$17,000	$18,500	$24,000	$37,500	—
Auctions: $21,150, MS-61, March 2014; $22,913, MS-61, August 2014; $15,275, AU-58, August 2014; $12,338, AU-55, August 2014													
1832, Proof	2–4	0	n/a		*(unique, in the Bass Foundation Collection)*								
Auctions: No auction records available.													

a. The 1825 quarter eagle might not exist in Proof; see the *Encyclopedia of U.S. Gold Coins, 1795–1933.* **b.** Proofs have been reported, but none have been authenticated. **c.** Proof 1827 quarter eagles almost certainly were made, but none are known to exist. **d.** Examples identified as Proofs are extremely rare, many are impaired, and none have been certified.

	Mintage	Cert	Avg	%MS	F-12	VF-20	EF-40	AU-50	AU-55	AU-58	MS-60	MS-63	MS-65
												PF-63	PF-64
1833	4,160	45	59.2	53%	$6,000	$7,500	$9,500	$13,000	$17,000	$18,500	$24,000	$35,000	$95,000
Auctions: $41,125, MS-63, August 2013; $15,275, AU-58, August 2014													
1833, Proof	2–4	0	n/a					*(extremely rare; 3–4 known)*					
Auctions: No auction records available.													
1834, With Motto	4,000	8	54.4	13%	$10,000	$15,000	$20,000	$30,000	$40,000	$45,000	$60,000	$125,000	
Auctions: $19,975, AU-50, November 2014; $64,625, EF-45, August 2014													
1834, With Motto, Proof	4–8	0	n/a					*(extremely rare; 3–5 known)*					
Auctions: No auction records available.													

CLASSIC HEAD, NO MOTTO ON REVERSE (1834–1839)

Designer: *William Kneass.* **Weight:** *4.18 grams.*
Composition: *.8992 gold, .1008 silver and copper (changed to .900 gold in 1837).*
Diameter: *18.2 mm.* **Edge:** *Reeded.* **Mints:** *Philadelphia, Charlotte, Dahlonega, and New Orleans.*

Circulation Strike
Breen-6151.

*Mintmark location
is on the obverse,
above the date.*

Proof

History. Gold quarter eagles had not circulated at face value in the United States since 1821, as the price of bullion necessitated more than $2.50 worth of gold to produce a single coin. Accordingly, they traded at their bullion value. The Act of June 28, 1834, provided lower weights for gold coins, after which the issues (of new designs to differentiate them from the old) circulated effectively. The Classic Head design by William Kneass is an adaptation of the head created by John Reich for the cent of 1808. The reverse illustrates a perched eagle. The motto E PLURIBUS UNUM, seen on earlier gold coins, no longer is present. These coins circulated widely until mid-1861 (for this reason, many show extensive wear). After that, they were hoarded by the public because of financial uncertainty during the Civil War.

Striking and Sharpness. Weakness is often seen on the higher areas of the hair curls. Also check the star centers. On the reverse, check the rims. The denticles usually are well struck.

Availability. Most coins range from VF to AU or lower ranges of MS. Most MS coins are of the first three years. MS-63 to 65 examples are rare. Good eye appeal can be elusive. Proofs were made in small quantities, and today probably only a couple dozen or so survive, most bearing the 1834 date.

GRADING STANDARDS

MS-60 to 70 (Mint State). *Obverse:* At MS-60, some abrasion and contact marks are seen on the portrait, most noticeably on the cheek, as the hair details are complex on this type. Luster is present, but may be dull or lifeless, and interrupted in patches. Many low-level Mint State coins have grainy surfaces. At MS-63, contact marks are few, and abrasion is very light. Abrasion is even less at MS-64. An MS-65 coin has hardly any abrasion, and contact marks are minute. Luster should be full and rich and is often more intense on the

1834. Graded MS-65.

obverse. Grades above MS-65 are defined by having fewer marks as perfection is approached. *Reverse:* Comments apply as for the obverse, except that abrasion is most noticeable on the eagle's neck and the highest area of the wings.

Illustrated coin: This coin is especially well struck.

AU-50, 53, 55, 58 (About Uncirculated). *Obverse:* Friction is seen on the higher parts, particularly the cheek and hair (under magnification) of Miss Liberty. Friction and scattered marks are in the field, ranging from extensive at AU-50 to minimal at AU-58. Luster may be seen in protected areas, minimal at AU-50 but more visible at AU-58. On an AU-58 coin the field retains some luster as well. *Reverse:* Comments as for Mint State,

1837. Graded AU-55.

except that the eagle's neck, the top of the wings, the leaves, and the arrowheads now show noticeable wear, as do other features. Luster ranges from perhaps 40% remaining in protected areas at AU-50 to nearly full mint bloom at AU-58. Often the reverse of this type retains much more luster than does the obverse.

Illustrated coin: The coin has light wear overall, but traces of luster can be seen here and there.

EF-40, 45 (Extremely Fine). *Obverse:* Wear is seen on the portrait overall, with reduction or elimination of some separation of hair strands, especially in the area close to the face. The cheek shows light wear. Luster is minimal or nonexistent at EF-40, and may survive in among the letters of LIBERTY at EF-45. *Reverse:* Wear is greater than on an About Uncirculated coin. On most (but not all) coins the eagle's neck lacks some feather

1834. Graded EF-40.

detail on its highest points. Feathers have lost some detail near the edges and tips of the wings. Some areas of the horizontal lines in the shield may be blended together. Some traces of luster may be seen, more so at EF-45 than at EF-40.

Illustrated coin: This coin is well struck.

VF-20, 30 (Very Fine). *Obverse:* Wear on the portrait has reduced the hair detail, especially to the right of the face and the top of the head, but much can still be seen. *Reverse:* Wear is greater, including on the shield and wing feathers. Generally, Classic Head gold at this grade level lacks eye appeal.

The Classic Head quarter eagle is seldom collected in grades lower than VF-20.

Illustrated coin: This coin was lightly

1836. Graded VF-30.

cleaned. It is lightly struck at the centers, although at this grade level that is not important.

PF-60 to 70 (Proof). *Obverse and Reverse:* PF–60 to 62 coins have extensive hairlines and may have nicks and contact marks. At PF-63, hairlines are prominent, but the mirror surface is very reflective. PF-64 coins have fewer hairlines. At PF-65, hairlines should be minimal and mostly seen only under magnification. There should be no nicks or marks. PF-66 and higher coins should have no marks or hairlines visible to the unaided eye.

1836. Graded PF-65 Cameo.

1836, Script 8

1836, Block 8

	Mintage	Cert	Avg	%MS	F-12	VF-20	EF-40	AU-50	AU-55	AU-58	MS-60	MS-63	MS-65
											PF-60	PF-63	PF-65
1834, No Motto	112,234	1,004	56.2	32%	$365	$600	$800	$1,300	$1,650	$2,250	$3,500	$10,000	$42,500
Auctions: $3,525, MS-61, February 2015; $1,645, AU-58, June 2015; $1,293, AU-50, June 2015; $794, EF-40, January 2015													
1834, No Motto, Proof	15–25	6	64.3								$35,000	$100,000	$275,000
Auctions: $138,000, PF-64Cam, January 2011													
1835	131,402	318	54.1	29%	$365	$600	$800	$1,300	$1,650	$2,350	$3,800	$10,000	$50,000
Auctions: $7,050, MS-63, January 2015; $1,770, AU-58, August 2015; $1,528, AU-55, June 2015; $1,116, AU-53, July 2015													
1835, Proof	5–8	1	65.0								$35,000	$100,000	$300,000
Auctions: No auction records available.													
1836, All kinds	547,986												
1836, Script 8 (a)		514	51.8	21%	$365	$600	$800	$1,300	$1,650	$2,250	$3,500	$10,500	$42,500
Auctions: $7,638, MS-63, September 2015; $3,055, MS-61, October 2015; $1,424, AU-50, June 2015; $423, VF-30, January 2015													
1836, Block 8		463	50.3	16%	$365	$600	$800	$1,300	$1,650	$2,250	$3,500	$10,500	$42,500
Auctions: $9,400, MS-64, January 2015; $3,290, MS-61, September 2015; $999, AU-50, October 2015; $764, EF-45, January 2015													
1836, Proof	5–8	7	65.0								$35,000	$115,000	$300,000
Auctions: $195,500, PF-64Cam, April 2012													
1837	45,080	267	52.3	18%	$385	$625	$1,200	$2,000	$2,500	$3,500	$5,250	$13,500	$55,000
Auctions: $11,750, MS-63, January 2014; $2,585, MS-60, August 2014; $3,055, AU-58, November 2014; $1,528, AU-50, October 2014													
1837, Proof (b)	3–5	2	64.5								$32,500	$125,000	$350,000
Auctions: No auction records available.													
1838	47,030	288	53.4	23%	$385	$625	$1,000	$1,500	$1,750	$2,600	$4,250	$11,500	$47,500
Auctions: $2,468, AU-58, August 2015; $1,469, AU-55, August 2015; $1,058, AU-50, January 2015; $541, VF-35, January 2015													
1838, Proof	2–4	0	n/a		*(unique, in the Bass Foundation Collection)*								
Auctions: No auction records available.													
1838-C	7,880	65	55.6	18%	$1,450	$2,500	$3,800	$8,000	$11,750	$16,000	$26,500	$50,000	
Auctions: $7,050, AU-53, August 2014; $3,055, AU-50, June 2015; $6,756, EF-40, January 2015; $2,350, EF-40, January 2014													

Note: So-called 9 Over 8 varieties for Philadelphia, Charlotte, and Denver mints were made from defective punches. **a.** Also known as the "Head of 1835." **b.** Two Proofs of 1837 are known; one is in the Smithsonian's National Numismatic Collection. A third example has been rumored, but its existence is not verified.

	Mintage	Cert	Avg	%MS	F-12	VF-20	EF-40	AU-50	AU-55	AU-58	MS-60	MS-63	MS-65
											PF-60	PF-63	PF-65
1839	27,021	87	52.2	14%	$400	$650	$1,300	$2,250	$2,900	$5,500	$6,500	$19,500	
	Auctions: $28,200, MS-61, August 2013; $4,700, AU-58, January 2015; $3,701, AU-58, January 2015; $1,116, AU-50, June 2015												
1839, Proof (c)	4–6	1	62.0					*(extremely rare)*					
	Auctions: $136,679, PF-62, August 2006												
1839-C	18,140	217	52.7	8%	$1,400	$2,350	$3,250	$5,000	$7,500	$15,000	$22,500	$55,000	
	Auctions: $7,403, MS-60, January 2015; $7,050, AU-55, June 2015; $2,585, AU-50, July 2015; $3,878, VF-30, January 2015												
1839-D	13,674	113	48.8	11%	$1,500	$2,500	$4,250	$8,500	$10,000	$17,500	$27,500	$50,000	
	Auctions: $105,750, MS-64, January 2013; $19,975, AU-58, November 2014; $8,813, $6,756, AU-50, August 2014; $4,230, VF-30, February 2015												
1839-O	17,781	318	53.0	19%	$650	$950	$1,500	$2,500	$3,800	$6,000	$8,500	$25,000	
	Auctions: $32,900, MS-64, September 2015; $11,163, AU-58, August 2015; $3,995, AU-53, July 2015; $2,350, EF-45, August 2015												

c. Three Proofs of 1839 are reported to exist; only two are presently accounted for.

LIBERTY HEAD (1840–1907)

Designer: *Christian Gobrecht.* **Weight:** *4.18 grams.*
Composition: *.900 gold, .100 copper (net weight .12094 oz. pure gold).* **Diameter:** *18 mm.*
Edge: *Reeded.* **Mints:** *Philadelphia, Charlotte, Dahlonega, New Orleans, and San Francisco.*

Circulation Strike

Mintmark location is on the reverse, above the denomination.

Proof

History. The Liberty Head quarter eagle debuted in 1840 and was a workhorse of American commerce for decades, being minted until 1907. Christian Gobrecht's design closely follows those used on half eagles and eagles of the same era.

In 1848, about 230 ounces of gold were sent to Secretary of War William L. Marcy by Colonel R.B. Mason, military governor of California. The gold was turned over to the Philadelphia Mint and made into quarter eagles. The distinguishing mark CAL. was punched above the eagle on the reverse of these coins, while they were in the die. Several pieces with prooflike surfaces are known.

A modified reverse design (with smaller letters and arrowheads) was used on Philadelphia quarter eagles from 1859 through 1907, and on San Francisco issues of 1877, 1878, and 1879. A few Philadelphia Mint pieces were made in 1859, 1860, and 1861 with the old Large Letters reverse design.

Striking and Sharpness. On the obverse, check the highest points of the hair, and the star centers. On the reverse, check the eagle's neck, and the area to the lower left of the shield and the lower part of the eagle. Examine the denticles on both sides. Branch-mint coins struck before the Civil War often are lightly struck in areas and have weak denticles. Often, a certified EF coin from the Dahlonega or Charlotte mint will not appear any sharper than a VF coin from Philadelphia. There are exceptions, and some C and D coins are sharp. The careful study of photographs is useful in acquainting you with the peculiarities of a given date or mint. Most quarter eagles from the 1880s to 1907 are sharp in all areas. Tiny copper staining spots (from improperly mixed alloy) can be a problem. Cameo contrast is the rule for Proofs prior to 1902, when the portrait was polished in the die (a few years later cameo-contrast coins were again made).

Availability. Early dates and mintmarks are generally scarce to rare in MS and very rare in MS–63 to 65 or finer, with only a few exceptions. Coins of Charlotte and Dahlonega (all of which are especially avidly collected) are usually EF or AU, or overgraded low MS. Rarities for the type include 1841, 1854-S, and 1875. Coins of the 1860s onward generally are seen with sharper striking and in higher average grades. Typically, San Francisco quarter eagles are in lower average grades than are those from the Philadelphia Mint, as Philadelphia coins did not circulate at par in the East and Midwest from late December 1861 until December 1878, and thus did not acquire as much wear. MS coins are readily available for the early-1900s years, and usually have outstanding eye appeal. Proofs exist relative to their original mintages; all prior to the 1890s are rare.

Note: Values of common-date gold coins have been based on the current bullion price of gold, $1,150 per ounce, and may vary with the prevailing spot price.

Grading Standards

MS-60 to 70 (Mint State). *Obverse:* At MS-60, some abrasion and contact marks are evident, most noticeably on the hair to the right of Miss Liberty's forehead, and on the jaw. Luster is present, but may be dull or lifeless, and interrupted in patches. At MS-63, contact marks are few, and abrasion is very light. An MS-65 coin has hardly any abrasion, and contact marks are so minute as to require magnification. Luster should be full and rich.

1859-S. Graded MS-65.

Grades above MS-65 are usually found late in the series and are defined by having fewer marks as perfection is approached. *Reverse:* Comments apply as for the obverse, except that abrasion and contact marks are most noticeable on the eagle's neck and to the lower left of the shield.

   Illustrated coin: Sharply struck, bright, and with abundant luster and great eye appeal, this is a "just right" coin for the connoisseur.

AU-50, 53, 55, 58 (About Uncirculated). *Obverse:* Light wear is seen on the face, the hair to the right of the face, and the highest area of the hair bun, more so at AU-50 than at AU–53 or 55. An AU-58 coin has minimal traces of wear. An AU-50 coin has luster in protected areas among the stars and letters, with little in the open fields or on the portrait. At AU-58, most luster is present in the fields, but is worn away on the highest parts

1855-D. Graded AU-55.

of the motifs. *Reverse:* Comments apply as for the preceding, except that the eagle shows wear in all of the higher areas, as well as the leaves and arrowheads. Luster ranges from perhaps 40% remaining in protected areas at AU-50 to nearly full mint bloom at AU-58. Often the reverse of this type retains more luster than the obverse.

   Illustrated coin: The example has the bold rims often seen on Dahlonega Mint coins of this denomination.

EF-40, 45 (Extremely Fine). *Obverse:* Wear is evident on all high areas of the portrait, including the hair to the right of the forehead, the tip of the coronet, and the hair bun. The stars show light wear at their centers. Luster, if present at all, is minimal and in protected areas such as between the star points. *Reverse:* Wear is greater than on an AU coin. The eagle's neck is nearly smooth, much detail is lost on the right wing, and there is flatness at the lower left of the shield, and on the leaves and arrowheads. Traces of luster may be seen, more so at EF-45 than at EF-40. Overall, the reverse appears to be in a slightly higher grade than the obverse.

1860-C. Graded EF-40.

Illustrated coin: This is an attractive coin with medium wear.

VF-20, 30 (Very Fine). *Obverse:* The higher-relief areas of hair are worn flat at VF-20, less so at VF-30. The hair to the right of the coronet is merged into heavy strands. The stars are flat at their centers. *Reverse:* Much of the eagle is flat, with less than 50% of the feather detail remaining. The vertical shield stripes, being deeply recessed, remain bold.

The Liberty Head quarter eagle is seldom collected in grades lower than VF-20.

1843-O, Small Date, Crosslet 4. Graded VF-20.

PF-60 to 70 (Proof). *Obverse and Reverse:* PF–60 to 62 coins have extensive hairlines and may have nicks and contact marks. At PF-63, hairlines are prominent, but the mirror surface is very reflective. PF-64 coins have fewer hairlines; PF-65, minimal hairlines mostly seen only under magnification, and no nicks or marks. PF-66 and higher coins should have no marks or hairlines visible to the unaided eye.

1895. Graded PF-66.

Illustrated coin: This is an exceptional gem in rich yellow-orange gold.

	Mintage	Cert	Avg	%MS	VF-20	EF-40	AU-50	AU-55	AU-58	MS-60	MS-62	MS-63 PF-63
1840	18,859	103	50.0	13%	$350	$850	$2,400	$3,000	$4,250	$6,000	$8,000	$11,000 (a)
Auctions: $2,468, AU-58, April 2013; $1,777, AU-53, October 2014; $564, AU-50, July 2015; $999, VF-30, June 2015												
1840, Proof	3–6	0	n/a			*(extremely rare; 3 known)*						
Auctions: No auction records available.												
1840-C	12,822	140	51.6	11%	$1,500	$2,100	$4,250	$6,250	$7,500	$10,000	$18,000	$25,000
Auctions: $3,525, AU-58, March 2015; $1,087, AU-50, February 2015; $2,115, EF-45, October 2014; $1,645, VF-25, June 2015												
1840-D	3,532	43	48.5	5%	$3,500	$8,000	$12,000	$18,000	$25,000	$35,000	$75,000	
Auctions: $10,575, AU-53, March 2014												
1840-O	33,580	112	51.4	13%	$450	$900	$1,850	$2,650	$5,000	$9,500	$14,000	$25,000
Auctions: $14,100, MS-62, April 2014; $7,344, MS-61, October 2014; $4,113, AU-58, July 2015; $270, VF-20, August 2014												

a. Value in MS-64 is $22,500.

1843-C, Small Date, Crosslet 4	1843-C, Large Date, Plain 4	1843-O, Small Date, Crosslet 4	1843-O, Large Date, Plain 4

	Mintage	Cert	Avg	%MS	VF-20	EF-40	AU-50	AU-55	AU-58	MS-60	MS-62	MS-63
												PF-63
1841 (b)	*unknown*	0	n/a		$65,000	$105,000	$125,000	$150,000	$175,000	$225,000		
Auctions: $105,800, EF-45, March 2012												
1841, Proof	*15–20*	5	57.0									$250,000
Auctions: $149,500, PF-55, April 2012												
1841-C	10,281	102	51.4	6%	$1,500	$2,250	$3,250	$5,500	$8,500	$14,000	$25,000	
Auctions: $28,200, MS-62, March 2014; $5,875, AU-58, November 2014; $3,055, AU-50, June 2015; $2,468, EF-45, January 2015												
1841-D	4,164	53	46.5	6%	$2,100	$4,000	$9,000	$12,000	$15,000	$25,000	$40,000	$50,000
Auctions: $7,638, AU-55, April 2013												
1842	2,823	23	49.7	4%	$1,200	$2,750	$6,000	$8,000	$10,000	$17,500	$35,000	
Auctions: $15,275, MS-60, January 2014; $7,931, AU-55, August 2015; $7,050, AU-55, July 2014; $3,819, EF-40, November 2014												
1842, Proof	*2–3*	0	n/a		*(unique, in the Smithsonian's National Numismatic Collection)*							
Auctions: No auction records available.												
1842-C	6,729	59	47.5	5%	$1,750	$3,250	$7,250	$9,250	$12,500	$22,500	$35,000	
Auctions: $8,813, AU-55, September 2014; $5,581, AU, February 2014; $3,760, EF-45, January 2015; $1,645, VF-20, January 2015												
1842-D	4,643	65	48.3	6%	$2,200	$4,500	$9,500	$14,000	$18,500	$32,500	$55,000	
Auctions: $13,513, AU-58, September 2015; $9,400, AU-55, June 2015; $6,463, AU-53, November 2014 $5,875, EF-40, January 2015												
1842-O	19,800	146	48.8	10%	$525	$1,400	$2,500	$4,250	$7,000	$10,500	$15,000	$27,500
Auctions: $7,638, MS-61, August 2015; $3,760, AU-58, October 2015; $1,293, EF-45, September 2015; $259, F-12, November 2015												
1843	100,546	191	54.1	10%	$360	$450	$800	$900	$1,250	$2,500	$4,000	$6,500 **(c)**
Auctions: $3,231, MS-62, January 2015; $764, AU-58, January 2015; $470, AU-53, July 2015; $376, AU-50, January 2015												
1843, Proof	*4–8*	3	64.3		*(extremely rare; 5–6 known)*							
Auctions: No auction records available.												
1843-C, Small Date, Crosslet 4	2,988	51	51.9	10%	$2,500	$5,250	$7,500	$10,000	$14,000	$24,000	$50,000	
Auctions: $4,406, MS-63, August 2014; $499, MS-60, July 2014; $646, AU-55, July 2014; $441, AU-55, October 2014												
1843-C, Large Date, Plain 4	23,076	198	48.2	9%	$1,500	$2,000	$3,000	$4,500	$5,750	$8,000	$12,500	$18,500
Auctions: $4,230, AU-58, August 2015; $3,525, AU-53, January 2015; $2,115, EF-45, January 2015; $764, VF-20, January 2015												
1843-D, Small Date, Crosslet 4	36,209	264	49.9	8%	$1,500	$2,000	$3,000	$4,500	$6,000	$7,500	$16,000	$27,500
Auctions: $14,100, MS-62, February 2015; $2,940, AU-55, March 2015; $2,820, AU-53, October 2015; $2,585, VF-35, July 2015												
1843-O, Small Date, Crosslet 4	288,002	514	53.0	16%	$385	$400	$500	$750	$1,000	$1,750	$3,000	$6,500
Auctions: $4,465, MS-63, June 2015; $764, AU-58, September 2015; $317, AU-50, October 2015; $259, F-15, August 2015												
1843-O, Large Date, Plain 4	76,000	133	53.7	14%	$425	$750	$1,750	$2,750	$4,000	$6,250	$13,000	$20,000
Auctions: $15,275, MS-62, February 2014; $5,875, MS-61, June 2015; $3,525, AU-55, August 2015												
1844	6,784	53	51.7	9%	$500	$775	$2,000	$3,250	$4,250	$8,500	$13,500	
Auctions: $15,275, MS-61, January 2014												
1844, Proof	*3–6*	1	66.0		*(extremely rare; 4–5 known)*							
Auctions: No auction records available.												
1844-C	11,622	119	48.7	11%	$1,350	$2,500	$6,000	$7,500	$8,500	$13,500	$25,000	$40,000
Auctions: $14,100, MS-61, January 2014; $6,756, AU-58, July 2015; $2,350, AU-50, August 2014; $3,055, VF-30, June 2015												
1844-D	17,332	167	52.6	13%	$1,500	$2,500	$3,000	$4,000	$5,000	$7,500	$14,000	$25,000
Auctions: $17,038, MS-63, April 2014; $1,645, AU-50, January 2015; $2,585, EF-45, August 2014												

b. Values are for circulated Proofs; existence of circulation strikes is unclear. **c.** Value in MS-64 is $13,500.

	Mintage	Cert	Avg	%MS	VF-20	EF-40	AU-50	AU-55	AU-58	MS-60	MS-62	MS-63 PF-63
1845	91,051	245	55.7	30%	$360	$385	$500	$650	$850	$1,250	$2,250	$4,750 **(d)**
	Auctions: $18,800, MS-65, January 2014; $14,100, MS-65, October 2014; $1,410, MS-61, March 2015; $235, AU-50, May 2015											
1845, Proof	*4–8*	2	67.0		*(extremely rare; 4–5 known)*							
	Auctions: No auction records available.											
1845-D	19,460	159	51.2	6%	$1,500	$2,350	$3,250	$4,250	$7,000	$11,000	$22,500	$35,000
	Auctions: $35,250, MS-63, January 2014											
1845-O	4,000	59	50.0	2%	$1,300	$2,500	$6,000	$8,500	$11,500	$22,500	$30,000	$50,000
	Auctions: $5,875, AU-50, January 2014											
1846	21,598	132	55.6	18%	$360	$550	$1,000	$1,600	$2,500	$5,000	$15,000	$20,000
	Auctions: $3,760, MS-61, August 2015; $1,293, AU-58, July 2015; $734, AU-53, October 2015; $646, AU-50, January 2015											
1846, Proof	*4–8*	1	64.0		*(extremely rare; 4–5 known)*							
	Auctions: $106,375, PF-64Cam, January 2011											
1846-C	4,808	64	50.7	9%	$1,700	$2,750	$7,500	$9,500	$12,500	$18,000	$25,000	$40,000
	Auctions: $15,275, MS-62, April 2014											
1846-D	19,303	167	51.5	9%	$1,750	$2,500	$3,250	$4,500	$6,250	$9,000	$13,500	$28,500
	Auctions: $7,638, MS-61, June 2013; $1,528, AU-50, August 2014; $3,055, EF-45, February 2015; $3,408, EF-40, July 2015											
1846-D, D Over D	**(e)**	3	51.0	0%		$2,750	$3,750	$6,500	$9,000	$15,000		
	Auctions: $5,175, AU-55, November 2011											
1846-O	62,000	279	51.1	9%	$400	$525	$1,200	$2,000	$3,500	$5,500	$12,500	$18,500
	Auctions: $4,700, MS-61, February 2013; $423, AU-50, August 2015; $552, EF-45, June 2015; $400, EF-40, June 2015											
1847	29,814	124	54.9	19%	$360	$400	$750	$1,200	$1,650	$3,000	$4,500	$8,000
	Auctions: $3,055, MS-61, November 2014; $1,175, AU-58, June 2013											
1847, Proof	*2–3*	0	n/a		*(unique, in the Smithsonian's National Numismatic Collection)*							
	Auctions: No auction records available.											
1847-C	23,226	246	52.3	14%	$1,500	$2,350	$3,000	$4,000	$5,000	$6,000	$8,000	$15,000
	Auctions: $3,525, AU-58, August 2015; $2,820, AU-50, July 2015; $2,364, AU-50, September 2015; $1,821, AU-50, January 2015											
1847-D	15,784	164	52.7	13%	$1,650	$2,500	$3,250	$5,000	$5,500	$8,750	$13,500	$24,000
	Auctions: $9,404, MS, February 2014; $2,820, AU-53, August 2014; $2,350, AU-50, January 2015											
1847-O	124,000	322	50.0	10%	$385	$475	$1,000	$1,750	$2,750	$4,000	$10,000	$15,000
	Auctions: $1,645, AU-55, January 2015; $764, AU-53, February 2015; $376, EF-40, May 2015; $259, VF-20, January 2015											

d. Value in MS-64 is $8,500. **e.** Included in 1846-D mintage figure.

1848, CAL. Above Eagle

	Mintage	Cert	Avg	%MS	VF-20	EF-40	AU-50	AU-55	MS-60	MS-62	MS-63 PF-60	MS-64 PF-63	MS-65 PF-65
1848	6,500	60	54.8	30%	$550	$900	$1,750	$2,500	$5,000	$8,500	$15,000	$25,000	
	Auctions: $5,640, AU-55, September 2015; $2,585, AU-50, February 2014; $823, AU-50, July 2014												
1848, CAL. Above Eagle	1,389	45	57.0	44%	$35,000	$45,000	$52,500	$55,000	$80,000	$115,000	$125,000	$150,000	$200,000
	Auctions: $176,250, MS-64, January 2014; $13,513, AU-50, August 2014												
1848, Proof	*3–6*	0	n/a		*(extremely rare; 3–4 known)*								
	Auctions: $96,600, PF-64, January 2008												
1848-C	16,788	159	50.3	9%	$1,500	$2,500	$3,500	$4,500	$12,500	$20,000	—		
	Auctions: $15,275, MS-62, March 2014												
1848-D	13,771	148	53.6	13%	$1,500	$2,500	$3,500	$4,250	$8,000	$13,500	$28,000		
	Auctions: $25,850, MS-63, April 2014												

	Mintage	Cert	Avg	%MS	VF-20	EF-40	AU-50	AU-55	MS-60	MS-62	MS-63	MS-64	MS-65
											PF-60	PF-63	PF-65
1849	23,294	133	55.1	17%	$375	$500	$975	$1,250	$2,500	$3,750	$7,500	$14,000	
	Auctions: $3,525, MS-62, March 2014; $3,055, MS-62, January 2015; $999, AU-55, July 2014; $764, AU-55, October 2015												
1849-C	10,220	93	50.9	9%	$1,500	$2,500	$4,500	$8,000	$17,500	$40,000	—		
	Auctions: $15,275, MS-61, January 2014; $3,290, AU-53, January 2015; $1,645, AU-50, September 2014; $2,350, EF-45, July 2014												
1849-D	10,945	135	53.1	8%	$1,500	$2,500	$3,750	$5,500	$15,000	$23,500	—		
	Auctions: $18,800, MS-62, August 2014; $4,935, AU-58, July 2015; $3,202, AU-53, October 2013												
1850	252,923	466	56.5	25%	$360	$380	$400	$500	$1,050	$2,000	$3,500	$7,500	
	Auctions: $940, MS-61, January 2015; $423, AU-58, September 2015; $376, AU-53, May 2015; $259, EF-40, July 2015												
1850, Proof	2–4	0	n/a		*(extremely rare; 1–2 known)*								
	Auctions: $41,250, PF-62, June 1995												
1850-C	9,148	135	51.4	15%	$1,500	$2,500	$3,500	$4,750	$11,000	$25,000	$32,500		
	Auctions: $8,879, MS-61, August 2014; $8,813, MS-61, October 2014; $12,925, MS-60, March 2014; $881, EF-40, January 2015												
1850-D	12,148	133	52.4	9%	$1,600	$2,750	$3,750	$5,500	$12,500	$27,500	$47,500		
	Auctions: $23,500, MS-62, April 2014												
1850-O	84,000	331	50.9	3%	$400	$575	$1,250	$1,800	$4,000	$6,500	$15,000		
	Auctions: $1,645, AU-58, March 2015; $1,410, AU-58, June 2015; $764, EF-45, August 2015; $447, EF-45, February 2015												
1851	1,372,748	852	59.0	55%	$360	$380	$385	$400	$550	$750	$1,100	$2,500	$5,500
	Auctions: $9,400, MS-66, February 2015; $376, MS-61, October 2015; $400, AU-58, March 2015; $266, AU-53, May 2015												
1851-C	14,923	108	50.7	14%	$1,500	$2,450	$3,750	$5,500	$9,500	$22,500	$32,500		
	Auctions: $5,640, MS-61, September 2015; $3,290, AU-53, January 2015; $2,820, AU-53, January 2015; $2,115, EF-40, July 2015												
1851-D	11,264	80	51.0	6%	$1,500	$2,500	$4,000	$5,500	$10,750	$17,500	$35,000	$50,000	
	Auctions: $7,638, AU-58, December 2013; $2,115, AU-50, September 2014												
1851-O	148,000	440	53.5	10%	$400	$475	$950	$2,000	$4,000	$7,500	$11,500	$23,500	
	Auctions: $3,539, MS-61, February 2015; $2,143, AU-58, January 2015; $823, AU-55, October 2015; $646, AU-50, January 2015												
1852	1,159,681	1,021	59.7	59%	$360	$380	$385	$400	$550	$950	$1,300	$2,500	$5,500
	Auctions: $4,818, MS-65, June 2015; $1,998, MS-64, February 2015; $588, MS-62, June 2015; $329, AU-58, July 2015												
1852-C	9,772	91	52.6	9%	$1,500	$2,500	$3,850	$5,750	$12,500	$22,500	$32,500		
	Auctions: $6,463, AU-58, August 2015; $4,465, AU-55, July 2015; $3,525, AU-53, October 2015; $4,935, AU-50, February 2015												
1852-D	4,078	54	53.5	9%	$1,850	$3,000	$6,000	$8,000	$15,750	$30,000	$42,500	$65,000	
	Auctions: $8,813, AU-53, August 2013												
1852-O	140,000	507	52.7	6%	$400	$450	$950	$1,250	$4,500	$8,000	$11,000		
	Auctions: $4,465, MS-61, August 2015; $1,410, AU-58, July 2015; $764, AU-55, January 2015; $617, AU-53, July 2015												
1853	1,404,668	1,448	59.8	59%	$350	$355	$365	$385	$550	$600	$1,200	$2,000	$5,000
	Auctions: $9,988, MS-66, June 2015; $676, MS-62, March 2015; $306, AU-58, June 2015; $247, AU-50, January 2015												
1853-D	3,178	49	52.7	14%	$1,800	$3,250	$4,750	$5,750	$13,500	$30,000	$45,000		
	Auctions: $25,850, MS-62, January 2014; $12,338, MS-61, October 2014; $13,513, MS-61, November 2014; $4,113, AU-50, July 2014												
1854	596,258	705	59.1	52%	$350	$355	$365	$385	$550	$1,100	$1,250	$2,500	$6,000
	Auctions: $4,230, MS-65, January 2015; $470, MS-61, January 2015; $294, AU-55, August 2015; $376, AU-50, February 2015												
1854, Proof	2–4	0	n/a		*(unique, in the Bass Foundation Collection)*								
	Auctions: No auction records available.												
1854-C	7,295	109	53.8	19%	$1,500	$2,600	$4,350	$6,500	$12,000	$22,500	$37,500		
	Auctions: $9,988, MS-61, June 2013; $4,994, AU-58, August 2014; $4,230, AU-53, August 2015; $3,525, EF-45, January 2015												
1854-D	1,760	22	48.9	18%	$3,500	$7,500	$12,000	$16,000	$27,500	$40,000	$70,000		
	Auctions: $15,275, AU-55, March 2014; $9,467, AU-53, August 2014; $5,875, AU-50, November 2014												
1854-O	153,000	507	53.7	7%	$385	$400	$575	$800	$1,500	$4,500	$9,000	$15,000	
	Auctions: $2,585, MS-61, February 2015; $435, MS-60, September 2015; $329, AU-53, January 2015; $329, EF-45, October 2015												
1854-S	246	7	35.3	0%	$275,000	$400,000	$500,000	—					
	Auctions: $282,000, EF-35, October 2013												

Old Reverse (Pre-1859)   **New Reverse**

	Mintage	Cert	Avg	%MS	VF-20	EF-40	AU-50	AU-55	MS-60	MS-62	MS-63 / PF-60	MS-64 / PF-63	MS-65 / PF-65
1855	235,480	396	59.5	55%	$360	$365	$375	$385	$550	$1,100	$1,600	$3,250	$7,000
Auctions: $2,585, MS-64, October 2015; $764, MS-62, July 2015; $447, MS-61, July 2015; $329, AU-58, April 2015
1855-C	3,677	72	54.7	24%	$1,850	$3,250	$5,500	$10,000	$20,000	$27,500	$42,500		
Auctions: $23,500, MS-62, January 2014
1855-D	1,123	24	53.3	13%	$4,500	$8,000	$15,000	$20,000	$46,500				
Auctions: $25,850, AU-55, July 2014; $8,225, EF-45, March 2015
1856	384,240	618	59.5	55%	$350	$365	$375	$385	$550	$1,000	$1,250	$3,500	$5,500
Auctions: $3,995, MS-65, July 2015; $1,234, MS-63, July 2015; $376, AU-58, March 2015; $282, AU-53, May 2015
1856, Proof	6–8	0	n/a								$40,000	$75,000	$135,000
Auctions: No auction records available.
1856-C	7,913	88	52.1	14%	$1,500	$2,600	$4,000	$6,500	$11,500	$20,000	$25,000		
Auctions: $6,463, AU-58, April 2013; $4,465, AU-58, August 2015; $4,230, AU-55, August 2015; $1,410, AU-50, October 2014
1856-D	874	16	52.4	25%	$8,000	$12,500	$30,000	$35,000	$70,000				
Auctions: $55,813, AU-58, March 2014
1856-O	21,100	139	53.5	10%	$385	$700	$1,500	$2,100	$7,500	$25,000			
Auctions: $7,050, MS-61, August 2013
1856-S	72,120	201	51.8	14%	$385	$450	$1,200	$1,500	$5,000	$8,000	$12,000	$15,000	$27,500
Auctions: $2,585, AU-58, September 2015; $1,821, AU-58, September 2015; $1,410, AU-58, June 2015; $1,058, AU-50, January 2015
1857	214,130	457	59.6	56%	$360	$365	$375	$385	$550	$1,050	$1,350	$3,250	$6,500
Auctions: $5,904, MS-65, July 2015; $423, MS-61, January 2015; $282, MS-60, November 2015; $282, AU-55, May 2015
1857, Proof	6–8	0	n/a								$35,000	$57,500	$125,000
Auctions: No auction records available.
1857-D	2,364	61	56.5	28%	$1,600	$2,800	$4,000	$5,500	$12,000	$22,000	$30,000		
Auctions: $18,800, MS-62, April 2014; $4,935, AU-55, June 2015; $1,586, AU-50, January 2015; $1,528, AU-50, July 2014
1857-O	34,000	271	55.2	20%	$385	$400	$1,250	$1,850	$4,250	$7,500	$13,000	$20,000	
Auctions: $6,463, MS-62, April 2014; $4,113, MS-61, November 2014; $1,998, AU-58, January 2015; $823, AU-53, January 2015
1857-S	69,200	180	51.7	12%	$385	$475	$1,200	$2,000	$5,500	$7,500	$13,500	$25,000	
Auctions: $5,875, MS-61, June 2015; $1,775, AU-58, July 2015; $1,293, AU-55, January 2015; $317, VF-35, July 2014
1858	47,377	191	58.3	37%	$375	$390	$450	$550	$1,100	$1,850	$3,000	$6,000	$13,500
Auctions: $999, MS-61, January 2015; $564, AU-58, October 2015; $376, AU-55, February 2015; $353, AU-53, May 2015
1858, Proof	6–8	3	65.3								$25,000	$45,000	$115,000
Auctions: $82,250, PF, March 2014
1858-C	9,056	134	54.7	28%	$1,500	$2,250	$3,000	$4,250	$8,000	$14,000	$25,000		
Auctions: $11,163, MS-62, January 2014; $4,113, AU-58, November 2014; $3,525, AU-58, November 2014
1859, Old Reverse	39,364	130	58.0	35%	$375	$500	$850	$1,000	$2,500	$4,000	$7,000	$10,000	
Auctions: $1,102, AU, February 2014; $456, AU-50, November 2014; $411, EF-40, August 2014
1859, New Reverse	(a)	45	58.2	20%	$360	$370	$500	$700	$1,200	$2,000	$3,000	$7,250	$11,000
Auctions: $3,290, MS-63, October 2014; $3,055, MS-63, August 2015; $1,998, MS-62, November 2014; $2,879, MS, January 2014
1859, Proof (b)	80	2	63								$15,000	$30,000	$75,000
Auctions: $80,500, PF-66, July 2005

a. Included in circulation-strike 1859, Old Reverse, mintage figure. **b.** Nearly all 1859 Proofs are of the Old Reverse style.

1862, 2 Over 1

1873, Close 3

1873, Open 3

	Mintage	Cert	Avg	%MS	VF-20	EF-40	AU-50	AU-55	MS-60	MS-62	MS-63	MS-64	MS-65
											PF-60	PF-63	PF-65
1859-D	2,244	89	54.9	15%	$2,200	$3,250	$4,750	$6,500	$20,000	$40,000			
Auctions: $24,675, MS-62, August 2015; $13,513, MS-60, September 2015; $3,819, AU-55, October 2014; $2,233, AU-50, July 2015													
1859-S	15,200	87	49.5	10%	$475	$950	$2,000	$3,000	$6,000	$10,000	$16,000		
Auctions: $4,994, MS-61, April 2014; $4,847, MS-61, August 2014; $3,290, AU-58, October 2014; $2,585, AU-58, July 2014													
1860, Old Reverse	22,563	29	57.2	34%	$1,250	$2,000	$2,750	$4,000	$5,000	$6,500	$12,500		
Auctions: $6,463, MS-62, April 2013													
1860, New Reverse	(c)	52	58.8	46%	$360	$370	$450	$600	$1,000	$1,600	$2,750	$7,500	$13,500
Auctions: $1,763, MS-60, August 2013													
1860, Proof (d)	112	9	63.8								$14,000	$22,500	$40,000
Auctions: $11,550, PF-64Cam, October 1993													
1860-C	7,469	111	51.5	10%	$1,650	$2,500	$4,000	$6,500	$15,000	$25,000	$35,000		
Auctions: $25,850, MS-63, January 2014; $14,100, MS-61, June 2015; $8,813, AU-58, September 2015; $1,586, AU-50, August 2014													
1860-S	35,600	119	47.8	8%	$425	$675	$1,150	$1,750	$3,500	$7,000	$15,000		
Auctions: $6,756, MS-62, August 2013; $317, EF-40, November 2014													
1861, Old Reverse	1,283,788	120	58.3	39%	$525	$1,100	$1,800	$2,350	$4,000	$8,000	$12,500		
Auctions: $11,163, MS-64, October 2015; $1,763, AU-58, September 2015; $881, AU-50, September 2014; $823, EF-45, June 2015													
1861, New Reverse	(e)	1,415	59.6	57%	$360	$370	$375	$600	$1,250	$1,750	$3,000	$5,500
Auctions: $9,400, MS-66, January 2015; $646, MS-61, July 2015; $353, AU-55, September 2015; $329, AU-50, September 2015													
1861, Proof (f)	90	3	65.5								$12,000	$20,000	$40,000
Auctions: $44,850, PF-65DCam, September 2005													
1861-S	24,000	95	46.4	7%	$400	$825	$2,500	$4,250	$7,250	$20,000			
Auctions: $5,875, AU-58, April 2013													
1862, 2 Over 1	(g)	55	54.5	15%	$1,000	$1,850	$3,000	$4,750	$8,000	$12,500			
Auctions: $9,400, MS-61, January 2014; $558, AU-50, July 2014													
1862	98,508	184	56.4	32%	$400	$600	$1,000	$1,750	$4,750	$6,500	$11,000	$18,500	
Auctions: $8,225, MS-63, August 2015; $4,700, MS-62, October 2015; $2,381, AU-58, January 2015; $1,116, AU-50, January 2015													
1862, Proof	35	11	64.7								$12,000	$20,000	$40,000
Auctions: $46,000, PF-65UCam, February 2007													
1862-S	8,000	138	47.1	9%	$1,000	$1,750	$3,000	$5,000	$16,000	$24,000	$35,000		
Auctions: $23,500, MS-62, January 2014													
1863, Proof (h)	30	7	64.4								$50,000	$75,000	$125,000
Auctions: $45,531, PF-58, April 2014													
1863-S	10,800	76	46.7	11%	$700	$1,350	$3,500	$5,000	$13,000	$20,000	$30,000		
Auctions: $3,290, EF-45, March 2013													
1864	2,824	8	53.4	25%	$7,500	$15,000	$27,500	$47,500	$75,000				
Auctions: $48,469, AU-55, March 2014													
1864, Proof	50	15	64.7								$12,000	$25,000	$45,000
Auctions: $30,550, PF-64Cam, April 2014													
1865	1,520	17	53.5	0%	$4,500	$8,500	$20,000	$27,500	$40,000	$45,000	$60,000		
Auctions: $15,891, AU-55, June 2013; $11,163, EF-45, August 2015; $4,113, VF-20, November 2014													
1865, Proof	25	13	63.9								$13,500	$20,000	$45,000
Auctions: $48,875, PF-65UCam, January 2012													
1865-S	23,376	96	45.8	5%	$400	$650	$1,250	$2,000	$4,500	$7,500	$11,000		
Auctions: $1,998, AU-53, March 2014													

c. Included in 1860, Old Reverse, mintage figure. **d.** All known 1860 Proofs are of the New Reverse style. **e.** Included in 1861, Old Reverse, mintage figure. **f.** All 1861 Proofs were struck in the New Reverse style. **g.** Included in circulation-strike 1862 mintage figure. **h.** Proof only.

	Mintage	Cert	Avg	%MS	VF-20	EF-40	AU-50	AU-55	MS-60	MS-62	MS-63 / PF-60	MS-64 / PF-63	MS-65 / PF-65
1866	3,080	35	51.2	17%	$1,150	$3,000	$5,250	$7,500	$12,500	$20,000	$25,000	$35,000	
	Auctions: $7,050, AU-58, February 2013												
1866, Proof	30	14	64.0								$10,000	$17,500	$32,500
	Auctions: $23,500, PF-64Cam, April 2014												
1866-S	38,960	193	47.5	5%	$400	$750	$1,700	$3,500	$7,500	$12,500	$25,000		
	Auctions: $7,050, MS-61, August 2015; $1,880, AU-58, July 2015; $470, EF-45, January 2015; $376, VF-25, January 2015												
1867	3,200	37	54.9	27%	$400	$650	$1,200	$1,700	$4,500	$6,000	$12,000	$13,500	$35,000
	Auctions: $1,544, AU-55, July 2014; $1,645, AU-55, May 2013												
1867, Proof	50	11	64.1								$10,000	$16,000	$30,000
	Auctions: $35,250, PF-65DCam, October 2015; $18,800, PF-64DCam, October 2014; $99,875, PF, August 2013												
1867-S	28,000	163	47.3	6%	$400	$650	$1,250	$1,600	$3,850	$5,000	$12,000	$15,000	
	Auctions: $1,163, AU-50, September 2015; $940, EF-45, August 2015; $541, EF-45, January 2015; $306, VF-30, November 2015												
1868	3,600	144	56.9	22%	$350	$425	$700	$800	$2,000	$4,000	$7,500	$15,000	
	Auctions: $3,290, MS-61, August 2014; $1,998, MS-61, November 2014; $1,880, AU-58, July 2015; $881, AU-58, February 2015												
1868, Proof	25	5	63.4								$9,500	$16,500	$35,000
	Auctions: $43,700, PF-65Cam, January 2009												
1868-S	34,000	247	52.0	6%	$350	$425	$950	$1,400	$4,000	$6,000	$10,000	$16,000	
	Auctions: $2,820, AU-58, August 2015; $999, AU-55, January 2015; $529, AU-50, July 2015; $447, EF-45, June 2015												
1869	4,320	146	56.7	23%	$350	$425	$700	$1,150	$2,750	$5,000	$10,000	$20,000	
	Auctions: $19,975, MS-64, August 2014; $1,058, AU-58, January 2015; $881, AU-55, July 2015; $940, AU-50, June 2015												
1869, Proof	25	18	64.2								$6,500	$14,000	$30,000
	Auctions: $12,650, PF-63, October 2011												
1869-S	29,500	229	51.8	8%	$350	$475	$1,000	$1,500	$4,000	$6,000	$9,250	$13,000	
	Auctions: $3,525, MS-62, October 2015; $1,645, AU-58, January 2015; $1,528, AU-58, August 2015; $1,528, AU-58, June 2015												
1870	4,520	95	56.9	21%	$350	$400	$600	$1,250	$3,250	$5,500	$8,500		
	Auctions: $4,994, MS-61, January 2014; $3,525, MS-61, January 2015; $3,760, MS-60, August 2015; $1,645, AU-58, August 2015												
1870, Proof	35	5	63.8								$6,500	$14,000	$30,000
	Auctions: $70,500, PF-66DCam, January 2014												
1870-S	16,000	144	51.2	10%	$350	$400	$900	$1,500	$4,000	$7,000	$13,500	$17,500	
	Auctions: $8,225, MS-62, January 2014; $1,528, AU-58, July 2014; $1,645, AU-50, October 2015; $447, AU-50, September 2015												
1871	5,320	119	56.4	25%	$350	$400	$550	$1,000	$2,000	$2,750	$4,000	$8,000	
	Auctions: $999, AU-58, July 2015; $705, AU-55, October 2015; $646, AU-55, July 2015; $306, AU-50, January 2015												
1871, Proof	30	9	64.4								$6,500	$14,000	$27,500
	Auctions: $19,975, PF-64DCam, August 2014												
1871-S	22,000	200	52.5	12%	$350	$400	$550	$1,000	$2,000	$3,000	$4,350	$9,000	$17,500
	Auctions: $1,087, AU-55, August 2015; $517, AU-53, June 2015; $423, AU-53, February 2015; $282, VF-30, November 2015												
1872	3,000	68	56.1	18%	$425	$700	$1,100	$2,000	$4,350	$9,000	$14,000	$25,000	
	Auctions: $2,596, AU-58, March 2014												
1872, Proof	30	9	64.8								$6,500	$14,000	$27,500
	Auctions: $34,075, PF-65Cam, March 2013												
1872-S	18,000	185	50.7	9%	$350	$400	$950	$1,350	$4,000	$6,000	$10,500	$13,500	
	Auctions: $3,594, MS-61, April 2012												
1873, Close 3	55,200	590	59.9	63%	$350	$375	$400	$425	$600	$1,100	$1,750	$2,750	$5,500
	Auctions: $3,525, MS-65, June 2015; $1,763, MS-64, June 2015; $1,293, MS-64, September 2015; $705, MS-63, July 2015												
1873, Open 3	122,800	512	60.8	75%	$325	$365	$375	$385	$585	$700	$800	$1,250	$4,500
	Auctions: $11,750, MS-66, July 2015; $1,116, MS-64, October 2015; $400, MS-62, August 2015; $329, AU-58, July 2015												
1873, Close 3, Proof	25	11	62.7								$7,500	$14,000	$30,000
	Auctions: $23,500, PF-63Cam, August 2014; $19,388, PF, August 2013												
1873-S	27,000	258	50.2	9%	$350	$425	$975	$1,300	$2,300	$4,750	$6,500	$13,500	
	Auctions: $11,750, MS-64, August 2015; $3,525, MS-62, October 2015; $620, AU-55, February 2015; $447, EF-45, May 2015												

	Mintage	Cert	Avg	%MS	VF-20	EF-40	AU-50	AU-55	MS-60	MS-62	MS-63	MS-64	MS-65
											PF-60	PF-63	PF-65
1874	3,920	114	57.0	26%	$350	$400	$650	$1,050	$2,000	$4,000	$6,000	$9,500	$25,000
	Auctions: $3,525, MS-62, August 2013												
1874, Proof	20	11	64.4								$7,500	$15,000	$45,000
	Auctions: $38,188, PF-64DCam, August 2014												
1875	400	30	57.1	20%	$5,500	$7,500	$12,500	$15,000	$27,500	$30,000	$45,000		
	Auctions: $25,850, MS-61, January 2015; $25,850, MS-61, August 2013; $15,275, AU-58, October 2014												
1875, Proof	20	10	63.6								$15,000	$35,000	$75,000
	Auctions: $94,000, PF, October 2013												
1875-S	11,600	177	54.2	17%	$350	$400	$650	$1,100	$3,500	$5,000	$7,250	$12,000	
	Auctions: $5,581, MS-63, October 2014; $1,087, AU-58, July 2015; $999, AU-58, June 2015; $676, AU-53, August 2014												
1876	4,176	132	53.9	14%	$375	$625	$950	$1,750	$3,000	$4,000	$6,500	$12,000	
	Auctions: $5,581, MS-62, March 2014; $3,055, MS-61, September 2015; $2,350, MS-60, October 2015; $823, AU-53, October 2015												
1876, Proof	45	16	64.4								$6,500	$13,500	$30,000
	Auctions: $39,950, PF, January 2013												
1876-S	5,000	136	54.2	17%	$350	$525	$950	$1,350	$3,000	$4,000	$8,000		
	Auctions: $8,225, MS-63, January 2014; $2,820, MS-61, August 2014; $1,880, AU-58, November 2015; $734, AU-53, June 2015												
1877	1,632	109	56.8	32%	$400	$750	$1,000	$1,500	$3,000	$4,000	$8,500	$15,000	
	Auctions: $4,406, MS-62, April 2014; $3,055, MS-61, August 2014; $1,763, AU-58, June 2015; $884, AU-50, March 2015												
1877, Proof	20	6	64.0								$6,500	$13,500	$30,000
	Auctions: $8,050, PF-55, November 2011												
1877-S	35,400	403	58.8	47%	$350	$365	$375	$400	$650	$1,500	$2,350	$4,000	$9,000
	Auctions: $376, AU-58, June 2015; $259, AU-58, January 2015; $282, AU-53, May 2015; $329, AU-50, May 2015												
1878	286,240	2,345	60.8	74%	$350	$365	$375	$385	$500	$650	$850	$1,300	$2,500
	Auctions: $12,925, MS-67, July 2015; $999, MS-64, August 2015; $541, MS-62, February 2015; $329, AU-58, June 2015												
1878, Proof	20	11	64.4								$6,500	$13,500	$30,000
	Auctions: $50,313, PF-65DCam, April 2012												
1878-S	178,000	706	59.3	54%	$350	$365	$375	$385	$535	$1,000	$1,800	$3,500	$12,000
	Auctions: $12,925, MS-66, January 2015; $423, MS-61, June 2015; $353, AU-58, October 2015; $353, AU-53, September 2015												
1879	88,960	938	60.7	74%	$350	$365	$375	$425	$535	$875	$1,100	$1,500	$3,500
	Auctions: $7,638, MS-66, September 2015; $940, MS-64, January 2015; $423, MS-61, October 2015; $282, AU-58, May 2015												
1879, Proof	30	8	65.0								$6,000	$13,000	$30,000
	Auctions: $40,250, PF-67Cam, January 2011												
1879-S	43,500	214	54.0	9%	$350	$365	$550	$1,000	$1,750	$3,500	$4,800	$12,500	
	Auctions: $423, MS-60, January 2015; $400, MS-60, February 2015; $617, AU-58, July 2015; $259, EF-45, January 2015												
1880	2,960	144	58.8	47%	$375	$425	$650	$800	$1,500	$2,000	$3,750	$6,000	$12,500
	Auctions: $2,820, MS-62, October 2013; $1,410, MS-61, February 2015; $1,410, AU-58, November 2014; $999, AU-58, January 2015												
1880, Proof	36	15	63.4								$6,500	$12,500	$27,500
	Auctions: $3,244, PF-55, January 2011												
1881	640	73	56.8	27%	$2,250	$3,000	$5,000	$6,000	$10,000	$14,000	$20,000	$30,000	
	Auctions: $7,931, MS-60, June 2013; $5,875, AU-58, August 2014; $5,875, AU-50, August 2015; $4,994, AU-50, July 2014												
1881, Proof	51	21	64.0								$6,500	$13,500	$27,500
	Auctions: $34,075, PF-65DCam, August 2013; $14,100, PF-64DCam, July 2014												
1882	4,000	174	59.7	54%	$375	$425	$575	$700	$925	$1,500	$2,750	$4,000	$9,000
	Auctions: $9,400, MS-66, November 2014; $1,058, AU-58, July 2015; $282, AU-50, July 2015; $259, AU-50, July 2015												
1882, Proof	67	14	65.3								$4,500	$9,500	$22,500
	Auctions: $9,487, PF-64, May 2006												
1883	1,920	60	58.1	33%	$375	$450	$900	$1,000	$1,750	$2,350	$6,500	$6,750	$9,000
	Auctions: $4,994, MS-61, June 2014												
1883, Proof	82	22	64.8								$4,500	$9,500	$22,500
	Auctions: $28,200, PF, March 2014												

1891, Doubled-Die Reverse
FS-G2.5-1891-801.

	Mintage	Cert	Avg	%MS	VF-20	EF-40	AU-50	AU-55	MS-60	MS-62	MS-63	MS-64	MS-65
											PF-60	PF-63	PF-65
1884	1,950	122	60.0	63%	$375	$400	$700	$800	$1,500	$1,900	$3,000	$3,500	$5,000
	Auctions: $18,800, MS-65, June 2015; $2,468, MS-62, June 2014; $1,645, MS-61, June 2015; $1,058, AU-58, August 2014												
1884, Proof	73	25	64.0								$4,500	$9,500	$22,500
	Auctions: $82,250, PF, August 2013												
1885	800	50	58.6	46%	$1,100	$2,000	$2,750	$3,000	$5,000	$6,500	$10,000	$15,000	$25,000
	Auctions: $13,513, MS-63, March 2014; $1,423, AU-50, July 2014												
1885, Proof	87	22	64.2								$5,000	$9,000	$27,500
	Auctions: $56,160, PF, September 2013												
1886	4,000	146	59.5	54%	$375	$400	$550	$600	$1,000	$1,750	$3,000	$7,000	$12,000
	Auctions: $1,528, MS-62, July 2014; $823, AU-58, September 2015; $823, AU-58, July 2015; $518, AU-53, June 2015												
1886, Proof	88	32	64.3								$4,500	$9,500	$22,500
	Auctions: $40,538, PF, August 2013												
1887	6,160	209	60.0	66%	$375	$400	$450	$500	$800	$1,250	$2,750	$4,500	$15,000
	Auctions: $15,275, MS-65, August 2015; $881, MS-62, February 2015; $764, AU-58, January 2015; $329, AU-50, October 2015												
1887, Proof	122	26	64.1								$4,500	$9,500	$22,500
	Auctions: $58,750, PF, August 2013												
1888	16,001	453	61.9	88%	$360	$365	$375	$400	$550	$800	$1,300	$1,475	$5,500
	Auctions: $8,225, MS-66, August 2015; $1,234, MS-64, January 2015; $541, MS-62, January 2015; $376, MS-61, August 2015												
1888, Proof	97	31	64.5								$4,500	$8,500	$22,500
	Auctions: $25,850, PF-65Cam, February 2013; $6,463, PF-63, November 2014; $5,288, PF-62, August 2014												
1889	17,600	397	61.5	87%	$360	$365	$375	$400	$525	$800	$1,350	$1,425	$5,500
	Auctions: $6,463, MS-65, July 2014; $441, MS-61, August 2014; $341, AU-58, October 2014; $329, AU-58, July 2015												
1889, Proof	48	17	64.9								$4,500	$8,500	$22,500
	Auctions: $31,792, PF-65DCam, August 2014												
1890	8,720	227	60.8	69%	$360	$375	$385	$400	$600	$900	$1,350	$2,750	$9,000
	Auctions: $9,400, MS-65, July 2015; $940, MS-62, August 2015; $646, AU-58, May 2015; $400, AU-55, June 2015												
1890, Proof	93	51	64.6								$4,500	$8,500	$20,000
	Auctions: $19,388, PF-65DCam, June 2014; $29,458, PF-65, October 2014												
1891	10,960	316	60.9	75%	$365	$385	$400	$450	$550	$800	$1,450	$1,850	$6,000
	Auctions: $2,233, MS-64, November 2014; $1,645, MS-64, June 2015; $447, MS-61, February 2015; $411, AU-58, May 2015												
1891, Doubled-Die Reverse	(i)	0	n/a					$450	$750	$1,250	$1,750	$3,000	$5,500
	Auctions: $823, MS-63, November 2014												
1891, Proof	80	27	65.4								$4,500	$8,000	$20,000
	Auctions: $30,550, PF, April 2013												
1892	2,440	137	61.2	81%	$365	$400	$475	$525	$900	$1,100	$2,250	$4,000	$8,000
	Auctions: $21,150, MS-67, November 2013; $8,527, MS-66, August 2014; $7,931, MS-66, November 2014; $1,998, MS-63, October 2014												
1892, Proof	105	30	64.5								$4,500	$8,000	$20,000
	Auctions: $111,625, PF, February 2013												
1893	30,000	877	62.3	91%	$360	$365	$375	$400	$550	$800	$1,300	$1,475	$2,250
	Auctions: $7,050, MS-67, January 2015; $3,290, MS-66, January 2015; $494, MS-62, April 2015; $259, MS-60, January 2015												
1893, Proof	106	38	65.1								$4,500	$7,500	$20,000
	Auctions: $21,150, PF-66DCam, September 2014; $44,063, PF, August 2013												

i. Included in circulation-strike 1891 mintage figure.

	Mintage	Cert	Avg	%MS	VF-20	EF-40	AU-50	AU-55	MS-60	MS-62	MS-63	MS-64	MS-65
											PF-60	PF-63	PF-65
1894	4,000	243	61.9	87%	$360	$365	$375	$475	$750	$1,000	$1,650	$2,000	$5,500
	Auctions: $3,525, MS-65, January 2015; $1,410, MS-62, July 2015; $833, MS-61, January 2015; $823, MS-61, August 2015												
1894, Proof	122	64	64.6								$4,500	$7,500	$20,000
	Auctions: $21,150, PF-66DCam, September 2014; $44,063, PF, August 2013												
1895	6,000	265	62.5	92%	$360	$365	$375	$450	$600	$725	$1,100	$1,350	$3,750
	Auctions: $8,519, MS-66, March 2013												
1895, Proof	119	69	65.0								$4,500	$7,500	$20,000
	Auctions: $23,500, PF-66DCam, January 2014; $28,200, PF-66DCam, August 2014; $9,400, PF-64DCam, January 2015												
1896	19,070	697	62.6	94%	$325	$355	$375	$400	$500	$700	$950	$1,100	$2,500
	Auctions: $7,344, MS-67, March 2014; $1,998, MS-65, September 2014; $940, MS-64, March 2015; $306, AU-58, July 2015												
1896, Proof	132	68	64.8								$4,500	$7,500	$20,000
	Auctions: $3,819, PF-62, March 2015; $3,055, PF-62, November 2014; $21,150, PF, October 2013												
1897	29,768	1,022	62.7	95%	$325	$355	$375	$400	$500	$575	$825	$900	$1,850
	Auctions: $7,638, MS-67, January 2015; $3,055, MS-66, July 2015; $881, MS-64, October 2015; $447, MS-62, January 2015												
1897, Proof	136	83	64.8								$4,500	$7,500	$20,000
	Auctions: $27,025, PF, March 2014												
1898	24,000	771	63.2	97%	$300	$315	$325	$350	$475	$525	$675	$750	$1,650
	Auctions: $7,638, MS-67, January 2015; $2,879, MS-66, August 2015; $364, MS-61, September 2015; $294, MS-60, April 2015												
1898, Proof	165	117	64.4								$4,500	$7,500	$20,000
	Auctions: $25,850, PF-66DCam, September 2014; $25,850, PF-66DCam, September 2014; $5,941, PF-64Cam, June 2015												
1899	27,200	802	62.8	97%	$300	$315	$325	$350	$475	$525	$675	$725	$1,200
	Auctions: $2,585, MS-66, June 2015; $1,998, MS-65, July 2015; $1,414, MS-65, June 2015; $969, MS-64, June 2015												
1899, Proof	150	135	64.5								$4,500	$7,500	$20,000
	Auctions: $36,425, PF, August 2013												
1900	67,000	1,967	63.0	96%	$300	$315	$325	$350	$475	$525	$675	$725	$1,200
	Auctions: $3,290, MS-67, June 2015; $940, MS-65, January 2015; $705, MS-64, October 2015; $541, MS-62, July 2015												
1900, Proof	205	193	64.0								$4,500	$7,500	$16,000
	Auctions: $56,400, PF-68DCam+, October 2015; $37,600, PF-68UCam, June 2015; $64,625, PF-68DCam, November 2014												
1901	91,100	2,324	62.9	96%	$300	$315	$325	$350	$475	$525	$675	$725	$1,200
	Auctions: $4,700, MS-67, August 2014; $1,351, MS-65, January 2015; $541, MS-63, January 2015; $447, MS-62, January 2015												
1901, Proof	223	139	64.4								$4,500	$7,500	$16,000
	Auctions: $28,200, PF-67DCam, October 2014; $16,450, PF-66Cam+, June 2015; $11,750, PF-64Cam, September 2014												
1902	133,540	3,402	63.0	97%	$300	$315	$325	$350	$475	$525	$675	$725	$1,200
	Auctions: $5,405, MS-67, January 2015; $646, MS-64, August 2015; $329, MS-61, April 2015; $282, MS-60, January 2015												
1902, Proof	193	102	64.0								$4,500	$7,500	$16,000
	Auctions: $5,640, PF-64, June 2015; $3,290, PF-62, June 2015; $2,585, PF-61, January 2015; $1,528, PF-50, August 2015												
1903	201,060	6,003	63.0	96%	$300	$315	$325	$350	$475	$525	$675	$725	$1,200
	Auctions: $9,400, MS-68, January 2015; $2,350, MS-67, January 2015; $376, MS-62, February 2015; $235, MS-60, June 2015												
1903, Proof	197	124	63.2								$4,500	$7,500	$16,000
	Auctions: $12,925, PF-65, January 2015; $7,050, PF-64, August 2014; $3,173, PF-62, November 2014; $3,055, PF-62, March 2015												
1904	160,790	4,556	63.0	96%	$300	$315	$325	$350	$475	$525	$675	$725	$1,200
	Auctions: $28,200, MS-68, January 2013; $3,290, MS-67, July 2015; $2,585, MS-67, November 2014; $1,351, MS-66, November 2014												
1904, Proof	170	119	64.0								$4,500	$7,500	$16,000
	Auctions: $4,700, PF-63, January 2015; $1,293, MS-66, October 2015; $270, MS-60, January 2015; $259, AU-55, January 2015												
1905 (j)	217,800	6,353	63.1	96%	$300	$315	$325	$350	$475	$525	$675	$725	$1,200
	Auctions: $3,995, MS-67, August 2015; $1,528, MS-66, August 2015; $329, MS-62, July 2015; $282, AU-58, February 2015												
1905, Proof	144	118	63.6								$4,500	$7,500	$16,000
	Auctions: $8,225, PF-64, October 2014; $6,463, PF-64, July 2015; $6,463, PF-64, February 2015; $1,058, PF, March 2015												

j. Pieces dated 1905-S are counterfeit.

| | Mintage | Cert | Avg | %MS | VF-20 | EF-40 | AU-50 | AU-55 | MS-60 | MS-62 | MS-63 | MS-64 | MS-65 |
											PF-60	PF-63	PF-65
1906	176,330	5,349	63.0	97%	$300	$315	$325	$350	$475	$525	$675	$725	$1,200
	Auctions: $21,150, MS-68, October 2015; $1,528, MS-66, January 2015; $353, MS-61, June 2015; $306, AU-58, June 2015												
1906, Proof	160	135	64.5								$4,500	$7,500	$16,000
	Auctions: $7,638, PF-64Cam, August 2014; $8,225, PF-64Cam, September 2014; $44,063, PF, August 2013												
1907	336,294	8,994	63.1	97%	$300	$315	$325	$350	$475	$525	$675	$725	$1,200
	Auctions: $12,925, MS-68, January 2015; $1,351, MS-66, June 2015; $494, MS-62, January 2015; $282, MS-60, June 2015												
1907, Proof	154	111	64.7								$4,500	$7,500	$16,000
	Auctions: $32,900, PF-68, April 2013; $21,738, PF-65+, January 2015; $4,700, PF-63Cam, September 2014												

INDIAN HEAD (1908–1929)

Designer: *Bela Lyon Pratt.* **Weight:** *4.18 grams.*
Composition: *.900 gold, .100 copper (net weight .12094 oz. pure gold).*
Diameter: *18 mm.* **Edge:** *Reeded.* **Mints:** *Philadelphia and Denver.*

Circulation Strike   *Mintmark is on the reverse, to the left of arrows.*   **Sandblast Finish Proof**   **Satin Finish Proof**

History. The Indian Head design—used on both the quarter eagle and the half eagle—is unusual in that the lettering and motifs are in sunken relief. (The design sometimes is erroneously described as incuse.) The designer, sculptor Bela Lyon Pratt, was chosen by President Theodore Roosevelt after Augustus Saint-Gaudens died before beginning his own design. Pratt modeled the head on Chief Hollow Horn Bear of the Lakota. The "standing eagle" reverse design was based on the reverse of Saint-Gaudens's Indian Head $10 gold coin of 1907; Pratt was a pupil of the famous sculptor.

Some Americans worried that the sunken designs of the Indian Head quarter eagle would accumulate dirt and germs—an unfounded fear. As the smallest gold denomination of the era, these coins were popular for use as souvenirs and gifts, but they did not circulate as money except in the West.

Striking and Sharpness. The striking quality of Indian Head quarter eagles varies. On many early issues the rims are flat, while on others, including most of the 1920s, they are slightly raised. Some have traces of a wire rim, usually on the reverse. Look for weakness on the high parts of the Indian's bonnet (particularly the garland of flowers) and in the feather details in the headdress. On the reverse, check the feathers on the highest area of the wing, the top of the shoulder. On some issues of the 1911-D, the D mintmark can be weak.

Availability. This design was not popular with collectors, and they saved relatively few of the coins. However, many coins were given as gifts and preserved in high quality. The survival of MS-63 and better coins is a matter of chance, especially for the issues dated from 1909 to 1915. The only scarce issue is 1911-D. Luster can range from deeply frosty to grainy. As the fields are the highest areas of the coin, luster diminished quickly as examples were circulated or jostled with others in bags. The Indian Head quarter eagle is one of the most challenging series for professional graders, and opinions can vary widely.

Proofs. Sandblast (also called Matte) Proofs were made in 1908 and 1911 to 1915, while Satin (also called Roman Finish) Proofs were made in 1909 and 1910. The Sandblast issues are usually somewhat dull, while the Satin Proofs are usually of a light-yellow gold. In their time the Proofs of both styles, made for all gold series, were not popular with numismatists. Today, they are in strong demand. As a class these are significantly more readily available than half eagles of the same date and style of finish.

Most are in grades from PF-63 upward. At lower levels coins can show light contact marks. Some microscopic bright flecks may have been caused by the sandblasting process and, although they do not represent handling, usually result in a coin being assigned a slightly lower grade.

Note: Values of common-date gold coins have been based on the current bullion price of gold, $1,150 per ounce, and may vary with the prevailing spot price.

GRADING STANDARDS

MS-60 to 70 (Mint State). *Obverse:* On MS–60 to 62 coins there is abrasion in the field, this representing the highest part of the coin. Abrasion is also evident on the head-dress. Marks and, occasionally, a microscopic pin scratch may be seen. At MS-63, there may be some abrasion and some tiny marks. Luster is irregular. At MS-64, abrasion is less. Luster is rich. At MS-65 and above, luster is deep and frosty. No marks at all are visible

1911-D. Graded MS-64.

without magnification at MS-66 and higher. *Reverse:* At MS–60 to 62, there is abrasion in the field, this representing the highest part of the coin. Abrasion is also evident on the eagle's wing. Otherwise, the same comments apply as for the obverse.

   Illustrated coin: This lustrous example has excellent eye appeal.

AU-50, 53, 55, 58 (About Uncirculated). *Obverse:* Friction on the cheek is very noticeable at AU-50, progressively less at higher levels to AU-58. The headdress shows light wear, most evident on the ribbon above the forehead and on the garland. Luster is minimal at AU-50 and scattered and incomplete at AU-58. Nicks and contact marks are to be expected. *Reverse:* Friction on the wing and neck is very noticeable at AU-50, increasingly

1911-D. Graded AU-55.

less at higher levels to AU-58. Otherwise, the same comments apply as for the obverse.

   Illustrated coin: Much of the original luster remains in the incuse areas but not in the fields, which are the highest points on this design.

EF-40, 45 (Extremely Fine). *Obverse:* Light wear characterizes the portrait and headdress. Luster is gone. Marks and tiny scratches are to be expected, but not distracting. *Reverse:* Light wear is most evident on the eagle's head and wing, although other areas are lightly worn as well. Luster is gone. Marks and tiny scratches are to be expected, but not distracting.

1911-D. Graded EF-40.

VF-20, 30 (Very Fine). *Obverse:* Many details of the ribbon above the forehead and the garland are worn away. Many feather vanes are blended together. The field is dull and has contact marks. *Reverse:* The neck and the upper part of the wing show extensive wear, other areas less so. The field is dull and has contact marks.

The Indian Head quarter eagle is seldom collected in grades lower than VF-20.

1912. Graded VF-20.

PF-60 to 70 (Proof). *Obverse and Reverse:* At PF–60 to 63, there is light abrasion and some contact marks; the lower the grade, the higher the quantity. On Sandblast Proofs these show up as visually unappealing bright spots. At PF-64 and higher levels, marks are fewer, with magnification needed to see any at PF-65. At PF-66, there should be none at all.

Illustrated coin: This is a Sandblast Proof of exceptionally high quality.

1913, Sandblast Finish. Graded PF-66.

| | Mintage | Cert | Avg | %MS | VF-20 | EF-40 | AU-50 | MS-60 | MS-62 | MS-63 | MS-64 | MS-65 |
										PF-60	PF-63	PF-65
1908	564,821	9,465	61.6	84%	$300	$325	$350	$450	$675	$1,150	$1,825	$4,000
	Auctions: $7,931, MS-66, August 2015; $1,645, MS-64, July 2015; $353, MS-61, February 2015; $235, AU-50, August 2015											
1908, Sandblast Finish Proof	236	135	65.2							$3,750	$9,000	$25,000
	Auctions: $49,938, PF-68, April 2014; $70,500, PF-67, January 2015; $38,188, PF-66, August 2014; $5,170, PF-58, February 2015											
1909	441,760	7,493	61.2	80%	$300	$325	$350	$450	$845	$1,500	$2,750	$6,000
	Auctions: $11,750, MS-66, October 2015; $2,115, MS-64, January 2015; $317, MS-60, August 2015; $282, AU-58, January 2015											
1909, Satin Finish Proof	139	48	64.3							$4,000	$9,000	$27,500
	Auctions: $57,500, PF-67, January 2011											
1910	492,000	8,705	61.5	85%	$300	$325	$350	$450	$675	$1,315	$2,350	$4,750
	Auctions: $2,938, MS-65, August 2015; $1,293, MS-64, June 2015; $376, MS-62, July 2015; $282, AU-58, March 2015											
1910, Satin Finish Proof	682	104	65.1							$4,000	$9,000	$27,500
	Auctions: $64,625, PF-67, January 2015; $23,500, PF-65, July 2015; $27,600, PF-64+, September 2011											
1910, Sandblast Finish Proof (a)	*unknown*	0	n/a					*(unique)*				
	Auctions: $47,000, PF-66, August 2014											
1911	704,000	12,980	61.2	81%	$300	$325	$350	$450	$600	$1,000	$1,500	$5,000
	Auctions: $3,525, MS-65, January 2015; $470, MS-62, June 2015; $423, AU-58, March 2015; $306, AU-55, June 2015											
1911, Sandblast Finish Proof	191	97	65.8							$3,750	$9,000	$25,000
	Auctions: $27,025, PF-66, January 2014											
1911-D (b)	55,680	5,039	59.8	58%	$2,850	$4,000	$4,750	$8,500	$11,000	$15,000	$25,000	$62,500
	Auctions: $52,875, MS-65, August 2015; $5,581, MS-60, March 2015; $3,290, AU-50, August 2015; $2,938, VF-30, February 2015											
1911-D, Weak D	(c)	207	54.0	3%	$1,000	$1,500	$2,500	$4,000				
	Auctions: $2,645, AU-55, April 2012											

a. The sole known example is part of a complete 1910 Sandblast Finish Proof gold set. Other examples may exist, but have not yet been confirmed. **b.** Beware of counterfeit and altered pieces. **c.** Included in 1911-D mintage figure.

	Mintage	Cert	Avg	%MS	VF-20	EF-40	AU-50	MS-60	MS-62	MS-63	MS-64	MS-65
										PF-60	PF-63	PF-65
1912	616,000	9,232	60.8	75%	$300	$325	$350	$475	$745	$1,690	$3,375	$16,000
	Auctions: $14,100, MS-65, October 2015; $2,350, MS-64, September 2015; $400, MS-61, July 2015; $282, AU-55, February 2015											
1912, Sandblast Finish Proof	197	46	65.7							$3,750	$10,000	$25,000
	Auctions: $35,250, PF-66, October 2014; $41,125, PF-66, September 2013											
1913	722,000	12,511	61.1	80%	$300	$325	$350	$475	$575	$1,015	$1,550	$4,750
	Auctions: $3,290, MS-65, January 2015; $499, MS-62, February 2015; $264, AU-58, February 2015; $259, AU-50, February 2015											
1913, Sandblast Finish Proof	165	56	65.9							$3,750	$9,000	$25,000
	Auctions: $31,050, PF-67, January 2012											
1914	240,000	7,903	60.7	75%	$315	$350	$450	$750	$2,300	$3,715	$6,750	$25,000
	Auctions: $16,450, MS-65, August 2015; $588, MS-61, August 2015; $282, AU-55, June 2015; $235, AU-50, August 2015											
1914, Sandblast Finish Proof	117	75	65.1							$3,750	$10,000	$25,000
	Auctions: $12,650, PF-64, April 2012											
1914-D	448,000	10,851	61.2	80%	$300	$325	$350	$475	$810	$1,755	$3,750	$25,000
	Auctions: $15,275, MS-65, August 2015; $2,233, MS-64, June 2015; $376, MS-61, September 2015; $282, AU-55, November 2015											
1915	606,000	11,880	61.3	82%	$300	$325	$350	$450	$575	$945	$1,620	$4,590
	Auctions: $25,850, MS-66, October 2015; $1,058, MS-64, January 2015; 4$376, AU-58, March 2015; $259, AU-50, June 2015											
1915, Sandblast Finish Proof	100	42	65.1							$4,000	$12,000	$30,000
	Auctions: $41,688, PF-66, January 2012											
1925-D	578,000	20,546	62.3	93%	$300	$325	$350	$450	$500	$610	$850	$1,650
	Auctions: $6,500, MS-66, January 2015; $881, MS-64, January 2015; $329, MS-61, June 2015; $376, AU-58, March 2015											
1926	446,000	18,673	62.3	95%	$300	$325	$350	$450	$500	$610	$850	$1,650
	Auctions: $5,875, MS-66, January 2015; $705, MS-64, January 2015; $329, MS-61, January 2015; $259, MS-60, June 2015											
1927	388,000	15,258	62.3	95%	$300	$325	$350	$450	$500	$610	$850	$1,650
	Auctions: $14,688, MS-66, October 2015; $447, MS-63, November 2015; $306, MS-61, March 2015; $311, AU-58, July 2015											
1928	416,000	16,487	62.4	97%	$300	$325	$350	$450	$500	$610	$850	$1,650
	Auctions: $8,225, MS-66, September 2015; $764, MS-64, July 2015; $376, MS-62, March 2015; $247, AU-50, March 2015											
1929	532,000	20,196	62.4	98%	$300	$325	$350	$450	$500	$610	$850	$3,500
	Auctions: $7,638, MS-65, October 2015; $764, MS-64, August 2015; $376, MS-62, August 2015; $353, MS-60, October 2015											

Three-Dollar Gold Pieces
1854–1889

AN OVERVIEW OF THREE-DOLLAR GOLD PIECES

The three-dollar gold coin denomination was conceived in 1853 and first produced for circulation in 1854. Although there were high hopes for it at the outset, and mintages were generous, the value was redundant given the $2.50 quarter eagle then in circulation. Mintages declined, and although pieces were struck each year through 1889, very few actually circulated after the 1850s.

Although many different three-dollar dates are available at reasonable prices, most numismatists opt to acquire either a circulated or Mint State 1854 (significant as the first year of issue; also, in this year the word DOLLARS is in smaller letters than on later issues) or a Mint State coin from the low-mintage era of 1879–1889. Similar to the situation for gold dollars, although the mintages of these later pieces were low, they were popularly saved at the time, and many more have survived in high quality than might otherwise be the case.

Some numismatists have observed that $3 gold pieces might have been commonly used to purchase sheets of 100 3¢ stamps.

FOR THE COLLECTOR AND INVESTOR: THREE-DOLLAR GOLD PIECES AS A SPECIALTY

Collecting three-dollar pieces by date and mint would at first seem to be daunting, but it is less challenging than expected, outside of a handful of pieces. The 1870-S is unique (in the Harry W. Bass Jr. Collection on loan to the American Numismatic Association), the 1875 and 1876 were made only in Proof format to the extent of 20 and 45 pieces respectively, and the 1873 is quite rare. Beyond that, examples of coins in grades such as EF and AU (including some varieties with very low mintages) can be purchased for reasonable prices.

Choice examples can be elusive, this being particularly true of branch-mint issues of the 1854–1860 years. Generally, Mint State Philadelphia pieces are rare after 1855, but then come on the market with frequency for 1861 and later, with dates in the 1860s being scarcer than later issues. Coins of the years 1878 and 1879 were made in larger quantities, with the 1878 in particular being easy to find today, although examples usually are quite bag-marked. The low-mintage three-dollar pieces of 1879 through 1889 were popular at the time of issue, many were saved, and today Mint State pieces exist to a greater extent than would otherwise be the case.

INDIAN PRINCESS HEAD (1854–1889)

Designer: *James B. Longacre.* **Weight:** *5.015 grams.*
Composition: *.900 gold, .100 copper (net weight .14512 oz. pure gold).* **Diameter:** *20.5 mm.*
Edge: *Reeded.* **Mints:** *Philadelphia, Dahlonega, New Orleans, and San Francisco.*

Circulation Strike

Mintmark location is on the reverse, below the wreath.

Proof

History. The three-dollar gold coin was designed by U.S. Mint chief engraver James B. Longacre, and first struck in 1854. The quarter eagle and half eagle had already been in use for a long time, and the reason for the creation of this odd new denomination is uncertain, although some numismatists note it could have been used to buy a sheet of current 3¢ postage stamps or a group of 100 silver trimes. After a large initial mintage in 1854, the coins were struck in smaller annual quantities. These coins were more popular on the West Coast, but, even in that region, use of this denomination dropped off sharply by the 1870s.

Striking and Sharpness. Points to observe on the obverse include the tips of the feathers in the headdress, and the hair details below the band inscribed LIBERTY. Focal points on the reverse are the wreath details (especially the vertical division in the ribbon knot), and the two central date numerals. Many of the later issues—particularly those of the early 1880s—are prooflike.

Availability. In circulated grades the issues of 1854 to 1860 survive in approximate proportion to their mintages. MS coins are plentiful for the first-year Philadelphia issue, 1854, but are scarce to rare for other years and for all branch-mint issues. For the 1860s and 1870s most are in grades such as EF, AU, and low MS, except for 1874 and in particular 1878, easily found in MS. Dates from 1879 to 1889 have a higher survival ratio and are mostly in MS, often at MS-65.

Proofs. Proofs were struck of all years. All prior to the 1880s are very rare today, with issues of the 1850s being exceedingly so. Coins of 1875 and 1876 were made only in Proof format, with no related circulation strikes. Most often seen in the marketplace are the higher-mintage Proofs of the 1880s. Some have patches of graininess or hints of non-Proof surface on the obverse, or an aura or "ghosting" near the portrait, an artifact of striking.

GRADING STANDARDS

MS-60 to 70 (Mint State). *Obverse:* On MS–60 to 62 coins there is abrasion on the hair below the band lettered LIBERTY (an area that can be weakly struck as well) and on tips of the feather plumes. At MS-63, there may be slight abrasion. Luster can be irregular. At MS-64, abrasion is less. Luster is rich on most coins, less so on the 1854-D (which is often overgraded). At MS-65 and above,

1879. Graded MS-64.

luster is deep and frosty, with no marks at all visible without magnification at MS-66 and higher. *Reverse:* On MS–60 to 62 coins there is abrasion on the 1, the highest parts of the leaves, and the ribbon knot. Otherwise, the same comments apply as for the obverse.

Illustrated coin: Satiny luster and partial mirror surfaces yield excellent eye appeal.

AU-50, 53, 55, 58 (About Uncirculated).
Obverse: Light wear on the hair below the coronet, the cheek, and the tips of the feather plumes is very noticeable at AU-50, increasingly less at higher levels to AU-58. Luster is minimal at AU-50 and scattered and incomplete at AU-58. Some tiny nicks and contact marks are to be expected and should be mentioned if they are distracting. *Reverse:* Light wear on the 1, the wreath, and the ribbon knot characterize an AU-50 coin, increasingly less at higher levels to AU-58. Otherwise, the same comments apply as for the obverse.

1854. Graded AU-55.

Illustrated coin: Most of the original luster is gone, but perhaps 15% remains in the protected areas.

EF-40, 45 (Extremely Fine). *Obverse:* Medium wear is seen on the hair below the coronet and on the feather plume tips. Detail is partially gone on the hair. Luster is gone on most coins. *Reverse:* Light wear is seen overall, and the highest parts of the leaves are flat, but detail remains elsewhere. Luster is gone on most coins.

1854-D. Graded EF-40.

Illustrated coin: Note the mushy denticles (as seen on all but one specimen of this, the only Dahlonega variety in the series).

VF-20, 30 (Very Fine). *Obverse:* Most hair detail is gone, except at the back of the lower curls. The feather plume ends are flat. *Reverse:* The wreath and other areas show more wear. Most detail is gone on the higher-relief leaves.

Three-dollar gold pieces are seldom collected in grades lower than VF-20.

1874. Graded VF-20.

PF-60 to 70 (Proof). *Obverse and Reverse:* PF–60 to 62 coins have extensive hairlines and may have nicks and contact marks. At PF-63, hairlines are prominent, but the mirror surface is very reflective. PF-64 coins have fewer hairlines. At PF-65, hairlines should be minimal and mostly seen only under magnification. There should be no nicks or marks. PF-66 and higher coins should have no marks or hairlines visible to the unaided eye.

1876. Graded PF-61.

Illustrated coin: Extensive friction is visible in the fields, but the mirror surface can be seen in protected areas. This is still a desirable example of a date of which only 45 were minted.

	Mintage	Cert	Avg	%MS	VF-20	EF-40	AU-50	AU-55	MS-60	MS-62 / PF-60	MS-63 / PF-63	MS-65 / PF-65
1854	138,618	4,027	55.5	22%	$825	$1,100	$1,400	$1,500	$2,450	$3,650	$5,500	$20,000
Auctions: $17,050, MS-66, January 2015; $1,293, AU-58, January 2015; $999, EF-45, January 2015; $447, VF-20, May 2015												
1854, Proof	15–20	7	62.0							$30,000	$80,000	$175,000
Auctions: $164,500, PF-64Cam, November 2013												
1854-D	1,120	99	51.0	9%	$18,500	$27,500	$38,500	$45,000	$80,000	$175,000		
Auctions: $52,875, EF-35, March 2013												
1854-O	24,000	824	49.4	3%	$2,200	$3,250	$5,250	$7,500	$30,000	$70,000	$100,000	
Auctions: $8,225, AU-55, July 2015; $4,406, AU-53, October 2015; $3,995, AU-50, August 2015; $2,820, EF-45, July 2015												
1855	50,555	1,242	54.3	19%	$850	$1,250	$1,600	$1,750	$3,000	$4,500	$8,500	$40,000
Auctions: $5,170, MS-63, July 2015; $1,645, AU-58, October 2015; $794, EF-40, January 2015; $541, VF-20, June 2015												
1855, Proof	4–8	0	n/a							$30,000	$95,000	$200,000
Auctions: $75,900, PF-64Cam, November 2003												
1855-S	6,600	166	42.8	2%	$1,750	$3,000	$7,000	$12,000	$25,000	$55,000	$95,000	
Auctions: $17,625, AU-58, November 2013; $2,820, EF-45, August 2015; $1,763, EF-40, March 2015; $1,998, VF-30, October 2015												
1855-S, Proof	unknown	1	64.0									
Auctions: $1,322,500, PF-64Cam, August 2011												
1856	26,010	768	55.1	20%	$850	$1,200	$1,500	$1,850	$3,250	$6,000	$8,500	$35,000
Auctions: $1,645, AU-58, August 2015; $999, AU-50, June 2015; $823, EF-45, October 2015; $494, VG-10, September 2015												
1856, Proof	8–10	2	63.5							$19,500	$45,000	$100,000
Auctions: $28,750, PF-62Cam, March 2011												
1856-S (a)	34,500	553	45.7	4%	$1,000	$1,700	$2,750	$4,000	$12,000	$20,000	$30,000	
Auctions: $2,115, AU-55, October 2015; $1,116, AU-50, July 2015; $1,175, EF-40, July 2015; $552, VF-20, July 2015												
1857	20,891	637	54.9	19%	$850	$1,200	$1,800	$1,900	$3,500	$7,000	$9,500	$35,000
Auctions: $14,100, MS-64, August 2015; $7,050, MS-63, June 2015; $1,175, AU-50, June 2015; $617, EF-40, October 2015												
1857, Proof	8–12	1	64.0							$17,500	$30,000	$100,000
Auctions: No auction records available.												
1857-S	14,000	194	43.3	2%	$1,650	$3,500	$6,000	$11,000	$21,500	$45,000	$60,000	$100,000
Auctions: $12,925, AU-58, November 2014; $6,463, AU-55, April 2013; $2,115, EF-45, January 2015; $999, VF-25, October 2015												
1858	2,133	107	52.6	8%	$1,300	$3,000	$3,750	$5,500	$12,000	$15,000	$22,500	
Auctions: $7,931, AU-58, August 2013												
1858, Proof	8–12	4	65.0							$15,000	$30,000	$95,000
Auctions: $85,188, PF-65Cam, April 2013; $94,000, PF-65, October 2014; $91,063, PF-65, January 2015												
1859	15,558	580	55.5	22%	$900	$1,250	$1,750	$1,850	$3,000	$5,500	$7,500	$25,000
Auctions: $38,188, MS-66, June 2013; $10,575, MS-64, July 2014; $9,988, MS-64, August 2014; $9,400, MS-64, September 2014												
1859, Proof	80	10	64.4							$8,500	$20,000	$60,000
Auctions: $59,925, PF-65DCam, April 2014												
1860 (b)	7,036	325	55.5	23%	$950	$1,300	$1,800	$1,950	$3,500	$6,500	$8,500	$30,000
Auctions: $5,875, MS-63, January 2015; $1,645, MS-60, October 2015; $1,763, AU-53, January 2015; $940, AU-50, June 2015												
1860, Proof	119	14	64.6							$8,000	$16,000	$55,000
Auctions: $88,125, PF-67Cam, September 2014; $67,563, PF-66Cam, August 2013												
1860-S	7,000	148	42.5	3%	$1,300	$2,500	$7,000	$11,500	$25,000	$50,000	—	
Auctions: $22,325, MS-61, January 2015; $21,150, AU-58, August 2015; $5,170, AU-50, January 2015; $999, F-15, October 2015												
1861	5,959	268	55.3	26%	$1,000	$1,650	$2,500	$3,500	$6,500	$11,000	$11,500	$35,000
Auctions: $17,625, MS-64, September 2015; $6,169, AU-58, January 2015; $2,115, AU-50, August 2014; $2,585, VF-35, September 2015												
1861, Proof	113	5	64.8							$8,000	$16,000	$55,000
Auctions: $37,375, PF-64Cam, January 2011												
1862	5,750	207	54.9	23%	$1,000	$1,650	$2,500	$3,500	$6,500	$11,000	$13,500	$40,000
Auctions: $6,463, AU-58, August 2015; $4,230, AU-53, October 2015; $1,293, AU-50, January 2015; $423, VG-8, July 2015												
1862, Proof	35	9	64.9							$8,000	$16,000	$55,000
Auctions: $74,750, PF-66UCam, August 2009												

a. Collectors recognize three mintmark sizes: Large (very rare); Medium (common), and Small (rare). b. Of the already low 1860 Philadelphia mintage, 2,592 coins were melted at the Mint.

	Mintage	Cert	Avg	%MS	VF-20	EF-40	AU-50	AU-55	MS-60	MS-62 / PF-60	MS-63 / PF-63	MS-65 / PF-65
1863	5,000	243	55.6	23%	$1,050	$1,750	$2,650	$4,500	$7,500	$11,250	$15,000	$35,000
Auctions: $61,700, MS-67, July 2015; $28,200, MS-66, August 2015; $8,225, MS-61, June 2015; $3,055, AU-50, October 2015												
1863, Proof	39	10	63.4							$8,000	$16,000	$50,000
Auctions: $80,500, PF-66UCam, March 2011												
1864	2,630	156	56.2	28%	$1,200	$2,000	$3,000	$5,000	$8,000	$13,000	$15,000	$38,000
Auctions: $5,584, AU-58, June 2015; $4,935, AU-55, January 2015; $3,560, EF-45, October 2015; $588, VF-20, July 2015												
1864, Proof	50	17	63.4							$8,000	$16,000	$47,500
Auctions: $48,875, PF-64DCam, April 2012												
1865	1,140	72	56.3	36%	$2,250	$3,500	$7,000	$9,500	$15,000	$23,500	$30,000	$55,000
Auctions: $70,500, MS-66, January 2014; $3,290, VF-25, November 2014												
1865, Proof	25	8	63.8							$8,500	$20,000	$50,000
Auctions: $46,000, PF-64Cam, March 2006												
1865, Proof Restrike (c)	5	0	n/a		*(extremely rare)*							
Auctions: No auction records available.												
1866	4,000	172	56.0	27%	$1,100	$1,500	$2,400	$3,000	$5,500	$7,500	$11,000	$35,000
Auctions: $12,925, MS-64, June 2015; $7,638, MS-63, November 2014; $2,115, AU-55, October 2015; $1,116, AU-50, August 2015												
1866, Proof	30	9	63.7							$8,000	$16,500	$50,000
Auctions: $46,000, PF-64DCam, April 2011												
1867	2,600	121	56.4	21%	$1,100	$1,500	$2,400	$3,000	$5,500	$9,500	$13,500	$35,000
Auctions: $141,000, MS-67, January 2014												
1867, Proof	50	10	62.8							$8,000	$16,500	$50,000
Auctions: $19,388, PF-63DCam, October 2014; $52,875, PF-66Cam, August 2014; $64,625, PF-66Cam, August 2013												
1868 (d)	4,850	365	56.7	26%	$950	$1,250	$2,000	$2,750	$4,250	$7,500	$10,000	$30,000
Auctions: $6,463, MS-63, January 2015; $3,290, AU-55, September 2015; $940, AU-50, August 2015; $823, VF-20, October 2015												
1868, Proof	25	9	64.3							$8,000	$16,500	$50,000
Auctions: $57,500, PF-65Cam, January 2011												
1869 (d)	2,500	176	54.4	16%	$950	$1,250	$2,200	$2,800	$4,750	$9,000	$13,500	$45,000
Auctions: $9,988, MS-63, August 2014; $3,525, MS-61, January 2015; $2,350, AU-55, March 2015; $1,763, AU-53, October 2015												
1869, Proof	25	4	64.5							$8,000	$16,500	$50,000
Auctions: $57,500, PF-65UCam, February 2009												
1870	3,500	275	54.2	12%	$1,000	$1,350	$2,500	$3,000	$5,000	$10,500	$15,000	
Auctions: $51,700, MS-65, January 2015; $2,820, AU-58, June 2015; $1,293, AU-50, January 2015; $823, EF-40, July 2015												
1870, Proof	35	10	62.9							$8,000	$16,500	$50,000
Auctions: $55,813, PF-64Cam, January 2014												
1870-S (e)		0	n/a		*(unique, in the Bass Foundation Collection)*							
Auctions: $687,500, EF-40, October 1982												
1871	1,300	190	56.7	23%	$1,100	$1,350	$2,250	$3,000	$4,750	$9,000	$12,750	$35,000
Auctions: $9,400, MS-63, November 2014; $6,463, MS-62, October 2014; $3,055, AU-58, October 2015; $1,880, AU-53, September 2015												
1871, Proof	30	5	62.2							$8,000	$16,500	$55,000
Auctions: $19,550, PF-63Cam, September 2007												
1872	2,000	200	56.2	22%	$1,100	$1,350	$2,250	$3,000	$4,750	$8,500	$12,500	
Auctions: $7,638, MS-62, August 2014; $7,050, MS-62, November 2014; $4,700, MS-62, February 2015; $3,290, AU-58, January 2015												
1872, Proof	30	22	62.8							$8,000	$16,500	$47,500
Auctions: $9,400, MS-62, November 2013; $7,638, AU-58, July 2014; $5,581, AU-58, November 2014; $2,115, AU-50, August 2014												

c. Sometime around 1873, the Mint restruck a small number of 1865 three-dollar pieces using an obverse die of 1872 and a newly created reverse with the date slanting up to the right (previously listed in *United States Pattern Coins* as Judd-440). Two examples are known in gold. Versions were also made in copper (Judd-441) for interested collectors. **d.** Varieties showing traces of possible overdating include 1868, 8 Over 7; 1869, 9 Over 8; and 1878, 8 Over 7. **e.** A second example of the 1870-S is rumored to exist in the cornerstone of the San Francisco Mint, but the precise location of the cornerstone has long been unknown.

	Mintage	Cert	Avg	%MS	VF-20	EF-40	AU-50	AU-55	MS-60	MS-62	MS-63	MS-65
										PF-60	PF-63	PF-65
1873, Close 3	(f)	51	56.6	20%	$4,250	$7,500	$13,500	$18,500	$32,500	$40,000	$55,000	
	Auctions: $61,688, MS-63, January 2014; $52,875, MS-63, August 2014; $8,813, AU-50, October 2015; $2,585, EF-40, August 2015											
1873, Open 3 (Original), Proof (g)	25	6	64.0							$25,000	$32,500	$70,000
	Auctions: $212,750, PF-65DCam, September 2008											
1873, Close 3, Proof	(h)	0	n/a							$25,000	$37,500	$75,000
	Auctions: $37,375, PF-61, January 2011											
1874	41,800	2,875	56.6	28%	$850	$1,150	$1,400	$1,500	$2,500	$3,500	$4,500	$15,000
	Auctions: $14,100, MS-66, October 2015; $1,998, MS-61, June 2015; $705, AU-50, July 2015; $564, F-15, September 2015											
1874, Proof	20	9	64.3							$12,500	$28,000	$60,000
	Auctions: $54,625, PF-65Cam, January 2012											
1875, Proof (i)	20	7	63.0							$80,000	$150,000	$250,000
	Auctions: $218,500, PF-64, January 2012											
1876, Proof (i)	45	29	63.9							$25,000	$50,000	$85,000
	Auctions: $76,375, PF-65Cam, June 2013											
1877	1,468	36	56.9	22%	$3,000	$6,000	$13,000	$20,000	$28,500	$35,000	$50,000	
	Auctions: $22,325, MS-61, August 2013; $18,800, AU-58, September 2015; $17,625, AU-58, July 2015; $12,992, AU-55, January 2015											
1877, Proof	20	14	63.1							$12,500	$30,000	$55,000
	Auctions: $64,400, PF-65DCam, November 2011											
1878 (d)	82,304	5,354	59.4	57%	$850	$1,150	$1,400	$1,450	$2,250	$2,750	$4,000	$9,500
	Auctions: $23,500, MS-66, January 2015; $999, AU-55, February 2015; $646, EF-40, September 2015; $423, AG-3, February 2015											
1878, Proof	20	8	63.8							$12,500	$27,500	$55,000
	Auctions: $877, PF, June 2014											
1879	3,000	406	60.8	67%	$1,000	$1,300	$2,000	$2,750	$3,750	$5,500	$7,000	$19,500
	Auctions: $19,975, MS-66, February 2015; $4,935, MS-64, July 2015; $2,233, AU-58, October 2015; $881, AU-50, September 2015											
1879, Proof	30	12	64.7							$10,000	$17,000	$42,500
	Auctions: $14,375, PF-63Cam, October 2011											
1880	1,000	122	62.1	89%	$1,200	$2,000	$3,500	$3,750	$5,000	$7,000	$9,000	$20,000
	Auctions: $16,450, MS-65, January 2015; $5,875, MS-62, June 2015; $3,995, MS-62, October 2015; $2,820, MS-60, October 2015											
1880, Proof	36	16	64.0							$10,000	$17,000	$42,500
	Auctions: $51,113, PF, August 2013											
1881	500	103	57.7	40%	$2,500	$4,500	$7,500	$8,500	$12,000	$15,000	$18,500	
	Auctions: $35,250, MS-64, September 2014; $14,100, MS-62, February 2015; $6,463, AU-55, January 2015; $3,290, EF-40, January 2015											
1881, Proof	54	30	64.2							$10,000	$17,000	$42,500
	Auctions: $32,200, PF-64Cam, January 2011											
1882	1,500	273	59.1	55%	$1,250	$1,500	$2,350	$3,000	$4,250	$6,750	$10,000	$25,000
	Auctions: $22,325, MS-65, August 2015; $3,643, MS-61, August 2015; $2,950, AU-58, September 2015; $705, AU-50, June 2015											
1882, Proof	76	33	63.2							$7,500	$13,500	$35,000
	Auctions: $38,188, PF-65DCam, September 2014; $28,200, PF-64DCam, March 2014											
1883	900	136	58.6	58%	$1,400	$2,000	$3,000	$3,500	$5,500	$7,500	$10,000	$30,000
	Auctions: $21,150, MS-65, June 2015; $3,760, MS-61, February 2015; $4,465, MS-60, July 2015; $2,820, AU-53, January 2015											
1883, Proof	89	39	64.3							$7,500	$13,500	$35,000
	Auctions: $70,500, PF-66Cam+, November 2014; $38,188, PF-65Cam, April 2013											
1884	1,000	53	60.3	66%	$1,500	$2,000	$3,250	$4,000	$5,500	$7,500	$10,000	$27,500
	Auctions: $7,931, MS-62, August 2013											
1884, Proof	106	39	63.9							$7,500	$13,500	$35,000
	Auctions: $30,550, PF-65DCam, September 2014; $23,500, PF-64DCam, August 2013											

d. Varieties showing traces of possible overdating include 1868, 8 Over 7; 1869, 9 Over 8; and 1878, 8 Over 7. **f.** The mintage figure for the 1873, Close 3, coins is unknown. Research suggests that only Proofs may have been struck (none for circulation), and those perhaps as late as 1879. **g.** Mint records report 25 Proof coins (with no reference to the style, Open or Close, of the number 3 in the date). The actual mintage may be as high as 100 to 1,000 coins. **h.** Included in 1873, Open 3 (Original), Proof, mintage figure. **i.** Proof only.

| | Mintage | Cert | Avg | %MS | VF-20 | EF-40 | AU-50 | AU-55 | MS-60 | MS-62 | MS-63 | MS-65 |
										PF-60	PF-63	PF-65
1885	801	149	59.5	56%	$1,650	$2,150	$3,750	$4,500	$6,000	$9,000	$15,000	$32,500
Auctions: $27,025, MS-65, January 2015; $7,638, MS-62+, August 2014; $4,700, AU-58, January 2015; $3,995, AU-58, October 2015
1885, Proof	109	55	63.5							$7,500	$13,500	$35,000
Auctions: $10,281, PF-63, November 2014; $8,813, PF-62, October 2014; $76,050, PF, September 2013
1886	1,000	157	57.9	44%	$1,500	$1,950	$2,750	$3,750	$5,000	$7,500	$13,500	$40,000
Auctions: $11,163, MS-63, January 2015; $4,465, MS-61, September 2015; $2,233, MS-60, August 2015; $1,293, AU-50, January 2015
1886, Proof	142	72	64.0							$7,500	$13,500	$35,000
Auctions: $38,188, PF-65DCam, April 2013
1887	6,000	222	60.6	68%	$900	$1,350	$2,250	$2,750	$3,500	$4,750	$10,500	$17,500
Auctions: $11,750, MS-65, August 2015; $3,995, MS-63, January 2015; $1,410, AU-53, October 2015; $953, AU-50, September 2015
1887, Proof	160	68	63.8							$7,500	$13,500	$35,000
Auctions: $64,625, PF-67Cam, August 2013
1888	5,000	510	60.9	73%	$850	$1,150	$1,750	$1,850	$3,000	$4,500	$5,500	$12,500
Auctions: $7,638, MS-65, October 2015; $4,935, MS-64, January 2015; $3,599, MS-63, January 2015; $3,055, MS-61, October 2015
1888, Proof	291	96	64.1							$7,500	$12,500	$32,500
Auctions: $38,188, PF-66Cam, November 2013; $15,863, PF-64Cam+, November 2014; $9,988, PF-63Cam, October 2015
1889	2,300	312	60.6	67%	$850	$1,150	$1,750	$2,250	$2,900	$4,500	$5,500	$12,500
Auctions: $15,275, MS-65, February 2015; $5,170, MS-63, January 2015; $3,760, MS-60, October 2015; $2,350, AU-58, October 2015
1889, Proof	129	51	63.8							$7,500	$12,500	$35,000
Auctions: $25,850, PF-65Cam, January 2014; $7,050, PF-62, November 2014

Four-Dollar Gold Pieces
1879–1880

AN OVERVIEW OF FOUR-DOLLAR GOLD PIECES

The four-dollar pattern gold coin, or Stella, is not widely collected, simply because of its rarity. For type-set purposes some numismatists opt to acquire a single example of the only issue readily available, Charles Barber's 1879 Flowing Hair, although these are expensive. However, the Coiled Hair style is a different type, much rarer, and a collector with the means might acquire an example of that design as well.

FOR THE COLLECTOR AND INVESTOR: FOUR-DOLLAR GOLD PIECES AS A SPECIALTY

Over the past century perhaps two dozen numismatists have put together complete sets of one of each gold striking of the 1879 and 1880 Flowing Hair and Coiled Hair Stella, this being made possible by collections being dispersed and sold to others, as it is unlikely that even as many as 20 complete sets could exist at one time.

John A. Kasson, a former Iowa congressman, originally proposed the four-dollar gold piece, or "Stella."

STELLA, FLOWING HAIR AND COILED HAIR (1879–1880)

Designers: *Charles E. Barber (Flowing Hair, and common reverse); George T. Morgan (Coiled Hair).*
Weight: *7.0 grams.* **Composition:** *Approximately .857 gold, .042 silver, .100 copper.*
Diameter: *22 mm.* **Edge:** *Reeded.* **Mint:** *Philadelphia.*

Flowing Hair

Coiled Hair

History. The four-dollar gold Stellas of 1879 and 1880 are Proof-only patterns, not regular issues. However, as they have been listed in popular references for decades, collectors have adopted them into the regular gold series. The obverse inscription notes the coins' metallic content in proportions of gold, silver, and copper in the metric system, intended to facilitate their use in foreign countries, where the value could be quickly determined. The Stella was proposed by John A. Kasson (formerly a U.S. representative from Iowa and chairman of the House Committee on Coinage, Weights, and Measures; in 1879 serving as envoy extraordinary and minister plenipotentiary to Austria-Hungary). It is believed that Charles E. Barber designed the Flowing Hair type (as well as the reverse common to both types), and George T. Morgan designed the Coiled Hair. Those dated 1879 were struck for congressional examination; popular testimony of the era suggests that the Flowing Hair Stella became a favorite gift for congressmen's lovers in the Washington demimonde. The only issue produced in quantity was the 1879, Flowing Hair. The others were made in secret and sold privately by Mint officers and employees. The Coiled Hair Stella was not generally known to the numismatic community until they were illustrated in *The Numismatist* in the early 20th century. Stellas are cataloged by their Judd numbers, assigned in the standard reference, *United States Pattern Coins*.

Striking and Sharpness. On nearly all examples the high parts of the hair are flat, often with striations. The other areas of the coin are typically well struck. Tiny planchet irregularities are common.

Availability. The 1879 Flowing Hair is often available on the market—usually in PF–61 to 64, although higher-condition examples come on the market with regularity (as do lightly handled and impaired coins). The 1880 Flowing Hair is typically found in PF-63 or higher. Both years of Coiled Hair Stellas are great rarities; typical grades are PF–63 to 65, with a flat strike on the head and with some tiny planchet flaws.

GRADING STANDARDS

PF-60 to 70 (Proof). *Obverse and Reverse:* PF–60 to 62 coins have extensive hairlines and may have nicks and contact marks. At PF-63, hairlines are prominent, but the mirror surface is very reflective. PF-64 coins have fewer hairlines. At PF-65, hairlines should be minimal and mostly seen only under magnification. There should be no nicks or marks. PF-66 and higher coins should have no marks or hairlines visible to the unaided eye.

1879, Flowing Hair; J-1657. Graded PF-62.

 Illustrated coin: A nick above the head and some light friction define the grade, but the coin has nice eye appeal overall.

PF-60 to 70 (Proof). *Obverse and Reverse:*
PF–60 to 62 coins have extensive hairlines and
may have nicks and contact marks. At PF-63,
hairlines are prominent, but the mirror surface is very reflective. PF-64 coins have fewer
hairlines. At PF-65, hairlines should be minimal and mostly seen only under magnification. There should be no nicks or marks.
PF-66 and higher coins should have no marks
or hairlines visible to the unaided eye.

1879, Coiled Hair; J-1660. Graded PF-65.

	Mintage	Cert	Avg	%MS	PF-40	PF-50	PF-60	PF-63	PF-64	PF-65	PF-66	PF-67
1879, Flowing Hair, Proof	425+	231	63.8		$75,000	$85,000	$105,000	$145,000	$170,000	$205,000	$235,000	$350,000
Auctions: $199,750, MS-65, August 2015; $182,125, PF-65, November 2014; $165,675, PF-64, October 2014; $44,650, VF-20, June 2015												
1879, Coiled Hair, Proof	12–15 known	13	65.1				$275,000	$400,000	$500,000	$750,000	$900,000	$1,150,000
Auctions: $1,041,300, PF, September 2013												
1880, Flowing Hair, Proof	17–20 known	20	64.9				$165,000	$237,500	$300,000	$425,000	$550,000	$725,000
Auctions: $959,400, PF, September 2013												
1880, Coiled Hair, Proof	8–10 known	12	64.9				$600,000	$775,000	$875,000	$1,250,000	$1,600,000	$2,000,000
Auctions: $2,574,000, PF, September 2013												

Note: Many individual high-value rare coins are submitted for certification and grading multiple times over the years, which can inflate
the number of certifications above the number of coins actually minted.

Gold Half Eagles ($5) 1795–1929

AN OVERVIEW OF GOLD HALF EAGLES

The half eagle was the first gold coin actually struck for the United States. The five-dollar gold piece was authorized by the Act of April 2, 1792, and the first batch was minted in 1795.

Forming a type set of half eagles is a daunting but achievable challenge—if a collector has the finances and some determination. Examples of the first type, with Capped Bust to Right (conical cap obverse), and with an eagle on a palm branch on the reverse, regularly come up on the market, usually of the date 1795. Typical grades range from EF to lower Mint State levels. Such pieces are scarce, and the demand for them is strong. The next type, the Heraldic Eagle motif, first struck in 1798, but also known from a 1795-dated die used later, was produced through 1807, and is easily enough obtained today. Again, typical grades range from EF to Mint State. MS-63 and better coins are available, but are in the distinct minority.

The short-lived Capped Bust to Left style, 1807–1812, can be found in similar grades, although such pieces did not circulate as extensively, and AU and Mint State levels are the rule, with VF pieces being unusual. Then follows the era of rarities. The Capped Head to Left, stars surrounding head, large diameter, 1813–1829 style is available largely courtesy of the first date of issue, 1813. This is the only date seen with some frequency. When available, examples tend to be choice. The later stretch of this series includes some formidable rarities, among which are the famous 1815 and the even rarer 1822, along with a whole string of other seldom-seen varieties in the 1820s. The same style, but of reduced diameter, 1829–1834, also is rare; examples of the 1830s turn up with some regularity, but these often lack eye appeal. For some reason, half eagles of the early 1830s are often heavily marked and abraded, which is not true at all for coins of the 1820s.

William Woodin, secretary of the Treasury under Franklin D. Roosevelt, built upon the findings of J. Colvin Randall in his research of half eagle die varieties.

Classic Head half eagles, capless and without the motto E PLURIBUS UNUM, first minted in August 1834, are easily enough obtained. Those seen in today's marketplace are usually of the first several dates, and less frequently of 1837 or 1838.

Grades range from VF upward, reflecting their extensive use in circulation. Mint State coins can be found on occasion and are scarce. Choice and gem pieces are rare.

With just a few exceptions, Liberty Head half eagles of the 1839–1866 type without the motto IN GOD WE TRUST are very plentiful in worn grades, including certain of the higher-mintage issues from the popular Charlotte and Dahlonega mints (permitting interesting varieties to be added to a type set). Mint State coins are scarce, and when seen are usually in lower levels such as MS–60 and 62. Gems of any date are rare. Then follow the Liberty Head pieces with the motto IN GOD WE TRUST on the reverse, 1866 through 1908; the earlier years are mostly encountered in worn grades, the later ones are easy enough to find in Mint State. Proofs were made of all Liberty Head half eagle dates, and today they are generally collectible from about 1860 onward.

With two exceptions (1909-O and 1929), the Indian Head half eagles of 1908 to 1929 are common enough in worn grades as well as low Mint State levels, but true gems, accurately graded and with lustrous, frosty surfaces, are quite rare. The field is the highest area of the coin and thus is quite susceptible to scuffs and marks. Probably the most readily available dates in higher grades are 1908 and 1909, with the 1909-D being plentiful due to a hoard that came on the market a generation ago.

FOR THE COLLECTOR AND INVESTOR: GOLD HALF EAGLES AS A SPECIALTY

While in the annals of American numismatics dozens of old-time numismatists collected half eagles by date (or, less often, by date *and* mint), today rarities are so widely scattered and are so expensive that few collectors can rise to the challenge.

Early half eagles can be collected by dates and basic varieties, and also by die varieties. The year 1795 in particular is rich in the latter, and years ago several scholars described such varieties, beginning with J. Colvin Randall in the 1870s, continuing to William H. Woodin in the early 1900s, then Edgar H. Adams, Thomas Ollive Mabbott, and Walter Breen. In more recent times Robert Miller, Harry W. Bass Jr., John Dannreuther, and others have added their research to the literature.

Among early half eagles there are two unique varieties: the 1797 with a 16-star obverse, and the 1797 with a 15-star obverse, both with the Heraldic Eagle reverse, likely struck in 1798. Of the later 1822, just three are known, two of which are in the National Numismatic Collection at the Smithsonian Institution. Of all early half eagles the 1815 was far and away the most famous during the 19th century. (In the 1880s a publication on the Mint Collection stated that the two highlights there were the 1815 half eagle and the unique 1849 double eagle.) At the time the rarer 1822 was not recognized for its elusive nature. Today an estimated 11 examples of the 1815 half eagles exist, mostly in higher circulated grades, including those in museums. There are only two known of the 1825, 5 Over 4, overdate, but it is not at all famous, probably because it is an overdate variety, not a single date on its own. Half eagles of 1826 through 1829 all are rare, with the 1829 being particularly well known. The latter date includes early pieces with regular diameter and later ones with the diameter reduced. Generally, all half eagles from 1815 through 1834 are scarce, some of them particularly so.

Classic Head half eagles of 1834 to 1838 include the scarce 1838-C and 1838-D, the first of the Charlotte and Dahlonega mints respectively; none are prohibitively rare. Generally, the higher-grade pieces are found toward the beginning of the Classic Head series, especially bearing the date 1834.

Liberty Head half eagles are readily available of most dates and mints from 1839 to 1908, save for the one great rarity, the 1854-S, of which just three are known (one is in the Smithsonian). There is a vast panorama of Charlotte and Dahlonega issues through 1861, most of which were made in fairly large quantities, as this was the highest denomination ever struck at each of these mints (larger-capacity presses were not on hand). Accordingly, they are highly collectible today. Some varieties are scarce, but none are completely out of reach. Typical grades range from VF to EF and AU, occasionally Mint State, though not often MS-63 or higher.

Among San Francisco half eagles most of the early issues are scarce, as such pieces circulated extensively and there was no thought to saving numismatic examples. However, there are not many specialists in the field, and for some varieties it can be said that collectors are harder to find than are the coins themselves, yielding the opportunity to purchase truly rare pieces for significantly less than would otherwise be the case. Carson City half eagles were minted beginning in 1870 and continuing intermittently through 1893. Most of the early issues range from scarce to rare, the 1870-CC being particularly well known in this regard. Proofs of the Liberty Head type are generally collectible from the 1860s onward, with most on the market being of the higher-mintage issues of the 1890s and 1900s.

Among Indian Head half eagles, 1908 to 1929, the 1909-O is the rarest of the early coins, and when seen is usually worn. A choice or gem Mint State 1909-O is an incredible rarity. However, enough worn 1909-O half eagles exist, including many brought from overseas hoards in recent decades, that a piece in VF or so grade presents no problem. Half eagles of 1929, of which just 662,000 were minted, were mostly melted, it seems. A couple hundred or so exist today, nearly all of which are Mint State, but nicked and with bagmarks, MS–60 to 62 or 63. Truly high-quality gems are exceedingly rare.

CAPPED BUST TO RIGHT, SMALL EAGLE REVERSE (1795–1798)

Designer: *Robert Scot.* **Weight:** *8.75 grams.*
Composition: *.9167 gold, .0833 silver and copper.*
Diameter: *Approximately 25 mm.* **Edge:** *Reeded.* **Mint:** *Philadelphia.*

Bass-Dannreuther–2.

History. Half eagles of this style, the first federal gold coins, were introduced in July 1795. The obverse features Miss Liberty wearing a conical cap, a design generally called Capped Bust to Right. The reverse depicts a "small" eagle perched on a palm branch. The same motif was used on contemporary $10 gold coins. No Proofs or presentation strikes were made of this type.

Striking and Sharpness. On the obverse, check the star centers and the hair details. On the reverse, check the feathers of the eagle, particularly on the breast. Examine the denticles on both sides. Adjustment marks (from Mint workers filing down overweight planchets to acceptable standards) often are visible, but are not explicitly noted by the grading services.

Availability. Typical grades range from EF to AU and low MS. MS-63 and better coins are rare; when seen, they usually are of the 1795 date (of which many different die varieties exist). Certain varieties are rare, most famously the 1798 with Small Eagle reverse.

GRADING STANDARDS

MS-60 to 70 (Mint State). *Obverse:* At MS-60, some abrasion and contact marks are evident, most noticeably on the hair to the left of Miss Liberty's forehead and on the higher-relief areas of the cap. Luster is present, but may be dull or lifeless, and interrupted in patches. At MS-63, contact marks are few, and abrasion is very light. An MS-65 coin has hardly any abrasion, and contact marks are so minute as to require magnifica-

1795, S Over D in STATES; BD-6. Graded MS-63.

tion. Luster should be full and rich. Grades above MS-65 for this type are more often theoretical than actual—but they do exist and are defined by having fewer marks as perfection is approached. *Reverse:* Comments apply as for the obverse, except that abrasion and contact marks are most noticeable on the breast and head of the eagle. The field area is mainly protected by the eagle, branch, and lettering.

Illustrated coin: This is the error die with the second S over an erroneous D in STATES (which originally read as STATED).

AU-50, 53, 55, 58 (About Uncirculated). *Obverse:* Light wear is seen on the cheek, the hair immediately to the left of the face, and the cap, more at AU-50 than at AU–53 or 55. An AU-58 coin has minimal traces of wear. An AU-50 coin has luster in protected areas among the stars and letters, with little in the open fields or on the portrait. At AU-58, most luster is present in the fields but is worn away on the highest parts of the motifs.

1795; BD-7. Graded AU-58.

Reverse: Comments as preceding, except that the eagle shows light wear on the breast and head in particular, but also at the tip of the wing on the left and elsewhere. Luster ranges from perhaps 40% remaining in protected areas (at AU-50) to nearly full mint bloom (at AU-58).

EF-40, 45 (Extremely Fine). *Obverse:* Wear is evident all over the portrait, with some loss of detail in the hair to the left of Miss Liberty's face. Excellent detail remains in low-relief areas of the hair, such as the front curl and at the back of her head. The stars show wear, as do the date and letters. Luster, if present at all, is minimal and in protected areas. *Reverse:* Wear is greater than on an About Uncirculated coin. The breast, neck, and legs of the

1795; BD-4. Graded EF-40.

eagle lack nearly all feather detail. More wear is seen on the edges of the wing. Some traces of luster may be seen, more so at EF-45 than at EF-40.

VF-20, 30 (Very Fine). *Obverse:* The higher-relief areas of hair are well worn at VF-20, less so at VF-30. The stars are flat at their centers. *Reverse:* Wear is greater, the eagle is flat in most areas, and about 40% to 60% of the wing feathers can be seen.

1795. Graded VF-20.

The Capped Bust to Right half eagle with Small Eagle reverse is seldom collected in grades lower than VF-20.

Illustrated coin: While exhibiting typical wear for a VF-20 coin, this specimen also shows rim damage from having been mounted as jewelry at some point in time.

1796, 6 Over 5

1797, 15-Star Obverse

1797, 16-Star Obverse

	Mintage	Cert	Avg	%MS	F-12	VF-20	EF-40	AU-50	AU-55	MS-60	MS-62	MS-63	MS-64
1795	8,707	222	55.2	30%	$21,500	$25,000	$32,500	$40,000	$47,500	$70,000	$95,000	$155,000	$250,000 (a)
Auctions: $587,500, MS-66H, January 2015; $64,625, MS-61, February 2013; $64,625, AU-58, August 2014; $52,875, AU-58, August 2014													
1795, S Over D in STATES (b)	(c)	0	n/a					$42,000	$50,000	$75,000			
Auctions: $345,000, MS-65PL, July 2009													
1796, 6 Over 5	6,196	38	55.3	42%	$20,000	$25,000	$40,000	$60,000	$75,000	$110,000	$150,000	$215,000	$300,000
Auctions: $67,563, AU-58, February 2014; $45,531, AU-55, October 2014; $52,875, AU-53, August 2014; $15,863, EF-40, October 2014													
1797, All kinds	3,609												
1797, 15-Star Obverse		4	56.5	25%	$27,000	$45,000	$65,000	$125,000	$155,000	$275,000			
Auctions: $152,750, AU-53, January 2014													
1797, 16-Star Obverse		6	56.7	17%	$25,000	$40,000	$55,000	$87,500	$145,000	$300,000			
Auctions: $411,250, MS-61, August 2013													
1798, Small Eagle (d)	unknown	2	50.0	0%		$375,000	$575,000	$850,000	$1,250,000	—			
Auctions: No auction records available.													

a. Value in MS-65 is $525,000. **b.** The final S in STATES is punched over an erroneous D. **c.** Included in 1795, Small Eagle, mintage figure. **d.** The reverse of the 1798, Small Eagle, was from a 1795 die. The obverse has an arched die crack or flaw beneath the date. 7 examples are known, and the finest is an AU-55 from the collection of King Farouk of Egypt.

CAPPED BUST TO RIGHT, HERALDIC EAGLE REVERSE (1795–1807)

Designer: *Robert Scot.* **Weight:** *8.75 grams.*
Composition: *.9167 gold, .0833 silver and copper.*
Diameter: *Approximately 25 mm.* **Edge:** *Reeded.* **Mint:** *Philadelphia.*

BD-13.

History. For this type, the obverse design is the same as that of the preceding. The reverse features a heraldic eagle, as used on other silver and gold coins of the era. Some half eagles of the Heraldic Eagle Reverse design are dated 1795, but these were actually struck in 1798, from a leftover obverse coinage die. The *Encyclopedia of U.S. Gold Coins, 1795–1933* notes that "No Proofs were made, but one 1795 half eagle with a Heraldic Eagle reverse has been certified as a Specimen."

Striking and Sharpness. On the obverse, check the star centers and the hair details. On the reverse, check the upper part of the shield, the lower part of the eagle's neck, the eagle's wing, the stars above the eagle, and the clouds. Inspect the denticles on both sides. Adjustment marks (from overweight planchets being filed down to correct standards by Mint workers) can be an aesthetic problem and are not explicitly identified by the grading services.

Availability. Although there are many rare die varieties, as a type this half eagle is plentiful. Typical grades are EF to lower MS. MS-63 and higher coins are seen with some frequency and usually are dated from 1802 to 1807. Sharply struck coins without adjustment marks are in the minority.

GRADING STANDARDS

MS-60 to 70 (Mint State). *Obverse:* At MS-60, some abrasion and contact marks are evident, most noticeably on the hair to the left of Miss Liberty's forehead and on the higher-relief areas of the cap. Luster is present, but may be dull or lifeless, and interrupted in patches. At MS-63, contact marks are few, and abrasion is very light. An MS-65 coin has hardly any abrasion, and contact marks are so minute as to require magnifica-

1802, 2 Over 1. Graded MS-62.

tion. Luster should be full and rich. Grades above MS-65 are not often seen but are defined by having fewer marks as perfection is approached. *Reverse:* Comments apply as for the obverse, except that abrasion and contact marks are most noticeable on the upper part of the eagle and the clouds. The field area is complex, with not much open space, given the stars above the eagle, the arrows and olive branch, and other features. Accordingly, marks are not as noticeable as on the obverse.

Illustrated coin: This is an attractive coin with rich luster. Some friction is visible on the higher points and in the obverse field.

AU-50, 53, 55, 58 (About Uncirculated).
Obverse: Light wear is seen on the cheek, the hair immediately to the left of the face, and the cap, more at AU-50 than at AU–53 or 55. An AU-58 coin has minimal traces of wear. An AU-50 coin has luster in protected areas among the stars and letters, with little in the open fields or on the portrait. At AU-58, most luster is present in the fields, but is worn away on the highest parts of the motifs.

1804. Graded AU-58.

Reverse: Comments as preceding, except that the eagle's neck, the tips and top of the wings, the clouds, and the tail now show noticeable wear, as do other features. Luster ranges from perhaps 40% remaining in protected areas (at AU-50) to nearly full mint bloom (at AU-58). Often the reverse of this type retains much more luster than the obverse.

Illustrated coin: An abrasion in the left obverse field keeps this otherwise lustrous and attractive coin below the Mint State level.

EF-40, 45 (Extremely Fine). *Obverse:* Wear is evident all over the portrait, with some loss of detail in the hair to the left of Miss Liberty's face. Excellent detail remains in low-relief areas of the hair, such as the front curl and at the back of her head. The stars show wear, as do the date and letters. Luster, if present at all, is minimal and in protected areas. *Reverse:* Wear is greater than on an About Uncirculated coin. The neck lacks feather detail on its

1804, Small 8 Over Large 8; BD-7. Graded EF-45.

highest points. Feathers have lost some detail near the edges of the wings, and some areas of the horizontal lines in the shield may be blended together. Some traces of luster may be seen, more so at EF-45 than at EF-40. Overall, the reverse appears to be in a slightly higher grade than the obverse.

VF-20, 30 (Very Fine). *Obverse:* The higher-relief areas of hair are well worn at VF-20, less so at VF-30. The stars are flat at their centers. *Reverse:* Wear is greater, including on the shield and wing feathers. The star centers are flat. Other areas have lost detail as well. E PLURIBUS UNUM may be light or worn away in areas.

The Capped Bust to Right half eagle with Heraldic Eagle reverse is seldom collected in grades lower than VF-20.

1798, Large 8, 13-Star Reverse; BD-4. Graded VF-20.

1797, 16-Star Obverse   **1797, 15-Star Obverse**

1797, 7 Over 5   **1798, Small 8**   **1798, Large 8**

1798, 13-Star Reverse   **1798, 14-Star Reverse**   **1799, Small Reverse Stars**   **1799, Large Reverse Stars**

	Mintage	Cert	Avg	%MS	F-12	VF-20	EF-40	AU-50	AU-55	MS-60	MS-62	MS-63	MS-64
1795	(a)	19	60.2	68%	$20,000	$25,000	$40,000	$60,000	$75,000	$100,000	$150,000	$200,000	$300,000
Auctions: $15,275, AU-50, January 2014													
1797, 7 Over 5	(a)	4	58.8	50%	$17,500	$30,000	$45,000	$75,000	$115,000	$200,000			
Auctions: $126,500, AU-58, September 2005													
1797, 16-Star Obverse	(a)	0	n/a		*(unique, in Smithsonian's National Numismatic Collection)*								
Auctions: No auction records available.													
1797, 15-Star Obverse	(a)	0	n/a		*(unique, in Smithsonian's National Numismatic Collection)*								
Auctions: No auction records available.													
1798, All kinds	24,867												
1798, Small 8		23	56.2	26%	$6,000	$8,000	$12,500	$18,500	$22,000	$32,500	$50,000	$77,500	
Auctions: $18,800, AU-53, April 2014													
1798, Large 8, 13-Star Reverse		71	54.2	23%	$5,000	$6,000	$10,000	$17,000	$21,000	$30,000	$40,000	$60,000	
Auctions: $21,150, AU-55, August 2014; $19,975, AU-55, November 2014; $16,450, AU-53, August 2014; $12,925, AU-50, January 2014													
1798, Large 8, 14-Star Reverse		18	54.3	6%	$5,500	$7,000	$15,000	$25,000	$35,000	$100,000			
Auctions: $32,900, AU-55, August 2014; $25,850, AU-55, October 2014; $25,850, AU, February 2014													
1799, All kinds	7,451												
1799, Small Reverse Stars		10	59.7	50%	$5,000	$7,000	$10,000	$14,000	$18,000	$27,500	$37,500	$65,000	$100,000
Auctions: $47,000, MS-62, February 2013; $19,975, AU-58, August 2014; $13,513, AU-55, September 2014; $4,711, EF-40, August 2014													
1799, Large Reverse Stars		17	58.1	59%	$5,000	$7,000	$10,000	$14,000	$18,000	$27,500	$37,500	$65,000	$100,000
Auctions: $70,500, MS-63, January 2014; $16,450, AU-55, August 2014; $11,750, AU-53, August 2014													

a. The 1795 and 1797 Heraldic Eagle half eagles are thought to have been struck in 1798 and are included in that year's mintage figure of 24,867.

| 1800, Pointed 1 | 1800, Blunt 1 | 1800, 8 Arrows | 1800, 9 Arrows |

| 1802, 2 Over 1 FS-G5-1802/1-301. | 1803, 3 Over 2 | 1804, Small 8 | 1804, Small 8 Over Large 8 |

1806, Pointed-Top 6, Stars 8 and 5   Closeup of Pointed-Top 6   1806, Round-Top 6, Stars 7 and 6   Closeup of Round-Top 6

	Mintage	Cert	Avg	%MS	F-12	VF-20	EF-40	AU-50	AU-55	MS-60	MS-62	MS-63	MS-64
1800	37,628	258	56.8	41%	$4,500	$5,500	$7,750	$11,000	$12,500	$16,000	$21,000	$35,000	$80,000
	Auctions: $16,100, MS-62, April 2012; $11,750, AU-55, January 2015												
1800, Pointed 1 (b)	(c)	0	n/a					$21,000	$24,000	$28,000			
	Auctions: $25,850, MS-63, November 2014; $21,150, MS-62, November 2013; $12,338, MS-61, October 2014												
1800, 9 Arrows (d)	(c)	0	n/a					$17,500	$21,500				
	Auctions: No auction records available.												
1802, 2 Over 1	53,176	276	57.6	39%	$4,000	$5,000	$7,000	$10,000	$12,000	$16,000	$18,500	$35,000	$57,500 (e)
	Auctions: $58,750, MS-64, January 2014; $16,450, MS-62, October 2014; $11,750, AU-58, September 2014; $5,141, AU, March 2015												
1803, 3 Over 2	33,506	321	57.4	44%	$4,000	$5,000	$7,000	$10,000	$12,500	$19,500	$25,000	$42,500	$80,000 (f)
	Auctions: $12,925, MS-62, October 2014; $14,100, MS-62, November 2014; $20,563, MS-62, October 2013; $10,575, AU-58, August 2014												
1804, All kinds	30,475												
1804, Small 8		36	60.2	67%	$4,000	$5,000	$7,000	$10,000	$11,500	$15,500	$22,000	$32,500	$60,000
	Auctions: $18,800, MS-62, January 2014; $10,575, AU-58, August 2014; $12,925, AU-55, August 2014; $5,875, AU-50, August 2014												
1804, Small 8 Over Large 8 (g)		64	59.4	56%	$4,000	$5,000	$7,000	$10,000	$12,500	$19,500	$25,000	$42,500	$75,000
	Auctions: $32,900, MS-63, January 2014; $8,813, AU-53, August 2014; $8,813, AU-53, November 2014; $5,581, AU-50, September 2014												
1805	33,183	186	59.4	60%	$4,500	$5,500	$7,750	$11,000	$12,500	$16,000	$21,000	$35,000	$60,000 (h)
	Auctions: $15,275, MS-62, August 2014; $14,688, MS-61, November 2014; $16,450, MS, February 2014; $12,925, AU-58, November 2014												
1806, Pointed-Top 6	9,676	75	57.5	52%	$4,000	$5,000	$7,000	$10,000	$12,000	$16,500	$20,000	$36,500	$60,000 (h)
	Auctions: $15,275, MS-61, August 2014; $15,275, MS-60, August 2014; $4,406, AU, March 2015; $7,638, EF-45, August 2013												
1806, Rounded-Top 6	54,417	178	58.4	52%	$4,000	$5,000	$7,000	$10,000	$11,500	$15,500	$19,000	$32,500	$50,000 (h)
	Auctions: $111,625, MS-65, March 2013; $48,469, MS-64, August 2014; $19,388, MS-62, August 2014; $18,213, MS-62, October 2014												

b. 4 to 6 examples are known. **c.** Included in 1800 mintage figure. **d.** 18 to 25 examples are known. **e.** Value in MS-65 is $135,000. **f.** Value in MS-65 is $125,000. **g.** Created when the engraver mistakenly used an 8 punch intended for $10 gold coins, then corrected the error by overpunching with a much smaller 8. **h.** Value in MS-65 is $120,000.

**1807, Small
Reverse Stars**

**1807, Large
Reverse Stars**

	Mintage	Cert	Avg	%MS	F-12	VF-20	EF-40	AU-50	AU-55	MS-60	MS-62	MS-63	MS-64
1807, All kinds	32,488												
1807, Small Reverse Stars		0	n/a					$10,000	$11,500	$15,500	$18,000	$32,500	$50,000
Auctions: $44,563, MS-64, January 2012													
1807, Large Reverse Stars		0	n/a					$10,000	$11,500	$15,500	$18,000	$32,500	$50,000
Auctions: $21,850, MS-63, January 2012; $1,880, F-12, October 2015													

DRAPED BUST TO LEFT (1807–1812)

Designer: *John Reich.* **Weight:** *8.75 grams.*
Composition: *.9167 gold, .0833 silver and copper.*
Diameter: *Approximately 25 mm.* **Edge:** *Reeded.* **Mint:** *Philadelphia.*

BD-8.

History. This half eagle motif, designed by John Reich and stylistically related to his Capped Bust half dollar of 1807, was used for several years in the early 1800s. Quantities minted were high, and the coins saw wide circulation. No Proof examples were made of this type.

Striking and Sharpness. The striking usually is quite good and is significantly better than on earlier half eagle types. Adjustment marks (from overweight planchets being filed down to acceptable weight) are seen only occasionally. On the obverse, check the star centers and the hair details. On the reverse, check the eagle, particularity at the shield and the lower left. Examine the denticles on both sides.

Availability. After 1821 gold coins of this standard no longer circulated, as their bullion value exceeded their face value. Accordingly, they never sustained extensive wear, and nearly all examples are in EF or higher grades (coins used as pocket pieces or incorporated into jewelry are exceptions). As a type this issue is readily available in grades up to MS-63, although MS–64 and 65 coins are seen on occasion. Most have excellent eye appeal.

GRADING STANDARDS

MS-60 to 70 (Mint State). *Obverse:* At MS-60, some abrasion and contact marks are seen on the cheek, the hair below the LIBERTY inscription, and the highest-relief folds of the cap. Luster is present, but may be dull or lifeless, and interrupted in patches. At MS-63, contact marks are few, and abrasion is very light. At MS-64, abrasion is even less. An MS-65 coin has hardly any abrasion, and contact marks are minute. Luster should be

1808. Graded MS-60.

full and rich and is often more intense on the obverse. Grades above MS-65 are defined by having fewer marks as perfection is approached. *Reverse:* Comments apply as for the obverse, except that abrasion is most noticeable on the eagle's neck and the highest area of the wings.

Illustrated coin: This attractive Draped Bust to Left half eagle has nice luster.

AU-50, 53, 55, 58 (About Uncirculated). *Obverse:* Light wear is seen on the cheek and the higher-relief areas of the hair and cap. Friction and scattered marks are in the field, ranging from extensive at AU-50 to minimal at AU-58. Luster may be seen in protected areas, minimal at AU-50 but more evident at AU-58. On an AU-58 coin the field retains some luster as well. *Reverse:* Comments as preceding, except that the eagle's neck, the

1811, Tall 5. Graded AU-58.

top of the wings, the leaves, and the arrowheads now show noticeable wear, as do other features. Luster ranges from perhaps 40% remaining in protected areas (at AU-50) to nearly full mint bloom (at AU-58). Often the reverse of this type retains much more luster than the obverse, as the motto, eagle, and lettering protect the surrounding flat areas.

Illustrated coin: This lustrous example is well struck.

EF-40, 45 (Extremely Fine). *Obverse:* More wear is seen on the portrait, the hair, the cap, and the drapery near the clasp. Luster is minimal or nonexistent at EF-40, and may be slight at EF-45. *Reverse:* Wear is more extensive on the eagle, including the top of the wings, the head, the top of the shield, and the claws. Some traces of luster may be seen, more so at EF-45 than at EF-40.

1807; BD-8. Graded EF-40.

VF-20, 30 (Very Fine). *Obverse:* Wear on the portrait has reduced the hair detail, especially to the right of the face and the top of the head, but much can still be seen. *Reverse:* Wear on the eagle is greater, and details of feathers near the shield and near the top of the wings are weak or missing. All other features show wear, but most are fairly sharp. Generally, Draped Bust gold coins at this grade level lack eye appeal.

1807; BD-8. Graded VF-20.

The Draped Bust to Left half eagle is seldom collected in grades lower than VF-20.

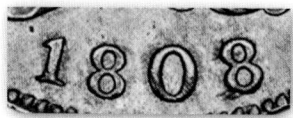

1808, 8 Over 7

1808, Normal Date

1809, 9 Over 8

1810, Small Date

1810, Large Date

Small 5

Large 5

Tall 5

	Mintage	Cert	Avg	%MS	F-12	VF-20	EF-40	AU-50	AU-55	MS-60	MS-62	MS-63	MS-64
1807	51,605	249	58.7	52%	$3,250	$4,750	$5,750	$8,250	$9,750	$14,000	$16,500	$27,000	$37,500 (a)
Auctions: $76,375, MS-65, April 2013; $19,975, MS-63, October 2014; $11,750, MS-62, August 2014; $12,338, MS-62, November 2014													
1808, All kinds	55,578												
1808, 8 Over 7		47	58.7	57%	$3,250	$5,000	$6,500	$9,000	$11,500	$18,500	$25,000	$35,000	$65,000
Auctions: $24,675, MS-62, August 2014; $19,388, MS-61, June 2014													
1808		181	58.1	53%	$3,000	$4,500	$5,500	$8,000	$9,500	$13,500	$15,500	$28,500	$35,500 (b)
Auctions: $25,850, MS-63, March 2013; $12,925, MS-60, October 2014; $4,113, MS, March 2015; $7,638, AU-58, November 2014													
1809, 9 Over 8	33,875	184	58.6	55%	$3,000	$4,500	$5,500	$9,250	$10,500	$14,000	$16,500	$27,500	$52,500
Auctions: $51,406, MS-64, January 2014; $11,750, MS-61, August 2014; $8,001, AU-53, August 2014													
1810, All kinds	100,287												
1810, Small Date, Small 5		6	54.8	33%	$20,000	$40,000	$55,000	$90,000	$110,000	$180,000	$200,000		
Auctions: $18,800, AU-50, January 2014													
1810, Small Date, Tall 5		83	57.7	52%	$3,000	$4,500	$5,500	$8,000	$9,500	$14,000	$16,000	$30,000	$55,000
Auctions: $12,925, MS-62, January 2014; $12,925, MS-62, August 2014; $12,925, AU-58, September 2014													
1810, Large Date, Small 5		83	57.7	53%	$30,000	$45,000	$75,000	$110,000	$130,000	$200,000			
Auctions: No auction records available.													
1810, Large Date, Large 5		258	59.2	63%	$3,000	$4,500	$5,500	$8,000	$9,500	$13,000	$14,500	$26,000	$40,000 (c)
Auctions: $32,900, MS-64, January 2014; $11,750, MS-62, November 2014; $8,813, AU-58, August 2014; $9,988, AU-55, March 2015													

a. Value in MS-65 is $100,000. **b.** Value in MS-65 is $127,500. **c.** Value in MS-65 is $100,000.

	Mintage	Cert	Avg	%MS	F-12	VF-20	EF-40	AU-50	AU-55	MS-60	MS-62	MS-63	MS-64
1811, All kinds	99,581												
1811, Small 5		27	55.7	44%	$3,000	$4,500	$5,500	$8,000	$9,500	$13,000	$14,500	$26,000	$40,000 **(c)**
	Auctions: $64,625, MS-64, August 2013; $10,575, MS-61, July 2014; $4,994, MS-60, October 2014; $3,836, AU-50, September 2014												
1811, Tall 5		46	60.4	65%	$3,000	$4,500	$5,500	$8,000	$9,500	$13,000	$14,500	$26,000	$40,000 **(c)**
	Auctions: $76,375, MS-65, August 2013; $9,400, AU-58, August 2014; $1,880, EF-40, July 2014; $3,055, EF-40, September 2014												
1812	58,087	221	59.0	65%	$3,000	$4,500	$5,500	$8,000	$9,500	$13,000	$14,500	$26,000	$40,000
	Auctions: $30,550, MS-64, November 2014; $61,688, MS-64, August 2013; $4,465, MS-60, August 2015												

c. Value in MS-65 is $100,000.

CAPPED HEAD TO LEFT (1813–1834)

Designer: *John Reich (design modified by William Kneass in 1829).*
Weight: *8.75 grams.* **Composition:** *.9167 gold, .0833 silver and copper.*
Diameter: *25 mm (reduced to 23.8 mm in 1829).* **Edge:** *Reeded.*

Circulation Strike
BD-1.

Proof
BD-3.

History. Half eagles of the Capped Head to Left design are divided into issues of 1813 to 1829 (with a larger diameter), and issues of 1829 to 1834 (with a smaller diameter, and smaller letters, dates, and stars). Those dated 1813 to 1815 are in bold relief and sometimes collected as a separate variety.

Striking and Sharpness. On the obverse, check the star centers and the hair details (these details are usually less distinct on the 1829–1834 smaller-diameter coins). On the reverse, check the eagle. Most examples are well struck. Adjustment marks (from overweight planchets being filed down to acceptable specifications at the mint) are not often encountered. Proof coins were struck on a limited basis for inclusion in sets and for numismatists. Over the years some prooflike Mint State pieces have been classified as Proofs.

Availability. The 1813 and 1814, 4 Over 3, are seen with some frequency and constitute the main supply available for assembling type sets. Other dates range from very rare to extremely rare, with the 1822 topping the list (just three are known, two of which are in the Smithsonian Institution). As gold coins did not circulate after 1821, issues of 1813 to 1820 are usually seen in high-level AU or in MS, and those of the 1820s in MS. The half eagles of the early 1830s are exceptions; these usually show light wear and are much rarer in high-level MS. All Proofs are exceedingly rare.

GRADING STANDARDS

MS-60 to 70 (Mint State). *Obverse:* At MS-60, some abrasion and contact marks are seen on the cheek, the hair below the LIBERTY inscription, and the highest-relief folds of the cap. Luster is present, but may be dull or lifeless, and interrupted in patches. At MS-63, contact marks are few, and abrasion is very light. At MS-64, abrasion is even less. An MS-65 coin has hardly any abrasion, and

1832, 13 Obverse Stars; BD-1. Graded MS-63.

contact marks are minute. Luster should be full and rich and is often more intense on the obverse. Grades above MS-65 are defined by having fewer marks as perfection is approached. *Reverse:* Comments apply as for the obverse, except that abrasion is most noticeable on the eagle's neck and the highest area of the wings.

AU-50, 53, 55, 58 (About Uncirculated).
Obverse: Light wear is seen on the cheek and the higher-relief areas of the hair and cap. Friction and scattered marks are in the field, ranging from extensive at AU-50 to minimal at AU-58. Luster may be seen in protected areas, minimal at AU-50 but more evident at AU-58. On an AU-58 coin the field retains some luster as well. *Reverse:* Comments as preceding, except that the eagle's neck, the

1813; BD-1. Graded AU-50.

top of the wings, the leaves, and the arrowheads now show noticeable wear, as do other features. Luster ranges from perhaps 40% remaining in protected areas (at AU-50) to nearly full mint bloom (at AU-58). Often the reverse of this type retains much more luster than the obverse, as the motto, eagle, and lettering protect the surrounding flat areas.

EF-40, 45 (Extremely Fine). *Obverse:* More wear is seen on the portrait, the hair, the cap, and the drapery near the clasp. Luster is minimal or nonexistent at EF-40, and may be slight at EF-45. *Reverse:* Wear is more extensive on the eagle, including the top of the wings, the head, the top of the shield, and the claws. Some traces of luster may be seen, more so at EF-45 than at EF-40.

The Capped Head half eagle is seldom collected in grades lower than EF-40.

1813; BD-1. Graded EF-45.

PF-60 to 70 (Proof). *Obverse and Reverse:* PF–60 to 62 coins have extensive hairlines and may have nicks and contact marks. At PF-63, hairlines are prominent, but the mirror surface is very reflective. PF-64 coins have fewer hairlines. At PF-65, hairlines should be minimal and mostly seen only under magnification. There should be no nicks or marks. PF-66 and higher coins should have no marks or hairlines visible to the unaided eye.

1829, Small Date, Reduced Diameter; BD-2. Proof.

1820, Curved-Base 2	1820, Square-Base 2	1820, Small Letters	1820, Large Letters

	Mintage	Cert	Avg	%MS	F-12	VF-20	EF-40	AU-50	AU-55	MS-60	MS-62 / PF-63	MS-63 / PF-64	MS-64 / PF-65
1813	95,428	281	58.7	57%	$4,750	$5,750	$7,000	$10,000	$11,000	$15,000	$17,500	$28,500	$40,000 **(a)**
Auctions: $49,350, MS-64, January 2013; $15,863, MS-62, August 2014; $6,463, MS-60, September 2014; $9,400, AU-55, October 2014													
1814, 4 Over 3	15,454	63	59.8	67%	$5,500	$7,000	$9,000	$12,000	$13,000	$20,000	$27,500	$40,000	$60,000
Auctions: $14,688, AU-58, January 2014; $11,764, AU-55, November 2014													
1815 (b)	635	4	57.8	50%			$200,000	$275,000	$325,000	$475,000	$600,000	$750,000	
Auctions: $460,000, MS-64, January 2009													
1818, All kinds	48,588												
1818		40	59.6	63%	$5,000	$6,000	$7,500	$15,500	$18,500	$25,000	$30,000	$47,000	$75,000 **(c)**
Auctions: $38,188, MS-62, November 2014; $19,388, MS-62, November 2014; $15,863, AU-50, September 2013													
1818, STATESOF one word		41	60.3	71%	$5,500	$7,000	$9,000	$14,000	$17,000	$22,500	$30,000	$50,000	$77,500
Auctions: $23,500, MS-62, January 2014; $4,994, AU-50, September 2014													
1818, 5-D Over 50		6	62.5	100%	$5,000	$6,500	$8,000	$11,000	$15,000	$30,000	$35,000	$70,000	$75,000 **(d)**
Auctions: $135,125, MS-65, January 2014													
1819, All kinds	51,723												
1819		3	51.7	33%			$65,000	$80,000	$95,000	$150,000			
Auctions: $38,188, AU-50, August 2014													
1819, 5-D Over 50		7	55.6	29%			$50,000	$65,000	$80,000	$125,000	$175,000	$225,000	
Auctions: $67,563, AU-55, January 2014													
1820, All kinds	263,806												
1820, Curved-Base 2, Small Letters		1	62.0	100%	$5,250	$7,000	$11,000	$14,000	$20,000	$27,500	$32,500	$65,000	$170,000
Auctions: $172,500, MS-64, January 2012													
1820, Curved-Base 2, Large Letters		1	64.0	100%	$5,000	$6,750	$8,500	$12,500	$17,500	$25,000	$27,500	$37,500	$75,000
Auctions: $19,975, MS-60, January 2014; $11,750, MS-60, September 2014													
1820, Square-Base 2		5	62.2	100%	$5,500	$7,000	$11,000	$16,000	$20,000	$27,500	$32,500	$45,000	$60,000
Auctions: $31,725, MS-63, January 2014													
1820, Square-Base 2, Proof (e)	2–3	1	64.0		*(unique, in the Bass Foundation Collection)*								
Auctions: No auction records available.													
1821	34,641	5	57.0	60%	$25,000	$35,000	$60,000	$100,000	$150,000	$215,000	$265,000	$400,000	
Auctions: $540,000, MS-63+, January 2015; $141,000, AU-55, January 2014													
1821, Proof (f)	3–5	0	n/a		*(extremely rare)*								
Auctions: No auction records available.													
1822 (g)	17,796	2	45.0	0%					$6,000,000				
Auctions: No auction records available.													
1822, Proof (h)	unknown	0	n/a		*(extremely rare)*								
Auctions: No auction records available.													

a. Value in MS-65 is $95,000. **b.** 11 examples are known. **c.** Value in MS-65 is $135,000. **d.** Value in MS-65 is $140,000. **e.** Some experts have questioned the Proof status of this unique piece; the surface of the coin is reflective, but it is not as convincing as other true Proofs of the type. Prior claims that as many as four Proofs exist of this date have not been substantiated. **f.** 2 examples are known. One is in the Harry W. Bass Jr. Foundation Collection, and another is in the Smithsonian's National Numismatic Collection. **g.** 3 examples are known. **h.** 3 examples are known, though the Proof status of these pieces has been questioned.

1825, 5 Over Partial 4 | **1825, 5 Over 4** | **1828, 8 Over 7**

1829, Large Date
BD-1.

1829, Small Date
BD-2.

	Mintage	Cert	Avg	%MS	F-12	VF-20	EF-40	AU-50	AU-55	MS-60	MS-62 / PF-63	MS-63 / PF-64	MS-64 / PF-65
1823	14,485	24	56.8	46%	$8,500	$10,000	$15,000	$20,000	$25,000	$35,000	$40,000	$65,000	$85,000
Auctions: $82,250, MS-64, January 2014; $29,375, MS-62, August 2014													
1823, Proof (i)	unknown	0	n/a										
Auctions: No auction records available.													
1824	17,340	16	60.4	63%	$14,000	$21,000	$30,000	$37,500	$50,000	$75,000	$95,000	$130,000	$150,000 (j)
Auctions: $199,750, MS-65, January 2014													
1824, Proof (k)	unknown	0	n/a										
Auctions: No auction records available.													
1825, 5 Over Partial 4 (l)	29,060	7	61.4	86%	$14,000	$20,000	$30,000	$37,500	$47,500	$75,000	$100,000	$130,000	$150,000
Auctions: $99,875, MS-61, January 2014													
1825, 5 Over 4 (m)	(n)	2	56.5	50%			$550,000	$750,000					
Auctions: $690,000, AU-50, July 2008													
1825, 5 Over Partial 4, Proof (o)	1–2	0	n/a		(unique, in the Smithsonian's National Numismatic Collection)								
Auctions: No auction records available.													
1826	18,069	6	63.8	100%	$10,000	$15,000	$20,000	$30,000	$40,000	$70,000	$80,000	$115,000	
Auctions: $546,000, MS-66, January 2015; $763,750, MS-66, January 2014													
1826, Proof	2–4	0	n/a		(unique, in the Smithsonian's National Numismatic Collection)								
Auctions: No auction records available.													
1827	24,913	14	62.9	93%	$20,000	$25,000	$30,000	$40,000	$50,000	$65,000	$75,000	$125,000	$150,000
Auctions: $141,000, MS-64, January 2014													
1827, Proof (p)	unknown	0	n/a										
Auctions: No auction records available.													
1828, 8 Over 7 (q)	(r)	3	63.3	100%					$175,000	$300,000	$400,000	$500,000	$750,000
Auctions: $632,500, MS-64, January 2012													
1828	28,029	3	60.7	67%		$50,000	$70,000	$90,000	$125,000	$200,000	$225,000	$325,000	$450,000
Auctions: $499,375, MS-64, April 2013													
1828, Proof	1–2	0	n/a		(unique, in the Smithsonian's National Numismatic Collection)								
Auctions: No auction records available.													
1829, Large Date	57,442	2	66.0	100%			—	—		$225,000	$300,000	$425,000	$600,000
Auctions: No auction records available.													
1829, Large Date, Proof	2–4	0	n/a								$1,400,000		
Auctions: No auction records available.													

i. The only auction references for a Proof 1823 half eagle are from 1885 and 1962. Neither coin (assuming they are not the same specimen) has been examined by today's standards to confirm its Proof status. **j.** Value in MS-65 is $275,000. **k.** No 1824 Proof half eagles are known to exist, despite previous claims that the Smithsonian's Mint collection specimen (actually an MS-62 circulation strike) is a Proof. **l.** Sometimes called 1825, 5 Over 1. **m.** 2 examples are known. **n.** Included in circulation-strike 1825, 5 Over Partial 4, mintage figure. **o.** The Smithsonian's example is a PF-67 with a mirrored obverse and frosty reverse. A second example, reported to have resided in King Farouk's collection, has not been confirmed. **p.** Two purported 1827 Proofs have been revealed to be circulation strikes: the Smithsonian's example is an MS-64, and the Bass example is prooflike. **q.** 5 examples are known. **r.** Included in circulation-strike 1828 mintage figure.

Small 5 D.

Large 5 D.

1832, Curved-Base 2, 12-Star Obverse

1832, Curved-Base 2, 13-Star Obverse

1833, Large Date

1833, Small Date

1834, Plain 4

1834, Crosslet 4

	Mintage	Cert	Avg	%MS	F-12	VF-20	EF-40	AU-50	AU-55	MS-60 / PF-63	MS-62 / PF-64	MS-63 / PF-65
1829, Sm Dt, Reduced Diameter (a)	(a)	2	61.5	100%	$60,000	$90,000	$150,000	$200,000	$250,000	$375,000	$450,000	$500,000
Auctions: $431,250, MS-61, January 2012												
1829, Small Date, Proof (b)	2–4	0	n/a		*(extremely rare)*							
Auctions: No auction records available.												
1830, Small or Large 5 D. (c)	126,351	21	60.0	71%	$20,000	$27,500	$40,000	$45,000	$52,500	$75,000	$80,000	$100,000
Auctions: $73,438, MS-63, January 2014; $47,000, AU-58, August 2014; $41,125, AU-58, October 2014												
1830, Proof (d)	2–4	2	63.5		*(extremely rare)*							
Auctions: No auction records available.												
1831, Small or Large 5 D. (e)	140,594	11	60.6	64%	$20,000	$27,500	$40,000	$45,000	$52,500	$75,000	$80,000	$100,000
Auctions: $82,250, MS-61, January 2014												
1832, Curved-Base 2, 12 Stars (f)	(g)	2	60.5	50%		$300,000	$350,000	$450,000				
Auctions: No auction records available.												
1832, Square-Base 2, 13 Stars	157,487	12	61.8	75%	$20,000	$27,500	$40,000	$45,000	$55,000	$95,000	$110,000	$125,000 (h)
Auctions: $176,250, MS-65, January 2014												
1832, Square-Base 2, 13 Stars, Proof	2–3	0	n/a		*(extremely rare)*							
Auctions: No auction records available.												
1833, Large Date	196,630	2	63.0	100%	$20,000	$27,500	$40,000	$45,000	$52,500	$75,000	$80,000	$100,000 (i)
Auctions: $29,375, AU-50, April 2014												
1833, Small Date (j)	(k)	1	61.0	100%	$20,000	$27,500	$40,000	$45,000	$52,500	$70,000	$100,000	$125,000 (l)
Auctions: $126,500, MS-63 PQ, May 2006												
1833, Proof (m)	4–6	4	61.3		*(extremely rare)*							
Auctions: $977,500, PF-67, January 2005												
1834, All kinds	50,141											
1834, Plain 4		17	58.3	53%	$20,000	$27,500	$40,000	$45,000	$52,500	$75,000	$80,000	$100,000
Auctions: $143,750, MS-65, August 2011												
1834, Crosslet 4		9	57.6	56%	$21,500	$30,000	$40,000	$47,500	$57,000	$85,000	$110,000	$140,000
Auctions: $45,531, AU-55, January 2014												

a. Included in circulation-strike 1829, Large Date, mintage figure (see chart on page 1036). **b.** 2 examples are known. One is in the Harry W. Bass Jr. Foundation Collection, and another of equal quality (PF-66) is in the Smithsonian's National Numismatic Collection. **c.** The 1830, Small 5 D. is slightly rarer than the Large 5 D. Certified population reports are unclear, and auction-lot catalogers typically do not differentiate between the two varieties. **d.** 2 examples are known. One is in the Byron Reed collection at the Durham Museum, Omaha, Nebraska. **e.** The 1831, Small 5 D. is estimated to be three to four times rarer than the Large 5 D. Both are extremely rare. **f.** 5 examples are known. **g.** Included in circulation-strike 1832, Square-Base 2, 13 Stars, mintage figure. **h.** Value in MS-64 is $140,000. **i.** Value in MS-64 is $150,000. **j.** The 1833 Small Date is slightly scarcer than the Large Date. **k.** Included in 1833, Large Date, mintage figure. **l.** Value in MS-64 is $175,000. **m.** 4 or 5 examples are known.

CLASSIC HEAD, NO MOTTO ON REVERSE (1834–1838)

Designer: *William Kneass.* **Weight:** *8.36 grams.*
Composition: *(1834–1836) .8992 gold, .1008 silver and copper; (1837–1838) .900 gold.*
Diameter: *22.5 mm.* **Edge:** *Reeded.* **Mints:** *Philadelphia, Charlotte, Dahlonega.*

Circulation Strike
Breen-6518.

Mintmark location is on the obverse, above the date.

Proof

History. U.S. Mint chief engraver William Kneass based the half eagle's Classic Head design on John Reich's cent of 1808. Minted under the Act of June 28, 1834, the coins' reduced size and weight encouraged circulation over melting or export, and they served American commerce until hoarding became extensive during the Civil War. Accordingly, many show considerable wear.

Striking and Sharpness. On the obverse, weakness is often seen on the higher areas of the hair curls. Also check the star centers. On the reverse, check the rims. The denticles are usually well struck.

Availability. Most coins range from VF to AU or lower grades of MS. Most MS coins are dated 1834. MS-63 and better examples are rare. Good eye appeal can be elusive. Proofs of the Classic Head type were made in small quantities, and today probably only a couple dozen or so survive, most bearing the 1834 date.

GRADING STANDARDS

MS-60 to 70 (Mint State). *Obverse:* At MS-60, some abrasion and contact marks are seen on the portrait, most noticeably on the cheek, as the hair details are complex on this type. Luster is present, but may be dull or lifeless, and interrupted in patches. Many low-level Mint State coins have grainy surfaces. At MS-63, contact marks are few, and abrasion is very light. Abrasion is even less at MS-64. An MS-65 coin will have hardly any

1834, Plain 4. Graded MS-65.

abrasion, and contact marks are minute. Luster should be full and rich and is often more intense on the obverse. Grades above MS-65 are defined by having fewer marks as perfection is approached. *Reverse:* Comments apply as for the obverse, except that abrasion is most noticeable in the field, on the eagle's neck, and on the highest area of the wings. Most Mint State coins in the marketplace are graded liberally, with slight abrasion on both sides of MS-65 coins.

Illustrated coin: This well-struck coin has some light abrasion, most evident in the reverse field.

AU-50, 53, 55, 58 (About Uncirculated). *Obverse:* Friction is seen on the higher parts, particularly the cheek and the hair (under magnification) of Miss Liberty. Friction and scattered marks are in the field, ranging from extensive at AU-50 to minimal at AU-58. Luster may be seen in protected areas, minimal at AU-50, more evident at AU-58. On an AU-58 coin the field retains some luster as well. *Reverse:* Comments as preceding, except

1834, Crosslet 4. Graded AU-50.

that the eagle's neck, the top of the wings, the leaves, and the arrowheads now show noticeable wear, as do other features. Luster ranges from perhaps 40% remaining in protected areas (at AU-50) to nearly full mint bloom (at AU-58). Often the reverse of this type retains much more luster than the obverse.

EF-40, 45 (Extremely Fine). *Obverse:* Wear is seen on the portrait overall, with reduction or elimination of some separation of hair strands, especially in the area close to the face. The cheek shows light wear. Luster is minimal or nonexistent at EF-40, and may survive in among the letters of LIBERTY at EF-45. *Reverse:* Wear is greater than on an About Uncirculated coin. On most (but not all) coins the neck lacks some feather detail

1837, Script 8. Graded EF-40.

on its highest points. Feathers have lost some detail near the edges and tips of the wings, and some areas of the horizontal lines in the shield may be blended together. Some traces of luster may be seen, more so at EF-45 than at EF-40.

VF-20, 30 (Very Fine). *Obverse:* Wear on the portrait has reduced the hair detail, especially to the right of the face and the top of the head, but much can still be seen. *Reverse:* Wear is greater, including on the shield and the wing feathers. Generally, Classic Head gold at this grade level lacks eye appeal.

The Classic Head half eagle is seldom collected in grades lower than VF-20.

1835, Block 8. Graded VF-30.

PF-60 to 70 (Proof). *Obverse and Reverse:* PF–60 to 62 coins have extensive hairlines and may have nicks and contact marks. At PF-63, hairlines are prominent, but the mirror surface is very reflective. PF-64 coins have fewer hairlines. At PF-65, hairlines should be minimal and mostly seen only under magnification. There should be no nicks or marks. PF-66 and higher coins should have no marks or hairlines visible to the unaided eye.

1834, Plain 4. Graded PF-65.

1834, Plain 4   1834, Crosslet 4

	Mintage	Cert	Avg	%MS	VF-20	EF-40	AU-50	AU-55	MS-60	MS-62	MS-63	MS-64
										PF-63	PF-64	PF-65
1834, Plain 4 (a)	657,460	2,129	51.3	13%	$675	$800	$1,350	$1,900	$4,500	$6,750	$11,500	$20,000
Auctions: $4,230, MS-61, February 2015; $1,704, AU-55, September 2015; $824, EF-45, July 2015; $447, VF-20, May 2015												
1834, Crosslet 4	(b)	88	46.4	10%	$2,250	$4,000	$6,000	$9,500	$23,500	$27,500	$55,000	$100,000
Auctions: $14,688, MS-61, January 2015; $6,463, AU-55, January 2015; $5,581, AU-50, January 2015; $3,995, EF-45, September 2015												
1834, Plain 4, Proof	8–12	5	63.2							$85,000	$135,000	$200,000
Auctions: $109,250, PF-63Cam, January 2011												
1835 (a)	371,534	709	51.4	15%	$675	$900	$1,450	$1,900	$4,500	$6,500	$11,000	$25,000
Auctions: $9,988, MS-63, September 2015; $2,115, AU-58, September 2015; $1,058, AU-53, August 2015; $517, F-12, November 2015												
1835, Proof (c)	4–6	1	68.0							$100,000	$150,000	$250,000
Auctions: $690,000, PF-67, January 2005												
1836	553,147	1,187	50.2	12%	$675	$900	$1,450	$1,900	$4,500	$6,500	$11,000	$25,000
Auctions: $3,353, MS-61, January 2015; $1,175, AU-55, October 2015; $631, EF-40, March 2015; $588, VF-30, August 2015												
1836, Proof (d)	4–6	2	67.0					*(extremely rare)*				
Auctions: No auction records available.												
1837 (a)	207,121	443	50.7	12%	$675	$975	$1,550	$2,100	$4,750	$8,500	$18,500	$35,000
Auctions: $21,738, MS-63, October 2013; $3,525, MS-61, October 2015; $1,763, AU-55, August 2014; $999, EF-45, January 2015												
1837, Proof	4–6	0	n/a				*(unique, in the Smithsonian's National Numismatic Collection)*					
Auctions: No auction records available.												
1838	286,588	683	51.8	13%	$375	$975	$1,500	$2,050	$4,500	$7,000	$11,500	$27,500
Auctions: $2,233, AU-58, August 2015; $1,645, AU-55, January 2015; $940, EF-45, June 2015; $447, EF-40, January 2015												
1838, Proof	2–3	1	65.0				*(unique, in the Bass Foundation Collection)*					
Auctions: No auction records available.												
1838-C	17,179	103	44.4	4%	$5,000	$7,250	$12,500	$20,000	$42,500	$60,000	$100,000	
Auctions: $10,575, EF-40, August 2013; $5,405, EF-40, June 2015; $1,645, VF-20, November 2014												
1838-D	20,583	132	49.9	8%	$4,250	$7,500	$12,500	$18,500	$35,000	$50,000	$85,000	
Auctions: $21,150, MS-60, January 2014; $21,738, AU-55, August 2014; $8,225, EF-45, August 2015; $1,880, VF-20, November 2014												

a. Varieties have either a script 8 or block-style 8 in the date. (See illustrations of similar quarter eagles on page 978.) **b.** Included in circulation-strike, 1838, Plain 4, mintage figure. **c.** 3 or 4 examples are known. **d.** 3 or 4 examples are known.

LIBERTY HEAD (1839–1908)

Designer: *Christian Gobrecht.* **Weight:** *8.359 grams.*
Composition: *.900 gold, .100 copper (net weight .24187 oz. pure gold).*
Diameter: *(1839–1840) 22.5 mm; (1840–1908) 21.6 mm.* **Edge:** *Reeded.*
Mints: *Philadelphia, Charlotte, Dahlonega, Denver, New Orleans, San Francisco, and Carson City.*

| **Circulation Strike** | Mintmark location, 1839, is on the obverse, above the date. | Mintmark location, 1840–1908, is on the reverse, below the eagle. | **Proof** |

History. Christian Gobrecht's Liberty Head half eagle design was introduced in 1839. The mintmark (for branch-mint coins) in that year was located on the obverse; for all later issues it was relocated to the reverse. The motto IN GOD WE TRUST was added to the reverse in 1866.

Striking and Sharpness. On the obverse, check the highest points of the hair and the star centers; the reverse, the eagle's neck, the area to the lower left of the shield, and the lower part of the eagle. Generally, the eagle on the $5 coins is better struck than on quarter eagles. Examine the denticles on both sides. Branch-mint coins struck before the Civil War are often lightly struck in areas. San Francisco half eagles are in lower average grades than are those from the Philadelphia Mint, as Philadelphia coins did not circulate at par in the East and Midwest from late December 1861 until December 1878, thus acquiring less wear. Most late 19th- and early 20th-century coins are sharp in all areas; for these issues, tiny copper staining spots (from improperly mixed coinage alloy) can be a problem. Cameo contrast is the rule for Proofs prior to 1902. Beginning that year the portrait was polished in the die, although a few years later cameo-contrast coins were again made.

Availability. Early dates and mintmarks are typically scarce to rare in MS, very rare in MS–63 to 65. Charlotte and Dahlonega coins are usually EF or AU, or overgraded as low MS, as seen with quarter eagles. The 1854-S and several varieties in the 1860s and 1870s are rare. Coins from 1880 onward are seen in higher than average grades. Proof coins exist in relation to their original mintages; issues prior to the 1890s are rare.

Note: Values of common-date gold coins have been based on the current bullion price of gold, $1,150 per ounce, and may vary with the prevailing spot price.

GRADING STANDARDS

MS-60 to 70 (Mint State). *Obverse:* At MS-60, some abrasion and contact marks are evident, most noticeably on the hair to the right of Miss Liberty's forehead and on the jaw. Luster is present, but may be dull or lifeless, and interrupted in patches. At MS-63, contact marks are few, and abrasion is very light. An MS-65 coin has only slight abrasion, and contact marks are so minute as to require

1848-C. Graded MS-63.

magnification. Luster should be full and rich. Grades above MS-65 are defined by having fewer marks as perfection is approached. *Reverse:* Comments apply as for the obverse, except that abrasion and contact marks are most noticeable on the eagle's neck and to the lower left of the shield.

Illustrated coin: Friction is seen in the obverse fields amid luster; on the reverse, luster is nearly complete.

AU-50, 53, 55, 58 (About Uncirculated). *Obverse:* Light wear is seen on the face, the hair to the right of the face, and the highest area of the hair bun, more so at AU-50 than at AU–53 or 55. An AU-58 coin has minimal traces of wear. An AU-50 coin has luster in protected areas among the stars and letters, with little in the open fields or on the portrait. At AU-58, most luster is present in the fields, but is worn away on the highest parts

1840. Graded AU-55.

of the motifs. Striking must be taken into consideration, for a lightly struck coin can be About Uncirculated, but be weak in the central areas. *Reverse:* Comments as preceding, except that the eagle shows wear in all of the higher areas, as well as the leaves and arrowheads. From 1866 to 1908 the motto IN GOD WE TRUST helped protect the field, with the result that luster is more extensive on this side in comparison to the obverse. Luster ranges from perhaps 50% remaining in protected areas (at AU-50) to nearly full mint bloom (at AU-58).

EF-40, 45 (Extremely Fine). *Obverse:* Wear is evident on all high areas of the portrait, including the hair to the right of the forehead, the tip of the coronet, the back of the head, and the hair bun. The stars show light wear at their centers (unless protected by a high rim). Luster, if present at all, is minimal and in protected areas such as between the star points. *Reverse:* Wear is greater than on an About Uncirculated coin, and flatness is

1844. Graded EF-40.

seen on the feather ends, the leaves, and elsewhere. Some traces of luster may be seen, more so at EF-45 than at EF-40. Overall, the reverse appears to be in a slightly higher grade than the obverse on coins from 1866 to 1908 (With Motto).

Illustrated coin: This coin is well struck on both sides.

VF-20, 30 (Very Fine). *Obverse:* The higher-relief areas of hair are worn flat at VF-20, less so at VF-30. The hair to the right of the coronet is merged into heavy strands. The stars are flat at their centers. *Reverse:* Feather detail is mostly worn away on the neck and legs, less so on the wings. The vertical shield stripes, being deeply recessed, remain bold.

The Liberty Head half eagle is seldom collected in grades lower than VF-20.

1858-C. Graded VF-20.

PF-60 to 70 (Proof). *Obverse and Reverse:* PF–60 to 62 coins have extensive hairlines and may have nicks and contact marks. At PF-63, hairlines are prominent, but the mirror surface is very reflective. PF-64 coins have fewer hairlines. At PF-65, hairlines should be minimal and mostly seen only under magnification. There should be no nicks or marks. PF-66 and higher coins should have no marks or hairlines visible to the unaided eye.

1872. Graded PF-55.

| | Mintage | Cert | Avg | %MS | VF-20 | EF-40 | AU-50 | AU-55 | MS-60 | MS-63 | MS-64 | MS-65 |
										PF-63	PF-64	PF-65
1839	118,143	234	51.1	14%	$500	$800	$1,200	$1,450	$4,000	$25,000	$45,000	
Auctions: $11,764, MS-62, January 2015; $3,760, AU-58, August 2015; $1,528, AU-55, January 2015; $1,410, AU-50, September 2015												
1839, Proof (a)	2–3	1	61.0		*(extremely rare)*							
Auctions: $184,000, PF-61, January 2010												
1839-C	17,205	86	49.0	15%	$2,250	$3,500	$6,000	$9,750	$20,000	$57,500		
Auctions: $23,500, MS-61, January 2014; $16,450, MS-60, January 2015; $8,813, AU-53, February 2015; $3,290, EF-40, August 2014												
1839-D	18,939	112	46.2	5%	$2,750	$4,000	$7,000	$12,500	$23,500			
Auctions: $9,400, AU-53, September 2013; $4,700, AU-50, July 2015; $4,700, EF-45, February 2015; $2,350, EF-40, November 2014												
1840 (b)	137,382	327	51.1	9%	$550	$625	$1,000	$1,600	$3,250	$9,000	$25,000	
Auctions: $2,585, AU-58, October 2015; $2,115, AU-58, June 2015; $999, AU-53, January 2015; $646, EF-45, January 2015												
1840, Proof	2–3	0	n/a		*(unique, in the Smithsonian's National Numismatic Collection)*							
Auctions: No auction records available.												
1840-C	18,992	91	48.1	11%	$2,000	$3,000	$5,250	$6,500	$16,000	$55,000	$85,000	
Auctions: $28,200, MS-62, January 2014; $5,581, AU-55, February 2015; $4,700, AU-50, August 2015; $1,645, VF-20, August 2014												
1840-D	22,896	73	50.5	19%	$2,250	$3,500	$5,750	$7,250	$14,000	$42,500		
Auctions: $14,100, MS-61, December 2013; $881, F-12, August 2014												
1840-O (b)	40,120	150	51.2	11%	$600	$900	$1,500	$2,500	$8,500	$32,500		
Auctions: $5,405, AU-58, June 2015; $2,350, AU-55, October 2015; $1,763, AU-55, January 2015; $764, AU-50, January 2015												
1841	15,833	67	52.8	27%	$550	$700	$1,250	$1,650	$4,500	$10,000	$20,000	$37,500
Auctions: $1,763, AU-55, December 2013												
1841, Proof (c)	2–3	1	63.0		*(extremely rare)*							
Auctions: No auction records available.												
1841-C	21,467	88	48.6	8%	$1,850	$2,500	$3,500	$5,750	$12,000	$40,000	$80,000	
Auctions: $5,581, AU-58, January 2014; $4,230, AU-55, September 2015; $1,939, EF-40, January 2015; $1,705, VF-35, August 2014												
1841-D	27,492	100	49.9	22%	$2,000	$2,750	$3,250	$5,000	$10,000	$22,000	$45,000	
Auctions: $9,988, MS-61, January 2014; $8,578, MS-60, August 2014												
1841-O (d)	50	0	n/a									
Auctions: No auction records available.												

a. 2 or 3 examples are known. **b.** Scarce varieties of the 1840 coins have the fine edge-reeding and wide rims of the 1839 issues. This is referred to as the broad-mill variety. **c.** 2 examples are known. One is in the Smithsonian's National Numismatic Collection; the other is ex Eliasberg Collection. **d.** Official Mint records report 8,350 coins struck at the New Orleans Mint in 1841. However, most—if not all—were actually dated 1840. No 1841-O half eagle has ever appeared on the market.

Small Letters   **Large Letters**

Small Date   **Large Date**

	Mintage	Cert	Avg	%MS	VF-20	EF-40	AU-50	AU-55	MS-60	MS-63	MS-64	MS-65
										PF-63	PF-64	PF-65
1842, All kinds	27,578											
1842, Small Letters		24	54.8	21%	$550	$1,000	$2,500	$4,000	$10,000	$22,000	$32,500	$60,000
	Auctions: $15,275, MS-62, January 2014											
1842, Large Letters		21	48.6	0%	$725	$1,600	$4,250	$6,500	$12,500	$25,000		
	Auctions: $4,113, AU-55, April 2014; $4,700, AU-55, August 2014											
1842, Small Letters, Proof (e)	4–6	1	64.0					*(extremely rare)*				
	Auctions: $172,500, PF-64Cam★, January 2009											
1842-C, All kinds	27,432											
1842-C, Small Date		25	51.5	20%	$7,500	$15,500	$25,000	$32,500	$70,000	$125,000		
	Auctions: $111,625, MS-63, January 2015; $49,938, AU-58, July 2014; $20,563, AU-53, January 2015; $12,925, EF-40, October 2015											
1842-C, Large Date		104	50.8	14%	$2,000	$2,550	$3,750	$5,000	$14,500	$30,000	$47,500	
	Auctions: $25,850, MS-63, September 2013; $11,750, MS-61, November 2014											
1842-D, All kinds	59,608											
1842-D, Small Date		160	46.2	6%	$2,000	$2,750	$3,750	$5,000	$10,500	$30,000		
	Auctions: $16,450, MS-62, April 2014; $3,995, AU-55, October 2015; $2,350, EF-45, July 2014; $764, F-12, January 2015											
1842-D, Large Date		26	44.4	8%	$3,000	$5,500	$11,000	$18,500	$37,500			
	Auctions: $7,050, MS-60, January 2014											
1842-O	16,400	49	45.1	4%	$2,500	$4,000	$9,500	$13,500	$20,000	$45,000		
	Auctions: $7,638, AU-53, January 2014; $734, VF-20, January 2015; $646, VF-20, August 2014; $823, F-12, January 2015											
1843	611,205	529	53.5	15%	$450	$500	$575	$600	$1,400	$9,500	$17,500	$37,500
	Auctions: $1,410, MS-61, January 2015; $1,175, MS-60, September 2015; $535, AU-55, January 2015; $447, EF-45, September 2015											
1843, Proof (f)	4–8	4	64.0					*(extremely rare)*				
	Auctions: $34,500, PF-58, August 2009											
1843-C	44,277	156	44.9	8%	$2,000	$2,500	$4,250	$6,000	$9,000	$25,000	$55,000	
	Auctions: $8,813, MS-61, October 2015; $3,084, AU-53, February 2015; $2,838, AU-50, November 2014; $2,233, EF-45, January 2015											
1843-D	98,452	223	46.6	9%	$2,000	$2,500	$3,500	$4,750	$10,000	$20,000	$50,000	
	Auctions: $19,975, MS-63, April 2013; $4,406, MS-60, November 2014; $5,434, AU-58, September 2014; $1,998, AU-50, August 2015											
1843-D, Proof (g)	*unknown*	1	65.0									—
	Auctions: No auction records available.											
1843-O, Small Letters	19,075	73	46.9	8%	$850	$1,650	$2,500	$4,500	$17,500	$35,000	$50,000	$65,000
	Auctions: $5,940, AU-58, January 2015; $2,585, AU-50, October 2014; $3,760, EF-45, September 2015; $1,116, EF-40, November 2014											
1843-O, Large Letters	82,000	114	49.9	19%	$650	$1,250	$2,000	$3,500	$9,500	$25,000	$35,000	
	Auctions: $19,975, MS-62, January 2014; $5,875, AU-58, March 2015; $5,170, AU-58, July 2015; $797, EF-40, August 2014											

e. Of the examples known today, one is in the Smithsonian's National Numismatic Collection, and another is ex Pittman Collection.
f. 4 or 5 examples are known. **g.** One non-circulation example of the 1843-D half eagle, probably a presentation strike of some sort, has been certified by NGC as a Specimen (rated Specimen-65).

**1846-D, High
Second D Over D**

	Mintage	Cert	Avg	%MS	VF-20	EF-40	AU-50	AU-55	MS-60	MS-63 / PF-63	MS-64 / PF-64	MS-65 / PF-65
1844	340,330	331	53.3	13%	$450	$500	$550	$625	$1,950	$8,500	$18,000	$55,000
Auctions: $3,525, MS-62, October 2015; $564, AU-53, June 2015; $494, AU-50, January 2015; $388, VF-30, September 2015												
1844, Proof (h)	3–5	1	64.0		*(extremely rare)*							
Auctions: No auction records available.												
1844-C	23,631	88	45.9	8%	$2,150	$3,000	$4,250	$7,000	$12,500	$30,000		
Auctions: $4,230, AU-55, January 2015; $3,290, AU-55, January 2015; $2,957, VF-35, March 2015; $999, G-6, October 2015												
1844-D	88,982	245	46.6	8%	$2,000	$2,750	$3,750	$4,500	$8,500	$25,000	$40,000	
Auctions: $7,638, MS-61, June 2015; $6,000, MS-60, January 2015; $5,405, EF-40, July 2015; $1,763, VF-35, September 2015												
1844-O	364,600	662	50.4	10%	$550	$600	$825	$1,200	$4,000	$12,500	$23,500	$45,000
Auctions: $1,880, AU-58, June 2015; $646, EF-45, July 2015; $494, EF-45, September 2015; $400, EF-40, October 2015												
1844-O, Proof (i)	1	0	n/a		*(unique)*							
Auctions: No auction records available.												
1845	417,099	367	53.7	13%	$500	$550	$600	$650	$2,000	$8,000	$16,000	
Auctions: $12,925, MS-64, July 2015; $1,235, AU-58, July 2015; $447, AU-53, January 2015; $470, EF-45, July 2015												
1845, Proof (j)	5–8	3	64.7		*(extremely rare)*							
Auctions: $149,500, PF-66UCam, August 2004												
1845-D	90,629	292	50.0	8%	$2,000	$2,650	$3,500	$4,500	$9,500	$21,500	$37,500	$85,000
Auctions: $7,050, MS-61, June 2015; $4,230, AU-58, January 2015; $2,056, EF-45, January 2015; $1,058, VG-8, October 2015												
1845-O	41,000	140	50.7	12%	$750	$1,000	$2,500	$4,750	$9,750	$30,000		
Auctions: $6,463, AU-58, December 2013												
1846, All kinds	395,942											
1846, Large Date		197	53.5	13%	$450	$500	$550	$600	$2,000	$12,500	$16,500	
Auctions: $16,450, MS-63, January 2015; $11,456, MS-63, September 2015; $1,058, MS-60, September 2015; $400, EF-45, June 2015												
1846, Small Date		89	54.3	17%	$475	$550	$700	$1,000	$2,500	$13,000	$20,000	
Auctions: $3,055, MS-61, October 2015; $2,585, MS-60, January 2015; $1,528, AU-58, July 2014; $388, EF-40, July 2014												
1846, Proof (k)	6–10	1	64.0		*(extremely rare)*							
Auctions: $161,000, PF-64Cam, January 2011												
1846-C	12,995	69	48.8	10%	$2,000	$2,750	$4,750	$6,500	$13,500	$47,500	$80,000	
Auctions: $10,575, MS-60, January 2014												
1846-D, All kinds	80,294											
1846-D (l)		121	47.6	3%	$2,150	$2,750	$3,750	$4,750	$12,000			
Auctions: $3,055, AU-53, August 2014; $5,640, AU-50, July 2015; $2,350, EF-45, September 2015; $1,058, EF-40, August 2014												
1846-D, High Second D Over D		124	49.8	6%	$1,750	$2,500	$4,000	$5,000	$11,000	$23,500		
Auctions: $21,150, MS-63, January 2014; $2,115, EF-45, August 2014; $2,115, EF-40, January 2015; $1,763, VF-25, January 2015												
1846-O	58,000	148	49.5	5%	$675	$1,000	$2,900	$4,500	$10,000	$25,000		
Auctions: $9,400, MS-61, January 2014; $4,230, AU-55, October 2015; $1,528, EF-45, July 2015; $881, EF-40, July 2014												

h. 2 examples are known. One is in the Smithsonian's National Numismatic Collection; the other is ex Pittman Collection. **i.** This unique coin first sold in 1890; pedigree is ex Seavy, Parmelee, Woodin, Newcomer, Farouk, Kosoff; current location unknown. **j.** 4 or 5 examples are known. **k.** 4 or 5 examples are known. Of the 20 or so Proof sets made in 1846, experts believe only 4 or 5 contained the year's gold coinage. **l.** The 1846-D half eagle with a normal mintmark actually is rarer than the variety with a boldly repunched D Over D mintmark.

1847, Top of Extra 7
Very Low at Border
FS-G5-1847-301.

1848-D, D Over D

1850-C, Normal C

1850-C, Weak C

	Mintage	Cert	Avg	%MS	VF-20	EF-40	AU-50	AU-55	MS-60	MS-63	MS-64	MS-65
										PF-63	PF-64	PF-65
1847, All kinds	915,981											
1847		750	54.5	18%	$450	$525	$575	$600	$1,650	$6,500	$15,000	
	Auctions: $2,820, MS-62, June 2015; $940, AU-58, September 2015; $517, AU-53, September 2015; $388, EF-45, January 2015											
1847, Top of Extra 7 Very Low at Border		164	55.1	16%	$525	$575	$675	$1,100	$2,150	$8,500	$13,000	
	Auctions: $3,173, MS-62, October 2013; $1,998, MS-61, November 2014; $705, AU-53, October 2015											
1847, Proof	2–3	0	n/a		*(unique, in the Smithsonian's National Numismatic Collection)*							
	Auctions: No auction records available.											
1847-C	84,151	257	46.3	6%	$2,000	$2,500	$3,500	$4,500	$9,250	$25,000	$35,000	$75,000
	Auctions: $4,406, AU-58, April 2014; $3,525, AU-55, October 2015; $2,350, EF-45, July 2014; $1,763, EF-40, August 2014											
1847-D	64,405	154	48.1	10%	$2,000	$2,500	$3,500	$4,500	$8,500	$16,000		
	Auctions: $3,995, AU-55, October 2015; $3,995, AU-55, January 2015; $4,261, AU-50, January 2015; $2,056, EF-45, January 2015											
1847-O	12,000	46	44.2	4%	$2,500	$5,000	$9,500	$13,500	$27,000			
	Auctions: $14,100, AU-53, January 2014; $11,163, AU-53, January 2015; $4,113, AU-50, August 2014											
1848	260,775	333	53.4	12%	$450	$525	$575	$600	$1,750	$9,000	$25,000	
	Auctions: $1,058, MS-60, April 2013; $705, AU-58, August 2015; $564, AU-53, September 2015; $515, EF-45, July 2014											
1848, Proof (m)	6–10	0	n/a		*(extremely rare)*							
	Auctions: No auction records available.											
1848-C	64,472	186	46.4	4%	$2,000	$2,500	$3,500	$6,000	$10,500	$32,500	$65,000	
	Auctions: $3,055, AU-53, January 2015; $2,115, AU-50, June 2015; $1,880, AU-50, June 2015; $1,586, VF-30, January 2015											
1848-D	47,465	115	48.6	6%	$1,900	$2,500	$3,500	$6,500	$13,500	$42,500	$67,500	
	Auctions: $5,640, AU-58, February 2015; $4,113, AU-55, April 2014; $2,241, EF-45, August 2014; $2,115, EF-40, July 2014											
1848-D, D Over D	(n)	0	n/a					$9,000	$20,000			
	Auctions: $29,900, MS-62, May 2008											
1849	133,070	204	53.0	15%	$450	$525	$675	$825	$2,750	$12,500	$15,000	
	Auctions: $2,585, MS-61, August 2014; $5,288, MS-61, April 2013; $911, AU-55, August 2014; $705, AU-53, November 2014											
1849-C	64,823	223	50.1	11%	$2,000	$2,500	$3,250	$4,750	$10,000	$23,500	$40,000	
	Auctions: $4,230, AU-55, September 2015; $2,585, AU-53, February 2015; $1,645, AU-50, February 2015; $2,233, EF-45, August 2015											
1849-D	39,036	138	49.2	5%	$2,000	$2,500	$3,250	$4,500	$10,000	$27,500		
	Auctions: $5,288, AU-58, April 2013; $2,233, AU-50, September 2015; $2,585, EF-45, August 2014											
1850	64,491	141	49.9	4%	$450	$525	$975	$1,250	$3,000	$12,500	$32,000	$75,000
	Auctions: $1,293, AU-58, October 2014; $1,028, AU-55, April 2014; $705, AU-50, October 2015; $499, EF-40, August 2014											
1850-C	63,591	164	47.8	12%	$1,900	$2,350	$3,250	$4,250	$8,500	$16,000	$37,500	
	Auctions: $8,813, MS-61, February 2013; $3,995, AU-50, January 2015; $2,056, AU-50, August 2015; $1,763, VF-35, August 2015											
1850-C, Weak C (o)	(p)	42	49.4	10%	$1,200	$1,500	$2,000	$2,500	$4,500			
	Auctions: $3,819, MS-61, August 2014; $1,293, EF-45, July 2014; $1,116, EF-45, October 2015; $1,058, VF-35, January 2015											
1850-D	43,984	131	48.6	3%	$2,000	$2,750	$3,500	$5,250	$20,000			
	Auctions: $5,640, AU-58, October 2015; $5,170, AU-53, February 2015; $1,293, AU-50, August 2015; $2,115, EF-45, August 2014											

m. 2 examples are known. One is in the Smithsonian's National Numismatic Collection; the other is ex Pittman Collection.
n. Included in 1848-D mintage figure **o.** Several branch-mint half eagles of the early 1850s can exhibit weak (sometimes very weak or almost invisible) mintmarks; such coins generally trade at deep discounts. **p.** Included in 1850-C mintage figure.

1851-D, Normal D

1851-D, Weak D

1854, Doubled-Die Obverse
FS-G5-1854-101.

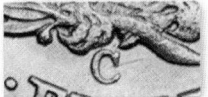
1854-C, Normal C

1854-C, Weak C

1854-D, Normal D

1854-D, Weak D

	Mintage	Cert	Avg	%MS	VF-20	EF-40	AU-50	AU-55	MS-60	MS-63 / PF-63	MS-64 / PF-64	MS-65 / PF-65
1851	377,505	404	54.6	16%	$450	$525	$575	$600	$2,500	$8,000	$22,500	
	Auctions: $2,820, MS-61, February 2015; $705, AU-55, June 2015; $447, AU-53, February 2015; $353, EF-40, July 2015											
1851-C	49,176	140	48.5	11%	$2,000	$2,500	$3,500	$4,750	$10,000	$42,500	$60,000	
	Auctions: $30,550, MS-63, April 2013; $3,760, AU-55, January 2015; $2,820, AU-53, February 2015; $1,175, EF-40, August 2014											
1851-D	62,710	115	49.4	7%	$2,000	$2,500	$3,750	$5,500	$12,000	$25,000	$45,000	
	Auctions: $16,450, MS-62, January 2014											
1851-D, Weak D (o)	(q)	10	56.9	40%	$1,200	$1,500	$2,000	$2,500				
	Auctions: $2,185, AU-50, July 2009											
1851-O	41,000	131	47.3	2%	$800	$1,400	$3,250	$5,500	$9,500	$20,000	$60,000	
	Auctions: $11,163, MS-61, October 2014; $6,463, AU-58, June 2013; $3,055, AU-50, July 2014; $447, EF-40, January 2015											
1852	573,901	714	54.8	16%	$450	$500	$575	$600	$1,500	$6,500	$12,500	$27,500
	Auctions: $9,400, MS-64, January 2015; $3,055, MS-62, August 2015; $646, AU-55, October 2015; $477, AU-55, May 2015											
1852-C	72,574	240	49.4	16%	$2,000	$2,500	$3,500	$4,250	$6,000	$18,500	$27,500	
	Auctions: $28,200, MS-64, August 2013; $9,694, MS-62, January 2015; $2,585, MS-60, November 2014; $2,468, EF-45, January 2015											
1852-D	91,584	264	48.7	8%	$2,000	$2,600	$3,700	$5,000	$9,500	$22,000		
	Auctions: $3,290, AU-55, June 2015; $3,290, AU-53, August 2015; $2,233, EF-45, June 2015; $1,645, VF-25, January 2015											
1853	305,770	541	54.4	16%	$450	$500	$575	$600	$1,700	$5,750	$14,500	$60,000
	Auctions: $15,863, MS-64, October 2015; $2,115, MS-62, March 2015; $1,528, MS-61, June 2015; $423, EF-40, January 2015											
1853-C	65,571	169	49.3	15%	$2,000	$2,500	$3,500	$4,250	$7,000	$21,500	$50,000	
	Auctions: $8,225, MS-62, January 2015; $1,998, MS-60, January 2015; $4,406, AU-58, August 2014; $852, VF-20, February 2015											
1853-D	89,678	335	51.3	12%	$2,000	$2,600	$3,700	$4,500	$6,500	$16,000	$55,000	
	Auctions: $13,513, MS-63, October 2015; $6,463, MS-61, January 2015; $3,290, AU-55, June 2015; $2,233, EF-45, October 2015											
1854	160,675	341	54.6	16%	$450	$500	$575	$850	$2,000	$8,500	$16,500	
	Auctions: $764, AU-58, August 2015; $530, AU-55, June 2015; $470, AU-50, June 2015; $423, AU-50, April 2015											
1854, Doubled-Die Obverse	(r)	31	54.1	10%				$1,350	$2,500			
	Auctions: $1,998, AU-55, October 2014											
1854, Proof (s)	*unknown*	0	n/a									
	Auctions: No auction records available.											
1854-C	39,283	102	48.8	8%	$2,000	$2,500	$3,750	$5,000	$12,000	$35,000		
	Auctions: $35,250, MS-63, April 2014; $3,819, AU-50, March 2015; $1,998, AU-50, January 2015; $2,115, EF-40, January 2015											
1854-C, Weak C (o)	(t)	40	49.7	15%	$1,200	$1,500	$1,750	$2,500	$6,500	$12,000		
	Auctions: $12,338, MS-63, January 2014; $4,584, MS-60, September 2014											
1854-D	56,413	217	53.4	23%	$2,000	$2,500	$3,500	$4,500	$8,000	$23,500	$42,500	$75,000
	Auctions: $8,813, MS-62, June 2013; $3,825, AU-55, March 2015; $3,055, EF-45, January 2015; $940, VF-30, January 2015											
1854-D, Weak D (o)	(u)	14	50.6	7%	$1,200	$1,500	$1,750	$2,500	$4,500			
	Auctions: $5,581, MS-61, September 2014; $1,998, AU-55, April 2014											

o. Several branch-mint half eagles of the early 1850s can exhibit weak (sometimes very weak or almost invisible) mintmarks; such coins generally trade at deep discounts. **q.** Included in 1851-D mintage figure. **r.** Included in circulation-strike 1854 mintage figure **s.** According to Walter Breen, a complete 1854 Proof set was presented to dignitaries of the sovereign German city of Bremen who visited the Philadelphia Mint. The set resided in Bremen until it disappeared almost 100 years later, during World War II. **t.** Included in 1854-C mintage figure. **u.** Included in 1854-D mintage figure.

	Mintage	Cert	Avg	%MS	VF-20	EF-40	AU-50	AU-55	MS-60	MS-63	MS-64	MS-65
										PF-63	PF-64	PF-65
1854-O	46,000	176	51.0	6%	$650	$800	$1,500	$2,250	$6,500	$22,500		
	Auctions: $2,585, AU-58, October 2015; $1,234, AU-53, June 2015; $764, EF-40, January 2015; $494, VF-30, January 2015											
1854-S (v)	268	1	58.0	0%			—	$5,000,000	—			
	Auctions: No auction records available.											
1855	117,098	251	53.8	12%	$450	$500	$575	$600	$1,750	$7,500	$18,500	
	Auctions: $2,115, MS-61, October 2015; $588, AU-58, October 2015; $470, AU-53, August 2014; $388, AU-53, November 2014											
1855-C	39,788	138	50.0	10%	$2,250	$2,600	$3,750	$4,500	$10,500	$35,000	$65,000	
	Auctions: $9,694, MS-61, April 2013; $7,638, AU-58, January 2015; $1,763, AU-50, January 2015; $1,998, EF-40, August 2014											
1855-D	22,432	83	51.1	8%	$2,000	$2,600	$3,600	$5,000	$13,500	$38,000		
	Auctions: $15,275, MS-61, January 2014; $3,819, MS-60, August 2014; $2,820, EF-45, July 2014; $5,640, VF-30, July 2015											
1855-O	11,100	54	49.6	6%	$1,000	$2,000	$4,000	$6,000	$17,000			
	Auctions: $8,225, AU-58, January 2015; $4,700, AU-50, September 2014; $3,290, AU-50, November 2014; $3,525, EF-40, January 2015											
1855-S	61,000	112	48.5	4%	$600	$1,300	$2,500	$4,000	$12,500			
	Auctions: $3,055, AU-58, September 2015; $2,115, AU-53, July 2014; $940, AU-50, August 2014; $1,351, EF-45, July 2014											
1856	197,990	388	54.0	12%	$450	$500	$550	$575	$2,000	$10,000	$17,000	$42,500
	Auctions: $6,182, MS-63, October 2015; $2,115, MS-61, September 2015; $470, AU-55, August 2015; $317, AU-50, June 2015											
1856-C	28,457	137	51.1	9%	$2,000	$2,500	$3,750	$6,000	$12,500	$45,000		
	Auctions: $17,625, MS-62, January 2014; $3,055, AU-50, September 2015; $2,820, AU-50, February 2015; $1,351, AU-50, January 2015											
1856-D	19,786	107	49.7	14%	$2,000	$2,500	$3,750	$5,750	$10,000	$30,000	$50,000	
	Auctions: $12,925, MS-62, January 2014; $3,878, AU-53, August 2015; $3,878, AU-53, January 2015; $1,880, VF-25, July 2014											
1856-O	10,000	51	49.2	10%	$1,000	$1,850	$4,250	$6,250	$12,500			
	Auctions: $10,575, MS-60, April 2014											
1856-S	105,100	154	47.9	5%	$575	$700	$1,250	$2,000	$7,500	$23,500	$38,000	
	Auctions: $4,700, AU-58, January 2014; $1,763, AU-55, January 2015; $1,116, AU-55, November 2014; $951, AU-53, July 2014											
1857	98,188	293	55.4	16%	$450	$475	$525	$575	$1,750	$7,000	$15,000	
	Auctions: $5,170, MS-63, January 2015; $1,528, MS-61, January 2015; $1,293, MS-61, September 2015; $705, AU-58, October 2015											
1857, Proof (w)	3–6	1	65.0		*(extremely rare)*							
	Auctions: $230,000, PF-65Cam, January 2007											
1857-C	31,360	168	52.9	16%	$2,000	$2,500	$3,500	$4,750	$7,250	$25,000		
	Auctions: $22,325, MS-63, January 2014; $8,813, MS-61, August 2015; $6,756, AU-55, July 2015; $2,115, EF-45, July 2014											
1857-D	17,046	100	52.3	15%	$2,000	$2,600	$3,750	$4,750	$10,000	$27,500		
	Auctions: $9,988, MS-61, January 2014; $5,581, AU-58, October 2014; $5,405, AU-58, January 2015; $1,586, VF-25, August 2014											
1857-O	13,000	85	49.1	4%	$1,000	$1,700	$3,750	$5,500	$12,000	$42,500		
	Auctions: $41,125, MS-63, April 2014; $3,672, AU-53, October 2014											
1857-S	87,000	123	47.3	5%	$600	$800	$1,500	$2,500	$10,500	$20,000		
	Auctions: $2,820, AU-58, September 2015; $2,350, AU-58, September 2015; $881, AU-55, August 2014; $1,528, AU-55, September 2014											
1858	15,136	81	53.9	21%	$550	$575	$750	$1,250	$3,000	$8,000	$12,500	$35,000
	Auctions: $14,100, MS-64, June 2015; $4,935, MS-62, August 2015; $1,410, AU-55, August 2014; $881, EF-40, August 2015											
1858, Proof (x)	4–6	5	65.6							$75,000	$100,000	$150,000
	Auctions: $195,500, PF-66UCamH, March 2006											
1858-C	38,856	195	51.4	12%	$2,000	$2,500	$3,750	$4,500	$9,000	$27,500		
	Auctions: $9,400, MS-61, August 2013; $3,055, AU-55, August 2014; $2,585, EF-40, January 2015; $1,175, EF-40, August 2015											
1858-D	15,362	123	51.6	9%	$2,000	$2,500	$3,750	$4,750	$10,500	$32,500	$45,000	
	Auctions: $17,625, MS-61, June 2013; $9,988, MS-61, February 2015; $7,638, MS-61, August 2014; $3,525, AU-55, June 2015											
1858-S	18,600	58	47.3	0%	$1,000	$2,600	$5,750	$9,000	$25,000			
	Auctions: $7,050, AU-55, March 2014											

v. 3 examples are known. **w.** 2 examples are known. **x.** 4 or 5 examples are known today. One resides in the Smithsonian's National Numismatic Collection, another in the collection of the American Numismatic Society. In recent decades the collections of Eliasberg, Trompeter, and Bass have included examples.

	Mintage	Cert	Avg	%MS	VF-20	EF-40	AU-50	AU-55	MS-60	MS-63	MS-64	MS-65
										PF-63	PF-64	PF-65
1859	16,734	99	50.7	8%	$550	$750	$1,000	$1,750	$5,000	$20,000		
Auctions: $2,585, AU-58, August 2015; $2,115, AU-55, October 2015; $1,410, AU-50, January 2015; $823, EF-45, August 2014												
1859, Proof	80	4	63.5							$45,000	$75,000	$125,000
Auctions: No auction records available.												
1859-C	31,847	153	50.8	9%	$2,000	$2,500	$3,500	$4,750	$11,750	$32,500		
Auctions: $8,225, MS-61, January 2014; $4,113, AU-55, August 2014; $1,645, AU-50, July 2014; $1,469, VF-25, August 2014												
1859-D	10,366	112	52.6	13%	$2,000	$2,750	$3,750	$5,000	$12,500	$35,000		
Auctions: $19,975, MS-62, January 2014; $2,938, MS-60, July 2014; $7,050, AU-58, June 2015; $2,115, AU-50, January 2015												
1859-S	13,220	33	47.9	3%	$1,500	$3,250	$4,250	$6,500	$23,500			
Auctions: $8,695, AU-58, October 2013; $6,463, AU-53, August 2014; $4,230, EF-45, October 2015												
1860	19,763	118	52.8	7%	$550	$575	$975	$1,350	$3,500	$15,000	$25,000	
Auctions: $4,700, AU-58, January 2014; $2,233, AU-58, August 2014; $646, AU-50, July 2014												
1860, Proof	62	5	64.6							$37,500	$65,000	$100,000
Auctions: $103,500, PF-66CamH, January 2012												
1860-C	14,813	118	53.0	17%	$2,000	$2,750	$4,000	$6,250	$11,000	$27,500	$45,000	
Auctions: $20,124, MS-63, April 2013; $4,113, AU-50, August 2014; $3,525, AU-50, June 2015; $2,585, EF-40, October 2014												
1860-D	14,635	131	51.8	14%	$2,250	$3,500	$4,500	$6,500	$12,500	$40,000	$75,000	
Auctions: $14,100, MS-62, March 2014; $5,405, AU-58, June 2015; $3,760, AU-53, February 2015; $3,760, EF-45, September 2015												
1860-S	21,200	58	45.8	2%	$1,100	$2,150	$4,750	$7,750	$26,000			
Auctions: $19,975, AU-58, April 2014; $4,994, AU-53, October 2014; $2,585, EF-45, September 2014												
1861	688,084	1,759	55.5	16%	$450	$475	$525	$575	$1,750	$6,000	$10,500	$30,000
Auctions: $32,900, MS-65, January 2015; $2,820, MS-62, January 2015; $1,528, AU-55, January 2015; $376, EF-40, June 2015												
1861, Proof	66	2	65.0							$35,000	$55,000	$87,500
Auctions: No auction records available.												
1861-C	6,879	78	51.3	9%	$4,000	$6,500	$10,000	$16,000	$30,000	$100,000		
Auctions: $25,850, MS-61, January 2014; $6,463, AU-50, January 2015; $3,290, AU-50, August 2014; $9,694, EF-45, January 2015												
1861-D	1,597	36	53.6	11%	$18,500	$22,500	$35,000	$55,000	$85,000	$175,000		
Auctions: $99,875, MS-62, January 2014												
1861-S	18,000	46	44.2	0%	$2,000	$4,000	$7,500	$10,500				
Auctions: $11,163, AU-53, March 2014; $9,988, AU-53, January 2015; $8,813, AU-53, January 2015; $4,259, VF-35, August 2014												
1862	4,430	35	51.5	3%	$2,500	$4,000	$6,500	$7,500	$22,000			
Auctions: $14,702, AU-58, August 2014; $17,625, AU-55, April 2013												
1862, Proof	35	8	64.5							$35,000	$55,000	$87,500
Auctions: $92,000, PF-65UCam, August 2011												
1862-S	9,500	42	40.7	5%	$4,000	$6,000	$12,500	$20,000	$40,000			
Auctions: $15,275, AU-53, March 2014; $4,406, VF-25, August 2014												
1863	2,442	18	53.1	11%	$3,000	$5,500	$11,500	$22,500	$40,000			
Auctions: $30,550, AU-58, January 2014												
1863, Proof	30	4	65.3							$35,000	$52,500	$85,000
Auctions: $69,000, PF-64DCam, November 2005												
1863-S	17,000	52	41.7	0%	$3,000	$4,500	$11,000	$16,000	$35,000			
Auctions: $16,450, AU-55, March 2014												
1864	4,170	53	50.9	8%	$3,000	$5,000	$7,500	$11,000	$17,500			
Auctions: $12,925, AU-55, January 2014; $10,575, AU-55, June 2015; $10,281, AU-55, October 2015												
1864, Proof	50	17	64.6							$35,000	$50,000	$77,500
Auctions: $103,500, PF-65UCam, October 2011												
1864-S	3,888	9	39.3	0%	$12,500	$37,500	$55,000	$75,000				
Auctions: $79,313, EF-45, March 2014												

	Mintage	Cert	Avg	%MS	VF-20	EF-40	AU-50	AU-55	MS-60	MS-63	MS-64	MS-65
										PF-63	PF-64	PF-65
1865	1,270	24	53.5	17%	$4,000	$10,000	$18,000	$22,500	$35,000			
Auctions: $17,626, AU-55, August 2014; $18,800, AU-53, January 2014; $17,625, AU-53, August 2015												
1865, Proof	25	13	64.5							$35,000	$50,000	$77,500
Auctions: $86,250, PF-65UCam, April 2012												
1865-S	27,612	87	43.4	6%	$3,000	$4,500	$6,000	$9,000	$17,500	$40,000	$60,000	
Auctions: $8,813, AU-55, March 2014; $5,875, EF-45, August 2014												
1866-S, No Motto	9,000	53	37.8	0%	$2,000	$3,500	$7,500	$11,000	$30,000			
Auctions: $14,688, AU-58, March 2014; $14,100, AU-58, January 2015; $5,581, AU-50, August 2014; $2,350, VF-20, August 2014												
1866, Motto Above Eagle	6,700	42	53.9	14%	$900	$2,000	$3,000	$4,250	$10,000	$40,000		
Auctions: $34,075, MS-63, February 2013; $12,338, MS-61, January 2015; $3,290, AU-55, August 2014; $3,055, EF-40, September 2015												
1866, Motto Above Eagle, Proof	30	6	61.8							$25,000	$35,000	$60,000
Auctions: $80,500, PF-66UCamH, August 2010												
1866-S, Motto Above Eagle	34,920	47	38.0	2%	$925	$2,500	$7,000	$10,000	$25,000			
Auctions: $4,994, AU-50, June 2013; $2,585, EF-45, August 2014; $1,469, VF-30, October 2014												
1867	6,870	53	49.4	2%	$600	$1,250	$3,000	$4,000	$9,500			
Auctions: $16,450, MS-61, September 2014; $8,813, MS-60, January 2014; $881, AU-50, August 2014												
1867, Proof	50	5	63.4							$25,000	$35,000	$60,000
Auctions: $21,150, PF-63Cam, August 2014												
1867-S	29,000	80	39.5	0%	$1,100	$1,800	$5,000	$7,500				
Auctions: $1,351, EF-40, January 2015; $1,293, VF-30, October 2015; $1,058, VF-20, June 2015; $458, F-12, January 2015												
1868	5,700	51	51.2	4%	$600	$1,250	$2,500	$4,750	$10,000			
Auctions: $16,450, MS-61, April 2013; $5,405, AU-58, October 2015; $4,935, AU-55, July 2015; $2,233, AU-50, August 2014												
1868, Proof	25	4	64.0							$25,000	$35,000	$60,000
Auctions: $69,000, PF-64DCam, June 2008												
1868-S	52,000	111	44.0	5%	$525	$1,250	$2,750	$4,250	$21,000			
Auctions: $18,213, MS-61, June 2015; $23,500, MS-60, March 2014; $1,645, AU-53, October 2014; $1,827, AU-50, July 2014												
1869	1,760	39	52.6	10%	$1,200	$2,500	$5,000	$8,500	$12,500	$27,000	$37,500	
Auctions: $9,400, AU-55, April 2014; $4,700, AU-53, February 2015; $2,267, EF-40, August 2014												
1869, Proof	25	5	63.8							$25,000	$35,000	$60,000
Auctions: $69,000, PF-65Cam, April 2012												
1869-S	31,000	117	41.6	3%	$575	$1,500	$3,000	$5,500	$18,000			
Auctions: $17,625, MS-61, July 2014; $2,233, AU-50, September 2015; $1,998, EF-45, August 2014												
1870	4,000	50	49.3	0%	$900	$2,000	$3,750	$4,750	$13,500			
Auctions: $7,640, AU-58, September 2014; $8,225, AU-55, January 2014; $2,180, VF-30, October 2015; $1,410, VF-30, October 2014												
1870, Proof	35	2	65.0							$25,000	$35,000	$60,000
Auctions: $82,250, PF-64, January 2014												
1870-CC	7,675	43	33.4	2%	$18,500	$26,500	$37,500	$60,000	$110,000			
Auctions: $47,000, AU-53, January 2014												
1870-S	17,000	94	39.7	0%	$850	$1,850	$5,500	$9,500	$22,500			
Auctions: $12,925, AU-58, August 2014; $1,763, AU-50, September 2015; $2,115, EF-40, July 2014; $1,116, VF-25, August 2014												
1871	3,200	49	53.3	8%	$750	$1,250	$2,500	$4,500	$10,000			
Auctions: $15,275, MS-61, September 2013; $3,525, AU-55, August 2014; $2,820, AU-53, August 2014												
1871, Proof	30	8	62.0							$25,000	$35,000	$60,000
Auctions: $73,438, PF-66Cam, August 2015; $70,500, PF-65Cam, September 2014												
1871-CC	20,770	91	37.3	2%	$3,200	$6,500	$12,000	$20,000	$50,000	$75,000		
Auctions: $48,469, MS-61, April 2013; $2,115, EF-40, July 2014; $5,288, EF-40, September 2014; $3,173, VF-30, August 2014												
1871-S	25,000	102	45.8	3%	$525	$850	$2,500	$4,000	$12,500			
Auctions: $35,250, MS-63, August 2014; $25,850, MS-61, March 2014; $2,364, AU-50, August 2015; $2,585, VF-25, August 2014												

1873, Close 3　　　　**1873, Open 3**

	Mintage	Cert	Avg	%MS	VF-20	EF-40	AU-50	AU-55	MS-60	MS-63 / PF-63	MS-64 / PF-64	MS-65 / PF-65
1872	1,660	26	54.3	15%	$850	$1,350	$2,500	$4,250	$10,500	$17,500	$22,500	
Auctions: $5,434, AU-58, April 2014												
1872, Proof	30	7	62.6							$22,500	$35,000	$60,000
Auctions: $7,188, PF-55, March 2012												
1872-CC	16,980	68	34.2	0%	$3,000	$6,750	$13,500	$23,500				
Auctions: $28,200, AU-58, March 2014; $11,764, AU-50, August 2014; $1,175, F-12, November 2014												
1872-S	36,400	114	42.8	3%	$575	$800	$2,500	$3,750	$12,000			
Auctions: $3,055, AU-55, October 2014; $2,233, AU-50, August 2015; $1,998, AU-50, February 2015; $1,880, AU-50, October 2015												
1873, Close 3	112,480	297	55.8	26%	$375	$400	$475	$550	$1,000	$4,500	$7,500	$20,000
Auctions: $5,875, MS-64, December 2013; $3,055, MS-63, July 2015; $852, MS-61, September 2014; $470, AU-58, August 2014												
1873, Open 3	112,505	327	55.9	25%	$375	$400	$450	$500	$700	$3,500	$6,500	$15,000
Auctions: $5,875, MS-64, September 2013; $2,703, MS-63, May 2015; $363, AU-58, August 2015; $317, EF-40, October 2014												
1873, Close 3, Proof	25	10	64.5							$22,500	$35,000	$60,000
Auctions: $24,675, PF-63Cam, August 2014; $12,338, PF-58, January 2014												
1873-CC	7,416	35	33.1	3%	$5,000	$11,500	$21,500	$32,500	$65,000	$180,000		
Auctions: $11,750, AU-50, August 2014; $21,150, AU-50, January 2013; $5,581, F-12, August 2014												
1873-S	31,000	109	42.0	1%	$600	$1,100	$2,250	$4,500	$18,500			
Auctions: $2,233, AU-55, August 2014; $3,173, AU-53, January 2014; $823, VF-35, January 2015; $376, VF-20, November 2015												
1874	3,488	59	50.3	8%	$550	$1,000	$2,250	$3,000	$10,000	$22,500		
Auctions: $4,700, AU-58, January 2014; $3,290, AU-55, August 2014												
1874, Proof	20	4	65.8							$27,500	$40,000	$65,000
Auctions: $54,625, PF-65CamH, August 2011												
1874-CC	21,198	129	39.1	1%	$2,500	$3,500	$10,000	$17,000	$35,000			
Auctions: $21,738, AU-58, August 2014; $14,100, AU-55, August 2015; $4,348, VF-35, February 2015; $734, F, March 2015												
1874-S	16,000	93	41.7	0%	$800	$1,500	$2,750	$4,500				
Auctions: $3,760, AU-55, August 2015; $2,820, AU-55, January 2015; $2,820, AU-53, September 2015; $1,645, EF-45, October 2015												
1875	200	2	50.0	0%	$75,000	$100,000	$155,000	$230,000				
Auctions: $211,500, AU-55, April 2014												
1875, Proof (y)	20	6	61.2							$150,000	$175,000	$225,000
Auctions: $176,250, PF-65Cam, January 2014												
1875-CC	11,828	90	39.0	1%	$3,000	$5,000	$12,500	$15,000	$45,000	$115,000		
Auctions: $17,625, AU-58, January 2014												
1875-S	9,000	68	42.6	3%	$775	$2,000	$3,750	$8,000	$18,500			
Auctions: $8,813, AU-58, August 2014; $3,819, AU-55, August 2014; $2,585, AU-50, August 2014; $3,055, AU-50, August 2013												
1876	1,432	27	55.7	19%	$1,000	$3,250	$4,500	$6,750	$11,000	$24,000	$32,000	$40,000
Auctions: $19,975, MS-63, March 2013												
1876, Proof	45	18	64.0							$20,000	$25,000	$47,500
Auctions: $48,469, PF-65Cam, February 2013												
1876-CC	6,887	72	39.0	1%	$2,500	$4,750	$13,500	$18,000	$40,000			
Auctions: $21,150, AU-58, March 2014; $4,113, VF-25, July 2014												
1876-S	4,000	22	39.5	5%	$1,150	$3,500	$8,500	$13,000	$30,000			
Auctions: $18,800, AU-58, March 2014												

y. The mintages of only 200 circulation strikes and 20 Proofs for the year 1875 combine to make the Proof a high-demand coin; hence its strong market value.

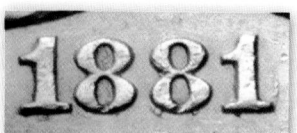

1881, Final 1 Over 0
FS-G5-1881-301.

1881, Recut 1881 Over 1881
FS-G5-1881-303.

	Mintage	Cert	Avg	%MS	VF-20	EF-40	AU-50	AU-55	MS-60	MS-63	MS-64	MS-65
										PF-63	PF-64	PF-65
1877	1,132	43	54.2	23%	$1,700	$3,000	$4,500	$6,000	$12,500			
Auctions: $7,638, AU-58, April 2014; $1,645, AU-50, June 2015; $1,469, AU-50, August 2015; $3,525, EF-45, July 2014												
1877, Proof	20	4	65.0							$22,500	$32,500	$57,500
Auctions: $51,750, PF-63, June 2005												
1877-CC	8,680	99	39.5	0%	$2,000	$4,000	$12,000	$14,000	$45,000			
Auctions: $14,688, AU-55, November 2014; $11,163, AU-53, July 2014; $8,871, AU-50, January 2015; $3,760, AU-50, August 2015												
1877-S	26,700	125	45.0	2%	$475	$600	$1,500	$3,000	$6,750	$18,500	$30,000	
Auctions: $1,645, AU-55, February 2015; $1,293, AU-53, August 2014; $1,175, EF-45, August 2014; $411, EF-40, June 2015												
1878	131,720	387	59.0	53%	$375	$400	$425	$435	$600	$1,750	$4,000	$10,000
Auctions: $8,813, MS-65, January 2015; $8,225, MS-65, September 2015; $3,525, MS-64, August 2014; $400, AU-58, March 2015												
1878, Proof	20	9	64.2							$22,500	$32,500	$57,500
Auctions: $31,725, PF-63DCam, June 2014												
1878-CC	9,054	53	44.7	4%	$5,000	$11,000	$18,000	$32,000	$75,000			
Auctions: $47,000, AU-58, March 2014												
1878-S	144,700	480	56.2	23%	$375	$400	$425	$435	$775	$4,000	$7,000	
Auctions: $423, AU-58, August 2015; $400, AU-55, March 2015; $323, AU-50, September 2015; $341, EF-45, August 2015												
1879	301,920	685	59.3	56%	$375	$400	$425	$435	$500	$1,500	$3,600	$8,500
Auctions: $6,463, MS-65, September 2014; $4,406, MS-64, September 2014; $2,115, MS-64, March 2015												
1879, Proof	30	7	64.1							$22,500	$30,000	$55,000
Auctions: $63,250, PF-65Cam, April 2012												
1879-CC	17,281	164	44.9	4%	$1,500	$2,500	$3,750	$7,500	$22,500			
Auctions: $21,150, MS-60, March 2014; $8,813, AU-58, August 2014; $1,116, VG-8, June 2015; $764, G-6, July 2014												
1879-S	426,200	729	57.1	26%	$375	$400	$425	$450	$600	$1,750	$6,000	$25,000
Auctions: $1,058, MS-63, January 2015; $541, MS-61, February 2015; $376, AU-58, January 2015; $282, AU-50, July 2015												
1880	3,166,400	2,898	60.0	73%	$375	$400	$425	$450	$525	$900	$1,250	$4,500
Auctions: $10,575, MS-66, October 2015; $4,348, MS-65, August 2015; $705, MS-63, July 2015; $376, EF-40, February 2015												
1880, Proof	36	7	65.7							$17,500	$30,000	$52,500
Auctions: $72,702, PF-67Cam, August 2006												
1880-CC	51,017	322	46.3	4%	$1,000	$1,350	$2,000	$4,500	$12,500	$40,000		
Auctions: $11,750, MS-61, January 2014; $705, VF-20, January 2015; $1,058, F-15, January 2015; $734, VG-8, February 2015												
1880-S	1,348,900	2,204	61.0	84%	$375	$400	$425	$450	$525	$700	$1,300	$5,000
Auctions: $1,410, MS-64, January 2015; $940, MS-64, January 2015; $400, MS-62, January 2015; $329, AU-55, February 2015												
1881, Final 1 Over 0 (z)	(aa)	109	58.3	52%	$475	$500	$550	$675	$1,350	$3,000	$8,000	
Auctions: $2,233, MS-63, January 2014; $646, AU-55, August 2014; $499, EF-40, July 2014												
1881, Recut 1881 Over 1881	(aa)	0	n/a					$535	$625	$1,325		
Auctions: $705, MS-63, August 2014; $1,528, MS-62, April 2014												
1881	5,708,802	16,515	61.5	92%	$375	$400	$425	$450	$500	$700	$1,100	$4,000
Auctions: $1,058, MS-64, June 2015; $435, MS-62, March 2015; $423, MS-61, July 2015; $329, AU-55, July 2015												
1881, Proof	42	10	65.8							$16,500	$25,000	$40,000
Auctions: $37,375, PF-65Cam, January 2011												
1881-CC	13,886	84	45.3	8%	$1,350	$3,000	$7,000	$10,500	$22,500	$55,000		
Auctions: $32,900, MS-62, May 2013; $3,055, EF-40, August 2014; $1,763, VF-30, July 2014; $1,293, F-15, August 2014												
1881-S	969,000	1,870	61.3	89%	$375	$400	$425	$450	$500	$750	$1,250	$4,000
Auctions: $1,058, MS-64, January 2015; $969, MS-64, February 2015; $687, MS-63, January 2015; $494, MS-62, January 2015												

z. The last digit of the date is repunched over the remnants of a zero; this is easily visible with the naked eye, making the 1 Over 0 a popular variety. **aa.** Included in circulation-strike 1881 mintage figure.

	Mintage	Cert	Avg	%MS	VF-20	EF-40	AU-50	AU-55	MS-60	MS-63	MS-64	MS-65
										PF-63	PF-64	PF-65
1882	2,514,520	7,504	61.5	91%	$375	$400	$425	$450	$500	$700	$1,500	$3,500
Auctions: $2,468, MS-65, May 2015; $999, MS-64, August 2015; $588, MS-63, August 2015; $454, MS-62, February 2015												
1882, Proof	48	12	64.3							$15,500	$25,000	$40,000
Auctions: $9,085, PF-63Cam, February 2010												
1882-CC	82,817	560	51.0	6%	$1,000	$1,250	$1,800	$3,500	$10,000	$35,000		
Auctions: $18,800, MS-62, February 2015; $1,175, AU-50, February 2015; $1,116, AU-50, January 2015; $734, EF-40, February 2015												
1882-S	969,000	2,345	61.6	92%	$375	$400	$425	$450	$500	$750	$1,300	$4,250
Auctions: $3,408, MS-65, January 2015; $999, MS-64, January 2015; $823, MS-64, January 2015; $447, MS-62, January 2015												
1883	233,400	469	60.3	71%	$375	$400	$425	$450	$500	$1,500	$2,250	$12,500
Auctions: $17,625, MS-67, February 2013; $1,410, MS-64, September 2015; $1,116, MS-63, June 2015; $411, AU-58, August 2014												
1883, Proof	61	10	64.3							$15,500	$25,000	$40,000
Auctions: $5,288, PF-55, September 2014												
1883-CC	12,598	123	50.1	7%	$950	$1,600	$3,200	$6,500	$18,500	$45,000		
Auctions: $18,213, MS-61, August 2014; $7,638, AU-58, August 2015; $5,875, AU-55, January 2015; $1,821, VF-25, January 2015												
1883-S	83,200	228	58.0	51%	$375	$400	$425	$450	$750	$1,775	$7,000	
Auctions: $7,050, MS-64, August 2013; $706, MS-61, July 2015; $382, AU-58, January 2015; $1,058, AU-53, August 2014												
1884	191,030	448	59.1	57%	$375	$400	$425	$450	$550	$1,650	$3,000	$9,000
Auctions: $2,468, MS-64, February 2013; $881, MS-62, July 2015; $588, MS-62, November 2015; $588, MS-61, August 2015												
1884, Proof	48	8	64.5							$15,500	$25,000	$40,000
Auctions: $39,100, PF-66UCam, November 2010												
1884-CC	16,402	167	49.8	4%	$950	$1,500	$3,500	$6,000	$20,000			
Auctions: $8,225, AU-58, January 2014; $8,519, AU-58, October 2014; $4,994, AU-55, August 2014												
1884-S	177,000	455	59.8	68%	$375	$400	$425	$450	$500	$1,150	$2,300	$9,000
Auctions: $999, MS-63, August 2015; $940, MS-63, June 2015; $588, MS-62, October 2015; $541, MS-62, August 2015												
1885	601,440	1,353	61.3	85%	$375	$400	$425	$450	$500	$750	$1,250	$4,500
Auctions: $1,528, MS-64, July 2015; $676, MS-63, July 2015; $517, MS-62, May 2015; $400, AU-53, February 2015												
1885, Proof	66	19	64.6							$15,500	$25,000	$40,000
Auctions: $70,500, PF-67UCam, August 2015; $56,400, PF-66UCam, January 2015; $31,725, PF-65DCam, August 2014												
1885-S	1,211,500	4,237	61.9	94%	$375	$400	$425	$450	$500	$750	$1,250	$4,000
Auctions: $5,170, MS-66, January 2015; $705, MS-63, August 2015; $458, MS-61, January 2015; $376, AU-55, July 2015												
1886	388,360	702	60.1	69%	$375	$400	$425	$450	$500	$750	$2,250	$5,500
Auctions: $5,288, MS-65, June 2013; $573, MS-63, August 2014; $499, MS-61, July 2014												
1886, Proof	72	12	64.3							$15,500	$25,000	$40,000
Auctions: $57,281, PF, March 2014												
1886-S	3,268,000	8,260	61.4	93%	$375	$400	$425	$450	$500	$750	$1,250	$3,000
Auctions: $2,350, MS-65, January 2015; $823, MS-64, October 2015; $458, MS-62, January 2015; $400, MS-60, October 2015												
1887, Proof (bb)	87	19	63.4							$65,000	$80,000	$115,000
Auctions: $54,050, PF, August 2013												
1887-S	1,912,000	3,275	61.2	91%	$375	$400	$425	$450	$500	$750	$1,500	$5,000
Auctions: $1,410, MS-64, January 2015; $940, MS-64, July 2015; $881, MS-64, July 2015; $470, MS-62, June 2015												
1888	18,201	157	59.8	68%	$375	$400	$425	$450	$600	$2,250	$3,500	$7,500
Auctions: $1,775, MS-63, January 2014; $764, MS-61, January 2015; $588, MS-60, August 2014												
1888, Proof	95	19	64.7							$13,500	$20,000	$32,500
Auctions: $34,500, PF-65DCam, October 2008												
1888-S	293,900	340	55.0	22%	$375	$400	$425	$450	$600	$3,000		
Auctions: $2,350, MS-64, August 2013; $1,116, MS-63, October 2014; $470, AU-53, July 2014; $368, EF-40, August 2014												
1889	7,520	151	58.1	42%	$500	$600	$700	$950	$1,400	$4,500	$6,000	
Auctions: $4,406, MS-63, June 2014; $1,763, MS-62, September 2015; $1,058, AU-55, July 2015; $1,175, AU-53, August 2014												
1889, Proof	45	13	64.3							$14,000	$22,500	$35,000
Auctions: $29,900, PF-65Cam, January 2011												

bb. Proof only.

	Mintage	Cert	Avg	%MS	VF-20	EF-40	AU-50	AU-55	MS-60	MS-63	MS-64	MS-65
										PF-63	PF-64	PF-65
1890	4,240	72	55.6	29%	$550	$675	$800	$1,000	$1,750	$7,250	$11,500	$15,000
Auctions: $5,581, MS-62, June 2014; $1,000, AU-55, July 2014; $823, AU-50, August 2014												
1890, Proof	88	30	64.9							$14,000	$22,500	$35,000
Auctions: $24,675, PF-64DCam, January 2014												
1890-CC	53,800	621	57.3	48%	$800	$950	$1,100	$1,300	$1,850	$12,000	$17,500	$45,000
Auctions: $11,750, MS-64, June 2015; $2,820, MS-62, June 2015; $1,410, AU-55, January 2015; $1,058, AU-50, January 2015												
1891	61,360	367	60.5	78%	$375	$400	$425	$450	$500	$1,750	$3,000	$12,000
Auctions: $4,700, MS-64, February 2013; $499, MS-61, August 2014; $400, AU-58, August 2015; $353, AU-53, September 2015												
1891, Proof	53	18	64.9							$13,500	$20,000	$32,500
Auctions: $19,550, PF-64DCam, January 2010												
1891-CC	208,000	2,065	58.0	52%	$750	$850	$950	$1,100	$2,750	$5,000	$7,500	$27,500
Auctions: $5,875, MS-64, January 2015; $1,175, AU-58, June 2015; $823, EF-45, July 2015; $764, VF-30, October 2015												
1892	753,480	2,023	61.5	92%	$375	$400	$425	$450	$500	$750	$1,100	$3,250
Auctions: $3,760, MS-66, July 2015; $2,585, MS-65, September 2015; $823, MS-63, January 2015; $329, AU-50, September 2015												
1892, Proof	92	18	64.4							$13,500	$18,000	$32,500
Auctions: $6,325, PF-62Cam, December 2011												
1892-CC	82,968	751	53.9	20%	$750	$850	$900	$1,200	$2,500	$9,500	$17,500	$30,000
Auctions: $2,511, MS-61, February 2015; $1,058, AU-55, January 2015; $881, EF-45, January 2015; $541, VG-8, January 2015												
1892-O	10,000	40	57.6	43%	$1,000	$1,500	$1,750	$2,000	$4,250	$11,000	$16,000	
Auctions: $8,225, MS-62, December 2013; $3,290, AU-58, July 2014; $3,290, AU-58, August 2014												
1892-S	298,400	443	57.8	44%	$375	$400	$425	$450	$500	$1,800	$4,250	$7,500
Auctions: $4,230, MS-64, January 2015; $2,350, MS-63, April 2013; $823, MS-62, August 2015; $400, MS-60, October 2015												
1893	1,528,120	7,572	61.9	96%	$375	$400	$425	$450	$500	$600	$1,000	$2,500
Auctions: $4,230, MS-66, June 2015; $3,995, MS-66, January 2015; $940, MS-64, September 2015; $852, MS-64, January 2015												
1893, Proof	77	20	64.8							$13,500	$18,000	$32,500
Auctions: $70,500, PF, August 2013												
1893-CC	60,000	675	55.6	27%	$850	$950	$1,250	$1,800	$2,700	$10,000	$17,500	$27,500
Auctions: $24,675, MS-64, August 2015; $2,115, AU-58, June 2015; $1,410, AU-53, July 2015; $969, EF-40, February 2015												
1893-O	110,000	436	58.8	50%	$400	$450	$500	$550	$1,000	$5,000	$8,500	
Auctions: $7,638, MS-64, January 2014; $1,880, MS-62, July 2015; $541, MS-60, August 2015; $529, AU-58, August 2014												
1893-S	224,000	1,051	61.0	84%	$375	$400	$425	$450	$500	$900	$2,200	$8,500
Auctions: $1,645, MS-64, October 2015; $999, MS-64, July 2015; $482, MS-62, October 2015; $447, MS-61, October 2015												
1894	957,880	3,459	61.7	96%	$365	$385	$425	$450	$500	$675	$1,100	$3,300
Auctions: $3,760, MS-65, January 2015; $1,058, MS-64, June 2015; $458, MS-62, August 2015; $329, MS-60, July 2015												
1894, Proof	75	27	64.1							$13,500	$18,500	$32,500
Auctions: $58,750, PF-67DCam, October 2014; $37,600, PF-66UCam, August 2015; $29,375, PF-64UCam, August 2015												
1894-O	16,600	328	57.6	33%	$425	$450	$550	$800	$1,600	$7,000		
Auctions: $3,525, MS-62, June 2014; $1,888, MS-61, July 2014; $1,175, AU-58, September 2015; $823, AU-55, November 2014												
1894-S	55,900	229	53.3	13%	$400	$425	$450	$650	$2,500	$8,500	$16,000	
Auctions: $3,819, MS-62, March 2015; $2,938, MS-62, July 2015; $2,350, MS-60, February 2015; $881, AU-58, August 2014												
1895	1,345,855	7,998	61.8	95%	$365	$385	$400	$425	$485	$600	$1,000	$2,750
Auctions: $19,975, MS-67, January 2015; $7,931, MS-66, February 2015; $564, MS-63, July 2015; $423, MS-61, May 2015												
1895, Proof	81	26	64.8							$12,500	$18,000	$30,000
Auctions: $6,233, PF-60, February 2014												
1895-S	112,000	319	53.4	8%	$375	$425	$450	$650	$2,250	$5,500	$12,000	$23,000
Auctions: $2,350, MS-62, September 2015; $1,645, MS-61, September 2015; $1,586, MS-61, June 2015; $447, AU-53, October 2015												
1896	58,960	481	61.8	93%	$365	$385	$400	$425	$485	$600	$1,500	$5,500
Auctions: $1,410, MS-64, August 2015; $1,293, MS-64, June 2015; $1,293, MS-64, January 2015; $382, AU-55, August 2014												
1896, Proof	103	32	64.8							$12,500	$18,000	$30,000
Auctions: $35,250, PF-65DCam, September 2014												
1896-S	155,400	387	54.5	19%	$365	$385	$400	$575	$1,150	$5,500	$8,500	$20,000
Auctions: $7,064, MS-64, January 2015; $4,230, MS-63, July 2015; $3,525, MS-63, August 2015; $2,233, MS-62, January 2015												

1901-S, Final 1 Over 0
FS-G5-1901S-301.

	Mintage	Cert	Avg	%MS	VF-20	EF-40	AU-50	AU-55	MS-60	MS-63 PF-63	MS-64 PF-64	MS-65 PF-65
1897	867,800	4,141	61.6	92%	$365	$385	$400	$425	$485	$600	$1,000	$2,750
	Auctions: $8,225, MS-66, January 2015; $1,175, MS-64, August 2015; $505, MS-62, July 2015; $388, AU-58, July 2015											
1897, Proof	83	25	64.5							$12,500	$18,000	$30,000
	Auctions: $9,988, PF-63, June 2014											
1897-S	354,000	414	56.3	26%	$365	$385	$400	$625	$900	$5,000	$7,500	
	Auctions: $15,275, MS-66, March 2015; $1,645, MS-62, July 2014; $499, MS-61, August 2014; $388, AU-58, November 2015											
1898	633,420	2,435	61.6	93%	$365	$385	$400	$425	$485	$600	$1,500	$3,500
	Auctions: $8,225, MS-66, June 2015; $3,643, MS-65, June 2015; $1,028, MS-64, June 2015; $447, MS-62, August 2015											
1898, Proof	75	39	64.7							$12,500	$18,000	$30,000
	Auctions: $105,750, PF-67UCam, August 2015; $29,375, PF-65DCam, September 2014; $18,800, PF-64DCam+, August 2015											
1898-S	1,397,400	676	59.3	67%	$365	$385	$400	$425	$500	$1,100	$2,750	$7,500
	Auctions: $70,500, MS-68, June 2015; $5,434, MS-65, June 2014; $7,050, MS-65, October 2014; $4,406, MS-64, August 2014											
1899	1,710,630	12,879	62.5	98%	$365	$385	$400	$425	$485	$600	$800	$2,750
	Auctions: $2,938, MS-66, June 2015; $2,585, MS-65, January 2015; $447, MS-62, January 2015; $388, AU-55, June 2015											
1899, Proof	99	30	64.5							$12,500	$18,000	$30,000
	Auctions: $134,550, PF, September 2013											
1899-S	1,545,000	951	59.5	70%	$365	$385	$400	$450	$500	$1,000	$1,750	$7,500
	Auctions: $1,410, MS-64, January 2015; $764, MS-63, January 2015; $734, MS-62, August 2015; $447, MS-62, March 2015											
1900	1,405,500	16,089	62.1	96%	$365	$385	$400	$425	$485	$600	$800	$2,500
	Auctions: $5,875, MS-66, January 2015; $2,820, MS-65, September 2015; $423, MS-62, July 2015; $329, MS-60, July 2015											
1900, Proof	230	62	64.2							$12,500	$18,000	$30,000
	Auctions: $35,250, PF-65DCam, September 2013											
1900-S	329,000	517	60.1	69%	$365	$385	$400	$450	$500	$1,000	$1,350	$9,500
	Auctions: $1,293, MS-64, March 2013; $940, MS-64, January 2015; $705, MS-63, August 2014; $529, MS-62, August 2014											
1901	615,900	5,314	61.9	93%	$365	$385	$400	$425	$485	$600	$800	$2,500
	Auctions: $16,450, MS-67, January 2015; $881, MS-64, July 2015; $823, MS-64, June 2015; $423, MS-62, May 2015											
1901, Proof	140	44	64.3							$12,500	$18,000	$30,000
	Auctions: $28,200, PF-65DCam, August 2014											
1901-S, All kinds	3,648,000											
1901-S, Final 1 Over 0		361	60.6	70%	$425	$450	$475	$500	$575	$1,250	$1,750	$4,500
	Auctions: $1,645, MS-64, January 2015; $1,116, MS-63, August 2014; $470, MS-62, October 2014; $401, AU-55, March 2015											
1901-S		7,315	62.0	92%	$365	$385	$400	$425	$485	$600	$800	$2,500
	Auctions: $2,585, MS-66, January 2015; $999, MS-64, June 2015; $705, MS-64, June 2015; $564, MS-63, August 2015											
1902	172,400	1,467	61.8	94%	$365	$385	$400	$425	$485	$600	$800	$2,500
	Auctions: $18,800, MS-67, October 2015; $2,820, MS-65, August 2015; $646, MS-63, June 2015; $535, MS-63, August 2015											
1902, Proof	162	29	63.1							$12,500	$18,000	$30,000
	Auctions: $12,925, PF-64, April 2013											
1902-S	939,000	2,605	62.1	91%	$365	$385	$400	$425	$485	$600	$800	$2,500
	Auctions: $23,500, MS-67, January 2014; $1,998, MS-65, January 2015; $588, MS-63, July 2015; $436, MS-62, March 2015											
1903	226,870	1,813	61.6	91%	$365	$385	$400	$425	$485	$600	$800	$2,500
	Auctions: $3,290, MS-66, July 2014; $3,819, MS-65, February 2014; $2,820, MS-65, September 2015; $423, MS-62, August 2015											
1903, Proof	154	57	63.9							$12,500	$18,000	$30,000
	Auctions: $32,900, PF-65, October 2014; $30,550, PF-65, August 2015; $66,975, PF, March 2014											
1903-S	1,855,000	4,340	62.1	92%	$365	$385	$400	$425	$485	$600	$800	$2,500
	Auctions: $2,585, MS-66, June 2015; $1,763, MS-65, January 2015; $764, MS-64, February 2015; $881, MS-63, September 2015											

	Mintage	Cert	Avg	%MS	VF-20	EF-40	AU-50	AU-55	MS-60	MS-63	MS-64	MS-65
										PF-63	PF-64	PF-65
1904	392,000	3,969	62.0	94%	$365	$385	$400	$425	$485	$600	$800	$2,500
Auctions: $5,170, MS-66, August 2015; $2,128, MS-65, July 2015; $482, MS-63, October 2015; $353, AU-58, June 2015												
1904, Proof	136	59	64.0							$12,500	$18,000	$30,000
Auctions: $31,725, PF-66Cam, June 2013												
1904-S	97,000	275	57.4	35%	$365	$385	$400	$475	$850	$2,250	$3,500	$8,500
Auctions: $4,113, MS-64, April 2013; $2,056, MS-63, January 2015; $423, AU-58, August 2015; $470, AU-55, October 2015												
1905	302,200	2,724	61.9	94%	$365	$385	$400	$425	$485	$600	$800	$2,500
Auctions: $2,350, MS-65, July 2015; $1,880, MS-65, February 2015; $999, MS-64, January 2015; $793, MS-64, June 2015												
1905, Proof	108	33	62.5							$12,500	$18,000	$30,000
Auctions: $23,000, PF-65Cam, October 2010												
1905-S	880,700	917	57.4	31%	$365	$385	$400	$475	$675	$1,500	$2,500	$8,000
Auctions: $764, MS-62, July 2015; $411, MS-61, March 2015; $347, AU-58, April 2015; $341, AU-53, March 2015												
1906	348,735	2,827	61.8	92%	$365	$385	$400	$425	$485	$600	$800	$2,500
Auctions: $7,050, MS-66, January 2015; $1,293, MS-64, September 2015; $517, MS-61, June 2015; $447, AU-55, January 2015												
1906, Proof	85	58	63.8							$12,500	$18,000	$30,000
Auctions: $64,625, PF-66Cam, August 2013												
1906-D	320,000	2,677	62.1	94%	$365	$385	$400	$425	$485	$600	$800	$2,500
Auctions: $4,935, MS-66, January 2015; $940, MS-64, August 2015; $823, MS-64, August 2015; $423, MS-60, February 2015												
1906-S	598,000	664	60.1	72%	$365	$385	$400	$450	$525	$1,000	$1,650	$4,500
Auctions: $793, MS-63, January 2015; $646, MS-63, February 2015; $470, MS-62, January 2015; $517, MS-61, June 2015												
1907	626,100	8,926	62.2	96%	$365	$385	$400	$425	$485	$600	$800	$2,500
Auctions: $7,638, MS-67, June 2015; $4,230, MS-66, August 2015; $1,175, MS-64, August 2015; $1,058, MS-64, August 2015												
1907, Proof	92	43	64.0							$12,500	$18,000	$30,000
Auctions: $24,675, PF-65Cam, April 2014												
1907-D	888,000	4,470	62.0	94%	$365	$385	$400	$425	$485	$600	$800	$2,500
Auctions: $1,704, MS-65, February 2015; $1,410, MS-64, September 2015; $423, MS-62, February 2015; $396, MS-61, July 2015												
1908	421,874	6,305	62.4	96%	$365	$385	$400	$425	$485	$600	$800	$2,500
Auctions: $4,465, MS-66, January 2015; $2,585, MS-65, August 2015; $999, MS-64, January 2015; $617, MS-63, January 2015												

INDIAN HEAD (1908–1929)

Designer: *Bela Lyon Pratt.* **Weight:** *8.359 grams.*
Composition: *.900 gold, .100 copper (net weight .24187 oz. pure gold).* **Diameter:** *21.6 mm.*
Edge: *Reeded.* **Mints:** *Philadelphia, Denver, New Orleans, and San Francisco.*

Circulation Strike   **Sandblast Finish Proof**   **Satin Finish Proof**

*Mintmark location
is on the reverse, to
the left of the arrows.*

History. The Indian Head half eagle made its first appearance in 1908; it was minted continuously through 1916, and again in 1929. Its design elements are in sunken relief (sometimes imprecisely called "incuse"), like those of the similar quarter eagle; the mintmark is raised. On most examples the rims are flat, while on others they are slightly raised. These coins saw limited circulation in the West, and were rarely encountered elsewhere.

Striking and Sharpness. Striking quality of Indian Head half eagles varies. Look for weakness on the high parts of the Indian's bonnet and in the feather details in the headdress. On the reverse, check the feathers on the highest area of the wing.

Proofs. Sandblast (also called Matte) Proofs were made in 1908 and from 1911 to 1915, while Satin (also called Roman Finish) Proofs were made in 1909 and 1910. At lower levels, these coins can show light contact marks. Some microscopic bright flecks may be caused by the sandblasting process and, although they do not represent handling, usually result in a coin being assigned a slightly lower grade.

Availability. Indian Head half eagles were not popular with numismatists of the time, who saved very few. Rare issues include the 1909-O, which usually is seen with evidence of circulation (often extensive) and the 1929, most of which are in MS. Luster can range from deeply frosty to grainy. Because the fields are the highest areas of the coin, luster diminished quickly as the coins were circulated or jostled with others in bags. When Proof examples are seen, they are usually in higher Proof grades, PF-64 and above. As a class these half eagles are rarer than quarter eagles of the same date and style of finish.

Note: Values of common-date gold coins have been based on the current bullion price of gold, $1,150 per ounce, and may vary with the prevailing spot price.

GRADING STANDARDS

MS-60 to 70 (Mint State). *Obverse:* At MS–60 to 62, there is abrasion in the field, this representing the highest part of the coin. Abrasion is also evident on the headdress. Marks and, occasionally, a microscopic pin scratch may be seen. At MS-63, there may be some abrasion and some tiny marks. Luster is irregular. At MS-64, abrasion is less. Luster is rich. At MS-65 and above, luster is deep and frosty, with no marks at all visible with-

1911-D. Graded MS-62.

out magnification at MS-66 and higher. *Reverse:* At MS–60 to 62 there is abrasion in the field, this representing the highest part of the coin. Abrasion is also evident on the eagle's wing. Otherwise, the same comments apply as for the obverse.

   Illustrated coin: This example is lustrous and attractive. Most of the luster in the fields (the highest-relief area of this unusual design) is still intact.

AU-50, 53, 55, 58 (About Uncirculated). *Obverse:* Friction on the cheek is very noticeable at AU-50, increasingly less at higher levels to AU-58. The headdress shows light wear, most evident on the ribbon above the forehead and on the garland. Luster is minimal at AU-50 and scattered and incomplete at AU-58. Nicks and contact marks are to be expected. *Reverse:* Friction on the wing and neck is very noticeable at AU-50, increasingly

1911. Graded AU-50.

less noticeable at higher levels to AU-58. Otherwise, the same comments apply as for the obverse.

EF-40, 45 (Extremely Fine). *Obverse:* Light wear will characterize the portrait and head-dress. Luster is gone. Marks and tiny scratches are to be expected, but not distracting. *Reverse:* Light wear is most evident on the eagle's head and wing, although other areas are lightly worn as well. Luster is gone. Marks and tiny scratches are to be expected, but not distracting.

1909-O. Graded EF-40.

VF-20, 30 (Very Fine). *Obverse:* Many details of the garland and of the ribbon above the forehead are worn away. Many feather vanes are blended together. The field is dull and has contact marks. *Reverse:* The neck and the upper part of the wing show extensive wear, other areas less so. The field is dull and has contact marks.

The Indian Head half eagle is seldom collected in grades lower than VF-20.

Illustrated coin: Some bumps are seen on the top obverse rim and should be mentioned in a description.

1909. Graded VF-25.

PF-60 to 70 (Proof). *Obverse and Reverse:* At PF–60 to 63, there is light abrasion and some contact marks (the lower the grade, the higher the quantity). On Sandblast Proofs these show up as visually unappealing bright spots. At PF-64 and higher levels, marks are fewer, with magnification needed to see any at PF-65. At PF-66, there should be none at all.

Illustrated coin: This is a particularly nice example.

1911, Sandblast Finish. Graded PF-67.

	Mintage	Cert	Avg	%MS	VF-20	EF-40	AU-50	AU-55	AU-58	MS-60	MS-62	MS-63	MS-65
											PF-63	PF-64	PF-65
1908	577,845	7,621	61.4	85%	$400	$420	$440	$460	$475	$525	$600	$1,150	$10,500
Auctions: $51,700, MS-67, January 2015; $911, MS-62, August 2015; $558, AU-58, February 2015; $376, AU-55, March 2015													
1908, Sandblast Finish Proof	167	85	65.2								$13,000	$18,000	$35,000
Auctions: $152,750, PF, August 2013													
1908-D	148,000	2,794	62.3	94%	$400	$420	$440	$460	$475	$525	$600	$1,500	$35,000
Auctions: $3,290, MS-64, September 2015; $1,351, MS-63, June 2015; $705, MS-61, August 2015; $470, AU-58, July 2015													
1908-S	82,000	541	57.7	43%	$575	$700	$1,000	$1,350	$1,650	$2,500	$4,500	$8,500	$20,000
Auctions: $47,000, MS-67, August 2014; $17,625, MS-65, January 2015; $7,344, MS-63, January 2015; $1,175, AU-55, July 2015													

	Mintage	Cert	Avg	%MS	VF-20	EF-40	AU-50	AU-55	AU-58	MS-60	MS-62 / PF-63	MS-63 / PF-64	MS-65 / PF-65
1909	627,060	6,936	61.0	83%	$400	$420	$440	$460	$475	$525	$600	$1,350	$10,000
Auctions: $7,638, MS-65, February 2015; $2,115, MS-64, October 2015; $676, MS-62, October 2015; $764, MS-61, July 2015													
1909, Satin Finish Proof	78	37	65.3								$13,000	$20,000	$37,500
Auctions: $82,250, PF-67, August 2014; $55,813, PF-66, August 2014; $99,875, PF-66, February 2013													
1909, Sandblast Finish Proof (a)	unknown	1	67										
Auctions: No auction records available.													
1909-D	3,423,560	31,910	61.5	87%	$400	$420	$440	$460	$475	$525	$600	$1,150	$10,000
Auctions: $2,350, MS-64, March 2015; $764, MS-62, June 2015; $552, MS-61, September 2015; $353, EF-40, April 2015													
1909-O (b)	34,200	979	55.4	15%	$4,500	$6,500	$9,500	$15,000	$25,000	$30,000	$65,000	$85,000	$400,000
Auctions: $35,250, MS-61, August 2015; $9,988, AU-53, October 2015; $6,463, AU-50, June 2015; $3,525, EF-40, January 2015													
1909-S	297,200	720	56.7	29%	$425	$450	$475	$550	$725	$1,500	$3,750	$12,500	$55,000
Auctions: $5,640, MS-62, January 2015; $3,410, MS-61, January 2015; $529, AU-55, March 2015; $400, EF-40, February 2015													
1910	604,000	7,013	60.9	80%	$400	$420	$440	$460	$475	$525	$600	$1,350	$12,000
Auctions: $17,625, MS-65, August 2015; $1,998, MS-64, February 2015; $999, MS-63, October 2015; $447, MS-60, May 2015													
1910, Satin Finish Proof	250	47	65.3								$13,000	$20,000	$37,500
Auctions: $146,250, PF, September 2013													
1910, Sandblast Finish Proof (c)	unknown	0	n/a										
Auctions: No auction records available.													
1910-D	193,600	1,171	60.4	75%	$400	$420	$440	$460	$475	$525	$600	$3,500	$30,000
Auctions: $7,050, MS-64, January 2015; $1,029, MS-62, January 2015; $617, MS-61, June 2015; $400, AU-55, May 2015													
1910-S	770,200	1,534	57.0	28%	$425	$450	$475	$500	$800	$1,750	$3,500	$9,500	$65,000
Auctions: $3,290, MS-62, March 2015; $2,056, MS-61, January 2015; $676, AU-58, August 2015; $517, AU-55, August 2015													
1911	915,000	10,867	60.7	77%	$400	$420	$440	$460	$475	$525	$600	$1,450	$12,000
Auctions: $8,225, MS-65, January 2015; $1,880, MS-64, January 2015; $529, MS-61, September 2015													
1911, Sandblast Finish Proof	139	54	65.7								$13,000	$18,000	$35,000
Auctions: $99,875, PF-67, April 2013													
1911-D	72,500	1,419	55.9	15%	$750	$1,000	$1,400	$2,500	$3,500	$10,000	$17,500	$40,000	$225,000
Auctions: $12,925, MS-62, August 2015; $8,813, MS-61, January 2015; $4,700, AU-58, January 2015; $1,998, AU-53, July 2015													
1911-S	1,416,000	2,704	57.2	36%	$425	$450	$475	$500	$600	$850	$2,500	$4,500	$35,000
Auctions: $12,925, MS-64, January 2015; $1,175, MS-61, July 2015; $494, AU-55, June 2015; $376, EF-45, March 2015													
1912	790,000	10,327	60.9	81%	$400	$420	$440	$460	$475	$525	$600	$1,350	$12,000
Auctions: $7,050, MS-65, January 2015; $2,820, MS-64, June 2015; $447, MS-61, October 2015; $482, AU-58, July 2015													
1912, Sandblast Finish Proof	144	38	66.4								$13,000	$18,000	$35,000
Auctions: $58,750, PF-66, September 2013													
1912-S	392,000	1,543	56.1	17%	$425	$450	$475	$600	$900	$2,500	$5,000	$15,000	$150,000
Auctions: $5,405, MS-62, August 2015; $2,820, MS-61, October 2015; $1,293, AU-58, August 2015; $449, AU-53, March 2015													
1913	915,901	11,874	61.0	82%	$400	$420	$440	$460	$475	$525	$600	$1,350	$10,000
Auctions: $2,585, MS-64, March 2015; $1,058, MS-63, October 2015; $764, MS-61, June 2015; $423, AU-58, July 2015													
1913, Sandblast Finish Proof	99	26	66.2								$13,000	$18,000	$35,000
Auctions: $51,750, PF-67, July 2011													
1913-S	408,000	1,866	56.5	23%	$525	$575	$625	$800	$1,000	$2,500	$7,500	$17,500	$125,000
Auctions: $4,600, MS-62, January 2015; $823, AU-58, July 2015; $470, AU-53, February 2015; $340, EF-40, February 2015													
1914	247,000	2,807	60.8	77%	$400	$420	$440	$460	$475	$525	$600	$1,850	$13,500
Auctions: $9,400, MS-65, January 2015; $5,170, MS-64, August 2015; $1,028, MS-62, June 2015; $541, MS-61, March 2015													
1914, Sandblast Finish Proof	125	32	65.8								$13,000	$18,000	$35,000
Auctions: $93,600, PF, September 2013													
1914-D	247,000	2,615	60.6	72%	$400	$420	$440	$460	$475	$600	$600	$2,250	$22,500
Auctions: $3,760, MS-64, October 2015; $1,880, MS-63, July 2015; $1,058, MS-61, February 2015; $470, AU-58, February 2015													
1914-S	263,000	1,497	57.8	35%	$425	$450	$475	$525	$850	$1,750	$4,500	$12,500	$100,000
Auctions: $16,450, MS-63, August 2015; $2,115, AU-58, September 2015; $470, AU-53, May 2015; $382, VF-35, June 2015													

a. This unique coin is certified by NGC as PF-67. **b.** Beware spurious "O" mintmark. **c.** This unique coin is part of the unique complete 1910 Sandblast Finish Proof gold set.

	Mintage	Cert	Avg	%MS	VF-20	EF-40	AU-50	AU-55	AU-58	MS-60	MS-62	MS-63	MS-65
											PF-63	PF-64	PF-65
1915 (d)	588,000	6,397	60.8	76%	$400	$420	$440	$460	$475	$525	$600	$1,600	$10,000
Auctions: $9,988, MS-65, August 2015; $3,760, MS-64, September 2015; $764, MS-62, August 2015; $646, MS-61, June 2015													
1915, Sandblast Finish Proof	75	22	65.2								$15,000	$25,000	$45,000
Auctions: $47,000, PF-66, June 2014													
1915-S	164,000	1,310	56.3	22%	$425	$450	$500	$700	$1,000	$2,500	$5,500	$17,000	$120,000
Auctions: $5,640, MS-62, January 2015; $3,525, MS-61, January 2015; $1,116, AU-58, October 2015; $364, AU-50, March 2015													
1916-S	240,000	2,053	58.9	48%	$450	$485	$525	$625	$725	$1,000	$2,500	$6,500	$32,000
Auctions: $41,126, MS-65, August 2015; $1,410, MS-61, October 2015; $400, AU-55, March 2015; $376, AU-50, October 2015													
1929	662,000	230	62.3	91%	$18,500	$20,000	$25,000	$27,500	$30,000	$35,000	$41,000	$45,000	$95,000
Auctions: $54,050, MS-64, January 2015; $51,700, MS-64, January 2015; $37,600, MS-62, August 2015; $24,675, AU-53, October 2015													

d. Pieces dated 1915-D are counterfeit.

Gold Eagles ($10)
1795–1933

AN OVERVIEW OF GOLD EAGLES

The ten-dollar gold coin, or *eagle*, was first produced in 1795. Coinage authority for the denomination, including its weight and fineness, had been specified by the Act of April 2, 1792.

The Capped Bust to Right with Small Eagle reverse is the rarest of the early ten-dollar coin types. However, when seen they tend to be in higher grades such as EF, AU, or low levels of Mint State. The Heraldic Eagle reverse issues from 1797 through 1804 are much more readily available and in slightly higher average grade.

The Liberty Head eagles without the motto IN GOD WE TRUST, minted from 1838 through 1865, are elusive in any Mint State grade, although VF and EF pieces are plentiful, and there are enough AU coins to easily satisfy collector demands. Some collectors have considered the 1838 and 1839, 9 Over 8, with the head of Miss Liberty tilted forward in relation to the date, to be a separate type. Eagles with IN GOD WE TRUST on the reverse, produced from 1866 to 1907, are plentiful in high grades, including choice and gem Mint State. Some of these were repatriated from overseas bank vaults beginning in the second half of the 20th century.

The Saint-Gaudens eagles of 1907, of the style with periods between and flanking the words E PLURIBUS UNUM, exist in the Wire Rim and Rounded Rim varieties. These can be collected as a distinct type, or not. Most readily available is the Wire Rim style, of which somewhat more than 400 are likely to exist today, nearly all in Mint State, often choice or gem. These coins were made as regular issues but soon became numismatic delicacies for Treasury officials to distribute as they saw fit. Some were to have gone to museums, but in reality most were secretly filtered out through favored coin dealers. Then comes the 1907–1908 style, without periods, easily available in EF, AU, and lower Mint State levels, although gems are elusive.

The final eagle type, the 1908–1933 style with IN GOD WE TRUST on the reverse, is readily obtained in grades from EF through MS-63. Higher-grade pieces are elusive, and

This pattern eagle of 1878, struck in copper and designated J-1580, was designed by George Morgan and strongly resembles the silver dollar design that bears his name.

when seen are often dated 1932, a year in which 4,463,000 were struck—more than any other coin in the history of the denomination.

FOR THE COLLECTOR AND INVESTOR: GOLD EAGLES AS A SPECIALTY

Collecting ten-dollar gold coins by die varieties is unusual, as the series includes so many scarce and rare coins. However, unlike other denominations, none is in the "impossible" category, and with some patience a full set of significant varieties, as listed in this book, can be obtained.

The early issues with a Small Eagle reverse, minted from 1795 through 1797, and those with the Heraldic Eagle reverse of 1797 through 1804, can be collected and studied by die varieties, with *United States Ten Dollar Gold Eagles 1795–1804*, by Anthony Teraskza, being one useful guide. *Early U.S. Gold Coin Varieties: A Study of Die States, 1795–1834*, by John W. Dannreuther and Harry W. Bass Jr., offers an abundance of information and enlarged photographs for study. In addition to the regular issues, a few 1804 restrike ten-dollar pieces exist from 1804-dated dies newly created in 1834.

Liberty Head eagles from 1838 through 1866 (without the motto IN GOD WE TRUST) comprise many scarce dates and mintmarks. Years ago the 1858, of which only 2,521 were minted, was highly acclaimed as a landmark issue, but since then the publicity has faded. In any event, although certain date-and-mintmark varieties are rare, the number of numismatists collecting them by date sequence is very small, and thus opportunities exist to acquire very elusive pieces at a much smaller proportionate premium than would be possible in, say, the gold dollar series. No full set of Mint State early eagles has ever been formed; probably none ever will be. EF and AU are typically the grades of choice, with Mint State pieces added when available.

Later Liberty Head eagles of the 1866–1907 style (with the motto IN GOD WE TRUST) include some low-mintage issues, but again these are not impossible to collect. The most famous is the 1875 Philadelphia coin, of which just 100 circulation strikes were made. Although smaller numbers exist for Proof-only mintages, in terms of those made for commerce the 1875 sets a record. The low-mintage 1879-O (1,500 made) and 1883-O (800) also have attracted much attention. Again, these pieces, while rare, are available to the specialist, as there is not a great deal of competition.

Among Indian Head eagles the 1907, With Periods, Wire Rim, is famous, popular, and rare. Examples come on the market with regularity but are expensive due to the demand they attract. The Rounded Rim style is much rarer and when seen is usually in choice Mint State.

The regular without-periods 1907 and 1908 eagles are easy enough to obtain in Mint State, although gems are elusive. The varieties from 1908 through 1916 include no great rarities, although some are scarcer than others. Not many such pieces were saved at the time they were issued, and, accordingly, gems are elusive. However, grades such as AU and low Mint State will present no problem. Among later eagles, the 1920-S, 1930-S, and 1933 are rarities. In particular the 1920-S is difficult to find in choice and gem Mint State. The 1933 eagle is usually found in Mint State, but is expensive due to the publicity given to it. Readily available at reasonable prices are the 1926 and 1932.

CAPPED BUST TO RIGHT, SMALL EAGLE REVERSE (1795–1797)

Designer: *Robert Scot.* **Weight:** *17.50 grams.*
Composition: *.9167 gold, .0833 silver and copper.*
Diameter: *Approximately 33 mm.* **Edge:** *Reeded.* **Mint:** *Philadelphia.*

Bass-Dannreuther–1.

History. Eagles of this style, the first in the denomination, debuted in the autumn of 1795. The obverse features Miss Liberty dressed in a conical cap. The reverse shows a "small" eagle perched on a palm branch and holding a laurel in his beak. The same motif was used on contemporary gold half eagles.

Striking and Sharpness. On the obverse, check the star centers and the hair details. On the reverse, check the feathers of the eagle. In particular, the breast feathers often are weakly struck. Examine the denticles on both sides. Adjustment marks (from a Mint worker filing an overweight planchet down to the correct weight) often are visible, but are not noted by the grading services.

Availability. Typical grades range from EF to AU and low MS. MS-63 and higher coins are rare; when seen, they usually are of the 1795 or 1796 dates. Certain varieties are rare. While no Proofs of this type were made, certain eagles of 1796 have prooflike surfaces and are particularly attractive if in high grades.

GRADING STANDARDS

MS-60 to 70 (Mint State). *Obverse:* At MS-60, some abrasion and contact marks are evident, most noticeably on the hair to the left of Miss Liberty's forehead and on the higher-relief areas of the cap. Luster is present, but may be dull or lifeless, and interrupted in patches. At MS-63, contact marks are few, and abrasion is very light. An MS-65 coin has hardly any abrasion, and contact marks are so minute as to require magnifica-

1795, 13 Leaves; BD-5. Graded MS-63.

tion. Luster should be full and rich. On prooflike coins in any Mint State grade, abrasion and surface marks are much more noticeable. Coins above MS-65 exist more in theory than in reality for this type— but they do exist, and are defined by having fewer marks as perfection is approached. *Reverse:* Comments apply as for the obverse, except that abrasion and contact marks are most noticeable on the breast and head of the eagle. The field area is mainly protected by the eagle, branch, and lettering.

AU-50, 53, 55, 58 (About Uncirculated).
Obverse: Light wear is seen on the cheek, the hair immediately to the left of the face, and the cap, more so at AU-50 than at AU–53 or 55. An AU-58 coin has minimal traces of wear. An AU-50 coin has luster in protected areas among the stars and letters, with little in the open fields or on the portrait. At AU-58, most luster is present in the fields, but is worn away on the highest parts of the motifs.

1796. Graded AU-58.

Reverse: Comments as preceding, except that the eagle shows light wear on the breast and head in particular, but also at the tip of the wing on the left and elsewhere. Luster ranges from perhaps 40% remaining in protected areas (at AU-50) to nearly full mint bloom (at AU-58).

Illustrated coin: This example shows light wear overall, with hints of original luster in protected areas.

EF-40, 45 (Extremely Fine). *Obverse:* Wear is evident all over the portrait, with some loss of detail in the hair to the left of Miss Liberty's face. Excellent detail remains in low-relief areas of the hair, such as the front curl and at the back of her head. The stars show wear, as do the date and letters. Luster, if present at all, is minimal and in protected areas. *Reverse:* Wear is greater than on an About Uncirculated coin. The breast, neck, and legs of the

1795, 9 Leaves; BD-3. Graded EF-45.

eagle lack nearly all feather detail. More wear is seen on the edges of the wing. Some traces of luster may be seen, more so at EF-45 than at EF-40.

VF-20, 30 (Very Fine). *Obverse:* The higher-relief areas of hair are well worn at VF-20, less so at VF-30. The stars are flat at their centers. *Reverse:* Wear is greater, the eagle is flat in most areas, and about 40% to 60% of the wing feathers can be seen.

The Capped Bust to Right eagle coin with Small Eagle reverse is seldom collected in grades lower than VF-20.

1795, 13 Leaves; BD-2. Graded VF-30.

1795, 13 Leaves   **1795, 9 Leaves**

	Mintage	Cert	Avg	%MS	F-12	VF-20	EF-40	AU-50	AU-55	MS-60	MS-62	MS-63
1795, 13 Leaves Below Eagle	5,583	49	55.3	29%	$25,000	$35,000	$45,000	$55,000	$67,500	$100,000	$150,000	$300,000 (a)
Auctions: $881,250, MS-65, August 2014; $152,750, MS-62, November 2014; $16,450, AU, March 2015; $49,938, EF-45, August 2014											
1795, 9 Leaves Below Eagle †	(b)	15	56.9	20%	$40,000	$55,000	$77,500	$120,000	$165,000	$250,000	$350,000	$500,000
Auctions: $146,875, EF-45, August 2014; $47,000, EF-40, January 2014											
1796	4,146	68	56.8	25%	$32,500	$42,500	$55,000	$60,000	$75,000	$125,000	$225,000	$350,000
Auctions: $164,500, MS-62, April 2014; $82,250, AU-55, August 2014											
1797, Small Eagle	3,615	28	55.1	32%	$37,500	$55,000	$75,000	$115,000	$130,000	$215,000	$325,000	$450,000
Auctions: $164,500, AU-58, August 2014; $76,375, EF-45, February 2014; $47,000, EF-40, August 2014											

† Ranked in the *100 Greatest U.S. Coins* (fourth edition). **a.** Value in MS-64 is $475,000. **b.** Included in 1795, 13 Leaves Below Eagle, mintage figure.

CAPPED BUST TO RIGHT, HERALDIC EAGLE REVERSE (1797–1804)

Designer: *Robert Scot.* **Weight:** *17.50 grams.*
Composition: *.9167 gold, .0833 silver and copper.*
Diameter: *Approximately 33 mm.* **Edge:** *Reeded.* **Mint:** *Philadelphia.*

Circulation Strike
BD-10.

Proof

History. Gold eagles of this type combine the previous obverse style with the Heraldic Eagle—a modification of the Great Seal of the United States—as used on other silver and gold coins of the era. Regarding the Proofs dated 1804: There were no Proofs coined in the era in which this type was issued, and all eagle and silver dollar production was suspended by President Thomas Jefferson in 1804. Years later, in 1834, the Mint made up new dies with the 1804 date (this time featuring a Plain 4 rather than a Crosslet 4) and struck a number of Proofs (the quantity unknown today, but perhaps a dozen or so) for inclusion in presentation Proof sets for foreign dignitaries.

Striking and Sharpness. On the obverse, check the star centers and the hair details. On the reverse, check the upper part of the shield, the lower part of the eagle's neck, the eagle's wing, the stars above the eagle, and the clouds. Inspect the denticles on both sides. Adjustment marks (from where an overweight planchet was filed down to correct specifications) can be problematic; these are not identified by the grading services.

Availability. Mintages of this type were erratic. Eagles of 1797 appear in the market with some regularity, while those of 1798 are rare. Usually seen are the issues of 1799 through 1803. Typical grades range from EF to lower MS. MS-62 and higher coins are seen with some frequency and usually are dated 1799 and later. The 1804 circulation strike is rare in true MS. Sharply struck coins without planchet adjustment marks are in the minority. Only a handful of the aforementioned 1804 Proofs survive today.

GRADING STANDARDS

MS-60 to 70 (Mint State). *Obverse:* At MS-60, some abrasion and contact marks are evident, most noticeably on the hair to the left of Miss Liberty's forehead and on the higher-relief areas of the cap. Luster is present, but may be dull or lifeless, and interrupted in patches. At MS-63, contact marks are few, and abrasion is very light. An MS-65 coin has even less abrasion (most observable in the right field), and contact marks are so

1799, Large Stars; BD-10. Graded MS-65.

minute as to require magnification. Luster should be full and rich. Coins graded above MS-65 are more theoretical than actual for this type—but they do exist, and are defined by having fewer marks as perfection is approached. Large-size eagles are usually graded with slightly less strictness than the lower gold denominations of this type. *Reverse:* Comments apply as for the obverse, except that abrasion and contact marks are most noticeable on the upper part of the eagle and the clouds. The field area is complex, without much open space, given the stars above the eagle, the arrows and olive branch, and other features. Accordingly, marks are not as noticeable as on the obverse.

Illustrated coin: This coin has an exceptionally sharp strike overall, but with some lightness on the eagle's dexter (viewer's left) talon. Note some trivial abrasion in the right obverse field.

AU-50, 53, 55, 58 (About Uncirculated). *Obverse:* Light wear is seen on the cheek, the hair immediately to the left of the face, and the cap, more so at AU-50 than at AU–53 or 55. An AU-58 coin has minimal traces of wear. An AU-50 coin has luster in protected areas among the stars and letters, with little in the open fields or on the portrait. At AU-58, most luster is present in the fields, but is worn away on the highest parts of the

1799, Small Stars; BD-7. Graded AU-50.

motifs. *Reverse:* Comments as preceding, except that the eagle's neck, the tips and top of the wings, the clouds, and the tail now show noticeable wear, as do other features. Luster ranges from perhaps 40% remaining in protected areas (at AU-50) to nearly full mint bloom (at AU-58). Often the reverse of this type retains much more luster than the obverse.

Illustrated coin: Note some lightness of strike at the center of the obverse. Significant luster remains.

EF-40, 45 (Extremely Fine). *Obverse:* Wear is evident all over the portrait, with some loss of detail in the hair to the left of Miss Liberty's face. Excellent detail remains in low-relief areas of the hair, such as the front curl and at the back of her head. The stars show wear as do the date and letters. Luster, if present at all, is minimal and in protected areas. *Reverse:* Wear is greater than on the preceding. The neck lacks some feather detail on its highest

1801; BD-2. Graded EF-45.

points. Feathers have lost some detail near the edges of the wings, and some areas of the horizontal lines in the shield may be blended together. Some traces of luster may be seen, more so at EF-45 than at EF-40. Overall, the reverse appears to be in a slightly higher grade than the obverse.

VF-20, 30 (Very Fine). *Obverse:* The higher-relief areas of hair are well worn at VF-20, less so at VF-30. *Reverse:* Wear is greater, including on the shield and wing feathers. The star centers are flat. Other areas have lost detail as well. E PLURIBUS UNUM may be faint in areas, but is usually sharp.

The Capped Bust to Right eagle coin with Heraldic Eagle reverse is seldom collected in grades lower than VF-20.

1799, Small Stars; BD-7. Graded VF-30.

PF-60 to 70 (Proof). *Obverse and Reverse:* PF–60 to 62 coins have extensive hairlines and may have nicks and contact marks. At PF-63, hairlines are prominent, but the mirror surface is very reflective. PF-64 coins have fewer hairlines. At PF-65, hairlines should be minimal and mostly seen only under magnification. There should be no nicks or marks.

1804, Plain 4; BD-2. Proof.

1798, 8 Over 7,
9 Stars Left, 4 Right

1798, 8 Over 7,
7 Stars Left, 6 Right

1799, Small
Obverse Stars

1799, Large
Obverse Stars

1803, Small
Reverse Stars

1803, Large
Reverse Stars

	Mintage	Cert	Avg	%MS	F-12	VF-20	EF-40	AU-50	AU-55	MS-60	MS-62	MS-63	MS-64
											PF-63	PF-64	PF-65
1797, Heraldic Eagle	10,940	165	55.8	29%	$12,500	$15,000	$20,000	$27,500	$37,500	$52,500	$85,000	$125,000	$200,000
	Auctions: $117,500, MS-63, April 2014; $44,063, MS-61, November 2014; $41,125, AU-58, August 2014; $34,075, AU-58, August 2014												
1798, 8 Over 7, 9 Stars Left, 4 Stars Right †	900	28	56.7	32%	$22,500	$30,000	$40,000	$55,000	$70,000	$125,000	$215,000	$300,000	
	Auctions: $176,250, MS-62, April 2014												
1798, 8 Over 7, 7 Stars Left, 6 Stars Right †	842	4	52.5	25%	$40,000	$55,000	$87,500	$165,000	$195,000	$325,000	$450,000		
	Auctions: $161,000, AU-55, January 2005; $176,250, AU-50, August 2014												
1799, Small Obverse Stars	37,449	27	57.6	48%	$8,750	$12,500	$16,000	$20,000	$23,500	$32,500	$42,500	$67,500	$135,000
	Auctions: $9,988, AU-58, September 2014; $25,850, AU-58, August 2014; $24,675, AU-55, January 2014; $15,275, AU-50, August 2014												
1799, Large Obverse Stars	(a)	31	59.5	61%	$8,750	$12,500	$16,000	$20,000	$23,500	$32,500	$42,500	$67,500	$115,000
	Auctions: $32,900, MS-62, October 2014; $19,975, AU-58, August 2014; $16,450, AU-53, November 2014; $9,400, AU, March 2015												
1800	5,999	109	57.4	43%	$9,000	$13,000	$16,500	$21,500	$24,500	$35,000	$52,500	$85,000	$160,000
	Auctions: $117,500, MS-64, January 2014; $32,900, MS-61, August 2014; $15,275, AU-50, August 2014; $7,638, AU-50, July 2014												
1801	44,344	411	58.6	52%	$8,750	$11,000	$15,000	$18,500	$21,500	$30,000	$40,000	$65,000	$125,000
	Auctions: $88,125, MS-64, March 2013; $48,763, MS-63, August 2014; $45,535, MS-63, August 2014; $29,375, MS-61, October 2014												
1803, Small Reverse Stars	15,017	18	56.4	44%	$9,500	$12,000	$16,000	$21,500	$23,500	$37,500	$50,000	$65,000	$135,000
	Auctions: $28,200, MS-61, January 2014; $15,875, AU-55, November 2014; $17,625, AU-55, August 2014; $13,513, AU-55, August 2014												
1803, Large Reverse Stars (b)	(c)	7	58.1	43%	$9,500	$12,000	$16,000	$21,500	$23,500	$37,500	$50,000	$65,000	$135,000
	Auctions: $99,875, MS-64, January 2014; $42,594, MS-62, August 2014; $24,675, AU-53, August 2014												
1804, Crosslet 4	3,757	52	58.8	50%	$20,000	$25,000	$37,500	$50,000	$65,000	$85,000	$100,000	$175,000	
	Auctions: $73,438, MS-61, January 2014; $64,625, MS-60, August 2014; $58,750, AU-58, August 2014												
1804, Plain 4, Proof † (d)	5–8	2	65.0								$4,000,000	$4,500,000	$5,000,000
	Auctions: $73,438, MS-61, January 2014												

† Ranked in the *100 Greatest U.S. Coins* (fourth edition). **a.** Included in 1799, Small Obverse Stars, mintage figure. **b.** A variety without the tiny 14th star in the cloud is very rare; 6 or 7 examples are known. It does not command a significant premium. **c.** Included in 1803, Small Reverse Stars, mintage figure. **d.** These coins were minted in 1834 (from newly created dies with the date 1804) for presentation sets for foreign dignitaries. 3 or four 4 are known today.

LIBERTY HEAD (1838–1907)

Designer: *Christian Gobrecht.* **Weight:** *16.718 grams.*
Composition: *.900 gold, .100 copper (net weight: .48375 oz. pure gold).* **Diameter:** *27 mm.*
Edge: *Reeded.* **Mints:** *Philadelphia, Carson City, Denver, New Orleans, and San Francisco.*

No Motto Above Eagle (1838–1866)

No Motto Above Eagle, Proof

Motto Above Eagle (1866–1907)

Motto Above Eagle, Proof

History. Production of the gold eagle, suspended after 1804, started up again in 1838 with the Liberty Head design. The coin's weight and diameter was reduced from the specifications of the earlier type. For the first time in the denomination's history, its value, TEN D., was shown. Midway through 1839 the style was modified slightly, including in the letters (made smaller) and in the tilt of Miss Liberty's portrait. In 1866 the motto IN GOD WE TRUST was placed on a banner above the eagle's head.

Striking and Sharpness. On the obverse, check the highest points of the hair and the star centers. On the reverse, check the eagle's neck, and the area to the lower left of the shield and the lower part of the eagle. Examine the denticles on both sides. Branch-mint coins issued before the Civil War often are lightly struck in areas, and some Carson City coins of the early 1870s can have areas of lightness. Most late 19th-century and early 20th-century coins are sharp in all areas. Tiny copper staining spots (from improperly mixed alloy) can be a problem for those issues. Cameo contrast is the rule for Proofs prior to 1902. Beginning that year the portrait was polished in the die, imparting a mirror finish across the entire design, although a few years later cameo-contrast coins were again made.

Availability. Early dates and mintmarks are generally scarce to rare in MS and very rare in MS-63 and better grades, with only a few exceptions. These were workhorse coins in commerce; VF and EF grades are the rule for dates through the 1870s, and for some dates the finest known grade can be AU. In MS, Liberty Head eagles as a type are rarer than either quarter eagles or half eagles of the same design. Indeed, the majority of Mint State examples were only discovered in recent decades, resting in European banks, and some varieties are not known to exist at this level. Eagles of the 1880s onward generally are seen in higher average grades. Proof coins exist in relation to their original mintages, with all issues prior to the 1890s being very rare.

Note: Values of common-date gold coins have been based on the current bullion price of gold, $1,150 per ounce, and may vary with the prevailing spot price.

GRADING STANDARDS

MS-60 to 70 (Mint State). *Obverse:* At MS-60, some abrasion and contact marks are evident, most noticeably on the hair to the right of Miss Liberty's forehead and on the jaw. Luster is present, but may be dull or lifeless, and interrupted in patches. At MS-63, contact marks are few, and abrasion is very light. An MS-65 coin has hardly any abrasion, and contact marks are so minute as to require magnification. Luster should be full and rich.

1880. Graded MS-63.

For most dates, coins graded above MS-65 exist more in theory than in actuality—but they do exist, and are defined by having fewer marks as perfection is approached. *Reverse:* Comments apply as for the obverse, except that abrasion and contact marks are most noticeable on the eagle's neck and to the lower left of the shield.

   Illustrated coin: This coin is brilliant and lustrous with scattered marks in the field, as is typical for this grade.

AU-50, 53, 55, 58 (About Uncirculated). *Obverse:* Light wear is seen on the face, the hair to the right of the face, and the highest area of the hair bun, more so at AU-50 than at AU–53 or 55. An AU-58 coin has minimal traces of wear. An AU-50 coin has luster in protected areas among the stars and letters, with little in the open fields or on the portrait. At AU-58 most luster is present in the fields, but is worn away on the highest parts

1839, Large Letters, 9 Over 8. Graded AU-53.

of the motifs. *Reverse:* Comments as preceding, except that the eagle shows wear in all of the higher areas, as well as the leaves and arrowheads. Luster ranges from perhaps 40% remaining in protected areas (at AU-50) to nearly full mint bloom (at AU-58). Often the reverse of this type retains more luster than the obverse.

EF-40, 45 (Extremely Fine). *Obverse:* Wear is evident on all high areas of the portrait, including the hair to the right of the forehead, the tip of the coronet, and the hair bun. The stars show light wear at their centers. Luster, if present at all, is minimal and in protected areas such as between the star points. *Reverse:* Wear is greater than on an About Uncirculated coin. On the $10 coins (in contrast to the $2.50 and $5 of the same design), most of the details on

1868. Graded EF-40.

the eagle are sharp. There is flatness on the leaves and arrowheads. Some traces of luster may be seen, more so at EF-45 than at EF-40.

   Illustrated coin: Note the many contact marks on both sides.

VF-20, 30 (Very Fine). *Obverse:* The higher-relief areas of hair are worn flat at VF-20, less so at VF-30. The hair to the right of the coronet is merged into heavy strands. The stars are flat at their centers. *Reverse:* The eagle is worn further, with most neck feathers gone and with the feathers in the wing having flat tips. The branch leaves have little or no detail. The vertical shield stripes, being deeply recessed, remain bold.

1838. Graded VF-25.

The Liberty Head eagle is seldom collected in grades lower than VF-20.

PF-60 to 70 (Proof). *Obverse and Reverse:* PF–60 to 62 coins have extensive hairlines and may have nicks and contact marks. At PF-63, hairlines are prominent, but the mirror surface is very reflective. PF-64 coins have fewer hairlines. At PF-65, hairlines should be minimal and mostly seen only under magnification. There should be no nicks or marks. PF-66 and higher coins should have no marks or hairlines visible to the unaided eye.

1862. Graded PF-65.

Illustrated coin: This is a museum-quality gem, with cameo-contrast motifs and mirror fields.

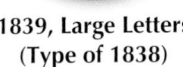

1839, Large Letters (Type of 1838)   **1839, Small Letters (Type of 1840)**

	Mintage	Cert	Avg	%MS	VF-20	EF-40	AU-50	AU-55	AU-58	MS-60 / PF-63	MS-63 / PF-64	MS-65 / PF-65
1838	7,200	59	47.9	3%	$2,750	$6,000	$13,000	$22,500	$35,000	$45,000	$125,000	
Auctions: $41,125, AU-58, August 2014; $7,638, EF-40, August 2015; $5,875, EF-40, June 2015; $5,288, VF-25, July 2014												
1838, Proof † (a)	4–6	1	65.0	*(extremely rare)*								
Auctions: $500,000, ChPF, May 1998												
1839, Large Letters (b)	25,801	162	50.6	10%	$1,500	$3,750	$6,500	$10,500	$16,000	$35,000	$85,000	$350,000
Auctions: $10,575, AU-58, September 2015; $9,694, AU-55, August 2015; $4,759, AU-50, August 2015; $6,169, EF-45, January 2015												
1839, Small Letters	12,447	37	46.9	3%	$1,850	$3,750	$8,500	$20,000	$30,000	$45,000	$135,000	
Auctions: $47,000, AU-58, February 2014												
1839, Large Letters, Proof (c)	4–6	1	67.0	*(extremely rare)*								
Auctions: $1,610,000, PF-67UCam, January 2007												

† Ranked in the *100 Greatest U.S. Coins* (fourth edition). **a.** 3 examples are known. **b.** The Large Letters style is also known as the "Type of 1838," because of the distinct style of the 1838 Liberty Head motif. The Small Letters style (or "Type of 1840") was used on subsequent issues. **c.** 3 examples are known.

1842, Small Date   **1842, Large Date**

	Mintage	Cert	Avg	%MS	VF-20	EF-40	AU-50	AU-55	AU-58	MS-60	MS-63	MS-65
										PF-63	PF-64	PF-65
1840	47,338	176	49.3	3%	$1,000	$1,100	$1,550	$2,750	$6,000	$12,000		
	Auctions: $35,250, MS-62, August 2014; $15,275, MS-61, June 2015; $1,528, AU-53, June 2015; $1,645, EF-40, September 2015											
1840, Proof (d)	1–2	0	n/a		*(unique, in the Smithsonian's National Numismatic Collection)*							
	Auctions: No auction records available.											
1841	63,131	195	49.7	7%	$1,000	$1,050	$1,250	$2,500	$4,500	$8,500		
	Auctions: $9,400, MS-61, February 2014; $4,230, AU-58, August 2015; $1,645, AU-55, February 2015; $1,116, AU-53, June 2015											
1841, Proof (e)	4–6	1	61.0		*(extremely rare)*							
	Auctions: No auction records available.											
1841-O	2,500	49	44.5	0%	$7,000	$15,000	$22,500	$35,000	$45,000			
	Auctions: $25,850, AU-53, January 2014; $14,688, AU-50, October 2014											
1842, Small Date	18,623	94	51.3	6%	$1,000	$1,050	$1,750	$3,000	$7,500	$13,500	$40,000	
	Auctions: $12,925, MS-61, June 2015; $2,115, AU-55, January 2015; $1,175, AU-50, February 2015; $940, AU-50, January 2015											
1842, Large Date	62,884	98	51.2	5%	$1,000	$1,050	$1,650	$2,500	$5,000	$15,000	$35,000	$125,000
	Auctions: $2,233, MS-60, January 2014											
1842, Small Date, Proof (f)	2	0	n/a		*(extremely rare)*							
	Auctions: No auction records available.											
1842-O	27,400	260	48.2	2%	$1,150	$1,250	$2,750	$6,500	$13,500	$25,000	$75,000	
	Auctions: $8,825, AU-55, March 2014; $4,230, AU-53, August 2015; $999, AU-50, July 2015; $823, EF-45, January 2015											
1843	75,462	185	49.4	3%	$950	$1,050	$1,750	$3,000	$5,000	$13,000		
	Auctions: $3,055, AU-55, October 2015; $1,763, AU-50, August 2015; $1,058, EF-40, January 2015; $1,011, VF-30, March 2015											
1843, Doubled Die	(g)	0	n/a									
	Auctions: No auction records available.											
1843, Proof (h)	6–8	3	62.7		*(extremely rare)*							
	Auctions: No auction records available.											
1843-O	175,162	411	49.5	2%	$1,050	$1,100	$1,800	$3,250	$5,500	$12,500		
	Auctions: $7,050, AU-58, February 2015; $2,585, AU-53, July 2015; $1,175, AU-50, January 2015; $1,058, VF-35, January 2015											
1844	6,361	38	49.2	5%	$1,200	$2,500	$4,750	$7,500	$10,000	$15,000	$50,000	
	Auctions: $24,170, AU-55, January 2014											
1844, Proof (i)	6–8	1	63.0		*(extremely rare)*							
	Auctions: No auction records available.											
1844-O	118,700	369	50.8	5%	$1,050	$1,100	$1,850	$3,250	$8,000	$15,000		
	Auctions: $7,931, AU-58, June 2013; $2,585, AU-53, July 2015; $2,585, AU-53, March 2015; $1,293, EF-45, November 2014											
1844-O, Proof †	1	1	65.0									
	Auctions: No auction records available.											
1845	26,153	109	48.7	3%	$950	$1,050	$2,000	$2,500	$6,000	$12,500		
	Auctions: $4,994, AU-55, April 2013											
1845, Proof (j)	6–8	1	65.0		*(extremely rare)*							
	Auctions: $120,750, PF-64, August 1999											
1845-O	47,500	232	49.7	5%	$1,050	$1,150	$2,750	$5,000	$8,000	$15,000	$50,000	
	Auctions: $2,820, AU-53, November 2014; $881, AU-50, October 2014; $3,819, AU, March 2014; $764, EF-40, January 2015											

† Ranked in the *100 Greatest U.S. Coins* (fourth edition). **d.** While there is only one known example known of this coin, it is possible that other 1840 Proof eagles were made, given that duplicates are known of the quarter eagle and half eagle denominations. **e.** 3 examples are known. **f.** 2 examples are known. **g.** Included in circulation-strike 1843 mintage figure. **h.** 5 examples are known. **i.** 3 or 4 examples are known. **j.** 4 or 5 examples are known.

1846-O, 6 Over 5   **1850, Large Date**   **1850, Small Date**

	Mintage	Cert	Avg	%MS	VF-20	EF-40	AU-50	AU-55	AU-58	MS-60 / PF-63	MS-63 / PF-64	MS-65 / PF-65
1846	20,095	93	48.1	4%	$1,050	$1,250	$3,500	$6,500	$10,000	$20,000		
	Auctions: $4,994, AU-55, September 2014; $4,406, AU-55, September 2014; $8,225, AU-55, January 2014; $3,760, AU-50, June 2015											
1846, Proof (k)	6–8	1	64.0		*(extremely rare)*							
	Auctions: $161,000, PF-64Cam, January 2011											
1846-O, All kinds	81,780											
1846-O		142	45.6	1%	$1,050	$1,200	$3,200	$6,000	$8,500	$13,500		
	Auctions: $2,820, AU-50, January 2014											
1846-O, 6 Over 5		12	55.1	8%	$1,100	$1,400	$4,000	$7,500	$10,000	$25,000		
	Auctions: $3,525, AU-50, January 2014											
1847	862,258	1,057	52.2	6%	$850	$950	$1,000	$1,050	$1,450	$3,500	$21,500	
	Auctions: $894, AU-55, June 2015; $823, AU-53, February 2015; $764, AU-50, January 2015; $881, EF-40, July 2015											
1847, Proof	1–2	0	n/a		*(unique, in the Smithsonian's National Numismatic Collection)*							
	Auctions: No auction records available.											
1847-O	571,500	891	49.9	2%	$950	$1,050	$1,150	$1,350	$2,500	$6,000	$25,000	
	Auctions: $2,056, AU-58, August 2015; $1,528, AU-55, October 2015; $1,058, AU-50, July 2015; $881, VF-30, January 2015											
1848	145,484	365	51.7	7%	$850	$950	$1,000	$1,050	$1,600	$4,500	$22,500	
	Auctions: $64,625, MS-64, October 2014; $3,760, MS-60, June 2015; $940, AU-53, June 2015; $881, EF-45, January 2015											
1848, Proof (l)	3–5	1	64.0		*(extremely rare)*							
	Auctions: No auction records available.											
1848-O	35,850	182	49.1	4%	$1,000	$1,500	$3,000	$6,000	$8,500	$15,000	$35,000	$85,000
	Auctions: $51,700, MS-64, January 2015; $2,820, MS-60, October 2014; $3,525, AU-50, September 2015; $2,820, AU-50, June 2015											
1849	653,618	944	50.4	5%	$850	$950	$1,000	$1,050	$1,750	$3,750	$13,500	
	Auctions: $4,467, MS-61, June 2015; $999, AU-55, August 2015; $1,058, EF-45, August 2015; $676, VF-25, October 2015											
1849, Recut 1849 Over 849	(m)	35	50.6	9%				$3,000	$5,500			
	Auctions: $978, EF-40, May 2011											
1849-O	23,900	229	47.7	2%	$1,100	$2,250	$5,000	$6,500	$11,000	$25,000		
	Auctions: $5,875, AU-53, October 2013											
1850, All kinds	291,451											
1850, Large Date		445	50.7	5%	$850	$950	$1,000	$1,050	$1,750	$4,000	$20,000	
	Auctions: $3,525, MS-60, September 2015; $1,116, AU-55, February 2015; $1,058, AU-53, August 2015; $940, AU-50, October 2015											
1850, Small Date		133	49.1	5%	$950	$1,100	$2,250	$3,000	$4,500	$8,000	$30,000	
	Auctions: $10,575, MS-61, August 2015; $1,528, AU-53, October 2015; $1,058, EF-45, July 2015; $999, EF-40, February 2015											
1850-O	57,500	203	47.6	1%	$1,050	$1,300	$3,500	$5,500	$8,500	$20,000		
	Auctions: $6,169, AU-58, November 2014; $3,967, AU-55, March 2015; $1,293, VF-35, January 2015; $1,293, VF-30, September 2015											
1851	176,328	274	52.0	7%	$800	$1,000	$1,050	$1,250	$1,750	$4,000	$26,000	
	Auctions: $852, AU-50, September 2014; $881, AU-50, August 2014; $3,819, MS-61, September 2013; $734, VF-30, October 2014											
1851-O	263,000	940	50.9	2%	$950	$1,100	$1,600	$2,750	$3,750	$6,500	$27,500	
	Auctions: $18,800, MS-61, January 2015; $2,820, AU-55, January 2015; $1,293, EF-45, August 2015; $705, VF-20, January 2015											
1852	263,106	615	52.8	6%	$800	$1,000	$1,050	$1,250	$1,500	$5,000		
	Auctions: $3,995, MS-61, July 2015; $1,146, AU-55, July 2015; $940, AU-50, July 2015; $823, VF-35, February 2015											
1852-O	18,000	103	49.7	2%	$1,100	$1,600	$3,750	$8,500	$15,000	$35,000		
	Auctions: $7,638, AU-55, August 2015; $3,290, AU-53, November 2014; $18,800, AU, February 2014											

k. 4 examples are known. **l.** 2 examples are known. **m.** Included in circulation-strike 1849 mintage figure.

1853, 3 Over 2	1854-O, Large Date	1854-O, Small Date

	Mintage	Cert	Avg	%MS	VF-20	EF-40	AU-50	AU-55	AU-58	MS-60 / PF-63	MS-63 / PF-64	MS-65 / PF-65
1853, All kinds	201,253											
1853, 3 Over 2		150	52.1	3%	$1,150	$1,500	$1,750	$3,250	$7,500			
Auctions: $14,688, MS-61, June 2015; $11,779, MS-60, August 2015; $5,875, AU-58, October 2014; $2,350, AU-55, June 2015												
1853		644	53.7	7%	$800	$900	$1,050	$1,200	$1,500	$4,000	$17,000	
Auctions: $34,075, MS-64, October 2014; $3,819, MS-61, November 2014; $999, AU-55, January 2015; $793, AU-53, January 2015												
1853-O	51,000	252	51.0	3%	$1,000	$1,150	$1,250	$3,000	$6,500	$15,000		
Auctions: $16,450, MS-61, November 2014; $9,400, MS-60, June 2015; $6,463, AU-58, October 2014; $881, AU-50, January 2015												
1853-O, Proof (n)	1	1	61.0									
Auctions: No auction records available.												
1854	54,250	257	52.4	5%	$800	$900	$1,050	$1,500	$2,750	$6,500	$27,500	
Auctions: $2,350, AU-58, September 2015; $2,115, AU-58, August 2015; $1,410, AU-55, June 2015; $1,293, AU-55, May 2015												
1854, Proof (o)	*unknown*	1	55.0									
Auctions: No auction records available.												
1854-O, Large Date (p)	52,500	157	53.7	9%	$950	$1,100	$1,750	$3,250	$4,500	$10,500		
Auctions: $10,869, MS-60, August 2013; $1,998, AU-53, November 2014; $2,585, EF-40, September 2015												
1854-O, Small Date (q)	(r)	114	53.0	1%	$950	$1,100	$1,750	$3,250	$4,700	$10,500		
Auctions: $1,821, AU-55, August 2013												
1854-S	123,826	469	50.3	2%	$950	$1,050	$1,350	$3,000	$5,500	$12,500		
Auctions: $4,935, AU-58, June 2015; $3,290, AU-55, June 2015; $1,998, AU-53, January 2015; $1,293, AU-50, August 2015												
1855	121,701	533	54.2	11%	$875	$950	$1,050	$1,200	$2,000	$4,750	$17,500	
Auctions: $7,115, MS-62, September 2015; $2,233, AU-58, August 2015; $1,058, AU-53, August 2015; $881, EF-45, January 2015												
1855, Proof (s)	*unknown*	0	n/a									
Auctions: No auction records available.												
1855-O	18,000	108	49.2	0%	$1,050	$1,800	$5,000	$8,250	$12,000	$25,000		
Auctions: $17,625, AU-58, January 2014												
1855-S	9,000	33	48.9	0%	$1,350	$2,250	$5,500	$8,750	$16,000			
Auctions: $17,625, AU-58, March 2014												
1856	60,490	304	53.9	12%	$875	$950	$1,050	$1,200	$1,500	$4,000	$15,000	
Auctions: $3,995, MS-61, January 2015; $2,242, AU-58, January 2015; $881, AU-53, February 2015; $793, EF-45, February 2015												
1856, Proof (s)	*unknown*	0	n/a									
Auctions: No auction records available.												
1856-O	14,500	107	49.8	4%	$1,050	$1,500	$4,250	$7,000	$9,000	$16,500		
Auctions: $4,406, AU-55, January 2014												
1856-S	68,000	273	50.2	1%	$875	$950	$1,400	$2,500	$4,000	$9,000	$25,000	
Auctions: $9,988, MS-61, April 2014; $3,290, AU-58, November 2014; $1,763, AU-55, October 2015; $1,116, AU-53, June 2015												

n. The 1853-O Proof listed here is not a Proof from a technical standpoint. This unique coin has in the past been called a presentation piece and a branch-mint Proof. "Although the piece does not have the same convincing texture as the 1844-O Proof eagle, it is clearly different from the regular-issue eagles found for the year and mint" (*Encyclopedia of U.S. Gold Coins, 1795–1933*, second edition). **o.** According to Walter Breen, in July 1854 a set of Proof coins was given by the United States to representatives of the sovereign German city of Bremen. Various Proof 1854 gold dollars, quarter eagles, and three-dollar gold pieces have come to light, along with a single gold eagle. **p.** The Large Date variety was made in error, when the diesinker used a date punch for a silver dollar on the much smaller ten-dollar die. **q.** The Small Date variety is scarce in AU. Only 3 or 4 MS examples are known, none finer than MS-60. **r.** Included in 1854-O, Large Date, mintage figure. **s.** No Proof 1855 or 1856 eagles have been confirmed, but Wayte Raymond claimed to have seen one of each some time prior to 1949.

	Mintage	Cert	Avg	%MS	VF-20	EF-40	AU-50	AU-55	AU-58	MS-60 PF-63	MS-63 PF-64	MS-65 PF-65
1857	16,606	115	51.5	6%	$875	$1,000	$1,950	$3,750	$5,500	$12,000		
	Auctions: $4,406, AU-58, April 2014; $1,293, EF-45, September 2014											
1857, Proof	2–3	1	66.0									
	Auctions: No auction records available.											
1857-O	5,500	59	51.8	0%	$1,500	$2,500	$4,000	$7,500	$15,000			
	Auctions: $22,325, AU-58, August 2014; $8,225, AU-55, February 2014											
1857-S	26,000	71	47.5	3%	$1,000	$1,250	$2,500	$4,500	$6,000	$11,000	$25,000	
	Auctions: $8,225, AU-58, July 2014; $5,875, AU-55, January 2015; $3,378, EF-45, August 2014; $4,465, EF-40, September 2015											
1858 (t)	2,521	32	48.9	6%	$6,000	$7,500	$12,500	$17,500	$25,000	$40,000		
	Auctions: $15,275, AU-53, February 2014											
1858, Proof (u)	4–6	2	64.0				*(extremely rare)*					
	Auctions: No auction records available.											
1858-O	20,000	194	51.5	4%	$1,050	$1,150	$1,850	$3,500	$5,000	$9,000	$32,500	
	Auctions: $6,463, AU-58, January 2015; $2,585, AU-55, January 2015; $1,293, AU-50, October 2015; $1,645, EF-45, January 2015											
1858-S	11,800	50	51.1	0%	$1,800	$3,000	$5,000	$12,000	$22,500			
	Auctions: $15,275, AU-58, April 2013; $3,055, EF-45, November 2014; $2,820, EF-40, October 2015; $2,115, EF-40, November 2014											
1859	16,013	150	51.0	7%	$900	$1,000	$1,300	$2,000	$3,750	$9,000	$40,000	
	Auctions: $41,125, MS-62, November 2014; $47,000, MS-62, April 2014; $1,175, EF-45, July 2015; $734, VF-20, January 2015											
1859, Proof	80	3	64.3							$75,000	$150,000	$200,000
	Auctions: No auction records available.											
1859-O	2,300	21	50.6	5%	$5,000	$10,000	$25,000	$35,000	$55,000			
	Auctions: $28,200, AU-50, December 2013											
1859-S	7,000	38	43.7	3%	$3,000	$7,500	$20,000	$22,500	$27,500	$50,000		
	Auctions: $14,100, AU-53, October 2014; $3,525, AU-50, June 2015; $6,463, EF-45, October 2015; $3,290, EF-40, August 2014											
1860	15,055	136	51.6	9%	$900	$1,100	$1,750	$2,700	$3,000	$7,500	$25,000	
	Auctions: $70,500, MS-64, February 2013; $14,100, MS-62, June 2015; $1,645, AU-50, September 2014; $1,293, EF-45, January 2015											
1860, Proof	50	5	63.6							$50,000	$80,000	$135,000
	Auctions: $142,175, PF-64DCam, April 2014											
1860-O	11,100	130	51.5	5%	$1,050	$1,450	$2,500	$5,000	$6,500	$15,000		
	Auctions: $8,814, AU-About Uncirculated, March 2014											
1860-S	5,000	22	48.4	9%	$3,000	$5,500	$13,000	$30,000	$45,000	$60,000		
	Auctions: $28,200, AU-55, March 2014											
1861	113,164	614	54.9	15%	$925	$1,050	$1,100	$2,500	$4,000	$6,500	$20,000	
	Auctions: $8,225, MS-62, August 2015; $7,652, MS-62, January 2015; $4,113, AU-58, July 2014; $940, AU-50, January 2015											
1861, Proof	69	6	64.2							$45,000	$70,000	$125,000
	Auctions: $129,250, PF-64Cam, March 2013											
1861-S	15,500	82	49.9	1%	$3,500	$5,500	$11,000	$16,000	$23,000	$47,500		
	Auctions: $25,850, AU-58, March 2014; $9,400, AU-53, August 2015; $7,638, AU-53, September 2014; $6,463, EF-40, June 2015											
1862	10,960	100	51.9	12%	$950	$1,750	$3,000	$8,500	$11,000	$18,500	$37,500	
	Auctions: $18,800, MS-61, October 2015; $7,050, AU-55, January 2015; $6,169, AU-53, July 2015; $4,935, AU-50, September 2015											
1862, Proof	35	5	64.4							$42,500	$70,000	$125,000
	Auctions: $152,750, PF-65DCam, August 2013											
1862-S	12,500	45	45.9	0%	$2,750	$4,000	$7,000	$12,500	$20,000	$40,000		
	Auctions: $21,150, AU-58, October 2014; $5,581, EF-35, February 2014											
1863	1,218	16	52.0	19%	$9,000	$16,000	$30,000	$40,000	$55,000	$75,000		
	Auctions: $49,938, AU-53, January 2014											
1863, Proof	30	12	64.2							$42,500	$70,000	$125,000
	Auctions: $299,000, PF-65DCam, August 2011											
1863-S	10,000	29	45.1	3%	$5,000	$15,000	$30,000	$35,000	$40,000	$45,000		
	Auctions: $32,900, AU-53, February 2014; $12,925, AU-50, October 2015; $15,275, EF-45, October 2014; $5,875, F-12, November 2014											

t. Beware of fraudulently removed mintmark. **u.** 4 or 5 examples are known.

1865-S, 865
Over Inverted 186

	Mintage	Cert	Avg	%MS	VF-20	EF-40	AU-50	AU-55	AU-58	MS-60 / PF-63	MS-63 / PF-64	MS-65 / PF-65
1864	3,530	24	50.0	17%	$5,000	$10,000	$20,000	$27,500	$32,500	$42,500		
Auctions: $41,125, AU-55, October 2014; $28,200, AU-55, January 2014												
1864, Proof	50	17	63.8							$42,500	$70,000	$125,000
Auctions: $138,000, PF-64UCam, October 2011												
1864-S	2,500	7	42.9	0%	$32,500	$65,000	$100,000	$150,000				
Auctions: $146,875, AU-53, March 2014												
1865	3,980	33	50.5	6%	$5,000	$9,000	$15,000	$20,000	$27,500	$47,500	$90,000	
Auctions: $15,275, AU-53, October 2014; $18,800, AU-53, January 2014; $13,513, AU-50, October 2014; $12,925, AU-50, August 2015												
1865, Proof	25	13	64.1							$42,500	$70,000	$125,000
Auctions: $528,750, PF, August 2013												
1865-S, All kinds	16,700											
1865-S		33	39.1	3%	$8,000	$12,500	$17,500	$30,000	$37,500	$65,000		
Auctions: $6,756, F-12, February 2013												
1865-S, 865 Over Inverted 186		37	42.4	3%	$7,500	$15,000	$21,000	$27,500	$35,000	$45,000		
Auctions: $20,563, AU-55, January 2015; $27,025, AU-53, March 2014; $9,400, EF-45, October 2015; $1,880, VG-8, August 2014												
1866-S, No Motto	8,500	33	46.8	3%	$3,000	$4,000	$12,000	$20,000	$27,500	$55,000		
Auctions: $14,950, EF-45, August 2011												
1866, With Motto	3,750	47	49.9	13%	$1,500	$2,000	$5,000	$8,000	$17,500	$30,000		
Auctions: $32,900, MS-61, January 2015; $14,100, AU-55, September 2013; $4,054, AU-50, August 2015; $1,763, EF-40, January 2015												
1866, Proof	30	9	64.1							$32,500	$50,000	$85,000
Auctions: $66,125, PF-64UCam+H, January 2012												
1866-S, With Motto	11,500	39	49.1	0%	$1,500	$3,250	$7,250	$10,000	$17,500			
Auctions: $15,275, AU-58, March 2014; $9,988, AU-55, August 2014; $4,230, EF-45, July 2015; $4,230, VF-35, January 2015												
1867	3,090	60	49.9	3%	$1,500	$2,500	$4,500	$10,000	$20,000	$35,000		
Auctions: $30,550, AU-58, August 2013												
1867, Proof	50	6	64.5							$32,500	$50,000	$85,000
Auctions: $64,625, PF-65Cam, August 2014; $64,625, PF-64Cam+, February 2015; $54,344, PF-64Cam, October 2014												
1867-S	9,000	34	46.8	0%	$2,250	$5,500	$9,000	$14,500	$25,000			
Auctions: $9,988, AU-53, June 2013												
1868	10,630	152	50.7	5%	$850	$950	$1,700	$3,500	$6,000	$17,500		
Auctions: $5,875, AU-58, February 2015; $4,700, AU-58, July 2015; $1,645, AU-50, January 2015; $2,350, EF-45, September 2015												
1868, Proof	25	4	64.8							$32,500	$50,000	$85,000
Auctions: $24,150, PF-62Cam, June 2005												
1868-S	13,500	74	48.5	0%	$1,250	$2,250	$4,000	$5,500	$8,500			
Auctions: $5,875, AU-58, August 2014; $4,700, AU-55, July 2015; $1,469, AU-50, August 2015; $2,115, EF-40, August 2014												
1869	1,830	42	50.6	7%	$1,500	$2,350	$4,750	$11,500	$18,000	$30,000		
Auctions: $14,100, AU-58, August 2013												
1869, Proof	25	8	63.8							$32,500	$50,000	$80,000
Auctions: $161,000, PF-67UCam+H, February 2012												
1869-S	6,430	36	46.9	3%	$1,500	$2,350	$4,750	$8,500	$18,500	$30,000		
Auctions: $16,450, AU-58, January 2015; $11,163, AU-55, August 2015; $7,638, AU-55, January 2015; $1,528, EF-40, October 2015												

	Mintage	Cert	Avg	%MS	VF-20	EF-40	AU-50	AU-55	AU-58	MS-60 / PF-63	MS-63 / PF-64	MS-65 / PF-65
1870	3,990	68	49.1	1%	$950	$1,250	$2,500	$6,000	$11,000	$18,500		
Auctions: $10,575, AU-55, January 2014												
1870, Proof	35	4	64.5							$32,500	$50,000	$80,000
Auctions: $97,750, PF-65UCam, January 2010												
1870-CC	5,908	32	41.8	0%	$30,000	$50,000	$80,000	$145,000				
Auctions: $135,125, AU-55, March 2014; $36,719, VF-35, August 2014; $28,200, VG-10, August 2015												
1870-S	8,000	60	42.0	0%	$1,050	$2,000	$5,500	$11,000	$15,000	$27,500		
Auctions: $12,925, AU-58, March 2014												
1871	1,790	47	50.7	0%	$1,400	$2,400	$3,750	$8,500	$15,000	$22,500		
Auctions: $15,275, AU-58, September 2013; $9,400, AU-55, March 2015; $4,583, AU-50, July 2015; $3,290, EF-40, August 2014												
1871, Proof	30	5	63.2							$32,500	$50,000	$80,000
Auctions: $76,375, PF-64DCam, August 2013												
1871-CC	8,085	71	46.6	3%	$4,000	$10,000	$18,000	$27,000	$42,500	$75,000		
Auctions: $35,250, AU-58, October 2014; $14,100, AU-53, January 2015; $5,170, AU-50, June 2015; $9,106, VF-35, August 2015												
1871-S	16,500	90	43.6	0%	$1,150	$1,850	$5,000	$7,500	$12,500			
Auctions: $10,281, AU-58, March 2014; $2,115, AU-50, July 2014; $1,116, AU-50, October 2015; $2,231, EF-45, February 2015												
1872	1,620	23	51.4	4%	$2,000	$3,250	$9,000	$12,000	$17,500	$40,000		
Auctions: $38,188, AU-58, August 2014; $16,450, AU-55, August 2015; $16,450, AU-55, February 2015; $6,169, EF-45, July 2015												
1872, Proof	30	7	64.7							$32,500	$50,000	$80,000
Auctions: $48,875, PF-64DCam, June 2012												
1872-CC	4,600	52	43.4	0%	$5,500	$16,000	$30,000	$40,000	$57,500			
Auctions: $47,000, AU, February 2014, $9,988, EF-40, August 2014												
1872-S	17,300	151	47.7	1%	$900	$1,050	$1,500	$4,250	$8,500	$17,500		
Auctions: $8,225, AU-58, October 2014; $7,050, AU-58, March 2014; $5,640, AU-58, January 2015; $1,645, EF-45, July 2015												
1873	800	21	50.0	0%	$6,500	$15,000	$20,000	$45,000	$55,000	$75,000		
Auctions: $55,813, AU-55, January 2014; $21,738, AU-53, January 2015; $16,450, EF-40, July 2014; $12,925, EF-40, January 2015												
1873, Proof	25	9	63.7							$37,500	$55,000	$85,000
Auctions: $74,750, PF-65Cam+, February 2012												
1873-CC	4,543	38	41.0	0%	$10,000	$18,000	$35,000	$80,000	$100,000			
Auctions: $58,750, AU-53, March 2014												
1873-S	12,000	83	43.2	0%	$1,000	$2,250	$4,250	$7,000	$12,000	$20,000		
Auctions: $4,700, AU-53, March 2013												
1874	53,140	340	56.1	21%	$750	$850	$900	$925	$950	$1,500	$7,500	
Auctions: $1,410, MS-61, September 2014; $1,058, AU-58, August 2015; $940, AU-58, September 2015; $999, AU-50, October 2014												
1874, Proof	20	1	62.0							$32,500	$55,000	$85,000
Auctions: $29,500, PF-64Cam, September 2006												
1874-CC	16,767	156	42.3	1%	$2,000	$4,000	$8,500	$17,500	$32,500	$50,000	$200,000	
Auctions: $30,550, AU-58, May 2013; $3,643, VF-35, June 2015; $2,585, F-15, January 2015; $1,410, VG-8, February 2015												
1874-S	10,000	95	42.5	0%	$1,450	$2,500	$5,000	$8,000	$13,500			
Auctions: $12,338, AU-58, July 2014; $2,644, EF-45, August 2014; $940, VF-20, February 2015												
1875	100	7	45.4	0%	$150,000	$185,000	$225,000	$375,000				
Auctions: $211,500, AU-50, February 2014												
1875, Proof	20	4	64.5							$155,000	$200,000	$275,000
Auctions: $164,500, PF-50, January 2014												
1875-CC	7,715	72	39.9	3%	$6,000	$10,000	$15,000	$35,000	$60,000	$80,000	$150,000	
Auctions: $8,225, EF-45, February 2014												

	Mintage	Cert	Avg	%MS	VF-20	EF-40	AU-50	AU-55	AU-58	MS-60	MS-63	MS-65
										PF-63	PF-64	PF-65
1876	687	20	51.0	5%	$4,500	$9,500	$17,000	$32,500	$50,000	$75,000		
	Auctions: $70,500, AU-58, January 2015; $28,200, AU-55, June 2015; $22,325, AU-53, August 2015; $18,800, AU-53, July 2014											
1876, Proof	45	16	63.5							$30,000	$45,000	$75,000
	Auctions: $100,625, PF-65Cam, April 2011											
1876-CC	4,696	96	41.7	0%	$5,000	$12,000	$18,500	$35,000	$55,000			
	Auctions: $14,100, AU-50, October 2013											
1876-S	5,000	50	45.3	0%	$1,250	$1,750	$5,500	$8,500	$20,000			
	Auctions: $22,325, AU-55, October 2013											
1877	797	30	54.1	0%	$3,000	$5,000	$10,000	$13,500	$18,500	$30,000		
	Auctions: $64,625, MS-61, March 2015; $11,163, AU-55, July 2014; $11,163, AU-55, January 2014; $3,290, EF-40, February 2015											
1877, Proof	20	3	64.7							$32,500	$45,000	$75,000
	Auctions: $39,100, PF-64Cam, April 2002											
1877-CC	3,332	41	40.4	0%	$5,500	$12,500	$24,000	$40,000	$65,000			
	Auctions: $10,575, EF-45, April 2014											
1877-S	17,000	166	46.8	2%	$850	$900	$1,800	$4,500	$11,000	$25,000		
	Auctions: $3,290, AU-55, September 2015; $881, AU-50, September 2015; $1,116, EF-45, September 2015; $1,116, EF-45, June 2015											
1878	73,780	363	57.9	43%	$675	$700	$725	$750	$850	$1,100	$6,500	
	Auctions: $1,410, MS-62, July 2015; $881, MS-61, September 2015; $852, MS-61, September 2015; $823, MS-61, January 2015											
1878, Proof	20	4	63.8							$27,500	$45,000	$75,000
	Auctions: $25,300, PF-63, August 2011											
1878-CC	3,244	45	46.1	2%	$5,500	$9,000	$18,000	$35,000	$55,000	$85,000		
	Auctions: $28,200, AU-55, March 2014											
1878-S	26,100	218	47.8	2%	$850	$950	$1,750	$2,000	$3,500	$10,500	$25,000	
	Auctions: $2,938, AU-58, October 2015; $1,410, AU-55, February 2015; $1,293, AU-50, October 2015; $646, EF-40, September 2014											
1879	384,740	946	58.9	53%	$675	$700	$725	$825	$875	$1,000	$4,000	
	Auctions: $2,585, MS-63, July 2015; $940, MS-61, August 2015; $711, MS-60, October 2015; $646, AU-58, January 2015											
1879, Proof	30	7	63.3							$25,000	$37,500	$65,000
	Auctions: $52,875, PF-65Cam, February 2013											
1879-CC	1,762	40	42.6	3%	$10,000	$17,500	$40,000	$45,000	$60,000			
	Auctions: $41,125, AU-50, March 2014											
1879-O	1,500	46	49.1	2%	$5,500	$12,500	$20,000	$35,000	$55,000	$75,000		
	Auctions: $88,125, MS-61, June 2014											
1879-S	224,000	467	57.0	25%	$675	$700	$725	$825	$875	$1,150	$6,000	
	Auctions: $1,410, MS-62, January 2015; $881, MS-60, June 2015; $999, AU-58, August 2015; $705, AU-55, October 2015											
1880	1,644,840	2,114	60.0	82%	$675	$750	$775	$800	$825	$950	$1,800	
	Auctions: $19,975, MS-65, August 2013; $764, MS-61, June 2015; $705, VF-35, February 2015; $646, AG-3, January 2015											
1880, Proof	36	5	64.2							$22,500	$35,000	$60,000
	Auctions: $32,200, PF-64, October 1999											
1880-CC	11,190	189	50.6	5%	$1,200	$1,500	$2,500	$5,500	$9,000	$17,500		
	Auctions: $2,761, AU-53, August 2013; $1,175, EF-40, July 2014											
1880-O	9,200	180	51.8	5%	$1,000	$1,150	$2,000	$3,000	$4,500	$10,000		
	Auctions: $3,760, AU-55, August 2015; $4,230, AU-50, September 2015; $2,233, AU-50, August 2015; $4,113, EF-40, June 2014											
1880-S	506,250	1,028	60.2	78%	$675	$750	$775	$800	$825	$900	$2,250	
	Auctions: $4,465, MS-64, October 2015; $1,293, MS-63, July 2015; $1,175, MS-62, August 2015; $764, MS-61, September 2015											
1881	3,877,220	12,517	60.9	94%	$675	$750	$775	$800	$825	$875	$1,200	$10,000
	Auctions: $2,115, MS-64, February 2015; $999, MS-63, January 2015; $705, MS-62, October 2014; $676, MS-61, January 2015											
1881, Proof	40	5	65.2							$22,500	$32,500	$55,000
	Auctions: $56,063, PF-65, October 2011											
1881-CC	24,015	339	52.4	14%	$1,200	$1,400	$1,750	$3,100	$4,500	$8,500		
	Auctions: $12,925, MS-62, April 2013; $4,113, AU-58, January 2015; $1,116, AU-50, July 2014; $1,763, EF-40, January 2015											
1881-O	8,350	189	52.3	7%	$1,000	$1,250	$1,650	$3,000	$6,500	$12,500		
	Auctions: $12,338, MS-60, January 2014											
1881-S	970,000	2,486	60.6	90%	$675	$750	$775	$800	$825	$875	$3,000	
	Auctions: $2,585, MS-63, January 2015; $1,763, MS-63, October 2015; $764, MS-62, January 2015; $734, MS-62, June 2015											

	Mintage	Cert	Avg	%MS	VF-20	EF-40	AU-50	AU-55	AU-58	MS-60 PF-63	MS-63 PF-64	MS-65 PF-65
1882	2,324,440	13,579	61.2	96%	$675	$750	$775	$800	$825	$875	$1,200	
Auctions: $1,175, MS-63, August 2015; $823, MS-62, August 2015; $881, MS-61, June 2015; $777, MS-61, September 2015											
1882, Proof	40	9	64.2							$20,000	$32,500	$55,000
Auctions: $43,125, PF-65Cam, October 2009											
1882-CC	6,764	151	52.6	3%	$1,250	$1,800	$4,000	$11,500	$17,500	$23,500		
Auctions: $25,850, MS-60, July 2014; $7,344, AU-55, February 2015; $4,935, EF-45, July 2015; $1,645, EF-40, January 2015											
1882-O	10,820	196	52.5	10%	$950	$1,050	$1,500	$2,500	$4,000	$7,500	$45,000	
Auctions: $30,550, MS-62, January 2014; $2,389, AU-53, September 2014; $1,410, VF-35, September 2015											
1882-S	132,000	350	60.6	85%	$675	$750	$775	$800	$825	$875	$3,000	
Auctions: $1,880, MS-63, January 2015; $1,293, MS-62, October 2015; $1,234, MS-62, August 2015; $1,087, MS-62, October 2015											
1883	208,700	1,364	61.2	95%	$675	$750	$775	$800	$825	$875	$1,500	
Auctions: $3,995, MS-64, January 2015; $1,880, MS-63, October 2015; $1,293, MS-63, August 2015; $881, MS-62, July 2015											
1883, Proof	40	9	64.3							$20,000	$32,500	$55,000
Auctions: $8,813, PF-60, July 2014											
1883-CC	12,000	335	49.3	4%	$1,325	$1,950	$3,250	$7,750	$16,500	$35,000		
Auctions: $41,125, MS-61, October 2014; $3,055, AU-50, October 2015; $2,820, EF-40, June 2015; $1,586, VF-20, January 2015											
1883-O	800	19	51.0	5%	$10,000	$25,000	$40,000	$72,500	$85,000	$125,000		
Auctions: $82,250, AU-58, August 2014; $70,500, AU-58, January 2015; $70,500, AU-55, February 2014; $47,000, AU-50, October 2014											
1883-S	38,000	137	56.0	39%	$675	$750	$775	$800	$825	$875	$7,500	
Auctions: $11,163, MS-63, February 2013; $2,056, MS-62, January 2015; $1,293, MS-61, August 2015; $823, AU-58, November 2014											
1884	76,860	359	58.3	43%	$675	$750	$775	$800	$825	$875	$4,250	
Auctions: $846, MS-61, July 2014; $823, AU-55, February 2014											
1884, Proof	45	7	64.6							$20,000	$32,500	$55,000
Auctions: $37,375, PF-64DCam, March 2012											
1884-CC	9,925	175	51.6	5%	$1,250	$1,750	$3,000	$5,250	$11,000	$20,000	$55,000	
Auctions: $17,625, AU-58, February 2014; $3,760, AU-55, August 2015; $2,291, EF-45, July 2014											
1884-S	124,250	541	59.4	67%	$675	$750	$775	$800	$825	$875	$5,500	
Auctions: $4,994, MS-63, July 2014; $1,175, MS-62, September 2015; $1,116, MS-62, September 2015; $1,175, MS-61, October 2015											
1885	253,462	645	60.5	82%	$675	$750	$775	$800	$825	$875	$2,750	$20,000
Auctions: $1,880, MS-63, October 2013; $1,528, MS-63, November 2014; $1,410, MS-63, July 2015; $823, MS-60, August 2014											
1885, Proof	65	12	63.5							$20,000	$32,500	$52,500
Auctions: $57,500, PF-66UCam, January 2012											
1885-S	228,000	843	60.7	87%	$675	$750	$775	$800	$825	$875	$1,750	
Auctions: $5,875, MS-64, August 2014; $4,406, MS-63, August 2013; $705, MS-62, October 2014; $881, MS-62, July 2014											
1886	236,100	640	59.3	63%	$675	$750	$775	$800	$825	$875	$3,000	
Auctions: $1,998, MS-63, June 2015; $764, MS-61, October 2015; $823, AU-58, June 2015; $564, VF-30, October 2015											
1886, Proof	60	15	63.0							$18,500	$32,500	$52,500
Auctions: $39,656, PF-64DCam, April 2014											
1886-S	826,000	2,992	61.3	95%	$675	$750	$775	$800	$825	$875	$1,250	
Auctions: $1,116, MS-63, January 2015; $999, MS-63, January 2015; $969, MS-63, May 2015; $852, MS-63, July 2015											
1887	53,600	285	57.9	44%	$675	$750	$775	$800	$825	$875	$4,500	
Auctions: $4,465, MS-63, June 2015; $1,351, MS-62, February 2015; $881, MS-61, January 2015; $999, AU-58, August 2015											
1887, Proof	80	17	63.9							$18,500	$32,500	$52,500
Auctions: $64,625, PF-65DCam, April 2014											
1887-S	817,000	1,470	60.8	90%	$675	$750	$775	$800	$825	$875	$1,600	
Auctions: $3,819, MS-64, January 2015; $1,293, MS-63, January 2015; $1,234, MS-63, February 2015; $1,116, MS-63, January 2015											
1888	132,921	476	58.8	57%	$675	$750	$775	$800	$825	$875	$4,500	
Auctions: $2,820, MS-63, January 2015; $1,175, MS-62, February 2015; $1,028, MS-62, August 2015; $940, MS-61, September 2015											
1888, Proof	75	11	64.1							$18,500	$32,500	$52,500
Auctions: $17,250, PF-63DCam, February 2009											
1888-O	21,335	627	60.2	81%	$725	$800	$850	$1,000	$1,100	$1,250	$6,000	
Auctions: $21,150, MS-64, August 2013; $999, MS-62, October 2014; $1,293, MS-61, July 2014; $734, MS-60, January 2015											
1888-S	648,700	1,765	60.7	89%	$675	$750	$775	$800	$825	$875	$1,500	
Auctions: $1,763, MS-63, August 2015; $1,528, MS-63, July 2015; $881, MS-62, January 2015; $764, AU-58, January 2015											

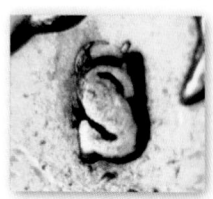

1889-S, Repunched Mintmark
FS-G10-1889S-501.

	Mintage	Cert	Avg	%MS	VF-20	EF-40	AU-50	AU-55	AU-58	MS-60 / PF-63	MS-63 / PF-64	MS-65 / PF-65
1889	4,440	120	58.7	56%	$875	$925	$950	$1,200	$1,350	$2,500	$10,000	
Auctions: $4,935, MS-62, June 2015; $3,995, MS-61, August 2015; $1,998, AU-58, June 2015; $1,528, AU-50, January 2015												
1889, Proof	45	4	64.3							$18,000	$32,500	$52,500
Auctions: $23,500, PF-64Cam, August 2014; $4,994, PF-60, April 2013												
1889-S	425,400	1,255	60.8	89%	$675	$750	$775	$800	$825	$875	$1,350	
Auctions: $999, MS-63, January 2015; $764, MS-62, February 2015; $823, MS-61, July 2015; $676, AU-55, June 2015												
1889-S, Repunched Mintmark	(v)	1	45.0	0%				$900	$975	$1,025	$1,850	
Auctions: $1,035, MS-63, August 2006												
1890	57,980	439	59.0	62%	$675	$750	$775	$800	$825	$875	$4,000	$12,500
Auctions: $2,820, MS-63, July 2014; $1,058, MS-62, November 2014; $1,116, MS-62, September 2014; $764, MS-60, October 2015												
1890, Proof	63	24	63.8							$16,500	$25,000	$47,500
Auctions: $29,900, PF-64UCam, January 2012												
1890-CC	17,500	368	57.0	40%	$1,100	$1,200	$1,500	$2,000	$2,750	$4,000	$22,500	
Auctions: $7,050, MS-62, August 2015; $4,935, MS-61, June 2015; $2,585, AU-55, January 2015; $2,233, AU-55, February 2015												
1891	91,820	710	61.1	95%	$675	$750	$775	$800	$825	$875	$2,500	
Auctions: $7,344, MS-64, November 2013; $1,998, MS-63, August 2014; $1,410, MS-62, July 2014; $716, MS-62, October 2015												
1891, Proof	48	20	64.2							$16,500	$25,000	$47,500
Auctions: $54,625, PF-65Cam, February 2012												
1891-CC	103,732	2,381	58.4	58%	$1,100	$1,200	$1,300	$1,850	$2,250	$2,500	$7,000	
Auctions: $14,688, MS-64, June 2015; $2,115, MS-61, July 2015; $1,763, AU-55, August 2015; $1,410, AU-50, August 2015												
1892	797,480	8,481	61.4	98%	$675	$750	$775	$800	$825	$875	$1,200	$7,500
Auctions: $6,756, MS-65, October 2013; $1,028, MS-63, July 2014; $652, MS-62, October 2014; $852, MS-62, August 2014												
1892, Proof	72	12	63.7							$16,500	$25,000	$47,500
Auctions: $4,406, PF-55, January 2014												
1892-CC	40,000	488	52.6	9%	$1,100	$1,250	$1,600	$1,850	$2,500	$4,250	$27,500	
Auctions: $1,763, AU-53, August 2014; $1,528, EF-45, February 2015; $823, EF-40, October 2015; $1,528, VF-35, January 2015												
1892-O	28,688	698	60.2	79%	$725	$800	$850	$900	$975	$1,150	$8,000	
Auctions: $1,998, MS-62, August 2015; $1,763, MS-62, September 2015; $1,410, MS-60, July 2015; $764, AU-55, January 2015												
1892-S	115,500	308	59.5	66%	$675	$750	$775	$800	$825	$875	$2,500	
Auctions: $940, MS-62, July 2015; $852, MS-62, January 2015; $764, MS-61, January 2015; $764, AU-58, January 2015												
1893	1,840,840	34,992	61.8	99%	$675	$750	$775	$800	$825	$875	$1,000	$5,500
Auctions: $1,645, MS-64, August 2015; $1,528, MS-63, July 2015; $734, MS-62, August 2015; $705, MS-61, June 2015												
1893, Proof	55	16	63.2							$16,500	$25,000	$47,500
Auctions: $30,550, PF-64DCam, August 2014; $58,750, PF, March 2014												
1893-CC	14,000	232	52.2	6%	$1,150	$1,400	$2,250	$3,750	$5,000	$15,000		
Auctions: $18,800, MS-61, January 2014; $6,463, AU-58, July 2015; $4,465, AU-55, September 2015; $4,465, AU-55, July 2015												
1893-O	17,000	436	59.8	70%	$725	$800	$850	$975	$1,000	$1,200	$5,000	
Auctions: $4,465, MS-63, June 2015; $1,293, MS-61, September 2014; $4,406, AU-58, September 2013; $823, AU-53, January 2015												
1893-S	141,350	627	60.2	79%	$675	$750	$775	$800	$825	$875	$2,500	
Auctions: $999, MS-62, July 2015; $940, MS-62, July 2015; $881, MS-62, February 2015; $823, MS-62, March 2015												

v. Included in 1889-S mintage figure.

	Mintage	Cert	Avg	%MS	VF-20	EF-40	AU-50	AU-55	AU-58	MS-60 PF-63	MS-63 PF-64	MS-65 PF-65
1894	2,470,735	36,569	61.7	99%	$675	$750	$775	$800	$825	$875	$1,000	$7,500
Auctions: $5,942, MS-65, October 2015; $1,528, MS-64, October 2015; $705, MS-62, June 2015; $650, MS-60, January 2015												
1894, Proof	43	11	64.1							$16,500	$25,000	$47,500
Auctions: $105,750, PF-65, January 2014												
1894-O	107,500	867	57.3	34%	$725	$800	$850	$975	$1,000	$1,200	$5,500	
Auctions: $1,410, MS-61, July 2015; $940, AU-58, August 2015; $823, AU-53, June 2015; $705, AU-50, January 2015												
1894-S	25,000	158	53.7	13%	$750	$775	$950	$1,100	$1,800	$3,500		
Auctions: $9,988, MS-61, March 2014; $1,058, AU-55, September 2014; $1,293, AU-50, September 2015												
1895	567,770	11,277	61.7	99%	$675	$750	$775	$800	$825	$875	$1,000	$11,000
Auctions: $9,400, MS-65, June 2015; $1,410, MS-64, January 2015; $1,058, MS-63, November 2015; $764, AU-58, June 2015												
1895, Proof	56	18	63.8							$16,000	$25,000	$47,500
Auctions: $51,750, PF-65UCam, January 2012												
1895-O	98,000	705	58.8	50%	$750	$775	$850	$975	$1,000	$1,200	$6,000	
Auctions: $9,400, MS-63, February 2013; $940, AU-55, July 2015; $764, AU-55, January 2015; $705, EF-45, January 2015												
1895-S	49,000	221	52.5	9%	$900	$950	$975	$1,000	$1,250	$2,000	$8,000	
Auctions: $5,875, MS-62, October 2014; $4,700, MS-62, November 2014; $966, AU-55, May 2015; $846, AU-55, September 2014												
1896	76,270	1,431	61.7	99%	$675	$750	$775	$800	$825	$875	$1,200	$12,000
Auctions: $1,293, MS-63, July 2015; $911, MS-63, May 2015; $881, MS-62, July 2015; $823, MS-62, October 2015												
1896, Proof	78	18	64.1							$16,000	$25,000	$47,500
Auctions: $89,125, PF-66DCam, April 2012; $70,500, PF-66, September 2014												
1896-S	123,750	469	54.1	15%	$750	$775	$800	$875	$925	$1,750	$8,000	
Auctions: $2,233, MS-62, January 2015; $823, AU-55, September 2015; $617, AU-50, October 2015; $705, EF-45, June 2015												
1897	1,000,090	9,833	61.6	98%	$675	$750	$775	$800	$825	$875	$1,000	$6,000
Auctions: $5,875, MS-65, August 2015; $2,233, MS-64, September 2015; $1,528, MS-64, October 2015; $764, MS-62, February 2015												
1897, Proof	69	12	64.3							$16,000	$25,000	$47,500
Auctions: $19,975, PF, August 2013												
1897-O	42,500	386	58.8	47%	$750	$775	$800	$950	$1,000	$1,050	$5,000	$27,500
Auctions: $6,169, MS-63, March 2013; $2,350, MS-62, June 2015; $1,880, AU-58, July 2014; $999, AU-55, January 2015												
1897-S	234,750	354	57.3	35%	$675	$750	$775	$800	$825	$875	$4,500	$25,000
Auctions: $1,058, MS-62, February 2015; $823, MS-61, July 2015; $823, MS-60, October 2015; $734, AU-55, September 2015												
1898	812,130	4,069	61.3	94%	$675	$750	$775	$800	$825	$875	$1,200	$6,500
Auctions: $5,599, MS-65, August 2015; $2,056, MS-64, August 2015; $1,293, MS-63, February 2015; $999, MS-63, January 2015												
1898, Proof	67	27	65.2							$16,000	$25,000	$47,500
Auctions: $58,750, PF-66DCam, September 2014; $85,188, PF-66DCam, April 2013												
1898-S	473,600	452	60.3	85%	$675	$750	$775	$800	$825	$875	$2,500	$15,000
Auctions: $3,290, MS-63, January 2014; $1,116, MS-62, October 2015; $870, MS-61, July 2014; $764, MS-61, October 2015												
1899	1,262,219	20,914	62.1	98%	$675	$750	$775	$800	$825	$875	$1,000	$3,000
Auctions: $25,850, MS-67, June 2015; $17,625, MS-66, January 2015; $1,175, MS-63, September 2015; $764, MS-62, October 2015												
1899, Proof	86	37	64.4							$15,000	$23,500	$45,000
Auctions: $76,375, PF-67DCam, September 2014; $56,400, PF, March 2014												
1899-O	37,047	236	59.3	52%	$750	$775	$800	$950	$1,000	$1,250	$7,000	
Auctions: $7,638, MS-63, October 2015; $2,115, MS-62, July 2015; $1,763, MS-62, January 2015; $940, AU-55, July 2014												
1899-S	841,000	680	60.2	80%	$675	$750	$775	$800	$825	$875	$2,000	$15,000
Auctions: $3,525, MS-64, January 2015; $1,293, MS-63, May 2015; $1,028, MS-63, July 2015; $764, EF-40, July 2015												
1900	293,840	6,532	62.1	99%	$675	$750	$775	$800	$825	$875	$1,100	$4,000
Auctions: $3,643, MS-65, January 2015; $2,500, MS-65, January 2015; $1,351, MS-64, July 2015; $940, MS-63, August 2014												
1900, Proof	120	50	64.4							$15,000	$23,500	$45,000
Auctions: $1,880, PF, February 2014												
1900-S	81,000	181	57.9	39%	$675	$750	$775	$800	$825	$875	$5,500	
Auctions: $6,169, MS-63, September 2013; $658, AU-58, November 2014; $705, AU-58, July 2014												

	Mintage	Cert	Avg	%MS	VF-20	EF-40	AU-50	AU-55	AU-58	MS-60 / PF-63	MS-63 / PF-64	MS-65 / PF-65
1901	1,718,740	24,176	62.3	98%	$675	$750	$775	$800	$825	$875	$1,000	$3,000
	Auctions: $7,931, MS-66, October 2015; $3,200, MS-65, January 2015; $999, MS-63, January 2015; $940, MS-62, June 2015											
1901, Proof	85	47	63.9							$15,000	$23,500	$45,000
	Auctions: $48,875, PF-66Cam, January 2012											
1901-O	72,041	434	60.0	68%	$750	$775	$800	$925	$975	$1,250	$3,250	$15,000
	Auctions: $6,169, MS-64, June 2014											
1901-S	2,812,750	17,653	62.9	99%	$675	$750	$775	$800	$825	$875	$1,000	$3,000
	Auctions: $19,975, MS-67, January 2015; $3,290, MS-65, August 2015; $1,146, MS-64, March 2015; $1,251, MS-63, August 2015											
1902	82,400	697	61.1	89%	$675	$750	$775	$800	$825	$875	$1,750	$9,000
	Auctions: $1,528, MS-63, June 2015; $1,293, MS-63, September 2015; $1,645, MS-62, August 2015; $712, AU-58, February 2015											
1902, Proof	113	26	63.5							$15,000	$23,500	$45,000
	Auctions: $61,688, PF-67, February 2013											
1902-S	469,500	2,837	62.8	99%	$675	$750	$775	$800	$825	$875	$1,000	$3,000
	Auctions: $8,519, MS-66, February 2014; $1,058, MS-63, September 2014; $1,058, MS-63, August 2014											
1903	125,830	1,016	61.3	92%	$675	$750	$775	$800	$825	$875	$1,250	$7,000
	Auctions: $1,116, MS-64, October 2014; $6,463, MS-65, January 2014; $1,058, MS-63, October 2014; $1,058, MS-63, August 2014											
1903, Proof	96	43	64.4							$15,000	$23,500	$45,000
	Auctions: $39,950, PF, October 2013											
1903-O	112,771	1,140	60.2	72%	$750	$775	$800	$925	$1,000	$1,200	$3,000	$17,500
	Auctions: $1,175, MS-62, January 2015; $999, MS-61, January 2015; $940, AU-58, September 2015; $646, AU-50, January 2015											
1903-S	538,000	924	62.3	92%	$675	$750	$775	$800	$825	$875	$1,000	$3,500
	Auctions: $9,106, MS-66, September 2015; $4,935, MS-66, July 2015; $4,935, MS-65, January 2015; $2,350, MS-64, June 2015											
1904	161,930	1,157	61.3	92%	$675	$750	$775	$800	$825	$875	$1,500	$8,500
	Auctions: $1,763, MS-64, October 2015; $1,293, MS-64, July 2015; $999, MS-63, June 2015; $999, MS-63, April 2015											
1904, Proof	108	37	63.1							$15,000	$23,500	$45,000
	Auctions: $64,625, PF-66Cam, June 2013											
1904-O	108,950	649	60.1	69%	$750	$775	$800	$925	$1,000	$1,200	$3,000	$20,000
	Auctions: $19,975, MS-65, January 2015; $1,410, MS-62, July 2015; $734, AU-58, January 2015; $764, AU-55, February 2015											
1905	200,992	2,244	61.6	94%	$675	$750	$775	$800	$825	$875	$1,200	$5,500
	Auctions: $24,675, MS-67, September 2015; $1,880, MS-64, June 2015; $1,880, MS-64, February 2015; $1,528, MS-64, June 2015											
1905, Proof	86	35	63.6							$15,000	$23,500	$45,000
	Auctions: $76,050, PF, September 2013											
1905-S	369,250	581	57.0	26%	$675	$750	$775	$800	$825	$875	$5,000	$30,000
	Auctions: $1,645, MS-62, July 2015; $940, MS-61, July 2015; $705, AU-58, January 2015; $617, AU-55, October 2015											
1906	165,420	1,516	61.2	91%	$675	$750	$775	$800	$825	$875	$1,750	$9,500
	Auctions: $1,998, MS-64, July 2015; $1,058, MS-63, July 2015; $1,058, MS-63, December 2014; $652, MS-61, October 2014											
1906, Proof	77	35	64.2							$15,000	$23,500	$45,000
	Auctions: $41,125, PF, February 2013											
1906-D	981,000	3,822	61.4	91%	$675	$750	$775	$800	$825	$875	$1,100	$6,500
	Auctions: $2,938, MS-64, June 2015; $1,058, MS-63, August 2015; $881, MS-62, September 2015; $764, MS-61, January 2015											
1906-O	86,895	351	60.3	69%	$750	$775	$800	$925	$1,000	$1,100	$4,750	$20,000
	Auctions: $21,150, MS-65, October 2014; $5,875, MS-64, August 2014; $1,645, MS-62, January 2015; $1,175, MS-62, October 2014											
1906-S	457,000	576	58.1	45%	$675	$750	$775	$800	$825	$875	$4,000	$16,500
	Auctions: $12,925, MS-64, February 2015; $1,998, MS-63, January 2015; $1,880, MS-63, January 2015; $1,528, MS-63, June 2015											
1907	1,203,899	24,168	62.0	98%	$675	$750	$775	$800	$825	$875	$1,000	$5,000
	Auctions: $3,525, MS-65, October 2015; $1,645, MS-64, October 2015; $764, MS-62, June 2015; $913, MS-61, July 2015											
1907, Proof	74	54	64.1							$15,000	$23,500	$45,000
	Auctions: $54,050, PF-65Cam, January 2015; $33,638, PF-65Cam, March 2012; $29,375, PF-64Cam, August 2014											
1907-D	1,030,000	545	61.4	88%	$675	$750	$775	$800	$825	$875	$1,750	$13,500
	Auctions: $2,585, MS-64, August 2015; $2,233, MS-64, January 2015; $1,821, MS-63, November 2014; $823, MS-61, August 2014											
1907-S	210,500	365	58.9	56%	$675	$750	$775	$800	$825	$875	$4,000	$20,000
	Auctions: $1,880, MS-62, September 2015; $969, MS-62, August 2015; $881, MS-61, January 2015; $823, MS-61, February 2015											

INDIAN HEAD (1907–1933)

Designer: *Augustus Saint-Gaudens.* **Weight:** *16.718 grams.*
Composition: *.900 gold, .100 copper (net weight: .48375 oz. pure gold).*
Diameter: *27 mm.* **Edge:** *1907–1911—46 raised stars; 1912–1933—48 raised stars.*
Mints: *Philadelphia, Denver, and San Francisco.*

No Motto (1907–1908)

Mintmark location, 1908-D (No Motto), is on the reverse, at the tip of the branch.

Mintmark location, 1908 (With Motto)–1930, is on the reverse, to the left of the arrows.

With Motto (1908–1933)

With Motto, Sandblast Finish Proof

With Motto, Satin Finish Proof

History. The Indian Head eagle, designed by sculptor Augustus Saint-Gaudens and championed by President Theodore Roosevelt, was struck from 1907 to 1916, and again in intermittent issues through the 1920s and early 1930s. Saint-Gaudens's original design proved impractical to strike and thus was modified slightly by Charles Barber before any large quantities were produced. Not long after (in July 1908), the motto IN GOD WE TRUST was added to the reverse, where it remained to the end of the series. These coins were widely used until 1918, in circulation in the American West and for export.

Striking and Sharpness. On the obverse, check the hair details and the vanes in the feathers. On the reverse, check the shoulder of the eagle. As well-struck coins are available for all varieties, avoid those that are weakly struck. Some examples may exhibit a pink-green color or rust-red "copper spots." Luster varies, but is often deeply frosty. On other coins, particularly from 1910 to 1916, it may be grainy.

Proofs. Sandblast (also called Matte) Proofs were made each year from 1907 through 1915. These have dull surfaces, much like fine-grained sandpaper. Satin (also called Roman Finish) Proofs were made in 1908, 1909, and 1910; they have satiny surfaces and are bright yellow.

Availability. Key rarities in this series are the rolled (or round) rim and wire rim 1907 coins, and the 1920-S, 1930-S, and 1933. Others are generally more readily available. MS-63 and higher coins are generally scarce to rare for the mintmarked issues. The Indian Head eagle is a very popular series. Most such coins in collectors' hands were exported in their time, then brought back to America after World War II. All of the Proofs are rare today.

Note: Values of common-date gold coins have been based on the current bullion price of gold, $1,150 per ounce, and may vary with the prevailing spot price.

GRADING STANDARDS

MS-60 to 70 (Mint State). *Obverse:* At MS-60, some abrasion and contact marks are evident, most noticeably on the hair to the left of Miss Liberty's forehead and in the left field. Luster is present, but may be dull or lifeless, and interrupted in patches. At MS-63, contact marks are few, and abrasion is very light. An MS-65 coin has hardly any abrasion, and contact marks are minute. Luster should be full and rich. Grades above MS-65 are defined by

1907. Graded MS-62.

having fewer marks as perfection is approached. *Reverse:* Comments apply as for the obverse, except that abrasion and contact marks are most noticeable on the front of the left wing and in the left field.

Illustrated coin: This is a brilliant and lustrous example.

AU-50, 53, 55, 58 (About Uncirculated). *Obverse:* Light wear is seen on the cheek, the hair to the right of the face, and the headdress, more so at AU-50 coin than at AU–53 or 55. An AU-58 coin has minimal traces of wear. An AU-50 coin has luster in protected areas among the stars and in the small field area to the right. At AU-58, most luster is present in the fields but is worn away on the highest parts of the Indian. *Reverse:* Com-

1908-D. Graded AU-58.

ments as preceding, except that the eagle's left wing, left leg, neck, and leg show light wear. Luster ranges from perhaps 40% (at AU-50) to nearly full mint bloom (at AU-58).

Illustrated coin: With nearly full original luster, this coin has remarkable eye appeal.

EF-40, 45 (Extremely Fine). *Obverse:* More wear is evident on the hair to the right of the face, and the feather vanes lack some details, although most are present. Luster, if present at all, is minimal. *Reverse:* Wear is greater than on the preceding. The front edge of the left wing is worn and blends into the top of the left leg. Some traces of luster may be seen, more so at EF-45 than at EF-40.

1907. Graded EF-40.

VF-20, 30 (Very Fine). *Obverse:* The Indian's forehead blends into the hair to the right. Feather-vane detail is gone except in the lower areas. *Reverse:* Wear is greater on the eagle, with only a few details remaining on the back of the left wing and the tail.

The Indian Head eagle is seldom collected in grades lower than VF-20.

1908-S. Graded VF-25.

PF-60 to 70 (Proof). *Obverse and Reverse:* At PF–60 to 63, there is light abrasion and some contact marks (the lower the grade, the higher the quantity). On Sandblast Proofs these show up as visually unappealing bright spots. At PF-64 and higher levels, marks are fewer, with magnification needed to see any at PF-65. At PF-66, there should be none at all.

1915. Sandblast Finish. Graded PF-65.

No Periods **Periods**

	Mintage	Cert	Avg	%MS	VF-20	EF-40	AU-50	AU-55	MS-60	MS-62 / PF-63	MS-63 / PF-64	MS-65 / PF-65
1907, Wire Rim, Periods	500	177	63.5	93%		$23,500	$25,000	$26,000	$30,000	$35,000	$42,500	$65,000
Auctions: $67,563, MS-65, October 2015; $58,750, MS-65, August 2015; $55,225, MS-64, January 2015												
1907, Rounded Rim, Periods Before and After •E•PLURIBUS•UNUM• † (a)	50	29	62.6	83%		$60,000	$65,000	$75,000	$85,000	$100,000	$150,000	$275,000
Auctions: $470,000, MS-67, August 2013												
1907, No Periods	239,406	6,294	61.5	82%	$750	$800	$850	$900	$1,150	$2,000	$3,250	$9,500
Auctions: $35,250, MS-67, August 2015; $5,170, MS-64, June 2015; $1,293, AU-58, January 2015; $999, AU-50, February 2015												
1907, Wire Rim, Periods, Plain Edge, Proof (b)	*unknown*	0	n/a									
Auctions: $359,375, PF-62, August 2010												
1907, Rounded Rim, Periods, Satin Finish Proof	*unknown*	0	n/a			*(extremely rare)*						
Auctions: $2,185,000, PF-67, January 2011												
1907, Sandblast Finish Proof (c)	*unknown*	0	n/a			*(extremely rare)*						
Auctions: No auction records available.												

† Ranked in the *100 Greatest U.S. Coins* (fourth edition). **a.** All but 50 of the 31,500 coins were melted at the mint. **b.** According to the *Encyclopedia of U.S. Gold Coins, 1795–1933*, the only confirmed example may be from the Captain North set of 1907 and 1908 gold coins sold by Stack's in the 1970s. **c.** 2 or 3 examples are known.

	Mintage	Cert	Avg	%MS	VF-20	EF-40	AU-50	AU-55	MS-60	MS-62	MS-63	MS-65
										PF-63	PF-64	PF-65
1908, No Motto	33,500	697	60.9	75%	$800	$850	$875	$925	$1,500	$2,750	$5,500	$17,500
	Auctions: $19,975, MS-66, October 2015; $7,050, MS-64, January 2015; $3,055, MS-62, October 2015; $1,763, AU-58, June 2015											
1908-D, No Motto	210,000	882	59.4	52%	$750	$825	$850	$875	$1,275	$2,800	$7,500	$35,000
	Auctions: $13,513, MS-64, January 2015; $2,233, MS-61, February 2015; $1,234, AU-58, August 2015; $734, EF-45, October 2015											
1908, With Motto	341,370	4,616	60.8	79%	$700	$725	$750	$775	$1,100	$1,500	$2,500	$10,000
	Auctions: $32,900, MS-66, October 2015; $1,998, MS-63, March 2015; $1,058, AU-58, August 2015; $764, EF-45, February 2015											
1908, With Motto, Sandblast Finish Proof	116	53	65.2							$16,500	$25,000	$50,000
	Auctions: $69,000, PF-66, January 2012; $79,313, PF-65, August 2014; $61,688, PF-65, January 2015											
1908, With Motto, Satin Finish Proof (d)	(e)	1	64.0		*(extremely rare)*							
	Auctions: No auction records available.											
1908-D, With Motto	836,500	790	59.2	57%	$700	$725	$750	$775	$1,150	$2,750	$7,500	$26,000
	Auctions: $5,640, MS-63, January 2015; $3,525, MS-62, October 2015; $1,293, MS-61, January 2015; $999, AU-58, August 2015											
1908-S	59,850	787	54.6	21%	$975	$1,100	$1,200	$1,500	$3,500	$7,500	$15,000	$25,000
	Auctions: $35,251, MS-66, October 2015; $14,100, MS-64, March 2015; $4,113, AU-58, September 2015; $999, EF-45, February 2015											
1909	184,789	2,182	60.5	73%	$700	$725	$750	$775	$1,100	$1,750	$4,750	$15,000
	Auctions: $5,640, MS-64, June 2015; $3,290, MS-63, January 2015; $1,058, MS-62, March 2015; $940, MS-61, June 2015											
1909, Satin Finish Proof	74	0	n/a							$17,500	$25,000	$55,000
	Auctions: $48,875, PF-65, July 2011											
1909, Sandblast Finish Proof (f)	(g)	0	n/a		*(extremely rare)*							
	Auctions: No auction records available.											
1909-D	121,540	1,075	59.5	57%	$800	$850	$925	$975	$1,500	$4,500	$7,500	$32,500
	Auctions: $4,113, MS-63, January 2015; $2,115, MS-62, March 2015; $999, AU-58, August 2015; $940, AU-55, August 2015											
1909-S	292,350	861	57.4	34%	$700	$725	$750	$775	$1,250	$4,250	$8,000	$17,500
	Auctions: $7,638, MS-64, October 2015; $1,880, MS-61, September 2015; $1,116, AU-58, June 2015; $800, AU-53, August 2015											
1910	318,500	6,397	61.5	89%	$700	$725	$750	$775	$1,000	$1,100	$1,550	$8,000
	Auctions: $17,625, MS-66, January 2015; $1,645, MS-64, January 2015; $940, MS-61, September 2015; $676, MS-60, October 2015											
1910, Satin Finish Proof	204	27	65.4							$17,500	$30,000	$65,000
	Auctions: $80,500, PF-67, January 2012											
1910, Sandblast Finish Proof (h)	(i)	1	66.0									
	Auctions: No auction records available.											
1910-D	2,356,640	12,592	61.6	90%	$700	$725	$750	$775	$1,000	$1,050	$1,500	$8,000
	Auctions: $13,513, MS-66, October 2015; $1,998, MS-64, January 2015; $837, MS-60, June 2015; $705, AU-58, October 2015											
1910-S	811,000	1,874	57.0	32%	$700	$725	$750	$775	$1,200	$3,750	$10,500	$50,000
	Auctions: $12,925, MS-64, January 2015; $1,645, MS-61, August 2015; $1,410, AU-58, January 2015; $823, AU-58, August 2015											
1911	505,500	10,217	61.5	86%	$700	$725	$750	$775	$1,000	$1,050	$1,500	$6,000
	Auctions: $30,550, MS-67, August 2015; $9,988, MS-66, September 2015; $1,293, MS-63, February 2015; $705, AU-55, August 2015											
1911, Sandblast Finish Proof	95	23	66.3							$16,000	$24,000	$50,000
	Auctions: $152,750, PF-67, November 2013; $76,375, PF-66, August 2015; $74,025, PF-66, October 2014											
1911-D	30,100	917	54.8	17%	$1,250	$1,500	$2,200	$3,500	$12,500	$17,500	$35,000	$175,000
	Auctions: $23,500, MS-63, October 2015; $6,169, AU-58, January 2015; $3,525, AU-53, January 2015; $1,998, EF-40, January 2015											
1911-S	51,000	374	56.9	30%	$800	$850	$925	$975	$1,750	$6,000	$10,000	$24,000
	Auctions: $24,793, MS-65, October 2015; $3,525, MS-61, October 2015; $2,820, AU-58, September 2015; $1,645, AU-50, February 2015											

d. 3 or 4 examples are known. **e.** Included in 1908, With Motto, Matte Proof, mintage figure. **f.** 2 or 3 examples are known. **g.** Included in 1909, Satin Finish Proof, mintage figure. **h.** The only example known is part of the unique complete 1910 Matte Proof gold set. **i.** Included in 1910, Satin Finish Proof, mintage figure.

| | Mintage | Cert | Avg | %MS | VF-20 | EF-40 | AU-50 | AU-55 | MS-60 | MS-62 | MS-63 | MS-65 |
										PF-63	PF-64	PF-65
1912	405,000	6,971	61.3	86%	$700	$725	$750	$775	$1,000	$1,100	$1,500	$8,500
	Auctions: $54,050, MS-67, January 2015; $3,290, MS-64, January 2015; $881, MS-61, September 2015; $705, AU-55, August 2015											
1912, Sandblast Finish Proof	83	21	65.6							$16,000	$24,000	$50,000
	Auctions: $99,875, PF, March 2014											
1912-S	300,000	1,185	57.2	28%	$725	$750	$775	$825	$1,250	$5,000	$8,500	$45,000
	Auctions: $12,402, MS-64, October 2015; $1,116, AU-58, August 2015; $734, AU-50, February 2015; $705, EF-45, January 2015											
1913	442,000	6,189	61.1	83%	$700	$725	$750	$775	$1,000	$1,100	$1,500	$8,000
	Auctions: $14,100, MS-66, January 2015; $3,408, MS-64, February 2015; $881, MS-62, June 2015; $705, AU-58, July 2015											
1913, Sandblast Finish Proof	71	24	65.5							$16,000	$24,000	$50,000
	Auctions: $63,250, PF-66, January 2012											
1913-S	66,000	968	55.0	13%	$1,000	$1,100	$1,200	$2,250	$10,000	$14,000	$30,000	$100,000
	Auctions: $22,325, MS-63, January 2015; $4,243, AU-58, February 2015; $1,528, AU-53, June 2015; $852, EF-40, January 2015											
1914	151,000	2,302	61.1	81%	$700	$725	$750	$775	$1,000	$1,050	$2,250	$11,000
	Auctions: $10,869, MS-65, October 2015; $2,832, MS-64, January 2015; $1,998, MS-63, January 2015; $881, MS-62, May 2015											
1914, Sandblast Finish Proof	50	33	65.6							$16,000	$24,000	$50,000
	Auctions: $96,938, PF, October 2013											
1914-D	343,500	2,842	60.7	74%	$700	$725	$750	$775	$1,000	$1,100	$2,400	$15,000
	Auctions: $9,988, MS-65, October 2015; $1,998, MS-63, January 2015; $887, MS-61, June 2015; $764, AU-55, October 2015											
1914-S	208,000	1,082	58.4	40%	$700	$725	$750	$825	$1,250	$3,750	$10,000	$30,000
	Auctions: $16,450, MS-64, October 2015; $1,645, AU-58, January 2015; $705, AU-53, August 2015; $709, EF-45, August 2015											
1915	351,000	4,472	61.1	80%	$700	$725	$750	$775	$1,000	$1,150	$2,000	$8,000
	Auctions: $6,463, MS-65, January 2015; $2,350, MS-63, January 2015; $823, MS-60, September 2015; $823, AU-58, September 2015											
1915, Sandblast Finish Proof	75	17	65.7							$17,500	$25,000	$55,000
	Auctions: $94,000, PF, August 2013											
1915-S	59,000	429	57.4	28%	$900	$1,000	$1,050	$1,750	$4,750	$9,500	$22,000	$65,000
	Auctions: $19,975, MS-62, September 2015; $6,611, MS-61, August 2015; $3,408, AU-58, January 2015; $1,058, AU-50, January 2015											
1916-S	138,500	910	59.1	51%	$950	$985	$1,000	$1,050	$1,250	$2,750	$6,500	$25,000
	Auctions: $7,050, MS-63, August 2015; $1,763, MS-61, October 2015; $1,528, AU-58, August 2015; $764, AU-50, September 2015											
1920-S	126,500	52	59.5	54%	$16,500	$20,000	$25,000	$32,500	$55,000	$75,000	$105,000	$225,000
	Auctions: $70,500, MS-62, September 2015; $64,625, MS-61, October 2015; $47,000, AU-58, January 2015; $15,863, AU-50, January 2015											
1926	1,014,000	40,328	62.5	99%	$700	$725	$750	$775	$925	$975	$1,150	$3,000
	Auctions: $7,638, MS-66, October 2015; $1,469, MS-64, October 2015; $823, MS-61, June 2015; $646, MS-60, July 2015											
1930-S	96,000	64	63.6	95%	$15,000	$17,500	$22,500	$24,500	$35,000	$40,000	$55,000	$85,000
	Auctions: $85,188, MS-65, September 2014; $70,500, MS-64, March 2014; $17,625, MS-60, January 2015											
1932	4,463,000	59,942	62.9	100%	$700	$725	$750	$775	$925	$975	$1,150	$3,000
	Auctions: $10,869, MS-66, January 2015; $2,482, MS-65, March 2015; $1,528, MS-63, August 2015; $793, MS-60, July 2015											
1933 † (j)	312,500	11	64.4	100%					$275,000	$325,000	$400,000	$650,000
	Auctions: $367,188, MS-64, August 2013											

† Ranked in the *100 Greatest U.S. Coins* (fourth edition). **j.** Nearly all were melted at the mint.

Gold Double Eagles ($20)
1850–1933

AN OVERVIEW OF GOLD DOUBLE EAGLES

Congress authorized the double eagle, or twenty-dollar coin—the largest denomination of all regular U.S. coinage issues—by the Act of March 3, 1849, in response to the huge amounts of gold coming from California.

Double eagles are at once large and impressive to own. Many gold collectors form a type set of the six major double eagle designs (with the 1861 Paquet added as a sub-type if desired). Thanks to overseas hoards repatriated since the 1950s, finding choice and gem Mint State examples is no problem at all for the later types.

The first double eagle type, the Liberty Head of 1850 to 1866 without the motto IN GOD WE TRUST, is generally available in grades from VF up. Mint State pieces were elusive prior to the 1990s, but the market supply was augmented by more than 5,000 pieces—including some gems—found in the discovery of the long-lost treasure ship SS *Central America*. The SS *Brother Jonathan*, lost at sea in 1865, was recovered in the 1990s and yielded hundreds of Mint State 1865-S double eagles, along with some dated 1864 and a few earlier. The wreck of the SS *Republic*, lost in 1865 while on a voyage from New York City to New Orleans and salvaged in 2003, also yielded some very attractive Mint State double eagles of this first Liberty Head type.

The Liberty Head type from 1866 through 1876, with the motto IN GOD WE TRUST above the eagle and with the denomination expressed as TWENTY D., is the rarest in MS-63 and higher grades. Many EF and AU coins have been repatriated from overseas holdings, as have quite a few in such grades as MS–60 through 62. However, true gems are hardly ever seen.

Liberty Head double eagles of the 1877–1907 type with the IN GOD WE TRUST motto and with the denomination spelled out as TWENTY DOLLARS are exceedingly plentiful in just about any grade desired, with gems being readily available of certain issues of the early 20th century. While it is easy to obtain a gem of a common date, some collectors of type coins have opted to acquire a coin of special historical interest, such as a Carson City issue.

The famous Saint-Gaudens MCMVII High Relief double eagle of 1907 was saved in quantity by the general public as well as by numismatists, and today it is likely that at least 5,000 to 6,000 exist, representing about half of the mintage. Most of these are in varying degrees of Mint State, with quite a few graded as MS–64 and 65. Those in lower grades such as VF and EF often were used for jewelry or were polished, or have other problems. This particular design is a great favorite with collectors, and although the coins are not rarities, they are hardly inexpensive.

The so-called Arabic Numerals 1907–1908 Saint-Gaudens design is available in nearly any grade desired, with MS-60 through MS-63 or MS-64 pieces being plentiful and inexpensive. Double eagles of the final type, 1908–1933, are abundant in any grade desired, with choice and gem coins being plentiful.

FOR THE COLLECTOR AND INVESTOR: GOLD DOUBLE EAGLES AS A SPECIALTY

Collecting double eagles by date and mint is more popular than one might think. Offhand, one might assume that these high denominations, laden with a number of rare dates, would attract few enthusiasts. However, over a long period of years more collectors have specialized in double eagles than have specialized in five-dollar or ten-dollar pieces.

Two particularly notable collections of double eagles by date and mint, from the earliest times to the latest, were formed by Louis E. Eliasberg of Baltimore, and Jeff Browning of Dallas. Both have been dispersed across the auction block. The first was cataloged by Bowers and Ruddy in 1982, and the second was offered by Stack's and Sotheby's in 2001. In addition, dozens of other collections over the years have had large numbers of double eagles, some specializing in the Liberty Head types of 1850–1907, others only with the Saint-Gaudens types from 1907 onward, and others addressing the entire range.

Among rarities in the double eagle series are the 1854-O and 1856-O, each known only to the extent of a few dozen pieces; the 1861 Philadelphia Mint coins with Paquet reverse (two known); the Proof-only issues of 1883, 1884, and 1887; several other low-mintage varieties of this era; the famous Carson City issue of 1870-CC; and various issues from 1920 onward, including 1920-S, 1921, mintmarked coins after 1923, and all dates after 1928. Punctuating these rarities is a number of readily available pieces, including the very common Philadelphia issues from 1922 through 1928 inclusive.

LIBERTY HEAD (1850–1907)

Designer: *James B. Longacre.* **Weight:** *33.436 grams.*
Composition: *.900 gold, .100 copper (net weight: .96750 oz. pure gold).* **Diameter** *34 mm.*
Edge: *Reeded.* **Mints:** *Philadelphia, Carson City, Denver, New Orleans, and San Francisco.*

No Motto (1849–1866)   No Motto, Proof

Mintmark location is on
the reverse, below the eagle.

With Motto (1866–1907)   With Motto, Proof

History. The twenty-dollar denomination was introduced to circulation in 1850 (after a unique pattern, which currently resides in the Smithsonian's National Numismatic Collection, was minted in 1849). The large new coin was ideal for converting the flood of California gold rush bullion into federal legal tender. U.S. Mint chief engraver James B. Longacre designed the coin. A different reverse, designed by Anthony Paquet with taller letters than Longacre's design, was tested in 1861 but ultimately not used past that date. In 1866 the motto IN GOD WE TRUST was added to the reverse. In 1877 the denomination on the reverse, formerly given as TWENTY D., was changed to TWENTY DOLLARS. The double eagle denomination proved to be very popular, especially for export. By 1933, more than 75 percent of the American gold used to strike coins from the 1850s onward had been used to make double eagles. Oddly, some of the coins of 1850 to 1858 appear to have the word LIBERTY misspelled as LLBERTY.

Striking and Sharpness. On the obverse, check the star centers and the hair details. As made, the hair details are less distinct on many coins of 1859 (when a slight modification was made) through the 1890s, and knowledge of this is important. Later issues usually have exquisite detail. The reverse usually is well struck, but check the eagle and other features. The denticles are sharp on nearly all coins, but should be checked. Proofs were made in all years from 1858 to 1907, and a few were made before then. Proofs of 1902 onward, particularly 1903, have the portrait polished in the die, imparting a mirror finish across the design, and lack the cameo contrast of earlier dates.

Availability. Basic dates and mintmarks are available in proportion to their mintages. Key issues include the 1854-O, 1856-O, 1861 Paquet Reverse, 1861-S Paquet Reverse, 1866 No Motto, 1870-CC, 1879-O, and several Philadelphia Mint dates of the 1880s The vast majority of others are readily collectible. Among early coins, MS examples from about 1854 to 1857 are available, most notably the 1857-S and certain varieties of the 1860s. Most varieties of the 1880s onward, and particularly of the 1890s and 1900s, are easily available in MS, due to the repatriation of millions of coins that had been exported overseas. Proofs dated through the 1870s are all very rare today; those of the 1880s are less so; and those of the 1890s and 1900s are scarce. Many Proofs have been mishandled. Dates that are Proof-only (and those that are very rare in circulation-strike form) are in demand even if impaired. These include 1883, 1884, 1885, 1886, and 1887.

Note: Values of common-date gold coins have been based on the current bullion price of gold, $1,150 per ounce, and may vary with the prevailing spot price.

GRADING STANDARDS

MS-60 to 70 (Mint State). *Obverse:* At MS-60, some abrasion and contact marks are evident, most noticeably on the hair to the right of Miss Liberty's forehead and on the cheek. Luster is present, but may be dull or lifeless, and interrupted in patches. At MS-63, contact marks are few, and abrasion is light. An MS-65 coin has little abrasion, and contact marks are minute. Luster should be full and rich. Grades above MS-65 are defined by

1876-S. Graded MS-64.

having fewer marks as perfection is approached. *Reverse:* Comments apply as for the obverse, except that abrasion and contact marks are most noticeable on eagle's neck, wingtips, and tail.

AU-50, 53, 55, 58 (About Uncirculated). *Obverse:* Light wear is seen on the face, the hair to the right of the face, and the highest area of the hair behind the coronet, more so at AU-50 than at AU–53 or 55. An AU-58 coin has minimal traces of wear. An AU-50 coin has luster in protected areas among the stars and letters, with little in the open fields or on the portrait. At AU-58 most luster is present in the fields, but is worn away on the

1856-S. Graded AU-53.

highest parts of the motifs. *Reverse:* Comments as preceding, except that the eagle and ornaments show wear in all of the higher areas. Luster ranges from perhaps 40% remaining in protected areas (at AU-50) to nearly full mint bloom (at AU-58). Often the reverse of this type retains more luster than the obverse.

    Illustrated coin: Much of the original luster still remains at this grade level, especially on the reverse.

EF-40, 45 (Extremely Fine). *Obverse:* Wear is evident on all high areas of the portrait, including the hair to the right of the fore-head, the tip of the coronet, and hair behind the coronet. The curl to the right of the neck is flat on its highest-relief area. Luster, if present at all, is minimal and in protected areas such as between the star points. *Reverse:* Wear is greater than on an About Uncircu-lated coin. The eagle's neck and wingtips

1855-S. Graded EF-45.

show wear, as do the ornaments and rays. Some traces of luster may be seen, more so at EF-45 than at EF-40. Overall, the reverse appears to be in a slightly higher grade than the obverse.

VF-20, 30 (Very Fine). *Obverse:* The higher-relief areas of hair are worn flat at VF-20, less so at VF-30. The hair to the right of the coronet is merged into heavy strands and is flat at the back, as is part of the bow. The curl to the right of the neck is flat. *Reverse:* The eagle shows further wear on the head, the tops of the wings, and the tail. The ornament has flat spots.

1857-S. Graded VF-20.

    The Liberty Head double eagle is seldom collected in grades lower than VF-20.

    Illustrated coin: Note the small test cut or mark on the top rim.

PF-60 to 70 (Proof). *Obverse and Reverse:* PF–60 to 62 coins have extensive hairlines and may have nicks and contact marks. At PF-63, hairlines are prominent, but the mirror surface is very reflective. PF-64 coins have fewer hairlines. At PF-65, hairlines should be relatively few. These large and heavy coins reveal hairlines more readily than do the lower denominations, mostly seen only under magnification. PF-66 and higher coins should have no marks or hairlines visible to the unaided eye.

1903. Graded PF-64.

Illustrated coin: A beautiful Proof, this is just a few hairlines away from a higher level.

Value TWENTY D.
(1849–1876)

Value TWENTY DOLLARS
(1877–1907)

1853, So-called 3 Over 2
Note rust under LIBERTY.
FS-G20-1853-301.

	Mintage	Cert	Avg	%MS	VF-20	EF-40	AU-50	AU-55	MS-60	MS-62	MS-63	MS-65
					PF-63					PF-63	PF-64	PF-65
1849, Proof (a)	1	0	n/a		*(unique; in the Smithsonian's National Numismatic Collection)*							
Auctions: No auction records available.												
1850	1,170,261	1,372	50.3	6%	$2,000	$3,000	$5,500	$8,500	$12,500	$37,500	$55,000	$200,000
Auctions: $42,300, MS-62, August 2015; $7,344, AU-55, August 2015; $4,465, AU-50, June 2015; $2,585, EF-40, January 2015												
1850, Proof (b)	1–2	0	n/a									
Auctions: No auction records available.												
1850-O	141,000	319	47.0	2%	$2,350	$5,750	$14,500	$25,000	$65,000	$150,000		
Auctions: $58,750, MS-61, January 2015; $21,150, AU-55, January 2015; $9,400, EF-45, August 2015; $4,465, VF-25, August 2015												
1851	2,087,155	1,088	51.3	8%	$1,500	$2,000	$2,750	$3,750	$6,750	$16,000	$22,500	
Auctions: $14,100, MS-62, July 2015; $5,170, AU-55, August 2015; $1,645, EF-40, January 2015; $1,772, VF-35, June 2015												
1851-O	315,000	722	49.6	3%	$2,100	$4,250	$7,000	$12,500	$28,000	$55,000	$125,000	
Auctions: $13,513, AU-58, August 2015; $7,638, AU-53, October 2015; $6,463, AU-50, January 2015; $4,818, EF-45, October 2015												
1852	2,053,026	1,815	51.6	7%	$1,500	$2,000	$2,900	$3,750	$6,500	$15,000	$22,500	
Auctions: $10,600, MS-62, October 2015; $3,819, AU-58, March 2015; $1,704, AU-50, January 2015; $1,998, EF-40, January 2015												
1852-O	190,000	594	51.3	4%	$2,500	$4,500	$7,500	$13,500	$35,000	$50,000	$95,000	$300,000
Auctions: $27,061, AU-58, August 2015; $5,640, AU-50, September 2015; $3,408, EF-40, July 2015; $2,291, VF-20, August 2015												
1853, All kinds	1,261,326											
1853, So-called 3 Over 2 (c)		189	52.6	3%	$3,000	$4,500	$7,500	$13,500	$42,500	$65,000		
Auctions: $17,625, AU-58, April 2014; $28,200, AU-58, August 2014; $28,200, AU-58, October 2014												
1853		1,253	52.5	5%	$1,600	$2,250	$2,750	$3,750	$8,500	$18,000	$30,000	
Auctions: $7,638, MS-61, February 2015; $6,169, AU-58, January 2015; $2,848, AU-53, January 2015; $1,880, EF-40, August 2015												
1853-O	71,000	238	49.9	2%	$2,750	$4,500	$10,500	$15,000	$37,500			
Auctions: $14,100, AU-55, August 2015; $11,750, AU-55, January 2015; $10,575, AU-50, January 2015; $7,638, EF-45, August 2015												

a. An unknown quantity of Proof 1849 double eagles was struck as patterns; all but two were melted. One (current location unknown) was sent to Treasury secretary W.M. Meredith; the other was placed in the Mint collection in Philadelphia, and transferred with that collection to the Smithsonian in 1923. **b.** Although no examples currently are known, it is likely that a small number of Proof 1850 double eagles were struck. For the years 1851 to 1857, no Proofs are known. **c.** Although overlaid photographs indicate this is not a true overdate, what appear to be remnants of a numeral are visible beneath the 3 in the date. This variety also shows a rust spot underneath the R of LIBERTY.

1854, Small Date   **1854, Large Date**

	Mintage	Cert	Avg	%MS	VF-20	EF-40	AU-50	AU-55	MS-60	MS-62	MS-63	MS-65
										PF-63	PF-64	PF-65
1854, All kinds	757,899											
1854, Small Date		587	52.2	4%	$1,600	$2,250	$2,850	$3,750	$9,000	$18,000	$35,000	
Auctions: $11,163, MS-61, January 2015; $4,714, AU-55, January 2015; $2,233, EF-45, October 2015; $1,645, VF-30, August 2015												
1854, Large Date		120	53.2	8%	$2,500	$3,500	$7,500	$15,000	$37,500	$55,000	$65,000	
Auctions: $55,813, MS-61, August 2014; $19,975, AU-58, October 2014; $9,988, AU-53, September 2015; $9,400, AU-50, August 2015												
1854-O † (d)	3,250	17	53.2	0%	$145,000	$275,000	$400,000	$475,000	—			
Auctions: $440,625, AU-55, April 2014; $340,750, AU-55, August 2015; $329,000, AU-50, August 2014												
1854-S	141,468	209	52.8	23%	$3,500	$4,500	$10,000	$15,000	$27,500	$35,000	$45,000	$85,000
Auctions: $16,450, AU-55, August 2015; $21,738, AU-53, February 2015; $14,688, AU-53, July 2015; $12,338, AU-53, January 2015												
1854-S, Proof † (e)	*unknown*	0	n/a	*(unique; in the Smithsonian's National Numismatic Collection)*								
Auctions: No auction records available.												
1855	364,666	365	52.8	5%	$1,750	$2,350	$3,000	$4,500	$12,000	$23,500	$65,000	
Auctions: $5,170, AU-58, September 2015; $3,878, AU-55, February 2015; $2,820, AU-53, August 2015; $2,350, AU-50, January 2015												
1855-O	8,000	46	50.5	9%	$8,750	$27,500	$50,000	$67,500	$125,000			
Auctions: $141,000, MS-61, January 2014; $70,500, AU-58, August 2015; $58,750, AU-55, August 2014; $28,200, AU-50, October 2014												
1855-S	879,675	1,043	51.4	4%	$1,500	$1,950	$2,750	$4,000	$8,000	$13,750	$25,000	
Auctions: $11,163, MS-61, July 2015; $3,819, AU-58, March 2015; $1,704, EF-40, June 2015; $1,528, VF-20, August 2015												
1856	329,878	340	52.4	6%	$1,900	$2,250	$3,000	$4,500	$10,000	$22,500	$35,000	
Auctions: $7,050, AU-58, October 2015; $4,465, AU-55, June 2015; $3,290, AU-53, January 2015; $3,995, AU-50, August 2015												
1856-O † (f)	2,250	10	51.7	0%	$145,000	$275,000	$450,000	$500,000				
Auctions: $340,750, AU-55, August 2015; $425,938, AU-53, August 2014; $164,500, AU-50, August 2014; $381,875, EF-45, January 2014												
1856-O, Proof (g)	*unknown*	1	63									
Auctions: $1,437,500, SP-63, May 2009												
1856-S	1189750	1,180	51.3	4%	$1,500	$1,950	$2,750	$3,500	$6,500	$11,000	$16,000	$65,000
Auctions: $7,344, MS-61, June 2015; $4,935, AU-58, September 2015; $5,170, AU-53, January 2015; $2,115, EF-40, September 2015												
1857	439,375	497	53.4	10%	$1,750	$2,000	$3,250	$4,000	$7,000	$15,000	$30,000	
Auctions: $5,875, MS-60, January 2015; $3,760, AU-58, January 2015; $2,350, AU-53, September 2015; $2,585, EF-45, January 2015												
1857-O	30,000	149	52.5	6%	$2,500	$5,500	$12,500	$22,500	$55,000	$85,000	$150,000	
Auctions: $21,150, AU-53, August 2015; $11,163, AU-50, January 2015; $7,050, EF-40, October 2015; $2,585, VF-20, September 2015												
1857-S † (h)	970,500	1,451	54.6	28%	$1,500	$1,950	$2,500	$3,250	$5,750	$7,500	$10,000	$16,500
Auctions: $15,863, MS-65, September 2015; $5,405, AU-58, August 2015; $2,233, AU-53, July 2015; $2,233, EF-40, January 2015												
1858	211,714	442	52.3	8%	$1,950	$2,250	$3,250	$4,500	$9,000	$25,000	$45,000	
Auctions: $19,975, MS-62, January 2015; $4,935, AU-58, October 2015; $2,820, AU-53, October 2015; $3,055, EF-45, August 2015												
1858, Proof (i)	*unknown*	0	n/a	*(extremely rare)*								
Auctions: No auction records available.												
1858-O	35,250	135	51.1	6%	$3,250	$6,750	$17,500	$30,000	$65,000	$77,500		
Auctions: $164,500, MS-63, January 2015; $44,650, AU-58, August 2015; $9,988, AU-50, August 2015; $7,050, AU-50, January 2015												
1858-S	846,710	1,047	50.9	2%	$1,750	$2,000	$2,750	$3,750	$10,000	$15,000	$45,000	
Auctions: $8,225, MS-60, October 2015; $7,638, AU-58, January 2015; $2,879, AU-53, June 2015; $1,528, EF-40, January 2015												

† Ranked in the *100 Greatest U.S. Coins* (fourth edition). **d.** Probably fewer than 35 exist, most in VF and EF. **e.** This unique coin, perhaps more accurately described as a presentation strike than a Proof, was sent to the Mint collection in Philadelphia by San Francisco Mint superintendent Lewis A. Birdsall. It may have been the first coin struck for the year, set aside to recognize the opening of the San Francisco Mint. **f.** Probably fewer than 25 exist, most in VF and EF. **g.** This prooflike presentation strike is unique. **h.** The treasure of the shipwrecked SS *Central America* included thousands of 1857-S double eagles in high grades. Different size mintmark varieties exist; the Large S variety is rarest. **i.** 3 or 4 examples are known.

1861-S, Normal Reverse   **1861-S, Paquet Reverse**
Note taller letters.

	Mintage	Cert	Avg	%MS	VF-20	EF-40	AU-50	AU-55	MS-60	MS-62	MS-63	MS-65
										PF-63	PF-64	PF-65
1859	43,597	129	51.6	5%	$1,900	$4,000	$9,500	$15,000	$32,000	$45,000		
Auctions: $17,625, AU-55, August 2015; $12,925, AU-50, August 2015; $3,290, AU-50, August 2014; $7,050, EF-40, October 2015												
1859, Proof (j)	80	5	62.6							$175,000	$325,000	$500,000
Auctions: $210,600, PF, June 2014												
1859-O	9,100	60	50.5	2%	$12,500	$27,500	$50,000	$65,000	$125,000			
Auctions: $28,200, MS-60, August 2014; $76,375, AU-58, August 2014; $51,700, AU-55, August 2015; $21,150, AU, March 2015												
1859-S	636,445	795	50.8	3%	$1,750	$2,250	$2,800	$4,500	$12,500	$30,000	$57,500	
Auctions: $9,400, AU-58, August 2015; $3,995, AU-55, July 2015; $2,820, AU-53, October 2015; $2,585, EF-45, September 2015												
1860	577,670	926	53.9	12%	$1,750	$2,000	$2,850	$3,500	$7,500	$12,000	$22,500	
Auctions: $10,575, MS-61, August 2015; $3,301, AU-58, January 2015; $2,644, AU-55, June 2015; $2,585, AU-53, January 2015												
1860, Proof (k)	59	9	64.3							$100,000	$185,000	$350,000
Auctions: $367,188, PF-66Cam, August 2014												
1860-O	6,600	59	51.2	2%	$12,500	$30,000	$50,000	$67,500				
Auctions: $64,625, AU-58, August 2015; $55,813, AU-53, August 2014; $30,550, EF-40, January 2015												
1860-S	544,950	722	51.1	3%	$1,750	$2,000	$2,750	$4,000	$11,000	$18,500	$32,500	
Auctions: $7,050, AU-58, January 2015; $3,673, AU-55, January 2015; $3,760, AU-53, August 2015												
1861	2,976,453	3,193	54.3	17%	$1,500	$1,850	$2,500	$3,250	$6,000	$10,000	$18,500	$52,500
Auctions: $8,813, MS-62, July 2015; $4,465, AU-58, February 2015; $1,998, AU-50, July 2015; $2,115, EF-40, January 2015												
1861, Proof (l)	66	2	64.0							$95,000	$185,000	$325,000
Auctions: $483,000, PF-67UCam, August 2006												
1861-O	17,741	115	48.2	4%	$13,500	$27,500	$55,000	$67,500	$135,000	$150,000		
Auctions: $51,406, AU-50, March 2015; $44,650, AU-50, August 2015; $11,163, AU-50, January 2015; $16,450, AU, March 2015												
1861-S	768,000	854	50.7	3%	$1,750	$2,000	$3,250	$5,000	$15,000	$25,000	$45,000	
Auctions: $3,525, MS-60, October 2015; $4,935, AU-58, January 2015; $2,350, AU-50, July 2015; $2,115, EF-45, August 2015												
1861, Paquet Rev (Tall Ltrs) † (m)	*unknown*	1	67.0	100%					$1,750,000			
Auctions: $1,645,000, MS-61, August 2014												
1861-S, Paquet Rev (Tall Ltrs) † (n)	19,250	74	48.5	0%	$65,000	$80,000	$120,000	$150,000	$250,000			
Auctions: $223,250, AU-58, April 2014; $164,500, AU-58, August 2015; $152,750, AU-58, August 2015												
1862	92,133	99	52.1	15%	$2,000	$5,750	$13,500	$20,000	$35,000	$47,500	$65,000	
Auctions: $70,500, MS-62, August 2014; $49,938, MS-62, August 2014; $28,200, AU-58, August 2015												
1862, Proof (o)	35	6	64.2							$85,000	$150,000	$300,000
Auctions: $381,875, PF-65Cam, April 2014												
1862-S	854,173	1,018	51.1	5%	$1,750	$2,250	$3,200	$5,000	$13,500	$27,500	$47,500	
Auctions: $9,400, AU-58, January 2015; $3,995, AU-55, October 2015; $2,470, AU-50, August 2015												

† Ranked in the *100 Greatest U.S. Coins* (fourth edition). **j.** 7 or 8 examples are known. **k.** Fewer than 10 examples are known. **l.** 5 or 6 examples are known. **m.** Once thought to be a pattern; now known to have been intended for circulation. 2 examples are known. **n.** Approximately 100 examples are known, most in VF and EF. **o.** Approximately 12 examples are known.

	Mintage	Cert	Avg	%MS	VF-20	EF-40	AU-50	AU-55	MS-60	MS-62 / PF-63	MS-63 / PF-64	MS-65 / PF-65
1863	142,790	195	52.9	12%	$2,000	$3,500	$8,500	$15,000	$32,500	$42,500	$60,000	
	Auctions: $85,188, MS-63, January 2015; $21,150, AU-58, September 2015; $20,563, AU-58, January 2015; $17,625, AU-55, August 2015											
1863, Proof (p)	30	8	64.3							$85,000	$150,000	$300,000
	Auctions: $381,875, PF-66Cam, August 2014; $345,150, PF, September 2013											
1863-S	966,570	1,363	51.4	9%	$1,750	$2,150	$3,000	$3,750	$8,500	$18,500	$32,000	
	Auctions: $5,405, AU-58, August 2015; $4,230, AU-55, August 2015; $2,115, EF-45, August 2015; $1,880, VF-30, January 2015											
1864	204,235	298	52.5	9%	$1,950	$2,500	$6,750	$9,000	$20,000	$45,000	$67,500	
	Auctions: $282,000, MS-65, April 2014; $8,813, AU-53, August 2015; $4,230, EF-40, August 2015; $3,760, EF-40, January 2015											
1864, Proof (q)	50	10	64.4							$85,000	$150,000	$250,000
	Auctions: $199,750, PF-64Cam, April 2014											
1864-S	793,660	977	51.3	13%	$1,850	$2,000	$2,750	$3,500	$11,000	$17,500	$42,500	$110,000
	Auctions: $19,975, MS-62, August 2015; $4,935, AU-53, February 2015; $1,998, EF-45, August 2015; $1,763, VF-35, July 2015											
1865	351,175	760	57.0	43%	$1,850	$2,100	$2,850	$3,750	$7,500	$13,500	$22,500	$65,000
	Auctions: $45,825, MS-65, October 2015; $3,290, AU-55, March 2015; $2,350, AU-50, January 2015; $2,115, EF-45, August 2015											
1865, Proof (r)	25	7	64.9							$85,000	$150,000	$250,000
	Auctions: $440,625, PF-66DCam, April 2014											
1865-S	1,042,500	1,342	53.9	35%	$1,750	$2,000	$2,750	$3,500	$6,750	$11,000	$13,500	$27,500
	Auctions: $25,850, MS-65, September 2015; $10,588, MS-62, August 2015; $2,233, AU-53, January 2015; $2,350, EF-45, August 2015											
1866-S, No Motto	120,000	157	47.5	4%	$4,750	$16,500	$36,500	$65,000	$155,000	$240,000		
	Auctions: $30,550, AU-50, October 2015; $28,200, AU-50, July 2015; $35,250, EF-45, August 2015; $8,225, VF-20, October 2015											

p. Approximately 12 examples are known. **q.** 12 to 15 examples are known. **r.** Fewer than 10 examples are known.

**1866, With Motto,
Doubled-Die Reverse**
FS-G20-1866-801.

	Mintage	Cert	Avg	%MS	VF-20	EF-40	AU-50	AU-55	MS-60	MS-62 / PF-63	MS-63 / PF-64	MS-64 / PF-65
1866, With Motto	698,745	589	53.3	8%	$1,600	$1,650	$2,500	$4,250	$11,000	$32,500	$65,000	$125,000
	Auctions: $25,850, MS-61, January 2015; $9,400, AU-58, August 2015; $3,995, AU-55, January 2015; $3,055, AU-50, September 2015											
1866, With Motto, Doubled-Die Reverse	(a)	0	n/a						$4,000	$6,000		
	Auctions: $12,650, MS-61, August 2010											
1866, With Motto, Proof (b)	30	7	64.6							$57,500	$125,000	$200,000
	Auctions: $126,500, PF-64, May 2007											
1866-S, With Motto	842,250	773	49.5	3%	$1,600	$1,650	$3,500	$9,500	$20,000	$45,000		
	Auctions: $15,275, AU-58, August 2015; $9,400, AU-55, February 2015; $3,760, AU-50, January 2015; $2,820, EF-40, August 2015											
1867	251,015	388	57.0	43%	$1,500	$1,600	$1,800	$3,500	$7,500	$15,000	$32,500	
	Auctions: $258,500, MS-66, November 2014; $9,400, MS-61, August 2015; $7,638, MS-61, August 2015; $6,492, AU-58, August 2015											
1867, Proof (c)	50	5	65.0							$57,500	$125,000	$200,000
	Auctions: $129,250, PF-64DCam, January 2015; $129,250, PF-64DCam, August 2014; $38,188, PF-61Cam, August 2014											
1867-S	920,750	1,149	50.8	2%	$1,500	$1,700	$2,000	$4,000	$15,000	$30,000		
	Auctions: $17,038, MS-61, January 2015; $8,225, AU-58, July 2015; $2,115, AU-53, January 2015; $1,763, EF-45, August 2015											

a. Included in circulation-strike 1866 mintage figure. **b.** Approximately 15 examples are known. **c.** 10 to 12 examples are known.

Open 3   Close 3

	Mintage	Cert	Avg	%MS	VF-20	EF-40	AU-50	AU-55	MS-60	MS-62	MS-63	MS-64
										PF-63	PF-64	PF-65
1868	98,575	187	52.0	5%	$1,850	$2,000	$3,500	$6,500	$22,500	$45,000	$75,000	
Auctions: $44,063, MS-62, August 2014; $18,800, AU-58, August 2015; $8,813, AU-53, June 2015; $4,113, EF-45, August 2014												
1868, Proof (d)	25	7	64.4							$65,000	$125,000	$200,000
Auctions: $149,500, PF-64DCam Plus, August 2011												
1868-S	837,500	1,401	51.7	3%	$1,500	$1,650	$1,800	$3,750	$15,000	$35,000		
Auctions: $16,450, MS-61, January 2015; $7,050, AU-58, January 2015; $1,645, AU-50, February 2015; $1,410, EF-45, January 2015												
1869	175,130	326	52.9	3%	$1,500	$1,650	$1,800	$4,000	$10,000	$20,000	$37,500	$65,000
Auctions: $108,688, MS-64, January 2014; $9,988, MS-60, January 2015; $2,115, AU-53, February 2015; $3,290, AU-50, August 2015												
1869, Proof (e)	25	7	65.0							$65,000	$125,000	$200,000
Auctions: $106,375, PF-64DCam, February 2009												
1869-S	686,750	1,354	52.2	5%	$1,500	$1,650	$1,750	$4,000	$10,000	$25,000	$42,500	$75,000
Auctions: $37,600, MS-62, August 2015; $7,638, AU-58, June 2015; $2,705, AU-55, February 2015; $1,880, AU-53, July 2015												
1870	155,150	265	54.0	15%	$1,500	$1,650	$2,500	$5,500	$16,000	$27,500	$50,000	
Auctions: $22,325, MS-61, June 2015; $14,688, MS-60, June 2015; $7,638, AU-58, August 2015; $6,463, AU-55, August 2015												
1870, Proof (f)	35	5	65.2							$65,000	$125,000	$200,000
Auctions: $503,100, PF, September 2013												
1870-CC † (g)	3,789	33	40.5	0%	$210,000	$250,000	$325,000	$475,000				
Auctions: $411,250, AU-53, March 2014; $58,815, EF-40, August 2014; $188,000, VF-30, October 2014; $182,125, VF-30, August 2015												
1870-S	982,000	1,314	52.3	4%	$1,500	$1,650	$1,750	$2,500	$9,000	$27,500	$50,000	
Auctions: $10,869, MS-61, September 2015; $2,000, AU-55, January 2015; $1,528, AU-50, January 2015; $1,410, EF-40, September 2015												
1871	80,120	253	53.3	5%	$1,500	$1,650	$2,500	$4,500	$10,000	$27,500	$45,000	$75,000
Auctions: $4,935, AU-58, January 2015; $4,848, AU-55, August 2015; $2,585, AU-50, September 2015; $2,820, EF-45, July 2015												
1871, Proof (h)	30	6	63.8							$65,000	$125,000	$200,000
Auctions: $26,450, PF-62Cam, August 2004												
1871-CC	17,387	177	48.9	3%	$17,500	$32,500	$50,000	$60,000	$115,000			
Auctions: $111,625, MS-60, August 2015; $56,400, AU-53, January 2015; $30,550, AU-50, September 2015; $42,300, EF-40, July 2015												
1871-S	928,000	1,594	54.0	9%	$1,500	$1,600	$1,750	$2,250	$5,750	$12,000	$27,500	$50,000
Auctions: $10,575, MS-62, August 2015; $2,471, AU-58, July 2015; $1,528, AU-50, August 2015; $1,351, EF-45, January 2015												
1872	251,850	691	55.3	13%	$1,500	$1,600	$1,750	$2,200	$6,500	$17,500	$35,000	$75,000
Auctions: $28,200, MS-63, January 2015; $2,820, AU-58, October 2015; $2,291, AU-53, January 2015; $1,528, EF-40, October 2015												
1872, Proof (i)	30	5	63.6							$65,000	$125,000	$200,000
Auctions: $135,125, PF-64, October 2014												
1872-CC	26,900	423	49.5	3%	$3,500	$5,500	$12,500	$22,500	$55,000			
Auctions: $94,000, MS-61, August 2015; $54,050, AU-58, January 2015; $13,513, AU-50, August 2015; $7,050, EF-40, January 2015												
1872-S	780,000	1,462	54.3	9%	$1,500	$1,600	$1,750	$1,850	$5,000	$13,500	$30,000	
Auctions: $25,850, MS-63, February 2015; $4,700, MS-61, March 2015; $1,880, AU-55, August 2015; $1,645, EF-45, August 2015												
1873, Close 3	1,709,825	374	54.3	11%	$1,500	$1,600	$1,750	$2,000	$4,500	$14,000		
Auctions: $3,525, MS-60, July 2015; $2,115, AU-55, January 2015; $1,880, AU-55, August 2015; $1,586, AU-55, October 2015												
1873, Open 3	(j)	7,512	58.6	52%	$1,500	$1,550	$1,600	$1,650	$2,500	$3,500	$7,500	$35,000
Auctions: $6,463, MS-63, January 2015; $1,645, AU-58, August 2015; $1,322, AU-53, September 2015; $1,234, EF-45, May 2015												
1873, Close 3, Proof (k)	25	7	63.9							$65,000	$125,000	$200,000
Auctions: $230,000, PF-65UCam, April 2011												

† Ranked in the *100 Greatest U.S. Coins* (fourth edition). **d.** Approximately 12 examples are known. **e.** Approximately 12 examples are known. **f.** Approximately 12 examples are known. **g.** An estimated 35 to 50 examples are believed to exist; most are in VF with extensive abrasions. **h.** Fewer than 10 examples are known. **i.** Fewer than 12 examples are known. **j.** Included in circulation-strike 1873, Close 3, mintage figure. **k.** 10 to 12 examples are known.

	Mintage	Cert	Avg	%MS	VF-20	EF-40	AU-50	AU-55	MS-60	MS-62	MS-63	MS-64
										PF-63	PF-64	PF-65
1873-CC, Close 3	22,410	398	52.2	5%	$4,500	$6,500	$12,500	$22,500	$50,000	$85,000	$150,000	
	Auctions: $25,850, AU-55, August 2015; $18,800, AU-55, January 2015; $15,863, AU-53, August 2015; $7,050, EF-40, October 2015											
1873-S, Close 3	1,040,600	1,472	54.7	14%	$1,500	$1,600	$1,675	$1,750	$2,650	$8,000	$27,500	
	Auctions: $7,638, MS-61, August 2015; $2,115, AU-58, February 2015; $1,410, AU-53, October 2015; $1,528, EF-45, September 2015											
1873-S, Open 3	(l)	799	54.2	11%	$1,500	$1,725	$1,775	$2,750	$9,500			
	Auctions: $14,100, MS-61, September 2015; $4,230, AU-58, August 2015; $1,528, AU-53, June 2015; $1,293, EF-45, September 2015											
1874	366,780	1,028	57.2	27%	$1,500	$1,550	$1,600	$1,650	$3,000	$13,000	$20,000	$55,000
	Auctions: $39,950, MS-64, August 2015; $3,760, MS-60, January 2015; $2,585, AU-55, August 2015; $1,351, AU-50, January 2015											
1874, Proof (m)	20	5	63.6							$75,000	$135,000	$225,000
	Auctions: $218,500, PF-64UCamH, January 2012											
1874-CC	115,085	1,323	48.9	1%	$3,000	$3,500	$5,000	$9,500	$25,000	$55,000		
	Auctions: $21,150, AU-58, August 2015; $5,640, AU-53, October 2015; $3,760, EF-45, July 2015; $2,350, VF-30, January 2015											
1874-S	1,214,000	3,126	56.2	20%	$1,500	$1,550	$1,600	$1,700	$2,500	$7,000	$28,500	
	Auctions: $7,050, MS-62, June 2015; $1,998, MS-60, January 2015; $1,645, AU-55, February 2015; $1,293, EF-45, January 2015											
1875	295,720	1,388	59.3	59%	$1,500	$1,550	$1,600	$1,700	$2,250	$3,500	$10,000	$40,000
	Auctions: $8,225, MS-63, September 2015; $2,585, MS-60, August 2015; $1,528, AU-58, January 2015; $1,351, AU-55, January 2015											
1875, Proof (n)	20	5	63.8							$100,000	$150,000	$250,000
	Auctions: $94,300, PF-63Cam, August 2009											
1875-CC	111,151	1,715	53.4	29%	$3,000	$3,250	$3,500	$4,250	$12,500	$20,000	$35,000	$75,000
	Auctions: $28,200, MS-63, January 2015; $7,344, AU-58, July 2015; $2,585, AU-50, January 2015; $2,820, EF-45, March 2015											
1875-S	1,230,000	3,790	56.9	28%	$1,500	$1,550	$1,600	$1,700	$2,500	$4,500	$15,000	$40,500
	Auctions: $16,450, MS-63, July 2015; $1,645, AU-58, August 2015; $1,410, AU-53, October 2015; $1,293, VF-35, January 2015											
1876	583,860	2,405	57.9	37%	$1,500	$1,550	$1,600	$1,700	$2,500	$4,000	$10,000	$38,000
	Auctions: $3,995, MS-62, January 2015; $1,410, AU-55, September 2015; $1,351, AU-53, January 2015; $1,528, EF-40, September 2015											
1876, Proof (o)	45	13	63.8							$55,000	$75,000	$135,000
	Auctions: $152,750, PF-64DCam, February 2013											
1876-CC	138,441	2,037	52.3	13%	$2,750	$3,000	$4,000	$5,500	$12,000	$25,000	$45,000	
	Auctions: $12,925, MS-60, October 2015; $8,813, AU-58, August 2015; $3,995, AU-50, October 2015; $2,585, VF-20, August 2015											
1876-S	1,597,000	5,981	57.1	31%	$1,500	$1,550	$1,600	$1,700	$2,500	$3,750	$10,000	$37,500
	Auctions: $42,300, MS-64, August 2015; $2,291, MS-61, August 2015; $1,528, AU-55, September 2015; $1,528, AU-50, October 2015											

l. Included in 1873-S, Close 3, mintage figure. **m.** Fewer than 10 examples are known. **n.** 10 to 12 examples are known.
o. Approximately 15 examples are known.

	Mintage	Cert	Avg	%MS	VF-20	EF-40	AU-50	AU-55	MS-60	MS-62	MS-63	MS-65
										PF-63	PF-64	PF-65
1877	397,650	1,005	59.3	66%	$1,400	$1,450	$1,550	$1,600	$2,100	$5,000	$20,000	
	Auctions: $3,995, MS-62, January 2015; $3,055, MS-61, August 2015; $2,000, MS-61, January 2015; $1,880, MS-61, July 2015											
1877, Proof (a)	20	8	63.5							$40,000	$75,000	$135,000
	Auctions: $21,150, PF-58, February 2013											
1877-CC	42,565	856	49.2	3%	$2,500	$3,660	$5,520	$11,700	$28,200	$60,000		
	Auctions: $24,675, AU-58, September 2015; $9,400, AU-55, August 2015; $4,700, AU-50, August 2015; $3,525, EF-40, January 2015											
1877-S	1,735,000	2,235	58.9	60%	$1,400	$1,425	$1,475	$1,500	$2,000	$5,000	$19,000	$30,000
	Auctions: $5,170, MS-62, February 2015; $1,998, MS-61, December 2015; $1,528, MS-60, February 2015; $1,645, AU-58, August 2015											
1878	543,625	1,579	59.8	69%	$1,400	$1,425	$1,475	$1,500	$2,000	$4,200	$15,000	
	Auctions: $9,400, MS-63, September 2015; $1,998, MS-61, July 2015; $1,645, AU-58, August 2015; $1,645, AU-55, August 2015											
1878, Proof (b)	20	8	64.5							$40,000	$65,000	$135,000
	Auctions: $69,000, PF-64Cam, April 2011											
1878-CC	13,180	339	46.9	2%	$3,500	$9,500	$13,000	$21,000	$45,000	$65,000		
	Auctions: $19,975, AU-55, August 2015; $9,400, EF-45, August 2015; $7,638, EF-40, July 2015; $6,169, VF-35, January 2015											
1878-S	1,739,000	1,524	58.2	55%	$1,400	$1,425	$1,475	$1,500	$1,950	$6,500	$23,500	
	Auctions: $6,169, MS-62, September 2015; $1,763, MS-60, August 2015; $1,763, AU-58, July 2015; $1,351, AU-55, January 2015											

a. 10 to 12 examples are known. **b.** Fewer than 10 examples are known.

	Mintage	Cert	Avg	%MS	VF-20	EF-40	AU-50	AU-55	MS-60	MS-62	MS-63	MS-65
										PF-63	PF-64	PF-65
1879	207,600	608	58.3	44%	$1,400	$1,425	$1,475	$1,500	$1,950	$6,500	$22,000	
Auctions: $3,290, MS-61, September 2015; $2,585, MS-61, February 2015; $2,350, MS-60, August 2015; $2,115, AU-58, September 2015												
1879, Proof (c)	30	5	64.0							$40,000	$65,000	$135,000
Auctions: $57,500, PF-64, July 2009												
1879-CC	10,708	325	50.0	3%	$3,000	$10,000	$15,000	$27,500	$42,000	$60,000		
Auctions: $28,200, AU-55, July 2015; $4,230, AU-50, August 2015; $11,899, EF-45, January 2015; $3,055, EF-40, October 2015												
1879-O	2,325	82	49.4	11%	$20,000	$30,000	$35,000	$60,000	$135,000	$155,000	$200,000	
Auctions: $135,125, MS-60, January 2014; $70,500, AU-58, August 2015; $35,250, AU-50, August 2014												
1879-S	1,223,800	1,302	57.3	30%	$1,400	$1,425	$1,475	$1,500	$2,500	$16,500	$42,500	
Auctions: $4,714, MS-61, January 2015; $2,585, AU-58, July 2015; $1,316, AU-55, January 2015; $1,539, AU-53, August 2015												
1880	51,420	394	55.3	15%	$1,475	$1,500	$1,575	$1,750	$10,500	$27,500	$37,500	
Auctions: $15,275, MS-61, August 2015; $3,525, AU-58, February 2015; $3,760, AU-55, August 2015; $2,820, AU-53, September 2015												
1880, Proof (d)	36	4	64.3							$40,000	$65,000	$135,000
Auctions: $217,375, PF-65DCam, August 2014; $235,000, PF, March 2014												
1880-S	836,000	903	58.0	39%	$1,400	$1,425	$1,475	$1,500	$1,800	$8,500	$27,500	
Auctions: $5,405, MS-62, January 2015; $4,700, MS-61, August 2015; $1,645, AU-58, June 2015; $1,645, AU-53, August 2015												
1881	2,199	31	54.0	19%	$15,000	$25,000	$40,000	$60,000	$100,000			
Auctions: $141,000, MS-61, August 2015; $141,000, MS-61, January 2015; $56,400, AU-58, August 2015; $28,214, EF-45, January 2015												
1881, Proof (e)	61	7	63.7							$40,000	$75,000	$135,000
Auctions: $172,500, PF-65Cam, January 2011												
1881-S	727,000	741	58.6	52%	$1,400	$1,425	$1,475	$1,500	$1,950	$7,500	$23,500	
Auctions: $10,575, MS-62, January 2015; $1,998, MS-61, February 2015; $2,233, AU-58, August 2015; $3,055, AU-55, September 2015												
1882	571	12	54.8	8%	$17,500	$37,500	$70,000	$95,000	$135,000	$140,000	$200,000	
Auctions: $94,000, AU-58, January 2014; $129,250, AU-55, August 2014												
1882, Proof (f)	59	6	63.7							$40,000	$75,000	$125,000
Auctions: $161,000, PF-64Cam, January 2011												
1882-CC	39,140	944	53.3	6%	$2,500	$3,500	$4,500	$7,000	$16,500	$37,500		
Auctions: $12,925, AU-58, July 2015; $7,050, AU-55, January 2015; $5,288, AU-53, September 2015; $3,055, EF-45, February 2015												
1882-S	1,125,000	1,399	58.9	60%	$1,400	$1,425	$1,475	$1,500	$2,000	$5,000	$18,500	
Auctions: $12,925, MS-63, June 2015; $3,995, MS-62, September 2015; $1,528, MS-60, July 2015; $1,552, AU-58, October 2015												
1883, Proof (g)	92	12	63.9							$115,000	$150,000	$200,000
Auctions: $282,000, PF-65DCam, January 2014; $158,625, PF-64DCam, August 2014												
1883-CC	59,962	1,275	52.6	8%	$2,250	$3,500	$4,500	$6,500	$15,000	$27,500	$40,000	
Auctions: $19,975, MS-61, January 2015; $11,750, AU-58, June 2015; $5,875, AU-53, August 2015; $2,820, EF-45, February 2015												
1883-S	1,189,000	2,127	59.7	73%	$1,400	$1,425	$1,475	$1,500	$1,950	$2,500	$8,500	
Auctions: $14,100, MS-64, June 2015; $1,528, MS-61, March 2015; $1,469, AU-55, January 2015; $1,293, EF-45, January 2015												
1884, Proof (h)	71	11	63.2							$110,000	$150,000	$200,000
Auctions: $246,750, PF-65DCam, January 2015; $235,000, PF-65DCam, August 2014; $246,750, PF-66Cam, April 2014												
1884-CC	81,139	1,694	54.1	18%	$2,250	$3,300	$4,500	$6,500	$11,000	$25,000	$37,500	
Auctions: $28,200, MS-62, June 2015; $5,244, AU-55, August 2015; $3,290, EF-40, July 2015; $3,525, VG-10, August 2015												
1884-S	916,000	2,573	60.5	82%	$1,400	$1,425	$1,475	$1,500	$1,900	$2,500	$6,500	$45,000
Auctions: $3,761, MS-63, January 2015; $1,998, MS-61, August 2015; $1,396, MS-60, January 2015; $1,351, AU-58, January 2015												
1885	751	52	55.7	27%	$12,500	$15,000	$25,000	$65,000	$90,000	$110,000	$135,000	
Auctions: $82,250, MS-62, October 2014; $14,100, MS-60, November 2014; $58,750, AU-58, January 2014; $49,390, AU-55, August 2015												
1885, Proof (i)	77	11	64.1							$40,000	$85,000	$120,000
Auctions: $35,250, PF-61DCam, September 2014												
1885-CC	9,450	296	50.8	7%	$3,750	$11,000	$15,500	$25,000	$40,000	$42,500	$75,000	
Auctions: $61,688, MS-62, March 2015; $37,600, MS-61, January 2015; $23,500, AU-55, August 2015; $3,055, AU-50, June 2015												
1885-S	683,500	2,257	60.8	86%	$1,400	$1,425	$1,475	$1,500	$1,900	$2,600	$5,500	
Auctions: $3,995, MS-63, January 2015; $1,998, MS-62, August 2015; $1,998, MS-61, August 2015; $1,528, AU-58, August 2015												

c. 10 to 12 examples are known. **d.** 10 to 12 examples are known. **e.** Fewer than 20 examples are known. **f.** 12 to 15 examples are known. **g.** Proof only. Approximately 20 examples are known. **h.** Proof only. Approximately 20 examples are known. **i.** 15 to 20 examples are known.

1888, Doubled-Die Reverse
FS-G20-1888-801.

	Mintage	Cert	Avg	%MS	VF-20	EF-40	AU-50	AU-55	MS-60	MS-62 PF-63	MS-63 PF-64	MS-65 PF-65
1886	1,000	28	54.9	7%	$22,500	$37,500	$60,000	$75,000	$125,000	$145,000	$195,000	
	Auctions: $129,250, MS-60, January 2014; $111,625, AU-58, August 2014; $76,375, AU-53, August 2015; $73,438, EF-45, August 2015											
1886, Proof (j)	106	18	64.3							$42,500	$75,000	$115,000
	Auctions: $19,975, PF-60, January 2014											
1887, Proof (k)	121	10	65.1							$67,500	$85,000	$125,000
	Auctions: $258,500, PF-66, January 2014; $123,375, PF-65Cam, August 2014; $117,500, PF-65Cam, August 2015											
1887-S	283,000	918	60.1	74%	$1,400	$1,425	$1,475	$1,500	$1,900	$6,000	$15,000	
	Auctions: $9,694, MS-63, January 2015; $4,935, MS-62, January 2015; $4,700, MS-62, August 2015; $2,585, MS-61, October 2015											
1888	226,161	1,057	60.1	73%	$1,400	$1,425	$1,475	$1,500	$1,900	$4,000	$12,000	$30,000
	Auctions: $4,465, MS-62, June 2015; $2,115, MS-61, September 2015; $1,763, MS-60, August 2015; $1,469, AU-55, January 2015											
1888, Doubled-Die Reverse	(l)	19	59.7	74%					$2,750	$3,500		
	Auctions: $3,819, MS-62, April 2013											
1888, Proof (m)	105	20	64.3							$27,500	$45,000	$85,000
	Auctions: $126,500, PF-65DCam, April 2012											
1888-S	859,600	2,506	60.7	84%	$1,400	$1,425	$1,475	$1,500	$1,900	$2,500	$5,000	
	Auctions: $5,640, MS-63, August 2015; $2,291, MS-62, February 2015; $1,998, MS-61, August 2015; $1,557, AU-58, August 2015											
1889	44,070	529	60.5	82%	$1,400	$1,425	$1,475	$1,500	$1,950	$5,000	$17,500	
	Auctions: $5,405, MS-62, August 2015; $2,585, MS-61, February 2015; $1,880, AU-55, August 2015; $1,645, AU-50, September 2015											
1889, Proof (n)	41	10	63.5							$27,500	$45,000	$85,000
	Auctions: $352,500, PF-65, January 2014											
1889-CC	30,945	842	52.5	8%	$2,500	$3,750	$5,000	$7,000	$13,500	$25,000	$35,000	
	Auctions: $16,450, MS-61, January 2015; $14,688, MS-60, June 2015; $7,638, AU-55, August 2015; $5,699, AU-53, August 2015											
1889-S	774,700	1,922	60.6	82%	$1,400	$1,425	$1,475	$1,500	$1,950	$2,600	$6,000	
	Auctions: $21,150, MS-65, January 2015; $2,115, MS-62, July 2015; $1,998, MS-61, September 2015; $1,410, AU-50, January 2015											
1890	75,940	640	60.6	81%	$1,400	$1,425	$1,475	$1,500	$1,950	$3,250	$12,500	$30,000
	Auctions: $7,931, MS-63, January 2015; $2,820, MS-62, October 2015; $2,115, AU-58, August 2015; $2,115, AU-50, September 2015											
1890, Proof (o)	55	14	65.4							$27,500	$45,000	$85,000
	Auctions: $92,000, PF-65UCam, August 2011											
1890-CC	91,209	2,200	53.0	10%	$2,250	$3,750	$4,500	$6,500	$10,500	$25,200	$45,000	
	Auctions: $25,850, MS-62, June 2015; $10,575, AU-58, August 2015; $5,875, AU-50, February 2015; $3,055, EF-40, October 2015											
1890-S	802,750	1,758	60.0	74%	$1,400	$1,425	$1,475	$1,500	$1,900	$2,500	$7,000	
	Auctions: $21,150, MS-65, January 2015; $3,995, MS-63, June 2015; $2,056, MS-62, June 2015; $1,586, MS-61, September 2015											
1891	1,390	41	55.1	12%	$8,000	$13,500	$22,500	$35,000	$65,000	$100,000		
	Auctions: $82,250, MS-61, January 2014; $52,875, AU-58, August 2014											
1891, Proof (p)	52	28	63.8							$27,500	$45,000	$85,000
	Auctions: $655,200, PF, September 2013											
1891-CC	5,000	245	54.0	15%	$6,500	$15,000	$20,000	$25,000	$42,500	$65,000	$85,000	
	Auctions: $41,125, MS-61, March 2015; $38,775, MS-60, January 2015; $23,500, AU-55, July 2015; $15,275, EF-45, August 2015											
1891-S	1,288,125	5,467	61.1	91%	$1,400	$1,425	$1,475	$1,500	$1,900	$1,950	$3,000	
	Auctions: $4,935, MS-64, July 2015; $2,468, MS-63, January 2015; $1,998, MS-62, July 2015; $1,880, MS-62, August 2015											

j. 20 to 25 examples are known. **k.** Proof only. More than 30 examples are known. **l.** Included in circulation-strike 1888 mintage figure. **m.** 20 to 30 examples are known. **n.** 10 to 12 examples are known. **o.** Approximately 15 examples are known. **p.** 20 to 25 examples are known.

	Mintage	Cert	Avg	%MS	VF-20	EF-40	AU-50	AU-55	MS-60	MS-62	MS-63	MS-65
										PF-63	PF-64	PF-65
1892	4,430	117	56.3	32%	$3,000	$4,500	$10,000	$14,500	$22,500	$45,000	$50,000	$85,000
Auctions: $32,900, MS-62, August 2015; $5,640, MS-60, July 2015; $11,788, AU-55, August 2014; $9,400, AU-53, September 2015											
1892, Proof (q)	93	15	64.3							$27,500	$45,000	$85,000
Auctions: $188,000, PF-66DCam, January 2014											
1892-CC	27,265	818	54.5	22%	$2,250	$3,500	$4,500	$7,000	$15,000	$37,500	$50,000	
Auctions: $35,250, MS-63, August 2015; $9,988, AU-58, July 2015; $4,465, AU-53, July 2015; $3,055, EF-40, July 2015											
1892-S	930,150	4,332	61.1	91%	$1,400	$1,425	$1,475	$1,500	$1,575	$1,600	$4,000	$28,500
Auctions: $17,625, MS-65, January 2015; $8,225, MS-64, August 2015; $1,592, MS-62, August 2015; $1,351, AU-55, January 2015											
1893	344,280	5,865	61.6	98%	$1,400	$1,425	$1,475	$1,500	$1,575	$1,600	$3,000	
Auctions: $3,643, MS-63, February 2015; $2,826, MS-63, October 2015; $1,998, MS-62, August 2015; $1,410, MS-60, October 2015											
1893, Proof (r)	59	5	63.4							$27,500	$45,000	$85,000
Auctions: $15,525, PF-60Cam, August 2011											
1893-CC	18,402	747	57.8	50%	$2,650	$4,000	$5,500	$7,500	$12,500	$27,500	$42,500	
Auctions: $19,975, MS-62, August 2015; $17,625, MS-62, July 2015; $14,688, MS-61, June 2015; $12,338, AU-58, October 2015											
1893-S	996,175	5,146	61.0	92%	$1,450	$1,475	$1,485	$1,600	$1,700	$1,750	$4,000	
Auctions: $3,290, MS-63, February 2015; $2,820, MS-63, January 2015; $1,763, MS-62, August 2015; $1,645, MS-62, July 2015											
1894	1,368,940	15,080	61.4	97%	$1,400	$1,425	$1,475	$1,500	$1,575	$1,600	$2,500	$25,000
Auctions: $22,325, MS-65, January 2015; $4,700, MS-64, February 2015; $1,645, MS-62, September 2015; $1,351, AU-55, January 2015											
1894, Proof (s)	50	13	63.8							$27,500	$45,000	$85,000
Auctions: $54,625, PF-64Cam, January 2005											
1894-S	1,048,550	5,575	61.2	93%	$1,400	$1,425	$1,475	$1,500	$1,575	$1,600	$3,000	$23,000
Auctions: $4,935, MS-64, January 2015; $2,585, MS-63, February 2015; $1,763, MS-62, August 2015; $1,351, MS-61, January 2015											
1895	1,114,605	21,476	61.7	98%	$1,400	$1,425	$1,475	$1,500	$1,575	$1,600	$2,500	$21,000
Auctions: $3,055, MS-64, January 2015; $1,880, MS-63, August 2015; $1,528, MS-62, August 2015; $1,293, AU-58, February 2015											
1895, Proof	51	11	64.2							$27,500	$45,000	$85,000
Auctions: $82,250, PF-65Cam, September 2014											
1895-S	1,143,500	7,088	61.3	93%	$1,400	$1,425	$1,475	$1,500	$1,575	$1,600	$2,500	$17,500
Auctions: $9,583, MS-65, January 2015; $3,878, MS-64, February 2015; $1,763, MS-62, October 2015; $1,293, MS-60, June 2015											
1896	792,535	10,085	61.7	97%	$1,400	$1,425	$1,475	$1,500	$1,575	$1,600	$2,250	$18,000
Auctions: $3,290, MS-64, September 2015; $2,056, MS-63, January 2015; $1,763, MS-62, July 2015; $1,704, MS-62, September 2015											
1896, Proof (t)	128	38	63.9							$27,500	$45,000	$85,000
Auctions: $97,750, PF-65DCam, April 2012											
1896-S	1,403,925	8,966	61.3	94%	$1,400	$1,425	$1,475	$1,500	$1,575	$1,600	$2,500	$25,000
Auctions: $3,055, MS-63, January 2015; $2,468, MS-63, February 2015; $1,645, MS-62, September 2015; $1,528, MS-61, January 2015											
1897	1,383,175	17,776	61.7	98%	$1,400	$1,425	$1,475	$1,500	$1,575	$1,600	$2,500	$22,800
Auctions: $2,585, MS-64, January 2015; $2,115, MS-63, August 2015; $1,763, MS-62, September 2015; $1,351, MS-61, January 2015											
1897, Proof (u)	86	23	64.1							$27,500	$45,000	$85,000
Auctions: $73,438, PF-64Cam, August 2014; $30,550, PF-62Cam, April 2013											
1897-S	1,470,250	12,512	61.6	95%	$1,400	$1,425	$1,475	$1,500	$1,575	$1,600	$2,600	$18,000
Auctions: $16,450, MS-65, January 2015; $3,643, MS-64, June 2015; $1,763, MS-62, August 2015; $1,351, MS-61, January 2015											
1898	170,395	1,699	61.2	89%	$1,400	$1,425	$1,475	$1,500	$2,750	$3,000	$5,500	
Auctions: $4,818, MS-63, October 2015; $2,585, MS-62, August 2015; $1,410, MS-61, January 2015; $1,410, AU-58, January 2015											
1898, Proof (v)	75	36	64.1							$27,500	$45,000	$85,000
Auctions: $52,875, PF-64DCam, September 2014; $117,500, PF-65Cam, April 2013											
1898-S	2,575,175	22,218	61.7	96%	$1,400	$1,425	$1,475	$1,500	$1,575	$1,600	$2,750	$8,500
Auctions: $9,400, MS-65, June 2015; $1,645, MS-62, September 2015; $1,351, AU-58, January 2015; $1,351, AU-55, January 2015											

q. Approximately 25 examples are known. **r.** 15 to 20 examples are known. **s.** 15 to 20 examples are known. **t.** 45 to 50 examples are known. **u.** 20 to 25 examples are known. **v.** 35 to 40 examples are known.

	Mintage	Cert	Avg	%MS	VF-20	EF-40	AU-50	AU-55	MS-60	MS-62 / PF-63	MS-63 / PF-64	MS-65 / PF-65
1899	1,669,300	23,553	62.0	98%	$1,400	$1,425	$1,475	$1,500	$1,575	$1,600	$1,650	$10,000
Auctions: $7,638, MS-65, September 2015; $4,113, MS-64, June 2015; $1,410, MS-61, October 2015; $1,528, AU-58, August 2015												
1899, Proof (w)	84	29	64.2							$27,500	$45,000	$85,000
Auctions: $76,375, PF, March 2014												
1899-S	2,010,300	9,118	61.3	91%	$1,400	$1,425	$1,475	$1,500	$1,575	$1,600	$2,750	$20,000
Auctions: $2,291, MS-63, September 2015; $1,939, MS-63, February 2015; $1,763, MS-62, August 2015; $1,645, MS-62, August 2015												
1900	1,874,460	49,070	62.4	99%	$1,400	$1,425	$1,475	$1,500	$1,575	$1,600	$1,650	$5,000
Auctions: $7,344, MS-65, August 2015; $2,820, MS-64, August 2015; $1,821, MS-62, June 2015; $1,293, MS-60, July 2015												
1900, Proof (x)	124	30	64.6							$27,500	$45,000	$85,000
Auctions: $88,125, PF, March 2014												
1900-S	2,459,500	7,562	61.1	92%	$1,400	$1,425	$1,475	$1,500	$1,575	$1,600	$2,750	$25,000
Auctions: $3,055, MS-63, August 2015; $1,763, MS-62, August 2015; $1,422, MS-60, August 2015; $1,410, AU-58, October 2015												
1901	111,430	5,075	62.9	99%	$1,400	$1,425	$1,475	$1,500	$1,575	$1,600	$1,650	$4,000
Auctions: $3,290, MS-65, January 2015; $2,115, MS-64, August 2015; $1,880, MS-63, February 2015; $1,645, MS-62, August 2015												
1901, Proof (y)	96	41	62.9							$27,500	$45,000	$85,000
Auctions: $68,150, PF, February 2013												
1901-S	1,596,000	3,046	61.1	93%	$1,400	$1,425	$1,475	$1,500	$1,575	$1,600	$4,250	$22,500
Auctions: $3,525, MS-63, February 2015; $2,938, MS-63, September 2015; $2,115, MS-62, August 2015; $2,350, MS-61, August 2015												
1902	31,140	514	59.9	68%	$1,400	$1,425	$1,475	$1,500	$2,500	$6,000	$15,000	
Auctions: $4,700, MS-62, July 2015; $3,995, MS-61, August 2015; $2,350, MS-61, January 2015; $2,820, AU-58, August 2015												
1902, Proof (z)	114	28	63.1							$27,500	$45,000	$85,000
Auctions: $9,400, PF-50, January 2014												
1902-S	1,753,625	4,423	61.0	94%	$1,400	$1,425	$1,475	$1,500	$1,575	$1,600	$3,750	$25,000
Auctions: $28,200, MS-65, October 2015; $3,525, MS-63, January 2015; $1,410, MS-60, January 2015; $1,351, AU-58, June 2015												
1903	287,270	12,338	62.9	100%	$1,400	$1,425	$1,475	$1,500	$1,575	$1,600	$1,650	$4,000
Auctions: $3,290, MS-65, January 2015; $2,585, MS-64, August 2015; $1,645, MS-63, August 2015; $1,410, MS-61, January 2015												
1903, Proof (aa)	158	40	62.8							$27,500	$45,000	$85,000
Auctions: $63,450, PF, March 2014												
1903-S	954,000	6,345	61.8	98%	$1,400	$1,425	$1,475	$1,500	$1,575	$1,600	$2,250	$16,000
Auctions: $3,290, MS-64, September 2015; $2,174, MS-63, June 2015; $1,481, MS-62, August 2015; $1,422, AU-55, August 2015												
1904	6,256,699	221,635	62.6	99%	$1,400	$1,425	$1,475	$1,500	$1,575	$1,600	$1,650	$3,000
Auctions: $5,875, MS-66, October 2015; $4,818, MS-65, March 2015; $1,528, MS-62, August 2015; $1,351, MS-60, June 2015												
1904, Proof (bb)	98	41	63.7							$27,500	$45,000	$85,000
Auctions: $146,875, PF-67Cam, August 2013												
1904-S	5,134,175	24,126	62.4	98%	$1,400	$1,425	$1,475	$1,500	$1,575	$1,600	$1,650	$4,500
Auctions: $4,465, MS-65, January 2015; $2,350, MS-64, January 2015; $1,645, MS-62, August 2015; $1,293, AU-58, January 2015												
1905	58,919	793	59.3	60%	$1,400	$1,425	$1,475	$1,500	$2,500	$6,000	$16,200	$60,000
Auctions: $6,463, MS-62, August 2015; $5,405, MS-62, July 2015; $1,763, AU-58, June 2015; $1,763, AU-53, August 2015												
1905, Proof (cc)	92	26	62.8							$27,500	$45,000	$85,000
Auctions: $10,005, PF-58, January 2012												
1905-S	1,813,000	2,284	61.1	89%	$1,400	$1,425	$1,475	$1,500	$1,575	$1,600	$4,500	$24,000
Auctions: $4,935, MS-64, July 2015; $3,525, MS-63, January 2015; $2,468, MS-62, August 2015; $1,645, MS-61, September 2015												

w. Fewer than 30 examples are known. **x.** Approximately 50 examples are known. **y.** 40 to 50 examples are known. **z.** Fewer than 50 examples are known. **aa.** 40 to 50 examples are known. **bb.** Approximately 50 examples are known. **cc.** 30 to 40 examples are known.

	Mintage	Cert	Avg	%MS	VF-20	EF-40	AU-50	AU-55	MS-60	MS-62	MS-63	MS-65
										PF-63	PF-64	PF-65
1906	69,596	683	60.4	75%	$1,500	$1,550	$1,650	$1,700	$1,800	$5,000	$8,500	$36,600
Auctions: $14,361, MS-64, August 2015; $4,230, MS-62, August 2015; $3,760, MS-61, August 2015; $3,055, AU-58, August 2015											
1906, Proof (dd)	94	45	63.4							$27,500	$45,000	$85,000
Auctions: $85,188, PF, August 2013											
1906-D	620,250	1,802	61.8	96%	$1,400	$1,425	$1,475	$1,500	$1,575	$1,600	$4,000	$24,000
Auctions: $10,575, MS-64, August 2015; $3,525, MS-63, January 2015; $3,760, MS-62, August 2015; $1,410, MS-61, January 2015											
1906-D, Proof (ee)	6	0	n/a		*(extremely rare)*							
Auctions: No auction records available.											
1906-S	2,065,750	4,501	61.5	95%	$1,400	$1,425	$1,475	$1,500	$1,575	$1,600	$2,500	$25,000
Auctions: $25,850, MS-65, January 2015; $4,935, MS-64, October 2015; $1,645, MS-62, August 2015; $1,645, EF-45, August 2015											
1907	1,451,786	31,144	61.9	99%	$1,400	$1,425	$1,475	$1,500	$1,575	$1,600	$1,650	$10,000
Auctions: $2,820, MS-64, July 2015; $1,471, MS-62, August 2015; $1,351, MS-60, January 2015; $1,351, AU-55, January 2015											
1907, Proof (ff)	78	51	63.6							$27,500	$45,000	$85,000
Auctions: $40,250, PF-64Cam, January 2012											
1907-D	842,250	2,265	62.4	96%	$1,400	$1,425	$1,475	$1,500	$1,575	$1,600	$3,500	$9,000
Auctions: $8,813, MS-65, March 2015; $4,230, MS-64, January 2015; $1,998, MS-62, September 2015; $1,528, MS-61, January 2015											
1907-D, Proof (gg)	unknown	1	62									
Auctions: $71,875, PF-62, January 2004											
1907-S	2,165,800	3,441	61.8	95%	$1,400	$1,425	$1,475	$1,500	$1,575	$1,600	$3,000	$22,500
Auctions: $17,625, MS-65, June 2015; $5,875, MS-64, March 2015; $2,820, MS-63, August 2015; $1,410, MS-61, January 2015											

dd. 45 to 50 examples are known. **ee.** Six 1906-D presentation strikes were made to commemorate the first coinage of double eagles at the Denver Mint. The coins were well documented at the time; however, at present only two are accounted for. **ff.** 25 to 50 examples are known. **gg.** Believed to have once been part of the collection of King Farouk of Egypt; cleaned.

SAINT-GAUDENS, HIGH RELIEF AND ULTRA HIGH RELIEF, MCMVII (1907)

Designer: *Augustus Saint-Gaudens.* **Weight:** *33.436 grams.*
Composition: *.900 gold, .100 copper (net weight: .96750 oz. pure gold).*
Diameter *34 mm.* **Edge:** *E PLURIBUS UNUM with words divided by stars*
(one specimen of the high-relief variety with plain edge is known). **Mint:** *Philadelphia.*

Circulation Strike

Proof, Ultra High Relief Pattern

History. Created by famous artist Augustus Saint-Gaudens under a commission arranged by President Theodore Roosevelt, this double eagle was first made (in pattern form) with ultra high relief, sculptural in its effect, on both sides and the date in Roman numerals. The story of its production is well known and has been described in several books, notably *Renaissance of American Coinage, 1905–1908* (Burdette) and *Striking Change: The Great Artistic Collaboration of Theodore Roosevelt and August Saint-Gaudens* (Moran). After the Ultra High Relief patterns of 1907, a modified High Relief version was developed to facilitate production. Each coin required three blows of the press to strike up properly. Most featured a flat rim (now known as the Flat Rim variety), but planchet metal would occasionally be squeezed up between the collar and the die, resulting in the Wire Rim variety; this can exist around part of or the entire circumference of the coin. The coins were made on a medal press in December 1907 and January 1908, to the extent of fewer than 13,000 pieces. In the meantime, production was under way for low-relief coins, easier to mint in quantities sufficient for commerce—these dated 1907 rather than MCMVII. Today the MCMVII double eagle is a favorite among collectors, and when surveys are taken of beautiful and popular designs (as in *100 Greatest U.S. Coins*, by Garrett and Guth), it always ranks near the top.

Striking and Sharpness. The striking usually is good. Check the left knee of Miss Liberty, which sometimes shows lightness of strike and, most often, shows flatness or wear (sometimes concealed by post-mint etching or clever tooling). Check the Capitol at the lower left. On the reverse, check the high points at the top of the eagle. The surface on all is a delicate matte texture, grainy rather than deeply frosty. Under examination the fields show myriad tiny raised curlicues and other die-finish marks. There is no record of any MCMVII double eagles being made as *Proofs*, nor is there any early numismatic record of any being sold as Proofs. Walter Breen in the 1960s made up some guidelines for Proofs, which some graders have adopted. Some homemade "Proofs" have been made by pickling or sandblasting the surface of regular coins—*caveat emptor*.

Availability. Half or more of the original mintage still exist today, as many were saved, and these grade mostly from AU-50 to MS-62. Circulated examples often have been cleaned, polished, or used in jewelry. Higher-grade coins are seen with some frequency, up to MS-65. Overgrading is common.

GRADING STANDARDS

MS-60 to 70 (Mint State). *Obverse:* At MS-60, some abrasion and contact marks are seen on Liberty's chest. The left knee is flat on lower Mint State coins and all circulated coins. Scattered marks and abrasion are in the field. Satiny luster is present, but may be dull or lifeless, and interrupted in patches. Many coins at this level have been cleaned. At MS-63, contact marks are fewer, and abrasion is light, but the knee still has a flat spot. An MS-65 coin

MCMVII (1907), High Relief. Graded MS-63.

has little abrasion and few marks. Grades above MS-65 are defined by having fewer marks as perfection is approached. *Reverse:* Comments apply as for the obverse, except that abrasion and contact marks are most noticeable on the side of the eagle's body and the top of the left wing.

Illustrated coin: This is a splendid choice striking.

AU-50, 53, 55, 58 (About Uncirculated). *Obverse:* Light wear is seen on the chest, the left leg, and the field, more so at AU-50 than at AU–53 or 55. An AU-58 coin has fewer traces of wear. An AU-50 coin has satiny luster in protected areas among the rays, with little in the open field above. At AU-58, most luster is present. *Reverse:* Comments as preceding, except that the side of the eagle below the front of the wing, the top of the wing, and the field

MCMVII (1907), High Relief. Graded AU-55.

show light wear. Satiny luster ranges from perhaps 40% (at AU-50) to nearly full mint bloom (at AU-58).

EF-40, 45 (Extremely Fine). *Obverse:* Wear is seen on all the higher-relief areas of the standing figure and on the rock at the lower right. Luster is minimal, if present at all. Eye appeal is apt to be lacking. Nearly all Extremely Fine coins have been cleaned. *Reverse:* The eagle shows more wear overall, especially at the bottom and on the tops of the wings.

MCMVII (1907), High Relief. Graded EF-45.

VF-20, 30 (Very Fine). *Obverse:* Most details of the standing figure are flat, her face is incomplete, and the tips of the rays are weak. Eye appeal is usually poor. As these coins did not circulate to any extent, a Very Fine coin was likely carried as a pocket piece. *Reverse:* Wear is greater overall, but most evident on the eagle. Detail is good at the center of the left wing, but worn away in most other areas of the bird.

MCMVII (1907), High Relief. Graded VF-30.

The MCMVII (1907) High Relief double eagle is seldom collected in grades lower than VF-20.

	Mintage	Cert	Avg	%MS	VF-20	EF-40	AU-50	AU-55	MS-60	MS-62	MS-63	MS-65
									PF-63	PF-64	PF-65	PF-67
1907, High Relief, MCMVII, Wire Rim † (a)	12,367	1,362	62.2	90%	$9,000	$11,000	$12,000	$13,000	$15,000	$20,000	$24,000	$47,500
	Auctions: $71,675, MS-66, October 2015; $18,800, AU-55, August 2015; $9,988, AU-50, January 2015; $5,875, VF-20, August 2015											
1907, High Relief, MCMVII, Flat Rim †	(b)	566	62.5	87%	$9,000	$11,000	$12,000	$13,500	$15,000	$20,000	$24,000	$50,000
	Auctions: $117,500, MS-67, January 2015; $16,450, AU-58, September 2015; $6,463, AU-50, January 2015; $5,640, EF-40, January 2015											
1907, High Relief, MCMVII, Wire or Flat Rim, Proof	*unknown*	0	n/a						$32,500	$40,000	$75,500	
	Auctions: $32,900, PF-64, February 2013											
1907, Ultra High Relief, Plain Edge, Proof	(c)	0	n/a									
	Auctions: No auction records available.											
1907, Ultra High Relief, Inverted Edge, Proof	(c)	0	n/a									
	Auctions: No auction records available.											
1907, Ultra High Relief, Lettered Edge, Proof †	*16–22*	3	67.3								$2,250,000	$2,500,000
	Auctions: $2,115,000, PF-68, January 2015; $1,840,000, PF-68, January 2007											

† Ranked in the *100 Greatest U.S. Coins* (fourth edition). **a.** The Wire Rim and Flat Rim varieties were the result of different collars used in the minting process. The Flat Rim is considered slightly scarcer, but this has not led to large value differentials, as both varieties are very popular among collectors. **b.** Included in 1907, High Relief, MCMVII, Wire Rim, mintage figure. **c.** Included in 1907, Ultra High Relief, Lettered Edge, Proof, mintage figure.

SAINT-GAUDENS, FLAT RELIEF, ARABIC NUMERALS (1907–1933)

Designer: *Augustus Saint-Gaudens.* **Weight:** *33.436 grams.*
Composition: *.900 gold, .100 copper (net weight: .96750 oz. pure gold).*
Diameter: *34 mm.* **Edge:** *E PLURIBUS UNUM with words divided by stars.*
Mints: *Philadelphia, Denver, and San Francisco.*

No Motto (1907–1908)

*Mintmark location is on
the obverse, above the date.*

With Motto (1908–1933)

With Motto, Proof

History. In autumn 1907 U.S. Mint chief engraver Charles E. Barber modified Augustus Saint-Gaudens's design by lowering its relief and substituting Arabic (not Roman) numerals. Coins of this type were struck in large quantities from 1907 to 1916 and again from 1920 to 1933. In July 1908 the motto IN GOD WE TRUST was added to the reverse. Coins dated 1907 to 1911 have 46 stars on the obverse; coins of 1912 to 1933 have 48 stars. Sandblast (also called Matte) Proofs were made in 1908 and from 1911 to 1915; Satin (also called Roman Finish) Proofs were made in 1909 and 1910.

The vast majority of these coins were exported. Since World War II millions have been repatriated, supplying most of those in numismatic hands today.

Striking and Sharpness. The details are often light on the obverse. Check the bosom of Miss Liberty, the covering of which tends to be weak on 1907 and, especially, 1908 No Motto coins. Check the Capitol building and its immediate area at the lower left. The reverse usually is well struck, but check the feathers on the eagle and the top of the wings. The Matte Proofs have dull surfaces, much like fine-grained sandpaper, while the Satin Proofs have satiny surfaces and are bright yellow.

Availability. Most dates and mintmarks range from very common to slightly scarce, punctuated with scarce to very rare issues such as 1908-S, 1920-S, 1921, mintmarked coins from 1924 to 1927, and all issues of 1929 to 1933. From their initial mintages, most of the double eagles of the 1920s were returned to the Mint and melted in the 1930s. Some, however, were unofficially saved by Treasury employees. Estimates of the quantities saved range from a few dozen to several hundred thousand, depending on the date; this explains the high values for coins that, judged only by their initial mintages, should otherwise be more common. Probably a million or more MS coins exist of certain dates, most notably 1908 No Motto, 1924, 1925, 1926, and 1928 (especially common). Quality varies, as many have contact marks.

Philadelphia Mint coins from 1922 onward usually are seen with excellent eye appeal. Common varieties are not usually collected in grades below MS. All of the Proofs are rare today.

Note: Values of common-date gold coins have been based on the current bullion price of gold, $1,150 per ounce, and may vary with the prevailing spot price.

GRADING STANDARDS

MS-60 to 70 (Mint State). *Obverse:* At MS-60, some abrasion and contact marks are seen on Liberty's chest and left knee, and scattered marks and abrasion are in the field. Luster is present, but may be dull or lifeless, and interrupted in patches. At MS-63, contact marks are fewer, and abrasion is light. An MS-65 coin has little abrasion and few marks, although quality among certified coins can vary. On a conservatively graded coin the lus-

1924. Graded MS-65.

ter should be full and rich. Grades above MS-65 are defined by having fewer marks as perfection is approached. Generally, Mint State coins of 1922 onward are choicer and more attractive than the earlier issues. *Reverse:* Comments apply as for the obverse, except that abrasion and contact marks are most noticeable on the eagle's left wing.

AU-50, 53, 55, 58 (About Uncirculated). *Obverse:* Light wear is seen on the chest, the left knee, the midriff, and across the field, more so at AU-50 than at AU–53 or 55. An AU-58 coin has minimal traces of wear. An AU-50 coin has luster in protected areas among the rays, with little in the open field above. At AU-58, most luster is present. *Reverse:* Comments as preceding, except that the side of the eagle below the front of the wing, the top of

1909, 9 Over 8. Graded AU-50.

the wing, and the field show light wear. Luster ranges from perhaps 40% (at AU-50) to nearly full mint bloom (at AU-58).

EF-40, 45 (Extremely Fine). *Obverse:* Wear is seen on all the higher-relief areas of the standing figure and on the rock at the lower right. Luster is minimal, if present at all. Eye appeal is apt to be lacking. *Reverse:* The eagle shows more wear overall, especially at the bottom and on the tops of the wings.

1908-S. Graded EF-40.

VF-20, 30 (Very Fine). *Obverse:* Most details of the standing figure are flat, her face is incomplete, and the tips of the rays are weak. Eye appeal is usually poor. *Reverse:* Wear is greater overall, but most evident on the eagle. Detail is good at the center of the left wing, but worn away in most other areas of the bird.

The Saint-Gaudens double eagle is seldom collected in grades lower than VF-20.

PF-60 to 70 (Proof). *Obverse and Reverse:* At PF–60 to 63, there is light abrasion and some contact marks (the lower the grade, the higher the quantity). On Sandblast Proofs these show up as visually unappealing bright spots. At PF-64 and higher levels, marks are fewer, with magnification needed to see any at PF-65. At PF-66, there should be none at all.

1914. Graded VF-20.

1909, Satin Finish. Graded PF-66.

	Mintage	Cert	Avg	%MS	VF-20	EF-40	AU-50	AU-55	MS-60	MS-62 / PF-63	MS-63 / PF-64	MS-65 / PF-65
1907, Arabic Numerals	361,667	10,229	62.7	97%	$1,400	$1,450	$1,475	$1,500	$1,850	$1,875	$2,100	$4,000
Auctions: $5,170, MS-66, January 2015; $4,113, MS-65, January 2015; $2,585, MS-64, August 2015; $1,645, MS-62, February 2015												
1907, Proof (a)	*unknown*	0	n/a		*(extremely rare)*							
Auctions: $40,250, PF-64Cam, January 2012												
1908, No Motto	4,271,551	133,775	63.3	100%	$1,300	$1,325	$1,350	$1,375	$1,425	$1,450	$1,475	$2,000
Auctions: $6,463, MS-67, June 2015; $4,700, MS-66, February 2015; $1,763, MS-63, September 2015; $1,469, MS-61, September 2015												
1908-D, No Motto	663,750	4,314	62.4	97%	$1,300	$1,325	$1,350	$1,375	$1,600	$1,700	$2,000	$9,500
Auctions: $9,400, MS-65, August 2015; $2,820, MS-64, August 2015; $1,586, MS-63, February 2015; $1,528, MS-62, September 2015												
1908, With Motto	156,258	2,111	62.0	95%	$1,400	$1,550	$1,650	$1,750	$1,875	$1,900	$2,500	$19,500
Auctions: $5,170, MS-64, January 2015; $2,233, MS-63, March 2015; $1,645, MS-62, October 2015; $1,645, MS-60, July 2015												
1908, With Motto, Sandblast Finish Proof	101	77	65.3							$30,000	$43,500	$72,500
Auctions: $57,500, PF-66+, June 2012												
1908, With Motto, Satin Finish Proof (b)	*unknown*	0	n/a		*(extremely rare)*							
Auctions: $152,750, PF, August 2013												
1908-D, With Motto	349,500	2,242	62.5	93%	$1,300	$1,325	$1,350	$1,375	$1,425	$1,450	$2,000	$5,000
Auctions: $21,150, MS-66, June 2015; $7,050, MS-65, January 2015; $3,525, MS-64, October 2015; $1,880, MS-62, July 2015												
1908-S, With Motto	22,000	520	56.1	33%	$2,500	$3,750	$6,000	$7,000	$11,500	$15,000	$22,500	$50,000
Auctions: $21,150, MS-63, August 2015; $4,935, AU-53, July 2015; $3,878, EF-45, February 2015; $3,055, VF-35, August 2015												

a. 2 or 3 examples are known. **b.** 3 or 4 examples are known.

1909, 9 Over 8

	Mintage	Cert	Avg	%MS	VF-20	EF-40	AU-50	AU-55	MS-60	MS-62 / PF-63	MS-63 / PF-64	MS-65 / PF-65
1909, All kinds	161,282											
1909, 9 Over 8 (c)		1,682	59.3	57%	$1,500	$1,550	$1,600	$1,650	$2,000	$3,000	$5,000	$42,000
Auctions: $14,153, MS-64, July 2015; $4,700, MS-63, January 2015; $1,880, AU-58, September 2015; $1,645, AU-50, August 2015												
1909		1,386	60.7	77%	$1,300	$1,325	$1,350	$1,375	$1,550	$1,850	$2,500	$40,000
Auctions: $35,250, MS-65, June 2015; $1,586, MS-61, April 2015; $1,469, AU-58, January 2015; $1,593, AU-53, July 2015												
1909, Satin Finish Proof	67	32	65.3							$28,500	$43,500	$80,000
Auctions: $184,860, PF, September 2013												
1909-D	52,500	511	59.8	61%	$1,600	$1,700	$1,750	$1,950	$3,250	$4,500	$6,500	$40,000
Auctions: $11,750, MS-64, July 2015; $5,640, MS-63, February 2015; $2,820, AU-58, September 2015; $1,528, AU-50, July 2015												
1909-S	2,774,925	5,746	62.6	96%	$1,300	$1,325	$1,350	$1,375	$1,425	$1,450	$1,750	$4,500
Auctions: $22,913, MS-66, July 2015; $2,938, MS-64, January 2015; $1,763, MS-63, June 2015; $1,645, MS-62, January 2015												
1910	482,000	8,211	62.3	98%	$1,300	$1,325	$1,350	$1,375	$1,425	$1,450	$1,750	$8,500
Auctions: $6,463, MS-65, September 2015; $3,055, MS-64, January 2015; $1,704, MS-63, August 2015; $1,704, MS-62, January 2015												
1910, Satin Finish Proof	167	0	n/a							$30,000	$43,500	$80,000
Auctions: $76,375, PF-65, August 2014; $56,063, PF-65, June 2012												
1910, Sandblast Finish Proof (d)	*unknown*	37	65.6					*(unique)*				
Auctions: No auction records available.												
1910-D	429,000	6,861	62.9	97%	$1,300	$1,325	$1,350	$1,375	$1,425	$1,450	$1,600	$3,000
Auctions: $9,400, MS-66, January 2015; $2,350, MS-65, July 2015; $1,763, MS-64, October 2015; $1,469, MS-62, September 2015												
1910-S	2,128,250	4,369	61.7	90%	$1,300	$1,325	$1,350	$1,375	$1,425	$1,450	$1,750	$6,000
Auctions: $88,125, MS-67, January 2015; $3,760, MS-64, January 2015; $1,998, MS-63, August 2015; $1,528, MS-62, October 2015												
1911	197,250	2,702	61.9	90%	$1,300	$1,325	$1,350	$1,375	$1,500	$1,600	$2,000	$13,500
Auctions: $17,038, MS-66, January 2015; $4,935, MS-64, June 2015; $1,763, MS-62, August 2015; $1,528, EF-45, September 2015												
1911, Sandblast Finish Proof	100	45	66.1							$27,500	$43,500	$75,000
Auctions: $157,950, PF, September 2013												
1911-D	846,500	11,622	63.4	98%	$1,300	$1,325	$1,350	$1,375	$1,425	$1,450	$1,600	$2,500
Auctions: $3,760, MS-66, January 2015; $2,644, MS-64, August 2015; $1,586, MS-63, July 2015; $1,469, MS-62, September 2015												
1911-S	775,750	5,347	62.8	97%	$1,300	$1,325	$1,350	$1,375	$1,425	$1,450	$1,650	$4,000
Auctions: $11,221, MS-66, October 2015; $5,758, MS-65, January 2015; $1,880, MS-63, February 2015; $1,469, MS-62, September 2015												
1912	149,750	2,447	61.5	89%	$1,300	$1,325	$1,350	$1,375	$1,500	$1,600	$2,250	$22,000
Auctions: $19,975, MS-65, September 2015; $5,640, MS-64, January 2015; $1,528, MS-61, February 2015; $1,469, AU-58, January 2015												
1912, Sandblast Finish Proof	74	54	66.0							$27,500	$43,500	$75,000
Auctions: $211,500, PF-67, August 2013												
1913	168,780	2,658	61.4	89%	$1,300	$1,325	$1,350	$1,375	$1,550	$1,800	$2,750	$47,500
Auctions: $11,750, MS-64, January 2015; $1,763, MS-62, July 2015; $1,645, MS-61, October 2015; $1,410, AU-58, January 2015												
1913, Sandblast Finish Proof	58	51	65.5							$27,500	$43,500	$75,000
Auctions: $79,313, PF, August 2013												
1913-D	393,500	3,842	62.5	95%	$1,300	$1,325	$1,350	$1,375	$1,450	$1,600	$1,700	$5,000
Auctions: $22,325, MS-66, February 2015; $6,463, MS-65, August 2015; $2,585, MS-64, October 2015; $2,350, MS-63, September 2015												
1913-S	34,000	1,140	61.6	86%	$1,800	$1,850	$1,800	$2,000	$2,350	$3,000	$4,500	$35,000
Auctions: $9,400, MS-64, January 2015; $3,055, MS-62, January 2015; $2,233, MS-61, July 2015; $2,585, AU-58, September 2015												

c. This is one of the few Saint-Gaudens double eagle die varieties that commands a premium over the regular coin. d. Part of the unique complete 1910 Sandblast Finish Proof gold set.

1922, Doubled-Die Reverse

	Mintage	Cert	Avg	%MS	VF-20	EF-40	AU-50	AU-55	MS-60	MS-62 / PF-63	MS-63 / PF-64	MS-65 / PF-65
1914	95,250	1,734	62.0	91%	$1,300	$1,325	$1,350	$1,375	$1,500	$1,600	$3,500	$17,500
	Auctions: $7,638, MS-64, January 2015; $7,050, MS-64, January 2015; $2,585, MS-63, August 2015; $2,115, MS-62, July 2015											
1914, Sandblast Finish Proof	70	28	65.5							$27,500	$43,500	$75,000
	Auctions: $60,375, PF-66, June 2012											
1914-D	453,000	6,545	63.0	97%	$1,300	$1,325	$1,350	$1,375	$1,425	$1,450	$1,700	$2,750
	Auctions: $3,055, MS-65, August 2015; $2,140, MS-64, September 2015; $1,788, MS-64, January 2015; $1,645, MS-63, October 2015											
1914-S	1,498,000	21,243	63.1	99%	$1,300	$1,325	$1,350	$1,375	$1,425	$1,450	$1,700	$2,400
	Auctions: $4,583, MS-66, December 2015; $1,763, MS-64, September 2015; $1,410, MS-61, September 2015; $1,293, MS-60, June 2015											
1915	152,000	2,248	61.7	88%	$1,300	$1,325	$1,350	$1,375	$1,500	$1,650	$1,800	$20,000
	Auctions: $5,170, MS-64, January 2015; $3,055, MS-63, September 2015; $1,586, MS-61, July 2015; $1,410, AU-55, January 2015											
1915, Sandblast Finish Proof	50	41	64.8							$30,000	$47,500	$85,000
	Auctions: $63,250, PF-66, August 2011											
1915-S	567,500	15,756	63.3	99%	$1,300	$1,325	$1,350	$1,375	$1,425	$1,450	$1,700	$2,250
	Auctions: $4,700, MS-66, June 2015; $1,528, MS-64, October 2015; $1,528, MS-63, June 2015; $1,410, MS-62, September 2015											
1916-S	796,000	4,233	63.4	97%	$1,300	$1,325	$1,350	$1,375	$1,425	$1,450	$1,700	$3,000
	Auctions: $4,935, MS-66, January 2015; $2,233, MS-64, January 2015; $1,763, MS-63, September 2015; $1,469, AU-58, January 2015											
1920	228,250	6,833	62.1	99%	$1,300	$1,325	$1,350	$1,375	$1,425	$1,450	$1,700	$55,000
	Auctions: $5,170, MS-64, January 2015; $4,348, MS-64, August 2015; $2,233, MS-63, January 2015; $1,528, MS-62, September 2015											
1920-S	558,000	75	60.8	73%	$16,500	$20,000	$25,000	$32,500	$50,000	$70,000	$80,000	$275,000
	Auctions: $99,875, MS-64, January 2015; $70,500, MS-63, January 2015; $30,198, AU-58, August 2014; $30,550, AU-53, June 2015											
1921	528,500	71	59.1	56%	$25,000	$37,500	$55,000	$65,000	$100,000	$125,000	$175,000	$600,000
	Auctions: $164,500, MS-63, January 2014; $105,750, MS-62, August 2014; $94,000, MS-62, January 2015; $99,875, MS-61, October 2014											
1921, Proof † (e)	unknown	1	64.0		*(extremely rare)*							
	Auctions: $1,495,000, PF-64+, 2006; $203,500, PF, 2000											
1922	1,375,500	53,851	62.6	100%	$1,300	$1,325	$1,350	$1,375	$1,425	$1,450	$1,650	$4,000
	Auctions: $11,750, MS-66, August 2015; $3,290, MS-65, January 2015; $2,585, MS-64, August 2015; $1,351, MS-61, September 2015											
1922, DblDie Rev	(f)	4	63.3	100%			$2,000	$2,200	$2,500	$2,750	$3,500	
	Auctions: $2,115, MS-64, December 2013											
1922-S	2,658,000	922	62.6	97%	$1,850	$1,900	$2,000	$2,150	$2,650	$3,000	$5,000	$40,000
	Auctions: $9,988, MS-64, July 2015; $3,408, MS-63, January 2015; $3,290, MS-62, January 2015; $3,290, MS-61, July 2015											
1923	566,000	29,543	62.5	100%	$1,300	$1,325	$1,350	$1,375	$1,425	$1,450	$1,500	$4,000
	Auctions: $3,760, MS-65, January 2015; $2,350, MS-64, August 2015; $2,115, MS-64, June 2015; $1,528, MS-63, July 2015											
1923-D	1,702,250	5,926	64.3	100%	$1,300	$1,325	$1,350	$1,375	$1,425	$1,450	$1,500	$2,150
	Auctions: $11,750, MS-67, February 2015; $2,585, MS-66, October 2015; $2,350, MS-65, February 2015; $1,469, MS-62, March 2015											
1924	4,323,500	304,629	63.4	100%	$1,300	$1,325	$1,350	$1,375	$1,425	$1,450	$1,475	$2,000
	Auctions: $6,463, MS-67, January 2015; $3,760, MS-66, June 2015; $1,528, MS-62, October 2015; $1,293, MS-60, February 2015											
1924-D	3,049,500	453	61.9	88%	$2,200	$2,500	$2,650	$3,250	$4,500	$5,500	$8,500	$75,000
	Auctions: $12,925, MS-64, August 2015; $3,290, MS-60, July 2015; $1,998, AU-53, August 2015; $1,763, AU-50, January 2015											
1924-S	2,927,500	480	62.5	93%	$2,200	$2,500	$2,650	$3,250	$4,500	$5,500	$10,000	$65,000
	Auctions: $16,450, MS-64, January 2015; $9,106, MS-63, January 2015; $3,173, MS-60, January 2015; $2,233, MS-60, January 2015											

† Ranked in the *100 Greatest U.S. Coins* (fourth edition). **e.** Prior to the first public auction of a 1921 presentation-strike double eagle (a lightly cleaned specimen) in summer 2000, this variety was unknown to the numismatic community at large. That example reportedly was struck in 1921 to celebrate the birth of Joseph Baker, nephew of U.S. Mint director Raymond T. Baker. In 2006 a second example (this one with original, uncleaned surfaces) was discovered and subsequently auctioned. **f.** Included in 1922 mintage figure.

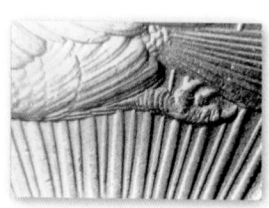

1925, Doubled-Die Reverse

1933 Saint-Gaudens Double Eagle

	Mintage	Cert	Avg	%MS	VF-20	EF-40	AU-50	AU-55	MS-60	MS-62 / PF-63	MS-63 / PF-64	MS-65 / PF-65
1925	2,831,750	52,811	63.2	100%	$1,300	$1,325	$1,350	$1,375	$1,425	$1,450	$1,475	$2,000
	Auctions: $4,230, MS-66, August 2015; $1,528, MS-64, June 2015; $1,293, MS-62, June 2015; $1,421, MS-60, October 2015											
1925, Doubled-Die Reverse (g)	(h)	19	63.9	100%			$2,000	$2,500	$2,750	$3,000	$3,500	
	Auctions: $3,055, MS-65, December 2013											
1925-D	2,938,500	317	62.6	98%	$2,600	$3,200	$3,750	$4,250	$5,500	$7,500	$11,000	$75,000
	Auctions: $64,625, MS-65, June 2015; $12,925, MS-64, August 2014; $7,638, MS-62, June 2015; $4,465, MS-61, August 2015											
1925-S	3,776,500	432	59.3	58%	$2,250	$3,000	$3,750	$5,250	$9,500	$12,000	$16,500	$100,000
	Auctions: $11,456, MS-63, August 2015; $8,225, MS-61, January 2015; $5,170, AU-58, January 2015; $5,405, AU-55, August 2015											
1926	816,750	23,294	63.6	100%	$1,300	$1,325	$1,350	$1,375	$1,425	$1,450	$1,475	$2,000
	Auctions: $1,821, MS-65, August 2015; $1,645, MS-64, June 2015; $1,528, MS-64, October 2015; $1,469, MS-63, March 2015											
1926-D	481,000	115	61.4	90%	$8,000	$12,000	$14,000	$15,500	$17,500	$30,000	$40,000	$150,000
	Auctions: $47,000, MS-64, March 2014; $22,325, MS-63, June 2015; $14,100, MS-62, September 2015; $11,163, AU-58, September 2015											
1926-S	2,041,500	682	63.1	97%	$2,150	$2,450	$2,750	$2,950	$3,500	$4,000	$5,500	$25,000
	Auctions: $18,277, MS-65, October 2015; $8,226, MS-64, June 2015; $5,170, MS-63, February 2015; $2,115, MS-60, January 2015											
1927	2,946,750	141,550	63.5	100%	$1,300	$1,325	$1,350	$1,375	$1,425	$1,450	$1,475	$2,000
	Auctions: $3,525, MS-66, September 2015; $2,585, MS-65, June 2015; $1,351, MS-61, September 2015; $1,410, MS-60, October 2015											
1927-D †	180,000	5	64.0	80%			$500,000	$550,000	$750,000	$850,000	$1,300,000	$1,600,000
	Auctions: $1,997,500, MS-66, January 2014											
1927-S	3,107,000	122	61.3	75%			$14,000	$16,000	$26,000	$37,500	$45,000	$110,000
	Auctions: $105,750, MS-65, March 2014; $25,850, MS-62, June 2015; $17,625, AU-55, January 2015; $10,575, AU-50, August 2014											
1928	8,816,000	48,552	63.3	100%	$1,300	$1,325	$1,350	$1,375	$1,425	$1,450	$1,475	$2,000
	Auctions: $18,800, MS-67, August 2015; $4,818, MS-66, September 2015; $1,998, MS-64, June 2015; $1,379, MS-60, August 2015											
1929	1,779,750	129	63.1	96%			$13,500	$15,500	$20,000	$30,000	$35,000	$75,000
	Auctions: $57,281, MS-65, August 2014; $37,600, MS-64, January 2015; $32,900, MS-63, September 2015; $15,863, MS-60, August 2014											
1930-S	74,000	21	64.1	100%			$42,000	$45,000	$65,000	$75,000	$90,000	$175,000
	Auctions: $176,382, MS-65, March 2014; $164,500, MS-65, September 2014; $164,500, MS-63, August 2014											
1931	2,938,250	33	64.3	100%			$22,500	$25,000	$35,000	$50,000	$65,000	$100,000
	Auctions: $76,375, MS-65, March 2014; $105,751, MS-65, September 2014; $64,625, MS-64, August 2014											
1931-D	106,500	41	63.3	98%			$22,500	$25,000	$35,000	$50,000	$65,000	$100,000
	Auctions: $129,250, MS-65, September 2014; $99,875, MS-64, January 2014; $64,625, MS-62, August 2014											
1932	1,101,750	71	63.9	100%			$22,500	$25,000	$35,000	$50,000	$65,000	$95,000
	Auctions: $108,688, MS-66, March 2014; $99,875, MS-66, August 2014; $94,000, MS-64, August 2014											
1933 † (i)	445,500	0	n/a					*(extremely rare)*				
	Auctions: $7,590,000, Gem BU, July 2002											

† Ranked in the *100 Greatest U.S. Coins* (fourth edition). **g.** Doubling is evident on the eagle's feathers, the rays, and IN GOD WE TRUST. **h.** Included in 1925 mintage figure. **i.** All but a few 1933 double eagles were to have been melted at the mint. Today 13 examples are known to have survived. Only one, said to have previously been in the collection of King Farouk of Egypt, has ever been sold at auction. The federal government has ruled that others are illegal to own privately.

Commemoratives
1892–1954
and 1982 to Date

AN OVERVIEW OF CLASSIC COMMEMORATIVES

Commemorative coins have been popular since the time of ancient Greece and Rome. In the beginning they recorded and honored important events and passed along the news of the day. Today commemorative coins, which are highly esteemed by collectors, have been issued by many modern nations—none of which has surpassed the United States when it comes to these impressive mementoes.

The unique position occupied by commemoratives in the United States coinage is largely due to the fact that, with few exceptions, all commemorative coins have real historical significance. The progress and advance of people in the New World are presented in an interesting and instructive manner on our commemorative coins. Such a record of history artistically presented on U.S. gold, silver, and other memorial issues appeals strongly to the collector who favors the romantic, storytelling side of numismatics. It is the historical features of our commemoratives, in fact, that create interest among many people who would otherwise have little interest in coins, and would not otherwise consider themselves collectors.

Concepts for commemorative issues are reviewed by two committees of Congress: the Committee on Banking, Housing, and Urban Affairs; and the Committee on Banking and Financial Services of the House; as well as by the Citizens Coinage Advisory Committee. Congress is guided to a great extent by the reports of these committees when considering bills authorizing commemorative coins.

These special coins are usually issued either to commemorate events or to help pay for monuments, programs, or celebrations that commemorate historical persons, places, or things. Pre-1982 commemorative coins were offered in most instances by a commission in charge of the event to be commemorated and sold at a premium over face value.

Commemorative coins are popularly collected either by major types or in sets with mintmark varieties. The pieces covered in this section of the *Guide Book of United States Coins, Deluxe Edition,* are those of the "classic" era of U.S. commemoratives, 1892 to 1954. All commemoratives are of the standard weight and fineness of their regular-issue 20th-century gold and silver counterparts, and all are legal tender.

A note about mintages and distribution numbers: Unless otherwise stated, the coinage figures given in each "Distribution" column represent the total released mintage: the total mintage (including assay coins), minus the quantity of unsold coins. In many cases, larger quantities were minted but not all were sold. Unsold coins usually were returned to the mint and melted, although sometimes quantities were placed in circulation at face value. A limited number of Proof strikings or presentation pieces were made for some of the classic commemorative issues.

A note about price performance: It has mostly been in recent decades that the general public has learned about commemorative coins. They have long been popular with coin collectors who enjoy the artistry and history associated with them, as well as the profit to be made from owning these rare pieces. Very few of them ever reached circulation because they were all originally sold above face value, and because they are all so rare. Most of the early issues were of the half dollar denomination, often made in quantities of fewer than 20,000 pieces. This is minuscule when compared to the regular half dollar coins that are made by the millions each year, and still rarely seen in circulation.

At the beginning of 1988, prices of classic commemoratives in MS-65 condition had risen so high that most collectors had to content themselves with pieces in lower grades. Investors continued to apply pressure to the high-quality pieces, driving prices even higher, while the collector community went after coins in grades from AU to MS-63. For several months the pressure from both influences caused prices to rise very rapidly (for all issues and grades) without even taking the price-adjustment breather that usually goes along with such activity.

By 1990, prices dropped to the point that several of the commemoratives began to look like bargains once again. Many of the MS-65 pieces held firm at price levels above the $3,000 mark, but others were still available at under $500 even for coins of similar mintage. Coins in MS–63 or 64 were priced at but a fraction of the MS-65 prices, which would seem to make them reasonably priced because the demand for these pieces is universal, and not keyed simply to grade, rarity, or speculator pressure.

Historically, the entire series of commemorative coins has frequently undergone a roller-coaster cycle of price adjustments. These cycles have usually been of short duration, lasting from months to years, with prices always recovering and eventually exceeding previous levels.

See page 1148 for discussion of modern commemorative coins of 1982 to date, page 1239 for pricing of government commemorative sets, and page 1502 for an alphabetical cross-reference list of all commemoratives.

WORLD'S COLUMBIAN EXPOSITION HALF DOLLAR (1892–1893)

Designers: *Charles E. Barber (obverse), George T. Morgan (reverse).* **Weight:** *12.50 grams.*
Composition: *.900 silver, .100 copper (net weight .3617 oz. pure silver).*
Diameter: *30.6 mm.* **Edge:** *Reeded.* **Mint:** *Philadelphia.*

The first U.S. commemorative coin was the Columbian half dollar sold at the World's Columbian Exposition—also known as the Chicago World's Fair—during 1893. The event celebrated the 400th anniversary of Christopher Columbus's arrival in the New World. A great many of the coins remained unsold and a substantial quantity was later released for circulation at face value or melted.

Designs. *Obverse:* Charles Barber's conception of Christopher Columbus, derived from a plaster model by Olin Levi Warner, taken from the explorer's portrait on an 1892 Spanish medal. The medal's portrait was inspired by a statue by Jeronimo Suñel, which itself was from an imagined likeness by Charles Legrand. *Reverse:* A sailing ship atop two globes representing the Old World and the New World. The vessel is from a plaster model by Olin Levi Warner, taken from a model made in Spain of Columbus's flagship, the *Santa Maria.*

Mintage and Melting Data. *Maximum authorized*—5,000,000 (both years combined). *Number minted*—1892: 950,000 (including an unknown number of assay coins; approximately 100 Proofs were struck as well); 1893: 4,052,105 (including 2,105 assay coins). *Number melted*—1893: 2,501,700. *Net distribution*—1892: 950,000; 1893: 1,550,405.

Original Cost and Issuer. Sale price $1. Issued by the Exposition.

Key to Collecting. Both dates are common in all grades through MS-65, and are often available in MS-66 and higher. The typical high-grade coin is lustrous and frosty; some have attractive, original light-blue or iridescent toning. Well-worn examples are very common, as the Treasury Department eventually released large quantities into circulation at face value. Striking usually is good. Some coins can be weak at the center—on the higher areas of the portrait and, on the reverse, in the details of the ship's sails. Most have contact marks from handling and distribution. High-grade 1892 coins typically are better struck than those of 1893. Approximately 100 brilliant Proofs were struck for each date; they vary widely in quality and eye appeal.

First Points of Wear. *Obverse:* The eyebrow, the cheek, and the hair at the back of the forehead. (The hair area sometimes is flatly struck.) *Reverse:* The top of the rear sail, and the right side of the Eastern Hemisphere.

	Distribution	Cert	Avg	%MS	AU-50	MS-60	MS-62	MS-63	MS-64 PF-63	MS-65 PF-64	MS-66 PF-65
1892	950,000	5,580	63.2	95%	$25	$30	$50	$85	$140	$375	$1,000
	Auctions: $11,163, MS-67, January 2015; $2,115, MS-66, January 2015; $423, MS-65, October 2015; $259, MS-64, January 2015										
1892, Proof	100	38	64.0						$5,750	$7,000	$13,000
	Auctions: $8,225, PF-65, November 2013										
1893	1,550,405	5,943	62.4	89%	$25	$30	$50	$85	$120	$375	$1,000
	Auctions: $8,229, MS-67, June 2015; $1,293, MS-66, July 2015; $400, MS-65, January 2015; $118, MS-64, August 2015										
1893, Proof	3–5	1	63.0								
	Auctions: $15,275, PF-66, January 2014; $5,830, PF-64, September 1993										

Note: Various repunched dates exist for both dates; these command little or no premium in the marketplace. For more information, see the *Cherrypickers' Guide to Rare Die Varieties*, sixth edition, volume II.

WORLD'S COLUMBIAN EXPOSITION ISABELLA QUARTER (1893)

Designer: *Charles E. Barber.* **Weight:** *6.25 grams.* **Composition:** *.900 silver, .100 copper (net weight .18084 oz. pure silver).* **Diameter:** *24.3 mm.* **Edge:** *Reeded.* **Mint:** *Philadelphia.*

In 1893 the Board of Lady Managers of the World's Columbian Exposition (also known as the Chicago World's Fair) petitioned for a souvenir quarter dollar. Authority was granted March 3, 1893, for the coin, which is known as the *Isabella quarter.*

Designs. *Obverse:* Crowned profile portrait of Spain's Queen Isabella, who sponsored Christopher Columbus's voyages to the New World. *Reverse:* A lady kneeling with a distaff and spindle, symbolic of the industry of American women.

Mintage and Melting Data. Authorized on March 3, 1893. *Maximum authorized*—40,000. *Number minted*—40,023 (including 23 assay coins). *Number melted*—15,809. *Net distribution*—24,214.

Original Cost and Issuer. Sale price $1. Issued by the Board of Lady Managers, World's Columbian Exposition.

Key to Collecting. Most examples in the marketplace are in Mint State, including many choice and gem pieces. Most are well struck and show full details, with richly lustrous fields. Connoisseurs avoid darkly toned, stained, and recolored coins. Many lower-grade Mint State examples have marks on Isabella's cheek and on the higher parts of the reverse design. The left obverse field often has marks made from contact with other coins during minting, storage, and distribution. The certification services have classified some coins with mirrored fields as Proofs, although no official records exist for the production of such.

First Points of Wear. *Obverse:* Isabella's cheekbone, and the center of the lower part of the crown. *Reverse:* The strand of wool at the lower-left thigh.

	Distribution	Cert	Avg	%MS	AU-50	MS-60	MS-62	MS-63	MS-64	MS-65	MS-66
									PF-63	PF-64	PF-65
1893	24,214	3,718	62.5	89%	$400	$475	$525	$600	$1,100	$2,400	$4,500
	Auctions: $17,625, MS-67, January 2015; $329, AU-58, February 2015; $306, EF-40, July 2015; $235, VF-30, February 2015										
1893, Proof	*100–105*	48	63.8						$4,750	$7,750	$13,000
	Auctions: $6,463, PF-64, July 2015; $5,640, PF-64, June 2015; $5,288, PF-64, October 2014										

LAFAYETTE DOLLAR (1900)

Designer: *Charles E. Barber.* **Weight:** *26.73 grams.* **Composition:** *.900 silver, .100 copper (net weight .7736 oz. pure silver).* **Diameter:** *38.1 mm.* **Edge:** *Reeded.* **Mint:** *Philadelphia.*

This issue—which was the first commemorative coin of one-dollar denomination, as well as the first authorized U.S. coin to bear a portrait of a U.S. president—commemorated the erection of a statue of Marquis de Lafayette in Paris in connection with the 1900 Paris Exposition (Exposition Universelle).

Designs. *Obverse:* Conjoined portraits of the marquis de Lafayette and George Washington. *Reverse:* Side view of the equestrian statue erected by the youth of the United States in honor of Lafayette. This view was based on an early model of the statue; the final version that was erected in Paris is slightly different.

Mintage and Melting Data. Authorized on March 3, 1899. *Maximum authorized*—50,000. *Number minted*—50,026 (including 26 assay coins). *Number melted*—14,000. *Net distribution*—36,026.

Original Cost and Issuer. Sale price $2. Issued by the Lafayette Memorial Commission through the American Trust & Savings Bank of Chicago.

Key to Collecting. Most surviving examples show evidence of circulation or other mishandling. The typical grade is AU. In Mint State, most are MS–60 to 63, and many are dull or unattractive, having been dipped or cleaned multiple times. Many have marks and dings. Properly graded MS–64 coins are very scarce, and MS–65 or higher gems are very rare, especially if with good eye appeal. Several die varieties exist and are collected by specialists.

Varieties. *Obverse varieties:* (1) Small point on the bust of Washington. The tip of Lafayette's bust is over the top of the L in DOLLAR. The AT in STATES is cut high. (2) The left foot of the final A in AMER-ICA is recut, and the A in STATES is high. The second S in STATES is repunched (this is diagnostic). (3) The AT in STATES is recut and the final S is low. The letter F in OF and in LAFAYETTE is broken from the lower tip of the crossbar and to the right base extension, and AMERICA is spaced A ME RI C A. The period after OF is close to the A of AMERICA. The tip of Lafayette's vest falls to the right of the top of the first L in DOLLAR. (4) The C in AMERICA is repunched at the inside top (this is diagnostic). The CA in AMERICA is spaced differently from the obverses previously described. *Reverse varieties:* (A) There are 14 long leaves and a long stem. The tip of the lowest leaf is over the 1 in 1900. (B) There are 14 shorter leaves and a short stem. The tip of the lowest leaf is over the space between the 1 and 9 in 1900. (C) There are 14 medium leaves and a short, bent stem. The tip of the lowest leaf is over the 9 in 1900. (D) There are 15 long leaves and a short, bent stem. The tip of the lowest leaf is over the 9 in 1900. (E) The tip of the lowest leaf is over the space to the left of the 1 in 1900.

First Points of Wear. *Obverse:* Washington's cheekbone, and Lafayette's lower hair curl. *Reverse:* The fringe of Lafayette's epaulet, and the horse's blinder and left rear leg bone.

	Distribution	Cert	Avg	%MS	AU-50	MS-60	MS-62	MS-63	MS-64	MS-65	MS-66
1900	36,026	2,559	62.0	88%	$600	$900	$1,250	$1,900	$3,000	$10,500	$18,000

Auctions: $73,438, MS-67, January 2015; $564, AU-58, January 2015; $376, EF-40, November 2015; $329, VF-30, July 2015

LOUISIANA PURCHASE EXPOSITION JEFFERSON GOLD DOLLAR (1903)

Designer: *Charles E. Barber (assisted by George T. Morgan).* **Weight:** *1.672 grams.*
Composition: *.900 gold, .100 copper (net weight .04837 oz. pure gold).*
Diameter: *15 mm.* **Edge:** *Reeded.* **Mint:** *Philadelphia.*

The first commemorative U.S. gold coins were authorized for the Louisiana Purchase Exposition, held in St. Louis in 1904. The event commemorated the 100th anniversary of the United States' purchase of the Louisiana Territory from France, an acquisition overseen by President Thomas Jefferson.

Designs. *Obverse:* Bewigged profile portrait of Thomas Jefferson, inspired by an early-1800s medal by John Reich, after Jean-Antoine Houdon's bust. *Reverse:* Inscription and branch.

Mintage and Melting Data. Authorized on June 28, 1902. *Maximum authorized*—250,000 (both types combined). *Number minted*—250,258 (125,000 of each type; including 258 assay coins comprising both types). *Number melted*—215,250 (total for both types; no account was kept of the portraits; 250 assay coins were melted). *Net distribution*—35,000 (estimated at 17,500 of each type).

Original Cost and Issuer. Sale price $3. Issued by the Louisiana Purchase Exposition Company, St. Louis, Missouri (sales through Farran Zerbe). Some were sold as mounted in spoons, brooches, and stick pins; 100 certified Proofs of each design were made, mounted in an opening in a rectangular piece of imprinted cardboard.

Key to Collecting. Market demand is strong, from collectors and investors alike, as most surviving examples are in choice or gem Mint State, with strong eye appeal. Most specimens are very lustrous and frosty. An occasional coin is prooflike. Avoid any with copper stains (from improper mixing of the gold/copper alloy). Proofs enter the market rarely and garner much publicity.

First Points of Wear. *Obverse:* Portrait's cheekbone and sideburn. *Reverse:* Date and denomination.

	Distribution	Cert	Avg	%MS	AU-50	MS-60	MS-62	MS-63	MS-64	MS-65	MS-66
									PF-63	PF-64	PF-65
1903	17,500	2,240	63.9	94%	$600	$700	$800	$900	$1,100	$1,500	$2,500
	Auctions: $5,993, MS-67, July 2015; $1,293, MS-64, July 2015; $470, AU-58, January 2015; $329, AU-50, January 2015										
1903, Proof (a)	100	31	64.9								
	Auctions: $37,375, PF-67UCam★, January 2012										

a. The first 100 Jefferson gold dollars were struck in brilliant Proof format. True Proofs exhibit deeply mirrored fields and are sharply struck. Many also have frosted devices, giving them a cameo appearance. "Although many of the coins seen today have been certified and lack original packaging, they were originally housed in cardboard holders certifying each coin as having been one of the first 100 impressions from the dies. The original holders are quite interesting, with the coin covered by a small piece of wax paper and a piece of string sealed by dark red wax. The coins are difficult to see behind the wax paper, and the author has seen holders with a circulation-strike example substituted for the Proof piece. Caution should be used when purchasing an example of this extreme rarity" (*Encyclopedia of U.S. Gold Coins, 1795–1933*, second edition).

Louisiana Purchase Exposition McKinley Gold Dollar (1903)

Designer: *Charles E. Barber (assisted by George T. Morgan).* **Weight:** *1.672 grams.*
Composition: *.900 gold, .100 copper (net weight .04837 oz. pure gold).*
Diameter: *15 mm.* **Edge:** *Reeded.* **Mint:** *Philadelphia.*

President William McKinley—who had been assassinated while in office two years before the Louisiana Purchase Exposition—was remembered on a gold dollar issued alongside the aforementioned coin featuring Thomas Jefferson. Like Jefferson, McKinley oversaw expansion of U.S. territory, with the acquisition of Puerto Rico, Guam, and the Philippines, as well as the annexation of Hawaii.

Designs. *Obverse:* Bareheaded profile portrait of William McKinley, derived from his presidential medal (designed, like this coin, by Charles Barber). *Reverse:* Inscriptions and branch.

Mintage and Melting Data. Authorized on June 28, 1902. *Maximum authorized—*250,000 (both types combined). *Number minted—*250,258 (125,000 of each type; including 258 assay coins comprising both types). *Number melted—*215,250 (total for both types; no account was kept of the portraits; 250 assay coins were melted). *Net distribution—*35,000 (estimated at 17,500 of each type).

Original Cost and Issuer. Sale price $3. Issued by the Louisiana Purchase Exposition Company, St. Louis, Missouri (sales through Farran Zerbe). Some were sold as mounted in spoons, brooches, and stick pins; 100 certified Proofs of each design were made, mounted in an opening in a rectangular piece of imprinted cardboard.

Key to Collecting. Market demand is strong, from collectors and investors alike, as most surviving examples are in choice or gem Mint State, with strong eye appeal. Most specimens are very lustrous and frosty. An occasional coin is prooflike. Avoid any with copper stains (from improper mixing of the gold/copper alloy). Proofs enter the market rarely and garner much publicity.

First Points of Wear. *Obverse:* Portrait's cheekbone and sideburn. *Reverse:* Date and denomination.

	Distribution	Cert	Avg	%MS	AU-50	MS-60	MS-62	MS-63	MS-64	MS-65	MS-66
									PF-63	PF-64	PF-65
1903	17,500	2,129	63.9	96%	$600	$700	$725	$750	$950	$1,500	$2,500
	Auctions: $8,813, MS-68, January 2015; $1,763, MS-66, January 2015; $517, MS-63, January 2015; $376, AU-58, August 2015										
1903, Proof (a)	100	27	64.3								
	Auctions: $14,950, PF-65Cam, April 2012										

a. Like the Jefferson issue, the first 100 McKinley gold dollars were struck as Proofs, and packaged as such. "Prooflike circulation strikes are quite common for the issue, and true Proofs can be distinguished by deeply mirrored surfaces and cameo devices. Certification is highly recommended" (*Encyclopedia of U.S. Gold Coins, 1795–1933*, second edition).

LEWIS AND CLARK EXPOSITION GOLD DOLLAR (1904–1905)

Designer: *Charles E. Barber.* **Weight:** *1.672 grams.* **Composition:** *.900 gold, .100 copper (net weight .04837 oz. pure gold).* **Diameter:** *15 mm.* **Edge:** *Reeded.* **Mint:** *Philadelphia.*

A souvenir issue of gold dollars was struck to mark the Lewis and Clark Centennial Exposition, held in Portland, Oregon, in 1905. The sale of these coins financed the erection of a bronze memorial of the Shoshone Indian guide Sacagawea, who assisted in the famous expedition.

Designs. *Obverse:* Bareheaded profile portrait of Meriwether Lewis. *Reverse:* Bareheaded profile portrait of William Clark. These portraits were inspired by works of Charles Willson Peale.

Mintage and Melting Data. Authorized on April 13, 1904. *Maximum authorized*—250,000 (both years combined). *Number minted*—1904: 25,028 (including 28 assay coins); 1905: 35,041 (including 41 assay coins). *Number melted*—1904: 15,003; 1905: 25,000. *Net distribution*—1904: 10,025; 1905: 10,041.

Original Cost and Issuer. Sales price $2 (some at $2.50); many were probably discounted further. Issued by the Lewis and Clark Centennial and American Pacific Exposition and Oriental Fair Company, Portland, Oregon (sales through Farran Zerbe and others).

Key to Collecting. Most surviving examples show evidence of handling. Some exhibit die problems (a rough raised area of irregularity at the denticles). Most range from AU–50 to 58, with an occasional MS–60 to 63. MS-64 coins are scarce, and MS-65 rare. Pristine examples are very rare. Most MS coins have areas of prooflike finish; some are deeply lustrous and frosty. The 1905-dated issue is noticeably scarcer than the 1904.

First Points of Wear. *Obverse:* Lewis's temple. *Reverse:* Clark's temple.

	Distribution	Cert	Avg	%MS	AU-50	MS-60	MS-62	MS-63	MS-64	MS-65	MS-66
									PF-63	PF-64	PF-65
1904	10,025	1,269	63.5	95%	$1,000	$1,100	$1,400	$1,800	$2,500	$6,000	$8,500
	Auctions: $15,275, MS-67, January 2015; $6,580, MS-66, January 2015; $734, MS-61, February 2015; $400, AU-50, May 2015										
1904, Proof	2–3	2	63.5								
	Auctions: No auction records available.										
1905	10,041	1,268	62.8	92%	$1,000	$1,400	$1,600	$2,000	$3,500	$11,000	$19,000
	Auctions: $35,250, MS-67, January 2015; $19,388, MS-66, January 2015; $1,880, MS-63, January 2015; $705, MS-60, June 2015										

PANAMA-PACIFIC EXPOSITION HALF DOLLAR (1915)

Designers: *Charles E. Barber (obverse), George T. Morgan (assisting Barber on reverse).*
Weight: *12.50 grams.* **Composition:** *.900 silver, .100 copper (net weight .3617 oz. pure silver).*
Diameter: *30.6 mm.* **Edge:** *Reeded.* **Mint:** *San Francisco.*

The Panama-Pacific Exposition held in San Francisco in 1915 celebrated the opening of the Panama Canal, as well as the revival of the Bay Area following the 1906 earthquake and fire. Five commemorative coins in four different denominations, including a half dollar, were issued in conjunction with the event.

Designs. *Obverse:* Columbia scattering flowers, alongside a child holding a cornucopia, representing the bounty of the American West; the Golden Gate in the background. *Reverse:* A spread-winged eagle perched on a shield, with branches of oak and olive.

Mintage and Melting Data. Authorized by the Act of January 16, 1915. *Maximum authorized*—200,000. *Number minted*—60,030 (including 30 assay coins). *Number melted*—32,896 (including the 30 assay coins; 29,876 were melted on September 7, 1916 and the balance on October 30, 1916). *Net distribution*—27,134.

Original Cost and Issuer. Sale price $1. Issued by the Coin and Medal Department (Farran Zerbe), Panama-Pacific International Exposition, San Francisco, California (combination offers included a set of four coins, including the buyer's choice of one $50, in a leather case, for $100; and a set of five coins in a copper frame for $200).

Key to Collecting. The half dollar does not have the typical deep mint frost associated with earlier silver issues. Most are satiny in appearance with the high parts in particular having a microscopically grainy finish. Many pieces have an inner line around the perimeter near the rim, a die characteristic. On the reverse of all known coins, the eagle's breast feathers are indistinct, which sometimes gives MS coins the appearance of having light wear. Most surviving coins grade from AU-50 to MS-63.

First Points of Wear. *Obverse:* Columbia's left shoulder. *Reverse:* The eagle's breast.

	Distribution	Cert	Avg	%MS	AU-50	MS-60	MS-62	MS-63	MS-64	MS-65	MS-66
1915-S	27,134	2,722	63.4	93%	$450	$525	$650	$850	$950	$1,500	$3,000

Auctions: $13,513, MS-67, August 2015; $646, MS-61, October 2015; $247, AU-50, July 2015; $165, VF-25, February 2015

PANAMA-PACIFIC EXPOSITION GOLD DOLLAR (1915)

Designer: *Charles Keck.* **Weight:** *1.672 grams.* **Composition:** *.900 gold, .100 copper (net weight .04837 oz. pure gold).* **Diameter:** *15 mm.* **Edge:** *Reeded.* **Mint:** *San Francisco.*

Coin dealer and entrepreneur Farran Zerbe conceived of a program of five different commemorative coins across four denominations (including the gold dollar) in conjunction with the Panama-Pacific Exposition in 1915. The event was held in what eventually constituted a miniature city, whose sculptures and impressive architecture were intended to remind one of Rome or some other distant and romantic place, but which at night was more apt to resemble Coney Island.

Designs. *Obverse:* Capped profile portrait of a Panama Canal laborer. *Reverse:* Two dolphins, symbolizing the Atlantic and Pacific oceans, and legends.

Mintage and Melting Data. Authorized by the Act of January 16, 1915. *Maximum authorized*—25,000. *Number minted*—25,034 (including 34 assay coins). *Number melted*—10,034 (including the 34 assay coins; melted at the San Francisco Mint on October 30, 1916). *Net distribution*—15,000.

Original Cost and Issuer. Sale price $2 (and a few at $2.25). Issued by the Coin and Medal Department (Farran Zerbe), Panama-Pacific International Exposition, San Francisco, California (combination offers included, among others, a set of four coins, with the buyer's choice of one fifty-dollar coin, in a leather case, for $100; and a set of five coins in a copper frame for $200).

Key to Collecting. Most examples are in Mint State. Many exhibit deep mint frost. Friction is common, especially on the obverse.

First Points of Wear. *Obverse:* The peak of the laborer's cap. *Reverse:* The heads of the dolphins, and the denomination.

	Distribution	Cert	Avg	%MS	AU-50	MS-60	MS-62	MS-63	MS-64	MS-65	MS-66
1915-S	15,000	3,741	63.6	94%	$550	$650	$700	$850	$950	$1,500	$1,900

Auctions: $3,538, MS-67, January 2015; $1,733, MS-64, August 2015; $441, AU-55, April 2015; $329, EF-40, April 2015

PANAMA-PACIFIC EXPOSITION QUARTER EAGLE (1915)

Designer: *Charles E. Barber (obverse), George T. Morgan (reverse).* **Weight:** *4.18 grams.* **Composition:** *.900 gold, .100 copper (net weight .12094 oz. pure gold).* **Diameter:** *18 mm.* **Edge:** *Reeded.* **Mint:** *San Francisco.*

The 1915 Panama-Pacific International Exposition—a name chosen to reflect the recently completed Panama Canal, as well as Pacific Ocean commerce—was planned to be the ultimate world's fair. Foreign countries, domestic manufacturers, artists, concessionaires, and others were invited to the 10-month event, which drew an estimated 19 million visitors. This quarter eagle was among the five coins issued to commemorate the celebration.

Designs. *Obverse:* Columbia seated on a hippocampus, holding a caduceus, symbolic of Medicine's triumph over yellow fever in Panama during the canal's construction. *Reverse:* An eagle, standing on a plaque inscribed E PLURIBUS UNUM, with raised wings.

Mintage and Melting Data. Authorized by the Act of January 16, 1915. *Maximum authorized*—10,000. *Number minted*—10,017 (including 17 assay coins). *Number melted*—3,268 (including the 17 assay coins; melted at the San Francisco Mint on October 30, 1916). *Net distribution*—6,749.

Original Cost and Issuer. Sale price $4. Issued by the Coin and Medal Department (Farran Zerbe), Panama-Pacific International Exposition, San Francisco, California (combination offers included, among others, a set of four coins, with the buyer's choice of one fifty-dollar coin, in a leather case, for $100; and a set of five coins in a copper frame for $200).

Key to Collecting. Most grade from AU-55 to MS-63. MS-64 coins are elusive, and MS-65 rare. Most MS pieces show a satiny, sometimes grainy luster.

First Points of Wear. *Obverse:* Columbia's head, breast, and knee. *Reverse:* The torch band and the eagle's leg.

	Distribution	Cert	Avg	%MS	AU-50	MS-60	MS-62	MS-63	MS-64 PF-63	MS-65 PF-64	MS-66 PF-65
1915-S	6,749	2,023	64.5	97%	$1,750	$2,250	$3,000	$4,500	$5,500	$6,000	$7,000
	Auctions: $12,925, MS-67, January 2015; $6,463, MS-66, February 2015; $5,405, MS-64, January 2015; $2,233, AU-50, August 2015										
1915-S, Proof (a)	*unique*	0	n/a								
	Auctions: No auction records available.										

a. This unique Satin Finish Proof resides in the National Numismatic Collection of the Smithsonian Institution.

PANAMA-PACIFIC EXPOSITION FIFTY-DOLLAR GOLD PIECE (1915)

Designer: *Robert Aitken.* **Weight:** *83.59 grams.* **Composition:** *.900 gold, .100 copper (net weight 2.4186 oz. pure gold).* **Diameter:** *43 mm (round), 44.9 mm (octagonal, measured point to point).* **Edge:** *Reeded.* **Mint:** *San Francisco.*

Both round and octagonal $50 gold pieces were struck as part of the series commemorating the Panama-Pacific International Exposition in 1915. These coins, along with the half dollars in the same series, were the first U.S. commemoratives to feature the motto IN GOD WE TRUST.

Designs. Round: *Obverse:* Helmeted profile portrait of Minerva, with shield and armor. *Reverse:* An owl, symbolic of wisdom, vigilant on a pine branch, with pinecones. Octagonal: *Obverse and reverse:* Same as the round coin, but with dolphins in the eight angled exergues on obverse and reverse.

Mintage and Melting Data. Authorized by the Act of January 16, 1915. Round: *Maximum authorized*—Round: 1,500; Octagonal:

1,500. *Number minted* (including 10 assay coins)—Round: 1,510 (including 10 assay coins); Octagonal: 1,509 (including 9 assay coins). *Number melted*—Round: 1,027; Octagonal: 864. *Net distribution*—Round: 483; Octagonal: 645.

Original Cost and Issuer. Round and octagonal: Sale price, each, $100. Coin and Medal Department (Farran Zerbe), Panama-Pacific International Exposition, San Francisco, California. Combination offers included a set of four coins (buyer's choice of one fifty-dollar coin) in a leather case for $100, and a set of five coins in a copper frame for $200, this issued after the Exposition closed.

Key to Collecting. Because such small quantities were issued, these hefty gold commemoratives today are rare in any grade. The round coins trade hands slightly less frequently than the octagonal. Typical grades are MS–63 or 64 for coins kept in an original box or frame over the years, or AU-58 to MS-63 if removed. Coins that have been cleaned or lightly polished exhibit a multitude of tiny hairlines; such pieces are avoided by connoisseurs.

First Points of Wear. *Obverse:* Minerva's cheek. *Reverse:* The owl's upper breast.

	Distribution	Cert	Avg	%MS	AU-50	MS-60	MS-62	MS-63	MS-64	MS-65	MS-66
1915-S, Round	483	420	63.4	95%	$55,000	$75,000	$80,000	$90,000	$100,000	$175,000	$225,000
	Auctions: $176,250, MS-65, August 2015; $79,313, MS-63, January 2015; $64,625, MS-61, July 2015; $51,700, MS-60, January 2015										
1915-S, Octagonal	645	456	63.1	95%	$55,000	$70,000	$77,500	$90,000	$110,000	$165,000	$235,000
	Auctions: $258,500, MS-67, January 2015; $123,375, MS-65, August 2015; $70,500, MS-62, September 2015; $55,225, AU-55, September 2015										

MCKINLEY MEMORIAL GOLD DOLLAR (1916–1917)

Designers: *Charles E. Barber (obverse) and George T. Morgan (reverse).* **Weight:** *1.672 grams.*
Composition: *.900 gold, .100 copper (net weight .04837 oz. pure gold).*
Diameter: *15 mm.* **Edge:** *Reeded.* **Mint:** *Philadelphia.*

The sale of the William McKinley dollars aided in paying for a memorial building at Niles, Ohio, the martyred president's birthplace.

Designs. *Obverse:* Bareheaded profile portrait of William McKinley. *Reverse:* Artist's rendition of the proposed McKinley Birthplace Memorial intended to be erected in Niles, Ohio.

Mintage and Melting Data. Authorized on February 23, 1916. *Maximum authorized*—100,000 (both years combined). *Number minted*—1916: 20,026 (including 26 assay coins); 1917: 10,014 (including 14 assay coins). *Number melted*—1916: 5,000 (estimated); 1917: 5,000 (estimated). *Net distribution*—1916: 15,000 (estimated); 1917: 5,000 (estimated).

Original Cost and Issuer. Sale price $3. Issued by the National McKinley Birthplace Memorial Association, Youngstown, Ohio.

Key to Collecting. The obverse of the 1916 issue often displays friction while its reverse can appear as choice Mint State. Prooflike fields are common. Some are highly prooflike on both sides. The 1917 issue is much harder to find than the 1916; examples usually are in higher grades with rich luster on both sides, and often exhibit a pale yellow color.

First Points of Wear. *Obverse:* McKinley's temple area, and the hair above his ear. *Reverse:* The pillar above the second 1 in the date; and the bottom of the flagpole.

	Distribution	Cert	Avg	%MS	AU-50	MS-60	MS-62	MS-63	MS-64	MS-65	MS-66
									PF-63	PF-64	PF-65
1916	*15,000*	2,582	63.7	96%	$550	$600	$625	$650	$850	$1,400	$1,800
	Auctions: $4,465, MS-67, August 2015; $1,528, MS-66, July 2015; $376, MS-61, January 2015; $447, AU-58, October 2015										
1916, Proof	*3–6*	1	63								
	Auctions: $37,375, PF-63, January 2012										
1917	*5,000*	1,499	63.7	95%	$600	$700	$750	$900	$1,100	$1,700	$2,250
	Auctions: $7,344, MS-67, January 2015; $2,585, MS-66, July 2015; $541, MS-62, October 2015; $306, MS-60, May 2015										

ILLINOIS CENTENNIAL HALF DOLLAR (1918)

Designers: *George T. Morgan (obverse) and John R. Sinnock (reverse).* **Weight:** *12.50 grams.*
Composition: *.900 silver, .100 copper (net weight .3617 oz. pure silver).*
Diameter: *30.6 mm.* **Edge:** *Reeded.* **Mint:** *Philadelphia.*

This coin was authorized to commemorate the 100th anniversary of the admission of Illinois into the Union, and was the first souvenir piece for such an event. The head of Abraham Lincoln on the obverse was based on that of a statue of the celebrated president by Andrew O'Connor in Springfield, Illinois.

Designs. *Obverse:* Bareheaded, beardless profile portrait of Abraham Lincoln, facing right.
Reverse: A fierce eagle atop a crag, clutching a shield and carrying a banner; from the Illinois state seal.

Mintage Data. Authorized on June 1, 1918. *Maximum authorized*—100,000. *Number minted*—100,000 (plus 58 assay coins).

Original Cost and Issuer. Sale price $1. Issued by the Illinois Centennial Commission, through various outlets.

Key to Collecting. Examples were struck with deep, frosty finishes, giving Mint State pieces an unusually attractive appearance. The obverse typically shows contact marks or friction on Lincoln's cheek and on other high parts of his portrait. The field typically shows contact marks. The reverse usually grades from one to three points higher than the obverse, due to the protective nature of its complicated design. Most examples are lustrous and frosty, although a few are seen with partially prooflike fields.

First Points of Wear. *Obverse:* The hair above Lincoln's ear. *Reverse:* The eagle's breast. (Note that the breast was sometimes flatly struck; look for differences in texture or color of the metal.)

	Distribution	Cert	Avg	%MS	AU-50	MS-60	MS-62	MS-63	MS-64	MS-65	MS-66
1918	100,058	4,277	63.9	98%	$140	$150	$160	$175	$225	$325	$850
	Auctions: $5,640, MS-67, January 2015; $823, MS-66, January 2015; $212, MS-64, February 2015; $84, AU-55, February 2015										

MAINE CENTENNIAL HALF DOLLAR (1920)

Designer: *Anthony de Francisci.* **Weight:** *12.50 grams.* **Composition:** *.900 silver, .100 copper (net weight .3617 oz. pure silver).* **Diameter:** *30.6 mm.* **Edge:** *Reeded.* **Mint:** *Philadelphia.*

Congress authorized the Maine Centennial half dollar on May 10, 1920, to be sold at the centennial celebration at Portland. They were received too late for this event and were sold by the state treasurer for many years.

Designs. *Obverse:* Arms of the state of Maine, with the Latin word DIRIGO ("I Direct"). *Reverse:* The centennial inscription enclosed by a wreath.

Mintage Data. Authorized on May 10, 1920. *Maximum authorized—*100,000. *Number minted—*50,028 (including 28 assay coins).

Original Cost and Issuer. Sale price $1. Issued by the Maine Centennial Commission.

Key to Collecting. Relatively few Maine half dollars were sold to the hobby community; the majority of coins distributed saw careless handling by the general public. Most examples show friction or handling marks on the center of the shield on the obverse. The fields were not completely finished in the dies and always show tiny raised lines or die-finishing marks; at first glance these may appear to be hairlines or scratches, but they have no effect on the grade. Appealing examples in higher Mint State levels are much more elusive than the high mintage might suggest.

First Points of Wear. *Obverse:* The left hand of the scythe holder; the right hand of the anchor holder. (Note that the moose and the pine tree are weakly struck.) *Reverse:* The bow knot.

	Distribution	Cert	Avg	%MS	AU-50	MS-60	MS-62	MS-63	MS-64	MS-65	MS-66
1920	50,028	2,917	64.2	98%	$130	$150	$155	$160	$200	$350	$550
	Auctions: $10,575, MS-68, January 2015; $3,290, MS-67, September 2015; $200, MS-64, January 2015; $74, EF-40, September 2015										

PILGRIM TERCENTENARY HALF DOLLAR (1920–1921)

Designer: *Cyrus E. Dallin.* **Weight:** *12.50 grams.* **Composition:** *.900 silver, .100 copper (net weight .3617 oz. pure silver).* **Diameter:** *30.6 mm.* **Edge:** *Reeded.* **Mint:** *Philadelphia.*

To commemorate the landing of the Pilgrims at Plymouth, Massachusetts, in 1620, Congress authorized a special half dollar on May 12, 1920. The first issue had no date on the obverse. The coins struck in 1921 show that date in addition to 1620–1920.

Designs. *Obverse:* Artist's conception of a partial standing portrait of Governor William Bradford holding a book. *Reverse:* The *May-flower* in full sail.

Mintage and Melting Data. Authorized on May 12, 1920. *Maximum authorized*—300,000 (both years combined). *Number minted*—1920: 200,112 (including 112 assay coins); 1921: 100,053 (including 53 assay coins). *Number melted*—1920: 48,000; 1921: 80,000. *Net distribution*—1920: 152,112; 1921: 20,053.

Original Cost and Issuer. Sale price $1. Issued by the Pilgrim Tercentenary Commission.

Key to Collecting. The 1920 issue is common, and the 1921 slightly scarce. Coins grading MS-64 and higher usually have excellent eye appeal, though many exceptions exist. Most coins have scattered contact marks, particularly on the obverse. Nearly all 1921 coins are this way. Many coins (particularly coins which are early impressions from the dies) show tiny raised lines in the obverse field, representing die finish marks; these are not to be confused with hairlines or other evidences of friction (which are recessed).

First Points of Wear. *Obverse:* Cheekbone, hair over ear, and the high areas of Governor Bradford's hat. *Reverse:* The ship's rigging and stern, the crow's nest, and the rim.

	Distribution	Cert	Avg	%MS	AU-50	MS-60	MS-62	MS-63	MS-64	MS-65	MS-66
1920	152,112	4,716	63.8	97%	$85	$100	$105	$110	$115	$225	$550
	Auctions: $6,756, MS-67, September 2015; $543, MS-66, October 2015; $153, MS-64, September 2015; $80, MS-62, September 2015										
1921, With Added Date	20,053	2,100	64.3	99%	$170	$190	$195	$200	$225	$300	$900
	Auctions: $5,876, MS-67, January 2015; $1,880, MS-66, July 2015; $447, MS-64, February 2015; $141, AU-58, March 2015										

MISSOURI CENTENNIAL HALF DOLLAR (1921)

Designer: *Robert Aitken.* **Weight:** *12.50 grams.* **Composition:** *.900 silver, .100 copper (net weight .3617 oz. pure silver).* **Diameter:** *30.6 mm.* **Edge:** *Reeded.* **Mint:** *Philadelphia.*

The 100th anniversary of the admission of Missouri to the Union was celebrated in the city of Sedalia during August 1921. To mark the occasion, Congress authorized the coinage of a fifty-cent piece.

Designs. *Obverse:* Coonskin-capped profile portrait of a frontiersman. One variety has 2★4 in the field; the other is plain. *Reverse:* Standing figures of a frontiersman and an Indian looking westward, against a starry field; SEDALIA (the location of the Missouri centennial exposition) incused below.

Mintage and Melting Data. Authorized on March 4, 1921. *Maximum authorized*—250,000 (both varieties combined). *Number minted*—50,028 (both varieties combined; including 28 assay coins). *Number melted*—29,600. *Net distribution*—20,428 (estimated; 9,400 for 1921 2★4 and 11,400 for 1921 Plain).

Original Cost and Issuer. Sale price $1. Issued by the Missouri Centennial Committee, through the Sedalia Trust Company.

Key to Collecting. Most grade from AU-55 to MS-63; have friction and contact marks on the higher areas of the design; and are lightly struck at the center of the portrait of Boone on the obverse, and at the torsos of the two figures on the reverse. MS-65 and higher coins with sharply struck centers are rarities.

First Points of Wear. *Obverse:* The hair in back of the ear. *Reverse:* The frontiersman's arm and shoulder.

	Distribution	Cert	Avg	%MS	AU-50	MS-60	MS-62	MS-63	MS-64	MS-65	MS-66
									PF-63	PF-64	PF-65
1921, "2★4" in Field	9,400	1,640	63.7	98%	$650	$725	$850	$1,100	$1,200	$2,100	$8,000
	Auctions: $6,169, MS-66, January 2015; $2,291, MS-65, August 2015; $705, MS-62, September 2015; $646, AU-58, September 2015										
1921, "2★4" in Field, Matte Proof	*1–2*	0	n/a								
	Auctions: No auction records available.										
1921, Plain	11,400	1,982	63.3	95%	$425	$550	$650	$850	$1,000	$2,400	$7,500
	Auctions: $5,640, MS-66, September 2015; $2,468, MS-65, January 2015; $353, AU-58, January 2015; $259, AU-50, November 2015										

ALABAMA CENTENNIAL HALF DOLLAR (1921)

Designer: *Laura Gardin Fraser.* **Weight:** *12.50 grams.* **Composition:** *.900 silver, .100 copper (net weight .3617 oz. pure silver).* **Diameter:** *30.6 mm.* **Edge:** *Reeded.* **Mint:** *Philadelphia.*

The Alabama half dollars were authorized in 1920 and struck until 1921 for the statehood centennial, which was celebrated in 1919. The coins were offered first during President Warren Harding's visit to Birmingham, October 26, 1921. T.E. Kilby's likeness on the obverse was first instance of a living person's portrait on a United States coin.

Designs. *Obverse:* Conjoined bareheaded profile portraits of William Wyatt Bibb, the first governor of Alabama, and Thomas Kilby, governor at the time of the centennial. *Reverse:* A dynamic eagle perched on a shield, clutching arrows and holding a banner; from the Alabama state seal.

Mintage and Melting Data. Authorized on May 10, 1920. *Maximum authorized*—100,000. *Number minted*—70,044 (including 44 assay coins). *Number melted*—5,000. *Net distribution*—2X2: estimated as 30,000; Plain: estimated as 35,000.

Original Cost and Issuer. Sale price $1. Issued by the Alabama Centennial Commission.

Key to Collecting. Most of these coins were sold to citizens of Alabama, and of those, few were acquired by numismatists. Many are in circulated grades (typical being EF or AU), with most surviving pieces grading MS-63 or less. Those grading MS-65 or finer are rare. Nearly all show friction or contact marks on Governor Kilby's cheek on the obverse, and many are flatly struck on the eagle's left leg and talons on the reverse. These coins were produced carelessly, and many lack sharpness and luster (sharply struck examples are very rare). Nicks and marks from the original planchets are often found on the areas of light striking. The eagle's upper leg is often lightly struck, particularly on the plain variety. The 2X2 coins usually are better struck than the plain variety.

First Points of Wear. *Obverse:* Kirby's forehead and the area to the left of his earlobe. *Reverse:* The eagle's lower neck and the top of its wings.

	Distribution	Cert	Avg	%MS	AU-50	MS-60	MS-62	MS-63	MS-64	MS-65	MS-66
1921, "2X2" in Field	6,006	1,694	63.5	95%	$325	$350	$400	$450	$600	$1,400	$3,000
	Auctions: $11,750, MS-67, August 2015; $3,525, MS-66, July 2015; $411, MS-63, September 2015; $188, AU-50, February 2015										
1921, Plain	16,014	2,010	62.8	90%	$200	$225	$300	$425	$500	$1,300	$2,500
	Auctions: $19,975, MS-67, January 2015; $5,405, MS-66, January 2015; $235, MS-62, March 2015; $141, AU-58, August 2015										

GRANT MEMORIAL HALF DOLLAR (1922)

Designer: *Laura Gardin Fraser.* **Weight:** *12.50 grams.* **Composition:** *.900 silver, .100 copper (net weight .3617 oz. pure silver).* **Diameter:** *30.6 mm.* **Edge:** *Reeded.* **Mint:** *Philadelphia.*

This half dollar (along with the Grant Memorial gold dollar) was struck during 1922 as a centenary souvenir of Ulysses S. Grant's birth. The Ulysses S. Grant Centenary Memorial Association originally planned celebrations in Clermont County, Ohio; the construction of community buildings in Georgetown and Bethel; and the laying of a five-mile highway from New Richmond to Point Pleasant in addition to the coins, but the buildings and highway never came to fruition.

Designs. *Obverse:* Bareheaded profile portrait of Ulysses S. Grant in a military coat. One variety has a star above GRANT. *Reverse:* View of the house Grant was born in (Point Pleasant, Ohio), amidst a wooded setting.

Mintage Data. Authorized on February 2, 1922. *Number minted*—With Star: 5,016 (including 16 assay coins); No Star: 5,000. *Net distribution*—10,016 (both varieties combined).

Original Cost and Issuer. Sale price $3 for either variety. Issued by the U.S. Grant Centenary Memorial Commission (mail orders were serviced by Hugh L. Nichols, chairman, Batavia, Ohio).

Key to Collecting. Almost all known specimens are MS–63 to 65 or better. MS–66 and 67 examples are easy to find. Some lower-grade coins show friction on Grant's cheek and hair. Some specimens have dull surfaces; these are avoided by connoisseurs.

First Points of Wear. *Obverse:* Grant's cheekbone and hair. *Reverse:* The leaves of the tree under the U in TRUST.

	Distribution	Cert	Avg	%MS	AU-50	MS-60	MS-62	MS-63	MS-64	MS-65	MS-66
1922, Star in Obverse Field	4,256	1,316	63.6	97%	$950	$1,300	$1,500	$1,800	$2,750	$6,500	$12,000
	Auctions: $37,600, MS-67, January 2015; $12,926, MS-66, July 2015; $764, AU-53, August 2015; $646, EF-40, August 2015										
1922, No Star in Obverse Field	67,405	3,582	63.7	97%	$120	$125	$135	$150	$250	$600	$1,000
	Auctions: $3,760, MS-67, September 2015; $2,115, MS-66, August 2015; $165, MS-61, February 2015; $60, AU-58, February 2015										

GRANT MEMORIAL GOLD DOLLAR (1922)

Designer: *Laura Gardin Fraser.* **Weight:** *1.672 grams.* **Composition:** *.900 gold, .100 copper (net weight .04837 oz. pure gold).* **Diameter:** *15 mm.* **Edge:** *Reeded.* **Mint:** *Philadelphia.*

The Ulysses S. Grant Centenary Memorial Association, incorporated in 1921, marked the 100th birth anniversary of the Civil War general and U.S. president with this gold dollar (as well as a commemorative half dollar).

Designs. *Obverse:* Bareheaded profile portrait of Ulysses S. Grant in a military coat. One variety has a star above GRANT. *Reverse:* View of the house Grant was born in (Point Pleasant, Ohio), amidst a wooded setting.

Mintage Data. Authorized on February 2, 1922. *Number minted*—With Star: 5,016 (including 16 assay coins); No Star: 5,000. *Net distribution*—10,016 (both varieties combined).

Original Cost and Issuer. Sale price $3 for either type. Issued by the U.S. Grant Centenary Memorial Commission (mail orders were serviced by Hugh L. Nichols, chairman, Batavia, Ohio).

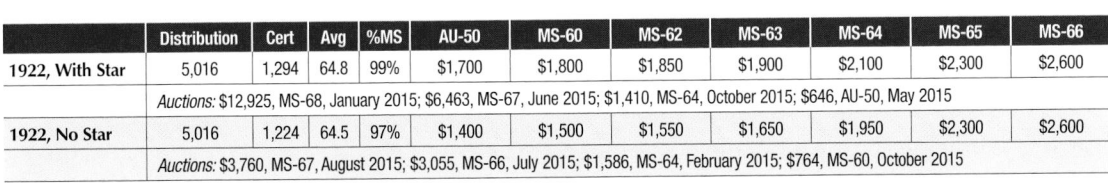

Key to Collecting. Almost all known specimens are MS–63 to 65 or better. MS–66 and 67 examples are easy to find. Some lower-grade coins show friction on Grant's cheek and hair. Some specimens have dull surfaces; these are avoided by connoisseurs.

First Points of Wear. *Obverse:* Grant's cheekbone and hair. *Reverse:* The leaves of the tree under the U in TRUST.

	Distribution	Cert	Avg	%MS	AU-50	MS-60	MS-62	MS-63	MS-64	MS-65	MS-66
1922, With Star	5,016	1,294	64.8	99%	$1,700	$1,800	$1,850	$1,900	$2,100	$2,300	$2,600
	Auctions: $12,925, MS-68, January 2015; $6,463, MS-67, June 2015; $1,410, MS-64, October 2015; $646, AU-50, May 2015										
1922, No Star	5,016	1,224	64.5	97%	$1,400	$1,500	$1,550	$1,650	$1,950	$2,300	$2,600
	Auctions: $3,760, MS-67, August 2015; $3,055, MS-66, July 2015; $1,586, MS-64, February 2015; $764, MS-60, October 2015										

MONROE DOCTRINE CENTENNIAL HALF DOLLAR (1923)

Designer: *Chester Beach.* **Weight:** *12.50 grams.* **Composition:** *.900 silver, .100 copper (net weight .3617 oz. pure silver).* **Diameter:** *30.6 mm.* **Edge:** *Reeded.* **Mint:** *San Francisco.*

The California film industry promoted this issue in conjunction with a motion-picture exposition held in June 1923. The coin purportedly commemorated the 100th anniversary of the Monroe Doctrine, which warned that European countries that interfered with countries in the Western Hemisphere or established new colonies there would be met with disapproval or worse from the U.S. government.

Designs. *Obverse:* Conjoined bareheaded profile portraits of presidents James Monroe and John Quincy Adams. *Reverse:* Stylized depiction of the continents of North and South America as female figures in the outlines of the two land masses.

Mintage Data. Authorized on January 24, 1923. *Maximum authorized*—300,000. *Number minted*—274,077 (including 77 assay coins). *Net distribution*—274,077.

Original Cost and Issuer. Sale price $1. Issued by the Los Angeles Clearing House, representing backers of the First Annual American Historical Revue and Motion Picture Industry Exposition.

Key to Collecting. Most examples show friction or wear. MS coins are common. Evaluating the numerical grade of MS–60 to 63 coins is difficult because of the design's weak definition. Low-magnification inspection usually shows nicks and graininess at the highest point of the obverse center; these flaws are from the original planchets. Many examples of this coin have been doctored and artificially toned in attempts to earn higher grades upon certification; these are avoided by connoisseurs.

First Points of Wear. *Obverse:* Adams's cheekbone. *Reverse:* The upper figure, underneath the CT in DOCTRINE.

	Distribution	Cert	Avg	%MS	AU-50	MS-60	MS-62	MS-63	MS-64	MS-65	MS-66
1923-S	274,077	3,646	63.1	96%	$65	$80	$100	$130	$220	$1,250	$3,000
	Auctions: $11,163, MS-67, August 2015; $5,640, MS-66, January 2015; $1,645, MS-65, January 2015; $84, MS-62, July 2015										

HUGUENOT-WALLOON TERCENTENARY HALF DOLLAR (1924)

Designer: *George T. Morgan (with model modifications by James Earle Fraser).*
Weight: *12.50 grams.* **Composition:** *.900 silver, .100 copper (net weight .3617 oz. pure silver).*
Diameter: *30.6 mm.* **Edge:** *Reeded.* **Mint:** *Philadelphia.*

Settling of the Huguenots and Walloons in the New World was the occasion commemorated by this issue. New Netherland, now New York, was founded in 1624 by this group of Dutch colonists. Interestingly, the persons represented on the obverse were not directly concerned with the occasion; both Admiral Gaspard de Coligny and Prince William the Silent were dead long before the settlement.

Designs. *Obverse:* Hat-clad profile portraits representing Admiral Gaspard de Coligny and Prince William the Silent, first stadtholder of the Netherlands. *Reverse:* The ship *Nieuw Nederland* in full sail.

Mintage Data. Authorized on February 26, 1923. *Maximum authorized—300,000. Number minted—142,080 (including 80 assay coins). Net distribution—142,080.*

Original Cost and Issuer. Sale price $1. Issued by the Huguenot-Walloon New Netherland Commission, Inc., and designated outlets.

Key to Collecting. This coin is readily available on the market, with most examples in MS–60 to 63. Those grading MS–64 and 65 are also found quite often; MS-66 coins are scarcer. Relatively few worn pieces exist. Friction and contact marks are sometimes seen on the cheek of Admiral Coligny on the obverse, and on the masts and ship's rigging on the reverse. Many coins have been cleaned or repeatedly dipped. Connoisseurs avoid deeply toned or stained coins, even those certified with high numerical grades. MS coins usually have satiny (rather than deeply lustrous or frosty) surfaces, and may have a gray appearance. High in the reverse field of most coins is a "bright" spot interrupting the luster, from a touch of polish in the die.

First Points of Wear. *Obverse:* Coligny's cheekbone. *Reverse:* The rim near the F in FOUNDING and over the RY in TERCENTENARY; the lower part of the highest sail; the center of the ship's stern.

	Distribution	Cert	Avg	%MS	AU-50	MS-60	MS-62	MS-63	MS-64	MS-65	MS-66
1924	142,080	3,300	64.2	99%	$140	$145	$155	$170	$190	$250	$650
Auctions: $15,275, MS-68, August 2015; $6,756, MS-67, September 2015; $100, MS-60, January 2015; $89, AU-58, January 2015											

LEXINGTON-CONCORD SESQUICENTENNIAL HALF DOLLAR (1925)

Designer: *Chester Beach.* **Weight:** *12.50 grams.* **Composition:** *.900 silver, .100 copper (net weight .3617 oz. pure silver).* **Diameter:** *30.6 mm.* **Edge:** *Reeded.* **Mint:** *Philadelphia.*

The Battle of Lexington and Concord—fought in 1775 just one day after Paul Revere's famous ride—is commemorated on this coin. Sculptor James Earle Fraser of the Commission of Fine Arts approved Beach's designs, but protested that the local committees had made a poor choice of subject matter.

Designs. *Obverse:* A view of *The Concord Minute Man of 1775* statue, by Daniel Chester French, located in Concord, Massachusetts. *Reverse:* Lexington's Old Belfry, whose tolling bell roused the Minute Men to action in 1775.

Mintage and Melting Data. Authorized on January 14, 1925. *Maximum authorized—300,000. Number minted—162,099 (including 99 assay coins). Number melted—86. Net distribution—162,013.*

Original Cost and Issuer. Sale price $1. Issued by the U.S. Lexington-Concord Sesquicentennial Commission, through local banks.

Key to Collecting. Examples are easily found in all grades, with most being in high AU or low MS grades, although eye appeal can vary widely. MS-65 coins are scarce in comparison to those in MS–60 through 64. Some specimens are deeply frosty and lustrous, whereas others have partially prooflike fields.

First Points of Wear. *Obverse:* The thighs of the Minuteman. *Reverse:* The top edge of the belfry.

	Distribution	Cert	Avg	%MS	AU-50	MS-60	MS-62	MS-63	MS-64	MS-65	MS-66
1925	162,013	4,118	63.6	97%	$75	$90	$95	$100	$140	$375	$800
	Auctions: $6,463, MS-67, July 2015; $1,645, MS-66, January 2015; $106, MS-63, June 2015; $69, AU-58, October 2015										

STONE MOUNTAIN MEMORIAL HALF DOLLAR (1925)

Designer: *Gutzon Borglum.* **Weight:** *12.50 grams.* **Composition:** *.900 silver, .100 copper (net weight .3617 oz. pure silver).* **Diameter:** *30.6 mm.* **Edge:** *Reeded.* **Mint:** *Philadelphia.*

The first of these half dollars were struck at Philadelphia on January 21, 1925, Confederate general Stonewall Jackson's birthday. Funds received from the sale of this large issue were devoted to the expense of carving figures of Confederate leaders and soldiers on Stone Mountain in Georgia. The coin's designer, Gutzon Borglum, was the original sculptor for that project, but left due to differences with the Stone Mountain Confederate Monumental Association. Augustus Lukeman took over in his stead, and the carving was completed and dedicated in 1970; Borglum would meanwhile go on to create the presidents' heads at Mount Rushmore.

Designs. *Obverse:* Equestrian portraits of Civil War generals Robert E. Lee and Thomas "Stonewall" Jackson. *Reverse:* An eagle perched on a cliff with wings in mid-spread.

Mintage and Melting Data. *Maximum authorized—5,000,000. Number minted—2,314,709* (including 4,709 assay coins). *Number melted—1,000,000. Net distribution—1,314,709.*

Original Cost and Issuer. Sale price $1. Issued by the Stone Mountain Confederate Monumental Association through many outlets, including promotions involving pieces counterstamped with abbreviations for Southern states.

Key to Collecting. This is the most plentiful commemorative from the 1920s. Examples are easily found in grades ranging from lightly worn through gem Mint State (many with outstanding eye appeal). Circulated coins are also found, as well as those that were counterstamped for special fundraising sales. The typical coin has very lustrous and frosty surfaces, although the reverse field may be somewhat satiny.

First Points of Wear. *Obverse:* Lee's elbow and leg. *Reverse:* The eagle's breast.

	Distribution	Cert	Avg	%MS	AU-50	MS-60	MS-62	MS-63	MS-64	MS-65	MS-66
1925	1,314,709	8,287	63.9	96%	$65	$70	$75	$85	$140	$190	$375
	Auctions: $3,055, MS-67, January 2015; $564, MS-66, August 2015; $182, MS-64, March 2015; $50, AU-58, September 2015										

CALIFORNIA DIAMOND JUBILEE HALF DOLLAR (1925)

Designer: *Jo Mora.* **Weight:** *12.50 grams.* **Composition:** *.900 silver, .100 copper*
(net weight .3617 oz. pure silver). **Diameter:** *30.6 mm.* **Edge:** *Reeded.* **Mint:** *San Francisco.*

The celebration for which these coins were struck marked the 75th anniversary of the admission of California into the Union. Notably, James Earle Fraser of the Commission of Fine Arts criticized Jo Mora's designs at the time. Art historian Cornelius Vermeule, however, called the coin "one of America's greatest works of numismatic art" in his book *Numismatic Art in America.*

Designs. *Obverse:* A rustic miner, squatting to pan for gold. *Reverse:* A grizzly bear, as taken from the California state flag.

Mintage and Melting Data. Authorized on February 24, 1925, part of the act also providing for the 1925 Fort Vancouver and 1927 Vermont half dollars. *Maximum authorized—300,000. Number minted—150,200 (including 200 assay coins). Number melted—63,606. Net distribution—86,594.*

Original Cost and Issuer. Sale price $1. Issued by the San Francisco Citizens' Committee through the San Francisco Clearing House Association and the Los Angeles Clearing House.

Key to Collecting. This coin's design is such that even a small amount of handling produces friction on the shoulder and high parts of the bear, in particular. As a result, most grade in the AU-55 to MS-62 range, and higher-level MS examples are rare. This issue exists in two finishes: frosty/lustrous, and the rarer "chrome-like" or prooflike. The frosty-finish pieces display some lack of die definition of the details. The prooflike pieces have heavily brushed and highly polished dies. Many specimens certified in high grades are toned, sometimes deeply, which can mask evidence of friction. Coins with no traces of friction are rarities.

First Points of Wear. *Obverse:* The folds of the miner's shirt sleeve. *Reverse:* The shoulder of the bear.

	Distribution	Cert	Avg	%MS	AU-50	MS-60	MS-62	MS-63	MS-64 PF-63	MS-65 PF-64	MS-66 PF-65
1925-S	86,594	4,197	63.9	96%	$190	$200	$205	$210	$375	$525	$1,000
	Auctions: $12,925, MS-68, January 2015; $4,465, MS-67, September 2015; $165, MS-62, October 2015; $129, AU-55, March 2015										
1925-S, Matte Proof	1–2	1	65								
	Auctions: No auction records available.										

FORT VANCOUVER CENTENNIAL HALF DOLLAR (1925)

Designer: *Laura Gardin Fraser.* **Weight:** *12.50 grams.* **Composition:** *.900 silver, .100 copper*
(net weight .3617 oz. pure silver). **Diameter:** *30.6 mm.* **Edge:** *Reeded.* **Mint:** *San Francisco.*

The sale of these half dollars at $1 each helped to finance the pageant staged for the celebration of the 100th anniversary of the construction of Fort Vancouver. As part of the publicity, pilot Oakley G. Kelly made a round-trip flight from Vancouver to San Francisco and back again to pick up and deliver the entire issue—which weighed 1,462 pounds.

Designs. *Obverse:* Bareheaded profile portrait of Dr. John McLoughlin, who built Fort Vancouver (Washington) on the Columbia River in 1825. *Reverse:* A pioneer in buckskin with a musket in his hands, with Fort Vancouver in the background.

Mintage and Melting Data. Authorized on February 24, 1925. *Maximum authorized—*300,000. *Number minted* (including 28 assay coins)—50,028. *Number melted*—35,034. *Net distribution*—14,994.

Original Cost and Issuer. Sale price $1. The Fort Vancouver Centennial Corporation, Vancouver, Washington.

Key to Collecting. This coin's design is such that even a small amount of handling produced friction on the higher spots. As a result, higher-level MS examples are rare.

First Points of Wear. *Obverse:* McLoughlin's temple area. *Reverse:* The pioneer's right knee.

	Distribution	Cert	Avg	%MS	AU-50	MS-60	MS-62	MS-63	MS-64	MS-65	MS-66
									PF-63	PF-64	PF-65
1925	14,994	2,261	64.0	97%	$325	$350	$360	$375	$475	$650	$1,000
	Auctions: $4,772, MS-67, September 2015; $2,115, MS-66, September 2015; $212, AU-53, March 2015; $129, EF-40, September 2015										
1925, Matte Proof	2–3	0	n/a								
	Auctions: No auction records available.										

SESQUICENTENNIAL OF AMERICAN INDEPENDENCE HALF DOLLAR (1926)

Designer: *John R. Sinnock.* **Weight:** *12.50 grams.* **Composition:** *.900 silver, .100 copper (net weight .3617 oz. pure silver).* **Diameter:** *30.6 mm.* **Edge:** *Reeded.* **Mint:** *Philadelphia.*

The 150th anniversary of the signing of the Declaration of Independence was the occasion for an international fair held in Philadelphia in 1926. To help raise funds for financing the fair, special issues of half dollars (as well as quarter eagles, below) were authorized by Congress. The use of Calvin Coolidge's likeness marked the first time a portrait of a president appeared on a coin struck during his own lifetime.

Designs. *Obverse:* Conjoined profile portraits of bewigged George Washington and bareheaded Calvin Coolidge. *Reverse:* The Liberty Bell.

Mintage and Melting Data. Authorized on March 23, 1925. *Maximum authorized—*1,000,000. *Number minted*—1,000,528 (including 528 assay coins). *Number melted*—859,408. *Net distribution*—141,120.

Original Cost and Issuer. Sale price $1. Issued by the National Sesquicentennial Exhibition Association.

Key to Collecting. Accurate grading can be problematic for this coin. Many examples certified at high grades have mottled or deeply toned surfaces that obfuscate examination, and others have been recolored. Most have graininess—marks from the original planchet—on the highest part of the portrait.

First Points of Wear. *Obverse:* Washington's cheekbone. *Reverse:* The area below the lower inscription on the Liberty Bell.

	Distribution	Cert	Avg	%MS	AU-50	MS-60	MS-62	MS-63	MS-64	MS-65	MS-66
1926	141,120	4,427	63.1	96%	$80	$100	$110	$130	$225	$2,000	$7,500
	Auctions: $5,288, MS-66, July 2015; $1,880, MS-65, January 2015; $112, MS-62, February 2015; $84, AU-55, July 2015										

SESQUICENTENNIAL OF AMERICAN INDEPENDENCE QUARTER EAGLE (1926)

Designer: *John R. Sinnock.* **Weight:** *4.18 grams.* **Composition:** *.900 gold, .100 copper (net weight .12094 oz. pure gold).* **Diameter:** *18 mm.* **Edge:** *Reeded.* **Mint:** *Philadelphia.*

This quarter eagle, along with a related half dollar, was sold to finance the National Sesquicentennial Exposition in Philadelphia (which marked the 150th anniversary of the signing of the Declaration of Independence). Note that though the issuer was known as the National Sesquicentennial *Exhibition* Association, the event was primarily billed with *Exposition* in its name.

Designs. *Obverse:* Miss Liberty standing, holding in one hand a scroll representing the Declaration of Independence and in the other, the Torch of Freedom. *Reverse:* A front view of Independence Hall in Philadelphia.

Mintage and Melting Data. Authorized on March 23, 1925. *Maximum authorized—200,000. Number minted—200,226 (including 226 assay coins). Number melted—154,207. Net distribution—46,019.*

Original Cost and Issuer. Sale price $4. National Sesquicentennial Exhibition Association.

Key to Collecting. Nearly all examples show evidence of handling and contact from careless production at the Mint, and from later indifference by their buyers. Most coins range from AU-55 to MS-62 in grade, and have scattered marks in the fields. MS-65 examples are rare. Well-struck coins are seldom seen. Some pieces show copper stains; connoisseurs avoid these.

First Points of Wear. *Obverse:* The bottom of the scroll held by Liberty. *Reverse:* The area below the top of the tower; and the central portion above the roof.

	Distribution	Cert	Avg	%MS	AU-50	MS-60	MS-62	MS-63	MS-64 / PF-63	MS-65 / PF-64	MS-66 / PF-65
1926	46,019	7,560	63.0	93%	$450	$525	$600	$750	$1,000	$2,000	$7,500
	Auctions: $25,850, MS-67, January 2015; $6,463, MS-66, January 2015; $494, MS-62, January 2015; $282, AU-55, September 2015										
1926, Matte Proof (a)	*unique*	1	65								
	Auctions: No auction records available.										

a. "The coin is unique and displays a matte surface similar to the Proof gold coins of 1908 to 1915. The coin was reportedly from the estate of the designer, John R. Sinnock, who is best known for his Roosevelt dime and Franklin half dollar designs. The piece was in the possession of coin dealer David Bullowa in the 1950s. Another example is rumored by Breen, but the whereabouts or existence of the coin is unknown" (*Encyclopedia of U.S. Gold Coins, 1795–1933,* second edition).

OREGON TRAIL MEMORIAL HALF DOLLAR (1926–1939)

Designers: *James Earle Fraser and Laura Gardin Fraser.* **Weight:** *12.50 grams.*
Composition: *.900 silver, .100 copper (net weight .3617 oz. pure silver).*
Diameter: *30.6 mm.* **Edge:** *Reeded.* **Mints:** *Philadelphia, San Francisco, and Denver.*

These coins—the longest-running series of commemoratives—were struck in commemoration of the Oregon Trail and in memory of the pioneers, many of whom lie buried along the famous 2,000-mile highway of history. This was the first commemorative to be struck at more than one Mint facility, and also the first commemorative to be struck at the Denver Mint.

Designs. *Obverse:* A pioneer family in a Conestoga wagon, heading west into the sunset. *Reverse:* A standing Indian with a bow, arm outstretched, and a map of the United States in the background.

Mintage and Melting Data. *Maximum authorized*—6,000,000 (for the entire series from 1926 onward). *Number minted*—1926: 48,030 (including 30 assay coins); 1926-S: 100,055 (including 55 assay coins); 1928: 50,028 (including 28 assay coins); 1933-D: 5,250 (including an unrecorded number of assay coins); 1934-D: 7,006 (including 6 assay coins); 1936: 10,006 (including 6 assay coins); 1936-S: 5,006 (including 6 assay coins); 1937-D: 12,008 (including 8 assay coins); 1938-P: 6,006 (including 6 assay coins); 1938-D: 6,005 (including 5 assay coins); 1938-S: 6,006 (including 6 assay coins). *Number melted*—1926: 75 (defective coins); 1926-S: 17,000; 1928: 44,000; 1933-D: 242 (probably defective coins). *Net distribution*—1926: 47,955; 1926-S: 83,055; 1928: 6,028; 1933-D: 5,008; 1934-D: 7,006; 1936: 10,006; 1936-S: 5,006; 1937-D: 12,008; 1938-P: 6,006; 1938-D: 6,005; 1938-S: 6,006.

Original Cost and Issuer. Sale price $1; later raised. Issued by the Oregon Trail Memorial Association, Inc.; some sold through Scott Stamp & Coin Co., Inc., and some sold through Whitman Centennial, Inc., Walla Walla, Washington. From 1937 onward, distributed solely by the Oregon Trail Memorial Association, Inc.

Key to Collecting. Although most of the later issues have low mintages, they are not rare in the marketplace, because the majority were originally sold to coin collectors and dealers. As a result, most surviving coins are in MS. The quality of the surface finish varies, with earlier issues tending to be frosty and lustrous and later issues (particularly those dated 1938 and 1939) having somewhat grainy or satiny fields. Grading requires care. Look for friction or contact marks on the high points of the Indian and the Conestoga wagon, but, more importantly, check both surfaces carefully for scattered cuts and marks. All three mints had difficulty in striking up the rims properly, causing many rejections. Those deemed acceptable and shipped out usually had full rims, but it is best to check when buying.

First Points of Wear. *Obverse:* The hip of the ox, and high points of the wagon (note that the top rear of the wagon was weakly struck in some years). *Reverse:* The Indian's left thumb and fingers (note that some pieces show flatness on the thumb and first finger, due to a weak strike).

	Distribution	Cert	Avg	%MS	AU-50	MS-60	MS-62	MS-63	MS-64 PF-63	MS-65 PF-64	MS-66 PF-65
1926	47,955	2,154	64.4	98%	$140	$175	$180	$190	$210	$260	$325
	Auctions: $999, MS-67, June 2015; $412, MS-66, November 2015; $235, MS-63, May 2015; $112, MS-61, February 2015										
1926, Matte Proof	*1–2*	1	65								
	Auctions: No auction records available.										
1926-S	83,055	3,005	64.6	98%	$140	$175	$180	$190	$210	$260	$350
	Auctions: $14,100, MS-68, January 2015; $1,998, MS-67, January 2015; $247, MS-65, June 2015; $129, MS-60, May 2015										
1928 (same as 1926)	6,028	1,320	65.3	100%	$160	$190	$195	$200	$260	$300	$450
	Auctions: $1,410, MS-67, September 2015; $400, MS-66, September 2015; $306, MS-65, February 2015; $223, MS-64, January 2015										
1933-D	5,008	1,031	65.1	100%	$375	$400	$410	$420	$425	$450	$575
	Auctions: $1,880, MS-67, June 2015; $564, MS-66, January 2015; $329, MS-65, August 2015; $329, MS-64, May 2015										
1934-D	7,006	1,319	64.8	100%	$190	$200	$205	$210	$215	$300	$450
	Auctions: $1,175, MS-67, September 2015; $376, MS-66, August 2015; $212, MS-65, August 2015; $188, MS-63, October 2015										
1936	10,006	1,596	65.3	100%	$160	$180	$190	$210	$220	$260	$300
	Auctions: $11,163, MS-68, September 2015; $1,293, MS-67, July 2015; $341, MS-66, February 2015; $200, MS-64, February 2015										
1936-S	5,006	1,125	65.5	100%	$170	$180	$190	$200	$225	$260	$350
	Auctions: $1,763, MS-68, November 2014; $10,575, MS-68, January 2013; $670, MS-67+, October 2014; $425, MS-67, November 2014										
1937-D	12,008	2,354	65.9	100%	$170	$200	$205	$210	$225	$260	$310
	Auctions: $4,935, MS-68, January 2015; $1,116, MS-67, September 2015; $353, MS-66, February 2015; $200, MS-64, February 2015										
1938 (same as 1926)	6,006	1,248	65.4	100%	$180	$190	$195	$200	$225	$275	$375
	Auctions: $1,410, MS-67, January 2015; $306, MS-66, June 2015; $259, MS-65, February 2015; $153, MS-63, May 2015										
1938-D	6,005	1,422	65.8	100%	$180	$190	$195	$200	$225	$275	$350
	Auctions: $5,405, MS-68, January 2015; $764, MS-67, August 2015; $306, MS-66, October 2015; $129, MS-63, May 2015										
1938-S	6,006	1,276	65.5	100%	$180	$190	$195	$200	$225	$300	$350
	Auctions: $6,933, MS-68, March 2015; $1,293, MS-67, January 2015; $306, MS-66, January 2015; $182, MS-64, September 2015										
Set of 1938 P-D-S					$570	$585	$600	$675	$850	$1,075	
	Auctions: $2,070, MS-67/67/67, February 2012; $617, MS-64/64/64, March 2015										
1939	3,004	768	65.5	100%	$475	$500	$525	$550	$600	$650	$750
	Auctions: $2,350, MS-67, January 2015; $823, MS-66, January 2015; $564, MS-65, January 2015; $494, MS-64, October 2015										
1939-D	3,004	801	65.8	100%	$475	$500	$525	$550	$600	$625	$675
	Auctions: $9,400, MS-68, January 2015; $1,880, MS-67, January 2015; $541, MS-65, January 2015; $353, AU-50, September 2015										
1939-S	3,005	793	65.5	100%	$475	$500	$525	$550	$600	$650	$750
	Auctions: $4,230, MS-68, January 2015; $1,410, MS-67, August 2015; $881, MS-66, January 2015; $588, MS-64, October 2015										
Set of 1939 P-D-S					$1,500	$1,575	$1,650	$1,800	$1,925	$2,175	
	Auctions: $5,175, MS-67/67/67, January 2012; $1,528, MS-65/65/65, March 2015										

VERMONT SESQUICENTENNIAL HALF DOLLAR (1927)

Designer: *Charles Keck.* **Weight:** *12.50 grams.* **Composition:** *.900 silver, .100 copper (net weight .3617 oz. pure silver).* **Diameter:** *30.6 mm.* **Edge:** *Reeded.* **Mint:** *Philadelphia.*

This souvenir issue commemorates the 150th anniversary of the Battle of Bennington and the independence of Vermont. Authorized in 1925, it was not coined until 1927. The Vermont Sesquicentennial Commission intended that funds derived would benefit the study of history.

Designs. *Obverse:* Profile portrait of a bewigged Ira Allen. *Reverse:* A catamount walking left.

Mintage and Melting Data. Authorized by the Act of February 24, 1925. *Maximum authorized—*40,000. *Number minted—*40,034 (including 34 assay coins). *Number melted—*11,892. *Net distribution—*28,142.

Original Cost and Issuer. Sale price $1. Issued by the Vermont Sesquicentennial Commission (Bennington Battle Monument and Historical Association).

Key to Collecting. The Vermont half dollar was struck with the highest relief of any commemorative issue to that date. Despite the depth of the work in the dies, nearly all of the coins were struck up properly and show excellent detail. Unfortunately, the height of the obverse portrait encourages evidence of contact at the central points, and nearly all coins show some friction on Allen's cheek. Most are in grades of MS–62 to 64 and are deeply lustrous and frosty. Cleaned examples are often seen—and are avoided by connoisseurs.

First Points of Wear. *Obverse:* Allen's cheek, and the hair above his ear and in the temple area. *Reverse:* The catamount's upper shoulder.

	Distribution	Cert	Avg	%MS	AU-50	MS-60	MS-62	MS-63	MS-64	MS-65	MS-66
1927	28,142	3,106	63.9	97%	$275	$300	$310	$325	$350	$450	$800
	Auctions: $3,290, MS-67, August 2015; $1,293, MS-66, January 2015; $282, MS-64, February 2015; $176, AU-53, January 2015										

HAWAIIAN SESQUICENTENNIAL HALF DOLLAR (1928)

Designer: *Juliette M. Fraser.* **Weight:** *12.50 grams.* **Composition:** *.900 silver, .100 copper (net weight .3617 oz. pure silver).* **Diameter:** *30.6 mm.* **Edge:** *Reeded.* **Mint:** *Philadelphia.*

This issue was struck to commemorate the 150th anniversary of the arrival on the Hawaiian Islands of Captain James Cook in 1778. The coin's $2 price was the highest ever for a commemorative half dollar up to that point.

Designs. *Obverse:* Portrait of Captain James Cook. *Reverse:* A Hawaiian chieftain standing with arm outstretched and holding a spear.

Mintage Data. Authorized on March 7, 1928. *Maximum authorized—*10,000. *Number minted—*10,008 (including 8 assay coins and 50 Sandblast Proofs). *Net distribution—*10,008.

Original Cost and Issuer. Sale price $2. Issued by the Captain Cook Sesquicentennial Commission, through the Bank of Hawaii, Ltd.

Key to Collecting. This is the scarcest of classic U.S. commemorative coins. It is elusive in all grades, and highly prized. Most are AU-55 to MS-62 or slightly finer; those grading MS-65 or above are especially difficult to find. Most examples show contact or friction on the higher design areas. Some coins have a somewhat satiny surface, whereas others are lustrous and frosty. Many undipped pieces have a yellowish tint. Beware of coins which have been repeatedly dipped or cleaned. Problem-free examples are rarer even than the low mintage would suggest. Fake "Sandblast Proofs" exist; these are coins dipped in acid.

First Points of Wear. *Obverse:* Cook's cheekbone. *Reverse:* The chieftain's legs; his fingers and the hand holding the spear.

	Distribution	Cert	Avg	%MS	AU-50	MS-60	MS-62	MS-63	MS-64 PF-63	MS-65 PF-64	MS-66 PF-65
1928	10,008	1,704	63.7	98%	$1,800	$2,250	$2,500	$2,750	$3,000	$4,250	$7,000
	Auctions: $17,625, MS-67, August 2015; $9,988, MS-66, January 2015; $4,230, MS-65, January 2015; $1,410, MS-60, June 2015										
1928, Proof (a)	50	27	64.1						$20,000	$30,000	$50,000
	Auctions: No auction records available.										

a. Sandblast Proof presentation pieces. "Of the production figure, 50 were Sandblast Proofs, made by a special process which imparted a dull, grainy finish to the pieces, similar to that used on certain Mint medals of the era as well as on gold Proof coins circa 1908–1915" (*Guide Book of United States Commemorative Coins*).

MARYLAND TERCENTENARY HALF DOLLAR (1934)

Designer: *Hans Schuler.* **Weight:** *12.50 grams.* **Composition:** *.900 silver, .100 copper (net weight .3617 oz. pure silver).* **Diameter:** *30.6 mm.* **Edge:** *Reeded.* **Mint:** *Philadelphia.*

The 300th anniversary of the founding of the Maryland Colony by Cecil Calvert (known as Lord Baltimore) was the occasion for this special coin. The profits from the sale of this issue were used to finance the celebration in Baltimore during 1934. John Work Garrett, distinguished American diplomat and well-known numismatist, was among the citizens of Maryland who endorsed the commemorative half dollar proposal on behalf of the Maryland Tercentenary Commission of Baltimore.

Designs. *Obverse:* Three-quarter portrait of Cecil Calvert, Lord Baltimore. *Reverse:* The state seal and motto of Maryland.

Mintage Data. Authorized on May 9, 1934. *Maximum authorized—25,000. Number minted—25,015* (including 15 assay coins). *Net distribution—25,015.*

Original Cost and Issuer. Sale price $1. Issued by the Maryland Tercentenary Commission, through various outlets.

Key to Collecting. The coin's field has an unusual "rippled" appearance, similar to a sculptured plaque, so nicks and other marks that would be visible on a coin with flat fields are not as readily noticed. Most examples grade MS–62 to 64. Finer pieces, strictly graded, are elusive. This issue was not handled with care at the time of mintage and distribution, and nearly all show scattered contact marks. Some exist struck from a reverse die broken from the right side of the shield to a point opposite the upper right of the 4 in the date 1634.

First Points of Wear. *Obverse:* Lord Baltimore's nose (the nose usually appears flatly struck; also check the reverse for wear). *Reverse:* The top of the coronet on top of the shield, and the tops of the draperies.

	Distribution	Cert	Avg	%MS	AU-50	MS-60	MS-62	MS-63	MS-64 PF-63	MS-65 PF-64	MS-66 PF-65
1934	25,015	3,431	64.7	100%	$140	$150	$160	$175	$200	$225	$350
	Auctions: $2,115, MS-67, January 2015; $447, MS-66, August 2015; $212, MS-65, January 2015; $119, MS-60, February 2015										
1934, Matte Proof	2–4	2	63								
	Auctions: No auction records available.										

TEXAS INDEPENDENCE CENTENNIAL HALF DOLLAR (1934–1938)

Designer: *Pompeo Coppini.* **Weight:** *12.50 grams.*
Composition: *.900 silver, .100 copper (net weight .3617 oz. pure silver).*
Diameter: *30.6 mm.* **Edge:** *Reeded.* **Mints:** *Philadelphia, Denver, and San Francisco.*

This issue commemorated the independence of Texas in 1836. Proceeds from the sale of the coin were intended to finance the Centennial Exposition, which was eventually held in Dallas. Sales were lower than expected, but the event was still held and attracted about 7 million visitors.

Designs. *Obverse:* A perched eagle with a large five-pointed star in the background.
Reverse: The goddess Victory kneeling, with medallions and portraits of General Sam Houston and Stephen Austin, founders of the republic and state of Texas, along with other Texan icons.

Mintage and Melting Data. Authorized on June 15, 1933. *Maximum authorized*—1,500,000 (for the entire series 1934 onward). 1934: *Number minted*—1934: 205,113 (including 113 assay coins); 1935-P: 10,008 (including 8 assay coins); 1935-D: 10,007 (including 7 assay coins); 1935-S: 10,008 (including 8 assay coins); 1936-P: 10,008 (including 8 assay coins); 1936-D: 10,007 (including 7 assay coins); 1936-S: 10,008 (including 8 assay coins); 1937-P: 8,005 (including 5 assay coins); 1937-D: 8,006 (including 6 assay coins); 1937-S: 8,007 (including 7 assay coins); 1938-P: 5,005 (including 5 assay coins); 1938-D: 5,005 (including 5 assay coins); 1938-S: 5,006 (including 6 assay coins). *Number melted*—1934: 143,650; 1935-P: 12 (probably defective coins); 1936-P: 12 (probably defective coins); 1937-P: 1,434; 1937-D: 1,401; 1937-S: 1,370; 1938-P: 1,225; 1938-D: 1,230; 1938-S: 1,192. *Net distribution*—1934: 61,463; 1935-P: 9,996; 1935-D: 10,007; 1935-S: 10,008; 1936-P: 9,996; 1936-D: 10,007; 1936-S: 10,008; 1937-P: 6,571; 1937-D: 6,605; 1937-S: 6,637; 1938-P: 3,780; 1938-D: 3,775; 1938-S: 3,814.

Original Cost and Issuer. Sale price $1; later raised. Issued by the American Legion Texas Centennial Committee, Austin, Texas, from 1934 through 1936; issued by the Texas Memorial Museum Centennial Coin Campaign in 1937 and 1938.

Key to Collecting. The typical example grades MS–64 or 65. Early issues are very lustrous and frosty; those produced toward the end of the series are more satiny.

First Points of Wear. *Obverse:* The eagle's upper breast and upper leg. *Reverse:* The forehead and knee of Victory.

	Distribution	Cert	Avg	%MS	AU-50	MS-60	MS-62	MS-63	MS-64	MS-65	MS-66
1934	61,463	2,487	64.5	98%	$140	$150	$155	$160	$175	$210	$325
	Auctions: $1,293, MS-67, July 2015; $306, MS-66, January 2015; $129, MS-64, September 2015; $100, MS-60, June 2015										
1935 (same as 1934)	9,996	1,574	65.6	100%	$140	$150	$155	$160	$175	$225	$290
	Auctions: $3,525, MS-68, January 2015; $1,998, MS-67, August 2015; $188, MS-65, September 2015; $106, MS-60, May 2015										
1935-D	10,007	1,611	65.5	100%	$140	$150	$155	$160	$175	$225	$300
	Auctions: $3,290, MS-68, September 2015; $1,410, MS-67, June 2015; $235, MS-66, May 2015; $153, MS-60, May 2015										
1935-S	10,008	1,343	65.2	100%	$140	$150	$155	$160	$175	$225	$290
	Auctions: $705, MS-67, January 2015; $259, MS-66, May 2015; $212, MS-65, August 2015; $129, MS-63, October 2015										
Set of 1935 P-D-S					$450	$465	$480	$525		$675	$880
	Auctions: $940, MS-67/67/67, March 2015; $871, MS-66/66/66, December 2011; $470, MS-65/65/65, April 2015										

	Distribution	Cert	Avg	%MS	AU-50	MS-60	MS-62	MS-63	MS-64	MS-65	MS-66
1936 (same as 1934)	8,911	1,444	65.4	100%	$140	$150	$155	$160	$175	$225	$290
Auctions: $14,100, MS-68, July 2015; $823, MS-67, June 2015; $382, MS-66, January 2015; $141, MS-64, January 2015											
1936-D	9,039	1,659	65.7	100%	$140	$150	$155	$160	$175	$225	$290
Auctions: $2,820, MS-68, July 2015; $705, MS-67, August 2015; $329, MS-66, March 2015; $123, MS-64, May 2015											
1936-S	9,055	1,351	65.3	100%	$140	$150	$155	$160	$175	$225	$290
Auctions: $1,058, MS-67, October 2015; $282, MS-66, September 2015; $176, MS-65, September 2015; $123, MS-64, March 2015											
Set of 1936 P-D-S					$450	$465	$480	$525	$675	$870	
Auctions: $863, MS-66/66/66, December 2011; $705, MS-65/65/65, March 2015											
1937 (same as 1934)	6,571	1,187	65.2	100%	$140	$150	$155	$160	$175	$225	$375
Auctions: $12,925, MS-68, August 2015; $2,585, MS-67, August 2015; $200, MS-65, April 2015; $147, MS-63, October 2015											
1937-D	6,605	1,225	65.4	100%	$140	$150	$155	$160	$175	$225	$350
Auctions: $3,760, MS-68, January 2015; $1,175, MS-67, September 2015; $129, MS-62, October 2015; $89, MS-60, January 2015											
1937-S	6,637	1,246	65.3	100%	$140	$150	$155	$160	$175	$225	$350
Auctions: $1,880, MS-67, February 2015; $329, MS-66, February 2015; $259, MS-66, September 2015; $200, MS-65, October 2015											
Set of 1937 P-D-S					$450	$465	$480	$525	$675	$1,075	
Auctions: $625, MS-66/66/66, April 2012; $617, MS-66/66/66, March 2015; $541, MS-65/65/65, September 2015											
1938 (same as 1934)	3,780	844	65.1	100%	$225	$240	$245	$250	$275	$475	$750
Auctions: $1,645, MS-67, January 2015; $823, MS-66, January 2015; $400, MS-65, July 2015; $176, MS-63, October 2015											
1938-D	3,775	888	65.4	100%	$225	$240	$245	$250	$275	$450	$625
Auctions: $1,880, MS-67, August 2015; $447, MS-66, January 2015; $447, MS-66, January 2015; $294, MS-64, October 2015											
1938-S	3,814	880	65.4	100%	$225	$240	$245	$250	$275	$450	$625
Auctions: $2,233, MS-67, January 2015; $646, MS-66, January 2015; $329, MS-65, October 2015; $176, MS-63, October 2015											
Set of 1938 P-D-S					$720	$735	$750	$825	$1,375	$2,000	
Auctions: $604, MS-64/65/64, June 2012											

DANIEL BOONE BICENTENNIAL HALF DOLLAR (1934–1938)

Designer: *Augustus Lukeman.* **Weight:** *12.50 grams.*
Composition: *.900 silver, .100 copper (net weight .3617 oz. pure silver).*
Diameter: *30.6 mm.* **Edge:** *Reeded.* **Mints:** *Philadelphia, Denver, and San Francisco.*

This coin type, which was minted for five years, was first struck in 1934 to commemorate the 200th anniversary of the birth of Daniel Boone, famous frontiersman, trapper, and explorer. Coinage covered several years, similar to the schedule for the Texas issues; 1934 coins are the only examples with true bicentennial status.

Designs. *Obverse:* Artist's conception of Daniel Boone in a profile portrait. *Reverse:* Standing figures of Boone and Blackfish, war chief of the Chillicothe band of the Shawnee tribe. (In 1935 the date 1934 was added to the reverse design.)

Mintage and Melting Data. Authorized on May 26, 1934 and, with "1934" added to modify the design, on August 26, 1935. *Maximum authorized*—600,000 (for the entire series from 1934 onward). *Number minted*—1934: 10,007 (including 7 assay coins); 1935-P: 10,010 (including 10 assay coins); 1935-D: 5,005 (including 5 assay coins); 1935-S: 5,005 (including 5 assay coins); 1935-P, "Small 1934": 10,008 (including 8 assay coins); 1935-D, "Small 1934": 2,003; 1935-S, "Small 1934": 2,004; 1936-P: 12,012 (including 12 assay coins); 1936-D: 5,005 (including 5 assay coins); 1936-S: 5,006 (including 6 assay coins); 1937-P: 15,010 (including 10 assay coins); 1937-D: 7,506 (including 6 assay coins); 1937-S: 5,006 (including 6 assay coins); 1938-P: 5,005 (including 5 assay coins); 1938-D: 5,005 (including 5 assay coins); 1938-S: 5,006 (including 6 assay coins). *Number melted*—1937-P: 5,200; 1937-D: 5,000; 1937-S: 2,500; 1938-P: 2,905; 1938-D: 2,905; 1938-S: 2,906. *Net distribution*—1934: 10,007; 1935-P: 10,010; 1935-D: 5,005; 1935-S: 5,005; 1935-P, "Small 1934": 10,008 (including 8 assay coins); 1935-D, "Small 1934": 2,003; 1935-S, "Small 1934": 2,004; 1936-P: 12,012; 1936-D: 5,005; 1936-S: 5,006; 1937-P: 9,810; 1937-D: 2,506; 1937-S: 2,506; 1938-P: 2,100; 1938-D: 2,100; 1938-S: 2,100.

Original Cost and Issuer. Sale prices varied by mintmark, from a low of $1.10 per 1935-P coin to a high of $5.15 per 1937-S coin. Issued by Daniel Boone Bicentennial Commission (and its division, the Pioneer National Monument Association), Phoenix Hotel, Lexington, Kentucky (C. Frank Dunn, "sole distributor").

Key to Collecting. Most collectors desire just a single coin to represent the type, but there are enough specialists who want one of each date and mintmark to ensure a ready market whenever the scarcer sets come up for sale. Most surviving coins are in MS, with MS–64 to 66 pieces readily available for most issues. Early issues in the series are characterized by deep frosty mint luster, whereas issues toward the end of the run, particularly 1937 and 1938, often are seen with a satin finish and relatively little luster (because of the methods of die preparation and striking). The 1937-S is very often seen with prooflike surfaces, and the 1938-S occasionally so. In general, the Boone commemoratives were handled carefully at the time of minting and distribution, but scattered contact marks are often visible.

First Points of Wear. *Obverse:* The hair behind Boone's ear. *Reverse:* The left shoulder of the Indian.

	Distribution	Cert	Avg	%MS	AU-50	MS-60	MS-62	MS-63	MS-64	MS-65	MS-66
1934	10,007	1,032	64.8	100%	$130	$135	$140	$150	$160	$225	$275
Auctions: $1,528, MS-67, January 2015; $569, MS-66, January 2015; $165, MS-65, September 2015; $94, MS-60, January 2015											
1935	10,010	1,167	64.7	100%	$130	$135	$140	$150	$175	$200	$250
Auctions: $1,175, MS-67, January 2015; $200, MS-66, January 2015; $176, MS-65, January 2015; $94, MS-62, February 2015											
1935-D	5,005	663	64.6	100%	$130	$135	$140	$150	$200	$225	$350
Auctions: $2,115, MS-67, January 2015; $201, MS-65, October 2015; $175, MS-65, March 2015; $153, MS-64, January 2015											
1935-S	5,005	840	65.0	100%	$130	$135	$140	$150	$175	$200	$275
Auctions: $1,116, MS-67, October 2015; $376, MS-66, January 2015; $176, MS-65, February 2015; $106, MS-60, July 2015											
Set of 1935 P-D-S					$405	$420	$450	$500	$625	$875	
Auctions: $380, MS-64/64/64, December 2011											
1935, With Small 1934	10,008	1,308	64.9	100%	$140	$150	$155	$160	$175	$200	$300
Auctions: $1,528, MS-67, July 2015; $282, MS-66, January 2015; $188, MS-65, April 2015; $106, MS-60, May 2015											
1935-D, Same type	2,003	505	65.2	100%	$250	$275	$300	$325	$375	$550	$700
Auctions: $6,463, MS-68, January 2015; $881, MS-66, January 2015; $646, MS-65, January 2015; $306, MS-64, January 2015											
1935-S, Same type	2,004	506	64.8	100%	$250	$275	$300	$325	$375	$550	$1,000
Auctions: $4,230, MS-67, January 2015; $1,528, MS-66, September 2015; $541, MS-65, January 2015; $248, MS-64, April 2015											
Set of 1935 P-D-S, With Added Date					$800	$865	$910	$925	$1,300	$2,000	
Auctions: $925, MS-65/63/64, May 2012											
1936	12,012	1,486	64.8	100%	$130	$135	$140	$150	$175	$180	$275
Auctions: $7,050, MS-68, October 2015; $940, MS-67, January 2015; $306, MS-66, January 2015; $100, MS-63, February 2015											
1936-D	5,005	851	65.0	100%	$130	$135	$140	$150	$175	$190	$300
Auctions: $1,293, MS-67, June 2015; $235, MS-66, September 2015; $188, MS-65, July 2015; $100, MS-63, February 2015											
1936-S	5,006	894	65.1	100%	$130	$135	$140	$150	$175	$190	$350
Auctions: $11,163, MS-68, January 2015; $705, MS-67, August 2015; $353, MS-66, September 2015; $102, MS-63, August 2015											
Set of 1936 P-D-S					$405	$420	$450	$525	$560	$925	
Auctions: $920, MS-66/66/66 Plus, November 2011											

	Distribution	Cert	Avg	%MS	AU-50	MS-60	MS-62	MS-63	MS-64	MS-65	MS-66
1937	9,810	1,376	64.9	100%	$140	$150	$155	$160	$175	$200	$325
	Auctions: $2,585, MS-67, October 2015; $376, MS-66, March 2015; $200, MS-65, February 2015; $100, MS-60, September 2015										
1937-D	2,506	559	64.9	100%	$240	$250	$260	$275	$325	$400	$500
	Auctions: $1,528, MS-67, October 2015; $376, MS-66, April 2015; $294, MS-65, January 2015; $212, MS-64, January 2015										
1937-S	2,506	683	65.0	100%	$240	$250	$260	$275	$325	$400	$500
	Auctions: $1,645, MS-67, January 2015; $470, MS-66, May 2015; $353, MS-65, January 2015; $118, MS-63, August 2015										
Set of 1937 P-D-S					$650	$675	$710	$825	$1,000	$1,325	
	Auctions: $564, MS-66/65/64, November 2011										
1938	2,100	459	64.8	100%	$325	$340	$345	$350	$375	$500	$750
	Auctions: $2,585, MS-67, July 2015; $946, MS-66, January 2015; $306, MS-65, September 2015; $236, MS-63, February 2015										
1938-D	2,100	485	65.1	100%	$325	$340	$345	$350	$375	$500	$750
	Auctions: $7,050, MS-67, January 2015; $823, MS-66, January 2015; $423, MS-65, February 2015; $259, MS-63, February 2015										
1938-S	2,100	492	64.8	100%	$325	$340	$345	$350	$375	$500	$750
	Auctions: $1,410, MS-67, August 2015; $1,087, MS-66, January 2015; $235, MS-63, July 2015; $188, AU-50, November 2015										
Set of 1938 P-D-S					$1,120	$1,135	$1,150	$1,225	$1,500	$2,250	
	Auctions: $4,312, MS-66/66/65, September 2011										

CONNECTICUT TERCENTENARY HALF DOLLAR (1935)

Designer: *Henry Kreiss.* **Weight:** *12.50 grams.* **Composition:** *.900 silver, .100 copper (net weight .3617 oz. pure silver).* **Diameter:** *30.6 mm.* **Edge:** *Reeded.* **Mint:** *Philadelphia.*

In commemoration of the 300th anniversary of the founding of the colony of Connecticut, a souvenir half dollar was struck. According to legend, the Royal Charter of the colony was secreted in the Charter Tree (seen on the coin's reverse) during the reign of King James II, who wished to revoke it. The charter was produced after the king's overthrow in 1688, and the colony continued under its protection.

Designs. *Obverse:* A modernistic eagle, standing. *Reverse:* The Charter Oak.

Mintage Data. Authorized on June 21, 1934. *Maximum authorized*—25,000. *Number minted*—25,018 (including 18 assay coins). *Net distribution*—25,018.

Original Cost and Issuer. Sale price $1. Issued by the Connecticut Tercentenary Commission.

Key to Collecting. Most examples survive in upper AU and lower MS grades. Higher-grade coins such as MS-65 are elusive. Friction and/or marks are often obvious on the broad expanse of wing on the obverse, and, in particular, at the ground or baseline of the oak tree on the reverse. Examples that are otherwise lustrous, frosty, and very attractive, often have friction on the wing.

First Points of Wear. *Obverse:* The top of the eagle's wing. *Reverse:* The ground above ON and TI in CONNECTICUT.

	Distribution	Cert	Avg	%MS	AU-50	MS-60	MS-62	MS-63	MS-64	MS-65	MS-66
									PF-63	PF-64	PF-65
1935	25,018	3,480	64.5	99%	$225	$230	$235	$240	$250	$400	$600
	Auctions: $2,350, MS-67, January 2015; $823, MS-66, October 2015; $376, MS-65, January 2015; $188, MS-60, July 2015										
1935, Matte Proof	*1–2*	1	65								
	Auctions: No auction records available.										

ARKANSAS CENTENNIAL HALF DOLLAR (1935–1939)

Designer: *Edward E. Burr.* **Weight:** *12.50 grams.*
Composition: *.900 silver, .100 copper (net weight .3617 oz. pure silver).*
Diameter: *30.6 mm.* **Edge:** *Reeded.* **Mints:** *Philadelphia, Denver, and San Francisco.*

This souvenir issue marked the 100th anniversary of the admission of Arkansas into the Union. The 1936 through 1939 issues were the same as those of 1935 except for the dates. The coin's four-year lifespan was intended to maximize profits, and sluggish sales contributed to the crash of the commemorative market and subsequent suspension of commemorative coinage in 1939.

Designs. *Obverse:* An eagle with outstretched wings, stars, and other elements of the Arkansas state seal. *Reverse:* Portraits of a Liberty in a Phrygian cap and an Indian chief of 1836.

Mintage and Melting Data. Authorized on May 14, 1934. *Maximum authorized*—500,000 (for the entire series from 1935 onward). *Number minted* (including 5, 5, and 6 assay coins)—1935-P: 13,012 (including 5 assay coins); 1935-D: 5,505 (including 5 assay coins); 1935-S: 5,506 (including 6 assay coins); 1936-P: 10,010 (including 10 assay coins); 1936-D: 10,010 (including 10 assay coins); 1936-S: 10,012 (including 12 assay coins); 1937-P: 5,505 (including 5 assay coins); 1937-D: 5,505 (including 5 assay coins); 1937-S: 5,506 (including 6 assay coins); 1938-P: 6,006 (including 6 assay coins); 1938-D: 6,005 (including 5 assay coins); 1938-S: 6,006 (including 6 assay coins); 1939-P: 2,140 (including 4 assay coins); 1939-D: 2,104 (including 4 assay coins); 1939-S: 2,105 (including 5 assay coins). *Number melted*—1936-P: 350; 1936-D: 350; 1936-S: 350; 1938-P: 2,850; 1938-D: 2,850; 1938-S: 2,850. *Net distribution*—1935-P: 13,012; 1935-D: 5,505; 1935-S: 5,506; 1936-P: 9,660; 1936-D: 9,660; 1936-S: 9,662; 1937-P: 5,505; 1937-D: 5,505; 1937-S: 5,506; 1938-P: 3,156; 1938-D: 3,155; 1938-S: 3,156; 1939-P: 2,104; 1939-D: 2,104; 1939-S: 2,105.

Original Cost and Issuer. Sale prices varied by mintmark, from a low of $1 per coin to $12 for a set of three. Issued by the Arkansas Centennial Commission in 1935, 1936, 1938, and 1939 (note that dealer B. Max Mehl bought quantities and retailed them at higher prices in 1935). Issued by Stack's of New York City in 1937.

Key to Collecting. The coin sets were produced with a satiny, almost "greasy" finish; even freshly minted coins appeared as if they had been dipped or repeatedly cleaned. Issues of 1937 to 1939 are usually more satisfactory but still are not deeply lustrous. The prominence of the girl's portrait on the center of the obverse renders that part of the coin prone to receiving bagmarks, scuffs, and other evidence of handling. As a result, relatively few pieces have great eye appeal. The obverse area where the ribbon crosses the eagle's breast is often very weak. Some examples are lightly struck on the eagle just behind its head.

First Points of Wear. *Obverse:* The eagle's head and the top of the left wing. *Reverse:* The band of the girl's cap, behind her eye.

	Distribution	Cert	Avg	%MS	AU-50	MS-60	MS-62	MS-63	MS-64	MS-65	MS-66
									PF-63	PF-64	PF-65
1935	13,012	1,151	64.4	100%	$90	$100	$105	$110	$120	$160	$450
Auctions: $1,116, MS-67, September 2014; $1,528, MS-67 Plus, July 2014; $400, MS-66, December 2014; $558, MS-66, October 2014											
1935-D	5,505	846	64.7	100%	$90	$100	$105	$110	$120	$160	$450
Auctions: $1,880, MS-67, January 2015; $400, MS-66, August 2015; $153, MS-65, January 2015; $100, MS-64, September 2015											
1935-S	5,506	845	64.6	100%	$90	$100	$105	$110	$120	$180	$575
Auctions: $1,939, MS-67, January 2015; $705, MS-66, September 2015; $100, MS-64, January 2015; $74, MS-62, February 2015											
Set of 1935 P-D-S					$270	$300	$315	$330	$360	$500	$1,475
Auctions: $322, MS-64/64/64 Plus, April 2012											
1936	9,660	1,000	64.3	100%	$90	$100	$105	$110	$120	$170	$550
Auctions: $1,998, MS-67, September 2015; $1,116, MS-66, July 2015; $120, MS-64, September 2015; $79, MS-60, August 2015											
1936-D	9,660	958	64.5	100%	$90	$100	$105	$110	$120	$170	$500
Auctions: $2,585, MS-67, January 2015; $353, MS-66, January 2015; $259, MS-65, July 2015; $100, MS-63, January 2015											
1936-S	9,662	978	64.4	100%	$90	$100	$105	$110	$120	$170	$800
Auctions: $1,528, MS-67, January 2015; $282, MS-66, September 2015; $153, MS-65, September 2015; $94, MS-63, October 2015											
Set of 1936 P-D-S					$270	$300	$315	$330	$360	$510	$1,850
Auctions: $300, MS-64/64/65, December 2011											
1937	5,505	749	64.3	100%	$110	$115	$120	$125	$130	$175	$375
Auctions: $2,585, MS-67, June 2015; $541, MS-66, January 2015; $129, MS-64, January 2015; $118, MS-63, August 2015											
1937-D	5,505	803	64.6	100%	$110	$115	$120	$125	$130	$175	$500
Auctions: $2,233, MS-67, January 2015; $494, MS-66, January 2015; $165, MS-64, September 2015; $79, MS-63, April 2015											
1937-S	5,506	646	64.2	100%	$110	$115	$120	$125	$130	$375	$825
Auctions: $999, MS-66, September 2015; $940, MS-66, September 2015; $200, MS-65, May 2015; $79, MS-63, January 2015											
Set of 1937 P-D-S					$330	$345	$360	$375	$490	$725	$1,700
Auctions: $600, MS-65/65/65, January 2012											
1938	3,156	528	64.3	100%	$140	$145	$150	$160	$170	$325	$800
Auctions: $3,290, MS-67, August 2015; $705, MS-66, January 2015; $306, MS-65, February 2015; $106, MS-63, April 2015											
1938-D	3,155	561	64.4	100%	$140	$145	$150	$160	$170	$300	$800
Auctions: $3,055, MS-67, January 2015; $881, MS-66, January 2015; $259, MS-64, June 2015; $123, MS-63, February 2015											
1938-S	3,156	510	64.3	100%	$140	$145	$150	$160	$170	$375	$900
Auctions: $1,058, MS-66, July 2015; $999, MS-66, September 2015; $282, MS-65, January 2015; $153, MS-64, April 2015											
Set of 1938 P-D-S					$420	$435	$450	$480	$510	$1,000	$2,500
Auctions: $2,900, MS-66/66/66, April 2012; $411, MS-63/63/63, October 2015											
Set of 1938 P-D-S, Matte Proof	1–2										
Auctions: No auction records available.											
1939	2,104	441	64.2	100%	$240	$250	$260	$275	$325	$650	$2,250
Auctions: $1,880, MS-66, June 2015; $1,763, MS-66, July 2015; $610, MS-65, January 2015; $306, MS-64, September 2015											
1939-D	2,104	458	64.4	100%	$240	$250	$260	$275	$325	$650	$1,500
Auctions: $3,995, MS-67, August 2015; $1,146, MS-66, January 2015; $470, MS-65, January 2015; $270, MS-63, March 2015											
1939-S	2,105	498	64.5	100%	$240	$250	$260	$275	$325	$650	$1,400
Auctions: $3,760, MS-67, August 2015; $1,939, MS-66, January 2015; $764, MS-65, January 2015; $294, MS-64, April 2015											
Set of 1939 P-D-S					$720	$750	$780	$825	$975	$1,950	$5,150
Auctions: $1,610, MS-65/65/65, February 2012											

ARKANSAS CENTENNIAL—ROBINSON HALF DOLLAR (1936)

Designers: *Henry Kreiss (obverse) and Edward E. Burr (reverse).* **Weight:** *12.50 grams (net weight .3617 oz. pure silver).* **Composition:** *.900 silver, .100 copper.* **Diameter:** *30.6 mm.* **Edge:** *Reeded.* **Mints:** *Philadelphia, Denver, San Francisco.*

A new reverse design for the Arkansas Centennial coin (see preceding coin) was authorized by the Act of June 26, 1936. Senator Joseph T. Robinson was still living at the time his portrait was used. Note that though it is normally true that portraits appear on the obverse of coins, the side bearing Robinson's likeness is indeed technically the reverse of this coin.

Designs. *Obverse:* An eagle with outstretched wings, stars, and other elements of the Arkansas state seal. *Reverse:* Bareheaded profile portrait of Senator Joseph T. Robinson.

Mintage Data. Authorized on June 26, 1936. *Maximum authorized*—50,000 (minimum 25,000). *Number minted*—25,265 (including 15 assay coins). *Net distribution*—25,265.

Original Cost and Issuer. Sale price $1.85. Issued by Stack's of New York City.

Key to Collecting. Most known coins are in MS, as most or all were originally sold to collectors and coin dealers. Examples are plentiful in the marketplace, usually grading MS–62 to 64. The coins were not handled with care during production, so many have contact marks on Robinson's portrait and elsewhere. Some examples are lightly struck on the eagle, just behind the head.

First Points of Wear. *Obverse:* The eagle's head and the top of the left wing. *Reverse:* Robinson's cheekbone.

	Distribution	Cert	Avg	%MS	AU-50	MS-60	MS-62	MS-63	MS-64	MS-65	MS-66
1936	25,265	2,701	64.3	100%	$140	$175	$185	$200	$225	$375	$700
	Auctions: $3,290, MS-67, August 2015; $617, MS-66, January 2015; $212, MS-65, February 2015; $112, MS-63, January 2015										

HUDSON, NEW YORK, SESQUICENTENNIAL HALF DOLLAR (1935)

Designer: *Chester Beach.* **Weight:** *12.50 grams.* **Composition:** *.900 silver, .100 copper (net weight .3617 oz. pure silver).* **Diameter:** *30.6 mm.* **Edge:** *Reeded.* **Mint:** *Philadelphia.*

This souvenir half dollar marked the 150th anniversary of the founding of Hudson, New York, which was named after the explorer Henry Hudson. The area was actually settled in 1662, but not given its permanent name and formally incorporated until 1785. The distribution of these coins was widely criticized, as certain dealers were allowed to purchase large quantities at $1 or less and then resold them at dramatically inflated prices.

Designs. *Obverse:* The ship *Half Moon*, captained by Henry Hudson, in full sail. *Reverse:* The ocean god Neptune seated backward on a whale (derived from the seal of the city of Hudson); in the background, a mermaid blowing a shell.

Mintage Data. Approved May 2, 1935. *Maximum authorized*—10,000. *Number minted*—10,008 (including 8 assay coins). *Net distribution*—10,008.

Original Cost and Issuer. Sale price $1. Issued by the Hudson Sesquicentennial Committee, through the First National Bank & Trust Company of Hudson.

Key to Collecting. Examples are readily available in the marketplace. Note that deep or artificial toning, which can make close inspection impossible, has led some certified coins to certified grades that are higher than they should be. True gems are very rare. These coins were struck at high speed and with little care to preserve their quality; by the time they were originally distributed most pieces showed nicks, contact marks, and other evidence of handling. Most are lustrous and frosty (except on the central devices), and grade in the lower MS levels. MS–62 to 64 are typical. Carefully graded MS-65 coins are scarce, and anything higher is very rare.

First Points of Wear. *Obverse:* The center of the lower middle sail. *Reverse:* The motto on the ribbon, and the figure of Neptune (both of which may also be lightly struck).

	Distribution	Cert	Avg	%MS	AU-50	MS-60	MS-62	MS-63	MS-64	MS-65	MS-66
1935	10,008	1,981	64.1	98%	$750	$800	$850	$900	$950	$1,250	$1,600

Auctions: $8,519, MS-67, July 2015; $2,350, MS-66, September 2015; $1,087, MS-65, September 2015; $588, MS-60, January 2015

CALIFORNIA PACIFIC INTERNATIONAL EXPOSITION HALF DOLLAR (1935–1936)

Designer: *Robert Aitken.* **Weight:** *12.50 grams.* **Composition:** *.900 silver, .100 copper (net weight .3617 oz. pure silver).* **Diameter:** *30.6 mm.* **Edge:** *Reeded.* **Mints:** *San Francisco and Denver.*

Congress approved the coinage of souvenir half dollars for the California Pacific International Exposition on May 3, 1935. The event—held in San Diego's Balboa Park—was attended by only 4 million people, and interest in the coin was not particularly strong.

Designs. *Obverse:* Minerva seated, holding a spear and shield, with a grizzly bear to her right (from California's state seal). *Reverse:* The Chapel of St. Francis and the California Tower, at the California Pacific International Exposition in San Diego.

Mintage and Melting Data. Originally authorized on May 3, 1935; 1936-D issues authorized on May 6, 1936 (for recoinage of melted 1935-S issues). *Maximum authorized*—1935-S: 250,000; 1936-D: 180,000. *Number minted*—1935-S: 250,132 (including 132 assay coins); 1936-D: 180,092 (including 92 assay coins). *Number melted*—1935-S: 180,000; 1936-D: 150,000. *Net distribution*—1935-S: 70,132; 1936-D: 30,092.

Original Cost and Issuer. Sale prices $1 (1935-S; increased to $3 in 1937; dropped to $2 in 1938) and $1.50 (1936-D; increased to $3 in 1937; reduced to $1 in 1938). Issued by the California Pacific International Exposition Company.

Key to Collecting. Both the 1935-S and 1936-D issues were coined with deeply frosty and lustrous surfaces. The eye appeal usually is excellent. The design made these coins susceptible to bagmarks, and most survivors, even in higher MS grades, show evidence of handling. Minerva, in particular, usually displays some graininess or contact marks, even on coins given high numerical grades. Most coins are deeply lustrous and frosty. On the 1935 San Francisco coins the S mintmark usually is flat, and on the Denver coins the California Tower is often lightly struck at the top.

First Points of Wear. *Obverse:* The bosom and knees of Minerva. *Reverse:* The top right edge of the tower. (The 1936-D was flatly struck in this area; examine the texture of the surface to determine if actual wear exists.)

	Distribution	Cert	Avg	%MS	AU-50	MS-60	MS-62	MS-63	MS-64	MS-65	MS-66
1935-S	70,132	4,705	64.9	100%	$105	$110	$115	$120	$130	$150	$200
	Auctions: $2,115, MS-67, September 2015; $223, MS-66, September 2015; $153, MS-65, August 2015; $106, MS-60, February 2015										
1936-D	30,092	2,749	64.9	100%	$110	$130	$135	$140	$150	$225	$250
	Auctions: $1,528, MS-67, January 2015; $188, MS-66, September 2015; $176, MS-65, February 2015; $106, MS-64, September 2015										

OLD SPANISH TRAIL HALF DOLLAR (1935)

Designer: *L.W. Hoffecker.* **Weight:** *12.50 grams.* **Composition:** *.900 silver, .100 copper (net weight .3617 oz. pure silver).* **Diameter:** *30.6 mm.* **Edge:** *Reeded.* **Mint:** *Philadelphia.*

This coin commemorated the 400th anniversary of the overland trek of the Alvar Nuñez Cabeza de Vaca Expedition through the Gulf states in 1535. The coin's designer and distributor, L.W. Hoffecker, is known to have had his hands in many of this era's commemoratives (and the exploitative practices surrounding them).

Designs. *Obverse:* The head of a steer, inspired by the explorer's last name: Cabeza de Vaca translates to "head of cow." *Reverse:* A map of the Southeastern states and a yucca tree.

Mintage Data. Authorized on June 5, 1935. *Maximum authorized—10,000. Number minted—10,008.*

Original Cost and Issuer. Sale price $2. Issued by L.W. Hoffecker, trading as the El Paso Museum Coin Committee.

Key to Collecting. These coins were handled with care during their production and shipping—still, most show scattered contact marks. The typical grade is MS-65 and higher. The fields are usually somewhat satiny and gray, not deeply lustrous and frosty.

First Points of Wear. *Obverse:* The top of the cow's head. *Reverse:* The lettering at the top.

	Distribution	Cert	Avg	%MS	AU-50	MS-60	MS-62	MS-63	MS-64	MS-65	MS-66
1935	10,008	1,852	65.0	100%	$1,100	$1,150	$1,175	$1,200	$1,250	$1,400	$1,800
	Auctions: $2,468, MS-67, September 2015; $1,763, MS-66, January 2015; $1,410, MS-65, January 2015; $764, MS-60, June 2015										

PROVIDENCE, RHODE ISLAND, TERCENTENARY HALF DOLLAR (1936)

Designers: *Arthur G. Carey and John H. Benson.* **Weight:** *12.50 grams.*
Composition: *.900 silver, .100 copper (net weight .3617 oz. pure silver).*
Diameter: *30.6 mm.* **Edge:** *Reeded.* **Mints:** *Philadelphia, Denver, and San Francisco.*

The 300th anniversary of Roger Williams's founding of Providence was the occasion for this special half dollar in 1936. Interestingly, no mention of Providence is to be found on the coin. The distribution of this coin, like that of many other commemoratives of the 1930s, was wrapped in controversy—phony news releases reported that the coin was sold out when it was indeed not, and certain dealers procured large amounts at low prices only to resell for tidy profits.

Designs. *Obverse:* Roger Williams, the founder of Rhode Island, being welcomed by an Indian. *Reverse:* Elements from the Rhode Island state seal, including the anchor of Hope and a shield.

Mintage Data. Authorized on May 2, 1935. *Maximum authorized—50,000. Number minted—1936-P: 20,013 (including 13 assay coins); 1936-D: 15,010 (including 10 assay coins); 1936-S: 15,011 (including 11 assay coins). Net distribution—1936-P: 20,013; 1936-D: 15,010; 1936-S: 15,011.*

Original Cost and Issuer. Sale price $1. Issued by the Rhode Island and Providence Plantations Tercentenary Committee, Inc.

Key to Collecting. These coins are readily available singly and in sets, with typical grades being MS–63 to 65. Contact marks are common. Higher-level coins, such as MS–66 and 67, are not hard to find, but are elusive in comparison to the lesser-condition pieces. The 1936 (in particular) and 1936-S are sometimes found with prooflike surfaces. Most specimens have a combination of satiny/frosty surface. Many are light gray in color.

First Points of Wear. *Obverse:* The prow of the canoe, and the Indian's right shoulder. *Reverse:* The center of the anchor, and surrounding areas.

	Distribution	Cert	Avg	%MS	AU-50	MS-60	MS-62	MS-63	MS-64	MS-65	MS-66
1936	20,013	2,386	64.7	100%	$100	$110	$115	$120	$135	$175	$250
	Auctions: $823, MS-67, July 2015; $165, MS-66, August 2015; $212, MS-65, May 2015; $79, MS-60, February 2015										
1936-D	15,010	1,774	64.7	100%	$100	$110	$115	$120	$135	$175	$250
	Auctions: $969, MS-67, November 2015; $435, MS-66, January 2015; $176, MS-65, August 2015; $100, MS-64, May 2015										
1936-S	15,011	1,511	64.6	100%	$100	$110	$115	$120	$135	$175	$300
	Auctions: $2,820, MS-67, January 2015; $470, MS-66, November 2015; $112, MS-64, May 2015; $69, EF-45, September 2015										
Set of 1936 P-D-S					$330	$345	$350	$410	$525	$800	
	Auctions: $2,185, MS-66/66/66, January 2012										

CLEVELAND CENTENNIAL / GREAT LAKES EXPOSITION HALF DOLLAR (1936)

Designer: *Brenda Putnam.* **Weight:** *12.50 grams.* **Composition:** *.900 silver, .100 copper (net weight .3617 oz. pure silver).* **Diameter:** *30.6 mm.* **Edge:** *Reeded.* **Mint:** *Philadelphia.*

A special coinage of fifty-cent pieces was authorized in commemoration of the centennial celebration of Cleveland, Ohio, on the occasion of the Great Lakes Exposition held there in 1936. Numismatic entrepreneur Thomas G. Melish was behind the coins' production and distribution—though he served as the Cleveland Centennial Commemorative Coin Association's treasurer while based in Cincinnati.

Designs. *Obverse:* Bewigged profile portrait of Moses Cleaveland. *Reverse:* A map of the Great Lakes region with nine stars marking various cities, and a compass point at the city of Cleveland.

Mintage Data. Authorized on May 5, 1936. *Maximum authorized*—50,000 (minimum 25,000). *Number minted*—50,030 (including 30 assay coins). *Net distribution*—50,030.

Original Cost and Issuer. Sale prices: one coin for $1.65; two for $1.60 each; three for $1.58 each; five for $1.56 each; ten for $1.55 each; twenty for $1.54 each; fifty for $1.53 each; one hundred for $1.52 each. Issued by the Cleveland Centennial Commemorative Coin Association (Thomas G. Melish, Cincinnati).

Key to Collecting. The Cleveland half dollar is the most readily available issue from 1936—a bumper-crop year for U.S. commemoratives. Nearly all coins are in Mint State, typically from MS–63 to 65, and most are very lustrous and frosty. This issue was not handled with care at the Mint, and scattered contact marks are typically found on both obverse and reverse.

First Points of Wear. *Obverse:* The hair behind Cleaveland's ear. *Reverse:* The top of the compass, and the land (non-lake) areas of the map.

	Distribution	Cert	Avg	%MS	AU-50	MS-60	MS-62	MS-63	MS-64	MS-65	MS-66
1936	50,030	4,814	64.6	100%	$100	$110	$120	$130	$135	$160	$250

Auctions: $3,995, MS-68, June 2015; $1,293, MS-67, September 2015; $247, MS-66, November 2015; $65, MS-62, March 2015

WISCONSIN TERRITORIAL CENTENNIAL HALF DOLLAR (1936)

Designer: *David Parsons.* **Weight:** *12.50 grams.* **Composition:** *.900 silver, .100 copper (net weight .3617 oz. pure silver).* **Diameter:** *30.6 mm.* **Edge:** *Reeded.* **Mint:** *Philadelphia.*

The 100th anniversary of the Wisconsin territorial government was the occasion for this issue. Benjamin Hawkins, a New York artist, made changes to the original designs by University of Wisconsin student David Parsons so that the piece conformed to technical requirements.

Designs. *Obverse:* A badger on a log, from the state emblem; and arrows representing the Black Hawk War of the 1830s. *Reverse:* A miner's arm holding a pickaxe over a mound of lead ore, derived from Wisconsin's territorial seal.

Mintage Data. Authorized on May 15, 1936. *Minimum authorized*—25,000 (unlimited maximum). *Number minted*—25,015 (including 15 assay coins). *Net distribution*—25,015.

Original Cost and Issuer. Sale price $1.50 plus 7¢ postage for the first coin, 2¢ postage for each additional coin (later sold for $1.25 each in lots of 10 coins, and still later sold for $3 per coin). Issued by the Wisconsin Centennial Coin Committee (also known as the Coinage Committee of the Wisconsin Centennial Commission). Unsold remainders were distributed, into the 1950s, by the State Historical Society.

Key to Collecting. Examples are readily available in the marketplace. Most grade MS–62 to 64— although higher grades are not rare—and are very lustrous and frosty, except for the higher areas of the design (which often have a slightly polished appearance).

First Points of Wear. *Obverse:* The flank and shoulder of the badger. *Reverse:* The miner's hand.

	Distribution	Cert	Avg	%MS	AU-50	MS-60	MS-62	MS-63	MS-64	MS-65	MS-66
1936	25,015	3,854	65.3	100%	$180	$190	$195	$200	$210	$225	$280
	Auctions: $3,055, MS-68, January 2015; $881, MS-67, January 2015; $235, MS-65, August 2015; $129, MS-60, November 2015										

CINCINNATI MUSIC CENTER HALF DOLLAR (1936)

Designer: *Constance Ortmayer.* **Weight:** *12.50 grams.*
Composition: *.900 silver, .100 copper (net weight .3617 oz. pure silver).*
Diameter: *30.6 mm.* **Edge:** *Reeded.* **Mints:** *Philadelphia, Denver, and San Francisco.*

Although the head of Stephen Foster, "America's Troubadour," dominates the obverse of this special issue, the anniversary celebrated bears little to no relation to him. Foster did live in Cincinnati for a time, but never worked in music while there. The coins were supposedly struck to commemorate the 50th anniversary in 1936 of Cincinnati as a center of music, but the issue was really a personal project of numismatist Thomas G. Melish.

Designs. *Obverse:* Bareheaded profile portrait of Stephen Foster, "America's Troubadour." *Reverse:* A woman playing a lyre, personifying Music.

Mintage Data. Authorized on March 31, 1936. *Maximum authorized*—15,000. *Number minted*—1936-P: 5,005 (including 5 assay coins); 1936-D: 5,005 (including 5 assay coins); 1936-S: 5,006 (including 6 assay coins). *Net distribution*—1936-P: 5,005; 1936-D: 5,005; 1936-S: 5,006.

Original Cost and Issuer. Sale price $7.75 per set of three (actually $7.50 plus 25¢ for the display container with cellophane slide front). Issued by the Cincinnati Musical Center Commemorative Coin Association, Ohio (Thomas G. Melish).

Key to Collecting. Nearly all sets of these coins were bought by collectors and investors, thus most still exist in Mint State, primarily MS–63 to 65. Conservatively graded MS–65 and finer pieces are rare. Most coins were carelessly handled at the mints, and nearly all show scattered contact marks. This issue has a somewhat satiny or "greasy" surface, instead of fields with deep luster and frost. Denver Mint coins are typically found in slightly higher grades than their Philadelphia and San Francisco Mint companions.

First Points of Wear. *Obverse:* The hair at Foster's temple. *Reverse:* The left breast, and the skirt, of the female figure.

	Distribution	Cert	Avg	%MS	AU-50	MS-60	MS-62	MS-63	MS-64	MS-65	MS-66
1936	5,005	877	64.4	100%	$300	$310	$340	$375	$380	$425	$700
	Auctions: $4,700, MS-67, January 2015; $2,115, MS-66, January 2015; $423, MS-65, September 2015; $329, MS-64, January 2015										
1936-D	5,005	1,231	64.9	100%	$300	$310	$340	$375	$380	$500	$1,400
	Auctions: $3,290, MS-67, September 2015; $940, MS-66, January 2015; $705, MS-65, January 2015; $188, MS-60, November 2015										
1936-S	5,006	890	64.1	100%	$300	$310	$340	$375	$380	$425	$700
	Auctions: $3,055, MS-66, January 2015; $470, MS-65, January 2015; $329, MS-64, January 2015; $306, MS-63, January 2015										
Set of 1935 P-D-S					$900	$930	$1,020	$1,125	$1,140	$1,350	$2,800
	Auctions: $4,198, MS-66/66/66, February 2012										

LONG ISLAND TERCENTENARY HALF DOLLAR (1936)

Designer: *Howard K. Weinman.* **Weight:** *12.50 grams.* **Composition:** *.900 silver, .100 copper (net weight .3617 oz. pure silver).* **Diameter:** *30.6 mm.* **Edge:** *Reeded.* **Mint:** *Philadelphia.*

This souvenir issue was authorized to commemorate the 300th anniversary of the first white settlement on Long Island, which was made at Jamaica Bay by Dutch colonists. This was the first issue for which a date was specified (1936) irrespective of the year minted or issued, as a safeguard against extending the coinage over a period of years. This measure proved effective in preventing many of the profiteering problems that arose with other commemorative issues of the era.

Designs. *Obverse:* Conjoined profile portraits of a Dutch settler and an Algonquin Indian. *Reverse:* A Dutch vessel with full-blown sails.

Mintage and Melting Data. Authorized on April 13, 1936. *Maximum authorized*—100,000. *Number minted*—100,053 (including 53 assay coins). *Number melted*—18,227. *Net distribution*—81,826.

Original Cost and Issuer. Sale price $1. Issued by the Long Island Tercentenary Committee, through various banks and other outlets.

Key to Collecting. These are among the most plentiful survivors from the commemorative issues of the 1930s, and examples grading MS–64 to 66 are readily obtainable. The coins were minted and handled carelessly, and at the time of distribution most showed nicks, bagmarks, and other evidence of contact; these grade from AU-50 to MS-60. Most coins have, as struck, a satiny or slightly "greasy" luster and are not deeply frosty.

First Points of Wear. *Obverse:* The hair and the cheekbone of the Dutch settler. *Reverse:* The center of the lower middle sail.

	Distribution	Cert	Avg	%MS	AU-50	MS-60	MS-62	MS-63	MS-64	MS-65	MS-66
1936	81,826	4,460	64.2	99%	$85	$100	$110	$120	$130	$200	$400
	Auctions: $9,988, MS-67, September 2015; $1,293, MS-66, January 2015; $129, MS-64, February 2015; $52, EF-40, July 2015										

YORK COUNTY, MAINE, TERCENTENARY HALF DOLLAR (1936)

Designer: *Walter H. Rich.* **Weight:** *12.50 grams.* **Composition:** *.900 silver, .100 copper (net weight .3617 oz. pure silver).* **Diameter:** *30.6 mm.* **Edge:** *Reeded.* **Mint:** *Philadelphia.*

A souvenir half dollar was authorized by Congress upon the 300th anniversary of the founding of York County, Maine. While the commemorated event was considered somewhat obscure, the proposing and distributing group—the York County Tercentenary Commemorative Coin Commission, led by ardent numismatist Walter P. Nichols—was lauded for its diligence and proper handling of the release.

Designs. *Obverse:* Brown's Garrison, on the Saco River (site of the original settlement in York County in 1636). *Reverse:* An adaptation of the seal of York County.

Mintage Data. *Maximum authorized*—30,000. *Number minted*—25,015 (including 15 assay coins).

Original Cost and Issuer. Sale price $1.50 ($1.65 postpaid by mail to out-of-state buyers). Issued by the York County Tercentenary Commemorative Coin Commission, York National Bank, Saco, Maine.

Key to Collecting. This issue was well handled at the Mint and in distribution, so most examples are in higher grades and are relatively free of marks. On the reverse, the top of the shield is a key point. Some coins have been brushed and have a myriad of fine hairlines; these can be detected by examining the coin at various angles to the light. MS–64 and 65 coins are readily found in the marketplace.

First Points of Wear. *Obverse:* The mounted sentry near the corner of the fort; the stockade; and the rim of the coin. *Reverse:* The pine tree in the shield; the top-right area of the shield; and the rim.

	Distribution	Cert	Avg	%MS	AU-50	MS-60	MS-62	MS-63	MS-64	MS-65	MS-66
1936	25,015	3,431	65.4	100%	$160	$165	$170	$175	$180	$225	$260

Auctions: $1,763, MS-68, August 2015; $881, MS-67, September 2015; $259, MS-66, January 2015; $121, MS-60, January 2015

BRIDGEPORT, CONNECTICUT, CENTENNIAL HALF DOLLAR (1936)

Designer: *Henry Kreiss.* **Weight:** *12.50 grams.* **Composition:** *.900 silver, .100 copper (net weight .3617 oz. pure silver).* **Diameter:** *30.6 mm.* **Edge:** *Reeded.* **Mint:** *Philadelphia.*

In commemoration of the 100th anniversary of the incorporation of the city of Bridgeport, a special fifty-cent piece was authorized on May 15, 1936. The city—actually originally founded in 1639—served as an important center in the 17th and 18th centuries.

Designs. *Obverse:* Bareheaded profile portrait of P.T. Barnum, Bridgeport's most famous citizen. *Reverse:* An art deco eagle, standing.

Mintage Data. Authorized on May 15, 1936. *Minimum authorized*—25,000 (unlimited maximum). *Number minted*—25,015 (including 15 assay coins). *Net distribution*—25,015.

Original Cost and Issuer. Sale price $2. Issued by Bridgeport Centennial, Inc., through the First National Bank and Trust Co. and other banks.

Key to Collecting. These coins are readily available in the marketplace. Most grade from MS–62 to 64. Many have been cleaned or lightly polished, but pristine MS–65 pieces are readily available. Obvious friction rub and/or marks are often seen. Some coins were struck from dies with lightly polished fields and have a prooflike or partially prooflike appearance in those areas.

First Points of Wear. *Obverse:* Barnum's cheek. *Reverse:* The eagle's wing.

	Distribution	Cert	Avg	%MS	AU-50	MS-60	MS-62	MS-63	MS-64	MS-65	MS-66
1936	25,015	3,088	64.6	100%	$125	$130	$135	$140	$150	$180	$325
	Auctions: $1,880, MS-67, September 2015; $353, MS-66, February 2015; $235, MS-65, August 2015; $106, MS-60, May 2015										

LYNCHBURG, VIRGINIA, SESQUICENTENNIAL HALF DOLLAR (1936)

Designer: *Charles Keck.* **Weight:** *12.50 grams.* **Composition:** *.900 silver, .100 copper (net weight .3617 oz. pure silver).* **Diameter:** *30.6 mm.* **Edge:** *Reeded.* **Mint:** *Philadelphia.*

The issuance of a charter to the city of Lynchburg in 1786 was commemorated in 1936 by a special coinage of half dollars. Interestingly, Lynchburg native Senator Carter Glass objected to the use of portraits of living persons on coins, but was featured on the issue anyway. It was considered that a portrait of John Lynch—for whom the city was named—would be used, but no such likeness existed.

Designs. *Obverse:* Bareheaded profile portrait of Senator Carter Glass, a native of Lynchburg and former secretary of the Treasury. *Reverse:* A figure of Miss Liberty standing before the old Lynchburg courthouse.

Mintage Data. Authorized on May 28, 1936. *Maximum authorized*—20,000. *Number minted*—20,013 (including 13 assay coins). *Net distribution*—20,013.

Original Cost and Issuer. Sale price $1. Issued by the Lynchburg Sesqui-Centennial Association.

Key to Collecting. Most of these half dollars are in higher grades; MS–65 and 66 examples are readily available in the marketplace. Some show graininess (from striking) on the high areas of the obverse portrait and on the bosom and skirt of Miss Liberty, or show evidences of handling or contact in the same areas. Surfaces are often somewhat satiny, instead of deeply lustrous and frosty. Often the reverse field is semi-prooflike. This issue must have been handled with particular care at the Mint.

First Points of Wear. *Obverse:* The hair above Glass's ear. *Reverse:* The hair of Miss Liberty, the folds of her gown, and her bosom.

	Distribution	Cert	Avg	%MS	AU-50	MS-60	MS-62	MS-63	MS-64	MS-65	MS-66
1936	20,013	2,609	64.8	100%	$225	$230	$235	$240	$280	$320	$375
	Auctions: $2,820, MS-67, January 2015; $294, MS-66, June 2015; $170, MS-63, October 2015; $118, AU-58, August 2015										

Elgin, Illinois, Centennial Half Dollar (1936)

Designer: *Trygve Rovelstad.* **Weight:** *12.50 grams.* **Composition:** *.900 silver, .100 copper (net weight .3617 oz. pure silver).* **Diameter:** *30.6 mm.* **Edge:** *Reeded.* **Mint:** *Philadelphia.*

The 100th anniversary of the founding of Elgin, Illinois, was marked by a special issue of half dollars in 1936. The year 1673 (seen on the obverse) bears no relation to the event but refers to the year in which Louis Joliet and Jacques Marquette entered Illinois Territory.

Designs. *Obverse:* The fur-capped profile of a bearded pioneer (a close-up view of the statue depicted on the reverse). *Reverse:* The Pioneer Memorial statuary group, whose creation was financed by the sale of these coins.

Mintage and Melting Data. Authorized on June 16, 1936. *Maximum authorized—25,000. Number minted—25,015 (including 15 assay coins). Number melted—5,000. Net distribution—20,015.*

Original Cost and Issuer. Sale price $1.50. Issued by the Elgin Centennial Monumental Committee, El Paso, Texas (L.W. Hoffecker in charge), through banks in and near Elgin, including the First National Bank of Elgin, the Elgin National Bank, and the Union National Bank.

Key to Collecting. Elgin half dollars are fairly plentiful in today's marketplace. They seem to have been handled with particular care at the time of minting, as most have fewer bagmarks than many other commemoratives of the same era. Typical coins grade MS–64 to 66. The surfaces often have a matte-like appearance (seemingly a combination of a lustrous circulation strike and a Matte Proof) quite different from other commemorative issues of 1936. Some coins are fairly frosty. On many a bright spot is evident on the reverse below the A of AMERICA, the result of an inadvertent polishing on a small area of the die. Chief Engraver John Sinnock made a few Matte Proofs, perhaps as many as 10, by pickling coins in acid at the Mint.

First Points of Wear. *Obverse:* The cheek of the pioneer. *Reverse:* The rifleman's left shoulder. (Note that a lack of detailed facial features is the result of striking, not wear, and that the infant is always weakly struck.)

	Distribution	Cert	Avg	%MS	AU-50	MS-60	MS-62	MS-63	MS-64	MS-65	MS-66
1936	20,015	3,310	65.0	100%	$180	$185	$190	$195	$200	$225	$300

Auctions: $3,995, MS-68, January 2015; $1,880, MS-67, September 2015; $200, MS-65, April 2015; $165, MS-60, February 2015

Albany, New York, Charter Half Dollar (1936)

Designer: *Gertrude K. Lathrop.* **Weight:** *12.50 grams.* **Composition:** *.900 silver, .100 copper (net weight .3617 oz. pure silver).* **Diameter:** *30.6 mm.* **Edge:** *Reeded.* **Mint:** *Philadelphia.*

The 250th anniversary of the granting of a charter to the city of Albany—an event of strictly local significance—was the occasion for this commemorative half dollar. Amusingly, designer Gertrude K. Lathrop kept a live beaver in her studio (courtesy of the state Conservation Department) during her work.

Designs. *Obverse:* A plump beaver gnawing on a maple branch—fauna and flora evocative of Albany and New York State, respectively. *Reverse:* A scene with Albany's first mayor, Peter Schuyler, and his secretary, Robert Livingston, accepting the city's charter in 1686 from Governor Thomas Dongan of New York.

Mintage and Melting Data. Authorized on June 16, 1936. *Maximum authorized*—25,000. *Number minted*—25,013 (including 13 assay coins). *Number melted*—7,342. *Net distribution*—17,671.

Original Cost and Issuer. Sale price $1. Issued by the Albany Dongan Charter Coin Committee.

Key to Collecting. This issue was fairly carefully handled during production and distribution, and most examples are relatively free of marks in the fields. Most specimens are lustrous and frosty, although the frost has satiny aspects. Albany half dollars are readily available on the market. The typical example grades from MS–63 to 65 and has at least minor friction and marks.

First Points of Wear. *Obverse:* The hip of the beaver (nearly all coins show at least minor evidence of contact here). *Reverse:* The sleeve of Dongan (the figure at left).

	Distribution	Cert	Avg	%MS	AU-50	MS-60	MS-62	MS-63	MS-64	MS-65	MS-66
1936	17,671	2,944	64.8	100%	$225	$230	$235	$240	$250	$275	$450

Auctions: $1,293, MS-67, September 2015; $470, MS-66, February 2015; $282, MS-65, June 2015; $176, MS-60, September 2015

SAN FRANCISCO–OAKLAND BAY BRIDGE OPENING HALF DOLLAR (1936)

Designer: *Jacques Schnier.* **Weight:** *12.50 grams.* **Composition:** *.900 silver, .100 copper (net weight .3617 oz. pure silver).* **Diameter:** *30.6 mm.* **Edge:** *Reeded.* **Mint:** *San Francisco.*

The opening of the San Francisco Bay Bridge was the occasion for a special souvenir fifty-cent piece. The bear depicted on the obverse was a composite of animals in local zoos.

Designs. *Obverse:* A stylized grizzly bear standing on all fours and facing the viewer. *Reverse:* A fading-to-the-horizon view of the San Francisco–Oakland Bay Bridge and part of San Francisco.

Mintage and Melting Data. Authorized on June 26, 1936. *Maximum authorized*—200,000. *Number minted*—100,055 (including 55 assay coins). *Number melted*—28,631. *Net distribution*—71,424.

Original Cost and Issuer. Sale price $1.50. Issued by the Coin Committee of the San Francisco–Oakland Bay Bridge Celebration.

Key to Collecting. These coins are readily available in today's marketplace, with most grading MS–62 to 64, typically with contact marks on the grizzly bear. The reverse design, being complex with many protective devices, normally appears free of marks, unless viewed at an angle under a strong light. The grade of the reverse for a given coin often is a point or two higher than that of the obverse. The fields of this coin often have a "greasy" appearance, rather than being deeply lustrous and frosty.

First Points of Wear. *Obverse:* The bear's body, in particular the left shoulder. *Reverse:* The clouds.

	Distribution	Cert	Avg	%MS	AU-50	MS-60	MS-62	MS-63	MS-64	MS-65	MS-66
1936-S	71,424	3,699	64.6	99%	$150	$155	$160	$165	$175	$225	$350

Auctions: $1,763, MS-67, January 2015; $764, MS-66, September 2015; $153, MS-64, January 2015; $129, AU-58, January 2015

COLUMBIA, SOUTH CAROLINA, SESQUICENTENNIAL HALF DOLLAR (1936)

Designer: *A. Wolfe Davidson.* **Weight:** *12.50 grams.*
Composition: *.900 silver, .100 copper (net weight .3617 oz. pure silver).*
Diameter: *30.6 mm.* **Edge:** *Reeded.* **Mints:** *Philadelphia, Denver, and San Francisco.*

Souvenir half dollars were authorized to help finance the extensive celebrations marking the sesquicentennial of the founding of Columbia, South Carolina, in 1786. The pieces had not been minted by the time of the actual celebrations, which took place in late March 1936, and only reached collectors (which the Columbia Sesqui-Centennial Commission expressed desire to sell to instead of to dealers) in December.

Designs. *Obverse:* Justice, with sword and scales, standing before the state capitol of 1786 and the capitol of 1936. *Reverse:* A palmetto tree, the state emblem, with stars encircling.

Mintage Data. Authorized on March 18, 1936. *Maximum authorized*—25,000. *Number minted*—1936-P: 9,007; 1936-D: 8,009; 1936-S: 8,007. *Net distribution*—1936-P: 9,007; 1936-D: 8,009; 1936-S: 8,007.

Original Cost and Issuer. Sale price $6.45 per set of three (single coins $2.15 each). Issued by the Columbia Sesqui-Centennial Commission.

Key to Collecting. These coins were widely distributed at the time of issue, and examples are readily obtainable today. Most grade from MS–63 to 65. They were treated carefully in their minting and distribution, so most coins exhibit lustrous surfaces with very few handling marks. Nearly all, however, show friction on the bosom of Justice and, to a lesser extent, on the high areas of the palmetto-tree foliage on the reverse.

First Points of Wear. *Obverse:* The right breast of Justice. *Reverse:* The top of the palmetto tree.

	Distribution	Cert	Avg	%MS	AU-50	MS-60	MS-62	MS-63	MS-64	MS-65	MS-66
1936	9,007	1,549	65.2	100%	$180	$185	$190	$200	$210	$225	$325
	Auctions: $2,585, MS-68, June 2015; $705, MS-67, May 2015; $235, MS-64, July 2015; $376, MS-62, October 2015										
1936-D	8,009	1,627	65.7	100%	$180	$185	$190	$200	$210	$225	$325
	Auctions: $705, MS-67, June 2015; $294, MS-66, February 2015; $212, MS-65, August 2015; $194, MS-63, July 2015										
1936-S	8,007	1,536	65.4	100%	$180	$185	$190	$200	$210	$225	$325
	Auctions: $7,638, MS-68, August 2015; $999, MS-67, September 2015; $306, MS-66, January 2015; $165, MS-63, October 2015										
Set of 1936 P-D-S					$540	$555	$570	$600	$630	$775	$975
	Auctions: $690, MS-65/66/65, February 2012										

DELAWARE TERCENTENARY HALF DOLLAR (1936)

Designer: *Carl L. Schmitz.* **Weight:** *12.50 grams.* **Composition:** *.900 silver, .100 copper (net weight .3617 oz. pure silver).* **Diameter:** *30.6 mm.* **Edge:** *Reeded.* **Mint:** *Philadelphia.*

The 300th anniversary of the landing of the Swedes in Delaware was the occasion for a souvenir issue of half dollars—as well as a two-krona coin issued in Sweden. The colonists landed on the spot that is now Wilmington and established a church, which is the oldest Protestant church in the United States still used for worship. Carl L. Schmitz's designs were chosen through a competition. These coins were authorized in 1936 and struck in 1937, but not released until 1938, as the Swedes' arrival was actually in 1638.

Designs. *Obverse:* Old Swedes Church. *Reverse:* The ship *Kalmar Nyckel.*

Mintage and Melting Data. Authorized on May 15, 1936. *Minimum authorized*—25,000 (unlimited maximum). *Number minted*—25,015 (including 15 assay coins). *Number melted*—4,022. *Net distribution*—20,993.

Original Cost and Issuer. Sale price $1.75. Issued by the Delaware Swedish Tercentenary Commission, through the Equitable Trust Company of Wilmington.

Key to Collecting. Most examples in today's marketplace grade MS–64 or 65, though they typically exhibit numerous original planchet nicks and marks. Most coins are very lustrous and frosty.

First Points of Wear. *Obverse:* The roof above the church entrance. (Note that the triangular section at the top of the entrance is weakly struck, giving an appearance of wear.) *Reverse:* The center of the lower middle sail (also often shows graininess and nicks from the original planchet).

	Distribution	Cert	Avg	%MS	AU-50	MS-60	MS-62	MS-63	MS-64	MS-65	MS-66
1936	20,993	2,957	64.7	100%	$210	$215	$220	$230	$240	$270	$375
	Auctions: $881, MS-67, January 2015; $541, MS-66, October 2015; $188, MS-63, September 2015; $176, MS-60, August 2015										

BATTLE OF GETTYSBURG ANNIVERSARY HALF DOLLAR (1936)

Designer: *Frank Vittor.* **weight:** *12.50 grams.* **Composition:** *.900 silver, .100 copper (net weight .3617 oz. pure silver).* **Diameter:** *30.6 mm.* **Edge:** *Reeded.* **Mint:** *Philadelphia.*

On June 16, 1936, Congress authorized a coinage of fifty-cent pieces in commemoration of the 75th anniversary of the 1863 Battle of Gettysburg. Similar to the previously mentioned Delaware Tercentenary coins, the coins were authorized two years before the event commemorated, and were minted a year early as well (in 1937). Paul L. Roy, secretary of the Pennsylvania State Commission, desired for the pieces to be struck at multiple mints—so as to sell more expensive sets of three coins, rather than just Philadelphia issues—but no coins were struck in Denver or San Francisco in the end.

Designs. *Obverse:* Uniformed profile portraits of a Union soldier and a Confederate soldier. *Reverse:* Union and Confederate shields separated by a fasces.

Mintage and Melting Data. Authorized on June 16, 1936. *Maximum authorized—50,000. Number minted—50,028 (including 28 assay coins). Number melted—23,100. Net distribution—26,928.*

Original Cost and Issuer. Sale price $1.65. Issued by the Pennsylvania State Commission, Hotel Gettysburg, Gettysburg. The price was later raised to $2.65 for coins offered by the American Legion, Department of Pennsylvania.

Key to Collecting. Examples are fairly plentiful in the marketplace. The typical coin grades from MS–63 to 65, is deeply frosty and lustrous, and shows scattered contact marks, which are most evident on the cheeks of the soldiers on the obverse and, on the reverse, on the two shields (particularly at the top of the Union shield on the left side of the coin).

First Points of Wear. *Obverse:* The cheekbones of each soldier. *Reverse:* The three ribbons on the fasces, and the top of the Union shield.

	Distribution	Cert	Avg	%MS	AU-50	MS-60	MS-62	MS-63	MS-64	MS-65	MS-66
1936	26,928	3,338	64.5	99%	$425	$430	$440	$450	$575	$850	$1,050

Auctions: $2,703, MS-67, January 2015; $1,763, MS-66, July 2015; $541, MS-64, September 2015; $423, AU-55, September 2015

Norfolk, Virginia, Bicentennial Half Dollar (1936)

Designers: *William M. and Marjorie E. Simpson.* **Weight:** *12.50 grams.*
Composition: *.900 silver, .100 copper (net weight .3617 oz. pure silver).*
Diameter: *30.6 mm.* **Edge:** *Reeded.* **Mint:** *Philadelphia.*

To provide funds for the celebration of Norfolk's anniversary of its growth from a township in 1682 to a royal borough in 1736, Congress first passed a law for the striking of medals. The proponents, however, being dissatisfied, finally succeeded in winning authority for half dollars commemorating the 300th anniversary of the original Norfolk land grant and the 200th anniversary of the establishment of the borough. In a strange twist, none of the five dates on these coins actually reflects the year of the coins' actual striking (1937).

Designs. *Obverse:* The seal of the city of Norfolk, Virginia, with a three-masted ship at center. *Reverse:* The city's royal mace, presented by Lieutenant Governor Robert Dinwiddie in 1753.

Mintage and Melting Data. Authorized on June 28, 1937. *Maximum authorized—25,000. Number minted—25,013 (including 13 assay coins). Number melted—8,077. Net distribution—16,936.*

Original Cost and Issuer. Sale price $1.50 locally ($1.65 by mail for the first coin, $1.55 for each additional). Issued by the Norfolk Advertising Board, Norfolk Association of Commerce.

Key to Collecting. Examples are fairly plentiful in today's marketplace, with most in high MS grades. The cluttered nature of the design had a positive effect: all of the lettering served to protect the fields and devices from nicks and marks, with the result that MS–65 and 66 coins are plentiful.

First Points of Wear. *Obverse:* The sails of the ship, especially the lower rear sail. *Reverse:* The area below the crown on the royal mace.

	Distribution	Cert	Avg	%MS	AU-50	MS-60	MS-62	MS-63	MS-64	MS-65	MS-66
1936	16,936	2,762	65.9	100%	$300	$305	$310	$315	$325	$350	$380

Auctions: $1,175, MS-68, September 2015; $482, MS-67, August 2015; $388, MS-66, May 2015; $306, MS-64, August 2015

ROANOKE ISLAND, NORTH CAROLINA, 350TH ANNIVERSARY HALF DOLLAR (1937)

Designer: *William M. Simpson.* **Weight:** *12.50 grams.* **Composition:** *.900 silver, .100 copper (net weight .3617 oz. pure silver).* **Diameter:** *30.6 mm.* **Edge:** *Reeded.* **Mint:** *Philadelphia.*

A celebration was held in Old Fort Raleigh in 1937 to commemorate the 350th anniversary of Sir Walter Raleigh's "Lost Colony" and the birth of Virginia Dare, the first white child born in British North America. Interestingly, Raleigh himself never actually visited America, but only sent ships of colonists who eventually founded a city in his name.

Designs. *Obverse:* Profile portrait of Sir Walter Raleigh in plumed hat and fancy collar. *Reverse:* Ellinor Dare and her baby, Virginia, the first white child born in the Americas to English parents.

Mintage and Melting Data. *Minimum authorized*—25,000 (unlimited maximum). *Number minted*—50,030 (including 30 assay coins). *Number melted*—21,000. *Net distribution*—29,030.

Original Cost and Issuer. Sale price $1.65. Issued by the Roanoke Colony Memorial Association of Manteo.

Key to Collecting. Most of these coins were handled with care during their minting, and today are in high grades. MS-65 pieces are plentiful. Most coins are lustrous and frosty. Partially prooflike pieces are occasionally seen (sometimes offered as "presentation pieces" or "prooflike presentation pieces").

First Points of Wear. *Obverse:* Raleigh's cheek and the brim of his hat. *Reverse:* The head of Ellinor Dare.

	Distribution	Cert	Avg	%MS	AU-50	MS-60	MS-62	MS-63	MS-64	MS-65	MS-66
1937	29,030	3,897	65.1	100%	$160	$165	$170	$175	$180	$200	$260
	Auctions: $5,170, MS-68, October 2015; $940, MS-67, August 2015; $188, MS-64, September 2015; $112, AU-50, November 2015										

BATTLE OF ANTIETAM ANNIVERSARY HALF DOLLAR (1937)

Designer: *William M. Simpson.* **Weight:** *12.50 grams.* **Composition:** *.900 silver, .100 copper (net weight .3617 oz. pure silver).* **Diameter:** *30.6 mm.* **Edge:** *Reeded.* **Mint:** *Philadelphia.*

A souvenir half dollar was struck in 1937 to commemorate the 75th anniversary of the famous Civil War battle to thwart Robert E. Lee's invasion of Maryland. The Battle of Antietam, which took place on September 17, 1862, was one of the bloodiest single-day battles of the war, with more than 23,000 men killed, wounded, or missing.

Designs. *Obverse:* Uniformed profile portraits of generals Robert E. Lee and George B. McClellan, opponent commanders during the Battle of Antietam. *Reverse:* Burnside Bridge, an important tactical objective of the battle.

Mintage and Melting Data. Authorized on June 24, 1937. *Maximum authorized*—50,000. *Number minted*—50,028 (including 28 assay coins). *Number melted*—32,000. *Net distribution*—18,028.

Original Cost and Issuer. Sale price $1.65. Issued by the Washington County Historical Society, Hagerstown, Maryland.

Key to Collecting. Antietam half dollars were handled with care during production. More often seen are scattered small marks, particularly on the upper part of the obverse. Most examples are very lustrous and frosty. MS-65 and finer coins are plentiful in the marketplace.

First Points of Wear. *Obverse:* Lee's cheekbone. *Reverse:* The leaves of the trees; the bridge; and the rim of the coin.

	Distribution	Cert	Avg	%MS	AU-50	MS-60	MS-62	MS-63	MS-64	MS-65	MS-66
1937	18,028	2,686	65.1	100%	$575	$600	$625	$650	$700	$750	$800

Auctions: $4,935, MS-68, January 2015; $1,411, MS-67, February 2015; $705, MS-65, September 2015; $447, AU-50, January 2015

NEW ROCHELLE, NEW YORK, 250TH ANNIVERSARY HALF DOLLAR (1938)

Designer: *Gertrude K. Lathrop.* **Weight:** *12.50 grams.* **Composition:** *.900 silver, .100 copper (net weight .3617 oz. pure silver).* **Diameter:** *30.6 mm.* **Edge:** *Reeded.* **Mint:** *Philadelphia.*

To observe the founding of New Rochelle in 1688 by French Huguenots, a special half dollar was issued in 1938. The title to the land that the Huguenots purchased from John Pell provided that a fattened calf be given away every year on June 20; this is represented the obverse of the coin.

Designs. *Obverse:* John Pell, who sold the French Huguenots the land for New Rochelle, and a fatted calf, an annual provision of the sale. *Reverse:* A fleur-de-lis, adapted from the seal of the city.

Mintage and Melting Data. Authorized on May 5, 1936. *Maximum authorized*—25,000. *Number minted*—25,015 (including 15 assay coins). *Number melted*—9,749. *Net distribution*—15,266.

Original Cost and Issuer. Sale price $2. Issued by the New Rochelle Commemorative Coin Committee, through the First National Bank of New Rochelle, New Rochelle, New York.

Key to Collecting. These half dollars received better-than-average care and handling during the minting and distribution process. The typical coin grades MS-64 or higher. Some examples show very light handling marks, but most are relatively problem-free. Some show areas of graininess or light striking on the high spots of the calf on the obverse, and on the highest area of the iris on the reverse. The majority of pieces have lustrous, frosty surfaces, and a few are prooflike (the latter are sometimes offered as "presentation pieces").

First Points of Wear. *Obverse:* The hip of the calf. *Reverse:* The bulbous part of the fleur-de-lis. (Note that on the central petal the midrib is flatly struck.)

	Distribution	Cert	Avg	%MS	AU-50	MS-60	MS-62	MS-63	MS-64	MS-65	MS-66
									PF-63	PF-64	PF-65
1938	15,266	2,544	65.0	100%	$300	$310	$315	$320	$325	$350	$400

Auctions: $1,410, MS-67, July 2015; $494, MS-66, September 2015; $400, MS-65, January 2015; $317, MS-64, January 2015

	Distribution	Cert	Avg								
1938, Proof	1–2	2	61								

Auctions: No auction records available.

IOWA CENTENNIAL HALF DOLLAR (1946)

Designer: *Adam Pietz.* **Weight:** *12.50 grams.* **Composition:** *.900 silver, .100 copper (net weight .3617 oz. pure silver).* **Diameter:** *30.6 mm.* **Edge:** *Reeded.* **Mint:** *Philadelphia.*

This half dollar, commemorating the 100th anniversary of Iowa's statehood, was sold first to the residents of Iowa and only a small remainder to others. Numismatists of the time, having largely forgotten the deceptions and hucksterism of the 1930s (and also seen the values of previously issued commemoratives rebound from a low point in 1941), were excited to see the first commemorative coin struck in some years. Nearly all of the issue was disposed of quickly, except for 500 that were held back to be distributed in 1996, and another 500 slated for 2046.

Designs. *Obverse:* The Old Stone Capitol building at Iowa City. *Reverse:* An eagle with wings spreading, adapted from the Iowa state seal.

Mintage Data. Authorized on August 7, 1946. *Maximum authorized—100,000. Number minted—100,057* (including 57 assay coins).

Original Cost and Issuer. Sale price $2.50 to in-state buyers, $3 to those out of state. Issued by the Iowa Centennial Committee, Des Moines, Iowa.

Key to Collecting. Most coins are in varying degrees of Mint State, and are lustrous and frosty. MS–63 to 66 are typical grades. The nature of the design, without open field areas, is such that a slight amount of friction and contact is usually not noticeable.

First Points of Wear. *Obverse:* The clouds above the Capitol, and the shafts of the building near the upper-left and upper-right windows. *Reverse:* The back of the eagle's head and neck. (Note that the head sometimes is flatly struck.)

	Distribution	Cert	Avg	%MS	AU-50	MS-60	MS-62	MS-63	MS-64	MS-65	MS-66
1946	100,057	5,927	65.5	100%	$90	$95	$100	$105	$125	$150	$175

Auctions: $4,700, MS-68, January 2015; $270, MS-67, August 2015; $212, MS-66, October 2015; $84, MS-63, August 2015

BOOKER T. WASHINGTON MEMORIAL HALF DOLLAR (1946–1951)

Designer: *Isaac S. Hathaway.* **Weight:** *12.50 grams.*
Composition: *.900 silver, .100 copper (net weight .3617 oz. pure silver).*
Diameter: *30.6 mm.* **Edge:** *Reeded.* **Mints:** *Philadelphia, Denver, and San Francisco.*

This commemorative coin was issued to perpetuate the ideals and teachings of African-American educator and presidential advisor Booker T. Washington and to construct memorials to his memory. Issued from all mints, it received wide distribution from the start. Unfortunately, the provision that the coins could be minted over several years led to many of the same problems seen with the Arkansas, Boone, Oregon Trail, and Texas pieces from the prior decade.

Designs. *Obverse:* Bareheaded three-quarters profile portrait of Booker T. Washington. *Reverse:* The Hall of Fame at New York University and a slave cabin.

Mintage Data. Authorized on August 7, 1946. *Maximum authorized*—5,000,000 (for the entire series 1946 onward). *Number minted*—1946-P: 1,000,546 (including 546 assay coins); 1946-D: 200,113 (including 113 assay coins); 1946-S: 500,279 (including 279 assay coins); 1947-P: 100,017 (including 17 assay coins); 1947-D: 100,017 (including 17 assay coins); 1947-S: 100,017 (including 17 assay coins); 1948-P: 20,005 (including 5 assay coins); 1948-D: 20,005 (including 5 assay coins); 1948-S: 20,005 (including 5 assay coins); 1949-P: 12,004 (including 4 assay coins); 1949-D: 12,004 (including 4 assay coins); 1949-S: 12,004 (including 4 assay coins); 1950-P: 12,004 (including 4 assay coins); 1950-D: 12,004 (including 4 assay coins); 1950-S: 512,091 (including 91 assay coins); 1951-P: 510,082 (including 82 assay coins); 1951-D: 12,004 (including 4 assay coins); 1951-S: 12,004 (including 4 assay coins). *Net distribution*—1946-P: 700,546 (estimated); 1946-D: 50,000 (estimated); 1946-S: 500,279 (estimated); 1947-P: 6,000 (estimated); 1947-D: 6,000 (estimated); 1947-S: 6,000 (estimated); 1948-P: 8,005; 1948-D: 8,005; 1948-S: 8,005; 1949-P: 6,004; 1949-D: 6,004; 1949-S: 6,004; 1950-P: 6,004; 1950-D: 6,004; 1950-S: 62,091 (estimated); 1951-P: 210,082 (estimated); 1951-D: 7,004; 1951-S: 7,004.

Original Cost and Issuer. Original sale price $1 per coin for Philadelphia and San Francisco, $1.50 for Denver, plus 10¢ postage per coin. In 1946, issued by the Booker T. Washington Birthplace Memorial Commission, Inc., Rocky Mount, Virginia (Dr. S.J. Phillips in charge); Stack's of New York City; and Bebee Stamp & Coin Company (a.k.a. Bebee's). For later issues, costs and distributors varied.

Key to Collecting. Of all commemorative half dollar issues produced up to this point, the Booker T. Washington half dollars were made with the least amount of care during the coining process at the mints. At the time of release, nearly all were poorly struck on the obverse and were marked with abrasions and nicks. Many have graininess and marks on Washington's cheek, from the original planchet surface that did not strike up fully. Many coins grade from MS–60 to (liberally graded) 65. Some have natural or artificial toning that masks the true condition and facilitates gem certification. Prooflike coins are sometimes seen, including for 1947-S (in particular), 1948-S, 1949, and 1951-S. These are not at all mirror-like, but still have surfaces different from the normal mint frost.

First Points of Wear. *Obverse:* Washington's cheekbone. *Reverse:* The center lettering (FROM SLAVE CABIN TO HALL OF FAME, etc.).

	Distribution	Cert	Avg	%MS	AU-50	MS-60	MS-62	MS-63	MS-64	MS-65	MS-66
1946	700,546	2,791	64.7	99%	$18	$20	$21	$25	$35	$60	$125
	Auctions: $1,293, MS-67, January 2015; $705, MS-67, March 2015; $141, MS-66, June 2015; $60, MS-65, March 2015										
1946-D	50,000	1,636	64.8	100%	$18	$20	$21	$25	$35	$60	$140
	Auctions: $5,405, MS-68, July 2015; $1,410, MS-67, August 2015; $286, MS-66, October 2015; $32, MS-64, April 2015										
1946-S	500,279	2,303	64.9	99%	$18	$20	$21	$25	$35	$60	$80
	Auctions: $4,113, MS-68, March 2015; $1,645, MS-67, August 2015; $123, MS-66, March 2015; $259, MS-64, November 2015										
Set of 1946 P-D-S					$54	$60	$63	$75	$105	$180	$345
	Auctions: $110, MS-65/65/65, May 2012										
1947	6,000	873	64.9	100%	$18	$20	$21	$25	$35	$60	$300
	Auctions: $3,525, MS-67, July 2015; $400, MS-66, January 2015; $259, MS-66, February 2015; $54, MS-65, January 2015										
1947-D	6,000	674	65.0	100%	$18	$20	$21	$25	$35	$60	$300
	Auctions: $1,645, MS-67, June 2015; $494, MS-66, January 2015; $329, MS-66, August 2015; $84, MS-65, September 2015										
1947-S	6,000	890	65.1	100%	$18	$20	$21	$25	$35	$60	$160
	Auctions: $2,585, MS-67, January 2015; $176, MS-66, November 2015; $64, MS-65, April 2015; $69, MS-64, January 2015										
Set of 1947 P-D-S					$54	$60	$63	$75	$105	$180	$760
	Auctions: $196, MS-65/65/65, January 2012										

	Distribution	Cert	Avg	%MS	AU-50	MS-60	MS-62	MS-63	MS-64	MS-65	MS-66
1948	8,005	795	65.2	100%	$18	$20	$21	$25	$35	$75	$150
Auctions: $999, MS-67, June 2015; $282, MS-66, September 2015; $235, MS-66, February 2015; $79, MS-65, February 2015											
1948-D	8,005	809	65.2	100%	$18	$20	$21	$25	$35	$75	$150
Auctions: $1,028, MS-67, February 2015; $176, MS-66, November 2015; $94, MS-65, January 2015; $36, MS-64, April 2015											
1948-S	8,005	949	65.3	100%	$18	$20	$21	$25	$35	$75	$150
Auctions: $1,293, MS-67, February 2015; $212, MS-66, February 2015; $70, MS-65, February 2015; $38, MS-64, April 2015											
Set of 1948 P-D-S					$54	$60	$63	$75	$105	$225	$450
Auctions: $220, MS-66/65/65, June 2012											
1949	6,004	807	65.2	100%	$18	$20	$21	$25	$35	$100	$130
Auctions: $2,233, MS-67, January 2015; $400, MS-66, February 2015; $141, MS-65, April 2015; $84, MS-64, January 2015											
1949-D	6,004	770	65.2	100%	$18	$20	$21	$25	$35	$100	$130
Auctions: $1,058, MS-67, October 2015; $165, MS-66, April 2015; $112, MS-65, April 2015; $74, MS-64, January 2015											
1949-S	6,004	839	65.5	100%	$18	$20	$21	$25	$35	$100	$110
Auctions: $940, MS-67, October 2015; $212, MS-66, September 2015; $188, MS-65, September 2015; $79, MS-64, February 2015											
Set of 1949 P-D-S					$54	$60	$63	$75	$105	$300	$370
Auctions: $320, MS-65/66/66, May 2012											
1950	6,004	620	65.2	100%	$20	$21	$22	$25	$35	$60	$150
Auctions: $541, MS-67, October 2015; $300, MS-66, May 2015; $200, MS-66, October 2015; $74, MS-65, May 2015											
1950-D	6,004	604	65.1	100%	$20	$21	$22	$25	$35	$60	$150
Auctions: $1,763, MS-67, February 2015; $282, MS-66, August 2015; $212, MS-66, September 2015; $84, MS-65, January 2015											
1950-S	62,091	1,254	65.2	100%	$20	$21	$22	$25	$35	$60	$150
Auctions: $940, MS-67, January 2015; $764, MS-67, August 2015; $141, MS-66, August 2015; $34, MS-65, April 2015											
Set of 1950 P-D-S					$60	$150	$160	$170	$190	$250	$2,250
Auctions: $725, MS-66/66/66, April 2012											
1951	210,082	1,273	64.6	100%	$18	$20	$21	$25	$35	$100	$140
Auctions: $1,528, MS-67, June 2015; $376, MS-66, January 2015; $147, MS-65, March 2015; $40, MS-64, April 2015											
1951-D	7,004	663	65.3	100%	$18	$20	$21	$25	$35	$100	$140
Auctions: $764, MS-67, January 2015; $259, MS-66, September 2015; $141, MS-65, January 2015; $56, MS-63, April 2015											
1951-S	7,004	766	65.6	100%	$18	$20	$21	$25	$35	$100	$175
Auctions: $764, MS-67, September 2015; $646, MS-67, September 2015; $170, MS-66, July 2015; $165, MS-66, November 2015											
Set of 1951 P-D-S					$54	$60	$63	$75	$105	$300	$455
Auctions: $475, MS-66/66/66, May 2012; $153, MS-66/66/66, March 2015											

CARVER / WASHINGTON COMMEMORATIVE HALF DOLLAR (1951–1954)

Designer: *Isaac S. Hathaway.* **Weight:** *12.50 grams.*
Composition: *.900 silver, .100 copper (net weight .3617 oz. pure silver).*
Diameter: *30.6 mm.* **Edge:** *Reeded.* **Mints:** *Philadelphia, Denver, and San Francisco.*

Designed by Isaac Scott Hathaway, this coin portrays the conjoined busts of two prominent black Americans. Booker T. Washington was a lecturer, educator, and principal of Tuskegee Institute. He urged training to advance independence and efficiency for his race. George Washington Carver was an agricultural chemist who worked to improve the economy of the American South. He spent part of his life teaching crop improvement and new uses for soybeans, peanuts, sweet potatoes, and cotton waste. Controversy erupted when it came to light that money obtained from the sale of these commemoratives was to be used "to oppose the spread of communism among Negroes in the interest of national defense."

Designs. *Obverse:* Conjoined bareheaded profile portraits of George Washington Carver and Booker T. Washington. *Reverse:* A map of the United States, with legends.

Mintage Data. Signed into law by President Harry S Truman on September 21, 1951. *Maximum authorized*—3,415,631 (total for all issues 1951 onward; consisting of 1,581,631 undistributed Booker T. Washington coins which could be converted into Carver-Washington coins, plus the unused 1,834,000 earlier authorization for Booker T. Washington coins). The following include author's estimates: 1951-P-D-S: *Number minted* (including 18, 4, and 4 assay coins)—110,018; 10,004; 10,004. *Net distribution*—20,018 (estimated); 10,004 (estimated); 10,004 (estimated). 1952-P-D-S: *Number minted* (including 292, 6, and 6 assay coins)—2,006,292; 8,006; 8,006. *Net distribution*—1,106,292 (estimated); 8,006 (estimated); 8,006 (estimated). 1953-P-D-S: *Number minted* (including 3, 3, and 20 assay coins)—8,003; 8,003; 108,020. *Net distribution*—8,003 (estimated); 8,003 (estimated); 88,020 (estimated). 1954-P-D-S: *Number minted* (including 6, 6, and 24 assay coins)—12,006; 12,006; 122,024. *Net distribution*—12,006 (estimated); 12,006 (estimated); 42,024 (estimated).

Original Cost and Issuer. 1951-P-D-S: $10 per set. 1952-P-D-S: $10 per set; many Philadelphia coins were sold at or near face value through banks. 1953-P-D-S: $10 per set; some 1953-S coins were distributed at or near face value (Bebee's prices $9 until January 15, 1952, $10 after that date). 1954-P-D-S: Official sale price: $10 per set; some 1954-S coins were paid out at face value (Bebee's prices for sets $9 until January 20, 1954, $12 after that date). Issued mainly by the Carver-Washington Coin Commission acting for the Booker T. Washington Birthplace Memorial Foundation (Booker Washington Birthplace, Virginia) and the George Washington Carver National Monument Foundation (Diamond, Missouri). Also, for some issues, these dealers: Stack's, Bebee Stamp & Coin Company, Sol Kaplan, and R. Green.

Key to Collecting. Nearly all coins of this issue were handled casually at the mints and also during the distribution process. Most were not fully struck up, with the result that under magnification many tiny nicks and marks can be seen on the higher parts, originating from planchet marks that were not obliterated during the striking process. Many MS examples are available on the market.

First Points of Wear. *Obverse:* Carver's cheekbone. (Note that some pieces were struck poorly in this area; check the reverse also for wear.) *Reverse:* The lettering U.S.A. on the map.

	Distribution	Cert	Avg	%MS	AU-50	MS-60	MS-62	MS-63	MS-64	MS-65	MS-66
1951	20,018	1,001	64.1	100%	$18	$20	$21	$25	$100	$250	$650
	Auctions: $940, MS-66, August 2015; $705, MS-66, January 2015; $141, MS-65, August 2015; $36, MS-64, April 2015										
1951-D	10,004	643	64.6	100%	$18	$20	$21	$25	$35	$65	$400
	Auctions: $376, MS-66, February 2015; $89, MS-65, January 2015; $84, MS-65, January 2015; $79, MS-65, August 2015										
1951-S	10,004	823	65.1	100%	$18	$20	$21	$25	$35	$75	$225
	Auctions: $1,763, MS-67, August 2015; $400, MS-66, August 2015; $275, MS-66, November 2015; $112, MS-65, August 2015										
Set of 1951 P-D-S					$54	$60	$63	$75	$170	$390	$1,275
	Auctions: $140, MS-64/64/64, June 2012										
1952	1,106,292	3,897	64.2	98%	$18	$20	$21	$25	$35	$50	$225
	Auctions: $2,820, MS-67, January 2015; $1,880, MS-67, August 2015; $306, MS-66, September 2015; $26, MS-60, August 2015										
1952-D	8,006	506	64.5	100%	$18	$20	$21	$25	$35	$65	$650
	Auctions: $764, MS-66, January 2015; $517, MS-66, September 2015; $106, MS-65, August 2015; $30, MS-64, April 2015										
1952-S	8,006	683	65.1	100%	$18	$20	$21	$25	$35	$65	$210
	Auctions: $3,200, MS-67, January 2015; $282, MS-66, September 2015; $84, MS-65, August 2015; $50, MS-64, August 2015										
Set of 1952 P-D-S					$54	$60	$63	$75	$105	$180	$1,085
	Auctions: $230, MS-65/65/65, March 2012										

	Distribution	Cert	Avg	%MS	AU-50	MS-60	MS-62	MS-63	MS-64	MS-65	MS-66
1953	8,003	581	64.7	100%	$18	$20	$21	$25	$35	$65	$475
Auctions: $259, MS-66, January 2015; $94, MS-65, September 2015; $89, MS-65, October 2015; $36, MS-64, May 2015											
1953-D	8,003	472	64.4	100%	$18	$20	$21	$25	$35	$65	$750
Auctions: $376, MS-65, July 2015; $84, MS-65, May 2015; $48, MS-64, August 2015; $30, MS-64, August 2015											
1953-S	88,020	1,275	64.8	100%	$18	$20	$21	$25	$35	$50	$475
Auctions: $3,290, MS-67, August 2015; $3,055, MS-67, March 2015; $282, MS-66, October 2015; $170, MS-65, May 2015											
Set of 1953 P-D-S					$54	$60	$63	$75	$105	$180	$1,700
Auctions: $300, MS-65/65/65, May 2012											
1954	12,006	794	64.6	100%	$18	$20	$21	$25	$35	$50	$475
Auctions: $282, MS-66, November 2015; $94, MS-65, July 2015; $79, MS-65, February 2015; $46, MS-64, April 2015											
1954-D	12,006	699	64.4	100%	$18	$20	$21	$25	$35	$50	$650
Auctions: $676, MS-66, February 2015; $423, MS-66, August 2015; $100, MS-65, August 2015; $82, MS-65, January 2015											
1954-S	42,024	1,165	64.6	100%	$18	$20	$21	$25	$35	$50	$350
Auctions: $1,998, MS-67, June 2015; $306, MS-66, August 2015; $84, MS-65, August 2015; $34, MS-64, August 2015											
Set of 1954 P-D-S					$54	$60	$63	$75	$105	$150	$1,475
Auctions: $316, MS-65/65/65, March 2012											

AN OVERVIEW OF MODERN COMMEMORATIVES

No commemorative coins were made by the U.S. Mint from 1955 through 1981. As the years went by, the numismatic community missed having new commemoratives to collect, and many endorsements for events and subjects worthy of the honor were made through letters to congressmen and other officials, which were often reprinted in pages of *The Numismatist*, the *Numismatic Scrapbook Magazine*, *Numismatic News*, and *Coin World*.

Finally, in 1982, the Treasury Department issued the first commemorative coin since 1954—a silver half dollar celebrating the 250th anniversary of the birth of George Washington. This time around, distribution was placed in the hands of the Bureau of the Mint (today called the U.S. Mint) rather than with a commission or private individuals. The profits accrued to the Treasury Department and the U.S. government. The issue was well received in the numismatic community, with more than seven million of the half dollars sold nationwide.

Then came the 1983 and 1984 Los Angeles Olympiad coins, minted in the subject years for the Los Angeles Olympiad held in 1984. These comprised a diverse and somewhat experimental series, with dollars of two different designs and, for the first time, a commemorative ten-dollar gold coin. Sales were satisfactory, and the supply easily met the demand from collectors and investors.

The concept of a surcharge, or built-in fee, was introduced, with a certain amount per coin going to a congressionally designated beneficiary—in the instance of the Olympic coins, the Los Angeles Olympic Organizing Committee. These and related surcharges became controversial with collectors, some of whom resented making involuntary donations when they bought coins. Today the practice continues, though without as much controversy. Surcharges are the spark that has ignited most commemorative programs, as potential recipients of the earmarked profits launch intense lobbying campaigns in Congress.

In 1986 the 100th anniversary of the completion of the Statue of Liberty was commemorated by the issuance of a copper-nickel–clad half dollar (first of its kind in the commemorative series), a silver dollar, and a five-dollar gold coin, with varied motifs, each depicting on the obverse the Statue of Liberty or an element therefrom. Unprecedented millions of coins were sold.

Then followed a lull in commemorative purchases, although the Mint continued to issue coins celebrating more Olympic Games, various national anniversaries, and significant people, places, events, and other subjects. Some years saw four or five or more individual commemorative programs. Some were well received by the hobby community, but sales of most fell far short of projections. In certain cases these low sales would eventually prove beneficial for collectors who placed orders from the Mint. An example is the 1995 five-dollar commemorative honoring baseball star and Civil Rights hero Jackie Robinson. Only 5,174 Uncirculated pieces were sold, creating a modern rarity.

Most modern commemorative coins have seen only modest secondary-market appreciation, if any. Beyond their retail values, however, the coins will always have significant historical, cultural, and sentimental value. The 2001 American Buffalo silver dollar created a sensation with its bold design harkening back to the classic Buffalo nickel of 1913 to 1938; the issue sold out quickly and soon was commanding high premiums in the collector market. It remains popular and valuable today. In 2014, the National Baseball Hall of Fame commemoratives (a three-coin suite in copper-nickel, silver, and gold) captured mainstream-media headlines and national TV news coverage. Other modern commemoratives have honored American inventors and explorers, branches of the U.S. military, Boy Scouts and Girl Scouts, the Civil Rights Act of 1964, and other important themes, continuing a tradition of special coinage dating back to 1892 and giving today's collectors a broad spectrum of issues to study and cherish.

See page 1239 for pricing of government commemorative sets and page 1502 for an alphabetical cross-reference list of all commemoratives.

GEORGE WASHINGTON 250TH ANNIVERSARY OF BIRTH HALF DOLLAR (1982)

Designer: *Elizabeth Jones.* **Weight:** *12.50 grams.*
Composition: *.900 silver, .100 copper (net weight .3617 oz. pure silver).*
Diameter: *30.6 mm.* **Edge:** *Reeded.* **Mints:** *Denver (Uncirculated) and San Francisco (Proof).*

This coin, the first commemorative half dollar issued since 1954, celebrated the 250th anniversary of the birth of George Washington. It was also the first 90% silver coin produced by the U.S. Mint since 1964.

Designs. *Obverse:* George Washington on horseback. *Reverse:* Mount Vernon.

Mintage Data. Authorized by Public Law 97-014, signed by President Ronald Reagan on December 23, 1981. *Maximum authorized*—10,000,000. *Number minted*—1982-D: 478,716; 1982-S: 868,326. *Net distribution*—1982-D: 2,210,458 Uncirculated; 1982-S: 4,894,044 Proof.

Original Cost. Sale prices originally $8.50 (Uncirculated) and $10.50 (Proof), later raised to $10 and $12, respectively.

Key to Collecting. Today, Uncirculated 1982-D and Proof 1982-S Washington half dollars are plentiful on the market and are readily available in as-issued condition. They are popular and highly regarded as part of the modern commemorative series.

	Distribution	Cert	Avg	%MS	MS-67
					PF-67
1982-D	2,210,458	4,478	66.9	100%	$12
Auctions: $123, MS-69, June 2014					
1982-S, Proof	4,894,044	9,734	69.0		$10
Auctions: $110, PF-70, June 2014; $106, PF-70, September 2015; $106, PF-70, November 2014; $74, PF-70UCam, June 2015					

LOS ANGELES OLYMPIAD DISCUS THROWER SILVER DOLLAR (1983)

Designer: *Elizabeth Jones.* **Weight:** *26.73 grams.* **Composition:** *.900 silver, .100 copper (net weight .7736 oz. pure silver).* **Diameter:** *38.1 mm.* **Edge:** *Reeded.*
Mints: *Philadelphia and Denver (Uncirculated), San Francisco (Uncirculated and Proof).*

Three distinctive coins were issued to commemorate the 1984 Los Angeles Summer Olympic Games. The 1983 Discus Thrower dollar was the first commemorative silver dollar since the 1900 Lafayette issue.

Designs. *Obverse:* Representation of the traditional Greek discus thrower inspired by the ancient work of the sculptor Myron. *Reverse:* The head and upper body of an American eagle.

Mintage Data. Authorized by Public Law 97-220, signed by President Ronald Reagan on July 22, 1982. *Maximum authorized*—50,000,000 totally for 1983 and 1984. *Number minted*—1983-P: 294,543 Uncirculated; 1983-D: 174,014 Uncirculated; 1983-S: 174,014 Uncirculated and 1,577,025 Proof.

Original Cost. Sale prices $28 (Uncirculated) and $24.95 (Proof, ordered in advance); Proof raised later to $29, and still later to $32. Part of the $10 surcharge per coin went to the U.S. Olympic Committee and the Los Angeles Olympic Organizing Committee.

Key to Collecting. These pieces in both Uncirculated and Proof format can be found today for prices near their issue cost. The vast quantities issued (never mind that 52 million were not sold) made them common. Nearly all surviving coins are in superb gem preservation. Today the aftermarket is supported by coin collectors, not by Olympic sports enthusiasts.

	Distribution	Cert	Avg	%MS	MS-67
					PF-67
1983-P	294,543	2,276	69.0	100%	$30
Auctions: $499, MS-70, September 2014					
1983-D	174,014	1,701	69.0	100%	$30
Auctions: $7,638, MS-70, April 2013					
1983-S	174,014	1,770	69.0	100%	$30
Auctions: $8,813, MS-70, April 2013					
1983-S, Proof	1,577,025	4,878	69.0		$30
Auctions: $1,175, PF-70DCam, April 2014					

LOS ANGELES OLYMPIAD OLYMPIC COLISEUM SILVER DOLLAR (1984)

Designer: *John Mercanti.* **Weight:** *26.73 grams.* **Composition:** *.900 silver, .100 copper (net weight .7736 oz. pure silver).* **Diameter:** *38.1 mm.* **Edge:** *Reeded.*
Mints: *Philadelphia and Denver (Uncirculated), San Francisco (Uncirculated and Proof).*

This coin became a reality at the insistence of the Los Angeles Olympic Organizing Committee. The semi-nude figures on the obverse created some controversy.

Designs. *Obverse:* Robert Graham's headless torso sculptures at the entrance of the Los Angeles Memorial Coliseum. *Reverse:* Perched eagle looking back over its left wing.

Mintage Data. Authorized by Public Law 97-220, signed by President Ronald Reagan on July 22, 1982. *Maximum authorized*—50,000,000 totally for 1983 and 1984. *Number minted*—1984-P: 217,954 Uncirculated; 1984-D: 116,675 Uncirculated; 1984-S: 116,675 Uncirculated and 1,801,210 Proof.

Original Cost. Sales prices $28 (Uncirculated) and $32 (Proof); Proof later raised to $35. Part of the $10 surcharge per coin went to the U.S. Olympic Committee and the Los Angeles Olympic Organizing Committee.

Key to Collecting. These pieces in both Uncirculated and Proof format can be found today for close to what they cost at the time of issue. The vast quantities issued (never mind that 52 million were not sold) made them common. Nearly all surviving coins are in superb gem preservation. Today, the aftermarket is supported by coin collectors, not by Olympic sports enthusiasts.

	Distribution	Cert	Avg	%MS	MS-67 PF-67
1984-P	217,954	1,681	69.0	100%	$30
	Auctions: $705, MS-70, September 2013; $456, MS-70, September 2014; $447, MS-70, August 2015				
1984-D	116,675	1,214	68.9	100%	$32
	Auctions: $4,994, MS-70, April 2013				
1984-S	116,675	1,219	68.9	100%	$32
	Auctions: $9,400, MS-70, April 2013				
1984-S, Proof	1,801,210	4,180	68.9		$30
	Auctions: $411, PF-70DCam, September 2014; $558, PF-70DCam, April 2013				

LOS ANGELES OLYMPIAD $10 GOLD COIN (1984)

Designer: *John Mercanti.* **Weight:** *16.718 grams.* **Composition:** *.900 gold, .100 copper (net weight .4837 oz. pure gold).* **Diameter:** *27 mm.* **Edge:** *Reeded.*

Mints: *Philadelphia, Denver, and San Francisco (Proof); West Point (Uncirculated and Proof).*

This ten-dollar coin was the first commemorative to be struck in gold since the 1926 Sesquicentennial $2.50 gold pieces. Mint engraver John Mercanti based the obverse design on a sketch by James Peed of the Bureau of the Mint's Washington office.

Designs. *Obverse:* Two runners holding aloft the Olympic torch. *Reverse:* Adaptation of the Great Seal of the United States.

Mintage Data. Authorized by Public Law 97-220, signed by President Ronald Reagan on July 22, 1982. *Maximum authorized*—2,000,000. *Number minted*—1984-P: 33,309 Proof; 1984-D: 34,533 Proof; 1984-S: 48,551 Proof; 1984-W: 75,886 Uncirculated and 381,085 Proof.

Original Cost. Sales prices $339 (Uncirculated) and $353 (Proof). Part of the $35 surcharge per coin went to the U.S. Olympic Committee and the Los Angeles Olympic Organizing Committee.

Key to Collecting. These coins are necessarily expensive due to their gold content, but are still quite reasonable. Nearly all surviving coins are in superb gem preservation. Today, the aftermarket is supported by coin collectors, not by Olympic sports enthusiasts.

	Distribution	Cert	Avg	%MS	MS-67 / PF-67
1984-W	75,886	1,599	69.3	100%	$800
Auctions: $764, MS-70, September 2014; $893, MS-70, April 2013; $611, MS-69, October 2014					
1984-P, Proof	33,309	1,850	69.0		$700
Auctions: $1,763, PF-70DCam, April 2013; $823, PF-70DCam, September 2014; $624, PF-69DCam, October 2014; $588, PF-69, June 2015					
1984-D, Proof	34,533	1,892	69.1		$700
Auctions: $1,116, PF-70DCam, April 2013; $617, PF-69DCam, October 2014; $611, PF-69DCam, October 2014; $564, PF-69, June 2015					
1984-S, Proof	48,551	1,812	69.2		$700
Auctions: $823, PF-70DCam, April 2013; $618, PF-69DCam, October 2014; $588, PF-69, June 2015					
1984-W, Proof	381,085	5,753	69.1		$700
Auctions: $646, PF-70UCam, January 2015; $646, PF-70UCam, July 2015; $646, PF-70UCam, July 2015; $588, PF-69, June 2015					

STATUE OF LIBERTY CENTENNIAL HALF DOLLAR (1986)

Designer: *Edgar Z. Steever IV (obverse), Sherl Winter (reverse).* **Weight:** *11.34 grams.* **Composition:** *.9167 copper, .0833 nickel.* **Diameter:** *30.61 mm.* **Edge:** *Reeded.* **Mints:** *Denver (Uncirculated) and San Francisco (Proof).*

The 100th anniversary of the dedication of the Statue of Liberty in New York City harbor in 1886 furnished the occasion for the issuance of three different commemorative coins in 1986. The clad half dollar was the first U.S. commemorative issued in copper-nickel format.

Designs. *Obverse:* Ship of immigrants steaming into New York harbor, with the Statue of Liberty greeting them in the foreground and the New York skyline in the distance. *Reverse:* Scene of an immigrant family with their belongings on the threshold of America.

Mintage Data. Authorized by the Act of July 9, 1985. *Maximum authorized*—25,000,000. *Number minted*—1986-D: 928,008 Uncirculated; 1986-S: 6,925,627 Proof.

Original Cost. Sale prices $5 (Uncirculated, pre-order) and $6.50 (Proof, pre-order); Uncirculated later raised to $6, and Proof later raised to $7.50.

Key to Collecting. So many 1986 Statue of Liberty half dollars were issued that the aftermarket affords the possibility of purchasing the coins not much above the original offering price. Nearly all are superb gems.

	Distribution	Cert	Avg	%MS	MS-67
					PF-67
1986-D	928,008	2,801	69.0	100%	$5
Auctions: $411, MS-70, April 2013					
1986-S, Proof	6,925,627	11,628	69.0		$5
Auctions: $84, PF-69DCam, January 2015; $129, PF-67, October 2015					

STATUE OF LIBERTY CENTENNIAL SILVER DOLLAR (1986)

Designer: *John Mercanti.* **Weight:** *26.73 grams.* **Composition:** *.900 silver, .100 copper (net weight .7736 oz. pure silver).* **Diameter:** *38.1 mm.* **Edge:** *Reeded.*
Mints: *Philadelphia (Uncirculated) and San Francisco (Proof).*

These coins, which are also known as Ellis Island silver dollars, feature an excerpt from Emma Lazarus's poem, *The New Colossus.*

Designs. *Obverse:* Statue of Liberty in the foreground, with the Ellis Island immigration center behind her. *Reverse:* Liberty's torch, along with the words GIVE ME YOUR TIRED, YOUR POOR, YOUR HUDDLED MASSES YEARNING TO BREATHE FREE.

Mintage Data. Authorized by the Act of July 9, 1985. *Maximum authorized*—10,000,000. *Number minted*—1986-P: 723,635 Uncirculated; 1986-S: 6,414,638 Proof.

Original Cost. Sale prices $20.50 (Uncirculated, pre-order) and $22.50 (Proof, pre-order); Uncirculated later raised to $22, and Proof later raised to $24.

Key to Collecting. Nearly all coins of this issue are superb gems.

	Distribution	Cert	Avg	%MS	MS-67
					PF-67
1986-P	723,635	3,872	69.0	100%	$25
Auctions: $170, MS-70, January 2013; $27, MS-69, August 2014					
1986-S, Proof	6,414,638	12,295	69.0		$25
Auctions: $141, PF-70DCam, April 2014; $106, PF-70DCam, April 2013; $70, PF-69DCam, August 2014; $188, PF-69DCam, November 2014					

STATUE OF LIBERTY CENTENNIAL $5 GOLD COIN (1986)

Designer: *Elizabeth Jones.* **Weight:** *8.359 grams.* **Composition:** *.900 gold, .100 copper (net weight .242 oz. pure gold).* **Diameter:** *21.6 mm.* **Edge:** *Reeded.* **Mint:** *West Point.*

The designs on these five-dollar gold coins created a sensation in the numismatic community and were widely discussed, and the coin received Krause Publications' Coin of the Year Award. The entire authorization of a half million coins was spoken for—the only complete sellout of any commemorative coin of the 1980s.

Designs. *Obverse:* Face and crown of the Statue of Liberty. *Reverse:* American eagle in flight.

Mintage Data. Authorized by the Act of July 9, 1985. *Maximum authorized*—500,000. *Number minted*—95,248 Uncirculated and 404,013 Proof.

Original Cost. Sale prices $160 (Uncirculated, pre-order) and $170 (Proof, pre-order); Uncirculated later raised to $165, and Proof later raised to $175.

Key to Collecting. So many 1986 Statue of Liberty commemoratives were issued that the aftermarket affords the possibility of purchasing the coins at prices near bullion value. Nearly all coins of this issue are superb gems.

	Distribution	Cert	Avg	%MS	MS-67
					PF-67
1986-W	95,248	3,829	69.5	100%	$325
	Auctions: $353, MS-70, August 2014; $329, MS-70, September 2014; $329, MS-70, November 2014; $441, MS-70, February 2013				
1986-W, Proof	404,013	10,737	69.3		$325
	Auctions: $306, PF-70, September 2015; $306, MS-70, April 2015; $282, PF-70, October 2015; $329, PF-69DCam, October 2014				

CONSTITUTION BICENTENNIAL SILVER DOLLAR (1987)

Designer: *Patricia Lewis Verani.* **Weight:** *26.73 grams.*
Composition: *.900 silver, .100 copper (net weight .7736 oz. pure silver).*
Diameter: *38.1 mm.* **Edge:** *Reeded.* **Mints:** *Philadelphia (Uncirculated) and San Francisco (Proof).*

In connection with the 200th anniversary of the U.S. Constitution, observed in 1987, Congress held a competition to design both a silver dollar and a five-dollar gold coin.

Designs. *Obverse:* Quill pen, a sheaf of parchment, and the words WE THE PEOPLE. *Reverse:* Cross-section of Americans from various periods representing various lifestyles.

Mintage Data. Authorized by Public Law 99-582, signed by President Ronald Reagan on October 29, 1986. *Maximum authorized*—1,000,000. *Number minted*—1987-P: 451,629 Uncirculated; 1987-S: 2,747,116 Proof.

Original Cost. Sale prices $22.50 (Uncirculated, pre-issue) and $24 (Proof, pre-issue); Uncirculated later raised to $26, and Proof later raised to $28. A $7 surcharge per coin went toward reducing the national debt.

Key to Collecting. Today, these coins remain inexpensive. Nearly all are superb gems.

	Distribution	Cert	Avg	%MS	MS-67 PF-67
1987-P	451,629	3,392	69.1	100%	$25
Auctions: $90, MS-70, January 2013					
1987-S, Proof	2,747,116	5,732	68.9		$25
Auctions: $115, PF-70DCam, April 2013					

CONSTITUTION BICENTENNIAL $5 GOLD COIN (1987)

Designer: *Marcel Jovine.* **Weight:** *8.359 grams.* **Composition:** *.900 gold, .100 copper (net weight .242 oz. pure gold).* **Diameter:** *21.6 mm.* **Edge:** *Reeded.* **Mint:** *West Point.*

A modernistic design by Marcel Jovine was selected for the five-dollar gold coin honoring the bicentennial of the U.S. Constitution.

Designs. *Obverse:* Stylized eagle holding a massive quill pen. *Reverse:* Large quill pen with nine stars to the left (symbolizing the first colonies to ratify the Constitution) and four to the right (representing the remaining original states).

Mintage Data. Authorized by Public Law 99-582, signed by President Ronald Reagan on October 29, 1986. *Maximum authorized*—1,000,000. *Number minted*—214,225 Uncirculated and 651,659 Proof.

Original Cost. Sale prices $195 (Uncirculated, pre-issue) and $200 (Proof, pre-issue); Uncirculated later raised to $215, and Proof later raised to $225.

Key to Collecting. Nearly all coins of this issue are superb gems.

	Distribution	Cert	Avg	%MS	MS-67 PF-67
1987-W	214,225	7,451	69.7	100%	$325
Auctions: $353, MS-70, August 2015; $317, MS-70, August 2015; $306, MS-70, August 2015; $300, MS-70, September 2015					
1987-W, Proof	651,659	16,436	69.5		$325
Auctions: $376, PF-70UCam, September 2015; $353, PF-70UCam, January 2015; $329, PF-70UCam, October 2015					

SEOUL OLYMPIAD SILVER DOLLAR (1988)

Designer: *Patricia Lewis Verani (obverse), Sherl Winter (reverse).* **Weight:** *26.73 grams.*
Composition: *.900 silver, .100 copper (net weight .7736 oz. pure silver).*
Diameter: *38.1 mm.* **Edge:** *Reeded.* **Mints:** *Denver (Uncirculated) and San Francisco (Proof).*

The holding of the 1988 Summer Olympic Games in Seoul, Republic of South Korea, furnished the opportunity for the issuance of this silver dollar (as well as a five-dollar gold coin; see next entry).

Designs. *Obverse:* One hand holding an Olympic torch as another hand holds another torch to ignite it. *Reverse:* Olympic rings surrounded by a wreath.

Mintage Data. Authorized by Public Law 100-141, signed by President Ronald Reagan on October 28, 1987. *Maximum authorized*—10,000,000. *Number minted*—1988-D: 191,368 Uncirculated; 1988-S: 1,359,366 Proof.

Original Cost. Sale prices $22 (Uncirculated, pre-issue) and $23 (Proof, pre-issue); Uncirculated later raised to $27, and Proof later raised to $29. The surcharge of $7 per coin went to the U.S. Olympic Committee.

Key to Collecting. These coins are inexpensive. The numismatic market, representing actual buyers and sellers, is not extensive enough to maintain large premiums over the price of hundreds of thousands of coins purchased by the non-numismatic public and then later sold when their novelty passed. Nearly all coins are superb gems.

	Distribution	Cert	Avg	%MS	MS-67 PF-67
1988-D	191,368	2,048	69.0	100%	$25
	Auctions: $247, MS-70, September 2014				
1988-S, Proof	1,359,366	4,679	68.9		$25
	Auctions: $135, PF-70DCam, September 2014; $141, PF-70DCam, April 2013				

SEOUL OLYMPIAD $5 GOLD COIN (1988)

Designer: *Elizabeth Jones (obverse), Marcel Jovine (reverse).* **Weight:** *8.359 grams.*
Composition: *.900 gold, .100 copper (net weight .242 oz. pure gold).*
Diameter: *21.6 mm.* **Edge:** *Reeded.* **Mint:** *West Point.*

Elizabeth Jones's five-dollar obverse design is considered by many to be the high point of commemorative coinage art of the late 20th century. Some observers suggested that, because the event was not held in the United States, the Seoul Olympics were not an appropriate subject for American coinage; regardless, the gold coin was praised to the skies.

Designs. *Obverse:* Nike, goddess of Victory, wearing a crown of olive leaves. *Reverse:* Stylized Olympic flame.

Mintage Data. Authorized by Public Law 100-141, signed by President Ronald Reagan on October 28, 1987. *Maximum authorized*—1,000,000. *Number minted*—62,913 Uncirculated and 281,465 Proof.

Original Cost. Sale prices $200 (Uncirculated, pre-issue) and $205 (Proof, pre-issue); Uncirculated later raised to $225, and Proof later raised to $235. The surcharge of $35 per coin went to the U.S. Olympic Committee.

Key to Collecting. Examples are readily available today.

	Distribution	Cert	Avg	%MS	MS-67
					PF-67
1988-W	62,913	2,339	69.5	100%	$325
	Auctions: $306, MS-69, August 2014; $423, MS-69, March 2013				
1988-W, Proof	281,465	9,587	69.4		$325
	Auctions: $447, PF-70UCam, March 2015; $376, PF-70UCam, March 2015; $353, PF-70UCam, October 2015; $317, PF-70UCam, April 2015				

CONGRESS BICENTENNIAL HALF DOLLAR (1989)

Designer: *Patricia Lewis Verani (obverse), William Woodward (reverse).*
Weight: *11.34 grams.* **Composition:** *.9167 copper, .0833 nickel.* **Diameter:** *30.61 mm.*
Edge: *Reeded.* **Mints:** *Denver (Uncirculated) and San Francisco (Proof).*

The 200th anniversary of the operation of Congress under the U.S. Constitution was observed in 1989, and a suite of commemorative coins was authorized to observe the bicentennial, among them this copper-nickel half dollar.

Designs. *Obverse:* The head of the *Freedom* statue (erected on top of the Capitol dome in 1863) is shown at the center, with inscriptions around, including LIBERTY in oversize letters at the bottom border. *Reverse:* A distant front view of the Capital is shown, with arcs of stars above and below, with appropriate lettering.

Mintage Data. Authorized by Public Law 100-673, signed by President Ronald Reagan on November 17, 1988. The coins were to be dated 1989 and could be minted through June 30, 1990. *Maximum authorized*—4,000,000. *Number minted*—1989-D: 163,753 Uncirculated; 1989-S: 767,897 Proof.

Original Cost. Sale prices $5 (Uncirculated, pre-issue) and $7 (Proof, pre-issue); Uncirculated later raised to $6, and Proof later raised to $8. The surcharge of $1 per coin went to the Capitol Preservation Fund.

Key to Collecting. Not popular with numismatists in 1989, these coins still languish in the marketplace. Exceptions are coins certified in ultra-high grades. The Uncirculated 1989-D half dollar exists with a misaligned reverse, oriented in the same direction as the obverse, instead of the usual 180 degree separation. These are rare and valuable, but are not widely known. Likely, some remain undiscovered in buyers' hands.

	Distribution	Cert	Avg	%MS	MS-67
					PF-67
1989-D	163,753	1,141	69.0	100%	$10
	Auctions: $4,113, MS-70, April 2013				
1989-S, Proof	767,897	2,683	69.0		$10
	Auctions: $382, PF-70, September 2014				

Congress Bicentennial Silver Dollar (1989)

Designer: *William Woodward.* **Weight:** *26.73 grams.*
Composition: *.900 silver, .100 copper (net weight .7736 oz. pure silver).*
Diameter: *38.1 mm.* **Edge:** *Reeded.* **Mints:** *Denver (Uncirculated) and San Francisco (Proof).*

To inaugurate the Congress Bicentennial coins, four coining presses weighing seven tons each were brought from the Philadelphia Mint to the east front of the Capitol building, where in a special ceremony on June 14, 1989, the first silver dollars and five-dollar gold coins were struck (but no half dollars).

Designs. *Obverse:* The statue of *Freedom* full length, with a cloud and rays of glory behind. Lettering around the border. *Reverse:* The mace of the House of Representatives, which is in the House Chamber when that body is in session.

Mintage Data. Authorized by Public Law 100-673, signed by President Ronald Reagan on November 17, 1988. The coins were to be dated 1989 and could be minted through June 30, 1990. *Maximum authorized*—3,000,000. *Number minted*—1989-D: 135,203 Uncirculated; 1989-S: 762,198 Proof.

Original Cost. Sale prices $23 (Uncirculated, pre-issue) and $25 (Proof, pre-issue): Uncirculated later raised to $26, and Proof later raised to $29. Surcharge of $7 per coin went to the Capitol Preservation Fund.

Key to Collecting. Not popular with numismatists in 1989, these coins today can be found for prices close to bullion value. Exceptions are coins certified in ultra-high grades.

	Distribution	Cert	Avg	%MS	MS-67 PF-67
1989-D	135,203	2,412	69.0	100%	$28
Auctions: $646, MS-70, September 2014; $940, MS-70, April 2013					
1989-S, Proof	762,198	3,673	68.9		$30
Auctions: $457, PF-70DCam, May 2013; $42, PF-69DCam, July 2014; $106, PF-69DCam, November 2014; $940, PF-70, March 2013					

Congress Bicentennial $5 Gold Coin (1989)

Designer: *John Mercanti.* **Weight:** *8.359 grams.* **Composition:** *.900 gold, .100 copper (net weight .242 oz. pure gold).* **Diameter:** *21.6 mm.* **Edge:** *Reeded.* **Mint:** *West Point.*

To diversify the motifs of the three Congress Bicentennial commemorative coins, 11 artists from the private sector were invited to submit designs, as were members of the Mint's Engraving Department staff. The designs for this five-dollar gold coin were praised in the *Annual Report of the Director of the Mint,* 1989, which stated that the obverse displayed "a spectacular rendition of the Capitol dome," while the reverse "center[ed] around a dramatic portrait of the majestic eagle atop the canopy overlooking the Old Senate Chamber."

Designs. *Obverse:* The dome of the Capitol is shown, with lettering around. *Reverse:* The eagle in the old Senate chamber is depicted, with lettering surrounding.

Mintage Data. Authorized by Public Law 100-673, signed by President Ronald Reagan on November 17, 1988. The coins were to be dated 1989 and could be minted through June 30, 1990. *Maximum authorized*—1,000,000. *Number minted*—46,899 Uncirculated and 164,690 Proof.

Original Cost. Sale prices $185 (Uncirculated, pre-issue) and $195 (Proof, pre-issue); Uncirculated later raised to $200, and Proof later raised to $215. Surcharge of $35 per coin went to the Capitol Preservation Fund.

Key to Collecting. Not popular with numismatists in 1989, these coins today can be purchased in the secondary marketplace for prices close to their bullion value. Exceptions are coins certified in ultra-high grades.

	Distribution	Cert	Avg	%MS	MS-67 PF-67
1989-W	46,899	2,241	69.5	100%	$325
	Auctions: $646, MS-70, September 2014; $376, MS-70, May 2015; $400, MS-69, April 2013				
1989-W, Proof	164,690	5,489	69.4		$325
	Auctions: $341, PF-70UCam, October 2015; $341, PF-70, July 2015; $323, PF-70DCam, April 2015; $306, PF-70DCam, January 2015				

EISENHOWER CENTENNIAL SILVER DOLLAR (1990)

Designer: *John Mercanti (obverse), Marcel Jovine (reverse).* **Weight:** *26.73 grams.*
Composition: *.900 silver, .100 copper (net weight .7736 oz. pure silver).* **Diameter:** *38.1 mm.*
Edge: *Reeded.* **Mints:** *West Point (Uncirculated) and Philadelphia (Proof).*

Five outside artists as well as the artists on the Mint Engraving Department staff were invited to submit designs for this silver dollar. In August 1989, secretary of the Treasury Nicholas F. Brady made the final selections.

This is the only U.S. coin to feature two portraits of the same person on the same side. The reverse shows Eisenhower's retirement residence, identified as EISENHOWER HOME.

Designs. *Obverse:* Profile of President Eisenhower facing right, superimposed over his own left-facing profile as a five-star general. *Reverse:* Eisenhower retirement home at Gettysburg, a national historic site.

Mintage Data. Authorized by Public Law 100-467, signed by President Ronald Reagan on October 3, 1988. *Maximum authorized*—4,000,000. *Number minted*—1990-W: 241,669 Uncirculated; 1990-P: 1,144,461 Proof.

Original Cost. Sale prices $23 (Uncirculated, pre-issue) and $25 (Proof, pre-issue; Uncirculated later raised to $26, and Proof later raised to $29. Surcharge of $7 per coin went to reduce public debt.

Key to Collecting. Eisenhower Centennial dollars are appreciated as a fine addition to the commemorative series. Examples are plentiful and inexpensive in the marketplace. Nearly all are superb gems.

	Distribution	Cert	Avg	%MS	MS-67 PF-67
1990-W	241,669	2,150	69.1	100%	$35
	Auctions: $206, MS-70, March 2013				
1990-P, Proof	1,144,461	4,029	69.0		$30
	Auctions: $135, PF-70DCam, September 2014; $201, PF-70DCam, March 2013; $42, PF-69DCam, July 2014; $165, PF-68DCam, March 2015				

KOREAN WAR MEMORIAL SILVER DOLLAR (1991)

Designer: *John Mercanti (obverse), James Ferrell (reverse).* **Weight:** *26.73 grams.*
Composition: *.900 silver, .100 copper (net weight .7736 oz. pure silver).*
Diameter: *38.1 mm.* **Edge:** *Reeded.* **Mints:** *Denver (Uncirculated) and Philadelphia (Proof).*

In the annals of commemoratives, one of the more curious entries is the 1991 silver dollar observing the 38th anniversary of the end of the Korean War, struck to honor those who served there. The 38th anniversary was chosen—rather than the 50th or some other typical anniversary—because, during that war, the 38th degree of latitude on the map defined the division between North and South Korea.

Buyers reacted favorably to the coin, and more than 800,000 were produced.

Designs. *Obverse:* Two F-86 Sabrejet fighter aircraft flying to the right, a helmeted soldier carrying a backpack climbing a hill, and the inscriptions: THIRTY EIGHTH / ANNIVERSARY / COMMEMORATIVE / KOREA / IN GOD WE TRUST / 1953 / 1991. At the bottom of the coin are five Navy ships above the word LIBERTY. *Reverse:* Outline map of North and South Korea, divided. An eagle's head (representing the United States) is depicted to the right. Near the bottom is the symbol of Korea.

Mintage Data. Authorized by Public Law 101-495 of October 31, 1990. *Maximum authorized—*1,000,000. *Number minted—*1991-D: 213,049 Uncirculated; 1991-P: 618,488 Proof.

Original Cost. Sale prices $23 (Uncirculated, pre-issue) and $28 (Proof, pre-issue); Uncirculated later raised to $26, and Proof later raised to $31. A surcharge of $7 went to fund the Korean War Veterans Memorial.

Key to Collecting. Gem Uncirculated and Proof coins are readily available in the marketplace.

	Distribution	Cert	Avg	%MS	MS-67
					PF-67
1991-D	213,049	2,285	69.1	100%	$35
	Auctions: $76, MS-70, July 2014; $106, MS-70, January 2013; $69, MS-70, May 2015				
1991-P, Proof	618,488	2,953	68.9		$35
	Auctions: $382, PF-70DCam, September 2014; $505, PF-70DCam, March 2013				

MOUNT RUSHMORE GOLDEN ANNIVERSARY HALF DOLLAR (1991)

Designer: *Marcel Jovine (obverse), T. James Ferrell (reverse).* **Weight:** *11.34 grams.*
Composition: *.9167 copper, .0833 nickel.* **Diameter:** *30.61 mm.* **Edge:** *Reeded.*
Mints: *Denver (Uncirculated) and San Francisco (Proof).*

This half dollar was part of a trio of coins struck to mark the Mount Rushmore National Memorial's 50th anniversary. Surcharges from their sale were divided between the Treasury Department and the Mount Rushmore National Memorial Society of Black Hills, North Dakota, with money going toward restoration work on the landmark.

Designs. *Obverse:* View of Mount Rushmore with rays of the sun behind. *Reverse:* An American bison with the words GOLDEN ANNIVERSARY.

Mintage Data. Authorized by the Mount Rushmore National Memorial Coin Act (Public Law 101-332, July 16, 1990). *Maximum authorized—2,500,000. Number minted—*1991-D: 172,754 Uncirculated; 1991-S: 753,257 Proof.

Original Cost. Sale prices $6 (Uncirculated) and $8.50 (Proof); Uncirculated later raised to $7, and Proof later raised to $9.50. Fifty percent of the surcharge of $1 per coin went to the Mount Rushmore National Memorial Society of Black Hills; the balance went to the U.S. Treasury.

Key to Collecting. Examples are easily available today. The coins were carefully struck, with the result that nearly all are superb gems.

	Distribution	Cert	Avg	%MS	MS-67
					PF-67
1991-D	172,754	1,695	69.1	100%	$15
Auctions: $306, MS-70, September 2014; $823, MS-70, March 2013					
1991-S, Proof	753,257	3,138	69.1		$12
Auctions: No auction records available.					

MOUNT RUSHMORE GOLDEN ANNIVERSARY SILVER DOLLAR (1991)

Designer: *Marika Somogyi (obverse), Frank Gasparro (reverse).* **Weight:** *26.73 grams.*
Composition: *.900 silver, .100 copper (net weight .7736 oz. pure silver).* **Diameter:** *38.1 mm.*
Edge: *Reeded.* **Mints:** *Philadelphia (Uncirculated) and San Francisco (Proof).*

The Mount Rushmore silver dollar displays the traditional portraits of presidents George Washington, Thomas Jefferson, Theodore Roosevelt, and Abraham Lincoln as sculpted on the mountain by Gutzon Borglum. The reverse was by former chief sculptor-engraver of the U.S. Mint Frank Gasparro.

Designs. *Obverse:* View of Mount Rushmore with an olive wreath prominently below.
Reverse: The Great Seal of the United States, surrounded by a sunburst, above an outline map of the continental part of the United States inscribed SHRINE OF / DEMOCRACY.

Mintage Data. Authorized by the Mount Rushmore National Memorial Coin Act (Public Law 101-332, July 16, 1990). *Maximum authorized—2,500,000. Number minted—*1991-P: 133,139 Uncirculated; 1991-S: 738,419 Proof.

Original Cost. Sale prices $23 (Uncirculated, pre-issue) and $28 (Proof, pre-issue); Uncirculated later raised to $28, and Proof later raised to $31. Fifty percent of the surcharge of $7 per coin went to the Mount Rushmore National Memorial Society of Black Hills; the balance went to the U.S. Treasury.

Key to Collecting. Examples are easily available today. The coins were carefully struck, with the result that nearly all are superb gems.

	Distribution	Cert	Avg	%MS	MS-67
					PF-67
1991-P	133,139	1,790	69.3	100%	$40
Auctions: $80, MS-70, July 2014; $92, MS-70, January 2013					
1991-S, Proof	738,419	3,675	69.0		$35
Auctions: $194, PF-70DCam, September 2014; $176, PF-70DCam, June 2013; $174, PF-70DCam, February 2013; $53, PF-69DCam, July 2014					

MOUNT RUSHMORE GOLDEN ANNIVERSARY $5 GOLD COIN (1991)

Designer: *John Mercanti (obverse), William Lamb (reverse).* **Weight:** *8.359 grams.*
Composition: *.900 gold, .100 copper (net weight .242 oz. pure gold).*
Diameter: *21.6 mm.* **Edge:** *Reeded.* **Mint:** *West Point.*

The reverse of the five-dollar Mount Rushmore coin consisted solely of lettering, with no emblems or motifs, the first such instance in the history of U.S. commemorative coins.

Designs. *Obverse:* An American eagle flying above the monument with LIBERTY and date in the field. *Reverse:* MOUNT RUSHMORE NATIONAL MEMORIAL in script type.

Mintage Data. Authorized by the Mount Rushmore National Memorial Coin Act (Public Law 101-332, July 16, 1990). *Maximum authorized—* 500,000. *Number minted—*31,959 Uncirculated and 111,991 Proof.

Original Cost. Sale prices $185 (Uncirculated, pre-issue) and $195 (Proof, pre-issue); Uncirculated later raised to $210, and Proof later raised to $225. Fifty percent of the surcharge of $35 per coin went to the Mount Rushmore National Memorial Society of Black Hills; the balance went to the U.S. Treasury.

Key to Collecting. Examples are easily available today. The coins were carefully struck, with the result that nearly all are superb gems.

	Distribution	Cert	Avg	%MS	MS-67 / PF-67
1991-W	31,959	1,614	69.6	100%	$325
	Auctions: $653, MS-70, September 2014; $573, MS-70, November 2014; $353, MS-70, May 2015; $353, MS-70, April 2015				
1991-W, Proof	111,991	4,065	69.4		$325
	Auctions: $456, PF-70DCam, February 2013; $423, PF-70DCam, May 2015; $306, PF-69DCam, October 2014				

UNITED SERVICE ORGANIZATIONS SILVER DOLLAR (1991)

Designer: *Robert Lamb (obverse), John Mercanti (reverse).* **Weight:** *26.73 grams.*
Composition: *.900 silver, .100 copper (net weight .7736 oz. pure silver).*
Diameter: *38.1 mm.* **Edge:** *Reeded.* **Mints:** *Denver (Uncirculated) and San Francisco (Proof).*

The United Service Organizations is a congressionally chartered nonprofit group that provides services, programs, and live entertainment to U.S. military troops and their families. The 50th anniversary of the USO was commemorated with this silver dollar in 1991.

Designs. *Obverse:* Consists entirely of lettering, except for a banner upon which appears USO. Inscriptions include IN GOD WE TRUST, 50th ANNIVERSARY (in script), USO (on a banner, as noted; with three stars to each side), and LIBERTY 1991. *Reverse:* Illustrates an eagle, facing right, with a ribbon inscribed USO in its beak, perched atop a world globe. An arc of 11 stars is in the space below the globe. The legends include FIFTY YEARS / SERVICE (on the left side of the coin), TO SERVICE / PEOPLE (on the right side of the coin).

Mintage Data. Authorized by Public Law 101-404, October 2, 1990. *Maximum authorized*—1,000,000. *Number minted*—1991-D: 124,958 Uncirculated; 1991-S: 321,275 Proof.

Original Cost. Sale prices $23 (Uncirculated, pre-issue) and $28 (Proof, pre-issue); Uncirculated later raised to $26, and Proof later raised to $31. Fifty percent of the surcharge of $7 per coin went to the USO; the balance went toward reducing the national debt.

Key to Collecting. Mintages were low compared to other recent commemorative silver dollars. Today these coins can be purchased for slightly more than their bullion value.

	Distribution	Cert	Avg	%MS	MS-67
					PF-67
1991-D	124,958	2,054	69.1	100%	$35
	Auctions: $92, MS-70, March 2013; $86, MS-70, July 2014; $66, MS-70, May 2015				
1991-S, Proof	321,275	2,246	69.0		$30
	Auctions: $881, PF-70DCam, September 2014; $235, PF-70DCam, September 2014; $382, PF-70DCam, April 2013				

CHRISTOPHER COLUMBUS QUINCENTENARY HALF DOLLAR (1992)

Designer: *T. James Ferrell.* **Weight:** *11.34 grams.* **Composition:** *.9167 copper, .0833 nickel.* **Diameter:** *30.61 mm.* **Edge:** *Reeded.* **Mints:** *Denver (Uncirculated) and San Francisco (Proof).*

The 500th anniversary of Christopher Columbus's first trip to the new world was observed in 1992 by a suite of commemoratives, including this clad half dollar. The numismatic tradition fit in nicely with the World's Columbian Exposition coins of a century earlier—the first commemorative half dollars issued in 1892 and 1893.

Designs. *Obverse:* A full-length figure of Columbus walking ashore, with a rowboat and the flagship *Santa Maria* in the background. *Reverse:* The reverse shows Columbus's three ships—the *Nina*, *Pinta*, and *Santa Maria*.

Mintage Data. Authorized by Public Law 102-281, signed by President George H.W. Bush on May 13, 1992. *Maximum authorized*—6,000,000. *Number minted*—1992-D: 135,702 Uncirculated; 1992-S: 390,154 Proof.

Original Cost. Sale prices $6.50 (Uncirculated, pre-issue) and $8.50 (Proof, pre-issue); Uncirculated later raised to $7.50, and Proof later raised to $9.50. A surcharge of $1 per coin went to the Christopher Columbus Quincentenary Coins and Fellowship Foundation.

Key to Collecting. Examples in the marketplace remain reasonably priced. Nearly all are superb gems.

	Distribution	Cert	Avg	%MS	MS-67
					PF-67
1992-D	135,702	937	69.2	100%	$10
	Auctions: $86, MS-70, April 2013				
1992-S, Proof	390,154	2,507	69.1		$10
	Auctions: No auction records available.				

CHRISTOPHER COLUMBUS QUINCENTENARY SILVER DOLLAR (1992)

Designer: *John Mercanti (obverse), Thomas D. Rogers Sr. (reverse).* **Weight:** *26.73 grams.*
Composition: *.900 silver, .100 copper (net weight .7736 oz. pure silver).*
Diameter: *38.1 mm.* **Edge:** *Reeded.* **Mints:** *Denver (Uncirculated) and Philadelphia (Proof).*

Representative Frank Annunzio, a Democrat from Illinois who was prominent in coin legislation for some time, introduced the bill that led to these commemoratives. Interestingly, on the approved sketch for this silver dollar's obverse design, Columbus was depicted holding a telescope—but after it was pointed out that such instrument had not been invented yet in 1492, it was changed to a scroll on the final coin.

Designs. *Obverse:* Columbus standing, holding a flag in his right hand, with a scroll in his left hand, and with a globe on a stand. Three ships are shown in the distance, in a panel at the top border. *Reverse:* A split image is shown, depicting exploration in 1492 at the left, with half of a sailing vessel, and in 1992 at the right, with most of a space shuttle shown in a vertical position, with the earth in the distance.

Mintage Data. Authorized by Public Law 102-281, signed by President George H.W. Bush on May 13, 1992. *Maximum authorized*—4,000,000. *Number minted*—1992-D: 106,949 Uncirculated; 1992-P: 385,241 Proof.

Original Cost. Sale prices $23 (Uncirculated, pre-issue) and $27 (Proof, pre-issue); Uncirculated later raised to $28, and Proof later raised to $31. A surcharge of $7 per coin went to the Christopher Columbus Quincentenary Coins and Fellowship Foundation.

Key to Collecting. Examples in the marketplace remain reasonably priced. Nearly all are superb gems.

	Distribution	Cert	Avg	%MS	MS-67 PF-67
1992-D	106,949	1,708	69.2	100%	$40
	Auctions: $135, MS-70, March 2013; $86, MS-70, July 2014; $62, MS-70, September 2015				
1992-P, Proof	385,241	2,635	69.0		$35
	Auctions: $441, PF-70DCam, September 2014; $418, PF-70DCam, June 2013; $96, PF-70DCam, April 2013				

CHRISTOPHER COLUMBUS QUINCENTENARY $5 GOLD COIN (1992)

Designer: *T. James Ferrell (obverse), Thomas D. Rogers Sr. (reverse).* **Weight:** *8.359 grams.*
Composition: *.900 gold, .100 copper (net weight .242 oz. pure gold).*
Diameter: *21.6 mm.* **Edge:** *Reeded.* **Mint:** *West Point.*

No portrait from the life of Christopher Columbus is known to exist, so the five-dollar gold commemorative features T. James Ferrell's artistic imagining of the explorer's profile.

Designs. *Obverse:* The artist's conception of Columbus's face is shown gazing to the left toward an outline map of the New World. *Reverse:* The crest of the Admiral of the Ocean Sea and a chart dated 1492 are depicted.

Mintage Data. Authorized by Public Law 102-281, signed by President George H.W. Bush on May 13, 1992. *Maximum authorized*—1,000,000. *Number minted*—24,329 Uncirculated and 79,730 Proof.

Original Cost. Sale prices $180 (Uncirculated, pre-issue) and $190 (Proof, pre-issue); Uncirculated later raised to $210, and Proof later raised to $225. A surcharge of $35 per coin went to the Christopher Columbus Quincentenary Coins and Fellowship Foundation.

Key to Collecting. Examples in the marketplace remain reasonably priced. Nearly all are superb gems.

	Distribution	Cert	Avg	%MS	MS-67 PF-67
1992-W	24,329	1,310	69.6	100%	$325
Auctions: $447, MS-70, June 2014; $646, MS-70, September 2014; $317, MS-69, August 2014; $306, MS-69, August 2014					
1992-W, Proof	79,730	2,792	69.5		$325
Auctions: $353, PF-70DCam, May 2015; $329, PF-70DCam, May 2015; $435, PF-69DCam, April 2013; $306, PF-69DCam, August 2014					

XXV OLYMPIC GAMES HALF DOLLAR (1992)

Designer: *William Cousins (obverse), Steven M. Bieda (reverse).*
Weight: *11.34 grams.* **Composition:** *.9167 copper, .0833 nickel.* **Diameter:** *30.61 mm.*
Edge: *Reeded.* **Mints:** *Philadelphia (Uncirculated) and San Francisco (Proof).*

In 1992 the XXV Winter Olympic Games were held in Albertville and Savoie, France, while the Summer Games took place in Barcelona, Spain. Although the events did not take place in the United States, the rationale for a commemorative coin issue was, in part, to raise money to train American athletes. The same line of reasoning had been used for the coins made in connection with the 1988 Olympic Games held in Seoul, South Korea.

Designs. *Obverse:* A pony-tailed female gymnast doing the stretch against a background of stars and stripes. *Reverse:* The Olympic torch and an olive branch, with CITIUS / ALTIUS / FORTIUS nearby in three lines, Latin for "faster, higher, stronger."

Mintage Data. Authorized by the 1992 Olympic Commemorative Coin Act, Public Law 101-406, signed by President George H.W. Bush on October 3, 1990. *Maximum authorized*—6,000,000. *Number minted*—1992-P: 161,607 Uncirculated; 1992-S: 519,645 Proof.

Original Cost. Sale prices $6 (Uncirculated, pre-issue) and $8.50 (Proof, pre-issue); Uncirculated later raised to $7.50, and Proof later raised to $9.50. The surcharge of $1 per coin went to the U.S. Olympic Committee.

Key to Collecting. Examples are easily available today. Nearly all are gems.

	Distribution	Cert	Avg	%MS	MS-67 PF-67
1992-P	161,607	1,095	69.3	100%	$10
Auctions: $59, MS-70, January 2013					
1992-S, Proof	519,645	2,517	69.2		$10
Auctions: No auction records available.					

XXV Olympic Games Silver Dollar (1992)

Designer: *John R. Deecken (obverse), Marcel Jovine (reverse).* **Weight:** *26.73 grams.*
Composition: *.900 silver, .100 copper (net weight .7736 oz. pure silver).* **Diameter:** *38.1 mm.*
Edge: *Lettered (Uncirculated), reeded (Proof).* **Mints:** *Denver (Uncirculated) and San Francisco (Proof).*

The image on this coin's obverse fit closely that of Fleer's card showing popular baseball player Nolan Ryan, of the Texas Rangers, but the designer denied there was any connection when queried on the subject by the Treasury Department. The Denver Mint Uncirculated dollars have XXV OLYMPIAD incuse four times around the edge, alternately inverted, on a reeded background; these are the first lettered-edge U.S. coins since the 1933 double eagle.

Designs. *Obverse:* A pitcher is shown about to throw a ball to a batter. *Reverse:* A shield, intertwined Olympic rings, and olive branches make up the main design.

Mintage Data. Authorized by the 1992 Olympic Commemorative Coin Act, Public Law 101-406, signed by President George H.W. Bush on October 3, 1990. *Maximum authorized—4,000,000. Number minted—1992-D:* 187,552 Uncirculated; 1992-S: 504,505 Proof.

Original Cost. Sale prices $24 (Uncirculated, pre-issue) and $28 (Proof, pre-issue); Uncirculated later raised to $28, and Proof later raised to $32. The surcharge of $1 per coin went to the U.S. Olympic Committee.

Key to Collecting. Examples are easily available today. Nearly all are gems.

	Distribution	Cert	Avg	%MS	MS-67 PF-67
1992-D	187,552	3,625	69.0	100%	$38
	Auctions: $247, MS-70, April 2013				
1992-S, Proof	504,505	2,787	68.9		$35
	Auctions: $588, PF-70DCam, September 2013; $84, PF-70, February 2013; $30, PF-69UCam, January 2015				

XXV Olympic Games $5 Gold Coin (1992)

Designer: *James Sharpe (obverse), James Peed (reverse).* **Weight:** *8.359 grams.*
Composition: *.900 gold, .100 copper (net weight .242 oz. pure gold).*
Diameter: *21.6 mm.* **Edge:** *Reeded.* **Mint:** *West Point.*

The five-dollar entry in the XXV commemorative coin program features a dynamic sprinter against a backdrop of the U.S. flag. Sales were relatively low compared to other recent gold commemoratives.

Designs. *Obverse:* A sprinter running forward with a vertical U.S. flag in the background. *Reverse:* A heraldic eagle with five Olympic rings and USA above.

Mintage Data. Authorized by the 1992 Olympic Commemorative Coin Act, Public Law 101-406, signed by President George H.W. Bush on October 3, 1990. *Maximum authorized*—500,000. *Number minted*—27,732 Uncirculated and 77,313 Proof.

Original Cost. Sale prices $185 (Uncirculated, pre-issue) and $195 (Proof, pre-issue); Uncirculated later raised to $215, and Proof later raised to $230. The surcharge of $35 per coin went to the U.S. Olympic Committee.

Key to Collecting. Examples are easily available today. Nearly all are gems.

	Distribution	Cert	Avg	%MS	MS-67 / PF-67
1992-W	27,732	1,561	69.7	100%	$325
Auctions: $376, MS-70, May 2015; $364, MS-70, May 2015; $350, MS-70, April 2015; $329, MS-70, June 2015					
1992-W, Proof	77,313	3,098	69.5		$325
Auctions: $423, PF-70UCam, March 2015; $364, PF-70UCam, April 2015; $358, PF-70UCam, March 2015; $333, PF-70UCam, May 2015					

WHITE HOUSE 200TH ANNIVERSARY SILVER DOLLAR (1992)

Designer: *Edgar Z. Steever IV (obverse), Chester Y. Martin (reverse).* **Weight:** *26.73 grams.*
Composition: *.900 silver, .100 copper (net weight .7736 oz. pure silver).*
Diameter: *38.1 mm.* **Edge:** *Reeded.* **Mints:** *Denver (Uncirculated) and West Point (Proof).*

This coin is one of few depicting Washington buildings that sold out its full authorized limit. Foliage, two trees, and a fountain were in the original sketch, but were removed at the suggestion of the Fine Arts Commission, yielding a clean and crisp design.

Designs. *Obverse:* The north portico of the White House is shown in a plan view, without shrubbery or background. *Reverse:* James Hoban, architect of the first White House, in a half-length portrait with the original entrance door.

Mintage Data. Authorized by Public Law 102-281, signed by President George H.W. Bush on May 13, 1992. *Maximum authorized*—500,000. *Number minted*—1992-D: 123,803 Uncirculated; 1992-W: 375,851 Proof.

Original Cost. Sale prices (pre-issue only) $23 (Uncirculated) and $28 (Proof). The surcharge of $10 per coin went towards the preservation of public rooms within the White House.

Key to Collecting. The White House dollar has remained popular ever since its issuance. Examples are readily available today and are nearly always found in superb gem preservation, as issued.

	Distribution	Cert	Avg	%MS	MS-67 / PF-67
1992-D	123,803	1,998	69.2	100%	$28
Auctions: $108, MS-70, January 2013					
1992-W, Proof	375,851	2,846	69.0		$35
Auctions: $194, PF-70DCam, April 2013					

BILL OF RIGHTS HALF DOLLAR (1993)

Designer: *T. James Ferrell (obverse), Dean McMullen (reverse).* **Weight:** *12.5 grams.*
Composition: *.900 silver, .100 copper.* **Diameter:** *30.6 mm.* **Edge:** *Reeded.*
Mints: *West Point (Uncirculated) and San Francisco (Proof).*

This silver half dollar, as well as the silver dollar and five-dollar gold coin issued alongside it, honored James Madison and the Bill of Rights, added to the Constitution in 1789 and intended to give basic rights and freedoms to all Americans. These were the first half dollars to be composed of 90% silver since the George Washington 250th Anniversary of Birth coins in 1982.

Designs. *Obverse:* James Madison seated at a desk, penning the Bill of Rights. Montpelier, Madison's Virginia home, is shown in the distance. *Reverse:* A hand holds a flaming torch, with inscriptions to each side.

Mintage Data. Authorized by Public Law 101-281, part of the White House Commemorative Coin Act, on May 13, 1992. *Maximum authorized—1,000,000. Number minted—1993-W:* 193,346 Uncirculated; *1993-S:* 586,315 Proof.

Original Cost. Sale prices $9.75 (Uncirculated, pre-issue) and $12.50 (Proof, pre-issue); Uncirculated later increased in $11.50, and Proof later increased to $13.50. The surcharge went to the James Madison Memorial Scholarship Trust Fund.

Key to Collecting. Following the pattern of other commemoratives of the early 1990s, these coins are readily available on the market, typically in superb gem preservation.

	Distribution	Cert	Avg	%MS	MS-67
					PF-67
1993-W	193,346	1,179	69.2	100%	$20
	Auctions: $82, MS-70, April 2013				
1993-S, Proof	586,315	2,728	69.0		$15
	Auctions: $441, PF-70DCam, April 2013; $382, PF-70DCam, April 2013				

BILL OF RIGHTS SILVER DOLLAR (1993)

Designer: *William Krawczewicz (obverse), Dean McMullen (reverse).* **Weight:** *26.73 grams.*
Composition: *.900 silver, .100 copper (net weight .7736 oz. pure silver).*
Diameter: *38.1 mm.* **Edge:** *Reeded.* **Mints:** *Denver (Uncirculated) and San Francisco (Proof).*

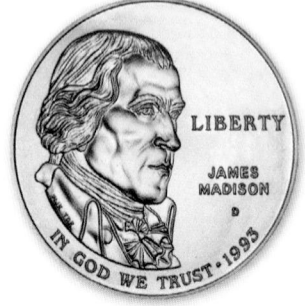 

On June 1, 1992, U.S. Treasurer Catalina Vasquez Villalpando announced a nationwide competition seeking designs for the James Madison / Bill of Rights Commemorative Coin Program, with all entries to be received by August 31. Secretary of the Treasury Nicholas F. Brady selected his favorite motifs from 815 submissions, which were then sent to the Commission of Fine Arts for review.

Many changes were suggested, including simplifying the appearance of Madison's residence, Montpelier.

Designs. *Obverse:* Portrait of James Madison facing right and slightly forward. *Reverse:* Montpelier.

Mintage Data. Authorized by Public Law 101-281, part of the White House Commemorative Coin Act, on May 13, 1992. *Maximum authorized*—900,000. *Number minted*—1993-D: 98,383 Uncirculated; 1993-S: 534,001 Proof.

Original Cost. Sale prices $22 (Uncirculated, pre-issue) and $25 (Proof, pre-issue); Uncirculated later raised to $27, and Proof later raised to $29. The surcharge went to the James Madison Memorial Scholarship Trust Fund.

Key to Collecting. Following the pattern of other commemoratives of the early 1990s, these coins are readily available on the market, typically in superb gem preservation.

	Distribution	Cert	Avg	%MS	MS-67
					PF-67
1993-D	98,383	1,363	69.1	100%	$40
Auctions: $182, MS-70, January 2013					
1993-S, Proof	534,001	2,337	68.9		$35
Auctions: No auction records available.					

BILL OF RIGHTS $5 GOLD COIN (1993)

Designer: *Scott R. Blazek (obverse), Joseph D. Peña (reverse).* **Weight:** *8.359 grams.*
Composition: *.900 gold, .100 copper (net weight .242 oz. pure gold).*
Diameter: *21.6 mm.* **Edge:** *Reeded.* **Mint:** *West Point.*

The coin project that resulted in this five-dollar gold coin (and the related half dollar and silver dollar) was encouraged by the Madison Foundation.

Designs. *Obverse:* Portrait of Madison, waist up, reading the Bill of Rights. *Reverse:* Quotation by Madison with an eagle above and small torch and laurel branch at the border below.

Mintage Data. Authorized by Public Law 101-281, part of the White House Commemorative Coin Act, on May 13, 1992. *Maximum authorized*—300,000. *Number minted*—23,266 Uncirculated and 78,651 Proof.

Original Cost. Sale prices $175 (Uncirculated, pre-issue) and $185 (Proof, pre-issue); Uncirculated later raised to $205, and Proof later raised to $220. The surcharge of $10 per coin went to the James Madison Memorial Scholarship Trust Fund.

Key to Collecting. Following the pattern of other commemoratives of the early 1990s, these coins are readily available on the market, typically in superb gem preservation.

	Distribution	Cert	Avg	%MS	MS-67
					PF-67
1993-W	23,266	1,336	69.6	100%	$325
Auctions: $329, MS-70, August 2014; $652, MS-70, September 2014; $400, MS-69, March 2013					
1993-W, Proof	78,651	3,246	69.4		$325
Auctions: $306, PF-70DCam, November 2014; $435, PF-70DCam, March 2013; $317, PF-69DCam, August 2014; $329, PF-69DCam, October 2014					

50TH ANNIVERSARY OF WORLD WAR II HALF DOLLAR (1991–1995)

Designer: *George Klauba (obverse), Bill J. Leftwich (reverse).* **Weight:** *11.34 grams.*
Composition: *.9167 copper, .0833 nickel.* **Diameter:** *30.61 mm.* **Edge:** *Reeded.* **Mint:** *Philadelphia.*

These half dollars and the other World War II 50th-anniversary coins were issued in 1993 and dated 1991–1995. Despite the importance of the war commemorated, the coins met with a lukewarm response by purchasers.

Designs. *Obverse:* The heads of a soldier, sailor, and airman are shown superimposed on a V (for victory), with a B-17 bomber flying overhead. *Reverse:* An American Marine is shown in action during the takeover of a Japanese-held island in the South Pacific. A carrier-based fighter plane flies overhead.

Mintage Data. Authorized by Public Law 102-414, signed by President William J. Clinton on October 14, 1992. *Maximum authorized*—2,000,000. *Number minted*—197,072 Uncirculated and 317,396 Proof.

Original Cost. Sale prices $8 (Uncirculated, pre-issue) and $9 (Proof, pre-issue); Uncirculated later raised to $9, and Proof later raised to $10. The surcharge of $2 per coin was split between the American Battle Monuments Commission (to aid in the construction of the World War II Monument in the nation's capital) and the Battle of Normandy Foundation (to assist in the erection of a monument in France).

Key to Collecting. Examples are easily enough found in the marketplace today and are nearly always of superb gem quality.

	Distribution	Cert	Avg	%MS	MS-67
					PF-67
1991–1995 (1993-P)	197,072	1,220	69.1	100%	$15
	Auctions: $165, MS-70Cam, September 2014; $529, MS-70Cam, April 2013; $153, MS-70, June 2013				
1991–1995 (1993-P), Proof	317,396	2,024	69.0		$15
	Auctions: No auction records available.				

50TH ANNIVERSARY OF WORLD WAR II SILVER DOLLAR (1991–1995)

Designer: *Thomas D. Rogers Sr.* **Weight:** *26.73 grams.*
Composition: *.900 silver, .100 copper (net weight .7736 oz. pure silver).*
Diameter: *38.1 mm.* **Edge:** *Reeded.* **Mints:** *Denver (Uncirculated) and West Point (Proof).*

The designs for these silver dollars and the related half dollars and five-dollar gold coins were the result of a competition. The works of five artists were selected (only one of them, Thomas D. Rogers Sr., being from the Mint staff). It was mandated that the dollar use the Battle of Normandy as a theme.

Designs. *Obverse:* An American soldier is shown as he runs ashore on the beach in Normandy during the D-Day invasion on June 6, 1944, which launched from England to liberate France. *Reverse:* The reverse illustrates the shoulder patch used on a uniform of Dwight D. Eisenhower's Supreme Headquarters Allied Expeditionary Force, with a quotation from Eisenhower.

Mintage Data. Authorized by Public Law 102-414, signed by President William J. Clinton on October 14, 1992. *Maximum authorized*—1,000,000. *Number minted*—1993-D: 107,240 Uncirculated; 1993-W: 342,041 Proof.

Original Cost. Sale prices $23 (Uncirculated, pre-issue) and $27 (Proof, pre-issue); Uncirculated later raised to $28, and Proof later raised to $31. The surcharge of $2 per coin was split between the American Battle Monuments Commission (to aid in the construction of the World War II Monument in the nation's capital) and the Battle of Normandy Foundation (to assist in the erection of a monument in France).

Key to Collecting. Examples are easily enough found in the marketplace today and are nearly always of superb gem quality.

	Distribution	Cert	Avg	%MS	MS-67 PF-67
1991–1995 (1993-D)	107,240	1,946	69.3	100%	$45
	Auctions: $118, MS-70, January 2013; $86, MS-70, July 2014; $74, MS-70, August 2015; $74, MS-70, May 2015				
1991–1995 (1993-W), Proof	342,041	3,082	69.0		$45
	Auctions: $206, PF-70DCam, September 2014				

50TH ANNIVERSARY OF WORLD WAR II $5 GOLD COIN (1991–1995)

Designer: *Charles J. Madsen (obverse), Edward Southworth Fisher (reverse).*
Weight: *8.359 grams.* **Composition:** *.900 gold, .100 copper (net weight .242 oz. pure gold).*
Diameter: *21.6 mm.* **Edge:** *Reeded.* **Mint:** *West Point.*

The approval of the American Legion, Veterans of Foreign Wars of the United States, American Veterans of World War, Korea and Vietnam (AMVETS), and the Disabled American Veterans, was required for the designs of all three 50th Anniversary of World War II commemoratives. The five-dollar coin was mandated to reflect the Allied victory in the war.

Designs. *Obverse:* An American soldier holds his rifle and raises his arm to indicate victory. *Reverse:* A large V (for victory) is at the center, with three dots and a dash over it, the Morse code for that letter. Branches are to each side.

Mintage Data. Authorized by Public Law 102-414, signed by President William J. Clinton on October 14, 1992. *Maximum authorized*—300,000. *Number minted*—23,672 Uncirculated and 67,026 Proof.

Original Cost. Sale prices $170 (Uncirculated, pre-issue) and $185 (Proof, pre-issue); Uncirculated later raised to $185, and Proof later raised to $220. The surcharge of $35 per coin was split between the American Battle Monuments Commission (to aid in the construction of the World War II Monument in the nation's capital) and the Battle of Normandy Foundation (to assist in the erection of a monument in France).

Key to Collecting. Examples are easily enough found in the marketplace today and are nearly always of superb gem quality.

	Distribution	Cert	Avg	%MS	MS-67	
					PF-67	
1991–1995 (1993-W)	23,672	1,411	69.6	100%	$400	
	Auctions: $646, MS-70, September 2014; $411, MS-70, April 2013; $353, MS-69, August 2014					
1991–1995 (1993-W), Proof	67,026	2,497	69.3		$400	
	Auctions: $458, PF-70DCam, April 2013; $382, PF-70DCam, April 2013; $333, PF-69DCam, August 2014					

THOMAS JEFFERSON SILVER DOLLAR (1993)

Designer: *T. James Ferrell.* **Weight:** *26.73 grams.*
Composition: *.900 silver, .100 copper (net weight .7736 oz. pure silver).*
Diameter: *38.1 mm.* **Edge:** *Reeded.* **Mints:** *Philadelphia (Uncirculated) and San Francisco (Proof).*

The 250th anniversary in 1993 of the birth of Thomas Jefferson in 1743 furnished the occasion for a commemorative silver dollar. The obverse portrait was based on an 1805 painting by Gilbert Stuart.

Designs. *Obverse:* Profile bust of President Thomas Jefferson. *Reverse:* Monticello, Jefferson's home.

Mintage Data. Authorized under Public Law 103-186, signed by President William J. Clinton on December 14, 1993. *Maximum authorized*—600,000. *Number minted*—1993-P: 266,927 Uncirculated; 1993-S: 332,891 Proof.

Original Cost. Sale prices $27 (Uncirculated, pre-issue) and $31 (Proof, pre-issue); Uncirculated later raised to $32, and Proof later raised to $35. The surcharge of $10 per coin went to the Jefferson Endowment Fund.

Key to Collecting. Although the Jefferson dollar was a popular sellout in its time, examples are easily found in the numismatic marketplace and are nearly always of superb gem quality. Most in demand, from the enthusiasm of five-cent piece collectors, are the special sets issued with the frosty Uncirculated 1994-P Jefferson nickel.

	Distribution	Cert	Avg	%MS	MS-67	
					PF-67	
1993-P	266,927	2,905	69.2	100%	$30	
	Auctions: $86, MS-70, January 2013					
1993-S, Proof	332,891	2,557	69.0		$20	
	Auctions: $400, PF-70DCam, March 2013					

U.S. CAPITOL BICENTENNIAL SILVER DOLLAR (1994)

Designer: *William Cousins (obverse), John Mercanti (reverse).* **Weight:** *26.73 grams.*
Composition: *.900 silver, .100 copper (net weight .7736 oz. pure silver).*
Diameter: *38.1 mm.* **Edge:** *Reeded.* **Mints:** *Denver (Uncirculated) and San Francisco (Proof).*

These silver dollars commemorated the 200th anniversary of the U.S. Capitol in Washington, D.C. Although the Federal City, as it was called, was laid out in the 1790s, it was not until 1800 that the federal government relocated there from Philadelphia. In honor of the recently deceased first president, the name was changed to Washington City, or, in popular use, Washington. The Capitol building design represented the work of several architects and artists, among them Benjamin Latrobe, Charles Bulfinch, and Constantino Brumidi.

Designs. *Obverse:* Dome of the Capitol with stars surrounding the *Freedom* statue. *Reverse:* Shield with four American flags, branches, and surmounted by an eagle, a motif based on the center area of a stained-glass window near the House and Senate grand staircases (produced by J. & G. Gibson, of Philadelphia, in 1859 and 1860).

Mintage Data. Authorized by Public Law 103-186, signed by President William J. Clinton on December 14, 1993. *Maximum authorized*—500,000. *Number minted*—1994-D: 68,332 Uncirculated; 1994-S: 279,579 Proof.

Original Cost. Sale prices $32 (Uncirculated, pre-issue) and $36 (Proof, pre-issue; Uncirculated later raised to $37, and Proof later raised to $40. The surcharge of $15 per coin went to the United States Capitol Preservation Commission. A Mint announcement noted that this was to go "for the construction of the Capitol Visitor Center" (itself the subject of a 2001 commemorative dollar).

Key to Collecting. Superb gem Mint State and Proof coins are easily available.

	Distribution	Cert	Avg	%MS	MS-67
					PF-67
1994-D	68,332	1,546	69.4	100%	$40
	Auctions: $101, MS-70, January 2013; $100, MS-70, August 2015; $80, MS-70, July 2014				
1994-S, Proof	279,579	1,800	69.0		$35
	Auctions: $294, PF-70DCam, April 2013; $270, PF-70DCam, September 2014; $217, PF-70DCam, August 2014				

U.S. Prisoner of War Memorial Silver Dollar (1994)

Designer: *Tom Nielsen (obverse), Edgar Z. Steever IV (reverse).* **Weight:** *26.73 grams.*
Composition: *.900 silver, .100 copper (net weight .7736 oz. pure silver).*
Diameter: *38.1 mm.* **Edge:** *Reeded.* **Mints:** *West Point (Uncirculated) and Philadelphia (Proof).*

The proposed National Prisoner of War Museum set the stage for the issuance of a silver dollar observing the tribulations of prisoners held by foreign military powers. The obverse designer, Nielsen, was a decorated former prisoner of war employed by the Bureau of Veterans Affairs.

Designs. *Obverse:* An eagle with a chain on one leg flies through a circle of barbed wire, representing flight to freedom. *Reverse:* Plan view, with landscaping, of the proposed National Prisoner of War Museum.

Mintage Data. Authorized by Public Law 103-186, signed by President William J. Clinton on December 14, 1993. *Maximum authorized*—500,000. *Number minted*—1994-W: 54,893 Uncirculated; 1994-P: 224,449 Proof.

Original Cost. Sale prices $27 (Uncirculated, pre-issue) and $31 (Proof, pre-issue); Uncirculated later raised to $32, and Proof later raised to $35. The surcharge of $10 per coin went toward the construction of the museum.

Key to Collecting. The 1994-W dollar is in special demand due to its relatively low mintage. Both varieties are seen with frequency in the marketplace and are nearly always superb gems.

	Distribution	Cert	Avg	%MS	MS-67
					PF-67
1994-W	54,893	1,844	69.4	100%	$80
	Auctions: $129, MS-70, January 2014; $100, MS-70, February 2015; $94, MS-70, January 2015; $87, MS-70, May 2015				
1994-P, Proof	224,449	2,398	68.9		$45
	Auctions: $1,116, PF-70DCam, September 2014; $999, PF-70DCam, September 2014; $1,763, PF-70DCam, January 2013				

Women in Military Service Memorial Silver Dollar (1994)

Designer: *T. James Ferrell.* **Weight:** *26.73 grams.*
Composition: *.900 silver, .100 copper (net weight .7736 oz. pure silver).*
Diameter: *38.1 mm.* **Edge:** *Reeded.* **Mints:** *West Point (Uncirculated) and Philadelphia (Proof).*

These coins were issued to honor women in the military and help fund the Women in Military Service for America Memorial at the ceremonial entrance to Arlington National Cemetery (which became a reality and opened in October 1997 on a 4.2-acre site).

Designs. *Obverse:* Servicewomen from the Army, Marine Corps, Navy, Air Force, and

Coast Guard, with the names of these branches around the border. *Reverse:* A diagonal view of the front of the proposed the Women in Military Service for America Memorial.

Mintage Data. Authorized by Public Law 103-186, signed by President William J. Clinton on December 14, 1993. *Maximum authorized—500,000. Number minted—1994-W:* 69,860 Uncirculated; 1994-P: 241,278 Proof.

Original Cost. Sale prices $27 (Uncirculated, pre-issue) and $31 (Proof, pre-issue); Uncirculated later raised to $32, and Proof later raised to $35. The surcharge of $10 per coin went towards the construction of the memorial.

Key to Collecting. Mirroring the situation for other commemoratives of the era, these are easily enough found on the market and are usually in superb gem grades.

	Distribution	Cert	Avg	%MS	MS-67 PF-67
1994-W	69,860	3,221	69.3	100%	$35
Auctions: $72, MS-70, April 2013					
1994-P, Proof	241,278	2,168	68.9		$40
Auctions: $646, PF-70DCam, April 2013					

Vietnam Veterans Memorial Silver Dollar (1994)

Designer: *John Mercanti (obverse), Thomas D. Rogers Sr. (reverse).* **Weight:** *26.73 grams.*
Composition: *.900 silver, .100 copper (net weight .7736 oz. pure silver).*
Diameter: *38.1 mm.* **Edge:** *Reeded.* **Mints:** *West Point (Uncirculated) and Philadelphia (Proof).*

In Washington, D.C., the Vietnam Veterans Memorial, often called the Memorial Wall, has been one of the city's prime attractions since it was dedicated in 1984.

Designs. *Obverse:* A hand touching the Wall. In the distance to the right is the Washington Monument. *Reverse:* Three military medals and ribbons surrounded with lettering.

Mintage Data. Authorized by Public Law 103-186, signed by President William J. Clinton on December 14, 1993. *Maximum authorized—500,000. Number minted—1994-W:* 57,290 Uncirculated; 1994-P: 227,671 Proof.

Original Cost. Sale prices $27 (Uncirculated) and $31 (Proof); Uncirculated later raised to $32, and Proof later raised to $35. The surcharge of $10 per coin went towards the construction of a visitor's center near the Memorial.

Key to Collecting. Gem specimens are easily available. The aftermarket price for this dollar is stronger than for most others of the early 1990s.

	Distribution	Cert	Avg	%MS	MS-67 PF-67
1994-W	57,290	1,741	69.3	100%	$80
Auctions: $141, MS-70, January 2013; $103, MS-70, July 2014; $84, MS-70, May 2015					
1994-P, Proof	227,671	2,968	68.9		$65
Auctions: $2,115, PF-70DCam, April 2013; $793, PF-70DCam, August 2015; $770, PF-70DCam, September 2014					

WORLD CUP TOURNAMENT HALF DOLLAR (1994)

Designer: *Richard T. LaRoche (obverse), Dean McMullen (reverse).* **Weight:** *11.34 grams.*
Composition: *.9167 copper, .0833 nickel.* **Diameter:** *30.61 mm.* **Edge:** *Reeded.*
Mints: *Denver (Uncirculated) and Philadelphia (Proof).*

The United States' hosting of the XV FIFA World Cup playoff—the culmination of soccer games among 141 nations—was commemorated with this copper-nickel half dollar, as well as a silver dollar and a five-dollar gold coin.

Designs. *Obverse:* A soccer player in action, on the run with a ball near his feet. *Reverse:* The World Cup USA logo at the center, flanked by branches.

Mintage Data. Authorized by Public Law 102-281, signed by President George H.W. Bush on May 13, 1992. *Maximum authorized*—5,000,000. *Number minted*—1994-D: 168,208 Uncirculated; 1994-P: 609,354 Proof.

Original Cost. Sale prices $8.75 (Uncirculated, pre-issue) and $9.75 (Proof, pre-issue); Uncirculated later raised to $9.50, and Proof later raised to $10.50. The surcharge of $1 per coin went to the World Cup Organizing Committee.

Key to Collecting. The World Cup coins are reasonably priced in the secondary market. Nearly all are superb gems.

	Distribution	Cert	Avg	%MS	MS-67
					PF-67
1994-D	168,208	927	69.1	100%	$10
Auctions: $212, MS-70, September 2014					
1994-P, Proof	609,354	2,775	69.0		$10
Auctions: $411, PF-70, September 2014; $558, PF-70, April 2013					

WORLD CUP TOURNAMENT SILVER DOLLAR (1994)

Designer: *Dean McMullen.* **Weight:** *26.73 grams.*
Composition: *.900 silver, .100 copper (net weight .7736 oz. pure silver).*
Diameter: *38.1 mm.* **Edge:** *Reeded.* **Mints:** *Denver (Uncirculated) and San Francisco (Proof).*

In terms of mintage goals, this program was one of the greatest failures in the history of American commemorative coinage. The U.S. Mint stated it lost $3.5 million in the effort, noting that there simply were too many commemorative programs in progress, each with excessive mintage expectations. The only winner in the World Cup scenario seemed to be the recipient of the surcharge.

Designs. *Obverse:* Two competing soccer players converge on a soccer ball in play. *Reverse:* The World Cup USA logo at the center, flanked by branches.

Mintage Data. Authorized by Public Law 102-281, signed by President George H.W. Bush on May 13, 1992. *Maximum authorized—5,000,000. Number minted—*1994-D: 81,524 Uncirculated; 1994-S: 577,090 Proof.

Original Cost. Sale prices $23 (Uncirculated, pre-issue) and $27 (Proof, pre-issue); Uncirculated later raised to $28, and Proof later raised to $31. The surcharge of $7 per coin went to the World Cup Organizing Committee.

Key to Collecting. The World Cup coins are reasonably priced in the secondary market. Nearly all are superb gems.

	Distribution	Cert	Avg	%MS	MS-67 PF-67
1994-D	81,524	1,280	69.0	100%	$45
Auctions: $329, MS-70, September 2014; $764, MS-70, April 2013					
1994-S, Proof	577,090	2,579	69.0		$35
Auctions: $170, PF-70DCam, September 2014; $294, PF-70DCam, April 2013					

WORLD CUP TOURNAMENT $5 GOLD COIN (1994)

Designer: *William J. Krawczewicz (obverse), Dean McMullen (reverse).* **Weight:** *8.359 grams.* **Composition:** *.900 gold, .100 copper (net weight .242 oz. pure gold).* **Diameter:** *21.6 mm.* **Edge:** *Reeded.* **Mint:** *West Point.*

The U.S. Mint's many recent commemoratives had caused buyer fatigue by the time the World Cup Tournament coins came out. Collectors blamed the Mint for creating coins that few people wanted. The complaints should have gone to Congress instead. Faced with so many coins to produce, often with very short deadlines, the Mint simply had no time to call for designs to be submitted from leading artists.

Designs. *Obverse:* The World Cup trophy. *Reverse:* The World Cup USA logo at the center, flanked by branches.

Mintage Data. Authorized by Public Law 102-281, signed by President George H.W. Bush on May 13, 1992. *Maximum authorized—750,000. Number minted—*22,447 Uncirculated and 89,614 Proof.

Original Cost. Sale prices $170 (Uncirculated, pre-issue) and $185 (Proof, pre-issue); Uncirculated later raised to $200, and Proof later raised to $220. The surcharge of $35 per coin went to the World Cup Organizing Committee.

Key to Collecting. The World Cup coins are reasonably priced in the secondary market. Nearly all are superb gems.

	Distribution	Cert	Avg	%MS	MS-67 PF-67
1994-W	22,447	1,062	69.5	100%	$400
Auctions: $382, MS-70, September 2014; $382, MS-70, November 2014; $448, MS-70, April 2013; $306, MS-69, November 2014					
1994-W, Proof	89,614	2,145	69.3		$400
Auctions: $470, PF-70DCam, June 2013; $295, PF-69DCam, October 2014; $306, PF-68DCam, February 2015					

XXVI Olympiad Basketball Half Dollar (1995)

Designer: *Clint Hansen (obverse), T. James Ferrell (reverse).* **Weight:** *11.34 grams.*
Composition: *.9167 copper, .0833 nickel.* **Diameter:** *30.61 mm.* **Edge:** *Reeded.* **Mint:** *San Francisco.*

Men's basketball has been an Olympic sport since the 1936 Summer Games in Berlin. The 1996 U.S. team, also known as "Dream Team III," won the gold medal at the Summer Games in Atlanta.

Designs. *Obverse:* Three basketball players. *Reverse:* Symbol of the Atlanta Committee for the Olympic Games superimposed over the Atlantic Ocean as viewed from space.

Mintage Data. Authorized by Public Law 102-390, signed by President George H.W. Bush on October 6, 1992. *Maximum authorized*—2,000,000. *Number minted*—171,001 Uncirculated and 169,655 Proof.

Original Cost. Sale prices $10.50 (Uncirculated, pre-issue) and $11.50 (Proof, pre-issue); Uncirculated later raised to $11.50, and Proof later raised to $12.50. The surcharge per coin went to the Atlanta Olympic Committee.

Key to Collecting. Enough 1995 and 1996 Olympics coins are on the aftermarket that finding designs of choice, or forming a set, will be no problem. The obverse designs are varied, and in total the collection is an excellent representation of this quadrennial worldwide competition.

	Distribution	Cert	Avg	%MS	MS-67 PF-67
1995-S	171,001	1,427	69.3	100%	$20
	Auctions: $118, MS-70, July 2014; $76, MS-70, July 2013				
1995-S, Proof	169,655	2,005	69.1		$15
	Auctions: No auction records available.				

XXVI Olympiad Baseball Half Dollar (1995)

Designer: *Edgar Z. Steever IV (obverse), T. James Ferrell (reverse).* **Weight:** *11.34 grams.*
Composition: *.9167 copper, .0833 nickel.* **Diameter:** *30.61 mm.* **Edge:** *Reeded.* **Mint:** *San Francisco.*

Baseball was an official Olympic sport at each Summer Games between 1992 and 2008, but was voted out of the 2012 London Olympics and will remain off the docket until at least 2024 following a 2013 International Olympic Committee vote. The team representing Cuba took home the gold medal at the 1996 Atlanta Olympics.

Designs. *Obverse:* Batter at the plate with catcher and umpire. *Reverse:* Symbol of the Atlanta Committee for the Olympic Games superimposed over the Atlantic Ocean as viewed from space.

Mintage Data. Authorized by Public Law 102-390, signed by President George H.W. Bush on October 6, 1992. *Maximum authorized*—2,000,000. *Number minted*—164,605 Uncirculated and 118,087 Proof.

Original Cost. Sale prices $10.50 (Uncirculated, pre-issue) and $11.50 (Proof, pre-issue); Uncirculated later raised to $11.50, and Proof later raised to $12.50. The surcharge per coin went to the Atlanta Olympic Committee.

Key to Collecting. Enough 1995 and 1996 Olympics coins are on the aftermarket that finding designs of choice, or forming a set, will be no problem. The obverse designs are varied, and in total the collection is an excellent representation of this quadrennial worldwide competition.

	Distribution	Cert	Avg	%MS	MS-67 PF-67
1995-S	164,605	1,100	69.3	100%	$20
	Auctions: $130, MS-70, April 2013				
1995-S, Proof	118,087	1,561	69.1		$20
	Auctions: $329, PF-70DCam, September 2014; $200, PF-70DCam, September 2014				

XXVI OLYMPIAD GYMNASTICS SILVER DOLLAR (1995)

Designer: *James C. Sharpe (obverse), William Krawczewicz (reverse).* **Weight:** *26.73 grams.*
Composition: *.900 silver, .100 copper (net weight .7736 oz. pure silver).*
Diameter: *38.1 mm.* **Edge:** *Reeded.* **Mints:** *Denver (Uncirculated) and Philadelphia (Proof).*

The men's gymnastics competition has been held at each Olympic Summer Games since the birth of the modern Olympic movement in 1896. Russia won the gold medal in the team all-around event at the 1996 Games in Atlanta.

Designs. *Obverse:* Men's gymnastics. *Reverse:* Clasped hands of two athletes with torch above.

Mintage Data. Authorized by Public Law 102-390, signed by President George H.W. Bush on October 6, 1992. *Maximum authorized*—750,000. *Number minted*—1995-D: 42,497 Uncirculated; 1995-P: 182,676 Proof.

Original Cost. Sale prices $27.95 (Uncirculated, pre-issue) and $30.95 (Proof, pre-issue); Uncirculated later raised to $31.95, and Proof later raised to $34.95. The surcharge per coin went to the Atlanta Olympic Committee.

Key to Collecting. Enough 1995 and 1996 Olympics coins are on the aftermarket that finding designs of choice, or forming a set, will be no problem. The obverse designs are varied, and in total the collection is an excellent representation of this quadrennial worldwide competition.

	Distribution	Cert	Avg	%MS	MS-67 PF-67
1995-D	42,497	1,496	69.2	100%	$50
	Auctions: $90, MS-70, April 2013				
1995-P, Proof	182,676	2,135	69.0		$35
	Auctions: No auction records available.				

XXVI Olympiad Track and Field Silver Dollar (1995)

Designer: *John Mercanti (obverse), William Krawczewicz (reverse).* **Weight:** *26.73 grams.*
Composition: *.900 silver, .100 copper (net weight .7736 oz. pure silver).*
Diameter: *38.1 mm.* **Edge:** *Reeded.* **Mints:** *Denver (Uncirculated) and Philadelphia (Proof).*

Track and field—grouped with road running and racewalking in the overarching "athletics" category—has been a part of the Olympics from the birth of the modern Games and traces its roots to the ancient Greek Olympics. At the 1996 Summer Games in Atlanta, the United States took home 13 gold medals between its men's and women's track and field teams, easily the most of any nation.

Designs. *Obverse:* Men competing in track and field. *Reverse:* Clasped hands of two athletes with torch above.

Mintage Data. Authorized by Public Law 102-390, signed by President George H.W. Bush on October 6, 1992. *Maximum authorized—750,000. Number minted—1995-D:* 24,976 Uncirculated; 1995-P: 136,935 Proof.

Original Cost. Sale prices $27.95 (Uncirculated, pre-issue) and $30.95 (Proof, pre-issue); Uncirculated later raised to $31.95, and Proof later raised to $34.95. The surcharge per coin went to the Atlanta Olympic Committee.

Key to Collecting. Enough 1995 and 1996 Olympics coins are on the aftermarket that finding designs of choice, or forming a set, will be no problem. The obverse designs are varied, and in total the collection is an excellent representation of this quadrennial worldwide competition.

	Distribution	Cert	Avg	%MS	MS-67
					PF-67
1995-D	24,976	793	69.3	100%	$75
	Auctions: $159, MS-70, July 2014				
1995-P, Proof	136,935	1,448	69.0		$35
	Auctions: $411, PF-70DCam, September 2014				

XXVI Olympiad Cycling Silver Dollar (1995)

Designer: *John Mercanti (obverse), William Krawczewicz (reverse).* **Weight:** *26.73 grams.*
Composition: *.900 silver, .100 copper (net weight .7736 oz. pure silver).*
Diameter: *38.1 mm.* **Edge:** *Reeded.* **Mints:** *Denver (Uncirculated) and Philadelphia (Proof).*

Part of the Summer Games from the inception of the modern Olympic movement in 1896, cycling has been expanded over the years to include more track races, mountain biking, and BMX racing. France dominated the podium at the 1996 Olympics in Atlanta, taking home the most gold medals (five) and total medals (nine).

Designs. *Obverse:* Men cycling. *Reverse:* Clasped hands of two athletes with torch above.

Mintage Data. Authorized by Public Law 102-390, signed by President George H.W. Bush on October 6, 1992. *Maximum authorized*—750,000. *Number minted*—1995-D: 19,662 Uncirculated; 1995-P: 118,795 Proof.

Original Cost. Sale prices $27.95 (Uncirculated, pre-issue) and $30.95 (Proof, pre-issue); Uncirculated later raised to $31.95, and Proof later raised to $34.95. The surcharge per coin went to the Atlanta Olympic Committee.

Key to Collecting. Enough 1995 and 1996 Olympics coins are on the aftermarket that finding designs of choice, or forming a set, will be no problem. The obverse designs are varied, and in total the collection is an excellent representation of this quadrennial worldwide competition.

	Distribution	Cert	Avg	%MS	MS-67
					PF-67
1995-D	19,662	883	69.3	100%	$140
	Auctions: $206, MS-70, July 2014; $200, MS-70, April 2013; $112, MS-69, November 2014				
1995-P, Proof	118,795	1,415	69.0		$40
	Auctions: $707, PF-70DCam, September 2014				

PARALYMPICS BLIND RUNNER SILVER DOLLAR (1995)

Designer: *James C. Sharpe (obverse), William Krawczewicz (reverse).* **Weight:** *26.73 grams.*
Composition: *.900 silver, .100 copper (net weight .7736 oz. pure silver).*
Diameter: *38.1 mm.* **Edge:** *Reeded.* **Mints:** *Denver (Uncirculated) and Philadelphia (Proof).*

Track and field events (under the umbrella of "athletics") have been a part of the Summer Paralympic Games since 1960. Spanish athletes took home a number of medals in the track events for visually impaired athletes at the 1996 Summer Paralympic Games, including the gold in two of the men's 100-meter dash events (Júlio Requena in the T-10 race, and Juan Antônio Prieto in the T-11 race) and both of the women's 100-meter dash events (Purificación Santamarta in the T-10 race, and Beatríz Mendoza in the T-11 race).

Designs. *Obverse:* Blind runner tethered to a seeing companion in a race. *Reverse:* Clasped hands of two athletes with torch above.

Mintage Data. Authorized by Public Law 102-390, signed by President George H.W. Bush on October 6, 1992. *Maximum authorized*—750,000. *Number minted*—1995-D: 28,649 Uncirculated; 1995-P: 138,337 Proof.

Original Cost. Sale prices $27.95 (Uncirculated, pre-issue) and $30.95 (Proof, pre-issue); Uncirculated later raised to $31.95, and Proof later raised to $34.95. The surcharge per coin went to the Atlanta Olympic Committee.

Key to Collecting. Enough 1995 and 1996 Olympics coins are on the aftermarket that finding designs of choice, or forming a set, will be no problem. The obverse designs are varied, and in total the collection is an excellent representation of this quadrennial worldwide competition.

	Distribution	Cert	Avg	%MS	MS-67			
					PF-67			
1995-D	28,649	1,250	69.3	100%	$35			
	Auctions: No auction records available.							
1995-P, Proof	138,337	1,599	69.0		$40			
	Auctions: No auction records available.							

XXVI Olympiad Torch Runner $5 Gold Coin (1995)

Designer: *Frank Gasparro.* **Weight:** *8.359 grams.*
Composition: *.900 gold, .100 copper (net weight .242 oz. pure gold).*
Diameter: *21.6 mm.* **Edge:** *Reeded.* **Mint:** *West Point.*

Whereas the concept of the Olympic flame dates from the ancient Games of ancient Greece, the torch relay has only been a tradition since 1936, when Carl Diem introduced the concept for the Berlin Summer Games. The 1996 Olympic torch relay spanned 112 days, approximately 18,030 miles, and 13,267 torch bearers before ending in Atlanta on July 19, 1996.

Designs. *Obverse:* Olympic runner carrying a torch. *Reverse:* Bald eagle with a banner in its beak with the Olympic Centennial dates 1896–1996.

Mintage Data. Authorized by Public Law 102-390, signed by President George H.W. Bush on October 6, 1992. *Maximum authorized*—175,000. *Number minted*—14,675 Uncirculated and 57,442 Proof.

Original Cost. Sale prices $229 (Uncirculated, pre-issue) and $239 (Proof, pre-issue); Uncirculated later raised to $249, and Proof later raised to $259. The surcharge per coin went to the Atlanta Olympic Committee.

Key to Collecting. Enough 1995 and 1996 Olympics coins are on the aftermarket that finding designs of choice, or forming a set, will be no problem. The obverse designs are varied, and in total the collection is an excellent representation of this quadrennial worldwide competition.

	Distribution	Cert	Avg	%MS	MS-67			
					PF-67			
1995-W	14,675	1,002	69.7	100%	$575			
	Auctions: $646, MS-70, February 2015; $447, MS-70, May 2015; $423, MS-70, May 2015; $353, MS-69, January 2015							
1995-W, Proof	57,442	1,836	69.3		$325			
	Auctions: No auction records available.							

XXVI Olympiad Stadium $5 Gold Coin (1995)

Designer: *Marcel Jovine (obverse), Frank Gasparro (reverse).* **Weight:** *8.359 grams.*
Composition: *.900 gold, .100 copper (net weight .242 oz. pure gold).*
Diameter: *21.6 mm.* **Edge:** *Reeded.* **Mint:** *West Point.*

Centennial Olympic Stadium was constructed in Atlanta for the 1996 Summer Games. The 85,000-seat venue hosted the track and field events, as well as the closing ceremony, and then was reconstructed into Turner Field, home of Major League Baseball's Atlanta Braves for two decades.

Designs. *Obverse:* Aerial view of the Olympic Stadium from a distance to the side. *Reverse:* Same as described for the Olympic Torch Runner $5 gold coin.

Mintage Data. Authorized by Public Law 102-390, signed by President George H.W. Bush on October 6, 1992. *Maximum authorized*—175,000. *Number minted*—10,579 Uncirculated and 43,124 Proof.

Original Cost. Sale prices $229 (Uncirculated, pre-issue) and $239 (Proof, pre-issue); Uncirculated later raised to $249, and Proof later raised to $259. The surcharge per coin went to the Atlanta Olympic Committee.

Key to Collecting. Enough 1995 and 1996 Olympics coins are on the aftermarket that finding designs of choice, or forming a set, will be no problem. The obverse designs are varied, and in total the collection is an excellent representation of this quadrennial worldwide competition.

	Distribution	Cert	Avg	%MS	MS-67
					PF-67
1995-W	10,579	955	69.6	100%	$1,100
	Auctions: $823, MS-70, February 2015; $764, MS-70, January 2015; $823, MS-69, February 2015; $646, MS-69, February 2015				
1995-W, Proof	43,124	1,821	69.4		$325
	Auctions: $499, PF-70DCam, June 2014; $470, PF-70DCam, June 2014				

XXVI Olympiad Swimming Half Dollar (1996)

Designer: *William Krawczewicz (obverse), Malcolm Farley (reverse).* **Weight:** *11.34 grams.*
Composition: *.9167 copper, .0833 nickel.* **Diameter:** *30.61 mm.* **Edge:** *Reeded.* **Mint:** *San Francisco.*

Swimming—an Olympic sport since the modern Games began in 1896—was dominated by U.S. athletes at the 1996 Summer Games in Atlanta. Americans took home a total of 26 medals (more than double the 12 each of Russia and Germany, which come next on the list), and swept all six relay events across the men's and women's competitions.

Designs. *Obverse:* Male swimmer. *Reverse:* Symbols of the Olympic games, including flame, torch, rings, Greek column, and 100 (the latter to observe the 100th anniversary of the modern Olympic games inaugurated with the 1896 Games in Athens).

Mintage Data. Authorized by Public Law 102-390, signed by President George H.W. Bush on October 6, 1992. *Maximum authorized*—3,000,000. *Number minted*—49,533 Uncirculated and 114,315 Proof.

Original Cost. Sale prices $10.50 (Uncirculated, pre-issue) and $11.50 (Proof, pre-issue); Uncirculated later raised to $11.50, and Proof later raised to $12.50. The surcharge per coin went to the Atlanta Olympic Committee.

Key to Collecting. Enough 1995 and 1996 Olympics coins are on the aftermarket that finding designs of choice, or forming a set, will be no problem. The obverse designs are varied, and in total the collection is an excellent representation of this quadrennial worldwide competition.

	Distribution	Cert	Avg	%MS	MS-67
					PF-67
1996-S	49,533	844	69.1	100%	$125
	Auctions: $499, MS-70, September 2013				
1996-S, Proof	114,315	973	69.1		$30
	Auctions: No auction records available.				

XXVI OLYMPIAD SOCCER HALF DOLLAR (1996)

Designer: *Clint Hansen (obverse), Malcolm Farley (reverse).* **Weight:** *11.34 grams.*
Composition: *.9167 copper, .0833 nickel.* **Diameter:** *30.61 mm.* **Edge:** *Reeded.* **Mint:** *San Francisco.*

Women's soccer debuted as an Olympic sport at the 1996 Summer Games in Atlanta. The host nation's team—featuring such names as Mia Hamm, Brandi Chastain, and Briana Scurry—was victorious in the gold medal game.

Designs. *Obverse:* Women playing soccer. *Reverse:* Symbols of the Olympic games, including flame, torch, rings, Greek column, and 100.

Mintage Data. Authorized by Public Law 102-390, signed by President George H.W. Bush on October 6, 1992. *Maximum authorized*—3,000,000. *Number minted*—52,836 Uncirculated and 112,412 Proof.

Original Cost. Sale prices $10.50 (Uncirculated, pre-issue) and $11.50 (Proof, pre-issue); Uncirculated later raised to $11.50, and Proof later raised to $12.50. The surcharge per coin went to the Atlanta Olympic Committee.

Key to Collecting. Enough 1995 and 1996 Olympics coins are on the aftermarket that finding designs of choice, or forming a set, will be no problem. The obverse designs are varied, and in total the collection is an excellent representation of this quadrennial worldwide competition.

	Distribution	Cert	Avg	%MS	MS-67
					PF-67
1996-S	52,836	617	69.3	100%	$110
	Auctions: $147, MS-70, July 2014; $170, MS-70, August 2013				
1996-S, Proof	112,412	956	69.0		$75
	Auctions: $294, PF-70DCam, September 2014				

XXVI Olympiad Tennis Silver Dollar (1996)

Designer: *James C. Sharpe (obverse), Thomas D. Rogers Sr. (reverse).* **Weight:** *26.73 grams.*
Composition: *.900 silver, .100 copper (net weight .7736 oz. pure silver).*
Diameter: *38.1 mm.* **Edge:** *Reeded.* **Mints:** *Denver (Uncirculated) and Philadelphia (Proof).*

Women's tennis was first a part of the Olympics in 1900, and singles competition was regularly held for the Summer Games between 1908 and 1924. Subsequent disputes between the International Lawn Tennis Federation and the International Olympic Committee led to both men's and women's tennis being removed from the Games for more than 60 years, but the sport returned permanently in 1988. U.S. athletes took both the women's singles gold medal (Lindsay Davenport) and women's doubles gold medal (Gigi Fernandez and Mary Joe Fernandez) at the 1996 Games in Atlanta.

Designs. *Obverse:* Woman playing tennis. *Reverse:* Atlanta Committee for the Olympic Games logo with torch and flame.

Mintage Data. Authorized by Public Law 102-390, signed by President George H.W. Bush on October 6, 1992. *Maximum authorized*—1,000,000. *Number minted*—1996-D: 15,983 Uncirculated; 1996-P: 92,016 Proof.

Original Cost. Sale prices $27.95 (Uncirculated, pre-issue) and $30.95 (Proof, pre-issue); Uncirculated later raised to $31.95, and Proof later raised to $34.95. The surcharge per coin went to the Atlanta Olympic Committee.

Key to Collecting. Enough 1995 and 1996 Olympics coins are on the aftermarket that finding designs of choice, or forming a set, will be no problem. The obverse designs are varied, and in total the collection is an excellent representation of this quadrennial worldwide competition.

	Distribution	Cert	Avg	%MS	MS-67
					PF-67
1996-D	15,983	746	69.1	100%	$225
	Auctions: $206, MS-70, September 2014; $482, MS-70, April 2013; $170, MS-69, July 2014; $170, MS-69, November 2014				
1996-P, Proof	92,016	1,275	68.9		$75
	Auctions: $355, PF-69DCam, November 2014				

XXVI OLYMPIAD ROWING SILVER DOLLAR (1996)

Designer: *Bart Forbes (obverse), Thomas D. Rogers Sr. (reverse).* **Weight:** *26.73 grams.*
Composition: *.900 silver, .100 copper (net weight .7736 oz. pure silver).*
Diameter: *38.1 mm.* **Edge:** *Reeded.* **Mints:** *Denver (Uncirculated) and Philadelphia (Proof).*

Rowing has been an official Olympic sport from the first modern Games in 1896, though coincidentally the competition was cancelled for that event due to weather concerns. At the 1996 Summer Olympics in Atlanta, Australia won the most medals (six, two gold).

Designs. *Obverse:* Men rowing. *Reverse:* Atlanta Committee for the Olympic Games logo with torch and flame.

Mintage Data. Authorized by Public Law 102-390, signed by President George H.W. Bush on October 6, 1992. *Maximum authorized*—1,000,000. *Number minted*—1996-D: 16,258 Uncirculated; 1996-P: 151,890 Proof.

Original Cost. Sale prices $27.95 (Uncirculated, pre-issue) and $30.95 (Proof, pre-issue); Uncirculated later raised to $31.95, and Proof later raised to $34.95. The surcharge per coin went to the Atlanta Olympic Committee.

Key to Collecting. Enough 1995 and 1996 Olympics coins are on the aftermarket that finding designs of choice, or forming a set, will be no problem. The obverse designs are varied, and in total the collection is an excellent representation of this quadrennial worldwide competition.

	Distribution	Cert	Avg	%MS	MS-67 / PF-67
1996-D	16,258	703	69.2	100%	$225
Auctions: $382, MS-70, April 2013; $153, MS-69, November 2014; $147, MS-69, November 2014					
1996-P, Proof	151,890	1,260	68.9		$70
Auctions: $6,169, PF-70DCam, September 2014					

XXVI OLYMPIAD HIGH JUMP SILVER DOLLAR (1996)

Designer: *Calvin Massey (obverse), Thomas D. Rogers Sr. (reverse).* **Weight:** *26.73 grams.*
Composition: *.900 silver, .100 copper (net weight .7736 oz. pure silver).*
Diameter: *38.1 mm.* **Edge:** *Reeded.* **Mints:** *Denver (Uncirculated) and Philadelphia (Proof).*

High jump has been one of the Olympic track and field program's events since the inaugural modern Games in 1896. At the 1996 Atlanta Olympics, the United States' Charles Austin won the gold medal in the men's competition with a height cleared of 2.39 meters.

Designs. *Obverse:* Athlete doing the "Fosbury Flop" maneuver. *Reverse:* Atlanta Committee for the Olympic Games logo with torch and flame.

Mintage Data. Authorized by Public Law 102-390, signed by President George H.W. Bush on October 6, 1992. *Maximum authorized*—1,000,000. *Number minted*—1996-D: 15,697 Uncirculated; 1996-P: 124,502 Proof.

Original Cost. Sale prices $27.95 (Uncirculated, pre-issue) and $30.95 (Proof, pre-issue); Uncirculated later raised to $31.95, and Proof later raised to $34.95. The surcharge per coin went to the Atlanta Olympic Committee.

Key to Collecting. Enough 1995 and 1996 Olympics coins are on the aftermarket that finding designs of choice, or forming a set, will be no problem. The obverse designs are varied, and in total the collection is an excellent representation of this quadrennial worldwide competition.

	Distribution	Cert	Avg	%MS	MS-67
					PF-67
1996-D	15,697	689	69.1	100%	$250
	Auctions: $441, MS-70, April 2013; $147, MS-69, July 2014; $165, MS-69, November 2014				
1996-P, Proof	124,502	1,321	68.9		$45
	Auctions: No auction records available.				

PARALYMPICS WHEELCHAIR SILVER DOLLAR (1996)

Designer: *James C. Sharpe (obverse), Thomas D. Rogers Sr. (reverse).* **Weight:** *26.73 grams.*
Composition: *.900 silver, .100 copper (net weight .7736 oz. pure silver).*
Diameter: *38.1 mm.* **Edge:** *Reeded.* **Mints:** *Denver (Uncirculated) and Philadelphia (Proof).*

Wheelchair racing events have comprised part of the Paralympic track and field program since 1960. Several countries were represented on the podium, though the United States' Shawn Meredith (gold medals in the T-51 400-meter and 800-meter), France's Claude Issorat (gold medals in the T-53 200-meter and 800-meter), and Switzerland's Heinz Frei (gold medals in the T52-53 1,500-meter and 10,000-meter) had particularly strong showings.

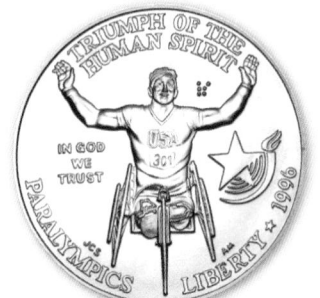

Designs. *Obverse:* Athlete in a racing wheelchair competing in a track and field competition. *Reverse:* Atlanta Committee for the Olympic Games logo with torch and flame.

Mintage Data. Authorized by Public Law 102-390, signed by President George H.W. Bush on October 6, 1992. *Maximum authorized*—1,000,000. *Number minted*—1996-D: 14,497 Uncirculated; 1996-P: 84,280 Proof.

Original Cost. Sale prices $27.95 (Uncirculated, pre-issue) and $30.95 (Proof, pre-issue); Uncirculated later raised to $31.95, and Proof later raised to $34.95. The surcharge per coin went to the Atlanta Olympic Committee.

Key to Collecting. Enough 1995 and 1996 Olympics coins are on the aftermarket that finding designs of choice, or forming a set, will be no problem. The obverse designs are varied, and in total the collection is an excellent representation of this quadrennial worldwide competition.

	Distribution	Cert	Avg	%MS	MS-67 PF-67
1996-D	14,497	823	69.2	100%	$240
Auctions: $499, MS-70, April 2013; $223, MS-70, June 2015; $153, MS-69, November 2014; $129, MS-69, November 2014					
1996-P, Proof	84,280	1,374	69.0		$70
Auctions: No auction records available.					

XXVI Olympiad Flag Bearer $5 Gold Coin (1996)

Designer: *Patricia Lewis Verani (obverse), William Krawczewicz (reverse).*
Weight: *8.359 grams.* **Composition:** *.900 gold, .100 copper (net weight .242 oz. pure gold).*
Diameter: *21.6 mm.* **Edge:** *Reeded.* **Mint:** *West Point.*

For the opening and closing ceremonies of each Olympic Games, each participating nation selects two flagbearers from among its athletes to lead its delegation in the Parade of Nations (opening) and Parade of Flags (closing). Wrestler Bruce Baumgartner served as the United States's flagbearer for the opening ceremony of the 1996 Summer Games, and show jumper Michael Matz was awarded the honor for the closing ceremony.

Designs. *Obverse:* Athlete with a flag followed by a crowd. *Reverse:* Atlanta Committee for the Olympic Games logo within laurel leaves.

Mintage Data. Authorized by Public Law 102-390, signed by President George H.W. Bush on October 6, 1992. *Maximum authorized*—300,000. *Number minted*—9,174 Uncirculated and 32,886 Proof.

Original Cost. Sale prices $229 (Uncirculated, pre-issue) and $239 (Proof, pre-issue); Uncirculated later raised to $249, and Proof later raised to $259. The surcharge per coin went to the Atlanta Olympic Committee.

Key to Collecting. Enough 1995 and 1996 Olympics coins are on the aftermarket that finding designs of choice, or forming a set, will be no problem. The obverse designs are varied, and in total the collection is an excellent representation of this quadrennial worldwide competition.

	Distribution	Cert	Avg	%MS	MS-67 PF-67
1996-W	9,174	712	69.5	100%	$550
Auctions: $881, MS-70, October 2015; $881, MS-70, February 2015; $494, MS-69, January 2015; $329, MS-69, September 2015					
1996-W, Proof	32,886	1,321	69.3		$325
Auctions: No auction records available.					

XXVI Olympiad Cauldron $5 Gold Coin (1996)

Designer: *Frank Gasparro (obverse), William Krawczewicz (reverse).*
Weight: *8.359 grams.* **Composition:** *.900 gold, .100 copper (net weight .242 oz. pure gold).*
Diameter: *21.6 mm.* **Edge:** *Reeded.* **Mint:** *West Point.*

The tradition of maintaining an Olympic flame hearkens to the ancient Greek Olympics, during which a fire was kept burning to represent the theft of fire from Zeus by Prometheus. The concept became part of the modern Games in 1928 and now serves as the culmination of the Olympic torch relay. At the 1996 Summer Games in Atlanta, boxing legend and American icon Muhammad Ali (himself a gold medalist at the 1960 Olympics) was the final torch bearer and lit the cauldron.

Designs. *Obverse:* Lighting of the Olympic flame. *Reverse:* Atlanta Committee for the Olympic Games logo within laurel leaves.

Mintage Data. Authorized by Public Law 102-390, signed by President George H.W. Bush on October 6, 1992. *Maximum authorized*—300,000. *Number minted*—9,210 Uncirculated and 38,555 Proof.

Original Cost. Sale prices $229 (Uncirculated, pre-issue) and $239 (Proof, pre-issue); Uncirculated later raised to $249, and Proof later raised to $259. The surcharge per coin went to the Atlanta Olympic Committee.

Key to Collecting. Enough 1995 and 1996 Olympics coins are on the aftermarket that finding designs of choice, or forming a set, will be no problem. The obverse designs are varied, and in total the collection is an excellent representation of this quadrennial worldwide competition.

	Distribution	Cert	Avg	%MS	MS-67
					PF-67
1996-W	9,210	803	69.4	100%	$1,150
Auctions: $1,116, MS-70, February 2015; $940, MS-70, October 2015; $823, MS-69, January 2015; $705, MS-69, November 2014					
1996-W, Proof	38,555	2,226	69.3		$325
Auctions: $505, PF-70UCam, March 2015; $423, PF-70UCam, March 2015; $353, PF-70UCam, May 2015					

Civil War Battlefield Preservation Half Dollar (1995)

Designer: *Don Troiani (obverse), T. James Ferrell (reverse).* **Weight:** *11.34 grams.*
Composition: *.9167 copper, .0833 nickel.* **Diameter:** *30.61 mm.* **Edge:** *Reeded.* **Mint:** *San Francisco.*

Preserving battlefields associated with the Civil War (1861–1865) formed the topic for a suite of three commemorative coins, including this copper-nickel half dollar.

Designs. *Obverse:* Drummer standing. *Reverse:* Cannon overlooking battlefield with inscription above.

Mintage Data. Authorized by Public Law 102-379. *Maximum authorized—2,000,000. Number minted—* 119,520 Uncirculated and 330,002 Proof.

Original Cost. Sale prices $9.50 (Uncirculated, pre-issue) and $10.75 (Proof, pre-issue); Uncirculated later raised to $10.25, and Proof later raised to $11.75. The surcharge of $2 per coin went to the Civil War Trust for the preservation of historically significant battlefields.

Key to Collecting. This coin, as well as those two issued alongside it, are readily available in the marketplace today. Most are superb gems.

	Distribution	Cert	Avg	%MS	MS-67
					PF-67
1995-S	119,520	977	69.3	100%	$40
	Auctions: $206, MS-70, May 2014; $153, MS-70, July 2014; $112, MS-70, June 2015				
1995-S, Proof	330,002	1,770	69.0		$30
	Auctions: $188, PF-68DCam, November 2014				

CIVIL WAR BATTLEFIELD PRESERVATION SILVER DOLLAR (1995)

Designer: *Don Troiani (obverse), John Mercanti (reverse).* **Weight:** *26.73 grams.*
Composition: *.900 silver, .100 copper (net weight .7736 oz. pure silver).*
Diameter: *38.1 mm.* **Edge:** *Reeded.* **Mints:** *Philadelphia (Uncirculated) and San Francisco (Proof).*

Civil War history attracts millions of followers, and books on the subject are always very popular. While total sales of the Civil War Battlefield Preservation silver dollar didn't approach the million coins authorized, sales of the Proof version were stronger than those of many recent silver dollars.

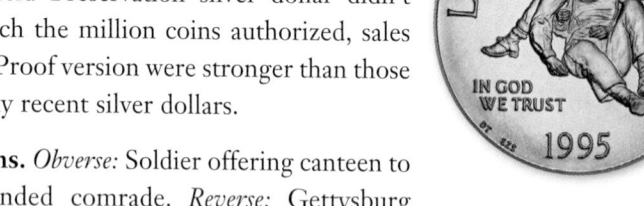

Designs. *Obverse:* Soldier offering canteen to a wounded comrade. *Reverse:* Gettysburg landscape with a quotation from Joshua Chamberlain, hero in that battle.

Mintage Data. Authorized by Public Law 102-379. *Maximum authorized—1,000,000. Number minted—* 1995-P: 45,866 Uncirculated; 1995-S: 437,114 Proof.

Original Cost. Sale prices $27 (Uncirculated, pre-issue) and $30 (Proof, pre-issue); Uncirculated later raised to $30, and Proof later raised to $34. The surcharge of $7 per coin went to the Civil War Trust for the preservation of historically significant battlefields.

Key to Collecting. This coin, as well as those two issued alongside it, are readily available in the marketplace today. Most are superb gems.

	Distribution	Cert	Avg	%MS	MS-67
					PF-67
1995-P	45,866	1,238	69.1	100%	$50
	Auctions: $247, MS-70, April 2013				
1995-S, Proof	437,114	3,080	69.0		$45
	Auctions: $435, PF-70DCam, March 2013; $306, PF-70DCam, April 2013				

CIVIL WAR BATTLEFIELD PRESERVATION $5 GOLD COIN (1995)

Designer: *Don Troiani (obverse), Alfred F. Maletsky (reverse).* **Weight:** *8.359 grams.*
Composition: *.900 gold, .100 copper.* **Diameter:** *21.6 mm.* **Edge:** *Reeded.* **Mint:** *West Point.*

Troiani, the designer of this coin's obverse as well as those of the other two Civil War Battlefield Preservation commemoratives, is an artist in the private sector well known for his depictions of battle scenes.

Designs. *Obverse:* Bugler on horseback sounding a call. *Reverse:* Eagle perched on a shield.

Mintage Data. Authorized by Public Law 102-379. *Maximum authorized*—300,000. *Number minted*—12,735 Uncirculated and 55,246 Proof.

Original Cost. Sale prices $180 (Uncirculated, pre-issue) and $195 (Proof, pre-issue); Uncirculated later raised to $190, and Proof later raised to $225. The surcharge of $35 per coin went to the Civil War Trust for the preservation of historically significant battlefields.

Key to Collecting. This coin, as well as those two issued alongside it, are readily available in the marketplace today. Most are superb gems.

	Distribution	Cert	Avg	%MS	MS-67
					PF-67
1995-W	12,735	809	69.7	100%	$450
	Auctions: $517, MS-70, January 2015; $494, MS-70, April 2015; $482, MS-70, January 2015; $329, MS-69, August 2015				
1995-W, Proof	55,246	1,896	69.3		$400
	Auctions: $482, PF-70DCam, July 2015; $306, PF-69UCam, October 2015; $329, PF-69DCam, October 2015; $306, PF-69DCam, August 2015				

SPECIAL OLYMPICS WORLD GAMES SILVER DOLLAR (1995)

Designer: *T. James Ferrell from a portrait by Jamie Wyeth (obverse), Thomas D. Rogers Sr. (reverse).*
Weight: *26.73 grams.* **Composition:** *.900 silver, .100 copper (net weight .7736 oz. pure silver).*
Diameter: *38.1 mm.* **Edge:** *Reeded.* **Mints:** *West Point (Uncirculated) and Philadelphia (Proof).*

This silver dollar's subject, Eunice Kennedy Shriver, was not only the first living female on U.S. coinage, but also the sister of former president John F. Kennedy and the aunt of Joseph F. Kennedy II, the House representative who sponsored the bill that created the coin. She is credited on the silver dollar as the founder of the Special Olympics.

Designs. *Obverse:* Portrait of Eunice Shriver.
Reverse: Representation of a Special Olympics medal, a rose, and a quotation by Shriver.

Mintage Data. Authorized by Public Law 103-328, signed by President William J. Clinton on September 29, 1994. *Maximum authorized*—800,000. *Number minted*—1995-W: 89,301 Uncirculated; 1995-P: 351,764 Proof.

Original Cost. Sale prices $30 (Uncirculated, pre-issue) and $33 (Proof, pre-issue); Uncirculated later raised to $32, and Proof later raised to $37. The surcharge of $10 per coin went to the Special Olympics to support the 1995 World Summer Games.

Key to Collecting. These coins are plentiful in the marketplace. Most are superb gems.

	Distribution	Cert	Avg	%MS	MS-67
					PF-67
1995-W	89,301	910	69.2	100%	$40
Auctions: $135, MS-70, April 2013					
1995-P, Proof	351,764	1,429	69.0		$35
Auctions: $360, PF-70DCam, March 2013					

NATIONAL COMMUNITY SERVICE SILVER DOLLAR (1996)

Designer: *Thomas D. Rogers Sr. from a medal by Augustus Saint-Gaudens (obverse), William C. Cousins (reverse).* **Weight:** *26.73 grams.* **Composition:** *.900 silver, .100 copper (net weight .7736 oz. pure silver).* **Diameter:** *38.1 mm.* **Edge:** *Reeded.* **Mint:** *San Francisco.*

In 1996 the National Community Service dollar was sponsored by Representative Joseph D. Kennedy of Massachusetts, who also sponsored the Special Olympics World Games dollar.

Designs. *Obverse:* Standing figure of Liberty. *Reverse:* SERVICE FOR AMERICA in three lines, with a wreath around, and other lettering at the border.

Mintage Data. Authorized by Public Law 103-328, signed by President William J. Clinton on September 29, 1994. *Maximum authorized*—500,000. *Number minted*—23,500 Uncirculated and 101,543 Proof.

Original Cost. Sale prices $30 (Uncirculated, pre-issue) and $33 (Proof, pre-issue); Uncirculated later raised to $32, and Proof later raised to $37. The surcharge of $10 per coin went to the National Community Service Trust.

Key to Collecting. Uncirculated examples are scarce by virtue of their low mintage, but demand is scarce as well, with the result that they can be purchased easily enough. Both formats are usually seen in superb gem preservation.

	Distribution	Cert	Avg	%MS	MS-67
					PF-67
1996-S	23,500	1,053	69.3	100%	$125
Auctions: $153, MS-70, August 2014; $129, MS-70, June 2015; $88, MS-69, July 2014; $86, MS-69, November 2014					
1996-S, Proof	101,543	1,986	69.1		$35
Auctions: $195, PF-70DCam, April 2013					

SMITHSONIAN INSTITUTION 150TH ANNIVERSARY SILVER DOLLAR (1996)

Designer: *Thomas D. Rogers Sr. (obverse), John Mercanti (reverse).* **Weight:** *26.73 grams.*
Composition: *.900 silver, .100 copper (net weight .7736 oz. pure silver).* **Diameter:** *38.1 mm.*
Edge: *Reeded.* **Mints:** *Denver (Uncirculated) and Philadelphia (Proof).*

This silver dollar, as well as a five-dollar gold coin, marked the 150th anniversary of Congress establishing the Smithsonian Institution in Washington, D.C., on August 10, 1846. Named for James Smithson—an English scientist whose will funded the entity—the institution quickly became America's national museum.

Designs. *Obverse:* The "Castle" building on the Mall in Washington, the original home of the Smithsonian Institution. Branches to each side. *Reverse:* Goddess of Knowledge sitting on top of a globe. In her left hand she holds a torch, in the right a scroll inscribed ART / HISTORY / SCIENCE. In the field to the right in several lines is FOR THE INCREASE AND DIFFUSION OF KNOWLEDGE.

Mintage Data. Authorized by Public Law 104-96, signed by President William J. Clinton on January 10, 1996. *Maximum authorized—650,000. Number minted—1996-D:* 31,320 Uncirculated; 1996-P: 129,152 Proof.

Original Cost. Sale prices $30 (Uncirculated, pre-issue) and $33 (Proof, pre-issue); Uncirculated later raised to $32, and Proof later raised to $37. The surcharge of $10 per coin went to the Smithsonian Board of Regents.

Key to Collecting. This silver dollar and the five-dollar gold coin issued alongside it have risen in value considerably since their release. Today examples can be found readily in the marketplace and are nearly always superb gems.

	Distribution	Cert	Avg	%MS	MS-67
					PF-67
1996-D	31,320	1,050	69.4	100%	$75
	Auctions: $119, MS-70, July 2014; $100, MS-70, February 2015; $89, MS-70, February 2015; $65, MS-69, October 2014				
1996-P, Proof	129,152	1,826	69.0		$40
	Auctions: $447, PF-70DCam, March 2013				

Smithsonian Institution 150th Anniversary $5 Gold Coin (1996)

Designer: *Alfred F. Maletsky (obverse), T. James Ferrell (reverse).* **Weight:** *8.359 grams.*
Composition: *.900 gold, .100 copper (net weight .242 oz. pure gold).*
Diameter: *21.6 mm.* **Edge:** *Reeded.* **Mint:** *West Point.*

The U.S. Mint offered the two 1996 Smithsonian commemorative coins via several new options, including the 50,000-set Young Collectors Edition and incorporated in jewelry items.

Designs. *Obverse:* Bust of James Smithson facing left. *Reverse:* Sunburst with SMITHSONIAN below.

Mintage Data. Authorized by Public Law 104-96, signed by President William J. Clinton on January 10, 1996. *Maximum authorized*—100,000. *Number minted*—9,068 Uncirculated and 21,772 Proof.

Original Cost. Sale prices $180 (Uncirculated, pre-issue) and $195 (Proof, pre-issue); Uncirculated later raised to $205, and Proof later raised to $225. The surcharge of $10 per coin went to the Smithsonian Board of Regents.

Key to Collecting. Both Smithsonian Institution 150th Anniversary coins have risen in value considerably since their release. Today examples can be found readily in the marketplace and are nearly always superb gems.

	Distribution	Cert	Avg	%MS	MS-67
					PF-67
1996-W	9,068	843	69.4	100%	$400
	Auctions: $646, MS-70, September 2014; $541, MS-70, January 2015; $447, MS-70, April 2015; $382, MS-69, August 2014				
1996-W, Proof	21,772	1,284	69.2		$325
	Auctions: $706, PF-70DCam, April 2013; $588, PF-70DCam, September 2014; $529, PF-70DCam, September 2014				

U.S. Botanic Garden Silver Dollar (1997)

Designer: *Edgar Z. Steever IV (obverse), William C. Cousins (reverse).* **Weight:** *26.73 grams.*
Composition: *Silver .900, copper .100 (net weight .7736 oz. pure silver).*
Diameter: *38.1 mm.* **Edge:** *Reeded.* **Mint:** *Philadelphia.*

These coins were purportedly struck to celebrate the 175th anniversary of the United States Botanic Garden (which would have been 1995), but they were dated on one side as 1997. The authorizing legislation that created the coins specified that the French façade of the U.S. Botanic Garden be shown on the obverse and a rose on the reverse.

Designs. *Obverse:* Façade of the United States Botanic Garden in plan view without landscaping. *Reverse:* A rose at the center with a garland of roses above. The inscription below includes the anniversary dates 1820–1995. Note that some listings designate the rose side as the obverse.

Mintage Data. Authorized by Public Law 103-328, signed by President William J. Clinton on September 29, 1994. *Maximum authorized*—500,000. *Number minted*—58,505 Uncirculated and 189,671 Proof.

Original Cost. Sale prices $30 (Uncirculated, pre-issue) and $33 (Proof, pre-issue); Uncirculated later raised to $33, and Proof later raised to $37. The surcharge of $10 per coin went to the National Fund for the Botanic Garden.

Key to Collecting. These coins are readily available on the market today. Nearly all are superb gems. Ironically, the most popular related item is the Mint package containing the 1997-P special-finish Jefferson nickel, the demand coming from collectors of five-cent pieces! Only 25,000 sets were sold. This is *déjà vu* of the 1993 Jefferson dollar offer.

	Distribution	Cert	Avg	%MS	MS-67 PF-67
1997-P	58,505	1,525	69.1	100%	$30
Auctions: $159, MS-70, July 2014; $170, MS-70, April 2013					
1997-P, Proof	189,671	1,449	69.0		$45
Auctions: $441, PF-70DCam, April 2013; $306, PF-70UCam, February 2015; $306, PF-70DCam, September 2014					

NATIONAL LAW ENFORCEMENT OFFICERS MEMORIAL SILVER DOLLAR (1997)

Designer: *Alfred F. Maletsky (obverse from a photograph by Larry Ruggieri).* **Weight:** *26.73 grams.*
Composition: *.900 silver, .100 copper (net weight .7736 oz. pure silver).*
Diameter: *38.1 mm.* **Edge:** *Reeded.* **Mint:** *Philadelphia.*

The National Law Enforcement Officers Memorial at Judiciary Square in Washington, D.C., dedicated on October 15, 1991, was the subject of this commemorative. The monument honors more than 14,000 men and women who gave their lives in the line of duty.

Designs. *Obverse:* United States Park Police officers Robert Chelsey and Kelcy Stefansson making a rubbing of a fellow officer's name. *Reverse:* Shield with a rose across it, evocative of the sacrifices made by officers.

Mintage Data. Authorized by Public Law 104-329, signed by President William J. Clinton on October 20, 1996. *Maximum authorized*—500,000. *Number minted*—28,575 Uncirculated and 110,428 Proof.

Original Cost. Sale prices $30 (Uncirculated, pre-issue) and $33 (Proof, pre-issue); Uncirculated later raised to $32, and Proof later raised to $37.

Key to Collecting. Once the distribution figures were published, the missed opportunity was realized—collectors saw that these coins would be a modern rarity. The market price rose to a sharp premium, where it remains today. Nearly all coins approach perfection in quality.

	Distribution	Cert	Avg	%MS	MS-67 PF-67
1997-P	28,575	797	69.3	100%	$125
Auctions: $259, MS-70, May 2013; $206, MS-70, August 2014; $84, MS-69, February 2015					
1997-P, Proof	110,428	1,569	69.0		$65
Auctions: $353, PF-70DCam, April 2013; $243, PF-70DCam, September 2014; $60, PF-69DCam, January 2015					

JACKIE ROBINSON SILVER DOLLAR (1997)

Designer: *Alfred F. Maletsky (obverse), T. James Ferrell (reverse).* **Weight:** *26.73 grams.*
Composition: *.900 silver, .100 copper (net weight .7736 oz. pure silver).*
Diameter: *38.1 mm.* **Edge:** *Reeded.* **Mint:** *San Francisco.*

This silver dollar and a concurrently issued five-dollar gold coin commemorated the 50th anniversary of the first acceptance of a black player in a major league baseball game, Jack ("Jackie") Robinson being the hero. The watershed event took place at Ebbets Field on April 15, 1947.

Designs. *Obverse:* Robinson in game action stealing home plate, evocative of a 1955 World Series play in a contest between the New York Yankees and the Brooklyn Dodgers. *Reverse:* 50th anniversary logotype of the Jackie Robinson Foundation (a motif worn by all Major League Baseball players in the 1997 season) surrounded with lettering of two baseball accomplishments.

Mintage Data. Authorized on October 20, 1996, by Public Law 104-329, part of the United States Commemorative Coin Act of 1996, with a provision tied to Public Law 104-328 (for the Botanic Garden dollar). Coins could be minted for a full year beginning July 1, 1997. *Maximum authorized*—200,000. *Number minted*—30,180 Uncirculated and 110,002 Proof.

Original Cost. Sale prices $30 (Uncirculated, pre-issue) and $33 (Proof, pre-issue); Uncirculated later raised to $32, and Proof later raised to $37. The surcharge of $10 per coin went to the Jackie Robinson Foundation.

Key to Collecting. Although the Jackie Robinson coins were losers in the sales figures of the U.S. Mint, the small quantities issued made both coins winners in the return-on-investment sweepstakes. Today, each of these can be found without a problem, and nearly all are in superb gem preservation.

	Distribution	Cert	Avg	%MS	MS-67 PF-67
1997-S	30,180	1,165	69.1	100%	$90
Auctions: $411, MS-70, October 2014; $682, MS-70, January 2013					
1997-S, Proof	110,002	2,039	69.0		$65
Auctions: $999, PF-70DCam, September 2014; $646, PF-70DCam, September 2013					

JACKIE ROBINSON $5 GOLD COIN (1997)

Designer: *William C. Cousins (obverse), James Peed (reverse).* **Weight:** *8.359 grams.*
Composition: *.900 gold, .100 copper (net weight .242 oz. pure gold).*
Diameter: *21.6 mm.* **Edge:** *Reeded.* **Mint:** *West Point.*

The U.S. Mint's marketing of the Jackie Robinson coins was innovative, as it had been in recent times. One promotion featured a reproduction of a rare baseball trading card, with the distinction of being the first such card ever issued by the U.S. government. But no matter how important Robinson's legacy was, buyers voted with their pocketbooks, and sales were low—making the Uncirculated gold coin a modern rarity.

Designs. *Obverse:* Portrait of Robinson in his later years as a civil-rights and political activist. *Reverse:* Detail of the seam on a baseball, Robinson's 1919–1972 life dates, and the inscription "Life of Courage."

Mintage Data. Authorized on October 20, 1996, by Public Law 104-329, part of the United States Commemorative Coin Act of 1996, with a provision tied to Public Law 104-328 (for the Botanic Garden dollar). Coins could be minted for a full year beginning July 1, 1997. *Maximum authorized*—100,000. *Number minted*—5,174 Uncirculated and 24,072 Proof.

Original Cost. Sale prices $180 (Uncirculated, pre-issue) and $195 (Proof, pre-issue); Uncirculated later raised to $205, and Proof later raised to $225. The surcharge of $35 per coin went to the Jackie Robinson Foundation.

Key to Collecting. The Jackie Robinson five-dollar gold coin takes top honors as the key issue among modern commemoratives. Especially rare and valuable is the Uncirculated version.

	Distribution	Cert	Avg	%MS	MS-67 / PF-67
1997-W	5,174	822	69.3	100%	$1,600
	Auctions: $3,290, MS-70, February 2015; $3,055, MS-70, June 2015; $1,763, MS-69, February 2015; $1,645, MS-69, February 2015				
1997-W, Proof	24,072	1,486	69.3		$550
	Auctions: $376, PF-69DCam, April 2015; $376, PF-69DCam, January 2015; $367, PF-69UCam, February 2015				

FRANKLIN D. ROOSEVELT $5 GOLD COIN (1997)

Designer: *T. James Ferrell (obverse), James Peed (reverse).* **Weight:** *8.359 grams.*
Composition: *.900 gold, .100 copper (net weight .242 oz. pure gold).*
Diameter: *21.6 mm.* **Edge:** *Reeded.* **Mint:** *West Point.*

Considering that newly inaugurated President Franklin D. Roosevelt suspended the mintage and paying out of U.S. gold coins in 1933, it was ironic that he should later have a gold coin commemorating his life. The year 1997 does not seem to have been a special anniversary date of any kind, as it was 115 years after his birth, 64 years after his inauguration, and 52 years after his death.

Designs. *Obverse:* Upper torso and head of Roosevelt facing right, based on one of the president's favorite photographs, taken when he was reviewing the U.S. Navy fleet in San Francisco Bay. *Reverse:* Presidential seal displayed at Roosevelt's 1933 inaugural.

Mintage Data. Authorized by Public Law 104-329, signed by President William J. Clinton on October 20, 1996. *Maximum authorized*—100,000. *Number minted*—11,894 Uncirculated and 29,474 Proof.

Original Cost. Sale prices $180 (Uncirculated, pre-issue) and $195 (Proof, pre-issue); Uncirculated later raised to $205, and Proof later raised to $225. A portion of the surcharge of $35 per coin went to the Franklin Delano Roosevelt Memorial Commission.

Key to Collecting. Since the mintages for both Uncirculated and Proof formats were low, their values rose substantially on the aftermarket. Examples are easily available today and are nearly always in superb gem preservation.

	Distribution	Cert	Avg	%MS	MS-67	
					PF-67	
1997-W	11,894	856	69.5	100%	$475	
	Auctions: $705, MS-70, August 2014; $611, MS-70, August 2014; $541, MS-70, April 2015; $535, MS-70, April 2015					
1997-W, Proof	29,474	1,738	69.3		$325	
	Auctions: $447, PF-69DCam, March 2013					

BLACK REVOLUTIONARY WAR PATRIOTS SILVER DOLLAR (1998)

Designer: *John Mercanti (obverse), Ed Dwight (reverse).* **Weight:** *26.73 grams.*
Composition: *.900 silver, .100 copper (net weight .7736 oz. pure silver).*
Diameter: *38.1 mm.* **Edge:** *Reeded.* **Mint:** *San Francisco.*

This coin commemorates black Revolutionary War patriots and the 275th anniversary of the birth of Crispus Attucks, the first patriot killed in the infamous Boston Massacre in 1770 (an event predating the Revolutionary War, one among many incidents that inflamed the pro-independence passions of Americans).

Designs. *Obverse:* U.S. Mint engraver John Mercanti's conception of Crispus Attucks.
Reverse: A black patriot family, a detail from the proposed Black Patriots Memorial.

Mintage Data. Authorized by Public Law 104-329, signed by President William J. Clinton on October 20, 1996. *Maximum authorized*—500,000. *Number minted*—37,210 Uncirculated and 75,070 Proof.

Original Cost. Sale prices $30 (Uncirculated, pre-issue) and $33 (Proof, pre-issue); Uncirculated later raised to $32, and Proof later raised to $37. A portion of the surcharge of $10 per coin went to the Black Revolutionary War Patriots Foundation to fund the construction of the Black Patriots Memorial in Washington, D.C.

Key to Collecting. These coins became highly desirable when the low mintage figures were published. Examples remain valuable today, and deservedly so. Nearly all are superb gems.

	Distribution	Cert	Avg	%MS	MS-67	
					PF-67	
1998-S	37,210	1,210	69.2	100%	$90	
	Auctions: $176, MS-70, April 2013					
1998-S, Proof	75,070	1,413	69.0		$60	
	Auctions: $353, PF-70DCam, April 2013					

ROBERT F. KENNEDY SILVER DOLLAR (1998)

Designer: *Thomas D. Rogers Sr.* **Weight:** *26.73 grams.*
Composition: *.900 silver, .100 copper (net weight .7736 oz. pure silver).*
Diameter: *38.1 mm.* **Edge:** *Reeded.* **Mint:** *San Francisco.*

These coins marked the 30th anniversary of the death of Robert F. Kennedy, attorney general of the United States appointed by his brother, President John F. Kennedy.

Designs. *Obverse:* Portrait of Robert F. Kennedy. *Reverse:* Eagle perched on a shield with JUSTICE above, Senate seal to lower left.

Mintage Data. Authorized by Public Law 103-328, signed by President William J. Clinton on September 29, 1994. *Maximum authorized*—500,000. *Number minted*—106,422 Uncirculated and 99,020 Proof.

Original Cost. Sale prices $30 (Uncirculated, pre-issue) and $33 (Proof, pre-issue); Uncirculated later raised to $32, and Proof later raised to $37. A portion of the surcharge of $10 per coin went to the Robert F. Kennedy Memorial.

Key to Collecting. Upon their publication the mintage figures were viewed as being attractively low from a numismatic viewpoint. Examples are easily found today and are usually superb gems.

	Distribution	Cert	Avg	%MS	MS-67 / PF-67
1998-S	106,422	3,020	69.3	100%	$40
Auctions: $70, MS-70, July 2014; $129, MS-70, April 2013					
1998-S, Proof	99,020	1,480	69.0		$75
Auctions: $282, PF-70DCam, September 2014; $270, PF-70DCam, September 2014					

DOLLEY MADISON SILVER DOLLAR (1999)

Designer: *Tiffany & Co.* **Weight:** *26.73 grams.*
Composition: *.900 silver, .100 copper (net weight .7736 oz. pure silver).*
Diameter: *38.1 mm.* **Edge:** *Reeded.* **Mint:** *Philadelphia.*

If the myth that Martha Washington was the subject for the 1792 silver half disme is discarded, Dolley Madison, wife of President James Madison, became the first of the first ladies to be depicted on a legal-tender U.S. coin with this silver dollar. The designs by Tiffany & Co. were modeled by T. James Ferrell (obverse) and Thomas D. Rogers Sr. (reverse). Note the T&Co. logo in a flower petal on the obverse and at the base of the trees to the right on the reverse.

Designs. *Obverse:* Portrait of Dolley Madison as depicted near the ice house (in the style of classic pergola) on the grounds of the family estate, Montpelier. A bouquet of cape jasmines is to the left. *Reverse:* Angular view of the front of Montpelier, complete with landscaping.

Mintage Data. Authorized by Public Law 104-329, signed by President William J. Clinton on October 20, 1996. *Maximum authorized*—500,000. *Number minted*—89,104 Uncirculated and 224,403 Proof.

Original Cost. Sale prices $30 (Uncirculated, pre-issue) and $33 (Proof, pre-issue); Uncirculated later raised to $32, and Proof later raised to $37. A portion of the surcharge of $10 per coin went to the National Trust for Historic Preservation.

Key to Collecting. The Dolley Madison dollars have been popular with collectors ever since they were first sold. Examples can be obtained with little effort and are usually superb gems.

	Distribution	Cert	Avg	%MS	MS-67 PF-67
1999-P	89,104	2,155	69.4	100%	$35
Auctions: $90, MS-70, April 2013					
1999-P, Proof	224,403	2,568	69.2		$35
Auctions: $106, PF-70DCam, April 2013					

GEORGE WASHINGTON DEATH BICENTENNIAL $5 GOLD COIN (1999)

Designer: *Laura Garden Fraser.* **Weight:** *8.359 grams.*
Composition: *.900 gold, .100 copper (net weight .242 oz. pure gold).*
Diameter: *21.6 mm.* **Edge:** *Reeded.* **Mint:** *West Point.*

The 200th anniversary of George Washington's death was commemorated with this coin. In 1932 Laura Garden Fraser's proposed Washington portrait for the quarter dollar had been rejected in favor of the portrait design by John Flanagan, but it was resurrected for this commemorative gold coin.

Designs. *Obverse:* A portrait of Washington inspired by the bust modeled in 1785 for French sculptor Jean Antoine Houdon. *Reverse:* A perched eagle with feathers widely separated at left and right.

Mintage Data. Authorized on October 20, 1996, by Public Law 104-329, part of the United States Commemorative Coin Act of 1996. *Maximum authorized*—100,000 pieces (both formats combined). *Number minted*—22,511 Uncirculated and 41,693 Proof.

Original Cost. Sale prices $180 (Uncirculated, pre-issue) and $195 (Proof, pre-issue); Uncirculated later raised to $195, and Proof later raised to $225. A portion of the surcharge went to the Mount Vernon Ladies' Association, which cares for Washington's home today.

Key to Collecting. This coin is readily available in any high grade desired.

	Distribution	Cert	Avg	%MS	MS-67 PF-67
1999-W	22,511	1,471	69.5	100%	$325
Auctions: $423, MS-70, April 2015; $423, MS-70, April 2015; $400, MS-70, April 2015; $353, MS-70, April 2015					
1999-W, Proof	41,693	2,042	69.4		$325
Auctions: $705, PF-70DCam, March 2013; $400, PF-70UCam, April 2015; $382, PF-69DCam, July 2014					

YELLOWSTONE NATIONAL PARK SILVER DOLLAR (1999)

Designer: *Edgar Z. Steever IV (obverse), William C. Cousins (reverse).* **Weight:** *26.73 grams.*
Composition: *.900 silver, .100 copper (net weight .7736 oz. pure silver).*
Diameter: *38.1 mm.* **Edge:** *Reeded.* **Mint:** *Philadelphia.*

This coin commemorated the 125th anniversary of the establishment of Yellowstone National Park. Technically, it came out and was dated two years later than it should have, as the park was founded in 1872 (and therefore the 125th anniversary would have been in 1997, not 1999).

Designs. *Obverse:* An unidentified geyser (not the famed Old Faithful, for the terrain is different) is shown in action. YELLOWSTONE is above, with other inscriptions to the left center and below, as illustrated. *Reverse:* A bison is shown, facing left. In the background is a mountain range with sun and resplendent rays (an adaptation of the seal of the Department of the Interior).

Mintage Data. Authorized on October 20, 1996, by Public Law 104-329, part of the United States Commemorative Coin Act of 1996. The catch-all legislation authorized seven commemoratives to be issued from 1997 to 1999. *Maximum authorized*—500,000 (both formats combined). *Number minted*—82,563 Uncirculated and 187,595 Proof.

Original Cost. Sale prices $30 (Uncirculated, pre-issue) and $33 (Proof, pre-issue); Uncirculated later raised to $32, and Proof later raised to $37.

Key to Collecting. Easily obtainable in the numismatic marketplace, nearly always in high grades. Investors are attracted to coins certified as MS-70 or PF-70, but few can tell the difference between these and coins at the 69 level. Only a tiny fraction of the mintage has ever been certified.

	Distribution	Cert	Avg	%MS	MS-67 PF-67
1999-P	82,563	1,853	69.3	100%	$55
	Auctions: No auction records available.				
1999-P, Proof	187,595	2,165	69.0		$50
	Auctions: $282, PF-70UCam, July 2015				

LIBRARY OF CONGRESS BICENTENNIAL SILVER DOLLAR (2000)

Designer: *Thomas D. Rogers Sr. (obverse), John Mercanti (reverse).* **Weight:** *26.73 grams.*
Composition: *.900 silver, .100 copper (net weight .7736 oz. pure silver).*
Diameter: *38.1 mm.* **Edge:** *Reeded.* **Mint:** *Philadelphia.*

The Library of Congress, located across the street from the U.S. Capitol in Washington, celebrated its 200th anniversary on April 24, 2000; these silver dollars and a ten-dollar bimetallic coin were issued to honor the milestone.

Designs. *Obverse:* An open book, with its spine resting on a closed book, with the torch of the Library of Congress dome behind. *Reverse:* The dome part of the Library of Congress.

Mintage Data. Authorized by Public Law 105-268, signed by President William J. Clinton on October 19, 1996. *Maximum authorized*—500,000. *Number minted*—53,264 Uncirculated and 198,503 Proof.

Original Cost. Sale prices $25 (Uncirculated, pre-issue) and $28 (Proof, pre-issue); Uncirculated later raised to $27, and Proof later raised to $32. A portion of the surcharges went to the Library of Congress Trust Fund Board.

Key to Collecting. The Library of Congress silver dollar (as well as the ten-dollar bimetallic coin issued alongside it) is readily available in the marketplace today, nearly always of the superb gem quality, as issued.

	Distribution	Cert	Avg	%MS	MS-67
					PF-67
2000-P	53,264	1,604	69.4	100%	$30
Auctions: $108, MS-70, April 2013; $76, MS-70, July 2014; $74, MS-70, October 2015					
2000-P, Proof	198,503	1,929	69.0		$30
Auctions: $188, PF-70DCam, September 2014; $635, PF-70DCam, April 2013					

LIBRARY OF CONGRESS BICENTENNIAL $10 BIMETALLIC COIN (2000)

Designer: *John Mercanti (obverse), Thomas D. Rogers Sr. (reverse).*
Weight: *16.259 grams.* **Composition:** *.480 gold, .480 platinum, .040 alloy.*
Diameter: *27 mm.* **Edge:** *Reeded.* **Mint:** *West Point.*

This coin was the U.S. Mint's first gold/platinum bimetallic coin. The Library of Congress—the original location of which was burned by the British, but which was resurrected using Thomas Jefferson's personal book collection—is today a repository that includes 18 million books and more than 100 million other items, including periodicals, films, prints, photographs, and recordings.

Designs. *Obverse:* The torch of the Library of Congress dome. *Reverse:* An eagle surrounded by a wreath.

Mintage Data. Authorized by Public Law 105-268, signed by President William J. Clinton on October 19, 1996. *Maximum authorized*—200,000. *Number minted*—7,261 Uncirculated and 27,445 Proof.

Original Cost. Sale prices $380 (Uncirculated, pre-issue) and $395 (Proof, pre-issue); Uncirculated later raised to $405, and Proof later raised to $425. A portion of the surcharges went to the Library of Congress Trust Fund Board.

Key to Collecting. The Library of Congress ten-dollar bimetallic coin (as well as the silver dollar issued alongside it) is readily available in the marketplace today, nearly always of the superb gem quality as issued.

	Distribution	Cert	Avg	%MS	MS-67
					PF-67
2000-W	7,261	1,364	69.7	100%	$1,400
Auctions: $2,115, MS-70, June 2015; $1,998, MS-70, August 2015; $1,293, MS-69, October 2015; $1,175, MS-69, June 2015					
2000-W, Proof	27,445	3,079	69.2		$1,100
Auctions: $2,115, PF-70DCam, September 2015; $1,763, PF-70UCam, October 2015; $881, PF-69UCam, October 2015					

LEIF ERICSON MILLENNIUM SILVER DOLLAR (2000)

Designer: *John Mercanti (obverse), T. James Ferrell (reverse).* **Weight:** *26.73 grams.*
Composition: *.900 silver, .100 copper (net weight .7736 oz. pure silver).*
Diameter: *38.1 mm.* **Edge:** *Reeded.* **Mint:** *Philadelphia.*

This silver dollar was issued in cooperation with a foreign government, the Republic of Iceland, which also sponsored its own coin, struck at the Philadelphia Mint (but with no mintmark), a silver 1,000 krónur. Both commemorated the millennium of the year 1000, the approximate departure date of Leif Ericson and his crew from Iceland to the New World.

Designs. *Obverse:* Portrait of Leif Ericson, an artist's conception, as no actual image survives—based on the image used on the Iceland 1 krónur coin. The helmeted head of the explorer is shown facing right. *Reverse:* A Viking long ship with high prow under full sail, FOUNDER OF THE NEW WORLD above, other inscriptions below.

Mintage Data. Authorized under Public Law 106-126. *Maximum authorized—500,000. Number minted—* 28,150 Uncirculated and 144,748 Proof.

Original Cost. Sale prices $30 (Uncirculated, pre-issue) and $33 (Proof, pre-issue); Uncirculated later raised to $32, and Proof later raised to $37. The surcharge of $10 per coin went to the Leifur Eiriksson Foundation for funding student exchanges between the United States and Iceland.

Key to Collecting. These coins are readily available in the marketplace today.

	Distribution	Cert	Avg	%MS	MS-67 PF-67
2000-P	28,150	1,268	69.4	100%	$75
	Auctions: $223, MS-70, June 2015; $212, MS-70, January 2013; $176, MS-70, July 2014				
2000-P, Proof	144,748	2,159	69.0		$60
	Auctions: $999, PF-70DCam, September 2014; $999, PF-70DCam, April 2013				

AMERICAN BUFFALO SILVER DOLLAR (2001)

Designer: *James Earle Fraser.* **Weight:** *26.73 grams.*
Composition: *.900 silver, .100 copper (net weight .7736 oz. pure silver).*
Diameter: *38.1 mm.* **Edge:** *Reeded.* **Mints:** *Denver (Uncirculated) and Philadelphia (Proof).*

James Earle Fraser's design, originally used on nickels from 1913 to 1938, was modified slightly by Mint engravers for this silver dollar. Commonly called the "American Buffalo Commemorative," the coin debuted at the groundbreaking for the Smithsonian Institution's National Museum of the American Indian and was very well received.

Designs. *Obverse:* Portrait of a Native American facing right. *Reverse:* An American bison standing, facing left.

Mintage Data. Authorized by Public Law 106-375, October 27, 2000. *Maximum authorized*—500,000. *Number minted*—2001-D: 227,131 Uncirculated; 2001-P: 272,869 Proof.

Original Cost. Sale prices (pre-issue only) $30 (Uncirculated) and $33 (Proof). The surcharge of $10 per coin went to the National Museum of the American Indian.

Key to Collecting. Both the Uncirculated and Proof of the 2001 American Buffalo were carefully produced to high standards of quality. Nearly all examples today grade at high levels, including MS-70 and PF-70, these ultra-grades commanding a sharp premium for investors. Coins grading 68 or 69 often have little or any real difference in quality and would seem to be the best buys.

	Distribution	Cert	Avg	%MS	MS-67
					PF-67
2001-D	227,131	14,526	69.1	100%	$175
Auctions: $259, MS-70, February 2015; $235, MS-70, July 2015; $259, MS-69, June 2015; $165, MS-69, January 2015					
2001-P, Proof	272,869	15,277	69.1		$175
Auctions: $376, PF-70DCam, February 2015; $353, PF-70DCam, January 2015; $153, PF-69DCam, June 2015					

U.S. Capitol Visitor Center Half Dollar (2001)

Designer: *Dean McMullen (obverse), Alex Shagin and Marcel Jovine (reverse).* **Weight:** *11.34 grams.* **Composition:** *.9167 copper, .0833 nickel.* **Diameter:** *30.61 mm.* **Edge:** *Reeded.* **Mint:** *Philadelphia.*

In 1991 Congress voted on a Visitor Center to be established near the U.S. Capitol building. This copper-nickel half dollar, as well as a silver dollar and a ten-dollar gold coin, were decided upon to provide the funds through sale surcharges. The center and the coins did not become a reality until more than a decade later, though.

Designs. *Obverse:* The north wing of the original U.S. Capitol (burned by the British in 1814) is shown superimposed on a plan view of the present building. *Reverse:* Within a circle of 16 stars are inscriptions referring to the first meeting of the Senate and House.

Mintage Data. Authorized by Public Law 106-126, signed by President William J. Clinton on December 6, 1999. *Maximum authorized*—750,000. *Number minted*—99,157 Uncirculated and 77,962 Proof.

Original Cost. Sale prices $7.75 (Uncirculated, pre-issue) and $10.75 (Proof, pre-issue); Uncirculated later raised to $8.50, and Proof later raised to $11.50. The $3 surcharge per coin went towards the construction of the Visitor Center.

Key to Collecting. Today, this half dollar is readily available on the market, nearly always in the same gem quality as issued.

	Distribution	Cert	Avg	%MS	MS-67
					PF-67
2001-P	99,157	3,422	69.5	100%	$20
Auctions: $153, MS-70, August 2013					
2001-P, Proof	77,962	1,350	69.0		$16
Auctions: No auction records available.					

U.S. CAPITOL VISITOR CENTER SILVER DOLLAR (2001)

Designer: *Marika Somogyi (obverse), John Mercanti (reverse).* **Weight:** *26.73 grams.*
Composition: *.900 silver, .100 copper (net weight .7736 oz. pure silver).*
Diameter: *38.1 mm.* **Edge:** *Reeded.* **Mint:** *Philadelphia.*

The U.S. Capitol Visitor Center, as first proposed, was to offer free exhibits and films, and it was believed that the center would eliminate lengthy waits to view the Capitol proper. However, presumably many would still want to visit the Capitol itself, and no further plan to eliminate waiting time was presented. After the September 11, 2001, terrorist attack on the World Trade Center in New York City and the Pentagon in the District of Columbia, security at the Capitol was heightened—and the concept of the Visitor Center became even more important.

Designs. *Obverse:* The original Capitol is shown with the date 1800, and a much smaller later Capitol, with the date 2001—a variation on the same theme as used on the half dollar. *Reverse:* An eagle reminiscent of Mint engraver John Mercanti's reverse for the 1986 silver bullion "Eagle" dollar. In the present incarnation, the national bird wears a ribbon lettered U.S. CAPITOL VISITOR CENTER.

Mintage Data. Authorized by Public Law 106-126, signed by President William J. Clinton on December 6, 1999. *Maximum authorized*—500,000. *Number minted*—35,380 Uncirculated and 143,793 Proof.

Original Cost. Sale prices $27 (Uncirculated, pre-issue) and $29 (Proof, pre-issue); Uncirculated later raised to $29, and Proof later raised to $33. The $10 surcharge per coin went towards the construction of the Visitor Center.

Key to Collecting. Today, this silver dollar is readily available on the market, nearly always in the same gem quality as issued.

	Distribution	Cert	Avg	%MS	MS-67 PF-67
2001-P	35,380	1,796	69.3	100%	$40
	Auctions: $129, MS-70, April 2013				
2001-P, Proof	143,793	2,176	69.0		$60
	Auctions: $294, PF-70DCam, February 2014; $4,113, PF-70DCam, April 2013				

U.S. CAPITOL VISITOR CENTER $5 GOLD COIN (2001)

Designer: *Elizabeth Jones.* **Weight:** *8.359 grams.* **Composition:** *.900 gold, .100 copper (net weight .242 oz. pure gold).* **Diameter:** *21.6 mm.* **Edge:** *Reeded.* **Mint:** *West Point.*

If there was a potential highlight for what proved to be yet another underperforming commemorative issue—with sales far below projections—it was that Elizabeth Jones, former chief engraver at the Mint, was tapped to do the obverse of the $5 gold coin in the Capitol Visitor Center series. The result might not be a showcase for her remarkable talent, given the nature of the subject, but it rounds out the suite of three commemorative coins with detailed architectural motifs.

Designs. *Obverse:* Section of a Corinthian column. *Reverse:* The 1800 Capitol (interestingly, with slightly different architectural details and proportions than seen on the other coins).

Mintage Data. Authorized by Public Law 106-126, signed by President William J. Clinton on December 6, 1999. *Maximum authorized*—100,000. *Number minted*—6,761 Uncirculated and 27,652 Proof.

Original Cost. Sale prices $175 (Uncirculated, pre-issue) and $177 (Proof, pre-issue); Uncirculated later raised to $200, and Proof later raised to $207. The $35 surcharge per coin went towards the construction of the Visitor Center.

Key to Collecting. Of all the Capitol Visitor Center commemoratives, the Uncirculated five-dollar gold coin is least often seen. After the distribution figure of only 6,761 was released for that coin, buyers clamored to acquire them, and the price rose sharply. Today, it still sells at one of the greatest premiums of any modern commemorative.

	Distribution	Cert	Avg	%MS	MS-67 / PF-67
2001-W	6,761	2,029	69.5	100%	$1,100
	Auctions: $1,087, MS-70, July 2014; $1,058, MS-70, August 2014; $881, MS-70, January 2015; $764, MS-70, June 2015				
2001-W, Proof	27,652	1,862	69.4		$325
	Auctions: No auction records available.				

SALT LAKE CITY OLYMPIC WINTER GAMES SILVER DOLLAR (2002)

Designer: *John Mercanti (obverse), Donna Weaver (reverse).* **Weight:** *26.73 grams.*
Composition: *.900 silver, .100 copper (net weight .7736 oz. pure silver).*
Diameter: *38.1 mm.* **Edge:** *Reeded.* **Mint:** *Denver (Uncirculated) and Philadelphia (Proof).*

In February 2002, Salt Lake City, Utah, was the focal point for the XIX Olympic Winter Games, a quadrennial event. Congress authorized both this silver dollar and a five-dollar gold coin to commemorate the competition.

Designs. *Obverse:* A stylized geometric figure representing an ice crystal. Five interlocked Olympic rings and inscriptions complete the picture, including XIX OLYMPIC WINTER GAMES. *Reverse:* The skyline of Salt Lake City is shown with exaggerated dimensions, with the rugged Wasatch Mountains in the distance. XIX OLYMPIC GAMES is repeated on the reverse.

Mintage Data. Authorized by Public Law 106-435, the Salt Lake Olympic Winter Games Commemorative Coin Act, signed by President William J. Clinton on November 6, 2000. *Maximum authorized*—400,000. *Number minted*—2002-D: 40,257 Uncirculated; 2002-P: 166,864 Proof.

Original Cost. Sale prices $30 (Uncirculated, pre-issue) and $33 (Proof, pre-issue); Uncirculated were later raised to $32, and Proof were later raised to $37. The surcharge of $10 per coin went to the Salt Lake Organizing Committee for the Olympic Winter Games of 2002 and the United States Olympic Committee.

Key to Collecting. As might be expected, coins encapsulated as MS-70 and PF-70 sell for strong prices to investors and Registry Set compilers. Most collectors are nicely satisfied with 68 and 69 grades, or the normal issue quality, since the coins are little different in actual appearance.

	Distribution	Cert	Avg	%MS	MS-67
					PF-67
2002-D	40,257	1,556	69.5	100%	$45
	Auctions: $94, MS-70, January 2013				
2002-P, Proof	166,864	2,146	69.1		$40
	Auctions: $217, PF-70DCam, April 2013				

SALT LAKE CITY OLYMPIC WINTER GAMES $5 GOLD COIN (2002)

Designer: *Donna Weaver.* **Weight:** *8.359 grams.*
Composition: *.900 gold, .100 copper (net weight .242 oz. pure gold).*
Diameter: *21.6 mm.* **Edge:** *Reeded.* **Mint:** *West Point.*

The design of the 2002 Olympic Winter Games commemoratives attracted little favorable notice outside of advertising publicity, and, once again, sales were low—all the more surprising, for Olympic coins often attract international buyers.

Designs. *Obverse:* An ice crystal dominates, superimposed over a geometric creation representing "Rhythm of the Land," but not identified. Also appearing are the date and SALT LAKE. *Reverse:* The outline of the Olympic cauldron is shown, with geometric sails above representing flames.

Mintage Data. Authorized by Public Law 106-435, the Salt Lake Olympic Winter Games Commemorative Coin Act, signed by President William J. Clinton on November 6, 2000. *Maximum authorized—* 80,000. *Number minted—*10,585 Uncirculated and 32,877 Proof.

Original Cost. Sale prices $180 (Uncirculated, pre-issue) and $195 (Proof, pre-issue); Uncirculated were later raised to $205, and Proof were later raised to $225. The surcharge of $10 per coin went to the Salt Lake Organizing Committee for the Olympic Winter Games of 2002 and the United States Olympic Committee.

Key to Collecting. Although the mintage of the Uncirculated $5 in particular was quite low, there was not much interest in the immediate aftermarket. Coins graded MS-70 and PF-70 sell for strong prices to investors and Registry Set compilers.

	Distribution	Cert	Avg	%MS	MS-67
					PF-67
2002-W	10,585	1,186	69.5	100%	$325
	Auctions: $499, MS-70, August 2013; $397, MS-70, September 2014; $353, MS-70, April 2015				
2002-W, Proof	32,877	1,216	69.5		$325
	Auctions: $400, PF-70UCam, May 2015; $376, PF-70UCam, April 2015; $108, PF-70DCam, April 2013; $33, PF-69DCam, August 2014				

West Point (U.S. Military Academy) Bicentennial Silver Dollar (2002)

Designer: *T. James Ferrell (obverse), John Mercanti (reverse).* **Weight:** *26.73 grams.*
Composition: *.900 silver, .100 copper (net weight .7736 oz. pure silver).*
Diameter: *38.1 mm.* **Edge:** *Reeded.* **Mint:** *West Point.*

The 200th anniversary of the U.S. Military Academy at West Point, New York, was celebrated with this coin. The Cadet Chapel is shown on the obverse of the dollar.

Designs. *Obverse:* A fine depiction of the Academy color guard in a parade, with Washington Hall and the Cadet Chapel in the distance—and minimum intrusion of lettering—projects this to the forefront of commemorative designs of the era. *Reverse:* The West Point Bicentennial logotype is shown, an adaptation of the Academy seal, showing at the center an ancient Greek helmet with a sword and shield.

Mintage Data. Authorized several years earlier by Public Law 103-328, signed by President William J. Clinton on September 29, 1994. *Maximum authorized*—500,000. *Number minted*—103,201 Uncirculated and 288,293 Proof.

Original Cost. Sale prices $30 (Uncirculated, pre-issue) and $32 (Proof, pre-issue); Uncirculated later raised to $32, and Proof later raised to $37. The surcharge of $10 per coin went to the Association of Graduates.

Key to Collecting. The scenario is familiar: enough coins were struck to satisfy all comers during the period of issue, with the result that there was no unsatisfied demand. Coins certified at the MS-70 level appeal to a special group of buyers and command strong premiums.

	Distribution	Cert	Avg	%MS	MS-67
					PF-67
2002-W	103,201	4,442	69.5	100%	$35
Auctions: No auction records available.					
2002-W, Proof	288,293	5,532	69.3		$35
Auctions: No auction records available.					

First Flight Centennial Half Dollar (2003)

Designer: *John Mercanti (obverse), Norman E. Nemeth (reverse).* **Weight:** *11.34 grams.*
Composition: *.9167 copper, .0833 nickel.* **Diameter:** *30.61 mm.* **Edge:** *Reeded.* **Mint:** *Philadelphia.*

To celebrate the 100th anniversary of powered aircraft flight by Orville and Wilbur Wright in 1903, Congress authorized a set of 2003-dated commemoratives, including this copper-nickel half dollar.

Designs. *Obverse:* Wright Monument at Kill Devil Hill on the North Carolina seashore. *Reverse:* Wright Flyer biplane in flight.

Mintage Data. Authorized by Public Law 105-124, as an amendment and tag-on to the 50 States Commemorative Coin Program Act (which authorized the State quarters), signed by President William J. Clinton on December 1, 1997. *Maximum authorized—750,000. Number minted—57,122* Uncirculated and 109,710 Proof.

Original Cost. Sale prices $9.75 (Uncirculated, pre-issue) and $12.50 (Proof, pre-issue); Uncirculated later raised to $10.75, and Proof later raised to $13.50. The surcharge of $1 per coin went to the First Flight Centennial Foundation, a private nonprofit group founded in 1995.

Key to Collecting. Values fell after sales concluded. In time, they recovered. Today, all the coins in this set sell for a premium. Superb gems are easily enough found.

	Distribution	Cert	Avg	%MS	MS-67
					PF-67
2003-P	57,122	2,183	69.5	100%	$15
Auctions: $50, MS-70, April 2013					
2003-P, Proof	109,710	2,049	69.1		$17
Auctions: No auction records available.					

First Flight Centennial Silver Dollar (2003)

Designer: *T. James Ferrell (obverse), Norman E. Nemeth (reverse).* **Weight:** *26.73 grams.*
Composition: *.900 silver, .100 copper (net weight .7736 oz. pure silver).*
Diameter: *38.1 mm.* **Edge:** *Reeded.* **Mint:** *Philadelphia.*

The release of this coin and the two other First Flight Centennial commemoratives with it marked the third straight year that a coin featuring the Wrights' plane was featured on a U.S. coin. In 2001, the North Carolina State quarter had portrayed the Wright Flyer, and the Ohio State quarter did the same in 2002 (though an astronaut was also incorporated).

Designs. *Obverse:* Conjoined portraits of Orville and Wilbur Wright. *Reverse:* The Wright brothers' plane in flight.

Mintage Data. Authorized by Public Law 105-124, as an amendment and tag-on to the 50 States Commemorative Coin Program Act (which authorized the State quarters), signed by President William J. Clinton on December 1, 1997. *Maximum authorized—500,000. Number minted—53,533* Uncirculated and 190,240 Proof.

Original Cost. Sale prices $31 (Uncirculated, pre-issue) and $33 (Proof, pre-issue); Uncirculated later raised to $33, and Proof later raised to $37. The surcharge of $1 per coin went to the First Flight Centennial Foundation, a private nonprofit group founded in 1995.

Key to Collecting. Values fell after sales concluded, but they did recover in time. Today, all the coins in this program sell for a premium. Superb gems are easily enough found.

	Distribution	Cert	Avg	%MS	MS-67
					PF-67
2003-P	53,533	3,134	69.4	100%	$45
Auctions: $94, MS-70, May 2013					
2003-P, Proof	190,240	3,076	69.0		$45
Auctions: $423, PF-70DCam, March 2013; $141, PF-70DCam, April 2013					

FIRST FLIGHT CENTENNIAL $10 GOLD COIN (2003)

Designer: *Donna Weaver (obverse), Norman E. Nemeth (reverse).* **Weight:** *16.718 grams.*
Composition: *.900 gold, .100 copper (net weight .4837 oz. pure gold).*
Diameter: *27 mm.* **Edge:** *Reeded.* **Mint:** *West Point.*

None of the First Flight Centennial commemoratives sold particularly well. The redundancy of the motifs undoubtedly contributed to this: each had the same reverse motif of the Wright brothers' plane, and the two largest denominations each pictured the Wright brothers.

Designs. *Obverse:* Portraits of Orville and Wilbur Wright. *Reverse:* Wright Brothers' plane in flight with an eagle overhead.

Mintage Data. Authorized by Public Law 105-124, as an amendment and tag-on to the 50 States Commemorative Coin Program Act (which authorized the State quarters), signed by President William J. Clinton on December 1, 1997. *Maximum authorized*—100,000. *Number minted*—10,009 Uncirculated and 21,676 Proof.

Original Cost. Sale prices $340 (Uncirculated, pre-issue) and $350 (Proof, pre-issue); Uncirculated later raised to $365, and Proof later raised to $375. The surcharge of $1 per coin went to the First Flight Centennial Foundation, a private nonprofit group founded in 1995.

Key to Collecting. Values fell after sales concluded, but they did recover in time. Today, all the coins in this commemorative program sell for a premium. Superb gems are easily enough found.

	Distribution	Cert	Avg	%MS	MS-67 / PF-67
2003-W	10,009	1,898	69.8	100%	$900
	Auctions: $823, MS-70, July 2015; $793, MS-70, January 2015; $617, MS-69, July 2015; $588, MS-69, June 2015				
2003-W, Proof	21,676	1,606	69.3		$700
	Auctions: $823, PF-70DCam, July 2014; $1,293, PF-70DCam, April 2013				

THOMAS ALVA EDISON SILVER DOLLAR (2004)

Designer: *Donna Weaver (obverse), John Mercanti (reverse).* **Weight:** *26.73 grams.*
Composition: *.900 silver, .100 copper (net weight .7736 oz. pure silver).*
Diameter: *38.1 mm.* **Edge:** *Reeded.* **Mint:** *Philadelphia.*

The 125th anniversary of the October 21, 1879, demonstration by Thomas Edison of his first successful electric light bulb was the event commemorated with this silver dollar. Despite sales falling far short of the authorized amount, the Edison dollar was well received by collectors. Interestingly, several proposals had earlier been made for commemoratives to be issued in 1997 to observe the 150th anniversary of Edison's February 11, 1847, birth in Milan, Ohio.

Designs. *Obverse:* Waist-up portrait of Edison holding a light bulb in his right hand. *Reverse:* Light bulb of the 1879 style mounted on a base, with arcs surrounding.

Mintage Data. Authorized by Public Law 105-331, signed by President William J. Clinton on December 6, 1999. *Maximum authorized*—500,000. *Number minted*—92,510 Uncirculated and 211,055 Proof.

Original Cost. Sale prices $31 (Uncirculated, pre-issue) and $33 (Proof, pre-issue); Uncirculated later raised to $33, and Proof later raised to $37. The surcharge of $10 per coin was to be divided evenly among the Port Huron (Michigan) Museum of Arts and History, the Edison Birthplace Association, the National Park Service, the Edison Plaza Museum, the Edison Winter Home and Museum, the Edison Institute, the Edison Memorial Tower, and the Hall of Electrical History.

Key to Collecting. Examples are plentiful. Nearly all are superb gems. As was the situation for many other U.S. Mint issues of the period, promoters who had coins encased in certified holders marked MS-70 or PF-70 were able to persuade, or at least imply, to investors (but not to seasoned collectors) that coins of such quality were rarities, and obtained strong prices for them. Smart buyers simply purchased examples remaining in original Mint holders, of which many were just as nice as the "70" coins.

	Distribution	Cert	Avg	%MS	MS-67 / PF-67
2004-P	92,510	2,778	69.3	100%	$35
Auctions: $90, MS-70, April 2013					
2004-P, Proof	211,055	3,330	69.1		$35
Auctions: $78, PF-70DCam, July 2014; $141, PF-70DCam, March 2013					

LEWIS AND CLARK BICENTENNIAL SILVER DOLLAR (2004)

Designer: *Donna Weaver.* **Weight:** *26.73 grams.*
Composition: *.900 silver, .100 copper (net weight .7736 oz. pure silver).*
Diameter: *38.1 mm.* **Edge:** *Reeded.* **Mint:** *Philadelphia.*

This was one of the most successful commemorative programs, despite the fact that many events across the nation celebrating the bicentennial were flops. Note that the Lewis and Clark Expedition had previously been commemorated with gold dollars dated 1903 for the Louisiana Purchase Exposition (St. Louis World's Fair held in 1904) and those of 1904 and 1905 for the Lewis and Clark Exposition (Portland, Oregon, 1905).

Designs. *Obverse:* Meriwether Lewis and William Clark standing with a river and foliage in the distance as a separate motif. Lewis holds the barrel end of his rifle in one hand and a journal in the other and is looking at Clark, who is gazing to the distance in the opposite direction. *Reverse:* Copy of the reverse of the Jefferson Indian Peace medal designed by John Reich and presented to Indians on the expedition (the identical motif was also revived for use on one variety of the 2004 Jefferson nickel). Feathers are to the left and right, and 17 stars are above.

Mintage Data. Authorized by Public Law 106-136, signed by President William J. Clinton on December 6, 1999. *Maximum authorized*—500,000. *Number minted*—142,015 Uncirculated and 351,989 Proof.

Original Cost. Sale prices $33 (Uncirculated, pre-issue) and $35 (Proof, pre-issue); Uncirculated later raised to $35, and Proof later raised to $39. Two-thirds of the surcharge of $10 per coin went to the National Council of the Lewis and Clark Bicentennial, while one-third went to the National Park Service for the bicentennial celebration.

Key to Collecting. Superb gem coins are readily available.

	Distribution	Cert	Avg	%MS	MS-67 PF-67
2004-P	142,015	4,084	69.4	100%	$35
	Auctions: $90, MS-70, April 2013				
2004-P, Proof	351,989	5,569	69.1		$35
	Auctions: $88, PF-70DCam, February 2013				

MARINE CORPS 230TH ANNIVERSARY SILVER DOLLAR (2005)

Designer: *Norman E. Nemeth (obverse), Charles L. Vickers (reverse).* **Weight:** *26.73 grams.*
Composition: *.900 silver, .100 copper (net weight .7736 oz. pure silver).*
Diameter: *38.1 mm.* **Edge:** *Reeded.* **Mint:** *Philadelphia.*

The widespread appreciation of the heritage of the Marine Corps plus the fame of the obverse design taken from Joe Rosenthal's photograph of the flag-raising at Iwo Jima, propelled this coin to remarkable success. For the first time in recent memory, pandemonium reigned in the coin market, as prices rose, buyers clamored to find all they could, and most dealers were sold out. Within a year, interest turned to other things, and the prices dropped, but not down to the issue levels.

Designs. *Obverse:* Marines raising the Stars and Stripes over Iwo Jima as shown on the famous photograph by Joe Rosenthal. *Reverse:* Eagle, globe, and anchor emblem of the Marine Corps.

Mintage Data. Authorized under Public Law 108-291, signed by President George W. Bush on August 6, 2004. *Maximum authorized*—500,000, later increased to 600,000. *Number minted*—49,671 Uncirculated and 548,810 Proof.

Original Cost. Sale prices $33 (Uncirculated, pre-issue) and $35 (Proof, pre-issue); Uncirculated later raised to $35, and Proof later raised to $39. The surcharge of $10 per coin went toward the construction of the Marine Corps Heritage Center at the base in Quantico, Virginia.

Key to Collecting. Superb gem coins are readily available.

	Distribution	Cert	Avg	%MS	MS-67 PF-67
2005-P	49,671	11,672	69.6	100%	$50
	Auctions: $89, MS-70, January 2015; $76, MS-70, July 2014; $62, MS-70, August 2014				
2005-P, Proof	548,810	14,083	69.2		$50
	Auctions: $165, PF-70DCam, November 2013				

CHIEF JUSTICE JOHN MARSHALL SILVER DOLLAR (2005)

Designer: *John Mercanti (obverse), Donna Weaver (reverse).* **Weight:** *26.73 grams.*
Composition: *.900 silver, .100 copper (net weight .7736 oz. pure silver).*
Diameter: *38.1 mm.* **Edge:** *Reeded.* **Mint:** *Philadelphia.*

Chief Justice John Marshall, who served 34 years in that post in the U.S. Supreme Court, was the subject for this commemorative dollar. Mint engravers submitted designs for the coin, with six depictions of Marshall inspired by a painting by Saint-Mèmin, ten from an oil painting by Rembrandt Peale, and three from a statue by William W. Story. It was John Mercanti's interpretation of the Saint-Mèmin work that was selected.

Designs. *Obverse:* Portrait of Marshall, adapted from a painting made in March 1808 by Charles-Balthazar-Julien Fevret de Saint-Mèmin, of France. *Reverse:* The old Supreme Court Chamber within the Capitol.

Mintage Data. Authorized by Public Law 108-290, signed by President George W. Bush on August 9, 2004. *Maximum authorized—*400,000. *Number minted—*67,096 Uncirculated and 196,753 Proof.

Original Cost. Sale prices $33 (Uncirculated, pre-issue) and $35 (Proof, pre-issue); Uncirculated later raised to $35, and Proof later raised to $39. The surcharge of $10 per coin went to the Supreme Court Historical Society.

Key to Collecting. Superb gem coins are available in the marketplace.

	Distribution	Cert	Avg	%MS	MS-67
					PF-67
2005-P	67,096	2,357	69.6	100%	$45
	Auctions: $106, MS-70, January 2013				
2005-P, Proof	196,753	3,238	69.3		$35
	Auctions: $86, PF-70DCam, July 2014; $92, PF-70DCam, March 2013				

BENJAMIN FRANKLIN TERCENTENARY SCIENTIST SILVER DOLLAR (2006)

Designer: *Norman E. Nemeth (obverse), Charles L. Vickers (reverse).* **Weight:** *26.73 grams.*
Composition: *.900 silver, .100 copper (net weight .7736 oz. pure silver).*
Diameter: *38.1 mm.* **Edge:** *Reeded.* **Mint:** *Philadelphia.*

Two silver dollars were issued to commemorate the 300th anniversary of Benjamin Franklin's birth. This version celebrated Franklin's scientific accomplishments, which included discoveries in fields from electricity to oceanography to demographics.

Designs. *Obverse:* Franklin standing with a kite on a string, evocative of his experiments with lightning in June 1752. *Reverse:* Franklin's political cartoon, featuring a snake cut apart, titled "Join, or Die," reflecting the sentiment that the colonies should unite during the French and Indian War (and which had nothing to do with perceived offenses by the British, at this early time). This appeared in Franklin's *Pennsylvania Gazette* on May 9, 1754.

Mintage Data. Authorized by Public Law 104-463, the Benjamin Franklin Tercentenary Act, and signed by President George W. Bush on December 21, 2004. *Maximum authorized—250,000. Number minted—58,000 Uncirculated, 142,000 Proof.*

Original Cost. Sale prices $33 (Uncirculated, pre-issue) and $35 (Proof, pre-issue); Uncirculated later raised to $35, and Proof later raised to $39. The surcharge of $10 per coin went to the Franklin Institute.

Key to Collecting. Superb gems are easily found in the marketplace.

	Distribution	Cert	Avg	%MS	MS-67
					PF-67
2006-P	58,000	7,631	69.7	100%	$35
	Auctions: $76, MS-70, January 2013				
2006-P, Proof	142,000	9,836	69.4		$45
	Auctions: No auction records available.				

BENJAMIN FRANKLIN TERCENTENARY
FOUNDING FATHER SILVER DOLLAR (2006)

Designer: *Don Everhart (obverse), Donna Weaver (reverse).* **Weight:** *26.73 grams.*
Composition: *.900 silver, .100 copper (net weight .7736 oz. pure silver).*
Diameter: *38.1 mm.* **Edge:** *Reeded.* **Mint:** *Philadelphia.*

The bill authorizing the issue of this silver dollar and its counterpart (see previous coin) took note of many of his accomplishments, stating he was "the only Founding Father to sign all of our Nation's organizational documents," who printed "official currency for the colonies of Pennsylvania, Delaware, New Jersey and Maryland," and helped design the Great Seal of the United States.

Designs. *Obverse:* Head and shoulders portrait of Franklin facing forward slightly to the viewer's right, with his signature reproduced below. *Reverse:* Copy of a 1776 Continental dollar within a frame of modern lettering. The mottoes on this coin were suggested by Franklin.

Mintage Data. Authorized by Public Law 104-463, the Benjamin Franklin Tercentenary Act, and signed by President George W. Bush on December 21, 2004. *Maximum authorized—250,000. Number minted—58,000 Uncirculated, 142,000 Proof.*

Original Cost. Sale prices $33 (Uncirculated, pre-issue) and $35 (Proof, pre-issue); Uncirculated later raised to $35, and Proof later raised to $39. The surcharge of $10 per coin went to the Franklin Institute.

Key to Collecting. Superb gems are easily found in the marketplace.

	Distribution	Cert	Avg	%MS	MS-67
					PF-67
2006-P	58,000	8,211	69.8	100%	$35
	Auctions: $90, MS-70, April 2013				
2006-P, Proof	142,000	10,104	69.7		$35
	Auctions: $96, PF-70DCam, January 2013; $103, PF-70DCam, April 2013				

SAN FRANCISCO OLD MINT CENTENNIAL SILVER DOLLAR (2006)

Designer: *Sherl J. Winter (obverse), Joseph Menna after George T. Morgan (reverse).*
Weight: *26.73 grams.* **Composition:** *.900 silver, .100 copper (net weight .7736 oz. pure silver).*
Diameter: *38.1 mm.* **Edge:** *Reeded.* **Mint:** *San Francisco.*

This coin and the five-dollar gold coin issued alongside it celebrated the 100th anniversary of the second San Francisco Mint surviving the 1906 Bay Area earthquake and fire.

Designs. *Obverse:* The Second San Francisco Mint as viewed from off the left front corner. *Reverse:* Copy of the reverse of a standard Morgan silver dollar of the era 1878–1921, said to have been taken from a 1904-S.

Mintage Data. Authorized by Public Law 109-230, the San Francisco Old Mint Commemorative Act, signed by President George W. Bush in June 2006. *Maximum authorized*—500,000. *Number minted*—67,100 Uncirculated and 160,870 Proof.

Original Cost. Sale prices $33 (Uncirculated, pre-issue) and $35 (Proof, pre-issue); Uncirculated later raised to $35, and Proof later raised to $39. The surcharge of $10 per coin went to the "San Francisco Museum and Historical Society for rehabilitating the Historic Old Mint as a city museum and an American Coin and Gold Rush Museum."

Key to Collecting. Superb gems are easily found in the marketplace.

	Distribution	Cert	Avg	%MS	MS-67
					PF-67
2006-S	67,100	4,529	69.6	100%	$45
	Auctions: $94, MS-70, January 2013				
2006-S, Proof	160,870	8,409	69.2		$35
	Auctions: No auction records available.				

SAN FRANCISCO OLD MINT CENTENNIAL $5 GOLD COIN (2006)

Designer: *Charles L. Vickers (obverse), Don Everhart after Christian Gobrecht (reverse).*
Weight: *8.359 grams.* **Composition:** *.900 gold, .100 copper (net weight .242 oz. pure gold).*
Diameter: *21.6 mm.* **Edge:** *Reeded.* **Mint:** *San Francisco.*

The designs of this coin and the corresponding silver dollar both had obverses showing the same subject (albeit from a different view), and reverses being copies of old coinage designs.

Designs. *Obverse:* Front view of the portico of the Second San Francisco Mint, with a portion of the building to each side. Modeled after an 1869 construction drawing by Supervising Architect A.B. Mullet. *Reverse:* Copy of the reverse of the Liberty Head half eagle with motto IN GOD WE TRUST, as regularly used from 1866 to 1907.

Mintage Data. Authorized by Public Law 109-230, the San Francisco Old Mint Commemorative Act, signed by President George W. Bush in June 2006. *Maximum authorized*—100,000. *Number minted*—17,500 Uncirculated and 44,174 Proof.

Original Cost. Sale prices $220 (Uncirculated, pre-issue) and $230 (Proof, pre-issue); Uncirculated later raised to $245, and Proof later raised to $255. The surcharge of $35 per coin went to the "San Francisco Museum and Historical Society for rehabilitating the Historic Old Mint as a city museum and an American Coin and Gold Rush Museum."

Key to Collecting. Superb gems are easily found in the marketplace.

	Distribution	Cert	Avg	%MS	MS-67 PF-67
2006-S	17,500	2,776	69.7	100%	$325
Auctions: $329, MS-70, October 2014; $294, MS-70, July 2015; $306, MS-69, July 2015; $282, MS-69, October 2015					
2006-S, Proof	44,174	3,861	69.5		$325
Auctions: $376, PF-70UCam, February 2015; $353, PF-70UCam, July 2015; $341, PF-70UCam, February 2015					

JAMESTOWN 400TH ANNIVERSARY SILVER DOLLAR (2007)

Designer: *Donna Weaver (obverse), Susan Gamble (reverse).* **Weight:** *26.73 grams.*
Composition: *.900 silver, .100 copper (net weight .7736 oz. pure silver).*
Diameter: *38.1 mm.* **Edge:** *Reeded.* **Mint:** *Philadelphia.*

Note that Jamestown was also honored on the 2000 Virginia State quarter.

Designs. *Obverse:* Captain John Smith is shown with an Indian man and woman. *Reverse:* Three sailing ships are shown, elements already seen from the 2000 State quarter, but differently arranged.

Mintage Data. Authorized by Public Law 108-289, the Jamestown 400th Anniversary Commemorative Coin Act, signed by President George W. Bush on August 6, 2004. *Maximum authorized*—500,000. *Number minted*—81,034 Uncirculated and 260,363 Proof.

Original Cost. Sale prices $33 (Uncirculated, pre-issue) and $35 (Proof, pre-issue); Uncirculated later raised to $35, and Proof later raised to $39. The surcharge of $20 per coin went to fund the public observance of the anniversary.

Key to Collecting. Superb gem coins are readily available.

	Distribution	Cert	Avg	%MS	MS-67 PF-67
2007-P	81,034	7,640	69.6	100%	$40
Auctions: $90, MS-70, April 2013					
2007-P, Proof	260,363	10,754	69.5		$35
Auctions: $100, PF-70DCam, April 2013					

JAMESTOWN 400TH ANNIVERSARY $5 GOLD COIN (2007)

Designer: *John Mercanti (obverse), Susan Gamble (reverse).* **Weight:** *8.359 grams.*
Composition: *.900 gold, .100 copper (net weight .242 oz. pure gold).*
Diameter: *21.6 mm.* **Edge:** *Reeded.* **Mint:** *West Point.*

Susan Gamble, who designed the reverse of both this coin and the silver dollar issued alongside it, was a participant in the Mint's Artistic Infusion Program, which was created to bring artists in from the private sector to upgrade the quality of coin designs.

Designs. *Obverse:* Captain John Smith is shown with Indian chief Powhatan, who holds a bag of corn. *Reverse:* Ruins of the old church at Jamestown.

Mintage Data. Authorized by Public Law 108-289, the Jamestown 400th Anniversary Commemorative Coin Act, signed by President George W. Bush on August 6, 2004. *Maximum authorized*—100,000. *Number minted*—18,623 Uncirculated and 47,123 Proof.

Original Cost. Sale prices $33 (Uncirculated, pre-issue) and $35 (Proof, pre-issue); Uncirculated later raised to $35, and Proof later raised to $39. The surcharge of $35 per coin went to fund the public observance of the anniversary.

Key to Collecting. Superb gem coins are readily available.

	Distribution	Cert	Avg	%MS	MS-67 PF-67
2007-W	18,623	3,209	69.8	100%	$325
	Auctions: $353, MS-70, April 2015; $329, MS-70, November 2014; $306, MS-70, July 2015; $294, MS-70, July 2015				
2007-W, Proof	47,123	4,117	69.6		$325
	Auctions: $341, PF-70DCam, July 2014; $317, PF-70DCam, August 2014; $306, PF-70UCam, July 2015				

LITTLE ROCK CENTRAL HIGH SCHOOL DESEGREGATION SILVER DOLLAR (2007)

Designer: *Richard Masters (obverse), Don Everhart (reverse).* **Weight:** *26.73 grams.*
Composition: *.900 silver, .100 copper (net weight .7736 oz. pure silver).*
Diameter: *38.1 mm.* **Edge:** *Reeded.* **Mint:** *Philadelphia.*

This coin commemorated the 50th anniversary of the desegregation of Little Rock Central High School, which was the result of the landmark U.S. Supreme Court case *Brown v. the Board of Education.*

Designs. *Obverse:* The feet of the "Little Rock Nine" students are shown, escorted by a soldier. *Reverse:* Little Rock Central High School as it appeared in 1957.

Mintage Data. Authorized by Public Law 109-146, the Little Rock Central High School Desegregation 50th Anniversary Commemorative Coin Act, signed by President George W. Bush on December 22, 2005. *Maximum authorized*—500,000. *Number minted*—66,093 Uncirculated and 124,678 Proof.

Original Cost. Sale prices $33 (Uncirculated, pre-issue) and $35 (Proof, pre-issue); Uncirculated later raised to $35, and Proof later raised to $39. The surcharge of $10 per coin went toward improvements at the Little Rock Central High School National Historic Site.

Key to Collecting. Superb gem coins are readily available.

	Distribution	Cert	Avg	%MS	MS-67 / PF-67
2007-P	66,093	2,633	69.7	100%	$35
Auctions: $79, MS-70, October 2014; $90, MS-70, April 2013					
2007-P, Proof	124,678	3,033	69.5		$35
Auctions: $80, PF-70DCam, July 2014; $113, PF-70DCam, April 2013					

BALD EAGLE RECOVERY AND NATIONAL EMBLEM HALF DOLLAR (2008)

Designer: *Susan Gamble (obverse), Donna Weaver (reverse).* **Weight:** *11.34 grams.*
Composition: *.9167 copper, .0833 nickel.* **Diameter:** *30.61 mm.* **Edge:** *Reeded.* **Mint:** *San Francisco.*

This copper-nickel half dollar, as well as the silver dollar and five-dollar gold coin issued alongside it, was issued to commemorate the recovery of the bald eagle species, the 35th anniversary of the Endangered Species Act of 1973, and the removal of the bald eagle from the Endangered Species List.

Designs. *Obverse:* Two eaglets and an egg in a bald eagle nest. *Reverse:* "Challenger," a non-releasable bald eagle in the care of the American Eagle Foundation and the first of his species to be trained to free-fly into major sporting events during the National Anthem.

Mintage Data. Authorized by Public Law 108-486, the Bald Eagle Commemorative Coin Act, signed by President George W. Bush on December 23, 2004. *Maximum authorized*—750,000. *Number minted*—120,180 Uncirculated and 220,577 Proof.

Original Cost. Sale prices $7.95 (Uncirculated, pre-issue) and $9.95 (Proof, pre-issue); Uncirculated later raised to $8.95, and Proof later raised to $10.95. The surcharge of $3 per coin went to the American Eagle Foundation of Tennessee for the purposes of continuing its work to save and protect bald eagles nationally.

Key to Collecting. Superb gem coins are readily available.

	Distribution	Cert	Avg	%MS	MS-67 / PF-67
2008-S	120,180	6,784	69.8	100%	$15
Auctions: $30, MS-70, April 2013					
2008-S, Proof	220,577	8,800	69.7		$16
Auctions: No auction records available.					

BALD EAGLE RECOVERY AND NATIONAL EMBLEM SILVER DOLLAR (2008)

Designer: *Joel Iskowitz (obverse), Jim Licaretz (reverse).* **Weight:** *26.73 grams.*
Composition: *.900 silver, .100 copper (net weight .7736 oz. pure silver).*
Diameter: *38.1 mm.* **Edge:** *Reeded.* **Mint:** *Philadelphia.*

The bald eagle, selected in 1782 by the Second Continental Congress as the national emblem of the United States, was common at the time of the nation's establishment. Through the years, however, poaching, habitat destruction, pesticides, and food-source contamination reduced the number of nesting pairs from approximately 100,000 to just more than 400 in the early 1960s. Fortunately, conservationists have saved the species in the past five decades.

Designs. *Obverse:* Bald eagle in flight, mountains in background. *Reverse:* The Great Seal of the United States used from 1782 to 1841.

Mintage Data. Authorized by Public Law 108-486, the Bald Eagle Commemorative Coin Act, signed by President George W. Bush on December 23, 2004. *Maximum authorized*—500,000. *Number minted*—119,204 Uncirculated and 294,601 Proof.

Original Cost. Sale prices $35.95 (Uncirculated, pre-issue) and $39.95 (Proof, pre-issue); Uncirculated later raised to $37.95, and Proof later raised to $43.95. The surcharge of $10 per coin went to the American Eagle Foundation of Tennessee for the purposes of continuing its work to save and protect bald eagles nationally.

Key to Collecting. Superb gem coins are readily available.

	Distribution	Cert	Avg	%MS	MS-67 PF-67
2008-P	119,204	9,043	69.7	100%	$30
Auctions: $90, MS-70, April 2013					
2008-P, Proof	294,601	13,474	69.3		$35
Auctions: $92, PF-70DCam, July 2014; $89, PF-70UCam, July 2015; $79, PF-70DCam, July 2014					

BALD EAGLE RECOVERY AND NATIONAL EMBLEM $5 GOLD COIN (2008)

Designer: *Susan Gamble (obverse), Don Everhart (reverse).* **Weight:** *8.359 grams.*
Composition: *.900 gold, .100 copper (net weight .242 oz. pure gold).*
Diameter: *21.6 grams.* **Edge:** *Reeded.* **Mint:** *West Point.*

Government entities, private organizations, and citizens were all part of the bald eagle's recovery from near-extinction in the middle of the 1900s. Bans on certain pesticides, protections granted under the Endangered Species Act of 1973, and captive-breeding and nest-watch programs have been crucial and have led to the removal of the national emblem from the Endangered Species List.

Designs. *Obverse:* Two bald eagles perched on a branch. *Reverse:* The current Great Seal of the United States.

Mintage Data. Authorized by Public Law 108-486, the Bald Eagle Commemorative Coin Act, signed by President George W. Bush on December 23, 2004. *Maximum authorized*—100,000. *Number minted*—15,009 Uncirculated and 59,269 Proof.

Original Cost. Sale prices $284.95 (Uncirculated, pre-issue) and $294.95 (Proof, pre-issue); Uncirculated later raised to $309.95, and Proof later raised to $319.95. The surcharge of $35 per coin went to the American Eagle Foundation of Tennessee for the purposes of continuing its work to save and protect bald eagles nationally.

Key to Collecting. Superb gem coins are readily available.

	Distribution	Cert	Avg	%MS	MS-67 PF-67
2008-W	15,009	1,049	69.9	100%	$325
	Auctions: $458, MS-70, January 2013				
2008-W, Proof	59,269	1,782	69.8		$325
	Auctions: $442, PF-70DCam, March 2014; $427, PF-70DCam, September 2014; $306, PF-70UCam, July 2015				

ABRAHAM LINCOLN BICENTENNIAL SILVER DOLLAR (2009)

Designer: *Justin Kunz (obverse), Phebe Hemphill (reverse).* **Weight:** *26.73 grams.*
Composition: *.900 silver, .100 copper (net weight .7736 oz. pure silver).*
Diameter: *38.1 mm.* **Edge:** *Reeded.* **Mint:** *Philadelphia.*

These coins, issued to mark the 200th anniversary of President Abraham Lincoln's birth, were extremely popular with collectors. The 450,000 pieces allocated to individual coin sales sold out after a month. Note that this anniversary was also commemorated with the release of four different reverse designs for the 2009 Lincoln cents.

Designs. *Obverse:* A portrait of Abraham Lincoln in three-quarter view. *Reverse:* The final 43 words of President Lincoln's Gettysburg Address, surrounded by a laurel wreath.

Mintage Data. Authorized Public Law 109-285, the Abraham Lincoln Commemorative Coin Act, signed by President George W. Bush on September 27, 2006. *Maximum authorized*—500,000. *Number minted*—125,000 Uncirculated and 325,000 Proof.

Original Cost. Sale prices $31.95 (Uncirculated, pre-issue) and $37.95 (Proof, pre-issue); Uncirculated later raised to $33.95, and Proof later raised to $41.95. The surcharge of $10 per coin went to the Abraham Lincoln Bicentennial Commission.

Key to Collecting. Superb gem coins are readily available.

	Distribution	Cert	Avg	%MS	MS-67 PF-67
2009-P	125,000	10,087	69.8	100%	$35
	Auctions: $96, MS-70, February 2014; $60, MS-70, June 2015; $56, MS-70, July 2014				
2009-P, Proof	325,000	18,100	69.4		$35
	Auctions: $353, PF-70DCam, November 2014; $90, PF-70DCam, August 2014; $74, PF-70DCam, June 2015				

LOUIS BRAILLE BICENTENNIAL SILVER DOLLAR (2009)

Designer: *Joel Iskowitz (obverse), Phebe Hemphill (reverse).* **Weight:** *26.73 grams.*
Composition: *.900 silver, .100 copper (net weight .7736 oz. pure silver).*
Diameter: *38.1 mm.* **Edge:** *Reeded.* **Mint:** *Philadelphia.*

The 200th anniversary of the birth of Louis Braille—the inventor of the eponymous system which is used by the blind to read and write—furnished the occasion for this commemorative. Fittingly, this was the first U.S. coin to feature readable Braille.

Designs. *Obverse:* A forward-facing portrait of Louis Braille. *Reverse:* The word Braille (in Braille code, abbreviated Brl) above a child reading a book in Braille.

Mintage Data. Authorized by Public Law 109-247, the Louis Braille Bicentennial–Braille Literacy Commemorative Coin Act, signed by President George W. Bush on July 27, 2006. *Maximum authorized*—400,000. *Number minted*—82,639 Uncirculated and 135,235 Proof.

Original Cost. Sale prices $31.95 (Uncirculated, pre-issue) and $37.95 (Proof, pre-issue); Uncirculated later raised to $33.95, and Proof later raised to $41.95. The surcharge of $10 per coin went to the National Federation of the Blind.

Key to Collecting. Superb gem coins are readily available.

	Distribution	Cert	Avg	%MS	MS-67 / PF-67
2009-P	82,639	3,404	69.5	100%	$30
	Auctions: $90, MS-70, April 2013				
2009-P, Proof	135,235	4,409	69.1		$30
	Auctions: $94, PF-70DCam, July 2014; $94, PF-70DCam, April 2013				

AMERICAN VETERANS DISABLED FOR LIFE SILVER DOLLAR (2010)

Designer: *Don Everhart.* **Weight:** *26.73 grams.*
Composition: *.900 silver, .100 copper (net weight .7736 oz. pure silver).*
Diameter: *38.1 mm.* **Edge:** *Reeded.* **Mint:** *West Point.*

This coin honored those members of the U.S. Armed Forces who have made extraordinary personal sacrifices in defense of the country.

Designs. *Obverse:* The legs and boots of three veterans, one of whom is using a pair of crutches. *Reverse:* The words "Take This Moment to Honor Our Disabled Defenders of Freedom," surrounded by a laurel wreath with a forget-me-not (widely known as a symbol for those who fought and became disabled in World War I) at its base.

Mintage Data. Authorized by Public Law 110-277, the American Veterans Disabled for Life Commemorative Coin Act, signed by President George W. Bush on July 17, 2008. *Maximum authorized*—350,000. *Number minted*—78,301 Uncirculated and 202,770 Proof.

Original Cost. Sale prices $33.95 (Uncirculated, pre-issue) and $39.95 (Proof, pre-issue); Uncirculated later raised to $35.95, and Proof later raised to $43.95. The surcharge of $10 per coin went to the Disabled Veterans' LIFE Memorial Foundation for the purpose of constructing the American Veterans' Disabled for Life Memorial in Washington, D.C.

Key to Collecting. Superb gem coins are readily available.

	Distribution	Cert	Avg	%MS	MS-67
					PF-67
2010-W	78,301	3,946	69.8	100%	$35
	Auctions: $70, MS-70, May 2013				
2010-W, Proof	202,770	5,055	69.7		$30
	Auctions: $78, PF-70DCam, May 2013; $42, PF-70DCam, September 2014				

BOY SCOUTS OF AMERICA CENTENNIAL SILVER DOLLAR (2010)

Designer: *Donna Weaver (obverse), Jim Licaretz from the universal logo of the Boy Scouts of America (reverse).*
Weight: *26.73 grams.* **Composition:** *.900 silver, .100 copper (net weight .7736 oz. pure silver).*
Diameter: *38.1 mm.* **Edge:** *Reeded.* **Mint:** *Philadelphia.*

The 100th anniversary of the establishment of the Boy Scouts of America was celebrated with this silver dollar. The design was somewhat controversial due to its inclusion of a female but was specifically requested by the organization itself so as to portray the evolution of the Boy Scouts over time to include all American youth.

Designs. *Obverse:* A Cub Scout, a female member of the Venturer Program, and a Boy Scout saluting. *Reverse:* The universal logo of the Boy Scouts of America, featuring an eagle bearing a shield on a fleur-de-lis.

Mintage Data. Authorized by Public Law 110-363, the Boy Scouts of America Centennial Commemorative Coin Act, signed by President George W. Bush on October 8, 2008. *Maximum authorized*—350,000. *Number minted*—105,020 Uncirculated and 244,693 Proof.

Original Cost. Sale prices $33.95 (Uncirculated, pre-issue) and $39.95 (Proof, pre-issue); Uncirculated later raised to $35.95, and Proof later raised to $43.95. The surcharge of $10 per coin went to the National Boy Scouts of America Foundation; the funds were then meant to be made available to local councils in the form of grants for the extension of Scouting in hard-to-serve areas.

Key to Collecting. Superb gem coins are readily available.

	Distribution	Cert	Avg	%MS	MS-67
					PF-67
2010-P	105,020	7,259	69.8	100%	$30
	Auctions: $82, MS-70, March 2013				
2010-P, Proof	244,963	8,132	69.4		$35
	Auctions: $82, PF-70DCam, March 2013				

U.S. ARMY HALF DOLLAR (2011)

Designer: *Donna Weaver (obverse), Thomas Cleveland (reverse).* **Weight:** *11.34 grams.*
Composition: *.9167 copper, .0833 nickel.* **Diameter:** *30.61 mm.*
Edge: *Reeded.* **Mints:** *Denver (Uncirculated) and San Francisco (Proof).*

This copper-nickel half dollar was one of three commemoratives released in honor of the U.S. Army in 2011, by which time the entity had already defended the nation for 236 years. The reverse design was praised by the Citizens Coinage Advisory Committee (CCAC) and the Commission of Fine Arts.

Designs. *Obverse:* Three scenes split in a "storyboard" fashion (from left to right): a soldier surveying; two servicemen laying a flood wall; the Redstone Army rocket at takeoff. *Reverse:* A Continental with a musket, with 13 stars (representing the first states) in an arc above.

Mintage Data. Authorized by Public Law 110-450, the United States Army Commemorative Coin Act of 2008, signed by President George W. Bush on December 1, 2008. *Maximum authorized*—750,000. *Number minted*—2011-D: 39,442 Uncirculated; 2011-S: 68,332 Proof.

Original Cost. Sale prices $15.95 (Uncirculated, pre-issue) and $17.95 (Proof, pre-issue); Uncirculated later raised to $19.95, and Proof raised to $21.95. The surcharge of $5 went toward the yet-to-be-constructed National Museum of the United States Army.

Key to Collecting. Superb gem coins are readily available.

	Distribution	Cert	Avg	%MS	MS-67 PF-67
2011-D	39,442	2,547	69.0	100%	$70
	Auctions: No auction records available.				
2011-S, Proof	68,332	2,447	69.5		$35
	Auctions: No auction records available.				

U.S. ARMY SILVER DOLLAR (2011)

Designer: *Richard Masters (obverse), Susan Gamble (reverse).* **Weight:** *26.73 grams.*
Composition: *.900 silver, .100 copper (net weight .7736 oz. pure silver).* **Diameter:** *38.1 mm.*
Edge: *Reeded.* **Mints:** *San Francisco (Uncirculated) and Philadelphia (Proof).*

The act authorizing this silver dollar (as well as the related copper-nickel half dollar and five-dollar gold coin) called for the coins to be "emblematic of the traditions, history, and heritage of the U.S. Army and its role in American society from the Colonial period to today."

Designs. *Obverse:* A male and female soldier back-to-back in front of a globe. *Reverse:* The Great Seal of the United States (which appears on Army uniforms) inside a ring that bears the seven core values of the Army (Loyalty, Duty, Respect, Selfless Service, Honor, Integrity, and Personal Courage).

Mintage Data. Authorized by Public Law 110-450, the United States Army Commemorative Coin Act of 2008, signed by President George W. Bush on December 1, 2008. *Maximum authorized*—500,000. *Number minted*—2011-S: 43,512 Uncirculated; 2011-P: 119,829 Proof.

Original Cost. Sale prices $49.95 (Uncirculated, pre-issue) and $54.95 (Proof, pre-issue); Uncirculated later raised to $54.95, and Proof later raised to $59.95. The surcharge of $10 per coin went toward the yet-to-be-constructed National Museum of the United States Army.

Key to Collecting. Superb gem coins are readily available.

	Distribution	Cert	Avg	%MS	MS-67 PF-67
2011-S	43,512	2,333	69.7	100%	$50
	Auctions: No auction records available.				
2011-P, Proof	119,829	3,834	69.5		$45
	Auctions: $80, PF-70DCam, April 2013				

U.S. ARMY $5 GOLD COIN (2011)

Designer: *Joel Iskowitz (obverse), Joseph Menna from the U.S. Army emblem (reverse).*
Weight: *8.359 grams.* **Composition:** *.900 gold, .100 copper (net weight .242 oz. pure gold).*
Diameter: *21.6 mm.* **Edge:** *Reeded.* **Mints:** *Philadelphia (Uncirculated) and West Point (Proof).*

By depicting soldiers from five distinct eras in U.S. history, the obverse of this five-dollar gold coin symbolizes the "continuity of strength and readiness" of the Army.

Designs. *Obverse:* Five U.S. Army soldiers representing various eras (from left to right): Revolutionary War, Civil War, modern era, World War II, and World War I. *Reverse:* The U.S. Army emblem, which features various items representative of home life and war time and the phrase "This We'll Defend" on a banner.

Mintage Data. Authorized by Public Law 110-450, the United States Army Commemorative Coin Act of 2008, signed by President George W. Bush on December 1, 2008. *Maximum authorized*—100,000. *Number minted*—2011-P: 8,052 Uncirculated; 2011-W: 17,148 Proof.

Original Cost. Sale prices $439.95 (Uncirculated, pre-issue) and $449.95 (Proof, pre-issue); Uncirculated later raised to $444.95, and Proof later raised to $454.95. The surcharge of $35 per coin went toward the yet-to-be-constructed National Museum of the United States Army.

Key to Collecting. Superb gem coins are readily available.

	Distribution	Cert	Avg	%MS	MS-67 PF-67
2011-P	8,052	433	69.9	100%	$425
	Auctions: $560, MS-70, September 2013				
2011-W, Proof	17,148	550	69.8		$425
	Auctions: $353, PF-69DCam, May 2014				

MEDAL OF HONOR SILVER DOLLAR (2011)

Designer: *Jim Licaretz (obverse), Richard Masters (reverse).* **Weight:** *26.73 grams.*
Composition: *.900 silver, .100 copper (net weight .7736 oz. pure silver).*
Diameter: *38.1 mm.* **Edge:** *Reeded.* **Mints:** *San Francisco (Uncirculated) and Philadelphia (Proof).*

The 150th anniversary of the creation of the Medal of Honor—the highest award for valor in action in the U.S. Armed Forces—was the impetus for this commemorative silver dollar, as well as a five-dollar gold coin.

Designs. *Obverse:* From left to right, the Medals of Honor of the Army, Navy, and Air Force. *Reverse:* An infantry soldier carrying a wounded soldier to safety on his back.

Mintage Data. Authorized by Public Law 111-91, the Medal of Honor Commemorative Coin Act of 2009, signed by President Barack Obama on November 6, 2009. *Maximum authorized*—500,000. *Number minted*—2011-S: 44,752 Uncirculated; 2011-P: 112,833 Proof.

Original Cost. Sale prices $49.95 (Uncirculated, pre-issue) and $54.95 (Proof, pre-issue); Uncirculated later raised to $54.95, and Proof later raised to $59.95. The surcharge of $10 per coin went to the Congressional Medal of Honor Foundation to help finance its educational, scholarship, and outreach programs.

Key to Collecting. Superb gem coins are readily available.

	Distribution	Cert	Avg	%MS	MS-67
					PF-67
2011-S	44,752	2,916	69.6	100%	$50
	Auctions: $100, MS-70, April 2013				
2011-P, Proof	112,833	2,194	69.3		$45
	Auctions: $123, PF-70DCam, March 2013				

MEDAL OF HONOR $5 GOLD COIN (2011)

Designer: *Joseph Menna (obverse), Joel Iskowitz (reverse).* **Weight:** *8.359 grams.*
Composition: *.900 gold, .100 copper (net weight .242 oz. pure gold).* **Diameter:** *21.6 mm.*
Edge: *Reeded.* **Mints:** *Philadelphia (Uncirculated) and West Point (Proof).*

This coin and the silver dollar issued alongside it were created in recognition of the Medal of Honor, the Navy's greatest personal award, first authorized by Congress in 1861. Though counterparts are now given in the Army and Air Force as well, fewer than 3,500 Medals of Honor have ever been awarded to date.

Designs. *Obverse:* The original Medal of Honor, the Navy's highest individual decoration. *Reverse:* Minerva, holding a shield and the U.S. flag on a staff, in front of munitions and a Civil War–era cannon.

Mintage Data. Authorized by Public Law 111-91, the Medal of Honor Commemorative Coin Act of 2009, signed by President Barack Obama on November 6, 2009. *Maximum authorized*—100,000. *Number minted*—2011-P: 8,233 Uncirculated; 2011-W: 17,999 Proof.

Original Cost. Sale prices $439.95 (Uncirculated, pre-issue) and $449.95 (Proof, pre issue); Uncirculated later raised to $444.95, and Proof later raised to $454.95. The surcharge of $35 per coin went to the Congressional Medal of Honor Foundation to help finance its educational, scholarship, and outreach programs.

Key to Collecting. Superb gem coins are readily available.

	Distribution	Cert	Avg	%MS	MS-67
					PF-67
2011-P	8,233	484	69.8	100%	$550
	Auctions: $470, MS-70, November 2014; $470, MS-70, August 2014; $400, MS-70, January 2015; $400, MS-69, January 2015				
2011-W, Proof	17,999	509	69.6		$425
	Auctions: $646, PF-70DCam, February 2015; $646, PF-70DCam, November 2014; $558, PF-70DCam, July 2014				

INFANTRY SOLDIER SILVER DOLLAR (2012)

Designer: *Joel Iskowitz (obverse), Ronald D. Sanders (reverse).* **Weight:** *26.73 grams.*
Composition: *.900 silver, .100 copper (net weight .7736 oz. pure silver).*
Diameter: *38.1 mm.* **Edge:** *Reeded.* **Mint:** *West Point.*

This coin recognizes the long history and crucial role of the U.S. Army Infantry. The infantry has accounted for more than half of all the Medals of Honor awarded, despite being just one of many branches of the Army.

Designs. *Obverse:* An infantry soldier advancing and motioning for others to follow. *Reverse:* The infantry insignia of two crossed rifles.

Mintage Data. Authorized by Public Law 110-357, the National Infantry Museum and Soldier Center Commemorative Coin Act, signed by President George W. Bush on October 8, 2008. *Maximum authorized*—350,000. *Number minted*—44,352 Uncirculated and 161,218 Proof.

Original Cost. Sale prices $44.95 (Uncirculated, pre-issue) and $49.95 (Proof, pre-issue); Uncirculated later raised to $49.95, and Proof later raised to $54.95. The surcharge of $10 per coin went to an endowment to support the maintenance of the National Infantry Museum and Solider Center in Columbus, Georgia.

Key to Collecting. Superb gem coins are readily available.

	Distribution	Cert	Avg	%MS	MS-67
					PF-67
2012-W	44,348	1,975	69.8	100%	$45
	Auctions: $69, MS-70, April 2013				
2012-W, Proof	161,151	2,895	69.2		$50
	Auctions: $74, PF-70DCam, April 2013				

STAR-SPANGLED BANNER SILVER DOLLAR (2012)

Designer: *Joel Iskowitz (obverse), William C. Burgard II (reverse).* **Weight:** *26.73 grams.*
Composition: *.900 silver, .100 copper (net weight .7736 oz. pure silver).*
Diameter: *38.1 mm.* **Edge:** *Reeded.* **Mint:** *Philadelphia.*

The 200th anniversary of the War of 1812—particularly the Battle of Baltimore, which is recounted in the U.S. National Anthem—was commemorated with this silver dollar, as well as a five-dollar gold coin issued alongside it.

Designs. *Obverse:* Miss Liberty waving the 15-star version of the U.S. flag with Fort McHenry in the background. *Reverse:* A waving modern U.S. flag.

Mintage Data. Authorized by Public Law 111-232, the Star-Spangled Banner Commemorative Coin Act, signed by President Barack Obama on August 16, 2010. *Maximum authorized*—500,000. *Number minted*—41,686 Uncirculated and 169,065 Proof.

Original Cost. Sale prices $44.95 (Uncirculated, pre-issue) and $49.95 (Proof, pre-issue); Uncirculated later raised to $49.95, and Proof later raised to $54.95. The surcharge of $10 per coin went to the Maryland War of 1812 Bicentennial Commission for the purpose of supporting bicentennial activities, educational outreach activities, and preservation and improvement activities pertaining to the sites and structures relating to the War of 1812.

Key to Collecting. Superb gem coins are readily available.

	Distribution	Cert	Avg	%MS	MS-67
					PF-67
2012-P	41,686	2,028	69.8	100%	$50
Auctions: $100, MS-70, April 2013; $94, MS-70, October 2014					
2012-P, Proof	169,065	3,160	69.4		$50
Auctions: $94, PF-70DCam, April 2013; $153, PF-69DCam, November 2014					

STAR-SPANGLED BANNER $5 GOLD COIN (2012)

Designer: *Donna Weaver (obverse), Richard Masters (reverse).* **Weight:** *8.359 grams.*
Composition: *.900 gold, .100 copper (net weight .242 oz. pure gold).*
Diameter: *21.6 mm.* **Edge:** *Reeded.* **Mint:** *West Point.*

The reverse of this commemorative coin features the first five words of the Star-Spangled Banner in the handwriting of Francis Scott Key, the man who penned it. On September 7, 1814, Key visited the British fleet in the Chesapeake Bay to secure the release of his friend Dr. William Beanes. Key secured Beanes's release, but the two were held by the British during the bombardment of Fort McHenry. It was on the morning of September 14, 1814, that the shelling stopped and Key saw through the smoke the massive American flag, flying above the U.S. fort, that would inspire his song.

Designs. *Obverse:* A naval battle, with a U.S. ship in the foreground and a British vessel in the background. *Reverse:* The words "O say can you see" over an arrangement of 13 stripes and 15 stars, representing the U.S. flag.

Mintage Data. Authorized by Public Law 111-232, the Star-Spangled Banner Commemorative Coin Act, signed by President Barack Obama on August 16, 2010. *Maximum authorized*—100,000. *Number minted*—7,027 Uncirculated and 18,313 Proof.

Original Cost. Sale prices $519.30 (Uncirculated, pre-issue) and $529.30 (Proof, pre-issue); both prices later increased by a base of $5 plus the change in gold market value. The surcharge of $35 per coin went to the Maryland War of 1812 Bicentennial Commission for the purpose of supporting bicentennial activities, educational outreach activities, and preservation and improvement activities pertaining to the sites and structures relating to the War of 1812.

Key to Collecting. Superb gem coins are readily available.

	Distribution	Cert	Avg	%MS	MS-67 PF-67
2012-W	7,027	631	69.9	100%	$500
Auctions: $618, MS-70, September 2013					
2012-W, Proof	18,313	469	69.8		$400
Auctions: $470, PF-70DCam, April 2014					

GIRL SCOUTS OF THE U.S.A. CENTENNIAL SILVER DOLLAR (2013)

Designer: *Barbara Fox (obverse), Chris Costello (reverse).* **Weight:** *26.73 grams.*
Composition: *.900 silver, .100 copper (net weight .7736 oz. pure silver).*
Diameter: *38.1 mm.* **Edge:** *Reeded.* **Mint:** *West Point.*

This commemorative silver dollar was issued as part of the celebration of the Girl Scouts of the United States of America's 100th anniversary of establishment. The Citizens Coinage Advisory Committee was particularly enthusiastic about this beautiful design.

Designs. *Obverse:* Three Girl Scouts of varying ages and ethnicities. The three girls are meant to reflect the organization's diversity. *Reverse:* The iconic Girl Scouts trefoil symbol.

Mintage Data. Authorized by Public Law 111-86, the 2013 Girl Scouts of the USA Centennial Commemorative Coin Program, signed by President Barack Obama on October 29, 2009. *Maximum authorized*—350,000. *Number minted*—31,714 Uncirculated and 86,353 Proof.

Original Cost. Sale prices $50.95 (Uncirculated, pre-issue) and $54.95 (Proof, pre-issue); Uncirculated later raised to $55.95, and Proof later raised to $59.95. The surcharge of $10 per coin went to the Girl Scouts of the United States of America.

Key to Collecting. Superb gem coins are readily available.

	Distribution	Cert	Avg	%MS	MS-67
					PF-67
2013-W	31,714	995	69.9	100%	$45
Auctions: No auction records available.					
2013-W, Proof	86,353	1,760	69.3		$55
Auctions: No auction records available.					

5-STAR GENERALS HALF DOLLAR (2013)

Designer: *Phebe Hemphill.* **Weight:** *11.34 grams.* **Composition:** *.9167 copper, .0833 nickel.*
Diameter: *30.61 mm.* **Edge:** *Reeded.* **Mints:** *Denver (Uncirculated) and San Francisco (Proof).*

The 5-star generals of the U.S. Army—as well as the institution that they each graduated from, the U.S. Army Command and General Staff College—were commemorated with this half dollar, as well as a silver dollar and five-dollar gold coin issued as part of the program.

Designs. *Obverse:* Side-by-side portraits of General Henry "Hap" Arnold and General Omar N. Bradley, 5-star insignia at center.
Reverse: Heraldic crest of Fort Leavenworth, home of the U.S. Army Command and General Staff College.

Mintage Data. Authorized by Public Law 111-262, the 5-Star Generals Commemorative Coin Act, signed by President Barack Obama on October 8, 2010. *Maximum authorized*—750,000. *Number minted*—2013-D: 38,191 Uncirculated; 2013-P: 47,337 Proof.

Original Cost. Sale prices $16.95 (Uncirculated, pre-issue) and $17.95 (Proof, pre-issue); Uncirculated later raised to $20.95, and Proof later raised to $21.95. The surcharge of $5 per coin went to the Command and General Staff College Foundation.

Key to Collecting. Superb gem coins are readily available.

	Distribution	Cert	Avg	%MS	MS-67
					PF-67
2013-D	38,181	1,054	69.0	100%	$40
Auctions: No auction records available.					
2013-S, Proof	47,337	2,270	69.4		$30
Auctions: No auction records available.					

5-STAR GENERALS SILVER DOLLAR (2013)

Designer: *Richard Masters (obverse), Barbara Fox (reverse).* **Weight:** *26.73 grams.*
Composition: *.900 silver, .100 copper (net weight .7736 oz. pure silver).*
Diameter: *38.1 mm.* **Edge:** *Reeded.* **Mints:** *West Point (Uncirculated) and Philadelphia (Proof).*

Each of the 5-star generals was given one appearance across this series of three commemoratives. Note that Dwight Eisenhower, who is featured on this silver dollar along with George C. Marshall, had previously appeared on another commemorative silver dollar that marked the centennial of his birth in 1990.

Designs. *Obverse:* Side-by-side portraits of General George C. Marshall and General Dwight D. Eisenhower against a striped background, 5-star insignia at top center. *Reverse:* The Leavenworth Lamp, a symbol of the Command and General Staff College.

Mintage Data. Authorized by Public Law 111-262, the 5-Star Generals Commemorative Coin Act, signed by President Barack Obama on October 8, 2010. *Maximum authorized*—500,000. *Number minted*—2013-W: 34,639 Uncirculated; 2013-P: 69,290 Proof.

Original Cost. Sale prices $50.95 (Uncirculated, pre-issue) and $54.95 (Proof, pre-issue); Uncirculated later raised to $55.95, and Proof later raised to $59.95. The surcharge of $10 per coin went to the Command and General Staff College Foundation.

Key to Collecting. Superb gem coins are readily available.

	Distribution	Cert	Avg	%MS	MS-67 PF-67
2013-W	34,639	1,650	69.9	100%	$90
Auctions: No auction records available.					
2013-P, Proof	69,290	2,660	69.7		$70
Auctions: No auction records available.					

5-STAR GENERALS $5 GOLD COIN (2013)

Designer: *Ronald D. Sanders (obverse), Barbara Fox (reverse).* **Weight:** *8.359 grams.* **Composition:** *.900 gold, .100 copper (net weight .242 oz. pure gold).* **Diameter:** *21.6 mm.* **Edge:** *Reeded.* **Mints:** *Philadelphia (Uncirculated) and West Point (Proof).*

The Leavenworth Lamp, seen on the reverse of this coin as well as that of the silver dollar in this series, is a symbol of the Command and General Staff College. The institution celebrated its 132nd anniversary in the year these coins were released.

Designs. *Obverse:* A portrait of General Douglas MacArthur and the 5-star insignia to the right. *Reverse:* The Leavenworth Lamp, a symbol of the Command and General Staff College.

Mintage Data. Authorized by Public Law 111-262, the 5-Star Generals Commemorative Coin Act, signed by President Barack Obama on October 8, 2010. *Maximum authorized*—100,000. *Number minted*—2013-P: 5,674 Uncirculated; 2013-W: 15,949 Proof.

Original Cost. Sale prices $480.50 (Uncirculated, pre-issue) and $485.50 (Proof, pre-issue); both prices later increased by a base of $5 plus the change in gold market value. The surcharge of $35 per coin went to the Command and General Staff College Foundation.

Key to Collecting. Superb gem coins are readily available.

	Distribution	Cert	Avg	%MS	MS-67 PF-67
2013-P	5,674	477	69.9	100%	$1,000
Auctions: No auction records available.					
2013-W, Proof	15,949	541	69.8		$500
Auctions: $499, PF-70DCam, September 2014					

NATIONAL BASEBALL HALL OF FAME HALF DOLLAR (2014)

Designer: *Cassie McFarland (obverse), Don Everhart (reverse).* **Weight:** *11.34 grams.*
Composition: *.9167 copper, .0833 nickel.* **Diameter:** *30.61 mm.* **Edge:** *Reeded.*
Mints: *Denver (Uncirculated) and San Francisco (Proof).*

This half dollar and the silver dollar and five-dollar gold coin issued alongside it were the first "curved" coins to be produced by the U.S. Mint—that is, the obverse is concave, and the reverse is convex. The three commemorated the 75th anniversary of the National Baseball Hall of Fame in Cooperstown, New York.

Designs. *Obverse:* A baseball glove, concave.
Reverse: A baseball, convex.

Mintage Data. Authorized by Public Law 112-152, the National Baseball Hall of Fame Commemorative Coin Act, signed by President Barack Obama on August 3, 2012. *Maximum authorized*—750,000. *Number minted*—2014-D: 147,934 Uncirculated; 2014-S: 258,643.

Original Cost. Sale prices $18.95 (Uncirculated, pre-issue) and $19.95 (Proof, pre-issue); Uncirculated later raised to $22.95, and Proof later raised to $23.95. The surcharge of $5 per coin went to the National Baseball Hall of Fame.

Key to Collecting. Superb gem coins are readily available.

	Distribution	Cert	Avg	%MS	MS-67 PF-67
2014-D	147,934	9,778	69.5	100%	$40
Auctions: No auction records available.					
2014-S, Proof	258,643	33,957	69.6		$30
Auctions: No auction records available.					

NATIONAL BASEBALL HALL OF FAME SILVER DOLLAR (2014)

Designer: *Cassie McFarland (obverse), Don Everhart (reverse).* **Weight:** *26.73 grams.*
Composition: *.900 silver, .100 copper (net weight .7736 oz. pure silver).*
Diameter: *38.1 mm.* **Edge:** *Reeded.* **Mint:** *Philadelphia.*

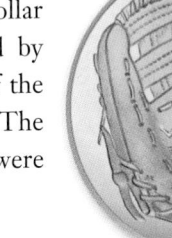 

Coins shaped like this silver dollar (as well as the corresponding half dollar and five-dollar gold coin) had previously been minted by Monnaie de Paris in commemoration of the 2009 International Year of Astronomy. The National Baseball Hall of Fame coins were the first curved issues for the U.S. Mint.

Designs. *Obverse:* A baseball glove, concave.
Reverse: A baseball, convex.

Mintage Data. Authorized by Public Law 112-152, the National Baseball Hall of Fame Commemorative Coin Act, signed by President Barack Obama on August 3, 2012. *Maximum authorized*—400,000. *Number minted*—137,909 Uncirculated and 268,076 Proof.

Original Cost. Sale prices $47.95 (Uncirculated, pre-issue) and $51.95 (Proof, pre-issue); Uncirculated later raised to $52.95, and Proof later raised to $56.95. The surcharge of $10 per coin went to the National Baseball Hall of Fame.

Key to Collecting. Superb gem coins are readily available.

	Distribution	Cert	Avg	%MS	MS-67
					PF-67
2014-P	137,909	17,411	69.7	100%	$75
Auctions: No auction records available.					
2014-P, Proof	268,076	4,201	69.9		$75
Auctions: No auction records available.					

NATIONAL BASEBALL HALL OF FAME $5 GOLD COIN (2014)

Designer: *Cassie McFarland (obverse), Don Everhart (reverse).* **Weight:** *8.359 grams.*
Composition: *.900 gold, .100 copper (net weight .242 oz. pure gold).*
Diameter: *21.6 mm.* **Edge:** *Reeded.* **Mint:** *West Point.*

The common obverse design for these coins was selected through a national competition, and the Department of the Treasury chose California artist Cassie McFarland's submission after input from the National Baseball Hall of Fame, the U.S. Commission of Fine Arts, and the Citizens Coinage Advisory Committee.

Designs. *Obverse:* A baseball glove, concave.
Reverse: A baseball, convex.

Mintage Data. Authorized by Public Law 112-152, the National Baseball Hall of Fame Commemorative Coin Act, signed by President Barack Obama on August 3, 2012. *Maximum authorized*—50,000. *Number minted*—18,000 Uncirculated and 32,495 Proof.

Original Cost. Sale prices $431.90 (Uncirculated, pre-issue) and $436.90 (Proof, pre-issue); Uncirculated later raised to $436.90, and Proof later raised to $441.90. The surcharge of $35 per coin went to the National Baseball Hall of Fame.

Key to Collecting. Superb gem coins are readily available.

	Distribution	Cert	Avg	%MS	MS-67
					PF-67
2014-W	18,000	2,282	69.9	100%	$850
Auctions: No auction records available.					
2014-W, Proof	32,495	4,253	69.9		$800
Auctions: No auction records available.					

CIVIL RIGHTS ACT OF 1964 SILVER DOLLAR (2014)

Designer: *Justin Kunz (obverse), Donna Weaver (reverse).* **Weight:** *26.73 grams.*
Composition: *.900 silver, .100 copper (net weight .7736 oz. pure silver).*
Diameter: *38.1 mm.* **Edge:** *Reeded.* **Mint:** *Philadelphia.*

This silver dollar commemorated the 50th anniversary of the Civil Rights Act of 1964, which greatly expanded American civil rights protections; outlawed racial segregation in public places and places of public accommodation; and funded federal programs.

Designs. *Obverse:* Three people holding hands at a Civil Rights march; man on left holding sign that reads WE SHALL OVERCOME. *Reverse:* Three intertwined flames representing freedom of education, freedom to vote, and freedom to control one's own destiny. Inspired by a quote by Dr. Martin Luther King Jr.

Mintage Data. Authorized by Public Law 110-451, the Civil Rights Act of 1964 Commemorative Coin Act, signed by President George W. Bush on December 2, 2008. *Maximum authorized*—350,000. *Number minted*—24,720 Uncirculated and 61,992 Proof.

Original Cost. Sale prices $44.95 (Uncirculated, pre-issue) and $49.95 (Proof, pre-issue); Uncirculated later raised to $49.95, and Proof later raised to $54.95. The surcharge of $10 per coin went to the United Negro College Fund, which has provided scholarships and internships for minority students for the past 70 years.

Key to Collecting. Superb gem coins are readily available.

	Distribution	Cert	Avg	%MS	MS-67
					PF-67
2014-P	24,720	817	69.6	100%	$80
	Auctions: No auction records available.				
2014-P, Proof	61,992	910	69.5		$70
	Auctions: No auction records available.				

U.S. MARSHALS SERVICE 225TH ANNIVERSARY HALF DOLLAR (2015)

Designer: *Joel Iskowitz (obverse), Susan Gamble (reverse).* **Weight:** *11.34 grams.*
Composition: *.9167 copper, .0833 nickel.* **Diameter:** *30.61 mm.*
Edge: *Reeded.* **Mints:** *Denver (Uncirculated) and San Francisco (Proof).*

The 225th anniversary of the establishment of the U.S. Marshals Service was commemorated with the release of a series including this half dollar as well as a silver dollar and five-dollar gold coin. The actual anniversary—September 24, 2014—was marked with a celebration in Washington, D.C., and the issuance of 35 special preview sets to employees of the Service.

Designs. *Obverse:* An Old West marshal and his horse at left, and a modern marshal in tactical gear at right. *Reverse:* Lady Justice holding scales and the U.S. Marshals Service star and standing over a copy of the Constitution, a stack of books, handcuffs, and a whiskey jug, each representing areas of responsibility of the Service in the past or present.

Mintage Data. Authorized by Public Law 112-104, the United States Marshals Service 225th Anniversary Commemorative Coin Act, signed into law by President Barack Obama on April 2, 2012. *Maximum authorized*—750,000. *Number minted*—2015-D: 29,400 Uncirculated; 2015-S: 60,763 Proof (as of press time).

Original Cost. Sale prices $13.95 (Uncirculated, pre-issue) and $14.95 (Proof, pre-issue); Uncirculated later raised to $17.95, and Proof later raised to $18.95. The surcharge of $3 per coin went to the U.S. Marshals Museum.

Key to Collecting. Superb gem coins are readily available.

	Distribution	Cert	Avg	%MS	MS-67 PF-67
2015-D	29,400	0	n/a		$20
	Auctions: No auction records available.				
2015-S, Proof	60,763	0	n/a		$20
	Auctions: No auction records available.				

U.S. MARSHALS SERVICE 225TH ANNIVERSARY SILVER DOLLAR (2015)

Designer: *Richard Masters (obverse), Frank Morris (reverse).* **Weight:** *26.73 grams.*
Composition: *.900 silver, .100 copper (net weight .7736 oz. pure silver).*
Diameter: *38.1 mm.* **Edge:** *Reeded.* **Mint:** *Philadelphia.*

The first federal law-enforcement officers of the United States, the U.S. Marshals were created under section 27 of the Act of Congress entitled "Chapter XX—An Act to Establish the Judicial Courts of the United States." The original 13 men to serve were confirmed on September 26, 1789.

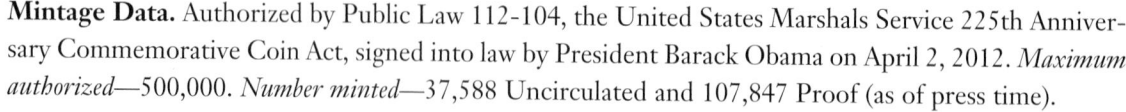

Designs. *Obverse:* U.S. marshals riding on horseback under the U.S. Marshals Service star. *Reverse:* A U.S. marshal of the frontier era holding a "wanted" poster.

Mintage Data. Authorized by Public Law 112-104, the United States Marshals Service 225th Anniversary Commemorative Coin Act, signed into law by President Barack Obama on April 2, 2012. *Maximum authorized*—500,000. *Number minted*—37,588 Uncirculated and 107,847 Proof (as of press time).

Original Cost. Sale prices $43.95 (Uncirculated, pre-issue) and $46.95 (Proof, pre-issue): Uncirculated later raised to $48.95, and Proof later raised to $51.95. The surcharge of $10 went to the U.S. Marshals Museum.

Key to Collecting. Superb gem coins are readily available.

	Distribution	Cert	Avg	%MS	MS-67 PF-67
2015-P	37,588	0	n/a		$50
	Auctions: No auction records available.				
2015-P, Proof	107,847	0	n/a		$50
	Auctions: No auction records available.				

U.S. Marshals Service 225th Anniversary $5 Gold Coin (2015)

Designer: *Donna Weaver (obverse), Paul C. Balan (reverse).* **Weight:** *8.359 grams.*
Composition: *.900 gold, .100 copper (net weight .242 oz. pure gold).*
Diameter: *21.6 mm.* **Edge:** *Reeded.* **Mint:** *West Point.*

The U.S. Marshals officially became the U.S. Marshals Service in 1969 by order of the Department of Justice. The Service achieved Bureau status in 1974 and today is the primary agency for fugitive operations, as well as protection of officers of the court and court buildings.

Designs. *Obverse:* The U.S. Marshals Service star superimposed on a mountain range. *Reverse:* An eagle, shield on chest, holding a banner and draped flag.

Mintage Data. Authorized by Public Law 112-104, the United States Marshals Service 225th Anniversary Commemorative Coin Act, signed into law by President Barack Obama on April 2, 2012. *Maximum authorized*—100,000. *Number minted*—6,592 Uncirculated and 9,671 Proof (as of press time)

Original Cost. Sale prices $395.45 (Uncirculated, pre-issue) and $400.45 (Proof, pre-issue): Uncirculated later raised to $400.45, and Proof later raised to $405.45. The surcharge of $35 per coin went to the U.S. Marshals Museum.

Key to Collecting. Superb gem coins are readily available.

	Distribution	Cert	Avg	%MS	MS-67
					PF-67
2015-W	6,592	0	n/a		$400
	Auctions: No auction records available.				
2015-W, Proof	9,671	0	n/a		$400
	Auctions: No auction records available.				

March of Dimes 75th Anniversary Silver Dollar (2015)

Designer: *Paul C. Balan (obverse), Don Everhart (reverse).* **Weight:** *26.73 grams.*
Composition: *.900 silver, .100 copper (net weight .7736 oz. pure silver).*
Diameter: *38.1 mm.* **Edge:** *Reeded.* **Mints:** *Philadelphia (Uncirculated) and West Point (Proof).*

Inspired by his own struggle with polio, President Franklin Delano Roosevelt created the National Foundation for Infantile Paralysis, now known as the March of Dimes, on January 3, 1938. This coin celebrated the organization's 75th anniversary (despite coming out after the actual date of said event) and recognized its accomplishments, which included the funding of research which resulted in Dr. Jonas Salk and Dr. Albert Sabin's polio vaccines.

Designs. *Obverse:* A profile view of President Franklin Delano Roosevelt and Dr. Jonas Salk. *Reverse:* A sleeping baby cradled in its parent's hand.

Mintage Data. Authorized by Public Law 112-209, the March of Dimes Commemorative Coin Act of 2012, signed into law by President Barack Obama on December 18, 2012. *Maximum authorized*—500,000. *Number minted*—2015-D: 24,387 Uncirculated; 2015-W: 56,718 Proof (as of press time)

Original Cost. Sale prices $43.95 (Uncirculated, pre-issue) and $46.95 (Proof, pre-issue): Uncirculated later raised to $48.95, and Proof later raised to $51.95. The surcharge of $10 per coin went to the March of Dimes to help finance research, education, and services aimed at improving the health of women, infants, and children.

Key to Collecting. Superb gem coins are readily available.

	Distribution	Cert	Avg	%MS	MS-67 PF-67
2015-P	24,387	0	n/a		$50
	Auctions: No auction records available.				
2015-W, Proof	56,718	0	n/a		$50
	Auctions: No auction records available.				

MARK TWAIN SILVER DOLLAR (2016)

Designer: *Chris Costello (obverse), Patricia Lucas-Morris (reverse).* **Weight:** *26.73 grams.* **Composition:** *.900 silver, .100 copper (net weight .7736 oz. pure silver).* **Diameter:** *38.1 mm.* **Edge:** *Reeded.* **Mint:** *Philadelphia.*

Samuel Langhorne Clemens—better known by his pen name, Mark Twain—is among the most celebrated authors in U.S. history. His *Adventures of Huckleberry Finn*, originally published in 1885, is often referred to as "The Great American Novel."

Designs. *Obverse:* A portrait of Mark Twain holding a pipe, with the smoke forming a silhouette of Huck Finn and Jim on their raft. *Reverse:* Depictions of several characters from Mark Twain's works, including the knight and horse from *A Connecticut Yankee in King Arthur's Court*, the frog from *The Celebrated Jumping Frog of Calaveras County*, and Huck and Jim from *Adventures of Huckleberry Finn*.

Mintage Data. Authorized by Public Law 112-201, the Mark Twain Commemorative Coin Act, signed into law by President Barack Obama on December 4, 2012. *Maximum authorized*—350,000. *Number minted*—To be determined.

Original Cost. Sale prices $44.95 (Uncirculated, pre-issue) and $45.95 (Proof, pre-issue). Uncirculated later raised to $49.95, and Proof later raised to $50.95. The surcharge of $10 per coin is to be distributed evenly between the Mark Twain House & Museum in Hartford, Conn.; the University of California, Berkeley, for the benefit of the Mark Twain Project at the Bancroft Library; Elmira College in New York; and the Mark Twain Boyhood Home and Museum in Hannibal, Missouri.

Key to Collecting. Superb gem coins are readily available.

	Distribution	Cert	Avg	%MS	MS-67 PF-67
2016-P	0	n/a			$45
	Auctions: No auction records available.				
2016-P, Proof	0	n/a			$45
	Auctions: No auction records available.				

Mark Twain $5 Gold Coin (2016)

Designer: *Benjamin Sowers (obverse), Ronald D. Sanders (reverse).* **Weight:** *8.359 grams.*
Composition: *.900 gold, .100 copper (net weight .242 oz. pure gold).*
Diameter: *21.6 mm.* **Edge:** *Reeded.* **Mint:** *West Point.*

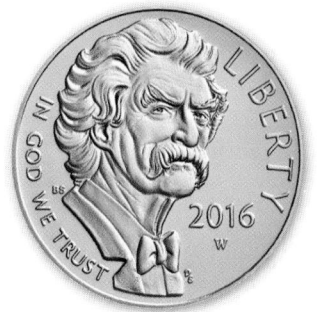 

The designs for the Mark Twain commemorative coins were unveiled two days before the 180th anniversary of his birth, November 30, 2015. Interestingly, Twain was born shortly after a visit by Halley's Comet, and he later predicted that he would "go out with it," too. He passed away two days after the comet returned.

Designs. *Obverse:* A portrait of Mark Twain.
Reverse: A steamboat on the Mississippi River.

Mintage Data. Authorized by Public Law 112-201, the Mark Twain Commemorative Coin Act, signed into law by President Barack Obama on December 4, 2012. *Maximum authorized*—100,000. *Number minted*—To be determined.

Original Cost. Sale prices $359 (Uncirculated, pre-issue) and $364 (Proof, pre-issue). Uncirculated later raised to $364, and Proof later raised to $369. The surcharge of $35 per coin is to be distributed evenly between the Mark Twain House & Museum in Hartford, Conn.; the University of California, Berkeley, for the benefit of the Mark Twain Project at the Bancroft Library; Elmira College in New York; and the Mark Twain Boyhood Home and Museum in Hannibal, Missouri.

Key to Collecting. Superb gem coins are readily available.

	Distribution	Cert	Avg	%MS	MS-67 PF-67
2016-W		0	n/a		$376
	Auctions: No auction records available.				
2016-W, Proof		0	n/a		$370
	Auctions: No auction records available.				

NATIONAL PARK SERVICE 100TH ANNIVERSARY HALF DOLLAR (2016)

Designer: *Barbara Fox (obverse), Thomas Hipschen (reverse).* **Weight:** *11.34 grams.*
Composition: *.9167 copper, .0833 nickel.* **Diameter:** *30.61 mm.*
Edge: *Reeded.* **Mints:** *Denver (Uncirculated) and San Francisco (Proof).*

The National Parks Service was created through the National Park Service Organic Act, signed into law by President Woodrow Wilson on August 25, 1916. Today the agency employs approximately 20,000 people and operates on a budget of nearly $3 billion.

Designs. *Obverse:* A hiker taking in a mountain landscape above a child observing a frog. *Reverse:* The National Parks service logo.

Mintage Data. Authorized by Public Law 113-291, signed into law by President Barack Obama on December 19, 2014. *Maximum authorized*—750,000. *Number minted*—To be determined.

Original Cost. Sale prices $20.95 (Uncirculated, pre-issue) and $21.95 (Proof, pre-issue). Uncirculated later raised to $24.95, and Proof later raised to $25.95. The surcharge of $5 per coin is assigned to the National Parks Foundation.

Key to Collecting. Superb gem coins are readily available.

	Distribution	Cert	Avg	%MS	MS-67 PF-67
2016-D		0	n/a		$21
	Auctions: No auction records available.				
2016-S, Proof		0	n/a		$22
	Auctions: No auction records available.				

NATIONAL PARK SERVICE 100TH ANNIVERSARY SILVER DOLLAR (2016)

Designer: *Joseph Menna (obverse), Chris Costello (reverse).* **Weight:** *26.73 grams.*
Composition: *.900 silver, .100 copper (net weight .7736 oz. pure silver).*
Diameter: *38.1 mm.* **Edge:** *Reeded.* **Mint:** *Philadelphia.*

The United States' National Parks range from Alaska's Gates of the Arctic National Park—an expanse of pristine wilderness devoid of any actual park facilities—to American Samoa National Park, which features coral reefs, rainforests, and volcanic mountains.

Designs. *Obverse:* Yellowstone National Park's Old Faithful geyser with a bison in the foreground. *Reverse:* A Latina Folklórico dancer and the National Parks Service logo.

Mintage Data. Authorized by Public Law 113-291, signed into law by President Barack Obama on December 19, 2014. *Maximum authorized*—500,000. *Number minted*—To be determined.

Original Cost. Sale prices $44.95 (Uncirculated, pre-issue) and $45.95 (Proof, pre-issue). Uncirculated later raised to $49.95, and Proof later raised to $50.95. The surcharge of $10 per coin is assigned to the National Parks Foundation.

Key to Collecting. Superb gem coins are readily available.

	Distribution	Cert	Avg	%MS	MS-67 PF-67
2016-P		0	n/a		$50
Auctions: No auction records available.					
2016-P, Proof		0	n/a		$51
Auctions: No auction records available.					

NATIONAL PARK SERVICE 100TH ANNIVERSARY $5 GOLD COIN (2016)

Designer: *Don Everhart.* **Weight:** *8.359 grams.* **Composition:** *.900 gold, .100 copper (net weight .242 oz. pure gold).* **Diameter:** *21.6 mm.* **Edge:** *Reeded.* **Mint:** *West Point.*

The National Parks Service acts as the steward of 409 official "units," which includes the 59 National Parks as well as the country's National Monuments, National Preserves, National Historic Sites, and more.

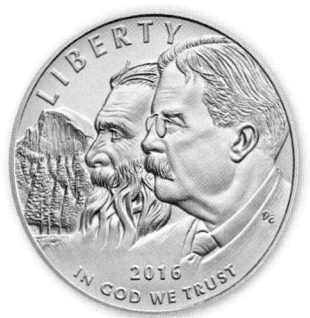 

Designs. *Obverse:* Profiles of John Muir and Theodore Roosevelt with Yosemite National Park's Half Dome in the background. *Reverse:* The National Parks Service logo.

Mintage Data. Authorized by Public Law 113-291, signed into law by President Barack Obama on December 19, 2014. *Maximum authorized*—100,000. *Number minted*—To be determined.

Original Cost. Sale prices to be determined. The surcharge of $35 per coin is assigned to the National Parks Foundation.

Key to Collecting. Superb gem coins are readily available.

	Distribution	Cert	Avg	%MS	MS-67 PF-67
2016-W		0	n/a		$375
Auctions: No auction records available.					
2016-W, Proof		0	n/a		$370
Auctions: No auction records available.					

GOVERNMENT COMMEMORATIVE SETS

	Value
(1983–1984) LOS ANGELES OLYMPIAD	
1983 and 1984 Proof silver dollars	$65
1983 and 1984 6-coin set. One each of 1983 and 1984 silver dollars, both Proof and Uncirculated gold $10 (a)	$1,550
1983 3-piece collector set. 1983 P, D, and S Uncirculated silver dollars	$90
1984 3-piece collector set. 1984 P, D, and S Uncirculated silver dollars	$90
1983 and 1984 gold and silver Uncirculated set. One each of 1983 and 1984 Uncirculated silver dollars and one 1984 Uncirculated gold $10	$800
1983 and 1984 gold and silver Proof set. One each of 1983 and 1984 Proof silver dollars and one 1984 Proof gold $10	$800

a. Packaged in cherrywood box.

	Value
(1986) STATUE OF LIBERTY	
2-coin set. Proof silver dollar and clad half dollar	$25
3-coin set. Proof silver dollar, clad half dollar, and gold $5	$400
2-coin set. Uncirculated silver dollar and clad half dollar	$35
2-coin set. Uncirculated and Proof gold $5	$750
3-coin set. Uncirculated silver dollar, clad half dollar, and gold $5	$400
6-coin set. One each of Proof and Uncirculated half dollar, silver dollar, and gold $5 (a)	$800
(1987) CONSTITUTION	
2-coin set. Uncirculated silver dollar and gold $5	$425
2-coin set. Proof silver dollar and gold $5	$450
4-coin set. One each of Proof and Uncirculated silver dollar and gold $5 (a)	$800
(1988) SEOUL OLYMPIAD	
2-coin set. Uncirculated silver dollar and gold $5	$400
2-coin set. Proof silver dollar and gold $5	$450
4-coin set. One each of Proof and Uncirculated silver dollar and gold $5 (a)	$800
(1989) CONGRESS	
2-coin set. Proof clad half dollar and silver dollar	$35
3-coin set. Proof clad half dollar, silver dollar, and gold $5	$400
2-coin set. Uncirculated clad half dollar and silver dollar	$35
3-coin set. Uncirculated clad half dollar, silver dollar, and gold $5	$400
6-coin set. One each of Proof and Uncirculated clad half dollar, silver dollar, and gold $5 (a)	$850
(1991) MOUNT RUSHMORE	
2-coin set. Uncirculated clad half dollar and silver dollar	$50
2-coin set. Proof clad half dollar and silver dollar	$45
3-coin set. Uncirculated clad half dollar, silver dollar, and gold $5	$425
3-coin set. Proof half dollar, silver dollar, and gold $5	$400
6-coin set. One each of Proof and Uncirculated clad half dollar, silver dollar, and gold $5 (a)	$900
(1992) XXV OLYMPIAD	
2-coin set. Uncirculated clad half dollar and silver dollar	$50
2-coin set. Proof clad half dollar and silver dollar	$40
3-coin set. Uncirculated clad half dollar, silver dollar, and gold $5	$425
3-coin set. Proof half dollar, silver dollar, and gold $5	$400
6-coin set. One each of Proof and Uncirculated clad half dollar, silver dollar, and gold $5 (a)	$900
(1992) CHRISTOPHER COLUMBUS	
2-coin set. Uncirculated clad half dollar and silver dollar	$50
2-coin set. Proof clad half dollar and silver dollar	$45
3-coin set. Uncirculated clad half dollar, silver dollar, and gold $5	$425
3-coin set. Proof half dollar, silver dollar, and gold $5	$400
6-coin set. One each of Proof and Uncirculated clad half dollar, silver dollar, and gold $5 (a)	$900
(1993) BILL OF RIGHTS	
2-coin set. Uncirculated silver half dollar and silver dollar	$60
2-coin set. Proof silver half dollar and silver dollar	$50
3-coin set. Uncirculated silver half dollar, silver dollar, and gold $5	$450
3-coin set. Proof half dollar, silver dollar, and gold $5	$400
6-coin set. One each of Proof and Uncirculated silver half dollar, silver dollar, and gold $5 (a)	$900
"Young Collector" set. Silver half dollar	$35
Educational set. Silver half dollar and James Madison medal	$35
Proof silver half dollar and 25-cent stamp	$20

a. Packaged in cherrywood box.

	Value
(1993) WORLD WAR II	
2-coin set. Uncirculated clad half dollar and silver dollar	$60
2-coin set. Proof clad half dollar and silver dollar	$45
3-coin set. Uncirculated clad half dollar, silver dollar, and gold $5	$425
3-coin set. Proof clad half dollar, silver dollar, and gold $5	$400
6-coin set. One each of Proof and Uncirculated clad half dollar, silver dollar, and gold $5 (a)	$900
"Young Collector" set. Clad half dollar	$30
Victory Medal set. Uncirculated clad half dollar and reproduction medal	$40
(1993) THOMAS JEFFERSON	
3-piece set (issued in 1994). Silver dollar, Jefferson nickel, and $2 note	$110
(1994) WORLD CUP SOCCER	
2-coin set. Uncirculated clad half dollar and silver dollar	$50
2-coin set. Proof clad half dollar and silver dollar	$45
3-coin set. Uncirculated clad half dollar, silver dollar, and gold $5	$425
3-coin set. Proof clad half dollar, silver dollar, and gold $5	$400
6-coin set. One each of Proof and Uncirculated clad half dollar, silver dollar, and gold $5 (a)	$900
"Young Collector" set. Uncirculated clad half dollar	$20
"Special Edition" set. Proof clad half dollar and silver dollar	$50
(1994) U.S. VETERANS	
3-coin set. Uncirculated POW, Vietnam, and Women in Military Service silver dollars	$200
3-coin set. Proof POW, Vietnam, and Women in Military Service silver dollars	$150
(1995) SPECIAL OLYMPICS	
2-coin set. Proof Special Olympics silver dollar, 1995-S Kennedy half dollar	$150
(1995) CIVIL WAR BATTLEFIELD PRESERVATION	
2-coin set. Uncirculated clad half dollar and silver dollar	$100
2-coin set. Proof clad half dollar and silver dollar	$90
3-coin set. Uncirculated clad half dollar, silver dollar, and gold $5	$650
3-coin set. Proof clad half dollar, silver dollar, and gold $5	$500
6-coin set. One each of Proof and Uncirculated clad half dollar, silver dollar, and gold $5 (a)	$1,150
"Young Collector" set. Uncirculated clad half dollar	$50
2-coin "Union" set. Clad half dollar and silver dollar	$125
3-coin "Union" set. Clad half dollar, silver dollar, and gold $5	$550
(1995–1996) CENTENNIAL OLYMPIC GAMES	
4-coin set #1. Uncirculated clad half dollar (Basketball), silver dollars (Gymnastics, Paralympics), gold $5 (Torch Bearer)	$800
4-coin set #2. Proof clad half dollar (Basketball), silver dollars (Gymnastics, Paralympics), gold $5 (Torch Bearer)	$600
2-coin set #1: Proof silver dollars (Gymnastics, Paralympics)	$80
"Young Collector" set. Uncirculated Basketball clad half dollar	$35
"Young Collector" set. Uncirculated Baseball clad half dollar	$35
"Young Collector" set. Uncirculated Swimming clad half dollar	$200
"Young Collector" set. Uncirculated Soccer clad half dollar	$175
1995–1996 16-coin Uncirculated set. One each of all Uncirculated coins (a)	$7,500
1995–1996 16-coin Proof set. One each of all Proof coins (a)	$1,800
1995–1996 8-coin Proof silver dollars set	$400
1995–1996 32-coin set. One each of all Uncirculated and Proof coins (a)	$7,000
(1996) NATIONAL COMMUNITY SERVICE	
Proof silver dollar and Saint-Gaudens stamp	$100
(1996) SMITHSONIAN INSTITUTION 150TH ANNIVERSARY	
2-coin set. Proof silver dollar and gold $5	$400
4-coin set. One each of Proof and Uncirculated silver dollar and gold $5 (a)	$950
"Young Collector" set. Proof silver dollar	$100

a. Packaged in cherrywood box.

	Value
(1997) U.S. BOTANIC GARDEN	
"Coinage and Currency" set. Uncirculated silver dollar, Jefferson nickel, and $1 note	$250
(1997) JACKIE ROBINSON	
2-coin set. Proof silver dollar and gold $5	$600
4-coin set. One each of Proof and Uncirculated silver dollar and gold $5 (a)	$2,000
3-piece "Legacy" set. Baseball card, pin, and gold $5 (a)	$750
(1997) FRANKLIN D. ROOSEVELT	
2-coin set. One each of Proof and Uncirculated gold $5	$900
(1997) NATIONAL LAW ENFORCEMENT OFFICERS MEMORIAL	
Insignia set. Silver dollar, lapel pin, and patch	$200
(1998) ROBERT F. KENNEDY	
2-coin set. RFK silver dollar and JFK silver half dollar	$200
2-coin set. Proof and Uncirculated RFK silver dollars	$110
(1998) BLACK REVOLUTIONARY WAR PATRIOTS	
2-coin set. Proof and Uncirculated silver dollars	$150
"Young Collector" set. Uncirculated silver dollar	$150
Black Revolutionary War Patriots set. Silver dollar and four stamps	$150
(1999) DOLLEY MADISON	
2-coin set. Proof and Uncirculated silver dollars	$75
(1999) GEORGE WASHINGTON DEATH	
2-coin set. One each of Proof and Uncirculated gold $5	$800
(1999) YELLOWSTONE NATIONAL PARK	
2-coin set. One each of Proof and Uncirculated silver dollars	$100
(2000) LEIF ERICSON MILENNIUM	
2-coin set. Proof silver dollar and Icelandic 1,000 kronur	$100
(2000) MILENNIUM COIN AND CURRENCY SET	
3-piece set. Uncirculated 2000 Sacagawea dollar; Uncirculated 2000 Silver Eagle; George Washington $1 note, series 1999	$100
(2001) AMERICAN BUFFALO	
2-coin set. One each of Proof and Uncirculated silver dollars	$350
"Coinage and Currency" set. Uncirculated American Buffalo silver dollar, face reprint of 1899 $5 Indian Chief Silver Certificate, 1987 Chief Red Cloud 10¢ stamp, 2001 Bison 21¢ stamp	$200
(2001) U.S. CAPITOL VISITOR CENTER	
3-coin set. Proof clad half dollar, silver dollar, and gold $5	$400
(2002) SALT LAKE OLYMPIC GAMES	
2-coin set. Proof silver dollar and gold $5	$400
4-coin set. One each of Proof and Uncirculated silver dollar and gold $5	$900
(2003) FIRST FLIGHT CENTENNIAL	
3-coin set. Proof clad half dollar, silver dollar, and gold $10	$1,125
(2003) LEGACIES OF FREEDOM	
Uncirculated 2003 $1 American Eagle silver bullion coin and an Uncirculated 2002 £2 Silver Britannia coin	$75
(2004) THOMAS A. EDISON	
Edison set. Uncirculated silver dollar and light bulb	$75
(2004) LEWIS AND CLARK	
Coin and Pouch set. Proof silver dollar and beaded pouch	$200
"Coinage and Currency" set. Uncirculated silver dollar, Sacagawea golden dollar, two 2005 nickels, replica 1901 $10 Bison note, silver-plated Peace Medal replica, three stamps, two booklets	$100
(2004) WESTWARD JOURNEY NICKEL SERIES	
Westward Journey Nickel Series™ Coin and Medal set. Proof Sacagawea golden dollar, two 2004 Proof nickels, silver-plated Peace Medal replica	$60
(2005) WESTWARD JOURNEY NICKEL SERIES	
Westward Journey Nickel Series™ Coin and Medal set. Proof Sacagawea golden dollar, two 2005 Proof nickels, silver-plated Peace Medal replica	$40

a. Packaged in cherrywood box.

	Value
(2005) CHIEF JUSTICE JOHN MARSHALL	
"Coin and Chronicles" set. Uncirculated silver dollar, booklet, BEP intaglio portrait	$65
(2005) AMERICAN LEGACY	
American Legacy Collection. Proof Marine Corps silver dollar, Proof John Marshall silver dollar, 11-piece Proof set	$100
(2005) MARINE CORPS 230TH ANNIVERSARY	
Marine Corps Uncirculated silver dollar and stamp set	$100
(2006) BENJAMIN FRANKLIN	
"Coin and Chronicles" set. Uncirculated "Scientist" silver dollar, four stamps, *Poor Richard's Almanack* replica, intaglio print	$75
(2006) AMERICAN LEGACY	
American Legacy Collection. Proof 2006-P Benjamin Franklin, Founding Father silver dollar; Proof 2006-S San Francisco Old Mint silver dollar; Proof cent, nickel, dime, quarter, half dollar, and dollar	$90
(2007) AMERICAN LEGACY	
American Legacy Collection. 16 Proof coins for 2007: five state quarters; four Presidential dollars; Jamestown and Little Rock Central High School Desegregation silver dollars; Proof cent, nickel, dime, half dollar, and dollar	$140
(2007) LITTLE ROCK CENTRAL HIGH SCHOOL DESEGREGATION	
Little Rock Coin and Medal set. Uncirculated 2007-P silver dollar, bronze medal	$175
(2008) BALD EAGLE	
3-piece set. Proof clad half dollar, silver dollar, and gold $5	$400
Bald Eagle Coin and Medal Set. Uncirculated silver dollar, bronze medal	$70
"Young Collector" set. Uncirculated clad half dollar	$18
(2008) AMERICAN LEGACY	
American Legacy Collection. 15 Proof coins for 2008: cent, nickel, dime, half dollar, and dollar; five state quarters; four Presidential dollars; Bald Eagle silver dollar	$150
(2009) LOUIS BRAILLE	
Uncirculated silver dollar in tri-folded package	$50
(2009) ABRAHAM LINCOLN COIN AND CHRONICLES	
Four Proof 2009-S cents and Abraham Lincoln Proof silver dollar	$150
(2012) STAR-SPANGLED BANNER	
2-coin set. Proof silver dollar and gold $5	$450
(2013) 5-STAR GENERALS	
3-coin set. Proof clad half dollar, silver dollar, and gold $5	$600
Profile Collection. Uncirculated half dollar and silver dollar, replica of 1962 General MacArthur Congressional gold medal	$80
(2013) THEODORE ROOSEVELT COIN AND CHRONICLES	
Theodore Roosevelt Proof Presidential dollar, silver Presidential medal, National Wildlife Refuge System Centennial bronze medal, and Roosevelt print	$60
(2013) GIRL SCOUTS OF THE U.S.A.	
"Young Collector" set. Uncirculated silver dollar	$60
(2014) NATIONAL BASEBALL HALL OF FAME	
"Young Collector" set. Uncirculated silver dollar	
(2015) MARCH OF DIMES SPECIAL SILVER SET	
Proof dime and March of Dimes silver dollar, Reverse Proof dime	
(2015) HARRY S TRUMAN COIN AND CHRONICLES	
Harry S. Truman Reverse Proof Presidential dollar, silver Presidential medal, one stamp, information booklet	
(2015) DWIGHT D. EISENHOWER COIN AND CHRONICLES	
Dwight D. Eisenhower Reverse Proof Presidential dollar, silver Presidential medal, one stamp, information booklet	
(2015) JOHN F. KENNEDY COIN AND CHRONICLES	
John F. Kennedy Reverse Proof Presidential dollar, silver Presidential medal, one stamp, information booklet	
(2015) LYNDON B. JOHNSON COIN AND CHRONICLES	
Lyndon B. Johnson Reverse Proof Presidential dollar, silver Presidential medal, one stamp, information booklet	
(2016) NATIONAL PARK SERVICE 100TH ANNIVERSARY	
3-piece set. Proof clad half dollar, silver dollar, and gold $5	

Proof and Mint Sets
1936 to Date

AN OVERVIEW OF PROOF AND MINT SETS

PROOF COINS AND SETS

A Proof is a specimen coin struck for presentation, souvenir, exhibition, or numismatic purposes. Before 1968, Proofs were made only at the Philadelphia Mint, except in a few rare instances in which presentation pieces were struck at branch mints. Today Proofs are made at the San Francisco and West Point mints.

The term *Proof* refers not to the condition of a coin, but to its method of manufacture. Regular-production coins (struck for circulation) in Mint State have coruscating, frosty luster; soft details; and minor imperfections. A Proof coin can usually be distinguished by its sharpness of detail, high wire edge, and extremely brilliant, mirrorlike surface. All Proofs are originally sold by the Mint at a premium.

Very few Proof coins were made prior to 1856. Because of their rarity and infrequent sales, they are not all listed in the regular edition of the *Guide Book of United States Coins*. However, here, in the *Deluxe Edition*, you will find them listed individually within their respective denominations.

Frosted Proofs were issued prior to 1936 and starting again in the late 1970s. These have a brilliant, mirrorlike field with contrasting dull or frosted design.

Matte Proofs have a granular, "sandblast" surface instead of the mirror finish. Matte Proof cents, nickels, and gold coins were issued from 1908 to 1916; a few 1921 and 1922 silver dollars and a 1998-S half dollar were also struck in this manner.

Brilliant Proofs have been issued from 1936 to date. These have a uniformly brilliant, mirrorlike surface and sharp, high-relief details.

Reverse Proofs were first struck for bullion coins in 2006, and regularly denominated, silver-struck coins have also been made with this finish since 2014. As their name implies, the devices, not the field, have a brilliant, mirrorlike finish, while the field has a matte finish.

"Prooflike" coins are occasionally seen. These are examples struck from dies that were lightly polished, often inadvertently during the removal of lines, contact marks, and other marks in the fields. In other instances, such as with certain New Orleans gold coins of the 1850s, the dies were polished in the machine shop of the mint. They are not true Proofs, but may have most of the characteristics of a Proof coin and generally command a premium. Collectors should beware of coins that have been buffed to look like Proofs; magnification will reveal polishing lines and loss of detail.

After a lapse of some 20 years, Proof coins were struck at the Philadelphia Mint from 1936 to 1942, inclusive. During these years the Mint offered Proof coins to collectors for individual sale, rather than in officially packaged sets, as such.

In 1942, when the composition of the five-cent piece was changed from copper-nickel to copper-silver-manganese, there were two Proof types of this denomination available to collectors.

The striking of all Proof coins was temporarily suspended from 1943 through 1949, and again from 1965 through 1967; during the latter period, Special Mint Sets were struck (see page 1246). Proof sets were resumed in 1968.

Sets from 1936 through 1972 included the cent, nickel, dime, quarter, and half dollar; from 1973 through 1981 the dollar was also included, and again from 2000 on. Regular Proof sets issued from 1982 to 1998 contain the cent through the half dollar. Specially packaged Prestige sets containing commemorative coins were sold from 1983 through 1997 at an additional premium. From 1999 to 2009, sets contain five different Statehood or Territorial quarters, and from 2010 to 2021, different National Parks quarters. In 1999 Proof dollars were sold separately. Four-piece Presidential dollar sets have been issued since 2007.

As part of a memorial John F. Kennedy half dollar set released in 2014, Reverse Proofs struck in silver at West Point were introduced. The Philadelphia mint first struck Reverse Proofs in 2015, also in silver, for inclusion in the March of Dimes commemorative set. Additionally, Coin and Chronicles sets of 2015 include Philadelphia-struck Reverse Proofs of the Presidential dollars of the year.

With the recent State and Territorial quarters programs, as well as the ongoing National Park quarters and Presidential dollars programs, the U.S. Mint has offered Proof sets featuring each of the designs issued for a particular year.

From time to time the Mint issues special Proof sets. One recent example is the four-piece 2009-S Lincoln Bicentennial set, which included each of the special cent designs issued that year, but coined in 95% copper (the Lincoln cent's original 1909 alloy).

Collectors are encouraged to consult David W. Lange's *Guide Book of Modern United States Proof Coin Sets* for detailed coverage and illustrations of Proof sets from 1936 to date.

How Modern Proof Coins Are Made

Selected dies are inspected for perfection and are highly polished and cleaned. They are again wiped clean or polished after every 15 to 25 impressions and are replaced frequently to avoid imperfections from wear. Coinage blanks for Proof coins are polished and cleaned to ensure high quality in striking. They are then hand fed into the coinage press one at a time, each blank receiving two or more blows from the dies to bring up sharp, high-relief details. The coinage operation is done at slow speed with extra pressure. Finished Proofs are individually inspected and are handled with gloves or tongs. They also receive a final inspection by packers before being sonically sealed in special plastic cases.

Mint Sets

Official Uncirculated Mint sets are specially packaged by the government for sale to collectors. They contain Uncirculated examples of each year's coins for every denomination issued from each mint. Before 2005, the coins were the same as those normally intended for circulation and were not minted with any special consideration for quality. From 2005 to 2010, however, Mint sets were made with a satin finish rather than the traditional Uncirculated luster. As in the past, coins struck only as Proofs are not included.

Uncirculated Mint sets sold by the Treasury from 1947 through 1958 contained two examples of each regular-issue coin. These were packaged in cardboard holders that did not protect the coins from tarnish. Nicely preserved early sets generally command a 10 to 20% premium above average values. Since 1959, sets have been sealed in protective plastic envelopes.

Privately assembled Mint sets, and Souvenir sets produced for sale at the Philadelphia or Denver mints for special occasions, are valued according to the individual pieces they contain. Only the official, government-packaged full sets are included in the following list. No Mint Sets were produced in 1950, 1982, or 1983, though Souvenir sets were sold in the latter two years (see the final section of this overview).

From time to time the Mint issues special Mint sets. One recent example is the 1996-P-D Mint set, which also included a 1996-W dime (released only in those sets).

Special Mint Sets

In mid-1964 the Treasury department announced that the Mint would not offer Proof sets or Mint sets the following year. This was prompted by a nationwide shortage of circulating coins, which was wrongly blamed on coin collectors.

In 1966 the San Francisco Assay Office began striking coins dated 1965, for inclusion in so-called United States Special Mint Sets. These were issued in pliofilm packaging similar to that of recent Proof sets. The coins in early 1965 Special Mint Sets are semi-brilliant or satiny (distinctive, but not equal in quality to Proofs); the coins in later 1965 sets feature very brilliant fields (but again not reaching Proof brilliance).

The San Francisco Assay Office started striking 1966-dated coins in August of that year, and its Special Mint Sets were packaged in rigid, sonically sealed plastic holders. The coins were struck once on unpolished planchets, unlike Proof coins (which are struck at least twice on polished planchets). Also unlike Proofs, the SMS coins were allowed to come into contact with each other during their production, which accounts for minor contact marks and abrasions. To achieve a brilliant finish, Mint technicians overpolished the coinage dies. The result was a tradeoff: most of the coins have prooflike brilliance, but many are missing polished-off design details, such as Frank Gasparro's initials on the half dollar.

All 1967-dated coinage was struck in that calendar year. Nearly all SMS coins of 1967 have fully brilliant, prooflike finishes. This brilliance was achieved without overpolishing the dies, resulting in coins that approach the quality of true Proofs. Sales of the 1967 sets were lackluster, however. The popularity of coin collecting had dropped from its peak in 1964. Also, collectors and speculators did not anticipate much secondary-market profit from the sets, which had an issue price of $4.00, compared to $2.10 for a 1964 Proof set. As a result, fewer collectors bought multiples of the 1967 sets, and today they are generally worth more than those of 1965 and 1966.

Similar SMS coins dated 1964 exist as single pieces and in sets. Like the 1965 through 1967 SMS coins, they have a semi-brilliant or satiny finish but are not equal in quality to Proofs. They are referred to as SP (Special Strike) coins and command much higher prices than their regular SMS counterparts.

SOUVENIR SETS

Uncirculated Souvenir sets were packaged and sold in gift shops at the Philadelphia and Denver mints in 1982 and 1983 in place of the "official Mint sets," which were not made in those years. A bronze Mint medal is packaged with each set. Similar sets were also made in other years.

1936 Proof Set
Liberty Walking half dollar, Washington quarter dollar, Mercury or Winged Liberty dime, Buffalo nickel, and Lincoln cent with Wheat Ears reverse.

1938 Proof Set
Buffalo nickel replaced with the new Jefferson nickel.

1950 Proof Set
There was a seven-year hiatus (1943–1949) before Proof sets were issued again after World War II. By 1950 the Liberty Walking half dollar had been replaced by the Franklin half dollar (introduced 1948), and the Mercury dime by the Roosevelt dime (introduced 1946).

1955 Proof Set
Issued in traditional individual envelopes, or in the new pliofilm package (pictured), with a Philadelphia Mint embossed paper seal with a metallic finish.

MODERN PROOF SETS (1936 TO DATE)

	Mintage	Issue Price	Face Value	Current Value
1936	3,837	$1.89	$0.91	$7,000
1937	5,542	$1.89	$0.91	$3,500
1938	8,045	$1.89	$0.91	$1,900
1939	8,795	$1.89	$0.91	$1,750
1940	11,246	$1.89	$0.91	$1,500
1941	15,287	$1.89	$0.91	$1,400
1942, Both nickels	21,120	$1.89	$0.96	$1,400
1942, One nickel	(a)	$1.89	$0.91	$1,350

a. Included in 1942, Both nickels, mintage figure.

	Mintage	Issue Price	Face Value	Current Value
1950	51,386	$2.10	$0.91	$600
1951	57,500	$2.10	$0.91	$600
1952	81,980	$2.10	$0.91	$250
1953	128,800	$2.10	$0.91	$200
1954	233,300	$2.10	$0.91	$110
1955, Box pack	378,200	$2.10	$0.91	$110
1955, Flat pack	**(b)**	$2.10	$0.91	$140
1956	669,384	$2.10	$0.91	$65
1957	1,247,952	$2.10	$0.91	$25
1958	875,652	$2.10	$0.91	$35
1959	1,149,291	$2.10	$0.91	$35
1960, With Large Date cent	1,691,602	$2.10	$0.91	$35
1960, With Small Date cent	**(c)**	$2.10	$0.91	$35
1961	3,028,244	$2.10	$0.91	$30
1962	3,218,019	$2.10	$0.91	$25
1963	3,075,645	$2.10	$0.91	$25
1964	3,950,762	$2.10	$0.91	$30
1968-S	3,041,506	$5	$0.91	$8
1968-S, With No S dime	**(d)**	$5	$0.91	$15,500
1969-S	2,934,631	$5	$0.91	$8
1970-S	2,632,810	$5	$0.91	$12
1970-S, With Small Date cent	**(e)**	$5	$0.91	$90
1970-S, With No S dime *(estimated mintage: 2,200)*	**(e)**	$5	$0.91	$900
1971-S	3,220,733	$5	$0.91	$4
1971-S, With No S nickel *(estimated mintage: 1,655)*	**(f)**	$5	$0.91	$1,250
1972-S	3,260,996	$5	$0.91	$5
1973-S	2,760,339	$7	$1.91	$9
1974-S	2,612,568	$7	$1.91	$11
1975-S, With 1976 quarter, half, and dollar	2,845,450	$7	$1.91	$10
1975-S, With No S dime	**(g)**	$7	$1.91	$260,000
1976-S	4,149,730	$7	$1.91	$8
1976-S, Silver clad, 3-piece set	3,998,621	$15	$1.75	$25
1977-S	3,251,152	$9	$1.91	$7
1978-S	3,127,781	$9	$1.91	$7
1979-S, Type 1	3,677,175	$9	$1.91	$7
1979-S, Type 2	**(h)**	$9	$1.91	$55
1980-S	3,554,806	$10	$1.91	$5
1981-S, Type 1	4,063,083	$11	$1.91	$6
1981-S, Type 2 (all six coins in set)	**(i)**	$11	$1.91	$275
1982-S	3,857,479	$11	$0.91	$5
1983-S	3,138,765	$11	$0.91	$5
1983-S, With No S dime	**(j)**	$11	$0.91	$750
1983-S, Prestige set (Olympic dollar)	140,361	$59	$1.91	$50
1984-S	2,748,430	$11	$0.91	$5
1984-S, Prestige set (Olympic dollar)	316,680	$59	$1.91	$30
1985-S	3,362,821	$11	$0.91	$4
1986-S	2,411,180	$11	$0.91	$7
1986-S, Prestige set (Statue of Liberty half, dollar)	599,317	$48.50	$2.41	$25

b. Included in 1955, Box pack, mintage figure. **c.** Included in 1960, With Large Date cent, mintage figure. **d.** Included in 1968-S mintage figure. **e.** Included in 1970-S mintage figure. **f.** Included in 1971-S mintage figure. **g.** Included in 1975-S, With 1976 quarter, half, and dollar, mintage figure. **h.** Included in 1979-S, Type 1, mintage figure. **i.** Included in 1981-S, Type 1, mintage figure. **j.** Included in 1983-S mintage figure.

	Mintage	Issue Price	Face Value	Current Value
1987-S	3,792,233	$11	$0.91	$5
1987-S, Prestige set (Constitution dollar)	435,495	$45	$1.91	$25
1988-S	3,031,287	$11	$0.91	$6
1988-S, Prestige set (Olympic dollar)	231,661	$45	$1.91	$35
1989-S	3,009,107	$11	$0.91	$5
1989-S, Prestige set (Congressional half, dollar)	211,807	$45	$2.41	$35
1990-S	2,793,433	$11	$0.91	$6
1990-S, With No S cent	3,555	$11	$0.91	$5,000
1990-S, With No S cent (Prestige set)	(k)	$45	$1.91	$5,500
1990-S, Prestige set (Eisenhower dollar)	506,126	$45	$1.91	$30
1991-S	2,610,833	$11	$0.91	$5
1991-S, Prestige set (Mt. Rushmore half, dollar)	256,954	$59	$2.41	$40
1992-S	2,675,618	$11	$0.91	$5
1992-S, Prestige set (Olympic half, dollar)	183,293	$56	$2.41	$50
1992-S, Silver	1,009,586	$11	$0.91	$20
1992-S, Silver Premier set	308,055	$37	$0.91	$25
1993-S	2,409,394	$12.50	$0.91	$6
1993-S, Prestige set (Bill of Rights half, dollar)	224,045	$57	$2.41	$45
1993-S, Silver	570,213	$21	$0.91	$30
1993-S, Silver Premier set	191,140	$37.50	$0.91	$40
1994-S	2,308,701	$12.50	$0.91	$5
1994-S, Prestige set (World Cup half, dollar)	175,893	$57	$2.41	$40
1994-S, Silver	636,009	$21	$0.91	$30
1994-S, Silver Premier set	149,320	$37.50	$0.91	$40
1995-S	2,010,384	$12.50	$0.91	$12
1995-S, Prestige set (Civil War half, dollar)	107,112	$57	$2.41	$100
1995-S, Silver	549,878	$21	$0.91	$65
1995-S, Silver Premier set	130,107	$37.50	$0.91	$65
1996-S	1,695,244	$12.50	$0.91	$8
1996-S, Prestige set (Olympic half, dollar)	55,000	$57	$2.41	$375
1996-S, Silver	623,655	$21	$0.91	$30
1996-S, Silver Premier set	151,366	$37.50	$0.91	$35
1997-S	1,975,000	$12.50	$0.91	$9
1997-S, Prestige set (Botanic dollar)	80,000	$57	$1.91	$65
1997-S, Silver	605,473	$21	$0.91	$40
1997-S, Silver Premier set	136,205	$37.50	$0.91	$40
1998-S	2,086,507	$12.50	$0.91	$12
1998-S, Silver	638,134	$21	$0.91	$25
1998-S, Silver Premier set	240,658	$37.50	$0.91	$30
1999-S, 9-piece set	2,543,401	$19.95	$1.91	$10
1999-S, 5-piece quarter set	1,169,958	$13.95	$1.25	$4
1999-S, Silver 9-piece set	804,565	$31.95	$1.91	$115
2000-S, 10-piece set	3,082,572	$19.95	$2.91	$6
2000-S, 5-piece quarter set	937,600	$13.95	$1.25	$3
2000-S, Silver 10-piece set	965,421	$31.95	$2.91	$40
2001-S, 10-piece set	2,294,909	$19.95	$2.91	$12
2001-S, 5-piece quarter set	799,231	$13.95	$1.25	$5
2001-S, Silver 10-piece set	889,697	$31.95	$2.91	$50
2002-S, 10-piece set	2,319,766	$19.95	$2.91	$8
2002-S, 5-piece quarter set	764,479	$13.95	$1.25	$4
2002-S, Silver 10-piece set	892,229	$31.95	$2.91	$40

k. Included in 1990-S mintage figure.

	Mintage	Issue Price	Face Value	Current Value
2003-S, 10-piece set	2,172,684	$19.95	$2.91	$7
2003-S, 5-piece quarter set	1,235,832	$13.95	$1.25	$3
2003-S, Silver 10-piece set	1,125,755	$31.95	$2.91	$35
2004-S, 11-piece set	1,789,488	$22.95	$2.96	$12
2004-S, 5-piece quarter set	951,196	$15.95	$1.25	$4
2004-S, Silver 11-piece set	1,175,934	$37.95	$2.96	$35
2004-S, Silver 5-piece quarter set	593,852	$23.95	$1.25	$25
2005-S, 11-piece set	2,275,000	$22.95	$2.96	$5
2005-S, 5-piece quarter set	987,960	$15.95	$1.25	$3
2005-S, Silver 11-piece set	1,069,679	$37.95	$2.96	$35
2005-S, Silver 5-piece quarter set	608,970	$23.95	$1.25	$20
2006-S, 10-piece set	2,000,428	$22.95	$2.91	$9
2006-S, 5-piece quarter set	882,000	$15.95	$1.25	$3
2006-S, Silver 10-piece set	1,054,008	$37.95	$2.91	$35
2006-S, Silver 5-piece quarter set	531,000	$23.95	$1.25	$20
2007-S, 14-piece set	1,702,116	$26.95	$6.91	$15
2007-S, 5-piece quarter set	672,662	$13.95	$1.25	$6
2007-S, 4-piece Presidential set	1,285,972	$14.95	$4	$6
2007-S, Silver 14-piece set	875,050	$44.95	$6.91	$40
2007-S, Silver 5-piece quarter set	672,662	$25.95	$1.25	$22
2008-S, 14-piece set	1,405,674	$26.95	$6.91	$30
2008-S, 5-piece quarter set	672,438	$13.95	$1.25	$45
2008-S, 4-piece Presidential set	869,202	$14.95	$4	$12
2008-S, Silver 14-piece set	763,887	$44.95	$6.91	$45
2008-S, Silver 5-piece quarter set	429,021	$25.95	$1.25	$20
2009-S, 18-piece set	1,482,502	$29.95	$7.19	$25
2009-S, 6-piece quarter set	630,976	$14.95	$1.50	$5
2009-S, 4-piece Presidential set	629,585	$14.95	$4	$9
2009-S, Silver 18-piece set	697,365	$52.95	$7.19	$55
2009-S, Silver 6-piece quarter set	299,183	$29.95	$1.50	$25
2009-S, 4-piece Lincoln Bicentennial set	201,107	$7.95	$0.04	$10
2010-S, 14-piece set	1,103,815	$31.95	$6.91	$35
2010-S, 5-piece quarter set	276,296	$14.95	$1.25	$13
2010-S, 4-piece Presidential set	535,397	$15.95	$4	$20
2010-S, Silver 14-piece set	585,401	$56.95	$6.91	$60
2010-S, Silver 5-piece quarter set	274,034	$32.95	$1.25	$25
2011-S, 14-piece set	1,098,730	$31.95	$6.91	$40
2011-S, 5-piece quarter set	152,032	$14.95	$1.25	$15
2011-S, 4-piece Presidential set	299,846	$19.95	$4	$30
2011-S, Silver 14-piece set	574,103	$67.95	$6.91	$75
2011-S, Silver 5-piece quarter set	147,895	$39.95	$1.25	$30
2012-S, 14-piece set	792,568	$31.95	$6.91	$150
2012-S, 5-piece quarter set	148,498	$14.95	$1.25	$15
2012-S, 4-piece Presidential set	249,111	$18.95	$4	$80
2012-S, Silver 14-piece set	395,149	$67.95	$6.91	$250
2012-S, Silver 8-piece Limited Edition set	44,952	$149.95	$2.85	$275
2012-S, Silver 5-piece quarter set	162,488	$41.95	$1.25	$30
2013-S, 14-piece set	802,478	$31.95	$6.91	$35
2013-S, 5-piece quarter set	128,377	$14.95	$1.25	$15
2013-S, 4-piece Presidential set	266,730	$18.95	$4	$25

	Mintage	Issue Price	Face Value	Current Value
2013-S, Silver 14-piece set	419,739	$67.95	$6.91	$75
2013-S, Silver 8-piece Limited Edition set	48,344	$139.95	$2.85	$150
2013-S, Silver 5-piece quarter set	138,451	$41.95	$1.25	$30
2014-S, 14-piece set	712,177	$31.95	$6.91	$35
2014-S, 5-piece quarter set	114,774	$14.95	$1.25	$18
2014-S, 4-piece Presidential set	228,806	$18.95	$4	$25
2014-S, Silver 14-piece set	429,529	$67.95	$6.91	$65
2014-S, Silver 8-piece Limited Edition set	41,609	$139.95	$2.85	
2014-S, Silver 5-piece quarter set	118,711	$41.95	$1.25	$40
2015-S, 14-piece set	600,140	$32.95	$6.91	
2015-S, 5-piece quarter set	91,531	$14.95	$1.25	
2015-S, 4-piece Presidential set	213,131	$18.95	$4	
2015-S, Silver 14-piece set	337,508	$53.95	$6.91	
2015-S, Silver 5-piece quarter set	92,544	$41.95	$1.25	
2016-S, 14-piece set		$32.95	$6.91	
2016-S, 5-piece quarter set		$14.95	$1.25	
2016-S, 4-piece Presidential set		$18.95	$4	
2016-S, Silver 14-piece set		$53.95	$6.91	
2016-S, Silver 5-piece quarter set		$41.95	$1.25	

UNCIRCULATED MINT SETS (1947 TO DATE)

	Mintage	Issue Price	Face Value	Current Value
1947 P-D-S	5,000	$4.87	$4.46	$2,900
1948 P-D-S	6,000	$4.92	$4.46	$1,700
1949 P-D-S	5,000	$5.45	$4.96	$2,250
1951 P-D-S	8,654	$6.75	$5.46	$1,800
1952 P-D-S	11,499	$6.14	$5.46	$1,600
1953 P-D-S	15,538	$6.14	$5.46	$1,250
1954 P-D-S	25,599	$6.19	$5.46	$650
1955 P-D-S	49,656	$3.57	$2.86	$400
1956 P-D	45,475	$3.34	$2.64	$450
1957 P-D	34,324	$4.40	$3.64	$700
1958 P-D	50,314	$4.43	$3.64	$425
1959 P-D	187,000	$2.40	$1.82	$55
1960 P-D	260,485	$2.40	$1.82	$45
1961 P-D	223,704	$2.40	$1.82	$45
1962 P-D	385,285	$2.40	$1.82	$45
1963 P-D	606,612	$2.40	$1.82	$40
1964 P-D	1,008,108	$2.40	$1.82	$30
1968 P-D-S	2,105,128	$2.50	$1.33	$8
1969 P-D-S	1,817,392	$2.50	$1.33	$8
1970 P-D-S, With Large Date cent	2,038,134	$2.50	$1.33	$20
1970 P-D-S, Small Date cent	(a)	$2.50	$1.33	$55
1971 P-D-S (no Ike dollar)	2,193,396	$3.50	$1.83	$5
1972 P-D-S (no Ike dollar)	2,750,000	$3.50	$1.83	$5
1973 P-D-S	1,767,691	$6	$3.83	$12
1974 P-D-S	1,975,981	$6	$3.83	$8
1975 P-D, With 1976 quarter, half, dollar	1,921,488	$6	$3.82	$10
1976, Silver clad, 3-piece set	4,908,319	$9	$1.75	$20
1976 P-D	1,892,513	$6	$3.82	$8
1977 P-D	2,006,869	$7	$3.82	$8
1978 P-D	2,162,609	$7	$3.82	$8

	Mintage	Issue Price	Face Value	Current Value
1979 P-D (b)	2,526,000	$8	$3.82	$8
1980 P-D-S	2,815,066	$9	$4.82	$8
1981 P-D-S	2,908,145	$11	$4.82	$10
1984 P-D	1,832,857	$7	$1.82	$5
1985 P-D	1,710,571	$7	$1.82	$5
1986 P-D	1,153,536	$7	$1.82	$8
1987 P-D	2,890,758	$7	$1.82	$5
1988 P-D	1,646,204	$7	$1.82	$5
1989 P-D	1,987,915	$7	$1.82	$5
1990 P-D	1,809,184	$7	$1.82	$5
1991 P-D	1,352,101	$7	$1.82	$5
1992 P-D	1,500,143	$7	$1.82	$5
1993 P-D	1,297,431	$8	$1.82	$5
1994 P-D	1,234,813	$8	$1.82	$5
1995 P-D	1,038,787	$8	$1.82	$5
1996 P-D, Plus 1996-W dime	1,457,949	$8	$1.92	$20
1997 P-D	950,473	$8	$1.82	$5
1998 P-D	1,187,325	$8	$1.82	$5
1999 P-D (18 pieces) (c)	1,243,867	$14.95	$3.82	$10
2000 P-D (20 pieces)	1,490,160	$14.95	$5.82	$10
2001 P-D (20 pieces)	1,116,915	$14.95	$5.82	$10
2002 P-D (20 pieces)	1,139,388	$14.95	$5.82	$10
2003 P-D (20 pieces)	1,001,532	$14.95	$5.82	$10
2004 P-D (22 pieces)	842,507	$16.95	$5.92	$10
2005 P-D (22 pieces)	1,160,000	$16.95	$5.92	$10
2006 P-D (20 pieces)	847,361	$16.95	$5.82	$10
2007 P-D (28 pieces)	895,628	$22.95	$13.82	$20
2008 P-D (28 pieces)	745,464	$22.95	$13.82	$50
2009 P-D (36 pieces)	784,614	$27.95	$14.38	$25
2010 P-D (28 pieces)	583,897	$31.95	$13.82	$25
2011 P-D (28 pieces)	533,529	$31.95	$13.82	$25
2012 P-D (28 pieces)	392,224	$27.95	$13.82	$80
2013 P-D (28 pieces)	*376,844*	$27.95	$13.82	$25
2014 P-D (28 pieces)	*344,383*	$27.95	$13.82	$25
2015 P-D (28 pieces)	*282,878*	$28.95	$13.82	
2016 P-D (28 pieces)		$28.95	$13.82	

b. S-mint dollar not included. **c.** Dollar not included.

SPECIAL MINT SETS (1965–1967)

	Mintage	Issue Price	Face Value	Current Value
1965	2,360,000	$4	$0.91	$12
1966	2,261,583	$4	$0.91	$12
1967	1,863,344	$4	$0.91	$12

See page 1246 for details on the similar 1964 Special Strike coins. Values for these coins are approximately $13,000 for each denomination.

SOUVENIR SETS (1982–1983)

	Issue Price	Face Value	Current Value
1982-P	$4	$0.91	$60
1982-D	$4	$0.91	$60
1983-P	$4	$0.91	$80
1983-D	$4	$0.91	$80

POPULAR DIE VARIETIES FROM PROOF AND MINT SETS

As noted in the *Cherrypickers' Guide to Rare Die Varieties*, "Beginning with those modern Mint sets from 1947, and Proof sets from 1950, there are many years of one or the other that are absent of a significant variety. Not all of the known varieties are significant." The following are some popular die varieties from Proof and Mint sets; for more information and additional examples, consult the *Cherrypickers' Guide*.

DIE VARIETIES IN PROOF SETS

Year	Denomination	Variety	Year	Denomination	Variety
1951	5¢	doubled-die obverse	1968-S	10¢	doubled-die obverse
1952	25¢	"Superbird" variety	1968-S	10¢	doubled-die reverse
1953	5¢	doubled-die obverse	1968-S	25¢	doubled-die reverse
1955	5¢	tripled-die reverse	1968-S	50¢	doubled-die obverse
1957	5¢	quadrupled-die obverse	1969-S	25¢	repunched mintmark
1960	1¢	doubled-die obverse (a)	1970-S	10¢	No S
1960	10¢	doubled-die reverse	1971-S	5¢	No S
1960	25¢	doubled-die reverse	1975-S	10¢	No S
1961	50¢	doubled-die reverse	1983-S	10¢	No S
1963	10¢	doubled-die reverse	1990-S	1¢	No S

a. Check for both Large Over Small Date, and Small Over Large Date, varieties.

DIE VARIETIES IN MINT SETS

Year	Denomination	Variety	Year	Denomination	Variety
1949	5¢	D/S—over mintmark (a)	1970	50¢	D—doubled-die reverse (d)
1954	25¢	doubled-die reverse (b)	1971	5¢	D/D—repunched mintmark
1960	5¢	(P)—doubled-die obverse (c)	1971	10¢	D/D—repunched mintmark
1960	25¢	(P)—doubled-die obverse (c)	1971	10¢	D—doubled-die reverse
1961	50¢	D/D—repunched mintmark	1971	50¢	D—doubled-die obverse
1963	10¢	(P)—doubled-die obverse	1971	50¢	D—doubled-die reverse
1963	25¢	(P)—doubled-die obverse	1972	1¢	(P)—doubled-die obverse
1963	25¢	(P)—doubled-die reverse	1972	5¢	D—doubled-die reverse
1963	50¢	(P)—doubled-die obverse	1972	50¢	D—doubled-die reverse
1963	50¢	(P)—doubled-die reverse	1973	50¢	(P)—doubled-die obverse
1968	10¢	(P)—doubled-die obverse	1973	50¢	D—doubled-die obverse
1968	25¢	D—doubled-die reverse	1974	50¢	D—doubled-die obverse
1969	5¢	D/D—repunched mintmark	1981	5¢	D—doubled-die reverse
1969	10¢	D/D—repunched mintmark	1984	50¢	D/D—repunched mintmark
1969	25¢	D/D—repunched mintmark	1987	5¢	D/D—repunched mintmark
1969	50¢	D—doubled-die reverse	1987	10¢	D/D—repunched mintmark
1970	1¢	D/D—repunched mintmark	1989	5¢	D—doubled-die reverse
1970	1¢	D—doubled-die obverse	1989	10¢	P—doubled-die reverse
1970	10¢	D—doubled-die reverse	1989	50¢	D/D—repunched mintmark
1970	25¢	D—doubled-die reverse	1991	5¢	D—doubled-die obverse

a. Although known, most have already been removed from their Mint-packaged sets. b. Small Date. c. Found in sets labeled as Small Date. d. Small Date.

U.S. Mint Bullion Coins

AN OVERVIEW OF U.S. MINT BULLION COINS

The United States' bullion-coin program was launched in 1986. Since then, American Eagle and other U.S. silver, gold, and platinum coins have provided investors with convenient vehicles to add physical bullion to their investment portfolios, not to mention their value as numismatic collectibles.

In addition to regular investment-grade strikes, the U.S. Mint offers its bullion coins in various collectible formats. Proofs are created in a specialized minting process: a polished coin blank is manually fed into a press fitted with special dies; the blank is struck multiple times "so the softly frosted yet detailed images seem to float above a mirror-like field" (per Mint literature); a white-gloved inspector scrutinizes the coin; and it is then sealed in a protective plastic capsule and mounted in a satin-lined velvet presentation case along with a certificate of authenticity. Members of the public can purchase Proofs directly from the Mint, at fixed prices.

Burnished (called Uncirculated by the Mint) coins are also sold directly to the public. These coins have the same design as other bullion coins, but are distinguished from regular bullion strikes by a W mintmark (for West Point), and by their distinctive finish (the result of burnished coin blanks). Their blanks are individually fed by hand into specially adapted coining presses. After striking, each Burnished specimen is carefully inspected, encapsulated in plastic, and packaged in a satin-lined velvet presentation case, along with a certificate of authenticity.

In recent years the Mint has also broadened its collectible bullion offerings with Reverse Proof and Enhanced Uncirculated formats. Various bullion coins have been offered in collector sets, as well.

Since the inception of the bullion-coin program in 1986, the Mint has marked several anniversaries with special issues and sets.

Regular bullion-strike coins are bought in bulk by Mint-authorized purchasers (wholesalers, brokerage companies, precious-metal firms, coin dealers, and participating banks). These authorized purchasers in turn sell them to secondary retailers, who then make them available to the general public. Authorized purchasers are required to meet financial and professional criteria, attested to by an internationally accepted accounting firm. They must be an experienced and established market-maker in bullion coins; provide a liquid two-way market for the coins; be audited annually; have an established and broad retail-customer base for distribution; and have a tangible net worth of $5 million (for American Silver Eagles) or $50 million (for gold and platinum American Eagles). Authorized purchasers of gold must have sold more than 100,000 ounces of gold bullion coins over any 12-month period since 1990. For gold and platinum, the initial order must be for at least 1,000 ounces, with reorders in increments of 500 ounces. For American Eagles, an authorized purchaser's cost is based on the market value of the bullion, plus a premium to cover minting, distribution, and other overhead expenses. For ASEs, the premium is $1.50 per coin. For gold, the premiums are 3% (for the one-ounce coin), 5% (1/2 ounce), 7% (1/4 ounce), and 9% (1/10 ounce). For platinum: 4% (for the one-ounce coin), 6% (1/2 ounce), 10% (1/4 ounce), and 15% (1/10 ounce).

Note that the U.S. Mint does not release bullion mintage data on a regular basis; the numbers given herein reflect the most recently available official data.

The listed values of uncertified, average Mint State coins have been based on bullion prices of silver ($17 per ounce), gold ($1,200 per ounce), and platinum ($1,400 per ounce).

For more detailed coverage of these coins, readers are directed to *American Silver Eagles: A Guide to the U.S. Bullion Coin Program* (Mercanti), *American Gold and Platinum Eagles: A Guide to the U.S. Bullion Coin Programs* (Moy), and *American Gold and Silver: U.S. Mint Collector and Investor Coins and Medals, Bicentennial to Date* (Tucker).

AMERICAN SILVER EAGLES (1986 TO DATE)

Designers: *Adolph A. Weinman (obverse) and John Mercanti (reverse).*
Weight: *31.101 grams.* **Composition:** *.9993 silver, .0007 copper (net weight 1 oz. pure silver).*
Diameter: *40.6 mm.* **Edge:** *Reeded.* **Mints:** *Philadelphia, San Francisco, and West Point.*

Regular Finish

Burnished Finish

Enhanced Uncirculated Finish
This special format incorporates elements with a brilliant mirrored finish, a light frosted finish, and a heavy frosted finish.

Reverse Lettering Style of 1986–2007
Note the lack of spur or stem at bottom right of U.

Reverse Lettering Style of 2008 to Date
Note the spur at bottom right of U.

Proof
Finish

Reverse
Proof Finish

History. The American Silver Eagle (face value $1, actual silver weight one ounce) is a legal-tender bullion coin with weight, content, and purity guaranteed by the federal government. It is one of the few silver coins allowed in individual retirement accounts (IRAs). The obverse design features Adolph A. Weinman's Liberty Walking, as used on the circulating half dollar of 1916 to 1947. Weinman's initials appear on the hem of Miss Liberty's gown. The reverse design, by John Mercanti, is a heraldic eagle.

From 1986 to 1999 all American Silver Eagles were struck at the Philadelphia and San Francisco mints (with the exception of the 1995 West Point Proof). In 2000 they were struck at both Philadelphia (Proofs) and the U.S. Mint's West Point facility (bullion strikes). From 2001 to 2010, West Point was their sole producer (with one exception in 2006), making regular bullion strikes (without mintmarks) and Proof and "Burnished" specimens (with mintmarks). (The exception is the 2006 Reverse Proof, which was struck in Philadelphia.) In 2011, for the 25th anniversary of the American Eagle bullion program, the mints at West Point, San Francisco, and Philadelphia were all put into production to make several collectible formats of the coins. Since 2012, both West Point and San Francisco have minted the American Silver Eagle.

In addition to the individually listed coins, American Silver Eagles were issued in two 2006 "20th Anniversary" sets (see page 1272) and in several other special bullion coin sets (see pages 1260, 1271, and 1272).

Striking and Sharpness. Striking is generally sharp. The key elements to check on the obverse are Miss Liberty's left hand, the higher parts and lines of her skirt, and her head. On the reverse, the eagle's breast is a main focal point.

Availability. The American Silver Eagle is one of the most popular silver-investment vehicles in the world. Between the bullion coins and various collectible formats, more than 400 million have been sold since 1986. The coins are readily available in the numismatic marketplace and from some banks, investment firms, and other non-numismatic channels.

MS-60 to 70 (Mint State). *Obverse and Reverse:* At MS-60, some abrasion and contact marks are evident on the higher design areas (Miss Liberty's left arm, her hand, and the areas of the skirt covering her left leg). Luster may be dull or lifeless at MS–60 to 62, but there should be deep frost at MS-63 and better, particularly in the lower-relief areas. At MS-65 and above, the luster should be full and rich. These guidelines are more academic than practical, as American Silver Eagles are not intended for circulation, and nearly all are in high Mint State grades.

PF-60 to 70 (Proof). *Obverse and Reverse:* Proofs that are extensively cleaned and have many hairlines are lower level, such as PF–60 to 62. Those with fewer hairlines or flaws are deemed PF–63 to 65. (These exist more in theory than actuality, as nearly all Proof ASEs have been maintained in their original high condition by collectors and investors.) Given the quality of modern U.S. Mint products, even PF–66 and 67 are unusually low levels for ASE Proofs.

AMERICAN SILVER EAGLES

	Mintage	MS	MS-69	MS-70
		PF	PF-69	PF-70
1986 ‡ (a,b)	5,393,005	$44	$50	$800
1986-S, Proof	1,446,778	$65	$80	$500
1987 (a,c)	11,442,335	$28	$34	$1,700
1987-S, Proof	904,732	$65	$80	$800
1988 (a,d)	5,004,646	$30	$35	$2,500
1988-S, Proof	557,370	$65	$80	$550
1989 (a)	5,203,327	$32	$37	$1,500
1989-S, Proof	617,694	$65	$80	$325
1990 (a)	5,840,210	$34	$40	$1,500
1990-S, Proof	695,510	$65	$80	$250
1991 (a,e)	7,191,066	$34	$40	—
1991-S, Proof	511,925	$65	$80	$500
1992 (a,f)	5,540,068	$34	$40	$1,600
1992-S, Proof	498,654	$65	$80	$400
1993 (a,g)	6,763,762	$34	$40	$2,900
1993-P, Proof (h)	405,913	$120	$135	$1,500
1994 (a,i)	4,227,319	$42	$50	$4,000
1994-P, Proof ‡ (j)	372,168	$180	$195	$1,900
1995 (a)	4,672,051	$40	$45	$1,100
1995-P, Proof	438,511	$90	$105	$400
1995-W, Proof ‡ (k)	30,125	$3,800	$4,750	—
1996 ‡ (a,l)	3,603,386	$70	$85	—
1996-P, Proof	500,000	$80	$95	$400
1997 (a)	4,295,004	$32	$38	$900
1997-P, Proof	435,368	$80	$95	$500
1998 (a)	4,847,549	$32	$38	$1,700
1998-P, Proof	450,000	$70	$85	$250
1999 (a,m)	7,408,640	$34	$40	—
1999-P, Proof	549,769	$70	$85	$350
2000 (n,o)	9,239,132	$30	$35	$3,200
2000-P, Proof	600,000	$70	$85	$425
2001 (n)	9,001,711	$30	$35	$800
2001-W, Proof	746,398	$65	$80	$175
2002 (n)	10,539,026	$27	$32	$250
2002-W, Proof	647,342	$65	$80	$150
2003 (n)	8,495,008	$25	$30	$150
2003-W, Proof	747,831	$65	$80	$120
2004 (n)	8,882,754	$25	$30	$135
2004-W, Proof	801,602	$65	$80	$125
2005 (n)	8,891,025	$25	$30	$160
2005-W, Proof	816,663	$65	$80	$125

Note: For more information, consult American Silver Eagles: A Guide to the U.S. Bullion Coin Program, 3rd edition (Mercanti). MS values are for uncertified Mint State coins of average quality, in their complete original U.S. Mint packaging. PF values are for uncertified Proof coins of average quality, in their complete original U.S. Mint packaging. ‡ Ranked in the *100 Greatest U.S. Modern Coins*. **a.** Minted at Philadelphia, without mintmark. **b.** Auction: $1,028, MS-70, September 2015. **c.** Auction: $999, MS-70, August 2015. **d.** Auction: $1,704, MS-70, August 2015. **e.** Auction: $3,760, MS-70, August 2015. **f.** Auction: $1,528, MS-70, June 2015. **g.** Auction: $3,760, MS-70, June 2015. **h.** Auction: $1,528, PF-70UCam, March 2015. **i.** Auction: $4,700, MS-70, June 2015. **j.** Auction: $1,293, PF-70DCam, September 2015. **k.** Auction: $14,100, PF-70UCam, June 2015. **l.** Auction: $5,640, MS-70, August 2015. **m.** Auction: $4,935, MS-70, June 2015. **n.** Minted at West Point, without mintmark. **o.** Auction: $1,293, MS-70, July 2015.

| | Mintage | MS | MS-69 | MS-70 |
		PF	PF-69	PF-70
2006 (n)	10,676,522	$25	$30	$160
2006-W, Burnished (p)	468,020	$100	$110	$225
2006-W, Proof	1,092,477	$65	$80	$125
2006-P, Reverse Proof ‡ (q,r,s)	248,875	$250	$305	$395
2007 (n)	9,028,036	$25	$30	$95
2007-W, Burnished	621,333	$35	$40	$75
2007-W, Proof	821,759	$65	$80	$100
2008 (n)	20,583,000	$24	$30	$95
2008-W, Burnished	533,757	$70	$75	$100
2008-W, Burnished, Reverse of 2007 ‡ (t,u)	*47,000*	$600	$650	$1,250
2008-W, Proof	700,979	$75	$90	$100
2009 (n)	30,459,000	$24	$30	$95
2010 (n)	34,764,500	$23	$28	$85
2010-W, Proof (v)	*849,861*	$65	$80	$100
2011 (n,w)	40,020,000	$23	$28	$95
2011-W, Burnished	409,776	$50	$60	$125
2011-W, Proof	947,355	$65	$80	$100
2011-P, Reverse Proof (r,x)	99,882	$325	$340	$450
2011-S, Burnished (y)	99,882	$290	$315	$350
2012 (n,w)	33,742,500	$23	$28	$80
2012-W, Burnished	226,120	$70	$75	$100
2012-W, Proof	869,386	$65	$85	$125
2012-S, Proof	285,184	$75	$90	$165
2012-S, Reverse Proof (r)	224,981	$125	$140	$175
2013 (n,w)	42,675,000	$23	$28	$80
2013-W, Burnished	222,091	$65	$70	$95
2013-W, Enhanced Uncirculated	281,310	$90	$115	$150
2013-W, Proof	934,812	$65	$75	$125
2013-W, Reverse Proof	281,310	$90	$105	$150
2014 (n,w)	44,006,000	$22	$27	$80
2014-W, Burnished	253,169	$65	$75	$80
2014-W, Proof	944,757	$65	$80	$100
2015 (n,w)	47,000,000	$22	$27	$80
2015-W, Burnished	223,879	$65	$75	$80
2015-W, Proof	707,518	$65	$80	$100
2016 (n,w)		$22	$27	$80
2016-W, Burnished		$65	$75	$80
2016-W, Proof		$65	$80	$100

Note: For more information, consult *American Silver Eagles: A Guide to the U.S. Bullion Coin Program*, 3rd edition (Mercanti). MS values are for uncertified Mint State coins of average quality, in their complete original U.S. Mint packaging. PF values are for uncertified Proof coins of average quality, in their complete original U.S. Mint packaging. ‡ Ranked in the *100 Greatest U.S. Modern Coins*. **n.** Minted at West Point, without mintmark. **p.** In celebration of the 20th anniversary of the Bullion Coinage Program, in 2006 the W mintmark was used on bullion coins produced in sets at West Point. **q.** The 2006-P Reverse Proof coins were issued to mark the 20th anniversary of the Bullion Coinage Program. **r.** Reverse Proofs have brilliant devices, and their background fields are frosted (rather than the typical Proof format of frosted devices and mirror-like backgrounds). **s.** Auction: $329, PF-70, February 2015. **t.** Reverse dies of 2007 and earlier have a plain U in UNITED. Modified dies of 2008 and later have a small spur at the bottom right of the U. **u.** Auction: $940, MS-70, August 2015. **v.** The U.S. Mint did not strike any Proof American Silver Eagles in 2009. **w.** Minted at San Francisco, without mintmark. **x.** Auction: $376, PF-70, September 2015. **y.** Auction: $306, MS-70, October 2015.

AMERICAN SILVER EAGLE COIN SETS

	Uncertified	69	70
1997 Impressions of Liberty set (a)	$3,300	$3,400	$6,200
2006 20th Anniversary Three-Coin Set. Silver dollars, Uncirculated, Proof, Reverse Proof	$425	$500	$750
2006-W 20th Anniversary 1-oz. Gold- and Silver-Dollar Set. Uncirculated	$1,600	$1,700	$2,100
2011 25th Anniversary Five-Coin Set	$750	$850	$1,100
2012-S 75th Anniversary of San Francisco Mint Two-Coin Set. Proof, Reverse Proof	$200	$240	$340
2013-W 75th Anniversary of West Point Depository Two-Coin Set. Reverse Proof, Enhanced Uncirculated	$180	$230	$280

Note: Uncertified values are for uncertified sets of average quality, in their complete original U.S. Mint packaging. **a.** This set contains a $100 platinum, $50 gold, and a $1 silver piece.

AMERICA THE BEAUTIFUL 5-OUNCE SILVER BULLION COINS (2010–2021)

Designers: *See image captions on pages 785–790 for designers.* **Weight:** *155.517 grams.*
Composition: *.999 silver, .001 copper (net weight 5 oz. pure silver).*
Diameter: *76.2 mm.* **Edge:** *Lettered.* **Mint:** *Philadelphia.*

Bullion
Strike

History. In conjunction with the National Park quarter dollars, the U.S. Mint issues silver-bullion coins based on each of the "America the Beautiful" program's circulation-strike coins. The coinage dies are cut on a CNC milling machine, bypassing a hubbing operation, which results in finer details than seen on the smaller quarter dollars. The bullion coins are made of .999 fine silver, have a diameter of three inches, weigh five ounces, and carry a face value of 25 cents. The fineness and weight are incused on each coin's edge. The Mint's German-made Gräbener press strikes 22 coins per minute, with two strikes per coin at 450 to 500 metric tons of pressure. In December 2010, the Mint announced it would produce Uncirculated and Specimen versions for collectors. Detailed information on each issue is in *American Gold and Silver: U.S. Mint Collector and Investor Coins and Medals, Bicentennial to Date* (Tucker).

Specimen
Strike

Mintmark location is
on the obverse, to the
right of the hair ribbon.

Details of the incused edge markings.

**Details on 2014 Great Smoky Mountains
National Park 5-ounce silver bullion coin (left)
and quarter dollar (right). Note differences
on window, cabin, and grass in foreground.**

Striking and Sharpness. Striking is generally sharp.

Availability. The National Park silver bullion coins are distributed through commercial channels similar to those for the Mint's American Silver Eagle coins. Production of the 2010 coins was delayed (finally starting September 21) as the Mint worked out the technical details of striking such a large product. Production and distribution have been smoother since then.

MS-65 to 70 (Mint State). *Obverse and Reverse:* At MS-65, some abrasion and contact marks are evident on the higher design areas. Luster may be dull or lifeless at MS–65 to 66, but there should be deep frost at MS-67 and better, particularly in the lower-relief areas. At MS-68 and above, the luster should be full and rich. These guidelines are more academic than practical, as these coins are not intended for circulation, and nearly all are in high Mint State grades.

SP-68 to 70 (Specimen). *Obverse and Reverse:* These pieces should be nearly perfect and with full luster, in their original Mint packaging. Any with imperfections due to careless handling or environmental damage are valued lower.

The U.S. Mint produces the America the Beautiful™ 5-ounce silver coins in bullion and numismatic versions. The bullion version, which lacks the P mintmark, has a brilliant Uncirculated finish and is sold only through dealers. The numismatic version, with the mintmark, has a matte or burnished finish. These coins are designated "Specimens" (SP) by most collectors and grading services. They are sold directly to the public by the Mint.

25¢ AMERICA THE BEAUTIFUL 5-OUNCE SILVER BULLION COINS

	Mintage	MS / SP	MS-69 / SP-69	MS-70 / SP-70
2010, Hot Springs National Park	26,788	$135	$170	—
2010-P, Hot Springs National Park, Specimen	33,000	$155	$185	$270
2010, Yellowstone National Park	26,711	$135	$170	—
2010-P, Yellowstone National Park, Specimen	33,000	$155	$185	$270
2010, Yosemite National Park	26,716	$135	$170	—
2010-P, Yosemite National Park, Specimen	33,000	$155	$185	$270
2010, Grand Canyon National Park	25,967	$135	$170	—
2010-P, Grand Canyon National Park, Specimen	33,000	$155	$185	$270
2010, Mt. Hood National Forest	26,637	$135	$170	—
2010-P, Mt. Hood National Forest, Specimen	33,000	$155	$185	$270
2011, Gettysburg National Military Park	24,625	$120	$155	—
2011-P, Gettysburg National Military Park, Specimen (a)	126,700	$255	$290	$550
2011, Glacier National Park	20,805	$120	$155	—
2011-P, Glacier National Park, Specimen (b)	126,700	$155	$190	$350
2011, Olympic National Park	18,345	$120	$155	—
2011-P, Olympic National Park, Specimen (c)	95,600	$155	$190	$350
2011, Vicksburg National Military Park	18,528	$120	$155	—
2011-P, Vicksburg National Military Park, Specimen (d)	41,200	$155	$185	$400
2011, Chickasaw National Recreational Area	16,746	$120	$155	—
2011-P, Chickasaw National Recreational Area, Specimen (e)	31,400	$215	$250	$450
2012, El Yunque National Forest	17,314	$215	$250	—
2012-P, El Yunque National Forest, Specimen (f)	21,900	$400	$435	$600
2012, Chaco Culture National Historical Park	17,146	$235	$270	—
2012-P, Chaco Culture National Historical Park, Specimen (g)	20,000	$355	$390	$600
2012, Acadia National Park	14,978	$350	$385	—
2012-P, Acadia National Park, Specimen (h)	25,400	$550	$585	$875
2012, Hawai'i Volcanoes National Park	14,863	$350	$385	—
2012-P, Hawai'i Volcanoes National Park, Specimen (i)	20,000	$650	$685	$1,500
2012, Denali National Park and Preserve	15,225	$235	$270	—
2012-P, Denali National Park and Preserve, Specimen	20,000	$475	$515	$700
2013, White Mountain National Forest	20,530	$125	$135	—
2013-P, White Mountain National Forest, Specimen	35,000	$165	$200	$250
2013, Perry's Victory and International Peace Memorial	17,707	$125	$135	—
2013-P, Perry's Victory and International Peace Memorial, Specimen	30,000	$165	$200	$250
2013, Great Basin National Park	17,792	$125	$135	—
2013-P, Great Basin National Park, Specimen	30,000	$165	$200	$250
2013, Ft. McHenry Nat'l Mon & Historic Shrine	19,802	$125	$135	—
2013-P, Ft. McHenry Nat'l Mon & Historic Shrine, Specimen	30,000	$165	$200	$250
2013, Mount Rushmore National Monument	23,547	$125	$135	—
2013-P, Mount Rushmore National Monument, Specimen	35,000	$165	$200	$250
2014, Great Smoky Mountains National Park	24,710	$130	$165	—
2014-P, Great Smoky Mountains National Park, Specimen	33,000	$125	$160	$210
2014, Shenandoah National Park	28,451	$130	$165	—
2014-P, Shenandoah National Park, Specimen	25,000	$125	$160	$210
2014, Arches National Park	28,434	$130	$165	—
2014-P, Arches National Park, Specimen	22,000	$130	$165	$210

Note: MS values are for uncertified Mint State coins of average quality, in their complete original U.S. Mint packaging. SP values are for uncertified Specimen coins of average quality, in their complete original U.S. Mint packaging. **a.** Auction: $341, SP-70, May 2015. **b.** $376, SP-70, September 2014. **c.** Auction: $188, SP-69, December 2015. **d.** $212, SP-69, October 2014. **e.** Auction: $353, SP-70, September 2014. **f.** Auction: $206, SP-69, December 2015. **g.** Auction: $306, SP-70, December 2014. **h.** Auction: $529, SP-70, September 2014. **i.** Auction: $776, SP-70, December 2014.

| | Mintage | MS | MS-69 | MS-70 |
		SP	SP-69	SP-70
2014, Great Sand Dunes National Park	24,103	$130	$165	—
2014-P, Great Sand Dunes National Park, Specimen	22,000	$130	$165	$210
2014, Everglades National Park	22,732	$130	$165	—
2014-P, Everglades National Park, Specimen	34,000	$125	$160	$210
2015, Homestead National Monument of America	20,602	$130	$165	—
2015-P, Homestead National Monument of America, Specimen	35,000	$130	$165	$210
2015, Kisatchie National Forest	19,168	$130	$165	—
2015-P, Kisatchie National Forest, Specimen	42,000	$130	$165	$210
2015, Blue Ridge Parkway	17,461	$130	$165	—
2015-P, Blue Ridge Parkway, Specimen	45,000	$130	$165	$210
2015, Bombay Hook National Wildlife Refuge	17,339	$130	$165	—
2015-P, Bombay Hook National Wildlife Refuge, Specimen	45,000	$130	$165	$210
2015, Saratoga National Historic Park	17,457	$130	$165	—
2015-P, Saratoga National Historic Park, Specimen	45,000	$130	$165	$210
2016(P), Shawnee National Forest		$130	$165	—
2016-P, Shawnee National Forest, Specimen		$130	$165	$210
2016(P), Cumberland Gap National Historical Park		$130	$165	—
2016-P, Cumberland Gap National Historical Park, Specimen		$130	$165	$210
2016(P), Harpers Ferry National Historical Park		$130	$165	—
2016-P, Harpers Ferry National Historical Park, Specimen		$130	$165	$210
2016(P), Theodore Roosevelt National Park		$130	$165	—
2016-P, Theodore Roosevelt National Park, Specimen		$130	$165	$210
2016(P), Fort Moultrie (Fort Sumter National Monument)		$130	$165	—
2016-P, Fort Moultrie (Fort Sumter National Monument), Specimen		$130	$165	$210

Note: MS values are for uncertified Mint State coins of average quality, in their complete original U.S. Mint packaging. SP values are for uncertified Specimen coins of average quality, in their complete original U.S. Mint packaging.

AMERICAN GOLD EAGLES (1986 TO DATE)

Designers: *Augustus Saint-Gaudens (obverse) and Miley Busiek (reverse).*
Weight: *$5 1/10 oz.—3.393 grams; $10 1/4 oz.—8.483 grams; $25 1/2 oz.—16.966 grams; $50 1 oz.—33.931 grams.* **Composition:** *.9167 gold, .03 silver, .0533 copper.*
Diameter: *$5 1/10 oz.—16.5 mm; $10 1/4 oz.—22 mm; $25 1/2 oz.—27 mm; $50 1 oz.—32.7 mm.* **Edge:** *Reeded.* **Mints:** *Philadelphia and West Point.*

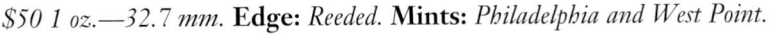

Regular Finish
Obverse design common to all denominations.

Burnished Finish

Mintmark location is on the obverse, below the date.

See additional images on next page.

Proof Finish   **Reverse Proof Finish**

History. American Eagle gold bullion coins are made in four denominations: $5 (1/10 ounce pure gold), $10 (1/4 ounce), $25 (1/2 ounce), and $50 (1 ounce). Each shares the same obverse and reverse designs: a modified rendition of Augustus Saint-Gaudens's famous Liberty (as depicted on the double eagle of 1907 to 1933), and a "family of eagles" motif by sculptor Miley Tucker-Frost (nee Busiek). From 1986 to 1991 the obverse bore a Roman numeral date, similar to the first Saint-Gaudens double eagles of 1907; this was changed to Arabic dating in 1992. The coins are legal tender—with weight, content, and purity guaranteed by the federal government—and are produced from gold mined in the United States. Investors can include them in their individual retirement accounts.

"American Eagles use the durable 22-karat standard established for gold circulating coinage over 350 years ago," notes the U.S. Mint. "They contain their stated amount of pure gold, plus small amounts of alloy. This creates harder coins that resist scratching and marring, which can diminish resale value."

Since the Bullion Coin Program started in 1986, these gold pieces have been struck in Philadelphia and West Point, in various formats similar to those of the American Silver Eagles—regular bullion strikes, Burnished, Proof, and Reverse Proof. Unlike their silver counterparts, none of the American Gold Eagles have been struck at San Francisco.

In addition to the individual coins listed below, American Eagle gold bullion coins have been issued in various sets (see pages 1271 and 1272).

Striking and Sharpness. Striking is generally sharp. The key elements to check on the obverse are Liberty's chest and left knee, and the open fields.

Availability. American Gold Eagles are the most popular gold-coin investment vehicle in the United States. The coins are readily available in the numismatic marketplace as well as from participating banks, investment firms, and other non-numismatic channels.

MS-60 to 70 (Mint State). *Obverse and Reverse:* At MS-60, some abrasion and contact marks are evident on the higher design areas (in particular, Miss Liberty's chest and left knee) and the open fields. Luster may be dull or lifeless at MS–60 to 62, but there should be deep frost at MS–63 and better, particularly in the lower-relief areas. At MS-65 and above, the luster should be full and rich. Contact marks and abrasion are less and less evident at higher grades. These guidelines are more academic than practical, as these coins are not intended for circulation, and nearly all are in high Mint State grades.

PF-60 to 70 (Proof). *Obverse and Reverse:* Proofs that are extensively cleaned and have many hairlines are lower level, such as PF–60 to 62. Those with fewer hairlines or flaws are deemed PF–63 to 65. (These exist more in theory than actuality, as nearly all Proof American Eagle gold bullion coins have been maintained in their original high condition by collectors and investors.) Given the quality of modern U.S. Mint products, even PF–66 and 67 are unusually low levels for these Proofs.

$5 1/10-OUNCE AMERICAN GOLD EAGLES

	Mintage	MS / PF	MS-69 / PF-69	MS-70 / PF-70
$5 MCMLXXXVI (1986)	912,609	$165	$195	$800
$5 MCMLXXXVII (1987)	580,266	$170	$195	$1,300
$5 MCMLXXXVIII (1988) (a)	159,500	$175	$240	$4,000
$5 MCMLXXXVIII (1988)-P, Proof	143,881	$190	$205	$325
$5 MCMLXXXIX (1989) (b)	264,790	$170	$195	$3,100
$5 MCMLXXXIX (1989)-P, Proof	84,647	$175	$190	$375
$5 MCMXC (1990) (c)	210,210	$200	$220	$4,000
$5 MCMXC (1990)-P, Proof	99,349	$175	$190	$350
$5 MCMXCI (1991) (d)	165,200	$220	$240	$1,200
$5 MCMXCI (1991)-P, Proof	70,334	$175	$190	$400
$5 1992	209,300	$170	$185	$1,400
$5 1992-P, Proof	64,874	$165	$180	$450
$5 1993	210,709	$170	$185	$400
$5 1993-P, Proof	58,649	$165	$180	$350
$5 1994	206,380	$170	$185	$400
$5 1994-W, Proof	62,849	$165	$180	$350
$5 1995	223,025	$150	$175	$975
$5 1995-W, Proof	62,667	$165	$180	$450
$5 1996	401,964	$145	$160	$550
$5 1996-W, Proof	57,047	$165	$180	$450
$5 1997	528,266	$145	$160	$450
$5 1997-W, Proof	34,977	$165	$180	$750
$5 1998	1,344,520	$145	$160	$300
$5 1998-W, Proof	39,395	$165	$180	$450
$5 1999	2,750,338	$145	$160	$275
$5 1999-W, Unc made from unpolished Proof dies ‡ (e,f)	14,500	$1,200	$1,300	$4,000
$5 1999-W, Proof	48,428	$165	$180	$400
$5 2000	569,153	$145	$160	$275
$5 2000-W, Proof	49,971	$165	$180	$400
$5 2001	269,147	$145	$160	$245
$5 2001-W, Proof	37,530	$165	$180	$500
$5 2002	230,027	$160	$175	$350
$5 2002-W, Proof	40,864	$165	$180	$500
$5 2003	245,029	$145	$160	$250
$5 2003-W, Proof	40,027	$165	$180	$500
$5 2004	250,016	$145	$160	$250
$5 2004-W, Proof	35,131	$165	$180	$450
$5 2005	300,043	$135	$155	$220
$5 2005-W, Proof	49,265	$165	$180	$400

Note: MS values are for uncertified Mint State coins of average quality, in their complete original U.S. Mint packaging. PF values are for uncertified Proof coins of average quality, in their complete original U.S. Mint packaging. ‡ Ranked in the *100 Greatest U.S. Modern Coins*. **a.** Auction: $159, MS-69, October 2014. **b.** Auction: $141, MS-69, October 2014. **c.** Auction: $141, MS-69, October 2014. **d.** Auction: $2,115, MS-70, January 2016. **e.** Unpolished Proof dies were used to mint some 1999 $5 gold coins, resulting in a regular bullion-strike issue bearing a W mintmark (usually reserved for Proofs). A similar error exists in the $10 (1/4-ounce) series. The mintage listed is an estimate. Other estimates range from 6,000 to 30,000 pieces. **f.** Auction: $764, MS-69, July 2015.

	Mintage	MS	MS-69	MS-70
		PF	PF-69	PF-70
$5 2006	285,006	$135	$155	$180
$5 2006-W, Burnished	20,643	$210	$225	$255
$5 2006-W, Proof	47,277	$165	$180	$240
$5 2007	190,010	$135	$155	$240
$5 2007-W, Burnished	22,501	$340	$345	$450
$5 2007-W, Proof	58,553	$165	$180	$300
$5 2008	305,000	$135	$155	$240
$5 2008-W, Burnished (g)	12,657	$340	$345	$450
$5 2008-W, Proof	28,116	$165	$180	$300
$5 2009	270,000	$135	$155	$210
$5 2010	*435,000*	$135	$155	$180
$5 2010-W, Proof	*54,285*	$165	$180	$300
$5 2011	*350,000*	$165	$155	$180
$5 2011-W, Proof	*42,697*	$170	$185	$300
$5 2012	315,000	$135	$155	$180
$5 2012-W, Proof	20,637	$190	$205	$250
$5 2013	535,000	$135	$155	$180
$5 2013-W, Proof	21,738	$190	$205	$235
$5 2014	565,000	$135	$155	$180
$5 2014-W, Proof	22,725	$170	$185	$210
$5 2015	980,000	$135	$155	$180
$5 2015-W, Proof	*26,761*	$170	$185	$210

Note: MS values are for uncertified Mint State coins of average quality, in their complete original U.S. Mint packaging. PF values are for uncertified Proof coins of average quality, in their complete original U.S. Mint packaging. **g.** Auction: $352, MS-70, November 2014.

$10 1/4-OUNCE AMERICAN GOLD EAGLES

	Mintage	MS	MS-69	MS-70
		PF	PF-69	PF-70
$10 MCMLXXXVI (1986) (a)	726,031	$500	$550	$1,500
$10 MCMLXXXVII (1987) (b)	269,255	$500	$550	—
$10 MCMLXXXVIII (1988) (c)	49,000	$600	$675	$3,000
$10 MCMLXXXVIII (1988)-P, Proof	98,028	$375	$405	$700
$10 MCMLXXXIX (1989) (d)	81,789	$600	$675	$1,500
$10 MCMLXXXIX (1989)-P, Proof	54,170	$375	$405	$850
$10 MCMXC (1990) (e)	41,000	$740	$775	$4,000
$10 MCMXC (1990)-P, Proof	62,674	$375	$405	$600
$10 MCMXCI (1991) (f)	36,100	$740	$775	$2,250
$10 MCMXCI (1991)-P, Proof	50,839	$375	$405	$700
$10 1992 (g)	59,546	$550	$600	$2,000
$10 1992-P, Proof	46,269	$375	$405	$750

Note: MS values are for uncertified Mint State coins of average quality, in their complete original U.S. Mint packaging. PF values are for uncertified Proof coins of average quality, in their complete original U.S. Mint packaging. **a.** Auction: $1,058, MS-70, January 2016. **b.** Auction: $306, MS-68, November 2015. **c.** Auction: $3,290, MS-70, August 2014. **d.** Auction: $3,290, MS-70, October 2015. **e.** Auction: $16,450, MS-70, October 2015. **f.** Auction: $1,293, MS-70, October 2014. **g.** Auction: $9,400, MS-70, September 2015.

| | Mintage | MS | MS-69 | MS-70 |
		PF	PF-69	PF-70
$10 1993 (h)	71,864	$550	$600	$2,250
$10 1993-P, Proof	46,464	$375	$405	$750
$10 1994 (i)	72,650	$550	$600	$2,500
$10 1994-W, Proof	48,172	$375	$405	$700
$10 1995 (j)	83,752	$550	$600	$2,000
$10 1995-W, Proof	47,526	$375	$405	$700
$10 1996 (k)	60,318	$550	$600	$2,100
$10 1996-W, Proof	38,219	$375	$405	$550
$10 1997	108,805	$325	$345	$2,000
$10 1997-W, Proof	29,805	$375	$405	$900
$10 1998	309,829	$325	$345	$2,200
$10 1998-W, Proof	29,503	$375	$405	$900
$10 1999	564,232	$325	$345	$3,000
$10 1999-W, Unc made from unpolished Proof dies ‡ (l,m)	10,000	$1,800	$1,900	—
$10 1999-W, Proof	34,417	$375	$405	$750
$10 2000	128,964	$325	$345	$900
$10 2000-W, Proof	36,036	$375	$405	$750
$10 2001	71,280	$550	$600	$650
$10 2001-W, Proof	25,613	$375	$405	$750
$10 2002	62,027	$550	$575	$600
$10 2002-W, Proof	29,242	$375	$405	$575
$10 2003	74,029	$325	$345	$500
$10 2003-W, Proof	30,292	$375	$405	$575
$10 2004	72,014	$325	$345	$500
$10 2004-W, Proof	28,839	$375	$405	$600
$10 2005	72,015	$325	$345	$500
$10 2005-W, Proof	37,207	$375	$405	$550
$10 2006	60,004	$325	$345	$500
$10 2006-W, Burnished (n)	15,188	$650	$675	$700
$10 2006-W, Proof	36,127	$375	$405	$550
$10 2007	34,004	$550	$600	$650
$10 2007-W, Burnished (o)	12,766	$700	$725	$750
$10 2007-W, Proof	46,189	$375	$405	$600
$10 2008	70,000	$325	$345	$500
$10 2008-W, Burnished (p)	8,883	$1,650	$1,700	$1,750
$10 2008-W, Proof	18,877	$450	$500	$700
$10 2009	110,000	$325	$345	$475
$10 2010	86,000	$325	$345	$400
$10 2010-W, Proof	44,507	$375	$405	$525
$10 2011	80,000	$325	$345	$400
$10 2011-W, Proof	28,782	$375	$405	$525
$10 2012	76,000	$325	$345	$400
$10 2012-W, Proof	13,926	$450	$475	$550

Note: MS values are for uncertified Mint State coins of average quality, in their complete original U.S. Mint packaging. PF values are for uncertified Proof coins of average quality, in their complete original U.S. Mint packaging. ‡ Ranked in the *100 Greatest U.S. Modern Coins.* **h.** Auction: $3,055, MS-70, June 2014. **i.** $5,640, MS-70, February 2015. **j.** Auction: $505, MS-69, March 2014. **k.** Auction: $306, MS-68, October 2015. **l.** Unpolished Proof dies were used to mint some 1999 $10 gold coins, resulting in a regular bullion-strike issue bearing a W mintmark (usually reserved for Proofs). A similar error exists in the $5 (1/10-ounce) series. The mintage listed is an estimate. Other estimates range from 6,000 to 30,000 pieces. **m.** $1,763, MS-69, July 2015. **n.** Auction: $646, MS-70, October 2015. **o.** Auction: $376, MS-70, October 2015. **p.** Auction: $1,528, MS-70, July 2015.

| | Mintage | MS | MS-69 | MS-70 |
		PF	PF-69	PF-70
$10 2013	122,000	$325	$345	$400
$10 2013W, Proof	12,782	$450	$475	$525
$10 2014	118,000	$325	$345	$400
$10 2014W, Proof	14,790	$450	$475	$525
$10 2015	158,000	$325	$345	$400
$10 2015-W, Proof	15,775	$450	$475	$525

Note: MS values are for uncertified Mint State coins of average quality, in their complete original U.S. Mint packaging. PF values are for uncertified Proof coins of average quality, in their complete original U.S. Mint packaging.

$25 1/2-Ounce American Gold Eagles

| | Mintage | MS | MS-69 | MS-70 |
		PF	PF-69	PF-70
$25 MCMLXXXVI (1986) (a)	599,566	$900	$950	$1,500
$25 MCMLXXXVII (1987) (b)	131,255	$1,300	$1,350	$2,000
$25 MCMLXXXVII (1987)-P, Proof	143,398	$800	$850	$2,000
$25 MCMLXXXVIII (1988) (c)	45,000	$1,950	$2,000	$5,000
$25 MCMLXXXVIII (1988)-P, Proof	76,528	$800	$850	$1,600
$25 MCMLXXXIX (1989) (d)	44,829	$2,100	$2,150	$4,000
$25 MCMLXXXIX (1989)-P, Proof	44,798	$950	$1,000	—
$25 MCMXC (1990) (e)	31,000	$2,450	$2,500	$5,000
$25 MCMXC (1990)-P, Proof	51,636	$725	$775	—
$25 MCMXCI (1991) ‡ (f)	24,100	$3,500	$3,550	—
$25 MCMXCI (1991)-P, Proof	53,125	$725	$775	$1,500
$25 1992 (g)	54,404	$1,500	$1,550	$3,800
$25 1992-P, Proof	40,976	$725	$775	$1,500
$25 1993 (h)	73,324	$1,000	$1,100	$3,500
$25 1993-P, Proof	43,819	$725	$775	—
$25 1994 (i)	62,400	$1,000	$1,100	—
$25 1994-W, Proof	44,584	$725	$775	$1,500
$25 1995 (j)	53,474	$1,600	$1,650	$1,500
$25 1995-W, Proof	45,388	$725	$775	$1,500
$25 1996 (k)	39,287	$1,650	$1,700	$4,500
$25 1996-W, Proof	35,058	$725	$775	$1,500
$25 1997 (l)	79,605	$1,000	$1,100	$2,800
$25 1997-W, Proof	26,344	$725	$775	$1,500
$25 1998	169,029	$645	$670	$1,250
$25 1998-W, Proof	25,374	$725	$775	$1,500

Note: MS values are for uncertified Mint State coins of average quality, in their complete original U.S. Mint packaging. PF values are for uncertified Proof coins of average quality, in their complete original U.S. Mint packaging. ‡ Ranked in the *100 Greatest U.S. Modern Coins.* **a.** Auction: $646, MS-68, October 2015. **b.** Auction: $999, MS-69, January 2016. **c.** Auction: $1,528, MS-69, October 2015. **d.** Auction: $9,400, MS-70, September 2015. **e.** Auction: $9,694, MS-70, September 2015. **f.** Auction: $2,820, MS-69, October 2015. **g.** Auction: $3,966, MS-70, July 2014. **h.** Auction: $4,964, MS-70, January 2015. **i.** Auction: $705, MS-68, October 2015. **j.** Auction: $5,875, MS-70, August 2015. **k.** Auction: $1,293, MS-69, September 2015. **l.** Auction: $1,293, MS-69, September 2015.

| | Mintage | MS | MS-69 | MS-70 |
		PF	PF-69	PF-70
$25 1999 (m)	263,013	$1,100	$1,150	$3,000
$25 1999-W, Proof	30,427	$725	$775	$1,500
$25 2000	79,287	$1,000	$1,050	—
$25 2000-W, Proof	32,028	$725	$775	$1,500
$25 2001 (n)	48,047	$1,400	$1,500	$1,800
$25 2001-W, Proof	23,240	$725	$775	$1,500
$25 2002	70,027	$1,000	$1,050	—
$25 2002-W, Proof	26,646	$725	$775	$1,500
$25 2003	79,029	$750	$775	$900
$25 2003-W, Proof	28,270	$725	$775	$1,500
$25 2004	98,040	$645	$670	$900
$25 2004-W, Proof	27,330	$725	$775	$1,600
$25 2005	80,023	$645	$670	$900
$25 2005-W, Proof	34,311	$725	$775	$1,000
$25 2006	66,005	$645	$670	$900
$25 2006-W, Burnished (o)	15,164	$1,100	$1,150	$1,350
$25 2006-W, Proof	34,322	$725	$775	$950
$25 2007	47,002	$1,000	$1,050	$1,150
$25 2007-W, Burnished (p)	11,455	$1,100	$1,150	$1,700
$25 2007-W, Proof	44,025	$725	$775	$950
$25 2008	61,000	$645	$670	$870
$25 2008-W, Burnished (q)	15,682	$1,000	$1,050	$1,400
$25 2008-W, Proof	22,602	$1,000	$1,050	$1,200
$25 2009	110,000	$645	$670	$870
$25 2010	*81,000*	$645	$670	$950
$25 2010-W, Proof	*44,527*	$725	$775	$950
$25 2011	*70,000*	$645	$670	$870
$25 2011-W, Proof	*26,781*	$770	$790	$950
$25 2012	71,000	$645	$670	$870
$25 2012-W, Proof	12,919	$800	$820	$950
$25 2013	58,000	$645	$670	$870
$25 2013-W, Proof	12,716	$800	$820	$950
$25 2014	46,000	$645	$670	$870
$25 2014-W, Proof	14,693	$770	$795	$950
$25 2015	75,000	$645	$670	$870
$25 2015-W, Proof	*15,287*	$770	$795	$950

Note: MS values are for uncertified Mint State coins of average quality, in their complete original U.S. Mint packaging. PF values are for uncertified Proof coins of average quality, in their complete original U.S. Mint packaging. **m.** Auction: $646, MS-69, November 2014. **n.** Auction: $1,763, MS-69, July 2014. **o.** Auction: $705, MS-70, October 2015. **p.** Auction: $646, MS-69, October 2015. **q.** Auction: $1,175, MS-70, November 2015.

$50 1-OUNCE AMERICAN GOLD EAGLES

| | Mintage | MS | MS-69 | MS-70 |
		PF	PF-69	PF-70
$50 MCMLXXXVI (1986) (a)	1,362,650	$1,250	$1,275	$5,500
$50 MCMLXXXVI (1986)-W, Proof	446,290	$1,600	$1,650	$2,200
$50 MCMLXXXVII (1987) (b)	1,045,500	$1,250	$1,275	$5,000
$50 MCMLXXXVII (1987)-W, Proof	147,498	$1,600	$1,650	$2,200
$50 MCMLXXXVIII (1988) (c)	465,000	$1,250	$1,275	$11,000
$50 MCMLXXXVIII (1988)-W, Proof	87,133	$1,600	$1,650	$2,200
$50 MCMLXXXIX (1989)	415,790	$1,250	$1,275	—
$50 MCMLXXXIX (1989)-W, Proof	54,570	$1,600	$1,650	$2,250
$50 MCMXC (1990) (d)	373,210	$1,250	$1,275	$5,500
$50 MCMXC (1990)-W, Proof	62,401	$1,600	$1,650	$2,200
$50 MCMXCI (1991) (e)	243,100	$1,250	$1,275	$5,500
$50 MCMXCI (1991)-W, Proof	50,411	$1,600	$1,650	$3,000
$50 1992	275,000	$1,230	$1,250	$2,100
$50 1992-W, Proof (f)	44,826	$1,550	$1,600	$3,000
$50 1993	480,192	$1,230	$1,250	$2,600
$50 1993-W, Proof (g)	34,369	$1,600	$1,650	$3,500
$50 1994 (h)	221,633	$1,230	$1,250	$6,500
$50 1994-W, Proof	46,674	$1,550	$1,600	$2,500
$50 1995	200,636	$1,230	$1,250	—
$50 1995-W, Proof	46,368	$1,550	$1,600	$2,500
$50 1996	189,148	$1,230	$1,250	—
$50 1996-W, Proof	36,153	$1,600	$1,750	$2,500
$50 1997 (i)	664,508	$1,230	$1,250	$5,000
$50 1997-W, Proof	32,999	$1,600	$1,650	$2,500
$50 1998	1,468,530	$1,230	$1,250	$2,300
$50 1998-W, Proof (j)	25,886	$1,600	$1,650	$4,000
$50 1999	1,505,026	$1,230	$1,250	$2,300
$50 1999-W, Proof	31,427	$1,500	$1,550	$3,000
$50 2000	433,319	$1,230	$1,250	$2,500
$50 2000-W, Proof	33,007	$1,500	$1,550	$2,500
$50 2001 (k)	143,605	$1,230	$1,250	$3,000
$50 2001-W, Proof ‡ (l)	24,555	$1,550	$1,600	$5,000
$50 2002	222,029	$1,230	$1,250	$2,800
$50 2002-W, Proof	27,499	$1,550	$1,600	$2,200
$50 2003	416,032	$1,230	$1,250	$2,500
$50 2003-W, Proof	28,344	$1,550	$1,600	$2,200
$50 2004	417,019	$1,230	$1,250	$2,500
$50 2004-W, Proof	28,215	$1,550	$1,600	$2,200
$50 2005	356,555	$1,230	$1,250	$2,000
$50 2005-W, Proof	35,246	$1,500	$1,550	$2,150
$50 2006	237,510	$1,230	$1,250	$1,700
$50 2006-W, Burnished	45,053	$1,450	$1,500	$1,900
$50 2006-W, Proof	47,092	$1,500	$1,550	$2,100
$50 2006-W, Reverse Proof ‡ (m,n)	9,996	$2,900	$3,100	$3,650

Note: MS values are for uncertified Mint State coins of average quality, in their complete original U.S. Mint packaging. PF values are for uncertified Proof coins of average quality, in their complete original U.S. Mint packaging. ‡ Ranked in the *100 Greatest U.S. Modern Coins*. **a.** Auction: $2,585, MS-70, June 2015. **b.** Auction:$1,351, MS-68, August 2014. **c.** Auction: $1,303, MS-68, December 2013. **d.** Auction: $1,469, MS-69, March 2014. **e.** Auction: $1,293, MS-69, July 2015. **f.** Auction: $2,056, PF-70UCam, July 2015. **g.** Auction: $2,233, PF-70UCam, June 2015. **h.** Auction: $2,820, MS-69, April 2014. **i.** Auction: $1,645, MS-69, April 2014. **j.** $2,233, PF-70UCam, September 2015. **k.** Auction: $1,351, MS-69, October 2014. **l.** Auction: $2,820, PF-70UCam, January 2015. **m.** The 2006-W Reverse Proof coins were issued to mark the 20th anniversary of the Bullion Coinage Program. They have brilliant devices, and their background fields are frosted (rather than the typical Proof format of frosted devices and mirror-like backgrounds). **n.** Auction: $4,935, PF-70, September 2015.

| | Mintage | MS | MS-69 | MS-70 |
		PF	PF-69	PF-70
$50 2007	140,016	$1,230	$1,250	$1,950
$50 2007-W, Burnished	18,066	$1,600	$1,650	$2,050
$50 2007-W, Proof	51,810	$1,500	$1,550	$2,100
$50 2008	710,000	$1,230	$1,250	$1,950
$50 2008-W, Burnished (o)	11,908	$2,200	$2,250	$2,300
$50 2008-W, Proof	30,237	$1,600	$1,650	$2,500
$50 2009	1,493,000	$1,230	$1,250	$1,750
$50 2010	1,125,000	$1,230	$1,250	$1,550
$50 2010-W, Proof	59,480	$1,500	$1,550	$2,100
$50 2011	857,000	$1,230	$1,250	$1,550
$50 2011-W, Burnished (p)	8,729	$2,200	$2,250	$2,600
$50 2011-W, Proof	48,306	$1,600	$1,650	$2,100
$50 2012	667,000	$1,230	$1,250	$1,550
$50 2012-W, Burnished (q)	6,118	$2,400	$2,450	$3,100
$50 2012-W, Proof	23,805	$1,700	$1,750	$2,100
$50 2013	743,500	$1,230	$1,250	$1,600
$50 2013-W, Burnished	7,293	$1,650	$1,700	$2,200
$50 2013-W, Proof	24,709	$1,700	$1,750	$2,100
$50 2014	415,300	$1,230	$1,250	$1,500
$50 2014-W, Burnished		$1,650	$1,700	$1,750
$50 2014-W, Proof	28,703	$1,600	$1,650	$2,100
$50 2015	220,500	$1,230	$1,250	$1,500
$50 2015-W, Proof	16,593	$1,600	$1,700	$2,100

Note: MS values are for uncertified Mint State coins of average quality, in their complete original U.S. Mint packaging. PF values are for uncertified Proof coins of average quality, in their complete original U.S. Mint packaging. ‡ Ranked in the *100 Greatest U.S. Modern Coins*. **o.** Auction: $1,293, MS-69, July 2015. **p.** Auction: $1,998, MS-70, June 2015. **q.** Auction: $2,585, MS-70, February 2015.

AMERICAN GOLD EAGLE PROOF COIN SETS

	PF	PF-69	PF-70
1987 Gold Set. $50, $25	$2,400	$2,450	$4,200
1988 Gold Set. $50, $25, $10, $5	$2,850	$3,000	$4,850
1989 Gold Set. $50, $25, $10, $5	$3,000	$3,250	—
1990 Gold Set. $50, $25, $10, $5	$2,850	$3,000	—
1991 Gold Set. $50, $25, $10, $5	$2,850	$3,000	$5,600
1992 Gold Set. $50, $25, $10, $5	$2,800	$2,950	$5,700
1993 Gold Set. $50, $25, $10, $5	$2,850	$3,000	—
1993 Bicentennial Gold Set. $25, $10, $5, Silver Eagle, and medal (a)	$1,350	$1,450	—
1994 Gold Set. $50, $25, $10, $5	$2,800	$2,950	$5,000
1995 Gold Set. $50, $25, $10, $5	$2,800	$2,950	$5,000
1995 Anniversary Gold Set. $50, $25, $10, $5, and Silver Eagle (b)	$6,550	$7,700	—
1996 Gold Set. $50, $25, $10, $5	$2,850	$3,000	$5,000
1997 Gold Set. $50, $25, $10, $5	$2,850	$3,000	$5,600
1997 Impressions of Liberty Set. $100 platinum, $50 gold, Silver Eagle (c)	$3,300	$3,400	$6,200
1998 Gold Set. $50, $25, $10, $5	$2,850	$3,000	$6,850
1999 Gold Set. $50, $25, $10, $5	$2,750	$2,900	$5,600
2000 Gold Set. $50, $25, $10, $5	$2,750	$2,900	$5,100
2001 Gold Set. $50, $25, $10, $5	$2,800	$2,950	$7,700

Note: PF values are for uncertified Proof sets of average quality, in their complete original U.S. Mint packaging. **a.** The 1993 set was issued to commemorate the bicentennial of the first coins struck by the U.S. Mint in Philadelphia. **b.** The 1995 set marked the 10th anniversary of the passage of the Liberty Coin Act, which authorized the nation's new bullion coinage program. **c.** The Impressions of Liberty set was issued in the first year that platinum coins were added to the Mint's bullion offerings.

	PF	PF-69	PF-70
2002 Gold Set. $50, $25, $10, $5	$2,800	$2,950	$4,450
2003 Gold Set. $50, $25, $10, $5	$2,800	$2,950	$4,450
2004 Gold Set. $50, $25, $10, $5	$2,800	$2,950	$4,800
2005 Gold Set. $50, $25, $10, $5	$1,800	$1,950	$3,800
2006 Gold Set. $50, $25, $10, $5	$2,800	$2,950	$3,900
2007 Gold Set. $50, $25, $10, $5	$2,800	$2,950	$3,900
2008 Gold Set. $50, $25, $10, $5	$3,000	$3,250	$4,700
2010 Gold Set. $50, $25, $10, $5 (d)	$2,800	$2,950	$3,800
2011 Gold Set. $50, $25, $10, $5	$2,850	$3,000	$3,850
2012 Gold Set. $50, $25, $10, $5	$2,950	$3,200	$3,850
2013 Gold Set. $50, $25, $10, $5	$2,950	$3,200	$3,800
2014 Gold Set. $50, $25, $10, $5	$2,950	$3,100	$3,800
2015 Gold Set. $50, $25, $10, $5	$2,950	$3,100	$3,800

Note: PF values are for uncertified Proof sets of average quality, in their complete original U.S. Mint packaging. **d.** The U.S. Mint did not issue a 2009 gold set.

2006 AMERICAN GOLD EAGLE 20TH-ANNIVERSARY COIN SETS

	Uncertified	69	70
2006-W $50 Gold Set. Uncirculated, Proof, and Reverse Proof	$5,900	$6,000	$7,500
2006-W 1-oz. Gold- and Silver-Dollar Set. Uncirculated	$1,550	$1,600	$2,100

Note: Uncertified values are for uncertified sets of average quality, in their complete original U.S. Mint packaging.

GOLD BULLION BURNISHED SETS

	Uncertified	69	70
2006-W Burnished Gold Set. $50, $25, $10, $5	$3,700	$4,000	$5,000
2007-W Burnished Gold Set. $50, $25, $10, $5	$4,000	$4,250	$5,500
2008-W Burnished Gold Set. $50, $25, $10, $5	$5,350	$5,500	$7,000

Note: Uncertified values are for uncertified sets of average quality, in their complete original U.S. Mint packaging.

AMERICAN BUFFALO .9999 FINE GOLD BULLION COINS (2006 TO DATE)

Designer: *James Earle Fraser.* **Weight:** *$5 1/10 oz.—3.393 grams; $10 1/4 oz.—8.483 grams; $25 1/2 oz.—16.966 grams; $50 1 oz.—31.108 grams.* **Composition:** *.9999 gold.* **Diameter:** *$5 1/10 oz.—16.5 mm; $10 1/4 oz.—22 mm; $25 1/2 oz.—27 mm; $50 1 oz.—32.7 mm.* **Edge:** *Reeded.* **Mint:** *West Point.*

Regular Finish   **Burnished Finish**

Obverse design common to all denominations.

Mintmark location is on the obverse, behind the neck.

Proof Finish

Reverse Proof Finish

History. American Buffalo gold bullion coins, authorized by Congress in 2005 and produced since 2006, are the first 24-karat (.9999 fine) gold coins made by the U.S. Mint. They are coined, by mandate, of gold derived from newly mined sources in America. They feature an adaptation of James Earle Fraser's iconic Indian Head / Buffalo design, first used on circulating five-cent pieces of 1913 to 1938.

Only 1-ounce ($50 face value) coins were struck in the American Buffalo program's first two years, 2006 and 2007. For 2008, the Mint expanded the coinage to include fractional pieces of 1/2 ounce ($25), 1/4 ounce ($10), and 1/10-ounce ($5), in various finishes, individually and in sets.

The coins are legal tender, with weight, content, and purity guaranteed by the federal government. Investors can include them in some individual retirement accounts. Proofs and Burnished (*Uncirculated*, in the Mint's wording) pieces undergo special production processes, similar to the American Eagle gold-bullion coinage, and can be purchased directly from the Mint. As with other products in the Mint's bullion program, regular bullion-strike pieces are distributed through a network of authorized distributors.

All American Buffalo gold bullion coins (Proofs, Burnished, and regular bullion pieces) are struck at the U.S. Mint's West Point facility.

Striking and Sharpness. Striking is generally sharp.

Availability. American Buffalo .9999 fine gold bullion coins are a popular way to buy and sell 24-karat gold. The coins are readily available in the numismatic marketplace as well as from participating banks, investment firms, and other non-numismatic channels.

MS-60 to 70 (Mint State). *Obverse and reverse:* At MS-60, some abrasion and contact marks are evident on the higher design areas and the open areas of the design. Luster may be dull or lifeless at MS–60 to 62, but there should be deep frost at MS-63 and better, particularly in the lower-relief areas. At MS-65 and above, the luster should be full and rich. Contact marks and abrasion are less and less evident at higher grades. These guidelines are more academic than practical, as these coins are not intended for circulation, and nearly all are in high Mint State grades, as struck.

PF-60 to 70 (Proof). *Obverse and reverse:* Proofs that are extensively cleaned and have many hairlines are lower level, such as PF–60 to 62. Those with fewer hairlines or flaws are deemed PF–63 to 65. (These exist more in theory than actuality, as nearly all Proof American Buffalo gold coins have been maintained in their original high condition by collectors and investors.) Given the quality of modern U.S. Mint products, even PF–66 and 67 are unusually low levels for these Proofs.

AMERICAN BUFFALO .9999 FINE GOLD BULLION COINS

$5 1/10-oz.   **$10 1/4-oz.**   **$25 1/2-oz.**

$50 1-oz.

	Mintage	MS	MS-69	MS-70
		PF	PF-69	PF-70
$5 2008-W, Burnished (a)	17,429	$500	$535	$650
$5 2008-W, Proof (b)	18,884	$500	$535	$350
$10 2008-W, Burnished ‡ (c)	9,949	$1,275	$1,350	$1,500
$10 2008-W, Proof (d)	13,125	$1,100	$1,250	$1,550
$25 2008-W, Burnished (e)	16,908	$1,250	$1,300	$1,700
$25 2008-W, Proof (f)	12,169	$1,450	$1,500	$1,800
$50 2006	337,012	$1,230	$1,280	$1,400
$50 2006-W, Proof	246,267	$1,300	$1,350	$1,500
$50 2007	136,503	$1,230	$1,280	$1,400
$50 2007-W, Proof	58,998	$1,300	$1,350	$1,500
$50 2008	214,058 (g)	$1,250	$1,300	$1,500
$50 2008-W, Burnished (h)	9,074	$2,350	$2,400	$3,200
$50 2008-W, Proof ‡ (i)	18,863	$3,100	$3,200	$3,400
$50 2009	200,000	$1,230	$1,280	$1,400
$50 2009-W, Proof	49,306	$1,350	$1,400	$1,500
$50 2010	209,000	$1,230	$1,280	$1,400
$50 2010-W, Proof	49,263	$1,300	$1,350	$1,500
$50 2011	174,500	$1,230	$1,280	$1,500
$50 2011-W, Proof	28,693	$1,400	$1,450	$1,650
$50 2012	132,000	$1,400	$1,450	$1,550
$50 2012-W, Proof	19,765	$1,800	$1,850	$2,200
$50 2013	239,000	$1,350	$1,400	$1,550
$50 2013-W, Proof	18,594	$1,550	$1,600	$2,100
$50 2013-W, Reverse Proof	47,836	$1,500	$1,550	$2,000
$50 2014	177,500	$1,230	$1,280	$1,550
$50 2014-W, Proof	20,557	$1,600	$1,650	$1,750
$50 2015	220,500	$1,230	$1,280	$1,400
$50 2015-W, Proof	16,593	$1,400	$1,450	$1,500

Note: MS values are for uncertified Mint State coins of average quality, in their complete original U.S. Mint packaging. PF values are for uncertified Proof coins of average quality, in their complete original U.S. Mint packaging. ‡ Ranked in the *100 Greatest U.S. Modern Coins*. **a.** Auction: $447, MS-70, September 2015. **b.** Auction: $705, PF-70DCam, June 2015. **c.** Auction: $1,116, MS-70, August 2015. **d.** Auction: $823, PF-70DCam, January 2015. **e.** Auction: $764, MS-69, November 2015. **f.** Auction: $1,528, PF-70UCam, August 2015. **g.** 24,558 sold as Lunar New Year Celebration coins. **h.** Auction: $2,703, MS-70, June 2015. **i.** Auction: $3,525, PF-70DCam, July 2015.

AMERICAN BUFFALO .9999 FINE GOLD BULLION COIN SETS

	Uncertified	MS-69 PF-69	MS-70 PF-70
2008-W Four-coin set ($5, $10, $25, $50), Proof	$6,100	$6,450	$7,400
2008-W Four-coin set ($5, $10, $25, $50), Burnished	$5,350	$5,500	$7,000
2008-W Double Prosperity set (Unc. $25 American Buffalo gold and $25 American Gold Eagle coins)	$2,250	$2,350	$3,100

Note: Uncertified values are for uncertified sets of average quality, in their complete original U.S. Mint packaging.

FIRST SPOUSE $10 GOLD BULLION COINS (2007 TO DATE)

Designers: *See image captions for designers.* **Weight:** *8.483 grams.*
Composition: *.9999 gold.* **Diameter:** *26.5 mm.* **Edge:** *Reeded.* **Mint:** *West Point.*

Burnished Finish
The first coin in the series, featuring Martha Washington.

Mintmark location is on the obverse, below the date.

Proof Finish

History. The U.S. Mint's First Spouse bullion coins are struck in .9999 fine (24-karat) gold. Each weighs one-half ounce and bears a face value of $10. The coins honor the nation's first spouses on the same schedule as the Mint's Presidential dollars program. Each features a portrait on the obverse, and on the reverse a unique design symbolic of the spouse's life and work. In cases where a president held office widowed or unmarried, the coin bears "an obverse image emblematic of Liberty as depicted on a circulating coin of that era and a reverse image emblematic of themes of that president's life." All First Spouse gold bullion coins (Proofs and Burnished pieces) are struck at the U.S. Mint's West Point facility.

Note that the Mint does not release bullion mintage data on a regular basis; the numbers given herein reflect the most recently available official data.

Striking and Sharpness. Striking is generally sharp.

Availability. These coins are readily available in the numismatic marketplace. They can be purchased by the public, in both Burnished and Proof formats, directly from the U.S. Mint. Sales of recent issues have been low, leading to some issues being ranked among the 100 Greatest U.S. Modern Coins.

MS-60 to 70 (Mint State). *Obverse and Reverse:* At MS-60, some abrasion and contact marks are evident on the higher design areas and the open areas of the design. Luster may be dull or lifeless at MS–60 to 62, but there should be deep frost at MS-63 and better, particularly in the lower-relief areas. At MS-65 and above, the luster should be full and rich. Contact marks and abrasion are less and less evident at higher grades. These guidelines are more academic than practical, as these coins are not intended for circulation, and nearly all are in high Mint State grades, as struck.

PF-60 to 70 (Proof). *Obverse and Reverse:* Proofs that are extensively cleaned and have many hairlines are lower level, such as PF–60 to 62. Those with fewer hairlines or flaws are deemed PF–63 to 65. (These exist more in theory than actuality, as nearly all Proof First Spouse gold coins have been maintained in their original high condition by collectors and investors.) Given the quality of modern U.S. Mint products, even PF–66 and 67 are unusually low levels for these Proofs.

FIRST SPOUSE $10 GOLD BULLION COINS

Martha Washington
Designers:
obverse—Joseph Menna;
reverse—Susan Gamble.

Abigail Adams
Designers:
obverse—Joseph Menna;
reverse—Thomas Cleveland.

Jefferson's Liberty
Designers: obverse—
Robert Scot / Phebe Hemphill;
reverse—Charles Vickers.

Dolley Madison
Designers:
obverse—Don Everhart;
reverse—Joel Iskowitz.

	Mintage	MS	MS-69	MS-70
		PF	PF-69	PF-70
$10 2007-W, M. Washington	17,661	$650	$675	$700
$10 2007-W, M. Washington, Proof	19,167	$650	$675	$700
$10 2007-W, A. Adams	17,142	$650	$675	$700
$10 2007-W, A. Adams, Proof	17,149	$650	$675	$700
$10 2007-W, Jefferson's Liberty	19,823	$650	$675	$700
$10 2007-W, Jefferson's Liberty, Proof	19,815	$650	$675	$700
$10 2007-W, D. Madison	12,340	$650	$675	$700
$10 2007-W, D. Madison, Proof	17,943	$650	$675	$700

Note: MS values are for uncertified Mint State coins of average quality, in their complete original U.S. Mint packaging. PF values are for uncertified Proof coins of average quality, in their complete original U.S. Mint packaging.

Elizabeth Monroe
Designers:
obverse—Joel Iskowitz;
reverse—Donna Weaver.

Louisa Adams
Designers:
obverse—Susan Gamble;
reverse—Donna Weaver.

Jackson's Liberty
Designers:
obverse—John Reich;
reverse—Justin Kunz.

Van Buren's Liberty
Designer:
obverse—Christian Gobrecht;
reverse—Thomas Cleveland.

	Mintage	MS	MS-69	MS-70
		PF	PF-69	PF-70
$10 2008-W, E. Monroe	4,462	$800	$850	$1,000
$10 2008-W, E. Monroe, Proof	7,800	$750	$800	$1,250
$10 2008-W, L. Adams	3,885	$900	$950	$1,000
$10 2008-W, L. Adams, Proof	6,581	$800	$850	$1,250

Note: MS values are for uncertified Mint State coins of average quality, in their complete original U.S. Mint packaging. PF values are for uncertified Proof coins of average quality, in their complete original U.S. Mint packaging.

	Mintage	MS	MS-69	MS-70
		PF	PF-69	PF-70
$10 2008-W, Jackson's Liberty ‡ (a)	4,609	$1,200	$1,250	$1,400
$10 2008-W, Jackson's Liberty, Proof	7,684	$850	$900	$1,400
$10 2008-W, Van Buren's Liberty	3,826	$1,250	$1,300	$1,450
$10 2008-W, Van Buren's Liberty, Proof (b)	6,807	$1,250	$1,300	$1,600

Note: MS values are for uncertified Mint State coins of average quality, in their complete original U.S. Mint packaging. PF values are for uncertified Proof coins of average quality, in their complete original U.S. Mint packaging. ‡ Ranked in the *100 Greatest U.S. Modern Coins.* **a.** Auction: $999, MS-69, February 2015. **b.** Auction: $1,058, PF-70DCam, January 2015.

Anna Harrison
Designers:
obverse—Donna Weaver;
reverse—Thomas Cleveland.

Letitia Tyler
Designers:
obverse—Phebe Hemphill;
reverse—Susan Gamble.

Julia Tyler
Designer:
obverse and reverse—
Joel Iskowitz.

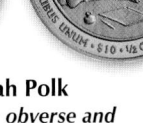

Sarah Polk
Designer: obverse and
reverse—Phebe Hemphill.

Margaret Taylor
Designers: obverse—Phebe Hemphill;
reverse—Mary Beth Zeitz.

	Mintage	MS	MS-69	MS-70
		PF	PF-69	PF-70
$10 2009-W, A. Harrison	3,645	$1,100	$1,150	$1,350
$10 2009-W, A. Harrison, Proof (c)	6,251	$1,000	$1,050	$1,350
$10 2009-W, L. Tyler	3,240	$1,300	$1,350	$1,500
$10 2009-W, L. Tyler, Proof (d)	5,296	$1,200	$1,250	$1,350
$10 2009-W, J. Tyler (e)	3,143	$1,300	$1,350	$1,500
$10 2009-W, J. Tyler, Proof (f)	4,844	$1,200	$1,250	$1,350
$10 2009-W, S. Polk	3,489	$925	$975	$1,400
$10 2009-W, S. Polk, Proof	5,151	$800	$850	$1,000
$10 2009-W, M. Taylor	3,627	$850	$900	$1,025
$10 2009-W, M. Taylor, Proof	4,936	$750	$800	$1,050

Note: MS values are for uncertified Mint State coins of average quality, in their complete original U.S. Mint packaging. PF values are for uncertified Proof coins of average quality, in their complete original U.S. Mint packaging. **c.** Auction: $646, PF-69DCam, June 2015. **d.** Auction: $881, PF-70DCam, June 2015. **e.** Auction: $1,293, MS-70, June 2015. **f.** Auction: $764, PF-69DCam, June 2015.

Abigail Fillmore
Designers:
obverse—Phebe Hemphill;
reverse—Susan Gamble.

Jane Pierce
Designer:
obverse and reverse—
Donna Weaver.

Buchanan's Liberty
Designers:
obverse—Christian Gobrecht;
reverse—David Westwood.

Mary Lincoln
Designers:
obverse—Phebe Hemphill;
reverse—Joel Iskowitz.

	Mintage	MS	MS-69	MS-70
		PF	PF-69	PF-70
$10 2010-W, A. Fillmore	3,482	$1,000	$1,050	$1,150
$10 2010-W, A. Fillmore, Proof	6,130	$900	$950	$1,025
$10 2010-W, J. Pierce	3,338	$1,000	$1,025	$1,100
$10 2010-W, J. Pierce, Proof	4,775	$900	$925	$1,200
$10 2010-W, Buchanan's Liberty	5,162	$800	$850	$1,050
$10 2010-W, Buchanan's Liberty, Proof	7,110	$900	$950	$1,200
$10 2010-W, M. Lincoln	3,695	$900	$950	$1,100
$10 2010-W, M. Lincoln, Proof	6,861	$900	$950	$1,250

Note: MS values are for uncertified Mint State coins of average quality, in their complete original U.S. Mint packaging. PF values are for uncertified Proof coins of average quality, in their complete original U.S. Mint packaging.

Eliza Johnson
Designers:
obverse—Joel Iskowitz;
reverse—Gary Whitley.

Julia Grant
Designers:
obverse—Donna Weaver;
reverse—Richard Masters.

Lucy Hayes
Designers:
obverse—Susan Gamble;
reverse—Barbara Fox.

Lucretia Garfield
Designers:
obverse—Barbara Fox;
reverse—Michael Gaudioso.

	Mintage	MS	MS-69	MS-70
		PF	PF-69	PF-70
$10 2011-W, E. Johnson	2,905	$900	$950	$1,625
$10 2011-W, E. Johnson, Proof	3,887	$950	$1,000	$1,200
$10 2011-W, J. Grant	2,892	$900	$950	$1,175
$10 2011-W, J. Grant, Proof	3,943	$950	$1,000	$1,150

Note: MS values are for uncertified Mint State coins of average quality, in their complete original U.S. Mint packaging. PF values are for uncertified Proof coins of average quality, in their complete original U.S. Mint packaging.

	Mintage	MS	MS-69	MS-70
		PF	PF-69	PF-70
$10 2011-W, L. Hayes (g)	2,196	$1,300	$1,350	$1,800
$10 2011-W, L. Hayes, Proof	3,868	$950	$1,000	$1,350
$10 2011-W, L. Garfield	2,168	$1,350	$1,400	$2,650
$10 2011-W, L. Garfield, Proof	3,653	$950	$1,000	$1,250

Note: MS values are for uncertified Mint State coins of average quality, in their complete original U.S. Mint packaging. PF values are for uncertified Proof coins of average quality, in their complete original U.S. Mint packaging. **g.** Auction: $1,763, MS-70, January 2015.

Alice Paul
Designers:
obverse—Susan Gamble;
reverse—Phebe Hemphill.

Frances Cleveland (Type 1)
Designers:
obverse—Joel Iskowitz;
reverse—Barbara Fox.

Caroline Harrison
Designers:
obverse—Frank Morris;
reverse—Donna Weaver.

Frances Cleveland (Type 2)
Designers:
obverse—Barbara Fox;
reverse—Joseph Menna.

	Mintage	MS	MS-69	MS-70
		PF	PF-69	PF-70
$10 2012-W, Alice Paul	2,798	$850	$900	$950
$10 2012-W, Alice Paul, Proof	3,505	$875	$925	$1,000
$10 2012-W, Frances Cleveland, Variety 1	2,454	$850	$900	$950
$10 2012-W, Frances Cleveland, Variety 1, Proof	3,158	$875	$925	$1,000
$10 2012-W, Caroline Harrison	2,436	$850	$900	$1,150
$10 2012-W, Caroline Harrison, Proof	3,046	$875	$925	$1,000
$10 2012-W, Frances Cleveland, Variety 2	2,425	$850	$900	$950
$10 2012-W, Frances Cleveland, Variety 2, Proof	3,104	$875	$925	$1,000

Note: MS values are for uncertified Mint State coins of average quality, in their complete original U.S. Mint packaging. PF values are for uncertified Proof coins of average quality, in their complete original U.S. Mint packaging.

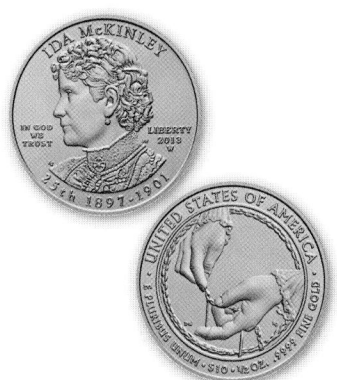

Ida McKinley
Designers:
obverse—Susan Gamble;
reverse—Donna Weaver.

Edith Roosevelt
Designers:
obverse—Joel Iskowitz;
reverse—Chris Costello.

Helen Taft
Designers:
obverse—William C. Burgard;
reverse—Richard Masters.

Ellen Wilson
Designers: obverse—Frank Morris;
reverse—Don Everhart.

Edith Wilson
Designers: obverse—David Westwood;
reverse—Joseph Menna.

	Mintage	MS	MS-69	MS-70
		PF	PF-69	PF-70
$10 2013-W, I. McKinley	2,008	$825	$875	$975
$10 2013-W, I. McKinley, Proof	2,724	$875	$925	$1,000
$10 2013-W, E. Roosevelt	2,027	$825	$875	$975
$10 2013-W, E. Roosevelt, Proof	2,840	$875	$925	$1,000
$10 2013-W, H. Taft	1,993	$825	$875	$975
$10 2013-W, H. Taft, Proof	2,598	$875	$925	$1,000
$10 2013-W, Ellen Wilson	1,980	$825	$875	$975
$10 2013-W, Ellen Wilson, Proof	2,511	$875	$925	$1,000
$10 2013-W, Edith Wilson	1,974	$825	$875	$975
$10 2013-W, Edith Wilson, Proof	2,464	$875	$925	$1,000

Note: MS values are for uncertified Mint State coins of average quality, in their complete original U.S. Mint packaging. PF values are for uncertified Proof coins of average quality, in their complete original U.S. Mint packaging.

Florence Harding
Designer:
obverse and reverse—
Thomas Cleveland.

Grace Coolidge
Designers:
obverse—Joel Iskowitz;
reverse—Frank Morris.

Lou Hoover
Designers:
obverse—Susan Gamble;
reverse—Richard Masters.

Eleanor Roosevelt
Designer:
obverse and reverse—
Chris Costello.

	Mintage	MS	MS-69	MS-70
		PF	PF-69	PF-70
$10 2014-W, F. Harding	1,801	$800	$850	$950
$10 2014-W, F. Harding, Proof	2,372	$875	$925	$1,000
$10 2014-W, G. Coolidge	1,797	$800	$850	$950
$10 2014-W, G. Coolidge, Proof	2,315	$875	$925	$1,000
$10 2014-W, L. Hoover	1,779	$800	$850	$950
$10 2014-W, L. Hoover, Proof	2,299	$875	$925	$1,000
$10 2014-W, E. Roosevelt	1,886	$800	$850	$950
$10 2014-W, E. Roosevelt, Proof	2,377	$875	$925	$1,000

Note: MS values are for uncertified Mint State coins of average quality, in their complete original U.S. Mint packaging. PF values are for uncertified Proof coins of average quality, in their complete original U.S. Mint packaging.

Bess Truman
Designer:
obverse and reverse—
Joel Iskowitz.

Mamie Eisenhower
Designers:
obverse—Richard Masters;
reverse—Barbara Fox.

Jacqueline Kennedy
Designers:
obverse—Susan Gamble;
reverse—Benjamin Sowards.

Claudia "Lady Bird" Johnson
Designers:
obverse—Linda Fox;
reverse—Chris Costello.

| | Mintage | MS | MS-69 | MS-70 |
		PF	PF-69	PF-70
$10 2015-W, B. Truman	1,654	$800	$850	$950
$10 2015-W, B. Truman, Proof	2,367	$875	$925	$1,000
$10 2015-W, M. Eisenhower	1,725	$800	$850	$950
$10 2015-W, M. Eisenhower, Proof	2,595	$875	$925	$1,000
$10 2015-W, J. Kennedy	5,491	$800	$850	$950
$10 2015-W, J. Kennedy, Proof	11,123	$875	$925	$1,000
$10 2015-W, Lady Bird Johnson	1,475	$800	$850	$950
$10 2015-W, Lady Bird Johnson, Proof	2,285	$875	$925	$1,000

Note: MS values are for uncertified Mint State coins of average quality, in their complete original U.S. Mint packaging. PF values are for uncertified Proof coins of average quality, in their complete original U.S. Mint packaging.

| | Mintage | MS | MS-69 | MS-70 |
		PF	PF-69	PF-70
$10 2016-W, P. Nixon		$800	$850	$950
$10 2016-W, P. Nixon, Proof		$875	$925	$1,000
$10 2016-W, B. Ford		$800	$850	$950
$10 2016-W, B. Ford, Proof		$875	$925	$1,000
$10 2016-W, N. Reagan		$800	$850	$950
$10 2016-W, N. Reagan, Proof		$875	$925	$1,000

Note: MS values are for uncertified Mint State coins of average quality, in their complete original U.S. Mint packaging. PF values are for uncertified Proof coins of average quality, in their complete original U.S. Mint packaging.

MMIX ULTRA HIGH RELIEF GOLD COIN (2009)

Designer: *Augustus Saint-Gaudens;* **Weight:** *31.101 grams.*
Composition: *.9999 gold (actual gold weight 1 oz.).*
Diameter: *27 mm.* **Edge:** *Lettered.* **Mint:** *Philadelphia.*

MMIX Ultra High Relief Gold Coin
Photographed at an angle to show the edge (lettered
E PLURIBUS UNUM), the thickness (4 mm), and the depth of relief.

History. In 2009 the U.S. Mint produced a modern collector's version of the first Saint-Gaudens double eagle. When the original debuted in 1907, the Mint had been unable to strike large quantities for circulation—the ultra high relief design was artistic, but difficult to coin. (It was modified later in 1907 to a lower relief suitable for commercial production.) Just over 100 years later, the 2009 version was a showcase coin: a tangible demonstration of the Mint's 21st-century ability to combine artistry and technology to make an outstanding numismatic treasure.

Like its predecessor, the new coin was dated in Roman numerals (with 2009 as MMIX). The Mint digitally mapped Saint-Gaudens's original plasters and used the results in the die-making process. The date was changed, and four additional stars were inserted, to represent the nation's current 50 states. Augustus Saint-Gaudens's striding Liberty occupied the obverse. On the reverse was his flying eagle, with the addition of IN GOD WE TRUST, a motto not used in the original design. The 2009 version was made in a smaller diameter (27 mm instead of 34), with a thickness of 4 mm, and composed of 24-karat (.9999 fine) gold, thus making it easier to strike and stay true to the ultra high relief design.

As with other bullion products of the U.S. Mint, the coins are legal tender and their weight, content, and purity are guaranteed by the federal government. They were packaged in a fancy mahogany box and sold directly to the public, instead of through a network of distributors.

Note that the Mint does not release bullion mintage data on a regular basis; the number given here reflects the most recently available official data.

Striking and Sharpness. Striking is sharp.

Availability. The coins are available in the numismatic marketplace for a premium above their gold bullion value.

MS-60 to 70 (Mint State). *Obverse and Reverse:* At MS-60, some abrasion and contact marks are evident on the higher design areas and the open areas of the design. Luster may be dull or lifeless at MS–60 to 62, but there should be deep frost at MS-63 and better, particularly in the lower-relief areas. At MS-65 and above, the luster should be full and rich. Contact marks and abrasion are less and less evident at higher grades. These guidelines are more academic than practical, as these coins are not intended for circulation, and presumably all are in high Mint State grades, as struck.

MMIX ULTRA HIGH RELIEF GOLD COIN

	Mintage	MS	MS-69	MS-70
MMIX Ultra High Relief $20 Gold Coin ‡ (a)	114,427	$2,150	$2,200	$2,750

Note: MS values are for uncertified Mint State coins of average quality, in their complete original U.S. Mint packaging. ‡ Ranked in the *100 Greatest U.S. Modern Coins.* **a.** Auction: $2,820, MS-70, October 2015.

AMERICAN PLATINUM EAGLES
(1997 TO DATE)

Designers: *John M. Mercanti (obverse), Thomas D. Rogers Sr. (original reverse)*
(see image captions for other reverse designers). **Weight:** *$10 1/10 oz.—3.112 grams;*
$25 1/4 oz.—7.780 grams; $50 1/2 oz.—15.560 grams; $100 1 oz.—31.120 grams.
Composition: *.9995 platinum.* **Diameter:** *$10 1/10 oz.—16.5 mm; $25 1/4 oz.—22 mm;*
$50 1/2 oz.—27 mm; $100 1 oz.—32.7 mm. **Edge:** *Reeded.* **Mints:** *Philadelphia and West Point.*

Regular Finish

Burnished Finish
Burnished coins of all denominations feature the year's
Proof reverse design. Mintmark location varies by design.

Proof Finish
First-year Proof coins featured the original
reverse design, which is still in use on bullion
strikes. See pages 1287–1289 for illustrations
of Proof reverse designs from 1998 to date.

Reverse Proof Finish
Reverse Proofs were only struck in 2007,
and only in the $50 1/2-oz. denomination.

Frosted FREEDOM
This variety is seen,
very rarely, for 2007
Proof coins of the
$25, $50, and $100
denominations.

History. Platinum American Eagles (face values of $10 to $100) are legal-tender bullion coins with weight, content, and purity guaranteed by the federal government. They were added to the U.S. Mint's program of silver and gold bullion coinage in 1997.

In their debut year, Proofs had the same reverse design as regular bullion strikes. Since then, the regular strikes have continued with the 1997 reverse, while the Proofs have featured new reverse designs each year. From 1998 through 2002, these special Proof designs comprised a "Vistas of Liberty" subset, with eagles flying through various American scenes. Since 2003, they have featured patriotic allegories and symbolism. From 2006 to 2008 the reverse designs honored "The Foundations of Democracy"—the nation's legislative branch (2006), executive branch (2007), and judicial branch (2008). In 2009 the Mint introduced a new six-year program of reverse designs, exploring the core concepts of American democracy as embodied in the preamble to the Constitution. The designs—which were based on narratives by John Roberts, chief justice of the United States—began with *To Form a More Perfect Union* (2009), which features four faces representing the nation's diversity, with the hair and clothing interweaving symbolically. The tiny eagle privy mark is from an original coin punch from the Philadelphia Mint's archives. This design is followed by *To Establish Justice* (2010), *To Insure Domestic Tranquility* (2011), *To Provide for the Common Defence* (2012), *To Promote the General Welfare* (2013), and *To Secure the Blessings of Liberty to Ourselves and Our Posterity* (2014). In 2015, the Mint issued the first of a two-year series of new reverse designs emblematic of the core values of liberty and freedom called *Liberty Nurtures Freedom*.

The Philadelphia Mint strikes regular bullion issues, which are sold to the public by a network of Mint-authorized precious-metal firms, coin dealers, banks, and brokerages. The West Point facility strikes Burnished pieces (called *Uncirculated* by the Mint, and featuring the reverse design of the Proof coins), which are sold directly to collectors. Proofs are also struck at West Point and, like the Burnished coins, are sold by the Mint to the public, without middlemen. Similar to their gold-bullion cousins, the platinum Proofs and Burnished coins bear a W mintmark and are specially packaged in plastic capsules and fancy presentation cases.

In addition to the individual coins listed below, platinum American Eagles were issued in the 1997 "Impressions of Liberty" bullion coin set (see page 1271); in 2007 "10th Anniversary" sets; and in annual platinum-coin sets.

Striking and Sharpness. Striking is generally sharp.

Availability. The platinum American Eagle is one of the most popular platinum-investment vehicles in the world. The coins are readily available in the numismatic marketplace and through some banks, investment firms, and other non-numismatic channels.

MS-60 to 70 (Mint State). *Obverse and Reverse:* At MS-60, some abrasion and contact marks are evident on the higher design areas. Luster may be dull or lifeless at MS–60 to 62, but there should be deep frost at MS-63 and better, particularly in the lower-relief areas. At MS-65 and above, the luster should be full and rich. These guidelines are more academic than practical, as platinum American Eagles are not intended for circulation, and nearly all are in high Mint State grades.

PF-60 to 70 (Proof). *Obverse and Reverse:* Proofs that are extensively cleaned and have many hairlines are lower level, such as PF–60 to 62. Those with fewer hairlines or flaws are deemed PF–63 to 65. (These exist more in theory than actuality, as nearly all Proof American Eagle platinum bullion coins have been maintained in their original high condition by collectors and investors.) Given the quality of modern U.S. Mint products, even PF–66 and 67 are unusually low levels for these Proofs.

$10 1/10-Ounce American Platinum Eagles

	Mintage	MS	MS-69	MS-70
		PF	PF-69	PF-70
$10 1997 (a)	70,250	$185	$210	$1,250
$10 1997-W, Proof	36,993	$200	$225	$350
$10 1998 (b)	39,525	$190	$215	$1,450
$10 1998-W, Proof (c)	19,847	$200	$225	$650
$10 1999 (d)	55,955	$180	$205	$800
$10 1999-W, Proof (c)	19,133	$200	$225	$400

Note: MS values are for uncertified Mint State coins of average quality, in their complete original U.S. Mint packaging. PF values are for uncertified Proof coins of average quality, in their complete original U.S. Mint packaging. **a.** Auction: $4,230, MS-70, January 2015. **b.** Auction: $223, MS-69, January 2013. **c.** Burnished and Proof coins from 1998 on featured the designs illustrated on pages 1287–1289. **d.** Auction: $170, MS-69, August 2014.

| | Mintage | MS | MS-69 | MS-70 |
		PF	PF-69	PF-70
$10 2000	34,027	$180	$205	$400
$10 2000-W, Proof (c)	15,651	$200	$225	$400
$10 2001	52,017	$180	$205	$325
$10 2001-W, Proof (c)	12,174	$200	$225	$425
$10 2002	23,005	$180	$205	$300
$10 2002-W, Proof (c)	12,365	$200	$225	$400
$10 2003	22,007	$180	$205	$300
$10 2003-W, Proof (c,e)	9,534	$240	$265	$450
$10 2004	15,010	$180	$205	$300
$10 2004-W, Proof (c,f)	7,161	$400	$425	$650
$10 2005	14,013	$180	$205	$300
$10 2005-W, Proof (c,g)	8,104	$260	$285	$400
$10 2006	11,001	$180	$205	$300
$10 2006-W, Burnished (c,h)	3,544	$410	$435	$450
$10 2006-W, Proof (c)	10,205	$190	$215	$350
$10 2007 (i)	13,003	$160	$190	$325
$10 2007-W, Burnished (c,j)	5,556	$220	$260	$300
$10 2007-W, Proof (c)	8,176	$190	$215	$400
$10 2008	17,000	$160	$190	$300
$10 2008-W, Burnished (c,k)	3,706	$335	$360	$375
$10 2008-W, Proof (c,l)	5,138	$400	$425	$550

Note: MS values are for uncertified Mint State coins of average quality, in their complete original U.S. Mint packaging. PF values are for uncertified Proof coins of average quality, in their complete original U.S. Mint packaging. **c.** Burnished and Proof coins from 1998 on featured the designs illustrated on pages 1287–1289. **e.** Auction: $176, PF-69DCam, December 2014. **f.** Auction: $447, PF-69DCam, February 2015. **g.** Auction: $212, PF-70UCam, February 2015. **h.** Auction: $441, MS-70, June 2013. **i.** Auction: $153, MS-70, September 2015. **j.** $364, MS-70, May 2015. **k.** Auction: $282, MS-69, September 2015. **l.** $376, PF-70UCam, January 2015.

$25 1/4-OUNCE AMERICAN PLATINUM EAGLES

| | Mintage | MS | MS-69 | MS-70 |
		PF	PF-69	PF-70
$25 1997 (a)	27,100	$375	$400	$2,200
$25 1997-W, Proof	18,628	$400	$425	$575
$25 1998	38,887	$375	$400	$1,200
$25 1998-W, Proof (b)	14,873	$400	$425	$700
$25 1999 (c)	39,734	$375	$400	$2,750
$25 1999-W, Proof (b)	13,507	$400	$425	$700
$25 2000	20,054	$375	$400	$800
$25 2000-W, Proof (b)	11,995	$400	$425	$700
$25 2001 (d)	21,815	$375	$400	$2,300
$25 2001-W, Proof (b)	8,847	$400	$425	$750
$25 2002	27,405	$375	$400	$575
$25 2002-W, Proof (b)	9,282	$400	$425	$750

Note: MS values are for uncertified Mint State coins of average quality, in their complete original U.S. Mint packaging. PF values are for uncertified Proof coins of average quality, in their complete original U.S. Mint packaging. **a.** Auction: $7,638, MS-70, January 2015. **b.** Burnished and Proof coins from 1998 on featured the designs illustrated on pages 1287–1289. **c.** Auction: $411, MS-68, October 2012. **d.** Auction: $374, MS-68, June 2012.

	Mintage	MS	MS-69	MS-70
		PF	PF-69	PF-70
$25 2003	25,207	$375	$400	$550
$25 2003-W, Proof (b)	7,044	$400	$425	$750
$25 2004	18,010	$375	$400	$550
$25 2004-W, Proof (b,e)	5,193	$950	$1,000	$1,600
$25 2005	12,013	$375	$400	$550
$25 2005-W, Proof (b,f)	6,592	$600	$635	$1,100
$25 2006	12,001	$375	$400	$550
$25 2006-W, Burnished (b,g)	2,676	$650	$675	$850
$25 2006-W, Proof (b)	7,813	$400	$425	$750
$25 2007	8,402	$450	$475	$550
$25 2007-W, Burnished (b,h)	3,690	$575	$600	$650
$25 2007-W, Proof (b)	6,017	$400	$425	$750
$25 2007-W, Frosted FREEDOM, Proof (b)	21	—		
$25 2008	22,800	$375	$400	$575
$25 2008-W, Burnished (b,i)	2,481	$650	$675	$950
$25 2008-W, Proof (b,j)	4,153	$650	$675	$1,000

Note: MS values are for uncertified Mint State coins of average quality, in their complete original U.S. Mint packaging. PF values are for uncertified Proof coins of average quality, in their complete original U.S. Mint packaging. **b.** Burnished and Proof coins from 1998 on featured the designs illustrated on pages 1287–1289. **e.** Auction: $764, PF-70DCam, July 2015. **f.** Auction: $564, PF-70DCam, January 2015. **g.** Auction: $306, MS-69, November 2015. **h.** Auction: $598, MS-70, August 2014. **i.** Auction: $764, MS-70, September 2015. **j.** Auction: $470, PF-70UCam, June 2015.

$50 1/2-OUNCE AMERICAN PLATINUM EAGLES

	Mintage	MS	MS-69	MS-70
		PF	PF-69	PF-70
$50 1997 (a)	20,500	$675	$700	$2,250
$50 1997-W, Proof	15,431	$725	$750	$925
$50 1998 (b)	32,415	$675	$700	$3,500
$50 1998-W, Proof (c)	13,836	$725	$750	$1,200
$50 1999 (d)	32,309	$675	$700	$3,500
$50 1999-W, Proof (c)	11,103	$725	$750	$1,350
$50 2000 (e)	18,892	$675	$700	$4,000
$50 2000-W, Proof (c)	11,049	$725	$750	$1,350
$50 2001 (f)	12,815	$675	$700	$3,750
$50 2001-W, Proof (c)	8,254	$725	$750	$1,400
$50 2002	24,005	$675	$700	$1,700
$50 2002-W, Proof (c)	8,772	$725	$750	$1,400
$50 2003	17,409	$375	$700	$1,100
$50 2003-W, Proof (c)	7,131	$725	$750	$1,400

Note: MS values are for uncertified Mint State coins of average quality, in their complete original U.S. Mint packaging. PF values are for uncertified Proof coins of average quality, in their complete original U.S. Mint packaging. **a.** Auction: $870, MS-69, July 2014. **b.** Auction: $881, MS-68, October 2012. **c.** Burnished and Proof coins from 1998 on featured the designs illustrated on pages 1287–1289. **d.** Auction: $823, MS-69, April 2014. **e.** Auction: $823, MS-69, November 2012. **f.** Auction: $796, MS-69, July 2014.

	Mintage	MS	MS-69	MS-70
		PF	PF-69	PF-70
$50 2004	13,236	$675	$700	$1,100
$50 2004-W, Proof (c,g)	5,063	$1,400	$1,450	$1,850
$50 2005	9,013	$675	$700	$1,100
$50 2005-W, Proof (c,h)	5,942	$1,150	$1,200	$1,450
$50 2006	9,602	$675	$700	$950
$50 2006-W, Burnished (c)	2,577	$925	$975	$1,300
$50 2006-W, Proof (c)	7,649	$725	$750	$1,300
$50 2007	7,001	$700	$725	$950
$50 2007-W, Burnished (c)	3,635	$850	$875	$1,000
$50 2007-W, Proof (c)	25,519	$725	$750	$1,200
$50 2007-W, Reverse Proof (c)	19,583	$900	$930	$1,200
$50 2007-W, Frosted FREEDOM, Proof (c)	21	—		
$50 2008	14,000	$675	$700	$1,000
$50 2008-W, Burnished ‡ (c,i)	2,253	$1,200	$1,225	$2,400
$50 2008-W, Proof ‡ (c,j)	4,020	$1,200	$1,250	$1,675

Note: MS values are for uncertified Mint State coins of average quality, in their complete original U.S. Mint packaging. PF values are for uncertified Proof coins of average quality, in their complete original U.S. Mint packaging. ‡ Ranked in the *100 Greatest U.S. Modern Coins.* **c.** Burnished and Proof coins from 1998 on featured the designs illustrated on pages 1287–1289. **g.** Auction: $1,058, PF-70DCam, July 2015. **h.** Auction: $705, PF-70UCam, February 2015. **i.** Auction: $1,528, MS-70, October 2015. **j.** Auction: $1,234, PF-70UCam. October 2015.

$100 1-Ounce American Platinum Eagles

**Proof Reverse, 1998:
Eagle Over New England.**
*Vistas of Liberty series.
Designer: John Mercanti.*

**Proof Reverse, 1999:
Eagle Above
Southeastern Wetlands.**
*Vistas of Liberty series.
Designer: John Mercanti.*

	Mintage	MS	MS-69	MS-70
		PF	PF-69	PF-70
$100 1997 (a)	56,000	$1,450	$1,475	—
$100 1997-W, Proof	20,851	$1,650	$1,700	$3,300
$100 1998 (b)	133,002	$1,450	$1,475	—
$100 1998-W, Proof	14,912	$1,650	$1,700	$3,500
$100 1999 (c)	56,707	$1,450	$1,475	—
$100 1999-W, Proof (d)	12,363	$1,650	$1,700	$4,150

Note: MS values are for uncertified Mint State coins of average quality, in their complete original U.S. Mint packaging. PF values are for uncertified Proof coins of average quality, in their complete original U.S. Mint packaging. **a.** Auction: $1,821, MS-69, July 2014. **b.** Auction: $1,704, MS-68, October 2012. **c.** Auction: $1,660, MS-69, November 2012. **d.** Auction: $1,645, PF69-UCam, March 2015.

Proof Reverse, 2000: Eagle Above America's Heartland.
Vistas of Liberty series.
Designer: Alfred Maletsky.

Proof Reverse, 2001: Eagle Above America's Southwest.
Vistas of Liberty series.
Designer: Thomas D. Rogers Sr.

Proof Reverse, 2002: Eagle Fishing in America's Northwest.
Vistas of Liberty series.
Designer: Alfred Maletsky.

Proof Reverse, 2003.
Designer: Alfred Maletsky.

Proof Reverse, 2004.
Designer: Donna Weaver.

Proof Reverse, 2005.
Designer: Donna Weaver.

Proof Reverse, 2006: Legislative Branch.
The Foundations of Democracy series.
Designer: Joel Iskowitz.

Proof Reverse, 2007: Executive Branch.
The Foundations of Democracy series.
Designer: Thomas Cleveland.

	Mintage	MS	MS-69	MS-70
		PF	PF-69	PF-70
$100 2000 (e)	10,003	$1,450	$1,475	—
$100 2000-W, Proof (f)	12,453	$1,650	$1,700	$2,500
$100 2001 (g)	14,070	$1,450	$1,475	—
$100 2001-W, Proof	8,969	$1,650	$1,700	$4,600
$100 2002 (h)	11,502	$1,450	$1,475	—
$100 2002-W, Proof (i)	9,834	$1,650	$1,700	$4,600
$100 2003	8,007	$1,450	$1,475	$3,750
$100 2003-W, Proof (j)	8,246	$1,650	$1,700	$4,600
$100 2004	7,009	$1,450	$1,475	$2,500
$100 2004-W, Proof (k)	6,007	$2,100	$2,150	$4,000
$100 2005	6,310	$1,450	$1,475	$2,500
$100 2005-W, Proof (l)	6,602	$2,300	$2,350	$3,300
$100 2006	6,000	$14,450	$1,475	$2,200
$100 2006-W, Burnished ‡ (m)	3,068	$2,100	$2,150	$2,200
$100 2006-W, Proof	9,152	$1,650	$1,700	$2,700
$100 2007	7,202	$1,450	$1,500	$2,100
$100 2007-W, Burnished	4,177	$2,000	$2,050	$2,150
$100 2007-W, Proof	8,363	$1,650	$1,700	$2,700
$100 2007-W, Frosted FREEDOM, Proof	12	—		

Note: MS values are for uncertified Mint State coins of average quality, in their complete original U.S. Mint packaging. PF values are for uncertified Proof coins of average quality, in their complete original U.S. Mint packaging. ‡ Ranked in the *100 Greatest U.S. Modern Coins.* **e.** Auction: $1,553, MS-69, June 2012. **f.** Auction: $1,410, PF-70UCam, April 2015. **g.** Auction: $4,994, MS-69, April 2014. **h.** Auction: $1,645, MS-69, September 2012. **i.** Auction: $1,880, PF-70DCam, February 2015. **j.** Auction: $1,880, PF-70DCam, April 2015. **k.** Auction: $2,291, PF-70UCam, January 2015. **l.** Auction: $1,998, PF-70UCam, October 2015. **m.** Auction: $1,351, MS-69, November 2015.

Proof Reverse, 2008: Judicial Branch.
The Foundations of Democracy series.
Designer: Joel Iskowitz.

Proof Reverse, 2009: "To Form a More Perfect Union."
Preamble series.
Designer: Susan Gamble.

Proof Reverse, 2010: "To Establish Justice."
Preamble series.
Designer: Donna Weaver.

Proof Reverse, 2011: "To Insure Domestic Tranquility."
Preamble series.
Designer: Joel Iskowitz.

Proof Reverse, 2012: "To Provide for the Common Defence."
Preamble series.
Designer: Barbara Fox.

Proof Reverse, 2013: "To Promote the General Welfare."
Preamble series.
Designer: Joel Iskowitz.

Proof Reverse, 2014: "To Secure the Blessings of Liberty to Ourselves and Our Posterity."
Preamble series.
Designer: Susan Gamble.

Proof Reverse, 2015: Liberty Nurtures Freedom.
Designer: Joel Iskowitz.

| | Mintage | MS | MS-69 | MS-70 |
		PF	PF-69	PF-70
$100 2008	21,800	$1,450	$1,500	$1,950
$100 2008-W, Burnished (n)	2,876	$2,200	$2,250	$2,900
$100 2008-W, Proof (o)	4,769	$2,350	$2,400	$3,500
$100 2009-W, Proof ‡	7,945	$2,100	$2,150	$2,250
$100 2010-W, Proof	14,790	$1,800	$1,850	$2,400
$100 2011-W, Proof	14,835	$1,800	$1,850	$2,100
$100 2012-W, Proof	10,084	$1,650	$1,700	$2,200
$100 2013-W, Proof	5,746	$1,900	$1,950	$2,250
$100 2014	16,900	$1,450	$1,475	$1,800
$100 2014-W, Proof	4,596	$1,900	$1,950	$2,700
$100 2015-W, Proof	3,881	$1,800	$1,850	$2,100

Note: MS values are for uncertified Mint State coins of average quality, in their complete original U.S. Mint packaging. PF values are for uncertified Proof coins of average quality, in their complete original U.S. Mint packaging. ‡ Ranked in the 100 Greatest U.S. Modern Coins. n. Auction: $1,880, MS-70, October 2015. o. Auction: $2,291, PF-70UCam, October 2015.

AMERICAN PLATINUM EAGLE BULLION COIN SETS

	MS	MS-69	MS-70
1997 Platinum Set. $100, $50, $25, $10	$2,700	$2,750	—
1998 Platinum Set. $100, $50, $25, $10	$2,650	$2,750	—
1999 Platinum Set. $100, $50, $25, $10	$2,600	$2,750	—
2000 Platinum Set. $100, $50, $25, $10	$2,650	$2,800	—
2001 Platinum Set. $100, $50, $25, $10	$2,600	$2,750	—
2002 Platinum Set. $100, $50, $25, $10	$2,650	$2,750	—

Note: MS values are for uncertified Mint State sets of average quality, in their complete original U.S. Mint packaging.

	MS	MS-69	MS-70
2003 Platinum Set. $100, $50, $25, $10	$2,600	$2,750	$5,700
2004 Platinum Set. $100, $50, $25, $10	$2,600	$2,750	$4,450
2005 Platinum Set. $100, $50, $25, $10	$2,600	$2,750	$4,450
2006 Platinum Set. $100, $50, $25, $10	$2,600	$2,750	$4,000
2006-W Platinum Burnished Set. $100, $50, $25, $10	$4,050	$4,200	$4,800
2007 Platinum Set. $100, $50, $25, $10	$2,700	$2,850	$3,900
2007-W Platinum Burnished Set. $100, $50, $25, $10	$3,600	$3,750	$4,000
2008 Platinum Set. $100, $50, $25, $10	$2,650	$2,800	$3,800
2008-W Platinum Burnished Set. $100, $50, $25, $10	$4,350	$4,500	$6,500

Note: MS values are for uncertified Mint State sets of average quality, in their complete original U.S. Mint packaging.

AMERICAN PLATINUM EAGLE PROOF COIN SETS

	PF	PF-69	PF-70
1997-W Platinum Set. $100, $50, $25, $10	$2,950	$3,100	$5,150
1998-W Platinum Set. $100, $50, $25, $10	$2,950	$3,100	$6,000
1999-W Platinum Set. $100, $50, $25, $10	$2,950	$3,100	$6,500
2000-W Platinum Set. $100, $50, $25, $10	$2,950	$3,100	$4,950
2001-W Platinum Set. $100, $50, $25, $10	$2,950	$3,100	$7,150
2002-W Platinum Set. $100, $50, $25, $10	$2,950	$3,100	$7,100
2003-W Platinum Set. $100, $50, $25, $10	$2,950	$3,100	$7,200
2004-W Platinum Set. $100, $50, $25, $10	$4,850	$5,000	$8,100
2005-W Platinum Set. $100, $50, $25, $10	$4,350	$4,400	$6,200
2006-W Platinum Set. $100, $50, $25, $10	$2,900	$3,050	$5,100
2007-W Platinum Set. $100, $50, $25, $10	$2,950	$3,100	$5,050
2008-W Platinum Set. $100, $50, $25, $10	$4,600	$4,750	$6,700

Note: PF values are for uncertified Proof sets of average quality, in their complete original U.S. Mint packaging. The Proof $100 American Platinum Eagle of 1997 is also included in the 1997 Impressions of Liberty set, listed on page 1271.

2007 AMERICAN PLATINUM EAGLE 10TH-ANNIVERSARY PROOF COIN SETS

	PF	PF-69	PF-70
2007 Two-Coin Set (a)	$1,600	$1,650	$2,400

a. This two-coin set, housed in a mahogany-finish hardwood box, includes one half-ounce Proof (with the standard cameo-finish background and frosted design elements) and one half-ounce Reverse Proof (with frosted background fields and mirrored raised elements) dated 2007-W.

Significant U.S. Patterns

Pattern coins are a fascinating part of numismatics that encompass thousands of designs and experimental pieces made by the U.S. Mint to test new motifs, alloys, coin sizes, and other variables. Most were official creations—products of the research-and-development process that takes a coin from congressionally authorized concept to finished pocket change. Some were made in secret, outside the normal day-to-day work of the Mint. The book *United States Pattern Coins*, by J. Hewitt Judd, gives extensive details of the history and characteristics of more than 2,000 different pattern varieties from 1792 to the present era.

Patterns provide students and collectors a chronology of the continuing efforts of engravers and artists to present their work for approval. Throughout the 220-plus years of federal coinage production, concepts meant to improve various aspects of circulating coins have been proposed and given physical form in patterns. In some instances, changes have been prompted by an outcry for higher aesthetics, a call for a more convenient denomination, or a need to overcome striking deficiencies. In many other instances, workers or officials at the Mint simply created special coins for the numismatic trade—often controversial in their time, but enthusiastically collected today. Certain patterns, bearing particular proposed designs or innovations, provided tangible examples for Mint and Treasury Department officials or members of Congress to review and evaluate. If approved and adopted, the pattern design became a familiar regular-issue motif; those that were rejected have become part of American numismatic history.

The patterns listed and illustrated in this section are samples from a much larger group. Such pieces generally include die and hub trials, off-metal Proof strikings of regular issues, and various combinations of dies that were sometimes struck at a later date. Certain well-known members of this extended pattern family historically have been included with regular issues in many popular, general-circulation numismatic reference books. The four-dollar gold Stellas of 1879 and 1880; certain Gobrecht dollars of 1836, 1838, and 1839; the transitional half dimes and dimes of 1859 and 1860; and the Flying Eagle cents of 1856 are examples. No official mintage figures of patterns and related pieces were recorded in most instances, and the number extant of each can usually only be estimated from auction appearances and from those found in museum holdings and important private collections. Although most patterns are very rare, the 2,000-plus distinct varieties make them unexpectedly collectible—not by one of each, but by selected available examples from favorite types or categories. Curiously, the most common of all patterns is the highly sought and expensive 1856 Flying Eagle cent!

Unlike regular coin issues that were emitted through the usual channels of commerce, and Proofs of regular issues that were struck expressly for sale to collectors, patterns were not intended to be officially sold. Yet as a matter of Mint practice, often against stated policy and law, countless patterns were secretly and unofficially sold and traded to favorite dealers (most notably William K. Idler and his son-in-law John W. Haseltine) and collectors, disseminated to government officials, and occasionally made available to numismatic societies. Not until mid-1885 did an incoming new director of the Mint enforce stringent regulations prohibiting their sale and distribution, although there had been many misleading statements to this effect earlier. In succeeding decades the Mint, while not making patterns available to numismatists, did place certain examples in the Mint Collection, now called the National Numismatic Collection, in the Smithsonian Institution. On other occasions, selected patterns were obtained by Mint and Treasury officials, or otherwise spared from destruction. Today, with the exception of certain cents and five-cent pieces of 1896, all pattern coins dated after 1885 are extremely rare.

The private possession of patterns has not been without its controversy. Most significant was the 1910 seizure by government agents of a parcel containing some 23 pattern pieces belonging to John W. Haseltine, a leading Philadelphia coin dealer with undisclosed private ties to Mint officials. The government asserted that the patterns had been removed from the Mint without authority, and that they remained the property of the United States. Haseltine's attorney successfully used the Mint's pre-1887 policies in his defense, and recovered the patterns a year after their confiscation. This set precedent for ownership, at least for the patterns minted prior to 1887, as all of the pieces in question predated that year. Today pattern coins can be legally held, and, in fact, they were inadvertently made legal tender (as was the earlier demonetized silver trade dollar) by the Coinage Act of 1965.

Among the grandest impressions ever produced at the U.S. Mint are the two varieties of pattern fifty-dollar gold pieces of 1877. Officially titled half unions, these large patterns were created at the request of certain politicians with interests tied to the gold-producing state of California. Specimens were struck in copper, and one of each variety was struck in gold. Both of the gold pieces were purchased around 1908 by numismatist William H. Woodin (who, years later, in 1933, served as President Franklin D. Roosevelt's first secretary of the Treasury). The sellers were John W. Haseltine and Stephen K. Nagy, well known for handling many rarities that few others could obtain from the Mint. The Mint desired to re-obtain the pieces for its own collection, and through a complex trade deal for quantities of other patterns, did so, adding them to the Mint Collection. Now preserved in the Smithsonian Institution, these half unions are regarded as national treasures.

The following resources are recommended for additional information, descriptions, and complete listings:

United States Pattern Coins, 10th edition, J. Hewitt Judd, edited by Q. David Bowers, 2009.

United States Patterns and Related Issues, Andrew W. Pollock III, 1994. (Out of print)

www.harrybassfoundation.org

www.uspatterns.com

Judd-52

J-67

	PF-60	PF-63	PF-65
1836 Two-cent piece (J-52, billon) (a)	$2,750	$5,000	$10,000
Auctions: $8,625, PF-65, January 2009			
1836 Gold dollar (J-67, gold) (b)	$10,000	$17,500	$25,000
Auctions: $24,725, PF-65, November 2010			

a. This proposal for a two-cent coin is one of the earliest collectible patterns. It was designed by Christian Gobrecht. An estimated 21 to 30 examples are known. **b.** Gobrecht styled the first gold dollar pattern after the familiar "Cap and Rays" design used on Mexican coins, which at the time were legal tender in the United States. An estimated 31 to 75 pieces are known.

J-164   **J-177**

	PF-60	PF-63	PF-65
1854 Cent (J-164, bronze) (a)	$1,500	$2,750	$6,750
Auctions: $16,100, PF-67BN, March 2005			
1856 Half cent (J-177, copper-nickel) (b)	$3,000	$4,500	$7,000
Auctions: $6,038, PF-64, January 2006			

a. Beginning in 1850, the Mint produced patterns for a reduced-weight cent. Among the designs were ring-style, Liberty Head, and Flying Eagle motifs. These experiments culminated with the 1856 Flying Eagle cent. An estimated 31 to 75 examples of J-164 are known. Those with red mint luster are worth more than the values listed here. **b.** Before producing copper-nickel small-size cents in 1856, the Mint experimented with that alloy using half-cent dies. An estimated 31 to 75 examples are known.

J-204   **J-239**

	PF-60	PF-63	PF-65
1858 Cent (J-204, copper-nickel) (a)	$1,600	$2,500	$4,000
1859 Half dollar (J-239, silver) (b)	$1,500	$2,000	$3,750

a. This pattern cent's flying eagle differs from the one adopted for regular coinage of the one-cent piece. An estimated 31 to 75 pieces are known. **b.** This design proposal for a new half dollar features James Longacre's French Liberty Head design. An estimated 76 to 200 pieces are known.

J-305

	PF-60	PF-63	PF-65
1863 Washington two-cent piece (J-305, copper) (a)	$1,500	$2,250	$4,000

a. Before the two-cent coin was introduced to circulation, two basic designs were considered. If this George Washington portrait design had been adopted, it would have been the first to depict a historical figure. An estimated 76 to 200 pieces are known.

J-349

J-407

J-470

	PF-60	PF-63	PF-65
1863 Eagle (J-349, gold) (a)		$450,000	
1865 Bimetallic two-cent piece (J-407, silver and copper) (b)	$6,000	$11,000	$19,500
1866 Five-cent piece (J-470, nickel) (c)	$1,650	$2,500	$4,500

a. This unique gold eagle features IN GOD WE TRUST on a scroll on the reverse. This feature would not appear on regular eagle coinage until 1866. The obverse is from the regular 1863 die. b. This experimental piece is the first "clad" coin. It consists of an irregular and streaky layer of silver fused to copper. The experiment was unsuccessful. An estimated 4 to 6 pieces are known. c. Another of George Washington's early pattern appearances was on five-cent pieces of 1866. An estimated 21 to 30 are known.

J-486

J-611

	PF-60	PF-63	PF-65
1866 Lincoln five-cent piece (J-486, nickel) (a)	$5,000	$9,000	$19,000
1868 Cent (J-611, copper) (b)	$17,500	$25,000	$35,000
Auctions: $36,800, PF-66BN, March 2005			

a. A number of pattern nickels were produced in 1866, including one designed to depict the recently assassinated President Abraham Lincoln. An estimated 7 to 12 examples are known. b. There is no known reason for the minting of this unusual piece, which mimics the original large cents that had last been made in 1857. There was no intent to resume the coinage of old-style copper "large" cents in 1868. Accordingly, this variety is regarded as a rarity created for collectors. Fewer than 15 examples are believed to exist.

J-1195

J-1235

	PF-60	PF-63	PF-65
1872 Amazonian quarter (J-1195, silver) (a)	$25,000	$40,000	$75,000
Auctions: $80,500, PF-66Cam, January 2009			
1872 Amazonian gold $3 (J-1235, gold) (b)	—	—	$1,250,000

a. Many of the most popular patterns have been given colorful nicknames by collectors in appreciation of their artistry. This design is by Chief Engraver William Barber. An estimated 7 to 12 examples are known. b. This unique piece was contained in the Mint's only uniform gold set using the same design from the gold dollar to the double eagle.

J-1373

	PF-60	PF-63	PF-65
1874 Bickford eagle (J-1373, gold) (a)	—	$500,000	$1,250,000

a. Dana Bickford, a New York City manufacturer, proposed a ten-dollar gold coin that would be exchangeable at set rates with other world currencies. Patterns were made, but the idea proved impractical. 2 examples are known.

J-1392

	PF-60	PF-63	PF-65
1875 Sailor Head twenty-cent piece (J-1392, silver) (a)	$3,000	$5,500	$9,500

a. Chief Engraver William Barber's "Sailor Head" is one of the most elegant of several rejected designs for a twenty-cent coin. The same head was used on other patterns, including proposals for trade dollars. An estimated 21 to 30 examples of J-1392 are known.

J-1507

J-1512   J-1528

	PF-60	PF-63	PF-65
1877 Morgan half dollar (J-1507, copper) (a)	$18,000	$29,000	$50,000
1877 Morgan half dollar (J-1512, silver) (b)	$15,000	$28,000	$45,000
1877 Half dollar (J-1528, silver) (c)	$17,000	$33,000	$50,000

a. A year before his famous and eponymous dollar design was adopted for regular coinage, engraver George Morgan's Liberty Head appeared on several varieties of pattern half dollars, all of which are rare today. J-1507 pairs the well-known obverse with an indented shield design. 2 examples are known. **b.** The half dollar pattern cataloged as J-1512 pairs Morgan's "silver dollar style" obverse with a dramatic "Defiant Eagle" reverse. 6 examples are known. **c.** This is one of several 1877 pattern half dollars by Chief Engraver William Barber. 4 are known.

J-1549

1877 Half union (J-1549, copper) (a)	PF-60	PF-63	PF-65
	$100,000	$175,000	$350,000
Auctions: $575,000, PF-67BN, January 2009			

a. This famous fifty-dollar pattern by Chief Engraver William Barber would have been the highest denomination ever issued by the Mint up to that time. The gold impression (J-1548) is unique and resides in the Smithsonian's National Numismatic Collection, but copper specimens (J-1549, which are priced here and are sometimes gilt) occasionally come to the market. Varieties exist with a somewhat larger or smaller head.

J-1590

1879 Quarter dollar (J-1590, silver) (a)	PF-60	PF-63	PF-65
	$6,000	$10,000	$18,000
Auctions: $34,500, PF-68, January 2007			

a. Referred to as the "Washlady" design, this was Charles Barber's first attempt at a uniform silver design. An estimated 13 to 20 examples are known.

J-1609

1879 Dollar (J-1609, copper) (a)	PF-60	PF-63	PF-65
	$20,000	$35,000	$75,000
Auctions: $74,750, PF-66RB, September 2006			

a. The "Schoolgirl" design by George T. Morgan is a widespread favorite among pattern collectors. Examples are rare, with only 7 to 12 known.

J-1643

	PF-60	PF-63	PF-65
1879 Metric double eagle (J-1643, gold) (a)	$325,000	$600,000	$1,000,000

a. James Longacre's Liberty Head design was the same as that used on regular-issue double eagles, but with an added inscription indicating the coin's specifications in metric units. 5 are known.

J-1667   J-1669   J-1673

	PF-60	PF-63	PF-65
1881 One-cent piece (J-1667, aluminum) (a)	$2,025	$3,780	$6,440
1881 Three-cent piece (J-1669, copper) (a)	$2,000	$3,750	$6,000
1881 Five-cent piece (J-1673, aluminum) (a)	$2,300	$4,800	$9,000

a. These patterns by Chief Engraver Charles Barber represent an attempt at a uniform set of minor coins; if adopted, they would have been struck in nickel for circulation. An estimated 7 to 20 examples are known of each of the illustrated patterns.

J-1698

	PF-60	PF-63	PF-65
1882 Quarter dollar (J-1698, silver) (a)	$17,500	$34,000	$55,000

a. George Morgan's "Shield Earring" design was made in patterns of quarter, half, and dollar denominations. 7 to 12 of the quarter dollar patterns are known.

J-1761   J-1770

	PF-60	PF-63	PF-65
1891 Barber quarter (J-1761, silver) (a)	—	—	—
1896 Shield nickel (J-1770, nickel) (b)	$1,500	$2,750	$4,000

a. Charles Barber prepared various pattern dimes, quarters, and half dollars in 1891. The quarter illustrated is similar to the design adopted for regular coinage in 1892. Two pieces are known, both in the Smithsonian's National Numismatic Collection. b. In 1896 the Mint struck experimental cents and nickels with similar designs, by Charles Barber. 21 to 30 examples of J-1770 are known.

J-1905

	PF-60	PF-63	PF-65
1907 Indian Head double eagle (J-1905, gold) (a)			*$10,000,000*

a. Designed by Augustus Saint-Gaudens, this pattern is unique and extremely valuable. A variation of the reverse of this design was used on the double eagles struck for circulation from 1907 through 1933.

J-1992

	PF-60	PF-63	PF-65
1916 Liberty Walking half dollar (J-1992, silver) (a)	$55,000	$80,000	$150,000
Auctions: $115,000, PF-65, July 2008			

a. Various pattern Mercury dimes, Standing Liberty quarters, and Liberty Walking half dollars were struck, all dated 1916. All are extremely rare, but a few found their way into circulation.

J-2063

	PF-60	PF-63	PF-65
1942 Experimental cent (J-2051 through J-2069, several metallic and other compositions) (a)	$1,750	$3,500	$6,000

a. Before settling on the zinc-coated steel composition used for the Lincoln cents of 1943, the Mint considered various alternative compositions, including plastics. Most were struck by outside contractors using specially prepared dies provided by the Mint. An estimated 7 to 12 examples are known of most types and colors.

Private and Territorial Gold

The expression *private gold*, used with reference to coins struck outside the United States Mint, is a general term. In the sense that no state or territory had authority to coin money, *private gold* simply refers to those necessity pieces of various shapes, denominations, and degrees of intrinsic worth that were coined by facilities other than official U.S. mints and circulated in isolated areas of the United States by assayers, bankers, and other private individuals and organizations. Some numismatists use the terms *territorial gold* and *state gold* to cover certain issues because they were coined and circulated in a territory or state. While the state of California properly sanctioned the ingots stamped by F.D. Kohler as state assayer, in no instance (except for the Mormon issues of Salt Lake City) were any of the gold pieces struck by authority of any of the territorial governments.

The stamped fifty-dollar and other gold coins, sometimes called *ingots*, but in coin form, were made by Augustus Humbert, the United States Assayer of Gold, but were not receivable at face value for government payments, despite the fact that Humbert was an official agent selected by the Treasury Department. However, such pieces circulated widely in commerce.

Usually, private coins were circulated due to a shortage of regular federal coinage. In the Western states particularly, official money became so scarce that gold itself—the very commodity the pioneers had come so far to acquire—was converted into a local medium of exchange.

Ephraim Brasher's New York doubloons of 1786 and 1787 are also private American gold issues and are described on page 125.

TEMPLETON REID

GEORGIA GOLD, 1830

The first private gold coinage in the 19th century was struck by Templeton Reid, a jeweler and gunsmith, in Milledgeville, Georgia, in July 1830. To be closer to the mines he moved some 120 miles northwest to Gainesville, where most of his coins were made. Although their weights were accurate, Reid's assays were not and his coins were slightly short of their claimed value. He was severely attacked in the newspapers by a determined adversary, and soon lost the public's confidence. He closed his mint before the end of October in 1830; his output had amounted to only about 1,600 coins. Denominations struck were $2.50, $5, and $10. All are great rarities today.

	VF	EF	AU
1830 $2.50	$125,000	$175,000	$300,000
1830 $5 (a)	$350,000	$475,000	$575,000

a. 7 examples are known.

	EF	AU
1830 TEN DOLLARS (a)	$700,000	$975,000
(No Date) TEN DOLLARS (b)	$775,000	$1,200,000

a. 6 examples are known. **b.** 3 examples are known.

CALIFORNIA GOLD, 1849

The enigmatic later issues of Templeton Reid, dated 1849 and marked CALIFORNIA GOLD, were probably made from California gold late in that year when bullion from California arrived in quantity in the East. Reid, who never went to California, was by then a cotton-gin maker in Columbus, Georgia (some 160 miles southwest of his former location of Gainesville), where he would die in 1851. The coins were in denominations of ten and twenty-five dollars. Struck copies of both exist in various metals.

The only example known of the twenty-five–dollar piece was stolen from the cabinet of the U.S. Mint on August 16, 1858. It was never recovered.

1849 TEN DOLLAR CALIFORNIA GOLD	*(unique, in Smithsonian collection)*
1849 TWENTY-FIVE DOLLARS CALIFORNIA GOLD	*(unknown)*

THE BECHTLERS, RUTHERFORD COUNTY, NORTH CAROLINA, 1831–1852

A skilled German metallurgist, Christopher Bechtler, assisted by his son August and his nephew, also named Christopher, operated a private mint in Rutherford County, North Carolina. Rutherford County and other areas in the Piedmont region of North Carolina and Georgia (from the coastal plain to the mountains of north Georgia) were the principal sources of the nation's gold supply from the early 1800s until the California gold strikes in 1848.

The coins minted by the Bechtlers were of only three denominations, but they covered a wide variety of weights and sizes. Rotated dies are common throughout the series. In 1831, the Bechtlers produced the first gold dollar in the United States. (The Philadelphia Mint made patterns in 1836 and struck its first circulating gold dollar in 1849.) Bechtler coins were well accepted by the public and circulated widely in the Southeast without interference from the government.

The legend AUGUST 1. 1834 on several varieties of five-dollar pieces has a special significance. The secretary of the Treasury recommended to the director of the U.S. Mint that gold coins of the reduced weight introduced in 1834 bear the authorization date. This ultimately was not done on federal gold coinage, but the elder Christopher Bechtler evidently acted on the recommendation to avoid potential difficulty with Treasury authorities.

CHRISTOPHER BECHTLER

	VF	EF	AU	Unc.
ONE GOLD DOLLAR N. CAROLINA, 30.G., Star	$2,800	$4,300	$6,750	$15,000
ONE GOLD DOLLAR N. CAROLINA, 28.G Centered, No Star	$5,000	$6,000	$11,500	$26,000
ONE GOLD DOLLAR N. CAROLINA, 28.G High, No Star	$9,000	$15,000	$23,000	$35,000

	VF	EF	AU	Unc.
ONE DOLLAR CAROLINA, 28.G, N Reversed	$2,500	$3,200	$4,750	$8,250
2.50 NORTH CAROLINA, 20 C. Without 75 G.	$28,000	$38,500	$57,500	$120,000

	VF	EF	AU	Unc.
2.50 NORTH CAROLINA, 75 G., 20 C. RUTHERFORD in a Circle. Border of Large Beads	$26,000	$36,000	$52,500	$115,000
2.50 NORTH CAROLINA, 20 C. Without 75 G., CAROLINA above 250 instead of GOLD (a)				—
2.50 NORTH CAROLINA, 20 C. on Obverse, 75 G. and Star on Reverse. Border Finely Serrated	—	—	—	

a. This piece is unique.

	VF	EF	AU	Unc.
2.50 CAROLINA, 67 G., 21 CARATS	$6,500	$11,000	$15,000	$28,000
2.50 GEORGIA, 64 G., 22 CARATS (Uneven "22")	$7,000	$11,500	$15,500	$30,000
2.50 GEORGIA, 64 G., 22 CARATS (Even "22")	$9,000	$15,000	$22,000	$45,000
2.50 CAROLINA, 70 G., 20 CARATS	$6,500	$11,000	$15,000	$28,000

	VF	EF	AU	Unc.
5 DOLLARS NORTH CAROLINA GOLD, 150 G., 20.CARATS	$27,000	$39,000	$70,000	$120,000
Similar, Without 150.G. (a)		—	—	

a. 1 or 2 examples are known.

CHRISTOPHER BECHTLER, CAROLINA

	VF	EF	AU	Unc.
5 DOLLARS CAROLINA, RUTHERFORD, 140 G., 20 CARATS, Plain Edge	$5,750	$8,250	$12,500	$26,000
5 DOLLARS CAROLINA, RUTHERFORD, 140 G., 20 CARATS, Reeded Edge	$18,000	$30,000	$45,000	$65,000
5 DOLLARS CAROLINA GOLD, RUTHERF., 140 G., 20 CARATS, AUGUST 1, 1834	$10,000	$18,000	$30,000	$50,000
Similar, but "20" Distant From CARATS	$6,250	$10,000	$15,000	$27,500
5 DOLLARS CAROLINA GOLD, 134 G., 21 CARATS, With Star	$5,500	$8,000	$12,000	$24,000

CHRISTOPHER BECHTLER, GEORGIA

	VF	EF	AU	Unc.
5 DOLLARS GEORGIA GOLD, RUTHERFORD, 128 G., 22 CARATS	$8,000	$11,500	$15,000	$32,000
5 DOLLARS GEORGIA GOLD, RUTHERFORD, 128 G:, 22 CARATS, With Colon After G	$15,000	$26,000	$38,500	
5 DOLLARS GEORGIA GOLD, RUTHERF., 128 G., 22 CARATS	$8,000	$11,500	$16,000	$32,000

AUGUST BECHTLER, CAROLINA

	VF	EF	AU	Unc.
1 DOL:, CAROLINA GOLD, 27.G., 21.C	$1,750	$2,400	$3,200	$5,500
5 DOLLARS, CAROLINA GOLD, 134.G:, 21 CARATS	$6,000	$8,750	$15,000	$36,000
5 DOLLARS, CAROLINA GOLD, 134 G:, 21 CARATS, Reverse of C. Bechtler as Shown Above	—	—		

	VF	EF	AU	Unc.
5 DOLLARS, CAROLINA GOLD, 128.G., 22 CARATS	$15,000	$18,000	$27,500	$45,000
5 DOLLARS, CAROLINA GOLD, 141.G., 20 CARATS	$12,500	$17,000	$25,000	$40,000

Note: Restrikes in "Proof" of this type using original dies were made about 1920.

NORRIS, GREGG & NORRIS, SAN FRANCISCO, 1849

Collectors consider this piece the first of the California private gold coins. A newspaper account dated May 31, 1849, described a five-dollar gold coin, struck at Benicia City, though with the imprint of San Francisco. It mentioned the private stamp of Norris, Gregg & Norris, the California branch of a New York City plumbing and hardware firm.

	F	VF	EF	AU	Unc.
1849 Half Eagle, Plain Edge	$4,750	$7,000	$12,000	$17,000	$37,000
1849 Half Eagle, Reeded Edge	$4,750	$7,000	$12,000	$17,000	$37,000
1850 Half Eagle, With STOCKTON Beneath Date (a)		—			

a. This unique piece is housed in the Smithsonian's National Numismatic Collection.

MOFFAT & CO., SAN FRANCISCO, 1849–1853

The firm of Moffat & Co. (principals John Little Moffat, Joseph R. Curtis, Philo H. Perry, and Samuel H. Ward) was the most important of the California private coiners. The assay office they conducted became semi-official in character starting in 1851. The successors to this firm, Curtis, Perry, and Ward, later sold their coining facility to the Treasury Department, which in March 1854 reopened it as the branch mint of San Francisco.

In June or July 1849, Moffat & Co. began to issue small, rectangular ingots of gold in response to lack of coin in the locality, in values from $9.43 to $264. The $9.43, $14.25, and $16.00 varieties are the only types known today. A similar ingot was made by the firm of Meyers & Company at this same time.

$9.43 Ingot (a)	—
$14.25 Ingot (a)	—
$16.00 Ingot	$175,000
$18.00 Meyers Ingot (b)	—

a. This unique piece is housed in the Smithsonian's National Numismatic Collection. b. This piece is unique.

The dies for the five-dollar and ten-dollar Moffat & Co. pieces were cut by a Bavarian engraver, Albrecht Küner, who had moved to the United States in October 1848. On the coronet of Miss Liberty appear the words MOFFAT & CO., instead of the word LIBERTY as in regular U.S. issues.

	F	VF	EF	AU	Unc.
1849 FIVE DOL. (a)	$1,850	$3,000	$4,350	$7,000	$15,000
1850 FIVE DOL. (a)	$1,900	$3,100	$4,500	$7,500	$17,500
1849 TEN DOL.	$3,750	$6,500	$12,500	$22,500	$38,000
1849 TEN D.	$4,000	$7,000	$13,500	$25,000	$45,000

a. Multiple varieties exist.

UNITED STATES ASSAY OFFICE

AUGUSTUS HUMBERT, UNITED STATES ASSAYER OF GOLD, 1851

Augustus Humbert, a New York watchcase maker, was appointed United States assayer by the Treasury Department in 1850 and arrived in California in early 1851. He placed his name and the government stamp on the ingots of gold issued by Moffat & Co., but without the Moffat imprint. The assay office, a provisional government mint, was a temporary expedient to accommodate the Californians until the establishment of a permanent federal branch mint.

The fifty-dollar gold piece was accepted by most banks and merchants as legal tender on a par with standard U.S. gold coins and was known variously as a *slug*, *quintuple eagle*, *five-eagle piece*, or *adobe* (the latter a type of construction brick). It was officially termed an *ingot*.

LETTERED-EDGE VARIETIES

  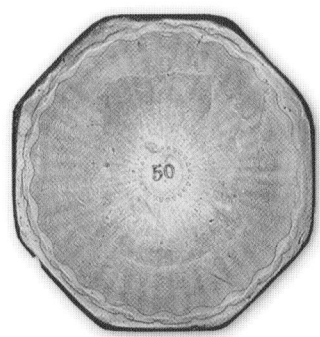

	F	VF	EF	AU	Unc.
1851 50 D C 880 THOUS., No 50 on Reverse. Sunk in Edge: AUGUSTUS HUMBERT UNITED STATES ASSAYER OF GOLD, CALIFORNIA 1851	$22,500	$36,000	$60,000	$90,000	$200,000
Auctions: $546,250, MS-63, August 2010					
1851 50 D C 880 THOUS., Similar to Last Variety, but 50 on Reverse	$30,000	$56,000	$82,500	$150,000	$300,000
1851 50 D C, 887 THOUS., With 50 on Reverse	$26,000	$47,500	$72,500	$110,000	$250,000

REEDED-EDGE VARIETIES

 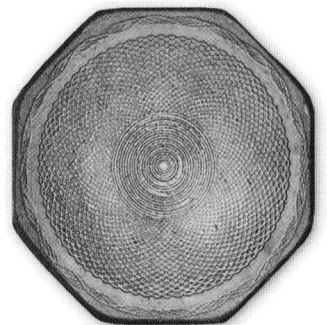

	F	VF	EF	AU	Unc.
1851 FIFTY DOLLS, 880 THOUS., "Target" Reverse	$16,500	$25,000	$40,000	$52,000	$100,000
Auctions: $460,000, MS-65, September 2008					
1851 FIFTY DOLLS, 887 THOUS., "Target" Reverse	$16,500	$25,000	$40,000	$52,000	$100,000
1852 FIFTY DOLLS, 887 THOUS., "Target" Reverse	$17,000	$27,000	$42,000	$55,000	$110,000

MOFFAT-HUMBERT

In 1851, certain issues of the Miners' Bank, Baldwin, Pacific Company, and others were discredited, some unfairly, by newspaper accounts stating they were of reduced gold value. This provided an enhanced opportunity for Moffat and the U.S. Assay Office of Gold. Supplementing privately struck gold pieces and federal issues, coins of almost every nation were being pressed into service by the Californians, but the supply was too small to help to any extent. Moffat & Co. proceeded in January 1852 to issue a new ten-dollar gold piece bearing the stamp MOFFAT & CO.

Close Date **Wide Date**

	F	VF	EF	AU	Unc.
1852 TEN D. MOFFAT & CO., Close Date	$4,200	$7,000	$15,000	$35,000	$77,500
1852 TEN D. MOFFAT & CO., Wide Date	$4,200	$7,000	$15,000	$35,000	$77,500
Auctions: $940,000, SP-63, January 2014					

1852, Normal Date **1852, 2 Over 1**

	F	VF	EF	AU	Unc.
1852 TEN DOLS.	$2,750	$4,250	$7,500	$12,000	$27,500
Auctions: $1,057,500, MS-68, April 2013					
1852 TEN DOLS. 1852, 2 Over 1	$2,850	$5,250	$9,500	$16,000	$35,000

	F	VF	EF	AU	Unc.
1852 TWENTY DOLS., 1852, 2 Over 1	$8,000	$13,000	$26,000	$42,500	$140,000
Auctions: $434,500, PF-64, October 1990					

UNITED STATES ASSAY OFFICE OF GOLD, 1852

The firm of Moffat & Co. was dissolved in 1852 and a newly reorganized company known as the United States Assay Office of Gold took over the contract. Principals in the firm were Joseph Curtis, Philo Perry, and Samuel Ward.

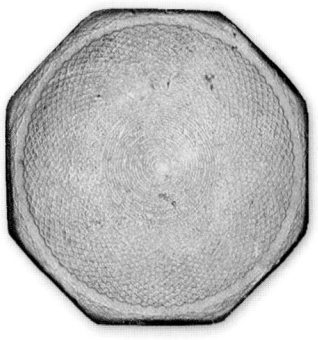

	F	VF	EF	AU	Unc.
1852 FIFTY DOLLS., 887 THOUS.	$16,500	$25,000	$40,000	$52,000	$100,000
1852 FIFTY DOLLS., 900 THOUS.	$17,500	$27,000	$42,000	$55,000	$110,000

	F	VF	EF	AU	Unc.
1852 TEN DOLS., 884 THOUS.	$2,000	$3,500	$5,250	$7,750	$20,000
1853 TEN D., 884 THOUS.	$7,500	$15,000	$27,500	$38,500	$75,000
1853 TEN D., 900 THOUS.	$4,500	$6,500	$10,000	$16,000	$24,000

	F	VF	EF	AU	Unc.
1853 TWENTY D., 884 THOUS.	$7,750	$11,000	$18,000	$30,000	$65,000

	F	VF	EF	AU	Unc.
1853 TWENTY D., 900 THOUS.	$2,250	$3,300	$4,750	$6,500	$13,000

Note: Modern prooflike forgeries exist.

MOFFAT & CO. GOLD, 1853

The last Moffat & Co. issue, an 1853 twenty-dollar piece, is very similar to the U.S. double eagle of that period. It was struck after John L. Moffat retired from the Assay Office. The circumstances of its issue are unclear, but many were coined.

	F	VF	EF	AU	Unc.
1853 TWENTY D.	$4,500	$6,500	$11,000	$17,000	$37,500

J.H. BOWIE, 1849

Joseph H. Bowie joined his cousins in San Francisco in 1849 and possibly produced a limited coinage of gold pieces. A trial piece of the dollar denomination is known in copper, but may never have reached the coinage stage. Little is known about the company or the reason for considering these pieces.

1849 1 DOL., copper pattern	—

CINCINNATI MINING & TRADING CO., 1849

The origin and location of this company are unknown.

	EF	Unc.
1849 FIVE DOLLARS (a)		
1849 TEN DOLLARS (b)	$750,000	—

Note: Beware of spurious specimens cast in base metal with the word TRACING in place of TRADING. **a.** This piece is unique. **b.** 5 examples are known.

MASSACHUSETTS AND CALIFORNIA COMPANY, 1849

This company was organized in Northampton, Massachusetts, in May 1849. Years later fantasy and copy dies were made and coins struck in various metals including gold. Pieces with the denomination spelled as 5D are not genuine.

	VF	EF
1849 FIVE D. (a)	$175,000	$275,000

a. 5 to 7 examples are known.

MINERS' BANK, SAN FRANCISCO, 1849

The institution of Wright & Co., exchange brokers located in Portsmouth Square, San Francisco, was known as the Miners' Bank. The firm issued a ten-dollar gold piece in the autumn of 1849, and it saw wide use in commerce. However, the firm's coinage was ephemeral, and it was dissolved on January 14, 1850. Unlike the gold in most California issues, the gold in these coins was alloyed with copper.

	VF	EF	AU	Unc.
(1849) **TEN D.**	$18,000	$32,000	$50,000	$110,000

J.S. ORMSBY, SACRAMENTO, 1849

The initials J.S.O., which appear on certain issues of California privately coined gold pieces, represent the firm of J.S. Ormsby & Co., located in Sacramento. They struck five- and ten-dollar denominations, all undated.

	VF
(1849) **5 DOLLS, Plain Edge** (a)	—
(1849) **5 DOLLS, Reeded Edge** (b)	—
(1849) **10 DOLLS** (c)	$450,000

a. This piece may be unique. **b.** This unique piece is housed in the Smithsonian's National Numismatic Collection. **c.** 4 examples are known.

PACIFIC COMPANY, SAN FRANCISCO, 1849

The origin of the Pacific Company is very uncertain. All data regarding the firm are based on conjecture.

Edgar H. Adams wrote that he believed that the coins bearing the stamp of the Pacific Company were produced by the coining firm of Broderick and Kohler. The coins were probably hand struck with the aid of a sledgehammer. Trial pieces exist in silver. All are rarities today.

	EF	AU	Unc.
1849 1 DOLLAR (a)			$300,000
1849 5 DOLLARS (b)	$400,000	$700,000	
Auctions: $763,750, AU-58, April 2014			
1849 10 DOLLARS (c)	$600,000	$800,000	$1,000,000

a. 2 examples are known. **b.** 4 examples are known. **c.** 4 examples are known.

F.D. KOHLER, CALIFORNIA STATE ASSAYER, 1850

The State Assay Office was authorized on April 12, 1850. That year, Governor Peter Burnett appointed to the position of state assayer Frederick D. Kohler, who thereupon sold his assaying business to Baldwin & Co. Kohler served at both the San Francisco and Sacramento offices. The State Assay Offices were discontinued at the time the U.S. Assay Office was established, on February 1, 1851.

Ingots issued ranged from $36.55 to $150. An Extremely Fine specimen sold in the Garrett Sale, 1980, for $200,000. Each is unique.

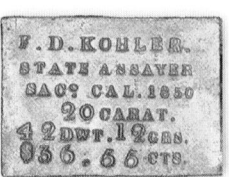

$36.55 Sacramento	—
$37.31 San Francisco	—
$40.07 San Francisco	—
$45.34 San Francisco	—
$50.00 San Francisco	—
$54.00 San Francisco	—

Note: A $40.07 ingot was stolen from the Mint Cabinet in 1858 and never recovered.

DUBOSQ & COMPANY, SAN FRANCISCO, 1850

Theodore Dubosq Sr., a Philadelphia jeweler, took melting and coining equipment to San Francisco in 1849 and minted five-dollar gold pieces.

	VF
1850 FIVE D. (a)	$300,000
Auctions: $329,000, MS-60, April 2014	
1850 TEN D. (b)	$300,000

a. 3 to 5 examples are known. **b.** 8 to 10 examples are known.

BALDWIN & CO., SAN FRANCISCO, 1850–1851

George C. Baldwin and Thomas S. Holman were in the jewelry business in San Francisco and were known as Baldwin & Co. They were the successors to F.D. Kohler & Co., taking over its machinery and other equipment in May 1850. The firm ceased minting coins in early 1851, at which time newspaper accounts stated that its coins fell short of their stated gold value. The 1850 Vaquero or Horseman ten-dollar design is one of the most famous of the California gold issues.

	F	VF	EF	AU	Unc.
1850 FIVE DOL.	$7,500	$13,000	$25,000	$35,000	$75,000
1850, TEN DOLLARS, Horseman Type	$45,000	$75,000	$125,000	$165,000	$275,000

	F	VF	EF	AU	Unc.
1851 TEN D.	$16,000	$32,500	$48,000	$80,000	$190,000

The Baldwin & Co. twenty-dollar piece was the first of that denomination issued in California. Baldwin coins are believed to have contained about 2% copper alloy.

	EF	Unc.
1851 TWENTY D. (a)	$625,000	—
Auctions: $646,250, EF-45, April 2014		

a. 4 to 6 examples are known.

SCHULTZ & COMPANY, SAN FRANCISCO, 1851

The firm of Schultz & Co., a brass foundry, was operated by Judge G.W. Schultz and William T. Garratt. The surname is misspelled as SHULTZ on the coins.

	F	VF	EF	AU	Unc.
1851 FIVE D.	$32,500	$57,500	$90,000	$150,000	$350,000

DUNBAR & COMPANY, SAN FRANCISCO, 1851

Edward E. Dunbar operated the California Bank in San Francisco. He later returned to New York City and organized the famous Continental Bank Note Co.

	VF	EF
1851 FIVE D. (a)	$250,000	$425,000

a. 4 to 6 examples are known.

WASS, MOLITOR & CO., SAN FRANCISCO, 1852–1855

The gold-smelting and assaying plant of Wass, Molitor & Co. was operated by two Hungarian patriots exiled after the Revolution of 1848, Count Samu Wass and A.P. Molitor. They maintained an excellent laboratory and complete apparatus for analysis and coinage of gold.

The company struck five-, ten-, twenty-, and fifty-dollar coins. In 1852 they produced a ten-dollar piece similar in design to the five-dollar denomination. The difference is in the reverse legend, which reads: S.M.V. [Standard Mint Value] CALIFORNIA GOLD TEN D.

No pieces were coined in 1853 or 1854, but they brought out the twenty- and fifty-dollar pieces in 1855. A considerable number of the fifty-dollar coins were made. There was a ten-dollar piece issued in 1855 also, with the Liberty Head design and small close date.

Small Head, Rounded Bust   **Large Head, Pointed Bust**

	F	VF	EF	AU	Unc.
1852 FIVE DOLLARS, Small Head, With Rounded Bust	$5,500	$11,000	$22,500	$40,000	$80,000
1852 FIVE DOLLARS, Large Head, With Pointed Bust	$4,700	$9,500	$18,000	$35,000	$67,500

Large Head

Small Head   **Small Date**   **1855**

	F	VF	EF	AU	Unc.
1852 TEN D., Large Head	$2,750	$4,500	$8,000	$14,000	$32,500
1852 TEN D., Small Head	$6,200	$8,000	$19,000	$32,000	$80,000
1852 TEN D., Small Close Date	$12,500	$28,000	$47,000	$90,000	
1855 TEN D.	$9,500	$16,000	$22,000	$29,000	$52,500

Large Head   **Small Head**

	F	VF	EF	AU	Unc.
1855 TWENTY DOL., Large Head (a)	—	—	$550,000	—	—
	Auctions: $558,125, AU-53, April 2014				
1855 TWENTY DOL., Small Head	$12,000	$25,000	$35,000	$55,000	$125,000

a. 4 to 6 examples are known. A unique piece with the Large Head obverse and the reverse used on the Small Head coins (which differs in the position of the eagle's left wing) also exists.

	F	VF	EF	AU	Unc.
1855 50 DOLLARS	$25,000	$36,000	$55,000	$85,000	$180,000

KELLOGG & CO., SAN FRANCISCO, 1854–1855

John G. Kellogg went to San Francisco on October 12, 1849, from Auburn, New York. At first he was employed by Moffat & Co., and remained with that organization when control passed to Curtis, Perry, and Ward. When the U.S. Assay Office was discontinued, December 14, 1853, Kellogg became associated with George F. Richter, who had been an assayer in the U.S. Assay Office of Gold. These two set up business as Kellogg & Richter on December 19, 1853.

When the U.S. Assay Office ceased operations, a period ensued during which no private firm was striking gold. The new San Francisco branch mint did not produce coins for some months after Curtis & Perry took the contract for the government (Ward having died). The lack of coin was again keenly felt by businessmen, who petitioned Kellogg & Richter to "supply the vacuum" by issuing private coin. Their plea was soon answered: on February 9, 1854, Kellogg & Co. placed their first twenty-dollar piece in circulation.

The firm dissolved late in 1854 and reorganized as Kellogg & Humbert. The latter partner was Augustus Humbert, for some time identified as U.S. assayer of gold in California. Regardless of the fact that the San Francisco branch mint was then producing coins, Kellogg & Humbert issued twenty-dollar coins in 1855 in a quantity greater than before. On September 12, 1857, hundreds of the firm's rectangular gold ingots in transit to New York City were lost in the sinking of the SS *Central America*. They were the most plentiful of bars aboard the ill-fated ship from several different assayers.

	F	VF	EF	AU	Unc.
1854 TWENTY D.	$3,250	$4,750	$6,500	$10,000	$24,000

The 1855 Kellogg & Co. twenty-dollar piece is similar to that of 1854. The letters on the reverse are larger and the arrows longer on one 1854 variety. There are die varieties of both.

	F	VF	EF	AU	Unc.
1855 TWENTY D.	$3,500	$5,000	$6,750	$11,000	$27,500

In 1855, Ferdinand Grüner cut the dies for a round-format fifty-dollar gold coin for Kellogg & Co., but coinage seems to have been limited to presentation pieces in Proof format. Only 10 to 12 pieces are known to exist. A "commemorative restrike" was made in 2001 using transfer dies made from the original and gold recovered from the SS *Central America*. These pieces have the inscription S.S. CENTRAL AMERICA GOLD, C.H.S. on the reverse ribbon.

	PF
1855 FIFTY DOLLS. (a)	$600,000
Auctions: $763,750, PF-64Cam, April 2014; $747,500, PF-64, January 2007	

a. 13 to 15 examples are known.

OREGON EXCHANGE COMPANY, OREGON CITY, 1849

THE BEAVER COINS OF OREGON

Upon the discovery of gold in California, a great exodus of Oregonians joined in the hunt for the precious metal. Soon, gold seekers returned with their gold dust, which became an accepted medium of exchange. As in other Western areas at that time, the uncertain qualities of the gold and weighing devices tended to irk tradespeople, and petitions were made to the legislature for a standard gold coin issue.

On February 16, 1849, the territorial legislature passed an act providing for a mint and specified five- and ten-dollar gold coins without alloy. Oregon City, the largest city in the territory with a population of about 1,000, was designated as the location for the mint. At the time this act was passed, Oregon had been brought into the United States as a territory by act of Congress. When the new governor arrived on March 2, he declared the coinage act unconstitutional.

The public-spirited people, however, continued to work for a convenient medium of exchange and soon took matters into their own hands by starting a private mint. Eight men of affairs, whose names were Kilborne, Magruder, Taylor, Abernethy, Willson, Rector, Campbell, and Smith, set up the Oregon Exchange Company.

The coins struck were of virgin gold as specified in the original act. Ten-dollar dies were made slightly later.

	F	VF	EF	AU	Unc.
1849 5 D.	$32,000	$48,500	$75,000	$125,000	$275,000

	F	VF	EF	AU	Unc.
1849 TEN.D.	$80,000	$145,000	$270,000	$350,000	—

MORMON GOLD PIECES, SALT LAKE CITY, UTAH, 1849–1860

The first name given to the organized Mormon Territory was the "State of Deseret," the last word meaning "honeybee" in the Book of Mormon. The beehive, which is shown on the reverse of the five-dollar 1860 piece, was a favorite device of the followers of Joseph Smith and Brigham Young. The clasped hands appear on most Mormon coins and exemplify strength in unity. HOLINESS TO THE LORD was an inscription frequently used.

Brigham Young was the instigator of the coinage system and personally supervised the mint, which was housed in a little adobe building in Salt Lake City. The mint was inaugurated late in 1848 as a public convenience and to make a profit for the church. Each coin had substantially less gold than the face value stated.

	F	VF	EF	AU	Unc.
1849 TWO.AND.HALF.DO.	$12,500	$23,000	$35,000	$57,000	$90,000
1849 FIVE.DOLLARS	$9,500	$18,000	$30,000	$40,000	$75,000

	F	VF	EF	AU	Unc.
1849 TEN.DOLLARS	$275,000	$450,000	$550,000	$750,000	$950,000
	Auctions: $705,000, AU-58, April 2014				

	F	VF	EF	AU	Unc.
1849 TWENTY.DOLLARS (a)	$92,500	$175,000	$275,000	$375,000	$525,000
Auctions: $558,125, MS-62, April 2014					

a. The first coin of the twenty-dollar denomination to be struck in the United States.

	F	VF	EF	AU	Unc.
1850 FIVE DOLLARS	$13,000	$22,000	$34,000	$47,500	$85,000

	F	VF	EF	AU	Unc.
1860 5.D.	$20,000	$32,000	$42,000	$65,000	$90,000

COLORADO GOLD PIECES

CLARK, GRUBER & CO., DENVER, 1860–1861

Clark, Gruber & Co. was a well-known private minting firm in Denver, Colorado, in 1860 and 1861, formed by bankers from Leavenworth, Kansas Territory. In 1862 their operation was purchased by the Treasury Department and thenceforth operated as an assay office.

	F	VF	EF	AU	Unc.
1860 2 1/2 D.	$1,800	$2,750	$4,000	$5,500	$13,500
1860 FIVE D.	$2,100	$3,250	$4,500	$6,250	$14,500

	F	VF	EF	AU	Unc.
1860 TEN D.	$9,000	$14,000	$20,000	$30,000	$55,000
1860 TWENTY D.	$70,000	$135,000	$250,000	$385,000	$650,000
	Auctions: $690,000, MS-64, January 2006				

The $2.50 and $5 pieces of 1861 follow closely the designs of the 1860 issues. The main difference is found in the legends. The reverse side now has CLARK GRUBER & CO. DENVER. On the obverse, PIKES PEAK now appears on the coronet of Miss Liberty.

	F	VF	EF	AU	Unc.
1861 2 1/2 D.	$1,900	$3,000	$4,400	$7,500	$14,000
1861 FIVE D.	$2,300	$3,700	$5,750	$10,500	$37,500
1861 TEN D.	$2,400	$4,000	$6,500	$11,000	$28,500

	F	VF	EF	AU	Unc.
1861 TWENTY D.	$20,000	$37,500	$57,500	$95,000	$225,000

JOHN PARSONS & COMPANY, TARRYALL MINES, COLORADO, 1861

Very little is known regarding the mint of John Parsons and Co., although it is reasonably certain that it operated in the South Park section of Park County, Colorado, near the original town of Tarryall, in the summer of 1861.

	VF	EF
(1861) Undated 2 1/2 D. (a)	$200,000	$300,000
(1861) Undated FIVE D. (b)	$275,000	$375,000

a. 6 to 8 examples are known. b. 5 or 6 examples are known.

J.J. Conway & Co., Georgia Gulch, Colorado, 1861

Records show that the Conway mint operated for a short while in 1861. As in all gold-mining areas the value of gold dust caused disagreement among the merchants and the miners. The firm of J.J. Conway & Co. solved this difficulty by bringing out its gold pieces in August 1861.

	VF	EF
(1861) Undated 2 1/2 DOLL'S (a)	$155,000	$200,000
(1861) Undated FIVE DOLLARS (b)	$225,000	$300,000

a. 8 to 12 examples are known. **b.** 5 to 8 examples are known.

(1861) Undated TEN DOLLARS (a)	—

a. 3 examples are known.

CALIFORNIA SMALL-DENOMINATION GOLD

There was a scarcity of small coins during the California gold rush. Starting in 1852, quarter, half, and dollar coins were privately minted from native gold to alleviate the shortage. The commercial acceptability of these hard-to-handle, underweight coins was always limited, but they soon became popular as souvenirs. Early coins contained up to 85% of face value in gold. The amount and quality of gold in the coins soon decreased, and some later issues are merely gold plated.

The Coinage Act of April 22, 1864, made private coinage illegal, but the law was not fully enforced until 1883. In compliance with the law, non-denominated tokens were made, and from 1872 until 1883 both coins and tokens were produced. After 1883, most of the production was tokens. To circumvent the law, and to make them more acceptable, some pieces made after 1881 were backdated to the 1850s or 1860s.

Early issues have Liberty heads; later issues have Indian heads and often are prooflike. Most have a wreath on the reverse, but some have original designs. About 35,000 pieces are believed to exist. Numismatists have identified more than 570 different varieties, many of them very rare. The quality of strike and edge treatment is inconsistent. Many bear their makers' initials: D, DERI, DERIB, DN, FD, G, GG, GL, H, L, N, or NR. Major denominated coins are listed below; values are for the most common variety of each type. Non-denominated tokens are not included in these listings. They are much less valuable. ***Beware of extremely common modern replicas*** (often having a bear in the design), which have little numismatic value.

The values in the following charts are only for coins made before 1883 with the denomination on the reverse expressed as CENTS, DOL., DOLL., or DOLLAR.

QUARTER DOLLAR, OCTAGONAL

	EF	AU	Unc.
Large Liberty Head / Value and Date in Wreath	$175	$250	$450
Large Liberty Head / Value and Date in Beaded Circle	$175	$275	$470
Large Liberty Head / Value and CAL in Wreath	$175	$230	$350
Small Liberty Head / Value and Date in Wreath	$170	$230	$320
Small Liberty Head / Value and Date in Beaded Circle	$175	$250	$340
Small Liberty Head / Value in Shield, Date in Wreath	$175	$250	$375
Small Liberty Head / Value and CAL in Wreath	$175	$250	$425
Small Liberty Head, date below / Value in Wreath	$175	$230	$320
Large Indian Head / Value in Wreath	$215	$310	$475
Large Indian Head / Value and CAL in Wreath	$200	$280	$450
Small Indian Head / Value and CAL in Wreath	$500	$625	$975
Washington Head 1872 / Value and CAL in Wreath	$775	$1,350	$2,000

QUARTER DOLLAR, ROUND

	EF	AU	Unc.
Liberty Head / Value in Wreath	$150	$250	$425
Large Liberty Head / Value and Date in Wreath	$190	$310	$450
Large Liberty Head / Value and CAL in Wreath	$150	$250	$400
Small Liberty Head / 25 CENTS in Wreath	$320	$500	$800
Small Liberty Head / Value and Date in Wreath	$180	$300	$435
Small Liberty Head / Value in Shield, Date in Wreath	$180	$315	$550
Small Liberty Head / Value and CAL in Wreath	$180	$225	$400
Large Indian Head / Value in Wreath	$350	$520	$825
Large Indian Head / Value and CAL in Wreath	$300	$400	$675
Small Indian Head / Value and CAL in Wreath	$375	$525	$850
Washington Head 1872 / Value and CAL in Wreath	$725	$1,000	$1,600

HALF DOLLAR, OCTAGONAL

	EF	AU	Unc.
Large Liberty Head / Value and Date in Wreath	$300	$370	$690
Large Liberty Head / Value and Date in Beaded Circle	$170	$210	$450
Large Liberty Head / Value and CAL in Wreath	$210	$425	$650
Large Liberty Head / Legend Surrounds Wreath	$400	$600	$1,000
Small Liberty Head / Value and Date in Wreath	$200	$375	$575
Small Liberty Head / Value and CAL in Wreath	$185	$320	$475
Small Liberty Head / Small Eagle With Rays	$1,300	$2,000	$3,250
Small Liberty Head / Large Eagle With Raised Wings	$1,500	$2,200	$3,250
Large Indian Head / Value in Wreath	$210	$400	$675
Large Indian Head / Value and CAL in Wreath	$235	$350	$575
Small Indian Head / Value in Wreath	$250	$425	$700
Small Indian Head / Value and CAL in Wreath	$450	$585	$975

HALF DOLLAR, ROUND

	EF	AU	Unc.
Liberty Head / Value in Wreath	$180	$325	$500
Liberty Head / Value and Date in Wreath	$180	$325	$500
Liberty Head / Value and CAL in Wreath	$225	$350	$575
Liberty Head / CALIFORNIA GOLD Around Wreath	$225	$375	$600
Large Indian Head / Value in Wreath	$210	$325	$525
Large Indian Head / Value and CAL in Wreath	$200	$300	$465
Small Indian Head / Value and CAL in Wreath	$200	$330	$525

DOLLAR, OCTAGONAL

	EF	AU	Unc.
Liberty Head / Value and Date in Wreath	$500	$750	$1,350
Liberty Head / Value and Date in Beaded Circle	$500	$800	$1,500
Liberty Head / Legend Around Wreath	$500	$825	$1,550
Liberty Head / Large Eagle	$2,150	$3,150	$5,250
Large Indian Head / Value in Wreath	$725	$1,150	$2,100
Small Indian Head / Value and CAL in Wreath	$725	$1,150	$2,100

DOLLAR, ROUND

	EF	AU	Unc.
Liberty Head / CALIFORNIA GOLD. Value and Date in Wreath	$1,750	$2,600	$4,500
Liberty Head / Date Beneath Head	$2,300	$3,200	$5,100
Indian Head / Date Beneath Head	$2,000	$3,100	$5,000

COINS OF THE GOLDEN WEST

Small souvenir California gold pieces were made by several manufacturers in the early 20th century. A series of 36 pieces, in the size of 25¢, 50¢, and $1 coins, was sold by the M.E. Hart Company of San Francisco to honor Alaska and various Western states. The Hart Company also marketed the official commemorative Panama-Pacific gold coins from the 1915 Exposition and manufactured plush copper cases for them. Similar cases were acquired by Farran Zerbe, who mounted 15 complete sets of what he termed "Coins of the Golden West." Intact, framed 36-piece sets are rare; individual specimens are among the most popular of all souvenir pieces of that era.

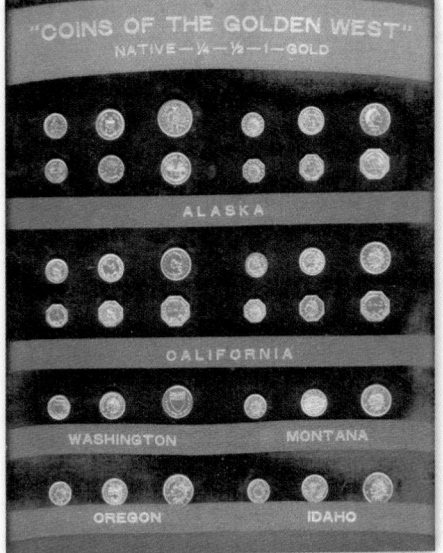

	AU	MS-63
Alaska Pinch, 25¢, octagonal, 1902	$350	$650
Alaska Pinch, 50¢, octagonal, 1900	$400	$700
Alaska Pinch, $1, octagonal, 1898	$500	$850
Alaska Pinch, 25¢, round, 1901	$350	$650
Alaska Pinch, 50¢, round, 1899	$400	$700
Alaska Pinch, $1, round, 1897	$500	$850
Alaska Parka, 25¢, round, 1911	$1,200	$1,900
Alaska Parka, 50¢, round, 1911	$1,300	$2,250
Alaska Parka, $1, round, 1911	$1,500	$2,650
Alaska AYPE, 25¢, round, 1909	$175	$300
Alaska AYPE, 50¢, round, 1909	$200	$350
Alaska AYPE, $1, round, 1909	$250	$400
California Minerva, 25¢, octagonal, 1915	$200	$350
California Minerva, 50¢, octagonal, 1915	$250	$400
California Minerva, $1, octagonal, 1915	$300	$500
California Minerva, 25¢, round, 1915	$200	$350
California Minerva, 50¢, round, 1915	$250	$400
California Minerva, $1, round, 1915	$300	$500
California 25¢, octagonal, 1860 or 1902	$500	$1,200
California 50¢, octagonal, 1900	$600	$1,350
California $1, octagonal, 1898	$700	$1,600
California 25¢, round, 1849, 1860, 1871, or 1901	$550	$1,250
California 50¢, round, 1849 or 1899	$650	$1,500
California $1, round, 1849	$800	$1,750
Idaho, 25¢, round, 1914	$650	$1,150
Idaho, 50¢, round, 1914	$750	$1,250
Idaho, $1, round, 1914	$850	$1,500
Montana, 25¢, round, 1914	$650	$1,150
Montana, 50¢, round, 1914	$750	$1,250
Montana, $1, round, 1914	$850	$1,500
Oregon, 25¢, round, 1914	$600	$1,100
Oregon, 50¢, round, 1914	$700	$1,200
Oregon, $1, round, 1914	$800	$1,400
Washington, 25¢, round, 1914	$600	$1,100
Washington, 50¢, round, 1914	$700	$1,200
Washington, $1, round, 1914	$800	$1,400

CALIFORNIA GOLD INGOT BARS

During the Gold Rush era, gold coins, ingots, and "dust" (actually flakes and nuggets) were sent by steamship from San Francisco to other ports, most importantly to New York City and London, where the gold was sold or, in some instances, sent to mints for conversion into coins. The typical procedure in the mid-1850s was to send the gold by steamship from San Francisco to Panama, where it was transported across 48 miles of territory by small water craft and pack animals from 1849 until the Panama Railroad opened in 1855, then loaded aboard another ship at the town of Aspinwall on the Atlantic side. On September 12, 1857, the SS *Central America*, en route from Aspinwall to New York City with more than 475 passengers, over 100 crew members, and an estimated $2.6 million in gold (in an era in which pure gold was valued at $20.67 per ounce) was lost at sea. Miraculously, more than 150 people, including all but one of the women and children, were rescued by passing ships. The *Central America* went to the bottom of the Atlantic Ocean off the Carolina coast.

In the 1980s a group of researchers secured financing to search for the long-lost ship. After much study and many explorations, they discovered the wreck of the *Central America* 7,200 feet below the surface. They used the robotic *Nemo*, a sophisticated device weighing several tons, to photograph the wreck and to carefully bring to the surface many artifacts. A king's ransom in gold ingots was found, along with more than 7,500 coins, the latter mostly consisting of Mint State 1857-S double eagles.

The 500-plus gold ingots furnished a unique opportunity to study specimens that, after conservation, were essentially in the same condition as they had been in 1857. These bore the imprints of five different California assayers, who operated seven offices. With few exceptions, each ingot bears individual stamps, indicating its maker, a serial number, the weight in ounces, the fineness (expressed in thousandths, e.g., .784 indicating 784/1000 pure gold), and the 1857 value in dollars. The smallest bar found was issued by Blake & Co., weighed 4.95 ounces, was .795 fine, and was stamped with a value of $81.34. The largest ingot, dubbed the "Eureka bar," bore the imprint of Kellogg & Humbert, and was stamped with a weight of 933.94 ounces, .903 fine, and a value of $17,433.57.

Blake & Co., Sacramento, California: From December 28, 1855, to May 1858, Blake & Co. was operated by Gorham Blake and W.R. Waters. • 34 ingots recovered. Serial numbers in the 5,100 and 5,200 series. Lowest weight and value: 4.95 ounces, $81.34. Highest weight and value: 157.40 ounces, $2,655.05. These bars have beveled or "dressed" edges and may have seen limited use in California commerce.

Harris, Marchand & Co., Sacramento and Marysville: This firm was founded in Sacramento in 1855 by Harvey Harris and Desiré Marchand, with Charles L. Farrington as the "& Co." The Marysville office was opened in January 1856. Serial numbers in the 6000 series are attributed to Sacramento, comprising 36 bars; a single bar in the 7000 series (7095) is attributed to Marysville. The Marchand bars each have a circular coin-style counterstamp on the face. Lowest weight and value (Sacramento): 9.87 ounces, $158.53. Highest weight and value (Sacramento): 295.20 ounces, $5,351.73. • Unique Marysville bar: 174.04 ounces, $3,389.06.

Henry Hentsch, San Francisco: Hentsch, a Swiss, was an entrepreneur involved in banking, real estate, assaying, and other ventures. In February 1856, he opened an assay office as an annex to his bank. It is likely that many of his ingots were exported to Europe, where he had extensive banking connections. • 33 ingots recovered. Lowest weight and value: 12.52 ounces, $251.82. Highest weight and value: 238.84 ounces, $4,458.35.

Justh & Hunter, San Francisco and Marysville: Emanuel Justh, a Hungarian, was a lithographer in San Francisco in the early 1850s. In 1854 and 1855 he worked as assistant assayer at the San Francisco Mint. Solomon Hillen Hunter came to California from Baltimore. The Justh & Hunter partnership was announced in May 1855. • Although study is continuing, the 60 ingots in the 4000 series are tentatively attributed to San Francisco, and the 26 ingots in the 9000 series are attributed to Marysville. • San Francisco—Lowest weight and value: 5.24 ounces, $92.18. Highest weight and value: 866.19 ounces, $15,971.93. • Marysville—Lowest weight and value: 19.34 ounces, $356.21. Highest weight and value: 464.65 ounces, $8,759.90.

Kellogg & Humbert, San Francisco: John Glover Kellogg and Augustus Humbert, two of the most famous names in the minting of California gold coins, formed the partnership of Kellogg & Humbert in spring 1855. The firm was one of the most active of all California assayers during the mid-1850s. • 346 ingots recovered, constituting the majority of those found. • Lowest weight and value: 5.71 ounces, $101.03. Highest weight and value: 933.94 ounces, $17,433.57.

A selection of gold ingots from the SS *Central America* treasure (with an 1857-S double eagle shown for scale, near lower left). (1) Harris, Marchand & Co., Marysville office, serial number 7095, 174.04 ounces, .942 fine, $3,389.06 (all values as stamped in 1857). (2) Henry Hentsch, San Francisco, serial number 3120, 61.93 ounces, .886 fine, $1,134.26. (3) Kellogg & Humbert, San Francisco, serial number 215, .944 fine, $1,045.96. (4) Blake & Co., Sacramento, 19.30 ounces, .946 fine, $297.42. (5) Another Blake & Co. ingot, serial number 5216, .915 fine, $266.12. (6) Justh & Hunter, Marysville office, serial number 9440, 41.79 ounces, $761.07. (7) Justh & Hunter, San Francisco office, serial number 4243, 51.98 ounces, .916 fine, $984.27. (8) Harris, Marchand & Co., Sacramento office, serial number 6514, 35.33 ounces, .807 fine, $589.38. (9) Harris, Marchand & Co., Sacramento office, serial number 6486, 12.64 ounces, .950 fine, $245.00.

Private Tokens

Privately issued tokens are by no means an American invention. They were common to most capitalist nations in the 1800s (and known even earlier), created and circulated by businessmen and others in periods of economic weakness or uncertainty, during financial panics, depressions, and times of war. Sometimes they were handed out as advertising trinkets or political propaganda pieces; more often they passed as makeshift currency when few real coins were available to make small change. Unlike real coins, which are government-issued as legal tender, tokens are minted by private citizens and companies. Commonly made of metal, usually round in shape, coins and tokens are very similar in appearance, but a token lacks a coin's official status as government-backed currency. Typically it would only have trade value, and then only in the vicinity in which it was issued (if, for example, a local merchant was prepared to redeem it in goods or services).

This section describes several of the more commonly encountered American tokens of the 1800s.

HARD TIMES TOKENS (1832–1844)

Hard Times tokens, as they are called, are pieces of Americana dating from the era of presidents Andrew Jackson and Martin Van Buren. They are mostly the size of a contemporary large copper cent. Privately minted from 1832 to 1844, they display diverse motifs reflecting political campaigns and satire of the era as well as carrying advertisements for merchants, products, and services. For many years these have been a popular specialty within numismatics, helped along with the publication of *Hard Times Tokens* by Lyman H. Low (1899; revised edition, 1906) and later works, continuing to the present day (see the *Guide Book of Hard Times Tokens*, 2015). In 1899 Low commented (adapted) that "the issues commonly called Hard Times tokens . . . had no semblance of authority behind them. They combine the character of political pieces with the catch-words of party cries; of satirical pieces with sarcastic allusions to the sentiments or speeches of the leaders of opposing parties; and in some degree also of necessity pieces, in a time when, to use one of the phrases of the day, 'money was a cash article,' hard to get for daily needs."

Although examples from the earlier 1830s are designated as Hard Times tokens, the true Hard Times period started in a serious way on May 10, 1837, when banks began suspending specie payments and would no longer exchange paper currency for coins. This date is memorialized on some of the token inscriptions. Difficult economic conditions continued through 1843; the first full year of recovery was 1844. From March 1837 to March 1841, President Martin Van Buren vowed to "follow in the steps of my illustrious predecessor," President Andrew Jackson, who had been in office from March 1829 until Van Buren's inauguration. Jackson was perhaps the most controversial president up to that time. His veto in 1832 of the impending (1836) recharter of the Bank of the United States set off a political firestorm, and the flames were fanned when his administration shifted deposits to favored institutions, derisively called "pet banks."

The Jackson era was one of unbridled prosperity. Due to sales of land in the West, the expansion of railroads, and a robust economy, so much money piled up in the Treasury that distributions were made in 1835 to all of the states. Seeking to end wild speculation, Jackson issued the "Specie Circular" on July 11, 1836, mandating that purchases of Western land, often made on credit, by paper money of uncertain worth, or by non-cash means, had to be paid in silver or gold coins. Almost immediately, the land boom settled and prices stabilized. A chill began to spread across the economy, which worsened in early 1837. Finally, many banks ran short of ready cash, causing the specie suspension.

After May 10, 1837, silver and gold coins completely disappeared from circulation. Copper cents remained, but were in short supply. Various diesinkers and others produced a flood of copper tokens. These were sold at discounts to merchants and banks, with $6 for 1,000 tokens being typical. Afterward, they were paid out in commerce and circulated for the value of one cent.

The actions of Jackson, the financial tribulations that many thought he precipitated, and the policies of Van Buren inspired motifs for a class of Hard Times tokens today known as "politicals." Several hundred other varieties were made with the advertisements of merchants, services, and products and are known as "store cards" or "merchants' tokens." Many of these were illustrated with elements such as a shoe, umbrella, comb, coal stove, storefront, hotel, or carriage.

One of the more famous issues depicts a slave kneeling in chains, with the motto "Am I Not a Woman & a Sister?" This token was issued in 1838, when abolition was a major rallying point for many Americans in the North. The curious small-size Feuchtwanger cents of 1837, made in Feuchtwanger's Composition (a type of German silver), were proposed to Congress as a cheap substitute for copper cents, but no congressional action was taken. Lewis Feuchtwanger produced large quantities on his own account and circulated them extensively (see page 1328).

As the political and commercial motifs of Hard Times tokens are so diverse, and reflect the American economy and political scene of their era, numismatists have found them fascinating to collect and study. Although there are major rarities in the series, most of the issues are very affordable. Expanded information concerning more than 500 varieties of Hard Times tokens can be found in Russell Rulau's *Standard Catalog of United States Tokens, 1700–1900* (fourth edition). Collectors and researchers are also encouraged to consult *A Guide Book of Hard Times Tokens* (Bowers). A representative selection is illustrated here.

L1, HT1

L57, HT76

L4, HT6

L56, HT75

	VF	EF	AU
L1, HT1. Andrew Jackson. Copper	$5,000	$8,500	—
L57, HT76. Van Buren, facing left. Brass	$2,200	$3,250	$4,250
L4, HT6. Jackson President of the U.S. Brass	$135	$275	$750
L56, HT75. Van Buren facing left. Copper	$80	$160	$375

L66, HT24

L54, HT81

L55, HT63

L31, HT46

L8, HT9

L18, HT32

L51, HT70

L47, HT66

L60, HT18

L44, HT69

	VF	EF	AU
L66, HT24. Agriculture. Copper	$225	$350	$650
L54, HT81. A Woman & A Sister. Copper	$180	$275	$400
L55, HT63. Loco Foco, 1838. Copper	$55	$160	$275
L31, HT46. Not One Cent, Motto. Copper	$45	$60	$135
L8, HT9. My Victory / Jackson. Copper	$30	$90	$125
L18, HT32. Executive Experiment. Copper	$25	$65	$110
L51, HT70. Roman Firmness. Copper	$35	$70	$125
L47, HT66. Phoenix / May Tenth. Copper	$25	$65	$110
L60, HT18. Ship/Lightning. Copper	$25	$65	$110
L44, HT69. Ship/Jackson. Copper	$25	$70	$125

L59, HT17

L65, HT23

	VF	EF	AU
L59, HT17. Ship / Wreath Border. Copper	$25	$65	$110
L65, HT23. Ship / Liberty Head. Copper	$100	$200	$350

FEUCHTWANGER TOKENS (1837–1864)

Lewis Feuchtwanger, a German-born chemist, moved to the United States in 1829 and settled in New York City. He produced a variety of German silver (an alloy of metals not including any actual silver) consisting of nickel, copper, and some zinc. Feuchtwanger suggested to Congress as early as 1837 that his metal be substituted for copper in U.S. coinage, and he made one-cent and three-cent trial pieces that circulated freely during the coin shortage of 1836 through 1844.

	VF	EF	AU	Unc.
1837 One Cent, Eagle	$130	$210	$300	$500
1837 Three-Cent, New York Coat of Arms	$750	$1,600	$2,750	$5,250
1837 Three-Cent, Eagle	$1,700	$3,600	$5,500	$13,000
1864 Three-Cent, Eagle	$1,300	$2,800	$3,800	$7,500

LESHER REFERENDUM DOLLARS (1900–1901)

Distributed in 1900 and 1901 by Joseph Lesher of Victor, Colorado, these private tokens manufactured in Denver were used in trade to some extent, and stocked by various merchants who redeemed them in goods. Lesher was an Ohio-born Civil War veteran and, after the war, an early pioneer of Colorado's mining fields. His coins, octagonal in shape, were numbered and a blank space left at bottom of 1901 issues, in which were stamped names of businessmen who bought them. All are quite rare; many varieties are extremely rare. Their composition is .950 fine silver (alloyed with copper).

	EF	AU	Unc.
1900 First type, no business name	$3,400	$4,200	$6,750
1900 A.B. Bumstead, with or without scrolls (Victor)	$1,800	$2,500	$3,800
1900 Bank type	$20,000	$32,000	—
1901 Imprint type, no name	$2,000	$3,000	$4,500
1901 Imprint type, Boyd Park. Denver	$2,000	$3,000	$4,600
1901 Imprint type, Slusher. Cripple Creek	$2,500	$3,500	$5,250
1901 Imprint type, Mullen. Victor	$4,000	$6,500	$10,500
1901 Imprint type, Cohen. Victor	$7,250	$11,000	$15,000
1901 Imprint type, Klein. Pueblo	$8,500	$13,500	$18,000
1901 Imprint type, Alexander. Salida	$9,500	$15,000	$21,000
1901 Imprint type, White. Grand Junction	$19,000	$27,000	—
1901 Imprint type, Goodspeeds. Colorado Springs	$34,000	$45,000	—
1901 Imprint type, Nelson. Holdrege, Nebraska	$32,000	$42,000	—
1901 Imprint type, A.W. Clark (Denver) (a)		$40,000	

a. This piece is unique.

CIVIL WAR TOKENS (1860s)

Early Friday morning, April 12, 1861, the Confederate States Army fired shells from 10-inch siege mortars into the Union's Fort Sumter in Charleston Bay, South Carolina, touching off the American Civil War. The ensuing turmoil would bring many changes to America's financial and monetary systems, including a dramatic reworking of the banking structure, federalization of paper money, bold innovations in taxation, tariffs, and land grants, and radical government experiments in new kinds of currency. For the man on the street, one daily noticeable development of the war was the large-scale hoarding of coins, which began in late 1861 and early 1862—people squirreled away first their gold, then silver coins, and finally, as the war dragged on that summer, even small copper-nickel cents. This caused trouble for day-to-day commerce. There were no coins to buy a newspaper or a glass of soda, to get a haircut, or tip a doorman. The situation gave birth to the humble but ubiquitous Civil War token.

Tokens were a familiar sight on the American scene by the time the Civil War was ignited. In fact, Americans had been using tokens as monetary substitutes since the colonial era, during the early days of the new nation, and throughout the 1800s. Two main kinds of tokens entered into American commerce during the war: *patriotics*, so called for their political and nationalistic themes; and *store cards*, or merchant tokens. An estimated 50 million or more were issued—more than two for every man, woman, and child in the Union. Civil War tokens were mostly a Northern phenomenon; not surprising, considering that New York State alone produced four times as much manufacturing as the entire Confederacy at the start of the war. Southerners had to make do with weak government-backed paper money, which quickly depreciated in value; Yankee tradesmen had the industrial base and financial means to produce a hard-money substitute that at least *looked* like money, even if it was backed by nothing more substantial than a local grocery store's promise to accept it at the value of one cent.

Most Civil War tokens were made of copper, some were brass, and rare exceptions were struck in copper-nickel or white metal. In addition to patriotics and store cards, some issuers crafted *numismatic* tokens during the war. These were struck for collectors rather than for day-to-day commerce, and made in the typical alloys as well as (rarely) in silver and other metals. Some were overstruck on dimes or copper-nickel cents.

Many kinds of tokens and medals were issued during the war. This sometimes leads to the question, "What, exactly, counts as a *Civil War token?*" How about the small hard-rubber checks and tickets, in various shapes, of that era? Or encased postage stamps, another small-change substitute of the war years? Or sutler tokens, issued by registered vendors who supplied the Union Army and traveled with the troops? These and more are sometimes collected along with the main body of about 10,000 varieties of store cards and patriotics. There is a long tradition of collecting Civil War tokens, dating back to even before the end of the war, and the hobby community has developed various habits and traditions over the years. Ultimately what to include in a collection is up to the individual collector. The Civil War Token Society (www.cwtsociety.com), the preeminent club for today's collector, suggests that to be "officially" considered a Civil War token, a piece must be between 18 and 25 mm in diameter. (Most of the copper tokens issued to pass as currency during the war were 18 or 19 mm, the size of the federal government's relatively new Flying Eagle and Indian Head cents, introduced in the late 1850s.)

Civil War tokens can be collected by state and by city, by type of issuer (druggist, saloonkeeper, doctor, etc.), or by any number of designs and themes. If you live in New York City and would like to study store cards issued by local shops and businesses, you have hundreds to choose from. You might hail from a small town and still be able to find a Civil War token from where you grew up. In 1863 in Oswego, New York, M.L. Marshall—a general-store seller of the unlikely combination of toys, fancy goods, fishing tackle, and rare coins—issued a cent-sized copper token featuring a fish! Undertakers issued store cards with tiny coffins advertising their services. Booksellers, bootmakers, beer brewers, hat dealers, and hog butchers all pictured their products on small copper tokens. On the patriotic side, Civil War tokens show Abraham Lincoln, various wartime presidential candidates, national heroes, cannons at the ready, unfurled flags, defiant eagles, and soldiers on horseback. They shout out the slogans of the day, warning the South of the strength of THE ARMY & NAVY, urging Americans to STAND BY THE FLAG, and insisting that THE FEDERAL UNION MUST AND SHALL BE PRESERVED.

Many tokens were more or less faithful imitations of the federal copper-nickel Indian Head cent. A few of this type have the word NOT in small letters above the words ONE CENT. For a time the legal status of the Civil War tokens was uncertain. Mint Director James Pollock thought they were illegal; however, there was no law prohibiting the issue of tradesmen's tokens or of private coins not in imitation of U.S. coins. Finally a law was passed April 22, 1864, prohibiting the private issue of any one- or two-cent coins, tokens, or devices for use as money, and on June 8 another law was passed that abolished private coinage of every kind. By that summer the government's new bronze Indian Head cents, minted in the tens of millions, were plentiful in circulation.

Today, Civil War tokens as a class are very accessible for collectors. Store-card tokens of Illinois, Massachusetts, Michigan, New York, Ohio, Pennsylvania, and Wisconsin are among those most frequently seen. A collector seeking special challenges will hunt for tokens from Iowa, Kansas, Maryland, and Minnesota—and, on the Confederate side, from Alabama, Louisiana (a counterstamped Indian Head cent), and Tennessee.

Three pieces of advice will serve the beginning collector. First, read the standard reference books, including *Patriotic Civil War Tokens* and *U.S. Civil War Store Cards*, both classics by George and Melvin Fuld, and the *Guide Book of Civil War Tokens*, by Q. David Bowers. These books lay the foundation and offer inspiration for building your own collection. Second, join the Civil War Token Society. This will put you in touch with other collectors who offer mentoring, friendship, and information. Third, visit a coin show and start looking for Civil War tokens in the inventories of the dealers there. Above all, enjoy the hobby and the many paths and byways it can lead you on through this important and turbulent era of American history.

Values shown are for the most common tokens in each composition.

	F	VF	EF	MS-63
Copper or brass	$15	$25	$35	$125
Nickel or German silver	$55	$75	$130	$290
White metal	$80	$125	$150	$275
Copper-nickel	$75	$125	$175	$325
Silver	$200	$300	$500	$1,200

PATRIOTIC CIVIL WAR TOKENS

Patriotic Civil War tokens feature leaders such as Abraham Lincoln; military images such as cannons or ships; and sociopolitical themes popular in the North, such as flags and slogans. Thousands of varieties are known.

	F	VF	AU	MS-63
Lincoln	$35	$70	$150	$300
Monitor	$30	$50	$125	$225
"Wealth of the South" (a)	$200	$400	$600	$1,000
Various common types	$15	$25	$45	$125

a. Dated 1860, but sometimes collected along with Civil War tokens.

CIVIL WAR STORE CARDS

Tradesmen's tokens of the Civil War era are often called store cards. These are typically collected by geographical location or by topic. The Fuld text (see bibliography) catalogs store cards by state, city, merchant, die combination, and metal. Values shown below are for the most common tokens for each state. Tokens from obscure towns or from merchants who issued only a few can be priced into the thousands of dollars and are widely sought.

	F	VF	EF	MS-63
Alabama	$1,500	$3,000	$4,000	$6,500
Connecticut	$10	$25	$50	$125
Washington, D.C.	—	$1,000	$1,400	$2,000
Idaho	$400	$700	$1,300	—
Illinois	$10	$25	$50	$125
Indiana	$10	$25	$50	$135
Iowa	$150	$450	$550	$1,250
Kansas	$900	$2,500	$3,500	$5,500
Kentucky	$50	$125	$200	$350
Louisiana	$2,000	$3,500	$4,500	—
Maine	$50	$100	$175	$275
Maryland	$150	$350	$550	$1,000
Massachusetts	$15	$35	$60	$140
Michigan	$10	$25	$50	$125
Minnesota	$150	$450	$550	$750
Missouri	$40	$100	$150	$250
New Hampshire	$80	$130	$175	$275
New Jersey	$10	$25	$50	$135
New York	$10	$25	$50	$125
Ohio	$10	$25	$50	$125
Pennsylvania	$10	$25	$50	$125
Rhode Island	$10	$25	$50	$135
Tennessee	$300	$650	$1,200	$1,750
Virginia	$250	$500	$1,000	—
West Virginia	$45	$100	$175	$400
Wisconsin	$15	$30	$60	$130
Sutlers' (a)	$185	$375	$500	$700

a. Sutler tokens were issued by registered contractors who operated camp stores that traveled with the military. These were made by coiners who also produced Civil War tokens, including John Stanton, Shubael Childs, and Francis X. Koehler. Each had a denomination, typically 5 cents to 50 cents. Some used on one side a die also used on Civil War tokens.

DC500A-1h

IN190D-3a

	VG	VF	AU	MS-63
DC500a-1h. H.A. Hall, Washington, D.C.	—	$1,000	$1,400	$2,200
IN190D-3a. J.L. & G.F. Rowe, Corunna, IN, 1863	$15	$40	$75	$175

MI865A-1a

MN980A-1a

MO910A-2a

NY630AQ-4a

NY630Z-1a

OH165M-1a

NY630BJ-1a

WI510M-1a

PA750F-1a

WV890D-4a

	VG	VF	AU	MS-63
MI865A-1a, W. Darling, Saranac, MI, 1864	$7,500	$12,000	$15,000	—
MN980A-1a. C. Benson, Druggist, Winona, MN	$300	$700	$900	$1,500
M0910A-4a. Drovers Hotel, St. Louis, MO, 1863	$125	$300	$600	$1,250
NY630AQ-4a. Gustavus Lindenmueller, New York, 1863	$15	$25	$50	$125
NY630Z-1a. Fr. Freise, Undertaker, New York, 1863	$20	$35	$85	$135
OH165M-1a. B.P. Belknp., "Teeth Extracted Without Pain"	$125	$250	$400	$600
NY630BJ-1a. Sanitary Commission, New York, 1864	$400	$850	$1,100	$1,750
WI510M-1a. Goes & Falk Malt House & Brewery, Milwaukee, WI, 1863	$25	$65	$100	$175
PA750F-1a. M.C. Campbell's Dancing Academy, Philadelphia, PA	$20	$35	$50	$130
WV890D-4a. R.C. Graves, News Dealer, Wheeling, WV, 1863	$45	$100	$175	$400

Confederate Issues

The Confederate States of America proclaimed itself in February 1861, a few weeks after Abraham Lincoln was elected president of the United States in November 1860. The newly formed nation based its monetary system on the Confederate dollar. Its paper currency was backed not by hard assets (such as gold) but by the promise to pay the bearer after the war was over—assuming Southern victory and independence. In addition to paper money, the Confederacy also explored creating its own coinage for day-to-day circulation. While this goal never came to fruition, interesting relics remain as testaments to the effort.

CONFEDERATE CENTS

Facts about the creation of the original Confederate cents are shrouded in mystery. However, a plausible storyline has developed based on research and recollections, through telling and retelling over the years. An order to make cents for the Confederacy is said to have been placed with Robert Lovett Jr., an engraver and diesinker of Philadelphia, through Bailey & Co., a jewelry firm of that city. Fearing arrest by the United States government for assisting the enemy, Lovett decided instead to hide the coins and the dies in his cellar. Captain John W. Haseltine, well known for finding numismatic rarities unknown to others, claimed that a bartender had received one of the coins over the counter and sold it to him. Haseltine recognized it as the work of Lovett, called on him, learned that he had struck 12 of the coins, and bought the remaining 11 and the dies. In 1874 Haseltine made restrikes in copper, silver, and gold.

Circa 1961, the dies were copied and additional pieces made by New York City coin dealer Robert Bashlow. These show die cracks and rust marks that distinguish them from earlier examples.

	Mintage	Unc.
		PF
1861 Cent, Original, Copper-Nickel, Unc.	13–16	$150,000
1861 Cent, Haseltine Restrike, Copper, Proof	55	$20,000
1861 Cent, Haseltine Restrike, Gold, Proof	7	$75,000
1861 Cent, Haseltine Restrike, Silver, Proof	12	$50,000

CONFEDERATE HALF DOLLARS

According to records, only four original Confederate half dollars were struck (on a hand press). Regular silver planchets were used, as well as a regular federal obverse die. One of the coins was given to Secretary of the Treasury Christopher G. Memminger, who passed it on to President Jefferson Davis for his approval. Another was given to Professor John L. Riddell of the University of Louisiana. Edward Ames of New Orleans received a third specimen. The last was kept by chief coiner Benjamin F. Taylor. Lack of bullion prevented the Confederacy from coining more pieces.

The Confederate half dollar was unknown to collectors until 1879, when a specimen and its reverse die were found in Taylor's possession in New Orleans. E. Mason Jr., of Philadelphia, purchased both and later sold them to J.W. Scott and Company of New York. J.W. Scott acquired 500 genuine 1861-O half dollars, routed or otherwise smoothed away the reverses, and then restamped them with the Confederate die. Known as restrikes, these usually have slightly flattened obverses. Scott also struck some medals in white metal using the Confederate reverse die and an obverse die bearing this inscription: 4 ORIGINALS STRUCK BY ORDER OF C.S.A. IN NEW ORLEANS 1861 / ******* / REV. SAME AS U.S. (FROM ORIGINAL DIE•SCOTT)

Confederate Reverse **Scott Obverse**

	Mintage	VF-20	EF-40	Unc.
1861 HALF DOL. (a)		—	$650,000	—
Auctions: $881,250, VF, January 2015				
1861 HALF DOL., Restrike	500	$6,500	$7,500	$15,000
1861 Scott Obverse, Confederate Reverse	500	$2,500	$3,750	$5,500

a. 4 examples are known.

Hawaiian and Puerto Rican Issues

Although the following issues of Hawaii and Puerto Rico were not circulating U.S. coins, they have political, artistic, and sentimental connections to the United States. Generations of American numismatists have sought them for their collections.

HAWAIIAN ISSUES

Five official coins were issued for the Kingdom of Hawaii. These include the 1847 cent issued by King Kamehameha III and the 1883 silver dimes, quarters, halves, and dollars of King Kalakaua I. The silver pieces were all designed by U.S. Mint chief engraver Charles E. Barber and struck at the San Francisco Mint. The 1883 eighth-dollar piece is a pattern. The 1881 five-cent piece is an unofficial issue.

The Hawaiian dollar was officially valued equal to the U.S. dollar. After Hawaii became a U.S. territory in 1900, the legal-tender status of these coins was removed and most were withdrawn from circulation and melted.

1847, One Cent

1881, Five Cents
Unofficial issue.

1883, Ten Cents

1883, Eighth Dollar

1883, Quarter Dollar

1883, Half Dollar

1883, Dollar

	Mintage	F-12	VF-20	EF-40	AU-50	MS-60	MS-63
							PF-63
1847 Cent (a)	100,000	$350	$450	$675	$850	$1,100	$2,000
Auctions: $2,585, MS-64BN, August 2014; $3,056, MS-64BN, November 2014; $2,350, MS-63RB, August 2014							
1881 Five Cents		$7,000	$10,000	$15,000	$17,500	$20,000	$27,000
Auctions: $14,688, MS-63, August 2014							
1881 Five Cents, Proof (b)							$8,000
Auctions: $2,185, PF-62, June 2001							
1883 Ten Cents	249,974	$70	$120	$275	$425	$1,000	$2,500
Auctions: $1,528, MS-63, July 2014; $823, MS-62, September 2014; $282, AU-55, September 2014; $206, EF-45, July 2014							
1883 Ten Cents, Proof	26						$12,000
Auctions: $12,690, PF-64, August 2014; $11,750, PF-63, November 2014							
1883 Eighth Dollar, Proof	20						$50,000
Auctions: $8,800, PF-50, July 1994							
1883 Quarter Dollar	499,974	$65	$90	$150	$175	$250	$400
Auctions: $9,400, MS-67, July 2014; $1,293, MS-66, August 2014; $823, MS-65, August 2014; $646, MS-65, August 2014							
1883 Quarter Dollar, Proof	26						$17,000
Auctions: $11,750, PF-62, November 2014							
1883 Half Dollar	699,974	$120	$175	$325	$500	$1,000	$2,500
Auctions: $17,625, MS-66, August 2014; $5,875, MS-65, August 2014; $2,350, MS-64, August 2014; $2,115, MS-64, August 2014							
1883 Half Dollar, Proof	26						$20,000
Auctions: $14,100, PF-63, November 2014							
1883 Dollar	499,974	$350	$450	$650	$1,100	$3,500	$10,000
Auctions: $10,575, MS-64, July 2014; $6,463, MS-63, August 2014; $1,087, AU-55, July 2014; $823, EF-45, August 2014							
1883 Dollar, Proof	26						$38,000
Auctions: $22,325, PF-61, November 2014							

a. Values shown are for the most common of the six known varieties. b. All Proofs of the 1881 five-cent coins are later restrikes, circa 1900.

PLANTATION TOKENS

During the 1800s, several private firms issued tokens for use as money in Hawaiian company stores. These are often referred to as Plantation tokens. The unusual denomination of 12-1/2 cents was equivalent to a day's wages in the sugar plantations, and was related to the fractional part of the Spanish eight-reales coin.

(1860) Undated, Waterhouse Token

(1871) Undated, Wailuku Plantation

1880, Wailuku Plantation

1882, Haiku Plantation

1891, Kahului Railroad

	F-12	VF-20	EF-40	AU-50
Waterhouse / Kamehameha IV, ca. 1860	$1,500	$3,000	$4,500	$6,750
Wailuku Plantation, 12-1/2 (cents), (1871), narrow starfish	$750	$2,000	$3,750	$6,000
Similar, broad starfish	$900	$2,250	$4,500	$7,250
Wailuku Plantation, VI (6-1/4 cents), (1871), narrow starfish	$1,800	$4,750	$7,000	$9,500
Similar, broad starfish	$2,200	$5,500	$7,500	$10,500
Wailuku Plantation, 1 Real, 1880	$750	$1,800	$3,500	$8,000
Wailuku Plantation, Half Real, 1880	$2,200	$5,000	$8,000	$11,500
Thomas H. Hobron, 12-1/2 (cents), 1879	$600	$850	$1,200	$1,500
Similar, two stars on both sides	$1,600	$2,800	$5,250	$9,000
Thomas H. Hobron, 25 (cents), 1879 (a)			$50,000	$60,000
Haiku Plantation, 1 Rial, 1882	$800	$1,250	$1,800	$2,500
Grove Ranch Plantation, 12-1/2 (cents), 1886	$1,400	$2,600	$4,600	$6,600
Grove Ranch Plantation, 12-1/2 (cents), 1887	$2,250	$4,500	$8,000	$10,500
Kahului Railroad, 10 cents, 1891	$2,100	$4,000	$7,500	$9,500
Kahului Railroad, 15 cents, 1891	$2,100	$4,000	$7,500	$9,500
Kahului Railroad, 20 cents, 1891	$2,100	$4,000	$7,500	$9,500
Kahului Railroad, 25 cents, 1891	$2,100	$4,000	$7,500	$9,500
Kahului Railroad, 35 cents, 1891	$2,100	$4,000	$7,500	$9,500
Kahului Railroad, 75 cents, 1891	$2,100	$4,000	$7,500	$9,500

a. 3 examples are known.

PUERTO RICAN ISSUES

Puerto Rico, the farthest east of the Greater Antilles, lies about 1,000 miles southeast of Florida between the Atlantic Ocean and the Caribbean Sea. Settled by Spain in 1508, the island was ceded to the United States after the Spanish-American War in 1898. Puerto Ricans were granted U.S. citizenship in 1917. Today Puerto Rico is a self-governing territory of the United States with commonwealth status.

The Puerto Rican coins of 1895 and 1896 were minted at the Casa de Moneda de Madrid, in Spain. The peso was struck in .900 fine silver, and the others were .835 fine. The portrait is of King Alfonso XIII, and the arms are of the Bourbons, the royal house of Spain. These coins were in circulation at the time of the Spanish-American War of 1898, which ended with U.S. victory and with Spain's loss of sovereignty over Cuba (along with its cession of the Philippine Islands, Puerto Rico, and Guam to the United States for $20 million). Puerto Rico's Spanish coins continued to circulate after the war.

Collectors of United States coins often include Puerto Rican coins in their collections, even though they are not U.S. issues. After the Spanish-American War, exchange rates were set for these coins relative to the U.S. dollar, and the island transitioned to a dollar-based currency. Today in Puerto Rico the dollar is still popularly referred to as a "peso."

1896, 5 Centavos

1896, 10 Centavos

1895, 20 Centavos

1896, 40 Centavos   1895, One Peso

	Mintage	F-12	VF-20	EF-40	AU-50	Unc.
1896 5 Centavos	600,000	$30	$50	$100	$150	$200
	Auctions: $56, EF-45, September 2014					
1896 10 Centavos	700,000	$40	$85	$135	$200	$300
	Auctions: $170, AU-55, September 2014; $212, AU-55, January 2014					
1895 20 Centavos	3,350,000	$45	$100	$150	$250	$400
	Auctions: No auction records available.					
1896 40 Centavos	725,002	$180	$300	$900	$1,700	$2,900
	Auctions: $705, AU-55, January 2015; $352, EF-45, January 2015					
1895 1 Peso	8,500,021	$200	$400	$950	$1,900	$3,250
	Auctions: $3,819, MS-63, September 2014; $1,380, AU-55, June 2006					

Philippine Issues

In April 1899, control of the Philippine Islands was officially transferred from Spain to the United States, as a condition of the treaty ending the Spanish-American War. The U.S. military suppressed a Filipino insurgency through 1902, and partway through that struggle, in July 1901, the islands' military government was replaced with a civilian administration led by American judge William Howard Taft. One of its first tasks was to sponsor a new territorial coinage that was compatible with the old Spanish issues, but also legally exchangeable for American money at the rate of two Philippine pesos to the U.S. dollar. The resulting coins—which bear the legend UNITED STATES OF AMERICA but are otherwise quite different in design from regular U.S. coins—today can be found in many American coin collections, having been brought to the States as souvenirs by service members after World War II or otherwise saved. The unusual designs, combined with the legend, have sometimes caused them to be confused with standard federal United States coins.

The coins, introduced in 1903, were designed by Filipino silversmith, sculptor, engraver, and art professor Melecio Figueroa, who had earlier worked for the Spanish *Casa de Moneda*, in Manila. They are sometimes called "Conant coins" or "Conants," after Charles Arthur Conant, an influential American journalist and banking expert who served on the commission that brought about the Philippine Coinage Act of March 2, 1903. "Both in the artistic quality of the designs and in perfection of workmanship, they compare favorably with anything of the kind ever done in America," wrote Secretary of War Elihu Root in his annual report to President Theodore Roosevelt. Figueroa died of tuberculosis on July 30, 1903, age 61, shortly after seeing his coins enter circulation.

Following Spanish custom, the dollar-sized peso was decimally equivalent to 100 centavos. Silver fractions were minted in denominations of fifty, twenty, and ten centavos, and minor coins (in copper-nickel and bronze) included the five-centavo piece, the centavo, and the half centavo.

In addition to the name of the United States, the coins bear the Spanish name for the islands: FILIPI-NAS. The silver coins feature a female personification of the Philippines, holding in one hand a hammer that she strikes against an anvil, and in the other an olive branch, with the volcanic Mount Mayon (northeast of the capital city of Manila) visible in the background. The minor coinage shows a young Filipino man, bare-chested and seated at an anvil with a hammer, again with Mount Mayon seen in the distance. The first reverse design, shared across all denominations, shows a U.S. federal shield surmounted by an eagle with outstretched wings, clutching an olive branch in its right talon and a bundle of arrows in its left. This reverse design was changed in 1937 to a new shield emblem derived from the seal of the 1936 Commonwealth.

Dies for the coins were made at the Philadelphia Mint by the U.S. Mint's chief engraver, Charles E. Barber. Mintmarks were added to the dies, as needed, at the branch mints. From 1903 to 1908 the coins were struck at the Philadelphia Mint (with no mintmark) and the San Francisco Mint (with an S mintmark). From

1909 through 1919, they were struck only at San Francisco. In the first part of 1920, one-centavo coins were struck in San Francisco; later in the year a new mint facility, the Mint of the Philippine Islands, was opened in Manila, and from that point into the early 1940s Philippine coins of one, five, ten, twenty, and fifty centavos were struck there. The coins produced at the Manila Mint in 1920, 1921, and 1922 bore no mintmark. No Philippine coins were struck in 1923 or 1924. The Manila Mint reopened in 1925; from then through 1941 its coinage featured an M mintmark. The Denver and San Francisco mints would be used for Philippine coinage in the final years of World War II, when the islands were under Japanese occupation.

Rising silver prices forced reductions in the fineness and weight for each Philippine silver denomination beginning in 1907, and subsequent issues are smaller in diameter. The new, smaller twenty-centavo piece was very close in size to the five-centavo piece (20.0 mm compared to 20.5 mm), resulting in a mismatching of dies for these two denominations in 1918. A small number of error coins were minted from this accidental combination, with some finding their way into circulation (often with the edge crudely reeded to induce them to pass as twenty-centavo coins). A solution was found by reducing the diameter of the five-centavo piece beginning in 1930.

It should be noted that, in addition to normal coins and paper currency, special token money in the form of coins and printed currency was made for use in the Culion Leper Colony. The token coinage saw six issues from 1913 to 1930, some produced at the Manila Mint. The leper colony was set up in May 1906 on the small island of Culion, one of the more than 7,000 islands comprising the Philippines, and the coinage was intended to circulate only there.

In 1935 the United States, responding to popular momentum for independence, approved the establishment of the Commonwealth of the Philippines, with the understanding that full self-governing independence would be recognized after a ten-year transition period. In 1936 a three-piece set of silver commemorative coins was issued to mark the transfer of executive power.

An adaptation of the new commonwealth's seal, introduced on the 1936 commemorative coins, was used for the reverse design of all circulating Philippine issues beginning in 1937. For their obverses, the Commonwealth coins retained the same Figueroa designs as those struck from 1903 to 1936. (A final transitional issue of more than 17 million 1936-dated one-centavo coins was minted using the federal-shield reverse design, rather than the new Commonwealth shield.)

After the bombing of Pearl Harbor, Japanese military forces advanced on the Philippines in late 1941 and early 1942, prompting the civil government to remove much of the Philippine treasury's bullion to the United States. Nearly 16 million pesos' worth of silver remained, mostly in the form of one-peso pieces of 1907 through 1912. These coins were hastily crated and dumped into Manila's Caballo Bay to prevent their capture by Japan. The Japanese occupied the Philippines, learned of the hidden treasure, and managed to recover some of the sunken coins (probably fewer than half a million). After the war, over the course of several years, more than 10 million of the submerged silver pesos were retrieved under the direction of the U.S. Treasury and, later, the Central Bank of the Philippines. Most of them show evidence of prolonged salt-water immersion, with dark corrosion that resists cleaning. This damage to so many coins has added to the scarcity of high-grade pre-war silver pesos.

Later during World War II, in 1944 and 1945, the U.S. Mint struck coins for the Philippines at its Philadelphia, Denver, and San Francisco facilities. These coins were brought over and entered circulation as U.S. and Philippine military forces fought to retake the islands from the Japanese.

After the war, the Commonwealth of the Philippines became an independent republic, on July 4, 1946, as had been scheduled by the Constitution of 1935. Today the Philippine coins of 1903 to 1945, including the set of commemoratives issued in 1936, remain significant mementoes of a colorful and important chapter in U.S. history and numismatics. They are a testament to the close ties and special relationship between the United States of America and the Republic of the Philippines.

PHILIPPINES UNDER U.S. SOVEREIGNTY (1903–1936)

The Philippine Islands were governed under the sovereignty of the United States from 1899 until early 1935. (In the latter year a largely self-governing commonwealth was established, followed by full independence in 1946.) Coinage under U.S. sovereignty began in 1903. There was a final issue of centavos dated 1936, minted in the style of 1903–1934, after which the design of all circulating coins changed to the new Commonwealth style.

BRONZE COINAGE

HALF CENTAVO (1903–1908)

Designer: *Melecio Figueroa.* **Weight:** *2.35 grams.* **Composition:** *.950 copper, .050 tin and zinc.* **Diameter:** *17.5 mm.* **Edge:** *Plain.* **Mint:** *Philadelphia.*

History. In 1903 and 1904 the United States minted nearly 18 million half centavos for the Philippines. By March of the latter year, it was obvious that the half centavo was too small a denomination, unneeded in commerce despite the government's attempts to force it into circulation. The recommendation of Governor-General Luke Edward Wright—that the coin be discontinued permanently—was approved, and on April 18, 1904, a new contract was authorized to manufacture one-centavo blanks out of unused half-centavo blanks. In April 1908, Governor-General James Francis Smith received permission to ship 37,827 pesos' worth of stored half centavos (7,565,400 coins) to the San Francisco Mint to be re-coined into one-centavo pieces. Cleared from the Philippine Treasury's vaults, the coins were shipped to California in June 1908, and most of them were melted and made into 1908 centavos.

Striking and Sharpness. Half centavos typically are well struck, except for the 1903 issue, of which some coins may show weak numerals in the date. Reverses sometimes show light flattening of the eagle's wing tips.

Half Centavo, 1903–1908

High Points of Wear. *Obverse Checkpoints:* 1. Figure's left hand. 2. Figure's right hand. 3. Face and frontal hair just above ear. 4. Edge of anvil. *Reverse Checkpoints:* 1. Eagle's wing tips. 2. Eagle's breast feathers. 3. Upper points of shield. 4. Eagle's right leg.

Proofs. The Philadelphia Mint struck small quantities of Proof half centavos for collectors throughout the denomination's existence, for inclusion in Proof sets (except for 1907, when no Proof sets were issued).

	Mintage	EF	MS-60	MS-63
		PF-60	PF-63	PF-65
1903	12,084,000	$2.25	$20	$40
	Auctions: $138, MS-65RD, September 2012; $247, MS-65RB, September 2013; $103, MS-65RB, September 2012			
1903, Proof	2,558	$50	$110	$150
	Auctions: $447, PF-67RB, October 2014; $282, PF-66RD, October 2014			
1904	5,654,000	$3.50	$25	$60
	Auctions: $270, MS-65RD, July 2013; $200, MS-65BN, January 2013; $65, MS-64RB, July 2013			
1904, Proof	1,355	$75	$135	$200
	Auctions: $382, PF-66RB, November 2014			
1905, Proof (a)	471	$175	$250	$500
	Auctions: $253, PF-64RB, June 2007; $207, PF-62BN, January 2012			
1906, Proof (a)	500	$150	$250	$450
	Auctions: $323, PF-65BN, January 2012; $374, PF-64RB, June 2007			
1908, Proof (a)	500	$150	$250	$450
	Auctions: $282, PF-64RB, April 2014; $230, PF-64RB, January 2012			

Note: The half centavo was unpopular in circulation. More than 7,500,000 were withdrawn and melted to be recoined as one-centavo pieces in 1908. **a.** Proof only.

ONE CENTAVO (1903–1936)

Designer: *Melecio Figueroa.* **Weight:** *4.7 grams.* **Composition:** *.950 copper, .050 tin and zinc.*
Diameter: *24 mm.* **Edge:** *Plain.* **Mints:** *Philadelphia, San Francisco, and Manila.*

Mintmark location is on the
reverse, to the left of the date.

History. Unlike the half centavo, the bronze centavo was a popular workhorse of Philippine commerce from the start of its production. Nearly 38 million coins were minted in the denomination's first three years. In 1920 the centavo was struck for circulation by two different mints (the only year this was the case). San Francisco produced the coins during the first part of 1920; later in the year, the coins were struck at the Manila Mint, after that facility opened. From that point forward all centavos struck under U.S. sovereignty were products of the Manila Mint. Those dated 1920, 1921, and 1922 bear no mint-mark identifying their origin. Manila produced no coins (of any denomination) in 1923 and 1924.

Coin collectors, notably educator, writer, and American Numismatic Association member Dr. Gilbert S. Perez, urged Manila Mint officials to include an M mark on their coinage—similar to the way that, for example, San Francisco coins were identified by an S—and this change was made starting with the coinage of 1925.

Coinage of the centavo continued through the late 1920s and early 1930s. U.S. sovereignty was significantly altered in 1935 with the establishment of the Commonwealth of the Philippines, and this change was reflected in all Philippine currency. A final mintage of 1936-dated centavos (17,455,463 pieces) was struck using the federal-shield reverse of the denomination's 1903–1934 coinage. The coin then switched over to the Commonwealth shield design in 1937.

Several centavo die varieties exist to give the specialist a challenge. Among them is the 1918-S, Large S, whose mintmark appears to be the same size and shape of that used on fifty-centavo pieces of the era.

Striking and Sharpness. On the obverse, the figure's right hand (holding the hammer) is almost always found flatly struck. The reverse, especially of later-date centavos, often shows flattening of the eagle's breast and of the left part of the shield. Issues of the Manila Mint, especially of 1920, often are lightly struck. Those of San Francisco typically are better struck, with only occasional light strikes. On centavos of 1929 to 1936, the M mintmark often is nearly unidentifiable as a letter.

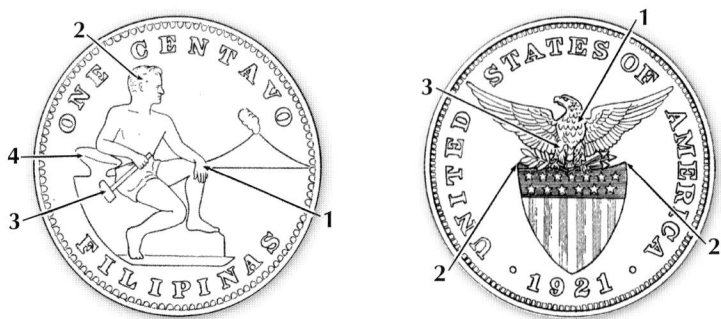

One Centavo, 1903–1936

High Points of Wear. *Obverse Checkpoints:* 1. Figure's left hand. 2. Frontal hair just above ear. 3. Head of hammer. 4. Left part of anvil. *Reverse Checkpoints:* 1. Eagle's breast feathers. 2. Upper points of shield. 3. Eagle's right leg.

Proofs. One-centavo Proofs were struck at the Philadelphia Mint for annual Proof sets in 1903, 1904, 1905, 1906, and 1908. Proof centavos of 1908 bear a date with numerals noticeably larger than those of circulation-strike 1908-S coins.

1908-S, S Over S

	Mintage	VF	EF	MS-60	MS-63
				PF-60	PF-63
1903	10,790,000	$1.25	$3	$15	$35
Auctions: $247, MS-66BN, January 2014					
1903, Proof	2,558			$60	$120
Auctions: $408, PF-65RB, April 2010; $212, PF-65RB, October 2015					
1904	17,040,400	$1.25	$3	$25	$45
Auctions: $94, MS-65BN, July 2015					
1904, Proof	1,355			$75	$125
Auctions: $217, PF-65RD, August 2013; $141, PF-64RB, April 2014					
1905	10,000,000	$1.25	$3.50	$30	$45
Auctions: $76, MS-64BN, June 2014					
1905, Proof	471			$175	$275
Auctions: $441, PF-65RB, April 2014; $805, PF-65RB, April 2010; $235, PF-64RD, August 2013					
1906, Proof (a)	500			$150	$250
Auctions: $423, PF-64RD, February 2014					
1908, Proof (a)	500			$150	$275
Auctions: $411, PF-66RD, October 2014; $499, PF-65RB, January 2014; $400, PF-65RB, August 2015					
1908-S	2,187,000	$4	$8	$40	$100
Auctions: $141, MS-65RB, April 2014; $129, MS-65RB, February 2014; $84, MS-64RB, December 2015					
1908-S, S Over S	(b)	$30	$50	$135	$300
Auctions: $558, MS-64RB, January 2014					

a. Proof only. **b.** Included in 1908-S mintage figure.

1918-S, Normal S   1918-S, Large S

	Mintage	VF	EF	MS-60	MS-63
1909-S	1,737,612	$10	$20	$110	$225
	Auctions: $317, MS-65RB, August 2014; $153, MS-64RB, December 2015; $62, MS-64BN, March 2014				
1910-S	2,700,000	$4.50	$9	$35	$60
	Auctions: $881, MS-66RD, April 2015; $118, MS-65RB, April 2014; $80, MS-64RB, April 2014				
1911-S	4,803,000	$2.50	$5	$25	$60
	Auctions: $90, MS-65RB, April 2014; $64, MS-64RB, March 2014				
1912-S	3,001,000	$7.50	$15	$75	$125
	Auctions: $118, MS-65BN, March 2014; $90, MS-64BN, June 2014				
1913-S	5,000,000	$4	$7	$35	$75
	Auctions: $270, MS-65BN, November 2014; $79, MS-63BN, January 2014; $62, MS-63BN, April 2015				
1914-S	5,000,500	$3.50	$5	$35	$70
	Auctions: $84, MS-64BN, November 2014; $113, MS-64BN, May 2014				
1915-S	2,500,000	$40	$90	$525	$1,250
	Auctions: $805, MS-63BN, June 2011; $647, MS-62BN, January 2014				
1916-S	4,330,000	$7.50	$12.50	$90	$150
	Auctions: $135, MS-64BN, July 2014; $159, MS-63RB, June 2014				
1917-S	7,070,000	$4	$10	$75	$150
	Auctions: $176, MS-65RD, February 2014; $53, MS-62BN, September 2014				
1917-S, 7 Over 6	(c)	$50	$160	$500	
	Auctions: No auction records available.				
1918-S	11,660,000	$5	$12	$100	$200
	Auctions: $212, MS-65BN, January 2015; $229, MS-64RB, June 2014				
1918-S, Large S	(d)	$150	$250	$1,000	$1,900
	Auctions: $2,585, MS-62BN, January 2016; $306, EF-45, January 2014				
1919-S	4,540,000	$5	$15	$75	$125
	Auctions: $110, MS-64BN, June 2014; $128, MS-64BN, January 2014				
1920	3,552,259	$3.50	$20	$50	$175
	Auctions: $259, MS-65RB, January 2014; $353, MS-65BN, June 2014				
1920-S	2,500,000	$8	$20	$125	$225
	Auctions: $236, MS-64BN, January 2014; $90, MS-62BN, March 2014				
1921	7,282,673	$2.50	$5	$35	$85
	Auctions: $153, MS-65RB, January 2014				
1922	3,519,100	$3	$6	$30	$70
	Auctions: $223, MS-65RB, January 2014; $52, MS-64BN, March 2014				
1925-M	9,325,000	$3	$7	$35	$65
	Auctions: $68, MS-64BN, May 2014				
1926-M	9,000,000	$2.50	$5	$30	$55
	Auctions: $89, MS-65BN, January 2015; $30, MS-64RB, March 2014				
1927-M	9,279,000	$2	$4	$25	$45
	Auctions: $212, MS-66RD, April 2014; $165, MS-66RB, January 2014				
1928-M	9,150,000	$2	$5	$30	$75
	Auctions: $141, MS-65RD, October 2015; $75, MS-64RD, April 2014; $50, MS-64RB, May 2014				
1929-M	5,657,161	$3	$6	$40	$85
	Auctions: $141, MS-65RD, January 2014; $106, MS-65RB, October 2015; $43, MS-63BN, March 2014				

c. Included in 1917-S mintage figure. **d.** Included in 1918-S mintage figure.

	Mintage	VF	EF	MS-60	MS-63
1930-M	5,577,000	$2	$4.50	$30	$50
	Auctions: $69, MS-65BN, January 2014; $75, MS-64RD, August 2014				
1931-M	5,659,355	$2.25	$5	$40	$60
	Auctions: $100, MS-65RB, December 2015; $40, MS-65RB, March 2014; $89, MS-65RB, January 2014				
1932-M	4,000,000	$3	$7	$50	$75
	Auctions: $112, MS-65RD, April 2014; $95, MS-65RD, January 2014				
1933-M	8,392,692	$2	$3	$20	$50
	Auctions: $147, MS-66RD, January 2014; $80, MS-66RB, March 2014; $141, MS-65RB, December 2015				
1934-M	3,179,000	$2.50	$4.50	$50	$75
	Auctions: $200, MS-66RD, April 2014; $112, MS-65RB, January 2014				
1936-M	17,455,463	$2.50	$4	$35	$65
	Auctions: $37, MS-64BN, March 2014				

COPPER-NICKEL COINAGE
FIVE CENTAVOS (1903–1935)

Designer: *Melecio Figueroa.* **Weight:** *1903–1928, 5 grams; 1930–1935, 4.75 grams.*
Composition: *.750 copper, .250 nickel.* **Diameter:** *1903–1908, 20.5 mm; 1930–1935, 19 mm.*
Edge: *Plain.* **Mints:** *Philadelphia, San Francisco, and Manila.*

Five Centavos, Large Size
(1903–1928, 20.5 mm)

Mintmark location is on the reverse, to the left of the date.

Five Centavos, Reduced Size
(1930–1935, 19 mm)

History. Five-centavo coins were minted under U.S. sovereignty for the Philippines from 1903 to 1935, with several gaps in production over the years. Circulation strikes were made in Philadelphia in 1903 and 1904, then coinage resumed in 1916, this time at the San Francisco Mint. The newly inaugurated Manila Mint took over all five-centavo production starting in 1920, continuing through the end of direct U.S. administration, and under the Commonwealth government beginning in 1937.

The Manila Mint coins of 1920 and 1921 bore no mintmark indicating their producer, a situation noticed by coin collectors of the day. Gilbert S. Perez, superintendent of schools for Tayabas in the Philippines (and a member of the American Numismatic Association), wrote to Assistant Insular Treasurer Salvador Lagdameo in June 1922: "Several members of numismatic societies in Europe and America have made inquiries as to why the Manila mint has no distinctive mint mark. Some do not even know that there is a mint in the Philippine Islands and that the mint is operated by Filipinos." He recommended the letter M be used to identify Manila's coins. Lagdameo replied later that month, thanking Perez and informing him: "It is now being planned that the new dies to be ordered shall contain such mark, and it is hoped that the coins of 1923 and subsequent years will bear the distinctive mint mark suggested by you." Coinage would not resume at the Manila facility until 1925, but from that year forward the mintmark would grace the coins struck in the Philippines.

The diameter of the five-centavo coin was 20.5 mm diameter from 1903 to 1928. This was very close to the 20 mm diameter of the twenty-centavo coin of 1907 to 1929. By 1928 there had been two separate instances where a reverse die of one denomination was "muled" to an obverse of the other. In 1918 this occurred by accident when a small quantity of five-centavo pieces was struck in combination with the reverse die of the twenty centavos (identifiable by its wider shield and a smaller date, compared to the normal five-centavo reverse). This error was known to numismatists by 1922, by which time it was recognized as a scarce variety. The second instance of muling, in 1928, is discussed under twenty-centavo pieces. In 1930, to clearly differentiate the sizes of the coins, the diameter of the five-centavo piece was reduced from 20.5 to 19.0 mm.

Five-centavo coinage under U.S. sovereignty continued to 1935. From 1937 on, the Manila Mint's production of five-centavo coins would use the new Commonwealth shield design on the reverse.

Striking and Sharpness. The obverse of the 1918 and 1919 San Francisco Mint issues often is weakly struck, with considerable loss of detail. The Manila Mint started production in 1920, and many five-centavo coins from that year lack sharpness in the rims and have weak details overall.

Five Centavos, 1903–1928

High Points of Wear. *Obverse Checkpoints:* 1. Figure's right hand. 2. Frontal hair just above ear. 3. Figure's left hand. *Reverse Checkpoints:* 1. Eagle's breast feathers. 2. Eagle's wing tip (to viewer's right). 3. Upper points of shield.

Five Centavos, 1930–1935

High Points of Wear. *Obverse Checkpoints:* 1. Figure's right hand. 2. Frontal hair just above ear. 3. Edge of anvil. *Reverse Checkpoints:* 1. Eagle's breast feathers. 2. Eagle's wing tip (to viewer's right).

Proofs. Five-centavo Proofs were struck at the Philadelphia Mint for annual Proof sets in 1903, 1904, 1905, 1906, and 1908.

| | Mintage | VF | EF | MS-60 | MS-63 |
				PF-60	PF-63
1903	8,910,000	$1.25	$2.50	$18	$30
	Auctions: $247, MS-66, July 2013; $200, MS-65, August 2013; $242, MS-65, December 2012; $123, MS-65, January 2015				
1903, Proof	2,558			$75	$130
	Auctions: $270, PF-66, August 2013; $223, PF-65, October 2015; $200, PF-65, November 2013				

	Mintage	VF	EF	MS-60 PF-60	MS-63 PF-63
1904	1,075,000	$2.50	$4	$20	$40
Auctions: $82, MS-64, June 2013; $76, MS-64, May 2013					
1904, Proof	1,355			$90	$150
Auctions: $235, PF-65, August 2013; $153, PF-64, October 2014; $153, PF-64, August 2013					
1905, Proof (a)	471			$200	$300
Auctions: $952, PF-67, August 2012; $476, PF-65, August 2013; $382, PF-64, August 2013					
1906, Proof (a)	500			$175	$250
Auctions: $617, PF-66, October 2014; $670, PF-66, August 2013; $400, PF-65, August 2013					
1908, Proof (a)	500			$200	$300
Auctions: $505, PF-66, October 2014; $969, PF-66, August 2013; $500, PF-66, August 2013					
1916-S	300,000	$85	$150	$800	$1,300
Auctions: $4,465, MS-65, January 2016; 240, MS-62, January 2014; $235, MS-62, February 2014					
1917-S	2,300,000	$5	$12	$130	$300
Auctions: $423, MS-65, April 2014; $447, MS-64, August 2014					
1918-S	2,780,000	$8	$15	$140	$300
Auctions: $306, MS-63, August 2014; $188, MS-62, January 2014					
1918-S, S Over S	(b)	$20	$100	$500	$1,000
Auctions: No auction records available.					
1918-S, Mule (c)	(b)	$575	$1,750	$4,750	$9,750
Auctions: $14,100, MS-61, January 2016; $544, VF-30, April 2014					
1919-S	1,220,000	$15	$30	$175	$450
Auctions: $588, MS-64, September 2014; $499, MS-63, January 2014					
1920	1,421,078	$8.50	$30	$175	$375
Auctions: $141, MS-63, January 2014; $200, MS-63, July 2013					
1921	2,131,529	$9	$20	$110	$200
Auctions: $212, MS-63, August 2013; $212, MS-63, July 2013; $153, MS-63, August 2014					
1925-M	1,000,000	$12	$30	$175	$300
Auctions: $575, MS-64, November 2011; $423, MS-63, December 2015; $217, MS-63, January 2014					
1926-M	1,200,000	$5	$20	$120	$200
Auctions: $112, MS-62, January 2014					
1927-M	1,000,000	$5	$10	$70	$100
Auctions: $259, MS-65, January 2014; $129, MS-64, June 2014					
1928-M	1,000,000	$7	$14	$70	$125
Auctions: $259, MS-65, January 2014; $259, MS-63, November 2015; $96, MS-63, June 2014					
1930-M	2,905,182	$2.50	$6	$45	$80
Auctions: $353, MS-65, September 2014; $71, MS-64RD, July 2014; $153, MS-64, August 2013					
1931-M	3,476,790	$2.50	$6	$75	$150
Auctions: $108, MS-64, June 2014; $74, MS-64, October 2015; $86, MS-63, June 2014					
1932-M	3,955,861	$2	$4	$50	$130
Auctions: $143, MS-64, June 2014; $65, MS-62, January 2014					
1934-M	2,153,729	$3.50	$9	$75	$200
Auctions: $306, MS-64, September 2014; $170, MS-63, June 2014; $88, MS-63, July 2013					
1934-M, Recut 1	(d)	$10	$35	$125	$250
Auctions: No auction records available.					
1935-M	2,754,000	$2.50	$8	$85	$225
Auctions: $282, MS-64, September 2014; $100, MS-63, January 2014					

a. Proof only. b. Included in 1918-S mintage figure. c. Small Date Reverse of twenty centavos. d. Included in 1934-M mintage figure.

SILVER COINAGE

TEN CENTAVOS (1903–1935)

Designer: *Melecio Figueroa.* **Weight:** *1903–1906, 2.7 grams (.0779 oz. ASW);
1907–1935, 2 grams (.0482 oz. ASW).* **Composition:** *1903–1906, .900 silver, .100 copper;
1907–1935, .750 silver, .250 copper.* **Diameter:** *1903–1906, 17.5 mm; 1907–1935, 16.5 mm.*
Edge: *Reeded.* **Mints:** *Philadelphia, San Francisco, and Manila.*

**Ten Centavos, Large Size
(1903–1906, 17.5 mm)**   *Mintmark location is on the
reverse, to the left of the date.*   **Ten Centavos, Reduced Size
(1907–1935, 16.5 mm)**

History. The Philippine ten-centavo coin was minted from 1903 to 1935, in several facilities and with occasional interruptions in production.

In 1907 the silver ten-centavo coin's fineness was reduced from .900 to .750, and at the same time its diameter was decreased. This was in response to the rising price of silver, with the goal of discouraging exportation and melting of the silver coins. The net effect was nearly 40 percent less silver, by actual weight, in the new ten-centavo piece. The older coins continued to be removed from circulation, and by June 30, 1911, it was reported that only 35 percent of the ten-centavo pieces minted from 1903 to 1906 still remained in the Philippines.

The Manila Mint took over ten-centavo production from San Francisco in 1920. The ten-centavo coins of 1920 and 1921 bear no mintmark identifying them as products of Manila (this was the case for all Philippine coinage of those years, and of 1922). The efforts of Philippine numismatists, including American Numismatic Association member Gilbert S. Perez, encouraged mint officials to add the M mintmark when the facility reopened in 1925 after a two-year hiatus for all coinage.

Ten-centavo production after 1921 consisted of 1 million pieces struck in 1929 and just less than 1.3 million in 1935. The next ten-centavo mintage would be under the Commonwealth, not U.S. sovereignty.

Die varieties include a 1912-S with an S Over S mintmark, and date variations of the 1914-S.

Striking and Sharpness. The ten-centavo coins of 1903 to 1906 generally are well struck, although some show slight weakness of features. Those of 1907 to 1935 also are generally well struck; some obverses may have slight flattening of the hair just above the ear and on the upper part of the figure. On the reverse, check the eagle's breast feathers for flatness.

Ten Centavos, 1903–1906

High Points of Wear. *Obverse Checkpoints:* 1. Figure's left bosom. 2. Figure's right knee. 3. Figure's left knee. 4. Edge of anvil. *Reverse Checkpoints:* 1. Eagle's breast feathers. 2. Upper points of shield. 3. Eagle's wing tips. 4. Eagle's right leg.

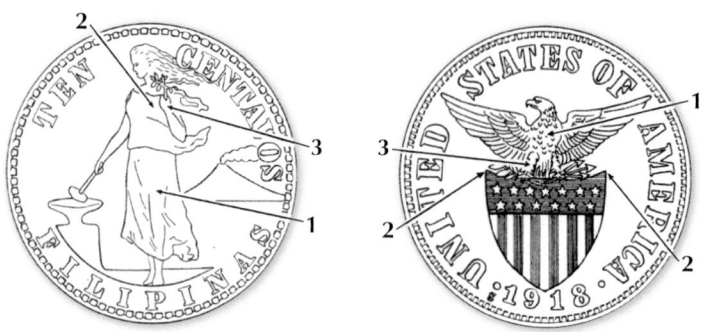

Ten Centavos, 1907–1935

High Points of Wear. *Obverse Checkpoints:* 1. Figure's left thigh. 2. Figure's left bosom. 3. Figure's left hand. *Reverse Checkpoints:* 1. Eagle's breast feathers. 2. Upper points of shield. 3. Eagle's right leg.

Proofs. Ten-centavo Proofs were struck at the Philadelphia Mint for annual Proof sets in 1903, 1904, 1905, 1906, and 1908.

	Mintage	VF	EF	MS-60	MS-63
				PF-60	PF-63
1903	5,102,658	$4	$5	$35	$75
	Auctions: $188, MS-65, January 2015; $100, MS-64, October 2014; $76, MS-64, July 2013				
1903, Proof	2,558			$100	$150
	Auctions: $270, PF-65, May 2014; $153, PF-63, September 2015; $70, PF-60, June 2013				
1903-S	1,200,000	$25	$45	$350	$950
	Auctions: $1,645, MS-62, January 2014				
1904	10,000	$20	$35	$80	$140
	Auctions: $397, MS-66, September 2014; $223, MS-65, July 2013; $100, MS-64, November 2014				
1904, Proof	1,355			$110	$150
	Auctions: $388, PF-66, October 2014; $259, PF-64, April 2015; $153, PF-64, October 2014; $88, PF-62, June 2014				
1904-S	5,040,000	$4	$9	$55	$120
	Auctions: $92, MS-64, June 2014; $59, MS-62, November 2014				
1905, Proof (a)	471			$150	$275
	Auctions: $259, PF-63, June 2004; $299, PF-62, April 2011				
1906, Proof (a)	500			$135	$225
	Auctions: $470, PF-65, April 2014; $212, PF-61, January 2014				
1907	1,500,781	$4	$5	$60	$115
	Auctions: $223, MS-65, April 2014; $188, MS-65, January 2014; $118, MS-65, August 2013				
1907-S	4,930,000	$2	$5	$40	$70
	Auctions: $170, MS-64, June 2014; $90, MS-63, May 2014				
1908, Proof (a)	500			$150	$200
	Auctions: $617, PF-66, October 2014; $353, PF-65, January 2014; $207, PF-63, January 2012				
1908-S	3,363,911	$2	$5	$40	$70
	Auctions: $306, MS-65, September 2014; $112, MS-64, January 2014				
1909-S	312,199	$30	$65	$450	$1,200
	Auctions: $2,350, MS-65, April 2015; $752, MS-62, May 2014; $382, MS-61, January 2014				
1911-S	1,000,505	$10	$15	$150	$500
	Auctions: $588, MS-63, January 2014				

a. Proof only.

| 1912-S, S Over S | 1914-S, Short Crossbar | 1914-S, Long Crossbar |

| | Mintage | VF | EF | MS-60 | MS-63 |
				PF-60	PF-63
1912-S	1,010,000	$6	$12	$125	$275
Auctions: $306, MS-63, April 2014					
1912-S, S Over S	**(b)**		$85	$200	$500
Auctions: $646, MS-63, September 2014					
1913-S	1,360,693	$9	$13	$85	$175
Auctions: $558, MS-65, September 2014, $270, MS-63, June 2014					
1914-S (c)	1,180,000	$6	$12	$125	$300
Auctions: $411, MS-63, May 2014; $374, MS-63, April 2010					
1915-S	450,000	$25	$40	$250	$750
Auctions: $1,234, MS-64, January 2014; $200, AU-58, January 2014					
1917-S	5,991,148	$2	$3	$20	$65
Auctions: $247, MS-65, June 2014; $447, MS-64, July 2014; $129, MS-64, October 2015					
1918-S	8,420,000	$2	$3	$20	$50
Auctions: $188, MS-65, December 2015; $129, MS-65, January 2013; $306, MS-63, July 2014					
1919-S	1,630,000	$2.50	$5	$30	$110
Auctions: $182, MS-64, June 2014					
1920	520,000	$6	$16	$95	$200
Auctions: $494, MS-64, June 2014					
1921	3,863,038	$2	$3	$25	$50
Auctions: $182, MS-65, June 2014; $153, MS-63, July 2014					
1929-M	1,000,000	$2	$3	$25	$45
Auctions: $176, MS-65, December 2015; $123, MS-65, June 2014					
1935-M	1,280,000	$2	$4	$20	$50
Auctions: $182, MS-65, June 2014					

b. Included in 1912-S mintage figure. **c.** Varieties exist with a short or long crossbar in the 4 of 1914. The Long Crossbar is scarcer.

TWENTY CENTAVOS (1903–1929)

Designer: *Melecio Figueroa.* **Weight:** *1903–1906, 5.385 grams (.1558 oz. ASW);*
1907–1929, 4 grams (.0964 oz. ASW). **Composition:** *1903–1906, .900 silver, .100 copper;*
1907–1929, .750 silver, .250 copper. **Diameter:** *1903–1906, 23 mm; 1907–1929, 20 mm.*
Edge: *Reeded.* **Mints:** *Philadelphia, San Francisco, and Manila.*

Twenty Centavos, Large Size
(1903–1906, 23 mm)

Mintmark location is on the
reverse, to the left of the date.

Twenty Centavos, Reduced
Size (1907–1929, 20 mm)

History. In the early 1900s the rising value of silver was encouraging exportation and melting of the Philippines' silver twenty-centavo coins. As was the case with the ten-centavo piece, in 1907 the diameter of the twenty-centavo coin was reduced and its silver fineness decreased from .900 to .750. The net effect was about 40 percent less silver, by actual weight, in the new smaller coins. Attrition continued to draw the older coins out of circulation and into the melting pot, as their silver value exceeded their face value. A report of June 30, 1911, held that only about 25 percent of the twenty-centavo coins minted from 1903 to 1906 still remained in the Philippines.

Circulation strikes were made at the Philadelphia and San Francisco mints through 1919. In July 1920, a new "Mint of the Philippine Islands," located in Manila, started production. Its output during the period of U.S. sovereignty included twenty-centavo pieces in 1920, 1921, 1928, and 1929. (Production of the coins later continued under the Commonwealth, with a slightly modified design.) The first two years of coinage did not feature a mintmark identifying Manila as the producer of the coins. This was noticed by collectors of Philippine coins; they protested the oversight, and later coinage dies had an M mintmark added.

In 1928 a rush order for twenty-centavo coins was received at the Manila Mint—by that time the only producer of the denomination. Manila had not minted the coins since 1921, and the Philadelphia Mint had not shipped any new reverse dies (which would have featured their 1928 date). Under pressure to produce the coins, workers at the Manila Mint married a regular twenty-centavo obverse die with the 1928-dated reverse die of the five-centavo denomination, which was only .5 mm larger. As a result, the entire mintage of 100,000 1928 twenty centavos consists of these "mule" (mismatched-die) coins. The reverse of the 1928 coins, compared with others of 1907 to 1929, has a narrower shield and a larger date.

Striking and Sharpness. Most twenty centavos of 1903 to 1906 are well struck. The 1904-S usually shows weak striking on the figure's left bosom, the frontal hair just above her ear, and her left hand. Most of the coins of 1907 to 1929 show flattening of the figure's hair, sometimes extending into the area of her left bosom and her left hand.

Twenty Centavos, 1903–1906

High Points of Wear. *Obverse Checkpoints:* 1. Figure's left thigh and knee. 2. Figure's left bosom. 3. Figure's left hand. *Reverse Checkpoints:* 1. Eagle's breast feathers. 2. Upper points of shield. 3. Eagle's right leg.

Twenty Centavos, 1907–1929

High Points of Wear. *Obverse Checkpoints:* 1. Figure's left thigh. 2. Edge of anvil. 3. Figure's left bosom. 4. Figure's left hand. *Reverse Checkpoints:* 1. Eagle's breast feathers. 2. Eagle's right leg. 3. Upper points of shield.

Proofs. Twenty-centavo Proofs were struck at the Philadelphia Mint for annual Proof sets in 1903, 1904, 1905, 1906, and 1908.

	Mintage	VF	EF	MS-60 / PF-60	MS-63 / PF-63
1903	5,350,231	$5	$8	$45	$100
Auctions: $88, MS-64, July 2014; $86, AU-55, July 2014					
1903, Proof	2,558			$100	$150
Auctions: $482, PF-66, October 2014; $129, PF-63, September 2014; $123, PF-63, September 2014					
1903-S	150,080	$25	$50	$600	$1,900
Auctions: $447, AU-58, May 2014					
1904	10,000	$30	$45	$125	$200
Auctions: $529, MS-66, June 2014; $194, MS-64, May 2014; $200, MS-63, January 2016; $188, MS-62, January 2015					
1904, Proof	1,355			$110	$175
Auctions: $200, PF-65, July 2014; $153, PF-63, May 2014; $200, PF-61, January 2014					
1904-S	2,060,000	$7.50	$11	$110	$200
Auctions: $223, MS-64, January 2015; $211, MS-64, March 2014; $411, MS-63, January 2014					
1905, Proof (a)	471			$225	$375
Auctions: $470, PF-64, January 2013; $282, PF-61, January 2014					
1905-S	420,000	$20	$35	$400	$1,250
Auctions: No auction records available.					
1906, Proof (a)	500			$175	$325
Auctions: $541, PF-66, October 2014; $564, PF-64, April 2015; $329, PF-62, November 2014; $329, PF-62, October 2014					
1907	1,250,651	$6	$13.50	$200	$450
Auctions: $881, MS-63, April 2015; $558, MS-63, September 2014					
1907-S	3,165,000	$4.50	$10	$75	$200
Auctions: $3,525, MS-65, April 2015; $374, MS-63, January 2010; $247, MS-62, June 2014					
1908, Proof (a)	500			$175	$325
Auctions: $397, PF-64, January 2014; $299, PF-63, January 2012					
1908-S	1,535,000	$4.50	$10	$100	$300
Auctions: $1,880, MS-64, September 2015; $2,233, MS-63, September 2014					
1909-S	450,000	$25	$50	$400	$1,500
Auctions: $5,640, MS-66, April 2015; $4,113, MS-64, April 2014; $1,528, MS-64, January 2013					
1910-S	500,259	$30	$60	$400	$1,000
Auctions: $9,988, MS-66, April 2015; $3,450, MS-64, April 2012; $2,070, MS-63, April 2012					
1911-S	505,000	$25	$45	$300	$900
Auctions: $2,350, MS-64, September 2013					
1912-S	750,000	$12	$30	$200	$400
Auctions: $294, MS-63, July 2014					
1913-S	795,000	$10	$15	$150	$200
Auctions: $235, MS-63, July 2014; $247, MS-62, June 2014					
1914-S	795,000	$10	$30	$200	$450
Auctions: $353, MS-63, January 2014					
1915-S	655,000	$20	$50	$400	$1,600
Auctions: $1,116, MS-63, January 2014; $270, AU-58, May 2014					
1916-S (b)	1,435,000	$10	$15	$125	$300
Auctions: No auction records available.					
1917-S	3,150,655	$5	$8	$75	$200
Auctions: $1,293, MS-66, September 2014; $646, MS-65, September 2014					
1918-S	5,560,000	$4	$6	$50	$125
Auctions: $188, MS-64, January 2014; $66, MS-63, June 2014					
1919-S	850,000	$7	$13	$125	$225
Auctions: $1,880, MS-66, January 2014; $106, MS-61, November 2014					

a. Proof only. **b.** Tilted 6 and Straight 6 varieties exist.

	Mintage	VF	EF	MS-60	MS-63
1920	1,045,415	$8	$20	$135	$225
Auctions: $411, MS-63, September 2014					
1921	1,842,631	$3	$7	$50	$90
Auctions: $79, MS-63, January 2014; $48, AU-58, May 2014					
1928-M, Mule (c)	100,000	$15	$65	$900	$1,800
Auctions: $3,055, MS-65, April 2014; $3,525, MS-64, January 2016; $2,233, MS-64, January 2013					
1929-M	1,970,000	$3	$5	$40	$100
Auctions: $92, MS-64, June 2014; $21, AU-55, May 2014					
1929-M, 2 Over 2 Over 2	(d)		$100	$250	$400
Auctions: No auction records available.					

c. Reverse of 1928 five centavos. d. Included in 1929-M mintage figure.

Fifty Centavos (1903–1921)

Designer: *Melecio Figueroa.* **Weight:** *1903–1906, 13.48 grams (.3900 oz. ASW);
1907–1921, 10 grams (.2411 oz. ASW).* **Composition:** *1903–1906, .900 silver, .100 copper;
1907–1921, .750 silver, .250 copper.* **Diameter:** *1903–1906, 30 mm; 1907–1921, 27 mm.*
Edge: *Reeded.* **Mints:** *Philadelphia, San Francisco, and Manila.*

**Fifty Centavos, Large Size
(1903–1906, 30 mm)**

*Mintmark location is
on the reverse, to
the left of the date.*

**Fifty Centavos, Reduced Size
(1907–1921, 27 mm)**

History. After four years of fifty-centavo coinage, in 1907 the denomination's silver fineness was lowered from .900 to .750, and its diameter was reduced by ten percent. This action was in response to rising silver prices. The new smaller coins contained 38 percent less silver, by actual weight, than their 1903–1906 forebears, making them unprofitable to melt for their precious-metal content. Gresham's Law being what it is ("Bad money will drive out good"), the older, heavier silver coins were quickly pulled from circulation; by June 30, 1911, it was officially reported that more than 90 percent of the 1903–1906 coinage had disappeared from the Philippines.

The reduced-size coins of the U.S. sovereignty type were minted from 1907 to 1921. The Manila Mint took over their production from the Philadelphia and San Francisco mints in 1920, using coinage dies shipped from Philadelphia. The fifty centavos was the largest denomination produced at the Manila Mint. Neither the 1920 nor the 1921 coinage featured a mintmark identifying Manila as its producer.

Production of the fifty-centavo denomination would again take place, in 1944 and 1945, in San Francisco, using the Commonwealth design introduced for circulating coins in 1937.

Striking and Sharpness. On fifty-centavo coins of 1903 to 1906, many obverses show slight flattening of the frontal hair just above the figure's ear. The reverses sometimes show slight flattening of the eagle's breast feathers. On the reverse, a high spot on the shield is the result of an unevenness in striking. The coins of 1907 to 1921 often show notable flatness of strike in the figure's hair just above her ear, and sometimes on her left hand. A flat strike on the abdomen and left leg should not be mistaken for circulation wear. The reverses are quite unevenly struck; observe the top part of the shield, which has a depressed middle and raised sides. The right side is slightly higher than the left and may show some flattening.

Fifty Centavos, 1903–1906

High Points of Wear. *Obverse Checkpoints:* 1. Edge of anvil. 2. Figure's left thigh and knee. 3. Figure's right knee. 4. Figure's right bosom. *Reverse Checkpoints:* 1. Part of shield just to left of lower-right star. 2. Eagle's breast feathers. 3. Eagle's right leg and claws.

Fifty Centavos, 1907–1921

High Points of Wear. *Obverse Checkpoints:* 1. Figure's left thigh and lower leg. 2. Mid-drapery. 3. Figure's left bosom. 4. Edge of anvil. *Reverse Checkpoints:* 1. Eagle's breast feathers. 2. Eagle's right leg. 3. Part of shield just to left of lower-right star.

Proofs. Fifty-centavo Proofs were struck at the Philadelphia Mint for annual Proof sets in 1903, 1904, 1905, 1906, and 1908. Proofs of 1908 often are found with considerable flatness in the frontal hair above Miss Liberty's hair and sometimes with flatness in her left hand.

	Mintage	VF	EF	MS-60 / PF-60	MS-63 / PF-63
1903	3,099,061	$10	$15	$75	$115
	Auctions: $259, MS-64, May 2014; $165, MS-64, September 2013; $129, MS-62, January 2014				
1903, Proof	2,558			$100	$175
	Auctions: $764, PF-66, January 2016; $734, PF-66, October 2014; $189, PF-64, September 2014; $411, PF-64, January 2014				
1903-S (a)			$30,000		
	Auctions: No auction records available.				
1904	10,000	$50	$100	$150	$260
	Auctions: $1,234, MS-66+, June 2014; $329, MS-64, September 2015; $223, MS-63, November 2014; $247, MS-63, May 2014				
1904, Proof	1,355			$125	$250
	Auctions: $476, PF-65, September 2012; $470, PF-64, April 2015; $247, PF-63, February 2014				
1904-S	216,000	$12	$25	$125	$225
	Auctions: $881, MS-65, September 2014; $443, MS-64, May 2014				
1905, Proof (b)	471			$275	$425
	Auctions: $3,760, PF-65, January 2016; $764, PF-63, January 2015; $411, PF-63, April 2014				
1905-S	852,000	$20	$50	$700	$2,100
	Auctions: $1,058, MS-62, April 2014; $206, AU-55, June 2014				

a. 2 examples are known. **b.** Proof only.

	Mintage	VF	EF	MS-60 PF-60	MS-63 PF-63
1906, Proof (b)	500			$225	$375
Auctions: $2,820, PF-67, October 2014; $940, PF-65, April 2014; $353, PF-61, November 2014					
1907	1,200,625	$15	$40	$150	$325
Auctions: $1,763, MS-64, April 2014; $427, MS-62, September 2014					
1907-S	2,112,000	$11	$30	$150	$325
Auctions: $5,640, MS-66, August 2015; $499, MS-63, September 2014; $427, MS-62, September 2014					
1908, Proof (b)	500			$200	$350
Auctions: $1,645, PF-66, January 2016; $499, PF-64, April 2014; $499, PF-64, January 2014					
1908-S	1,601,000	$15	$40	$325	$1,500
Auctions: $2,820, MS-63, January 2014; $823, MS-62, September 2014					
1909-S	528,000	$20	$60	$350	$850
Auctions: $4,230, MS-65, April 2015; $1,645, MS-64, April 2014; $1,528, MS-63, January 2014					
1917-S	674,369	$12.50	$35	$200	$550
Auctions: $541, MS-63, December 2015; $294, MS-63, January 2014; $411, MS-62, September 2014					
1918-S	2,202,000	$7.50	$15	$125	$190
Auctions: $129, MS-62, June 2014; $176, MS-61, January 2014					
1918-S, S Over Inverted S	(c)	$7.50	$15	$80	$160
Auctions: No auction records available.					
1919-S	1,200,000	$7.50	$15	$125	$225
Auctions: $353, MS-64, July 2014; $129, MS-62, January 2015					
1920	420,000	$8	$12	$70	$100
Auctions: $211, MS-64, January 2014; $212, MS-62, July 2014					
1921	2,316,763	$7.50	$11	$50	$85
Auctions: $588, MS-65, January 2016; $62, MS-63, October 2014; $94, MS-63, July 2014; $82, MS-63, July 2013					

b. Proof only. **c.** Included in 1918-S mintage figure.

ONE PESO (1903–1912)

Designer: *Melecio Figueroa.* **Weight:** *1903–1906, 26.96 grams (.7800 oz. ASW);
1907–1912, 20 grams (.5144 oz. ASW).* **Composition:** *1903–1906, .900 silver, .100 copper;
1907–1912, .800 silver, .200 copper.* **Diameter:** *1903–1906, 38 mm; 1907–1912, 35 mm.*
Edge: *Reeded.* **Mints:** *Philadelphia and San Francisco.*

Peso, Large Size
(1903–1906, 38 mm)

Peso, Reduced Size
(1907–1912, 35 mm)

*Mintmark location is on the
reverse, to the left of the date.*

History. The Philippine silver peso was struck under U.S. sovereignty from 1903 to 1912. The key date among those struck for circulation is the issue of 1906-S. Although the San Francisco Mint produced more than 200,000 of the coins that year, nearly all of them were held back from circulation. They were instead stored and then later sold as bullion.

By 1906 natural market forces were driving the Philippine silver pesos out of commerce and into the melting pot: the rising price of silver made the coins worth more as precious metal than as legal tender. In 1907 the U.S. Mint responded by lowering the denomination's silver fineness from .900 to .800 and reducing its diameter from 38 mm to 35. The resulting smaller coins had about one-third less silver, by actual weight, than those of 1903 to 1906, guaranteeing that they would stay in circulation. The older coins, meanwhile, were still profitable to pull aside and melt for their silver value. An official report of June 30, 1911, disclosed that less than ten percent of the heavier silver coins still remained in the Philippines.

The new smaller pesos were minted every year from 1907 to 1912, with the San Francisco Mint producing them for commerce and the Philadelphia Mint striking a small quantity of Proofs in 1907 and 1908. Millions of the coins were stored as backing for Silver Certificates (and, later, Treasury Certificates) in circulation in the Philippines. Although the Manila Mint started operations in 1920, the silver peso was never part of its production for circulation.

In December 1941, Imperial Japan, immediately after attacking Pearl Harbor, began a fierce assault on the Philippines. Manila fell on January 2, 1942, and General Douglas MacArthur, commander of U.S. Army Forces in the Far East, fell back to the Bataan Peninsula. In late February President Franklin Roosevelt ordered him to leave the Philippines for Australia, prompting the general's famous promise to the Philippine people: "I shall return!" Not long after the fighting erupted it had become apparent that the Japanese would overtake the islands, and early in 1942 the U.S. military dumped crates holding 15,700,000 silver pesos, mostly of 1907–1912 coinage, into the sea near Corregidor, to avoid their seizure. Many millions of these coins were salvaged by the U.S. Treasury and the Central Bank of the Philippines after the war, with all but about five million pieces being reclaimed by 1958. Today a great majority of the salvaged "war pesos" show clear evidence of their prolonged submersion in saltwater. A typical effect is a dark corrosion strongly resistant to any manner of cleaning or conservation.

Striking and Sharpness. The silver pesos of 1903 to 1906 generally have well-struck obverses, but occasionally with some flattening of the figure's frontal hair above her ear, and sometimes her left bosom and hand. On the reverse, the feathers on the eagle's breast are indistinctly cut, and the wing tips can sometimes be found slightly flatly struck. Of the silver pesos of 1907 to 1912, some but not all exhibit flattened frontal hair, and sometimes a flattened left hand. On the reverse, the eagle's breast feathers are not clearly defined. On some examples the reverses are quite unevenly struck; check the top part of the shield, which has a depressed middle and raised sides, and the right side, which is slightly higher than the left and may show some flattening.

One Peso, 1903–1906

High Points of Wear. *Obverse Checkpoints:* 1. Figure's upper-left leg and knee. 2. Figure's right knee. 3. Figure's left bosom. 4. Frontal hair just above ear. *Reverse Checkpoints:* 1. Eagle's breast feathers. 2. Eagle's right leg. 3. Eagle's wing tips.

One Peso, 1907–1912

High Points of Wear. *Obverse Checkpoints:* 1. Figure's upper-left leg and knee. 2. Figure's lower-left leg. 3. Figure's left hand. 4. Frontal hair just above ear. *Reverse Checkpoints:* 1. Eagle's breast feathers. 2. Eagle's right leg.

Proofs. Proof pesos were struck at the Philadelphia Mint for annual Proof sets in 1903, 1904, 1905, 1906, and 1908. Unlike the smaller denominations, Proof pesos of 1907 also are known—but only to the extent of two examples.

1905-S, Curved Serif on "1" **1905-S, Straight Serif on "1"**

	Mintage	VF	EF	MS-60	MS-63
				PF-60	PF-63
1903	2,788,901	$35	$45	$190	$550
	Auctions: $3,290, MS-64, January 2016; $552, MS-63, October 2014				
1903, Proof	2,558			$200	$350
	Auctions: $3,525, PF-67, October 2014; $999, PF-65, January 2016; $200, PF-62, September 2014				
1903-S	11,361,000	$30	$40	$150	$325
	Auctions: $690, MS-63, March 2011; $188, MS-60, January 2014; $129, AU-58, September 2015				
1904	11,355	$85	$110	$300	$625
	Auctions: $3,995, MS-65, January 2016; $705, MS-64, January 2014; $329, MS-63, August 2013				
1904, Proof	1,355			$250	$450
	Auctions: $7,050, PF-67, January 2016; $3,525, PF-67, October 2014; $3,290, PF-67, October 2014; $881, PF-64, September 2014				
1904-S	6,600,000	$35	$50	$175	$375
	Auctions: $440, MS-63, September 2014; $282, MS-62, May 2015; $188, MS-62, January 2015				
1905, Proof (a)	471			$750	$1,500
	Auctions: $11,163, PF-67, January 2013; $5,875, PF-65, January 2016; $911, PF-63, October 2014				
1905-S, Curved Serif on "1"	6,056,000	$40	$60	$350	$750
	Auctions: $764, MS-61, January 2014				
1905-S, Straight Serif on "1"	(b)	$50	$75	$900	$3,500
	Auctions: $3,819, MS-63, September 2014				
1906, Proof (a)	500			$700	$1,200
	Auctions: $3,819, PF-67, October 2014; $3,525, PF-67, October 2014; $6,463, PF-66, January 2016; $1,880, PF-63, April 2014				
1906-S	201,000	$1,500	$3,200	$17,500	$32,500
	Auctions: $7,050, AU-55, October 2014; $7,638, AU-55, April 2014				

Note: Philippine silver pesos of 1907–1912 that were corroded from submersion in Caballo Bay during World War II are worth considerably less than their problem-free counterparts, but are avidly collected for their historical value. **a.** Proof only. **b.** Included in 1905-S, Curved Serif on "1," mintage figure.

	Mintage	VF	EF	MS-60 PF-60	MS-63 PF-63
1907, Proof (a,c)					$160,000
Auctions: $189,750, PF, June 2012					
1907-S	10,278,000	$17	$22	$90	$250
Auctions: $940, MS-64, October 2014; $447, MS-63, March 2015; $188, MS-62, December 2014; $112, MS-60, January 2014					
1908, Proof (a)	500			$650	$1,000
Auctions: $2,585, PF-66, January 2016; $1,763, PF-64, January 2015; $940, PF-64, August 2014; $999, PF-64, January 2014					
1908-S	20,954,944	$17	$22	$90	$275
Auctions: $881, MS-64, January 2016; $852, MS-64, January 2015; $705, MS-64, September 2014					
1909-S	7,578,000	$18	$24	$115	$300
Auctions: $4,935, MS-65, April 2015; $1,058, MS-64, October 2014; $235, MS-62, January 2014					
1909-S, S Over S	(d)	$35	$100	$175	$600
Auctions: No auction records available.					
1910-S	3,153,559	$24	$35	$225	$450
Auctions: $5,170, MS-65, April 2015; $489, MS-63, January 2010					
1911-S	463,000	$40	$75	$750	$4,250
Auctions: $5,875, MS-62, January 2016					
1912-S	680,000	$50	$80	$2,000	$5,000
Auctions: $9,988, MS-63, October 2014; $5,875, MS-61, April 2014; $999, AU-58, April 2014					

Note: Philippine silver pesos of 1907–1912 that were corroded from submersion in Caballo Bay during World War II are worth considerably less than their problem-free counterparts, but are avidly collected for their historical value. **a.** Proof only. **c.** 2 examples are known. **d.** Included in 1909-S mintage figure.

MANILA MINT OPENING MEDAL (1920)

Designer: *Clifford Hewitt.* **Composition:** *bronze; silver; gold.*
Diameter: *38 mm.* **Edge:** *Plain.* **Mint:** *Manila.*

Bronze

Silver

Gold

History. During U.S. sovereignty, much of the civilian government of the Philippines was administered by the Bureau of Insular Affairs, part of the War Department. Most heads or secretaries of Philippine government departments were appointed by the U.S. governor general, with the advice and consent of the Philippine Senate. In 1919, the chief of the Bureau of the Insular Treasury (part of the Department of Finance) was Insular Treasurer Albert P. Fitzsimmons, formerly a mayor of Tecumseh, Nebraska, and member of the municipal board of Manila. Fitzsimmons, a surgeon who had served in the U.S. Army Medical Corps in Cuba and the Philippines, was active in civil affairs, and had been in charge of U.S. government bond issues in the Philippines during the Great War. On May 20, 1919, he was named director ad interim of the Mint of the Philippine Islands, which was then being organized.

The genesis of this new mint started on February 8, 1918, when the Philippine Legislature passed an appropriations bill for construction of its machinery. The war in Europe was interfering with shipments from the San Francisco Mint, where Philippine coinage was produced, and a local mint was seen as more expedient and economical. In addition, a mint in Manila would serve the United States' goal of preparing the Philippines for its own governance and infrastructure.

The mint was built in Manila in the Intendencia Building, which also housed the offices and hall of the Senate, and the offices and vaults of the Philippine Treasury. Its machinery was designed and built in Philadelphia under the supervision of U.S. Mint chief mechanical engineer Clifford Hewitt, who also oversaw its installation in Manila. The facility was opened, with formalities and machine demonstrations, on July 15, 1920. The fanfare included the production of an official commemorative medal, the first example of which was struck by Speaker of the House of Representatives Sergio Osmeña.

The medal has since come to be popularly known as the "Wilson Dollar" (despite not being a legal-tender coin), because of its size and its bold profile portrait of Woodrow Wilson on the obverse, surrounded by the legend PRESIDENT OF THE UNITED STATES. The reverse features the ancient Roman goddess Juno Moneta guiding a youth—representing the fledgling mint staff of the Philippines—in the art of coining. She holds a pair of metallurgical scales. The reverse legend is TO COMMEMORATE THE OPENING OF THE MINT / MANILA P.I., along with the date, 1920. The medal was designed by Hewitt, the mint's supervising engineer from Philadelphia. Its dies were made by U.S. Mint chief engraver George T. Morgan, whose initial, M, appears on the obverse on President Wilson's breast and on the reverse above the goddess's sandal.

The issue was limited to 2,200 silver medals (2,000 of which were struck on the first day), sold to the public at $1 apiece; and 3,700 in bronze, sold for 50¢. In addition, at least five gold specimens were reportedly struck. These included one for presentation to President Wilson and one for U.S. Secretary of War Newton Baker. The other gold medals remained in the Philippines and were lost during World War II. Of the medals unsold and still held by the Treasury in the early 1940s, some or all were dumped into Caballo Bay in April 1942 along with millions of silver pesos, to keep them from the approaching Japanese forces. The invaders learned of the coins and in May attempted to recover the sunken silver coins using the labor of Filipino divers. Although skilled divers, the Filipinos were not experienced in deep-sea diving, and the coins were at the bottom of the bay, 120 feet below the surface. After three deaths the Filipinos refused to participate in further recovery efforts. The Japanese then forced U.S. prisoners of war who were experienced deep-sea divers to recover the coins and medals. The American divers conspired to salvage only small quantities of the sunken treasure. They repeatedly sabotaged the recovery process, and smuggled a significant number of recovered silver coins to the Philippine guerrillas. Only about 2 to 3 percent of the dumped coinage was recovered before the Japanese ceased recovery operations. Following the war the United States brought up much of the coinage that had been dumped into the sea. Many of the recovered silver and bronze Wilson dollars in grades VF through AU bear evidence of saltwater corrosion.

The Manila Mint Opening medal is popular with collectors of Philippine coins and of American medals. It is often cataloged as a *So-Called Dollar*, a classification of historic dollar-sized souvenir medals, some of which were struck by the U.S. Mint and some produced privately. The Manila Mint Opening medal is valued for its unique connections to the United States and to American numismatics.

	Mintage	VF-20	EF-40	AU-50	MS-60	MS-63	MS-65
Manila Mint medal, 1920, bronze	3,700	$35	$80	$235	$785	$1,350	$4,500
Manila Mint medal, 1920, silver	2,200	$85	$250	$525	$875	$1,850	$3,200

Note: VF, EF, and AU examples in bronze and silver often show signs of saltwater corrosion. The values above are for problem-free examples.

	Mintage	AU-55	MS-62
Manila Mint medal, 1920, gold	5	$44,000	$75,000

COMMONWEALTH ISSUES FOR CIRCULATION (1937–1945)

The Philippine Islands were largely self-governed, as a commonwealth of the United States, from 1935 until full independence was recognized in 1946. Coinage under the Commonwealth began with three commemorative coins in 1936 (see next section). Circulating issues were minted from 1937 to 1941 (in Manila) and in 1944 and 1945 (in Philadelphia, Denver, and San Francisco).

The Commonwealth coinage retained the obverse motifs designed by Melecio Figueroa and used on the coinage of 1903 to 1936. Its new reverse design featured a shield derived from the official seal of the government of the Philippines, with three stars symbolizing Luzon, Mindanao, and the Visayas, the islands' three main geographical regions. In the oval set in the shield's center is a modification of the colonial coat of arms of the City of Manila: a fortress tower above with a heraldic crowned *morse* or sea-lion (half dolphin, half lion) below. An eagle with outstretched wings surmounts the entirety of the shield design, and beneath is a scroll with the legend COMMONWEALTH OF THE PHILIPPINES.

World War II forced the Commonwealth government to operate in exile during the Japanese occupation of 1942 to 1945. A pro-Japan puppet government was set up in Manila in 1943; it issued no coins of its own, and in fact during the Japanese occupation many coins were gathered from circulation to be melted and remade into Japanese coins. Barter and low-denomination emergency paper money took their place in day-to-day commerce. (Much of the money used in the Philippines during World War II consisted of hastily printed "guerrilla" currency.) The United States military knew of the local need for circulating coins, and the U.S. and Philippine governments included new coinage in the plans to liberate the islands. The U.S. Treasury Department used its Philadelphia, San Francisco, and Denver mints to produce brass, copper-nickel-zinc, and silver coins in 1944 and 1945, to be shipped to the Philippines during and after the liberation.

Note that mintage figures given for 1938, 1939, 1940, and 1941 are estimates, as many Manila Mint records were lost during the war.

BRONZE AND BRASS COINAGE
ONE CENTAVO (1937–1944)

Designer: *Melecio Figueroa (obverse).* **Weight:** *5.3 grams.*
Composition: *.950 copper, .050 tin and zinc (except for 1944-S: .950 copper, .050 zinc).*
Diameter: *24 mm.* **Edge:** *Plain.* **Mints:** *Manila and San Francisco.*

  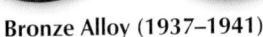   

Bronze Alloy (1937–1941)

Mintmark location is on the reverse, to the left of the date.

Brass Alloy (1944)

History. The Manila Mint struck one-centavo coins for the Commonwealth of the Philippines every year from 1937 through 1941. This production was brought to an end by the Japanese invasion that started in December 1941, immediately after the bombing of Pearl Harbor. Part of the United States–Commonwealth plan to retake the islands included the San Francisco Mint's 1944 striking of 58 million one-centavo coins—a quantity greater than all of Manila's centavo output since 1937. Like the federal Lincoln cents of 1944 to 1946, these coins were made of *brass* rather than bronze—their alloy was derived in part from recycled cartridge cases, and their composition included copper and zinc, but no tin (a vital war material). The coins were transported to the islands to enter circulation as U.S. and Philippine military forces fought back the Japanese invaders. This would be the final mintage of centavos until the Republic of the Philippines, created on July 4, 1946, resumed the denomination's production in 1958.

The centavo was a popular coin that saw widespread circulation. As a result, many of the coins today are found with signs of wear or damage, exacerbated by corrosion and toning encouraged by the islands' tropical climate.

Striking and Sharpness. Well-struck examples are uncommon. Obverses of the Commonwealth centavos usually have very flat or depressed strikes in the left shoulder of the seated figure, and part of the face and chest. His right hand is better struck than in the coins struck under U.S. sovereignty. The left side of the anvil's edge is slightly rounded. On the reverse, many Uncirculated coins have flatness on the lower and central sections of the coat of arms, and some or most of the words COMMONWEALTH OF THE PHILIPPINES are unreadable.

On a perfectly struck coin, the eagle surmounting the Commonwealth shield would have a pattern of feathers visible on its breast; this level of detail is rarely evident, with the breast instead appearing smooth or flat.

Many 1937-M centavos have a barely readable mintmark. Issues of 1938 to 1941 used a narrow M mintmark, rather than a square version of the letter, resulting in better legibility.

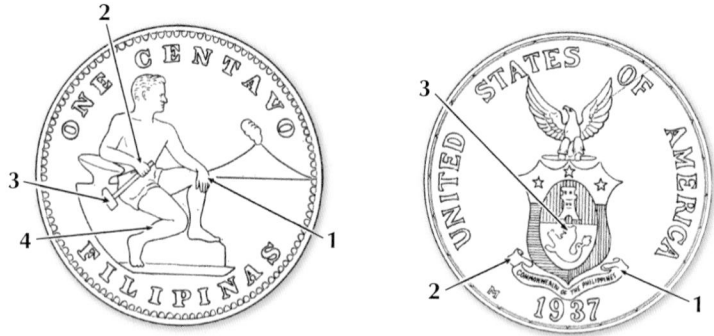

One Centavo, 1937–1944

High Points of Wear. *Obverse Checkpoints:* 1. Figure's left hand. 2. Figure's right hand. 3. Head of hammer. 4. Figure's right calf. *Reverse Checkpoints:* 1. Inner-right fold of ribbon. 2. Outer-left fold of ribbon. 3. Center of coat of arms.

	Mintage	VF	EF	MS-60	MS-63
1937-M	15,790,492	$2	$3	$20	$45
	Auctions: $153, MS-65RD, December 2015				
1938-M	10,000,000	$1.50	$2.50	$15	$35
	Auctions: $66, MS-65RB, March 2014; $94, MS-64RB, January 2014				
1939-M	6,500,000	$2.50	$3.50	$17.50	$50
	Auctions: $223, MS-66RD, April 2014				

	Mintage	VF	EF	MS-60	MS-63
1940-M	*4,000,000*	$1.25	$3	$15	$25
	Auctions: $50, MS-65RB, May 2014; $30, MS-64RD, March 2014				
1941-M	*5,000,000*	$3	$7.50	$20	$45
	Auctions: $59, MS-65RD, March 2014				
1944-S	*58,000,000*	$0.25	$0.50	$2	$4
	Auctions: $32, MS-65RD, March 2014				

COPPER-NICKEL AND COPPER-NICKEL-ZINC COINAGE
FIVE CENTAVOS (1937–1945)

Designer: *Melecio Figueroa (obverse).* **Weight:** *1937–1941, 4.8 grams; 1944–1945, 4.92 grams.*
Composition: *1937–1941, .750 copper, .250 nickel; 1944–1945, .650 copper, .230 zinc, .120 nickel.*
Diameter: *19 mm.* **Edge:** *Plain.* **Mints:** *Manila, Philadelphia, and San Francisco.*

**Copper-Nickel
(1937–1941)**

*Mintmark location is on the reverse,
to the left of the date (Manila and San
Francisco issues only; Philadelphia
issues have no mintmark).*

**Copper-Nickel-Zinc
(1944–1945)**

*Manila mintmark style of 1937
and 1941 (wide, with midpoint
not extending to baseline).*

*Manila mintmark style of 1938
(narrow, with midpoint
extending to baseline).*

History. The Manila Mint switched its coinage of five-centavo pieces to the Commonwealth reverse design in 1937. Production of the coins increased in 1938, then skipped two years. The 1941 output would be Manila's last for the type; the Japanese invasion at year's end stopped all of its coinage.

Philippine commerce was starved for coins during the war. As part of the broader strategy for liberating the Philippines from Japanese occupation, the U.S. Treasury Department swung its mints into production of five-centavo coins in 1944 (Philadelphia and San Francisco) and 1945 (San Francisco alone). This effort dwarfed that of the Commonwealth's late-1930s coinage, producing in those two years more than ten times the combined output of 1937, 1938, and 1941. In order to help save copper and nickel for military use, the U.S. Mint reduced the proportions of those metals in the five-centavo coinage, making up for them with the addition of zinc. This substitution saved more than 4.2 million pounds of nickel and 3.2 million pounds of copper for the war effort. The Philadelphia and San Francisco coins were shipped to the islands during the combined American-Filipino military operations against Japan.

Striking and Sharpness. Most pre-war five-centavo coins are poorly struck. On the obverse, the seated figure's left hand is flat, and the left shoulder can be as well. The left side of the pedestal and the right side of Mount Mayon can be poorly detailed. The obverse rim typically lacks sharpness. On the reverse, the ribbon usually is flat, with its wording partially or completely illegible, and the coat of arms can lack detail especially at the top-left side. On a perfectly struck coin, the eagle surmounting the Commonwealth shield would have a pattern of feathers visible on its breast; this level of detail is rarely evident, with the breast instead appearing smooth or flat.

The mintmark style of 1937 and 1941—a wide M, with the middle point not descending to the letter's baseline—usually did not strike clearly, making it difficult to read. The mintmark style of 1938 was narrower, with the middle point descending to the base, and typically is more legible.

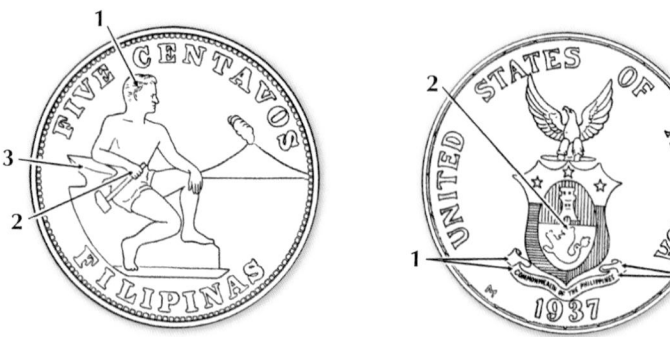

Five Centavos, 1937–1945

High Points of Wear. *Obverse Checkpoints:* 1. Frontal hair just above ear. 2. Figure's right hand. 3. Edge of anvil. *Reverse Checkpoints:* 1. Inner and outer folds of ribbon. 2. Center of coat of arms.

	Mintage	VF	EF	MS-60	MS-63
1937-M	2,493,872	$5	$7	$50	$75
Auctions: $188, MS-65, September 2013					
1938-M	4,000,000	$1	$2.25	$20	$45
Auctions: $92, MS-65, July 2014; $112, MS-65, September 2013					
1941-M	2,750,000	$4	$8	$70	$150
Auctions: $282, MS-65, January 2014; $88, MS-64, September 2013					
1944 (a)	21,198,000	$0.50	$1	$2	$3
Auctions: $46, MS-65, June 2013; $29, MS-64, April 2013					
1944-S (a)	14,040,000	$0.25	$0.50	$1	$2
Auctions: $165, MS-67, September 2013; $200, MS-67, August 2013; $188, MS-67, August 2013					
1945-S (a)	72,796,000	$0.25	$0.50	$1	$2
Auctions: No auction records available.					

a. Copper-nickel-zinc alloy.

SILVER COINAGE
TEN CENTAVOS (1937–1945)

Designer: *Melecio Figueroa.* **Weight:** *2 grams (.0482 oz. ASW).* **Composition:** *.750 silver, .250 copper.* **Diameter:** *16.5 mm.* **Edge:** *Reeded.* **Mints:** *Manila and Denver.*

Mintmark location is on the
reverse, to the left of the date.

History. As with its production of other denominations, the Manila Mint under Commonwealth governance struck ten-centavo coins in 1937 and 1938, followed by a hiatus of two years, and a final coinage in 1941. Normal mint functions were interrupted in 1941 when Imperial Japan invaded the Philippines as part of its war with the United States. The Japanese puppet government of 1943–1945 would not produce any of its own coins, and the Manila Mint, damaged by bombing during the Japanese assault, was later used as part of the invaders' defensive fortifications on the Pasig River.

Japan's wartime exportation of Philippine coins resulted in scarcity of coinage in day-to-day commerce. The U.S. Treasury geared up the Denver Mint for a massive production of Philippine ten-centavo coins in 1944 and 1945, to be shipped overseas and enter circulation as American and Philippine troops liberated the islands. The 1945 coinage was particularly heavy: more than 130 million ten-centavo coins, compared to the Denver Mint's production of just over 40 million Mercury dimes that year. This large mintage of silver coins continued to circulate in the Philippines into the 1960s.

Striking and Sharpness. Well-struck examples of the Commonwealth ten-centavo coin are unusual. Part of the figure's bust is nearly always flatly struck, especially along the left side. The hair and left arm may also be poorly struck. On the reverse, the coat of arms usually lacks detail, and COMMONWEALTH OF THE PHILIPPINES, on the ribbon, often is only partly legible. On a perfectly struck coin, the eagle surmounting the Commonwealth shield would have a pattern of feathers visible on its breast; this level of detail is rarely evident, with the breast instead appearing smooth or flat.

The Denver coinage of 1944 and 1945 often is weakly struck on the obverse, with loss of detail. The reverse typically is weakly struck on the ribbon, with indistinct lettering.

The mintmark style of 1937 and 1941—a wide M, with the middle point not descending to the letter's baseline—usually did not strike clearly, making it difficult to read. The mintmark style of 1938 was narrower, with the middle point descending to the base, and typically is more legible.

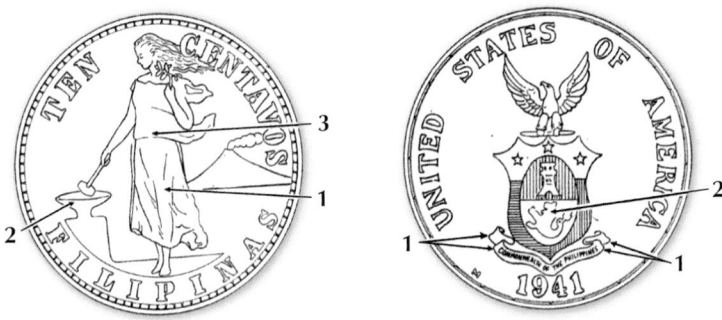

Ten Centavos, 1937–1945

High Points of Wear. *Obverse Checkpoints:* 1. Figure's left leg. 2. Edge of anvil. 3. Mid-drapery area. *Reverse Checkpoints:* 1. Inner and outer folds of ribbon. 2. Center of coat of arms.

	Mintage	VF	EF	MS-60	MS-63
1937-M	3,500,000	$2.25	$3.50	$15	$30
	Auctions: $500, MS-67, January 2013				
1938-M	3,750,000	$1.75	$2.25	$12	$25
	Auctions: $36, MS-63, August 2009				
1941-M	2,500,000	$1.50	$2	$7	$15
	Auctions: $36, MS-65, August 2009				
1944-D	31,592,000	$1	$2	$2.50	$4
	Auctions: No auction records available.				
1945-D	137,208,000	$1	$2	$2.50	$4
	Auctions: No auction records available.				
1945-D, D Over D	(a)	$8.50	$15	$25	$50
	Auctions: $470, AU-50, April 2014				

a. Included in 1945-D mintage figure.

TWENTY CENTAVOS (1937–1945)

Designer: *Melecio Figueroa (obverse).* **Weight:** *4 grams (.0964 oz. ASW).*
Composition: *.750 silver, .250 copper.* **Diameter:** *20 mm.*
Edge: *Reeded.* **Mints:** *Manila and Denver.*

Mintmark location is on the
reverse, to the left of the date.

History. The twenty-centavo piece was the largest circulating coin struck by the Commonwealth of the Philippines at the Manila Mint. Production commenced in 1937 and 1938, followed by a hiatus of two years, and a final year of output in 1941 before Japan's December invasion put a halt to all coinage. During their occupation, the Japanese pulled many twenty-centavo pieces out of circulation and melted them as raw material for new imperial coins.

Anticipating driving the Japanese military out of the islands, the United States and Commonwealth governments planned an impressive production of coinage for the Philippines in 1944 and 1945. The Denver Mint was the source for twenty-centavo pieces, and its output was immense, in 1945 exceeding even the Philadelphia Mint's production of Washington quarters for domestic use. 111 million of the coins were shipped overseas to accompany the U.S. military as Americans and Filipinos fought to liberate the islands. The need was great, as legal-tender coins had largely disappeared from circulation. Most day-to-day commerce was transacted with small-denomination scrip notes and paper money issued by guerrilla military units, local governments, or anti-Japanese military and civilian currency boards.

Striking and Sharpness. Well-struck twenty-centavo Commonwealth coins are a challenge to locate. Nearly all obverses have flattened hair on the figure's head. On the reverse, the coat of arms usually lacks detail, and COMMONWEALTH OF THE PHILIPPINES, on the ribbon, often is only partly legible. The Denver coins typically lack sharp details on the obverse and have the same reverse weakness as earlier Manila issues.

On a perfectly struck coin, the eagle surmounting the Commonwealth shield would have a pattern of feathers visible on its breast; this level of detail is rarely evident, with the breast instead appearing smooth or flat.

The mintmark style of 1937 and 1941—a wide M, with the middle point not descending to the letter's baseline—usually did not strike clearly, making it difficult to read. The mintmark style of 1938 was narrower, with the middle point descending to the base, and typically is more legible.

Twenty Centavos, 1937–1945

High Points of Wear. *Obverse Checkpoints:* 1. Figure's left thigh and knee. 2. Figure's left hand. 3. Edge of anvil. *Reverse Checkpoints:* 1. Inner folds of ribbon. 2. Center of coat of arms.

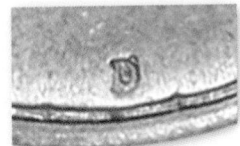

1944-D, D Over S

	Mintage	VF	EF	MS-60	MS-63
1937-M	2,665,000	$3	$5	$35	$50
	Auctions: No auction records available.				
1938-M	3,000,000	$3	$3.50	$15	$30
	Auctions: $40, MS-64, August 2009; $32, MS-64, August 2009				
1941-M	*1,500,000*	$3	$3.50	$12.50	$20
	Auctions: No auction records available.				
1944-D	28,596,000	$2	$2.75	$3	$5
	Auctions: No auction records available.				
1944-D, D Over S	(a)	$5	$9	$25	$50
	Auctions: $403, MS-66, January 2010				
1945-D	82,804,000	$2	$2.75	$3	$5
	Auctions: No auction records available.				

a. Included in 1944-D mintage figure.

FIFTY CENTAVOS (1944–1945)

Designer: *Melecio Figueroa.* **Weight:** *10 grams (.2411 oz. ASW).*
Composition: *.750 silver, .250 copper.* **Diameter:** *27 mm.*
Edge: *Reeded.* **Mint:** *San Francisco.*

Mintmark location is on the reverse, to the left of the date.

History. No fifty-centavo coins were struck at the Manila Mint for the Commonwealth of the Philippines. The denomination's first issue was a wartime production of the San Francisco Mint, in 1944, to the extent of some 19 million coins, or double that facility's production of Liberty Walking half dollars for the year. This was followed by a similar mintage in 1945. These coins were intended to enter circulation after being shipped overseas with the U.S. military during the liberation of the Philippines from Imperial Japan's 1942–1945 occupation. They were readily accepted in the coin-starved wartime economy and continued to circulate in the islands into the 1960s.

Striking and Sharpness. Many Commonwealth fifty-centavo coins are lightly struck, but they typically show flattening less severe than that of the 1907–1921 issues struck under U.S. sovereignty. On the reverse, the coat of arms usually is weakly struck, with COMMONWEALTH OF THE PHILIPPINES rarely completely legible. On a perfectly struck coin, the eagle surmounting the Commonwealth shield would have a pattern of feathers visible on its breast; this level of detail is rarely evident, with the breast instead appearing smooth or flat.

Fifty Centavos, 1944–1945

High Points of Wear. *Obverse Checkpoints:* 1. Figure's left thigh and lower leg. 2. Mid-drapery area. 3. Figure's left bosom. 4. Edge of anvil. *Reverse Checkpoints:* 1. Inner folds of ribbon. 2. Center of coat of arms.

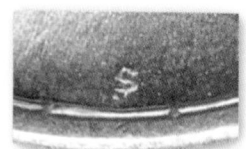

1945-S, S Over S

	Mintage	VF	EF	MS-60	MS-63
1944-S	19,187,000	$5	$6	$8	$12
	Auctions: $94, MS-66, July 2015; $44, MS-64, March 2013				
1945-S	18,120,000	$5	$6	$8	$12
	Auctions: $100, MS-66, January 2014				
1945-S, S Over S	(a)	$12	$30	$80	$180
	Auctions: $306, MS-66, May 2014; $118, MS-62, October 2015				

a. Included in 1945-S mintage figure.

COMMONWEALTH COMMEMORATIVE ISSUES

The American territory of the Philippines was governed by the U.S. military from 1899 to mid-1901. Its executive branch was managed by the Bureau of Insular Affairs (part of the War Department) from mid-1901 to 1935. In the latter year the Philippines' status was changed to that of a commonwealth—a type of organized but unincorporated dependent territory, self-governed (except in defense and foreign policy) under a constitution of its own adoption, whose right of self-government would not be unilaterally withdrawn by Congress. This was a step in the direction of complete independence, scheduled to be recognized after an additional ten years of "nation building."

To celebrate this transfer of government, the Manila Mint in 1936 produced a set of three silver commemorative coins—one of the fifty-centavo denomination, and two of the one-peso. These were designed by Ambrosio Morales, professor of sculpture at the University of the Philippines School of Fine Arts.

The fifty-centavo coin and one of the set's pesos feature busts of Philippine president Manuel L. Quezon and the last U.S. governor-general, Frank Murphy, who served (largely ceremonially) as the first U.S. high commissioner to the Commonwealth of the Philippines. On the fifty-centavo piece the two men face each other with the rising sun between them; on the peso, they appear jugate (in conjoined profile portraits). The other peso has busts of Quezon and U.S. president Franklin D. Roosevelt. This was a rare instance of a living American president appearing on a coin, the only precedent being the 1926 Sesquicentennial commemorative half dollar, which showed President Calvin Coolidge.

On each of the three coins appears the date November 15, 1935, when the new commonwealth's government was inaugurated on the steps of the Legislative Building in Manila, witnessed by 300,000 people in attendance.

The set's issue price was $3.13, or about 2.5 times the coins' face value expressed in U.S. dollars. Commemorative coins were popular in the United States at the time, but still these sets sold poorly, and thousands remained within the Philippine Treasury at the onset of World War II. In early 1942 many if not all of the remainders were crated and thrown into Caballo Bay, to keep them (along with millions of older silver pesos) from being captured by the approaching forces of Imperial Japan. Today many of the coins are found with corrosion caused by their long exposure to saltwater before being salvaged.

FIFTY CENTAVOS (1936)

Designer: *Ambrosio Morales (obverse).* **Weight:** *10 grams (.2411 oz. ASW).*
Composition: *.750 silver, .250 copper.* **Diameter:** *27.5 mm.* **Edge:** *Reeded.* **Mint:** *Manila.*

Striking and Sharpness. This issue typically is found well struck.

	Mintage	VF	EF	MS-60	MS-63
1936-M, Silver fifty centavos	20,000	$25	$50	$100	$155
	Auctions: $1,528, MS-66, January 2016; $206, MS-64, January 2014; $112, MS-63, December 2014				

ONE PESO (1936)

Designer: *Ambrosio Morales (obverse).* **Weight:** *20 grams (.5144 oz. ASW).*
Composition: *.800 silver, .200 copper.* **Diameter:** *35 mm.* **Edge:** *Reeded.* **Mint:** *Manila.*

One Peso, Busts of Murphy and Quezon   One Peso, Busts of Roosevelt and Quezon

Striking and Sharpness. Sharply struck gems of the Murphy/Quezon peso can be a challenge to locate. Weak strike is evident on the reverse in particular, where the sea-lion can be softly detailed. On some pieces, tiny bubbles resulting from improper fabrication of the planchet can be observed among the letters surrounding the rim.

The Roosevelt/Quezon peso typically is found well struck.

	Mintage	VF	EF	MS-60	MS-63
1936-M, Silver one peso, busts of Murphy and Quezon	10,000	$70	$85	$200	$300
	Auctions: $940, MS-66, October 2014; $764, MS-66, October 2014; $176, MS, May 2015				
1936-M, Silver one peso, busts of Roosevelt and Quezon	10,000	$70	$85	$200	$300
	Auctions: $823, MS-66, January 2016; $359, MS-65, August 2013; $329, MS-65, January 2013				

Alaska Tokens

ALASKA RURAL REHABILITATION CORPORATION TOKENS OF 1935

Before the Roosevelt Administration's dramatic New Deal response to the Great Depression, it was the states themselves, rather than the federal government, that organized and funded the relief of their citizens in need. This changed with the Federal Emergency Relief Act of 1933, by which Congress appropriated $250 million for states to use in their relief efforts, with the same amount funded for federal programs. Other relief acts would follow. The states were to use their 1933 FERA grant money "to aid in meeting the costs of furnishing relief and in relieving the hardship and suffering caused by unemployment in the form of money, service, materials, and/or commodities to provide the necessities of life to persons in need as a result of the present emergency, and/or their dependents, whether resident, transient, or homeless," as well as to "aid in assisting cooperative and self-help associations for the barter of goods and services."

Americans living in cities benefited from direct relief grants as well as employment in work-relief projects. Those in rural areas, however, had a stronger need for *rehabilitation* programs rather than relief as such. In April 1934 a special Rural Rehabilitation Division was set up. This helped establish rural camps where people made homeless by the Depression could find shelter and assistance until conditions improved. Nonprofits called *rural rehabilitation corporations* were devised to carry this effort forward. One function of the corporations was to buy large expanses of farmland to divide into 40- or 60-acre plots. These would be mortgaged to displaced farm families who agreed to develop and farm the land in exchange for low-interest loans and other assistance. One community developed under this plan was the Matanuska Valley Colony at Palmer, about 45 miles northeast of Anchorage, in the territory of Alaska. For the Alaska program some 203 families were recruited from Michigan, Minnesota, and Wisconsin. Those states were targeted not only because they had a very high percentage of displaced farmers on social-assistance relief, but also because their cold-weather climates were similar to Alaska's.

A suite of (undated) 1935 tokens was issued by the U.S. government for the use of the Midwesterners who relocated to the colonization project. These aluminum and brass tokens (nicknamed "bingles") would supply the settlers with much-needed federal aid, being paid out for work at the rate of 50¢ per hour. In theory this wage payment in tokens, rather than regular coinage, would also discourage the workers from spending their money unwisely, as the bingles were redeemable only at Alaska Rural Rehabilitation Corporation stores. In addition to use as wages, the tokens were issued based on immediate need and according to the size of the family. A family of two would receive a monthly allowance of $45; a family of three, $55; a family of four, $75; and a family of five, $85. The bingles were in use only about six months, during the winter of 1935 and 1936. The colony's managers were unable to restrict their use to the purchase of necessities in corporation-run stores—other merchants, including the local saloon, realized they could also accept them as currency. Eventually the tokens were recalled and redeemed for regular U.S. money. Practically all of the circulated tokens were destroyed after redemption.

Of the $23,000 face value minted, about $18,000 worth of tokens were issued in the months they were in active use. The unissued tokens were later made into souvenir sets for collectors. Some 250 complete sets were thus preserved in unused condition, in addition to about 100 "short" sets consisting of the one-cent, five-cent, and ten-cent pieces.

Each token is similar in size to the corresponding U.S. coin of the same denomination (one cent through ten dollars), with the exception of the one-cent piece, which is octagonal. The design is the same on both sides of each denomination.

Even after leaving hardship in the Midwest, and even with this federal aid, the Alaska colonists faced ongoing challenges. Potatoes and other crops were successfully grown, but the farming seasons were short, markets were far away, and the expense of shipping was high. More than half of the Alaska colonists left the Matanuska Valley within five years, and thirty years later only twenty of the original families were still farming there. Still, the New Deal colony helped the Matanuska Valley to slowly grow into Alaska's most productive agricultural region.

For more information on these and other Alaska-related coins and tokens, see *Alaska's Coinage Through the Years*, by Maurice Gould, Kenneth Bressett, and Kaye and Nancy Dethridge.

ALUMINUM

	Mintage	EF	Unc.
One Cent	5,000	$100	$185
Five Cents	5,000	$100	$185
Ten Cents	5,000	$100	$185
Twenty-Five Cents	3,000	$150	$275
Fifty Cents	2,500	$150	$275
One Dollar	2,500	$250	$325

BRASS

	Mintage	EF	Unc.
Five Dollars	1,000	$250	$375
Ten Dollars	1,000	$275	$450

APPENDIX A

Misstrikes and Errors

With the production of millions of coins each year, it is natural that a few abnormal pieces escape inspection and are inadvertently released for circulation, usually in original bags or rolls of new coins. These are not considered regular issues because they were not made intentionally. They are all eagerly sought by collectors for the information they shed on minting techniques, and as a variation from normal date and mint series collecting.

MISSTRUCK COINS AND ERROR PIECES

Nearly every misstruck or error coin is unique in some way, and prices may vary from coin to coin. They may all be classified in general groups related to the kinds of errors or manufacturing malfunctions involved. Collectors value these pieces according to the scarcity of each kind of error for each type of coin. Non-collectors usually view them as curios, and often believe that they must be worth much more than normal coins because they look so strange. In reality, the value assigned to various types of errors by collectors and dealers reflects both supply and demand, and is based on recurring transactions between willing buyers and sellers.

The following listings show current average values for the most frequently encountered kinds of error coins. In each case, the values shown are for coins that are unmarred by serious marks or scratches, and in Uncirculated condition for modern issues, and Extremely Fine condition for obsolete types. Exceptions are valued higher or lower. Error coins of rare-date issues generally do not command a premium beyond their normal values. In most cases each of these coins is unique in some respect and must be valued according to its individual appearance, quality, and eye appeal.

There are many other kinds of errors and misstruck coins beyond those listed in this guide book. Some are more valuable, and others less valuable, than the most popular pieces that are listed here as examples of what this interesting field contains. The pieces illustrated are general examples of the types described.

Early in 2002 the mints changed their production methods to a new system designed to eliminate deformed planchets, off-center strikes, and similar errors. They also changed the delivery system of bulk coinage, and no longer shipped loose coins in sewn bags to be counted and wrapped by banks or counting rooms, where error coins were often found and sold to collectors. Under the new system, coins are packaged in large quantities and go directly to automated counters that filter out deformed coins. The result has been that very few error coins have entered the market since late 2002, and almost none after that date. The values shown in these listings are for pre-2002 coins; those dated after that, with but a few exceptions, are valued considerably higher.

For additional details and information about these coins, the following books are recommended:

Margolis, Arnold, and Fred Weinberg. *The Error Coin Encyclopedia* (4th ed.). 2004.

Herbert, Alan. *Official Price Guide to Minting Varieties and Errors.* New York, 1991.

Fivaz, Bill, and J.T. Stanton. *The Cherrypickers' Guide to Rare Die Varieties.* Atlanta, GA, updated regularly.

The coins discussed in this section must not be confused with others that have been mutilated or damaged after leaving the mint. Examples of such pieces include coins that have been scratched, hammered, engraved, impressed, acid etched, or plated by individuals to simulate something other than a normal coin. Those pieces have no numismatic value, and can only be considered as altered coins not suitable for a collection.

TYPES OF ERROR COINS

Clipped Planchet—**An incomplete coin, missing 10 to 25% of the metal.** Incomplete planchets result from accidents when the steel rods used to punch out blanks from the metal strip overlap a portion of the strip already punched. There are curved, straight, ragged, incomplete, and elliptical clips. Values may be greater or less depending on the nature and size of the clip. Coins with more than one clip usually command higher values.

Multiple Strike—**A coin with at least one additional image from being struck again off center.** Value increases with the number of strikes. These minting errors occur when a finished coin goes back into the press and is struck again with the same dies. The presence of a date can bring a higher value.

No Rim   With Rim

Blank or Planchet—**A blank disc of metal intended for coinage but not struck with dies.** In the process of preparation for coinage, the blanks are first punched from a strip of metal and then milled to upset the rim. In most instances, first-process pieces (blanks without upset rims) are slightly more valuable than the finished planchets. Values shown are for the most common pieces.

Defective Die—**A coin showing raised metal from a large die crack, or small rim break.** Coins that show evidence of light die cracks, polishing, or very minor die damage are generally of little or no value. Prices shown here are for coins with very noticeable, raised die-crack lines, or those for which the die broke away, producing an unstruck area known as a *cud*.

Off Center—**A coin that has been struck out of collar and incorrectly centered, with part of the design missing.** Values are for coins with approximately 10 to 20% of design missing from obsolete coins, or 20 to 60% missing from modern coins. These are misstruck coins that were made when the planchet did not enter the coinage press properly. Coins that are struck only slightly off center, with none of the design missing, are called broadstrikes (see the next category). Those with nearly all of the impression missing are generally worth more, but those with a readable date and mint are the most valuable.

Broadstrike—**A coin that was struck outside the retaining collar.** When coins are struck without being contained in the collar die, they spread out larger than normal pieces. All denominations have a plain edge.

Lamination—**A flaw whereby a fragment of metal has peeled off the coin's surface.** This defect occurs when a foreign substance, such as gas oxides or dirt, becomes trapped in the strip as it is rolled out to the proper thickness. Lamination flaws may be missing or still attached to the coin's surface. Minor flaws may only decrease a coin's value, while a clad coin that is missing the full surface of one or both sides is worth more than the values listed here.

Brockage—**A mirror image of the design impressed on the opposite side of the same coin.** These errors are caused when a struck coin remains on either die after striking, and impresses its image into the next blank planchet as it is struck, leaving a negative or mirror image. Off-center and partial brockage coins are worth less than those with full impression. Coins with negative impressions on both sides are usually mutilated pieces made outside the mint by the pressing together of coins.

Wrong Planchet—**A coin struck on a planchet intended for another denomination or of the wrong metal.** Examples of these are cents struck on dime planchets, nickels on cent planchets, or quarters on dime planchets. Values vary depending on the type of error involved. Those struck on coins of a different denomination that were previously struck normally are of much greater value. A similar kind of error occurs when a coin is struck on a planchet of the correct denomination but wrong metal. One famous example is the 1943 cent struck in bronze (pictured), rather than in that year's new steel composition. (Fewer than three dozen are thought to exist.) Such errors presumably occur when an older planchet is mixed in with the normal supply of planchets and goes through the minting process.

Mint-Canceled Coins

In mid-2003, the U.S. Mint acquired machines to eliminate security concerns and the cost associated with providing Mint police escorts to private vendors for the melting of scrap, substandard struck coins, planchets, and blanks. Under high pressure, the rollers and blades of these machines cancel the coins and blanks in a manner similar in appearance to the surface of a waffle, and they are popularly known by that term. This process has effectively kept most misstruck coins produced after 2003 from becoming available to collectors. Waffled examples are known for all six 2003-dated coin denominations, from the Lincoln cent through the Sacagawea dollar. The Mint has not objected to these pieces' trading in the open market because they are not considered coins with legal tender status.

Misstruck and Error Pieces

	Clipped Planchet	Multiple Strike	Blank, No Raised Rim	Planchet, Raised Rim	Defective Die	Off Center	Broadstrike	Lamination	Brockage
Large Cent	$60	$1,000	$200	$350	$25	$600	$100	$25	$1,100
Indian Head 1¢	$15	$600	—	—	$25	$150	$60	$15	$400
Lincoln 1¢ (95% Copper)	$3	$65	$4	$3	$12	$12	$8	$3	$35
Steel 1¢	$30	$250	$30	$40	$15	$60	$35	$15	$200
Lincoln 1¢ (Zinc)	$4	$35	$3	$2	$15	$8	$5	$15	$40
Liberty 5¢	$20	$700	—	$250	$35	$200	$110	$25	$450
Buffalo 5¢	$20	$2,500	—	$350	$40	$500	$300	$35	$850
Jefferson 5¢	$3	$50	$15	$10	$15	$12	$10	$15	$40
Wartime 5¢	$10	$400	$400	$350	$25	$175	$70	$15	$200
Barber 10¢	$50	$750	—	—	$75	$300	$85	$15	$400
Mercury 10¢	$20	$800	—	—	$35	$175	$55	$15	$275
Roosevelt 10¢ (Silver)	$12	$250	$50	$40	$35	$150	$45	$12	$100
Roosevelt 10¢ (Clad)	$3	$65	$3	$4	$15	$10	$10	$16	$40

	Clipped Planchet	Multiple Strike	Blank, No Raised Rim	Planchet, Raised Rim	Defective Die	Off Center	Broadstrike	Lamination	Brockage
Washington 25¢ (Silver)	$20	$400	$175	$150	$25	$350	$200	$15	$300
Washington 25¢ (Clad)	$5	$150	$7	$5	$12	$70	$20	$25	$50
Bicentennial 25¢	$35	$350	—	—	$65	$150	$50	$50	$250
State 25¢	$20	$500	—	—	$25	$100	$40	$400	$350
Franklin 50¢	$40	$1,800	—	—	$150	$1,800	$500	$25	$750
Kennedy 50¢ (40% Silver)	$25	$1,000	$185	$135	$70	$450	$200	$40	$450
Kennedy 50¢ (Clad)	$20	$600	$135	$100	$50	$250	$75	$25	$300
Bicentennial 50¢	$45	$700	—	—	$90	$300	$95	$40	$650
Silver $1	$50	$5,000	$1,750	$1,600	$950	$2,500	$1,000	$50	—
Eisenhower $1	$40	$1,200	$175	$100	$500	$600	$150	$50	$950
Bicentennial $1	$60	$2,000	—	—	$750	$850	$200	$50	$1,250
Anthony $1	$25	$600	$160	$120	$100	$275	$75	$30	$300
Sacagawea $1	$85	$1,800	$275	$85	$50	$1,500	$300	$50	$500

WRONG PLANCHETS

	Zinc 1¢	Copper 1¢	Steel 1¢	5¢	Silver 10¢	Copper-Nickel Clad 10¢	Silver 25¢	Copper-Nickel Clad 25¢	Copper-Nickel Clad 50¢
Indian Head 1¢	(a)	—	(a)	(a)	$8,500	(a)	(a)	(a)	(a)
Lincoln 1¢	—	—	—	(a)	$1,000	$350	(a)	(a)	(a)
Buffalo 5¢	(a)	$4,000	(a)	—	$5,000	(a)	(a)	(a)	(a)
Jefferson 5¢	$300	$275	$2,500	—	$450	$375	(a)	(a)	(a)
Wartime 5¢	(a)	$2,500	$3,500	—	$2,000	(a)	(a)	(a)	(a)
Washington 25¢ (Silver)	(a)	$950	$7,000	$500	$1,800	—	—	—	(a)
Washington 25¢ (Clad)	—	$750	(a)	$225	—	$350	—	—	(a)
Bicentennial 25¢	(a)	$3,000	(a)	$2,500	—	$3,500	—	—	(a)
State 25¢ (b)	—	$4,500	(a)	$750	(a)	$4,000	(a)	—	(a)
Walking Liberty 50¢	(a)	—	—	—	—	(a)	$25,000	(a)	(a)
Franklin 50¢	(a)	$5,000	(a)	$5,000	$6,000	(a)	$1,500	(a)	(a)
Kennedy 50¢ (c)	(a)	$3,000	(a)	$1,250	—	$2,000	—	$650	—
Bicentennial 50¢	(a)	$4,000	(a)	$2,750	—	—	—	$1,200	—
Eisenhower $1	(a)	$12,500	(a)	$9,500	—	$11,000	—	$6,000	$2,750
Anthony $1	(a)	$3,500	(a)	$5,000	(a)	—	—	$1,000	(a)
Sacagawea $1	$10,000	(a)	(a)	$10,000	(a)	$10,000	(a)	$3,000	(a)

Note: Coins struck over other coins of different denominations are usually valued three to five times higher than these prices. Coins made from mismatched dies (State quarter obverse combined with Sacagawea dollar reverse) are extremely rare. **a.** Not possible. **b.** Values for State quarter errors vary with each type and state, and are generally much higher than for other quarters. **c.** The Kennedy fifty-cent piece struck on an Anthony one-dollar planchet is very rare.

A GALLERY OF SIGNIFICANT U.S. MINT ERROR COINS

Every high-production manufacturing facility makes a certain percentage of "factory irregulars." The U.S. Mint—which for decades has produced billions of coins annually—is no exception. Today's Mint, though, has cutting-edge machinery and quality-control procedures that keep errors and misstruck coins to a minimum. When such coins *do* come into being, the Mint's sophisticated safeguards (such as riddlers that filter aside odd-shaped coins) prevent nearly all of them from leaving its facilities. Over the course of its 220-plus years of making and issuing coins, however, the Mint has produced some amazing and unusual coins that have made their way into collectors' hands. This gallery highlights a selection of collectible, significant, and valuable errors and misstruck coins.

Some early U.S. Mint coins might appear to be misstrikes when in fact they simply illustrate the standard operating procedures of the time. For example, many 1795 and 1797 half cents show faint evidence of the design of Talbot, Allum & Lee tokens. These are not highly prized double-denominations, but rather regular federal coins intentionally struck on planchets made from cut-down tokens. Other examples exist, such as "spoiled" (misstruck) large cents salvaged and cut down into planchets for half cents.

The introduction of steam-driven coining presses in the 1830s ushered in what today's collector might consider a golden age of misstruck coins. Two competing factors were at work: improved minting techniques and quality control helped curb (or at least catch) most errors and misstrikes, but dramatically increasing mintages naturally led to a greater quantity of such mistakes.

The 1900s and 2000s saw continuing modernization of the mints and a gradual conversion from older presses to new higher-speed presses, eventually capable of striking up to 750 coins per minute. In addition to their speed, today's presses strike coins horizontally, allowing highly efficient and consistently accurate production. As discussed earlier, major misstrikes and coinage errors from 2002 to the present are very rare. Currently, only a handful of new significant pieces enter the market each year.

Error and misstruck coins are a growing specialty in the rare-coin market. Their appeal and value lie in their rarity, their unusual appearance, and the insight they provide into the minting process. When major specimens appear at auction, they bring excitement and active bidding. While no misstrike or error coin has yet sold for a million dollars, several have sold for six-figure sums.

This gallery illustrates a variety of such pieces not typically seen. Some of the featured coins reside in museums or other permanent collections. Each is a classic representation of its type (e.g., wrong planchet or double strike). In many cases, they are unique; for the rest, only a few such pieces are known. The valuations are approximate, based on recent sales and market conditions. For misstruck and error coins, the grade, type, and eye appeal are important factors in market pricing.

Special credit is due to Nicholas P. Brown, David J. Camire, and Fred Weinberg, authors of *100 Greatest U.S. Error Coins*, for contributing to this feature.

1904 Lewis and Clark Exposition gold dollar (partial collar with reverse brockage). This specimen, part of the Smithsonian's National Numismatic Collection, is unique among commemorative gold coinage. It was created when a struck coin failed to fully eject from the press. A new planchet entered and came to rest partially atop the coin; when they were struck together, a reverse image was transferred to the error coin. The obstruction also prevented the planchet from being fully enclosed by the collar. *Value:* $25,000 or more.

1943 Lincoln cent struck over a struck 1943 Mercury dime (double denomination). This piece is unique for the date, and one of only a handful known in silver for the series. It occurred when 1943-dated cent dies struck a 1943 dime instead of a steel cent planchet. *Value:* $16,000 or more.

1999-P Anthony dollar struck on a 2000 Sacagawea planchet (wrong planchet–transitional). About six examples of this kind are known, most acquired from Mint rolls and bags. During transitions in a coin series (e.g., in metal content or design), wrong planchets may accidentally be used in production. This transitional error shows a "golden dollar" planchet that was used to strike an Anthony dollar. *Value:* $16,000 or more.

1863 Indian Head cent (obverse capped die). This dramatic piece is unique for the date and the series. The coin was struck multiple times by the obverse die against a planchet that rested atop the reverse die. Since the planchet was not properly seated in the collar, the force of the strike spread the planchet (cracking it in the process) until it was larger than a quarter dollar. *Value:* $55,000 or more.

1906 Indian Head cent struck on a quarter eagle planchet (wrong planchet). This error is unique for the date, and one of perhaps four known in the series. Somehow a gold quarter-eagle planchet made its way into the coining chamber for cent production. Some theorize that this and similar specimens were intentionally struck, but most show light to moderate wear that suggests they entered circulation. *Value:* $150,000 or more.

1860 Liberty Seated quarter struck on a cent planchet (wrong planchet). This specimen is unique for the date and the series. Its bright bronze color (from the copper-nickel Indian Head cent planchet) and Mint State grade give it great visual appeal. *Value:* $50,000 or more.

1837 Capped Bust half dollar struck on a struck large cent (double denomination). This misstrike is unique for the date and the series. It was made when the steam press had been in use for half dollars only a little more than a year. The coin appears to have circulated for a while before being placed into a collection. Much detail still shows from both strikes. *Value:* $50,000 or more.

Peace dollar struck on a Standing Liberty quarter planchet (wrong planchet). This error is unique for the date and the series. Judging from its Mint State grade, it was probably placed into a collection after being found in a bag or roll of coins. *Value:* $75,000 or more.

   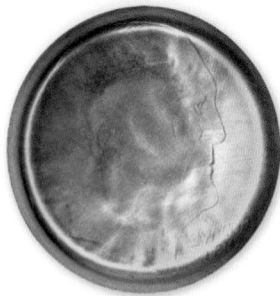

1909 Indian Head cent struck on a struck 1906 Barber dime (double denomination). This piece is unique for the date and the series. Considerable detail shows from both strikes. *Value:* $25,000 or more.

1976-D Eisenhower dollar (obverse die cap). This specimen is unique for the date, and one of only a couple known in the series. It occurred when a struck coin adhered to the die, essentially becoming a die itself. Each subsequent strike caused the planchet to bend around the die, forming a deep, bottle cap–shaped coin. *Value:* $25,000 or more.

1976-D Washington quarter (double strike). A few such specimens are known, in varying degrees of off-center double striking. This misstrike has a second strike 40% off center from the first, and is die-struck on both sides. *Value:* $2,750 or more.

1923 Peace dollar (double strike). This misstrike is unique for the date and the series. Apparently the coin was struck about 45% off center, then repositioned and struck a second time, centered normally. *Value:* $75,000 or more.

1977 Jefferson nickel struck on a 1976 Lincoln cent (double denomination–dual date). Two examples of this error are known for the date, among a half dozen in the series. Both dates are clearly visible. *Value:* $8,000 or more.

(1976 or 1977) Lincoln cent struck off center on a Philippine five-sentimos planchet (wrong planchet–multiple error). This error is unique for the series as an off center; several are known struck on center. The Philadelphia Mint struck almost 99 million five-sentimo coins for the Philippines in 1976, and more than 1 million in 1977. Only a few U.S. coins are known accidentally struck on their planchets. *Value:* $2,750 or more.

(1960) Jefferson nickel struck on a 1960 Peruvian five-centavos coin (double denomination–dual country). This error is unique for the date and the series. Interestingly, Mint records do not indicate any coins of Peru were struck at the Philadelphia Mint in 1960. *Value:* $10,000 or more.

Lincoln cent struck off center on a Roosevelt dime (double denomination–off center). Only a few off-center double denominations are known for this series. This is a full dime that was struck off-center by cent dies. *Value:* $5,500 or more.

1943 Lincoln cent struck on a bronze planchet (wrong planchet–transitional). About a dozen of these well-known errors have been confirmed. They came about when bronze planchets left over from 1942 cent production were mixed with the regular 1943 steel planchets. All but one were found in circulation. This error was voted among the *100 Greatest U.S. Coins* (Garrett and Guth). *Value:* $100,000 or more.

(2000) Washington quarter obverse muled with a Sacagawea dollar reverse (mule). About two dozen of these dramatic errors are known to have been struck at Philadelphia, in three die pairings. They have received nationwide publicity in the mainstream press. *Value:* $100,000 or more.

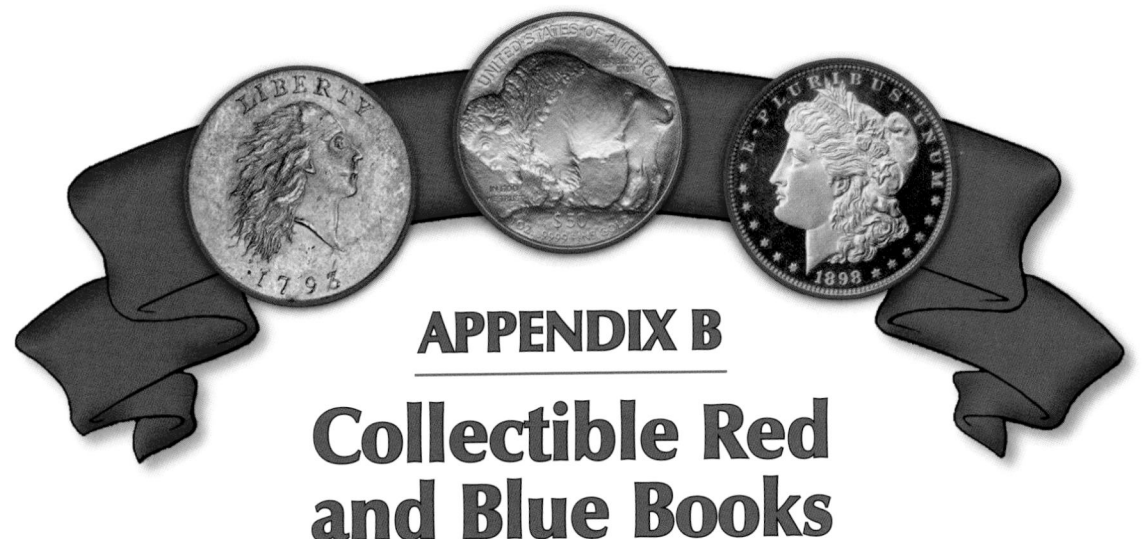

APPENDIX B

Collectible Red and Blue Books

The book you are reading is the *Deluxe Edition* of a classic hobby reference, the *Guide Book of United States Coins*, popularly known as the "Red Book." More than 23 million copies of the Red Book have been sold since 1946, making it one of the best-selling nonfiction titles in American publishing history. By 1959 more than 100,000 copies were being printed annually. The 1965 (18th) edition, published in 1964, reached a peak of 1,200,000 copies. That year the Red Book was ranked fifth on the list of best-selling nonfiction—ahead of Dale Carnegie's classic *How to Win Friends and Influence People* (at number 6) and John F. Kennedy's *Profiles in Courage* (at number 9).

The idea for the Red Book started in the 1940s with R.S. Yeoman. Employed by Whitman Publishing Company (part of Western Publishing), Yeoman at first created the "Blue Book" (official title, the *Handbook of United States Coins With Premium List*), which gave hobbyists an overview of American coinage and a detailed guide to the prices that dealers were paying for collectible coins. The first edition was published in 1942. Yeoman saw that collectors wanted even more information, and he began compiling data and records for an expanded *retail* version of the Blue Book (showing how much a collector could expect to pay a dealer for coins). After World War II ended, Yeoman and his team introduced the new volume, the *Guide Book of United States Coins*, soon nicknamed the Red Book because of its distinctive cover color.

Numismatist Kenneth E. Bressett joined the Red Book in 1956 as a freelance editor. He has continued to work on the annually published book, and other Whitman projects, ever since. He took a full-time editorial position with Whitman Publishing in 1959, and assumed full editorship of the Red Book in 1975. Today Bressett serves as the Red Book's senior editor, assisted by research editor Q. David Bowers, valuations editor Jeff Garrett, and a panel of more than 100 coin dealers, researchers, and other specialists.

THE RED BOOK AS A COLLECTIBLE

The *Guide Book of United States Coins* holds the record as the longest-running annual retail coin-price guide. It has passed its 65th anniversary, and collectors seem to be almost as interested in assembling sets of old Red Books as of old coins. The demand for old Red Books has created a solid market. Some who collect these old editions maintain reference libraries of all kinds of coin publications. To them, having one of each edition is essential, because that is the way old books are collected. Others are speculators who believe that the value of old editions will go up as interest and demand increase. Many people who save old Red Books do so to maintain a record of coin prices going back further than any other source.

Following price trends in old Red Books is a good indicator of how well individual coins are doing in comparison to each other. The price information published in each year is an average of what collectors are paying for each coin. It is a valuable benchmark, showing how prices have gone up or down over the years. Information like this often gives investors an edge in predicting what the future may hold.

Old Red Books are also a handy resource on collecting trends. They show graphically how grading has changed over the years, what new coins have been discovered and added to the listings, and which areas are growing in popularity. Studying these old books can be educational as well as nostalgic. It's great fun to see what your favorite coins sold for 15 or 25 years ago or more—and a bit frustrating to realize what might have been if we had only bought the right coins at the right time in years past.

Many collectors have asked about the quantities printed of each edition. That information has never been published, and now no company records exist specifying how many were made. The original author, R.S. Yeoman, told inquirers that the first press run in November 1946 was for 9,000 copies. In February 1947 an additional 9,000 copies were printed to satisfy the unexpected demand.

There was a slight but notable difference that can be used to differentiate between the first and second printings. The wording in the first printing at the bottom of page 135 reads, "which probably accounts for the scarcity of *this* date." Those last few words were changed to "the scarcity of *1903 O*" in the second printing.

The second edition had a press run of 22,000. The printing of each edition thereafter gradually increased, with the highest number ever being reached with the 18th edition, dated 1965 and published in 1964. At the top of a booming coin market, a whopping 1,200,000 copies were produced. Since that time the numbers have decreased, but the Red Book still maintains a record of being the world's largest-selling coin publication each year.

In some years a very limited number of Red Books were made for use by price contributors. Those were interleaved with blank pages. No more than 50 copies were ever made for any one year. Perhaps fewer than 20 were made in the first few years. Three of these of the first edition, and one of the second edition, are currently known. Their value is now in four figures. Those made in the 1960s sell for about $300–$500 today.

There are other unusual Red Books that command exceptional prices. One of the most popular is the 1987 special edition that was made for, and distributed only to, people who attended the 1986 American Numismatic Association banquet in Milwaukee. Only 500 of those were printed with a special commemorative cover.

Error books are also popular with collectors. The most common is one with double-stamped printing on the cover. The second most frequently seen are those with an upside-down cover. Probably the best known of the error books is the 1963 16th edition with a missing page. For some uncanny reason, page 239 is duplicated in some of those books, and page 237 is missing. The error was corrected on most of the printing.

The terminology used to describe book condition differs from that utilized in grading coins. A "Very Fine" book is one that is nearly new, with minimal signs of use. Early editions of the Red Book are rarely if ever found in anything approaching "New" condition. Exceptionally well-preserved older editions command a substantial premium and are in great demand. Nice used copies that are still clean and in good shape, but slightly worn from use, are also desirable. Only the early editions are worth a premium in badly worn condition.

For a more detailed history and edition-by-edition study of the Red Book, see Frank J. Colletti's *A Guide Book of The Official Red Book of United States Coins* (Whitman, 2009).

VALUATION GUIDE FOR PAST EDITIONS OF THE RED BOOK
CLASSIC HARDCOVER BINDING
See page 1385 for special editions in the classic hardcover binding.

Year/Edition	Issue Price	VG	F	VF	New
1947 (1st ed.), 1st Printing	$1.50	$350	$650	$1,000	$2,500 (a)
1947 (1st ed.), 2nd Printing	$1.50	$300	$600	$900	$2,000 (a)
1948 (2nd ed.)	$1.50	$80	$150	$225	$450 (a)
1949 (3rd ed.)	$1.50	$80	$150	$350	$520 (a)
1951/52 (4th ed.)	$1.50	$55	$110	$175	$300 (a)
1952/53 (5th ed.)	$1.50	$150	$250	$450	$1,500 (a)
1953/54 (6th ed.)	$1.75	$45	$65	$100	$150
1954/55 (7th ed.)	$1.75	$40	$50	$100	$120
1955 (8th ed.)	$1.75	$30	$45	$90	$115
1956 (9th ed.)	$1.75	$20	$35	$60	$110
1957 (10th ed.)	$1.75	$10	$20	$35	$50
1958 (11th ed.)	$1.75		$8	$12	$25
1959 (12th ed.)	$1.75		$8	$12	$25
1960 (13th ed.)	$1.75		$7	$9	$20
1961 (14th ed.)	$1.75		$4	$6	$17
1962 (15th ed.)	$1.75		$4	$6	$10
1963 (16th ed.)	$1.75		$4	$6	$10
1964 (17th ed.)	$1.75		$4	$5	$7
1965 (18th ed.)	$1.75		$3	$4	$7
1966 (19th ed.)	$1.75		$3	$4	$7
1967 (20th ed.)	$1.75		$3	$5	$8
1968 (21st ed.)	$2		$3	$5	$10
1969 (22nd ed.)	$2		$3	$5	$10
1970 (23rd ed.)	$2.50		$3	$6	$11
1971 (24th ed.)	$2.50		$3	$4	$7
1972 (25th ed.)	$2.50		$5	$8	$10
1973 (26th ed.)	$2.50		$4	$5	$7
1974 (27th ed.)	$2.50		$3	$4	$7
1975 (28th ed.)	$3			$4	$6
1976 (29th ed.)	$3.95			$4	$7
1977 (30th ed.)	$3.95			$4	$6
1978 (31st ed.)	$3.95			$4	$6
1979 (32nd ed.)	$3.95			$4	$7
1980 (33rd ed.)	$3.95			$4	$9
1981 (34th ed.)	$4.95			$2	$5
1982 (35th ed.)	$4.95			$2	$5
1983 (36th ed.)	$5.95			$2	$5
1984 (37th ed.)	$5.95			$2	$5
1985 (38th ed.)	$5.95			$2	$5
1986 (39th ed.)	$5.95			$2	$5
1987 (40th ed.)	$6.95			$2	$5
1988 (41st ed.)	$6.95			$2	$5
1989 (42nd ed.)	$6.95			$3	$7
1990 (43rd ed.)	$7.95			$2	$6
1991 (44th ed.)	$8.95			$2	$5
1992 (45th ed.)	$8.95			$2	$5

Note: Values are for unsigned books. Those signed by R.S. Yeoman are worth substantially more. **a.** Values are for books in Near Mint condition, as truly New copies are effectively nonexistent.

Year/Edition	Issue Price	VG	F	VF	New
1993 (46th ed.)	$9.95			$2	$5
1994 (47th ed.)	$9.95			$1	$4
1995 (48th ed.)	$10.95			$1	$4
1996 (49th ed.)	$10.95			$1	$4
1997 (50th ed.)	$11.95			$1	$4
1998 (51st ed.)	$11.95				$3
1999 (52nd ed.)	$11.95				$3
2000 (53rd ed.)	$12.95				$3
2001 (54th ed.)	$13.95				$3
2002 (55th ed.)	$14.95				$3
2003 (56th ed.)	$15.95				$2
2004 (57th ed.)	$15.95				$2
2005 (58th ed.)	$15.95				$2
2006 (59th ed.)	$16.95				$3
2007 (60th ed.)	$16.95				$3
2008 (61st ed.)	$16.95				$3
2009 (62nd ed.)	$16.95				$3
2010 (63rd ed.)	$16.95				$3
2011 (64th ed.)	$16.95				$2
2012 (65th ed.)	$16.95				$2
2013 (66th ed.)	$16.95				$2
2014 (67th ed.)	$16.95				$2
2015 (68th ed.)	$16.95				
2016 (69th ed.)	$16.95				

Note: Values are for unsigned books. Those signed by R.S. Yeoman are worth substantially more.

SOFTCOVERS (1993–2007)

The first softcover (trade paperback) Red Book was the 1993 (46th) edition. The softcover binding was offered (alongside other formats) in the 1993, 1994, 1995, and 1996 editions; again in the 1998 edition; and from 2003 through 2007. All are fairly common and easily collectible today. Values in New condition range from $2 up to $3–$4 for the earlier editions.

SPIRALBOUND SOFTCOVERS (1997 TO DATE)

The first spiralbound softcover Red Book was the 1997 (50th) edition. The spiralbound softcover format was next available in the 1999 edition, and it has been an annually offered format every edition since then. Today the spiralbound softcovers all are easily collectible. The 1997 edition is worth $4 in New condition, and later editions are valued around $2.

SPIRALBOUND HARDCOVERS (2008 TO DATE)

The first spiralbound hardcover Red Book was the 2008 (61st) edition. The format has been available (alongside other formats) every edition since. All spiralbound hardcovers are readily available to collectors, and are valued from $2 to $4.

JOURNAL EDITION (2009)

The large-sized Journal Edition, featuring a three-ring binder, color-coded tabbed dividers, and removable pages, was issued only for the 2009 (62nd) edition. Today it is valued at $5 in VF and $30 in New condition.

LARGE PRINT EDITIONS (2010 TO DATE)

The oversized Large Print format of the Red Book has been offered annually since the 2010 (63rd) edition. All editions are readily available to collectors and are valued at $5 in New condition.

LEATHER LIMITED EDITIONS (2005 TO DATE)

Year/Edition	Print Run	Issue Price	New
2005 (58th ed.)	3,000	$69.95	$75
2006 (59th ed.)	3,000	$69.95	$75
2007 (60th ed.)	3,000	$69.95	$100
2007 1947 Tribute Edition	500	$49.95	$135
2008 (61st ed.)	3,000	$69.95	$60
2008 (61st ed.), Numismatic Literary Guild (a)	135 (b)		$1,000
2008 (61st ed.), American Numismatic Society (c)	250 (b)		$750
2009 (62nd ed.)	3,000	$69.95	$75
2010 (63rd ed.)	1,500	$69.95	$75
2011 (64th ed.)	1,500	$69.95	$75
2012 (65th ed.)	1,000	$69.95	$80
2013 (66th ed.)	1,000	$69.95	$75
2014 (67th ed.)	1,000	$69.95	$75
2015 (68th ed.)	500	$99.95	$100
2016 (69th ed.)	500	$99.95	$100
2017 (70th ed.)	250	$99.95	

a. One hundred thirty-five imprinted copies of the 2008 leather Limited Edition were created. Of these, 125 were distributed to members of the NLG at its 2007 literary awards ceremony; the remaining 10 were distributed from Whitman Publishing headquarters in Atlanta. b. Included in total print-run quantity. c. Two hundred fifty copies of the 2008 leather Limited Edition were issued with a special bookplate honoring the 150th anniversary of the ANS. They were distributed to attendees of the January 2008 celebratory banquet in New York.

SPECIAL EDITIONS

Year/Edition	Print Run	Issue Price	VF	New
1987 (40th ed.), American Numismatic Association 95th Anniversary	500		$700	$1,400
1992 (45th ed.), American Numismatic Association 100th Anniversary	600		$150	$250
1997 (50th ed.), Red Book 50th Anniversary	1,200	$24.95	$50	$100
2002 (55th ed.), American Numismatic Association "Target 2001"	500	$100	$35	$50
2002 (55th ed.), SS Central America		$35	$25	$35
2005 (58th ed.), FUN (Florida United Numismatists) 50th Anniversary	1,100		$45	$100
2007 (60th ed.), American Numismatic Association 115th Anniversary	500		$50	$125
2007 (60th ed.), Michigan State Numismatic Society 50th Anniversary	500		$50	$125
2007 (1st ed.), 1947 Tribute Edition		$17.95	$5	$20
2008 (61st ed.), ANA Milwaukee World's Fair of Money	1,080		$30	$50
2008 (61st ed.), Stack's Rare Coins			$4	$18
2010 (63rd ed.), Hardcover, Philadelphia Expo (a)		$24.95	$18	$35
2011 (64th ed.), Boston Numismatic Society		$85	$50	$85
2012 (65th ed.), American Numismatic Association	800	$100	$25	$75
2013 (66th ed.), American Numismatic Society (b)	250		$75	$250
2015 (68th ed.), Central States Numismatic Society	500	$15		
2016 (69th ed.) American Numismatic Association 125th Anniversary				

a. Two thousand and nine copies of a special 2010 hardcover edition were made for distribution to dealers at the premiere Whitman Coin and Collectibles Philadelphia Expo (September 2009). Extra copies were sold at $50 apiece with proceeds benefiting the National Federation for the Blind. b. Two hundred fifty copies of the 2013 hardcover were issued with a special bookplate honoring ANS Trustees' Award recipient (and Red Book research contributor) Roger Siboni.

THE BLUE BOOK AS A COLLECTIBLE

The precursor to the Red Book was the *Handbook of United States Coins With Premium List*, popularly known as the "Blue Book." Its mastermind was R.S. Yeoman, who had been hired by Western Publishing as a commercial artist in 1932. He distributed Western's Whitman line of "penny boards" to coin collectors, promoting them through department stores, along with children's books and games. He eventually arranged for Whitman to expand the line into other denominations, giving them the reputation of a numismatic endeavor rather than a "game" of filling holes with missing coins. He also developed these flat boards into a line of popular folders.

Yeoman began to compile coin-mintage data and market values to aid collectors. This research grew into the Blue Book: now collectors had a coin-by-coin guide to the average prices dealers would pay for U.S. coins. The first two editions were both published in 1942.

In the first edition of the Red Book, Whitman Publishing would describe the Blue Book as "a low-priced standard reference book of United States coins and kindred issues" for which there had been "a long-felt need among American collectors."

The Blue Book has been published annually (except in 1944 and 1950) since its debut. Past editions offer valuable information about the hobby of yesteryear as well as developments in numismatic research and the marketplace. Old Blue Books are collectible; most editions after the 12th can be found for a few dollars in VF or better condition. Major variants were produced for the third, fourth, and ninth editions, including perhaps the only "overdate" books in American numismatic publishing. Either to conserve the previous years' covers or to correct an error in binding, the cloth on some third-edition covers was overstamped "Fourth Edition," and a number of eighth-edition covers were overstamped "Ninth Edition." The third edition was produced in several shades of blue ranging from light to dark. Some copies of the fourth edition were also produced in black cloth—the only time the Blue Book was bound in other than blue.

VALUATION GUIDE FOR SELECT PAST EDITIONS OF THE BLUE BOOK

Edition	Date (a)		VF	New
	Title Page	Copyright		
1st	1942	1942	$100	$460
2nd	1943	1942	$45	$75
3rd	1944	1943	$35	$85
4th	none	1945	$40	$85
5th	none	1946	$20	$35
6th	1948	1947	$15	$30
7th	1949	1948	$12	$25
8th	1950	1949	$10	$20
9th	1952	1951	$5	$10
10th	1953	1952	$5	$8
11th	1954	1953	$3	$7
12th	1955	1954	$3	$7

a. During its early years of production, the Blue Book's date presentation was not standardized. Full information is given here to aid in precise identification of early editions.

APPENDIX C

Bullion Values

These charts show the bullion values of silver and gold U.S. coins. These are intrinsic values and do not reflect any numismatic premium a coin might have. The weight listed under each denomination is its actual silver weight (ASW) or actual gold weight (AGW).

In recent years, the bullion price of silver has fluctuated considerably. You can use the following chart to determine the approximate bullion value of many 19th- and 20th-century silver coins at various price levels—or you can calculate the approximate value by multiplying the current spot price of silver by the ASW for each coin, as indicated. Dealers generally purchase common silver coins at around 15% below bullion value, and sell them at around 15% above bullion value.

Nearly all U.S. gold coins have an additional premium value beyond their bullion content, and thus are not subject to minor bullion-price variations. The premium amount is not necessarily tied to the bullion price of gold, but is usually determined by supply and demand levels in the numismatic market-place. Because these factors can vary significantly, there is no reliable formula for calculating "percentage below and above bullion" prices that would remain accurate over time. The gold chart lists bullion values based on AGW only; consult a coin dealer to ascertain current buy and sell prices.

BULLION VALUES OF SILVER COINS

Silver Price Per Ounce	Wartime Nickel .05626 oz.	Dime .07234 oz.	Quarter .18084 oz.	Half Dollar .36169 oz.	Silver Clad Half Dollar .14792 oz.	Silver Dollar .77344 oz.
$8.00	$0.45	$0.58	$1.45	$2.89	$1.18	$6.19
$8.50	$0.48	$0.61	$1.54	$3.07	$1.26	$6.57
$9.00	$0.51	$0.65	$1.63	$3.26	$1.33	$6.96
$9.50	$0.53	$0.69	$1.72	$3.44	$1.41	$7.35
$10.00	$0.56	$0.72	$1.81	$3.62	$1.48	$7.73
$10.50	$0.59	$0.76	$1.90	$3.80	$1.55	$8.12
$11.00	$0.62	$0.80	$1.99	$3.98	$1.63	$8.51
$11.50	$0.65	$0.83	$2.08	$4.16	$1.70	$8.89
$12.00	$0.68	$0.87	$2.17	$4.34	$1.78	$9.28
$12.50	$0.70	$0.90	$2.26	$4.52	$1.85	$9.67
$13.00	$0.73	$0.94	$2.35	$4.70	$1.92	$10.05
$13.50	$0.76	$0.98	$2.44	$4.88	$2.00	$10.44

Note: The U.S. bullion coins first issued in 1986 are unlike the older regular issues. They contain the following amounts of pure metal: silver $1, 1 oz.; gold $50, 1 oz.; gold $25, 1/2 oz.; gold $10, 1/4 oz.; gold $5, 1/10 oz.

Silver Price Per Ounce	Wartime Nickel .05626 oz.	Dime .07234 oz.	Quarter .18084 oz.	Half Dollar .36169 oz.	Silver Clad Half Dollar .14792 oz.	Silver Dollar .77344 oz.
$14.00	$0.79	$1.01	$2.53	$5.06	$2.07	$10.83
$14.50	$0.82	$1.05	$2.62	$5.24	$2.14	$11.21
$15.00	$0.84	$1.09	$2.71	$5.43	$2.22	$11.60
$15.50	$0.87	$1.12	$2.80	$5.61	$2.29	$11.99
$16.00	$0.90	$1.16	$2.89	$5.79	$2.37	$12.38
$16.50	$0.93	$1.19	$2.98	$5.97	$2.44	$12.76
$17.00	$0.96	$1.23	$3.07	$6.15	$2.51	$13.15
$17.50	$0.98	$1.27	$3.16	$6.33	$2.59	$13.54
$18.00	$1.01	$1.30	$3.26	$6.51	$2.66	$13.92
$18.50	$1.04	$1.34	$3.35	$6.69	$2.74	$14.31
$19.00	$1.07	$1.37	$3.44	$6.87	$2.81	$14.70
$19.50	$1.10	$1.41	$3.53	$7.05	$2.88	$15.08
$20.00	$1.13	$1.45	$3.62	$7.23	$2.96	$15.47
$20.50	$1.15	$1.48	$3.71	$7.41	$3.03	$15.86
$21.00	$1.18	$1.52	$3.80	$7.60	$3.11	$16.24
$21.50	$1.21	$1.56	$3.89	$7.78	$3.18	$16.63
$22.00	$1.24	$1.59	$3.98	$7.96	$3.25	$17.02
$22.50	$1.27	$1.63	$4.07	$8.14	$3.33	$17.40
$23.00	$1.29	$1.66	$4.16	$8.32	$3.40	$17.79
$23.50	$1.32	$1.70	$4.25	$8.50	$3.48	$18.18
$24.00	$1.35	$1.74	$4.34	$8.68	$3.55	$18.56
$24.50	$1.38	$1.77	$4.43	$8.86	$3.62	$18.95
$25.00	$1.41	$1.81	$4.52	$9.04	$3.70	$19.34
$25.50	$1.43	$1.84	$4.61	$9.22	$3.77	$19.72
$26.00	$1.46	$1.88	$4.70	$9.40	$3.85	$20.11
$26.50	$1.49	$1.92	$4.79	$9.58	$3.92	$20.50
$27.00	$1.52	$1.95	$4.88	$9.77	$3.99	$20.88
$27.50	$1.55	$1.99	$4.97	$9.95	$4.07	$21.27
$28.00	$1.58	$2.03	$5.06	$10.13	$4.14	$21.66
$28.50	$1.60	$2.06	$5.15	$10.31	$4.22	$22.04
$29.00	$1.63	$2.10	$5.24	$10.49	$4.29	$22.43
$29.50	$1.66	$2.13	$5.33	$10.67	$4.36	$22.82
$30.00	$1.69	$2.17	$5.43	$10.85	$4.44	$23.20
$30.50	$1.72	$2.21	$5.52	$11.03	$4.51	$23.59
$31.00	$1.74	$2.24	$5.61	$11.21	$4.59	$23.98
$31.50	$1.77	$2.28	$5.70	$11.39	$4.66	$24.36
$32.00	$1.80	$2.31	$5.79	$11.57	$4.73	$24.75
$32.50	$1.83	$2.35	$5.88	$11.75	$4.81	$25.14
$33.00	$1.86	$2.39	$5.97	$11.94	$4.88	$25.52
$33.50	$1.88	$2.42	$6.06	$12.12	$4.96	$25.91
$34.00	$1.91	$2.46	$6.15	$12.30	$5.03	$26.30
$34.50	$1.94	$2.50	$6.24	$12.48	$5.10	$26.68
$35.00	$1.97	$2.53	$6.33	$12.66	$5.18	$27.07
$35.50	$2.00	$2.57	$6.42	$12.84	$5.25	$27.46
$36.00	$2.03	$2.60	$6.51	$13.02	$5.33	$27.84
$36.50	$2.05	$2.64	$6.60	$13.20	$5.40	$28.23
$37.00	$2.08	$2.68	$6.69	$13.38	$5.47	$28.62
$37.50	$2.11	$2.71	$6.78	$13.56	$5.55	$29.00
$38.00	$2.14	$2.75	$6.87	$13.74	$5.62	$29.39

Note: The U.S. bullion coins first issued in 1986 are unlike the older regular issues. They contain the following amounts of pure metal: silver $1, 1 oz.; gold $50, 1 oz.; gold $25, 1/2 oz.; gold $10, 1/4 oz.; gold $5, 1/10 oz.

BULLION VALUES OF GOLD COINS

Gold Price Per Ounce	$5.00 Liberty Head 1839–1908 Indian Head 1908–1929 .24187 oz.	$10.00 Liberty Head 1838–1907 Indian Head 1907–1933 .48375 oz.	$20.00 1849–1933 .96750 oz.
$850	$205.59	$411.19	$822.38
$875	$211.64	$423.28	$846.56
$900	$217.68	$435.38	$870.75
$925	$223.73	$447.47	$894.94
$950	$229.78	$459.56	$919.13
$975	$235.82	$471.66	$943.31
$1,000	$241.87	$483.75	$967.50
$1,025	$247.92	$495.84	$991.69
$1,050	$253.96	$507.94	$1,015.88
$1,075	$260.01	$520.03	$1,040.06
$1,100	$266.06	$532.13	$1,064.25
$1,125	$272.10	$544.22	$1,088.44
$1,150	$278.15	$556.31	$1,112.63
$1,175	$284.20	$568.41	$1,136.81
$1,200	$290.24	$580.50	$1,161.00
$1,225	$296.29	$592.59	$1,185.19
$1,250	$302.34	$604.69	$1,209.38
$1,275	$308.38	$616.78	$1,233.56
$1,300	$314.43	$628.88	$1,257.75
$1,325	$320.48	$640.97	$1,281.94
$1,350	$326.52	$653.06	$1,306.13
$1,375	$332.57	$665.16	$1,330.31
$1,400	$338.62	$677.25	$1,354.50
$1,425	$344.66	$689.34	$1,378.69
$1,450	$350.71	$701.44	$1,402.88
$1,475	$356.76	$713.53	$1,427.06
$1,500	$362.81	$725.63	$1,451.25
$1,525	$368.85	$737.72	$1,475.44
$1,550	$374.90	$749.81	$1,499.63
$1,575	$380.95	$761.91	$1,523.81
$1,600	$386.99	$774.00	$1,548.00
$1,625	$393.04	$786.09	$1,572.19
$1,650	$399.09	$798.19	$1,596.38
$1,675	$405.13	$810.28	$1,620.56
$1,700	$411.18	$822.38	$1,644.75
$1,725	$417.23	$834.47	$1,668.94
$1,750	$423.27	$846.56	$1,693.13
$1,775	$429.32	$858.66	$1,717.31
$1,800	$435.37	$870.75	$1,741.50
$1,825	$441.41	$882.84	$1,765.69
$1,850	$447.46	$894.94	$1,789.88
$1,875	$453.51	$907.03	$1,814.06
$1,900	$459.55	$919.13	$1,838.25
$1,925	$465.60	$931.22	$1,862.44
$1,950	$471.65	$943.31	$1,886.63
$1,975	$477.69	$955.41	$1,910.81
$2,000	$483.74	$967.50	$1,935.00

Note: The U.S. bullion coins first issued in 1986 are unlike the older regular issues. They contain the following amounts of pure metal: silver $1, 1 oz.; gold $50, 1 oz.; gold $25, 1/2 oz.; gold $10, 1/4 oz.; gold $5, 1/10 oz.

APPENDIX D

Top 250 U.S. Coin Prices Realized at Auction

Rank	Price	Coin	Grade	Firm	Date
1	$10,016,875	$1(s), 1794, Silver Plug, B-1 BB-1	PCGS SP-66	Stack's Bowers	January 2013
2	$7,590,020	$20, 1933	Gem BU	Sotheby's/Stack's	July 2002
3	$4,993,750	$1(s), 1794	PCGS MS-66+	Sotheby's/Stack's Bowers	September 2015
4	$4,582,500	Prefed, 1787, Brasher dbln, EB on Wing	NGC MS-63	Heritage	January 2014
5	$4,140,000	$1(s), 1804, Class I	PCGS PF-68	B&M	August 1999
6	$3,877,500	$1(s), 1804, Class I	PCGS PF-62	Heritage	August 2013
7	$3,737,500	5¢, 1913, Liberty Head (A)	NGC PF-64	Heritage	January 2010
8	$3,737,500	$1(s), 1804, Class I	NGC PF-62	Heritage	April 2008
9	$3,290,000	5¢, 1913, Liberty Head (A)	NGC PF-64	Heritage	January 2014
10	$3,172,500	5¢, 1913, Liberty Head	PCGS PF-63	Heritage	April 2013
11	$2,990,000	Prefed, 1787, Brasher, EB on Breast (B)	NGC EF-45	Heritage	January 2005
12	$2,990,000	$20, MCMVII, Ultra HR, LE (C)	PCGS PF-69	Heritage	November 2005
13	$2,760,000	$20, MCMVII, Ultra HR, LE (C)	PCGS PF-69	Stack's Bowers	June 2012
14	$2,585,000	$10, 1795, 13 Leaves, BD-4	PCGS MS-66+	Sotheby's/Stack's Bowers	September 2015
15	$2,585,000	Pattern 1¢, 1792, Birch Cent, LE, J-4	NGC MS-65RB	Heritage	January 2015
16	$2,574,000	$4, 1880, Coiled Hair (D)	NGC PF-67Cam	Bonhams	September 2013
17	$2,415,000	Prefed, 1787, Brasher, EB on Wing	NGC AU-55	Heritage	January 2005
18	$2,350,000	$2.50, 1808	PCGS MS-65	Sotheby's/Stack's Bowers	May 2015
19	$2,350,000	1¢, 1793, Chain AMERICA, S-4	PCGS MS-66BN	Heritage	January 2015
20	$2,300,000	$1(s), 1804, Class III	PCGS PF-58	Heritage	April 2009
21	$2,232,500	Pattern 25¢, 1792, copper, J-12	NGC MS-63BN	Heritage	January 2015
22	$2,185,000	$10, 1907, Rounded Rim	NGC Satin PF-67	Heritage	January 2011
23	$2,115,000	$20, MCMVII, Ultra HR, LE	PCGS PF-68	Heritage	January 2015
24	$1,997,500	10¢, 1894-S	PCGS PF-66	Heritage	January 2016
25	$1,997,500	Pattern 1¢, 1792 Silver Center, J-1	PCGS MS-64BN	Heritage	August 2014
26	$1,997,500	$20, 1927-D	NGC MS-66	Heritage	January 2014
27	$1,897,500	$20, 1927-D	PCGS MS-67	Heritage	November 2005
28	$1,880,000	$1(s), 1804, Class III	NGC PF-55	Stack's Bowers	August 2014
29	$1,840,000	10¢, 1873-CC, No Arrows	PCGS MS-65	Stack's Bowers	August 2012
30	$1,840,000	5¢, 1913, Liberty Head	NGC PF-66	Superior	March 2008
31	$1,840,000	$20, MCMVII, Ultra HR, LE	PCGS PF-68	Heritage	January 2007
32	$1,840,000	$1(s), 1804, Class I (E)	PCGS PF-64	Stack's	October 2000

Rank	Price	Coin	Grade	Firm	Date
33	$1,821,250	$4, 1880, Coiled Hair	NGC PF-67	Heritage	April 2015
34	$1,815,000	$1(s), 1804, Class I	PF-63	B&M/Stack's	April 1997
35	$1,725,000	$2.50, 1796, No Stars (F)	PCGS MS-65	Heritage	January 2008
36	$1,725,000	$10, 1920-S	PCGS MS-67	Heritage	March 2007
37	$1,645,000	$20, 1861, Paquet Reverse (G)	PCGS MS-61	Heritage	August 2014
38	$1,610,000	$10, 1839/8, Type of 1838, Lg Letters (H)	NGC PF-67UCam	Heritage	January 2007
39	$1,610,000	$20, 1861, Paquet Reverse (G)	PCGS MS-61	Heritage	August 2006
40	$1,552,500	10¢, 1894-S	PCGS PF-64	Stack's	October 2007
41	$1,527,500	25¢, 1796, B-2	PCGS MS-66	Sotheby's/Stack's Bowers	May 2015
42	$1,527,500	50¢, 1797, O-101a	PCGS MS-66	Sotheby's/Stack's Bowers	May 2015
43	$1,527,500	Prefed, 1776, Cont. $1 Silver, N-3D	NGC MS-62	Heritage	January 2015
44	$1,527,500	Prefed, 1776, Cont. $1 Silver, N-1C	NGC EF-40	Heritage	January 2015
45	$1,527,500	25¢, 1796, B-2	NGC MS-67+	Heritage	November 2013
46	$1,495,000	$20, 1927-D	PCGS MS-66	Heritage	January 2010
47	$1,495,000	$20, 1921	PCGS MS-63	B&M	August 2006
48	$1,485,000	5¢, 1913, Liberty Head	Gem PF-66	B&M/Stack's	May 1996
49	$1,437,500	$20, 1856-O	NGC SP-63	Heritage	May 2009
50	$1,410,000	Prefed, 1776, Cont. $1 Silver, N-3D	NGC MS-63	Heritage	May 2014
51	$1,410,000	Pattern 1¢, 1792, Silver Center, J-1	NGC MS-63BN+	Heritage	May 2014
52	$1,410,000	Pattern half disme, 1792, J-7 (I)	PCGS SP-67	Heritage	January 2013
53	$1,380,000	$5, 1829, Large Date	PCGS PF-64	Heritage	January 2012
54	$1,380,000	1¢, 1793, Chain AMERICA, S-4	PCGS MS-65BN	Heritage	January 2012
55	$1,380,000	50¢, 1797, O-101a (J)	NGC MS-66	Stack's	July 2008
56	$1,380,000	$2.50, 1796, No Stars (F)	PCGS MS-65	Stack's (ANR)	June 2005
57	$1,322,500	$3, 1855-S	NGC PF-64Cam	Heritage	August 2011
58	$1,322,500	Pattern half disme, 1792, J-7 (I)	PCGS SP-67	Heritage	April 2006
59	$1,322,500	$20, 1927-D	NGC MS-65	Heritage	January 2006
60	$1,322,500	10¢, 1894-S	NGC PF-66	DLRC	March 2005
61	$1,292,500	Pattern half disme, 1792, J-7 (I)	PCGS SP-67	Heritage	August 2014
62	$1,292,500	50¢, 1797, O-101a	PCGS MS-65+	Heritage	August 2014
63	$1,265,000	Pattern $10, 1874, Bickford, J-1373	PCGS PF-65DCam	Heritage	January 2010
64	$1,265,000	1¢, 1795, Reeded Edge, S-79 (K)	PCGS VG-10	Goldberg	September 2009
65	$1,265,000	$1(s), 1795, Flowing Hair, B-7, BB-18	V Ch Gem MS	Bullowa	December 2005
66	$1,210,000	$20, MCMVII, Ultra HR, LE (L)	PCGS PF-67	Goldberg	May 1999
67	$1,207,500	$1(s), 1794	NGC MS-64	B&M	August 2010
68	$1,207,500	$1(s), 1866, No Motto	NGC PF-63	Stack's (ANR)	January 2005
69	$1,207,500	$1(s), 1804, Class III (M)	PCGS PF-58	B&M	July 2003
70	$1,175,000	$5, 1798, Small Eagle, BD-1	PCGS AU-55	Sotheby's/Stack's Bowers	September 2015
71	$1,175,000	Pattern 1¢, 1792, Birch Cent, LE, J-4	PCGS AU-58	Stack's Bowers	March 2015
72	$1,175,000	Prefed, 1783, quint, T-II, Nova Const.	PCGS AU-53	Heritage	April 2013
73	$1,175,000	$1(s), 1796, Sm Dt, Sm Ltrs, B-2,BB-63	NGC MS-65	Heritage	April 2013
74	$1,150,000	1/2¢, 1794, C-7	PCGS MS-67RB	Goldberg	January 2014
75	$1,150,000	Pattern 1¢, 1792, Silver Center Cent, J-1	PCGS MS-61BN	Heritage	April 2012
76	$1,150,000	$1(s), 1794	NGC MS-64	Stack's (ANR)	June 2005
77	$1,145,625	Pattern half disme, 1792, J-7	NGC MS-68	Stack's Bowers	January 2013
78	$1,121,250	1/2¢, 1811, C-1	PCGS MS-66RB	Goldberg	January 2014
79	$1,116,250	$4, 1880, Coiled Hair	PCGS PF-65	Heritage	June 2015
80	$1,092,500	$20, 1921	PCGS MS-66	Heritage	November 2005
81	$1,092,500	$1(s), 1870-S	BU PL	Stack's	May 2003
82	$1,057,500	$10, 1795, 9 Leaves, BD-3	PCGS MS-63+	Sotheby's/Stack's Bowers	September 2015
83	$1,057,500	Pattern disme, 1792, copper, J-11	NGC MS-64RB	Heritage	January 2015
84	$1,057,500	Terr, 1852, Humbert, $10, K-10	NGC MS-68	Heritage	April 2013

Rank	Price	Coin	Grade	Firm	Date
85	$1,057,500	$20, MCMVII, Ultra HR, LE of 06	PCGS PF-58	Heritage	August 2012
86	$1,041,300	$4, 1879, Coiled Hair (N)	NGC PF-67Cam	Bonhams	September 2013
87	$1,035,000	10¢, 1894-S	PCGS PF-65	Heritage	January 2005
88	$1,012,000	$20, 1921 (O)	PCGS MS-65 PQ	Goldberg	September 2007
89	$1,006,250	$2.50, 1796, Stars, Bass-3003, BD-3 (P)	NGC MS-65	Heritage	January 2008
90	$1,006,250	$1 Trade, 1885	NGC PF-62	DLRC	November 2004
91	$998,750	Pattern disme, 1792, J-9	NGC AU-50	Heritage	January 2015
92	$998,750	$1 Trade, 1884	PCGS PF-65	Heritage	January 2014
93	$998,750	1¢, 1793, Chain, S-2	PCGS MS-65BN	Stack's Bowers	January 2013
94	$990,000	$1(s), 1804, Class I (E)	Choice Proof	Rarcoa	July 1989
95	$977,500	1¢, 1799, S-189	NGC MS-62BN	Goldberg	September 2009
96	$977,500	$4, 1880, Coiled Hair (D)	NGC PF-66Cam	Heritage	January 2005
97	$977,500	$5, 1833, Large Date	PCGS PF-67	Heritage	January 2005
98	$966,000	50¢, 1797, O-101a (J)	NGC MS-66	Stack's (ANR)	March 2004
99	$962,500	5¢, 1913, Liberty Head	Proof	Stack's	October 1993
100	$959,400	$4, 1880, Flowing Hair	NGC PF-67	Bonhams	September 2013
101	$948,750	Terr, 1852, Moffat & Co., $10, Wide Date, K-9	PCGS SP-67	Stack's (ANR)	August 2006
102	$940,000	Terr, 1852, Moffat & Co., $10, Wide Date, K-9	PCGS SP-63	Heritage	January 2014
103	$920,000	1/2¢, 1793, C-4	PCGS MS-66BN	Goldberg	January 2014
104	$920,000	$1(s), 1802, Restrike	PCGS PF-65Cam	Heritage	April 2008
105	$920,000	$20, 1907, Small Edge Letters	PCGS PF-68	Heritage	November 2005
106	$920,000	$1 Trade, 1885	NGC PF-61	Stack's	May 2003
107	$910,625	$1(s), 1795, Draped, Off-Ctr, B-14, BB-51	NGC MS-66+	Heritage	November 2013
108	$907,500	$1 Trade, 1885	Gem PF-65	B&M/Stack's	April 1997
109	$891,250	1/2¢, 1796, No Pole, C-1	PCGS MS-65BN	Goldberg	January 2014
110	$891,250	10¢, 1873-CC, No Arrows (Q)	NGC MS-65	B&M	July 2004
111	$881,250	$4, 1879, Coiled Hair	PCGS PF-65	Heritage	April 2015
112	$881,250	Confed, 1861, Original 50¢	NGC PF-30	Heritage	January 2015
113	$881,250	25¢, 1796, B-1	PCGS SP-66	Heritage	August 2014
114	$881,250	$10, 1795, BD-5	PCGS MS-65	Heritage	August 2014
115	$881,250	10¢, 1796, JR-1	PCGS MS-67	Heritage	June 2014
116	$881,250	$1(s), 1889-CC	PCGS MS-68	Stack's Bowers	August 2013
117	$881,250	1¢, 1794, Head of 93, S-18b	PCGS MS-64BN	Stack's Bowers	January 2013
118	$874,000	$1(s), 1804, Class III (M)	PCGS PF-58	B&M	November 2001
119	$862,500	1¢, 1793, Strawberry Leaf, NC-3	NGC F-12	Stack's	January 2009
120	$862,500	Pattern $4, 1879, Quintuple Stella, J-1643, P-1843	PCGS PF-62	Heritage	January 2007
121	$862,500	$2.50, 1796, Stars, Bass-3003, BD-3 (P)	NGC MS-65	Heritage	January 2007
122	$851,875	$4, 1879, Coiled Hair	PCGS PF-66	Heritage	January 2014
123	$851,875	$1(s), 1803, Restrike	PCGS PF-66	Heritage	January 2013
124	$851,875	$1(s), 1802, Restrike	PCGS PF-65Cam	Heritage	August 2012
125	$825,000	$20, MCMVII, Ultra HR, LE	Proof	Sotheby's	December 1996
126	$824,850	Pattern half disme, 1792, copper, J-8	NGC AU-55	Heritage	January 2015
127	$822,500	$1(s), 1795, Flowing Hair, B-7, BB-18	PCGS MS-66	Sotheby's/Stack's Bowers	September 2015
128	$822,500	50¢, 1796, 16 Stars, O-102	PCGS MS-66	Sotheby's/Stack's Bowers	May 2015
129	$822,500	$2.50, 1796, No Stars, BD-2	PCGS MS-62	Sotheby's/Stack's Bowers	May 2015
130	$822,500	$10, 1933	PCGS MS-65	Heritage	April 2015
131	$822,500	$1(s), 1795, Flowing Hair, B-2, BB-20	NGC SP-64	Stack's Bowers	August 2014
132	$822,500	$1(s), 1799, B-5, BB-157	NGC MS-67	Heritage	November 2013
133	$822,500	Pattern 1¢, 1792, Silver Center Cent, J-1 (R)	NGC MS-61BN+	Heritage	April 2013
134	$805,000	$1(s), 1870-S	NGC EF-40	Heritage	April 2008
135	$805,000	$20, 1921	PCGS MS-65	Heritage	November 2005
136	$793,125	10¢, 1796, JR-6	PCGS MS-68	Heritage	August 2014

Rank	Price	Coin	Grade	Firm	Date
137	$793,125	Pattern half disme, 1792, J-7	PCGS MS-66	Stack's Bowers	August 2013
138	$763,750	50¢, 1794, O-101a	PCGS MS-64	Sotheby's/Stack's Bowers	May 2015
139	$763,750	$2.50, 1798, BD-1	PCGS MS-65	Sotheby's/Stack's Bowers	May 2015
140	$763,750	Terr, 1849, Pacific Company, $5, K-1	PCGS AU-58	Heritage	April 2014
141	$763,750	Terr, 1855, Kellogg & Co., $50	PCGS PF-64Cam	Heritage	April 2014
142	$763,750	50¢, 1838-O	NGC PF-64	Heritage	January 2014
143	$763,750	$1(s), 1870-S	PCGS EF-40	Heritage	January 2014
144	$763,750	$5, 1826, BD-2 **(S)**	PCGS MS-66	Heritage	January 2014
145	$747,500	1¢, 1793, Chain, S-3	NGC MS-66BN	Stack's Bowers	August 2012
146	$747,500	$20, 1921	PCGS MS-66	Heritage	January 2012
147	$747,500	Terr, 1855, Kellogg & Co., $50	PCGS PF-64	Heritage	January 2007
148	$747,500	$1(s), 1794	NGC MS-61	Heritage	June 2005
149	$734,375	50¢, 1838-O	PCGS PF-64	Heritage	January 2013
150	$725,000	Prefed, 1787, Brasher, EB on Wing	MS-63	B&R	November 1979
151	$718,750	1/2¢, 1793, C-3	PCGS MS-65BN	Goldberg	January 2014
152	$718,750	1/2¢, 1796, With Pole, C-2	PCGS MS-65RB+	Goldberg	January 2014
153	$718,750	$10, 1933	Unc	Stack's	October 2004
154	$705,698	$1(s), 1870-S	VF-25	B&M	February 2008
155	$705,000	$1(s), 1795, Flowing Hair, B-7, BB-18	PCGS MS-65+	Sotheby's/Stack's Bowers	September 2015
156	$705,000	$10, 1798/7, 7x6 Stars, BD-2	PCGS MS-61	Sotheby's/Stack's Bowers	September 2015
157	$705,000	25¢, 1827, Original	PCGS PF-66Cam+	Sotheby's/Stack's Bowers	May 2015
158	$705,000	50¢, 1794, O-109	NGC VF-25	Heritage	April 2015
159	$705,000	Pattern 1¢, 1792, Silver Center Cent, J-1 **(R)**	NGC MS-61BN+	Heritage	September 2014
160	$705,000	Prefed, 1783, Nova Const., PE Bit, W-1820	NGC AU-55	Heritage	May 2014
161	$705,000	Terr, 1849, Morman, $10, K-3	NGC AU-58	Heritage	April 2014
162	$705,000	$1(s), 1803, Large 3, B-6, BB-255	NGC MS-65+	Heritage	November 2013
163	$690,300	$5, 1836	NGC PF-67UCam	Bonhams	September 2013
164	$690,000	$5, 1909-O **(T)**	PCGS MS-66	Heritage	January 2011
165	$690,000	1¢, 1796, Liberty Cap, S-84	PCGS MS-66RB	Goldberg	September 2008
166	$690,000	Pattern disme, 1792, copper, RE, J-10 **(U)**	NGC PF-62BN	Heritage	July 2008
167	$690,000	$5, 1825, 5 Over 4	NGC AU-50	Heritage	July 2008
168	$690,000	$20, MCMVII, Ultra HR, LE of 06	NGC PF-58	Stack's	July 2008
169	$690,000	Terr, 1860, Clark, Gruber & Co., $20	NGC MS-64	Heritage	January 2006
170	$690,000	Prefed, 1742 (1786), Lima Brasher	NGC EF-40	Heritage	January 2005
171	$690,000	$5, 1835	PCGS PF-67	Heritage	January 2005
172	$690,000	$1(g), 1849-C, Open Wreath	NGC MS-63 PL	DLRC	July 2004
173	$690,000	$20, MCMVII, Ultra HR, LE	Proof	Sotheby's/Stack's	October 2001
174	$690,000	$10, 1839, 9/8, Type of 1838, Lg Letters **(H)**	NGC PF-67	Goldberg	September 1999
175	$687,500	$3, 1870-S	EF-40	B&R	October 1982
176	$687,500	$5, 1822	VF-30/EF-40	B&R	October 1982
177	$675,525	$10, 1795, BD-5	NGC MS-65	Heritage	August 2013
178	$672,750	$1(s), 1803, Restrike	PF-66	B&M	February 2007
179	$661,250	1¢, 1804, S-266c	PCGS MS-63BN	Goldberg	September 2009
180	$661,250	1/2 dime, 1870-S	NGC MS-63 PL	B&M	July 2004
181	$660,000	$20, MCMVII, Ultra HR, LE **(L)**	PF-67	B&M	January 1997
182	$660,000	$20, 1861, Paquet Reverse	MS-67	B&M	November 1988
183	$655,500	$4, 1879, Coiled Hair **(N)**	NGC PF-67Cam	Heritage	January 2005
184	$655,200	$20, 1891	NGC PF-68UCam	Bonhams	September 2013
185	$646,250	$5, 1795, Small Eagle, BD-3	PCGS MS-65	Sotheby's/Stack's Bowers	September 2015
186	$646,250	50¢, 1838-O	NGC PF-64	Heritage	May 2015
187	$646,250	Confed, 1861, Original 50¢	NGC EF-40	Stack's Bowers	March 2015
188	$646,250	$1(s), 1893-S	PCGS MS-65	Legend	October 2014

Rank	Price	Coin	Grade	Firm	Date
189	$646,250	Prefed, (1652), NE 6 Pence, N-1-A, S-1-A	NGC AU-58	Heritage	May 2014
190	$646,250	Terr, 1851, Baldwin & Co., $20, K-5	PCGS EF-45	Heritage	April 2014
191	$646,250	1¢, 1795, Reeded Edge, S-79 (K)	PCGS VG-10	Heritage	January 2014
192	$646,250	$5, 1909-O (T)	PCGS MS-66	Heritage	January 2014
193	$646,250	$1(s), 1795, 3 Leaves, B-5, BB-27	NGC MS-65	Heritage	November 2013
194	$646,250	$4, 1879, Coiled Hair	PCGS PF-64Cam	Stack's Bowers	May 2013
195	$632,500	$5, 1828, 8 Over 7	NGC MS-64	Heritage	January 2012
196	$632,500	$1(s), 1870-S	PCGS EF-40	B&M	August 2010
197	$632,500	10¢, 1804, 14 Star Reverse, JR-2	NGC AU-58	Heritage	July 2008
198	$632,500	1¢, 1793, Liberty Cap, S-13, B-20	PCGS AU-55	Heritage	February 2008
199	$632,500	1¢, 1794, Starred Reverse, S-48, B-38	PCGS AU-50	Heritage	February 2008
200	$632,500	50¢, 1838-O	PCGS PF-63 BM	Heritage	February 2008
201	$632,500	Prefed, 1652, Willow Tree Threepence, N-1A	VF	Stack's	October 2005
202	$632,500	50¢, 1838-O	PCGS PF-64 BM	Heritage	June 2005
203	$632,500	Confed, 1861, Original 50¢	VF	Stack's	October 2003
204	$632,500	10¢, 1873-CC, No Arrows (Q)	PCGS MS-64	Heritage	April 1999
205	$625,000	Prefed, 1787, Brasher, EB on Breast (B)	VF	B&R	March 1981
206	$618,125	$4, 1880, Coiled Hair	NGC PF-63	Superior	July 2005
207	$605,000	$2.50, 1796, No Stars	Choice BU	Stack's	November 1995
208	$603,750	1/2¢, 1852, Large Berries	PCGS PF-65RD	Goldberg	January 2014
209	$603,750	$20, 1854-O	PCGS AU-55	Heritage	October 2008
210	$603,750	Pattern 1¢, 1792, No Silver Center Cent, J-2	PCGS VF-30	Heritage	January 2008
211	$603,750	$1 Trade, 1884	PCGS PF-65	Heritage	November 2005
212	$587,500	$1(s), 1901	PCGS MS-66	Legend	October 2015
213	$587,500	$10, 1933	PCGS MS-65	Heritage	June 2015
214	$587,500	50¢, 1796, 15 Stars, O-101	PCGS SP-63	Sotheby's/Stack's Bowers	May 2015
215	$587,500	$2.50, 1807, BD-1	PCGS MS-65	Sotheby's/Stack's Bowers	May 2015
216	$587,500	Prefed, 1652, Willow Tree Threepence, N-1A	PCGS AU-50	Stack's Bowers	March 2015
217	$587,500	$5, 1795, Small Eagle, BD-1	NGC MS-66	Heritage	January 2015
218	$587,500	Pattern disme, 1792, copper, RE, J-10 (U)	NGC PF-62BN	Heritage	October 2012
219	$587,500	$20, 1921 (O)	PCGS MS-65	Heritage	August 2012
220	$586,500	$5, 1795, Small Eagle, BD-1	PCGS MS-65	Stack's	June 2008
221	$583,000	$5, 1795, Small Eagle	NGC MS-65 PL	Bullowa	January 2007
222	$577,500	$20, 1927-D	PCGS MS-65	Akers	May 1998
223	$577,500	$1(s), 1794	Gem BU	Stack's	November 1995
224	$576,150	$20, 1856-O	NGC AU-58	Heritage	October 2008
225	$575,000	$20, 1920-S	PCGS MS-66	Heritage	January 2012
226	$575,000	$1(s), 1794	PCGS AU-58 PQ	Goldberg	May 2011
227	$575,000	$4, 1880, Coiled Hair	NGC PF-62	Heritage	January 2009
228	$575,000	Pattern $50, 1877, copper, J-1549	NGC PF-67BN	Heritage	January 2009
229	$575,000	$1(s), 1895-O	PCGS MS-67	Heritage	November 2005
230	$575,000	$20, MCMVII, HR, WR	PCGS MS-69	Heritage	November 2005
231	$575,000	$20, 1927-D	NGC MS-62	DLRC	July 2004
232	$573,300	$20, MCMVII, HR, WR	NGC PF-69	Bonhams	September 2013
233	$564,000	Pattern 1¢, 1792, Birch Cent, LE, J-5	NGC MS-61BN	Heritage	January 2015
234	$564,000	$5, 1826, BD-2 (S)	PCGS MS-66	Heritage	January 2015
235	$564,000	20¢, 1876-CC	PCGS MS-65	Stack's Bowers	January 2013
236	$558,125	$2.50, 1821, BC-1	PCGS MS-66+	Sotheby's/Stack's Bowers	September 2015
237	$558,125	Terr, 1849, Morman, $20, K-4	NGC MS-62	Heritage	April 2014
238	$558,125	Terr, 1855, Wass, Molitor & Co., $20 Lg. Head	NGC AU-53	Heritage	April 2014
239	$558,125	1¢, 1793, Wreath, S-9	PCGS MS-69BN	Stack's Bowers	January 2013
240	$552,000	$10, 1933	PCGS MS-65	Heritage	January 2008

Rank	Price	Coin	Grade	Firm	Date
241	$552,000	$1(s), 1870-S	VF-20	Stack's	October 2007
242	$550,000	$10, 1838	Choice Proof	Akers	May 1998
243	$550,000	10¢, 1873-CC, No Arrows **(Q)**	Gem MS-65	B&M/Stack's	May 1996
244	$550,000	25¢, 1901-S	NGC MS-68	Superior	May 1990
245	$546,250	Prefed, 1776, Cont. $1, pewter, N-3D	NGC MS-67	Heritage	January 2012
246	$546,250	$1(s), 1893-S	NGC MS-67	Heritage	August 2011
247	$546,250	Terr, 1851, Humb't, $50, 880 Thous., No 50 on Rev	PCGS MS-63	Heritage	August 2010
248	$546,250	$4, 1880, Coiled Hair	NGC PF-62	Heritage	July 2009
249	$546,250	$10, 1795, 13 Leaves, BD-1, T-1	PCGS MS-64	Stack's	July 2008
250	$546,250	$10, 1933	PCGS MS-65	Heritage	January 2007

KEY

Price: The sale price of the coin, including the appropriate buyer's fee.

Coin: The denomination/classification, date, and description of the coin, along with pertinent catalog or reference numbers. B = Baker (for pre-federal), Bolender (for silver dollars), Breen (for gold), or Browning (for quarter dollars); BB = Bowers/Borckardt; BD = Bass-Dannreuther; Confed = Confederate States of America issue; dbln = doubloon; HR = High Relief; J = Judd; JR = John Reich Society; LE = Lettered Edge; N = Newman; NC = Non-Collectible; O = Overton; P = Pollock; Pattern = a pattern, experimental, or trial piece; Prefed = pre-federal issue; S = Sheldon; T = Taraskza; Terr = territorial issue. Letters in parentheses, **(A)** through **(U)**, denote instances in which multiple sales of the same coin rank within the Top 250.

Grade: The grade of the coin, plus the name of the grading firm (if independently graded). BM = branch mint; NGC = Numismatic Guaranty Corporation of America; PCGS = Professional Coin Grading Service; PQ = premium quality.

Firm: The auction firm (or firms) that sold the coin. ANR = American Numismatic Rarities; B&R = Bowers & Ruddy; DLRC = David Lawrence Rare Coins; Stack's Bowers = Stack's Bowers Galleries (name under which Stack's and B&M merged in 2010; also encompasses the merger of Stack's and ANR in 2006).

Date: The month and year of the auction.

Auction records compiled and edited by P. Scott Rubin.

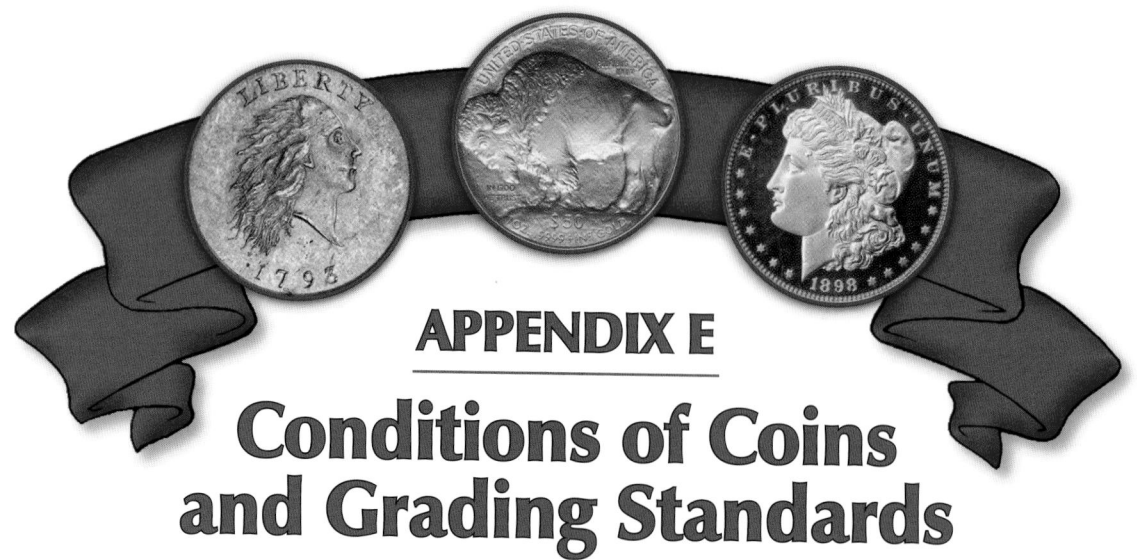

APPENDIX E

Conditions of Coins and Grading Standards

ESSENTIAL ELEMENTS OF THE AMERICAN NUMISMATIC ASSOCIATION GRADING STANDARDS

Proof—A specially made coin distinguished by sharpness of detail and usually with a brilliant, mirrorlike surface. *Proof* refers to the method of manufacture and is not a grade. The term implies superior condition unless otherwise noted.

> **Gem Proof (PF-65)**—Surfaces are brilliant, with no noticeable blemishes or flaws. A few scattered, barely noticeable marks or hairlines.

> **Choice Proof (PF-63)**—Surfaces are reflective, with only a few blemishes in secondary focal places. No major flaws.

> **Proof (PF-60)**—Surfaces may have several contact marks, hairlines, or light rubs. Luster may be dull and eye appeal lacking.

Mint State—The terms *Mint State (MS)* and *Uncirculated (Unc.)* are interchangeable and refer to coins showing no trace of wear from circulation. Such coins may vary slightly because of minor surface imperfections, as described in the following subdivisions:

> **Perfect Uncirculated (MS-70)**—Perfect new condition, showing no trace of wear. The finest quality possible, with no evidence of scratches, handling, or contact with other coins. Very few circulation-issue coins are ever found in this condition.

> **Gem Uncirculated (MS-65)**—An above-average Uncirculated coin that may be brilliant or lightly toned and that has very few contact marks on the surface or rim.

> **Choice Uncirculated (MS-63)**—A coin with some distracting contact marks or blemishes in prime focal areas. Luster may be impaired.

> **Uncirculated (MS-60)**—A coin that has no trace of wear, but which may show a number of marks from contact with other coins during minting, storage, or transportation, and whose surface may be spotted or lack some luster.

Choice About Uncirculated (AU-55)—Evidence of friction on high points of design. Most of the mint luster remains.

About Uncirculated (AU-50)—Traces of light wear on many of the high points. At least half of the mint luster is still present.

Choice Extremely Fine (EF-45)—Light overall wear on the highest points. All design details are very sharp. Some of the mint luster is evident.

Extremely Fine (EF-40)—Light wear on the design throughout, but all features are sharp and well defined. Traces of luster may show.

Choice Very Fine (VF-30)—Light, even wear on the surface and highest parts of the design. All lettering and major features are sharp.

Very Fine (VF-20)—Moderate wear on design high points. All major details are clear.

Fine (F-12)—Moderate to considerable even wear. The entire design is bold with an overall pleasing appearance.

Very Good (VG-8)—Well worn with main features clear and bold, although rather flat.

Good (G-4)—Heavily worn, with the design visible but faint in areas. Many details are flat.

About Good (AG-3)—Very heavily worn with portions of the lettering, date, and legend worn smooth. The date may be barely readable.

Important: Undamaged coins are worth more than bent, corroded, scratched, holed, nicked, stained, or mutilated ones. Flawless Uncirculated coins are generally worth more than values quoted in this book. Slightly worn coins ("sliders") that have been cleaned and conditioned ("buffed") to simulate Uncirculated luster are worth considerably less than perfect pieces.

Unlike damage inflicted after striking, manufacturing defects do not always lessen values. Examples include colonial coins with planchet flaws or weakly struck designs; early silver or gold coins with weight-adjustment "file marks" (parallel cuts made on the planchet prior to striking); and coins with "lint marks" (surface marks due to the presence of dust or other foreign matter during striking).

Note that while grading *standards* strive to be precise, interpretations are subjective and can vary among collectors, dealers, and certification services.

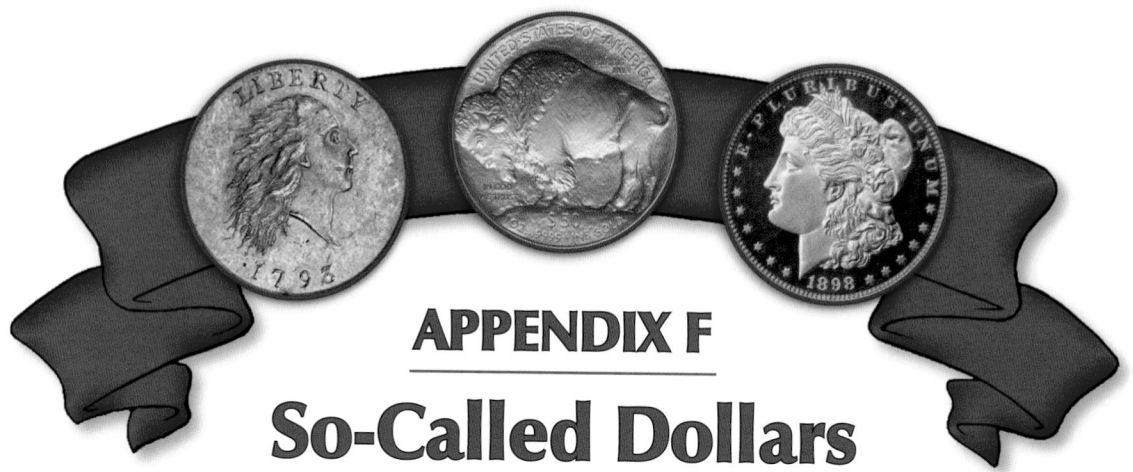

APPENDIX F

So-Called Dollars

The contents of this section are based on the work and research of Jeff Shevlin.

AN OVERVIEW OF SO-CALLED DOLLARS

So-Called Dollars are U.S. medals approximately the size of a silver dollar that were struck to commemorate a historical subject. A collection of So-Called Dollars is strikingly different from a typical collection of U.S. coins assembled by date and mintmark, in that each piece in the collection has a uniquely different design. There are more than 750 different design types, and when different metal compositions are considered, there are more than 1,500 varieties to consider collecting. So-Called Dollars were struck in virtually every metal composition conceivable, including gold, silver, copper, bronze, brass, aluminum, nickel, white metal, German silver, gutta-percha, gold-plated, and silver-plated.

These collectibles were cataloged in the illustrated standard reference book *So-Called Dollars*, authored by Harold Hibler and Charles Kappen and published in 1963. This book, which is widely considered as the most definitive reference on So-Called Dollars, was revised and edited by Tom Hoffman, Dave Hayes, Jonathan Brecher, and John Dean in 2008.

So-Called Dollars were struck by the U.S. Mint as well as by private mints (and one was struck by the Manila Mint while the Philippines was an American territory). Many of the most famous engravers of U.S. coins also engraved So-Called Dollars, including William and Charles Barber, George T. Morgan, Augustus Saint-Gaudens, and others. Some of the designs and artwork on these pieces match or surpass these artists' other work in coin and medal design.

Historical medals come in all sizes. To be classified as a So-Called Dollar one must be approximately the size of a silver dollar, between 33 and 45 mm in diameter (a silver dollar is 38.1 mm), although collectors traditionally include a few specific exceptions such as the 1939 Charbneau medals (see the gallery, which follows).

From national events and celebrations to local anniversaries, from great successes to major disasters, bits and pieces of the history of the United States are chronologically depicted on these fascinating historical medals.

About half of the So-Called Dollars are related to a Fair or Exposition with the other half commemorating important events in U.S. history. Expositions played a significant part in the development of the United States. Local communities, often with federal funding support, would begin to plan years ahead of time and build enormous halls and buildings for their expositions, which would last anywhere from a few months to a few years. Millions of people would travel to attend these grand events and see things they had never seen before, often visiting for days, sometimes weeks.

Throngs of tourists entering the Electrical Building at the World's Columbian Exposition.

When the city of Chicago hosted the World's Columbian Exposition in 1893, its population was slightly greater than a million people. More than five years were spent in the exposition's planning and construction on a 700-acre site on the shore of Lake Michigan. President Benjamin Harrison invited all of the nations of the earth to take part by sending exhibits that most fully illustrated their resources, their industries, and their progress in civilization. Every state and territory of the United States and more than 50 foreign countries were represented, many erecting their own buildings. Exhibits exceeded 50,000, including one set up by the U.S. Mint. Attendance at the exposition was 27,500,000, and by the end of the 1890s Chicago's population had grown to 1,700,000, making it one of the fastest-growing cities in the history of mankind and the fifth or sixth largest city in the world. More than 100 So-Called Dollars were struck commemorating the World's Columbian Exposition, its events, and its structures—the last remaining of which, originally called the "Palace of Fine Arts," now serves as Chicago's Museum of Science and Industry.

When Philadelphia hosted the Centennial Exposition in 1876, the first United States International Exhibition of the arts, manufacturers, and products, the country was showing the world the progress it had made in the past 100 years. The United States was, for the first time being recognized as one of the leading nations in the world. Until then, the young nation had focused on material problems, with art playing a less significant part in American life. Approximately 10,000,000 people attended the exposition and were not only exposed to the latest machines, mechanical progress, and industrial expansion, but also electrified by displays of art by the world's greatest artists throughout time. After the exposition numerous art schools and societies were formed, and there was a rush of American students to art schools in Paris. The impact on the emphasis for the arts in American culture was dramatic and everlasting. There are close to 50 different So-Called Dollars related to the 1876 Centennial Exposition.

The U.S. Mint had a presence at many of the expositions, often setting up presses and striking souvenir medals to sell to the attendees. The medals produced by the Mint were always designated as the official exposition medal and were usually struck in a variety of metals including silver.

Outside of fairs and expositions, the other half of the series of So-Called Dollars covers a broad range of topics. From the completion of the Erie Canal in 1826 and the completion of the first Transcontinental Railroad in 1869 through the centennial of the Pony Express in 1961, So-Called Dollars celebrate and remember hundreds of national, regional, and local events.

FOR THE COLLECTOR AND INVESTOR: SO-CALLED DOLLARS AS A SPECIALTY

So-Called Dollars as a specialty can be exciting, fascinating, and controversial, and they are collected in hundreds of different ways. Some collectors aspire to collect the entire series, and some collect specific metal compositions. Many collectors have an interest in one or more of the major expositions or other significant events in U.S. history that are portrayed on these medals. Some collect medals from local or regional areas, while others have an interest in those with a U.S. Mint relationship, which includes a broad area of different designs. In addition to marking battles of the Revolutionary War and the Civil War, as well as other military events, So-Called Dollars were struck that address the gold-versus-silver political controversy of the late 1800s and early 1900s. Lesher dollars; silver Bryan dollars; Pedley-Ryan dollars; and others struck by professor Montroville Dickeson, coin dealer Thomas Elder, numismatic historian Q. David Bowers, and other famous personalities are all popular collector categories.

So-Called Dollars range in rarity from very common to exceptionally rare. For many types only one example or very few are known to exist; for others there are thousands. Many So-Called Dollars are considerably rarer than U.S. coins. One of the most common So-Called Dollars is the 1931 McCormick Reaper Centennial Dollar, of which there were possibly as many as 5,000 struck. Compare that to the 1909-S V.D.B. Lincoln cent, of which 484,000 were minted. While the Lincoln cent in MS-63 would sell for $1,500, the McCormick Reaper in the same grade sells for around $20 despite being 100 times rarer. The following rarity scale is used for So-Called Dollars in this appendix:

R-1	More than 5000 known
R-2	2001–5000 known
R-3	501–2000 known
R-4	201–500 known
R-5	76–200 known
R-6	21–75 known
R-7	11–20 known
R-8	5–10 known
R-9	2–4 known
R-10	1 known (unique)

Hundreds of different So-Called Dollars in MS-63 can be purchased for less than $100. All of the major third-party grading firms, including NGC, PCGS, ANACS, and ICG, grade So-Called Dollars. Professional grading and slabbing of So-Called Dollars has had a significant impact on collector interest and prices realized when they appear in auction. Many of today's advanced collectors want the finer and higher-grade pieces, and if the medals are certified by a major grading firm, their confidence in the value goes up. Higher prices paid today for rare So-Called Dollars are a direct result of this increase in buyers' confidence.

So-Called Dollars have a broad appeal to today's collectors. Similar to most series of U.S. coinage, there are many interesting and historically significant pieces available to the beginning collector at relatively low introductory prices. There are literally hundreds of different types available in Uncirculated and Choice Uncirculated grades in the $25 to $75 range. There are also many highly desired rare varieties from the 1800s that are beautiful pieces of art, struck in bronze and with high relief, that the more advanced collectors appreciate. At the upper end of the So-Called Dollar market—those that sell for $1,000 or more—collectors are treated to exceptionally rare and significant pieces.

1826, Erie Canal
Completion

1826, U.S.
Semicentennial

1857, Dr. Elisha Kent Kane

1859, Nassau Water Works

| | Rarity | HK# | VF-20 | EF-40 | AU-50 | MS-60 | MS-63 | MS-65 |
						PF-60	PF-63	PF-65
1826, Erie Canal Completion. Gold Proof §	R-9	1001		$63,000			$200,000	
1826, Erie Canal Completion. Silver	R-6	1000	$900	$1,100	$1,400	$2,550	$4,500	$9,000
1826, Erie Canal Completion. White Metal	R-6	1	$250	$575	$900	$1,950	$3,800	
1826, Erie Canal Completion. Gold-Plated	R-8	UNL	$425	$625	$1,750	$2,600	$4,500	—
1826, U.S. Semicentennial. Silver	R-9	2	$3,450	$4,200	$5,000	—	—	—
1826, U.S. Semicentennial. Copper	R-9	3	$3,000	$3,800	$4,450	—	—	—
1826, U.S. Semicentennial. White Metal	R-8	4	$2,800	$3,950	$4,500	$5,200	—	—
1857, Dr. Elisha Kent Kane. Bronze	R-7	756	—	—	$575	$800	$1,150	$1,400
1857, Dr. Elisha Kent Kane. White Metal	R-7	757	—	—	$600	$850	$1,250	$1,550
1859, Nassau Water Works. Silver	R-8	589C	—	—	$2,000	$2,850	$4,250	$5,750
1859, Nassau Water Works. Silver Proof	R-8	589C				$3,300	$4,750	—
1859, Nassau Water Works. Bronze	R-7	589A	$500	$625	$800	$950	$1,250	$2,300
1859, Nassau Water Works. Bronze Proof	R-8	589A						$2,600
1859, Nassau Water Works. White Metal	R-6	589B	$185	$225	$395	$510	$575	—
1859, Nassau Water Works. White Metal Proof	R-8	589B				$1,050	$1,450	—

§ Ranked in the *100 Greatest American Medals and Tokens*. **UNL** = Unlisted.

1826, Erie Canal Completion (HK–1, 1000, and 1001): This piece was struck to celebrate the completion of the Erie Canal, the greatest and most expensive U.S. engineering achievement yet undertaken. Pan and Neptune appear with cornucopias on the obverse; an eagle on the reverse sits atop the New York State coat of arms. Engraved by Charles Cushing Wright. **1826, U.S. Semicentennial (HK–2 to 4):** Struck to commemorate the 50th anniversary of the Declaration of Independence. An eagle perches on a shield on the obverse; the reverse legend refers to the Declaration of Independence dramatically stating; "For the support of this we pledge to each other our lives, our fortunes and our sacred honor." **1857, Dr. Elisha Kent Kane (HK–756 to 757):** The bust of Elisha Kent Kane, commander of the Second Grinnell Expedition, is on the obverse. In the early 1800s the British encouraged attempts to find the Northwest Passage, an ocean route hoped to connect the Atlantic and Pacific oceans via the Arctic. Kane commanded an unsuccessful recovery effort in 1850 to rescue two vessels that were lost in an attempt to find the passage. **1859, Nassau Water Works (HK–589A to 589C):** Neptune moves a lever with his right arm, which causes water to gush out of a vase or pipe held in his left. In July of 1858 public water was first introduced to Brooklyn, New York, and celebrated in April of 1859, at which time this medal was struck. Engraved by F.B. Smith & Hartmann.

1861, Bombardment of Fort Sumter

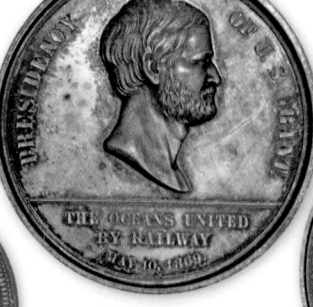

1869, Grant Transcontinental Railway Completion

1873, San Francisco Mint Coining Press

1875, Battle of Lexington Centennial

	Rarity	HK#	VF-20	EF-40	AU-50	MS-60 / PF-60	MS-63 / PF-63	MS-65 / PF-65
1861, Bombardment of Fort Sumter. Copper	R-7	11C	$450	$650	$975	$1,650	$2,650	$3,680
1861, Bombardment of Fort Sumter. Brass	R-8	11B	—	—	—	—	$2,250	—
1861, Bombardment of Fort Sumter. White Metal	R-7	11	$200	$350	$550	$950	$1,700	$2,400
1869, Grant Transcontinental Railway Completion. Silver Proof	R-7	12A	$600	$950	$1,500	$2,200	$4,850	$6,750
1869, Grant Transcontinental Railway Completion. Bronze	R-6	12	$85	$175	$300	$600	$800	$1,200
1869, Grant Transcontinental Railway Completion. Gilt Bronze	R-9	12B	—	—	$2,500	$3,500	—	—
1869, Grant Transcontinental Railway Completion. Yellow Bronze. Restrike	R4	UNL	$25	$40	$65	$85	$120	$160
1873, San Francisco Mint Coining Press. Silver Proof	R-9	1003	—	—	$3,800	$5,200	$7,500	$7,800
1873, San Francisco Mint Coining Press. Copper	R-9	1003A	—	$875	$1,200	$1,500	—	—
1875, Battle of Lexington Centennial. Gold	R-9	1004					—	
1875, Battle of Lexington Centennial. Silver	R-9	16					$2,700	$5,500
1875, Battle of Lexington Centennial. Silver Proof	R-7	16				$2,600	$3,100	$5,500
1875, Battle of Lexington Centennial. Bronze	R-5	17	$200	$250	$375	$475	$575	$675
1875, Battle of Lexington Centennial. Bronze Proof	R-7	17				$700	$850	
1875, Battle of Lexington Centennial. White Metal	R-6	18			$135	$350	$475	$575
1875, Battle of Lexington Centennial. White Metal not holed	R-8	18	—	—	$500	$1,100	$1,700	—
1875, Battle of Lexington Centennial. White Metal Proof	R-7	18			$195	$425	$500	$750

UNL = Unlisted.

1861, Bombardment of Fort Sumter (HK–11 to 11C): A battle scene on the obverse depicts exploding bombs and smoke as Fort Sumter is attacked by the South Carolina Rebels—the initial engagement of the Civil War. The reverse legend elaborates how 75 men in the fort held off 8,000 Southern Confederate Rebels for 30 hours. **1869, Grant Transcontinental Railway Completion (HK–12 to 12B):** The completion of the first transcontinental railroad was a major technological accomplishment. Only 20 years after the California Gold Rush there was now an economical way to transport people and goods from coast to coast. Dies made by William Barber and struck at the Philadelphia Mint. **1873, San Francisco Mint Coining Press (HK–1003 and 1003A):** The mint in San Francisco dropped the word "Branch" from its title to become the United States Mint at San Francisco on April 1, 1873. On October 14, 1873, this medal was struck to celebrate the delivery of the largest and most powerful coining press in the world to the San Francisco Mint. **1875, Battle of Lexington Centennial (HK–16 to 18 and 1004):** "What a glorious morning for America," Samuel Adams exclaimed after the Battle of Lexington, April 19, 1775, which marked the beginning of the Revolutionary War. The gold, silver, and bronze medals were struck at the Philadelphia Mint; the white-metal pieces were privately minted later. Dies by Henry Mitchell from designs by Edward Griffin Porta.

1876, Centennial Exposition Nevada

1876, Centennial Exposition Official Medal

1876, Centennial Exposition Liberty Bell / Independence Hall

1876, Centennial Exposition Liberty Seated / Colonial Soldiers

	Rarity	HK#	VF-20	EF-40	AU-50	MS-60 / PF-60	MS-63 / PF-63	MS-65 / PF-65
1876, Centennial Exposition Nevada. Silver	R-5	19	$175	$350	$475	$550	$795	$900
1876, Centennial Exposition Nevada. Silver Proof	R-6	19				$675	$950	$1,150
1876, Centennial Exposition Nevada. Copper	R-9	19A				—	—	—
1876, Centennial Exposition Nevada. White Metal	R-9	UNL				—	—	—
1876, Centennial Exposition Official Medal. Silver §	R-4	20	$65	$120	$145	$325	$545	$725
1876, Centennial Exposition Official Medal. Silver Proof	R-6	20				$400	$750	$1,250
1876, Centennial Exposition Official Medal. Copper	R-6	UNL	$60	$85	$125	$225	$325	$475
1876, Centennial Exposition Official Medal. Bronze	R-4	21	$55	$85	$140	$210	$325	$495
1876, Centennial Exposition Official Medal. Bronze Proof	R-7	21				$195	$375	$575
1876, Centennial Exposition Official Medal. White Metal	R-9	22A				$1,500		
1876, Centennial Exposition Official Medal. Gilt	R-4	22	$25	$50	$70	$115	$265	$535
1876, Centennial Exposition Liberty Bell/Independence Hall. Silver Proof	R-9	23				$6,900		
1876, Centennial Exposition Liberty Bell/Independence Hall. Copper	R-6	25	$25	$45	$75	$145	$245	$425
1876, Centennial Exposition Liberty Bell/Independence Hall. Bronze	R-6	24	$25	$45	$75	$125	$215	$450
1876, Centennial Exposition Liberty Bell/Independence Hall. White Metal	R-5	26	$20	$40	$80	$150	$375	$525
1876, Centennial Exposition Liberty Bell/Independence Hall. Gold-Plated	R-9	UNL	—	—	$1,500	$2,500	—	—
1876, Centennial Exposition Liberty Seated/Colonial Soldiers. Silver	R-9	56	—	—	$1,500	$2,250	$4,200	$7,800
1876, Centennial Exposition Liberty Seated/Colonial Soldiers. Copper	R-9	57	—	—	$550	$750	—	—
1876, Centennial Exposition Liberty Seated/Colonial Soldiers. White Metal	R-7	59	—	—	—	$800	$1,200	—
1876, Centennial Exposition Liberty Seated/Colonial Soldiers. Gold-Plated	R-6	58	$175	$275	$450	$700	$1,100	$1,375

§ Ranked in the *100 Greatest American Medals and Tokens*. **UNL** = Unlisted.

1876, Centennial Exposition Nevada (HK–19 and 19A): Made of pure silver crushed from Nevada ores at the Nevada quartz mill located in the Centennial Exposition and later refined and struck at the Philadelphia Mint and sold at the 1876 Centennial Exposition. Dies engraved by William Barber. **1876, Centennial Exposition Official Medal (HK–20 to 22A):** This medal depicts the United States rising in importance to be recognized as a world power, grasping a sword in her right hand to enforce her demands. The medal was designed and engraved by William Barber, struck at the Philadelphia Mint, and sold at the 1876 Centennial Exposition. **1876, Centennial Exposition Liberty Bell / Independence Hall (HK–23 to 26):** The Centennial Exposition held in Philadelphia had the Liberty Bell on display, as depicted on the obverse. Independence Hall is on the reverse. The medal was engraved by William H. Key, assistant engraver to William Barber, 1864–1885. **1876, Centennial Exposition Liberty Seated / Colonial Soldiers (HK–56 to 59):** A seated woman, similar to James Longacre's one-dollar patterns, represents America. The reverse depicts an interesting scene of colonial soldiers preparing for battle. This is one of many So-Called Dollars engraved by George B. Soley, who was an engraver for the U.S. Mint from 1859 until his death in 1908.

1876, Centennial Exposition Washington Bust / Declaration of Independence

1876, Centennial Exposition Lovett Battle of Moores Creek Bridge

1876, Dickeson Continental Dollar

1876, Dickeson Perseverando / Confederation

	Rarity	HK#	VF-20	EF-40	AU-50	MS-60 PF-60	MS-63 PF-63	MS-65 PF-65
1876, Centennial Expo Declaration of Independence/Washington. Silver	R-9	75A	—	—	$1,650	$2,500	—	—
1876, Centennial Expo Declaration of Independence/Washington. Bronze	R-7	75	—	—	—	$325	$625	$975
1876, Centennial Expo Declaration of Independence/Washington. White Metal	R-7	76	—	—	—	$625	$875	$1,100
1876, Centennial Exposition Lovett Battle of Moores Creek Bridge. Silver	R-9	90			$2,000	$2,900	$4,500	$5,900
1876, Centennial Exposition Lovett Battle of Moores Creek Bridge. Bronze	R-8	91	$200	$400	$625	$1,000	$1,800	$2,500
1876, Centennial Exposition Lovett Battle of Moores Creek Bridge. White Metal	R-6	92	$50	$110	$160	$275	$475	$675
1876, Dickeson Continental Dollar. Gold, struck on gold $20	R-10	852B					—	
1876, Dickeson Continental Dollar. Silver	R-8	852					$2,300	$3,850
1876, Dickeson Continental Dollar. Silver, struck on silver $1	R-10	UNL					$4,500	
1876, Dickeson Continental Dollar. Copper	R-7	853	$350	$500	$650	$1,200	$1,400	$1,900
1876, Dickeson Continental Dollar. White Metal	R-6	854	$125	$190	$300	$450	$780	$1,540
1876, Dickeson Continental Dollar. Lead	R-9	856	—	—	—	—	—	—
1876, Dickeson Continental Dollar. Bowers White Metal	R-4	854A	$15	$20	$30	$40	$55	$80
1876, Dickeson Continental Dollar. Bashlow Silver	R-5	852A	$50	$65	$85	$115	$180	$245
1876, Dickeson Continental Dollar. Bashlow Bronze	R-4	853A	$15	$20	$35	$50	$65	$90
1876, Dickeson Continental Dollar. Bashlow Goldine	R-4	856A	$15	$20	$35	$45	$60	$85
1876, Dickeson Perseverando/Confederation. Copper	R-8	866B				$1,200	$1,500	
1876, Dickeson Perseverando/Confederation. White Metal	R-9	UNL				$1,250	$1,600	

UNL = Unlisted.

1876, Centennial Exposition Washington Bust / Declaration of Independence (HK–75 to 77): The obverse by George Hampden Lovett features a naked bust of George Washington with an ornamental border depicting cavalry and infantry. Abraham Demarest's reverse features a copy of John Trumbull's painting of the 1776 Congress Committee of Five making its report on the Declaration of Independence. **1876, Centennial Exposition Lovett Battle of Moores Creek Bridge (HK–90 to 92):** The first in a series of eight medals engraved and issued by George Hampden Lovett to commemorate the Revolutionary Battles of 1776. On February 27, 1776, the American victory ended British authority in North Carolina and greatly boosted patriotic morale. Less than two months later North Carolina became the first colony to vote in favor of independence from Britain. **1876, Dickeson Continental Dollar and Modern Restrikes (HK–852 to 856A):** Prominent numismatist Professor Montroville Dickeson, publisher of the *American Numismatic Manual of 1859,* had dies made and struck copies of the Continental Dollar as souvenirs for the 1876 Centennial Exposition. In the 20th century Robert Bashlow used the Dickeson dies to restrike medals. **1876, Dickeson Perseverando / Confederation (HK–866B):** For the obverse, Dickeson adopted a vignette from the Perseverando $6 bills issued by the 1775–1778 Continental Congress: the all-seeing eye above casts rays down upon a flaming altar surrounded by 13 stars. A vignette depicting a beaver gnawing on what is likely a palmetto tree, from the Confederation $40 bills issued by the 1778–1779 Continental Congress, was adopted for the reverse.

1878, Wyoming Battle and Massacre Centennial

1878, Washington Valley Forge Centennial

1881, Battle of Groton Heights Centennial

1882, William Penn Pennsylvania Bicentennial Official Medal

| | Rarity | HK# | VF-20 | EF-40 | AU-50 | MS-60 | MS-63 | MS-65 |
						PF-60	PF-63	PF-65
1878, Wyoming Battle & Massacre Centennial. Gold	R-9	120D			—	—	—	—
1878, Wyoming Battle & Massacre Centennial. Silver	R-8	120A	$350	$550	$725	$2,650	$3,450	
1878, Wyoming Battle & Massacre Centennial. Bronze	R-6	120	$75	$160	$250	$380	$600	$825
1878, Wyoming Battle & Massacre Centennial. Brass	R-9	120B	—	—	—	$750	—	—
1878, Wyoming Battle & Massacre Centennial. White Metal	R-6	121	$50	$95	$175	$350	$475	$700
1878, Wyoming Battle & Massacre Centennial. White Metal Proof	R-7	121				$425	$550	$825
1878, Wyoming Battle & Massacre Centennial. Gold-Plated	R-7	120C	$100	$220	$350	$1,050	$1,650	—
1878, Washington Valley Forge Centennial. Silver	R-7	136			$1,800	$3,800	$5,200	$6,495
1878, Washington Valley Forge Centennial. Silver Proof	R-7	136				$3,800	$4,900	$6,495
1878, Washington Valley Forge Centennial. Bronze	R-6	137	$200	$325	$425	$600	$825	$1,200
1878, Washington Valley Forge Centennial. Yellow Bronze. Restrike	R-5	UNL	$20	$35	$45	$60	$75	$145
1881, Battle of Groton Heights Centennial. Silver Proof	R-8	125C					$3,850	
1881, Battle of Groton Heights Centennial. Bronze	R-6	125B	$75	$140	$195	$325	$495	$795
1881, Battle of Groton Heights Centennial. White Metal	R-6	125	$75	$135	$185	$320	$465	$725
1881, Battle of Groton Heights Centennial. White Metal Proof	R-6	125				$440	$600	$1,000
1882, William Penn Pennsylvania Bicentennial Official Metal. Gold-Plated Brass	R-7	138	$90	$150	$235	$350	$500	$700

UNL = Unlisted.

1878, Wyoming Battle and Massacre Centennial (HK–120 to 121): The scene on the obverse depicts Indians, with tomahawks raised in their hands, attacking a family of settlers. On the reverse is a memorial monument with the legend "Dulce et decorum est pro patria mori," which translated means: "It is a sweet and noble thing to die for one's country." Dies engraved by George T. Morgan. **1878, Washington Valley Forge Centennial (HK–136 and 137):** Engraved by William Barber, the medal commemorates the departure of the Continental Army from Valley Forge on June 19, 1778. A large naked bust of George Washington adorns the obverse. Struck originally in 1880 at the Philadelphia Mint, this is one of the medals in the U.S. Mint Medal Series. **1881, Battle of Groton Heights Centennial (HK–125, 125B, and 125C):** The obverse shows two American soldiers reloading and firing their muskets while being attacked by the British at the Fort Griswold Massacre. Their determination echoes the legend: "We will not give up the fort, let the consequence be what they may." The outline of Fort Griswold is displayed on the piece's reverse. **1882, William Penn Pennsylvania Bicentennial Official Medal (HK-138):** This medal celebrates the 200th anniversary of the founding of Pennsylvania and the landing of William Penn. A bust of William Penn is on the obverse, and anniversary dates are on the reverse. Engraved by George T. Morgan.

1884, World's Industrial and Cotton Centennial Exposition Official Medal

1891, South Carolina General Assembly Centennial

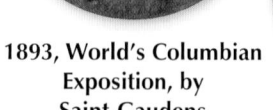 

1893, World's Columbian Exposition Official Medal, Large Letters

1893, World's Columbian Exposition, by Saint-Gaudens

	Rarity	HK#	VF-20	EF-40	AU-50	MS-60 PF-60	MS-63 PF-63	MS-65 PF-65
1884, World's Industrial & Cotton Centennial Expo Official Metal. Copper	R-8	142A						
1884, World's Industrial & Cotton Centennial Expo Official Metal. White Metal	R-7	142	$125	$210	$300	$450	$695	$850
1884, World's Industrial & Cotton Centennial Expo Official Metal. Gold-Plated	R-8	UNL					$480	
1891, South Carolina General Assembly Centennial. Silver, struck on silver $1	R-10	UNL					$2,750	
1891, South Carolina General Assembly Centennial. Copper	R-8	621				$750	$950	$1,250
1891, South Carolina General Assembly Centennial. White Metal	R-8	622				$1,500	$2,000	
1893, World's Columbian Expo Official Medal Large Letters. Silver Proof	R-9	154B					$3,600	
1893, World's Columbian Expo Official Medal Large Letters. Struck on silver $1	R-10	UNL					$2,500	
1893, World's Columbian Expo Official Medal Large Letters. Brass (a)	R-5	UNL	$20	$30	$60	$70	$150	$195
1893, World's Columbian Expo Official Medal Large Letters. Aluminum Proof	R-9	154A					$4,800	
1893, World's Columbian Expo Official Medal Large Letters. Gilted Brass	R-3	154	$9	$13	$17	$28	$60	$125
1893, World's Columbian Expo Official Medal Large Letters. Silver-Plated	R-6	UNL	$65	$125	$225	$375	$825	—
1893, World's Columbian Expo Official Medal Large Letters. Struck on Large Cent	R-10	UNL					$2,500	
1893, World's Columbian Exposition Saint-Gaudens. Copper C. Emmerich §	R-5	223	$35	$60	$90	$125	$210	$375
1893, World's Columbian Exposition Saint-Gaudens. Copper Chas Emmerich	R-7	223	$60	$90	$125	$265	$350	$485
1893, World's Columbian Exposition Saint-Gaudens. White Metal	R-10	223A						$2,825
1893, World's Columbian Exposition Saint-Gaudens. Gold-Plated	R-10	UNL						$1,750

§ Ranked in the *100 Greatest American Medals and Tokens*. **a.** Originally issued in Brass, replaced with the more common Gilted Brass. **UNL** = Unlisted.

1884, World's Industrial and Cotton Centennial Exposition Official Medal (HK–142 and 142A): Engraved by George T. Morgan and struck in the U.S. Mint Exhibit at the exposition. The Cotton Centennial Exposition was held in 1884 and 1885 to commemorate the first shipment of cotton exported to England and to promote the cotton industry. **1891, South Carolina General Assembly Centennial (HK–621 and 622):** This piece celebrates the centennial of the "Start of South Carolina," which occurred in 1791 with the first meeting of the General Assembly (legislature) of the state. The state's seal is on the obverse, and the reverse legend describes the date and location of the meeting. **1893, World's Columbian Exposition Official Medal, Large Letters (HK–154 and 154A):** This is the official medal from the Columbian Exposition held to commemorate the 400th anniversary of the discovery of America by Columbus and to tell the story of the world's progress for the past four centuries. On the obverse, large letters are found in the legend U.S. GOVT BUILDING. Engraved by George T. Morgan and struck at the Exposition. **1893, World's Columbian Exposition, by Saint-Gaudens (HK–223 and 223A):** The obverse portrays a smaller version of the Official Award Medal engraved by Augustus Saint-Gaudens, featuring Columbus wearing a cloak and armor; his head is upraised and arms spread as if giving thanks for finding land. The obverse was designed by Saint-Gaudens, and the detailed reverse by Charles Barber. Struck at the Philadelphia Mint.

1894, California Midwinter Exposition Official Medal

1894, California Midwinter Exposition Grizzly Bear / Exposition View

1895, Cotton States and International Exposition Official Medal

1897, Tennessee Centennial Exposition Official Medal

| | Rarity | HK# | VF-20 | EF-40 | AU-50 | MS-60 | MS-63 | MS-65 |
						PF-60	PF-63	PF-65
1894, California Midwinter Exposition Official Medal. Copper	R-9	UNL	$85	$125	$175	—	—	—
1894, California Midwinter Exposition Official Medal. Brass	R-5	245	$35	$45	$60	$120	$210	$325
1894, California Midwinter Exposition Official Medal. Gold-Plated	R-7	UNL	$45	$80	$135	$325	$495	$750
1894, California Midwinter Exposition Official Medal. Silver-Plated	R-8	UNL	$50	$90	$150	—	—	—
1894, California Midwinter Exposition Grizzly Bear/Expo View. Aluminum	R-6	259	$65	$120	$150	$290	$475	$750
1895, Cotton States & International Exposition Official Medal. Gold-Plated Brass	R-4	268	$25	$40	$60	$95	$125	$175
1897, Tennessee Centennial Exposition Official Medal. Gold-Plated Brass	R-5	274	$35	$45	$60	$125	$190	$300

UNL = Unlisted.

1894, California Midwinter Exposition Official Medal (HK-245): The exposition official medal was struck in the Mechanics Building at the exposition under contract by agent J.W. Ewing of the U.S. Department of the Interior. The exposition's purpose was to showcase to the world the great wealth and riches of California. Dies were engraved by Charles E. Barber and produced by the Philadelphia Mint. Gold-plated medals were struck on opening day. **1894, California Midwinter Exposition Grizzly Bear / Exposition View (HK-259):** The obverse shows a California grizzly bear on a crag high atop a mountain looking down over a detailed bird's-eye view of the exposition grounds. The reverse legend expounds the numerous benefits of aluminum, a popular metal that could now be produced inexpensively due to the invention of electricity. Engraved, struck, and signed by Noble Chicago along the lower rim on the reverse. **1895, Cotton States and International Exposition Official Medal (HK-268):** Designed by Philip Martinez and struck at the Philadelphia Mint. The medal symbolizes that Atlanta and the South had "risen from its fires and ashes" after the Civil War. **1897, Tennessee Centennial Exposition Official Medal (HK-274):** The official medal designed by Charles E. Barber was struck and sold in the U.S. Mint Exhibit at the Exposition. The exposition celebrated the 100th anniversary of statehood for Tennessee and was meant to attract business to the state and increase its population.

1898, Trans-Mississippi and International Exposition Official Medal

1900, Bryan Dollar Cartwheel With Legend

1901, Pan-American Exposition Official Medal

1901, South Carolina Exposition Official Medal

	Rarity	HK#	VF-20	EF-40	AU-50	MS-60 PF-60	MS-63 PF-63	MS-65 PF-65
1898, Trans-Mississippi & International Expo Official Medal. Gold	R-9	UNL				—	—	—
1898, Trans-Mississippi & International Expo Official Medal. Silver	R-5	281	$60	$85	$195	$340	$575	$925
1898, Trans-Mississippi & International Expo Official Medal. Silver Proof	R-9	281				—	—	$2,000
1898, Trans-Mississippi & International Expo Official Medal. Bronze (a)	R-7	282	$90	$140	$225	$300	$380	$475
1898, Trans-Mississippi & International Expo Official Medal. Gold-Plated Brass	R-4	283	$30	$50	$70	$125	$175	$325
1898, Trans-Mississippi & International Expo Official Medal. White Metal Proof	R-9	UNL				—	—	—
1900, Bryan Dollar Cartwheel with Legend. Silver	R-6	782	$400	$625	$710	$800	$950	$1,250
1901, Pan-American Exposition Official Medal. Silver	R-6	287	$235	$295	$360	$495	$635	$1,150
1901, Pan-American Exposition Official Medal. Copper	R-8	288	$100	$250	$495	$850	$1,600	$2,530
1901, Pan-American Exposition Official Medal. Gold-Plated Copper	R-4	289	$15	$55	$75	$90	$115	$185
1901, South Carolina Exposition Official Medal. Silver	R-8	294A	—	—	—	—	—	—
1901, South Carolina Exposition Official Medal. Nickel	R-8	295A	—	—	—	—	—	—
1901, South Carolina Exposition Official Medal. White Metal	R-8	295	—	—	—	$1,200	$1,500	—
1901, South Carolina Exposition Official Medal. Gold-Plated Bronze	R-5	294	$125	$210	$285	$495	$950	$1,250

a. Reported copper strikings appear to be bronze. **UNL** = Unlisted.

1898, Trans-Mississippi and International Exposition Official Medal (HK–281 to 283A): On the obverse, a composite picture of the most beautiful women in the Trans-Mississippi county portion of the country celebrates past 50 years of expansion west of the Mississippi since the discovery of gold in California in 1848. T.R. Kimball proposed the use of the well-known picture "The Wild Huntsman" as inspiration for the reverse. The medal was designed and the models were prepared by Emil Fuchs. The official medal was struck in the U.S. Mint Exhibit at the exposition from dies made at the Philadelphia Mint. **1900, Bryan Dollar Cartwheel With Legend (HK–782):** A satirical piece struck to discredit Democratic congressman William Jennings Bryan during his 1900 presidential campaign. Bryan ran unsuccessfully against William McKinley on the Free Silver platform, supporting the coining of silver and gold at the legal ratio of sixteen to one. The cartwheel is the size of a silver dollar, and its oversize shows how unmanageably large a silver dollar would have to be to have the silver value Bryan proposed. **1901, Pan-American Exposition Official Medal (HK–287 to 289):** Designed by G.T. Brewster, the dies were engraved at the Philadelphia Mint, and the medals were struck in Buffalo, New York, in the U.S. Mint Exhibit at the exposition. The purpose of the exposition was to promote trade and social relations with our Pan-American neighbors. Tragedy overtook the nation when President McKinley was assassinated while greeting citizens in the Temple of Music at the exposition. **1901, South Carolina Exposition Official Medal (HK–294 to 295A):** The winged female standing on a globe with ships, trains, buildings, and agriculture in the background promotes Charleston's well-situated shipping port and the potential for trade with the West Indies, Central America, and South America. Designed by George T. Morgan and struck in the U.S. Mint Exhibit at the Exposition.

1904, Louisiana Purchase Exposition Official Medal

1902, Wells Fargo Semicentennial

1904, Louisiana Purchase Exposition Napoleon and Jefferson / Good Luck

1905, Louis and Clark Centennial Exposition Official Medal

	Rarity	HK#	VF-20	EF-40	AU-50	MS-60	MS-63	MS-65
						PF-60	PF-63	PF-65
1902, Wells Fargo Semicentennial. Silver	R-5	296	$450	$600	$900	$1,200	$1,500	$2,100
1902, Wells Fargo Semicentennial. Brown leatherette box of issue	R-6	UNL	$250	$350	$500			
1904, Louisiana Purchase Exposition Official Medal. Gold	R-10	299A				—	—	—
1904, Louisiana Purchase Exposition Official Medal. Silver (a)	R-4	299	$50	$70	$110	$170	$240	$385
1904, Louisiana Purchase Exposition Official Medal. Copper	R-6	301	$30	$60	$120	$165	$250	$290
1904, Louisiana Purchase Exposition Official Medal. Bronze	R-4	303	$15	$40	$55	$95	$275	$290
1904, Louisiana Purchase Exposition Official Medal. Yellow Bronze (Brass)	R-3	302	$15	$35	$45	$75	$100	$225
1904, Louisiana Purchase Exposition Official Medal. Gold-Plated Bronze (b)	R-3	300/304	$15	$30	$45	$95	$125	$185
1904, Louisiana Purchase Exposition Napoleon & Jefferson/Good Luck. Gold	R-10	310B	$7,250					
1904, Louisiana Purchase Exposition Napoleon & Jefferson/Good Luck. Silver	R-9	311A			$1,450	$1,800	$3,800	
1904, Louisiana Purchase Exposition Napoleon & Jefferson/Good Luck. Brass	R-5	310	$20	$35	$50	$125	$170	$240
1904, Louisiana Purchase Exposition Napoleon & Jefferson/Good Luck. Aluminum	R-6	311	$25	$40	$55	$135	$175	$250
1905, Louis and Clark Centennial Exposition Official Medal. Silver	R-5	325	$295	$350	$425	$650	$750	$895
1905, Louis and Clark Centennial Exposition Official Medal. Bronze (c)	R-5	327	$45	$65	$135	$180	$225	$350
1905, Louis and Clark Centennial Exposition Official Medal. Gold-Plated Bronze	R-6	326	$50	$90	$115	$190	$350	$475

a. * There is a rare "no star reverse" variety that is found in several different compositions and is considerably more valuable.
b. Gold-Plated Bronze and Gilt are combined. **c.** Reported brass strikings appear to be bronze. **UNL** = Unlisted.

1902, Wells Fargo Semicentennial (HK–296 and 296A): Struck in silver in 1902, the medal was given to each employee of Wells Fargo who had worked there for one year or more. The obverse displays a fascinating design of a stagecoach with guns firing at robbers above and a Pony Express rider being attacked by Indians below. The reverse depicts ships, trains, and various symbols of industry and progress. **1904, Louisiana Purchase Exposition Official Medal (HK–299 to 304):** The design depicts and commemorates the 100th anniversary of the Louisiana Purchase by Thomas Jefferson from Napoleon Bonaparte for $15,000,000. Designed by George T. Morgan and struck in the U.S. Mint Exhibit at the exposition. **1904, Louisiana Purchase Exposition Napoleon and Jefferson / Good Luck (HK–310 to 311B):** Conjoined busts of Napoleon and Jefferson are depicted on the obverse with an inscription around, stating, "– NAPOLEON SOLD IT – APRIL 30th – JEFFERSON BOUGHT IT – 1803." For good luck, a horseshoe with entwined ribbon and a four-leaf clover are shown together on the reverse. **1905, Lewis and Clark Centennial Exposition Official Medal (HK–325 to 327):** In the arms of a female figure representing America, captains Meriwether Lewis and William Clark sight the Pacific Ocean at the western termination of their Northwest Expedition. Westward the course of the empire takes its way. On the reverse is a topographical map of the American West showing the states, major cities, and shipping routes from Seattle, Portland, and San Francisco. Designed by George T. Morgan and struck in the U.S. Mint Exhibit at the Exposition.

1905, Louis and Clark Centennial Expo, Conjoined Busts

1905, Denver Mint Opening

1906, Pike's Peak Southwest Centennial Exposition Official Medal

1907, Jamestown Tercentennial Exposition Official Medal

	Rarity	HK#	VF-20 PF-60	EF-40 PF-63	AU-50 PF-65	MS-60	MS-63	MS-65
1905, Louis and Clark Centennial Expo Conjoined Busts, 34 mm. Silver	R-7	UNL	$45	$80	$150	$295	$370	$550
1905, Louis and Clark Centennial Expo Conjoined Busts, 34 mm. Silver antiqued	R-5	328	$30	$70	$135	$275	$350	$510
1905, Louis and Clark Centennial Expo Conjoined Busts, 34 mm. Bronze	R-6	329	$30	$60	$95	$190	$250	$375
1905, Louis and Clark Centennial Expo Conjoined Busts, 34 mm. Gold-Plated Bronze	R-7	330	$45	$70	$120	$220	$300	$425
1905, Denver Mint Opening. Silver	R-9	876A	—	—	—	$3,500	$5,000	
1905, Denver Mint Opening. Bronze	R-6	876	$300	$450	$950	$1,100	$1,500	$2,025
1906, Pike's Peak Southwest Centennial Exposition Official Medal. Silver	R-6	UNL	$90	$190	$270	$350	$500	$625
1906, Pike's Peak Southwest Centennial Exposition Official Medal. Silver oxidized	R-5	336	$30	$50	$75	$115	$195	$395
1906, Pike's Peak Southwest Centennial Exposition Official Medal. Silver Proof	R-6	335	$90	$150	$225	$325	$625	$800
1906, Pike's Peak Southwest Centennial Exposition Official Medal. Bronze	R-4	338	$15	$30	$50	$60	$85	$150
1906, Pike's Peak Southwest Centennial Exposition Official Medal. Gold-Plated	R-8	337	$175	$350	$850	$1,150	$1,750	$2,530
1907, Jamestown Tercentennial Exposition Official Medal. Silver	R-5	344	$95	$150	$195	$325	$495	$725
1907, Jamestown Tercentennial Exposition Official Medal. Bronze	R-4	346	$35	$50	$75	$125	$225	$350
1907, Jamestown Tercentennial Exposition Official Medal. Gold-Plated Bronze	R-4	347	$30	$45	$60	$95	$175	$235
1907, Jamestown Tercentennial Exposition Official Medal. Silver-Plated Bronze	R-7	345	$85	$140	$180	$285	$375	$595

UNL = Unlisted.

1905, Lewis and Clark Centennial Exposition, Conjoined Busts, 34 mm (HK–328 to 331B): Captain Meriwether Lewis and Captain William Clark grace this unofficial medal struck by Joseph Mayer & Brothers of Seattle. This issue was struck in several sizes as well as different die varieties and metal compositions. A view of the Government Building at the exposition is shown on the reverse. **1905, Denver Mint Opening (HK–876 and 876A):** As the first product of the Denver Mint, this type was struck to test the new machinery and, some believe, new dies for a $20 gold piece. It was issued as a souvenir at the official opening ceremonies of the mint in early 1906. **1906, Pike's Peak Southwest Centennial Exposition Official Medal (HK–335 to 338):** Designed by Charles E. Barber and struck at the Philadelphia Mint, this medal commemorates the 100th anniversary of the discovery of Pike's Peak by Lt. Zebulon Montgomery Pike during his Southwest Expedition of 1806–1807, which followed the Louisiana Purchase and Lewis and Clark's expedition with the Corp of Discovery. **1907, Jamestown Tercentennial Exposition Official Medal (HK–344 to 347):** With Pocahontas on the obverse and Captain John Smith's ship on the reverse, this medal commemorates the 300th anniversary of the Jamestown settlement in North America by English-speaking people. Designed by George T. Morgan and struck in the U.S. Mint Exhibit at the Exposition.

1908, Bryan the Great Commoner, by Thomas Elder

1909, Alaska-Yukon-Pacific Exposition Official Medal

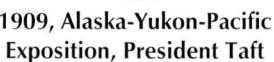 

1909, Alaska-Yukon-Pacific Exposition, President Taft

1910, Brian Boru

	Rarity	HK#	VF-20	EF-40	AU-50	MS-60 / PF-60	MS-63 / PF-63	MS-65 / PF-65
1908, Bryan the Great Commoner by Thomas Elder. Silver	R-9	805						$2,500
1908, Bryan the Great Commoner by Thomas Elder. Copper	R-9	807						$2,530
1908, Bryan the Great Commoner by Thomas Elder. Brass	R-9	808						$2,780
1908, Bryan the Great Commoner by Thomas Elder. Aluminum	R-9	809						$1,610
1908, Bryan the Great Commoner by Thomas Elder. German-silver	R-9	806						$3,300
1909, Alaska-Yukon-Pacific Exposition Official Medal. Silver	R-5	353	$80	$95	$130	$195	$425	$575
1909, Alaska-Yukon-Pacific Exposition Official Medal. Copper	R-5	355	$25	$35	$65	$75	$110	$245
1909, Alaska-Yukon-Pacific Exposition Official Medal. Bronze	R-4	354	$25	$35	$60	$95	$145	$265
1909, Alaska-Yukon-Pacific Exposition Official Medal. Bronze sandblast finish	R-7	UNL	$45	$65	$115	$180	$235	$295
1909, Alaska-Yukon-Pacific Exposition Official Medal. Gold-Plated	R-7	356	$140	$200	$250	$360	$435	$475
1909, Alaska-Yukon-Pacific Exposition President Taft. Gold-Plated Silver	R-8	361					$7,800	
1910, Brian Boru. Silver	R-6	390	$275	$465	$600	$950	$1,400	$1,900
1910, Brian Boru. Bronze	R-9	391						$6,400
1910, Brian Boru. Aluminum	R-5	392	$150	$200	$270	$315	$375	$525

UNL = Unlisted.

1908, Bryan the Great Commoner, by Thomas Elder (HK–805 to 809): William Jennings Bryan, who virtually controlled the Democratic Party for 30 years, ran unsuccessfully for the U.S. presidency in 1896, 1900, and 1908. After his unsuccessful campaign in 1900 against William McKinley, Bryan edited a weekly political journal, The Commoner, after which he became known as "The Great Commoner." Thomas L. Elder, a coin dealer in New York City, struck this satirical Bryan medal. **1909, Alaska-Yukon-Pacific Exposition Official Medal (HK–353 to 356):** The exposition and official medal were designed to promote the "enormous value of Alaska" and the "greatness" of Seattle's sea port. U.S. Mint die engraver George T. Morgan designed the official medal based on Adelaide Hanscomb's official logo for the exposition and the Seattle City seal. The medals were struck at the exposition by the U.S. Mint and sold through Joseph Mayer & Brothers of Seattle. **1909, Alaska-Yukon-Pacific Exposition, President Taft (HK-361):** The visit of President William H. Taft to Seattle on September 30, 1909, is commemorated on this gold-plated, .900-fine silver medal designed and produced by Joseph Mayer & Brothers Jewelry Company in Seattle. A variation of the exposition logo surrounded by an ornate wreath is depicted on the obverse. The reverse has commemorative text with an olive branch, a Mayer signature, and .900 indicating the piece's composition along with SILVER imprinted on the edge. **1910, Brian Boru (HK–390 to 392):** Brian Boru was king of Ireland from 1002–1014 A.D. Considered the George Washington of Ireland, at the age of 88 he broke Danish power over Ireland at the Battle of Clontart, where he was slain. The medal was issued by Thomas Elder, a coin dealer in New York City, to pay "tribute to the indomitable spirit of the Irish race."

1910, Ohio Valley Exposition Official Medal

1915, Panama Pacific International Exposition Official Medal

1915, Panama-California Exposition Official Medal

1920, Manila Mint Opening ("Wilson Dollar")

	Rarity	HK#	VF-20 / PF-60	EF-40 / PF-63	AU-50 / PF-65	MS-60 PF-60	MS-63 PF-63	MS-65 PF-65
1910, Ohio Valley Exposition Official Medal. Silver	R-6	393	$175	$225	$300	$425	$500	$625
1910, Ohio Valley Exposition Official Medal. Copper	R-6	394	$75	$105	$145	$200	$325	$595
1910, Ohio Valley Exposition Official Medal. Bronze	R-6	395	$75	$100	$135	$210	$325	$540
1910, Ohio Valley Exposition Official Medal. Gold-Plated	R-8	UNL	$175	$225	$300	$425	$500	$625
1915, Panama Pacific International Exposition Official Medal. Silver §	R-5	399	$50	$110	$225	$290	$350	$925
1915, Panama Pacific International Exposition Official Medal. Bright Bronze	R-5	400	$25	$55	$70	$90	$225	$425
1915, Panama Pacific International Exposition Official Medal. Statuary Bronze	R-6	UNL	$30	$60	$85	$120	$275	$485
1915, Panama Pacific International Exposition Official Medal. Antiqued Bronze	R-7	UNL	$30	$60	$90	$135	$310	$500
1915, Panama Pacific International Exposition Official Medal. Oxidized Bronze	R-7	UNL	$30	$60	$90	$135	$310	$500
1915, Panama Pacific International Exposition Official Medal. Gold-Plated Bronze	R-5	401	$40	$55	$90	$175	$325	$525
1915, Panama Pacific International Exposition Official Medal. Silver-Plated Bronze	R-6	UNL	$125	$175	$250	$325	$475	$595
1915, Panama-California Exposition Official Medal. Silver	R-5	426	$75	$125	$225	$275	$425	$675
1915, Panama-California Exposition Official Medal. Bronze	R-5	427	$35	$80	$110	$160	$295	$460
1915, Panama-California Exposition Official Medal. Gold-Plated Bronze	R-4	428	$30	$70	$95	$130	$235	$310
1915, Panama-California Exposition Official Medal. Silver-Plated Bronze	R-6	UNL	$55	$110	$140	$185	$320	$450
1920, Wilson Dollar Manila Mint Opening. Gold	R-8	1031			$44,000	$60,000	$75,000	
1920, Wilson Dollar Manila Mint Opening. Silver (a)	R-4	449	$85	$250	$525	$875	$1,850	$3,200
1920, Wilson Dollar Manila Mint Opening. Bronze (a)	R-5	450	$35	$80	$235	$785	$1,350	$4,500

§ Ranked in the *100 Greatest American Medals and Tokens*. **a.** VF and EF show signs of sea salvage. **UNL** = Unlisted.

1910, Ohio Valley Exposition Official Medal (HK–393 to 395): The exposition and official medal promoted the "industrial prowess of Ohio Valley," a century of "steamboat navigation on Ohio River," and the "commercial strength of South." Designed by George T. Morgan and struck in the U.S. Mint Exhibit at the exposition. **1915, Panama-Pacific International Exposition Official Medal (HK–399 to 401):** The official medal celebrates the opening of the Panama Canal. Winged Mercury opens the canal locks with the ship Argo, the symbol of navigation, passing through. Two women, entwined around the globe holding cornucopias, represent the two hemispheres on the reverse. Designed by Robert Aitken, who also designed the official $50 gold commemorative coins for the exposition, the medal was struck in the U.S. Mint Exhibit at the exposition. **1915, Panama-California Exposition Official Medal (HK–426 to 428):** On the obverse Uncle Sam, in front of North and Central America, holds a shovel with its handle overlaying the Panama Canal. Designed by *Washington Star* cartoonist C.K. Berryman, engraved by Charles E. Barber, and struck in the U.S. Mint Exhibit at the exposition. **1920, Manila Mint Opening ("Wilson Dollar") (HK–449, 450, and 1031):** This medal was struck at the opening of the Manila Mint in the Philippines. President Woodrow Wilson's bust is on the obverse; the goddess Juno Moneta guides a child striking medals in a coining press on the reverse—an apparent reference to the relationship between the United States and the Philippines. Many examples were dumped into Manila Bay just days prior to the Japanese invasion of the Philippines during WWII. Design concept by Clifford Hewitt and dies engraved by George T. Morgan.

1933, Century of Progress Exposition Official Medal

1926, U.S. Sesquicentennial Exposition

1939, Golden Gate International Exposition, by Charbneau (shown at 200%)

1950, Washington, D.C., Sesquicentennial

	Rarity	HK#	VF-20	EF-40	AU-50 MS-60	MS-63	MS-65
					PF-60	PF-63	PF-65
1926, U.S. Sesquicentennial Exposition. Bronze	R-5	451/452	$20	$45	$65	$95	$140	$195
1926, U.S. Sesquicentennial Exposition. Bronze high relief antiqued	R-6	UNL	$45	$80	$120	$165	$265	$350
1926, U.S. Sesquicentennial Exposition. Nickel	R-4	454	$15	$45	$67	$75	$130	$165
1926, U.S. Sesquicentennial Exposition. Gold-Plated Bronze	R-4	453	$15	$45	$65	$75	$135	$175
1933, Century of Progress Exposition Official Medal. Bronze	R-4	463	$15	$20	$40	$50	$95	$125
1933, Century of Progress Exposition Official Medal. Bronze antiqued	R-6	UNL	$20	$35	$65	$95	$150	$245
1939, Golden Gate International Expo Charbneau. J1 Gold 1 D SOLID GOLD	R-6	488			$1,780	$2,185	$2,350	$2,950
1939, Golden Gate International Expo Charbneau. J14 Gold 1 D SOLID GOLD stamped 10K & 40	R-9	UNL			$2,400	$2,700	$2,950	$3,300
1939, Golden Gate International Expo Charbneau. J2 Gold 1 D 10K SOLID GOLD	R-8	UNL			$1,850	$2,300	$2,450	$2,950
1939, Golden Gate International Expo Charbneau. J3 Gold 1 * 10K SOLID GOLD	R-7	UNL			$1,900	$2,350	$2,600	$3,000
1939, Golden Gate International Expo Charbneau. J4 Gold 1 * 22 over 10K SOLID GOLD	R-8	UNL			$2,100	$2,750	$3,350	$3,600
1939, Golden Gate International Expo Charbneau. J5 Gold 1 D 10K SOLID GOLD stamped 40	R-8	UNL			$2,100	$2,400	$2,600	$2,750
1939, Golden Gate International Expo Charbneau. J6 STERLING	R-6	487			$1,200	$1,495	$1,975	$2,400
1939, Golden Gate International Expo Charbneau. J7 STERLING Gold-Plated	R-7	487C			$1,300	$1,550	$2,100	$2,600
1939, Golden Gate International Expo Charbneau. J8 STERLING stamped 40	R-8	487B			$1,900	$2,400	$2,650	$2,750
1939, Golden Gate International Expo Charbneau. J9 Copper	R-9	UNL			$2,500	$2,700	$3,000	$3,600
1939, Golden Gate International Expo Charbneau. J10 Copper Gold-Plated	R-6	490			$850	$975	$1,450	$2,250
1940, Golden Gate International Expo Charbneau. J11 Gold 1 * 10K SOLID GOLD	R-8	489			$1,800	$1,950	$2,350	$2,750
1940, Golden Gate International Expo Charbneau. J12 Gold 1 * 22 over 10K SOLID GOLD	R-8	UNL			$1,650	$1,700	$2,100	$2,300
1940, Golden Gate International Expo Charbneau. J13 STERLING	R-6	487A			$1,350	$1,650	$2,100	$2,550

§ Ranked in the *100 Greatest American Medals and Tokens*. **UNL** = Unlisted.

1926, U.S. Sesquicentennial Exposition Official Medal (HK–451 to 454): For the 150th anniversary of the Declaration of Independence. The obverse displays a bust of George Washington, with Liberty riding a Pegasus and holding a torch on the reverse. Designed by Albin Polasek and struck in the U.S. Mint Exhibit at the exposition. **1933, Century of Progress Exposition Official Medal (HK–463):** A semi-nude male stretches his arms over Research and Industry on the obverse, with a topographical map of Chicago fairgrounds on the reverse. Designed by Emil Robert Zettler, dies made by Medallic Art Company, and struck in the U.S. Mint Exhibit at the exposition. **1939–1940, Golden Gate International Exposition, by Charbneau (HK–488):** Designed by Jules Charbneau and sold as souvenirs. Fourteen varieties were struck in gold, silver, and copper. All are the size of a U.S. gold dollar. The exposition statue Pacifica adorns the obverse, with the Tower of the Sun edifice, Portals of the Pacific, and the Golden Gate Bridge on the reverse.

Chart continued on next page.

| | Rarity | HK# | VF-20 | EF-40 | AU-50 | MS-60 | MS-63 | MS-65 |
						PF-60	PF-63	PF-65
1950, Washington, D.C. Sesquicentennial. Silver oxidized	R-5	507	$50	$65	$95	$275	$325	$485
1950, Washington, D.C. Sesquicentennial. Copper oxidized	R-4	508	$10	$20	$30	$50	$80	$120
1950, Washington, D.C. Sesquicentennial. Gold-Plated Copper	R-8	UNL	—	—	—	—	—	—

1950, Washington, D.C., Sesquicentennial (HK–507 and 508): For the 150th anniversary of Washington, D.C., as the seat of the federal government. The obverse displays the Statue of Freedom on the dome of the U.S. Capitol. On the reverse President John Adams addresses the 6th Congress, resulting in the city becoming the permanent capital. Designed by Thomas Hudson Jones and struck at the Philadelphia Mint.

1954, Cradle of the Union Celebration

1959, Nevada Silver Centennial

1959, Colorado Rush to the Rockies Centennial

1959, Oregon Statehood Centennial / Buchanan-Eisenhower

| | Rarity | HK# | VF-20 | EF-40 | AU-50 | MS-60 | MS-63 | MS-65 |
						PF-60	PF-63	PF-65
1954, Cradle of the Union Celebration. Gold Proof	R-7	511				$3,900	$4,900	$6,550
1954, Cradle of the Union Celebration. Silver oxidized	R-5	510	$65	$125	$275	$325	$380	$545
1954, Cradle of the Union Celebration. Bronze oxidized	R-4	512	$10	$25	$40	$55	$65	$90
1959, Nevada Silver Centennial. Silver	R-5	552	$110	$125	$150	$225	$345	$425
1959, Nevada Silver Centennial. Nickel holed	R-6	552A	$30	$45	$70	$115	$165	$195
1959, Colorado Rush to the Rockies Centennial. Silver	R-3	542	$15	$20	$35	$50	$65	$95
1959, Oregon Statehood Centennial Buchanan-Eisenhower. Gold Proof	R-8	554				—	$5,000	$8,000
1959, Oregon Statehood Centennial Buchanan-Eisenhower. Silver antiqued	R-9	553	$250	$360	$500	$625	$750	$1,200
1959, Oregon Statehood Centennial Buchanan-Eisenhower. Aluminum	R-6	555	—	—	—	—	—	—
1959, Oregon Statehood Centennial Buchanan-Eisenhower. Uniface Gold-Plated	R-9	UNL				$700	$950	$1,500

UNL = Unlisted.

1954, Cradle of the Union Celebration (HK–510 to 512): This medal honors the 200th anniversary of the Albany, New York, Congress of 1754—historically the First American Congress—where Benjamin Franklin presented his plan for a federal union. Albany's first public building, known as the Stadt Huys, later to be City Hall and the Courthouse, is depicted on the obverse. The reverse design is based on Franklin's famous cartoon, first published in 1754, of a segmented serpent representing the Colonies with a message "Join, or Die." Dies were engraved by Gilroy Roberts and struck at the Philadelphia Mint. **1959, Nevada Silver Centennial (HK–552 and 552A):** The State Seal of Nevada with a mining scene, train, and agricultural implements, is depicted on the obverse. The legend on the reverse mentions Virginia City, which was a boomtown in 1859 due to the Comstock Lode (the first major silver-deposit discovery in the United States) bestowing Virginia City the title of "Richest City in America." **1959, Colorado Rush to the Rockies Centennial (HK–542):** Oxen pulling a covered wagon heading west, being escorted by a cowboy on horseback, adorn the obverse. The reverse depicts the U.S. Air Force Academy logo in tribute to its First Commencement and Official Dedication by President Dwight Eisenhower. Designed by Arthur Roy Mitchell, modeled by Frank Gasparro, and struck at the Philadelphia Mint. **1959, Oregon Statehood Centennial / Buchanan-Eisenhower (HK–553 to 555):** The conjoined busts of the 15th president, James Buchanan, and the 34th president, Dwight D. Eisenhower, grace the obverse. The official Oregon Centennial emblem is depicted on the reverse. Issued by Northwestern Specialty Sales Co.

1960, Pony Express Centennial

1961, Kansas Statehood Centennial

1961, Mobile, Alabama 250th Anniversary

1961, Pony Express Termination Centennial

	Rarity	HK#	VF-20	EF-40	AU-50	MS-60	MS-63	MS-65
						PF-60	PF-63	PF-65
1960, Pony Express Centennial. Silver	R-3	582	$25	$30	$35	$50	$60	$75
1960, Pony Express Centennial. Bronze	R-2	583	$5	$7	$10	$12	$25	$70
1961, Kansas Statehood Centennial. Silver	R-3	586	$25	$30	$35	$50	$60	$85
1961, Mobile, Alabama 250th Anniversary. Silver	R-3	587	$25	$30	$35	$55	$70	$90
1961, Pony Express Termination Centennial. Silver	R-3	588	$25	$30	$35	$50	$65	$85
1961, Pony Express Termination Centennial. Silver	R-2	589	$5	$7	$10	$12	$25	$50

1960, Pony Express Centennial (HK–582 and 583): This piece was struck to commemorate the 100th anniversary of the famed Pony Express, which delivered mail from St. Joseph, Montana, to Sacramento, California, from April 3, 1860, to October 24, 1861. The medal displays busts of the Pony Express founders Russel, Majors, and Waddell on the obverse. The reverse depicts the famous painting by Herman Hansen depicting a Pony Express rider on horseback. **1961, Kansas Statehood Centennial (HK-586):** Issued for the Kansas Centennial, the medal's obverse shows a covered-wagon train being pulled by oxen, with mountains and a setting sun in the background. Its reverse depicts a vertical stalk of wheat over a sunflower. With its design a composite resulting from the work of Topeka artists and Treasury Department experts, this medal was struck at the Philadelphia Mint. **1961, Mobile, Alabama, 250th Anniversary (HK-587):** A bust of Sieur de Bienville, who founded the city in 1711 as the French capital of Louisiana, graces the obverse. The official seal of the anniversary is shown on the reverse along with six flags, representing the six countries that ruled Mobile. **1961, Pony Express Termination Centennial (HK-588 and 589):** The Pony Express was discontinued when the transcontinental telegraph was completed in late 1861. President Abraham Lincoln characterized the Pony Express as "an immortal service to the Union." A telegraph key and a riderless horse are on the obverse. The reverse depicts a dismounted Pony Express rider leading his horse away, walking with his back to us, with telegraph wires in the background.

APPENDIX G

Scouting and Numismatics: A Celebration

This consideration of 2010 and 2013 Boy Scouts and Girl Scouts commemorative coins benefited greatly from the knowledge and historical research of George Cuhaj.

The Boy Scouts of America and Girls Scouts of the USA commemorative silver dollars of 2010 and 2013 pay tribute to the centennials of two iconic organizations that have been woven into the fabric of American life for generations. While it's not unusual for commemoratives to honor individuals or institutions that have positively impacted our shared experience as a nation, these particular coins are special in that they also represent the culmination of Scouting's long history of engagement with coin collecting and with prominent numismatic associations.

ESTABLISHMENT OF THE SCOUTS

Formed in 1910 by W.D. Boyce, the Boy Scouts of America borrowed elements from earlier Scouting entities established by Ernest Thompson Seton in the United States and Lord Robert Baden-Powell in England. Aiming to instill self-reliance, courage, patriotism, and a strong sense of ethics in young boys, the Scouts adopted the following oath to be recited by its members: "On my honor I will do my best, To do my duty to God and my country and to obey the Scout Law; To help other people at all times; To keep myself physically strong, mentally awake, and morally straight." The Scout Law goes on to classify the ideal scout as someone who is "Trustworthy, Loyal, Helpful, Friendly, Courteous, Kind, Obedient, Cheerful, Thrifty, Brave, Clean, and Reverent." An Act of Congress signed into law by President Woodrow Wilson in 1916 gave the organization its federal charter.

A system of merit badges was instated, allowing Scouts to earn patches for achieving proficiency in a wide variety of skills, from wilderness survival and first aid to reading and public speaking. There have been more than 111 million participants in the Boy Scouts since its start; today it is the largest youth organization in the United States, boasting 2.8 million youth members and 1.1 million adult leaders.

The Girl Scouts were created shortly afterward on March 12, 1912, by Juliette Gordon Low. Low was similarly inspired by an encounter with Robert Baden-Powell, and sought to set up an organization that would inspire girls to develop "self-reliance and resourcefulness" in nature and in their communities. A system of pins and badges was developed, and in little more than a decade the organization grew to 125,738 members across every state in America. Congress granted the Girl Scouts of the USA its official charter in 1950, and today there are more than 3.2 million members throughout the United States and its territories. Marilyn Reback, former senior editor of *The Numismatist* (the magazine of the American Numismatic Association) and one-time Girl Scout, says, "Members of Girl Scouts of the USA are part of an international family of 10 million girls and adults. Today it is the world's preeminent leadership organization dedicated solely to girls, building character and skills for success."

THE SCOUTS EMBRACE NUMISMATICS

The Boy Scouts and Girl Scouts instituted their first merit badges for coin collecting in the late 1930s. Since then, the relationship between Scouting and collecting has grown, as George Cuhaj, numismatist and coauthor of the Boy Scouts' requirements for the coin-collecting merit badge, describes:

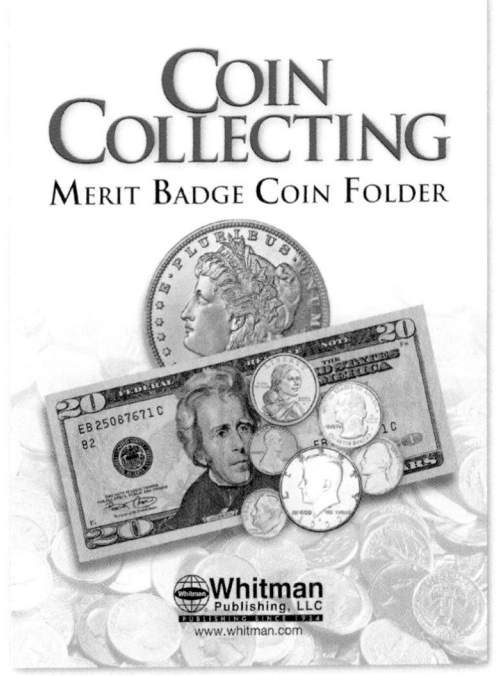

Coin collecting was not the first hobby badge (that was stamp collecting), but it has maintained a steady popularity since its 1938 introduction. That first merit-badge book was authored by William L. Clark of the American Numismatic Society in New York City and topped out at 84 pages. The design of the badge at the time was a modified rendering of a helmeted Athena head with a bronze or golden tone.

With the wartime conservation of paper, the book cover was changed to a white and red cover, then a red cover with a photo, and finally it was time for a full-photo cover in the 1960s.

With these revisions and the circulating coin changes brought about with the replacement of silver circulating dimes, quarters, and half dollars, as well as the impending national Bicentennial celebrations, Kenneth Bressett, editor of the *Guide Book of United States Coins*, was tapped to write the new merit-badge book to go along with the new requirements. The cover featured the three circulating Bicentennial coins on the cover. It was also at this time that the merit-badge design was changed to that of the obverse of the Washington quarter.

This era saw the American Numismatic Association begin to engage in more activities for young numismatists. At the 1973 National Scout Jamboree, the ANA was represented by a Merit Badge Midway booth, and it maintained a similar presence at all Jamborees through 2010.

With the circulating coin changes of the 1980s and 1990s, it was time for a review of the requirements again, and, once approved by the national advancement committee, I prepared a new book with the assistance of several Midway booth staff members. This was introduced in 2003 and a color version was released in 2010. Whitman Publishing also introduced a two-page folder for use by Scouts in housing the coins required for the badge.

AN ONGOING COLLABORATION

The Girl Scouts embraced coin collecting with similar gusto and have been keen to nurture the hobby over the decades, readily updating badge programs to remain in step with the realities of modern numismatics. The Scouts' approach to coin collecting evolves as part of a decades-old partnership that continues to flourish in unexpected ways.

Or, as Marilyn Reback points out, "Much like Girl Scouting itself, which offers troop or neighborhood settings or individual girl memberships, numismatists can enjoy the hobby through organized groups or shows, or at home through books, the Internet, or email connections. Both are global in scope, and offer camaraderie of shared interests."

These and other commonalities surface time and again, establishing the basis for a decades-long relationship between Scouting and coin collecting—one that eventually found its highest expression in the halls of Congress and the hands of the U.S. Mint's engravers and production professionals.

SUPPORT FROM THE ANA

The American Numismatic Association has been instrumental in cultivating and maintaining strong relationships between Scouting and numismatic organizations, setting up a host of programs and initiatives in an effort to support Scouts' budding numismatic interests and talents. In recent decades, the ANA has also played an important role in the establishment of standards for merit badges, as well as in the promotion of promising young collectors.

Jeff Swindling is an Eagle Scout who served on the ANA's board of governors from 2013 to 2015. Now closely involved with the upkeep and implementation of standards for coin-collecting merit badges, he was deeply influenced by his association with the ANA during his time as a Boy Scout:

> Despite earning 81 merit badges in my Scouting career, my heart was always with my very first—Coin Collecting. I eagerly shared things I learned about coins with my fellow Scouts, friends, and schoolmates. The merit-badge program has many opportunities for Scouts to learn and grow; Family Life taught me about budgeting and saving for things I wanted to buy, Public Speaking helped me be more comfortable sharing my knowledge with others, Art taught me to appreciate the aesthetic qualities of my favorite coin designs, and Metalwork helped me gain a deeper understanding of the process of how coins are made. The Scout Oath and Scout Law were my guiding principles (Thrifty always helps when building a collection, but Clean is something you should never do to coins!) on my way to building skills in leadership and volunteering.

Swindling went on to have unusual success as a Scout and numismatist, earning a host of prestigious awards from both communities, including the National Eagle Scout Association's National Outstanding Eagle Scout Award and the ANA's 2003 Outstanding Young Numismatist of the Year. This may be unusual, but it is not exactly an accident; the ANA offers several awards and programs to encourage exceptional boys and girls, and it tends to value applicants demonstrating many of the qualities nurtured by the Scouts.

As with Swindling's case, Marilyn Reback made a similar journey from Scout-collector to active numismatist. She helped oversee the development of the "Fun with Money" patch, developed by the Girl Scouts to give numismatics a badge distinct from the larger category of "Collecting Hobbies." She tells the story of the badge's development, goals, and requirements:

> The ANA offered workshops and resources to help Junior Girl Scouts earn their Collecting Hobbies badge locally starting in 1992, and held its first national convention workshop in Spring 1993. However, the Association sought a recognition focusing specifically on the world of numismatics.
>
> Representing the ANA, I began working on a patch program with the Girl Scouts Wagon Wheel Council (now part of Girl Scouts of Colorado) in Colorado Springs, Colorado, in 1992. The resulting "Fun with Money" patch was approved in 1993. The patch itself pictures a Peace dollar, reflecting not only a global theme, but also making a connection to the ANA's role in obtaining approval for issuance of the Peace dollar following World War I. The ANA is responsible for updating the requirements.

The Fun with Money patch requirements are broken down into age-appropriate activities. Through hands-on participation, use of the senses, and creative thinking, girls explore money and its relationship to history, culture, economics, and art. They touch on unfamiliar subjects as well. How do monetary forms and designs reflect a nation's history and values? Have they noticed recent changes in paper currency and new coinage issues? Where is our money made?

Fun with Money Patch Workshops are offered at every ANA show. They are, as the name implies, fun events. Whether or not they were collectors before the workshop, Scouts expand their knowledge of the money we use every day and perhaps discover the benefits of and a passion for the hobby. Active participation is key to learning. Generous donations allow us to provide examples of a variety of numismatic items, such as world coins and paper money, medals, and tokens.

Girls make connections with other area troops, as well as with Scouts attending the convention with family from out of state, broadening their sense of belonging to a world organization. Parents and leaders are encouraged to join in. If they like, Scouts stand up and describe the coin designs they created before coming to the workshop; their ideas tell us all about what young people value about our nation. The Scouts' input and their participation are always impressive; they are truly becoming tomorrow's leaders. The adults support their interest and curiosity by bringing them to the workshops and participating alongside them.

Eugene Freeman is a Boy Scout Merit Badge Counselor who served as the local Scouting Committee Chair of the Planning Committee for the ANA's World's Fair of Money from 2011 through 2015. He details another important numismatic program for scouts called "Scouting at the ANA":

For the last three years of the World's Fair of Money, there has been another program, which has been open to Boy Scouts, Girl Scouts, and uniformed adult Scout leaders of all ages. This is the "Scouting at the ANA" program. In this program, the participants could earn a center patch with a Liberty Walking design, and a segment patch with "Chicago" and the applicable year. I designed this program, and obtained approval for it (and its requirements) from the ANA and from the Northwest Suburban Area Council BSA.

The program was sponsored by the Chicago Coin Club and the Illinois Numismatic Association. This program is different from the other programs, in that all the requirements are fulfilled on the show floor. (At times, Scouts have come to the patch clinics, earned the patches, and left, without ever experiencing what can be learned by actually attending the show itself.)

MAKINGS OF A COMMEMORATIVE

All of this collaboration was bound to bear fruit, and in 2001, with the centennials of the Boy Scouts and Girl Scouts on the horizon in 2007 and 2013, respectively, Jeff Swindling had an idea while discussing new ideas for the Coin Collecting Merit Badge with George Cuhaj.

"The National Scout Jamboree is held once every four years and is the pinnacle of all that is Scouting," said Swindling. "While serving on the staff of the Coin Collecting Merit Badge booth, I met George Cuhaj, who had led the booth since 1980. He asked me to help him brainstorm refreshed requirements for the new edition of the CCMB booklet he was writing, and I happily obliged. While discussing potential new requirements, I mentioned that 2007 was the upcoming 100th anniversary of the Scouting program, and that it would be really cool if we had a U.S. Mint commemorative coin to celebrate the occasion. I communicated this idea back to the ANA headquarters, who had contacts within Congress needed to get the idea off the ground."

The ANA moved forward with the proposal, but that didn't mean Congress would find the motivation necessary to grant the commemorative program its approval. Swindling continued, "The ANA's contacts originally weren't able to drum up enough support, and I got a call in 2005 saying that the bill was not likely to pass in enough time to have a coin made in 2007. I was extremely disappointed, because many other nations around the world were planning coins to commemorate the 100th anniversary of Scouting in 2007.

"Luckily, I had an ace up my sleeve—although Baden-Powell created the Scouting program in England in 2007, the Boy Scouts of America was not chartered by Congress until 1910. This time, the coin was approved by Congress and signed into law by the president in 2008. 350,000 silver dollars were authorized to be minted, with a $10 surcharge on each which would go to the Boy Scouts of America.

"In 2009, the Citizens Coinage Advisory Committee (CCAC) held a meeting at the ANA's annual Summer Seminar, where I was invited to review the proposed designs created by the U.S. Mint engravers. I got to provide feedback on approximately 20 obverse designs and 10 reverse designs."

DESIGN CONSIDERATIONS

The Boys Scouts of America Centennial silver dollar was released by the U.S. Mint in 2010. Its obverse features an image of three Scouts saluting under the inscription CONTINUING THE JOURNEY. The centennial dates of 1910 and 2010 are included in the field, and IN GOD WE TRUST and LIBERTY appear along the rim near the bottom of the design.

Donna Weaver, a designer in the U.S. Mint's Artistic Infusion Program, and creator of the image, noted that she paid careful attention to the pose, salute, and composition of the figures. "It is a permanent representation," she said of the design, "so it's important to be correct."

Jeff Swindling notes that "the original design we proposed had a 2010 Scout helping a 1910 Scout climb up a mountain—I loved the symbolism and allegory in the design. The design which was chosen actually has representatives of Boy Scouting, Cub Scouting, and Venture Scouting. Many people are surprised when they see a female Venture Scout on the Boy Scout Centennial commemorative coin."

Weaver detailed the process of creating the design, saying, "Adding the Venture Scout was a suggested option, and I liked what the Venture Scouts stood for and did. The roughs worked out well, gave a nice variation to the group I submitted, so I finished the design and submitted it." Interestingly, Weaver recruited members of her family to serve as early models for the poses and figures, though features were altered in accordance with Mint standards to prevent recognizable models appearing on U.S. coinage.

The coin's reverse was designed by U.S. Mint medallic sculptor Jim Licaretz. This design employs the Boys Scouts of America's emblem which places a bald eagle over a fleur-de-lis. Inscribed on this side of the coin are UNITED STATES OF AMERICA, BOY SCOUTS OF AMERICA, E PLURIBUS UNUM, BE PREPARED, and the coin's denomination of ONE DOLLAR. Licaretz has sculpted many coin and medal designs since 1986, including the reverse of the 2008 Bald Eagle silver dollar, the image of Andrew Jackson on the obverse of the 2008 Andrew Jackson Presidential dollar, and the reverse of the 2012 Denali National Park America the Beautiful quarter.

Three years later, in 2013, the Mint issued the 2013 Girl Scouts of the USA Centennial silver dollar in time for the organization's 100th anniversary. The obverse design for the issue featured the portraits of three girls of varying ages, with the inscriptions COURAGE, CONFIDENCE, CHARACTER, LIBERTY, IN GOD WE TRUST, 100, and 2013, and the West Point Mint's W mintmark.

Barbara Fox, a designer in the U.S. Mint's Artistic Infusion Program, told her story of working out the design:

> The three models live in my community. The young woman in the back was a high-school student at the time she posed for me. She was a member of Girl Scouts at the time, and her mother has been a Girl Scout leader in our area for over 25 years. Needless to say, they were thrilled to be connected to this commemorative coin. I thought she represented not only the older Girl Scout, but also the valuable lessons learned in the organization as a girl matures to adulthood. She has a calm and poised demeanor, in contrast to the two young girls who are smiling and laughing. I like to think those two enjoy the fun, adventure, and camaraderie that Girl Scouts can provide.
>
> I want my designs to have an emotional appeal when appropriate, and in this case I drew each of the girls as a real person, not a generic representation. I would like to point out that although I used three girls as models for this design, the U.S. Mint requires that their features are changed so as not to be recognizable as the model. I made this clear to the model and her parents when they were hired, but everyone was still very excited to play a part in the development of this coin.

The coin's reverse bears the logo of Girl Scouts of the USA with the inscriptions UNITED STATES OF AMERICA, GIRL SCOUTS, E PLURIBUS UNUM, and $1 placed in the field and along the rim. It was designed by U.S. Mint Artistic Infusion Program designer Chris Costello, who said of the layout, "The trefoil logo is a very striking and attractive graphic and I wanted to bring it to life by incorporating it as part of a larger dynamic composition. I was excited about the possibilities of working with bold and simple graphic forms that would complement the logo and enhance its message of unity, leadership, and self-confidence. My intent was to show the Girl Scouts logo emerging from its past with a proud legacy to the left, and have the girls' profiles looking forward to a bright future, represented by the mirror surface to the right. The final composition, sculpted as a coin, provided the energy needed to amplify the theme of the logo while giving it depth, vibrancy, and life."

CENTENNIALS AND BEYOND

When the Boy Scouts commemorative silver dollar was unveiled in 2010, Jeff Swindling was there.

"When I was contacted by the BSA National Office and invited to speak with the director of the Mint and the Chief Scout Executive at the official launch ceremony, I could barely contain my enthusiasm," he said. "I went through probably 100 versions of my speech, trying to write something which could express to the world everything that Scouting and coin collecting had done for me.

"At the ceremony, I presented both the director and the Chief Scout Executive with one of my personal wooden nickels, which I had made for my Eagle Scout Court of Honor. A few weeks later, I got a signed and personalized photo in a very official-looking envelope from the U.S. Department of the Treasury. Mint Director Ed Moy was smiling, standing next to me and Bob Mazzucca, holding up the coin I had given him. I still have it hanging in a place of honor in my office."

Girl Scouts of the USA CEO Anna Maria Chavez was similarly enthused upon the release of the Girls Scouts Centennial commemorative coin in 2013. "It is a beautiful coin, and a fitting tribute to our 100-year legacy of instilling the values of leadership, confidence, and character in girls across America," she said. "We enter our second century of service to girls poised for even greater things, and I can't imagine a better way to launch our next 100 years than with the minting of our commemorative coin."

APPENDIX H

American Arts Gold Medallions

This essay is adapted from sections of Dennis Tucker's American Gold and Silver:
U.S. Mint Collector and Investor Coins and Medals, Bicentennial to Date.

The early-1980s American Arts medals were a bridge between the era of federally outlawed gold and the U.S. Mint's dynamic and popular American Eagle bullion program that started in 1986.

During the Great Depression, various federal orders had made it illegal for the average American to buy and own gold. Their intent was to strengthen the U.S. economy by discouraging hoarding. In the 1930s nearly all privately owned gold was cashed in and held for decades by the Treasury Department. The executive orders were finally revoked in 1974, and Congress explored ways to sell the Treasury's gold reserves. Various programs were proposed to offer the metal in formats affordable for the average American family to invest in.

From 1980 to 1984, the U.S. Mint struck congressionally mandated half-ounce and one-ounce .900 fine gold bullion pieces. Unlike South Africa's Krugerrand and Canada's Maple Leaf, the American Arts Commemorative Series medals were not legal tender. In fact, at first they were designed specifically not to resemble federal coins: for the first two years, the medals bore no marks of content, fineness, or weight, and their edges were smooth. Although they honored popular American writers, singers, and other artists, the medals sold poorly. The Treasury tinkered with new features in 1982 to make them appear more coin-like, and launched new marketing efforts, but sales remained lackluster. Eventually hundreds of thousands were melted by wholesale buyers. In some cases today's surviving quantities are mere fractions of their original mintages and quantities sold. (For detailed information, see *American Gold and Silver: U.S. Mint Collector and Investor Coins and Medals, Bicentennial to Date.*)

Note: Values based on gold bullion price of $1,150 per ounce.

Date and Subject	Mintage	Quantity Sold	Estimated Surviving*	Value
1980, Marian Anderson (singer) half ounce	1,000,000	281,624	*225,000*	$595
1980, Grant Wood (artist) one ounce	500,000	312,709	*250,000*	$1,170
1981, Willa Cather (writer) half ounce	200,000	97,331	*83,000*	$575
1981, Mark Twain (writer) one ounce	141,000	116,371	*99,000*	$1,170
1982, Frank Lloyd Wright (architect) half ounce	360,000	348,305	*51,000*	$575
1982, Louis Armstrong (musician) one ounce	420,000	409,098	*60,000*	$1,180
1983, Alexander Calder (artist) half ounce	410,000	75,571	*8,000*	$595
1983, Robert Frost (poet) one ounce	500,000	390,669	*41,000*	$1,170
1984, John Steinbeck (writer) half ounce	35,000	32,572	*32,000*	$585
1984, Helen Hayes (actress) one ounce	35,000	33,546	*33,000*	$1,250

*After melting and other attrition.

Marian Anderson (1980)

Grant Wood (1980)

Willa Cather (1981)

Mark Twain (1981)

Frank Lloyd Wright (1982)

Louis Armstrong (1982)

Alexander Calder (1983)

Robert Frost (1983)

John Steinbeck (1984)

Helen Hayes (1984)

APPENDIX I

Modern U.S. Mint Gold and Silver Medals

This essay is adapted from sections of Dennis Tucker's American Gold and Silver:
U.S. Mint Collector and Investor Coins and Medals, Bicentennial to Date.

During the American Revolution, the Continental Congress authorized official medals to be designed and struck (often in Paris) to honor heroes of the emerging new nation. One famous example is the Washington Before Boston medal, awarded in 1776 to thank General George Washington, his officers, and his soldiers after their victorious bombardment of Boston and the British evacuation of the city.

The national mint of the United States was established in 1792, and since the early 1800s it has issued medals for commemorative and historical purposes. These have celebrated everything from acts of heroic lifesaving to famous entertainers and wildlife conservation. "The United States Mint produces a variety of national medals to commemorate significant historical events or sites and to honor those whose superior deeds and achievements have enriched U.S. history or the world," the Mint says. "Some of these are bronze duplicates of Congressional Gold Medals authorized by Congress under separate public laws, while others are produced under the secretary of the Treasury's authority to strike national medals."

The following is a sampling of silver and gold medals struck by the U.S. Mint since the early 1970s. These and more are studied in detail in *American Gold and Silver: U.S. Mint Collector and Investor Coins and Medals, Bicentennial to Date* (Tucker).

AMERICAN REVOLUTION BICENTENNIAL MEDALS (1972–1976)

Congress passed a law on February 15, 1972, to authorize national medals to commemorate the bicentennial of the American Revolution and "historical events . . . in the continuing progress of the United States of America toward life, liberty, and the pursuit of happiness." Medals were issued each year from 1972 to 1976, in various bronze, silver, and gold formats.

	Distribution*	Value
1972, G. Washington, Liberty Tree, bronze, dated	672,200	$4
(1972) G. Washington, Liberty Tree, bronze, undated (a)	791,000	$6
1973, P. Henry and S. Adams, Committees of Correspondence, bronze, dated	237,790	$4
(1973) P. Henry and S. Adams, Committees of Correspondence, bronze, undated (a)	475,812	$6
1973, P. Henry and S. Adams, Committees of Correspondence, silver (pictured)	208,120	$25
1974, J. Adams, First Continental Congress, bronze, dated	188,308	$4
(1974) J. Adams, First Continental Congress, bronze, undated (a)	511,428	$6
1974, J. Adams, First Continental Congress, silver	150,428	$25
1975, P. Revere, Lexington/Concord, bronze, dated	327,677	$4
(1975) P. Revere, Lexington/Concord, bronze, undated (a)	668,419	$6
1975, P. Revere, Lexington/Concord, silver	212,542	$25
1976, T. Jefferson, Declaration of Independence, bronze, dated	98,408	$4
(1976) T. Jefferson, Declaration of Independence, bronze, undated (a)	446,939	$6
1976, T. Jefferson, Declaration of Independence, silver	98,677	$25
1976, Statue of Liberty, We the People, 1.5-inch, bronze	438,971	$5
1976, Statue of Liberty, We the People, 1.5-inch, gilt bronze	45,163	$10
1976, Statue of Liberty, We the People, 1.5-inch, silver	211,772	$25
1976, Statue of Liberty, We the People, 3-inch, silver	8,824	$325
1976, Statue of Liberty, We the People, .906-inch, gold (pictured)	29,468	$600
1976, Statue of Liberty, We the People, 1.31-inch, gold	5,396	$2,000
1976, Statue of Liberty, We the People, 3-inch, gold	423	$26,000

* There are discrepancies in Mint and other government records as to the exact mintages and quantities sold of some medals. **a.** Issued as part of a Philatelic-Numismatic Combination or PNC (medal, postage stamp, and first-day cover).

COLORADO STATEHOOD CENTENNIAL MEDAL (1976)

Colorado was the only state to join the Union in the national centennial year of 1876, and therefore was the only one to celebrate its 100th anniversary during the national Bicentennial in 1976. Congress authorized a medal—struck in various alloys at the Denver Mint—to mark the anniversary.

	Mintage	Value
1976, Colorado Centennial, bronze	41,000	$6
1976, Colorado Centennial, bronze, mule (a)	*	$6
1976, Colorado Centennial, gilt bronze	5,000	$8
1976, Colorado Centennial, silver	20,200	$32
1976, Colorado Centennial, gold (pictured)	100	$5,200
1976, Colorado Centennial, three-piece set (b)	1,876	$45

* Included in number above. **a.** The mule variety has the standard centennial logo reverse combined with a Denver Mint obverse (showing the mint building). **b.** Issued in a hard plastic case containing one each of the bronze, gilt bronze, and silver medals.

VALLEY FORGE MEDAL (1978)

Congress authorized this medal to be struck for the United States Capitol Historical Society. It was designed by Chief Engraver Frank Gasparro and struck in several formats at the Philadelphia Mint.

	Mintage	Value
1978, Valley Forge, 3-inch, bronze	2,500	$45
1978, Valley Forge, 1.5-inch, gilt bronze	5,000	$15
1978, Valley Forge, 1.5-inch, silver	1,999	$50
1978, Valley Forge, 3-inch, silver (pictured)	1,000	$600
1978, Valley Forge, 1.31-inch, gold	339	$5,000

YOUNG ASTRONAUTS MEDALS (1988)

Three different designs were created for bronze, silver, and gold medals by students in the Young Astronauts program (a White House initiative that encouraged proficiency and interest in science, math, and technology). The medals were executed by U.S. Mint sculptor-engravers and struck in Philadelphia in 1988.

Common Reverse	Bronze	Silver	Gold

	Mintage	Value
1988, Young Astronauts, bronze, Unc.	28,700	$10
1988, Young Astronauts, bronze, Proof	(17,250)	$15
1988, Young Astronauts, silver, 1.5-inch, Unc.	15,400	$45
1988, Young Astronauts, silver, 1.5-inch, Proof	(33,250)	$50
1988, Young Astronauts, silver, 3-inch, 6-ounce, Unc.	1,075	$350
1988, Young Astronauts, silver, 3-inch, 12-ounce, Unc.	3,700	$600

	Mintage	Value
1988, Young Astronauts, gold, .875-inch, Unc.	13,000	$600
1988, Young Astronauts, gold, .875-inch, Proof	(3,400)	$700
1988, Young Astronauts, gold, 3-inch	38	$20,500
1988, Young Astronauts, three-piece set, Unc. (a)		$650

a. Bronze, small silver, and small gold medals in Unc. format in a blue box. Other two- and three-medal sets were issued as well; each is worth about the combined retail value of the medals it contains.

BENJAMIN FRANKLIN FIREFIGHTERS MEDAL (1993)

This medal was authorized as part of the Benjamin Franklin National Memorial Commemorative Medal and Fire Service Bill of Rights Act. Franklin organized the country's first fire company in Philadelphia in 1736. The medals were struck at the Philadelphia Mint on American Eagle silver planchets.

	Mintage	Value
1993, Franklin Firefighters, Unc.	26,011	$38
1993, Franklin Firefighters, Proof	(89,311)	43

PHILADELPHIA MINT COINAGE BICENTENNIAL MEDAL (1993)

This 1993 silver medal was issued in "The Philadelphia Set," a special packaging of the year's half-ounce, quarter-ounce, and tenth-ounce American Gold Eagle coins, plus the American Silver Eagle (struck at Philadelphia for the first time that year). The medal celebrates the bicentennial of the Philadelphia Mint's first coinage in 1793.

	Mintage	Value
1993, Philadelphia Mint Coinage Bicentennial, Proof	(12,869)	$125

NATIONAL WILDLIFE REFUGE SYSTEM CENTENNIAL MEDALS (2003)

In 2003 the U.S. Mint released a series of prooflike silver national medals to celebrate the 100th anniversary of the National Wildlife Refuge System, founded in 1903 by President Theodore Roosevelt. They were the first Mint products created using laser technology (for texturing the dies).

Common Obverse

	Mintage	Value
2003, Bald Eagle, bronze	(a)	$5
2003, Bald Eagle, silver	35,000	$27
2003, Salmon, silver	25,000	$29
2003, Elk, silver	25,000	$29
2003, Canvasback Duck, silver	25,000	$28

a. The Mint established no production limit for the bronze Bald Eagle medal. Mintage has been ongoing into the early 2010s, with the medal sold individually and packaged in various sets.

SEPTEMBER 11, 2011, NATIONAL MEDAL (2011)

This silver medal was authorized to mark the 10th anniversary of the September 11, 2001, terror attacks in New York City; Washington, D.C.; and Shanksville, Pennsylvania. A surcharge from each sale benefited the National September 11 Memorial & Museum at the World Trade Center site in New York.

	Distribution*	Value
2011-P, September 11	67,928	$60
2011-W, September 11	109,365	$55

* Quantities sold by the end of sale in December 2012.

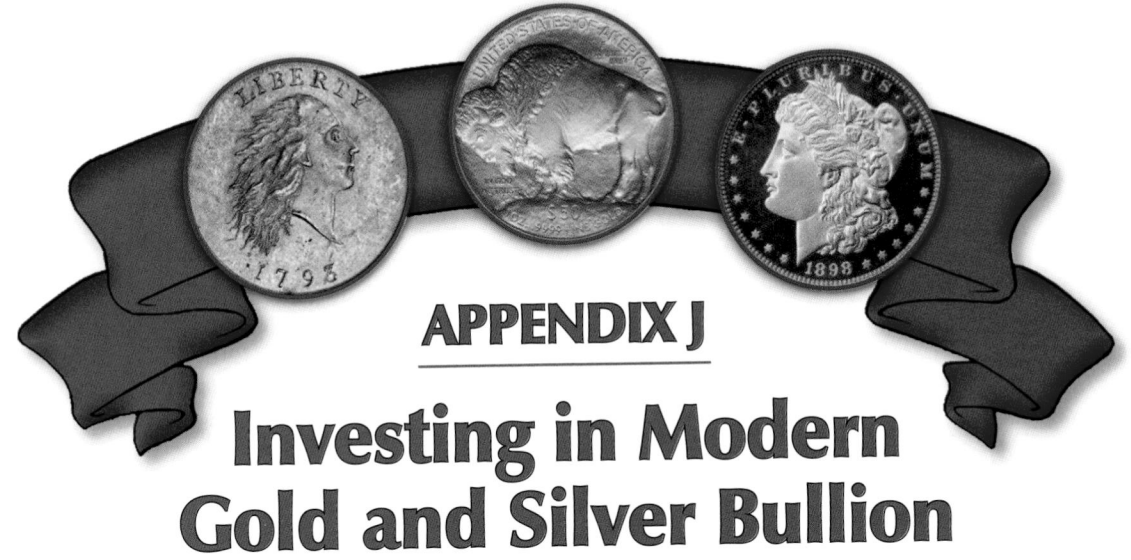

APPENDIX J

Investing in Modern Gold and Silver Bullion

This essay is adapted from appendix A and other sections of Dennis Tucker's American Gold and Silver: U.S. Mint Collector and Investor Coins and Medals, Bicentennial to Date.

Silver and gold can be intelligent choices for a diversified portfolio of investments. As with any investment, there is a level of risk involved in buying, holding, and selling precious metals. General caveats that apply to all investing naturally apply to the bullion and rare-coin markets, along with some warnings unique to these fields. The advice in this appendix is derived from guidelines recommended by the Securities and Exchange Commission, the Commodity Futures Exchange Commission, and other federal and state regulatory agencies, as well as the insight and experience of professional coin dealers and numismatists. This advice is addressed mainly toward the investor in *gold*, but it applies to silver, platinum, palladium, and other precious metals as well.

SOME GUIDELINES FOR PRECIOUS-METAL INVESTORS

Keep a healthy level of skepticism. It's the oldest advice in the investment world: If something appears too good to be true, it probably is. If an insider had access to a fail-safe investment, or an incredible bargain, or a guaranteed profit, why would he offer it to anyone else? Carefully investigate any claims of "secret," "new," or unusual ways of extracting or mining gold. Beware sensationalistic hard-sell tactics that rely on fear, e.g., threats of the federal government seizing privately owned gold, or the imminent collapse of civilization leading to the U.S. dollar losing all value.

Use common sense. Just as you would be suspicious of a door-to-door salesman who appeared on your front step offering expensive investments, you should be wary of unsolicited mail, email, or telephone offers to sell you bullion or gold-investment products (such as rare coins or certificates or stock in gold mines). Be skeptical of get-rich-quick schemes. Take common-sense steps to avoid identity theft (for example, never giving your Social Security number, bank-account information, or other financial details over the phone to unknown parties). Even if you establish a relationship with a seller, remember that private information given to a third party might not be kept secret.

Deal with people and firms you trust. Deal only with professional sellers you feel comfortable with, and whom you've vetted for trustworthiness. Get neutral, third-party advice from a knowledgeable and trusted friend or associate. Investigate a seller's membership in business organizations such as the

Professional Numismatists Guild (www.PNGdealers.com). Are they registered with the SEC or a state securities agency? Has the Better Business Bureau logged any complaints about them? If you search for their name on the Internet plus the word *lawsuit*, do you find anything disturbing?

Learn as much as you can. Don't give in to pressure to make an immediate buying decision, or to make a decision with information missing. Take your time and learn before you buy ("Investigate before you invest"). Almost any "opportunity" offered today will still be available next week or next month, and the same opportunity may be offered at a lower price elsewhere. If possible, ascertain the seller's profit margin (how much they buy gold for, versus their selling price). Verify claims made by the seller through your own research, and if you have questions, ask for clarification.

Look for guarantees of quality. Most gold bullion coins bear marks of their fineness and weight, as do many bars, ingots, rounds, and similar non–legal-tender gold instruments. Ask potential sellers if they guarantee the fineness and weight of their products.

Understand the terms and details of your investment. Some sellers add hidden fees and expenses to the base cost of the gold bullion and coins they sell. Refining and assay charges, shipping and handling fees, storage fees, insurance fees, and sales commissions are some ways a seller might increase your expense. (Of course, some of these added costs can be legitimate; and it should be noted that gold coins and ingots normally sell for a premium over the precious metal's *spot price*—that is, its commodity price set by the marketplace.) Study all terms of sale and understand delivery and other details.

Be mindful of taxes and reporting. Your state might charge a sales tax or a use tax on gold bullion purchases. Also be aware that the IRS has reporting requirements for large sales of precious metals (more than 20 ounces). A tax professional will be able to guide you on current laws and how they apply to your situation. Some bullion coins can be included in Individual Retirement Accounts; others are not eligible.

Know your own comfort level with risk. Analyze whether you can afford to invest in a tangible asset such as gold, and to risk a reasonable potential loss. The price of precious metals has risen in some periods and has fallen in others. Remember that coins and precious metals do not pay interest or dividends. The "play" is solely in a hoped-for increase in value.

Look for a two-way market. Modern bullion coins such as those produced by the U.S. Mint are readily *sold* as well as being easily *bought*. Other forms of gold, such as privately minted medallions, or scrap gold, might be harder to sell after you buy them, or might be sold easily only for a discount. If a non-standard form of gold needs to be assayed before you can sell it, the expense will eat into any profits.

Always take possession. Some firms will offer to sell you gold and then securely store it for you. While this might seem like a good idea, most professional coin dealers encourage taking physical possession of your gold and storing it yourself, in a bank safe deposit box or other secure place under your personal control. This allows you to avoid fraud—in the case of a seller who oversells his actual inventory—and gives you more immediate access to your gold in emergencies. Insurance for safe deposit boxes in banks with FDIC registration is inexpensive.

Make sure your precious metals are secure. A safe deposit box in an FDIC-recognized bank is very secure, can hold a large bullion investment in a small space, and is affordable. If you must store your gold or silver at home, take common-sense security precautions: install an alarm system and strong locks, secure your doors and windows, invest in a good fireproof safe, and don't let people know that you keep coins or bullion at home.

Know the pros and cons of different forms of precious metal. Some of these are discussed in chapter 3 of *American Gold and Silver*. Modern bullion coins—legal-tender gold or silver pieces minted by a government and guaranteed as to weight and fineness—often are bought, sold, and traded much more easily than ingots, bars, medals, jewelry, nuggets, and the like. Larger gold *bars* will sometimes require an independent assay for resale, to authenticate their gold content. Smaller bars, weighing one ounce or up to five ounces, can have higher liquidity, especially those manufactured by a recognized refiner such as Credit Suisse or Engelhard. Older foreign gold coins often trade similarly to bullion, with a buy-sell spread based on their gold content (with no additional numismatic value despite their age).

Purchase strategically. If you invest in the stock market through a mutual fund or other means, you're probably familiar with the concept of dollar cost-averaging. This is a strategy that reduces the impact of volatility on large purchases by dividing the total sum of your investment into smaller amounts put into the market at regular intervals. Taking a steady, long-term approach to bullion purchases won't always maximize profits, but it helps reduce downside risk. For example, if you invest a lump sum of $12,000 to buy 10 ounces of gold at $1,200 per ounce, you risk the metal's spot value slowly declining to, say, $900 per ounce over the course of 12 months. This brings a costly downside when you sell a year later. However, if you invest $1,000 per month for 12 months, you'll be buying along with the market, and by the end of the same period your $1,000 will purchase more than one ounce of gold. You'll lose less money when selling than you would have with the single investment of $12,000 at the market's peak.

SCHEMES TO LOOK OUT FOR

The Securities and Exchange Commission has warned investors about scams involving gold since the metal in bullion and modern coin form was made legal to buy again in the early 1970s. "The areas which are fraught with the greatest potential for fraud are representations concerning the existence, amount, and purity of gold, accuracy of assays and geological surveys, and secret refining processes," the SEC reported in December 1974. The following are some schemes that it described at that time, some of which still are concerns today.

> **False mining claims** were used to inflate a company's financial position and to tout its investment merit. Bogus or speculative geological surveys by a purported expert or misleading ore samples were used by the company as the basis for unwarranted high estimates of mineral value.

> Purportedly large quantities of gold located outside of the United States and obtained from underdeveloped countries were being offered in the form of **certificates of ownership** through offshore banks.

> An unscrupulous assayer conspired with a seller to certify that **bars of almost pure lead** were pure gold.

> Gold coins of **low purity** were issued by small foreign entities.

> **Secret processes** were promoted as promising to extract gold from ore previously labeled as worthless. Investors were induced to finance the construction of the secret-process machinery necessary for the production of the gold.

To these old schemes we might add: the growing danger of counterfeit and debased gold "coins," being sold even in what appear to be genuine third-party slabs; deceptive print ads that show dramatically enlarged pictures of American Gold Eagles, when what are being sold are small tenth-ounce coins; base-metal medallions advertised as "coins," especially those layered or plated in 24-karat gold (an insubstantial and basically worthless coating); and other frauds.

The SEC recommends that victims of fraud consult an attorney to assert and protect their rights if possible, and to report at the federal level to the SEC (which regulates public interstate offerings of and trading in securities related to gold), the Federal Trade Commission (which enforces laws prohibiting unfair or deceptive acts in interstate commerce), the Commodity Futures Trading Commission, the U.S. Postal Service (for mail fraud), and the Department of Justice. On the state and local level, fraud victims can contact the Consumer Protection Division of their state Attorney General's Office, the state Securities Commissioner, and the local Better Business Bureau. Although these agencies cannot intervene in your behalf or offer legal representation to obtain redress of your individual rights, your complaint may prevent others from being defrauded. In any event, it is far more costly and time-consuming to try to recover from a fraud than it is to be careful when buying.

INVESTING IN GOLD AND SILVER COLLECTOR COINS

As described in the coin-by-coin catalog in *American Gold and Silver*, the U.S. Mint's modern bullion coins often have a kind of "split personality" in the marketplace and within the hobby community. This can lead to pitfalls for uneducated buyers.

Coins struck purely as *bullion* (not in a limited-edition numismatic format) are intended to be sold for their precious-metal content plus a very small markup, as investments, hedges against inflation, a store of value, etc. The U.S. Mint will produce as many bullion coins as the public demands. In essence they should be regarded as commodities, each individual bullion coin being as valuable as every other—no more valuable, no less—just as one bushel of wheat or one barrel of oil is comparable to every other. However, sometimes hobbyists collect these bullion coins more like rare coins: they assemble them into one-per-year or one-of-each-variety coin collections, the way they might collect old Morgan silver dollars or Buffalo nickels—and they seek the finest grades they can find. Third-party grading firms like NGC, PCGS, ICG, and ANACS grade and slab the bullion coins just as they do old Liberty Head and Saint-Gaudens double eagles—this despite the fact that the modern coins are struck by the tens or hundreds of thousands (or millions), their quality from coin to coin is nearly perfect and nearly identical, and they're distributed as commodities rather than collectibles.

At the same time, collectors and investors often discuss the Mint's *numismatic* coins—limited-edition Burnished pieces, Proofs, and the like—as if they were bullion. On the aftermarket many of these coins trade at close to their precious-metal value, sometimes despite having very low mintages. When they're first released, the Mint prices them according to sliding scales based on the market value of their precious metal (a premium is added, but the basis is their spot value). And collectors often perceive the coins' numismatic values more closely in relation to their current bullion values than they would an old Mint State silver dollar or rare-date gold coin.

This blurry kinship between the bullion value and the numismatic value of the Mint's modern silver and gold coins requires you, as a buyer, to be savvy to the modern marketplace. The following caveats are made by professional numismatists:

"Buy the coin, and not its holder." Professional third-party grading firms sometimes release autographed holders, special labels, and slabs that signify a coin was issued at a particular coin convention or other venue, or is an "early strike" or has some other seemingly exotic feature. This kind of special packaging has limited premium value over the long run, in the secondary marketplace. A slab autographed by a coin designer or other famous person might have personal sentimental value, but ask yourself if other collectors will pay a premium for it in the future, and let your own buying be guided by the answer. Usually coin collectors consider only the alphanumeric certified grade (MS-69, PF-70, and the like) and pay little or no premium for extra adjectives.

Shop around. Sellers who advertise in non-numismatic media—for example, in full-page mainstream newspaper ads, or on television shopping programs—sometimes have overhead expenses that result in higher retail prices. (In one instance in 2015, a television offer of $700 for a modern U.S. Mint item was five times the price the same item could be bought for on eBay!) Even among numismatic sellers, coin prices can vary. Shop around for competitive pricing; get offers from your local coin shop and from professional coin dealers who advertise in *The Numismatist* (www.money.org/the-numismatist), *Coin World* (www.coinworld.com), *Numismatic News* (www.numismaticnews.net), and other hobby publications.

Don't overvalue high-grade coins. The U.S. Mint's modern products, on the whole, enjoy very high production quality. The difference between an MS-69 and MS-70 coin, each professionally graded by a third-party firm, can be visually indistinguishable for the average collector. If you pay a huge premium for the one graded 70, are you getting real value for your money, or are you buying into a fragile bubble that will burst? Older coins struck for circulation, before the mid-1900s, can be very expensive and rare in grades such as MS–68, 69, or 70. Many modern U.S. Mint products such as commemoratives coins and numismatic versions of bullion coins are extremely common in such grades. Be aware of the difference between modern and old.

Be mindful of collecting vs. investing. You can collect coins for pleasure, to enjoy their artistry, history, and educational and cultural significance. If you do, as the *Guide Book of United States Coins* advises, "A secondary consideration is that of investment, the profits from which are usually realized over the long term based on careful purchases." In other words, enjoy the hobby and don't expect or worry too much about profiting financially (although it's normal to think about such things).

If, on the other hand, you consider yourself solely to be an *investor* in modern bullion coins: Keep an open mind, learn about the coins you're investing in, and spend some time studying their designs. You might get bitten by the "coin bug" and become a *collector* as well!

A Note on "First Strike," "First Release," and "Early Release" Designations

The U.S. Mint does not have a program or designation for the first or earliest coins struck by a set of dies, or for the coins produced first or earliest in a particular year or series. Still, terms such as First Strike, Early Strike, and Early Release have sometimes been used in retailers' advertising, often centered around the Mint's bullion programs. In 2006 the Mint released the following clarification regarding coins popularly described in marketing literature as being "First Strike":

> The United States Mint has received inquiries from consumers regarding use of the term "first strike." The term has appeared in connection with the advertising and grading of 2005 and 2006 silver, gold, and platinum Proof and bullion American Eagle coins, and the new 2006 24-karat Proof and bullion American Buffalo gold coins. Currently, there is no widely accepted and standardized numismatic industry definition of "first strike." Coin dealers and grading services may use this term in varying ways. Some base its use on dates appearing on United States Mint product packaging or packing slips, or on the dates of product releases or ceremonial coin strike events. Consumers should carefully review the following information along with each dealer's or grading service's definition of "first strike" when considering a purchase of coins with this designation.
>
> The United States Mint has not designated any 2005 or 2006 American Eagle coins or 2006 American Buffalo coins as "first strikes," nor do we track the order in which we mint such coins during their production. The United States Mint held a launch ceremony for the 2006 American Buffalo Gold Coin on June 20, 2006, two days before its release on June 22, at which two Proof coins and two Burnished coins were ceremonially struck. However, those coins were not individually identified and were put in

regular inventory after the ceremony. The United States Mint did not hold any striking ceremonies for the 2005 or 2006 American Eagle coins.

The United States Mint strives to produce coins of consistently high quality throughout the course of production. Our strict quality controls assure that coins of this caliber are produced from each die set throughout its useful life. Our manufacturing facilities use a die set as long as the quality of resulting coins meets United States Mint standards, and then replace the dies, continually changing sets throughout the production process. For bullion American Eagle and American Buffalo coins, the United States Mint makes an average of about 6,000 coins from one die set. For Proof versions of the 2006 American Buffalo coins, the yield is an average of about 1,500 coins per die set. For Proof versions of the American Eagle coins, the yield is an average of about 300–500 coins per die set. This means that coins may be minted from new die sets at any point and at multiple times while production of a coin is ongoing, not just the first day or at the beginning of production. To put this in context, in 2005 the United States Mint produced approximately 356,500 one-ounce gold, 8,891,000 silver, and 6,300 one-ounce platinum American Eagle bullion coins.

American Eagle and American Buffalo coins are not individually numbered and the United States Mint does not keep track of the order or date of minting of individual bullion or Proof coins. The United States Mint begins production several weeks before these coins are scheduled to be released. By the release dates for 2005 and 2006 bullion coins, the United States Mint had already minted approximately 50% of the projected sales numbers for these coins. Any dates on shipping boxes containing Uncirculated bullion coins sent to Authorized Purchasers are strictly for quality control and accounting purposes at the United States Mint at West Point. The date on the box represents the date that the box was packed, verified as 500 ounces, and sealed, and the date of packaging does not necessarily correlate with the date of manufacture. The date on shipping labels and packing slips for Proof coins, which are sent directly to United States Mint customers from our fulfillment center, is the date the item was packed and shipped by the fulfillment center. The other numbers on the shipping label and packing slip are used to track the order and for quality control.

PCGS and NGC state their positions on their Web sites.

PCGS says, "The PCGS First Strike program designates coins issued in the first 30 days of the Mint's release. This designation not only adds value to modern coins, but takes modern coin collecting to another level with multiple Mint releases each year. There are two ways to obtain the First Strike designation: 1. The package mailed to PCGS has a postmark date prior to the PCGS cutoff date for that particular coin/issue. Only the coins need to be mailed to PCGS and received within the first 30 days of issue. 2. Submit the coins in the original unopened shipping box from the U.S. Mint with a postmark date prior to the specified PCGS cutoff date." The firm charges an additional fee per coin for the First Strike designation, and offers a bulk submission program.

NGC says, "NGC offers the Early Releases designation for selected coins received by NGC or an NGC-approved depository during the first 30 days of release. The term EARLY RELEASES will be noted as part of the description on the special blue Early Releases label. Other special and series-specific labels available from NGC may also be used in combination with the Early Releases designation. To qualify for Early Releases, all coins must generally be received by NGC or an NGC-approved depository within 30 days of their release. Coins being sent directly to NGC do not need to be accompanied by original packaging or shipped in sealed Mint boxes, but must arrive within the time period described above. The Early Releases request must be noted on the submission invoice, and additional service fees apply for the special label and designation verification. This is the default label for coins received within their first 30 days of issue. Alternatively, NGC offers the First Releases designation, which has the same definition as Early Releases."

BERNARD BARUCH AND THE 10 RULES OF INVESTING

American financier, stock investor, philanthropist, and statesman Bernard Baruch, in his two-volume 1957 memoir, *My Own Story*, admitted he was hesitant to lay down any magisterial "rules" on investing. However, he did list some points of advice for investing and speculating wisely and with self-discipline:

1. Don't speculate unless you can make it a full-time job.
2. Beware of barbers, beauticians, waiters—or anyone—bringing gifts of "inside" information or "tips."
3. Before you buy a security, find out everything you can about the company, its management and competitors, its earnings and possibilities for growth.
4. Don't try to buy at the bottom and sell at the top. This can't be done—except by liars.
5. Learn how to take your losses quickly and cleanly. Don't expect to be right all the time. If you have made a mistake, cut your losses as quickly as possible.
6. Don't buy too many different securities. Better have only a few investments which can be watched.
7. Make a periodic reappraisal of all your investments to see whether changing developments have altered their prospects.
8. Study your tax position to know when you can sell to greatest advantage.
9. Always keep a good part of your capital in a cash reserve. Never invest all your funds.
10. Don't try to be a jack of all investments. Stick to the field you know best.

Baruch encapsulated this advice in two lessons that experience had taught him: "getting the facts of a situation before acting is of crucial importance," and "getting these facts is a continuous job which requires eternal vigilance."

Today's coin collectors and investors in gold and silver will profit from this shared wisdom.

APPENDIX K

Building a Registry Set

This interview was obtained with the assistance of Q. David Bowers.

REGISTRY-SET COMPETITION—GET READY! GET SET! GO!

In recent years registry-set competitions conducted by the Professional Coin Grading Service (PCGS) and the Numismatic Guaranty Corporation (NGC) have profoundly affected the rare coin market. In brief, participants select a category of interest, learn the rules, and set about acquiring coins, keeping track of the numerical grade of each—such as 20 for VF-20, etc. It is only the grade number that counts—with other aspects such as sharpness of strike and eye appeal being irrelevant. Connoisseurs among the participants do indeed seek quality in addition to numbers, adding to the resale value of their collections, but this effort is not necessary for registry-set competition.

For certain key scarce and rare coins a multiplier is added to the number, per the rules to increase the worth of the rare piece in the registry. Participants as well as PCGS and NGC keep track of the cumulative totals. The winners in different categories are recognized and identified, usually under a "stage name" the coin owners choose.

This has been a stimulating pursuit for thousands of people. In the meantime, the activity of registry-set participants has created an unprecedented demand for coins—old as well as modern, common (in lower grades) and rare—that never existed before.

We asked PCGS and NGC to respond to our questions. Their answers (as of December18, 2015) are given below.

NUMISMATIC GUARANTY CORPORATION (NGC)

When did your registry-set program start, and what is the program's formal name?
The NGC Registry is a free online platform where collectors can register their coins, share images and descriptions with their fellow collectors, and join a fun and friendly competition for the best sets. Every January awards are given for the best sets in each category, and several top-ranking sets are selected for the most prestigious awards, which include Best Classic Sets, Best Modern Sets, and Best World Sets.

Established in 2001, today the NGC Registry has more than 8,400 participants who have registered more than 650,000 coins in nearly 80,000 different sets.

What categories do you offer (for American issues only), and what are the guidelines? What coins are allowed?

The NGC Registry offers categories for all U.S. coin series from colonial and early-American issues to the present. This includes set categories for classic and modern commemoratives, bullion issues, territorial gold, Proof and mint sets, and other issues. There are also a number of options for type collectors.

The NGC Registry accepts U.S. coins that are certified by NGC or PCGS, a reflection of the fact that many collectors purchase coins graded by either of the two major third-party coin-grading services.

What, in order, are the top five or ten most popular sets?

The most popular categories in the NGC Registry closely mirror the most widely collected U.S. coin series. These sets are:

> American Silver Eagles, 1986 to date, Mint State issues – 2,386 registered sets
> Morgan dollars, 1878–1921, circulation issues – 1,970 registered sets
> American Silver Eagles, 1986 to date, Proof issues – 1,501 registered sets
> Presidential dollars, 2007 to date, Proof issues – 1,194 registered sets
> Statehood quarters, 1999–2008, Clad and Silver, Proof issues – 1,067 registered sets
> Peace dollars, 1921–1935, circulation issues – 870 registered sets
> Kennedy half dollars, 1964 to date, Proof issues – 840 registered sets
> Sacagawea dollars, 2000 to date, Proof issues – 810 registered sets
> Franklin half dollars, 1948–1963, circulation issues – 690 registered sets
> Modern commemorative silver dollars, 1983 to date, Mint State and Proof issues – 683 registered sets

How many people participate in your registry-set program overall?

Overall, the NGC Registry has more than 8,000 people with at least one U.S. coin registry set. Collectively, these users have registered more than 400,000 NGC-certified U.S. coins in nearly 1,100 U.S. coin set categories.

What seems to be the longevity of interest of the typical participant?

NGC Registry users often participate over a long period of time as they work to complete a set. One of the many advantages of the NGC Registry is that it can help collectors to define goals—they can more easily visualize what coins are needed to complete a set.

These set categories have varying difficulties, and more challenging sets can take years to complete— if it is even possible to find all of the key dates. In modern coin registry sets slots are added each year for new releases, which keeps these interesting for collectors year after year.

NGC Registry users will often complete a set but then continue to look for upgrades to improve their set and its ranking in the NGC Registry. Other times NGC Registry users will complete a set in one category and then start a set in a different category.

The NGC Registry gives collectors a lot of options, and, as a result, many stay active in the NGC Registry for a number of years.

How many people build multiple sets?

The majority of NGC Registry users have more than one set, and some of the most prolific users have dozens of sets with thousands of coins.

Do builders of PCGS sets also build NGC sets and vice versa?

Yes, the NGC Registry allows both NGC and PCGS-certified US coins because many, if not most, collectors buy coins graded by both major third-party coin grading services. According to our data, 54% of NGC Registry users have U.S. coins that are graded by both NGC and PCGS, 41% have U.S. coins that are graded by NGC only, and 6% have U.S. coins that are graded by PCGS only.

What effect has this had on market prices?

The NGC Registry has been an important catalyst for expanding the hobby. It gives new collectors an introduction to the hobby with an easy-to-use collecting platform. It encourages collectors to be more active in the hobby and also to expand their interests.

Every month thousands of new coins are added to the NGC Registry. These active buyers have a tremendously positive impact on the coin market.

Why should readers investigate registry sets?

The NGC Registry has something for everyone, whether you are new to the hobby or an advanced collector. There are set categories for virtually every interest. It can be a lot of fun to view other people's sets and register your own to see how it stacks up. You can see some of the world's greatest collections and learn about some of the world's rarest coins. The NGC Registry is also an easy way to keep your collection organized and establish collecting goals.

PROFESSIONAL COIN GRADING SERVICE (PCGS)

When did your registry-set program start and what is the program's formal name?

The program started in February, 2001, and it is formally called the PCGS Set Registry®.

What categories do you offer (for American issues only), and what are the guidelines? What coins are allowed?

The PCGS Set Registry offers composites in all U.S. categories. Guidelines vary from set to set. We follow five basic set definitions:

Date Set: The Date Set includes one coin for each year in the series. Any mintmark and any variety can be used as the "date" in your set. For example, a Morgan dollar Date Set could have an 1899-S, 1900-O/CC, and a 1901 for the 1899, 1900, and 1901 in the Date Set.

Basic Set (Date and Mintmark): The Basic Set includes one of each date and mintmark in the series. For most of the Basic Sets, varieties can be used in place of a non-variety coin.

Classic Set (Date, Mintmark, and Major Varieties): The Classic Set includes one of each date, mintmark, and major variety, with the major varieties being those that have been recognized since the early 1970s. Examples of these long time recognized varieties would be the three-legged Buffalo nickel, the 1955 Doubled-Die Lincoln cent, and the 1918/7-S Standing Liberty quarter. These sets are dated through 1964. The purpose of the Classic Set is to allow your current collection to be compared to the great collections of the past, such as the Louis E. Eliasberg collection, the only "complete" collection of U.S. coins ever assembled.

Major Variety Set (Date, Mintmark, and Major Varieties): The Major Variety Set includes one of each date, mintmark, and major variety currently recognized by PCGS. Major varieties are defined as coins that are easily recognized as having major differences from other coins of the same design, type, date, and mint. Generally, major varieties are significant and can be easily seen with the naked eye. When there are various "states" to a variety, the major variety is the state which is considered the strongest by the collecting community. For example, there are three states, or types, for the 1936 Doubled-Die Obverse Lincoln cent. Only the Type One, the strongest and most apparent of the three states, is considered a major variety and is included in the PCGS Major Variety Set for Lincoln cents.

Note that new varieties are recognized each year and the number of coins needed for a Major Variety Set may increase over time. Also note that it is possible for varieties to be "delisted," *i.e.*, removed from inclusion in the Major Variety set. Sometimes varieties are misattributed by the numismatic community. For example, for years the pricing guides listed an 1869/8 overdate Indian cent. Experts now state that this is not a 9 Over 8, but "recut 9," or "9 Over 9.' This minor recutting is a much more common occurring variety and is not considered major. Accordingly, it does not qualify for inclusion in a Major Variety Set.

Complete Variety Set (Date, Mintmark, and all Varieties): The Complete Variety Set includes one of each date, mintmark, and all major and minor varieties recognized by PCGS. In regards to the Major Variety Set, only the Type One (using the example of the 1936 DDO previously mentioned) is allowed in and is necessary for the set. The Complete Variety Set, however, requires all three types of 1936 DDO Lincoln cents for the set. Note that for early series, such as large cents, Capped Bust half dollars, half cents, etc., the Complete Variety Set includes all die varieties as listed in the most recognized reference books.

Within these 5 types of sets, we have sets that are circulation strikes only, Proof only, SP (Specimen) only, and combination sets. We also offer type sets, as well as an area called the "Collectors Showcase" which allows collectors to build their own undefined set. Genuine-graded coins can be used to fill slots and are assigned a grade of one. Only PCGS-graded coins are allowed in competitive sets and the showcase. The PCGS Set Registry does not allow raw coins or coins graded by other services, but members may add those coins to their inventory in order to keep track of costs, purchase prices and sources, populations, market prices, and sales information.

What, in order, are the top five or ten most popular sets?

We have included only major sets and not specialty sets in this list. The counts also include retired sets:

Eisenhower Dollars with Major Varieties, Proof (1971–1978) – 720 participants
Morgan Dollars Basic Set, circulation strikes (1878–1921) – 622 participants
Sacagawea Dollars, Proof (2000–present) – 616 participants
Silver Eagles, circulation strikes (1986–present) – 587 participants
Morgan Dollars Date Set, circulation strikes (1878–1921) – 547 participants
Silver Eagles, Proof (1986–present) – 517 participants
Susan B. Anthony Dollars with Major Varieties, Proof (1979–1981, 1999) – 476 participants
Presidential Dollars, Proof (2007–2016) – 470 participants
Peace Dollars, circulation strikes (1921–1935) – 440 participants
Washington Statehood Quarters Basic Set, Proof (1999–2008) – 435 participants

How many people participate in your registry-set program overall?

There are 2,725 individuals who have or are currently participating in the top ten sets above. To date, a total of 10,064 collectors have at one time or another registered a set in the PCGS Set Registry. Currently, 6,548 members are active with sets.

In total there are 11,986 active members in the Registry. An active member is defined as having an active inventory and may or may not have active sets.

What seems to be the longevity of interest of the typical participant?

Just like the coin market in general, some people are lifetime collectors. Others are interested only for a brief time. The PCGS Set Registry has members who were active in 2001 and are still participating today. Every summer we recognize the top sets in the PCGS Set Registry. Some winners have gone platinum, which means they have received top honors for five years in a row, are still ranked number one, and are still active. 197 registered sets have won Ten Year Anniversary awards, meaning they have been in the top spot in active status for at least ten years in a row.

While many of the same people win awards every year, there is always an influx of new collectors who are also recognized. Some of these collectors burst onto the scene with outstanding, noteworthy sets, and within a year are ranked number one. The typical collector, however, takes a number of years to build his or her set to the world-class level.

How many people build multiple sets?

6,548 members have registered sets. Of the 6,548 members, 67.5% of them have built more than one set.

Do builders of PCGS sets also build NGC sets and vice versa?

Builders of PCGS sets also build sets in the NGC Registry because that registry allows users to add PCGS-graded coins to their sets. Builders of NGC-graded sets, however, cannot participate in the PCGS Registry because it is exclusive to PCGS-graded coins.

What effect has this had on market prices?

Early on the PCGS Set Registry became the ultimate "check list" for building sets. As a result, collectors became keenly aware of which coins they needed to fill the holes in their collections. Through the Registry's unique "What if?" feature, collectors learned what the addition of a coin would do to their rankings, which grade would be needed to rank number one, and what that coin would cost. As competition increased in certain sets in the Registry, so did the prices. This was especially apparent for modern coinage, which saw prices jump as demand for high quality coins increased.

Why should readers investigate registry sets?

It's a digital world and the PCGS Set Registry® (www.pcgs.com/setregistry) provides you with a powerful way to organize and virtually display your PCGS-certified rare coins. Since 2001, the Set Registry has been a free service for collectors interested in electronically maintaining their inventory with purchase dates, sources, costs, images, personal and public notes, and population data in a secure, online environment. Market prices are automatically uploaded from the number one pricing source on the Internet, the PCGS Price Guide (www.pcgs.com/prices). In addition, want lists can be created for items that are needed. When an item is sold, you can keep accurate records by adding the date sold, the buyer, and price realized.

Once inventory is listed, collectors can build sets and enjoy friendly competition with others who share their joy of collecting. For the beginner, the Set Registry program is a great way to watch a collection grow as it helps you to see which items are needed for a set. And, with the built-in www.Collectors.com Shop feature, finding coins that are needed for sets is only a click or two away. The Registry software is very simple and easy to use. Loading inventory is just a matter of typing certification numbers into an online form and images can be uploaded directly into your inventory. When you are ready to begin building a set, the software indicates which set can be started based on your inventory. Sets can be public so that you can share your sets with others, or sets can remain private.

For the advanced collector, you will find links to your grading submissions and can upload items directly into your Registry inventory and sets after the items have been graded. You can also use the "What if?" feature which helps determine what the addition of a certain item will do to the overall ranking of your set. In the PCGS Set Registry, coins in each inventory are linked to CoinFacts (www.pcgscoinfacts.com/), the number one online coin encyclopedia which delivers auction prices realized, pricing and populations for different grades of the same coin, rarity and survival estimates, and expert commentaries.

All levels of collectors will enjoy the Set Registry's newest feature, the PCGS Digital Album (www.pcgs.com/digitalalbumguide). These albums are reminiscent of the days when collectors maintained cardboard albums to store their collections. You now have a beautiful way to share your coin sets with the world while your inventory remains safely stored in safe deposit boxes. Albums are built from the images of items in sets which you have created in the Set Registry. Six different color pallets are offered and your personal set description can be added to the albums' inside cover. The albums are printable and sharing can easily be done through any number of different social media venues.

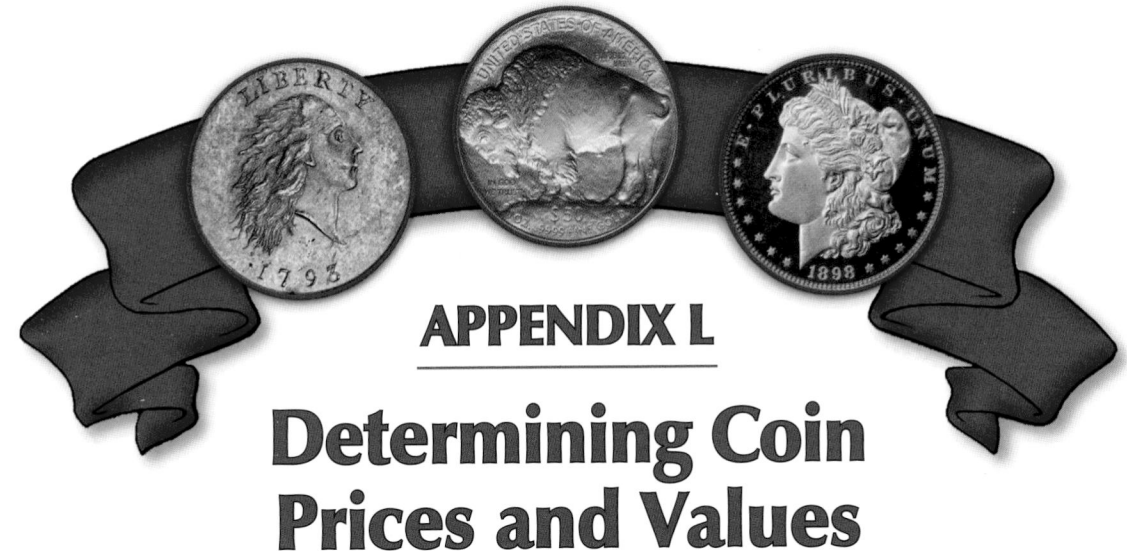

APPENDIX L

Determining Coin Prices and Values

This essay is adapted from sections of Q. David Bowers's
Expert's Guide to Collecting and Investing in Rare Coins.

The science of numismatics is a paying investment if a collection be formed with some judgment. An important and scientific collection of anything cannot be formed unless the collector is intensely interested in the subject and willing to devote much time to the study of all matters closely connected to the line he has selected. He must be an enthusiast. . . . I do want to thoroughly impress the fact on everyone that the time to form collections of things is when no one is collecting that particular series. I have made all kinds of mistakes in collecting . . . but I did manage to form a collection of United States gold when not many were interested in it. . . .

—*William H. Woodin, May 1911*

DETERMINANTS OF VALUE

The market price of a rare coin, token, medal, or currency note is dependent upon several factors, no one of which can stand alone. It is appropriate to say that price can be one thing and value another. I'll discuss market prices, and along the way suggest that some prices can represent better values than others. Of course, if a coin sells at auction for $20,000, it is also correct to say that at that moment it was valued at that sum. In the marketplace a comment such as "this coin has a market price of $20,000" is interchangeable with "this coin has a market value of $20,000."

Common, but expensive: the MCMVII (1907) High-Relief $20 gold double eagle is not a great rarity, for more than 6,000 are estimated to exist, most of which are in Mint State. However, such a Mint State coin is valued well into five, even six, figures.

A coin can be a great rarity, but have a low market price. A coin can be common, but have a relatively high price. Some gem Mint State coins have low prices, and some well-worn pieces have high prices.

The factors I mention here are the fundamentals. Your knowledge of them can be vastly expanded by further research.

RARITY

The rarity of a coin is an important element of value. Rarity refers to the specific number of coins known to exist in numismatic hands. As new discoveries are made and as some coins become lost, a rating of rarity can change. However, for most U.S. coins, estimates of rarity are well established.

Of the 1838-O (New Orleans Mint) half dollar, only about 12 to 15 are known today.

Of the 1970-D Kennedy half dollar, 2,150,000 were struck, all of which were sold in special sets to collectors. Accordingly, its rarity can be estimated at 2,000,000 or so Mint State coins in existence today, assuming that 150,000 may have strayed or been lost or spent.

Of the 1776–1976 Bicentennial half dollar, 234,308,000 were made for circulation. Most of these were issued, but half dollars were not often seen in circulation then, nor are they now. How many survive today is anyone's guess. In the absence of having any figures as to the government melting or destroying of such pieces, an estimate of 200,000,000 or so is reasonable.

The estimates reiterated, plus prices in the *Guide Book of United States Coins, Deluxe Edition*, Second Edition (referred to henceforth as *MEGA RED*, Second Edition), for each of the three preceding examples are as follows:

> **1838-O half dollar** (*estimated 20 known*)—MS-60: $500,000; MS-63: $750,000.
>
> **1970-D half dollar** (*estimated 2,150,000 known*)—MS-63: $20.
>
> **1776–1976 half dollar** (*estimated 234,308,000 known*)—MS-63: $3.

So within the half dollar series, a coin of which fewer than 20 are known can be worth hundreds of thousands of dollars, while one of which a couple hundred million are known is worth about face value (plus a slight premium for the effort in handling), never mind that the latter coin is more than a quarter century old and is in Mint State.

MEGA RED, Second Edition also lists values for certain Civil War tokens of common varieties, in each of several metals. Most of these were struck in copper, and many were made in brass. Tokens in other metals are scarcer. Within this series, a common die variety, such as a Dix, Not One Cent, or Monitor issue, typically exists to the extent of an estimated 1,000 to 5,000 or so examples. On the other hand, many if not most silver Civil War tokens are one of a kind for their die variety, or one of just a handful.

Adapting *MEGA RED*, Second Edition prices to die varieties (descriptions and estimates added by me, and assuming "Unc." to be MS-63) for certain metal listings, we get this:

> **1863 Civil War token, copper or brass** (*estimated 1,000 to 5,000 known of a given common die variety*)—F-12: $15; VF-20: $25; EF-40: $35; MS-63: $125.
>
> **1863 Civil War token, silver** (*estimated 1–5 known of a given die variety*)—F-12: $200; VF-20: $300; EF-40: $500; MS-63: $1,200.

Unlike the situation for popular U.S. series, prices for Civil War tokens often require a lot of digging to find. Accordingly, here are some actual market prices I have paid for certain Civil War tokens:

> **1863 Civil War token, copper; cloaked head on obverse; flag, liberty cap, etc., on reverse; die variety Fuld-36/340a** (*estimated 500–1,000 known*)—MS-65 red and brown: Common, but not among the most common. I paid $45 on September 29, 1997. Formerly from the Cindy Grellman Collection.
>
> **1863 Civil War token, silver, cloaked head on obverse; flag, liberty cap, etc., on reverse; Fuld-36/340f** (*estimated 2–4 known*)—MS-64, planchet lamination on obverse: Bought for $600 on August 8, 1998, from Rich Hartzog. Pedigreed to an auction held by George Fuld, June 1979, Lot 2715, where it sold for $24.

The foregoing illustrates that relative rarity is important *within the context of a given series*, but that if a series is not widely collected, extremely rare coins can be inexpensive. Conversely, in a very popular series, coins that exist in quantity can be expensive—and worth the cost—as the market is broad and there is a strong demand. Stated another way, an 1838-O half dollar, of which an estimated 12 to 15 are known, is valued at $750,000 in MS-63 grade, because it is rare and also part of a very popular and widely collected series. A silver Civil War token, of greater rarity (only 2–4 known) and in higher grade, is worth $1,200, because it is in a specialty niche, with relatively few collectors seeking it.

Another set of prices, these involving numismatic items that are believed to be unique (just one known) in collectors' hands, demonstrates the same thing—that well-known rarities bring far better prices than do pieces known only to specialists:

1822 $5 gold half eagle *(unique in collectors' hands)*—AU-55: $7,500,000 (*MEGA RED*, Second Edition price).

1792 pattern Birch cent, white metal *(unique in collectors' hands)*—Unc: $1,500,000 (*United States Pattern Coins*, Tenth Edition price).

1737 Higley "The Wheele Goes Round" copper *(unique in collectors' hands)*—VF: $376,000 (*MEGA RED*, Second Edition price).

1837 Feuchtwanger token in silver, Rulau HT-268-A, Low-120, in silver rather than Feuchtwanger's composition *(unique in collectors' hands)*—MS-60: $5,000 (actual transaction, 2001; related pieces, but not in rare silver, are listed in *MEGA RED*, Second Edition).

1863 Civil War token issued by Roswell Barnes, Brighton, Michigan; Fuld-MS-085A-03d; copper-nickel *(unique in collectors' hands)*—MS-65: $550 (actual transaction by Rossa & Tanenbaum, 1997).

By way of explanation, the 1822 $5 gold piece is one of three extant, the other two being held by the Smithsonian Institution. Although *MEGA RED*, Second Edition lists it at $5,000,000, a check for twice this amount would not buy the coin if the owner did not want to sell. This prompts me to state that *the rarer the coin, the less fixed or standard are the market values*. Those with great rarities can name their own prices, and if a buyer is at hand, they might be successful.

The 1792 Birch cent was sold years ago; there are no modern prices. Although *MEGA RED*, Second Edition gives $1,500,000 as a current estimate, if auctioned it would likely bring far more. The 1776 Janus copper is in the same category. I cataloged this in the late 1970s as part of the Garrett Collection for The Johns Hopkins University, and it has not been seen on the market since. Ditto for the 1737 Higley copper, in recent years a prized possession of an eastern specialist.

The 1837 Feuchtwanger token in silver sold for the high price of $5,000 years ago. However, because the Ford Collection of Hard Times tokens (Stack's 2004) did not have an example, and because many pieces of which two to four are known sold for much more than $10,000 each (some for more than $50,000) at that event, the silver Feuchtwanger would probably bring more if offered today.

The last coin on the list, the Civil War token, is a classic and could be called priceless, but it is part of a niche market without many players. In such specialized markets, rarities tend to be inexpensive.

As can be seen from time to time, a coin can be common in one grade, such as Good-4, but rare in MS-65. A coin that is rare in a certain high grade, but not in lower ranges, is sometimes called a *condition rarity*. One cannot say that a 1901 Morgan silver dollar is rare, for 6,912,183 were minted, and well over 50,000 well-worn coins exist today. In VF-20 *MEGA RED*, Second Edition prices the 1901 for $50. However, in gem MS-65 only a handful exist, and the listed price is $475,000. Accordingly, as a date the 1901 is common, but in MS-65 it is a condition rarity.

Rarity is important, but only in connection with other factors.

GRADE

Generally, for a given *coin*, the higher the grade, the higher the value. The 1901 Morgan dollar discussed previously, worth $50 in VF-20 grade but $475,000 in MS-65, is an example. This is not always true for certain other numismatic items, as I shall explain. Most numismatic rules have exceptions.

Often, a very small difference in a grading number can mean a very big difference in market price. Consider another Morgan dollar:

The 1896-O Morgan silver dollar is common and inexpensive in lower grades, but emerges as an expensive rarity in MS-65 preservation. As the price differentials between grades are so great, much care must be taken to determine what grade is suitable for you, and, later, to assure proper quality, grade, and eye appeal when you select a coin.

1896-O Morgan silver dollar—VF-20: $39; EF-40: $43; AU-50: $160; MS-60: $1,500; MS-63: $8,000; MS-64: $42,000; MS-65: $175,000.

For some other coins, such differences are not as important to price. Here is the 1936 Elgin (Illinois) Centennial commemorative half dollar, these being the prices listed in *MEGA RED*, Second Edition:

1936 Elgin Centennial commemorative half dollar—AU-50: $180; MS-60: $185; MS-63: 195; MS-65: $225; MS-66: $300.

Most of the 20,000 Elgin commemorative half dollars struck in 1936 still exist today, and nearly all are in Mint State. Gems are common. Selecting a gem MS-65 for your collection is, as they say, a "no-brainer."

No matter how much money you may have to spend, if you are seeking a Mint State 1896-O dollar, you will want to be very careful—for a tiny difference in grade can make a huge difference in market price. On the other hand, for the 1936 Elgin half dollar, go ahead and buy an MS-65. You don't have to do much thinking about it. To buy an MS-60 1896-O dollar might be quite worthwhile, in view of much higher prices for grades beyond that. However, buying an MS-60 1936 Elgin half dollar would seem to make no sense at all! (Perhaps without realizing it you are already well on your way to becoming a smart buyer!)

As to those exceptions I mentioned, in some instances the evidence that a numismatic item has been actually used for its intended purpose can make it far more valuable than one that was preserved in Mint State. For example:

An Indian Peace medal known to have been awarded to an Indian chief is more valuable than one made from the same dies but for a collector's cabinet.

A silver award medal given as an exposition or competition prize may be worth, say, $50, if blank and not awarded, but in Mint State. However, if it is engraved with the name of a recipient, such as to Samuel F.B. Morse for improvements in the telegraph, it might be worth hundreds or thousands of dollars.

In the *Guide Book of Double Eagle Gold Coins*, I included the following, and cannot resist restating it here:

The most exciting recent example of a used (in this case, very well used to the point of being damaged) item being worth more than a Mint State one involves an otherwise ordinary $20 gold coin recovered in 2000 from the wreck of the Confederate submarine Hunley, which had sunk in 1864.

The piece was dated 1860 and was disfigured from being hit by a bullet that might otherwise have killed its owner, George Dixon, who later carried it as a good luck piece while commanding the Hunley. Salvagers said that this coin, worth, say, a few hundred dollars if in VF grade, was worth $500,000 because of how it was used!

Examples of Indian Peace medals, old bank notes, and the *Hunley* artifact are exceptions to the rule that higher grades are the most valuable. Such exceptions will probably not be relevant to what you collect, but it is worth knowing about such things. Besides, you can keep such situations in mind in case you want to stump someone in a quiz at a coin-club meeting!

POPULARITY

Popularity is probably the single most important determinant of value. I could devote pages upon pages to the subject, but as it isn't particularly abstruse, these few paragraphs should suffice.

Basically, if rarities and grades are comparable, a numismatic item in a widely collected series will bring a much higher price than will one in a narrow, specialized series with few adherents. Thousands of Mint State 1889-CC Morgan silver dollars exist, and yet *MEGA RED*, Second Edition prices an example in minimum MS-60 grade for $26,000. In contrast, not more than a few hundred 1935 Alaska Rural Rehabilitation Corporation twenty-five-cent tokens exist, but a Mint State coin is priced at just $275.

The difference is due to popularity. Well over 100,000 enthusiasts, perhaps far more, aspire to collect Morgan silver dollars by date and mint. Although thousands of Mint State 1889-CC dollars exist, they are expensive because they are rare in relation to the demand for them. On the other hand, probably not more than a few hundred collectors aspire to gather the Alaska tokens, and a year or two can elapse before my company receives "want-list" requests for them.

This aspect also appeared under "Rarity" earlier—the unique 1822 $5 half eagle is listed at $7,500,000, while unique items in series that are not popular can be bought for very modest sums.

This general rule is true all across numismatics.

Popularity can be adjusted, manipulated, and revised. While rarity tends to remain constant, popularity can change over a period of time. Even entire collecting *fields* can change, sometimes dramatically. Birds' eggs and tobacco tags, widely collected in the 19th century, are hardly ever heard of in this context today. A friend in the stamp business mused the other day about the future of that hobby, what with memberships in societies declining and stamps seeing less use over the years.

However, as I see it, this negative thinking does not apply to numismatics—money is not going to go out of style anytime soon. Many new America the Beautiful quarters and commemoratives are coming down the pike—enough to keep us all busy for a long time—and membership in the American Numismatic Association (ANA) has increased significantly in the past decade.

What makes a coin or an entire series popular? The following sections contain some of my thoughts on the subject.

LISTINGS IN THE RED BOOK

If a particular variety is listed in a frequently used or cited reference, its value will be enhanced. Years ago, beginning in 1934, *The Standard Catalogue of United States Coins* was the arbiter of what to collect.

Many used the various editions of this text to compile lists of what they needed. If a coin was listed in the *Standard Catalogue*, it was desired. If it was rare, desirable, interesting, or anything else, but was not listed, it was not added to "want lists."

Today, the *Standard Catalogue* has lapsed into history, with the last (18th) edition being published in 1958. In the meantime, the *Guide Book of United States Coins* (known as the *Red Book*), and now the deluxe edition, *MEGA RED*, have become far and away the most widely used books on prices. Hence, a coin listed in one of these becomes more popular. Of course, basic dates and mintmarks are necessarily listed in the interest of completeness. However, the addition of repunched dates, curious mintmarks, doubled dies, and so on is not at all consistent, and some are listed while others are not.

Here are some examples of curious varieties listed in *MEGA RED*, Second Edition, and their prices, together with a related regular issue:

1936 Lincoln cent, Doubled-Die obverse—MS-60BN: $500.

1936 Lincoln cent, regular—MS-60BN: $5.

1892-O Barber half dollar, "Micro O" mintmark—MS-60: $28,000.

1892-O Barber half dollar, regular—MS-60: $900.

Overall view of an 1876-CC trade dollar. On a few of these coins the reverse is seen to be the Doubled-Die variety, with doubling of certain features, such as the branch at the lower right. Bill Fivaz, co-author (with J.T. Stanton) of the *Cherrypickers' Guide to Rare Die Varieties*, considers this to be the most spectacular doubled die in the American series.

Although a super-dedicated collector could search out these varieties by reading specialized texts, they would not be generally known if it were not for their inclusion in the *Red Book*.

Focus on "Numismatic Delicacies"

There are some famous American rarities that were made after a regular series ended. These were created as delicacies for collectors. Included are the 1913 Liberty Head nickel (the series otherwise ended in 1912), the 1866 without-motto silver quarter, half dollar, and dollar (that type ended in 1865), and the 1884 and 1885 trade dollars (the series ended in 1883).

Each of these is worth a lot of money, at least hundreds of thousands of dollars apiece, and for some, more than a million dollars. There is another post-issue rarity of equal importance, in my opinion: the 1868-dated large copper cent, the exact type as last regularly minted in 1857, but made in 1868 as a rarity for collectors. About a dozen exist.

This 1868 large copper cent is identical in design and appearance to a regular issue copper cent of the 1843 to 1857 Braided Hair style except for the date. Made as a delicacy for the numismatic trade, only about a dozen or so pieces are believed to exist today. (Hogan Pond Collection)

The pattern $4 gold pieces ("Stellas") of 1879 and 1880 are just that: patterns. They are not regular issues, but are strictly a part of the series of more than 1,800 patterns described in the tenth edition of *United States Pattern Coins*, by Dr. J. Hewitt Judd. However, as they are listed in the *Red Book*, the demand for them is multiples of what it would be if they were listed only in the Judd book.

There are other strictly pattern coins that are listed among regular issues in the *Guide Book*, and, accordingly, they have gained great popularity. The 1856 Flying Eagle cent and the 1838 Gobrecht silver dollar are just two examples.

The 1879 pattern $4 gold Stella (enlarged), the variety with Flowing Hair listed as J-1635 in the Judd book on patterns, is known to the extent of hundreds of specimens, from a mintage of somewhat more than 700 pieces. As a pattern coin it is one of the most plentiful of all varieties. However, because it is listed in the *Red Book* it plays to a much wider audience and, accordingly, is in strong demand and very expensive.

Listing a variety in the *Guide Book of United States Coins* is the equivalent of listing a common stock on the New York Stock Exchange. It (the variety or stock) becomes important and widely known.

To a lesser extent, listings in other places, such as the value guides published by *Coin World*, *Numismatic News*, the *Coin Dealer Newsletter*, and the *Certified Coin Dealer Newsletter*, help as well.

OTHER ASPECTS OF POPULARITY

The inclusion of a variety in a Whitman, Littleton, Dansco, or other widely sold coin holder or folder can increase its popularity and hence the demand for it. In the 1930s, Wayte Raymond published his "National" album pages for many series. For large copper cents of 1793 to 1857 he included openings for the basic dates and overdates, then a selection of other varieties such as letter sizes. Those varieties he chose became desired by a generation of numismatists, and important varieties for which there were no gaping holes to be filled were ignored by most.

News coverage can influence popularity. The demand for the 2004-D Wisconsin State quarters with Extra Leaf High and Extra Leaf Low was previously very strong, as they had been given wide play in *Numismatic News*, *Coin World*, and dealer advertisements since their discovery in December 2004. While they may no longer be as popular as when they were found, grading services have added these varieties to their listings of significant issues.

Over the years, certain current issues have been darlings of the press, and nationwide demand arose for them—such as the Liberty Head nickel without CENTS made and publicized in 1883, and the Small Date cent of 1960. Another example is the 1979-S Anthony dollar with "Filled S" mintmark and "Clear S." *MEGA RED*, Second Edition lists the former for $7 in Proof-65 grade and the latter for $70. In contrast, a Filled S vis-à-vis a Clear S on a Morgan silver dollar would attract little attention, and certainly not such a differential in market price!

Auction appearances generate publicity and increase desire. Every time my company has a nice MCMVII (1907) High Relief double eagle in a sale, something is said about its history, romance, and beauty in addition to its rarity and grade. When a spectacular rarity comes up for sale, its availability and publicity combine to draw potential buyers out of the woodwork—and someone who is not an active coin collector might jump in with both feet and buy it. I have seen this happen many times. The same is true for the 1879 $4 Flowing Hair Stella mentioned previously.

In other times, a collector of one series will jump ship and through a catalog description decide to plunge into another specialty entirely—based on an auction presentation. I recall spending quite some time researching and describing the early American medals in Part I of the Harry W. Bass, Jr., Collection in 1999. A North Carolina numismatist who did not specialize in medals and had not a single one in his collection—in fact, his main interest was *banjos* (the musical instruments)—became enchanted with the history of the Libertas Americana medal in silver. Although he was going on a trip to New Zealand, he kept in touch while away so as to participate in

A Libertas Americana medal dated July 1776, made in Paris in 1782, commisioned by Benjamin Franklin. The dies, by Augustin Dupré, feature Miss Liberty with a liberty cap and pole—the first depiction of a motif later used on some U.S. coins, starting with copper half cents and cents in 1793. The reverse shows America fighting off the British lion with the help of the French (represented by fleur de lis emblems on the shield)—an allegory illustrating the Revolutionary War.

the bidding for it. (He tried, but lost in the competition.) I could mention dozens, probably even hundreds, of instances in which a nice "spread" in an auction catalog on the gold coins of the Charlotte and Dahlonega mints, or a beautiful 1879 Schoolgirl pattern silver dollar, or an obscure colonial, served as the launch pad for a collector entering a completely new series.

The earlier-mentioned concept of "registry sets," initiated a few years ago by David Hall of Professional Coin Grading Service (PCGS) and soon joined by Numismatic Guaranty Corporation of America (NGC), has increased the demand for certain high-grade coins in these sets—with points being awarded to coins that are among the highest certified of their variety.

Market fads, trends, and cycles are exceedingly important aspects of a coin's popularity and, in consequence, of a coin's price. And yet, relatively few buyers know about these things.

Here are some vignettes from coin-market history, including the most popular items or series at the time—coins that everyone was talking about and that were leading the market. You may be surprised at some of the listings:

1860: Medals with the portrait of George Washington. Even the Mint collected them!

1899: Hard Times tokens of the 1830s. More popular at the time than were Morgan dollars!

1935: 1935-D and -S Boone half dollars with small "1934." The price skyrocketed in a matter of weeks.

1956: Proof sets of 1936 to 1942, and 1950 to 1955. Prices sometimes rose hourly, as posted on "bid and ask" boards at coin shows.

1960: Small Date Philadelphia cent of this year. A media event par excellence. A $50 sack of freshly minted cents sold for more than $12,000!

1962: 1903-O Morgan dollar, a market sensation when a long-hidden cache was found.

1963: 1950-D Jefferson nickels, the dazzling sensation of a great bull market in coins.

1975: Franklin Mint medals sold to the general public, who could not buy them fast enough.

1989: Certified MS-65 or finer silver and gold coins for investors. Prices went up and up and up some more.

2000s: High-grade certified coins for registry sets. Never mind whether a similar coin that is a grade-notch or so lower is as common as can be.

Each one of these hot spots in the market was riding a popularity crest and drew many new players into numismatics.

FAME

Many coins have significant value based on their *fame*. I am not quite sure you could call the 1804 silver dollar (the "King of American Coins") *popular*, as only 15 exist, and few people have the financial wherewithal to buy an example. Certainly, reading about this coin is a popular pursuit—more ink, including that in two books, is devoted to this particular variety than to any other single rarity in the U.S. series. However, the coin itself is not a popular item in the context of widespread acquisition. Most known examples show signs of wear, and, accordingly, grade and scarcity alone do not determine its price. Its value rests on its *fame*.

There are many other famous coins in American numismatics, their fame resting on a combination of historical importance, beauty, market price, rarity, and press agentry over the years.

If a coin hits the headlines with a value of a million dollars, as a rare 1866 no-motto Liberty Seated silver dollar did in 2004 when John Kraljevich and John Pack located the coin, long missing, in the hands of a non-collector, and returned it to its rightful owner, the coin will become famous. This particular coin, not well known previously (only two are known to exist), was showcased on television programs, in newspaper articles, and elsewhere. The ANA, whose museum was the coin's destination, featured it in publicity. For a time it was the talk of the hobby. Had it been for sale (it was not), chances are good it would have fetched a record price, due to its massive exposure in the media. In January 2005, the *other* specimen of this variety, the only one in private hands, was consigned by a Texas estate and was sold by American Numismatic Rarities (ANR) for more than $1 million.

A list of famous American coins with interesting stories would be a long one, but, for starters, would surely include the 1652 Massachusetts Pine Tree shilling, 1799 copper cent, 1856 Flying Eagle cent, 1943 error cent (struck in copper instead of the steel otherwise used this year), 1913 Liberty Head nickel, 1792 half disme, and 1851 Augustus Humbert $50 gold "slug."

As a professional numismatist, I know well that if someone consigned an 1851 Humbert $50 "slug," direct from the height of the California Gold Rush, it could be sold in a wink to just about anyone who could afford it—no matter whether they collected gold coins. All it takes is for someone to write about or tell of its romantic history!

Similarly, the *Mona Lisa*, in the Louvre in Paris, may or may not be the most beautiful of all paintings, and certainly *any* painting shares its one-of-a-kind status. Nonetheless, the *Mona Lisa* is the most famous of all paintings in the world and, consequently, probably the most valuable. If it should come on the market (theoretically, of course, as it is a French national treasure), I imagine the bidding audience would include many people who didn't own any other classic art, but wanted this icon.

PROVENANCE

The provenance, or identities of previous owners, can contribute to a coin's value. Often a common coin, if offered as part of a famous collection, will bring a very high price, simply because it affords the opportunity to own a coin with an illustrious background. I recall that in the Garrett Collection series of sales, 1979 to 1981, a common, worn 1913 Buffalo nickel, worth perhaps $12, brought several hundred dollars because it was from this collection.

Famous collectors of the past are many, and such names as McCoy, Maris, Randall, Parmelee, Mills, Stickney, Ten Eyck, and dozens more from generations ago add value to coins attributed to these collections today. Since 1950, dozens of other famous collectors have joined the Hall of Fame, including, in no particular order, and mentioning just a few (and deliberately excluding those who formed collections that I've helped sell), Farouk, Anderson-Dupont (agents), Robinson, Wolfson, Trompeter, Donlon, Gilhousen, Hydeman, Halpern, Gaskill, Wilkison, Hydeman, Buss, Miles, Black, Miller, Carter, Bloomfield, Benson, Browning, Naftzger, Bloomfield, Ryder, Ford, Kern, Robison, Judd, Price, Pittman, Starr, and Hawn. As to my own involvement, you can add Garrett, Norweb, Eliasberg, Bass, and a string of others.

Provenance listings for specific coins can be fascinating. The following is a listing for one of the 15 known 1804 silver dollars.

ADAMS SPECIMEN OF THE *1804* DOLLAR

John W. Haseltine was the first person to exhibit this specimen, a Class-III or restrike variety, early in 1876, with the story that it had been located by a private English source. This coin was purchased by Phinehas Adams of Manchester, New Hampshire. For a long time it was known as the "Lyman" dollar, after a later owner.

The following provenance is conjectural before circa 1875:

1858–1872: Believed to have been struck at the Philadelphia Mint during this period.

1875–1876: Captain John W. Haseltine, Philadelphia dealer.

1876: Phinehas Adams, Manchester, New Hampshire.

1880 (circa): Henry Ahlborn, Boston coin dealer and publisher of coin premium lists; the handling of this coin was a bright feather in his publicity cap.

1880: John P. Lyman, Boston, Massachusetts, who bought this as part of a "full set of dollars." Consigned with the rest of his collection to the following.

1913 (November 7): S. Hudson Chapman, Lyman Collection, Lot 16.

1913: Waldo C. Newcomer, Baltimore, Maryland. Displayed at the American Numismatic Society, 1914, and illustrated on Plate 17 of the catalog titled *Exhibition of United States and Colonial Coins, January 17th to February 18, 1914.*

1932: B. Max Mehl, on consignment from Newcomer.

1932: Colonel Edward H.R. Green.

1936–1943 (circa): Colonel Green estate. As of March 1943, the 1804 dollar was still in the Green estate, which was being administered by the Chase National Bank, New York City.

1943 (circa): A.J. Allen, Plainfield, New Jersey; the coin changed hands for a reported $3,200.

1946 (circa): Frederick C.C. Boyd, East Orange, New Jersey. Boyd must have acquired it for the satisfaction of having owned this famous rarity, holding it but briefly, after which he put it up for sale. By this time his main collection of U.S. silver coins had already been sold (by Numismatic Gallery, under the title of "The World's Greatest Collection," 1945).

1946: Numismatic Gallery (Abe Kosoff and Abner Kreisberg), on consignment from Boyd.

1946: Percy A. Smith, Portland, Oregon. Displayed by Smith on September 14, 1946, at the Oregon Numismatic Society meeting. Sold privately to the following.

1949–1950: B. Max Mehl, who had it in his inventory by October 1949.

1950 (May 23): B. Max Mehl, Golden Jubilee Sale (Jerome Kern and other collections), Lot 804.

1950: Amon G. Carter Sr., Fort Worth, Texas.

1955: Amon G. Carter Jr.; descended to him after the passing of his father.

1982–1984: Amon G. Carter Jr., estate, to his family.

1984 (January 18–21): Stack's, Carter Collection, Lot 241.

1984: John Nelson Rowe III, agent for the following.

1984–1989: L.R. French Jr., Texas numismatist.

1989 (January 18): Stack's, L.R. French Jr., Family Collection, Lot 15.

1989: Rarities Group, Inc. (Martin B. Paul).

1989: National Gold Exchange (Mark Yaffe), Tampa, Florida.

1989: Heritage Rare Coin Galleries (Jim Halperin and Steve Ivy), Dallas, Texas.

1989–November 1993: Indianapolis collection. In May 1992, the owner commissioned Farmington Valley Rare Coin Co., New Hartford, Connecticut (Tony Scirpo, owner), to find a buyer. At this time the coin was certified as EF-45 by PCGS.

1993 (November): Acquired by a private buyer located by Farmington Valley Rare Coin Co. Subsequently sold to the following.

1994: David Liljestrand.

1994–1998: Midwest collection.

1998: David Liljestrand.

1998: National Gold Exchange and Kenneth Goldman.

1998: Legend Numismatics, Inc. (Laura Sperber).

1998: Private collection. Now certified as AU-58.

The compilation of provenance involves some guesswork in instances in which coins were not illustrated in catalogs, or when they were sold privately without announcement. Generally, any extensive provenance is subject to updating and revision by modern scholars as more information becomes available. Until recently, the first name of Adams, in the above provenance, was spelled as "Phineas," in the style of Phineas T. Barnum. However, in reviewing some biographical information about Adams, who was also prominent in New Hampshire banking, I learned that the correct spelling is *Phinehas*.

In recent years, members of the Numismatic Bibliomania Society and others have done a great deal of provenance research, Saul Teichman and P. Scott Rubin prominent among them. The late Carl W.A. Carlson enjoyed compiling provenance lists, and in 1991 contributed "Tracker: An Introduction to Pedigree Research in the Field of Rare American Coins" to the *American Numismatic Association Centennial Anthology*.

METAL

Precious metals have a special appeal and are often attractive to buyers. A newcomer to the market will find it easier to be enticed by a sparkling Mint State gold $20 coin of a common date (e.g., 1901) than by a well worn but very rare copper cent of 1799.

In some series within such specialties as tokens, pattern coins, and medals, the same dies were used to strike coins in different metals. For example, certain Standard Silver pattern coins of 1869 and 1870 were made in copper, aluminum, and silver. Generally, in such instances, copper is the least valuable striking, followed by aluminum, then silver. An 1879 pattern Schoolgirl silver dollar can be found in copper and silver, with silver being the more valuable.

Exceptions abound, and for strikings of off-metal coins from regular-issue Proof dies (not pattern designs), a half dollar struck in aluminum or copper is worth more than one in silver, and an Indian Head cent struck in aluminum (such as in 1872) is worth more than a bronze impression.

Civil War tokens were struck in various metals, some of the same die pairs in copper, brass, German silver (a nickel composition), and silver—with this also being the order of value. In all instances, a silver impression of such a token is worth more than a copper one. For 19th century medals, it is generally true that a gold impression is worth more than a silver one, and a silver medal commands a higher market price than does one in copper.

For the numismatic specialist in gold double eagles the 1904-S is considered to be very common, and hundreds of thousands exist in Mint State. Of course, every specialized collection needs an example, but beyond this most of the demand for such plentiful issues is with investors. More than just a few people have bought a 1904-S or related common date as an investment item, have become piqued with its design and history, have investigated further, and have gone on to become serious collectors.

An 1872 Indian Head cent (enlarged) struck from regular Proof dies, but in aluminum instead of the normal bronze—a numismatic delicacy listed in the Judd pattern text as J-1181, although it is not a pattern, strictly speaking.

INVESTMENT DEMAND

Every now and then the coin market comes into sharp focus outside of the numismatic community. Investors in stocks and bonds learn about the historically excellent (mostly) returns shown by rare coins, and want to get into the action. Focus is usually on series in silver and gold, and in higher grades. Sometimes the values of precious metals plays a part in investment demand. A run-up in the price of gold bullion nearly always increases the demand for gold coins.

A large influx of investor money results in a sharp rise in price for the series affected. After the passion fades, as it usually does, prices subside—but usually settle at figures somewhat higher than when the action began.

Sometimes the advent of large numbers of investors lifts the spirit of the market across many series. Dealers who make large profits selling bulk double eagles might spend their earnings on other series of personal interest, or to acquire a trophy rarity for the pride of possession. Conversely, a mass exodus of investors can dampen the spirit of a market, as dealers scramble to get cash to pay their obligations and are forced to cut back on overhead expenses.

DIE VARIETY

Concluding my comment on basic aspects determining a coin's value I mention die varieties. These are examples of a regular date or mintmark issue, but with some subtle difference from the ordinary. While major varieties are listed in the *Red Book* and even more varieties are listed in *MEGA RED*, most minor varieties are not listed in either. To learn about minute differences between the dies used to strike dozens of varieties of copper cents dated 1794, you must consult Sheldon's *Early American Cents* and its revision, *Penny Whimsy*. To distinguish die varieties among half cents of 1804, you need a copy of either the Cohen or the Breen text on this denomination.

Interesting and rare die varieties offer a fertile field once you gain experience as a numismatist. Valuable finds are constantly being made. The September 13, 2004, issue of *Coin World*, told of an entirely new die variety of 1807 Draped Bust silver half dollar, unknown to Haseltine, Beistle, or Overton—each of whom wrote a book on the subject. It was discovered in June 2004, was given the new listing of "Overton-115," and was then added on to the end of already known varieties. In August of the same year a second specimen of O-115 was found in VF-20 grade, reported by Sheridan Downey and Dr. Glenn Peterson. At the time, a "regular" (not rare die variety) 1807 Draped Bust half dollar listed for $400 in the *Red Book*. Although the market value of each of the two newly discovered O-115 halves was not stated, I am probably safe in saying that each is worth quite a few thousand dollars.

The collector of die varieties can appreciate this well-worn example, certified as Fine-12, of the 1793 Strawberry Leaf large copper cent. Although it is in low grade, the other three pieces, one of which is in the American Numismatic Society collection, are in far lower preservation. This particular coin appeared in the 1890 sale of the Lorin G. Parmelee Collection, and years later, in the early 1940s, was sold to a New England numismatist. In 2004, it crossed the auction block at $412,000, setting the all-time record for any United States one-cent piece of any variety in any grade.

In the very same issue of *Coin World*, Rick Snow, dealer specialist in Flying Eagle and Indian Head cents, reported cherrypicking a rare die variety of the 1856 Flying Eagle cent. The coin was misattributed and offered as a common issue, in an auction held by a Midwest firm. "His winning bid, including 15% buyer's fee, was $9,200, for what he said could easily have been a $20,000 coin."

In December 2004, one of the most famous of all die varieties of large copper cents, the 1793 Strawberry Leaf, Sheldon NC-3 ("Non-Collectible" No. 3), crossed the auction block. Although it was only in Fine-12 grade, this was far higher than any of the other three known specimens, which hover in the Fair to G-4 range. Had it been an ordinary die variety of a 1793 cent, a rare date, it might have squeaked past the $1,000 mark. However, this rare variety soared to a remarkable $412,000!

A die variety, if rare, can add considerably to the value of a coin. Of course, while good fortune strikes now and then, most such things are already identified by the time you buy them. However, hope springs eternal!

SOURCES FOR PRICING INFORMATION

INTRODUCTION

In the field of stocks, if you want to learn the current price of a share of Intel, General Motors, or Compudyne, all you need to do is know its abbreviation and your Internet stock broker's URL, and push a button. There is no single source for pricing information on all coins. If there were, then we could all refer to a given book, Internet listing, or other location and save a lot of time!

This is the case with rare coins (and stamps, and old cars, and paintings, and real estate, and unrestored "warbird" airplanes). To most enthusiasts, the seeking of price information adds to the excitement.

As a professional numismatist, *experience* is my main source—but that does not do *you* much good, unless you ask me and I want to share my ideas. Even with a great deal of experience, I have to constantly look up prices, as they are always changing. Then I have to determine which price listings are useful and which are not. Every once in a while a *book* is written as a guide to prices, but proves to be unreliable. Some years ago a volume on what are termed *so-called dollars* (medals of dollar size) offered prices that for many issues were wildly unrealistic, and the same happened with a book on small-denomination California gold. Still other books may have prices on the low side. Generally, for most rare coins needed for customers' "want lists" I will pay more than the prices listed in the popular *Handbook of United States Coins* (the wholesale price guide known as the *Blue Book*) published annually by Whitman. (However, the book remains generally useful as to what typical buyers will pay for average quality coins.)

A few years ago I had an 1878-CC silver trade dollar I graded as MS-65. Try as I might, I could not find any information for a recent sale at that level. Then I encountered a market-value listing for $150,000 in a popular coin periodical. Seeking the basis for the figure, I telephoned the compiler, only to be told that he could not find a price either, and guessed that $150,000 was about right. I did some more checking, some thinking, some extrapolations beyond the prices that MS-63 coins had sold for, and figured it was worth $35,000. I mentioned my methodology to several specialists in the field, and they agreed that was about right (but none offered to buy it for $35,000!). I did price it for $35,000, and it sold right away. The new owner was quite happy.

The opposite situation might be true for a 1787, Bust Left, Vermont copper. I have not handled more than five examples of this coin in my career. It is not listed in many places at all. In G-4 grade *MEGA RED*, Second Edition suggests $4,500. Based on my experience I would pay $5,000, perhaps more, if one were offered to me this minute!

These instances demonstrate that prices published in well-known locations are not always indicative of what I might buy or sell a coin for. However, most standard sources are at least in the ballpark.

Just as a real estate agent might investigate several sources to put a price on 100 acres of land in Vermont, bordering on Lake Champlain, and the sources might be different from those used to evaluate a cottage three blocks in from the sea at Wildwood Crest, New Jersey, and still different from a resale condominium in Trump Tower in Manhattan. No single price guide fits all numismatic situations.

In the course of business I use many sources and then add my own thoughts based on experience. In brief, published listings are usually just fine for actively traded coins in popular series, in grades in which many are known, and for which there are not many problems relating to strike, eye appeal, or other aspects of quality. For coins requiring a degree of connoisseurship to buy, published guides are only a part of the story.

PUBLISHED GUIDES

The *Guide Book of United States Coins*, issued yearly, has served as my basic reference for many years. Amos Press and Krause Publications also issue market guides that contain much valuable information. *Coin World* and *Numismatic News* each publish magazine-style listings, often including a wider range of grades than can be found in the *Guide Book*.

Ever since 1963, the *Coin Dealer Newsletter* has published "bid" prices on selected coins, expanding the coverage in recent years through the *Certified Coin Dealer Newsletter*. Prices in these two newsletters are generally for generic coins, and it is carefully noted that high-quality examples within a given grade often bring much more money.

NGC and PCGS publish reports showing the numbers of coins each has certified in various grades, a very valuable resource in determining the number of *submission events* (prices are not listed) of certain certified coins in certain grades. The number of *different coins* involved is often far different from the number of *submission events* for such pieces. To look at population reports, you might get the (wrong) idea that a Proof 1879 $4 gold Stella is fairly common, for there are hundreds of listings, while a VF-20 1916 cent is extremely rare, as listings are few (more about certified coin populations later).

Specialized series often have their own price guides, sometimes updated infrequently. Russell Rulau's *Standard Catalog of United States Tokens* is a foundation reference for that field, while *Paper Money of the United States*, created by the Friedberg family, is essential to the valuation of its title subject (as is the most recent edition of Whitman title, *A Guide Book of United States Paper Money*, using Friedberg numbers). The tenth edition of Dr. J. Hewitt

What a difference 70 editions make! Shown at right is the listing for Liberty Seated quarter dollars in the first edition of the *Guide Book of United States Coins*, copyright 1946, with a cover date of 1947. Shown on the next page is the same series in the latest (70th) edition, 2017. Today, the *Guide Book* stands as the longest continuously published retail price guide in the hobby, with no close competition.

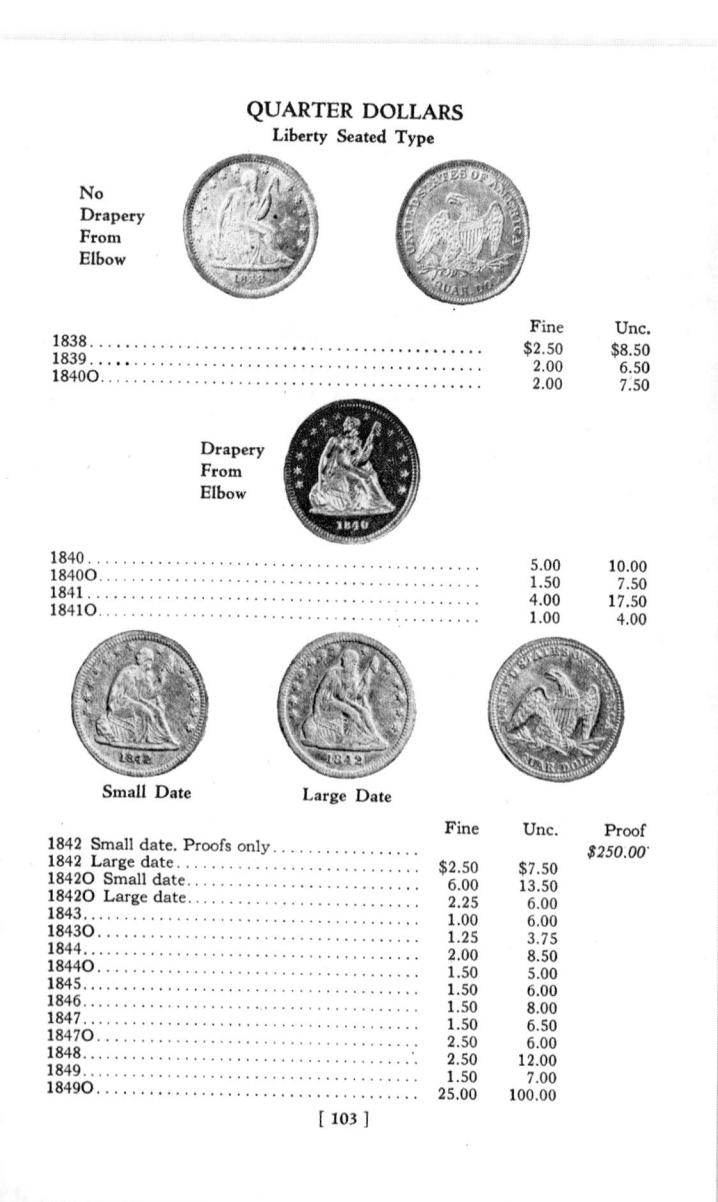

QUARTER DOLLARS
Liberty Seated Type

No Drapery From Elbow

	Fine	Unc.
1838	$2.50	$8.50
1839	2.00	6.50
1840O	2.00	7.50

Drapery From Elbow

1840	5.00	10.00
1840O	1.50	7.50
1841	4.00	17.50
1841O	1.00	4.00

Small Date   Large Date

	Fine	Unc.	Proof
1842 Small date. Proofs only			$250.00
1842 Large date	$2.50	$7.50	
1842O Small date	6.00	13.50	
1842O Large date	2.25	6.00	
1843	1.00	6.00	
1843O	1.25	3.75	
1844	2.00	8.50	
1844O	1.50	5.00	
1845	1.50	6.00	
1846	1.50	8.00	
1847	1.50	6.50	
1847O	2.50	6.00	
1848	2.50	12.00	
1849	1.50	7.00	
1849O	25.00	100.00	

[103]

Judd's *United States Pattern Coins* covers that series with values in several grades plus auction records. Many other examples could be given.

ELECTRONIC MEDIA

Numismedia, a service conducted by Dennis Baker, combines data from the two titles in the *Coin Dealer Newsletter* series, plus population data, as well as other information. It is available to online users for a subscription fee. Many dealers use this as a handy source for actively traded coins and for up-to-the-minute prices—a valuable resource as, in areas such as in the trading of gold bullion coins, prices can change rapidly, sometimes several times within a single day.

Beyond standard sources, browsing the Internet will reveal many listings of prices, sometimes for coins being offered for sale, sometimes estimated auction values.

AUCTION DATA

Years ago, lists of auction "prices realized" often included items that were bought back or otherwise did not find buyers. Today, most (but not all) auction houses omit prices for lots that did not sell. Sometimes a coin will "sell" back to its owner, or someone connected with the owner, in order to establish a price—perhaps through a special arrangement with the auction house. In other instances a coin may have been bid on by mistake, or found to be wrongly listed, or have a defect in its title, and the sale rescinded after the list of prices was published.

Auction prices are useful only to a limited extent, as they often represent certified coins for which not much information is available other than the grades on the holders. Studies show that often the same company can sell two coins, certified in the same grade, in the same auction, for two significantly varying prices. However, some outside knowledge (perhaps gained by a study of the photographs in the catalogs) can help you gather more information as to why the prices were so different. In the instance of significant rarities or other expensive coins, recent auction records are particularly useful in combination with other data.

| FEDERAL ISSUES | | | | | | QUARTER DOLLARS |

LIBERTY SEATED (1838–1891)

Designer Christian Gobrecht.

G-4 Good—Scant rim. LIBERTY on shield worn off. Date and letters legible.
VG-8 Very Good—Rim fairly defined, at least three letters in LIBERTY evident.
F-12 Fine—LIBERTY complete, but partly weak.
VF-20 Very Fine—LIBERTY strong.
EF-40 Extremely Fine—Complete LIBERTY and edges of scroll. Shoulder clasp on Liberty's gown clear.
AU-50 About Uncirculated—Slight wear on Liberty's knees and breast and on eagle's neck, wing tips, and claws.
MS-60 Uncirculated No trace of wear. Light blemishes.
MS-63 Choice Uncirculated Some distracting contact marks or blemishes in prime focal areas. Impaired luster possible.

Variety 1 – No Motto Above Eagle (1838–1853)

Weight 6.68 grams; composition .900 silver, .100 copper; diameter 24.3 mm; reeded edge; mints: Philadelphia, New Orleans.

| No Drapery From Elbow | Drapery From Elbow | Large Date |

Mintmark location is on reverse, below eagle.

	Mintage	G-4	VG-8	F-12	VF-20	EF-40	AU-50	MS-60	MS-63
1838, No Drapery	466,000	$35	$40	$60	$100	$375	$750	$2,000	$6,750
1839, No Drapery	491,146	35	40	60	100	375	750	1,850	5,000
$517,500, PF-65, Heritage auction, April 2008									
1840O, No Drapery	382,200	40	45	70	120	400	800	2,000	8,000
1840, Drapery	188,127	25	30	55	100	180	300	950	4,500
1840O, Drapery	43,000	30	50	70	110	210	500	1,300	4,000
1841	120,000	45	70	100	150	250	325	900	2,500
1841O	452,000	30	45	60	80	175	320	800	1,900
1842, Sm Date (Pf only)									60,000
1842, Large Date	88,000	75	100	160	250	350	650	1,750	4,500
1842O, All kinds	769,000								
1842O, Small Date		350	550	1,000	1,900	3,750	7,500	20,000	75,000
1842O, Large Date		30	50	70	110	220	600	1,750	4,500
1843	645,600	25	30	35	45	85	175	450	1,250
1843O	968,000	30	45	60	125	250	800	2,250	8,500
1844	421,200	25	30	35	45	85	175	525	1,500
1844O	740,000	30	45	60	85	200	360	1,500	3,000
1845	922,000	25	30	35	45	80	160	450	1,250
1846	510,000	25	30	35	50	85	180	600	1,500
1847	734,000	25	30	35	45	80	160	575	1,500
1847O	368,000	35	50	75	150	800	800	4,500	12,500
1848	146,000	25	35	60	100	175	300	1,150	4,000
1849	340,000	25	30	45	75	160	250	800	2,000
1849O	*	450	600	1,100	2,400	6,000	7,750	15,000	20,000
1850	190,800	30	45	65	95	175	240	1,000	3,500
$460,000, PF-68, Heritage auction, January 2008									
1850O	412,000	30	45	65	95	175	475	1,600	3,500

* Included in 1850-O mintage.

Chart continued on next page.

169

OFFERS AND AVAILABILITY

Published price lists, "Buy It Now" offers on eBay, Internet inventory listings, and catalogs are all rich sources of prices, as are advertisements in the leading numismatic periodicals. In many instances these are more valuable than listings of market values in a book, or of auction prices realized—for if you like the price, and the quality checks out, you can own the coin right away. In contrast, while reading the *Guide Book of United States Coins* or another reference source you can contemplate all of those interesting listings and prices for colonial coins, or gold dollars, or commemoratives, but you cannot reach out and buy them.

One caveat is that some dealers emphasize price but sacrifice quality. If a choice specimen of a gold coin or a silver dollar has a standard value of, say, $1,000, the chances are that a coin advertised at a bargain $700 will be below par. Many buyers specialize in "bargains," but when they sell their collections they often find that few people want to buy or bid on them, and then only at low prices.

In my opinion it is better to pay more for a high-quality coin than to buy an average or subpar piece at a discount. In coins, as in the rest of life, you get what you pay for.

JUST ASK—THE PERSONAL TOUCH

Most dealers are willing to discuss the derivation of prices in their inventories. If a coin is priced at $15,000 and the *Red Book* suggests $11,000, and listings by *Coin World* and *Numismatic News* suggest $10,500 and $12,000, ask the seller how he or she figured the $15,000 number. In the course of buying obscure things such as Civil War tokens and obsolete paper money, where no current price guides are available, I often ask questions if I cannot figure out the answer myself.

It is okay to discuss price levels of a dealer's own stock offerings, but it is *not* cricket to go to Dealer A at a convention and ask him or her to go over a string of asking prices from Dealer B. If you are a beginner and say so, and you seek information, a dealer may or may not be willing to help (but collectors usually are). Also, if at a coin show you ask a lot of questions about a lot of coins, it is good form to buy a few! Although most in the trade are willing to assist well-meaning newcomers with information, they are not in the business of giving extensive free appraisals—any more than an attorney would welcome you into his office and give you free legal opinions, or a doctor would make an appointment to see you for a free medical checkup. I don't mean to sound overly commercial here, but dealers do have expenses (employees, travel, rent, insurance, interest on loans, etc.), and they do need to show a profit to remain in business.

Also, if a dealer is busy at a coin show, stop by later at a quiet moment and ask questions then. Most shows have their slow moments, and that is a good time to pull up a chair and chat.

By human nature, some dealers are willing to share, to help others, to educate, to give talks, to serve as club officers, and more, while others are strictly merchants and are not the slightest bit interested in doing anything that does not result in a sale. Accept this—it is true in all hobbies and businesses—and, as you learn about buying and collecting coins, find someone who will share information and time.

SURPRISE ENDINGS

Sometimes, unexpectedly, such sharing can lead to more business for a dealer than simply trying to sell can ever do. Two instances come to mind as I write this.

In one instance, a young lad walked into the Stack's store in New York City, with a blue Whitman coin folder in his hand. He was seeking some inexpensive Lincoln "pennies" to add to those he had found in pocket change. His dad was with him. This story, related to me by Harvey Stack, played out this way:

Since it was a quiet time at the sales counter, Harvey stopped by to talk with the boy and ask him about his collection and to see what he had been able to find in circulation. Then his father joined the

How much is this 1879 three-dollar gold coin (enlarged) worth? Commercially graded as MS-64, the coin has excellent eye appeal due to a satiny luster and partial mirror surfaces. But what about the price? Determining what is just right to achieve a good buy will take some studying and, perhaps, "asking around."

In contrast, the 1883-CC Morgan silver dollar exists in large quantities, is usually seen in high-quality Mint State, and has a current market price easier to determine, for they are listed just about everywhere.

conversation and introduced himself. His name was Samuel Wolfson. He asked for a few catalogs, developed his own interest in coins, and went on to form one of the greatest collections ever—including such rarities as an 1804 dollar. Years later, Stack's auctioned his magnificent holding.

In the second situation, a friend asked me about California gold coins. He was a native of that state, knew about the Gold Rush, and had heard there were some coins associated with that memorable event in American history. Although he was not a numismatist and had no intention of becoming one, he wanted to know whether I could direct him to a museum with such items on display. He simply wanted to see what they looked like.

Not knowing of any local or regional institutions with these coins on view, I gave him a copy of the *Guide Book of United States Coins* so he could read about them, and said I'd let him know the next time I bought a $50 octagonal gold "slug" so he could stop by to see it. I found a nice 1851 Augustus Humbert $50, called him, and he came to look it over, bought it, and went on to form a marvelous collection of U.S. coins from half cents to double eagles—plus a specialized collection of California gold! A few years later, he consigned the collection to one of our sales, and doubled his money on his investment.

APPENDIX M

Coin Clubs

Joining a coin club is an important part of your hobby fulfillment. Membership brings many advantages, most important of which are camaraderie and the accumulation of knowledge. We all need both.

Even if you can't travel to meeting locations and shows, most clubs produce newsletters that are highly educational and encourage members to contribute articles. This is one of the best ways to learn about a specific numismatic subject. With every article you write, you'll travel new avenues of research and add to your numismatic knowledge. It never fails.

Many specialized coin clubs have been born in the virtual environment of the Internet. These clubs often are interactive, offering all members a great opportunity to ask questions of specialists, share knowledge, and meet others with similar interests.

This appendix lists numismatic organizations dedicated to subjects that should interest most of our readers. The information noted, including membership fees and addresses, is as accurate as possible at the time of publication. A visit to a group's Web site can provide the latest information.

NATIONWIDE CLUBS AND GROUPS

The American Numismatic Association. This is the largest coin-collecting group in the world. The monthly magazine, *The Numismatist*, contains articles submitted by members on a wide array of topics. Additionally, the ANA's library is second to none and is available to all members. Other great benefits are also included as a part of your membership.

American Numismatic Association
818 N. Cascade Ave.
Colorado Springs, CO 80903-3279
Phone: 800-367-9723
Fax: 719-634-4085
E-mail: ana@money.org
Web site: www.money.org

CONECA (Combined Organizations of Numismatic Error Collectors of America). CONECA is a worldwide organization that specializes in the study of errors and varieties. Its bimonthly newsletter, *ErrorScope*, is filled with educational topics. Additionally, CONECA's Web site has a huge listing with descriptions of several thousand repunched mintmarks and doubled dies. And access to that is free to all! Finally, there are also members-only sections with still more for your error and variety education.

CONECA
c/o Rachel Irish
3807 Belmont Rd.
Coeur d'Alene, ID 83815
Web site: www.conecaonline.org

SPECIALIZED CLUBS AND GROUPS

Barber Coin Collectors' Society. Serving collectors of the many U.S. coins designed by Charles Barber, chief engraver of the Mint from 1879 to 1917, this group offers myriad resources for the interested numismatist. It publishes the *Journal of the Barber Coin Collectors' Society* on a quarterly basis. A membership application is available via its Web site.

Dave Earp
BCCS Membership
P.O. Box 1723
Decatur, IL 62525

Early American Coppers. Founded in 1967, this not-for-profit numismatic organization serves as a point of contact for collectors of early U.S. copper coins, including colonial issues and Hard Times tokens in addition to U.S. half cents and large cents. The group's publication, *Penny-Wise*, is renowned as a great source of information. A membership application is available via its Web site.

EAC
P.O. Box 2462
Heath, OH 43056
Web site: www.eacs.org

Fly-In Club. This specialty group, formed in 1991, is for collectors of Flying Eagle and Indian Head small cents. *Longacre's Ledger* is the group's award-winning publication. A membership application is available via its Web site.

Fly-In Club
P.O. Box 559
Sandwich, IL 60548
Web site: www.fly-inclub.org

John Reich Collectors Society. The purpose of the John Reich Collectors Society is to encourage the study of numismatics, particularly United States gold and silver coins minted before the introduction of the Liberty Seated design, and to provide technical and educational information concerning such coins. JRCS has a great newsletter and conducts meetings at various times throughout the year.

John Reich Collectors Society
Attn: Stephen A. Crain
P.O. Box 1680
Windham, ME 04062
Web site: http://logan.com/jrcs

Liberty Seated Collectors Club. LSCC is one of the strongest groups dedicated to any coin design or series. LSCC members receive the quarterly *Gobrecht Journal*, which is filled with some of the most educational numismatic articles available anywhere.

LSCC
Dennis Fortier
LSCC New Member Dues
P.O. Box 1841
Pawtucket, RI 02862
Web site: www.lsccweb.org

Lincoln Cent Forum. An active online community for Lincoln cent collectors to discuss America's smallest circulating denomination, this forum also provides various resources for Lincoln cent collectors, including detailed explanation of the series and various aspects of the design, a glossary, and tips on coin photography. Creating an account is free.

Web site: www.lincolncentforum.com

Shield Nickels. This is another excellent online group, this one for enthusiasts of Shield nickels. Like many of the others, the discussion groups are filled with excellent information. There is no better discussion group available for the variety enthusiast. And best of all, you can join free!

Web site: groups.yahoo.com/group/
Shield_Nickels

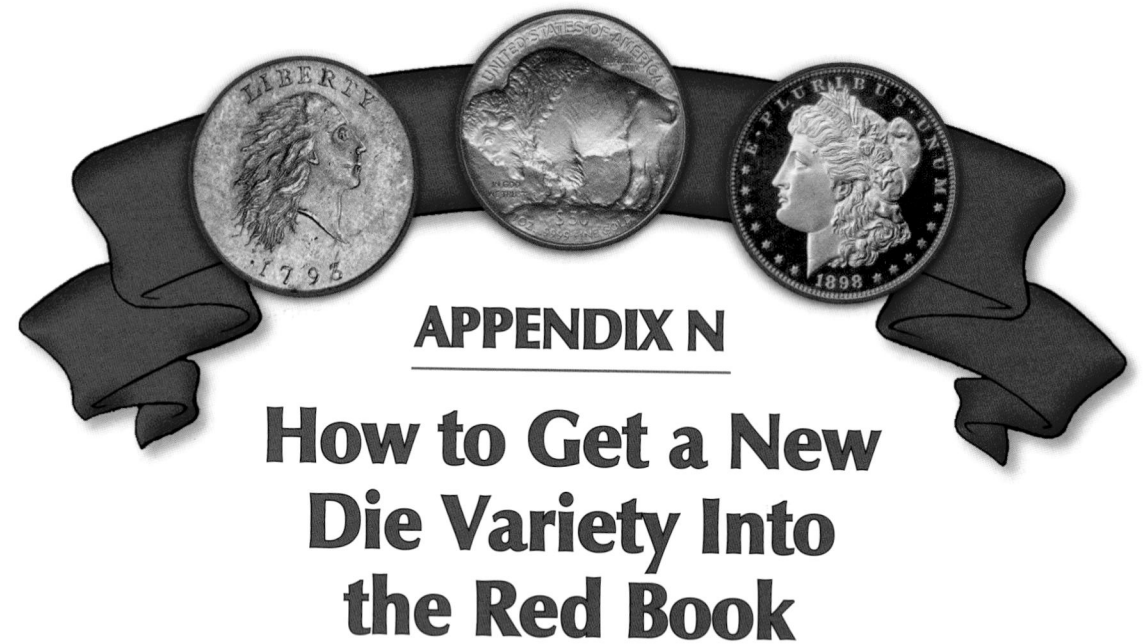

APPENDIX N

How to Get a New Die Variety Into the Red Book

A version of this article by Whitman publisher Dennis Tucker first appeared in the **Journal of the Barber Coin Collector's Society.**

In the Summer 2015 issue of the *Journal of the Barber Coin Collectors' Society*, member Bob Duzan shared his firsthand observations of some interesting Barber dime varieties ("A Variety Challenge," volume 26, no. 2). In his article he asked, "What should be the criteria for listing a coin variety in the 'Red Book' or other coin publications?"

That's a very good question, and one we think about quite a bit at Whitman Publishing. Having worked on 12 editions of the *Guide Book of United States Coins* (the "Red Book") and counting, I know that sometimes collectors and dealers can be very bullish on getting a favorite coin listed, in an attempt to increase popular interest (perhaps hoping to watch the value of their holdings climb higher, or simply as a way to share their enthusiasm for the coin). I explain to them that the Red Book *reports* on the market and collector trends; it doesn't seek to spearhead popular interest in any particular die variety or other coin. If the Red Book's editors (Senior Editor Kenneth Bressett, Research Editor Q. David Bowers, and Valuations Editor Jeff Garrett) observe strong, broad interest within the hobby community for a particular variety, it has a much better chance of being included in the book.

"Strong, broad interest" can be measured many ways. If we see a number of letters to the editors of the hobby newspapers . . . or receive letters and emails ourselves . . . and hear people talking about the variety at coin shows, club meetings, and online . . . and read articles and possibly even books being written by collectors, dealers, and other numismatists . . . and observe the growth of a healthy and vibrant secondary market, with buy-sell-and-trade prices actively published and discussed . . . all of these things point toward a robust and popular interest in a particular die variety.

Do the editors and publisher of the Red Book have a vested interest in drumming up popular interest in any given variety? No. But do we want to report on well-developed trends that show signs of long-term "here to stay" activity within the hobby community? Definitely yes!

As Bob Duzan pointed out in his Summer 2015 article, the regular-edition Red Book includes two Barber dime varieties in its listings. For Barber quarters, the Red Book lists only regular issues (circulation strikes and Proofs) by date and mintmark. And for Barber half dollars, we include a single die variety.

Adding a new die variety to the Red Book is somewhat akin to Abraham Lincoln's description of his own learning style: "My mind is like a piece of steel—very hard to scratch anything on it, and almost impossible after you get it there to rub it out." This is traditionally how the editors of the Red Book have approached new irregular listings (overdates, doubled dies, repunched mintmarks, and the like): with a high level of scrutiny, knowing that once a coin is deemed significant enough to be listed, the hobby community expects it to *stay* listed.

The Red Book is meant as a reference guide. It's not comprehensive or encyclopedic, but it strives to provide as much valuable information as possible to as many readers as possible. Longtime senior editor Kenneth Bressett and I have had many conversations about his editorial philosophy, honed and sharpened since he first started working with hobby legend R.S. Yeoman in the late 1950s. "The Red Book has to be somewhat selective," Ken says, "and perhaps even a bit arbitrary, in deciding which minor varieties are listed in the book. The reasons for this are twofold: First, it must remain true to the title *Guide Book*, and not attempt to be an encyclopedic listing of every known variety. And secondly, minor variations are generally excluded from separate listing unless there is a wide variation in value, or a conspicuous collector demand for the item."

With the larger-format *Professional Edition* Red Book, published from 2009 to 2014, we took a more relaxed approach. Where the regular-edition Red Book seeks to be an overview *guide* to U.S. coins, the *Professional Edition* went above and beyond the basic date-and-mintmark and major variety listings. It wasn't as meaty as the *Cherrypickers' Guide to Rare Die Varieties*, of course, but it included more die varieties than the regular-edition Red Book for many coin types.

We stopped publishing the *Professional Edition* after the sixth edition (2014) in order to focus on an even bigger new book: the *Guide Book of United States Coins, Deluxe Edition*, which you're reading right now. The first edition came out in March 2015, and it quickly became popularly known as "MEGA RED." This 1,504-page volume carries forward the *Professional Edition*'s focus on including more die varieties.

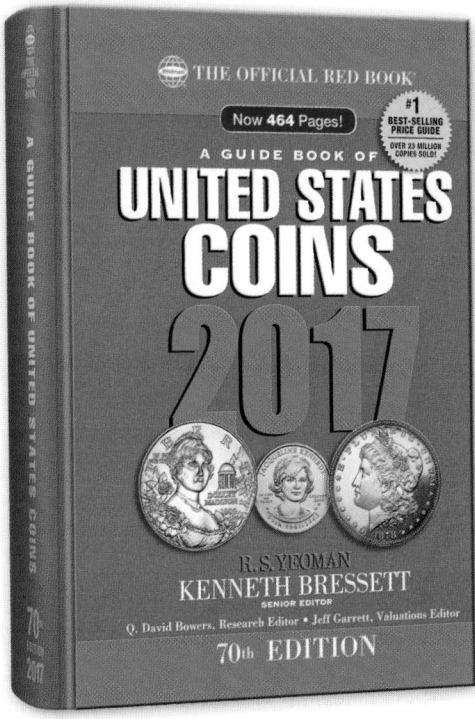

The regular-edition 2017 Red Book.

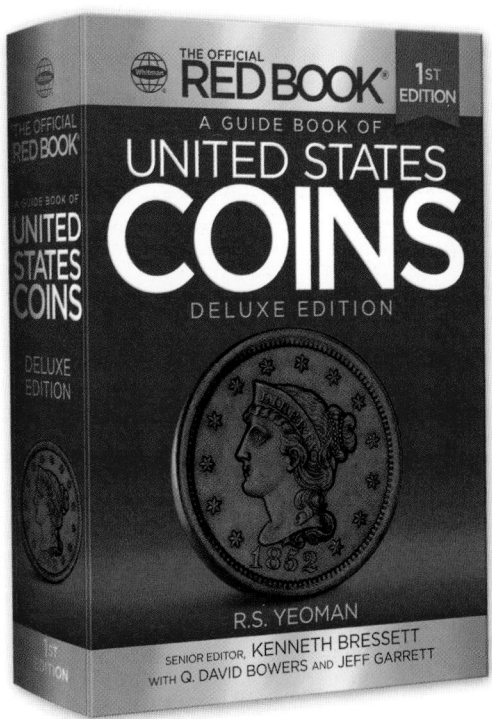

The first edition of the Deluxe Edition Red Book (MEGA RED).

Here's how the regular-edition Red Book and the current edition of MEGA RED compare, using as a case study the circulating coins designed by U.S. Mint Chief Engraver Charles E. Barber:

Number of Die Varieties, by Coin Type (Designs by Charles E. Barber)		
	Regular-Edition Red Book	MEGA RED
Liberty Head nickel	0	2
Barber dime	3	5
Barber quarter	0	0*
Barber half dollar	1	3

* But see below, under "Barber Quarters."

Liberty Head Nickels. The regular-edition Red Book lists only the standard dates and mintmarks among circulation strikes and Proofs. This includes both Variety 1 (Without CENTS) and Variety 2 (With CENTS) of the 1883 coin, which are not die varieties in the traditionally accepted sense, but rather a Mint-authorized design change. It also lists the 1913 Liberty Head nickels—not regular Mint issues, as they were never placed into circulation, but historically studied alongside their regular-issue kin.

MEGA RED lists two Liberty Head nickel die varieties: the 1899 Repunched Date (FS-05-1899-301, illustrated with close-ups of both an Early Die State and a Late Die State), and the 1900 Doubled-Die Reverse (FS-05-1900-801).

Barber Dimes. The regular-edition Red Book includes line-item listings for the 1893 So-Called 3 Over 2, and the 1905-O Micro O. It also includes a chart note about the 1893-S with a boldly doubled mintmark being valued slightly higher than the normal coin. I count these as three die-variety listings, even though only two of them have line items in the charts.

In addition to those varieties, MEGA RED includes listings and illustrations for the 1897 Repunched Date (FS-10-1897-301) and the 1912-S Doubled-Die Obverse (FS-10-1912S-101). It also shows comparative images of the Normal O and the Micro O mintmarks in the 1905-O issue.

Barber Quarters. The regular-edition Red Book focuses solely on normal dates and mintmarks for the Barber quarter series, listing no die varieties.

MEGA RED currently has no line-item listings for Barber quarter die varieties, but it does illustrate the two kinds of 1892 reverse (Variety 1, with the eagle's wing covering only half of the E in UNITED; and Variety 2, where the wing covers most of the E). It also describes the two varieties in a narrative chart note, and delineates their relative scarcity.

Barber Half Dollars. In the regular-edition Red Book, the 1892-O Micro O is the sole die-variety listing.

In MEGA RED additional listings include the 1909-S Inverted Mintmark (FS-50-1909S-501) and the 1911-S Repunched Mintmark (FS-50-1911S-501). These are illustrated with close-up photographs, as are the 1892-O Normal and Micro O mintmarks.

Now, circling back to Bob Duzan's query: How were these extra six die varieties chosen to be included in MEGA RED? Using the *Cherrypickers' Guide* as a reference, and checking with collectors, dealers, and other numismatists, we studied each series and its major varieties. The following questions guided our decision-making: How rare is a particular variety? How much demand is there for it within the hobby community—is it desired by a considerable number of collectors? Among those collectors, are most of them die-variety specialists, or are more casual collectors aware of the variety as well? What about its liquidity—how quickly and easily does it sell when offered at auction or private transaction? Does it sell right away, commanding full or even higher-than-expected value? Or does it sell fairly quickly, at commonly listed values; or perhaps it sells over time, at a discounted price, or only to a specialist who happens to be in the market at the right moment? Further regarding the retail value: Is there a large differential between the regular coin's value and that of the die variety? Or are they fairly close in price?

The inverted mintmark on the 1909-S Barber half dollar, FS-50-1909S-501, featured in the Deluxe Edition Red Book.

The 1911-S Repunched Mintmark Barber half dollar, FS-50-1911S-501.

If a particular die variety has a) a high interest factor, b) a high liquidity factor, and c) a strong premium over the normal coin, it has a better chance of being listed, described, and illustrated in MEGA RED. If it's unique or extremely rare, which limits its availability in the marketplace, or if collectors simply aren't excited about it, a variety probably won't be listed. And, as with the *Cherrypickers' Guide*, if these factors change over time—specifically, if collector interest wanes—a die variety is more likely to be delisted from MEGA RED (contrary to the regular-edition Red Book's "scratched in steel" approach).

With all of this in mind, we invite you to submit your proposals for new coin die varieties to include in future editions of MEGA RED. I can be contacted by email at dennis.tucker@whitman.com, or by mail at Whitman Publishing, Attn: Dennis Tucker, 3101 Clairmont Road, Suite G, Atlanta GA 30329.

We look forward to hearing from you!

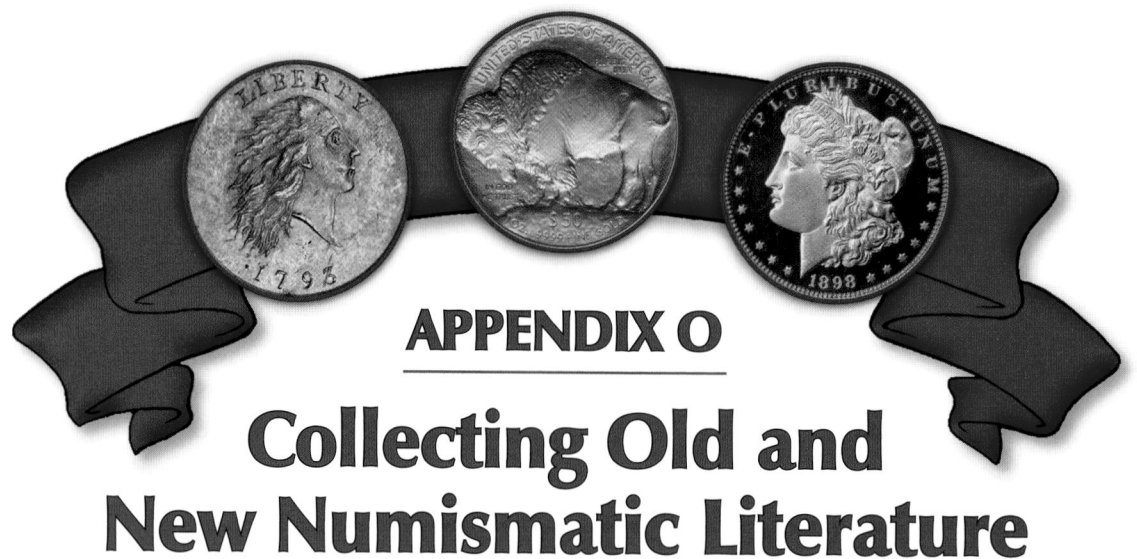

APPENDIX O

Collecting Old and New Numismatic Literature

This appreciation of numismatic literature was drawn from the experiences of Q. David Bowers.

"I cannot live without books," stated Thomas Jefferson. Indeed, many of his books went on to form the Library of Congress.

"Books are a uniquely portable magic," Stephen King, modern author, stated.

"Buy the book before the coin" is an adage popularized by Aaron Feldman, a dealer in numismatic books in the 1960s and 1970s.

Of course, we can all live without books, just as we can live without ice cream or music, but books make life more enjoyable.

If there is one item that costs very little but pays for itself many times over in the collecting of coins, tokens, medals, and paper money, it is an interesting and information-filled numismatic reference book. The most popular and perhaps the single most useful title of all time is Whitman's own *A Guide Book of United States Coins*, better known as the Red Book. Within its covers is information on coins ranging from the first Massachusetts silver coins of 1652 to the latest offerings of the United States Mint—truly everything "from A to Z."

It may come as a surprise to learn that it was not until 1934, when Wayte Raymond published the first hardbound *Standard Catalogue of United States Coins*, that there was a useful and regularly issued book listing varieties, mintages, and prices. Prior to that, generations of collectors from the 19th century onward had to learn about pricing by reading advertisements and lists of auction results. Today a complete set of 18 editions of the Standard Catalogue can be assembled with patience—though it will take a bit longer if original dust jackets are desired.

There is room in every library for at least a few stray copies of the *Standard Catalogue*. Copies of the *Guide Book* from across time—say from each decade—give a nice view of market history if your ambition falls short of owning each and every one. The 1946 edition comes in two slightly different typographical variations. A choice example of either can cross the $1,000 mark.

AFFORDABLE 19TH-CENTURY CLASSICS

The first important and numismatically useful book to be published in America debuted in 1839 and was titled *An Historical Account of Massachusetts Currency*, by Joseph Barlow Felt. This 248-page work was not intended for collectors but, as the title indicates, dealt with the history of money and media of exchange of the Massachusetts colony. Nevertheless, it was highly valuable and informative to numismatists.

Nearly all of the information presented then in 1839 is relevant and very useful today. Not many people know about this work, so if you are lucky enough to track down a copy, it will not cost much.

The second book with numismatic significance to come out, *A Manual of Gold and Silver Coins of All Nations*, by Jacob R. Eckfeldt and William E. DuBois, was published by the Assay Department of the Philadelphia Mint in 1842. Like Felt's book, this volume did not directly deal with numismatics. Rather, it was an illustrated text describing the characteristics of the title-subject coins, most useful to bullion dealers and exchange offices who handled such coins in an era in which many foreign issues were legal tender in America. It, too, is of modest cost today.

In 1846 the 138-page *Pledges of History: A Brief Account of the Collection of Coins Belonging to the Mint of the United States*, by Mint Cabinet co-curator William E. DuBois, was published. The second and expanded edition of this work was issued in 1851 and described many private and territorial coins made in California during the early years of the Gold Rush. Both of these are harder to find than the two books mentioned before.

Also on the list of important early numismatic books is the *American Numismatical Manual*, by Montroville W. Dickeson, published in 1859. It was later re-issued with a slightly revised title, *American Numismatic Manual*, in editions of 1860 and 1865. This impressive volume is illustrated in color with metallic-tone plates and lists different coins from the colonial era. As the work was a first effort for the hobby and created mostly from scratch, it contained many errors (such as the assertion that the C mintmark stood for California rather than the Charlotte Mint). Widely distributed, the book did much to create interest in numismatics, which at the time was becoming increasingly dynamic.

In 1860, *A Description of Ancient and Modern Coins, in the Cabinet Collection at the Mint of the United States*, by Mint Director James Ross Snowden, was published. It was followed in 1861 by Snowden's *A Description of the Medals of Washington*, and in that same year *Coins, Medals, and Seals*, by W.C. Prime, enjoyed wide sales. By this time *Historical Magazine*, launched in 1857, had also furnished much numismatic information, as had auction catalogs.

Each of the aforementioned books can be purchased today from sellers of antiquarian books, including several who specialize in numismatic titles. Reading through them will give you an appreciation of the cradle days of coin collecting in America, which makes for an interesting in-print excursion.

From that point continuing up to the present day, hundreds of numismatic books have been published. Two from the late 19th century are standard references still useful today. The first is *Early Coins of America*, by Sylvester S. Crosby, published in 1875. Crosby, a Boston-area dealer, collector, and scholar, spent several years visiting and corresponding with collectors, researching early legislation of the various colonies regarding coins, and photographing many specimens. This is a "must-have" title for any basic library.

The second is somewhat obscure, except to those who appreciate a rich combination of numismatics and world history: *American Colonial History Illustrated by Contemporary Medals*, by C. Wyllys Betts, published posthumously in 1894. This richly detailed work tells of hundreds of medals, most of which were issued in Europe, that depict scenes in and center on themes of what is now the United States in the New World. This is one book that has never been superseded, even though many new discoveries have been made. Used copies are readily available in the marketplace.

Other useful books related to large copper cents, silver coins from quarters to dollars, Hard Times tokens, medals, and other subjects were published before the turn of the century, but have been rendered obsolete information-wise by later studies. Still, many of these books are worth owning. Today the Numismatic Bibliomania Society serves the many enthusiasts who collect out-of-print as well as new literature. Information is also available on the Internet, where the free *eSylum*, edited by Wayne Homren and sponsored by the Society, is presented each week.

INTO THE TWENTIETH CENTURY AND BEYOND

Into the 20th century you will find hundreds of books on numismatics. Currently useful titles are listed in the present book in the bibliography. The Whitman Publishing Web site (www.whitman.com) lists titles that are currently available. The 100 Greatest™ series is especially popular, with each page detailing the story of a different coin, token, medal, or piece of currency—a veritable numismatic smorgasbord.

Among out-of-print titles, one of the most interesting and most important is Early American Cents, by Dr. William H. Sheldon, published in 1958. It introduced the numerical grading system of 1 to 70 adopted and revised by the American Numismatic Association, and used as the standard today. It also established the Sheldon Rarity Scale, which ranges from Rarity-1 (common, 1,000 or more coins known) to Rarity-8 (just 2 or 3 known) and Unique (1 known). A revised edition titled *Penny Whimsy* was issued in 1958 with Walter Breen and Dorothy I. Paschal as co-authors. While it only deals with large copper cents of the 1793 to 1814 years, it is especially valuable for its overall philosophies.

A BIBLIOPHILE'S RECOMMENDATIONS

We invited Dr. Joel Orosz, long-time collector of numismatic literature, author, and columnist, to give a list of his favorite and recommended books:

Walter Breen, *Walter Breen's Complete Encyclopedia of U.S. Coinage*, 1988. The only book to try to cover *everything* in American numismatics. Inevitably some mistakes were made, but where else can you become an instant expert about "Hancock's Revenge" and Kempson's halfpence by reading just two consecutive pages?

Q. David Bowers, *The History of United States Coinage as Illustrated by the Garrett Collection*, 1979. The collection of the Garrett family had almost everything a collector could desire, and Bowers has filled in the rest with his immensely readable research. I'll bet you a Bungtown copper you just can't put this book down!

Don Taxay, *The U.S. Mint and Coinage*, 1966. Everything that you ever wanted to know about all four United States Mint facilties in Philadelphia, including the startling fact that the biggest building of the first Mint had less than 3,500 square feet: about half the size of a contemporary suburban "McMansion."

Augustus G. Heaton, *Mint Marks*, 1893. Believe it or not, hardly anyone collected U.S. coins by mintmarks—until, that is, this little book came along to point out how rare some mintmarked coins are. Not many books change the hobby completely, but this one did.

Neil Carothers, *Fractional Money*, 1930. The title refers to fractions of a dollar, so this book is about small coins and fractional paper currency. It's full of fascinating information you can't find elsewhere: for example, the origin of nicknames for coins like "levy" or "fip" and stories of strange pricing (a Pittsburgh newspaper sold for six and a quarter cents as late as 1841).

Eric P. Newman, *The Early Paper Money of America*, 1967. Still in print today and in its fifth edition, this book brought order out of chaos for Continental currency collectors in the 1960s. *Early Paper Money* is bursting with amazing facts. For Pennsylvania alone, did you know that some notes were printed by John Dunlap, the printer of the Declaration of Independence, while a note of 1783 was signed by David Rittenhouse, the first director of the U.S. Mint?

J. Hewitt Judd, M.D., *United States Pattern, Trial and Experimental Pieces*, 1959. This original edition made the complicated world of pattern coins comprehensible for collectors, and makes it easy to love "what might have been" in American coinage—although you can still start a healthy argument over the question: "Is a 1792 half disme a regular issue coin, or a pattern?" Today the 10th edition, now titled United States Patterns, remains the standard reference.

Eric P. Newman and Kenneth Bressett, *The Fantastic 1804 Dollar*, 1962. Today it's hard to believe that one of the most valuable coins in American numismatics, the 1804 dollar, used to be a mystery as impenetrable as the fate of Amelia Earhart. Yet it was until this book, which reads like a mystery thriller, revealed the truth about why and when they were struck—and then restruck. Spoiler alert: neither the first nor the second strikes actually took place in 1804!

R.W. Julian, *Medals of the United States Mint*, 1977. The Mint strikes all of the nation's coins, of course, but it also has struck beautiful and historical medals. The subjects range from the high and mighty (presidents and generals) to the surprisingly mundane (a Baltimore couple's 50th wedding anniversary). Julian covers them all, including a case of dies long thought to be lost at sea that later turned up as paperweights in the Department of the Navy!

John W. Adams, *United States Numismatic Literature*, volumes 1 and 2, 1982 and 1990. The bible of numismatic auction catalog collectors, these volumes also reveal much about the colorful personalities of the great coin dealers. If you want to know which dealers were brilliant and which were blowhards, Adams pulls no punches in his assessments. He exposes one famous 19th-century dealer for perpetrating a "massive, deliberate fraud" in his 137th catalog (which didn't stop that same dealer from issuing 38 more catalogs over the next five years)!

Q. David Bowers, *Louis Eliasberg Collection Sales*, 1982, 1996, 1997. Only one collector has ever collected every United States coin by date and mintmark, and only one dealer has ever cataloged each and every one of these coins for sale. The first auction, in 1982, was offered with the title of *The United States Gold Coin Collection* by Bowers and Ruddy Galleries, and the last two, in 1996 and 1997, with the Eliasberg name under the auspices of Bowers and Merena Galleries. This achievement was unprecedented in American numismatic history and will be virtually impossible to duplicate in the future, so these catalogs belong on every collector's shelves. Where else can you buy a listing of a complete collection of United States coins for less than a hundred dollars? For good measure, you might also enjoy Dave's related book: *Louis E. Eliasberg, Sr.: King of Coins*.

COINS IN NEWSPAPERS AND MAGAZINES

From colonial times, newspapers and general-interest magazines have had many news articles, notices, and other entries relating to coins in circulation, the various mints, discoveries of lost treasure, and the like. In the late 1850s 17-year-old Augustus B. Sage in the *New-York Dispatch* in New York City and seasoned collector Jeremiah Colburn in the *Evening Transcript* in Boston each wrote extensive articles on rare coins. Today the Internet offers the possibility to search for such items. Similarly, later magazines have had many feature articles of interest to numismatists, such as illustrated features on minting in *Harper's Monthly Magazine* in 1860 and various articles on sculptor Augustus Saint-Gaudens and his coins in issues of *Century* magazine, as well as many others.

In the *New York Sun* in the early 20th century, Edgar H. Adams, a leading scholar of his time, presented detailed articles on rare coins each week. Single copies of these newspapers and magazines are nice additions to an advanced specialized numismatic library.

Regarding magazines with significant or exclusive numismatic content, the first was the earlier-mentioned *Historical Magazine*. Launched in 1857, this monthly journal contained many numismatic items, often responses to queries. At the time there were no handy sources for general information. *Norton's Literary Letter*, published from 1857 to 1860, was another magazine with numismatic items, as well as much other material.

THE *AMERICAN JOURNAL OF NUMISMATICS*

A giant step forward took place in May 1866, when the American Numismatic and Archaeological Society published the first issue of the *American Journal of Numismatics*. Accordingly, it merits an expanded commentary. Here for the first time was a magazine mainly devoted to rare coins and related subjects, although for a while it was thought that information on archaeology would broaden the membership of the society and the readership of its magazine. For the first four years it was issued monthly. The periodical was laden with interesting news, tidbits of information, specialized articles (including some about Civil War tokens and numismatic auction catalogs), and the like. Here, indeed, was a "fun" publication. However, there was a dichotomy between collectors who enjoyed collecting and scholars who were more interested in academics and abstruse subjects.

In 1958, Society historian Howard L. Adelson wrote the following about the *American Journal of Numismatics*: "It contained published notices of short, rather popularized articles. The scientific aspects of numismatics were still not the primary interest of the Society, which was for the most part composed of collectors, not scholars." One can readily imagine that if *popularizing* the hobby was not wanted, and that *collectors* were not wanted either, much would be lost!

In the first several years of the publication's history, there was infighting among editors,. To start, there was a single editor—Frank Norton—but he was later joined by two more to make a triumvirate. Not helping matters was the fact that the magazine was losing money. After the issue of April 1870, the New York group gave up the project and announced that the Journal had been transferred to the Boston Numismatic Society and would be published quarterly. In 1907 it was transferred back to the American Numismatic Society, recently renamed from American Numismatic and Archaeological Society. The group had found a financial angel in Archer Huntington, an heir to a railroad fortune. In 1908 a beautiful stone headquarters paid for by Archer opened on Audubon Terrace in New York City. Over the years the "American" in American Numismatic Society faded, and for a long period of time the organization was primarily devoted to ancient and world coins. After 1912 the *Journal* was issued at irregular intervals in the form of specialized monographs.

In the meantime a number of periodicals were issued by dealers. From 1867 to 1872 Ebenezer Locke Mason Jr. published *Mason's Coin and Stamp Collectors' Magazine* (the title varied) and later other magazines, most with interesting comments on news of the day and his (mostly) uninformed and less ethical competitors, and so on. The Scott Stamp & Coin Company issued the *Coin Collector's Journal*, and Édouard Frossard issued the chatty *Numisma*. Other titles could be mentioned. Any and all of these make interesting reading today and are worthwhile additions to an advanced library.

POPULAR PERIODICALS WITH EXTENDED RUNS

In 1888 George F. Heath, M.D., published the first issue of *The American Numismatist*. He soon learned that a New Jersey magazine of the same name had been issued in 1886 and thus changed the name of his periodical—to avoid confusion, one word was dropped, and *The Numismatist* continued production. The American Numismatic Association was formed in 1891, and later in that decade Heath's publication became the official magazine of the organization, except for a brief time when the ANA was inactive and its officers were not answering mail.

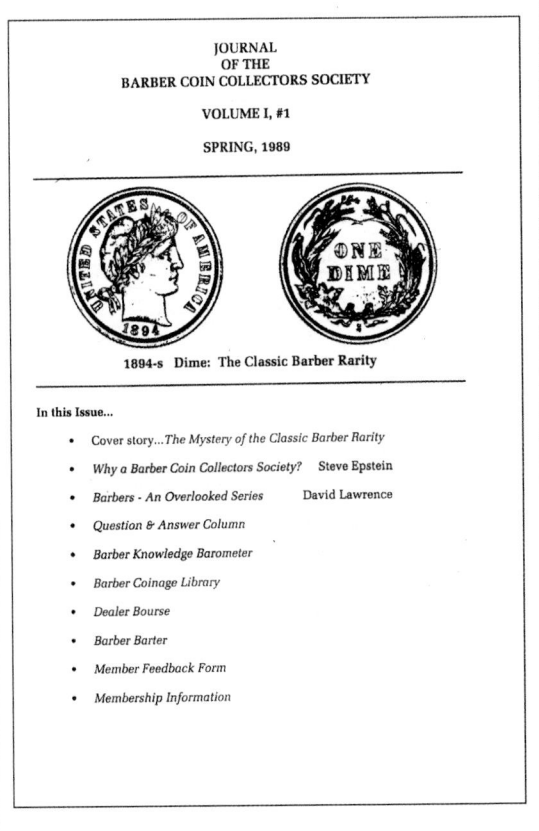

Cover of the first issue of the *Journal of the Barber Coin Collectors' Society,* spring 1989.

The cover of the January 1917 issue of *The Numismatist,* starting its thirtieth year of publication.

On a monthly basis, with some combined double-issues in the early days, *The Numismatist* sounded the heart strings of collectors, published popular articles alongside research and technical items, gave current news, told of club and society meetings, and became essential to the growth of the hobby. Today it is larger and better than ever and is edited by Barbara Gregory at ANA Headquarters in Colorado Springs.

In 1935 Lee F. Hewitt, an Illinois publisher, launched the *Numismatic Scrapbook Magazine.* Each monthly issue was filled with advertisements, news, reports of finding scarce coins in circulation, and the like, with little in the way of technical articles. It became very popular and for a long time eclipsed *The Numismatist* in circulation. It continued to be issued until 1976, by which time the weekly *Numismatic News* and *Coin World* dominated coin publishing.

Numismatic News was founded as a monthly by Chet Krause in Iola, Wisconsin, in 1952. It was originally devoted mostly to classified advertising, but that changed as the years went on. Clifford Mishler joined the management, and into the 1960s Krause Publications became an empire with many different periodicals ranging in topic from automobiles to sports and more. *Numismatic News* shifted to a weekly schedule and contained advertising, news, and features. Krause Publications also launched *Coins* magazine, and it quickly became a favorite, as did the company's *The Bank Note Reporter.* David Harper has been a key editor of multiple Krause offerings for a long time.

Coin World made its debut in the spring of 1960, when J. Oliver Amos of the Sidney (Ohio) Printing and Publishing Company decided to issue a hobby or leisure-time publication. After due contemplation, antiques, bowling, and coins were the three top favorites for the periodical's subject. Coins got the nod, and under the editorship of D. Wayne Johnson the newspaper far exceeded expectations and climbed to an unbelievable circulation of more than 100,000. Fueling this were two factors: the nationwide excitement about newly issued Lincoln cents with a "Small Date" (a $50 bag of Philadelphia coins became worth $12,000 or more) and nationwide publicity that rare coins were one of the best investments ever. After a relatively short tenure, Johnson resigned and was replaced by Margo Russell as editor. In 1985, Beth Deisher took over the position; she was later succeeded by Steve Roach, who in turn was succeeded by Bill Gibbs.

The rare-coin market rush ended in 1964 and prices dropped, as did circulation of all periodicals and memberships in clubs. *Coin World* has continued to chronicle the events in the hobby. Other periodicals such as *The Coin Dealer Newsletter* and *COINage* have had their share of subscribers as well. Journals of specialized collectors' societies play to their members and back issues are often sought.

Today, back issues of *The Numismatist* and the *Numismatic Scrapbook* are widely collected, the modern newspapers less so. In the present age of digitizing editorial content, much valuable information can be easily accessed, with more to come.

VINTAGE AUCTION CATALOGS

Catalogs issued by auction houses and rare-coin dealers have been eagerly sought for a long time. In terms of prices paid, these have led the way among numismatic bibliophiles. Here I address vintage catalogs up to the 1950s.

In 1859 the first rare-coin auctions prepared by a professional numismatist and billed as such took place. Earlier, several notable sales had taken place, including those of the Roper Collection in 1851 and the Flandin and the Kline sales in 1855, but these were prepared by art and antique auction houses. In contrast, the 1859 sales, three in number, were prepared by and bore the name of coin dealer Augustus B. Sage, who the year before had been the key person in organizing the American Numismatic Society. The Bogert Collection crossed the block from February 28 to March 5, 1859, the Foskett Collection followed on June 7, and the Whitmore Collection was sold on November 2 and 3.

In 1860 W. Elliott Woodward, a Roxbury, Massachusetts pharmacist and casual dealer in coins, wrote his first auction catalog. A gentleman who could be called a polymath in today's terminology, Woodward was well versed not only in rare coins, but in the arts, literature, and other endeavors. His reference library contained more than a thousand volumes. In 1863 and 1864, the Woodward sales set a high standard. The *American Journal of Numismatics* later called him "the lion of the day." Today, individual Woodward catalogs, which extended into the 1890s, are highly prized, and fortunate is the owner of an extensive run.

Woodward's main competitor in the auction venue was Edward Cogan, a Philadelphian who ran an art shop and in 1858 issued a small mail-bid list of old cents. He claimed this gave him the cachet of being the first rare-coin dealer in America—a true statement if you don't count John Allan (a dealer in New York City from the 1820s onward) and a half dozen or more others. Cogan, hardly a scholar but an enthusiastic champion of the hobby, issued many catalogs that today are valuable for their content, if not for scholarly content.

John W. Haseltine, whose rare-coin shop was the largest in Philadelphia, produced many catalogs, some of which offered previously unknown rarities that officers had slipped out of the Mint. In the mid-1870s S. Hudson Chapman (born in 1857) and Henry Chapman (1859) were employed by Haseltine, and in 1878 the brothers hung out their own shingle as numismatists and antiquarians. The Charles I. Bushnell estate collection was consigned to them, and in 1882 they delighted collectors and dismayed their competitors by issuing a large catalog of coins and medals, one edition with photographic plates, that was offered for the high sum of five dollars. The Bushnell sale gave the Chapmans overnight success.

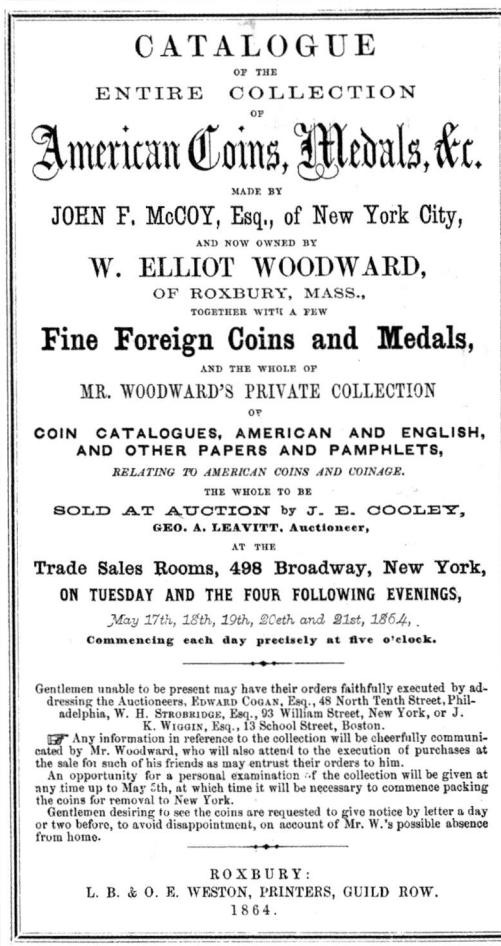

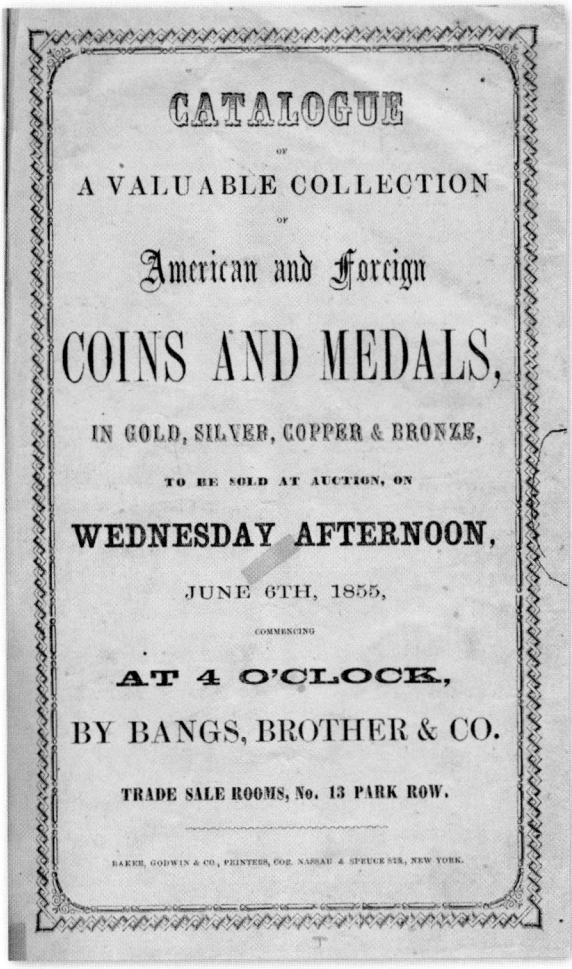

The catalog title page from W. Elliot Woodward's sale of the McCoy Collection in 1864.

Cover panel of the Flandin Collection catalog, June 6, 1855.

From then until 1906, they turned out some of the most important auction catalogs in American history up to that time, many in deluxe editions. By that time W. Elliot Woodward was no longer active, and the brothers were at the top of the profession.

Other auction catalogs of interest and importance were issued during the 19th century by William Strobridge, John W. Haseltine, Edouard Frossard, Scott Stamp & Coin Company, New York Coin and Stamp Company, Lyman H. Low, and others. Two comprehensive books by John W. Adams study auction catalogs and are described above on the list given by Dr. Joel Orosz.

CLASSIC CATALOGS OF THE EARLY 20TH CENTURY

During the early part of 20th century, B. Max Mehl, of Fort Worth, Texas, rose into great prominence as a rare-coin dealer. He had two parallel businesses. The first and larger was selling copies of *The Star Rare Coin Encyclopedia* to the general public. With some good luck, a rare 1913 Liberty Head nickel or 1804-dated silver dollar might be found in an attic, resulting in a large check from Mehl. No such coins were ever found hidden outside of numismatic circles, but millions of *Encyclopedia* copies were sold. At one time Mehl even had his own radio program.

His second business was rare-coin auctions—actually mail-bid sales, as none were ever held in a gallery with in-person attendance. Over a long period of years he handled some of the finest collections ever—the Manning, Ten Eyck, Slack, Dunham, Neil, Atwater, and many others laden with rarities. A run of these is an interesting addition to a library today. Most of these and other 20th century catalogs are rather inexpensive, some limited editions with photographic plates excepted.

Catalogs issued by Thomas L. Elder early in the century and into the 1930s were thrown together hastily (Elder claimed he could catalog 1,000 lots per day), but upon analysis yield many treasures. Of the extensive series of catalogs of this era, his are the least studied, mainly due to the difficulty of assembling a long run of copies.

In 1906 S. Hudson and Henry Chapman dissolved their partnership. After that time each conducted memorable sales, including some described in photographic-plate catalogs that are highly desired today. M.H. Bolender, an Illinois dealer, produced many mail-bid catalogs, mostly from the 1930s to the 1950s, the same time frame in which Barney Bluestone, of Syracuse, New York, also conducted many sales.

In the 1930s and 1940s Wayte Raymond and James G. Macallister conducted auctions under the otherwise anonymous name of J.C. Morgenthau & Company. Although Raymond in particular had excellent writing skills, the catalogs have some of the barest listings of any firm of the era. Stack's, formed by brothers Joseph and Morton Stack in New York City in 1933, conducted their first auction in 1935, inaugurating a dazzling run of "name" sales of major collections laden with rarities that continue into the present century. The New Netherlands Coin Company, established in New York City in 1936, hit its auction stride in 1952 when John J. Ford Jr., who was associated with the firm, and Walter H. Breen, an employee and later contract cataloger, produced some of the most information-filled catalogs in American auction history, a series that continued into the 1960s.

The Numismatic Gallery, established by Abe Kosoff in 1937 with Abner Kreisberg as a partner beginning in 1944, was another notable issuer of catalogs through 1953, including that of the F.C.C. Boyd Collection in 1945 and 1946 and other memorable events.

Beyond the era of vintage catalogs, into the present era, many new personalities and companies are involved beyond the scope of the present essay. Suffice it to say that many modern catalogs with beautiful illustrations on quality stock exceed in appearance most of those of years past. The auction venue has also gone beyond collectible catalogs in print to include virtual presentations on the Internet. What will the future hold?

Notes

SMALL CENTS

1. After having had some bad experiences, including a RD Proof becoming stained and blotchy while in its holder, PCGS no longer guarantees the stability of color in its holders.

2. David W. Lange, communication with Q. David Bowers, September 15, 2015.

3. Communication with Q. David Bowers, July 12, 2007.

4. Coin World, "Collectors' Clearinghouse," February 19, 1986. Also supported by Ken Potter, in communications with Q. David Bowers, January 2007, including information from a 1985 correspondence with Jerry Yellin, then chief of the Assay Division at the U.S. Mint.

5. David W. Lange, communication with Q. David Bowers, September 15, 2015.

6. Communication to Q. David Bowers by an interested party, July 5, 2007.

7. Today it is more popular to state the diameter as 19.1 mm, obscuring the "useful" diameter originally intended.

8. Director Snowden, in *A Description of Ancient and Modern Coins, in the Cabinet Collection at the Mint of the United State Mint*, 1860, p. 120, specifically called this a cereal wreath. In the 19th century it was occasionally called a tobacco wreath.

9. Breen mistakenly described these as maple leaves in his encyclopedia of Proofs, but Snow correctly identified the wreath details with numismatic as well as botanical images on p. 23 of the *Flying Eagle & Indian Cent Attribution Guide*, third edition, volume 1.

10. Although the top ends of the wreath do not particularly resemble corn ears, this is what they were intended to be. Thomas K. DeLorey, in a communication with Q. David Bowers, June 3, 1996, commented: "The original wax model for the agricultural wreath, now in my possession, shows the detail of the two corn ears at the tops of the wreath as long, feathery fronds, signifying the tassel normally found on a corn ear. However, none of this detail survived the transfer to the various incarnations of this wreath, and in each case Longacre was forced to replace it with a series of dots resembling kernels of corn themselves." Hence, this figure does not—as posited in Breen's encyclopedia of Proofs—represent an "open wheat stalk."

11. Perhaps the most elegant and varied array of new art created in a short period of time at the Mint is found among silver pattern half dollars of the year 1877.

12. However, millions were taken north to Canada, and in the early and mid-1860s large cents circulated actively there at a time when they were no longer plentiful in everyday transactions in the United States, having been mostly replaced by copper-nickel cents.

13. Rick Snow, communication with Q. David Bowers, September 22, 2015.

14. *The Numismatist*, April 1944. Most of the text is directly from this article, although writer. David Bowers has edited it and in some instances expanded the information.

15. Rick Snow, communication with Q. David Bowers, September 22, 2015.

16. Mint records are often incomplete, and this finding of two die pairs does not preclude the possibility that other dies were made as well.

17. The same is true of 1858 pattern cents, all of which were made for pattern or numismatic purposes, but most of which have incompletely polished surfaces; some call these "circulation strikes," which is a misnomer, and others routinely call them Proofs.

18. Rick Snow, communication with Q. David Bowers, September 22, 2015.

19. Estimates are from Rick Snow, in a communication with Q. David Bowers, September 22, 2015. Bill Fivaz, in a communication with Q. David Bowers, September 15, estimated 20 to 35 MS–60 to 64, 8 to 12 MS-65 and higher, and 100 to 150 in circulated grades. "These are plentiful, and I still run across them unattributed," Bill stated.

20. *Walter Breen's Encyclopedia of United States and Colonial Proof Coins, 1722–1977*, p. 104.

21. Rick Snow, communication with Q. David Bowers, April 18, 1996.

22. 1858 *Mint Report*, p. 86.

23. This description of the dies was adapted from Rick Snow, *Flying Eagle & Indian Cent Attribution Guide*, third edition, volume 1, p. 46.

24. Bill Fivaz, "Definitely a Difference," *Longacre's Ledger*, Summer 1994. A follow-up in the same publication's Fall 1994 issue suggests that Robert E. Guiles may have been the first to notice this. Fivaz further supported the initial point in a letter to Q. David Bowers on March 30, 1996.

25. The inscription UNITED STATES OF AMERICA in three different punch font sizes (apparently intended for the dime, quarter dollar, and half dollar denominations) attributed to Paquet, is seen on Pollock-3131, a one-sided trial striking.

26. Communication with Q. David Bowers, April 10, 1996.

27. Rick Snow, communication with Q. David Bowers, September 22, 2015.

28. These few leaves have been called olive leaves by some, including by the 1858 correspondent Howard subsequently quoted, but the berries among the leaves are round, as laurel leaves are, not elongated, as olive leaves would be; on the other hand, Heraldic Eagle silver and gold coins of the 1790s and early 1800s have an eagle holding an olive branch with incorrectly styled round berries. However, the olive branch held by Miss Liberty on the 1873 trade dollar, designed by William Barber, does appear to have elongated olives, the same as the olives on the branch on the reverse of the trade dollar. On August 20, 1858, Longacre called the reverse an "olive wreath" in correspondence; while on November 4, 1858, Director Snowden called it a "plain laurel wreath."

29. This sketch can be identified as Associative/Decorative Object No. A/D NPG 77.50.24, and it has been described as: "Reverse design; wreath of olives, probably for one-cent piece. Maker: James B. Longacre."

30. In some 19th-century literature these are called olive leaves; the Mint used both terms.

31. Snowden, *A Description of Ancient and Modern Coins, in the Cabinet Collection at the Mint of the United State Mint*, 1860, p. 120.

32. This information and more can also be found in Larry Steve and Kevin Flynn's *The F.ind.ers Report: A Comprehensive Guide to Selected Rare Flying Eagle and Indian Cent Die Varieties*, p. 213.

33. R.W. Julian, communication with Q. David Bowers, April 16, 1996. Additional information on the subject came from Walter Breen, in a communication with Q. David Bowers, February 12, 1992. Also, a letter from R.W. Julian, March 20, 1992. Robert Coulton Davis was one of the earliest specialists in pattern coins and wrote the first serious study on them, which appeared serially in *The Coin Collector's Journal*, from 1885 to 1887. His collection was cataloged by David U. Proskey and auctioned by the New York Coin & Stamp Co., January 20–24, 1890. Davis had an 1804 silver dollar which the Mint had obligingly certified not only as genuine and original, but actually struck in the year 1804. It was Davis who, circa 1858, informed Director Snowden that someone at the Mint was secretly restriking 1804 dollars and peddling them to coin dealers; these were the plain-edge varieties subsequently bought back by the Mint (for details of the plain-edge coins see *The Fantastic 1804 Dollar* by Eric Newman and Kenneth Bressett). Davis also owned a set of 1866 silver coins without the IN GOD WE TRUST motto, probably struck to his order. Walter Breen stated that druggist Davis secretly supplied laudanum to employees in the Mint Medal Department and in return received many special restrikes and mulings. However, as at the time it was perfectly legal to buy opiates at any drug store, and the supplying of such would not have been a rare favor, it seems unlikely that this would have been a major factor.

34. R.W. Julian, communication with Q. David Bowers, April 24, 1996.

35. Information from Dr. George R. Conger, "The Controversial Feathered Headdress," *Longacre's Ledger*, April 1992, and Joy Goforth, "Who Came First? Goddess, Sarah, or Indian?" *Coin World*, January 4, 1984 (reprinted there from Goforth's article in the November 1983 issue of *Mint Press*, there titled "Goddess of Liberty").

36. *Walter Breen's Encyclopedia of United States and Colonial Proof Coins, 1722–1977*, p. 217, locates the statue "in a Philadelphia museum." Cornelius Vermeule, in *Numismatic Art in America*, is the source for the Vatican location. Could there be two versions of the statue? The Sarah Longacre

biographical and portrait information is adapted from "An Argument Favoring Sarah as Longacre's Model," *Longacre's Ledger*, July 1992, which in turn was based upon several cited sources.

37. George and Melvin Fuld, *Patriotic Civil War Tokens*, 4th edition, p. 17.

38. Communication with Q. David Bowers, May 15, 1996.

39. R.W. Julian, "Notes on U.S. Proof Coinage, Silver and Minor," *Numismatic Scrapbook Magazine*, March 1966; also a letter to Q. David Bowers, April 24, 1996.

40. Snowden's account was primarily directed toward the coinage of precious metals as related in extensive parts of his commentary not reprinted here; certain aspects including die life may have been different for copper-nickel cents.

41. Communication with Q. David Bowers, April 10, 1996.

42. R.W. Julian, "Notes on U.S. Proof Coinage, Silver and Minor," *Numismatic Scrapbook Magazine*, March 1966.

43. *Annual Report of the Director of the Mint*, 1861.

44. Rick Snow, letters to Q. David Bowers, April 10 and 18, 1996.

45. From the Massachusetts periodical the *Worcester Palladium*, May 28, 1862, provided for research courtesy of Don Munro.

46. No documentation of this has been found, but the Scovill archives include a collection of encased postage stamps.

47. However, in 1864 the legislation was dusted off and threats were made against several token issuers.

48. This was also printed as "Large Coinage of Cents," *Bankers Magazine*, November 1862.

49. Adapted from R.W. Julian, "The Cent Becomes Bronze: 1864," *FUN-Topics*, Summer 1987.

50. Alfred Ernest Barlow, *A Report on the Origin, Geological Relations and Composition of the Nickel and Copper Deposits of the Sudbury Mining District, Ontario, Canada*, 1907, p.172.

51. Theodore Fleitmann was at one time a business associate of Joseph Wharton in Camden, New Jersey; about 1869 he left Wharton and went on to set up facilities for making nickel and nickel-alloy products in the Ruhr section of Germany.

52. Catalog copy furnished by Frank Campbell of the American Numismatic Society, New York City.

53. Rick Snow, in a communication with Q. David Bowers, April 10, 1996, the quantity of 200 Proof cents is suggested. However, R.W. Julian, in a communication with Q. David Bowers, April 24,

1996, notes, "Only a small number of 1862 cents were found in the mid-1870s, not about 200. Also, the large number of Proof cents that piled up [in numismatic hands] were the result of volume buying by dealers, not a Mint action."

54. 1925 *Mint Report*, p. 10.

55. Information in this and the following paragraph is adapted from R.W. Julian, "The Cent Becomes Bronze: 1864," *FUN-Topics*, Summer 1987.

56. The English word *nickel* comes from the German word *Kupfernickel*, meaning "copper demon." Nickel was viewed as a "demon" which prevented miners from obtaining the metal they were truly after, copper.

57. If they were exchanged by weight—which is unlikely due to the logistics and fluctuating values involved—the number was smaller (as the price of copper had risen to the point at which each old cent had more than one cent's worth of the metal).

58. Rick Snow, letters, April 10 and 18, 1996.

59. R.W. Julian, "The Cent Becomes Bronze: 1864." *FUN-Topics*, Summer 1987.

60. R.W. Julian, "The Cent Becomes Bronze: 1864." *FUN-Topics*, Summer 1987. Separately (in a letter, April 19, 1996), R.W. Julian advised that the total mintage for cents this year was 51,795,000 (from a calendar-year statement located among Mint data in the National Archives) against a combined *Guide Book of United States Coins* total of 52,973,714. This information was also shared in a communication with Q. David Bowers, April 24, 1996.

61. R.W. Julian, communication with Q. David Bowers, April 24, 1996.

62. R.W. Julian, "The Cent Becomes Bronze: 1864," *FUN-Topics*, Summer 1987.

63. Certain additional information is from R.W. Julian, in a communication with Q. David Bowers, April 24, 1996.

64. R.W. Julian, "The Cent Becomes Bronze: 1864," *FUN-Topics*, Summer 1987.

65. Rick Snow, communication with Q. David Bowers, September 22, 2015.

66. See note 60.

67. *Walter Breen's Complete Encyclopedia of U.S. and Colonial Coins*, p. 220.

68. Further, R.W. Julian, on April 24, 1996, commented that Treasury records do not show bronze coins shipped to England in 1864 or any other year.

69. Communication with Q. David Bowers, April 15, 1996.

70. Rick Snow, communication with Q. David Bowers, September 26, 2015.

71. Breen in *Dies & Coinage*, p. 26, described the Boulton & Watt (Birmingham, England) method of bronzing: "[Matthew] Boulton was also responsible for innovations in proofing. Specifically, he began the practice (later carried over to the Philadelphia Mint for medals and some patterns) of striking Proofs on pre-gilded or pre-patinated (bronzed) blanks. Bronzing of copper for this purpose was done by coating the blanks with some copper compound and heating them. [Apparently, Breen drew most if not all of this information from C. Wilson Peck, *English Copper, Tin and Bronze Coins*, 1960, pp. 220–221, etc.] A very large number of Soho Mint Proofs are bronzed, as are most of the GOD OUR TRUST patterns of 1861–1863 and some others from the Philadelphia Mint." Of course, this period encompasses the same year (1863) that the 1863 pattern bronze Indian cents were struck.

72. Rick Snow, communication with Q. David Bowers, April 10, 1996.

73. Rick Snow, communication with Q. David Bowers, April 10, 1996.

74. Die Pair 1 and Die Pair 2 are described by Rick Snow in "The 1864 With L Proof," *Longacre's Ledger*, Summer 1994. Breen's 1977 description in his *Complete Encyclopedia of U.S. and Colonial Coins*, p. 123, is ambiguous and seems to combine features of both dies; apparently, he did not know there were two different pairs: "Date is about centered, peak of 1 nearly even with bust point (unusual), left base of 1 above space between denticles, right base of 4 above center of denticle. Spine slants down to left, about 1.5 mm in length, from curl below ear into neck. Doubling on much of legend. Reverse: Spine to left from a round leaf tip at very top of right branch. Heavy letters, base of N in ONE not as strong as other serifs, left base stronger than right base (respectively rounded and pointed)."

75. Rick Snow, communication with Q. David Bowers, April 10, 1996.

76. Die Pair 1 is equivalent to Die Pair 2 in Richard E. Snow's Flying Eagle & Indian Cents book, 1st edition, 1992; the 3rd edition will has the pairings numbered as in the present text. (Per Rick Snow, communication with Q. David Bowers, May 3, 1996.)

77. Rick Snow in "The 1864 With L Proof," *Longacre's Ledger*, Summer 1994.

78. Rick Snow, communication with Q. David Bowers, April 10, 1996.

79. Communication with Q. David Bowers, May 13, 1996.

80. Rick Snow, communication with Q. David Bowers, April 10, 1996. Die pairs are listed per current designations and are the opposite of Pair 1 and Pair 2 in Snow's 1992 book, as noted in note 76.

81. As quoted by Don Taxay, *The U.S. Mint and Coinage: An Illustrated History from 1776 to the Present*, p. 244.

82. Similar "Plain" and "Fancy" 5 varieties exist among 1865 two-cent pieces and are from the same four-digit date logotype punches.

83. *Walter Breen's Complete Encyclopedia of U.S. and Colonial Coins*, p. 221.

84. This is a departure from the norm; those regions did not usually desire to use minor coins. Could the new demand have been from Northern occupation or Reconstruction? (Suggestion of Thomas K. DeLorey, communication with Q. David Bowers, April 15, 1996).

85. Thomas K. DeLorey, communication with Q. David Bowers, April 15, 1996.

86. Larry R. Steve, communication with Q. David Bowers, April 12, 1996.

87. Rick Snow, communication with Q. David Bowers, September 22, 2015.

88. "Collectors' Clearinghouse" column. Article titled "Clashed Dies: Usually Common, There Are Some Bizarre Varieties to Seek."

89. Communication with Q. David Bowers, April 12, 1996.

90. For further information: Chris Pilliod, "What Error Coins Can Teach Us About Die Settings," *The Numismatist*, April 1996.

91. R.W. Julian, "Notes on U.S. Proof Coinage, Silver and Minor." *Numismatic Scrapbook Magazine*, March 1966.

92. "Proof Die Identification for Indian Cents." *Longacre's Ledger*, Fall 1994.

93. Many dozens of photographs of 1871 nickel three-cent pieces and Shield nickels were examined; all of these were made using different and considerably smaller logotype punches.

94. For a detailed exposition see Rick Snow, "President's Report," *Longacre's Ledger*, April 1992.

95. *American Journal of Numismatics*, July 1871, p. 24.

96. Jim Reardon, of Littleton Coin Co., communication with Q. David Bowers, May 3, 1996. Littleton is one of America's largest-volume sellers of circulated Indian Head cents.

97. Larry R. Steve, "THE F.IND.ERS REPORT," *Longacre's Ledger*, Winter 1995.

98. Letter, February 17, 1996.

99. A copy of this letter is reproduced in *The F.ind.ers Report: A Comprehensive Guide to Selected Rare Flying Eagle and Indian Cent Die Varieties*, by Larry R. Steve and Kevin Flynn, pp. 55, 56.

100. No precision intended—this figure is the result of deducting an estimated two million pieces (for the Close 3 variety) from the overall mintage figure.

101. Rick Snow, communication with Q. David Bowers, September 22, 2015.

102. Rick Snow, communication with Q. David Bowers, May 3, 1996, noted: "I believe all [1874] Proofs have defective dates. I have never seen a perfect date Proof 1874. The 'normal die' listing was an error in my 1992 book."

103. Larry R. Steve, communication with Q. David Bowers, April 12, 1996. The Proofs are the Snow-1 variety; the circulation strikes are S-2.

104. See "The Case of the Disappearing Cent," *Numismatic Scrapbook Magazine*, May 1972, by R.W. Julian, and the commentary by Q. David Bowers in *Flying Eagle and Indian Head Cents, a Buyer's and Enthusiast's Guide*, 1996.

105. Larry R. Steve, communication with Q. David Bowers, April 12, 1996.

106. Rick Snow, communication with Q. David Bowers, April 10, 1996; additional comments May 3, 1996.

107. *Mint Report*; also *American Journal of Numismatics*, July 1876, p. 12 (latter citation suggested by Michael Hodder, communication with Q. David Bowers, May 14, 1996).

108. Reported by John Dannreuther, communication with Q. David Bowers, May 16, 1996; a similar roll of 1878 cents was dispersed at the same time.

109. *Walter Breen's Complete Encyclopedia of U.S. and Colonial Coins*, p. 223.

110. Rick Snow, communication with Q. David Bowers, September 22, 2015.

111. Bill Fivaz, communication with Q. David Bowers, March 30, 1996.

112. Rick Snow, communication with Q. David Bowers, September 22, 2015.

113. Rick Snow. "Proof Die Identification for Indian Cents." *Longacre's Ledger*, Fall 1994; updated and revised by a letter, on April 10, 1996.

114. Rick Snow, communication with Q. David Bowers, April 10, 1996.

115. Rick Snow, communication with Q. David Bowers, April 10, 1996.

116. Reported by John Dannreuther, communication with Q. David Bowers, May 16, 1996; a similar roll of 1876 cents was dispersed at the same time.

117. Rick Snow, communication with Q. David Bowers, September 22, 2016.

118. Rick Snow. "Proof Die Identification for Indian Cents." *Longacre's Ledger*, Fall 1994; number of dies modified to 4 in a letter to Q. David Bowers, April 10, 1996.

119. Communication with Q. David Bowers, April 10, 1996.

120. Observation of John Dannreuther in reference to coins submitted to PCGS for grading; letter, May 16, 1996.

121. Communication with Q. David Bowers, May 16, 1996.

122. In the article "Collect Indian Head Cents for Pleasure and Profit."

123. Edward Hungerford in his book, *The Romance of a Great Store*, as quoted by *The Numismatic Scrapbook Magazine*, April 1944, p. 312. Why a telephone call wasn't placed to Washington or a telegram sent was not explained. However, it makes a good story.

124. Rick Snow, Communication with Q. David Bowers, April 10, 1996.

125. Rick Snow, communication with Q. David Bowers, April 10, 1996.

126. Observation of John Dannreuther regarding coins submitted to PCGS for grading; letter, May 16, 1996.

127. Observation of John Dannreuther regarding coins submitted to PCGS for grading; letter, May 16, 1996.

128. Communication with Q. David Bowers, May 3, 1996.

129. Communication with Q. David Bowers, May 16, 1996.

130. Larry R. Steve, communication with Q. David Bowers, April 12, 1996.

131. Subsequently the discovery was published in several places including *The Numismatist*, April 1970, p. 531.

132. At one time examples of Snow-8 were called Type 2 1888/7 overdate. Today the overdate status is not recognized. Rick Snow, in a communication with Q. David Bowers, September 22, 2015.

133. 1889 *Mint Report*, p. 18.

134. Rick Snow, communication with Q. David Bowers, September 22, 2015.

135. 1890 *Mint Report*, p. 19. Other contracts were let during this era, including others let to Scovill; this citation is representative.

136. 1891 *Mint Report*, p. 69.

137. 1892 *Mint Report*, p. 24.

138. Henry T. Hettger, "Collusive Bidding on Indian Head Cent Planchets in 1892," *Longacre's Ledger*, October 1991.

139. 1894 *Mint Report*, pp. 11–12.

140. Citation located by Henry T. Hettger; printed in *Longacre's Ledger*, Fall 1993.

141. 1896 *Mint Report*, p. 203.

142. Called MPDs (misplaced dates) hundreds of such anomalies occur in coinage of this era across various denominations, and they have been studied by Bill Fivaz, J.T. Stanton, Kevin Flynn, John Wexler, and others and have been described in society journals.

143. Better not look too closely at the above hyperbolic calculations and try to compare the heights of the Statue of Liberty and the Eiffel Tower, the latter apparently being about 1/40th as tall as the New York statue.

144. About the cent-grabbing devices: The Kinetoscope (properly capitalized) was an Edison device showing a short "movie" via a film strip. Similarly, the American Mutoscope Company had "movies" via a series of photographic flip cards viewed in rapid succession. While several brands of coin-operated music boxes were in vogue, the market leader was the Regina Music Box Co., of Rahway, New Jersey. Candy and chewing gum vendors were very popular, especially the latter; Zeno was a popular gum brand sold this way. Weighing machines such as the National (a brand which was especially popular in the first decade of the 20th century) were typically made of cast iron and placed on the sidewalk in front of stores, taverns, hotels, railroad stations, and other public places where they could ingest Indian cents 24 hours a day.

145. John Craig, *The Mint: A History of the London Mint from A.D. 287 to 1948*, 1953, p. 332.

146. Rick Snow, communication with Q. David Bowers, April 10, 1996.

147. Michael Hodder, communication with Q. David Bowers, May 14, 1996, reported the knowledge of three pieces, all personally seen, with weights ranging from 65.8 to 67.1 grains.

148. 1900 *Mint Report*, p. 6; 1901 *Mint Report*, p. 5. Later pleas could be cited as well.

149. Rick Snow, communication with Q. David Bowers, April 10, 1996.

150. Communication with Q. David Bowers, April 10, 1996, modified with better information on September 22, 2016.

151. Communication with Q. David Bowers, May 16, 1996.

152. 1902 *Mint Report*, p. 26.

153. Rick Snow, communication with Q. David Bowers, April 10, 1996.

154. Rick Snow, "Proof Die Identification for Indian Cents," *Longacre's Ledger*, Fall 1994.

155. Communication with Q. David Bowers, May 16, 1996.

156. Heritage Auctions, Long Beach Sale, September 2015.

157. 1906 *Mint Report*, p. 36.

158. Michael Hodder, communication with Q. David Bowers, May 14, 1996, who reported he had personally inspected the coin.

159. Rick Snow, communication with Q. David Bowers, April 10, 1996.

160. 1907 *Mint Report*, p. 35.

161. Rick Snow, communication with Q. David Bowers, April 10, 1996.

162. *Catalogue of Coins, Tokens and Medals in the Numismatic Collection of the Mint of the United States at Philadelphia, Pa*, 1914, p. 82.

163. Commodore Eaton also did important work on 1857 Flying Eagle cents.

164. 1909 *Mint Report*, p. 43.

165. Rick Snow, communication with Q. David Bowers, April 10, 1996. He further commented: "The only one I have ever seen with full feather tips was certified as MS-65RD, but I informed [a leading certification service] that the S was added later." The service bought the coin from him.

166. David W. Lange, communication with Q. David Bowers, September 17, 2015.

167. Roger W. Burdette, correspondence, July 1, 2007, drawing upon Mint correspondence 1907–1912 and a letter to the Mint director, February 4, 1913.

168. Interview with Q. David Bowers in Owego, New York, August 1960. By that time Ziemer was a well-known dealer in antiques. His numismatic interest was still strong, with a specialty in gold coins.

169. Courtesy of Roger W. Burdette. The full text of this letter and other correspondence appears in *Renaissance of American Coinage, 1909–1915*.

170. As cited in *Renaissance of American Coinage, 1909–1915*, pp. 56–57.

171. Published in *The Numismatist*, double issue of September and October 1909.

172. C.R. Morey, "Sculpture Since the Centennial," in *The Pageant of America*, vol. XII, Yale University Press, 1927, p. 208.

173. David W. Lange, communication with Q. David Bowers, September 17, 2015.

174. Kevin Flynn, *Lincoln Cent Matte Proofs*, p. 118. Also see that text for related correspondence.

175. Communication with Q. David Bowers, September 17, 2017.

176. Communication with Q. David Bowers, September 22, 2015, part of a discussion about huge price variations among certified coins in the same grades—a subject rarely discussed openly in the marketplace.

177. Letter to Q. David Bowers, July 5, 2007.

178. Kevin Flynn, *Lincoln Cent Matte Proofs*, pp. 120–121.

179. James Wiles, communication with Q. David Bowers, September 15, 2015.

180. Q. David Bowers's discussion with Pukall about Matte Proofs and Proof remainders in the 1950s.

181. *Colorado Springs Gazette*, November 29, 1914. The same article also included this misinformation: "According to officials at the United States Mint in Denver all pennies are coined in Philadelphia and shipped through the local mint and Sub-Treasury for distribution."

182. David W. Lange, communication with Q. David Bowers, September 17, 2015.

183. Communication with Q. David Bowers, September 22, 2015.

184. See James Wiles, varietyvista.com, for more information.

185. This was not a practical suggestion as the vast majority of coin-in-the-slot machines were owned by route operators who placed them in locations and visited them at pre-set intervals.

186. David W. Lange, communication with Q. David Bowers, September 17, 2015. This estimate is a revision of that given in his 1996 book on the series.

187. David W. Lange, communication with Q. David Bowers, September 17, 2015.

188. Sent to Q. David Bowers, July 2007. Also used in Lange's "USA Coin Album" column in the *Numismatist*, April 2005.

189. James Wiles, communication with Q. David Bowers, September 11, 2015.

190. David W. Lange, communication with Q. David Bowers, September 17, 2015. This estimate is a revision of that given in his 1996 book on the series.

191. John A. Wexler and Kevin Flynn. *The Authoritative Reference on Lincoln Cents*, devotes pp. 250-358 to these.

192. See *Numismatic News*, October 5, 2010. Laura Sperber sold it for $1.7 million to Andy Skrabalak, owner of Angel Dee's Coins and Collectibles, who was acting as an agent for a private collector.

193. *Coin World*, October 2012, related that Bob R. Simpson, co-chairman of the Texas Rangers, paid Legend Numismatics $1 million for the finest-known (MS-62 PCGS) bronze 1943-S Lincoln cent, an upgrade from the AU-58 PCGS example previously in his PCGS Registry set. Simpson now owns the all-time finest PCGS Registry Set of off-metal Lincoln cent circulation strikes dated 1943 and 1944.

194. In the course of studying prices, economics, and prevailing attitudes in the numismatic marketplace from the late 1930s through the early 1950s, in the 1960s Q. David Bowers interviewed Abe Kosoff, Abner Kreisberg, Arthur M. Kagin, and others in depth.

195. For one of the earlier accounts on a variety that would engender endless coverage in print see Bowers, *Coins and Collectors*, 1964.

196. Spadone also published *The Flying Eaglet*, a coin newspaper until 1959 (the last two issues were titled Coin News), which was sold to Krause Publications in Iola, WI.

197. An interesting comment as the office of the director of the Mint was in Washington. Interviews with various Mint artists over the years reveals that few had traveled widely, either to the director's office in Washington or to the branch mints.

198. David W. Lange, communication with Q. David Bowers, September 15, 2015.

199. David W. Lange, "Mint Keeps Some Coins Secret," *Coin World*, November 23, 1992.

200. Eric von Klinger, "PCGS Buys Back Proof-70 1963 Cent," *Coin World*, January 26, 2004.

201. Third-party grading services decline to guarantee color stability for this and other reasons.

202. David W. Lange, communication with Q. David Bowers, September 19, 2015.

203. David W. Lange, communication with Q. David Bowers, September 19, 2015.

204. David W. Lange, communication with Q. David Bowers, September 15, 2015.

205. David W. Lange, communication with Q. David Bowers, September 18, 2005.

206. James Wiles, communication with Q. David Bowers, September 17, 2015.

207. Michael Ellis, communication with Q. David Bowers, September 9, 2015.

208. James Wiles, communication with Q. David Bowers, September 17, 2015.

209. *Coin World*, October 23, 2006.

210. David W. Lange, communication with Q. David Bowers, September 18, 2005.

211. Issue of March 25, 2008.

212. Issue of June 30, 2008.

213. Special arrangements were made by Tom Jurkowsky of the U.S. Mint. David Sundman, Dennis Tucker, Lee Bowers, and John Dannreuther accompanied Q. David Bowers on the trip, April 7, 2015.

Glossary

Over the years coin collectors have developed a special jargon to describe their coins. The following list includes terms that are used frequently by coin collectors or that have a special meaning other than their ordinary dictionary definitions. You will find them useful when you want to discuss or describe your coins.

alloy—A combination of two or more metals.

altered date—A false date on a coin; a date altered to make a coin appear to be one of a rarer or more valuable issue.

bag mark—A surface mark, usually a small nick, acquired by a coin through contact with others in a mint bag.

billon—A low-grade alloy of silver (usually less than 50%) mixed with another metal, typically copper.

blank—The formed piece of metal on which a coin design will be stamped.

bronze—An alloy of copper, zinc, and tin.

bullion—Uncoined gold or silver in the form of bars, ingots, or plate.

cast coins—Coins that are made by pouring molten metal into a mold, instead of in the usual manner of striking blanks with dies.

cent—One one-hundredth of the standard monetary unit. Also known as a *centavo, centimo,* or *centesimo* in some Central American and South American countries; *centime* in France and various former colonies in Africa; and other variations.

certified coin—A coin that has been graded, authenticated, and encapsulated in plastic by an independent (neither buyer nor seller) grading service.

cherrypicker—A collector who finds scarce and unusual coins by carefully searching through unattributed items in old accumulations or dealers' stocks.

circulation strike—An Uncirculated coin intended for eventual use in commerce, as opposed to a Proof coin.

clad coinage—Issues of the United States dimes, quarters, halves, and some dollars made since 1965. Each coin has a center core of pure copper and a layer of copper-nickel or silver on both sides.

collar—The outer ring, or die chamber, that holds a blank in place in the coinage press while the coin is impressed by the obverse and reverse dies.

contact marks—Minor abrasions on an Uncirculated coin, made by contact with other coins in a bag or roll.

countermark—A stamp or mark impressed on a coin to verify its use by another government or to indicate revaluation.

crack-out—A coin that has been removed from a grading service holder.

crown—Any dollar-size coin (c. 38 mm in diameter) in general, often struck in silver; specifically, one from the United Kingdom and some Commonwealth countries.

cud—An area of raised metal at the rim of a coin where a portion of the die broke off, leaving a void in the design.

designer—The artist who creates a coin's design. An engraver is the person who cuts a design into a coinage die.

die—A piece of metal, usually hardened steel, with an incuse reverse image, engraved with a design and used for stamping coins.

die crack—A fine, raised line on a coin, caused by a broken die.

die defect—An imperfection on a coin, caused by a damaged die.

die variety—Any minor alteration in the basic design of a coin.

dipped, dipping—Refers to chemical cleaning of a coin to remove oxidation or foreign matter.

double eagle—The United States twenty-dollar gold coin.

doubled die—A die that has been given two misaligned impressions from a hub; also, a coin made from such a die.

doubloon—Popular name for a Spanish gold coin originally valued at $16.

eagle—A United States ten-dollar gold coin; also refers to U.S. silver, gold, and platinum bullion pieces made from 1986 to the present.

edge—Periphery of a coin, often with reeding, lettering, or other decoration.

electrotype—A reproduction of a coin or medal made by the electrodeposition process. Electrotypes are frequently used in museum displays.

electrum—A naturally occurring mixture of gold and silver. Some of the world's first coins were made of this alloy.

encapsulated coins—Coins that have been authenticated, graded, and sealed in plastic by a professional service.

engrailed edge—A coin edge marked with small curved notches.

engraver—The person who engraves or sculpts a model for use in translating to a coin die.

error—A mismade coin not intended for circulation.

exergue—That portion of a coin beneath the main design, often separated from it by a line, and typically bearing the date.

field—The background portion of a coin's surface not used for a design or inscription.

filler—A coin in worn condition but rare enough to be included in a collection.

fineness—The purity of gold, silver, or any other precious metal, expressed in terms of one thousand parts. A coin of 90% pure silver is expressed as .900 fine.

flan—A blank piece of metal in the size and shape of a coin; also called a *planchet*.

gem—A coin of exceptionally high quality, typically considered MS-65 or PF-65 or better.

gripped edge—An edge with irregularly spaced notches.

half eagle—The United States five-dollar gold coin minted from 1795 to 1929.

hub—A positive-image punch to impress the coin's design into a die for coinage.

incuse—The design of a coin that has been impressed below the coin's surface. A design raised above the coin's surface is in relief.

inscription—The legend or lettering on a coin.

intrinsic value—Bullion or "melt" value of the actual precious metal in a numismatic item.

investment grade—Promotional term; generally, a coin in grade MS-65 or better.

junk silver—Common-date silver coins taken from circulation; worth only bullion value.

key coin—One of the scarcer or more valuable coins in a series.

laureate—Head crowned with a laurel wreath.

legal tender—Money that is officially issued and recognized for redemption by an authorized agency or government.

legend—A principal inscription on a coin.

lettered edge—The edge of a coin bearing an inscription, found on some foreign and some older United States coins, modern Presidential dollars, and the MMIX Ultra High Relief gold coin.

luster—The brilliant or "frosty" surface quality of an Uncirculated (Mint State) coin.

milled edge—The raised rim around the outer surface of a coin, not to be confused with the reeded or serrated narrow edge of a coin.

mint error—Any mismade or defective coin produced by a mint.

mint luster—Shiny "frost" or brilliance on the surface of an Uncirculated or Mint State coin.

mintmark—A small letter or other mark on a coin, indicating the mint at which it was struck.

Mint set—A set of Uncirculated coins packaged and sold by the Mint. Each set contains one of each of the coins made for circulation at each of the mints that year.

motto—An inspirational word or phrase used on a coin.

mule—A coin struck from two dies not originally intended to be used together.

obverse—The front or face side of a coin.

overdate—Date made by superimposing one or more numerals on a previously dated die.

overgraded—A coin in poorer condition than stated.

overstrike—An impression made with new dies on a previously struck coin.

patina—The green or brown surface film found on ancient copper and bronze coins, caused by oxidation over a long period of time.

pattern—Experimental or trial coin, generally of a new design, denomination, or metal.

pedigree—The record of previous owners of a rare coin.

planchet—The blank piece of metal on which a coin design is stamped.

Proof—Coins struck for collectors by the Mint using specially polished dies and planchets.

Proof set—A set of each of the Proof coins made during a given year, packaged by the Mint and sold to collectors.

quarter eagle—The United States $2.50 gold coin.

raw—A coin that has not been encapsulated by an independent grading service.

reeded edge—The edge of a coin with grooved lines that run vertically around its perimeter, as seen on modern United States silver and clad coins.

regula—The bar separating the numerator and the denominator in a fraction.

relief—Any part of a coin's design that is raised above the coin's field is said to be in relief. The opposite of relief is incuse, meaning sunk into the field.

restrike—A coin struck from genuine dies at a later date than the original issue.

reverse—The back side of a coin.

rim—The raised portion of a coin that protects the design from wear.

round—A round one-ounce silver medal or bullion piece.

series—A set of one coin of each year of a specific design and denomination issued from each mint. For example, Lincoln cents from 1909 to 1959.

slab—A hard plastic case containing a coin that has been graded and encapsulated by a professional service.

spot price—The daily quoted market value of precious metals in bullion form.

token—A privately issued piece, typically with an exchange value for goods or services, but not an official government coin.

trade dollar—Silver dollar issued especially for trade with a foreign country. In the United States, trade dollars were first issued in 1873 to stimulate commerce with the Orient. Many other countries have also issued trade dollars.

truncation—The sharply cut-off bottom edge of a bust or portrait.

type—A series of coins defined by a shared distinguishing design, composition, denomination, and other elements. For example, Barber dimes or Franklin half dollars.

type set—A collection consisting of one representative coin of each type, of a particular series or period.

Uncirculated—A circulation-strike coin that has never been used in commerce, and has retained its original surface and luster; also called Mint State.

unique—An item of which only one specimen is known to exist.

variety—A coin's design that sets it apart from the normal issue of that type.

wheaties—Lincoln cents with the wheat ears reverse, issued from 1909 to 1958.

year set—A set of coins for any given year, consisting of one of each denomination issued that year.

Bibliography

COLONIAL ISSUES

Bowers, Q. David. *Whitman Encyclopedia of Colonial and Early American Coins.* Atlanta, GA, 2009.

Breen, Walter. *Walter Breen's Complete Encyclopedia of U.S. and Colonial Coins.* New York, NY, 1988.

Carlotto, Tony. *The Copper Coins of Vermont.* Chelsea, MI, 1998.

Crosby, S.S. *The Early Coins of America.* Boston, 1875. Reprint, 1945, 1965, 1974, and 1983.

Demling, Michael. *New Jersey Coppers.* 2011.

Kessler, Alan. *The Fugio Cents.* Newtonville, MA, 1976.

Maris, Edward. *A Historic Sketch of the Coins of New Jersey.* Philadelphia, 1881. Reprint, 1965, 1974, and 1987.

Martin, Syd. *The Hibernia Coinage of William Wood (1722–1724).* 2007.

Martin, Syd. *The Rosa Americana Coinage of William Wood.* Ann Arbor, MI, 2011.

Miller, Henry C., and Ryder Hillyer. *The State Coinages of New England.* New York, NY, 1920.

Nelson, Philip. *The Coinage of William Wood, 1722–1733.* London, 1903. Reprint, 1959.

Newman, Eric P. *Coinage for Colonial Virginia.* New York, NY, 1956.

Newman, Eric P. *The United States Fugio Copper Coinage of 1787.* Ypsilanti, MI, 2007.

Newman, Eric P., and Richard G. Doty. *Studies on Money in Early America.* New York, NY, 1976.

Noe, Sydney P. *The New England and Willow Tree Coinage of Massachusetts.* New York, NY, 1943; *The Oak Tree Coinage of Massachusetts.* New York, NY, 1947; and *The Pine Tree Coinage of Massachusetts.* New York, NY, 1952. Combined reprint as *The Silver Coins of Massachusetts.* New York, NY, 1973.

Noyes, William C. *United States Large Cents, 1816–1857.* Ypsilanti, MI, 2012.

Rulau, Russell, and George Fuld. *Medallic Portraits of Washington.* Iola, WI, 1999.

Salmon, Christopher J. *The Silver Coins of Massachusetts.* New York, NY, 2010.

Vlack, Robert. *An Illustrated Catalogue of the French Billon Coinage in the Americas.* Boston, NY, 2004.

HALF CENTS

Bowers, Q. David. *A Guide Book of Half Cents and Large Cents.* Atlanta, GA, 2015.

Breen, Walter. *Walter Breen's Encyclopedia of United States Half Cents 1793–1857.* South Gate, CA, 1983.

Cohen, Roger S., Jr. *American Half Cents—The "Little Half Sisters"* (2nd ed.). 1982.

Eckberg, William, Robert Fagaly, Dennis Fuoss, and Raymond Williams. *Grading Guide for Early American Copper Coins.* Heath, OH, 2014.

Fivaz, Bill, and J.T. Stanton. *The Cherrypickers' Guide to Rare Die Varieties* (6th ed., vol. I). Atlanta, GA, 2015.

Frossard, Édouard. *United States Cents and Half Cents Issued Between the Years of 1793 and 1857.* Irvington, NY, 1879.

Manley, Ronald P. *The Half Cent Die State Book, 1793–1857.* United States, 1998.

Robinson, Jack H. *Copper Quotes by Robinson* (20th ed.). 2011.

LARGE CENTS

Bowers, Q. David. *A Guide Book of Half Cents and Large Cents*. Atlanta, GA, 2015.

Breen, Walter. *Walter Breen's Encyclopedia of Early United States Cents, 1793–1814*. Wolfeboro, NH, 2001.

Eckberg, William, Robert Fagaly, Dennis Fuoss, and Raymond Williams. *Grading Guide for Early American Copper Coins*. Heath, OH, 2014.

Fivaz, Bill, and J.T. Stanton. *The Cherrypickers' Guide to Rare Die Varieties* (6th ed., vol. I). Atlanta, GA, 2015.

Frossard, Édouard. *United States Cents and Half Cents Issued Between the Years of 1793 and 1857*. Irvington, NY, 1879.

Grellman, J.R. *Attribution Guide for United States Large Cents, 1840–1857* (3rd ed.). Bloomington, MN, 2002.

Newcomb, H.R. *United States Copper Cents, 1816–1857*. New York, NY, 1944. Reprint, 1983.

Noyes, William C. *United States Large Cents, 1793–1794*. Ypsilanti, MI, 2006.

Noyes, William C. *United States Large Cents, 1793–1814*. Bloomington, MN, 1991.

Noyes, William C. *United States Large Cents, 1795–1797*. Ypsilanti, MI, 2007.

Noyes, William C. *United States Large Cents, 1816–1839*. Bloomington, MN, 1991.

Penny-Wise. Official publication of Early American Coppers, Inc.

Robinson, Jack H. *Copper Quotes by Robinson* (20th ed.). 2011.

Sheldon, William H. *Penny Whimsy (1793–1814)*. New York, NY, 1958. Reprint, 1965 and 1976.

Wright, John D. *The Cent Book, 1816–1839*. Bloomington, MN, 1992.

SMALL CENTS

Anderson, Shane M. *The Complete Lincoln Cent Encyclopedia*. Iola, WI, 1996.

Bowers, Q. David. *A Buyer's and Enthusiast's Guide to Flying Eagle and Indian Head Cents*. Wolfeboro, NH, 1996.

Bowers, Q. David. *A Guide Book of Lincoln Cents*. Atlanta, GA, 2008.

Burdette, Roger W. *Renaissance of American Coinage 1909–1915*. Great Falls, VA, 2008.

Daughtrey, Charles D. *Looking Through Lincoln Cents: Chronology of a Series*. (2nd ed.). Irvine, CA, 2005.

Fivaz, Bill, and J.T. Stanton. *The Cherrypickers' Guide to Rare Die Varieties* (6th ed., vol. I). Atlanta, GA, 2015.

Lange, David W. *The Complete Guide to Lincoln Cents*. Wolfeboro, NH, 1996.

Linderman, Henry R. *Money and Legal Tender*. New York, NY, 1877.

Manley, Stephen G. *The Lincoln Cent*. Muscatine, IA, 1981.

Snow, Richard. *Flying Eagle and Indian Cent Attribution Guide, 1856–1909* (3rd ed.). Tuscon, AZ, 2014.

Snow, Richard. *A Guide Book of Flying Eagle and Indian Head Cents* (3rd ed.). Atlanta, GA, 2016.

Steve, Larry, and Kevin Flynn. *Flying Eagle and Indian Cent Die Varieties*. Jarretteville, MD, 1995.

Taylor, Sol. *The Standard Guide to the Lincoln Cent*. Anaheim, CA, 1999.

Wagnon, Gary, Karen Peterson, and Kevin Flynn. *A Quick Reference to the Top Lincoln Cent Die Varieties*. Rancocas, NJ, 1997.

Wexler, John A. *The Lincoln Cent Doubled Die*. 1984.

Wexler, John, and Kevin Flynn. *The Authoritative Reference on Lincoln Cents*. Rancocas, NJ, 1996.

TWO-CENT PIECES

Fivaz, Bill, and J.T. Stanton. *The Cherrypickers' Guide to Rare Die Varieties* (6th ed., vol. I). Atlanta, GA, 2015.

Flynn, Kevin. *Getting Your Two Cents Worth*. Rancocas, NJ, 1994.

Leone, Frank. *Longacre's Two Cent Piece Die Varieties and Errors*. College Point, NY, 1991.

NICKEL FIVE-CENT PIECES

Bowers, Q. David. *A Guide Book of Buffalo and Jefferson Nickels*. Atlanta, GA, 2007.

Bowers, Q. David. *A Guide Book of Shield and Liberty Head Nickels*. Atlanta, GA, 2006.

Fivaz, Bill, and J.T. Stanton. *The Cherrypickers' Guide to Rare Die Varieties* (6th ed., vol. I). Atlanta, GA, 2015.

Fletcher, Edward L., Jr. *The Shield Five Cent Series.* Ormond Beach, FL, 1994.

Lange, David W. *The Complete Guide to Buffalo Nickels.* Virginia Beach, VA, 2006.

Nagengast, Bernard. *The Jefferson Nickel Analyst* (2nd ed.). Sidney, OH, 1979.

Peters, Gloria, and Cynthia Mahon. *The Complete Guide to Shield and Liberty Head Nickels.* Virginia Beach, VA, 1995.

Wescott, Michael. *The United States Nickel Five-Cent Piece.* Wolfeboro, NH, 1991.

HALF DISMES

Judd, J. Hewitt. *United States Pattern Coins* (10th ed.), edited by Q. David Bowers. Atlanta, GA, 2009.

Logan, Russell, and John McCloskey. *Federal Half Dimes, 1792–1837.* Manchester, MI, 1998.

Newlin, H.P. *The Early Half-Dimes of the United States.* Philadelphia, PA, 1883. Reprint, 1933.

Valentine, D.W. *The United States Half Dimes.* New York, NY, 1931. Reprint, 1975.

HALF DIMES

Blythe, Al. *The Complete Guide to Liberty Seated Half Dimes.* Virginia Beach, VA, 1992.

Breen, Walter. *United States Half Dimes: A Supplement.* New York, NY, 1958.

Fivaz, Bill, and J.T. Stanton. *The Cherrypickers' Guide to Rare Die Varieties* (5th ed., vol. II). Atlanta, GA, 2012.

Logan, Russell, and John McCloskey. *Federal Half Dimes, 1792–1837.* Manchester, MI, 1998.

Newlin, Harold P. *The Early Half-Dimes of the United States.* Philadelphia, PA, 1883. Reprint, 1933.

Valentine, D.W. *The United States Half Dimes.* New York, NY, 1931. Reprint, 1975.

DIMES

Ahwash, Kamal M. *Encyclopedia of United States Liberty Seated Dimes, 1837–1891.* Kamal Press, 1977.

Bowers, Q. David. *A Guide Book of Barber Silver Coins.* Atlanta, GA, 2015.

Bowers, Q. David. *A Guide Book of Mercury Dimes, Standing Liberty Quarters, and Liberty Walking Half Dollars.* Atlanta, GA, 2015.

Davis, David, Russell Logan, Allen Lovejoy, John McCloskey, and William Subjack. *Early United States Dimes, 1796–1837.* Ypsilanti, MI, 1984.

Fivaz, Bill, and J.T. Stanton. *The Cherrypickers' Guide to Rare Die Varieties* (5th ed., vol. II). Atlanta, GA, 2012.

Flynn, Kevin. *The 1894-S Dime: A Mystery Unraveled.* Rancocas, NJ, 2005.

Flynn, Kevin. *The Authoritative Reference on Roosevelt Dimes.* Brooklyn, NY, 2001.

Greer, Brian. *The Complete Guide to Liberty Seated Dimes.* Virginia Beach, VA, 2005.

Lange, David W. *The Complete Guide to Mercury Dimes* (2nd ed.). Virginia Beach, VA, 2005.

Lawrence, David. *The Complete Guide to Barber Dimes.* Virginia Beach, VA, 1991.

TWENTY-CENT PIECES

Brunner, Lane J., and John M. Frost. *Double Dimes: The United States Twenty-Cent Piece.* Hanover, PA, 2014.

Flynn, Kevin. *The Authoritative Reference on Twenty Cents.* Lumberton, NJ, 2013.

QUARTER DOLLARS

Bowers, Q. David. *A Guide Book of Barber Silver Coins.* Atlanta, GA, 2015.

Bowers, Q. David. *A Guide Book of Mercury Dimes, Standing Liberty Quarters, and Liberty Walking Half Dollars.* Atlanta, GA, 2015.

Bowers, Q. David. *A Guide Book of Washington and State Quarters.* Atlanta, GA, 2006.

Bressett, Kenneth. *The Official Whitman Statehood Quarters Collector's Handbook.* New York, NY, 2000.

Briggs, Larry. *The Comprehensive Encyclopedia of United States Seated Quarters.* Lima, OH, 1991.

Browning, Ard W. *The Early Quarter Dollars of the United States, 1796–1838.* New York, NY, 1925. Reprint, 1992.

Cline, J.H. *Standing Liberty Quarters* (4th ed.). 2007.

Duphorne, R. *The Early Quarter Dollars of the United States.* 1975.

Fivaz, Bill, and J.T. Stanton. *The Cherrypickers' Guide to Rare Die Varieties* (5th ed., vol. II). Atlanta, GA, 2012.

Haseltine, J.W. *Type Table of United States Dollars, Half Dollars and Quarter Dollars*. Philadelphia, PA, 1881. Reprint, 1927 and 1968.

Kelman, Keith N. *Standing Liberty Quarters*. 1976.

Lawrence, David. *The Complete Guide to Barber Quarters*. Virginia Beach, VA, 1989.

Rea, Rory, Flenn Peterson, Bradley Karoleff, and John Kovach. *Early Quarter Dollars of the U.S. Mint, 1796–1838*. 2010.

Tompkins, Steve M. *Early United States Quarters, 1796–1838*. Sequim, WA, 2010.

HALF DOLLARS

Bowers, Q. David. *A Guide Book of Barber Silver Coins*. Atlanta, GA, 2015.

Bowers, Q. David. *A Guide Book of Mercury Dimes, Standing Liberty Quarters, and Liberty Walking Half Dollars*. Atlanta, GA, 2015.

Fivaz, Bill, and J.T. Stanton. *The Cherrypickers' Guide to Rare Die Varieties* (5th ed., vol. II). Atlanta, GA, 2012.

Flynn, Kevin. *The Authoritative Reference on Barber Half Dollars*. Brooklyn, NY, 2005.

Fox, Bruce. *The Complete Guide to Walking Liberty Half Dollars*. Virginia Beach, VA, 1993.

Haseltine, J.W. *Type Table of United States Dollars, Half Dollars and Quarter Dollars*. Philadelphia, PA, 1881. Reprint, 1927 and 1968.

Lawrence, David. *The Complete Guide to Barber Halves*. Virginia Beach, VA, 1991.

Overton, Al C. *Early Half Dollar Die Varieties, 1794–1836* (3rd ed.), edited by Donald Parlsey, 1990. Colorado Springs, CO, 1967.

Peterson, Glenn R. *The Ultimate Guide to Attributing Bust Half Dollars*. Rocky River, OH, 2000.

Tomaska, Rick. *A Guide Book of Franklin and Kennedy Half Dollars* (2nd ed.). Atlanta, GA, 2012.

Wiley, Randy, and Bill Bugert. *The Complete Guide to Liberty Seated Half Dollars*. Virginia Beach, VA, 1993.

SILVER DOLLARS

Bolender, M.H. *The United States Early Silver Dollars From 1794 to 1803* (5th ed.). Iola, WI, 1987.

Bowers, Q. David. *The Encyclopedia of United States Silver Dollars, 1794–1804*. Irvine, CA, 2013.

Bowers, Q. David. *The Rare Silver Dollars Dated 1804*. Wolfeboro, NH, 1999.

Bowers, Q. David. *Silver Dollars and Trade Dollars of the United States: A Complete Encyclopedia*. Wolfeboro, NH, 1993.

Bowers, Q. David. *A Guide Book of Morgan Silver Dollars* (5th ed.). Atlanta, GA, 2016.

Burdette, Roger W. *A Guide Book of Peace Dollars* (3rd ed.). Atlanta, GA, 2016.

Fey, Michael S., and Jeff Oxman. *The Top 100 Morgan Dollar Varieties*. Morris Planes, NJ, 1997.

Fivaz, Bill, and J.T. Stanton. *The Cherrypickers' Guide to Rare Die Varieties* (5th ed., vol. II). Atlanta, GA, 2012.

Haseltine, J.W. *Type Table of United States Dollars, Half Dollars and Quarter Dollars*. Philadelphia, PA, 1881. Reprint, 1927 and 1968.

Judd, J. Hewitt. *United States Pattern Coins* (10th ed.), edited by Q. David Bowers. Atlanta, GA, 2009.

Logies, Martin A. *The Flowing Hair Silver Dollars of 1794*. 2004.

Newman, Eric P., and Kenneth E. Bressett. *The Fantastic 1804 Dollar, Tribute Edition*. Atlanta, GA, 2009.

Standish, Michael "Miles," and John B. Love. *Morgan Dollar: America's Love Affair With a Legendary Coin*. Atlanta, GA, 2014.

Van Allen, Leroy C., and A. George Mallis. *Comprehensive Catalogue and Encyclopedia of U.S. Morgan and Peace Silver Dollars*. New York, NY, 1997.

TRADE DOLLARS

Bowers, Q. David. *Silver Dollars and Trade Dollars of the United States: A Complete Encyclopedia*. Wolfeboro, NH, 1993.

Fivaz, Bill, and J.T. Stanton. *The Cherrypickers' Guide to Rare Die Varieties* (5th ed., vol. II). Atlanta, GA, 2012.

Willem, John M. *The United States Trade Dollar* (2nd ed.). Racine, WI, 1965.

MODERN DOLLARS

Bowers, Q. David. *Silver Dollars and Trade Dollars of the United States: A Complete Encyclopedia.* Wolfeboro, NH, 1993.

Fivaz, Bill, and J.T. Stanton. *The Cherrypickers' Guide to Rare Die Varieties* (5th ed., vol. II). Atlanta, GA, 2012.

Judd, J. Hewitt. *United States Pattern Coins* (10th ed.), edited by Q. David Bowers. Atlanta, GA, 2009.

GOLD DOLLARS

Akers, David W. *Gold Dollars (and Other Gold Denominations).* Englewood, OH, 1975–1982.

Bowers, Q. David. *A Guide Book of Gold Dollars* (2nd ed.). Atlanta, GA, 2011.

Bowers, Q. David. *United States Gold Coins: An Illustrated History.* Wolfeboro, NH, 1982.

Breen, Walter. *Major Varieties of U.S. Gold Dollars (and Other Gold Denominations).* Chicago, IL, 1964.

Fivaz, Bill. *United States Gold Counterfeit Detection Guide.* Atlanta, GA, 2005.

Fivaz, Bill, and J.T. Stanton. *The Cherrypickers' Guide to Rare Die Varieties* (5th ed., vol. II). Atlanta, GA, 2012.

Garrett, Jeff, and Ron Guth. *Encyclopedia of U.S. Gold Coins, 1795–1933* (2nd ed.). Atlanta, GA, 2008.

GOLD QUARTER EAGLES

Akers, David W. *Gold Dollars (and Other Gold Denominations).* Englewood, OH, 1975–1982.

Bowers, Q. David. *United States Gold Coins: An Illustrated History.* Wolfeboro, NH, 1982.

Breen, Walter. *Major Varieties of U.S. Gold Dollars (and Other Gold Denominations).* Chicago, IL, 1964.

Dannreuther, John W., and Harry W. Bass. *Early U.S. Gold Coin Varieties.* Atlanta, GA, 2006.

Fivaz, Bill. *United States Gold Counterfeit Detection Guide.* Atlanta, GA, 2005.

Fivaz, Bill, and J.T. Stanton. *The Cherrypickers' Guide to Rare Die Varieties* (5th ed., vol. II). Atlanta, GA, 2012.

Garrett, Jeff, and Ron Guth. *Encyclopedia of U.S. Gold Coins, 1795–1933* (2nd ed.). Atlanta, GA, 2008.

THREE-DOLLAR GOLD PIECES

Akers, David W. *Gold Dollars (and Other Gold Denominations).* Englewood, OH, 1975–1982.

Bowers, Q. David. *United States Gold Coins: An Illustrated History.* Wolfeboro, NH, 1982.

Bowers, Q. David, and Douglas Winter. *United States $3 Gold Pieces, 1854–1889.* Wolfeboro, NH, 2005.

Breen, Walter. *Major Varieties of U.S. Gold Dollars (and Other Gold Denominations).* Chicago, IL, 1964.

Fivaz, Bill. *United States Gold Counterfeit Detection Guide.* Atlanta, GA, 2005.

Fivaz, Bill, and J.T. Stanton. *The Cherrypickers' Guide to Rare Die Varieties* (5th ed., vol. II). Atlanta, GA, 2012.

Garrett, Jeff, and Ron Guth. *Encyclopedia of U.S. Gold Coins, 1795–1933* (2nd ed.). Atlanta, GA, 2008.

FOUR-DOLLAR GOLD PIECES

Akers, David W. *Gold Dollars (and Other Gold Denominations).* Englewood, OH, 1975–1982.

Bowers, Q. David. *United States Gold Coins: An Illustrated History.* Wolfeboro, NH, 1982.

Breen, Walter. *Major Varieties of U.S. Gold Dollars (and Other Gold Denominations).* Chicago, IL, 1964.

Garrett, Jeff, and Ron Guth. *Encyclopedia of U.S. Gold Coins, 1795–1933* (2nd ed.). Atlanta, GA, 2008.

Judd, J. Hewitt. *United States Pattern Coins* (10th ed.), edited by Q. David Bowers. Atlanta, GA, 2009.

GOLD HALF EAGLES

Akers, David W. *Gold Dollars (and Other Gold Denominations).* Englewood, OH, 1975–1982.

Bowers, Q. David. *United States Gold Coins: An Illustrated History.* Wolfeboro, NH, 1982.

Breen, Walter. *Major Varieties of U.S. Gold Dollars (and Other Gold Denominations).* Chicago, IL, 1964.

Dannreuther, John W., and Harry W. Bass. *Early U.S. Gold Coin Varieties.* Atlanta, GA, 2006.

Fivaz, Bill. *United States Gold Counterfeit Detection Guide.* Atlanta, GA, 2005.

Fivaz, Bill, and J.T. Stanton. *The Cherrypickers' Guide to Rare Die Varieties* (5th ed., vol. II). Atlanta, GA, 2012.

Garrett, Jeff, and Ron Guth. *Encyclopedia of U.S. Gold Coins, 1795–1933* (2nd ed.). Atlanta, GA, 2008.

Miller, Robert W., Sr. *United States Half Eagle Gold Coins, 1795–1834.* 1997.

GOLD EAGLES

Akers, David W. *Gold Dollars (and Other Gold Denominations).* Englewood, OH, 1975–1982.

Bowers, Q. David. *United States Gold Coins: An Illustrated History.* Wolfeboro, NH, 1982.

Breen, Walter. *Major Varieties of U.S. Gold Dollars (and Other Gold Denominations).* Chicago, IL, 1964.

Dannreuther, John W., and Harry W. Bass. *Early U.S. Gold Coin Varieties.* Atlanta, GA, 2006.

Fivaz, Bill. *United States Gold Counterfeit Detection Guide.* Atlanta, GA, 2005.

Fivaz, Bill, and J.T. Stanton. *The Cherrypickers' Guide to Rare Die Varieties* (5th ed., vol. II). Atlanta, GA, 2012.

Garrett, Jeff, and Ron Guth. *Encyclopedia of U.S. Gold Coins, 1795–1933* (2nd ed.). Atlanta, GA, 2008.

Teraskza, Anthony. *United States Ten Dollar Gold Eagles, 1795–1804.*

GOLD DOUBLE EAGLES

Akers, David W. *Gold Dollars (and Other Gold Denominations).* Englewood, OH, 1975–1982.

Bowers, Q. David. *A Guide Book of Double Eagle Gold Coins.* Atlanta, GA, 2004.

Bowers, Q. David. *United States Gold Coins: An Illustrated History.* Wolfeboro, NH, 1982.

Bowers, Q. David. *U.S. Liberty Head $20 Double Eagles: The Gilded Age of Coinage.* Irvine, CA, 2014.

Fivaz, Bill. *United States Gold Counterfeit Detection Guide.* Atlanta, GA, 2005.

Fivaz, Bill, and J.T. Stanton. *The Cherrypickers' Guide to Rare Die Varieties* (5th ed., vol. II). Atlanta, GA, 2012.

Garrett, Jeff, and Ron Guth. *Encyclopedia of U.S. Gold Coins, 1795–1933* (2nd ed.). Atlanta, GA, 2008.

Moran, Michael. *Striking Change: The Great Artistic Collaboration of Theodore Roosevelt and Augustus Saint-Gaudens.* Atlanta, GA, 2008.

Moran, Michael, and Jeff Garrett. *1849: The Philadelphia Mint Strikes Gold.* Atlanta, GA, 2016.

COMMEMORATIVES

Bowers, Q. David. *A Guide Book of United States Commemorative Coins.* Atlanta, GA, 2008.

Bullowa, David M. *The Commemorative Coinage of the United States, 1892–1938.* New York, NY, 1938.

Fivaz, Bill, and J.T. Stanton. *The Cherrypickers' Guide to Rare Die Varieties* (5th ed., vol. II). Atlanta, GA, 2012.

Flynn, Kevin. *The Authoritative Reference on Commemorative Coins, 1892–1954.* Roswell, GA, 2008.

Mosher, Stuart. *The Commemorative Coinage of the United States, 1892–1938.* New York, NY, 1940.

Slabaugh, Arlie. *United States Commemorative Coinage.* Racine, WI, 1975.

Swiatek, Anthony. *Encyclopedia of the Commemorative Coins of the United States.* Chicago, IL, 2012.

Swiatek, Anthony, and Walter Breen. *The Encyclopedia of United States Silver and Gold Commemorative Coins, 1892–1954.* New York, NY, 1981.

Taxay, Don. *An Illustrated History of U.S. Commemorative Coinage.* New York, NY, 1967.

PROOF AND MINT SETS

Lange, David W. *A Guide Book of Modern United States Proof Coin Sets* (2nd ed.). Atlanta, GA, 2010.

U.S. MINT BULLION COINS

Mercanti, John M., and Michael Standish. *American Silver Eagles: A Guide to the U.S. Bullion Coin Program* (2nd ed.). Atlanta, GA, 2013.

Moy, Edmund. *American Gold and Platinum Eagles: A Guide to the U.S. Bullion Coin Programs.* Atlanta, GA, 2013.

Tucker, Dennis. *American Gold and Silver: U.S. Mint Collector and Investor Coins and Medals, Bicentennial to Date.* Atlanta, GA, 2016.

TOKENS AND MEDALS

Bowers, Q. David. *A Guide Book of Civil War Tokens* (2nd ed.). Atlanta, GA, 2015.

Bowers, Q. David. *A Guide Book of Hard Times Tokens.* Atlanta, GA, 2015.

Fuld, George, and Melvin Fuld. *Patriotic Civil War Tokens.* Ypsilanti, MI, 1982.

Fuld, George, and Melvin Fuld. *U.S. Civil War Store Cards* (3rd ed.). 2015.

Gould, Maurice, Kenneth Bressett, and Kaye and Nancy Dethridge. *Alaska's Coinage Through the Years.* Racine, WI, 1960.

Jaeger, Katherine. *A Guide Book of United States Tokens and Medals.* Atlanta, GA, 2008.

Jaeger, Katherine, and Q. David Bowers. *100 Greatest American Medals and Tokens.* Atlanta, GA, 2007.

Rulau, Russell. *Standard Catalog of United States Tokens, 1700–1900.* Iola, WI, 1997.

PATTERNS

Judd, J. Hewitt. *United States Pattern Coins* (10th ed.), edited by Q. David Bowers. Atlanta, GA, 2008.

PRIVATE AND TERRITORIAL GOLD

Adams, Edgar H. *Official Premium Lists of Private and Territorial Gold Coins.* Brooklyn, NY, 1909.

Adams, Edgar H. *Private Gold Coinage of California, 1849–1855.* Brooklyn, NY, 1913.

Bowers, Q. David. *A California Gold Rush History Featuring Treasure from the S.S.* Central America. Wolfeboro, NH, 2001.

Bowers, Q. David. *The History of United States Coinage as Illustrated by the Garrett Collection.* Los Angeles, CA, 1979.

Breen, Walter, and Ronald Gillio. *California Pioneer Fractional Gold* (2nd ed.). Santa Barbara, CA, 1983.

Clifford, Henry H. "Pioneer Gold Coinage in the West—1848–1861," reprint from *The Westerners Brand Book—Book Nine.* Los Angeles, CA, 1961.

Griffin, Clarence. *The Bechtlers and Bechtler Coinage and Gold Mining in North Carolina, 1814–1830.* Spindale, NC, 1929.

Kagin, Donald H. *Private Gold Coins and Patterns of the United States.* New York, NY, 1981.

Lee, Kenneth W. *California Gold—Dollars, Half Dollars, Quarter Dollars.* Santa Ana, CA, 1979.

Owens, Dan. *California Coiners and Assayers.* Wolfeboro, NH, and New York, NY, 2000.

Seymour, Dexter C. "The 1830 Coinage of Templeton Reid." *American Numismatic Society Museum Notes 22.* New York, NY, 1977.

WORLD ISSUES

Allen, Lyman L. *U.S. Philippine Coins.* Oakland Park, FL: Lyman Allen Numismatic Services, 1998.

Haxby, James. *A Guide Book of Canadian Coins and Tokens.* Atlanta, GA, 2012.

Medcalf, Donald, and Ronald Russell. *Hawaiian Money Standard Catalog* (2nd ed.). Mill Creek, WA, 1991.

Perez, Gilbert S. *The Mint of the Philippine Islands.* New York, NY, 1921.

Shafer, Neil. *United States Territorial Coinage for the Philippine Islands.* 1961.

TYPE COINS

Bowers, Q. David. *A Guide Book of United States Type Coins* (2nd ed.). Atlanta, GA, 2008.

Garrett, Jeff, and Ron Guth. *100 Greatest U.S. Coins* (3rd ed.). Atlanta, GA, 2008.

Guth, Ron, and Jeff Garrett. *United States Coinage: A Study by Type.* Atlanta, GA, 2005.

MISSTRIKES AND ERRORS

Fivaz, Bill, and J.T. Stanton. *The Cherrypickers' Guide to Rare Die Varieties* (6th ed., vol. I). Atlanta, GA, 2015.

Fivaz, Bill, and J.T. Stanton. *The Cherrypickers' Guide to Rare Die Varieties* (5th ed., vol. II). Atlanta, GA, 2012.

Herbert, Alan. *Official Price Guide to Minting Varieties and Errors.* New York, NY, 1991.

Margolis, Arnold, and Fred Weinberg. *The Error Coin Encyclopedia* (4th ed.). 1991.

Collectible Red and Blue Books

Colletti, Frank J. *A Guide Book of the Official Red Book of United States Coins*. Atlanta, GA, 2009.

Journal Articles, Periodicals, and Lectures Pertaining to Small Cents

Abbott, Waldo. "Making Money: The Mint at Philadelphia." *Harper's New Monthly Magazine*, March 1861.

Adams, Edgar H. Untitled commentary about pattern cents in *The Numismatist*, July 1912, pp. 246–247.

American Journal of Numismatics. New York, NY. Various 19th century issues as cited.

Annual Report of the Director of the Mint. Various years 1850s to date.

Ballou's Pictorial Drawing-Room Companion, Vol. XII. Boston: 1857.

Barber, Charles E. "Manufacture of Dies." *Twenty-Fourth Annual Report of the Director of the Mint to the Secretary of the Treasury. For the Fiscal Year Ended June 30, 1896*. Washington, D.C.: 1897.

——— Letter about the origins of Longacre's Indian motif as used on the 1859 cent. *The Numismatist*. March 1910, p. 75.

Boyd, F.C.C. "Engravers of the U.S. Mint In Philadelphia." *The Numismatist*. July 1940.

Breen, Walter H. "More About Longacre's Indian Cent Model." *Numismatic Scrapbook Magazine*. April 1951.

——— "Blundered Dies of U.S. and Colonial Coins." *Empire Topics*. October 1958.

Cherrypickers' News. Savannah, GA: May 1996.

Coin Dealer Newsletter. Various locations, 1963 to date.

Coin World Almanac. Sidney, OH: 1976 and later editions.

Coin World. Sidney, OH: Various issues.

COINage. Ventura, CA: Various issues.

Coins magazine. Iola, WI: Various issues.

CONECA. Combined Organizations of Numismatic Error Collectors of America. Die Variety Master Listings (Variety Vista). CONECA Errorscope, CONECA forum, and other features on the Internet at conecaonline.org.

Conger, George R. "The Controversial Feathered Headdress," *Longacre's Ledger*. April 1992.

——— "An Argument Favoring Sarah as Longacre's Model." *Longacre's Ledger*. July 1992.

Davis, Robert Coulton. "Pattern and Experimental Issues of the United States Mint." *The Coin Collector's Journal*. Series beginning in July 1885; issue of September 1885 includes information on cent patterns of the 1850s.

DeLorey, Thomas K. "Was Mischief Afoot in 1857 Die Clashes?," "Collectors' Clearinghouse," *Coin World*. July 1, 1977.

——— "Longacre, Unsung Engraver of the U.S. Mint." *Longacre's Ledger*, January 1992.

Downing, A.W. Notebook of dies at the Philadelphia Mint each year 1880–1886. Downing was general foreman of the Coining Department and kept the notebook; certain pages were countersigned at the bottom by A.W. Straub, a machinist in the Engraving Department (who by 1884 identified himself as foreman of the Die Makers' Room). Copy furnished by Dr. Richard Doty, Smithsonian Institution.

Eaton, W.C. "The Eagle Cents of 1858." *The Numismatist*. January 1916.

——— "The Eagle Cents of 1858." *The Numismatist*. November 1920 (update of 1916 article).

——— "The Eagle Cents of 1858." *The Numismatist*. March 1921 (further update of 1916 article).

——— "The Eagle Cents of 1857." *The Numismatist*. May 1921. Most research for this article was done by F.R. Alvord.

Errorscope. Journal of the Combined Organizations of Numismatic Error Collectors of America (CONECA).

Fivaz, Bill. "Never In My Wildest Dreams." *Rare Coin Review*. No. 62. Description of the discovery of the 1857 Flying Eagle cent with clash marks from a Liberty Seated quarter dollar.

——— "Definitely a Difference!" *Longacre's Ledger*. Summer 1994. Description of the differences in the neck feathers on the letter size varieties of the 1858 Flying Eagle cent.

Flynn, Kevin. "Two Obverse Types Used on 1858 Flying Eagle Cents." *Numismatic News*. April 2, 1996.

Gerhardt, Paul W. "Proof Cents and Nickels, 1878–1916." *Numismatic Scrapbook Magazine*, February 1946.

Goforth, Joy. "Goddess of Liberty." *Mint Press*, November 1983; reprinted as "Who Came First? Goddess, Sarah, or Indian?" *Coin World*, January 4, 1984. Discussion of the Indian headdress motif on the cent including citations from Mint correspondence.

Harper's New Monthly Magazine. New York City, NY: various issues circa 1856–1862.

Harper's Weekly. New York City, NY: various issues circa 1857–1887.

Hettger, Henry T. "Collusive Bidding on Indian Head Cent Planchets in 1892." *Longacre's Ledger.* October 1991.

Hewitt, Lee F. "Cent Design Changed in 1886." *Numismatic Scrapbook Magazine.* June 1949.

———— "Feuchtwanger Bid on Making 3-Cent Nickel Blanks." *Numismatic Scrapbook Magazine.* February 1963.

Indian Central. Seahurst, WA. Various issues 1995 and 1996.

Jones, John F. "The 1856 Flying Eagle Cent." *The Numismatist.* April 1944.

Julian, R.W. "Notes on U.S. Proof Coinage: Silver and Minor." *Numismatic Scrapbook Magazine.* March 1966.

———— "Philadelphia Coinage Statistics, 1853–1873, The Half Dollar." *Numismatic Scrapbook Magazine.* October 1966.

———— "The Case of the Disappearing Cent." *Numismatic Scrapbook Magazine.* May 1972.

———— "The Flying Eagle Cent." *COINage.* October 1987.

———— "The Indian Head Cent." *COINage.* May 1988.

———— "The Cent Becomes Bronze: 1864." *FUN-Topics.* Summer 1987.

———— "The 1877 Indian Head Cent." *Coins Magazine.* October 1992.

Kreisberg, Abner, and Jerry Cohen. John A. Beck Collection auction sale catalogs, 1975 and 1976. Offerings of 1856 Flying Eagle cents.

Longacre's Ledger. Journal of the Fly-In Club. Contains much information on die varieties, rarity ratings, etc.

McGirk, Charles E., M.D. "Varieties of 1871 Indian Cents." *The Numismatist.* April 1910.

Numismatic Guaranty Corporation of America Census Report. Sarasota, FL: Various issues.

Numismatic News. Iola, WI: Various issues.

Numismatic Scrapbook Magazine. Chicago, IL, and Sidney, OH: 1935–1976.

Numismatist, The. Current address: Colorado Springs, CO; other addresses earlier. Various issues 1888 to date.

Penny Talk. Newsletter. Scarborough, Maine.

Pilliod, Chris. "What Error Coins Can Teach Us About Die Settings." *The Numismatist.* April 1996. Description of the 1870 Shield nickel with Indian Head cent clash marks; also a valuable discussion of die positions in coining presses. This was an exceedingly important article which influenced the thinking of Q. David Bowers on the mystery of the 1857 clashed-die cents.

PCGS Population Report, Newport Beach, CA: various issues.

Pollock, Andrew W. III. *United States Patterns and Related Issues.* Wolfeboro, NH: 1994.

Rare Coin Review. Wolfeboro, NH: Various issues.

Rosen, Maurice. *Rosen Numismatic Advisory.* October–November 1995 issue.

Schultz, William J. "The Flying Eagle Cent of 1856; The Origin of the Copper-Nickel Half Cent." *The Numismatist,* October 1938.

Sholley, Craig B. "Inexperience, Not Die Steel, Caused Problems at Early U.S. Mint." *Penny-Wise.*

Sinnock, John R. "Making Dies At the Philadelphia Mint." *The Numismatist.* October 1941.

Snow, Richard. "The Midnight Minter." *Longacre's Ledger.* January 1991.

———— "High Leaves, Low Leaves." *Longacre's Ledger.* April 1991.

———— Rick Snow's Variety Sale No. 1. Tucson, AZ: January 16, 1993. Contains report of the Floyd Starr group of Flying Eagle cents.

Snow, Richard, and Brian Wagner. "Pricing Proof-65RD Small Cents (1856–1909)." *Longacre's Ledger.* Fall 1993.

Steve, Larry R. "THE F.IND.ERS REPORT." *Longacre's Ledger.* Various issues. Reports and updates concerning new discoveries and significant varieties.

Thompson, Walter. "The Copper Nickel Cent." *Numismatic Scrapbook Magazine.* September 1960.

———— "The Adoption of [the] Indian Cent." *Numismatic Scrapbook Magazine.* July 1961.

2 Times Numismatic Newsletter. College Point, NY: May 1996. Contains discussion of the so-called "clashed die" 1868 nickel three-cent piece in which the writer believes it is not clashed with an Indian Head cent die.

Wagner, Brian, and Richard E. Snow. "Pricing MS-65 RED Bronze Indian Cents." *Longacre's Ledger.* Winter 1993.

White, W.O. "A Population Report Rarity Review." *Longacre's Ledger.* Spring 1995.

Wysong, Jerry. "A Third 1857 F.E. Cent Obverse Die." *Longacre's Ledger.* Summer 1993.

———— "How Many Are There, Anyway?" Article in *Longacre's Ledger,* Winter 1996.

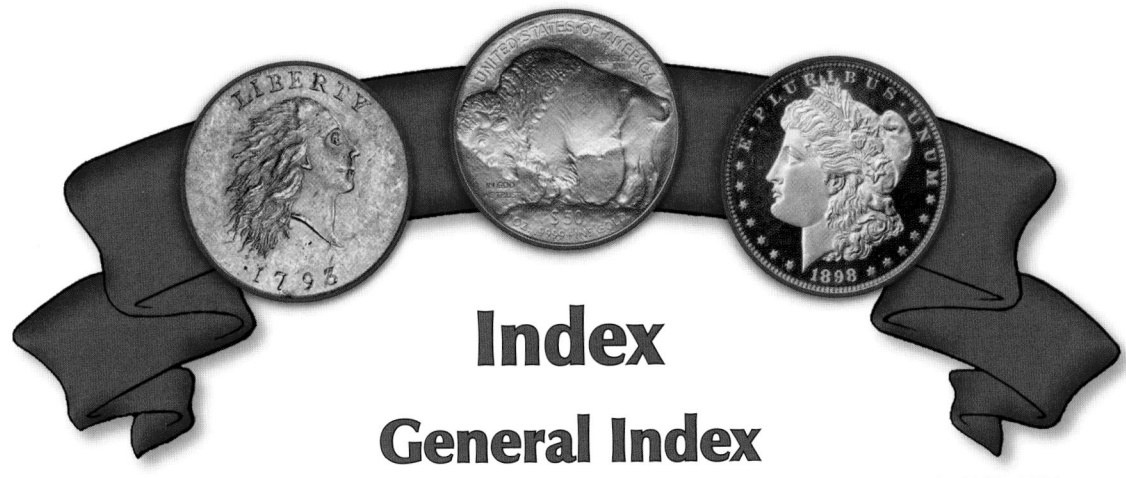

Index

General Index

abbreviations, used in this book, 17

Adams, Eva, 461, 472, 473, 474, 475

African Head copper, 121

Alaska Rural Rehabilitation Corporation, 1370, 1371

Alaska, coinage of, 14, 1370, 1371

Albany Church pennies, 136

altered coins, 23, 24, 596, 689, 914, 915, 993, 1373

America the Beautiful™ bullion, 1260–1263

America the Beautiful™ quarter dollars, 783–790

American Buffalo bullion coinage, 1272–1274

American Gold Eagle (AGE), 1263–1271

American Numismatic Association (ANA), 13, 19, 21, 356, 413, 466,471, 488, 495, 902, 995, 1343, 1346, 1349, 1382, 1385, 1396

   grading standards of, 19, 557, 680, 688, 712, 746, 760, 796, 837, 1396

American Plantations tokens, 101

American Platinum Eagle (APE), 1283–1290

American Silver Eagle (ASE), 24, 1255–1259

ANACS, 19

Anthony dollars, 86, 925, 930, 931, 1378

Articles of Confederation, 48, 54, 56, 134

Atlee, James F., 117, 127, 128

auction prices, top 250 U.S., 1390

Auctori Plebis tokens, 135

authentication, 23, 24, 150, 756

Baltimore Find, 31

Bailey, John, 117, 125, 127, 129

Baldwin & Co., 66

Baltimore, Lord, 42, 99

Bank of New York hoard, 29

bank notes, national, 63, 73, 80, 82

bank notes, private, 63, 64, 72

Bar coppers, 135

Barber, Charles E., 76, 78, 83, 357, 358, 367, 686, 715, 744, 745, 792, 836, 905, 916, 917, 1002, 1003, 1067, 1089, 1096–1103, 1105, 1296, 1297, 1336, 1340

Barber, William, 295, 710, 711, 946, 1045, 1294–1296

Barnum, P.T., 1135, 1136

Barry, Standish, 124, 136

barter system, 40, 42, 44, 46, 56

Bechtler, August, 65, 70

Bechtler, Christopher, 65, 70

Bechtler gold, 65, 70

Bermuda (Sommer Islands), 94, 95

Bicentennial coinage, 82, 87, 88, 715, 717, 758, 769, 856, 857, 924, 926, 927, 1123, 1124, 1141, 1154, 1155, 1157, 1158, 1173, 1200–1202, 1208,

1211, 1212, 1220, 1221, 1227, 1228, 1246, 1251, 1376

billon coinage, 113

bimetallism, 75

Birch cent, 154, 155

Birch, Robert, 58, 59, 154, 616

Bishop, Samuel, 121

bit, 151

Bland-Allison Act, 28, 74, 945, 946

blanks, 36, 61, 102, 113, 872, 873, 877, 883, 932, 1246, 1255, 1342, 1373, 1375

Blue Books

   collectible, 1381

   See also Handbook of United States Coins

Boudinot, Elias, 61, 62

Boulton and Watt, 138

branch mints, 22, 69, 70, 72–74, 563, 575, 679, 871, 955, 1244, 1304, 1305, 1314, 1340, 1395

Brasher, Ephraim, 52, 124, 125, 127, 129

Brasher doubloons, 52, 124, 125, 129

Breen, Walter, 13, 65, 109, 157, 182, 244, 251, 253, 254, 270, 275, 282, 290, 293, 305, 314, 340, 416, 580, 595, 725, 870, 917, 976, 1006, 1022, 1031, 1058, 1087, 1117, 1395

Brenner, Victor D., 25, 77, 83, 352, 353, 354, 355–369, 456, 457, 534, 545

Alphabetical Index of Dates for Commemoratives

* See also "Government Commemorative Sets" on page 1240.

* See also "Government Commemorative Sets" on page 1240.

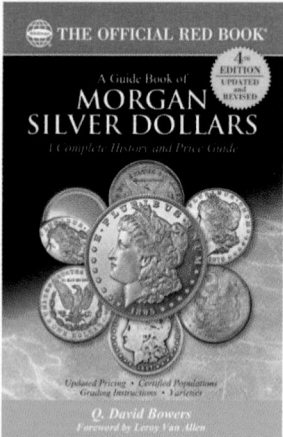
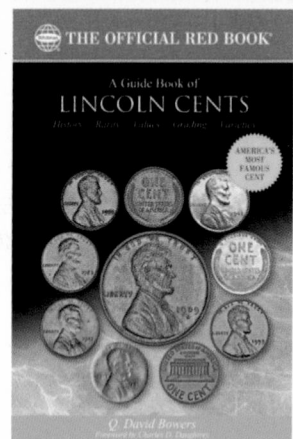

Three Valuable Books for Every Stage of Your Hobby

In *Pleasure and Profit: 100 Lessons for Building and Selling a Collection of Rare Coins*, Robert W. Shipee shares hands-on hobby advice, but his text is also about golf, whisky, friendships, and other good things in life that are attached to the experience of collecting coins. His relaxed, storyteller's wit makes the lessons fun and interesting. Q. David Bowers says, *"Pleasure and Profit* is one of the most useful books in American numismatics. It will change your buying strategies." **320 pages, 6 x 9 inches, full color • $9.95**

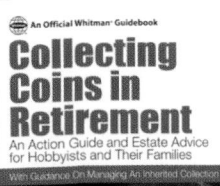
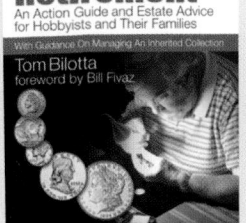

"Coin collecting during retirement poses specialized challenges and opportunities," says numismatist Tom Bilotta. In *Collecting Coins in Retirement*, he covers these issues in depth and guides you toward building your enjoyment of the hobby. Bill Fivaz calls it "comprehensive," "user-friendly," and "a must-read." **256 pages, 6 x 9 inches, full color • $19.95**

Don't leave your heirs in the dark. *Cash In Your Coins: Selling the Rare Coins You've Inherited* is for anyone who's inherited or found a collection of old coins. How rare are they? What are they worth? Should you sell? Where do you even begin? If you're a coin collector, you want your heirs to make smart, confident decisions—and avoid expensive mistakes! Keep a copy of this book with your collection for the benefit of your loved ones. Updated and expanded 2nd edition. **304 pages, 6 x 9 inches, full color • $9.95**

Order individually, or....... *SPECIAL OFFER* for readers of the *Red Book*—get all three books, a $39.85 value, for just $30 postpaid. Use promo code: 16

Whitman.com   Order by phone at 1-866-546-2995, online at Whitman.com, or email customerservice@Whitman.com